DEDICATION

The book is dedicated to my wife Elizabeth Langer and our two sons, Ben and Sam. I hope all who read this volume have the good fortune to spend a major portion of their lives with people as supportive and wonderful as them.

PREFACE

This book is designed to accomplish three things. First, learning the basic rules and concepts of property should not be difficult. The most important and challenging goal is to explore their cultural and social significance. Second, exploration of the cultural and social significance of property rules and concepts should be interesting. That is more likely if the teaching materials tell stories about the development of law over time and relate those stories to events in contemporary life. History can be fascinating in its own right; it becomes quite useful if it improves our understanding of how contemporary law is structured. Finally, legal teaching materials should not be boring. Making this volume tractable, engaging, and provocative should produce its own rewards.

These three goals led me to structure the book with certain clear cut divisions and sections. Many chapters or parts of chapters begin with a section that summarizes either a set of standard legal doctrines or a set of ideas and themes common to the cases and other materials that follow. Some of these opening sections end with a set of problems. If you feel you need additional reading to fully grasp the basic legal rules and concepts explored in these segments, I also provide page references to relevant sections of commonly used hornbooks and other helpful sources. The hope is that these portions of the text will provide you with a grounding in the basic rules and concepts taken up in the rest of the chapter. The next part of each chapter tells a story about the development of a set of legal rules and concepts over time. Each chapter ends with materials on the contemporary status of the rules and concepts being explored. Chapter I, for example, opens with some background materials on the importance of property in early America, then explores several classic Native American land claim cases, and concludes with readings on contemporary reservation land use issues and adverse possession disputes.

The book is organized both historically and substantively. Various portions of property law have been highly controversial at various points in our history. Those nodes of legal attentiveness provide structure to the materials. As already noted, Native American land claims is the subject of Chapter 1. Resolution of such disputes was an important feature of early American history. Chapter 2 covers family property law, which was subjected to searching review beginning in the first half of the nineteenth century. It opens with a section on common law rules about concurrent and family ownership of property, then tells a story about the gradual reform of rules restricting ownership of property by married women and ends with materials on present-day family property law. Exploration of the historical materials should give you a sophisticated understanding of the structure of modern legal debates about family property law. Chapters 3 and 4 cover the structure of property ownership by large organizations. There were many large sectarian and religious communes in the mid-nineteenth century. They are the focus of Chapter 3, which ends with materials on contemporary religious sects. Chapter 4 describes the late nineteenth century appearance of corporate and other forms of business organization, and ends with materials on ownership of property by present-day corporations. Chapters 5 and 6 deal with the gradual opening of property ownership to African Americans after the Civil War. Chapter 5 covers the classic rules on estates in land and future interests by looking at the way these rules were used to discriminate on the grounds of race. The following chapter reviews the law of easements and covenants, and the early law of zoning by focusing on the way they encouraged housing segregation.

The post-World War II era spawned some dramatic rethinking about the meaning of property. The growth of the administrative state became the object of intense scrutiny, first by a group of scholars known as the "Legal Process School" and somewhat later by a bevy of movements interested in wealth redistribution. These events are the focus of Chapter 7, which reviews the ways in which property was partially redefined to include administrative benefits and the consequences for land owners of the growth in federal programs intended to benefit the poor. This chapter lays out much of the theoretical basis for property reforms that occurred after the post-World War II years. Landlord-tenant law is taken up in Chapter 8. Debates about rental housing were quite intense among Progressives at the beginning of the twentieth century, but major reforms did not occur until the 1960s and 1970s. The chapter looks at the adoption of tenement house acts early in the century, and then moves to more contemporary efforts to reform tort and eviction rules in rental settings. Chapter 9 covers land transfer. Though many of the parameters of modern residential land sales were established by reforms enacted during the Great Depression, they did not spawn massive suburban growth until the post-World War II housing boom. The massive growth of suburbs in the last forty years, along with more contemporary problems of land transfer, is reviewed in this chapter.

The book ends with three chapters on contemporary thinking about property law. These materials cover the law of waste and nuisance with the help of the law and economics school, the constitutional law of takings through the prism of jurisprudes writing about the impact of history on the justice of contemporary legal structures, and the law of property in human beings with the guidance of recent thinkers on individualism and community.

The structure of this book has been heavily influenced by two streams of experience in my own career–teaching and writing about legal history and participating in Georgetown University Law Center's experimental first year curriculum. My work in legal history has given me a deep appreciation for the ways in which we continue to play out the dramas of our ancestors and for the importance of good stories in legal education. The experimental curriculum (now actually a permanent feature of first year life for twenty percent of each entering class) has provided me with a richer understanding of the ways modes of legal thought have evolved over time. It not only has allowed me to organize these materials in accordance with the historical periods in which various property doctrines were the focus of attention, but also to integrate materials about modes of legal thought popular at various times into each chapter.

We no longer (if we ever did) live in a world in which there is general agreement about the nature of legal institutions, the theoretical justifications for legal actions, or the roles lawyers should play in society. This lack of uniform, systematic understandings has led to a milieu in which lots of people are vying for your intellectual attention. Participants in this vibrant debate take it for granted that non-legal disciplines have something to say about the nature and purpose of legal institutions in an administrative state. Economics, philosophy, and history have become much more important parts of legal discourse and education in the last few decades. While this volume has its economic and philosophical moments, it largely is designed as an historical adventure. I hope you enjoy the journey.

If you have comments or questions about this book, please let me know. Send mail to me at:

Georgetown University Law Center
600 New Jersey Avenue, N.W.
Washington, DC 20001

or email me at chused@law.georgetown.edu.

Richard H. Chused
June, 1999

SUMMARY TABLE OF CONTENTS

DETAILED TABLE OF CONTENTS

Chapter 1
PROPERTY AND THE STATE

Chapter 2
GENDER, FAMILY AND CONCURRENT PROPERTY OWNERSHIP

Chapter 3
COMMUNAL LIVING AND THE LAW OF GENEROSITY

Chapter 4
BUSINESS OWNERSHIP OF PROPERTY

Chapter 5
ESTATES IN LAND, THE TIMING OF OWNERSHIP AND RACIAL CONDIDITIONS

Chapter 6
EMERGENCE OF HOUSING DEVELOPMENTS IN THE TWENTIETH CENTURY: SERVITUDES, REALISM, CLASS AND RACE

Chapter 7
PROPERTY AND THE POST-WORLD WAR II ADMINISTRATIVE STATE

Chapter 8
LANDLORD-TENANT LAW: FROM THE PRIVATE TO THE REGULATED SPHERE

Chapter 9

REAL ESTATE TRANSFERS: THE SUBURBAN EXPLOSION, CONSUMER PROTECTIONS, AND HOME SALES

Chapter 10
WASTE AND NUISANCE LAW: ECONOMICS AND THE LAW OF
PROPERTY

Chapter 11
PROPERTY THEORY AND THE SUPREME COURT SINCE THE NEW DEAL

Chapter 12
AUTONOMY AND COMMUNITY: PROPERTY IN HUMAN BEINGS

CHAPTER 1

PROPERTY AND THE STATE

§ 1.01 Introduction

Property is often thought of as a way of defining a domain of self-control—"a shield for the individual against the intrusions of the collective." But the creation and maintenance of property—something of value that you may restrain others from using—requires the blessing and protection of state power. Property is a creature of the state. As Jennifer Nedelsky notes, it "requires collective recognition and enforcement."[1] You should immediately see the potential for conflict. If property is both a creature of the state and a shield against arbitrary exercise of power by the collective, the state itself may be asked to implement inconsistent goals. To protect one person's property may require it to impinge on another's interests in other property. The preferences of one group about one set of assets may have negative consequences for the property of others.

Zoning land for commercial use, for example, may make farming more difficult on neighboring parcels. Requiring those constructing buildings to dig their foundations in ways that prevent neighboring structures from collapsing may increase construction costs. Requiring owners of historic buildings to maintain them for public benefit may raise the cost of ownership. In each of these cases the reverse may also be true. Zoning land for agricultural use to protect farmers may reduce the value of land an owner hoped to use for a shopping center. Allowing those constructing buildings to dig foundations that undermine nearby structures may lead to the collapse of a neighbor's building. And allowing historic buildings to fall into disrepair may lead to a loss of important cultural landmarks. It is these sorts of conflicts that leads Jennifer Nedelsky and others to argue that the single-minded definition of property as a shield of individual liberty is misguided, that such a notion should be replaced with a set of ideals about property as relational, about property as interconnectedness, about property as mediator (not separator) between the interests of people and the state.

The importance of state power to the definition and maintenance of property ownership is made painfully obvious by the fate of those occupying America before the Europeans colonized these shores. Native Americans living here before 1600 certainly believed they had the blessings of their elders to occupy, use and "own" this land in accordance with their settled customs and understandings. When their governing structures lost power to European colonizers and then the United States, the native legal claims to ownership fell apart.

There is a set of fundamental ironies at work here. Many of those governing America during its founding decades claimed that one of the primary duties of government was to protect the

---

[1] Both quotes are from Jennifer Nedelsky, *Law, Boundaries, and the Bounded Self*, *in* LAW AND THE ORDER OF CULTURE 162, 165 (Robert Post, ed., 1991).

interests of the landed, to insure that government would not interfere with the privileges of ownership. But many of the same people were perfectly prepared to use government power to extinguish the interests of a putatively incompatible group claiming the same land. The Native American land claim cases are a metaphor for much of what is discussed in this book. Everything you will be exploring involves this fundamental contradiction between property as a device for explaining individual or group identity and property as a creature of the state.

Many members of the elite class governing this country in the years just before and after 1800 had a particular set of perspectives on the importance of property to the definition of self and state. The Republicans and the Federalists held one important idea in common. They both believed that property was an aspect of personality, of individuality, that helped define every person's cultural role. Stanley Katz has argued that Jefferson, at least initially, believed that each person owned the products of his (and I use the masculine intentionally) labor, that a stake in ownership was central to the development of a moral, civically responsible, citizenry.[2] (It is, by the way, this notion of civic responsibility in early Republicanism that is now the focus of attention in a present day movement, discussed some in the final chapters of this book, to revisit notions of public responsibility as part of a modern system of legal thought about property.) Hamilton, however, tartly observed that "as luxury prevails in society, virtue will be in a greater degree considered as only a graceful appendage of wealth, and the tendency will be to depart from the Republican standard . . . . It is a common misfortune, that awaits our state constitution, as well as all others."[3] And so Hamilton, not believing with Jefferson that property makes for civility, made the more straightforward argument that wealth, something every individual craved, must be protected from the grasp of the impoverished by government structures. In sum, Jefferson contended that the minimal state would function well so long as participants in that state had a stake in its wealth. Hamilton argued that the state's purpose was to protect private property from redistribution. But regardless of their differences, Jefferson and Hamilton, as well as many other founders, believed that the scope of individual ownership of property was a central problem for the state to consider.

The common views of Jefferson and Hamilton about the importance of land ownership as a defining element of Republican citizenship meant there was widespread agreement that only property owners should be allowed to participate in running the government. Prior to 1820, property ownership was a prerequisite to male suffrage throughout the land. Membership in state legislatures was similarly restricted. And both the federal and the various state senates were appointive rather than elective bodies, with members of the landed elites usually selected for service. Until the 17th amendment was adopted in 1913, United States Senators were appointed by a method chosen by each state. Early in our history, state governors or state senates usually made the appointment. (I suspect most of you have not read the 17th amendment let alone the entire constitution. You should read it. A copy is available for your perusal in the appendices of this text.) While this part of our political history began to change during the Jacksonian era, it was part of the general understanding of our early politicians that government was in large part created to protect the interests of the landed aristocracy.

Though both Jefferson and the Republicans and Hamilton and the Federalists believed in the importance of property's relation to proper governance of the state, there were some important

---

[2] Stanley N. Katz, *Thomas Jefferson and the Right to Property in Revolutionary America*, 19 J.L. & ECON. 467 (1976).

[3] Alexander Hamilton, *Address Before the New York Ratifying Convention of Poughkeepsie, New York, June 21, 1788, in* 5 PAPERS OF ALEXANDER HAMILTON 36 (Howard C. Syrett ed., 1962).

differences. One involved their attitudes about expanding the size of the landed class. Jefferson believed in encouraging the growth of a civically responsible class of yeoman farmers by distributing land to the landless. Hamilton cared less about that as a matter of political theory, though he did see that *sale* of land might be a way of raising money for the state. This is crucial to understanding a case like *Johnson v. McIntosh*, the first case in this text. Given the importance of land ownership as a defining element of both the state and the right to participate in it, Chief Justice Marshall, a Federalist, was confronted with a dispute between two aristocratic groups, each claiming the right to property in the Northwest Territory. It was not just a case about the right of Native Americans to claim participatory rights in the new republic as owners of land, but about the machinery the state had to use to resolve property disputes among the European descendants then running the nation. When all was said and done, the Supreme Court not only confirmed the secondary status of native claims, but also affirmed the validity of federal structures for distributing lands west of the original thirteen states.

As a Federalist, Marshall also believed in the central role of the national government as the arbiter of property rights. Fearing the clamor of the masses in the unwieldy diversity of states that created confusion under the Articles of Confederation, the Federalists thought it crucial to develop a strong central government to control the major features of the new republic. That belief created another conflict for Marshall. What was he supposed to do with Native American communities, such as the Cherokees and others in the southeast, that had adopted many of the core political, Republican notions espoused by both Hamilton and Jefferson?

Jefferson, while president, established a policy for Native Americans that encouraged them to drop their nomadic habits in favor of a static agricultural life and to adopt governing structures mimicking those of the United States. Two commentaries Jefferson wrote explain why this happened. The first is an 1803 letter he wrote to William H. Harrison, Governor of the Indiana Territory from 1801-1812 and later the ninth President of the United States. In this letter, which was not meant for general circulation, Jefferson, in fairly Machiavellian prose, described his "Indian policy." Though obviously not a believer in equality as we now think of it, he did wish to follow through on his Republican idea that property ownership has civilizing effects:

> Our system is to live in perpetual peace with the Indians, to cultivate an affectionate attachment from them, by everything just and liberal which we can do for them within the bounds of reason, and by giving them effectual protection against wrongs from our own people. The decrease of game rendering their subsistence by hunting insufficient, we wish to draw them to agriculture, to spinning and weaving. The latter branches they take up with great readiness, because they fall to the women, who gain by quitting the labors of the field for those which are exercised within doors. When they withdraw themselves to the culture of a small piece of land, they will perceive how useless to them are their extensive forests, and will be willing to pare them off from time to time in exchange for necessaries for their farms and families. To promote this disposition to exchange lands, which they have to spare and we want, we shall push our trading uses, and be glad to see the good and influential individuals among them run in debt, because we observe that when these debts get beyond what the individuals can pay, they become willing to lop them off by a cession of lands. At our trading houses, too, we mean to sell so low as merely to repay us cost and charges, so as neither to lessen or enlarge our capital. This is what private traders cannot do, for they must gain; they will consequently retire from the competition, and we shall thus get clear of this pest without giving offence or umbrage to the Indians. In this way our settlements will gradually circumscribe

and approach the Indians, and they will in time either incorporate with us as citizens of the United States, or remove beyond the Mississippi. The former is certainly the termination of their history most happy for themselves; but, in the whole course of this, it is essential to cultivate their love. As to their fear, we presume that our strength and their weakness is now so visible that they must see we have only to shut our hand to crush them, and that all our liberalities to them proceed from motives of pure humanity only.[4]

The second excerpt is from an address Jefferson delivered in 1808 to several "Indian chiefs." Here Jefferson more politely and publicly described the aims of his policy.

Scanty and unwholesome food produce diseases and death among young children, and hence you have raised few and your numbers have decreased. Frequent wars, too, and the abuse of spirituous liquors, have assisted in lessening your numbers. The whites, on the other hand, are in the habit of cultivating the earth, of raising stocks of cattle, hogs, and other domestic animals, in much greater numbers than they could kill of deer and buffalo. Having always a plenty of food and clothing they raise abundance of children, they double their numbers every twenty years, the new swarms are continually advancing upon the country like flocks of pigeons, and so they will continue to do. Now, my children, if we wanted to diminish our numbers, we would give up the culture of the earth, pursue the deer and buffalo, and be always at war; this would soon reduce us to be as few as you are, and if you wish to increase your numbers you must give up the deer and buffalo, live in peace, and cultivate the earth. You see then, my children, that it depends on yourselves alone to become a numerous and great people. Let me entreat you, therefore, on the lands now given you to begin to give every man a farm; let him enclose it, cultivate it, build a warm house on it, and when he dies, let it belong to his wife and children after him. Nothing is so easy as to learn to cultivate the earth; all your women understand it, and to make it easier, we are always ready to teach you how to make ploughs, hoes, and necessary utensils. If the men will take the labor of the earth from the women they will learn to spin and weave and to clothe their families. In this way you will also raise many children, you will double your numbers every twenty years, and soon fill the land your friends have given you, and your children will never be tempted to sell the spot on which they have been born, raised, have labored and called their own. When once you have property, you will want laws and magistrates to protect your property and persons, and to punish those among you who commit crimes. You will find that our laws are good for the purpose; you will wish to live under them, you will unite yourselves with us, join in our Great Councils and form one people with us, and we shall all be Americans; you will mix with us by marriage, your blood will run in our veins, and will spread with us over this great island. Instead, then, my children, of the gloomy prospect you have drawn of your total disappearance from the face of the earth, which is true, if you continue to hunt the deer and buffalo and go to war, you see what a brilliant aspect offered to our future history, if you give up war and hunting.[5]

It is fascinating how Jefferson paternalistically extended his views about expanding the number of white land owners to the Native American "children" then dependent upon American policy for survival. The combination of Jefferson's respect for yeoman farmers and land ownership,

[4] Letter to Governor William H. Harrison (Feb. 27, 1803) in THOMAS JEFFERSON, WRITINGS 1118 (Library of America, 1984).

[5] Advice to Indian Chiefs To Captain Hendrick, the Delawares, Mohicans, and Munries (Washington, Dec. 21, 1808), in LETTERS AND ADDRESSES OF THOMAS JEFFERSON 189-90 (Unit Book ed. 1905).

the connections between morality and cultivation of property, and the relationship between governance and property ownership is palpable in these excerpts. And, in light of Jefferson's ownership of slaves and our troubled history of race relations, his assumption that property ownership would lead to intermarriage is remarkable. As a result of Jefferson's policy, a number of southeastern tribes developed agricultural habits, established governing structures emulating those of the United States, and settled down for what they hoped was the long term. What you are about to do is investigate what happened to such tribes. While it is easy to predict the fate of the small minority of native communities that fought for their land, we will be looking at disputes not involving warring peoples. *Johnson v. McIntosh* sets the legal stage, and the *Cherokee Cases* conclude the early part of this ongoing tale.

The history of American policy toward its native people can be roughly divided into three large stages. During the first period, which lasted until the Adoption of the Dawes Act in 1887, most native communities were removed from their homelands. Many died in battles or from diseases brought for the first time to these shores by European settlers. Those who survived were forced into reservations, most located west of the Mississippi River. The *Johnson* and *Cherokee* cases deal with this epoch's disputes over land and tribal claims of sovereignty. During the Dawes Act, or General Allotment Act,[6] period, the federal government embarked on an ill-fated attempt to gradually shift federal ownership of reservation lands into the private ownership system typical in most of the United States. Members of tribes were given an allotment of land which had to remain in the hands of an Indian owner for 25 years. After that waiting period, the land could be sold to anyone. Lands not subject to allotment were declared to be surplus property open to general sale by the government. During the Dawes Act era, the amount of land under tribal jurisdiction decreased by about two-thirds. The results were disastrous. Many tribal members became landless. Reservations lost their coherence as they became checkerboarded with lands owned by outsiders. Tribal governance became more difficult. The depression greatly exacerbated the problems and the allotment system was repealed by the Indian Reorganization Act of 1934.[7] This act reestablished the reservation system, restricted the further disposal of allotted Indian lands to outsiders and barred the further sale of surplus lands. Though the scope of authority left in the hands of tribal governments has ebbed and flowed over the years, the Reorganization Act system has remained largely intact to this day.

§ 1.02 Source Materials

[1] Outside Reading

For a basic review of the history of Native American land law, *see* ch. 67 in POWELL ON REAL PROPERTY (Matthew Bender).

For nicely written works on the history of the *Johnson* and *Cherokee* litigation, *see* Reid Chambers, *Judicial Enforcement of the Federal Trust Responsibility to Indians*, 27 STAN. L. REV. 1213 (1975); Joseph C. Burke, *The Cherokee Cases: A Study in Law, Politics, and Morality*, 21 STAN. L. REV. 500 (1969). The three basic eras of native land treatment are covered in Scott Gould, *The Consent Paradigm: Tribal Sovereignty at the Millennium*, 96 COLUM. L. REV. 809, 810-837 (1996). The history and impact of the General Allotment or Dawes Act is well covered in Judith Royster, *The Legacy of Allotment*, 27 ARIZ. ST. L.J. 1 (1995). A good critique of the

---

[6] Ch. 119, 24 Stat. 388 (1887).

[7] Ch. 576, 48 Stat. 984 (1934); 25 U.S.C. §§ 461-479.

development of law on Indian title may be found in Joseph Singer, *Sovereignty and Property*, 86 Nw. U. L. Rev. 1 (1991).

[2]   Readings from Chused, A Property Anthology (2d ed. 1997);

At pp. 18-23, 25-39, there are excerpts from the following works on early Republicanism and property: Stanley N. Katz, *Thomas Jefferson and the Right to Property in Revolutionary America*, 19 J.L. & Econ. 467 (1976); Robert J. Steinfeld, *Property and Suffrage in the Early American Republic*, 41 Stan. L. Rev. 335 (1989); Jennifer Nedelsky, *Law, Boundaries and the Bounded Self*, *in* Law and the Order of Culture 162 (1991).

At pp. 40-61, there are excerpts from the following works on Native American land claims: Robert Williams, the American indian in Western Legal Thought (1990); Phillip P. Frickey, *Marshaling Past and Present: Colonialism, Constitutionalism, and Interpretation in Federal Indian Law*, 107 Harv. L. Rev. 381 (1993).

§ 1.03 Early Native American Land Claim Cases

[1]   Johnson v. McIntosh

[a]   Background of the Case

In 1609 King James I of England granted to "The Treasurer and Company of Adventurers and Planters of the City of London, for the First Colony of Virginia" all the lands in the area known as Virginia. This grant included all the area to the west and northwest of a 200-mile segment of the Atlantic Ocean coast. Prior to 1609, this land was held, in full ownership and sovereignty, by various native tribes. In 1624, this corporation of "Adventurers" was dissolved, leaving the Colony of Virginia under the control of the English crown. Segments of this crown colony were later given over to the control of other colonial groups under new charters. During the years before 1756, the French government also laid claim to portions of Virginia west of the Allegheny and Appalachian Mountains, and took possession of certain parts of it. The international dispute led to the French and Indian War. During the war, the Iroquois, or Six Nations, allied themselves with Great Britain, while the Illinois, or Kaskaskias, and the Wabash, or Piankeshaw, tribes, residing in the territory northwest of the Virginia coast and west of the mountains, allied themselves with France. At the conclusion of the French and Indian War in 1763, the northwest tribes signed treaties of peace with Great Britain and the Six Nations. France's claims to the land east of the Mississippi River and northwest of the mountains were ended.

On July 5, 1773, certain Chiefs of the Illinois tribes delivered a deed to a group of British colonial subjects, led by William Murray, for two large tracts of land, one along the Kaskaskia and Ohio Rivers, and the other along the Mississippi River. The sum of $24,000 was paid to the tribe for the land. On October 18, 1775, certain chiefs of the Wabash deeded another two tracts of land to another group headed by Lewis Viviat. This land, transferred for $31,000, ran along the Wabash, Cat, White, and Ohio Rivers. On May 6, 1776, the Colony of Virginia declared itself independent of Great Britain. On October 5, 1778, the armies of the Virginia Colony took possession of the lands northwest of Virginia from Britain. The Virginia Assembly authorized the transfer of these northwest lands to the United States on December 20, 1783. This was part of the general cession to the central government of claims to western lands made by a number of the original thirteen states. The formal transfer of Virginia's western land claims to the United States, then organized under the Articles of Confederation, occurred on March 1, 1784, with

Thomas Jefferson, Samuel Hardy, Arthur Lee, and James Monroe acting on behalf of Virginia as the state's representatives to Congress.

Despite the formal transfer of the northwestern lands to the central government, it took some time before many settlers migrated west. The Northwest Ordinance, under which the Northwest Territory was organized, was adopted in 1787, but it took quite a bit of time before land was surveyed, Native land claims extinguished, hostile tribes removed, and land bureaucracies organized to handle the flow of title documents to the new settlers.[8] On July 20, 1818, the United States issued a patent to William McIntosh for a parcel of over 11,000 acres, which parcel, the parties to the case claimed, was within the area conveyed by the Wabash to the Lewis Viviat group in 1775.[9] Thomas Johnson, one of the grantees in the Viviat group, died on October 1, 1819. He was a member of the Continental Congress, the first Governor of Maryland after it became a state, and an Associate Justice on the Supreme Court during the 1790s. His will's *residuary clause*[10] bestowed most of his real estate on his son Joshua Johnson and his grandson Thomas Graham, the lessors in *McIntosh*. Joshua Johnson and Thomas Graham, and their lessee, were citizens of Maryland. William McIntosh was a citizen of Illinois, established as a state in 1818. The Murray and Viviat groups petitioned to Congress many times to confirm their title claims, but without success. The case itself was brought to "test" the various title claims. The plaintiffs, Johnson and Graham's lessee and others, brought an *ejectment*[11] action in the Illinois District Court. The case came before the courts on a statement of facts agreed to by the parties. In modern parlance, the case was decided at the trial level on the equivalent of a *motion for a summary judgment*.[12] Judgment below was for the defendants, and the plaintiffs appealed.

---

[8] While it seems obvious, don't forget that communication was very difficult at the end of the eighteenth century. The mails, if they worked at all, were extremely slow. Moving documents back and forth between the new territories and the land bureaucrats in Washington, D.C. took months. Final distribution of land patents, the name given deeds issued by the United States, usually took years after the initial land claims were made.

[9] In a ground breaking study, Eric Kades has reconstructed the flow of property documents in the *Johnson* case. He argues that McIntosh probably obtained much of his land through fraud, bribery or trickery. His claims were perfected several years before the patent was issued at a time when the area was not open for general settlement. Kades has also unearthed evidence that the land at issue in the case was never actually within the areas claimed by the Murray and Viviat groups. The case, he claims, was a feigned dispute designed by the last remnants of a largely dispirited and sometimes impoverished group of land investors to recoup their losses. Eric Kades, *The Dark Side of Efficiency:* Johnson v. M'Intosh *and the Expropriation of Indian Lands* (1997) (unpublished manuscript in author's files).

[10] The *residuary clause* is usually the final granting clause of a will and disposes of all property not dealt with by other provisions in the will.

[11] An *ejectment* action tries the right of the parties to claim possession to the land. While deciding the right to possess *may* also resolve issues as to who owns the land, that is not always so. Think, for example, about a tenant. A tenant has the right to possess a place, and to eject others who claim a right to that possession. But a tenant does not own the rented land. Though neither party was actually living on the land during the *McIntosh* litigation, both claimed the right to do so. It was the right, more than the reality, that was being tested.

[12] *See* FED. R. CIV. P. 56. A *motion for summary judgment* may be granted if there are no material facts in dispute in the claim. The motion therefore makes it possible to decide a case without a trial.

[b]   The United States Supreme Court Opinion

Johnson & Graham's Lessee v. William McIntosh
United States Supreme Court
21 U.S. (8 Wheat.) 543, 5 L. Ed. 681 (1823)

March 10th, 1823. MARSHALL, CH. J., delivered the opinion of the court. — The plaintiffs in this cause claim the land in their declaration mentioned, under two grants, purporting to be made, the first in 1773, and the last in 1775, by the chiefs of certain Indian tribes, constituting the Illinois and the Piankeshaw nations; and the question is, whether this title can be recognized in the courts of the United States? The facts, as stated in the case agreed, show the authority of the chiefs who executed this conveyance, so far as it could be given by their own people; and likewise show, that the particular tribes for whom these chiefs acted were in rightful possession of the land they sold. The inquiry, therefore, is, in a great measure, confined to the power of Indians to give, and of private individuals to receive, a title, which can be sustained in the courts of this country.

As the right of society to prescribe those rules by which property may be acquired and preserved is not, and cannot, be drawn into question; as the title to lands, especially, is, and must be, admitted, to depend entirely on the law of the nation in which they lie; it will be necessary, in pursuing this inquiry, to examine, not simply those principles of abstract justice, which the Creator of all things has impressed on the mind of his creature man, and which are admitted to regulate, in a great degree, the rights of civilized nations, whose perfect independence is acknowledged; but those principles also which our own government has adopted in the particular case, and given us as the rule for our decision.

On the discovery of this immense continent, the great nations of Europe were eager to appropriate to themselves so much of it as they could respectively acquire. Its vast extent offered an ample field to the ambition and enterprise of all; and the character and religion of its inhabitants afforded an apology for considering them as a people over whom the superior genius of Europe might claim an ascendancy. The potentates of the old world found no difficulty in convincing themselves, that they made ample compensation to the inhabitants of the new, by bestowing on them civilization and Christianity, in exchange for unlimited independence. But as they were all in pursuit of nearly the same object, it was necessary, in order to avoid conflicting settlements, and consequent war with each other, to establish a principle, which all should acknowledge as the law by which the right of acquisition, which they all asserted, should be regulated, as between themselves. This principle was, that discovery gave title to the government by whose subjects, or by whose authority, it was made, against all other European governments, which title might be consummated by possession. The exclusion of all other Europeans, necessarily gave to the nation making the discovery the sole right of acquiring the soil from the natives, and establishing settlements upon it. It was a right with which no Europeans could interfere. It was a right which all asserted for themselves, and to the assertion of which, by others, all assented. Those relations which were to exist between the discoverer and the natives, were to be regulated by themselves. The rights thus acquired being exclusive, no other power could interpose between them.

In the establishment of these relations, the rights of the original inhabitants were, in no instance, entirely disregarded; but were, necessarily, to a considerable extent, impaired. They were admitted to be the rightful occupants of the soil, with a legal as well as just claim to retain possession of it, and to use it according to their own discretion; but their rights to complete sovereignty, as independent nations, were necessarily diminished, and their power to dispose of the soil, at their own will, to whomsoever they pleased, was denied by the original fundamental principle, that discovery gave exclusive title to those who made it. While the different nations of Europe respected the right of the natives, as occupants, they asserted the ultimate dominion to be in themselves; and claimed and exercised, as a consequence of this ultimate dominion, a power to grant the soil, while yet in possession of the natives. These grants have been understood by all, to convey a title to the grantees, subject only to the Indian right of occupancy.

No one of the powers of Europe gave its full assent to this principle, more unequivocally than England. The documents upon this subject are ample and complete. So early as the year 1496, her monarch granted a commission to the Cabots, to discover countries then unknown to Christian people, and to take possession of them in the name of the king of England. Two years afterwards, Cabot proceeded on this voyage, and discovered the continent of North America, along which he sailed as far south as Virginia. To this discovery, the English trace their title. In this first effort made by the English government to acquire territory on this continent, we perceive a complete recognition of the principle which has been mentioned. The right of discovery given by this commission, is confined to countries "then unknown to all Christian people;" and of these countries, Cabot was empowered to take possession in the name of the king of England. Thus asserting a right to take possession, notwithstanding the occupancy of the natives, who were heathens, and, at the same time, admitting the prior title of any Christian people who may have made a previous discovery. The same principle continued to be recognized. The charter granted to Sir Humphrey Gilbert, in 1578, authorizes him to discover and take possession of such remote, heathen and barbarous lands, as were not actually possessed by any Christian prince or people. This charter was afterwards renewed to Sir Walter Raleigh, in nearly the same terms.

By the charter of 1606, under which the first permanent English settlement on this continent was made, James I. granted to Sir Thomas Gates and others, those territories in America, lying on the sea-coast, between the 34th and 45th degrees of north latitude, and which either belonged to that monarch, or were not then possessed by any other Christian prince or people. The grantees were divided into two companies, at their own request. The first, or southern colony, was directed to settle between the 34th and 41st degrees of north latitude; and the second, or northern colony, between the 38th and 45th degrees. In 1609, after some expensive and not very successful attempts at settlement had been made, a new and more enlarged charter was given by the crown to the first colony, in which the king granted to the "Treasurer and Company of Adventurers of the city of London for the first colony in Virginia," in absolute property, the lands extending along the sea-coast four hundred miles, and into the land throughout from sea to sea. This charter, which is a part of the special verdict in this cause, was annulled, so far as respected the rights of the company, by the judgment of the court of king's bench, on a writ of *quo warranto*; but the whole effect allowed to this judgment was, to revest in the crown the powers of government, and the title to the lands within its limits.

At the solicitation of those who held under the grant to the second or northern colony, a new and more enlarged charter was granted to the Duke of Lenox and others, in 1620, who were denominated the Plymouth Company, conveying to them in absolute property all the lands between the 40th and 48th degrees of north latitude. Under this patent, New England has been in a great measure settled. The company conveyed to Henry Rosewell and others, in 1627, that territory which is now Massachusetts; and in 1628, a charter of incorporation, comprehending the powers of government, was granted to the purchasers. Great part of New England was granted by this company, which, at length, divided their remaining lands among themselves; and in 1635, surrendered their charter to the crown. A patent was granted to Gorges, for Maine, which was allotted to him in the division of property. All the grants made by the Plymouth Company, so far as we can learn, have been respected.

. . . .

Thus has our whole country been granted by the crown, while in the occupation of the Indians. These grants purport to convey the soil as well as the right of dominion to the grantees. In those governments which were denominated royal, where the right to the soil was not vested in individuals, but remained in the crown, or was vested in the colonial government, the king claimed and exercised the right of granting lands, and of dismembering the government, at his will. The grants made out of the two original colonies, after the resumption of their charters by the crown, are examples of this. The governments of New England, New York, New Jersey, Pennsylvania, Maryland, and a part of Carolina, were thus created. In all of them, the soil, at the time the grants were made, was occupied by the Indians. Yet almost every title within those governments is dependent on these grants. In some instances, the soil was conveyed by the crown, unaccompanied by the powers of government, as in the case of the northern neck of Virginia. It has never been objected to this, nor to any other similar grant, that the title as well as possession was in the Indians when it was made, and that it passed nothing on that account.

These various patents cannot be considered as nullities; nor can they be limited to a mere grant of the powers of government. A charter intended to convey political power only, would never contain words expressly granting the land, the soil and the waters. Some of them purport to convey the soil alone; and in those cases in which the powers of government, as well as the soil, are conveyed to individuals, the crown has always acknowledged itself to be bound by the grant. Though the power to dismember regal governments was asserted and exercised, the power to dismember proprietary governments was not claimed; and in some instances, even after the powers of government were revested in the crown, the title of the proprietors to the soil was respected. Charles II. was extremely anxious to acquire the property of Maine, but the grantees sold it to Massachusetts, and he did not venture to contest the right of that colony to the soil. The Carolinas were originally proprietary governments. In 1721, a revolution was effected by the people, who shook off their obedience to the proprietors, and declared their dependence immediately on the crown. The king, however, purchased the title of those who were disposed to sell. One of them, Lord Carteret, surrendered his interest in the government, but retained his title to the soil. That title was respected until the revolution, when it was forfeited by the laws of war.

Further proofs of the extent to which this principle has been recognized, will be found in the history of the wars, negotiations and treaties, which the different nations, claiming territory in America, have carried on, and held with each other. The contests between the cabinets of Versailles and Madrid, respecting the territory on the northern coast of the gulf of Mexico, were fierce and bloody; and continued, until the establishment of a Bourbon on the throne of Spain, produced such amicable dispositions in the two crowns, as to suspend or terminate them. Between France and Great Britain, whose discoveries as well as settlements were nearly contemporaneous, contests for the country, actually covered by the Indians, began, as soon as their settlements approached each other, and were continued until finally settled in the year 1763, by the treaty of Paris.

. . . .

These conflicting claims produced a long and bloody war, which was terminated by the conquest of the whole country east of the Mississippi. In the treaty of 1763, France ceded and guaranteed to Great Britain, all Nova Scotia or Acadie, and Canada, with their dependencies; and it was agreed, that the boundaries between the territories of the two nations, in America, should be irrevocably fixed by a line drawn from the source of the Mississippi, through the middle of that river and the lakes Maurepas and Ponchartrain, to the sea. This treaty expressly cedes, and has always been understood to cede, the whole country, on the English side of the dividing line, between the two nations, although a great and valuable part of it was occupied by the Indians. Great Britain, on her part, surrendered to France all her pretensions to the country west of the Mississippi. It has never been supposed, that she surrendered nothing, although she was not in actual possession of a foot of land. She surrendered all right to acquire the country; and any after-attempt to purchase it from the Indians, would have been considered and treated as an invasion of the territories of France. By the 20th article of the same treaty, Spain ceded Florida, with its dependencies, and all the country she claimed east or south-east of the Mississippi, to Great Britain. Great part of this territory also was in possession of the Indians. By a secret treaty, which was executed about the same time, France ceded Louisiana to Spain; and Spain has since retroceded the same country to France. At the time both of its cession and retrocession, it was occupied, chiefly, by the Indians. Thus, all the nations of Europe, who have acquired territory on this continent, have asserted in themselves, and have recognized in others, the exclusive right of the discoverer to appropriate the lands occupied by the Indians. Have the American states rejected or adopted this principle?

By the treaty which concluded the war of our revolution, Great Britain relinquished all claim, not only to the government, but to the "propriety and territorial rights of the United States," whose boundaries were fixed in the second article. By this treaty, the powers of government, and the right to soil, which had previously been in Great Britain, passed definitively to these states. We had before taken possession of them, by declaring independence; but neither the declaration of independence, nor the treaty confirming it, could give us more than that which we before possessed, or to which Great Britain was before entitled. It has never been doubted, that either the United States, or the several states, had a clear title to all the lands within the boundary lines described in the treaty, subject only to the Indian right of occupancy, and that the exclusive power to extinguish that right, was vested in that government which might constitutionally exercise it.

Virginia, particularly, within whose chartered limits the land in controversy lay, passed an act, in the year 1779, declaring her "exclusive right of pre-emption from the Indians, of all the lands within the limits of her own chartered territory, and that no person or persons whatsoever, have, or ever had, a right to purchase any lands within the same, from any Indian nation, except only persons duly authorized to make such purchase; formerly for the use and benefit of the colony, and lately for the commonwealth." The act then proceeds to annul all deeds made by Indians to individuals, for the private use of the purchasers. Without ascribing to this act the power of annulling vested rights, or admitting it to countervail the testimony furnished by the marginal note opposite to the title of the law, forbidding purchases from the Indians, in the revisals of the Virginia statutes, stating that law to be repealed, it may safely be considered as an unequivocal affirmance, on the part of Virginia, of the broad principle which had always been maintained, that the exclusive right to purchase from the Indians resided in the government. In pursuance of the same idea, Virginia proceeded, at the same session, to open her land-office, for the sale of that country which now constitutes Kentucky, a country, every acre of which was then claimed and possessed by Indians, who maintained their title with as much persevering courage as was ever manifested by any people.

The states, having within their chartered limits different portions of territory covered by Indians, ceded that territory, generally, to the United States, on conditions expressed in their deeds of cession, which demonstrate the opinion, that they ceded the soil as well as jurisdiction, and that in doing so, they granted a productive fund to the government of the Union. The lands in controversy lay within the chartered limits of Virginia, and were ceded with the whole country north-west of the river Ohio. This grant contained reservations and stipulations, which could only be made by the owners of the soil; and concluded with a stipulation, that "all the lands in the ceded territory, not reserved, should be considered as a common fund, for the use and benefit of such of the United States as have become, or shall become, members of the confederation," &c., "according to their usual respective proportions in the general charge and expenditure, and shall be faithfully and *bona fide* disposed of for that purpose, and for no other use or purpose whatsoever." The ceded territory was occupied by numerous and warlike tribes of Indians; but the exclusive right of the United States to extinguish their title, and to grant the soil, has never, we believe, been doubted.

. . . .

The United States, then, have unequivocally acceded to that great and broad rule by which its civilized inhabitants now hold this country. They hold, and assert in themselves, the title by which it was acquired. They maintain, as all others have maintained, that discovery gave an exclusive right to extinguish the Indian title of occupancy, either by purchase or by conquest; and gave also a right to such a degree of sovereignty, as the circumstances of the people would allow them to exercise. The power now possessed by the government of the United States to grant lands, resided, while we were colonies, in the crown or its grantees. The validity of the titles given by either has never been questioned in our courts. It has been exercised uniformly over territory in possession of the Indians. The existence of this power must negative the existence of any right which may conflict with and control it. An absolute title to lands cannot exist, at the same time, in different persons, or in different governments. An absolute, must be an exclusive title, or at least a title which excludes all others not compatible with it. All our institutions recognise the absolute title of the crown, subject only to the Indian right of occupancy, and recognise the absolute title of the crown to extinguish that right. This is incompatible with an absolute and complete title in the Indians.

We will not enter into the controversy, whether agriculturists, merchants and manufacturers, have a right, on abstract principles, to expel hunters from the territory they possess, or to contract their limits. Conquest gives a title which the courts of the conqueror cannot deny, whatever the private and speculative opinions of individuals may be, respecting the original justice of the claim which has been successfully asserted. The British government, which was then our government, and whose rights have passed to the United States, asserted a title to all the lands occupied by Indians, within the chartered limits of the British colonies. It asserted also a limited sovereignty over them, and the exclusive right of extinguishing the titles which occupancy gave to them. These claims have been maintained and established as far west as the river Mississippi, by the sword. The title to a vast portion of the lands we now hold, originates in them. It is not for the courts of this country to question the validity of this title, or to sustain one which is incompatible with it.

Although we do not mean to engage in the defence of those principles which Europeans have applied to Indian title, they may, we think, find some excuse, if not justification, in the character and habits of the people whose rights have been wrested from them. The title by conquest is acquired and maintained by force. The conqueror prescribes its limits. Humanity, however, acting on public opinion, has established, as a general rule, that the conquered shall not be wantonly oppressed, and that their condition shall remain as eligible as is compatible with the objects of the conquest. Most usually, they are incorporated with the victorious nation, and become subjects or citizens of the government with which they are connected. The new and old members of the society mingle with each other; the distinction between them is gradually lost, and they make one people. Where this incorporation is practicable, humanity demands, and a wise policy requires, that the rights of the conquered to property should remain unimpaired; that the new subjects should be governed as equitably as the old, and that confidence in their security should gradually banish the painful sense of being separated from their ancient connections, and united by force to strangers. When the conquest is complete, and the conquered inhabitants can be blended with the conquerors, or safely governed as a distinct people, public opinion, which not even the conqueror can disregard, imposes these restraints upon him; and he cannot neglect them, without injury to his fame, and hazard to his power.

But the tribes of Indians inhabiting this country were fierce savages, whose occupation was war, and whose subsistence was drawn chiefly from the forest. To leave them in possession of their country, was to leave the country a wilderness; to govern them as a distinct people, was impossible, because they were as brave and as high-spirited as they were fierce, and were ready to repel by arms every attempt on their independence. What was the inevitable consequence of this state of things? The Europeans were under the necessity either of abandoning the country, and relinquishing their pompous claims to it, or of enforcing those claims by the sword, and by the adoption of principles adapted to the condition of a people with whom it was impossible to mix, and who could not be governed as a distinct society, or of remaining in their neighborhood, and exposing themselves and their families to the perpetual hazard of being massacred. Frequent and bloody wars, in which the whites were not always the aggressors, unavoidably ensued. European policy, numbers and skill prevailed; as the white population advanced, that of the Indians necessarily receded; the country in the immediate neighborhood of agriculturists became unfit for them; the game fled into thicker and more unbroken forests, and the Indians followed. The soil, to which the crown originally claimed title, being no longer occupied by its ancient inhabitants, was parceled out according to the will of the sovereign power, and taken possession of by persons who claimed immediately from the crown, or mediately, through its grantees or deputies.

That law which regulates, and ought to regulate in general, the relations between the conqueror and conquered, was incapable of application to a people under such circumstances. The resort to some new and different rule, better adapted to the actual state of things, was unavoidable. Every rule which can be suggested will be found to be attended with great difficulty. However extravagant the pretension of converting the discovery of an inhabited country into conquest may appear; if the principle has been asserted in the first instance, and afterwards sustained; if a country has been acquired and held under it; if the property of the great mass of the community originates in it, it becomes the law of the land, and cannot be questioned. So too, with respect to the concomitant principle, that the Indian inhabitants are to be considered merely as occupants, to be protected, indeed, while in peace, in the possession of their lands, but to be deemed incapable of transferring the absolute title to others. However this restriction may be opposed to natural right, and to the usages of civilized nations, yet, if it be indispensable to that system under which the country has been settled, and be adapted to the actual condition of the two people, it may, perhaps, be supported by reason, and certainly cannot be rejected by courts of justice.

Another view has been taken of this question, which deserves to be considered. The title of the crown, whatever it might be, could be acquired only by a conveyance from the crown. If an individual might extinguish the Indian title, for his own benefit, or, in other words, might purchase it, still he could acquire only that title. Admitting their power to change their laws or usages, so far as to allow an individual to separate a portion of their lands from the common stock, and hold it in severalty, still it is a part of their territory, and is held under them, by a title dependent on their laws. The grant derives its efficacy from their will; and, if they choose to resume it, and make a different disposition of the land, the court of the United States cannot interpose for the protection of the title. The person who purchases lands from the Indians, within their territory, incorporates himself with them, so far as respects the property purchased; holds their title under their protection, and subject to their laws. If they annul the grant, we know of no tribunal which can revise and set aside the proceeding. We know of no principle which can distinguish this case from a grant made to a native Indian, authorizing him to hold a particular tract of land in severalty. As such a grant could not separate the Indian from his nation, nor give a title which our courts could distinguish from the title of his tribe, as it might still be conquered from, or ceded by his tribe, we can perceive no legal principle which will authorize a court to say, that different consequences are attached to this purchase, because it was made by a stranger. By the treaties concluded between the United States and the Indian nations, whose title the plaintiffs claim, the country comprehending the lands in controversy has been ceded to the United States, without any reservation of their title. These nations had been at war with the United States, and had an unquestionable right to annul any grant they had made to American citizens. Their cession of the country, without a reservation of this land, affords a fair presumption, that they considered it as of no validity. They ceded to the United States this very property, after having used it in common with other lands, as their own, from the date of their deeds to the time of cession; and the attempt now made, is to set up their title against that of the United States.

The proclamation issued by the king of Great Britain, in 1763, has been considered, and we think, with reason, as constituting an additional objection to the title of the plaintiffs. By that proclamation, the crown reserved under its own dominion and protection, for the use of the Indians, "all the land and territories lying to the westward of the sources of the rivers which fall into the sea from the west and north-west," and strictly forbade all British subjects from making any purchases or settlements whatever, or taking possession of the reserved lands. In Virginia, therefore, as well as elsewhere in the British dominions, the complete title of the crown to vacant lands was acknowledged. So far as respected the authority of the crown, no distinction was taken between vacant lands and lands occupied by the Indians. The title, subject only to the right of occupancy by the Indians, was admitted to be in the king, as was his right to grant that title. The lands, then, to which this proclamation referred, were lands which the king had a right to grant, or to reserve for the Indians.

According to the theory of the British constitution, the royal prerogative is very extensive, so far as respects the political relations between Great Britain and foreign nations. The peculiar situation of the Indians, necessarily considered, in some respects, as a dependent, and in some respects, as a distinct people, occupying a country claimed by Great Britain, and yet too powerful and brave not to be dreaded as formidable enemies, required, that means should be adopted for the preservation of peace; and that their friendship should be secured by quieting their alarms for their property. This was to be effected by restraining the encroachments of the whites; and the power to do this was never, we believe, denied by the colonies to the crown.

. . . .

Much reliance is also placed on the fact, that many tracts are now held in the United States, under the Indian title, the validity of which is not questioned. Before the importance attached to this fact is conceded, the circumstances under which such grants were obtained, and such titles are supported, ought to be considered. These lands lie chiefly in the eastern states. It is known that the Plymouth Company made many extensive grants, which, from their ignorance of the country, interfered with each other. It is also known, that Mason, to whom New Hampshire, and Gorges, to whom Maine was granted, found great difficulty in managing such unwieldy property. The country was settled by emigrants, some from Europe, but chiefly from Massachusetts, who took possession of lands they found unoccupied, and secured themselves in that possession by the best means in their power. The disturbances in England, and the civil war and revolution which followed those disturbances, prevented any interference on the part of the mother country, and the proprietors were unable to maintain their title. In the meantime, Massachusetts claimed the country and governed it. As her claim was adversary to that of the proprietors, she encouraged the settlement of persons made under her authority, and encouraged, likewise, their securing themselves in possession, by purchasing the acquiescence and forbearance of the Indians.

After the restoration of Charles II., Gorges and Mason, when they attempted to establish their title, found themselves opposed by men, who held under Massachusetts, and under the Indians. The title of the proprietors was resisted; and though, in some cases compromises were made, and in some, the opinion of a court was given ultimately in their favor, the juries found uniformly against them. They became wearied with the struggle, and sold their property. The titles held under the Indians, were sanctioned by length of possession; but there is no case, so far as we are informed, of a judicial decision in their favor.

. . . .

After bestowing on this subject a degree of attention which was more required by the magnitude of the interest in litigation, and the able and elaborate arguments of the bar, than by its intrinsic difficulty, the court is decidedly of opinion, that the plaintiffs do not exhibit a title which can be sustained in the courts of the United States; and that there is no error in the judgment which was rendered against them in the district court of Illinois.

Judgment affirmed, with costs.

[c] Explanatory Notes and Questions

[*i*] *The Title Claims.* The two sides in the *McIntosh* case claimed their land through different chains of title. Johnson and Graham's lessee claimed through the tribes, arguing that England lacked authority under the Peace Treaty of 1763 to disturb titles granted to English citizens and that later Virginia legislation had not disturbed their interests. McIntosh argued that his title originated in the sovereign rights of England which had been legitimately taken over as part of the spoils of the Revolutionary War by the individual states and then by the United States. The Supreme Court made it clear that any title claims arising out of the supposed sovereign authority of tribes over land in their possession were at risk and that, once the various states

had ceded to the central government their claims to the western territories, control over the disposition of property in the territories rested with Congress and the President.

Title conflicts are typically resolved quite differently from the *McIntosh* dispute. In order to place the world on notice of a land title change, written instruments, or *deeds*,[13] which describe the transfer are recorded and indexed in centralized public offices. Anyone dealing with land is presumed to know the contents of the recorded deeds related to the parcel in question. The recording system makes it difficult for a seller to transfer property to A, and then fraudulently sell the same parcel later to B. A, upon recording the deed, will be unaffected by B's claim. It is presumed that B will find A's deed by making the appropriate search in the recording system's records. B, having failed to make the search, and having proceeded with the purchase, will not be able to obtain relief from A, but will be able to sue the seller who fraudulently sold the land a second time, assuming B can find and recover money from the nefarious soul.

In the *McIntosh* setting, the land transfer system did not work quite the same way. Two chains of title, each claimed by parties to the case to be *the* authentic chain, developed side by side, as if in different recording systems. Everyone argued they were acting in good faith, though the persons buying from the tribes knew, after vainly seeking redress in Congress for many years, that they were in troubled waters. While the Supreme Court probably had to select one of the chains simply so everyone would know what the rules of the game were, was there anything inherently "better" or "more just" about one chain or the other? The Supreme Court wrote, p. 13 above, that the "Indian inhabitants are to be considered merely as occupants, to be protected, indeed, while in peace, in the possession of their lands, but to be deemed incapable of transferring the absolute title to others." Does this suggest that even if the plaintiffs' titles were flawed, their right to possession should have been upheld? If you believe that the Court was correct in relying upon the sovereign authority of the United States as the basis for resolving the title conflict, should the sovereign decide to uphold the earliest arising title claim made by a private party? Was the Supreme Court in a position to do this? What of Congress? Should the debate have been over the scope of the discovery principle or over the appropriate powers of courts and legislatures to resolve land disputes?

[*ii*]   *The Meaning of Possessory Interests.* Many of you may assume that having possession of something is the same as owning it. The old saw about possession being nine-tenths of the law speaks accurately to many situations. But the fact that possession and ownership frequently coalesce does not mean they are the same. Parties in possession of an asset do not always have full dominion and control over it. Trustees holding an asset for the benefit of a minor are limited in what they may do. Tenants may not sell the apartment building in which they live. A thief may be obligated to return stolen property to its rightful owners.

In the *McIntosh* setting, the government was said to have the sovereign right to full ownership of the land, subject to tribal possessory interests. The tribal interests were terminable at the will of the sovereign. McIntosh, a claimant tracing title to the sovereign, was the instrument by which the tribal possessory claims were terminated. But all this is not to say that the tribal possessory interest was without any content. The Supreme Court was quite careful to note that Johnson and Graham's lessee did own something prior to the sale to McIntosh. It just turned out that this "something" was only what the tribe had, and what the tribe had was subject to termination by the sovereign. Though tribal possessory interests were terminated over most of the United States

---

[13] When a deed transfers title from the federal government to a private party, it is often called a *patent.*

during the nineteenth century, much of the land within present day reservations is still held in *McIntosh* form. In addition, many recent Native American land claim cases involved a demand that tribal possessory rights, not full title, be restored on the ground that Indian title—the possessory rights left with tribes after *McIntosh*—were unlawfully terminated.

So if a native community retains possession of land, what may that community do? May the tribal government arrest and try a non-member of the community who breaks tribal law? May it require non-members to pay taxes on goods purchased on tribal lands? May it open a gambling house in a state that does not allow gambling? Can you think of other similar sorts of problems?

[iii] ***Long Term Possession and Ownership Claims.*** Near the end of his opinion, Justice Marshall noted that certain land claims rooted in tribal possessory rights "were sanctioned by length of possession." It is in fact possible for persons in possession of land for a long time to eventually claim ownership rights. The doctrinal basis for such claims, known as *adverse possession* or *prescription*,[14] will be studied in the second part of this chapter. Adverse possession rules emerge from state statutes which require that property title disputes must be brought before the courts within a certain period of time or be forever lost. These *statutes of limitation*, or laws setting a time limit on the bringing of lawsuits, permit parties behaving as if they owned property to successfully claim title if the "true" owner does nothing for the period set by the statute. Was Marshall referring to adverse possession in his opinion? And if he was, why couldn't Johnson and Graham's lessee claim the benefits of such a rule? May individuals adversely possess land against federal or state governments?

[iv] ***Organizing the Territories and the Respective Powers of the Federal and State Governments.*** The *McIntosh* case was, in one sense, a simple historical sketch about the spoils of war. The United States claimed title under authority obtained by the sword from England. But the case is not as simple as it may seem. For example, define the "property" relationship between the United States, the State of Illinois, and the Wabash tribes. Did Illinois have any role to play in *McIntosh*? What is presently Illinois was part of the Indiana Territory when the area was first organized in 1800. The Illinois Territory was established in 1809 and Illinois became a state in 1818, the year McIntosh alleged he first went into possession of the land he claimed. Suppose Illinois passed a statute in 1818 declaring that all prior titles granted to American or British subjects by the Illinois and Wabash tribes were valid and superior to the titles of those claiming under later deeds from the United States. Would the Supreme Court have validated such a statute? What impact might the Constitution have? Before reading the *Cherokee Cases*, look at these clauses in the Constitution: the Supremacy Clause, Article VI, Clause [2]; the Indian Commerce Clause, Article I, Section 8, Clause [3]; and the Territories Clause, Article IV, Section 3, Clause [2].

[d]   Some Thoughts on the Significance of *Johnson v. McIntosh*

In the notes before the *Johnson v. McIntosh* opinion, I suggested that many of the men founding the nation were nurtured on a set of political beliefs that closely integrated concepts of citizenship and property. Noting with displeasure both the tight control exercised by European monarchical systems of governance and the disorder created by the gradual demise of such a system in the colonies, the founders wished to establish a new vision of political stability by relying both upon

---

[14] *Adverse possession* deals with claims over full title to a piece of land. *Prescription* deals with claims to easements, usually rights of way like roads, paths, sidewalks and driveways.

a structure of government giving no particular power block a monopoly on control and upon the civic responsibility of those participating in governing the nation. Property, they thought, provided something more than a stake in the action. It created a sense of responsibility, a concern about the stability of the government, and a lack of dependence on others, all crucial characteristics of an intelligent, voting population.

Parts of this theory, especially those dealing with the political rights of working but landless men, began to break down early in the nineteenth century. But any theory relying upon wealth as a basis for categorizing political rights created winners and losers. Those lacking property were left outside the political process. Some propertied men welcomed that outcome as one that guaranteed the long term protection of their wealth. Women, presumed destined to marry and thereby become dependent souls, the propertyless lower classes and slaves could not participate in the political process. While Native Americans—"dependent" nations, in the language of Chief Justice Marshall—were deemed unworthy of political rights, their claimed right to govern themselves using institutions similar to but separate from the United States, raised fundamental questions for our young nation.

Johnson v. McIntosh was the first important case about native property claims to reach the Supreme Court. It has set the tone for hundreds of cases decided in the succeeding 175 years. Begin your review of the litigation by exploring the meaning of the central tenet of the case—the discovery principle. "Discovery," Marshall wrote, "gave title to the government by whose subjects, or by whose authority, it was made, against all other European governments, which title might be consummated by possession." Once the colonial era ended, the states, followed by the Articles of Confederation and Constitutional United States, became the successors in interest to those European sovereignties "discovering" these already occupied shores.

"Consummated by possession" is a meaningful and important phrase. For those at war, force of arms would do the trick. Treaties of cession, which usually ended up in the form of statutes subject to later amendment by Congress, followed by occupancy by an agent of the United States, also served to consummate possession. Indeed, throughout the nineteenth century, the United States paid careful attention to the need to terminate so-called "Indian title" prior to opening western lands for settlement. Before statutes granting railroads and canal companies title to vast areas of the west or allowing citizens to claim lands were adopted, Congress routinely passed statutes terminating Indian title in whatever lands were being transferred into private hands. To this day, those lands still occupied by Native Americans are usually nothing more than territories where Indian title has never been terminated.

There was no obvious source of law to support Marshall's reliance on the discovery principle in *Johnson v. McIntosh*. With the exception of the non-intercourse acts, which barred purchase of lands by private parties without government approval, statutes on the issues did not really exist. The Constitution had clauses about commerce with the Indians and governance of the territories, but nothing in the Constitution told him which lands were owned by the United States or its successors in interest and which were not. The Articles of Confederation contained hopelessly vague language about the relationships between the central, state, and native governments.[15] Marshall had to resolve the case by creating some sort of federal common law rule.

---

[15] Section 4 of Article IX of the Articles of Confederation provided:

　　The United States, in Congress assembled, shall have the sole and exclusive right and power of . . . regulating the trade and managing of all affairs with the Indians, not members of any of the States; provided that the legislative right of any State, within its own limits, be not infringed or violated . . . .

Despite the apparent freedom to use whatever basis for rule making he wished, Marshall had little room within which to maneuver. The political reality of the time obviously precluded a decision that would return the land then occupied by the United States to those claiming under a chain of title beginning with indigenous peoples. All that was open to the exercise of judicial authority was some determination of the scope of authority the government had over those natives living in peace, the realm of sovereignty, if any, to be left to the Native Americans, and the nature of the governmental authority—federal, state, or local—that would have primary responsibility for implementing these policies.

While Marshall began to explore these governance questions in *Johnson*, he was not compelled to fully explicate his views until the *Cherokee Cases* were before him. *Johnson* does tell us that federal chains of title took priority over chains originating in ownership by tribes. And we also know that a native people occupying land under Indian title had something of potential value. As long as their right of occupancy was not terminated, they maintained possessory interests. Marshall also told us that tribal possession had some meaning, for white people claiming to hold Indian title must make recourse to tribal remedies, not to the courts of the United States, to protect their interests.

Before going on to the *Cherokee Cases*, think about Marshall's precatory language—that is, his wishful thinking language—in *McIntosh* about how those indigenous people living in peace should be treated. Where peace reins, Marshall wrote, p. 13 above, that conquered peoples often

> are incorporated with the victorious nation, and become subjects or citizens of the government with which they are connected. The new and old members of the society mingle with each other; the distinction between them is gradually lost, and they make one people. Where this incorporation is practicable, humanity demands, and a wise policy requires, that the rights of the conquered to property should remain unimpaired; that the new subjects should be governed as equitably as the old, and that confidence in their security should gradually banish the painful sense of being separated from their ancient connections, and united by force to strangers.

This phrasing has a Civic Republican cast. Part of the idea of governance held by those founding the nation—and Marshall was part of that group—was a sense of responsibility both for the nation and the dependent souls living within its boundaries. I don't want to overplay this card. Slaves don't fit into such a framework. Native Americans were also harshly treated at times. By the time of the Revolutionary War most Native American communities living on the east coast when the Europeans arrived had been moved west, killed off or ravaged by poverty and disease. Indian wars on the frontier were common in the decades after the revolution. But a claim may be made that Marshall tried to exercise a paternalistic sense of responsibility for the well being of the "peaceful" tribes living along the east coast willing to cede land, adopt American government structures and thereby subject themselves to the possibility of assimilation. In that sense he, and other Federalists, were in agreement with the Jeffersonian sentiments we have already explored. It was not until the founding generation lost its grasp on the reigns of power in 1828 when Andrew Jackson ascended to the presidency, that the political treatment of Native Americans approached its nadir.

It is this path from the somewhat paternalistic and protective regime of the Republicans and Federalists to the extremely harsh regime of the Jacksonian Democrats that will be explored next. Investigating this shift requires that we explore the way in which government power to deal with

---

The courts have never deciphered the meaning of this phrasing.

native claims was to be distributed among the various levels and branches of government in the then young United States. The *Cherokee Cases* will open that inquiry.

[2] Origins of the Trust Relationship: The Cherokee Removal Cases

[a] The Growth of Pressure to Move the Southeastern Tribes West

When Marshall wrote in *Johnson v. McIntosh* that Native Americans were "necessarily considered, in some respects, as a dependent, and in some respects, as a distinct people"[16] he was surely aware of the difficulties such an ambiguous status might cause both his Court and the tribes litigating before him. Though Georgia and other southern states had been seeking extinguishment of tribal possessory rights for some time, it was just about the time *McIntosh* was decided that the scope of the potential conflict over tribal rights began to emerge. Indeed, in the very year Marshall issued his now famous opinion in *McIntosh*, the Cherokees asserted that, "It is the fixed and unalterable determination of this nation never again to cede one foot more of our land."[17]

The Cherokee's resistance to further cessions surfaced in response to a Commission appointed by President Monroe to negotiate a treaty for the cession of the Cherokee lands to the United States. To re-emphasize their position, the Cherokees sent a delegation to Washington to see the President.

The Cherokee delegation was received at Washington in 1824 with diplomatic courtesy, and its representatives attended to as those of a foreign power. The Congressional Representatives of Georgia viewed the matter from the standpoint of their State. They accordingly remonstrated with the President, March 10, 1824, against the practice of showing diplomatic courtesy to the Cherokees. They said that too much time had been wasted, while the Indians were further than ever from removal. If a peaceable purchase of the Cherokee land could not be made, they demanded that the nation be peremptorily ordered to remove and be suitably indemnified for their pains.

Mr. Monroe replied in a message to Congress on March 30 that the United States had done its best in the past to carry out the agreement of 1802, and that the Government was under no obligation to use other means than peaceable and reasonable ones. Governor Troup entered his protest against the message on April 24, urging that Georgia had the sole right to the lands, and denying that the Indians were privileged to refuse when a cession was demanded. The Cherokees, for their part, held to their contention for national rights, appealing to the clause in the Declaration of Independence "that all men are created equal," and reiterating their determination to give up not an inch of their land. As far as concerned results, the Cherokees had the best of the argument. The effort to drive them west was given up for the time.[18]

---

[16] Johnson v. McIntosh, p. 14 above.

[17] U. Phillips, *Georgia & State Rights,* 2 ANNUAL REPORT OF THE AMERICAN HISTORICAL ASSOCIATION 69-74 (1902). [Hereinafter cited as Phillips.]

[18] *Id.* The agreement of 1802 mentioned by Phillips was contained in a cession of western land claims by Georgia. In return for the cession, the central government agreed to try to extinguish tribal land claims within Georgia. Section 4 of the agreement provided:

> That the United States shall at their own expense extinguish for the use of Georgia, as early as the same can be peaceably obtained on reasonable terms, the Indian title to the [lands] . . . ; for which several objects the President of the United States has directed that a treaty shall be immediately held with the Creeks, and that the United States shall in the same manner extinguish the Indian title to all the other lands within the State of Georgia.

The Cherokees' refusal to cede further land was in part the natural consequence of United States government policy. Since Jefferson's presidency, the southeastern tribes[19] had been encouraged to substitute a stable agricultural existence for nomadic and hunting customs. The very success of this policy "attached them to their lands, created in them a sense of property, and made the wild lands west of the Mississippi seem uninviting."[20] In 1827 the Cherokees adopted a constitution modeled after that of the United States and declared themselves an independent nation with complete sovereignty over their soil. This new "nation" was not a minor civilization. According to an 1825 census, the eastern Cherokee Nation numbered 13,563 "citizens," along with 220 white men and women who had married Cherokees, and 1,277 slaves.[21]

Georgia responded forcefully to the Cherokee declaration of independence. A series of statutes were enacted in 1828 and 1829 that distributed Cherokee lands among several counties in northwestern Georgia and extended the laws of Georgia over the Cherokee lands as of June 1, 1830. The Cherokee constitution, as well as all tribal laws and customs, were said to be null after that date. Delaying the effective date until 1830 provided the new President, Andrew Jackson, with some time to remove the Cherokees from Georgia and thereby avoid a constitutional crisis.

Jackson, like John Quincy Adams and James Monroe before him, believed that the Cherokees could not remain permanently in Georgia. But:

[A] vital difference remained between their policy and that of Jackson. While Monroe and Adams had urged removal by every kind of inducement, officially they continued to treat the tribes as more or less sovereign nations and to respect their right to remain on the treaty lands. Whereas circumstances had permitted them to postpone decision on the Indian question, the intransigence of Georgia and the Cherokees did not allow Jackson such a luxury.[22] The Cherokee delegation in Washington received a letter from John Eaton, Jackson's Secretary of War, in April of 1829, declaring that the Cherokees did not have the right to set up an independent nation in Georgia. The Cherokees either had to move west or submit themselves to Georgia law. A bill was submitted to Congress setting aside territory west of the Mississippi for the Cherokees.

The Cherokees and their allies, mostly anti-Jacksonian politicians, along with Quakers and other religious groups in the Northeast, mounted an intensive lobbying and public relations effort against the proposed legislation. The crucial test vote came in the Senate when an amendment calling upon the federal government to respect the Cherokees' political and property rights

---

An Act To Ratify and Confirm Certain Articles of Agreement and Cession Entered into on the 24th Day of April, 1802. Between the Commissioners of the State of Georgia on the One Part, and the Commissioners of the United States on the Other Part, as found in Augustin S. Clayton, A compilation of the laws of the State of Georgia, Passed by the Legislature Since the Political Year 1800 to the Year 1810, Inclusive 48, 49-50 (1813).

[19] In addition to the Cherokees, significant areas of the Southeast were occupied by members of the Choctaw, Creek, Chickasaw and Seminole tribes.

[20] Joseph C. Burke, *The Cherokee Cases: A Study in Law, Politics, and Morality,* 21 Stan. L. Rev. 500, 503 (1969). [Hereinafter cited as Burke.]

[21] Phillips, note 17 above.

[22] Burke, note 20 above, at 504. Copyright 1969 by the Board of Trustees of the Leland Stanford Junior University. Reprinted by permission of the Stanford Law Review.

pending their decision on whether to move west failed by a 27-20 vote. The bill passed the House by only five votes and was signed by Jackson on May 28, 1830.[23]

Three other events made a constitutional conflict inevitable. First, in July of 1829, gold was discovered in the Cherokee lands. Hordes of fortune hunters descended on the area. Order was difficult, if not impossible, to maintain, even with federal troops present. Needless to say, the white miners had little sympathy for the tribal land claims. Second, the Cherokees, their legislative hopes dashed, hired William Wirt to pursue any available judicial remedy. Finally, the Georgia legislative, executive and judicial authorities, now with the support of federal legislation calling for the Cherokees' removal, asked for federal troops to be withdrawn and pledged never to obey any judicial decree calling into question their authority over the Cherokee lands. The resolution of Georgia authorities was made crystal clear when George Tassel, convicted by a Georgia court of a murder committed within Cherokee territory, was executed despite the issuance of a writ of error from the Supreme Court of the United States staying the execution pending review in the high court.[24]

Tassel's execution shortly before the Supreme Court arguments in *Cherokee Nation v. Georgia* underscored the difficulty of Wirt's position as counsel for the Cherokees. Wirt had served as Attorney General for both John Quincy Adams and James Monroe and was a political foe of Jackson. But he had a widespread reputation as a man of integrity, and was a strong believer in maintaining the authority of the federal courts. His concern about the potential impact of the Cherokee situation on the power of the Supreme Court led him to make widespread inquiries about the best way to present the tribal claims. Wirt contacted a number of prominent lawyers, asking for their views on the legal issues in the Cherokee situation. He even wrote a lengthy letter ruminating about the case to his friend Judge Dabney Carr of the Virginia Court of Appeals and asked Carr to show it to Chief Justice John Marshall![25]

The possibility of conflict between the Supreme Court on one side and Georgia and the President on the other prompted this request, for Wirt believed that the State would resist and the President would refuse to enforce a decision favorable to the Indians. Answers from the Chief Justice might prevent mischief, for if the Cherokees had "no hope from the Supreme Court," they would move west rather than submit to Georgia law. [Wirt asked] Carr . . . [to] tell Marshall that while no case was pending one might be started if the past opinions of the Supreme Court did not prevent it.[26]

Marshall, though evincing sympathy for the Cherokee's situation, declined to comment on the legal issues.

Wirt had few strategic options. The state courts were not an inviting forum. He could have waited for another criminal case to arise and taken any conviction to the Supreme Court, but that both removed his control over the timing of the litigation and subjected him to the difficulties

---

[23] *Id.* at 506-508. Burke noted that the legislation barely was adopted despite a large Jacksonian majority in the House. A number of northeastern Jacksonians, particularly from Quaker dominated areas of Pennsylvania, did not support him on this issue.

[24] Burke, note 20 above, at 512.

[25] The letter of June 21, 1830, may be found in 2 JOHN P. KENNEDY, MEMOIRS OF WILLIAM WIRT 253-258 (1849). Today such contacts with judges outside the normal course of litigation would subject an attorney to the possibility of severe discipline.

[26] Burke, note 20 above, at 510.

of *Tassel*-like obstacles.[27] He could have had John Ross, the Cherokee Chief, sue a Georgia state official in a lower federal court or bring suit directly in the Supreme Court on behalf of the tribe against the State of Georgia.[28] In either case, Wirt had to convince the courts that the Cherokees were a foreign state. Given the importance of the issue, and the likelihood that the Supreme Court would eventually have to hear the case, it was not surprising that Wirt opted to file his case as an original action in the High Court. Indeed, the fate of Tassel suggested that he had no other option. So in a supreme irony, the Cherokee Nation filed suit in the highest court of the very sovereign having the power, according to *Johnson v. McIntosh*, to dispossess them.

Argument of the case occurred in March, 1831, shortly after the papers were filed. Georgia, declining to submit to the "indignity" of making an appearance in the Supreme Court, did not send any counsel to argue at the hearing. Wirt and his co-counsel had the podium to themselves. Only four days after the arguments closed, Marshall read the decision of the Court; Justices Baldwin and Johnson delivered their concurring opinions at the same Court session. The dissents of Justices Thompson and Story, neither of whom were present when the other three opinions were read, appeared later.[29]

[b]   The United States Supreme Court Opinions

Cherokee Nation v. State of Georgia
United States Supreme Court
30 U.S. (5 Pet.) 1, 8 L. Ed. 25 (1831)

MARSHALL, Ch. J., delivered the opinion of the court. — This bill is brought by the Cherokee nation, praying an injunction to restrain the state of Georgia from the execution of certain laws of that state, which, as is alleged, go directly to annihilate the Cherokee as a political society, and to seize for the use of Georgia, the lands of the nation which have been assured to them by the United States, in solemn treaties repeatedly made and still in force.

If courts were permitted to indulge their sympathies, a case better calculated to excite them can scarcely be imagined. A people, once numerous, powerful, and truly independent, found by

---

[27] The reasons why Wirt's legal options were so limited are buried deep in the history of the limited jurisdiction of the federal courts. Look, for example, at the 11th Amendment to the Constitution, which declares that the judicial power of the federal courts does not extend "to any suit . . . commenced or prosecuted against one of the United States by Citizens of another State, or by Citizens or Subjects of any Foreign State." This provision barred a suit against the State of Georgia by a citizen of another state negatively affected by the attempts of Georgia to take control of Cherokee lands. But it was construed not to bar a case, such as a criminal prosecution, brought by Georgia. Thus, the federal courts could not have heard a case brought by George Tassel against Georgia, but they could hear an appeal of Georgia's criminal prosecution of Tassel.

[28] To continue the short lesson in federal court jurisdiction begun in the previous note, you can look at Article III, Section 2, Clause [1] of the United States Constitution which provides for suits between foreign citizens and a citizen of a state. Ross suing an official of Georgia (not the State of Georgia for that was barred by the 11th Amendment) would have raised jurisdictional issues about nationhood like those in the *Cherokee Nation* case, only at the trial court level. In addition, Article III, Section 2, Clause [2] grants original jurisdiction in the Supreme Court to hear suits between a foreign state and a state of the United States. Using this provision had the advantage of an immediate hearing before the Supreme Court. General jurisdiction to hear all cases arising under the constitution, laws and treaties of the United States did not exist at this time. Although the Constitution extended the federal judicial power to such cases, Congress had not yet enacted a statute implementing this power. Except for the original jurisdiction of the Supreme Court, Article III's definition of the judicial power has not been read as self-implementing.

[29] Burke, note 20 above, at 514.

our ancestors in the quiet and uncontrolled possession of an ample domain, gradually sinking beneath our superior policy, our arts and our arms, have yielded their lands, by successive treaties, each of which contains a solemn guarantee of the residue, until they retain no more of their formerly extensive territory than is deemed necessary to their comfortable subsistence. To preserve this remnant, the present application is made.

Before we can look into the merits of the case, a preliminary inquiry presents itself. Has this court jurisdiction of the cause? The third article of the constitution describes the extent of the judicial power. The second section closes an enumeration of the cases to which it is extended, with "controversies" "between a state or citizens thereof, and foreign states, citizens or subjects." A subsequent clause of the same section gives the supreme court original jurisdiction, in all cases in which a state shall be a party. The party defendant may then unquestionably be sued in this court. May the plaintiff sue in it? Is the Cherokee nation a foreign state, in the sense in which that term is used in the constitution? The counsel for the plaintiffs have maintained the affirmative of this proposition with great earnestness and ability. So much of the argument as was intended to prove the character of the Cherokees as a state, as a distinct political society, separated from others, capable of managing its own affairs and governing itself, has, in the opinion of a majority of the judges, been completely successful. They have been uniformly treated as a state, from the settlement of our country. The numerous treaties made with them by the United States, recognize them as a people capable of maintaining the relations of peace and war, of being responsible in their political character for any violation of their engagements, or for any aggression committed on the citizens of the United States, by any individual of their community. Laws have been enacted in the spirit of these treaties. The acts of our government plainly recognise the Cherokee nation as a state, and the courts are bound by those acts.

A question of much more difficulty remains. Do the Cherokees constitute a *foreign* state in the sense of the constitution? The counsel have shown conclusively, that they are not a state of the Union, and have insisted that, individually, they are aliens, not owing allegiance to the United States. An aggregate of aliens composing a state must, they say, be a foreign state; each individual being foreign, the whole must be foreign.

This argument is imposing, but we must examine it more closely, before we yield to it. The condition of the Indians in relation to the United States is, perhaps, unlike that of any other two people in existence. In general, nations not owing a common allegiance, are foreign to each other. The term *foreign* nation is, with strict propriety, applicable by either to the other. But the relation of the Indians to the United States is marked by peculiar and cardinal distinctions which exist nowhere else. The Indian territory is admitted to compose a part of the United States. In all our maps, geographical treatises, histories and laws, it is so considered. In all our intercourse with foreign nations, in our commercial regulations, in any attempt at intercourse between Indians and foreign nations, they are considered as within the jurisdictional limits of the United States, subject to many of those restraints which are imposed upon our own citizens. They acknowledge themselves, in their treaties, to be under the protection of the United States; they admit, that the United States shall have the sole and exclusive right of regulating the trade with them, and managing all their affairs as they think proper; and the Cherokees in particular were allowed by the treaty of Hopewell, which preceded the constitution, "to send a deputy of their choice, whenever they think fit, to congress." Treaties were made with some tribes, by the state of New York, under a then unsettled construction of the confederation, by which they ceded all their lands to that state, taking back a limited grant to themselves, in which they admit their dependence.

Though the Indians are acknowledged to have an unquestionable, and heretofore unquestioned, right to the lands they occupy, until that right shall be extinguished by a voluntary cession to our government; yet it may well be doubted, whether those tribes which reside within the acknowledged boundaries of the United States can, with strict accuracy, be denominated foreign nations. They may, more correctly, perhaps, be denominated domestic dependent nations. They occupy a territory to which we assert a title independent of their will, which must take effect in point of possession, when their right of possession ceases. Meanwhile, they are in a state of pupilage; their relation to the United States resembles that of a ward to his guardian. They look to our government for protection; rely upon its kindness and its power; appeal to it for relief to their wants; and address the president as their great father. They and their country are considered by foreign nations, as well as by ourselves, as being so completely under the sovereignty and dominion of the United States, that any attempt to acquire their lands, or to form a political connection with them, would be considered by all as an invasion of our territory and an act of hostility. These considerations go far to support the opinion, that the framers of our constitution had not the Indian tribes in view, when they opened the courts of the Union to controversies between a state or the citizens thereof and foreign states.

In considering this subject, the habits and usages of the Indians, in their intercourse with their white neighbors, ought not to be entirely disregarded. At the time the constitution was framed, the idea of appealing to an American court of justice for an assertion of right or a redress of wrong, had perhaps never entered the mind of an Indian or of his tribe. Their appeal was to the tomahawk, or to the government. This was well understood by the statesmen who framed the constitution of the United States, and might furnish some reason for omitting to enumerate them among the parties who might sue in the courts of the Union. Be this as it may, the peculiar relations between the United States and the Indians occupying our territory are such, that we should feel much difficulty in considering them as designated by the term foreign state, were there no other part of the constitution which might shed light on the meaning of these words. But we think that in construing them, considerable aid is furnished by that clause in the eighth section of the first article, which empowers congress to "regulate commerce with foreign nations, and among the several states, and with the Indian tribes." In this clause, they are as clearly contradistinguished, by a name appropriate to themselves, from foreign nations, as from the several states composing the Union. They are designated by a distinct appellation; and as this appellation can be applied to neither of the others, neither can the appellation distinguishing either of the others be, in fair construction, applied to them. The objects to which the power of regulating commerce might be directed, are divided into three distinct classes—foreign nations, the several states, and Indian tribes. When forming this article, the convention considered them as entirely distinct. We cannot assume that the distinction was lost, in framing a subsequent article, unless there be something in its language to authorize the assumption.

. . . .

The court has bestowed its best attention on this question, and, after mature deliberation, the majority is of opinion, that an Indian tribe or nation within the United States is not a foreign state, in the sense of the constitution, and cannot maintain an action in the courts of the United States.

A serious additional objection exists to the jurisdiction of the court. Is the matter of the bill the proper subject for judicial inquiry and decision? It seeks to restrain a state from the forcible exercise of legislative power over a neighboring people, asserting their independence; their right to which the state denies. On several of the matters alleged in the bill, for example, on the laws making it criminal to exercise the usual powers of self-government in their own country, by the Cherokee nation, this court cannot interpose; at least, in the form in which those matters are presented.

That part of the bill which respects the land occupied by the Indians, and prays the aid of the court to protect their possession, may be more doubtful. The mere question of right might, perhaps, be decided by this court, in a proper case, with proper parties. But the court is asked to do more than decide on the title. The bill requires us to control the legislature of Georgia, and to restrain the exertion of its physical force. The propriety of such an interposition by the court may be well questioned; it savors too much of the exercise of political power, to be within the proper province of the judicial department. But the opinion on the point respecting parties makes it unnecessary to decide this question.

If it be true, that the Cherokee nation have rights, this is not the tribunal in which those rights are to be asserted. If it be true, that wrongs have been inflicted, and that still greater are to be apprehended, this is not the tribunal which can redress the past or prevent the future. The motion for an injunction is denied.

JOHNSON, Justice.— In pursuance of my practice, in giving an opinion on all constitutional questions, I must present my views on this. With the morality of the case, I have no concern; I am called upon to consider it as a legal question.

The object of this bill is to claim the interposition of this court, as the means of preventing the state of Georgia, or the public functionaries of the state of Georgia, from asserting certain rights and powers over the country and people of the Cherokee nation. It is not enough, in order to come before this court for relief, that a case of injury, or of cause to apprehend injury, should be made out. Besides having a cause of action, the complainant must bring himself within that description of parties, who alone are permitted, under the constitution, to bring an original suit to this court. It is essential to such suit, that a state of this Union should be a party; so says the second member of the second section of the third article of the constitution; the other party must, under the control of the eleventh amendment, be another state of the Union, or a foreign state. In this case, the averment is, that the complainant is a foreign state.

. . . .

I cannot but think that there are strong reasons for doubting the applicability of the epithet "state," to a people so low in the grade of organized society as our Indian tribes most generally are. I would not here be understood as speaking of the Cherokees, under their present form of government; which certainly must be classed among the most approved forms of civil government. Whether it can be yet said to have received the consistency which entitles that people to admission into the family of nations is, I conceive, yet to be determined by the executive of these states. Until then, I must think, that we cannot recognise it as an existing state, under any other character than that which it has maintained hitherto as one of the Indian tribes or nations.

. . . .

In the very treaty of Hopewell, the language or evidence of which is appealed to, as the leading proof of the existence of this supposed state, we find the commissioners of the United States expressing themselves in these terms. "The commissioners plenipotentiary of the United States give peace to all the Cherokees, and receive them into the favor and protection of the United States on the following conditions." This is certainly the language of sovereigns and conquerors, and not the address of equals to equals. And again, when designating the country they are to be confined to, comprising the very territory which is the subject of this bill, they say, "Art. 4. The boundary allotted to the Cherokees for their hunting-grounds" shall be as therein described. Certainly, this is the language of concession on our part, not theirs; and when the full bearing and effect of those words, "for their hunting-grounds," is considered, it is difficult to think, that they were then regarded as a state, or even intended to be so regarded. It is clear, that it was intended to give them no other rights over the territory than what were needed by a race of hunters; and it is not easy to see, how their advancement beyond that state of society could ever have been promoted, or, perhaps, permitted, consistently with the unquestioned rights of the states, or United States, over the territory within their limits. The preemptive right, and exclusive right of conquest in case of war, was never questioned to exist in the states, which circumscribed the whole or any part of the Indian grounds or territory. To have taken it from them by direct means, would have been a palpable violation of their rights. But every advance, from the hunter state to a more fixed state of society, must have a tendency to impair that pre-emptive right, and ultimately to destroy it altogether, both by increasing the Indian population, and by attaching them firmly to the soil. The hunter state bore within itself the promise of vacating the territory, because when game ceased, the hunter would go elsewhere to seek it. But a more fixed state of society would amount to a permanent destruction of the hope, and, of consequence, of the beneficial character of the pre-emptive right.

But it is said, that we have extended to them the means and inducement to become agricultural and civilized. It is true, and the immediate object of that policy was so obvious, as probably to have intercepted the view of ulterior consequences. Independently of the general influence of humanity, these people were restless, warlike, and signally cruel in their irruptions, during the revolution. The policy, therefore, of enticing them to the arts of peace, and to those improvements which war might lay desolate, was obvious; and it was wise, to prepare them for what was probably then contemplated, to wit, to incorporate them in time into our respective governments; a policy which their inveterate habits and deep-seated enmity has altogether baffled. But the project of ultimately organizing them into states, within the limits of those states which had not ceded or should not cede to the United States the jurisdiction over the Indian territory within their bounds, could not possibly have entered into the contemplation of our government. Nothing but express authority from the states could have justified such a policy, pursued with such a view.

. . . .

However, I will enlarge no more upon this point; because I believe, in one view, and in one only, if at all, they are or may be deemed a state, though not a sovereign state, at least, while they occupy a country within our limits. Their condition is something like that of the Israelites, when inhabiting the deserts. Though without land that they can call theirs in the sense of property, their right of personal self-government has never been taken from them; and such a form of government may exist, though the land occupied be in fact that of another. The right to expel them may exist in that other, but the alternative of departing, and retaining the right of self-government, may exist in them. And such they certainly do possess; it has never been questioned, nor any attempt made at subjugating them as a people, or restraining their personal liberty, except as to their land and trade . . . . But in no sense can they be deemed a foreign state, under the judiciary article.

. . . .

But had I been sitting alone in this cause, I should have waived the consideration of personal description altogether; and put my rejection of this motion upon the nature of the claim set up, exclusively. I cannot entertain a doubt, that it is one of a political character altogether, and wholly unfit for the cognisance of a judicial tribunal. There is no possible view of the subject, that I can perceive, in which a court of justice can take jurisdiction of the questions made in the bill. The substance of its allegations may be thus set out. That the complainants have been, from time immemorial, lords of the soil they occupy. That the limits by which they hold it have been solemnly designated and secured to them by treaty, and by laws of the United States. That within those limits, they have rightfully exercised unlimited jurisdiction, passing their own laws and administering justice in their own way. That in violation of their just rights, so secured to them, the state of Georgia has passed laws, authorizing and requiring the executive and judicial powers of the state to enter their territory and put down their public functionaries. That in pursuance of those laws the functionaries of Georgia have entered their territory with an armed force, and put down all powers legislative, executive and judicial, exercised under the government of the Indians.

What does this series of allegations exhibit, but a state of war, and the fact of invasion? They allege themselves to be a sovereign independent state, and set out that another sovereign state has, by its laws, its functionaries, and its armed force, invaded their state and put down their authority. This is war, in fact; though not being declared with the usual solemnities, it may perhaps be called war in disguise. And the contest is distinctly a contest for empire. It is not a case of *meum* and *tuum*, in the judicial, but in the political sense. Not an appeal to laws, but to force. A case in which a sovereign undertakes to assert his right upon his sovereign responsibility; to right himself, and not to appeal to any arbiter but the sword, for the justice of his cause . . . . In the exercise of sovereign right, the sovereign is sole arbiter of his own justice. The penalty of wrong is war and subjugation.

But there is still another ground, in this case, which alone would have prevented me from assuming jurisdiction; and that is, the utter impossibility of doing justice, at least, even-handed justice, between the parties. As to restoring the complainant to the exercise of jurisdiction, it will be seen at once, that this is no case for the action of a court; and as to quieting him in possession of the soil, what is the case on which the complainant would have this court to act? Either the Cherokee nation are a foreign state, or they are not. If they are not, then they cannot come here; and if they are, then how can we extend our jurisdiction into their country?

. . . .

I vote for rejecting the motion.

BALDWIN, Justice.— As jurisdiction is the first question which must arise in every cause, I have confined my examination of this, entirely to that point, and that branch of it which relates to the capacity of the plaintiffs to ask the interposition of this court. I concur in the opinion of the court, in dismissing the bill, but not for the reasons assigned. In my opinion, there is no plaintiff in this suit; and this opinion precludes any examination into the merits of the bill, or the weight of any minor objections. My judgment stops me at the threshold, and forbids me to examine into the acts complained of.

As the reasons for the judgment of the court seem to me more important than the judgment itself, in its effects on the peace of the country, and the condition of the complainants, and as I stand alone on one question of vital concern to both; I must give my reasons in full. The opinion of this court is of high authority in itself; and the judge who delivers it has a support as strong in moral influence over public opinion, as any human tribunal can impart. The judge, who stands alone in decided dissent on matters of the infinite magnitude which this case presents, must sink under the continued and unequal struggle; unless he can fix himself by a firm hold on the constitution and laws of the country. He must be presumed to be in the wrong, until he proves himself to be in the right. Not shrinking even from this fearful issue, I proceed to consider the only question which I shall ever examine in relation to the rights of Indians to sue in the federal courts, until convinced of my error in my present convictions.

. . . .

Indians have rights of occupancy to their lands, as sacred as the fee-simple, absolute title of the whites; but they are only rights of occupancy, incapable of alienation, or being held by any other than common right, without permission from the government . . . . In the case of *Johnson v. McIntosh*, the nature of the Indian title to lands on this continent, throughout its whole extent, was most ably and elaborately considered; leading to conclusions satisfactory to every jurist, clearly establishing that, from the time of discovery under the royal government, the colonies, the states, the confederacy and this Union, their tenure was the same occupancy, their rights occupancy, and nothing more; that the ultimate absolute fee, jurisdiction and sovereignty was in the government, subject only to such rights; that grants vested soil and dominion, and the powers of government, whether the land granted was vacant or occupied by Indians.

. . . .

If their jurisdiction within their boundaries has been unquestioned, until this controversy; if rights have been exercised, which are directly repugnant to those now claimed; the judicial power cannot divest the states of rights of sovereignty, and transfer them to the Indians, by decreeing them to be a nation, or foreign state, pre-existing and with rightful jurisdiction and sovereignty over the territory they occupy. This would reverse every principle on which our government have acted for fifty-five years; and force, by mere judicial power, upon the other departments of this government, and the states of this Union, the recognition of the existence of nations and states, within the limits of both, possessing dominion and jurisdiction paramount to the federal and state constitutions. It will be a declaration, in my deliberate judgment, that the sovereign power of the people of the United States and Union must hereafter remain incapable of action over territory to which their rights in full dominion have been asserted with the most rigorous authority, and bow to a jurisdiction hitherto unknown; unacknowledged by any department of the government; denied by all, through all time; unclaimed till now; and now declared to have been called into exercise, not by any change in our constitution, the laws of the Union or the states; but pre-existent and paramount over the supreme law of the land.

I disclaim the assumption of a judicial power so awfully responsible. No assurance or certainty of support in public opinion can induce me to disregard a law so supreme; so plain to my judgment and reason. Those who have brought public opinion to bear on this subject, act under a mere moral responsibility; under no oath, which binds their movements to the straight and narrow line drawn by the constitution. Politics or philanthropy may impel them to pass it; but when their objects can be effectuated only by this court, they must not expect its members to diverge from it, when they cannot conscientiously take the first step, without breaking all the high obligations under which they administer the judicial power of the constitution. The account of my executorship cannot be settled before the court of public opinion or any human tribunal. None can release the balance which will accrue by the violation of my solemn conviction of duty.

THOMPSON, Justice. (*Dissenting*)—Entertaining different views of the questions now before us in this case, and having arrived at a conclusion different from that of a majority of the court, and considering the importance of the case and the constitutional principle involved in it; I shall proceed, with all due respect for the opinion of others, to assign the reasons upon which my own has been formed.

In the opinion pronounced by the court, the merits of the controversy between the state of Georgia and the Cherokee Indians have not been taken into consideration. The denial of the application for an injunction has been placed solely on the ground of want of jurisdiction in this court to grant the relief prayed for. It became, therefore, unnecessary to inquire into the merits of the case. But thinking as I do, that the court has jurisdiction of the case, and may grant relief, at least, in part; it may become necessary for me, in the course of my opinion, to glance at the merits of the controversy; which I shall, however, do very briefly, as it is important only so far as relates to the present application.

Before entering upon the examination of the particular points which have been made and argued, and for the purpose of guarding against any erroneous conclusions, it is proper that I should state, that I do not claim for this court, the exercise of jurisdiction upon any matter properly falling under the denomination of political power. Relief to the full extent prayed by the bill may be beyond the reach of this court. Much of the matter therein contained, by way of complaint, would seem to depend for relief upon the exercise of political power; and as such, appropriately devolving upon the executive, and not the judicial, department of the government. This court can grant relief so far only as the rights of person or property are drawn in question, and have been infringed.

It would very ill become the judicial station which I hold, to indulge in any remarks upon the hardship of the case, or the great injustice that would seem to have been done to the complainants, according to the statement in the bill, and which, for the purpose of the present motion, I must assume to be true. If they are entitled to other than judicial relief, it cannot be admitted, that in a government like ours, redress is not to be had in some of its departments; and the responsibility for its denial must rest upon those who have the power to grant it. But believing as I do, that relief to some extent falls properly under judicial cognisance, I shall proceed to the examination of the case . . . .

. . . .

That a state of this Union may be sued by a foreign state, when a proper case exists and is presented, is too plainly and expressly declared in the constitution, to admit of doubt; and the first inquiry is, whether the Cherokee nation is a foreign state, within the sense and meaning of the constitution . . . . Every nation that governs itself, under what form soever, without any dependence on a foreign power, is a sovereign state. Its rights are naturally the same as those of any other state . . . . It is sufficient, if it be really sovereign and independent; that is, it must govern itself by its own authority and laws. We ought, therefore, to reckon in the number of sovereigns those states that have bound themselves to another more powerful, although by an unequal alliance. The conditions of these unequal alliances may be infinitely varied; but whatever they are, provided the inferior ally reserves to itself the sovereignty or the right to govern its own body, it ought to be considered an independent state. Consequently, a weak state, that, in order to provide for its safety, places itself under the protection of a more powerful one, without stripping itself of the right of government and sovereignty, does not cease, on this account, to be placed among the sovereigns who acknowledge no other power

. . . .

Testing the character and condition of the Cherokee Indians by these rules, it is not perceived how it is possible to escape the conclusion, that they form a sovereign state. They have always been dealt with as such by the government of the United States; both before and since the adoption of the present constitution.

. . . .

They have never been, by conquest, reduced to the situation of subjects to any conqueror, and thereby lost their separate national existence, and the rights of self-government, and become subject to the laws of the conqueror. Whenever wars have taken place, they have been followed by regular treaties of peace, containing stipulations on each side, according to existing circumstances; the Indian nation always preserving its distinct and separate national character. And notwithstanding we do not recognize the right of the Indians to transfer the absolute title of their lands to any other than ourselves, the right of occupancy is still admitted to remain in them, accompanied with the right of self-government, according to their own usages and customs; and with the competency to act in a national capacity, although placed under the protection of the whites, and owing a qualified subjection, so far as is requisite for public safety. But the principle is universally admitted, that this occupancy belongs to them as a matter of right, and not by mere indulgence. They cannot be disturbed in the enjoyment of it, or deprived of it, without their free consent; or unless a just and necessary war should sanction their dispossession.

In this view of their situation, there is as full and complete recognition of their sovereignty, as if they were the absolute owners of the soil. The progress made in civilization by the Cherokee Indians cannot surely be considered as in any measure destroying their national or foreign character, so long as they are permitted to maintain a separate and distinct government; it is their political condition that constitutes their foreign character, and in that sense must the term foreign be understood, as used in the constitution. It can have no relation to local, geographical or territorial position. It cannot mean a country beyond sea. Mexico or Canada is certainly to be considered a foreign country, in reference to the United States. It is the political relation in which one government or country stands to another, which constitutes it foreign to the other. The Cherokee territory being within the chartered limits of Georgia, does not affect the question. When Georgia is spoken of as a state, reference is had to its political character, and not to boundary; and it is not perceived, that any absurdity or inconsistency grows out of the circumstance, that the jurisdiction and territory of the state of Georgia surround or extend on every side of the Cherokee territory. It may be inconvenient to the state, and very desirable, that the Cherokees should be removed; but it does not at all affect the political relation between Georgia and those Indians. Suppose, the Cherokee territory had been occupied by Spaniards, or any other civilized people, instead of Indians, and they had, from time to time, ceded to the United States portions of their lands, precisely in the same manner as the Indians have done, and in like manner, retained and occupied the part now held by the Cherokees, and having a regular government established there; would it not only be considered a separate and distinct nation or state, but a foreign nation, with reference to the state of Georgia or the United States?

. . . .

And what possible objection can lie to the right of the complainants to sustain an action? The treaties made with this nation purport to secure to it certain rights. These are not gratuitous obligations assumed on the part of the United States. They are obligations founded upon a consideration paid by the Indians, by cession of part of their territory. And if they, as a nation, are competent to make a treaty or contract, it would seem to me, to be a strange inconsistency, to deny to them the right and the power to enforce such a contract. And where the right secured by such a treaty forms a proper subject for judicial cognisance, I can perceive no reason why this court has not jurisdiction of the case. The constitution expressly gives to the court jurisdiction, in all cases of law and equity arising under treaties made with the United States. No suit will lie against the United States, upon such treaty, because no possible case can exist, where the United States can be sued. But not so with respect to a state: and if any right secured by treaty has been violated by a state, in a case proper for judicial inquiry, no good reason is perceived, why an action may not be sustained for violation of a right secured by treaty, as well as by contract under any other form. The judiciary is certainly not the department of the government authorized to enforce all rights that may be recognized and secured by treaty. In many instances, these are mere political rights with which the judiciary cannot deal. But when the question relates to a mere right of property, and a proper case can be made between competent parties, it forms a proper subject for judicial inquiry.

. . . .

The twelfth article of the treaty of Hopewell contains a full recognition of the sovereign and independent character of the Cherokee nation. To impress upon them full confidence in the justice of the United States respecting their interest, they have a right to send a deputy of their choice to congress. No one can suppose, that such a deputy was to take his seat as a member of congress, but that he would be received as the agent of that nation. It is immaterial, which such agent is called, whether minister, commissioner or deputy; he is to represent his principal. There could have been no fitness or propriety in any such stipulation, if the Cherokee nation had been considered in any way incorporated with the state of Georgia, or as citizens of that state.

. . . .

If this be a just view of . . . the character, state and condition of the Cherokee nation of Indians . . . we may safely conclude, that they are not citizens, and must, of course, be aliens: and if aliens in their individual capacities, it will be difficult to escape the conclusion, that, as a community, they constitute a foreign nation or state, and thereby become a competent party to maintain an action in this court, according to the express terms of the constitution.

. . . .

The next inquiry is, whether such a case is made out in the bill, as to warrant this court in granting any relief?

. . . .

That the Cherokee nation of Indians have, by virtue of . . . treaties, an exclusive right of occupancy of the lands in question, and that the United States are bound, under their guarantee, to protect the nation in the enjoyment of such occupancy, cannot, in my judgment, admit of a doubt; and that some of the laws of Georgia set out in the bill are in violation of, and in conflict with, those treaties, and the act of 1802, is, to my mind, equally clear. But a majority of the court having refused the injunction, so that no relief whatever can be granted, it would be a fruitless inquiry for me to go at large into an examination of the extent to which relief might be granted by this court, according to my own view of the case. I, certainly, as before observed, do not claim, as belonging to the judiciary, the exercise of political power; that belongs to another branch of the government. The protection and enforcement of many rights, secured by treaties, most certainly do not belong to the judiciary. It is only where the rights of persons or property are involved, and when such rights can be presented under some judicial form of proceedings, that courts of justice can interpose relief. This court can have no right to pronounce an abstract opinion upon the constitutionality of a state law. Such law must be brought into actual or threatened operation, upon rights properly falling under judicial cognisance, or a remedy is not to be had here.

The laws of Georgia, set out in the bill, if carried fully into operation, go the length of abrogating all the laws of the Cherokees, abolishing their government, and entirely subverting their national character. Although the whole of these laws may be in violation of the treaties made with this nation, it is probable, this court cannot grant relief to the full extent of the complaint. Some of them, however, are so directly at variance with these treaties and the laws of the United States, touching the rights of property secured to them, that I can perceive no objection to the application of judicial relief. The state of Georgia certainly could not have intended these laws as declarations of hostility, or wish their execution of them to be viewed, in any manner whatever, as acts of war; but merely as an assertion of what is claimed as a legal right: and in this light ought they to be considered by this court.

. . . .

Upon the whole, I am of opinion: 1. That the Cherokees compose a foreign state, within the sense and meaning of the constitution, and constitute a competent party to maintain a suit against the state of Georgia. 2. That the bill presents a case for judicial consideration, arising under the laws of the United States, and treaties made under their authority with the Cherokee nation, and which laws and treaties have been, and are threatened to be still further violated by the laws of the state of Georgia referred to in this opinion. 3. That an injunction is a fit and proper writ to be issued, to prevent the further execution of such laws, and ought, therefore, to be awarded. And I am authorized by my brother STORY to say, that he concurs with me in this opinion.

[c] Analysis of the Opinions

[i] *The Court Lineup.* The Supreme Court split three ways in *Cherokee Nation v. State of Georgia.* Although Justices Johnson and Baldwin concurred with Chief Justice Marshall's opinion, they had quite different views on some issues. Justice McLean, who did not write a separate opinion, agreed with the views of Chief Justice Marshall. Justice Thompson, with whom Justice Story agreed, wrote a dissent. The Court therefore voted 2-2-2 in the case.[30] Careful reading of the four opinions provides some fairly strong clues about the reasons for the divisive votes.

[ii] *Chief Justice Marshall's Opinion.* Chief Justice Marshall did not hide his views about Jackson's position on the Cherokees. The second and last paragraphs of his opinion suggest quite strongly that if the jurisdiction problems had been overcome, Marshall would have voted with the Cherokees on the merits of the case. He recognized that the tribes had "an unquestionable, and heretofore unquestioned, right to the lands they occupy, until that right shall be extinguished by a voluntary cession." Their existence as "domestic dependent nations" suggested a relation of "a ward to his guardian" in which the ward naturally looked to the guardian for protection. Such phrases were hardly designed to mollify those favoring the Cherokee Nation's removal to the west.

---

[30] The Court actually had seven members at the time this case was heard. Justice Duvall, however, was absent. The Court has not always had nine members as it does now. The Constitution does not establish the size of the Supreme Court. Congress has enacted statutes from time to time modifying the Court's size.

[*iii*]   *The Concurring Opinions.* When the case was being discussed among the judges privately in chambers, Justices Johnson and Baldwin must have known that the Court's votes were split 4-2 in favor of denying the Cherokee Nation the status of a foreign state for purposes of construing the Supreme Court's original jurisdiction, but 4-2 against the validity of Georgia's claim of authority over the Cherokees, should that issue ever be presented on the merits to the Court. That surely had something to do with their writing separate opinions, and strongly worded ones at that. Justice Baldwin even labeled himself as a dissenter, hardly the statement of a fully satisfied judge. Johnson and Baldwin both took the position that the Court lacked jurisdiction to hear the Cherokee claims, and that if the jurisdictional problems were avoided in another case, the Cherokees should still lose. Johnson believed that the Cherokee claim of independence placed them in a state of war with the United States. Baldwin used the opinion of Chief Justice Marshall in *Johnson v. McIntosh* to argue that sovereignty over the lands of the Cherokees rested originally with Georgia, and after the cession of lands to the central government by Georgia in 1802, with the United States.

[*iv*]   *Justice Thompson's Dissent.* Justice Thompson, though agreeing with Wirt that the Cherokees were a foreign state and that the treaties signed with the Cherokees gave them sovereign authority over their lands until a voluntary cession was made to the United States, wrote an opinion full of cautions. Thompson, like the rest of the Court, knew full well that any decision upholding the Cherokee's claims would be met with strong resistance by authorities in both Georgia and the White House. Perhaps he hoped to create some public support by placing the blame for any future conflict on the President. Or perhaps he hoped his opinion would serve as a warning to the Cherokees not to press their claims too far if they hoped to maintain the Court as an available option in the future.

[d]   Problems

[*i*]   *What is a Treaty?* The Cherokees claimed the benefit of the Treaty of Hopewell. Normally the United States only enters into treaties with foreign states. Does that mean that the Hopewell agreement really was not a treaty?

[*ii*]   *The Impact of a Treaty.* Suppose the United States enters into a treaty with a foreign state called Otherland requiring reduction in emission of green-house gases from electrical generating facilities. Also assume that the treaty says nothing about using courts to enforce its terms. If the United States violated the treaty, could a citizen of Otherland seek relief in a court of the United States? Suppose that the treaty with Otherland also contained a specific clause granting citizens of Otherland access to courts of the United States to enforce the treaty. If Congress refused to amend our federal court jurisdictional statutes to allow such law suits to be brought here, could the courts compel Congress to act? Suppose Congress ratified the treaty, but 20 years later adopted a statute altering its meaning. Could anyone prevent that by suing in a United States court? While the United States would presumably be subject to whatever internationally orchestrated penalties are established by the treaty or other sources of international law, doesn't it seem difficult to imagine that the power of Congress to legislate on the same subject is withdrawn by our accession to an international agreement? Does that mean that even if the Treaty of Hopewell was a treaty, Congress could change its terms whenever it wished?

[e]   Events Leading to *Worcester v. Georgia*

The Supreme Court was given a second opportunity to review the Cherokee situation due to an arrest occurring only one day after Wirt argued *Cherokee Nation v. State of Georgia* in the

Court. Invasions of the gold country in Georgia had gotten so out of hand during 1830 that even Georgia authorities moved to place some controls over movement of whites into the lands claimed by the Cherokees. In December, 1830, a state statute was enacted prohibiting whites from residing among the Cherokees without a license from the state of Georgia, unless they were agents of the United States government.

One week later the whole body of missionaries within the Cherokee country took a step that so enraged Governor Gilmer that he decided so to interpret the recent enactment that *they* might be brought within its operation. Their offense was [that] they had held a meeting at New Echota and, while exonerating themselves for meddling in politics, declared their conviction that the Cherokees as a people were averse to emigration and that the extension of Georgian jurisdiction would work "an immense and irreparable injury." Soon they were called upon to retract or remove. Refusal to do either brought about the arrest of three of their number—two ordained missionaries, S.A. Worcester and John Thompson, and one missionary teacher, Isaac Proctor. An application for a writ of habeas corpus was successful,[31] and when the case came up for hearing before the superior court for Gwinnett County, Judge Clayton (another of Wirt's relatives, but a man of confessedly different opinions upon the doctrine of State Rights), ordered the release of the prisoners, not upon the plea of their counsel that the late law was unconstitutional, but upon the assumption, that, by the indulgence of Georgia, they were exempt from its operation, because as dispensers of the civilization fund, they were nominally agents of the United States.[32]

But events did not end there.

The missionaries, who had deliberately courted prosecution in order to bring the question of Cherokee sovereignty before the Supreme Court, had tried to avoid this result by refusing to plead that they were federal officials. When Worcester and the other missionar[ies] still refused to leave the Indian country, the Governor persuaded President Jackson to deny that they were federal employees and to remove Worcester as Postmaster of New Echota. With these obstacles removed Georgia again arrested them and a state court in September convicted all the missionaries of violating the licensing law and sentenced them to four years of hard labor. Nine of them accepted pardons, but Worcester and Elizur Butler rejected offers of freedom in order to get the Cherokees their second day in court.[33]

The Supreme Court heard arguments in *Worcester v. Georgia* on February 20, 1832. Once again Georgia refused to send counsel to argue the case before the Supreme Court. Two weeks later the opinions were rendered.

---

[31] To say that a writ of habeas corpus was "successful" does not mean that the petitioner was released. It only means that the person being held against his will was brought before the court and given an opportunity to present reasons why his confinement should be ended. [Ed.]

[32] Abel, *The History of the Events Resulting in Indian Consolidation West of the Mississippi*, 1 AM. HIST. ASS'N FOR 1906, at 233, 396-401 (1908).

[33] Burke, note 20 above, at 519-520.

[f]   The United States Supreme Court Opinions

Samuel A. Worcester v. State of Georgia
United States Supreme Court
31 U.S. (6 Pet.) 515, 8 L. Ed. 483 (1832)

MARSHALL, Ch. J., delivered the opinion of the court.— This cause, in every point of view in which it can be placed, is of the deepest interest. The defendant is a state, a member of the Union, which has exercised the powers of government over a people who deny its jurisdiction, and are under the protection of the United States. The plaintiff is a citizen of the state of Vermont, condemned to hard labor for four years in the penitentiary of Georgia; under color of an act which he alleges to be repugnant to the constitution, laws and treaties of the United States. The legislative power of a state, the controlling power of the constitution and laws of the United States, the rights, if they have any, the political existence of a once numerous and powerful people, the personal liberty of a citizen, are all involved in the subject now to be considered.

. . . .

America, separated from Europe by a wide ocean, was inhabited by a distinct people, divided into separate nations, independent of each other, and of the rest of the world, having institutions of their own, and governing themselves by their own laws. It is difficult to comprehend the proposition, that the inhabitants of either quarter of the globe could have rightful original claims of dominion over the inhabitants of the other, or over the lands they occupied; or that the discovery of either, by the other, should give the discoverer rights in the country discovered, which annulled the pre-existing right of its ancient possessor. After lying concealed for a series of ages, the enterprise of Europe, guided by nautical science, conducted some of her adventurous sons into this western world. They found it in possession of a people who had made small progress in agriculture or manufactures, and whose general employment was war, hunting and fishing. Did these adventurers, by sailing along the coast, and occasionally landing on it, acquire for the several governments to whom they belonged, or by whom they were commissioned, a rightful property in the soil, from the Atlantic to the Pacific, or rightful dominion over the numerous people who occupied it? Or has nature, or the great Creator of all things, conferred these rights over hunters and fishermen, on agriculturists and manufacturers? But power, war, conquest, give rights, which, after possession, are conceded by the world; and which can never be controverted by those on whom they descend. We proceed, then, to the actual state of things, having glanced at their origin; because holding it in our recollection might shed some light on existing pretensions.

The great maritime powers of Europe discovered and visited different parts of this continent, at nearly the same time. The object was too immense for any one of them to grasp the whole; and the claimants were too powerful to submit to the exclusive or unreasonable pretensions of any single potentate. To avoid bloody conflicts, which might terminate disastrously to all, it was necessary for the nations of Europe to establish some principle which all would acknowledge, and which should decide their respective rights as between themselves. This principle, suggested by the actual state of things, was, "that discovery gave title to the government by whose subjects, or by whose authority, it was made, against all other European governments, which title might be consummated by possession." *Johnson v. McIntosh*, 8 Wheat. 573. This principle, acknowledged by all Europeans, because it was the interest of all to acknowledge it, gave to the nation making the discovery, as its inevitable consequence, the sole right of acquiring the soil and of making settlements on it. It was an exclusive principle, which shut out the right of competition among those who had agreed to it; not one which could annul the previous rights of those who had not agreed to it. It regulated the right given by discovery among the European discoverers; but could not affect the rights of those already in possession, either as aboriginal occupants, or as occupants by virtue of a discovery made before the memory of man. It gave the exclusive right to purchase, but did not found that right on a denial of the right of the possessor to sell. The relation between the Europeans and the natives was determined in each case, by the particular government which asserted and could maintain this pre-emptive privilege in the particular place. The United States succeeded to all the claims of Great Britain, both territorial and political; but no attempt, so far as is known, has been made to enlarge them. So far as they existed merely in theory, or were in their nature only exclusive of the claims of other European nations, they still retain their original character, and remain dormant. So far as they have been practically exerted, they exist in fact, are understood by both parties, are asserted by the one, and admitted by the other.

Soon after Great Britain determined on planting colonies in America, the king granted charters to companies of his subjects, who associated for the purpose of carrying the views of the crown into effect, and of enriching themselves. The first of these charters was made, before possession was taken of any part of the country. They purport, generally, to convey the soil, from the Atlantic to the South Sea. This soil was occupied by numerous and warlike nations, equally willing and able to defend their possessions. The extravagant and absurd idea, that the feeble settlements made on the sea-coast, or the companies under whom they were made, acquired legitimate power by them to govern the people, or occupy the lands from sea to sea, did not enter the mind of any man. They were well understood to convey the title which, according to the common law of European sovereigns respecting America, they might rightfully convey, and no more. This was the exclusive right of purchasing such lands as the natives were willing to sell. The crown could not be understood to grant what the crown did not affect to claim; nor was it so understood.

. . . .

The general views of Great Britain, with regard to the Indians, were detailed by Mr. Stuart, superintendent of Indian affairs, in a speech delivered at Mobile, in presence of several persons of distinction, soon after the peace of 1763. Towards the conclusion he says, "Lastly, I inform you that it is the king's order to all his governors and subjects, to treat Indians with justice and humanity, and to forbear all encroachments on the territories allotted to them; accordingly, all individuals are prohibited from purchasing any of your lands; but as you know that, as your white brethren cannot feed you when you visit them, unless you give them ground to plant, it is expected that you will cede lands to the king for that purpose. But whenever you shall be pleased to surrender any of your territories to his majesty, it must be done, for the future, at a public meeting of your nation, when the governors of the provinces, or the superintendent shall be present, and obtain the consent of all your people. The boundaries of your hunting-grounds will be accurately fixed, and no settlement permitted to be made upon them. As you may be assured that all treaties with your people will be faithfully kept, so it is expected that you, also, will be careful strictly to observe them."

The proclamation issued by the King of Great Britain, in 1763, soon after the ratification of the articles of peace, forbids the governors of any of the colonies to grant warrants of survey, or pass patents upon any lands whatever, which, not having been ceded to, or purchased by, us (the king), as aforesaid, are reserved to the said Indians, or any of them. The proclamation proceeds: "And we do further declare it to be our royal will and pleasure, for the present, as aforesaid, to reserve, under our sovereignty, protection and dominion, for the use of the said Indians, all the lands and territories lying to the westward of the sources of the rivers which fall into the sea, from the west and northwest as aforesaid; and we do hereby strictly forbid, on pain of our displeasure, all our loving subjects from making any purchases or settlements whatever, or taking possession of any of the lands above reserved, without our special leave and license for that purpose first obtained. And we do further strictly enjoin and require all persons whatever, who have, either wilfully or inadvertently, seated themselves upon any lands within the countries above described, or upon any other lands which, not having been ceded to, or purchased by us, are still reserved to the said Indians, as aforesaid, forthwith to remove themselves from such settlements."

. . . .

This was the settled state of things when the war of our revolution commenced. The influence of our enemy was established; her resources enabled her to keep up that influence; and the colonists had much cause for the apprehension, that the Indian nations would, as the allies of Great Britain, add their arms to hers. This, as was to be expected, became an object of great solicitude to congress. Far from advancing a claim to their lands, or asserting any right of dominion over them, congress resolved, "that the securing and preserving the friendship of the Indian nations appears to be a subject of the utmost moment to these colonies." The early journals of congress exhibit a most anxious desire to conciliate the Indian nations. Three Indian departments were established; and commissioners appointed in each, "to treat with the Indians, in their respective departments, in the name and on the behalf of the united colonies, in order to preserve peace and friendship with the said Indians, and to prevent their taking any part in the present commotions." The most strenuous exertions were made, to procure those supplies on which Indian friendships were supposed to depend; and everything which might excite hostility was avoided.

. . . .

During the war of the revolution, the Cherokees took part with the British. After its termination, the United States, though desirous of peace, did not feel its necessity so strongly as while the war continued. Their political situation being changed, they might very well think it advisable to assume a higher tone, and to impress on the Cherokees the same respect for congress which was before felt for the King of Great Britain. This may account for the language of the treaty of Hopewell. There is the more reason for supposing that the Cherokee chiefs were not very critical judges of the language, from the fact, that every one makes his mark; no chief was capable of signing his name. It is probable, the treaty was interpreted to them.

The treaty is introduced with the declaration, that "the commissioners plenipotentiary of the United States give peace to all the Cherokees, and receive them into the favor and protection of the United States of America, on the following conditions." When the United States gave peace, did they not also receive it? Were not both parties desirous of it? If we consult the history of the day, does it not inform us, that the United States were at least as anxious to obtain it as the Cherokees? We may ask further, did the Cherokees come to the seat of the American government to solicit peace; or, did the American commissioners go to them to obtain it? The word "give," then, has no real importance attached to it . . . . The third article acknowledges the Cherokees to be under the protection of the United States of America, and of no other power. This stipulation is found in Indian treaties, generally. It was introduced into their treaties with Great Britain; and may probably be found in those with other European powers. Its origins may be traced to the nature of their connection with those powers; and its true meaning is discerned in their relative situation.

The general law of European sovereigns, respecting their claims in America, limited the intercourse of Indians, in a great degree, to the particular potentate whose ultimate right of domain was acknowledged by the others. This was the general state of things, in time of peace. It was sometimes changed in war. The consequence was, that their supplies were derived chiefly from that nation, and their trade confined to it. Goods, indispensable to their comfort, in the shape of presents, were received from the same hand. What was of still more importance, the strong hand of government was interposed to restrain the disorderly and licentious from intrusions into their country, from encroachments on their lands, and from those acts of violence which were often attended by reciprocal murder. The Indians perceived in this protection only what was beneficial to themselves—an engagement to punish aggressions on them. It involved, practically, no claim to their lands—no dominion over their persons. It merely bound the nation to the British crown, as a dependent ally, claiming the protection of a powerful friend and neighbor, and receiving the advantages of that protection, without involving a surrender of their national character. This is the true meaning of the stipulation, and is, undoubtedly, the sense in which it was made. Neither the British government nor the Cherokees ever understood it otherwise.

The same stipulation, entered into with the United States, is undoubtedly to be construed in the same manner. They receive the Cherokee nation into their favor and protection. The Cherokees acknowledge themselves to be under the protection of the United States, and of no other power. Protection does not imply the destruction of the protected.

. . . .

The Indian nations were, from their situation, necessarily dependent on some foreign potentate, for the supply of their essential wants, and for their protection from lawless and injurious intrusions into their country. That power was naturally termed their protector. They had been arranged under the protection of Great Britain; but the extinguishment of the British power in their neighborhood, and the establishment of that of the United States in its place, led naturally to the declaration, on the part of the Cherokees, that they were under the protection of the United States, and of no other power. They assumed the relation with the United States, which had before subsisted with Great Britain. This relation was that of a nation claiming and receiving the protection of one more powerful; not that of individuals abandoning their national character, and submitting, as subjects, to the laws of a master.

. . . .

From the commencement of our government, Congress has passed acts to regulate trade and intercourse with the Indians, which treat them as nations, respect their rights, and manifest a firm purpose to afford that protection which treaties stipulate. All these acts, and especially that of 1802, which is still in force, manifestly consider the several Indian nations as distinct political communities, having territorial boundaries, within which their authority is exclusive, and having a right to all the lands within those boundaries, which is not only acknowledged, but guaranteed by the United States.

In 1819, Congress passed an Act for promoting those humane designs of civilizing the neighboring Indians, which had long been cherished by the executive. It enacts, "that, for the purpose of providing against the further decline and final extinction of the Indian tribes, adjoining to the frontier settlements of the United States, and for introducing among them the habits and arts of civilization, the President of the United States shall be, and he is hereby authorized, in every case where he shall judge improvement in the habits and condition of such Indians practicable, and that the means of instruction can be introduced, with their own consent, to employ capable persons, of good moral character, to instruct them in the mode of agriculture suited to their situation; and for teaching their children in reading, writing and arithmetic; and for performing such other duties as may be enjoined, according to such instructions and rules as the president may give and prescribe for the regulation of their conduct in the discharge of their duties." This act avowedly contemplates the preservation of the Indian nations as an object sought by the United States, and proposes to effect this object by civilizing and converting them from hunters into agriculturists. Though the Cherokees had already made considerable progress in this improvement, it cannot be doubted, that the general words of the act comprehend them. Their advance in the "habits and arts of civilization," rather encouraged perseverance in the laudable exertions still further to meliorate their condition. This act furnishes strong additional evidence of a settled purpose to fix the Indians in their country, by giving them security at home.

The treaties and laws of the United States contemplate the Indian territory as completely separated from that of the states; and provide that all intercourses with them shall be carried on exclusively by the government of the Union. Is this the rightful exercise of power, or is it usurpation?

. . . .

The Indian nations had always been considered as distinct, independent, political communities, retaining their original natural rights, as the undisputed possessors of the soil, from time immemorial, with the single exception of that imposed by irresistible power, which excluded them from intercourse with any other European potentate than the first discoverer of the coast of the particular region claimed; and this was a restriction which those European potentates imposed on themselves, as well as on the Indians. The very term "nation," so generally applied to them, means "a people distinct from others." The constitution, by declaring treaties already made, as well as those to be made, to be the supreme law of the land, has adopted and sanctioned the previous treaties with the Indian nations, and consequently, admits their rank among those powers who are capable of making treaties. The words "treaty" and "nation," are words of our own language, selected in our diplomatic and legislative proceedings, by ourselves, having each a definite and well-understood meaning. We have applied them to Indians, as we have applied them to the other nations of the earth; they are applied to all in the same sense.

Georgia, herself, has furnished conclusive evidence, that her former opinions on this subject concurred with those entertained by her sister states, and by the government of the United States. Various acts of her legislature have been cited in the argument, including the contract of session made in the year 1802, all tending to prove her acquiescence in the universal conviction that the Indian nations possessed a full right to the lands they occupied, until that right should be extinguished by the United States, with their consent; that their territory was separated from that of any state, within whose chartered limits they might reside, by a boundary line, established by treaties; that within their boundary, they possessed rights with which no state could interfere; and that the whole power of regulating the intercourse with them was vested in the United States. A review of these acts on the part of Georgia, would occupy too much time, and is the less necessary, because they have been accurately detailed in the argument at the bar. Her new series of laws, manifesting her abandonment of these opinions, appears to have commenced in December 1828.

. . . .

The Cherokee nation, then, is a distinct community, occupying its own territory, with boundaries accurately described, in which the laws of Georgia can have no force, and which the citizens of Georgia have no right to enter, but with the assent of the Cherokees themselves, or in conformity with treaties, and with the acts of congress. The whole intercourse between the United States and this nation, is, by our constitution and laws, vested in the government of the United States. The act of the state of Georgia, under which the plaintiff in error was prosecuted, is, consequently void, and the judgment a nullity. Can this court revise and reverse it?

If the objection to the system of legislation, lately adopted by the legislature of Georgia, in relation to the Cherokee nation, was confined to its extra-territorial operation, the objection, though complete, so far as respected mere right, would give this court no power over the subject. But it goes much further. If the view which has been taken be correct, and we think it is, the acts of Georgia are repugnant to the constitution, laws and treaties of the United States. They interfere forcibly with the relations established between the United States and the Cherokee nation, the regulation of which, according to the settled principles of our constitution, are committed exclusively to the government of the Union. They are in direct hostility with treaties, repeated in a succession of years, which mark out the boundary that separates the Cherokee country from Georgia; guaranty to them all the land within their boundary; solemnly pledge the faith of the United States to restrain their citizens from trespassing on it; and recognise the pre-existing power of the nation to govern itself. They are in hostility with the acts of congress for regulating this intercourse, and giving effect to the treaties. The forcible seizure and abduction of the plaintiff in error, who was residing in the nation, with its permission, and by authority of the President of the United States, is also a violation of the acts which authorize the chief magistrate to exercise this authority.

Will these powerful considerations avail the plaintiff in error? We think they will. He was seized, and forcibly carried away, while under guardianship of treaties guarantying the country in which he resided, and taking it under the protection of the United States. He was seized, while performing, under the sanction of the chief magistrate of the Union, those duties which the humane policy adopted by congress had recommended. He was apprehended, tried and condemned, under color of a law which has been shown to be repugnant to the constitution, laws and treaties of the United States. Had a judgment, liable to the same objections, been rendered for property, none would question the jurisdiction of this court. It cannot be less clear, when the judgment affects personal liberty, and inflicts disgraceful punishment—if punishment could disgrace, when inflicted on innocence. The plaintiff in error is not less interested in the operation of this unconstitutional law, than if it affected his property. He is not less entitled to the protection of the constitution, laws and treaties of his country . . . .

It is the opinion of this court, that the judgment of the Superior Court for the County of Gwinnett, in the State of Georgia, condemning Samuel A. Worcester to hard labor in the penitentiary of the State of Georgia, for four years, was pronounced by that court under color of a law which is void, as being repugnant to the constitution, treaties and laws of the United States, and ought, therefore, to be reversed and annulled.

[The concurring opinion of Justice McLean has been omitted.]

Baldwin, Justice, dissented, stating that . . . his opinion remained the same as was expressed by him in the case of the *Cherokee Nation v. State of Georgia*, at the last term. The opinion of Mr. Justice Baldwin was not delivered to the reporter.

[g] Events Subsequent to the *Cherokee Cases*: Worcester's Release and the Trail of Tears

The fate of Worcester after the Supreme Court ordered his release by the State of Georgia is told in Abel, *The History of Events Resulting in Indian Consolidation West of the Mississippi*, 1 AM. HIST. ASS'N FOR 1906, at 233, 401-403, note c (1908):[34]

"Immediately after the decision of the Supreme Court of the United States" [had been rendered] . . . "the mandate of that Court was . . . laid before the court of Georgia, by which they [the missionaries] had been tried and sentenced, and a motion made by the counsel for the missionaries that the court reverse its decision. But after the case had been argued at length, the motion was rejected. The court also refused to permit the motion, or its own decision upon it, or anything by which it might appear that such a motion had ever been made, to be entered on its records. The counsel then made an affidavit, stating that the mandate of the Supreme Court had been presented to the court in Georgia, and the motion made to reverse the decision of the latter, in obedience to the mandate. This affidavit was signed by the counsel for the missionaries, and acknowledged by the judge, and would have been used before the Supreme Court of the United States, instead of the record of the court in Georgia, had a motion been made there for further proceedings at its present session.

"On the 4th of April last, immediately subsequent to this refusal of the Court in Georgia to obey the mandate of the Supreme Court, the counsel for the prisoners presented a memorial in their behalf to his excellency Wilson Lumpkin, governor of the state, showing in what manner the mandate of the Supreme Court had been rejected by the state court, and praying him to use the executive power intrusted to him, and discharge the prisoners. To this the governor refused to give any written reply, but stated verbally that the prayer of the memorialists would not be complied with.

"In this state, so far as any legal proceedings are concerned, the case remained until the 27th of November, when Messrs. Worcester and Butler were informed that, if any motion were to be made before the Supreme Court of the United States for further proceedings in their case at its next approaching session, notice to that effect must be served on the governor and attorney general of Georgia without delay. They had no time to deliberate or consult their patrons on the subject. Knowing, however, that, if the notice should be served, and they should afterwards decide that it was inexpedient to prosecute their case further, the notice could be withdrawn, and the process arrested; while, if they neglected to serve the notice till it should be too late, the motion in their behalf before the Supreme Court could not be sustained, however desirable it might seem, but must be deferred another year. Placed in this predicament, they decided to give notice of the intended motion, leaving the question whether that motion should be actually made open to further consideration.

"Messrs. Worcester and Butler immediately informed the Prudential Committee (of the American Board) of what they had done, and requested their advice on the point, whether they should prosecute their case further before the Supreme Court of the United States or not . . . .

---

[34] The first segment of this excerpt is a Statement of the American Board for Foreign Missions, which was the conduit for federal funding of efforts to "civilize" the Cherokees after 1819. This statement was published in the *Missionary Herald*, XXIX, at 109-111. When the close quotation marks appear at the end of the statement, commentary by Abel continues. For a much more detailed summary of the events after the Supreme Court issued its opinions in *Worcester v. Georgia, see* Burke, note 20 above, at 524-531.

"It should also be remarked, before proceeding further with this statement, that Messrs. Worcester and Butler, very soon after they were placed in the penitentiary, were visited by a number of highly respectable gentlemen, who urged them, not to appeal to the Supreme Court of the United States, but to accept of a pardon from the governor of the state, and promise not to return to the Cherokee nation—the condition on which pardon was offered them immediately after their sentence was pronounced. This they steadily refused to do, deeming it of great importance, in its bearing on their own characters and the cause in which they were engaged, to obtain the opinion of that Court whether the law of the state of Georgia, extending her jurisdiction over the Cherokee country, was or was not contrary to the constitution, laws, and treaties of the United States; and whether they had or had not been lawfully arrested and subjected to an ignominious punishment for disregarding that law . . . . But as the missionaries were at first, from their own view of their rights, confident that they had been guilty of no crime, and would not, therefore, accept a *pardon*; so now, having obtained the decision of the Supreme Court in their favor, they were still less inclined to do anything which might imply that they had not a just claim to an unconditional discharge, without the stigma of being pardoned criminals . . . .

"More recently, however, and especially subsequent to giving the notice of the intended motion in the Supreme Court, the subject was presented to the minds of the missionaries in a somewhat different aspect; which, together with the posture of our national affairs, induced them to examine the whole subject anew, and to lay the arguments in favor of withdrawing their suit, which had been suggested to them by others, or had occurred to their own minds, before the committee, which they did in a letter from which the subjoined paragraphs are extracted. Doct. Butler being at the time unwell, Mr. Worcester, after mentioning that they had given notice of the intended motion, with some account of the interviews which they had had with gentlemen on the subject, presents the following interrogations as containing the substance of the arguments presented by them.

"What then are we to gain by the further prosecution of the case? Our personal liberty? There is much more prospect of gaining it by yielding than by perseverance. And if not, it is not worthy of account in comparison with the interests of our country.

"Freedom from the stigma of being pardoned criminals? That also is a consideration of personal feeling not to be balanced against the public good.

"The maintenance of the authority of the Supreme Court? It is argued against us that, if we yield, the authority of the court is not prostrated—only not tested; that, if it be put to the test now, it is almost certain to fail; that the probability of prostrating its authority is far greater than of maintaining it; that, if it were to be put to the test, it ought to be done at a more favorable time.

"The prevention of the violation of the public faith? That faith, it appears to us, is already violated; and, as far as we can see, our perseverance has no tendency to restore it.

"The arresting of the hand of oppression? It is already decided that such a course cannot arrest it.

"The privilege of preaching the gospel to the Cherokees? That privilege is at least as likely to be restored by our yielding as by our perseverance.

"The reputation of being firm and consistent men? Firmness degenerates into obstinacy, if it continues when the prospect of good ceases; and the reputation of doing right is dearly purchased by doing wrong . . . .

"In view of the foregoing considerations and some others which occurred to their minds, all tending to convince them that little good was to be hoped from further prosecution of the case: they were much more likely to be speedily restored to their labors among the Cherokees by withdrawing their suit, than by carrying it to the extremity, the Committee expressed to Messrs. Worcester and Butler the opinion, that it was inexpedient for them to prosecute their case further before the Supreme Court. It seemed to them also the part of Christian forbearance in the missionaries, in the present agitated state of the country, to yield rights, which, in other circumstances, it might have been their duty to claim, rather than to prosecute them tenaciously at the expense of hazarding the public interests . . . ."

Worcester wrote Wirt on January 8, 1833, instructing him to stop all legal proceedings. At the same time Worcester wrote Governor Lumpkin to inform him of this—in effect, to request a pardon, but still with a note of defiance.

"We beg leave respectfully to state to your Excellency that we have not been led to the adoption of this measure by any change of views in regard to the principles on which we have acted, or by any doubt of the justice of our perfect right to a legal discharge in accordance with the decision of the Supreme Court, in our favor already given, but by the apprehension that the further prosecution of the controversy under existing circumstances, might be attended with consequences injurious to our beloved country."

Governor Lumpkin considered this an insult. Hearing this, Worcester quickly wrote a second letter.

"We are sorry to be informed that some expressions in our communication of yesterday were regarded by your Excellency as an indignity offered to the State or its authorities. Nothing could be further from our design. In the course we have now taken it has been our intention simply to forbear the prosecution of our case and to leave the question of the continuance of our confinement to the magnanimity of the State."

Niles Register, XLII, Feb. 16, 1833.

Lumpkin did not send a letter in response but signed a proclamation on January 14, 1833 ordering release.

After their release, Worcester and Butler stayed with the Cherokees. Many years later, Georgia atoned a bit for its actions. In 1992 the Georgia Board of Pardons and Appeals acted "to remove a stain on the history of criminal justice in Georgia" by pardoning the two missionaries. Thirteen years before, in 1979, the state legislature formally repealed the statutes found unconstitutional in *Worcester*.[35] These deeds could not make up for the disaster that befell the Cherokees and other southeastern tribes a few years after *Worcester* was decided. Pressure from state authorities against the Cherokees continued throughout the 1830s. A "treaty" ceding the Georgia lands was "ratified" by the Senate in 1834 by a single vote, even though the tribal representative body turned it down. Eventually, approximately 17,000 members of the tribe were forcefully removed to western lands. Many died on the way. Worcester and Butler marched with the Cherokees and continued their work after reaching Oklahoma. The removals of the Cherokees and other southeastern tribes are well described in the literature. WILLIAM G. MCLOUGHLIN, AFTER THE TRAIL OF TEARS, THE CHEROKEES STRUGGLE FOR SOVEREIGNTY, 1839-1880 (1993); ALVIN M. JOSEPHY, JR., THE INDIAN HERITAGE OF AMERICA 294-343 (1968); VIRGIL J. VOGEL, A DOCUMENTARY HISTORY OF THE AMERICAN INDIAN 103-148 (1972); GRANT FOREMAN, INDIAN

---

[35] Georgia to Pardon Missionaries Jailed in 1830s, WASHINGTON POST, Nov. 23, 1992, at A5, col. 1.

REMOVAL (1932). Foreman wrote poignantly of the removals in his Preface to INDIAN REMOVAL: [36]

> While this book is not written to excite sympathy for the Indians, this tragic phase of American history is best understood if one will remember that for the most part the southern Indians were people of fixed habits and tastes. They were not nomads like some western Indians; they were less inclined to wander to strange places than white people. They loved their fields and herbs, their homes and firesides, families and friends; they were rooted in the soil as the Choctaw chief Pushmataha said, "where we have grown-up as the herbs of the woods." More than white people they cherished a passionate attachment for the earth that held the bones of their ancestors and relatives. Few white people either understood or respected this sentiment. The trees that shaded their homes, the cooling spring that ministered to every family, friendly water-courses, familiar trails and prospects, busk grounds, and council houses were their property and their friends; these simple possessions filled their lives; their loss was cataclysmic. It is doubtful if white people with their readier adaptability can understand the sense of grief and desolation that overwhelmed the Indians when they were compelled to leave all these behind forever and begin the long sad journey toward the setting sun which they called the Trail of Tears.

[h]   Analysis of *Worcester*

[i]   *The Court Opinion.* Chief Justice Marshall's opinion in *Worcester v. Georgia* is subtly different from the one he wrote in *Johnson v. McIntosh*. For example, near the beginning of his opinion, Marshall recited the *McIntosh* holding that discovery gave "title to the government by whose subject, or by whose authority, it was made, against all other European governments, which title might be consummated by possession." He then went on to note that this principle "regulated the right given by discovery among the European discoverers; but could not affect the rights of those already in possession, either as aboriginal occupants, or as occupants by virtue of a discovery made before the memory of man. It gave the exclusive right to purchase, but did not found that right on a denial of the right of the possessor to sell." This last phrase connotes authority in the tribes themselves that is not to be found in the language of *McIntosh*. Indeed, it arguably conflicts directly with the theories expressed in the earlier case, particularly since the Illinois and Wabash tribes never ceded their right to dispose of their land to England, Virginia, or the United States before McIntosh took possession under a deed from the United States. Such shifts in phraseology frequently occur while areas of the law are under development. When viewed in that light, *Worcester* is hardly unusual. On the other hand, this case represents one of the few settings in which the Supreme Court's authority to interpret the Constitution has been seriously challenged by another branch of the government. Marshall and the other judges certainly knew of this. Viewed in this light, any such shift in viewpoint must have represented a conscious choice to enter the political maelstrom. Later in the text, you should compare the *Worcester* Court's handling of its Constitutional crisis with the path taken decades later in *Dred Scott v. Sanford*, p. 1081 below.

[ii]   *The Trust Relationship.* *Worcester v. Georgia* is now viewed by most commentators as the foundation case for defining a "trust relationship" between the United States and the still extant Native American tribes. A review of some of the literature may be found in William

---

[36] GRANT FOREMAN, INDIAN REMOVAL: THE EMIGRATION OF THE FIVE CIVILIZED TRIBES OF INDIANS (1932). Copyright 1932, 1953 by the University of Oklahoma Press. Reprinted by permission of the University of Oklahoma Press.

Walters, *Review Essay: Preemption, Tribal Sovereignty, and Worcester v. Georgia*, 62 OR. L. REV. 127 (1983). It is easy to see how the trust view of *Worcester* could blossom. Despite the actual outcome of the case, in which the defendants never were able to use the Supreme Court's judgment to save the Cherokee lands, the opinion placed the ability of states to regulate the tribes within their boundaries in a secondary position to the structure established by the United States Constitution and federal statutory and treaty provisions. The language in the *Worcester* opinion arguably created a duty in the Office of the President to prevent states from encroaching on tribal rights. Marshall's use of the "guardian and ward" analogy in his *Cherokee Nation* opinion also created trust-like images. But what sort of trust relationship is involved?

The question may be easier to grapple with if the guardian and ward image is made a bit clearer. There are a number of situations in which courts or legislative bodies impose special obligations upon one person or group to care for another person or group. Individuals or groups may also establish such caring relationships by voluntarily creating a trust, in which the trust instruments would name a trustee and describe the duties of that trustee to care for the property of the beneficiary. A common example is the parent-child relationship. If a child owns property, parents are normally given the responsibility of caring for that property until the child reaches adulthood. Trusts are often formally created when children have significant amounts of property. Such family relationships also involve dependency; a child is generally viewed as needing the help of an adult to cope with property ownership. Guardian and ward relationships are of this sort. A ward could be a child or an ill adult incapable of handling his or her affairs. A guardian would be designated to care for any property owned by the ward. Guardians and trustees are also bound by strict fiduciary obligations in handling the assets placed in their control. They may not commingle trust assets with other property, use trust property for their own benefit, or allow third parties to improperly use trust holdings.

Is the trust relationship between a tribe and the United States the same as the standard obligation of a trustee to properly care for the assets of a child, incompetent person or ward? Here is one now classic description of the trust relationship taken from Reid P. Chambers, *Judicial Enforcement of the Federal Trust Responsibility to Indians*, 27 STAN. L. REV. 1213, 1246-1249 (1975):[37]

[T]he enduring teaching of the Cherokee cases is their perception of the underlying purposes of the trust relationship. Construing the early treaties as territorial arrangements among sovereign entities, Marshall correctly discerned that the basic guarantee of the United States was the territorial and governmental integrity of the tribes. The cases at the turn of the [twentieth] century emphasize the power derived by Congress from the trust relationship. [More recent cases represent] . . . a return to the Marshallian analysis, but with the additional suggestion that federal officials can be judicially restrained from actions contrary to their fiduciary duties to Indians—actions which contravene the ordinary proprietary obligations of a fiduciary to a trust beneficiary—even if they are not contrary to any treaty, statute, or agreement. The underlying theory . . . is that such actions are outside the general statutory authority of such officials.

It is premature to confirm that the case law definitively confirms these later principles, or to announce the existence of a cause of action for breach of trust . . . . The trend, however, seems to be a sound one given the purposes of the trust responsibility emphasized by

Marshall—the federal guarantee of the tribe's self-governing status. Given this objective, the property-related fiduciary standards appear to be an appropriate and probably necessary means toward achieving the end. Tribal autonomy will almost certainly be frustrated unless the option to continue a separate existence on a territorially secure reservation is protected, and legal remedies alone offer little protection.

It must be acknowledged, of course, that this analysis of the trust relationship has not been the exclusive one. Congress has at times adopted a narrower conception of the trust responsibility—that it is a transition period to cushion the assimilation of Indians into the dominant culture. This model of the trust relationship views the Indian as an "incompetent" requiring a period of education prior to assimilation, rather than the proprietor of federally guaranteed permanent rights. The courts have upheld congressional power to terminate the trust relationship or constrict its purposes, and while [this outcome] . . . seems questionable, it is unlikely to be overruled.

If one rejects the broad Marshallian purposes of the trust relationship in favor of a more limited one, the case for judicial enforcement through equitable remedies is weakened. But the different approaches to the purposes of the trust responsibility can be reconciled to permit judicial enforcement as long as a distinction is observed between executive and congressional action. Reading all the cases together, the principle that emerges is that Congress intends specific adherence to the trust responsibility by executive officials unless it has expressly provided otherwise. Such a formulation preserves the role of Congress as the ultimate umpire of the purposes of the trust relationship while requiring strict executive compliance with the terms of the trust.

[i]   Problems on the Trust Relationship

[*i*]   *The Nature of the Trust.* In *Worcester*, did Marshall really argue that the United States had a fiduciary obligation to care for the assets of the Cherokees? Or did he argue that the Cherokees were, though not a foreign state, a state nonetheless, with the competence and obligation to govern their own property? If Marshall held the latter view, and there is certainly much language in the Cherokee removal opinions to support that position, was a trust really at stake? Is Chambers, in the excerpt quoted above, justified in saying that cases suggesting that the United States has a fiduciary responsibility to the tribes are a logical extension of the *Worcester* dispute? Or should he have spoken of a dramatic shift in the ideology of Native American relationships with the United States from that of two nations working out their differences on an international law model to that of a trustee deciding how best to care for a beneficiary? Chambers, perhaps reflecting the confusion of the culture at large in dealing with Native American problems, does not make his argument about the trust relationship unambiguously. The basic nature of trust theory, he suggests, is still not totally clear. How do you picture the status of modern Native Americans? Are they foreign nationals? Are they independent or dependent? What is the role of the majority culture in Native American affairs?

[*ii*]   *Modern Contexts.* Chambers wrote his article in an era when the Supreme Court was rendering opinions highly protective of tribal interests. The present, more conservative, Supreme Court has rendered a series of opinions allowing significant parts of tribal life to be subjected to state and local regulation. How would you work out the balance of power between the federal government, state and local governments and tribes in the following situations:

(a) A state seeks to require members of a tribe who own property allotted to their families between 1887 and 1934 to pay local property taxes and the tribal members resist.

(b) A state seeks to require a tribe to pay local property taxes on lands held as trust lands for the tribe's use by the federal government.

(c) A tribe seeks to require non-tribal members purchasing items at a tribally owned store to pay a tribal sales tax.

(d) A state seeks to require a tribe running a store to collect and pay to the state a sales tax on all sales in the store.

(e) A tribal rule provides that husbands control the management of all family property in a state whose family property rules call for joint management of family property.

[*iii*]   *The Non–Intercourse Acts.* In *McIntosh* and the *Cherokee Cases*, Justice Marshall referred to the Indian non-intercourse acts. Shortly after the Constitution took effect in 1789, Congress adopted legislation barring sales of land by tribes to any person or state of the United States unless the transaction was "made and duly executed at some public treaty, held under the auspices of the United States." [38] This non-intercourse act mimicked earlier enactments adopted by England, the original colonies, and, between 1776 and 1789, the newly independent states of the United States. Despite the passage of the non-intercourse act by Congress, states and private parties continued to "buy" Indian lands. While title conflicts arose from time to time, many of the supposedly illegal transactions were forgotten in the mists of time.

In the middle of the twentieth century, Native Americans, like women, African Americans and others, began to mount protests on a variety of issues and make demands for change. This prompted a number of people to search for ways to reassert long dormant claims that Indian title had been illegally terminated decades earlier. Claims eventually were filed under the non-intercourse act by a number of tribes, mostly in the east.

The longest lived and most complex of these claims involved the Oneida Indian Nation in New York. The Oneidas claimed that New York had unlawfully obtained cessions of a large tract of their land in western New York extending from the Pennsylvania border north to Lake Ontario. Four years after the case was filed, it reached the Supreme Court for the first time. The Court directed the federal district court to hear the case, reversing an appellate court ruling that the federal courts lacked subject matter jurisdiction over the claim. [39]

Eleven years later the case found its way back to the Supreme Court a second time. A variety of issues were presented. Perhaps the most interesting involved whether the claim was barred by the passage of time, either because of a state statute of limitations or because of a state laches rule. In federal cases where Congress has not enacted a statute of limitations, the federal courts normally use a state statute dealing with an area similar to the federal claim. No federal statute of limitations existed with respect to the Oneida claim. Should the Court have "borrowed" the New York adverse possession or laches statute of limitations? The Court, in a 5-4 decision, declined to do so, opining that Indian title issues were distinctly federal in nature and that use of state limitations statutes would contradict the *McIntosh* holding that state law could not be

---

[38] An Act to Regulate Trade and Intercourse with the Indian Tribes, 1 Stat. 137 (1790). This non-intercourse act was re-enacted in 1793, 1 Stat. 329, and is now codified at 25 U.S.C. § 177.

[39] Oneida Indian Nation v. County of Oneida, 414 U.S. 661 (1974). The Court concluded that the land dispute arose under the laws, treaties and constitution of the United States and therefore stated a federal question claim.

used to terminate Indian title. How would you have resolved this issue? After reading *Brendale*, the next case, and the notes that follow it, ask yourself whether the contemporary Supreme Court would have decided the statute of limitations question the same way as the *Oneida* Court.

Congress adopted a statute of limitation for the non-intercourse act claims in 1982. Further filing of ancient claims is now barred. Most of the claims filed in the 1970s have now been settled under the terms of federal, state and tribal legislation. But a number, including the Oneida claim and several others in New York, are still pending. Settlement negotiations have failed to produce a solution after over 20 years of litigation in the Oneida case. The tribe recently added about 20,000 land owners in the area as defendants in an effort to spur officials in state and local offices in New York to bargain more seriously. Discussions apparently are focusing on some land transfers to the tribes, permissions to open more gambling and other business facilities, and monetary payments in return for the tribe releasing their claims against private land owners. The passage of time also has revealed another interesting twist. The tribe has become quite well-to-do over the years. Gambling has proven to be quite a boon. The Oneida Indian Nation is now the largest employer in the area with over 3,000 employees working in their business facilities.[40]

§ 1.04 Contemporary Consequences of the Dawes Act Era

[1] Introduction

Consistency has hardly been the watchword of Indian property law. At times a desire to defend tribal sovereignty has dominated policy making; at other times the goal has been to assimilate tribal communities into the larger culture. During the decades following the presidency of Andrew Jackson, the federal government's primary goal was to isolate native peoples from the rest of the population. Reservations were established in largely unsettled areas of the country. The motivations for this system were diverse. "In part, like the removal policy, the reservation policy was intended to ease hostilities and tensions between tribes and settlers by segregating the two groups from one another. Moreover, reservations were designed to preserve the tribes from destruction and, at the same time, to provide a laboratory for teaching Indians the virtues of agriculture and civilization."[41]

After the middle of the nineteenth century, a movement grew to undo the reservation system and replace it with an overtly assimilationist policy. Some Indian treaties agreed to after 1850 provided for allotting land to individual members of tribes. Government officials began to recommend the adoption of an allotment system. In 1871, Congress passed legislation barring the further use of treaties to resolve Indian land claims, stating that no tribe was to be "recognized as an independent nation, tribe or power with whom the United States may contract by treaty."[42] Just the year before the Supreme Court had made it clear that Congress may, by statute, alter the terms of pre-existing treaties.[43]

In 1887 the General Allotment Act, commonly known as the Dawes Act,[44] was adopted. Private ownership of land was to become the tool to force native communities to assimilate into the

---

[40] James Dao, *Anxiety Growing Over Indian Claim in New York State*, N.Y. TIMES, Jan. 13, 1999, at A.1, col. 4.

[41] Judith Royster, *The Legacy of Allotment*, 27 ARIZ. ST. L.J. 1, 8 (1995).

[42] Ch. 120, § 1, 16 Stat. 566 (Mar. 3, 1871).

[43] The Cherokee Tobacco, 78 U.S. 616 (1870).

[44] Ch. 119, 24 Stat. 388 (1887).

larger culture. Spurred on by powerful political currents advocating minimal use of government regulation and reliance on market forces to generate wealth,[45] Congress totally restructured Indian policy. Rather than following Jefferson's plan allowing each native community to develop its own internal system for allocating tribal lands for agricultural use, the Dawes Act required the distribution of land to tribal members, and, after a 25 year transition period,[46] subjected the land to state civil law systems and allowed it to be sold to anyone. By the end of the allotment period in 1934, over two-thirds of all allotted lands had fallen into the hands of non-Indians.[47]

Land not needed for allotments was treated as surplus lands and made available for settlement by the general population. Though the General Allotment Act provided that tribal consent was necessary to treat reservation lands as surplus, Congress adopted a number of acts designating lands of particular native communities as surplus without tribal consent. In a 1903 case, *Lone Wolf v. Hitchcock*,[48] the Supreme Court validated such designations in spite of the terms of the Allotment Act or of specific treaties that required tribal consent. Between the allotment and surplus land systems, about two-thirds of all reservation lands fell into non-Indian hands.[49]

Concern about the effects of the allotment and surplus lands systems began to surface in the 1920s. The Secretary of the Department of the Interior, Hubert Work, requested that a study be made. The Meriam Report, put together by Lewis Meriam for the Brookings Institution, described a wide ranging series of problems and called for dramatic changes in Indian policy.[50] The report generated much public sympathy and helped create a shift in mood toward reform. When Franklin Roosevelt became President in 1933, his new Commissioner of Indian Affairs, John Collier, ordered a halt to issuance of certificates of competency, effectively halting further disposition of allotted lands to non-tribal members, and successfully sought legislation to repeal the Dawes Act.

Adoption of the Indian Reorganization Act in 1934[51] barred further allotments of tribal lands, made permanent the trust status of any lands previously allotted to Indians and not disposed of to outsiders, ended the designation of reservation lands as surplus, and returned lands designated as surplus but not yet sold to reservation trust status. What the act did not do, however, was restore to tribal ownership allotted lands still held by tribal members or make any definitive statements about the respective authority of federal, state, local and tribal governments over lands held in various forms. That muddled situation still bedevils us. Though successive administrations since President Johnson have all attempted to implement policies supporting a significant degree of tribal sovereignty over reservation lands, the courts have been confronted with a variety of disputes over the treatment of the remaining reservation lands, allotted lands held by Indians, and allotted or surplus lands held by non-Indians.

---

[45] More complete discussion of the impact of laisez faire policy on property law in the late nineteenth and early twentieth centuries may be found in Chapters 2, 4, 5 and 6.

[46] In 1906 this waiting period rule was altered to allow immediate conveyance of lands by Indians deemed capable of managing their own affairs. Applications to make use of this provision were rarely denied.

[47] Royster, note 41 above, at 12.

[48] 187 U.S. 553 (1903).

[49] Twenty-seven million acres were lost via allotment and 60 million through disposition as surplus land. Royster, note 41 above, at 13.

[50] INSTITUTE FOR GOVERNMENT RESEARCH OF THE BROOKINGS INSTITUTION, THE PROBLEM OF INDIAN ADMINISTRATION (1928).

[51] 48 Stat. 984 (1934).

Controversies about the Yakama[52] Indian Reservation have produced some recent indications that the consequences of the Dawes Act era are still having a profound impact on land use policy. The reservation was established by treaty in 1855. It covers approximately 1.3 million acres in southeastern Washington State.

[2]   The United States Supreme Court Opinions

Brendale v. Confederated Tribes and Bands of Yakima Indian Nation
Wilkinson v. Confederated Tribes and Bands of Yakima Indian Nation
County of Yakima v. Confederated Tribes and Bands of Yakima Indian Nation
United States Supreme Court
492 U.S. 408, 109 S. Ct. 2994, 106 L. Ed. 2d 343 (1989)

JUSTICE WHITE, joined by THE CHIEF JUSTICE, JUSTICE SCALIA and JUSTICE KENNEDY, delivered an opinion announcing the judgment of the Court in Nos. 87-1697 [*Wilkinson*] and 87-1711 [*County of Yakima*] and dissenting in No. 87-1622 [*Brendale*].

The issue presented by these three consolidated cases is whether the Yakima Indian Nation or the County of Yakima, a governmental unit of the State of Washington, has the authority to zone fee lands owned by nonmembers of the Tribe located within the boundaries of the Yakima Reservation.

I

A

The Confederated Bands and Tribes of the Yakima Indian Nation are composed of 14 originally distinct Indian Tribes that banded together in the mid-1800's to negotiate with the United States. The result of those negotiations was a treaty signed in 1855 and ratified by the Senate in 1859. Treaty between the United States and the Yakima Nation of Indians (Treaty with the Yakimas), 12 Stat. 951. By the terms of the treaty, the Yakima Nation ceded vast areas of land to the United States but retained an area, the Yakima Indian Reservation, for its "exclusive use and benefit."[1]

The Reservation is located in the southeastern part of the State of Washington. Approximately 1.3 million acres of land are located within its boundaries. Of that land, roughly 80% is held in trust by the United States for the benefit of the Yakima Nation or individual members of the Tribe. The remaining 20% of the land is owned in fee by Indian or non-Indian owners. Most of the fee land is found in Toppenish, Wapato, and Harrah, the three incorporated towns located in the northeastern part of the Reservation. The remaining fee land is scattered throughout the Reservation in a "checkerboard" pattern.

The parties to this litigation, as well as the District Court and the Court of Appeals, have treated the Yakima Reservation as divided into two parts: a "closed area" and an "open area." The closed area consists of the western two-thirds of the Reservation and is predominantly forest land. Of the approximately 807,000 acres of land in the closed area, 740,000 acres are located in Yakima

---

[52] After the case was decided, the Yakima Indian Nation asked Congress to change its name to the Yakama Indian Nation. The change was made. So I have used "Yakama" in my text, but left the Court's opinion as it was written.

[1] The treaty further provides that no "white man, excepting those in the employment of the Indian Department, [shall] be permitted to reside upon the said reservation without permission of the tribe and the superintendent and agent." 12 Stat. 951, 952 (1855).

County. Twenty-five thousand acres of the seven hundred and forty thousand acres are fee land. The closed area is so-named because it has been closed to the general public at least since 1972 when the Bureau of Indian Affairs restricted the use of federally maintained roads in the area to members of the Yakima Nation and to its permittees, who must be record land owners or associated with the Tribe.[2] Access to the open area, as its name suggests, is not likewise restricted to the general public. The open area is primarily rangeland, agricultural land, and land used for residential and commercial development. Almost half of the land in the open area is fee land.

B

The Yakima Nation adopted its first zoning ordinance in 1970. The ordinance was amended to its present form in 1972. By its terms, the Yakima Nation ordinance applies to all lands within the Reservation boundaries, including fee lands owned by Indians or non-Indians. Yakima County adopted its present comprehensive zoning ordinance in 1972, although the county had regulated land use as early as 1946. The County ordinance applies to all real property within county boundaries, except for Indian trust lands. The ordinance establishes a number of use districts, which generally govern agricultural, residential, commercial, industrial, and forest watershed uses. The particular zoning designations at issue are "forest watershed" and "general rural."

The fee lands located in the closed area are zoned by the county ordinance as forest watershed. That designation permits development of single family dwellings, commercial camp grounds, small overnight lodging facilities, restaurants, bars, general stores and souvenir shops, service stations, marinas, and saw mills. The minimum lot size is one-half acre. None of these uses would be permitted by the zoning designation "reservation restricted area," which applies to the closed area under the Yakima Nation zoning ordinance.

The general rural zoning designation, applicable to land in the open area, is one of three use districts governing agricultural properties. The minimum lot size for land zoned general rural is smaller than that specified for agricultural land in the Yakima Nation ordinance, although the other county use districts for agricultural properties have larger minimum lot sizes than the Yakima Nation ordinance.

C

1

Petitioner Philip Brendale, who is part-Indian but not a member of the Yakima Nation, owns a 160-acre tract of land near the center of the forested portion of the closed area. The parcel was originally allotted to Brendale's great aunt, a member of the Yakima Nation. The land passed by inheritance to Brendale's mother and grandfather, who were issued a fee patent in 1963, and

---

[2] At oral argument, counsel arguing for petitioners represented that a decision by the Bureau of Indian Affairs in April 1988, after the Court of Appeals issued its opinion here, has reopened the roads in the closed area to the public. Tr. of Oral Arg. 17. See App. to Brief for Petitioner Brendale 1a. According to counsel, there is no longer a closed area on the Reservation. Tr. of Oral Arg. 17. Counsel for respondent agreed with this characterization, describing what had formerly been the closed area as the "reservation reserved area," based on the Yakima Nation's zoning designation for the area. *Id.*, at 28. Despite these developments, Justice Stevens persists in treating the two areas differently, a position that is rejected by seven Members of the Court, and continues to rely on the District Court's findings of fact regarding the Brendale property, which are undermined by the change in circumstances. This opinion will continue to refer to the respective areas as the closed area and the open area, but for convenience only.

then, on his·mother's death in 1972, to Brendale. The land is zoned as reservation restricted area by the Yakima Nation. It is zoned forest watershed by Yakima County.

In January 1982, Brendale filed four contiguous "short plat" applications with the Yakima County Planning Department. After determining that the short platting did not require an Environmental Impact Statement (EIS), the department issued a Declaration of Non-Significance. The department requested comments from the Yakima Nation, and after the Tribe did not respond, the short plats were approved.

Brendale then submitted in April 1983 a "long plat" application to divide one of his platted 20-acre parcels into ten 2-acre lots to be sold as summer cabin sites. Each lot is to have an individual well and a septic tank. Electric generators would provide electricity. The proposed plat is bordered on the north and east by other lands owned by Brendale, on the south by lands owned in fee by the St. Regis Paper Company, and on the west by lands held in trust by the United States. The proposed development would not have been permissible under the Yakima Nation ordinance.

The county planning department again issued a Declaration of Non-Significance. The Yakima Nation appealed the Declaration of Non-Significance to the Yakima County Board of Commissioners on the grounds that the county had no zoning authority over the land and that an EIS was necessary. The Commissioners concluded that the appeal was properly before the Board but reversed the planning department and ordered that an EIS be prepared.[3]

2

Petitioner Stanley Wilkinson, a non-Indian and a nonmember of the Yakima Nation, owns a 40-acre tract of land in the open area of the Reservation. The tract is located less than a mile from the northern boundary of the Reservation and is on a slope overlooking the Yakima Municipal Airport and the city of Yakima. The land is bordered on the north by trust land and on the other three sides by fee land, and is currently vacant sagebrush property. It is zoned agricultural by the Yakima Nation and general rural by Yakima County.

In September 1983, Wilkinson applied to the Yakima County Planning Department to subdivide 32 acres of his land into 20 lots. The lots range in size from 1.1 acres to 4.5 acres. Each is to be used for a single family home and will be served by individual wells and septic systems. The proposed development would not have been permissible under the Yakima Nation ordinance.

The planning department initially indicated that an EIS needed to be prepared for the project, but later, after Wilkinson modified his proposal, the department issued a Declaration of Non-Significance. The Yakima Nation thereafter appealed the Declaration of Non-Significance, again challenging the county's authority to zone the land and alleging that an EIS was necessary. The County Board of Commissioners concluded that the appeal was properly before it and affirmed the planning department's conclusion that an EIS was not necessary.

D

The Yakima Nation then filed separate actions in United States District Court challenging the proposed development of the Brendale and Wilkinson properties and the county's exercise of zoning authority over the land. The complaints sought a declaratory judgment that the Yakima

---

[3] Preparation of the EIS was underway when the Yakima Nation filed the present action in District Court.

Nation had exclusive authority to zone the properties at issue and an injunction barring any action or the approval of any action on the land inconsistent with the land-use regulations of the Yakima Nation.

The District Court held that the Yakima Nation had exclusive zoning authority over the Brendale property, but concluded that the Tribe lacked authority over the Wilkinson property. The District Court looked to this Court's opinion in *Montana v. United States*, 450 U.S. 544 (1981), as controlling whether an Indian tribe has authority to regulate activities of nonmembers of the tribe on fee lands. The District Court determined that there was no evidence of any "consensual relationship" between the Yakima Nation and Wilkinson and Brendale that would extend the authority of the Tribe to the fee lands. But after making detailed findings of fact,[5] the court concluded that "Brendale's proposed development does indeed pose a threat to the political integrity, the economic security and the health and welfare of the Yakima Nation" and therefore the Tribe has authority to impose its zoning regulations on that property. The District Court then proceeded to determine that Yakima County was pre-empted from exercising concurrent zoning authority over the land in the closed area because its interests in regulating the land were minimal while the Tribe's interests were substantial. But because Wilkinson's proposed development did not impose a similar threat, the Tribe had no authority whatsoever over that property.

On appeal, the Ninth Circuit consolidated the cases and affirmed as to the Brendale property but reversed as to the Wilkinson property. In upholding the Yakima Nation's zoning authority, the Court of Appeals did not disturb or rely on the findings of the District Court. Instead, it concluded that zoning ordinances by their very nature attempt "to protect against the damage caused by uncontrolled development, which can affect all of the residents and land of the reservation." According to the Court of Appeals, zoning ordinances are within the police power of local governments precisely because they promote the health and welfare of the community. Moreover, a "major goal" of zoning is coordinated land use planning. Because fee land is located throughout the reservation in a checker-board pattern, denying the Yakima Nation the right to zone fee land "would destroy their capacity to engage in comprehensive planning, so fundamental to a zoning scheme." This the court was "unwilling" to do.

Brendale, Wilkinson, and Yakima County each petitioned for writ of certiorari. We granted the petitions and consolidated the cases for argument.

II

The present actions were brought by the Yakima Nation to require development occurring on property within the boundaries of its Reservation to proceed in accordance with the Yakima Nation zoning ordinance. The Tribe is necessarily contending that it has the exclusive authority to zone all of the property within the Reservation, including the projects at issue here. We

---

[5] The District Court found that Brendale's proposed development would disrupt soil conditions; cause a deterioration of air quality; change drainage patterns; destroy some trees and natural vegetation; cause a deterioration of wildlife habitat; alter the location and density of human population in the area; increase traffic, light, and the use of fuel wood; and require added police and fire protection as well as new systems for waste disposal. The Court also found that a number of places of religious and cultural significance were located in the closed area and that much of the Tribe's income comes from lumber harvested from lands within the closed area. Unlike the closed area, however, the District Court found that the open area had no unique religious or spiritual importance to the Yakima Nation and that the trust land in the vicinity of the proposed Wilkinson development did not provide a significant source of food for the Tribe.

therefore examine whether the Yakima Nation has the authority, derived either from its treaty with the United States or from its status as an independent sovereign, to zone the fee lands owned by Brendale and Wilkinson.

A

The Yakima Nation argues first that its treaty with the United States establishes its authority to regulate fee land within the Reservation but owned by nonmembers of the Tribe. By its terms, the Treaty with the Yakima provides that the land retained by the Yakima Nation "shall be set apart . . . for the exclusive use and benefit" of the Tribe, and no "white man, excepting those in the employment of the Indian Department, [shall] be permitted to reside upon the said reservation without permission of the tribe. The Yakima Nation contends that this power to exclude provides the source for its authority over the land at issue here.

We disagree. The Yakima Nation no longer retains the "exclusive use and benefit" of all the land within the Reservation boundaries established by the Treaty with the Yakima. Under the Indian General Allotment Act of 1887, significant portions of the Yakima Reservation, including the tracts of land at issue here, were allotted to individual members of the Tribe. The land was held in trust for a period of years, generally 25 although the period was subject to extension, after which fee patents were issued. Over time, through sale and inheritance, nonmembers of the Tribe, such as petitioners Brendale and Wilkinson, have come to own a substantial portion of the allotted land.

We analyzed the effect of the Allotment Act on an Indian Tribe's treaty rights to regulate activities of nonmembers on fee land in *Montana v. United States.* The treaty language there was virtually identical to the language in the Treaty with the Yakima, and we concluded that "treaty rights with respect to reservation lands must be read in light of the subsequent alienation of those lands." In *Montana,* as in the present cases, the lands at issue had been alienated under the Allotment Act, and the Court concluded that "[i]t defies common sense to suppose that Congress would intend that non-Indians purchasing allotted lands would become subject to tribal jurisdiction when an avowed purpose of the allotment policy was the ultimate destruction of tribal government."

The Yakima Nation argues that we should not consider the Allotment Act because it was repudiated in 1934 by the Indian Reorganization Act. But the Court in *Montana* was well aware of the change in Indian policy engendered by the Indian Reorganization Act and concluded that this fact was irrelevant. Although the Indian Reorganization Act may have ended the allotment of further lands, it did not restore to the Indians the exclusive use of those lands that had already passed to non-Indians or prevent already allotted lands for which fee patents were subsequently issued from thereafter passing to non-Indians.

Justice Stevens acknowledges that the Allotment Act eliminated tribal authority to exclude nonmembers from fee lands they owned. Yet he concludes that Brendale and Wilkinson are somehow subject to a tribal power to "determine the character of the tribal community," unless the tribe has voluntarily surrendered that power. This view of tribal zoning authority as a sort of equitable servitude is wholly unsupported by precedent.[8]

---

[8] Furthermore, the practical consequences of Justice Stevens' approach will be severe. Justice Stevens' conception of tribal zoning authority allows Indian tribes to obtain the power to zone by defining areas on their reservations that contain only a "small percentage" of fee lands. The uncertainty that would result from the necessarily case-by-case

. . . .

We would follow *Montana* and conclude that, for the reasons stated there, any regulatory power the Tribe might have under the treaty "cannot apply to lands held in fee by non-Indians."

B

An Indian tribe's treaty power to exclude nonmembers of the tribe from its lands is not the only source of Indian regulatory authority . . . . [T]ribes have inherent sovereignty independent of that authority arising from their power to exclude. Prior to the settlement of the New World, Indian tribes were self-governing sovereign political communities, and they still retain some elements of 'quasi-sovereign' authority after ceding their lands to the United States and announcing their dependence on the Federal Government. Thus, an Indian tribe generally retains sovereignty by way of tribal self-government and control over other aspects of its internal affairs.

A tribe's inherent sovereignty, however, is divested to the extent it is inconsistent with the tribe's dependent status, that is, to the extent it involves a tribe's "external relations." *United States v. Wheeler*, 435 U.S. 313, 326. Those cases in which the Court has found a tribe's sovereignty divested generally are those "involving the relations between an Indian tribe and nonmembers of the tribe." For example, Indian tribes cannot freely alienate their lands to non-Indians, *Oneida Indian Nation v. Oneida County*, 414 U.S. 661, 667-668 (1974), cannot enter directly into commercial or governmental relations with foreign nations, *Worcester v. Georgia*, 6 Pet. 515 (1832), and cannot exercise criminal jurisdiction over non-Indians in tribal courts, *Oliphant v. Suquamish Indian Tribe*, 435 U.S. 191 (1978).

This list is by no means exclusive, as *Montana* makes clear. In *Montana*, the Crow Tribe sought to prohibit hunting and fishing within its Reservation by anyone not a member of the Tribe. The Court held that the Tribe's inherent sovereignty did not support extending the prohibition on hunting and fishing to fee lands owned by non-Indians. It recognized the general principle that the "exercise of tribal power beyond what is necessary to protect tribal self-government or to control internal relations is inconsistent with the dependent status of the tribes, and so cannot survive without express congressional delegation." Because regulation of hunting and fishing on fee lands owned by nonmembers of the Tribe did not bear any "clear relationship to tribal self-government or internal relations," this general principle precluded extension of tribal jurisdiction to the fee lands at issue.

The Yakima Nation contends that the Court's insistence in *Montana* on an express congressional delegation of tribal power over nonmembers is inconsistent with language in *Washington v. Confederated Tribes of the Colville Indian Reservation*, 447 U.S. 134, 153 (1980), that tribal powers are divested by implication only when "the exercise of tribal sovereignty would be inconsistent with the overriding interests of the National Government." We do not see this language as inconsistent with *Montana*. As the opinion in *Colville* made clear, that case involved "[t]he power to tax transactions occurring on trust lands and significantly involving a tribe or its members." It did not involve the regulation of fee lands, as did *Montana*. Moreover, the Court in *Montana* itself reconciled the two cases, citing *Colville* as an example of the sort of "consensual relationship" that might even support tribal authority over nonmembers on fee lands.

determination of which regulatory body (or bodies) have zoning jurisdiction over such land, not to mention the uncertainty as to when a tribe will attempt to assert such jurisdiction, would be far worse than that resulting from the scheme discussed . . . [here], in which the contours of the zoning authority are clearly defined and resort to the courts to protect tribal interests should not often be required.

Justice Blackmun takes a slightly different approach, relying particularly on *Colville* and *Wheeler* for the proposition that "tribal sovereignty is not implicitly divested except in those limited circumstances principally involving external powers of sovereignty where the exercise of tribal authority is necessarily inconsistent with their dependent status." But Justice Blackmun ignores what the Court made clear in *Wheeler*, in a passage immediately preceding the one he cites: that regulation of "the relations between an Indian tribe and nonmembers of the tribe" is necessarily inconsistent with a tribe's dependent status, and therefore tribal sovereignty over such matters of "external relations" is divested. Indeed, it is precisely this discussion that the Court relied upon in *Montana* as "distinguish[ing] between those inherent powers retained by the tribes and those divested."

There is no contention here that Congress has expressly delegated to the Yakima Nation the power to zone fee lands of nonmembers of the Tribe. Therefore under the general principle enunciated in *Montana*, the Yakima Nation has no authority to impose its zoning ordinance on the fee lands owned by petitioners Brendale and Wilkinson.

C

Our inquiry does not end here because the opinion in *Montana* noted two "exceptions" to its general principle. First, "[a] tribe may regulate, through taxation, licensing, or other means, the activities of nonmembers who enter consensual relationships with the tribe or its members, through commercial dealing, contracts, leases, or other arrangements." Second, "[a] tribe may also retain inherent power to exercise civil authority over the conduct of non-Indians on fee lands within its reservation when that conduct threatens or has some direct effect on the political integrity, the economic security, or the health or welfare of the tribe."

The parties agree that the first *Montana* exception does not apply in this case. Brendale and Wilkinson do not have a "consensual relationship" with the Yakima Nation simply by virtue of their status as landowners within reservation boundaries, as *Montana* itself necessarily decided. The Yakima Nation instead contends that the Tribe has authority to zone under the second *Montana* exception. We disagree.

Initially, we reject as overbroad the Ninth Circuit's categorical acceptance of tribal zoning authority over lands within reservation boundaries. We find it significant that the so-called second *Montana* exception is prefaced by the word "may"—"[a] tribe *may* also retain inherent power to exercise civil authority over the conduct of non-Indians on fee lands within its reservation" (emphasis added). This indicates to us that a tribe's authority need not extend to all conduct that "threatens or has some direct effect on the political integrity, the economic security, or the health or welfare of the tribe," but instead depends on the circumstances. The Ninth Circuit, however, transformed this indication that there may be other cases in which a tribe has an interest in activities of nonmembers on fee land into a rule describing every case in which a tribe has such an interest. Indeed, the Ninth Circuit equated an Indian tribe's retained sovereignty with a local government's police power, which is contrary to *Montana* itself. *Montana* rejected tribal sovereignty to regulate hunting and fishing on fee land owned by non-Indians, which clearly is a power within the police power of local governments.[11]

---

[11] Justice Blackmun contends that upholding zoning authority does not necessarily "entai[l] a finding of inherent authority for all police powers," reasoning that "[a]s *Montana* itself demonstrates, there may be cases in which tribes assert the power to regulate activities as to which they have no valid interest." The errors in this reasoning are twofold. First, Justice Blackmun characterizes the decision in *Montana* incorrectly. The Court did not hold in *Montana* that

It is also evident that a literal application of the second exception would make little sense in the circumstances of this case. To hold that the tribe has authority to zone fee land when the activity on that land has the specified effect on Indian properties would mean that the authority would last only so long as the threatening use continued. If it ceased, zoning power would revert to the country. Under the District Court's interpretation of *Montana*, not only would regulatory authority depend in the first instance on a factual inquiry into how a tribe's interests are affected by a particular use of fee land, but as circumstances changed over time, so, too, would the authority to zone. Conceivably, in a case like this, zoning authority could vest variously in the county and the tribe, switching back and forth between the two, depending on what uses the county permitted on the fee land at issue. Uncertainty of this kind would not further the interests of either the tribe or the county government and would be chaotic for landowners.[12]

Montana should therefore not be understood to vest zoning authority in the tribe when fee land is used in certain ways. The governing principle is that the tribe has no authority itself, by way of tribal ordinance or actions in the tribal courts, to regulate the use of fee land. The inquiry thus becomes whether and to what extent the tribe has a protectable interest in what activities are taking place on fee land within the reservation and, if it has such an interest, how it may be protected. Of course, under ordinary law, neighbors often have a protectable interest in what is occurring on adjoining property and may seek relief in an appropriate forum, judicial or otherwise. *Montana* suggests that in the special circumstances of checkerboard ownership of lands within a reservation, the tribe has an interest under federal law, defined in terms of the impact of the challenged uses on the political integrity, economic security, or the health or welfare of the tribe. But, as we have indicated above, that interest does not entitle the tribe to complain or obtain relief against every use of fee land that has some adverse effect on the tribe. The impact must be demonstrably serious and must imperil the political integrity, economic security or the health and welfare of the tribe. This standard will sufficiently protect Indian tribes while at the same time avoiding undue interference with state sovereignty and providing the certainty needed by property owners.

Since the tribes' protectable interest is one arising under federal law, the Supremacy Clause requires state and local governments, including Yakima County zoning authorities, to recognize and respect that interest in the course of their activities. The Tribe in this case, as it should have, first appeared in the county zoning proceedings, but its submission should have been, not that the county was without zoning authority over fee land within the Reservation, but that its tribal interests were imperiled. The federal courts had jurisdiction to entertain the Tribe's suit for declaratory and injunctive relief, but given that the county has jurisdiction to zone fee lands on the Reservation and would be enjoinable only if it failed to respect the rights of the Tribe under

---

the Tribe had no interest in regulating non-Indian fishing and hunting on fee land. Instead, it held that the Tribe lacked an interest sufficient "to justify tribal regulation." Second, Justice Blackmun's reasoning confirms, rather than disproves, that recognizing zoning authority here will equate tribal retained sovereignty with the police power. Under Justice Blackmun's view, tribes evidently lack authority to exercise a power within the police power only when they have no legitimate interest in the regulation. But this is a meaningless limitation because to be a valid exercise of the police power in the first instance a government regulation must be rationally related to a legitimate state interest.

[12] Justice Blackmun asserts that his position, that "the general and longer-term advantages of comprehensive land management" justify tribal zoning of fee land, avoids this uncertainty. But this broad position would also authorize the Yakima Nation to zone all fee land within reservation boundaries, including that within the incorporated towns of Toppenish, Wapato, and Harrah. Although Justice Blackmun purports to avoid this "difficult question," there appears to be no principled basis on which to exclude the incorporated towns from the Tribe's zoning authority without leading to the very uncertainty Justice Blackmun attempts to dismiss as hypothetical.

federal law, the proper course for the District Court in the Brendale phase of this case would have been to stay its hand until the zoning proceedings had been completed. At that time, a judgment could be made as to whether the uses that were actually authorized on Brendale's property imperiled the political integrity, the economic security, or the health or welfare of the Tribe. If due regard is given to the Tribe's protectable interest at all stages of the proceedings, we have every confidence that the nightmarish consequences predicted by Justice Blackmun will be avoided. Of course if practice proves otherwise, Congress can take appropriate action.

III

The District Court found that Yakima County's exercise of zoning power over the Wilkinson property would have no direct effect on the Tribe and would not threaten the Tribe's political integrity, economic security, or health and welfare. On the basis of these findings, it is clear that the Wilkinson development and the county's approval of that development do not imperil any interest of the Yakima Nation. Therefore, I would reverse the judgment of the Ninth Circuit as to the Wilkinson property.

The Brendale property presents a different situation. At the time the Tribe filed its suit, the County had agreed with the Tribe that an EIS was required before Brendale's development could go forward. The zoning proceedings had thus not been concluded, and the District Court's judgment was that the county had no power to go forward. That judgment was infirm under the approach outlined in this opinion. The zoning proceedings should have been allowed to conclude and it may be that those proceedings would adequately recognize tribal interests and make unnecessary further action in the District Court. If it were otherwise, the District Court could then decide whether the uses the State permits on the Brendale property would do serious injury to and clearly imperil the protectable tribal interests identified in this opinion. This part of the case in my view should therefore be returned to District Court. A majority of this Court, however, disagrees with this conclusion.

Accordingly, since with respect to the Wilkinson property, Justice Stevens and Justice O'Connor agree that the judgment of the Court of Appeals . . . should be reversed, that is the judgment of the Court in those cases. With respect to the Brendale property, I would vacate the judgment of the Court of Appeals and remand the case to the Court of Appeals with instructions to vacate the judgment of the District Court and to remand the case to that Court for further proceedings. Because the Court instead affirms the judgment of the Court of Appeals in . . . [the Brendale case], I dissent as to that case.

JUSTICE STEVENS, joined by JUSTICE O'CONNOR, delivered an opinion announcing the judgment of the Court in No. 87-1622 [Brendale] and concurring in the judgment in Nos. 87-1697 [Wilkinson] and 87-1711 [Yakima County].

The United States has granted to many Indian tribes, including the Yakima Nation, "a power unknown to any other sovereignty in this Nation: a power to exclude nonmembers entirely from territory reserved for the tribe." *Merrion v. Jicarilla Apache Tribe*, 455 U.S. 130, 160 (1982) (Stevens, J., dissenting). That power necessarily must include the lesser power to regulate land use in the interest of protecting the tribal community. Thus, the proper resolution of these cases depends on the extent to which the Tribe's virtually absolute power to exclude has been either diminished by federal statute or voluntarily surrendered by the Tribe itself. The facts of record, which are summarized in Justice White's opinion, dictate a different answer as to the two tracts of land at issue.

I

Zoning is the process whereby a community defines its essential character. Whether driven by a concern for health and safety, esthetics, or other public values, zoning provides the mechanism by which the polity ensures that neighboring uses of land are not mutually, or more often unilaterally, destructive. As Justice Sutherland observed for the Court in the landmark case of *Euclid v. Ambler Realty Co.*, 272 U.S. 365 (1926), the power to zone closely parallels the common law of nuisance and thus finds guidance in "the maxim *sic utere tuo ut alienum non laedas*"—use your own property in such a manner as not to injure that of another. Hence, a community reasonably might conclude that a factory has no place in an otherwise exclusively residential section or that an amusement park does not belong in an area devoted to quiet parks, libraries, and schools. As in nuisance law, the issue is ultimately one of whether the proposed land use is, "like a pig in the parlor instead of the barnyard," "merely a right thing in the wrong place."

An Indian tribe's power to exclude nonmembers from a defined geographical area obviously includes the lesser power to define the character of that area . . . . It is difficult to imagine a power that follows more forcefully from the power to exclude than the power to require that nonmembers, as a condition of entry, not disturb the traditional character of the reserved area.

At one time, the Yakima Nation's power to exclude nonmembers from its reservation was near-absolute. This power derived from two sources: The Tribe's aboriginal sovereignty over vast reaches of land in the Pacific Northwest and the express provisions of its 1855 treaty with the United States. Even in the absence of a treaty provision expressly granting such authority, Indian tribes maintain the sovereign power of exclusion unless otherwise curtailed. *See Worcester v. Georgia*, 6 Pet. 515 (1832); F. Cohen, Handbook of Federal Indian Law 252 (1982) (hereinafter Cohen). As is the case with many tribes, the Yakima Nation's power to exclude was confirmed through an express treaty provision. Through the 1855 treaty, which was ratified by the Senate and proclaimed by President Buchanan in 1859, the Yakima Nation ceded to the United States millions of acres of land east of the main ridge of the Cascade Mountains in exchange for the guarantee that a defined area of approximately 1.3 million acres would be reserved from the ceded lands "for the use and occupation of the aforesaid confederated tribes and bands of Indians." Treaty between the United States and the Yakima Indian Nation, 12 Stat. 951-952. The treaty provided that the entire "tract shall be set apart . . . for the exclusive use and benefit of said confederated tribes and bands of Indians, as an Indian reservation," and that no "white man, excepting those in the employment of the Indian Department [shall] be permitted to reside upon said reservation without permission of the tribe and the superintendent and agent." Thus, as of 1859, the Tribe's power to exclude was firmly established. The power to regulate land use ran parallel to the power to exclude. Just as the Tribe had authority to limit absolutely access to the Reservation, so it could also limit access to persons whose activities would conform to the Tribe's general plan for land use.

The Indian General Allotment Act of 1887 (Dawes Act), 24 Stat. 388, however, to some extent reworked fundamental notions of Indian sovereignty. Under the Dawes Act, the President was authorized to allot reservation lands in severalty to resident Indians. Allotted lands were held in trust for members of the Tribe for a period of at least 25 years, after which the members received fee patents and could freely transfer the land to nonmembers. "When all the lands had been allotted and the trusts expired, the reservation could be abolished." *Mattz v. Arnett*, 412 U.S. 481 (1973); *Moe v. Confederated Salish and Kootenai Tribes*, 425 U.S. 463 (1976). In this manner, the Dawes Act was designed ultimately to abolish Indian reservations while attempting to bring "security and civilization to the Indian." D. Otis, The Dawes Act and the Allotment of Indian Lands 32 (1973). But, not long after the Act took effect it became apparent that its beneficent purpose had failed and, in 1934, the Indian Reorganization Act, 48 Stat. 984, repudiated the allotment policy. In the interim, however, large portions of reservation lands were conveyed to nonmembers such as petitioners Wilkinson and Brendale.

The Dawes Act did not itself transfer any regulatory power from the Tribe to any state or local governmental authority. Nonetheless, by providing for the allotment and ultimate alienation of reservation land, the Act in some respects diminished tribal authority. As we recognized in *Montana v. United States*, "treaty rights with respect to reservation lands must be read in light of the subsequent alienation of those lands." A statute that authorizes the sale of a parcel of land in a reservation must implicitly grant the purchaser access to that property. In addition, to the extent that large portions of reservation land were sold in fee, such that the Tribe could no longer determine the essential character of the region by setting conditions on entry to those parcels, the Tribe's legitimate interest in land use regulation was also diminished. Although it is inconceivable that Congress would have intended that the sale of a few lots would divest the Tribe of the power to determine the character of the tribal community, it is equally improbable that Congress envisioned that the Tribe would retain its interest in regulating the use of vast ranges of land sold in fee to nonmembers who lack any voice in setting tribal policy.

Since the Dawes Act provided that individual allotments would be held in trust by the United States for members of the Tribe for a period of at least 25 years, it is evident that the tribal authority over land use within the Reservation remained undiminished during that period and at least until actual transfers of land to nonmembers began to occur. The record does not contain a chronology of conveyances of trust lands to nonmembers of the Tribe, but it does disclose the extent of fee ownership of reservation lands at the time these lawsuits began. Most significantly, it establishes that as early as 1954 the Tribe had divided its Reservation into two parts, which the parties and the District Court consistently described as the "closed area" and the "open area," and that it continues to maintain the closed area as a separate community. That division, which was made many years before either petitioner Brendale or petitioner Wilkinson acquired title to reservation land, is of critical importance and requires a different disposition of their respective cases.[2]

II

Resolutions adopted by the Tribal Council of the Yakima Nation have created what is known officially as the "Reservation restricted area," and commonly referred to as the "closed area." Relying on language in the 1855 treaty assuring the Tribe "exclusive use and benefit" of reservation lands, the Council in a 1954 resolution declared "that the open range and forested area of the Yakima Indian Reservation is to *remain* closed to the general public" to protect the area's "grazing, forest, and wildlife resources." Resolution of Yakima Tribal Council (Aug. 4, 1954) (emphasis supplied). Under the 1954 resolution, entry into this area was "restricted to enrolled members of the Yakima Tribe, official agency employees, persons with *bona fide* property or business interests," close relatives of enrolled members, members of certain other

---

[2] The labels "closed area" and "open area" are, of course, irrelevant to my analysis. What is important is that the Tribe has maintained a defined area in which only a very small percentage of the land is held in fee and another defined area in which approximately half of the land is held in fee.

tribes, and certain permittees. In addition, the resolution provided that "[e]ntry into closed areas is forbidden all persons while under the influence of liquor."

Although the closed area occupies about 807,000 acres, consisting of almost two-thirds of the entire Reservation, only 25,000 acres are owned in fee. For the most part this area consists of forests, which provide the major source of income to the Tribe. Virtually all of the fee land is owned by lumber companies whose operations are subject to regulation by the Bureau of Indian Affairs (BIA). Excluding the land owned by these lumber companies, the remaining fee land constitutes less than one percent of the closed area. There are no permanent inhabitants of the Yakima County portion of the closed area. One state-maintained highway traverses a portion of the area and several roads maintained by the BIA provide access to the closed area's interior. Apparently, however, the county does not maintain any roads in this portion of the reservation.

The Tribe operates a "courtesy permit system" that allows selected groups of visitors access to the closed area. In order to protect the area's "'natural foods, medicines,'" and other natural resources, the activities of visitors "are limited to sightseeing, hiking, camping and tribal, BIA or family related business or activity." Visitors are expressly "prohibited from hunting, fishing, boating, drinking, operating vehicles off established roads, camping at other than designated campsites and removing flora, fauna, petrified wood, other valuable rocks or minerals or artifacts." Tribal police and game officers enforce the courtesy permit system by monitoring ingress and egress at four guard stations and by patrolling the interior of the closed area.

Until recently the BIA supported the Tribe's policy of denying entry into the closed area by restricting use of BIA roads to members of the Tribe and a narrowly defined class of permittees. In litigation with the Government, petitioner Brendale eventually succeeded in establishing a right of access to his own property over BIA roads. Moreover, in 1988 the BIA ultimately decided to allow the public to use BIA roads because they had been constructed with public funds. Contrary to the suggestion in Justice White's opinion, however, the fact that nonmembers may now drive on these roads does not change the basic character of the closed area or undermine the Tribe's historic and consistent interest in preserving the pristine character of this vast, uninhabited portion of its Reservation.

Petitioner Brendale's property is located in the heart of this closed portion of the Reservation. He inherited the property in 1972 from his mother, who had been an enrolled member of the Yakima Nation. In 1982, Brendale filed a proposal with the Yakima County zoning authorities for the development of a 20-acre subdivision consisting of ten 2-acre lots. BIA roads provide the only access to the property, the nearest county road being more than 20 miles away. The proposal contemplates the construction of recreational summer cabins, on-site sewage disposal systems, and interior access roads that would be maintained by a homeowners' association. The District Court found that the proposal would have a number of adverse environmental consequences and that the only interest that Yakima County possessed in overseeing the use of the Brendale property was that of "providing regulatory functions to its taxpaying citizens." The county did not appeal from the District Court's decision holding that the Tribe has the exclusive authority to regulate land use in the closed area.

Although the logging operations, the construction of BIA roads, and the transfer of ownership of a relatively insignificant amount of land in the closed area unquestionably has diminished the Tribe's power to exclude non-Indians from that portion of its Reservation, this does not justify the conclusion that the Tribe has surrendered its historic right to regulate land use in the restricted portion of the Reservation. By maintaining the power to exclude nonmembers from entering all but a small portion of the closed area, the Tribe has preserved the power to define the essential character of that area. In fact, the Tribe has exercised this power, taking care that the closed area remains an undeveloped refuge of cultural and religious significance, a place where tribal members "may camp, hunt, fish, and gather roots and berries in the tradition of their culture." Amended Zoning Regulations of the Yakima Indian Nation, Resolution No. 1-98-72, § 23 (1972).

The question is then whether the Tribe has authority to prevent the few individuals who own portions of the closed area in fee from undermining its general plan to preserve the character of this unique resource by developing their isolated parcels without regard to an otherwise common scheme. More simply, the question is whether the owners of the small amount of fee land may bring a pig into the parlor. In my opinion, just as Congress could not possibly have intended in enacting the Dawes Act that tribes would maintain the power to exclude *bona fide* purchasers of reservation land from that property, it could not have intended that tribes would lose control over the character of their reservations upon the sale of a few, relatively small parcels of land. Neither proposition is explicit in the Dawes Act, yet both appear necessary to a reasonable operation of the allotment process . . . . In this sense, the Tribe's power to zone is like an equitable servitude; the burden of complying with the Tribe's zoning rules runs with the land without regard to how a particular estate is transferred.

. . . .

[T]he Court's decision in *Montana v. United States*, 450 U.S. 544 (1981), require a different result. First, the *Montana* case involved a discriminatory land use regulation. The Tribe's regulation prohibited non-Indians from hunting or fishing on their own property while members of the Tribe were free to engage in those activities. In contrast, petitioners do not suggest that a member of the Tribe would be allowed to undertake the development Brendale proposes. It is Brendale who seeks a special, privileged status. Second, in the *Montana* case we were careful to point out that the conduct of the non-Indians on their fee lands posed no threat to the welfare of the Tribe. In sharp contrast, in this case the District Court expressly found that Brendale's

"planned development of recreational housing places critical assets of the Closed Area in jeopardy . . . . [O]f paramount concern to this court is the threat to the Closed Area's cultural and spiritual values. To allow development in this unique and undeveloped area would drastically diminish those intangible values. That in turn would undoubtedly negatively affect the general health and welfare of the Yakima Nation and its members. This court must conclude therefore that the Yakima Nation may regulate the use that Brendale makes of his fee land within the Reservation's Closed Area."

Finally, in holding in the *Montana* case that the Tribe could not regulate non-Indian fishing and hunting on fee land within the reservation, we stressed that the State of Montana, and not the Tribe, stocked the river with fish and provided a portion of the game found on the reservation. In addition, we held that the State owned the bed of the Big Horn River and thus rejected the Tribe's contention that it was entitled to regulate fishing and duck hunting in the river based on its purported ownership interest. No such state or county interest is asserted in this case.

In my view, the fact that a very small proportion of the closed area is owned in fee does not deprive the Tribe of the right to ensure that this area maintains its unadulterated character. This is particularly so in a case such as this in which the zoning rule at issue is neutrally applied, is necessary to protect the welfare of the Tribe, and does not interfere with any significant state or county interest. Although application of the pre-emption analysis advocated by Justice White provides some assurance that the Reservation will not be overrun by various uses inconsistent with important tribal interests, it does not provide a means by which the Tribe can continue to define the character of the restricted area. The incremental shifts in the texture and quality of the surrounding environment occasioned by discrete land-use decisions within an expansive territory are not readily monitored or regulated by considering "whether the uses that were actually authorized on [the relevant] property imperiled the political integrity, the economic security, or the health or welfare of the Tribe."

I therefore agree with Justice Blackmun that the Tribe may zone the Brendale property. The judgment of the Court of Appeals is accordingly affirmed in No. 87-1622.

III

The authority of the Tribe to enact and enforce zoning ordinances applicable in the open area—where petitioner Wilkinson's property is located—requires a different analysis. Although the Tribe originally had the power to exclude non-Indians from the entire Reservation, the "subsequent alienation" of about half of the property in the open area has produced an integrated community that is not economically or culturally delimited by reservation boundaries. Because the Tribe no longer has the power to exclude nonmembers from a large portion of this area, it also lacks the power to define the essential character of the territory. As a result, the Tribe's interest in preventing inconsistent uses is dramatically curtailed. For this reason, I agree with Justice White that the Tribe lacks authority to regulate the use of Wilkinson's property. So long as the land is not used in a manner that is pre-empted by federal law, the Tribe has no special claim to relief. It, of course, retains authority to regulate the use of trust land, and the county does not contend otherwise.

Unlike the closed area, the Tribe makes no attempt to control access to the open area. In this respect, the District Court found that "access to the area is not limited by the Yakima Nation and non-tribal members move freely throughout the area." The county has constructed and maintained 487 miles of road, all of which are equally accessible to reservation residents and the general public. Although the Tribe has asserted that it has the authority to regulate land use in the three incorporated towns, it has never attempted to do so. In "sharp contrast to the pristine, wilderness-like character of the 'Closed Area,'" the open area is marked by "residential and commercial developmen[t]."

Members of the Yakima Nation represent less than 20 percent of the open area's total population.[4] Indians and non-Indians alike are eligible to vote in County elections. Only enrolled members of the Tribe, however, are entitled to participate in Tribal elections. Similarly, while the county provides police protection, public education, and other social services to both Indians and non-Indians, government services provided by the Tribe—although theoretically available to all residents—are in practice generally used only by members of the Tribe. Furthermore, the District Court found that the county has a substantial interest in regulating land use in the open area—and in particular in protecting "the county's valuable agricultural land"—and that the open area lacks "a unique religious or spiritual significance to the members of the Yakima Nation."

In contrast to the closed area, almost half of the land in the open area is owned in fee. The majority of the fee land is located in three incorporated towns in the open area, where

---

[4] According to the 1980 Census, the total population of the portion of the Yakima reservation within Yakima County is 24,750, of whom 4,908 are Indians. U.S. Dept. of Commerce, Bureau of Census, 1980 Census of Population 49-460 (Table 192) (1983).

approximately 10,000 of the open area's 25,000 residents live. The remaining portion of the open area, which includes approximately 143,000 acres of irrigated farm land, is largely devoted to agriculture. About 63,179 acres of this farm land are owned in fee by nonmembers. Another 67,466 acres of this land are owned by the Yakima Nation or its members, but are leased to non-Indians. Only 12,355 acres are farmed by tribal members. Petitioner "Wilkinson's property is bordered to the north by trust land and to the east, south and west by fee land." The 40 acre lot overlooks the Yakima Municipal Airport and is composed of unfarmed, sagebrush land.

Given that a large percentage of the land in the open area is owned in fee by nonmembers—and that an additional portion is leased to nonmembers—even if the Tribe had exercised its power to exclude nonmembers from trust land, it would have been unable thereby to establish the essential character of the region. In such circumstances, allowing a nonmember to use his or her land in a manner that might not be approved by the Tribal Council does not upset an otherwise coherent scheme of land use. The Tribe cannot complain that the nonmember seeks to bring a pig into the parlor, for, unlike the closed area, the Tribe no longer possesses the power to determine the basic character of the area. Moreover, it is unlikely that Congress intended to give the Tribe the power to determine the character of an area that is predominantly owned and populated by nonmembers, who represent 80 percent of the population yet lack a voice in tribal governance. Finally, to the extent the open area has lost its character as an exclusive tribal resource, and has become, as a practical matter, an integrated portion of the county, the Tribe has also lost any claim to an interest analogous to an equitable servitude. Under the "change of neighborhood" doctrine, an equitable servitude lapses when the restriction, as applied to "the general vicinity and not merely a few parcels," has "become outmoded," has "lost its usefulness," or has become "'inequitable' to enforce." R. Cunningham, W. Stoebuck, & D. Whitman, Law of Property § 8.20, pp. 482-483 (1984). Because the open area no longer maintains the character of a unique tribal asset and because the Tribe accordingly lacks a substantial interest in governing land use, the power to zone has "become outmoded."

I therefore agree with Justice White's conclusion that the Tribe lacks authority to zone the Wilkinson property.

IV

My conclusion that the dramatically different facts of these two cases should produce different results is subject to the obvious criticism that it does not identify a bright-line rule. The primary responsibility for line-drawing, however, is vested in the legislature. Moreover, line-drawing is inherent in the continuum that exists between those reservations that still maintain their status as distinct social structures and those that have become integrated in other local polities. Any difficulty courts may encounter in drawing the line between "closed" and "open" portions of reservations simply reflects that the factual predicate to these cases is itself complicated. Indeed, Justice White's rule does little to avoid the difficulty of drawing lines and making subtle distinctions. Just as it is neither possible nor appropriate in this case to set a fixed percentage of fee ownership that will govern every case that may arise, so is it impossible to articulate precise rules that will govern whenever a tribe asserts that a land use approved by a county board is preempted by federal law. And although the rule that Justice Blackmun proposes would provide an obvious answer in most cases, he recognizes that "[i]t may be that on some reservations, including the Yakima reservation, there are essentially self-contained, definable, areas in which non-Indian fee lands so predominate that the tribe has no significant interest in controlling land use." Finally, it would be fundamentally unfair to deny appropriate relief to either party in this case, which involves no difficulty in discerning the proper line, simply because a future case may be more difficult.

Accordingly, in No. 87-1622, the judgment of the Court of Appeals is affirmed. I concur in the judgment in Nos. 87-1697 and 87-1711, reversing the judgment of the Court of Appeals.

JUSTICE BLACKMUN, with whom JUSTICE BRENNAN and JUSTICE MARSHALL join, concurring in the judgment in No. 87-1622 and dissenting in Nos. 87-1697 and 87-1711.

The Court's combined judgment in these consolidated cases—splitting tribal zoning authority over non-Indian fee lands between the so-called "open" and "closed" areas of the Yakima Indian Reservation—is Solomonic in appearance only. This compromise result arises from two distinct approaches to tribal sovereignty, each of which is inconsistent with this Court's past decisions and undermines the Federal Government's longstanding commitment to the promotion of tribal autonomy. Because the Court's judgment that the tribe does not have zoning authority over non-Indian fee lands in the "open" area of its reservation is wrong, in my view, as a matter of law and fashions a patently unworkable legal rule, I dissent in Nos. 87-1697 and 87-1711. Because Justice Stevens' opinion reaches the right result for the wrong reason with respect to the tribe's authority to zone non-Indian fee lands in the closed portion of the Reservation, I concur in the judgment in No. 87-1662.

. . . .

I

Eight years ago, this Court decided *Montana v. United States*, 450 U.S. 544 (1981). In that case, it was ruled that an Indian tribe did not have the inherent authority to prohibit non-Indian hunting and fishing on fee lands located on a reservation and owned by a non-Indian, where the tribe did not assert that any right or interest was infringed or affected by the non-Indian conduct. Today, with what seems to me to be no more than a perfunctory discussion of this Court's decisions both before and after *Montana*, Justice White's opinion reads that case as establishing a general rule, modified only by two narrow exceptions, that Indian tribes have no authority over the activities of non-Indians on their reservations absent express congressional delegation.

Applying this rule, Justice White further suggests that *Montana*'s "second exception," which recognizes inherent tribal authority over non-Indian conduct that "threatens or has some direct effect on the political integrity, the economic security, or the health or welfare of the tribe," does not extend to the right of an Indian tribe to make rational and comprehensive land-use decisions for its reservation. Such a holding would guarantee that adjoining reservation lands would be subject to inconsistent and potentially incompatible zoning policies, and for all practical purposes would strip tribes of the power to protect the integrity of trust lands over which they enjoy unquestioned and exclusive authority.

Montana need not, and should not, be read to require such an absurd result. When considered in the full context of the Court's other relevant decisions, it is evident that *Montana* must be read to recognize the inherent authority of tribes to exercise civil jurisdiction over non-Indian activities on tribal reservations where those activities, as they do in the case of land use, implicate a significant tribal interest.

A

Justice White's opinion reiterates a "general principle" it finds in *Montana* that Indian tribes have no authority over the activities of non-Indians absent express congressional delegation. Concededly, the Court in *Montana* suggested that the "exercise of tribal power beyond what is necessary to protect tribal self-government or to control internal relations is inconsistent with the dependent status of the tribes, and so cannot survive without express congressional delegation." But *Montana* is simply one, and not even the most recent, of a long line of our decisions discussing the nature of inherent tribal sovereignty. These cases, landmarks in 150 years of Indian-law jurisprudence, establish a very different "general principle" governing inherent tribal sovereignty—a principle according to which tribes retain their sovereign powers over non-Indians on reservation lands unless the exercise of that sovereignty would be "inconsistent with the overriding interests of the National Government." *See, e.g., Washington v. Confederated Tribes of Colville Indian Reservation*, 447 U.S. 134, 153 (1980). *Montana*, and specifically the two "exceptions" that *Montana* recognizes to its anomalous "general principle," must be read against the rich and extensive background of these cases. When so considered, it is clear to me that nothing in *Montana* precludes, and indeed *Montana* contemplates, the exercise of civil jurisdiction over non-Indian activities on a tribal reservation, including the power to zone fee lands, where those non-Indian reservation activities implicate a significant tribal interest.

1

The crucial step in the process of interpreting *Montana*, and the step that Justice White's opinion neglects, is to place that case in the spectrum of what came before and after it. From a time long before the 13 Colonies declared their independence from England, European nations recognized the native tribes of this continent as self-governing, sovereign, political communities. From this Court's earliest jurisprudence immediately after the American Revolution, it followed the settled understanding of international law that the sovereignty of the individual tribes, "domestic dependent nations" that placed themselves under the protection of the United States, survived their incorporation within the United States, except as necessarily diminished.[1] In the landmark *Cherokee Cases*, this Court, through Chief Justice Marshall, held that the dependent status of the tribes divested them only of those aspects of their sovereignty—in particular the authority to engage in governmental relations with foreign powers and the power to alienate land to non-Indians—that were inherently inconsistent with the paramount authority of the United States.[2]

Our approach to inherent tribal sovereignty remained essentially constant in all critical respects in the century and a half between John Marshall's first illumination of the subject and this Court's *Montana* decision. Time and again we stated that, while Congress retains the authority to abrogate tribal sovereignty as it sees fit, tribal sovereignty is not implicitly divested except in those limited circumstances principally involving external powers of sovereignty where the exercise of tribal

---

[1] F. Cohen, Handbook of Federal Indian Law 235 (1982 ed.). *See also* Worcester v. Georgia, 6 Pet. 515, 560-561 (1832): "[T]he settled doctrine of the law of nations is, that a weaker power does not surrender its independence—its right to self-government, by associating with a stronger, and taking its protection. A weak state, in order to provide for its safety, may place itself under the protection of one more powerful, without stripping itself of the right of government, and ceasing to be a state."

[2] *See* Cherokee Nation v. Georgia, 5 Pet. 1 (1831); Worcester v. Georgia, 6 Pet. 515 (1832); *see also* Johnson v. McIntosh, 8 Wheat. 543 (1823).

authority is necessarily inconsistent with their dependent status. *See, e.g., United States v. Wheeler*, 435 U.S. 313 (1978).

. . . .[3]

Indeed, what is most remarkable about this Court's jurisprudence of inherent tribal sovereignty is that, except for those few aspects of sovereignty recognized in the *Cherokee Cases* as necessarily divested, the Court only once prior to *Montana* (and never thereafter) has found an additional sovereign power to have been relinquished upon incorporation. In *Oliphant v. Suquamish Indian Tribe*, 435 U.S. 191 (1978), we held that tribes have no inherent criminal jurisdiction over non-Indians in tribal court. In light of the nearly universal understanding dating from the origins of this country's dealings with the tribes that they do not possess criminal jurisdiction over non-Indians except as permitted by treaty, and in light of the Federal Constitution's extraordinary protections against intrusions on personal liberty, we concluded that inherent criminal jurisdiction over non-Indians is inconsistent with the dependent status of the tribes. But . . . nothing in *Oliphant* negates our historical understanding that the tribes retain substantial civil jurisdiction over non-Indians.

. . . .

2

Given this background, how should we read *Montana* where the Court held that the tribe had no inherent authority to prohibit non-Indians from hunting and fishing on fee lands within the

---

[3] Justice White's opinion asserts that *Wheeler* "made clear" that all tribal regulatory authority over relations with non-Indians is necessarily inconsistent with their dependent status and, therefore, divested. *Wheeler* says no such thing, as is clear when Justice White's opinion's selective quotation is placed in context. The issue in *Wheeler* was whether the conviction of an Indian in tribal court on a charge of contributing to the delinquency of a minor was a federal prosecution such that a second criminal proceeding arising from the same incident would be barred under the Double Jeopardy Clause. The resolution of this issue turned on whether the Tribe's criminal jurisdiction over the Indian defendant stemmed from its own inherent authority or, instead, from federal authority delegated to the Tribe by Congress. After discussing at some length the general rule that Indian tribes still possess those aspects of sovereignty not withdrawn by treaty or statute, or by implication as a necessary result of their dependent status, the Court held that the Tribe retained inherent authority to punish Indian offenders. The Court first noted that Congress, far from divesting tribes of this power, had consistently recognized it. The Court then turned to the question whether criminal jurisdiction was necessarily divested by virtue of the dependent status of the tribes. The Court stated:

"[T]he sovereign power of a tribe to prosecute its members for tribal offenses does not fall within that part of sovereignty which the Indians implicitly lost by virtue of their dependent status. The areas in which such implicit divestiture of sovereignty has been held to have occurred are those involving the relations between an Indian tribe and nonmembers of the tribe. Thus, Indian tribes can no longer freely alienate to non-Indians the land they occupy. They cannot enter into direct commercial or governmental relations with foreign nations. And, as we have recently held, they cannot try nonmembers in tribal courts.

These limitations rest on the fact that the dependent status of Indian tribes within our territorial jurisdiction is necessarily inconsistent with their freedom independently to determine their external relations. But the power of self-government, including the power to prescribe and enforce internal criminal laws, are of a different type. They involve only the relations among members of a tribe."

Clearly, nothing in this discussion suggests that tribes have lost all inherent sovereignty over tribal relations with non-Indians. (Indeed, the Court in *Wheeler* had no cause to address this issue.) *Wheeler* simply stands for the uncontroversial proposition that those specific aspects of inherent sovereignty that necessarily have been divested (criminal jurisdiction over non-Indians, alienation of land, and foreign relations) involve tribal relations with non-Indians. Notably, Justice White's proposed reading of *Wheeler* is in direct conflict with *Montana*, which explicitly recognizes that tribes retain some inherent authority over non-Indians.

reservation? With respect to *Montana*'s "general principle" creating a presumption against tribal civil jurisdiction over non-Indians absent express congressional delegation, I find it evident that the Court simply missed its usual way. Although the Court's opinion reads as a restatement, not as a revision, of existing doctrine, it contains language flatly inconsistent with its prior decisions defining the scope of inherent tribal jurisdiction. Notably, in support of its anomalous "general principle," the *Montana* opinion relies mainly on a line of state-law pre-emption cases that address the issue—irrelevant to the issue of inherent tribal sovereignty—as to when States may exercise jurisdiction over non-Indian activities on a reservation. Not surprisingly, and of critical importance for deciding the instant case, the *Montana* presumption has found no place in our subsequent decisions discussing inherent sovereignty.

But to recognize that *Montana* strangely reversed the otherwise consistent presumption in favor of inherent tribal sovereignty over reservation lands is not to excise the decision from our jurisprudence. Despite the reversed presumption, the plain language of *Montana* itself expressly preserves substantial tribal authority over non-Indian activity on reservations, including fee lands, and, more particularly, may sensibly be read as recognizing inherent tribal authority to zone fee lands.

Montana explicitly recognizes that tribes "retain inherent sovereign power to exercise some forms of civil jurisdiction over non-Indians on their reservations, even on non-Indian fee lands." Specifically, *Montana* holds that tribes have civil jurisdiction over non-Indians who enter "contracts, leases or other arrangements" with the tribe, and over non-Indian conduct which "threatens or has some direct effect on the political integrity, the economic security, or the health or welfare of the tribe," even if that conduct occurs on fee lands. Thus, despite *Montana*'s reversal of the usual presumption in favor of inherent sovereignty over reservation activity, the decision reasonably may be read, and, in my view, should be read, to recognize that tribes may regulate the on-reservation conduct of non-Indians whenever a significant tribal interest is threatened or directly affected. So construed, *Montana* fits with relative ease into the constellation of this Court's sovereignty jurisprudence.

Under this approach, once the tribe's valid regulatory interest is established, the nature of land ownership does not diminish the tribe's inherent power to regulate in the area. This, too, is consistent with our cases. The Court has affirmed and reaffirmed that tribal sovereignty is in large part geographically determined . . . . We have held that lands obtained under the allotment policy, which permitted non-Indians to purchase lands located within reservations, remain part of those reservations unless Congress explicitly provides to the contrary, *e.g., Mattz v. Arnett*, 412 U.S. 481 (1973), and that tribal jurisdiction cannot be considered to vary between fee lands and trust lands; the resulting "impractical pattern of checkerboard jurisdiction" would be contrary to federal statute and policy. *Moe v. Confederated Salish and Kootenai Tribes*, 425 U.S. 463 (1976).

. . . .

It would be difficult to conceive of a power more central to "the economic security, or the health or welfare of the tribe," *Montana*, than the power to zone . . . . This fundamental sovereign power of local governments to control land use is especially vital to Indians, who enjoy a unique historical and cultural connection to the land. And how can anyone doubt that a tribe's inability to zone substantial tracts of fee land within its own reservation—tracts that are inextricably intermingled with reservation trust lands—would destroy the tribe's ability to engage in the systematic and coordinated utilization of land that is the very essence of zoning authority? . . . I am hard pressed to find any reason why zoning authority, a critical aspect of self-government and the ultimate instrument of "territorial management," should not be deemed to lie within the inherent sovereignty of the tribes . . . . Thus, if *Montana* is to fit at all within this Court's Indian sovereignty jurisprudence, zoning authority—even over fee lands—must fall within the scope of tribal jurisdiction under *Montana*.

. . . .

3

Justice White's opinion rejects this reading of *Montana* for several reasons, none of which withstands scrutiny. First, his opinion notes that *Montana*'s recognition of tribal sovereignty over non-Indian conduct that threatens the political and economic integrity or health or welfare of the tribe is prefaced by the word "may"—a linguistic turn that the majority reads as suggesting that such tribal sovereignty is not always retained. Read in context, I think it clear that the Court's use of the word "may" was not an expression of doubt about the existence of tribal sovereignty under the enumerated circumstances, but, rather, was a reflection of the obvious fact that the comment was pure dictum. A more definitive statement on an issue not presented in the case surely would have been inappropriate.

Second, Justice White's opinion suggests that applying *Montana*'s language literally to the problem of zoning fee lands would create the peculiar, and untenable, situation of having zoning authority vary over time between the tribe and the State depending on what effect a proposed land use might have on the tribe. This hypothetical problem is entirely of Justice White's own creation. *Montana*'s literal language does not require, as he claims, a parcel-by-parcel, use-by-use determination whether a proposed use of fee land will threaten the political integrity, economic security, or health or welfare of the tribe. The threat to the tribe does not derive solely from the proposed uses of specific parcels of fee lands (which admittedly would vary over time and place). The threat stems from the loss of the general and longer-term advantages of comprehensive land management.

What the majority offers the tribes falls far short of meeting their legitimate needs. Justice White's opinion fashions a newfangled federal nuisance-type cause of action by which the tribe may bring suit in federal court to enjoin a particular proposed land use that seriously imperils the political integrity, economic security, or health or welfare of the tribe. While resort to this proposed cause of action may ultimately prevent blatantly abusive non-Indian uses of reservation lands, the opportunity to engage in protracted litigation over every proposed land use that conflicts with tribal interests does nothing to recognize the tribe's legitimate sovereign right to regulate the lands within its reservation, with the view to the long-term, active management of land use that is the very difference between zoning and case-by-case nuisance litigation.

Justice White's opinion also claims that it is acting here to protect the expectations of landowners. I agree that the need for certainty in zoning laws is a valid concern. But if Justice White's true concern were with practical consequences, he would never adopt the rule he proposes today. Because we know that the tribe, and only the tribe, has authority to zone the trust lands within the reservation, Justice White's opinion, and a majority of the Court with respect to the "open" area, have established a regime that guarantees that neither the State nor the Tribe will be able to establish a comprehensive zoning plan. Although under the majority's rule landowners may be certain as to which zoning authority controls the use of their land, adjoining parcels of land throughout the "open" area of the reservation (and throughout the entire reservation under

Justice White's theory) will be zoned by different zoning authorities with competing and perhaps inconsistent land-use priorities. This, in practice, will be nothing short of a nightmare, nullifying the efforts of both sovereigns to segregate incompatible land uses and exacerbating the already considerable tensions that exist between local and tribal governments in many parts of the Nation about the best use of reservation lands.

In any event, Justice White's opinion does not really explain why the general inability of a tribe to control land use on numerous tracts of land interspersed across its reservation does not inherently threaten the political integrity, economic security, or health or welfare of the tribe. Instead, the opinion claims that to hold that tribes have inherent zoning power over non-Indian fee lands would be to hold that tribes can exercise every police power over such lands, and that such a holding is contrary to the result in *Montana* itself.

This concern is misplaced. It does not necessarily follow that a finding of inherent zoning authority over fee lands on a checkerboarded reservation, an authority indispensable to the fulfillment of a tribe's uncontested right to zone its trust lands, also entails a finding of inherent authority for all police powers. As *Montana* itself demonstrates, there may be cases in which tribes assert the power to regulate activities as to which they have no valid interest. Zoning is clearly not such a case.

4

In short, it is my view that under all of this Court's inherent sovereignty decisions, including *Montana*, tribes retain the power to zone non-Indian fee lands on the reservation. Justice White's opinion presents not a single thread of logic for the proposition that such zoning power is inconsistent with the overriding interest of the National Government, and therefore necessarily divested, or that such zoning power is not fundamental to the political and economic security of the tribe, and therefore reserved to the tribe by the plain language of *Montana*. Instead, at the expense of long-recognized tribal rights, many of our precedents, and 150 years of federal policy, Justice White's opinion replaces sovereignty with a form of legal tokenism: the opportunity to sue in court has replaced the opportunity to exercise sovereign authority. This substitution is without sound basis in law, and without practical value.

B

While Justice White's opinion misreads the Court's decisions defining the limits of inherent tribal sovereignty, Justice Stevens' opinion disregards those decisions altogether. By grounding the tribe's authority to zone non-Indian fee lands exclusively in its power to exclude non-Indians from the reservation, and by refusing even to consider whether the Tribe's inherent authority might support the zoning of non-Indian fee lands in the "open area," Justice Stevens' opinion appears implicitly to conclude that tribes have no inherent authority over non-Indians on reservation lands. As is evident from my discussion of Justice White's opinion, this conclusion stands in flat contradiction to every relevant Indian sovereignty case that this Court has decided.

Justice Stevens' opinion also is at odds with this Court's reservation disestablishment decisions. Justice Stevens distinguishes between the "open" and "closed" areas of the Reservation on the ground that Congress, in enacting the Dawes Act, could not have intended for tribes to maintain zoning authority over non-Indian fee lands where, as in the "open area" of the Yakima Reservation, the allotment of reservation lands "has produced an integrated community that is not economically or culturally delimited by reservation boundaries." I fail to see how this distinction can be squared with this Court's decisions specifically rejecting arguments that those reservation areas where the Dawes Act has resulted in substantial non-Indian land ownership should be treated differently for jurisdictional purposes from those areas where tribal holdings predominate. And I do not see how Justice Stevens' theory can be squared with the unequivocal holdings of our cases that the Dawes Act did not diminish the reservation status of reservation lands alienated to non-Indian owners even where that part of the reservation had "lost its [Indian] identity."

Precedents aside, Justice Stevens' opinion points to no authority, either in the text of the Dawes Act or its legislative history, in support of its critical conjecture that "it is inconceivable that Congress would have intended that the sale of a few lots would divest the Tribe of the power to determine the character of the tribal community, it is equally improbable that Congress envisioned that the Tribe would retain its interest in regulating the use of vast ranges of land sold in fee to nonmembers who lack any voice in setting tribal policy." Moreover, even if Justice Stevens is right about congressional intent at the time of the Dawes Act, why should this matter? "The policy of allotment and sale of surplus reservation land was repudiated in 1934 by the Indian Reorganization Act, 48 Stat. 984, now amended and codified as 25 U.S.C. § 461 et seq." *Mattz.* Surely, in considering whether Congress intended tribes to enjoy civil jurisdiction, including zoning authority, over non-Indian fee lands in reservation areas where non-Indian ownership predominates, this Court should direct its attention not to the intent of the Congress that passed the Dawes Act, but rather to the intent of the Congress that repudiated the Dawes Act, and established the Indian policies to which we are heir. This 1934 Congress, as definitively interpreted by the Executive Branch at the time, intended that tribal civil jurisdiction extend over "all of the lands of the reservation, whether owned by the tribe, by members thereof, or by outsiders."

On a practical level, Justice Stevens' approach to zoning authority poses even greater difficulties than Justice White's approach. Justice Stevens' opinion not only would establish a self-defeating regime of "checkerboard" zoning authority in "open" areas of every reservation, but it would require an intrinsically standardless threshold determination as to when a section of a reservation contains sufficient non-Indian land holdings to warrant an "open" classification. Justice Stevens' opinion suggests no benchmark for making this determination, and I can imagine none.

Moreover, to the extent that Justice Stevens' opinion discusses the characteristics of a reservation area where the Tribe possesses authority to zone because it has preserved the "essential character of the reservation," these characteristics betray a stereotyped and almost patronizing view of Indians and reservation life. The opinion describes the "closed area" of the Yakima Reservation as "pristine," and emphasizes that it is spiritually significant to the tribe and yields natural foods and medicines. The opinion then contrasts this unadulterated portion of the reservation with the "open area," which is "marked by 'residential and commercial developmen[t].' " In my view, even under Justice Stevens' analysis, it must not be the case that tribes can retain the "essential character" of their reservations (necessary to the exercise of zoning authority), only if they forgo economic development and maintain those reservations according to a single, perhaps quaint, view of what is characteristically "Indian" today.

In sum, because Justice Stevens' opinion proposes an approach to tribal authority radically different from, and inconsistent with, our past decisions, because this approach rests on irrelevant conjecture about congressional intent, and because the approach is generally unsound, I cannot concur even partially in Justice Stevens' opinion, however partially attractive its results. Our past decisions and common sense compel a finding that the tribe has zoning authority over all the lands within its reservation.

II

Having concluded that the tribe has the inherent authority to zone non-Indian fee lands, the question remains whether this authority is exclusive or whether it is coextensive with the authority of the State acting through the county. This is not the place for an extended discussion of Indian pre-emption law. Suffice it to say that our cases recognize that the States have authority to exercise jurisdiction over non-Indian activities on the reservation, but that this authority is pre-empted if it either unlawfully infringes on the right of reservation Indians to make their own laws and be ruled by them, or interferes or is incompatible with federal and tribal interests reflected in federal law, unless the state interests at stake are sufficient to justify the assertion of state authority. Applying this test, the Court has recognized coextensive state and tribal civil jurisdiction where the exercise of concurrent authority does not do violence to the rights of either sovereign.

In my view, however, concurrent zoning jurisdiction by its very nature is unworkable. Concurrent zoning authority has the practical effect of nullifying the zoning authority of both sovereigns in every instance where the two establish different permissible land uses for the same tract of land. Presumably, under a scheme of concurrent jurisdiction, every proposed land use would have to satisfy the more stringent of the two competing zoning codes. Such a system obviously would defeat the efforts of both sovereigns to establish comprehensive plans for the systematic use of the lands within their respective jurisdictions.[9]

. . . .

Unlike the Court of Appeals, I find no room here for a remand to consider more closely the nature of the county's conflicting interests. When it is determined that the tribe, which is the one entity that has the power to zone trust lands, also has the power to zone fee lands, the inherent unworkability of concurrent zoning requires the conclusion that the tribe's power to zone, once it chooses to exercise that power, is exclusive. No further balancing of interests is required. Thus, I would hold that, as to both "open" and "closed" lands, the county of Yakima is without authority to zone reservation lands, including fee lands.

[3] Analysis of the Opinions

McIntosh, *Worcester* and *Brendale* obviously are related. I assume you were not surprised when cites to the earlier cases showed up in the *Brendale* opinions. But there were subtle and not so subtle differences in the logic of the opinions in the three cases. *McIntosh* emphasized the discovery principle and the sovereign authority created by military power. *Worcester*

---

[9] It may be that on some reservation, including the Yakima reservation, there are essentially self-contained, definable, areas in which non-Indian fee lands so predominate that the tribe has no significant interest in controlling land use. I note that the Yakima reservation includes three incorporated towns—Harrah, Toppenish, and Wapato—that comprise almost exclusively non-Indian fee lands. Since the tribe never has attempted to zone lands within the incorporated towns, this litigation does not present the difficult question whether the tribe's interest in comprehensive zoning is sufficient to justify its exercise of zoning authority over a discrete portion of the reservation which includes no appreciable percentage of trust lands.

continued to evoke the discovery principle, but with additional rhetorical flourishes about voluntary cessions and tribal control over the sale of tribal possessory rights. In *Brendale*, the three way split among the justices produced three different visions of tribal sovereignty. All of the Court's members assumed that tribal trust lands were rightly zoned by the Yakamas, a genuflection to the central features of the *McIntosh-Worcester* line of cases leaving control over possessory interests in land with the tribes until terminated by the federal government. But the authors of the three opinions differed in quite significant ways on other questions.

Justice White, using ownership of specific parcels of land as a test to define governmental authority, allowed the Yakamas to control land use policy on non-trust fee lands only if they could prove, in a non-tribal administrative forum, that the plans of a specific developer on a specific site posed demonstrably serious threats to the political integrity of the tribe. That burden is obviously difficult, if not impossible, for the tribe to meet. It suggests that, for White, the obligation of the United States to protect tribal sovereignty is narrow, easily circumscribed by Congress and the states, especially when those without the right to participate in the political system of tribal governance are affected by tribal regulations. It also suggests a basic willingness to broaden the area of state and local control over tribal affairs.

Justice Stevens, focusing not on the ownership of any specific site, but on the general cultural flavor of a large area, concluded that authority to zone followed cultural ownership patterns. Thus the closed area, still largely primitive, undeveloped, and held as trust lands, could be zoned by the tribe. Stevens, of course, risked censure in taking this view. As Blackmun noted in dissent, why should a primitive and undeveloped flavor be the crucial definitional content of tribal culture? An argument may certainly be made that the more developed town areas represent the future cultural milieu of the tribe and that development in those areas on fee lands threatened tribal sovereignty much more directly than did construction in the middle of the closed area's wilderness.

Be that as it may, Stevens' vision of sovereignty was more culturally based than White's. Rather than focusing on land ownership and the inability of those outside a tribe's political structure to participate in the decisions affecting their assets, Stevens concentrated on the way in which actions on land might alter tribal culture. Stevens tried hard to find a compromise between the Marshall-era view granting large areas of sovereignty to tribes and the Dawes Act era in which such sovereignty was significantly reduced by Congressional action.

Justice Blackmun, looking more to the Marshall-era historical roots of Native American property law as a basis for his opinion, found the appropriate arena of power in the boundaries of the reservation rather than in any of its cultural divisions, political structures, or plots of individually owned land. Though limited by the impact of the allotment acts, Blackmun strove to retain as large a realm of tribal sovereignty as history, politics and circumstances allowed. Like the Viviat group of an earlier time, those claiming rights inside reservation boundary lines were relegated by Blackmun to pleading their case with tribal authorities. Rather than forcing the tribe to pursue its interests in external fora, as White wished, Blackmun asked those outside the tribe seeking to use reservation assets to subject themselves to tribal administrative and judicial procedures. Lack of political participation by non-Indians in tribal governance was not as important for Blackmun as safeguarding the cultural integrity of the Yakama nation. Presumably, a Blackmun oriented rule would require those not belonging to the Yakama nation dealing in land within reservation boundaries to sacrifice political influence in return for economic reward. While that might create a disincentive to investment by outsiders, perhaps that is exactly what Blackmun wished to do.

All the justices in *Brendale* professed to be acting faithfully within the structure of rules established by the *Cherokee Cases.* Perhaps they all paid homage to the old cases to avoid the charge that their decisions were motivated simply by political preferences rather than well reasoned, fair legal rules. Perhaps they have succeeded in fending off those who criticize the Court when it appears to act for political reasons, but there can be little doubt that significant political differences motivated the logic of their opinions.

The opinion of Justice White, for example, suggests that he favored the power of the state of Washington over that of the tribes, that his preference for state authority arose out of a fundamental distrust of central government, and that he wished to integrate the tribes into the larger American culture by reducing their sovereignty.

Justice Stevens, at least if we are to believe Blackmun's dissent, was adopting a paternalistic view of the trust, one looking to the dominant culture's vision of what tribal culture should be like as the defining influence on the role of the United States as trustee. Perhaps Stevens, similar to the role played by a guardian defining the ward's life, was defining the meaning of tribal culture and asking the central authority to protect it.

Justice Blackmun's opinion suggests that he distrusted states more than the central government, that he believed that the only way to provide power to the less powerful in this setting was to reduce the authority of Yakima County and the State of Washington, and that he felt integration of tribes into the dominant culture was less important than the cultural and economic integrity of the tribes themselves.

It is interesting that none of the opinions paid much attention to the importance of voting, political influence and electoral participation—the importance of approval by the supposedly "political" branches of government (executive and legislative as opposed to judicial) to the legitimacy of any legal norm.[53] Justice White, for example, could have argued that it was inappropriate to allow the tribe to zone fee lands owned by non-members of the Yakama Nation because they could not vote in tribal elections. Put another way, White could have used land ownership as a proxy for the right to vote, allowing land use regulation of any particular site only by a government that "represented" the interests of the person owning the property.

Perhaps White was reluctant to use such a theory because he sat in an institution which itself lacked the direct support of the electorate. Or perhaps such an argument would undermine the authority of the United States itself in claiming control over the reservation system and the right to terminate Indian title at the drop of a Congressional hat. Or perhaps he was unwilling to make the argument because others had powerful critiques. Blackmun, for example, might have argued that, given the run of American history, it was the tribe, not Yakima County, that needed representational bolstering and easy access to political power. Or he could have claimed that those dealing in tribal lands must run the risks associated with buying property in an area where they have no political clout, just as any absentee property owner who lives in one county but owns property in another must accede to a regulatory regime in which the owner has no electoral voice. Such logic would allow Blackmun to claim that the real issue was not linking political influence with voting power, but finding a way to give support to the long challenged integrity of tribal authority.

Allow me one final set of thoughts about these cases. The *Brendale* debate over the meaning of tribal sovereignty echoes the older debates about Civic Republicanism. Just as the founding

---

[53] Justice Stevens briefly mentioned that the Yakamas could vote in county elections, while non-Yakamas could not vote in tribal elections. But he did not use that fact for any logical purpose.

generation used property ownership as a way of guaranteeing responsible behavior by voters, the opinions of White, Stevens and Blackmun give us a debate about the relationships between culture, land ownership and regulation. Just as Jefferson assumed that turning the Cherokees into an agricultural people would hasten their adoption of "civilized" behavior, so White, Stevens and Blackmun argued about the links between land and the survival of culture. Integration and separation, cultural mix and cultural preservation—these ancient debates find continued meaning for us now. While we rarely draw links between the land rules governing the life of surviving Native American peoples and the vast redefinition of citizenship for African Americans that has occurred in the last 135 years, it should be clear to all of you that the links are there. For who among us can deny the power of cultural forces that both push us together and pull us apart, that force us to wonder about how each of us may comfortably claim membership in both ethnic and national communities.

[4] Problems of Tribal Sovereignty

[a] Any Practical Problems Generated by the Outcome of *Brendale?*

The land use decision making process left behind by *Brendale* is two-headed. Non-tribally owned fee lands in the closed area are largely under the control of the Yakama Nation, while those in the open area are generally governed by Yakima County regulations. The reservation covers a variety of land areas, from the ridges of the Cascade Mountains on the west to the Yakima River Valley on the east. The closed area covers the forested and mountainous areas to the west. Tribal guard stations, I am told, still prevent unwanted persons from venturing into the closed area along the few back country roads traversing the area. When zoning was first adopted in the area, the tribe largely adopted the county's ordinance. After the state adopted growth management legislation in 1990 requiring much more detailed local planning regimes, the tribal and county plans diverged significantly. Nonetheless, not much confusion has resulted. Land owners and officials of the Yakama Nation and Yakima County generally know whether a parcel of fee land is in the open or closed area and most zoning decisions are made without much contact between the two governments. The Yakama Nation's desire to protect its sovereignty has generally militated against cooperative land use planning arrangements in the area. The tribe does get involved in approvals for development of some non-tribally owned parcels in the open area when requests are made for access to water or water rights retained by the Yakama Nation, but for the most part two differing conceptions of land use operate side by side. Neither the Brendale nor the Wilkinson parcel has been developed since *Brendale* was decided. Brendale's land in the closed area is very remote and not very suitable for development. The Wilkinson parcel might be developed in the future, but at the moment stands unused.[54]

[b] Other Recent United States Supreme Court Cases

The Supreme Court has rendered decisions recently in a number of other disputes about the authority of local and tribal governments. How would you have resolved each of them?

Mississippi Band of Choctaw Indians v. Holyfield, 490 U.S. 30 (1989), involved twin babies, fathered by a Choctaw, and born to a Choctaw woman in Gulfport, Mississippi, some 200 miles from the reservation on which both parents lived. The Choctaw parents each signed a consent-to-adoption form before the Chancery Court of Harrison County, a Mississippi state court. A petition seeking approval of the children's adoption was filed by Orrey and Vivian Holyfield before the

---

[54] Interview with Mr. Dick Anderwald, Yakima County Planning Director (Nov. 18, 1998).

same court. The petition was granted. Two months later the Choctaw Band filed a petition in the Mississippi courts to void the adoption on the ground that it violated the Indian Child Welfare Act of 1978, 25 U.S.C. §§ 1901-1963, which among other things vests in the tribe exclusive jurisdiction over the custody of any Indian child "who resides or is domiciled within the reservation of such tribe." 25 U.S.C. § 1911(a). The Mississippi courts found that the twins were not domiciled on the reservation and that the Holyfield adoption was therefore legitimate. The Supreme Court reversed. The normal assumption that the domicile of children is the same as that of their parents was said not to be disturbed by the consent-to-adoption forms signed off the reservation. Justice Stevens, Rehnquist and Kennedy dissented, preferring to allow the parents to abandon their children's domicile. Both opinions noted with regret that over three years had passed between the adoption and the Supreme Court's decision.

Duro v. Reina, 495 U.S. 676 (1990), concerned a habeas corpus petition filed to challenge the authority of a tribal court to try a member of another tribe on criminal charges. Albert Duro was a member of the Torres-Martinez Band of Cahuilla Mission Indians who had lived most of his life outside the limits of any reservation. While living with a woman member of the Pima-Maricopa Tribe on the Salt River Reservation, he was charged with the illegal firing of a firearm within the Salt River Reservation, an event that led to the death of a 14-year-old member of the Gila River Indian Tribe of Arizona. Reina filed a habeas corpus petition challenging the authority of the Pima-Maricopa Indian Community Court to try him. The Supreme Court held that the writ should be granted since the tribal court only had the authority to try members of its own tribe. Two prior cases, *Oliphant v. Suquamish Indian Tribe*, 435 U.S. 191 (1978) and *United States v. Wheeler*, 435 U.S. 313 (1978) refused to allow tribes to try non-Indians. In *Duro*, that rule was extended to encompass Indians who are not members of the tribe seeking jurisdiction over the criminal actions. Reina, though an Indian, was relegated to a trial in a state court. Justices Brennan and Marshall dissented.

Oklahoma Tax Commission v. Citizen Band Potawatomi Indian Tribe of Oklahoma, 498 U.S. 806 (1991), concerned the collection of taxes on the sales of goods to tribal members and non-members at a convenience store owned by the tribe and located on trust land. The Court prohibited Oklahoma from seeking to tax the sale of goods to tribal members. Although taxation of sales to non-members was theoretically permitted, a direct suit against the tribe by a state to collect the tax was prohibited. Oklahoma was relegated to a suit against individual officers of the tribe for damages. The state was also free to structure legislation to seek payment of a tax fairly prorated between likely sales to members and non-members from wholesalers supplying the tribal store.

County of Yakima v. Confederated Tribes and Bands of the Yakama Indian Nation, 502 U.S. 251 (1992), presented another taxation issue, this time between the same jurisdictions involved in *Brendale*. Yakima County imposed two taxes—a property tax on land and an excise tax on the transfer of land. Justice Scalia wrote an opinion for the eight Justice majority holding that Yakima County could impose a property tax on all fee lands, including those owned by members of the Yakama Nation, but could not impose an excise tax on the sale of fee lands on the reservation. The former tax, the Court said, was allowed by a provision in the General Allotment Act permitting the "taxation of . . . land," while the latter tax was not. The Allotment Act did not bar state regulation of fee lands, Justice Scalia opined, unless it caused significant disruption of tribal self-government. Property taxes did not do that, he argued, while excise taxes did. That was because property taxes were imposed *in rem*, that is, on the Indian owned fee land, while excise taxes were imposed *in personam*, that is, on the person of a tribal member. Justice

Blackmun dissented, claiming to be mystified by the willingness of the majority to apply the terms of the Allotment Act to Indian owned fee lands in the face of Congressional rejection of that Act's assimilationist policies by the Indian Reorganization Act of 1934. In its most recent pronouncement on the taxation question, the Supreme Court unanimously held that fee lands that have been repurchased by a tribe are also taxable. *Cass County v. Leech Lake Band of Chippewa Indians*, 118 S. Ct. 1904 (1998).

[c] The Taking Clause

Materials on the Constitution's Taking Clause appear near the end of the text in Chapter 11. But the *Brendale* case neatly poses a problem about the degree to which the Taking Clause in the Fifth Amendment of the United States Constitution, which proclaims that property may not "be taken for public use, without just compensation," applies to tribal and non-tribal lands. Would it be legitimate under the Taking Clause for a tribe to prohibit all development in areas it may zone, even though similar actions taken by a typical local zoning agency would be unlawful? Come back to this issue after reading the takings cases.

§ 1.05 Adverse Possession, Prescription and Customary Rights

The rules of adverse possession and prescription are among the most interesting and surprising bodies of law in property. Much like the outcome of *Johnson v. McIntosh*, they operate to give ownership of land or an interest in land to trespassers. The rules owe their existence to statutes of limitations—laws requiring persons to pursue their legal rights within a certain period of time or lose them forever. If, for example, you are hit and injured by a drunk driver, every state requires that you sue the driver within a certain period of time or forfeit your right to do so. At some point, the Damoclean Sword of a lawsuit must be lifted, permitting even the most negligent to get back to the business of living their lives. Similarly, statutes of limitations require that land ownership claims be brought within a certain period of time. They are part of a structure of land law designed to minimize the longevity of potential title conflicts.

This segment of the text contains three cases. The first is a fairly standard prescription case, the second involves a claim of adverse possession against a government, and the third a claim that long standing customary practices by significant numbers of people override the interests of land owners. Native Americans are involved in the first two of these cases. That provides an opportunity to consider the broad cultural implications of relationships between governments, tribes and other citizens and to investigate some features of state law that may be relevant to claims of tribal sovereignty. It also should allow you to carefully consider the significance of Justice Marshall's observations near the end of his *Johnson v. McIntosh* opinion that some titles "held under the Indians were sanctioned by length of possession, but there is no case, so far as we are informed, of a judicial decision in their favor."

[1] Introduction: Summary of Adverse Possession and Prescription

Adverse possession and prescription statutes exist in a profusion of formats. For example, the statutes of Montana, where the next case originated, provide that suits to recover property must be brought within five years of the time the right to sue arises.[55] The period varies from five

---

[55] MONT. CODE ANN. § 70-19-401 (1997) reads:

No action for the recovery of real property or for the possession thereof can be maintained unless it appear that the plaintiff, his ancestor, predecessor, or grantor was seized or possessed of the property in question within 5 years before the commencement of the action.

to 30 years in different states, with most of the shorter periods (10 years or less) in states west of the Mississippi River. The western states, burdened in the nineteenth century with large numbers of conflicts in land titles, adopted short statutes of limitation in an effort to more quickly clear up titles. Some states have also shortened the statutory period to benefit parties in possession who pay property taxes or claim title under an instrument that purported, but failed, to convey land.[56]

Though the statutory time limits seem clear on their face, the courts have developed elaborate bodies of law to decide whether the time limits have in fact passed. Only certain sorts of events will cause the statute of limitations clock to "run" or move forward. In the situation in which you were run over by a drunk driver, for example, suppose you were knocked into a coma by the accident and did not wake up for two years. Should you be required to sue while still in a coma if the relevant statute of limitations was two years or less? Or suppose it is not possible today to make a forecast about the permanence or extent of your injuries. Should you have to sue before you know what your damages are? In the case of adverse possession, judicial inquiry focuses on the sort of possessory actions evincing a claim of ownership. A minor trespass may not start the statute of limitations time period running. But if a person lives on land for a significant period of time and claims to own it, the issue of commencement of the running of the limitations period might be resolved quite differently.

A standard statement of the adverse possession rule is that a statute of limitations will bar a claim of land ownership by an owner if possession by another has been actual, open and notorious, exclusive, continuous and hostile for the statutory period. The meanings of these terms often overlap; in many cases the same facts will support a conclusion that more than one factor has been fulfilled. *Actual* possession requires some sort of physical use of the land. Construction or use of buildings, farming, grazing, construction of fences, or a multitude of other actions are evidence that possession has been actual. Often this issue turns out to be a boundary question. A possessor may live in a farmhouse and cultivate 40 acres of what was originally a parcel of 160 acres. If he fenced in the whole thing, maybe he actually possessed it all despite leaving 75% unused. But if there were no fences, maybe he actually used only the house and the 40 acres of cultivated fields. Fences may be more important in some cases than in others. In largely open areas, fences might tell us more about actual use than in areas where roads or natural features of the land are frequently used as boundary lines. As with much of adverse possession, figuring out if possession is actual may be heavily dependent on the ways land in the area is normally used.

The *open and notorious* possession requirement, like the actual possession norm, is designed to allow a shift of title only when a reasonable owner fails to discover trespassory activity that a standard inspection of the land would reveal. It is thought to be unfair to reward a secretive user. A recluse living in a cave or in a cabin located in difficult to reach terrain is unlikely to win an adverse possession claim. The bias here runs in favor of productive use rather than conservation of land.

Possession by a trespasser is *exclusive* when it is not shared with the true owner. Two trespassers acting in concert may share possession. If they later are deemed adverse users, they will end up owning the land together.

This section has been re-enacted, though with different section numbers, in all the major Montana statutory codifications in the twentieth century.

[56] These last variations on the adverse possession theme were in part adopted to protect people from lawyers' errors, one of the most common reasons for adverse possession litigation.

Continuity requires that there be no significant breaks in the adverse possession. This causes interesting problems in at least two settings. First, what should be done with seasonal or periodic usage patterns? If land is suitable for seasonal or periodic activity, then such use is likely to be deemed continuous. The other set of intriguing continuity cases involves use by different parties over time. If a primary feature of adverse possession law is to bar a claim when owners ignore obvious use of their land for a long period of time, then it should not make any difference if the adverse use is undertaken by one or by a series of trespassers. The courts generally conclude that successor trespassers may *tack* their period of use onto prior periods of use by others if there is documentary evidence of a transfer, succession of use within a family, or some other firm evidence that a transfer in possession between parties was intended.

Finally, possession must be *hostile* to be adverse. This is the nub of most cases. Everyone agrees that hostile possession is a legal "term of art"[57] that means something other than permissive presence. Owners who consent to the use or occupancy of their land by others do not risk loss of their property. Granting a *license*—a right of use terminable at the will of the owner—does not create an adverse possessor.[58] Landlords do not place their title at risk by agreeing to leases. Once beyond this widely accepted point, two quite different theories about the legal significance of hostility surface in the literature. If hostility is required to insure that a reasonable owner should discover the possessory activity before the statute of limitation runs, then hostility is much like the open and notorious requirement. On this theory, any activity which is actual, open and notorious to an objective viewer should be viewed as hostile. But some contend that the courts don't behave in accordance with this objective theory of hostility. They argue that the courts should and do treat possessors who know the land they are using belongs to another less kindly than they do parties trespassing on land they honestly think is theirs.[59] An acquisitive subjective intent, it is argued, will sometimes preclude a finding that possession is hostile. The hornbook and academic literature tends to say that the objective theory is the normal and better rule. But this conclusion should not be accepted without question.

There are other features of adverse possession law found in many jurisdictions. In some states, payment of property taxes not only serves as evidence of actual, open and hostile possession, but also lessens the adverse possession time period. Some states also reduce the adverse possession period if the claim is under *color of title*, that is under a claim of right based upon a written instrument. For example, suppose someone buys land disposed of at a sheriff's sale because property taxes were delinquent. If the procedures leading up to the sale were flawed, the sheriff's deed will be invalid, and the purchaser will hold possession under color of title. Documents in color of title cases may also help resolve boundary issues left open by the actual

---

[57] A "term of art" is a word or phrase that lawyers use in ways that are not the same as standard lay understandings. Here, for example, "hostile" does not mean "in anger," but in conflict with the legal interests of the true owner.

[58] Movie or sports event tickets are typical licenses. Granting permission to a tree surgeon to prune a neighbor's tree from a truck resting in your driveway is a license. Explicitly allowing kids in your neighborhood to go through your house lot to get to the school playground creates a license, though allowing kids to do the same thing without any sign of permission from you may run the risk of a prescriptive easement.

[59] The primary statement of this theory is in R. H. Helmholz, *Adverse Possession and Subjective Intent,* 61 WASH. U. L.Q. 331 (1983). After this article appeared, a debate ensued. *See* Roger A. Cunningham, *Adverse Possession and Subjective Intent: A Reply to Professor Helmholz,* 64 WASH. U. L.Q. 1 (1986); R. H. Helmholz, *More on Subjective Intent: A Response to Professor Cunningham,* 64 WASH. U. L.Q. 65 (1986); Roger A. Cunningham, *More on Adverse Possession: A Rejoinder to Professor Helmholz,* 64 WASH. U. L.Q. 1167 (1986). Both authors claim to have left the battlefield standing upright.

possession requirement. If the possessor uses only some of a parcel, but the flawed deed describes the entire tract, then the adverse possessor will be more likely to gain title to the whole thing.

In most states, prescription is much like adverse possession. The primary difference is in the property interests involved. Adverse possession almost always involves a dispute over a *fee simple absolute*, legal jargon for full title to a parcel of land.[60] A prescriptive user claims only an *easement*, or the right to use the land of another. Easements are often used to create driveways or other access routes, provide for installation of utility lines, and allow for the extraction of minerals. So, for example, if I routinely drive my car across your land to get to my garage, I might be able to claim a prescriptive easement after the statute of limitation period runs.

In some places, courts say that use rather than possession of another's land is presumed to be permissive. This rule may have survived in some places as a way of avoiding prescriptive easements in cases where it seems unfair to allow incidental, but long term use, to ripen into an easement. Should, for example, the use of your land as a pathway to the school playground across the creek running along in back of your house lead to the creation of a public right of way? In jurisdictions where use is presumed permissive, the party claiming a prescriptive easement will have a somewhat heightened burden of proving hostility. This may require explicit evidence that the true owner was put on notice that the user claimed something more than a permissive right to be on the land, or that the level of use was fairly extensive.[61]

Prescription requires some gentle shifts in the meaning of two pieces of the adverse possession puzzle. Exclusivity requires a showing in adverse possession cases that the claimant's use was not shared with the true owner. But the essence of an easement is sharing. One party is using the land of another. Exclusivity, therefore, is taken in prescription cases to mean that use by the prescriptive trespasser is compatible with use by the true owner. For example, two parties may not simultaneously use the same garage for their cars; those uses are incompatible. But the trespasser and the owner easily may use the same driveway to get to different garages; this use is compatible and therefore exclusive. The meaning of continuity may also shift just a bit. Use of an easement is almost always intermittent. But if the level of use is typical for the kind of easement being claimed, the continuity requirement will be fulfilled.

[2]   Adverse Possession and Prescription Source Materials

[a]   Outside Reading

For a basic hornbook review of adverse possession and prescription law *see* ROGER A. CUNNINGHAM, WILLIAM B. STOEBUCK & DALE A. WHITMAN, THE LAW OF PROPERTY 451-456, 807-815 (2d ed. 1993). For a more extensive look, read § 34.10 and ch. 91 in POWELL ON REAL PROPERTY (Matthew Bender).

---

[60] Theoretically it is possible to adversely possess something other than a fee simple absolute. If the party legally entitled to possession only owns an interest for life or a lease, then the trespasser may only end up with a property interest that lasts as long as that held by the legal possessor. Such cases are extremely rare.

[61] The significance of this burden is a bit unclear. Those claiming an interest in land by way of adverse possession almost always have the burden of showing they have fulfilled the requirements of the rule even though possession rather than use is usually presumed to be non-permissive. The proof obligations imposed on those claiming prescriptive rights in states presuming use to be permissive is sometimes stated in ways that seem much like the standard adverse possession burden of proof.

[b] Readings from CHUSED, A PROPERTY ANTHOLOGY (2d ed. 1997)

At pp. 285-302 there are excerpts from the following works on adverse possession: R. H. Helmholz, *Adverse Possession and Subjective Intent*, 61 WASH. U. L.Q. 331 (1983); John G. Sprankling, *The Antiwilderness Bias in American Property Law*, 63 U. CHI. L. REV. 519 (1996). There is also a helpful article on the importance of possession in property law excerpted, at pp. 9-15: Carol Rose, *Possession as the Origin of Property*, 52 U. CHI. L. REV. 73 (1985).

[3] An Adverse Possession Problem

Old Neighbor and Old Friend lived next to each other at 10 and 12 Main Street respectively. Their state's adverse possession statute of limitation required that suits to claim title to or easements in land be brought within 20 years. In 1987 they were chatting over their mutual back yard fence about how all the fencing in their two back yards was rotting away. They agreed to jointly contract for the rebuilding of all their fences and to split the cost of rebuilding that part of the fence running between their two lots.

The old fence between 10 and 12 Main Street was constructed in 1977 by the original developer of the area on the lot line shown on the architect's blue prints. The actual lot line written into the deeds for 10 and 12 Main Street by the developer's lawyer was different from the line on the blue prints. For some reason, the rear corner point between the two lots was two feet to the west of where the architect and developer intended. The architect's drawings would have created perfectly square lots. It later turned out that all the lots on this block had the same problem. When Old Neighbor and Old Friend rebuilt their fences, they instructed the new fence builder to put the new one in the exact same place as the old one. As a result, the new fence was located as the architect intended, but not as the deeds ordained.

Now it is 1997, and new owners are living in both 10 and 12 Main Street. They too noticed that their fences were rotting away and decided to have new ones built. By this time local building codes required that a survey be done before new fences were constructed in order to avoid land title conflicts. The survey, of course, revealed that the old fence was not located in accordance with the lot descriptions in both deeds. Not knowing where to build the fence, New Neighbor and New Friend took their problem to court for resolution. In fact, New Neighbor and New Friend had little choice. The mortgage instruments and title insurance policies on both parcels required that the lending banks and the insurance companies be notified of any problem about title so that they could take steps to protect their interests. Where should the court tell the parties to put their new fence?

Diagram of Neighbor-Friend Problem

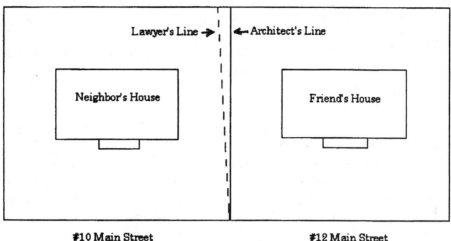

[4]   A Case of Tribal Possession and Use

[a]   Background to *Salish v. Vulles*[62]

The Flathead Reservation, established in 1855 by the Treaty of Hell Gate, negotiated at the same time as the Treaty of the Yakamas that created the reservation at issue in the *Brendale* litigation, is nestled between two mountain ranges—The Bitter Root Mountains to the west and the Rocky Mountains to the east. The flatlands in the middle of the two ranges are the best grazing lands in the area. During the Dawes Act era when the United States pursued an assimilationist policy, much reservation land was sold off.[63] In the case of the Salish and Kootenai, many parcels in the flatlands were among the first to be allotted and sold. By the time the allotment system was ended in 1934, the tribes owned a ring of land surrounding mostly private holdings.

Joseph Vanderburg's allotment separated tribal lands in the mountainous ring from other prime flatland in Range 5B which the tribes, as trust beneficiaries, had managed to retain during the Dawes Act era. For many years Range 5B was leased as pastureland to various cattlemen-owners of the Vanderburg allotment. James Gladden obtained a patent from the United States for the land in 1929. He and his wife Elizabeth Gladden sold it to J. Wallace and Genevieve Quinn in 1948, who in turn sold it to Mike Vulles and his son Vladimir in 1951. Success of cattlemen in the area frequently depended on their leasing some tribal grazing lands. In the early 1960s the tribes began to move into the large scale cattle raising business themselves. An Indian Cattlemen's Association was formed to promote tribal interests, a step seen by some non-tribal cattlemen as endangering their livelihood.[64]

---

[62] Documentary material for these notes was supplied by Richard A. Baenen, a Washington, D.C., attorney who represented the tribes in this litigation, and by the Confederated Salish and Kootenai Tribes of the Flathead Reservation. Mr. Baenen was also interviewed by telephone on July 11, 1986.

[63] The major federal legislation on this subject affecting the Flathead Reservation was adopted in 1904. An Act for the Survey and Allotment of Lands Now Embraced Within the Limits of the Flathead Indian Reservation, in the State of Montana, and the Sale and Disposal of All Surplus Lands After Allotment, 33 Stat. 302 (Apr. 23, 1904).

[64] Telephone interview with Eugene A. Mahoney of Thompson Falls, who represented Vulles (July 11, 1986).

Mike and Vladimir Vulles, like their predecessors, leased Range Unit 5B for grazing cattle after they purchased the Vanderburg allotment in 1951. When their grazing lease expired, a cattleman with Native American blood invoked a tribal rule directing that persons with Native blood have priority in the leasing of communally held tribal lands. The tribal claimant only needed to match the non-tribal cattleman's offer in order to obtain the lease. When this rule was invoked, the Vulleses lost their lease. In retaliation, Vulles locked the gate to the Vanderburg Truck Trail. When that failed to stop traffic, he felled a large tree across the trail. The trail was the primary path for driving cattle to and from Range Unit 5B. Although another route existed, it was sixteen miles longer, rougher, and frequently impassable because of rock slides.

This activity got the attention of the United States government. The local United States District Attorney filed suit against Vulles to have the trail declared a public road, although his primary interest appears to have been to maintain access to the fire watch tower in Range Unit 5B and to confirm access to the pastureland so that grazing leases would still produce significant funds for the tribal accounts. Vulles defended the action by arguing that the tribes had used the land with his permission and were therefore licensees. Vulles produced evidence that he had locked the gate before 1964 and had given a key to the United States, but the evidence was not believed.

Apparently because the United States Attorney was not pursuing matters the tribes considered important, they intervened. They argued that The Treaty of Hell Gate, signed in 1855, provided for tribal property rights in the area later sold off as the Vanderburg allotment, and that the right to move between various sections of the communally owned reservation that survived the allotment system was a right superior to the interests of any non-tribal owner of an allotment. This theory was rejected by the trial court.[65] Interestingly enough, the Ninth Circuit opinion you are about to read does not discuss this issue, using the narrower prescription theory to support tribal interests. Thus, even though the tribes won, they were not entirely pleased with the outcome.

[b]   Opinion of the United States Circuit Court of Appeals

Confederated Salish and Kootenai Tribes of Flathead Reservation v. Vulles

United States Court of Appeals, Ninth Circuit
437 F.2d 177 (1971)

HUFSTEDLER, CIRCUIT JUDGE:

This battle between the Indians and the white settlers began in 1964 when the settlers padlocked a gate across a road, traversing the settlers' property, that the Indians used to reach their tribal lands, and the Indians responded by shooting off the locks. The Indians are members of the Confederated Salish and Kootenai Tribes of the Flathead Reservation ("Tribes"), appellants; and the settlers are the Vulleses, appellees.

The United States, acting as trustee for the Confederated Tribes, sued to enjoin the Vulleses from obstructing the right of way and to recover lost revenue previously earned by leasing tribal grazing lands. After the court had denied the United States' request for a preliminary injunction, the Tribes intervened as plaintiffs. Judgment was entered in part favorably to the United States and the Tribes and in part favorably to the Vulleses. The Tribes alone appeal from that portion of a judgment denying them the use, as individual members of the Tribes, of a right of way

---

[65] United States of America v. Vulles, 282 F. Supp. 829 (D. Mont. 1968).

across the Vulles land for the purposes of hunting, berry hunting, or recreation on tribal lands lying beyond the Vulles property.

In 1855, by the Treaty of Hell Gate (12 Stat. 975), the Tribes ceded much of their land to the United States, reserving for their exclusive use and occupancy an area in Montana now known as the Flathead Indian Reservation. In 1904, Joseph Vanderburg, a member of the Tribes, received an allotment of land within the reservation. Ownership of that allotment passed by fee patent to one Gladden in 1927. The Vulleses obtained title in 1951.

The allotment separates one portion of the tribal lands from another designated as Range Unit 5B. Members of the Tribes and others reached the range via the right of way in question, known as the Vanderburg truck trail. The trail has existed in substantially its present location since 1933. In that year, the Bureau of Indian Affairs surveyed the road and made some improvements on portions lying beyond the Vulles land. The road crews took their automobiles and equipment over the trail, including that portion which crossed the Vulles property. In 1937 and 1938 the Civilian Conservation Corps further improved the entire length of the road. From then until the Vulleses blocked the road in 1964, the Bureau maintained the truck trail.

The Vanderburg truck trail was subjected to a variety of uses after it was improved. The Bureau of Indian Affairs and its employees used it to manage Range Unit 5B. The Bureau maintained the trail, using heavy equipment; it serviced the Vanderburg fire lookout by vehicle; and it managed timber development by vehicle. Other persons also used the trail in conjunction with their activities on Range Unit 5B: private contractors harvested tribal timber with logging trucks and caterpillar tractors, members of the Tribes removed Christmas trees, and lessees of grazing lands drove cattle to the range over the trail.

The successive owners of the Vanderburg allotment have maintained gates at the points where the trail entered and left the property since 1933. Except for a brief period when cattle guards supplemented the gates, users of the trail had to open the gates to enter the Vulles land. The gates were not locked, and for the most part the users closed the gates behind them.

The district court found that the truck trail was used continuously by the United States as trustee for the Tribes from 1933 until 1964. Its use was open, notorious, and nonpermissive. The court further found that there was no open, notorious, and continuous use of the road by the general public and that individual hunters, wood gatherers, and berry pickers made spasmodic use of the truck trail. The presence of the gates denied the use of the road to those members of the public who were not acquainted with the road. The court concluded that the United States had established a right of way by prescription prior to the Vulleses' acquisition of their land, but that members of the Tribes, as members of the general public, had not done so. The court decreed that employees of the United States and the Tribes have the right to use the truck trail for the purpose of managing Range Unit 5B, including maintaining the trail, leasing grazing rights and moving cattle to the range, and contracting for, or permitting, the harvesting and removal of timber, Christmas trees, and wood. But the order specifically excluded the Tribes from using the Vanderburg truck trail to reach Range Unit 5B for the purposes of hunting, berry picking, or recreation. The Vulleses were granted the same right to exclude members of the Tribes as they had to exclude members of the general public. Also, the Vulleses were permitted to lock their gate if they gave a key to the Bureau of Indian Affairs. Additionally, the United States as trustee was awarded damages for lost grazing revenue.

Although the evidence clearly and convincingly supports the court's finding that the United States has a right of way across the Vulles land, the court's finding that the Tribes had not established their independent right to use the Vanderburg truck trail is clearly erroneous in light of the applicable law and the evidence presented.

In order to establish a right of way by prescription, the claimant must prove that his use was adverse, open, notorious, exclusive, continuous, and uninterrupted throughout the statutory period. Continuous use does not mean constant use. Rather, if the claimant used the right of way whenever he desired, without interference by the owner of the servient estate, the use was continuous and uninterrupted. "Exclusive" means that the claimant's right to use the right of way is independent of a like right in another.

The evidence reveals continuous, uninterrupted, exclusive, and adverse use of the truck trail by individual members of the Tribes. Daniel Cole, husband of a tribal member, had worked on the trail in 1936 and testified at the hearing for a preliminary injunction that from 1938 until 1948 the road was used regularly by the public. Elmer Morigeau, who worked on improving and maintaining the road from 1933 until 1947, testified that following the improvements, "quite a few" used the road,[1] that he had used it himself to hunt, that in the fall both members and nonmembers of the Tribes, one or two at a time, used the truck trail to reach the range in order to hunt or gather wood, and that miners used the road to reach a mine located beyond the Vulles land. Orral Lake, employed in the harvesting of tribal timber in the late 1940's testified that he saw Indians and others in vehicles crossing the Vulles land on the truck trail.[2] Alexander Clairmont, a member of the Tribes employed by the Bureau of Indian Affairs, testified that from 1936 until 1958 he himself used the road a dozen times a year, that all tribal members used the road to cut Christmas trees, pick berries, or hunt on the range, and that the general public as well as members of the Tribes used the road to cut and gather wood on the range. Finally, appellee Vladimir Vulles admitted that since 1951 he had seen wood gatherers use the Vanderburg trail without his permission while hunters traveled the road with and without permission.[3] The

---

[1] Morigeau testified:

"Q Now, these people that were hunting in there, were they all traveling in vehicles; some of them on horseback; on foot?

A Most of them go up in there with vehicles.

Q But you assumed that they got in there on the same road you did?

A Well, I know some of them did."

[2] Lake's testimony supported Morigeau's as follows:

"Q Now, during the time that you worked up there, Mr. Lake, did you see persons and vehicles using the Vanderburg Truck Trail from Highway 10A on up through the Gladden place, other than Thornton Logging Company vehicles and people?

A Yes.

Q Do you know who any of these people were?

A Yes. Yes.

Q Who were they? Were they Indians?

A Yes, most of them.

Q And did you see persons other than the Thornton employees and Indians utilizing the Vanderburg Truck Trail from Highway 10A through the Gladden Ranch?

A I believe they were, but I couldn't name them now. A lot of fellows got wood up there.

Q In other words, it wasn't an unusual occurrence during your employment up there, to see Indians and other persons not employed by the Thornton Lumber Company going up through the Vanderburg Trail through the Gladden Ranch?

A Yes."

[3] Vulles testified:

only conflicting testimony was to the effect that few or no persons used the road for any purposes; the court clearly discredited this testimony when it held that the Government had established its right to use the truck trail to manage the range unit. The failure of the gates to deter tribal traffic confirms the adverse nature of the use.[4]

Our conclusion is reinforced by the court's holding that traffic moving across the Vulles land for the purpose of, or resulting from the management and development of the range's resources met the requirements of adverse, open, continuous, and uninterrupted use for the statutory period. The purpose of travel does not prescribe the right of way. The character and extent of the use (the type and intensity of traffic) determines the nature and extent of the servitude. The fact of travel and not the purpose of the travel delimits the right of way; the mode of travel determines the servient estate's burden. Movement over the Vanderburg truck trail established the users' right to utilize the trail independent of the reasons motivating the traffic. Consequently, the court erred in limiting the purposes for which the United States and the Tribes could use the Vanderburg truck trail. The only limitation is imposed by the use made of the right of way during the statutory period; subsequent use cannot exceed the prior burden. The Vulleses do not have the right to exclude members of the Tribes.

That portion of the judgment denying to the members of the Tribes the use of the Vanderburg truck trail for the purposes of hunting, berry picking, or recreation is reversed, and the cause is remanded for further proceedings consistent with the views herein expressed.

[c]   Analysis of *Vulles*

Why did Vulles lose? At one level the answer to that question is quite easy. The various parts of the prescription rule seem to fit like a glove. Use of the road by the United States and by members of the tribe in their own right was plain and long standing. Putting aside all of the academic rhetoric about objective and subjective tests of adversity, there can be little doubt that the actions of those not holding title to the land were visible, that everyone thought there was a road open for general use, and that the uses were widely known in the community. This is the stuff of adverse possession and prescription. Remember that this rule is based upon a statute of limitation and that such statutes generally begin to run when the party having the right to bring a law suit for trespass *knows or should know* that a cause of action exists. Vulles' predecessors in title certainly knew about the situation. And there is nothing obviously unfair about binding Vulles to the failures of his predecessors to take steps to avoid the prescriptive easement.[66] He purchased the land knowing of the existence of the road.

"Q Now, since you have purchased the property in August of 1951, have people gone in there to get wood?

A They have without permission.

Q And have hunters gone in through your property?

A Yes.

Q Did they ask permission, or do they go through there as a matter of right?

A Well, a lot of them did ask permission. Now, when I moved on this place, I couldn't very well keep it locked at the bottom, so I locked it on the upper gate, but I can't see that gate from the house; so oftentimes I did find the lock blowed off of there. "

[4] The unexplained, open use of a right of way for the statutory period creates the presumption that the use was adverse under claim of right. However, the presence of gates that must be opened by the user is strong evidence of a license to pass over the right of way. (Peasley v. Trosper (1973) 103 Mont. 401, 64 P.2d 109.) Here, the evidence of license was rebutted by Vulles himself. (See Scott v. Weinheimer (1962) 140 Mont. 554, 374 P.2d 91; note 3 supra.)

[66] There is not even need for use of the tacking rules here. The prescriptive easement found by the court had almost certainly come into existence long before Mike and Vladimir Vulles purchased the land.

Once past this seemingly straight forward application of the legal vocabulary, however, the case raises at least two interesting questions. First, though the facts may seem one-sided, they actually pose some hard problems about the meaning of hostility. Second, what does this case tell us about the basic purposes for the adverse possession and prescription rules? What cultural role do they play? What do they tell us about the nature of property?

The court tells us that "The successive owners of the Vanderburg allotment have maintained gates at the points where the trail entered and left the property." What do these gates have to say about the meaning of hostility? If we "read" the fence gate to say "keep out" and people still open it and use the road, perhaps the use is hostile. If we "read" the fence and gate to say "come in if you know about this road," then maybe a license has been granted. Since we wish to encourage people to let others use their land when it is helpful—generosity is something we like to see—permissive uses will not lead to title changes. This purpose is clear enough, but the rule is often ambiguous and hard to apply.

When thinking about such questions, courts and commentators usually adopt one of two approaches. The first, as suggested in the materials before the case on the general contours of adverse possession and prescription law, posits that the state of mind of the parties to the litigation, in addition to the nature of the adverse or prescriptive use, is important. The second claims that courts look objectively at the behavior of the adverse claimant in determining adversity. And before this analytical note is finished, I want to suggest a third approach that looks at the needs of the community or communities claiming rights in the property.

If adverse possession or prescription claimants have reasonable arguments that their trespassory activities are justifiable, some writers argue they ought to be rewarded for the economic investments and risks they take. If, however, someone makes a claim knowing that others actually hold legal title, the same writers have less sympathy for the trespasser's actions. In some cases, it may be possible to use this sort of test to help define hostility. Those claiming the land of another knowing that their claim has no legal basis or that another person actually owns the property will lose; those making a claim thinking they had the right to do so will prevail. As noted above at footnote 59, Professor Helmholz contends that this is how courts tend to resolve cases.

One problem with use of such a theory is that it may be difficult to tell when a party has the "proper" state of mind. In *Salish*, for example, tribal members surely believed in the historical correctness of their actions under the Treaty of Hell Gate. But they, at least in the beginning years of the truck trail, must also have known that the Dawes Act era undermined claims for general tribal sovereignty over all reservation lands and that non-Indians owned the Vanderburg allotment. Did the Salish act with acceptable or unacceptable intentions? Analysis of intention, it seems, may take us on some merry chases.

So if you wish to pay attention to the motivations of the parties in adverse possession and prescription cases, you may need to take some additional steps to figure out when a state of mind is legitimately hostile. In short, I think we often need to answer a second set of questions about hostility, to move beyond Professor Helmholz to questions of community expectations. In *Salish* it was certainly plausible to argue that Vulles, in felling a tree across the road, was disrupting long standing norms of cooperative use of the road. Even though his claim to holding the original title to the underlying land was obviously correct, he initiated a heated community battle. He knew about the tribal rules on access to grazing lands. He knew that Native Americans might give preferences to their members. He knew of the various uses the federal government made of the road. In a typical situation, property law tends not to sympathize much with those who disrupt land use patterns as a way of making political protests. There is a crucial, conservative, historical cast to the property world which prefers stability and predictability, and which assumes, ironically, that private economic growth in a market depends upon continuation of certain basic community norms of behavior. In this light, the Vulleses had to lose, even though arguments may be made that those claiming prescriptive use of the road against the Vulleses' predecessors knew full well they were using the land of another. They had to lose because too many segments of the community relied upon the road for too long a time to permit the Vulleses to obtain control over the access route. They had to lose even if their dislike of the grazing preferences given to Native Americans was shared by others in the area. Felling trees across roads used for a large array of purposes is not the sort of activity likely to be given much credence by the courts.

Community norms may also help solve the Neighbor-Friend problem posed earlier in the text. As in *Salish*, looking only at the intentions of the parties is not altogether helpful. For if we assume that the boundary line errors occurred in a number of deeds in the area, each land owner (except at the ends of the string of lots) in this hypothetical development is both an adverse claimant *and* a victim of another's adverse claim. Knowledge of one's own claim implies knowledge of the claims of one's neighbors. In such a setting, it is difficult to work out the contours of correct and incorrect states of mind. But there is also a community understanding here. The entire neighborhood has been operating since its creation on the assumption that the fences, not the deeds, delineated the correct property lines. There is no reason to upset that understanding. I would let the fences mark the lines, not because the facts objectively speak for themselves, or because one or another resident did or did not occupy the land of another with bad intention, but because the community has acted on that view for so long.

Paying attention to community expectations fits nicely into the various, oft-stated purposes for adverse possession rules. Obviously, these rules cut off litigation possibilities. Whatever the outcome of any particular case, the clarity and certitude of many property titles is enhanced just because stale claims are buried. Assuming private property is to exist, such an outcome is desirable. In addition, community expectation theories *may* enhance the likelihood that productive land use will be rewarded. I am not thinking only of the idea that adverse possession rules create a mild incentive to inspect and use land in order to avoid its loss to interlopers. Rather, I am suggesting that rewarding long standing community uses of land may protect the preferences of significant groups of people.

Such a look at community standards is also required by an objective theory of hostility. For as Professor Carol Rose wisely instructs us in her article *Possession as the Origin of Property*,[67] the idea of notice encompasses not only the ways in which communications are made, but also the meaning of those communications to the sender and receiver. In objective theories of adverse possession, which are really based on the idea that actions on land of a certain intensity have the effect of notifying true owners of problems on their property, we must also understand the implications of notice in the broader community. Some sorts of actions on land will be read by the community as providing notice of adverse possessory action; others will not. The idea of an "objective" theory of adverse possession must be dependent on a "subjective" community understanding about how various actions should be viewed by a reasonable property owner. It is therefore plausible to argue that the subjective and objective tests both investigate the same

---

[67] 52 U. CHI. L. REV. 73 (1985).

problem—the ways in which a community will be best served when conflicts over use of property come to the fore. Sometimes state of mind will help us resolve this conflict; sometimes actions on land will serve as notification of adversity. In both kinds of cases, however, community standards are relevant to the final resolution of the case.

Whether my preferred outcomes in *Salish* and the Neighbor-Friend problem are correct or not; whether my take on the cases is widely shared in the litigation and judicial worlds,[68] I think it is sensible to argue that operation of a market system of private property is heavily reliant on community understandings. And I mean "community" here not just in the simple sense that it takes a set of community or government rules to create, approve and maintain private property and markets—an idea that arose in the discussion of *McIntosh* and the *Cherokee Cases*—but in the more important sense of inter-dependency and mutual cooperation among individuals. The existence of private property depends upon both a set of legal rules giving it room to operate and upon community wide expectations and levels of cooperative behavior about the nature of use and transfer of assets. Particularly in a world as messy, fast paced, and technological as the one we all live in, community must exist in order for any of us to prosper. Working out the contours of this community is a central task for a property course. For more on this idea, you might want to read Stewart Sterk, *Neighbors in American Land Law*, 87 COLUM. L. REV. 55 (1987).

[d] Adverse Possession and Prescription Questions

[*i*] *The Prescription Claim by the Salish and Rights of the General Public.* The court granted easements to two different plaintiffs. The United States, as trustee of lands still held under Indian title, obtained an easement to use the truck trail to reach Range Unit 5B for grazing and timbering. The court also reversed the trial court and concluded that members of the tribe could use the trail for hunting, berry picking and recreation. The rights held by members of the tribe were in addition to any benefits to which they were entitled as beneficiaries of the trust held by the United States. If the court's conclusion granting tribal members hunting, berry picking and recreational rights was correct, then could members of the general public also have won a prescription case? Reread the testimony laid out in the footnotes to the *Salish* opinion. Did the witnesses carefully distinguish between use by the Salish and use by the general public?

[*ii*] *Exclusivity.* Suppose that the tribes claimed fee simple absolute title to the road and to some berry patches near the road. Would their claim succeed? Even if you conclude that such use was actual, open, notorious, continuous and hostile, was it exclusive? What if people, not members of the tribe, also picked from the same berry patches? Would the claim then be one of a fee simple held jointly with the other berry pickers or of an easement to pick berries?

[*iii*] *Continuity.* Did the berry picking claim of the Salish fulfill the continuity requirement? Presumably the activity was seasonal. And the notes do not contain evidence that berry picking occurred every year. Another interesting case raising very similar issues is *United States on Behalf of the Zuni Tribe v. Platt*, 730 F. Supp. 318 (D. Ariz. 1990). The court found a prescriptive easement over privately held lands to allow the Zuni to make a religious pilgrimage every four years on foot or horseback to a mountain area believed by the Zuni to be their place of origin. As in *Salish*, the tribe intervened in a case originally brought by the United States

---

[68] Those worlds certainly do not always walk my walk, so you should be careful in taking my ideas as a reflection of how the world actually operates.

on their behalf. The Zuni argued that the prescriptive easement was held by the tribe rather than the United States and that their pilgrimage rights were protected by the terms of the Treaty of Guadalupe Hidalgo. The Zuni got their prescriptive easement.

[*iv*] *Notice and Tacking.* Assume that a 20-year statute of limitations applied in *Salish.* The earliest facts giving rise to the prescription claims arose in 1933, the year the truck trail was surveyed and improved. When Vulles purchased the allotment in 1951, only two years were left to run under the presumed 20-year limitation period. While it may be appropriate to permit adverse possessors to "tack" their period of possession onto that of prior occupants, why do the courts apply the same tacking idea to the title chain of the true owners? To the degree that adverse possession rules take the likelihood of knowledge of the true owner into account, was not Vulles placed at a substantial disadvantage? Does that mean that the hostility issue must be less important than the community based reasons for the adverse possession and prescription rules?

Part of the reason for the rules allowing adverse claimants to tack together both their use to a prior possessor, and the ownership periods of prior title holders, lies in the notion that adverse possession is designed to cut off stale property claims. As long as a party should have notice of the claim, the length of their stay is thought to be irrelevant.

[*v*] *Adverse Possession, Licenses and Estoppel.* Uses which arise by permission usually begin as licenses. The party allowing the activity may halt licensed uses at any time. But after a long period of time, the original permissive quality of the activity becomes less and less relevant to a decision about whether the use should be allowed to continue. For example, suppose the truck trail in *Salish* was originally built by the government with the permission of the land owner. Over the years, with the expenditure of money by various parties and the development of community expectations about use of the trail, the original grant of permission to construct the road gradually becomes less germane to a decision about the future. Courts have responded to this problem by barring some owners from disputing adverse possession claims arising out of use that was originally authorized. The rationales are varied, but usually involve arguments that the owner is *estopped* from disputing the title of a possessor who has economically relied on the continued existence of the right to possess, or that the owner has somehow been put on notice that the possessor's claims have become adverse.[69]

[*vi*] *The Treaty Claim.* At the trial level the Salish claimed that the Treaty of Hell Gate guaranteed them sovereignty over their reservation, including the right to go from one area of tribal land to another over non-tribally owned land. While recognizing that the allotment system reduced their scope of control, the Salish argued they had the right to reasonable paths connecting the parts of the reservation still held under Indian title. The trial court held against the tribe and the appellate court did not discuss the issues. In light of the way the Supreme Court justices handled *Brendale*, how do you think they would have treated the Salish sovereignty claim had it reached the Court?

[*vii*] *Neighbor–Friend Problem.* Go back to the Neighbor-Friend problem. Under both an objective and a subjective approach to hostility, good arguments may be made that Neighbor

---

[69] *Estoppel* prevents a party from taking a position inconsistent with a position taken previously. In the license-to-adverse possession cases, the long term existence of originally permissive activity sometimes is deemed to create an estoppel. Courts will be particularly sympathetic to such adverse possession claims if large numbers of people have come to rely upon the use or persons have expended significant sums of money anticipating the continuation of the use.

would prevail in his claim against Friend. Assuming Neighbor wins, should he have to pay Friend the value of this land? Adverse possession law might give Neighbor the right to claim this land, but why should he get it for free? Thomas W. Merrill, in *Property Rules, Liability Rules, and Adverse Possession*, 79 Nw. U. L. Rev. 1122 (1985), took the position that adverse possessors acting in bad faith, but gaining title under an objective standard, ought be required to pay for their gain. This rule, he suggested, might deter bad faith possessors while permitting those who have relied in good faith on the validity of their title claims to perfect them. Merrill argued, at p. 1152 "that courts manipulate the common law doctrine of adverse possession in order to punish or deter those who intentionally dispossess others of their property. A less drastic means of achieving a similar end would be to apply a liability rule in cases of bad faith possession. A rule of limited indemnification would in effect impose a fine on bad faith dispossessors equal to the value of the property at the time of original entry. Squatters and thieves would know that, even if they could obtain title to property after the passage of the statute of limitations and the satisfaction of the common law's five elements, they would have to pay for their gain. Consequently, the incentives to engage in coerced transfers would be reduced." Do you agree? Is it better to deny bad faith trespassers the land or make them pay for it? If community needs are important to the resolution of adverse possession and prescription cases, does that reduce the need to worry about compensation?

[*viii*]   *Later Events.* Vladimir Vulles still lives on the land. The problem of access to the range has sorted itself out without a recurrence of the sort of problems that led to the *Salish* litigation. Though the range is still closed to those lacking Indian blood, the incidence of inter-racial marriages has increased in recent decades, making it easier for owners of landlocked allotments to find sympathetic property owners with useable pathways to the range lands.

[5]   Adverse Possession Between Co-Owners: Some More Rules and a Problem

Here is another problem. About 30 years ago, Herman and Belinda Woodmont moved to Southville and bought a retirement house together. By that time three of their four children were married and living quite prosperous lives with their families in other parts of the country. The remaining child, Allison Woodmont Needful, also lived in Southland. She, along with her disabled husband, struggled to get by on her first grade teacher's salary.

Herman Woodmont died 24 years ago. In his will, he left the retirement house to "my beloved wife Belinda for her life, and then to those of our children surviving Belinda." Belinda died four years later leaving a simple will giving all her property to her four children. All the children came together for her funeral. A day or so after the burial, the four children met at the house to divide up the personal property of their parents. Somehow the discussion turned to the difficult economic situation of Allison and her husband. The three out of town children all told Allison to give up her rental apartment and move into the house. With tears of gratitude streaming down her cheeks, Allison agreed.

And so the situation remained until last week. Allison and her husband lived in the house, maintained it, paid the property taxes, added on a small screen porch in the back, and successfully cared for a stream of foster children over the years. Last week, however, Allison was notified that the City of Southville planned to condemn the house and the land it was on for construction of a new neighborhood school. Assuming that the relevant statute of limitations period is 20 years, even when property taxes are paid by the parties in possession, who should get the money paid by Southville when they condemn the land? Should Allison get it all or should it be shared among all four Woodmont siblings?

Some legal rules might help with this problem. It is generally said that persons owning land together each have the right to possess the entire parcel of property, that possession is *undivided* rather than split up along geographical lines.[70] This understanding may have a distinct impact on adverse possession disputes between co-owners. In the Woodmont problem, for example, each of the four siblings owning the house after the death of Belinda has the right to possess the entire house. The possession of Allison therefore was not only permissive but required by law. Indeed, each of the siblings has an undivided right to possess the house. Can Allison overcome this rule and still claim that her possession was hostile? The hornbooks generally opine that in order for one co-owner to demonstrate hostility against other co-owners, she must show she has taken steps to oust the co-owners. Writing a letter to the siblings claiming complete ownership might do the trick. Imposing such a requirement on Allison would probably bar her from claiming adverse possession unless the courts wish to read her payment of property taxes, maintenance of the house and construction of the porch without seeking permission of her siblings as an ouster.

Take the case one step further and assume that Allison died with a will leaving the house to one of her foster children. At some point wouldn't you expect the courts to ignore the ouster requirement and ease up on the application of standard adverse possession rules? Perhaps they could analogize these sorts of problems to those cases in which licenses have ripened into title. Some courts have taken such a route in order to clear up title disputes after generations of informal passing on of property within families. This has been a particularly difficult problem for many black families in the south. *See* C. Scott Graber, *Heirs Property: The Problems and Possible Solutions*, 12 CLEARINGHOUSE REV. 273 (1978); *Collier v. Welker*, 19 N.C. App. 617, 199 S.E.2d 691 (1973).

Most courts, however, tend to require ouster to prove hostility in Woodmont type problems. *See, e.g., Commercial Union Assurance Company v. Pucci*, 523 F. Supp. 1310 (W.D. Pa. 1981), a case filed by an insurance company trying to figure out who to pay insurance proceeds to after a house was destroyed in a natural gas explosion. In the *Pucci* case, the court found that the sibling in possession could not automatically exclude her brothers and sisters from claiming part of the title. After the insurance litigation was over, however, the possessory sibling filed another case seeking to quiet title in herself. She eventually "won" that dispute because none of the surviving potential owners wished to even up the financial scoresheet. If the non-possessory siblings confirmed their ownership interests by prevailing in an adverse possession case, they would have had to contribute their share of the expenses born by the possessory sibling for the mortgage, capital improvements, and other required payments such as property taxes and insurance. As with much of law, the interaction of different bundles of legal rules—here adverse possession and payment contribution norms for concurrent owners—often determines the actual outcomes of human disputes.

[6] Adverse Possession and the Government

[a] Legal Summary

It is commonly said that adverse possession against the government is not possible. That adage originally was derived from English common law rules of sovereign immunity that barred claims against the crown. Similar constraints continued here after the Revolutionary War and still exist in some form in many jurisdictions. But during the twentieth century a number of federal and

---

[70] The law of joint ownership will be taken up in the next chapter. If you want to learn a bit more now, read the first section of Chapter 2 on the basic rules of concurrent estates.

state legislative enactments and judicial decisions have limited the impact of the old sovereign immunity rules. Though most states still appear to bar adverse possession claims for government land, some states have altered the traditional rule, particularly when state land is not being held for use by the general public.[71] Other jurisdictions permit such suits against local but not state governments. Trends are hard to discern. Some states have recently cut back on such cases, while others have begun to allow them.[72] To read more about adverse possession of government lands, take a look at ch. 91 in POWELL ON REAL PROPERTY (Matthew Bender).

The federal government has a variety of statutes concerning the lands it owns. One of the most important controls adverse possession claims against lands of the United States held by the Department of the Interior, the agency responsible for the administration of tribal lands. 43 U.S.C. § 1068 provides:

> The Secretary of the Interior (a) shall, whenever it shall be shown to his satisfaction that a tract of public land has been held in good faith and peaceful, adverse, possession by a claimant, his ancestors or grantors, under claim or color of title for more than twenty years, and that valuable improvements have been placed on such land or some part thereof has been reduced to cultivation, . . . *Provided,* That where the area so held is in excess of one hundred and sixty acres the Secretary may determine what particular subdivisions, not exceeding one hundred and sixty acres, may be patented hereunder; *Provided further,* That coal and all other minerals contained therein are hereby reserved to the United States; that said coal and other minerals shall be subject to sale or disposal by the United States under applicable leasing and mineral land laws, and permittees, lessees, or grantees of the United States shall have the right to enter upon said lands for the purpose of prospecting for and mining such deposits; *And provided further*, That no patent shall issue under the provisions of this chapter for any tract to which there is a conflicting claim adverse to that of the applicant, unless and until such claim shall have been fully adjudicated in favor of such applicant.

This statute is framed in ways that make it a close relative to a family of nineteenth century land laws allowing those who moved onto and cultivated land before it had been surveyed and formally opened up by the General Land Office for settlement to obtain preferences for land patents once the area was thrown open. And the limitation to 160 acres mirrors the area most commonly sold or given to citizens who obtained federal land patents in the west before 1900.

The federal statute has not been invoked very often. While conflicting title claims inundated the federal bureaucracy during the nineteenth century, they are much less common now. In addition, the requirement in § 1068 that the adverse possession claim be under color of title has been strictly construed to require written evidence of a grant of land from the federal government. The most interesting of the § 1068 cases follows.

---

[71] A recent example of such an outcome is Devins v. Borough of Bogota, 124 N.J. 570, 592 A.2d 199 (1991), which involved a dispute over unused publicly owned land that a neighbor fenced in, maintained, and used for recreation and play equipment.

[72] For a recent survey of cases, *see* Paula Latovic, *Adverse Possession Against the States: The Hornbooks Have it Wrong,* 29 U. MICH. J.L. REFORM 939 (1996).

[b]   Opinion of the United States Court of Appeals

United States of America v. Charles J. Schwarz, et al.

United States Court of Appeals, Seventh Circuit
460 F.2d 1365 (1972)

Before SWYGERT, Chief Judge, HASTINGS, Senior Circuit Judge, and KILEY, Circuit Judge.

HASTINGS, Senior Circuit Judge.

The United States of America filed this action seeking a decree to quiet title to certain real estate in Wisconsin on behalf of the heirs of a Chippewa Indian patentee of the land as the result of adverse claims and actions of an adjacent landowner. Following a trial to the court, without the intervention of a jury, the trial court . . . entered a judgment and decree . . . favorable to the plaintiff. Defendants Schwarz and Yeschek alone have appealed . . . . We affirm.

For purposes of clarity and identification we deem it advisable to set out in full the findings of fact made by the district court:

"Facts.

The subdivision lines in Township 40 North, Range 4 East, 4th Principal Meridian, Vilas County, in this Western District of Wisconsin, were surveyed from July 22, 1865, through July 31, 1865. The plat of survey for this township was approved October 15, 1865 and is the official plat of this township. There have been no subsequent official surveys or resurveys. Government Lots 4 and 5 were shown in said plat of survey as they appear in the following diagram:

Diagram A

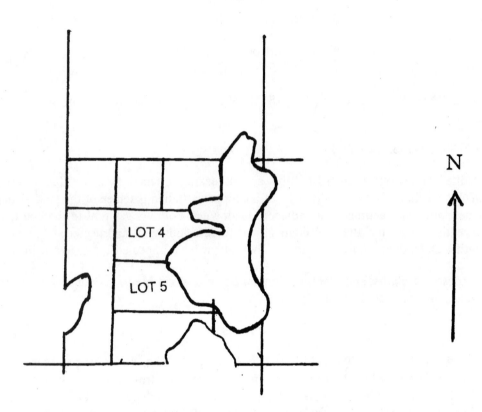

The acreage of Lot 4 is shown on the plat of survey as 57.7, and that of Lot 5 as 54.4. The line dividing Lots 4 and 5, as shown on the plat, coincides with the quarter-section line of Section 23. The irregularly shaped line along what appear to be the eastern edges of Lots 4 and 5 represents a rough approximation of the meander lines described in the surveyor's notes; the meander lines, in turn, were intended to assist in determining the approximate size of the said lots by indicating the approximate location of the shore line of a lake which has since come to be known as Tippecanoe Lake.

The actual boundary of Tippecanoe Lake as it existed in 1961, and at the time of trial, and the meander line as described in 1865, are as they appear in diagram B . . . .

Diagram B

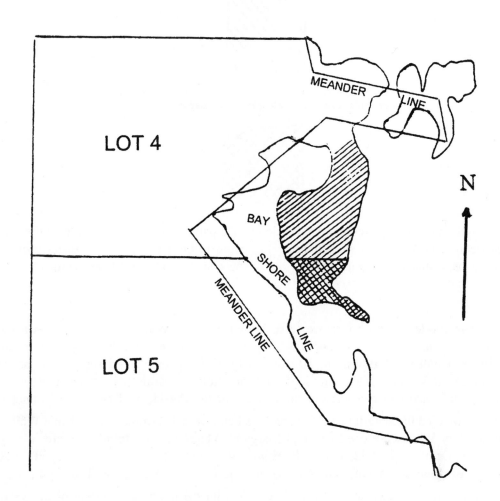

Lots 4 and 5 are riparian to Tippecanoe Lake.

On diagram B, a peninsula which extends into Tippecanoe Lake has been shaded, thus:

The dispute in this suit concerns that portion of the
peninsula which has also been cross-shaded, thus:

The cross-shaded area represents that portion of the peninsula which lies south of the dividing line between Lots 4 and 5 if said dividing line were to be extended in an easterly direction. The entire peninsula contains about 16.3 acres; the disputed portion of the peninsula contains about 3.8 acres.

. . . .

Lot 4 was allotted to Be bo ke we (also known as John Whitescott), a Chippewa Indian, pursuant to Article 3 of a treaty concluded September 30, 1854, with the Chippewa Indians of Lake Superior and the Mississippi, 10 Stat. 1109, and a patent was issued to Be bo ke we December 28, 1895. Said patent provided that the allottee and his heirs could not sell, lease, or otherwise alienate the tract without the consent of the President of the United States.

Be bo ke we died intestate July 5, 1919, and his heirs were determined to be Annie Whitescott, one-third, Mary Whitescott, one-third, and Margaret Whitescott, one-third. Margaret Whitescott died intestate October 13, 1932, and her heirs were determined to be Annie Whitescott (or Annie Whitescott Abraham), one-half, and Mary Whitescott (or Mary Whitescott Theobold), one-half.

Lot 5 was originally patented to an Indian who, with the necessary consent of the Secretary of the Interior, conveyed the property. The lot passed through a chain of title until it was conveyed in 1947, by warranty deed, to William Yeschek and Elsie Yeschek, who were the parents of William F. Yeschek, named as a defendant in this action; the deed described the property simply as Government Lot 5, and contained no express description of any portion of the peninsula. Yeschek, Sr., immediately built a road through Lot 5, west of Tippecanoe Lake, running in a northerly-southerly direction, and extended it into and across Lot 4 in an easterly direction and then down the peninsula, in a southerly direction, to that portion of the peninsula now in dispute. His intention was to use the road to service the now disputed portion of the peninsula, which he considered to be a part of Lot 5. The construction and use of this road by Yeschek, Sr., was well known to the Whitescotts, who owned Lot 4, and it was well known to representatives of the Great Lakes Indian Agency, of the United States Department of the Interior. However, the Agency advised Yeschek, Sr., in 1947, and again in 1952, of the Agency's opinion that the disputed portion of the peninsula was a part of Lot 4 and not a part of Lot 5.

The defendant in this action, William F. Yeschek, Jr. (hereinafter "defendant Yeschek") acquired Lot 5 from his parents, and in 1960 the defendants Yeschek conveyed the now disputed portion of the peninsula to the defendants Schwarz, for a consideration, by a warranty deed in which the property was described as a part of Lot 5.

. . . .

In 1969, while this action was pending in this court, the defendants Schwarz delivered a quit claim deed to the disputed property to the defendants Yeschek.

. . . .

One issue of fact, which may be pertinent, remains to be mentioned. Defendants Yeschek and Schwarz contend, and emphasize the contention, that in the 1865 government survey an island in Tippecanoe Lake located easterly from the northerly portion of Lot 4 was meandered and surveyed so as actually to have been included as a part of the mainland and as a part of Lot 4, whereas the entire peninsula in question was not. See diagram B, above. A finding of fact on this point is to be made only with great difficulty. The meander lines include a relatively small portion of the island in question, as it exists in fact. As against defendants' interpretation, it may be contended with equal force that the somewhat rectangular projection of the meander line in an easterly direction represents a crude attempt to outline the peninsula lying beneath it and pointing in a southerly direction. I am unable to make a finding either way. I expressly decline to find that the meander line was intended to include the island referred to by defendants. I do find that the peninsula was not intentionally omitted from the 1865 survey."

From our examination of the record in this case, . . . , we find and conclude that the facts as found by the district court are amply supported by the evidence and may not be set aside as clearly erroneous.

. . . .

As indicated in the trial court's finding, the current dispute began in 1947 when the senior Yeschek constructed a road through Lot 5, extending it across Lot 4 and then down through the peninsula in a southerly direction to the 3.8 acre portion of the peninsula now in dispute. This action was immediately challenged by letters to the senior Yeschek from the Superintendent of the Great Lakes Indian Agency, in 1947, and the Area Director of the Bureau of Indian Affairs, in 1952. These letters declared that no part of the peninsula was in Lot 5, but instead was a part of Lot 4, and was Indian owned.

The two ultimate issues to be determined on this appeal are (1) whether the district court erred in denying appellants' claim to the 3.8 acre tract at the southern end of the peninsula separated from Lot 5 by a bay in Lake Tippecanoe, a navigable lake; and (2) whether, either under the Color of Title Act, Title 43, U.S.C.A. § 1068, or under Wisconsin adverse possession statutes, the appellants acquired title to the 3.8 acre tract by adverse possession.

I.

As the district court noted in its memorandum opinion, all parties appear to concede "that the meander lines included in the 1865 survey were not intended to form the eastern boundaries of Lots 4 and 5." Appellants further agree with the court that the "initial question is to determine what the eastern boundary of Lot 5 was intended to be."

The Government contended that the eastern boundaries of the two lots coincided with the western shore of Lake Tippecanoe and appellants claimed they coincided with the eastern shore of the peninsula.

Appellants assert the trial court erred in concluding that the resolution of this controversy is a question of federal law and contend that Wisconsin law controls. Our examination of the authorities cited by both parties leads us to conclude that this case is controlled by federal law.

. . . .

In our judgment . . . a dispute over title to lands owned by the Federal Government is governed by federal law, although of course the Federal Government may, if it desires, choose to select a state rule as the federal rule. There is no showing that the Federal Government has elected to make such a choice in the case at bar . . . .

The evidence supports the district court's finding and conclusion that the peninsula was morphologically a part of Lot 4. Likewise, under applicable federal standards, the record shows that Lake Tippecanoe is a navigable waterway of the United States. There was a further finding that "the peninsula was not intentionally omitted from the 1865 survey," and, no such evidence having been offered, it follows that the survey was not fraudulent. There was no evidence tending to show that dry land ever connected Lot 5 with the peninsula at any point in 1865, or thereafter.

Under all the facts and circumstances presented here, we have concluded that, as a matter of law, all of the peninsula, shown on the plat as extending into a meandered lake, passed to the patentee of Lot 4 and not to the patentee of Lot 5 or appellants. It necessarily follows that the district court did not err in concluding that the eastern boundary of Lot 5 is defined by the western edge of the waters by the bay, which bay lies between the peninsula and the western shore of the lake.

. . . .

II.

Appellants' alternative claim of title by adverse possession is grounded either on the Wisconsin 10 and 20-year statutes, Wis. Stat. Ann., §§ 893.06 and 893.08, respectively, or on the federal 20-year Color of Title Act, 43 U.S.C.A. § 1068.

We find no merit in the contention concerning the state adverse possession statutes. As to Lot 4, the restrictions against alienation have not been removed. It has long been held that adverse possession under a state statute of limitations cannot run against Indians if the land is not alienable by them, so long as such restrictions exist. United States v. 7,405.3 Acres of Land, 4 Cir., 97 F.2d 417, 422-423 (1938). It has been noted that a similar holding was made by the court in the Western District of Wisconsin in a prior case concerning a restricted-fee patent granted to a Chippewa Indian pursuant to the same Chippewa treaty here involved. United States v. Raiche, D.C.W.D.Wis., 31 F.2d 624 (1928). There the court said at 628: "Furthermore, the [Wisconsin] statute of limitations cannot run against these plaintiffs, who, with respect to this land, are still under disability." . . .

. . . .

The Color of Title Act, supra, only governs "public lands." We have held, as the district court concluded, that the disputed 3.8 acres passed to the Indian patentee of Lot 4. The acreage and the lot were thereby removed from the "public land," as that term is used in 43 U.S.C.A. § 1068. It could not be alienated without the express consent of the President of the United States. It was not subject to a claim of adverse possession under the provisions of the Act sought to be involved.

As the Government aptly points out, if the disputed acreage did not pass to the patentee it remains instead a part of the Lac du Flambeau Indian Reservation as shown on the 1865 plat. It has long been established that Indian reservation land is not public land.

. . . .

For the foregoing reasons, the judgment of the district court in all things is affirmed.

Affirmed.

[c] Problems

[i] *Public Land.* What is the meaning of the phrase "public land" in 43 U.S.C. § 1068? The *Schwarz* court opined that the disputed land was not "public land" because it "passed to the Indian patentee of Lot 4" and was "thereby removed from the 'public land.'" What other sorts of land have been removed from the public land? How about national parks or national forests? Even though title to such areas is held by the United States, wouldn't you expect them to be deemed non-public for purposes of § 1068?

[ii] *Indian Land and Adverse Possession. Schwarz* involved tribal lands allotted during the Dawes Act era on which sale restrictions had never been lifted. Though such restrictions typically ended after 25 years (or earlier under a waiver system), the statutes for some reservation areas allowed the Department of the Interior to extend the sale restrictions. As a result, the Whitescott acreage was deemed removed from public land status because it had been allotted, but free of state adverse possession laws because transfer was still restricted. Can you figure out which of the following types of land *within the boundary lines of a reservation* would be subject to state adverse possession laws?

(a)   Trust lands held by the United States on behalf of a tribe.

(b)   Allotted land still subject to alienation restrictions.

(c)   Allotted land not subject to alienation restrictions but owned free of trust by the tribe itself in fee simple absolute.

(d)   Allotted land not subject to alienation restrictions but owned free of trust by a member of the tribe in fee simple absolute.

(e)   Allotted land not subject to alienation restrictions and owned by someone not belonging to the tribe in an area the *Brendale* court would deem "closed."

(f)   Allotted land not subject to alienation restrictions and owned by someone not belonging to the tribe in an area the *Brendale* court would deem "open."

[iii] *Tribal Artifacts.* With the permission of the person he thought was the owner of the land, Leonard Charrier, an amateur archaeologist, opened a "dig" in an area he suspected was the site of an ancient village of Tunica Indians. He uncovered 30 to 40 burial plots before being informed that the "permission" he had obtained was from the caretaker rather than the absentee owners of the land. Nonetheless he continued his work for three more years, excavating artifacts weighing over two tons from about 150 burial sites. When Charrier sought to sell the collection to the Peabody Museum at Harvard University, the museum demanded proof of ownership. In response, Charrier filed an action against the absentee owners of the site seeking to be declared the owner. The State of Louisiana then intervened in the action claiming it had

a duty to seek escheat of the artifacts in the absence of lawful heirs.[73] A bit later the State of Louisiana purchased the once artifact laden land from the absentee owners, along with any rights those owners had to the artifacts. The Tunica-Biloxi Indians of Louisiana also intervened in the action, claiming the artifacts for themselves. The Louisiana Court of Appeals held in favor of the tribe, concluding that burial with artifacts did not imply the artifacts were abandoned property free to be seized by anyone who found them. It also declined to award Charrier damages. He had claimed that if he lost his ownership claim, he should obtain remuneration for his time and effort; otherwise the true owner, he argued, would be unjustly enriched. *Charrier v. Bell*, 496 So. 2d 601 (La. Ct. App. 1986). What do you think of these results?

A similar sort of dispute has been brewing over the claim by another tribe that the fossil remains of an ancient Indian must be buried according to tribal custom rather than allowed to be studied by anthropologists and a variety of other claimants. The convoluted story of Kennewick Man is chronicled in detail at a web site maintained by the Tri-City Herald, a paper serving Kennewick, Pasco and Richland, Washington. The URL is *http://www.tri-cityherald.com/bones*. As this is written, arrangements are being made to send the bones to a laboratory equipped to determine if they are the remains of an Indian. After that study is completed, the court will resolve the ownership dispute. If you are interested in the broader issues about the propriety of returning ancient artifacts to Native Americans read Sarah Harding, *Justifying Repatriation of Native American Cultural Property*, 72 IND. L.J. 723 (1997). Can buried artifacts and bodies be adversely possessed by the user of the surface? Do the notice features of adverse possession law—notoriety, continuity and hostility—protect the interests of Native Americans in buried items?

[iv] *Dinosaurs.* In 1990, Sue Hendrickson, a research worker for the Black Hills Institute of Geological Research, uncovered "Sue," the most complete and valuable Tyrannosaurus Rex skeleton known. The find was made within the boundary lines of the Cheyenne River Sioux Reservation on land held by the United States in trust for Maurice Williams, a member of the Cheyenne River Sioux Tribe. The United States patented the land to Williams in 1969 under a deed providing that the trust status of the land would expire in 25 years. Shortly after the dinosaur was found and excavated, the Black Hills Institute paid Williams $5,000 "for title to the fossil and the right to excavate the fossil from his land." On May 11, 1992, the Justice Department sent 28 F.B.I. agents, federal officials and National Guardsmen to raid the Black Hills Institute, seize the plaster-encased fossils of Sue and other creatures, along with books and records. The Institute was later indicted for a variety of violations of federal law.[74] Litigation over ownership of "Sue" bounced around in the courts for years. Eventually it was decided that the sale of the fossil by Williams to the Institute was an attempt to convey "land" in violation of the terms of his trust deed, and that the United States owned the fossil in trust for Williams. *Black Hills Institute Geological Museum v. United States*, 12 F.3d 737 (8th Cir. 1994). On October 4, 1997, "Sue" was put up for auction at Sotheby's in New York City. Including the auction house premium, it fetched $8,362,000 from Chicago's Field Museum.[75] Who should get the $7,600,000 left over after Sotheby's takes its fee?

---

[73] When a person dies intestate, that is, without a will, state statutes provide directions on how the person's assets should be distributed. In the absence of any statutory takers, the property will escheat to the state.

[74] Malcolm W. Browne, *High Court Lets Stand Dinosaur Fossil Ruling*, NEW YORK TIMES, Oct. 4, 1994, at C6, col. 5.

[75] *Museum Pays $8.4 Million for T-Rex; 65-Million-Year-Old Fossil to Go on Display in Chicago in 2000,* WASHINGTON POST, Oct. 5, 1997, at A10.

[*v*] ***Historic Preservation.*** In 1992 the Historic Preservation Act was amended by Congress to require that the federal historic preservation apparatus apply to the preservation of "historic properties" of Indian tribes.[76] Among other things, that means that the status of sacred sites, burial grounds, ruins and other structures—both on and off of reservation lands—must be taken into account when the federal government undertakes construction projects or other major initiatives. As of 1998, regulations to enforce the program have still not been issued. They are bogged down in controversy over the level of influence tribal organizations and governments should have in writing the rules and administering the historic preservation system.[77] How much authority should each tribe have in controlling the fate of sites that are important to its historic traditions? Should on and off reservation sites be treated differently? Should sites on reservation trust lands be treated differently from sites on reservation fee lands?

[7] Customary and Habitual Land Use Patterns

[a] Rules of Implied Dedication, Public Trust and Custom

A variety of legal doctrines have been used to prevent public land from being used for private purposes, or to allow the public to make use of privately owned property. In addition to adverse possession and prescription, courts have invoked implied dedication, public trust, and custom doctrines to protect the public's interest in land, particularly in fragile or ecologically sensitive zones. Normally, land is dedicated to the public in a formal way. A writing is delivered to an appropriate public official with the authority to accept property for general use. But formality is not required in most places. Oral offers of land to the public may be made and accepted. And if the public is allowed to use property for a significant period of time, such as that normally required by the adverse possession statute, the intent to dedicate may be presumed. This sort of rule led to confirmation of public rights in beach land in California.[78] Public trust doctrine treats tidelands and some other areas as held in trust for citizens of the jurisdiction. Lands subject to a public trust may only be used for the public's benefit. While tidal lands have been the most prominent focus of these cases,[79] the theory has been applied to a variety of coastal areas and even some upland parcels with great public significance. Custom has been used most often to affirm public access to coastal areas long used for recreational or business purposes. While controversy over the wisdom of all these doctrines exists,[80] they form an interesting counterpoint to both adverse possession law and to contemporary controversies about Native American demands for access to traditional lands for customary religious and cultural observances. If you are interested in further reading about these areas, look at Carol Rose, *The Comedy of the Commons: Custom, Commerce and Inherently Public Property*, 53 U. CHI. L. REV. 711 (1986); Hope M. Babcock, *Has the U.S. Supreme Court Finally Drained the Swamp of Takings on Wetlands and Coastal Barrier Beaches*, 19 HARV. ENVTL. L. REV. 1, 26-49 (1995).

---

[76] National Historic Preservation Act Amendments of 1992, 106 Stat. 4753 (1992) (codified as amended at 16 U.S.C. § 470a(d)).

[77] William Claiborne, *U.S., Indians Fight Over Role in Protecting Sacred Sites,* WASHINGTON POST, Nov. 28, 1998, at A2, col. 1.

[78] Gion v. City of Santa Cruz, 2 Cal. 3d 29, 465 P.2d 50, 84 Cal. Rptr. 162 (1970).

[79] The Supreme Court has discussed the public trust in tidelands quite recently. *See* Phillips Petroleum Co. v. Mississippi, 484 U.S. 469 (1988).

[80] For example, an attempt to use all of these doctrines to affirm public access to beach areas between the low and high tide lines in Maryland failed. Department of Natural Resources v. Ocean City, 274 Md. 1, 332 A.2d 630 (1975).

[b]   A Public Trust Case: *Oregon ex rel. Thornton v. Hay*

The next case involved the dry sand area of a beach abutting the Surfsand Motel. Mr. William Hay and his wife Georgianna Hay built the small motel in the 1960s. In an effort to draw more customers, they installed some cabanas on the dry sand area of the beach. The Hays thought they had a right to do this because the deed for the motel land included land all the way to the mean high tide line. They soon discovered that motel guests were often unable to find an empty cabana. Non-guests, thinking some generous soul had added an amenity to the beach, were making use of the facilities. In response, Mr. Hay had some old telephone polls laid flat on the beach along his property lines about 100 feet west of the sand dunes and posted signs saying the beach was private property.[81] This got the attention of the Oregon State Highway Commission, which asked Hay to remove the polls and the signs.

The Highway Commission was drawn into the dispute because of a 1912 statute designating the seashore as a public highway. The statute, however, only protected the wet sand area, leaving Hay room to claim that the dry sand area belonged to him. In 1967, the Highway Commission, fearing that Oregon's beaches would be lost to the public, introduced a bill to include the dry sand areas within the terms of the old highway statute. The majority of the Republican dominated legislature opposed the bill, but their Republican Governor, Tom McCall strongly favored it. One morning in May, 1967, McCall flew into Cannon Beach with a bunch of reporters on two helicopters and held a "news conference" to demand passage of the bill. McCall quickly got his wish, but Hay continued to claim ownership of the beach.[82] It took litigation to settle the matter.

---

[81] Some of these details were provided by Mr. William Allread, son-in-law of Mr. William Hay, in a September 14, 1998 telephone interview.

[82] TERENCE O'DONNELL, CANNON BEACH: A PLACE BY THE SEA 105-106 (1996).

Governor Tom McCall in Front of Surfsand Motel[83]

State of Oregon, ex rel. Thornton v. Hay

Supreme Court of Oregon
254 Or. 584, 462 P.2d 671 (1969)

Before Perry, C.J., and McAllister, O'Connell, Goodwin, Denecke, and Holman, JJ. Goodwin, Justice.

William and Georgianna Hay, the owners of a tourist facility at Cannon Beach, appeal from a decree which enjoins them from constructing fences or other improvements in the dry-sand area between the sixteen-foot elevation contour line and the ordinary high-tide line of the Pacific Ocean.

The issue is whether the state has the power to prevent the defendant landowners from enclosing the dry-sand area contained within the legal description of their ocean-front property.

The state asserts two theories: (1) the landowners' record title to the disputed area is encumbered by a superior right in the public to go upon and enjoy the land for recreational purposes; and (2) if the disputed area is not encumbered by the asserted public easement, then the state has power to prevent construction under zoning regulations made pursuant to ORS 390.640.

---

[83] Reproduced with permission of the Oregon Historical Society (Negative Number 52610).

The defendant landowners concede that the State Highway Commission has standing to represent the rights of the public in this litigation and that all tideland lying seaward of the ordinary, or mean high-tide line is a state recreation area as defined in ORS 390.720.[1]

From the trial record, applicable statutes, and court decisions, certain terms and definitions have been extracted and will appear in this opinion. A short glossary follows:

ORS 390.720 refers to the "ordinary" high-tide line, while other sources refer to the "mean" high-tide line. For the purposes of this case the two lines will be considered to be the same. The mean hightide line in Oregon is fixed by the 1947 Supplement to the 1929 United States Coast and Geodetic Survey data.

The land area in dispute will be called the dry-sand area. This will be assumed to be the land lying between the line of mean high tide and the visible line of vegetation.

The vegetation line is the seaward edge of vegetation where the upland supports vegetation. It falls generally in the vicinity of the sixteen-foot-elevation contour line, but is not at all points necessarily identical with that line. Differences between the vegetation line and the sixteen-foot line are irrelevant for the purposes of this case.

The sixteen-foot line, which is an engineering line and not a line visible on the ground, is mentioned in ORS 390.640, and in the trial court's decree.

The extreme high-tide line and the highwater mark are mentioned in the record, but will be treated as identical with the vegetation line. While technical differences between extreme high tide and the highwater mark, and between both lines and the sixteen-foot line, might have legal significance in some other litigation, such differences, if any, have none in this case. We cite these variations in terminology only to point out that the cases and statutes relevant to the issues in this case, like the witnesses, have not always used the same words to describe similar topographical features.

Below, or seaward of, the mean high-tide line, is the state-owned foreshore, or wet-sand area, in which the landowners in this case concede the public's paramount right, and concerning which there is no justiciable controversy.

The only issue in this case, as noted, is the power of the state to limit the record owner's use and enjoyment of the dry-sand area, by whatever boundaries the area may be described.

The trial court found that the public had acquired, over the years, an easement for recreational purposes to go upon and enjoy the dry-sand area, and that this easement was appurtenant to the wet-sand portion of the beach which is admittedly owned by the state and designated as a "state recreation area."

Because we hold that the trial court correctly found in favor of the state on the rights of the public in the dry-sand area, it follows that the state has an equitable right to protect the public in the enjoyment of those rights by causing the removal of fences and other obstacles.

---

[1] ORS 390.720 provides:

"Ownership of the shore of the Pacific Ocean between ordinary high tide and extreme low tide, and from the Oregon and Washington state line on the north to the Oregon and California state line on the south, excepting such portions as may have been disposed of by the state prior to July 5, 1947, is vested in the State of Oregon, and is declared to be a state recreation area. No portion of such ocean shore shall be alienated by any of the agencies of the state except as provided by law."

It is not necessary, therefore, to consider whether ORS 390.640 would be constitutional if it were to be applied as a zoning regulation to lands upon which the public had not acquired an easement for recreational use.

In order to explain our reasons for affirming the trial court's decree, it is necessary to set out in some detail the historical facts which lead to our conclusion.

The dry-sand area in Oregon has been enjoyed by the general public as a recreational adjunct of the wet-sand or foreshore area since the beginning of the state's political history. The first European settlers on these shores found the aboriginal inhabitants using the foreshore for clam-digging and the dry-sand area for their cooking fires. The newcomers continued these customs after statehood. Thus, from the time of the earliest settlement to the present day, the general public has assumed that the dry-sand area was a part of the public beach, and the public has used the dry-sand area for picnics, gathering wood, building warming fires, and generally as a headquarters from which to supervise children or to range out over the foreshore as the tides advance and recede. In the Cannon Beach vicinity, state and local officers have policed the dry sand, and municipal sanitary crews have attempted to keep the area reasonably free from man-made litter.

Perhaps one explanation for the evolution of the custom of the public to use the dry-sand area for recreational purposes is that the area could not be used conveniently by its owners for any other purpose. The dry-sand area is unstable in its seaward boundaries, unsafe during winter storms, and for the most part unfit for the construction of permanent structures. While the vegetation line remains relatively fixed, the western edge of the dry-sand area is subject to dramatic moves eastward or westward in response to erosion and accretion. For example, evidence in the trial below indicated that between April 1966 and August 1967 the seaward edge of the dry-sand area involved in this litigation moved westward 180 feet. At other points along the shore, the evidence showed, the seaward edge of the dry-sand area could move an equal distance to the east in a similar period of time.

Until very recently, no question concerning the right of the public to enjoy the dry-sand area appears to have been brought before the courts of this state. The public's assumption that the dry sand as well as the foreshore was "public property" had been reinforced by early judicial decisions. See Shively v. Bowlby, 152 U.S. 1, 14 S. Ct. 548, 38 L. Ed. 331 (1894), which affirmed Bowlby v. Shively, 22 Or. 410, 30 P. 154 (1892). These cases held that landowners claiming under federal patents owned seaward only to the "high-water" line, a line that was then assumed to be the vegetation line.[3]

In 1935, the United States Supreme Court held that a federal patent conveyed title to land farther seaward, to the mean hightide line. Borax Consolidated, Ltd. v. Los Angeles, 296 U.S. 10, 56 S. Ct. 23, 80 L. Ed. 9 (1935). While this decision may have expanded seaward the record ownership of upland landowners, it was apparently little noticed by Oregonians. In any event, the Borax decision had no discernible effect on the actual practices of Oregon beachgoers and upland property owners.

---

[3] One of the issues in the Bowlby litigation was the right to wharf out from the upland. The state had sold to various private owners certain tidelands seaward of Shively's uplands. Shively, in an early plat, had overlapped his platted lots upon state-owned tidelands. The controversy concerned the foreshore generally. The litigants were not then particularly interested in "dry" versus "wet" sand, because a wharf must cross both "dry" and "wet" sand if such topography lies between the upland and deep water. The state's title to the tidelands was confirmed to the "highwater mark." Most private landowners in Oregon apparently assumed after Bowlby that their patented lands run seaward only to the "high-water mark," which is also, for all practical purposes, the vegetation line.

Recently, however, the scarcity of oceanfront building sites has attracted substantial private investments in resort facilities. Resort owners like these defendants now desire to reserve for their paying guests the recreational advantages that accrue to the dry-sand portions of their deeded property. Consequently, in 1967, public debate and political activity resulted in legislative attempts to resolve conflicts between public and private interests in the dry-sand area:

ORS 390.610 "(1) The Legislative Assembly hereby declares it is the public policy of the State of Oregon to forever preserve and maintain the sovereignty of the state heretofore existing over the seashore and ocean beaches of the state from the Columbia River on the North to the Oregon-California line on the South so that the public may have the free and uninterrupted use thereof.

"(2) The Legislative Assembly recognizes that over the years the public has made frequent and uninterrupted use of lands abutting, adjacent and contiguous to the public highways and state recreation areas and recognizes, further, that where such use has been sufficient to create easements in the public through dedication, prescription, grant or otherwise, that it is in the public interest to protect and preserve such public easements as a permanent part of Oregon's recreational resources.

"(3) Accordingly, the Legislative Assembly hereby declares that all public rights and easements in those lands described in subsection (2) of this section are confirmed and declared vested exclusively in the State of Oregon and shall be held and administered in the same manner as those lands described in ORS 390.720."

The state concedes that such legislation cannot divest a person of his rights in land, Hughes v. Washington, 389 U.S. 290, 88 S. Ct. 438, 19 L. Ed.2d 530 (1967), and that the defendants' record title, which includes the dry-sand area, extends seaward to the ordinary or mean high-tide line.

The landowners likewise concede that since 1899 the public's rights in the foreshore have been confirmed by law as well as by custom and usage. Oregon Laws 1899, p. 3, provided:

"That the shore of the Pacific ocean, between ordinary high and extreme low tides, and from the Columbia river on the north to the south boundary line of Clatsop county on the south, is hereby declared a public highway, and shall forever remain open as such to the public."

The disputed area is *sui generis*. While the foreshore is "owned" by the state, and the upland is "owned" by the patentee or record-title holder, neither can be said to "own" the full bundle of rights normally connoted by the term "estate in fee simple."

In addition to the *sui generis* nature of the land itself, a multitude of complex and sometimes overlapping precedents in the law confronted the trial court. Several early Oregon decisions generally support the trial court's decision, i.e., that the public can acquire easements in private land by long-continued use that is inconsistent with the owner's exclusive possession and enjoyment of his land. A citation of the cases could end the discussion at this point. But because the early cases do not agree on the legal theories by which the results are reached, and because this is an important case affecting valuable rights in land, it is appropriate to review some of the law applicable to this case.

One group of precedents relied upon in part by the state and by the trial court can be called the 'implied-dedication' cases. The doctrine of implied dedication is well known to the law in this state and elsewhere . . . . Dedication, however, whether express or implied, rests upon an intent to dedicate.[4] In the case at bar, it is unlikely that the landowners thought they had anything to dedicate, until 1967, when the notoriety of legislative debates about the public's rights in the dry-sand area sent a number of ocean-front landowners to the offices of their legal advisers.

A second group of cases relied upon by the state, but rejected by the trial court, deals with the possibility of a landowner's losing the exclusive possession and enjoyment of his land through the development of prescriptive easements in the public.

In Oregon, as in most common-law jurisdictions, an easement can be created in favor of one person in the land of another by uninterrupted use and enjoyment of the land in a particular manner for the statutory period, so long as the use is open, adverse, under claim of right, but without authority of law or consent of the owner. In Oregon, the prescriptive period is ten years. The public use of the disputed land in the case at bar is admitted to be continuous for more than sixty years. There is no suggestion in the record that anyone's permission was sought or given; rather, the public used the land under a claim of right. Therefore, if the public can acquire an easement by prescription, the requirements for such an acquisition have been met in connection with the specific tract of land involved in this case.

The owners argue, however, that the general public, not being subject to actions in trespass and ejectment, cannot acquire rights by prescription, because the statute of limitations is irrelevant when an action does not lie.

While it may not be feasible for a landowner to sue the general public, it is nonetheless possible by means of signs and fences to prevent or minimize public invasions of private land for recreational purposes. In Oregon, moreover, the courts and the Legislative Assembly have both recognized that the public can acquire prescriptive easements in private land, at least for roads and highways. See, e.g., Huggett et ux. v. Moran et ux., 201 Or. 105, 266 P.2d 692 (1954), in which we observed that counties could acquire public roads by prescription. And see ORS 368.405, which provides for the manner in which counties may establish roads. The statute enumerates the formal governmental actions that can be employed, and then concludes: "This section does not preclude acquiring public ways by adverse use."

. . . Consequently, we conclude that the law in Oregon . . . does not preclude the creation of prescriptive easements in beach land for public recreational use.

Because many elements of prescription are present in this case, the state has relied upon the doctrine in support of the decree below. We believe, however, that there is a better legal basis for affirming the decree. The most cogent basis for the decision in this case is the English doctrine of custom. Strictly construed, prescription applies only to the specific tract of land before the court, and doubtful prescription cases could fill the courts for years with tract-by-tract litigation. An established custom, on the other hand, can be proven with reference to a larger region. Ocean-front lands from the northern to the southern border of the state ought to be treated uniformly.

The other reason which commends the doctrine of custom over that of prescription as the principal basis for the decision in this case is the unique nature of the lands in question. This case deals solely with the dry-sand area along the Pacific shore, and this land has been used by the public as public recreational land according to an unbroken custom running back in time as long as the land has been inhabited.

---

[4] Because of the elements of public interest and estoppel running through the cases, intent to dedicate is sometimes "presumed" instead of proven. But conceptually, at least, dedication is founded upon an intent to dedicate.

. . . .

In 1 Blackstone, Commentaries *75-*78, Sir William Blackstone set out the requisites of a particular custom.

Paraphrasing Blackstone, the first requirement of a custom, to be recognized as law, is that it must be ancient. It must have been used so long "that the memory of man runneth not to the contrary." Professor Cooley footnotes his edition of Blackstone with the comment that "long and general" usage is sufficient. In any event, the record in the case at bar satisfies the requirement of antiquity. So long as there has been an institutionalized system of land tenure in Oregon, the public has freely exercised the right to use the dry-sand area up and down the Oregon coast for the recreational purposes noted earlier in this opinion.

The second requirement is that the right be exercised without interruption. A customary right need not be exercised continuously, but it must be exercised without an interruption caused by anyone possessing a paramount right. In the case at bar, there was evidence that the public's use and enjoyment of the dry-sand area had never been interrupted by private landowners.

Blackstone's third requirement, that the customary use be peaceable and free from dispute, is satisfied by the evidence which related to the second requirement.

The fourth requirement, that of reasonableness, is satisfied by the evidence that the public has always made use of the land in a manner appropriate to the land and to the usages of the community. There is evidence in the record that when inappropriate uses have been detected, municipal police officers have intervened to preserve order.

The fifth requirement, certainty, is satisfied by the visible boundaries of the dry-sand area and by the character of the land, which limits the use thereof to recreational uses connected with the foreshore.

The sixth requirement is that a custom must be obligatory; that is, in the case at bar, not left to the option of each landowner whether or not he will recognize the public's right to go upon the dry-sand area for recreational purposes. The record shows that the dry-sand area in question has been used, as of right, uniformly with similarly situated lands elsewhere, and that the public's use has never been questioned by an upland owner so long as the public remained on the dry sand and refrained from trespassing upon the lands above the vegetation line.

Finally, a custom must not be repugnant, or inconsistent, with other customs or with other law. The custom under consideration violates no law, and is not repugnant.

Two arguments have been arrayed against the doctrine of custom as a basis for decision in Oregon. The first argument is that custom is unprecedented in this state, and has only scant adherence elsewhere in the United States. The second argument is that because of the relative brevity of our political history it is inappropriate to rely upon an English doctrine that requires greater antiquity than a newly-settled land can muster. Neither of these arguments is persuasive.

The custom of the people of Oregon to use the dry-sand area of the beaches for public recreational purposes meets every one of Blackstone's requisites. While it is not necessary to rely upon precedent from other states, we are not the first state to recognize custom as a source of law.

On the score of the brevity of our political history, it is true that the Anglo-American legal system on this continent is relatively new. Its newness has made it possible for government to provide for many of our institutions by written law rather than by customary law.[6] This truism does not, however, militate against the validity of a custom when the custom does in fact exist. If antiquity were the sole test of validity of a custom, Oregonians could satisfy that requirement by recalling that the European settlers were not the first people to use the dry-sand area as public land.

Finally, in support of custom, the record shows that the custom of the inhabitants of Oregon and of visitors in the state to use the dry sand as a public recreation area is so notorious that notice of the custom on the part of persons buying land along the shore must be presumed. In the case at bar, the landowners conceded their actual knowledge of the public's long-standing use of the dry-sand area, and argued that the elements of consent present in the relationship between the landowners and the public precluded the application of the law of prescription. As noted, we are not resting this decision on prescription, and we leave open the effect upon prescription of the type of consent that may have been present in this case. Such elements of consent are, however, wholly consistent with the recognition of public rights derived from custom.

Because so much of our law is the product of legislation, we sometimes lose sight of the importance of custom as a source of law in our society. It seems particularly appropriate in the case at bar to look to an ancient and accepted custom in this state as the source of a rule of law. The rule in this case, based upon custom, is salutary in confirming a public right, and at the same time it takes from no man anything which he has had a legitimate reason to regard as exclusively his.

For the foregoing reasons, the decree of the trial court is affirmed.

Denecke, Justice (specially concurring).

I agree with the decision of the majority; however, I disagree with basing the decision upon the English doctrine of "customary rights." In my opinion the facts in this case cannot be fitted into the outlines of that ancient doctrine.

In my opinion the doctrine of "customary rights" is useful but only as an analogy. I am further of the opinion that "custom," as distinguished from "customary rights," is an important ingredient in establishing the rights of the public to the use of the dry sands.

I base the public's right upon the following factors: (1) long usage by the public of the dry sands area, not necessarily on all the Oregon beaches, but wherever the public uses the beach; (2) a universal and long held belief by the public in the public's right to such use; (3) long and universal acquiescence by the upland owners in such public use; and (4) the extreme desirability to the public of the right to the use of the dry sands. When this combination exists, as it does here, I conclude that the public has the right to use the dry sands.

---

[6] The English law on customary rights grew up in a small island nation at a time when most inhabitants lived and died without traveling more than a day's walk from their birthplace. Most of the customary rights recorded in English cases are local in scope. The English had many cultural and language groups which eventually merged into a nation. After these groups developed their own unique customs, the unified nation recognized some of them as law. Some American scholars, looking at the vast geography of this continent and the freshness of its civilization, have concluded that there is no need to look to English customary rights as a source of legal rights in this country. See, e.g., 6 Powell, Real Property s 934, note 5, at 362 (1949). Some of the generalizations drawn by the text writers from English cases would tend to limit customary rights to specific usages in English towns and villages. See Gray, The Rule Against Perpetuities ss 572—588 (1942). But it does not follow that a custom, established in fact, cannot have regional application and be enjoyed by a larger public than the inhabitants of a single village.

Admittedly, this is a new concept as applied to use of the dry sands of a beach; however, it is not new as applied to other public usages. In Luscher v. Reynolds, 153 Or. 625, 56 P.2d 1158 (1963), we held that regardless of who owns the bed of a lake, if it is capable of being boated, the public has the right to boat it.

. . . .

In Collins v. Gerhardt, 237 Mich. 38, 211 N.W. 115, 116 (1926), the defendant was wading Pine River and fishing. The plaintiff, who owned the land on both sides and the bed of Pine River, sued defendant for trespass. The court held for the defendant.

> "From this it follows that the common-law doctrine, viz., that the right of fishing in navigable waters follows the ownership of the soil, does not prevail in this state. It is immaterial who owns the soil in our navigable rivers. The trust remains. From the beginning the title was impressed with this trust for the preservation of the public right of fishing and other public rights which all citizens enjoyed in tidal waters under the common law . . . ."

These rights of the public in tidelands and in the beds of navigable streams have been called "jus publicum" and we have consistently and recently reaffirmed their existence. The right of public use continues although title to the property passes into private ownership and nothing in the chain of title reserves or notifies anyone of this public right.

In a recent treatise on waters and water rights the authors state:

> "The principle that the public has an interest in tidelands and banks of navigable waters and a right to use them for purposes for which there is a substantial public demand may be derived from the fact that the public won a right to passage over the shore for access to the sea for fishing when this was the area of substantial public demand. As time goes by, opportunities for much more extensive uses of these lands become available to the public. The assertion by the public of a right to enjoy additional uses is met by the assertion that the public right is defined and limited by precedent based upon past uses and past demand. But such a limitation confuses the application of the principle under given circumstances with the principle itself.

> "The law regarding the public use of property held in part for the benefit of the public must change as the public need changes. The words of Justice Cardozo, expressed in a different context nearly a half-century ago are relevant today in our application of this law: 'We may not suffer it to petrify at the cost of its animating principle.'" 1 Clark (ed-in-chief), Waters and Water Rights, at 202 (1967).

[c]　Questions

[i]　*Shifting Prescription Rights.* The *Hay* court judges used custom rules rather than prescription doctrines to resolve the case. They noted that prescription normally was used to deal with specific parcels of land. Litigating hundreds of prescription cases about shoreline access rights, the court added, was a cumbersome way to resolve beach ownership questions. But is it obvious that prescription applies only to specific, stable sites? If the beach moves because of wave and storm action and usage patterns follow the beach, why not allow prescription? Note that in most oceanfront states, public ownership extends up to the mean high tide line. If beach erosion causes the high tide line to move inside the boundaries of property that used to be completely behind the vegetation line, then the state ends up owning part of the previously private acreage. If state ownership follows the shifting fortunes of the high tide line, why shouldn't public

prescriptive rights behave in a similar fashion? For two cases deciding this question in opposite ways, compare *Feinman v. State of Texas*, 717 S.W.2d 106 (Tex. App. 1986), in which moving easements were found, with *Dept. of Natural Resources v. Mayor and City Council of Ocean City*, 274 Md. 1, 332 A.2d 630 (1975).

[*ii*]   ***Public Trust.*** Judge Denecke, concurring in *Hay*, wrote that he preferred the public trust doctrine over custom. Are there any significant differences between the two theories? Does it make any difference which one you use?

[*iii*]   ***Takings.*** If, as the *Hay* majority opined, the owners of beachfront property never intended to dedicate the dry sand areas to the public, did the decision to validate public ownership of the area by use of custom rules serve to take the dry sand areas in violation of the fifth amendment to the United States Constitution? This issue will be taken up at length in Chapter 11. In one of the cases in that chapter, *Lucas v. South Carolina Coastal Council*, 505 U.S. 1003 (1992), the Supreme Court relied heavily on background principles of property extant at the time regulatory regimes are first imposed in deciding upon the constitutional propriety of land use controls. If custom rules have been around since the founding of the nation, does that mean that public access to beaches should sometimes be affirmed despite the takings clause? In Oregon, the answer appears to be "yes." *Stevens v. City of Cannon Beach,* 317 Or. 131, 854 P.2d 449 (1993). The parcel of land at issue in *Stevens* is located right next door to the Surfsand Motel land that was the subject of *Hay*.[84] The United States Supreme Court declined to grant certiorari in *Stevens*. 510 U.S. 1207 (1994). Justice Scalia dissented from the denial of certiorari, arguing that *Hay* represented a significant change in Oregon law, that the court's construction of custom rules did not fulfill the requirements of the common law rule, and that a serious taking question was therefore presented for the court to review. Stevens then filed an action in federal court seeking compensation which he also lost, this time on the ground of res judicata.[85] *Stevens v. City of Cannon Beach,* 893 F. Supp. 944 (D. Or. 1995). The Supreme Court again refused to hear the case.

[*iv*]   ***Native Customary "Rights."*** Can the reasoning of *Hay* be used to affirm the validity of claims by Native Americans that they have rights of access to land that is culturally, historically or religiously important to their communities? Would it matter if they have been denied access to an area for quite some time despite repeated requests to use a disputed area?

[*v*]   ***Denouement.*** The Surfsand is no longer owned by the Hay family, but by the Steve Martin Management Company. It is now one of the largest resort hotels on the Oregon shore, complete with its own web site at http://www.surfsand.com.

---

[84] Telephone interview of William Allread, Sept. 14, 1998.

[85] A party is generally entitled to litigate a claim only once. In *Stevens,* the federal district court found that the compensation claim had been fully litigated and lost in the prior state action, and that it could not be relitigated in the federal courts.

CHAPTER 2

GENDER, FAMILY AND CONCURRENT PROPERTY OWNERSHIP

§ 2.01 Introduction

Concurrent estates are property holding forms designed for use by groups of two or more people. The most common varieties of concurrent estates—tenancies in common and joint tenancies with rights of survivorship—create packages of understandings about the use, management and disposition of property owned by groups of people. Since many parts of these packages of understanding may be modified by contract, concurrent estates can be structured to meet the specific needs of particular groups. A second set of concurrent ownership forms exists for married couples. This set includes tenancies by the entirety, marital property and community property. Finally, there is a collection of holding patterns, such as partnerships and corporations, used by businesses. This chapter discusses the first two sets of non-business holding patterns. Business ownership forms are taken up in Chapter 4.

The chapter is organized in three parts. The first is an introduction to the contemporary language of concurrent estates for unmarried groups. Mastering the material will provide a solid foundation for the second part of the chapter on the role gender has played in the development of property ownership rights held by married men and women. Since study of the early history of marital property mostly involves an inquiry into the limitations imposed on property ownership by wives, the first section on non-marital group ownership establishes the base line left behind by women upon marriage. The chapter concludes with materials on recent developments in the property law of non-marital couples and families.

§ 2.02 Ownership Forms Available to Non-Marital Groups

[1] Introduction

[a] Tenancy in Common

The simplest form of group ownership is a tenancy in common. Mike and Vladimir Vulles held their allotment land in this form in the *Vulles* litigation discussed at p. 83, et seq. above. Conveyances creating a tenancy in common take the form of a transfer to "A and B and their heirs as tenants in common" or simply "to A and B as tenants in common."[1] Transfers to groups of two or more unmarried people are presumed to be tenancies in common unless a contrary intent is shown. Therefore, a grant "to A and B" will usually be treated as a tenancy in common.

---

[1] The words "and their heirs" are words of *limitation*, rather than words of *purchase*. That is, they denote the length of time the interest may exist, not the parties taking the property. "And their heirs" means "forever." Using non-legalese, therefore, the granting language would read "to A and B forever as tenants in common." In most places now, a grant to "A and B as tenants in common" will be treated as if the "and their heirs" phrase is present unless the context clearly suggests that the grantor intended to convey a life estate.

Tenancies in common often arise when property is disposed of by will or intestate succession. The successors in interest, usually children, of the deceased person become tenants in common of the land left to them.

The central feature of a tenancy in common is unity of possession. This means that each of the owners has an undivided interest in the property[2] with the right to possess and use the entire parcel. Each owner also may transfer, lease or mortgage her or his share of the property to another party. If, for example, A and B hold property as tenants in common and A sells his interest to C, C then becomes a tenant in common with B.

Absent a statement to the contrary, each tenant in common takes an equal share of ownership. A grant "to A, B and C as tenants in common" will give each grantee a one-third share. That does not mean, however, that all tenants in common will hold the same shares. A grantor may create different shares by conveying an interest "to A and B as tenants in common, A holding a two-thirds interest and B a one-third interest." Odd fractions may also result when a tenant in common dies. So, for example, if A, B and C hold a parcel as tenants in common and A dies leaving her share to her children D and E, D and E will each take a one-sixth share.

Co-ownership is not always easy to manage. Administrative disputes and family quarrels often upset the apple cart. When one co-owner dies, leaving her share to the next generation, concurrent interests multiply, along with the probability for disagreements. The simplest way to end such disputes is for all the tenants in common to sell their interests to the same party and split the proceeds. The purchaser ends up with a fee simple absolute. If one concurrent owner does not wish to sell, however, the remaining owners are placed in a difficult position. Sale of a fractional interest in a piece of land rarely will fetch full fractional value. Who would want to buy and share land with a stranger? The only way for a concurrent owner to obtain the full value of their share is to force the physical division of the land among the owners or the sale of a fee simple over the objections of the other owners. This sort of property "divorce"—a partition—is allowed everywhere. But filing such an action will sometimes cause acrimonious family quarrels. A partition court will usually order the land to be sold at auction.[3] The costs of the sale will be deducted from the money obtained and the remaining funds will be distributed to the concurrent owners. The routine availability of the partition remedy, together with the significant cost of legal proceedings, creates a large disincentive to the withholding of permission for the sale of land held by quarrelsome concurrent owners.

[b]   Joint Tenancy with Rights of Survivorship

Many characteristics of a joint tenancy with rights of survivorship are like tenancies in common. Each owner takes an undivided right to possess the entire estate and partition is routinely available. The central difference between the two forms of concurrent ownership is survivorship. At the death of a tenant in common, that owner's share passes to takers designated by a will or by the intestate succession laws. When a joint tenant dies, that person's share is split among the other concurrent owners. So if A, B and C hold land as joint tenants with rights of survivorship and A dies, B and C will end up owning the entire asset as joint tenants with rights of survivorship.

---

[2] The word "undivided" is used to distinguish this idea from a geographical division using boundary lines.

[3] A partition court may also geographically divide the land and give each concurrent owner a fee simple absolute in part of the land. It is only fair to do this, however, if the parties can agree on a division or if all the land is of similar value and quality. In urban settings geographical division is almost always impossible without an agreement among the parties. In rural settings, it is sometimes possible to divide the land rather than sell it.

If A's will contains a provision giving his interest in the parcel to D, it will have no effect. The survivorship feature means that the property automatically passes to the still living owners. There is nothing left for the will to convey.

Because of the survivorship feature, joint tenancies are more likely than tenancies in common to be used in family situations. Since survivorship would be an irrational feature in many situations, tenancies in common are presumed when grants are ambiguous. A grant to "A and B as joint tenants" may be read as a tenancy in common in some situations. In order to insure that a joint tenancy is created, grantors commonly use boiler-plate language such as "to A and B as joint tenants with rights of survivorship and not as tenants in common."

At common law the centrality of survivorship to the joint tenancy was reinforced by a requirement that four unities—time, title, interest and possession—exist. Survivorship and its common use in family situations suggested that the parcel was to be held as a unity, not only in possession, but in organization and action. So joint tenants had to take their interest at the same time. Their title had to arise by the same deed or will. Each owner's interest had to be of equal value; different fractional shares were not allowed. And the source of possessory rights had to be the same for all owners; one owner could not hold an equitable share with a party holding a legal interest.[4] The four unities are still required in some places. That means that if A and B held land as joint tenants with rights of survivorship and they wished to remove B from ownership and replace her with C, they could not simply convey land from A and B to A and C as joint tenants with rights of survivorship. A and B would have to use a "straw party." That means that A and B would convey a fee simple to X, a trusted soul, and X would then convey the land to A and C as joint tenants with rights of survivorship. The ability to do that, along with the hassle of being required to do it, has led some states to remove the requirement that the time and title unities be met when a joint tenant wishes to restructure the ownership pattern into another joint tenancy.

As with tenancies in common, a joint tenant may unilaterally convey her interest. That may seem surprising given the centrality of the survivorship idea. But the need to allow easy exit is felt just as strongly here. Locking up property ownership in unbreakable joint tenancies is thought to be too large an inhibition on the marketability of land. So joint tenants may sell their shares before they die. (Death, of course, triggers the survivorship feature.) But if a joint tenant sells out, that removes the unities of time and title. The party purchasing a joint tenant's share, therefore, may not become a joint tenant with the non-selling owner or owners.

Here is an example. Suppose A, B and C hold property as joint tenants with rights of survivorship and that A sells her share to D. The sale severs the unities of time and title. That means that D may not be a joint tenant. B and C, however, still hold their interests in a way that meets the four unities. So B and C will be joint tenants in the two-thirds share of the land not sold to D. D will hold the other third as a tenant in common with the still unified joint tenant group of B and C.

[2] Outside Reading on Concurrent Estates

You can find additional materials on concurrent estates in JOHN E. CRIBBET & CORWIN W. JOHNSON, PRINCIPLES OF THE LAW OF PROPERTY 101-117 (3d ed. 1989); ROGER A. CUNNINGHAM, WILLIAM B. STOEBUCK & DALE A. WHITMAN, THE LAW OF PROPERTY 2d Ed. 69-77,

---

[4] This might occur most often in settings where the grantor wished to protect one of the owners, say a minor, by making him or her a beneficiary of a trust. That sort of division was not allowed.

187-202, 211-232 (1993). Treatise length materials are in Chs. 49-51, POWELL ON REAL PROPERTY (Matthew Bender).

[3] Readings from CHUSED, A PROPERTY ANTHOLOGY (2d ed. 1997)

At pp. 234-256 there is an excerpt from Evelyn Alicia Lewis, *Struggling with Quicksand: The Ins and Outs of Cotenant Possession, Value Liability and a Call for Default Rule Reform*, 1994 WIS. L. REV. 421 (1992). This work discusses the difficulties of mediating family ownership disagreements as the "homestead" descends to succeeding generations of tenants in common.

[4] Non-Marital Concurrent Estate Problems

Problem 1. In 1996, Ginny Grantor conveyed land to Abner Adams, Barbara Bailey, Conrad Caulkins and Darlene Dinkins by a deed reading as follows:

Ginny Grantor, a single woman, grants in fee simple to Abner Adams, Barbara Bailey, Conrad Caulkins and Darlene Dinkins the property known as 249 Merchant Street, N.W., in Washington, D.C., and described as follows: [formal legal description omitted].

a. Describe the form in which Adams, Bailey, Caulkins and Dinkins held the property after the 1996 conveyance.

b. Assume that in 1997, Dinkins sold her share to Ellen Elkton. Describe the form in which Ellen Elkton holds this share of the property.

c. Assume that in 1998, Barbara Bailey died. Who gets her interest? Describe the form in which the successor or successors to Barbara Bailey hold the Bailey share.

Problem 2. In 1996, Ginny Grantor conveyed land to Abner Adams, Barbara Bailey, Conrad Caulkins and Darlene Dinkins by a deed reading as follows:

Ginny Grantor, a single woman, grants in fee simple to Abner Adams, Barbara Bailey, Conrad Caulkins and Darlene Dinkins as joint tenants with rights of survivorship and not as tenants in common the property known as 249 Merchant Street, N.W., in Washington, D.C., and described as follows: [formal legal description omitted].

a. Describe the form in which Adams, Bailey, Caulkins and Dinkins held the property after the 1996 conveyance.

b. Assume that in 1997, Dinkins sold her share to Ellen Elkton. Describe the form in which Ellen Elkton holds this share of the property.

c. Assume that in 1998, Barbara Bailey died. Who gets her interest? Describe the form in which the successor or successors to Barbara Bailey hold the Bailey share.

Problem 3. In 1996, Ginny Grantor conveyed land to Abner Adams, Barbara Bailey, Conrad Caulkins and Darlene Dinkins by a deed reading as follows:

Ginny Grantor, a single woman, grants in fee simple to Abner Adams and Barbara Bailey as joint tenants with rights of survivorship and not as tenants in common a 50% undivided share, and to Conrad Caulkins and Darlene Dinkins as joint tenants with rights of survivorship and not as tenants in common a 50% undivided share, in the property known as 249 Merchant Street, N.W., in Washington, D.C., and described as follows: [formal legal description omitted].

a. Describe the form in which Adams, Bailey, Caulkins and Dinkins held the property after the 1996 conveyance.

b. Assume that in 1997, Dinkins sold her share to Ellen Elkton. Describe the form in which Ellen Elkton holds this share of the property.

c. Assume that in 1998, Barbara Bailey died. Who gets her interest? Describe the form in which the successor or successors to Barbara Bailey hold the Bailey share.

[5]   Case Materials on Non-Marital Concurrent Estates

[a]   Background to *Reilly v. Sageser*

On June 2, 1966, Mabel Reilly and her son Glen signed a contract to purchase a small farm outside Tacoma, Washington.[5] The place had two dwellings, one a bit larger than the other. The Reillys, people of very modest means, were interested in finding someone to help them pay the costs of holding and operating their new farm, including the monthly payments of $135 on the contract of purchase. A short time later they located a couple—Bernard and Marguerite Sageser—interested in making an investment. On October 31, 1966, the Reillys executed a quit claim deed for the farm to themselves and the Sagesers.[6]

The quit claim format was probably used for two reasons. First, the Reillys did not own a fee simple in the land. They held only a "vendee's interest" as the opinion reprinted below called it. That meant they had signed a contract to buy the land on installments, but would not get the fee simple until their payments were complete. A warranty deed, which typically guarantees to the vendees that good title is held by the transferors, would therefore have been inappropriate. Transferring land by installment contract will be taken up in greater detail in *Skendzel v. Marshall*, p. 774 below. Second, the Reillys conveyed to themselves and the Sagesers, a format in which title guarantees would be awkward to say the least. The deed is reproduced below.[7]

QUIT CLAIM DEED

THE GRANTORS, GLEN A. REILLY, a single person, and MABEL C. REILLY, a widow, for and in consideration of Ten Dollars and other valuable consideration, convey and quit claim

---

[5] D. Van Fredenberg, Esq. of Seattle, Washington, represented the Reillys in this litigation. He was kind enough to send me copies of the pleadings in the case and to describe by letter of Oct. 30, 1979, some of the actions taken during the litigation. He did not become involved until after the Agreement between the Reillys and the Sagesers had begun to fall apart.

[6] Such a deed conveyed whatever interest the grantor owned, making no guarantees that any interest was being transferred. The deed had to name the Reillys as well as the Sagesers if the survivorship portion of the joint tenancy was to operate. If the Reillys had simply conveyed a one-half interest to the Sagesers they would have severed the survivorship interest and ended up as tenants in common. The common law four unities requirement to establish a joint tenancy had been modified in Washington so that use of a straw party was not necessary.

[7] The description of the land will seem a bit strange unless you have done title work in the west before coming to law school. The descriptions refer to a survey made by the federal government when the land was first opened to settlement in the nineteenth century. A township contains 36 sections, each about one square mile (640 acres) in size. The sections are numbered starting with 1 in the upper northeast corner, going west to 6, then south to number 7 and heading back east to number 12, and continuing like a snake to number 36 in the southwest corner. W.M. are the initials of the main north-south survey line, or meridian, running through the area. Township 17 North, Range 4 East means the particular township in this case is located 17 tiers north of a survey base line and 4 columns of townships east of the meridian. So in this case, Parcel B is in Section 32 of this township (which is the section in the southernmost row two sections from the southwest corner of the township), but consists of only a half of a quarter of a quarter of 640 acres, or about 20 acres. (640 divided by (2 x 4 x 4) is 640 divided by 32, or 20.) The other parcels are lots whose sizes are not described that are recorded on a plat subdividing an area in a section just to the south of Parcel B. Section 5 is on the northern edge of Township 16, while Section 32 is just above it on the southern edge of Township 17.

to GLEN A. REILLY, a single person; MABEL C. REILLY, a widow, and BERNARD F. SAGESER and MARGUERITTE [*sic*] A. SAGESER, husband and wife, as joint tenants with the right of survivorship and not as tenants in common, the following described real estate, situated in the County of Pierce, State of Washington, including any interest therein which Grantors may hereafter acquire:

Parcel A: Government Lot 4, Section 5, Township 16 North, Range 4 East of the W.M. TOGETHER with shorelands of the second class as conveyed by the State of Washington. EXCEPT Lakeside Extension County Road.

Parcel B: West half of the Southeast quarter of the Southwest quarter of Section 32, Township 17 North, Range 4 East of the W.M.

Parcel C: West half of the West half of the West half of the West half of Government Lot 3, Section 5, Township 16 North, Range 4 East of the W.M. EXCEPT Lakeside Extension County Road.

DATED this *31th* [*sic* handwritten] day of October, 1966.

Glen A. Reilly [handwritten]

Mabel C. Reilly [handwritten]

STATE OF WASHINGTON
COUNTY OF PIERCE   } ss.

On this day personally appeared before me GLEN A. REILLY, and MABEL C. REILLY, to me known to be the individuals described in and who executed the within and foregoing instrument, and acknowledged that they signed the same as their free and voluntary act and deed, for the uses and purposes therein mentioned.

GIVEN under my hand and official seal this *31th* [*sic* handwritten] day of October, 1966.

Sadie L. Hughes [handwritten]

Notary Public in and for the State of Washington, residing at Puyallup.

———

The deal was completed the following month when the Sagesers paid the Reillys $1,500, representing one-half of the payments made by the Reillys on the land installment contract[8] and

---

[8] Yes, it is quite unusual to be paid after transferring an interest in land. This demonstrates the somewhat informal nature of the deals made in this case.

the parties signed a contract specifying how they were to organize the operation of the now jointly owned farm. The contract read as follows:

AGREEMENT

AGREEMENT made this *25th [handwritten]* day of *November [handwritten]*, 1966 between GLEN A. REILLY, a single person, and MABEL C. REILLY, his mother, and between BERNARD F. SAGESER and MARGUERITE A. SAGESER, his wife, wherein the parties mutually agree as follows: That

WHEREAS, the REILLYS have deeded to the four individuals herein named as joint tenants with right of survivorship the real estate described in a quit claim deed dated the 31st day of October, 1966; and,

WHEREAS, it is the purpose and intent of all parties that the REILLYS shall pay one-half of the principal, interest, taxes, insurance and other charges which are the purchaser's obligation under a real estate contract dated the 1st of June, 1966 covering the property described in said quit claim deed; now, therefore,

IT IS MUTUALLY AGREED BETWEEN THE PARTIES:

1. That the payments shall be made hereafter as set forth in this agreement.

2. That the cost of operation and upkeep of the property shall be borne equally between the REILLYS as to one-half and the SAGESERS as to one-half.

3. That the SAGESERS will move into the small home upon the described property, make their own improvements, pay their own charges of living therein.

4. That the REILLYS will occupy the larger home on the property without charge for rent, make their own improvements and pay their own costs of living.

5. That the deep well serving the property shall be a joint operation available to all parties.

6. That the costs of electricity through the meter on the dock shall be jointly shared by the parties.

7. That if the parties hereafter operate any business or joint venture upon the premises a formal partnership agreement shall be prepared and signed.

8. That if one side defaults in the obligations set forth in this agreement causing the other party to spend money for which such party is not obligated, such defaulted obligation shall be immediately due upon demand.

DATED this *[left blank!]* day of November, 1966.

_____

Glen A. Reilly

_____

Mabel C. Reilly

[all four signed]

_____

Bernard F. Sageser

_____

Marguerite A. Sageser

G.A.R. M.C.R. [handwritten initials]

[handwritten paragraph:]

If at any time in the future any party to this agreement desires to withdraw, or either Mr. Reilly or Mr. Sageser should become permanently disabled or die, then the surviving interest shall arrange to purchase the entire interest of Reillys or Sagesers, as the case may be, at the actual contract investment of the withdrawing party, plus cost of permant [*sic*] improvements invested by such withdrawing party, and such purchase shall be evidenced by standard real estate contract (form L138 of Commonwealth Title Co.) payable in equal monthly installments over 10 years, or sooner, at the option of the purchaser, payments to include interest at 6% on declining balances.

    B.F.S.   M.A.S. [handwritten initials]

The deal quickly fell apart. The Sagesers did not move into the smaller house, although they paid $67.50, one-half of the monthly contract payment of $135.00, through March, 1967. Beginning in April, the Reillys moved into the smaller house and agreed to forego the monthly contract payments from the Sagesers. The Reillys then rented out the larger house, initially for $125.00, but later for only $62.00, per month. On July 24, 1967, the Sagesers wrote the Reillys demanding possession of the little house by September 1, 1967. In August Mabel Reilly had a trailer moved onto the property and moved into it.[9]

There were also disputes over maintenance and other expenditures. The Reillys claimed that they received no contributions from the Sagesers for an insurance bill for $111.00, property taxes in the amount of $166.78, plumber's charges for bleeding the water pump twice in the amount of $27.10, installation of a new water pump pressure tank for $157.60, and propane gas for heating the smaller house during the winter of 1967-1968 costing $61.62.[10] They felt they were entitled to one-half of these amounts, or $262.05. In addition, the Reillys contended that they were entitled to demand resumption of payments by the Sagesers of one-half of the monthly contract installments since the Sagesers had demanded possession of the smaller house after September 1.

In February, 1968, the Reillys sued the Sagesers for $262.05 together with monthly contract charges of $67.50 for September, 1967, through March, 1968, or $472.50.[11] The handwritten

---

[9] There was a dispute between the parties as to when the smaller house was totally vacated. The Reillys contended that they both moved out before September 1, but the Sagesers argued that they were never given possession. The trial court ended up finding that possession of the small house was made available to the Sagesers by December 1, 1967. Apparently the parties were not in communication with each other, so notice of the house's availability was not given promptly to the Sagesers. The court arguably compromised by finding that the house was ready on December 1. Transcript of Unreported Oral Opinion Delivered, Reilly v. Sageser, Civ. No. 180740 (Wash. Super. Ct., Pierce Co., Oct. 16, 1968).

[10] This last amount was a bit strange. The Reillys apparently paid the Sagesers $61.62 after the latter paid for the propane. Later they sued for repayment of half of it (and got it).

[11] The original complaint only demanded payments through February, the month the complaint was filed. By the time of trial, the parties agreed that the monthly payments due from April, 1968 on were not owing, but that the March, 1968, payment was in dispute.

"buy out" clause in the parties Agreement was not invoked. As the Reilly's attorney, Mr. D. Van Fredenberg noted in a letter about the case, the strategy was quite deliberate:

> You asked us something about the parties. In addition to the Reillys wanting this property as a life-long home, and the Sagesers being interested only as an investment, the Sagesers are educated and intelligent people whereas the Reillys were the salt-of-the-earth types with little or no book larnin'. While the Reillys worked most of the time on the place, the Sagesers contributed practically nothing. Initially the Reillys wanted two things: to recover some contribution toward expenses as the agreement provides, and to get Sageser out of the picture by purchase or otherwise. However, looking at that "desires to withdraw" in the handwritten portion of the agreement, we didn't think that we should take a chance on asking for a partition or to try to force a sale from one to the other . . . . [W]e asked for money only in the Complaint, and Sageser obliged us by coming back and asking for a partition. That made it possible for us to start talking about getting Sageser out upon payment of his actual contract investment without any consideration of intrinsic value or appreciation of value of the property.[12]

As Mr. Van Fredenberg indicated, the Sagesers responded to the complaint by seeking to partition the property. They also filed a counterclaim for $3,000, alleging that they "were forced to find other living quarters and pasture for their cattle."[13] At trial, the Reillys obtained a judgment for $605.48, which included relief for all the tax, insurance and maintenance expenses, and five months of contract payments.[14] The court dismissed the Sagesers' counterclaim, noting that "there was no adequate proof presented of any damages sustained by defendants therein."[15] Apparently the Sagesers had been attempting to buy another place for their cattle before the dispute with the Reillys arose and their reluctance to move into the smaller house belied any allegations that they had been deprived of a place to live. Finally, the court ordered that the land be partitioned. If it is feasible to physically divide land, the normal partition remedy orders that result rather than a public auction and sale. In this case, the court ordered a physical division into northern and southern halves, with the Reillys to be given the first choice among the parcels. The water well was to be maintained as a joint facility for both parcels.

The Reillys, dissatisfied with the order to partition the property, appealed.

[b]   Opinion of the Washington Court of Appeals

Reilly v. Sageser

Washington Court of Appeals
2 Wash. App. 6, 467 P.2d 358 (1970)

PEARSON, J.—On June 1, 1966 the plaintiffs and appellants, Glen A. Reilly and Mabel C. Reilly, acquired a vendee's interest under a real estate contract of three parcels of real property

---

[12] Letter from D. Van Fredenberg to Richard Chused (Oct. 30, 1979).

[13] Answer and Cross-Complaint [sic], Reilly v. Sageser, Civ. No. 180740 (Wash. Super. Ct., Pierce Co., 1968).

[14] The months covered were December, 1967, through April, 1968. *See* note 11 above. Actually, the court made an arithmetical mistake. The tax, insurance and maintenance awards amounted to $262.05, leaving $343.43 for the monthly payments according to the court. Five monthly payments should have been $337.50 ($67.50 × 5) and the total award should have been $599.55.

[15] Findings of Fact and Conclusions of Law, Reilly v. Sageser, Civ. No. 180740 (Wash. Super. Ct., Pierce Co., Nov. 4, 1968).

in Pierce County, Washington. This property had two homes situated thereon, one of somewhat larger size than the other.

On October 31, 1966 the plaintiffs executed a quitclaim deed to themselves and to the defendants, Bernard F. Sageser and Marguerite A. Sageser, husband and wife. The deed specified that the parties were to be "joint tenants with the right of survivorship and not as tenants in common."

On November 25, 1966 the parties signed an agreement which recited the creation of the joint tenancy by quitclaim deed. The agreement provided that the parties would pay one-half of the principal, interest, taxes, insurance, and other purchaser's obligations under the real estate contract of June 1, 1966. Concurrently with the execution of the agreement, $1,500 was paid by the defendants as consideration for the transaction.

The agreement further provided that the cost of operation and upkeep of the properties would be borne equally between the Reillys and the Sagesers. It allowed the Sagesers to occupy the small home without rental, and the Reillys were permitted to occupy the larger home without rental. Each was to provide for his own property improvements and his own costs of living.

The agreement contains two provisions which are pertinent to this appeal. Paragraph 8 provided: "That if one side defaults in the obligations set forth in this agreement causing the other party to spend money for which such party is not obligated, such defaulted obligation shall be immediately due upon demand."

It appears that at the time the agreement was signed, the parties believed that an omission had occurred. Consequently, after the signature lines, and in the handwriting of the attorney for the defendants Sageser, appeared the following provision:

If at any time in the future any party to this agreement desires to withdraw, or if either Mr. Reilly or Mr. Sageser should become permanently disabled or die, then the surviving interest shall arrange to purchase the entire interest of Reillys or Sagesers, as the case may be, at the actual contract investment of the withdrawing party, plus cost of permant [sic] improvements invested by such withdrawing party, and such purchase shall be evidenced by standard real estate contract (Form L 138 of Commonwealth Title Co.) payable in equal monthly installments over 10 years, or sooner, at the option of the purchaser, payments to include interest at 6% on declining balances.

This handwritten paragraph was initialed by the parties.

In February, 1968 the plaintiffs, relying upon paragraph 8 of the agreement, commenced an action against the defendants in which the only relief sought was contribution for contract payments, taxes, and repairs to a water pump servicing the entire property. The complaint alleged that since the inception of the agreement, the defendants had paid nothing toward the expenses they had agreed to pay and had vacated the home which the defendants had agreed to occupy. There was nothing in the complaint, however, indicating that plaintiffs sought to withdraw from the agreement.

The defendants filed an answer and cross complaint, which in effect denied that any sums were due under the agreement and by way of cross complaint sought damages of $3,000 on account of the plaintiffs' refusal to permit them to occupy the smaller home, and other miscellaneous items of damages.

It was also alleged in the cross complaint that the plaintiffs had consented to relieve the defendants from the contract payments, since they were occupying the smaller house and inasmuch as they had rented out the larger home. The defendants asked that the complaint be dismissed, that they be given damages, and that the property be partitioned.

The trial court entered findings of fact that the plaintiffs were entitled to contribution in the sum of $605.48 for contract payments, insurance, taxes, pump repairs, and propane gas for heating the smaller home. This finding was supported by substantial evidence. The trial court further found that the defendants had not proved any damages with reference to the cross complaint and dismissed the same. Our review of the record convinces us that the trial court was correct in its oral ruling on this issue. . . .

The court further found that the parties "have been unable to agree as to the use and maintenance of the property and their respective responsibilities therefor . . . ." Because of the disagreements between the parties, the court concluded that the property should be partitioned as defendants claimed. Accordingly, the court effected a division of the real estate, apportioning the contract payment and taxes between the parties.

The plaintiffs' appeal contended that the trial court erred in refusing to give effect to the agreement of the parties and by directing a partition of the real property. The plaintiffs argue that the trial court was obliged, because of the agreement between the parties, to treat the cross complaint of the defendants as a "desire to withdraw" from the agreement and, consequently, to permit the plaintiffs to purchase the entire interest of defendants for the actual contract investment, plus cost of improvements, if any.

The issue involved in this case is whether or not the agreement altered the property interests created by the quitclaim deed to the extent that partition was not available as a remedy to the defendants. We must also ascertain whether or not the trial court's findings support the remedy of partition.

There is no doubt that the quitclaim deed created a joint tenancy between the parties . . . since it created a right of "survivorship and severability as at common law." However, the agreement entered into by the parties on November 25, 1966, and in particular the handwritten paragraph, destroyed the right of survivorship by providing that in the event of death, the survivor could purchase the deceased party's interest for the contract investment. Such an agreement, inconsistent with the common law survivorship under a joint tenancy, terminates such a tenancy.

A joint tenancy may be converted into a tenancy in common by agreement or by the failure of an attempt to create a joint tenancy . . . . This is . . . the result under RCW 64.28.020, which provides:

Every interest created in favor of two or more persons in their own right is an interest in common, unless acquired by them in partnership, for partnership purposes, or unless declared in its creation to be a joint tenancy, as provided in RCW 64.28.010, or unless acquired as community property or unless acquired by executors or trustees.

There was a unity of possession in the parties. They were entitled to equal use and possession of the property, subject only to the provision concerning the occupancy of the two houses on the property. . . .

Tenants in common are by RCW 7.52.010 granted the following right to partition:

When several persons hold and are in possession of real property as tenants in common, in which one or more of them have an estate of inheritance, or for life or years, an action may be maintained by one or more of such persons, for a partition thereof, according to the respective rights of the persons interested therein, and for sale of such property, or a part of it, if it appears that a partition cannot be made without great prejudice to the owners.

In an early case, the Supreme Court held that the right of partition under this statute is absolute, in the absence of an agreement to hold the property in such a tenancy for a definite and fixed time. *Hamilton v. Johnson*, 137 Wash. 92, 241 P. 672 (1925).

At common law, co-tenants were permitted by agreement to waive the right to partition, which was a normal incidence of a tenancy in common. We believe that the Supreme Court recently modified *Hamilton* and inferentially adopted the common law rule permitting co-tenants to waive the right to partition by agreement. [In] . . . *Carter v. Weowna Beach Com. Corp.*, 71 Wash. 2d 498, 429 P.2d 201 (1967), which holds that the remedy of partition by sale is not available where a co-tenant, by his own acts, is estopped or has waived his right by express or implied agreement . . . the Supreme Court stated:

> The plaintiffs in the instant case purchased their property with full knowledge of the rights and privileges of the other purchasers. They may not now claim the absolute right to sell the property in a manner destructive of these rights and in violation of their own agreement and the restrictions imposed on the estate by the original grantor through whom they claim.

We now come to the crucial question presented by this appeal. To what extent was the right of partition waived by the co-tenants by the handwritten paragraph of their agreement?

Partition is obviously inconsistent with the right of a remaining or surviving tenant to purchase at the contract investment the interest of his withdrawing, disabled or deceased co-tenant,[1] for if this right could be defeated by an action for partition, then it is without purpose or meaning.

It is therefore our conclusion that the result of the deed and agreement between the parties was the creation of a tenancy in common in which neither could, unilaterally, ask for a partition, nor could one of them convey his interest in the realty to a stranger. To this extent, the right of partition was waived by the agreement.

It is our opinion that the purchase agreement precludes a unilateral partition suit:

(1) Unless the agreement is mutually rescinded, in which case the tenancy in common would be without any contract restrictions, or

(2) Unless both parties evidence a desire to withdraw from the tenancy, either expressly or by their conduct, in which events the contract is silent, or

(3) Unless the wrongful conduct of one party, in substantial breach of the agreement, seeks to force a withdrawal by the other from the tenancy in order to gain the financial advantage of the purchase agreement. Such a repudiation of the contract should give the other a right to partition.

We believe the trial court would have been justified in allowing partition of the property under any of the above-mentioned circumstances.

This brings us to the question of whether or not the trial court's findings support the remedy of partition sought by the defendant. We are mindful of the rule that where conclusions of law are not supported by findings, the findings control.

In support of the partition, the court found that "the parties have been unable to agree as to the use and maintenance of the property and their respective responsibilities therefor . . . ." This

---

[1] Which is in effect an option to purchase under those circumstances.

finding is insufficient to support a partition under any of the circumstances set forth above. It does not delineate either a mutual rescission, a mutual desire to withdraw, or wrongful conduct on plaintiffs' part.

The trial court's other findings established that plaintiffs' conduct had not caused any damage to the defendants, while defendants had breached paragraph 8 of the agreement.

The trial court did not find, and we cannot say as a matter of law, that the conduct of both parties demonstrated a desire to withdraw from the tenancy. The problem is compounded somewhat by the posture both parties evidenced by the actions and cross actions they filed. Plaintiffs, on the one hand, in their complaint, sought enforcement of the agreement by seeking contribution for contract payments and other expenses. The defendants, on the other hand, sought, in effect, to terminate the tenancy by seeking a complete partition.

We think the findings made do not support a partition at defendants' request, but are more consistent with either a unilateral request for withdrawal by the defendants, dictating the application of the purchase agreement, or a partition if plaintiffs so request. On the other hand, we do not believe the findings (that the parties cannot agree as to the use and maintenance of the property) would be sufficient to support the relief which plaintiff requested on appeal,[2] namely, that the defendants should be forced to sell their interest at the contract investment amount. Had the trial court found that the differences were caused by the unilateral fault of the defendants and that their breach of the agreement was substantial, then plaintiffs' position would be well taken. Likewise, we do not think as a matter of law that defendants' cross complaint for partition establishes their "desire to withdraw" from the tenancy, although it is a persuasive factor which may lead the trial court to that finding.

We do believe that the findings of the trial court and judgment in favor of the plaintiffs for contribution are supported by substantial evidence and should be affirmed. Likewise, the court's finding against the defendants' cross complaint and the dismissal thereof should be affirmed.

. . . .

Accordingly, the judgment, and all parts thereof pertaining to a partition of the property, is reversed, and the trial court is directed to dismiss the defendants' action for a partition, unless the court finds that the conduct of both parties prior to the action manifested an intention of their desire to withdraw from the tenancy, in which case a partition would be warranted. If the court does not so find, then the court should make a determination as to whether or not the defendants' conduct prior to the action, together with their suit to partition, manifested a desire to withdraw from the agreement. If such a finding is made, then the court should ascertain the amount of the defendants' contract investment, plus improvements, if any, and apply the purchase agreement as though defendants are the withdrawing party.

In the event the court wishes to adhere to the findings entered, the judgment is affirmed, except as to the granting of a partition, which part of the judgment is reversed, with directions to dismiss the cross complaint for partition.

[c] Analytic Notes on Obligations of Concurrent Owners

[i] *Events After the* **Reilly** *Decision.* On remand, the trial court gave the Reillys all the relief they could have hoped for. The court's unreported opinion noted:

---

[2] Plaintiff urged on appeal that the court's findings, coupled with the relief asked for by the defendant, compelled the conclusion that defendant "desired to withdraw" from the agreement.

[T]he court finds that the differences between the parties during the existence of the tenancy and the agreement were caused by the unilateral fault of the defendants, and that their breach of the agreement was substantial. That while defendants' cross-complaint for partition may not have, as a matter of law, indicated their "desire to withdraw" from the tenancy, it was nevertheless a very persuasive factor in indicating such a desire, and that defendants' actions and conduct prior to the action, together with their suit for partition, manifested a desire to withdraw from the agreement.[16]

The court went on to find that the actual contract investment by the Sagesers was $2,201.06, consisting of the initial $1,500.00 payment, together with $601.06 in monthly contract payments and $100.00 for floor tiles installed in the small house. The Reillys paid this amount (less court costs[17] and the $599.55 previously found owing to the Reillys by the Sagesers) and that ended the matter.

[ii] *Nature of Tenancy Created in* **Reilly v. Sageser.** The court indicated that there was "no doubt that the quitclaim deed created a joint tenancy" among the Reillys and the Sagesers. Note that the four unities required at common law to establish a joint tenancy with rights of survivorship were not fulfilled by the deed from the Reillys to the Reillys and Sagesers. Washington, like a number of other states, has modified the common law rule, leaving only unity of possession as a requirement for the establishment of a joint tenancy with rights of survivorship.

Of more interest (though not discussed by the court) was the meaning of this finding. Before the November, 1966 agreement was signed, what would have happened if Mr. Sageser died? Would his interest be automatically split among the three survivors, or would Mrs. Sageser hold one-half of the property while the Reillys held the other half? The instrument is silent on this issue. If the normal rule were applied, each joint tenant would hold the same size share, and if an owner died the survivors would continue to hold the same (though larger) shares. But there is also logic to the notion that these parties intended to split their ownership equally by pairs, and that if one party died, the normal rule would be inapplicable. *See, e.g., Nelson v. Hotchkiss,* 601 S.W.2d 14 (Mo. 1980), where a similarly ambiguous deed was construed to create tenancies by the entireties for two married couples, with the couples holding their halves as joint tenants with rights of survivorship.

There is no clear answer to this problem in the *Reilly* setting, only a question. But it does suggest the need for very careful drafting on even the most basic of points when joint investments are made. If the parties wished to invest as couples, not as individuals, and still use the joint tenancy form, they could have written the quitclaim deed as follows:

THE GRANTORS, GLEN A. REILLY and MABEL C. REILLY, in consideration of $10 and other valuable consideration, convey and quit claim to GLEN A. REILLY and MABEL C. REILLY as joint tenants with rights of survivorship and not as tenants in common a one-half interest and to BERNARD F. SAGESER and MARGUERITE A. SAGESER as joint tenants with rights of survivorship and not as tenants in common a one-half interest, with the respective one-half interests of the REILLYS and the SAGESERS held as joint tenants with rights of survivorship and not as tenants in common, the following described real estate: . . . .

---

[16] Findings of Fact and Conclusions of Law, Reilly v. Sageser, Civ. No. 180740 (Wash. Super. Ct., Pierce Co., June 18, 1968).

[17] A court may, in its discretion, award a prevailing party court costs. These usually consist of filing fees, court reporter fees and the like, but not attorney fees. *See, e.g.,* Fed. R. Civ. P. 41(d), 54(d).

Perhaps the complexity (to say nothing of the prolixity) of such granting language suggests the wisdom of using a contract.

[iii] *Impact of the Agreement.* The timing of events in *Reilly* makes it easy to consider two related sets of problems in the operation of concurrent estates. The Agreement was signed and initialed on November 25, 1966, not quite one month after the quitclaim deed was signed, sealed and delivered. Absent some enforceable oral contractual obligations, the property management duties of the Reillys and Sagesers between October and November, 1966, as concurrent owners, would have been determined by the common law rules typically used when parties say nothing about their mutual obligations. After the Agreement was signed, the parties were bound by rules they created for themselves, rather than the presumptively operative common law rules. The rules called into play by the use of a set of "magic words"[18] like "joint tenancy with rights of survivorship" were altered by contractual understandings. The next two notes investigate the presumptive rules and the impact of the Agreement on their operation.

[iv] *Presumptive Rules for Governance of Concurrent Interests.* Marital or other family residential purchases aside, few people take title to real property as tenants in common or joint tenants with rights of survivorship as part of a detailed ownership plan. Those who plan frequently sign an agreement to govern their property-holding relationship. Most co-tenancies are thrust upon people, usually as takers of a class gift[19] in a will or an intestate disposition. The only sensible thing for such property owners to do is to agree on management principles or sell the assets held in common.

Therefore, when a tenancy in common or joint tenancy is created by the use of the appropriate "magic words," the presumptive rules will automatically be called into play only in those cases where parties are unable to agree upon a course of behavior. We have already looked at some of the presumptive rules operative in such settings, including the notion that each owner of an undivided interest is entitled to possession of the entire estate, or that a tenant in common or a joint tenant may almost always seek to partition the property, or that shares in a concurrent estate may be transferred. Other issues are also handled "automatically" including the ability to recover rents or other payments received by only one owner, or to charge non-cooperating owners for maintenance or other expenses on the property.

[A] *Possessory Value and Rent Receipts.* In the discussion of adverse possession between co-owners in Chapter 1, we saw that occupancy of property by one co-owner is usually presumed to be permissive. The right of an owner to possess property is not hostile, but in harmony with the common law notion that all concurrent owners have the right to possess the entire estate. But the lack of hostility does not mean that the party in possession gains nothing from the possession. Quite the contrary is true. Possession has value whether it arises out of permissive or hostile conduct. Nonetheless, the traditional rule was that the party in possession need not pay the other owners the value of his or her possession unless the other owners were ousted from possession and the adverse possession time limit had not run. In fact, the rule was carried so far that the possessory owner could rent the premises and pocket the proceeds without an obligation to pay the other owners their shares. This last result was changed by statute in England in the early 1700s. Most American jurisdictions permit a non-possessory owner to ask

---

[18] By "magic words," I mean legal phrases which automatically invoke a set of presumptive understandings about how the property holding system will work.

[19] A class gift is given to a group, such as "to my children."

for an accounting[20] and to recover an appropriate share of any profits derived from a *lease* to a third party. But the old rule permitting a *co-owner* not ousting her colleagues to occupy property "rent free" is still largely intact.[21]

As the *Reilly* background materials indicate, the larger house was rented out after the Reillys moved into the little house with the blessing of the Sagesers. Later, Mabel Reilly moved a trailer onto the site and lived there. The application of the rent contribution rules to these facts would probably have required the Reillys to pay the Sagesers a portion of the rents received from the lease of the larger house, subject, of course, to any contributions due the Reillys because of the Sagesers failure to pay other bills.

[*B*]   *Maintenance, Capital Improvements and Other Expenses.* The *Reilly* case involved a series of different sorts of expenses including contract payments, property taxes, insurance premiums, plumbing repairs, and propane heating costs. Somewhat different rules normally govern the ability of one co-owner to obtain contribution from other owners for such costs. For example, if one owner has made all the mortgage payments, he may usually obtain redress from the other owners in a partition action in which the affairs of the owners are always fully settled, or in a separate action for an accounting, or in an independent action for monetary contribution. These three forms of relief have somewhat different consequences. In a partition, of course, the land is divided or sold, a step not always desired by the owners even if they have monetary disagreements. In the other actions—an equitable accounting for rents or profits, or an action at law for contribution—the end result (monetary relief) may be the same, although the process of obtaining relief may be a bit more cumbersome in an accounting. In the *Reilly* setting, the Sagesers would probably have been bound by the presumptive rules to pay the monthly contract charges. Though the property was not being purchased with a mortgage, failure to pay the installments seriously endangered the interests of the owners. To whatever degree courts may be reluctant to impose unexpected costs on co-owners, this hesitancy would disappear if the continued existence of the ownership was threatened by the failure to pay. The same rationale suggests that the Reillys would have been able to obtain payment of the property taxes.

Regular maintenance expenses, which presumably would include insurance premiums[22] plumbing repairs, and propane bills are said not to be recoverable from a non-paying co-owner in an action for contribution, but only in an accounting for rents and profits, or in a partition action. In the *Reilly* setting, the availability of this relief under the presumptive rules would have been an interesting problem. The action was not filed as an action to account for rents and profits, but rents, and perhaps profits, there were. While the rules would not permit such an accounting for use value when an owner was in possession, there were third-party leases entered into by the Reillys. Some states have responded to the limitations of this presumptive rule by allowing independent contribution actions as well.

---

[20] An *accounting* is a traditional equitable remedy available in a number of settings in which a party seeks a share of the proceeds from a deal or transaction. If an accounting is deemed appropriate, the relevant financial books and records are reviewed, credits and debits are totaled, and an award is made.

[21] Another interesting dividing line is that between legitimate possession by a co-owner and waste. If actions of an owner permanently reduce the value of an asset, then the others may sue to recover their losses. Compare the next case, *Givens v. Givens.*

[22] Many mortgages require that the borrower maintain fire and casualty insurance on the property being used as collateral for the loan. Installment land contracts frequently have a similar clause. A good argument may therefore be made that lack of insurance also endangers the title of the owners.

Finally, the traditional rule as to capital improvements was that repayment for expenses made without the knowledge and consent of co-owners could only be obtained in a settling up of accounts in a partition action. By and large this presumptive rule is still in full force. The rationale appears to be that courts are unwilling to impose large expenses on unsuspecting owners. In the *Reilly* setting, the portion of the plumbing expenses undertaken to install a new pressure tank may have been treated as capital expenses and therefore not recoverable.

The rules as a group create something of a patchwork quilt set of remedies. If factual equities flow in a particular direction, it is arguably easy for a court to characterize an expenditure in such a way that contribution is made available. In addition, the rationales for the rules, which play off concern over imposition of expenses on unsuspecting owners with a willingness to aid owners whose title is in distress because of the failure of co-owners to pay their fair share, make it possible to stretch or alter the rules if a court feels it is necessary. In the background lurks the ever-present ability to obtain partition. Since those co-tenants unable to agree on a management strategy are also likely to be arguing over maintenance and repair payments, there is some logic in making partition the most encompassing remedy for contribution disputes.

[v] *The "Reilly Rules."* But the presumptive rules did not operate in *Reilly*. The November 25, 1966 agreement established a whole new set of principles to govern the relationship between the Reillys and the Sagesers. First, the court held that the basic nature of the joint tenancy established by the October 31, 1966 quitclaim deed was changed. Survivorship rights were severed, partition was unavailable, and transfer of a share was virtually impossible. Second, the rules about when one co-owner may obtain contribution from another co-owner were altered in fundamental ways. The Reillys were entitled to immediate payment for virtually all of their expenses.

[A] *Basic Nature of the Joint Tenancy.* Recall from the introductory notes that when joint tenants transfer their share of the property, survivorship rights are severed and the new owner becomes a tenant in common with the remaining owners. Thus if A, a joint tenant with B and C, sells her share to D, B and C are still joint tenants as between themselves, but D is a tenant in common with them. Something quite similar happened in *Reilly*. Though new owners were not brought in by the November Agreement, the death of Glen Reilly or Bernard Sageser was to lead to results quite different from those mandated by the presumptive joint tenancy survivorship rule. The Agreement served much like a deed, transforming the arrangement into a tenancy in common with contractual understandings about what was to happen at death. The Agreement had the effect of severing survivorship.

The Agreement also contained provisions sharply limiting the ability of any owner to transfer their interest or get out of the deal. The handwritten paragraph locked the parties together by giving one side of the deal the right to buy out the other side at a very low price. The court read this paragraph to ban partition or sale except in settings where one side was in such substantial breach of the agreement that the other side had the right to force a buy-out at the below-market, contract investment price. This combination of holdings demonstrates that the agreement itself was terribly drafted. Not only were the parties locked together quite closely, but the only way out was to take a financial beating.

[B] *Repair and Maintenance Contribution Rules.* The Agreement provided in very straightforward fashion that non-payment of any amount due under the contract created a right to immediate recovery. All of the traditional rules which delayed recovery to the time of a partition or an accounting for rents or profits were changed. The court had little difficulty granting the Reillys the monetary relief they requested. This part of the contract worked fine.

[C] *Rent Contribution Rules.* The Agreement allocated possessory rights of the Reillys and the Sagesers to the big and little houses. Later an oral understanding led the Reillys to move into the little house and rent the big one. A good argument may be made that under the Agreement, the Reillys did not owe the Sagesers any rent contributions. The larger house was contractually under the control of the Reillys, and the little house was under control of the Sagesers. Each couple was apparently free to do as they wished with their possessory interests. Thus, the argument goes, the Reillys used their rights to make money while the Sagesers waived their right to control their house by letting the Reillys live there. The Sagesers seemed to confirm this reading of events later when they demanded possession of the little house. Mabel Reilly then moved into a trailer she had brought onto the site and continued to collect rent from the larger house. The Sagesers must also have had the right to move a trailer onto the land and rent their house, but they did not do so. Is there a counter argument to all this?

[d] Problem Notes

[i] *Survivorship, Property Contracts and Wills.* The handwritten portion of the Agreement described how the property was to be divided upon the death of either Glen Reilly or Bernard Sageser. Did this portion of the Agreement function like a will? The survivorship rights of a joint tenancy operate automatically upon the death of an owner; the terms of a will have no impact. But if the court's holding that the Agreement transformed the joint tenancy into a tenancy in common was correct, then upon the death of an owner, that person's share of the property would become an asset of his or her estate, subject to disposition by will or intestate succession statute. If the agreement was, in part, a will, it would have had to meet the requirements of the local Statute of Wills.[23] It would also have been subject to revocation by any later written wills. This suggests that even if the agreement between the Reillys and the Sagesers served some of the functions of a will, it almost surely should be characterized as something else, like a contract. For what if Bernard Sageser, after signing this agreement, wrote a will giving all his property to X? Would that have terminated the right of the Reillys to buy out the Sagesers? The answer is surely not, but if the will had the effect of wiping out the Agreement, would there be a breach of contract case against the estate of Bernard Sageser for failing to write a will consistent with the Agreement? While cases are successfully brought against estates upon contracts providing that the deceased person was obligated to place certain provisions in a will, the *Reilly* Agreement did not contain a clause requiring that all wills of the parties be consistent with the terms of the Agreement.

[ii] *Drafting Problem.* Draft a contract which fulfills the needs of the Reillys and the Sagesers. At a minimum, the contract should contain terms dealing with the form of ownership, the right to receive contributions, the impact of death or disability, the right to withdraw, and, in any situation where a price must be paid, the method of determining the amount and the terms of payment. This is a difficult task. Compare the Harmony Society Articles of Agreement, p. 253 below.

---

[23] These statutes require certain formalities for wills, such as the number of people who must witness a will and the nature of the sworn statement the testator must make about his intentions in signing the document.

[*iii*] *Enforceability of Bad Deals.* The contractual agreement between the Reillys and the Sagesers certainly was a bad deal. Sometimes a deal is so bad that courts are unwilling to enforce it. But how bad must a deal be before the courts will intervene to protect a party? Think about this case: In 1952, Marjorie Thompson and Ida Pritchett purchased a small farm for recreational use as joint tenants with rights of survivorship. The deed contained the following paragraph:

> The grantees by the acceptance of this deed hereby covenant and agree with the grantor that in the event that they or either of them should at any time wish to sell or otherwise dispose of or convey her or their interest in the premises herein described, or in any event upon the death of the eventual survivor of them, the grantor shall have an option to repurchase said premises together with any improvements thereon, for the total purchase price of $5,000.00, to be payable within sixty days of receipt of notice of such desire to sell or dispose of such interest from the grantee or grantees or the survivor of them or in any event within sixty days of the decease of the survivor of them, real estate taxes to be prorated between the parties as of the date of transfer of title, and it is understood and agreed that the word "grantor," as used in this paragraph shall include the grantor, his heirs, executors, administrators or assigns.

Ida Pritchett died in 1965; Marjorie Thompson died in 1975. From 1952 to 1975, the value of the property skyrocketed. The plaintiff-grantor sued the heirs of Marjorie Thompson for specific performance of the repurchase agreement, and prevailed. After finding that the grantees fully understood the nature of their agreement, and intended to buy the property primarily for their own benefit, the court declared, "Specific performance cannot be denied to permit persons to avoid improvident agreements." *Emerson v. King*, 118 N.H. 684, 689-690, 394 A.2d 51, 55 (1978). Would you decide the case the same way? Suppose the parties understood the agreement, but never dreamed the value of the land would increase so much. What if the grantees never read the provision or were unrepresented by counsel? If you would void the agreement in any of these circumstances, is that fair to the plaintiff who carefully protected her interests?

[e] Background of *Givens v. Givens*

The *Givens* case is a bit more interesting than the factual statement in the opinion would have you believe. Indeed, the story involves a large number of deeds, leases, children and coal seams. There is even some indication that the Kentucky Court of Appeals was confused by it all. The story began with a deed by W.M. Givens to his wife Rilla Givens, not Willa Givens as the opinion stated.[24] The first deed between W.M. and Rilla[25] was made in 1937. It provided that Rilla was to take certain described land:

> To have and to hold to her assigns in during her natural life with the understanding that the party of the first part is to help manage the leasing and collecting rents and royalties and making leases in during his natural life after the death of both parties then the lands of whatever the parties have not transferred shall belong to the heirs of the party of the first part by kind and their assigns forever. R. Lee he has been paid.

---

[24] All the briefs and pleadings filed in the Kentucky Court of Appeals discuss Rilla (or Rella) Givens. Willa was nowhere to be found! The facts given here are gleaned from the Briefs filed by the parties in the case, File No. S-108-63 (Ky. App. Mar. 5, 1965).

[25] The opinion refers to both deeds but provides details only about the second.

Eleven years later a second deed for the *same* land was recorded in which W.M. Givens made the conveyance to Rilla mentioned in the court's opinion:

> To have and to hold to her in during her natural life, then the lands of whatever the parties have not transferred shall belong to the heirs of the party of the second part except R. Lee, Ray Givens, J.L. Givens and anybody else that W.M. Givens has deeded Fourty acres of land or coal they have been paid.

W.M. Givens died in 1953, and Rilla in 1960.

Litigation first arose among the family members in 1962 when the children and grandchildren of W.M. and Rilla Givens sued the children of W.M. Givens by his first wife.[26] W.M.'s "double deeding" of the land naturally led to a dispute over who actually owned it, since the first deed conveyed the land to the heirs of the party of the first part (that is, W.M.), while the second deed conveyed the land to the heirs of the party of the second party (that is, Rilla)! W.M. seemed to use deeds in place of wills! In addition, the parties disputed the validity of three coal leases and a timber lease. W.M. and Rilla Givens conveyed leases to various seams of coal to Vola Mae Givens on September 21, 1947, and January 20, 1948, and on March 31, 1948, granted Vola Mae Givens the right to strip mine these seams. Vola Mae was to pay W.M. and Rilla a royalty of 10 cents per ton. Vola Mae in turn assigned these leases to Green Mountain Coal Company (apparently run by John Nils Givens, one of Rilla's children) for a royalty of 25 cents a ton on April 8, 1960, just three weeks after Rilla died. On March 17, 1956, Rilla sold all of the timber on the land to Millet Hardwood Lumber Company for $4,500. The case was eventually settled, with the parties agreeing that the *second* deed acted to convey title to the land! The parties also agreed that all of the coal leases to Vola Mae Givens were valid, but that 16 cents of the 25-cent-per-ton royalty was to be paid to the children of Rilla and the remaining 9 cents per ton to Vola Mae Givens. The timber sale was also validated.[27] The array of coal lease arrangements apparently continued unabated after the death of W.M. Givens. Herbert Givens, Jr., the defendant in the case you are about to read, argued in his brief that Rilla made at least 50 leases between the death of W.M. in 1953 and her own death in 1960, and that the other children only began to contest the validity of some of them after Rilla was no longer around. The initial pleadings in the second piece of litigation originally involved the validity of three coal leases to Herbert Givens, but the settlement of the first case effectively resolved all ownership questions as to two of them.[28] After reading the *Givens* opinion, you may gain the impression that Herbert Givens somehow coerced or pressured his mother into granting him a coal lease while on her death bed. But the background facts suggest that the Givens clan was deeply involved in coal mining and that leases were exchanged with great regularity. The dispute apparently arose as part of the process of straightening out the family's finances after Rilla died.

---

[26] From the various court papers, it appears that Rilla Givens had nine children survive her—Herbert Givens, Theodore Joseph Givens, W.M. Givens, Jr., Goldie Marie Givens Robinson, Ruby Lucille Givens Kimsey, May Ola Givens Fuson, John Nils Givens and George Wilbur Givens. One other son predeceased her leaving two children—Charles Ray Givens and Jack Givens. The only child of W.M. Givens by his first wife named in the papers is Vola Mae Givens.

[27] Judgment, May Ola Fuson, et al. v. Charles Ray Givens, et al., Civ. Action No. 2623-11 (Ky. Cir. Ct. Bell Co. Jan. 7, 1963). This settlement simply shifted more of the coal revenues to the children of Rilla.

[28] John Nils Givens was also named as a defendant in the judgment entered by the trial court, but his name was dropped as a defendant in the appeal, apparently because the removal of two of the leases from the dispute had realigned his interests to be compatible with the plaintiffs.

[f]   Opinion of the Kentucky Court of Appeals

Givens v. Givens

Kentucky Court of Appeals
387 S.W.2d 851 (1965)

CLAY, COMMISSIONER.

This is a suit for a declaration of rights, the principal objective of which was to have declared void a long term coal lease appellee obtained from his mother. The Chancellor adjudged the lease valid. Appellants contend this was error, and in the alternative contend that the lease, if valid, should inure to their benefit.

In 1948 W.M. Givens deeded the real estate involved to his wife, Willa Givens, and the deed provided in part:

To have and to hold to her in during her natural life, then the lands of whatever the parties have not transferred shall belong to the heirs of the party of the second . . . .

The grantor had in 1937 conveyed the same property to his wife under somewhat similar terms, but the parties claim their rights under the last deed from which we have quoted. The grantee life tenant, Willa Givens, is dead and the appellants and appellee are her heirs and now own as co-tenants the fee in the property.

The parties agree that Willa Givens had a life estate with a power to encroach upon the corpus. Nine days before her death she executed a coal mining lease to appellee, her son. This lease had a term of 40 years.

Appellants' first contention is that a life tenant has no authority to execute a lease for a term longer than her lifetime. This is the accepted general rule. . . .. It is also recognized that a life tenant can make no oil and gas lease. . . .. Since the reason for the rule is that this would permit the life tenant to deplete or waste the estate of the remaindermen, the same principle would apply to a coal lease. This seems to be recognized by KRS 353.300, which provides for the appointment of a trustee to execute an oil, gas, coal or other mineral lease where present and future interests are involved.

It is the position of the appellee that the right of the life tenant to encroach upon the corpus authorized her to execute a long term mineral lease. The argument is that if the life tenant could convey the property, she could lease it. There is merit in this argument. The only authority we have been able to discover on the point is *Holland v. Bogardus-Hill Drug Co.*, 314 Mo. 214, 284 S.W. 121. Therein the court upheld a lease of business property which extended beyond the life-time of the life tenant who had a power of disposition. Even though the lease in the present case is of a different kind and will result in the depletion of the estate of the remaindermen, it seems that the life tenant's power to encroach (which is admitted) would authorize her to transfer in this manner an interest in the devised property. We so decide. It may be observed that the remaindermen will benefit from this lease.

. . . .

The next question is whether this lease inures to the benefit of appellee's cotenants. It is clear that after the death of the life tenant, when the remainder estates matured into a fee simple and the coremaindermen had become cotenants, appellee could not have acquired an outstanding interest against the property for his exclusive benefit. The accepted principle is thus stated in 54 A.L.R. 874, at page 875:

> Tenants in common and joint tenants are said to stand in confidential relations to each other in respect to their interests in the common property and the common title under which they hold; and the courts generally assert that it would be inequitable to permit one, without the consent of the others, to buy in an outstanding adversary claim to the common estate and assert it for his exclusive benefit to the injury or prejudice of his co-owners; and, if one cotenant actually does acquire such claim, he is regarded as holding it in trust for the benefit of all his cotenants, in proportion to their respective interests in the common property, who seasonably contribute their share of his necessary expenditures; the courts will not, ordinarily, permit one cotenant to acquire and set up for his exclusive benefit any claim adverse to the common rights; at least, where all the cotenants derive title from a common ancestor by descent, or from a common grantor by a single conveyance.

> . . . .

That rule is not specifically applicable here because appellee acquired his interest *prior* to the time the cotenancy relationship came into being. As a general rule the fiduciary duties of joint tenants or tenants in common are coextensive with the cotenancy.

As we have noted before, at the time appellee acquired this lease from his mother, the life tenant, she had a power of disposition of the corpus of the property. At that time appellants and appellee were not cotenants (because lacking the right to possession). They were, however, jointly vested with a defeasible remainder.

. . . It could be argued that when the life tenant executed the lease she thereby reduced appellants' remainder interest and they had no right in the benefits which subsequently accrued to appellee by virtue of this lease. (Those benefits consisted of profits accruing from a sublease of the property.)

Our problem is whether a fiduciary relationship exists between *coremaindermen* similar to that existing between *cotenants*. We think it does. Though there is lacking a unity of possession, there is a unity of title created by a single deed vesting equal remainder interests in appellants and appellee. As in the case of joint tenants or tenants in common, public policy dictates that a remainderman shall not impair the title or interests of his coremaindermen.

. . . .

This case points up the necessity for recognizing a fiduciary relationship between coremaindermen. Here appellee acquired from the life tenant, nine days before her death, a long term lease which affected the remainder interests of appellants and from which appellee has and will realize substantial benefits. The unity of title as remaindermen and the family relationship make it inequitable for appellee to obtain this advantage, against those who are now his cotenants, by so dealing with the property in which they had, since the execution of the original deed, a common interest. We hold that the benefits of this lease inure to the benefit of appellants as well as to appellee. Of course appellee is entitled to contribution for their rateable share of appellee's expenditures, if any, in the acquisition and exploitation of this lease.

The judgment is affirmed in part and reversed in part, with directions to modify the judgment consistent with this opinion.

[g] Analytic Notes: Fiduciary Obligations Among Co-Owners

[i] *The Property Interests at Stake in* Givens. The court stated that the holders of the future interests created under the deed from W.M. Givens to his wife Rilla Givens were "jointly vested with a defeasible remainder" at the time Rilla entered into the 40-year lease with her son. This language will seem a bit mysterious until you read about future interests in Chapter 5.[29] Part of the property holding structure needs to be deciphered now. At the time the lease was executed, Rilla Givens held a life estate and a power to dispose of all or some of the property without limitation as to reason.[30] The heirs held a remainder in whatever property was left over. The *power* held by Rilla gave her the authority to completely dispose of the land during her life. This sort of device is not uncommon. It is used not only to create flexibility in property disposition, but also in a variety of other situations in which one party wishes to give control over their property to another person. Spouses frequently sign documents giving their mates the power to control their property and make medical decisions in case of mental or physical disability. In the *Givens* setting, I suspect the existence of the power mirrored the way in which the family handled their mineral properties. W.M. often gave land to various family members. He probably assumed that Rilla would behave in a similar fashion, using grants to distribute her assets as she thought fair and appropriate. It's as if W.M. wrote his will to merely establish a presumptive testamentary pattern, leaving Rilla free to alter the pattern to meet any changing circumstances that might arise after W.M.'s death.

[ii] *Fiduciary Duties.* You have already read about other situations in which fiduciary duties are said to exist. Expressly created trusts, like those used to manage the property of children, automatically imposed special duties on the trustees to prudently manage the corpus of the trust. In addition, courts and legislatures have imposed trust-like obligations in a number of settings where express trusts do not exist. The *Givens* case is an example of the judicial construction of a fiduciary duty. The co-owners of the remainder interest, the court said, were subject to mutual duties of fair dealing, including the very traditional obligation to avoid self dealing to the exclusion of other owners.

Work through this example. Suppose that A, B and C purchased a piece of land as tenants in common, that they obtained a mortgage to finance most of the purchase price, that their development plans went sour, and that the property went into foreclosure. A, one of the co-tenants, sought out the help of new investors, D and E, and with their help purchased the property at the foreclosure sale. B and C found out about A's purchase of the land and sought judicial aid in imposing an obligation upon A to hold the property for the benefit of B and C. Most courts

---

[29] You might want to come back to this case later. When you do, consider the following. Presumably the *Givens* court felt that the heirs of Rilla held a vested remainder subject to defeasance. Was the court correct? There are two arguments for the proposition that the remainder was contingent. First, the deed used the word "heirs" as words of purchase designating takers. Technically, the heirs of a person are not known until the person dies. Thus, a grant to heirs is usually treated as contingent. If W.M. Givens meant "heirs" to be "children" (probable in this case) the interest would have been vested subject to open. Second, Rilla, according to all the parties in the case, had a power to encroach upon the corpus of the property. The language in the deed suggested that the grant of the remainder was contingent upon there being property left unexecuted under the power. All that being said, does it make any difference in *Givens* whether the remainders were vested or contingent?

[30] If there was any doubt about the scope of the power held by Rilla Givens, the settlement agreement in the first portion of this litigation, Fuson v. Givens, note above, effectively resolved that issue by legitimating leases written by Rilla after her husband's death.

would impose such an obligation on A, unless B and C were offered a chance to participate in the restructuring of the financial arrangements and declined to do so.

[*iii*] ***Relief in*** **Givens.** Note well that the *Givens* court did not void the 40-year coal lease. Rilla, the court said, had the power to dispose of such a coal lease to anybody in the world. That she happened to repose such beneficence on her son had no effect on the scope of *her* power to encroach upon the corpus of the asset. The problem, in other words, was not with Rilla's actions, but with those of her son. The son, after accepting the lease, was treated like A in the mortgage example in the prior note. The son, like A, was said to have taken an interest to the detriment of the other co-owners. The normal remedy in these cases is to impose a fiduciary obligation by requiring that the property be held for the benefit of the excluded co-owners. That, of course, is what the Kentucky court did.

[*iv*] ***Some Thoughts on Fiduciary Obligations of Co-Owners.*** *Givens* raises basic questions about appropriate property dealings during life, about the ways we should be permitted to encumber property while we live, and about the relationships between marketability and management of property by a community of owners. The court elected to give preference to obligations created by membership in a group, rather than validate the right of an individual within a group to exclude others from participating in an investment opportunity in the land that was jointly owned.

There were several factors that easily could have been used by the court to deny the solidity of Herbert's obligations to the group. First, the concurrent estate was not in possession of its owners at the time the gift was made; it was a future interest whose ultimate possessors were not yet completely known. Second, the creation of the group of owners of the future interest was "involuntary." That is, it was created by parental edict rather than "voluntary" agreement and purchase among the co-owners. The latter setting is more conducive to the establishment of cooperative norms like those embedded in the notion of a fiduciary obligation. Third, the opportunity for one co-owner to act independently of the other co-owners did not arise because of some nefarious plot to remove the others from an interest in the asset. Rather, it was a gift from the non-concurrent owner-parent to a child in a family quite accustomed to dividing assets in various ways among the various siblings.

In short, the court's decision breached the intentions of both W. M. Givens, who gave *carte blanche* conveyance authority to his wife Rilla under the power to encroach, and of Rilla Givens, who actually made the gift to one rather than all of the siblings holding the remainder. Indeed, in the grant itself some persons were excluded from the remainder because they had already obtained other assets from Rilla or W.M. Despite these factors, the court denied Herbert Givens the "right" to invest in and take profits from the coal lease without sharing them with his co-owning siblings. The court resolved the clash between individual preferences and group obligation by subordinating individual preference.

Indeed, the resolution of the case even made it more expensive to exploit the mineral source transferred to Herbert by Rilla. There were two different sets of decisions at stake in *Givens*—one made by Rilla when she conveyed the gift and the other made by Herbert when he decided how best to exploit the resource. The first choice was not the problem in the case, and it is not a problem here. For Rilla there was very little if any difference in the costs of making a gift to one or four people in a single instrument. The heart of the matter was the impact of the *Givens* rule on the cost of exploiting the resource. The court gave Herbert a choice. Either take the additional time (remember that time is in fact money, since delayed receipt of funds causes loss of interest, income or use rights) and energy to work with the other co-owners, or act unilaterally, thereby risking the costs of litigation and future payment of some of the profits to the other co-owners. If Herbert takes the steps necessary either to lawfully include or to permit exclusion of his fellow concurrent owners, he has to spend more money. Indeed, in some cases, people in positions like Herbert may have to spend a lot of money for attorney fees and other costs to work out a deal. While some forms of group organization may operate to create efficiencies of scale—that is, improvements in cost structures as the size of the enterprise increases— concurrent estates among individuals, particularly concurrent estates created among family members by parental fiat, are unlikely to do that. For in all non-business concurrent estate settings, each owner may demand a chunk of the decisional authority by threatening litigation if anyone tries to take unilateral action, while typical business arrangements, often using the monetary investments of many people, rely upon a management structure resting authority in the hands of a few. Business investors presumably are willing to forego control of the enterprise if they feel comfortable with the quality of its management. Using economic jargon, transaction costs, the costs associated with making and concluding deals, may be higher when decisions are made by small communities of individuals holding concurrent estates than when they are made by individuals on behalf of a group or by individuals for themselves alone.

Other concurrent estate rules, such as the *Reilly* rules about third party rents, make this even clearer. That is, the reduction in efficient exploitation of resources in group settings seems even clearer to me in the case of rents from third parties than it does in *Givens*. Consultations about tenants, rental policy and a host of other items are likely to impose significant costs on those concurrent owners wishing to rent an asset to a third party. *Reilly* surely describes this problem for us quite well, in terms of both the costs of negotiating an agreement and the potential costs of making a bad agreement. And if the concurrent owner with the clearest shot at renting the property to a third party takes the risk without group consultation, the investing owner will end up bearing all the down side risk and only part of the upside gain. For the co-owner not doing the leasing will sue the active owner *only if* a profit is forthcoming; who would sue to share in a loss? And if there is a loss, the active co-owner may not seek contribution from another owner if the active owner did not spend the time, effort and money necessary to obtain the cooperation of that party before the rental deal was made. The incentive to invest in a resource likely to make a profit is clearly reduced in such settings.

These outcomes draw lines based not on economic efficiency in a market, but on a reading of community expectations about the ways people in groups should behave. Groups are supposed to be able to decide upon use of the property among themselves. That is, we assume, the nature of such ownership. When all is said and done the *Givens* court stated a preference for resolving the case by recourse to distributional, not efficiency, concerns, that is, by recourse to notions of group interaction and equality, not economic value. The failure of Herbert to inform his colleagues about the coal lease was seen as a breach of group ethics, as a denial of the generosity presumed to operate among co-owners. The lopsided distribution of coal mining profits among the owners of the land that would result from a different conclusion was viewed as an unfair allocation of funds. The Herberts of this world must either openly deal with their co-owners or terminate the concurrent estate by seeking partition.

The outcome was really quite stunning. Not only did the court's imposition of a fiduciary duty validate a kind of concurrent owner equality principle, itself an interesting result, but it did so in the face of the clear intention of a grantor to breach that equality principle. The court first defined the relevant group for analysis purposes by looking to the concurrent owners rather than the grantor for guidance, and then enunciated a rule which insured that no concurrent owner would be made worse off by the ability of one owner to invest in the property owned by the group. Rather than searching for a rule which would guarantee the most efficient use of the land, it looked for a rule more likely to insure that each owner had an opportunity to better their economic position. There seems to be much common ground between the underlying principles of adverse possession[31] and concurrent estates.

[h]   Problem Notes

[i]   *Duty of Co-Owner.* What could Herbert have done to avoid the outcome in this case? Suppose he put all the other co-remainder holders on notice of the "investment opportunity" he had just acquired from his mother and asked how many wished to participate in mining the coal. If some of the others did not contribute their fair share of the mine start-up costs, could Herbert then decline to pay them any profits? What if some of his brothers and sisters were very poor and could not afford to contribute? What if some of the brothers and sisters objected to strip mining, but Herbert went ahead and stripped anyway? Would the others be able to either stop the stripping or obtain their fair share of the proceeds?

[ii]   *Problem Avoidance.* As a lawyer, one of your professional obligations often is to structure the lives of your clients so that problems are avoided. What actions could Rilla have taken to avoid the *Givens* problem? A will might have resolved the issue at her death. If the power she was given by W.M. also included the right to dispose of the property at her death (an open question) and Rilla gave the land in fee simple to Herbert, would that have avoided the problem? What if she gave the land to Herbert in fee simple during her life?

§ 2.03   Marriage and Property

[1]   Introduction

Married couples may hold property as tenants in common or as joint tenants with rights of survivorship, but if they do, special marital and community property rules will have an impact on the operation of those holding patterns at the time of divorce or death. In addition, about 40% of the states allow married couples to hold property as tenants by the entirety, a surviving remnant of old common law rules on property management by married couples. Marital property law has changed dramatically since its common law origins. Much of this section of materials is devoted to recounting the history of these changes by telling the story of Myra Bradwell's efforts to reform Illinois property law and to become a lawyer. The goal of this introductory segment is to summarize the contemporary state of marital property rules.

[a]   Tenancy by the Entirety

At common law real property conveyed to a husband and wife was presumptively treated as a tenancy by the entirety. In addition to the four unities required to establish a joint tenancy with rights of survivorship, a fifth unity—marriage—was required to establish a tenancy by the entirety. The central feature of this estate was indestructible survivorship. In contrast to a joint tenancy with rights of survivorship, neither concurrent owner of property held as tenants by the

[31] Compare the analytical notes on adverse possession, pp. 87–90 above.

entirety could unilaterally sever survivorship by selling or encumbering their ownership share. Nor could creditors of one party—virtually always the husband in common law days—seize entireties property to pay the debt.

This concurrent estate arose on the theory that husband and wife were a single, male dominated entity that could not be severed by either civil or religious action. This vision of coverture carried with it the idea that husbands managed all property held as tenants by the entirety. An often quoted passage from Chapter XV of BLACKSTONE'S COMMENTARIES, originally published in 1765, captures the central themes:

> By marriage, the husband and wife are one person in law: that is, the very being or legal existence of the woman is suspended during the marriage, or at least is incorporated and consolidated into that of the husband: under whose winge, protection and *cover*, she performs every thing; and is therefore . . . said to be *covert baron* or under the protection and influence of her husband, her *baron*, or lord; and her condition during marriage is called coverture.

During the second half of the nineteenth century and early decades of the twentieth century a multitude of reforms enlarging the capacity of married women to own and manage property were adopted. Many state legislatures and courts concluded that these enactments were so inconsistent with the Blackstonian vision of marital property that the tenancy by the entirety should be abolished. Today the tenancy by the entirety survives in about 40% of the states. Those jurisdictions still allowing the form have taken a variety of steps to insure that the tenancy by the entirety conforms to changes in marital property rules. Husbands, for example, have recently lost their unilateral management rights over tenancies by the entirety. Most states altered the debtor protection rules so that creditors of both spouses were barred from attaching the non-debtor's interest in entireties property. As a result, debts incurred by spouses together place entireties property at risk; whereas, debtors of one spouse will face limits on their ability to attach the non-indebted spouse's interest in the property. This debtor protection feature leads to high usage of tenancies by the entirety in jurisdictions where it is available.[32]

[b] Community Property

During the period in which married women's property acts were first being adopted, the United States invaded Mexico and, after prevailing in the Mexican American War, found itself holding vast areas of what is now the southwestern part of the United States. Much of the Spanish oriented civil law that had been used by Mexico to govern these lands, including the notion of community property, was absorbed into American law as states were carved out of the area. To this day, Arizona, California, Nevada, New Mexico, and Texas are community property jurisdictions. Idaho and Washington, as well as Louisiana, with its historical connections to both France and Spain, also adopted community property systems in the last century. In 1983, Wisconsin joined the group by adopting the Uniform Marital Property Act (9A U.L.A. 103).[33]

In these nine states, a distinct set of property allocation rules based on service to the marital community arose. All property accumulated during a marriage, except that obtained by way of gift, devise, bequest or inheritance, is presumed to be equally owned by both parties to the marital

---

[32] More details about the debtor protection area are taken up a bit later in the case of Sawada v. Endo. *See* p. 186 below.

[33] The Act went into effect in 1986. Most common listings of community property jurisdictions do not include Wisconsin. But, despite the name of the act, it is basically designed to function like a community property regime. Puerto Rico is also a community property jurisdiction.

community, not by one of them, regardless of who is designated as owner in a deed or other ownership document. A partnership-like system governs this regime. Wages, for example, as well as all property purchased with wages, are presumptively treated as community property regardless of who is the payee on the check or whose account the money is placed in. Assets owned before marriage are presumptively treated as non-community, or separate, property. These rules govern unless it is clear that both parties to the marriage intended to change the presumptive rules.

Community property regimes, like those in common law states, have undergone significant gender based reforms since the middle of the nineteenth century. A century ago, husbands were given the right to manage community property. Though they could not unilaterally convey real estate owned by their marital community, they could take the profits and otherwise manage community assets. These rules, like the husband dominated management rules in common law states, have been altered to allow mutual management by both marriage partners.

In the last century, the most profound impact of the community property system arose at the death of one spouse. Since property accumulated by the married couple was presumed to be equally owned by each partner, half of the marital community's assets would go to the estate of the deceased spouse and the other half to the surviving spouse. In case of divorce, the partnership rationale led to a presumption in most community property jurisdictions that the property of a marital community should be split when the marriage was terminated. These rules often led to outcomes quite different from those in common law states. Suppose, for example, that H and W each put their wages into their own bank accounts. At the death of one of them in a community property state, that person's bank account would be treated as community property unless the couple had expressly agreed to a contrary outcome. In a common law state, the account would be treated as the property of the deceased person and pass through that person's estate.

[c] Marital Property

The dramatic increase in divorce rates after World War II made other differences between community property and common law regimes very visible. When a couple divorced in a common law state, each partner was entitled to all property held in their names. Dependent spouses, usually wives, could claim alimony, but it was ordered in only a small proportion of the cases. In many instances, property held in the name of one spouse in a common law state would have been treated as community property in a community property state. Take the wage example from just above. At divorce in a common law state, the contents of each bank account would go to the named owner of each account, subject to possible alimony awards. In a community property state, the accounts were more likely to be split in half.[34]

Beginning in the late 1960s, in part as a response to the most recent women's movement, common law regimes adopted statutes calling for equitable division of "marital property" at divorce. Variations on this theme now exist in all common law jurisdictions. These reforms call for the property of a divorcing couple to be placed in two categories—marital and separate. The separate property is given to its owner. Marital property is equitably divided. The characterization of property as marital or separate mirrors the analogous division of property into community and separate in community property states. As a practical matter, the contemporary economic consequences of divorce are very much alike in common law and community property regimes.

---

[34] Community property states vary a bit on the solidity of the even split rule at divorce. Some strongly favor equal division. Others allow more judicial discretion. Alimony is still ordered sometimes if the amounts of separate property owned by the two spouses is disproportionate.

Note well that adoption of the new marital property regimes of the common law states had no effect on the distribution of property at death. A few jurisdictions have now adopted the 1990 version of the Uniform Probate Code (8 U.L.A. Parts I, II) which adopts the community property system's allocation of property at death. The lingering differences between common law and community property states will be taken up at the end of this segment of the chapter.

[2] Outside Readings on Marital Ownership

You can find additional materials on marital estates in JOHN E. CRIBBET & CORWIN W. JOHNSON, PRINCIPLES OF THE LAW OF PROPERTY 88-100 (3d ed. 1989); ROGER A. CUNNINGHAM, WILLIAM B. STOEBUCK & DALE A. WHITMAN, THE LAW OF PROPERTY 69-77, 202-208, 232-246 (2d ed. 1993). Treatise length materials are in Chs. 6 (¶¶ 109-110), 52-53, 85A, and 90 POWELL ON REAL PROPERTY (Matthew Bender).

[3] Readings from CHUSED, A PROPERTY ANTHOLOGY (2d ed. 1997)

At pp. 256-277 you will find excerpts from two articles: Joan C. Williams, *Women and Property* (1992) and Carol M. Rose, *Women and Property: Gaining and Losing Ground*, 78 VA. L. REV. 421 (1992). Williams discusses a bit of the history of women's rights to own property and suggests a marital property vision for the future. Rose's work takes a law and economics look at the difficulties women may have in making demands on their husbands or male lovers for access to wealth.

Other materials cover the interplay between concepts of Civic Republicanism, citizenship, developments in the Jacksonian and post-Civil War eras and gender. Reprinted at pp. 24-32, 73-83 are excerpts from *Letter From John Adams to James Sullivan* (1776); Robert J. Steinfeld, *Property and Suffrage in Early America*, 41 STAN. L. REV. 335 (1989); and Amy Dru Stanley, *Conjugal Bonds and Wage Labor: Rights of Contract in the Age of Emancipation*, 75 J. AMER. HIST. 471 (1988).

[4] Development of Marital Property Concepts Over Time

Enormous changes in the cultural and legal roles of women have taken place since the beginning of the nineteenth century. While most of you probably take for granted the ability of women to own, transfer and deal in all sorts of property, men sitting in law school classrooms only 30 years ago did not routinely harbor such notions. Even today, courts and legislatures are struggling to absorb the changes wrought by the modern movement to equalize property rights of men and women.

In Chapter 1, we explored some of the features of early Civic Republicanism—the interwoven ideas of government as a servant of the populace, the populace as servants of the government, the importance of moral citizenship to the operation of government, the importance of property as a stimulus for moral citizenship and the use of property ownership as a defining element of political citizenship from which Native Americans were generally excluded. Class divisions and inequality were built into such a belief structure. And of course, the likes of Alexander Hamilton and John Adams were well aware of that problem. "Power," Adams wrote in a letter to John Sullivan in 1776,[35] "always follows property." "If the multitude," Adams went on, "is possessed of the balance of real estate, the multitude will have the balance of power, and in that case the multitude will take care of the liberty, virtue and interest of the multitude, in all acts of

---

[35] IX WORKS OF JOHN ADAMS (C. Adams, ed.) 375 (1856).

government." On the other hand, if the multitude does not own property but does have the right to vote, watch out. For the masses will "demand an equal voice with any other in all acts of state. It tends to confound and destroy all distinction, and prostrate all ranks to one common level."

This sort of political structure caused problems when thinking about both class and women. Adams, like Jefferson, suggested that one way to spread the political wealth was to spread the western lands among the masses. Give them land and they will become independent political souls. Adams' thinking about women was not so clear. He merely noted that removing property ownership as a criterion of political citizenship would allow women to claim suffrage rights. But rather than arguing that they should be given land to compensate for their lack of independence, he simply used the conclusion that propertyless women might claim suffrage as a warning against easing property restrictions on suffrage generally. He could not bring himself to use the same reasoning structure for landless women that he used for landless men.

Adams' views about the family played a pivotal role in his gendered theories about citizenship, property and the state. The idea of family in the late eighteenth and early nineteenth centuries, like property ownership, was central to the structure of government. Under a monarchy, the ruling hierarchy was quite clear cut. The king was thought of in quite literal ways as the father of the country. Families on each rung down the ruling ladder owed duties to the next highest level and were owed duties by the level below. As late as the mid-eighteenth century, the vocabulary of English law mixed theories of family with ideas of governance. In the chapter on the common law rules of coverture in BLACKSTONE'S COMMENTARIES, published during the decade before the Revolutionary War, spouses are referred to as baron and femme, the lord and his wife.

Overt hierarchies like those in England were attenuated in the United States by the end of the eighteenth century, but the idea of families as governmental units working in unison survived. The family was thought of as a central feature of the political system. Its propertied head helped run the government. He also ran a small little government of his own. The family was set up not just for reasons of economic survival (though that was obviously important to the revolutionary generation), but also to support the husband as a political entity and to train the next generation of men for entry into the political system. That structure gave women a very definite governance role to play, even as it forbade any claims to participation in the actual selection of government leadership. Raising children was her government function; selecting senators was up to her husband. In short, the legal domains of men and women were thought of as quite different. Men were property owners and governors. Women were procreators and teachers of the next generation. That outcome made denial of property rights a straight forward result.

As a result, many of the traditional, Blackstonian rules of property ownership were closely followed in America just after the Revolutionary War. Eighteenth century women were treated as civilly dead persons. The political arena was closed to all women, single or married.[36] Married women were unable to own or control many forms of property, or to act as a party in litigation. Common law rules provided that upon marriage, almost all personal property owned by a woman became the property of her husband if he, in eighteenth century parlance, "reduced it to his possession."[37] Her real property became subject to the husband's "marital right," or *jure uxoris*,

---

[36] Women could not vote, serve on juries, or hold elective office, among other things.

[37] There was a quaint exception to this general rule for "paraphernalia," the intimate personal property of a married woman.

the right to manage, control, encumber and take the profits from her real estate during *coverture*.[38] If a child of the marriage was born, the husband's marital right in the real property of his wife was extended to a *tenancy by curtesy*, a life estate held by the husband.[39] The owner of a life estate has the right to possess, manage and take the profits of the asset, but is obligated to preserve the corpus of the asset for the benefit of the party holding the *remainder*, the ownership interest following the life estate.[40] Though the husband could manage his wife's real property, he could not sell a fee simple absolute without his wife's signature. Her ownership of the remainder interest precluded unilateral disposition.[41] Single women were theoretically able to hold and deal in all sorts of property, but the high probability of marriage during the nineteenth century made such rights of marginal utility for most women until they became widows.

Married women did have some common law property rights in the assets of their husbands. Upon her husband's death, *dower* gave a married woman the right to a life estate in one-third of the real estate[42] owned by her husband at any time during the marriage, free of the claims of all creditors of her husband. In contrast with the rights of husbands in their wives' property, dower took effect only upon death of the husband. That meant that wives had no management authority over their living husbands' lands. It did, however, mean that a husband had to obtain his wife's signature in order to convey an unencumbered fee simple absolute in his land to a third party.[43]

Many states adopted changes in the dower system early in the nineteenth century. In an effort to increase the alienability of land, some jurisdictions forced women to cash out their dower interest rather than claim a possessory interest for life. Others removed the priority of dower over the creditors of husbands. Most states also altered the rights of widows by requiring husbands to leave a certain percentage—usually one-third—of their entire estates to their surviving wives, and allowing wives to take this statutory share in lieu of the total amounts left to them under dower rules and their husbands' wills. These mandatory share statutes generally gave creditors of a deceased husband the first crack at the assets left behind. That meant that in jurisdictions where dower took priority over creditors, widows of bankrupt husbands who had real estate were better off taking their dower rights than insisting on their mandatory share. Some combination

---

[38] *Jure uxoris* literally means "law of the wife." *Coverture* is the period of time a man and woman are married. Coverture was usually terminated by the death of one partner since divorce was uncommon until well into the nineteenth century.

[39] The change to a life estate did not increase the husband's management rights in the land over that enjoyed under *jure uxoris*, but it did extend the period of husbandly control from that of the marriage to the life of the husband. Thus, if the wife of a marriage with children died before her husband, her property was not available to her heirs until after her husband's death. If there were no children and a wife died, her successors would get the property immediately.

[40] Mediating the interests of owners of life estates and remainders can be a challenging problem. This topic will be taken up in Chapter 10 on waste and nuisance law.

[41] The husband could, however, encumber his life estate and the income stream the land produced.

[42] The common law dower right applied only to land. The widow of a landless husband got nothing by way of dower.

[43] This requirement led to some interesting legal disputes. Most states required that all conveyances of land by a married women had to be reviewed by a judge or magistrate to insure that they were voluntary. The cases on enforcement of this system were in wild disarray. Some courts strictly construed the requirements surrounding approval of a wife's conveyance on the theory that their dependence mandated careful scrutiny. Other courts were quite lax, insisting that land should generally be transferable and that purchasers of land should not be injured by the failure of judicial officers to carefully do their jobs.

of dower, curtesy and mandatory share statutes exist in some form in all jurisdictions to this day. [44]

During the eighteenth century, one major exception developed to this male dominated system of marital property rights—the *equitable separate estate of a married woman*. A bit of English history will help here. There were two major types of courts in eighteenth century England—law and equity. Courts of law came to be seen as cumbersome, bound by rules, uncaring and sometimes harsh. Those not satisfied by the outcome in courts of law began to petition the king's chancellor for personal relief. When some of the petitions began to be granted, more people lined up. After a time, the monarchy established a procedure for applying to the chancellor for relief and appointed people to oversee the system. By the end of the colonial era in the United States, these chancery systems or equity courts were highly developed tribunals with different procedures and rules from the courts of law.

The married woman's separate estate originated in the courts of equity or chancery. The first separate estates for married women were trusts, usually set up by a father, husband or other male relative, with specific directions to a trustee on how to manage and control a married woman's property. By the end of the eighteenth century, English Chancery Courts permitted the creation of separate estates without the use of trustees, leaving married women fortunate enough to hold separate property free to manage part of their own financial affairs. The trustee-less separate estate did not necessarily provide for the total financial independence of married women, since the estates were usually created by men and often did not direct that the married woman holding the property be given total authority to manage it, [45] though dower and curtesy have been eliminated in about three-quarters of the states as part of the married women's property act reform movement described in the notes that follow. But almost without exception, separate estates were structured to insulate the property of married women from the debts of their husbands. The central "separate" feature of the estate insisted upon by those fathers and husbands using the device was to wall assets off from both economic uncertainty and the spendthrift habits of husbands. [46]

Though the evidence is in some conflict, [47] it appears that the married woman's separate estate was used with greater frequency in the United States as the first five decades of the nineteenth century passed. Growing familiarity with the separate estate idea eventually led to legislative

---

[44] Because of recent alterations in our understanding of equal protection, these property arrangements have been reconstructed so they create identical bundles of rights in husbands and wives. A typical scheme allows either spouse to claim some form of dower or curtesy. The word "curtesy" has disappeared from the statutes of some states. In these places dower has been altered to include husbands as well as wives and provides a surviving spouse with the right to take one half of the estate of the deceased spouse in lieu of dower and the property, if any, left to the survivor by will.

[45] For a summary of the English common law and equity developments in the eighteenth century, *see* MARYLYNN SALMON, WOMEN AND THE LAW OF PROPERTY IN EARLY AMERICA 84-119 (1986); Richard Chused, *Married Women's Property Law: 1800-1850*, 71 GEO. L.J. 1359, at 1364-1372, 1384-1389 (1983).

[46] Middle and upper class fathers were obviously concerned about protecting the value of assets they bestowed upon their daughters at marriage. Husbands sometimes used the separate estate to insulate their household wealth from business creditors. Some also were concerned about the well being of their wives in case they became widows and remarried.

[47] *See* Salmon, 46 note above; SUZANNE LEBSOCK, THE FREE WOMEN OF PETERSBURG: STATUS AND CULTURE IN A SOUTHERN TOWN, 1784-1860, at 60-78 (1984); Richard Chused, *Married Women's Property Law*, note 46 above, at 1381-1384; Richard Chused, *Married Women's Property and Inheritance by Widows in Massachusetts: A Study of Wills Probated Between 1800 and 1850*, 2 BERKELEY WOMEN'S L.J. 42, 85-87 (1987).

action. The first married women's act was adopted in 1835,[48] and most states had passed statutes by 1850. The single provision common to all this legislation was the insulation of some or all of the property of a married woman from seizure by the creditors of her husband. In fits and starts during the nineteenth and early twentieth centuries, the property ownership rights of wives began to approximate those of husbands. The married women's separate estate grew from a device created to protect property from husbands' creditors to a property holding device analogous to a husband's fee simple absolute. Why did these developments occur?

Despite the traditional contours of John Adams' Civic Republican ideology, it created openings for change as social and economic patterns shifted after the Revolutionary War. The pre-war domination of family life by men began to break down. More men, especially in towns and cities, became away-from-home workers, rather than stay-at-home family organizers. A new space for women to exercise control opened. Running the home is rarely thought of today as a source of authority. But at that time, granting women some measure of control over the home was a significant shift in emphasis. Furthermore, if government was to be run by citizens, however defined, rather than by monarchs, the right-thinking brains of those citizens had to be created. Men were not born capable of governing; they had to be shaped and molded. As part of their home based governance, women began to take over educational functions. Their sons had to be prepared for political citizenship. And—mark this well—when their daughters married they had to be capable of teaching their sons about the nature of a civic society. Both boys and girls therefore had to become literate, though for different reasons. In 1800 most women could not read. By 1850, women's literacy rate was about the same as that for men. Indeed, women took over the teaching profession as schools began to open in the early nineteenth century. Thousands of women taught for a time before they married. Studies suggest that by 1850, most women worked for some period of time before marriage outside their parents' homes in teaching, mills or some other service capacity.

These developments were crucial first steps in the gradual enlargement of women's role in the United States. Not only did women learn to read; they also learned to write. And write they did. From the publication of Wollstonecraft's *Vindication of the Rights of Women* in England in 1791 and its publication in the United States the following year, women produced thousands of tracts, books and novels. And they sometimes became political as they wrote. Literacy also allowed women to run their family economies. And run them they began to do. As men went off to work, women not only did the dishes and the laundry, but also the buying and the selling of consumer goods. They could legitimately begin to claim that their ability to run the family economy made them competent to handle their own economic lives as well.

Another important change in legal culture was occurring at the same time. Think about the consequences of a shift in legal authority from one system of law (England) to a multitude of systems (thirteen states soon augmented by new states and the federal government). The sense of certainty bred by a single legal system became frayed. Complaints began to arise that it was impossible to figure out what the law was or to find it in usable ways. Legal codes and reported cases were hard to find. By the 1820s a codification and treatise movement arose. Books appeared containing all of the laws of each state. Legislatures began to set aside an entire session every so often to issue logically written codes of all the laws rather than to pass new statutes. And

---

[48] Arkansas passed legislation in that year insulating married women's property from debts incurred by a husband before marriage. For a summary of the development of married women's acts, *see* Chused, *Married Women's Property Law,* note 46 above, at 1397-1409.

authors began to write treatises on American law. All of this activity was built on a premise that careful explication of legal sources would help unify legal doctrine and rationalize its content. And so BLACKSTONE'S COMMENTARIES were first published in the United States in 1803, with copious notes by an American on the differences between English and American law.[49] Many other English treatises were also reprinted with notes. In 1826, the first major American treatise, KENT'S COMMENTARIES ON AMERICAN LAW, appeared. And 10 years later, Joseph Story's famous COMMENTARIES ON EQUITY JURISPRUDENCE arrived. These developments were the first step in the establishment of a new structure of legal thought assuming that law could be rationalized, written down, and understood—the roots of what is commonly called Formalism or Classical Legal Thought.

The codification and treatise movement had a pronounced effect on coverture law. Though it may not be possible to rationalize a legal system with as many parts as ours, it is possible to popularize certain forms. Among the forms popularized by Story's treatise were those at equity. Seen as arms of the monarchy by many in New England, the northern colonies and states were reluctant to establish equity courts. Southern legal systems, much more like British systems in their operation, had no such problem. The widespread distribution of Story's treatise in the north helped popularize the system of equity in areas previously hostile to it.[50] It became part of a movement to establish equity courts throughout New England. Those interested in reforming women's property rules were among those behind the effort.[51] By 1850 equity courts were commonplace. With the acceptance of equity jurisprudence came greater acceptance of the married woman's separate estate.

A third set of legal changes—those involving inheritance patterns and statutes—was also important for women. Before the eighteenth century ended, all states had abolished rules requiring that estates pass only to male heirs. It was part of a widespread rejection of monarchy inspired hierarchies by the colonies. Primogeniture, which left assets to the eldest son, was rejected. As a result, some daughters became owners of property. Other influences accelerated the inheritance of property by women and enhanced the acceptability of the separate estate. Changes in the economy led not only to the separation of home and work, but also to a labor surplus. In the east, the division of farms over the generations led to smaller holdings and departure of some children to the west or to town. Agricultural efficiency also improved, beginning the lengthy process of turning children from economic assets to economic liabilities. This also caused children to leave home, either to move west to find new farmland, or to move to town to work. As a result, some men changed their will writing habits. Those unwilling to leave property to their departed sons, or to children living economically independent lives elsewhere, named their still dependent daughters and wives as beneficiaries. The shifts in inheritance patterns also led many states to either enact statutes requiring husbands to leave a certain share of their estates to their widows, or to alter preexisting systems by enlarging the size of the mandatory share.

As property ownership by women began to increase, so did acceptability of the married woman's separate estate. That estate, which commonly contained a provision making a married

---

[49] BLACKSTONE'S COMMENTARIES (St. George Tucker, ed., Philadelphia, 1803). In addition to notes by Tucker, Professor of Law at the University of William and Mary, the volume also contained some often critical notes by Edward Christian, a previous English editor.

[50] A good example of this development is Massachusetts. Chused, *Massachusetts*, note 48 above, at 48-58.

[51] For example, New York developments reflected both the codification and treatise movements. *See* PEGGY RABKIN, FATHERS TO DAUGHTERS: THE LEGAL FOUNDATIONS OF FEMALE EMANCIPATION (1980).

woman's property unavailable to creditors of the husband, was a nice legal device for protecting women's assets from the pitfalls of bad marriages and the vicissitudes of the economy. Testamentary gifts to surviving wives were sometimes placed in separate estates to protect the assets from any economic difficulties their future husbands might fall into. Daughters were protected in similar ways. As the rate of desertion by husbands grew in the first half of the nineteenth century, some fathers responded by embedding their testamentary and inter vivos gifts to daughters in separate estates.

There were a variety of other cultural forces at work before 1850 that helped create an environment sympathetic to mild changes in property rules. Economic troubles during the late 1830s and early 1840s heightened concerns about family security. Indeed, when married women's property acts began to be passed in the late 1830s, they all contained provisions protecting some property held by married women from the creditors of their husbands. Men also began to see the need for change. Fathers watched in dismay as their daughters were deserted by wayward husbands who took their wives' property with them. Husbands, recognizing their own mortality, saw the need to protect their widows against the possibility they would remarry less worthy husbands, or fall victim to economic panics. After reading the writings of Civic Republicans like John Adams, it is hard to imagine that reforms in married women's property law would be adopted by male legislatures until a significant number of men felt it was necessary.

Finally, women themselves began to make noises about property rules. Those married women who ran home-based businesses such as clothes making, inns and restaurants, like their male counterparts, began to move their work from home to town. Even if women business owners weren't more numerous, they became more visible, and sometimes more vocal. The declarations emanating from the first women's convention, at Seneca Falls in 1848, were full of protests about property rules. Women lobbied heavily at the New York State Constitutional Convention in 1846 and in the state legislature during the following years for legal reform. The moment was ripe for change. And it is the course of that change that this section of materials explores.

[5] Marital Ownership Problems

Assume that you are in a jurisdiction where the tenancy by the entirety still exists, where husbands and wives get curtesy or dower respectively at the death of their spouses in one-third of all real estate held at any time during marriage, that creditors of a deceased spouse are paid after dower and curtesy rights are determined, that upon the death of a spouse without a will the intestate succession statutes provide that the surviving spouse gets all of the estate, and that upon the death of a spouse with a will a surviving spouse may elect to take one half of the assets of the deceased spouse in lieu of the amounts provided by will and allocated by dower or curtesy.[52]

In addition, assume that Harold Husband and Wanda Wife own the following assets:

A House: The house is held by Husband and Wife as tenants by the entirety. It is valued at $250,000 and encumbered by a mortgage with an outstanding balance of $125,000. $25,000 of the downpayment Husband and Wife made on the house came from a gift made to Husband by his parents.

A Bank Account: The bank account, held in the name of Wanda Wife, contains $10,000. The funds came from Wife's earnings.

---

[52] Some form of mandatory spousal share statutes exist in all states. A bit of the history of these statutes is given in the prior section of materials.

Another Bank Account: This bank account, held in the names of Husband and Wife as joint tenants with rights of survivorship, contains $20,000. $10,000 of this amount was received by Wife as an inheritance and deposited in this account.

Husband and Wife each are employed. Husband earns $45,000 per year. Wife earns $55,000 per year.

Problem 1. If Husband and Wife divorced, which of the above assets would be treated as community or marital property and which as separate property?

Problem 2. Assume Husband dies in a common law state with a will leaving all of his property to the two children of Husband and Wife. What assets will Wife be able to claim? Reverse the situation and assume that Wife dies leaving a similar will. What assets will Husband be able to claim?

Problem 3. Suppose Husband drives negligently and injures X. If X obtains a judgment against Husband for $50,000, which assets will X be able to attach to satisfy the judgment?

[6] The Myra Bradwell Era: Changing Concepts of Property Ownership by Married Women

[a] Introduction: The Early Life of Myra Bradwell

Myra Colby was born in Manchester, Vermont, on February 12, 1831. Twelve years later her family moved west to Illinois. She went to school, as did a growing number of young women in the early nineteenth century, in a ladies seminary, hers being in Elgin, Illinois. Also like many of her nineteenth century peers, Colby left home and entered the school teaching ranks after finishing her seminary work. At one of several teaching posts she held in various towns, she met James Bradwell. In 1852 they married, and purchased and ran a school together in Memphis for a short time. The year after their marriage, James, who had been studying law while teaching, entered the Tennessee Bar. Two years later they moved back to Illinois and settled in Chicago. James then joined the Illinois Bar and opened a law office with Myra's brother.[53]

Three children were born to Myra and James, the first in 1854, followed by births in 1856 and 1861. Only the first two survived childhood. In 1868, Myra, with the full support of her husband, began publishing the CHICAGO LEGAL NEWS, a paper which became one of the most widely read legal publications in the region. The company she founded also published other legal materials, such as statutes and legal forms. This activity was certainly unusual for a woman in the middle of the nineteenth century. Even though Illinois had in 1861 adopted a statute providing that married women had the right to own property "free from the control and interference of her husband, and exempt from his debts,"[54] the long history of special regulations on women's legal status was hard to overcome, both legally and culturally.

---

[53] For a brief biography of Myra Bradwell, *see* JAMES, JAMES & BOYER, NOTABLE AMERICAN WOMEN: A BIO-GRAPHICAL DICTIONARY 1607-1950, at 223 (1971). The best available story of her life is Gilliam, *A Professional Pioneer: Myra Bradwell's Fight to Practice Law,* 5 L. & HIST. REV. 105 (1987). Some of the information in these notes is also taken from Hancock, *Myra Bradwell and the Struggle for Women's Legal Equality* (1983) (unpublished paper on file in author's office).

[54] 1861 ILL. LAWS 143 (1861). The act read as follows:

AN ACT to protect Married Women in their Separate Property.

Section 1. *Be it enacted by the People of the State of Illinois, represented in the General Assembly,* That all the property, both real and personal, belonging to any married woman, as her sole and separate property, or which

The 1861 Illinois Married Women's Act was construed narrowly in three decisions rendered by the state Supreme Court just before Bradwell began her business. The court held that the act did not protect women's *earnings* from husbandly debts.[55] Bradwell noted with displeasure the impact these decisions would have on the independence of her own business ventures. In 1869 she drafted a bill extending the 1861 act to cover earnings, lobbied for it in her newspaper and in the state legislature, and saw it adopted.[56] In addition, the legislature passed a private bill in the same session specifically protecting the separate estate nature of the earnings Bradwell might gain from her publishing business.[57]

[b]   The Impact of Property Reform

Bradwell's efforts to reform married women's property law in Illinois were grounded in a solid understanding of the limitations that common law coverture rules placed on the economic activity of wives. For example, in 1855, the year after James and Myra Bradwell moved back to Illinois from Tennessee, the state Supreme Court decided *Love v. Moynehan*, 16 Ill. 277 (1855). Ann Moynehan complained that the defendants had entered her dwelling and carried away her goods. The defendants countered that Moynehan's status as a married woman barred her from filing a lawsuit, and that the damages, if any, inflicted upon her were recoverable only in a suit brought by her husband. Moynehan, in turn, asserted that she had been abandoned by her husband in 1847, that she had supported herself since he left, and that the property taken by the defendants was purchased with funds she had accumulated since her husband left. She argued that the common law coverture rules should give way when wayward husbands left their wives to fend for themselves.

---

any woman hereafter married owns at the time of her marriage, or which any married woman, during coverture, acquires, in good faith, from any person, other than her husband, by descent, devise or otherwise, together with all the rents, issues, increase and profits thereof, shall, notwithstanding her marriage, be and remain, during coverture, her sole and separate property, under her sole control, and be held, owned, possessed and enjoyed by her the same as though she was sole and unmarried; and shall not be subject to the disposal, control or interference of her husband, and shall be exempt from execution or attachment for the debts of her husband.

Approved Feb. 21, 1861.

[55] Bear v. Hays, 36 Ill. 280 (1865); Farrell v. Patterson, 43 Ill. 52 (1867); Schwartz v. Sanders, 46 Ill. 18 (1867). This was a common problem in many states, leading eventually to adoption of legislation making married women's earnings their separate property.

[56] 1869 ILL. LAWS 255 (1869). Articles on the legislation may be found at 1 CHICAGO LEGAL NEWS 60 (1868); 1 CHICAGO LEGAL NEWS, 212 (1869). The act read as follows:

AN ACT in Relation to the Earnings of Married Women.

Section 1. *Be it Enacted by the People of the State of Illinois, represented in the General Assembly*, That a married woman shall be entitled to receive, use and possess her own earnings, and sue for the same in her own name, free from the interference of her husband or his creditors; *Provided*, this act shall not be construed to give to the wife any right to compensation for any labor performed for her minor children or husband.

Approved Mar. 24, 1869.

[57] Private bills are adopted for the benefit of specific persons or legal entities. They were quite common in the nineteenth century. The legislation in Bradwell's behalf was An Act to Incorporate the Chicago Legal News Company, 2 Private Laws of the State of Illinois 876 (Feb. 27, 1869). Section 4 of the act read in part as follows:

Section 4. . . . [A]nd all the real and personal estate of the said Myra Bradwell shall be liable for the debts of said company contracted while she is a stockholder therein; and all stock of said company owned by her and the earnings thereof shall be her sole and separate property, the same as if she were an unmarried woman; and she shall have the same right to hold any office or offices in said company or transact any of its business that a *femme sole* would have.

During the first half of the nineteenth century many states had adopted rules releasing abandoned wives from some coverture restraints in order to preclude long absent husbands from returning unannounced and demanding control over the assets their mates had managed to accumulate by themselves. That path was partly followed by the Illinois Supreme Court in *Moynehan*, which held that "where the husband compels the wife to live separate from him, either by abandoning her, or by forcing her . . . to leave him," and does not provide for her, "she may acquire property, control her person and acquisitions, and contract, sue and be sued in relation to them, as a *feme sole* during the continuance of such condition." Though Anne Moynehan regained her property, the court result provided little solace to other women in similar situations. For if a husband returned and wished to resume his married life, "such condition" of abandonment would end and so would *feme sole* status. In addition, the *Moynehan* court made it quite clear that if a court found a wife to blame for the spousal separation, she could lose everything. Indeed, Ann Moynehan ran that litigation risk. Her adversaries accused her of running a bawdy house, apparently in an effort to blame her for Mr. Moynehan's disappearance. Divorce might provide some relief to abandoned women, but it was difficult to obtain and in many quarters culturally risque. Though Chicago had a reputation as a divorce haven in the 1860s, the number of yearly divorce proceedings in the city numbered only a few hundred.[58] By statute, women could be released from the bonds of matrimony only on the grounds of adultery, willful desertion for two years, extreme and repeated cruelty, habitual drunkenness for two years, or conviction of a felony.[59] In the end, only husbands who had clearly breached their obligation to support their wives were likely to lose control over the property accumulated by their spouses.

Though Illinois had a long equity tradition and the married woman's separate estate was recognized by its courts well before 1850, it was clear to those like Bradwell that ameliorative legislation was needed. The state was among the last to adopt its first married women's property act. And that 1861 enactment was quite limited in scope. Though in the first case to reach the Illinois Supreme Court the statute was said to have made "a radical and thorough change in the condition of a *feme covert*,"[60] it wasn't long before more traditional sentiments dominated the court's discourse.

[c] A Case on Property Management After Reform

Solomon Cole v. Henry Van Riper

Supreme Court of Illinois
44 Ill. 58 (1867)

This was an action of ejectment brought by Henry Van Riper against Solomon Cole, in the La Salle County Court to recover possession of a tract of land situate in the town of Whitfield, in La Salle County.

The plaintiff, to prove title, called George Munroe, who was sworn as a witness. Showed the witness a deed from John R. Snyder, and Elizabeth H. Snyder, his wife, to James Van Riper,

[58] NELSON BLAKE, ROAD TO RENO: A HISTORY OF DIVORCE IN THE UNITED STATES 117-119 (1962).

[59] Ch. 33, STATUTES of ILLINOIS 214 (Gross ed. 1872).

[60] Emerson v. Clayton, 32 Ill. 493 (1863). *Emerson* tested only the limited question of whether a married woman could sue to protect her property in her own name or had to join with her husband. The court held that she could sue alone, even against her husband.

of all of block number nine in the town of Whitfield, in La Salle county, Illinois, dated July 22, A.D. 1862, and filed for record August 2, A.D. 1862.

James Van Riper went into possession, under that deed of a store building, which stood on the east part of the block, and moved a stable from the east side of the block.

Cole, the defendant, at that time and before, was in possession of the tavern stand on the west part of the block—on the part of the block now in controversy in this suit—as the tenant of John R. Snyder; so Cole told me.

The plaintiff then offered the deed in evidence to the jury. The defendant objected. The court overruled the objection, and the plaintiff read the deed in evidence to the jury.

The plaintiff then read in evidence to the jury a deed from James Van Riper and Hannah Van Riper, his wife, to Ellen Cole.

Plaintiff then offered in evidence a deed from Ellen Cole to himself.

It was agreed that the said Ellen Cole was the wife of the defendant at the date of said last mentioned deed.

The defendant objected to the giving of said deed in evidence to the jury, on the ground Ellen Cole, being a married woman at the date of the deed, could not convey real estate without her husband, the defendant, joining with her in the conveyance. The court overruled the objection and permitted the deed to be read in evidence to the jury, and the defendant excepted.

The plaintiff then called as a witness J. W. Brown, who testified:

The defendant was in possession of the premises in controversy at the time of the service of the declaration in this case on him; and just before the commencement of this suit I advised Cole to go out of this property, and he said that the property was his, and he should not go out until he was carried out.

The jury returned a verdict for the plaintiff.

The defendant moved for a new trial at common law, on the ground that the court erred in admitting in evidence the deed from Ellen Cole to the plaintiff, and in deciding that, by the laws of this State, a married woman can convey her own real estate without her husband joining with her in the conveyance.

The court then rendered judgment upon the verdict for the plaintiff.

The defendant then prayed an appeal, which was allowed on filing bond, as required by law.

Mr. Justice Lawrence delivered the opinion of the Court:

This was an action of ejectment, and one of the questions presented by the record is, whether under the law of 1861, known as the married woman's act, a married woman can convey real estate, acquired since that time, without the joinder of her husband. That act provides "that all the property, both real and personal, belonging to any married woman, as her sole and separate property, or which any woman hereafter married owns at the time of her marriage, or which any married woman, during coverture, acquires in good faith from any person other than her husband, by descent, devise or otherwise, together with all the rents, issues, increase and profits thereof, shall, notwithstanding her marriage, be and remain during coverture, her sole and separate property under her sole control, and be held, owned, possessed and enjoyed by her the same as though she was sole and unmarried; and shall not be subject to the disposal, control or interference of her husband, and shall be exempt from execution or attachment for the debts of her husband."

The legislature has here used very sweeping language, but it must be interpreted with reference to the evil intended to be cured, and in such manner as to be made to harmonize with other statutes which are left unrepealed, so far as such harmony can be secured without disregarding the legislative intent. It is a familiar maxim, that repeal by implication is never favored.

That this statute cannot be enforced according to its literal terms without impairing, to a very large extent, the strength of the marriage tie, will be evident on a moment's reflection. By the terms of the act, the property of a married woman is to be "under her sole control, and to be held, owned, possessed and enjoyed by her the same as though she was sole and unmarried." If this language is to receive a literal interpretation, a married woman, living with her husband and children in a house owned by her, would have the right to forbid her husband to enter upon the premises, and he would be a trespasser in case he should enter against her will, and would be liable to her in damages. Such would be her right as a *feme sole*. The wife would thus divorce her husband *a mensa et thoro*, without the aid of a court of chancery. Or, again, suppose in a house thus owned and occupied, the furniture is also the wife's property. Can she forbid the husband the use of such portion as she may choose, allow him to occupy only a particular chair, and to take from the shelves of the library a book only upon her permission? This would be all very absurd, and we know the legislature had no idea of enacting a law to be thus interpreted. It is simply impossible that a woman married should be able to control and enjoy her property as if she were sole, without leaving her at liberty, practically, to annul the marriage tie at pleasure; and the same is true of the property of the husband, so far as it is directly connected with the nurture and maintenance of his household. The statute cannot receive a literal interpretation.

The object of the legislature was, not to loosen the bonds of matrimony, or create an element of constant strife between husband and wife, but to protect the latter against the misfortunes, imprudence, or possible vice of the former, by enabling her to withhold her property from being levied on and sold for the payment of his debts, or squandered by him against her wishes. Before the passage of this law, the husband became the owner, by virtue of the marriage, of the personal property held by the wife at the date of the marriage, or which came to her after that time, as was reduced by the husband to possession, and he was also seized of an estate, during coverture, in lands held by the wife in fee. This estate was, in the eye of the law, a freehold, as it would continue during their joint lives, and might last during his life, and was liable to be sold on execution against the husband. The personal property reduced to possession, and this estate in the wife's land, were at the disposal of the husband, and liable to be sold at his pleasure, for his own use, or to be levied upon and sold by his creditors. These were the evils which the law was designed to cure, and has cured. Although we held in *Rose v. Sanderson*, 38 Ill. 247, that where the husband's estate in the wife's lands had vested before the passage of this law, it was not divested by the act, and might be sold by his creditors, yet where the marriage has occurred, or the land has been acquired by the wife, since that time, it would doubtless be held, that this species of estate, known as an estate during coverture, has been substantially abolished, because its existence is wholly irreconcilable with both the language and the objects of this law.

But besides this estate which the husband acquired, by virtue of the marriage, in the lands of his wife, he also, if there was issue of the marriage born alive, became tenant by the curtesy of all lands of the wife which such issue might by possibility inherit, and this estate, unlike the other, terminated only with his own life. The law termed this estate initiate on the birth of issue, and consummate only on the death of the wife, but the initiate estate could be seized and sold on execution against the husband. Up to the period of the wife's death, it was substantially the same thing as the estate during coverture above mentioned. Now, although this estate is greatly modified by the act of 1861, it is not totally destroyed. During the life of the wife, the husband can exercise no control over his wife's lands as tenant by the curtesy, nor has he an interest in them subject to execution. We refer, of course, to lands where no interest had vested before the passage of the law. This estate, then, would be totally abolished, like the estate during coverture, were it not that tenancy by the curtesy continued after the wife's death, and, indeed, at that period became most material to the husband, since, up to that time, he had the enjoyment of his wife's realty by virtue of the other species of estate. While, then, the one estate is annihilated by a necessary implication, the utmost that can be said in regard to the other is, that it is materially modified. This estate is as old as the common law. It has always been recognized as existing in this State. It is not expressly abolished by the act of 1861, and, so far from being abolished by implication, it may be recognized as taking effect on the death of the wife, without conflicting in the slightest degree with the letter, spirit, or object of that law. On the contrary, the law itself provides, that it is "during coverture" that the property of the wife is clothed with these new qualities, thus leaving the existing law unchanged, as to the disposition of the wife's property at her death. Moreover, it is hardly to be supposed, that the legislature would totally abolish this estate, without remodeling that of dower, or that they would work so important a change in our law of realty merely by implication. But, in fact, there is not even an implication that affects this estate after the death of the wife.

We have said thus much in regard to this estate, as a foundation for our opinion that this act does not enable the wife to convey her lands without the consent of her husband, manifested by joining in the deed. At common law the wife could only convey by fine or a common recovery, and a fine levied without the husband's consent was not binding upon him unless he was a party. A conveyance in which the husband unites has been substituted in this country, and is the mode . . . [provided for in our] statute of conveyances. The estate of the husband in the wife's lands could not, therefore, be destroyed or impaired by the sole act of the wife. If this section of our conveyance act is repealed by the act of 1861, it is repealed by implication, which, as already remarked, the law does not favor. But where is the implication? Not certainly in the language of the act, which gives the wife the right to hold, own, possess and enjoy her property, for the terms give only the *jus tenendi* and not the *jus disponendi*. The power to own and enjoy, is entirely different from the power to dispose of, and the latter is not necessary to the exercise of the former. Neither is the power of disposing implied in that phrase of the law directing that her property shall be under her sole control, because that term, although indefinite, must be construed in connection with the terms "own, hold, possess and enjoy." In order that she may hold and enjoy she must necessarily control. But the control of the use and enjoyment does not imply the power to sell. Strictly speaking, the land, when conveyed, would pass away from her control and enjoyment.

But the chief reliance seems to be placed on the provision, that she is to have the power of controlling and enjoying as if she were sole and unmarried, and hence it is contended she can convey as if she were sole, and her deed would have the same effect as the deed of a *feme sole*. If she can convey at all, because of the language in the act referring to the condition of a *feme sole*, her deed would undoubtedly have this effect, and would thus destroy the husband's estate by curtesy, and prevent him from resuming possession of the lands conveyed, after her death. We have already given the reasons why this act does not annihilate the estate of a tenant by the curtesy, or place it in the power of the wife to destroy it. If we are right in the conclusion, it necessarily follows, that it was not the intention of the legislature, when they gave her the power to enjoy as a *feme sole*, to give also the right to convey as a *feme sole,* and thereby destroy the husband's estate.

There is another reason for not holding that this act enables the wife to convey by her own deed. Before the passage of the law, acts similar in their general character had been passed in several of our sister States. The law of New York expressly gave the wife the power of conveyance. The laws of Pennsylvania and New Jersey did not, but employed terms of the same general character as our own. Our legislature chose to shape our law after the latter models. It is but a just inference, that the omission of any words, in our act, expressly giving the power to convey, was the result of design and not of accident.

The Supreme Courts of Pennsylvania and New Jersey have given to the acts of these States the same construction adopted in this opinion. *Walker v. Reamy,* 36 Pa. St. 410; *Naylor v. Field,* 5 Dutcher, 287.

We should add, in conclusion, that we have not considered the question of the power of the wife to dispose of her personal property. That may depend upon different considerations. The power to sell has sometimes been considered a necessary incident to the ownership of personal property, but a majority of the court are of opinion that the act of 1861 does not authorize a married woman to convey her realty in any other manner than that pointed out by the statute of conveyances. In holding this however, we do not question the rule laid down in *Emerson v. Clayton*, 32 Ill. 493, as to the right of a married woman to bring a suit in her own name. That right is a necessary incident to the law.

As the decision of this question disposes of this case, it is unnecessary to consider the other questions raised.

Judgment reversed.

BREESE, J., dissents.

[d]   Comments and Notes on *Van Riper*

[*i*]   *The* **Van Riper** *Story.* The pattern of land conveyances in *Van Riper* is a bit mysterious. John and Elizabeth Snyder apparently rented a building used as a tavern on the western part of block 9 in Whitfield to Solomon Cole. The Snyders then conveyed the entire block to James Van Riper who ran a store and a stable on the land. In a strange turnabout, James Van Riper and his wife Hannah joined together in transferring the block to Ellen Cole,[61] the wife of Solomon. The plaintiff, Henry Van Riper, obtained the land by a deed signed only by Ellen Cole. Van Riper then sued to eject Solomon Cole from the property, presumably at the end of his lease.[62] Solomon apparently responded that "the property was his" and that he wouldn't leave "until he was carried out."

This little tale suggests strongly that Solomon and Ellen Cole did not see eye to eye on their financial situation. It is certainly logical to argue that they may have been living apart though

---

[61] At one point in the opinion, Ellen Cole is referred to as Helen Cole. The language of the opinion makes it clear that Ellen and Helen are the same person.

[62] Don't be fooled by the fact that the name of the case seems to have Van Riper as a defendant. In many court systems, the party appealing from a trial court gets named first in the name of the appellate case. In this case, the trial proceedings were styled as *Van Riper v. Cole*, while the appellate proceedings were known as *Cole v. Van Riper.*

still married. Regardless of whether Solomon and Ellen were still living together, if Solomon was supporting Ellen, she could not seek to be treated as a *feme sole* under cases like *Love v. Moynehan*, discussed above at p. 151. As a result, the common law coverture rules, as modified by the 1861 Illinois Married Women's Property Act, still applied. So the question in the case boiled down to whether a married woman owning land in her name could convey it without the signature of her husband.

[*ii*]   ***Impact of the Married Women's Property Act on Unilateral Land Transfers.*** As the *Van Riper* court pointed out, the language of the 1861 married womens property legislation seemed to provide married women with full conveyancing power. A single woman—the ultimate *feme sole*—could convey her own land, so why not allow Ellen Cole to do the same? The court gave two reasons for its negative answer. The first was that allowing a married woman to sell her lands independently of her husband would allow her to "divorce her husband *a mensa et thoro*"[63] and to "annul the marriage tie at pleasure." The second relied on the Illinois conveyancing statutes, which barred unilateral sale of a fee simple in land by either spouse. The husband could not transfer a fee simple free of dower on his signature alone and a wife could not transfer complete title free of her husband's curtesy rights.

The second of these two reasons is the easiest to grasp. As long as all spouses automatically hold an interest in the land of their mates, it makes sense that unilateral conveyance of a fee simple absolute cannot be possible. That is the rule now and it was the rule when *Van Riper* was decided. At common law, a wife had to go through a bizarre process, called fine and recovery, to transfer her dower interest. But within a very short time after the Revolutionary War, all states had reformed their conveyancing laws to remove unnecessary bars to transfers. In the process, wives were allowed to sign deeds, often with some review by judge or magistrate to insure that the signature was voluntarily given. While these independent reviews of wives' signatures have long since disappeared, the basic rules barring unilateral transfers have survived.

The divorce based rationale is fascinating. It suggests the tight connections that existed between theories of family economic organization and wifely dependence. No one would have dared suggest that the broad authority of husbands to control the economic lives of their wives meant that the coverture rules should be modified to remove their ability to "annul the marriage tie at pleasure." Even though the conveyancing rules made it clear that unilateral transfer of land was not possible, the court still felt compelled to voice its alarm at the threat to traditional notions of marriage represented by coverture reforms.

[*iii*]   ***Impact on the Tenancy by the Entirety.*** There is language in *Van Riper* suggesting that the tenancy by the entirety was not consistent with the language of the 1861 married women's property legislation. The right of a husband to become "seized of an estate, during coverture, in lands held by the wife in fee," the court noted, "has been substantially abolished, because its existence is wholly irreconcilable with both the language and the objects of the law." The court did say that the estate by the curtesy which arose after the birth of a child was not abolished because the reform legislation had no impact on the allocation of marital estates after coverture

---

[63] Divorce *a mensa et thoro* is a divorce from bed and board, or a legal separation as it is sometimes called in modern parlance. Such a divorce proceeding settles up the economic, child custody, child support and alimony aspects of a divorce, but entry of the court judgment does not allow the parties to remarry. In the nineteenth century it was easier in many states to obtain a divorce *a mensa et thoro* than a divorce *a vinculo*, a divorce from the chains of marriage.

ended by death. These outcomes certainly left room to abolish the tenancy by the entireties. If the estate arising at marriage was inconsistent with the married women's property act, then why should a husband automatically get management rights in jointly owned property?

Despite the apparent inconsistency, Illinois never clearly abolished the tenancy by the entirety. Though dicta in some cases suggested the concurrent estate was no longer available, no clear outcome was ever reached.[64] The state legislature eventually resolved the ambiguity by creating a statutory tenancy by the entirety.

[iv]   *Management of Wives' Property.* The reasons for the ambiguity in the treatment of the tenancy by the entirety in Illinois may lie in the way the *Van Riper* court described the purposes for the reform legislation. "The object of the legislature was, not to loosen the bonds of matrimony, or create an element of constant strife between husband and wife," the court wrote, "but to protect the latter against the misfortunes, imprudence, or possible vice of the former, by enabling her to withhold her property from being levied on and sold for the payment of his debts, or squandered by him against her wishes." Illinois was not the only state to describe its first married women's property act as primarily a debtor protection measure. Many others made similar declarations. Narrowing the primary purpose to protection from creditors left intact the general understandings about the authority of husbands to govern the economy and behavior of their families. Abolition of the tenancy by the entirety would have required a declaration that husbands no longer had the authority to manage jointly held property. The judges were trying to protect the family governance prerogatives of men from the encroaching legislative reforms. The court's refusal to declare that wives had the right to dispose of their personal property, while simultaneously affirming their right to sue to obtain possession of it, fit the same mold.

[v]   *Relevance to* Bradwell *and a Few Questions.* The reasoning of the *Van Riper* court was consistent with other holdings that denied married women the right to control their wages, and hinted at the inability of women to contract about their property even if they held title. Do you think the Illinois courts unfairly narrowed the meaning of the 1861 reform legislation, or that they described its general tenor in a way that conformed with common understandings of the day? Were judges likely to be more conservative and traditional than legislators?

[e]   History of the *Bradwell* Litigation

During 1869, while she lobbied the Illinois state legislature to pass a second married women's property act and a private bill protecting her business enterprises, Bradwell was deeply involved in an array of other suffrage activities. Indeed the nature of the arguments made by both sides in the litigation over her application to join the Illinois bar makes it clear that cultural concerns about the appropriate role of women in the economy played a major role in the deliberations about suffrage.

The pages of her CHICAGO LEGAL NEWS were not used solely for the dry business of the legal world. She was hardly shy about publishing columns on the women's suffrage movement and other aspects of the nineteenth century women's movement. She also publicized the efforts of her husband in the state legislature, where he went as an elected representative in 1873. In fact, the opening of her newspaper in 1868 was a propitiously timed event. The Civil War had recently concluded, and much activity was afoot with regard to the passage of the Thirteenth,

---

[64] For a summary of the situation, *see* Comment, *Tenancy by the Entirety in Illinois: a Reexamination,* 1990 So. ILL. U. L.J. 83.

Fourteenth and Fifteenth Amendments to the United States Constitution. Bradwell, like many other feminists of her time, either assumed or hoped that the amendment of the Constitution to guarantee blacks the right to vote would be extended to cover women as well. Elizabeth Cady Stanton, Susan B. Anthony and other well known suffragists certainly worked toward that goal. They were sorely disappointed.

One of the first Congressional debates on women's suffrage focused on an attempt to amend a bill extending suffrage to blacks in the District of Columbia to include women as well. The Thirteenth Amendment abolishing slavery had been ratified in 1865, and discussion was progressing on other portions of the post-Civil War civil rights legislation. The District of Columbia suffrage debate, which took place in 1866, was part of that ongoing process. Attempts to include women's suffrage in the bill failed badly. Many abolitionists opposed the effort, fearing that the long fight over black suffrage would be lost if it was linked to the vote for women. A similar fate befell the women's movement when the Fifteenth Amendment came up for debate later. Fears that the Thirteenth Amendment did not provide adequate Constitutional support for the civil rights legislation of 1866 led to adoption of the next amendment, the Fourteenth, which was ratified in 1868. It became the first part of the Constitution to specifically limit a right to males, and efforts to delete such phraseology presaged the demise of all attempts to include women's suffrage as part of the voting protection provisions of the Fifteenth Amendment.

The linkage of race and gender issues in the post-Civil War suffrage debates actually continued well into the twentieth century, though with some ironic twists. After the onset of the Jim Crow era, many women suffragists eschewed arguments based on racial and gender equality and some openly noted that granting women suffrage should not become an occasion for easing state and local practices restricting access to the ballot by black citizens. Public discourse on women's suffrage focused more on the special moral and educational roles of women. Those favoring suffrage viewed these special roles as a needed political corrective; those opposed saw suffrage as the path to the destruction of the special role of women. In either case, blacks were left on the sidelines by most of those debating suffrage in the early twentieth century.

It may not be entirely coincidental that Myra Bradwell opened her paper in the same year that the effort to implant women's suffrage in the Constitution was dealt a blow not recovered from for 50 years. Nor is it surprising that she would apply for membership in the Illinois Bar the following year. She had been reading law with her husband for some time. Perhaps the legal difficulties of the women's movement of her time propelled her to action.[65] Or perhaps the application was a "pure" political statement. Given the scope of her other activities, it is not clear that she really wanted to practice law.

In any case, Bradwell applied for membership in the Illinois Bar in August, 1869. At the time of her application, Rule 76 of the Rules of the Supreme Court of Illinois provided that Bar applications "will be sufficient" upon presentation of a certificate signed by the Circuit Judge and State's Attorney of the circuit in which the applicant resided. Mrs. Bradwell filed the required certificate and, presumably because she expected problems, a brief supporting her application. This first brief (there were two more filed before the Illinois Supreme Court) focused solely on the notion that she could be admitted even though the pronoun "he" was used in the state statute regarding Bar admission. This argument was not without some support, since Arabella

---

[65] It is interesting that Bradwell was one of seven women who applied for membership in state bars in 1869. It is hard to believe this was entirely coincidental. There must have been "something in the air" that year. *See* Gilliam, note 53 above, at 107.

A. Mansfield had already become, in June of 1869, the first woman admitted to a state Bar, in her case Iowa, under a similarly worded statute.[66]

Bradwell's application was denied on October 6, 1869, the court clerk writing her:

Mrs. Myra Bradwell—Madam: The court instruct me to inform you that they are compelled to deny your application for a license to practice as an attorney-at-law in the courts of the state, upon the ground that you would not be bound by the obligations necessary to be assumed where the relation of attorney and client shall exist, by reason of the disability imposed by your married condition—it being assumed that you are a married woman.

Applications of the same character have occasionally been made by persons under twenty-one years of age, and have always been denied upon the same ground that they are not bound by their contracts, being under a legal disability in that regard.

Until such disability shall be removed by legislation, the court regards itself powerless to grant your application.

Very respectfully, your obedient servant,

N.L. Freeman.[67]

Bradwell responded rapidly. On October 18, 1869, she filed an additional brief with the court, arguing forcefully that the Illinois Married Women's Acts of 1861 and 1869 had removed her civil disabilities, and that even if the general legislation had not, the private bill in her favor accomplished the same end. She wrote:

This result can, in my opinion, only be reached by disregarding the liberal statutes of our state, passed for the sole purpose of extending the rights of married women, and forever removing from our law, relating to their power to contract in regard to their earnings and property, the fossil foot-prints of the feudal system, and following the strictest rules of the common law.[68]

The state court was not so quick to respond this time. An opinion did not appear for several months. In the meantime, the women's suffrage movement, frustrated in Congress, began to adopt new strategies. At a women's suffrage convention which met in St. Louis while Bradwell was framing her second brief to the Illinois Supreme Court, Francis Minor, the husband of Virginia Minor, President of the Missouri State Suffrage Association, submitted resolutions to the assembly calling for the construction of the new Fourteenth Amendment's Privileges and Immunities Clause as a definition of national rights superior in force to state law, and for inclusion of suffrage as a privilege and immunity of national citizenship for all persons, regardless of gender. The resolutions were adopted by the convention, and they set the strategic tone for women suffragists for the next several years.

Bradwell responded to the Minor Resolutions with a third and final brief to the Illinois Supreme Court. On December 31, 1869, she filed her papers contending that the Fourteenth Amendment's Privileges and Immunities Clause guaranteed her the right to practice the profession of her choice.

[66] ELIZABETH CADY STANTON, SUSAN B. ANTHONY, & MATILDA J. GAGE, 2 HISTORY OF WOMAN SUFFRAGE 606 (1882).

[67] 2 CHICAGO LEGAL NEWS 145 (1870). The letter may also be found in WOMAN SUFFRAGE, note 66 above, at 603.

[68] WOMAN SUFFRAGE, note 66 above, at 608.

A short time later the court issued its opinion. They did not respond to the Constitutional argument, contending instead that even if the state Married Women's Acts had removed some of Bradwell's common law disabilities, women could not practice law in the state. The court reaffirmed its recent holding that the state legislation granting married women control over their earnings did not give them the right to contract about non-marital property, something a lawyer must routinely do. The court also noted that its authority to admit members to the Bar was to be exercised so that only persons intended by the Legislature to be members could gain entry. The court went on to note:

> Whether, in the existing social relations between men and women, it would promote the proper administration of justice, and the general well-being of society, to permit women to engage in the trial of cases at the bar, is a question opening a wide field of discussion upon which it is not necessary for us to enter. It is sufficient to say that, in our opinion, the other implied limitation upon our power, to which we have referred, must operate to prevent our admitting women to the office of attorney-at-law. If we were to admit them, we should be exercising the authority conferred upon us in a manner which, we are fully satisfied, was never contemplated by the legislature.

> Upon this question, it seems to us neither this applicant herself, nor any unprejudiced and intelligent person, can entertain the slightest doubt.

> . . . .

> That God designed the sexes to occupy different spheres of action, and that it belonged to men to make, apply, and execute the laws, was regarded as an almost axiomatic truth. It may have been a radical error, and we are by no means certain it was not, but that this was the universal belief certainly admits of no denial. A direct participation in the affairs of government, in even the most elementary form, namely, the right of suffrage, was not then claimed, and has not yet been conceded, unless recently in one of the newly-settled territories of the west.

The sequence of letters, briefs and opinions in the state consideration of Bradwell's application to join the bar provide a telling glimpse into the way concepts of citizenship, property and gender worked together in the latter decades of the nineteenth century. The Illinois Supreme Court's statement that "God designed the sexes to occupy different spheres of action, and that it belonged to men to make, apply, and execute the laws" confirms that many found it unacceptable for women to participate in the public sphere—in governance, politics, economic decision making and law. But they took this position for reasons subtly different from those of John Adams earlier in the century.[69]

Adams certainly thought that women were best suited to domestic service, but he found political benefit in such a system by calling upon women to educate men to assume their role as citizens of the republic. However, by Bradwell's time, property ownership was no longer tightly linked to the concept of citizenship. As Robert Steinfeld makes clear,[70] by the middle of the century, the ability to exercise independent judgment and therefore to be a citizen, depended on employment status and income, not just on property ownership. While that shift in emphasis made it possible for property owning and employed women to claim that they should be treated as citizens, it also led traditionalists to redefine their vision of women's proper role to insure

---

[69] Adams' views on property and citizenship are discussed earlier in this chapter, at p. 144.

[70] Robert J. Steinfeld, *Property and Suffrage in the Early American Republic*, 41 STAN. L. REV. 335 (1989).

their continued dependence on others. Instead of being defined as participants in a civic state, they were said to best serve humanity by playing a private role and leaving the public sphere to men.

Bradwell's pursuit of her case to the United States Supreme Court was a direct challenge to the conception of middle class women as occupants of a private, non-governmental, sphere. The case was being briefed in the Supreme Court while the Victoria Woodhull Memorials were being debated in Congress, and while some women, fortified by the Minor Resolutions, attempted to vote in the 1870 elections. The contours of Bradwell's arguments, including reliance on the constitutional theory of the Minor Resolutions, made her challenge to long standing limitations on the economic role of married women a stalking horse for the suffrage movement.

In late 1870, Woodhull submitted a memorial to Congress asking for investigation of the Minor claim that the Fourteenth Amendment enfranchised women. The House Judiciary Committee issued a report on the question, finding that it would not be lawful for Congress to enforce the Fourteenth Amendment by adopting women's suffrage legislation. The report, however, was issued over a dissent by two committee members. Meanwhile, some women, in a genteel but forceful spate of civil disobedience, started to vote—Marilla Ricker in New Hampshire, and Nannette Gardner in Detroit for starters. Sara Andrews Spencer, along with about 70 other women, marched to the polls in the District of Columbia, but were turned aside. They sued in the Supreme Court of the District of Columbia in 1871, but their case was thrown out on a demurrer.[71] Other attempts to vote led to the celebrated cases involving Susan B. Anthony and Virginia Minor.[72]

The *Bradwell* case was first argued in the Supreme Court in December of 1871, just three months after Sara Spencer and her 70 colleagues filed their voting rights case in the District of Columbia courts and shortly after it had been dismissed. Bradwell's case was argued by Matthew H. Carpenter, an eminent Republican, then the party of the left, and United States Senator from Wisconsin.[73] Carpenter's presence in the case raises an intriguing mystery, for he also appeared as counsel in the *Slaughter Houses Cases*, which were argued only a week before *Bradwell*. A good argument can be made that he took opposite positions in the two cases.

The *Slaughter House Cases* involved an 1869 Louisiana statute chartering a slaughtering corporation and granting it a 25-year monopoly. Meat packers not included in the state monopoly challenged the Louisiana regulation, arguing that the brand new Privileges and Immunities Clause of the Fourteenth Amendment guaranteed them the right to participate in their chosen occupation. Carpenter, as counsel for Louisiana, argued that efforts to invalidate the monopoly would have the effect of repealing all laws "regulating and fixing the hours of labor and prohibiting the employment of children, women and men in particular occupations," and "depriving the legislature and state courts . . . from regulating and setting their internal affairs." For Bradwell, Carpenter contended that pursuit of an occupation was a privilege and immunity of federal citizenship. The exact role of Carpenter remains a mystery.

---

[71] *Spencer & Webster v. Board of Inspectors* is described in 2 WOMAN SUFFRAGE, note 66 above, at 597-599. Much of the rest of the material in this section is also discussed in this volume of the History.

[72] Anthony was indicted under a then recently enacted civil rights act for casting an illegal ballot! She was convicted in a widely publicized trial, but never paid her fine. Minor's efforts led to a formal declaration by the United States Supreme Court that women were not enfranchised by the Fourteenth Amendment. Minor v. Happersett, 88 U.S. (21 Wall.) 162 (1875).

[73] It was common in those days for Congressmen to earn extra money by arguing cases before the Court.

All the suffrage agitation occurring at the time Bradwell's case was working its way to the top must have put the Supreme Court justices on edge. Carpenter spent the first part of his brief and his oral argument contending that Bradwell's case was not a portender of women's suffrage. Given the similarity between her arguments and those of Minor, Carpenter's efforts were almost surely doomed to fail. The narrow question presented by the case, according to Carpenter, was "can a female citizen, duly qualified in respect of age, character and learning, claim under the Fourteenth Amendment, the privilege of earning a livelihood" by practicing law? There must have been certain rights guaranteed by the Privileges and Immunities Clause, he contended, or the insertion of the language in the Constitution would have been surplusage. Despite Carpenter's reassurances, all concerned must have known that a loss by Bradwell would virtually end any chance the Court would accept the Minor Resolution suffrage theory.

The decision in the *Slaughter House Cases* came down on April 14, 1873, after Susan B. Anthony had been arrested and charged with violating recently enacted civil rights legislation by attempting to cast an illegal ballot in the 1872 elections. The *Slaughter House* decision was rendered one and one-half years after the original oral argument before the Court. The case had to be re-argued when Justice Samuel Nelson resigned after an illness. The eventual 5-4 vote in the case suggests he was the swing vote. The rendering of the *Bradwell* decision was held up while the Court struggled with the Louisiana butchers. *Bradwell* was announced the day after *Slaughter House*. The majority opinion in *Slaughter House* gave a narrow construction to the Privileges and Immunities Clause. Only rights already protected by the federal Constitution were said to be protected by the new amendment.

Four judges dissented. Justice Field took the position that it was a privilege and immunity of United States citizenship to have the "right to pursue a lawful employment in a lawful manner." Justice Bradley and Chief Justice Chase joined in Field's opinion. Justice Bradley, in a second dissenting opinion, argued that pursuit of employment was a right protected by the Fourteenth Amendment's protection of liberty and property. Swayne also wrote a dissent strongly criticizing the majority for narrowly construing the post-Civil War Amendments. It is therefore understandable why Swayne, Field and Bradley felt compelled to write a separate opinion in *Bradwell*. After writing that the right to seek employment was a national right of citizenship, they most assuredly felt the need to explain why Bradwell lacked the same right they had attempted to create for Louisiana's male butchers. Chief Justice Chase did not write an opinion in *Bradwell*, though he arguably remained more consistent than some of his colleagues by dissenting. Bradley's concurring opinion in *Bradwell* has since become a classic of women's history.

[f]   The United States Supreme Court Opinions

Bradwell v. The State of Illinois

United States Supreme Court
83 U.S. (16 Wall.) 130, 21 L.Ed. 442 (1872)

Mr. Justice MILLER delivered the opinion of the court:

The plaintiff in error, residing in the state of Illinois, made application to the judges of the supreme court of that state for a license to practice law. She accompanied her petition with the usual certificate from an inferior court, of her good character, and that on due examination she had been found to possess the requisite qualifications. Pending this application, she also filed an affidavit to the effect "that she was born in the state of Vermont; that she was (had been) a citizen of that state; that she is now a citizen of the United States, and has been for many years past a resident of the city of Chicago in the state of Illinois." And with this affidavit she also filed a paper claiming that under the foregoing facts she was entitled to the license paid for, by virtue of the 2d section of the 4th article of the Constitution of the United States, and of the 14th article of Amendment of that instrument.

The statute of Illinois on this subject enacts that no person shall be permitted to practice as an attorney or counselor at law, or to commence, conduct, or defend any action, suit, or plaint, in which he is not a party concerned, in any court of record within this state, either by using or subscribing his own name or the name of any other person, without having previously obtained a license for that purpose from two justices of the supreme court, which license shall constitute the person receiving the same an attorney and counselor at law, and shall authorize him to appear in all the courts of record within this state and there to practice as an attorney and counselor at law according to the laws and customs thereof.

The supreme court denied the application apparently upon the ground that it was a woman who made it.

The record is not very perfect, but it may be fairly taken that the plaintiff asserted her right to a license on the grounds, among others, that she was a citizen of the United States, and that having been a citizen of Vermont at one time, she was, in the state of Illinois, entitled to any right granted to citizens of the latter state.

The court having overruled these claims of right founded on the clauses of the Federal Constitution before referred to, those propositions may be considered as properly before this court.

As regards the provision of the Constitution that citizens of each state shall be entitled to all the privileges and immunities of citizens in the several states, the plaintiff in her affidavit has stated very clearly a case to which it is inapplicable.

The protection designed by that clause, as has been repeatedly held, has no application to a citizen of the state whose laws are complained of. If the plaintiff was a citizen of the state of Illinois, that provision of the Constitution gave her no protection against its courts or its legislation.

The plaintiff seems to have seen this difficulty, and attempts to avoid it by stating that she was born in Vermont.

While she remained in Vermont that circumstance made her a citizen of that state. But she states, at the same time, that she is a citizen of the United States, and that she is now, and has been for many years past, a resident of Chicago, in the state of Illinois.

The 14th Amendment declares that citizens of the United States are citizens of the state within which they reside; therefore the plaintiff was, at the time of making her application, a citizen of the United States and a citizen of the state of Illinois.

We do not here mean to say that there may not be a temporary residence in one state, with intent to return to another, which will not create citizenship in the former. But plaintiff states nothing to take her case out of the definition of citizenship of a state as defined by the 1st section of the 14th Amendment.

In regard to that Amendment counsel for the plaintiff in this court truly says that there are certain privileges and immunities which belong to a citizen of the United States as such; otherwise it would be nonsense for the 14th Amendment to prohibit a state from abridging them, and he proceeds to argue that admission to the bar of a state, of a person who possesses the requisite learning and character, is one of those which a state may not deny.

In this latter proposition we are not able to concur with counsel. We agree with him that there are privileges and immunities belonging to citizens of the United States, in that relation and character, and that it is these and these alone which a state is forbidden to abridge. But the right to admission to practice in the courts of a state is not one of them. This right in no sense depends on citizenship of the United States. It has not, as far as we know, ever been made in any state or in any case to depend on citizenship at all. Certainly many prominent and distinguished lawyers have been admitted to practice, both in the state and Federal courts, who were not citizens of the United States or of any state. But, on whatever basis this right may be placed, so far as it can have any relation to citizenship at all, it would seem that, as to the courts of a state, it would relate to citizenship of the state, and as to Federal courts, it would relate to citizenship of the United States.

The opinion just delivered in the *Slaughter-House Cases*, from Louisiana, renders elaborate argument in the present case unnecessary; for, unless we are wholly and radically mistaken in the principles on which those cases are decided, the right to control and regulate the granting of license to practice law in the courts of a state is one of those powers which are not transferred for its protection to the Federal government, and its exercise is in no manner governed or controlled by citizenship of the United States in the party seeking such license.

It is unnecessary to repeat the argument on which the judgment in those cases is founded. It is sufficient to say, they are conclusive of the present case.

The judgment of the State Court is, therefore, affirmed.

Mr. Justice BRADLEY:

I concur in the judgment of the court in this case, by which the judgment of the supreme court of Illinois is affirmed, but not for the reasons specified in the opinion just read.

The claim of the plaintiff, who is a married woman, to be admitted to practice as an attorney and counselor at law, is based upon the supposed right of every person, man or woman, to engage in any lawful employment for a livelihood. The supreme court of Illinois denied the application on the ground that, by the common law, which is the basis of the laws of Illinois, only men were admitted to the bar, and the legislature had not made any change in this respect, but had simply provided that no person should be admitted to practice as attorney or counselor without having previously obtained a license for that purpose from two justices of the supreme court, and that no person should receive a license without first obtaining a certificate from the court of some county of his good moral character. In other respects it was left to the discretion of the court to establish the rules by which admission to the profession should be determined. The court, however, regarded itself as bound by at least two limitations. One was that it should establish such terms of admission as would promote the proper administration of justice, and the other that it should not admit any persons or class of persons not intended by the legislature to be admitted, even though not expressly excluded by statute. In view of this latter limitation the court felt compelled to deny the application of females to be admitted as members of the bar. Being contrary to the rules of the common law and the usages of Westminster Hall from time immemorial, it could not be supposed that the legislature had intended to adopt any different rule.

The claim that, under the 14th Amendment of the Constitution, which declares that no state shall make or enforce any law which shall abridge the privileges and immunities of citizens of the United States, . . . the statute law of Illinois, or the common law prevailing in that state, can no longer be set up as a barrier against the right of females to pursue any lawful employment for a livelihood (the practice of law included), assumes that it is one of the privileges and immunities of women as citizens to engage in any and every profession, occupation or employment in civil life. It certainly cannot be affirmed, as a historical fact, that this has ever been established as one of the fundamental privileges and immunities of the sex. On the contrary, the civil law, as well as nature herself, has always recognized a wide difference in the respective spheres and destinies of man and woman. Man is, or should be, woman's protector and defender. The natural and proper timidity and delicacy which belongs to the female sex evidently unfits it for many of the occupations of civil life. The constitution of the family organization, which is founded in the divine ordinance, as well as in the nature of things, indicates the domestic sphere as that which properly belongs to the domain and functions of womanhood. The harmony, not to say identity, of interests and views which belong or should belong to the family institution, is repugnant to the idea of a woman adopting a distinct and independent career from that of her husband. So firmly fixed was this sentiment in the founders of the common law that it became a maxim of that system of jurisprudence that a woman had no legal existence separate from her husband, who was regarded as her head and representative in the social state; and, notwithstanding some recent modifications of this civil status, many of the special rules of law flowing from and dependent upon this cardinal principle still exist in full force in most states. One of these is, that a married woman is incapable, without her husband's consent, of making contracts which shall be binding on her or him. This very incapacity was one circumstance which the supreme court of Illinois deemed important in rendering a married woman incompetent fully to perform the duties and trusts that belong to the office of an attorney and counselor.

It is true that many women are unmarried and not affected by any of the duties, complications, and incapacities arising out of the married state, but these are exceptions to the general rule. The paramount destiny and mission of woman are to fulfill the noble and benign offices of wife and mother. This is the law of the Creator. And the rules of civil society must be adapted to the general constitution of things, and cannot be based upon exceptional cases.

The humane movements of modern society, which have for their object the multiplication of avenues for woman's advancement, and of occupations adapted to her condition and sex, have my heartiest concurrence. But I am not prepared to say that it is one of her fundamental rights and privileges to be admitted into every office and position, including those which require highly special qualifications and demanding special responsibilities. In the nature of things it is not every citizen of every age, sex, and condition that is qualified for every calling and position. It is the prerogative of the legislator to prescribe regulations founded on nature, reason, and experience for the due admission of qualified persons to professions and callings demanding special skill and confidence. This fairly belongs to the police power of the state; and, in my opinion, in view of the peculiar characteristics, destiny, and mission of woman, it is within the province of the legislature to ordain what offices, positions, and callings shall be filled and discharged by men, and shall receive the benefit of those energies and responsibilities, and that decision and firmness which are presumed to predominate in the sterner sex.

For these reasons I think that the laws of Illinois now complained of are not obnoxious to the charge of abridging any of the privileges and immunities of citizens of the United States.

Mr. Justice FIELD and Mr. Justice SWAYNE; We concur in the opinion of Mr. Justice BRADLEY.

Dissenting, Mr. Chief Justice CHASE.

[g] Analytic Notes on the Importance of *Bradwell*

Bradwell was certainly disappointed by the 8-1 results in the Supreme Court. But all was not lost. Although she never reapplied for admission to the Illinois Bar, the state adopted legislation in March, 1872, just before the *Bradwell* opinion was rendered, removing the gender limitations on Bar membership.[74] Many other states adopted similar legislation shortly thereafter. In 1879, Congress followed the trend by permitting practice in The United States Supreme Court by women.[75] On motion of then Attorney General W.H. Miller, Bradwell was admitted to membership in the Bar of the United States Supreme Court in 1882. And the Illinois Supreme Court, on its own motion, admitted Bradwell to the state Bar in 1890, apparently the only time an attorney has ever been admitted to practice in Illinois on the motion of the Court rather than the applicant. She was then suffering from the cancer that would kill her four years later.

That Bradwell won her war after losing her battle suggests that some change in the status of women was occurring. The family protection motivations providing much of the support for the earlier married women's property acts had broadened enough to permit female entry to the Bar. However, her personal triumph and those of the handful of other women who became lawyers in the late nineteenth and early twentieth centuries was only an early signal of the profound change that was to come a century later. Even putting aside the limited roles many early women lawyers were permitted to play—their relegation to divorce and juvenile courts in many firms and to similar courses as teachers in the few law schools with female faculty—very few women joined the Bar until recently. In 1910, women made up only 1.1 percent of lawyers. The figure rose to 4.7 percent by 1970. Only in 1980 did the percentage rise to double figures—12 percent—for the first time.

The real importance of the case for purposes of family property law lies not so much in its compelling story about the significance of an early woman lawyer and suffragist, but in the signals it provides about changes in property theory in the last few decades of the nineteenth century.

When Bradwell was litigating her petition to join the Illinois bar in state court, she was told by the clerk of the state Supreme Court that the legal profession was not open to her because she "would not be bound by the obligations necessary to be assumed where the relation of attorney and client shall exist." Simply put, since she could not enter into a contract as a married woman, she could not practice law. Bradwell's response that the 1861 married woman's property act had removed such barriers based on the old coverture system was rebuffed. This little "debate" over the right to contract actually touched on a central theme of then ongoing debates over the meaning of property and the role of women in society.

As already noted, the concept of male citizenship for voting purposes changed in the first half of the nineteenth century. While independence from the economic clutches of another was retained as a central tenet of citizenship, independence was found not only among the landed gentry, but also among those with their own jobs and steady incomes.[76] After the Civil War, this view of an independent suffrage was subjected to some strain by the movement to enfranchise the recently freed slaves. Though slavery was gone, the idea that black men as a class were economically self sufficient souls was rejected by many whites. In addition, debates over the

---

[74] An Act to Secure to All Persons Freedom in the Selection of an Occupation, Profession or Employment, ILL. REV. STAT., Ch. 48, Section 3 (1874), was passed on Mar. 22, 1872.

[75] An Act to Relieve Certain Legal Disabilities of Women, 20 Stat. 292 (Feb. 15, 1879).

[76] *See* Robert Steinfeld, note 70 above.

meaning of slavery and emancipation cast the right to contract for one's labor as the antithesis of slavery and as an essential element of "freedom." Freedom to contract became a new indicia of full citizenship. The clerk's letter to Bradwell, therefore, was a statement denying her right to claim membership in a population of independent citizens capable of participating in the body politic.

While marriage was often thought of as a contractual relationship, the contract had become a private arrangement that was designed to assist men in fulfilling their public status as governors while reaffirming women as domestic, dependent persons. Rather than marriage establishing women as participants in the building of a Republican state, it placed them in a non-public space. The clerk's letter helps us discern the outlines of a debate about marriage as a private contract versus a public institution, about wives and mothers as independent actors or persons with a certain family status regulated for the benefit of the state. Private versus public. Contract versus status. Independent versus dependent. Perhaps you can see the beginning of a transition in legal thought from Civic Republicanism to what many label as Legal Formalism or Classical Legal Thought.

Some aspects of this transition from Republicanism to Formalism are wonderfully chronicled in an article by Amy Dru Stanley on the post-Civil War adoption of married women's property acts designating the wages of married women as their property.[77] She noted the contradictions in simultaneously declaring that wives' wages were their property while retaining the right of husbands to control the domestic labor of their wives and the wages of their wives from outside employment once those funds found their way back into family bank accounts. She could sue her boss for her pay, but she could not always deny her husband access to the money after the judgment was paid off. Even in some states where the old reduction to possession rules had been discarded for personal property, wages sometimes came to be seen as a different sort of asset still under husbandly control. Just as the early married women's property acts were usually construed to protect women's real and personal property from husbandly debts, but not to expand women's authority to manage their assets, so too women's wages were often left in a nether-nether land between contract and status.

Some important recent historical commentary has argued that American law was largely transformed during the nineteenth century from a law about civic status to a law about contract.[78] In many ways that was probably true. The legislation Stanley discussed played out that transformation in a limited way. But the continuing vision of women as dependent upon their husbands and obligated to their families prolonged the vitality of status concepts much longer in family property law than it did in other areas of American law. Recall that women were not really thought of as full citizens of the early republic. Men were the real Civic Republicans. Similarly, as the world of Legal Formalism and contract became more relevant to men in the second half of the nineteenth century, status formulae were often used to deny women access to the full benefits or burdens of the industrial and labor world of contract.

The *Bradwell* case fits into this mold. She, like other women of her time and like the recently freed slaves, was claiming the right to contract for her labor. Bradwell was allowed to work for a living and even to control the operation of her own corporation. But she was not allowed

---

[77] Amy Dru Stanley, *Conjugal Bonds and Wage Labor: Rights of Contract in the Age of Emancipation*, 76 J. AMER. HIST. 471 (1988).

[78] MORTON J. HORWITZ, THE TRANSFORMATION OF AMERICAN LAW, 1780-1860 (1977). The Horwitz book has spawned an industry of commentary about the nature of shifts in legal theory that occurred in the nineteenth century.

to practice law and the Illinois married women's acts she drafted were not construed to grant women management authority over their incomes once the funds hit the family coffers.

William Howard Taft, in a speech he gave at the 1894 University of Michigan Law School, lauded the "deep seated conviction that security of property and contract and liberty of the individual are indissolubly linked, as the main props of higher and progressive civilization." And he bemoaned the claim of workers for sympathy when they demanded "the right to compel another to employ him at his own price" amid a "bloody battle . . . against private property and its defenders."

These sorts of statements were typical of late nineteenth century Classical or Formalist Legal Thinkers. Although Taft was in some ways less rigid about his beliefs than many of his contemporaries—he evinced some sympathy for cooperative, intelligent unions, for example—his speech hit several important themes. First, note how he merged contract and property on the one hand with liberty on the other. This is significantly different from the linkage of property with virtue and citizenship that so dominated the thinking of Jefferson or Adams. They sought a theoretical *merger* of government, politics, property and citizenship. Taft wrote of a world in which government was *separate* from property and contract, in which the role of government was to protect contract and property from encroachment rather than to use them as a foundation for developing civic responsibility. The ability to earn a wage was not the definition of independence for purposes of entry *into* full citizenship, but the fulcrum of liberty *from* regulation. It was not the definition of responsibility and the central feature of participation *in* government, but the license for freedom *from* government.

A bevy of other contemporaneous developments confirmed the importance of the right to contract about property as an integral part of liberty. The industrial age arrived with vengeance after the Civil War, making the labor contract a central feature of American life for capitalist and worker alike. Darwinism flourished after publication of ON THE ORIGIN OF SPECIES in 1859. Survival of the fittest was applied by Social Darwinists to human "progress," to use Taft's word, as well as to evolution. Laissez faire became the mantra of the wealthy and an ideology felt by many to be in tune with Darwinism. Immigrants flooded to these shores in one of the largest international migrations in history. Those having an instinctive desire to denigrate the recent arrivals as less worthy of respect (an instinct, by the way, that Darwin explicitly rejected) made quick use of survival of the fittest theories in Social Darwinism. Racism against the recently freed slaves also fit neatly into the Social Darwinist mix.

What we ended up with was a culture where many had a vision of the world in which the role of law was to protect the right to contract about wealth, in which the right to contract was an integral part of the meaning of property, and in which preservation of property was the central tenet of liberty. But we also ended up with a world in which access to property was easy to restrict. For only certain people or groups of people were worthy of having access to it. Once the post-Civil War reconstruction period was over and Social Darwinist thought became popularized, it was easy for some to justify the continued existence of the lower classes by blaming them for their plight rather than helping them excel, or by affirming the legitimacy of all contracts about property without regard to their fairness.

Bradwell was decided during the beginnings of that transition. While recently freed slaves were free to contract for their labor, the Supreme Court was not yet willing to diminish the power of the state to control contracts about wealth or labor. Louisiana was still free to restrict access to the slaughtering industry and Illinois was still free to control access to the legal market. The idea of a minimalist state protecting a laissez faire world had not yet fully matured. What was clear, however, was that those three judges dissenting in *Slaughter House* and willing to read the privileges and immunities clause as an embodiment of the right to contract for one's labor without state interference were not willing to extend that idea to women. While the working and political worlds might value freedom of contract, women were still bound by their status as domestic, dependent persons, unable to manage their property free of state control. Indeed, their domestic status was central to Social Darwinist survival of the race. It was women's natural role to reproduce, care for men and take care of the young. The human species had survived because of it. White men, in the Formalist world, were juridical equals capable of contracting for their labor. Others were in different roles ordained by the need to survive.

As Classical Legal Thought, or Formalism, gathered steam in the latter decades of the nineteenth century, it took on certain basic characteristics. Science entered a "golden age" of respectability. Darwinism, industrial developments, and the proliferation of new inventions, such as electricity, automobiles, the telegraph and eventually the telephone, convinced many that the secrets of the world were knowable and rational. Everything became a science. Sociology got its start. Political theorists proliferated. Economics blossomed. Law, too, became scientific, at least for some. Following scientifically structured legal rules would lead to a rational, easily understood legal system. The right of contract became a natural right; it was preordained and scientific. Its long term historical existence provided the necessary cultural props. Government interference with it would only mess up the rational world. Private ordering became central, government secondary. The role of government was to protect the private order, not control it.

The result was a legal world of rules and dichotomies. Following scientifically derived precedent was all that was necessary for success. Studying cases—the Langdell method of legal studies that came to dominate law school pedagogy—became crucial to the understanding of scientific rules. Contract and property became private. Government was public. The domestic world was private. The world of work, politics and controversy was public. Men could participate in the public world, women were usually relegated to the private. Those intelligent enough to obtain good contracts survived; those that were deemed inferior, such as immigrants and African Americans, were simply in their proper, Social Darwinist places.

By the end of the nineteenth century the post-Civil War claim of African Americans and suffragists that their right to contract for their labor entitled them to the full privileges of citizenship had been turned upside down. The upper classes used the same rhetorical phrases to justify unfair labor contracts and to maintain women's domesticity. Labor contracts, as property, were not alterable by the state. And marriage contracts, though terminable by divorce, were based on scientific, rational understandings about the natural roles of women in perpetuation of the species. Surely by the time of *Lochner v. New York*,[79] the classic Supreme Court case embedding laissez faire theory into the Constitution by finding New York's attempt to limit the length of the work week for bakers to 60 hours a violation of the due process clause, the *Slaughter House Cases* would have come out the other way. *Bradwell*, however, would probably have passed by unchanged. As *Muller v. Oregon*[80] instructs us in Darwinist prose, "women's physical structure and the performance of maternal functions place her at a disadvantage in the struggle for subsistence . . . . This is especially true when the burdens of motherhood are upon her." Working conditions for women, therefore, may be regulated by the state. "Especial care," must

[79] 198 U.S. 45 (1908).
[80] 208 U.S. 412 (1908).

be taken the Court added, "that her rights may be preserved . . . . She is properly placed in a class by herself, and legislation designed for her protection may be sustained."

While all of this was going on, of course, counter currents were flowing through the culture. We have always been much too complicated a place for any one ideological fashion to totally dominate the scene. In Chapters 5 and 6, we will explore a cross section of attitudes about Legal Realism and property using race rather than gender as the analytical prism.

[h]   Married Women and Wages: *Hancett v. Rice*

As noted in the comments after *Bradwell*, many states adopted statutes after the Civil War allowing married women to claim ownership of their wages. The Illinois reform legislation of 1869 was such an enactment.[81] It was the subject of an interesting case decided by the Illinois Court of Appeals in 1886.

Seth F. Hancett v. Amelia Rice

Illinois Court of Appeals
22 Ill. App. 442 (1886)

Statement by MORAN, J. This was an action of repletion to recover possession of certain household furniture which had been taken by the Sheriff on a writ of attachment against one Isaac A. Rice, the husband of appellee, and which appellee claimed was her separate property purchased with her own money. It appeared from her evidence that she was married in Baltimore, Maryland, in 1854, and at once went to live with her husband in Richmond, Virginia. On the day of her marriage she received $1,000 from her parents, which she never gave to her husband, but which she invested in part in personal property in Richmond, and again disposing of the property, brought the money back to Baltimore where she lived with her husband some three years. During her residence in Baltimore she purchased a slave and sold him again, making some money by the transaction, and in 1859 or 1860 she came with her husband to this State and settled in Jacksonville. After a time the family removed to Winona, Illinois, where her husband conducted a business for some years. During the sojourn at Jacksonville and Winona she purchased real estate in her own name and sold it again, making a profit, and also purchased and sold county bonds. About 1867 or 1868 she moved with her husband to Hobart, Indiana, where they resided for a year, and she took the money with her to that place and kept it in her own possession until they came to this State again, and still retained the money in her possession, when the family went to Beloit, Wisconsin, where they lived for some time. While there she purchased some real estate and sold it again, making a profit, and then returned to this State, and to the City of Chicago, to live. While she was living in Winona with her husband, his brother was in partnership with her husband in the clothing business and the brother having gone into the army in 1861-2 employed her to take his place in the store and paid her $50 a month for her services until he returned from the war in 1865 or 1866. This money as well as the money that was given her at her marriage by her parents, she always kept in her own possession and control, and when she purchased property she did the business herself and in her own name, and her husband never at any time had possession of the money or claimed it as his, but left her to manage it as she liked. When she came to Chicago to live she had some $4,000 or $5,000 which was the money given her by her parents at the time of her marriage, and the money given

---

[81] You can find the terms of the statute at note 56 above.

her by her brother for services rendered while she was living with her husband in this State, between 1861 and 1866, and the increase of such money made by her investments and speculations. The furniture in controversy was purchased by her and paid for out of this fund, and was, at the time of the levy, in the house in which she resided with her husband and family. Upon these facts the appellant offering no evidence, the court instructed the jury to find a verdict in favor of appellee, to which instruction appellant duly excepted. There was a verdict for the appellee, a motion for a new trial which was overruled, and judgment; and the case comes to this court by appeal.

MORAN, J. the question presented by this record is whether the appellee established, by the evidence introduced, a title in the furniture replevied, which entitled her to recover it in an action at law against the creditor of her husband, who had levied upon it. By the common law the money and personal property of the wife, of which she was actually and beneficially possessed at the time of the marriage in her own right, and such goods and chattels as might come to her during marriage, became the absolute property of her husband, and the tangible property was transferred to him by operation of the law wherever it might be situated. For this purpose the possession of the wife was the possession of the husband, "as for example, if she has money in her pocket, and this money never comes within his personal control, still being under her control, it is therefore in law his money and not hers, and the principle applies to all other chattels." Bishop on the Law of Married Women, Sec. 64, and cases cited.

Such was the law of this State prior to the passage of the Act of 1861, and that act was designed to take from the husband that which belonged to him at the time of its passage.

When the appellee came into this State and lived with her husband prior to the passage of the Law of Married Woman's Act of 1861, the money which she had in possession was the money of her husband, and at law and so far at least as the rights of his creditors were concerned, it continued to be his after the passage of that act, and all property that she purchased with it was his, and throughout all the changes and speculations and purchases and sales, the money, as well as the increase thereof, was his. Farrell v. Patterson, 43 Ill. 52, is conclusive of this case upon this point. There, Sarah Ann Farrell claimed certain property which was levied upon by the Sheriff under execution against her husband, and a proceeding was had under the statute to try the right of property. There was an appeal from the verdict of the Sheriff's jury and on the trial in the Circuit Court, the claimant introduced evidence that she married in 1849; that after her marriage her father gave her some means and also gave her $500 by his will; that she had two negroes which were sold for $1,300 and also had some household furniture which she had received from her father; that she came with her husband to this State in 1859, and from that time had been keeping hotel, the entire business being carried on in her name. The property levied upon was purchased by her in her own name. The court, after alluding to the fact that the moneys which she claimed came from a source other than her husband came to her from her relations prior to the law of 1861, said: "these moneys then, by force of well known and well established principles of law governing marital relations, became the property of her husband, and the chattels purchased with it became his likewise. The statute of 1861 was never designed to take from the husband that which belonged to him as a consequence of the marriage, nor could it do so without violating those principles of right and justice no Legislature ever knowingly and of purpose disregarded and ignored. All the well recognized presumptions arising from the marital relation with respect to the title to property of the wife still remain notwithstanding this statute. The act is prospective only, and is not designed to change and could not change the title to property possessed by the wife prior to its passage and which by the marriage vested in her husband."

. . . .

So with reference to the money paid to appellee by her brother for services prior to 1866; that also became her husband's, and whatever chattels she purchased with it would be subject to the rights of his creditors.

It was not until the passage of the Act of 1869 that married women became entitled to their own earnings in this State. Hay v. Hayes, 56 Ill. 342; Jassoy v. Delius, 65 Ill. 469.

The fact that appellee went from this State to Indiana and also to Wisconsin, and resided in each of those States for a time with her husband, and there had the money in her possession and dealt with it, does not in any manner strengthen her position, but in fact rather makes against it under the evidence in this record. It is a presumption always indulged in by the courts that the common law prevails in such of the States of the Union as are formed from territory which once belonged to the colonies of England. Unless the contrary is proven as a fact to the court it will be presumed in this State that the common law prevails in Indiana and Wisconsin, as regards the marital rights of the husband. So when appellee proved that she resided in Indiana with her husband and had the money in her possession there, and that she also resided in Wisconsin and had this money there, and afterward came with it into this State, the presumption of law in the absence of proof that by statute a married woman could hold her own personal property in that State is, that the common law prevailed there, and that by virtue of that law the money there became her husband's and therefore remained her husband's when she came into this State with it, and so the furniture purchased with it was subject to the levy by his creditors. This principle has been declared and applied by the Supreme Court in the case of Tinkler v. Cox, 68 Ill. 119. There the plaintiff, a married woman, purchased a horse with her own means in the State of Indiana, in 1867, and removed with her husband to this State, bringing the horse with them. The husband, in 1872, mortgaged the horse and placed him in the possession of the mortgagee, and the wife brought replevin, claiming him as her separate property. The court said: "The proof is, Mrs. Cox purchased the horse in the State of Indiana, but it is not proved as it might have been, if the law was established in that State, that by the laws of that State property so purchased became the separate property of the wife, free from the control of her husband. In the absence of such proof we must presume that the common law was in force in 1867, at the time Mrs. Cox purchased the horse, and so presuming, by that law the title of the property became vested absolutely in her husband; being so vested in the husband, by no act of our Legislature could his title be divested." . . . The Married Woman's Act of 1861 was repealed by the general repealing act adopted in 1874, and appellee's rights were controlled at the time of the trial by the act to revise the law in relation to husband and wife, in force July 1, 1874. Section 9 of said act is as follows: "A married woman may own in her own right, real and personal property obtained by descent, gift or purchase, and manage, sell and convey the same to the same extent and in the same manner that the husband can property belonging to him: *provided*, that where husband and wife shall be living together, no transfer or conveyance of goods and chattels between such husband and wife shall be valid as against the rights and interests of any third person, unless such transfer or conveyance be in writing, and be acknowledged and recorded in the same manner as chattel mortgages are required to be acknowledged and recorded by the laws of this State, in cases where the possession of the property is to remain with mortgagor." It may be suggested that by the terms of this statute a married woman may obtain property from her husband by gift, and that the evidence would justify the inference that the husband meant to renounce all rights to the money or property which appellee held and to make a gift of the same to her. It may be that in equity the husband and his representatives would be estopped from claiming the property because of the manner in which it was treated by him, but at law, in a case in which appellee must recover upon the strength of her legal title, it is very clear that a gift or transfer of personal property from the husband to the wife could not be established unless the terms of the above statute were shown to have been complied with. A valid transfer of the husband's goods to the wife must be in writing, and acknowledged and recorded, as required by law. It is not pretended that this was done, nor indeed is it claimed that she held the property by gift from her husband. Contention is that the property never belonged to the husband, because he never reduced it into his possession. The rule with reference to reducing the personal property of the wife to possession has application only to the wife's choses in action. We have already seen that as to money and chattels, being choses in possession, the title to them vests in the husband absolutely under the common law, and that the wife's possession becomes his possession.

The furniture in question in this suit was in the house in which appellee resided with her husband. He is still regarded as the head of the family, and the household furniture in possession of the family is presumed to be his until the contrary is shown. The Act of 1874 was not designed, any more that the Act of 1861, to overcome this presumption of the common law, nor was it designed to take from husbands rights which had vested in them prior to its passage, or to take from them such as had been acquired in another State subsequent to its passage.

Appellee asserted that the legal title to the furniture was in her; that she bought and paid for it with her own money, and the *onus* was on her to prove it. Starting with the presumption that the furniture belonged to her husband, what has she shown to rebut the presumption? She has shown that she received money from her parents and brought it with her to this State before the Act of 1861. That goes for nothing; for as the law then was it became her husband's as soon as it was given to her, or as soon as she came with her husband to reside in this State. She further showed that, while living with her husband in this State, money was paid to her by her brother for services rendered between 1861 and 1866. That, too, became the money of her husband as the law then stood, and his ownership of it was not divested by any subsequent statute. She finally showed that she retained all the money in her possession and went with her husband to the State of Wisconsin and increased the amount of it by profitable investment and brought it back with her to the State of Illinois, and with a part of it purchased this furniture. Here again, as we have seen, the presumption is that money which was in her hands in the State of Wisconsin became vested in her husband by virtue of the common law, and that it remained his upon their coming into this State, and thus the conclusion of the law on the facts in evidence is that the furniture was purchased with the money of her husband, and was his property, and was, therefore, subject to attachment at the suit of his creditors. It follows that the court erred in instructing the jury to find a verdict for appellee, and the judgement must, therefore, be reversed and the case remanded.

Reversed and remanded.

[i] Comments and Problems

[*i*] *The* **Hancett** *Case.* The outcome of the *Hancett* case is a dramatic example of the impact common law coverture rules had on married women. Bringing cash to the marital home was a risky business, even when a husband like Isaac Rice was totally sympathetic with the

desire of his wife to manage her own economic affairs. Since the property belonged to Mr. Rice when he reduced it to his possession, his creditors could seize it over the objections of both spouses. Indeed, the Illinois courts' vision of the reduction to possession rule was harsher than many other states. Marriage alone was enough to transfer ownership from wife to husband unless the personal property was a chose in action.

[*ii*]   ***Impact of the 1861 Married Womens' Property Act.*** If the transactions in the *Hancett* case had occurred after 1861, would the outcome have changed? The terms of the 1861 act are reproduced above at footnote 54, p. 150. The terms of the act seem to cover the situation. But note the ambiguous comment in *Van Riper* that the court was leaving open the question of whether a married woman could sell her personal property without the permission of the husband. If she needed her husband's consent to sell the property, would that mean her husband's creditors could attach the asset? Over the years, courts in Illinois and elsewhere gradually enlarged the control of married women over their personal property, allowed them to dispose of it by themselves, established the principle that transformation of a wife's property from one form—say, a cow—to another form—cash—did not change its character as the property of a married woman, and barred attachment by creditors of the husband. Once all of these principles were established, the Amelia Rices of this world began to win their cases.

[*iii*]   ***Home Labor.*** Suppose a married woman ran a business out of her home. Would the profits of such a business be treated as her property under the 1869 reform legislation, reprinted above in footnote 56, p. 151? Many courts found such profits not to be wages under legislation like that adopted in Illinois. This was part of a larger set of problems about the way the courts treated the labor of married women in the home. Wives had no right to demand payment for their household labor and often lost control over the moneys they earned in home businesses such as inns, pubs, restaurants, tailoring, or laundries. While they could sue to obtain their wages earned in jobs outside the home, husbands were still thought to control labor in the home. For more on these issues, read Amy Dru Stanley's article on the wage acts, referred to above in footnote 77 p. 168. You might also look at Reva B. Siegel, *Home as Work: The First Woman's Rights Claims Concerning Wives' Household Labor, 1850-1880,* 103 Yale L.J. 1073 (1994); Reva B. Siegel, *The Modernization of Marital Status Law: Adjudicating Wives' Rights to Earnings, 1860-1930,* 82 Geo. L.J. 2127 (1994).

[*iv*]   ***Creditor Protection.*** After 1869, much of the property of a married woman was both subject to her control (except for the requirement that husbands had to agree to land transfers) and exempt from attachment by the creditors of her husband. If you, as a wife, were involved in a good, solid marriage in the 1870s in which your husband ran a sometimes risky business, and you trusted your mate completely, how would you title your property? Might you put as much of it as possible in your name in order to insulate the assets from your husband's business creditors? Couples began to do that more often after the Civil War. During the 1880s creditors began to complain that the special status of married women's separate property was being used unfairly. They began to argue that married women were just as capable of operating in the business world as men and that their property should not enjoy any special protections from creditors. States began to adopt legislation that removed the special debt protected status of married women's property. When that happened, married women's property matured into a form of property ownership that was for all practical purposes like a male fee simple absolute. And as that began to happen the unwillingness of courts to admit women to the bar began to look silly and old-fashioned.

§ 2.04 Contemporary Family Property Law

[1]   Recent Constitutional Law Developments

[a]   Developments Since *Bradwell*

Although most states adopted a number of married women's property reforms between the Civil War and the middle of the twentieth century, numerous differences in treatment between men and women remained in the property laws of most states. Neither legislatures nor courts took steps to eliminate those differences until the early 1970s. Indeed, a number of Supreme Court decisions made it quite clear that the Court had no intention of using the Constitution as a way of equalizing the civil law treatment of men and women. For example, commonly articulated sentiments about the weakness and fragility of women were used as a basis for upholding protective labor legislation for women while voiding such legislation for men.[82] Legislation excluding women from bartending jobs was also validated even though it was quite clear that the motivation for the legislation was to protect men's jobs, not women's morals.[83]

In the early 1970s, however, the Supreme Court began to chip away at the old jurisprudence. The line of cases began with *Reed v. Reed*,[84] in which a statute mandating a preference for males as administrators of estates was invalidated. This case was quickly followed by another which voided a statute making it virtually impossible for a father of an illegitimate child to obtain custody upon the death of its mother while giving the mother the protection of a judicial hearing before custody was lost under any circumstances.[85]

In neither case did the Court clearly articulate a Constitutional standard to guide future decision making on gender issues. The reason for that was made clear in 1973, when the Court voided a statute denying to female members of the military fringe benefits given to male members, but split on the standard of review.[86] Four members of the Court opined that gender was a "suspect classification" under the Equal Protection Clause, requiring a state to justify any distinction or classification it makes upon the basis of gender by demonstrating a compelling public interest in using the distinction. This is the same sort of standard used to this day to decide upon the validity of classifications based upon race. The other four justices sitting on the case declined to adopt that path, but still agreed that the statute was invalid. The judges wishing to use the suspect classification standard wrote:

> There can be no doubt that our Nation has had a long and unfortunate history of sex discrimination. Traditionally, such discrimination was rationalized by an attitude of "romantic paternalism" which, in practical effect, put women not on a pedestal but in a cage . . . . [O]ur statute books gradually became laden with gross, stereotyped distinctions between the sexes and, indeed, throughout much of the 19th century the position of women in our society was, in many respects, comparable to that of blacks under the pre-Civil War codes. Neither slaves nor women could hold office, serve on juries, or bring suit in their own names, and married women traditionally were denied the legal capacity to hold or convey property or to serve as legal guardians of their own children . . . .

---

[82] Muller v. Oregon, 208 U.S. 412 (1908).

[83] Goessart v. Cleary, 335 U.S. 464 (1946).

[84] 404 U.S. 71 (1971).

[85] Stanley v. Illinois, 405 U.S. 645 (1972).

[86] Frontiero v. Richardson, 411 U.S. 677 (1973).

It is true, of course, that the position of women in America has improved markedly in recent decades. Nevertheless, it can hardly be doubted that, in part because of the high visibility of the sex characteristic, women still face pervasive, although at times more subtle, discrimination in our education institutions, in the job market, and, perhaps most conspicuously, in the political arena.

The Court never adopted the suspect classification standard. Instead gender classifications must hold a "fair and substantial relation" to an important state interest in order to be valid. Using this standard, the Court approved the use of different mandatory discharge criteria for men and women by the Navy[87] but twice invalidated gender distinctions in the Social Security system.[88] That this standard was not the same as that used in race discrimination cases was made clear during the same term that *Kirchberg v. Feenstra*, the next case, was decided. In addition to its decision in *Kirchberg*, the Court also decided that it was constitutional for Congress to order only men to register for the draft, and for a state to create different ages of consent for men and women for purposes of statutory rape.[89] It is difficult to believe that the Court would also permit Congress to order only black or white males to register for the draft or allow states to create different statutory rape offenses for black and white persons. The Equal Rights Amendment, proposed by Congress but never ratified by sufficient states, was intended to create similar judicial standards for the evaluation of distinctions made on the basis of race and gender.

Despite the rapid change in constitutional law in the 1970s, many states still retained rules declaring that husbands had the rights to manage and control property jointly held by the spouses in a concurrent estate or as community property. The next case dealt with such a rule.

[b]   Background to *Kirchberg v. Feenstra*

Barbara Hausman-Smith first met Joan Paillot Feenstra in 1976 when Feenstra came to the offices of the New Orleans Legal Assistance Corporation (NOLAC) seeking help in collecting damages resulting from an automobile accident. Hausman-Smith was assigned Feenstra's case.[90] Joan Paillot, widowed when in her twenties, later married Harold Feenstra in the early 1960s and had a daughter early in the marriage. She was very poor, living in the outskirts of sprawling Orleans Parish on the rural, southeastern side of Lake Pontchartrain. She hitched a ride on a school bus to get to the NOLAC offices in 1976.

The Feenstras had purchased a small house in February, 1966, for about $3,000. To finance the purchase they signed mortgage deeds for two other lots located on either side of an unpaved road running alongside wetlands and a canal in an area known as the Irish Bayou. Joan Feenstra crabbed from one of the lots, which was located on the water, while her husband was off working in construction.

In October, 1974, Joan Feenstra filed a criminal complaint against her husband for molesting her daughter. He retained an attorney, Karl C. Kirchberg, to represent him in the criminal case. To guarantee payment of Kirchberg's legal fees, Harold Feenstra signed a promissory note for $3,000 secured by a mortgage on the Irish Bayou house. By October 22, 1974, only five days

---

[87] The *Frontiero* Four dissented. Schlesinger v. Ballard, 419 U.S. 498 (1975).

[88] Weinberger v. Weisenfeld, 420 U.S. 636 (1975); Califano v. Goldfarb, 430 U.S. 199 (1977).

[89] Michael M. v. Superior Court, 450 U.S. 464 (1981) (age of consent); Rostker v. Goldberg, 453 U.S. 57 (1981) (draft registration).

[90] Much of the information about this case was obtained in a telephone interview with Barbara Hausman-Smith on July 8, 1986.

after he retained Kirchberg, Harold Feenstra had paid off $984.72 on the note. Later that month, after the criminal charges were dropped, he left Louisiana for Florida. The Feenstras were then legally separated. One morning in February, 1976, Kirchberg knocked on Joan Feenstra's door, told her he owned her property and was planning to put a trailer park on the land, and demanded that she leave. Joan Feenstra called her new attorney at NOLAC and asked for help on this problem as well.

By 1976, the Louisiana Civil Code rule that the husband was the head and master of the marital community and controlled the property of the marriage was under attack from a number of directions. Louisiana was a community property state.[91] Prior to the 1970s, all community property regimes named the husband as the head of the community and the manager of its assets. Most of the other community property states had altered that rule by 1976, and Louisiana was under pressure to do the same.[92] Part of the pressure to change the old rule came from a recently formed group called the Association for Women Attorneys, which included among its members Joan Feenstra's attorney, Barbara Hausman-Smith. Indeed, so many bankers and other mainstream lenders feared that the Louisiana head and master rule was of dubious validity that most mortgage loans were made only with the signatures of both husband and wife. Kirchberg apparently had no such compunctions.

Despite the ongoing pressure to alter the head and master rule, Hausman-Smith did not immediately perceive the equal protection theory that could be used to attack it. When the state foreclosure hearing came up, she argued that Kirchberg was a creditor under the Federal Truth in Lending Act, was therefore required to disclose Harold Feenstra's mortgage deed to his wife, and was liable in damages for his failure to do so. For unclear reasons, Kirchberg then filed an action in federal court seeking a declaratory judgment that he was not a creditor under the Truth in Lending Act. It was while preparing the answer to this lawsuit that Hausman-Smith began to understand the Constitutional implications of her client's case.[93]

When motions for summary judgment were filed in the federal case, Judge Sear took the highly unusual step of writing a letter to the law schools in Louisiana and inviting faculty members to express their views on the head and master rule. None took him up on his offer. Nonetheless, Judge Sears, not known as being very sympathetic to attempts to gender-neutralize the Louisiana community property regime, relied in his opinion[94] on an article written by a proponent of the head and master rule teaching at the Tulane Law School.[95]

During this litigation, Hausman-Smith was sharing her research with her friend and fellow member in the Association for Women Attorneys, Dorothy Waldrup. At the time, Waldrup represented Selina K. Martin whose husband had defaulted on a mortgage signed by him alone. Mr. Martin's attempt to use his marital community's assets to pay off the debt on his mother's property caused the break up of his marriage and a lawsuit. While Feenstra lost her case before Judge Sear, Selina Martin won at the trial level in state court on February 14, 1978.

[91] For a summary of the community property system, turn back to p. 142.

[92] See Janet M. Riley, *Women's Rights in the Louisiana Matrimonial Regime*, 50 TUL. L. REV. 557 (1976); Janet M. Riley, *Equal Management in Louisiana—Some Flaws Still Exist*, 8 COMMUNITY PROP. J. 151 (1981).

[93] One of the articles she came across was George L. Bilbe, *Constitutionality of Sex Based Differentiations in the Louisiana Community Property Regime*, 19 LOY. L. REV. 373 (1973).

[94] Kirchberg v. Feenstra, 430 F. Supp. 642 (E.D. La. 1977).

[95] Robert A. Pascal, *Updating Louisiana's Community of Gains*, 49 TUL. L. REV. 555 (1975). There was scholarly literature on the other side of course. *See* Bilbe, note 93 above.

Martin's victory caused quite a stir. The Louisiana Attorney General, obligated under state law to step into any case in which a trial court declares a state law unconstitutional, immediately asked the state Supreme Court to review the matter in an expedited fashion. Only 15 days after the trial judge found in Selina Martin's favor, oral arguments were heard by the state's highest court. Only a month later, the decision came down reversing the trial court. The 4-3 result was based on the theory that a provision in the Civil Code permitting a wife to designate property as a family home and thereby barring it from sale or encumberment without her signature provided her with sufficient protection.[96] But the dissent took the remarkable step of saying that if the state legislature did not change the head and master rule in the upcoming session, the case would be reheard and the dissent would become the majority! On October 10, 1978, the United States Supreme Court denied Martin's petition for certiorari.[97] Though Selina Martin lost her individual battle, she won the Constitutional war. The 1979 session of the state legislature passed an "equal management" law while Feenstra's appeal was being briefed and argued in the Fifth Circuit Court of Appeals.[98] When the Fifth Circuit reversed Judge Sears, only Kirchberg pursued the case to the Supreme Court. The State of Louisiana was a party to the case because of the attack that was being made on the head and master rule, but given the legislature's recent adoption of an equal management rule, the state declined to appeal from the Fifth Circuit result. Perhaps if the Fifth Circuit had applied its rule retroactively, the state would also have appealed. The United States Supreme Court agreed to hear the case, even though it had declined only a short time before to accept Selina Martin's petition for certiorari. No one knows why the Court acted this way.

[c] United States Supreme Court Opinion in *Kirchberg v. Feenstra*

KIRCHBERG v. FEENSTRA

United States Supreme Court
450 U.S. 455, 101 S. Ct. 1195, 67 L. Ed. 2d 428 (1981)

Justice MARSHALL delivered the opinion of the Court.

In this appeal we consider the constitutionality of a now superseded Louisiana statute that gave a husband, as "head and master" of property jointly owned with his wife, the unilateral right to dispose of such property without his spouse's consent. Concluding that the provision violates the Equal Protection Clause of the Fourteenth Amendment, we affirm the judgment of the Court of Appeals for the Fifth Circuit invalidating the statute.

I

In 1974, appellee Joan Feenstra filed a criminal complaint against her husband, Harold Feenstra, charging him with molesting their minor daughter. While incarcerated on that charge, Mr. Feenstra retained appellant Karl Kirchberg, an attorney, to represent him. Mr. Feenstra signed a $3,000 promissory note in prepayment for legal services to be performed by appellant Kirchberg. As

---

[96] Corpus Christi Credit Union v. Martin, 358 So. 2d 295 (La. 1978).

[97] Martin v. Corpus Christi Credit Union, 439 U.S. 897 (1978).

[98] The legislation provided that both spouses had the right to manage the community, but that the concurrence of both spouses was required for the sale, encumbrance or lease of real property or other major assets. The new statute also permits a spouse to expressly renounce his or her management rights as to an asset for a stated period of time. LA. CIV. CODE ANN. art. 2346-2355.

security on this note, Mr. Feenstra executed a mortgage in favor of appellant on the home he jointly owned with his wife. Mrs. Feenstra was not informed of the mortgage, and her consent was not required because a state statute, former Art. 2404 of the Louisiana Civil Code Ann. (1971), gave her husband exclusive control over the disposition of community property.[1]

Mrs. Feenstra eventually dropped the charge against her husband. He did not return home, but instead obtained a legal separation from his wife and moved out of the State. Mrs. Feenstra first learned of the existence of the mortgage in 1976, when appellant Kirchberg threatened to foreclose on her home unless she paid him the amount outstanding on the promissory note executed by her husband. After Mrs. Feenstra refused to pay the obligation, Kirchberg obtained an order of executory process directing the local sheriff to seize and sell the Feenstra home.

Anticipating Mrs. Feenstra's defense to the foreclosure action, Kirchberg in March 1976 filed this action in the United States District Court for the Eastern District of Louisiana, seeking a declaratory judgment against Mrs. Feenstra that he was not liable under the Truth in Lending Act, 15 U.S.C. § 1601 *et seq.*, for any nondisclosures concerning the mortgage he held on the Feenstra home. In her answer to Kirchberg's complaint, Mrs. Feenstra alleged as a counterclaim that Kirchberg has violated the Act, but also included a second counterclaim challenging the constitutionality of the statutory scheme that empowered her husband unilaterally to execute a mortgage on their jointly owned home. The State of Louisiana and its Governor were joined as third-party defendants on the constitutional counterclaim. The governmental parties, joined by appellant, moved for summary judgment on this claim. The District Court, characterizing Mrs. Feenstra's counterclaim as an attack on "the bedrock of Louisiana's community property system," granted the State's motion for summary judgment.[2]

While Mrs. Feenstra's appeal from the District Court's order was pending before the Court of Appeals for the Fifth Circuit, the Louisiana Legislature completely revised its code provisions relating to community property. In so doing, the State abandoned the "head and master" concept embodied in Art. 2404, and instead granted spouses equal control over the disposition of community property. La.Civ.Code Ann., Art. 2346 (Supp. 1981).[3] The new code also provided that community immovables could not be alienated, leased, or otherwise encumbered without the concurrence of both spouses. La.Civ.Code Ann., Art. 2347 (Supp.1981).[4] These provisions, however, did not take effect until January 1, 1980, and the Court of Appeals was therefore required to consider whether Art. 2404, the Civil Code provision which had authorized Mr. Feenstra to mortgage his home in 1974 without his wife's knowledge or consent, violated the Equal Protection Clause of the Fourteenth Amendment. . . . .

---

[1] Article 2404, in effect at the time Mr. Feenstra executed the mortgage in favor of appellant, provided in pertinent part:

> The husband is the head and master of the partnership or community of gains; he administers its effects, disposes of the revenues which they produce, and may alienate them by an onerous title, without the consent and permission of his wife.

This provision has been repealed.

[2] After the District Court granted summary judgment against appellee Feenstra on her constitutional challenge to the head and master statute, she and appellant Kirchberg agreed to the dismissal with prejudice of their Truth in Lending Act claims.

[3] Article 2346 provides that "[e]ach spouse acting alone may manage, control, or dispose of community property unless otherwise provided by law."

[4] However, either spouse may renounce his or her right to concur in the disposition of community immovables. La.Civ.Code Ann., Art. 2348 (Supp.1981).

II

By granting the husband exclusive control over the disposition of community property, Art. 2404 clearly embodies the type of express gender-based discrimination that we have found unconstitutional absent a showing that the classification is tailored to further an important governmental interest. In defending the constitutionality of Art. 2404, appellant Kirchberg does not claim that the provision serves any such interest.[7] Instead, appellant attempts to distinguish this Court's decisions in cases . . . which struck down similar gender-based statutory classifications, by arguing that appellee Feenstra, as opposed to the disadvantaged individuals in those cases, could have taken steps to avoid the discriminatory impact of Art. 2404. Appellant notes that under Art. 2334 of the Louisiana Civil Code, in effect at the time Mr. Feenstra executed the mortgage, Mrs. Feenstra could have made a "declaration by authentic act" prohibiting her husband from executing a mortgage on her home without her consent.[8] By failing to take advantage of this procedure, Mrs. Feenstra, in appellant's view, became the "architect of her own predicament" and therefore should not be heard to complain of the discriminatory impact of Art. 2404.

By focusing on steps that Mrs. Feenstra could have taken to preclude her husband from mortgaging their home without her consent, however, appellant overlooks the critical question: Whether Art. 2404 substantially furthers an important government interest. As we have previously noted, the "absence of an insurmountable barrier" will not redeem an otherwise unconstitutionally discriminatory law. Instead the burden remains on the party seeking to uphold a statute that expressly discriminates on the basis of sex to advance an "exceedingly persuasive justification" for the challenged classification. Because appellant has failed to offer such a justification, and because the State, by declining to appeal from the decision below, has apparently abandoned any claim that an important government objective was served by the statute, we affirm the judgment of the Court of Appeals invalidating Art. 2404.[9]

III

Appellant's final contention is that even if Art. 2404 violates the Equal Protection Clause of the Fourteenth Amendment, the mortgage he holds on the Feenstra home is nonetheless valid

---

[7] Nor will this Court speculate about the existence of such a justification. "The burden . . . is on those defending the discrimination to make out the claimed justification . . . ." *Wengler v. Druggist Mutual Ins. Co.*, 446 U.S. 142 (1980). We note, however, that the failure of the State to appeal from the decision of the Court of Appeals and the decision of the Louisiana Legislature to replace Art. 2404 with a gender-neutral statute, suggest that appellant would be hard pressed to show that the challenged provision substantially furthered an important governmental interest.

[8] Article 2334, as it existed in 1974, provided:

Where the title to immovable property stands in the names of both the husband and the wife, it may not be leased, mortgaged or sold by the husband without the wife's consent where she has made a declaration by authentic act that her authority and consent are required for such lease, sale or mortgage and has filed such a declaration in the mortgage and conveyance records of the parish in which the property is situated.

This Article has been replaced with a new code provision prohibiting either spouse from alienating or encumbering community immovables without the consent of the other spouse. *See* n. 3, *supra*.

[9] In so ruling, we also reject appellant's secondary argument that the constitutional challenge to Art. 2404 should be rejected because the provision was an integral part of the State's community property law and its invalidation would call into question the constitutionality of related provisions of the Louisiana Civil Code. The issue before us is not whether the State's community property law, as it existed in 1974, could have functioned without Art. 2404, but rather whether that provision unconstitutionally discriminated on the basis of sex.

because the Court of Appeals limited its ruling to prospective application. Appellant asserts that the opinion of the Court of Appeals is ambiguous on whether the court intended to apply its prospective ruling to his mortgage, which was executed in 1974, or only to those dispositions of community property made pursuant to Art. 2404 between December 12, 1979, the date of the court's decision, and January 1, 1980, the effective date of Louisiana's new community property law. Appellant urges this Court to adopt the latter interpretation on the ground that a contrary decision would create grave uncertainties concerning the validity of mortgages executed unilaterally by husbands between 1974 and the date of the Court of Appeals' decision.

While it is clear that the Court is correct in holding that the judgment of the Court of Appeals applied to the particular mortgage executed by Mr. Feenstra, it is equally clear that court's explicit announcement that its holding was to apply only prospectively means that no other mortgage executed before the date of the decision of the Court of Appeals is invalid by reason of its decision.

We decline to address appellant's concerns about the potential impact of the Court of Appeals' decision on other mortgages executed pursuant to Art. 2404. The only question properly before us is whether the decision of the Court of Appeals applies to the mortgage in this case, and on that issue we find no ambiguity.[10]

This case arose not from any abstract disagreement between the parties over the constitutionality of Art. 2404, but from appellant's attempt to foreclose on the mortgage he held on the Feenstra home. Appellant brought this declaratory judgment action to further that end, and the counterclaim asserted by Mrs. Feenstra specifically sought as relief "a declaratory judgment that the mortgage executed on [her] home by her husband . . . is void as having been executed and recorded without her consent pursuant to an unconstitutional state statute." Thus, the dispute between the parties at its core involves the validity of a single mortgage, and in passing on the constitutionality of Art. 2404, the Court of Appeals clearly intended to resolve that controversy adversely to appellant.

Accordingly, the judgment of the Court of Appeals is affirmed.

Justice STEWART, with whom Justice REHNQUIST; joins, concurring in the result.

Since men and women were similarly situated for all relevant purposes with respect to the management and disposition of community property, I agree that Art. 2404 of the Louisiana Civil Code Ann. (West 1971), which allowed husbands but not wives to execute mortgages on jointly owned real estate without spousal consent, violated the Equal Protection Clause of the Fourteenth Amendment.

[d]   Events After the Case

Although the Supreme Court of the United States effectively nullified the mortgage deed signed by Harold Feenstra, several months passed before the mortgage was actually released. Releasing a mortgage requires the payment of various fees and no attorney in New Orleans would do the paperwork for a poor woman from the Irish Bayou. Barbara Hausman-Smith had left Louisiana to practice law in Wisconsin while Feenstra's case was on appeal to the Fifth Circuit. It took a couple of phone calls to her old employer, NOLAC, before the Legal Assistance Corporation filed the release papers on Joan Feenstra's behalf. The last time Barbara Hausman-Smith heard about Joan Feenstra she was seriously ill with a brain tumor.

---

[10] Indeed, appellant's view that some ambiguity exists concerning the applicability of the Fifth Circuit's decision to the mortgage he held on the Feenstra home appears to be of recent vintage. Appellant Kirchberg never sought clarification from the Court of Appeals on the scope of its decision, and apparently regarded the court's judgment to be sufficiently adverse and binding on him to warrant seeking review on the merits before this Court.

[e]   Comments and Problem Notes

[*i*]   *Necessaries.* A common law doctrine provided that if a husband refused to supply his wife with items necessary for the household, the wife could purchase the items on her husband's credit, but the husband could not purchase items on his wife's credit. Court decisions since *Kirchberg* dealing with this sort of rule have found it unconstitutional. *See, e.g., Medical Business Associates, Inc. v. Steiner*, 183 A.D.2d 86, 588 N.Y.S.2d 890 (1992); *Jersey Shore Medical Center-Fitkin Hospital v. Baum Estate*, 84 N.J. 137, 417 A.2d 1003 (1980). Suppose that in response to the *Kirchberg* decision, a state legislature modified this old rule so that both a husband and a wife were responsible for paying for any typical household item. In addition, suppose the new rule provided that in case the seller was not paid, the husband would be primarily liable and the wife secondarily liable. That means that assets of the husband would be taken by the creditor before assets of the wife. Assume this priority rule was established because women generally are economically less well off than men. Does the result in *Kirchberg* require that the creditor be given a free choice as to which assets to attach to recover the debt for the household goods? One case raising such an issue was *Sharpe Furniture, Inc. v. Buckstaff*, 99 Wis. 2d 114, 299 N.W.2d 219 (1980), in which the Wisconsin Supreme Court, sympathizing with the economic plight of many women, declined to void the preference for using a husband's assets first.

Suppose that the Wisconsin rules also contained a provision that in case of a marriage between a white person and a black person, the assets of the white person, regardless of gender, were primarily available for payment of necessaries and the assets of the black person secondarily available. Would this rule survive Constitutional scrutiny? If not, should the gender based rule survive?

[*ii*]   *Gender, Religion and Equal Protection.* It has already been noted that the tenancy by the entirety at common law was a male-managed method for married couples to hold property concurrently. Though many states had altered that aspect of the tenancy by the mid-1970s, Massachusetts still followed the common law rule. In *D'Ercole v. D'Ercole*, 407 F. Supp. 1377 (D. Mass. 1976), the constitutionality of the male management feature of the tenancy was challenged. The litigation arose after Mary D'Ercole left her home to live with relatives when her husband refused to leave. Then, for religious reasons, she told her husband she wanted a legal separation rather than a divorce. In a divorce, the parties are able to remarry. In a legal separation, the marriage is not formally ended, although property matters and child custody issues are resolved. Alghier D'Ercole, the husband, preferred a divorce and refused to leave the couple's home, which was held in tenancy by the entirety, unless his wife agreed to a divorce. Mary D'Ercole sued, asking for a separation and her share of the use value of the house if it was not sold or the value of the home if it was sold. The court declined to interfere with the male management features of the tenancy by the entirety on the ground that Mrs. D'Ercole voluntarily chose that method of holding the house when she and her husband purchased it. Mary D'Ercole was left in a bit of a pickle. If she continued to insist on a legal separation, then the house would still be held in a tenancy by the entirety which would be managed by her separated husband. If she agreed to go forward with a divorce she violated her religious scruples. Eventually the parties divorced and the assets of the couple were split up.

First, is it clear that if *D'Ercole* was litigated today, it would come out the other way? Was the D'Ercoles' use of a tenancy by the entirety any more voluntary than the Feenstras' use of the Louisiana community property scheme? In one sense it was. There were other devices the

D'Ercoles could have used to hold their house—tenancy in common or joint tenancy with rights of survivorship—while all couples in Louisiana were automatically covered by the community property system. But Massachusetts did not have a "tenancy by the female entirety" calling for wifely property management. If such a holding device was desired, specially drafted documents would have been required. Is that additional hurdle enough to invalidate the male management features of Massachusetts' tenancy by the entirety?

Finally, a divorce automatically ends a tenancy by entirety. The split couple will own the asset as tenants in common. That means that they may each sell their share of the property, absent a requirement to the contrary in their separation agreement. Couples holding religious scruples prohibiting divorce may not so easily free up their property. They must both sign any document transferring their house and may not terminate the survivorship aspect of the tenancy by the entirety without first transferring the property to another person. Should not persons holding such beliefs be treated the same as other persons for purposes of dividing their property, even if they opt not to divorce? Why isn't *D'Ercole* a case involving discrimination on the grounds of both gender and religion?

In 1980, Massachusetts adopted legislation responding to *D'Ercole* that made tenancy by the entirety a jointly managed estate. MASS. GEN. LAW ch. 209, § 1 now provides:

> The real and personal property of any person shall, upon marriage, remain the separate property of such person, and a married person may receive, receipt for, hold, manage and dispose of property, real and personal, in the same manner as if such person were sole. A husband and wife shall be equally entitled to the rents, products, income or profits and to the control, management and possession of property held by them as tenants by the entirety.

> The interest of a debtor spouse in property held as tenants by the entirety shall not be subject to seizure or execution by a creditor of such debtor spouse so long as such property is the principal residence of the nondebtor spouse; provided, however, both spouses shall be liable jointly or severally for debts incurred on account of necessaries furnished to either spouse or to a member of their family.

This section was later construed to mean that either a husband or a wife was free to encumber the tenancy by the entirety in their residence, even if it occurred without the permission of the other, but that any creditor desiring to attach one spouse's interest in the tenancy by the entirety would have to wait until the end of the marriage to actually seize that interest.[99] In the case of death, the creditor would get something only if the debtor survived. In the case of divorce, the creditor could claim a share once the divorce was final and the tenancy by the entirety became a tenancy in common.

[*iii*]   *The* Get. Under traditional Jewish law, only a man may institute a religious divorce proceeding. If a woman obtains a civil divorce and remarries, traditional Jewish law would consider her remarriage adulterous, and her children to be illegitimate and unable to marry within the faith. So a woman following orthodox tradition would be in some difficulty if her husband refused to give her a *get*, a letter of divorce. Given the bar on establishment of religion in the First Amendment, could a state legislature enact a law that would penalize a man who refused to provide his wife a *get* unless she gave up all economic and child custody rights she is entitled to under that state's divorce system?

---

[99] Coraccio v. Lowell Five Cents Savings Bank, 415 Mass. 145, 612 N.E.2d 650 (1993).

In the Conservative Jewish tradition a *ketubah*, or marriage contract, form is now used that requires a man refusing to provide a *get* to appear before a *Beth Din* (Jewish Court) where he would be strongly encouraged to change his mind in order to live his life in accordance with the standards of Jewish law. In one case, the *ketubah* was treated as a legally binding document, and a husband was required to appear before a *Beth Din* under the terms of the agreement. Arguments that enforcement of the contract violated the First Amendment failed. *Avitzur v. Avitzur*, 58 N.Y.2d 108, 446 N.E.2d 136, 459 N.Y.S.2d 572 (1983). The Supreme Court refused to take certiorari in the case. You can find additional material on the *get* problem in Jessica Davidson Miller, *The History of the* Agunah[100] *in America: A Clash of Religious Law and Social Progress*, 19 WOMEN'S RTS L. RPTR. 1 (1997).

[*iv*] *Compare Age Discrimination.* Racial, religious, and gender based distinctions are not the only ones made in property law. Young children are customarily not permitted to manage their own financial affairs. Parents or guardians usually have that responsibility. Is a distinction based upon age subject to the more searching constitutional scrutiny given to classifications based on race or gender? For example, would it be constitutional for a state legislature to forbid any child under the age of seven from owning any property and to bestow full ownership of any asset coming to such a child upon a parent or guardian?

[*v*] *Discrimination on the Grounds of Familial Status.* Congress has adopted rules prohibiting discrimination on the basis of "familial status." "Familial status" is defined in 42 U.S.C. § 3602(k):

(k) "Familial status" means one or more individuals (who have not attained the age of 18 years) being domiciled with:

(1) a parent or another person having legal custody of such individual or individuals; or

(2) the designee of such parent or other person having such custody, with the written permission of such parent or other person.

The protections afforded against discrimination on the basis of familial status shall apply to any person who is pregnant or is in the process of securing legal custody of any individual who has not attained the age of 18 years.

It is interesting to compare this definition of family with those found in local ordinances attempting to limit occupancy to traditional families. The Supreme Court has invalidated some of these local ordinances as violations of the right to privacy. Compare *Belle Terre v. Boraas* with *Moore v. City of East Cleveland*, discussed at p. 908 below. Is the decision of Congress to protect only certain sorts of families from discrimination subject to Constitutional challenge?

[2] Tenancy by the Entirety and Creditor Access

[a] Married Families, Their Creditors and the Tenancy by the Entirety

As noted previously,[101] the adoption of married women's property acts led to quite diverse treatment of the tenancy by the entirety among the states. Some states left the estate untouched, others found the purposes of the married women's acts so inconsistent with the purposes of the tenancy by the entirety that they abolished it, and still others retained the device but removed

---

[100] *Agunah* is Hebrew for "chained woman."

[101] A summary of the tenancy by the entirety may be found beginning at p. 140.

the male management features. In those states where the tenancy by the entirety was retained, creditors were also treated in a variety of ways. Some states removed the ability of married couples to insulate entireties property from their personal creditors; others modified the old rules; and still others left the old rules intact. In those jurisdictions still following the nineteenth-century rules, the married couple's interests in entireties property may be taken for the joint debts of a married couple or the personal debts of a husband or wife purchasing family necessaries, but not for other personal debts of a husband or a wife.[102] The existence of such rules creates a fairly powerful reason for married couples to repose property in the entireties form. A debtor's interest in property held as a tenancy in common or joint tenancy is reachable by his or her creditors regardless of who the co-owner may be. But both halves of a tenancy by the entirety may be insulated from the creditors of only one owner. Although there are other debtor protection benefits of marriage, such as the homestead acts, the tenancy by the entirety is particularly prone to create disputes and litigation between families and creditors.

Take, for example, the dispute between the Sawadas and the Endos. On November 30, 1968, Masako and Helen Sawada were struck and injured by a car while walking in a crosswalk in Wahiawa on the island of Oahu in Hawaii. The car was driven by Kokichi Endo. The following summer, the Sawadas filed tort suits against Endo, alleging that his negligent driving caused the accident. Helen Sawada filed her action on June 17; Masako Sawada on August 13. Between these two filings, Kokichi Endo and his wife Ume Endo, owners of a house as tenants by the entirety, conveyed the fee simple absolute in the house as a gift to their two sons, Samuel H. Endo and Toru Endo. Despite the gift, Kokichi and Ume Endo remained in possession. The complaints in the negligence actions were not served on Kokichi Endo until October 29, 1969.[103] His son Toru delivered the papers to their attorney the following week. Then on November 11, 1969, Kokichi and Ume Endo transferred their savings account at the Bank of Hawaii and an account at an outfit called Finance Factors to their two sons and a woman named Frances S. Todani. The next day (!) their attorney filed answers to the negligence complaints of Masako and Helen Sawada.[104] The cases went to trial in early 1971, and the Sawadas obtained judgments totaling $25,045.74, plus $190.75 in court costs. Shortly after the trial, Ume Endo died. Absent the prior conveyance of the family home to their sons, Ume Endo's death would have left unencumbered title in the house in Kokichi Endo. However, attempts to execute the judgment by seizing the Endo home failed because of the title switch. The following litigation then was brought.

---

[102] In addition, the husband's management interest in entireties property could be taken to pay his debts. The existence of this rule without a similar ability in the wife to manage the property is now unconstitutional. *See* Kirchberg v. Feenstra, p. 179 above.

[103] It is not clear from the briefs in the case why it took so long to obtain service on Endo. Perhaps it took time to find him.

[104] Opening Brief at 4-5, Sawada v. Endo, Civil No. 34936 (Oct. Term, 1973).

[b] Opinions of the Supreme Court of Hawaii in *Sawada v. Endo*

Sawada v. Endo

Hawaii Supreme Court
57 Haw. 608, 561 P.2d 1291 (1977)

MENOR, JUSTICE.

This is a civil action brought by the plaintiffs-appellants, Masako Sawada and Helen Sawada, in aid of execution of money judgments in their favor, seeking to set aside a conveyance of real property from judgment debtor Kokichi Endo to Samuel H. Endo and Toru Endo, defendants-appellees herein, on the ground that the conveyance as to the Sawadas was fraudulent.

On November 30, 1968, the Sawadas were injured when struck by a motor vehicle operated by Kokichi Endo. On June 17, 1969, Helen Sawada filed her complaint for damages against Kokichi Endo. Masako Sawada filed her suit against him on August 13, 1969. The complaint and summons in each case was served on Kokichi Endo on October 29, 1969.

On the date of the accident, Kokichi Endo was the owner, as a tenant by the entirety with his wife, Ume Endo, of a parcel of real property situated at Wahiawa, Oahu, Hawaii. By deed, dated July 26, 1969, Kokichi Endo and his wife conveyed the property to their sons, Samuel H. Endo and Toru Endo. This document was recorded in the Bureau of Conveyances on December 17, 1969. No consideration was paid by the grantees for the conveyance. Both were aware at the time of the conveyance that their father had been involved in an accident, and that he carried no liability insurance. Kokichi Endo and Ume Endo, while reserving no life interests therein, continued to reside on the premises.

On January 19, 1971, after a consolidated trial on the merits, judgment was entered in favor of Helen Sawada and against Kokichi Endo in the sum of $8,846.46. At the same time, Masako Sawada was awarded judgment on her complaint in the amount of $16,199.28. Ume Endo, wife of Kokichi Endo, died on January 29, 1971. She was survived by her husband, Kokichi. Subsequently, after being frustrated in their attempts to obtain satisfaction of judgment from the personal property of Kokichi Endo, the Sawadas brought suit to set aside the conveyance which is the subject matter of this controversy. The trial court refused to set aside the conveyance, and the Sawadas appeal.

I

The determinative question in this case is, whether the interest of one spouse in real property, held in tenancy by the entireties, is subject to levy and execution by his or her individual creditors. This issue is one of first impression in this jurisdiction.

A brief review of the present state of the tenancy by the entirety might be helpful. Dean Phipps, writing in 1951,[1] pointed out that only nineteen states and the District of Columbia continued to recognize it as a valid and subsisting institution in the field of property law.[2] Phipps divided

---

[1] Phipps, *Tenancy by Entireties*, 25 TEMPLE L.Q. 24 (1951).

[2] According to ch. 52 of POWELL ON REAL PROPERTY (Matthew Bender), Phipps' count of states is significantly low. 25 states and the District of Columbia clearly recognize the tenancy by the entirety. Another five mention the holding form in their statutes and lack any other indication that its use is barred. According to my research, one of these, Illinois, now allows the tenancy by the entirety. Only 13 have expressly abandoned tenancies by the entirety, according to Powell. Four have conflicting holdings on the point and three others have taken no position. Editor.

these jurisdictions into four groups. He made no mention of Alaska and Hawaii, both of which were then territories of the United States.

In the Group I states (Massachusetts, Michigan, and North Carolina) the estate is essentially the common law tenancy by the entireties, unaffected by the Married Women's Property Acts. As at common law, the possession and profits of the estate are subject to the husband's exclusive dominion and control. In all three states, as at common law, the *husband* may convey the entire estate subject only to the possibility that the wife may become entitled to the whole estate upon surviving him. As at common law, the obverse as to the wife does not hold true. Only in Massachusetts, however, is the estate in its entirety subject to levy by the husband's creditors. In both Michigan and North Carolina, the use and income from the estate is not subject to levy during the marriage for the separate debts of either spouse.

In the Group II states (Alaska, Arkansas, New Jersey, New York, and Oregon) the interest of the debtor spouse in the estate may be sold or levied upon for his or her separate debts, subject to the other spouse's contingent right of survivorship. Alaska, which has been added to this group, has provided by statute that the interest of a debtor spouse in any type of estate, except a homestead as defined and held in tenancy by the entirety, shall be subject to his or her separate debts.

In the Group III jurisdictions (Delaware, District of Columbia, Florida, Indiana, Maryland, Missouri, Pennsylvania, Rhode Island, Vermont, Virginia, and Wyoming) an attempted conveyance by either spouse is wholly void, and the estate may not be subjected to the separate debts of one spouse only.

In Group IV, the two states of Kentucky and Tennessee hold that the contingent right of survivorship appertaining to either spouse is separately alienable by him and attachable by his creditors during the marriage. The use and profits, however, may neither be alienated nor attached during coverture.

It appears, therefore, that Hawaii is the only jurisdiction still to be heard from on the question. Today we join that group of states and the District of Columbia which hold that under the Married Women's Property Acts, the interest of a husband or a wife in an estate by the entireties is not subject to the claims of his or her individual creditors during the joint lives of the spouses. In so doing, we are placing our stamp of approval upon what is apparently the prevailing view of the lower courts of this jurisdiction.

Hawaii has long recognized and continues to recognize the tenancy in common, the joint tenancy, and the tenancy by the entirety, as separate and distinct estates. That the Married Women's Property Act of 1888 was not intended to abolish the tenancy by the entirety was made clear by the language of Act 19 of the Session Laws of Hawaii, 1903 (now HRS § 509-1). *See also* HRS § 509-2. The tenancy by the entirety is predicated upon the legal unity of husband and wife, and the estate is held by them in single ownership. They do not take by moieties, but both and each are seized of the whole estate.

A joint tenant has a specific, albeit undivided, interest in the property, and if he survives his cotenant he becomes the owner of a larger interest than he had prior to the death of the other joint tenant. But tenants by the entirety are each deemed to be seized of the entirety from the time of the creation of the estate. At common law, this taking of the "whole estate" did not have the real significance that it does today, insofar as the rights of the wife in the property were concerned. For all practical purposes, the wife had no right during coverture to the use and enjoyment and exercise of ownership in the marital estate. All she possessed was her contingent right of survivorship.

The effect of the Married Women's Property Acts was to abrogate the husband's common law dominance over the marital estate and to place the wife on a level of equality with him as regards the exercise of ownership over the whole estate. The tenancy was and still is predicated upon the legal unity of husband and wife, but the Acts converted it into a unity of equals and not of unequals as at common law. No longer could the husband convey, lease, mortgage or otherwise encumber the property without her consent. The Acts confirmed her right to the use and enjoyment of the whole estate, and all the privileges that ownership of property confers, including the right to convey the property in its entirety, jointly with her husband, during the marriage relation. They also had the effect of insulating the wife's interest in the estate from the separate debts of her husband.

Neither husband nor wife has a separate divisible interest in the property held by the entirety that can be conveyed or reached by execution. A joint tenancy may be destroyed by voluntary alienation, or by levy and execution, or by compulsory partition, but a tenancy by the entirety may not. The indivisibility of the estate, except by joint action of the spouses, is an indispensable feature of the tenancy by the entirety.

. . . .

We are not persuaded by the argument that it would be unfair to the creditors of either spouse to hold that the estate by the entirety may not, without the consent of both spouses, be levied upon for the separate debts of either spouse. No unfairness to the creditor is involved here. We agree with the court in *Hurd v. Hughes*, 12 Del. Ch. 188, 109 A. 418 (1920):

> But creditors are not entitled to special consideration. If the debt arose prior to the creation of the estate, the property was not a basis of credit, and if the debt arose subsequently the creditor presumably had notice of the characteristics of the estate which limited his right to reach the property.

12 Del.Ch. at 193, 109 A. at 420.

We might also add that there is obviously nothing to prevent the creditor from insisting upon the subjection of property held in tenancy by the entirety as a condition precedent to the extension of credit. Further, the creation of a tenancy by the entirety may not be used as a device to defraud existing creditors.

Were we to view the matter strictly from the standpoint of public policy, we would still be constrained to hold as we have done here today. In *Fairclaw v. Forrest*, 130 F.2d 829 (1942), the court makes this observation:

> The interest in family solidarity retains some influence upon the institution [of tenancy by the entirety]. It is available only to husband and wife. It is a convenient mode of protecting a surviving spouse from inconvenient administration of the decedent's estate and from the other's improvident debts. It is in that protection the estate finds its peculiar and justifiable function. 130 F.2d at 833.

It is a matter of common knowledge that the demand for single-family residential lots has increased rapidly in recent years, and the magnitude of the problem is emphasized by the concentration of the bulk of fee simple land in the hands of a few. The shortage of single-family residential fee simple property is critical and government has seen fit to attempt to alleviate the problem through legislation. When a family can afford to own real property, it becomes their single most important asset. Encumbered as it usually is by a first mortgage, the fact remains that so long as it remains whole during the joint lives of the spouses, it is always available in its entirety for the benefit and use of the entire family. Loans for education and other emergency expenses, for example, may be obtained on the security of the marital estate. This would not be possible where a third party has become a tenant in common or a joint tenant with one of the spouses, or where the ownership of the contingent right of survivorship of one of the spouses in a third party has cast a cloud upon the title of the marital estate, making it virtually impossible to utilize the estate for these purposes.

If we were to select between a public policy favoring the creditors of one of the spouses and one favoring the interests of the family unit, we would not hesitate to choose the latter. But we need not make this choice for, as we pointed out earlier, by the very nature of the estate by the entirety as we view it, and as other courts of our sister jurisdictions have viewed it, "[a] unilaterally indestructible right of survivorship, an inability of one spouse to alienate his interest, and, importantly for this case, a broad immunity from claims of separate creditors remain among its vital incidents." *In re Estate of Wall*, 440 F.2d at 218.

Having determined that an estate by the entirety is not subject to the claims of the creditors of one of the spouses during their joint lives, we now hold that the conveyance of the marital property by Kokichi Endo and Ume Endo, husband and wife, to their sons, Samuel H. Endo and Toru Endo, was not in fraud of Kokichi Endo's judgment creditors.

Affirmed

KIDWELL, JUSTICE, dissenting.

This case has been well briefed, and the arguments against the conclusions reached by the majority have been well presented. It will not materially assist the court in resolving the issues for me to engage in an extensive review of the conflicting views. Appellants' position on the appeal was that tenancy by the entirety as it existed at common law, together with all of the rights which the husband had over the property of his wife by virtue of the common law doctrine of the unity of the person, was recognized by the early decisions; that the Married Women's Act of 1888 (now Ch. 573, HRS) destroyed the fictional unity of husband and wife; that the legislature has recognized the continuing existence of the estate of tenancy by the entirety, but has not defined the nature or the incidents of that estate, HRS § 509-1, 509-2; that at common law the interest of the husband in an estate by the entireties could be taken by his separate creditors on execution against him, subject only to the wife's right of survivorship; and that the Married Women's Act merely eliminated any inequality in the positions of the spouses with respect to their interests in the property, thus depriving the husband of his former power over the wife's interest, without thereby altering the nature and incidents of the husband's interest.

. . . .

The majority reaches its conclusion by holding that the effect of the Married Women's Act was to equalize the positions of the spouses by taking from the husband his common law right to transfer his interest, rather than by elevating the wife's right of alienation of her interest to place it on a position of equality with the husband's. I disagree. I believe that a better interpretation of the Married Women's Acts is that offered by the Supreme Court of New Jersey in *King v. Greene*, 30 N.J. 395, 412, 153 A.2d 49, 60 (1959):

It is clear that the Married Women's Act created an equality between the spouses in New Jersey, insofar as tenancies by the entirety are concerned. If as we have previously concluded, the husband could alienate his right of survivorship at common law, the wife, by virtue of the act, can alienate her right of survivorship. And it follows, that if the wife takes equal rights with the husband in the estate, she must take equal disabilities. Such are the dictates of common equality. Thus, the judgment creditors of either spouse may levy and execute upon their separate rights of survivorship.

One may speculate whether the courts which first chose the path to equality now followed by the majority might have felt an unexpressed aversion to entrusting a wife with as much control over her interest as had previously been granted to the husband with respect to his interest. Whatever may be the historical explanation for these decisions, I feel that the resultant restriction upon the freedom of the spouses to deal independently with their respective interests is both illogical and unnecessarily at odds with present policy trends. Accordingly, I would hold that the separate interest of the husband in entireties property, at least to the extent of his right of survivorship, is alienable by him and subject to attachment by his separate creditors, so that a voluntary conveyance of the husband's interest should be set aside where it is fraudulent as to such creditors, under applicable principles of the law of fraudulent conveyances.

[c] Explanatory Notes

[*i*] *Creditors and the Operation of Survivorship Rules.* In *Sawada*, Kokichi and Ume Endo conveyed their home to their sons, Samuel and Toru. This action prevented the normal operation of the tenancy by the entirety survivorship rule which would have given Kokichi Endo fee simple absolute ownership of the house when his wife died in January, 1971. If the court had voided the conveyance to the sons, the Sawadas would have been able to execute on the house to collect their judgments after the death of Ume Endo. The Endos knew they were being sued for negligence in the Sawada auto accident cases; they transferred their entireties property to their children in order to avoid attachment at some future date by the Sawadas. If the Endos had not transferred the property to their children, the creditors could have waited until one or the other party died and executed on the land. The case, therefore, involves not only the inability of creditors of one spouse to seize possessory interests in entireties property during the owners' marriage, but also the ability of both spouses to transfer their survivorship interests completely out of reach of all creditors while retaining use of the asset.

[*ii*] *The Tenancy by the Entirety and the Hawaii Married Women's Act.* The Hawaii Married Women's Act of 1888, mentioned in the *Sawada* opinion, was much like that adopted in a number of jurisdictions of the United States. It provided that the:

[R]eal and personal property of a woman shall, upon her marriage, remain her separate property, free from the management, control, debts and obligations of her husband; and a married woman may receive, receipt for, hold, manage and dispose of property, real and personal, in the same manner as if she were sole; Provided, however, that no sale or mortgage of her real estate shall be valid without the written consent of her husband.[105]

---

[105] Section 1884, Ch. 123, The Civil Laws of the Hawaiian Islands 705 (1897). Until 1984, this statute remained unchanged in the Hawaii Code. *See, e.g.,* HAW. REV. STAT. § 573-1 (1976). In 1984, the same code section was amended to read:

The real and personal property of a spouse, upon marriage, shall remain that spouse's separate property, free from the management, control, debts, and obligations of the other spouse; and a spouse may receive, receipt for, hold, manage, and dispose of property, real and personal, in the same manner as if that spouse were sole.

The amendment reflects the recent pressure to remove gender bias from property statutes.

The Hawaiian courts did not read the act to abolish the tenancy by the entirety. In addition, as the *Sawada* dissent noted, they continued to enforce the notion that a married woman's property (including her interest in a tenancy by the entirety) could not be reached by her husband's creditors. The *Sawada* court, confronted with the gender equity problem for the first time, was certainly concerned with equalizing the status of husbands and wives. But such equalization could have been obtained either by insulating some or all of a husband's interest from his wife's creditors or by abolishing the notion of creditor insulation altogether. The existence of a specific statute benefitting wives (the old married women's act) made it difficult to select the second equalization option. Indeed, the Hawaii property statutes also provided that the *separate*, non-marital, property of each spouse was unavailable to creditors of the other spouse except for necessaries of the household.[106] But *Sawada* involved a somewhat different problem. The debt was owed by the *husband*, and the separate property was the survivorship interest of the *husband*. Is it fair to suggest that the majority opinion did not grapple with the question of whether the tenancy by the entirety should be insulated from creditors not only when one spouse's interest is threatened by a debt of the other spouse but also when the interest of one spouse is endangered by his or her own obligation? Despite the court's failure to grapple with this issue, the *Sawada* opinion was in step with decisions rendered in some other jurisdictions. A number of the states which have retained the tenancy by the entirety make it unreachable by any creditors, unless both spouses have agreed to encumber the property or the debt is owed by both spouses jointly.

[*iii*]   *Tenancies by the Entirety and Bankruptcy.* Disputes between creditors and couples holding entireties property arise in a number of circumstances. Bankruptcy proceedings have been a particularly "rich" source for such litigation. Bankruptcy law normally denies creditors access to tenancy by the entirety property to the extent that state law bars attachment. But intriguing disputes still have arisen. Among the most interesting is *In re Oliver*, 38 Bankr. 407 (D. Mass. 1984). After the decision in *D'Ercole v. D'Ercole*, discussed at p. 183 above, Massachusetts adopted a statute which substantially altered the nature of that state's common law tenancy by the entirety. Management authority of husbands and wives was equalized. In addition, if the family home was held by the entirety, the interest of each spouse in the home became immune from attachment by creditors of one spouse unless the indebtedness was for the purchase of family necessaries. Before filing for bankruptcy, David Oliver and his wife owned their house as tenants by the entirety as that estate was defined *prior* to the new legislation. Under the old rules, the husband's—but not the wife's—interest in the estate could be taken by creditors, including those in the bankruptcy proceeding. In November, 1980, they conveyed their house to a straw-person (some trustworthy soul who took title and promised to immediately reconvey it). The straw conveyed it back to the Olivers as tenants by the entirety, but since the new statute governed all conveyances made after February 11, 1980, the new debtor protection provisions applied to this conveyance.

After Oliver filed for bankruptcy on February 13, 1981, the bankruptcy trustee, charged with the duty of gathering the assets of the bankrupt for use in paying off debts, charged that the November, 1980 conveyance was made in fraud of creditors. The trustee prevailed under a provision of the federal bankruptcy statute defining a transfer to be fraudulent if it occurred less than a year before the bankruptcy filing for less than a reasonable value, and if the debtor was insolvent at the time of the transfer. This result was possible only because the old Massachusetts

---

[106] HAW. REV. STAT. § 510-8 (1976). It is interesting to note that use of the tenancy by the entirety has the apparent effect of turning survivorship interests into separate property.

law provided that husbands held attachable interests in tenancies by the entirety, while wives did not. Was reliance on the old Massachusetts scheme constitutionally permissible in light of *Kirchberg v. Feenstra*, p. 179 above?

[*iv*] ***Retroactive Application of Modern Gender Neutral Property Reforms.*** Another interesting case is *Perry v. Perry*, 341 S.E.2d 53 (N.C. App. 1986), in which the court construed the North Carolina statute equalizing management rights of husbands and wives to apply retroactively and found such retroactive application constitutional. Judge Martin decided that husbandly management prerogatives were unconstitutional, and that husbands could not obtain judicial enforcement of "vested" property rights that were unconstitutionally discriminatory. In the nineteenth century, most courts refused to apply married women's property reforms retroactively, arguing that husbands' interests in the property of their wives were "vested" and therefore unreachable by legislation. When, however, legislatures narrowed the scope of dower rights, courts generally applied those changes retroactively, claiming that dower rights were "inchoate" and non-possessory, arising only upon the death of a husband. Compare these sorts of holdings with the takings cases in Chapter 11.

[d] Problem Notes

[*i*] ***Marriage, Families and Creditors.*** Is there any justification for insulating property from creditor access just because one of the parties owning the property is married? There may be a number of reasons why certain property should be exempt from seizure by creditors. Most states provide some universal exemptions so that people may preserve an ability to pay for shelter and food. Do any of the reasons you can conjure up for exempting property generally from attachment by creditors apply only to a married couple? Furthermore, if there is something about marriage which suggests a need to protect property, why not adopt legislation which provides such protection for all assets owned by all married people, not just for tenancy by the entireties property? Homestead acts are a good example of a debtor protection benefit extended to all married couples with homes. Note that property held by a married couple as tenants in common or as joint tenants is treated differently from entireties property. If Wife owns a share of land as a tenant in common with Husband and is indebted to Creditor, Creditor may go after her share but not her husband's. Is the difference in treatment simply an anomaly left over from the slow accretion and construction of married women's legislation which altered the nature of the tenancy by the entirety while leaving the other concurrent estates alone? If all property owned by a married couple were pooled in a community, would it be easier to rationalize the relationships between creditors and families? For a review of some of these problems, *see* Note, *Sharing Debts: Creditors and Debtors Under the Uniform Marital Property Act*, 69 MINN. L. REV. 111 (1984).

[*ii*] ***"Intentional" Adoption of a Property Holding Pattern by Laypersons.*** In *Kirchberg v. Feenstra*, p. 179 above, Karl Kirchberg, the attorney attempting to foreclose on Joan Feenstra's house, argued that she could have protected her separate interest in the property by filing a declaration barring her husband from unilaterally encumbering the assets. The Supreme Court refused to use that "out" as a basis for confirming the vitality of the husband-management features of the Louisiana community property regime, noting instead that gender equality required that the same hurdles must be jumped by both genders in order to obtain certain property rights. Underneath this sort of problem lies a basic question of how much we presume people know about property law and the steps they must take to protect themselves. For example, those using a tenancy by the entirety are not likely to realize the debt protection benefits they gain until

a crisis strikes. Selection of the tenancy by the entirety may well be made (or seriously influenced) by the real estate agent handling the transaction leading to a married couple's purchase of property. Similarly, those using a tenancy in common or joint tenancy are unlikely to know that use of a tenancy by the entirety might lead to different treatment of creditors. To the extent that people act in ignorance of legal consequences, the application of different hurdle jumping rules for men and women has real consequences.

Several questions, unrelated to gender issues, surface as a result of this lack of knowledge by most lay persons. First, does the legal system have an obligation to educate the public? Very little public education about law is done. Is this because lawyers are not interested in letting people know about simple areas of the legal system for fear of losing business? Second, if few people are likely to know about the differences between a tenancy by the entirety and a tenancy in common, should we remove the differences? Should law reflect common understandings, historical traditions, or the "wisdom" of those "in the know?" Third, when various property holding patterns are used by lay persons without a full understanding of the reasons for selecting one pattern over another, is there any justification for a court to make use of the "four corners" rule of construction—if the document is unambiguous on its face, contrary understandings of the parties are irrelevant? Should we be more concerned with what the document says in order to retain some certainty in the meaning of documents on file in a Recorder of Deeds Office, or with the "real" intentions of the parties in order to put into effect the result most likely to conform to the parties' needs?

[iii]   *Unilateral Transfer of Tenancy by Entirety by One Spouse.* The central features of a tenancy by the entirety are survivorship and the ban on unilateral transfer by one spouse. In one unusual case, the ban on unilateral transfer was altered. Chester and Helen Lampert were in their fifties when they married in 1965. They each had adult children from prior marriages. Five years later they signed a postnuptial property agreement in which they each waived their right to take an elective share of the other's estate, released all claims for dower and curtesy, and agreed not to contest the other's will. In addition, Chester promised to deed their Anchorage, Alaska home to Helen and Helen promised to give Chester a life estate in the house in her will. About 10 years later, they were advised that significant estate tax savings could be realized if Chester began a gift program. So he executed three quit claim deeds conveying all his right, title and interest in a Hawaii condominium unit (held as tenants by the entirety by Chester and Helen) to Helen's daughter, Grace Stauffer. The three deeds were designed to give Stauffer the condominium in increments as the tax laws required. Helen Lampert never signed the three quit claim deeds. In 1988, Helen Lampert secretly visited an attorney and, claiming that her rights were never fully explained to her, amended her will to delete Chester's life estate in the Anchorage house. Three months later Helen died. A short time after that Chester died too. The estates then fell into litigation over the various properties. In *Estate of Lampert v. Estate of Lampert*, 896 P.2d 214 (Alaska 1995), the Alaska Supreme Court held that Helen's reneging on her promise to provide Chester a life estate gave Chester the right to rescind the postnuptial agreement. That freed him to take the Anchorage house as the survivor of the tenancy by the entirety and to demand his statutory share of Helen's estate. But as to the Hawaii condo, the court estopped Chester from denying the validity of his transfer to Grace Stauffer. Since he was the survivor, his signature served to transfer the fee in the condo to Stauffer. Was this the correct outcome?

[iv]   *Torts.* In *Sawada*, payment of damages to the victims of negligent drivers depended upon the way property owned by the defendant was held. When viewed from the perspective of the party injured as a result of tortious action, does this outcome make any sense?

[3] Community and Marital Property

[a] Background to *Gibbons v. Gibbons:* What is Marital or Community Property?

As noted in the introductory materials for this part of the chapter,[107] there are a number of similarities between community and marital property. Though marital property regimes govern only the disposition of property at divorce, while community property systems cover all aspects of property law for married couples, the presumptive rules governing decisions about whether property is marital or separate are basically the same as those governing the distinction between community and separate assets. When common law states began adopting marital property statutes to govern distribution of assets at divorce, their courts naturally looked to community property precedents for guidance.

New Jersey was among the first of the common law states to adopt a marital property system to govern the distribution of property upon divorce. A Divorce Law Study Commission was established in 1967 by the state legislature to make recommendations about changing the 1907 divorce statute. The commission's report was submitted to the governor and legislature in the spring of 1970, and divorce reforms were adopted the following year. The Divorce Law Study Commission recommendations largely related to the grounds that should be available for obtaining a divorce; little attention was paid to property division. This made some sense. Most divorcing couples have little or no property to divide. The major reform recommended by the commission was to create a no-fault ground for divorce based on separation for 18 months. The hope was that rationalizing the grounds for divorce would make divorce courts "honest" without increasing divorce rates. For decades, couples desiring a divorce would agree that one or the other of them would file a complaint alleging some fault ground, that the non-filing party would not contest the allegations, and that the filing party would testify that the defendant's actions fulfilled some fault ground even if they did not. Divorce court judges usually went along, demanding minimal proof of a ground like cruelty, and granting the desired divorces. But every once in a while, a bitter divorce contest would unfold or a judge would apply the rules more strictly. To some extent getting a divorce became a bit of a lottery. Most of the reform statutes required proof either that a separation was long standing or that the parties were irreconcilable. These sorts of hurdles were thought to be at least as demanding as those required by the day-to-day operation of the fault system in most places.[108] New Jersey elected to adopt a ground requiring separation for 18 months.

Despite the somewhat narrow focus of the New Jersey Divorce Commission, the reform bill was amended when it came to the floor of the state legislature to include an important provision on property dispositions. Divorce courts were given the authority to:

> [M]ake such award or awards to the parties, in addition to alimony and maintenance, to effectuate an equitable distribution of the property, both real and personal, which was legally and beneficially acquired by them or either of them during the marriage.[109]

---

[107] A summary of community and marital property may be found beginning at p. 141 above.

[108] A similar motivation was behind adoption in 1969 of a no-fault system in California, another one of the earliest states to adopt reforms. The story is told in great detail by an author quite critical of no-fault divorce in J. HERBIE DIFONZO, BENEATH THE FAULT LINE: THE POPULAR AND LEGAL CULTURE OF DIVORCE IN TWENTIETH CENTURY AMERICA (1997).

[109] N.J. STAT. ANN. § 2A:34-23. For a review of the history of the divorce reform legislation, *see* Painter v. Painter, 65 N.J. 196, 320 A.2d 484 (1974).

The adoption of the "equitable distribution" principle for divorcing couples was much more significant, at least in theory, than its simple wording suggested. Most common law states placed substantial barriers in the way of any judicial inclination to award property titled in the name of one spouse to the other spouse upon divorce. While the law varied from state to state, many permitted non-owning spouses to recover some or all of the property only if they could prove that payment for the asset came from their funds. Although it was quite possible that the size of alimony, maintenance and child support awards was influenced by the relative wealth of the parties, the perception was quite widespread that the system operated unfairly. Equitable distribution permitted the New Jersey courts, like those in community property states, to base property division decisions on factors other than ownership. Similar changes have been adopted in all common law states since 1970.

When the new statute first came before the New Jersey Supreme Court, in *Painter v. Painter*,[110] the court construed the new statute broadly to give all property, including inherited wealth, acquired by the couple during marriage, the status of "marital property." But it did not indicate precisely what circumstances might justifiably lead to the *distribution* of marital property to a non-acquiring spouse. Instead a number of factors were listed for divorce courts to use in resolving property disputes, including earning capacity, duration of the marriage, the nature of property brought to the marriage, present incomes, present mental and physical health, and the size of any gifts made by the spouses to each other during the marriage. Some community property states apply a similar system—despite the general rule that community assets are owned equally by each spouse—in order to allow trial judges some discretion to deal with the particular needs of the parties and their children.

The use of a laundry list approach to equitable distribution gives enormous discretion to trial judges confronted with divorce cases. The New Jersey Supreme Court, in a companion case to *Painter,* using language quite reminiscent of that found in community property opinions, attempted to give some guidance on the exercise of discretion by lower court judges, writing that:

> The public policy sought to be served is at least twofold. Hitherto future financial support for a divorced wife has been available only by grant of alimony. Such support has always been inherently precarious. It ceases upon the death of the former husband and will cease or falter upon his experiencing financial misfortune disabling him from continuing his regular payments. This may result in serious misfortune to the wife and in some cases will compel her to become a public charge. An allocation of property to the wife at the time of the divorce is at least some protection against such an eventuality. In the second place the enactment seeks to right what many have felt to be a grave wrong. It gives recognition to the essential supportive role played by the wife in the home, acknowledging that as homemaker, wife and mother she should clearly be entitled to a share of family assets accumulated during the marriage. Thus the division of property upon divorce is responsive to the concept that marriage is a shared enterprise, a joint undertaking, that in many ways it is akin to a partnership. Only if it is understood that far more than economic factors are involved, will the resulting distribution be equitable within the true intent and meaning of the statute.[111]

Though helpful in describing the court's reasoning, trial judges were still left with the day-to-day obligation to exercise discretion under the new statute. Indeed, the court insisted that use

---

[110] 65 N.J. 196, 320 A.2d 484 (1974).

[111] Rothman v. Rothman, 65 N.J. 219, 228-229, 320 A.2d 496, 501-502 (1974).

of a specific or presumptive rule calling for marital property to be evenly split was inappropriate. Use of such a presumption "would import into our law concepts now held chiefly, if not solely, in those states where community property law principles have gained acceptance, and we foresee that it might readily lead to unjust results."[112]

In the case of Mary and Felton Gibbons, who filed for divorce in August, 1976, after almost 24 years of marriage, Judge Tams indicated at the first pretrial conference that he had a strong preference for dividing property of long-term marriages fifty-fifty.[113] The statement of this preference made settlement of the Gibbons' marital dispute impossible. It also made it highly advantageous for Felton Gibbon's attorney to drag out the litigation for as long a time as possible. Legislative consideration of whether inherited assets should be treated as marital property was ongoing; delay could only work to Felton's advantage. In any case, the important facts on the financial status of Felton and Mary Gibbons were stipulated. The major legal issues—the validity of a presumption that property of long term marriages should be evenly split and the status of inherited property at divorce—became the main focus of the litigation.

Despite the warnings by the state Supreme Court that presumptive formulae were inappropriate, Judge Tams acted in accordance with his preference for equal division, placed all of the property of the Gibbons' in one pot, and gave Mary and Felton each half. He made no distinction between property titled individually or jointly, or between property obtained through the labor of one or the other party or through inheritance. Judge Tams noted:

> What is meant by equitable [division], . . . is up to the judge that hears the case and the only things I can look to in this case to determine what is equitable is the contribution which is made by each party to the marriage. I can't find any difference in the kind of contribution they made. They both clearly admitted on their testimony that years were spent in equal effort and the defendant saying he agreed with the statement which the plaintiff testified to.[114]

When the case was appealed, the appellate division agreed that an even split of property in many long term marriage cases made sense and that inherited property should be included in the pot to be divided.[115] While the appeal was pending, the state legislature was considering an amendment to the 1971 divorce reform legislation to exclude property acquired by way of gift, devise or bequest from marital property subject to equitable distribution. As originally drafted, the legislation also provided that the exclusion of inherited assets from property to be equitably distributed would apply only to divorce cases filed after the effective date of the legislation. After the trial court decision in *Gibbons*, Alfred Ferguson, Felton Gibbons' attorney, registered as a lobbyist[116] and urged members of the Senate committee handling the matter to delete the provision making the new rule govern only those complaints filed after the effective date of the statute. Ferguson also argued that equitable division of inherited property created intolerable incentives in New Jersey's family property law. Consider, he asserted, the position

---

[112] *Id.* at 232, n. 6. Some writers disagreed strongly with these sentiments, warning that wholly discretionary distribution systems are likely to operate unfairly for women. *See, e.g.,* Mary Ann Glendon, *Family Law Reform in the 1980's,* 44 LA. L. REV. 1553 (1984).

[113] Telephone Interview with Alfred Ferguson (July 23, 1986). Ferguson represented Felton Gibbons.

[114] Oral Decision of Judge Tam, Transcript of Trial: Divorce Proceedings p. 157, Gibbons v. Gibbons, Docket No. M-25688-75 (N.J. Super., Ch. Div.—Matrimonial Branch, Mercer County, Oct. 23, 1978).

[115] Gibbons v. Gibbons, 174 N.J. Super. 107, 415 A.2d 1174 (App. Div. 1980).

[116] Registration was arguably not required since Ferguson was actually representing a single client rather than a large enterprise, but he decided to register as a precautionary measure. Telephone Interview (Sept. 22, 1986).

of a spouse in a long term marriage who was unsure whether she would be well treated by her mate's will. The common law rules provided that such a spouse would get only property held in a concurrent estate with survivorship rights[117] and dower rights. If equitable division normally meant an even split of all the property, then she should file for divorce before her husband dies. Ferguson was correct in noting that the use of equitable division rules at divorce created potential anomalies when compared with treatment of property at death. But was he correct that removing inherited wealth from the property subject to equitable division did away with the anomaly? Doesn't the problem go much deeper, suggesting that if the rules of property division at divorce needed changing, then many of the common law property rules on concurrent estates were also ripe for review?

In any case, the statute was amended without the provision on effective date,[118] and Felton Gibbons took another appeal, this time to the New Jersey Supreme Court. In the opinion reprinted next, that court agreed to apply the new statute to the *Gibbons* case and remanded for entry of a new property division scheme excluding the inherited property. Reading the opinion provides you with an opportunity to consider why the most important exception to the rule presumptively categorizing all property acquired during the course of a marriage as marital or community allows assets acquired by gift, devise or bequest to be treated as separate property.

[b]   Opinion of the New Jersey Supreme Court in *Gibbons v. Gibbons*

Gibbons v. Gibbons

New Jersey Supreme Court
86 N.J. 515, 432 A.2d 80 (1981)

PASHMAN, J.

N.J.S.A. 2A:34-23 authorizes the trial court in divorce actions to "make such award or awards to the parties, in addition to alimony and maintenance, to effectuate an equitable distribution of the property, both real and personal, which was legally and beneficially acquired by them or either of them during the marriage." On December 31, 1980, the Legislature . . . amended this statute by excluding from equitable distribution all property "acquired during the marriage by either party by way of gift, devise or bequest . . . except . . . interspousal gifts." In this case we must decide whether the provision of the statute excluding gifts, devises or bequests from equitable distribution is to be given retroactive application and thus governs this divorce action, which was instituted and tried, as well as heard in the Appellate Division, before the effective date of the amendment.

---

[117] And note that if the concurrent estate was a joint tenancy, the survivorship interest was severable.

[118] As presently codified, the relevant portion of N.J. STAT. ANN. § 2A:34-23 reads as follows:

In all actions where a judgment of divorce or divorce from bed and board is entered the court may make such award or awards to the parties, in addition to alimony and maintenance, to effectuate an equitable distribution of the property, both real and personal, which was legally and beneficially acquired by them or either of them during the marriage. However, all such property, real, personal or otherwise, legally or beneficially acquired during the marriage by either party by way of gift, devise, or intestate succession shall not be subject to equitable distribution, except that interspousal gifts shall be subject to equitable distribution.

The original phrase "by way of gift, devise or bequest" was amended in 1988 to make sure that property passing by intestate succession was also included in the exception.

For the reasons below, we hold that the statute as amended should be given limited retroactive application and therefore governs this case. Consequently, we reverse the judgment of the Appellate Division, which held that gift and inheritance assets of defendant Felton Lewis Gibbons were subject to equitable distribution, and remand the case to the trial court for determination of the proper distribution of the marital assets in accordance with our opinion.

I

Plaintiff Mary Weitzel Gibbons and defendant Felton Lewis Gibbons were married on November 15, 1952, shortly after their graduation from college. Following Felton's military service, both went to graduate school and Felton received a Ph.D. in 1961. Mary, however, terminated her graduate studies prematurely to care for the couple's two children who were born in 1957 and 1958.

After Felton received his degree, he was appointed an associate professor at Princeton University. The wealth of their respective families enabled Felton, Mary and their children to live at a far higher standard of living than Felton's income alone would have permitted. In addition to their house in Princeton, the Gibbonses purchased real estate in Italy and Rhode Island. They also acquired an art collection. Most of the family's expenses were paid out of the income from gift or inheritance assets that Felton had received from his family. In addition, Felton set up trusts to pay for the children's educational expenses.

The couple began to experience marital difficulties in the early 1970's. Their continuing difficulties led to separation and then to the institution of this divorce action by Mary in August 1976. The parties ultimately agreed to proceed with the divorce on no-fault grounds and the case was tried in October 1978.

The trial court granted a dual judgment of divorce and ordered that the couple's joint assets, valued at $421,500, be divided equally. The court also valued the couple's gift and inheritance assets available for distribution,[1] held that these assets should likewise be divided equally, and thus ordered Felton to transfer $575,000 to Mary.[2] Subsequently, the court modified its judgment to include equitable distribution of Felton's pension, with a resultant award of an additional $14,750 to Mary.

Felton appealed the trial court's judgment to the Appellate Division. In a decision dated May 12, 1980 a divided panel affirmed the trial court's modified judgment. Two members of the panel believed that the trial court had properly exercised its discretion in dividing the couple's gift and inheritance assets equally as part of its equitable distribution of marital assets. One member of the panel dissented, expressing the following view:

Although equitable jurisdiction over inherited and gifted assets is clearly desirable, . . . it should be exercised only upon a finding that failure to do so will result in grossly disparate and unfair inequality, or some other manifest injustice . . . . Further, if distribution of such assets is ordered, it should not be in an amount greater than what is articulably related to what is needed to repair the inequity or relieve the injustice.

. . . .

---

[1] The court valued these assets as follows: Felton, $2,167,000; Mary, $1,016,000.

[2] Initially, Mary had sought alimony but after the commencement of the action she dropped her alimony claim and sought only equitable distribution.

On December 31, 1980, the equitable distribution statute was, as noted above, amended to provide that

all . . . property, real, personal or otherwise, legally or beneficially acquired during the marriage by either party by way of gift, devise or bequest shall not be subject to equitable distribution, except that interspousal gifts shall be subject to equitable distribution.

According to the committee statement accompanying the amendment, the rationale for it was that

in the majority of instances, the gift, devise or bequest in question will be from the parents or other relative of the recipient. To permit a compulsory division of the asset between the recipient and his spouse is contrary to the marital expectations of the recipient and the giving parent or relative. Since the efforts of neither spouse resulted in the gift, devise or bequest, it need not be regarded as a marital asset under the partnership concept of marriage. [*Senate Judiciary Committee Statement to Assembly, No. 1229 of 1980.*]

However, the amendment contained no indication as to whether it was to be applied to pending cases or only prospectively, and the legislative history offers no clear guidance on this point.[4] This lack of direction led the Governor to state, at the time he signed the bill into law, that because of the statute's silence on the question of retroactivity and the absence of a consensus in the Legislature on the point, "I believe the courts are the more appropriate forum to resolve that issue. They will have to decide based on existing principles of law, the extent to which this new law will affect pending cases." We now undertake to resolve the retroactivity issue.

II

The courts of this State have long followed a general rule of statutory construction that favors prospective application of statutes.

The rationale for this rule has been succinctly stated as follows:

It is a fundamental principle of jurisprudence that retroactive application of new laws involves a high risk of being unfair. There is a general consensus among all people that notice or warning of the rules that are to be applied to determine their affairs should be given in advance of the actions whose effects are to be judged by them. The hackneyed maxim that everyone is held to know the law, itself a principle of dubious wisdom, nevertheless presupposes that the law is at least susceptible of being known. But this is not possible as to law which has not been made. [2 Sutherland, *Statutory Construction*, § 41.02 at 247 (4th ed. 1973)]

However, as we have said on at least one occasion, the rule favoring prospective application of statutes, while "a sound rule of statutory interpretation . . . is no more than a rule of statutory

---

[4] As originally introduced and passed by the Assembly, A. 1229 contained the following express disclaimer of retroactivity: "[T]his amendatory act does not apply to any judgment entered and any action for divorce or divorce from bed and board filed prior to the effective date of this act." The Assembly Committee explained that the amendment "is not retroactive and does not apply to any judgment entered or any divorce action filed prior to the effective date of the act." *Assembly Judiciary, Law, Public Safety and Defense Committee Statement to Assembly, No. 1229 of 1980.* The Senate Judiciary Committee, however, deleted the disclaimer of retroactivity and explained that the effect of the deletion "was to make the provisions of Assembly Bill No. 1229 applicable to pending actions." *Senate Judiciary Committee Statement to Assembly, No. 1229 of 1980.* The Senate and Assembly passed the Senate Committee's version without further comment.

interpretation" and is not to be applied mechanistically to every case. *Rothman v. Rothman*, 65 *N.J.* 219, 224, 320 *A.2d* 496 (1974). Thus, there are well-settled rules concerning the circumstances in which statutes should be applied retroactively, where there is no clear expression of intent by the Legislature that the statute is to be prospectively applied only.

First, there are those statutes in which the Legislature has expressed the contrary intent; *i.e.*, that the statute be applied retroactively. In such cases the court should, as Justice Schreiber has said, "apply the statute in effect at the time of its decision." *Kruvant v. Mayor of Cedar Grove*, 82 *N.J.* 435, 440, 414 *A.2d* 9 (1980). This expression of legislative intent may be either express, that is, stated in the language of the statute or in the pertinent legislative history, or implied, that is, retroactive application may be necessary to make the statute workable or to give it the most sensible interpretation . . . .

In *Rothman v. Rothman, supra*, for example, we held that the equitable distribution statute should be retroactively applied because we were

. . . unable to believe that the Legislature intended its grant of power to undertake an equitable distribution of marital assets to apply solely to property acquired on or after the effective date of the act. Were this construction to be adopted, it would, in each case, become necessary to determine the date of acquisition of each asset acquired during marriage, often a difficult if not impossible task. A further question would arise should the particular property interest under consideration, though acquired after the effective date of the act, have been purchased with, or received in exchange for, money or other property owned before that date. Moreover, if [the statute were to be prospectively applied,] it has been estimated, apparently without exaggeration, that the full effect of the statute would not be felt for at least a generation.

Another category of cases in which we have held that statutes may be given retroactive application is that in which the statute is ameliorative or curative. *In re Smigelski*, 30 *N.J.* 513, 527, 154 *A.2d* 1 (1959). In *Smigelski* this rule was applied to permit retroactive application of an amendatory statute that set limits to the duration of juvenile commitments.

. . . .

However, even if a statute may be subject to retroactive application, a final inquiry must be made. That is, will retroactive application result in "manifest injustice" to a party adversely affected by such an application of the statute? The essence of this inquiry is whether the affected party relied, to his or her prejudice, on the law that is now to be changed as a result of the retroactive application of the statute, and whether the consequences of this reliance are so deleterious and irrevocable that it would be unfair to apply the statute retroactively . . . .

Applying these principles to the statute at issue in the present case, we conclude that the amendment to *N.J.S.A.* 2A:34-23 should be applied retroactively. Consequently, it applies to this case and all other cases presently on direct appeal or in which a final judgment has not been entered.

As a preliminary matter, there is no clear expression of legislative intent that the amendatory statute be applied prospectively. Indeed, it can even fairly be inferred from the legislative history that the Legislature intended the amendment to apply retroactively.

Furthermore, the exceptions to the rule of prospectivity weigh in favor of retroactive application. First, the amendment in question, like that in *Smigelski, supra*, is curative insofar as it reflects the Legislature's attempt to improve a statutory scheme already in existence. Second, retroactive application will bring the law into harmony with the settled expectations of many donors and donees. As was noted by the Senate Judiciary Committee in the legislative statement quoted above, "[t]o permit a compulsory division of [gift or inheritance assets] between the recipient and his spouse is contrary to the marital expectations of the recipient and the giving parent or relative." *Senate Judiciary Committee Statement to Assembly, No. 1229 of 1980.* In view of this legislative statement, giving the statute retroactive application will fulfill the essential purpose of retroactivity, to effectuate the current policy declared by the legislative body.

Nor will retroactive application of the statute result in manifest injustice to the adversely affected party, in this case, Mary Weitzel Gibbons. She claims that it is inequitable to apply the amended statute to her because she relied upon the law as it existed at the time she brought her action. In particular, she says she chose to seek equitable distribution only and not alimony as well because of what she believed was the broad scope of assets subject to equitable distribution. But clearly no manifest injustice will result from retroactive application of the amendatory statute to her case since any orders pertaining to alimony or other support "may be revised and altered by the court from time to time as circumstances may require," *N.J.S.A.* 2A:34-23.

Accordingly, we reverse the judgment of the Appellate Division and remand this case to the trial court for determination of the correct equitable distribution in accordance with the statute as amended.

[c]   Explanatory Notes

[*i*]   *Retroactivity.* Did *Gibbons* really involve an issue of retroactivity? The case was pending at the time the legislature amended the divorce statute to exclude inherited property from the equitable division scheme. Suppose the "new" rule excluding inherited wealth was made by the New Jersey Supreme Court in this case, rather than by the legislature. The odds are quite high that the court would have applied the new rule to Mary and Felton Gibbons. Should it make any difference that the change in legal norms was announced by the legislature rather than by the courts?

In some sense every decision altering expectations of one of the parties to litigation has an element of retroactivity in it. Regardless of how the New Jersey Supreme Court decided *Gibbons*, this sort of retroactivity was present. Mary Gibbons argued that her legal strategy depended on the continued existence of the old rule. She claimed that she dropped her claim for alimony because she felt she was entitled to share the inherited wealth of her husband. Courts usually do not take this sort of retroactivity claim very seriously. Rather, it is treated as an unavoidable consequence of having a court system.

It is also fair to note that *Gibbons* was not the sort of serious retroactivity case in which long settled principles of property law are dramatically changed to the significant financial detriment of one of the litigants. All marital as well as community property regimes other than New Jersey treated inherited assets as individually rather than jointly held at the time *Gibbons* was litigated. The adoption by New Jersey of the standard used everywhere else was hardly an earth shaking event.

[*ii*]   *Marital Property.* The adoption of equitable division statutes like that in New Jersey has dramatically altered the language used in divorce actions in common law states. Before deciding upon the exact property division to be made, courts must first determine which assets are eligible for division and which are not. *Marital property* must be distinguished from *separate*

property. Thus, in *Gibbons* the court decided that inherited property was not subject to equitable division and remanded to the trial court for a recomputation of the property portion of the divorce decree. Other sorts of property may also be excluded from the marital property pie, including property held separately by the parties before their marriage. This entire structure is laid on top of the pre-existing common law scheme. The consequences of holding property in a tenancy in common, or any other device, may be altered for purposes of divorce by the new marital property concept, but not for death or other purposes. The legal pattern is a bit of a crazy quilt.

[*iii*]   *Community Property as a Model.* Despite the statements of the New Jersey Supreme Court describing the differences between common law and community law jurisprudence, marital property is like community property in some significant ways. Though some community property states presume that community property should be equally divided at divorce, while statutes in most marital property states call for equitable division, the process of labeling property as marital is almost identical to that used to denominate community property. It should not be surprising, therefore, that several common law states are beginning to seriously consider adopting a community property system rather than continue to patch their common law regimes.

In 1983, the National Conference of Commissioners on Uniform State Laws promulgated the Uniform Marital Property Act, 9A U.L.A. 97 (1987), which is basically a model community property statute, and recommended that states adopt it. So far, only Wisconsin has done so. Section 17 of the Uniform Act, dealing with division of property upon divorce, provides that after divorce, "each former spouse owns an undivided one-half interest in the former marital property as a tenant in common except as provided otherwise in a decree or written consent."

Two fundamental differences between common law systems and community property systems dominate contemporary property reform debates. First, in a community property system all assets of the married couple, except property owned before marriage and property received by way of gift, inheritance or devise, is presumed to be held by the marriage as a unit—a community. Specific agreements or actions evidencing a mutual intention to treat property as separate from the community are required to alter operation of the basic rule. This is the part of the community property regime that has been adopted by common law states using marital property systems at divorce. Second, the consequences of labeling an asset as part of the community is carried through all major family property events—transfer, divorce, and death. Commonality of ownership means that at death half of the community property goes to the surviving spouse and the other half passes through the estate of the deceased person, that transfer of an asset requires the agreement of both parties,[119] and that division of community property at divorce will generally be fifty-fifty.[120] The notion of marriage as an economic partnership rather than as a sharing of economically independent lives provides the theoretical basis for the community.

[*iv*]   *Reality of Divorce.* Whether community property systems actually operate to provide women greater protection from economic difficulties than common law systems is subject to great doubt. Divorce generally leaves women economically much less well off than their

[119] In a typical common law state, both parties' signatures are required to transfer real property because of dower and curtesy or their modern replacements, but personal property owned by one spouse may be freely transferred by a single signature even if it is marital property.

[120] Most of the community property states permit some variation from the community property norm at divorce, making the community and common law divorce systems now operating in the vast majority of states appear very similar. Whether they operate similarly is not really known.

ex-husbands in both common law and community property states.[121] There are a number of reasons for this. Most divorcing couples are not wealthy. Property division is largely an academic question for them. In such cases, post-divorce economic status depends on the ability to obtain income in the future. The lower average income of women automatically places property-less divorced females at an economic disadvantage. Even for couples with some assets, equal division of property accumulated during the marriage is not likely to leave women as well off as men. Women generally earn less than men. They also enter marriage with less property and therefore have less separate wealth than men. Finally, women still get custody of any children of their marriages in vastly greater proportions than men. Raising children is obviously expensive. Absent significant child support awards against non-custodial parents, dividing the capital assets of a marriage is unlikely to leave ex-husbands and ex-wives on an equal footing. This is not to say that husbands necessarily end up better off after a divorce than before. Setting up two households may leave both parties in worse shape. But there is much evidence that the movement to equally divide the accumulated assets of a marriage still is likely to leave ex-wives, particularly those with children, in significantly poorer economic condition than their ex-husbands.

This has led some women to advocate abolition of both the discretion oriented common law system and the more uniform community property system, at least for divorcing couples with children. States, the argument goes, should instead adopt a child oriented distribution system in which decisions are first made about the financial needs of the children, the appropriate treatment of the family home in light of the children's need for stability in living arrangements, and the best way to pay for the children's care from the assets and incomes of the divorcing couple. Assets left after these calculations would be split between the adults.[122]

[d]   Problem Notes

[i]   *The Nature of the Marital Community. Gibbons* is a typical case in many ways. Though it involved people much wealthier than the norm, it exemplified a basic thread of community and marital property law—the exclusion of inherited and donated property from common ownership by husbands and wives. Does this exclusion serve any significant social purposes? Presumably the argument is that family wealth should stay within blood lines unless a contrary intent appears. It is an atavistic sort of argument, one based on the assumption that ancestral lines should have continued force in present day culture. It is much like the contemporary drive to permit inheritance of publicity rights—the right to prevent others from making commercial use of your name, likeness or voice without your permission.[123] This argument

---

[121] The most commonly cited study on this issue is Lenore J. Weitzman, *The Economics of Divorce: Social and Economic Consequences of Property, Alimony and Child Support Awards*, 28 UCLA L. REV. 1181 (1981). Though Weitzman's treatment of the data has been strongly criticized as overstating the problem in books like SUSAN FALUDI, BACKLASH: THE UNDECLARED WAR AGAINST AMERICAN WOMEN (1991), there is general agreement that divorced women as a class have exited marriage worse off than their ex-husbands. Widowhood has not been as intensively studied.

[122] *See, e.g.*, Nanette K. Laughrey, *Uniform Marital Property Act: A Renewed Commitment to the American Family*, 65 NEB. L. REV. 120 (1986); Mary A. Glendon, *Family Law Reform in the 1980's*, 44 LA. L. REV. 1553 (1984); Martha Fineman, *Implementing Equality: Ideology, Contradiction and Social Change, A Study of Rhetoric and Results in the Regulation of the Consequences of Divorce*, 1983 WIS. L. REV. 789; Comment, *The Marital Home: Equal or Equitable Distribution?*, 50 U. CHI. L. REV. 1089 (1983) (Martha Davis). *See also*, Frances Olsen, *The Family and the Market: A Study of Ideology and Legal Reform*, 96 HARV. L. REV. 1497, 1540-1541 (1983). Some have even recommended that the institution of separate property be abolished. Richard Chused, *Family (Proper)ty*, 1 GREEN BAG 125 (1998).

[123] Publicity rights are taken up in the last chapter of the book.

creates a significant tension in the theory giving rise to the community property ideal. If two persons marry and thereby agree to establish an economic partnership, why should that partnership fail just because one or both partners came from a wealthy family? Compare this exception to the community or marital property norm with some other common practices:

Ante-nuptial and Post-nuptial Agreements. If the parties to a marriage agree to treat certain assets as outside (or inside) the marital community, they may do so. Strict enforcement of the presumption designating property as in the community will create a strong incentive for some parties to demand the signing of agreements by their future marital partners declaring certain property to be separate assets. Given the heightened incentive to draft contracts that would be created by presumptively including inherited assets within the community, why should the legislature care about narrowing the scope of the community by excluding inherited assets? On the other hand, why should we allow people to contract out of marital or community property regimes? If we truly believe that marriage is a partnership, why not create a body of law that treats marriage that way all of the time?

Tort Damages. In some states, damages earmarked as recovery of lost wages are generally treated as marital or community property, but those for pain and suffering are separate assets. It is as if pain can never be shared! Query? In a growing number of states all tort damages are subject to equitable division at divorce.[124]

Capital Gains and Losses. Gains and losses from investments generally "run with the property." If the gain is from community or marital property it is also community or marital; if it is from separate property it too is separate. Is that sensible? Why shouldn't gains accruing from separate property during marriage be treated as community assets?

Lottery Winnings. Luck of the draw money is probably community or marital property. Is there really any difference between winning a lottery and being lucky enough to be born into a family likely to leave you with a great deal of inherited wealth?

[ii]   Death and Marital Assets. A combination of techniques are used in the various common law states to guarantee a certain degree of economic security to surviving spouses. Dower and curtesy, where they still exist, provide a share of property for the life of the survivor. Mandatory share statutes require that a certain portion of an estate be left to a surviving spouse. Homestead or other exemption statutes may also provide continued access to the marital home or other property for the survivor. Testamentary freedom—the right to dispose of property as you wish through a will—is limited by all of these schemes. Community property states draw the line between concern for surviving spouses and testamentary freedom somewhat differently, requiring that half of the community go to the survivor unless that disposition is waived by agreement. How much latitude should a spouse have to deny property to her or his mate? If you think a surviving spouse should always be able to get at least some of the property of a dead partner, should ante-nuptial and post-nuptial contracts also be limited in their effect? For example, should it be possible for a widow to defeat an ante-nuptial contract that required all property earned by the husband during the marriage to be treated as separate property? Would it make any difference if the husband was also supporting children from a prior marriage?

---

[124] *See* Lopiano v. Lopiano, 247 Conn. 356 (1998).

[e] Spousal Elections at Death of a Spouse: *Carr v. Carr*

As noted in the introductory comments to this portion of the text,[125] the primary area of difference between community and marital property states involves treatment of property owned by married couples when one of them dies. In community property states a surviving spouse is entitled to half of the community property and, in some states, a share of the deceased spouse's separate property. If a deceased spouse's will does not leave the survivor the required amount, the survivor may reject the will and demand the statutory share. In common law states, even after their adoption of marital property regimes for divorce, the old inheritance rules usually were left intact. Property titled in the name of a deceased spouse would flow to that spouse's estate even if it was marital property. Though mandatory share statutes also exist in common law states, they do not require that half of the jointly accumulated property be left to the survivor.

The case reprinted here presents an example of how marital property and mandatory share statutes interact. When Mr. H. Thomas Carr fell ill shortly before his divorce case was scheduled to come to trial, his attorney sought and obtained a continuance. He died shortly thereafter, leaving Joyce Carr a widow rather than an ex-wife. The courts were left to sort out how to handle the property of a floundering marriage ended by death rather than divorce.

Joyce Carr v. H. Thomas Carr

Supreme Court of New Jersey
120 N.J. 336, 576 A.2d 872 (1990)

The opinion of the Court was delivered by

HANDLER, J.

In this case, a wife brought an action for divorce against her husband. Her husband's death before trial effectively terminated the divorce action. The issue arising from the death of the husband during the pendency of the divorce action is whether the wife is entitled either to statutory equitable distribution of the marital assets under the divorce laws or to a statutory elective share of her deceased husband's estate under the probate code. The courts below concluded that neither statutory scheme provided the surviving wife with an enforceable interest against marital assets legally held by the husband. The wife's plight, likened to a "black hole," gives rise to the ultimate issue: whether, in this situation, the surviving wife is entitled to any relief at all.

I.

Joyce and Thomas Carr were married on December 9, 1966. Thomas Carr owned and operated an engineering firm; Joyce Carr was a housewife. The Carrs did not have any children although Mr. Carr had children from a prior marriage. In June of 1983, after seventeen years of marriage, Mr. Carr left Mrs. Carr. On July 29, 1984, Mrs. Carr filed a complaint for divorce on the grounds of desertion, N.J.S.A. 2A:34-2(b), and sought alimony, equitable distribution of their marital assets, N.J.S.A. 2A:34-23, and counsel fees. She also filed a complaint for divorce from bed and board. N.J.S.A. 2A:34-3. Mrs. Carr was subsequently awarded pendente lite support of $125.00 per week plus medical, insurance, car, and household expenses.

Substitutions of defense counsel and extended discovery prolonged the divorce proceeding. Trial was set eventually for August 19, 1987. On that day, however, defendant did not appear,

---

[125] *See* p. 141 above.

and his attorney moved to adjourn the trial due to his client's hospitalization and illness. Five days later, Mr. Carr died. He left his entire estate to his children.

After Thomas Carr's death, Joyce Carr filed an order to show cause to substitute the executor of defendant's estate as a defendant, to restrain the disposition of the decedent's estate, to continue pendente lite support payments, and requested a hearing to resolve the issues of alimony, equitable distribution, and fees.

The Chancery Division, Family Part, held that the divorce action and claims for alimony and equitable distribution were terminated by Mr. Carr's death, and discontinued Mrs. Carr's pendente lite support. The court, however, viewed the action as essentially one of equity and allowed the plaintiff to amend her complaint to pursue alternate equitable remedies "to prevent a failure of justice." It denied defendant's motion to dismiss the plaintiff's actions, enjoined the executor from distributing the assets of the estate to its beneficiaries, and granted plaintiff's motion for attorneys' fees.

Plaintiff then filed an amended complaint seeking distribution of the marital assets based on equitable grounds. She also appealed the trial court's dismissal of the alimony and equitable distribution claims. The Appellate Division, in a reported decision, unanimously affirmed the trial court's opinion. *Carr v. Carr*, 229 N.J. Super. 370, 551 A.2d 989 (App. Div. 1988). The appellate court held that the trial court correctly construed the equitable distribution and elective share statutes to preclude statutory relief in these circumstances but that equitable relief was available to plaintiff. We granted defendant's petition for certification.

II.

In this case, plaintiff's initial recourse was to the equitable distribution statute, N.J.S.A. 2A:34-23, since she had brought an action for divorce that specifically included a claim for equitable distribution . . . .

The courts below, correctly in our view, concluded that the equitable distribution statute does not authorize the distribution of marital assets except upon the divorce of the parties. By the plain terms of the statute, a spouse's right to share in marital property by virtue of equitable distribution arises when "a judgment of divorce . . . is entered." The Court has consistently interpreted the statute to authorize a distribution of marital assets only on the condition that the marriage of the parties has been terminated by divorce. *Painter v. Painter*, 65 N.J. 196, 216 n. 5, 320 A.2d 484 (1974); *Rothman v. Rothman*, 65 N.J. 219, 228, 320 A.2d 496 (1974).

The current controversy arises because the marriage between the Carrs was terminated not by divorce, but by Mr. Carr's death. Divorce proceedings abate with the death of one of the parties. The lower courts held, and the plaintiff concedes, that the death of either party to a divorce terminates the cause of action as to the "status of the marriage relationship" between the parties. Thus, with the death of her husband, a judgment of divorce was no longer attainable by Mrs. Carr and, derivatively, equitable distribution under the statute also became unattainable.

Some New Jersey courts have recognized that in highly unusual circumstances some aspects of statutory equitable distribution and related forms of relief may precede a divorce judgment or survive a spouse's death before divorce. See, e.g., *Graf v. Graf*, 208 N.J. Super. 240, 505 A.2d 207 (Ch. Div. 1985) (prior to a judgment of divorce, court has authority to order sale of personalty when necessary to ensure maintenance and support of wife and children); *Fulton v. Fulton*, 204 N.J. Super. 544, 499 A.2d 542 (Ch. Div. 1985) (after death of husband, court allowed entry of final judgment of divorce based on previously-taken testimony); . . . *Jacobson v. Jacobson*, 146 N.J. Super. 491, 370 A.2d 65 (Ch. Div. 1976) (husband who murders wife during pendency of divorce action may not object to equitable distribution); *Olen v. Melia*, 141 N.J. Super. 111, 357 A.2d 310 (App. Div.) (final judgment of divorce entered after one party had died prior to the entry of the final order and where trial court had already issued an oral opinion and entered a judgment) . . . . The circumstances exemplified by these cases do not undermine the rule that, ordinarily, equitable distribution of marital assets arises only with the adjudication of divorce. This case, not surrounded by any of the circumstances that make a surviving spouse's claim unusual or exceptional, is governed by the general rule: statutory equitable distribution is conditioned on the termination of marriage by divorce.

The courts below also concluded that the elective-share provision of the probate code, N.J.S.A. 3B:8-1, did not afford relief to plaintiff. We agree.

In 1981, the Legislature adopted a modified version of the Uniform Probate Code (U.L.A.) §§ 1-101 to 8-102 (West 1983) governing the estates of intestate decedents. L.1981, c. 405; N.J.S.A. 3B:1-1 to 3B:29-1 ("code"). The new code included a major revision of the antecedent common-law right of dower. It provided a surviving spouse with an "elective share" or forced share of the estate in the event the spouse is "disinherited." N.J.S.A. 3B:8-1. The elective-share provision in part specifies:

> If a married person dies domiciled in this State . . . the surviving spouse has a right of election to take an elective share of one-third of the augmented estate under the limitations and conditions hereinafter stated . . . .

Under certain circumstances, a surviving spouse is not entitled to an elective-share. N.J.S.A. 3B:8-1 explicitly excludes a surviving spouse if (1) at the time of death decedent and surviving spouse are living separate and apart in separate habitations; or (2) decedent and surviving spouse had ceased to cohabit as man and wife, either as the result of (a) a judgment of divorce from bed and board; or (b) circumstances that would give rise to a cause of action for divorce or nullity of the marriage in New Jersey . . . . Thus, the elective-share statute prevents a spouse, if divorced, from claiming the right to share in decedent's estate, and also prevents a spouse from such an entitlement if the parties no longer live together . . . .

Moreover, it does not appear that the conditions restricting the class of persons entitled to the statutory elective share were enacted through legislative inadvertence or clearly lead to absurd, as opposed to harsh, results . . . .

Under an early draft of the elective-share statute, disentitlement would only occur if the parties had been living separate and apart in different habitations and had obtained a judgment of divorce, or ceased to cohabit as married under circumstances which would have given rise to a cause of action for divorce. This version was more similar than the enacted statute to the approach of the Uniform Probate Code, U.P.C. § 2-201(a), under which only a judgment of divorce will result in disqualification for an elective share. A committee changed the early draft's "and" to an "or." Senate Jud. Comm'n, Statement to A. 18 (Nov. 19, 1979). Hence, as enacted, a separation without a judgment of divorce or cause of action for divorce can remove a spouse from the class of persons entitled to an elective share.

We thus concur in the reasoning and conclusions of the lower courts. The wife's entitlement to equitable distribution under N.J.S.A. 2A:34-23 abated with the termination of the divorce action on her husband's death; and the wife, having separated from her husband and embarked on a divorce action with good cause prior to her husband's death, is not entitled to an elective share of his estate under N.J.S.A. 3B:8-1.

III.

The ultimate issue is whether judicial relief can be afforded a surviving wife who, at the time of her husband's death, is not statutorily entitled either to equitable distribution because she had not yet obtained a divorce or to an elective share because she was then obtaining a divorce. If she is not entitled to relief under either statute, a plight created by her husband's supervenient death, we must determine whether the dual statutory schemes express a design to deny any relief at all.[2]

. . . .

Statutory equitable distribution is based on the philosophy that marriage is a joint enterprise in which the interest in and entitlement to its underlying property is also joint and mutual. The entitlement to marital property is not dependent on economic contributions as such. Less tangible efforts are recognized as equally valuable to the overall prosperity of the familial entity.

. . . .

The distinctive interest vindicated by equitable distribution is highlighted by contrasting it with alimony, which "is awarded to defray the expenses of supporting a spouse post divorce, whereas, fundamentally, equitable distribution is awarded for recognized contributions that each spouse has made toward the accumulation of property during the time span of the viable coverture." *Mendell v. Mendell*, 162 N.J. Super. 469, 475-76 (1978). As stated by the Court in *Chalmers v. Chalmers*, 65 N.J. at 194, 320 A.2d 478 (1974), equitable distribution secures for the spouse "what really belongs to him or her."

The judiciary has been responsible for defining, explaining, and applying the doctrine of equitable distribution. When the Divorce Reform Act . . . was enacted [in 1971], the equitable distribution provision was inserted during passage with virtually no discussion or antecedent history. Much later, in 1988, after several years of judicial experience with the equitable distribution statute, the Legislature [amended the statute, adding language] . . . which provides in part that

[i]n making an equitable distribution of property, the court shall consider . . .

i. The contribution of each party to the acquisition, dissipation, preservation, depreciation or appreciation in the amount of value of the marital property, as well as the contribution of a party as a homemaker . . . .

It shall be a rebuttable presumption that each party made a substantial financial or nonfinancial contribution to the acquisition of property while the party was married.

Thus, the legislature in effect reconfirmed the judicial perception and articulation of the equitable principles that undergird the statutory entitlement to equitable distribution of marital assets.

---

[2] Stretching a metaphor, the parties and commentators characterize the surviving wife's plight in this setting as a "black hole." This term has come into common parlance and is derived from the astrophysical expression that describes an area of the universe created by collapsing stars, giving the appearance of a "black hole," in which the pull of gravity is irresistible and irreversible. The term is of recent origin. It was coined in 1969 by the American scientist, John Wheeler. Hawking, *A Brief History of Time* (Bantam: 1988) at 81.

We can thus discover in our matrimonial laws a confluence of legislative and judicial understanding, embodying a clear and strong public policy with respect to the cognizable rights of spouses in marital property. These rights arise from the marital relationship in which, presumptively, both parties contribute in varied ways to the creation, acquisition and preservation of their familial property and, thereby, secure a protectable interest to share, possess, and enjoy that property.

The underlying philosophy of the probate code, as it may address a married couple who had become estranged, is no less grounded in legislatively-sensed equities. The code recognizes that both the needs and the rights of a surviving spouse justify a forced or elective share against the decedent's estate. The history of the current elective share provision of the Code discloses a legislative recognition that the existing law allowed spouses to deplete their respective estates during their lifetimes by gift, or at death by other means, effectively resulting in a complete disinheritance of the surviving spouse. A clear purpose of the new code was to eliminate this unfairness. See, e.g., Assembly Jud., Law, Pub. Safety and Defense Comm'n, Statement to A. 28 (Feb. 23, 1978); Senate Jud. Comm'n, Statement to A. 18 (Nov. 19, 1979). However, some perceive that a public policy behind the elective-share provision implicitly acknowledges that "the contributions, whether financial or not, of a surviving spouse during marriage" justify resort to marital assets. See Reid, "Post-Mortem Divorce: Should a Spouse's Statutory Inheritance Rights Depend on Divorce Standards?", 5 *Seton Hall Legis. J.* 185, 186 (1982). This policy is consistent with the principle that in marriage each spouse contributes to and creates marital assets and thereby has an entitlement in such property that is protectable when the marriage ends.

We conclude, therefore, that the principle that animates both statutes is that a spouse may acquire an interest in marital property by virtue of the mutuality of efforts during marriage that contribute to the creation, acquisition, and preservation of such property. This principle, primarily equitable in nature, is derived from notions of fairness, common decency, and good faith. Further, we are convinced that these laws do not reflect a legislative intent to extinguish the property entitlements of a spouse who finds himself or herself beyond the reach of either statute because the marriage has realistically but not legally ended at the time of the other's death.

In the exercise of their common-law jurisdiction, courts should seek to effectuate sound public policy and mold the law to embody the societal values that are exemplified by such public policy. In this process, courts should be responsive to legislation as expressive of public policy, which can serve to shape and add content to the common law, even though such legislative expressions may not be directly applicable or binding in the given matter. Accordingly, we hold that marital property does not lose its essential and distinctive nature as property arising from the joint contributions of both spouses during marriage because of the death of one spouse during the pendency of divorce proceedings.

IV.

The trial court determined that plaintiff's peculiar status, for which statutory relief is unavailable, should be remedied through judicial exercise of its inherent equitable jurisdiction and invocation of "general equitable remedies." "Equities arise and stem from facts which call for relief from the strict legal effects of given situations." *Untermann v. Untermann*, 19 N.J. 507, 518, 117 A.2d 599 (1955) . . . . Courts have ordered the sequestering of any profits of real estate pending divorce proceedings, *Grange v. Grange*, supra, 160 N.J. Super. 153, 388 A.2d 1335, and have invoked equitable remedies, for example, to apportion premarital assets. *Rolle v. Rolle*, 219 N.J. Super. 528, 535-36, 530 A.2d 847 (Ch. Div. 1987); *Coney v. Coney*, 207 N.J. Super. 63, 74-76, 503 A.2d 912 (Ch. Div. 1985).

The constructive trust, we believe, is an appropriate equitable remedy in this type of case. Justice Cardozo described "[a] constructive trust [as] the formula through which the conscience of equity finds expression. When property has been acquired in such circumstances that the holder of the legal title may not in good conscience retain the beneficial interest, equity converts him into a trustee." *Beatty v. Guggenheim Exploration Co.*, 225 N.Y. 380, 386, 122 N.E. 378, 380 (1919).

. . . .

It has been recognized that "the general principles with reference to unjust enrichment which are at the basis of constructive trusts . . . are also at the basis of quasi-contractual obligations." 5 *Scott on Trusts* (3d ed.) § 461 at 3410. Quasi-contractual obligations are "imposed by law for the purpose of bringing about justice without reference to the intent of the parties." *St. Paul Fire & Marine Ins. Co. v. Indemnity Ins. Co.*, 32 N.J. 17, 22, 158 A.2d 825 (1960). As with constructive trusts, theories of quasi-contract and quantum meruit are not based on the actual intent of the parties, but "are arbitrarily imposed by the court to prevent an unjust enrichment." *Coney v. Coney*, 207 N.J. Super. 63, 503 A.2d 912 (Ch. Div. 1985). Such remedies have been invoked in the analogous context of unmarried cohabitants who may acquire rights as a result of enduring, intimate personal relationships founded on mutual trust, dependence, and raised expectations. E.g., *Crowe v. DeGoia*, 90 N.J. 126, 447 A.2d 173 (1982). In such cases, courts may presume that the parties "intended to deal fairly with one another [and will] employ the doctrine of quantum meruit, or equitable remedies such as constructive or resulting trusts" in order to ensure that one party has not been unjustly enriched, and the other unjustly impoverished, on account of their dealings. *Kozlowski v. Kozlowski*, 80 N.J. 378, 390-91, 403 A.2d 902 (Pashman, J., concurring).

In *Coney v. Coney, supra*, mentioning the equitable remedies of constructive trust, quasi-contract, and quantum meruit, the court stated: "There appears to be no reason why such equitable remedies, which are available to parties who cohabited but did not marry, are not also available to those parties who ultimately married . . . ." Extending this reasoning, we find no reason why equitable remedies available to cohabitants who did not marry, and available to cohabitants who ultimately did marry, and, by statute, available to married persons who have divorced, should not also be available to married persons who were in the process of divorcing but did not simply because one died.

We thus determine that Mrs. Carr should be afforded judicial relief . . . .

We are satisfied that, if warranted by the evidence, the equitable remedy of constructive trust should be invoked and imposed on the marital property under the control of the executor of Mr. Carr's estate. Further, principles of quasi-contract may be used since marital contributions and efforts in the creation and acquisition of marital assets are also relevant. These remedies, upon a sufficient evidentiary showing, should be applied to avoid the unjust enrichment that would occur if the marital property devolving to Mr. Carr's estate included the share beneficially belonging to Mrs. Carr.

V.

We affirm the judgment of the Appellate Division and remand the cause to the trial court for proceedings consistent with this opinion.

For affirmance and remandment — Justices HANDLER, POLLOCK, O'HERN, GARIBALDI and STEIN and Judges BILDER and ARNOLD M. STEIN — 7.

For reversal — None.

[f]   Comments

[i]   *The* **Carr** *Case.* After the case was remanded, the parties reached a settlement that mirrored standard outcomes in divorce cases.[126] According to Mrs. Carr's counsel, standard settlements usually split common property, such as houses, bank accounts, stocks and investments accumulated during the marriage. But the value of a business owned by one spouse is usually not halved. The speculative nature of business evaluations, together with practical concerns about maintaining stable ownership structures of closely held corporations often compel the non-owning spouse to compromise for a lesser share.

[ii]   *Recent Developments in the Terms of Mandatory Share Statutes.* The National Conference of Commissioners on Uniform State Laws[127] first proposed the Uniform Probate Code for adoption by the states in 1969. It was the provisions of that proposal that New Jersey adopted and that were in controversy in the *Carr* case. In 1990,[128] the Commissioners proposed some significant changes in those parts of Article II of the Uniform Probate Code dealing with intestate succession and mandatory shares. The changes in intestacy rules suggested giving a surviving spouse the entire estate of her or his deceased mate, even when children of the marriage survived.[129] This recommendation was based on studies finding that wills of married people tended to leave all the property to a surviving spouse rather than splitting it between spouse and children. In an important and dramatic shift from prior recommendations, the Commissioners also suggested that provisions based on community property theory be adopted to govern mandatory shares.[130] The new recommendations require that all the property owned by both spouses—marital and separate—be pooled into an "augmented estate" and then split. The surviving spouse may reject a will and take a percentage of the augmented estate based on the length of the marriage. A marriage of one to two years would lead to a mandatory share of only 3%. One lasting 15 years or more would yield a 50% share. In the comments to these sections, the Commissioners stated that their intention was "to implement a partnership or marital-sharing theory. Under that theory, there is a fifty/fifty split of the property acquired by *both* spouses." Widespread adoption of the new provisions of the Uniform Probate Code would work a major revision in the theory and practice of common law jurisdictions. Such jurisdictions would begin to look very much like their community property sisters. To date five states—Alaska, Arizona, Montana, New Mexico and North Dakota—have adopted the new intestacy and mandatory share provisions of the Uniform Probate Code.

[iii]   *Medical Expenses.* Medical expenses may seriously deplete the size of an estate. Before any assets are distributed from an estate to a surviving spouse, the debts of the deceased

---

[126] Telephone Interview with Mr. John A. Craner (Oct. 20, 1998). Mr. Craner represented Joyce Carr.

[127] The Commission, formed in 1892, is composed of members (four per state on average) selected according to statutes of the various states to sit for three year terms. The members then oversee the development of model codes that are presented to state legislatures for adoption.

[128] Further changes were recommended in 1993, but they were mostly clarifying amendments.

[129] Uniform Probate Code § 2-102 (8, pt. I, U.L.A. 81). The provision provides for a lesser share in the surviving spouse when children of a prior marriage of the deceased survive.

[130] Uniform Probate Code §§ 2-202 to 2-207 (8, pt. I, U.L.A. 102-121).

party must be paid. Think about a situation analogous to *Carr* involving medical expenses rather than splitting marital property or applying mandatory share statutes. For example, in *St. Mary's Hospital Medical Center v. Brody*, 186 Wis. 2d 100, 519 N.W.2d 706 (1994), Cynthia and Forest Brody married in 1981 and divorced in 1990. About nine months before the divorce judgment was entered, Forest Brody was hospitalized. After the divorce, the hospital sued both Forest and Cynthia for the unpaid part of the hospital bill. The court treated the hospital debt as a "necessary" for which both spouses were liable. Since the doctrine of necessaries had been gender-neutralized to make each spouse liable for the basic needs of their mate, the court's conclusion meant that the hospital could seek payment of the judgment out of the couple's marital estate or the separate property of either of them. Outcomes in similar disputes around the country vary. Some courts, perhaps gagging at imposing enormous hospital costs on separated or surviving spouses, have abolished the common law necessaries rule rather than expanding it to cover medical care and applying it to both spouses. *Schilling v. Bedford Co. Memorial Hospital*, 225 Va. 539, 303 S.E.2d 905 (1983); *Condore v. Prince George's Co.*, 289 Md. 516, 425 A.2d 1011 (1981). Others have adopted Wisconsin's approach. *Forsyth Memorial Hospital, Inc. v. Chisholm*, 342 N.C. 616, 467 S.E.2d 88 (1996); *North Carolina Baptist Hospitals v. Harris*, 319 N.C. 347, 354 S.E.2d 471 (1987); *Jersey Shore Medical Center-Fitkin Hospital v. Baum Estate*, 84 N.J. 137, 417 A.2d 1003 (1980).

[4]   Non-Marital Families and Property Ownership

[a]   The Non-Traditional Family: Introduction and Suggested Additional Reading

"Traditional" families with working husbands, housekeeping wives, and young children now constitute a minority of American households. Recent decades have witnessed a dramatic increase in the number of unmarried parents, single parent families, and unmarried cohabitants. Homosexual men and women, even if not greater in numbers than in prior periods of history, have become more willing to publicly discuss their sexual preferences and openly form households.

The modern diversity of family structures creates particular difficulties for property law. Recall from the discussion surrounding *Kirchberg v. Feenstra*, p. 179 above, the importance of the presumptive models property law relies upon. Traditional male dominated marital households were given credence by the common law tenancy by the entirety and the severe restrictions on married women's legal status. It has taken over a century to structure a new set of presumptions to govern ownership of property by married women, and the job is still not finished. We are just now beginning to reconsider the presumptive rules applicable to non-marital families. Significant differences exist between the property presumptions typically made when people are married and when they are not. Community and marital property regimes, dower and curtesy, homestead laws, intestate succession statutes, and social security survivor benefits, among others, depend upon the validity of drawing a distinction between married couples and all other couples.

Two major sorts of tactics have been adopted by various unmarried couples to overcome any perceived disadvantages from their unwillingness or inability to marry. First, litigation has arisen over the obligations of partners to each other both upon separation and upon death. These "divorce" cases, initially made famous by the widespread notoriety of *Marvin v. Marvin*, have become a staple of modern family law. Second, the inability to call upon the marital model has led a number of couples to sign agreements describing how various situations are supposed to be handled, from treatment of property upon "divorce" to appointment of guardians in case of serious medical problems. The notes after *Marvin* contain an example of such an agreement.

For additional reading on non-marital families in RICHARD H. CHUSED, A PROPERTY ANTHOLOGY (2d ed. 1998), look at pp. 277-285 for the article by William Reppy, *Property and Support Rights of Unmarried Cohabitants: A Proposal for Creating a New Legal Status*, 44 LA. L. REV. 1678 (1984). Another quite interesting article is Barbara Bennett Woodhouse, *Toward a Communitarian Theory of the "Nontraditional" Family*, 1996 UTAH L. REV. 569.

[b] Opinions of the California Supreme Court in *Marvin v. Marvin*

Marvin v. Marvin

California Supreme Court, En Banc
18 Cal. 3d 660, 557 P.2d 106, 134 Cal. Rptr. 815 (1976)

TOBRINER, J.

During the past 15 years, there has been a substantial increase in the number of couples living together without marrying.[1] Such nonmarital relationships lead to legal controversy when one partner dies or the couple separates. Courts of Appeal, faced with the task of determining property rights in such cases, have arrived at conflicting positions: two cases (*In re Marriage of Cary* (1973) 34 Cal. App. 3d 345 [109 Cal. Rptr. 862]; *Estate of Atherley* (1975) 44 Cal. App. 3d 758 [119 Cal. Rptr. 41]) have held that the Family Law Act (Civ. Code, § 4000 et seq.) requires division of the property according to community property principles, and one decision (*Beckman v. Mayhew* (1975) 49 Cal. App. 3d 529 [122 Cal. Rptr. 604]) has rejected that holding. We take this opportunity to resolve that controversy and to declare the principles which should govern distribution of property acquired in a nonmarital relationship.

We conclude: (1) The provisions of the Family Law Act do not govern the distribution of property acquired during a nonmarital relationship; such a relationship remains subject solely to judicial decision. (2) The courts should enforce express contracts between nonmarital partners except to the extent that the contract is explicitly founded on the consideration of meretricious sexual services. (3) In the absence of an express contract, the courts should inquire into the conduct of the parties to determine whether that conduct demonstrates an implied contract, agreement of partnership or joint venture, or some other tacit understanding between the parties. The courts may also employ the doctrine of *quantum meruit*, or equitable remedies such as constructive or resulting trusts, when warranted by the facts of the case.

In the instant case plaintiff and defendant lived together for seven years without marrying; all property acquired during this period was taken in defendant's name. When plaintiff sued to enforce a contract under which she was entitled to half the property and to support payments, the trial court granted judgment on the pleadings for defendant, thus leaving him with all property accumulated by the couple during their relationship. Since the trial court denied plaintiff a trial on the merits of her claim, its decision conflicts with the principles stated above, and must be reversed.

1. *The factual setting of this appeal.*

Since the trial court rendered judgment for defendant on the pleadings, we must accept the allegations of plaintiff's complaint as true, determining whether such allegations state, or can

---

[1] "The 1970 census figures indicate that today perhaps eight times as many couples are living together without being married as cohabited ten years ago." (Comment, *In re Cary: A Judicial Recognition of Illicit Cohabitation* (1974) 25 HASTINGS L.J. 1226.)

be amended to state, a cause of action. We turn therefore to the specific allegations of the complaint.

Plaintiff avers that in October of 1964 she and defendant "entered into an oral agreement" that while "the parties lived together they would combine their efforts and earnings and would share equally any and all property accumulated as a result of their efforts whether individual or combined." Furthermore, they agreed to "hold themselves out to the general public as husband and wife" and that "plaintiff would further render her services as a companion, homemaker, housekeeper and cook to . . . defendant."

Shortly thereafter plaintiff agreed to "give up her lucrative career as an entertainer [and] singer" in order to "devote her full time to defendant . . . as a companion, homemaker, housekeeper and cook;"in return defendant agreed to "provide for all of plaintiff's financial support and needs for the rest of her life."

Plaintiff alleges that she lived with defendant from October of 1964 through May of 1970 and fulfilled her obligations under the agreement. During this period the parties as a result of their efforts and earnings acquired in defendant's name substantial real and personal property, including motion picture rights worth over $1 million. In May of 1970, however, defendant compelled plaintiff to leave his household. He continued to support plaintiff until November of 1971, but thereafter refused to provide further support.

On the basis of these allegations plaintiff asserts two causes of action. The first, for declaratory relief, asks the court to determine her contract and property rights; the second seeks to impose a constructive trust upon one half of the property acquired during the course of the relationship.

Defendant demurred unsuccessfully, and then answered the complaint. Following extensive discovery and pretrial proceedings, the case came to trial. Defendant renewed his attack on the complaint by a motion to dismiss. Since the parties had stipulated that defendant's marriage to Betty Marvin did not terminate until the filing of a final decree of divorce in January 1967, the trial court treated defendant's motion as one for judgment on the pleadings augmented by the stipulation.

After hearing argument the court granted defendant's motion and entered judgment for defendant. Plaintiff moved to set aside the judgment and asked leave to amend her complaint to allege that she and defendant reaffirmed their agreement after defendant's divorce was final. The trial court denied plaintiff's motion, and she appealed from the judgment.

2. *Plaintiff's complaint states a cause of action for breach of an express contract.*

In *Trutalli v. Meraviglia* (1932) 215 Cal. 698 [12 P.2d 430] we established the principle that nonmarital partners may lawfully contract concerning the ownership of property acquired during the relationship. We reaffirmed this principle in *Vallera v. Vallera* (1943) 21 Cal. 2d 681, 685 [134 P.2d 761], stating that "If a man and woman [who are not married] live together as husband and wife under an agreement to pool their earnings and share equally in their joint accumulations, equity will protect the interests of each in such property."

In the case before us plaintiff, basing her cause of action in contract upon these precedents, maintains that the trial court erred in denying her a trial on the merits of her contention. Although that court did not specify the ground for its conclusion that plaintiff's contractual allegations stated no cause of action,[3] defendant offers some theories to sustain the ruling; we proceed to examine them.

Defendant first and principally relies on the contention that the alleged contract is so closely related to the supposed "immoral" character of the relationship between plaintiff and himself that the enforcement of the contract would violate public policy.[4] He points to cases asserting that a contract between nonmarital partners is unenforceable if it is "involved in" an illicit relationship, or made in "contemplation" of such a relationship. A review of the numerous California decisions concerning contracts between nonmarital partners, however, reveals that the courts have not employed such broad and uncertain standards to strike down contracts.

. . . .

Although the past decisions hover over the issue in the somewhat wispy form of the figures of a Chagall painting, we can abstract from those decisions a clear and simple rule. The fact that a man and woman live together without marriage, and engage in a sexual relationship, does not in itself invalidate agreements between them relating to their earnings, property, or expenses. Neither is such an agreement invalid merely because the parties may have contemplated the creation or continuation of a nonmarital relationship when they entered into it. Agreements between nonmarital partners fail only to the extent that they rest upon a consideration of meretricious sexual services. Thus the rule asserted by defendant, that a contract fails if it is "involved in" or made "in contemplation" of a nonmarital relationship, cannot be reconciled with the decisions.

The . . . cases cited by defendant which have *declined* to enforce contracts between nonmarital partners involved consideration that *was* expressly founded upon an illicit sexual service. In *Hill v. Estate of Westbrook*, 95 Cal. App. 2d 599, the woman promised to keep house for the man, to live with him as man and wife, and to bear his children; the man promised to provide for her in his will, but died without doing so. Reversing a judgment for the woman based on the reasonable value of her services, the Court of Appeal stated that "the action is predicated upon a claim which seeks, among other things, the reasonable value of living with decedent in meretricious relationship and bearing him two children . . . . The law does not award compensation for living with a man as a concubine and bearing him children . . . . As the judgment is at least in part, for the value of the claimed services for which recovery cannot be had, it must

---

[3] The colloquy between court and counsel at argument on the motion for judgment on the pleadings suggests that the trial court held the 1964 agreement violated public policy because it derogated the community property rights of Betty Marvin, defendant's lawful wife. Plaintiff, however, offered to amend her complaint to allege that she and defendant reaffirmed their contract after defendant and Betty were divorced. The trial court denied leave to amend, a ruling which suggests that the court's judgment must rest upon some other ground than the assertion that the contract would injure Betty's property rights.

[4] Defendant also contends that the contract was illegal because it contemplated a violation of former Penal Code section 269a, which prohibited living "in a state of cohabitation and adultery." (§ 269a was repealed by Stats. 1975, ch. 71, eff. Jan. 1, 1976.) Defendant's standing to raise the issue is questionable because he alone was married and thus guilty of violating section 269a. Plaintiff, being unmarried could neither be convicted of adulterous cohabitation nor of aiding and abetting defendant's violation. (See *In re Cooper* (1912) 162 Cal. 81, 85-86 [121 P. 318].)

The numerous cases discussing the contractual rights of unmarried couples have drawn no distinction between illegal relationships and lawful nonmarital relationships. (*Cf. Weak v. Weak* (1962) 202 Cal. App. 2d 632, 639 [21 Cal. Rptr. 9] (bigamous marriage).) Moreover, even if we were to draw such a distinction—a largely academic endeavor in view of the repeal of section 269a—defendant probably would not benefit; his relationship with plaintiff continued long after his divorce became final, and plaintiff sought to amend her complaint to assert that the parties reaffirmed their contract after the divorce.

be reversed." Upon retrial, the trial court found that it could not sever the contract and place an independent value upon the legitimate services performed by claimant. We therefore affirmed a judgment for the estate. (*Hill v. Estate of Westbrook* (1952) 39 Cal. 2d 458 [247 P.2d 19].).. . .[6]

. . . .

The principle that a contract between nonmarital partners will be enforced unless expressly and inseparably based upon an illicit consideration of sexual services not only represents the distillation of the decisional law, but also offers a far more precise and workable standard than that advocated by defendant . . . .

[I]n the present case a standard which inquires whether an agreement is "involved" in or "contemplates" a nonmarital relationship is vague and unworkable. Virtually all agreements between nonmarital partners can be said to be "involved" in some sense in the fact of their mutual sexual relationship, or to "contemplate" the existence of that relationship. Thus defendant's proposed standards, if taken literally, might invalidate all agreements between nonmarital partners, a result no one favors. Moreover, those standards offer no basis to distinguish between valid and invalid agreements. By looking not to such uncertain tests, but only to the consideration underlying the agreement, we provide the parties and the courts with a practical guide to determine when an agreement between nonmarital partners should be enforced.

Defendant secondly relies upon the ground suggested by the trial court: that the 1964 contract violated public policy because it impaired the community property rights of Betty Marvin, defendant's lawful wife. Defendant points out that his earnings while living apart from his wife before rendition of the interlocutory decree were community property under 1964 statutory law (former Civ. Code, §§ 169, 169.2)[7] and that defendant's agreement with plaintiff purported to transfer to her a half interest in that community property. But whether or not defendant's contract with plaintiff exceeded his authority as manager of the community property (see former Civ. Code, § 172), defendant's argument fails for the reason that an improper transfer of community property is not void *ab initio*, but merely voidable at the instance of the aggrieved spouse.

In the present case Betty Marvin, the aggrieved spouse, had the opportunity to assert her community property rights in the divorce action. The interlocutory and final decrees in that action fix and limit her interest. Enforcement of the contract between plaintiff and defendant against property awarded to defendant by the divorce decree will not impair any right of Betty's, and thus is not on that account violative of public policy.[8]

---

[6] Although not cited by defendant, the only California precedent which supports his position is *Heaps v. Toy* (1942) 54 Cal. App. 2d 178 [128 P.2d 813]. In that case the woman promised to leave her job, to refrain from marriage, to be a companion to the man, and to make a permanent home for him; he agreed to support the woman and her child for life. The Court of Appeal held the agreement invalid as a contract in restraint of marriage (Civ. Code, § 1676) and, alternatively, as "contrary to good morals" (Civ. Code, § 1607). The opinion does not state that sexual relations formed any part of the consideration for the contract, nor explain how—unless the contract called for sexual relations—the woman's employment as a companion and housekeeper could be contrary to good morals.

The alternative holding in *Heaps v. Toy, supra*, finding the contract in that case contrary to good morals, is inconsistent with the numerous California decisions upholding contracts between nonmarital partners when such contracts are not founded upon an illicit consideration, and is therefore disapproved.

[7] Sections 169 and 169.2 were replaced in 1970 by Civil Code section 5118. In 1972 section 5118 was amended to provide that the earnings and accumulations of *both* spouses "while living separate and apart from the other spouse, are the separate property of the spouse."

[8] Defendant also contends that the contract is invalid as an agreement to promote or encourage divorce. (See 1 Witkin, *Summary of Cal. Law* (8th ed.) pp. 390-392 and cases there cited.) The contract between plaintiff and defendant

. . . .

In summary, we base our opinion on the principle that adults who voluntarily live together and engage in sexual relations are nonetheless as competent as any other persons to contract respecting their earnings and property rights. Of course, they cannot lawfully contract to pay for the performance of sexual services, for such a contract is, in essence, an agreement for prostitution and unlawful for that reason. But they may agree to pool their earnings and to hold all property acquired during the relationship in accord with the law governing community property; conversely they may agree that each partner's earnings and the property acquired from those earnings remain the separate property of the earning partner.[10] So long as the agreement does not rest upon illicit meretricious consideration, the parties may order their economic affairs as they choose, and no policy precludes the courts from enforcing such agreements.

In the present instance, plaintiff alleges that the parties agreed to pool their earnings, that they contracted to share equally in all property acquired, and that defendant agreed to support plaintiff. The terms of the contract as alleged do not rest upon any unlawful consideration. We therefore conclude that the complaint furnishes a suitable basis upon which the trial court can render declaratory relief. The trial court consequently erred in granting defendant's motion for judgment on the pleadings.

3. Plaintiff's complaint can be amended to state a cause of action founded upon theories of implied contract or equitable relief.

As we have noted, both causes of action in plaintiff's complaint allege an express contract; neither assert any basis for relief independent from the contract. In *In re Marriage of Cary, supra,* 34 Cal. App. 3d 345, however, the Court of Appeal held that, in view of the policy of the Family Law Act, property accumulated by nonmarital partners in an actual family relationship should be divided equally. Upon examining the *Cary* opinion, the parties to the present case realized that plaintiff's alleged relationship with defendant might arguably support a cause of action independent of any express contract between the parties. The parties have therefore briefed and discussed the issue of the property rights of a nonmarital partner in the absence of an express contract. Although our conclusion that plaintiff's complaint states a cause of action based on an express contract alone compels us to reverse the judgment for defendant, resolution of the *Cary* issue will serve both to guide the parties upon retrial and to resolve a conflict presently manifested in published Court of Appeal decisions.

Both plaintiff and defendant stand in broad agreement that the law should be fashioned to carry out the reasonable expectations of the parties. Plaintiff, however, presents the following contentions: that the decisions prior to *Cary* rest upon implicit and erroneous notions of punishing a party for his or her guilt in entering into a nonmarital relationship, that such decisions result in an inequitable distribution of property accumulated during the relationship, and that *Cary*

---

did not, however, by its terms require defendant to divorce Betty, nor reward him for so doing. Moreover, the principle on which defendant relies does not apply when the marriage in question is beyond redemption (*Glickman v. Collins* (1975) 13 Cal. 3d 852, 858-859 [120 Cal. Rptr. 76, 533 P.2d 204]); whether or not defendant's marriage to Betty was beyond redemption when defendant contracted with plaintiff is obviously a question of fact which cannot be resolved by judgment on the pleadings.

[10] A great variety of other arrangements are possible. The parties might keep their earnings and property separate, but agree to compensate one party for services which benefit the other. They may choose to pool only part of their earnings and property, to form a partnership or joint venture, or to hold property acquired as joint tenants or tenants in common, or agree to any other such arrangement. (See generally Weitzman, *Legal Regulation of Marriage: Tradition and Change* (1974) 62 CAL. L. REV. 1169.)

correctly held that the enactment of the Family Law Act in 1970 overturned those prior decisions. Defendant in response maintains that the prior decisions merely applied common law principles of contract and property to persons who have deliberately elected to remain outside the bounds of the community property system.[11] *Cary,* defendant contends, erred in holding that the Family Law Act vitiated the force of the prior precedents.

As we shall see from examination of the pre-*Cary* decisions, the truth lies somewhere between the positions of plaintiff and defendant. The classic opinion on this subject is *Vallera v. Vallera, supra,* 21 Cal. 2d 681. Speaking for a four-member majority, Justice Traynor posed the question: "whether a woman living with a man as his wife but with no genuine belief that she is legally married to him acquires by reason of cohabitation alone the rights of a co-tenant in his earnings and accumulations during the period of their relationship." (21 Cal. 2d at p. 684.) . . . In the absence of express contract, *Vallera* concluded, the woman is entitled to share in property jointly accumulated only "in the proportion that her funds contributed toward its acquisition." (p. 685.) Justice Curtis, dissenting, argued that the evidence showed an implied contract under which each party owned an equal interest in property acquired during the relationship.

The majority opinion in *Vallera* did not expressly bar recovery based upon an implied contract, nor preclude resort to equitable remedies. But Vallera's broad assertion that equitable considerations "are not present" in the case of a nonmarital relationship (21 Cal. 2d at p. 685) led the Courts of Appeal to interpret the language to preclude recovery based on such theories.

Consequently, when the issue of the rights of a nonmarital partner reached this court in *Keene v. Keene* (1962) 57 Cal. 2d 657 [21 Cal. Rptr. 593, 371 P. 2d 329], the claimant forwent reliance upon theories of contract implied in law or fact. Asserting that she had worked on her partner's ranch and that her labor had enhanced its value, she confined her cause of action to the claim that the court should impress a resulting trust on the property derived from the sale of the ranch. The court limited its opinion accordingly, rejecting her argument on the ground that the rendition of services gives rise to a resulting trust only when the services aid in acquisition of the property, not in its subsequent improvement. (57 Cal. 2d at p. 668.) Justice Peters, dissenting, attacked the majority's distinction between the rendition of services and the contribution of funds or property; he maintained that both property and services furnished valuable consideration, and potentially afforded the ground for a resulting trust.

This failure of the courts to recognize an action by a nonmarital partner based upon implied contract, or to grant an equitable remedy, contrasts with the judicial treatment of the putative spouse. Prior to the enactment of the Family Law Act, no statute granted rights to a putative spouse.[13] The courts accordingly fashioned a variety of remedies by judicial decision. Some cases

---

[11] We note that a deliberate decision to avoid the strictures of the community property system is not the only reason that couples live together without marriage. Some couples may wish to avoid the permanent commitment that marriage implies, yet be willing to share equally any property acquired during the relationship; others may fear the loss of pension, welfare, or tax benefits resulting from marriage (*see Beckman v. Mayhew, supra,* 49 Cal. App. 3d 529). Others may engage in the relationship as a possible prelude to marriage. In lower socio-economic groups the difficulty and expense of dissolving a former marriage often leads couples to choose a nonmarital relationship; many unmarried couples may also incorrectly believe that the doctrine of common law marriage prevails in California, and thus that they are in fact married. Consequently we conclude that the mere fact that a couple have not participated in a valid marriage ceremony cannot serve as a basis for a court's inference that the couple intend to keep their earnings and property separate and independent; the parties' intention can only be ascertained by a more searching inquiry into the nature of their relationship.

[13] The Family Law Act, in Civil Code section 4452, classifies property acquired during a putative marriage as "quasi-marital property," and requires that such property be divided upon dissolution of the marriage in accord with Civil Code section 4800.

permitted the putative spouse to recover half the property on a theory that the conduct of the parties implied an agreement of partnership or joint venture. Others permitted the spouse to recover the reasonable value of rendered services, less the value of support received. Finally, decisions affirmed the power of a court to employ equitable principles to achieve a fair division of property acquired during putative marriage.[15]

Thus in summary, the cases prior to *Cary* exhibited a schizophrenic inconsistency. By enforcing an express contract between nonmarital partners unless it rested upon an unlawful consideration, the courts applied a common law principle as to contracts. Yet the courts disregarded the common law principle that holds that implied contracts can arise from the conduct of the parties. Refusing to enforce such contracts, the courts spoke of leaving the parties "in the position in which they had placed themselves" just as if they were guilty parties *in pari delicto*.

Justice Curtis noted this inconsistency in his dissenting opinion in *Vallera*, pointing out that "if an express agreement will be enforced, there is no legal or just reason why an implied agreement to share the property cannot be enforced." (see Bruch, *Property Rights of De Facto Spouses Including Thoughts on the Value of Homemakers' Services* (1976) 10 FAMILY L.Q. 101, 117-121.) And in *Keene v. Keene, supra*, Justice Peters observed that if the man and woman "were not illegally living together . . . it would be a plain business relationship and a contract would be implied." (Dis. opn.)

Still another inconsistency in the prior cases arises from their treatment of property accumulated through joint effort. To the extent that a partner had contributed *funds* or *property*, the cases held that the partner obtains a proportionate share in the acquisition, despite the lack of legal standing of the relationship. Yet courts have refused to recognize just such an interest based upon the contribution of *services*. As Justice Curtis points out "Unless it can be argued that a woman's services as cook, housekeeper, and homemaker are valueless, it would seem logical that if, when she contributes money to the purchase of property, her interest will be protected, then when she contributes her services in the home, her interest in property accumulated should be protected." (*Vallera v. Vallera, supra*, 21 Cal. 2d 681, 686-687 (dis. opn.); see Bruch, *op. cit., supra*, 10 FAMILY L.Q. 101, 110-114; Article, *Illicit Cohabitation: The Impact of the Vallera and Keene Cases on the Rights of the Meretricious Spouse* (1973) 6 U.C. DAVIS L. REV. 354, 369-370; Comment (1972) 48 WASH. L. REV. 635, 641.)

Thus as of 1973, the time of the filing of *In re Marriage of Cary, supra*, the cases apparently held that a nonmarital partner who rendered services in the absence of express contract could assert no right to property acquired during the relationship. The facts of *Cary* demonstrated the unfairness of that rule.

Janet and Paul Cary had lived together, unmarried, for more than eight years. They held themselves out to friends and family as husband and wife, reared four children, purchased a home and other property, obtained credit, filed joint income tax returns, and otherwise conducted themselves as though they were married. Paul worked outside the home, and Janet generally cared for the house and children.

---

[15] The contrast between principles governing nonmarital and putative relationships appears most strikingly in *Lazzarevich v. Lazzarevich, supra*, 88 Cal. App. 2d 708. When Mrs. Lazzarevich sued her husband for divorce in 1945, she discovered to her surprise that she was not lawfully married to him. She nevertheless reconciled with him, and the Lazzareviches lived together for another year before they finally separated. The court awarded her recovery for the reasonable value of services rendered, less the value of support received, until she discovered the invalidity of the marriage, but denied recovery for the same services rendered after that date.

In 1971 Paul petitioned for "nullity of the marriage."[17] Following a hearing on that petition, the trial court awarded Janet half the property acquired during the relationship, although all such property was traceable to Paul's earnings. The Court of Appeal affirmed the award.

Reviewing the prior decisions which had denied relief to the homemaking partner, the Court of Appeal reasoned that those decisions rested upon a policy of punishing persons guilty of cohabitation without marriage. The Family Law Act, the court observed, aimed to eliminate fault or guilt as a basis for dividing marital property. But once fault or guilt is excluded, the court reasoned, nothing distinguishes the property rights of a nonmarital "spouse" from those of a putative spouse. Since the latter is entitled to half the " 'quasi marital property' " (Civ. Code, § 4452), the Court of Appeal concluded that, giving effect to the policy of the Family Law Act, a nonmarital cohabitator should also be entitled to half the property accumulated during an "actual family relationship."[18]

Cary met with a mixed reception in other appellate districts. In *Estate of Atherley, supra*, the Fourth District agreed with *Cary* that under the Family Law Act a nonmarital partner in an actual family relationship enjoys the same right to an equal division of property as a putative spouse. In *Beckman v. Mayhew, supra*, however, the Third District rejected *Cary* on the ground that

[17] The Court of Appeal opinion in *In re Marriage of Cary, supra*, does not explain why Paul Cary filed his action as a petition for nullity. Briefs filed with this court, however, suggest that Paul may have been seeking to assert rights as a putative spouse. In the present case, on the other hand, neither party claims the status of an actual or putative spouse. Under such circumstances an action to adjudge "the marriage" in the instant case a nullity would be pointless and could not serve as a device to adjudicate contract and property rights arising from the parties' nonmarital relationship. Accordingly, plaintiff here correctly chose to assert her rights by means of an ordinary civil action.

[18] The court in *Cary* also based its decision upon an analysis of Civil Code section 4452, which specifies the property rights of a putative spouse. Section 4452 states that if the "court finds that either party or both parties believed in good faith that the marriage was valid, the court should declare such party or parties to have the status of a putative spouse, and, . . . shall divide, in accordance with Section 4800, that property acquired during the union . . . ." Since section 4800 requires an equal division of community property, *Cary* interpreted section 4452 to require an equal division of the property of a putative marriage, so long as one spouse believed in good faith that the marriage was valid. Thus under section 4452, *Cary* concluded, the "guilty spouse" (the spouse who knows the marriage is invalid) has the same right to half the property as does the "innocent" spouse.

Cary then reasoned that if the "guilty" spouse to a putative marriage is entitled to one-half the marital property, the "guilty" partner in a nonmarital relationship should also receive one-half of the property. Otherwise, the court stated, "We should be obliged to presume a legislative intent that a person, who by deceit leads another to believe a valid marriage exists between them, shall be legally guaranteed half of the property they acquire even though most, or all, may have resulted from the earnings of the blameless partner. At the same time we must infer an inconsistent legislative intent that two persons who, candidly with each other, enter upon an unmarried family relationship, shall be denied any judicial aid whatever in the assertion of otherwise valid property rights."

This reasoning in *Cary* has been criticized by commentators. (See Note, *op. cit. supra*, 25 HASTINGS L.J. 1226, 1234-1235; Comment, *In re Marriage of Carey [sic]: The End of the Putative-Meretricious Spouse Distinction in California* (1975) 12 SAN DIEGO L. REV. 436, 444-446.) The commentators note that Civil Code section 4455 provides that an "innocent" party to a putative marriage can recover spousal support, from which they infer that the Legislature intended to give only the "innocent" spouse a right to one-half of the quasimarital property under section 4452.

We need not now resolve this dispute concerning the interpretation of section 4452. Even if *Cary* is correct in holding that a "guilty" putative spouse has a right to one-half of the marital property, it does not necessarily follow that a nonmarital partner has an identical right. In a putative marriage the parties will arrange their economic affairs with the expectation that upon dissolution the property will be divided equally. If a "guilty" putative spouse receives one-half of the property under section 4452, no expectation of the "innocent" spouse has been frustrated. In a nonmarital relationship, on the other hand, the parties may expressly or tacitly determine to order their economic relationship in some other manner, and to impose community property principles regardless of such understanding may frustrate the parties' expectations.

the Family Law Act was not intended to change California law dealing with nonmarital relationships.

If *Cary* is interpreted as holding that the Family Law Act requires an equal division of property accumulated in nonmarital "actual family relationship," then we agree with *Beckman v. Mayhew* that *Cary* distends the act. No language in the Family Law Act addresses the property rights of nonmarital partners, and nothing in the legislative history of the act suggests that the Legislature considered that subject.[19] The delineation of the rights of nonmarital partners before 1970 had beenfixed entirely by judicial decision; we see no reason to believe that the Legislature, by enacting the Family Law Act, intended to change that state of affairs.

But although we reject the reasoning of *Cary* and *Atherley*, we share the perception of the *Cary* and *Atherley* courts that the application of former precedent in the factual setting of those cases would work an unfair distribution of the property accumulated by the couple. Justice Friedman in *Beckman v. Mayhew, supra*, also questioned the continued viability of our decisions in *Vallera* and *Keene*; commentators have argued the need to reconsider those precedents.[20] We should not, therefore, reject the authority of *Cary* and *Atherley* without also examining the deficiencies in the former law which led to those decisions.

The principal reason why the pre-*Cary* decisions result in an unfair distribution of property inheres in the court's refusal to permit a nonmarital partner to assert rights based upon accepted principles of implied contract or equity. We have examined the reasons advanced to justify this denial of relief, and find that none have merit.

First, we note that the cases denying relief do not rest their refusal upon any theory of "punishing" a "guilty" partner. Indeed, to the extent that denial of relief "punishes" one partner, it necessarily rewards the other by permitting him to retain a disproportionate amount of the property. Concepts of "guilt" thus cannot justify an unequal division of property between two equally "guilty" persons.[21]

Other reasons advanced in the decisions fare no better. The principal argument seems to be that "[e]quitable considerations arising from the reasonable expectation of . . . benefits attending the status of marriage . . . are not present [in a nonmarital relationship]." (*Vallera v. Vallera, supra*) But, although parties to a nonmarital relationship obviously cannot have based any

---

[19] Despite the extensive material available on the legislative history of the Family Law Act neither *Cary* nor plaintiff cites any reference which suggests that the Legislature ever considered the issue of the property rights of nonmarital partners, and our independent examination has uncovered no such reference.

[20] See Bruch, *op. cit., supra*, 10 FAMILY L.Q. 101, 113; Article, *op. cit., supra*, 6 U.C. DAVIS L. REV. 354; Comment (1975) 6 GOLDEN GATE L. REV. 179, 197-201; Comment, *op. cit., supra*, 12 SAN DIEGO L. REV. 436; Note, *op. cit., supra*, 25 HASTINGS L.J. 1226, 1246.

[21] Justice Finely of the Washington Supreme Court explains: "Under such circumstances [the dissolution of a nonmarital relationship], this court and the courts of other jurisdictions have, in effect, sometimes said, 'We will wash our hands of such disputes. The parties should and must be left to their own devices, just where they find themselves.' To me, such pronouncements seem overly fastidious and a bit fatuous. They are unrealistic and, among other things, ignore the fact that an unannounced (but nevertheless effective and binding) rule of law is inherent in any such terminal statements by a court of law. The unannounced but inherent rule is simply that the party who has title, or in some instances who is in possession, will enjoy the rights of ownership of the property concerned. The rule often operates to the great advantage of the cunning and the shrewd, who wind up with possession of the property, or title to it in their names, at the end of a so-called meretricious relationship. So, although the courts proclaim that they will have nothing to do with such matters, the proclamation in itself establishes, as to the parties involved, an effective and binding rule of law which tends to operate purely by accident or perhaps by reason of the cunning, anticipatory designs of just one of the parties." (*West v. Knowles* (1957) 50 Wash. 2d 311 [311 P.2d 689, 692] (conc. opn.).)

expectations upon the belief that they were married, other expectations and equitable considerations remain. The parties may well expect that property will be divided in accord with the parties'
own tacit understanding and that in the absence of such understanding the courts will fairly
apportion property accumulated through mutual effort. We need not treat nonmarital partners
as putatively married persons in order to apply principles of implied contract, or extend equitable
remedies; we need to treat them only as we do any other unmarried persons.[22]

The remaining arguments advanced from time to time to deny remedies to the nonmarital
partners are of less moment. There is no more reason to presume that services are contributed
as a gift than to presume that funds are contributed as a gift; in any event the better approach
is to presume, as Justice Peters suggested, "that the parties intend to deal fairly with each other."
(*Keene v. Keene, supra*, (dissenting opn.); see Bruch, *op. cit., supra*, 10 FAMILY L.Q. 101, 113.)

The argument that granting remedies to the nonmarital partners would discourage marriage
must fail; as *Cary* pointed out, "with equal or greater force the point might be made that the
pre-1970 rule was calculated to cause the income-producing partner to avoid marriage and thus
retain the benefit of all of his or her accumulated earnings." Although we recognize the well-
established public policy to foster and promote the institution of marriage, perpetuation of judicial
rules which result in an inequitable distribution of property accumulated during a nonmarital
relationship is neither a just nor an effective way of carrying out that policy.

In summary, we believe that the prevalence of nonmarital relationships in modern society and
the social acceptance of them, marks this as a time when our courts should by no means apply
the doctrine of the unlawfulness of the so-called meretricious relationship to the instant case.
As we have explained, the nonenforceability of agreements expressly providing for meretricious
conduct rested upon the fact that such conduct, as the word suggests, pertained to and
encompassed prostitution. To equate the nonmarital relationship of today to such a subject matter
is to do violence to an accepted and wholly different practice.

We are aware that many young couples live together without the solemnization of marriage,
in order to make sure that they can successfully later undertake marriage. This trial period,[23]
preliminary to marriage, serves as some assurance that the marriage will not subsequently end
in dissolution to the harm of both parties. We are aware, as we have stated, of the pervasiveness
of nonmarital relationships in other situations.

The mores of the society have indeed changed so radically in regard to cohabitation that we
cannot impose a standard based on alleged moral considerations that have apparently been so
widely abandoned by so many. Lest we be misunderstood, however, we take this occasion to
point out that the structure of society itself largely depends upon the institution of marriage, and
nothing we have said in this opinion should be taken to derogate from that institution. The joining
of the man and woman in marriage is at once the most socially productive and individually
fulfilling relationship that one can enjoy in the course of a lifetime.

We conclude that the judicial barriers that may stand in the way of a policy based upon the
fulfillment of the reasonable expectations of the parties to a nonmarital relationship should be
removed. As we have explained, the courts now hold that express agreements will be enforced
unless they rest on an unlawful meretricious consideration. We add that in the absence of an

---

[22] In some instances a confidential relationship may arise between nonmarital partners, and economic transactions
between them should be governed by the principles applicable to such relationships.

[23] Toffler, *Future Shock* (Bantam Books, 1971) page 253.

express agreement, the courts may look to a variety of other remedies in order to protect the parties' lawful expectations.[24]

The courts may inquire into the conduct of the parties to determine whether that conduct demonstrates an implied contract or implied agreement of partnership or joint venture, or some other tacit understanding between the parties. The courts may, when appropriate, employ principles of constructive trust or resulting trust. Finally, a nonmarital partner may recover in quantum meruit for the reasonable value of household services rendered less the reasonable value of support received if he can show that he rendered services with the expectation of monetary reward.[25]

Since we have determined that plaintiff's complaint states a cause of action for breach of an express contract, and, as we have explained, can be amended to state a cause of action independent of allegations of express contract,[26] we must conclude that the trial court erred in granting defendant a judgment on the pleadings.

The judgment is reversed and the cause remanded for further proceedings consistent with the views expressed herein.

Wright, C.J., McComb, J., Mosk, J., Sullivan, J., and Richardson, J., concurred.

CLARK, J., Concurring and Dissenting.

The majority opinion properly permits recovery on the basis of either express or implied in fact agreement between the parties. These being the issues presented, their resolution requires reversal of the judgment. Here, the opinion should stop.

This court should not attempt to determine all anticipated rights, duties and remedies within every meretricious relationship—particularly in vague terms. Rather, these complex issues should be determined as each arises in a concrete case.

The majority broadly indicate that a party to a meretricious relationship may recover on the basis of equitable principles and in quantum meruit. However, the majority fail to advise us of the circumstances permitting recovery, limitations on recovery, or whether their numerous remedies are cumulative or exclusive. Conceivably, under the majority opinion a party may recover half of the property acquired during the relationship on the basis of general equitable principles, recover a bonus based on specific equitable considerations, and recover a second bonus in quantum meruit. The general sweep of the majority opinion raises but fails to answer several questions. First, because the Legislature specifically excluded some parties to a meretricious relationship from the equal division rule of Civil Code section 4452, is this court now free to create an equal division rule? Second, upon termination of the relationship, is it equitable to impose the economic obligations of lawful spouses on meretricious parties when the latter may

---

[24] We do not seek to resurrect the doctrine of common law marriage, which was abolished in California by statute in 1895. (See *Norman v. Thomson* (1898) 121 Cal. 620, 628 [54 P. 143]; *Estate of Abate* (1958) 166 Cal. App.2d 282, 292 [333 P.2d 200].) Thus we do not hold that plaintiff and defendant were "married," nor do we extend to plaintiff the rights which the Family Law Act grants valid or putative spouses; we hold only that she has the same rights to enforce contracts and to assert her equitable interest in property acquired through her effort as does any other unmarried person.

[25] Our opinion does not preclude the evolution of additional equitable remedies to protect the expectations of the parties to a nonmarital relationship in cases in which existing remedies prove inadequate; the suitability of such remedies may be determined in later cases in light of the factual setting in which they arise.

[26] We do not pass upon the question whether, in the absence of an express or implied contractual obligation, a party to a nonmarital relationship is entitled to support payments from the other party after the relationship terminates.

have rejected matrimony to avoid such obligations? Third, does not application of equitable principles—necessitating examination of the conduct of the parties—violate the spirit of the Family Law Act of 1969, designed to eliminate the bitterness and acrimony resulting from the former fault system in divorce? Fourth, will not application of equitable principles reimpose upon trial courts the unmanageable burden of arbitrating domestic disputes? Fifth, will not a quantum meruit system of compensation for services—discounted by benefits received—place meretricious spouses in a better position than lawful spouses? Sixth, if a quantum meruit system is to be allowed, does fairness not require inclusion of all services and all benefits regardless of how difficult the evaluation?

When the parties to a meretricious relationship show by express or implied in fact agreement they intend to create mutual obligations, the courts should enforce the agreement. However, in the absence of agreement, we should stop and consider the ramifications before creating economic obligations which may violate legislative intent, contravene the intention of the parties, and surely generate undue burdens on our trial courts.

By judicial overreach, the majority perform a nunc pro tunc marriage, dissolve it, and distribute its property on terms never contemplated by the parties, case law or the Legislature.

[c]   Explanatory Notes

[i]   *Events After the California Supreme Court Decision.* The trial after remand in *Marvin v. Marvin* was something of a circus. Papers all over the country printed daily stories of the proceedings as the "dirty laundry" of the couple was hung out to dry. Tales of drinking, pettiness, frequent arguing, broken promises, abortions, attempted suicides and intrigue titillated the public.[131] Michelle and Lee had diametrically opposite stories to tell the court. Michelle testified that Lee professed to love her and promised to take care of her for the rest of her life. Lee said that he wanted to get rid of Michelle almost from the beginning of their relationship, but was afraid she would attempt to commit suicide and wash all their dirty linen in public.

The trial court concluded that Michelle Marvin failed to prove the existence of either an express or implied contract to share property. Nor did the court find that a resulting trust or a constructive trust existed. That is, there was no proof that Lee held in his name assets purchased with Michelle's funds, or that Lee unjustly enriched himself by using Michelle's assets. Finally, the court refused to award Michelle money because of her homemaking role. The growth of Lee's wealth was not deemed to be a result of mutual effort. In addition, the funds and assets given to Michelle during her relationship with Lee were found to be sufficient compensation for whatever services Michelle performed. However, in somewhat cryptic prose, the court decided to award Michelle $104,000. The reasoning was as follows:

The court is aware that Footnote 25, *Marvin v. Marvin*, urges the trial court to employ whatever equitable remedy may be proper under the circumstances. The court is also aware of the recent resort of plaintiff to unemployment insurance benefits to support herself and of the fact that a return of plaintiff to a career as a singer is doubtful. Additionally, the court knows that the market value of defendant's property at time of separation exceeded $1,000,000.

---

[131] A lengthy story appeared in the *Washington Post* on January 10, 1979, the day after their trial began. *Marvin vs. Marvin*: The Price of Living Together, at D1. Further coverage appeared regularly in the *Post* for the next several months. *See, e.g.*, Marvin's "Idle Male Promises," D3 (Jan. 27, 1979); 3 Pregnancies Alleged, at B1 (Jan. 30, 1979); *Marvin v. Marvin*, at B4 (Feb. 1, 1979); 'Til Millions Do Them Part, at C1 (Feb. 9, 1979); The Split Decision, at B1 (Apr. 19, 1979).

In view of these circumstances, the court in equity awards plaintiff $104,000[132] for rehabilitation purposes so that she may have the economic means to re-educate herself and to learn new, employable skills or to refurbish those utilized, for example, during her most recent employment[133] and so that she may return from her status as a companion of a motion picture star to a separate, independent but perhaps more prosaic existence.[134]

Lee Marvin appealed the award of $104,000 and won in a 2-1 decision. *Marvin v. Marvin*, 122 Cal. App. 3d 871, 176 Cal. Rptr. 555 (1981). The court noted that the plaintiff's amended complaint failed to ask for rehabilitative relief and that the award was therefore outside the scope of the pleadings. In addition, such an obligation must be supported, the court opined, by "some recognized underlying obligation in law or in equity." The finding of fact by the trial court that Lee had undertaken no actual or implied obligation to Michelle meant there was no basis for the award. Even the dissent noted that the award was without support in the findings of fact made by the trial judge. Rather than dismissing the case, however, he preferred to remand for correction of the inconsistencies in the judge's findings and conclusions. The California Supreme Court refused to review the case again.

[*ii*]   *Other Non-Marital Settings.* Post-*Marvin* litigation has arisen all over the country. Most states confronting situations like that in the *Marvin* case have permitted the enforcement of contracts between cohabiting adults, although some have required that such contracts be express rather than implied. A small number of states have refused to enforce such contracts at all. Cases have also raised a wide variety of related questions, including unsuccessful attempts by cohabitants to sue for wrongful death of a mate, to recover damages for loss of consortium, or to obtain homestead rights. Courts have used *Marvin* as a basis for distributing property accumulated by a divorcing couple while they were living together before their marriage, or property gathered by a couple cohabiting after their divorce. These results demonstrate quite forcefully the continued vitality of the distinction between married and unmarried couples for property law purposes.

[*iii*]   *Cohabitation and Death.* Among the most interesting post-*Marvin* cases are those dealing with claims against estates. Contractual claims against estates for services rendered but not paid for prior to the death of the estate's subject have long been available. But a few cases have presented some interesting twists on this old theme. Reported cases include successful claims by a woman who left a husband and two children to live with an older man whom she later cared for as he died of a brain tumor,[135] by a mistress against the estate of her deceased lover,[136] and by a mate against the estate of a man whose will contained a clause terminating the inheritance of any party who contested the will.[137]

---

[132] [Court footnote number 18]: Plaintiff should be able to accomplish rehabilitation in less than two years. The sum awarded would be approximately equivalent to the highest scale that she ever earned as a singer, $1,000 per week, for two years.

[133] [Court footnote number 19]: While part of the funds may be used for living expenses, the primary intent is that they be employed for retraining purposes.

[134] 5 Fam. L. Rep. 3077, 3085 (Apr. 19, 1979).

[135] Matter of Steffes' Estate, 95 Wis. 2d 490, 290 N.W.2d 697 (1980).

[136] Donovan v. Scuderi, 51 Md. App. 217, 443 A.2d 121 (1982).

[137] Estate of Black, 160 Cal. App. 3d 582, 206 Cal. Rptr. 663 (1984). The court argued that a "contest" is a direct challenge to the will itself, while the *Marvin* claim is one for moneys not properly belonging to the estate at all. The issue as to whether a will with a clause wiping out an inheritance in case a *Marvin* claim is filed against the estate would be enforced was left for another day.

In *In re Estate of Eriksen*, 337 N.W.2d 671 (Minn. 1983), Pamela Potvin filed a claim against the estate of her deceased mate. Potvin and Jorgen Eriksen began living together in June, 1977. In the spring of 1979 they decided to buy a house together with joint funds. The title, however, was placed in Eriksen's name. Potvin, though separated from her husband, was still legally married. If the house was titled partly in her name, her husband would automatically have obtained statutory inchoate rights in the property analogous to curtesy and the mortgagee would have demanded his signature. In addition, Potvin would have lost some welfare benefits if she took an interest in the house. Potvin obtained a divorce on January 8, 1981, but Eriksen died a few months later. When he died, the proceeds of a life insurance policy paid $48,334.63, virtually all the remaining mortgage indebtedness on the house. During their time together, Potvin and Eriksen shared all expenses in running the house, including the premiums on the life insurance policy.

The probate court awarded Potvin half of the house, noting that the estate of Eriksen would have been "unjustly enriched" if it took the entire property.[138] This result was affirmed despite the existence of Minnesota statutes adopted in 1980 just after the *Marvin* trial which arguably restricted the availability of *Marvin* relief. MINN. STAT. § 513.075 then provided:

If sexual relations between the parties are contemplated, a contract between a man and a woman who are living together in this state out of wedlock, or who are about to commence living together in this state out of wedlock, is enforceable as to terms concerning the property and financial relations of the parties only if:

(1) the contract is written and signed by the parties, and

(2) enforcement is sought after termination of the relationship. The court construed this statute to apply only "where the sole consideration for a contract between cohabiting parties is their" contemplation of sexual relations.

[iv] *Proof of Implied Contract.* Though the *Marvin* court approved the use of implied contract theory between cohabitants, Michelle Marvin failed in her effort to take advantage of that holding. What sorts of evidence might prove an implied contract? The mere fact of living together only implies that two parties agreed to share living space. More evidence is necessary before the actions of the parties might lead a court to imply an agreement to support each other, split their estates, or to adopt the rules of community or marital property regimes. In one of the few reported cases in which an implied contract was successfully proven, Milian v. De Leon, 181 Cal. App. 3d 1185, 226 Cal. Rptr. 831 (1986), Arthur Milian and Sylvia Ann Sanchez De Leon were involved in a partition action over a house. De Leon and Milian dated for eight years, commingled significant amounts of money and jointly agreed to purchase the house. They both signed the escrow agreement papers and took title as joint tenants with rights of survivorship. Milian claims he had never promised to marry De Leon. De Leon claimed that she only purchased the house with Milian because they planned to marry. When he refused to wed, she refused to move into the house and broke off their relationship. Milian wanted a partition, along with extra credits reflecting that payments made toward the purchase of the house were mostly his. De Leon asked for a partition that evenly split the house. The court concluded that the parties contemplated marriage, took title as equal owners and each contributed significant amounts toward various expenses under a plan calling for each to pay what they could. This story was sufficient to give rise to an implied contract to share their assets equally.

---

[138] The actual remedy was in the form of a constructive trust, a device commonly used to control property titled in one name that has been paid for with funds from another source.

[d] Problem Notes

[i] Cohabitation and "Necessaries." In an earlier note, the obligation for one spouse to pay for medical expenses of the other was discussed.[139] Suppose in a case like *Milian v. De Leon*, discussed just above, that one of the cohabitants was hospitalized and the resulting bill was not paid. Could the hospital prove that the two parties had an implied agreement to share all expenses and use that contract to collect a judgment from either or both of the parties?

[ii] Anything New Under the Sun? Did the *Marvin* case do anything new? The remedies listed in the opinion have been available in one guise or another for a long time. Constructive or purchase money trusts have long been imposed on parties using other people's money to purchase property when there is no indication that a gift was intended. Express contracts are certainly old hat. Implied contracts, or perhaps better put, contracts provable circumstantially, have also been around quite a while. It is certainly arguable that contract law was simply used as it has always been used. What may have changed was the *Marvin* court's unwillingness to continue use of (outmoded?) moral precepts to evaluate the propriety of any particular remedy. The advent of no fault divorce during the decade prior to *Marvin* may have been a precursor for the trend to remove some aspects of moral evaluation from other areas of "family" law. Have the courts traveled too far down this path?

[iii] Family Community. Are there good reasons for distinguishing between married families and other families? Is there any reason to believe that unmarried couples are any less likely than married couples to wish the survivor of them to take all their joint property? Should we create a tenancy by the entirety, including its debtor protection features, for unmarried couples who wish to link their property responsibilities quite closely? Should intestate succession statutes be amended to leave property to surviving unmarried cohabitants ahead of children, as is frequently done for husbands or wives dying with children? What of communes? If you began to adopt property models for unmarried cohabitants, how would you treat larger "family" groups? Barbara Woodhouse, in *Toward a Communitarian Theory of the "Nontraditional" Family,* 1996 UTAH L. REV. 569, 576 argues that we should treat as a "family" any household "when its members are bound together by a powerful sense of specific obligation—legal, cultural, religious and/or moral." What changes would the legal system have to make to accommodate such a notion of family?

Legal searches for the meaning of family have occurred in a number of settings not involving the resolution of property disputes after cohabiting couples split up. Here are three of particular interest:

Right to Continue Occupancy of a Rent Controlled Apartment. A gay New York man lived in a rent controlled apartment. Regulations required the landlord to allow family members to continue occupancy of the unit after the tenant named in the lease dies. When the gay tenant died, should his companion be allowed to stay? The court said "Yes" in *Braschi v. Stahl Associates Company,* 74 N.Y.2d 201, 543 N.E.2d 49, 544 N.Y.S.2d 784 (1989).

Condominium Restrictions Limiting Occupancy of Housing Units to Family Use. A number of cases have arisen in which condominium home owner associations attempt to enforce rules about family use of houses against group homes occupied by small groups of psychologically or physically handicapped persons. The decisions go both ways. In *Hill v. Community of Damien*

---

[139] *See* p. 213 above.

of Molokai, 121 N.M. 353, 911 P.2d 861 (1996) an attempt to bar a group of four AIDS patients under a covenant limiting use of the house to a "single family" failed. But, in *Shaver v. Hunter*, 626 S.W.2d 574 (Tex. App. 1981) a group of seriously handicapped persons was not permitted to live in a house covered by a similar restriction.

Zoning Ordinances Limiting Use to Single Families. Zoning ordinances limiting occupancy to single family use have been challenged as violations of constitutional rights to privacy and free association. The results have been mixed, with the Court extending some constitutional protection to extended families, while leaving room for zoning controls to operate against other unrelated groups of people. *Moore v. City of East Cleveland*, 431 U.S. 494 (1977).

How would you resolve these various disputes?

[*iv*]   *Cohabitants and Marriage.* Why shouldn't we declare that two people who live together in an intimate relationship for a reasonable period of time or have a child together are married? Common law marriage once existed everywhere, but is now used in less than half the states. It was eliminated both for moral reasons and to force everyone to get a venereal disease blood test prior to marriage. Now that both rationales for doing away with common law marriage have little relevance, why not reinstitute it? Is it possible that we and our children would be better off if some legal structure based on an assumption that intimate relationships lasted a long time were applied to cohabitants and parents?

[e]   Cohabitation Agreement

Because of the unsettled nature of the law governing relationships between unmarried persons, a growing number of couples have signed contracts. Their terms are quite varied. A simple agreement is reprinted here so that you may evaluate both the wisdom of using such a device and the sorts of terms you might include in such an agreement were you asked to write one. You might also wish to compare this agreement with that in *Reilly v. Sageser*, p. 121 above.

RELATIONSHIP AGREEMENT[140]

This Agreement is made on _____ day of_____, _____ by _____ [Party 1] and _____ [Party 2] regarding their house at _____ [Address] in _____ [City and State], any other real property they may own in the future ("real property"), and jointly and individually owned personal property they presently own or may own in the future ("personal property").

---

[140] A relationship agreement might well be signed at the same time that wills are executed to cover property owned at death and not disposed of by the agreement, powers of attorney are signed giving the cohabiting partners authority to manage their mate's property in case of serious disability or incompetency and to make decisions on medical treatment in case mates become incompetent to handle their own affairs, and guardianship choices are made for children. Married partners are routinely given responsibility for their children, and disabled or incompetent spouses. But some couples, particularly homosexual ones, find that outsiders to their relationships are called upon by courts to fill such roles.

The parties have enjoyed each other's companionship over the past years and have shared jointly their incomes and property, in a spirit of partnership. In consideration of the mutual promises made in this agreement, the parties make the following contract:

I. REAL PROPERTY

1. The parties agree that they are joint tenants with rights of survivorship and not tenants in common, with each party holding an equal interest, in their real property. Each of the parties shall have the right to reside in or possess their real property and each shall have equal rights and responsibilities for day to day management of their real property.

2. Each of the parties has and shall continue to contribute equally to the purchase, operation, repair and improvement of the real property. Such contributions include but are not limited to monthly mortgage payments, property taxes, and insurance payments. If either party shall, for any reason, not contribute equally to the payment of these expenses, her[141] interest in the property shall not be affected by her unequal contribution. The parties anticipate that one or both of them may at some time be financially unable to pay half of the real property expenses because of unemployment or other causes. Failure to pay half of the real property expenses shall not diminish that party's ownership interest in the real property.

3. In the event any or all of the real property is rented to a third party, the rent proceeds shall be distributed to each of the parties equally.

4. In the event the parties elect to sell any or all of their property to a third party, the net profit from the sale of the real property shall be divided equally between the parties regardless of each party's relative contributions to the purchase, operation, repair and improvement of the property. Net profit is the sale price of the real property less any outstanding debt financing on the real property, real estate broker's fees and other closing costs attributable to the parties as sellers.[142]

5. In the event the parties shall separate, the jointly owned real property shall be disposed of as follows:

a. *Right to Purchase:*

(1) Each party shall have the right to purchase some or all of the other party's interest in the real property. In that event, the parties shall in good faith establish a fair market price for the real property. If the parties are unable to agree on a fair market price, a price shall be established by an independent appraiser selected by the parties.

(2) The net price to be paid to the party selling her interest shall be the fair market price of the interest less one half of any costs required to close the transaction.

(3) Each party shall have 30 days from the time of separation to exercise, in writing, her option to purchase the other's interest in real property. The party exercising her option to purchase will then have 60 additional days to complete the purchase. Failure to complete the purchase within 60 days will result in the real property being placed on the open market for sale to a third party.

---

[141] This agreement is written as if it was to be signed by two women. But the gender of the pronouns may obviously be altered to serve any other sort of couple.

[142] The decision not to account for capital improvements in this calculation is obviously important. Some couples may wish the party making contributions to such improvements to be able to recapture some or all of them upon sale.

(4) The party exercising the option to purchase shall pay the net price either in cash from her own funds or, in good faith, attempt to obtain refinancing for the real property. The terms of any refinancing must be acceptable to the party retaining ownership of the real property, taking into account the financial ability of that party to make monthly mortgage payments. In case of disagreement over the acceptability of the refinancing, the disagreement shall be resolved in accordance with Part IV of this Agreement.

(5) If the party purchasing the real property is unable for any reason to pay the net price in cash or to obtain satisfactory refinancing, then the purchasing party shall execute for the benefit of the party selling a note and second mortgage for the balance owed, principal and interest payable monthly for fifteen years, with interest at the rate prevailing at the time the right to purchase is exercised.

(6) If within 30 days of the time of separation, both parties exercise, in writing, their right to purchase the same real property and the parties are unable to agree upon which of them will exercise their right of purchase, the real property shall be placed on the open market for sale to a third party after the 30 days have elapsed.

(7) If neither party exercises their right to purchase within 30 days of their separation the real property shall be placed on the open market for sale to a third party.

b. *Rental*: Both parties may agree, in lieu of a sale to one of themselves or to a third party, to rent any or all of their real property to a third party. In such a case the parties will divide any rents received equally and will share equally in the expenses required to maintain the property for rental. During the 30 day period prior to the expiration of any lease or, in the case of a month to month lease, at any time, either party may exercise their rights to purchase under paragraph 5.a.

c. *Retain the Property*: Both parties may agree, in lieu of sale or rental, that they wish to keep any or all of their real property and that one of the parties will reside in or possess the real property. In that case, the party in residence or possession will lease the property for a term of at least one year and pay to the other party rent at the fair market rate. During the 30 day period prior to the expiration of any such lease either party may exercise their rights to purchase under paragraph 5.a. The party not in residence or possession shall be entitled to depreciation for tax purposes. Both parties shall continue to share equally the expenses required to maintain the real property and each shall take half of the mortgage interest as a deduction on their tax returns.

d. *Maintenance Until Disposition*: Until the real property is sold, transferred or rented pursuant to paragraphs 5.a. or 5.b., the parties will attempt to agree as to which of them will occupy the real property. During the period of joint ownership of the real property pursuant to paragraphs 5.a. or 5.b., the parties will share equally in the payment of the mortgage, property taxes, insurance premiums and repairs required to preserve the integrity of the real property. The party in possession will pay the cost of utilities, upkeep and maintenance.

II. PERSONAL PROPERTY

6. The parties agree that they have in the past pooled all income earned, and shall in the future pool all income earned, and such income and all personal property purchased or accumulated from that income is and shall be held as joint tenants with the right of survivorship and not as tenants in common, with each party holding an equal interest in such personal property.

7. In the event that the parties separate in the future, each is entitled to one-half of the jointly held personal property. Neither party shall have any claim for support or for any other money or property from the other, except as provided in this Agreement. All liabilities presently owed, or any subsequently acquired liabilities of either or both parties, shall be discharged out of jointly held personal property at the time of the separation.[143] If such liability is in the name of one party, who prefers not to discharge it at that time, she shall be awarded the necessary amount out of the common funds prior to their division.

III. GIFTS AND INHERITANCES

8. Should either party receive real or personal property by gift or inheritance the property belongs absolutely to the person receiving it. Such property may not be transferred to the other party except by way of a gift evidenced by a writing signed by the donor.[144]

IV. MEDIATION AND ARBITRATION

9. Any controversy, dispute or question arising out of, or in connection with, this Agreement or any breach of this Agreement shall be determined by mediation conducted by a mediator mutually agreed to by both parties. If mediation fails, the parties agree that any controversy shall be determined by arbitration conducted in _____ [City and State] under the terms of the Uniform Arbitration Act.

V. RESTRICTIONS

10. Neither party shall sell, transfer, mortgage, or otherwise dispose of or encumber her undivided interest in the real or personal property of the parties except as provided for in Part I of this agreement.

11. No party shall, either directly or indirectly, make application or petition any court for a partition of the real property.[145]

VI. MISCELLANEOUS PROVISIONS

12. This Agreement has been drafted and executed in _____ [City and State] and shall be governed by the laws of the state of _____.

13. This Agreement represents the complete understanding regarding the parties' decision to live together and replaces any prior agreements on the same subject, written or oral. This Agreement may be rescinded or amended, but only by a writing signed by both parties.

14. It is agreed by the parties that all rights, remedies, and liabilities given to or imposed upon the parties to this Agreement shall be binding upon their respective heirs, legatees, executors, administrators, successors and assigns.

15. In the event that any part or provision of this Agreement shall be determined to be invalid or unenforceable under the laws of _____ [State], the remaining portions of this Agreement

---

[143] This provision may cause problems for some couples and is likely to vary in its terms considerably from agreement to agreement.

[144] *Compare* Gibbons v. Gibbons, p. 198 above.

[145] Note how this clause makes a joint tenancy similar to a tenancy by the entirety.

which can be separated from the invalid or unenforceable provision shall continue in full force and effect.

Signatures: [Both Parties and Witness for Each]

CHAPTER **3**

COMMUNAL LIVING AND THE LAW OF GENEROSITY

§ 3.01 Introduction

This introductory segment of materials begins with a review of the basic law governing gifts and wills, continues with discussion of the relationships between inheritance rules and the concept of Civic Republicanism previously reviewed in the discussion of materials on Native Americans and women, and concludes with two cases on gifts and wills. These materials form the basis for the rest of the chapter, which investigates the role—historical and contemporary—that donative rules play in the creation, maintenance and public oversight of charitable, religious and other non-profit cultural entities. The next section reviews the rise and collapse of The Harmony Society, one of the most successful of many communal groups that flourished during the nineteenth century. Some of these societies took seriously the egalitarian rhetoric of both the Revolutionary War era and the nineteenth century women's movement, and experimented openly with new ways of organizing work, families and reproduction. The size and wealth of several of the communes, including The Harmony Society, also led to use of new forms of business organization. The Harmony Society materials, therefore, both build on the learning about gender issues in Chapter 2 and introduce consideration of property ownership by businesses taken up more fully in the next chapter.

This chapter closes with materials on donative rules, duress and modern religious cults. Drawing on the materials in both this introductory segment and those on the Harmony Society will help you analyze how we should treat attempts of "donors" to regain control over "gifts" made to contemporary religious groups.

[1] Summary of Donative and Testamentary Transfers

The basic rules governing donative and testamentary transfers are simply stated. A gift must be an accomplished fact for it to have legal effect. Thus, a promise to make a gift is unenforceable. The delivery of an asset with a present intention to transfer an interest in the property, and the acceptance of the gift by the donee, will result in a legally recognized transfer. Most common gifts easily fulfill these requirements. Amos simply gives an object to Brenda and says, "Happy Birthday." In order to prevent fraud, courts generally opine that gifts are recognized only when delivery is complete. It is so easy for the dishonest to declare, "My friend Don said he would give that to me," that we ignore promises to make donations. The typical gift rules operate on the "uncivilized" presumption that gifts are unusual. They give ammunition to the more cynical among us who assert that charitable impulses are unexpected and should therefore be deemed present only when benevolence is clearly intended and fully executed. Despite the concern over fraud, gifts are extremely easy to make. As a day to day proposition, the state exercises remarkably little control over donations.

Wills are treated quite differently. They must usually be in writing and these writings must be prepared with certain formalities. Traditional rules required testators to acknowledge that the instruments they signed were their wills. In addition, at least two (or in a few states, three) witnesses also had to sign the will. Despite the formalities required to execute a will, the document has no legal effect until the death of the testator. Wills are said to be *ambulatory instruments*. That is, they may be changed at any time prior to death; they "walk around" with the author.

The statutes on will formalities in effect throughout the United States are descendants of the Statute of Wills adopted in England in 1540. The requirement of a writing, like that of a completed delivery for gifts, is generally justified as a measure to prevent fraud, here against the estates of deceased persons. Since wills by definition only operate at death, reliance on completion of the transfer as a device to weed out fraud is not possible. The only way to insure that the living know about the wishes of deceased persons is to require a writing.

Though the need for some sort of protection against fraud is clear, there is no longer complete agreement about the need for enforcement of strict will formality requirements in all cases. The Uniform Probate Code, for example, permits *holographic wills*, those written in the handwriting of the deceased, but not witnessed. The theory is that the handwriting in such a document provides independent evidence that the deceased person actually wrote it, while corroboration of a testator's intentions must be specifically provided when the will is a typed or printed document. The Uniform Probate Code provisions on will formalities, adopted by 16 states, read as follows:

§ 2-502. Execution; Witnessed Wills; Holographic Wills [*]

(a) Except as provided in subsection (b) . . . , a will must be:

(1) in writing;

(2) signed by the testator or in the testator's name by some other individual in the testator's conscious presence and by the testator's direction; and

(3) signed by at least two individuals, each of whom signed within a reasonable time after he or she witnessed either the signing of the will as described in paragraph (2) or the testator's acknowledgment of that signature or acknowledgment of the will.

(b) A will that does not comply with subsection (a) is valid as a holographic will, whether or not witnessed, if the signature and material portions of the document are in the testator's handwriting.

(c) Intent that the document constitute the testator's will can be established by extrinsic evidence, including, for holographic wills, portions of the document that are not in the testator's handwriting.

Some states also recognize a *nuncupative will*, an oral will stated just prior to death, or *in extremis*. Tennessee, for example, has adopted the following provision, which mirrors § 49 of the Model Probate Code:[1]

§ 32-1-106 Nuncupative will.

(a) A nuncupative will may be made only by a person in imminent peril of death, whether from illness or otherwise, and shall be valid only if the testator died as a result of the impending peril, and must be:

---

[*] Reprinted with permission of the National Conference of Commissioners on Uniform State Laws.

[1] Other states have more limited provisions. The District of Columbia, for example, permits nuncupative wills only for persons in military service or for mariners at sea. D.C. CODE ANN. § 18-107.

(1) Declared to be his will by the testator before two (2) disinterested witnesses;

(2) Reduced to writing by or under the direction of one (1) of the witnesses within thirty (30) days after such declaration; and

(3) Submitted for probate within six (6) months after the death of the testator.

(b) The nuncupative will may dispose of personal property only and to an aggregate value not exceeding one thousand dollars ($1,000), except that in the case of persons in active military, air or naval service in time of war the aggregate amount may be ten thousand dollars ($10,000).

(c) A nuncupative will neither revokes nor changes an existing written will.

Despite the loosening of formalities in many states, the existence of restrictions on will writing, together with the large institutional structure of probate courts and the use of other mechanisms to control the distribution of assets of the dead, suggests an abiding role for state regulation of inheritance. Indeed, restrictions on the devolution of property at death are much more pervasive than those on *inter vivos* gifts. In addition to the greater formalities imposed on will writing than on gift giving, dower and curtesy limit the testamentary disposition of property, as do homestead acts, and statutes requiring that a certain share of an estate be left to surviving family members. And, of course, property left behind by persons dying without wills is disposed of under state intestate succession statutes.

The legal distinctions made between gifts and wills have led to enormous amounts of litigation. In spite of the simplicity of the basic rules for making gifts and wills, the case digests are littered with hundreds of decisions on the legitimacy of purported donative and testamentary transfers. Think of Deborah leaving a package in her desk with a letter saying, "Give this to Betsy when I die." Is there a delivery of the gift? Is the letter an instrument of gift or an attempt to write a will without meeting the formalities required by state law? George gives an envelope to Melvin and says, "Give this to Sam if I get killed in the war." Is this a completed gift of the contents of the envelope conditioned on Melvin's death in the war, or an invalid oral will? William and Susan set up a joint bank account using Susan's funds without paying much attention to the legal effects of establishing a joint tenancy with rights of survivorship. Susan completely manages the account while alive. When she dies, should the account proceeds go to her estate on the ground that the gift of a survivorship interest to William was never delivered or should the entire account go to William under survivorship rules?

While some of the differences in treatment of gifts and dispositions at death are attributable to concerns about the greedy among us lying about the wishes of a donor or testator, or to the practical need to dispose of assets left behind by the dead, the dissimilarity in treatment also reflects important, and at times contradictory, cultural perceptions about the right of the state to control the disposition of property. At the most basic level, different feelings surround the donation of property before and after death. The presumptively high level of control exercised by living people over their assets creates a strong basis for opposition to high levels of state control of *inter vivos* transfers. Some of that opposition dissipates after a person dies and is no longer able to exercise independent control of his or her assets.

[2] Additional Reading on Gifts and Wills

Additional material on the basic rules of gifts and wills may be found in JOHN E. CRIBBET & CORWIN W. JOHNSON, PRINCIPLES OF THE LAW OF PROPERTY 152-158 (3d ed. 1989); §§ 85.13 and 85.21 of POWELL ON REAL PROPERTY (Matthew Bender).

[3]   Civic Republicanism and Disposition of Property at Death

State control over a person's disposition of property at death has a long political and cultural history in the United States. The treatment of inheritance during the late eighteenth and early nineteenth centuries revolved around many of the themes previously reviewed in the materials on early Native American land claims and the limited economic roles of nineteenth-century married women.[2] The following article beautifully tells part of this tale.

Stanley Katz, *Republicanism and the Law of Inheritance in the American Revolutionary Era* [*]

76 Mich. L. Rev. 1, 4-9, 11, 15-18, 26-29 (1977)

The context of the problem will perhaps be more apparent if we first examine the intellectual justifications for the concept of inheritance and then examine the Anglo-American legal tradition. Broadly speaking, two sorts of justification for the law of inheritance have been advanced: one is derived from the Romano-medieval natural rights tradition, and the other emerged out of modern—that is, eighteenth century—conceptions of popular sovereignty and legal positivism.

. . . .

[I]t was Locke who, in his *First Treatise*, written in 1689, gave the classic English account of the natural rights argument. According to Locke, "[i]f anyone had began, and made himself a Property in any particular thing," here referring to his labor theory of value, "that thing, that possession, if he dispos'd not otherwise of it by his positive Grant, descended Naturally to his Children, and they had a right to succeed to it, and possess it."[6] Locke recognized that the right of children to take such property was not self-evident, especially as natural resources ("the Creatures" in Locke's term) used by a person should return, upon his death, to the common stock of society. He rejected the easy answer that "common consent hath disposed of it, to the Children" for although "Common Practice" does indeed so provide, nevertheless

> the common consent of Mankind . . . hath never been asked, nor actually given: and if common tacit Consent hath establish'd it, it would make it but a positive and not a Natural Right of Children to Inherit the Goods of their Parents: But where the Practice is Universal, tis reasonable to think the Cause is Natural.

Locke found the true reason in the interlocking natural principles of self-preservation and procreation. Reproduction fulfills the human instincts to propagate the species and to achieve an immortality. But since children are incapable of maintaining themselves, their parents have an obligation, and an instinctual urge, to provide for their sustenance and comfort. To Locke, the principle of procreation "gives Children a Title, to share in the *Property* of their Parents, and a Right to Inherit their Possession." Locke even went so far as to say that children actually shared in the title to their parents' property:

> Men are not Proprietors of what they have meerly for themselves, their Children have a Title to part of it, and have their Kind of Right joyn'd with their Parents, in the Possession

---

[2] Compare the materials here with the attitudes of Thomas Jefferson toward Native Americans, discussed in Chapter 1 beginning at p. 2, and of John Adams towards women's rights, discussed in Chapter 2 beginning at p. 144.

[*] © Stanley Katz. Reprinted with the permission of the author.

[6] J. Locke, Two Treatises of Government § 87, at 224 (P. Laslett ed., 1960).

which comes to be wholly theirs, when death having put an end to their Parents use of it, hath taken them from their Possessions, and this we call Inheritance.

This natural rights justification for inheritance, with its deeply ingrained respect for private property rights and the familial organization of society, has always had an intuitive appeal in Anglo-American culture.

. . . .

[However,] the mainstream of our tradition is clearly marked by the positivist spirit of Blackstone and the theorists of legislative sovereignty. Blackstone explained the basis of inheritance in the first chapter of the second book of his *Commentaries on the Law of England* and flatly denied the natural rights theory:

We are apt to conceive at first view that it has nature on its side; yet we often mistake for nature what we find established by long and inveterate custom. It is certainly a wise and effectual, but clearly a political, establishment; since the permanent right of property, vested in the ancestor himself, was no *natural*, but merely a *civil*, right.

Blackstone argued that natural-law theory suggests that "on the death of the possessor the estate should again become common," that it should revert to its natural state and thereby be available to the first occupant and user. But any such process would, in his view, lead to enormous discord in a perpetual rush to lay claim to the properties of the recently deceased, and it was therefore "for the sake of civil peace" that society began to order inheritance by legislation. Thus

the universal law of almost every nation (which is a kind of secondary law of nature) has either given the dying person a power of continuing his property, by disposing of his possessions by will; or, in case he neglects to dispose of it, or is not permitted to make any disposition at all, the municipal law of the country then steps in, and declares who shall be the successor, representative or heir of the deceased; that is, who alone shall have a right to enter upon this vacant possession, in order to avoid that confusion which its becoming again common would occasion.

. . . .

Despite this . . . endorsement of the positivist theory . . . we still must acknowledge that the natural rights tradition formed an exceedingly important part of the intellectual ferment of the American Revolution. After all, the Declaration of Independence justified colonial separation from Great Britain on the basis of "the Laws of Nature and of Nature's God," and, in a Lockeian vein, went on to hold that "all men . . . are endowed by their Creator with certain unalienable Rights, that among these are Life, Liberty and the pursuit of Happiness."[25] Such natural rights thinking might have led in either of two directions with regard to the law of inheritance. On the one hand, it could simply have reinforced the right of inheritance and stood as an ultimate, constitutional guarantee against the legislative abolition of that right, in which case, . . . it might also have provided an even greater freedom of testation than Americans currently enjoy. On the other, the natural rights philosophy of the Declaration might have stimulated a radical egalitarianism ("all men are created equal") condemning the traditional law of inheritance as paternalistic and nonegalitarian. Thus the natural rights component of the Revolution provided relevant but ambiguous guidelines for the study of

---

[25] 1 T. JEFFERSON, THE PAPERS OF THOMAS JEFFERSON 429 (J. Boyd ed., 1950).

inheritance. I hope to show that in the end it was the theory of the positivist Blackstone that was used to support the conclusions of . . . Locke, while the more radical egalitarian potential was only fleetingly articulated and never realized.

. . . .

For the Revolutionary generation, the law of inheritance took on a new, strategic importance, since it appeared to symbolize the aristocratic aspects of English government against which the Revolution increasingly directed itself. The absence of dramatic change in the law of inheritance during the colonial period should not distract attention from the disparities in the settings of inheritance in England and America. The socioeconomic impact of inheritance, particularly as to real property, was far less in North America than in England, where land was scarce. Moreover, the social and political structure of the American colonies was vastly less aristocratic than that of the Mother Country, and nowhere did this fact have more obvious and profound consequences than in the institution of inheritance, which, after all, furnished the principle that defined the succession to the Crown and the peerage, thereby determining the membership of the governing elite.

. . . .

The most eloquent and thoroughgoing exponent of [reform] . . . was Thomas Jefferson. Jefferson's first great public project was the reform of Virginia's law, and the revision of the law of inheritance was the first item on his agenda. Reflecting on this episode in his autobiography, Jefferson explained the strategic significance of this portion of the law:

> I considered 4 of these bills . . . as forming a system by which every fibre would be eradicated of antient [sic] or future aristocracy; and a foundation laid for a government truly republican. The repeal of the laws of entail would prevent the accumulation and perpetuation of wealth in select families, and preserve the soil of the country from being daily more & more absorbed in Mortmain. The abolition of primogeniture, and equal partition of inheritances removed the feudal and unnatural distinctions which made one member of every family rich, and all the rest poor, substituting equal partition, the best of all Agrarian laws. [49]

Jefferson stressed the ease with which this portion of the aristocratic legal establishment could be altered: "To effect it no violence was necessary, no deprivation of natural right, but rather an enlargement of it by a repeal of the law." [50]

At this early stage in the development of Jefferson's social thought, he stressed that the creation and maintenance of a republic required not just barriers to aristocratic accumulation of property, but also a scheme to distribute at least small parcels of land to all members of the society. This view was reflected in a bill drafted by Jefferson in January 1778 in which he proposed that every freeborn Virginian who marries and resides in the state for one year receive "seventy five Acres of waste or unappropriated Land." The purpose of this measure, Jefferson explained, was to promote "the more equal Distribution of Lands, and to encourage Marriage and population."

. . . .

---

[49] T. JEFFERSON, AUTOBIOGRAPHY OF THOMAS JEFFERSON 1743-1790, at 77-78 (P. Ford ed., 1914). For an extended discussion of the subject, *see* Katz, *Thomas Jefferson and the Right to Property in Revolutionary America*, 19 J.L. & ECON. 467 (1976).

[50] T. JEFFERSON, *supra* note 49, at 58 . . . .

These were Jefferson's views at the beginning of the Revolution; his thinking, provoked by his experiences in France, developed further in the 1780s. Observing firsthand the stark contrast in Europe between the immense wealth of the landed elite and the destitution of the landless, he was convinced that only drastic redistribution of property would alleviate poverty. He attributed the widespread unemployment of able and willing workers, amid great reserves of uncultivated land, to the high concentration of land ownership. Because of their great wealth, the proprietors paid no attention to expanding production. Jefferson recognized "that an equal division of property is impracticable." "But," he told James Madison in a famous letter written at Fountainbleu in October 1785, "the consequences of this enormous inequality producing so much misery to the bulk of mankind, legislators cannot invent too many devices for subdividing property, only taking care to let their subdivisions go hand in hand with the natural affections of the human mind."[53] Specifically, Jefferson recommended that the rules of inheritance require wide distribution of a decedent's estate among his relations and that the state levy progressive estate taxes on large estates.[54]

In this and in a second letter to Madison, written in September 1789, Jefferson set forth his philosophical approach to the law of inheritance. In 1785 he had concluded that

> [w]henever there is in any country, uncultivated lands and unemployed poor, it is clear that the laws of property have been so far extended as to violate natural right. The earth is given as a common stock for man to labour and live on [and] . . . [i]f, for the encouragement of industry we allow it to be appropriated, we must take care that other employment be furnished to those excluded from the appropriation. If we do not the fundamental right to labour the earth returns to the unemployed.[55]

Jefferson returned, with greater confidence, to the same theme in his remarkable letter of 1789, which represents the culmination of his thinking on the problem of the intergenerational transmission of wealth. In this letter he proposed to Madison the "self evident" proposition "'that the earth belongs in usufruct to the living' that the dead have neither powers nor rights over it." The critical passage is worth quoting in full:

> The portion occupied by an individual ceases to be his when himself ceases to be, and reverts to the society. If the society has formed no rules for the appropriation of it's lands in severality, it will be taken by the first occupants. These will generally be the wife and children of the decedent. If they have formed rules of appropriation, those rules may give it to the wife and children, or to some one of them, or to the legatee of the deceased. So they may give it to his creditor. But the child, the legatee, or creditor takes it, not by any natural right, but by a law of the society of which they are members, and to which they are subject. Then no man can, by *natural right*, oblige the lands he occupied, or the persons who succeed him in that occupation, to the paiment [*sic*] of debts contracted by him. For if he could, he might, during his own life, eat up the usufruct of the lands for several generations to come, and then the lands would belong to the dead, and not to the living, which would be the reverse of our principle.

We are thus confronted with the fascinating spectacle of a natural rights thinker escaping from a natural rights tradition. Jefferson was perfectly aware that inheritance had generally been

---

[53] 8 T. JEFFERSON *supra* note 25, at 682; 8 J. MADISON, THE PAPERS OF JAMES MADISON 386 (R. Rutland & W. Rachal eds., 1973). Note the response from Madison on June 19, 1786, in 9 *id.* at 76.

[54] 8 T. JEFFERSON, *supra* note 25, at 682.

[55] *Id.*

considered a natural right, but of course his own conclusions are precisely those of Blackstone and the positivists. He therefore favored legislation prescribing a just distribution of intestate property. Yet, the real logic of his self-evident proposition might well have led him to advocate the total abolition of inheritance. If the earth truly belongs to the living, the right of the dead to stipulate by will the disposition of their property is not easily justified, and the legitimacy of intestate succession seems insecure as well. Of course, by 1789 Jefferson was both geographically and politically far removed from the affairs of state government, and he never again concerned himself with inheritance legislation. Nevertheless, it is significant that at least one influential Revolutionary American perceived that the logic of republican revolution pointed toward radical reevaluation of the law of inheritance.

Jefferson's flirtation with radical theories of economic redistribution upon death is another reminder of the relationships between concepts of Civic Republicanism and property ownership that were discussed in Chapter 1. Considering ways to prevent land from being tied up over many generations in large aristocratic estates was a reaction not only to the English class system, but also to a desire to spread land ownership widely to guarantee the presence of a large group of civically responsible citizens.

[4] A Case on Gifts and Wills

Jefferson's contention that death was an appropriate moment for using egalitarian legislation to redistribute wealth emphatically demonstrates the potential differences between pre-and post-death transfers. While the intricacies of donative and testamentary transfers must be left for advanced courses in probate, trusts and wills, this section of materials has the modest goal of investigating basic tensions in the way we treat efforts to give things away. One case—*Gruen v. Gruen*—has been selected for this purpose. It inquires into the differences between a completed gift of a future interest with the donor retaining a life estate and an invalid attempt to transfer an asset at death without writing a will. This common problem allows discussion of the various purposes served by *inter vivos* and testamentary transfers and the circumstances in which one legal device, such as a gift, should be permitted to substitute for another, like a will.

Gruen involved a family dispute over ownership of a painting by the well known artist, Gustav Klimt. The plaintiff, Michael S. Gruen, initially pursued his claim for the work in Austrian courts where his step-mother lived. The Austrian legal system found it quite strange that anyone would pursue a claim that a gift of personal property had been made by the delivery of a letter. Their law required much more formal documentation that passed through a government approval process. Only when Mr. Gruen convinced the court that American law should be applied to the case, did he make any headway. He eventually got an injunction giving him control over the painting, but he was never able to enforce it. The New York case you are about to read was part of his continuing attempt to obtain relief.[3]

---

[3] Some of the background about *Gruen* was obtained in a telephone interview with Michael S. Gruen on Oct. 27, 1998.

[a] Opinions of the Court of Appeals of New York in *Gruen v. Gruen*

Michael Gruen v. Kemija Gruen

New York Court of Appeals
68 N.Y.2d 48, 496 N.E.2d 869, 505 N.Y.S.2d 849 (1986)

Paul G. Whitby and Helen J. Williamson, New York City, for appellant.

Michael S. Gruen, *pro se.*

Victor P. Muskin, New York City, for Michael S. Gruen, respondent.

OPINION OF THE COURT

SIMONS, Judge.

Plaintiff commenced this action seeking a declaration that he is the rightful owner of a painting which he alleges his father, now deceased, gave to him. He concedes that he has never had possession of the painting but asserts that his father made a valid gift of the title in 1963 reserving a life estate for himself. His father retained possession of the painting until he died in 1980. Defendant, plaintiff's stepmother, has the painting now and has refused plaintiff's requests that she turn it over to him. She contends that the purported gift was testamentary in nature and invalid insofar as the formalities of a will were not met or, alternatively, that a donor may not make a valid inter vivos gift of a chattel and retain a life estate with a complete right of possession. Following a seven-day nonjury trial, Special Term found that plaintiff had failed to establish any of the elements of an inter vivos gift and that in any event an attempt by a donor to retain a present possessory life estate in a chattel invalidated a purported gift of it. The Appellate Division held that a valid gift may be made reserving a life estate and, finding the elements of a gift established in this case, it reversed and remitted the matter for a determination of value. That determination has now been made and defendant appeals directly to this court, pursuant to CPLR 5601(d), from the subsequent final judgment entered in Supreme Court awarding plaintiff $2,500,000 in damages representing the value of the painting, plus interest. We now affirm.

The subject of the dispute is a work entitled "Schloss Kammer am Attersee II" painted by a noted Austrian modernist, Gustav Klimt. It was purchased by plaintiff's father, Victor Gruen, in 1959 for $8,000. On April 1, 1963 the elder Gruen, a successful architect with offices and residences in both New York City and Los Angeles during most of the time involved in this action, wrote a letter to plaintiff, then an undergraduate student at Harvard, stating that he was giving him the Klimt painting for his birthday but that he wished to retain the possession of it for his lifetime. This letter is not in evidence, apparently because plaintiff destroyed it on instructions from his father. Two other letters were received, however, one dated May 22, 1963 and the other April 1, 1963. Both had been dictated by Victor Gruen and sent together to plaintiff on or about May 22, 1963. The letter dated May 22, 1963 reads as follows:

Dear Michael:

I wrote you at the time of your birthday about the gift of the painting by Klimt.

Now my lawyer tells me that because of the existing tax laws, it was wrong to mention in that letter that I want to use the painting as long as I live. Though I still want to use it, this should not appear in the letter. I am enclosing, therefore, a new letter and I ask you to send the old one back to me so that it can be destroyed.

I know this is all very silly, but the lawyer and our accountant insist that they must have in their possession copies of a letter which will serve the purpose of making it possible for you, once I die, to get this picture without having to pay inheritance taxes on it.

Love, s/Victor.

Enclosed with this letter was a substitute gift letter, dated April 1, 1963, which stated:

Dear Michael:

The 21st birthday, being an important event in life, should be celebrated accordingly. I therefore wish to give you as a present the oil painting by Gustav Klimt of Schloss Kammer which now hangs in the New York living room. You know that Lazette and I bought it some 5 or 6 years ago, and you always told us how much you liked it.

Happy birthday again.

Love,

s/Victor.

Plaintiff never took possession of the painting nor did he seek to do so. Except for a brief period between 1964 and 1965 when it was on loan to art exhibits and when restoration work was performed on it, the painting remained in his father's possession, moving with him from New York City to Beverly Hills and finally to Vienna, Austria, where Victor Gruen died on February 14, 1980. Following Victor's death plaintiff requested possession of the Klimt painting and when defendant refused, he commenced this action.

The issues framed for appeal are whether a valid inter vivos gift of a chattel may be made where the donor has reserved a life estate in the chattel and the donee never has had physical possession of it before the donor's death and, if it may, which factual findings on the elements of a valid inter vivos gift more nearly comport with the weight of the evidence in this case, those of Special Term or those of the Appellate Division. The latter issue requires application of two general rules. First, to make a valid inter vivos gift there must exist the intent on the part of the donor to make a present transfer; delivery of the gift, either actual or constructive to the donee; and acceptance by the donee. Second, the proponent of a gift has the burden of proving each of these elements by clear and convincing evidence.

Donative Intent

There is an important distinction between the intent with which an inter vivos gift is made and the intent to make a gift by will. An inter vivos gift requires that the donor intend to make an irrevocable present transfer of ownership; if the intention is to make a testamentary disposition effective only after death, the gift is invalid unless made by will.

Defendant contends that the trial court was correct in finding that Victor did not intend to transfer any present interest in the painting to plaintiff in 1963 but only expressed an intention that plaintiff was to get the painting upon his death. The evidence is all but conclusive, however, that Victor intended to transfer ownership of the painting to plaintiff in 1963 but to retain a life estate in it and that he did, therefore, effectively transfer a remainder interest in the painting to plaintiff at that time. Although the original letter was not in evidence, testimony of its contents was received along with the substitute gift letter and its covering letter dated May 22, 1963. The three letters should be considered together as a single instrument and when they are they unambiguously establish that Victor Gruen intended to make a present gift of title to the painting at that time. But there was other evidence for after 1963 Victor made several statements orally and in writing indicating that he had previously given plaintiff the painting and that plaintiff owned it. Victor Gruen retained possession of the property, insured it, allowed others to exhibit it and made necessary repairs to it but those acts are not inconsistent with his retention of a life estate. Furthermore, whatever probative value could be attached to his statement that he had bequeathed the painting to his heirs, made 16 years later when he prepared an export license application so that he could take the painting out of Austria, is negated by the overwhelming evidence that he intended a present transfer of title in 1963. Victor's failure to file a gift tax return on the transaction was partially explained by allegedly erroneous legal advice he received, and while that omission sometimes may indicate that the donor had no intention of making a present gift, it does not necessarily do so and it is not dispositive in this case.

Defendant contends that even if a present gift was intended, Victor's reservation of a lifetime interest in the painting defeated it. She relies on a statement from *Young v. Young*, 80 N.Y. 422, that "any gift of chattels which expressly reserves the use of the property to the donor for a certain period, or . . . as long as the donor shall live, is ineffectual." The statement was dictum, however, and the holding of the court was limited to a determination that an attempted gift of bonds in which the donor reserved the interest for life failed because there had been no delivery of the gift, either actual or constructive . . . . The court expressly left undecided the question "whether a remainder in a chattel may be created and given by a donor by carving out a life estate for himself and transferring the remainder" (*Young v. Young, supra*). We answered part of that question in *Matter of Brandreth*, 169 N.Y. 437, 62 N.E. 563, when we held that "[in] this state a life estate and remainder can be created in a chattel or a fund the same as in real property." The case did not require us to decide whether there could be a valid gift of the remainder.

Defendant recognizes that a valid inter vivos gift of a remainder interest can be made not only of real property but also of such intangibles as stocks and bonds. Indeed, several of the cases she cites so hold. That being so, it is difficult to perceive any legal basis for the distinction she urges which would permit gifts of remainder interests in those properties but not of remainder interests in chattels such as the Klimt painting here. The only reason suggested is that the gift of a chattel must include a present right to possession. The application of *Brandreth* to permit a gift of the remainder in this case, however, is consistent with the distinction, well recognized in the law of gifts as well as in real property law, between ownership and possession or enjoyment. Insofar as some of our cases purport to require that the donor intend to transfer both title and possession immediately to have a valid inter vivos gift, they state the rule too broadly and confuse the effectiveness of a gift with the transfer of the possession of the subject of that gift. The correct test is "whether the maker intended the [gift] to have *no effect* until after the maker's death, or whether he intended it to transfer *some present interest*." (*McCarthy v. Pieret*, 281 N.Y. 407, 409, 24 N.E.2d 102.) As long as the evidence establishes an intent to make a present and irrevocable transfer of title or the right of ownership, there is a present transfer of some interest and the gift is effective immediately . . . .

Defendant suggests that allowing a donor to make a present gift of a remainder with the reservation of a life estate will lead courts to effectuate otherwise invalid testamentary dispositions of property. The two have entirely different characteristics, however, which make them distinguishable. Once the gift is made it is irrevocable and the donor is limited to the rights of a life tenant not an owner. Moreover, with the gift of a remainder title vests immediately in the donee and any possession is postponed until the donor's death whereas under a will neither title nor possession vests immediately. Finally, the postponement of enjoyment of the gift is produced by the express terms of the gift not by the nature of the instrument as it is with a will.

Delivery

In order to have a valid inter vivos gift, there must be a delivery of the gift, either by a physical delivery of the subject of the gift or a constructive or symbolic delivery such as by an instrument of gift, sufficient to divest the donor of dominion and control over the property. As the statement of the rule suggests, the requirement of delivery is not rigid or inflexible, but is to be applied in light of its purpose to avoid mistakes by donors and fraudulent claims by donees. Accordingly, what is sufficient to constitute delivery must be tailored to suit the circumstances of the case. The rule requires that the delivery necessary to consummate a gift must be as perfect as the nature of the property and the circumstances and surroundings of the parties will reasonably permit.

Defendant contends that when a tangible piece of personal property such as a painting is the subject of a gift, physical delivery of the painting itself is the best form of delivery and should be required. Here, of course, we have only delivery of Victor Gruen's letters which serve as instruments of gift. Defendant's statement of the rule as applied may be generally true, but it ignores the fact that what Victor Gruen gave plaintiff was not all rights to the Klimt painting, but only title to it with no right of possession until his death. Under these circumstances, it would be illogical for the law to require the donor to part with possession of the painting when that is exactly what he intends to retain.

Nor is there any reason to require a donor making a gift of a remainder interest in a chattel to physically deliver the chattel into the donee's hands only to have the donee redeliver it to the donor. As the facts of this case demonstrate, such a requirement could impose practical burdens on the parties to the gift while serving the delivery requirement poorly. Thus, in order to accomplish this type of delivery the parties would have been required to travel to New York for the symbolic transfer and redelivery of the Klimt painting which was hanging on the wall of Victor Gruen's Manhattan apartment. Defendant suggests that such a requirement would be stronger evidence of a completed gift, but in the absence of witnesses to the event or any written confirmation of the gift it would provide less protection against fraudulent claims than have the written instruments of gift delivered in this case.

Acceptance

Acceptance by the donee is essential to the validity of an inter vivos gift, but when a gift is of value to the donee, as it is here, the law will presume an acceptance on his part. Plaintiff did not rely on this presumption alone but also presented clear and convincing proof of his acceptance of a remainder interest in the Klimt painting by evidence that he had made several contemporaneous statements acknowledging the gift to his friends and associates, even showing some of them his father's gift letter, and that he had retained both letters for over 17 years to verify the gift after his father died. Defendant relied exclusively on affidavits filed by plaintiff in a matrimonial action with his former wife, in which plaintiff failed to list his interest in the painting as an asset. These affidavits were made over 10 years after acceptance was complete and they do not even approach the evidence in *Matter of Kelly* (285 N.Y. 139, 33 N.E.2d 62) where the donee, immediately upon delivery of a diamond ring, rejected it as "too flashy." We agree with the Appellate Division that interpretation of the affidavit was too speculative to support a finding of rejection and overcome the substantial showing of acceptance by plaintiff.

Accordingly, the judgment appealed from and the order of the Appellate Division brought up for review should be affirmed, with costs.

WACHTLER, C.J., and MEYER, KAYE, ALEXANDER, TITONE and HANCOCK, JJ., concur.

[b]   Explanatory Notes

[i]   *Giving Away Future Interests.* The *Gruen* case is your first exposure to *future interests*, or interests in property that are owned in the present but will not be possessed by the owner until some time in the future. If, for example, T writes a will giving a house to X for life, and then to the children of X, the children of X have a future interest until X dies.[4] Giving away future interests is a bit different from giving away complete, possessory, ownership of a tangible asset. When Arnold gives Brenda a nicely wrapped present and says, "Happy Birthday," possession and complete ownership of the gift are simultaneously transferred. As the *Gruen* court went to some pains to articulate, disposing of future interests necessarily transfers only ownership, leaving possession in the hands of the donor until a later time. Whether delivery of a gift of a future interest has been made will frequently become an issue when possession of the object remains with the donor. Michael Gruen was lucky enough to have possession of letters from his father evidencing the senior Gruen's intent to give him a future interest in the Klimt painting. Delivery of the letters served as a symbolic substitute for delivery of the painting itself. Try to decide *Gruen* on the assumption that all the discussions about the painting between Victor and Michael Gruen were oral. Would the court have decided the oral version the same way as the real case?

[ii]   *Some Other Examples.* There are so many gift cases that describing a few runs the risk of painting a distorted picture of judicial activities. But even if only a couple, perhaps abstract, dabs of paint are put on the canvas, perhaps you will be able to arrive at some interpretation of reality.

[A]   *Future Interests. Speelman v. Pascal*, 10 N.Y.2d 313, 178 N.E.2d 723, 222 N.Y.S.2d 324 (1961), was another "gift-of-future-interest" case. Gabriel Pascal, a theatrical producer, owned 98% of the stock in Gabriel Pascal Enterprises, which held the exclusive world rights to prepare and produce a musical play to be based on George Bernard Shaw's play *Pygmalion*, provided that arrangements to produce the musical were made by 1956. Pascal made a number of unsuccessful attempts to arrange with well-known composers to write the music and arrange to produce it. It was not until after his death in July, 1954, that his executor made arrangements for the highly successful production of *My Fair Lady*. On February 22, 1954, just a few months before he died, Pascal delivered a letter to Marianne Kingman:[5]

I give you from my shares of profits of the Pygmalion Musical stage version five per cent (5%) in England, and two per cent (2%) of my shares of profits in the United States. From the film version, five per cent (5%) from my profit shares all over the world.

---

[4] Chapter 5 takes up future interests in some detail.

[5] By the time of the litigation she had apparently married and changed her name to Marianne Speelman.

As soon as the contracts are signed, I will send a copy of this letter to my lawyer, Edwin Davies, in London, and he will confirm to you this arrangement in a legal form.

This participation in my shares of profits is a present to you, in recognition for your loyal work for me as my Executive Secretary.

At the time this letter was delivered, the rights to the musical version of Pygmalion were unexercised and subject to termination in 1956; there were, therefore, no profits to distribute. The court found that a completed gift was made. Even though there were no funds to distribute when the letter was written, the court had little difficulty holding that an expectancy of royalties, like a future interest in land or a painting, can be the subject of a gift.

[B] *Joint Tenancies With Rights of Survivorship.* Another realm in which gift problems frequently arise is joint tenancies with rights of survivorship. *Neuschafer v. McHale*, 76 Or. App. 360, 709 P.2d 734 (Or. App. 1985) is a nice example. In 1963, Eulalia Neuschafer and her daughter Eulalia James owned 1,103 and 416 shares respectively of stock in AT&T. With the help of a local banker, Eulalia Neuschafer named James McHale, her grandson, as a joint tenant with rights of survivorship in 498 of her AT&T shares. Eulalia James did the same with all of her shares. New stock certificates were issued in the joint names. The two Eulalias, however, continued to hold the certificates, vote the shares, receive the dividends and report the dividends as theirs on tax returns. Such generosity was not without precedent. Eulalia Neuschafer had bestowed numerous gifts upon McHale over the years, paid for his college education and given him the down payment for his first house. In 1981, just after McHale retired and moved back to Oregon, Eulalia James asked McHale to remove his name from "her" AT&T shares so she could do some estate planning. He complied. Shortly thereafter, Eulalia Neuschafer became seriously ill. McHale then claimed as his the July and October, 1981, dividend checks paid on the block of 498 shares still jointly named as his and Neuschafer's. Neuschafer reluctantly complied, but the episode caused a serious breach in relations among the parties. Litigation ensued to determine ownership of the 498 shares still jointly named. The court found that McHale had no interest in the stock. At trial, Neuschafer testified as follows:

Q. What was your reason for making this stock joint with . . . [McHale]?

A. Because they said when I passed on, it wouldn't have to go through Probate Court. It would go directly to . . . [him]. That is the reason I put the names on like that.

Q. At that time, did you intend on making a complete and absolute gift of this stock . . . to Jim [McHale] . . . ?

A. Yes, after I've died, it was to go to them.

Q. But at that time, at that time in 1963, while you are still alive, what was your understanding and intent as to who owned the stock?

A. I owned it.

Q. And did you at that time mean by putting Jim's name on the stock he had the right to take the dividends?

A. No. I didn't give them any right to the dividends.

Q. Did you at that time feel that you could, if you like, change whoever was on that stock, besides yourself, change the name on it?

A. Well, I saw no reason for changing the name then.

Q. Okay. Did you feel at that time you were giving the stock away to Jim, the 498 shares at that time back in 1963?

A. I didn't feel like I was giving the stock to him. I never felt like giving that stock as long as I lived because that is my protection, I needed that money to live on.

Review the above testimony carefully. The court found no absolute gift of a joint interest to McHale, holding instead that Neuschafer's attempt to create an interest in McHale was intended to take effect only upon her death and that such a testamentary disposition was void because it lacked the formalities required for a will. The court viewed a wish to "avoid probate" as evidence of an intention to make a testamentary disposition rather than to make an *inter vivos* gift. Did the court err in not finding that Neuschafer gave away a future interest, keeping the life estate for herself? Even if you can find an intent to give away a future interest, can you find a delivery? You should see how joint accounts, despite the formal language used to create them, may end up being treated in a variety of different ways. For a case coming out differently and confirming joint ownership, *see Estate of Brown v. Fulp*, 718 S.W.2d 588 (Mo. 1986).

[*iii*] *Gifts as Will Substitutes.* Many people naturally view their *inter vivos* gifts and testamentary dispositions as parts of a general plan of caring for relatives, friends and charities.[6] The *Gruen* case is a perfect example of that tendency. Michael's father apparently decided to give a bit more property to his favorite son than his will bestowed. Despite the possibility that *inter vivos* and testamentary dispositions may be part of the same process, there are a number of non-tax legal structures which treat gifts and wills quite differently. We have already seen how gift giving is viewed less formalistically than will writing and how that may cause difficulty when future interests are at issue.

Another interesting way in which gifts and testamentary dispositions are treated differently is the level of protection afforded spouses. As mentioned in Chapter 2 on married women's property law, many states have statutes permitting a spouse to reject a mate's will in favor of taking a certain share of the estate. But note well that the size of an estate may be significantly affected by the size and number of gifts delivered during life. In some states, an action may be brought by the surviving spouse to claim for the estate assets distributed during the deceased's life in "fraud of marital rights." Section 2-205 of the Uniform Probate Code, for example, includes in the value of an estate for mandatory share purposes gifts made by a deceased spouse during the two years before death "to the extent the aggregate transfers to any one donee in either of the two years exceeded $10,000."

Missouri statutes contain the following provision:

§ 474.150. Gifts in fraud of marital rights—presumptions on conveyances

1. Any gift made by a person, whether dying testate or intestate, in fraud of the marital rights of his surviving spouse to share in his estate, shall, at the election of the surviving spouse, be treated as a testamentary disposition and may be recovered from the donee and persons taking from him without adequate consideration and applied to the payment of the spouse's share, as in case of his election to take against the will.

2. Any conveyance of real estate made by a married person at any time without the joinder or other written express assent of his spouse, made at any time, duly acknowledged, is deemed

---

[6] Indeed, with some important exceptions, federal law now treats *inter vivos* and testamentary gifts as part of the same pie for purposes of figuring gift and estate tax levels. The most important exception for present purposes is the right of donors to make tax free *inter vivos* gifts of up to $10,000 per year per donee.

to be in fraud of the marital rights of his spouse, if the spouse becomes a surviving spouse, unless the contrary is shown.

This statute was used in *Estate of Catherine Bernskoetter*, 693 S.W.2d 249 (Mo. 1985), to force Charlene Kixmiller, the daughter of Hubert and Catherine Bernskoetter, to return over $65,000 to her mother's estate. For over 20 years, Catherine Bernskoetter put her monthly paychecks into an account named jointly in her's and her daughter's names. When his wife died, Hubert Bernskoetter claimed to be surprised both that the amount saved by his wife had gotten so large and that his daughter was named as joint tenant. The court ordered the funds placed in Catherine Bernskoetter's estate, noting that the transfer to her daughter was gratuitous, that Catherine Bernskoetter had retained control over the funds during her life, that the amounts were disproportionately large in relation to the rest of her estate, and that the savings were not openly and frankly disclosed to her spouse.[7]

The *Bernskoetter* litigation is a particularly interesting commentary on gender roles. Over the last two centuries, many married women maintained "rainy-day" funds. They provided a sense of security in a world fraught with economic risk in case a husband died, left home or fell on hard times. In some cases, these funds were passed along to daughters. While Catherine Bernskoetter's rainy-day fund was quite large, it was certainly not unusual. Indeed, it is difficult to believe that Hubert Bernskoetter didn't know his wife was putting her paycheck aside every month. In any case, are there any strong policy reasons for denying Catherine's daughter access to this entire fund? Would the Uniform Probate Code provision barring large transfers during the two years prior to death produce a more equitable result?

[c] Problem Notes

[i] *Divorce and Testamentary Dispositions.* Suppose Clara wrote a will naming her husband James as her principal beneficiary, and James wrote a similar will naming Clara as his primary beneficiary. At the same time they both changed the beneficiary designations on their retirement plans and all their insurance policies, naming each other as primary beneficiaries. Twelve years later, Clara and James divorced. James remarried shortly thereafter, named his new wife as primary beneficiary and wrote a new will to the same effect. Clara did not remarry. She did change the beneficiary designations on her retirement plan and insurance policies, but neglected to write a new will. When she dies, may her now remarried husband claim the bulk of her assets under her old will? Section 2-804 of the Uniform Probate Court says "No." Many states have similar provisions. Do you agree with them?

[ii] *Survivorship Rights.* As the above notes suggest, there is a tendency to ignore survivorship rights where evidence outside the joint tenancy itself supporting an intention to make a gift is lacking. This tendency is especially pronounced in bank account, stock certificate and certificate of deposit cases. The issue turns up much less frequently in real property settings. It is true that joint bank accounts are very easy to establish, but should we be so quick to ignore the establishment of survivorship rights? Or take the other tack. If gifts of survivorship rights in personal property are given a tenuous status, why treat real property survivorship interests differently?

---

[7] A similar problem also may arise with regard to homestead rights. For example, in *Estate of Johnson*, 397 So.2d 970 (Fla. App. 1981), the family home was conveyed to an *inter vivos* trust over which the deceased retained control during his life. The designation of the party to take the home upon Johnson's death in the trust was overridden in favor of guaranteeing rights in the homestead to the surviving spouse and children.

[iii] **Wealth Redistribution and Inheritance Rights.** Compare *Gruen* with *Martin Luther King, Jr., Center for Social Change v. American Heritage Products*, found in Chapter 12 (*see* p. 1130), the trends to reform the Rule Against Perpetuities discussed in Chapter 5 (*see* p. 381), and *Gibbons v. Gibbons*, taken up in Chapter 2 (*see* p. 198). In combination these cases suggest strongly that the scope of control given people over the disposition of their property at death has significantly increased in this century. Though large gifts carefully detailed in writing, as in *Gruen*, may certainly be made during life, the *King*, Perpetuities reform and *Gibbons* situations each guaranteed greater authority to the scrivener of wills. Intangible rights in one's personality affirmed by *King* may be inherited, perpetuities reform allows a testator to control property for a longer period of time, and spouses are excluded from inherited property at both death and divorce absent quite specific proof of an *inter vivos* gift by the spouse receiving the inheritance to her or his mate. Additional controls have been awarded to testators by the significant reduction in estate taxes adopted in recent decades. To whatever degree death has historically been viewed as an appropriate moment for significant redistribution of wealth, that view appears to be on the decline. Is that a trend you support?

[iv] **Gifts and Theft.** One of my students told me a story about her grandfather who painted a portrait of John F. Kennedy and gave it to Jacqueline Kennedy on behalf of Hungarian immigrants in the United States. She accepted the painting and hung it in the White House library. For a few months, friends of the artist who visited the White House told the artist they had seen it. After that, visitors reported it was no longer hanging in the library. The artist's family tried to track down what had happened to it without success. Twenty years later a man called the artist asking about the painting. He said that Mrs. Evelyn Lincoln, President Kennedy's secretary, had given the work to his father-in-law two decades ago and that his father-in-law later gave it to his daughter, the caller's wife. It turns out the call was made to obtain background information about the painting for use by Sotheby's when it was put on auction. The artist's family tried to get those possessing the painting to either return it to the White House or give it to the painter without success. So the artist's son went to the auction, purchased it, and gave it to the artist as a birthday present. Who actually owned the painting when it went up for auction?

§ 3.02 Nineteenth Century Utopian Religious Communities: The Harmony Society

[1] Introduction

Frederick Jackson Turner, the famous nineteenth-century historian, argued that the frontier, more than any other force, forged the American character.[8] Turner's belief that the trait of individualism could be traced to the pioneer's response to the frontier has become a classic topic of American intellectual history debates. Regardless of the validity of Turner's thesis as a description of the general American community, rugged individualism hardly described all early frontier settlements. A significant number of Christian communist churches and other utopian groups transplanted their concepts of collective social structure and communal ownership of property to the American frontier long before the country, as a whole, matured economically. The Amana ranges and refrigerators in kitchens, the Oneida silverware on your table and the Ambridge steel girders in the Empire State Building all find their origins in these early communal settlements. Indeed the nineteenth century was littered with various utopian and religious groups.

---

[8] Turner, *The Significance of the Frontier in American History*, PROCEEDINGS OF THE FORTY-FIRST ANNUAL MEETING OF THE STATE HISTORICAL SOCIETY OF WISCONSIN (1894).

The "sect"-tarianism of recent decades is minor in comparison with that of a century and a half ago.

Many of these communities arose at the same time that the first women's movement was beginning to flower. Questions were being posed throughout the culture about the roles of women, the nature of childhood, the importance of family to the development of a civic society, and the nature of life in an increasingly commercial world. While most people attempted to integrate new cultural developments into their established patterns of life, a significant minority experimented with dramatically different forms of living. Spurred on during the 1830s by deep economic dislocations, flare-ups of religious revivalism, and the arrival of large waves of immigrants, utopian and religious groups took off to the frontiers to set up ideal communities.

This section of materials tells part of the story of one of the earliest and most prosperous of such groups—the Harmony Society of Economy, Pennsylvania. The story itself is quite fascinating; it is worth reading for its own sake. But along the way, some basic problems about gifts and property ownership by groups are evoked. As you know from studying Chapters 2 and 3, property may be donated to and held by groups in a variety of different ways. In all these settings, those giving money to a community may wish to get it back if they withdraw for some reason, whether it be divorce, bankruptcy, sheer pettiness, or death. This section of materials surveys some of the intriguing issues that surround the creation and break up of communities of people. Most groups holding property eventually disband. One consequence is that courts are often forced to decide when total dissolution is appropriate and who should get the assets of the defunct group. While much time is devoted to problems of withdrawal in later courses on partnerships and corporations, study of the Harmony Society will permit you to focus on the same basic issues without knowing a great deal about forms of business organization.

Finally, looking at problems of creation, withdrawal from and termination of groups holding property should help you understand how difficult it is to establish a group. Anticipating future difficulties is a crucial consideration in drafting legal documents and accepting gifts. Doing it well is extremely difficult. An example may help. Very few of those among you who are married thought about divorce, death, property division, or serious illness prior to the wedding. Most people simply do not think of unpleasant events if they don't have to. But even if you think about unpleasantness at happy moments in your life, writing documents which anticipate how you would like to handle misfortune is hard. You may guess wrong about your future wishes. Future events may render prior decisions useless. Rigidly drafted documents may make it impossible to alter strategies over time; loosely drafted documents may make it too easy to alter intentions later.

Problems of property donation and transfer, withdrawal, dissolution and document drafting recur at a number of spots throughout the course. For now, simply recognize that these sort of problems are endemic in property law while working through the ways in which one communal group—the Harmony Society—attempted to handle them.

[2]   The Early History of the Harmony Society

[a]   The George Rapp Era

The Harmony Society was established in 1805 by a group of German religious separatists who pooled their resources into a common fund and purchased land in Butler County, Pennsylvania. Unable to practice their religion freely in their native province of Wurtemburg, Germany, the group came to the United States under the patriarchal leadership of its founder and "prophet," the Reverend George Rapp, in search of land upon which to found a church consecrated to total Christianity. The members adopted the community structure of the early Christian church. Property was communally owned and church members were subject to a social compact which articulated publicly the rights and obligations of both the member and the society. By Article 1 of the agreement all members agreed to "deliver up, renounce and remit all our estate and property, consisting of cash, lands and chattels or whatever it may be, to George Rapp and his associates in Harmony, Butler Co. . . .as a free gift and donation for the benefit and use of the community there" and bound themselves, their heirs, and descendants, "to make free renunciation thereof, and to leave the same at the disposal of the superintendents of the community" as if the member "never had nor possessed it."

In Article 2 the members pledged obedience and submission to the Society and promised "to promote the good and interest of the community," and to that they pledged their children and families. Recognizing that human frailty might make it difficult for certain members to "stand it in the community," each member also promised, in Article 3, never to demand any reward for themselves or their children for "labor or services," and declared whatever they should do would be "as a voluntary service for our brethren." In consideration of this renunciation of property and dedication of labor and services, George Rapp and his associates promised to supply the subscribers to the contract with all the necessaries of life, not only in their "healthful days, but when they should become sick or unfit for labor." And if, after a "short or long period," a member should die or otherwise depart from the community, "being the father or mother of a family," such family should "not be left widows and orphans but partakers of the same rights and maintenance."[9]

Article 5 read as follows:

And if, as above stated, the case should happen that one or several of the subscribers after a short or long period should abstain from their promise and could or would not submit to the laws and regulations of the church or congregation, and for this or another cause would leave the Harmonie, George Rapp and his Society promise to refund him or them, the property brought into the Harmonie without interest, and that in one, two or three annual installments, as the sum may be, large or small; and if one or more of them was poor and brought nothing into the congregation, they shall, provided they depart openly and orderly, receive a donation in cash, according to their conduct while here, or as their circumstances and needs may require, which George Rapp and his Society shall determine at his or their departure.[10]

In 1807 and 1808, a deep religious feeling pervaded the newly founded community and brought the entire congregation into ferment. At this time, the Society, under the spiritual influence of George Rapp, adopted the practice of celibacy in order to approach the pure virgin image of God necessary to become a true follower of Christ. The adoption of this practice, which was later to create great tension in the community and lead many otherwise loyal members to withdraw, caused the first lawsuits to be brought against the Society. These suits, which sought the refund of withdrawing members' money from the common treasury, were settled quickly and quietly by Rapp.

By 1814, the Society, with an emphasis on development through the harmonious balance of agriculture and industry, achieved self-sufficiency and owned about 7,000 acres. The settlement

---

[9] Schwartz v. Duss, 187 U.S. 8, 16-17 (1902).

[10] K.J.R. ARNDT, GEORGE RAPP'S HARMONY SOCIETY, 1785-1847, at 74 (1971). [Hereinafter cited as Arndt I.]

of neighboring tracts of land, however, upset the secluded environment Rapp felt so essential to the religious harmony of the community. Rapp arranged for the sale of the land for $100,000 and moved the Society to Indiana. There, a second agreement, renewing the commitment of 1805, was entered into on January 20, 1821. This agreement also expressed the submission of the subscribers to the Society, the dedication of their service and labor, and the communal promise of continuing support. After building a new settlement on the Wabash River, the Society found the climate, especially the hot, humid summers, disagreeable. They moved again in 1825 to a tract of land along the Ohio River in Beaver County, Pennsylvania. The land left behind on the Wabash was sold to Robert Owen, a famous Scottish social reformer, who envisioned the creation of a new social state in the town he named New Harmony. In his first address to his new community, Owen stated his aims: "I am come to this country to introduce an entire new State of society; to change it from the ignorant, selfish system, to an enlightened social system which shall gradually unite all interest into one and remove all cause for contest between individuals."[11] New Harmony was also to be a place where women's full rights were to exist and where the individual would be able to achieve physical, intellectual and spiritual unity. Plagued by too many aspirations and too little organization, Owen's dream lasted only two years. Lack of selectivity in the choice of members and absence of strict discipline hastened the collapse of this bold social experiment. The failure of New Harmony reinforced Rapp's determination to continue his system of patriarchal rule.

The new home of the Harmony Society was ideally situated on a fertile plateau overlooking the Ohio River. The settlement became known as Economy and it was here that the Society was to blossom into the "divine economy" envisioned by Rapp. In keeping with this advancement, the Articles of Agreement were rewritten in 1827 to bind the members of the "divine economy" together more clearly and to emphasize more explicitly the patriarchal management of the Society. Drafting of the new agreement was also spurred by a lawsuit filed by a former Society member who challenged the prior Articles of Agreement.

By the first article the members gave, granted and forever conveyed to "George Rapp and his associates, their heirs and assigns, all of our property, real, personal and mixed, whether it be lands and tenements, goods and chattels, money or debts due to us, jointly or severally, in possession or in remainder or in reversion, or in expectancy, whatsoever or whensoever, without evasion or qualification, or reserve, as a free gift or donation, for the benefit and use of said association or community." Members were to be obedient to superintendents, were bound to promote the interests and welfare of the community, and were to receive support and instruction. Article 5 of the 1805 Agreement dealing with withdrawal, became, with only slight changes, Article 6 of the 1827 Agreement.

According to later testimony of members of the Society, George Rapp was able to get the members to sign the document only by straining his spiritual powers to the utmost.[12] On the one hand, the patriarchal system of government was essential to the faith of the primitive church. The individual was but a member of the body which is Christ, according to Rapp, and as a member could exist only under the direction of the head, here represented through the patriarch, George Rapp. On the other hand, with the building of a third settlement and the passing of 20 years in service of the community, the equity of the individuals in the Society was greater than ever before. Since those who succumbed to nature's temptations were subjected to a feeling of

---

[11] *Id.* at 325.

[12] *Id.* at 357.

inferiority which usually resulted in their "voluntary withdrawal" from the Society, the members had reason to be hesitant in signing an agreement that would increase Rapp's ability to deny them the benefits of their toils. These tensions over the arduous path of celibacy and Rapp's dictatorial rule were intensified by the arrival of Count De Leon in 1832.

The visit of Count De Leon, a man of mysterious origins and questionable background, was preceded by a series of letters which heralded the self-styled "lion of Judah" as a prophet the equal of Rapp. The arrival of the Count and his followers marked a major event in the history of the Society. As the Count's stay progressed, the contrast between his generosity and sensitivity to injustice and Rapp's demand for a more ascetic way of life split the community. As many as one-third of the Harmonists, in open dissension, signed a document calling for Rapp to produce a full accounting, for the "overthrow" of George Rapp and Frederick Rapp, the Society's financial manager, and for the election of Count De Leon as the new patriarch. These dissenters established a committee of 12 which drew up a formal declaration denouncing Rapp for departing from the spiritual basis of an association formed by contract on apostolic principles for the common good. In the end, Rapp won this power struggle. Two hundred and fifty departing members followed Count De Leon to a new settlement 12 miles away, called Phillipsburgh. They received a "settlement" of $110,000 in return for the signing of a release granting to George Rapp and his associates all their right and title in any of the property belonging to the Society.

In 1836, the Articles of Agreement received their first thorough judicial test when the *Schriber* suit,[13] begun in 1827, was decided by the Pennsylvania Supreme Court. Jacob Schriber, the son of one of the original contributing members, frustrated by his inability to persuade Rapp to remove the group to Palestine to await the coming of the Lord, withdrew from the Society in 1826. His father, Peter, who had contributed property totaling about $8,000 to the original common fund, remained a member and died intestate in the Society. Jacob, as heir, sued for an accounting of property of his father in the Society's hands. He predicated his right to recover on the grounds that the Society was a partnership, that the defendants were joint partners and, as to real estate, tenants in common with the intestate, and that the Articles of Agreement executed by the intestate at Harmony on the Wabash and at Economy were fraudulently procured. The court found that the Articles were not inconsistent with Constitutional rights, moral precepts, or public policy, and ruled that:

> [A]n association by which each surrendered his property into common stock, for the mutual benefit of all, during their joint lives, with the right of survivorship, reserving to each the privilege to secede at any time during his life is not prohibited by law . . . and that the right of secession is not transmissible to the personal representative of a party to such agreement, so as to enable him to recover the property of his intestate, so put into the common stock . . . [and] . . . that a member of a religious society cannot avoid a contract with it on the basis of its peculiar faith by setting up the supposed extravagance of its doctrines as a proof that he was entrapped.[14]

Prompted by the outcome of the *Schriber* case and the bitter lessons of the Count De Leon secession, Rapp decided to revise the Articles again in 1836 to eliminate the last vestige of personal claim to property and the last temptation to leave the Society. The life of the Society, at this time, was marked by an inward movement. Membership was closed to outsiders and a church fund of over $500,000 in gold and silver coins was sealed away. Revision of the Articles

---

[13] Schriber v. Rapp, 5 Watts 351, 30 Am. Dec. 327 (Pa. 1836).

[14] *Id.* at 351.

was the last step in this process—an attempt to stop any possible loophole which might make the outside world more desirable to members within. The new agreement, which revoked Article 6 of the 1827 Agreement (Article 5 of the Agreement of 1805), read in part as follows:

And whereas, The provisions of the said 6th article, though assented to at the time, manifestly depart from the great principle of a community of goods and may tend to foster and perpetuate a feeling of inequality at variance with the true spirit and objects of the association;

And whereas, The principle of restoration of property, besides its pernicious tendency, is one which cannot now be enforced with uniformity and fairness, inasmuch as the members of the association in the year 1816, under a solemn conviction of the truth of what is above recited, did destroy all record and memorial of the respective contributions up to that time;

And whereas, Continued happiness and prosperity of the association, a more intimate knowledge of each other, have removed from the minds of all members the least apprehension of injustice and bad faith:

Now, therefore, Be it known by these presents that the undersigned, with a view to carry out fully the great principles of our union, and in consideration of the benefits to be derived therefrom, do hereby solemnly enter into covenants, and agree with each other as follows:

1st. The said 6th article is entirely annulled and made void, as if it had never existed; all others remain in full force as heretofore.

2nd. All the property of the society, real, personal and mixed, in law or equity, and howsoever contributed or acquired shall be deemed now and forever joint and indivisible stock. Each individual is to be considered to have finally and irrevocably parted with all his former contributions, whether in land, goods, money or labor; and the same rule shall apply to all future contributions whatever they may be.

3d. Should any individual withdraw from the society, or depart this life, neither he in the one case nor his representatives in the other, shall be entitled to demand in account of said contributions, whether in land, goods, money or labor, or to claim anything from the society as matter of right. But it shall be left altogether to the discretion of the superintendent to decide whether any, and if any, what allowance shall be made to such member or his representatives as a donation.[15]

Prior to this agreement all contributions of property were for the use and benefit of the community on the condition that any members withdrawing were to receive the original value of their contributions. After 1836, the Society's property would no longer be held subject to reclamation on the basis of its original value.

With the revision of 1836 and the closing off of membership to outsiders, George Rapp became the undisputed patriarch of a purified and purged congregation of saints. His last 11 years of life were spent watching his Society prosper and grow. During this time, the Community's wool and silk industries were among the nation's best. The Society began to receive world-wide acclaim for its remarkable achievements in agriculture and industry. At his death in 1847, Rapp remained steadfast in his belief that his mission was heaven sent: "If I did not so fully believe that the Lord has designed me to place our society before his presence in the land of Canaan I would consider this my last."[16] After Rapp's death, the members of the Society renewed the Articles

---

[15] Schwartz v. Duss, 187 U.S. 8, 32-33 (1902).

[16] Arndt I, note 10 above, at 599.

and reaffirmed their commitment to hold firm until Christ should make his personal appearance or until the death of each member. To remedy the governmental void created by Rapp's death, the Council of Elders was formed, and two Trustees, Jacob Henrici and Romelius Baker, were appointed to conduct the affairs of the Society.

Although prosperity continued to visit the Society in the time after Rapp's death, some of the problems which had existed during his lifetime surfaced in the form of a lawsuit which would plague the Society with investigations and court battles for eight years. An incident in 1846 provided the factual background for the case. Many of those who had left the Society during the Count De Leon secession still lived in the area and harbored great resentment towards Rapp for the paltry sum he had offered them in settlement of their interests. As the wealth of the Harmonists grew, the seceders approached Rapp through intermediaries in an effort to increase the settlement. Rapp, however, stood fast by his legal release and refused to see the seceders.

With rumors circulating throughout the area of a possible march on Economy and memories of the riotous departure of Count De Leon reawakening, a group of former members approached Joshua Nachtrieb, a member of the Society and foreman of the outdoor crew, while he was serving jury duty in a neighboring town. The seceders requested information on the likelihood of an adjustment in the $110,000 settlement. Nachtrieb responded that he personally did not know but would arrange a meeting with a group of knowledgeable members the next week in a field adjacent to Economy. Able to persuade only one other member, Elijah Lemix, to accompany him, Nachtrieb met with the seceders for a few moments and reported to them that he had not received any new information. Hearing of this meeting Rapp called the two members to his house and expelled them from the Society. Nachtrieb "unwillingly" left the community after receiving $200 from Rapp in exchange for a written release of all his interest in the Society. He married and had children shortly after leaving Economy. But, at age 48, he found life outside Economy difficult without a small amount of capital to make a new start. With this in mind, he brought suit, in 1849, for an accounting and partition of property.

[b] Opinion of the United States Circuit Court in *Nachtrieb v. The Harmony Settlement*

Nachtrieb v. The Harmony Settlement

United States Circuit Court, Western District of Pennsylvania

17 F. Cas. 1139 (1855) (No. 10,003)

. . . .

Joshua Nachtrieb had joined the society, without any property, in 1819; and had remained a peaceful and useful member for twenty-seven years. In 1846 certain seceding members, who professed to have claims against the society, and had given Rapp a good deal of anxiety, met Nachtrieb, with one or two others, and held a few short conversations with them on the subject of their demands and discontents. They inquired of Nachtrieb whether the society was willing to do anything for those who had left it and got nothing—whether Rapp had brought their request before the society; matters to which Nachtrieb answered that nothing had been done or said in the society about their getting anything. Rapp hearing of the meeting and colloquy, proceeded to discipline. Nachtrieb and the others were summoned to Rapp's house. "When Rapp came in," said the testimony, "he commenced on Joshua and said, 'Now let us give them fellows our judgment—Joshua, you are to blame for all this.' Joshua said, 'He did not know it was wrong or he would not have done it.' Rapp said, 'You intended to raise a mob.' Joshua said, 'No; if I had thought it was wrong to go there, I would not have done it.' Rapp then said, 'You must go right off and leave the town.' Joshua pleaded off, said he was sorry, said he would not go. Rapp said, 'No; we won't have you—you must go.' A night or two after this, the society being all present at a religious meeting, one of the elders, when the services were over, said to Rapp, 'There is something to be said.' Rapp then observed from the pulpit, 'Something has taken place lately—it is this: Joshua Nachtrieb and some others have gone out and conversed with their friends who left us. He must now leave the society; we cannot have such men.' Rapp then asked if he was present. Nachtrieb said, 'Yes, father, I am here.' Rapp said, 'What are you doing here? I thought you had gone.' Nachtrieb said. 'He was sorry if he had done anything wrong, and that if it had happened it should not happen again.' Rapp answered, 'Any fool can speak so; we cannot use such men; you must leave the society; you must be off.' Rapp then inquired of the society if they agreed with him—they said yes. Rapp then said to Nachtrieb, 'Now you know what you have to do: thy father himself, don't want you any longer.' Nachtrieb went away two days after, having previously received from Rapp $200, and signed this receipt, which it was not shown had been obtained by any specific fraud or misrepresentation: To-day I have withdrawn myself from the Harmony Society, and ceased to be a member thereof. I have also received from George Rapp, two hundred dollars as a donation, agreeably to the contract. Joshua Nachtrieb. Harmony, 18th June, 1846."

Soon after this Nachtrieb declared to several of the members, that he was glad to go away—was tired of the society—and that he did not depart from any compulsion. The property of the concern at this time amounted to $901,723.42, and there were 321 members. So that if Nachtrieb had received a full share of the concern, as on a division, he would have got about $2,809.10.

In this state of things, Nachtrieb having married after his departure, and got children, now filed a bill in chancery—this suit—against the Harmony elders or trustees, setting forth his joining the society in 1819, being then 21 years old; his faithful and diligent labors in its business, receiving nothing in return but a bare maintenance; and that in June, 1846, being then 48 years old, and worn out with labor, he was wrongfully excluded from the society, turned out of its possessions, and deprived of participation in its property and effects, by the fraud, &c., of Rapp and his associates. The bill prayed an account "of the sums due complainant, for his labor and services in said association, and of the share he was justly entitled to, in the property and estates of said association, and the profits accrued during his membership, and that the same may be decreed to him."

The respondents, in their answer, admitted that the complainant was a member of the association, as stated in his bill, and that up to 1846 he had labored diligently in the affairs and business of the association, increasing its wealth and promoting its interest agreeably to the terms and spirit of their mutual compact—and that the association had prospered in its temporal affairs, having, from small beginnings, become the owner of property to a considerable amount.

It then averred that the complainant, during the period of his membership, enjoyed all the benefits, advantages, and comforts, individual, social, and religious, which were enjoyed by the fellow members, and all that were contemplated in forming the association and to which he was entitled by the terms and spirit of their agreements, and was entitled to be maintained, cherished, &c., by the association; one of the objects of the society being that of making old age comfortable and free from cares or the necessity of labor. But it denied that the defendant was wrongfully and unjustly excluded from the association. On the contrary, it averred that the complainant voluntarily and of his own free will separated himself from and abandoned said association, and consequently, according to the terms of their articles of association, was not entitled to any compensation for his labor and services, other than that which he received in his support and maintenance, instruction, &c., while he remained a member.

On this case, two questions arose:

1. A question of fact: Whether Nachtrieb had "withdrawn" from the society; and so, under the articles of compact, lost his right to demand any account of its property, and bound himself to take such allowance as "the discretion of the superintendent might decide should be made to him as a donation?" or whether he was improperly expelled, and had some further rights against the society?

2. A question of law: Supposing the last to be the case, viz., that he had been improperly expelled, what was the exact nature and extent of the remedy to be awarded him? Whether he was entitled to compensation for his labor during the time that he had been in the community? or whether he was entitled to a share of the profits made since he was there? or whether he was entitled to an equal and separated share of the whole property as it stood at the time of such expulsion? or finally, whether under so peculiar a kind of contract and arrangement as that which lay at the base of this community, he could, under any circumstances, ask more than a restoration to his ancient membership and its rights.

The whole capital of the Harmony Society when Nachtrieb entered, in 1819, was $368,690.92, and when he was expelled in 1846, it had increased, as has been already stated to $901,723.42. A numerical share being 1/321 part, in this last sum would be $2,809.10. His labor, if paid for during the twenty-seven years, at what was proved to be the ordinary rate of labor, would give him $4,290, and this last, as giving him the largest compensation, was what he claimed. If the court, disallowing this claim, and thinking further that he was not entitled to a share of the capital of 1846, should think him entitled to profits only since he came in, then he regarded as profits the increase between 1819 and 1846, on the capital as found at these two dates, that is to say, $533,032.50, and claimed as his share of them the 1/321 part.

. . . .

Grier, Circuit Justice. On the first question; the question of fact: Although by the contract and agreement of the several members of this association, each had an equal right to and interest in their common property and had estopped himself from even setting up any claim for property or labor contributed to the common stock, in case of a voluntary withdrawal from the society; yet it contained no enumeration of offences by which a member should forfeit his rights and interest in their common property; it pointed out no tribunal which had a power to inflict the punishment of expulsion or forfeiture of all title to an immense property gained by their common contributions and labor. In dealing with rights to persons and property, the court can only look at the agreements of the parties, as written and signed by themselves. In these we have found no power conferred on Rapp to expel, at his mere whim and caprice, any unoffending or even offending member, and divest his title to the common property, after the labor of a life, spent in assisting to accumulate it. If he could expel one member in this way, he could another, and thus get rid of all the partners but himself, and retain the property for his own use.

That parties wrongfully expelled would have a right to the interference of courts of justice, has not been disputed. Nor has it been pretended that the evidence shows any case which could justify the expulsion of the complainant. He had been a faithful, diligent and laborious member of the association for thirty of the best years of his life, obeying every command and ordinance of Rapp, even to that of enforced celibacy. The only offence charged against him was holding a few minutes' conversation with some of his friends out of the society, who were anxious for some information as to the fortune of certain claims which they had made on the Harmony Society. No charge seems to have been made against him, save that of thinking and speaking about the concerns of the society to which he belonged.

We come, therefore, to the point on which this case turns. Did the complainant voluntarily and of his own accord abandon and forsake the society? or was he wrongfully and unjustly excluded or expelled therefrom? As we have seen, there was no proof of any act of the complainant which would justify his expulsion. The argument has therefore turned entirely on the fact of expulsion or voluntary abandonment.

Nachtrieb's receipt, in which he in terms declared that he has withdrawn from the society, is much relied on; and so have his own declarations soon after he went away, that he had left the society voluntarily.

In regard to the receipt, when we consider the nature and extent of the authority exercised by Rapp, over his followers—their reverence and fear of him, and their unbounded submission to his command—it must be evident that the signature of such a receipt would be but slender evidence that the complainant acted voluntarily in withdrawing himself from the society. It is plain that if Rapp commanded him to go, he would feel bound to go, and that unless, after a servitude of thirty years, he was willing to go penniless, he must sign the receipt. It was the consideration for the means of departing without being reduced to beggary. As yet the complainant was not free from the shackles of the spiritual and temporal slavery to which he had been all his life subject; a power which forbade him to learn English, to marry, or if married, denied him intercourse with his wife. Free will can hardly be predicated of actions, performed at the command of a ruler believed to possess the keys both in this world and the next, and who taught that disobedience to his orders was a sin against the Holy Ghost, not to be forgiven, here or hereafter.

If the complainant departed from the society in obedience to the commands of Rapp, it may be said he obeyed them voluntarily, as there was no physical compulsion. But we may easily conceive of a social or spiritual excommunication, or a combination of both, which would leave as little choice to the party who feared them, as the rack or the inquisition. So also the declarations of the complainant, that he went away voluntarily, can have very little or no weight against the clear evidence of his expulsion. This sort of testimony is seldom worthy of any reliance. It cannot be contradicted. Conversations are always but partially recollected, never truly stated, and often purposely misrepresented. Besides, if the conversations stated, were literally and strictly true they amount to nothing. I presume every member of this society felt uneasy, as to what would be the state of it after Rapp's death; and may well have doubted, whether a community of property can well exist without an infallible apostle with patriarchal or absolute power, so that unity may be attained by having but one will in the society. That the complainant after his expulsion, may have exulted in his first taste of the sweets of liberty; that he may have frequently said that he came away of his own accord, may well be admitted. Probably there are few instances, where a man has been expelled from any respectable society, in which his personal vanity would not soften the word expulsion into withdrawal, in speaking of his change of connection with it. An expelled member seldom expresses much respect for those who have wrongfully ejected him, or affects to regret the loss of their society.

The plaintiff is therefore entitled to a decree, and the only question which remains is, what is the character and the extent of the relief which we shall give him. We shall not consider the objection to the form of the pleadings; for the case having been argued and considered on the merits, without objections, until a late time as to that point, we shall not go back to decide a game of sharps between the parties.

On the second question; the question of law: The complainant demands pay for his labor during the time he was a member. This would be the extreme and longest rate of compensation. The defendants, on the contrary, without tendering in their answer a reconciliation with the complainant, and a restoration of him to his rights, or intimating a willingness to receive his wife and children as members, now insist that the court can decree no other remedy than restoration to his rights as a member. Such a decree would compel him, perhaps, to forsake his wife and children, for the small hope of the survivorship in the tontine. This, we think, would be rendering very scant justice or recompense to a man for half his life's labor. The Pennsylvania case cited has no resemblance to the present. That was a corporation for benevolent purposes, where membership and not the ownership and enjoyment of property to the corporator's own use, was the object. Its members accumulated to give away, or to expend on charitable purposes. These accumulated for themselves. They have, by joint labor, accumulated property of great value, which they hold as joint owners. The complainant had an equal ownership with his three hundred and twenty partners. By their contract, it is to remain joint and indivisible stock forever, but the complainant has his right to enjoy it equally with his fellows. Their articles of partnership or association provide for the case of any partner who chooses to withdraw or depart from it; but makes no provision for those who are unjustly driven away and expelled. Whether the society be governed by prophet, priest, king, or majority, they are subject to the law of the land; and if the complainant has been wrongfully deprived of valuable rights of property, the law should afford him a remedy. I know of no other measure of satisfaction or compensation more just than to give the expelled and injured party his several share of their joint assets. The dissolution of the partnership by the wrongful act of the majority of the firm or association, necessarily dissolves, inter sese, viz., as between the expelled and the remaining partners, the covenants as to the indivisibility of their joint property. If this were otherwise, a majority could at any time expel the minority, and retain all the joint property. They who break the agreement as to perpetuity of the benefits of membership cannot be heard to allege it as to destination of the property. By their wrongful expulsion of the complainant, the whole power and force of the articles as between them is broken, and inter sese, annulled; and the complainant has a right to the separate use of his heretofore undivided interest in the property, because he is wrongfully deprived of his joint use of it. The wrong done to plaintiff, is capable of a compensation in money, without compelling him to leave his family, and spend his days among those who have injured him. And the proper measure of his compensation is the amount of his interest or share at the time of his expulsion. It is not like a mere corporate privilege or office, to which a court of equity may restore a corporator who has been wrongfully expelled. It is a question of the enjoyment of property. His copartners have ejected him from his joint use and enjoyment of their common property; they have severed the tenure, as between him and themselves, and he has a right to his share in severalty. This is the proper measure of the complainant's compensation, and not wages for his labor during the time of his membership. Let the decree be for the 1/321 part of the whole property of the society, $901,723.42, at the time of his expulsion, with interest from that date; deducting what the complainant has received.

Decree accordingly.

———

The court reporter for the *Nachtrieb* case added a note at the end of the opinion, describing the fate of Elijah Lemix:

In a case brought by another complainant against these same defendants, there being imperfect evidence of any expulsion, and the defendants by their answer, "conceding the complainant's perfect right and liberty to return to the enjoyment of all the privileges, benefits, and advantages contemplated by the association, he discharging the duties incumbent on him as a member of it," the court refused to grant the complainant any relief, but dismissed his bill with costs. *Lemix v. Harmony Society* [unreported].

[c]   Problem Notes: Forms of Group Ownership

[*i*]   *Magic Words.* One interesting quality of property law is the ability to use pre-established forms of ownership rather than writing new ones for each transaction. Much of Chapter 2 was taken up with problems of various pre-established forms for holding property. We discovered that by using some "magic" words—tenancy in common, joint tenancy with rights of survivorship or tenancy by the entirety—all sorts of rules about formation of, withdrawal from, and termination of group holdings are called into play. These rules may be altered, of course, if the group does not wish to use magic words, but for typical transactions, well understood phrases may be perfectly adequate. Were any such magic words used by the Harmony? The court repeatedly used the magic word "partnership" to describe the Society holding pattern, but it is not clear that description was accurate.

[*ii*]   *Partnerships.* A partnership is a form of co-ownership particularly suited to the needs of business. The essential needs of a business are flexibility in management methods, assurance of a proper method for sharing profits and losses, and protection from unwarranted creditor and tort liability. The Uniform Partnership Act defines a partnership as "an association of two or more persons to carry on as co-owners a business for profit formed under Section 202 . . . ."[17] Section 202 provides:

§ 202. Formation of Partnership.*

(a) Except as otherwise provided in subsection (b), the association of two or more persons to carry on as co-owners a business for profit forms a partnership, whether or not the persons intend to form a partnership.

. . . .

(c) In determining whether a partnership is formed, the following rules apply:

(1) Joint tenancy, tenancy in common, tenancy by the entireties, joint property, common property, or part ownership does not by itself establish a partnership, even if the persons sharing them have a joint or common right or interest in property from which the returns are derived.

---

[17] Unif. Partnership Act § 101, 6 U.L.A. 10 (1996).

* Reprinted with permission of the National Conference of Commissioners on Uniform State Law.

(2) The sharing of gross returns does not by itself establish a partnership, even if the persons sharing them have a joint or common right or interest in property from which the returns are derived.

(3) A person who receives a share of the profits of a business is presumed to be a partner in the business, unless the profits were received in payment:

(i) of a debt by installments or otherwise;

(ii) for services as an independent contractor or of wages or other compensation to an employee;

(iii) of rent;

(iv) of an annuity or other retirement or health benefit to a beneficiary, representative, or designee of a deceased or retired partner;

(v) of interest or other charge on a loan . . . ; or

(vi) for the sale of goodwill of a business or other property by installments or otherwise. Elsewhere in the Uniform Partnership Act, it is made quite clear that any written partnership agreement governs operation of the partnership, except for certain non-waivable duties to provide information to partners and to behave with fiduciary loyalty to the partnership.

The effect of this definition is to establish a legal entity separate from the individual partners themselves. Once a partnership is established the various partners take on a double status. They function economically in society both as individuals and as partners. Does the definition in the Uniform Partnership Act accurately reflect the intentions of those creating the Harmony Society? Can you have a non-business partnership?

[*iii*] **The Tontine.** In *Nachtrieb*, the court talked of a "*tontine*" in discussing the amount of property to be distributed to the survivors of those jointly holding property. The most common form of property ownership creating a tontine—the joint tenancy with rights of survivorship—was reviewed in the prior chapter. It is pretty clear that the Harmony did not create a typical joint tenancy tontine. Given the contents of the articles establishing the group, it is hard to imagine that any single owner was to survive to take all the assets of the Harmony. In addition, members did not have the right to alienate or devise their interest in the Harmony. If a tontine was created, and the Harmony community ended, who was to get the property? If no one was named and the Harmony terminated, perhaps it should all have gone to the state of Pennsylvania. *See Schwartz v. Duss*, reprinted at p. 271 below.

[*iv*] **Trust.** Perhaps the Harmony was just a trust, with George Rapp, and later the Board of Elders, acting as trustees for the benefit of all the members. In that case, did Nachtrieb have a cause of action for breach of fiduciary responsibilities by Rapp?

[*v*] **Does the Holding Pattern Matter?** At bottom it is not clear what holding pattern best described the Harmony Society. Perhaps it did not make any difference. Regardless of the presumptive rules that operate when "magic" words are used to create a property interest, the parties involved may draft and agree to contracts which alter the presumptive understandings. Thus, even if property is said to be held in a certain form, a contract may be used to alter the operation of that form, or even to effectively create a different form. *See, e.g., Reilly v. Sageser* at p. 123 in Chapter 2.

[*vi*]   *Property Forms and Contract Law.* Contracts still form a crucial part of property holding devices. Each condominium, for example, has peculiar characteristics which require special agreements in order for the organized development to work properly. In fact, certain parts of a condominium, usually called the "common areas" are "locked" together with the housing units in order to avoid diffuse ownership, just as Nachtrieb's right to use the Harmony assets may have been locked together with membership in the community. It would be silly if the stairwell, elevator, swimming pool or mailboxes, all jointly owned by all the residents in a condominium, could be split up as in joint tenancy. Thus, each owner of a condominium unit holds a fee simple in the chunk of space in which his unit is contained as well as a share of the common areas which may be transferred only when the condominium unit itself is transferred. Would it be stretching things too much to call the Harmony Society a condominium? For more information on condominiums and cooperatives, *see Centex v. Boag*, p. 746 in Chapter 9.

[*vii*]   *Gifts and Property Holding Forms.* Should the ability of someone like Nachtrieb to get money from an ownership community upon withdrawal depend upon whether his initial contribution of money or assets was by way of gift? If you give money to a charity that disbands, should you be able to get your money back? If you invest money in a business that closes, should you be able to get back a fair share of any money left when the business shuts down? Can you articulate any reasons why these last two questions might be answered differently?

[d]   Opinions of the United States Supreme Court in *Nachtrieb*

The Society leadership, not at all pleased with the outcome of the *Nachtrieb* case at the Circuit Court level, took the dispute to the Supreme Court, which reversed in the following opinion.

Baker and Henrici, Trustees of the Harmony Society
v. Nachtrieb

United States Supreme Court

60 U.S. (19 How.) 126, 15 L. Ed. 2d 528 (1856)

MR. JUSTICE CAMPBELL delivered the opinion of the court.

The appellee, who describes himself as a member in the common and joint-stock association for mutual benefit and advantage, and for the mutual acquisition and enjoyment of property, called the "Harmony Society," filed a bill in the Circuit Court against the appellants, as the trustees and managers of its business and estate. The object of the bill is to obtain for the plaintiff a decree for an account of the share to which he is entitled in the property of the society, or compensation for his labor and service during the time he was a member.

. . . .

The organic law of the society, in regard to their property, is contained in two sections of the articles of association, adopted in 1827 by the associates, of whom the plaintiff was one. They are as follows:

> All the property of the society, real, personal, and mixed, in law or equity, and howsoever contributed and acquired, shall be deemed, now and forever, joint and indivisible stock; each individual is to be considered to have finally and irrevocably parted with all his former contributions, whether in land, goods, money, or labor, and the same rule shall apply to all future contributions, whatever they may be.

Should any individual withdraw from the society, or depart this life, neither he, in the one case, nor his representatives, in the latter, shall be entitled to demand an account of said contributions, whether in land, goods, money, or labor; or to claim anything from the society as matter of right. But it shall be left altogether to the discretion of the superintendent to decide whether any, and, if any, what allowance shall be made to such member, or his representatives, as a donation.

The defendants, admitting . . . that the plaintiff, until 1846, was a contented member of the association, answer and say, that during that year he became disaffected; used violent threats against the associates; made repeated declarations of his intentions to leave the society, and in that year fulfilled his design by a voluntary withdrawal and separation from the society, receiving at the same time from George Rapp two hundred dollars as a donation. They exhibit, as a part of the answer, a writing, signed by the plaintiff, to the following effect:

To day I have withdrawn myself from the Harmony Society, and ceased to be a member thereof; I have also received of George Rapp two hundred dollars as a donation, agreeably to contract.

JOSHUA NACHTRIEB.

ECONOMY, June 18, 1846.

This statement of the pleadings shows that no issue was made in them upon the merit of the doctrines, social or religious, which form the basis of this association; nor any question in reference to the religious instruction and ministration, or the domestic economy or physical discipline which their leader and the other managers have adopted and enforced. Nor do they suggest any inquiry into the condition of the members, and whether they have experienced hardship, oppression, or undue mortification, from the ambition, avarice, or fanaticism, of their guides and administrators.

The bill depends on the averments, that the plaintiff approved the constitution of the society; submitted to its government; obeyed its regulations, and prized the advantage of being a member. The burden of his complaint is, that he was wrongfully, and without any fault or consent on his part, deprived of his station through the combination of the leader and his assistants. And the defendants concede the character the plaintiff claims for himself; they concede that the plaintiff was an approved and blameless member of the association, and was entitled to whatever its constitution and order provided for the temporal good or the eternal felicity of the members, and assert that he enjoyed them until he became disaffected and repining, and finally surrendered to a spirit of discontent, which moved him to abandon his condition and privileges. As an evidence of this, they produce a writing, signed by him, in which he acknowledges a voluntary secession from the society, and claims that the case has arisen to authorize him to make an appeal to the bounty of the superintendent, and that the superintendent has answered that appeal by a donation. The value of this writing is now to be considered. The power of the superintendent to subtract from the otherwise "joint and indivisible stock" of the society a portion for the individual use of a seceding member, depends upon the concession that the member has withdrawn voluntarily. He cannot supply one who is the victim of covin or combination. The evidence shows that the mind of the plaintiff, in June, 1846, was disquieted in consequence of his connection with the association, and that he contemplated a change in his condition; that he made inquiries upon the expediency of a removal from Economy, and made some preparations for his departure; that the leader of the society, suspecting his discontent, and discovering some deviation by him from the rules of the society, rebuked him with harshness, and menaced him with a sentence of expulsion. Some of the witnesses testify to such a sentence, while the testimony of others reduces the expressions to an admonition and menace. But two days after the occurrence of the last of these scenes, and before any removal had taken place, the writing in the record was executed by him, embodying his decision to leave the society, and to accept the bounty the constitution permitted the superintendent to bestow. This writing would have much probative force, if we were simply to treat it as an admission of the statements it contains, when considered in connection with other evidence in the record. But, we think, this writing is something more than an admission, and stands in a different light from an ordinary receipt. The writing must be treated as the contract of dissolution, between the plaintiff and the society, of their mutual obligations and engagements to each other. No evidence of prior declarations or antecedent conduct is admissible to contradict or to vary it.

It was prepared to preserve the remembrance of what the parties had prescribed to themselves to do, and expresses their intention in their own language; and that such was its object, is corroborated by the fact that for three years there is no evidence of a contrary sentiment. Treating this writing as an instrument of evidence of this class, it is clear that the bill has not made a case in which its validity can be impeached. To enable the plaintiff to show that the rule of the leader, (Rapp,) instead of being patriarchal, was austere, oppressive, or tyrannical; his discipline vexatious and cruel; his instructions fanatical, and, upon occasions, impious; his system repugnant to public order, and the domestic happiness of its members; his management of their revenues and estate rapacious, selfish, or dishonest; and that the condition of his subjects was servile, ignorant, and degraded, so that none of them were responsible for their contracts or engagements to him, from a defect of capacity and freedom, as has been attempted by him in the testimony collected in this cause, it was a necessary prerequisite that his bill should have been so framed as to exhibit such aspects of the internal arrangements and social and religious economy of the association. This was not done; and for this cause the evidence cannot be considered. . . .

Decree reversed. Bill dismissed.

[e]   Explanatory Notes

[*i*]   ***Why did the Supreme Court Reverse?*** First, the Court called the signed receipt a contract. In return for Nachtrieb's departure from the Society, the Society gave him $200 in settlement of all claims to the Harmony's assets. Such a contract could not be reformed by presentation of parole, or outside, evidence unless it was ambiguous or some other special circumstance arose. The trial court discussed some possible special circumstances, especially duress at the signing of the separation contract. The Supreme Court did not hold that duress proofs were always inadmissible to vary the terms of a signed contract. Rather, the Court held that in Nachtrieb's case, the bill, or original complaint, did not sufficiently allege duress, and that the evidence admitted at trial was improperly accepted because it varied from the terms of the complaint. The result was procedural. Why the Court chose this path is not clear. The Court even ignored statements made by the trial court that were highly critical of the "sharp" practices used by the Harmony's lawyers in trying to win the case on the same pleading theory. The trial judge noted:

We shall not consider the objection to the form of the pleadings; for the case having been argued and considered on the merits, without objections, until a late time as to that point, we shall not go back to decide a game of sharps.

The procedural outcome meant that even though the Harmony Society won the case, they could not be sure that future cases would be resolved the same way.

Simply as a matter of curiosity you might be interested to know that most present day rules of civil procedure permit a complaint to be amended to conform to the proofs at trial, provided that no unfairness would result. *See* Fed. R. Civ. P. 15(b). The application of such a rule in the *Nachtrieb* dispute would probably have altered the outcome.

[*ii*] *Other Communal Disputes.* Harmony was not the only communal settlement to be sued by a former member or heirs of a former member. The Shakers, Hutterites, Society of Zoar, and the Oneida Community all faced court battles over the validity of their written agreements. *Waite v. Merrill*, 4 Me. (4 Greenl.) 102, 16 Am. Dec. 238 (1826) (Shakers); *Gass v. Wilhite*, 32 Ky. (2 Dana) 170, 26 Am. Dec. 446 (1834) (Shakers); *Goesele v. Bimeler*, 55 U.S. (14 How.) 589 (1852) (Society of Zoar); *Gasely v. Separatists' Society of Zoar*, 13 Ohio St. 144 (1862); *Burt v. Oneida Community*, 16 N.Y.S. 289 (1891); *Hofer v. Hofer*, 59 D.L.R.2d 723 (Manitoba Q.B. 1966) (Hutterites). In all of these cases, the courts upheld the interest of the community over that of the individual. Until it was reversed by the Supreme Court, the Circuit Court opinion in *Nachtrieb* stood alone in granting a former member of a communal society his interest in the community's property.

[f] Problem Notes

[*i*] *Freedom of Religion and Property Disputes.* Problems of withdrawing members of groups are difficult enough in average cases. The religious overtones of the *Nachtrieb* dispute make it both more interesting and more difficult. Should a court hesitate to interfere with property disputes in religious societies? The First Amendment, in somewhat cryptic prose, prohibits the adoption of laws "respecting an establishment of religion, or prohibiting the free exercise thereof." In *Serbian Eastern Orthodox Diocese for the United States and Canada v. Milivojevich*, 426 U.S. 696 (1976), the Supreme Court reversed a judgment of the Illinois Supreme Court on the grounds that detailed judicial inquiry into "matters of ecclesiastical cognizance and polity" violated the First Amendment.

In 1963, the Holy Assembly of Bishops and the Holy Synod of the Serbian Orthodox Church removed Milivojevich as Bishop of the American-Canadian diocese. He was later defrocked. Milivojevich then sued to regain both his position and control of the property and assets of the diocese. The dispute arose out of a church reorganization, which split the American-Canadian diocese into three parts, leaving Milivojevich in control of only one part. His refusal to accept the reorganization led to his dismissal and defrocking. The Illinois courts set aside the dismissal and defrocking as arbitrary and not conducted in accordance with church law. The Supreme Court held that the decisions of church ecclesiastical bodies were binding on civil courts, and that matters of purely internal church discipline, such as defrockings, were not for civilian authorities to resolve.

If the Harmony dispute arose today, would Rapp's decision to remove Nachtrieb be deemed to have been made by an appropriate ecclesiastical body? Was the Harmony Society a church or a religion for First Amendment purposes?

[*ii*] *Nature of the Harmony "Church."* In *Milivojevich*, the church property was owned by a corporation and held in trust for the members of the church. If the property was held directly by the church members and a dispute arose over its disposition, could the courts resolve it? Which

was *Nachtrieb* closer to—a property dispute or an ecclesiastical power struggle? Note that Rapp originally held the fee in the property of the Society. Later Baker and Henrici were overtly named as trustees. Assuming that Rapp, like his successors, was a trustee, what were his obligations to Nachtrieb and the other members? Could it be argued that a withdrawing member was not entitled to anything since the trustees were obligated to act in the best interests of the remaining members?

[*iii*] *Judicial Neutrality and Religious Property Disputes.* Is it possible for the courts to "abstain" from making decisions as the Supreme Court opined it was doing in *Milivojevich*? Is not abstention itself a decision? Can rules about property and religion be rationally framed on a theory requiring the use of "neutral" rules which neither encourage nor discourage the practice of religious beliefs?

[*iv*] *Religion and Community Control.* Consider one last problem. Suppose that a religious group moves into a community, that members of the religious group run for office in various local political campaigns, and that these members take control of all the major elective offices and bodies in the community. May a state then decline to recognize the community as an official municipality on the ground that continued existence of the polity would be an establishment of religion? Such a dispute arose in Oregon with the town of Rajneeshpuram. *See State of Oregon v. City of Rajneeshpuram*, 598 F. Supp. 1208 (D. Or. 1984). The dispute was never fully litigated and decided because the religious community fell apart in early 1986. Should Salt Lake City be de-recognized if it is controlled by Mormons? Should Utah be returned to territorial status for the same reasons?

[3] The Post-Rapp Period

[a] The Beginning of the End

The period from 1847 to 1868 marked a transition in the Society from communal work to communal investment. During this time the Harmonists became pioneers, along with Edwin L. Drake, in the oil industry in the Tidioute area of Pennsylvania. Their refined oil came to be considered the best in the region because of the way it was prepared and marketed. The Society also built one of the first oil pipelines, owned coal mines, and founded the Economy Savings Bank. In addition, it participated in the building of several railroads, and provided the major financing for one of them—the Pittsburgh and Lake Erie Railroad.[18] As a result of all these activities, the Harmony Society became an immensely wealthy capitalist.

As the Society's wealth grew so did the generosity of its senior trustee, Jacob Henrici. Henrici used the Society's millions to help other religious communities here and abroad. His contributions to charitable causes, both large and small, kept thousands of Americans from becoming unemployed. Such generosity, which outdid even Carnegie and Vanderbilt, with whom Henrici did business, soon became famous throughout the world. The saying "as rich as an Economist" became proverbial among Americans. Unfortunately, the welfare state which Henrici created took its toll on the Harmony Society's assets. By 1890, cash reserves were depleted, and debts of over $400,000 were outstanding.

The year 1890 was a watershed in the Society's history. Besides the financial difficulties created by Henrici's failure to account for the wealth he dispensed, the membership of the still celibate

---

[18] K.J.R. ARNDT, GEORGE RAPP'S SUCCESSORS AND MATERIAL HEIRS, 1847-1916, at 66-69 (1971). [Hereinafter cited as Arndt II.]

Society had dwindled to less than 20. The fear of dissolution had become a reality. In December, 1889, and January, 1890, a series of sudden deaths took the lives of three Harmony Society pioneers—Gertrude Rapp, Jonathan Lenz and George Kirschbaum. Soon after these deaths, 20 new members were admitted to the Society, among them John and Susie Duss and Dr. Benjamin Feucht, a former member, and his family. Although the Dusses and the Feuchts soon were to emerge as heads of rival factions in a fight for control of the Society, the battle for the Society's millions did not immediately become acute. In April, 1890, the members, in a display of unity, reaffirmed the Articles of Agreement, after a 40-year lapse, and ratified the interim acts of the Board of Elders and Trustees, Jacob Henrici and Ernst Woelfel. The signing of this document brought external harmony to the Society for a short time. But in July, 1890, Woelfel, the junior trustee, died and John Duss was elected in his place.

In 1891, as his first act as trustee, John Duss persuaded the Board of Elders to request an accounting from Henrici. Soon thereafter, with the long term purpose of transferring the Society's assets to a corporation, Duss began rearranging the affairs of the community. He hired a professional accountant and numerous lawyers to advise him on the most prudent path to take towards liquidation. It was important to Duss not to begin the process of liquidation too quickly. Moves clearly contrary to the Society's purposes would provide evidence of dissolution beneficial to the claims of former members and their heirs. Because of this, his attorneys advised him to proceed with patience and use his position as trustee to control the future of the Society. With Henrici nearing death in 1892, Duss had the Society revise the Articles again. He drew up a statement of membership which defined the rights and powers of the trustees. This statement, signed by all the members except the Feuchts, bestowed power of attorney upon Duss and Henrici to act on behalf of the Society in the sale or mortgage of its property. Since Henrici, on his death bed, was *non compos mentis*, Duss gained complete control of the Society. He immediately secured a $400,000 mortgage on the Society's assets and paid off the accumulated debt.

The Feucht faction objected to Duss' assumption of power and filed a bill in equity in the Beaver County Court of Common Pleas asking that a receiver be appointed for the Harmony Society.[19] The Feucht bill charged, among other things, that, under Duss, the Society was mismanaged financially and spiritually, that Duss had sold, assigned, and disposed of dividend paying stocks in the amount of nearly two million dollars, that the Society as a religious organization had ceased to exist, that the majority of the Board of Elders now consisted of "confirmed and common drunkards" and that through coercion and misrepresentation Duss, on December 21, 1892, obtained the signatures on the document giving him power to sell or mortgage the property of the Society. The Feuchts requested the court to decree a dissolution of the Society and a division of the property "amongst the parties legally and equitably entitled thereto." After a long court battle, in which the financial affairs of the Society were laid bare, the case was settled. On June 5, 1893, the Feuchts agreed to accept $28,000 and a seven acre parcel of land in return for their withdrawal from the Society. Impatience and age had caused them to sell their interest in the Society for a small sum.

During this time, Duss made many payoffs of $5,000 to withdrawing, aging members. The Society "lost" so many members through this process that it faced a shortage of males to serve on the Board of Elders. A proposal was made to fill vacancies with women and, as a result, Duss' wife, Susie, age 33, and two other women in their seventies, were elected to the Board

---

[19] *Id.* at 230.

of Elders. With two Dusses on the Board, John Duss solidified his domination over the remaining members of the Society.

Shortly after the *Feucht* case was settled, another suit was brought against Duss by heirs and former members to enjoin the further sale or donation of the property of the Harmony Society by its trustees. The *Schwartz* bill, filed in 1894 in the Circuit Court of the United States for the Western District of Pennsylvania, contained 26 complaints of which the 20th, 25th and 26th were the most significant:

20th. That on the 12th day of April, 1894, the said Duss, without any authority from the members of the Harmony Society, and in the utmost disregard to his trust secretly entered into an arrangement with said Hice, Reeves and one James Dickson, whereby he, the said Duss, agreed to convey the town of Economy, the surrounding properties and certain other lands of the Harmony Society, situate in Allegheny County, to the Union Company, an alleged corporation created under the laws of the State of Pennsylvania. And your orators allege that a conveyance has been made by said Duss for the lands as aforesaid and that the same was made without the knowledge of your orators or any members of the said Society, excepting possibly Susie C., wife of said Duss and Gottlieb Riethmueller. That by the said pretended conveyance and sale of the home of the Harmony Society and its other properties the said Duss has attempted to wholly terminate the existence of said Society, not only as to the government thereof by the Board of Elders, and by the members, but also as to the ownership of any property. That the said Union Company, in addition to said Duss and Riethmueller is composed of said Hice and Reeves, debtors of the said Harmony Society as herein before stated and one James Dickson, the private bookkeeper and confidential agent of said Duss whose interest in said corporation was acquired by gift from said Duss.

That your orators are advised that it was not competent for the said trustees to convey said properties to the said Union Company, but such transfer was a breach of trust and wholly invalid. Your orators therefore demand a full answer and disclosure as to said pretended sale and transfer and to whom the several shares therein have been issued and on what consideration.

25th. That recently said Harmony Society has become dissolved as aforesaid, that all of its property and practices established as aforesaid by the founder of said Society and by the ancestors of your orators have been abandoned, that the pursuit of agriculture no longer exists in said Society, that its chief assets consisting of bonds, stocks, and other securities and the town of Economy with its buildings and the adjacent lands of said Society, consisting of some 3,000 acres, and which constituted the basis of organization and business of said Society have been sold and conveyed away by the said Duss as aforesaid in fraud, however, of the rights of your orators and their cotenants, and that by reason of the facts hereinbefore set forth your orators and the said last members, except the said Duss and wife, are now tenants in common of all said lands and tenements and entitled to partition thereof, in proportion to their respective interests.

26th. That for some time past the members of said Harmony Society have been retiring therefrom and have received the amount of their interest in said association in the land or money, or both, the land being set apart in severalty to them and have released all of their rights and interests in said association in consideration for such payment or conveyance to them and that by said retirement and withdrawal the membership of said association has been reduced to the persons hereinbefore named members, that by common consent this association has ceased to exist as an association and that if the property thereof has ever been impressed with a trust (which your orators deny, as being contrary to public policy and void in law or equity) such trust has wholly ceased and the assets of such dissolved association have reverted to the donors thereof among whom were the ancestors and intestates of your orators as hereinbefore fully set forth.[20]

In the November term of 1894, the parties agreed to request the court to appoint a master. Much testimony was introduced for the purpose of proving that the members and trustees had voluntarily abandoned the original purposes of the trust, or Society, and that as an organization it had drifted so far away from the original plans upon which it was formed that it could no longer be recognized as the Harmony Society.

[b] Opinions of the United States Supreme Court in *Schwartz v. Duss*[21]

Schwartz v. Duss

United States Supreme Court

187 U.S. 8, 23 S. Ct. 4, 47 L. Ed. 53 (1902)

This suit was brought for the distribution of the property and assets of the Harmony Society, which the bill alleged had ceased to exist. The bill also prayed for an injunction against John S. Duss to restrain him from in anywise dealing with the property of the society, and also for a receiver. The bill was exceedingly voluminous.

. . . .

By agreement of the parties the case was referred to a master, with "authority to hear and take all the testimony, and to find all the issues of law and facts, and to report the testimony and such findings to the court, and if the report of such master shall suggest a decree that the plaintiffs or any of them are entitled to an account against the defendants or any of them, and the same be confirmed by the court, then the case shall be referred again to the master, to state such an account and report thereon to the court."

Under the orders of the court the master considered the following questions:

First. Have the plaintiffs, or any of them, such a proprietary right or interest in the property and assets of the Harmony Society as entitled them upon the dissolution of the society to any part of or share in such property or assets or as entitles them to the account prayed for in the bill?

Second. Has the Harmony Society been dissolved by the common consent of the members or by an abandonment of the purposes for which it was formed?

On both propositions the master reported adversely to the claim of the petitioners, and recommended a decree dismissing the bill. His conclusions of fact and law were approved and accepted by the Circuit Court, and a decree entered dismissing the bill. The decree was affirmed by the Circuit Court of Appeals. The case was then brought here by certiorari on petition of the plaintiffs in the Circuit Court . . . .

---

[20] *Id.* at 262-264.

[21] As noted in the opinions, Justices Gray and Shiras did not participate. Justice Gray's reasons are not known, but Justice Shiras was the father of the main attorney for the plaintiffs.

MR. JUSTICE MCKENNA, after making the foregoing statement, delivered the opinion of the court.

Two questions were submitted to the master: (1) Have the plaintiffs such a proprietary right or interest as would entitle them upon the dissolution of the society to share all its property or assets, or which entitles them to an accounting? (2) Has the society been dissolved by consent or by an abandonment of the purposes for which it was formed? A negative answer to either of the propositions determines the controversy against petitioners, and both were so answered by the master and by the Circuit Court and the Circuit Court of Appeals. The case, therefore, seems not to be as broad or as complex as presented in the argument of counsel. The case is certainly clear from any disputes of fact, and we may dismiss from consideration the accusations against Duss, not only as to his motives in joining the society, but also as to his motives and acts as a member and officer of it. We are concerned alone with the legal aspect and consequences of his acts and those of his associates. They, however, pertain more particularly to the second proposition.

. . . .

[A]s to the relations of the plaintiffs to the society the master found as follows:

1st. That none of the plaintiffs were ever members of the society.

2d. That all of those members of the society through whom Christian Schwartz claims as their heir, signed the agreements of 1836 and 1874, and continued members until their death.

3d. That Antony Koterba claims as heir of his father, Joseph Koterba, and his half-brother, Andreas Koterba; that Joseph Koterba joined in the organization of the society, and also signed the agreement of 1827, and afterwards, in 1827, withdrew from the society; and that Andreas Koterba signed the agreements of 1827, 1836 and 1847, and died a member of the society.

4th. That the grandparents of David Strohaker, viz., Christian Strohaker and wife, and Matthias Rief and wife, joined the society in 1805, and all remained members until their death—all dying between 1820 and 1825, except Mrs. Rief, who died between 1830 and 1836. That his father, Christopher Strohaker, signed the agreement of 1827, and withdrew from the society in 1827. That his aunt, Catharina Strohaker, signed the agreements of 1827, 1836 and 1847, and continued a member of the society until her death.

5th. That Lawrence Scheel and Jacob Scheel, ancestors of Allen and G. L. Shale, joined the society in 1805; that Lawrence withdrew in 1824 or 1826; that Jacob Scheel signed the agreement in 1827 and died a member, about 1837.

6th. That none of the parties through whom the plaintiffs claim contributed any money or property to the society.

He divided the persons from whom the plaintiffs claim as follows:

First. Those withdrawn from the society before the execution of the agreement of 1836.

Second. Those dying in the society before that time.

Third. Those who died members of the society after having joined in the agreements of 1836 and 1847.

Manifestly the plaintiffs cannot have other rights than their ancestors, and the rights of the latter depend upon the agreements they signed . . . . The signers of them certainly strove to express their meaning clearly, and, whenever occasion arose, declared their understanding, aims and purposes, and always substantially in the same way.

The cardinal principle of the society was self-abnegation. It was manifested not only by submission to a religious head, but by a community instead of individual ownership of property, and the dedication of their labor to the society. The possibility of some member or members not being able to "stand to it," to use the expressive phrase of the agreements, was contemplated, and provision was made for that event. But a very significant difference was made between a performance of service and the contribution of property. For the former it was covenanted by the members no reward should be demanded for themselves or their children or those belonging to them. As to the latter, George Rapp and his associates promised to refund the value of the property brought in without interest, in one, two or three annual installments, as the same might be large or small. It was, however, provided, as to those who "were poor and brought nothing to the community," that they should receive, if they departed openly and orderly, "a donation in money, according to his or their conduct while a member, or as his or their circumstances might require," as "George Rapp and his associates shall determine" (agreement of 1805); as "in the judgment of the superintendents of the association" (agreement of 1827).

Those provisions apply to those who withdrew from the society prior to 1836—the first class into which the master divided the plaintiffs, and need not much comment. None of the persons who so withdrew contributed property to the association. We are not informed by the record whether their conduct when in the society or whether their manner of withdrawing from it, entitled them to the consideration that the articles of agreement permitted as an indulgence to withdrawing members. If they could have exacted anything as a matter of right it would now be presumed that it had been demanded and the demand satisfied.

There was another class, the faithful and abiding members, but even these, the master found, contributed no property, and the decision of their rights becomes as easy as the decision of the right of those who "could not stand to it in the community" and withdrew. They promised, as we have seen, to endeavor by the labor of their hands "to promote the good and interest of the community," and to hold their "children and families to do the same." And for compensation they received instruction in church and school. They received assurance of maintenance "in healthful days" and days which might not be such, and assurance when death should come to them, that their families would be taken care of. It may be presumed that as the members were faithful to their covenants the society was faithful to its covenants, and there were no undischarged obligations or rights for distant relatives of deceased members to assert or claim against the community or its property. This seems to be conceded by counsel for petitioners, and we are brought to the consideration of the third class into which the master divided the persons from whom some of the petitioners claim to derive, those who died members of the society after having joined in the agreements of 1836 and 1847.

Counsel for petitioners say in their brief: "The article of 1836 is the only material article bearing upon the property rights of the plaintiffs, while the articles of 1805, 1821, 1827 and 1847 are material in considering the character of the trust, the purposes and principles of the society."

In other words, as we understand counsel by the propositions they have submitted and the arguments employed to support them, by the articles executed prior to October 31, 1836, those who joined the society made "a free gift and donation of all their property" to George Rapp and his associates, *for the use and benefit of the community,*" upon the condition, however, to have the property returned to them if they should withdraw from the society. But that "by the articles of October 31, 1836, all the members of the society agreed with each other to surrender this right of property restitution which each possessed, and to convey the same to all the members in equal shares." In other words, the gifts before 1836 were to the community; after 1836 to "all the members in equal shares." This difference in result in 1836 and afterwards was effected, it is claimed, by the following provision of the agreement of 1836:

All the property of the society, real, personal and mixed, in law or equity and howsoever constituted or acquired, shall be deemed, now and forever, joint and indivisible stock. Each individual is to be considered to have finally and irrevocably parted with all his former contributions, whether in lands, goods, money or labor, and the same rule shall apply to all future contributions, whatever they may be.

To the articles of 1836, it is also contended, that the society as such was not a party, but nevertheless the property became impressed with a trust for the use of the society, as such, "by those who then (1836) represented the ownership of this joint and indivisible stock," and as each new member came in "he became an owner of an equal share of the property, subject to the trust." And it is further contended that the members of 1836 and those who came in afterwards became *donors* of the property, and when the society or the trust failed from any cause the "corpus of the trust property" reverted to them "by way of resulting trust, . . . not to the surviving members as donees, or beneficiaries of the trust." In other words, the members became at once *donees* of each other and *donors* to the society, and the descendants of members who had not and might not bring a dollar to the society excluded from any interest in the reversion of its great properties the descendants of those from whom those properties came. And this through the doctrine of resulting trusts, whose fundamental principle is to recognize an equity only in them from whom the consideration has proceeded. And this, too, would result from granting the contentions of petitioners—a society whose chief purpose was to establish community of property would come back to the assertion and fact of individual ownership, and whose hope was self-sacrifice and self-abasement would encourage self-interest and self-assertion. Members could go into the society or go out of it, take nothing to it, serve it ever so little, and become ultimate sharers of its property. They might die in the society, or, having withdrawn, die out of it, and will or convey their titles or rights to others. No such right was ever conceived to exist and no such right was intended to be created. This is demonstrated by the quotations which we have made from the articles of agreement. The permanence of the community was provided for in the articles of 1805; it was continued in those of 1821 and 1827; and on account of the secession of Count De Leon and his followers it was asserted with emphasis in 1836. The article of that year became, and was intended to become, the complete and final consummation of community ownership—did not become, and was not intended to become the commencement of individual ownership. That article was but an incident in the life and evolution of the society. It asserted constancy to the principles of the association, and annulled the sixth article of 1825— fifth article of 1805, because that article manifestly departed "from the great principle of community of goods," and it was said that "with a view to carry out the great principles" of their union "and in consideration of the benefits to be derived therefrom," they entered into this covenant:

Should any individual withdraw from the society, or depart this life, neither he in the one case nor his representatives in the other shall be entitled to demand an account of said contributions, whether in land, goods, money or labor, or to claim anything from the society as matter of right. But it shall be left altogether to the discretion of the superintendent to decide whether any, and if any what, allowance shall be made to such member or his representatives as a donation.

The purpose was definite and clearly expressed. It was certainly thought to be clear enough by the men who framed it to declare and accomplish the "sacrifice of all narrow and selfish feelings to the true purposes of the association," as the articles fervidly declared. And it was provided that the member who withdrew from the society could make no demand against it "as a matter of right." The member who died left no right to his representatives. It needs no argument to show that as such members had no rights they could transmit none to the petitioners in this case.

No trust having been created by the agreement of 1836 different from that created by the other agreements, there is no necessity to consider the arguments based on the assumption of its invalidity . . . .

An analysis of the agreements of 1847, 1890 and 1892 is not necessary. They were made to meet particular exigencies, and expressly affirmed the prior agreements, except the sixth section of that of 1827.

The master, and both the Circuit Court and the Circuit Court of Appeals, found that the society had not been dissolved, either by the consent of its members or by the abandonment of the purposes for which it was founded. On account of this concurrence the disputed facts involved in that finding, under the rules of this court, and the circumstances of the record, we do not feel disposed to review. There is left, therefore, for consideration only the agreements of 1890 and 1892 and the changes in administration effected by them, and the conveyance of the property of the society to the Union Company. So far as those agreements affect the property rights of petitioners we have expressed an opinion of them, but their effect upon the question of the dissolution of the society, or the effect of the conveyance to the Union Company, we are not called upon to decide. In that question, we have seen, the petitioners have no concern.

Judgment affirmed.

MR. CHIEF JUSTICE FULLER, with whom concurred MR. JUSTICE BREWER, dissenting.

Assuming the validity of the trusts, the questions appear to be, whether the condition of things has resulted in failure to carry out, and of ability to carry out the principles and purposes of the society, and the defeat of the trusts; and, if so, whether the destination of the corpus of the trust property has, thereupon, become such that complainants or some of them have a *locus standi* to ask relief in a court of equity.

The courts below held that the society still existed in law and in fact, and that this case was not one of "dealing with the assets of a defunct or dissolved association"; or in other words, that the trusts had not been defeated; and the decrees rested on this conclusion. If erroneous, the inquiry then arises, to whom does the corpus of the trust property go in the event of the defeat of the trusts.

. . . .

[I]t appears that prior to October 31, 1836, all contributions of property were for the use and benefit of the community on the condition that any member withdrawing was to receive back the value of his contributions.

But that by the contract of 1836, the property then held in trust was no longer held subject to reclamation on the basis of original contribution, but the whole aggregate was made a common fund in which each member was equally interested, subject to the previously existing trust for the use and benefit of the society; that the corpus of the trust property included all future contributions, accretions and accumulations; and that the then and subsequently admitted members occupied the relation of donors and the society, as a society, of donee.

The joint and indivisible stock embraced all present and future property subject to the trusts declared in the articles of 1827, which were reaffirmed in 1836, except the sixth article. That trust was described "as a free gift or donation for the benefit and use of the said association." And by the agreement of 1847, the property was to be held and deemed the common property of said society, and each trustee disclaimed all personal interest therein "other than that of a member thereof."

If then the trusts are defeated I concur in the view that the trust property must go either to the owners or donors living, and to the heirs and legal representatives of those who are dead, by way of resulting trust; or to the surviving members of the society as joint tenants with right of survivorship, or by way of tontine.

It is true that the third clause of the agreement of 1836, provided that on withdrawal, or death, no member, or his representatives, should be entitled to an account or "to claim anything from the society as matter of right." But that clause referred to the society as a going concern, and this bill is not filed against the society, but proceeds on the ground of the termination of the trusts and the existence of a condition of things demanding the winding up of the society's affairs.

And if the system of patriarchal government has been abandoned; if for the communistic scheme, a capitalistic scheme has been substituted; if the society has become a trading community and lost all its distinctive attributes; if it is undergoing the process of liquidation; if all its property and assets have passed to a trading corporation and the power of carrying out its original principles has departed; if its membership has become practically incapable of perpetuation; it follows that the trusts have been defeated and the society ended to all intents and purposes.

Early in 1890, John S. Duss and two others, employees but not members of the society, were elected to fill vacancies in the Board of Elders.

In April, 1890, certain articles were executed, the number of members being stated to be 45.

The Junior Trustee having died, John S. Duss was elected to fill the vacancy, and soon after, with his wife and children, took possession of the official residence of the society. In 1892 the Senior Trustee died, and Duss was elected to that position, one Sieber, the town constable, who had a wife, being elected Junior Trustee. Later in that year other articles were entered into, describing the then number of members as 37.

In February, 1893, certain members of the society filed a bill for its dissolution, the winding up of its affairs and the distribution of its assets.

While the bill was pending, seventeen members received from the assets money and property to the amount of something over one hundred thousand dollars, and gave quitclaims and acknowledgments of full satisfaction of their interest or share in the property of the society. The grantors in nearly all of these instruments acknowledged in consideration of the money paid or land conveyed, that he or she does "hereby release, cancel and discharge any and all claims whatsoever, which I, my heirs, assigns or lawful representatives, may or could ever have against said society or its trustees, its property or assets, or any part thereof, I hereby declaring all such claims to be fully compensated, settled, released and discharged"; and, after reciting the various properties and assets, "I am entirely satisfied to accept as my full share and interest therein," etc.

Two of the deeds contained this paragraph: "While it may be that said society may have and be the possessor of several hundred thousand dollars worth of property after paying all debts, I am entirely satisfied to accept as my full share therein the sum of __ thousand dollars."

After these settlements began the bill was dismissed by consent.

In January, 1894, a corporation styled the Union Company was organized, under the state statute, "for the purpose of the purchase and sale of real estate, or for holding, leasing and selling real estate," its business "to be transacted in the borough of Beaver, county of Beaver, State of Pennsylvania."

On April 11, 1894, seventeen persons purporting to be all the then members of the society, executed a paper stating:

We the members of said Harmonie Society, do each hereby express our consent with and request that John S. Duss and Gottlieb Riethmueller, the present trustees of said society, shall forthwith sell, transfer and convey to the Union Company, a corporation duly created and organized under the laws of the State of Pennsylvania, all the lands, tenements and hereditaments situated in the Allegheny and Beaver Counties, Pennsylvania, now owned and held by said trustees for the benefit of the said society, to the end that all said lands, tenements and hereditaments may be owned, held and managed by said incorporated company, and be sold and otherwise disposed of from time to time in pursuance of proper corporate action as may be determined by the directors and officers of said incorporated company.

The capital stock of said incorporated company, however, to be owned and held by the said trustees for the benefit of the society, in accordance with, and on the terms and conditions of the articles of association of said society and the ratifications and modifications thereof, as the same now exists, to the extent of three hundred and ninety-seven thousand five hundred ($397,500) dollars, out of a total capital of four hundred thousand ($400,000) dollars.

The vast property of the society was conveyed to the Union Company, and the stock of that corporation assigned to the trustees.

Since April 11, 1894, nine of the seventeen subscribers have died, leaving eight, consisting of John S. Duss and his wife, one Gillman, 77 years of age, and unable to read or speak English; and five women of the ages of 80, 77, 58, 54 and 47, respectively.

Duss and Gillman became the sole remaining male members of the society and the women, with the exception of Mrs. Duss, were mostly old, infirm or ignorant.

No new member has been admitted since 1893. It is suggested that this was because none desired admission. This may be so, and this would explain the diminishing of over five hundred members in 1827 to two hundred and eighty-eight in 1847, and forty-five in 1890. But the result is the same. The eight remaining cannot reasonably be held to represent the great communistic scheme which the Wurtembergers of 1803 sought to found on "the basis of Christian Fellowship, the principles of which being faithfully derived from the sacred Scriptures include the government of the patriarchal age, united to the community of property adopted in the days of the Apostles, and wherein the single object sought is to approximate, so far as human imperfection may allow, to the fulfillment of the will of God, by the exercise of those affections, and the practice of those virtues which are essential to the happiness of man in time and throughout eternity."

As the membership diminished the wealth increased, but not from contributions by new members, and operations were carried on by hired labor.

Not one of the eight contributed to the three or four millions of property accumulated. It is conceded that Duss alone is the active member. But he is not the society, nor does the society in respect of its avowed principles any longer exist.

Moreover the transactions by which seventeen members of the society, not old and infirm, but vigorous and capable, were bought out, were in themselves acts of liquidation. It is idle to say that these payments were "donations" to withdrawing members. They were purchases, in terms, and in effect. They were settlements by agreement instead of through litigation.

Finally, substantially the entire property of the society and its affairs have been turned over to a corporation created under the laws of Pennsylvania, authorized to purchase and sell land. This corporation has none of the powers confided by the articles of 1847, to the Board of Elders and the Board of Trustees. It has no power to feed, lodge, maintain and support, or to care for the spiritual welfare of members of the society or to perform any of the duties imposed upon the boards. The trustees have no distinct title to the society's property, but only the rights pertaining to the stock of the Union Company. All the industries carried on in Economy are carried on by tenants and lessees of the Union Company, and the society has ceased to possess the power to carry out the purposes for which its property was accumulated.

The affairs of the Union Company must be wound up under the state statutes in that behalf, and proceeds derived from the lands by sale or otherwise would go to the stockholders by way of dividends. The legal effect of the transaction was the same as a sale, out and out, for cash, and it was irrevocable. And this point so arises on the record that it must be disposed of as matter of law.

The master found, as matter of law, that the society continued to exist because the surviving members had not formally declared it to be dissolved, and that the purposes and principles of the society could not be held to have been abandoned unless by the formal action of all its members. But this could only be so on the assumption that the scheme of the trust created a joint tenancy with the right of survivorship, or a system of tontine; and that a single surviving member might be the society although to the integrity of a community, numbers are essential. By the articles neither the members, nor the Board of Elders, nor the Board of Trustees, nor all together, possessed the power voluntarily to formally dissolve the association, and it is for a court of equity to adjudge whether a condition of dissolution or a condition requiring winding up is or is not created by acts done or permitted.

Such being, in my opinion, the condition here, the trust property must go, as I have said, either to the surviving members as joint tenants with right of survivorship, or by way of tontine; or to the owners or donors living, and to the heirs and legal representative of those who are dead by way of resulting trust.

Appellees contend for the first of these propositions. Their counsel says in his brief:

It is the society, as a society, which owns this property. It is the entire body as one whole. If at any time the society did dissolve, its property would go to the persons who then were its members. No one else has any legal or equitable claim to it except those members. To them, and to them alone, it would belong, and among them it would be divided.

It is inconceivable that the creators of the trust contemplated any such result, when they sought to perpetuate Christian fellowship by the renunciation of their property.

The present membership has shrunk to eight members, less than enough to fill the Board of Elders, and that board consists of Duss and his wife; an old man and five women, aged or ignorant. Practically Duss is the last survivor and he claims the ownership of this vast estate as such survivor. By the articles no period was fixed for the termination of the life of the society. There is no remainder over, nor provision of any kind for the disposition of the trust estate in the event of the society's extinction.

Joint tenancy with survivorship or tontine excluding all but living members and casting accumulations on the survivor, are neither of them to be presumed. They are the result of express agreement and there is none such in these documents.

On the contrary, this property was held in trust for the use and benefit of the society as a society, and not for the individual members. The trust was for the use and benefit of the society in the maintenance of its principles as declared by its constitution and laws. When the purposes of the society were abandoned, or could not be accomplished, or the society ceased to exist, the trust failed, and the property reverted by way of resulting trust to the owners, who subjected it to the trust, living, and to the heirs and legal representatives of those of them who are dead.

This conclusion does not involve the assertion of a reversion secured by the express terms of the contracts, but rests on the familiar principle of equity jurisprudence that when the trust clearly created by the documents terminated a resulting trust arose to the grantors or donors or their heirs.

. . . .

The titles held by the trustees in this case were held for the benefit and use of the society in the maintenance of its principles. When the purposes of the trusts failed the property reverted, not because of special provision to that effect, but because that was the result of the termination of the trusts.

Complainants, or some of them, are the heirs and next of kin of members who signed the articles of 1836 and 1847, and who died in fellowship. The service of one of these families is said to aggregate three hundred years of unrequited toil. They are entitled to invoke the aid of the court in the winding up of this concern, and these decrees ought to be reversed.

[c] Explanatory Notes

[i] *The Court Opinion.* Schwartz's theory was that the Society had ceased to exist, that the trust relationship between the Society's trustees and the members had terminated, and that the heirs of the members of the Society were the proper recipients of the Harmony's wealth. The Society allegedly ceased to exist for a variety of reasons, including loss of membership, transformation of the group's assets into shares of stock, and termination of the religious activities of The Harmony. The Supreme Court did not resolve the question of whether the Society had ceased to exist. Rather, it held that if the Society no longer existed, Schwartz was not a proper claimant. Normal trust rules provide that upon termination of a trust, the parties creating the trust, or their heirs, receive the property as a *resulting trust* unless the document creating the trust designates other successors. The resulting trust is basically a *reversionary interest*, an interest retained by a grantor when an interest in property is conveyed to another. If Schwartz's ancestors joined before 1836, they apparently contributed no assets. The resulting trust rules could not assist them, the Court held. If they joined after 1836, the articles of agreement, the Court said, explicitly defeated the possibility that the heirs of any member had rights in the assets of the

Society. This holding effectively reduced the possible claimants to the Society's wealth to the remaining members, the State of Pennsylvania in escheat, and the heirs of members who died or withdrew before 1836 after contributing assets to the Harmony. The *Schwartz* case contained no pre-1836 contributing claimants and none surfaced later. Thus, both the question of whether the Society had terminated, and, if so, who should get the money, was left hanging. But the effect of the decision was to leave Duss in control.

[*ii*] *Escheat.* The Harmony presents a difficult problem in determining who should get the assets if the Society was indeed terminated. The dissent contended that giving the assets to the remaining members was completely inconsistent with the purposes of the Society. But the dissent's suggestion that all past members share in the wealth was hardly more consistent. Each member renounced any such interest in the Harmony. If there is no taker of an asset, most states provide that it escheats to the public coffers. It does seem like the Harmony was a good escheat situation.

[*iii*] *Fraud.* The actions of Duss looked remarkably similar to classic land fraud. First he set up a corporation, The Union Company, an innocuous act by itself. In part that step reflected the easing of regulations on establishment of corporations that occurred in the second half of the nineteenth century. Legislative charters were generally required to establish corporations at the beginning of the nineteenth century. In part for this reason, the trust was used by many large business enterprises as the organizational structure of choice. By the end of the century the process of incorporation was handled bureaucratically in accordance with the terms of state corporation statutes. In any case, Duss arranged for the Society to hold the shares of stock, representative of ownership interests in the corporation, and transferred all the assets of the Society to The Union Company. Duss also set up a number of other land companies which purchased various tracts from The Union Company, probably at below market prices. This left Duss-controlled companies with the land and The Union Company, the Society-owned corporation, with cash. As the land was sold again by the land companies, the profits were retained by Duss-owned businesses. Even assuming that the Society had some potential lawsuits against Duss for breach of his fiduciary duties as a trustee of the Society and an officer of The Union Company, the internal operations of the Society made legal action impossible. In addition, many of the purchasers of the land were probably unaware of Duss' wheeling and dealing. If the Society had legal rights against Duss or The Union Company, such rights were probably cut off as against the ultimate buyers because of their status as innocent purchasers, or in legalese, their status as *bona fide purchasers for value without notice* of any title defects.

[d]　The Final Days of the Harmony

The end came very soon after the Supreme Court decision in *Schwartz.* Between April, 1894, when the *Schwartz* case started, and 1902, when the Supreme Court decision was announced, death claimed nine of the 17 members left in the Society. On April 16, 1903, the eight remaining members reduced the Board of Elders to two: John Duss and Franz Gillman. Three of the eight members then withdrew; each was granted a "donation" of $75,000. One month later, Duss himself withdrew in exchange for a "donation" of $500,000, so that he could continue to pursue his career as a world famous, if eccentric, bandleader—the rival, at least in publicity, of John Philip Sousa.

Duss' musical enterprises are in fact quite intriguing. The Harmony Society had always loved music and had always had a band. Traditionally, the band had led the Harmonists into the fields during the harvest. As membership declined, however, the band became only a vestige of its former self. When Duss took over as trustee he devoted considerable time and much money to rebuilding the community's band. He imported talent from other areas, dressed them in magnificent uniforms and housed them in the vacated dwellings of the Society. Under his direction, they became the best band in the Pittsburgh region.

In 1902, Duss accepted the offer of a theatrical agent to send the band to New York for the summer season. At this point, Duss' love for showmanship, his unlimited access to the Society's millions, a $100,000 publicity campaign, and the boredom of the people of New York, combined to catapult him into fame. Before Duss entered the City of New York, his public relations agent, C. E. Bradford, saturated the city with "Dussism." In a campaign reminiscent of P. T. Barnum, Bradford employed two giants and a dwarf, dressed them in striped suits with the name "Duss" emblazoned on their caps and paraded them through the streets of the city handing out 36-page booklets filled with photographs of John Duss and the band. With added attractions such as flower girls, perfumed fountains, refrigerated air and an automaton in the form of an overdressed woman offering flowers to feminine visitors, Duss' engagement at St. Nicholas Gardens captured the fascination of the city.

Underneath all of this camouflage, however, Duss' abilities as a conductor were suspect. To compensate for his lack of musical talent, Duss gave speeches between numbers of the program and, when conducting, faced the audience and burst into gyrations without notice. This spectacle stole the show and made Duss the main attraction of the evening. The 1902 season was a box office success. In 1903, Duss returned to New York. This time, however, he was set on becoming the greatest conductor of his age. As a backdrop, he bought the Metropolitan Opera House Orchestra, spent thousands of dollars transforming Madison Square Garden into a replica of the city of Venice and staged a new opera, "Night in Venice." Duss' ambition to become the greatest conductor was never fulfilled. Critics continually disparaged his lack of talent. After this strange interlude in the operatic world of New York, the normal standard of serene beauty returned to the stage. While Duss returned with his "Venice" for another season, the Metropolitan Opera House Orchestra was conspicuously absent. Gradually, he faded back into his role as heir apparent, along with his wife, to the Harmony Society millions.

By the time Duss' New York interludes were completed, the Society was almost finished. After Duss gave himself a "donation" of $500,000 only four members of the Society remained. On May 12, 1903, Susie Duss was elected to the position of trustee vacated by her husband. Two years later, with the deaths of Christina Rall and Barbara Boesch, only Susie Duss and Franz Gillman remained. On December 13, 1905, the Harmony Society was dissolved. The property was divided equally between the two survivors. Franz Gillman then gave his half of the Harmony Society property back to Susie Duss. The dissolution documents declared the Society's assets as worth $1.2 million, though much of the property of the Harmony had long since been conveyed out of reach.[22]

After dissolution, the Dusses faced one final legal hurdle. Throughout the latter part of the Society's history, two of its trustees, Henrici and Lenz, had provided, in their letters, full evidence of the following points:

(1) It was contrary to the religious teachings of the Harmony Society for any trustee, member, or members to dissolve the Society.

---

[22] Arndt II, note 18 above, at 330.

(2) It was contrary to the teachings of the Society ever to make a will.

(3) It was contrary to the teachings of the Society ever to convert the property of the Society into private property.

(4) If Christ should not come before the last member died, then the property was to go to the State of Pennsylvania.[23]

In 1910, after much delay, the Attorney General of the State of Pennsylvania instituted escheat proceedings against Susie Duss and her husband to recover all the property in the possession of the trustees at the time of the actual dissolution of the Harmony. The State predicated its case on the ground that the Harmony Society was a religious organization dedicated to religious or charitable work, that as such the society had ceased to exist and that under the laws of the state such property remaining at its dissolution accrued to the public treasury for public use.[24]

The Dusses, aware of the letters in the Society's archives and fearful of the possibility of losing all their wealth, agreed to a compromise, passed as a joint resolution by the General Assembly and approved by Governor Brumbaugh on June 17, 1915. The Dusses gave the state $15,000 in cash, approximately two city squares of buildings, and a park as a museum and memorial of the Society. While many factors led the State to accept this small sum in settlement of the escheat action, fear of chaos in hundreds of land titles was one of the important motivations.

One final, and perhaps desperate, attempt was made by descendants of George Rapp to obtain some of the Harmony assets while the escheat was pending. The plaintiffs in *Everitt v. Duss* argued they owned a share of the assets by way of a resulting trust as heirs of Rapp. They lost. The trial court opined that the Society's assets were held as a joint tenancy with rights of survivorship, a somewhat peculiar view.[25] On appeal, the Circuit Court of Appeals took a more intriguing view of the situation:

We do not find it necessary to decide precisely what kind of valuable interest George Rapp may have had in the society's property when he died in 1847. If he had any interest at all, we need not discriminate between a resulting trust and a base fee, nor do we need to explore other regions in the law of real property; this much at least seems clear: The interest could only have been contingent, but (if it existed at all) it was real enough to be capable of transfer. Call it what we will—a contingent right, a somnolent capacity, a budding estate, or any other fanciful name—it must at least have been alive at his death if it has developed since into a full-grown right, and if it were alive then we may safely conclude that it did not evade the intestate laws of Pennsylvania. These statutes act upon every property right of every name, nature, and description, and, if this particular possibility was then a part of George Rapp's possessions, it passed at his death to his daughter and grand daughter as his next of kin, and afterwards to his grand daughter alone; and, as she disposed of it by last will and testament in which the plaintiffs have no beneficial interest, they cannot maintain the present bill. They must themselves claim under the intestate laws of Pennsylvania as George Rapp's next of kin, but the claim must fail, because they were not his next of kin at the time of his death. It was then that his property rights passed—if he had any—and not 60 years afterward.[26]

---

[23] *Id.* at 158.

[24] *Id.* at 340-341.

[25] 197 F. 401 (W.D. Pa. 1912).

[26] 206 F. 590, 610 (3d Cir. 1913).

John Duss died a pauper in 1951. During the depression he lost the money (estimated by Arndt to have amounted to $7.5 million) he gained from his control of the Society's thousands of acres of land. Susie Duss, who died in 1949, kept her assets separate from her husband, and managed to die a woman of some means. The land areas controlled by the Society included much of what currently comprises the towns of Beaver Falls and Ambridge, Pennsylvania. The State operates a museum in Old Economy, just outside Ambridge. A significant area of Ambridge, which contains buildings from the Society era, has been declared an historic district. Some day, when you are traveling in the Pittsburgh area, take a 15 mile detour northwest along the Ohio River to visit the area that Rapp built.

[e]   Some Notes on Gifts and Non-Profit Organizations

[*i*]   *Gifts are Forever.* Making a gift, the Harmony saga tells us, is an irrevocable step, unless the donor places some restrictions on the use of the transferred assets or the gift was procured by fraud. You can't renege once the gift is complete any more than you can take back a sale after the deal has been performed.

[*ii*]   *Organization of Charities.* Another lesson from the Harmony tale is that organizations may construct themselves in almost any way their members wish. While use of common "magic" forms like concurrent estates is certainly allowed, most organizations have special needs that make the standard forms inappropriate. So the Harmony, by using a series of instruments signed by all the members of the community, managed its affairs and kept control of its wealth. By designating itself as a trust, the Harmony was able to appoint leaders, make investment decisions and place significant constraints on the economic decision making of its members.

[*iii*]   *Fraud.* The combination of gift irrevocability, flexible organization of charitable trusts and freedom of religion creates room for less than honest behavior. Gifts obtained by fraud by non-religious institutions may be recovered. But defining fraud in a religious context often is much more difficult than in other settings. Not only does the constitution bar unnecessary government intrusions into religion, but the presence of spiritual faith allows for the creation of off-beat belief structures that we are not allowed to question. The next case forces us to consider the meaning of fraud in the arena of faith.

§ 3.03 Gift Giving in Contemporary Culture

[1]   Charitable Donations and Religious Organizations

David Molko and Tracy Leal are two ex-members of the Unification Church who were "deprogrammed." They both sued, alleging causes of action in fraud, among other things, and sought restitution of assets they had given to the church. The California Supreme Court reversed the lower court's dismissal of the action, holding that the allegations in the complaint, if later proved true, were sufficient to overcome any freedom of religion claims made by the church.

[a]   Opinions of the California Supreme Court in *Molko v. Holy Spirit Association*

David Molko and Tracy Leal v. Holy Spirit

Association for the Unification of World Christianity

Supreme Court of California

46 Cal. 3d 1092, 762 P.2d 46, 252 Cal. Rptr. 122 (1988)

MOSK, J.

This case raises [the] . . . issue . . . [of] whether, consistently with the free exercise clause of the First Amendment of the United States Constitution . . . former members of a religious organization may sue that organization on various causes of action arising out of its allegedly deceptive recruitment practices . . . .

Appellants David Molko and Tracy Leal are former members of the Unification Church. While members of the Church, they were on separate occasions forcibly abducted from a public street by third parties and "deprogrammed" — *i.e.*, persuaded to relinquish their belief in and association with the Church. Thereafter Molko and Leal filed the present action against the Church, alleging they had been fraudulently induced to join the Church through a variety of deceptive tactics on the part of some of its members. Molko and Leal each asserted causes of action for fraud and deceit. Molko also sought restitution of a $6,000 gift he alleged the Church obtained from him by undue influence.

The Church filed a first amended cross-complaint against Molko and Neil Maxwell, alleging their deprogramming activities violated the Church's federal and state civil rights.[3] . . . .

The court granted summary judgment for the Church in the action brought by Molko and Leal, and entered a judgment of dismissal for Molko after sustaining his demurrer without leave to amend as to the Church's amended cross-complaint against him. Similarly, the court entered a judgment of dismissal for Maxwell after sustaining his demurrer without leave to amend as to the Church's amended cross-complaint against him.

Molko and Leal appealed from the summary judgment for the Church. The Church cross-appealed from the judgment of dismissal for Molko, and appealed from the judgment of dismissal for Maxwell and Alexander. The Court of Appeal consolidated all the appeals; it affirmed the summary judgment for the Church, but reversed the judgments of dismissal for Molko . . . [and] Maxwell . . . . We granted petitions by Molko and Leal to review the affirmance of summary judgment for the Church, and by Maxwell to review the reversal of his judgment of dismissal.[4]

As will appear, we conclude that (1) the summary judgment for the Church should be . . . reversed as to the causes of action for fraud, and restitution, and (2) the reversal of the judgment of dismissal for Maxwell should be affirmed.

---

[3] The Church alleged that Molko, after his own deprogramming, became involved in kidnaping and deprogramming other Church members.

[4] . . . Molko [did not seek] . . . review of the reversal of . . . [his] judgment of dismissal.

I. FACTS

A. *Facts as to David Molko*

In June 1978 27-year-old David Molko graduated from Temple University School of Law. A month later he took and passed the Pennsylvania bar examination. In spite of these educational successes, he was unsure about his future. He considered moving to California, and decided to visit San Francisco, perhaps to find a job or take the California bar examination. He arrived in San Francisco in early January 1979.

On Sunday, January 21, Mark Bush and Ernest Patton approached Molko as he waited at a bus stop in San Francisco. Bush and Patton told Molko they lived in an "international community" of socially conscious people from different occupations who met in the evenings to discuss important issues. They invited Molko to come to dinner that evening. Molko asked the two their occupations and was told they did social work and worked with environmental programs. He asked if Bush and Patton had a "religious connection." They said "no." Bush and Patton did not reveal to Molko that they were members of the Unification Church, or that their purpose in approaching him and inviting him to dinner was to recruit him into the Church.

Molko attended the dinner, at which there appeared to be a number of other invited guests. He was kept apart from the other guests, and during dinner was held in constant conversation with group members. After dinner there was a lecture on general social problems, followed by a slide show on "Boonville" — a "farm" a few hours to the north, owned by the group at the house. The slide show depicted Boonville as a rural getaway where people from the house went for relaxation and pleasure. When the presentation was concluded, all the dinner guests were invited to visit the farm. Bush, Patton, and another group member, David Hager, strongly urged Molko to accept the invitation, and told him a van would be leaving for Boonville in a few minutes. Molko said he had no personal belongings with him, and he preferred to think about it. The group members assured him they would provide for all his needs, and again urged him to go. Impressed by this hospitality and enthusiasm, Molko finally agreed to go. At their request he then filled out and signed a form declaring his name, address, and telephone number, and 15 minutes later was in a van on his way to Boonville. He did not know and was not told Boonville was an indoctrination facility for the Unification Church.

The van arrived at Boonville several hours later. Molko was given a sleeping bag and shown to a shelter where others were already sleeping. He quickly fell asleep, and awoke the next morning to discover that many more people than just the 12 from the van were sleeping in the large room. When he arose and walked to the bathroom, a group member arose and walked with him. Wherever he went, a group member accompanied him.

Molko expected to spend some relaxed time in the country, but soon learned the day's schedule was tightly planned and left him no time to himself. First came group calisthenics, then breakfast, then a lecture on moral and ethical issues, followed by small group discussions of the lecture. Next came lunch, more exercise, another lecture and discussion, then a break to take a shower. Finally came dinner, "testimonials" by individuals about their lives and their impressions of the day at Boonville, and group singing followed by yet another small group discussion. At the end of the day Molko was exhausted and quickly fell asleep.

Tuesday was a repeat of Monday, except that Molko became acquainted with group member Bethie Rubenstein. He asked her the name of the group, and she told him it was the "Creative Community Project." He asked if the group was associated with any religious organization, and she told him "no." By the end of Tuesday, Molko was tired, uncomfortable and concerned about the direction his life was taking. He informed Patton and Bush he desired to return to San Francisco. They told him he was free to leave and that a bus would depart at three o'clock in the morning, but they strongly urged him to stay and hear the important information that would be discussed in the days to come. Molko agreed to stay on a little longer.

Wednesday and Thursday were exactly like Monday and Tuesday — even the two-day cycle of lectures was repeated verbatim. The lecturers spoke of brotherly love and social problems, and included references to God and some amount of prayer. On Wednesday, Rubenstein informed Molko the group's teachings derived from many philosophical sources, including Aristotle, Jefferson, and Reverend Sun Myung Moon. She did not disclose that Reverend Moon was the group's spiritual leader.

On Friday night, Molko was told the group was about to leave Boonville for "Camp K" — another group-owned retreat used on weekends. Molko said he wanted to return to San Francisco, but again was urged to give the group a few more days. He agreed and made the trip to Camp K, still oblivious of his involvement with the Unification Church.

The exercise-lecture-discussion regimen continued throughout both the weekend at Camp K and the following week back at Boonville, during which Molko became increasingly disoriented and despairing of his future. On Friday — his 12th day of continuous group activity — Molko once again asked if the group was involved with any larger organization. Finally, a member named Gloria revealed to him for the first time that the group was part of the Unification Church. He was confused and angry, but was informed the deception was necessary because people who had heard negative stories about the Church tended to be unreceptive if they knew the group's identity before hearing what it had to say. He agreed to stay and try to work out his confusion.

That night he returned to Camp K, where he remained for approximately five to seven weeks of "advanced training." The same regimen and structure continued during this period. Molko's parents, concerned about his welfare, flew from Florida in late February to talk to him. They stayed a week, but saw their son for only a few hours, and only in the presence of church members. The parents urged him to come home briefly, but he refused. Molko — who by this time had been taught that his parents were agents of Satan trying to tempt him away from the Church—was confused by the visit, but remained with the Church. His parents returned to Florida.

On finishing his advanced training at Camp K, Molko was judged ready to go back to the city to sell flowers and "witness"[7] for the Church. Shortly thereafter, in early April, two Church leaders told Molko the Church desperately needed funds for taxes, and urged him to give money. He donated $6,000 to the Church. Sometime during this period he also became a formal Church member.

Church leaders advised Molko he could help the Church most by becoming a member of the bar, and promised that the Church would pay for his bar review course. He agreed, and studied for and took the California bar examination while living in the Church's San Francisco house. As he left the final session of the bar examination, however, Molko was abducted and taken to a motel by "deprogrammers" hired by his parents. After three days of deprogramming, Molko terminated his association with the Unification Church.

---

[7] "Witnessing" is the Unification Church's name for the process of recruiting new members on the street. Bush and Patton, for example, were witnessing when they persuaded Molko to come to dinner. Open and candid witnessing is employed by other religious denominations.

B. *Facts as to Tracy Leal*

[The facts as to Tracy Leal have been omitted. Their basic tenor is much like those for Molko.]

II. FRAUD AND DECEIT

A. *Standard of Review*

A motion for summary judgment "shall be granted if all the papers submitted show that there is no triable issue as to any material fact and that the moving party is entitled to a judgment as a matter of law." (Code Civ. Proc., § 437c, subd. (c).) The purpose of summary judgment is to penetrate evasive language and adept pleading and to ascertain, by means of affidavits, the presence or absence of triable issues of fact . . ..

Summary judgment is a drastic measure that deprives the losing party of a trial on the merits. It should therefore be used with caution, so that it does not become a substitute for trial. The affidavits of the moving party should be strictly construed, and those of the opponent liberally construed. Any doubts as to the propriety of granting the motion should be resolved in favor of the party opposing the motion.

A defendant is entitled to summary judgment if the record establishes as a matter of law that none of the plaintiff's asserted causes of action can prevail. To succeed, the defendant must conclusively negate a necessary element of the plaintiff's case, and demonstrate that under no hypothesis is there a material issue of fact that requires the process of a trial. We shall examine the grant of summary judgment in this case with the foregoing standard in mind.

B. *Nature of the Fraud Claim*

The necessary elements of fraud are: (1) misrepresentation (false representation, concealment, or nondisclosure); (2) knowledge of falsity (scienter); (3) intent to defraud (*i.e.*, to induce reliance); (4) justifiable reliance; and (5) resulting damage. Molko and Leal contend specified members of the Unification Church knowingly misrepresented the Church's identity with the intent to induce each of them to associate with and ultimately join the Church. Molko and Leal further contend they justifiably relied on those misrepresentations in unknowingly agreeing to participate in Church activities, and suffered psychological and financial damage as a result of their involvement with and membership in the Unification Church. They state they would not have chosen to associate with the Church had they known its true identity.

The Church concedes for pleading purposes its members knowingly misrepresented the Church's identity to Molko and Leal. It further concedes the misrepresentations were made with the intent to induce Molko and Leal first to associate with Church recruiters and later to continue participating in Church activities. Nor, finally, does the Church contest plaintiffs' claims that they suffered damages as a result of their involvement with the Church. The Church contends, however, that it is entitled to summary judgment because the undisputed facts conclusively negate the element of justifiable reliance.

Justifiable reliance exists when the misrepresentation or nondisclosure was an immediate cause of the plaintiff's conduct which alters his legal relations, and when without such misrepresentation or nondisclosure he would not, in all reasonable probability, have entered into the contract or other transaction. The Church contends that because Molko and Leal learned the Church's true identity prior to becoming formal members, the misrepresentations were "cured" and Molko and Leal could not have justifiably relied on them in deciding to join the Church.

Molko and Leal admit they were aware of the Church's identity at the time they formally joined. However, they contend that by the time the Church disclosed its true identity, the Church's agents had rendered them incapable of deciding not to join the Church, by subjecting them, without their knowledge or consent, to an intense program of coercive persuasion or mind control. They contend, in other words, that the Church deceived them into a setting in which they could be "brainwashed," and that the Church could not then "cure" the deception by telling them the truth after their involuntary indoctrination was accomplished.[11] 1 Molko and Leal therefore contend that a triable issue of fact remains as to whether the Church brainwashed them prior to disclosing its identity. If the answer is affirmative, they urge, they have established justifiable reliance.

. . . .

Brainwashing is "a forcible indoctrination to induce someone to give up basic political, social, or religious beliefs and attitudes and to accept contrasting regimented ideas." (*Webster's Ninth New Collegiate Dict.* (1987) p. 175.) The specific methods of indoctrination vary, but the basic theory is that brainwashing "is fostered through the creation of a controlled environment that heightens the susceptibility of a subject to suggestion and manipulation through sensory deprivation, physiological depletion, cognitive dissonance, peer pressure, and a clear assertion of authority and dominion. The aftermath of indoctrination is a severe impairment of autonomy and [of] the ability to think independently, which induces a subject's unyielding compliance and the rupture of past connections, affiliations, and associations." (*Peterson v. Sorlien* (Minn. 1981) 299 N.W.2d 123, 126.)

The brainwashing concept is controversial. Some highly respected authorities conclude brainwashing exists and is remarkably effective. (*See, e.g.*, Lifton, *Thought Reform and the Psychology of Totalism* (1961); Schein, *Coercive Persuasion* (1961).) Some commentators additionally conclude that certain religious groups use brainwashing techniques to recruit and control members. (*See, e.g.*, Delgado, *Religious Totalism: Gentle and Ungentle Persuasion Under the First Amendment* (1977), 51 So. Cal. L. Rev. 1, 3-9; Rudin & Rudin, *Prison or Paradise? The New Religious Cults* (1980) pp. 20-25; Clark et al., *Destructive Cult Conversion: Theory, Research and Treatment* (1979) pp. 1-15.) . . . .

To the contrary, other authorities believe brainwashing either does not exist at all (*see* Coleman, *New Religions and the Myth of Mind Control* (1984) Am. J. Orthopsychiatry 322, 323) or is effective only when combined with physical abuse or physical restraint (*see* Scheflein & Opton, *The Mind Manipulators* (1978) p. 23). We need not resolve the controversy; we need only conclude that the existence of such differing views compels the conclusion that Molko and Leal's theory indeed raises a factual question — *viz.*, whether Molko and Leal were brainwashed — which, if not prohibited by other considerations, precludes a grant of summary judgment for the Church.

. . . .

---

[11] The Court of Appeal mischaracterized the fraud claims when it stated that plaintiffs' contention was, "they justifiably relied on representations they *knew to be untrue* because those who made the false representations first stripped [Molko and Leal] of their independent judgment." (Italics added.) The contention is rather that Molko and Leal justifiably relied on representations they *believed* to be true, and as a result were subjected to a process by which they were stripped of their independent judgment.

D. Constitutional Issues

1. Applicable Principles

The First Amendment to the Constitution of the United States provides that "Congress shall make no law respecting an establishment of religion, or prohibiting the free exercise thereof . . . ." The provision creates two very different protections. The "establishment clause" guarantees the government will not impose religion on us; the "free exercise" clause guarantees the government will not prevent us from freely pursuing any religion we choose.

Because the First Amendment refers only to Congress, it originally did not apply to state and local governments. After the Civil War the states ratified the Fourteenth Amendment, and pursuant thereto the Supreme Court made the free exercise and establishment clauses federally enforceable against the states.

. . . .

The religion clauses protect only claims rooted in religious belief. The free exercise clause protects religious beliefs absolutely. While a court can inquire into the sincerity of a person's beliefs, it may not judge the truth or falsity of those beliefs. The government may neither compel affirmation of a religious belief nor penalize or discriminate against individuals or groups because of their religious beliefs, nor use the taxing power to inhibit the dissemination of particular religious views.

However, while religious belief is absolutely protected, religiously motivated conduct is not. Such conduct "remains subject to regulation for the protection of society." (*Cantwell v. Connecticut* (1940) 310 U.S. 296, 304.) Government action burdening religious conduct is subject to a balancing test, in which the importance of the state's interest is weighed against the severity of the burden imposed on religion. The greater the burden imposed on religion, the more compelling must be the government interest at stake. (*Compare Wisconsin v. Yoder* (1972) 406 U.S. 205, 221-235 [government's strong interest in education of citizens insufficient to justify educational requirement that threatened continued survival of Old Order Amish communities] *with Goldman v. Weinberger* (1986) 475 U.S. 503, 508 [government's reasonable interest in uniform military attire sufficient to justify mild burden on religious expression created by ban against Jewish officer wearing a yarmulke]. A government action that passes the balancing test must also meet the further requirements that (1) no action imposing a lesser burden on religion would satisfy the government's interest and (2) the action does not discriminate between religions, or between religion and nonreligion. (*Braunfield v. Brown* (1961) 366 U.S. 599, 607.)

Applying these criteria, the Supreme Court has allowed some religious conduct to be banned entirely (*see, e.g., Reynolds v. United States* (1878) 98 U.S. 145, 166 [upholding law against polygamy]; *Prince v. Massachusetts* (1944) 321 U.S. 158, 170-171 [permitting state to prohibit parents from allowing their children to distribute religious literature when necessary to protect children's health and safety]), and some conduct to be compelled in the face of religious objections (*see, e.g., Jacobson v. Massachusetts* (1905) 197 U.S. 11, 38 [upholding compulsory vaccinations for communicable diseases]; *United States v. Lee* (1982) 455 U.S. 252, 261 [upholding mandatory participation of Amish in Social Security system]).

Other religious conduct, though not banned, has been restricted. (*See, e.g., Heffron v. International Society for Krishna Consciousness, Inc.* (1981) 452 U.S. 640, 654 [upholding law restricting sale and distribution of literature and soliciting of funds at state fair to booths at specified locations]; *Cox v. New Hampshire* (1941) 312 U.S. 569, 575 [upholding license requirement for religious parades].) Still other religious conduct, though not banned or restricted, has been made more costly. (*See, e.g., Braunfield v. Brown, supra*, 366 U.S. 599, 605 [upholding Sunday closing law in spite of financial burden on Orthodox Jew who must refrain from working Saturday as well]; *Bob Jones University v. United States* (1983) 461 U.S. 574, 604 [upholding denial of tax-exempt status to private school practicing religiously motivated racial discrimination]; *Tony and Susan Alamo Foundation v. Secty. of Labor* (1985) 471 U.S. 290, 305 [holding minimum wage laws applicable to religious groups].)

While judicial sanctioning of tort recovery constitutes state action sufficient to invoke the same constitutional protections applicable to statutes and other legislative actions (*New York Times v. Sullivan* (1964) 376 U.S. 254, 265), religious groups are not immune from all tort liability. It is well settled, for example, that religious groups may be held liable in tort for secular acts. (*See, e.g., Malloy v. Fong* (1951) 37 Cal. 2d 356, 372 [232 P.2d 241] [religious corporation liable for negligent driving by employee].) Most relevant here, in appropriate cases courts will recognize tort liability even for acts that are religiously motivated. (*See, e.g., O'Moore v. Driscoll* (1933) 135 Cal. App. 770, 778 [28 P.2d 438] [allowing priest's action against his superiors for false imprisonment as part of their effort to obtain his confession of sins]; *Bear v. Reformed Mennonite Church* (1975) 107 462 Pa. 330 [341 A.2d 105, 107] [allowing action for interference with marriage and business interests when church ordered congregation to "shun" former member]; *Carrieri v. Bush* (1966) 69 Wash.2d 536 [419 P.2d 132, 137] [allowing action for alienation of affections when pastor counseled woman to leave husband who was "full of the devil"]; *Candy H. v. Redemption Ranch, Inc.* (M.D. Ala. 1983) 563 F. Supp. 505, 516 [allowing action for false imprisonment against religious group]; *Van Schaick v. Church of Scientology of Cal., Inc.* (D. Mass. 1982) 535 F. Supp. 1125, 1135 ["[c]auses of action based upon some proscribed conduct may, thus, withstand a motion to dismiss even if the alleged wrongdoer acts upon a religious belief or is organized for a religious purpose"].)

2. Constitutional Analysis of the Fraud Claim

While the Unification Church's standing as a church is not at issue, Molko and Leal contend the Church's misrepresentations were "entirely secular" and therefore not protected by the religion clauses. We disagree. Molko and Leal themselves claim the Church made its misrepresentations because of a belief in what they describe as "Heavenly Deception." According to Molko and Leal, that doctrine holds, in essence, that it is acceptable to lie to someone in order to give him the opportunity to hear Reverend Moon's teachings.[15] 5 As alleged by the plaintiffs, the Church's deceptions, although secular on the surface, are clearly "rooted in religious belief." (*Wisconsin v. Yoder, supra*, 406 U.S. at p. 215.) While this does not mean such Church misrepresentations are immune from government regulation, it does mean any such regulation must survive constitutional scrutiny.

Preliminarily, we note Molko and Leal do not contest the sincerity of what they understand to be the Church's beliefs; indeed, as just stated, they assert the Church's deceptions were the product of sincerely held beliefs. Our initial inquiry, then, is whether plaintiffs' actions for fraud implicate religious belief or religiously motivated conduct. If the former, the actions are barred. If the latter, further constitutional analysis is necessary.

Molko and Leal claim they do not challenge the truth or falsity of the Church's beliefs; they contend rather that they challenge only the Church's fraudulent conduct in implementing those

---

[15] At oral argument, the Church disavowed any such belief.

beliefs. The Court of Appeal disagreed, reasoning that it would be impossible to consider Molko and Leal's theory "without questioning the authenticity and force of the Unification Church's religious teachings and permitting a jury to do likewise, which is constitutionally forbidden." The court relied on *Katz v. Superior Court* (1977) 73 Cal. App. 3d 952, in reaching its conclusion, and the Church adopts this view. We therefore examine *Katz* to determine whether such reliance was properly placed.

Like the present case, *Katz* involved allegations of brainwashing against the Unification Church. The plaintiffs in *Katz*, however, were not former Church members but parents of current Church members. Claiming their adult children had been brainwashed, the parents sought and received orders from the superior court appointing them temporary conservators of the persons of their children. The parents' objective was to have their children deprogrammed and their children's association with the Unification Church terminated.

The Court of Appeal in *Katz* overturned the conservatorship orders, holding that in the absence of actions rendering the adult believers "gravely disabled," the processes of the state could not "be used to deprive the believer of his freedom of action and to subject him to involuntary treatment." The court declared the conservatorship orders violated the Church members' free exercise rights because the orders were based on a judgment regarding the truth or falsity of their beliefs. Likening the Church members' radical changes of lifestyle to the refusal of the Amish in *Yoder* to send their children to high school, the court found the situation one in which conduct could not be separated from beliefs. It queried "When the court is asked to determine whether that change [in lifestyle] was induced by faith or by coercive persuasion is it not in turn investigating and questioning the validity of that faith?"

The *Katz* court, of course, faced circumstances substantially different from those before us. The conservatorship orders, if allowed to stand, would have directly and severely burdened the Church members' absolute right to believe in the teachings of the Unification Church. Not only would the orders have allowed the parents to remove their adult children from the religious community they claimed to desire; the orders would have further allowed the parents to subject those individuals, against their will, to a program specifically intended to eradicate their current religious beliefs. Thus, the *Katz* court was correct — as in *Yoder*, the burden on the Church members' conduct was inseparable from the burden on their beliefs.

In sharp contrast, liability for fraud in the case at bar would burden no one's right to believe and no one's right to remain part of his religious community, nor would it subject anyone to involuntary deprogramming: the plaintiffs here are the former Church members themselves. It might, of course, somewhat burden the Church's efforts to recruit new members by deceptive means.

The *Katz* court also faced a legal question markedly different from that now posed: it considered whether a court could determine if an asserted religious conversion "was induced by faith or by coercive persuasion." In other words, the *Katz* court had to decide whether a court could "question the validity" of a person's stated faith because someone else claimed that person was brainwashed.

Again in contrast, the legal question here does not require a court to determine whether anyone's faith, current or past, is or was real. As stated above, Molko and Leal do not question the Church's beliefs. Neither do they challenge the "validity" of their former faith; they state quite plainly that their erstwhile beliefs in the Unification Church were sincere. The legal question is simply whether a religious organization can be held liable on a traditional cause of action in fraud for deceiving nonmembers into subjecting themselves, without their knowledge or consent, to coercive persuasion.

The Court of Appeal held that although *Katz* was different in certain ways, its analysis compelled the conclusion that to consider plaintiffs' fraud claims would require "questioning the authenticity and the force" of the Church's teachings. We disagree. The challenge here, as we have stated, is not to the Church's teachings or to the validity of a religious conversion. The challenge is to the Church's practice of misrepresenting or concealing its identity in order to bring unsuspecting outsiders into its highly structured environment. That practice is not itself belief — it is conduct "subject to regulation for the protection of society." (*Cantwell v. Connecticut, supra,* 310 U.S. at p. 304.)

Our next inquiry, then, is whether the state's interest in allowing tort liability for the Church's deceptive practices is important enough to outweigh any burden such liability would impose on the Church's religious conduct.

We turn first to the question whether tort liability for fraudulent recruiting practices imposes any burden on the free exercise of the Unification Church's religion. We think it does. While such liability does not impair the Church's right to believe in recruiting through deception, its very purpose is to discourage the Church from putting such belief into practice by subjecting the Church to possible monetary loss for doing so. Further, liability presumably impairs the Church's ability to convert nonbelievers, because some potential members who would have been recruited by deception will choose not to associate with the Church when they are told its true identity.

Yet these burdens, while real, are not substantial. Being subject to liability for fraud does not in any way or degree prevent or inhibit Church members from operating their religious communities, worshiping as they see fit, freely associating with one another, selling or distributing literature, proselytizing on the street, soliciting funds, or generally spreading Reverend Moon's message among the population. It certainly does not, like the educational requirement in *Yoder,* compel Church members to perform acts "at odds with fundamental tenets of their religious beliefs." At most, it potentially closes one questionable avenue for bringing new members into the Church.

We must next consider whether a compelling state interest justifies the marginal burden such liability imposes on the Church's free exercise rights. We have no difficulty in finding such an interest in the "substantial threat to public safety, peace or order" the Church's allegedly fraudulent conduct poses. For it is one thing when a person knowingly and voluntarily submits to a process involving coercive influence, as a novice does on entering a monastery or a seminary. (*See* Schein, *Coercive Persuasion* (1961) p. 272.) But it is quite another when a person is subjected to coercive persuasion without his knowledge or consent. While some individuals who experience coercive persuasion emerge unscathed, many others develop serious and sometimes irreversible physical and psychiatric disorders, up to and including schizophrenia, self-mutilation, and suicide. (*See generally* Delgado, *Religious Totalism: Gentle and Ungentle Persuasion Under the First Amendment, supra,* 51 So. Cal. L. Rev. 1, 10-25, and sources cited therein.) The state clearly has a compelling interest in preventing its citizens from being deceived into submitting unknowingly to such a potentially dangerous process.

The state has an equally compelling interest in protecting the family institution. (*See, e.g., Moore v. City of East Cleveland* (1977) 431 U.S. 494, 503-504 [plur. op.].) Since the family almost invariably suffers great stress and sometimes incurs significant financial loss when one of its members is unknowingly subjected to coercive persuasion, the state has a compelling interest in protecting families from suffering such impairments as a result of fraud and deception.

We conclude, therefore, that although liability for deceptive recruitment practices imposes a marginal burden on the Church's free exercise of religion, the burden is justified by the compelling state interest in protecting individuals and families from the substantial threat to public safety, peace and order posed by the fraudulent induction of unconsenting individuals into an atmosphere of coercive persuasion.

Our analysis cannot end here, however. A government action burdening free exercise, even though justified by a compelling state interest, is impermissible if any action imposing a lesser burden on religion would satisfy that interest. After careful consideration, we perceive no such less restrictive alternative available . . . . [B]rainwashing [could] be criminalized. This approach, which would invoke the coercive power of the state and could result in the jailing of church members, would clearly impose a greater burden on religion than would civil tort liability for fraud . . . . [T]he law [could] . . . authorize involuntary deprogramming of brainwashed individuals by their friends or families. But the potentially severe burdens on religion inherent in this approach are evident from our discussion of *Katz, supra.* Lastly, . . . proselytizers [could] be required to obtain informed consent prior to attempting to initiate religious conversions. To the extent such an approach would require the active dissemination of specific information about a religion's nature, activities and lifestyle, however, it would also burden religion to a greater extent than would simple passive liability for fraud. In short, it appears that to allow injured parties to bring private actions for fraud is the least restrictive means available for advancing the state's interest in protecting individuals and families from the harmful effects of fraudulent recruitment.

Finally, even though the state action is justified by a compelling state interest and imposes the minimum burden required to satisfy that interest, it can be upheld only if it (1) has the purpose and effect of advancing the state's secular goals and (2) does not discriminate between religions, or between religion and nonreligion. We find that judicial sanctioning of traditional tort liability for fraudulent recruitment satisfies these standards. First, its purpose and effect is plainly to advance the legitimate secular goal of protecting persons from being harmed by fraud. Second, it is nondiscriminatory: all organizations, religious or otherwise, may be held liable for damages caused by their fraudulent acts. Were a nonreligious organization —*e.g.*, a group espousing a political or social cause — to deceive a person into unknowingly submitting to coercive persuasion, the same liability would ensue.

We conclude that neither the federal nor state Constitution bars Molko and Leal from bringing traditional fraud actions against the Church for allegedly inducing them, by misrepresentation and concealment of its identity, into unknowingly entering an atmosphere in which they were then subjected to coercive persuasion. Because triable issues of fact exist as to (1) whether the forms Molko and Leal signed before going to Boonville put them on notice regarding the Church's identity and (2) whether Molko and Leal were, by means of coercive persuasion, rendered unable to respond independently upon learning they had been deceived, we hold that the Court of Appeal erred in affirming the summary judgment for the Church as to plaintiff's actions for fraud.

. . . .

V. RESTITUTION

Molko seeks restitution of his $6,000 gift to the Church. His claim arises directly out of his fraud theory: he asserts that the Church deceived him into unknowingly submitting to coercive persuasion, thereby obtaining undue influence over him which it later used to extract the gift.

The Court of Appeal held that Molko could not challenge the validity of the gift without challenging the validity of his former beliefs, which is constitutionally forbidden. We disagree. Molko's assertion is a natural extension of his fraud theory: he contends in effect, that one of his damages from the fraud was the $6,000 loss.

The Court of Appeal cited *Estate of Supple* (1966) 247 Cal. App. 2d 410, 414-415, to support its position. *Supple*, however, was not an undue influence case. In *Supple*, a lifelong church member left a portion of his estate to various church charities with which he had a longstanding association. His grandnephew challenged the will on the sole ground that the church's teachings were false, and hence the testator was in that sense tricked into leaving part of his estate to the church. Such a direct attack on the truth or falsity of religious beliefs was clearly prohibited by the First Amendment. However, as we explained above in distinguishing *Katz v. Superior Court*, Molko does not challenge the validity of his former beliefs. Therefore *Supple* is inapplicable.

Undue influence is "the use, by one in whom a confidence is reposed by another, or who holds a real or apparent authority over him, of such confidence or authority for the purpose of obtaining an unfair advantage over him." (Civ. Code, § 1575.) Stated another way, undue influence is that kind of influence or supremacy of one mind over another by which that other is prevented from acting according to his own wish or judgment; it occurs when one party uses its dominant psychological position in an unfair manner to induce the subservient party to consent to an agreement to which he would not otherwise have consented.

We have already concluded, in the context of Molko's fraud claim, that a triable issue of fact exists as to whether Molko lost his ability to make independent decisions as a result of being deceived into submitting unknowingly to coercive persuasion. It would be odd indeed, then, if we did not find that a triable issue of fact exists as to whether, by means of the alleged deception, the Church established and used its dominant psychological position and its confidential relationship with Molko "for the purpose of obtaining unfair advantage over him" with regard to his $6,000 gift.

. . . .

VI. THE CHURCH'S CROSS-COMPLAINT AGAINST MAXWELL

The Church alleged that Maxwell's deprogramming activities violated the federal and state civil rights of the Church and its members. (42 U.S.C. § 1985(3); Civ. Code, §§ 51.7, 52) . . . .

The trial court sustained without leave to amend Maxwell's demurrers to all three causes of action, and entered judgments of dismissal for him. The Court of Appeal reversed the judgments of dismissal on the state and federal civil rights causes of action, holding that the court abused its discretion by refusing leave to amend the complaint.

. . . .

[Discussion of the largely procedural issues involved in affirming the Court of Appeal's refusal to dismiss this claim is omitted.]

. . . .

LUCAS, C.J., BROUSSARD, J., ARGUELLES, J., EAGLESON, J., KAUFMAN, J., concurred. ANDERSON (CARL W.), JUSTICE, Concurring and Dissenting.

I . . . disagree with the reversal of summary judgment in connection with the fraud, intentional infliction of emotional distress and the restitution counts. I am strongly persuaded that the imposition of tort liability for "heavenly deception" in proselytizing and for its ensuing "systematic manipulation of social influences" (religious persuasion) runs counter to established legal precedents and the free exercise clause of the First Amendment. Furthermore, imposition of liability in such cases constitutes bad legal policy, since it unnecessarily projects the court into the arena of divining the truth or falsity of religious beliefs. I respectfully suggest that the trial court's thorough analysis and the Court of Appeal's well-reasoned affirmance thereof correctly apply the law.

I. Fraud

. . . .

[C]ontrary to the conclusion reached by the majority, I find appellants' fraud cause of action fatally defective for two fundamental reasons: (1) the record fails to show that the initial fraud committed by the proselytizers was relied upon by appellants at the crucial time of joining the Church; and (2) the immediate cause of appellants' damages was not the incipient fraud but rather the ensuing indoctrination and conversion (dubbed by the majority as "brainwashing"). However, the indoctrination achieved by persuasion absent physical force or violence is not unlawful; religious conversion is simply not subject to judicial review. It follows that neither of these questions creates a triable issue of fact which defeats the grant of summary judgment.

A. Reliance on Initial Misrepresentations

In granting summary judgment on the fraud cause of action, the trial court found that appellants, by their own admissions, joined the Unification Church (the Church) because that "Association satisfied personal concerns and anxieties both were experiencing"; it did not find they joined in reliance on the initial misrepresentations of the recruiters. This finding of the trial court is well supported by the record.

. . . .

[T]he majority maintains that appellants' behavior following the initial fraud did not negate the element of reliance (*i.e.*, the initial fraud was not "cured"); they conclude that as a result of the Church's initial "heavenly deception" (*i.e.*, fraudulent conduct), appellants were placed in a situation where they were "brainwashed" and thereby deprived of their independent judgment. The majority predicates this "brainwashing" theory primarily upon appellants' declarations that due to the rigid indoctrination, psychological and emotional pressure, they lost their ability to freely decide to stay with the group and, instead, they acted in a robot-like manner. Such conclusion fails to withstand critical analysis.

Under the widely adopted view, the fact that the religious belief does not originate in a voluntary choice does not, as a rule, raise a presumption of incapacity to affirm the belief as one's own. (Shapiro, *"Mind Control" or Intensity of Faith: The Constitutional Protection of Religious Beliefs* (1978) 13 Harv. Civ. Liberties L. Rev. 751, 789.) To the contrary, it has been said that "An intentional deception should not justify impinging upon a convert's ideas, so long as the convert has the ability to affirm his faith after the deception is realized. If he retains his personhood [*i.e.*, the capacity to evaluate the commitment], . . . he can still adopt or ratify the beliefs as his own." (Shapiro, *Of Robots, Persons and the Protection of Religious Beliefs* (1982-1983) 56 So. Cal. L. Rev. 1277, 1295.) By illustration, Mr. Shapiro points out that if the proselytizer had offered merely a self-improvement course and the subsequent banquet and lectures in fact had aimed at converting the recruit to a religion, the deceptiveness of the introduction would be immaterial as long as the convert would be still capable of adopting or affirming his belief.

The evidence before us, including appellants' depositions, clearly indicates that the Church's indoctrination did not render appellants mindless puppets or robot-like creatures. Instead, it shows that both before and after the disclosure of the group's true identity, both appellants retained their ability to think, to evaluate the events and to exercise their independent judgment.

. . . .

In view of [their] . . . sworn testimony, the unsupported allegations of brainwashing in appellants' pleadings and declarations should not be deemed sufficient to raise that triable issue of material fact which requires reversal of the grant of summary judgment.

B. Conversion Is the Immediate Cause of Damages

Reversal of summary judgment is improper for the additional reason that the immediate cause of damages was not the incipient fraud, *i.e.*, heavenly deception, but rather the ensuing introduction effected by "brainwashing" which ultimately resulted in appellants' conversion. That the gist of appellants' fraud complaint was that the conversion was achieved by actionable "brainwashing" is manifest. Indeed, the majority so defines the issue: "Molko and Leal therefore contend that a triable issue of fact remains as to whether the Church brainwashed them prior to disclosing its identity. If the answer is affirmative, they urge, they have established justifiable reliance." Again, the majority declares that appellants' "statements are consistent with the contention that they were deceived into a situation in which they were then brainwashed" and summary judgment on the fraud count must be overturned because the brainwashing theory advanced in appellants' declarations presented a triable issue of fact. This same notion not unsurprisingly has its genesis in appellants' briefs. For example, Molko asserts in his opening brief that "By means of deceits and deceptions utilized in order to place plaintiff in Boonville, plaintiff was abruptly thrust into an environment directed entirely toward the *conversion* of plaintiff's allegiance to accept Sun Myung Moon as the Messiah and to become a member of the Unification Church . . . . The conversion of plaintiff occurred in an unusual place." (Italics partially added.) Amici likewise emphasize that the immediate cause of damages was the process of conversion which has been known by many labels — brainwashing, thought reform, coercive persuasion, etc.

Identification of the indoctrination (*i.e.*, "brainwashing") and the conversion as the critical issues for determining the applicability of summary judgment carries far-reaching legal significance. For under settled law the indoctrination methods employed in obtaining conversion (including coercive persuasion, mind control and/or brainwashing) are not actionable *per se;* religious conversion is not subject to judicial scrutiny regardless of the methods used because such scrutiny necessarily entails the questioning of religious faith — scrutiny that is absolutely forbidden by the First Amendment. Moreover, even if judicial scrutiny were permitted, governmental interference in this case is not warranted.

. . . .

[R]eligious indoctrination, even if achieved by "brainwashing," is not tortious if unaccompanied by physical force or threat . . . . To the extent that the plaintiff alleges that the decedent was "brainwashed" as a result of the church's program, this claim must be viewed in the context of the situation as a whole, *i.e.*, as a method of religious indoctrination that is neither extreme nor outrageous . . . . It is important to note that no facts are set forth which would warrant the conclusion that the plaintiffs [were] . . . falsely imprisoned by the appellant or that [they were] . . . subjected to any form of violence, or physical or mental torture, as such. The claim of brainwashing is based upon the activities heretofore described, which . . . are commonly used by religious and other groups, and are accepted by society as legitimate means of indoctrination. They are not classifiable as so extreme or outrageous, or offensive to society, as to incur liability therefor.

. . . .

[Nor is] . . . the conversion . . . actionable. The majority concedes that the free exercise clause of the First Amendment provides absolute protection for religious beliefs; that the government cannot discriminate against individuals or groups because they hold views abhorrent to the authorities; and that while the court can inquire into the sincerity of an individual's beliefs, it may not judge the truth or falsity of those beliefs. However, the majority concludes that while religious belief is absolutely protected, religious conduct is not; that conduct even if religiously motivated is subject to regulation for the protection of society; and that the Church's initial fraud which led to the brainwashing of appellants was conduct which, under the balancing test required by the First Amendment, can be penalized with tort sanctions based upon a compelling state interest.

I respectfully submit that this reasoning is flawed. To begin with, the conduct which according to the majority constitutes a triable issue of fact is not only the initial fraud (an act clearly subject to proof), but also the subsequent "brainwashing" and conversion — matters comprising not only sociological or psychological phenomena, but also involving intangible elements of religious belief. It follows that brainwashing and conversion are so inextricably intertwined with religious faith that they cannot be scrutinized, much less proven, without questioning the authenticity of the religious teachings of the Church. Such inquiry is absolutely proscribed by the free exercise clause of the First Amendment.

The proposition that the act or conduct of a religious organization or its members is immune from judicial scrutiny if the proof thereof calls into question the truth or falsity of religious faith is well established in case law as well as in legal commentary.

United States v. Ballard (1944) 322 U.S. 78, the leading case defining the parameters of the constitutional protection of religious faith, dealt with prosecution of religious fraud. Therein it was alleged that respondents, founders of the "I am" movement, fraudulently represented that they were divine messengers; that they had miraculous powers to heal all diseases and, in fact, had cured hundreds of afflicted people; and that as a result of these misrepresentations, they obtained money from the public through the mail. The trial court excluded from jury consideration the issue of the truth or falsity of respondents' claim of divine designation and miraculous powers, and the case was submitted on the sole issue of whether respondents made those claims in good faith. In approving the trial court's ruling, the Supreme Court reasoned:

Freedom of thought, which includes freedom of religious belief, is basic in a society of free men. It embraces the right to maintain theories of life and of death and of the hereafter which are rank heresy to followers of the orthodox faiths. Heresy trials are foreign to our Constitution. Men may believe what they cannot prove. They may not be put to the proof of their religious doctrines or beliefs. Religious experiences which are as real as life to some may be incomprehensible to others. Yet the fact that they may be beyond the ken of mortals does not mean that they can be made suspect before the law. Many take their gospel from the New Testament. But it would hardly be supposed that they could be tried before a jury charged with the duty of determining whether those teachings contained false representations. The miracles of the New Testament, the Divinity of Christ, life after death, the power of prayer are deep in the religious convictions of many. If one could be sent to jail because a jury in a hostile environment found those teachings false, little indeed would be left of religious freedom . . . . The religious views espoused by respondents might seem incredible, if not preposterous, to most people. But if those doctrines are subject to trial before a jury charged with finding their truth or falsity, then the same can be done with the religious beliefs of any sect. When the triers of fact undertake that task, they enter a forbidden domain.

. . . .

Even more analogous to this case is *Katz v. Superior Court* (1977) 73 Cal. App. 3d 952 . . . . The majority's effort to distinguish *Katz* from the case at bench is not persuasive. While *Katz* arose, indeed, in a somewhat different legal setting . . . the pivotal issue was the same: were the children brainwashed by the church and was their brainwashing subject to proof in a court proceeding?

. . . .

The teachings of *Katz* that "brainwashing" and religious conversion are not really distinguishable; that the methods used in each are either identical or very similar; and that proof of the existence of each is virtually identical are well illustrated by the present case.

. . . .

Indeed, what [the majority] . . . characterizes as indicia of brainwashing or mind control, might very well be equated with the more popularly accepted symptoms of genuine religious conversion. Religious behavioral change induced by the mystery of faith cannot be proved or disproved by secular science, which limits its scope of inquiry to tangible, rational and logical phenomena, comprehensible and explainable by human reasons. As Mr. Shapiro states in his essay:

> Religious beliefs — whether held by adherents to new sects or by "mainstream" believers — may not be dictated by societal norms. Such norms can easily encourage labels that transform religious beliefs into illnesses. A religion becomes a cult; proselytization becomes brainwashing; persuasion becomes propaganda; missionaries become subversive agents; retreats, monasteries, and convents become prisons; holy ritual becomes bizarre conduct; religious observance becomes aberrant behavior; devotion and meditation become psychopathic trances. (Shapiro, *Of Robots, Persons, and the Protection of Religious Beliefs, supra*, 56 So. Cal. L. Rev. at pp. 1316-1317.)

. . . .

III. Restitution

Finally, I find myself in profound disagreement with the reversal of summary judgment on the restitution count. The majority's ruling as to this issue rests on the theory of fraud (fraudulent inducement to facilitate brainwashing) and undue influence. However, neither of these theories support the cause of action at issue.

The uncontroverted evidence provided by Molko clearly demonstrates that he made the gift of $6,000 out of a then held religious belief. Thus, Molko explained that he gave the money to the Church to please God, the Heavenly Father, and that he had not asked that the money be returned while a member of the Church, because he had been afraid of the evil forces and felt guilty of demanding back something he had given to God. I quite agree with the trial court's finding: "Careful review of Mr. Molko's deposition testimony negates the conclusionary allegations contained in the Complaint." Molko made his gift after careful consideration and consultation with one of the two Church members in whom he had the greatest confidence. That he did not part with all his savings further negates the conclusionary allegations of undue influence in his complaint and indisputably establishes the gift as a product of his free will.

Since this gift was indisputably prompted by religious beliefs, and the issue of fraudulent inducement cannot be determined without inquiring into the truth or falsity of such beliefs, the theory of fraud as a ground justifying restitution cannot be judicially entertained without transgressing the free exercise clause of the First Amendment.

. . . .

Members of this court may detest the practice of heavenly deception. We may abhor the results of the Church's selective (and successful) proselytization. We may condemn such practices as destructive of the integrity of the family. Yet, as judges we must resist the temptation to tread into this theological thicket. For it is neither for governments, nor their instrumentalities, the courts, to divine the truth of those teachings. That is the law to which we are all bound. I am satisfied that both the Court of Appeal and the trial court before it have correctly found the law and applied it to these appellants . . . .

[b]   Explanatory Notes

[i]   *Impact of the Free Exercise Clause on* **Molko.** After *Molko* was decided, the United States Supreme Court handed down the now leading case on the relationships between state law having an impact on religion and the Free Exercise of Religion Clause in the First Amendment of the federal constitution. *Employment Division, Department of Resources v. Smith,* 494 U.S. 872 (1990). Smith was a member of the Native American Church. Church ritual involved supervised consumption of peyote, a controlled substance under Oregon law. After Smith was fired from his job at a private drug rehabilitation clinic because of his consumption of peyote, he sought unemployment benefits. The benefits were denied because he had been fired for work related misconduct. The Oregon Supreme Court holding that the benefit denial violated the free exercise clause was reversed by the United States Supreme Court. The *Smith* court concluded that application of "neutral" state civil and criminal legal standards[27] is permissible even if they have an impact on religious observance.

The outcome in *Molko* arguably fits within the rational of *Smith.* Molko claimed that he lacked an intention to make a gift. Fraud and brainwashing, he alleged, removed his ability to make decisions about his money. Application of neutral fraud principles to Molko's situation, the

---

[27] In this context, "neutrality" means that the legal standard was established for non-religious reasons to govern some aspect of human behavior. As long as the standard is applied in the same way to both religious and non-religious activity, there will usually not be any constitutional difficulty.

Supreme Court would probably say, is permissible even though it has an impact on use of religious "deception." So long as religious observance is not substantially effected by the use of fraud rules, the state is allowed to enforce its tort principles.

[*ii*] *Heavenly Deception.* Does the *Smith* standard make sense in the *Molko* setting? If "Heavenly Deception" always runs the risk of being fraudulent under California law, then isn't the impact on some forms of religious belief quite substantial? Compare the *Molko* setting to the Harmony Society. Do you think the gifts made to Harmony were different in kind from those made by Molko? Is it possible to develop a coherent description of the differences? Can it be done without stepping too hard on religious toes?

[*iii*] *One More Example.* Perhaps one more example will further highlight the serious nature of the problems in *Molko.* Suppose the leader of a religious group claims he is a messenger from God, that the best way to insure continuation of his communications with God is to provide for his personal comfort and well being, that those donating money for such purposes will be praised in his communications with God, and that such praise will significantly increase the likelihood of the donors' salvation and ascent to Heaven. These claims are made both on television and in meetings carried on in frenzied environments. Suppose further that the leader claims to be able to heal physical maladies. If a person spends $6,000 to go to a religious gathering to be healed, and has the leader's hands laid upon him in prayer, but is not healed, can he or she recover the $6,000?

[2]   Substitute Donative Intent: Incompetence and Gift Giving

For those with significant assets, estate planning routinely involves a program of annual gift giving. Federal estate and gift taxes do not have to be paid on gifts as large as $10,000 made in any year to any one person. In addition, if a person dies without a will designating how to distribute their wealth and no surviving relatives, the assets will escheat to the state. Most people prefer to give their money away rather than let it fall into the hands of a government. If a wealthy person becomes incompetent before instituting a gift giving program or writing a will, intriguing questions arise about the ability of a guardian to make estate planning decisions. That is the problem in the next case.

[a]   Opinion of the Supreme Court of Massachusetts in *Wanda Jones*

In the Matter of Wanda W. Jones

Massachusetts Supreme Judicial Court

379 Mass. 826, 401 N.E.2d 351 (Mass. 1980)

Before QUIRICO, BRAUCHER, KAPLAN, WILKINS and ABRAMS, JJ.

ABRAMS, JUSTICE.

This case is before us on the reservation and report by a Probate Court judge of certain questions of law arising from a petition by a conservator for approval of an estate plan for his ward under G.L. c. 201, § 38.[1] The Probate Court judge reserved and reported questions concerning the

---

[1] General Laws c. 201, § 38, as amended through St. 1976, c. 515, §§ 25-26, reads as follows: "He shall manage the estate of his ward frugally and without waste, and shall, except as otherwise provided, apply the same, so far

estate plan to the Appeals Court pursuant to G.L. c. 215, § 13.[2] We transferred the case to this court on our own motion.

The proposed estate plan principally consists of the creation of two inter vivos trusts: one, a revocable trust, providing for distributions to or for the ward during her lifetime from income or principal as necessary or advisable for her health and comfortable support, with remainders to certain charitable organizations; the other, an irrevocable charitable remainder trust which provides for an annual payment to or for the ward, during her lifetime, of an amount equal to

---

as may be necessary, to the comfortable and suitable maintenance and support of the ward and his family. If the income and profits are insufficient for that purpose, he may sell the real estate upon obtaining a license therefore, and shall apply the proceeds of such sale, so far as may be necessary, for the maintenance and support of the ward and his family. Such license and the application therefore shall state whether the ward is married or single. He shall have custody of all wills, codicils, and other instruments purporting to be testamentary dispositions executed by his ward.

"The probate court, upon the petition of a conservator or guardian, other than the guardian of a minor, and after such notice to all other persons interested as it directs, may authorize such conservator or guardian to take such action, or to apply such funds as are not required for the ward's own maintenance and support, in such fashion as the court shall approve as being in keeping with the ward's wishes so far as they can be ascertained and as designed to minimize insofar as possible current or prospective state or federal income, estate and inheritance taxes, and to provide for gifts to such charities, relatives and friends as would be likely recipients of donations from the ward.

"Such action or application of funds may include but shall not be limited to the making of gifts, to the conveyance or release of the ward's contingent and expectant interests in property including marital property rights and any right of survivorship incident to joint tenancy or tenancy by the entirety, to the exercise or release of his powers as donee of a power of appointment, the making of contracts, the creation of revocable or irrevocable trusts of property of the ward's estate which may extend beyond his disability or life, the exercise of options of the ward to purchase securities or other property, the exercise of his rights to elect options and to change beneficiaries under insurance and annuity policies, and the surrendering of policies for their cash value, the exercise of his right to an elective share in the estate of his deceased spouse, and the renunciation or disclaimer of any interest acquired by testate or intestate succession or by inter-vivos transfer.

"The guardian or conservator in his petition shall briefly outline the action or application of funds for which he seeks approval, the results expected to be accomplished thereby and the tax savings expected to accrue. The proposed action or application of funds may include gifts of the ward's personal property or real estate, but transfers of real estate shall be subject to the requirements of chapter two hundred and two. Gifts may be for the benefit of prospective legatees, devisees or heirs apparent of the ward or may be made to individuals or charities in which the ward is believed to have an interest. The conservator or guardian shall also indicate in the petition that any planned disposition is consistent with the intentions of the ward insofar as they can be ascertained, and if the ward's intentions cannot be ascertained, the ward will be presumed to favor reduction in the incidence of the various forms of taxation and the partial distribution of his estate as herein provided. The conservator or guardian shall not, however, be required to include as a beneficiary any person whom he has reason to believe would be excluded by the ward."

[2] General Laws c. 215 § 13, as amended through St. 1975, c. 400, § 59, states in pertinent part that "[a] judge of the probate court by whom a case or matter is heard for final determination may reserve and report the evidence and all questions of law therein for consideration of the appeals court, and thereupon like proceedings shall be had as upon appeal." This statute is the sole source of authority under which a Probate Court judge can reserve and report a case. Second Bank-State St. Trust Co. v. Linsley, 341 Mass. 113, 116, 167 N.E.2d 624 (1960). Dunlop v. Claussen, 313 Mass. 715, 716, 48 N.E.2d 919 (1943). "This provision does not authorize a report of a part of a case or of specific questions of law arising therein. The report must be of the entire case and in such form that this court can enter or order the entry of a final decree disposing of the case." Petition of Curran, 314 Mass. 91, 94, 49 N.E.2d 432, 434 (1943).

The Probate Court judge "declined to issue judgment in accordance with the petition or any modification thereof pending resolution of certain questions." In view of the fact that specific questions were reported, the reservation and report does not comply with G.L. c. 215, § 13. The issues having been raised and briefed, however, we think it appropriate to respond to the judge's concerns.

nine per cent of the fair market value of the trust assets, determined annually, with remainders to certain charitable organizations.[3]

As we read the judge's reservation and report, three basic questions are presented: (1) whether the creation of revocable and irrevocable trusts specifying the ultimate distribution of trust assets to other than the estate of the ward is the same as making a will; (2) whether G.L. c. 201, § 38, as amended through St. 1976, c. 515, §§ 25-26, authorizes making a will; and (3) whether the proposed estate plan could be approved in a proceeding in which the Commonwealth's representation may have been neutralized by a conflict of interest, and in which the ward's next of kin were represented by a guardian ad litem for unborn and unascertained heirs.[4] Although not reported by the judge, the parties have also asked whether an estate plan which is found to be in accordance "with the ward's wishes so far as they can be ascertained, although speculative" complies with the requirements of G.L. c. 201, § 38.

We hold that the proposed estate plan is not a testamentary disposition and is authorized by the statute. Furthermore, we find no infirmities arising from representation of the next of kin by the guardian ad litem or of the Commonwealth by the Attorney General. Finally, we uphold the judge's finding that the estate plan complied with the statutory criteria.

We briefly summarize the evidence presented below and reported by the judge. Wanda W. Jones is a ninety-year-old woman residing at the McLean Hospital in Belmont. She was found to be incapacitated by reason of advanced age and mental weakness in 1975 conservatorship proceedings. She is mentally incompetent and is unlikely to recover sufficient mental capacity to execute a will.

The conservator was first introduced to the ward in 1950 by her husband, Dr. Stephen G. Jones. The conservator did occasional legal work for Dr. Jones until 1959, when Dr. Jones died. Thereafter the conservator became the ward's attorney. The conservator alleges that to the best of his knowledge, the ward has no husband, issue, or other kindred. On her death, unless it should ultimately prove to be the case that she has a will or next of kin, her estate would pass by escheat to the Commonwealth. The conservator believes his ward never made a will.

In 1968, the conservator drafted a will for the ward under which virtually all her estate would pass to various charities,[5] but she never executed the will. Although the ward refused to sign

---

[3] The estate plan also includes an inter vivos gift of $1,000 to the ward's brother-in-law.

[4] The questions formulated by the Probate Court judge were as follows: "The Court declined to issue judgment in accordance with the petition or any modification thereof pending the resolution of certain questions. First, it appeared to the court that the proposed trusts were substantially similar to making a will. In this regard, the first question is whether the creation of revocable and irrevocable trusts specifying remainders in favor of persons other than the estate of the ward is authorized by General Laws Chapter 201, Section 38, in the light of Strange v. Powers, 358 Mass. 126 [260 N.E.2d 704] . . . (1970), which holds that the statute in question does not authorize the making of a will. The second question is whether the doctrine of Strange v. Powers, as it might otherwise apply to this case, is superseded by the 1976 amendment of the statute (St. 1976, c. 515, § 25) which substantially modified the statute and, in particular, authorized the creation of revocable and irrevocable trusts and eliminated a provision under which an estate plan authorized by the Court was good only for a period of up to 12 months. Second, the Court was concerned as to whether a fundamental change in the probable devolution of the ward's estate could be effected in a proceeding in which the Commonwealth—the potential recipient of property upon escheat—was not actually heard and in which there was no representative of kindred. As to the Commonwealth, it appears that the Attorney General's advocacy may have been neutralized by the conflict between his duty to represent the interests of the Commonwealth and his duty to represent the interests of public charities. As to kindred, it was the Court's supposition that some relatives, no matter how remote, exists [sic]."

[5] The charities given cash bequests in the unexecuted will were: Pleasant Street Congregational Church, Arlington;

the will, she never repudiated the dispositive provisions. The ward claimed that she had consulted with unidentified advisors who told her that the will was not properly drafted.[7] There was no evidence as to the ward's competency at the time she refused to sign the will. Although the will was presented to the ward for signature only once, the conservator reminded her of it on several occasions, the last being either in 1974 or 1975. The conservator also testified that the ward made small annual gifts, shown in her tax returns, to the charities named in the draft will; however, no individual charitable gift exceeded seventy-five dollars.

Prior to the hearing on the petition, the judge ordered that notice be given to the Attorney General of the Commonwealth and to the Department of Mental Health, and both filed acknowledgments of notice. The Attorney General's acknowledgment stated that the Attorney General assented to the allowance of the petition. Pursuant to the court order, a notice of the proceedings was also published in a major Boston newspaper once a week for three successive weeks. The judge found that the conservator made no special effort to investigate the possible existence of kindred, but simply relied on his long-standing acquaintance with the ward and her deceased husband, the ward's statements to the conservator and others that she had no relatives, and the failure of any party claiming a relationship to have responded to the newspaper publication of notice in the conservatorship proceedings.[8] In addition, the conservator made inquiries of the ward's brother-in-law, and others who knew her well. All reported that they did not know of any person claiming a relationship to the ward. However, no professional heir search was undertaken.

The court below appointed a guardian ad litem for the ward. The guardian ad litem's report opposed the allowance of the petition in so far as the petition proposed that ninety per cent of the ward's property be transferred to the irrevocable trust and only ten percent to the revocable trust. The guardian ad litem for the ward recommended that fifty per cent of the ward's assets should be transferred to the revocable trust in order to assure the availability of sufficient funds, including principal, for the ward's needs. With that modification, the guardian ad litem for the ward recommended approval of the estate plan as making sufficient provision for the ward's own needs, as being in accordance with the ward's own wishes so far as they can be ascertained, and as reducing prospective State and Federal taxes by a large amount.

The court also appointed a guardian ad litem to represent the interests of the unascertained heirs. He filed a report opposing the allowance of the petition on the ground that heirs who might with reasonable diligence be discovered at the time of the ward's death would be deprived of any rights they might have under the laws governing the estates of deceased persons.

Symmes Hospital, Arlington; Massachusetts General Hospital, Boston; and New England Conservatory of Music, Boston. Phillips Andover Academy, Andover; Harvard University, Cambridge; and Harvard University Medical School, Cambridge, were named as charitable remaindermen in the unsigned will. These charities are beneficiaries under the proposed estate plan, which also makes Phillips Andover Academy, Harvard University and Harvard University Medical School remaindermen. Of these beneficiaries, Symmes Hospital and the Harvard University Medical School were both institutions with which Dr. Jones was professionally associated.

[7] The conservator speculated that the ward's failure to sign the will may have been based on the common superstition that as long as she did not sign the will she would live.

[8] General Laws c. 201, § 17, requires that notice of a petition to appoint a conservator be given to the heirs apparent or presumptive of the person who will be the ward, including a husband or wife, if any.

At the time of the conservatorship proceedings, notice was given to the ward and the Department of Mental Health. The conservator reported that there were no heirs at law known to the petitioner and no one appeared as a result of the notice by publication in the local newspaper.

The conservator moved for judgment in accordance with his petition, as modified by the recommendations of the guardian ad litem for the ward. The Probate Court judge declined to issue a judgment but instead reserved and reported certain questions to the Appeals Court. As part of the judge's reservation and report, the judge made the following findings. First, the proposed estate plan, modified as recommended by the guardian ad litem of the ward, includes adequate provision for the ward's own maintenance and support. Second, the estate plan is in keeping with the ward's wishes, so far as they can be ascertained, although speculative, and provides gifts to such charities, relatives and friends as would be likely recipients of donations from the ward. Third, the estate plan is designed to minimize in so far as possible current and prospective State and Federal income, estate and gift taxes.

The judge indicated that the plan might be substantially similar to making a will, and therefore not authorized by the statute, G.L. c. 201, § 38. We do not think the proposed estate plan is objectionable for that reason.

In *Strange v. Powers*, 358 Mass. 126, 260 N.E.2d 704 (1970), we held that the prior version of § 38[9] did not empower the court to approve the making of a will because that would involve "an unduly broad construction of the term 'estate plan.' " We think that the amendment to § 38 still does not permit a conservator to execute a will on behalf of his ward. The 1976 amendment to § 38 was largely drawn from § 5-408(3)[10] of the Uniform Probate Code, which specifically prohibits the conservator from making a will. We think that our decision in *Strange v. Powers* stands unimpaired. The omission of language prohibiting the making of a will from § 38 is not decisive. "[W]hen the same legislature, in a later statute, use the terms of an earlier one which has received a judicial construction, that construction is to be given to the later statute . . . . For if it were intended to exclude any known construction of a previous statute, the legal presumption is, that its terms would be so changed as to effect that intention." *Luacaw v. Fire Comm'r of Boston*, 350 Mass. 326, 329, 214 N.E.2d 734, 735 (1966), quoting *Commonwealth v. Hartnett*, 3 Gray 450, 451 (1855).

Moreover, our case law does not support the view that the creation of an inter vivos trust is "the making of a will." In *National Shawmut Bank v. Joy*, 315 Mass. 457, 53 N.E.2d 113 (1944), the validity of a revocable trust in which the settlor not only created a life interest for himself and another, but also retained a general power of appointment subject to two life estates was upheld despite the argument that the trust was testamentary in nature and did not comply

---

[9] The prior version of § 38 (as amended through St. 1969, c. 422), while authorizing a conservator to establish an estate plan for tax minimization purposes or for gifts to those charities and persons who would be likely donees of the ward, did not contain the specific list of permitted applications of funds contained in § 38 as most recently amended.

[10] The Uniform Probate Code, § 5-408(3) (Uniform Laws Annotated, Master ed. 1972), reads: "After hearing and upon determining that a basis for an appointment or other protective order exists with respect to a person for reasons other than minority, the Court has, for the benefit of the person and members of his household, all the powers over his estate and affairs which he could exercise if present and not under disability, except the power to make a will. These powers include, but are not limited to power to make gifts, to convey or release his contingent and expectant interests in property including marital property rights and any right of survivorship incident to joint tenancy or tenancy by the entirety, to exercise or release his powers as trustee, personal representative, custodian for minors, conservator, or donee of a power of appointment, to enter into contracts, to create revocable or irrevocable trusts of property of the estate which may extend beyond his disability or life, to exercise options of the disabled person to purchase securities or other property, to exercise his rights to elect options and change beneficiaries under insurance and annuity policies and to surrender the policies for their cash value, to exercise his right to an elective share in the estate of his deceased spouse and to renounce any interest by testate or intestate succession or by inter vivos transfer."

with the statute of wills. "The distinguishing feature of a testamentary disposition is that it remains ambulatory until the death of the one who makes it. Until he dies, his title remains unimpaired and unaffected . . . . If the interest in question passes from the owner presently, while he remains alive, the transfer is inter vivos and not testamentary." . . . .

The fact that a certain disposition of property, here the creation of revocable and irrevocable trusts with charitable remainders, is virtually a substitute for a will is unobjectionable. "If an owner of property can find a means of disposing of [the property] inter vivos that will render a will unnecessary for the accomplishment of his practical purposes, he has a right to employ it. The fact that the motive of a transfer is to obtain the practical advantages of a will without making one is immaterial." *National Shawmut Bank v. Joy*, 315 Mass. 457, 53 N.E.2d 113 (1944).

The amendment to § 38 grants the ward through a conservator most of the powers that the ward would have if the ward were of full capacity. "[T]he purpose is to carry out the ward's wishes so far as they can be ascertained, and not solely for tax minimization . . . ." Young, *Probate Reform*, 18 Boston B.J. No. 3, 7, 19 (1974) . . . . There is no reason not to allow the ward to use inter vivos trusts in estate planning. Given the legislative policy to carry out "the ward's wishes so far as they can be ascertained," the arguments of the guardian ad litem for unborn and unascertained heirs to the effect that authorization of the estate plan in question will undermine the well-established laws of this Commonwealth governing devolution and descent of property are not persuasive.

The most serious question raised by the reservation and report is the adequacy of the notice by publication to unascertained heirs.[11] Under § 38, the precise means of notice to interested persons is left to the discretion of the Probate Court judge. Generally, if a court's order for notice pursuant to § 38 has been followed, any ensuing judgment would bind the party affected. The guardian ad litem for persons unborn and unascertained complains that the notice by publication ordered by the court is constitutionally inadequate. We disagree.

Due process permits notice by publication for "[t]hose beneficiaries . . . whose interests or whereabouts could not with due diligence be ascertained." *Mullane v. Central Hanover Bank & Trust Co.*, 339 U.S. 306, 317 (1950). Notice by publication is prohibited "with respect to a person whose name and address are known or very easily ascertainable." *Schroeder v. City of N.Y.*, 371 U.S. 208, 212-213, (1962). Our cases hold that due process "does not demand the impossible. It is impossible to mail a copy of a citation to a person unborn, and as a practical matter it is impossible to mail one to a person whose identity cannot with reasonable diligence be ascertained." *Young v. Tudor*, 323 Mass. 508, 514, 83 N.E.2d 1, 5 (1948).

The judge found the conservator's belief that his ward had no kindred was based on his thirty-year friendship with the ward (and prior to 1959, with her deceased husband), her frequent statements to him and to others that she had no relatives, the lack of response to the newspaper publication of notice of the conservatorship proceedings,[12] and the lack of any contrary information from the ward's brother-in-law and two of her close friends. The record is clear

---

[11] The reservation and report phrases this issue in terms of "no representative of kindred." See note 4, *supra*. However, unascertained persons were, in fact, represented by a guardian ad litem. Thus we read the reservation and report as raising the issue of notice and this issue has been briefed by the parties.

[12] We do not suggest that notice of the conservatorship proceedings, if such notice had been received, would have been sufficient notice as to any subsequent proceedings.

that the conservator had no actual knowledge of the existence of any heirs, and furthermore, that he possessed no information which, if pursued, might have led to the discovery of kindred.[13]

The question then is whether the conservator is required to retain the services of a professional genealogist in this case. We think not.[14] It is not "unreasonable for the State to dispense with more certain notice to those beneficiaries whose interests are either conjectural or future or, although they could be discovered upon investigation, do not in due course of business come to knowledge of the common trustee . . . . [S]uch impracticable and extended searches are not required in the name of due process." *Mullane v. Central Hanover Bank & Trust Co., supra;* 339 U.S. at 317-318. . . .

Finally, it is by no means clear that the heirs' participation in the proceedings would affect the outcome. General Laws, c. 201, § 38, authorizes the conservator to exclude "as a beneficiary any person whom he has reason to believe would be excluded by the ward." Thus, the interest of any person whose existence was unknown to the ward or whose existence she denied in conversations with family and friends is very attenuated. There is no evidence that the ward ever intended to benefit her next of kin.

Under similar provisions of North Carolina law,[15] the North Carolina Supreme Court said persons who had a contingent or potential financial interest in the death of the incompetent are limited "to present[ing] to the court facts which will assist the court in determining whether the action proposed by the trustee is detrimental to the estate of the incompetent, or whether the incompetent, if then competent, would probably not act as the trustee proposes to act." *In re Kenan,* 262 N.C. 627, 638, 138 S.E.2d 547, 555 (1964). In the case at bar, the judge had appointed a guardian ad litem for persons unborn and unascertained, who very ably represented their interests. As a result, it is hard to imagine what further arguments could be presented on their behalf.

The reservation and report raises a question whether the Attorney General's representation of the Commonwealth might have been "neutralized by the conflict between his duty to represent the interests of the Commonwealth and his duty to represent the interests of public charities." Since the Legislature has determined that the public interest is served by enabling a conservator to dispose of the property of his ward "in keeping with the ward's wishes so far as they can be ascertained" and for tax minimization, G.L. c. 201 § 38, we find no conflict between the Commonwealth's interest and the Attorney General's position. The decision to assent to the estate plan is well within the authority of the Attorney General.

---

[13] If the ward's maiden name were known, the petitioner could have searched local phone directories, city directories, or tax rolls for persons with a similar name. See Cleaveland v. Draper, 194 Mass. 118, 121, 80 N.E. 227 (1907). Of course, persons who might be found through such sources are precisely those persons who, because of their local residence, are most likely to have been reached by the notice published in the newspaper.

[14] Our conclusion on this issue is influenced by the fact that none of the available information suggests more than a remote possibility that next of kin of the ward would be located, and in view of the ward's advanced age and ill health, we think the delay occasioned by a genealogical search would be unduly burdensome in this case.

[15] North Carolina General Statutes § 35-29.6(6)(b)(2) (1976), dealing generally with gifts of principal from an incompetent's estate for certain purposes, requires that where the incompetent has made no will, notice must be given to any person who would take in the event of intestacy. North Carolina General Statutes § 35-29.12 (1976), dealing with similar gifts of certain limited trust interests, contains a similar provision. Contrast N.C. Gen.Stat. § 35-23 (1976), dealing with advancements of surplus income to certain relatives of the incompetent, which requires that all persons who would be entitled to a distributive share of the incompetent's estate if he were then dead be made parties.

We have now disposed of the specific issues raised by the Probate Court judge. The remaining question briefed by the parties is whether an estate plan which is found to accord "with the ward's wishes, so far as they can be ascertained, although speculative" complies with the requirements of G.L. c. 201, § 38. We also address this issue. *See* note 2, *supra.*

The findings of a Probate Court judge will not be overturned unless they are plainly wrong. In a petition under § 38, the conservator is not required to prove that a proposed estate plan conforms with absolute certainty to the ward's wishes. The court is merely required to "approve [the estate plan] as being in keeping with the ward's wishes so far as they can be ascertained," and "as designed to minimize insofar as possible current or prospective state or federal income, estate and inheritance taxes." The plan may "provide for gifts to such charities, relatives and friends as would be likely recipients of donations from the ward . . . [*i.e.,* those] individuals or charities in which the ward is believed to have an interest."

The guardian ad litem for unascertained heirs argues that the estate plan sought to be established is substantially based on the terms of a will the ward refused to sign. While this is true, the evidence indicated that the will was drafted according to her instructions, instructions which were never changed. The ward continued to make modest annual gifts to the same charitable institutions named in the will. Where the record is not clear as to the ward's wishes, § 38 creates a presumption that the ward would favor a reduction in estate taxes and a distribution of her estate to achieve that goal . . . Although the evidence offered as to the ward's wishes is not conclusive, we cannot say that the Probate Court judge is plainly wrong in finding that the estate plan is "in keeping with the ward's wishes." *See* G.L. c. 201, § 38.

We summarize our answers to the questions raised by the judge's reservation and report and by the parties to this proceeding. Under G.L. c. 201, § 38, the Probate Court has authority to approve the estate plan proposed by the conservator, as modified in accordance with the report of the guardian ad litem for the ward. The findings made by the Probate Court judge relative to this petition are not plainly wrong. The proceedings are not open to attack either because the Commonwealth's interests were inadequately represented or because notice by publication to unknown heirs did not meet due process requirements. Thus, there is no legal impediment to the entry of a judgment approving the proposed estate plan as modified in accordance with the report of the guardian ad litem for the ward.

Since specific questions were reserved and reported, we remand the case to the Probate Court for consideration of the proposed estate plan in light of this opinion.

So ordered

[b]   Explanatory Notes

[i]   *The Impact of Procedure on the Handling of Wanda Jones' Case.* Putting aside the property problems in *Jones* for a moment, the procedural handling of the case presents a melange of interesting problems. In addition to the attorney representing the conservator, the court appointed a temporary *guardian ad litem* for the ward, Wanda Jones, and a second *guardian ad litem* for any unborn and unascertained heirs of Wanda Jones. This bevy of guardian-lawyers was gathered in part to protect the unascertainable interests of the incompetent ward. Since the court could never be sure that the intentions of the conservator were an appropriate substitute for those of the ward, the other attorneys were asked to provide additional input for review by the court.

The State of Massachusetts was also in a peculiar position. If the conservator could not legitimately create the *inter vivos* trust he drafted on behalf of Wanda Jones, and no other device was available to distribute her assets when she died, the estate would escheat to the state. *Compare* the denouement of the Harmony Society, discussed earlier in this chapter. Massachusetts, like most other states, has also given its Attorney General the obligation to represent the interests of public charities. Since the conservator's plan called for giving significant sums of money to various charities, the state had an interest in protecting the plan. Perhaps the court should also have appointed separate attorneys to represent the various conflicting interests of the State of Massachusetts. Some might counter that the government has the right (duty?) to decide which public policy should prevail in any case such as *Jones* and that Massachusetts effectively renounced its interest in escheat by enacting Chapter 201 of the General Laws.

Regardless of how the representation of the state should have been organized, the court obviously decided that an enormous amount of process was due for the protection of the assets of the incompetent ward. *Compare* the process found to be due to consumers of commercial products in the Supreme Court cases discussed in *Callen v. Sherman's, Inc.*, p. 622 below; or to the occupants of public housing in *Kutcher v. Housing Authority,* p. 684 below.

The use of all this process caused never-ending headaches for the conservator's attorney. Wanda Jones was very old and feeble by the time he got involved in the case. Every day's delay represented another significant chance that she would die. If the trust plan was not in effect when she died her considerable estate would have either escheated to Massachusetts or gone to then unknown relatives. A number of steps were taken to try to speed things up, including the interlocutory appeal to the Massachusetts Supreme Court on the propriety of the estate plan and the use of only newspaper notice to hunt for relatives. The alternative to a newspaper notice would have been to hire a professional genealogist for a lengthy search. Rather than undertake that search now, counsel preferred to make a minimal search so that the trust plan could be established and take the risk of a challenge to the plan at her death if any relatives appeared. That turned out to be a wise choice. When Wanda Jones died in 1983, one professional genealogist who regularly checks probate records to see if he might be able to get some clients, claimed he had found two cousins of Jones. The probate court refused to permit them to challenge the trust plan, but did permit them to try to prove their relationship to Jones so they could share in whatever assets were left in her estate. At her death, about $1.2 million was held in trust. About $40,000, held by the conservator when Jones died, fell into her estate.[28]

[ii]   *Gift Giving and Intention to Deliver Title.* The basic elements of a completed gift were outlined at the beginning of this chapter. There appears little doubt that Wanda Jones was unable to form an intention to make a gift, either to her trustee-conservator or to any other recipients of her wealth in the trust established by her conservator. State statutes simply filled in the doctrinal gap by granting to the conservator the power to "create" that intention, subject to review by the probate courts. The statute relied on the conservator to distribute the assets in accordance with his or her understanding of what the ward's wishes would have been if she was competent. The notion is that the various actors in the drama should strive to substitute for the mind of the ward. That was particularly difficult in *Jones* since the ward was of two

---

[28] Telephone Interview with Louis Hamel, Jr., Attorney for Conservator (July 9, 1987). The vast difference between the amounts in the trust and the estate was also a measure of the divergence in interests of the state of Massachusetts. The conflict between the state's role as overseer of charities and the state's role as taker of escheated funds involved over $1.2 million.

minds before being declared incompetent. When she was 68 years old she directed that a will be drafted, but then refused to sign it. The attorney for the conservator indicated that he had two suspicions as to why she declined to sign the will. There were some indications Jones was delusional, hearing voices. She did spend many years in psychiatric hospitals before being sent to a nursing home for her final years. The conservator also thought that Jones may have visited a bank trust officer who, in an effort to direct the trust management fees his way, told her the will was all wrong. Jones never told her conservator why she refused to execute the will.[29]

[iii] *Trusts as Will Substitutes.* Massachusetts statutes prohibited conservators from writing wills for their wards. The trust written for Wanda Jones contained provisions for taking care of the ward for the rest of her life. But it also contained precise instructions on how to distribute the corpus of the trust upon the death of the ward-beneficiary. When put into effect, these instructions operated like a will. Indeed, the conservator's attorney was quite open in saying that he wished to get court approval for the estate plan contained in Jones' unexecuted 1968 will in order to avoid escheat and reduce estate taxes. He took the position before the Massachusetts Supreme Court that no public policy was affronted by such an approach, that the intent to prevent fraud evidenced by the Statute of Wills formality requirements was unlikely to be frustrated by creation of judicially reviewed estate plans for wards.

The use of *inter vivos* trusts as a will substitute is fairly common among normal, competent people. The settlor of the trust turns over all or most of his or her assets to a trustee with instructions on how to use them while the settlor is alive and what to do with them upon the settlor's death. The trust instruments frequently give the settlor-beneficiary a significant amount of control over the assets while alive by naming the settlor as the trustee and including a right to revoke the trust. Such trusts have several advantages over wills. First, they normally have provisions in them describing what is to occur if the settlor-beneficiary becomes incompetent. These provisions effectively avoid guardianship proceedings and the substantial expense that goes along with them. Second, the use of a trust permits the settlor to pick an experienced asset manager rather than relying upon the predilections of a probate court or an executor. Finally, the use of *inter vivos* trusts avoids probate proceedings, and the expense of such proceedings, for most if not all of the estate.

Given the widespread use of trusts today as will substitutes, it may not be so odd that the Massachusetts Supreme Court viewed the writing of such a trust as within the conservator's authority to create an "estate plan" when the writing of a will was outside that authority. Perhaps the court was simply attempting to make room for will-like action as an end-run around the limitations it saw in the state's statutory structure. In any case, the Jones trust had its intended effect. As already noted, about $1.2 million was held in trust when Jones died, while only about $40,000 went into her estate.

[c] **Problem Notes**

[i] *Conservators and Wills.* Should Massachusetts give its conservators the authority to write wills? Or is there something so different about wills from other forms of dispositions taking effect at death that present practice should be continued? Are the differing formalities required for gifts, trusts and wills of any importance in a guardian-ward setting? If not, should the level of formality now required of a normal person to make a will also be reduced? Should a writing still be required?

---

[29] *Id.*

[*ii*]   *Compare Revocable Inter Vivos Trusts and Wills.* What is the difference between a revocable *inter vivos* trust and a will. Both may be changed virtually at will. *Inter vivos* trusts do require that property be bestowed upon a trustee, but addition of a revocability clause means that such trusts are almost as flexible as a will. What of statutes requiring that certain amounts of property from an estate must go to surviving spouses? Are funds in an *inter vivos* trust subject to the distribution required by these mandatory share statutes? Generally, the answer is yes. Given the similarities between the two forms, does it make sense to continue requiring strict formality for the signing of a will?

[*iii*]   *Substitution for the Mind of the Ward.* The general principle at work in *Jones* is that the state, with the aid of judges, conservators and guardians, should make every effort to recreate the gift giving desires of the ward. A similar theory is often used to decide upon the appropriate medical treatment to give to an incompetent person. Might other basic principles be used instead of this substitution rule? Do any of the following seem better:

(a) When giving away an incompetent ward's money, the inability to determine the wishes of the ward means that larger public policy pronouncements should govern the distribution of the wealth. Thus, conservators should be limited to caring for the ward during his or her life and upon the ward's death, all assets should pass under normal intestacy, and if there are no heirs, under escheat statutes.

(b) Substitution of intention is impossible. Therefore, the state ought simply create a board of ward overseers who will decide what to do with the property of wards who never wrote wills. Such decisions would be made in accordance with a priority list commanding that assets be given to various family members first, and lacking any family, to certain designated state programs.

(c) Problems like those presented in the *Jones* case are so intractable that all adults ought be required to file, with their yearly tax returns, a form stating either that they have written a will or elected to have their assets distributed in accordance with the intestate succession law of their state. The same form should provide various treatment options in case of medical problems and mental incapacity, and a box to check off if they wish to donate their organs for transplantation.

[*iv*]   *Inheritance Rights.* What sort of assets should be deemed inheritable and why? How about publicity rights—the right of a person to control the use of their name and likeness for commercial purposes? Take a look at *King v. American Heritage*, discussed in Chapter 12 (*see* p. 1130). May a will dispose of transplantable tissues? Should a guardian be allowed to approve the donation of a ward's transplantable tissue upon death?

CHAPTER 4

BUSINESS OWNERSHIP OF PROPERTY

§ 4.01 Introduction

Use of the major forms of business ownership—sole proprietorships, partnerships[1] and corporations—has changed significantly during the course of American history. At the dawn of the republic, most businesses were small, family owned and agricultural. Assets used for business purposes were often indistinguishable from personal assets. There was no particular reason to place a scythe in a special ownership form. Small commercial enterprises run by small groups were usually organized as partnerships. Relationships between partners were frequently informal. By the end of the nineteenth century, corporations, and the formalities required to run them, became much more prominent. The corporate form made it easier to create, finance and manage the array of medium and large scale industrial and commercial enterprises that emerged after the Civil War. In recent years, a variety of new forms of business organization have emerged as entrepreneurs developed new strategies to deal with federal and state tax laws, in addition to the traditional issues surrounding creation, financing and management of business enterprises.

A sole proprietorship is a commercial extension of a person. It does not have separate legal existence. Business contracts are individually signed by the proprietor, litigation is brought by or against the owner of the enterprise, and liability for debts runs to all of the assets held by the entrepreneur. In its simplest form, a general partnership is nothing more than a proprietorship run by more than one person. A writing is not required to establish a partnership. It can arise by the actions of the business owners. Over time, partly because the terms of typical partnership agreements describe in some detail the powers held by its members, the partnership came to be seen as a legal entity, capable of participating in litigation and entering into contracts over the signature of a partner given appropriate authority by a partnership agreement. But each partner still was left responsible for all the business debts.

Corporations were initially established by adoption of special or private legislative acts. Passage of private acts was commonplace before 1850. Legislatures dealt with an array of matters, from granting divorces and *feme sole* status to abandoned married women, to settling title disputes and establishing businesses. Mimicking the tradition of the English crown in handing out charters to settle what is now the eastern United States and to set up businesses in the colonies, the various state legislatures took over the activity of receiving applications for and granting corporate charters after the Revolutionary War. Most corporations chartered by the states early in the nineteenth century were transportation companies operating river navigation systems, turnpikes and toll bridges. Others ran banks or insurance companies or water supply systems. Very few

---

[1] An introduction to partnerships may be found in Chapter 3, at p. 262.

311

were general business corporations.[2] State corporate charters routinely provided certain benefits to entrepreneurs not available to proprietors or partners. They allowed the corporations to sue and be sued as a legal entity. The interests of shareholders could be transferred without disturbing the existence of the corporation.[3] And, in contrast to partners, shareholders were not individually responsible for corporate obligations to third parties.

The first major manufacturing enterprise to be organized as a corporation, The Boston Manufacturing Company, obtained its charter in 1813.[4] As corporations proliferated during the nineteenth century, pressure on state legislatures to remove themselves from the process grew. Some states amended their constitutions to bar legislatures from granting corporate charters or adopting other private acts. In other states, the legislature relinquished control over the chartering function by passing general incorporation statutes. New Jersey adopted a very broad incorporation statute in 1875, and all the other states gradually adopted similar practices. Large enterprises gradually incorporated, though many of the giant firms continued to operate much like partnerships into the beginning of the twentieth century. The Carnegie enterprises, for example, did not incorporate until 1892. When it did make the move, only 25 shareholders were created and all were barred from selling their shares to outsiders.[5] Such arrangements required the company to raise capital from its revenues or to use its assets as security for a loan. Much of this history is mirrored in the development of the Harmony Society described in the prior chapter. The creation of the Union Company in 1892, the first step in the process of dissolving the Harmony Society, allowed for the sale of most of the Society's assets to a corporation owned by those seeking to evade the restrictions of the trust arrangements then constraining Harmony's operations.[6]

While Carnegie and Harmony remained closely held, other companies began to publicly sell shares of stock, using the sale of new shares as a way of broadening financing alternatives to allow those wishing to invest in the business to purchase an ownership interest. Indeed, it is the ease of arranging for financing that was one of the primary motivations for establishing the modern, publicly traded, firm.[7]

By the end of the century, the status of corporations as special creatures of the state was disappearing. They were more likely to be seen as independent legal creatures, established by the will of entrepreneurs rather than licensed and constrained by governmental authority. Private acts chartering corporations early in the nineteenth century, as well as the first batch of general incorporation statutes adopted after the Civil War placed many restrictions on the freedom of action of corporate leaders. These restrictions were an inheritance from long standing objections to business corporations shared by many segments of society in the early years of the nation. The use of corporations in England to establish approved monopolies, fears that corporations created unchecked challenges to governmental order, and concern that corporations established

---

[2] James Willard Hurst, The Legitimacy of the Business Corporation 17 (1970).

[3] The default partnership rule was that a partnership ended when a partner died or left the business. Partnership agreements routinely contained provisions for continuing a business when a partner left or died, but the basic structure of a corporation took that result for granted.

[4] Adolf A. Berle & Gardiner C. Means, The Modern Corporation and Private Property 11 (1932).

[5] Herman E. Drooss & Charles Gilbert, American Business History 161 (1972).

[6] *See* pp. 268–271 above.

[7] For a review of the history of the formation of corporations, *see* Butler, *Nineteenth-Century Jurisdictional Competition in the Granting of Corporate Privileges*, 14 J. Legal. Stud. 129, 138-153 (1985).

new forms of dependency that undermined Civic Republican values slowed the acceptance of general incorporation statutes.[8] But by the end of the century, legislatures and courts alike were thinking of corporations as "independent" actors, capable not only of suing and being sued, but also of having "rights" and holding "freedoms."[9] Society came to see corporations as economic actors, rather than implementers of state policy. This trend was emphasized in Supreme Court decisions definitively affirming that corporations were not just legally recognized entities, but also "persons" capable of holding and claiming rights under the constitution.[10]

Recognition of corporations as rights-holders came at a propitious moment in the history of the United States. As noted in the discussion of the post-Civil War married women's earning statutes in Chapter 2, p. 167–171 above, Formalist or Classical Legal Thought was maturing at the end of the nineteenth century. Heavily reliant upon the importance of contracts about property as legal indicia of independence, freedom and individualism, classical legal thinkers looked to government to protect the right to contract about wealth, viewed the right to contract as an integral part of the meaning of property, and opined that preservation of property was a central tenet of liberty. Rather than viewing property ownership as a guarantee of civic responsibility like the early Republicans, Formalists viewed property ownership as an element of freedom. When large corporations emerged as independent holders of legal rights, sanctity of property ownership, and the laissez faire theory that went with it, became an important theoretical base for protecting corporate freedom of action.

Classical legal thinkers' reliance on contractual understandings as the backbone of freedom and the source of property rights also entailed a particular view about the role of law in society. Government was not the embodiment of civic responsibility, but the guarantor of liberty. Law's job was not to structure the interrelationships between citizen and state, but to stay neutral, allowing free citizens to structure their own interests. Courts were not to take sides, but only to apply neutral rules guaranteeing the enforcement of private obligations. In this view, the embodiment of rights to sue or to own property no longer hinged on models of responsible citizenship, but on the ability to make economic decisions. The fiction that a corporation was a legal "person," capable of suing and being sued, was a natural byproduct of such a view of law and rights. By the end of the nineteenth century, large property owning corporations had become full, largely unrestricted, actors in the legal system. And their claim of rights to hold property without interference from the government became a central feature of judicial decisions restricting the ability of states and the federal government to regulate corporate activities.[11] This issue will resurface later in discussion of the racial zoning statutes at issue in *Buchanan v. Warley*, p. 477 below, and of the mining subsidence regulations challenged in *Pennsylvania Coal v. Mahon*, p. 934 below.

---

[8] This history is nicely described in *Note, Incorporating the Republic: The Corporation in Antebellum Political Culture,* 102 Harv. L. Rev. 1883 (1989).

[9] A lengthy essay on these issues may be found in Hurst, note 2 above, at 58-111. A similar point is made in Peter Karsten, *Supervising the ' 'Spoiled Children of Legislation'': Judicial Judgments Involving Quasi-Public Corporations in the Nineteenth Century U.S.,* 41 Am. J. Legal Hist. 315 (1997).

[10] *See, e.g.,* Santa Clara County v. Southern Pacific Railroad Co., 118 U.S. 394, 396 (1886); Chicago, Milwaukee & St. Paul Railway Co. v. Minnesota, 134 U.S. 418 (1890).

[11] *See, e.g.,* Lochner v. New York, 198 U.S. 45 (1908), in which the Supreme Court found that a rule limiting the number of hours bakers could work each week violated the due process clause of the Fourteenth Amendment.

§ 4.02 Partnership and Corporation Basics

[1] Partnerships

Though the governance of most large partnerships is established by lengthy agreements, actions of persons in business together may lead to the creation of partnerships without formal writings. [12] Absent statements to the contrary in documents creating the business, enterprises owned by two or more persons will be treated as general partnerships. Creditors of such partnerships may seek payment for debts from assets owned by the business and, if those assets are inadequate, from each of the partners. Because of the rule that general partners are responsible for partnership obligations, general partnerships are usually established for reasons of business convenience or taxation policy. But the desire of some to establish barriers between their personal and business economies has led to the creation of an array of new partnership forms in this century.

Limited partnerships were quite popular in the 1970s and 1980s. A limited partnership has two classes of owners—general partners who are responsible for partnership obligations, and limited partners whose liability for debts is limited to the amount of their investment in the business. In general, partnerships are treated for tax purposes as conduits. Partnerships report each partner's share of income, deductions and losses to the Internal Revenue Service, but pay no taxes. Those seeking financing for tax sheltered enterprises used limited partnerships to offer investors a share in a tax shelter with no liability beyond their contribution to the business. The investors were usually passive owners, giving up any control over the operation of the partnership in return (hopefully) for profits and tax advantages.

The tax shelter-based attractions of limited partnerships were largely removed by the Tax Reform Act of 1986. In addition, two new business forms have arisen in the last decade that provide many of the tax and liability advantages of limited partnerships without their governance limitations. Limited liability corporations provide the tax treatment of partnerships, limited liability for all investors, and enormous flexibility in governance. And limited liability partnerships obtain traditional partnership tax treatment, allow all partners to participate in governance, and limit liability in particularized ways. Some limited liability partnerships constrain liability for professional malpractice. Others leave partners personally liable for business debts, but excuse them for negligence or misconduct. Despite the proliferation of partnership forms, limiting partnership liability does not guarantee that all partners will be able to make risk free business investments. Lenders worried about the credit worthiness of any business—proprietorship, partnership or corporation—often seek contractual agreements from individuals to pay debts from their personal assets in case of business failure.

Regardless of the sort of partnership used, issues may arise about property ownership. Parties seeking redress from a partnership with some form of limited liability will attempt to characterize a "borderline" asset as belonging to the partnership rather than to a partner. Those suing partners will do the opposite, arguing that assets are held privately rather than by the business. Related problems arise in disputes involving general partnerships. If a general partner, for some reason, cannot be reached from a particular jurisdiction, there may be advantages to characterizing property as a partnership asset. And if the partnership is distant, while the partner is local, the opposite impulse may reign. Finally, there may be times when a general partnership will claim

---

[12] The text of the Uniform Partnership Act provisions on partnership formation may be found in Chapter 3, pp. 262–263 above.

that a debt is not a partnership obligation, but a personal responsibility of one of the partners. That was the nature of the dispute in the first case in this chapter, *Olson v. Olson.*

[2] Corporations

Establishing a corporation is quite simple. The first step is to have incorporators. These individuals need not be parties who will ultimately own stock in the corporation. Many times, young attorneys working in the law firm drawing up the incorporation papers serve in this capacity. The next step is to secure from the state a charter, or certificate of incorporation pursuant to a statute which authorizes the creation of a corporation. This process is now handled by a state administrative agency, usually located in the state Secretary of State's office. This agency records the names of the business, the principals in the company, and the party to receive service of process in any future litigation, among other things. After the certificate of incorporation is issued by the state government, directors are chosen and a director's meeting is held at which shares of stock are issued in exchange for cash or property. The stock serves as evidence of ownership of the company. The holders of this stock periodically elect a board of directors who are charged with the management of the corporation. The directors make major policy decisions but do not run the corporation day-to-day. Officers, selected by the directors, perform these functions. The officers, directors, and to a lesser extent the major stockholders of the company,[13] owe fiduciary duties to the corporation, that is to the stockholders. Profits are distributed among the stockholders as dividends or retained in the business at the discretion of the directors. If retained, the stockholders theoretically enjoy the profits indirectly through an increase in the value of their stock. Unless restricted by provisions in the corporation's organizational documents, each stockholder is free to sell or transfer their interest in the corporation.[14] This ability to transfer shares permits the corporation to continue its separate legal existence without regard to the status of the shareholders. If, for example, a shareholder dies, that person's shares, not the business itself, become the property of the estate.

One advantage of the corporate form is the insulation of the shareholder owners from personal liability for the acts of the corporation. While use of a general partnership creates priorities for access to individual and partnership property, it does not insulate partners from business debts. With a corporation, the main investors may make contributions to the business without fear that their individual assets will always be available to creditors. When a corporation becomes the general partner in an otherwise limited partnership, the same limited liability rule is effectively transferred to the partnership as well. Recognition that traditional limited partnerships, which operated under a requirement that there be at least one general partner, could be transformed into completely limited enterprises by constructing the general partner as a corporation, has made it much easier for us to think of limited liability corporations and partnerships as mere variations on old themes.

The liability insulation rules of the corporation may well create a willingness to invest which would otherwise not arise. But at times, business proprietors use the rules in ways which strain judicial and legislative willingness to protect investors in heavily indebted corporations. In the taxi industry, for example, it is not uncommon for large fleet operators to create a slew of small

---

[13] Large stockholders are much more likely to owe fiduciary obligations to other shareholders in a close corporation setting, that is, one in which only a small number of stockholders (often members of the same family) exist. *Zaist v. Olson*, the second case in this chapter, involved just such a situation.

[14] Restrictions on sale of stock are most common in close corporations. Family owned businesses may have very strong reasons for attempting to keep newcomers out of the corporation.

corporations, each holding only a few cabs. The various corporations are all owned by the same people, but accident losses may not be spread among the whole fleet. The courts have sometimes responded to such tactics by *piercing the corporate veil*. Where a corporation is a fragment of a larger business enterprise which actually conducts the business, or where the corporation is a "front" for its individual stockholders who, in reality, carry on the business in their individual capacities for purely personal rather than corporate ends, creditors sometimes manage to avoid the corporate limited liability rule. Where a corporation is a fragment operated by a large enterprise, the fragment dissolves, leaving the larger company responsible; where the corporation is a front, the individual stockholders are made liable for the business obligations.

Zaist v. Olson is a well known example of veil piercing. It is included here not to teach corporate law, but to generate thought about the circumstances in which it is justifiable to separate individually owned property from business property. The issues raised by the case are closely related to those involved in deciding upon the propriety of separating marital from personal obligations. So it should be useful to compare the results in *Zaist* with those in *Sawada v. Endo* p. 186 above, and *Olson v. Olson*, p. 319 below.

[3] Additional Reading

For additional reading on the basics of partnerships and corporations, *see* ROBERT W. HAMILTON & RICHARD A. BOOTH, BUSINESS BASICS FOR LAW STUDENTS 257-304 (1998).

§ 4.03 Separating the Personal and Business Aspects of Property Ownership

[1] Introduction

The particular benefits married couples gain from use of a tenancy by the entirety were discussed in Chapter 2 (*see* p. 185 above). For families in economic distress, owning property in a form which insulates some or all of it from the clutches of creditors is of obvious benefit. The risk of a financial downfall confronts everyone. But the risk of difficulty is much higher for those running their own businesses. Even in small businesses, the amounts of money changing hands over the course of a year may dwarf the actual profit of the proprietor. It should therefore not surprise you that business forms have evolved which permit people to separate their private and business financial affairs.

In some ways the issues taken up here mimic those which surfaced with cotenancies and familial property ownership in Chapter 2 and the Harmony Society in Chapter 3. Creating ownership organizations, deciding on the form in which to purchase assets, running and maintaining property, and dissolving economic organizations cause problems in both personal and business dealings. The additional desire of persons establishing business entities to insulate their personal assets from the risks of running an enterprise instigates frequent controversy between creditors and the proprietors of firms. The two cases which follow—one involving a partnership and the other several corporations—illustrate the sorts of problems that may emerge when the interests of creditor, business and family collide.

[2]   Background to *Olson v. Olson*: The "Family" Partnership

Olson v. Olson was a divorce case. But it had many characteristics of a business breakup.[15] Ruby and Peter Olson were married August 21, 1948. At the time of their marriage, Ruby was a widow and had three children between the ages of two and six from her first marriage. Peter had a 10-year-old daughter from another marriage. In 1956, they had their first and only child, a daughter. They stayed together until the morning of March 1, 1964. When Peter went off to work that morning, Ruby left the house. There was quite a bit of testimony in the record that she had been beaten the night before (and on other occasions) by Peter and that Peter threatened her from time to time with a shotgun.[16] Ruby was granted a divorce, custody of their child, $20 per week in child support, and all the household furnishings in lieu of alimony. The trial court split their small joint bank account, their cars, the farm machinery, and the property tax and mortgage payments on the farm which came due before Ruby left the house. But Ruby's request that Peter have a continuing obligation to pay off the mortgage was denied.[17]

After the trial court entered its Decree of Divorce, Ruby Olson's attorney moved for a rehearing of "that portion of the above cause relating to the financial relationship of the parties, and for a modification of the decree."[18] Attached to the motion was an affidavit of Ruby Olson saying that she and Peter had signed a post-nuptial agreement on February 16, 1953, that she wished it introduced as "after discovered evidence," and that she "was not aware that such evidence was necessary or in any way required in the trial and consequently did not produce the same" at trial.[19] A copy of the agreement was attached to the affidavit. It provided that the parties wished to assure "their respective estates to their issue by their respective former marriages, in the event of death." They each waived any rights they might have as a result of their marriage in the property of the other. Ruby also agreed to pay $5,000 to Peter Olson's daughter by his first marriage, Karen Olson, in case Karen survived her father, Ruby survived Peter, and Peter died within five years of the signing of the post-nuptial agreement. Finally, the last paragraph of the agreement provided:

> Sixth: It is presently contemplated that the parties hereto shall carry on their farming operations as partners and that except as to bank accounts and other items, if any, which may be specifically controlled by a joint tenancy contract, and in the absence of other agreement or evidence to the contrary, each of the parties hereto shall own an undivided one half 1/2 interest in all livestock, grain and machinery which shall be possessed by said parties at the time of the first death of the parties. At the time of the death of one of said parties, the estate of such decedent shall bear one-half 1/2 of the then outstanding obligations which shall have been incurred by the said parties in connection with the operation of said farm real estate.[20]

The trial court agreed to supplement the record by accepting a copy of the post-nuptial agreement into evidence, but denied the motion to rehear the issue of whether Peter should be

---

[15] The facts in this narrative were gleaned from the trial and appellate records, which were obtained from the DeKalb County Circuit Court (General No. 64-215) and the Appellate Court of Illinois for the Second Judicial District (No. 65-66). Citations to these records often have been omitted. When referenced, the trial record is cited by [Name of Record], Trial, and the appellate record by [Name of Record], Appeal.

[16] Abstract of Record at 8-9, 24-27, 32-33, Appeal.

[17] Decree of Divorce, Trial. The factual statements in the case give a reasonably accurate picture of the family finances as they came out in the testimony. They are therefore not reviewed here in any detail.

[18] Post-Trial Motion, Trial.

[19] Affidavit in Support of Post-Trial Motion, Trial.

[20] Abstract of Record 46, Appeal.

obligated to help make monthly payments on the mortgage. Ruby Olson's attorney filed a notice of appeal on that issue. When the case was briefed on appeal, George Spitz, Ruby's attorney, argued as follows:

There is no question that the Olson marriage, farm operation and outside employment by Peter and Ruby, all were viewed as a joint venture or partnership. All contributed to the common fund, with an equal sharing of the profits and the losses, the ups and downs, as indeed should be done in every marriage . . . . As the [Illinois Supreme Court] stated in *Taylor v. Coffing*, 18 Ill. 422, 428 . . . .

The law does not deem that every partner shall lose the exact amount put in, in case of loss of capital; but, on the contrary, however unequal the amounts of capital advanced may be, its loss, or partial loss, is apportioned among the partners in the degree or proportion in which they may have agreed to share the losses, if any is fixed; otherwise, equally.

In effect, the chancellor recognized this rule of law when he awarded one-half the farm machinery to Peter, all of it acquired during the marriage, except for that contributed by Ruby, and much of it bought with at least a part of the borrowed monies. Should not Peter assume his half of the joint debt created by just such purchases?[21]

Daniel Cliffe, Peter's attorney, responded by arguing that a partnership did not exist, and if it did, that the land was not an asset held by the partnership:

The plaintiff has worked hard to impress a partnership relation upon the efforts of Ruby and Peter to successfully raise their families by farming Ruby Olson's farm . . . . Under the definition of partners or partnership in the laymen's dictionary we find husband and wife, but in this action we must use the definition found in [the] Illinois Revised Statute . . . . "A partnership is an association of two or more persons to carry on as co-owners of a business for profit."

An examination of this situation reveals that there cannot be a partnership in the light of the legal definition. Ruby did not contribute her property to an entity known as Olson and Olson. Her title to the farm was that of the beneficial owner of a land trust, legal title to which was held by DeKalb Trust and Savings Bank.[22] The mortgage in question was taken out by the DeKalb Trust and Savings Company as Trustee for Ruby Olson. Peter signed the note as husband of the beneficial owner at the insistence of the lending institution. He signed not as a partner in Olson and Olson but to insure the mortgagee that Peter's inchoate dower right or rights under the probate laws of Illinois, were properly subjected to the mortgage. One of the requisites of the legal partnership is the holding of property as co-owners with the other partners. This co-ownership never existed. Legal title remained in the trust institution, subject only to the order of Ruby Olson. At any time Ruby could have ordered the Trustee to sell and deliver to her the proceeds of the sale. There would have been no necessity on her part to account to Peter for any of the proceeds of the sale. A right to an accounting is inherent in a partnership.[23]

The Appellate Court later issued the following opinion.

---

[21] Brief and Argument for Appellant 10, Appeal.

[22] Illinois has a somewhat peculiar title holding system in which the "real" owners are often hidden behind the facade of a trust under which a bank or trust institution holds legal title for the benefit of the "owner."

[23] Brief and Argument for Defendant-Appellee 5-6, Appeal.

[3] Opinion of the Illinois Appellate Court

Ruby Olson v. Peter Olson

Illinois Appellate Court, Second District
66 Ill. App. 2d 227, 213 N.E.2d 95 (1965)

MR. JUSTICE DAVIS delivered the opinion of the court.

This is an appeal, by plaintiff, from a divorce decree entered in her favor, with reference to its provisions regarding property rights and alimony. Plaintiff seeks a reversal of that part of the decree which awarded the household furnishings to her in lieu of alimony, and which decreed that the last half of the 1963 taxes on plaintiff's 172-acre farm in DeKalb County and the interest on the mortgage thereon to March 1, 1964, were the joint obligations of both parties.

Plaintiff contends that the farm was operated as a partnership; that one-half of the mortgage indebtedness thereon, which was incurred during the marriage, is the defendant's obligation; and that the defendant should be decreed to pay one half thereof either as alimony or in settlement of property rights.

It is the defendant's contention that no partnership existed in connection with the operation of the farm; that the funds of the parties were so commingled that it was impossible to determine the amount of money spent for farm business purposes and for living expenses; that the mortgage indebtedness was the result of the plaintiff's personal expenditures and her contribution to the living expenses of the family unit; and that since the defendant has no interest in the farm, he should not be held liable for one half the mortgage thereon.

The plaintiff, a widow with three young daughters, and the defendant, who had one daughter, were married July 21, 1948. As issue of the marriage, a daughter, Deborah Olson, was born. They all lived together as a family unit, apparently without differentiation in the treatment of the children. The decree for divorce was entered December 9, 1964.

At the time of the marriage, plaintiff owned a 120-acre farm in DeKalb County, which she sold in 1952, for $54,000. In November of 1951, she purchased the 172-acre DeKalb County farm which she now owns, and title thereto was taken in the DeKalb Trust and Savings Bank, as Trustee, with plaintiff as the beneficiary under this land trust. Plaintiff had other funds and, with the aid of a temporary advancement from her father, paid for the farm with her own money. She testified that she had approximately $8,000 left after buying the 172-acre farm, which sum was deposited in her personal account, but eventually went into the common account of the parties; and that at the time of the trial the farm was probably worth $750 per-acre, or $129,000.

Thereafter, in 1954, plaintiff encumbered this farm for $25,000 without the knowledge or signature of the defendant, and used this money to buy a house, which was subsequently sold for $24,000. Plaintiff testified that this sum was likewise deposited in her personal account and subsequently transferred into the common account. To clear up the interest due on the $25,000 loan and to pay other outstanding debts, a new mortgage was placed on the farm in 1961, in the sum of $35,000. Both plaintiff and defendant signed this mortgage and note, and the balance presently due thereon is $33,000.

Plaintiff testified that she had a complete line of furniture when the parties were married in 1948; and that when she purchased the 172-acre farm in 1951, plaintiff and defendant purchased additional furniture located at the farm, and got a bill of sale for it. The record contains no further evidence concerning the acquisition of further items of furniture.

The parties operated the farm as a grain and stock farm. In addition, the plaintiff worked as a secretary, and the defendant did carpentry work between 1961 and 1963. These earnings also went into the common account. The defendant had no bank account other than the common account.

The testimony is at variance relative to the machinery which was purchased in connection with the operation of the farm, but it appears to have been a full line of farm machinery. The bulk of the machinery, which plaintiff owned at the time of the marriage, was old and obsolete. The new machinery was paid for from the common account.

The plaintiff kept the records and made the deposits, but she did not keep a set of books. While both parties drew checks on the common account, plaintiff also maintained a separate account. When she sold the house aforementioned, the proceeds were placed in her separate account. She testified that she transferred sums therefrom to the common account, from time to time, to meet family and farm expenses, but offered no evidence as to the time and amounts of such transfers.

The farm operation apparently did not prosper. In seven out of eleven years, for which tax returns were available, the farm operated at a loss. The losses were largely due to a break in prices which caused cattle feeders across the country to suffer financial difficulties. However, such losses also reflected depreciation on the buildings and equipment which accounted for about one half thereof.

The defendant built a 24' x 32' addition to the farm house on the 172-acre farm, which he estimated to cost $10,000. He was not paid for his work, and the materials were paid for from the common account. On the same basis, he repaired the corn crib and put a new roof on the machine shed. In certain instances he had to have help in connection with such work, and he repaid that labor in kind to the neighbors who assisted him.

During the marriage, the cost of a new car, farm machinery, insurance, cattle, feed, seed, fertilizer, living and medical expenses, personal items, the costs of four weddings for members of the family unit, as well as taxes, and principal and interest on the mortgage, were paid from the common account. The testimony indicates that neither plaintiff nor the defendant were extravagant in their personal expenditures.

Confronted with the maze of unidentified figures covering such expenses, and in the absence of books of account, the trial Court, after hearing and considering the evidence, entered a decree for divorce; awarded the custody of the minor child to plaintiff and directed the defendant to pay $20 per week for her support; set visitation hours for the defendant; awarded the plaintiff all of the household furnishings as her sole property in lieu of alimony; ordered the farm machinery owned by the parties to be their joint property, with each party having an undivided one half interest therein; ordered that the decree for divorce shall in no way affect the lease between the parties whereby plaintiff's farm was leased to defendant; ordered that the common bank account with a balance of $428.57 be divided equally between the parties; awarded the 1955 Oldsmobile to plaintiff and the 1951 Chevrolet to the defendant; and ordered that the last one half of the 1963 taxes and the interest payment on the mortgage to March 1, 1964, be the joint obligation of the parties—each party being liable for one half thereof.

As between the parties, the question of the existence of a partnership relation is largely one of intent. In the absence of a written partnership agreement, as in the case at bar, the question of whether it was the intention of the parties that an agreement or arrangement constitute a partnership, must be determined from the language and conduct of the parties and from all the facts and circumstances surrounding the transaction.

The following factors are material in determining the existence of a partnership: the manner in which the parties have dealt with each other; the mode in which each has, with the knowledge of the other, dealt with persons in a partnership capacity; whether they have filed with the county clerk, a certificate setting forth the name of the partnership, in the event the firm name does not include the true name of the persons transacting such partnership business; whether they have carried telephone listings and signs on trucks, etc., using the firm name; and whether they have shared the profits of the partnership.

The record is replete with evidence that no partnership existed or was contemplated by the parties. Plaintiff did not deal with defendant as a partner in the handling of funds, some of which were deposited in her personal account and others in the common account—according to her fancy. The account, as shown by the checks, was merely a joint account of plaintiff and defendant upon which either could draw checks. It was not a partnership account. Neither of the parties, with the knowledge of the other, dealt with others in a partnership capacity. There is no record of the parties doing business under any partnership name. They carried no listings, telephone or otherwise, and had no signs indicating a partnership business or the use of a firm name. The record does not show that they filed partnership income tax returns. There is no record of the sharing of any profits or losses. The maintenance of a personal bank account by plaintiff and her sole business operation in the purchase of the farm indicate that, to her, the farm venture was not a partnership. In addition, her complaint for divorce, by separate count, or otherwise, did not allege the existence of a partnership or seek its dissolution.

The plaintiff and defendant, as husband, and wife and parent, were engaged in the joint venture of supporting, rearing and educating a family. The funds for this purpose, part of which were kept in a common account, were derived from farming, cattle raising, and the personal endeavors of both plaintiff and defendant aside from their farm efforts. However, special agreements or arrangements, for particular joint undertakings and adventures, do not constitute a partnership.

Even if the parties were partners, the plaintiff could not maintain an action at law against the defendant upon a demand growing out of the partnership, until the partnership accounts had been settled and a balance struck. Such a procedure had not been attempted herein.

Plaintiff further urges that defendant should be ordered to discharge one half of the $33,000 mortgage debt on her farm. She argues that in the absence of such order, plaintiff must pay the debt and then demand contribution from defendant as co-obligor on the mortgage note.

However, we do not believe that it is within the contemplation of the divorce decree that, as between the parties, the defendant is liable in any respect with reference to the $33,000 farm mortgage. He did not know of the original mortgage or note on the farm until after their execution, and he did not sign them. It was only when the encumbrance was increased to $35,000 that the defendant was asked to sign. He had no interest in the farm, beneficial or otherwise, other than as husband of plaintiff and a party in possession. It is apparent that he signed the mortgage and note, as requested, to cut off any possible rights which he might have in and to said premises, and to further secure the payment of the note.

The mortgagee is not a party to this proceeding and the decree herein can have no binding effect on it with reference to the obligation of the parties to it, but as between themselves, we find that it was the intent of the decree to relieve the defendant of all obligation to pay any part of said note, by contribution or otherwise, except as therein provided. The question before us is the propriety of this portion of the decree.

We recognize that it has frequently been held that a cotenant, who pays more than his share of a debt, principal or interest, secured by a mortgage on the commonly owned property, is entitled to reimbursement by contribution from his cotenants to the extent to which he paid their share of the indebtedness. However, plaintiff and defendant here were not cotenants in the ownership of the farm. The plaintiff was the sole beneficial owner thereof and the defendant had no interest therein. Plaintiff has cited no law, and we have found none, holding that she is entitled to contribution under the facts of this case.

Plaintiff further urges that, under the equities of the case, the defendant should be ordered to pay one half of the mortgage in that after 16 years she ended up with a $33,000 jointly created debt against her farm. However, the defendant contributed to the worth of the farm through building an addition to the house and repairing its buildings, and he helped to support her and her three daughters and to educate the daughters. His gain from this venture was age and experience, while plaintiff acquired a 172-acre farm, which, according to her estimate, is worth $129,000, subject to an indebtedness of $33,000. At the time of the marriage of the parties, plaintiff owned a 120-acre farm, free of encumbrance, which she subsequently sold for $54,000. Thus, the existing equities do not make a very impressive case for the plaintiff.

The Court below acted within the powers vested in it in entering the decree appealed from herein, and the only question before us is the propriety of the provisions of the decree appealed from. The trial Court heard the evidence and saw the witnesses; it was its duty to make the necessary determination of facts; and its findings are presumed to be correct. The evidence was ample to support the findings of the trial Court and it is not for us to substitute our findings for those of the Court below unless such findings are clearly and manifestly against the weight of the evidence. Such is not the circumstance in the case at bar.

Accordingly, the decree of the Circuit Court is affirmed, and . . . the last paragraph of said decree is hereby expanded, and it is hereby ordered, as between plaintiff and defendant, that the defendant is relieved of all obligation to pay any part of the $35,000 mortgage note, upon which the balance remaining unpaid is $33,000, by contribution or otherwise, except as provided in said decree.

[4] Explanatory Notes

[a] "Family Partnerships"

Though marriage is often spoken of as a "partnership" in which difficulties and joys, as well as assets and liabilities are shared, many (most?) marriages are not partnerships in this ideal sense. Difficulties, joys, assets and liabilities are not always shared equally. Many of the difficulties inherent in divorce cases arise out of the tension between the ideal of sharing and the reality of unequal ownership and division of family duties. The *Olson* case displays this tension vividly. Ruby wanted her ex-husband to assume half of the family debts. Peter responded that the farm was not his, that Ruby was the wealthier of the parties to the marriage, and that he should not have to share in payment of the mortgage if he cannot share in the benefits of owning the land. Both sides made arguments based on notions of "equality." Defining "equality" in these circumstances was difficult, in part because one party was wealthier than the other when the marriage began.

The Olsons made some efforts to define their own property relationships, in part because they knew that Illinois dower rules would have led to unsatisfactory property dispositions. Their post-nuptial agreement provided that the property each of them brought to the marriage was to be maintained as separate property and that the farm operations were to be maintained as a business partnership. This combination of family and business "partnerships" made the Olson situation interesting. Though introduced into the litigation by Ruby's attorney, the terms of the agreement probably doomed her argument. If the farm land was her separate property, then it was not part of the assets of the partnership. The agreement itself said only that the "farming operations" were to be carried on as a partnership, and that "livestock, grain and machinery" were to be evenly split by the partners. Ruby could have put her land in the partnership, but she did not appear to do so, either under the language of the agreement or in the way she and her husband organized their lives. Note well that if she had placed the land into the business part of the family partnership, Peter would have been obligated on half of the debt, but he also would have gained half of the title to the land. In fact, you might wonder how Ruby could possibly have claimed that Peter should pay half of the mortgage debt when she was unwilling to let him share the value of the land. Even if she was justified in arguing that the portion of the land's value she brought to the marriage was her separate property, shouldn't she have to split the increase in the land's value that accrued during the life of the "partnership" if she wanted Peter to pay half of the debt?

[b]   Consequences of Finding that Property Is Held by a Business Partnership

The *Olson* case presented interesting problems about distinguishing "family" from "business" assets. Distinctly different legal rules would have been applied to the disposition of the farm if it had been found to be business property. In the actual case, all of the property was talked of as an indistinguishable mess, although the court's distribution actually followed the outlines of the post-nuptial agreement fairly closely. The Illinois statutes in effect when *Olson* was decided gave the courts wide discretion as to how to distribute property in divorce cases. Ill. Rev. Stat. ch. 40, § 17 (1963), provided that:

> Whenever a divorce is granted, if it shall appear to the court that either party holds the title to property equitably belonging to the other, the court may compel conveyance thereof to be made to the party entitled to the same, upon such terms as it shall deem equitable.

It was therefore predictable that the *Olson* court, once it concluded that a business partnership did not exist, would be reluctant to disturb the way in which the trial court exercised its discretion in splitting up the property.

If the court had concluded that a business partnership existed, the outcome might have been very different. The farm, as well as the farm equipment, livestock and grain, would have been owned by the business, which could have continued even if the marriage was over. In most cases, however, married persons in business together would not wish to continue their business relationship after the marriage terminated. If the Olsons wished to end the business they would have been forced to plow through another process calling for an accounting of the assets and liabilities of the business, payment of creditors and distribution of any remaining property to the partners. It is not at all clear that this would have turned out as well for Ruby as the actual case did. If the Olsons wished to continue the business, but not work together, they would have been forced to decide which of them should get the business and how to pay the non-participating person their share of the business' value. Compare *Gibbons v. Gibbons*, p. 198 above. If business property was jointly owned by the Olsons and the business was itself marital property, then the divorce court would have been forced to decide upon a method of including the business property in the distribution of the couple's assets. Illinois, like New Jersey, has adopted a marital property statute for divorce since *Olson* was decided. *See* 750 Ill. Comp. Stat. 5/503 (1998).

[c] Creditors and Partnerships

Problems of distinguishing partnership from non-partnership property arise in a number of circumstances outside of marriage. As with tenancy by the entirety cases, one common theme in such litigation involves the ability of creditors to gain access to one or another asset. In *Taber-Prang Art Co. v. Durant*, 189 Mass. 173, 75 N.E. 221 (1905), for example, creditors sued to have the proceeds from the sale of certain lands and buildings used by a partnership distributed among creditors of the partnership. The land and buildings were owned by A and B as tenants in common. They conducted a manufacturing business on the premises as partners under a firm name. A died and devised his half share of the tenancy in common to C. Thereafter, B and C carried on the business as partners under the same name as before. There was no conveyance of the land and buildings to themselves as a firm, nor was there an intention that the land and buildings should be regarded as partnership property. Upon bankruptcy of the partnership, the court was asked to decide whether the land and buildings belonged to the partnership or to the individual partners in order that the priority rights of the partnership and individual creditors could be established. After noting that the use of property for partnership purposes did not of itself convert the property into partnership assets, the court investigated the use of funds in connection with the purchase and the maintenance of the land and buildings. The court held that the land and the original buildings remained separate property subject, initially, to the claims of individual creditors. Buildings, fixtures, and other improvements added to the land with partnership funds and used for partnership purposes, the court held, were partnership property, subject first to the claims of partnership creditors. Note well that in cases like *Durant*, the division of property between business and individual may have dramatic effects on the ability of some creditors to recover their losses.

When disputes arise over the nature of property related to a partnership, courts will first look to any partnership agreement to determine the question of ownership. If the agreement is silent as to whether some assets are owned by the partnership, then the conduct of the parties in handling the property will be controlling. This is what occurred in *Durant*. Both partners were apparently general partners. However, the amount of individually owed debts was so large that partnership creditors were prevented from gaining access to those assets. The case was really a battle between creditors more than between creditors and partners.

[d] A First Primer on Mortgages

Two mortgages were taken out on the Olson farm. The first, for $25,000, was replaced a bit later with one for $35,000. Ruby Olson arranged for the first loan without the participation of her husband. The second loan was closed over the signatures of both spouses.[24] This difference should seem a bit strange to you and indeed it was. A mortgage is a special type of arrangement in which a land owner uses land as security or collateral for a loan. If the borrower defaults

---

[24] In a typical mortgage, two important documents are signed by the borrower. One is a mortgage deed which gives the lender an interest in the land allowing the lender to foreclose on the land and sell it in case of default. The other document is a note, a contract in which the borrower agrees to repay the loan. In the *Olson* case, Peter signed the mortgage deed and note for only the $35,000 loan.

on the mortgage loan, the lender may sell the land in an effort to pay off the indebtedness. Even when the borrower goes bankrupt, secured lenders are usually in preferred positions. They will gain access to the asset used to secure their loan before other unsecured creditors get their shot.

Now put the knowledge you gleaned from Chapter 2 to work. If a lender wants to make sure that it can sell the land used as security for a loan it makes to a married person, who should the lender require to sign the mortgage documents? If the loan is to the wife, as in the *Olson* case, and only she signs, then what will happen if she dies before her husband? The husband could demand that dower or curtesy rights be extended to him. While the Olsons' post-nuptial agreement might have precluded dower and curtesy, it is not at all clear that the bank was aware of its existence. It was not recorded. So if the lender wanted to make sure that "clean" security was provided for the Olson loan, the signatures of both parties should have been required. That apparently was done for the second loan, but not for the first. That means that Peter Olson was in fact responsible to the lender for repaying the $35,000 loan.

Then how could the court let Peter off the hook? Actually it didn't completely relieve him of all responsibility. Justice Days carefully noted that the mortgagee[25] was not a party to the case and that the decree relieving Peter of responsibility to Ruby was not binding on the lender. So if Ruby failed to pay off the loan and the bank sought relief from Peter, the lender would win. If Peter then sought contribution from Ruby, he would win. If, however, the lender sought and received payment from Ruby, she could not get any relief from Peter.

[5] Problem Notes

[a] *Olson* Under Contemporary Marital Property Regimes

The divorce aspects of the case followed the title of the property in the old common law world. Illinois had not adopted a marital property divorce statute at the time *Olson* was decided. Though the state did give its divorce courts discretion to divide property fairly at divorce, judicial practice at the time generally followed common law title. So the mish-mashed assets were divided by the trial court; those separately titled were given to the title holders. The results of the case might be different under a marital property system. For example, if Ruby's farm was commingled together with other assets, Peter might be able to claim a share. Or if the mortgage payments were made from marital assets, Peter might be responsible for some of the debt. How would you divide the Olson assets up under a marital property regime?

[b] Difference Between Partnerships and Concurrent Estates

Compare *Olson v. Olson* with *Reilly v. Sageser*, p. 123 above. Did *Reilly* involve a partnership agreement? The agreement did apportion responsibilities for operating the land, and prevented transfer of the land without first hurdling the "buyout" clause. Would it have made any difference whether the contract was read as a partnership agreement? If the agreement did create a partnership, could the court have wound up the affairs of the partnership without partitioning the property? Did *Reilly* involve a business relationship? While the Sagesers were investors, does

---

[25] Be careful in reading this sort of language. The lender is the *mortgagee*, not the *mortgagor*. The lender does transfer money to the borrower, a transaction which might make you think the lender should be called the *mortgagor*. But the use of the "or" ending doesn't follow the path of the money; it follows the path of the property instruments. In this case the borrower transfers a document to the lender giving the lender the right to sell the property in case of default. So the borrower is blessed with the "or" ending as *mortgagor*, and the lender, as recipient of the mortgage deed, is called a *mortgagee*.

that fact alone turn the relationship into a business? Regardless of your answers to these inquiries, note again how quickly one form of holding property may be changed into a different form. Purchasers and owners of property are always making choices, frequently untutored, that may have a major impact on the nature of the bundles of rights they hold.

[c]　Difference Between Partnership and Non-Marital "Partnerships"

Compare *Olson v. Olson* with *Marvin v. Marvin*, p. 214 above. Should non-marital family relationships be treated like business partnerships in which property held by the "partnership" would be equally divided upon death or termination of the relationship? Is there any justification for applying the special creditor access rules of partnerships to non-marital families? Compare *Sawada v. Endo*, p. 186 above, and the special creditor rules sometimes associated with tenancies by the entirety. Is it time to consider "uniform" legislation on the various creditor features of family property law?

[d]　Import of Using Business Rather than Family Based "Magic Words"

As was stated in the notes after *Gibbons v. Gibbons*, p. 203 above, the two major property systems extant in the United States—common law and community—have come closer to each other in recent years, particularly in the handling of property dispositions upon divorce. If it had been perfectly clear in *Olson* that the couple established a partnership for the entire farming business, including the land, how would you have handled the divorce? Which "construct" should govern the property—the applicable property system (common law or community) or the business system? To the extent splitting up a business follows more rigid notions of fairness, such as dividing the assets in accordance with the partnership interests described in a partnership agreement, a partnership may be used to avoid the more discretionary aspects of a divorce proceeding. Is this wise? Should married couples be allowed to vary their share of community or marital property by agreement?

[6]　Opinions of the Connecticut Supreme Court in *Zaist v. Olson*

Zaist v. Olson

Connecticut Supreme Court
154 Conn. 563, 227 A.2d 552 (1967)

ALCORN J.

The plaintiffs brought this action against Martin Olson, The East Haven Homes, Inc., and Martin Olson, Inc. The allegations of the complaint, briefly stated, are that the plaintiffs rendered services, supplied materials and furnished equipment to The East Haven Homes, Inc., for work on properties owned or leased by Martin Olson and Martin Olson, Inc., or by corporations subsequently merged into the latter; that the services, material and equipment were furnished at the instance and request of Martin Olson, who was an officer and director and the person in general charge of the affairs of The East Haven Homes, Inc.; that this corporation acted as the agent or instrumentality of Martin Olson and of Martin Olson, Inc., of which Martin Olson was also an officer and director and the person in general charge; that the services rendered and the material and equipment furnished inured to the benefit of Martin Olson and Martin Olson, Inc.; and that the plaintiffs were entitled to recover the amount due with interest.

The defendants' answer was a general denial, and, on stipulation of the parties, the court referred the case to a referee to hear the facts and to report. The referee filed his report, recommending a judgment in favor of the plaintiffs against Martin Olson and Martin Olson, Inc. The defendants made a massive attack on the report by a motion to correct, in response to which the referee made a limited number of corrections, whereupon the defendants filed with the court, and were heard on, exceptions to the report as corrected and a request for further corrections by the court. The court overruled the exceptions, refused to make the corrections sought, and rendered judgment on the referee's report. This appeal is from that judgment.

. . . .

These defendants once again attack, in wholesale fashion, the referee's finding of the facts upon which the judgment was rendered. A study of the evidence submitted in the appendices to the briefs satisfies us that no corrections in the referee's amended report are merited and that the court did not err in overruling the exceptions and objections to it or in refusing to make any corrections . . . . [T]he only issue . . . is the claim that the court erred in rendering judgment on the basis of the conclusions that the services, materials and equipment furnished by the plaintiffs inured to the benefit of Martin Olson and Martin Olson, Inc., and that those defendants acted through the agency or instrumentality of The East Haven Homes, Inc.

The essential facts, as found by the referee, may be summarized as follows: In 1943, Martin Olson, subsequently referred to as Olson, caused The East Haven Homes, Inc., which we shall call East Haven, to be incorporated. Two hundred shares of stock were issued, of which Olson received 198; the other two shares were issued, one each, to his lawyer and his bookkeeper. Olson was president, treasurer and a director. He continued as president until November, 1955, and as treasurer until November, 1962, and, throughout all the dealings hereinafter related, he controlled East Haven and was empowered to sign all checks for it.

During 1952 and 1953, Olson personally acquired land in Groton for the purpose of erecting a shopping center. In April, 1954, he requested the plaintiffs to submit, and the plaintiffs did submit, prices for clearing and grading this land. The terms were mutually agreeable, and the plaintiffs began the work, setting the account on their records under the heading "Martin Olson." Thereafter, and before any payment was made, Olson told the plaintiffs to send the bills to East Haven, and the plaintiffs did so, keeping their records variously in the names of Olson and East Haven.

In 1954, Olson caused Martin Olson, Inc., hereinafter called Olson, Inc., to be incorporated; in it he owned, personally or as trustee for three of his minor children, thirty-two of the forty shares of issued stock. Olson was president and treasurer and in full control of the corporation from its inception until October, 1959. He and two of his children were the directors, and a son was vice-president. Thereafter, Olson quitclaimed a substantial part of his Groton land to Olson, Inc., which also acquired additional adjoining land from private owners. The plaintiffs continued to work on the land, known to them only as the Groton shopping center, unaware of any change in title. Olson, or in his absence his son, directed the work. In 1955, Olson, Inc., reconveyed part of the land to Olson.

While the plaintiffs were at work on the Groton land, Olson and Olson, Inc., acquired land for a shopping center in New London. In 1955, Olson caused The New London Shopping Center, Inc., to be incorporated. Olson was president and treasurer of that corporation and held all the stock personally or as trustee for his three minor children. Thereafter, Olson, this time describing himself as either "of" or "acting for" East Haven, made three contracts with the plaintiffs for work to be done and materials to be furnished in developing the New London shopping center land.

Later, Olson, Inc., voted to sell a large part of its New London land to The New London Shopping Center, Inc., which then had little if any capital funds, for $177,000, and Olson, as president, signed the deed. Meantime, East Haven voted to contract with Olson, Inc., to erect a shopping center in Groton for not over $450,000 and to contract with The New London Shopping Center, Inc., to erect a shopping center in New London for not over $1,700,000, but no such contracts were ever executed. While this was going on, the plaintiffs were continually working on the properties both in Groton and New London; and East Haven, with fixed assets consisting of office furniture, a few small tools and cars and a truck of small value, had neither the funds nor the equipment to construct either of the shopping centers. Nevertheless, East Haven, acting by Olson or his son, the vice-president of Olson, Inc., engaged various contractors for both projects. Funds for the construction of both projects were provided by a bank loan of $1,700,000 secured by a mortgage given by The New London Shopping Center, Inc., the proceeds from which were paid over to East Haven. Neither corporation was able, with these funds, to complete the New London project, and Olson besought the lending bank for additional funds.

To meet the lending bank's demand, Olson caused Viking, Inc., to be formed, to which The New London Shopping Center, Inc., conveyed a part of its land, which Viking, Inc., on the same day mortgaged to the lending bank for a loan of $650,000. Olson controlled, and was president, treasurer and a majority stockholder of, Viking, Inc., and was authorized by it to borrow such sums as he deemed advisable. The proceeds of the $650,000 loan were paid over to East Haven and used to pay bills on the New London project, and Viking, Inc., acting by Olson as its president, reconveyed to The New London Shopping Center, Inc., the land which was mortgaged to secure, and was covered by, the $650,000 mortgage.

During the month after Viking, Inc., was formed, Olson, Inc., acquired a tract of land in Waterford on which the plaintiffs also worked under a contract with East Haven. Thereafter, The New London Shopping Center, Inc., was merged into Olson, Inc., the two corporations continuing under the name of Olson, Inc., which remained under the full control of Olson. A few months later Olson, Inc., quitclaimed a substantial portion of its Groton land to Olson after Olson had notified the plaintiffs that, owing to the financial status of East Haven, "we would not be in a position to discuss settlement with you for at least another four months." About two months before this suit was brought, Olson and his children conveyed their stock in Olson, Inc., to a syndicate, so that Olson no longer controls the corporation.

For five years subsequent to April, 1954, the plaintiffs had furnished labor, materials and equipment on the aforementioned lands in Groton, New London and Waterford to an amount in excess of $192,752.66, all of which labor, materials and equipment inured to the benefit of Olson and Olson, Inc. The plaintiffs had been paid $169,652.66 by checks of East Haven, of which an aggregate of $97,401.26 had been signed by Olson and the balance by his son as vice-president of East Haven. The balance owed to the plaintiffs as of December 31, 1959, was $23,100.

The offices maintained by Olson, Olson, Inc., East Haven, The New London Shopping Center, Inc., and Viking, Inc., were all at the same address, and Olson's secretary was also secretary and bookkeeper for Olson, Inc., and East Haven. East Haven was originally formed for the purpose of building homes and, prior to 1954, engaged in that and other construction work on property of Olson and others. During the period covered by the plaintiffs' work, East Haven maintained an office and a checking account, kept corporate and financial records, filed corporation returns, and had employees. The record is completely silent as to any similar activity or conduct on the part of any of the other corporations involved except for the single meeting of Olson, Inc., at which that corporation voted to sell land to The New London Shopping Center, Inc., for $177,000, and the single meeting of Viking, Inc., which authorized Olson to borrow such sums as he deemed advisable. The only corporate action found to have been taken by East Haven relating to these projects consists of the two votes authorizing contracts with Olson, Inc., which were never consummated, to erect shopping centers in Groton and New London.

The referee concluded that East Haven, in all its dealings, was the agent of Olson and Olson, Inc. The defendants not only denied this agency but also claimed that no services, materials or equipment furnished by the plaintiffs inured to the benefit of Olson or Olson, Inc., and that neither of those defendants was indebted to the plaintiffs. The court concluded, in substance, that the referee could reasonably find that Olson transacted business as an individual and also through corporate entities under his control and that all of the services rendered by the plaintiffs inured to the benefit of Olson or Olson, Inc. The second portion of this conclusion requires no discussion. The facts recited demonstrate clearly enough that Olson or Olson, Inc., received the benefit of the plaintiffs' services and the materials and equipment furnished by them. It is the first portion of the conclusion which poses the question for decision, namely, that Olson transacted the business as an individual and through corporate entities under his control.

Although Olson was the person with whom the plaintiffs dealt, he directed them to look to East Haven for payment, and the plaintiffs did so. All checks issued in payment of bills rendered were East Haven checks signed by either its vice-president or by Olson, who was its president. East Haven was, as a corporation, a separate legal entity. It must be assumed, from the facts found, that the plaintiffs undertook to deal with this corporation. The facts indicate that they were unaware of, and probably indifferent to, the identity of the owners of the property, who were to receive the actual benefit of their work. Nothing is indicated to warrant the conclusion that Olson ever enlightened them on this subject or that they ever asked him to do so. These circumstances did not prevent the plaintiffs, once they learned that their undertaking was for the benefit of Olson and Olson, Inc., from seeking to hold them, as they did in this action. So long as other requirements which justified a recovery were met, the plaintiffs were entitled to hold Olson and Olson, Inc., for the amount due them. And this brings us to the basic question of the plaintiffs' right to look beyond East Haven, the corporate entity with which they dealt, to Olson and Olson, Inc., for a recovery of the amount due them.

The referee and the court based this right on agency. No express agency was found to exist, and, consequently, either an implied agency was meant, or the term "agency" was loosely used, as is sometimes done, to pierce the shield of immunity afforded by the corporate structure in a situation in which the corporate entity has been so controlled and dominated that justice requires liability to be imposed on the real actor. The complaint alleged that East Haven was "the agent or instrumentality" of Olson and Olson, Inc. We think that it was the latter.

Courts will disregard the fiction of separate legal entity when a corporation is a mere instrumentality or agent of another corporation or individual owning all or most of its stock. Under such circumstances the general rule, which recognizes the individuality of corporate entities and the independent character of each in respect to their corporate transactions, and the obligations incurred by each in the course of such transactions, will be disregarded, where, as here, the interests of justice and righteous dealing so demand. The circumstance that control is exercised merely through dominating stock ownership, of course, is not enough. There must be such domination of finances, policies and practices that the controlled corporation has, so to speak, no separate mind, will or existence of its own and is but a business conduit for its principal.

In the present case, Olson, Inc., owned none of the stock of East Haven. On the other hand, Olson held a dominating stock interest in both East Haven and Olson, Inc., and was president, treasurer and a director of both corporations. It is not the fact that he held these positions which is controlling but rather the manner in which he utilized them. The essential purposes of the corporate structure, including stockholder immunity, must and will be protected when the corporation functions as an entity in the normal manner contemplated and permitted by law. When it functions in this manner, there is nothing insidious in stockholder control, inter-locking directorates or identity of officers. When, however, the corporation is so manipulated by an individual or another corporate entity as to become a mere puppet or tool for the manipulator, justice may require the courts to disregard the corporate fiction and impose liability on the real actor . . . .

The instrumentality rule requires, in any case but an express agency, proof of three elements: (1) Control, not mere majority or complete stock control, but complete domination, not only of finances but of policy and business practice in respect to the transaction attacked so that the corporate entity as to this transaction had at the time no separate mind, will or existence of its own; (2) that such control must have been used by the defendant to commit fraud or wrong, to perpetrate the violation of a statutory or other positive legal duty, or a dishonest or unjust act in contravention of plaintiff's legal rights; and (3) that the aforesaid control and breach of duty must proximately cause the injury or unjust loss complained of.

Complementing the instrumentality rule is the identity rule. Its application is illustrated in *Luckenbach S.S. Co. v. W.R. Grace & Co.*, 267 Fed. 676 (4th Cir.). In that case, Edgar F. Luckenbach owned 94 percent of the stock of the Luckenbach Steamship Company and almost 90 percent of the stock of the Luckenbach Company. The Luckenbach Steamship Company had a capital of $10,000 and owned no ships. The Luckenbach Company was capitalized at $800,000 and did own ships which it leased to the steamship company. Both corporations had the same officers and directors, and Luckenbach was president of and personally managed both. When the steamship company defaulted on a contract with W.R. Grace and Company, the latter, in a suit against the two corporations, was allowed recovery against the Luckenbach Company. The court said (p. 681): "For all practical purposes the two concerns are one and it would be unconscionable to allow the owner of this fleet of steamers, worth millions of dollars, to escape liability because it had turned them over a year before to a $10,000 corporation, which is simply itself in another form." The proposition has been otherwise expressed as follows: "If plaintiff can show that there was such a unity of interest and ownership that the independence of the corporations had in effect ceased or had never begun, an adherence to the fiction of separate identity would serve only to defeat justice and equity by permitting the economic entity to escape liability arising out of an operation conducted by one corporation for the benefit of the whole enterprise." *Mull v. Colt Co.*, 31 F.R.D. 154, 163 (S.D.N.Y.); *Walkovszky v. Carlton*, 24 App. Div. 2d 582, 583, 262 N.Y.S.2d 334.

The facts in the present case are, beyond question, that Olson caused the creation of both East Haven and Olson, Inc., and thereafter completely dominated and controlled not only them but his other corporate creations. All shared the same office. All the work and material furnished by the plaintiffs went into land which, after being juggled about, came to rest in Olson or Olson,

Inc. The record is significantly silent with regard to any formal corporate action by the directors or stockholders of any of the several corporations except in the insignificant instances specifically mentioned. East Haven had no sufficient funds of its own and acquired no funds for the work on its own initiative. It had no proprietary interest in the property on which the work was done, and, so far as appears, it gained nothing from whatever part it played in the transaction . . . . With no showing of any responsible corporate action of its own, it was used by Olson for the benefit of Olson and Olson, Inc. On the facts established, the cause of justice would not be served by denying to the plaintiffs the amount found due them and unpaid because of the inadequate resources of East Haven.

We do not wish to be understood to countenance, by anything we have said here, the imposition of the legitimate indebtedness of a corporation upon a majority stockholder in derogation of his legal immunity merely because of the corporate control inherent in his stock ownership. The present case presents a set of circumstances far different from that. The only reasonable meaning to attach to the transactions spread upon this record is that East Haven undertook no obligation of its own to the plaintiffs, was financially unable to cope with the actual transaction, and reaped no benefit from it. The undertaking throughout was Olson's, planned and carried out through his various other corporate creatures for his own and Olson, Inc.'s, enrichment, a part of which, if the plaintiffs were to be denied a recovery, would consist of the amount which East Haven, as the plaintiffs' ostensible debtor, is unable to pay because Olson and Olson, Inc., have not provided the final necessary funds.

On the basis of the referee's report, the court could properly conclude that Olson so completely controlled East Haven that that corporation had no separate mind, will or existence of its own; that the control was used to perpetrate an unjust act in contravention of the plaintiffs' rights; and that it caused the unjust loss complained of. Consequently, a judgment against Olson was warranted. The court could, with equal propriety, reach the conclusion that the identity of Olson and Olson, Inc., was such that judgment against Olson, Inc., was warranted. The court in fact rendered judgment for the full amount against both Olson and Olson, Inc. This aspect of the judgment is not in issue since neither of those defendants has claimed that the other is either solely or partially responsible for the amount found due. Indeed, each of those two defendants steadfastly denied that either was liable to the plaintiffs for anything.

. . . .

In this opinion KING, C.J., and RYAN, J., concurred.

HOUSE, J. (dissenting).

I have no quarrel with the statement of legal principles expounded in the majority opinion, but I do not agree that the facts found by the referee support a conclusion that the control which the defendants Martin Olson and Martin Olson, Inc., undoubtedly did exercise over The East Haven Homes, Inc., was used by them or either of them "to commit fraud or wrong, to perpetrate the violation of a statutory or other positive legal duty, or a dishonest and unjust act in contravention of" the plaintiffs' legal rights. As the majority opinion recognizes, proof that the controlled corporation was so used is a condition precedent to the imposition of liability on the controlling individual or corporation under the instrumentality rule . . . . The referee who heard the evidence in this case did not find that this essential element had been proven, nor, in my opinion, do the facts found support a conclusion that it existed. Accordingly, I believe that there was error in the judgment and it should be reversed.

COTTER, J. (dissenting).

I cannot agree with the conclusion of the majority that the "only reasonable meaning to attach to the transactions spread upon this record is that East Haven undertook no obligation of its own to the plaintiffs, [and] was financially unable to cope with the actual transaction." The East Haven Homes, Inc., was organized as a general contractor in 1943. Thereafter, and over a period of several years, it built a large number of individual homes, a fifty-seven unit apartment house, a bank building, and several other commercial structures. In 1954, eleven years after it had been formed, East Haven Homes engaged the plaintiffs to do certain clearing work. From then until June of 1959, it paid them $169,652.66 for services rendered. East Haven Homes then apparently became insolvent, with an unpaid balance of $23,100 on this account. These facts, together with others recited in the majority opinion, support a conclusion that Martin Olson used his corporations to engage in speculative business undertakings, that these corporations borrowed funds, exchanged properties and undertook obligations in a free and easy fashion, and even that Olson structured a corporate network with a weak capital foundation, but they do not reasonably support the conclusion, made for the first time in this court, that "control [by Olson] was used to perpetrate an unjust act in contravention of the plaintiffs' rights." Indeed, it appears equally possible that Olson's entire corporate empire went into eclipse in 1960 and that East Haven Homes was merely a victim of this general financial decline. In my opinion, the record does not justify overriding the principle of a shareholder's limited liability.

The practice of disregarding the corporate entity should be undertaken with great caution. This principle is fully applicable in situations where the corporation is dominated by a single individual. Persons dealing with such corporations may refuse to contract without a personal guarantee of payment from the principal. The plaintiffs in the present case, however, elected to deal with the corporation and in fact were paid substantial sums by the corporation over a long period of time.

The underlying rationale behind the statutory granting of stockholder immunity from corporate debts has been stated as follows: "Obviously the useful and beneficial role of the corporate concept in the economic and business affairs of the modern day world would be destroyed if the rule of freedom from individual liability for corporate obligations did not obtain. The protection of limited liability for venture or investment capital is essential to the efficient operation of a system of free enterprise. Such protection from individual liability encourages and promotes business, commerce, manufacturing and industry which provides employment, creates sales of goods and commodities and adds to the nation's economic and financial growth, stability and prosperity." *Johnson v. Kinchen*, 160 So. 2d 296, 299 (La.). The majority opinion in the present case, although not directly undermining this principle, casts a doubtful shadow in its direction.

The new rule which the majority had adopted as the test of the personal liability of a corporation's dominant shareholder is a broad one, will be difficult to apply realistically and is not warranted by the record in the present case. Close corporations, although individual entities from a legal standpoint, are normally no more than vehicles for the goals and motives of their principals. The law is not necessarily advanced by adopting a rule which includes a presumption that this kind of corporation may have a "separate mind, will, or existence of its own." Under the circumstances of this case, I would reaffirm the "fraudulent or illegal purposes" test . . . .

Zaist v. Olson: Transaction Diagram

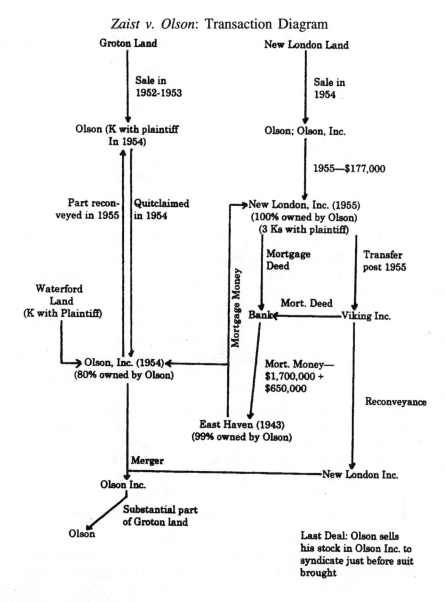

[7]　Explanatory Notes

[a]　Veil Piercing

Typical explanations of veil piercing suggest that courts look to a variety of factors in deciding whether to ignore corporation law's limited liability rules. Among the factors typically mentioned are commonality in various features of the businesses such as boards of directors, officers, and major shareholders, the degree to which the corporations were actually operated as separate legal entities, the likelihood that the corporation was under-capitalized and the tendency of the corporate actions to deceive the parties with whom they dealt. Why should any of these features be important?

　　[*i*]　*Commonality.* In *Zaist* all the corporations had very similar principals. For all practical purposes, Martin Olson fully controlled each of the entities—East Haven, Inc., Olson,

Inc., New London Shopping Center, Inc., and Viking, Inc. The court apparently argued that such facts meant that the corporations had no existence separate from Martin Olson. But can that really be correct? Was the real problem the way Olson behaved or the way Zaist behaved? For example, assume that the Zaist Company was the largest contractor in Connecticut, that it had branch offices all over the state, that it oversaw millions of dollars of construction projects yearly, and that its major officers were all lawyers well schooled in the intricacies of corporate law. Under these circumstances, wouldn't you find in favor of Olson on the theory that Zaist should have made a thorough investigation of East Haven before agreeing to receive payment through that corporate "shell?" In fact, wouldn't such a fact situation make you want to protect Olson from the overzealous attempts of a major corporation to recover debts from the family assets of a struggling shopping center developer? If so, then the presence of Martin Olson in all the entities can't be the most crucial factor, can it?

[*ii*]   *Operation as Separate Entities.* Running a corporation requires the maintenance of minutes of board meetings, account books and other streams of paper. All of these activities are supposed to provide some basis for evaluating the actions of a corporation. Since corporations are legal fictions created to serve certain perceived social needs, an artificial "life" is created to give substance to the fiction. But why should sloppy record keeping lead to a higher likelihood of piercing the corporate veil? Most persons who deal with corporations have no idea what goes on behind the corporate scene. If veil piercing is meant to protect some perceived unfairness associated with depriving creditors of access to assets outside the corporation, why should such hidden activities be relevant? If a corporate owner runs a messy shop, it may be that those dealing with the corporation would be unable to discover who they should be seeking money from even if they bothered to check out the business. But that suggests that the real issue is whether a party dealing with a corporation must check out the business. Again if Zaist was an enormous outfit and was therefore said to be the sort of business with a duty to check out those with whom it deals, would messiness make a difference? If the business was sloppy and its various corporate components could not be easily distinguished, would you give relief to Zaist if it dealt with Olson despite knowing of the problems? Unlikely. On the other hand, if Zaist was a small outfit, you might not even want to require Zaist to investigate Olson before granting Zaist relief.

[*iii*]   *Capitalization.* If a business is under-capitalized and therefore more likely than other businesses to get into financial difficulty, its seems (on the surface at least) that a party dealing with such a corporation ought to be able to recover a debt from a principal of the business. But if that were true, then the very basis of the limited liability rules of corporations is threatened. To the extent that veil piercing problems are much more likely to arise with weak businesses, the use of under capitalization as a factor undermines the rule. On the other hand, the financial health of the business is obviously relevant information for parties deciding on whether to make a deal. Perhaps the real issues are how to transfer that information, not the mere fact of financial health or ill health.

[*iv*]   *Deception.* Fraud is one thing. If a party is deceived by intentional misstatements of fact, it is almost impossible to discover the true state of affairs. That may be why fraud is universally thought to be a basis for a law suit regardless of the nature of the intentional misstatement causing harm. *Zaist,* however, did not involve fraud, at least as far as the proofs tell us anything about the actual setting. To the two dissenters in the case, the lack of proof of fraud provided a basis for suggesting the case should have been dismissed. But even if Zaist was not defrauded, he might not have known that East Haven was an almost worthless shell

into which Olson put money when he needed it and took it out when he had bills to pay. To the extent that Zaist was acting under a misapprehension of the true state of affairs when he agreed to bill East Haven for his excavation and sewer work, you might feel he should recover. But what if Zaist had a duty to check out the financial health of East Haven? If so, would he still have been "deceived?" Judge Cotter's position in dissent was that Zaist did have such a duty and that his failure to fulfill it should have been fatal to his case. Deception, it appears, is a sometime thing, dependent upon who has the burden of searching for information. It may be much easier to justify requiring a large business enterprise to search for information than a small struggling shop. If that be the case, then veil piercing may have much more to do with the relative financial power of the parties than with the sorts of things courts typically talk about in their opinions.

[b] The *Zaist* Decision

The *Zaist* decision is interesting in part because it does *not* talk at length about the sorts of factors typically mentioned in veil piercing cases. Though the commonality theme appears, there is little else of note. The three theories bandied about—agency, instrumentality and identity—seem remarkably interchangeable; it probably made little difference that the referee deciding the case below went off on an agency theory while the Connecticut Supreme Court relied upon instrumentality and identity language. In any case, the opinion is remarkably opaque. It is very difficult to discover what motivated a decision in Zaist's favor. If deception—or better put, the placement of the duty to search for information—was the key, then a decision in Zaist's favor required a conclusion that Zaist was not under an obligation to investigate Olson's affairs before signing the excavation contracts. From my review of all the pleadings in the case, it is difficult to conclude that Zaist and Olson were in dramatically different financial leagues. Under these circumstances should you decide the case on the basis of which party would have to spend the most money to obtain information on finances? If so, Zaist should win because it would be cheaper for Olson to reveal his status than for Zaist to search for it. But what about Olson doing business with Zaist? Should Zaist be under an obligation to reveal information to Olson? What is being unraveled by all of this are some of the inherent costs involved in transferring information associated with making any deal. Barriers to information exchange may be the reason why courts sometimes step in to protect people who made deals without information that was expensive to obtain. Compare *Zaist v. Olson* with *Reilly v. Sageser*, p. 123 above, which involved serious informational gaps on the part of at least one party. Or compare *Zaist* with *Commercial Union v. Pucci*, p. 93 above, where parties had lots of information and did not act on it!

[c] Another Piercing Example

One other very well known piercing case is *Bartle v. Home Owners Co-operative, Inc.*, 309 N.Y. 103, 127 N.E.2d 832 (1955). The Home Owners Co-operative (HOC) was organized in 1947 by veterans to construct low cost housing for its members. HOC, in turn, set up a subsidiary, Westerlea Builders, Inc., to actually undertake the construction. Westerlea was under-capitalized by HOC and got into financial difficulty. The creditors of Westerlea eventually took over the construction project and looked to HOC for payment of the debts. In *Bartle* the New York Court of Appeals refused to pierce Westerlea's corporate shield, saying that there was no evidence of fraud, misrepresentation or illegality. Judge Van Voorhis dissented. He argued that the organization of the building project made it impossible for Westerlea to make money. At best the company would break even. The entire capital of the company came from HOC which was owned by the people who eventually occupied the buildings. As a result of the majority's views, the members of HOC who bought the houses ended up benefiting from Westerlea's insolvency. Van Voorhis would have held Westerlea to be HOC's agent for building the houses and charged HOC's members with Westerlea's losses.

[8] Problem Notes

[a] Underlying Assumption of Limited Corporate Liability

Much of the structure of corporate law depends on the assumption that limiting liability of business enterprises increases the incentive to invest in new ventures and that such additional incentive is basic to the operation of the American economy. Is the assumption provably correct? Even if the incentive theory works, are there other ways to create the incentives without limiting the liability of corporate shareholders? Why not create government guarantees for some or all of the debts of businesses needing support? Are there any other devices that may be available? Does the incentive theory work for very large businesses? If there is a need to protect individuals from their business debts, can the same be said for large corporations setting up subsidiaries or small under-capitalized corporations acting as general partners in otherwise limited partnerships?

[b] Torts and Piercing

If *Zaist* and similar contract cases should be decided on the basis of some theory related to the cost of obtaining information, how should tort cases be resolved? A person injured by a truck owned by an insolvent subsidiary has no chance to discover the financial status of the company before the truck runs them over. Should the courts (as some appear to do) simply shift to a "tort-like" model in which the ability to bear the risk of loss becomes an important part of piercing analysis. In such a model, larger companies with insolvent subsidiaries will more likely be found responsible for the torts of their subsidiaries than for their contract breaches. If you think Zaist should have lost his case, how would you decide the matter if Zaist had been injured while using some excavating equipment due to the negligence of Olson, Inc. employees? Compare *Sawada v. Endo*, p. 186 above.

[c] Property Law

After studying lots of property holding devices in Chapter 2 and in this chapter and struggling through the definitional structures of each one, what emerges? Even if each device standing by itself is understandable, is there a definable "property" system? There certainly is a great deal of flexibility granted to those "in the know" and financially capable of using the multitude of devices to serve their own needs. It is possible to assemble packages of property holding devices designed to meet very specific needs. A corporation may act as a tenant in common or a partner. A partnership may hold stock in a corporation. Shell business entities may be created that are traps for the unwary.

But what about those who are not "in the know?" Is the system designed for the benefit of those least likely to understand the nature of the devices being studied? Even if the courts are willing to provide relief to unsophisticated participants in the marketplace, is litigation likely to be a useful technique for aiding the prevailing parties in such cases?

[9] Some Final Observations on *Olson v. Olson* and *Zaist v. Olson* and the Cultural Nature of "Risk"

In *Olson v. Olson*, the law was about the relationship between marital and partnership property law. But the cultural issue in the case was about the problems of simultaneously accommodating the wishes of people to isolate business and personal liabilities while providing creditors with a "fair" probability of recovering debts. The confusing state of the Olson's financial affairs and their failure to follow the basic, formal rituals associated with operating their supposed partnership made it hard for those dealing with the Olsons to figure out if their business and personal economic lives were separate.

The Olsons easily could have handled part of the economy of their marriage with a partnership. They could, for example, have placed their debts but not Ruby's farm land in a limited partnership, and made the least wealthy spouse the general partner. If this worked, creditors of the partnership would have access to all of the partnership property and to Peter's assets, but not to Ruby's larger stash of wealth. Creditors of each of the Olsons as individuals would have had access to their individual property (including Ruby's farm), and to their interest in the partnership, but partnership creditors would not have had access to Ruby's farm. In this note, I am asking you to think some about both the moral propriety of such techniques of property structuring and the wisdom of such legal rules.

In *Zaist*, the law was about piercing the corporate veil as an exception to the general limited liability rule for corporations. As with *Olson v. Olson*, Olson could have set up his life to minimize his economic risks. Setting up and running his corporations with all the appropriate legal formalities, insuring that all inter-corporate transactions were economically sound, and guaranteeing that money was not transferred between legal entities without transactional support would have made it virtually impossible for Zaist to recover. So *Zaist*, like *Olson v. Olson*, raises issues about the tensions between a property world modeled on incentive structures in which access to information is crucial and one based on moral, ethical, or community expectations about paying obligations and dealing fairly with fellow human beings. The cases are about the problems associated with creating legal rules for reasons thought economically "good" by many, while knowing that these same rules will be used by the devious among us as shelters for ethically troubling, if not fraudulent, behavior.

I suspect a lot of your reactions to the outcomes in these two cases depended heavily upon who you thought should have the obligation to gather information about credit worthiness. Most of you probably agreed with the partnership (not necessarily the property and divorce) outcome in *Olson v. Olson* because their economic lives were an undifferentiated mess. But assuming that the Olsons actually operated their partnership with the proper formalities and then got into trouble, you might change your mind. We could then assume that creditors of their limited partnership should have known that Ruby Olson's private, non-business property would be sealed off from their collection efforts. If the Olsons used partnership stationery, filed partnership tax returns, kept separate books and otherwise held themselves out to the world as a business, then those dealing with them, if sophisticated, would probably be aware that there was a difference between the married and business lives of the Olsons. Peter Olson would have been aware that the mortgage was a partnership debt. And those dealing with the Olsons, you might argue, would or should know that if they needed more financial support than the partnership could provide in order to extend credit, they should seek Ruby's agreement to use her individually owned property as collateral.

In *Zaist*, despite the inability of Zaist to prove fraud, many of you surely sympathized with him. Given the messy way Olson operated his affairs, how was Zaist to know anything? If Zaist was a small operator, why can't he assume he is dealing with Olson rather than the multitude of corporations flitting around? Zaist might have been able to find out, but why impose that cost of operation on Zaist when Olson could have easily told him what was up? If Olson actually managed to convince Zaist that everything was hunky-dory when it wasn't, a version of the facts approaching if not reaching fraud, it would seem unfair to refuse Zaist relief because he didn't skeptically inquire into his "friend" Olson's financial dealings.

If, however, Olson operated a squeaky clean shop, contracting and billing would have been much better organized. Zaist would have had a very clear understanding about which entity he was dealing with and who was paying his bills. And if his written contract (assuming he had one) was clearly with East Haven and his bills were clearly paid by East Haven, but East Haven was under-capitalized and unbonded, then your sympathies may have switched more easily to Olson.

Though your sympathies might float around a bit depending on the facts, your final resolution of these cases may be quite different from those of your fellow students. Some of you may react to organizing multiple business organizations primarily as a legal trick to fool the uninitiated or helpless. You would rather restrict or eliminate the liability rules than permit them to be used by the more powerful against the less powerful. For those of you with less strongly framed feelings about such matters, there may be pangs of concern about the ease with which rules designed to protect important personal assets—like houses and cars—from the tribulations and uncertainties of the business world may be used as shelters for fraud and corruption. Others of you may have little sympathy for people losing money in the market. If you make a deal you always take a chance. Be careful or take your losses.

This range of responses mirrors approaches to a wide range of difficult and important legal questions. They are responses to concerns about the appropriate outer limits of market operation, the cultural meaning of risk, the cultural meaning of notice, the nature of information transfer about the value of assets and the meaning of legal words used to describe various ways of owning assets, and the role of the state in regulating human behavior for the benefit of the community. It is important to note that cases like these may be framed in any of these ways. What is seen as an investment risk by some is seen as taking advantage of naive parties by others. The trouble we let people get into is as much culturally defined as are the various definitions of property, notice, and risk at issue throughout this text. You may never have thought of the idea of risk or the meaning of notice as a cultural concept, but I hope you will now.

For more on the notion that the concepts of risk and notice vary over time and are culturally defined, read Carol Rose's fascinating article, *Possession as the Origin of Property*, 52 U. CHI. L. REV. 73 (1985), *excerpted in* RICHARD H. CHUSED, A PROPERTY ANTHOLOGY 9-15 (2d. ed. 1997).

CHAPTER **5**

ESTATES IN LAND, THE TIMING OF OWNERSHIP AND RACIAL CONDITIONS

§ 5.01 Introduction

To this point, the text has reviewed various ways groups of people may hold property—concurrent estates, marital estates, trusts, partnerships and corporations. In this and the next two chapters, the focus slightly shifts to an examination of the various ways any person or group may structure the time during which ownership interests are held. This chapter covers *estates in land*—the devices that may be used to split the time line of ownership between those holding present possessory rights and those eligible to take over possession in the future. During the late nineteenth and early twentieth centuries some of these estates in land, or timing devices, were used to control the contours of real estate development and maintain racial segregation. We will take a look at some of those cases in this chapter.

Chapter 6, relying upon your knowledge of both group ownership patterns and estates in land, describes the development of the modern residential real estate development and early attempts to channel their contours through zoning. Antecedents to contemporary condominium housing systems and land use planning appeared during the first decades of the twentieth century, the era when the United States emerged as a racially segregated, but highly urbanized and mobile, society. Not surprisingly, the arrival of zoning and land use planning, and the maturation of legal structures, such as covenants and equitable servitudes, allowing for the flexible governance of private, residential developments, occurred in an atmosphere strained with anxiety about race. Like this chapter's journey through estates in land, a full understanding of the history of residential development patterns requires that attention be paid to the relationships between law and the contours of segregation in the early part of the twentieth century.

Chapter 7 takes up a special form of timed possession—the lease. The shape of landlord-tenant law has changed dramatically in this century, beginning with the adoption of housing and building codes during the Progressive Era, and ending with wholesale changes in the operation of eviction courts in the 1960s and 1970s. That history unfolds in the last of these three chapters on estates in land.

This chapter begins the journey through property and its operation over time by reviewing estates in land. This survey in part is an inquiry into the relevance of Formalist or Classical methods of legal analysis in the contemporary world of property law. In prior sections of the text on married women's earnings statutes, pp. 167–171 above, and the development of the corporation as a legal "person," pp. 311–313 above, there was discussion of Formalism as it was embodied in political movements and modes of legal analysis prevalent in the later decades of the nineteenth and the early decades of the twentieth centuries. The political movement was built largely on laissez faire economic analysis, relying on contracts as the best way to guarantee personal independence. The freedoms to contract about and to sell property came to be seen as central features of liberty in many segments of society. Those favoring the emancipation of slaves viewed the right to contract for one's labor as a prerequisite to liberty. Entrepreneurs in large scale commercial enterprises claimed the right to make agreements and transfer property without government constraint. Part of this debate also involved a mode of legal analysis. For in freedom of contract theory the highest obligation of the state was to protect liberty by enforcing agreements. And the best way to enforce agreements was to allow the intentions of the parties as expressed in their private arrangements to govern behavior.

In this sort of environment, the meaning of texts split apart from their place in a social milieu took on primary importance. The goal was to discern the meaning of contracts from the words used by the parties rather than by reference to government policy or the needs of large segments of society. In such a world, rules of construction of documents took on great weight. And incentives arose for industries regularly using contracts to develop legal terms of art which took on meanings that could be repetitively used in related transactions. This sort of legal analysis, without regard to the now century old political moment in which it was popular, is of great moment in property law. Systems relying on title documents, descriptions of property boundary lines, and agreements about management of real estate developments need understandings about the meanings of certain words in order to function efficiently.

Paradoxes arise in both arms of Formalist or Classical Legal Thought—the political and the analytical. Encouraging freedom of contract about property may easily lead to contractual arrangements that inhibit the liberty of the next generation. Favoring the freedom of action of the living will have an impact on the autonomy of those who follow. Similarly, reliance on the "neutral" or "clear" meaning of words in texts, or upon common rules of construction, may produce results that seem bizarre or unfair. The desire for certainty will sometimes clash with a preference for fairness. Such problems form the theoretical background for this and the next two chapters.

For some readings about the impact of Formalist modes of analysis on property law, read Carol Rose, *Crystals and Mud in Property Law*, 40 STAN. L. REV. 577 (1988), *excerpted in* RICHARD H. CHUSED, A PROPERTY ANTHOLOGY 307-320 (2d ed. 1997), and Gregory Alexander, *The Dead Hand and the Law of Trusts in the Nineteenth Century*, 37 STAN. L. REV. 1189 (1985), excerpted at the end of this chapter.

§ 5.02 The Basics of Estates in Land

Estates in land may be grouped into two categories—present possessory interests and future interests. Present possessory interests include the fee simple absolute, the maximum interest any person or group may hold in property, various fee simple estates with limitations, life estates and leases. Fee simples in all their guises and life estates are taken up here. Lease law is saved for Chapter 7. Future interests include any holding in which the owner takes possession of the asset in the future. All of the common future interests are covered here.

[1] Present Possessory Estates

Real property has traditionally been described with a somewhat cryptic vocabulary. But the basic concepts are not that difficult. First, the maximum interest that can be held in a piece of land is a *fee simple absolute*. A fee simple absolute defines an interest held by a single person or group lasting forever.[1] The "lasting forever" is important. Even though a person owning a fee simple absolute will not live forever, the definition of the interest guarantees that a transfer of a fee simple operates to transfer complete title—eternal ownership—from one entity to another. If fee simple absolute ownership ended at some point, it would be impossible to transfer full ownership from one person or group to another.

All other estates in land are time variations on the fee simple absolute theme. Some describe a period of time shorter than eternity. A *life estate*, a right to use and receive income from property for life, is a good example. A lease is usually even shorter, allowing possession for a period of months, a year, or perhaps a period of years. Other estates leave open the possibility of eternal ownership, while creating some circumstances in which ownership of the eternal interest will switch to another. These sorts of interests are fee simples subject to some sort of condition or limitation. Still other property instruments split ownership and possession, leaving possession in one person now, as with a life estate, while creating a separate *future interest* in another having the right to take possession in the future. *Remainders* are an example of a future interest.[2] This segment of the chapter concentrates on the various present possessory interests. The next segment takes up future interests.

[a]   Life Estates

Many wills contain provisions giving an asset to someone, often a spouse, for life, and then passing it on to others, such as children. Such a grant might read as follows:

G (for Grantor) to my husband H for his life, then to my children surviving my husband.[3]

We will take up future interests like that in the surviving children a bit later. The life estate itself is pretty straightforward. In this example, H holds the possessory interest in the asset until he dies. That interest gives him the right to use the property or to take its income. In the case of an investment asset, such as a bond, H gets the interest but not the principal. If the asset is land, H gets to use the land or to take income from it in the form of crop payments or rent.

You can easily see that a timing problem might emerge. Suppose H rents the asset to Samantha for five years. What happens if H dies before the lease expires? Samantha's lease will end, since H can only transfer an interest in the asset for the period of his ownership. Similarly, what happens if H sells his life estate to Gregory. Gregory gets an interest that will last only for H's life. If Gregory gets an interest for his life and he outlives H, the right of the surviving children to take their future interest in the property would be disturbed. In this sort of setting, Gregory is said to have a *life estate pur autre vie*, or a life estate for the life of another.

[b]   Fee Simple Absolutes and Use of the Word "Heirs"

Before getting to some examples of limited fee simple interests, you need to understand the ways the word "heirs" may be used in title documents. Consider two grants:

---

[1] The entity that holds a fee simple may take on a variety of forms. Groups, businesses, couples and individuals may all fill the bill. The consequences of placing a fee simple in one or another entity were taken up in the prior three chapters.

[2] A transfer to A for life, then to B, for example, creates a life estate in A and a remainder in B.

[3] It is common for wills with this sort of provision to limit the remainder interest to surviving children. In general, parents are not interested in making a gift to a dead person. If there are grandchildren, the instrument usually contains additional provisions protecting their interests.

G to A and his heirs.

G to A for life, then to the heirs of A and their heirs.

The word "heirs" is used in two different ways in these grants. The first grant is "hornbook" language creating a fee simple absolute in A. The words "and his heirs" denote the period of time—eternity—that the land is to be held by A or A's successors. In this grant "heirs" does *not* refer to any people. A's heirs, that is those who would take his estate under intestate succession laws, get nothing unless he dies without a will while still owning the property. When "and his heirs" is used to describe a period of time or when any other language, such as "for life," is used to denote an interval of time, the words are called *words of limitation.* Although most careful instrument drafters use the "and his heirs" language when creating a fee simple absolute, the presumption is that a simple grant like "G to A" creates a fee simple absolute in A even though the words of limitation are not used.

In the second grant, the first use of "heirs" in the language "to the heirs of A," describes the class of takers of A's land designated by intestate succession statutes. This group of takers is not within A's control in a will, since he only holds a life estate. Thus, the words "for life" are words of limitation, but the words "heirs of A" are *words of purchase,* that is, words designating takers of property. The second use of "heirs" in the phrase "and their heirs" represents words of limitation, just like the first grant to "A and his heirs."

One other note about the word "heirs" is appropriate. As mentioned above, when the word is used as a word of purchase, the correct meaning refers to intestate successors. But the word appears in many property documents, sometimes without much concern over technical meanings. People, for example, may use "heirs" to describe children or relatives generally. In addition, "heirs" are thought of by lay persons as any party getting property from the estate of a deceased person, whether it be through intestate succession laws or under a will. Technically, a taker of real property under a will is a *devisee* and a taker of personal property under a will is a *legatee.* Any time "heirs" is used, care must therefore be taken to discern how the person drafting the instrument intended to use the word.

[c]   Fee Simple Determinable

A typical *fee simple determinable* is written as follows:

G to A and her heirs so long as the land is used for church purposes, and should the land ever be used other than for church purposes, then it reverts automatically to G and his heirs.

The words of limitation—words of time—in this grant are "and her heirs so long as the land is used for church purposes." This is not quite an absolute grant for eternity. It may last forever in real life, but it need not. G retains an interest, the possibility that the land will revert if it is not used for church purposes. Just as the life estate in A terminates automatically in a grant "to A for life, then to B and his heirs," so the grant to A in this example terminates automatically and the land returns to G or G's successors in interest when church use ceases. All interests retained by grantors in this and later examples are called *reversions.* This particular kind of reversion is called a *possibility of reverter.*

Fee simple determinables may also be written so that the land passes to a third party rather than G upon the happening of the relevant event. If, in the above example, the last phrase of the grant read "then automatically to B and his heirs," the grant to A would still be a fee simple determinable, but G holds no reversion. B's interest is called an *executory interest,* an interest which defeats a pre-existing *freehold estate* (life estate or fee simple) or *vested remainder*. The definition of vested remainder will have to wait until the next set of examples. Also note that executory interests are subject to the Rule against Perpetuities, discussed later in this chapter.[4]

[d] Fee Simple Subject to a Condition Subsequent

A typical fee simple subject to a condition subsequent reads as follows:

G to A and his heirs, but if the land is ever used other than for church purposes, then G and her heirs may re-enter and take possession.

In this example the estate in A terminates only upon the action of G or her successors. G retains a slightly different reversion from a fee simple determinable. This one is called a *right of re-entry*, the *discretionary* right to take back the property. From the language, A is given a fee simple absolute; the only words of limitation are "and his heirs." This fee simple, however, may be taken back if the stated event occurs. The distinction between a determinable fee and a fee subject to a condition resides in the difference between "so long as" and "but if." In the first case, the words of limitation defining A's interest never grant a full fee simple. In the second, the words of limitation grant a full fee simple, but enable G to regain it upon the happening of an event. The language of the determinable fee creates a time for its existence based upon a stated event by using language such as "so long as" or "until." Technically, an entire fee simple absolute is never conveyed, but only that part of a fee simple prior to the happening of the stated event. In a fee subject to a condition subsequent, the language conveys an entire fee simple, subject to defeat later upon the happening of a condition subsequent.

The difference between the two fees is largely semantic, but then much of estate law is largely semantic. Often the semantic difference makes no difference. If, for example, the party violating the condition imposed by either a fee simple determinable or a fee simple subject to a condition subsequent fails to vacate the premises, legal action will be necessary regardless of the sort of fee involved. But the semantic difference may sometimes have consequences. In the world of adverse possession, the statute of limitations will start to run against the holder of a possibility of reverter as soon as the condition imposed by the fee simple determinable is violated. But it may not start to run when the holder of a right of re-entry gains the right to oust the party in possession under a fee simple subject to a condition subsequent. Possession is not wrongful or adverse until the party in possession is notified that the right of re-entry will be exercised. Some also thought that the distinction between automatic happening and discretionary action was important in *Charlotte Park Recreation Commission v. Barringer*, the first case in this chapter. After reading the opinion, you should consider whether the difference between an *automatically* operating possibility of reverter and a *discretionary* right of re-entry is important to analysis of the state action issue in the case.

[e] Fee Simple Subject to an Executory Limitation

A typical fee simple subject to an executory limitation reads as follows:

G to A and her heirs, but if the land is ever used other than for church purposes, then to B and his heirs.

The practical effect of this fee is the same as a fee simple determinable with the property going to a third party upon the termination of the determinable fee. The difference, again, is largely

---

[4] You will discover that the executory interest used as an example above would be void under the standard Rule Against Perpetuities.

semantic. The recipient of a determinable fee never gets a full fee simple. The recipient of a fee subject to an executory limitation gets the fee, but that fee may go to a third party on the happening of a stated event. It is much like a fee subject to a condition subsequent. In both fees, A gets the full fee but may lose it. But in a fee on a condition subsequent, it is the grantor who *may* claim it, and in a fee subject to an executory limitation, a third party gains the fee automatically on the happening of the stated event. In the above example, B, who has an interest which defeats the continued existence of a fee simple in the hands of A, has an executory interest. Should the land ever be used other than for church purposes, B's executory interest would ripen into a full fee simple in possession,[5] and A would have nothing. Note well that with the happening of events, the nature of the interests held by various persons may change.

Perhaps this table will help you organize your thoughts about the possessory estates.

Chart of Standard Present Estates in Land[6]

G to:	Interest in A	Interest in B	Reversionary Interest
A for life.	Life Estate	None	Remainder
A so long as [cond.], then to G.	Fee Simple Determinable	None	Possibility of Reverter
A, but if [cond.] then G may re-enter.	Fee Simple Subject to a Condition Subsequent	None	Right of Re-entry
A, but if [cond.], then to B.	Fee Simple Subject to an Executory Limitation	Executory Interest	None

[2] Future Interests

[a] Indefeasibly Vested Remainder

A typical grant with an indefeasibly vested remainder reads as follows:

G to A for life, then to B and his heirs.

A, of course, has a life estate. B has a vested remainder which will go into possession upon the death of A. The phrase "indefeasibly vested" connotes that this remainder is *owned*, at the instant of its creation,[7] without any limitations expressed *in the language* of the grant. Only possession is delayed. B owns a "concept," the right to take possession in the future, which he can sell, devise or encumber. Another example of an indefeasibly vested remainder is:

G to A for life, then to B for life.

Even though B gets nothing *in possession* if he dies before A, he *presently owns*, without any limitation imposed *in the language* of the grant by G, the right to take possession upon the death

---

[5] As with executory interests following a fee simple determinable, the Rule Against Perpetuities may void them.

[6] All entries written as "to A" or "to B" mean the same thing as "to A and his/her heirs" or "to B and her/his heirs." The table has been written as if the presumption that the language "and his/her heirs" is unnecessary to create a fee interest is operating in all cases. [Cond.] means some condition of the grantor's choice is inserted at that spot.

[7] Though the estate in this example is a vested remainder at the instant the conveyance occurs, indefeasibly vested remainders may also arise at other moments. Later examples of contingent remainders present settings in which a future interest begins as one type, and becomes a vested remainder on the happening of an event.

of A. Remember that labeling future interests is largely a semantic exercise, not necessarily related to the realities of life. So the following instrument creates a life estate in A, an indefeasibly vested remainder for life in B, and an indefeasibly vested remainder in fee simple absolute in C:

G to A for life, then to B for life, then to C and her heirs.

[b] Vested Remainder Subject to Defeasance

A typical grant with a vested remainder subject to defeasance reads as follows:

G to A for life, then to B and her heirs, but if B dies before A then the property reverts to G and his heirs.

Read this grant very literally. First G gives B a vested remainder in fee simple with the use of the words of limitation "and her heirs." No pre-conditions are contained in the language of the grant on B's ability to own the right to future possession of the property. However, if B dies before A, then her remainder in fee simple returns to G or his successors. In non-artistic language, G has given everything after A's life estate to B with one hand, but taken it back (perhaps) with the other. Such interests are vested remainders (I giveth) subject to defeasance (and taketh away). Other examples of such an interest are:

G to A for life, then to B and his heirs, but if B sells alcohol on the land, to C and her heirs.

or

G to A for life, then to B and her heirs, provided that if B subdivides the land or destroys the solar energy devices presently in place on the land, then to the City of Madison.

Focus again on the word *vested*. It does not connote immediate possession. Nor does it connote that the taker of the interest will *always* gain possession in the future. It *does* connote a *present intention* on the part of the grantor to *immediately* bestow a *future* right to possession upon the taker. A vested remainder subject to defeasance indicates that the grantor had such a present intention to depart with a future interest in land, subject to subsequent conditions.

[c] Executory Interests

Return to the last two examples in the prior paragraph. Recall the fee simple subject to an executory limitation from the notes on present estates just above. That fee simple estate is linguistically similar to the vested remainder subject to defeasance. If the life estates are removed from the examples of vested remainders subject to defeasance just above in this note, you are left with fee simples subject to executory limitations. Both the fee simples and the vested remainders are completely disposed of, only to be taken back (perhaps). Such *divesting* of a prior estate or vested interest is accomplished by the subsequent estate, called an executory interest.

[d] Contingent Remainders

Look at this example:

G to my wife for her life, then, if our daughter graduates college before the death of my wife, to our daughter.

The language of this conveyance places a pre-condition upon the gift from G to his daughter. There is no present intention to immediately bestow a future right to possession. The interest taking effect at the death of G is a contingent remainder. If the daughter graduates college before the death of G's wife, then the pre-condition will be fulfilled and the daughter's interest will become an indefeasibly vested remainder.[8]

[e] Compare a Contingent Remainder with a Vested Remainder Subject to Defeasance

Compare:

G to A for life, then to B and her heirs, but if B dies before A, then to C and his heirs.

with

G to A for life, then if B survives A, to B and her heirs, but if B does not survive A, then to C and his heirs.

As a practical matter, these two interests are likely to accomplish the same purposes. As a legal matter, they are different. The first example creates a vested remainder subject to defeasance in B; the second creates a contingent remainder in B. The first exemplifies a present intention to bestow a future right to possession, subject to a possibility of loss. The second places a pre-condition on the receipt of the future right to possession.

[f] Alternate Contingent Remainder

Look again at the examples in the last note. What of the interests of C? In the first example, C's interest divests a prior vested remainder and is therefore an executory interest. In the second example, however, the interest of C does not divest a vested interest since B has a contingent remainder. If you took a stab in the dark and guessed that C also has a contingent remainder in this example, you were right. In legalese B and C have *alternate contingent remainders*. What happens in the second example if at the death of A, B and C are both alive? Then B's interest vests (and, incidentally, goes into possession as well) and C's disappears. What if, while A is alive, B dies? Then B's interest is defeated, and the precondition upon C's interest has been met. Thus, under these circumstances, C's interest vests (but not in possession because A is still alive). Continuing this same example, what happens if, after B dies before A and C, C dies before A? C's interest does not disappear! Since it has vested in C and C's successors (remember the significance of the words of limitation "and his heirs"), C's will or the intestate succession laws will designate the final takers.

---

[8] Note that if the daughter already has graduated college at the moment the conveyance occurs, then the pre-condition has been fulfilled and the daughter immediately gets an indefeasibly vested remainder.

The following chart may be helpful in assembling the future interest jigsaw puzzle.

Chart of Future Interests[9]

G to A for life, then:	Interest in B	Interest in C	Reversionary Interest in G
to B.	Indefeasibly Vested Remainder	None	None
to B, but if [cond.] then to C.	Vested Remainder Subject to Defeasance	Executory Interest	None
if [cond.] then to B.	Contingent Remainder	None	Yes
if [cond. #1] then to B, but if [cond. #2] then to C.	Alternate Contingent Remainder	Alternate Contingent Remainder	Perhaps

[3]   Estates in Land Problems

Label the property interests held by the various parties in the following grants under the circumstances given in each example. Assume that G is a grantor of some sort. The sign "→" means "transfers" or "conveys."

1. *G → to A.*

2. *In a Will: G → to A for life, then to B for life, then to C and her heirs.*

   a. Assume that at the death of G, A, B and C are all alive.

   b. Assume that at the death of G, A is alive, B is dead and C is alive.

   c. Assume that at the death of G, A is alive, B is alive and C is dead.

   d. Assume that at the death of G, A is alive, but B and C are both dead.

3. *In a Will: G → to A for life, then, if B survives A, to B for life, then to C and her heirs.*

   a. Assume that at the death of G, A, B and C are all alive.

   b. Assume that at the death of G, A is alive, B is dead and C is alive.

   c. Assume that at the death of G, A is alive, B is alive and C is dead.

   d. Assume that at the death of G, A is alive, but B and C are both dead.

4. *By Inter Vivos Deed: G → to A and his heirs so long as A does not marry B, but if A does marry B, then to C forever.*

   a. Assume that after the grant is conveyed, A marries B and C is alive.

   b. Assume that after the grant is conveyed, A marries B and C is dead.

   c. What happens to the labels when B dies before A?

---

[9] All entries written as "to B" or "to C" mean the same thing as "to B and his/her heirs" or "to C and her/his heirs." The table has been written as if the presumption that the language "and his/her heirs" is unnecessary to create a fee interest is operating in all cases. [Cond.] means some condition of the grantor's choice is inserted at that spot.

5. *By Inter Vivos Deed: G → to The Main Street First Religion Church for use as a place of worship, but if the land is ever used other than as a place of worship, then to My Favorite University School of Law.*

    a. Assume that the Church is a "living" institution using the land for church purposes.

    b. Assume that the Church sells the land to the Second Street Congregation of God which then uses the land and building as a place of worship.

    c. Assume that the Church sells the land to the Oriental Religion Center for use as a place of meditation and education about Oriental religions.

    d. Assume that the Church ceases to exist and the building is left vacant for a year.

6. *In a Will: G → to A for life, then to the children of A, but if A dies without children surviving A, then to B and her heirs.*

    a. Assume that A is alive, but childless, and that B is alive.

    b. Assume that A is alive, has one child, and that B is alive.

    c. Assume that A is alive, has two children, and that B is dead.

    d. Assume that A is dead, leaving two living children, and that B is alive.

7. *In a Will: G → to A for life, then to the children of A alive at the death of A, but if A dies without children surviving A, then to B and his heirs.*

    a. Assume that A is alive, but childless, and that B is alive.

    b. Assume that A is alive, has one child, and that B is alive.

    c. Assume that A is alive, has two children, and that B is dead.

    d. Assume that A is dead, leaving two living children, and that B is alive.

8. *In a Will: G → to A for life, then to the children of B forever, but if B dies without children surviving him, then to the children of C forever.*

    a. Assume that A is alive, that B is childless and that C is childless.

    b. Assume that A is alive, that B has one child and that C is childless.

    c. Assume that A is alive, that B has two children and that C has one child.

    d. Assume that A dies before B, that at the death of A, B has two children and C has three children, and that after A dies, B has a third child.

    e. Assume that at the death of A, B is alive but childless and that C has one child.

    f. Assume that at the death of A, B is dead with two surviving children and that C is alive with two children.

9. *By Inter Vivos Deed: G → to A for life, then to the children of A reaching the age of 25 and their heirs.*

    a. Assume that A is alive and has three children ages 4, 7 and 10.

    b. Assume that A is alive and that A is childless.

10. *In a Will: G → to T in trust, T to distribute the income produced by the property to my surviving children in equal shares, provided that, upon the death of any child after my death, the still surviving children shall equally divide the income share of the deceased child, and that*

upon the death of my last surviving child, the corpus of the trust shall be distributed by T as follows:

1/10 to My Favorite University;

2/10 to my grandchildren surviving all of my children;

3/10 to my great-grandchildren surviving all of my grandchildren; and

4/10 to the children of Uncle George and Aunt Susan.

Make up your own questions for this problem.

11. Here is a problem that reprises the law of gifts, covered in Chapter 3, and marital property, discussed in Chapter 2, and also raises interesting estate problems. At a 1973 engagement party for their son James and Carol Posnick, Mr. and Mrs. Singer announced that they were giving the couple "a home to live in as a wedding gift." The elder Singers then retitled the home so it was owned by them and their son. Ms. Posnick's name did not appear on the title. The couple's plans to wed were then canceled, but they continued to live together in the house for six years. In 1979 they married. The couple later split and a divorce decree first was entered in 1990. The family court was confronted with the task of deciding what marital or separate property interests, if any, were held in the house by James and Carol. Note that the date upon which any interest held by Carol began will have an influence on the ownership interest she will get upon divorce. Would you:

a. Conclude that Carol held no interest in the house because there could be no gift unless the marriage occurred within a reasonable time from the engagement party?

b. Conclude that, if Carol got a gift in 1973 that it was:

i. a fee simple interest, subject to the condition subsequent that the Singers could reclaim the house if the marriage did not occur shortly after the engagement party?

ii. a contingent interest (remainder or executory interest) subject to the precondition that marriage occur shortly after the engagement party?

iii. a vested interest (remainder or executory interest) subject to defeasance upon the failure to marry shortly after the engagement party?

iv. any of i, ii or iii without the limitation that marriage must occur shortly after the engagement party?

c. If you selected b.i., did the failure of the elder Singers to exercise their right to retake Carol's interest in the house mean that she had a fee simple interest (as a tenant in common) from the time of the engagement party? You can learn more about this problem from the saga of *Singer v. Singer*, 636 A.2d 422 (D.C. 1994); 623 A.2d 1226 (D.C. 1993); 583 A.2d 689 (D.C. 1990).

[4] Additional Reading on Estates in Land

For additional material on estates in land, read ROGER A. CUNNINGHAM, WILLIAM B. STOEBUCK & DALE A. WHITMAN, THE LAW OF PROPERTY 26-156 (2d. ed. 1993); JOHN E. CRIBBET & CORWIN W. JOHNSON, PRINCIPLES OF THE LAW OF PROPERTY 21-82 (3d ed. 1989).

§ 5.03 Estates in Land and Racial Conditions

[1] History of *Charlotte Park Recreation Commission v. Barringer*

In 1929, four parcels of land were joined to form Revolution Park in Charlotte, North Carolina. Two years before, three transfers of land were made with the expectation that the City of Charlotte would provide a fourth parcel to complete the park. On August 31, 1927, W. T. Shore and T. C. Wilson offered to convey one parcel as a gift, Osmond L. Barringer a second, and Abbott Realty Corporation a third, provided that the City of Charlotte would also contribute a neighboring piece of land for the park. In addition, the offered gifts from Shore, Wilson, Barringer and Abbott Realty were conditioned upon the Charlotte Park and Recreation Commission using the four parcels "for white people's parks and playgrounds, parkways and municipal golf courses only," beautifying and maintaining the parks at a cost of not less than $5,000 annually for at least eight years after the gifts were made, and providing for the construction of driveways. The offers to donate the land were accepted by the Park and Recreation Commission on February 18, 1929. The City of Charlotte adopted a conforming ordinance three days later.

The three parcels of land were then conveyed to the Park and Recreation Commission. Osmond Barringer and his wife conveyed their parcel on May 22, 1929. The *granting clause*[10] conveyed the land "upon the terms and conditions, and for the uses and purposes, as hereinafter fully set forth." The *habendum clause*[11] then recited the conditions described in the offer to donate the land, followed by this language:

In the event that the said lands comprising the said Revolution Park area as aforesaid, being all of the lands hereinbefore referred to, shall not be kept and maintained as a park, playground and/or recreational area, at an average expenditure of five thousand dollars ($5,000) per year, for the eight-year period as aforesaid, and/or in the event that the said lands and all of them shall not be kept, used and maintained for park, playground and/or recreational purposes, for use by the white race only, and if such disuse or non-maintenance continue for any period as long as one year, and/or should the party of the second part, or its successors, fail to construct or have constructed the roadway above referred to, within the time specified above, then and in either one or more of said event, the lands hereby conveyed shall revert in fee simple to the said Osmond L. Barringer, his heirs or assigns; provided, however, that before said lands, in any such event, shall revert to the said Osmond L. Barringer and as a condition precedent to the reversion of the said lands in any such event, the said Osmond L. Barringer, his heirs or assigns, shall pay unto the party of the second part or its successors the sum of thirty-five hundred dollars ($3,500).

On the same day that the Barringers conveyed their parcel, W. T. Shore and his wife, and T. C. Wilson and his wife, tendered a deed much like the Barringers'. The only difference was that the Shore-Wilson deed did not contain the last phrase in the habendum clause of the Barringer deed requiring the payment of $3,500 as a condition to a reversion of the land. Some time later, a controversy arose between the Park and Recreation Commission and Shore-Wilson. In settlement of litigation brought against the Commission, the heirs of Wilson were paid $2,400 and Shore was paid $3,600. In return Shore and the heirs of Wilson delivered *quit claim deeds*[12]

---

[10] This is a clause in a deed declaring that an interest in land is to be transferred.

[11] The habendum clause in a deed describes the nature of the estate in land to be taken by the grantee.

[12] A *quit claim deed* conveys whatever interest the grantor has. If the grantor has no interest in the land, then the deed conveys nothing. If the grantor owns the complete title in the land, then the deed conveys that interest. Such

to the Commission in which they "remised, released and forever quitclaimed" to the Commission "all rights of reversion, forfeiture, entry, re-entry, title, interest, equity and estate and all other rights of every nature, kind and character" in the land.

Abbott Realty also delivered a deed to the Park and Recreation Commission on May 29, 1929. This deed was similar to the Barringers' deed, containing the same list of conditions, including the racial restriction. However, the reverter portion of the habendum clause in the Abbott Realty deed contained neither a provision calling for a reversion of the land if it was used by non-whites, nor a requirement that Abbott pay the Commission money as a condition precedent to a reversion. The omission of the racial reversion created a somewhat strange deed—one containing a conveyance conditioned on use of the land by whites only without a provision for what should happen to the land if non-whites used it. Finally, the City of Charlotte conveyed the last of the four parcels to the Commission, also on May 29. The deed contained a racial restriction in both the granting and reversionary portions of the instrument. Charlotte's conveyance completed the assembly of land necessary for construction of the park.

When the park was ready for use, it contained a municipal swimming pool, public tennis courts, and the Bonnie Brae Golf Course. The golf course, placed entirely on land donated by Shore and Wilson and the City of Charlotte, was the only public course in Charlotte. In December, 1951, a group of black residents of Charlotte sought to use the golf course. On being denied entry they presented a petition to the Commission stating that they had been denied the right to use the golf course in violation of their Constitutional rights and demanding to be allowed to play the course. In response, the Commission filed a lawsuit against the black petitioners and all the grantors of lands making up the park, except Shore and Wilson, asking for a *declaratory judgment*[13] as to what would happen if black persons were allowed to use the golf course. Shore and Wilson were omitted from the case because their quit claim deeds left their chunk of the park fully in the hands of the Commission. Pending the outcome of the litigation, the Commission declined to alter its whites-only policy.

The trial court then came to the following conclusions of law in the case:

The deeds from Osmond L. Barringer, and wife, and from Abbott Realty Company vested in plaintiff a valid determinable fee with the possibility of reverter in and to the lands described in the deeds.

In the event any one of the reverter provisions in the Barringer deed or the Abbott Realty Company deed be violated, then and in such event title to the lands conveyed in said deeds will by operation of law immediately revert title in the grantors; and the admission of negroes on the Bonnie Brae Golf Course to play golf will cause the reverter provisions in said deeds immediately to become operative, and title to revert.

---

a deed provides a handy way of transferring an interest when you are not exactly sure what you have. Most real estate transactions use *warranty deeds*, in which specific interests are conveyed with guarantees made by the grantor that such interests are owned by the grantor and available for transfer.

[13] Most plaintiffs sue either for money or an injunction. Those forms of relief, however, do not always meet the needs of litigants. In the situation of the Park Commission, they were not interested in money or an injunction. They simply wanted to know the consequences that would follow from removal of the whites-only policy on the golf course. If they tested the racial restrictions by letting blacks on the course, they risked losing the land immediately because of the deed restrictions. Procedural situations like this surface often enough that most states and the federal government have adopted *declaratory judgment* statutes that permit plaintiffs with real disputes to seek a statement of their rights in the situation giving rise to the problem.

The deed from the city of Charlotte vested in plaintiff a valid determinable fee with the possibility of reverter. That the use of Bonnie Brae Golf Course by negroes as players would not cause a reversion of the property conveyed by the city of Charlotte to plaintiff, for that [sic] the reversionary clause in the city's deed is, under such circumstances, void as being in violation of the 14th amendment to the U.S. Constitution.

The plaintiff is the owner in fee, free of any conditions, reservations or reverter provisions of the lands conveyed to it by Shore and Wilson.

Revolution Park was created as an integral area of land, and to permit negroes to play golf on any part of said land will cause the reverter provisions in the Barringer and Abbott Realty Company deeds immediately to become effective and result in the title of plaintiff terminating and the lands reverting to Barringer and Abbott Realty Company.[14]

The black defendants appealed.

[2] Opinion of the North Carolina Supreme Court in *Charlotte Park and Recreation Commission v. Barringer*

Charlotte Park and Recreation Commission v. Barringer

North Carolina Supreme Court
242 N.C. 311, 88 S.E.2d 114 (1955)

PARKER, JUSTICE.

. . . .

We shall discuss first the Barringer Deed . . . . The first question presented is: Does the Barringer Deed create a fee determinable on special limitations, as decided by the Trial Judge?

This Court said in *Hall v. Turner*, 110 N.C. 292, 14 S.E. 791:

Whenever a fee is so qualified as to be made to determine, or liable to be defeated, upon the happening of some contingent event or act, the fee is said to be base, qualified or determinable.

An estate in fee simple determinable, sometimes referred to as a base or a qualified fee, is created by any limitation which, in an otherwise effective conveyance of land, creates an estate in fee simple and provides that the estate shall automatically expire upon the occurrence of a stated event . . . No set formula is necessary for the creation of the limitation, any words expressive of the grantor's intent that the estate shall terminate on the occurrence of the event being sufficient . . . . So, when land is granted for certain purposes, as for a schoolhouse, a church, a public building, or the like, and it is evidently the grantor's intention that it shall be used for such purposes only, and that, on the cessation of such use, the estate shall end, without any re-entry by the grantor, an estate of the kind now under consideration is created. It is necessary, it has been said, that the event named as terminating the estate be such that it may by possibility never happen at all, since it is an essential characteristic of a fee that it may possibly endure forever. Tiffany: *Law of Real Property*, 3rd Ed., Sec 220.

. . . .

---

[14] *See* Charlotte Park and Recreation Commission v. Barringer, 242 N.C. 311, 315-316, 88 S.E.2d 114, 119 (1955).

In *First Universalist Society of North Adams v. Boland*, 155 Mass. 171, 29 N.E. 524, 15 L.R.A. 231, "the grant of the plaintiff was to have and to hold, etc., 'so long as said real estate shall by said society or its assigns be devoted to the uses, interests, and support of those doctrines of the Christian religion' as specified; 'and when said real estate shall by said society or its assigns be diverted from the uses, interests, and support aforesaid to any other interests, uses, or purposes than as aforesaid, then the title of said society or its assigns in the same shall forever cease, and be forever vested in the following named persons, etc.' " The Supreme Court of Connecticut in *Connecticut Junior Republic Association v. Litchfield*, has quoted the language of this case holding that the grant creates "'a determinable or qualified fee.' " Immediately after the quoted words, the Massachusetts Court used this language:

> The grant was not upon a condition subsequent, and no re-entry would be necessary; but by the terms of the grant the estate was to continue so long as the real estate should be devoted to the specified uses, and when it should no longer be so devoted then the estate would cease and determine by its own limitation.

. . . .

In the Barringer Deed in the granting clause the land is conveyed to plaintiff "upon the terms and conditions, and for the uses and purposes, as hereinafter fully set forth." The *habendum* clause reads, "to have and to hold the aforesaid tract or parcel of land . . . upon the following terms and conditions, and for the following uses and purposes, and none other, to-wit . . . . The lands hereby conveyed, together with the other tracts of land above referred to (the Shore, Wilson and City of Charlotte lands) "as forming Revolution Park, shall be held, used and maintained by the party of the second part" (the plaintiff here), ". . . as an integral part of a park, playground and recreational area, to be known as Revolution Park and to be composed of the land hereby conveyed and of the other tracts of land referred to above, said park and/or recreational area to be kept and maintained for the use of, and to be used and enjoyed by persons of the white race only." The other terms and conditions as to the use and maintenance, etc., of the land conveyed are omitted as not material. The pertinent part of the reverter provision of the deed reads: "In the event that the said lands comprising the said Revolution Park area as aforesaid, being all of the lands hereinbefore referred to . . . and/or in the event that the said lands and all of them shall not be kept, used and maintained for park, playground and/or recreational purposes, for use by the white race only . . . then, and in either one or more of said events, the lands hereby conveyed shall revert in fee simple to the said Osmond L. Barringer, his heirs and assigns," provided, however, that before said lands shall revert to Barringer, and as a condition precedent to the reversion, Barringer, his heirs or assigns, shall pay unto plaintiff or its successors $3,500.

Barringer by clear and express words in his deed limited in the granting clause and in the *habendum* clause the estate granted, and in express language provided for a reverter of the estate granted by him, to him or his heirs, in the event of a breach of the expressed limitations. It seems plain that his intention, as expressed in his deed, was that plaintiff should have the land as long as it was not used in breach of the limitations of the grant, and, if such limitations, or any of them, were broken, the estate should automatically revert to the grantor by virtue of the limitations of the deed. In our opinion, Barringer conveyed to plaintiff a fee determinable upon special limitations.

It is a distinct characteristic of a fee determinable upon limitation that the estate automatically reverts at once on the occurrence of the event by which it is limited, by virtue of the limitation in the written instrument creating such fee, and the entire fee automatically ceases and determines by its own limitations . . . .

No action on the part of the creator of the estate is required, in such event, to terminate the estate . . . .

According to the deed of gift "Osmond L. Barringer, his heirs and assigns" have a possibility of reverter in the determinable fee he conveyed to plaintiff. It has been held that such possibility of reverter is not void for remoteness, and does not violate the rule against perpetuities. 19 Am. Jur., Estates, Section 31; Tiffany: *Law of Real Property*, 3rd Ed., Section 314.

The land was Barringer's, and no rights of creditors being involved, and the gift not being induced by fraud or undue influence, he had the right to give it away if he chose, and to convey to plaintiff by deed a fee determinable upon valid limitations, and by such limitations provide that his bounty shall be enjoyed only by those whom he intended to enjoy it.

. . . .

We know of no law that prohibits a white man from conveying a fee determinable upon the limitation that it shall not be used by members of any race except his own, nor of any law that prohibits a negro from conveying a fee determinable upon the limitation that it shall not be used by members of any race, except his own.

If negroes use the Bonnie Brae Golf Course, the determinable fee conveyed to plaintiff by Barringer, and his wife, automatically will cease and terminate by its own limitation expressed in the deed, and the estate granted automatically will revert to Barringer, by virtue of the limitation in the deed, provided he complies with the condition precedent by paying to plaintiff $3,500, as provided in the deed. The operation of this reversion provision is not by any judicial enforcement by the State Courts of North Carolina, and *Shelley v. Kraemer*, 334 U.S. 1, has no application. We do not see how any rights of appellants under the 14th Amendment to the U.S. Constitution, Section 1, or any rights secured to them by Title 42 U.S.C.A. §§ 1981, 1983, are violated.

If negroes use Bonnie Brae Golf Course, to hold that the fee does not revert back to Barringer by virtue of the limitation in the deed would be to deprive him of his property without adequate compensation and due process in violation of the rights guaranteed to him by the 5th Amendment to the U.S. Constitution and by Art. 1, Sec. 17 of the N.C. Constitution, and to rewrite his deed by judicial fiat.

. . . .

Now as to the Abbott Realty Company deed. This deed conveyed as a gift certain lands to plaintiff upon the same terms and conditions, and for the same uses and purposes, and for the white race only, as set forth in the Barringer deed. This deed contains a reverter provision, if there is a violation of certain limitations of the estate conveyed, but the reverter provision does not provide that, if the lands of Revolution Park are used by members of a nonwhite race, the lands conveyed by Abbott Realty Company to plaintiff shall revert to the grantor. In our opinion, the estate conveyed by Abbott Realty Company to plaintiff is a fee determinable upon certain expressed limitations set forth in the deed, with a possibility of reverter to Abbott Realty Company if the limitations expressed in the deed are violated and the reverter provision states that such violations will cause a reverter. That was the conclusion of law of the Trial Judge, and the appellants' assignment of error No. 2 thereto is overruled. However, the reverter provision does not require a reverter to Abbott Realty Company, if the lands of Revolution Park are used by negroes. Therefore, if negroes use Bonnie Brae Golf Course, title to the lands conveyed by Abbott Realty Company to plaintiff will not revert to the grantor.

The Trial Judge concluded as a matter of law that if any of the reverter provisions in the Abbott Realty Company deed were violated, title would revert to Abbott Realty Company, and that if negroes use Bonnie Brae Golf Course, title to the land granted by Abbott Realty Company will revert to it. The appellants' assignments of error Nos. 5 and 6 are to this conclusion of law. These assignments of error are sustained to this part of the conclusion, that if negroes use Bonnie Brae Golf Course, title to the land will revert to Abbott Realty Company: and as to the other part of the conclusion the assignments of error are overruled.

The appellants' assignment of error No. 7 is to this conclusion of law of the Trial Judge, that the deed from the city of Charlotte to plaintiff created a valid determinable fee with the possibility of a reverter, and that as the city of Charlotte has only one municipal golf course, the use of Bonnie Brae Golf Course by negroes will not cause a reversion of title to the property conveyed by the city of Charlotte to plaintiff, for that said reversionary clause in said deed is, under such circumstances void as being in violation of the 14th Amendment to the U. S. Constitution.

From this conclusion of law the city of Charlotte and the plaintiff did not appeal. We do not see in what way appellants have been aggrieved by this conclusion of law, and their assignment of error thereto is overruled.

The appellants also include as part of their assignments of error Nos. 3, 4, 5 and 6 these conclusions of law of the Trial Judge numbered 7 and 8. No. 7, that the plaintiff is the owner in fee simple, free of any conditions, reservations or reverter provisions of the property which was conveyed to it by W. T. Shore and T. C. Wilson. The city of Charlotte has not appealed from this conclusion of law, and we are unable to see how appellants have been harmed, so their assignments of error thereto are overruled. No. 8, that Revolution Park, in which is located Bonnie Brae Golf Course, was created as an integral area of land, comprising the various contiguous tracts conveyed to plaintiff by Barringer, Abbott Realty Company, city of Charlotte, Shore and Wilson, and to permit negroes to use for golf any part of said land will cause the reverter provisions in the Barringer and Abbott Realty Company deeds immediately to become effective, and result in title of the plaintiff terminating, and the property reverting to Barringer and Abbott Realty Company. As to this conclusion of law the assignments of error are sustained as to that part which states that, if negroes use Bonnie Brae Golf Course, the reverter provision in the Abbott Realty Company deed will become effective and title will revert to Abbott Realty Company: as to the other parts the assignments of error are overruled.

Judgment will be entered below in accordance with this opinion.

Modified and affirmed.

[3] Notes on *Charlotte Park and Recreation Commission v. Barringer*

[a] Denouement

Revolution Park still exists and is operated as an integrated park. The Barringers never sought to enforce the restriction as to their segment of the park. By the time the litigation was concluded, Mr. Barringer was an old man in some need of funds. After the North Carolina Supreme Court decision, the Park Commission purchased the Barringer reversion for $18,000.[15]

---

[15] Telephone Interview, July 2, 1986, with Mr. Joe Grier, Jr., an attorney in Charlotte, N.C., who was on the Park Commission at the time of the litigation.

[b] Statement of the Problem in the *Charlotte Park* Case

The *Barringer* court wrote that the operation of the reversion provision in the Barringer deed "is not by any judicial enforcement by the State Courts of North Carolina, and *Shelley v. Kraemer*, 334 U.S. 1, has no application. We do not see how any rights of appellants under the 14th Amendment to the U.S. Constitution, Section 1, or any rights secured to them by Title 42 U.S.C.A. §§ 1981, 1983, are violated." *Shelley v. Kraemer*, a case you will read in the next chapter, involved the enforceability of clauses in deeds for residential property barring sale of the property to blacks or other minority purchasers. The *Shelley* Court noted that the racial covenants in the deeds were directed toward a "designated class of persons," and that the plaintiffs had available to them the "full coercive power of government" to forestall the performance of a deal between willing buyers and sellers. As a result, the Court concluded, enforcement of the racial covenants by a state court violated the Fourteenth Amendment provisions barring a state from violating the Equal Protection of the laws. The *Charlotte Park* restrictions were also directed toward a designated class. But there were at least two differences between this situation and *Shelley*. First, the impact of enforcing the restrictions was to close the park, a result which would have affected people of all races in Charlotte. Second, there was an argument available in *Charlotte Park* that the termination of the park would occur automatically. If the Barringer grant created a fee simple determinable, then, the argument went, use of state power was not required to enforce the racial restriction. These notes are designed to help you understand this argument.

[c] Two Examples of Fee Simple Estates in Operation

Before returning to the *Charlotte Park* case, study two other cases to see how the various fee simple estates may operate. In *Storke v. Penn Mutual Life Insurance Company*, 390 Ill. 619, 61 N.E.2d 552 (1945), land in Chicago was sold by Storke via a deed containing the following language:

> [To X and his heirs, party of the second part] . . . [T]he party of the second part his heirs and assigns hereby covenant and agree that no saloon shall be kept and no intoxicating liquors be sold or permitted to be sold on said premises herein conveyed or in any building erected upon said premises; and that in case of breach in these covenants or any of them said premises shall immediately revert to the grantors, and the said party of the second part shall forfeit all right, title and interest in and to said premises.

What kind of interest was transferred here—a fee simple absolute subject to a covenant, a fee simple determinable, or a fee simple subject to a condition subsequent? A covenant, which you will study in the next chapter, is a contractual undertaking which is also enforceable against persons purchasing the land from the original buyer. The court held that the language was ambiguous. If it was meant to create a fee simple determinable, the court held, it failed since automatic forfeitures are disfavored; determinable fees will not be said to exist unless the intention to create them is clear. If it was meant to create a fee simple subject to a condition subsequent, it also failed. As with the Abbott Realty deed in *Charlotte Park*, a right of re-entry was not expressly reserved. Finally, if it was meant to create a fee simple absolute subject to a covenant, as in *Shelley*, the covenant failed because the 40-acre neighborhood subject to deeds like this one was full of liquor establishments by the time of this litigation. The change in neighborhood circumstances supported an equitable decision to deny enforcement.[16]

---

[16] This result follows the general rule that covenants will not be enforced when the purposes for their creation may no longer be served. *See* Ginsberg v. Yeshiva of Far Rockaway, p. 465 below.

This opinion is a good example of the hostility courts sometimes show to all sorts of limitations on fee simple absolutes. Fee simple absolutes are preferred because they often are easier to transfer than conditioned fees. Among the conditioned fees, those subject to a condition subsequent are favored because they leave open the option in the grantor to waive enforcement. In this particular case, the long-term failure of anyone to seek enforcement of the restriction in the deeds was the crucial factor in the outcome. Even if you think the language created one or another sort of restriction on the fee, it is still understandable why the court was reluctant to enforce it.

Compare *Storke* with *Babb v. Rand*, 345 A.2d 496 (Me. 1975). The *Babb* court construed the following language as a fee simple subject to a condition subsequent:

That the share of the Estate of Henry Rand of the Town of Southport, Lincoln County, State of Maine, shall be left to John Freeman Rand in fee simple with the proviso that he shall never deny access or occupation to the several heirs hereinafter named during their lifetime.

The next paragraph in the will, apparently drafted without the aid of an attorney, named the five children and stepchildren of the deceased. The court had several options in construing this will. First, it could have given the named heirs life estates. But the instrument does use the magic words "fee simple," making it very difficult to adopt that choice. Second, it could have given one or another limited fee simple. This route was adopted by the court, which concluded that the testator created a fee simple subject to a condition subsequent. Finally, the court could have given Rand a fee simple absolute, as in *Storke*, because no reversionary interest was clearly delineated in the will. The court probably decided to enforce the interests of the named heirs because the will was drafted by a lay person and the intentions were pretty clear. In addition, there was no evident unfairness that would surface if the restriction was enforced. Remember that in *Storke* all sorts of inequities might have surfaced if the restrictions were suddenly reinvigorated.

These two cases make clear that *rules of construction*, or routinized judicial statements describing how an instrument should be construed, are not always rigidly applied. Various rules of construction may be called upon, depending on the circumstances. While hostility to restricted fees in unfair factual settings led to a narrow construction of the language in the *Storke* case, the opposite occurred in *Babb*. Lack of a clearly stated reversion will not always lead a court to haul out a rule of construction ignoring a restriction imposed on a fee simple in a document of conveyance.

[d]   Back to the *Charlotte Park* Case

The trial court construed the various deeds setting up Revolution Park as interrelated; if one reversionary interest was activated then all the land reverted. Even though the golf course was entirely on the Shore-Wilson and City segments, the court concluded that its use by blacks would cause the Barringer and Abbott reversions to operate. But, by the time the case got to court, only half of the park was really involved. The Shore-Wilson segment was long since owned in fee simple absolute by the Park Commission because of the settlement of prior litigation. The City of Charlotte segment was viewed by all sides as subject to the commands of the Fourteenth Amendment. Since an agency of the state owned the land, the enforcement of a racial restriction fulfilled the state action requirement and violated the Equal Protection clause. In addition, the state supreme court said that the lack of a racial reversion in the Abbott Realty deed meant that segment was in effect not restricted. The Park and Recreation Commission effectively held a fee simple absolute. The effect of all these holdings was that only the Barringer segment had an active racial restriction, and that only the Barringer segment would revert if blacks used *any* portion of the park.

Now, recall from the first note in this series the argument that the activation of the racial restriction in *Charlotte Park* occurred automatically, and that the state action required to find a violation of the Fourteenth Amendment was missing. From the notes and problems before the *Charlotte Park* case, you should understand that if the grant in the Barringer deed was a fee simple determinable, then the possibility of reverter would be triggered automatically. This was the conclusion the court ultimately reached. But was that conclusion justified? Answering that question is the main topic for the Problem Notes that follow.

[4]   Problem Notes

[a]   Did the Barringer Deed Create a Fee Simple Determinable?

Note that before Barringer or Barringer's successors could regain the land, they had to pay $3,500 to the Park Commission. This payment was presumably discretionary. If they made it, they got the land; if they didn't, ownership was left unchanged. Doesn't that mean the interest was really a fee simple subject to a condition subsequent?

[b]   State Action and the Fee Simple on a Condition Subsequent

Assume that the interest created by the Barringer deed was really a fee simple subject to a condition subsequent. Does that *really* make any difference in the outcome of the case? If a determinable fee does not trigger state action, why should a fee on a condition subsequent? Does the state need to undertake any action to activate the right of reentry in a fee simple subject to a condition subsequent situation? Does the fact that the case exists mean that state intervention is necessary regardless of the nature of the fee simple at issue? Is it fair to conclude that the court's dismissal of *Shelley v. Kraemer* in a single sentence was erroneous? If there be a trend in the cases, it seems to be that a fee simple subject to a condition subsequent implicates the Fourteenth Amendment, while a fee simple determinable does not. *See* Jonathan L. Entin, *Defeasible Fees, State Action and the Legacy of Massive Resistance,* 34 WM. & MARY L. REV. 769 (1993).

[5]   History of *Evans v. Abney*: Future Interests and Racial Conditions

Augustus O. Bacon died on February 14, 1914, leaving his home and estate, "Baconsfield," to the City of Macon as a park. Bacon was, to say the least, a very well known figure in Macon. After practicing law in Atlanta, and serving as a captain in the Confederate Army, Bacon married Virginia Lamar, moved to Macon, and developed a large legal practice. In 1870 he was elected to the Georgia House of Representatives, in which he served for 14 years. After a failed campaign for Governor, Bacon joined the United States Senate in 1894, where he served until his death.[17]

Bacon's will was quite complex, creating a number of trusts for various members of his family.[18] Item Nine of the will provided that Baconsfield be given in trust to named trustees for the benefit of his wife and two daughters, Mary Louise Bacon Sparks and Augusta Lamar Bacon Curry, for their joint use during their lives. The will then provided:

---

[17] 1 DICTIONARY OF AMERICAN BIOGRAPHY 473-474 (A. Johnson ed., 1964).

[18] The will was the subject of other litigation besides that over Baconsfield. In Curry v. Crump, 192 F.2d 279 (5th Cir. 1951), one of his grandchildren litigated an aspect of one of the family trusts.

When my wife, Virginia Lamar Bacon, and my two daughters, Mary Louise Bacon Sparks and Augusta Lamar Bacon Curry, shall all have departed this life, and immediately upon the death of the last survivor of them, it is my will that all right, title and interest in and to said property hereinbefore described and bounded, both legal and equitable, including all remainders and reversions and every estate in the same of whatsoever kind, shall thereupon vest in and belong to the Mayor and Council of the City of Macon, and to their successors forever, in trust for the sole, perpetual and unending, use, benefit and enjoyment of the white women, white girls, white boys and white children of the City of Macon to be by them forever used and enjoyed as a park and pleasure ground, subject to the restrictions, government, management, rules and control [of a Board of Managers of seven white persons, at least four of whom must be women.]

In addition, the will had a *residuary clause* [19] designating the takers of all of his property not otherwise disposed of by the will. These takers were Bacon's grandchildren, the four children of Mary Louise Bacon Sparks—A. O. B. Sparks, Willis B. Sparks, Jr., M. Garten Sparks, and Virginia Lamar Sparks—and the three children of Augusta Lamar Bacon Curry—Louise Curry Williams, Shirley Curry Cheatam, and Manley Lamar Curry. At the time litigation over Baconsfield began, the interests of the Curry grandchildren were held in trust; the Sparks grandchildren had charge of their shares of their grandfather's estate.

After Bacon died in 1914, the park was not immediately developed. The old farm was left largely wild. By 1931, his former home was being used, in accordance with Bacon's will, by several women's clubs for meetings, receptions, luncheons and dances. A wading pool was dedicated in 1931. During the depression, in part with federal funding from the Works Progress Administration, thousands of trees, flowering shrubs and flowers were planted and a women's clubhouse was constructed. A swimming pool and a zoo were constructed in the 1940s. [20]

By the early 1960s desegregation of public facilities was in full swing and black persons had begun to use Baconsfield. In response, Charles E. Newton and the other members of the Board of Managers of the park filed an action in May, 1963, against the residuary takers under Bacon's will and the City of Macon as trustee of the park. They alleged that the City was failing to obey the racial restrictions in Bacon's will and asked that new trustees be named to manage the park. The City of Macon's answer to the complaint asserted that as a public entity it could not enforce segregation in the park and asked that the court inform it of its obligations in the circumstances. [21] The residuary takers admitted the allegations of the complaint, asked that the City be removed as trustee, and argued that if the city was removed as trustee, the park property reverted to them!

Then things got really interesting. Reverend E. S. Evans and other black residents of Macon asked to intervene in the case, [22] arguing that the court could not consistently with the United

---

[19] This clause appears in virtually every will. It is frequently the most important clause, but its main function is to name the takers of all the property of the estate that is not specifically disposed of. Its function to get rid of all that is left suggests it is the "garbage" clause of will writers.

[20] Many details of the park's history and demise may be found in Mary Anne Berg Richardson, *Baconsfield Park: Macon's Lost Treasure*, MACON MAGAZINE 24 (July-Aug., 1990).

[21] This is a fairly common tactic for a trustee who does not know exactly what to do. Rather than take the chance of having to repay the trust for any damages occasioned by making an erroneous judgment, a trustee may file a petition seeking instructions from a court on how to behave. In *Evans*, the trustee was responding to a complaint filed by another party, but the idea is the same.

[22] Intervention is a procedural device permitting those claiming an interest in litigation to join a case filed by others. *See, e.g.,* FED. R. CIV. P. 24.

States Constitution appoint a private trustee in order to maintain Baconsfield as a segregated park and asking that the court reform the will of Bacon so as to permit the park to be integrated.[23] The City of Macon then resigned as trustee, and amended its pleadings by asking the court to accept its resignation and appoint new trustees. On March 10, 1964, the trial judge entered an order granting the black residents of Macon the right to intervene, but accepting the resignation of Macon as trustee, and appointing three private parties, Hugh Comer, Lawton Miller and B. L. Register, as the new trustees.

Reverend Evans and his black colleagues appealed, but the Georgia Supreme Court affirmed the trial judge.[24] The United States Supreme Court then agreed to review the case. In *Evans v. Newton*[25] the Court ruled that the appointment of private trustees could not magically transform the park from a state to a private entity and thereby avoid the constraints of the Fourteenth Amendment, and that the new trustees could not operate the facility in a segregated fashion. Signs of future difficulties abounded in the Court opinions. Justices Black, Harlan and Stewart dissented, arguing that private trustees were not controlled by the Constitution and could do as they pleased with the park. Justice White concurred on the narrow ground that the Georgia statute enabling Bacon to create a charitable trust for a segregated facility[26] created sufficient public involvement to fulfill state action requirements, and that the appointment of private trustees was therefore an unacceptable charade to avoid the Constitutional mandate to integrate public facilities. And Justice Douglas' opinion for a majority of only five said nothing about what would happen if the state chose to close the park if it could not be operated under the terms of Bacon's will.

The case then went back to the Georgia courts. The Georgia Supreme Court declared that integration of the park meant that the main purpose for the Bacon trust had failed, and remanded the case to the trial court for a determination as to whether the trust should be reformed or the assets of the estate given over to the residuary takers.[27] The trial court declined to reform the trust under the *cy pres* rules, and ordered the trust assets distributed to Guyton Abney and the other trustees of the three Curry grandchildren and to the four Sparks grandchildren. The Currys each took a 1/16 interest as beneficiaries of a trust and the Sparks each took a 1/8 interest. That result was also affirmed on appeal,[28] and the case went back to the Supreme Court a second time.

---

[23] Such reformation under the *cy pres* rules is discussed in the notes after the United States Supreme Court opinions in *Evans v. Abney.*

[24] Evans v. Newton, 220 Ga. 280, 138 S.E.2d 573 (1964).

[25] 382 U.S. 296 (1966).

[26] At the time of the litigation, GA. CODE ANN. §§ 69-504 and 69-505 provided for gifts to municipalities with racial restrictions and authorized municipalities to accept the gifts.

[27] Evans v. Newton, 221 Ga. 870, 148 S.E.2d 329 (1966).

[28] Evans v. Abney, 224 Ga. 826, 165 S.E.2d 160 (1968).

[6]   United States Supreme Court Opinions in *Evans v. Abney*

Evans v. Abney

United States Supreme Court
396 U.S. 435, 90 S. Ct. 628, 24 L. Ed. 2d 634 (1970)

Mr. Justice Black delivered the opinion of the Court.

Once again this Court must consider the constitutional implications of the 1911 will of United States Senator A. O. Bacon of Georgia which conveyed property in trust to Senator Bacon's home city of Macon for the creation of a public park for the exclusive use of the white people of that city. As a result of our earlier decision in this case which held that the park, Baconsfield, could not continue to be operated on a racially discriminatory basis, *Evans v. Newton*, 382 U.S. 296 (1966), the Supreme Court of Georgia ruled that Senator Bacon's intention to provide a park for whites only had become impossible to fulfill and that accordingly the trust had failed and the parkland and other trust property had reverted by operation of Georgia law to the heirs of the Senator. Petitioners, the same Negro citizens of Macon who have sought in the courts to integrate the park, contend that this termination of the trust violates their rights to equal protection and due process under the Fourteenth Amendment. We granted certiorari because of the importance of the questions involved. For the reasons to be stated, we are of the opinion that the judgment of the Supreme Court of Georgia should be, and it is, affirmed.

. . . .

We are of the opinion that in ruling as they did the Georgia courts did no more than apply well-settled general principles of Georgia law to determine the meaning and effect of a Georgia will. At the time Senator Bacon made his will Georgia cities and towns were, and they still are, authorized to accept devises of property for the establishment and preservation of "parks and pleasure grounds" and to hold the property thus received in charitable trust for the exclusive benefit of the class of persons named by the testator. Ga. Code Ann., c. 69-5 (1967); Ga. Code Ann. §§ 108-203, 108-207 (1959). These provisions of the Georgia Code explicitly authorized the testator to include, if he should choose, racial restrictions such as those found in Senator Bacon's will. The city accepted the trust with these restrictions in it. When this Court in *Evans v. Newton* held that the continued operation of Baconsfield as a segregated park was unconstitutional, the particular purpose of the Baconsfield trust as stated in the will failed under Georgia law. The question then properly before the Georgia Supreme Court was whether as a matter of state law the doctrine of *cy pres* should be applied to prevent the trust itself from failing. Petitioners urged that the *cy pres* doctrine allowed the Georgia courts to strike the racially restrictive clauses in Bacon's will so that the terms of the trust could be fulfilled without violating the Constitution.

The Georgia *cy pres* statutes upon which petitioners relied provide:

When a valid charitable bequest is incapable for some reason of execution in the exact manner provided by the testator, donor, or founder, a court of equity will carry it into effect in such a way as will as nearly as possible effectuate his intention.

Ga. Code Ann. § 108-202 (1959).

A devise or bequest to a charitable use will be sustained and carried out in this State; and in all cases where there is a general intention manifested by the testator to effect a certain purpose, and the particular mode in which he directs it to be done shall fail from any cause, a court of chancery may, by approximation, effectuate the purpose in a manner most similar to that indicated by the testator.

Ga. Code Ann. § 113-815 (1959). The Georgia courts have held that the fundamental purpose of these *cy pres* provisions is to allow the court to carry out the general charitable intent of the testator where this intent might otherwise be thwarted by the impossibility of the particular plan or scheme provided by the testator. But this underlying logic of the *cy pres* doctrine implies that there is a certain class of cases in which the doctrine cannot be applied. Professor Scott in his treatise on trusts states this limitation on the doctrine of *cy pres* which is common to many States as follows:

> It is not true that a charitable trust never fails where it is impossible to carry out the particular purpose of the testator. In some cases . . . it appears that the accomplishment of the particular purpose and only that purpose was desired by the testator and that he had no more general charitable intent and that he would presumably have preferred to have the whole trust fail if the particular purpose is impossible of accomplishment. In such a case the cy pres doctrine is not applicable.

4 A. Scott, *The Law of Trusts* § 399, p. 3085 (3d ed. 1967).

In this case, Senator Bacon provided an unusual amount of information in his will from which the Georgia courts could determine the limits of his charitable purpose. Immediately after specifying that the park should be for "the sole, perpetual and unending, use, benefit and enjoyment of the white women, white girls, white boys and white children of the City of Macon," the Senator stated that "the said property under no circumstances . . . (is) to be . . . at any time for any reason devoted to any other purpose or use excepting so far as herein specifically authorized." And the Senator continued:

> I take occasion to say that in limiting the use and enjoyment of this property perpetually to white people, I am not influenced by any unkindness of feeling or want of consideration for the Negroes, or colored people. On the contrary I have for them the kindest feeling, and for many of them esteem and regard, while for some of them I have sincere personal affection.

> I am, however, without hesitation in the opinion that in their social relations the two races . . . should be forever separate and that they should not have pleasure or recreation grounds to be used or enjoyed, together and in common.

The Georgia courts, construing Senator Bacon's will as a whole, concluded from this and other language in the will that the Senator's charitable intent was not "general" but extended only to the establishment of a segregated park for the benefit of white people. The Georgia trial court found that "Senator Bacon could not have used language more clearly indicating his intent that the benefits of Baconsfield should be extended to white persons only, or more clearly indicating that this limitation was an essential and indispensable part of his plan for Baconsfield." . . . The Baconsfield trust was therefore held to have failed, and, under Georgia law, "[w]here a trust is expressly created, but [its] uses . . . fail from any cause, a resulting trust is implied for the benefit of the grantor, or testator, or his heirs." Ga. Code Ann. § 108-106(4) (1959).[2] The Georgia

---

[2] Although Senator Bacon's will did not contain an express provision granting a reverter to any party should the trust fail, § 108-106(4) of the Georgia Code quoted in the text makes such an omission irrelevant under state law. At one point in the Senator's will he did grant "all remainders and reversions" to the city of Macon, but the Supreme Court of Georgia showed in its opinion that this language did not relate in any way to what should happen upon a failure of the trust but was relevant only to the initial vesting of the property in the city. The Georgia court said:

courts concluded, in effect, that Senator Bacon would have rather had the whole trust fail than have Baconsfield integrated.

When a city park is destroyed because the Constitution requires it to be integrated, there is reason for everyone to be disheartened. We agree with petitioners that in such a case it is not enough to find that the state court's result was reached through the application of established principles of state law. No state law or act can prevail in the face of contrary federal law, and the federal courts must search out the fact and truth of any proceeding or transaction to determine if the Constitution has been violated. Here, however, the action of the Georgia Supreme Court declaring the Baconsfield trust terminated presents no violation of constitutionally protected rights, and any harshness that may have resulted from the state court's decision can be attributed solely to its intention to effectuate as nearly as possible the explicit terms of Senator Bacon's will.

Petitioners first argue that the action of the Georgia court violates the United States Constitution in that it imposes a drastic "penalty," the "forfeiture" of the park, merely because of the city's compliance with the constitutional mandate expressed by this Court in *Evans v. Newton*. Of course, *Evans v. Newton* did not speak to the problem of whether Baconsfield should or could continue to operate as a park; it held only that its continued operation as a park had to be without racial discrimination. But petitioners now want to extend that holding to forbid the Georgia courts from closing Baconsfield on the ground that such a closing would penalize the city and its citizens for complying with the Constitution. We think, however, that the will of Senator Bacon and Georgia law provide all the justification necessary for imposing such a "penalty." The construction of wills is essentially a state-law question, *Lyeth v. Hoey*, 305 U.S. 188 (1938), and in this case the Georgia Supreme Court, as we read its opinion, interpreted Senator Bacon's will as embodying a preference for termination of the park rather than its integration. Given this, the Georgia court had no alternative under its relevant trust laws, which are long standing and neutral with regard to race, but to end the Baconsfield trust and return the property to the Senator's heirs.

A second argument for petitioners stresses the similarities between this case and the case in which a city holds an absolute fee simple title to a public park and then closes that park of its own accord solely to avoid the effect of a prior court order directing that the park be integrated as the Fourteenth Amendment commands. Yet, assuming *arguendo* that the closing of the park would in those circumstances violate the Equal Protection Clause, that case would be clearly distinguishable from the case at bar because there it is the State and not a private party which is injecting the racially discriminatory motivation. In the case at bar there is not the slightest indication that any of the Georgia judges involved were motivated by racial animus or discriminatory intent of any sort in construing and enforcing Senator Bacon's will. Nor is there any indication that Senator Bacon in drawing up his will was persuaded or induced to include

---

Senator Bacon devised a life estate in the trust property to his wife and two daughters, and the language pointed out by the intervenors appears in the following provision of the will: "When my wife, Virginia Lamar Bacon and my two daughters, Mary Louise Bacon Sparks and Augusta Lamar Bacon Curry, shall all have departed this life, and immediately upon the death of the last survivor of them, it is my will that all right, title and interest in and to said property hereinbefore described and bounded, both legal and equitable, including all remainders and reversions and every estate in the same of whatsoever kind, shall thereupon vest in and belong to the Mayor and Council of the City of Macon, and to their successors forever, in trust etc." This language concerned remainders and reversions prior to the vesting of the legal title in the City of Macon, as trustee, and not to remainders and reversions occurring because of a failure of the trust, which Senator Bacon apparently did not contemplate, and for which he made no provision.

racial restrictions by the fact that such restrictions were permitted by the Georgia trust statutes. On the contrary, the language of the Senator's will shows that the racial restrictions were solely the product of the testator's own full-blown social philosophy. Similarly, the situation presented in this case is also easily distinguishable from that presented in *Shelley v. Kraemer*, 334 U.S. 1 (1948), where we held unconstitutional state judicial action which had affirmatively enforced a private scheme of discrimination against Negroes. Here the effect of the Georgia decision eliminated all discrimination against Negroes in the park by eliminating the park itself, and the termination of the park was a loss shared equally by the white and Negro citizens of Macon since both races would have enjoyed a constitutional right of equal access to the park's facilities had it continued.

Petitioners also contend that since Senator Bacon did not expressly provide for a reverter in the event that the racial restrictions of the trust failed, no one can know with absolute certainty that the Senator would have preferred termination of the park rather than its integration, and the decision of the Georgia court therefore involved a matter of choice. It might be difficult to argue with these assertions if they stood alone, but then petitioners conclude: "Its [the court's] choice, the anti-Negro choice, violates the Fourteenth Amendment, whether it be called a 'guess,' an item in 'social philosophy,' or anything else at all." We do not understand petitioners to be contending here that the Georgia judges were motivated either consciously or unconsciously by a desire to discriminate against Negroes. In any case, there is, as noted above, absolutely nothing before this Court to support a finding of such motivation. What remains of petitioners' argument is the idea that the Georgia courts had a constitutional obligation in this case to resolve any doubt about the testator's intent in favor of preserving the trust. Thus stated, we see no merit in the argument. The only choice the Georgia courts either had or exercised in this regard was their judicial judgment in construing Bacon's will to determine his intent, and the Constitution imposes no requirement upon the Georgia courts to approach Bacon's will any differently than they would approach any will creating any charitable trust of any kind. Surely the Fourteenth Amendment is not violated where, as here, a state court operating in its judicial capacity fairly applies its normal principles of construction to determine the testator's true intent in establishing a charitable trust and then reaches a conclusion with regard to that intent which, because of the operation of neutral and nondiscriminatory state trust laws, effectively denies everyone, whites as well as Negroes, the benefits of the trust.

Another argument made by petitioners is that the decision of the Georgia courts holding that the Baconsfield trust had "failed" must rest logically on the unspoken premise that the presence or proximity of Negroes in Baconsfield would destroy the desirability of the park for whites. This argument reflects a rather fundamental misunderstanding of Georgia law. The Baconsfield trust "failed" under that law not because of any belief on the part of any living person that whites and Negroes might not enjoy being together but, rather, because Senator Bacon who died many years ago intended that the park remain forever for the exclusive use of white people.

Petitioners also advance a number of considerations of public policy in opposition to the conclusion which we have reached. In particular, they regret, as we do, the loss of the Baconsfield trust to the City of Macon, and they are concerned lest we set a precedent under which other charitable trusts will be terminated. It bears repeating that our holding today reaffirms the traditional role of the States in determining whether or not to apply their *cy pres* doctrines to particular trusts. Nothing we have said here prevents a state court from applying its *cy pres* rule in a case where the Georgia court, for example, might not apply its rule. More fundamentally, however, the loss of charitable trusts such as Baconsfield is part of the price we pay for permitting deceased persons to exercise a continuing control over assets owned by them at death. This aspect of freedom of testation, like most things, has its advantages and disadvantages. The responsibility of this Court, however, is to construe and enforce the Constitution and laws of the land as they are and not to legislate social policy on the basis of our own personal inclinations.

In their lengthy and learned briefs, the petitioners and the Solicitor General as *amicus curiae* have advanced several arguments which we have not here discussed. We have carefully examined each of these arguments, however, and find all to be without merit.

The judgment is

Affirmed.

MR. JUSTICE MARSHALL took no part in the consideration or decision of this case.

MR. JUSTICE DOUGLAS, dissenting.

Bacon's will did not leave any remainder or reversion in "Baconsfield" to his heirs. He left "all remainders and reversions and every estate in the same of whatsoever kind" to the City of Macon. He further provided that the property "under no circumstances, or by any authority whatsoever" should "be sold or alienated or disposed of, or at any time for any reason" be "devoted to any other purpose or use excepting so far as herein specifically authorized."

Giving the property to the heirs, rather than reserving it for some municipal use, does therefore as much violence to Bacon's purpose as would a conversion of an "all-white" park into an "all-Negro" park.

. . . .

Moreover, putting the property in the hands of the heirs will not necessarily achieve the racial segregation that Bacon desired. We deal with city real estate. If a theatre is erected, Negroes cannot be excluded. If a restaurant is opened, Negroes must be served. If office or housing structures are erected, Negro tenants must be eligible. If a church is erected, mixed marriage ceremonies may be performed. If a court undertook to attach a racial-use condition to the property once it became "private," that would be an unconstitutional covenant or condition.

Bacon's basic desire can be realized only by the repeal of the Fourteenth Amendment. So the fact is that in the vicissitudes of time there is no constitutional way to assure that this property will not serve the needs of Negroes.

The Georgia decision, which we today approve, can only be a gesture toward a state-sanctioned segregated way of life, now *passé*. It therefore should fail as the imposition of a penalty for obedience to a principle of national supremacy.

MR. JUSTICE BRENNAN, dissenting.

For almost half a century Baconsfield has been a public park. Senator Bacon's will provided that upon the death of the last survivor among his widow and two daughters title to Baconsfield would vest in the Mayor and Council of the City of Macon and their successors forever. Pursuant to the express provisions of the will, the Mayor and City Council appointed a Board of Managers to supervise the operation of the park, and from time to time these same public officials made appointments to fill vacancies on the Board. Senator Bacon also bequeathed to the city certain bonds which provided income used in the operation of the park.

The city acquired title to Baconsfield in 1920 by purchasing the interests of Senator Bacon's surviving daughter and another person who resided on the land. Some $46,000 of public money was spent over a number of years to pay the purchase price. From the outset and throughout the years the Mayor and City Council acted as trustees, Baconsfield was administered as a public park. T. Cleveland James, superintendent of city parks during this period, testified that when he first worked at Baconsfield it was a "wilderness . . . nothing there but just undergrowth everywhere, one road through there and that's all, one paved road." He said there were no park facilities at that time. In the 1930's Baconsfield was transformed into a modern recreational facility by employees of the Works Progress Administration, an agency of the Federal Government. WPA did so upon the city's representation that Baconsfield was a public park. WPA employed men daily for the better part of a year in the conversion of Baconsfield to a park. WPA and Mr. James and his staff cut underbrush, cleared paths, dug ponds, built bridges and benches, planted shrubbery, and, in Mr. James' words, "just made a general park out of it." Other capital improvements were made in later years with both federal and city money. The Board of Managers also spent funds to improve and maintain the park.

. . . .

No record could present a clearer case of the closing of a public facility for the sole reason that the public authority that owns and maintains it cannot keep it segregated. . . .

I have no doubt that a public park may constitutionally be closed down because it is too expensive to run or has become superfluous, or for some other reason, strong or weak, or for no reason at all. But under the Equal Protection Clause a State may not close down a public facility solely to avoid its duty to desegregate that facility . . . .

When it is as starkly clear as it is in this case that a public facility would remain open but for the constitutional command that it be operated on a nonsegregated basis, the closing of that facility conveys an unambiguous message of community involvement in racial discrimination. . . .

The Court, however, affirms the judgment of the Georgia Supreme Court on the ground that the closing of Baconsfield did not involve state action. The Court concedes that the closing of the park by the city "solely to avoid the effect of a prior court order directing that the park be integrated" would be unconstitutional. However, the Court finds that in this case it is not the State or city but "a private party which is injecting the racially discriminatory motivation." . . . The exculpation of the State and city from responsibility for the closing of the park is simply indefensible on this record. This discriminatory closing is permeated with state action: at the time Senator Bacon wrote his will Georgia statutes expressly authorized and supported the precise kind of discrimination provided for by him; in accepting title to the park, public officials of the City of Macon entered into an arrangement vesting in private persons the power to enforce a reversion if the city should ever incur a constitutional obligation to desegregate the park; it is a *public* park that is being closed for a discriminatory reason after having been operated for nearly half a century as a segregated *public* facility; and it is a state court that is enforcing the racial restriction that keeps apparently willing parties of different races from coming together in the park. That is state action in overwhelming abundance. I need emphasize only three elements of the state action present here.

First, there is state action whenever a State enters into an arrangement that creates a private right to compel or enforce the reversion of a public facility. Whether the right is a possibility of reverter, a right of entry, an executory interest, or a contractual right, it can be created only with the consent of a public body or official, for example the official action involved in Macon's acceptance of the gift of Baconsfield. The State's involvement in the creation of such a right is also involvement in its enforcement; the State's assent to the creation of the right necessarily contemplates that the State will enforce the right if called upon to do so. Where, as in this case, the State's enforcement role conflicts with its obligation to comply with the constitutional command against racial segregation the attempted enforcement must be declared repugnant to the Fourteenth Amendment.

. . . .

A finding of discriminatory state action is required here on a second ground. *Shelley v. Kraemer*, 334 U.S. 1 (1948), stands at least for the proposition that where parties of different races are willing to deal with one another a state court cannot keep them from doing so by enforcing a privately devised racial restriction . . . . Nothing in the record suggests that after our decision in *Evans v. Newton*, the City of Macon retracted its previous willingness to manage Baconsfield on a nonsegregated basis, or that the white beneficiaries of Senator Bacon's generosity were unwilling to share it with Negroes, rather than have the park revert to his heirs. Indeed, although it may be that the city would have preferred to keep the park segregated, the record suggests that, given the impossibility of that goal, the city wanted to keep the park open. The resolution by which the Mayor and Council resigned as trustees prior to the decision in *Evans v. Newton*, reflected, not opposition to the admission of Negroes into the park, but a fear that if Negroes were admitted the park would be lost to the city. The Mayor and Council did not participate in this litigation after the decision in *Evans v. Newton*. However, the Attorney General of Georgia was made a party after remand from this Court, and, acting "as *parens patriae* in all legal matters pertaining to the administration and disposition of charitable trusts in the State of Georgia in which the rights of beneficiaries are involved," he opposed a reversion to the heirs and argued that Baconsfield should be maintained "as a park for all the citizens of the State of Georgia." Thus, so far as the record shows, this is a case of a state court's enforcement of a racial restriction to prevent willing parties from dealing with one another. The decision of the Georgia courts thus, under *Shelley v. Kraemer*, constitutes state action denying equal protection.

Finally, a finding of discriminatory state action is required on a third ground. In *Reitman v. Mulkey*, 387 U.S. 369 (1967), this Court announced the basic principle that a State acts in violation of the Equal Protection Clause when it singles out racial discrimination for particular encouragement, and thereby gives it a special preferred status in the law, even though the State does not itself impose or compel segregation. This approach to the analysis of state action was foreshadowed in Mr. JUSTICE WHITE's separate opinion in *Evans v. Newton*. There MR. JUSTICE WHITE comprehensively reviewed the law of trusts as that law stood in Georgia in 1905, prior to the enactment of §§ 69-504 and 69-505 of the Georgia Code. He concluded that prior to the enactment of those statutes "it would have been extremely doubtful" whether Georgia law authorized "a trust for park purposes when a portion of the public was to be excluded from the park." 382 U.S. at 310. Sections 69-504 and 69-505 removed this doubt by expressly permitting dedication of land to the public for use as a park open to one race only. Thereby Georgia undertook to facilitate racial restrictions as distinguished from all other kinds of restriction on access to a public park. *Reitman* compels the conclusion that in doing so Georgia violated the Equal Protection Clause.

. . . .

I would reverse the judgment of the Supreme Court of Georgia.

[7] Notes on Charitable Trusts, Future Interests and Wills

[a] Charitable Trusts and the Social Preference for Alienability

Charitable trusts operate somewhat differently from other trusts. They may last longer than personal trusts[29] and are subject to reformation under the *cy pres* rules. These differences play an important role in cases like *Evans*.

A basic conflict exists between two important policies in American property law. On the one hand, an assumption exists that an asset ought to be transferable. Transferability, or *alienability* as it is often called by lawyers, is thought to increase the likelihood that productive use will be made of the property. On the other hand, a number of property rules and institutions, to say nothing of environmental controls, are designed to permit individuals or governments to limit alienability in order to protect future generations, the public welfare, or the ecology.

A will like that of Bacon presents the conflict directly. Even if the racial restriction is put aside, Bacon's will controlled large amounts of property for a long period of time. It delayed for a couple of generations the final distribution of those assets left to various members of his family and bestowed a large amount of property permanently (or so he hoped) on public authorities. The general preference to encourage the transfer of property was suspended for quite some time so that Bacon could control his clan's wealth.

Discord between the desire to transfer and the desire to let property owners dispose of property to private parties in wills is mediated by the Rule Against Perpetuities, discussed later in this chapter. For now, understand only that the perpetuities rules permit a person to control the disposition of property in private hands for about two generations into the future. With charitable trusts the preference to permit transfer is totally suspended in favor of encouraging gifts of property for the public use of this and future generations.

The permanence of charitable trusts may create serious problems. When shifts in social mores occur, some older charitable impulses will be viewed as tainted, inappropriate, out of date or impractical. The arrival of the Civil Rights Era, for example, caused serious tension in the operation of Baconsfield. Under such circumstances, you might predict that a set of rules would develop permitting courts to modify the terms of some charitable trusts to permit their continuance. The *cy pres* rules have taken on this role. Surprisingly, the rules are not cast in such a way that courts may alter any charitable trust to meet "modern" needs. Rather, the courts inquire, as in *Evans*, whether the *settlor*, the party establishing the trust, had a general charitable intent. If so, the court may, but need not, make modifications in the trust to permit this general charitable intent to continue operating. If, however, the charitable intent was specific, and the purposes of the trust may no longer be served, the trust is ended. This, of course, was the outcome in *Evans*. One way of thinking about *Evans* is to inquire whether the judicial use of the *cy pres* rules to forbid modification of a trust with racial restrictions fulfilled the state action requirement.

The focus of the *cy pres* rules on the intent of the settlor rather than upon the ability to modify the trust to meet modern social needs represents a compromise among the various cultural demands at issue. On the one hand, the desire to grant property owners control over the disposition of their assets suggests a need to constantly look at the intent of the grantor or settlor. Indeed,

---

[29] The rule against perpetuities, discussed later in this chapter, generally does not limit the length of time a charitable trust may continue to operate.

the cases on future interests and trusts all have ritualized references to the importance of the intention of the person establishing the trust. On the other hand, the desire to maintain charities for the benefit of future generations leads us to fiddle with such intent when it is said to be "general." Such an outcome satisfies our reluctance to simply throw away the generous instincts of somewhat picky donors. Only when the settlor quite specifically says that he or she does not wish to be charitable at all if certain events occur will we terminate the trust. Bacon's clear statements in his will indicating that he was a segregationist led the Georgia courts to close the park rather than alter the trust to meet contemporary social mores.

The final result in *Evans* was not a foregone conclusion. Other courts confronting similar situations have applied the *cy pres* rules to reform trusts. The best known such case probably is *Commonwealth of Pennsylvania v. Brown*, 392 F.2d 120 (3d Cir. 1967) involving the will of Stephen Girard which provided funds for establishing Girard College in 1831. Further information on the *cy pres* debate may be found in Jonathan Macey, *Private Trusts for the Provision of Private Goods*, 37 Emory L.J. 295 (1988).

[b]   Future Interests

The provisions in Bacon's will relevant to the *Evans* case may be paraphrased and rewritten as follows:

> *Bacon to my wife and two daughters for their lives, then upon the death of the last of my wife and two daughters, to the Mayor and City Council of Macon in trust for use as a park for white women and children.*

Use the notes at the beginning of this chapter to label the various interests in this version of the Bacon will. You should be able to discern that Bacon's will created life estates in his wife and daughters, followed by a vested remainder subject to defeasance in the Mayor and City Council of Macon. The Macon authorities acted as a trustee for the town's white people, who held beneficial or equitable interests that were also much like vested remainders subject to defeasance. There was, however, no executory interest. Instead, the park land reverted to Bacon and his heirs. In addition, note that the wife and daughters held their life estate as tenants in common.

[c]   Another *Evans*–Based Problem

Rewrite the Bacon will to read as follows:

> *To my wife and daughters for their lives, then if before the death of the last of my wife and daughters, the City of Macon builds a memorial to my memory costing no less than $1,000, to the City of Macon in trust for use as a park for white women and children.*

What interests does this conveyance create? The language places a pre-condition upon the gift from Bacon to the City of Macon. There is no present intention to immediately bestow a future right to possession. The interest taking effect at the death of Bacon is a contingent remainder. If Macon builds the memorial before the death of the wife and daughters, then the pre-condition will be fulfilled and the City of Macon's interest would become a vested remainder subject to defeasance.

[8]   Problem Notes

[a]   Denouement of *Evans*

Justice Douglas' dissent in *Evans* was a bit prophetic. After the United States Supreme Court sent the case back to the Georgia courts, the Baconsfield park was closed, and the land reverted to Bacon and his heirs. Since his will had a residuary clause distributing all assets not otherwise disposed of in his will, the reverted park passed to the residuary takers. They in turn sold the land for a tidy sum to various developers who have since constructed a large shopping center, McDonald's Restaurant, apartments, condominiums, row houses and office buildings. Part of the edge of the park also was used for an interstate highway. Black persons, at least in legal theory, must be allowed access to all of these facilities under present civil rights laws. Does this outcome mean that the Supreme Court decision came out the wrong way?

[b]   Formalism and Construction of Conveyance Documents

Recall the *Storke v. Penn Mutual* and *Babb v. Rand* cases discussed pp. 356–357 above. I made the point there that rigid use of rules of construction may well lead courts (and students) astray. A similar debate occurs in studying future interests. Though the categorization of interests in property has the appearance of ease of application, the vagaries of individual cases may cause a great deal of head scratching.

In re Estate of Houston, 414 Pa. 579, 201 A.2d 592 (1964), is one of the most famous head scratchers. Enormous sums of money rode on the construction of the last clause in an extremely complex will. The end of the clause read, "On the death of my last surviving child, I direct that the whole of the principal of the trust estate shall be distributed in equal portions to and among my grand-children, the children of any deceased grandchild taking their deceased parents share." By the time the last surviving child died, three of the testator's 12 grandchildren had also died. If the language quoted above was construed literally, these three dead grandchildren were entitled to a share of the estate. Such a literal construction was adopted by the court. That resulted in splitting the $145 million estate 12 ways, reopening estates of long dead persons, bestowing property on persons related to the testator only by marriage and not part of the rest of his estate plan, and forcing the payment of substantial estate taxes that would not otherwise have been paid. The dissenters argued that the quoted language should be construed to mean that assets were to go only to *surviving* grandchildren. That construction would have left only nine shares to the estate, prevented reopening the estates of long dead persons, and avoided the payment of huge taxes.

How literal would you be? What would convince you to construe the conveyance as one to surviving grandchildren? The outcome of the case was one reason a prominent academic wrote an article sharply criticizing the courts for being too quick to apply a standard rule of construction favoring vested over contingent interests. Edward Rabin, *The Law Favors Vesting of Estates. Why?*, 65 COLUM. L. REV. 467 (1965). This is part of a large and important debate in property law. The need for certainty in titles suggests that we should be quite Formalist in the way we use legal terms of art in documents of conveyance. That instinct is sorely tested when Formalism produces unfair results. Such was the nature of the debate between the majority and dissenting judges in *Houston*.

[c]   Use of Attorneys and Rules of Construction

At one point the *Houston* court noted that the will was carefully drafted by a lawyer. Is it appropriate to apply stricter rules of construction to such a will than to wills handwritten by untutored persons? In some jurisdictions, holographic wills—handwritten, unwitnessed, but signed, wills—are enforced upon the death of the maker. Do you suppose that courts are less prone to apply technical rules of construction, such as early vesting notions, to holographic wills? If so, why should Houston's will have been treated differently? After all, Houston's family, not the attorney, were the ones that took a licking in the case! Why should the sins of the lawyer be visited upon the client or the client's family? Should the court have noted that errors of this sort—leaving out the word "surviving"—are easy to overlook in long wills and then construed it with human frailty in mind? Or should lawyers, well paid for their time, be expected to deal perfectly with all the complexities of a will like Houston's? Was the attorney negligent? And if a lawyer drafts the will, can the court talk "honestly" about the intention of the testator when it construes the document? Do you think that Houston, or the testator of any other very complex will, really understood his will?

[d] Definition of Discrimination and "Neutral" State Legal Rules

The *Evans* court opined that the decision of the Georgia Supreme Court not to apply the *cy pres* rules to modify the Bacon trust involved no racial discrimination. Rather, the state court was applying old and well understood "neutral" property rules. Was the outcome in *Evans* really neutral? Baconsfield was established by a segregationist. Is enforcement of the intention of a segregationist "neutral?" What if Baconsfield was the park in town most convenient to largely black neighborhoods? Would the consequences of closing the park be "neutral?" Does the idea of "neutrality" in cases like this force us to divorce the technical meaning of legal rules involving estates in land from the social consequences of legal rules? If so, are you willing to do that?

[e] Definitions of Discrimination and State Action

Does it make any difference that in *Shelley v. Kraemer*, the case about enforcement of racial restrictions on sale of property, the operation of the restriction deprived only black persons of property, while in *Evans* both black and white people lost a park? In the *Evans* opinion, the Court assumed for purposes of argument that Macon could not close a facility, but held that it was Bacon, not Macon, that closed the park. Subsequent to the decision in *Evans*, the Supreme Court decided that public authorities could close a public facility rather than integrate it. Both races were equally affected, the Court opined. *Palmer v. Thompson*, 403 U.S. 217 (1971). Would you define "discrimination" to include outcomes based on an "intention" to treat persons differently, results that "affect" one group differently from another, or outcomes based on intent that also affect groups differently? If intent is the only requirement, was not *Palmer v. Thompson* wrongly decided?

[9] Some Further Notes on Estates in Land

There are a few other rules about future interests which sometimes trap the unwary.

[a] Destruction of Contingent Remainders

Consider this grant:

G to A for life, then to the heirs of B.

The heirs of B are not known until B dies. The interest is thus contingent upon the determination of the heirs.[30] Suppose that A dies before B. In such a situation we would not know the heirs

---

[30] Note that "heirs" is used here as a word of purchase describing takers, not as a word of limitation describing time. If "heirs" were used in both senses in this grant, it would read:

G to A for life, then to the heirs of B and their heirs.

of B until a later time. There is a "gap" in the flow of interests, and G would hold a reversion in the property between the time A and B die. At common law, such a gap caused the destruction of the contingent remainder. As Professor Jesse Dukeminier made clear in the article excerpted below, almost all states have done away with destructibility and permit such interests to take effect upon the death of B as executory interests.

[b] Other Relics

At common law, just like today, taxation led to tax avoidance schemes. As a general rule, passage of wealth through an estate was a heavily taxed event. Efforts were therefore made to avoid taxes by the use of various future interests. Courts sometimes responded with rules to circumscribe the tax avoidance. Two such old rules—the Rule in Shelley's Case and the Doctrine of Worthier Title—still haunt some jurisdictions.

The Rule in Shelley's Case involved the construction of the transfer:

G to A for life, then to the heirs of A.

If the interest in the heirs of A was deemed a contingent remainder at the moment G created these interests, then the land would not pass through A's estate upon his death. Instead, the property would automatically go to the heirs of A, determined at A's death. To insure tax collection, the courts construed this language to create a fee simple absolute in A. The heirs of A then collected as takers of the estate of A, not as transferees from G. Most jurisdictions have abolished the rule.

The Doctrine of Worthier Title involved construction of a transfer such as:

G to A for life, then to the heirs of G.

If the interest in the heirs of G was viewed as a contingent remainder, the interest would not pass through G's estate, but would arise automatically upon the death of A. The court found the interest void, requiring the heirs of G to take as devisees or intestate heirs rather than as *inter vivos* transferees. This rule, believe it or not, has not (at least in theory) been universally abolished. In most areas where it survives it operates as a "rule of construction," making it possible for a clear statement of intention in derogation of the rule to operate effectively.

[c] Class Gifts

Gifts of future interests to groups sometimes create intriguing little problems. Consider the following testamentary grant:

G to Zelda for life, then to the children of Zelda.

Suppose that upon the death of G, Zelda is alive but childless. Then the gift to the children of Zelda is a contingent remainder; its vesting depends upon the birth of a child. Now suppose that the year after G dies, Zelda has a child, Abe. Abe then becomes the proud owner of a vested remainder; the pre-condition that a child be born has been removed. But Zelda could have more children. These children would also be entitled to take a share in this remainder. So, assume that after Abe's birth, Zelda has two more children, Bertha and Carla. Then Abe, Bertha and Carla each are proud owners of a vested remainder. Until the death of Zelda, more children could be born. Though the interests of Abe, Bertha and Carla are vested they are said to be *vested remainders subject to open*, that is subject to the addition of more members of the class of takers known as the "children of Zelda." This sort of remainder is very much like a vested remainder subject to defeasance. But rather than being totally defeated, interests subject to open are reduced in size for each taker as the class expands. Class gifts are common.

[d] Gifts Per Capita and Per Stirpes

In the *Houston* case discussed above at p. 370, the will established a trust. Income produced by the assets held in the trust was to be distributed to the children of Houston in equal shares upon the death of Houston's wife. However, the income was to be distributed to grandchildren upon the death of a child, with the grandchildren splitting their parent's share. The first type of gift is made *per capita*, or per head; each taker gets an equal share. The second type of gift is *per stirpes*, meaning the share of the ancestor. Thus, the grandchildren split their parent's share. Various grandchildren may not get the same amount of income. In the *Houston* case, for example, the two surviving grandchildren of one child split her share of income in half, while the three surviving grandchildren of another split his share in thirds. This is a fairly common practice. Parents tend to make equal gifts to their children and then allow each child's share to be split among his or her descendants.

[10] Have Executory Interests Seen Their Day?

There is a great deal of reluctance to ignore old, and perhaps useless, rules of construction, or to discard old, and perhaps useless, property vocabulary. Our Formalist instinct is to hold on to any term of art that may provide precise guidance on the devolution of property. In a valiant effort to notify us of the tendency of outmoded words to obfuscate rather than enlighten our thinking, one commentator had little good to say about the continued use of the label "executory interest."

Jesse Dukeminier, *Contingent Remainders and Executory Interests: A Requiem For a Distinction*

43 MINN. L. REV. 13-14, 51-55 (1958)[31]

A few years ago James Thurber spun a whimsical yarn about a Duke who "limped because his legs were of different lengths. The right one had outgrown the left because, when he was young, he had spent his mornings place kicking pups and punting kittens. He would say to a suitor, 'What is the difference in the length of my legs?' and if the youth replied, 'Why, one is shorter than the other,' the Duke would run him through with the sword he carried in his swordcane and feed him to the geese. The suitor was supposed to say, 'Why, one is longer than the other.' Many a prince had been run through for naming the wrong difference."[1]

Many a student in future interests has been run through by his instructor for an error of equal magnitude: calling a contingent remainder an executory interest (or vice versa). We who pretend to some knowledge of future interests are wont to stress the importance of precise labeling, of carefully classifying the interest by the rigid and artificial criteria of the common law. But if the legal consequences which flow from the label "executory interest" are the same as the consequences which flow from "contingent remainder" then the student is likely to believe he is being impaled by a crotchet. Either label should do. And would, were it not for our professional love of being able to speak well the language of the dead.

---

[31] Reprinted by permission of the Minnesota Law Review and Jesse Dukeminier.
[1] THURBER, THE 13 CLOCKS 20 (1950).

The question is, is a contingent remainder an interest that differs in important ways from an executory interest? This must be answered "no" before we can dismiss proper labeling as a mere matter of good form. In order to answer it we shall have to look into the criteria for applying the labels and then examine the situations where it has been suggested the label matters. These situations are:

A. *Creation*

(1) Application of the Rule in Shelley's Case

(2) Application of the Rule Against Perpetuities

(3) Invalidity of gift over where first taker has power to alienate

B. *Termination of Possessory Estate*

C. *Rights Against Owner of Possessory Estate*

(1) Waste

(2) Security for personal property

D. *Alienation Inter Vivos*

There are many, many other problems that may arise concerning contingent future interests, such as: may the holder partition, sue a third party in tort, recover a portion of condemnation proceeds? What rights has he against a possessory owner who fails to pay taxes or interest on the mortgage? In these problems there is no evidence that the two interests might be treated substantially differently. Hence they are excluded from discussion.

If we conclude that executory interests and contingent remainders are treated alike in the seven situations discussed, the question then arises whether it is wise to preserve the two concepts in seemingly unchanged historic form or whether it would be better to revamp them to account for factors modern cases reveal to be important. If the concepts are too stubborn to change, they may have to be discarded altogether. I shall take up this question at the end of the article.

. . . .

Executory interests can be divided into two groups: (1) those that are in an ascertained person on an event certain to happen, and (2) those that are given to unascertained persons or on an uncertain event. Executory interests of the first type are rare. Examples are "to A 30 years from date," "to A after my death." The first is analogous to a vested remainder after a term of years, the second to a vested remainder after a life estate. These executory interests are treated like vested remainders under the Rule Against Perpetuities, and, although the cases are scarce, it is believed that they would also be treated as "vested" for other purposes as well. If they do not differ in consequences from vested remainders, they may as well be called vested future interests or vested remainders. And by a number of courts they have been. In this Article they have not been included within the term "executory interests" except where expressly stated or where the context has indicated otherwise. This exclusion was made to avoid repetition of the clumsy phrase, "contingent executory interests."

Executory interests of the second type are analogous to contingent remainders. It is with these executory interests that we have been primarily concerned. The foregoing analysis indicates there is no difference between them and contingent remainders except where the issue is destructibility and, possibly, where the Rule in Shelley's Case is involved. No court has refused to apply Shelley's Case to an executory interest because it was an executory interest, and for the reasons given above, the distinction between the two interests under the Rule in Shelley's Case is either nonexistent or, if theoretically existent, of no substantial importance. We are left with destructibility as the only distinguishing feature. That relic of feudalism exists in Florida and, viewed in the friendliest fashion, possibly, although certainly not probably, in less than a dozen other states. In three-quarters of the states destructibility has been wholly done away with. Thus, in at least three-quarters of the states, there is no discernible difference between executory interests and contingent remainders. Only in Florida are we sure of any difference between them.

Is there any reason for retaining two concepts that produce the same consequences? Of what value are the hours after hours spent teaching students to use labels properly, when they are functional equivalents? It is clear the concepts cannot be revamped in any useful way. The alternatives are keeping the two concepts separate and merging them under one label. It seems to me there are two arguments for the former alternative and two for the latter. I shall deal briefly with each of them.

The arguments for retaining the two concepts are both, in a sense, pedagogical. The first is that students must be taught to distinguish between the two interests because the different labels are currently used by judges and lawyers. The second suggests that while the distinction may be unimportant for contemporary purposes all the history wrapped up in it ("gaps in seisin," "destructibility" and so forth) is of educational value. The first seems fallacious in that it assumes that the labels are meaningfully used today by courts. There is no need to cite again the many cases wherein the labels are treated with utmost indifference, where the wrong label is applied or where the labels are used interchangeably.

The second has merit, and I am sure it could be stated with much greater effect by one who believes in it more strongly than I do. The great trouble I have with it is that it proves both too much and too little. All history has many insights to offer, but it cannot all be taught. When the emphasis shifts from the reasons for, and methods of, change and growth to technicalities, the value sharply diminishes. In this field all too often has the mind's eye skipped over the greatness of the common law as a process constantly adapting forms to changing circumstances and fixed uncritically on the technicalities: on the Rule in Shelley's Case, on destructibility, on contingent interests as "mere possibilities," on form rather than substance. What is justified as history becomes only training in the worst sort of artificial reasoning.

The first argument for abandoning the distinction is doctrinal simplification. Even John Chipman Gray, ruled though he was by a passion for rigid adherence to theorems, saw the need of paring off useless, artificial distinctions beyond the comprehension of the ordinary lawyer.

A serious objection to the continuance of the old doctrines of real property in the jurisprudence of today is that, while the judges are thoroughly familiar with and move at ease among the general doctrines of contract and equity which govern the ordinary transactions of modern life, it is impossible (or if not impossible at least very unlikely) that they should have at their fingers' ends the fundamental distinctions of a highly artificial system, and they are in danger of being unduly governed by "the *cantilena*[142] of lawyers" and of losing opportunities for the simplification of the law.[143]

Gray's genius was achieving insight within apparent complexity by discovering a simpler doctrinal order. His energy was fired by an *elan* to understand multiplicity in terms of a few basic ideas. If he was wrong in thinking that clear and rational doctrines could be built on such words as "vest,"[144] "condition precedent," "divest," he was right in thinking that, in order to be useful in advocacy and decisions, words have to have some meaning for the ordinary lawyer and judge.

Society, and by reflection the lawyer's practice, has become far more complex than in Gray's time. Lawyers are even less likely to "have at their fingers' ends the fundamental distinctions" between such things as contingent remainders and executory interests. If we are truthful we must admit that not too many students master the distinction and most of those forget about it in their first years of practice. If they think very, very hard they may remember that executory interests are "divesting" or "springing" or "shifting" interests, but that is about as far as their memory and understanding go. More often than not their "knowledge" of executory interests simply clutters up their minds with ambiguous verbalisms and half understood maxims, such as "there can be no remainder after a fee." (That particular maxim has led astray a good many lawyers and judges who did not realize all it means is that we call the gift over by another name.)

As a result of this surfeit of vaguely understood words, arguments in future interests cases are often remarkable for their vacuity and for their failure to come to grips with the fundamental problem. Many of the cases cannot be read without writhing.[145] Here, more than in any other field, there is a tendency to collect familiar quotations, glue them together and by sheer humbug make them applicable to the problem. It is hard for the lawyer to know why he has won and even harder for losing counsel to understand why he has lost. Thus the more profane practitioner

---

[142] For those who do not have a dictionary handy, the word means "melody." The phrase comes from *O'Connell v. The Queen*, 11 Cl. & Fin. 155, 8 All E.R. 1061, 1143 (1844).

[143] Gray [JOHN CHIPMAN GRAY, THE RULE AGAINST PERPETUITIES (1886)] § 782.

[144] Gray himself subsequently had doubts about the word "vest." *See* Gray, Appendix M §§ 970-74.

[145] A leading contender for honors is *Sands v. Fly*, 292 S.W.2d 706 (Tenn. 1956), 45 Ky.L.J. 704 (1957). Testatrix devised land to her only son Howard for his life, then to his children for their lives, and at the death of the last child of Howard in fee to named nieces and nephews, the issue of any deceased niece or nephew to take his or her share per stirpes, and if any niece or nephew be then dead without issue, his share to the surviving nieces and nephews or their issue. The court held the remainder in fee vested immediately and was entirely valid even though an event to happen later was said to be a "condition precedent" to the remainder's vesting. Counsel quoted Gray § 108, to the effect that a remainder is contingent where the conditional element is incorporated into the gift to the remaindermen. The court agreed that here "the conditional element was incorporated in the gift to the remaindermen," but, said the court, "it definitely and conclusively appears that this condition was satisfied at the time of the testatrix's death, all children of Howard J. Sands being alive at that time." Having survived living persons is undoubtedly a neat trick, but even more marvelous is having survived the unborn (for the court later conceded that some children of Howard "might be born after the death of the testatrix"). The best argument for invalidity—that the remainder in fee was a gift to a class which would not close until the death of Howard's children—was not mentioned by the court.

Other features of this bizarre case include an argument by Howard that the remainder in his children for life and the remainder in fee were alternative contingent remainders; a contention by the guardian *ad litem* of the children that his ward's remainder was void; and a finding of an alternative remainder after a vested remainder in fee. The court cited numerous cases as authority, not one of which was in point. The case is annotated in 57 A.L.R.2d 188 (1958) by an inapposite note entitled "Character of remainder limited to surviving children of life tenant."

comes to regard future interests as not a divine madness at all, but, like William James' algebra, a peculiarly low sort of cunning.

It is a reasonable assumption that two labels stand for two different things; and when they do not, when we have two labels for equivalent future interests, confusion is the natural result. Abandoning the distinction between contingent remainders and executory interests would not be a giant step toward improving this situation, but it would be a much larger step than some might imagine, for understanding the distinction requires at least a speaking acquaintance with "gaps in seisin" and "destructibility"—an acquaintance not likely to be quickly made. If the distinction goes, "gaps in seisin" and "destructibility," which make up a large part of the history of real property law, can go with it.

The second argument for abandonment is that emphasizing labels leads to an unfortunate type of reasoning. It makes form important and substance unimportant. It moves from words to label to result. Numerous examples of this type of reasoning have been exhibited in this Article, and especially in the parts dealing with waste and security. There distinctions were drawn by eminent scholars between executory interests after fees and contingent interests after life estates, between "to A but if A die without issue to B" and "to A for life, then to A's issue, but if A die without issue to B." B was said to be entitled to less protection in the latter case, irrespective of A's age or the existence of issue or of a host of other important variables. It was shown that in terms of results in the cases the distinctions were illusory. The right inference from this is that the labels had better be dispensed with in analysis of these problems; they are not an adequate substitute for analysis of the many factors that move decisions. The same thing may be said of other problems as well, for there is no proof that labels affect results except in one case (destructibility) in one state (Florida).

It is enchantment with labels that is the hidden cause of most of the law's failures in the field of future interests. So long as we concern ourselves with labels and purely verbal distinctions, we can have no doctrinal structure that is more than a play with words, no doctrines that can justify themselves in terms of policy, no doctrines that can recognize the important factors, that can give predictability. All in all, the way to a useful, critical analysis of future interests seems to lead, not through gaps in seisin, but around them.

§ 5.04 Dead Hand Control: Perpetuities and Restraints on Alienation

[1] Introduction

Earlier in this chapter, it was noted that there is a tension in American law between insuring that land is freely alienable and allowing for charitable impulses to operate without regard to alienability.[32] A related strain emerges in parsing our sometimes conflicting desires to allow each person the liberty to determine who will take their property after death and to insure that property is freely transferable. For if we allow a person to tie up an asset in a long string of future interests, there is a risk that the multiplicity of ownership interests will lead to both inefficient use of the asset and inability to sell it. Two closely related sets of rules have developed to grapple with this problem—bans on provisions limiting the transfer of property to large groups of potential buyers, and the Rule Against Perpetuities. Alienation restraints, which can arise in either donative or non-donative contexts, are taken up in the next chapter. The materials that follow work out the parameters of the Rule Against Perpetuities.

---

[32] *See* p. 368 above.

[2] Rule Against Perpetuities Basics

Before reading any litigation or commentary about the Rule Against Perpetuities, try to understand the rule. It is traditionally stated[33] as follows:

An interest is void unless it must totally vest or totally fail to vest not later than 21 years after the death of some life in being at the creation of the interest.

An array of proposals have surfaced in recent years to modify the common law rule, but let's first work on the meaning of its traditional configuration. To figure it out, work with this example:

G by will →To my wife and children for their lives, and upon the death of the last of my wife and children then the remainder shall go to my grandchildren, but if any grandchild dies with issue surviving then that grandchild's share shall go to the surviving issue.

From prior notes and some concentration, you should be able to reach the somewhat messy conclusion, asssuming at least one grandchild is living at the death of G, that the interest of the grandchildren was vested subject to open upon the birth of additional grandchildren and subject to defeasance upon death with issue surviving. Now work through the rule one phrase at a time.

[a] Total Vesting or Total Failure to Vest

The rule says that an interest *must totally* vest or *totally* fail to vest within a certain period of time. Forget what the required period of time is for a moment, and concentrate only on this *total* vesting language. *Total* vesting requires not only that the interest *must totally* vest or *totally* fail to vest within the rule period rather than remain contingent, but, if it is an interest held by a class, that the class members *must* all be known within the rule period. In legalese, in order for a class gift to *totally* vest, the *class must close*. It is also possible that the gift will *fail* to vest within the rule period. If a gift *must totally fail* to vest within the rule period, it also will not violate the rule. Thus a gift to George that is contingent upon George's surviving Sarah will either *totally* vest if Sarah dies before George or *totally fail* to vest if George dies before Sarah. Furthermore, we will always know if this gift has either *totally* vested or *totally failed* to vest at the latest when Sarah dies.

In the example given at the beginning of this note, the remainder to the grandchildren is vested, but since it is a class gift to grandchildren it is also subject to open. Thus, this gift could not *totally* vest until the class of grandchildren closes. This event will occur when the last child dies, since it is impossible to produce a new grandchild when the children are all dead. Thus, the gift to the grandchildren will *totally* vest when the last child dies. But you might say, this gift to grandchildren is also subject to defeasance. Does that defeat total vesting? In short, no. The rule requires class gifts to close, but does not require that all defeasance possibilities disappear. Pre-conditions on a contingent remainder must disappear, but post-conditions creating a defeasance need not.

In a sense, this distinction between class closing and defeasance is arbitrary; you have to draw the line somewhere. But it arguably follows the peculiar logic of future interests. Remember that linguistically, a vested remainder subject to defeasance provides for the future possession of a full fee simple to a known taker or group of takers and shifts that whole fee simple to another person or group upon the happening of the defeating event. To whatever degree the terms of

---

[33] The classic treatise on future interests and the Rule Against Perpetuities is JOHN CHIPMAN GRAY, THE RULE AGAINST PERPETUITIES (1886). The book was edited and reissued several times in later years.

the Rule Against Perpetuities are motivated by a desire to create certainty about the takers of property, that motivation is, linguistically at least, fulfilled by vested remainders subject to defeasance.

Note that in analyzing the nature of the future interests in the example problem, we not only looked for the appropriate labels to describe the interests, but also noted the *latest moment in time when total vesting or total failure to vest had to occur*. It is crucial to figure out that moment. The Rule Against Perpetuities does not require that the owners of future interests must actually go into possession of their interests within the rule period, but only that total vesting or total failure to vest must occur within the rule period.

[b]   Lives In Being and The Rule Period

The event of total vesting or total failure to vest must occur within 21 years after the death of some life in being at the creation of the interest. The notion of *life in being* is the one that usually causes the most difficulty for property students working with the Rule Against Perpetuities. It sounds so amorphous and changes in each case according to the nature of the future interests created. But there are some guidelines that will take care of almost all situations. First, the life or lives in being (yes, there can be more than one) must be people actually alive at the moment the interest in question is created. Second, the life or lives in being are usually, though not always, living persons of the generation before that of the eventual takers of the interest. Third, the life or lives in being are usually named in the instrument creating the interest, but they need not be. Fourth, the life or lives in being usually, but not always, hold possession of the property before the eventual takers. Together these guidelines create a pattern of rational relationships between the definition of the present and future estates.

Applying these notions to the example problem, assume that the persons alive when the will takes effect include the testator's wife, his three children and some grandchildren. The living persons from the generation before the eventual takers will be his three living children. They are, of course, actually named in the will and hold possession of the life estate. The lives in being are the children of the testator.[34]

When you think about it, the notion that the lives in being are the kids makes a lot of sense. The Rule basically functions to require that vesting decisions be made within two generations of the time a will or *inter vivos* deed takes effect. In this example, the first generation is the children; the testator, after all, is dead when the will is probated. The second generation is represented by the additional 21 years stated in the Rule Against Perpetuities.

[c]   Summary

If you put all this together, the Rule Against Perpetuities requires, in the example situation, that the vested class interest in the grandchildren must *totally vest and close* within the lives of the three children plus another 21 years. We have already discovered that the class gift to the grandchildren totally closes when the last child dies. Thus, the interest will totally vest (*and has to do so*) upon the death of the last life in being, well within the period of time represented by the life of the last life in being plus another 21 years. Put simply, there is not a Rule Against Perpetuities problem in the example.

---

[34] This statement is not quite accurate, but for introductory purposes it will do fine. Houston's wife may also be treated as a life in being. As you become more familiar with the rule's application, you will see that her addition to the list does not change the outcome of the analysis at all. It is for this reason that I have left her out. It simplifies matters a bit.

Consider another example.

G to A for life, then to the first child of A to reach age 22.

Assume that A is alive and childless at the time the interests are created by G. First, is the interest in the first child of A to reach age 22 vested or contingent? It is contingent upon both the birth of a child (A is childless) and the aging of that child for 22 years. Thus, this gift will *totally* vest upon the birth of a child that lives for 22 years. It will *totally* fail to vest upon the death of A childless or the death of all children of A before their 22nd birthdays. Who is the life in being? A looks good. A is of the generation before the taker, named in the instrument, in possession of the property first, and alive when G sets up these property interests. Must the event of *total* vesting or failure to vest occur within A's life plus 21 years? *No!* If A had a child the day after G created these interests and A died the day after that, the interest *might not* totally vest until 21 years, 364 days later, or 364 days longer than the period permitted by the Rule. Note well that the interest *might* vest within the rule period. But the traditional statement of the Rule requires that an interest *must always* vest or fail to vest, not that it might vest or fail to vest, within the period.

Change the facts of this last example slightly so that A is dead, but has one child, a 12-year-old daughter, when G creates these interests. Then the interest in the first child of A to reach age 22 is still contingent; the only child has 10 years to go before reaching the required age. (The interest, by the way, will take effect as an executory interest because G or G's successors holds a "gap" reversion in this example.) But this interest *must* either *totally* vest or fail to vest in 10 years. The daughter will either live or die. The vesting decision will therefore occur, on these facts, within the life of A (which is zero years since A is dead) plus 10 years. That means that there would not be a violation of the Rule Against Perpetuities.

Before going to the first case, work on three more problems.

(1) Change the opening example in this set of notes to read:

G by will → To my wife and children for their lives, and upon the death of the last of my wife and children then the remainder shall go to my surviving grandchildren, but if any grandchild dies with issue surviving before the death of the last of my wife and children then that grandchild's share shall go to the surviving issue.

Figure out why this grant does not violate the Rule Against Perpetuities.

(2) Assume that the gifts made in the problem just above are *inter vivos*, that is made while G is still alive. Figure out why such gifts violate the Rule Against Perpetuities.

(3) Consider this example:

G by will → to my wife for life, then, if she has any surviving children, to the children of my wife, but if she dies without children surviving, then to my grandchildren, share and share alike.

Why does the interest in this example not violate the Rule? Be careful with the complication caused by the alternative takers under the will being the children of the wife and the grandchildren of the testator. [35]

(4) Look at one final example:

---

[35] This example is taken from *Baker v. Weedon*, which you can find at p. 860 below.

G by will → to Place of Worship, so long as the land is used for religious purposes, but if the land is ever used for non-religious purposes, then G may re-enter and take possession of the land.

Though the policy of the Rule Against Perpetuities clearly applies to the possibility of reverter held by G and her heirs, American courts have consistently declined to apply the rule to such interests, or to rights of re-entry. These types of interests arose before the common law rule developed to constrain the transfer of contingent interests. Reversionary interests, which remain with the grantor after a transfer, were left unconstrained. In response, some states have adopted legislation limiting the lifetime of reversionary interests, either to the Rule Against Perpetuities period or to some definite term of years.

[d]   Hornbook Reading

For a basic hornbook review of the rule, look at ROGER A. CUNNINGHAM, WILLIAM B. STOEBUCK & DALE A. WHITMAN, THE LAW OF PROPERTY 126-148 (2d ed. 1993). There is a great deal of literature on the Rule. Among the most readable articles attempting to describe its workings are three by Barton Leach, *Perpetuities in a Nutshell*, 51 HARV. L. REV. 638 (1938); *Perpetuities: A Standard Saving Clause to Avoid Violations of the Rule*, 74 HARV. L. REV. 1141 (1961) (with Logan); and *Perpetuities: The Nutshell Revisited*, 78 HARV. L. REV. 973 (1965).

[3]   Twentieth Century Reforms of the Rule Against Perpetuities

[a]   Introduction

Since World War II, there has been an explosion in perpetuities reforms. For the most part, the changes have enlarged the dead hand authority of testators to control the disposition of their property. Alterations of the common law Rule Against Perpetuities have taken three different forms. Some states adopted statutes allowing courts to reform devises that violate the Rule Against Perpetuities under *cy pres* like rules. An example of such a technique is presented in the next case. Another reform technique permits courts to "wait and see" if an event that would normally cause a perpetuities problem actually occurs. If it does not, then the devise will be allowed to operate. The third technique sets a specific time limit, such as 90 years, within which an interest must either vest or fail to vest. This method eliminates much of the ambiguity associated with determining lives in being and avoids the insecurity of a long "wait and see" period.

The reform era was ushered in by Pennsylvania in 1947 when it adopted a "wait and see" statute. Momentum for change has increased in recent years with the promulgation in 1986 of the Uniform Statutory Rule Against Perpetuities and the integration of that uniform act into the 1990 version of the Uniform Probate Code. A significant number of states have adopted this code.[36] The most important features of the uniform act provide that an interest will be valid if it vests or fails to vest within 90 years of its creation, and that courts are given the power to reform interests so they will comply with the statutory formulation of the rule. The main provisions of the uniform act read as follows:

---

[36] As of 1998, 24 states had adopted the uniform proposals on the Rule Against Perpetuities, either by enacting the 1990 version of the Uniform Probate Code or by passing a stand alone version of the Uniform Statutory Rule Against Perpetuities Act.

§ 2-901. Statutory Rule Against Perpetuities[*]

(a) [Validity of Nonvested Property Interest.] A nonvested property interest is invalid unless:

(1) when the interest is created, it is certain to vest or terminate no later than 21 years after the death of an individual then alive; or

(2) the interest either vests or terminates within 90 years after its creation.

. . . .

(d) [Possibility of Post-death Child Disregarded.] In determining whether a nonvested property interest . . . is valid under section (a)(1) . . . the possibility that a child will be born to an individual after the individual's death is disregarded.

. . . .

§ 2-903. Reformation

Upon the petition of an interested person, a court shall reform a disposition in the manner that most closely approximates the transferor's manifested plan of distribution and is within the 90 years allowed by Section 2-901(a)(2) . . . if:

(1) a nonvested property interest . . . becomes invalid under Section 2-901 (statutory rule against perpetuities);

(2) a class gift is not but might become invalid under Section 2-901 (statutory rule against perpetuities) and the time has arrived when the share of any class member is to take effect in possession or enjoyment; or

(3) a nonvested property interest that is not invalidated by Section 2-901(a)(1) can vest but not within 90 years after its creation.[37]

The impact of perpetuities reforms like those in the Uniform Probate Code has been significantly magnified by demographic patterns. Increases in life expectancy, even without statutory changes in the rule, would have increased the dead hand authority of testators. Together, reform and demography have caused a stunning shift in the balance of power from recipients of largesse to donors and testators.

The changes mirror many other recent changes in property law enlarging control by the living over use of assets after death. A famous personality may now control the commercial use of her likeness and name during life and after death. This publicity right, which will be taken up in Chapter 12, has blossomed in the last 20 years. The ability of medical personnel to harvest the organs of a dead person for use in transplant surgery is constrained by the preferences of the donor rather than by the wishes of surviving members of the donor's family. As you will see in the next chapter, developers may create governing structures for housing developments that are quite difficult for later residents to change. Recent takings cases, discussed in Chapter 11, have diminished the authority of governments to alter pre-existing understandings about the nature of property ownership. All of these developments illustrate a pronounced trend in present-day culture favoring the interests of the living generation over the interests of those arriving in future generations. Currently popular theories of individualism pay more attention to the living

---

[*] Reprinted with the permission of the National Conference of Commissioners on Uniform State Laws.

[37] UNIF. PROBATE CODE (8, pt. I U.L.A. 226, 234) (1998). Section 2-904 excludes a number of interests from the rule, including nondonative transfers.

than to the unborn. The next case illustrates both the current desire of people to exercise extensive control over the lives of surviving family members and the willingness of legislatures and courts to sanction most of that control.

[b]   A Case Law Example of Perpetuities Reform: *Estate of Ghiglia*

In the Matter of the Estate of Frank P. Ghiglia

Court of Appeal, Fifth District, California
42 Cal. App. 3d 433, 116 Cal. Rptr. 827 (1974)

OPINION

FRANSON, Associate Justice.

Appellant, one of three surviving children of the testator, Frank P. Ghiglia, challenges the validity of a testamentary trust established for the benefit of appellant, his sister and their children (testator's grandchildren), on the ground that the gift to the grandchildren of a future interest in the trust estate, the possession of which is deferred until the youngest grandchild reaches age 35, is a class gift which includes any grandchild born after the testator's death, thus permitting the vesting of the interests of the class members beyond a life in being and 21 years in violation of the rule against perpetuities. We hold that, although the gift to the grandchildren violates the vesting rule, under the authority of Civil Code 715.5,[1] we should order the will reformed to require the vesting of the interests of all class members within the allowable period of time.

Frank P. Ghiglia died on January 1, 1972, a widower. He was survived by three grown children, Frank P. Ghiglia, Jr., Adeline Marguerite McClintock and Robert J. Ghiglia. Each child had two children. Frank P. Ghiglia, Jr. had two sons, Frank Joseph Ghiglia and George Frank Ghiglia. Adeline Marguerite McClintock, had a son, John Arthur McClintock, and a daughter, Nancy Ann [McClintock] Berge. Robert J. Ghiglia had two sons, William Joseph Ghiglia and John Robert Ghiglia. At the time of the testator's death, the testator's daughter, Adeline, who was divorced, was about 53 years of age, the testator's son Robert, was about 51 years of age, and Robert's wife was about 45 years of age; all of the testator's grandchildren were adults.

Decedent left a will which was admitted to probate. The testator's oldest son, Frank, was named executor in the will. The will provides that Frank shall receive one-third of the estate outright after certain household furniture, automobiles and personal belongings are divided equally among Frank and the other two children, Adeline and Robert. The will then provides in the fourth clause as follows:

". . . .

"B) The remaining two-thirds, IN TRUST—to Frank P. Ghiglia and the Bank of America National Trust and Savings Association, for the uses and purposes hereinafter set forth.

". . . .

---

[1] Civil Code section 715.5 provides: "No interest in real or personal property is either void or voidable as in violation of [the rule against perpetuities] if and to the extent that it can be reformed or construed within the limits of that [rule] to give effect to the general intent of the creator of the interest whenever that general intent can be ascertained. This section shall be liberally construed and applied to validate such interest to the fullest extent consistent with such ascertained intent."

"E) The NET INCOME of THE TRUST ESTATE shall be distributed as follows:

"1) One full share to my daughter Adeline Marguerite McClintock.

"2) One full share to my son Robert J. Ghiglia.

"3) The net income to my daughter Adeline Marguerite McClintock and my son Robert J. Ghiglia shall be distributed in convenient installments, not less frequently then quarterly during their lifetime.

"F) Upon the death of my daughter Adeline Marguerite McClintock, the Trustees shall apportion her share of the net income and pay the same to my grandchildren Nancy Ann McClintock and John Arthur McClintock, equally.

"G) Upon the death of my son Robert J. Ghiglia, the Trustees shall apportion his share of the net income and pay the same to my grandchildren William G. Ghiglia and John Ghiglia, equally.

"Upon the death of each of my children, Adeline Marguerite McClintock and Robert J. Ghiglia, the trust shall terminate *provided, however, if any of my grandchildren have not attained the age of thirty-five (35) years, the two trusts shall continue until all of the grandchildren have attained the age of thirty-five (35) years. In other words, each trust shall continue in full force and effect, until all of my grandchildren reach the age of thirty-five (35) years.* Upon such termination the entire Trust Estate, shall be distributed to the persons for whom said estate is then held in trust, in proportion to the trusts then held for such persons and, if there shall be no such persons surviving, then said Trust Estate shall be distributed to my heirs, to be determined according to the laws of California relating to the succession of separate property in force at the date of such termination."

On March 12, 1973, Robert Ghiglia filed a petition to determine the interests under the will. The petition sets forth the fact that the three children were the decedent's heirs-at-law and alleges that the grandchildren's interests under the trust violated the rule against perpetuities. Following a hearing, the trial court upheld the validity of the trust by deciding that the testator's use of "grandchildren" in the will had reference only to the four children of Adeline and Robert alive at the testator's death and, therefore, the gift to them did not violate the vesting rule. Robert Ghiglia appeals from that decision.

VIOLATION OF THE VESTING RULE

We commence our decision by reciting the general rules of law applicable to the questions before us. Civil Code section 715.2 codifies the common law rule against perpetuities; it provides that no interest in real or personal property is valid unless it must vest, if at all, not later than 21 years after some life in being at the creation of the interest. Civil Code section 715.6 sets forth an alternate period in gross; it provides that "No interest . . . which must vest, if at all, not later than 60 years after the creation of the interest violates Section 715.2 . . . ."

The determination as to whether a future interest vests within the time allowed is made as of the moment the instrument containing the limitation speaks; we are not permitted to wait and see what happens in order to determine its validity. (Estate of Gump, 16 Cal. 2d 535, 547, 107 P.2d 17.) Thus, the validity of an interest in a testamentary trust is determined at the time of the testator's death. Moreover, it is not the probability that a perpetuity may have been created that brings the rule into operation. If, at the time of the creation of the interest, there exists even a bare possibility that the interest involved may not vest within the prescribed period, the rule has been violated.

If the possession of a testamentary gift to a class is postponed to a future time, the class includes all persons coming within the description within the time to which possession is postponed. (Prob.Code, § 123.) If the gift is not of a specific sum to each member or subgroup in the class, then the gift violates the vesting rule because the interest of each member cannot be finally ascertained until the membership is fixed.

In determining whether the testator intended the trust estate eventually to go to his four named grandchildren or to all of his possible grandchildren as a class, we must look to the language of the will and the surrounding circumstances and, inasmuch as a will speaks from the date of the testator's death, we also must consider the state of things then existing.

In the instant case, the testator's language is ambiguous. In subparagraph "F)" and "G)" of paragraph "Fourth" of the will, he provides that upon the death of the life beneficiaries of the trust (his daughter, Adeline, and his son, Robert), the trustee shall pay the net income to his four named grandchildren. Subparagraph "G)" then provides among other things that the trust shall continue "until *all of my grandchildren* have attained the age of thirty-five (35) years. In other words, *each trust* shall continue . . . , until *all of my grandchildren* reach the age of thirty-five (35) years. Upon such termination the entire trust estate shall be distributed to the persons for whom said estate is then held in trust . . . ." (Emphasis added.)

The first question to be decided is whether the phrase "all of my grandchildren" was intended to include the testator's grandchildren by his oldest son, Frank. We think not, for Frank received his one-third of the estate free of the trust, and presumably the testator intended that Frank would support his children during their minority and that they would inherit his estate upon his death. That the testator had this in mind is borne out by the fact that upon the death of Adeline and Robert the income beneficiaries of the trust are only their respective children. Nor do we see any logical reason why the testator would use Frank's children, who are not named as beneficiaries of the trust, as measuring lives to determine when the trust corpus should be distributed to Adeline and Robert's children. Accordingly, we construe the phrase "all of my grandchildren" to exclude Frank's children.

The second question, admittedly more difficult to resolve, is whether the phrase "all of my grandchildren" used to describe the ultimate beneficiaries of the trust corpus was intended to include only the four grandchildren named as income beneficiaries, or whether it was intended to include any additional grandchild born after the testator's death. If we conclude that the gift of the trust corpus was not limited to the four grandchildren, then the gift was to a class and would include all persons coming within the class description before the time to which possession is postponed.

When the testator executed his will, his daughter, Adeline, then was about 47 years of age, his son, Robert, was about 45 years of age and Robert's wife was about 39 years of age. It is entirely possible that either Adeline or Robert could have had another child. We find nothing in the language of the will to suggest that the testator intended to cut off from his estate any child thereafter born to Adeline or Robert. The fact that the testator designated only his four grandchildren as income beneficiaries does not force another conclusion; this designation is explained simply by the fact that the four grandchildren were the only children of Adeline and Robert living at the time the testator executed his will, and he did not contemplate the birth of an additional child to either Adeline or Robert. This belief becomes even more apparent if we view the circumstances as of the time of the testator's death when Adeline was then 53 years of age and Robert and his wife were 51 and 45 years of age; the testator simply assumed that they would not have any more children.

However, our search to ascertain the testator's intent cannot stop at this point merely because the testator did not contemplate the possibility that additional children might be produced by Adeline or Robert. We must ask: what if the possibility had been brought to his attention—would he nonetheless have excluded an after-born grandchild from his estate: In the absence of contrary evidence, we believe the answer is self-evident—he would have wanted an after-born grandchild to share in his estate. The use of the term "all my grandchildren" in reference to Adeline and Robert's children indicates that he intended that final distribution of his trust corpus would be made to those who would be the natural recipients of his beneficent objectives. Interpreting a similar provision in a will, the court in Estate of Van Wyck, 185 Cal. 49, 57, 196 P. 50, 54, said: "Reading it as a provision for such grandchildren only as should be born prior to the testator's death, it is an unnatural and unreasonable provision, and one contrary to the natural meaning of the language used. We think it certain, therefore, that by 'youngest grandchild' the testator meant exactly what he said—his youngest grandchild, whether born before or after his death." For the reasons stated in *Van Wyck*, we conclude that a reasonable interpretation of the will before us, reading the particular language in the light of the entire testamentary scheme, is that the testator intended to make a gift of the trust corpus to all of his grandchildren, including any born after his death.

It is clear that the gift violates the rule against remoteness of vesting. Either Adeline or Robert, in the eyes of the law, possibly could have another child who might not reach age 35 within 21 years after their respective deaths. Moreover, the child could be born more than 25 years after the testator's death and would not reach age 35 within 60 years after the creation of the interest under the alternative period in gross provided by Civil Code section 715.6.

Can we sever the invalid portion from the valid portion, i.e., can we uphold the gift of the trust corpus to the four members of the class living at the testator's death and exclude only the gift to a future member born after his death? We think not, for, again, we find nothing in the will to suggest that had the testator foreseen the partial invalidity of his testamentary scheme that he nonetheless would have intended to exclude a member of the class in order to save the interests of the other members. The test of severability is "whether the two (parts) are so parts of a single plan or scheme or otherwise so dependent one upon the other, that by avoiding the invalid provisions and allowing the valid to stand there will result a disposition of the estate so different from what the testator contemplated or so unreasonable that it must be presumed that (he) would not have made the valid provisions if he had been aware of the invalidity of the others." (Estate of Van Wyck, *supra*, 185 Cal. at p. 62, 196 P. at p. 56) We hold the gift to the unborn members of the class inseparable from the gift to the living members of the class.

REFORMATION

Contrary to appellant's position, however, it does not follow that the trust should be declared void because the vesting of the grandchildren's interest exceeds the lawful period of perpetuity. The testator's general intent was to create a spendthrift trust under which his children, Adeline and Robert, would receive the income for their lives, but would not receive a fee interest in the corpus—only the grandchildren would receive such an interest after the death of Adeline and Robert. Appellant seeks to overthrow the dominant intention of the testator by having the trust declared entirely void for remoteness merely because the testator is unable to defer the vesting of the trust estate in his grandchildren as long as he wished.

Testamentary dispositions that are otherwise valid are not necessarily invalidated by illegal limitations. Moreover, Probate Code section 101 provides in part: "A will is to be construed according to the intention of the testator. Where his intention cannot have effect to its full extent, *it must have effect as far as possible*." (Emphasis added.)

Of particular importance in the present case is Civil Code section 715.5. While we have been unable to find a California case applying this statute to uphold a testamentary disposition in violation of the rule against perpetuities, courts in other jurisdictions have taken such an approach. In Edgerly v. Barker, 66 N.H. 434, 31 A. 900, the testator left property in trust to be distributed among the children of his living son and daughter when the youngest reached age 40. In order to achieve the testator's primary intent and at the same time conform the trust to the limitation imposed by the rule against perpetuities, the court applied the *cy pres* doctrine and held that the grandchildren's interest would vest at 21 rather than 40. More recently, in Carter v. Berry, 243 Miss. 321, 140 So.2d 843, the court applied the doctrine of "equitable approximation" to make an invalid gift to the testator's children at age 25 distributable at age 21. This approach is in accord with English law where the severity of the common law rule has been mitigated by a statute providing, "[T]he disposition should be treated for all purposes as if, instead of being limited by reference to the age in fact specified, it had been limited by reference to the age nearest to that age which would, if specified instead, have prevented the disposition from being so void." (Perpetuities and Accumulations Act of 1964, ch. 55, § 4.)

We recognize that the testator intended that the gift of the trust corpus to his grandchildren be delayed until the youngest was sufficiently mature to deal responsibly with his inheritance and that the testator believed that age 35 was a prudent age for this purpose. However, this does not mean that, if faced with the realization that by postponing the vesting in his grandchildren to age 35 he rendered the trust itself invalid, with the result that two-thirds of his estate would be taken outright by Adeline and Robert, he nonetheless would not have elected to set up a trust with the corpus vesting at the time the youngest grandchild reached age 21 rather then age 35. We believe that rather than forego his dominant testamentary plan of preserving two-thirds of his estate for Adeline and Robert's children, he would have intended to give his trust estate to their children within a permissible period of time.

Because it is the duty of the court to give effect to the testator's general intent to the fullest extent possible, we hold that the trial court must use its power as defined in Civil Code section 715.5 to reform the will so that distribution of the trust corpus will be made when the youngest grandchild reaches 21 with the result that all class interests must vest within the required time.

The order on the petition for determination of rights and distribution is reversed; the matter is remanded to the trial court with directions to reform the last will of Frank P. Ghiglia, Deceased, in accordance with this opinion.

GEO. A. BROWN, P.J., and GARGANO, J., concur.

[c]   Explanatory Notes

[*i*]   *The Family Tree.* Part of the Ghiglia family tree is reproduced below. Referring to it should make your analysis of the case a bit easier. Ghiglia had three children. He gave one third of his estate to Frank Ghiglia, Jr. without any restrictions. That branch of the estate

plan is not at issue in the case. To ease the analysis a bit, Frank, Jr.'s line is left out of the diagram. The numbers in parentheses represent the ages of the various members of the family at the death of Frank Ghiglia, Sr. The court's opinion notes that each of the grandchildren were adults when Frank, Sr. died. Though we don't know their exact ages, we do know they were all at least 18 years of age. The maximum number of years it would take for each of the grandchildren to reach the age of 35 after the death of Frank, Sr., therefore, was 17.

The Ghiglia Family Tree

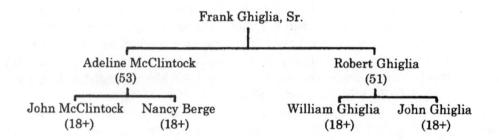

[*ii*]   **Work Out the Future Interests in Ghiglia.** Frank Ghiglia's will established two trusts. The income from one trust went to Ghiglia's daughter, Adeline Marguerite McClintock, for her life. When she died, the income was to be paid to her two children in equal amounts. Income from the other trust went to Ghiglia's son, Robert Ghiglia, for his life. When he died, his two children split his income stream. The two trusts were to be closed when the last of the grandchildren reached the age of 35. Paraphrasing, Ghiglia's will distributed a bunch of income interests and then provided:

> upon the death of my children Adeline and Robert, the trusts shall terminate and the assets shall be paid per stirpes to my grandchildren, provided that if the last of my grandchildren has not reached the age of 35, the trusts shall not terminate until the last of my grandchildren reaches the age of 35, but if no grandchild reaches the age of 35, then to my heirs at law.

This language created a contingent remainder in the grandchildren, which was also subject to defeasance.

[*iii*]   **Ghiglia and Class Gifts.** Before getting to the Rule Against Perpetuities, think about the court's conclusion that the contingent remainder in Ghiglia's will was a class gift to grandchildren. Despite the use of the open-ended word "grandchildren" in the will, the court quickly (and easily it noted) concluded that the children of Frank, Jr. were not included. At a minimum, therefore, it is fair to say that the testator did not actually mean to use the word "grandchildren" as a completely open designation of a class. Why then conclude that he intended to leave the class open for any additional children that might be parented by Adeline or Robert? Adeline and Robert's wife were probably past their child bearing years when Frank, Sr. died. Wouldn't it have made more sense to view the class gift as closed? The structure of the entire case actually depends on resolving this class gift issue, for as the next note indicates, there cannot possibly be a violation of the common law Rule Against Perpetuities if the gift is viewed as closed.

[iv] *Application of the Common Law Rule.* For starters, assume that the gift to the grandchildren was closed and included only the four living grandchildren of Frank, Sr.—John, Nancy, William and John. Then the gift could be rewritten as:

upon the death of my children Adeline and Robert, the trusts shall terminate and the assets shall be paid per stirpes to my grandchildren John, Nancy, William and John if the last of these four grandchildren has reached the age of 35, and if not all four have reached the age of 35, the trusts shall terminate when the last of them reaches the age of 35, but if none of John, Nancy, William or John reaches the age of 35, then to my heirs at law.

This interest would not violate the common law rule. Though it would be contingent when Frank, Sr. died if any of the four grandchildren had not yet reached age 35 that milestone would occur a maximum of 17 years after Frank, Sr.'s death. The interest would therefore vest less than 21 years after the death of Frank, Sr.

If the gift to the grandchildren is treated as an open class gift, then the gift is void under the common law rule. During the year after Frank, Sr.'s death, one of his children could have had another child. If Adeline and Robert then died, the new grandchild would not become 35 until more than 21 years after the death of Frank, Sr.'s children, the lives in being for purposes of applying the common law rule. Even if the couples were biologically incapable of having children, the interest would still be void. The common law cared not a bit about reality, but only about the theoretical possibility of vesting happening too late. Since the court found the gift to grandchildren to be open, the interest was void unless the statutory reform rule was applied to rescue it. That, of course, is exactly what the court did.

[d] Problem Notes

[i] *Ninety Years?* The Uniform Probate Code perpetuities provisions allow donors to allow contingent interests to survive for 90 years. And, of course, the end of contingency does not mean that the owners of interests will actually go into possession of the property. That step could be delayed for another quite substantial period of time. Why should any one person be able to control the disposition and use of property for such a long time? It is interesting to note that the standard terms for copyrights in the United States were recently enlarged and now last for the life of the author plus 70 years or, in the case of institutionally created works, for 90 years after the work is published.[38] Is there something about the 90 to 100 year range which is particularly important for modern property holders?

[ii] *Parents and Children.* Think about the different feelings of parents and children over the disposition of parental wealth. Should younger generations have as much to say about the distribution of property as older generations? Is it appropriate to allow one generation to so constrain the structure of property that later generations find it difficult to alter prior allocations of wealth?

[4] Future Interests and Perpetuities Reform: The Demise of Classical Legal Thought?

In the introduction to this chapter, the point was made that studying future interests and the Rule Against Perpetuities inevitably requires study of the role of formal or classical legal thought in American property law. Reliance on freedom of contract may be paradoxical in any setting in which donors are allowed to transfer property in ways that restrict the dispositional freedom

---

[38] 17 U.S.C. § 302.

of donees. In such settings one actor's freedom limits another's liberty. In a fascinating article on the nineteenth-century history of the perpetuities rule in the United States, Gregory Alexander describes the paradox.

Gregory S. Alexander, *The Dead Hand and the Law of Trusts in the Nineteenth Century*[39]

37 STAN. L. REV. 1189-91 (1985).

[There is] . . . a basic paradox at the core of liberal property law.[1] Individual freedom to dispose of consolidated bundles of rights cannot simultaneously be allowed and fully maintained. If the donor of a property interest tries to restrict the donee's freedom to dispose of that interest, the legal system, in deciding whether to enforce or void that restriction, must resolve whose freedom it will protect, that of the donor or that of the donee.

Although post-realist American property lawyers acknowledge this conflict, at least nominally, it did not emerge in legal consciousness in so starkly visible a form until the end of the nineteenth century. Several features of antebellum legal thought obscured the problem in the "dead hand" doctrines. Incident to the Classical, or late nineteenth century, effort to recategorize and rationalize private law rules on the basis of "scientific" principles that abandoned the old "feudal" policy supporting property's "technical" elements, these pre-Classical mediating devices began to erode. With the disintegration of the pre-Classical conceptual structure, Classical lawyers explicitly faced the problem of the freedom of disposition principle. Their effort to construct a synthesis that resolved the contradiction on an objective basis and that assimilated equitable with legal doctrine failed toward the end of the nineteenth century.

The demise of the Classical synthesis was signaled by the adoption in most jurisdictions of a pair of new trust law doctrines that reversed established trust rules. The spendthrift trust doctrine permitted trust transferors to tie up a beneficiary's interest by imposing direct restraints on its alienability. The *Claflin* doctrine soon thereafter immunized private trusts from attempts by beneficiaries to destroy them through premature termination. Far from being reconcilable with the conventional property rules which invalidate most restraints on legal interests, these doctrines placed trust and property, equity and law in fundamental conflict over the problem of freedom of disposition.

This doctrinal development and the changes in legal consciousness that underlay it are central to a historical understanding of the ideology of private property in liberal legal thought. Anglo-American lawyers have long identified the lifting of restraints on alienation as the major defining characteristic of a liberal commercial society as opposed to a feudal one. Along with liberty of contract, free alienation is one of the keystones of the twin policies of promoting individual autonomy and free exchange in competitive markets. Nineteenth century lawyers

[39] Republished with the permission of Gregory Alexander and the Stanford Law Review, 559 Nathan Abbott Way, Palo Alto, CA 94305. *The Dead Hand and the Law of Trusts in the Nineteenth Century*, G. Alexander, 1985, Vol. 37. Reproduced by permission of the publisher via Copyright Clearance Center, Inc.

[1] Two characteristics distinguish liberal property law. First, it promotes individual freedom of disposition as the basic mechanism for allocation. Second, it exhibits a strong preference for . . . [concentrating] in a single legal entity, usually an individual person, the relevant rights, privileges, and powers of possessing, using, and transferring discrete assets . . . .

conflated the distinction between state-imposed restrictions on alienation and privately imposed restraints, treating the policy underlying rules proscribing the latter as continuous with the policy opposed to the old feudal restraints. Their historical vision, which persists today, sees the development of the law of disposition as continuous and directional. Within this vision, modern lawyers have pushed the deviationist trust rules into a corner as aberrational or accommodated them on the basis of instrumentalist accounts of the doctrines as pragmatic responses to existing social "needs."

In the rest of his article, Alexander did two things with the freedom of alienation paradox he described. First, he tracked the development of the two areas of trust law noted above—the right of a donor to restrict the alienability of a beneficiary's interest in a trust, and the right of beneficiaries to terminate a trust prior to the date specified by the donor. At the opening of the nineteenth century, donors generally lacked the ability to restrain transfer of a beneficial interest in a trust, and beneficiaries were able to terminate their trusts. By the end of the century the rules had flipped, simultaneously increasing the dispositional authority of donors and decreasing that of donees.

Alexander also takes his readers on a lengthy journey through the corridors of judicial thought and legal commentary about these two changing areas of trust law. The large message is that the standard idea that progress in a liberal society may in part be measured by the solidity of rules about restraints on alienation is internally incoherent. New paradigms of thought, Alexander argued, based on "the recognition of the inevitability of interdependence" must be developed. Alexander constructed the constituent parts of his message by describing how various schools of legal thought in one way or another ignored the contradictions inherent in using freedom of alienation rhetoric to justify either the early or late nineteenth-century version of the trust rules. Early Republicans opining about perpetuities rules during the decades after the founding of the nation justified their rules by labeling dispositional control by beneficiaries as feudal or technical, and dispositional authority of donors as modern and liberal. And late nineteenth-century classical or formal thinkers, convinced that disposition of "clean" property bundles, unencumbered by conditions and limitations, was central to the maintenance of freedom, railed against the changes in trust rules. Both groups missed Alexander's central message—that reasoning about these rules by recourse to adages about alienability and liberalism was incoherent.

At one point in this discourse, Alexander wrote about the ways rhetoric about self-determination and protectionism was used by those attempting to justify the late nineteenth-century changes in trust doctrines.[40] Classical thinkers tended to measure freedom by the degree to which dispositional authority was protected by the state. Market participants were thought of as juridical equals, each capable of fully controlling their economic lives. Those outside of the market, however, such as dependent women and children, immigrants or blacks, were often discussed in quite different ways, evoking the need to protect them from the cruel vicissitudes of the economy, or cordon them off from economic influence. In fact, Alexander noted, the late

---

[40] The beginning of this discussion is found in 37 STAN. L. REV. at 1240.

nineteenth-century changes in trust rules were laden, not only with notions of protecting the dynasties of the wealthy, but also with paternalistic features designed to safeguard the well being of wives and children.

Alexander's description of the rhetoric surrounding nineteenth-century changes in trust perpetuities law conforms quite well with the history of the late nineteenth century. That era was replete with examples of law reform based on a mixture of dynastic and protectionist motivations. The cultural idea of generational replication—the desire of the middle and upper classes to maintain the social position of their offspring—requires that both social standing and wealth be passed in a protected way from generation to generation. Maintenance of the dynasty for the late nineteenth-century upper classes was heavily focused on children. From Anthony Comstock's anti-gambling crusades to anti-alcohol sit-ins by upper class women in Ohio in the 1870s, fear of immigration, the temptations of urban vice, and the loss of romantic visions of agricultural America led members of the upper classes to take steps to cordon off their children from the "frightful" images of city life. Boarding schools in the country side for children of the elite opened in droves, public prostitution and obscenity were subjected to constant diatribes, books thought to tempt children to adopt the vices of the lower classes were banned, and, lo and behold, trust rules were changed in ways that prevented children from altering their parents' economic preferences. This is indeed a case where the legal rhetoric about freedom of alienation for men and protectionism for women and children reflected deep currents of anxiety among those most concerned with the impacts of perpetuities rules. Perhaps similar fears also lay behind the contemporary enlargement of authority granted to members of the present generation to control the disposition of property by their successors.

The intellectual paradox Alexander discussed in his work was, therefore, mirrored in the social history of the late nineteenth century. Indeed, as the twentieth century opened, legal thinkers were beginning to openly note such contradictions, complain about classical reliance on freedom of contract and property alienation as central tenets of American political life, and construct new theories for justifying the existence and operation of regulatory regimes. The gradual unwinding of the political side of classical or formal modes of legal analysis is one of the subjects taken up in the next chapter on the rise of zoning, urban planning and land use regulation. And, of course, since history sometimes repeats itself, the paradox in nineteenth-century thought Alexander wrote about reappeared in recent decades as debates flowered over the wisdom of reforming the common law Rule Against Perpetuities. For part of that debate, *see* Jesse Dukeminier, *The Uniform Statutory Rule Against Perpetuities: Ninety Years in Limbo*, 34 UCLA L. REV. 1023 (1987).

CHAPTER 6

EMERGENCE OF HOUSING DEVELOPMENTS IN THE TWENTIETH
CENTURY: SERVITUDES, REALISM, CLASS AND RACE

§ 6.01 Introduction

This chapter is divided into two large parts. The first reviews interests that one party may hold in the land of another—easements, covenants and equitable servitudes, or *servitudes* as they are called in the tentative draft of the new Restatement Third of the Law of Property. The second investigates the early history of zoning and land use regulation. Both servitudes and zoning came into prominence during the decades just prior to the Great Depression. They are intimately linked to the contours of contemporary residential housing development. The use of servitudes and zoning to shape housing development, like the use of limited fee simple estates, emerged in an era in which racial segregation was a central feature of American life. Their early history is entangled with the cultural impacts of industrialization, urbanization, immigration, and migration of blacks from south to north that dominated life in the United States prior to the Depression. One goal of this chapter is to tell this complicated, but fascinating story.

The second overall object of this chapter is to explore some of the changes in legal thinking affecting property law that emerged in response to classical or Formalist legal thought. "By the end of the nineteenth century," Kenneth Vandevelde wrote in *The New Property of the Nineteenth Century*, "Blackstone's conception of property as absolute dominion over things had become fatally anachronistic, and was supplanted by a new form of property. This new property had been dephysicalized and thus consisted not of rights over things, but of any valuable right. It consisted not of an absolute or fixed constellation of rights, but of a set of rights which were limited according to the situation."[1] Property was no longer about things, but about legal relationships. This concept of property had the potential to encompass the entire legal world. The merger of contract and property accomplished after the Civil War was small potatoes compared to the potential scope of this new relational form of property, for any relationship involving something of actual or potential value could be said to involve property. In order to prevent such a property concept from becoming too imperialist, Vandevelde argued, those in authority established limiting principles to allow for the creation of property only when public policy demanded it. These policy based developments of property were said to be *realist,* firmly based in the realistic needs of the people.

A good argument may be made that some aspects of both Formalism and Realism fit Vandevelde's description of what property was becoming. For a Formalist believed that property rights arose when people contracted for their labor or made investments to increase their capital.

---

[1] Kenneth Vandevelde, *The New Property of the Nineteenth Century: The Development of the Modern Concept of Property,* 29 Buff. L. Rev. 325, 330 (1980).

These sorts of arrangements were certainly relational. They did not involve property as a thing, but as a set of relationships—formalized, rigid, pre-ordained, scientific and rational—but relational nonetheless. The major gloss added by the Realists was that this relationship was not independent of government but totally dependent upon and intertwined with government. Realist property was a creature of the state, developed to further some important public policy. And reliance on the social sciences—the newly developing disciplines designed to discover how society really functioned—was a central feature of Realist thought.

The Realists had an agenda quite different from the Formalists. The primary goal of the Realists was to break down the rationalist, scientific, pre-ordained characteristics of Formalist modes of thought. For the Realists, law was the implementation of public policy. Property and contracts were not privately ordered structures the state was duty bound to protect, but publicly ordained structures of wealth authorized by and subject to government authority and control. The right to contract for one's labor was not the *sine qua non* of liberty, but an opportunity for exploitation. White men were not juridical equals, each capable of protecting their interests in the market place, but realistically subject to differing sets of social forces and constraints. Government protection of private ordering was not the appropriate method for allowing the fittest to survive, but an abdication of responsibility to govern. The many judicial decisions during the last decades of the nineteenth and the first decades of the twentieth centuries invalidating—on freedom of contract grounds—statutes regulating the work place were viewed as a usurpation of the authority of legislative bodies to resolve important questions of public policy. Property, Morris Cohen argued in his famous article *Property and Sovereignty,* was a species of state legitimated authority exercised by owners over others.[2] He wrote:

Anyone who frees himself from the crudest materialism readily recognizes that as a legal term property denotes not material things but certain rights. In the world of nature apart from more or less organized society, there are things but clearly no property rights.

Further reflection shows that a property right is not to be identified with the fact of physical possession. Whatever technical definition of property we may prefer, we must recognize that a property right is a relation not between an owner and a thing, but between the owner and other individuals in reference to things. A right is always against one or more individuals. This becomes unmistakably clear if we take specifically modern forms of property such as franchises, patents, good will, etc., which constitute such a large part of the capitalized assets of our industrial and commercial enterprises.

The classical view of property as a right over things resolves it into component rights such as the *jus utendi, jus disponendi,* etc. But the essence of private property is always the right to exclude others. The law does not guarantee me the physical or social ability of actually using what it calls mine. By public regulations it may indirectly aid me by removing certain general hindrances to the enjoyment of property. But the law of property helps me directly only to exclude others from using the things which it assigns to me. If then somebody else wants to use the food, the house, the land, or the plow which the law calls mine, he has to get my consent. To the extent that these things are necessary to the life of my neighbor, the law thus confers on me a power, limited but real, to make him do what I want. If Laban has the sole disposal of his daughters and his cattle, Jacob must serve him if he desires to possess them. In a regime where land is the principal source of obtaining a livelihood, he who has

---

[2] Morris R. Cohen, *Property and Sovereignty,* 13 CORNELL L.Q. 11-12, 14 (1927). © 1927 by Cornell University. All rights reserved. Reprinted with the permission of Cornell Law Review and Fred B. Rothman & Co.

the legal right over the land receives homage and service from those who wish to live on it.

The character of property as sovereign power compelling service and obedience may be obscured for us in a commercial economy by the fiction of the so-called labor contract as a free bargain and by the frequency with which service is rendered indirectly through a money payment. But not only is there actually little freedom to bargain on the part of the steel worker or miner who needs a job, but in some cases the medieval subject had as much power to bargain when he accepted the sovereignty of his lord. Today I do not directly serve my landlord if I wish to live in the city with a roof over my head, but I must work for others to pay him rent with which he obtains the personal services of others. The money needed for purchasing things must for the vast majority be acquired by hard labor and disagreeable service to those to whom the law has accorded dominion over the things necessary for subsistence.

. . . .

[T]he recognition of private property as a form of sovereignty is not itself an argument against it. Some form of government we must always have. For the most part men prefer to obey and let others take the trouble to think out rules, regulations and orders. That is why we are always setting up authorities; and when we cannot find any we write to the newspaper as the final arbiter. While, however, government is a necessity, not all forms of it are of equal value. At any rate it is necessary to apply to the law of property all those considerations of social ethics and enlightened public policy which ought to be brought to the discussion of any just form of government.

The Realists, in short, had a clear cut agenda—to delegitimate the laissez faire ideology that went with the brand of Formalism prevalent in the late nineteenth century. The legitimization of urban planning, housing and building codes, and zoning was part of this agenda during the years before the Depression.

For additional readings on Realism and property, *see* Kenneth J. Vandevelde, *The New Property of the Nineteenth Century: The Development of the Modern Concept of Property,* 29 BUFF. L. REV. 325 (1980); Felix S. Cohen, *Dialogue on Private Property,* 9 RUTGERS L. REV. 357 (1954); Morris R. Cohen, *Property and Sovereignty,* 13 CORNELL L. Q. 8 (1927), all reprinted in RICHARD H. CHUSED, A PROPERTY ANTHOLOGY 83-104 (2d ed. 1997).

§ 6.02 Servitudes and Private Residential Developments

[1] Introduction

In the last chapter, you learned about limited fee simples. These devices were often used before 1920 as land use control devices. Today they have been replaced by easements, covenants and equitable servitudes. While the limited fees are still used in some documents making gifts for specific purposes to charities, they are rarely used in residential developments. The story of the switch from limited fees to servitudes is nicely told in an article by Timothy Jost excerpted here.

Timothy Jost, *The Defeasible Fee and the Birth of the Modern Residential Subdivision*

49 Mo. L. Rev. 695-714, 719-721, 724-726, 728-739 (1984)[*]

I. INTRODUCTION

In the late nineteenth and early twentieth centuries, the United States experienced an unprecedented building spree. With the quickened pace of housing construction came a dramatic innovation in residential housing development: the emergence of the modern restricted residential subdivision. Across the nation, developers large and small began to build blocks of uniformly spaced and similarly constructed houses, separated from industrial and commercial uses, and largely segregated by class and race.

Developers sought new legal tools to assure the restricted character of these subdivisions. Eventually, such tools emerged: real covenants, equitable servitudes, negative easements, and finally, zoning. But at the end of the mid-nineteenth century, public land use planning was largely non-existent. Even private restrictions were still nascent, undeveloped, and most important, unfamiliar to most lawyers. The lawyers advising the subdividers and developers of the period faced a not uncommon problem: how does the legal counselor and drafter satisfy the demand for new legal tools and doctrines emanating from changing social and economic needs? The drafter of the period, and, more to the point, the drafter's client, were not interested in providing a test case to extend the common law precedents. Though creation of new legal tools through legislation was a conceivable solution, legislation was not always politically possible, and was a less common approach to legal problems in the nineteenth century than it is now. Ideally, the drafter could have received direction from the treatise writers and law review commentators, who have always purported to guide the profession. But these sources were not only far more scarce a century ago than now, they were also even more out of touch with the needs of practitioners.

In the common law tradition, lawyers of the late nineteenth and early twentieth centuries looked to the existing cases and attempted to meet the needs of their clients, the developers and subdividers, through extension or new application of the tools they found. The defeasible fee was the tool chosen by many lawyers who first considered the problem of restricting the new subdivisions their clients were developing.[5] During the late nineteenth and early twentieth centuries, the defeasible fee became a common device for restricting land use in most jurisdictions, ubiquitous in a few. Thousands, perhaps millions, of deeds were written conveying property conditional on observance of various land use restrictions.

The choice of the defeasible fee was on the whole unfortunate, indeed, a disaster. The use of defeasible fees for restricting residential subdivisions caused innumerable problems, some of which continue to plague us to the present. Moreover, defeasible fee restrictions were seldom enforced by the courts, at least through forfeiture, and thus did not directly achieve their restrictive purpose. By the third decade of the twentieth century, the defeasible fee was by and large abandoned as a land use planning device, though it continues to surface in casebooks and treatises discussing private land use planning, and of course, continues to be useful in

---

[*] Copyright 1984 Curators of the University of Missouri. Reprinted with the permission of the Missouri Law Review and the author.

[5] The term defeasible fee is used here in accordance with the RESTATEMENT OF PROPERTY . . . to include the fee simple determinable, fee simple subject to a condition subsequent, and fee simple subject to an executory limitation. . ..

other contexts. Litigation involving the defeasible fee, however, seems to have helped point the way to other, more functional, forms of deed restrictions that matured as the use of the defeasible fee waned. In this respect, the defeasible fee may have played an important role in the development of modern private land use planning.

This article tells the story of the emergence and decline of the defeasible fee as a land use planning device. In doing so, it also examines the beginnings of private residential land use planning in the United States. Finally, it seeks to shed some light on the phenomenon of the development and dissemination of legal knowledge and customs in a non-litigation context in the late nineteenth and early twentieth centuries. The article is based not only on cases and literature from and about this period, but also on the author's review of deeds from subdivisions spanning the period of 1870 to 1930 from four American cities that were undergoing rapid expansion during the period.[12]

II. Urban Growth in the Late Nineteenth and Early Twentieth Centuries

Three eras have been identified in the history of American urban development.[13] During the first phase, from colonial times until about 1860, urban growth was constrained because the principal form of transportation in cities was walking. This made it necessary for most people to live close enough to walk to the places where they worked, shopped, and obtained services. The second phase of urban growth occurred during the second half of the nineteenth and early twentieth centuries, as developments in transportation technology made distinct and more widely spread residential districts possible. First, the horse-drawn trolley car and steam-powered train, and later the electric railway and the elevated subway, radically expanded the scale of urban development. The third phase began about 1920, as the rapid proliferation of the automobile further amplified the possibilities of suburban growth and contributed to the creation of the modern metropolis. This article focuses on the second stage of development, from 1870 to 1920, during which the modern residential subdivision was born.

Though innovations in transportation technology undoubtedly played a major role in giving rise to the modern residential subdivision, several other forces also converged to conceive and give a particular form to residential subdivision development. First, other technical and economic changes gave impetus to the building boom. In particular, the perfection of balloon frame construction made possible efficient mass construction of residential dwellings in the new subdivisions. Additionally, in the late nineteenth century, the development of institutions and methods to provide capital for residential development—in particular, for financing owner-occupied, single family dwellings—permitted unprecedented levels of residential construction and purchase.

Other social and intellectual conditions gave direction to the new form of development. Traditional American distaste for city living flowered during the nineteenth century. Urban concentration of population, while perhaps necessary for economic reasons, was believed to be unhealthy and morally degrading. Urban congestion was considered a major social evil. By contrast, country living was idealized. Suburban life partook of the best of both urban and rural environments, combining at once the open air and spaciousness of the country with the sanitary improvements, comforts, and associated life of the city.

---

[12] The author reviewed deeds found in the recording offices of Franklin County (Columbus), Ohio; Suffolk County (Boston), Massachusetts; Cook County (Chicago), Illinois; and the District of Columbia. . ..

[13] C. Glaab & A. Brown, A History of Urban America (1967); S. Warner, Streetcar Suburbs (1978).

. . . .

Finally, the late nineteenth century saw the emergence of American city planning, a development that had some influence on the nature of suburban growth. The era is best remembered for its grand urban designs: Burnham's plans for Chicago and San Francisco, and the plan of Burnham, Olmstead and others for Washington, D.C. However, some advocates of city planning also attended to development at the suburban level. Planned residential communities emerged in the United States as early as 1870. While speculative unplanned residential subdivision continued throughout the period, the planning movement contributed to the emergence of ordered and restricted subdivisions.

The decentralization of the nation's large urban areas, through the outward spread of residential subdivisions, began as early as the 1850's but became really significant only after 1870. By 1900, ten American cities of more than 50,000 population had decentralized and by 1930, 51 more had undergone this process. The character of the new residential neighborhoods that emerged in these decentralized urban areas varied somewhat by location, economic status of occupants, and time of construction. By the end of the nineteenth century, however, the basic model of residential development was established that would continue to the present: detached, single-family housing segregated from other uses and arranged on uniform blocks fronting on residential streets, usually laid out in a grid pattern.

III. LEGAL TOOLS FOR RESTRICTING SUBDIVISIONS

Developers and home buyers desired legal control mechanisms to protect and preserve this residential environment. A home buyer was often investing his or her life savings, and was vitally concerned with the protection of this investment. Moreover, the purchaser bought not only a piece of property, but also a way of life. Controls were necessary to assure that neighboring lots were not developed for commercial use or, worse yet, industrial uses that would destroy the homeowner's peaceful enjoyment of his property and diminish the value of his investment. The purchaser of a suburban lot desired exterior open space for access to light and air, provision for that great American institution, the lawn, and room for a garden for relaxation and for a place for the children to play. Even if this open space consisted of a pitifully few feet of grass between the house and the street and a slightly larger space to the rear between the house and the alley or the rear of an adjacent lot, it was still treasured. Purchasers in the new subdivisions also sought to protect the resale value of their investment through restrictions that would assure uniformity of building size, value, and architecture.

Until 1920, most residential real estate was controlled, if at all, only through private plat and deed restrictions.[33] Until late in the nineteenth century, however, even private law deed restrictions, as we know them today, were still immature. Though a number of devices for permitting one landowner to enjoy rights in the property of another had emerged earlier in a variety of contexts, none of these devices were ideally suited for restricting residential subdivisions.

The legal restriction needed for creating and preserving residential subdivisions had to meet certain specifications. First, it had to be enforceable against all subsequent purchasers (i.e.,

---

[33] Control over the development and use of property would, of course, be provided during the third, post-1920 stage of urban development by public zoning and subdivision controls. But zoning did not really take hold until the second decade of the twentieth century. New York, the first major city to adopt zoning, did so in 1916 . . . .. The legitimacy of zoning was not finally established until *Village of Euclid v. Ambler Realty Co.*, 272 U.S. 365 (1926).

the burden of the obligation had to run with the land). Second, the restriction had to be enforceable not only by the developer, but also by the subsequent purchasers (i.e., the benefit of the obligation had to run with the land). An initial purchaser could, of course, at the time of sale, take on obligations to the developer through a contract restricting the purchaser's development and use of his or her property. This was not adequate, however, since such a contract would not bind future owners of the restricted parcel or benefit purchasers of neighboring lots. What was needed was a device that created something more than contractual relationships between the developer and purchasers. A device was needed that would create durable property interests mutually enforceable by and against all owners of lots in the development.

The law as it existed at the outset of our period presented three tools used in other contexts, each of which met some of these specifications and could be adapted to the job of restricting property: the defeasible fee, the real covenant, and the negative easement. By the end of the nineteenth century, a fourth device, the equitable servitude, emerged as the tool preferred by the courts for subdivision restriction.

The real covenant was, by the nineteenth century, recognized by English property law in a variety of contexts. Covenants placed in deeds provided security of title. The earlier law of warranty had been, by this time, replaced by covenants of warranty, right to convey, seisin, quiet enjoyment, further assurances and against encumbrances. The benefits of these covenants of title attached to and ran with the estate of the covenantee. Covenants that attached to and ran with the estates of lessors and lessees were also utilized to govern landlord-tenant relationships.

For the covenant to be functional in creating restrictions in the residential subdivision context, however, it was necessary that the burden of the covenant obligation, as well as the benefit, attach to and run with the land in situations where privity of estate, in the sense of a landlord-tenant relationship, did not exist. This possibility was blocked in England where, by the early nineteenth century, courts had held that the burden of real covenants would not run at law in the absence of tenurial privity.[40] This restrictive definition of privity was early rejected by Judge Hare, the most influential commentator on real covenants in nineteenth century America, in favor of a broader definition, finding privity between any grantor and grantee of property. Most American courts that considered the issue concurred and permitted the burden of a real covenant to run whenever there was a grantor-grantee relationship between the initial covenantee and covenantor. Indeed, some courts permitted the burden of covenants to run even in the absence of privity of estate. . . . .

The receptivity of American courts and commentators to the running of real covenants no doubt contributed to the increasingly frequent use of real covenant language, by drafters of the period, in creating deed restrictions. By the early twentieth century, many deeds used the word "covenant," or specified that restrictions should "run with the land." Rarely, however, did cases address whether residential deed restrictions were enforceable as covenants at law.

This was true first, because the most controversial aspects of covenant doctrine were seldom at issue in the subdivision restriction context. The requirement that restrictions "touch and concern" burdened and benefited property, a much litigated aspect of covenant law, was not

---

[40] *Keppel v. Bailey*, 2 My. & K. 517, 39 Eng. Rep. 1042 (1834); *Webb v. Russell*, 3 Tem. Rep. 393, 106 Eng. Rep. 639 (1789). . ..

an issue because subdivision restrictions were almost exclusively negative in character, imposing limitations on the development of the burdened properties. Thus, they clearly touched and concerned affected properties by any definition. The negative nature of most subdivision restrictions also largely obviated consideration of the issue of privity, which during the nineteenth century came up as a problem almost exclusively in actions brought to enforce affirmative obligations.

Second, and more important, the paucity of decisions discussing deed restrictions as covenants is attributable to the fact that plaintiffs seeking to enforce subdivision restrictions normally brought actions for equitable relief. In these cases, the question of whether restrictions were enforceable at law as covenants was seldom dispositive. The few cases pronouncing deed restrictions to be covenants did so in the context of either saying the restrictions were not something else or as a predicate to enforcing them at equity.

Another candidate for the job of restricting residential subdivisions was the negative easement. An easement is an interest in land possessed by another which entitles the owner of the easement to limited use and enjoyment of the other's land. This interest is protected against interference by third parties and is capable of creation by conveyance. It is not subject to the will of the possessor of the servient property nor a normal incident of the possession of any other land of the owner of the dominant parcel. One common example of an easement is a right of way across the land of another. The negative easement by analogy created negative rights in the land of another. It entitled its owner to prevent the possessor of the land from using the land in specific ways otherwise within the possessor's rights. A number of early cases interpreting deed restrictions held that the restrictions created negative easements.

By the mid-nineteenth century, an extensive body of easement law existed in the United States. The negative easement was reluctantly acknowledged by English law, which recognized only four negative easements: the rights to air, light, support, and water in an artificial stream. But negative easements came to be used expansively in the United States, not only for protecting light and air, but also for enforcing setback lines and limiting noxious uses. The easement was superior to the covenant as a restricted tool because it was not subject to a requirement of privity. As deed restrictions became more complex and extended beyond establishing setback lines and limiting nuisances, however, they bore less resemblance to traditional easements and seemed increasingly fictive. Some American courts were hesitant to recognize negative easements for purposes not known to the common law. Moreover, while restrictions treated as easements were commonly enforced at equity, some courts expressed doubt whether they were enforceable at law. This suggests that such "equitable easements" were not in fact true easements. Perhaps because of these uncertainties, drafters of subdivision restrictions were less enamored with easement theory than were the courts. None of the deeds surveyed by the author denominated use restrictions as easements.

As actions for injunctions to enforce subdivision deed restrictions became more common, it became increasingly clear that courts were not particularly concerned with the legal classification of restrictions, only with whether the restrictions ought to be enforced at equity. Thus, a fourth kind of restriction enforceable at equity, variously called an equitable servitude, equitable easement, or sometimes an (equitable) negative easement, came to the fore as the primary tool the courts recognized for enforcing subdivision restrictions. Though this development is commonly traced to the English case of *Tulk v. Moxhay*,[66] American cases

---

[66] 2 Phi. Ch. 774 (1848).

enforcing restrictions at equity antedate *Tulk.*[67] The theories courts put forward for equitable enforcement of restrictions varied widely. Some courts believed that they were enforcing covenants at equity, others that they were specifically enforcing negative easements, still others that they were simply enforcing a promise against successors to a promisor with notice of the promise. Theory was a good deal less important to the courts than were the equities of the situation being litigated. The primary concern of the courts was identifying the obligor and beneficiary of a duty respecting a parcel of land.

The willingness of these courts to enforce virtually any form of restriction at equity made relatively unimportant the form of restriction drafters used. Nevertheless, drafters of subdivision deed restrictions generally attempted to use recognized legal devices. Most commonly, they used either covenant or condition rather than easement or equitable servitude language. This may be attributable to the relatively slow recognition and exploration of equitable servitudes in the cases and commentary, caution and fear of innovation on the part of the drafters, or a desire by drafters for remedial options other than the injunction, i.e., damages for forfeiture. Avoidance of equitable servitudes in a few situations may also have been due to the reluctance of some American jurisdictions to enforce affirmative obligations through equitable servitudes.

IV. The Defeasible Fee as a Land Use Planning Tool

While the law of real covenants, negative easements, and equitable servitudes was still in a formative stage until late in the nineteenth century, the drafter of deed restrictions of that period had ready access to an elaborate law of defeasible fees developed in closely related contexts, such as charitable or public donations, industrial development, family settlements, and support arrangements. It was natural for many developers to turn first to this body of law for models for drafting residential subdivision restrictions. It is not surprising, therefore, that use of defeasible fees for deed restrictions was widespread during the period from 1870 until 1920, appearing before other forms of restriction in many jurisdictions and becoming nearly universal in some areas.

For the benefit of those whose memory of first year property is now fuzzy, a quick review of the lore of defeasible fees is in order. The 1936 Restatement of Property distinguished three kinds of defeasible fees: the fee simple determinable—created by any limitation that establishes an estate in fee simple and provides that the estate shall automatically expire upon the occurrence of a stated event; the fee simple subject to a condition subsequent—created by any condition that establishes an estate in fee simple and provides that upon the occurrence of a stated event the grantor or his successor shall have the power to terminate the estate; and the fee simple subject to an executory limitation, which establishes an estate in fee simple in a grantee but provides that upon the occurrence of a stated event the grantee will be divested in favor of another transferee other than the grantor or his successor. A fee simple determinable would be created by a grant for so long as the property were used for residential purposes. A grant in fee, but subject to the condition that if the property were ever to be used for other than residential purposes, the grantor or his heirs could re-enter and take possession, would create a fee simple subject to a condition subsequent. Finally, a grant for so long as the property were used for residential purposes, but stipulating that if the property were ever used for other than residential purposes it would pass to a third party other than the grantor or grantee, would create a fee simple subject to an executory limitation. In each instance, the grant of a defeasible

---

[67] *Barrow v. Richard,* 8 Paige Ch. 351 (N.Y. Ch. 1840); *Hills v. Miller,* 3 Paige Ch. 254 (N.Y. Ch. 1832).

fee would create a future interest. The future interests that correspond to the three defeasible estates are: the possibility of reverter, the power of termination (or right of reentry), and the executory interest. The Restatement's classification of these three categories of defeasible fees is more or less in line with other modern sources, and on the whole consistent with the distinctions generally recognized by authorities in the nineteenth century.

These distinctions were of little practical importance to the drafters of deed restrictions in the late nineteenth and early twentieth centuries or to the courts interpreting those restrictions. The fee simple subject to executory limitation was not commonly used for deed restrictions. Though this type of defeasible fee could, in theory, have been used to transfer the responsibility of enforcement of restrictions from developers to neighbors or neighborhood associations who could have been granted the executory interest, the author discovered no examples of this kind of grant. This paucity of fees subject to executory limitation is no doubt attributable to the fact that these interests were subject to the Rule Against Perpetuities, and thus avoided by drafters who feared the many hazards of that Rule.

. . . .

More common were deeds expressly stipulating that breaches of conditions would cause the property to "revert to the grantor" or "work forfeiture of the estate," or cause the deed of conveyance to be void, or some combination of these terms. Though these terms seemed to contemplate the automatic reversion, a characteristic of determinable fees, the courts generally interpreted them as creating fees subject to condition subsequent rather than determinable fees. Occasionally, courts interpreted these terms as creating covenants, or described them by hybrid terms such as "conditional estate in the nature of a negative easement" or "right of reverter." A few courts stated that such language created a possibility of reverter, though exhibiting no awareness that the possibility of reverter was distinguishable from the right of entry.

. . . .

The defeasible fee differs dramatically from the other forms of restrictions in its remedy. Violation of one of the other forms of restrictions renders the violator liable for damages or injunctive relief. There is necessarily some relationship between the seriousness of the breach and the penalty, if any, imposed. Violation of a restriction imposed by the grant of a defeasible fee results, at least in theory, in forfeiture, a remedy that bears no necessary relationship to the nature of the breach, and that is, in fact, in most instances inappropriately draconian.

Undoubtedly, many developers and their attorneys turned to the defeasible fee as a tool for restricting subdivisions because of the common use of conditions for restricting the use of property in other contexts. However, it must have seemed, at the time, a propitious choice. First, restriction of a subdivision through uniform conditional deeds appeared to offer substantial protection to purchasers of subdivision lots. The threat of forfeiture impressed the legally unsophisticated purchaser of a lot worried about the enforceability of deed restrictions. The purchaser to whom the defeasible deed restriction was touted no doubt believed that if a neighbor built a slaughterhouse or a bay window projecting out beyond the setback line the neighbor's property would revert to the developer. Forfeiture appeared on its face a much more effective deterrent than the threat of a damage suit. Moreover, conditional restrictions enforced by forfeiture clearly ran with the land to bind future purchasers. A purchaser of land in a development did not have to worry that the burden of restrictions might be lifted once its lots began to change hands.

The defeasible fee also met the needs of the developer. Indeed, it yielded benefits not accessible through other forms of deed restrictions. The law was relatively clear that, in theory, restrictions applied through defeasible estates could exist in gross; therefore the power to enforce the restrictions could be held by a developer even though that developer did not retain any other property in the development. This was not clearly true with equitable servitudes or real covenants. Further, the use of defeasible fees appeared to allow the developer to market a subdivision at a premium as a restricted community without really limiting options for future development. Where the developer imposed a restriction through an equitable servitude contained in a deed to a purchaser in a subdivision, and the purchaser believed that the servitude would be imposed throughout the development as part of a common scheme, the developer might be obligated to include such a restriction in all future deeds in the development. The defeasible fee was more clearly a one way device. Technically, the developer who granted the defeasible fee retained an estate or a power, but was not in any way limited as to the development of other properties. If the development sold poorly, the developer could, without apparent liability, change the layout or even sell lots for commercial development. Further, the defeasible fee was well adapted for developers who retained property for themselves within the development or who felt strongly enough about some issues, such as the sale of alcohol or race restrictions, to desire continued control over the development even after their last lots had been sold. This control could be retained more effectively through defeasible fee restrictions than through alternative restrictive devices. Finally, some developers may have desired the gambler's chance of actually recovering property for resale if a condition was breached or the potential for future profit by sale of releases.

. . . .

VI. USES OF DEFEASIBLE FEE RESTRICTIONS

. . . .

Excessive use of alcohol was a serious social problem in the early nineteenth century . . . . By the end of the nineteenth century, the neighborhood bar represented the urban, South European Catholic immigrant influence from which many of those buying suburban property were escaping . . . . During the . . . pervasive temperance movement of the 1870's through the 1920's, . . . restrictions [against the sale or manufacture of alcohol] became nearly universal in some areas.

A broader use of conditional deed restrictions was to forbid uses regarded as nuisances in a residential district . . . . [Eventually] deeds appeared forbidding all nonresidential uses.

. . . .

A final conditional restriction, the racial exclusion, became common, indeed in some areas ubiquitous, in the 1890's and early 1900's. A great many deeds written during this period provided that if the property were sold or leased to or occupied by members of excluded racial groups, it would revert to the grantor. Blacks (referred to as Negroes, Africans, or Ethiopians) were the racial group most commonly excluded, but many deeds excluded all non-Caucasians, and others, particularly in the West, excluded Orientals (Mongolians).

Race restrictions were regarded at the time by some as essential for planned, restricted developments. They allowed developers to achieve through private restrictions what could not be done through zoning. . . . .

Courts uniformly enforced racial restrictions on occupancy (though not necessarily on sale) until the 1950's, finding them to violate neither the Constitution nor public policy. Indeed, the defeasible fee formed one of the last barricades of proponents of legal residential racial segregation. In 1948, the Supreme Court, in *Shelley v. Kraemer*[215] swept the records clear of all other forms of racially exclusive deed restrictions by holding that the fourteenth amendment forbade their enforcement through the state courts. Seven years later, the North Carolina Supreme Court, in *Charlotte Park and Recreation Commission v. Barringer,*[216] held that *Shelley v. Kraemer* did not apply to determinable fees limited by racial restrictions, since the determinable interest terminated automatically without state involvement if the racial limitation was violated. The Supreme Court denied certiorari. This decision provoked extensive commentary, most of it negative, but is of doubtful continuing effect. Developments in civil rights law and, it is hoped, in public morality have precluded a resurgence of defeasible fee limitations to enforce racial segregation.

. . . .

VII. Deficiencies of the Defeasible Fee as a Land Use Planning Device

The popularity of the defeasible fee as a land use planning device was relatively brief. It is not difficult to understand its demise. From the start, the courts were hostile to the use of forfeiture as a tool for land use planning. Traditional abhorrence of forfeitures disposed the courts against enforcing deed restrictions written in conditional language through defeasance. Judges found numerous ways of avoiding forfeiture. The simplest approach was to construe a condition strictly to avoid finding a violation. Other approaches attacked the use of defeasible fees more directly.

Courts frequently permitted defendants to interpose equitable defenses to avoid forfeiture. The most frequently sustained equitable defenses were estoppel, waiver and laches (or, closely related, failure to claim forfeiture within the statute of limitations) . . . . Others held that grantors could only enforce conditions if they retained property to which the restricted property was appurtenant, effectively creating a new rule that conditions could not exist in gross. Finally, some courts construed conditional restrictions as enforceable only for a reasonable period of time.

. . . .

Even when courts did not expressly refuse to enforce conditions or limitations through forfeiture, they frequently achieved the same result by construing conditional language to create covenants or equitable servitudes. The restrictions would then be enforced through injunctive relief rather than forfeiture. Courts were especially likely to interpret conditional language to create an equitable servitude or covenant rather than a defeasible fee if a deed contained no reversion or reentry clause — if the remedy of forfeiture was not explicitly reserved. Courts also frequently granted injunctions to enforce conditions in suits brought by neighbors of the violator. Such neighbors were, of course, interested in the equitable relief rather than forfeiture, and seldom held a right of entry or possibility of reverter. Neighbors could equitably enforce conditions reserved by a grantor under the theory that, by accepting a conditional deed, the grantee made a promise to abide by the conditions independently enforceable at equity.

[215] 334 U.S. 1 (1948).
[216] 242 N.C. 311, 88 S.E.2d 114 (1955) . . . .

Courts not only interpreted conditions as equitable servitudes, but some jurisdictions applied the changed conditions defense to enforcement of equitable servitudes to avoid enforcing conditions at all. The tendency of the courts to treat conditional restrictions as equitable interests, enforceable, if at all, only through injunctive relief, undoubtedly played a significant role in the development and education of the bar in the lore of equitable servitudes.

The reluctance of the judiciary to enforce conditions as such was not the only cause of the demise of the defeasible fee, which soon exhibited serious deficiencies as a land use planning device. First, it became clear that the defeasible fee was in fact of little value to purchasers in a subdivision. Forfeiture was not a remedy available to adjoining landowners, who in most instances had the only real interest in enforcing deed restrictions. The right to enforce a conditional restriction by forfeiture could not, in many jurisdictions, be transferred from the developer to interested residents in the subdivision or to a property owners' association. Even where transfer was permitted, difficulties with transfer to many parties of the essentially indivisible right of enforcement made this solution impractical. Further, the owner of the reversionary interest could at any time release it, rendering the residents of the subdivision without protection.

If violation of a restriction was enforced through forfeiture, further problems resulted. Once the property was forfeited to the developer for violation of a condition, the restriction ceased to exist, and the developer could resell or use the property for any other purpose. Moreover, rights upon forfeiture were unclear. Established doctrine, for example, did not clearly decide who should get the value of improvements if property was forfeited.

. . . .

Because conditional restrictions in theory made title depend on the manner in which the property was in fact used or developed, the defeasible fee made security of the title of an owner, potential purchaser, or mortgagee depend on facts extraneous to the title record. Indeed, some conditions such as alcohol or cost of improvement restrictions could be breached by activity not readily discovered by visual inspection or survey. This, of course, made subsequent purchasers who discovered a condition during a title search nervous and may have discouraged improvement by current owners. A much more important problem, however, was the impact of defeasible fees on lending institutions, which were understandably reluctant to finance the purchase of property subject to the potential of forfeiture for conduct over which they had little control. Indeed, laws regulating financial institutions in some states forbade loans on such insecure collateral. Some developers attempted to deal with this problem by expressly allowing mortgagees to cure violations of conditions prior to forfeiture. A more acceptable solution was to change to restrictions that did not threaten forfeiture.

Abandonment of the use of defeasible fee subdivision restrictions was counseled by more sophisticated planners and developers, who early recognized the limitations of conditions. Some aspirations of developers, like establishing permanent property owners' associations to manage maintenance fees collected under deed restrictions, could be accomplished only with difficulty through conditions. Because most jurisdictions at the time did not permit rights of entry or possibilities of reverter to be transferred, the developer could not transfer the rights to the property owners' association. The interest could have initially been created as an executory limitation in the property owners' association, but then would have been subject to the Rule Against Perpetuities. A well-advised developer could have created an executory limitation in a property owners' association with a duration of less than 21 years, but the author found no examples of this. Developers saddled with rights of entry chafed under the responsibility of enforcing deed restrictions. Other developers found they could restrict property more easily by placing restrictions in the original plat or in a declaration of restrictions, an approach possible with equitable servitudes but not with defeasible fees.

Ultimately, the defeasible fee gave way to the equitable servitude as the restrictive device of choice. For a host of reasons, conditions enforced by forfeiture were inferior to servitudes enforced by injunction for assuring compliance with deed restrictions. Perhaps the most important development contributing to the ascendancy of the equitable servitude was the maturation by the end of the nineteenth century of the doctrine of the equitable servitude common scheme, which permitted developers to impose restrictions on all properties in a subdivision for the benefit of all others. In the end, deed restrictions generally became less important because of the rise of public land use control.

. . . .

IX. The Clean Up of the Debris

By 1920, a substantial number of subdivision lots in many states were subject to forfeiture restrictions appearing somewhere in the chain of title. The possibility of forfeiture under most of these provisions was very remote. First, a court presented with the issue would almost always find a reason for not permitting a forfeiture. More to the point, the issue was seldom raised as developers, who technically held the power to enforce forfeitures, rarely had any interest in doing so. Few developers maintained much interest in their subdivisions once the lots were sold. Nevertheless, forfeiture provisions lurked insidiously in the background of many properties, perpetually clouding the title. The construction of a bay window or porch beyond the setback line, the opening of a professional office in the basement, the sale of the property to a black family, could raise the long dormant specter of forfeiture.

. . . .

The most obvious solution to these problems was legislation eliminating stale or useless defeasible fee restrictions. Such legislation existed in a few states from the nineteenth century, but did not really become popular until the 1940's. In the 1940's and 1950's, a number of states passed legislation limiting in various ways rights of entry and possibilities of reverter. This legislation took several basic forms. First, several statutes, following the lead of the early Michigan statute, purported to eliminate merely nominal conditions. Second, a number of statutes imposed specific time limits on the duration of defeasible fee limitations or for assertion of defeasance. One statute changed defeasible fee restrictions into covenants after a set period of time. Another subjected actions for enforcing conditions or limitations to defenses available against the enforcement or other forms of restriction.

. . . .

X. Conclusion

Though the defeasible fee emerged early as the legal tool for restricting residential development, its career was brief and far from glorious . . . . By the conclusion of our period, the flexible and easily enforced equitable servitude triumphed everywhere over the defeasible fee as the land use planning tool of choice. Even the real covenant, plagued though it was with labyrinthine legal complexities, and the negative easement, despite its fictive character, gained ascendancy over the defeasible fee. In the end, zoning, subdivision controls, and other public land use planning tools overshadowed private restrictions in shaping residential development.

. . . .

Wherever the defeasible fee was used as a land use planning device, generations of lawyers have struggled with the title problems left behind. In many jurisdictions, however, old forfeiture restrictions now have been rendered ineffective by reverter and marketable title legislation. Many other restrictions have receded beyond the horizons of interest of title insurance companies and opinion writers. The unfortunate defeasible fee chapter of the history of private land use planning in the United States is by and large closed.

[2] Easements, Covenants and Servitudes: The Basics

The American Law Institute's ongoing project to rewrite the Restatement of the Law of Property has recently produced a massive compendium of tentative drafts and commentaries on what the institute now calls *servitudes*. Much of the old learning and vocabulary dealing with easements, covenants and equitable servitudes has been discarded. The contours of the Restatement's tentative draft confirm in dramatic fashion that huge changes in the law of private land use controls have been made in this century. The roots for these legal shifts lay in the creation of residential subdivisions before and after the turn of the twentieth century.

At the turn of the century, there were three major classes of interests held by one party in the land of another—easements[3] and profits, covenants, and equitable servitudes. These were thought of as separate bundles of legal rights surrounded by different legal structures.

[a] Easements and Profits

Easements and profits (sometimes called *profits a prendre*) typically establish non-possessory rights to go upon the land of another. Common easements include driveways and other rights of way and access rights to install and maintain utility lines. Profits give their owners the right to remove minerals, timber or other resources from the land of another. Easements and profits are normally transferable, though it is not possible to sell the easement or profit apart from the lands they relate to. A driveway, for example, running from Main Street over the land of Sam to the land of Susan lying to the rear of Sam's is firmly linked to the parcels of Sam and Susan. Susan's land is *benefited* by the easement and Sam's land is *burdened*. If Sam sells his land, the buyer takes the property subject to the burden of the easement. Similarly, if Susan sells her land, the buyer takes the property along with the benefit of the easement. In settings like this, Sam owns the *servient tenement* and Susan owns the *dominant tenement*. The combined arrangement linking together the two parcels is called an *appurtenant easement*.

A typical mineral profit has a slightly different structure. If Mining Company owns the right to remove gravel from the land of Quarryman, the burden of the profit is imposed on the land of Quarryman. The benefit of the profit, however, is not linked to any particular property asset. Mining Company may sell the gravel to anyone it wishes. Such easements or profits are *in gross*. When Quarryman sells his land the burden will follow. Mining Company may sell their benefit to anyone. Most profits are in gross, as are most utility easements. Many rights of way are appurtenant, though easements creating public thoroughfares are in gross.

---

[3] Sometimes the old language "incorporeal herediment"—non-possessory but transferable—is used to describe an easement.

Traditional rules allow easements to be created in three sets of ways—by prescription, expressly in a document, and by implication. Prescription is covered in Chapter 1. Most typical easements are created by some formal arrangement manifested in conveyance documents. If, in the Sam and Susan example above, Susan paid Sam for the right of way, Sam would give Susan a deed of easement describing the metes and bounds of the easement boundaries, the nature of the permitted uses for the right of way, the duration of the easement,[4] and any other details agreed upon by the parties. Susan would then record the document in the local land records office. Use of the recording system is a crucial part of typical easement law, for anyone on actual or constructive notice of the content of the easement deed will be bound by its terms if they purchase lands benefited or burdened by the arrangement. Anyone purchasing land is presumed to know the contents of all properly recorded property documents related to that parcel.

Deeds of easements are sometimes badly drafted. Words or phrases like "convey," "transfer," or "provide a right of way" which might mean that a fee simple estate is being created should be avoided. The most precise prose will either *grant* or *reserve* an easement. The owner of land destined to become a servient tenement should *grant* an easement; the owner of land intended to be the dominant tenement should *reserve* an easement. In the Sam and Susan example above, the language to be used would depend on the way the driveway was created. If Sam sold the back lot to Susan, the deed transferring the land to her would also *grant* her an easement. If Susan was selling the front lot to Sam, she would *reserve* an easement for the benefit of the land she retains.

Easements may arise by implication in several ways—by plat, prior use or necessity. Easements implied from plats are quite similar to express easements. A number of decisions must be made about how structures and other uses will be laid out on the land whenever a real estate development is planned. In order to obtain zoning approvals and building permits, the developer will file a plat in the recording system, laying out lot lines, easement locations for streets and utility lines, and other related features. If the development as constructed conforms to the plat, those purchasing property will generally be both benefited and burdened by easements displayed on the recorded plat regardless of what their own house deeds say. Such easements by plat may result in the public holding rights in streets. Others may give residents access to streets, parks, playgrounds, alleys or other sites.

Easements implied by prior use are designed to deal with a specific situation of potential unfairness. Suppose Gardner owns a pretty large parcel with two houses on it, a main house in the front and a guest cottage in the back. There is a driveway that runs past the main house to the rear and terminates in a turnaround on the side of the guest cottage. To raise some money, Gardner decides to sell the cottage. Lucy buys it, getting a deed that precisely describes the lot lines of her parcel but neglects to say anything about the continued existence of the driveway. After the sale, Gardner puts a fence along the lot line between the two dwellings and installs a flower bed where the driveway used to enter what is now Lucy's land. If Lucy can't work something out with Gardner, she will get a very sympathetic judicial response. The court will make use of an old rule implying an easement when a parcel of land is split apart while there is a usage pattern on the land that is apparent and reasonably necessary for the enjoyment and possession of one or both segments of the parcel after it is divided. In this example, Gardner

---

[4] Easements, like other interests in land, will be conveyed with words of purchase and words of limitation. The same words of limitation, such as "and her heirs," or "for life" used in transferring possessory interests also may be used in easement deeds.

splits the land, the driveway is in existence when the split occurs and is reasonably necessary for Lucy's enjoyment of her cottage, and the driveway is clearly apparent to all parties at the time of the land transfer. The court will imply an appurtenant easement benefiting Lucy's lot and burdening the land of Gardner. This rule may also benefit Lucy even if she bought her cottage from someone other than Gardner if she can show that the driveway existed at some time in the past when both parts of the land were owned by the same party, and that the use of the driveway continued up until the time she arrived. To deprive Lucy of the driveway in these settings is highly likely to be unfair. Most of the litigation in cases like this involves disputes over whether the pre-existing use was apparent at the time the land was divided and whether continued existence of the use is reasonably necessary to the enjoyment and possession of the benefited parcel.

Easements by necessity deal with landlocked parcels, another setting where unfairness, to say nothing of inefficient use of resources, may result. If land is split in a way that provides no access to one of the resulting parcels, the purchaser of the landlocked parcel will be able to claim an access easement implied by necessity. The rule normally operates after a parcel is split into accessible and landlocked segments. The courts tend to state that the parties must have intended to create an easement in such settings.

[b] Covenants

Though the term "covenants" refers to contracts, property practitioners have long been interested in covenants relating to land that bind not only the original contracting parties, but also subsequent owners of the land. The most important common law arena for covenant law development involved leases. It was important to know, for example, whether the tenant's agreement to pay rent would also redound to the benefit of any person who might purchase the landlord's property or impose obligations on subtenants of the original tenant. Some fairly elaborate rules were developed to handle such issues. When large scale residential developments began to appear, real estate entrepreneurs were interested in establishing legal structures to help run the areas after construction was complete. After all the housing units were sold, private roads and common areas still needed to be managed and maintained. Many developers were also interested in finding ways to control the racial and ethnic composition of those who would live in the area.

Applying the old landlord-tenant covenant rules to these new residential settings caused some problems and anomalies. First, let's try to get a sense of the lease rules. Work with a simple situation diagramed as follows:

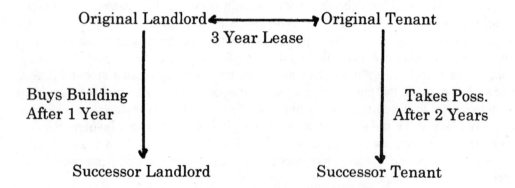

Original Landlord ⟵————————⟶ Original Tenant

3 Year Lease

Buys Building
After 1 Year

Takes Poss.
After 2 Years

Successor Landlord   Successor Tenant

Now, the issue we will play with is whether either one of the landlords may, during their period of ownership, sue either or both of the tenants if either defaults in the payment of rent.

Get the easy one out of the way first. If the Original Tenant defaults in the payment of rent shortly after taking possession, surely the Original Landlord may sue for the rent. The Original Landlord and the Original Tenant have a contractual agreement requiring the tenant to pay rent and that contract has been breached. The interesting questions surface in cases involving one or both of the successors. In this example, Original Landlord sells the building to Successor Landlord one year after the lease is agreed to. Can the Successor Landlord sue the Original Tenant if the Original Tenant defaults in the payment of rent? You surely would hope that the answer will usually be "Yes." When a rental building is sold, the new owner buys subject to all the existing leases. An owner can only transfer what she owns. In this case, possession has been transferred to a tenant for three years and that term can't be shortened by a sale. So if the tenant may retain possession under the lease, you would assume rent still has to be paid.

So how was this outcome described in legal terms? The old texts and cases came up with the label of *privity of estate* to describe a set of relationships in which successors in interest could obtain the benefit or be burdened by the terms of agreements reached by their predecessors in interest. Privity of estate was divided into two parts—*horizontal privity* and *vertical privity*. If both parts were fulfilled, then privity of estate was said to exist between the two parties in litigation and liability would flow. The rule about horizontal privity dealt with the relationship between the Original Landlord and the Original Tenant; the rule about vertical privity dealt with the relationships between either of the original parties and the successor in interest in ownership or possession at the time of the litigation.

The oldest version of the horizontal privity rule simply said that the parties were in horizontal privity if there was a landlord-tenant relationship! And the vertical privity rule was fulfilled if the successor party held the same property interest as the original party. So in the example, a lease exists between Original Landlord and Original Tenant, fulfilling the horizontal privity requirement. And Successor Landlord holds the same interest as the Original Landlord, satisfying the terms of the vertical privity rule. So Successor Landlord may sue Original Tenant in case of a default in the payment of rent.

Change the example in one more way. Now assume that the party defaulting in the payment of rent is the Successor Tenant, not the Original Tenant. Can the Successor Landlord sue for the rent? We know from the prior example that vertical privity exists on the landlord side and that horizontal privity exists between the original parties to the lease. So the only question left to answer is whether the Successor Tenant is in vertical privity with the Original Tenant. In landlord-tenant law, this is basically a definitional problem. A lease is said to be *assigned* if the new tenant takes possession for the entire remaining lease period under the same terms as Original Tenant. A *sublease* arises in all other subtenant settings. So if in our example, Successor Tenant stands in the shoes of Original Tenant, an assignment exists and vertical privity requirements are fulfilled. Otherwise, Successor Tenant is a sublessee not in vertical privity with Original Tenant. Putting all of this together, Successor Landlord may collect the rent from Successor Tenant if the lease was assigned, but not if it was subleased.[5] By the way, if you assume that the building was not sold and that Original Landlord still owned the building, the rental obligation rules come out the same way. Can you figure out why?[6]

Moving the landlord-tenant based privity rules to different transactional settings was not a straightforward transition. The easiest to deal with involved easements. If, for example, Sam grants an easement for a right of way to Susan living on the rear lot, they might also make covenants about sharing the costs for maintaining the driveway or taking steps to make sure that neither party blocks access by the other. Assuming that the easement and covenants are recorded, what happens after both Sam and Susan sell their houses? Courts began enforcing such arrangements using the old rules. Vertical privity was fairly easy to find since both successors held the same interests as their predecessors. And the courts analogized an easement to a lease by contending that both parties to the easement, like both parties to a lease, held interests in the same property that were created at the same time as the covenants were agreed to. Though it took longer, courts eventually found a way to use the same basic structure to allow for covenants encumbering fee simple transactions. The horizontal privity requirement that both sides to a covenant had to hold interests in the same parcel of land was replaced by the requirement that an agreement related to the land had to arise simultaneously with a transaction in which interests in land were conveyed. If vertical privity requirements were also met, privity of estate was said to exist.

In all of these settings—leases, easements and land transfers—there was also a need to separate personal agreements out from those related to land. That is not a problem with traditional easements, which by definition involved the use of specific parcels of land by a nonpossessory party. But covenants and equitable servitudes presented some different problems. No one, for

---

[5] This old common law rule has actually been modified almost everywhere so that any tenant in possession is liable for the rent to the owner of the building.

[6] The follow-up question in this setting asks if Successor Landlord may collect the rent from Original Tenant if Successor Tenant is the party actually defaulting on the rent obligation. First assume that Successor Tenant is a sublessee. In this case, we have discovered, the common law rules said that Successor Landlord could not recover the rent from the tenant in possession. Another way of thinking about this outcome is that there is still a landlord-tenant relationship between Successor Landlord and Original Tenant. The first part of this example tells us that the Original Tenant must therefore pay the rent. A further implication of this outcome is that Original Tenant may be thought of as Successor Tenant's landlord! A second lease, different from the original one has been entered into between Original and Successor Tenant. So Successor Tenant must pay the rent to Original Tenant, who then is obligated to pay it to the landlord.

Now what if the Successor Tenant is an assignee. We already know that Successor Tenant is obligated to pay the rent directly to the landlord. May the landlord also recover from Original Tenant if, for example, Successor Tenant is bankrupt? The answer is usually "Yes!" The theory supporting that result is usually found in contract law rather than property law. In contract, the original lease is not rescinded after an assignment and Successor Landlord is said to be a third party beneficiary of Original Tenant's promise to pay rent. Further details on these and related issues are taken up in Chapter 8 on landlord-tenant law.

example, was eager to allow a subtenant to take advantage of a promise by the original tenant to paint a portrait of the landlord in lieu of paying one month's rent. Two other requirements therefore arose. One required that the original parties to a covenant had to intend that it bind successors, or *run with the land,* in covenant lingo. This requirement was usually met by a statement in the covenant documents about intent. The other insisted that the covenant *touch and concern the land.* Early versions of this vague notion limited covenants to actions or events closely tied to use of the property. As demands of the industrial age developed, permissible subjects gradually expanded. In recent years, the touch and concern requirement has been dropped in some states, the courts concluding that its purpose was adequately fulfilled by an inquiry into the intentions of those establishing the servitude scheme, and altered in others, leaving only a requirement that enforcement of the servitude be reasonable.

For many settings, these covenant rules worked fine. But there were two limitations which created serious problems for developers. First, the covenant rules arose in courts of law. They were, after all, offshoots from contract actions for breach of lease contracts. Relief was therefore limited to damages. Injunctions were not available. Second, enforcement was by a suit between two property owners. Establishing a governing structure, like the contemporary managing boards of condominiums, to manage residential facilities and enforce the rules was not easily done.

[c] Equitable Servitudes

The hunt for alternative structures led to the widespread use of equitable servitudes. In traditional equitable servitudes land owners agreed not to behave in certain ways—*e.g.*, promises not to plant corn, build a factory, make a lot of noise, or construct houses smaller than 2,000 square feet in lots smaller than one-third of an acre.[7] Enforcement of such agreements operated under rules very much like easements. If a party owning land burdened by such a promise was on actual or constructive notice of the contents of the promise, they were bound by its terms. The recording system served to provide notice. Traditionally, findings that equitable servitudes were intended to bind successors and touched and concerned the land were also required. Since the primary concern of these rules was making sure that a party was on notice of the obligation, developers began to experiment with new enforcement systems, including use of resident management boards, to monitor compliance. By the 1920s, courts began to legitimate these strategies. One of the cases in this chapter, *Neponsit v. Emigrant Savings Bank,* is still viewed as a classic embodiment of the shift to equitable servitudes. While transition problems also arose in this shift—especially the willingness to enforce affirmative promises as well as promises not to undertake certain actions—the overall result left developers with a flexible, easily used technique for running residential and commercial projects.

[d] Restatement Third of Property (Servitudes)

Those drafting the Restatement Third are now confronted with a world in which easements are widely used, covenants at law are rarely if ever used,[8] and equitable servitudes dominate the creation of non-governmental management schemes for residential and commercial developments. Not surprisingly, they decided to eliminate covenants at law from the agenda and fold

---

[7] These early sorts of servitudes were often called "negative easements." That description is now largely obsolete.

[8] In my own research for both this book and the prior edition, I found virtually no interesting cases with discussion of covenants at law since World War II. The few that did show up were usually confused about the contours of the rules, wrongly applied privity of estate rules to equitable servitude situations, or involved suits for damages for violations of covenants not to compete.

everything else into variations on one central theme—the enforceability of servitudes against those owning burdened land and on notice of servitude terms. Rather than speaking of implied easements, the draft refers to implied servitudes. An indication of the trend is displayed in the following definitional provisions in the new Restatement:[9]

§ 1.1 Servitude Defined; Scope of Restatement

(1) A servitude is a legal device that creates a right or an obligation that runs with land or an interest in land.

(a) Running with land means that the right or obligation passes automatically to successive owners or occupiers of the land or the interest in land with which the right or obligation runs.

(b) A right that runs with land is called a "benefit" and the interest in land with which it runs may be called the "benefited" or "dominant" estate.

(c) An obligation that runs with the land is called a "burden" and the interest in land with which it runs may be called the "burdened" or "servient" estate.

(2) The servitudes covered by this Restatement are easements, profits and covenants.

. . . .

§ 1.2 Easement and *Profit a Prendre* Defined

An easement creates a nonpossessory right to enter and use land in the possession of another and obligates the possessor not to interfere with the uses authorized by the easement.

A *profit a prendre* is an easement that confers the right to enter and remove timber, minerals, oil, gas, game, or other substances from land in the possession of another. It is referred to as a "profit" in this Restatement.

The burden of an easement or profit is always appurtenant. The benefit may be either appurtenant or in gross.

. . . .

§ 1.3 Covenant Running with Land

. . . A covenant is a servitude if either the benefit or the burden runs with land. A covenant that is a servitude "runs with land."[10]

. . . .

[3]　Additional Readings on Servitudes

For additional reading on the basics of servitudes, *see* ROGER A. CUNNINGHAM, WILLIAM B. STOEBUCK & DALE A. WHITMAN, THE LAW OF PROPERTY 436-504 (2d ed. 1993); JOHN E. CRIBBET & CORWIN W. JOHNSON, PRINCIPLES OF THE LAW OF PROPERTY 368-396 (3d ed. 1989).

Additional materials on servitudes in RICHARD H. CHUSED, A PROPERTY ANTHOLOGY 337-377 (2d ed. 1997) include excerpts from Uriel Reichman, *Toward a Unified Concept of Servitudes,*

---

[9] © 1999 by The American Law Institute. Reprinted with permission.

[10] In this section the Restatement drafters are thinking of covenants as agreements. They become servitudes if they run.

55 S. CAL. L. REV. 1179 (1982); Stewart Sterk, *Neighbors in American Land Law,* 87 COLUM. L. Rev. 55 (1987); Glen O. Robinson, *Explaining Contingent Rights: The Puzzle of "Obsolete" Covenants,* 91 COLUM. L. REV. 546 (1991); and Gregory S. Alexander, *Freedom, Coercion, and the Law of Servitudes,* 73 CORNELL L. REV. 883 (1988).

[4] The Central Servitude Rule: Running of Burdens to Owners on Notice

[a] Background to *Gaskin v. Harris*

Dr. Payne S. Harris and his wife lived in a well-to-do residential subdivision in Santa Fe, New Mexico. Their house had a large, 30′ × 55′ courtyard containing a swimming pool, which they decided to enclose to reduce pool maintenance and make the area usable year round. In 1963, they hired an architect and began construction. The design created a swimming pool cover which rose above the roof of their house approximately one story, curving downward from a central beam much like a pagoda to facilitate drainage. The raised portion was necessary to obtain proper ventilation. It was made out of laminated wood beams and fiberglass material designed to admit diffused sunlight. Though the materials used sound tawdry, the structure, designed by Bob Plettenberg, won architectural awards and was featured in the November-December, 1964 issue of NEW MEXICO ARCHITECT. As the pictures below[11] suggest, the structure was visible from both the street and from the lots of the surrounding neighbors.[12] Although the homes in the neighborhood were located quite far apart and the lots were large, some neighbors disliked the courtyard pool enclosure's appearance and felt it violated a subdivision covenant which required that structures conform to the Old Santa Fe or Pueblo style of architecture. They decided to sue to force the Harrises to remove the enclosure.[13]

---

[11] These pictures were provided courtesy of the architect Bob Plettenberg.

[12] Appellants' Brief in Chief at 8-9, Gaskin v. Harris, No. 9027 (N. M. 1970). [Hereinafter cited as Appellants' Brief.]

[13] The successor in interest to the original developer also joined the lawsuit as a plaintiff, but the neighbors were the moving force behind the case. Telephone Interview with John Catron, Attorney for Dr. & Mrs. Harris (June 25, 1987).

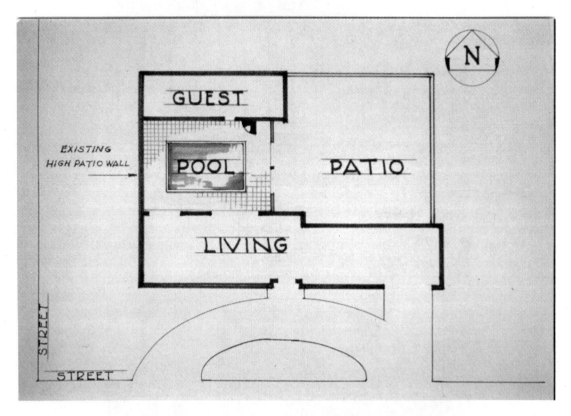

Site Plan for Harris House and Pool Enclosure

Looking East From Pool to Patio Area

Harris House and Pool Enclosure Viewed from the Southwest

The Harrises' subdivision, which contained 68 houses,[14] was originally developed in 1931.[15] The lots were each bound by a covenant which read as follows:

FIRST: That no building whatever except a private dwelling house with the necessary outbuildings, including a private garage, shall be erected, placed or permitted on said premises or any part thereof, and said dwelling house permitted on said premises shall be used as a private residence only and shall cost and be reasonably worth not less than Eight Thousand ($8,000.00) Dollars, excluding the cost of the necessary outbuildings, and shall be located not less than fifty (50) feet distance from the outer edge of any street, public road or highway now established, and no outbuilding shall be built or located closer than fifty (50) feet from the outer edge of any street, public road or highway now established; and said dwelling house and necessary outbuildings shall be in the style or form or appearance known as the Old Santa Fe or Pueblo-Spanish style of architecture; no billboards or advertising signs shall be erected or placed on said premises; and no windmill or similar machinery or structure shall be erected, placed or permitted on said premises.

SECOND: That no conveyance shall be made or granted of said premises, or any part thereof, to any person or persons of African or Oriental descent.[16]

. . . .

---

[14] Appellants' Brief at 12.

[15] Appellees' Answer Brief at 1, Gaskin v. Harris, No. 9027 (N. M. 1970). [Hereinafter cited as Appellees' Brief.]

[16] Appellants' Brief at 1-2. Compare the racial restrictions in this covenant with those in Shelley v. Kraemer, p. 445 below.

IT IS UNDERSTOOD AND AGREED that said covenants on the part of the grantee herein, shall attach to and run with the land hereby conveyed, and the party of the first part (the Company) or any owner of adjacent or abutting premises, shall have the right to enforce compliance with said covenants by injunction, or other legal proceedings . . . .[17]

The Harrises' displeased neighbors hired an attorney who sent a letter to the Harrises on December 31, 1963, demanding that construction on the pool and courtyard enclosure stop and that the structure be removed. The Harrises claimed this was the first they knew of the covenant, since the title opinion they received when they bought their house made no mention of building restrictions. By the time the demand letter was received, the enclosure was in the final stages of construction. It was too late to change the design. The Harrises elected to finish the job. The enclosure cost about $11,000, plus a 10% fee for the architect.

During the ensuing litigation, the Harrises made three arguments. First, they admitted that the pool enclosure did not conform to the Santa Fe or Pueblo Spanish style, but argued that so many other structures in the subdivision violated the style that it was no longer in the public interest to enforce the covenant. They attempted to define the nature of the style by using a definition contained in the zoning regulations of the Santa Fe City Code, which called for flat roofs with a slight slope, no roof eaves, windows no larger than 30 inches square, and walls of adobe or hard plaster.[18] Testimony of architects was introduced to show that the vast majority of houses in the subdivision did not comply with the definition.[19] The neighbors countered that the zoning ordinance was written in 1960, that the style referred to in the 1931 covenants was to be construed much more generally to encompass both very traditional and later developed styles common to the area.

The Harrises also argued that even if their pool and courtyard enclosure was covered by the covenant, it should not be applied in the particular circumstances of this case. Since they did not find out about the covenant until quite late in the game, spent a great deal of money and were sued after the structure was complete, it was unfair to require them to dismantle the enclosure. In balancing the interests of the Harrises, the neighbors and the community, the Harrises noted that the enclosure was used for functions by important community organizations, including the Santa Fe Opera Guild, the Garden Club Tour, the faculty of St. Michaels College, and the Sisters of Charity from St. Vincent.[20] Finally, their lack of notice of the covenant was said to preclude its enforcement against them. Both of these contentions were resisted on the theory that the Harrises were bound by the contents of the recorded covenants regardless of whether they *actually* knew of them.[21]

---

[17] Appellees' Brief at 2.

[18] Appellants' Brief at 5-6.

[19] *Id.* at 12-14.

[20] Appellants' Brief at 21.

[21] Appellees' Brief at 12-15.

[b] **Opinion of the New Mexico Supreme Court in *Gaskin v. Harris***

Gaskin v. Harris

New Mexico Supreme Court

82 N.M. 336, 481 P.2d 698 (1971)

OPINION

McManus, Justice.

Plaintiffs brought suit in the District Court of Santa Fe County to enjoin the defendants from constructing on their residential property a structure alleged to be in violation of an architectural restriction applicable to the property. The court entered judgment ordering removal of the offending structure, a swimming pool enclosure.

The plaintiffs, except for Mr. Gaskin who is successor to the interests of the original subdivider, are the owners of lots within the De Vargas Development Company Subdivision No. 2, a residential development in Santa Fe. The defendants are the owners of a lot within the same subdivision, on which lot they constructed the swimming pool cover in question. It is likewise undisputed that all of the property in the subdivision is subject to certain restrictive covenants containing building restrictions, the material parts of which provide:

FIRST: That no building whatever except a private dwelling house with the necessary outbuildings, including a private garage, shall be erected, placed or permitted on said premises or any part thereof, and said dwelling house permitted on said premises shall be used as a private residence only . . . ; and said dwelling house and necessary outbuildings shall be in the style or form or appearance known as the Old Santa Fe or Pueblo-Spanish style of architecture:

. . . .

IT IS UNDERSTOOD AND AGREED that said covenants on the part of the grantee herein, shall attach to and run with the land hereby conveyed, and the party of the first part (the Company) or any owner of adjacent or abutting premises, shall have the right to enforce compliance with the said covenants by injunction, or other legal proceedings . . . .

The defendants were in the process of constructing a swimming pool enclosure on their property which was visible from outside their property, and from the plaintiffs' lots. The plaintiffs complained that this structure violated the restrictive covenants of the deeds to the subdivision as it did not in any manner conform to the "Old Santa Fe or Pueblo-Spanish" style of architecture required by the covenants. Instead, the pool enclosure was in a modern style variously described as being of an oriental or pagoda style, but certainly in no way resembling the adobe style known to Santa Fe.

In their Point I, the defendants refer to change of condition as to architectural styles in their subdivision and the relative hardships that would be imposed upon them if they should be ordered to remove the structure in question. Yet, as to the alleged change of conditions, even the defendants' own architect, Plettenberg, conceded that the homes within the subdivision, even if not complying exactly with the definition of "Old Santa Fe or Pueblo-Spanish style of architecture," were of a consistent and uniform type of construction:

Q: In other words, these were quite consistent, quite uniform, what you chose to characterize as violations, in other words, the houses, whereas they don't conform to what you consider to be Old Santa Fe or Pueblo-Spanish, so at least conform with one another?

A: Yes, they do.

This testimony really does not show a "change" of conditions in the true sense of the phrase. All of the expert witnesses did however state that the structure involved was in violation of the architectural restriction applicable to this subdivision. Two of the expert witnesses testified, in part, as follows:

Q: Mr. Hill, in reference to the protruding addition, the so-called second story addition, if you will, that which protrudes above the main structure, in your professional opinion is the second story structure included in any way, shape or form in the terms of art Old Santa Fe style or Spanish pueblo?

A: I would say definitely not because the method of framing, the use of materials, such as the enclosing Fiberglass, plastic materials, are certainly far removed from what one would construe as being Old Santa Fe style.

Mr. Walker testified:

Q: Now, Mr. Walker, referring to this structure you have sketched on this Exhibit Thirteen and your view of it in your professional opinion as an architect, does it conform to either of the styles of architecture we have mentioned that is to say Old Santa Fe or Spanish pueblo? Now, I refer to the part which rises up above the main building only?

A: I would not consider the upper section in either of those categories.

The Historical Zoning Ordinance of Santa Fe, Sec. 28-43.6(a), Santa Fe City Code, was referred to during the trial and it was agreed that it was the only document containing a definition of "Old Santa Fe style" in writing. The trial court was the author of this ordinance and in his findings of fact in this cause said that except for the defendants' property, all lots in the subdivision ". . . have been improved with buildings in substantial conformity with the Old Santa Fe or Pueblo-Spanish styles of architecture." While it is true that this Court has held, in a case involving medical testimony, that uncontradicted evidence is conclusive upon the court as a trier of the facts, *see Ross v. Sayers Well Servicing Co.,* 76 N.M. 321, 414 P.2d 679 (1966), it is our opinion, considering the facts in this case as to the evidence presented by the expert witnesses and the aesthetic nature of the issues, that the trier of the facts may take the whole panorama into consideration, including his own knowledge of the area. Consequently, in this cause the fact finder may reject expert opinion evidence.

In their briefs and arguments before this Court, the defendants emphasized that they were not asking the court to extinguish the architectural restriction contained in the covenants but only not to enforce it in this case. In *Montoya v. Barreras,* 81 N.M. 749, 473 P.2d 363 (1970), the plaintiff sought to exclude residential restrictions from only the one lot owned by plaintiff in said subdivision. This Court held that absolution as to some, but not all, of the lots is not a valid construction of an instrument containing covenants where the language of the instrument manifests an intent for orderly neighborhood development. In the instant case the defendant would have the architectural restriction removed from his lot, while leaving the restriction on the rest of the subdivision. This cannot be done.

Finally, the defendants would argue relative hardship in that they had no actual notice of the restrictive covenants from the time they bought their lot, until after the swimming pool cover was substantially erected. Therefore, they contend that the trial court committed reversible error in failing to make findings to that effect as requested by the defendants. Yet, this Court has previously held, and we reaffirm the proposition, that it is not error to refuse requested findings of fact not material to the court's decision. In this case, the restrictive covenant does exist, and because of the aims and purposes of such covenants, as discussed above, the relative hardship to the defendants is far outweighed by the benefits to the community affected.

The judgment of the trial court is affirmed.

COMPTON, C.J., and TACKETT, J., concur.

[c]   Explanatory Notes

[i]   *Impact of the Opinion.* After the opinion in *Gaskin* was rendered a settlement was reached. The architect reports that the owners did not tear down the pagoda but "built an Aswan Dam in front of the gable and no doubt labeled it 'Adobe Style.'"[22] In short, they made the adobe wall around the pool area taller, altering quite substantially the architectural feel of the project. The architect was not particularly happy with the contours of the litigation. "I am sure," he wrote me, "that animosities were at work. As to whether they were petty or not depends on that person's point of view. People here in Santa Fe take their 'cityscape' pretty seriously. However, when I took a photo of the house across the street, there was a great plastic bubble skylight. As I turned to the house next door, there was a long plexiglass arcade with aluminum ribs spanning the distance from the garage to the house and, by golly, directly across the street from it was a plastic air-roof over the pool!"[23]

[ii]   *Notice and Intent to Run.* As indicated in the notes before *Gaskin,* servitudes are normally enforceable at equity if the burdened party is on notice that the servitude binds the owner's land, the original parties intended that the burden run with the land, and the servitude touches and concerns the land. In the last paragraph of the *Gaskin* opinion, the court dealt with the Harrises' defense that the covenants were unenforceable because they lacked *actual* notice of their existence. The court routinely rejected the claim. Property owners are presumed to know the contents of recorded documents in their chain of title; surely the covenant at issue in *Gaskin* was recorded. Intention of the original parties that the covenant should run was also not an issue; the covenant contained very clear language on this point. *Gaskin* makes quite clear how easy it is to enforce servitudes at equity. Whether that is always a wise outcome is the subject of some of the notes that follow.

[d]   Problem Notes

[i]   *Touch and Concern.* Does an architectural covenant touch and concern the land? Construction styles may affect land values, the most traditional basis for evaluating whether a covenant touches and concerns. But to the extent that the touch and concern requirement embodies public policy limitations on private land use controls, other issues may be relevant to a decision on enforceability of the covenant. For example, if Harris' religion required the construction of

---

[22] Letter from Bob Plettenberg to Richard Chused (Sept. 14, 1989).

[23] *Id.* The architect sent me pictures of these houses. The pool enclosure referred to with an air roof over it is also surrounded by a beige painted cinder block round wall!

a pagoda in his back yard, should covenants be permitted to interfere?[24] Or suppose Harris hired I. M. Pei or some other famous architect to design an addition to his house. Should the freedom of expression entailed in such a design be subject to the (potentially arbitrary?) review of others in the development? At times the courts take a close look at how architectural controls are used by neighbors. In *Riss v. Angel,* 131 Wash. 2d 612, 934 P.2d 669 (1997), those members of a homeowners association voting to stop construction of a house under a design control servitude for what the court found were unreasonable grounds were jointly and severally liable for the attorneys fees and court costs expended by the offended owners in defending their right to build their house.

[*ii*]   ***Who Can Enforce an Equitable Covenant?*** Look at the diagram of the *Gaskin* situation. Assume that all the present residents of the development were *not* the original home buyers. According to this diagram, the original contracting parties were DeVargas and Original Buyer F.

Gaskin Transaction Diagram

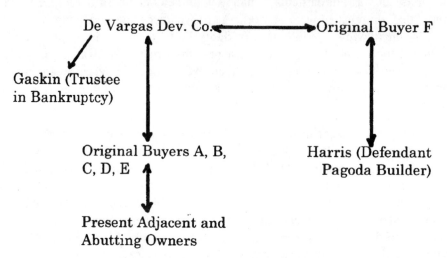

Gaskin was the trustee of the bankrupt corporation, DeVargas, that had built the subdivision over 30 years before the dispute arose. It was certainly not surprising that bankruptcy captured the developer after the passage of so much time. Should both Gaskin and the present adjacent and abutting owners be able to sue Harris? Here it is true that Gaskin succeeded to the contractual rights of DeVargas and that the present adjacent and abutting owners are the intended beneficiaries of the architectural covenant.[25] Could Gaskin have enforced the covenant after all the houses were sold? If not, could an association of residents in the development do so? Compare *Neponsit v. Emigrant Industrial Savings Bank,* the next case.

---

[24] Compare Serbian Eastern Orthodox Diocese v. Milivojevich, discussed at p. 267 above, and Ginsberg v. Yeshiva of Far Rockaway, p. 465 below.

[25] If any of these other owners had been in Harris' shoes because of their making unapproved alterations in their homes, then they would have been the burdened parties. The covenant in theory both benefited and burdened all the owners. But on the facts of this case, only Harris was burdened.

[*iii*] *Equitable "Privity"—Logical Nexus to the Burdened Property.* Consider the following case. S sells a grocery store to B, B agreeing not to sell certain products in the store as long as S owns another nearby business. B then sells his store to his wife without a covenant. B's wife then leases the store for 10 years to V (for victim), again with no covenants. Can S enforce the covenant not to compete against V in equity? First, is V on notice of the covenant? Is a lessee for a medium length term required to check the chain of title of the lessor? Second, is this a contract that touches and concerns the land or a personal contract between S and B? A similar covenant was enforced against a lessee like V in *Oliver v. Hewitt,* 191 Va. 163, 60 S.E.2d 1 (1950). Although the court was probably motivated by the shady dealings of B and his wife to avoid the impact of the covenant, was V fairly treated by the court? Could the court have denied equitable enforcement against V on the ground that the damage remedy at law of S against B and his wife was adequate?

[5]   Clearing Away the Common Law Underbrush: *Neponsit v. Emigrant Savings Bank*

[a]   Background to *Neponsit v. Emigrant Industrial Savings Bank*

As noted in the introductory notes on the basics of servitudes, the role of equity in this area became particularly important in the nineteenth century. Jost, in his article excerpted at the beginning of this chapter, commented that the extent of relief available in covenant enforcement actions in English courts of law was significantly narrowed in *Keppell v. Bailey,* 2 Myl. & K. 517, 39 Eng. Rep. 1042 (1834). In *Keppell,* which was emulated by some major American courts, it was decided that the running of burdens to owners in fee simple was a violation of the public policy encouraging freedom from restraints on alienation. Equity came to a partial rescue a few years later in *Tulk v. Moxhay,* 2 Phil. 774, 41 Eng. Rep. 1143 (Ch. 1848), holding that a subsequent owner on notice of a covenant could be enjoined from violating its terms. This decision was later limited to the enforcement of negative, as opposed to affirmative, obligations, placing a significant obstacle in the way of enforcing any servitude calling for the payment of money.

It was in this somewhat ambiguous environment that large scale urban land development began in the United States in the late nineteenth and early twentieth centuries. Among these early planned communities was Ocean Park lying north of Neponsit Beach in West Rockaway, Queens, New York. The plat for the development, filed by Neponsit Realty Company in January, 1911, covered a 34 square block area with about 1600 lots. The original plan called for the developer, and later an association of homeowners, to own and maintain all the common areas, including streets, parks and the beach, and required residents to pay up to $4.00 each year per lot for such maintenance. The residents were in turn granted the right to use the Ocean Park Beach and to use the streets to gain access to the beach.

In 1919, Neponsit Realty Company created the Neponsit Property Owners' Association. The Association was established "to preserve the settlement known as Neponsit on Rockaway Beach . . . as a highly restricted, well kept and properly maintained suburban home community."[26] One year later, when development of the project was mostly complete, the Realty Company conveyed all its interests in the common areas to the Association subject to the restrictions imposed by the covenants and easements for access to and use of the beach. The "exclusive" quality of the development did not last long. In 1926 most of the common areas and the beach were condemned by New York City, which then maintained them for use by all residents of the city. Though the homeowner association continued to function, it had a much reduced role.

---

[26] In re Public Beach, Borough of Queens, 269 N.Y. 64, 199 N.E. 5 (1935).

The condemnation aspect of the case was an interesting precursor to *Neponsit v. Emigrant Industrial Savings Bank*, the next case in the text. It involved a dispute over the value to be paid the residents of Ocean Park for their beach rights when New York City condemned the common elements in the area. In deciding that the residents were entitled to more than the six cents awarded by the trial court, the New York Court of Appeals implicitly affirmed the validity of the arrangements which had given the residents rights to use the beach. Though couched in easement terminology, the outcome suggested that the old beach rights had value, an outcome auguring well for Neponsit.[27]

The Depression led to a number of mortgage foreclosures in the area. Emigrant Industrial Savings Bank took over some of the foreclosed property, including five lots held by one Deyer sold at a judicial sale in 1935. Payments to the Property Owners' Association for these five lots had not been made since 1920 and Emigrant did not renew making payments after it bought the lots. On July 13, 1937, the Association sued Emigrant for $340, the 17 years of Association dues not paid for the five lots.[28] Emigrant defended the case on the grounds that the City, not the Property Owners' Association, owned the common areas, that the Association had performed no duties since it took title to the common areas in 1920, that New York City did all the maintenance in the area, and that the Association had waived its rights to enforce the covenant.[29] After the pleadings were filed, the Association successfully moved to strike the various defenses, while Emigrant's motion for judgment on the pleadings failed. When Emigrant appealed, the higher courts were obligated to assume for purposes of appeal that the allegations in plaintiff's complaint, including a contention that they had fully performed their obligations under the covenants, were true.

The procedural and factual setting of *Neponsit* suggests that some issue other than concerns about the validity of the covenants must have been motivating the litigants. It went up to the highest court in New York on the pleadings, removing all factual ambiguity from the legal proceedings, even though the defenses raised by Emigrant were susceptible to lots of factual development. In addition, the City's takeover of the common areas and beaches meant that the decision would have no dramatic impact on the Ocean Park neighborhood regardless of the outcome. The impact of the case on land use patterns was also minimal because the covenants were due to expire on their own terms only two years after the *Neponsit* opinion was rendered. Nonetheless, the case was pursued doggedly to the highest court in New York State.

The lawsuit was probably initiated because the Association was concerned about how to pay out the condemnation award it received from the city after the beach and common areas were condemned. After years of litigation over both the value of common areas and the rights of the property owners to share in the condemnation award, the Association was told to pay the various property owners of Ocean Park their shares of the condemnation award, less amounts owed the city for property taxes and amounts owed the Association in unpaid assessments.[30] Any lingering questions about the validity of the underlying covenants, therefore, had to be resolved before the condemnation award could be distributed to property owners in arrears in their Association

[27] Some additional information on the condemnation case may be found in Casenote, 24 CORNELL L. Q. 133 (1939).

[28] Complaint at 19, Papers on Appeal From Orders, Neponsit Property Owners' Association v. Emigrant Industrial Savings Bank, 278 N.Y. 248, 15 N.E.2d 793 (1938). The $340 amount consists of $4.00 per lot for five lots for 17 years, or $17 \times 5 \times \$4.00 = \$340.00$.

[29] *Id.*, Answer, at 28.

[30] In re Public Beach, City of New York, Borough of Queens, 258 A.D. 455, 17 N.Y.S.2d 2 (1940).

dues payments. Those running the Association, holding money as trustees for its members, were obligated to make sure that they gave the eminent domain funds to the appropriate parties in the proper amounts. There is therefore some irony in the fact that the opinion is now read by almost every property law student as a path breaking servitude case. Like many cases, *Neponsit* has probably taken on a role never dreamed of by its litigants.

Regardless of its history, *Neponsit* answered a series of extremely important questions about the scope of power equitable servitudes may grant to homeowners' associations. The results made possible the sorts of subdivision, cooperative and condominium developments we now take for granted.

[b]   Opinion of the New York Court of Appeals in *Neponsit v. Emigrant Savings Bank*

Neponsit Property Owners' Association, Inc. v. Emigrant Industrial Savings Bank

New York Court of Appeals
278 N.Y. 248, 15 N.E.2d 793 (1938)

LEHMAN, JUDGE.

The plaintiff, as assignee of Neponsit Realty Company, has brought this action to foreclose a lien upon land which the defendant owns. The lien, it is alleged, arises from a covenant, condition or charge contained in a deed of conveyance of the land from Neponsit Realty Company to a predecessor in title of the defendant. The defendant purchased the land at a judicial sale. The referee's deed to the defendant and every deed in the defendant's chain of title since the conveyance of the land by Neponsit Realty Company purports to convey the property subject to the covenant, condition or charge contained in the original deed. The answer of the defendant contains, in addition to denials of some of the allegations of the complaint, seven separate affirmative defenses and a counterclaim. The defendant moved for judgment on the pleadings, dismissing the complaint . . . . The plaintiff moved to dismiss the counterclaim . . . and to strike out the affirmative defenses contained in the answer . . . .

The motion of the plaintiff was granted and the motion of the defendant denied. The Appellate Division unanimously affirmed the order of the Special Term and granted leave to appeal to this court upon certified questions.

. . . Upon this appeal the defendant contends that the land which it owns is not subject to any lien or charge which the plaintiff may enforce. Its arguments are confined to serious questions of law. Some of these questions are properly raised by the defendant's challenge of the sufficiency of the complaint; other questions are raised by the plaintiff's challenge of the sufficiency of the separate defenses. The two motions, indeed, involve, in general, the same questions. The form in which the questions are raised is unimportant. On this appeal we may confine our consideration to the merits of these questions, and, in our statement of facts, we drew indiscriminately from the allegations of the complaint and the allegations of the answer.

It appears that in January, 1911, Neponsit Realty Company, as owner of a tract of land in Queens county, caused to be filed in the office of the clerk of the county a map of the land. The tract was developed for a strictly residential community, and Neponsit Realty Company conveyed lots in the tract to purchasers, describing such lots by reference to the filed map and to roads and streets shown thereon. In 1917, Neponsit Realty Company conveyed the land now owned by the defendant to Robert Oldner Deyer and his wife by deed which contained the covenant upon which the plaintiff's cause of action is based.

That covenant provides:

And the party of the second part for the party of the second part and the heirs, successors and assigns of the party of the second part further covenants that the property conveyed by this deed shall be subject to an annual charge in such an amount as will be fixed by the party of the first part, its successors and assigns, not, however exceeding in any year the sum of four ($4.00) Dollars per lot 20 × 100 feet. The assigns of the party of the first part may include a Property Owners' Association which may hereafter be organized for the purposes referred to in this paragraph, and in case such association is organized the sums in this paragraph provided for shall be payable to such association. The party of the second part for the party of the second part and the heirs, successors and assigns of the party of the second part covenants that they will pay this charge to the party of the first part, its successors and assigns on the first day of May in each and every year, and further covenants that said charge shall on said date in each year become a lien on the land and shall continue to be such lien until fully paid. Such charge shall be payable to the party of the first part or its successors or assigns, and shall be devoted to the maintenance of the roads, paths, parks, beach, sewers and such other public purposes as shall from time to time be determined by the party of the first part, its successors or assigns. And the party of the second part by the acceptance of this deed hereby expressly vests in the party of the first part, its successors and assigns, the right and power to bring all actions against the owner of the premises hereby conveyed or any part thereof for the collection of such charge and to enforce the aforesaid lien therefor.

These covenants shall run with the land and shall be construed as real covenants running with the land until January 31st, 1940, when they shall cease and determine.

Every subsequent deed of conveyance of the property in the defendant's chain of title, including the deed from the referee to the defendant, contained, as we have said, a provision that they were made subject to covenants and restrictions of former deeds of record.

There can be no doubt that Neponsit Realty Company intended that the covenant should run with the land and should be enforceable by a property owners association against every owner of property in the residential tract which the realty company was then developing. The language of the covenant admits of no other construction. Regardless of the intention of the parties, a covenant will run with the land and will be enforceable against a subsequent purchaser of the land at the suit of one who claims the benefit of the covenant, only if the covenant complies with certain legal requirements. These requirements rest upon ancient rules and precedents. The age-old essentials of a real covenant, aside from the form of the covenant, may be summarily formulated as follows: (1) It must appear that grantor and grantee intended that the covenant should run with the land; (2) it must appear that the covenant is one "touching" or "concerning" the land with which it runs; (3) it must appear that there is "privity of estate" between the promise or party claiming the benefit of the covenant and the right to enforce it, and the promisor or party who rests under the burden of the covenant. *Clark on Covenants and Interests Running with Land,* p. 74 . . . .

The covenant in this case is intended to create a charge or obligation to pay a fixed sum of money to be "devoted to the maintenance of the roads, paths, parks, beach, sewers and such other public purposes as shall from time to time be determined by the party of the first part [the grantor], its successors or assigns." It is an affirmative covenant to pay money for use in connection with, but not upon, the land which it is said is subject to the burden of the covenant. Does such a covenant "touch" or "concern" the land? These terms are not part of a statutory definition, a limitation placed by the State upon the power of the courts to enforce covenants *intended* to run with the land by the parties who entered into the covenants. Rather they are words used by courts in England in old cases to describe a limitation which the courts themselves created or to formulate a test which the courts have devised and which the courts voluntarily apply. In truth such a description or test so formulated is too vague to be of much assistance and judges and academic scholars alike have struggled, not with entire success, to formulate a test at once more satisfactory and more accurate. "It has been found impossible to state any absolute tests to determine what covenants touch and concern land and what do not. The question is one for the court to determine in the exercise of its best judgment upon the facts of each case." Clark, *op. cit.,* p. 76.

Even though that be true, a determination by a court in one case upon particular facts will often serve to point the way to correct decision in other cases upon analogous facts. Such guideposts may not be disregarded. It has been often said that a covenant to pay a sum of money is a personal affirmative covenant which usually does not concern or touch the land. Such statements are based upon English decisions which hold in effect that only covenants, which compel the covenantor to submit to some *restriction on the use* of his property, touch or concern the land, and that the burden of a covenant which requires the covenantor to do an affirmative act, even on his own land, for the benefit of the owner of a "dominant" estate, does not run with his land. *Miller v. Clary,* 210 N.Y. 127, 103 N.E. 1114. In that case the court pointed out that in many jurisdictions of this country the narrow English rule has been criticized and a more liberal and flexible rule has been substituted. In this State the courts have not gone so far. We have not abandoned the historic distinction drawn by the English courts. So this court has recently said: "Subject to a few exceptions not important at this time, there is now in this state a settled rule of law that a covenant to do an affirmative act, as distinguished from a covenant merely negative in effect, does not run with the land so as to charge the burden of performance on a subsequent grantee [citing cases]. This is so though the burden of such a covenant is laid upon the very parcel which is the subject-matter of the conveyance." *Guaranty Trust Co. of New York v. New York & Queens County Ry. Co.,* 253 N.Y. 190, 170 N.E. 887, opinion by Cardozo, Ch.J.

Both in that case and in the case of *Miller v. Clary, supra,* the court pointed out that there were some exceptions or limitations in the application of the general rule. Some promises to pay money have been enforced, as covenants running with the land, against subsequent holders of the land who took with notice of the covenant. It may be difficult to classify these exceptions or to formulate a test of whether a particular covenant to pay money or to perform some other act falls within the general rule that ordinarily an affirmative covenant is a personal and not a real covenant, or falls outside the limitations placed upon the general rule. At least it must "touch" or "concern" the land in a substantial degree, and though it may be inexpedient and perhaps impossible to formulate a rigid test or definition which will be entirely satisfactory or which can be applied mechanically in all cases, we should at least be able to state the problem and find a reasonable method of approach to it. It has been suggested that a covenant which runs with the land must affect the legal relations—the advantages and the burdens—of the parties to the covenant, as owners of particular parcels of land and not merely as members of the community in general, such as taxpayers or owners of other land. Clark, *op. cit.,* p. 76. *Cf.* Professor Bigelow's article on *The Contents of Covenants in Leases,* 12 Mich. L. Rev. 639; 30 Law Quarterly Review 319. That method of approach has the merit of Realism. The test is based on the effect of the covenant rather than on technical distinctions. Does the covenant impose, on the one hand, a burden upon an interest in land, which on the other hand increases the value of a different interest in the same or related land?

Even though we accept that approach and test, it still remains true that whether a particular covenant is sufficiently connected with the use of land to run with the land, must be in many cases a question of degree. A promise to pay for something to be done in connection with the promisor's land does not differ essentially from a promise by the promisor to do the thing himself, and both promises constitute, in a substantial sense, a restriction upon the owner's right to use the land, and a burden upon the legal interest of the owner. On the other hand, a covenant to perform or pay for the performance of an affirmative act disconnected with the use of the land cannot ordinarily touch or concern the land in any substantial degree. Thus, unless we exalt technical form over substance, the distinction between covenants which run with land and covenants which are personal, must depend upon the effect of the covenant on the legal rights which otherwise would flow from ownership of land and which are connected with the land. The problem then is: Does the covenant in purpose and effect substantially alter these rights?

. . . .

Looking at the problem presented in this case from the same point of view and stressing the intent and substantial effect of the covenant rather than its form, it seems clear that the covenant may properly be said to touch and concern the land of the defendant and its burden should run with the land. True, it calls for payment of a sum of money to be expended for "public purposes" upon land other than the land conveyed by Neponsit Realty Company to plaintiff's predecessor in title. By that conveyance the grantee, however, obtained not only title to particular lots, but an easement or right of common enjoyment with other property owners in roads, beaches, public parks or spaces and improvements in the same tract. For full enjoyment in common by the defendant and other property owners of these easements or rights, the roads and public places must be maintained. In order that the burden of maintaining public improvements should rest upon the land benefited by the improvements, the grantor exacted from the grantee of the land with its appurtenant easement or right of enjoyment a covenant that the burden of paying the cost should be inseparably attached to the land which enjoys the benefit. It is plain that any distinction or definition which would exclude such a covenant from the classification of covenants which "touch" or "concern" the land would be based on form and not on substance.

Another difficulty remains. Though between the grantor and the grantee there was privity of estate, the covenant provides that its benefit shall run to the assigns of the grantor who "may include a Property Owners' Association which may hereafter be organized for the purposes referred to in this paragraph." The plaintiff has been organized to receive the sums payable by the property owners and to expend them for the benefit of such owners. Various definitions have been formulated of "privity of estate" in connection with covenants that run with the land, but none of such definitions seems to cover the relationship between the plaintiff and the defendant in this case. The plaintiff has not succeeded to the ownership of any property of the grantor. It does not appear that it ever had title to the streets or public places upon which charges which are payable to it must be expended. It does not appear that it owns any other property in the residential tract to which any easement or right of enjoyment in such property is appurtenant. It is created solely to act as the assignee of the benefit of the covenant, and it has no interest of its own in the enforcement of the covenant.

The arguments that under such circumstances the plaintiff has no right of action to enforce a covenant running with the land are all based upon a distinction between the corporate property owners association and the property owners for whose benefit the association has been formed. If that distinction may be ignored, then the basis of the arguments is destroyed. How far privity of estate in technical form is necessary to enforce in equity a restrictive covenant upon the use of land, presents an interesting question. Enforcement of such covenants rests upon equitable principles, *Tulk v. Moxhay*, 2 Phillips, 774; at times, at least, the violation "of the restrictive covenant may be restrained at the suit of one who owns property or for whose benefit the restriction was established, irrespective of whether there were privity either of estate or of contract between the parties, or whether an action at law were maintainable." *Chesebro v. Moers*, 233 N.Y. 75, 80, 134 N.E. 842, 843, 21 A.L.R. 1270. The covenant in this case does not fall exactly within any classification of "restrictive" covenants, which have been enforced in this State and no right to enforce even a restrictive covenant has been sustained in this State where the plaintiff did not own property which would benefit by such enforcement so that some of the elements of an equitable servitude are present. In some jurisdictions it has been held that no action may be maintained without such elements.

We do not attempt to decide now how far the rule . . . will be carried, or to formulate a definite rule as to when, or even whether, covenants in a deed will be enforced, upon equitable principles, against subsequent purchasers with notice, at the suit of a party without privity of contract or estate. *Cf. Equitable Rights and Liabilities of Strangers to a Contract,* by Harlan F. Stone, 18 Columbia Law Review, 291. There is no need to resort to such a rule if the courts may look behind the corporate form of the plaintiff.

The corporate plaintiff has been formed as a convenient instrument by which the property owners may advance their common interests. We do not ignore the corporate form when we recognize that the Neponsit Property Owners' Association, Inc., is acting as the agent or representative of the Neponsit property owners. As we have said in another case: when Neponsit Property Owners' Association, Inc., "was formed, the property owners were expected to, and have looked to that organization as the medium through which enjoyment of their common right might be preserved equally for all." *Matter of City of New York, Public Beach, Borough of Queens,* 269 N.Y. 64, 75, 199 N.E. 5, 9. Under the conditions thus presented we said: "It may be difficult, or even impossible, to classify into recognized categories the nature of the interest of the membership corporation and its members in the land. The corporate entity cannot be disregarded, nor can the separate interests of the members of the corporation." Only blind adherence to an ancient formula devised to meet entirely different conditions could constrain the court to hold that a corporation formed as a medium for the enjoyment of common rights of property owners owns no property which would benefit by enforcement of common rights and has no cause of action in equity to enforce the covenant upon which such common rights depend. Every reason which in other circumstances may justify the ancient formula may be urged in support of the conclusion that the formula should not be applied in this case. In substance if not in form the covenant is a restrictive covenant which touches and concerns the defendant's land, and in substance, if not in form, there is privity of estate between the plaintiff and the defendant.

. . . .

The order should be affirmed, with costs, and the certified questions answered in the affirmative.

CRANE, C.J., and O'BRIEN, LOUGHRAN, FINCH, AND RIPPEY, JJ., concur.

HUBBS, J., took no part.

[c]   Explanatory Notes

[i]   **Neponsit.** Two important issues were resolved by the case—whether affirmative covenants to pay money touched and concerned land and whether home owners' associations could enforce covenants at equity. Other elements typically required for enforcement of covenants at equity were clearly present in *Neponsit*. The covenants contained specific statements about the intention to bind successors in interest and Emigrant was on notice of the contents of the deeds of record.

[ii]   *Affirmative Covenants.* Many courts had previously held that affirmative obligations to pay money were unenforceable because they did not touch and concern land. The *Neponsit* court, declining to follow the old cases, said that such covenants would touch and concern if they "impose, on the one hand, a burden upon an interest in land, which on the other hand increases the value of a different interest in the same or related land." The impact on value was found in the requirement that the funds received under the covenant be spent on improving and maintaining the common elements of the development.

[iii]   *Homeowners' Associations.* The following diagram may help your understanding of the problems raised by homeowners' associations. First, work on the enforceability of the *Neponsit* covenant at law. The difficulty, nay impossibility, of obtaining monetary relief under these rules was the reason an equitable structure of remedies was sought. Second, figure out why the *Neponsit* covenant was enforceable at equity even though the relief sought was monetary. Finally, consider the problems covenant enforcement met even at equity.

Neponsit **Diagram**

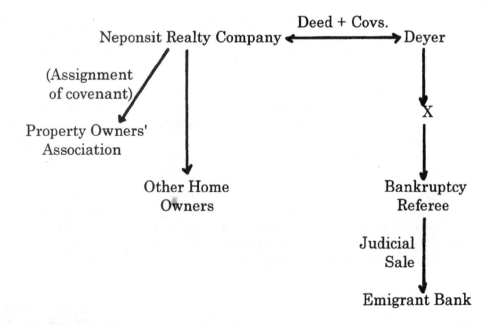

[A]   **Neponsit** *Covenants at Law.* Lack of privity was the major obstacle to enforcement of the *Neponsit* covenants at law. At the time of the litigation, the homeowners' association did not own a property interest in any portion of the development. The City had taken over the streets and the beach. It simply held an assignment of rights under the covenants from Neponsit Realty Company. While property owners other than Emigrant were in vertical privity with Neponsit Realty Company, the covenants did not give them a contractual right to receive the yearly payments.

[B]   *Equitable Obligations to Pay Money.* Go back to the first paragraph of the opinion and note the form of relief sought by the plaintiff. The action was brought to foreclose on a lien! The procedural nature of the case was much like an action to foreclose a mortgage. The underlying covenant in *Neponsit* provided that if the required payments were not made, the amount of the default became a lien on the property, a basic form of equitable relief. The hunt for an end run around the difficulties of enforcing obligations to pay money at law led nineteenth century scriveners to use the lien, an equitable technique that had the same practical effect as an obligation to pay money under a contract enforced at law.

[C]   *Homeowners' Associations at Equity.* Though equity courts did not use horizontal and vertical privity requirements, homeowners' associations still presented an intriguing problem. Ignoring the notion that a party enforcing a covenant had to hold the *same* interest as their predecessor in interest was one thing, but permitting enforcement by a party holding *no* interest in land was quite another. The *Neponsit* court, taking a step that was crucial to the development of the modern condominium, permitted enforcement of the covenants at equity because the association, acting as an agent for the owners, was "a convenient instrument by which the property owners may advance their common interests." In essence, the court pierced the corporate veil. Compare the outcome in *Zaist v. Olson,* discussed at p. 326 above.

[d]   Problem Notes

[i]   *Associations With Virtually No Connections with the Development.* Suppose a development is assembled and sold with an architectural covenant something like the one in *Gaskin v. Harris,* p. 419 above. But place enforcement of the covenant in the hands of a committee with the following characteristics:

a. No member of the committee may live in the development.

b. Of the five members of the committee one is appointed by the Mayor, one by the Chairperson of the Board of the largest bank in town, one by the religious leader of the largest church or temple in town, and two by the President of the local chapter of the American Institute of Architects.

c. All committee members serve without pay.

d. The committee has no other functions except to review requests to modify the buildings in the development and to seek injunctions against those who pursue building modifications without permission.

May a court of equity enforce the decisions of the committee?

[ii]   *Individual Versus Homeowner Association Enforcement of Covenants.* In the above example, if the committee approved a design, could a resident of the development sue at either law for damages or equity for injunctive relief if he or she believed the committee acted erroneously?[31] While decisions on these sorts of problems often depend on the wording of the

---

[31] For a case of this sort, *see* Hanson v. Salishan Properties, Inc., 267 Or. 199, 515 P.2d 1325 (1973).

covenants at issue, they reflect a constant theme of covenant litigation—the degree to which a property owner in a development gives up individual rights to enforce covenants to a homeowners' association.

[*iii*] *Servitude Towns.* Some "new" communities like the now well established Rouse development of Columbia, Maryland, use servitudes, rather than traditional forms of municipal government, to govern the entire community.

[e] *Neponsit,* Formalism and Realism

The *Neponsit* opinion is a fascinating historical document. Judge Lehman, overtly called the result realist, writing at 278 N.Y. p. 257, 15 N.E.2d p. 796:

> It has been suggested that a covenant which runs with the land must affect the legal relations—the advantages and the burdens—of the parties to the covenant, as owners of particular parcels of land and not merely as members of the community in general, such as taxpayers or owners of other land. [citing to Clark] That method of approach has the merit of realism. The test is based on the effect of the covenant rather than on technical distinctions.

Judge Lehman's citing of Clark's 1929 treatise, REAL COVENANTS AND OTHER INTERESTS WHICH "RUN WITH LAND," is an important signal about the mode of legal analysis driving the judge's decision-making. Charles E. Clark was a distinguished jurist and legal scholar. He began teaching at his alma mater, Yale Law School in 1919, where he was one of the leaders of the Realist Movement. He became Dean of Yale the same year he published his covenant treatise.[32]

Near the end of World War II, the American Law Institute began preparing a second edition of the servitudes portion of the Restatement of the Law of Property. The ALI, founded in 1923 as a center for the systemization and study of American law, was a response to widespread discontent with the lack of uniformity of American case law. The Restatement project aimed at increasing legal certainty by articulating "correct" legal rules culled from the confusing body of law of the states, thereby promoting doctrinal unity. The Institute asked Clark to serve as an advisor in the Restatement project, and appointed Professor Oliver S. Rundell as Reporter.[33] Rundell was a member of the University of Wisconsin Law School faculty, where he served as Dean from 1945-1953.

Clark and Rundell brought distinctly different perspectives to bear on their Restatement efforts. In an article published in the middle of the project, Clark launched a Realist attack on the Property Restatement, complaining that "the attempt to compress fluid law of many jurisdictions into one arbitrary statement is bound to mislead more than it clarifies."[34] A few years before, he launched a similar broadside against the Contract Restatement, arguing that it had "the rigidity of a code (with the added unreality that it is a declaration unsupported by . . . past precedent) and without the opportunity for reform and advance which a code affords."[35] The Restatement of Property

---

[32] Some of the ideas and comments in this note are taken from materials developed by my colleague at Georgetown, Professor Daniel Ernst. The particular segment used here was put together by his research assistant, Ms. Ashley Gable, J.D. 1998, Georgetown University Law Center. They have graciously allowed me to use their work.

[33] The Reporter is in charge of a restatement project, overseeing the drafting of the Restatement sections, along with all the commentary, running meetings, and organizing the project.

[34] Charles E. Clark, *The American Law Institute's Law of Real Covenants,* 52 YALE L.J. 699, 713 (1943).

[35] Charles E. Clark, *The Restatement of the Law of Contracts,* 42 YALE L.J. 646-647, 650 (1933). The Realist bias in favor of legislative action was rooted in antipathy to judicial attempts to invalidate economic regulations on freedom of contract grounds. The formalist, apolitical analytical techniques of the Restatement projects led to similar objections.

represented merely "property history," an excessive devotion to a past that was largely irrelevant to the concerns of the present. "Dicta repeating the rules of Lord Coke's time," he wrote, "without independent consideration of them are of comparatively little value."[36] Given these feelings, one wonders why Clark would wish to become involved in creating "the dry pulp of the pontifical and vague black letter generalities."[37] Perhaps he believed it was the best way to guarantee independent consideration of certain issues, such as the horizontal privity and "touch and concern" requirements.

Rundell, who uncritically accepted the Formalist mission of the American Law Institute, and Clark differed on major issues from the beginning of the Servitudes Restatement project.[38] The most controversial sections of the Proposed Final Draft of that Restatement[*] provided:

§ 82. Privity between Promisor and Promisee

The successor in interest to one who has made a promise respecting the use of his land is not liable as a promisor upon the promise, unless

(a) the promise is made in the adjustment of the mutual relationships arising out of the existence of an easement held by one of the parties to the promise in the land of another, or

(b) the transaction of which the promise is part includes a transfer of an interest either in the land benefited by or in the land burdened by the performance of the promise.

§ 85. Promise "Touching and Concerning" Land

A promise respecting the use of land of the promisor can bind as promisors the successors of the original promisor only if

(a) the performance of the promise will benefit the promisee or other beneficiary of the promise in the physical use or enjoyment of land possessed by him, or the consummation of the transaction of which it is a part will operate to benefit and is for the benefit of the promisor in the physical use or enjoyment of land possessed by him, and

(b) the burden on the land of the promisor bears a reasonable relation to the benefit received by the person benefited.

Once the basic drafting of the RESTATEMENT OF PROPERTY (SERVITUDES) was complete, Clark and Rundell tore into each other in the pages of the Yale Law Journal. Clark condemned the restrictions on running of burdens of covenants embodied in Sections 82 and 85. Although he thought it "doubtful how far we can judge our cause by what was done in feudal England seven or eight centuries ago," Clark insisted that Rundell's position was not founded on valid precedent. He deemed it "a result which is more bold in extending doubtful and overlapping lines of cases into a completely novel structure of prohibition than any other Institute product, and an unusually uncompromising adherence to a policy of outlawing parties' bargaining contrary to the trend of modern legal thinking."[39]

---

[36] Charles E. Clark, *Confidential Statement in re Restatement of the Law of Property,* quoted in LAURA KALMAN, LEGAL REALISM AT YALE, 1927-1960, at 27 (1986).

[37] Clark, note 35 above.

[38] Clark, note 34 above at 727.

[*] © The American Law Institute (1943). Reprinted with permission.

[39] *Id.,* at 722, 726.

Rundell acerbically responded that both the horizontal privity and touch and concern requirements were "in accord with both authority and sound policy." He steadfastly refused to acknowledge Clark's Realist skepticism of the rules he held dear. In his own Yale article, he formalistically opined that the rationale for the privity requirement was simple:

> The answer is that there is a rule of policy which can be expressed in the form of a rule of law that one man can not make another man legally responsible as a promisor; that there is an exception to that rule in the case of promises respecting the use of land; that that exception has limits; that those limits can be stated, and that [the horizontal privity requirement] is an attempt to state one of them.[40]

When the final draft of the servitudes Restatement came up for debate at the 1943 annual meeting of the American Law Institute, it was sent back to the drafters for further review. Minor revisions were made and the Institute, perhaps exhausted by the lengthy debates, finally approved the draft in 1944.[41]

The Clark-Rundell debate exemplified much more than tensions about the scope of servitude rules. Their differences also involved central features of the American judicial system. You have already read some materials about law and equity courts.[42] The traditional story is that equity arose as a creature of the English crown, designed to deal with perceived unfairness in the results reached by courts of law. Over the course of centuries two separate bodies of English law developed—one in law and one in equity or chancery. By the middle of the nineteenth century, all states in the United States had two separate court systems, one legal and the other equitable. Each system followed its own line of cases and did, as it were, its own thing. Pressure to change this structure arose almost as soon as it became standard practice. It just seemed silly to have two separate court systems with all the inefficiencies and costs that created. By the 1930s, pressures for reform were overwhelming. Realists were in the forefront of the reforms. They looked with favor on the equitable notion of fairness, found reliance on centuries of common law rules inappropriate in their fast-paced world, and strongly urged a merger of equity and law courts.

It is therefore hardly surprising that Clark was aware of and sympathetic with the equity cases, such as *Neponsit,* which allowed for changes in privity and touch and concern rules. Indeed a good argument may be made that the most important legacy of Clark's Realist Era, other than the new deal, was in the organization of our court systems, an organization which largely persists to this day. The Federal Rules of Civil Procedure were first promulgated in 1938. Separate courts of law and equity were merged into one system. Crucial decisions, including *Erie v. Tompkins,*[43] were made about the appropriate ways to apply state law in the federal courts. These reforms in the federal system quickly spread through the state courts as well. Courts of law and equity were merged in many places and state courts adopted procedural rules much like the new federal rules.

The fact that many courts of law and equity were merged did not, however, immediately do away with all of the old cases. The substantive law was not changed, only the place of its

---

[40] Oliver S. Rundell, *Judge Clark on the American Law Institute's Law of Real Covenants: A Comment,* 53 YALE L.J. 312, 325-326 (1944).

[41] § 82 became § 534 of the RESTATEMENT OF PROPERTY and § 85 became § 537. The changes made in late 1943 and early 1944 did not change the basic import of the Final Draft quoted in the text.

[42] Review the discussion of equity and the married woman's separate estate in Chapter 2, pp. 147–148 above.

[43] 304 U.S. 64 (1938).

application. Both legal and equitable forms of relief could be requested from the same court, but that court had to make decisions about when to use one body of law or the other. The result is a somewhat strange body of case law that still makes references to law or equity, that still makes decisions about which body of law to use. But it is also a system in which the merger of the two systems has allowed judges to be sloppy in their use of law and equity vocabulary, or to intentionally meld the two old systems into a new vision, or to select one line of cases and ignore another. I suspect that 50 or maybe 100 years from now, the idea that we still pay attention to law and equity will seem quaint.

In reading cases like *Neponsit,* decided in the same year the Federal Rules of Civil Procedure were first promulgated, you are studying how ancient bodies of law disappear. This, of course, is not the first time you have watched equity become a vehicle for undoing centuries of jurisprudence. The married woman's separate estate got its start as an equitable idea. Equitable notions were then imported into dozens of statutes and used as precedents by reform minded judges sitting in courts of law. Reform minded judges in law courts simply got rid of the idea that the separate estate could only be set up via a trust, an equitable institution, and declared that appropriate language would serve similar ends in a legal setting. Eventually, the separate estate was formalized into a fee simple-like concept, called upon by the mere incantation of a woman's name in a deed. It had turned into an interest in land much like the one that had been owned by men for centuries.

So too with covenants. The merged courts of law and equity began to call upon equitable concepts to resolve covenant cases. Developers saw the opening and drafted their documents to take advantage of the newer cases. The old rules at law have never been overruled. They were still out there, perhaps as traps for the unwary, but they were being used much less often. Equity was gradually taking over the field. Clark knew and liked this historical shift. Rundell paid it no heed.

The Clark-Rundell debate about the Servitudes Restatement project still resonates. Debates about Formalism and Realism often flourish in the halls of the American Law Institute. In every Restatement project, discussion arises about the utility of Restatements, the ability to rationally state a summary of trends in many jurisdictions, and the propriety of using Restatements to anticipate future developments rather than to merely document historical patterns. Though such debates continue, the most recent debates over the RESTATEMENT THIRD OF PROPERTY (SERVITUDES) at least have resolved the substantive legal differences between Clark and Rundell. The draft drops horizontal privity as a requirement for covenants to run and replaces the touch and concern requirement with a general rule barring enforcement when an arrangement is "illegal or unconstitutional or violates public policy."[44] Today we are, therefore, left in the ironic position of being able to claim, in a quite formalistic way, that Clark's Realist rule—a property owner on notice of the contents of a servitude is bound by its terms if its creators intended it to run to successors—now governs American property law.

While the vituperative qualities of the debate between Clark and Rundell may seem remote or even quaint to you, they illustrate the painful shifts in legal thought and policy that Realists were forcing upon the legal world in the first half of this century. Rundell was concerned with predictable rules and easy land transfer, hallmarks of pre-New Deal Formalism. Clark, with the

---

[44] RESTATEMENT (THIRD) OF PROPERTY (SERVITUDES) § 3.1 (Tentative Draft No. 7, 1998). The section and chapter then provides further details on specific areas that might limit enforcement of a servitude, including arbitrariness of terms, restraints on alienation or commerce, and unconscionability.

realistic needs of the legal system's clients in mind, focused on the freedom to bind one's successors in interest in order to efficiently develop structures for land planning and development. Rundell's policy, Clark believed, would discourage such useful devices as plans for the sharing of expenses of sanitation, sewer, and other community benefits. Rundell concluded, "In respect to the question of policy involved Judge Clark and I seem hopelessly at odds."[45] That, at least, was something the two men could agree on.

[6] Racial Covenants in the Realist Era

[a] Introduction to *Corrigan v. Buckley*

While the Realists helped make servitudes workable, they were not used only to make residential real estate development and planning possible. The flexibility of the device allowed people to impose an enormous array of restraints on use and occupancy of land, including ones that implemented Jim Crow in the late decades of the nineteenth and the opening decades of the twentieth centuries.

In the years immediately after the Civil War, important alterations in the Constitutional and statutory status of black persons were adopted. The Thirteenth Amendment abolishing slavery was ratified in 1865. Shortly thereafter, the Civil Rights Act of 1866[46] passed Congress. This act declared that all persons born in the United States were citizens of the United States, thereby overruling one of the central holdings of *Dred Scott v. Sanford,*[47] and provided that all citizens "of every race and color, without regard to any previous condition of slavery" had the "same right . . . to make and enforce contracts, to sue, be parties, and give evidence, to inherit, purchase, lease, sell, hold, and convey real and personal property . . . as is enjoyed by white citizens . . . ." During the Congressional debates on this act, doubts were expressed that the second section of the Thirteenth Amendment provided congress with authority to pass the bill. President Johnson, whose veto of the bill was overridden by Congress, expressed the same point of view.

Such expressions of doubt led Congress to draw up another amendment designed in part to validate the Civil Rights Act of 1866. The Fourteenth Amendment was passed by Congress and ratified by sufficient states by 1868. In 1870, the Fifteenth Amendment, or suffrage amendment, was ratified and Congress passed another civil rights act, mostly containing provisions enforcing the Fifteenth Amendment.[48] Further Civil Rights legislation was adopted in 1871 and 1875[49] before the election of Hayes in the close election of 1876 and the withdrawal of northern troops from the south shortly thereafter ended the Reconstruction Era. Not until 1957 was another major piece of Civil Rights legislation adopted by Congress.

While the major civil rights debates were raging in Congress and state legislative halls after the Civil War, a number of lesser noted legal difficulties were appearing for black persons in

---

[45] Oliver S. Rundell, *Judge Clark on the American Law Institute's Law of Real Covenants: A Comment*, 53 YALE L.J. 312, 325 (1944).

[46] An Act to Protect All Persons in the United States in Their Civil Rights, and Furnish the Means of Their Vindication, 14 Stat. 27 (1866). This act is presently codified at 42 U.S.C. §§ 1981, 1982 and 18 U.S.C. § 242.

[47] 60 U.S. (19 How.) 393 (1857). This case is excerpted and discussed in Chapter 12, p. 1081 below.

[48] An Act to Enforce the Rights of Citizens of the United States to Vote in the Several States of this Union, and for Other Purposes, 16 Stat. 140 (1870).

[49] An Act to Enforce the Provisions of the Fourteenth Amendment to the Constitution of the United States, and for Other Purposes, 17 Stat. 13 (1871); An Act to Protect All Citizens in Their Civil and Legal Rights, 18 Stat. 335 (1875). Part of the 1871 legislation is now codified at 42 U.S.C. § 1983 and provides the statutory basis for a substantial number of cases now filed each year in the federal courts.

their transition from slave to freed status. Since much of the normal legal structure was inapplicable to slaves, it was inevitable that the post-war era would create disputes over the status of slave marriages, the legitimacy of slave children, inheritance of property by slaves from Blacks freed before the war was over and countless other issues. But despite the array of legal problems, black ownership of rural land rose through the last decades of the nineteenth and opening decade of the twentieth centuries. There is some irony in the fact that black ownership of rural land was rising during the very era in which the Jim Crow laws were becoming firmly embedded in American culture. A combination of low land prices in the south and a strong agricultural economy permitted a substantial number of freed black tenant farmers to purchase land between 1860 and 1910. During that period, black persons accumulated almost 15 million acres of rural land. The figure has been falling ever since.[50] When the bottom fell out of the cotton market as World War I approached, the attractions of urban America drew huge numbers of rural southern black people north. A majority culture, unwilling to provide the same sort of assistance to black farmers as it provided to whites, stood by and watched the migration.

The legal backdrop for these developments began shortly after the last of the Civil War Amendments was added to the Constitution in 1870. As noted in Chapter 2 (pp. 162–163 above), in the *Slaughter House Cases,* 83 U.S. (16 Wall.) 36 (1873), the United Stated Supreme Court narrowly construed the Privileges and Immunities Clause of the Fourteenth Amendment. Justice Taney in his *Dred Scott* opinion, had concluded that black persons could not call upon any of the privileges or immunities of membership in the community of citizens. To reverse that holding, the Fourteenth Amendment, among other things, contained language forbidding states from abridging "the privileges or immunities of citizens of the United States." At the time of its adoption, this clause was thought by many to contain the most far reaching and important language in the Amendment. In *Slaughter House,* however, the Court opined that the Privileges and Immunities Clause created no new rights of federal citizenship, that its only purpose was to grant to black persons the same rights of federal citizenship that white persons had, and that federal citizenship only conferred rights explicitly granted in the Constitution. Thus, the rights to travel in interstate commerce, to have access to the writ of habeas corpus, or to use navigable waters were protected, but the right to participate in a profession of one's choice was not.

Before the century was over, the Supreme Court had imposed serious limitations on the criminal enforcement provisions of the Civil Rights Act of 1870,[51] found unconstitutional certain sections of the Civil Rights Act of 1875 integrating public accommodations,[52] and, as you probably know, declared that the Equal Protection Clause of the Fourteenth Amendment required no more than "equal but separate accommodations" for black and white persons.[53]

During the era just after "separate but equal" became the watchwords of the nation, major racially motivated riots by white persons in black neighborhoods rocked several cities. East St. Louis erupted in July, 1917, leaving 6000 black persons homeless. Chicago followed suit in July,

---

[50] United States Civil Rights Commission, The Decline of Black Farming in America 21-23 (1982); THE BLACK RURAL LANDOWNER—ENDANGERED SPECIES xv (L. McGee & Robert Boone eds., 1979); Graber, *Heirs Property: The Problems and Possible Solutions,* 12 CLEARINGHOUSE REV. 273 (1978).

[51] United States v. Cruikshank, 92 U.S. 542 (1875).

[52] Civil Rights Cases, 109 U.S. 3 (1883).

[53] Plessy v. Ferguson, 163 U.S. 537 (1896). The case involved the constitutionality of a Louisiana statute requiring separate accommodations for black and white railway passengers.

1919, following 25 other race riots around the nation in the first half of that year.[54] Lynching was still a major problem. Although the peak in the number of lynchings occurred late in the nineteenth century, several hundred persons were murdered between 1914 and 1918.[55]

While the structure of Jim Crow was being created, covenants restricting the transfer of property to black persons were placed in the deeds of innumerable real estate developments. These racial covenants were not imposed as a matter of legislative command, but as a matter of agreement among residents of a neighborhood or between real estate developers and the original purchasers of the housing units. Given the tenor of the times it is not surprising that the courts routinely validated the covenants. One of the most remarkable features of these cases is their lack of commentary on arcane issues like privity and touch and concern then dominating other servitude cases. Race dominated the agenda.

The next case is about the racial covenants which blanketed much of Washington, D.C.[56] The properties involved in the case were located on the 1700 block of S Street, N.W., in what is now the Dupont Circle Historic District in downtown Washington. The house of the plaintiff Buckley, a typical Washington Victorian bay front house, was constructed in 1905 and still stands at 1719 S Street, N.W.[57]

---

[54] BLACK PROTEST: HISTORY, DOCUMENTS, AND ANALYSES 175-179 (J. Grant ed., 1968); E.M. RUDWICK, RACE RIOT AT EAST ST. LOUIS JULY 2, 1917 (1964); S. DRAKE & H. CAYTON, 1 BLACK METROPOLIS: A STUDY OF NEGRO LIFE IN A NORTHERN CITY 65-76 (1962).

[55] NAACP, THIRTY YEARS OF LYNCHING (1919); JACQUELYN DOWD HALL, REVOLT AGAINST CHIVALRY: JESSIE DANIEL AMES AND THE WOMEN'S CAMPAIGN AGAINST LYNCHING 130-136 (1979).

[56] When my wife and I moved to Washington, D.C. in 1973 and bought our first house, the form deed given to our predecessors in title contained a racial covenant! We asked all concerned if they would mind not inserting similar language in the deed given to us. We knew these covenants were no longer enforceable because of the result in *Shelley v. Kraemer,* excerpted a bit later in this chapter, but wanted the language removed anyway. Everyone agreed to do so.

[57] The lot and block number for Corrigan's house are no longer used. That may mean either that the house is gone or that the lot's boundary lines have changed and a new number has been issued.

1719 S Street, N.W.
Washington, D.C.

[b]   Opinion of Court of Appeals in *Corrigan v. Buckley*

Corrigan v. Buckley

Court of Appeals of District of Columbia.

299 F. 899 (1924)

James A. Cobb, of Washington, D.C., for appellants.

James S. Easby-Smith, of Washington, D.C., for appellee.

Before ROBB and VAN ORSDEL, Associate Justices, and BARBER, Judge of the United States Court of Customs Appeals.

VAN ORSDEL, Associate Justice.

Appellee, plaintiff below, filed a bill of complaint to restrain defendant Corrigan from conveying to defendant Curtis certain real estate in the District of Columbia, and to prevent the latter from occupying the same, in violation of a covenant affecting the title to said land, and to compel specific performance of the covenant.

It is alleged in the bill that plaintiff owns an undivided interest in lot 74, square 152, improved by a dwelling house. Defendant Corrigan is the owner of lot 20, square 152, on which is situated a dwelling house; that on June 1, 1921, plaintiff and defendant Corrigan, together with 28 other persons, who were owners of land improved by dwelling houses adjacent to and in the same immediate neighborhood as the above property described, mutually executed and delivered a covenant which was recorded in the office of the recorder of deeds of the District of Columbia, which, after describing the location of the property as a whole, and expressing the desire of the parties to further the interests of said community and neighborhood, provided that:

"In consideration of the premises and the sum of five dollars ($5.00) each to the other in hand paid, the parties hereto do hereby mutually covenant, promise, and agree each to the other, and for their respective heirs and assigns, that no part of the land now owned by the parties hereto, a more detailed description of said property, being given after the respective signatures hereto, shall ever be used or occupied by, or sold, conveyed, leased, rented, or given to, negroes, or any person or persons of the negro race or blood. This covenant shall run with the land and bind the respective heirs and assigns of the parties hereto for the period of twenty-one (21) years from and after the date of these presents."

Plaintiff alleged that thereafter defendant Corrigan entered into a contract with defendant Curtis to sell to the latter a house and lot belonging to the former and included within the covenant; that defendant Curtis is a person of the negro race and blood, and before making the contract had knowledge of the existence and terms of the covenant; and that in executing the contract of sale plaintiff had acted in violation of the terms and conditions of the covenant. Plaintiff alleges that, if the conveyance is made in accordance with the contract of sale, irreparable injury will be done to plaintiff and to other persons who are parties to the indenture or covenant; that plaintiff is without any plain, adequate, and complete remedy at law; and that plaintiff is entitled to specific performance of the covenant by means of injunction preventing the defendant from carrying into effect the contract of sale.

Plaintiff accordingly prayed that defendant Corrigan be enjoined for 21 years from the date of the covenant, from carrying out the contract of sale with defendant Curtis, and that Curtis be permanently enjoined, during the same period of time, from taking title to the land, and from occupying, selling, conveying, leasing, renting, or giving the same to a negro, or permitting the same to be used or occupied by any negro.

Defendant Curtis filed a motion to dismiss the bill, on the ground that the covenant is void, in that it deprives defendant and others of property without due process of law, abridges the privileges and immunities of citizens of the United States, and denies the defendants equal protection of law. The court below denied the motion to dismiss the petition, and, defendants electing to stand upon their motion, a decree of injunction was entered, from which this appeal was taken.

Appellant seems to have misconceived the real question here involved. We are not dealing with the validity of a statute, or municipal law, or ordinance; nor are we concerned with the right of a negro to acquire, own, and use property; nor are we confronted with any preexisting rights which are affected by the covenant here in question. The sole issue is the power of a number of landowners to execute and record a covenant running with the land, by which they bind themselves, their heirs and assigns, during a period of 21 years, to prevent any of the land described in the covenant from being sold, leased to, or occupied by negroes.

The constitutional right of a negro to acquire, own, and occupy property does not carry with it the constitutional power to compel sale and conveyance to him of any particular private property. The individual citizen, whether he be black or white, may refuse to sell or lease his property to any particular individual or class of individuals. The state alone possesses the power to compel a sale or taking of private property, and that only for public use. The power of these property owners to exclude one class of citizens implies the power of the other class to exercise the same prerogative over property which they may own. What is denied one class may be denied the other. There is, therefore, no discrimination within the civil rights clauses of the Constitution. Such a covenant is enforceable, not only against a member of the excluded race, but between the parties to the agreement.

Our attention has not been called to any decision of the Supreme Court of the United States involving the exact question before us. It has, however, been before the courts of the states, where it has been held that similar covenants against ownership or occupancy by negroes are neither unconstitutional nor contrary to public policy. Parmalee et al. v. Morris, 218 Mich. 625, 188 N.W. 330; Queensboro Land Co. v. Cazeaux, 136 La. 724, 67 South. 641, L.R.A. 1916B, 1201, Ann. Cas. 1916D, 1248; Los Angeles Investment Co. v. Gary, 181 Cal. 680, 186 Pac. 596, 9 A.L.R. 115; Koehler v. Rowland, 275 Mo. 573, 205 S.W. 217, 9 A.L.R. 107.

It is unnecessary to consider the contention that the restriction amounts to a denial of equal protection of the laws under the Fourteenth Amendment, since the Supreme Court has held in numerous instances that the inhibition is upon the power of the state, and not to action by individuals in respect of their property. United States v. Cruikshank, 92 U.S. 542; Virginia v. Rives, 100 U.S. 313; United States v. Harris, 106 U.S. 629; Civil Rights Cases, 109 U.S. 31.

In Plessy v. Ferguson, 163 U.S. 537, the court, sustaining the validity of a statute of Louisiana, providing for separation of races in passenger cars, as not being repugnant to the provisions of the Fourteenth Amendment, said:

"The object of the amendment was undoubtedly to enforce the absolute equality of the two races before the law but in the nature of things it could not have been intended to abolish distinctions based upon color, or to enforce social, as distinguished from political, equality, or a commingling of the two races upon terms unsatisfactory to either. Laws permitting, and even requiring, their separation in places where they are liable to be brought into contact, do not necessarily imply the inferiority of either race to the other, and have been generally, if not universally, recognized as within the competency of the state Legislatures in the exercise of their police power."

The foregoing rule applies, not only to segregation in railway coaches, but to statutes requiring separate white and colored schools, as well as regulations providing for the segregation of the races in municipal playgrounds, municipal golf courses, municipal tennis courts, and municipal bathing beaches. The same general and settled public opinion controls in respect of the segregation of the races in churches, hotels, restaurants, lodging houses, apartment houses, theaters, and places of public amusement.

It follows that the segregation of the races, whether by statute or private agreement, where the method adopted does not amount to the denial of fundamental constitutional rights, cannot be held to be against public policy. Nor can the social equality of the races be attained, either by legislation or by the forcible assertion of assumed rights. As was said in People v. Gallagher, 93 N.Y. 438, 448 (45 Am.Rep. 232):

"This end can neither be accomplished nor promoted by laws which conflict with the general sentiment of the community upon whom they are designed to operate. When the government, therefore, has secured to each of its citizens equal rights before the law and equal opportunities for improvement and progress, it has accomplished the end for which it is organized, and performed all of the functions respecting social advantages with which it is endowed."

Defendant claims protection under certain legislation of Congress. As suggested in the opinion of the learned trial justice, this legislation was enacted to carry into effect the provisions of the Constitution. The statutes, therefore, can afford no more protection than the Constitution itself. If, therefore, there is no infringement of defendant's rights under the Constitution, there can be none under the statutes.

The decree is affirmed, with costs.

[c] Notes on *Corrigan*

[*i*] **Theory of the Case.** The rationale of Judge Van Orsdel was taken right from the pages of *Plessy v. Ferguson* and "separate but equal." "The power of these property owners to exclude one class of citizens," he wrote, "implies the power of the other class to exercise the same prerogative over property which they may own. What is denied one class may be denied the other. There is, therefore, no discrimination within the civil rights clauses of the Constitution." Furthermore, there could be no violation of the Constitution because the Fourteenth Amendment restrains only the exercise of state power. Since the racial covenants resulted from private conduct, the courts were powerless to intervene. These results were affirmed by the United States Supreme Court in *Corrigan v. Buckley,* 271 U.S. 323 (1924).

[*ii*] **Alienation Restraint.** In addition to the Rule Against Perpetuities, studied in Chapter 4, courts have long barred the enforcement of limitations on estates or of covenants which unreasonably restrain the transfer of land. Clauses in deeds which directly barred an owner from selling or transferring the property were deemed unenforceable. Other less drastic terms failed if they lacked a reasonable basis of support.[58] Why shouldn't the refusal of the courts to enforce this rule against racial covenants create sufficient state action to justify invoking the terms of the Fourteenth Amendment?

[*iii*] **Corrigan, *Formalism and Realism.*** There is a certain Formalist quality to the *Corrigan* opinion. It arises not just in the rote recitation of the separate but equal rule, but in its studious aversion to discussion of the reality of racial discrimination. The fact that both whites and blacks were allowed to bind themselves to racial covenants automatically made them equal. The theoretical ability to enter into a contract, devoid of any connection to the market power

---

[58] The modern view is laid out in §§ 3.4 and 3.5 of the Tentative Draft of the RESTATEMENT (THIRD) OF PROPERTY (SERVITUDES).

of one or another person to seek an agreement, fulfilled constitutional demands. The unwillingness of Realists, however, to protest such outcomes vividly displays the limitations of their views that law is an instrument of policy making. In an era of racial tension and segregation, reliance on legislatures as the primary tools for reform left little room for action on racial discrimination in the disposition of property.

[d]   Additional Materials on Early History of Racial Covenants

For a compelling story about the history of racial covenants and segregated housing patterns in Baltimore, read Garrett Power, *Apartheid Baltimore Style: The Residential Segregation Ordinances of 1910-1913,* 42 Md. L. Rev. 289 (1982), excerpted in Richard H. Chused, A Property Anthology 116-128 (2d ed.1997).

[7]   Race and Servitudes in Contemporary Life

[a]   Background to *Shelley v. Kraemer*

St. Louis, like most major cities in the first half of this century, was tightly segregated. Clear demarcation lines existed between white and black neighborhoods; white neighborhood associations were frequently active in taking steps to insure that the lines were not crossed. In northwest St. Louis, the Marcus Avenue Improvement Association, founded in 1910, began seeking signatures on racially restrictive covenants almost immediately after it was formed. By 1928, most of the neighborhood was covered by such agreements.[59]

From prior materials in this chapter, you know that servitudes have two qualities in addition to those of typical contracts which make them distinctive property arrangements. First, every properly drafted covenant has a clause in it which states that it is the intention of the parties to the covenant to benefit and burden all the future owners of the property subject to the agreement. Second, a covenant is a document which can be recorded along with deeds and other real property instruments, making it possible to notify future owners that the property they are interested in buying is in some way bound by a covenant. If these and other requirements are met, the covenant will bind all future owners of the property. While older covenant law required covenants to be entered into simultaneously with the transfer of some interest in land, cases decided early in this century, including *Neponsit v. Emigrant Savings Bank,* established guidelines for any property owner who wished to bind the property to a covenant. This development made it possible to use covenants for racial purposes.

Although the activity of the Marcus Avenue Improvement Association fell off during the early years of the depression, much of the neighborhood was recanvassed between 1937 and 1948 to make sure that the racial covenants were all up to date.[60] Cooperation between the Association and the St. Louis Real Estate Exchange was close. The Association also monitored real estate deals in the neighborhood and brought several law suits to enforce covenants before the *Shelley* case.[61] In 1945, the black population of St. Louis was about 116,000, or 13% of the city's population. Due to covenant restrictions on housing, virtually all of this population was crowded

---

[59] C. Vose, Caucasians Only: The Supreme Court, the NAACP, and the Restrictive Covenant Cases 100 (1959). [Hereinafter cited as Vose.]

[60] Vose, note 59 above, at 102. A number of the covenants had defined lifetimes, making it necessary to renew them periodically.

[61] *Id.* 105-109.

into seven percent of the city's housing stock.[62] The overcrowding led to high rents in the affected neighborhoods.[63] The pressure of unmet housing needs in the black community created constant pressure on black real estate agents to find available housing.

Robert Bishop was an agent for Bowers Real Estate Company, as well as the minister of J. D. Shelley and his wife. In 1945, the Shelleys informed Bishop that they were interested in buying a house. Bishop bought a duplex at 4600 Labadie Avenue a short time later from another real estate firm for $4,700, but acquired it under the name of a white "straw party," Geraldine Fitzgerald, because it was easier to obtain financing for the purchase when a white person fronted the deal. In addition, the use of a white front hid the possibility that an attempt to break the racial covenant covering 4600 Labadie Avenue might be made. Bishop then turned around and sold the duplex to the Shelleys for $5,700.[64]

Putting aside the racial aspects of the case for a moment, you should have some questions about the propriety of Bishop's quick profit. Real estate agents, like trustees, have trust-like responsibilities to deal fairly with their clients. The Shelleys were unaware that Bishop was making a profit on the deal. A good argument can be made that any profit greater than the normal real estate commission Bishop made should have been disgorged to the Shelleys.

In any case, the Shelleys moved in on September 11, 1945, and were served with papers in a lawsuit that evening. The plaintiffs were Fern and Lewis Kraemer, who lived at 3542 Labadie Avenue. Fern Kraemer inherited their house from her mother who had signed the original covenant documents.[65] The Shelleys' answer to the plaintiffs' complaint contended that the covenant, originally signed in 1911, was unenforceable because significant numbers of black persons already lived in the area affected by the agreement and because the agreement had not been signed by all property owners in the blocks it covered,[66] and that enforcement of the covenants violated provisions of both the state and federal constitutions.[67] On October 9, 1945, the trial judge restrained the Shelleys from taking possession of their house, but at the trial, he denied the plaintiffs permanent injunctive relief. The judge held that the covenant was unenforceable unless enough owners signed to make it an effective arrangement. The signatures of 30 of the 39 owners were not enough to meet that standard. In addition, the court held that the Shelleys lacked notice of the covenant. Bishop, whose interests were adverse to the Shelleys on this issue, never informed them of the covenant. The Constitutional issues were not reached.[68]

The Missouri Supreme Court reversed,[69] holding that all owners did not have to sign, that the lack of some signatures did not make the covenant an ineffective agreement, that the Shelleys were on constructive if not actual notice of the covenant because it had been recorded, and that the Constitutional rights of the Shelleys were not infringed by the covenant. Immediately after this opinion was announced, a number of black real estate agents in St. Louis formed the Real

---

[62] JAMIE GRAHAM, *SHELLEY V. KRAEMER*: A CELEBRATION 7 (1988).

[63] MARK TUSHNET, MAKING CIVIL RIGHTS LAW 88-89 (1994).

[64] *Id.* 109-111.

[65] *Id.* 111-113.

[66] There is a general covenant rule that renders them unenforceable if circumstances since the signing of the covenant have changed so much that the original purposes of the agreement may no longer be served. For more on this notion, *see* Ginsberg v. Yeshiva of Far Rockaway, p. 465 below.

[67] Vose, note 59 above, at 114-115.

[68] *Id.* at 116.

[69] Kraemer v. Shelley, 355 Mo. 814, 198 S.W.2d 679 (1946).

Estate Brokers Association of St. Louis to counter the influence of the white St. Louis Real Estate Exchange whose members had been supporting the litigation costs of the Kraemers. The Real Estate Brokers Association mounted a drive of their own to raise funds for an appeal to the Supreme Court.[70]

[b]   United States Supreme Court Opinions in *Shelley v. Kraemer*

Shelley v. Kraemer

United States Supreme Court
334 U.S. 1, 68 S. Ct. 836, 92 L. Ed. 1161 (1948)

George L. Vaughn[71] ; and *Herman Willer* argued the cause and filed a brief for petitioners in No. 72. Earl Susman was also of counsel.

Thurgood Marshall and *Loren Miller* argued the cause for petitioners in No. 87. With them on the brief were *Willis M. Graves, Francis Dent, William H. Hastie, Charles H. Houston, George M. Johnson, William R. Ming, Jr., James Nabrit, Jr., Marian Wynn Perry, Spottswood W. Robinson, III, Andrew Weinberger* and *Ruth Weyand.*

By special leave of Court, *Solicitor General Perlman* argued the cause for the United States, as *amicus curiae,* supporting petitioners. With him on the brief was *Attorney General Clark.*

Gerald L. Seegers argued the cause for respondents in No. 72. With him on the brief was *Walter H. Pollmann. Benjamin F. York* was also of counsel.

Henry Gilligan and *James A. Crooks* argued the cause and filed a brief for respondents in No. 87. *Lloyd T. Chockley* was also of counsel.

Briefs of *amici curiae* supporting petitioners were filed by *Perry W. Howard* for the Civil Liberties Department, Grand Lodge of Elks, I. B. P. O. E. W.; *Isaac Pacht, Irving Hill* and *Clore Warne*; *Robert McC. Marsh* and *Eugene Blanc, Jr.* for the Protestant Council of New York City; *Herbert S. Thatcher* and *Robert A. Wilson* for the American Federation of Labor; *Julius L. Goldstein* for the Non-Sectarian Anti-Nazi League to Champion Human Rights, Inc.; *Melville J. France* for the General Council of Congregational Christian Churches et al.; *Robert W. Kenny, O. John Rogge* and *Mozart G. Ratner* for the National Lawyers Guild; *Lee Pressman, Eugene Cotton, Frank Donner, John J. Abt, Leon M. Despres, M. H. Goldstein, Isadore Katz, David*

---

[70] Vose, note 59 above, at 119-121.

[71] Author's Note: In addition to the materials in the first textual note after the *Shelley* opinion, the book by J. CLAY SMITH, EMANCIPATION: THE MAKING OF THE BLACK LAWYER 1844-1944 (1993) provides information on some of the lawyers listed here. George L. Vaughn was a black practitioner in St. Louis, Missouri. Loren Miller graduated Washburn Law School in 1928, moved to California two years later and published the black newspaper the LOS ANGELES SENTINEL, in addition to practicing law. Francis Dent graduated Detroit College of Law in 1923 and was a leader in the black led but integrated Wolverine Bar Association. Ruth Weyand was a white lawyer who lobbied the American Bar Association to admit blacks and worked at the NLRB. Perry W. Howard chaired the math department at Alcorn University, received his law degree in 1904 from the predecessor to DePaul, served as a special assistant to the Attorney General in the 1920s, helped fund raise for the NAACP, and was very instrumental in establishing the National Bar Association. Earl B. Dickerson was the first black law graduate of the University of Chicago, became an assistant attorney general in Illinois, and in 1942 was appointed by Franklin Roosevelt to the United States Fair Employment Practice Committee. He also served on the national board of the National Lawyer's Guild. Richard E. Westbrooks was a lawyer in Chicago, successfully litigated an early case challenging segregation on the railroads before the Interstate Commerce Commission, and was involved in establishing the Cook County Bar Association.

Rein, Samuel L. Rothbard, Harry Sacher, William Standard and *Lindsay P. Walden* for the Congress of Industrial Organizations et al.; *Phineas Indritz, Irving R. M. Panzer* and *Richard A. Solomon* for the American Veterans *Committee; William Maslow, Shad Polier, Joseph B. Robison, Byron S. Miller* and *William Strong* for the American Jewish Congress; *Joseph M. Proskauer* and *Jacob Grumet* for the American Jewish Committee et al.; *William Strong* for the American Indian Citizens League of California, Inc.; *Francis M. Dent, Walter M. Nelson, Eugene H. Buder, Victor B. Harris, Luther Ely Smith* and *Harold I. Kahen* for the American Civil Liberties Union; *Earl B. Dickerson, Richard E. Westbrooks* and *Loring B. Moore* for the National Bar Association; *Alger Hiss, Joseph M. Proskauer* and *Victor Elting* for the American Association for the United Nations; and *Edward C. Park* and *Frank B. Frederick* for the American Unitarian Association.

Briefs of *amici curiae* supporting respondents were filed by *Roger J. Whiteford* and *John J. Wilson* for the National Association of Real Estate Boards; *Ray C. Eberhard* and *Elisabeth Eberhard Zeigler* for the Arlington Heights Property Owners Association et al.; and *Thomas F. Cadwalader* and *Carlyle Barton* for the Mount Royal Protective Association, Inc.

Mr. Chief Justice Vinson delivered the opinion of the Court.

These cases present for our consideration questions relating to the validity of court enforcement of private agreements, generally described as restrictive covenants, which have as their purpose the exclusion of persons of designated race or color from the ownership or occupancy of real property. Basic constitutional issues of obvious importance have been raised.

The first of these cases comes to this Court on certiorari to the Supreme Court of Missouri. On February 16, 1911, thirty out of a total of thirty-nine owners of property fronting both sides of Labadie Avenue between Taylor Avenue and Cora Avenue in the city of St. Louis, signed an agreement, which was subsequently recorded, providing in part:

> . . . the said property is hereby restricted to the use and occupancy for the term of Fifty (50) years from this date, so that it shall be a condition all the time and whether recited and referred to as [*sic*] not in subsequent conveyances and shall attach to the land as a condition precedent to the sale of the same, that hereafter no part of said property or any portion thereof shall be, for said term of Fifty-years, occupied by any person not of the Caucasian race, it being intended hereby to restrict the use of said property for said period of time against the occupancy as owners or tenants of any portion of said property for resident or other purpose by people of the Negro or Mongolian Race.

The entire district described in the agreement included fifty-seven parcels of land. The thirty owners who signed the agreement held title to forty-seven parcels, including the particular parcel involved in this case. At the time the agreement was signed, five of the parcels in the district were owned by Negroes. One of those had been occupied by Negro families since 1882, nearly thirty years before the restrictive agreement was executed. The trial court found that owners of seven out of nine homes on the south side of Labadie Avenue, within the restricted district and "in the immediate vicinity" of the premises in question, had failed to sign the restrictive agreement in 1911. At the time this action was brought, four of the premises were occupied by Negroes, and had been so occupied for periods ranging from twenty-three to sixty-three years. A fifth parcel had been occupied by Negroes until a year before this suit was instituted.

On August 11, 1945, pursuant to a contract of sale, petitioners Shelley, who are Negroes, for valuable consideration received from one Fitzgerald a warranty deed to the parcel in question.

The trial court found that petitioners had no actual knowledge of the restrictive agreement at the time of the purchase.

On October 9, 1945, respondents, as owners of other property subject to the terms of the restrictive covenant, brought suit in the Circuit Court of the city of St. Louis praying that petitioners Shelley be restrained from taking possession of the property and that judgment be entered divesting title out of petitioners Shelley and revesting title in the immediate grantor or in such other person as the court should direct. The trial court denied the requested relief on the ground that the restrictive agreement, upon which respondents based their action, had never become final and complete because it was the intention of the parties to that agreement that it was not to become effective until signed by all property owners in the district, and signatures of all the owners had never been obtained.

The Supreme Court of Missouri sitting *en banc* reversed and directed the trial court to grant the relief for which respondents had prayed. That court held the agreement effective and concluded that enforcement of its provisions violated no rights guaranteed to petitioners by the Federal Constitution. At the time the court rendered its decision, petitioners were occupying the property in question.

The second of the cases under consideration comes to this Court from the Supreme Court of Michigan. The circumstances presented do not differ materially from the Missouri case.

. . . .

Petitioners have placed primary reliance on their contentions, first raised in the state courts, that judicial enforcement of the restrictive agreements in these cases has violated rights guaranteed to petitioners by the Fourteenth Amendment of the Federal Constitution and Acts of Congress passed pursuant to that Amendment. Specifically, petitioners urge that they have been denied the equal protection of the laws, deprived of property without due process of law, and have been denied privileges and immunities of citizens of the United States. We pass to a consideration of those issues.

I.

. . . .

It is well, at the outset, to scrutinize the terms of the restrictive agreements involved in these cases. In the Missouri case, the covenant declares that no part of the affected property shall be "occupied by any person not of the Caucasian race, it being intended hereby to restrict the use of said property . . . against the occupancy as owners or tenants of any portion of said property for resident or other purpose by people of the Negro or Mongolian Race." Not only does the restriction seek to proscribe use and occupancy of the affected properties by members of the excluded class, but as construed by the Missouri courts, the agreement requires that title of any person who uses his property in violation of the restriction shall be divested. The restriction of the covenant in the Michigan case seeks to bar occupancy by persons of the excluded class. It provides that "This property shall not be used or occupied by any person or persons except those of the Caucasian race."

It should be observed that these covenants do not seek to proscribe any particular use of the affected properties. Use of the properties for residential occupancy, as such, is not forbidden. The restrictions of these agreements, rather, are directed toward a designated class of persons and seek to determine who may and who may not own or make use of the properties for residential purposes. The excluded class is defined wholly in terms of race or color; "simply that and nothing more."[6]

It cannot be doubted that among the civil rights intended to be protected from discriminatory state action by the Fourteenth Amendment are the rights to acquire, enjoy, own and dispose of property. Equality in the enjoyment of property rights was regarded by the framers of that Amendment as an essential pre-condition to the realization of other basic civil rights and liberties which the Amendment was intended to guarantee.[7] Thus, § 1978 of the Revised Statutes, derived from § 1 of the Civil Rights Act of 1866 which was enacted by Congress while the Fourteenth Amendment was also under consideration,[8] provides:

All citizens of the United States shall have the same right, in every State and Territory, as is enjoyed by white citizens thereof to inherit, purchase, lease, sell, hold, and convey real and personal property.[9]

This Court has given specific recognition to the same principle. *Buchanan v. Warley,* 245 U.S. 60 (1917).

It is likewise clear that restrictions on the right of occupancy of the sort sought to be created by the private agreements in these cases could not be squared with the requirements of the Fourteenth Amendment if imposed by state statute or local ordinance. We do not understand respondents to urge the contrary.

. . . .

But the present cases, unlike those just discussed, do not involve action by state legislatures or city councils. Here the particular patterns of discrimination and the areas in which the restrictions are to operate, are determined, in the first instance, by the terms of agreements among private individuals. Participation of the State consists in the enforcement of the restrictions so defined. The crucial issue with which we are here confronted is whether this distinction removes these cases from the operation of the prohibitory provisions of the Fourteenth Amendment.

Since the decision of this Court in the *Civil Rights Cases,* 109 U.S. 3 (1883), the principle has become firmly embedded in our constitutional law that the action inhibited by the first section of the Fourteenth Amendment is only such action as may fairly be said to be that of the States. That Amendment erects no shield against merely private conduct, however discriminatory or wrongful.

We conclude, therefore, that the restrictive agreements standing alone cannot be regarded as violative of any rights guaranteed to petitioners by the Fourteenth Amendment. So long as the purposes of those agreements are effectuated by voluntary adherence to their terms, it would appear clear that there has been no action by the State and the provisions of the Amendment have not been violated.

But here there was more. These are cases in which the purposes of the agreements were secured only by judicial enforcement by state courts of the restrictive terms of the agreements. The

[6] Buchanan v. Warley, 245 U.S. 60, 73 (1917).

[7] Slaughter-House Cases, 16 Wall. 36, 70, 81 (1873).

[8] In Oyama v. California, 332 U.S. 633, 640 (1948) the section of the Civil Rights Act herein considered is described as the federal statute, "enacted before the Fourteenth Amendment but vindicated by it." The Civil Rights Act of 1866 was reenacted in § 18 of the Act of May 31, 1870, subsequent to the adoption of the Fourteenth Amendment. 16 Stat. 144.

[9] 14 Stat. 27, 8 U.S.C. § 42.

respondents urge that judicial enforcement of private agreements does not amount to state action; or, in any event, the participation of the State is so attenuated in character as not to amount to state action within the meaning of the Fourteenth Amendment. Finally, it is suggested, even if the States in these cases may be deemed to have acted in the constitutional sense, their action did not deprive petitioners of rights guaranteed by the Fourteenth Amendment. We move to a consideration of these matters.

II.

That the action of state courts and judicial officers in their official capacities is to be regarded as action of the State within the meaning of the Fourteenth Amendment, is a proposition which has long been established by decisions of this Court . . . .

One of the earliest applications of the prohibitions contained in the Fourteenth Amendment to action of state judicial officials occurred in cases in which Negroes had been excluded from jury service in criminal prosecutions by reason of their race or color. These cases demonstrate, also, the early recognition by this Court that state action in violation of the Amendment's provisions is equally repugnant to the constitutional commands whether directed by state statute or taken by a judicial official in the absence of statute. Thus, in *Strauder v. West Virginia,* 100 U.S. 303 (1880), this Court declared invalid a state statute restricting jury service to white persons as amounting to a denial of the equal protection of the laws to the colored defendant in that case . . . .

The action of state courts in imposing penalties or depriving parties of other substantive rights without providing adequate notice and opportunity to defend, has, of course, long been regarded as a denial of the due process of law guaranteed by the Fourteenth Amendment. *Pennoyer v. Neff,* 95 U.S. 714 (1878).

. . . .

But the examples of state judicial action which have been held by this Court to violate the Amendment's commands are not restricted to situations in which the judicial proceedings were found in some manner to be procedurally unfair. It has been recognized that the action of state courts in enforcing a substantive common-law rule formulated by those courts, may result in the denial of rights guaranteed by the Fourteenth Amendment, even though the judicial proceedings in such cases may have been in complete accord with the most rigorous conceptions of procedural due process.[19] Thus, in *American Federation of Labor v. Swing,* 312 U.S. 321 (1941), enforcement by state courts of the common-law policy of the State, which resulted in the restraining of peaceful picketing, was held to be state action of the sort prohibited by the Amendment's guaranties of freedom of discussion. In *Cantwell v. Connecticut,* 310 U.S. 296 (1940), a conviction in a state court of the common-law crime of breach of the peace was, under the circumstances of the case, found to be a violation of the Amendment's commands relating to freedom of religion. In *Bridges v. California,* 314 U.S. 252 (1941), enforcement of the state's common-law rule relating to contempts by publication was held to be state action inconsistent with the prohibitions of the Fourteenth Amendment.

The short of the matter is that from the time of the adoption of the Fourteenth Amendment until the present, it has been the consistent ruling of this Court that the action of the States to

---

[19] In applying the rule of *Erie R. Co. v. Tompkins,* 304 U.S. 64 (1938), it is clear that the common-law rules enunciated by state courts in judicial opinions are to be regarded as a part of the law of the State.

which the Amendment has reference includes action of state courts and state judicial officials. Although, in construing the terms of the Fourteenth Amendment, differences have from time to time been expressed as to whether particular types of state action may be said to offend the Amendment's prohibitory provisions, it has never been suggested that state court action is immunized from the operation of those provisions simply because the act is that of the judicial branch of the state government.

III.

Against this background of judicial construction, extending over a period of some three-quarters of a century, we are called upon to consider whether enforcement by state courts of the restrictive agreements in these cases may be deemed to be the acts of those States; and, if so, whether that action has denied these petitioners the equal protection of the laws which the Amendment was intended to insure.

We have no doubt that there has been state action in these cases in the full and complete sense of the phrase. The undisputed facts disclose that petitioners were willing purchasers of properties upon which they desired to establish homes. The owners of the properties were willing sellers; and contracts of sale were accordingly consummated. It is clear that but for the active intervention of the state courts, supported by the full panoply of state power, petitioners would have been free to occupy the properties in question without restraint.

These are not cases, as has been suggested, in which the States have merely abstained from action, leaving private individuals free to impose such discriminations as they see fit. Rather, these are cases in which the States have made available to such individuals the full coercive power of government to deny to petitioners, on the grounds of race or color, the enjoyment of property rights in premises which petitioners are willing and financially able to acquire and which the grantors are willing to sell. The difference between judicial enforcement and non-enforcement of the restrictive covenants is the difference to petitioners between being denied rights of property available to other members of the community and being accorded full enjoyment of those rights on an equal footing.

The enforcement of the restrictive agreements by the state courts in these cases was directed pursuant to the common-law policy of the States as formulated by those courts in earlier decisions. In the Missouri case, enforcement of the covenant was directed in the first instance by the highest court of the State after the trial court had determined the agreement to be invalid for want of the requisite number of signatures. In the Michigan case, the order of enforcement by the trial court was affirmed by the highest state court. The judicial action in each case bears the clear and unmistakable imprimatur of the State. We have noted that previous decisions of this Court have established the proposition that judicial action is not immunized from the operation of the Fourteenth Amendment simply because it is taken pursuant to the state's common-law policy. Nor is the Amendment ineffective simply because the particular pattern of discrimination, which the State has enforced, was defined initially by the terms of a private agreement. State action, as that phrase is understood for the purposes of the Fourteenth Amendment, refers to exertions of state power in all forms. And when the effect of that action is to deny rights subject to the protection of the Fourteenth Amendment, it is the obligation of this Court to enforce the constitutional commands.

We hold that in granting judicial enforcement of the restrictive agreements in these cases, the States have denied petitioners the equal protection of the laws and that, therefore, the action of the state courts cannot stand. We have noted that freedom from discrimination by the States in the enjoyment of property rights was among the basic objectives sought to be effectuated by the framers of the Fourteenth Amendment. That such discrimination has occurred in these cases is clear. Because of the race or color of these petitioners they have been denied rights of ownership or occupancy enjoyed as a matter of course by other citizens of different race or color.

. . . .

Respondents urge, however, that since the state courts stand ready to enforce restrictive covenants excluding white persons from the ownership or occupancy of property covered by such agreements, enforcement of covenants excluding colored persons may not be deemed a denial of equal protection of the laws to the colored persons who are thereby affected. This contention does not bear scrutiny. The parties have directed our attention to no case in which a court, state or federal, has been called upon to enforce a covenant excluding members of the white majority from ownership or occupancy of real property on grounds of race or color. But there are more fundamental considerations. The rights created by the first section of the Fourteenth Amendment are, by its terms, guaranteed to the individual. The rights established are personal rights. It is, therefore, no answer to these petitioners to say that the courts may also be induced to deny white persons rights of ownership and occupancy on grounds of race or color. Equal protection of the laws is not achieved through indiscriminate imposition of inequalities.

Nor do we find merit in the suggestion that property owners who are parties to these agreements are denied equal protection of the laws if denied access to the courts to enforce the terms of restrictive covenants and to assert property rights which the state courts have held to be created by such agreements. The Constitution confers upon no individual the right to demand action by the State which results in the denial of equal protection of the laws to other individuals.

. . . .

The historical context in which the Fourteenth Amendment became a part of the Constitution should not be forgotten. Whatever else the framers sought to achieve, it is clear that the matter of primary concern was the establishment of equality in the enjoyment of basic civil and political rights and the preservation of those rights from discriminatory action on the part of the States based on considerations of race or color. Seventy-five years ago this Court announced that the provisions of the Amendment are to be construed with this fundamental purpose in mind.[30] Upon full consideration, we have concluded that in these cases the States have acted to deny petitioners the equal protection of the laws guaranteed by the Fourteenth Amendment. Having so decided, we find it unnecessary to consider whether petitioners have also been deprived of property without due process of law or denied privileges and immunities of citizens of the United States.

For the reasons stated, the judgment of the Supreme Court of Missouri and the judgment of the Supreme Court of Michigan must be reversed.

[c]   Explanatory Notes

[i]   *Importance of* **Shelley.** At the time *Shelley* was argued before the Supreme Court it was widely viewed as an extremely important test case. While the Supreme Court had given some prior indications it might be prepared to move away from the old separate but equal standard,[72] the growing civil rights community knew that *Shelley* was a crucial test of the justices'

---

[30] *Slaughter-House Cases*, 16 Wall. 36, 81 (1873); *Strauder v. West Virginia*, 100 U.S. 303 (1880).

[72] Missouri ex rel. Gaines v. Canada, 305 U.S. 337 (1937), for example, found it unconstitutional for the University of Missouri to deny Blacks admission to its law school while offering to pay tuition to an out of state institution. The state responded by creating a law school for Blacks only.

predilections. The list of attorneys involved in the case provides a telling indication of its importance. Those appearing for the NAACP were among the who's who of the black legal community. Many had connections with Howard University Law School, either as students or teachers. They included Thurgood Marshall, late Justice of the Supreme Court, William Hastie, who sat on the United States Court of Appeals for the Third Circuit, Charles H. Houston, a Dean of Howard Law School among other accomplishments, James Nabrit, President of Howard University, William R. Ming, the only black professor in the history of the University of Chicago Law School until very recent times and later a member of the Howard Law School faculty, and Spottswood W. Robinson III, who sat on the United States Court of Appeals for the District of Columbia Circuit. The Solicitor General of the United States, the officer in the Department of Justice responsible for all arguments of the United States before federal appellate courts, entered the case on the side of the black petitioners after President Harry Truman spoke out strongly about the need to redress racial inequalities after years of unfairness and the deaths of thousands of black soldiers in the recently ended World War. The Supreme Court took the extremely unusual step of allowing Solicitor General Perlman to actually appear and argue the case as an *amicus curiae,* indicating that the Court was quite aware of the significance of the issues. President Truman's Attorney General, Tom C. Clark, helped write the Solicitor General's brief. He later sat on the Supreme Court, and his son, Ramsey Clark was later Attorney General of the United States.[73] The list of attorneys writing and filing *amicus curiae* briefs was also impressive.

[*ii*]   ***Recusal of Justices in* Shelley.**   Justices Reed, Jackson and Rutledge did not participate in hearing or deciding *Shelley.* Judges do sometimes recuse themselves from a case in which they have a personal pecuniary or other stake. But it is very unusual for three judges to step aside at the same time. The reasons for their recusal are not really known; judges need not publicly state why they step aside. At the time of the case, there was some speculation that the three judges owned property subject to racial covenants, but speculation does not an answer provide.[74]

[*iii*]   ***More on Bishop's Role.***   To help work out Bishop's role in the case, consider the following example. Suppose Olivia Smith living in a far off place asks you to buy land for her with her money and hold it for her until her plans to move to your location are complete. You agree to do this favor for her, take her $10,000, make a down payment on a condominium unit, and use money she sends you monthly to pay the continuing bills as they come in for the condominium. Unfortunately for Olivia, you also take title to the unit in your name. There is little doubt that if Olivia could prove all this to a court of equity, your claim of ownership would fail. Absent proof that a gift was made, a person holding property paid for by another will be required to turn over the land to the true owner on demand. Fitzgerald played a similar role for Bishop, acting as his front person so Bishop could obtain financing and attempt to break the racial covenant. These sorts of arrangements were said by equity courts to create a *purchase money resulting trust.* That sounds complicated, but really isn't. The parties did not formally create a trust, but courts viewed the situation as one in which both parties assumed that the nominal title holder owed a high duty of care towards the actual owner's financial interests. A trust results because the party holding the title is said to have the title only for benefit of the

---

[73] For a more complete picture of the history of the Supreme Court litigation, *see* C. E. Vose, note 59 above, at 151-210.

[74] Vose, note 59 above, at 179.

party providing the purchase money. Fitzgerald almost surely owed such a duty of care to Bishop while she held the title.

A more modern example of a purchase money resulting trust problem is provided by *Edwards v. Woods,* 385 A.2d 780 (D.C. App.1978). An unmarried couple decided to buy a house on Capitol Hill in Washington, D.C. Edwards was an artist; Woods an airline stewardess. Woods applied for mortgage credit, took title in her name, and signed all the mortgage papers. Edwards used an accident claim settlement check to make the down payment. The post-occupancy expenditures of the two were a mass of confusion. When the couple split up, each claimed title to the house. On appeal, after the trial court decided that each owned half the house, the District of Columbia Court of Appeals held that it was appropriate to use resulting trust rules to resolve the case, but remanded for a trial on the shares to be held by each party. Edwards, the litigant claiming an interest not displayed by the title of record, was given the burden of proving the amount of his actual monetary contributions. *Compare Marvin v. Marvin,* p. 214 above.

[*iv*]   *State Action.* The wording of the Fourteenth Amendment appears to place limitations only on the authority of states to act. Defining what is meant by "state action" has been a difficult problem for the Supreme Court ever since the Amendment was adopted. Two basic themes about state action surface in the *Shelley* case—the sorts of legal issues that create state action problems and the meaning of the word "state" in the Fourteenth Amendment of the constitution.

[*A*]   *Legal Issues.* A myriad of legal issues create potential state action problems. If the *Shelley* opinion is to be taken seriously, then almost every case presents a potential constitutional issue. The theory goes like this: Among the rights guaranteed by the Fourteenth Amendment Due Process Clause is the right to be free from irrational or unreasonable action by the state. If a judge trying a case makes a decision without any factual support for the result, it is fair to label that decision unreasonable, arbitrary and capricious. Thus, any case involving factual disputes or arguments about the applicability of legal rules to the facts raises potential constitutional problems.

It is fair to say, however, that a deluge of such decisions has not been rendered by the Supreme Court, in part because *Shelley* itself has been largely, though not completely, ignored in later cases raising state action problems.[75] Judge made law has by itself not often formed the basis for a Court finding that state action existed. In most cases there is some further activity by executive or legislative authorities, usually enactment of legislation or administrative actions.

[*B*]   *What is a "State?"* Part of the difficulty in figuring out what creates state action arises because the Court has not created a clear theory of what a "state" is for purposes of the Constitution. One possible theory is that a state is a government, formally organized and operating directly to influence a situation. Another theory suggests that the word does not require the formal actions of governmental institutions, but only the presence of strong public policies.

Neither theory fits *Shelley* very neatly. In one sense, a government was formally operating; a court did order the Shelley family out of their home. But the moving forces behind the dispute were not those of formal government entities. The mere fact that a court is available to resolve

---

[75] The Court also has a great deal of discretion to decide which cases it will take; that discretion has been routinely used to turn aside review of almost all cases where the only constitutional issue raised was adequacy of the proofs submitted to the trial court.

a property or contract dispute does not necessarily mean the dispute itself is generated by the government. It is worth comparing *Shelley* to *Marsh v. Alabama,*[76] decided just two years before. *Marsh* involved a company town run by a shipping company. All the property in the town was owned by the company. Standard municipal facilities—police and fire protection, schools, and the like—also were provided by the firm. The main street looked like any other main street, with stores, restaurants and a post office. When Jehovah's Witnesses seeking converts in the town were barred access, the Supreme Court came to their rescue. In essence, the Court held that if the town looked like a town, acted like a town, and provided the services of a town, it was a town, bound by the terms of the Fourteenth Amendment. *Marsh* is still good law, but most commentators don't see a way to squeeze *Shelley* within its bounds.

If "state action" means a strong public policy impacting on a situation in a way otherwise prohibited by the Constitution, then the fit with *Shelley* is marginally better. Until the decision in the case, virtually every government and private housing program operated in a segregated fashion. But if that is the way to approach a state action problem, the inquiry boils down to a discussion of whether a particular outcome is one that should be countenanced by the courts. If, for example, state policy is to ban racial discrimination, then courts ought to follow that policy. That, you might contend, does violence to the "state action" terminology in the Constitutional text.

For now (perhaps forever), there is no need to resolve the definitional problem. But note carefully that litigation under a Constitution creates enormous room for the creation and revision of rules and public policies. Indeed, it is reasonable to argue that the outcome in *Shelley* reflected much more about changing views on race relations after World War II than it did about any well thought out view of the meaning of the Fourteenth Amendment.

[d] Problem Notes

[*i*] *A Shelley* Postscript. The *Shelley* case involved an attempt to use a covenant to obtain an injunction against the transfer of real estate. But a real covenant is nothing more than a "fancy" contract "running" to future generations of land holders. And contract law, of course, provides a basis for relief in damages in case a contract is breached. Now suppose that a racially restrictive covenant governed all the property in a particular development, that Mr. White sold his house to Mr. Black, much to the displeasure of Mr. Neighbor, that Neighbor sued White for monetary damages only, confessing after *Shelley* that the courts lacked authority to remove Mr. Black from his new house, and that Mr. Neighbor alleged the value of his house declined by $10,000 after Mr. Black moved in. Mr. White defended the contract action by arguing that enforcement of the contract against him violated the Equal Protection Clause of the Fourteenth Amendment. Note that a black person is not a litigant before the court. This was basically the fact situation in *Barrows v. Jackson,* 346 U.S. 249 (1953), in which the Supreme Court extended *Shelley* to prohibit such contract damage actions. Can you articulate a state action theory justifying that result?

[*ii*] *State Action and Common Law Rules.* Though the Missouri Supreme Court's decision to enforce the covenants in *Shelley* was not unusual for that period of history, there were several theories the court could have used to void the racial covenants. Courts generally frowned upon arrangements placing unreasonable restraints on alienation of property. Though

[76] 326 U.S. 501 (1946).

many public and private regulations affect both the ability of property owners to sell and the price they may obtain from a willing buyer, restraints severely reducing alienability or reducing alienability in an irrational way face rough sledding in the courts. A covenant like that in *Shelley* substantially reduced the size of the market in an arguably irrational way, but the Missouri Supreme Court failed to seize upon this opening to void the restriction. The state court could also have voided the covenant on the grounds that the circumstances leading to its creation in 1911 were no longer an appropriate basis for restricting land, both because of cultural changes in the acceptability of racial discrimination and because the neighborhood had changed so much that, as a practical matter, the covenant no longer served its original goals. It is, therefore, clear that the Missouri Supreme Court selected among a variety of possible theories to enforce one contract, the covenant, rather than the other, the contract of sale to the Shelleys. Did state action exist because such selection occurred?

[*iii*] ***Supreme Court and Social Science.*** The NAACP gathered a considerable body of social science evidence showing that restrictive covenants led to overcrowded neighborhoods, and increases in crime and infant mortality. This information played a significant role in the briefs, much discussed during the oral arguments in *Shelley* and probably played a role in convincing some organizations to file *amicus curiae* briefs supporting the NAACP.[77] The data was marshaled to support the proposition that the impact of the racially restrictive covenants was much like racial zoning which the Court had invalidated over 30 years before in *Buchanan v. Warley,* 245 U.S. 60 (1917) and that state action was therefore present. The Court, however, did not refer to the social science data. Though the justices do not rely often upon sociological studies in their opinions, they have done so in some very important cases. The famous Brandeis brief played an important role in *Muller v. Oregon,* 198 U.S. 45 (1908) upholding maximum hours legislation for women.[78] And the Court's opinion in *Brown v. Board of Education,* 347 U.S. 483 (1954) referred to studies suggesting that segregation has negative effects on black children. Should the Court have discussed the social science before it in its *Shelley* opinion? Would the Formalists or Realists have supported such a step?

[8] Contemporary Non-Racial Limitations on Servitude Enforcement

[a] Introduction

Servitudes may last indefinitely.[79] Though subject to rules against restraints on alienation, they are not constrained by the Rule Against Perpetuities. Given the impact servitudes may have on the use of land, you should not be surprised that mechanisms have surfaced to both limit the enforceability of some servitudes and allow for others to be terminated. This section of the chapter covers both types of limitations.

As already mentioned,[80] under the draft RESTATEMENT (THIRD) OF PROPERTY (SERVITUDES), the touch and concern requirement has been replaced by general unwillingness to enforce servitudes that are illegal, unconstitutional or unreasonable. The first case in this section provides

---

[77] Tushnet, note 63 above, at 88-89, 98.

[78] The "science" described in the Brandeis brief took the position that overwork endangered the ability of women to reproduce.

[79] Historically this was true for both easements and covenants running with the land. Though a contingent interest in an easement might fail under the Rule Against Perpetuities, contingent limitations on easements are almost unheard of.

[80] *See* p. 433 above.

you with an example of how this general principle might operate. Servitudes may also be modified or terminated in a series of ways. They may be abandoned. Just as an easement may be prescribed, it may also be prescribed out of existence. All of the parties bound by a servitude may agree to modify or end it.[81] Of most interest is a rule allowing for the modification or termination of servitudes due to changed circumstances. The Tentative Draft of the new Restatement contains this provision:

§ 7.10 Modification and Termination of Servitudes Because of Changed Conditions[*]

When a change has taken place since the creation of a servitude that makes it impossible as a practical matter to accomplish the purpose for which the servitude was created, a court may modify the servitude to permit the purpose to be accomplished. If modification is not practicable, a court may terminate the servitude.

If the purpose of a servitude can be accomplished, but because of changed conditions the servient estate is no longer suitable for any use permitted by the servitude, a court may modify the servitude to permit other uses under conditions designed to preserve the benefits of the original servitude.

Conservation and preservation servitudes are not subject to termination under this section.

The final case in this section invokes this rule.

[b]   Unreasonable Servitudes: New Jersey Superior Court Opinion in *Petersen v. Beekmere*

Petersen v. Beekmere, Inc.

New Jersey Superior Court, Chancery Division

117 N.J. Super. 155, 283 A.2d 911 (1971)

LORA, J.S.C.

This is a class action to construe a covenant compelling purchasers of property in a subdivision, known as Allison Acres, to purchase a share of stock in a community association Beekmere, Inc. Said action has been consolidated with a county district court suit instituted by Beekmere against each of the plaintiffs herein for $100 for a required stock subscription, and for $75 representing the 1969 annual assessment as against each of them.

The pertinent facts reveal that the original tract surrounding a small lake was owned by Glendale Investments Corp., which subdivided said tract into five sections, the fifth and final subdivision being filed March 18, 1968. The principal stockholders of Glendale, Charles and Elizabeth Decker, formed Beekmere, Inc., a corporation for profit . . . said corporation's ostensible purpose, as gleaned from its certificate of incorporation, being the development of land for recreational pursuits, the sale of merchandise incidental thereto, the operation of a private club for the limited membership of lot owners in various real estate developments, and to deal in lands generally.

---

[81] This action must be taken unanimously unless the terms of the servitude itself specifically allow for termination with less than unanimous agreement. Any other rule would make it very difficult to create long term governing institutions for developments.

[*] © The American Law Institute (1999). Reprinted with permission.

On January 31, 1961 Glendale conveyed to Beekmere the lake and a certain access lot to the lake in Section Two of the subdivision. A set of covenants, one of which is at issue herein, was not annexed to the deed. On June 29, 1962 Beekmere conveyed back to Glendale; no restrictions were involved. Thereafter, on October 16, 1967 Glendale reconveyed to Beekmere the lake and access lot together with an easement retained by the grantor over two lots with access to the lake in Section Five of the subdivision; no covenants were annexed to the deed.

Individual lots were conveyed by Glendale to purchasers who were predecessors in title of the within plaintiffs, and a copy of the covenants were annexed to all deeds in these original conveyances. In subsequent conveyances by these individual lot owners to plaintiffs, the covenants were not annexed to some of the deeds. The covenant in dispute, set forth in a document annexed to such deeds and entitled "Covenants for Insertion in Deeds 'Allison Acres,' Sections . . . ," recited:

Whereas, the Purchaser (hereinafter designated as the Owner), agrees to apply for membership in Beekmere, Incorporated (hereinafter designated as Beekmere), and member to purchase one share of the common stock of said Beekmere, for a sum not in excess of $100.00 and to comply with and conform to the Constitution and By-Laws of said Beekmere . . . .

The threshold question for the court is whether this covenant, being affirmative in nature, can be enforced at law through the medium of the county district court action, or in equity, by plaintiffs' action to construe the covenant. Plaintiffs argue that under the law of this State affirmative covenants cannot be enforced . . . .

. . . .

However, whether affirmative covenants are enforceable at law or in equity does not appear to be settled in this State.

. . . .

A view of other jurisdictions indicates that the weight of authority permits the enforcement of affirmative covenants, although courts have not distinguished between the rubrics under which such enforcement is effected, whether it be by covenant running with the land at law, or as an equitable servitude enforceable against a subsequent purchaser with notice.

. . . .

In New York the courts adhered to the old English rule that affirmative covenants did not run with the land so as to charge the burden of performance upon a subsequent grantee. *Miller v. Clary,* 210 N.Y. 127, 103 N.E. 1114 (Ct. App. 1913). However, such position has been eroded in that state due to recognized exceptions, and in subsequent cases that in all but letter appear to overrule *Miller v. Clary* . . . . In *Nicholson v. 300 Broadway Realty Corp.,* 7 N.Y. 2d 240, 164 N.E.2d 832, 835 (1959), which involved a covenant to furnish heat, the Appellate Division stated:

The burden of affirmative covenants may be enforced against subsequent holders of the originally burdened land whenever it appears that (1) the original covenantor and covenantee intended such a result; (2) there has been a continuous succession of conveyances between the original covenantor and the party now sought to be burdened; and (3) the covenant touches or concerns the land to a substantial degree.

The Appellate Division relied on a case very similar on its facts to the present one: *Neponsit Property Owners' Ass'n v. Emigrant Industrial Sav. Bank,* 278 N.Y.248, 15 N.E.2d 793 (Ct. App. 1938).

. . . .

It would thus appear, by the weight of authority and logic, that the distinction between "affirmative" and "negative" covenants is an anachronism which all too often precludes an analysis of the covenant itself in order to determine whether it should be enforced, whether at law as a covenant running with the land or in equity as an equitable servitude enforceable against the original grantee and all successors having notice. *See Caullett v. Stanley Stilwell & Sons, Inc.,* 67 N.J. Super.111, 116, 170 A.2d 52 (App. Div. 1961), where the . . . Appellate Division . . . set forth the requirements of a covenant directly restrictive of title to land. Of the primary requirement that it "touch and concern" the subject property, the court stated:

> To constitute a real rather than a personal covenant, the promise must exercise direct influence on the occupation, use or enjoyment of the premises. It must be a promise respecting the use of the land, that is, a use of identified land which is not merely casual and which is not merely an incident in the performance of the promise.

The meaning of the "touch and concern" requirement is unclear, especially with respect to affirmative covenants, in New Jersey. Although *Caullett v. Stanley Stilwell & Sons, Inc., supra,* and *Brewer v. Marshall and Cheeseman,* 19 N.J. Eq. 537 (E. & A. 1868), spoke in terms of the physical use of the land, both cases involved negative covenants (that the grantor reserved the right to build the original building on the premises, and a covenant not to sell marl) . . . .

The covenant here under consideration requires individual lot owners to purchase stock in a property owners' association, and make payment of assessments, which ostensibly will be put to use for the development and maintenance of the lake area. Under such a scheme both the burden and benefit of the covenant would be linked to each parcel found subject to the covenant.

As was stated in *Neponsit Property Owners' Ass'n v. Emigrant Industrial Sav. Bank, supra*:

> In order that the burden of maintaining public improvements should rest upon the land benefited by the improvements, the grantor exacted from the grantee of the land with its appurtenant easement or right of enjoyment a covenant that the burden of paying the cost should be inseparably attached to the land which enjoys the benefit. It is plain that any distinction or definition which would exclude such a covenant from the classification of covenants which "touch" or "concern" the land would be based on form and not on substance.

. . . .

Examining the covenant therein under consideration, the court in *Caullett v. Stanley Stilwell & Sons, Inc., supra,* stated that prerequisite to a conclusion that a covenant runs with the land at law is a finding that both burdened and benefited properties exist and were intended to be so affected by the contracting parties. That the properties were intended to be so affected in the present case appears evident by the incorporation of Beekmere with its ostensible purpose of subdivision development, together with the pattern of original conveyances by the grantor annexing the restrictions to all deeds. As to the existence of burdened and benefited properties, it would seem that both are merged into the individual lots of Allison Acres subject to the covenant, since they reap the benefits of lake area development and provide the source for necessary funds.

Although not discussed in *Caullett v. Stanley Stilwell & Sons, Inc., supra,* there perhaps is an additional requirement in order for a covenant to run at law, namely, privity of estate. Early cases in this State seem to require a tenurial relationship in order to constitute privity. *See Costigan v. Pennsylvania R.R., Co.,* 54 N.J.L. 233, 23 A. 810 (Sup. Ct. 1892) (negative duty held unenforceable in the absence of a landlord-tenant relationship); *The Inhabitants of City of Bordentown v. Anderson,* 81 N.J.L. 434, 79 A. 281 (E. & A. 1910) (burden of a covenant will not run with the land in the absence of lessor-lessee relationship). For a contrary view, *see* Clark, *Real Covenants and Other Interests Which "Run With the Land"* (2d ed. 1947), 111-137, which takes the position that logically and historically the only privity requirement is that between the promisor and the assignee which is satisfied by a succession to the estate of the promisor. While the covenant herein under consideration might perhaps fail at least as to the privity requirement, such is not a problem when the covenant is sought to be enforced in equity under a theory of equitable servitude.

> The English doctrine of equitable servitudes was based on notice. In that country (which had no recording system) notice had to mean principally actual notice. In this country which has had a well-developed recording system since its beginning, the record was deemed to be notice to the subsequent purchaser, and thus so long as the agreement was recorded, it was a stable and sure way to bind subsequent parties to private use arrangements. [Berger, *A Policy Analysis of Promises Respecting the Use of Land,* 55 Minn. L. Rev. 167, at 186 (1970).]

As to the privity requirement it has been stated that "Problems as to the existence of 'privity' have no significance when . . . [t]he controversy is in equity for the enforcement against a successor of the promisor of a promise with notice of which the ownership has been acquired . . . ." 5 Powell, *Real Property,* § 674 at 171, citing Restatement, Property, § 539, comment (a) (1944). Likewise, our courts have "consistently enforced the covenantal rights of an owner of benefited property against a successor, with notice, to the burdened land, even though the covenant did not run with the land at law." *Caullett v. Stanley Stilwell & Sons, Inc., supra.*

Thus, although the question whether an affirmative covenant is enforceable at law as a covenant running with the land is here expressly left open, it is the conclusion of this court that such a covenant is, in equity, enforceable as an equitable servitude against a subsequent grantee who takes with notice. That the covenant was not annexed to all of plaintiffs' deeds is of no consequence since they acquired title with notice of the covenant, its presence in their chain of title charging them with such notice.

The right to urge enforcement of a servitude against the burdened land "'depends primarily on the covenant's having been made for the benefit' of other land, either retained by the grantor or part of a perceptible neighborhood scheme." *Caullett v. Stanley Stilwell & Sons, Inc., supra.* Since Glendale Investments Inc. has conveyed all the lots in Sections One through Four of Allison Acres, and is likewise conveying out the lots of Section Five, equitable enforcement of the covenant herein under consideration is predicated on the finding of such a scheme.

As set forth in *Olson v. Jantausch,* 44 N.J. Super. 380, 130 A.2d 650 (App. Div. 1957), there must be a clear intent to establish a neighborhood scheme of restrictions. To be effective and enforceable, such a scheme must be (a) universal, the restrictions applying to all lots of like character brought within the scheme; (b) reciprocal, the restrictions constituting a benefit to all lots involved which are subject to the burden imposed, and (c) reasonably uniform as to the restrictions imposed; they need not be identical, but any variations must be such as not to create an inequitable burden or benefit.

. . . .

Plaintiffs contend that no neighborhood scheme exists or, alternatively, that the common grantor has abandoned it if one is found to exist. The evidence supports the conclusion that it was the *intent* of the common grantor, Glendale Investments Inc., to create an integrally related lake community as to all sections of Allison Acres. The tax map reveals that portions of Sections One, Two, Three and Five actually border on the lake and a part of Section Four is adjacent to the lake. In any event, the property furthest removed from the lake in Section Four is no further from the lake than its counterpart in Section Five. Easements over the two lake access lots in Section Five were reserved by the grantor and were to be used by the property owners for access to the lake on its easterly bank; a similar arrangement was created on the westerly bank where Beekmere retained the only unsold access lot. (It should be noted that in a separate action Beekmere has been ordered by judgment entered October 13, 1970 by another court to release its easements in Section Five except for the limited purpose of maintaining the lake.) The sheet of restrictions annexed to some of plaintiffs' deeds refers to Allison Acres, designating the sections thereof. Finally, Glendale has conveyed a number of lots in Section Five subject to the restrictions, these appearing in a document entitled "Covenants for the Insertion in Deeds 'Allison Acres', Sections 1, 2, 3 & 4 and 5."

However, it is stipulated and appears from a report of title examination before the court that not all lots sold by Glendale have been made subject to the covenant under consideration. The question then becomes whether this action by Glendale destroys the neighborhood scheme.

A neighborhood scheme may be created in a number of ways . . . . "The most complete way, of course, is by a reciprocal covenant, whereby the grantor covenants to insert, in apt language, like covenants in all deeds of his remaining lots or lands for the common benefit of all of his grantees and their assigns. Another way is for him to offer his lots for sale, and to sell them, on the representation that all lots will be conveyed subject to like covenants for the common benefit, in which case purchasers with notice or knowledge will be bound by the covenant. But, in the absence of either of these methods (as was the case here), the courts will only spell out such a scheme from a plan of lots and sales therefrom where all the deeds from the common grantor for the lots making up any particular neighborhood group of common benefit therefrom, are made subject to the common covenant. If, under these circumstances, the covenant is omitted from a deed of one lot so located that a violation on that lot of the provisions of the covenant would deprive the other lots of the benefit to be derived by them from the common observance of the restriction, there is, in the absence of knowledge or notice of the scheme on the part of the grantee in the deed for such omitted lot, a failure to make out a neighborhood scheme, at least as to that lot and as to such other lots as would lose the benefit of the scheme if it were violated on the lot not subjected to the covenant." [*Margate Park Protective Ass'n v. Abate,* 22 N.J. Super. 550, 554-555, 92 A.2d 110, 112 (Ch. Div. 1952).]

. . . .

[I]n order to prove an abandonment or modification of a neighborhood scheme, the materiality of the violations alleged is to be determined by the circumstances of each case, and the question to be resolved is whether the violations are such as to indicate an abandonment of the original general plan and to make its enforcement inequitable because of the changed conditions of the property.

The "neighborhood scheme" in Section Five of Allison Acres must fail due to the inconsistency of making only some similarly situated lots subject to the covenant. Further, since each section is an integral part of the entire lake community subdivision, the entire scheme must fail. It would be inequitable to enforce the burden of the covenant against only those lot owners who were unfortunate enough either to have had their predecessors in title or themselves purchase lots with the restrictions annexed to their deeds. The benefit of maintaining the lake, and indeed developing it further, accrues to all property owners throughout the subdivision. When some owners are released by the common grantor from sharing in the expense attached thereto, the other property owners are forced to tender larger proportionate amounts albeit such noncontributing neighbors will derive at least some if not all of the benefits of a well maintained lake.

Assuming *arguendo* that a neighborhood scheme were sustainable, the covenant herein would still be unenforceable due to its vagueness of terms and consequent restraint on alienation. Other jurisdictions have held that covenants similar to the one at hand have been enforced; however, their terms were far more precise . . . . *See Neponsit Property Owners' Ass'n v. Emigrant Industrial Sav. Bank, supra,* (covenant specified that the funds collected would be devoted to maintenance purposes).

. . . .

In the covenant before this court there is no formula by which to calculate future assessments, thus binding property owners to unspecified obligations and leaving open the possibility of inequitable assessments as to each member of the lake community. *See Moorestown Mgmt. v. Moorestown Bookshop,* 104 N.J. Super. 250, 249 A.2d 623 (Ch. Div.1969), in which a provision in a shopping center lease requiring tenants to become members of an incorporate association of all tenants, to pay dues and to be bound by the by-laws of the association, was not found invalid where the by-laws, which were incorporated by reference into the lease, provided a formula for establishing dues. Nor is there any limitation on the duration of the covenant in question, unlike covenants upheld in decisions in other jurisdictions . . . .

Beekmere, Inc., according to its certificate of incorporation, has perpetual existence. Further, there is no requirement that the assessment money must be spent on the land for which the funds were received. In Glendale's conveyances to Beekmere, the latter was not bound to the restrictions which attached to the individual property owners; the covenant itself does not require that the money must be expended for the development of Allison Acres, nor is there anything in Beekmere's certificate of incorporation or by-laws that requires the funds to be so expended. Indeed, Beekmere is not restricted to dealing solely with the subdivision known as Allison Acres. Finally, property owners are required to purchase a nontransferable share of stock in a corporation for profit. When they leave Allison Acres they cannot recover their capital investment nor transfer the stock to a new purchaser as part of the consideration. Having paid $100, they have no further interest or rights in the stock if they leave Allison Acres.

These ambiguities, uncertainties and shortcomings likewise militate against the enforcement of this covenant in equity.

[c] Explanatory Notes

[*i*] **Beekmere *as a Case at Law.*** First a review. Two lawsuits were consolidated in *Beekmere.* The residents sued to void the covenant in one case. Beekmere sued the residents for membership fees in the other. Take the second case first. Can Beekmere sue in law, under the traditional rules, to recover the money?[82] Your initial answer should be "No." Beekmere was not a party to any covenant; nor was Beekmere in any significant property relationship with the residents. Although Beekmere owned one access lot and held an easement over another,

---

[82] The court, after deciding in favor of the residents in the first, did not have to answer this question.

neither Glendale nor the residents held reciprocal interests in the lots. Beekmere could sue only if privity requirements at law were significantly reduced from the common law standard. There was one additional, and peculiar, twist. The back and forth conveyances between the two entities suggests that Beekmere and Glendale were probably owned by the same people. If the corporate veils were pierced, Beekmere/Glendale might become a single entity meeting the privity standards. Use of this theory would have required Beekmere to argue that its own veil should be pierced, a strange step to say the least.[83]

[ii]   *The* **Beekmere** *Issues.* The *Beekmere* court discussed three major issues— enforcement of affirmative covenants, neighborhood scheme, and limitations on enforcement of covenants. The affirmative covenant problem was resolved by a ritual citation to *Neponsit v. Emigrant Industrial Savings Bank,* the prior case in the text. The other two issues raised some very interesting questions.

[iii]   *Neighborhood Schemes.* Neighborhood scheme cases in servitude settings— covenant and easements alike—explore the settings in which inartfully drawn development plans may be rescued. To fully understand what the neighborhood plan rules accomplish, consider an example involving a three house development which Don Developer constructed and sold with a covenant restricting use of the land to single family residences. When the first house was sold Developer inserted a simple covenant in the deed to Owner #1 reading as follows:

> The grantee under this deed agrees to use his or her property only for single family residential purposes. This covenant is binding upon the successors and assigns of the grantee.

Later, sales of Houses #2 and #3 occurred, with similar covenants in the deeds. How would the relationships work out among these parties?

When the first sale was completed, House #1 was burdened by the covenant to use the land only for a single family residence. The land then owned by Developer, and later sold to Owners #2 and #3, benefited from the covenant. Thus, Owners #2 and #3 could enforce the covenant against Owner #1 or his successor. However, by the time Developer sold the third lot, he had no land left to benefit from the covenant imposed on House #3. No one could sue since no one retained land benefited by the agreement. How could this silly result be avoided?

One way was to insert reciprocal covenants in each deed. That is, in the first sale, Developer should have inserted a covenant that bound the land he retained as well as the land he transferred. Then Owner #1 could have sued all later buyers of houses in the development. For example, the Developer covenant could have been written as follows:

> The property purchased by the grantee under this deed, as well as all the rest of the property in Don Developer's development may only be used for single family residential purposes. This restriction is intended to run with the land and is binding upon the successors and assigns of all owners of property in the development.

Note that the *Beekmere* covenant was *not* reciprocal; it simply bound each purchaser to pay money to Beekmere.

---

[83] In fact, Beekmere was probably set up to separate the liabilities of the developer from those of the recreation facilities company. Given the financial difficulties Glendale apparently ran into, that turned out to be a wise decision. If Beekmere had argued that it sat in Glendale's shoes for purposes of the covenants, then Glendale's creditors might have responded by seeking relief from Beekmere.

In developments where the covenants were not reciprocal, the courts created another way to avoid the failure of covenant plans—the neighborhood scheme rule. Basically, the rule provides that covenants will be treated as reciprocal and binding on all owners when the restrictions are uniformly inserted in all the deeds, or where all buyers are on actual or constructive notice of the neighborhood plan. Notice may arise from the filing of a master deed or subdivision plat map containing indicia of the covenants, or from the uniform appearance of a development constructed in conformity with inartfully drafted covenants.[84] In *Beekmere,* the neighborhood scheme rule did not rescue the covenants because some buyers took deeds lacking covenants, and the plan was not obvious on the face of the land.

Easements, of course, may also be drafted inartfully. A set of deeds which granted a right of way over an access road to Owner #1, and to each successive buyer, would not create reciprocal rights. While Owner #1 would be able to traverse the right of way, later buyers would not be able to go upon land held by #1 because Developer did not own it at the time they took their deeds. The neighborhood scheme rule may be used to imply reciprocity in the right to use the way.

[iv]   *Reasonableness Limitations on Enforcement of Covenants.* Though the *Beekmere* court did not explicitly refer to the "touch and concern" requirement, it did find the covenant scheme unenforceable at equity even if a neighborhood scheme existed. The covenant contained no limitations on what Beekmere, a for-profit corporation, could do with the money. It didn't have to spend it on the recreation areas; no controls were placed on fee increases; and control of Beekmere was totally outside the hands of the residents. This is the sort of covenant that the more recent cases, discarding specific reliance on "touch and concern" language, have invalidated as unreasonable or arbitrary.

The *Beekmere* servitude also stretched the willingness to ignore old privity requirements to the breaking point. Beekmere, like the Neponsit Property Owners' Association, owned no interest in land in the development area. But at least the Neponsit Property Owners' Association was controlled by residents and significantly limited in its activities. Perhaps Beekmere was so far removed from the day-to-day activities of the residents that a sufficient nexus for *requiring* payment of fees to the recreation outfit was lacking. While the *Neponsit* court was willing to treat the home owners' corporation as an entity representing the interests of the residents, that rationale was unavailable in *Beekmere.*

[v]   *Control of Projects After Development is Complete. Beekmere* is representative of a long series of cases involving efforts by developers to retain control over portions of developments that are likely to produce good profits on a continuing basis after all the housing units have been sold. In addition to recreation, community and club facilities,[85] disputes have arisen over efforts to retain control over the Board of Directors of the home owners' association after most units were sold,[86] resale of apartment units,[87] maintenance services or management

---

[84] For an example of this last sort of neighborhood scheme, *see* Case v. Morisette, 475 F.2d 1300 (D.C. Cir. 1973).

[85] A reprise of *Beekmere* was played out in Berman v. Gurwicz, 189 N.J. Super. 89, 458 A.2d 1311 (1981). *See also* Raintree Corporation v. Rowe, 38 N.C. App. 664, 248 S.E.2d 904 (1978); Ebbe v. Senior Estates Golf and Country Club, 61 Or. App. 398, 657 P.2d 696 (1983).

[86] *See, e.g.,* Siegel v. Division of Florida Land Sales and Condominiums, Department of Business Regulation, 453 So.2d 414 (Fla. App. 1984). Most states require that developers yield control over the home owners' association as units are sold.

[87] *See, e.g.,* Berkeley Condominium Association, Inc. v. Berkeley Condominium Residences, Inc., 185 N.J. Super. 313, 448 A.2d 510 (1982); Connecticut v. Hossan-Maxwell, Inc., 436 A.2d 284 (1980).

contracts,[88] and (perhaps with an intent less tidy than a simple desire to make profit) obligations under notes and mortgages.[89] For example, in *Point East Management Corporation v. Point East One Condominium Corporation, Inc.*, 282 So.2d 628 (Fla. 1973), a condominium development corporation signed a 25-year non-revocable management contract with itself prior to selling the individual housing units. As manager, the developer also signed a 99-year lease with itself for certain community facilities to be retained by the developer. The residents' later effort to void these arrangements failed.

The prevalence of such practices led to the enactment of condominium and cooperative regulatory legislation all across the country. Legislation requiring developers to file documents with state officials and notify prospective purchasers of the nature of the binding obligations they accept if they buy a unit is commonplace.[90] Many states have also adopted statutes rendering unconscionable clauses in development deals unenforceable[91] and prohibiting practices like those in *Point East*. The Uniform Condominium Act contains the following provision:

§ 3-105. [Termination of Contracts and Leases of Declarant] *

If entered into before the executive board elected by the unit owners . . . takes office, (i) any management contract, employment contract, or lease of recreational or parking areas or facilities, (ii) any other contract or lease between the association and a declarant or an affiliate of a declarant, or (iii) any contract or lease that is not bona fide or was unconscionable to the unit owners at the time entered into under the circumstances then prevailing, may be terminated without penalty by the association at any time after the executive board elected by the unit owners . . . takes office upon not less than (90) days' notice to the other party. This section does not apply to any lease the termination of which would terminate the condominium or reduce its size, unless the real estate subject to that lease was included in the condominium for the purpose of avoiding the right of the association to terminate a lease under this section.

[d] Problem Note

Easements, Real Covenants and Equitable Servitudes. Under the old common law notions of easements, covenants at law and equitable servitudes, the provisions in the deeds at issue in *Beekmere* were covenants at law. The covenants did not create equitable liens upon the land of those residents buying stock in Beekmere and paying their annual fees. The only easement in the case was one held by Beekmere over an access lot to the lake. No covenants in the deeds

---

[88] *See, e.g.,* Point East Management Corporation v. Point East One Condominium Corporation, 282 So.2d 628 (Fla. 1973).

[89] *See, e.g.,* Wisconsin Avenue Associates, Inc. v. 2720 Wisconsin Avenue Cooperative Association, Inc., 441 A.2d 956 (D.C. App. 1982), involving notes signed by the developing corporation in favor of the developers prior to sale of housing units and without notice to the buyers. Breach of fiduciary obligations to the corporate owner of the building by the developers, among other legal theories, formed a basis for relief to the residents.

[90] A sample of that legislation may be found below in *Troy v. Renna*, p. 712, the constitutional challenge to New Jersey's Citizens and Disabled Protected Tenancy Act.

[91] *See, e.g.,* Section 1-112 of the UNIF. CONDOMINIUM ACT, 7 U.L.A. 421, 450 (1980). Section 3-103 of the Act also places limits on the developers right to control the home owners' association as units are sold. As of 1987, the Uniform Condominium Act has been adopted in eight states, but many others have crafted legislation of their own.

* Reprinted with the permission of the National Conference of Commissioners on Uniform State Laws.

of the residents referred to this easement. Obviously the entire plan was poorly crafted. How would you draft the plan to avoid the legal traps Beekmere fell into?

[e] Servitude Termination: Opinions of the New York Supreme Court, Appellate Division in *Ginsberg v. Yeshiva*

Ginsberg v. Yeshiva of Far Rockaway

New York Supreme Court, Appellate Division, Second Department
45 A.D.2d 334, 358 N.Y.S.2d 477 (1974)

Before GULOTTA, P.J., and LATHAM, COHALAN, BENJAMIN and MUNDER, JJ.

LATHAM, Justice.

In this action to enjoin the operation of a religious school on property subject to a private residential use covenant, the issue is whether there is a violation of the constitutional guarantees of religious freedom by the enforcement of the covenant against the defendant, which purchased with knowledge of the covenant and of the plaintiffs' intention to enforce it.

In 1908, a covenant was attached to six lots, three on the north side and three on the south side of a short dead-end street (now named Virginia Street) off Empire Avenue, which is a well-traveled two-lane street in Far Rockaway, Queens. The defendant's property is situated at the dead end, where all traffic, including emergency vehicles, turns around. The covenant provides in pertinent part that none of the six lots "shall be used except for one private residence" and that no "apartment buildings, boarding houses, stores, business houses, barns or stables" shall be "erected or maintained." Of the six restricted lots, the four corner ones are improved with single-family residences while the two middle lots are vacant. The surrounding area contains one-family homes in all directions, with the exception of a few two-family homes and a four-story apartment house, all of which have been there for many years.

Plaintiffs Dr. Stanley A. and Mrs. Susan K. Ginsberg own and reside in a single-family home on the *restricted* southeast corner lot. Dr. Ginsberg uses part of the house as a medical office 12 hours a week. His father, who was also a physician, lived and practiced in the house from 1932 on. Dr. Ginsberg started his practice in 1964, paying rent for the office first to his father and then, after his father's death, to his mother. In 1969, his mother transferred the house to the plaintiffs.

In or about 1963, an orthodox synagogue purchased the adjacent *unrestricted* property south of the plaintiffs', demolished two private dwellings, and erected its temple. At the same time, the synagogue bought the adjacent vacant *restricted* lot west of the plaintiffs', paved and lighted it, and used it as a parking lot without objection from the plaintiffs or their predecessors apart from minor complaints as to fencing and lighting which were modified pursuant to the plaintiffs' request. Synagogue traffic enters the parking lot through Virginia Street and exits directly onto Empire Avenue by the driveway on the *unrestricted* portion of the synagogue's premises, thus not clogging Virginia Street or substantially disturbing the one-family residential atmosphere. The Trial Justice believed Dr. Ginsberg's statement that the use of the lot for parking was not offensive to him.

In August, 1971, concededly with knowledge of the covenant and of the plaintiffs' intention to enforce it, the defendant, Yeshiva of Far Rockaway, apparently not affiliated with the synagogue, purchased the *restricted* northwest corner lot at the dead end of the block diagonally across from the plaintiffs. On the eve of purchase, the plaintiffs' attorneys advised the defendant of the plaintiffs' intention to enforce the covenant. In September, 1971, the defendant began to operate an all-day religious school in the former private dwelling for grades 9 through 12. The original nine rooms, unchanged, now serve as four classrooms, an office, a prayer room where the boys pray in the morning and the evening, and a kitchen, with two of the rooms used as a dormitory for three out-of-town boys. The hours are 9 to 6 P.M. Monday through Friday, with additional hours on Sunday mornings and meetings on Thursday evenings. There are 47 students ages 14 to 18 and some eight teachers. Dr. Ginsberg has been disturbed by the students playing roller skate hockey on the parking lot and in the street in the late afternoon and early evening and by the frequent failure of the school to remove some 8 to 10 garbage cans from the street for several days after collection.

The plaintiffs commenced this action to enforce the covenant on or about February 1, 1972. In or about March, 1972, the defendant purchased the adjoining vacant *restricted* lot. It plans to further expand the school. Though the record is barren with respect to a connection between the synagogue and the school, it is apparent that a synagogue and a yeshiva are both identified with the Jewish faith.

The trial court found that despite the synagogue's use of one lot as a parking lot and some deterioration in the residential character of the area, the area retains a residential character of substantial value. This value will be adversely affected by the presence of groups of students of high school age and by the use and servicing of the school property by persons other than private residents. In reliance on *Evangelical Lutheran Church v. Sahlem,* 254 N.Y. 161, 172 N.E. 455, the trial court enjoined the operation of the school.

On appeal, the defendant seeks to distinguish *Sahlem,* on the ground that in that case the covenanted area was exactly the same as when the restriction was placed on the land, while at bar, as contended by the defendant, there has been substantial change. The defendant *inter alia* argues that, in balancing the equities, religious corporations should be distinguished from commercial enterprises (*cf. Matter of Westchester Reform Temple v. Brown,* 22 N.Y.2d 488, 293 N.Y.S.2d 297, 239 N.E.2d 891).

. . . .

It has long been the rule in this and other jurisdictions that residential use covenants are enforceable against religious institutions such as churches and synagogues (*Evangelical Lutheran Church v. Sahlem, supra;* 12 Syracuse L. Rev. 347). Chief Judge Cardozo, speaking for the Court of Appeals, said: "Neither at law nor in equity is it written that a license has been granted to religious corporations, by reason of the high purpose of their being, to set covenants at naught. Indeed, if in such matters there can be degrees of obligation, one would suppose that a more sensitive adherence to the demands of plighted faith might be expected of them than would be looked for of the world at large." In that case, as at bar, the plaintiff, with knowledge of the restrictive covenants and of the defendant's opposition, purchased land opposite the defendant's and sought to build a church. In the absence of proof that "the character of the neighborhood has so changed as to defeat the object and purposes for which the restrictions were imposed," the Court of Appeals declared the covenants enforceable both at law and in equity. The facts at bar are entirely similar to those in *Sahlem,* with the added circumstance that the *purchaser here is a school, not a church or synagogue. Sahlem is clearly dispositive.*

The dissenters, ignoring the limits of both the briefs and the arguments before the trial court, attack the viability of *Sahlem* in the light of more recent decisions with regard to zoning and restrictive covenants.

Clearly, however, zoning is an aspect of the police power, asserted for the general welfare, and must bear a substantial relation to the public health, safety, morals, or general welfare (*Village of Euclid v. Ambler Realty Co.*, 272 U.S. 365, 47 S. Ct. 114, 71 L. Ed. 303). It is conceded that *all schools,* public and private, and religious institutions are protected from the full impact of *zoning* restrictions because of their contribution to the public welfare. While the Court of Appeals has stated that a municipality's lack of power to limit the use or erection of structures for churches and synagogues is founded on the constitutional guarantees of freedom of worship (*Matter of Community Synagogue v. Bates,* 1 N.Y.2d 445, 458, 154 N.Y.S.2d 15, 25, 136 N.E.2d 488, 496; *Matter of Westchester Reform Temple v. Brown, supra*), at the same time the court noted that appropriate restrictions may nevertheless be imposed on churches and schools and they may also be excluded.

There is a fundamental distinction between zoning restrictions and private covenants. Zoning is an *encroachment* on private property rights and its enforcement requires the justification of an overriding public interest. In contrast, the restrictive private covenant *is itself a property right and its subordination to the right of the purchaser is "condemnation without authority of law"* (*Christ's Methodist Church v. Macklanburg,* 198 Okl. 297, 300, 177 P.2d 1008 [emphasis added]).

Reliance by the dissenters on *Shelley v. Kraemer,* 334 U.S. 1, is completely misplaced. Unlike the restrictions at bar, the covenants considered in *Shelley* were racially discriminatory on their face . . . . Furthermore, the Supreme Court of the United States has shown little disposition to extend *Shelley*.

The dissenters' reliance on *Marsh v. Alabama,* 326 U.S. 501, is also misplaced. In *Marsh,* a company-owned town sought to ban the distribution of religious literature on a sidewalk in its shopping district. The town and its shopping district were accessible to and freely used by the public in general. In reversing a conviction for criminal trespass, the Supreme Court merely held that people who live in company towns have the obligations of all other citizens and the consequent need for uncensored information. The case is inapposite.

It must further be observed that even in zoning, exclusion of religious institutions is not impossible. The availability of alternative locations would be a highly relevant consideration (70 Harvard Law Review 1428, 1436). The ordinance may be constitutional while the particular application is not (*Matter of Westchester Reform Temple v. Brown, supra*).

To support their argument that the defendant's school is such an exercise of religion as renders unenforceable the plaintiffs' property right, the dissenters rely on a decision which held that parochial schools involve sufficient religious activity and purpose to invalidate State aid (*Lemon v. Kurtzman,* 403 U.S. 602). However, it requires very little religious activity to run afoul of the Establishment Clause. A short daily prayer is an impermissible religious activity for a public school (*School District of Abington Township, Pennsylvania v. Schempp,* 374 U.S. 203), but no one argues that the same daily prayer converts the public school to a religious school.

In the face of its conceded knowledge of the covenant and the warning on the eve of purchase that the plaintiffs would enforce their rights, the defendant purchased the *restricted* corner lot and immediately opened its school. Six months later, despite the commencement of this action, the defendant arrogantly purchased the adjoining *restricted* lot with admitted plans to expand.

The area subject to the covenant is limited to six lots on one short block terminating in a dead end. There is no claim by the defendant that it is excluded from a larger nearby area by the operation of similar restrictions. On the contrary, the neighboring synagogue purchased *unrestricted* property adjacent to the plaintiffs' and demolished two private residences to construct its building. Nor does the defendant school claim that the property in question is particularly suited to its purpose, that it possesses some unique advantage for the operation of its school. The facts are contrary. The probable need for emergency vehicles is much greater in an expanding school with a present population of some 60 students and teachers than it is in a one-family residence, while a building located at the blind end of a dead-end street is less accessible than one on an open street.

In this short dead-end street, noise pollution is magnified and contained. Should the plaintiffs and others who bought in reliance on the restrictive covenant be helpless to protect themselves? No balancing of constitutional rights can support such a conclusion on the facts at bar.

The judgment and order should be affirmed, with one bill of costs.

GULOTTA, P.J., and COHALAN J., concur.

BENJAMIN, J., dissents and votes to reverse and to grant judgment in favor of defendant, with an opinion, in which MUNDER, J., concurs.

BENJAMIN, JUSTICE (dissenting).

In this action to enjoin violation of a covenant limiting the use of each of six plots of land to "one private residence, to cost not less than $5,000" and barring the erection or maintenance on any of the plots of "any apartment buildings, boarding houses, stores, business houses, barns or stables," the defendant appeals from a judgment granting such injunction and from an order denying its motions to set aside the decision after trial.

The six plots are located three on each side of a short dead-end street, Virginia Street, which runs at right angles off Empire Avenue, a well traveled street. The plaintiffs are the owners and occupants of a one-family 14-room house on one corner of Empire Avenue and Virginia Street which they use as their family home, and the plaintiff husband, a urologist, also uses part for his office, the entrance to the office being on Empire Avenue and the main entrance to the house being on Virginia Street. The house had been owned by the plaintiff doctor's father, who had lived and practiced there from 1932 until his death in 1965. In 1964 the plaintiff doctor began to practice at the same premises, paying rent therefor first to his father and later to his mother until 1969, when his mother transferred the house to the plaintiffs.

In or about 1963, an orthodox synagogue purchased nonrestricted property adjacent to the plaintiffs' plot and the two other restricted plots adjoining it on the same side of Virginia Street and built a synagogue on the property. It also purchased the vacant restricted lot adjacent to the plaintiffs' and paved and lighted it and used it as a parking lot for those using the synagogue. In August, 1971, the defendant Yeshiva, concededly with knowledge of the restrictive covenant, purchased the home and plot at the inner end of Virginia Street on the side opposite the plaintiffs' home and began soon after to operate a full-time religious school in the one-family residence it had purchased. In or about March, 1972, after the instant action was commenced, the defendant purchased the vacant plot alongside the one it owns and it plans to expand its school.

The issue raised in this appeal is whether the State power may be invoked by way of injunction against the defendant Yeshiva to prevent it from using its premises, which are subject to the above-mentioned covenant restricting them to one-family residential use, to operate a religious school thereon. We believe such a use of State power violates the constitutionally protected status religious structures enjoy under the First Amendment made applicable to the States by the

Fourteenth Amendment. I therefore think the judgment and order appealed from should be reversed and that judgment should be granted in favor of the defendant.

In our State the question of the impact of the constitutional guarantees of the free exercise of religion and enjoyment of religious profession (N.Y.Const., art. I, § 3) on zoning ordinances limiting the use of real property in a designated area to residential use only has been considered in several cases. In those cases it has been held "that religious structures cannot be excluded, directly or indirectly, from residential zones" (*Matter of Westchester Reform Temple v. Brown*, 22 N.Y.2d 488, 239 N.E.2d 891) . . . .

In the instant case, however, we are not dealing with the constitutional validity of an exercise of the police power based upon a local legislative determination as to possible damage to the public health and welfare resulting from permitting a structure to be used for religious purposes to be located in an area reserved for residential use. Rather we are dealing with a demand by an owner of land subject to a restrictive covenant that the covenant be enforced against other land made subject to that convent by a previous owner. While the plaintiffs seeking the injunction stand primarily on the letter of their covenant, they do by their proof seek to establish that the operation of the defendant's school does somewhat inconvenience them in their use of their premises. Plaintiffs make no claim that the public welfare will be adversely affected by the operation of the defendant's religious school. The trial court found that the value of the plaintiffs' premises will be adversely affected by the presence of groups of students. But such a claim of inconvenience and possible adverse effect on the value of the plaintiff's premises, a conclusion not supported by any proof in the record, can hardly be given more weight in the balance against the preferred position given to the free exercise of religion by our Constitution than . . . a legislative finding that the public welfare will be disserved by the erection of a church and religious school in an area reserved for residential use.

It might be argued that we are faced here with a simple question of enforcing a private contract between private parties and hence the Fourteenth Amendment which is limited to State action cannot serve to raise the First Amendment issue of free exercise of religion. *Shelley v. Kraemer*, 334 U.S. 1, and its progeny, *Hurd v. Hodge*, 334 U.S. 24, and *Barrows v. Jackson*, 346 U.S. 249, dispose of that contention. *Shelley* established the doctrine that State court enforcement of a racially discriminatory restrictive covenant is State action subject to the Fourteenth Amendment, and any contention that *Shelley* is limited to matters of racial and even religious discrimination falls before *Marsh v. Alabama*, 326 U.S. 501, where the Supreme Court of the United States struck down an effort to use State power to compel compliance with a ban by a privately-owned town against distribution of religious literature on its streets, declaring it a violation of the First and Fourteenth Amendments and saying:

> When we balance the Constitutional rights of owners of property against those of the people to enjoy freedom of press and religion, as we must here, we remain mindful of the fact that the latter occupy a preferred position.

The foregoing authorities require us to reverse the judgment appealed from. Nor does *Evangelical Lutheran Church v. Sahlem*, 254 N.Y. 161, 172 N.E. 455, cited and relied on by the plaintiffs, compel a contrary conclusion. That case was decided in 1930, long before the doctrines of *Marsh v. Alabama* and *Shelley v. Kraemer* expanding the scope of the Fourteenth Amendment to the First Amendment guarantee of free exercise of religion and declaring State court enforcement of private agreements to be State action subject to the Fourteenth Amendment. Further, the issue of the constitutionality of a ruling against the plaintiff church was not raised in *Sahlem.* In our view the doctrine established in *Sahlem* no longer has application to the case before us.

View down Virginia Street, Ginsberg house is on the left;
Yeshiva house is through the trees in the right center

View from rear of Ginsberg House across Virginia Ave. Yeshiva House is at left

Front (Virginia Street) view of Yeshiva House

[f] Explanatory Notes

[*i*] **Ginsberg** *Diagram.* Here is a diagram of the *Ginsberg* venue for your use:

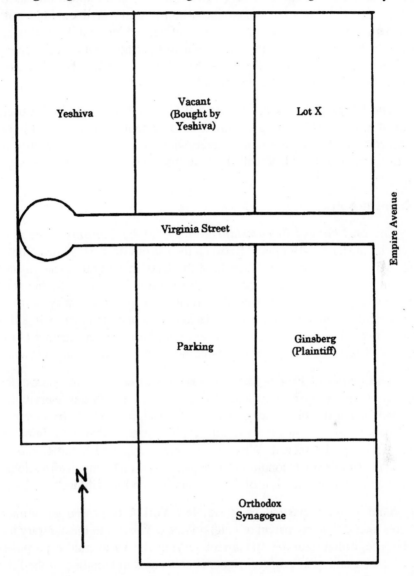

One of my students, whose home was in the area where *Ginsberg* arose, visited the site in the mid-1980s. He reported back that the house in which the Yeshiva was located was boarded up and abandoned, the school had constructed a new facility a short distance away, and the rest of the lots were still being used as described in the opinion.

[*ii*] *Operation of the Changed Circumstances Rule. Ginsberg* involved a small enclave of buildings. This presented certain problems in using the typical rule that servitudes are not enforceable if circumstances have so changed since the inception of the servitudes that their original purposes may no longer be served. Did the changes in the area have to occur on the land bound by the covenant scheme or could changes in the surrounding area also be considered?

There is very little discussion of this issue in judicial opinions, perhaps because the courts prefer to leave themselves some flexibility. In any case, the size of the judicial view may have a significant impact in cases like *Ginsberg*. The *Ginsberg* court apparently used a small view, ignoring the effect of the nearby synagogue which was located on land not bound by the covenants. Perhaps the court's choice of view was influenced by Yeshiva's insistence on pursuing its plans in the teeth of judicial action. You might wonder how many more changes in land use patterns would have to occur before the covenant would fail. If Ginsberg had not sued Yeshiva, might that have been the end of the covenant?

[*iii*] **The Dissent.** The dissent argued that *Shelley v. Kraemer* and restrictions on control of religious institutions combined to prohibit the enforcement of the covenant in *Ginsberg*. While it is fair to suggest that few courts would agree with the dissent, the majority hardly grappled with the issues the dissent raised. Recall the note discussion of state action beginning above at p. 453.

[g]　Problem Notes

[*i*]　**More on Changed Circumstances.** Why did the *Ginsberg* court so quickly dispose of the changed circumstances argument? Between the use of Ginsberg's house for doctors' offices, the long term existence of a parking lot behind the Ginsberg's house, the vacant lot across the street, and, finally, the Yeshiva, what purposes were still being served by the covenant scheme? Since Ginsberg used his house for other than residential purposes, why permit him to sue to enforce the covenant? Should either waiver or laches rules operate in cases like this? What might have happened if Yeshiva counterclaimed to enforce the covenant against Ginsberg? What if the owner of Lot X testified that he or she cared not a wit whether the covenant was enforced?

[*ii*]　**Termination of Future Interests and Servitudes.** Future interests terminate either by their own terms or the operation of the Rule Against Perpetuities. Servitudes terminate by intentional abandonment by the owner of the benefit, by prescription, by unanimous agreement of all effected parties, or by changes so significant in character that the original purposes of the covenant may no longer be served. What would have happened if the *Ginsberg* arrangement was set up using fee simples on a condition subsequent? Are there any justifications for continuing to use different rules for termination of future interests and servitudes?

[*iii*]　**State Action Revisited.** Suppose New York City passed an ordinance permitting religious schools to build on any parcel of land, private covenants to the contrary notwithstanding. Would this be a legitimate zoning enactment serving the valid public purpose of furthering religious worship or a taking of property rights in covenants in violation of the Fifth Amendment to the Constitution?

Compare another covenant termination case which raised the taking issue in a somewhat different context. *Blakely v. Gorin,* 365 Mass. 590, 313 N.E.2d 903 (1974). In *Blakely,* state legislation made it easier than at common law to terminate a covenant because of changed circumstances by preventing enforcement of a covenant unless it was of "actual and substantial benefit" to a person claiming enforcement rights. Even if an actual and substantial benefit existed, only damages were available if the covenant's purposes had been materially reduced by neighborhood change. Old covenants against mercantile and stable use were deemed unenforceable. The area involved was a prominent commercial zone in Boston and horse stables were a quaint relic of a few residents' memories. A right to receive light through an alley, however, was found to be enforceable, but only through relief in damages. The payment of damages avoided a holding that the statute operated as an unconstitutional taking without just compensation. The effect of the decision was to permit the Ritz Carlton Hotel to buy the servitude of access to light and build a 12-story addition to its hotel.

[*iv*] *Contemporary Tests for Religious Discrimination.* In recent cases, the United States Supreme Court has held that state regulatory schemes, which on their face are neutral about religion, are valid even if they have impacts on religious organizations.[92] In a case like *Ginsberg,* a neutral zoning scheme which indirectly limits the ability of religious institutions to construct facilities in certain areas, would be valid. Is a zoning scheme which lists the sorts of uses that may exist in certain zones "neutral?" Suppose, for example that churches, schools and offices of non-profit organizations are allowed in some zones but not in others. What would be the constitutional consequences?

§ 6.03 Zoning, Housing and Race

[1] Formalism, Land Use Planning and Racial Zoning in the Early Twentieth Century

[a] Background to *Buchanan v. Warley*

The chaos of urban growth in the early twentieth century, unprecedented levels of immigration, movement of Blacks north, the arrival of the automobile, and development of new building construction techniques generated enormous social conflicts. Muckraking books such as Lincoln Steffens' SHAME OF THE CITIES (1904) and Upton Sinclair's THE JUNGLE (1906) mirrored widespread concern about the state of urban America. A sense of the scale of the changes overtaking the United States may be gleaned by a quick glance at some demographic trends. The table below shows that the decade of the 1920's was the first era when more than half of the population of the country lived in urban areas and more than 10 million cars were registered with local authorities. In addition, major eastern cities were swamped with the millions of immigrants that crowded these shores before World War I. If ever there was a propitious time for city planners and Progressive Era reformers to have an impact on the policies of urban America, the early twentieth century was the time.

---

[92] *See, e.g.,* Employment Division v. Smith, 494 U.S. 872 (1990).

Demographic Trends

Census Year	Percent Population Urban[93]	Auto Registrations[94]	Immigration Rate[95]
1830	9%	—	2.4%
1840	11%	—	4.2%
1850	15%	—	12.4%
1860	20%	—	5.3%
1870	26%	—	8.1%
1880	29%	—	7.6%
1890	35%	—	7.3%
1900	40%	8,000	6.0%
1910	46%	468,500	11.0%
1920	51%	9,239,100	3.7%
1930	56%	26,749,800	1.7%
1970	73%	108,407,300	1.0%

From 1901, when the first major tenement house regulations were adopted by New York City, through World War I, virtually every major state and city in the country adopted apartment and building codes to ensure that new construction would meet certain minimum standards of health and safety.[96] Agitation for zoning statutes grew during the same period. The construction in 1902 of Daniel Burnham's[97] Flatiron Building, the first steel skeleton building in New York City, at the intersection of 23rd Street, Broadway and Fifth Avenue, caused a sensation in the city, leading many to voice concerns about the need for controls over building densities in the city.

At the same time that urbanization pressures created large reform constituencies, they also generated groups basing their politics on fear, anxiety, xenophobia and hatred. While Progressives fought over building codes and zoning reforms, the Klu Klux Klan became one of the most powerful political organizations in the country; a significant number of its members were elected to public office at the state and federal level. Pressures to curb immigration grew, and hatred of cities was expressed by many. These unsavory instincts merged with planning devices as a

---

[93] Data is taken from BUREAU OF THE CENSUS, DEPARTMENT OF COMMERCE, STATISTICAL HISTORY OF THE UNITED STATES FROM COLONIAL TIMES TO THE PRESENT 11-12 (1976).

[94] *Id.* at 716.

[95] *Id.* at 8, 105-106. The percentage rate listed in the table is the number of immigrants entering the United States as a percentage of the total population for a 10 year period beginning five years before the listed year and ending five years after the listed year. The number in the table is the sum of 10 years of data, with each year's contribution representing Total Immigration/Total Population for that year.

[96] Lawrence Veiller arguably was the most important tenement house reformist in the country. He was Secretary of the first Tenement House Commission established by the New York Tenement Inspection Law of 1901 and co-authored a major muckraking book on housing in 1903. R. W. DEFOREST & LAWRENCE VEILLER, THE TENEMENT HOUSE PROBLEM (1903). A bit later he wrote A MODEL TENEMENT HOUSE LAW (1910). For more on tenement house reform, *see* R. LUBOVE, THE PROGRESSIVES AND THE SLUMS: TENEMENT HOUSE REFORM IN NEW YORK CITY 1890-1917 (1962).

[97] Burnham was a Chicago architect and founder of one the most famous architecture firms in the history of the nation, Burnham & Root.

number of communities adopted laws that zoned neighborhoods by race.[98] The earliest such statute was probably one adopted in California to remove Chinese from their homes and confine them to an area set aside for slaughterhouses and other business establishments.[99] In 1910, Baltimore, Maryland, adopted a race based zoning scheme, followed in 1912 by Mooresville and Winston-Salem, North Carolina. Asheville, North Carolina; Atlanta, Georgia; Madisonville, Kentucky; Greenville, South Carolina; and Richmond, Norfolk and Roanoke, Virginia adopted ordinances in 1913, with St. Louis, Missouri; Birmingham, Alabama; and Louisville, Kentucky doing so a year later.[100] The Louisville ordinance, like the others, made it unlawful for a black family to move into a block with a majority of white residents or a white family to move into a block with a majority of black residents.

In one of the first test cases ever orchestrated by the NAACP, William Warley, president of the Louisville branch of the Association, contracted to buy a lot from Charles Buchanan, a white real estate agent. The lot was on a "white block," but was surrounded by black-owned residences. The contract contained the following ingenious clause:

> It is understood that I am purchasing the above property for the purpose of having erected thereon a house which I propose to make my residence, and it is a distinct part of this agreement that I shall not be required to accept a deed to the above property or to pay for said property unless I have the right under the laws of the State of Kentucky and the City of Louisville to occupy said property as a residence.

Warley then declined to perform the contract on the ground that because of the Louisville racial zoning ordinance he could not "occupy said property as a residence." Buchanan sued for *specific performance*[101] in what was a "friendly" lawsuit. The structure of the litigation created a role reversal, with Buchanan, the white real estate agent arguing that the ordinance was invalid and that the contract should be performed, and Warley, the black NAACP official contending that he should be excused from performance because the ordinance was valid. This strategy brought the contract claim of the white litigant front and center. Nonetheless, the Kentucky courts upheld the validity of the ordinance. The Supreme Court, however, unanimously reversed in the following opinion.

---

[98] For a summary of the various statutes adopted around the country, and a detailed description of the racial zoning policies of Baltimore, Maryland, in this epoch, *see* Garrett Power, *Apartheid Baltimore Style: The Residential Segregation Ordinances of 1910-1913*, 42 MD. L. REV. 289 (1982).

[99] The ordinance was invalidated in In re Lee Sing, 43 F. 359 (C.C.N.D. Cal. 1890).

[100] Garrett Power, *Apartheid Baltimore Style: The Residential Segregation Ordinances of 1910-1913*, 42 MD. L. REV. 289, 310 (1982).

[101] This remedy is commonly sought in broken property transactions. It is an equitable remedy asking that the court order a party to perform all the obligations of the contract. *See* Centex v. Boag, p. 746 below.

[b] Opinion of the Supreme Court in *Buchanan v. Warley*

Buchanan v. Warley

United States Supreme Court
245 U.S. 60, 38 S. Ct. 16, 62 L. Ed. 149

Argued April 10 and 11, 1916.

Restored to Docket, April 17, 1916, for Reargument.

Reargued April 27, 1917.

Decided Nov. 5, 1917.

Mr. Justice DAY delivered the opinion of the Court.

Buchanan, plaintiff in error, brought an action in the chancery branch of Jefferson circuit court of Kentucky for the specific performance of a contract for the sale of certain real estate situated in the city of Louisville at the corner of Thirty-seventh street and Pflanz avenue. The offer in writing to purchase the property contained a proviso:

"It is understood that I am purchasing the above property for the purpose of having erected thereon a house which I propose to make my residence, and it is a distinct part of this agreement that I shall not be required to accept a deed to the above property or to pay for said property unless I have the right under the laws of the state of Kentucky and the city of Louisville to occupy said property as a residence." This offer was accepted by the plaintiff.

To the action for specific performance the defendant by way of answer set up the condition above set forth, that he is a colored person, and that on the block of which the lot in controversy is a part, there are ten residences, eight of which at the time of the making of the contract were occupied by white people, and only two (those nearest the lot in question) were occupied by colored people, and that under and by virtue of the ordinance of the city of Louisville, approved May 11, 1914, he would not be allowed to occupy the lot as a place of residence.

In reply to this answer the plaintiff set up, among other things, that the ordinance was in conflict with the Fourteenth Amendment to the Constitution of the United States, and hence no defense to the action for specific performance of the contract.

In the court of original jurisdiction in Kentucky, and in the Court of Appeals of that state, the case was made to turn upon the constitutional validity of the ordinance. The Court of Appeals of Kentucky held the ordinance valid and of itself a complete defense to the action.

The title of the ordinance is: "An ordinance to prevent conflict and ill-feeling between the white and colored races in the city of Louisville, and to preserve the public peace and promote the general welfare, by making reasonable provisions requiring, as far as practicable, the use of separate blocks, for residences, places of abode, and places of assembly by white and colored people respectively."

By the first section of the ordinance it is made unlawful for any colored person to move into and occupy as a residence, place of abode, or to establish and maintain as a place of public assembly any house upon any block upon which a greater number of houses are occupied as residences, places of abode, or places of public assembly by white people than are occupied as residences, places of abode, or places of public assembly by colored people.

Section 2 provides that it shall be unlawful for any white person to move into and occupy as a residence, place of abode, or to establish and maintain as a place of public assembly any house upon any block upon which a greater number of houses are occupied as residences, places of abode or places of public assembly by colored people than are occupied as residences, places of abode or places of public assembly by white people.

Section 4 provides that nothing in the ordinance shall affect the location of residences, places of abode or places of assembly made previous to its approval; that nothing contained therein shall be construed so as to prevent the occupancy of residences, places of abode or places of assembly by white or colored servants or employees of occupants of such residences, places of abode or places of public assembly on the block on which they are so employed, and that nothing therein contained shall be construed to prevent any person who, at the date of the passage of the ordinance, shall have acquired or possessed the right to occupy any building as a residence, place of abode or place of assembly from exercising such a right; that nothing contained in the ordinance shall prevent the owner of any building, who when the ordinance became effective, leased, rented, or occupied it as a residence, place of abode or place of public assembly for colored persons, from continuing to rent, lease or occupy such residence, place of abode or place of assembly for such persons, if the owner shall so desire; but if such house should, after the passage of the ordinance, be at any time leased, rented or occupied as a residence, place of abode or place of assembly for white persons, it shall not thereafter be used for colored persons, if such occupation would then be a violation of section 1 of the ordinance; that nothing contained in the ordinance shall prevent the owner of any building, who when the ordinance became effective, leased, rented or occupied it as a residence, place of abode, or place of assembly for white persons from continuing to rent, lease or occupy such residence, place of abode or place of assembly for such purpose, if the owner shall so desire, but if such household, after the passage of the ordinance, be at any time leased, rented or occupied as a residence, place of abode or place of assembly for colored persons, then it shall not thereafter be used for white persons, if such occupation would then be a violation of section 2 thereof.

The ordinance contains other sections and a violation of its provisions is made an offense.

The assignments of error in this court attack the ordinance upon the ground that it violates the Fourteenth Amendment of the Constitution of the United States, in that it abridges the privileges and immunities of citizens of the United States to acquire and enjoy property, takes property without due process of law, and denies equal protection of the laws.

The objection is made that this writ of error should be dismissed because the alleged denial of constitutional rights involves only the rights of colored persons, and the plaintiff in error is a white person. This court has frequently held that while an unconstitutional act is no law, attacks upon the validity of laws can only be entertained when made by those whose rights are directly affected by the law or ordinance in question. Only such persons, it has been settled can be heard to attack the constitutionality of the law or ordinance. But this case does not run counter to that principle.

The property here involved was sold by the plaintiff in error, a white man, on the terms stated, to a colored man; the action for specific performance was entertained in the court below, and in both courts the plaintiff's right to have the contract enforced was denied solely because of the effect of the ordinance making it illegal for a colored person to occupy the lot sold. But for the ordinance the state courts would have enforced the contract, and the defendant would have been compelled to pay the purchase price and take a conveyance of the premises. The right of the plaintiff in error to sell his property was directly involved and necessarily impaired because it was held in effect that he could not sell the lot to a person of color who was willing and ready to acquire the property, and had obligated himself to take it. This case does not come within the class wherein this court has held that where one seeks to avoid the enforcement of a law or ordinance he must present a grievance of his own, and not rest the attack upon the alleged violation of another's rights. In this case the property rights of the plaintiff in error are directly and necessarily involved.

We pass then to a consideration of the case upon its merits. This ordinance prevents the occupancy of a lot in the city of Louisville by a person of color in a block where the greater number of residences are occupied by white persons; where such a majority exists colored persons are excluded. This interdiction is based wholly upon color; simply that and nothing more. In effect, premises situated as are those in question in the so-called white block are effectively debarred from sale to persons of color, because if sold they cannot be occupied by the purchaser nor by him sold to another of the same color.

This drastic measure is sought to be justified under the authority of the state in the exercise of the police power. It is said such legislation tends to promote the public peace by preventing racial conflicts; that it tends to maintain racial purity; that it prevents the deterioration of property owned and occupied by white people, which deterioration, it is contended, is sure to follow the occupancy of adjacent premises by persons of color.

The authority of the state to pass laws in the exercise of the police power, having for their object the promotion of the public health, safety and welfare is very broad as has been affirmed in numerous and recent decisions of this court. Furthermore the exercise of this power, embracing nearly all legislation of a local character is not to be interfered with by the courts where it is within the scope of legislative authority and the means adopted reasonably tend to accomplish a lawful purpose. But it is equally well established that the police power, broad as it is, cannot justify the passage of a law or ordinance which runs counter to the limitations of the federal Constitution; that principle has been so frequently affirmed in this court that we need not stop to cite the cases.

The Federal Constitution and laws passed within its authority are by the express terms of that instrument made the supreme law of the land. The Fourteenth Amendment protects life, liberty, and property from invasion by the states without due process of law. Property is more than the mere thing which a person owns. It is elementary that it includes the right to acquire, use, and dispose of it. The Constitution protects these essential attributes of property. *Holden v. Hardy,* 169 U. S. 366. Property consists of the free use, enjoyment, and disposal of a person's acquisitions without control or diminution save by the law of the land. 1 Blackstone's Commentaries (Cooley's Ed.) 127.

True it is that dominion over property springing from ownership is not absolute and unqualified. The disposition and use of property may be controlled in the exercise of the police power in the interest of the public health, convenience, or welfare. Harmful occupations may be controlled and regulated. Legitimate business may also be regulated in the interest of the public. Certain uses of property may be confined to portions of the municipality other than the resident district, such as livery stables, brickyards and the like, because of the impairment of the health and comfort of the occupants of neighboring property. Many illustrations might be given from the decisions of this court, and other courts, of this principle, but these cases do not touch the one at bar.

The concrete question here is: May the occupancy, and, necessarily, the purchase and sale of property of which occupancy is an incident, be inhibited by the states, or by one of its municipalities, solely because of the color of the proposed occupant of the premises? That one may dispose of his property, subject only to the control of lawful enactments curtailing that right in the public interest, must be conceded. The question now presented makes it pertinent to inquire into the constitutional right of the white man to sell his property to a colored man, having in view the legal status of the purchaser and occupant.

Following the Civil War certain amendments to the federal Constitution were adopted, which have become an integral part of that instrument, equally binding upon all the states and fixing certain fundamental rights which all are bound to respect. The Thirteenth Amendment abolished slavery in the United States and in all places subject to their jurisdiction, and gave Congress power to enforce the amendment by appropriate legislation. The Fourteenth Amendment made all persons born or naturalized in the United States, citizens of the United States and of the states in which they reside, and provided that no state shall make or enforce any law which shall abridge the privileges or immunities of citizens of the United States, and that no state shall deprive any person of life, liberty, or property without due process of law, nor deny to any person the equal protection of the laws.

The effect of these amendments was first dealt with by this court in *Slaughter House Cases*, 16 Wall. 36, 21 L. Ed. 394. The reasons for the adoption of the amendments were elaborately considered by a court familiar with the times in which the necessity for the amendments arose and with the circumstances which impelled their adoption. In that case Mr. Justice Miller, who spoke for the majority, pointed out that the colored race, having been freed from slavery by the Thirteenth Amendment, was raised to the dignity of citizenship and equality of civil rights by the Fourteenth Amendment, and the states were prohibited from abridging the privileges and immunities of such citizens, or depriving any person of life, liberty, or property without due process of law. While a principal purpose of the latter amendment was to protect persons of color, the broad language used was deemed sufficient to protect all persons, white or black, against discriminatory legislation by the states. This is now the settled law. In many of the cases since arising the question of color has not been involved and the cases have been decided upon alleged violations of civil or property rights irrespective of the race or color of the complainant. In *Slaughter House Cases* it was recognized that the chief inducement to the passage of the amendment was the desire to extend federal protection to the recently emancipated race from unfriendly and discriminating legislation by the states.

. . . .

In giving legislative aid to these constitutional provisions Congress enacted in 1866, chapter 31, § 1, 14 Stat. 27 (Comp. St. 1916, § 3931), that:

"All citizens of the United States shall have the same right, in every state and territory, as is enjoyed by white citizens thereof to inherit, purchase, lease, sell, hold and convey real and personal property."

And in 1870, by chapter 114, § 16, 16 Stat. 144 (Comp. St. 1916, § 3925), that:

"All persons within the jurisdiction of the United States shall have the same right in every state and territory to make and enforce contracts to sue, be parties, give evidence, and to the full and equal benefit of all laws and proceedings for the security of person and property as is enjoyed by white citizens, and shall be subject to like punishment, pains, penalties, taxes, licenses and exactions of every kind, and none other."

In the face of these constitutional and statutory provisions, can a white man be denied, consistently with due process of law, the right to dispose of his property to a purchaser by prohibiting the occupation of it for the sole reason that the purchaser is a person of color intending to occupy the premises as a place of residence?

The statute of 1866, originally passed under sanction of the Thirteenth Amendment, 14 Stat. 27, and practically re-enacted after the adoption of the Fourteenth Amendment, 16 Stat. 144, expressly provided that all citizens of the United States in any state shall have the same right to purchase property as is enjoyed by white citizens. Colored persons are citizens of the United States and have the right to purchase property and enjoy and use the same without laws discriminating against them solely on account of color. *Hall v. De Cuir,* 95 U. S. 485. These enactments did not deal with the social rights of men, but with those fundamental rights in property which it was intended to secure upon the same terms to citizens of every race and color. *Civil Rights Cases,* 109 U.S. 3, 22.The Fourteenth Amendment and these statutes enacted in furtherance of its purpose operate to qualify and entitle a colored man to acquire property without state legislation discriminating against him solely because of color.

The defendant in error insists that *Plessy v. Ferguson,* 163 U. S. 537, is controlling in principle in favor of the judgment of the court below. In that case this court held that a provision of a statute of Louisiana requiring railway companies carrying passengers to provide in their coaches equal but separate accommodations for the white and colored races did not run counter to the provisions of the Fourteenth Amendment. It is to be observed that in that case there was no attempt to deprive persons of color of transportation in the coaches of the public carrier, and the express requirements were for equal though separate accommodations for the white and colored races. In *Plessy v. Ferguson,* classification of accommodations was permitted upon the basis of equality for both races.

In the *Berea College Case,* 211 U. S. 45, 29 Sup. Ct. 33, 53 L. Ed. 81, a state statute was sustained in the courts of Kentucky, which, while permitting the education of white persons and negroes in different localities by the same incorporated institution, prohibited their attendance at the same place, and in this court the judgment of the Court of Appeals of Kentucky was affirmed solely upon the reserved authority of the Legislature of Kentucky to alter, amend, or repeal charters of its own corporations, and the question here involved was neither discussed nor decided.

. . . .

That there exists a serious and difficult problem arising from a feeling of race hostility which the law is powerless to control, and to which it must give a measure of consideration, may be freely admitted. But its solution cannot be promoted by depriving citizens of their constitutional rights and privileges.

As we have seen, this court has held laws valid which separated the races on the basis of equal accommodations in public conveyances, and courts of high authority have held enactments lawful which provide for separation in the public schools of white and colored pupils where equal privileges are given. But in view of the rights secured by the Fourteenth Amendment to the federal Constitution such legislation must have its limitations, and cannot be sustained where the exercise of authority exceeds the restraints of the Constitution. We think these limitations are exceeded in laws and ordinances of the character now before us.

It is the purpose of such enactments, and, it is frankly avowed it will be their ultimate effect, to require by law, at least in residential districts, the compulsory separation of the races on account of color. Such action is said to be essential to the maintenance of the purity of the races, although it is to be noted in the ordinance under consideration that the employment of colored servants in white families is permitted, and nearby residences of colored persons not coming within the blocks, as defined in the ordinance, are not prohibited.

The case presented does not deal with an attempt to prohibit the amalgamation of the races. The right which the ordinance annulled was the civil right of a white man to dispose of his property if he saw fit to do so to a person of color and of a colored person to make such disposition to a white person.

It is urged that this proposed segregation will promote the public peace by preventing race conflicts. Desirable as this is, and important as is the preservation of the public peace, this aim cannot be accomplished by laws or ordinances which deny rights created or protected by the federal Constitution.

It is said that such acquisitions by colored persons depreciate property owned in the neighborhood by white persons. But property may be acquired by undesirable white neighbors or put to disagreeable though lawful uses with like results.

We think this attempt to prevent the alienation of the property in question to a person of color was not a legitimate exercise of the police power of the state, and is in direct violation of the fundamental law enacted in the Fourteenth Amendment of the Constitution preventing state interference with property rights except by due process of law. That being the case, the ordinance cannot stand.

Reaching this conclusion it follows that the judgment of the Kentucky Court of Appeals must be reversed, and the cause remanded to that court for further proceedings not inconsistent with this opinion.

Reversed.

[c]   Some Thoughts on *Buchanan v. Warley*

The idea of racial zoning did not completely die with the outcome in *Buchanan v. Warley*. Birmingham, Alabama attempted to resurrect the idea after World War II with an ordinance that, with some minor exceptions made it "unlawful for a Negro to occupy property for residential purposes in an area zoned A-1 or white residential, or for a white person to occupy property for residential purposes in an area zoned B-1 or Negro residential."[102] Though the Fifth Circuit Court of Appeals invalidated the enactment (over a dissent by one member of the three judge panel!), the very existence of the case suggests the staying power of overt segregationist impulses in the United States well into this century. The reasons for this may lay in the strength of two quite powerful legal cross-currents that buffeted the Justices hearing, rehearing and finally deciding *Buchanan v. Warley*.[103] On the one hand, the freedom of contract arm of Classical Legal Thought often dominated the Supreme Court's jurisprudence in the early twentieth century and has continuing appeal for conservatives and libertarians. The "right" of Buchanan to sell his house, therefore, was presumably protected by the Constitution. On the other hand, another

---

[102] City of Birmingham v. Monk, 185 F.2d 859 (5th Cir. 1950).

[103] The *Warley* Court era was also buffeted by tumultuous race riots. As noted previously at p. 437–438, the case was decided while whites in a number of cities rioted, looted and killed in black neighborhoods.

line of cases beginning with *Plessy v. Ferguson*,[104] clearly had established that segregation, seemingly including residential segregation, was not only lawful but to be encouraged. Those sentiments also were very much alive in the 1950s.

In a fascinating little twist, the *Buchanan* Court began its analysis with the "elementary" proposition that rights in property included "the right to acquire, use and dispose of" assets, and supported that statement with a citation to *Holden v. Hardy*,[105] rather than to *Lochner v. New York*.[106] Both cases involved the legitimacy of statutes limiting the hours of workers—miners in *Holden* and bakers in *Lochner*. The limit on working hours for miners was upheld, while that for bakers was not. The Court was not prepared to treat racial zoning as an obvious and easy extension of *Lochner*. Justice Day went on to admit that property ownership rights are not absolute, that they may be controlled, as in *Holden*, by exercise of the police power "in the interest of public health, convenience or welfare." The issue, therefore, was whether regulations of property based on race could justify invocation of the police power. That was a hard question for the Court, for, Day wrote, "there exists a serious and difficult problem arising from a feeling of race hostility which the law is powerless to control, and to which it must give a measure of consideration."

The Court's conundrum was resolved by use of a distinction between civil rights and "social rights." The Constitution could be used to protect the former but not the latter. *Plessy* guaranteed civil rights by, at least in theory, treating both races equally. But nothing in *Plessy* or any other case ever guaranteed social rights—cultural equality among whites and blacks. "The case presented," Justice Day opined, "does not deal with an attempt to prohibit the amalgamation of the races. The right which the ordinance annulled was the civil right of a white man to dispose of his property if he saw fit to do so to a person of color and a colored person to make such disposition to a white person." While any statute barring intermarriage, sexual relationships across race lines, integrated seating on public transportation, or joint schooling was constitutional, the Louisville ordinance limiting the civil right to sell property was invalid.

The rubric "social rights" or "social equality" was used before the civil rights era as part of the standard rhetoric condemning those seeking just treatment for black citizens. In the *Buchanan* era very few people were concerned about white people selling property in a way that produced profits from payments out of the pockets of blacks. Rather, the basest of fears were over amalgamation of the races. It was the need to keep black men and white women apart that was central to the ideology of segregation. Signing Formalist contracts was one thing. Going to school together, sitting in the same bus seat together, and, god forbid, having dates, sex and marriage together, were beyond the pale. And white women were the linchpin of the entire structure. They, in a way perversely like their sisters in the era of Jeffersonian Republicanism, were the saviors of the entire body politic. Arch segregationists were serious when they argued that the entire fabric of society would crumble if black blood found its way into the veins of America's white women. Indeed the perceived need to preserve the purity of white women was the driving force behind the myriad false accusations during the lynching era that black men raped white women.

The Formalist justices of the *Buchanan* Court, though torn by two potentially opposing ideological constructs, resolved to protect the freedom of men to contract about their property and labor. That was the only way they could guarantee the ability of whites to profit by sales

---

[104] 163 U.S. 537 (1896).

[105] 169 U.S. 366 (1898)

[106] 198 U.S. 45 (1908).

of houses in black communities. In the long run, they did not find that outcome to be a threat to the continued existence of racial segregation. Indeed, the theory used by the Court actually validated the use of racially restrictive servitudes even as it struck down Louisville's zoning segregation ordinance. No one was surprised in 1926 when the justices affirmed the result in *Corrigan v. Buckley*,[107] the previously excerpted opinion affirming the legitimacy of racial covenants in Washington, D.C.

[2]   Land Use Zoning Statutes and the Realists

[a]   Background to *Village of Euclid v. Ambler Realty*

The Supreme Court's opinion in *Village of Euclid v. Ambler Realty Company* was eagerly awaited by important federal government officials, Progressive Era reformers, real estate developers and local government officials across the country. It was widely viewed as a crucial test of the validity of the Standard Zoning Enabling Act, adopted by 1925 in just under half of the states and under consideration in many others.

Shortly after Warren G. Harding assumed the Presidency in 1921, his Secretary of Commerce, Herbert Hoover, appointed an Advisory Committee on Zoning in the Department of Commerce. Hoover later claimed in his memoirs that encouraging the construction of more and better housing was among his most satisfying accomplishments.[108] Those serving on the Advisory Committee represented the real estate community and the Chamber of Commerce, in addition to well known city planning progressives. The group included Edward Bassett, Counsel for the Zoning Committee of New York; Alfred Bettman, Director of the National Conference on City Planning; Lawrence Veiller, Director of The National Housing Council;[109] and Frederick Law Olmsted, arguably the most famous landscape architect in the nation's history.[110] In 1924, the year following Harding's death and Calvin Coolidge's move to the White House, the Advisory Committee issued the Standard State Zoning Enabling Act and recommended its adoption by the states.[111] By the end of the following year, 19 states, including Ohio, had followed the Committee's advice. By the end of the decade, some or all localities in every state had been granted the power to zone.[112]

The Advisory Committee also reviewed the status of subdivision regulations in the various states. Some control of subdivisions had existed in many places well back into the nineteenth century. They were designed to assure that plat maps were correctly drawn and filed, and that engineering studies were appropriately completed. Other functions were gradually added, such as requiring that new streets tie into old ones and that utility lines be correctly laid. Shortly after

---

[107] 271 U.S. 323 (1926).

[108] THE MEMOIRS OF HERBERT HOOVER: THE CABINET AND THE PRESIDENCY 1920-1933 92-96 (1952).

[109] Veiller was probably the most important housing reformer in New York City in the early twentieth century. In addition to his zoning work, he was instrumental in gaining enactment of significant tenement house reforms.

[110] He designed Central Park in New York City, Prospect Park in Brooklyn, the U.S. Capitol Grounds, the Fenway in Boston, Stanford University, Forest Park in St. Louis, and the Colombian Exposition in Chicago, among many others.

[111] Virtually all persons favoring adoption of zoning argued that each municipality had separate and distinct problems and that actual implementation of zoning had to come at a local level. But most cities were then and are now legal creatures of state legislatures, limited in their authority to the powers granted in state legislation. It was therefore necessary for states to adopt legislation enabling city governments to adopt their own zoning schemes.

[112] NATIONAL COMMISSION ON URBAN PROBLEMS, BUILDING THE AMERICAN CITY, H.R. Doc. No. 34, 91st Cong., 1st Sess., 201 (1968).

Euclid was decided, the Advisory Committee published a Standard City Planning Enabling Act, making subdivision regulation a tool of comprehensive planning, placing administration of subdivision controls in the hands of local planning boards, and establishing certain guarantees that improvements planned in subdivisions were actually carried out. The Standard Act, or some other similar regulatory scheme, was eventually adopted by most states.[113] The two Standard Acts drafted by the Commerce Department are still the basic statutory structures used in many jurisdictions.

The Village of Euclid actually adopted its first zoning ordinance in 1922, two years before the Commerce Department published its final draft of the Standard Zoning Enabling Act.[114] Euclid followed in the footsteps of New York City which adopted its first zoning ordinance in 1916, two years after the New York State legislature adopted the nation's first zoning enabling statute,[115] and almost immediately after the zoning ordinance of the town next door, East Cleveland, was validated by an Ohio court.[116] When Euclid adopted its zoning ordinance, the town's 16 square miles of territory contained less than 4,000 people. It was mostly agricultural, though bordered by working class neighborhoods in East Cleveland. While some land speculators, including Ambler Realty, had bought up parcels of land in the town anticipating future industrial development, there were no factories in the Village of Euclid. Indeed, during the decade before Euclid adopted its zoning plan, Ambler sold off some tracts east of the 68 acre site that became the subject of litigation in *Euclid* and imposed covenants prohibiting commercial and industrial development.[117]

---

[113] *Id.*

[114] Timothy A. Fluck, Euclid v. Ambler: *A Retrospective*, 52 J. AMER. PLAN. ASS'N 326, 328 (1986). Fluck's article is a nice history of the case. *See also*, S. I. TOLL, ZONED AMERICAN 213-253 (1969). Euclid may have been ahead of the general trend because Alfred Bettman, who drafted the Standard Act for President Hoover, was from Ohio and deeply involved in development of land use legislation in the state.

[115] The most prominent entity seeking adoption of zoning enabling legislation in New York was the Fifth Avenue Commission established in 1913 by the Manhattan Borough President. The Commission was concerned about the growth of tall buildings in lower Manhattan and the negative effects of the garment industry. *See* TOLL, note 114 above, at 143-171 (1969).

[116] William M. Randle, *Professor, Reformers, Bureaucrats and Cronies: The Players in* Euclid v. Ambler, in CHARLES M. HAAR & JEROLD S. KAYDEN, ZONING AND THE AMERICAN DREAM: PROMISES STILL TO KEEP 31, 39-40 (1989).

[117] Fluck, note 114 above, at 327-328.

AMBLER REALTY SITE IN THE VILLAGE OF EUCLID[118]

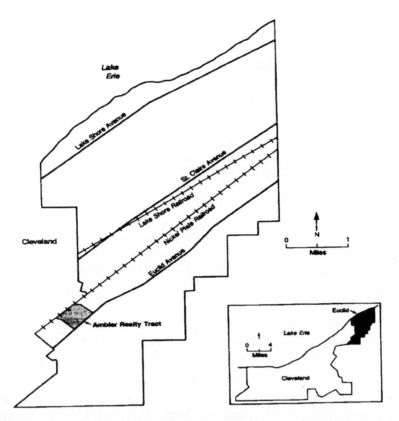

Aptly named Euclid Avenue was the major thoroughfare running through the town. As the map above indicates, Ambler's 68 acres sat between Euclid Avenue on the southeast and the Nickel Plate Railroad tracks and the Cleveland city limits on the northwest. Under the first version of Euclid's plan, Ambler's land was zoned industrial (U-6) for a distance of 500 feet to the southeast of the railroad tracks and two family residential (U-2) over the rest of the site. Ambler's protests led Euclid to modify the plan so that a two family residential zone covered the area 620 feet to the northwest of Euclid Avenue, apartment use (U-3) was permitted on the next 130 feet, and industrial use on the remainder. The two plans[119] are displayed below.

---

[118] *Id.* at 327. Reprinted by permission of the Journal of the American Planning Association, Vol. 52, No. 3, 1986.

[119] *Id.* at 329.

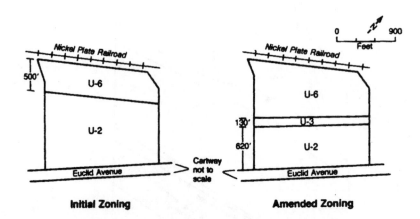

Initial Zoning

Amended Zoning

Despite the modifications creating a significantly larger industrial zone, Ambler filed suit. The Village attempted to have the case dismissed, arguing that Ambler was required to pursue available administrative remedies to its claimed deprivation of property before seeking judicial relief. The motion to dismiss was denied by Judge David Westenhaver, who was appointed to the federal bench by President Wilson in 1917. Westenhaver was appointed in large part because of the influence of Ambler's attorney, Newton Baker. Baker served as Wilson's Secretary of War and was a close friend of Westenhaver's.[120] A short time later, Westenhaver rendered his decision finding Euclid's ordinance unconstitutional.[121]

Even though Westenhaver had close ties to Baker, it is virtually impossible to contend that his decision distorted prior Supreme Court jurisprudence in Ambler's favor. Within the two years before Westenhaver's January, 1924, opinion appeared, the Court decided three cases in a manner quite adverse to the notion that states had broad authority to regulate land or the economy; Westenhaver relied upon all three. The most important of the three cases was *Pennsylvania Coal v. Mahon,*[122] which found that Pennsylvania's attempt to control subsidence of the surface from mining activities was a taking. Two other cases appeared in 1923, *Adkins v. Children's Hospital,*[123] invalidating a Washington, D.C., minimum wage statute, and *Wolff Co. v. Industrial Court,*[124] striking down a Kansas compulsory labor arbitration law. The tenor of Judge Westenhaver's *Euclid* opinion was revealed in the following excerpt:

[C]onfusion of thought appears to exist touching the nature and extent of the police power . . . . [C]ounsel [for Euclid] deduce . . . that since the ordinance in question does not take away plaintiff's title or oust it from physical possession, the power of eminent domain has not been exercised, but that the police power has been. This conception recognizes no distinction between police power and sovereign power. The power asserted is not merely sovereign, but is power unshackled by any constitutional limitation protecting life, liberty, and property from its despotic exercise. In defendant's view, the only difference between the police power and eminent domain is that the taking under the former may be done without

[120] *Id.*

[121] Ambler Realty Co. v. Village of Euclid, 297 F. 307 (N.D. Ohio 1924).

[122] 260 U.S. 393 (1922).

[123] 261 U.S. 525 (1923).

[124] 262 U.S. 522 (1923).

compensation and under the latter a taking must be paid for. It seems to be the further view that whether one power or the other is exercised depends wholly on what the legislative department may see fit to recite on that subject. Such, however, is not the law. If police power meant what is claimed, all private property is now held subject to temporary and passing phases of public opinion, dominant for a day, in legislative or municipal assemblies.[125]

It was a major surprise when the Supreme Court reversed Judge Westenhaver and upheld Euclid's zoning ordinance. The reasons for this result have never become entirely clear, although suggestions have been made by those writing about the case. The Court may have been influenced by the recommendations emerging from successive conservative Republican administrations that zoning statutes be adopted. These endorsements of land use controls reflected a widespread feeling that urbanization problems were getting out of hand, that skyscraper technology threatened the fabric of large cities, and that middle and upper income single family residential areas needed protection from high density apartment and industrial development, as well as from the influx of immigrant and black residents. The scale of urbanization, suggested in the data discussed earlier,[126] surely had an impact.

The *Euclid* Court was evidently troubled by these land use issues. After oral arguments were first heard during January of 1926, the case, like *Buchanan v. Warley* before it, was set down for reargument that fall. Reargument is a rare event. Since the Court never states reasons why a case is set down for further discussion, historians may only speculate about why it happened with *Euclid*. Several intriguing facts are known about the case which may help explain the situation. James Metzenbaum, Euclid's village counsel, requested and was granted the right to file a reply brief after the arguments; the other side was granted the same right. The month after these briefs were filed, the court announced it had set the case for reargument.[127] In addition, the National Conference on City Planning wished to file an *amicus curiae* brief in the case, but inadvertently missed the original filing deadline. Their counsel, Alfred Bettman, was a long time advocate of city planning, the draftsman of much of Ohio's zoning legislation and secretary to the Advisory Committee on Housing and Zoning of the Commerce Department that drafted the Standard Zoning Enabling Act.[128] He wrote to Justice Taft[129] the month after the oral arguments in *Euclid* explaining the importance of the case to city planners and asking if he could file an *amicus* brief. Taft replied that he had brought the matter up in conference with the Court and invited him to submit the brief. Finally, a law clerk to Justice Harlan Fiske Stone at this time has claimed that Justice Sutherland, while writing an opinion striking down Euclid's zoning ordinance, was shaken in his convictions about the case after talks with those who would have dissented from his opinion.[130] Justice Sutherland was also absent from the first oral arguments in *Euclid,* making it somewhat easier for him to justify rehearing the case. It may be of some importance that Justice Sutherland's three well known conservative colleagues—Justices Van Devanter, McReynolds and Butler—dissented from Sutherland's majority opinion when the *Euclid* case was finally decided. Perhaps Sutherland and another justice switched sides. The

---

[125] 297 F. at 313-14.

[126] *See* the Table of Demographic Trends, p. 476 above.

[127] Fluck, note 114 above, at 331.

[128] Bettman had also worked with the Attorney General during World War I helping to prosecute many Americans, including Eugene Debs, for violations of the Wartime Sedition and Espionage Acts. Fluck, note 114 above, at 332, suggests this gave Bettman added credibility with conservatives both on and off the Supreme Court.

[129] Bettman was an old friend of Taft's and a fellow Cincinnatian. *Id.*

[130] *Id.*

dissenters' failure to publish an opinion may indicate they were unwilling to publicly squabble with their conservative colleague. In any case, authorship of the opinion by Sutherland has been declared a "jurisprudential miracle."[131] He was a consistently conservative voice on the pre-New Deal Court, regularly using freedom of contract theories to place limitations on the ability of governments to regulate the economy.

[b]   Opinion of the United States Supreme Court in *Euclid v. Ambler*

Village of Euclid v. Ambler Realty Company

United States Supreme Court
272 U.S. 365, 47 S. Ct. 114, 71 L. Ed. 303 (1926)

MR. JUSTICE SUTHERLAND delivered the opinion of the Court.

The Village of Euclid is an Ohio municipal corporation. It adjoins and practically is a suburb of the City of Cleveland. Its estimated population is between 5,000 and 10,000, and its area from twelve to fourteen square miles, the greater part of which is farm lands or unimproved acreage. It lies, roughly, in the form of a parallelogram measuring approximately three and one-half miles each way. East and west it is traversed by three principal highways: Euclid Avenue, through the southerly border, St. Clair Avenue, through the central portion, and Lake Shore Boulevard, through the northerly border in close proximity to the shore of Lake Erie. The Nickel Plate railroad lies from 1,500 to 1,800 feet north of Euclid Avenue, and the Lake Shore railroad 1,600 feet farther to the north. The three highways and the two railroads are substantially parallel.

Appellee is the owner of a tract of land containing 68 acres, situated in the westerly end of the village, abutting on Euclid Avenue to the south and the Nickel Plate railroad to the north. Adjoining this tract, both on the east and on the west, there have been laid out restricted residential plats upon which residences have been erected.

On November 13, 1922, an ordinance was adopted by the Village Council, establishing a comprehensive zoning plan for regulating and restricting the location of trades, industries, apartment houses, two-family houses, single family houses, etc., the lot area to be built upon, the size and height of buildings, etc.

The entire area of the village is divided by the ordinance into six classes of height districts, denominated U-1 to U-6, inclusive; three classes of height districts, denominated H-1 to H-3, inclusive; and four classes of area districts, denominated A-1 to A-4, inclusive. The use districts are classified in respect of the buildings which may be erected within their respective limits, as follows: U-1 is restricted to single family dwellings, public parks, water towers and reservoirs, suburban and interurban electric railway passenger stations and rights of way, and farming, non-commercial greenhouse nurseries and truck gardening; U-2 is extended to include two-family dwellings; U-3 is further extended to include apartment houses, hotels, churches, schools, public libraries, museums, private clubs, community center buildings, hospitals, sanitariums, public playgrounds and recreation buildings, and a city hall and courthouse; U-4 is further extended to include banks, offices, studios, telephone exchanges, fire and police stations, restaurants, theaters and moving picture shows, retail stores and shops, sales offices, sample rooms, wholesale stores for hardware, drugs and groceries, stations for gasoline and oil (not exceeding 1,000 gallons storage) and for ice delivery, skating rinks and dance halls, electric substations, job and newspaper

---

[131] *Id.* at 333.

printing, public garages for motor vehicles, stables and wagon sheds (not exceeding five horses, wagons or motor trucks) and distributing stations for central store and commercial enterprises; U-5 is further extended to include billboards and advertising signs (if permitted), warehouses, ice and ice cream manufacturing and cold storage plants, bottling works, milk bottling and central distribution stations, laundries, carpet cleaning, dry cleaning and dyeing establishments, blacksmith, horseshoeing, wagon and motor vehicle repair shops, freight stations, street car barns, stables and wagon sheds (for more than five horses, wagons or motor trucks), and wholesale produce markets and salesrooms; U-6 is further extended to include plants for sewage disposal and for producing gas, garbage and refuse incineration, scrap iron, junk, scrap paper and rag storage, aviation fields, cemeteries, crematories, penal and correctional institutions, insane and feeble minded institutions, storage of oil and gasoline (not to exceed 25,000 gallons), and manufacturing and industrial operations of any kind other than, and any public utility not included in, a class U-1, U-2, U-3, U-4 or U-5 use. There is a seventh class of uses which is prohibited altogether.

Class U-1 is the only district in which buildings are restricted to those enumerated. In the other classes the uses are cumulative; that is to say, uses in class U-2 include those enumerated in the preceding class, U-1; class U-3 includes uses enumerated in the preceding classes, U-2 and U-1; and so on. In addition to the enumerated uses, the ordinance provides for accessory uses, that is, for uses customarily incident to the principal use, such as private garages. Many regulations are provided in respect of such accessory uses.

The height districts are classified as follows: In class H-1, buildings are limited to a height of two and one-half stories or thirty-five feet; in class H-2, to four stories or fifty feet; in class H-3, to eighty feet. To all of these, certain exceptions are made, as in the case of church spires, water tanks, etc.

The classification of area districts is: In A-1 districts, dwellings or apartment houses to accommodate more than one family must have at least 5,000 square feet for interior lots and at least 4,000 square feet for corner lots; in A-2 districts, the area must be at least 2,500 square feet for interior lots, and 2,000 square feet for corner lots; in A-3 districts, the limits are 1,250 and 1,000 square feet, respectively; in A-4 districts, the limits are 900 and 700 square feet, respectively. The ordinance contains, in great variety and detail, provisions in respect of width of lots, front, side and rear yards, and other matters, including restrictions and regulations as to the use of bill boards, sign boards and advertising signs.

A single family dwelling consists of a basement and not less than three rooms and a bathroom. A two-family dwelling consists of a basement and not less than four living rooms and a bathroom for each family; and is further described as a detached dwelling for the occupation of two families, one having its principal living rooms on the first floor and the other on the second floor.

Appellee's tract of land comes under U-2, U-3 and U-6. The first strip of 620 feet immediately north of Euclid Avenue falls in class U-2, the next 130 feet to the north, in U-3, and the remainder in U-6. The uses of the first 620 feet, therefore, do not include apartment houses, hotels, churches, schools, or other public and semi-public buildings, or other uses enumerated in respect of U-3 to U-6, inclusive. The uses of the next 130 feet include all of these, but exclude industries, theaters, banks, shops, and the various other uses set forth in respect of U-4 to U-6, inclusive.*

---

* The court below seemed to think that the frontage of this property on Euclid Avenue to a depth of 150 feet came under U-1 district and was available only for single family dwellings. An examination of the ordinance and subsequent amendments, and a comparison of their terms with the maps, shows very clearly, however, that this view was incorrect.

Annexed to the ordinance, and made a part of it, is a zone map, showing the location and limits of the various use, height and area districts, from which it appears that the three classes overlap one another; that is to say, for example, both U-5 and U-6 use districts are in A-4 area districts, but the former is in H-2 and the latter in H-3 height districts. The plan is a complicated one and can be better understood by an inspection of the map, though it does not seem necessary to reproduce it for present purposes.

The lands lying between the two railroads for the entire length of the village area and extending some distance on either side to the north and south, having an average width of about 1,600 feet, are left open, with slight exceptions, for industrial and all other uses. This includes the larger part of appellee's tract. Approximately one-sixth of the area of the entire village is included in U-5 and U-6 use districts. That part of the village lying south of Euclid Avenue is principally in U-1 districts. The lands lying north of Euclid Avenue and bordering on the long strip just described are included in U-1, U-2, U-3 and U-4 districts, principally in U-2.

The enforcement of the ordinance is entrusted to the inspector of buildings, under rules and regulations of the board of zoning appeals. Meetings of the board are public, and minutes of its proceedings are kept. It is authorized to adopt rules and regulations to carry into effect provisions of the ordinance. Decisions of the inspector of buildings may be appealed to the board by any person claiming to be adversely affected by any such decision. The board is given power in specific cases of practical difficulty or unnecessary hardship to interpret the ordinance in harmony with its general purpose and intent, so that the public health, safety and general welfare may be secure and substantial justice done. Penalties are prescribed for violations, and it is provided that the various provisions are to be regarded as independent and the holding of any provision to be unconstitutional, void or ineffective shall not affect any of the others.

The ordinance is assailed on the grounds that it is in derogation of § 1 of the Fourteenth Amendment to the Federal Constitution in that it deprives appellee of liberty and property without due process of law and denies it the equal protection of the law, and that it offends against certain provisions of the Constitution of the State of Ohio. The prayer of the bill is for an injunction restraining the enforcement of the ordinance and all attempts to impose or maintain as to appellee's property any of the restrictions, limitations or conditions. The court below held the ordinance to be unconstitutional and void, and enjoined its enforcement. 297 Fed. 307.

Before proceeding to a consideration of the case, it is necessary to determine the scope of the inquiry. The bill alleges that the tract of land in question is vacant and has been held for years for the purpose of selling and developing it for industrial uses, for which it is especially adapted, being immediately in the path of progressive industrial development; that for such uses it has a market value of about $10,000 per acre, but if the use be limited to residential purposes the market value is not in excess of $2,500 per acre; that the first 200 feet of the parcel back from Euclid Avenue, if unrestricted in respect of use, has a value of $150 per front foot, but if limited to residential uses, and ordinary mercantile business be excluded therefrom, its value is not in excess of $50 per front foot.

Appellee's brief correctly interpreted the ordinance: "The northerly 500 feet thereof immediately adjacent to the right of way of the New York, Chicago & St. Louis Railroad Company under the original ordinance was classed as U-6 territory and the rest thereof as U-2 territory. By amendments to the ordinance a strip 630 [620] feet wide north of Euclid Avenue is classed as U-2 territory, a strip 130 feet wide next north as U-3 territory and the rest of the parcel to the Nickel Plate right of way as U-6 territory."

It is specifically averred that the ordinance attempts to restrict and control the lawful uses of appellee's land so as to confiscate and destroy a great part of its value; that it is being enforced in accordance with its terms; that prospective buyers of land for industrial, commercial and residential uses in the metropolitan district of Cleveland are deterred from buying any part of this land because of the existence of the ordinance and the necessity thereby entailed of conducting burdensome and expensive litigation in order to vindicate the right to use the land for lawful and legitimate purposes; that the ordinance constitutes a cloud upon the land, reduces and destroys its value, and has the effect of diverting the normal industrial, commercial and residential development thereof to other and less favorable locations.

The record goes no farther than to show, as the lower court found, that the normal, and reasonably to be expected, use and development of that part of appellee's land adjoining Euclid Avenue is for general trade and commercial purposes, particularly retail stores and like establishments, and that the normal, and reasonably to be expected, use and development of the residue of the land is for industrial and trade purposes. Whatever injury is inflicted by the mere existence and threatened enforcement of the ordinance is due to restrictions in respect of these and similar uses; to which perhaps should be added—if not included in the foregoing—restrictions in respect of apartment houses. Specifically, there is nothing in the record to suggest that any damage results from the presence in the ordinance of those restrictions relating to churches, schools, libraries and other public and semipublic buildings. It is neither alleged nor proved that there is, or may be, a demand for any part of appellee's land for any of the last named uses; and we cannot assume the existence of facts which would justify an injunction upon this record in respect of this class of restrictions. For present purposes the provisions of the ordinance in respect of these uses may, therefore, be put aside as unnecessary to be considered. It is also unnecessary to consider the effect of the restrictions in respect of U-1 districts, since none of appellee's land falls within that class.

We proceed, then, to a consideration of those provisions of the ordinance to which the case as it is made relates, first disposing of a preliminary matter.

A motion was made in the court below to dismiss the bill on the ground that, because complainant [appellee] had made no effort to obtain a building permit or apply to the zoning board of appeals for relief as it might have done under the terms of the ordinance, the suit was premature. The motion was properly overruled. The effect of the allegations of the bill is that the ordinance of its own force operates greatly to reduce the value of appellee's lands and destroy their marketability for industrial, commercial and residential uses; and the attack is directed, not against any specific provision or provisions, but against the ordinance as an entirety. Assuming the premises, the existence and maintenance of the ordinance, in effect, constitutes a present invasion of appellee's property rights and a threat to continue it. Under these circumstances, the equitable jurisdiction is clear.

It is not necessary to set forth the provisions of the Ohio Constitution which are thought to be infringed. The question is the same under both Constitutions, namely, as stated by appellee: Is the ordinance invalid in that it violates the constitutional protection "to the right of property in the appellee by attempted regulations under the guise of the police power, which are unreasonable and confiscatory?"

Building zone laws are of modern origin. They began in this country about twenty-five years ago. Until recent years, urban life was comparatively simple; but with the great increase and concentration of population, problems have developed, and constantly are developing, which require, and will continue to require, additional restrictions in respect of the use and occupation of private lands in urban communities. Regulations, the wisdom, necessity and validity of which, as applied to existing conditions, are so apparent that they are now uniformly sustained, a century ago, or even half a century ago, probably would have been rejected as arbitrary and oppressive. Such regulations are sustained, under the complex conditions of our day, for reasons analogous to those which justify traffic regulations, which, before the advent of automobiles and rapid transit street railways, would have been condemned as fatally arbitrary and unreasonable. And in this there is no inconsistency, for while the meaning of constitutional guaranties never varies, the scope of their application must expand or contract to meet the new and different conditions which are constantly coming within the field of their operation. In a changing world, it is impossible that it should be otherwise. But although a degree of elasticity is thus imparted, not to the *meaning,* but to the *application* of constitutional principles, statutes and ordinances, which, after giving due weight to the new conditions, are found clearly not to conform to the Constitution, of course, must fall.

The ordinance now under review, and all similar laws and regulations, must find their justification in some aspect of the police power, asserted for the public welfare. The line which in this field separates the legitimate from the illegitimate assumption of power is not capable of precise delimitation. It varies with circumstances and conditions. A regulatory zoning ordinance, which would be clearly valid as applied to the great cities, might be clearly invalid as applied to rural communities. In solving doubts, the maxim *sic utere tuo ut alienum non laedas,* which lies at the foundation of so much of the common law of nuisances, ordinarily will furnish a fairly helpful clew. And the law of nuisances, likewise, may be consulted, not for the purpose of controlling, but for the helpful aid of its analogies in the process of ascertaining the scope of, the power. Thus the question whether the power exists to forbid the erection of a building of a particular kind or for a particular use, like the question whether a particular thing is a nuisance, is to be determined, not by an abstract consideration of the building or of the thing considered apart, but by considering it in connection with the circumstances and the locality. A nuisance may be merely a right thing in the wrong place,—like a pig in the parlor instead of the barnyard. If the validity of the legislative classification for zoning purposes be fairly debatable, the legislative judgment must be allowed to control.

There is no serious difference of opinion in respect of the validity of laws and regulations fixing the height of buildings within reasonable limits, the character of materials and methods of construction, and the adjoining area which must be left open, in order to minimize the danger of fire or collapse, the evils of overcrowding, and the like, and excluding from residential sections offensive trades, industries and structures likely to create nuisances.

Here, however, the exclusion is in general terms of all industrial establishments, and it may thereby happen that not only offensive or dangerous industries will be excluded, but those which are neither offensive nor dangerous will share the same fate. But this is no more than happens in respect of many practice-forbidding laws which this Court has upheld although drawn in general terms so as to include individual cases that may turn out to be innocuous in themselves. The inclusion of a reasonable margin to insure effective enforcement, will not put upon a law, otherwise valid, the stamp of invalidity. Such laws may also find their justification in the fact that, in some fields, the bad fades into the good by such insensible degrees that the two are not capable of being readily distinguished and separated in terms of legislation. In the light of these considerations, we are not prepared to say that the end in view was not sufficient to justify the general rule of the ordinance, although some industries of an innocent character might fall within the proscribed class . . . . Moreover, the restrictive provisions of the ordinance in this particular may be sustained upon the principles applicable to the broader exclusion from residential districts of all business and trade structures, presently to be discussed.

It is said that the Village of Euclid is a mere suburb of the City of Cleveland; that the industrial development of that city has now reached and in some degree extended into the village and, in the obvious course of things, will soon absorb the entire area for industrial enterprises; that the effect of the ordinance is to divert this natural development elsewhere with the consequent loss of increased values to the owners of the lands within the village borders. But the village, though physically a suburb of Cleveland, is politically a separate municipality, with powers of its own and authority to govern itself as it sees fit within the limits of the organic law of its creation and the State and Federal Constitutions. Its governing authorities, presumably representing a majority of its inhabitants and voicing their will, have determined, not that industrial development shall cease at its boundaries, but that the course of such development shall proceed within definitely fixed lines. If it be a proper exercise of the police power to relegate industrial establishments to localities separated from residential sections, it is not easy to find a sufficient reason for denying the power because the effect of its exercise is to divert an industrial flow from the course which it would follow, to the injury of the residential public if left alone, to another course where such injury will be obviated. It is not meant by this, however, to exclude the possibility of cases where the general public interest would so far outweigh the interest of the municipality that the municipality would not be allowed to stand in the way.

We find no difficulty in sustaining restrictions of the kind thus far reviewed. The serious question in the case arises over the provisions of the ordinance excluding from residential districts, apartment houses, business houses, retail stores and shops, and other like establishments. This question involves the validity of what is really the crux of the more recent zoning legislation, namely, the creation and maintenance of residential districts, from which business and trade of every sort, including hotels and apartment houses, are excluded. Upon that question this Court has not thus far spoken. The decisions of the state courts are numerous and conflicting; but those which broadly sustain the power greatly out number those which deny altogether or narrowly limit it; and it is very apparent that there is a constantly increasing tendency in the direction of the broader view.

. . . .

The decisions . . . in the first group . . . agree that the exclusion of buildings devoted to business, trade, etc., from residential districts, bears a rational relation to the health and safety of the community. Some of the grounds for this conclusion are—promotion of the health and security from injury of children and others by separating dwelling houses from territory devoted to trade and industry; suppression and prevention of disorder; facilitating the extinguishment of fires, and the enforcement of street traffic regulations and other general welfare ordinances; aiding the health and safety of the community by excluding from residential areas the confusion and danger of fire, contagion and disorder which in greater or less degree attach to the location of stores, shops and factories. Another ground is that the construction and repair of streets may be rendered easier and less expensive by confining the greater part of the heavy traffic to the streets where business is carried on.

. . . .

The matter of zoning has received much attention at the hands of commissions and experts, and the results of their investigations have been set forth in comprehensive reports. These reports, which bear every evidence of painstaking consideration, concur in the view that the segregation of residential, business, and industrial buildings will make it easier to provide fire apparatus suitable for the character and intensity of the development in each section; that it will increase the safety and security of home life; greatly tend to prevent street accidents, especially to children, by reducing the traffic and resulting confusion in residential sections; decrease noise and other conditions which produce or intensify nervous disorders; preserve a more favorable environment in which to rear children, etc. With particular reference to apartment houses, it is pointed out that the development of detached house sections is greatly retarded by the coming of apartment houses, which has sometimes resulted in destroying the entire section for private house purposes; that in such sections very often the apartment house is a mere parasite, constructed in order to take advantage of the open spaces and attractive surroundings created by the residential character of the district. Moreover, the coming of one apartment house is followed by others, interfering by their height and bulk with the free circulation of air and monopolizing the rays of the sun which otherwise would fall upon the smaller homes, and bringing, as their necessary accompaniments, the disturbing noises incident to increased traffic and business, and the occupation, by means of moving and parked automobiles, of larger portions of the streets, thus detracting from their safety and depriving children of the privilege of quiet and open spaces for play, enjoyed by those in more favored localities, —until, finally, the residential character of the neighborhood and its desirability as a place of detached residences are utterly destroyed. Under these circumstances, apartment houses, which in a different environment would be not only entirely unobjectionable but highly desirable, come very near to being nuisances.

If these reasons, thus summarized, do not demonstrate the wisdom or sound policy in all respects of those restrictions which we have indicated as pertinent to the inquiry, at least, the reasons are sufficiently cogent to preclude us from saying, as it must be said before the ordinance can be declared unconstitutional, that such provisions are clearly arbitrary and unreasonable, having no substantial relation to the public health, safety, morals, or general welfare.

It is true that when, if ever, the provisions set forth in the ordinance in tedious and minute detail, come to be concretely applied to particular premises, including those of the appellee, or to particular conditions, or to be considered in connection with specific complaints, some of them, or even many of them, may be found to be clearly arbitrary and unreasonable. But where the equitable remedy of injunction is sought, as it is here, not upon the ground of a present infringement or denial of a specific right, or of a particular injury in process of actual execution, but upon the broad ground that the mere existence and threatened enforcement of the ordinance, by materially and adversely affecting values and curtailing the opportunities of the market, constitute a present and irreparable injury, the court will not scrutinize its provisions, sentence by sentence, to ascertain by a process of piecemeal dissection whether there may be, here and there, provisions of a minor character, or relating to matters of administration, or not shown to contribute to the injury complained of, which, if attacked separately, might not withstand the test of constitutionality. In respect of such provisions, of which specific complaint is not made, it cannot be said that the land owner has suffered or is threatened with an injury which entitles him to challenge their constitutionality . . . .

The relief sought here is of the same character, namely, an injunction against the enforcement of any of the restrictions, limitations or conditions of the ordinance. And the gravamen of the complaint is that a portion of the land of the appellee cannot be sold for certain enumerated uses because of the general and broad restraints of the ordinance. What would be the effect of a restraint imposed by one or more of the innumerable provisions of the ordinance, considered apart, upon the value or marketability of the lands is neither disclosed by the bill nor by the evidence, and we are afforded no basis, apart from mere speculation, upon which to rest a conclusion that it or they would have any appreciable effect upon those matters. Under these circumstances, therefore, it is enough for us to determine, as we do, that the ordinance in its general scope and dominant features, so far as its provisions are here involved, is a valid exercise of authority, leaving other provisions to be dealt with as cases arise directly involving them.

And this is in accordance with the traditional policy of this Court. In the realm of constitutional law, especially, this Court has perceived the embarrassment which is likely to result from an attempt to formulate rules or decide questions beyond the necessities of the immediate issue. It has preferred to follow the method of a gradual approach to the general by a systematically guarded application and extension of constitutional principles to particular cases as they arise, rather than by out of hand attempts to establish general rules to which future cases must be fitted. This process applies with peculiar force to the solution of questions arising under the due process clause of the Constitution as applied to the exercise of the flexible powers of police, with which we are here concerned.

Decree reversed.

Mr. Justice Van Devanter, Mr. Justice McReynolds and Mr. Justice Butler, dissent. [The dissenters did not publish an opinion.]

[c] Explanatory Notes

[i] *Facial and As Applied Challenges to the Constitutionality of Statutes.* In order to pass Constitutional muster, condemnations and land use regulations must be enacted in pursuit of a valid public purpose. In addition, land use controls providing no compensation to the owner must avoid "taking" the regulated property without compensation in violation of the Fifth Amendment. Condemnations by government entities automatically require payment of compensation to the prior owner. In cases like *Euclid,* land owners argue that land use regulations have the same impact as an eminent domain proceeding and that compensation must, therefore, be paid if the regulations are enforced. "Facial" challenges to the constitutionality of land use controls attack the validity of the entire regulatory scheme. In such attacks it is usually possible to contest the validity of the public purpose underlying the curbs, but more difficult to argue that a taking has occurred. Taking analysis is almost always case specific since it is difficult to argue that a *de facto* eminent domain proceeding has occurred without detailed analysis of the impact of a regulation on a particular piece of property.

Ambler Realty probably made it easier for Justice Sutherland to approve zoning by bringing a *facial* challenge to the statute as a whole. The point was driven home repetitively in the briefs of both James Metzenbaum for the Village of Euclid and Alfred Bettman for *amicus curiae.* It was probably important that they did so because Ambler actually sought and obtained some relief from Euclid before suing. Ambler might have been able to argue that any further efforts to seek relief under the ordinance would have been fruitless and that their challenge was really to the zoning plan *as applied* to it. But there was no evidence in *Euclid* that the market for industrial land in the area was vibrant. Only residential construction was being done in the town.

If an as applied challenge was made, Ambler may simply have looked like a speculator taking a bad risk. In any case, it is intriguing that the Court said nothing about the alterations made to the zoning plan for Ambler's benefit. The stance of the litigants made it possible for Sutherland to write:

> What would be the effect of a restraint imposed by one or more of the innumerable provisions of the ordinance, considered apart, upon the value or marketability of the lands is neither disclosed by the bill nor by the evidence, and we are afforded no basis, apart from mere speculation, upon which to rest a conclusion that it or they would have any appreciable effect upon those matters. Under these circumstances, therefore, it is enough for us to determine, as we do, that the ordinance in its general scope and dominant features, . . . is a valid exercise of authority, leaving other provisions to be dealt with as cases arise directly involving them.

It was possible, however, that some individual property owners were harshly affected by Euclid's zoning statute even if the scheme as a whole was a reasonable police power undertaking. The Standard Zoning Enabling Act attempted to ameliorate potential difficulties caused to individual landowners by providing for *variances,* permitting *non-conforming uses* in existence prior to the zoning statute's enactment but inconsistent with it to continue in operation, and outlawing the use of *spot zones* conferring special benefits or imposing arbitrary burdens upon a single parcel. That these sorts of *as applied* problems raised serious constitutional problems was made clear by *Nectow v. City of Cambridge,* 277 U.S. 183 (1928), decided only two years after *Euclid.* In one of the very few Supreme Court cases to invalidate a zoning action before 1990, Justice Sutherland wrote the Court's opinion forbidding the application of a residence only zone to a parcel surrounded by existing factories and major streets.

The vast bulk of zoning litigation is handled in the state courts, where the problem of arbitrary individual treatment continues to surface on a regular basis. A fascinating description of the factors leading to judicial disapproval of zoning decisions in *as applied* challenges may be found in Haar, Sawyer & Commings, *Computer Power and Legal Reasoning: A Case Study of Judicial Decision Prediction in Zoning Amendment Cases,* 1977 AM. B. FOUND. RES. J. 651. Among the more interesting findings of this massive study was the authors' conclusion that zoning decisions were being reversed by the Connecticut courts less frequently after 1960 than before, and that the reasons for reversal had shifted from concern about arbitrary spot zoning, as in *Nectow,* to fear of physical hazards, street overloads, and adverse effects on neighboring owners. *Id.* at 723-727.

     [ii]   **Race and the Nuisance Rationale.** Nuisance disputes between two private parties did not provide an exact parallel to the broad brush attacks on zoning mounted by Ambler Realty. The Court, realizing that private disputes could not form a perfect model for Constitutional decision making, opined that nuisance law, "which lies at the foundation of so much of the common law . . . , ordinarily will furnish a fairly helpful clew" about the validity of a zoning scheme, "not for the purpose of controlling [decisions], but for the helpful aid of its analogies." The segment of the opinion describing the negative effects of industry and apartments on single family residential zones was an attempt to fit *Euclid* into the "nuisance analogy" mold. Thus, residence zones, the Court noted, guaranteed easier access for fire equipment, greater family safety, reduced traffic, less noise and fewer nervous disorders.

But the nuisance analogy was loose at best. The sorts of guarantees listed in *Euclid* were not the typical fare of public regulations that had previously come before the Supreme Court. Judge

Westenhaver, in his trial level opinion, noted that many of the prior cases involved statutes designed to prevent activities commonly viewed as nuisances, such as livery stables[132] and brick manufacturing plants[133] near residences. Though there were certainly some other examples that were hard for Westenhaver to deal with,[134] the recent cases gave significant support for his general thesis. Indeed, one of the most important cases for Westenhaver was *Buchanan v. Warley*, discussed here just before *Euclid*. If racial zoning was invalid, he argued, then certainly Euclid's plan had to fail. Comparing the *Buchanan* and *Euclid* ordinances, he wrote:

> It seems to me that no candid mind can deny that more and stronger reasons exist, having a real and substantial relation to the public peace, supporting . . . [the *Buchanan*] ordinance than can be urged under any aspect of the police power to support the present ordinance as applied to plaintiff's property. And no gift of second sight is required to foresee that if this Kentucky statute had been sustained, its provisions would have spread from city to city throughout the length and breadth of the land. And it is equally apparent that the next step in the exercise of this police power would be to apply similar restrictions for the purpose of segregating in like manner various groups of newly arrived immigrants. The blighting of property values and the congesting of population, whenever the colored or certain foreign races invade a residential section, are so well known as to be within the judicial cognizance.

But even if the Supreme Court did not closely follow then recent precedents limiting land use regulation to nuisance control, their reasoning paid homage to all the appropriate legal rhetoric. Though use of nuisance language disappeared from most later Supreme Court land use opinions, Sutherland probably felt compelled not to stray too far from understood standards. Indeed, the case was an interesting indication that old nuisance standards were losing their grip. The complexity of problems confronting urbanizing America in the 1920s made it more and more difficult to assume that noxious uses were easy to define and regulate. Large factories, closely knit urban land use patterns and high density population levels rendered agricultural era precedents involving livery stables and brick yards less useful. The Court admitted as much when it stated that regulations routinely upheld "would have been rejected as arbitrary and oppressive" 50 years earlier.

In the final analysis, Justice Sutherland probably used Judge Westenhaver's concerns about race to reach the opposite result. It is hard to separate Justice Sutherland's notion that apartment zones are potential nuisances from the images of tenement house districts crowded with immigrants and Blacks that so dominated public perceptions of urban America. Zoning enthusiasts, including many progressives, were fully aware of the potential for "neutrally framed" zoning statutes, combined with use of racially restrictive servitudes, to segregate people by income and, indirectly, by race and ethnicity.[135] Justice Sutherland surely was sympathetic with those results.

---

[132] Reinman v. Little Rock, 237 U.S. 171 (1915).

[133] Hadacheck v. Sebastian, 239 U.S. 394 (1915). *Hadacheck* actually presented much more difficult problems than its ritual citation in later opinions as a "get rid of the noxious use" case would suggest. The brick yard had been in the same location for many years. Over time, residential use came to the brickyard. The Court's approval of an ordinance banning the brickyard eliminated a long term use at obvious cost to the owner of the brickyard. Compare the nuisance cases, Boomer v. Atlantic Cement Co. p. 869 and Spur v. Del Webb p. 887 excerpted in Chapter 10.

[134] *See*, for example, Welch v. Swasey, 214 U.S. 91, 29 S. Ct. 567, 53 L. Ed. 923 (1909), which involved limitations on building height. Even recognizing that tall buildings and the light they block were a major concern of the New York legislature when they first adopted zoning statutes, Westenhaver could say only that the case involved "merely a reasonable regulation of the height of buildings." 297 F. at 315.

[135] *See* Randle, note 116 above.

The nuisance analogy was also loose because of the way the Court treated the authority of legislative bodies. Anticipating the sort of judicial restraint that would lead to the demise of Sutherland's conservative opposition to the New Deal 10 years later, the Court allowed a "reasonable margin" of breadth in the terms of the statute "to insure effective enforcement" and, given the facial attack on the zoning scheme, declined "to ascertain by a process of piecemeal dissection whether there may be, here and there, provisions of a minor character . . . which might not withstand the test of constitutionality." The legislature was given some room in which to define the need for public regulation. To some extent the scope of the loose nuisance analogy was left outside the control of judicial authority.

[d]   Some Thoughts on *Euclid*

Justice Sutherland clearly was influenced by the forces at work in his cultural moment. City growth, the City Beautiful Movement, tenement houses, large scale immigration, urban fire storms, and vicious race riots in many areas of the country all had an impact. While the *Euclid* Court seemed to pay scant heed to the property freedoms it validated in *Buchanan v. Warley,* it did use all of the ongoing urban cacophony to make zoning a public rather than private question. That was a major development, one that was not wholly consonant with Formalism.

The duality of the outcome—allowing freedom of contract to control racial policies with the help of public land use policy—is a stark reminder of the mixed blessing left behind by *Euclid.* Reading the case together with *Corrigan v. Buckley, Buchanan v. Warley,* and Judge Westenhaver's lower court opinion convinces me that zoning's legacy is fraught with difficulty. Those not represented in legislative and administrative halls of power became the subjects, rather than the beneficiaries of, planning. Leaving zoning power in the hands of each municipality, rather than in larger governmental entities like states or the federal government, allowed for the balkanization of land use planning. It permitted each town to wall itself off from its neighbors, zoning in "good" people and zoning out "bad" people. That is certainly what has happened in the 70 years since *Euclid* was first the subject of judicial inquiry

Justice Sutherland's acquiescence in zoning, therefore, is perfectly explicable. He could rationalize the outcome as one that left intact the "formalist" ability of his peers to invest in property while protecting those like him from outsiders. His peers, in fact, did well in both *Buchanan* and *Euclid.* In each case their perceived interests were protected.

The outcome of *Euclid* reflects some fundamental qualities of Realist as well as Formalist thought. For the Realists, once they came to dominate the Supreme Court in the late 1930s, used their power to enhance the authority of legislatures much as Sutherland did in *Euclid.* Reacting to years of judicially imposed right of contract limitations upon legislative action, Realists insisted that more democratically formed legislatures should be allowed to mold public policy. This move later came back to haunt them. Their insistence that legislatures should be allowed to handle matters of great public importance came acropper in the post World War II epoch, and later in the Civil Rights Era. Realist deference to legislative authority and skepticism about judicial power became difficult to justify when legislatures were adopting Jim Crow statutes and refusing to undo segregation after a war generated by the likes of Hitler had ended. Claims that legislatures were "democratic" and therefore due deference and respect did not fulfill the needs of those who were unable to fashion a majority, let alone to vote. Some Realist adherents, unable to cope with the need to challenge legislative primacy during the Civil Rights Era, lost credibility as the civil rights movement looked for guidance from new modes of legal thought. Put another way, cases like *Euclid,* which itself came under searing attack in the 1960s and 1970s, came to represent both the wisdom of administrative planning and the difficulties inherent in allowing the democratic majority to coerce the minority.

The undoing of Realist legitimacy during the Civil Rights Era has never been repaired. Nor has a new mode of legal thought emerged that captures the imagination of large segments of the legal and non-legal communities. We are still in a period of great jurisprudential disarray.

[e] A Problem on Zoning, Democracy and Allocation of Power

Although each local community was granted the power to zone by its state government, the terms of the Standard Zoning Enabling Act adopted in most jurisdictions and the outcome of *Euclid v. Ambler* left virtually all zoning decisions in the hands of local authorities. That created a form of competition among communities for the "better" land uses. In such a system, less favored uses were likely to be left in less attractive locations. The potential existed for zoning to create a vicious cycle—problem areas, unable to attract new uses, were made even less attractive as the zoning in other communities caused more businesses and people to leave.

This dynamic caused serious anomalies in the allocation of power and the operation of democracy. Decisions made by one democratic community had effects on other nearby communities even though those living in the effected communities had no voice in the land use decisions of its neighbor. Think about a city like Camden, New Jersey, for example, surrounded by numerous small suburban towns. The suburban towns zone themselves for single family residential and light industrial and commercial uses, gradually drawing businesses and middle and upper class residents from Camden. Despite the serious consequences of the flight to the suburbs, Camden has no voice in the zoning decisions made by the suburban towns. But if you attempt to remedy the situation by allowing Camden residents to participate in the decision making processes of the neighboring suburban communities, the neighbors justifiably complain that their electoral power is being diluted. Relegating zoning to local communities, therefore, inevitably creates anomalous effects. The problem is very similar to the representation problems in *Brendale v. Yakima Indian Nation,* which you read in Chapter 1 (*see* p. 51 above).

How would you handle these problems? Would you let Camden exercise some level of authority over the zoning decisions of its suburban neighbors? Would you regionalize planning at the state level in an effort to alter the political contour of land use debates and to provide a forum for Camden to influence policy making? If you want to regionalize planning, would you do so across state lines so that, for example, Philadelphia could have a voice in the zoning decisions made by its New Jersey suburban neighbors?

And what does all this tell us about the nature of democracy? Is it often true that the outcome of a political debate depends on the governmental level at which it occurs? Do agendas change when you move up and down the scale of political organization? Are there any standards that can be developed to help us decide at which level—local, regional, state or national—a debate should be held? The materials in the rest of this chapter focus on some of these questions.

[3] Race, Class and Zoning in Contemporary Life

Since the Supreme Court decisions in *Euclid v. Ambler* and *Shelley v. Kraemer,* two sets of cases have continued to raise questions about the relationships between race, class and zoning. In one set, challenges to a variety of housing practices favoring housing for the middle and upper classes—over-zoning for single family houses, under-zoning for apartments, over-zoning for "clean" businesses and under-zoning for "dirty" ones—were pursued under the Constitution and various federal civil rights statutes. The difficulty of successfully mounting challenges under standards tied to racial discrimination against zoning practices which on their face were class-based led other litigants to rely upon state constitutional provisions to challenge local zoning patterns. This section covers both sets of disputes. The next segment describes the contours of post-*Shelley* housing discrimination law and presents one case discussing the use of that law in a zoning context. The chapter ends with a state challenge to class based "Euclidean" zoning.

[a] Contemporary Zoning and Federal Race Discrimination Law

The debate over state action coursing through the opinions in *Charlotte Park v. Barringer,* p. 352 above, *Shelley v. Kraemer,* p. 445 above, and *Evans v. Abney,* p. 361 above, has changed dramatically in contemporary racial discrimination litigation involving real estate. During the years that the *Evans* dispute was bouncing back and forth between state and federal courts, other litigation was in progress that would significantly change the focus of the Supreme Court's jurisprudence. Not only were a number of new Civil Rights Acts adopted by Congress between 1957 and 1970, but the Supreme Court began to pay renewed attention to the old Civil Rights Acts adopted during the decade after the Civil War. In fact, the continuing difficulty with state action problems in federal Constitutional litigation led civil rights groups to investigate the possibility of a civil rights structure not at all dependent on the intervention of state authority as a prerequisite to federal judicial intervention.

Part of the search for a non-state action based civil rights legal structure involved lobbying intensively for new federal legislation. That work was rewarded with the adoption of a series of new measures, including significant fair housing legislation in 1968.[136] The other part of the search led to litigation attempting to re-invigorate the old Reconstruction Era Civil Rights Acts by arguing that they were adopted in accordance with authority granted to Congress in the second section of the *Thirteenth* Amendment, which does not contain any state action limitations.[137] This effort eventually led to the decision in *Jones v. Mayer*[138]

Joseph Lee Jones, who was black, and his wife, Barbara Jo Jones, who was white, filed a complaint in federal district court in St. Louis, Missouri, on September 2, 1965, alleging that Alfred H. Mayer Company had refused to sell them a house in the Paddock Woods subdivision in the suburbs of St. Louis because Mr. Jones was black. The complaint, among other things, alleged a cause of action under what is now 42 U.S.C. § 1982,[139] originally adopted as part of the Civil Rights Act of 1866. The federal district court dismissed the case, and the United States Court of Appeals for the Eighth Circuit affirmed the dismissal, both courts reasoning that

---

[136] The Civil Rights Commission was established in 1957. The same act contained voting rights provisions. Other voting measures passed in 1960 and 1965. The 1964 Civil Rights Act was a major enactment containing provisions on public accommodations, voting, school desegregation, and other matters. Further attempts to obtain passage of civil rights acts were filibustered to death in the Senate until the assassination of Martin Luther King and subsequent urban riots in 1968 loosed the floodgates. It was this act that contained the first major civil rights provisions directed at fair housing. Civil Rights Act of 1968, 82 Stat. 73 (1968).

[137] The state action limitation imposed on Congress by the *Civil Rights Cases* in 1883 was also dealt a serious blow by Congressional use of the commerce clause to support enactment of many of the civil rights acts adopted in the modern era. This tactic was legitimated by the Supreme Court in Heart of Atlanta Motel v. United States, 379 U.S. 241 (1964).

[138] 392 U.S. 409 (1968).

[139] The section provides that all citizens "shall have the same right . . . as is enjoyed by white citizens . . . to inherit, purchase, lease, sell, hold, and convey real and personal property."

the lack of state action prevented the federal courts from interfering with the refusal of Mayer to sell a house to Mr. and Mrs. Jones. The United States Supreme Court reversed, holding that Congress had the authority to adopt remedies to eradicate all badges and indicia of slavery under the Thirteenth Amendment, including private discriminatory acts against black persons.[140]

The Supreme Court opinion, released shortly after Martin Luther King Jr.'s assassination and the adoption by Congress of the Civil Rights Act of 1968, made it significantly easier to pursue federal remedies against racial discrimination in property transactions. A dispute like that in *Shelley v. Kraemer,* for example, could now be handled as a simple case of discrimination. Parties claiming to have acted in accordance with a racially restrictive covenant would find themselves subject to a federal court action for damages and injunctive relief. The *Evans* case, however, may not be so easy to rework. The Supreme Court opinion in *Evans* can be read as a state action holding, but it can also be read as a holding that the closing of the park did not result in discrimination against any particular group. In the latter case, alteration of the prerequisites for state action still might not change the result.

Despite the easing of the state action limitation on pursuit of federal housing discrimination cases, challenging class based zoning practices still faced a number of obstacles. The tone was set in two cases decided in the 1970s. The first, *Washington v. Davis,*[141] was not a housing case, but a challenge to a qualifying test administered to applicants for positions as police officers. While use of the test had a disproportionate and negative impact on black applicants, the Court refused to intervene in this Equal Protection challenge without a showing that the test was used with the intent to discriminate on the grounds of race. While acknowledging that circumstantial evidence might be used to prove that actions were taken with a discriminatory purpose, the Justices refused to create a presumption that the Constitution was violated when government actions had a disproportionate impact on blacks.

The *Davis* result was reaffirmed in *Village of Arlington Heights v. Metropolitan Housing Development Corp.,* 429 U.S. 252 (1977). Arlington Heights turned down a Metropolitan Housing Development Corporation (MHDC) request for a zoning variance so it could construct a 190 unit townhouse project for low and moderate income tenants. MHDC and others then sued the village under both the Constitution and federal civil rights statutes alleging that the denial was racially discriminatory. Their argument was that the denial had a significant negative impact on minority persons, and that this racial impact placed the burden on Arlington Heights to demonstrate a compelling reason for the variance denial. The Constitutionally based portion of this theory failed before the Supreme Court, which claimed it was unable to find any factual support for a finding that the variance denial was based on intentionally discriminatory behavior. The case was remanded for further proceedings under federal housing civil rights statutes.

On remand, the Seventh Circuit Court of Appeals heard arguments on whether the variance denial violated the federal Fair Housing Act, 42 U.S.C § 3601, *et seq.* They returned the case to the District Court for further hearings on the strength of the discriminatory effect of the variance denial, leaving open the possibility that an effects test might serve to meet the statutory rather than Constitutional test of discrimination.[142] The trial court was instructed to evaluate four factors

---

[140] The 1866 legislation relied on by the Joneses was first enacted under the authority of the Thirteenth Amendment. It was reenacted after the Fourteenth Amendment was ratified in 1868, in part out of concern that it stepped beyond the power granted Congress by the Thirteenth Amendment. Surprising as it may seem, the scope of Congressional authority under the Thirteenth Amendment was not fully explored until Jones v. Mayer.

[141] 426 U.S. 229 (1976).

[142] Metropolitan Housing Development Corp. v. Village of Arlington Heights, 558 F.2d 1283 (7th Cir. 1977).

in determining whether the discriminatory effect of Arlington Heights' denial of the zoning variance was permissible: the strength of the plaintiff's showing of discriminatory effect; the existence of any evidence of discriminatory intent short of that required to fulfill the Constitutional test of *Washington v. Davis;* the defendant's reasons for taking the action complained of; and whether the plaintiff seeks to compel the defendant to affirmatively provide housing for members of minority groups or merely to restrain the defendant from interfering with individual property owners who wish to provide such housing. The case was eventually settled by a strange contrivance. The Village of Arlington Heights annexed two parcels of land adjacent to the town but in unincorporated areas and zoned them for the construction of low income housing units. The opposition of Mt. Prospect, a neighboring community which then intervened in the litigation, failed to halt the settlement.[143]

After *Davis* and *Arlington Heights* those challenging zoning practices must show an intention to discriminate on the grounds of race in a Constitutional challenge, or significant discriminatory effects not supported by important public policies in a statutory dispute. In either case, it is very difficult to prevail in challenges to the structure of entire zoning schemes which have a discriminatory effect because of the class based distinctions buried in their land use plans. Plaintiffs are most likely to fair well when they bring challenges to specific decisions of zoning authorities having a racial effect. The next case provides an example.

[b]   Opinion of the Court of Appeals in *Huntington NAACP v. Town of Huntington*[144]

Huntington Branch, National Association for the Advancement of Colored People v. The Town of Huntington

United States Court of Appeals for the Second Circuit
844 F.2d 926 (1988)

Before KAUFMAN, OAKES, and NEWMAN, Circuit Judges.

IRVING R. KAUFMAN, Circuit Judge:

Twenty years ago, widespread racial segregation threatened to rip civil society asunder. In response, Congress adopted broad remedial provisions to promote integration. One such statute, Title VIII of the Civil Rights Act of 1968, 42 U.S.C. § § 3601-3631 ("Fair Housing Act"), was enacted "to provide, within constitutional limitations, for fair housing throughout the United States." 42 U.S.C. § 3601. Today, we are called upon to decide whether an overwhelmingly white suburb's zoning regulation, which restricts private multi-family housing projects to a largely minority "urban renewal area," and the Town Board's refusal to amend that ordinance to allow construction of subsidized housing in a white neighborhood violates the Fair Housing Act.

The Huntington Branch of the National Association for the Advancement of Colored People (NAACP), Housing Help, Inc. (HHI), and two black, low-income residents of Huntington appeal from an adverse judgment of the United States District Court for the Eastern District of New York . . . . Appellants allege that the Town violated Title VIII by restricting private construction of multi-family housing to a narrow urban renewal area and by refusing to rezone the parcel outside this area where appellants wished to build multi-family housing. Specifically, appellants

---

[143] Metropolitan Housing Development Corp. v. Village of Arlington Heights, 469 F. Supp. 836 (N.D. Ill. 1979).

[144] The United States Supreme Court affirmed this result in a per curiam opinion, Town of Huntington v. Huntington Branch, N.A.A.C.P., 488 U.S. 15 (1988).

sought to construct an integrated, multi-family subsidized apartment complex in Greenlawn/East Northport, a virtually all-white neighborhood. The Town's zoning ordinance, however, prohibited private construction of multi-family housing outside a small urban renewal zone in the Huntington Station neighborhood, which is 52% minority. Thus, appellants petitioned the Town to revise its code to accommodate the project. When the Town refused, appellants brought this class-action to compel the change under Title VIII.

. . . .

In the case currently appealed . . . [t]he district judge . . . incorrectly employed an intent-based standard for the disparate impact claim asserted here both in analyzing the showing of effect and in scrutinizing the validity of the Town's reasons for rejection. Accordingly, we reverse and, finding a Title VIII violation, grant appellants' request for site-specific relief . . . .

Huntington is a town of approximately 200,000 people located in the northwest corner of Suffolk County, New York. In 1980, 95% of its residents were white. Blacks comprised only 3.35% of the Town's population and were concentrated in areas known as Huntington Station and South Greenlawn. Specifically, 43% of the total black population lived in four census tracts in Huntington Station and 27% in two census tracts in the South Greenlawn area. Outside these two neighborhoods, the Town's population was overwhelmingly white. Of the 48 census tracts in the Town in 1980, 30 contained black populations of less than 1%.

The district court found that the Town has a shortage of affordable rental housing for low and moderate-income households. The Town's Housing Assistance Plan (HAP), which is adopted by the Town Board and filed with HUD as part of Huntington's application for federal community development funds, reveals that the impact of this shortage is three times greater on Blacks than on the overall population. Under the 1982-1985 HAP, for example, 7% of all Huntington families required subsidized housing, while 24% of black families needed such housing.

In addition, a disproportionately large percentage of families in existing subsidized projects are minority. In Gateway Gardens, a public housing project built in 1967, 38 of 40 units were occupied by Blacks and Hispanics in 1984. Seventy-four percent of those on the project's waiting list were minority. In Whitman Village, a 260-unit HUD subsidized development built in 1971, 56% of the families were minority in 1984. Lincoln Manor, which was built in 1980, is a 30-unit HUD Section 8 project. Thirty percent of the households and 45% of those on the waiting list were minority in 1984. Under a HUD Section 8 program, lower income families can obtain certificates to supplement their rent. Each family, however, must locate its own apartment. In January 1984, 68% of families holding certificates and 61% of those on the waiting list were minority.

Although a disproportionate number of minorities need low-cost housing, the Town has attempted to limit minority occupancy in subsidized housing projects. Michael Miness, the Director of Huntington's Community Development agency and responsible for developing the Town's low-cost housing, and Angela Sutton, Executive Director of the Huntington Housing Authority, repeatedly told whites opposing the Lincoln Manor project that they would impose a racial quota on occupancy. When HUD reviewed the project's management plan which established 5% minority occupancy, however, it advised the Huntington Housing Authority that it would not permit a racial quota at Lincoln Manor. The Town similarly attempted to impose racial quotas on occupancy at a proposed 150-unit subsidized housing project in Huntington Station on the Melville Industrial Associates (MIA) site. When Alan H. Wiener, HUD's Area Director, wrote Kenneth C. Butterfield, Town Supervisor, that "limitations on minority occupancy of housing on the Huntington Station site are not justifiable and will not be permitted," (Letter of June 19, 1981, E-18), the Town Board unanimously passed a resolution withdrawing its support for the project because they could not "ensure a particular ethnic mix." (Huntington Town Board Resolution re: Huntington Station Urban Renewal Project, June 23, 1981, E-17.)

Under the Town's zoning ordinance, multi-family housing is permitted only in an "R-3M Apartment District." . . . On its face . . . this provision limits private construction of multi-family housing to the Town's urban renewal area, where 52% of the residents are minority. It does permit the Huntington Housing Authority (HHA) to build multi-family housing townwide. But HHA's only project, Gateway Gardens, is in the urban renewal zone. The private housing projects are also in or nearby the urban renewal area. Whitman Village is adjacent to Gateway Gardens in census blocks that are over 40% minority. Lincoln Manor, only a few blocks from the projects in the urban renewal area, is also in a racially impacted census block.

The Town's zoning ordinance also includes a special category for multi-family housing for senior citizens called "R-RM Retirement Community District." Only one such development—Paumanack Village—has been built in Huntington. It is the only multi-family housing for low income people which is situated in an overwhelmingly white neighborhood. The development itself is largely white, having a black occupancy of 3%.

Only one vacant parcel of land in Huntington currently is zoned R-3M and thus would be eligible for the appellants' proposed development: the MIA site, which is at the northeast corner of Broadway and New York Avenue, is partially zoned C-6 and partially zoned R-3M. The Town in 1980 requested pre-approval for 150 units of Section 8 housing on this site.[5]

In response to the great need for subsidized housing in the Town, HHI decided to sponsor an integrated housing project for low-income families. HHI determined that the project could foster racial integration only if it were located in a white neighborhood outside the Huntington Station and South Greenlawn areas. This decision eliminated consideration of the MIA site, the only vacant R-3M property located in the urban renewal area.

In its effort to create racially integrated, low-cost housing, HHI actively sought the assistance of Town officials. Specifically, HHI's Executive Director, Marianne Garvin, and HHI Board members met repeatedly with Michael Miness. In response to Miness's suggestion that HHI pursue rehabilitating existing structures before focussing on new construction, HHI commissioned a study in 1979 to assess whether any of the vacant schools were suitable for the housing project. After narrowing the possibilities to the Green Meadow School, HHI determined that this location was inappropriate for a low-cost housing development. Throughout 1979, Miness assured HHI representatives that existing zoning should not impede their efforts because the Town Board would amend the zoning ordinance if it supported the organization's project.

After a lengthy search, HHI determined that a 14.8 acre parcel located at the corner of Elwood and Pulaski Roads in the Town was well suited for a 162-unit housing project. This flat, largely cleared and well-drained property was near public transportation, shopping and other services, and immediately adjacent to schools.

Ninety-eight percent of the population within a one-mile radius of the site is white. HHI set a goal of 25% minority occupants. The district court found that "a significant percentage of the

---

[5] Although pre-approval was granted, the project was delayed by community opposition and by an attempt by Butterfield to reserve 30 units for the elderly and to set a limit on black participation of 10%. In June 1981, Alan Weiner, HUD's Area Manager, suspended pre-approval.

tenants [at Matinecock Court] would have belonged to minority groups." *Huntington,* 668 F. Supp. at 785. HHI officials determined that the property was economically feasible and offered a lengthy option period.

Prior to purchasing the option for the property, Garvin asked Miness to visit the property and evaluate it. Garvin testified that, although Miness told Garvin he would not give an opinion before HHI secured an option, he assured her that the property's R-40 designation (single family homes on one-acre lots) should not be an obstacle because the Town Board, if it supported the project, would simply amend the zoning ordinance.

HHI obtained its option to purchase the Elwood-Pulaski parcel on January 23, 1980. Garvin again called Miness and invited him to visit the site. She testified that he responded that he was familiar with the property and believed it was a good location for development.

Throughout 1980, HHI sought to advance its project by gaining the approval of the Town Board to rezone the property to R-3M from its R-40 designation. The opinion below recites the multitudinous disputes which color the parties' versions of the events of those months, especially concerning the apparently "illegal" closed meeting between the Board and HHI on February 22, 1980. Certain facts, however, are not in contention. Robert Ralph, a director of HHI, addressed the Town Board on February 26, 1980, at a public hearing. The district court found that he filed a document requesting "a commitment by the Town to amend the zoning ordinance to allow multi-family rental construction by a private developer." *Huntington,* 668 F. Supp. at 784 (quoting Presentation to the Huntington Town Board at the Community Development Block Grant Hearing 2 (February 26, 1980)). In August 1980, HHI and National Housing Partnership, an owner-manager of federally subsidized housing, filed a joint application with HUD for Section 8 funding for the project.

At the time HHI applied for the Section 8 funding, Huntington had a Housing Assistance Plan, which had been approved by HUD. Pursuant to the provisions of the Housing and Community Development Act of 1974, 42 U.S.C. § § 5301-20 (1982 & Supp. III 1985), when a town has such a plan, HUD must refer a Section 8 application to the Town for comment. In an October 14, 1980, letter to Alan H. Weiner, HUD Area Manager, Town Supervisor Kenneth C. Butterfield set forth seven reasons why Huntington opposed the project. It reads, in pertinent part, as follows:

The Town's professional staff in the Planning, Legal and Community Development Departments have reviewed the proposal and have submitted the following comments:

1. The HUD-approved Housing Assistance Plan (both the three-year goal submitted with the Community Development Block Grant 1979-80 application and the annual goal submitted with the 1980-1981 Community Development Block Grant) contains no "new construction" units as a program goal.

2. The plan for development cannot be carried out within the existing single family R-40 (1 acre) zoning.

3. The development is located at the intersection of two heavily trafficked streets.

4. The site plan presents a poor parking plan in terms of location with respect to the units, substandard in size and the lack of streets results in very poor fire protection access.

5. The development is located adjacent to both the Long Island Railroad as well as a LILCO substation. This is in addition to the heavy traffic conditions.

6. The site plan shows recreation and/or play areas very inadequate for the number and type of dwelling units being proposed.

7. The three and four-bedroom units are quite undersized; have poor layout; bedrooms are much too small; living space is unrealistic; no storage; one full and two half-baths for a family of 6 to 8 is not realistic.

In conclusion, I do not recommend HUD approval of this proposal based on the material reviewed and the comments presented above.

When the proposal became public, substantial community opposition developed. A group called the Concerned Citizens Association was formed, and a petition containing 4,100 signatures against the proposal was submitted to the Town Board. A protest meeting in November drew about 2,000 persons. Supervisor Butterfield was the principal speaker and assured the audience of his opposition to the project. Matinecock Court came before the Town Board at a meeting on January 6, 1981. The Board rejected the proposed zoning change and adopted the following resolution:

WHEREAS, it has been proposed by HOUSING HELP, INC., a private non-profit group, that Huntington's zoning code be changed in order to build 162 federally-subsidized apartments for low to moderate income people at Elwood and Pulaski Roads in the Elwood section of the Town of Huntington; and

WHEREAS, the Town Board has studied the various aspects of the proposal for a zoning change for 162 apartments at the said location of Elwood and Pulaski Roads;

NOW, THEREFORE,

THE TOWN BOARD finds that although favoring housing for the senior citizens and others, in appropriate areas, that the location referred to herein is not an appropriate location due to lack of transportation, traffic hazard and disruption of the existing residential patterns in the Elwood area and requests that the Department of Housing and Urban Development (HUD) reject the application by HOUSING HELP, INC.

Huntington Town Board Resolution re: Housing at Elwood and Pulaski Roads (January 6, 1981).

The district court based its refusal to order rezoning on three alternative grounds: (1) appellants never formally applied for rezoning; (2) even if they had applied, they failed to make the requisite prima facie showing of discriminatory effect; and (3) even if they had demonstrated discriminatory effect, the city had rebutted it by articulating legitimate, non-pretextual justifications. We now consider each ground separately.

The district court, in its first alternative holding, found that appellants failed to exhaust their available remedies because they did not formally apply to rezone their parcel. . . . . Despite the myriad of factual disputes surrounding HHI's dealings with the Town Board, two facts are crystal clear: HHI requested the Town Board to amend the code to allow R-3M zoning townwide at a formal meeting on February 26, 1980, and the Board, in its resolution of January 6, 1981, deemed this application a "propos[al] . . . that Huntington's zoning code be changed in order to build 162 federally-subsidized apartments for low to moderate income people at Elwood and Pulaski Roads . . . ." . . . Both parties thus clearly understood that an application for a zoning change had been made. . . . . Moreover, the Town's refusal to amend the zoning code rendered meaningless a request to change the zoning on the Elwood-Pulaski property, as R-3M classifications were reserved for property within the urban renewal area, and there were no other multi-family housing designations.

In its second holding, the court adopted the four-prong disparate impact test set out in *Metropolitan Housing Dev. Corp. v. Village of Arlington Heights*, 558 F.2d 1283, 1287-90 (7th

Cir.1977), and concluded that, even if appellants applied for a rezoning change, they had failed to make out a prima facie case. The court considered:

> (1) how strong is the plaintiff's showing of discriminatory effect; (2) is there some evidence of discriminatory intent, though not enough to satisfy the constitutional standard of *Washington v. Davis;* (3) what is the defendant's interest in taking the action complained of; and (4) does the plaintiff seek to compel the defendant to affirmatively provide housing for members of minority groups or merely to restrain the defendant from interfering with individual property owners who wish to provide such housing.

On the first prong, the court found that the showing of discriminatory effect was "not particularly strong." *Huntington,* 668 F. Supp. at 786. Although the judge held that a shortage of rental housing existed, that a disproportionately large percentage of the households using subsidized rental units are minority, and, accordingly, that a "significant percentage" of Matinecock Court tenants would be minority, he compared the larger absolute number of white poor (22,160) with minority poor (3,671) and concluded that the beneficiaries "might not come disproportionately from minority groups." On the second factor, Judge Glasser found no proof of segregative intent, deeming this a plus in the Town's favor. In so holding, he determined that appellants had failed to prove that the Town was motivated by segregative intent when it confined subsidized housing to the urban renewal area. The third prong of *Arlington Heights,* he concluded, was satisfied by "legitimate, nondiscriminatory reasons for [the Town's] conduct." He deemed the fourth factor to cut in favor of appellants because they were not asking the Town to provide housing. Nevertheless, because the first three factors weighed in favor of appellees, he held that the appellants had failed to demonstrate a prima facie case.

In its third rationale, the court applied the test set forth in *McDonnell Douglas Corp. v. Green,* 411 U.S. 792 (1973), as a final determination on the merits for Title VII disparate treatment cases. According to this formula, if plaintiffs establish a prima facie case of disparate treatment, the "burden shifts to the defendant to articulate some legitimate, nondiscriminatory reason for the employee's rejection." If defendants meet this burden, plaintiffs must show that the legitimate justifications offered were pretextual and not the employer's true reasons. Applying this test, the court below found that, even if appellants had demonstrated a prima facie showing of discriminatory effect, the Town's justifications for rejecting the project were legitimate and non-discriminatory reasons which "have not been exposed as pretextual."

We find it convenient to discuss Judge Glasser's second and third holdings together. In considering them, we start by pointing out that this case requires what has been called "disparate impact" or "disparate effects" analysis, not "disparate treatment" analysis. A disparate impact analysis examines a facially-neutral policy or practice, such as a hiring test or zoning law, for its differential impact or effect on a particular group. Disparate treatment analysis, on the other hand, involves differential treatment of similarly situated persons or groups. The line is not always a bright one, but does adequately delineate two very different kinds of discrimination claims.

Here, appellees would collapse the distinction between disparate impact and disparate treatment by characterizing this as a "mixed" impact and treatment case. Thus, they argue, "treatment" analysis should be applied to the Town's refusal to rezone the Matinecock Court site, while "impact" analysis should be applied to the zoning ordinance's restriction of multi-family housing to the urban renewal area. Under appellees' methodology, however, every disparate impact case would include a disparate treatment component. This cannot be the case. There is always some discrete event (refusal to rezone property, refusal to hire someone because he did not graduate from high school) which touches off litigation challenging a neutral rule or policy.

. . . .

Under disparate impact analysis, as other circuits have recognized, a prima facie case is established by showing that the challenged practice of the defendant "actually or predictably results in racial discrimination; in other words that it has a discriminatory effect." *United States v. City of Black Jack,* 508 F.2d 1179, 1184-85 (8th Cir. 1974). The plaintiff need not show that the decision complained of was made with discriminatory intent. *United States v. Yonkers Board of Education,* 837 F.2d 1181, 1217 (2d Cir. 1987); *Resident Advisory Board v. Rizzo,* 564 F.2d 126, 146-48 (3d Cir. 1977); *Smith v. Anchor Bldg. Corp.,* 536 F.2d 231, 233 (8th Cir. 1976) . . . . In determining whether discriminatory effect is sufficient, we look to congressional purpose, as gleaned from the legislative history of Title VIII, related Title VII jurisprudence, and practical concerns. Although none of these considerations is alone determinative, taken together they strongly suggest that discriminatory impact alone violates Title VIII.

The Act's stated purpose to end discrimination requires a discriminatory effect standard; an intent requirement would strip the statute of all impact on de facto segregation. Congress appears not to have resolved this precise question. Nonetheless, the legislative history provides some indication that an intent standard was not contemplated. The *Rizzo* court attached significance to the Senate's rejection of an amendment that would have required "proof of discriminatory intent to succeed in establishing a Title VIII claim." The amendment, however, was far less sweeping than *Rizzo* suggests because it applied only to a single-family owner-occupied house. Nevertheless, its rejection does underscore congressional willingness to broaden Title VIII to encompass segregation resulting from the application of facially neutral rules, even in the absence of discriminatory intent.

More persuasive is the parallel between Title VII and Title VIII . . . . The two statutes are part of a coordinated scheme of federal civil rights laws enacted to end discrimination; the Supreme Court has held that both statutes must be construed expansively to implement that goal. *See, e.g., Trafficante v. Metropolitan Life Ins. Co.,* 409 U.S. 205 (1972) (Fair Housing Act must be generously construed to foster integration); *Griggs v. Duke Power Co.,* 401 U.S. 424 (1971) (Title VII should be interpreted broadly to achieve equal employment opportunity) . . . . [T]he two statutes require similar proof to establish a violation. Thus, just as the Supreme Court held that Title VII is violated by a showing of discriminatory effect [in] *Griggs,* we hold that a Title VIII violation can be established without proof of discriminatory intent.

Practical concerns also militate against inclusion of intent in any disparate impact analysis . . . . [C]lever men may easily conceal their motivations. . . . . This is especially persuasive in disparate impact cases where a facially neutral rule is being challenged. Often, such rules bear no relation to discrimination upon passage, but develop into powerful discriminatory mechanisms when applied. Second, inclusion of intent undermines the trial judge's inquiry into the impact of an action. The lower court's insistence on probing the "pretextual" nature of appellees' justifications vividly demonstrates the extent to which an intent-based standard can infect an analysis and draw it away from its proper focus. Accordingly, we will not require proof of discriminatory intent to establish a prima facie disparate impact case under Title VIII.

Confusion concerning the content of a prima facie disparate impact case under Title VIII has been engendered by the tendency of some courts to consider factors normally advanced as part of a defendant's justification for its challenged action in assessing whether the plaintiff has established a prima facie case. . . . . Though . . . we are not persuaded to adopt precisely the formulation of the *Arlington Heights* factors, we agree with the Third Circuit that factors such as those mentioned in *Arlington Heights* are to be considered in a final determination on the merits rather than as a requirement for a prima facie case. *See* Rizzo, 564 F.2d at 148 n. 32. Nothing in *Arlington Heights* indicates the court saw its test as anything but a final determination on the merits. Furthermore, treating the four factors as steps necessary to make out a prima facie case places too onerous a burden on appellants. The legislative history of the Fair Housing Act, although sparse, argues persuasively against so daunting a prima facie standard.

. . . .

Once a prima facie case of adverse impact is presented, as occurred here, the inquiry turns to the standard to be applied in determining whether the defendant can nonetheless avoid liability under Title VIII. The Third Circuit in *Rizzo* and the Seventh Circuit in *Arlington Heights* have both made useful contributions to this inquiry. Both circuits essentially recognize that in the end there must be a weighing of the adverse impact against the defendant's justification. As phrased by the Third Circuit [in *Rizzo*], the defendant must prove that its actions furthered, in theory and in practice, a legitimate, bona fide governmental interest and that no alternative would serve that interest with less discriminatory effect. . . . . The Seventh Circuit adds two other factors that can affect the ultimate determination on the merits. One factor is whether there is any evidence of discriminatory intent on the part of the defendant. Though we have ruled that such intent is not a requirement of the plaintiff's prima facie case, there can be little doubt that if evidence of such intent is presented, that evidence would weigh heavily on the plaintiff's side of the ultimate balance. The other factor is whether the plaintiff is suing to compel a governmental defendant to build housing or only to require a governmental defendant to eliminate some obstacle to housing that the plaintiff itself will build. In the latter circumstance, a defendant would normally have to establish a somewhat more substantial justification for its adverse action than would be required if the defendant were defending its decision not to build.

In this case, we are obliged to refine the standard for assessing a Title VIII defendant's justification somewhat beyond what was said in either *Rizzo* or *Arlington Heights*. In *Rizzo*, two of the defendants offered no justification for the adverse decision, and the municipal defendant offered only the entirely unacceptable apprehension of violence. The Third Circuit therefore did not have anything of substance to weigh on the defendants' side. In *Arlington Heights*, the consideration of the defendant's justification scarcely moved past inquiring whether the municipal defendant was acting within the scope of zoning authority granted by state law.

In considering the defendant's justification, we start with the framework of Title VII analysis. When an employer's facially neutral rule is shown to have a racially disproportionate effect on job applicants, that rule must be shown to be substantially related to job performance. In a zoning case, . . . however, . . . there is no single objective like job performance to which the legitimacy of the facially neutral rule may be related. A town's preference to maintain a particular zoning category for particular sections of the community is normally based on a variety of circumstances. The complexity of the considerations, however, does not relieve a court of the obligation to assess whatever justifications the town advances and weigh them carefully against the degree of adverse effect the plaintiff has shown. Though a town's interests in zoning requirements are substantial, they cannot, consistently with Title VIII, automatically outweigh significant disparate effects.

. . . With these principles in mind, we review Judge Glasser's findings in two areas: the strength of the discriminatory effect and the import of the Town's justifications.

The discriminatory effect of a rule arises in two contexts: adverse impact on a particular minority group and harm to the community generally by the perpetuation of segregation. In analyzing Huntington's restrictive zoning, however, the lower court concentrated on the harm to Blacks as a group, and failed to consider the segregative effect of maintaining a zoning ordinance that restricts private multi-family housing to an area with a high minority concentration. Yet, recognizing this second form of effect advances the principal purpose of Title VIII to promote, "open, integrated residential housing patterns." Otero v. New York Housing Authority, 484 F.2d 1122, 1134 (2d Cir. 1973).

Seventy percent of Huntington's black population reside in Huntington Station and South Greenlawn. Matinecock Court, with its goal of 25% minorities, would begin desegregating a neighborhood which is currently 98% white. Indeed, the district court found that a "significant percentage of the tenants" at Matinecock Court would belong to minority groups. The court, however, failed to take the logical next step and find that the refusal to permit projects outside the urban renewal area with its high concentration of minorities reinforced racial segregation in housing. This was erroneous. Similarly, the district court found that the Town has a shortage of rental housing affordable for low and moderate-income households, that a "disproportionately" large percentage of the households using subsidized rental units are minority citizens, and that a disproportionately large number of minorities are on the waiting lists for subsidized housing and existing Section 8 certificates. But it failed to recognize that Huntington's zoning ordinance, which restricts private construction of multi-family housing to the largely minority urban renewal area, impedes integration by restricting low-income housing needed by minorities to an area already 52% minority. We thus find that Huntington's refusal to amend the restrictive zoning ordinance to permit privately-built multi-family housing outside the urban renewal area significantly perpetuated segregation in the Town.

On the question of harm to blacks as a group, the district court emphasized that 22,160 whites and 3,671 minorities had incomes below 200% of the poverty line, a cutoff close to the Huntington Housing Authority's qualification standards. Thus, the district court focussed on the greater absolute number of poor whites compared with indigent minorities in Huntington. The district court, however, did not analyze the disproportionate burden on minorities as required by *Griggs v. Duke Power Co.*, 401 U.S. 424 (1971). By relying on absolute numbers rather than on proportional statistics, the district court significantly underestimated the disproportionate impact of the Town's policy. Thus, the district court perceived facts through a misapprehension of the applicable law and we must make our own findings at least as to the significance of the undisputed underlying facts.

The parties have stipulated that 28% of minorities in Huntington and 11% of whites have incomes below 200% of the poverty line. What they dispute is the meaning of these statistics. Judge Glasser found that, as the Town contends, there is no showing of discriminatory effect because a majority of the victims are white. We disagree for reasons analogous to those the Supreme Court enumerated in *Griggs*. The disparity is of a magnitude similar to that in Griggs, where the Court found discriminatory an employer's policy of hiring only high school graduates because 12% of black males in North Carolina had high school diplomas while 34% of white males were high school graduates. But the plaintiffs presented even stronger evidence reflecting the disparate impact of preventing the project from proceeding. Under the Huntington HAP for 1982-1985, 7% of all Huntington families needed subsidized housing, while 24% of the black families needed such housing. In addition, minorities constitute a far greater percentage of those currently occupying subsidized rental projects compared to their percentage in the Town's population. Similarly, a disproportionately high percentage (60%) of families holding Section 8 certificates from the Housing Authority to supplement their rents are minorities, and an equally disproportionate percentage (61%) of those on the waiting list for such certificates are minorities. Therefore, we conclude that the failure to rezone the Matinecock Court site had a substantial adverse impact on minorities.

In sum, we find that the disproportionate harm to Blacks and the segregative impact on the entire community resulting from the refusal to rezone create a strong prima facie showing of discriminatory effect—far more than the *Rizzo* test would require. Thus, we must consider the Town's asserted justifications.

. . . .

The *Rizzo* approach has two components: (1) whether the reasons are bona fide and legitimate; and (2) whether any less discriminatory alternative can serve those ends. For analytical ease, the second prong should be considered first. Concerns can usually be divided between "plan-specific" justifications and those which are "site-specific." "Plan-specific" problems can be resolved by the less discriminatory alternative of requiring reasonable design modifications. "Site-specific" justifications, however, would usually survive this prong of the test. Those remaining reasons are then scrutinized to determine if they are legitimate and bona fide. By that, we do not intend to devise a search for pretext. Rather, the inquiry is whether the proffered justification is of substantial concern such that it would justify a reasonable official in making this determination. Of course, a concern may be non-frivolous, but may not be sufficient because it is not reflected in the record.

Appellants challenge both the ordinance which restricts privately-built multi-family housing to the urban renewal area and the Town Board's decision to refuse to rezone the Elwood-Pulaski site. All the parties and the district court judge, however, focussed on the latter issue. Indeed, appellees below simply relied on the existence of the Housing Assistance Plan and the zoning ordinance and failed to present any substantial evidence indicating a significant interest in limiting private developers to the urban renewal area. On appeal, appellees now contend that the ordinance is designed to encourage private developers to build in the deteriorated area of Huntington Station. Although we believe that the Town's failure to raise this argument below precludes its consideration here, we briefly address this contention. The Town asserts that limiting multi-family development to the urban renewal area will encourage restoration of the neighborhood because, otherwise, developers will choose to build in the outlying areas and will bypass the zone. The Town's goal, however, can be achieved by less discriminatory means, by encouraging development in the urban renewal area with tax incentives or abatements. The Town may assert that this is less effective, but it may actually be more so.

Developers are not wed to building in Huntington; they are filling a perceived economic void. Developments inside the urban renewal area and outside it are not fungible. Rather, developers prevented from building outside the urban renewal area will more likely build in another town, not the urban renewal area. Huntington incorrectly assumes that developers limit their area of interest by political subdivision. In fact, the decision where to build is much more complex. Hence, if the Town wishes to encourage growth in the urban renewal area, it should do so directly through incentives which would have a less discriminatory impact on the Town.

We turn next to the Town's reasons rejecting the Elwood-Pulaski site. The 1980 letter written by Town Supervisor Butterfield detailed seven justifications for the Town's refusal to rezone:

(1) inconsistency with the Town's Housing Assistance Plan; (2) inconsistency with zoning; (3) traffic considerations; (4) parking and fire protection problems; (5) proximity to the railroad and Long Island Lighting Company substation; (6) inadequate recreation and play areas; and (7) undersized and unrealistic units. As the judge below noted, the first two beg the question because appellants are challenging the Town's zoning ordinance. More significantly, as we have already indicated, the Town simply relied on the existence of the Housing Assistance Plan and the zoning ordinance and failed to present any substantial evidence indicating why precluding plaintiff from building a multi-family housing project outside the urban renewal area would impair significant interests sought to be advanced by the HAP and the ordinance. The fourth, sixth and seventh problems are "plan-specific" issues which could presumably have been solved with reasonable design modifications at the time appellants applied for rezoning of the parcel. The fifth concern also is largely plan-specific because proper landscaping could shield the project from the railroad and substation.

Thus, only the traffic issue and health hazard from the substation are site-specific. At trial, however, none of Huntington's officials supported these objections. Butterfield, for example, was primarily concerned that the Matinecock Court project would "torpedo" the Town's plan to develop the site at Broadway and New York Avenue in the urban renewal area in Huntington Station. (Testimony of Kenneth C. Butterfield, JA-1752.) Moreover, Huntington's only expert, planner David Portman, set forth entirely different problems than were contained in Butterfield's letters. Specifically, he noted sewage concerns, lack of conformity with the low density of the surrounding neighborhood, and inaccessibility of the site to public transportation (Testimony of David J. Portman, JA-1508-11.) Once during his testimony, he did mention "the relationship [of the site] to the power station." (JA-1511) Never, however, did he raise any concern about a health hazard from the proximity to the substation. Indeed, appellees do not broach this issue in their brief to this court. Accordingly, we find the reasons asserted are entirely insubstantial.

The sewage problem was first raised at trial by appellees' expert Portman. Appellees now advance it as an additional concern. The district court, however, chose not to consider it. We agree. Post hoc rationalizations by administrative agencies should be afforded "little deference" by the courts, and therefore cannot be a bona fide reason for the Town's action. Moreover, the sewage concern could hardly have been significant if municipal officials only thought of it after the litigation began. If it did not impress itself on the Town Board at the time of rejection, it was obviously not a legitimate problem. In sum, the only factor in the Town's favor was that it was acting within the scope of its zoning authority, and thus we conclude that the Town's justifications were weak and inadequate.

In balancing the showing of discriminatory effect against the import of the Town's justifications, we note our agreement with the Seventh Circuit that the balance should be more readily struck in favor of the plaintiff when it is seeking only to enjoin a municipal defendant from interfering with its own plans rather than attempting to compel the defendant itself to build housing. . . . . Bearing in mind that the plaintiffs in this case seek only the freedom to build their own project, we conclude that the strong showing of discriminatory effect resulting from the Town's adherence to its R-3M zoning category and its refusal to rezone the Matinecock Court site far outweigh the Town's weak justifications. Accordingly, to recapitulate, we find that the Town violated Title VIII by refusing to amend the zoning ordinance to permit private developers to build multi-family dwellings outside the urban renewal area. We also find that the Town violated Title VIII by refusing to rezone the Matinecock Court site. We thus reverse the district court and direct entry of judgment in appellants' favor.

Appellees argue that we should deny site-specific relief because there are 64 "community development" sites available for low-cost multi-family housing in Huntington. . . . . Ordinarily, HHI would not be automatically entitled to construct its project at its preferred site. The Town might well have legitimate reasons for preferring some alternative site to the one preferred by HHI. On the other hand, the Town would not be permitted to select a site that suits the Town's preference if that site imposed undue hardships on the applicant, such as distance from public transportation or other services. Thus, we would ordinarily remand this case to the district court to afford the appellees an opportunity to identify an alternative site, outside the urban renewal area, that would be appropriate for HHI's project and eligible for the same financial arrangements and assistance available at the Matinecock Court site. If the Town identified such a site, it would then have the burden of persuading the district court that there were substantial reasons for using its preferred site and that those reasons did not impose undue hardships on the appellants. If the district court was not persuaded on balance of the benefits of an alternative site, it would then enter an appropriate judgment to enable HHI to proceed with its project at the Matinecock Court site.

This case, however, is not ordinary. First, we recognize the protracted nature of this litigation, which has spanned over seven years. Further delay might well prove fatal to this private developer's plans. Second, . . . the Town has demonstrated little good faith in assisting the development of low-income housing. After the Town began receiving federal community development funds, HUD found it necessary to pressure the Town continually to include commitments for construction of subsidized family housing in the Town's HAPs. Because of the Town's lack of progress in constructing such housing, HUD imposed special conditions on the Town's community development grants for the 1978 fiscal allocation. Thereafter, HUD continued to express its dissatisfaction with the Town's performance. This history, while it does not rise to a showing of discriminatory intent, clearly demonstrates a pattern of stalling efforts to build low-income housing.

. . . We therefore refuse to remand this case to the district court to determine the suitability of . . . sites outside the urban renewal area. Rather, we find that site-specific relief is appropriate in this case.

Accordingly, we direct the district court to include in its judgment provision ordering the Town to rezone the 14.8 acre Matinecock Court site located at the corner of Elwood and Pulaski Roads in Huntington Township to R-3M status. The judgment should also order the Town to strike from its R-3M zoning ordinance that portion which limits private multi-family housing projects to the urban renewal area.

[c]   A Problem

Racial Steering Plans. Suppose the Mayor of a community, in cooperation with local citizen groups and real estate agents, establishes a "voluntary" plan to avoid a speedy changeover of the community from white to black. The plan involves overt racial "steering" in which the citizen groups and real estate agents select a house for a prospective buyer or renter based on the racial composition of the neighborhood and block. If a particular block is mostly or all white, a black client will be steered to an available residence there; if a block is mostly or all black, a white family will be steered there. Part of the plan calls for the cooperating real estate agents to place advertisements in all local newspapers and in selected papers around the country "bragging" about the plan and urging persons interested in living in an integrated community to move to the area.

Finally, as part of the plan, the Mayor convinces the City Council to adopt an ordinance providing up to $10,000 in grants per real estate company, for use by cooperating companies in placing such "bragging" advertisements. Are any parts of this plan invalid, either under the Constitution or federal statutes? Note that the First Amendment may place limits on the ability to restrict speech on signs in front of houses. In *Linmark Associates v. Willingboro,* 431 U.S. 85 (1977), the Supreme Court invalidated an ordinance adopted by a town not experiencing massive white flight to the suburbs that totally banned all residential for sale signs anywhere in the community.

[d]　State Level Public Policy Constraints on Zoning

To this day, many suburban jurisdictions zone only for single family residences or light, non-polluting, industries. During the 1960s, the leadership of major civil rights groups, including the National Association for the Advancement of Colored People, the Urban League, and the National Committee Against Discrimination in Housing, noted with dismay that use of such zoning strategies left major inner cities with the task of handling the bulk of lower and lower middle class housing demand at the very time that service and other job opportunities were expanding in suburban communities. New Jersey, Pennsylvania and New York became the focus of litigation challenging, under state rather than federal standards, the legality of light industry-single family residence zoning plans.

In what has come to be called "Mt. Laurel" litigation, challenges were brought against such zoning schemes in a significant number of states. The plaintiffs based their cases on general clauses in either the state zoning enabling act or the state constitution requiring that state actions be taken for the "general welfare" of the people. The "Mt. Laurel" tag refers to the massive series of cases that worked their way through the New Jersey court system in the 1970s and 1980s.[145] The sheer bulk of the opinions makes them impossible to use in a textbook such as this.[146] But for anyone interested in the policy issues at stake in this area, they are must reading.

---

[145] The first opinion appeared in 1972, and was followed by a series of massive outpourings of judicial prose. Southern Burlington County N.A.A.C.P. v. Township of Mt. Laurel, 119 N.J. Super. 164, 290 A.2d 465 (1972); Southern Burlington County N.A.A.C.P. v. Township of Mt. Laurel, 67 N.J. 151, 336 A.2d 713 (1975); Southern Burlington County N.A.A.C.P. v. Township of Mt. Laurel, 92 N.J. 158, 456 A.2d 390 (1983).

[146] A sense of the scale of the litigation is provided by the following description of the oral arguments before the New Jersey Supreme Court in 1980: The actual opinion in the case was not issued until three years later and went on for hundreds of pages.

The October [1980] argument was as much a landmark in the annals of American legal process as the subsequent decision itself. Because individual presentations by all the parties would have been hopelessly unwieldy (four pages were required to list the attorney appearances in the final opinion), the parties were required by the court to form themselves into interest groups (towns, developers, and poor people) and only one attorney was permitted to speak, for the entire group, to any given portion of the twenty-four questions [under review]. A formal outline of the program, with designated speakers and time limitations, was presented to each visitor upon arrival, as at the opera. Under the ground rules announced by the Chief Justice, each speaker was bound to address the general question, rather than to advocate the facts or the law of his or her client's individual position.

The "argument" itself was as extraordinary as its setting. Because virtually all the lawyers involved were intimately familiar with the actual process of housing development, their arguments had the feel of testimony at a legislative hearing, rather than appellate advocacy. The members of the court in turn slipped readily into the role of legislators, peppering the speakers with well informed questions to elicit facts (seldom law) about housing economics and the mechanics of land development. One of the twenty-four questions, for instance, asked that the parties discuss the applicability of the "trickle down" theory of housing supply, hardly a typical subject of courtroom debate. John Payne, *From the Courts: Starting Over*—Mount Laurel II, 12 REAL EST. L.J. 85, 88 (1983). Reprinted by permission of Warren, Gorham & Lamont Inc. and John M. Payne. Copyright 1983. Warren, Gorham & Lamont Inc., 20 South Street, Boston, MA 02111. All Rights Reserved.

Vastly over simplifying what the New Jersey Courts did, every community in the state was required to absorb its fair share of least cost housing, remove building code and zoning requirements that barred or imposed unnecessary costs on the construction of least cost or prefabricated housing, and welcome proposals for the construction of subsidized residential complexes. After a great deal of controversy, the state legislature moved certain aspects of the planning and zoning process to the state level, adopted regulations for determining fair shares and established administrative methods for resolving disputes over compliance with fair share obligations.

While the New Jersey litigation is by far the most comprehensive, a number of other state courts have rendered decisions requiring local communities to alter their land use plans to accommodate least cost housing.[147] One of the more recent pieces of "Mt. Laurel" litigation resulted in the next opinion in the text. For more on exclusionary zoning in the state courts, *see* ROGER A. CUNNINGHAM, WILLIAM B. STOEBUCK & DALE A. WHITMAN, THE LAW OF PROPERTY 587-594 (2d ed. 1993).

[e]   Opinion of the New Hampshire Supreme Court in *Britton v. Town of Chester*

Wayne Britton, et al. v. Town of Chester

Supreme Court of New Hampshire
134 N.H. 434, 595 A.2d (1991)

New Hampshire Legal Assistance (Elliott Berry, on brief and orally, and Thomas Fredenburg on the brief), for plaintiff Wayne Britton and plaintiff class of low-and moderate-income plaintiffs.

Craig and Wenners P.A., Manchester (James W. Craig on the brief, and William H. Craig orally), for plaintiff Raymond Remillard.

Grinnell & Bureau, Derry (David R. Connell on the brief and orally), for defendant.

McSwiney, Jones, Semple, Bowers & Wise P.C., Concord (James B. Kazan on the brief), by brief for New Hampshire Housing Finance Authority, as amicus curiae.

Gallagher, Callahan & Gartrell P.A., Concord (Robert J. Finn on the brief), by brief for the Home Builders Ass'n of New Hampshire, as amicus curiae.

Donahue, McCaffrey & Tucker, Exeter (Charles F. Tucker on the brief), by brief for American Planning Ass'n, as amicus curiae.

H. Bernard Waugh, Jr., Legal Counsel, New Hampshire Mun. Ass'n, by brief for Association, as amicus curiae.

BATCHELDER, Justice.

In this appeal, the defendant, the Town of Chester (the town), challenges a ruling by the Master (*R. Peter Shapiro,* Esq.), approved by the Superior Court (*Gray,* J.), that the Chester Zoning

---

[147] The initial strategies to raise "Mt. Laurel" challenges focussed on New Jersey, New York and Pennsylvania. The latter two states also issued well known opinions conforming to the general tone of the New Jersey results. National Land & Investment Co. v. Kohn, 419 Pa. 504, 215 A.2d 597 (1965); In re Girsh, 437 Pa. 237, 263 A.2d 395 (1970); Appeal of Kit-Mar Builders, Inc., 439 Pa. 466, 268 A.2d 765 (1970); Township of Williston v. Chesterdale Farms, 462 Pa. 445, 341 A.2d 466 (1975); Surrick v. Zoning Hearing Bd., 476 Pa. 182, 382 A.2d 105 (1977); Berenson v. Town of New Castle, 38 N.Y.2d 102, 341 N.E.2d 236, 378 N.Y.S.2d 672 (1975). For a summary of the results around the nation, *see* § 79.07 in POWELL ON REAL PROPERTY (Matthew Bender).

Ordinance is invalid and unconstitutional. In addition, the town argues that the relief granted to plaintiff Remillard, permitting him to construct multi-family housing on a parcel not currently zoned for such development, violates the separation of powers provision of the New Hampshire Constitution, *N.H. CONST.* pt. I, art. 37, and creates an unreasonable use for this parcel. We modify the trial court's ruling that the ordinance as a whole is invalid, but we affirm the granting of specific relief to plaintiff Remillard as well as the court's ruling that the ordinance, on the facts of this case, is unlawful as applied.

The plaintiffs brought a petition in 1985, for declaratory and injunctive relief, challenging the validity of the multi-family housing provisions of the Chester Zoning Ordinance. The master's report, filed after a hearing, contains extensive factual findings which we summarize here. The town of Chester lies in the west-central portion of Rockingham County, thirteen miles east of the city of Manchester. Primary highway access is provided by New Hampshire Routes 102 and 121. The available housing stock is principally single-family homes. There is no municipal sewer or water service, and other municipal services remain modest. The town has not encouraged industrial or commercial development; it is a "bedroom community," with the majority of its labor force commuting to Manchester. Because of its close proximity to job centers and the ready availability of vacant land, the town is projected to have among the highest growth rates in New Hampshire over the next two decades.

The United States Department of Housing and Urban Development, having settled upon the median income for non-metropolitan Rockingham County as a yardstick, has determined that a low-income family in Chester is a household with annual earnings of $16,500 or less, and a moderate-income family has annual earnings of $16,501 to $25,680. Various federal and State government agencies have also determined that low-and moderate-income families should not pay in excess of 30% of their gross income for rent. Thus, a low-income family in Chester should pay less than $4,950 annually, and a moderate-income family in Chester should pay between $4,951 and $7,704 annually, for housing.

The plaintiffs in this case are a group of low -and moderate-income people who have been unsuccessful in finding affordable, adequate housing in the town, and a builder who, the master found, is committed to the construction of such housing. At trial, two plaintiffs testified as representative members of the group of low-and moderate-income people. Plaintiff George Edwards is a woodcutter who grew up in the town. He lives in Chester with his wife and three minor children in a one-bedroom, thirty-foot by eight-foot camper trailer with no running water. Their annual income is $14,040, which places them in the low-income category. Roger McFarland grew up and works in the town. He lives in Derry with his wife and three teenage children in a two-bedroom apartment which is too small to meet their needs. He and his wife both work, and their combined annual income is $24,000. Under the area standards, the McFarlands are a moderate-income family. Raymond Remillard is the plaintiff home builder. A long-time resident of the town, he owns an undeveloped twenty-three-acre parcel of land on Route 102 in the town's eastern section. Since 1979, he has attempted to obtain permission from the town to build a moderate-sized multi-family housing development on his land.

The zoning ordinance in effect at the beginning of this action in 1985 provided for a single-family home on a two-acre lot or a duplex on a three-acre lot, and it excluded multi-family housing from all five zoning districts in the town. In July, 1986, the town amended its zoning ordinance to allow multi-family housing. Article six of the amended ordinance now permits multi-family housing as part of a "planned residential development" (PRD), a form of multi-family housing required to include a variety of housing types, such as single-family homes, duplexes, and multi-family structures.

After a hearing, the master recommended that judgment be ordered for the plaintiffs; that the town's land use ordinances, including the zoning ordinance, be ruled invalid; and that plaintiff Remillard be awarded a "builder's remedy." . . .

We first turn to the ordinance itself, because it does, on its face, permit the type of development that the plaintiffs argue is being prohibited. The master found, however, that the ordinance placed an unreasonable barrier to the development of affordable housing for low-and moderate-income families. Under the ordinance, PRDs are allowed on tracts of not less than twenty acres in two designated "R-2" (medium-density residential) zoning districts. Due to existing home construction and environmental considerations, such as wetlands and steep slopes, only slightly more than half of all the land in the two R-2 districts could reasonably be used for multi-family development. This constitutes only 1.73% of the land in the town. This fact standing alone does not, in the confines of this case, give rise to an entitlement to a legal remedy for those who seek to provide multi-family housing. However, it does serve to point out that the two R-2 districts are, in reality, less likely to be developed than would appear from a reading of the ordinance. A reviewing court must read the entire ordinance in the light of these facts.

Article six of the ordinance also imposes several subjective requirements and restrictions on the developer of a PRD. Any project must first receive the approval of the town planning board as to "whether in its judgment the proposal meets the objectives and purposes set forth [in the ordinance] in which event the Administrator [i.e., the planning board] may grant approval to [the] proposal subject to reasonable conditions and limitations." Consequently, the ordinance allows the planning board to control various aspects of a PRD without reference to any objective criteria. One potentially onerous section permits the planning board to "retain, at the applicant's expense, a registered professional engineer, hydrologist, and any other applicable professional to represent the [planning board] and assist the [planning board] in determining compliance with [the] ordinance and other applicable regulations." The master found such subjective review for developing multi-family housing to be a substantial disincentive to the creation of such units, because it would escalate the economic risks of developing affordable housing to the point where these projects would not be realistically feasible. In addition, we question the availability of bank financing for such projects, where the developer is required to submit a "blank check" to the planning board along with his proposal, and where to do so could halt, change the character of, or even bankrupt the project.

The defendant first argues that the trial court erred in ruling that the zoning ordinance exceeds the powers delegated to the town by the zoning enabling legislation, RSA 674:16-30. In support of this argument, the town asserts that the zoning enabling act does not require it to zone for the low-income housing needs of the region beyond its boundaries. Further, the town maintains that even if it were required to consider regional housing needs when enacting its zoning ordinance, the Chester Zoning Ordinance is valid because it provides for an adequate range of housing types. These arguments fail to persuade us of any error in the master's proposed order.

RSA 674:16 authorizes the local legislative body of any city or town to adopt or amend a zoning ordinance "[f]or the purpose of promoting the health, safety, *or the general welfare of the community*." (Emphasis added.) The defendant asserts that the term "community" as used in the statute refers only to the municipality itself and not to some broader region in which the municipality is situated. We disagree.

The possibility that a municipality might be obligated to consider the needs of the region outside its boundaries was addressed early on in our land use jurisprudence by the United States Supreme Court, paving the way for the term "community" to be used in the broader sense. In *Village of Euclid v. Ambler Realty Co.*, 272 U.S. 365 (1926), the Court recognized "the possibility of cases where the general public interest would so far outweigh the interest of the municipality that the municipality would not be allowed to stand in the way." When an ordinance will have an impact beyond the boundaries of the municipality, the welfare of the entire affected region must be considered in determining the ordinance's validity. *Associated Home Builders v. City of Livermore*, 18 Cal. 3d 582, 557 P.2d 473, 487 (1976); *see also Berenson v. Town of New Castle*, 38 N.Y.2d 102, 110-11 341 N.E.2d 236, 242-43 (1975).

We have previously addressed the issue of whether municipalities are required to consider regional needs when enacting zoning ordinances which control growth. In *Beck v. Town of Raymond*, 118 N.H. 793, 394 A.2d 847 (1978), we held that "[growth] controls must not be imposed simply to exclude outsiders, *see Steel Hill Dev. v. Town of Sanbornton*, [469 F.2d 956 (1st Cir. 1972)]; *Nat'l Land and Inv. Co. v. Kohn*, 419 Pa. 504, 215 A.2d 597 (1965), especially outsiders of any disadvantaged social or economic group, *see S. Burlington County N.A.A.C.P. v. Township of Mount Laurel*, 67 N.J. 151, 336 A.2d 713 (1975)." We reasoned that "each municipality [should] bear its fair share of the burden of increased growth." Today, we pursue the logical extension of the reasoning in *Beck* and apply its rationale and high purpose to zoning regulations which wrongfully exclude persons of low- or moderate-income from the zoning municipality.

In *Beck*, this court sent a message to zoning bodies that "[t]owns may not refuse to confront the future by building a moat around themselves and pulling up the drawbridge." The town of Chester appears willing to lower that bridge only for people who can afford a single-family home on a two-acre lot or a duplex on a three-acre lot. Others are realistically prohibited from crossing.

Municipalities are not isolated enclaves, far removed from the concerns of the area in which they are situated. As subdivisions of the State, they do not exist solely to serve their own residents, and their regulations should promote the general welfare, both within and without their boundaries. Therefore, we interpret the general welfare provision of the zoning enabling statute, RSA 674:16, to include the welfare of the "community," as defined in this case, in which a municipality is located and of which it forms a part.

A municipality's power to zone property to promote the health, safety, and general welfare of the community is delegated to it by the State, and the municipality must, therefore, exercise this power in conformance with the enabling legislation. Because the Chester Zoning Ordinance does not provide for the lawful needs of the community, in that it flies in the face of the general welfare provision of RSA 674:16 and is, therefore, at odds with the statute upon which it is grounded, we hold that, as applied to the facts of this case, the ordinance is an invalid exercise of the power delegated to the town pursuant to RSA 674:16-30. We so hold because of the master's finding that "there are no substantial and compelling reasons that would warrant the Town of Chester, through its land use ordinances, from fulfilling its obligation to provide low[-] and moderate[-]income families within the community and a proportionate share of same within its region from a realistic opportunity to obtain affordable housing."

. . . .

The trial court's order declared the Chester Zoning Ordinance invalid and unconstitutional; as a result, but for this appeal, the town has been left "unzoned." To leave the town with no land use controls would be incompatible with the orderly development of the general community, and the court erred when it ruled the ordinance invalid. It is not, however, within the power of this court to act as a super zoning board. "Zoning is properly a legislative function, and courts are prevented by the doctrine of separation of powers from invasion of this field." *Godfrey v. Zoning Bd. of Adjustment,* 317 N.C. 51, 58, 344 S.E.2d 272, 276 (1986). Moreover, our decision today is limited to those sections of the zoning ordinance which hinder the construction of multi-family housing units. Accordingly, we defer to the legislative body of the town, within a reasonable time period, to bring these sections of its zoning ordinance into line with the zoning enabling legislation and with this opinion. Consequently, we will temporarily allow the zoning ordinance to remain in effect.

As to the specific relief granted to plaintiff Remillard, the town contends that the court's order effectively rezones the parcel in violation of the separation of powers provision found in part I, article 37 of the New Hampshire Constitution. It further asserts that, even if it were lawful for a court to rezone or grant specific relief, plaintiff Remillard's proposed development does not qualify for such a remedy.

The master found that the requirement that multi-family housing may be built only as part of a PRD containing a variety of housing types violated plaintiff Remillard's rights under the equal protection clause of the New Hampshire Constitution, part I, article 2. The master also found that plaintiff Remillard was "unalterably committed to develop [his] tract to accommodate low[-] and moderate[-]income families." Accordingly, he granted specific relief to plaintiff Remillard, ordering that the town allow him to build his development as proposed.

The trial court has the power, subject to our review for abuse of discretion, to order definitive relief for plaintiff Remillard. In *Soares v. Town of Atkinson,* 129 N.H. 313, 529 A.2d 867 (1987), we upheld the master's finding that granting a "builder's remedy," i.e., allowing the plaintiff builder to complete his project as proposed, is discretionary. Although we there upheld the decision that such relief was inappropriate, noting that the master determined that the ordered revision of the town ordinances would permit the building of the plaintiff's project, we did not reject such relief as a proper remedy in appropriate zoning cases. In this appeal, the master found such relief to be appropriate, and the town has not carried its burden on appeal to persuade us to the contrary. A successful plaintiff is entitled to relief which rewards his or her efforts in testing the legality of the ordinance and prevents retributive action by the municipality, such as correcting the illegality but taking pains to leave the plaintiff unbenefitted. The Pennsylvania Supreme Court reasoned in *Casey v. Zoning Board of Warwick Township,* 459 Pa. 219, 328 A.2d 464 (1974), that "[t]o forsake a challenger's reasonable development plans after all the time, effort and capital invested in such a challenge is grossly inequitable."

The master relied on *Southern Burlington County N.A.A.C.P. v. Township of Mount Laurel,* 92 N.J. 158, 456 A.2d 390 (1983), (*Mt. Laurel II*), in determining that plaintiff Remillard was entitled to build his development as proposed. In *Mount Laurel I*, the New Jersey Supreme Court held that the municipality's zoning ordinance violated the general welfare provision of its State Constitution by not affording a realistic opportunity for the construction of its "fair share" of the present and prospective regional need for low-and moderate-income housing. *So. Burlington Cty. N.A.A.C.P. v. Mt. Laurel Tp.,* 67 N.J. 151, 174, 336 A.2d 713, 724 (1975). *Mt. Laurel II* was a return to the New Jersey Supreme Court, eight years later, prompted by the realization that *Mt. Laurel I* had not resulted in realistic housing opportunities for low-and moderate-income people, but in "paper, process, witnesses, trials and appeals." The court noted that the "builder's remedy," which effectively grants a building permit to a plaintiff/developer, based on the development proposal, as long as other local regulations are followed, should be made more readily available to insure that low-and moderate-income housing is actually built.

Since 1979, plaintiff Remillard has attempted to obtain permission to build a moderate-sized multi-family housing development on his land in Chester. He is committed to setting aside a minimum of ten of the forty-eight units for low-and moderate-income tenants for twenty years. "Equity will not suffer a wrong without a remedy." 2 *Pomeroy's Equity Jurisprudence* § 423 (5th ed. 1941). Hence, we hold that the "builder's remedy" is appropriate in this case, both to compensate the developer who has invested substantial time and resources in pursuing this litigation, and as the most likely means of insuring that low-and moderate-income housing is actually built.

Although we determine that the "builder's remedy" is appropriate in this case, we do not adopt the *Mt. Laurel* analysis for determining whether such a remedy will be granted. Instead, we find the rule developed in *Sinclair Pipe Line Co. v. Richton Park,* 19 Ill. 2d 370, 167 N.E.2d 406 (1960), is the better rule as it eliminates the calculation of arbitrary mathematical quotas which *Mt. Laurel* requires. That rule is followed with some variation by the supreme courts of several other states, *see, e.g., Schwartz v. City of Flint,* 426 Mich. 295, 329, 395 N.W.2d 678, 692-93 (1986); *Union Oil Co. v. City of Worthington,* 62 Ohio St. 2d 263, 267, 405 N.E.2d 277, 280 (1980); *Casey v. Zoning Hearing Board of Warwick Township,* 459 Pa. 219, 328 A.2d 464 (1974); *City of Richmond v. Randall,* 215 Va. 506, 513, 211 S.E.2d 56, 62 (1975), and awards relief to the plaintiff builder if his development is found to be reasonable, i.e., providing a realistic opportunity for the construction of low-and moderate-income housing and consistent with sound zoning concepts and environmental concerns. Once an existing zoning ordinance is found invalid in whole or in part, whether on constitutional grounds or, as here, on grounds of statutory construction and application, the court may provide relief in the form of a declaration that the plaintiff builder's proposed use is reasonable, and the municipality may not interfere with it. The plaintiff must bear the burden of proving reasonable use by a preponderance of the evidence. Once the plaintiff's burden has been met, he will be permitted to proceed with the proposed development, provided he complies with all other applicable regulations.

The town's argument that the specific relief granted to plaintiff Remillard violates the separation of powers provision found in part I, article 37 of the New Hampshire Constitution, to the extent that the trial court exercised legislative power specifically delegated to the local zoning authority, is without merit. The rule we adopt today does not produce this result. . . . . This rule will permit the municipality to continue to control its own development, so long as it does so for the general welfare of the community. It will also accommodate the construction of low-and moderate-income housing that had been unlawfully excluded.

The town argues that plaintiff Remillard's proposed use of his property is not reasonable, and that the master erred in implicitly finding to the contrary, as it would be constructed atop a potential high-yield aquifer. During the hearing before the master, plaintiff Remillard's expert concluded that the proposed development would not adversely affect any aquifer, and the town's engineering expert agreed. The master made a specific finding that any wells, streams, and aquifers would be protected by the project as proposed. Because we determine that the master did not abuse his discretion or err as a matter of law, we uphold his finding with respect to the reasonableness of the proposed project.

The zoning ordinance evolved as an innovative means to counter the problems of uncontrolled growth. It was never conceived to be a device to facilitate the use of governmental power to prevent access to a municipality by "outsiders of any disadvantaged social or economic group." *Beck*, 118 N.H. at 801, 394 A.2d at 852. The town of Chester has adopted a zoning ordinance which is blatantly exclusionary. This court will not condone the town's conduct.

Affirmed in part and reversed in part.

All concurred.

[f] Explanatory Notes

[*i*] *Zoning Incentives and Exclusionary Land Use Policies.* While a desire to exclude certain sorts of persons provides one explanation for exclusionary zoning policies, economic incentives may have a similar impact. The New Jersey Supreme Court explained the phenomenon in *Mt. Laurel I*:

> There cannot be the slightest doubt that the reason for this course of conduct has been to keep down local taxes on *property* . . . and that the policy was carried out without regard for nonfiscal considerations with respect to *people,* either within or without its boundaries.
> . . . .
>
> This policy of land use regulation for a fiscal end derives from New Jersey's tax structure, which has imposed on local real estate most of the cost of municipal and county government and of the primary and secondary education of the municipality's children. The latter expense is much the largest, so, basically, the fewer the school children, the lower the tax rate. Sizable industrial and commercial ratables are eagerly sought and homes and the lots on which they are situated are required to be large enough, through minimum lot sizes and minimum floor areas, to have substantial value in order to produce greater tax revenues to meet school costs. Large families who cannot afford to buy large houses and must live in cheaper rental accommodations are definitely not wanted, so we find drastic bedroom restrictions for, or complete prohibition of, multifamily or other feasible housing for those of lesser income.
>
> This pattern of land use regulation has been adopted for the same purpose in developing municipality after developing municipality. Almost every one acts solely in its own selfish and parochial interest and in effect builds a wall around itself to keep out those people or entities not adding favorably to the tax base, despite the location of the municipality or the demand for varied kinds of housing.[148]

The fiscal pressure to zone in certain ways has also led those interested in broadening land use policy and increasing the funds available to urban school districts to challenge the legality of reliance on property taxes to fund education. The New Jersey Supreme Court was among the first to invalidate the state property tax system.[149] Other states have followed.[150] The fiscal motivations behind much of the nation's suburban zoning was one factor making race-based challenges to exclusionary zoning difficult to mount. Even if fiscal motivations create unfair

---

[148] Southern Burlington N.A.A.C.P. v. Township of Mt. Laurel, 67 N.J. 151, 170-171, 336 A.2d 713, 723 (1975).

[149] Robinson v. Cahill, 62 N.J. 473, 303 A.2d 273 (1973). The court relied on a clause in the state constitution guaranteeing every child a quality education. Twenty-seven years later the New Jersey Courts were finding fault with various parts of the legislative efforts to equalize educational tax burdens and expenditures in the state. Abbott v. Burke, 153 N.J. 480, 710 A.2d 450 (1998).

[150] By the end of 1997, 17 state court decisions invalidating some or all of their jurisdiction's property tax system had been rendered. And the pace seems to be accelerating with four of the decisions being rendered in 1997. James Martin, *North Carolina's Court Fails North Carolina's Children: Leandro v. State and the Case for Equal School Funding*, 33 WAKE FOREST L. REV. 745 (1998).

inequalities, they do not provide much evidence of intentional racial discrimination and make it easier to dilute the racial impact of zoning policy.

[*ii*]   *Inclusionary Zoning.* In the *Mt. Laurel* litigation, the New Jersey Supreme Court required communities to make use of some sort of inclusionary zoning technique to increase the likelihood that least cost housing would be constructed. Among the suggestions were programs granting incentives to developers for constructing low-cost houses or apartments, requiring that all developments of a certain size contain low-cost residences,[151] and zoning significant amounts of land for prefabricated and mobile housing units. All of these techniques (and others) are being used in various spots around the nation. For a recent summary, *see* Jennifer M. Morgan, *Zoning For All: Using Inclusionary Zoning Techniques to Promote Affordable Housing,* 44 EMORY L.J. 359 (1995).

In New Jersey, the onus of operating the fair share system has now been placed in a state agency, the Council on Affordable Housing. Under the terms of the Fair Housing Act establishing the agency, the Council has the power to establish fair share obligations, certify the compliance of local plans, and alter local plans not meeting state requirements. As part of the allocation of fair share obligations, the Council divided the state into six planning regions, established basic land use planning goals for each region and developed a fair share plan. Each locality is required to consider use of a series of inclusionary options listed in the Fair Housing Act:

(1) Rezoning for densities necessary to assure the economic viability of any inclusionary developments, either through mandatory set-asides or density bonuses, as may be necessary to meet all or part of the municipality's fair share;

(2) Determination of the total residential zoning necessary to assure that the municipality's fair share is achieved;

(3) Determination of measures that the municipality will take to assure that low and moderate income units remain affordable to low and moderate income households for an appropriate period of not less than six years;

(4) A plan for infrastructure expansion and rehabilitation if necessary to assure the achievement of the municipality's fair share of low and moderate income housing;

(5) Donation or use of municipally owned land or land condemned by the municipality for purposes of providing low and moderate income housing;

(6) Tax abatements for purposes of providing low and moderate income housing;

(7) Utilization of funds obtained from any State or federal subsidy toward the construction of low and moderate income housing; and

(8) Utilization of municipally generated funds toward the construction of low and moderate income housing.[152]

[g]   **Problem Notes**

[*i*]   *Decentralization of the Poor.* The benefits of "Mt. Laurel" litigation are presumed to lie in the decentralization of housing for the poor throughout populated areas in a state. The

---

[151] In Montgomery County, Maryland, just north of Washington, D.C., this sort of regulation has added 10,000 moderately priced housing units to the county's housing stock. Implementation of similar programs is being considered in a number of other areas. Jay Walljasper, *A Fair Share in Suburbia,* 268 THE NATION 15 (Jan. 25, 1999).

[152] N.J. STAT. ANN. § 52:27D-311.

common picture of run down, crime ridden, economically depressed inner cities convinced the New Jersey Supreme Court, as well as other state high courts, that it was both unfair and unwise to impose most of the problems of poor citizens upon the areas least able to deal with them. A somewhat different response, though perhaps motivated by the same basic desire to alleviate the distressed central cities, might have led to a vast increase in funding for urban areas rather than to the planned dispersal of their citizens in the suburbs. Are there political, cultural, economic or social reasons for preferring one remedy to the other?

[*ii*]   ***Taking Law and Inclusionary Zoning.*** Inclusionary zoning techniques now in use around the nation include over-zoning for lower income (and presumably high density) dwellings and set-aside plans. Presumably "over-zoned" land will be difficult to use once the needs of lower income people have been met. And, absent the infusion of federal, state or local subsidies, set-asides presumably require that prices for some units must rise if development is to be as profitable as it was before inclusionary zoning obligations were imposed. Does use of inclusionary zoning techniques raise any Taking Clause problems?

[*iii*]   ***Legislative and Judicial Roles.*** While the New Jersey Supreme Court sought legislative intervention to rid itself of *Mt. Laurel* litigation burdens, it also criticized the state legislature for doing nothing about the serious housing problems created by exclusionary zoning. Even if you think it generally inappropriate for courts to involve themselves in massive reform efforts, may they step in when legislative intervention seems highly unlikely? Compare *Mt. Laurel* litigation with other major judicially imposed reforms of recent history where legislative inaction was the rule, such as school integration and legislative reapportionment. When should courts step in and when should they refuse to act? How would the Realists react to "Mt. Laurel" litigation?

[*iv*]   ***Actual Construction of Low Income Housing.*** Is "Mt. Laurel" litigation likely to have an impact on the availability of housing for poor people? Housing subsidies have been among the federal programs most drastically curtailed in the recent past. Absent the infusion of subsidies for the construction and maintenance of below market rate housing, is housing for the poor unlikely to be built? Despite all the judicial rhetoric about fair shares of least cost housing, are the most fundamental policy questions about housing still in legislative hands?

CHAPTER 7

PROPERTY AND THE POST-WORLD WAR II ADMINISTRATIVE STATE

§ 7.01 Introduction

At this point in the text, it is worth pausing for a moment to speculate a bit about where you have been and what is to come. While there will be elements in some of the chapters to come that reach back to pre-World War II historical moments, much of the rest of the volume traces stories about property that have occurred in the last 50 years. Vast changes in landlord-tenant law occurred in the 1970s. Home sale transactions have become highly regulated and standardized. The growth of the administrative state after World War II, recent shifts in Constitutional jurisprudence and dramatic changes within your lifetimes in technology and the health sciences have led to new understandings about the relationships between process and property, the relevance of non-legal disciplines like economics, the meaning of the Takings Clause, and the nature of relationships between concepts of property and personal integrity.

Given the large shifts in our understanding about property, process, the relevance of non-legal disciplines, and the very nature of life itself, it would be highly unlikely that old jurisprudential movements like Formalism or Realism would continue to dominate legal discourse. Indeed, the post-World War II era brought a crisis in legal thinking that has not yet been resolved. Recall that a central tenet of Realist thought insisted that law in general and property law in particular was an instrument of political power. While that idea was quite successful in undermining Formalist claims that the good of society was best served by using government in a "neutral" fashion to affirm the validity of private contractual and property arrangements, it was not very successful in creating a new positive vision of the role of law in general or property in particular in society.

This difficulty was exacerbated by the nature of World War II and the political issues of the decade following the war. While the Realists were surely correct in teaching us that law represents an exercise of political authority, that sort of statement does nothing to legitimate exercise of any particular form of power. Observing that law is an instrument of authority does not tell us when use of one or another form of authority is justified. Fears about illegitimate use of power were rampant right after World War II. The Nazis, who consistently used the trappings of their legal system to justify their actions, were the worst nightmare for western legal theorists. Further concern about the relationships between law and legitimacy were raised by the rise of Communism to power in the Soviet Union, and by the challenges to "lawful" authority raised by the Civil Rights Movement that emerged in the 1950s.

In short, there was no post-war legal orthodoxy. Finding a new one has been quite difficult. Several candidates have emerged over the years. The Legal Process School, while in accord with the Realists that there could not be general agreement within the legal and political communities

527

on the goals of a system of law, sought to legitimate government decisions by allocating resolution of different sorts of problems to the system most likely to handle them fairly. The process of resolution, more than the actual outcomes, became the source of justification for the exercise of legal power.

Other patterns of analysis have also claimed our attention in recent decades. Some social science adherents, especially economists, have claimed an ability to systematically analyze the public welfare. Particular groups organized by gender, race, sexual orientation or wealth have asserted they have special spheres of understanding and knowledge that should be taken into account in the structuring of law. Critical Legal Studies has staked a claim to the Realist mantle. And new theories about community, privacy, and personal integrity have generated much interest in recent years. Describing recent modes of legal thought about property and analyzing their influence on legal developments is one of the tasks that will be worked on in the last half of this book.

This chapter begins by exploring some of the relationships between property, poverty, process and the role of the judiciary dealt with by the Legal Process School. The Due Process Clauses of the federal Constitution and similar clauses in state constitutions are the legal texts laying at the root of one wing of the debate. The federal Constitution contains two Due Process Clauses. The Fifth Amendment, binding Congress, provides that "No person shall . . . be deprived of life, liberty or property, without due process of law." And the Fourteenth Amendment states that "No state shall . . . deprive any person of life, liberty or property, without due process of law." We have already seen how these clauses became the repository for Formalist notions that the Constitution often barred the state from adopting regulations affecting contractual relationships and property ownership. These "substantive" due process decisions were widely castigated by the Realists. But their critiques did not leave the Due Process Clauses without content. The Legal Process Movement, imbued with the importance of process in a world lacking widespread agreement about the substantive content of "justice," laid the groundwork for reinvigoration of the procedural side of Due Process.

During the 1950s, a group of academics, mostly from Harvard,[1] met to figure out a post-realist agenda. They agreed with the Realists that there were no longer (if there ever were) a set of substantive legal principles that were widely shared by the entire culture. They, therefore, concluded that a new Formalist structure was not attainable. But they feared the possibility inherent in Realism that the exercise of law was no more than the mustering of raw political power. Seeing the outcome of such a system in Nazi Germany, they were unwilling to label a legal system as legitimate if it acted without any standards or guidance. The abuses of the McCarthy Era engendered similar concerns. Failing to find any coherent system of justice in substantive legal principles, they searched for appropriate institutional methods of settling disputes, looking in the structure of legal process for a way of legitimating law, for a way of justifying the use of legal power.

Starting from the idea that control of discretion was a central problem of the modern administrative state, they searched for the appropriate roles for judges, administrators and legislators. They ended up agreeing with the Realists that basic value choices ought to be made

---

[1] The two most prominent figures were Henry M. Hart and Albert M. Sacks, both professors at Harvard. They put together a set of materials called THE LEGAL PROCESS: BASIC PROBLEMS IN THE MAKING AND APPLICATION OF LAW (1958) which were distributed in duplicated format and used in classes all over the country. Indeed, they are still being used in some places.

by legislatures, not for "political" reasons (a charge they leveled at the Realists), but because legislatures are most competent at evaluating such large scale choices. Courts, they opined, are good places to resolve small disputes and to fill in the interstices left open by legislative action. Administrators might take on different roles, depending on their bureaucratic function, but the basic idea was the same—to look for general principles of Institutional Competence. In sum this idea came to be called the Principle of Institutional Settlement.

In one sense, Legal Process folks were clearly the descendants of the Realists. Like the Realists they did not believe that any single theory of the good existed that most people would ascribe to. And like the Realists, they bestowed a certain level of primacy on legislative action. Politics, or democracy, held the most sway in legislative halls. That, indeed, was the very reason they were institutionally competent to resolve questions of moral values or broad economic choice. But their preference for legislative action rested on somewhat different premises than those used by the Realists. The Realists claimed that judges were just as political as legislators and that courts, therefore, could not justify striking down legislation using rational, scientific principles. The Legal Process school was afraid of such a rationale. For if courts and legislatures were not really that different, there was no particular reason for anyone to imbue courts with the sense of respect necessary for long term support of their work. Instead they argued that legislatures were due respect as political bodies making value judgments and courts were due respect because they made fair minded, neutral adjudicative choices in individual cases.

I suspect these are ideas with which many of you may empathize. You may well have come to law school with a built-in sense that legislatures are messy, conflict ridden places where democracy rules, that courts are calm places where neutral arbiters dispense fairness, and that these images legitimate both institutions. They are doing what they are supposed to be doing.

As with Formalism and Realism, there is a part of many of us (all of us?) that finds these images useful in thinking about legal problems. But there are obvious problems with Legal Process theory. One of them appeared in *Euclid v. Ambler*, the object of much attention in Chapter 6. It is easy to see how the *Euclid* Court used the common feeling that politically driven legislatures are the proper location to resolve large public policy issues about urbanization and that neutral courts are best designed to resolve factually intense face-to-face disputes over the fairness of zoning rules as applied to particular parcels of land. But when you recognize that zoning decisions in one place have impacts in other places, some of the core values of the Legal Process School come under stress. Even assuming that we can tell the difference between adjudication and legislation often enough to make viable decisions about institutional competence, locating a legislative decision-making process in one place that has dramatic and serious effects upon other places doesn't fully satisfy the Institutional Settlement Principle. Legislative decision making becomes non-representational and loses some of its legitimacy as a democratic institution designed to resolve serious issues of public policy. The unrepresented cry out for an institution to serve their interests. That is one of the dilemmas of modern land use law. It is part of the heritage of the Standard Zoning Enabling Act and *Euclid v. Ambler*. Put more generally, agenda setting is sometimes arbitrary. It is dependent upon non-democratic processes, influenced by the governmental level at which the debate is held, and difficult to change across jurisdictional boundary lines.

Despite such problems, there are parts of the Legal Process School that sit quite comfortably with present-day attitudes about the legal system. When confronted with a dispute about loss of property rights, there is something attractive about concluding that "owners" adjudicating their "rights" need some protection, that one way to protect them is to regularize the adjudicative process used to terminate their interests, and that potentially abusive exercise of administrative discretion may be restrained by the imposition of procedural obligations. In short, we all talk like Legal Process people sometimes.

For a short time, the Legal Process School captured the imaginations of segments of the legal community, spurring some to use concepts of procedural unfairness as bases for litigation. A number of lawsuits challenging the procedural characteristics of administrative, legislative and judicial practices began to appear in the courts. During its 1970 term, in what was then viewed as a revolutionary development in legal thinking, the Supreme Court held that termination of welfare benefits without a prior administrative hearing violated the Due Process Clause. That decision in *Goldberg v. Kelly*, excerpted just below, spawned a long series of cases about the requirements of the Due Process Clause and the nature of the "property" interests it protects.[2]

§ 7.02 Welfare Benefits and Property Concepts in the Supreme Court

[1] Opinions of the United States Supreme Court in *Goldberg v. Kelly*

Jack R. Goldberg, Commissioner of Social Services of the City of New York v. John Kelly

Supreme Court of the United States
397 U.S. 254, 90 S. Ct. 10011, 25 L. Ed. 2d 287 (1970)

Mr. Justice BRENNAN delivered the opinion of the Court.

The question for decision is whether a State that terminates public assistance payments to a particular recipient without affording him the opportunity for an evidentiary hearing prior to termination denies the recipient procedural due process in violation of the Due Process Clause of the Fourteenth Amendment.

This action was brought in the District Court for the Southern District of New York by residents of New York City receiving financial aid under the federally assisted program of Aid to Families with Dependent Children (AFDC) or under New York State's general Home Relief program. Their complaint alleged that the New York State and New York City officials administering these programs terminated, or were about to terminate, such aid without prior notice and hearing, thereby denying them due process of law.[2] At the time the suits were filed there was no

---

[2] Some other aspects of these issues are taken up in Chapter 9's discussion of self-help remedies in landlord-tenant law. *See* p. 619, below.

[2] Two suits were brought and consolidated in the District Court. The named plaintiffs were 20 in number, including intervenors. Fourteen had been or were about to be cut off from AFDC, and six from Home Relief. During the course of this litigation most, though not all, of the plaintiffs either received a "fair hearing" or were restored to the rolls without a hearing. However, even in many of the cases where payments have been resumed, the underlying questions of eligibility that resulted in the bringing of this suit have not been resolved. For example, Mrs. Altagracia Guzman alleged that she was in danger of losing AFDC payments for failure to cooperate with the City Department of Social Services in suing her estranged husband. She contended that the departmental policy requiring such cooperation was inapplicable to the facts of her case. The record shows that payments to Mrs. Guzman have not been terminated, but there is no indication that the basic dispute over her duty to cooperate has been resolved, or that the alleged danger of termination has been removed. Home Relief payments to Juan DeJesus were terminated because he refused to accept counseling and rehabilitation for drug addiction. Mr. DeJesus maintains that he does not use drugs. His payments were restored the day after his complaint was filed. But there is nothing in the record to indicate that the underlying factual dispute in his case has been settled.

requirement of prior notice or hearing of any kind before termination of financial aid. However, the State and city adopted procedures for notice and hearing after the suits were brought, and the plaintiffs, appellees here, then challenged the constitutional adequacy of those procedures.

The State Commissioner of Social Services amended the State Department of Social Services' Official Regulations to require that local social services officials proposing to discontinue or suspend a recipient's financial aid do so . . . [only after] the giving of notice to the recipient of the reasons for a proposed discontinuance or suspension at least seven days prior to its effective date, with notice also that upon request the recipient may have the proposal reviewed by a local welfare official holding a position superior to that of the supervisor who approved the proposed discontinuance or suspension, and, further, that the recipient may submit, for purposes of the review, a written statement to demonstrate why his grant should not be discontinued or suspended. The decision by the reviewing official whether to discontinue or suspend aid must be made expeditiously, with written notice of the decision to the recipient. The section further expressly provides that "[a]ssistance shall not be discontinued or suspended prior to the date such notice of decision is sent to the recipient and his representative, if any, or prior to the proposed effective date of discontinuance or suspension, whichever occurs later."[3]

Pursuant to . . . [the new regulation a] caseworker who has doubts about the recipient's continued eligibility must first discuss them with the recipient. If the caseworker concludes that the recipient is no longer eligible, he recommends termination of aid to a unit supervisor. If the latter concurs, he sends the recipient a letter stating the reasons for proposing to terminate aid and notifying him that within seven days he may request that a higher official review the record, and may support the request with a written statement prepared personally or with the aid of an attorney or other person. If the reviewing official affirms the determination of ineligibility, aid is stopped immediately and the recipient is informed by letter of the reasons for the action. Appellees' challenge to this procedure emphasizes the absence of any provisions for the personal appearance of the recipient before the reviewing official, for oral presentation of evidence, and for confrontation and cross-examination of adverse witnesses. However, the letter does inform the recipient that he may request a post-termination "fair hearing." This is a proceeding before an independent state hearing officer at which the recipient may appear personally, offer oral evidence, confront and cross-examine the witnesses against him, and have a record made of the hearing. If the recipient prevails at the "fair hearing" he is paid all funds erroneously withheld. A recipient whose aid is not restored by a "fair hearing" decision may have judicial review. The recipient is so notified.

I

The constitutional issue to be decided, therefore, is the narrow one whether the Due Process Clause requires that the recipient be afforded an evidentiary hearing *before* the termination of benefits. The District Court held that only a pretermination evidentiary hearing would satisfy the constitutional command, and rejected the argument of the state and city officials that the combination of the post-termination "fair hearing" with the informal pre-termination review

---

[3] . . . A new HEW regulation, now scheduled to take effect in July 1970, would require continuation of AFDC payments until the final decision after a "fair hearing" and would give recipients a right to appointed counsel at "fair hearings." . . . Another recent regulation now in effect requires a local agency administering AFDC to give "advance notice of questions it has about an individual's eligibility so that a recipient has an opportunity to discuss his situation before receiving formal written notice of reduction in payment or termination of assistance."

disposed of all due process claims. The court said: "While post-termination review is relevant, there is one overpowering fact which controls here. By hypothesis, a welfare recipient is destitute, without funds or assets . . . . Suffice it to say that to cut off a welfare recipient in the face of . . . 'brutal need' without a prior hearing of some sort is unconscionable, unless overwhelming considerations justify it." Kelly v. Wyman, 294 F. Supp. 893, 899, 900 (1968). The court rejected the argument that the need to protect the public's tax revenues supplied the requisite "overwhelming consideration." "Against the justified desire to protect public funds must be weighed the individual's overpowering need in this unique situation not to be wrongfully deprived of assistance . . . . While the problem of additional expense must be kept in mind, it does not justify denying a hearing meeting the ordinary standards of due process. Under all the circumstances, we hold that due process requires an adequate hearing before termination of welfare benefits, and the fact that there is a later constitutionally fair proceeding does not alter the result." Although state officials were party defendants in the action, only the Commissioner of Social Services of the City of New York appealed. We noted probable jurisdiction, 394 U.S. 971, 89 S. Ct. 1469, 22 L. Ed. 2d 751 (1969) . . . . We affirm.

Appellant does not contend that procedural due process is not applicable to the termination of welfare benefits. Such benefits are a matter of statutory entitlement for persons qualified to receive them.[8] Their termination involves state action that adjudicates important rights. The constitutional challenge cannot be answered by an argument that public assistance benefits are "a 'privilege' and not a 'right.'" Shapiro v. Thompson, 394 U.S. 618 (1969). Relevant constitutional restraints apply as much to the withdrawal of public assistance benefits as to disqualification for unemployment compensation, Sherbert v. Verner, 374 U.S. 398, 83 S. Ct. 1790 (1963); or to denial of a tax exemption, Speiser v. Randall, 357 U.S. 513 (1958); or to discharge from public employment, Slochower v. Board of Higher Education, 350 U.S. 551 (1956). The extent to which procedural due process must be afforded the recipient is influenced by the extent to which he may be "condemned to suffer grievous loss," Joint Anti-Fascist Refugee Committee v. McGrath, 341 U.S. 123 (1951) (Frankfurter, J., concurring), and depends upon whether the recipient's interest in avoiding that loss outweighs the governmental interest in summary adjudication. Accordingly, as we said in Cafeteria & Restaurant Workers Union, etc. v. McElroy, 367 U.S. 886, 895 (1961), "consideration of what procedures due process may require under any given set of circumstances must begin with a determination of the precise nature of the government function involved as well as of the private interest that has been affected by governmental action."

---

[8] It may be realistic today to regard welfare entitlements as more like "property" than a "gratuity." Much of the existing wealth in this country takes the form of rights that do not fall within traditional common-law concepts of property. It has been aptly noted that

"(s)ociety today is built around entitlement. The automobile dealer has his franchise, the doctor and lawyer their professional licenses, the worker his union membership, contract, and pension rights, the executive his contract and stock options; all are devices to aid security and independence. Many of the most important of these entitlements now flow from government: subsidies to farmers and businessmen, routes for airlines and channels for television stations; long term contracts for defense, space, and education; social security pensions for individuals. Such sources of security, whether private or public, are no longer regarded as luxuries or gratuities; to the recipients they are essentials, fully deserved, and in no sense a form of charity. It is only the poor whose entitlements, although recognized by public policy, have not been effectively enforced." Reich, Individual Rights and Social Welfare: The Emerging Legal Issues, 74 Yale L.J. 1245, 1255 (1965). See also Reich, The New Property, 73 Yale L.J. 733 (1964).

It is true, of course, that some governmental benefits may be administratively terminated without affording the recipient a pre-termination evidentiary hearing.[10] But we agree with the District Court that when welfare is discontinued, only a pre-termination evidentiary hearing provides the recipient with procedural due process. For qualified recipients, welfare provides the means to obtain essential food, clothing, housing, and medical care. Thus the crucial factor in this context—a factor not present in the case of the blacklisted government contractor, the discharged government employee, the taxpayer denied a tax exemption, or virtually anyone else whose governmental entitlements are ended—is that termination of aid pending resolution of a controversy over eligibility may deprive an eligible recipient of the very means by which to live while he waits. Since he lacks independent resources, his situation becomes immediately desperate. His need to concentrate upon finding the means for daily subsistence, in turn, adversely affects his ability to seek redress from the welfare bureaucracy.

Moreover, important governmental interests are promoted by affording recipients a pre-termination evidentiary hearing. From its founding the Nation's basic commitment has been to foster the dignity and well-being of all persons within its borders. We have come to recognize that forces not within the control of the poor contribute to their poverty. This perception, against the background of our traditions, has significantly influenced the development of the contemporary public assistance system. Welfare, by meeting the basic demands of subsistence, can help bring within the reach of the poor the same opportunities that are available to others to participate meaningfully in the life of the community. At the same time, welfare guards against the societal malaise that may flow from a widespread sense of unjustified frustration and insecurity. Public assistance, then, is not mere charity, but a means to "promote the general Welfare, and secure the Blessings of Liberty to ourselves and our Posterity." The same governmental interests that counsel the provision of welfare, counsel as well its uninterrupted provision to those eligible to receive it; pre-termination evidentiary hearings are indispensable to that end.

Appellant does not challenge the force of these considerations but argues that they are outweighed by countervailing governmental interests in conserving fiscal and administrative resources. These interests, the argument goes, justify the delay of any evidentiary hearing until after discontinuance of the grants. Summary adjudication protects the public fisc by stopping payments promptly upon discovery of reason to believe that a recipient is no longer eligible. Since most terminations are accepted without challenge, summary adjudication also conserves both the fisc and administrative time and energy by reducing the number of evidentiary hearings actually held.

We agree with the District Court, however, that these governmental interests are not overriding in the welfare context. The requirement of a prior hearing doubtless involves some greater expense, and the benefits paid to ineligible recipients pending decision at the hearing probably cannot be recouped, since these recipients are likely to be judgment-proof. But the State is not without weapons to minimize these increased costs. Much of the drain on fiscal and administrative

---

[10] One Court of Appeals has stated: "In a wide variety of situations, it has long been recognized that where harm to the public is threatened, and the private interest infringed is reasonably deemed to be of less importance, an official body can take summary action pending a later hearing." R. A. Holman & Co. v. SEC, 112 U.S. App. D.C. 43, 47, 299 F.2d 127, 131 (1962) (suspension of exemption from stock registration requirement). See also, for example, Ewing v. Mytinger & Casselberry, Inc., 339 U.S. 594 (1950) (seizure of mislabeled vitamin product); North American Cold Storage Co. v. Chicago, 211 U.S. 306 (1908) (seizure of food not fit for human use); Yakus v. United States, 321 U.S. 414 (1944) (adoption of wartime price regulations); Gonzalez v. Freeman, 118 U.S. App. D.C. 180, 334 F.2d 570 (1964) (disqualification of a contractor to do business with the Government) . . ..

resources can be reduced by developing procedures for prompt pre-termination hearings and by skillful use of personnel and facilities. Indeed, the very provision for a post-termination evidentiary hearing in New York's Home Relief program is itself cogent evidence that the State recognizes the primacy of the public interest in correct eligibility determinations and therefore in the provision of procedural safeguards. Thus, the interest of the eligible recipient in uninterrupted receipt of public assistance, coupled with the State's interest that his payments not be erroneously terminated, clearly outweighs the State's competing concern to prevent any increase in its fiscal and administrative burdens. As the District Court correctly concluded, "[t]he stakes are simply too high for the welfare recipient, and the possibility for honest error or irritable misjudgment too great, to allow termination of aid without giving the recipient a chance, if he so desires, to be fully informed of the case against him so that he may contest its basis and produce evidence in rebuttal."

II

We also agree with the District Court, however, that the pre-termination hearing need not take the form of a judicial or quasi-judicial trial. We bear in mind that the statutory "fair hearing" will provide the recipient with a full administrative review. Accordingly, the pre-termination hearing has one function only: to produce an initial determination of the validity of the welfare department's grounds for discontinuance of payments in order to protect a recipient against an erroneous termination of his benefits. Thus, a complete record and a comprehensive opinion, which would serve primarily to facilitate judicial review and to guide future decisions, need not be provided at the pre-termination stage. We recognize, too, that both welfare authorities and recipients have an interest in relatively speedy resolution of questions of eligibility, that they are used to dealing with one another informally, and that some welfare departments have very burdensome caseloads. These considerations justify the limitation of the pre-termination hearing to minimum procedural safeguards, adapted to the particular characteristics of welfare recipients, and to the limited nature of the controversies to be resolved. We wish to add that we, no less than the dissenters, recognize the importance of not imposing upon the States or the Federal Government in this developing field of law any procedural requirements beyond those demanded by rudimentary due process.

. . . In the present context these principles require that a recipient have timely and adequate notice detailing the reasons for a proposed termination, and an effective opportunity to defend by confronting any adverse witnesses and by presenting his own arguments and evidence orally. These rights are important in cases such as those before us, where recipients have challenged proposed terminations as resting on incorrect or misleading factual premises or on misapplication of rules or policies to the facts of particular cases.[15]

We are not prepared to say that the seven-day notice currently provided by New York City is constitutionally insufficient per se, although there may be cases where fairness would require that a longer time be given. Nor do we see any constitutional deficiency in the content or form of the notice. New York employs both a letter and a personal conference with a caseworker to inform a recipient of the precise questions raised about his continued eligibility. Evidently the

---

[15] This case presents no question requiring our determination whether due process requires only an opportunity for written submission, or an opportunity both for written submission and oral argument, where there are no factual issues in dispute or where the application of the rule of law is not intertwined with factual issues.

recipient is told the legal and factual bases for the Department's doubts. This combination is probably the most effective method of communicating with recipients.

The city's procedures presently do not permit recipients to appear personally with or without counsel before the official who finally determines continued eligibility. Thus a recipient is not permitted to present evidence to that official orally, or to confront or cross-examine adverse witnesses. These omissions are fatal to the constitutional adequacy of the procedures.

The opportunity to be heard must be tailored to the capacities and circumstances of those who are to be heard. It is not enough that a welfare recipient may present his position to the decision maker in writing or second-hand through his caseworker. Written submissions are an unrealistic option for most recipients, who lack the educational attainment necessary to write effectively and who cannot obtain professional assistance. Moreover, written submissions do not afford the flexibility of oral presentations; they do not permit the recipient to mold his argument to the issues the decision maker appears to regard as important. Particularly where credibility and veracity are at issue, as they must be in many termination proceedings, written submissions are a wholly unsatisfactory basis for decision. The second-hand presentation to the decisionmaker by the caseworker has its own deficiencies; since the caseworker usually gathers the facts upon which the charge of ineligibility rests, the presentation of the recipient's side of the controversy cannot safely be left to him. Therefore a recipient must be allowed to state his position orally. Informal procedures will suffice; in this context due process does not require a particular order of proof or mode of offering evidence.

In almost every setting where important decisions turn on questions of fact, due process requires an opportunity to confront and cross-examine adverse witnesses. What we said in Greene v. McElroy, 360 U.S. 474, 496-497 (1959), is particularly pertinent here:

"Certain principles have remained relatively immutable in our jurisprudence. One of these is that where governmental action seriously injures an individual, and the reasonableness of the action depends on fact findings, the evidence used to prove the Government's case must be disclosed to the individual so that he has an opportunity to show that it is untrue. While this is important in the case of documentary evidence, it is even more important where the evidence consists of the testimony of individuals whose memory might be faulty or who, in fact, might be perjurers or persons motivated by malice, vindictiveness, intolerance, prejudice, or jealousy. We have formalized these protections in the requirements of confrontation and cross-examination. They have ancient roots. They find expression in the Sixth Amendment . . . . This Court has been zealous to protect these rights from erosion. It has spoken out not only in criminal cases, . . . but also in all types of cases where administrative . . . actions were under scrutiny."

Welfare recipients must therefore be given an opportunity to confront and cross-examine the witnesses relied on by the department.

"The right to be heard would be, in many cases, of little avail if it did not comprehend the right to be heard by counsel." Powell v. Alabama, 287 U.S. 45, 68-69 (1932). We do not say that counsel must be provided at the pre-termination hearing, but only that the recipient must be allowed to retain an attorney if he so desires. Counsel can help delineate the issues, present the factual contentions in an orderly manner, conduct cross-examination, and generally safeguard the interests of the recipient. We do not anticipate that this assistance will unduly prolong or otherwise encumber the hearing.

Finally, the decisionmaker's conclusion as to a recipient's eligibility must rest solely on the legal rules and evidence adduced at the hearing. To demonstrate compliance with this elementary requirement, the decision maker should state the reasons for his determination and indicate the evidence he relied on, though his statement need not amount to a full opinion or even formal findings of fact and conclusions of law. And, of course, an impartial decision maker is essential. We agree with the District Court that prior involvement in some aspects of a case will not necessarily bar a welfare official from acting as a decision maker. He should not, however, have participated in making the determination under review.

Affirmed.

Mr. Justice BLACK, dissenting.

In the last half century the United States, along with many, perhaps most, other nations of the world, has moved far toward becoming a welfare state, that is, a nation that for one reason or another taxes its most affluent people to help support, feed, clothe, and shelter its less fortunate citizens. The result is that today more than nine million men, women, and children in the United States receive some kind of state or federally financed public assistance in the form of allowances or gratuities, generally paid them periodically, usually by the week, month, or quarter. Since these gratuities are paid on the basis of need, the list of recipients is not static, and some people go off the lists and others are added from time to time. These ever-changing lists put a constant administrative burden on government and it certainly could not have reasonably anticipated that this burden would include the additional procedural expense imposed by the Court today.

The dilemma of the ever-increasing poor in the midst of constantly growing affluence presses upon us and must inevitably be met within the framework of our democratic constitutional government, if our system is to survive as such. It was largely to escape just such pressing economic problems and attendant government repression that people from Europe, Asia, and other areas settled this country and formed our Nation. Many of those settlers had personally suffered from persecutions of various kinds and wanted to get away from governments that had unrestrained powers to make life miserable for their citizens. It was for this reason, or so I believe, that on reaching these new lands the early settlers undertook to curb their governments by confining their powers within written boundaries, which eventually became written constitutions. They wrote their basic charters as nearly as men's collective wisdom could do so as to proclaim to their people and their officials an emphatic command that: "Thus far and no farther shall you go; and where we neither delegate powers to you, nor prohibit your exercise of them, we the people are left free."

Representatives of the people of the Thirteen Original Colonies spent long, hot months in the summer of 1787 in Philadelphia, Pennsylvania, creating a government of limited powers. They divided it into three departments—Legislative, Judicial, and Executive. The Judicial Department was to have no part whatever in making any laws. In fact proposals looking to vesting some power in the Judiciary to take part in the legislative process and veto laws were offered, considered, and rejected by the Constitutional Convention. In my judgment there is not one word, phrase, or sentence from the beginning to the end of the Constitution from which it can be inferred that judges were granted any such legislative power. True, Marbury v. Madison, 1 Cranch 137, 2 L. Ed. 60 (1803), held, and properly, I think, that courts must be the final interpreters of the Constitution, and I recognize that the holding can provide an opportunity to slide imperceptibly into constitutional amendment and law making. But when federal judges use this judicial power for legislative purposes, I think they wander out of their field of vested powers and transgress into the area constitutionally assigned to the Congress and the people. That is precisely what I believe the Court is doing in this case. Hence my dissent.

The more than a million names on the relief rolls in New York, and the more than nine million names on the rolls of all the 50 States were not put there at random. The names are there because state welfare officials believed that those people were eligible for assistance. Probably in the officials' haste to make out the lists many names were put there erroneously in order to alleviate immediate suffering, and undoubtedly some people are drawing relief who are not entitled under the law to do so. Doubtless some draw relief checks from time to time who know they are not eligible, either because they are not actually in need or for some other reason. Many of those who thus draw undeserved gratuities are without sufficient property to enable the government to collect back from them any money they wrongfully receive. But the Court today holds that it would violate the Due Process Clause of the Fourteenth Amendment to stop paying those people weekly or monthly allowances unless the government first affords them a full "evidentiary hearing" even though welfare officials are persuaded that the recipients are not rightfully entitled to receive a penny under the law. In other words, although some recipients might be on the lists for payment wholly because of deliberate fraud on their part, the Court holds that the government is helpless and must continue, until after an evidentiary hearing, to pay money that it does not owe, never has owed, and never could owe. I do not believe there is any provision in our Constitution that should thus paralyze the government's efforts to protect itself against making payments to people who are not entitled to them.

Particularly do I not think that the Fourteenth Amendment should be given such an unnecessarily broad construction. That Amendment came into being primarily to protect Negroes from discrimination, and while some of its language can and does protect others, all know that the chief purpose behind it was to protect ex-slaves. The Court, however, relies upon the Fourteenth Amendment and in effect says that failure of the government to pay a promised charitable installment to an individual deprives that individual of his own property, in violation of the Due Process Clause of the Fourteenth Amendment. It somewhat strains credulity to say that the government's promise of charity to an individual is property belonging to that individual when the government denies that the individual is honestly entitled to receive such a payment.

I would have little, if any, objection to the majority's decision in this case if it were written as the report of the House Committee on Education and Labor, but as an opinion ostensibly resting on the language of the Constitution I find it woefully deficient. Once the verbiage is pared away it is obvious that this Court today adopts the views of the District Court "that to cut off a welfare recipient in the face of . . . 'brutal need' without a prior hearing of some sort is unconscionable," and therefore, says the Court, unconstitutional. The majority reaches this result by a process of weighing "the recipient's interest in avoiding" the termination of welfare benefits against "the governmental interest in summary adjudication." Ante, at 1018. Today's balancing act requires a "pre-termination evidentiary hearing," yet there is nothing that indicates what tomorrow's balance will be. Although the majority attempts to bolster its decision with limited quotations from prior cases, it is obvious that today's result doesn't depend on the language of the Constitution itself or the principles of other decisions, but solely on the collective judgment of the majority as to what would be a fair and humane procedure in this case.

This decision is thus only another variant of the view often expressed by some members of this Court that the Due Process Clause forbids any conduct that a majority of the Court believes "unfair," "indecent," or "shocking to their consciences." See, e.g., Rochin v. California, 342 U.S.

165, 172, 72 S. Ct. 205, 209, 96 L. Ed. 183 (1952). Neither these words nor any like them appear anywhere in the Due Process Clause. If they did, they would leave the majority of Justices free to hold any conduct unconstitutional that they should conclude on their own to be unfair or shocking to them.[6] Had the drafters of the Due Process Clause meant to leave judges such ambulatory power to declare laws unconstitutional, the chief value of a written constitution, as the Founders saw it, would have been lost. In fact, if that view of due process is correct, the Due Process Clause could easily swallow up all other parts of the Constitution. And truly the Constitution would always be "what the judges say it is" at a given moment, not what the Founders wrote into the document.[7] A written constitution, designed to guarantee protection against governmental abuses, including those of judges, must have written standards that mean something definite and have an explicit content. I regret very much to be compelled to say that the Court today makes a drastic and dangerous departure from a Constitution written to control and limit the government and the judges and moves toward a constitution designed to be no more and no less than what the judges of a particular social and economic philosophy declare on the one hand to be fair or on the other hand to be shocking and unconscionable.

The procedure required today as a matter of constitutional law finds no precedent in our legal system. Reduced to its simplest terms, the problem in this case is similar to that frequently encountered when two parties have an ongoing legal relationship that requires one party to make periodic payments to the other. Often the situation arises where the party "owing" the money stops paying it and justifies his conduct by arguing that the recipient is not legally entitled to payment. The recipient can, of course, disagree and go to court to compel payment. But I know of no situation in our legal system in which the person alleged to owe money to another is required by law to continue making payments to a judgment-proof claimant without the benefit of any security or bond to insure that these payments can be recovered if he wins his legal argument. Yet today's decision in no way obligates the welfare recipient to pay back any benefits wrongfully received during the pretermination evidentiary hearings or post any bond, and in all "fairness" it could not do so. These recipients are by definition too poor to post a bond or to repay the benefits that, as the majority assumes, must be spent as received to insure survival.

The Court apparently feels that this decision will benefit the poor and needy. In my judgment the eventual result will be just the opposite. While today's decision requires only an administrative, evidentiary hearing, the inevitable logic of the approach taken will lead to constitutionally imposed, time-consuming delays of a full adversary process of administrative and judicial review. In the next case the welfare recipients are bound to argue that cutting off benefits before judicial review of the agency's decision is also a denial of due process. Since, by hypothesis, termination of aid at that point may still "deprive an eligible recipient of the very means by which to live while he waits," I would be surprised if the weighing process did not compel the conclusion that termination without full judicial review would be unconscionable. After all, at each step,

---

[6] I am aware that some feel that the process employed in reaching today's decision is not dependent on the individual views of the Justices involved, but is a mere objective search for the "collective conscience of mankind," but in my view that description is only a euphemism for an individual's judgment. Judges are as human as anyone and as likely as others to see the world through their own eyes and find the "collective conscience" remarkably similar to their own.

[7] To realize how uncertain a standard of "fundamental fairness" would be, one has only to reflect for a moment on the possible disagreement if the "fairness" of the procedure in this case were propounded to the head of the National Welfare Rights Organization, the president of the national Chamber of Commerce, and the chairman of the John Birch Society.

as the majority seems to feel, the issue is only one of weighing the government's pocketbook against the actual survival of the recipient, and surely that balance must always tip in favor of the individual. Similarly today's decision requires only the opportunity to have the benefit of counsel at the administrative hearing, but it is difficult to believe that the same reasoning process would not require the appointment of counsel, for otherwise the right to counsel is a meaningless one since these people are too poor to hire their own advocates. Cf. Gideon v. Wainwright, 372 U.S. 335, 344 (1963). Thus the end result of today's decision may well be that the government, once it decides to give welfare benefits, cannot reverse that decision until the recipient has had the benefits of full administrative and judicial review, including, of course, the opportunity to present his case to this Court. Since this process will usually entail a delay of several years, the inevitable result of such a constitutionally imposed burden will be that the government will not put a claimant on the rolls initially until it has made an exhaustive investigation to determine his eligibility. While this Court will perhaps have insured that no needy person will be taken off the rolls without a full "due process" proceeding, it will also have insured that many will never get on the rolls, or at least that they will remain destitute during the lengthy proceedings followed to determine initial eligibility.

For the foregoing reasons I dissent from the Court's holding. The operation of a welfare state is a new experiment for our Nation. For this reason, among others, I feel that new experiments in carrying out a welfare program should not be frozen into our constitutional structure. They should be left, as are other legislative determinations, to the Congress and the legislatures that the people elect to make our laws.

[The dissenting opinions of Justices Burger and Stewart have been omitted.]

[2] Property and Due Process for Justices Brennan and Black

In his majority opinion, Justice Brennan was very careful not to label welfare benefits as "property rights." The closest he came was in the first part of his opinion when he observed that Goldberg, the Commissioner of Social Services,

> does not contend that procedural due process is not applicable to the termination of welfare benefits. Such benefits are a matter of statutory entitlement for persons qualified to receive them . . . . The constitutional challenge cannot be answered by an argument that public assistance benefits are "a 'privilege' and not a 'right.'"

And then Justice Brennan dropped a fascinating footnote—number 8—in which he observed that "it may be realistic today to regard welfare entitlements as more like 'property' than a 'gratuity.'" The note proceeds with a long quote from an article by Charles Reich. Figuring out what all this was about is crucial to an understanding of the significance of *Goldberg v. Kelly*.

Start with Brennan's observation that the issues in the case could not be resolved by use of the distinction between privilege and right. In simple terms, this is the sort of statement a Realist would make. Indeed, the Realists critiqued a number of common legal distinctions. The observation, for example, that property was a creature of the state rather than a private creation protected by the state was part of a wide scale attack on the notion that public and private legal spheres were significantly different. The state action debate in a case like *Shelley v. Kraemer* was part of that attack. Arguments that governmental tolerance of widespread use of covenants was "state action" for constitutional purposes broke down the idea that "government" and "contract" were in different regulatory spheres.

Similarly, the Realists attacked the notion that "rights" and "privileges" were different things. If government guaranteed the presence of activity it was often labeled as a "right." But nothing inherent in the label automatically prevents that same government from altering or destroying the "right," thereby turning it into a "privilege." Similarly "privileges," when guaranteed by the state may easily be categorized as "rights." The decision about which label to deploy was a matter of public policy, the Realists argued, not an outcome intrinsic in the nature of any particular activity or asset.

This part of Justice Brennan's opinion was certainly realist in tone. That is certainly not surprising. He came to maturity during the height of the Realist era. But his *Goldberg* opinion also challenged that Realist mantle. He paid a great deal of attention to the plight of welfare recipients. He demonstrated an obvious empathy for the least well off. In other cases, he demonstrated the same sort of empathy for the disenfranchised or for those unable to muster a political majority. His vision of the judicial role engrafted a large "but if" exception upon the standard Realist deference to legislative decision making. Courts should defer to the political branches in most cases, he thought, but if persons or groups were unlikely to be able to muster much influence in such places, courts should be their protectors. Courts should reinforce the representation of the under-represented.[3] If Realism was designed to recognize the political nature of all legal machinery, then courts should inquire into the distribution of that power to insure that everyone had a forum in which their claims might be sympathetically heard. If the most radical of the Realists were correct that both judicial and legislative bodies were bastions of power allocation, someone had to watch how that power was deployed. Perhaps Brennan used *Goldberg* as a way of explicating a theory about the need to use judicial power to lessen the impact of majoritarian preferences upon the least politically powerful in society. In such a view, civil rights issues, first amendment questions, religious freedom disputes, minority voting claims, and similar disputes should get more sympathetic judicial review than other areas left largely in the hands of legislatures. Some Realists, like Justice Black, were unable to make the complete leap to creation of this large exception to their general desire to defer to legislative decision making. Others, like Brennan, were quite comfortable with the transition.

There were also other influences at work upon Justice Brennan's opinion in *Goldberg v. Kelly.* Much of what the Warren Court did was influenced by the Legal Process School. The Court

---

[3] In the academic literature, perhaps the best statement of such a judicial role is found in JOHN HART ELY, DEMOCRACY AND DISTRUST: A THEORY OF JUDICIAL REVIEW (1980). This work is an extended analysis of the consequences of a famous footnote—number 4—in Justice Stone's opinion in United States v. Carolene Products Co., 304 U.S. 144 (1938). The case was about the legality of a federal statute regulating shipment of certain milk products. But the judicial debate was about the role of the courts in reviewing Congressional legislation. The footnote read:

There may be narrower scope for operation of the presumption of constitutionality when legislation appears on its face to be within a specific prohibition of the Constitution, such as those of the first ten amendments, which are deemed equally specific when held to be embraced within the Fourteenth.

It is unnecessary to consider now whether legislation which restricts those political processes which can ordinarily be expected to bring about repeal of undesirable legislation, is to be subjected to more exacting judicial scrutiny under the general prohibitions of the Fourteenth Amendment than are most other types of legislation. [Examples may be] . . . restrictions upon the right to vote, . . . restraints upon the dissemination of information, . . . interferences with political organizations, [and] . . . prohibition of peaceable assembly.

Nor need we enquire whether similar considerations enter into the review of statutes directed at particular religious, or national, or racial minorities; whether prejudice against discrete and insular minorities may be a special condition, which tends seriously to curtail the operation of those political processes ordinarily to be relied upon to protect minorities, and which may call for a correspondingly more searching judicial inquiry.

took a number of criminal procedure cases and substantially changed the ways in which police, prosecutors and courts had to process those charged with crimes. Administrative law matured in that epoch, and much of the maturing had to do with the nature of the process agencies were required to use when they undertook their various rule making, investigative and adjudicative functions.

Despite the substantial increase in procedural protections created by the Court, it never fully adopted the analytical framework of the Legal Process School. Justice Brennan's opinion in *Goldberg v. Kelly*, for example, was not written as if there was a sharp dividing line between substance and process. He did not discuss the need for hearings in terms of institutional competence. He did not write an opinion saying that an adjudication was occurring and that, therefore, certain procedural safeguards were required in order to legitimate the outcome. Rather he wrote about the economic needs of welfare recipients, the harsh realities accompanying termination of benefits, and the potential for arbitrary and unfair behavior in welfare agencies acting without anyone reviewing their decisions. While, he, like the Legal Process adherents recognized the importance of fact finding hearings as a "neutral" device designed to increase the likelihood of fair decision making, he saw that protection as closely tied to his substantive concerns about the allocation of power between the governed and the governors, the haves and the have nots.

The tone of Justice Brennan's opinion is an indication of the limited influence of The Legal Process School. While quite influential in academic circles, its moment in the sun was brief. Like the Realists before them, Legal Process adherents had trouble with questions about race and poverty. While the Realists of the Roosevelt era could retain their hold on positions of power while refusing to respond to demands of African Americans for change, that was not possible after World War II. Since Legal Process advocates viewed large scale movements for social change as appropriate subjects for legislative inquiry, they were reluctant to embrace the judicial accommodations to the civil rights movement made by the Warren Court.[4] Others began to claim that if courts actually followed the lead of the Legal Process School, failure to meet head on the demands of the Civil Rights Movement would delegitimate the judicial system. Filibusters in the Senate killed a number of civil rights acts in the 1950s and 1960s.[5] The use of the filibuster to frustrate Congressional action was itself an affront to the Legal Process idea of a legislature as a democratic institution. If the courts did not respond, many argued, society could be torn apart. Judicial review of state and federal government actions on race issues came to the fore much as court oversight of economic regulations had dominated the Formalist Era. And that pressure forced a rethinking about the appropriate roles for courts and legislatures.

While all of these shifts in legal thinking may help explain the contours of Justice Brennan's opinion in *Goldberg v. Kelly*, they do not fully explain his fascinating footnote number 8 references to the work of Charles Reich. Reich, like Brennan, was certainly influenced by the Legal Process School. Reich's article, *The New Property*,[6] hit the legal world by storm. It was widely read in all segments of the legal community—bench, bar and the academy. It struck sympathetic chords in a wide variety of both conservative and liberal groups. He began his article with a long recitation of the many settings in which people had come to rely upon government largesse. Most people were in some way affected by subsidy payments to an array of businesses,

---

[4] *See, e.g.*, Herbert Wechsler, *Toward Neutral Principles of Constitutional Law*, 73 HARV. L. REV. 19 (1959).

[5] Shutting off debate in the Senate then required a two-thirds vote rather than the 60% we are now familiar with.

[6] Charles A. Reich, *The New Property*, 73 YALE L.J. 733 (1964).

organizations and individual recipients, licensing requirements, welfare benefits, unemployment compensation, social security payments or government jobs. The notion, Reich argued, that all of these programs created only "privileges," subject to arbitrary termination by the government, was untenable. Adherence to such a rule would result in tyranny, not democracy. Like Brennan's antipathy to the right/privilege distinction, Reich railed against cases where courts had allowed arbitrary government actions terminating one benefit or another to proceed unchecked.

But Reich's solution to the problem was not like Brennan's. Pointing out that deployment of the label "property" might be one way to create barriers to arbitrary government termination of its largesse, Reich, in a famous passage, wrote:

> Property is a legal institution the essence of which is the creation and protection of certain private rights in wealth of any kind. The institution performs many different functions. One of these functions is to draw a boundary between public and private power. Property draws a circle around the activities of each private individual or organization. Within that circle, the owner has a greater degree of freedom than without . . . .

> Thus, property performs the function of maintaining independence, dignity and pluralism in society by creating zones within which the majority has to yield to the owner.

In this view, property acts as a buffer between the state and the individual, protecting the individual from arbitrary actions. Process was the tool to be used to implement this idea. Creation of procedural protections against arbitrary behavior, Reich argued, acknowledged the Realist notions that property was a creature of the state and that "assets" distributed by the government were not mere "privileges," while guaranteeing the maximum freedom and liberty to individuals.

It is not hard to understand why so many types of people were attracted to Reich's article. Taking something from the Realists (debunking the right/privilege distinction and the public/private distinction, and bundling government and large businesses as the common foe of freedom), something from the Legal Process folks (the use of process as a way of implementing the idea of property as a buffer between state and individual), and something from the Formalists (government's obligation is to protect the individual from unnecessary state intrusion), Reich argued that the distribution of wealth by government and large institutions, regardless of the way in which that distribution occurred, should give rise to property like protections, to limits on the ability of government or large institutions to alter the reliance or dependency created by its distribution of wealth.

Though the article was thought by many to be a tour de force, Reich's use of property as the major metaphor in his writing did not find a totally receptive listener in Justice Brennan. Fearing the ways in which use of that metaphor might freeze government action and preclude future changes, Brennan preferred a more open display of empathy for the least fortunate in society. He recognized that use of the "property" label had enormous potential consequences. Use of property concepts in *Goldberg* might have forced him later to hold that receipt of welfare benefits was a right and that repeal of welfare laws violated the Takings Clause. Reich's decision to deploy the "property" label displayed his willingness to freeze certain aspects of the wealth distribution system in ways that might penalize future generations.

While the fame of Reich's work and his clearly articulated debunking of the right/privilege distinction led to Justice Brennan's footnote reference, Justice Black read the footnote as saying a great deal more than was probably intended. After claiming that the *Goldberg* majority was too broadly construing the Fourteenth Amendment to include an array of non-racially based claims, Black complained that the Court in effect says that failure of the government to pay a promised charitable installment to an individual deprives that individual of *his own property*, in violation of the Due Process Clause of the Fourteenth Amendment. It somewhat strains credulity to say that the government's promise of charity to an individual is property belonging to that individual when the government denies that the individual is honestly entitled to receive such a payment.

While Black's claim that the majority established a "property" claim in welfare was incorrect, he could not bring himself to quarrel with legislative decisions about the methods for distribution of largesse. "New experiments in carrying out a welfare program," he Realistically concluded, "should not be frozen into our constitutional structure. They should be left, as are other legislative determinations, to the Congress and the legislatures that the people elect to make our laws."

Presumably Justice Black, noting the phrasing of the Due Process Clauses limiting protection to "life, liberty or property," concluded that "life" and "liberty" were clearly not at stake and that the majority, therefore, had invoked the "property" label. I suspect Justice Brennan would have claimed he was invoking a "liberty" interest.

For additional readings on some of this material, *see* Charles A. Reich, *The New Property*, 73 YALE L.J. 733 (1964), excerpted in RICHARD CHUSED, A PROPERTY ANTHOLOGY, 136–144 (2d ed. 1997).

[3]   Explanatory Notes

[a]   Publicly Supported Housing

Some circuit courts applied *Goldberg v. Kelly* to limit evictions from public housing.[7] Was that a wholly logical extension of *Goldberg*? Welfare beneficiaries were provided an informal review only after their benefits were terminated. Tenants were removed only after a hearing in a landlord-tenant court. The use of *Goldberg*, however, made some sense because of the limited nature of the hearings provided in landlord-tenant courts before 1970. Many tenancies were terminable without any statement of reasons.[8] Was it appropriate to use *Goldberg* as a precedent to force public housing authorities to state and prove reasons prior to seeking the removal of a tenant? Before *Goldberg* was decided, the United States Supreme Court had taken a case to resolve some of these issues, but remanded it after the Department of Housing and Urban Development issued regulations requiring notification to tenants of the reasons for eviction and the evidence supporting those reasons.[9] For more on this area, *see* Chapter 8, below.

[b]   Consumer Protection and Process

In another series of cases, the Supreme Court placed some restraints on the seizure of goods by creditors seeking relief from defaulting buyers.[10] Two issues dominated the discourse in these

---

[7] Escalera v. New York City Housing Authority, 425 F.2d 853 (2d Cir. 1970); Caulder v. Durham Housing Authority, 433 F.2d 998 (4th Cir. 1970).

[8] You will learn a great deal more about this in the next chapter. For now, note that non-payment of rent cases involved an obvious cause for eviction. But many tenancies may be terminated on 30 days notice without the statement of any reasons. Many public housing agencies used such tenancies and routinely removed tenants without stating any cause. The hearing in landlord-tenant court would not explore such issues, but would simply inquire whether the formalities required to terminate a tenancy were correctly observed by the landlord.

[9] *See* Thorpe v. Housing Authority of the City of Durham, 393 U.S. 268 (1969).

[10] Sniadach v. Family Finance Corp., 395 U.S. 337 (1969); Fuentes v. Shevin, 407 U.S. 67 (1972); Mitchell v. W. T. Grant Co., 416 U.S. 600 (1974); North Georgia Finishing, Inc. v. Di-Chem, 419 U.S. 601 (1975).

cases. First, the Court evaluated the seriousness of the deprivation of rights in property accomplished by the various attachment systems. And second, the cases often turned on whether the Court found that the state was involved in the attachment process at a level significant enough to justify use of the Fourteenth Amendment. Despite the existence of statutes authorizing the attachment of property to pay debts, something more was said to be needed before the attachments could be deemed state action.

§ 7.03   Contemporary Views on Due Process and Property

[1]   Introduction

A series of cases have appeared since *Goldberg v. Kelly* evaluating the impact of the Due Process Clause on the deprivation of "property" rights. These disputes inquire into the nature of "property" and the scope of "process" required to protect it. Two years after *Goldberg*, the Court took two companion cases involving teachers at state-run institutions of higher education.

Board of Regents of State Colleges v. Roth,[11] involved a teacher hired under a one-year contract as an assistant professor without tenure. Roth was informed that he would not be rehired. No reasons were given and no hearing was provided. He claimed a Due Process violation, but lost in the Supreme Court. Justice Stewart, writing for the majority, opined that the Court had rejected the "wooden distinction" between "rights" and "privileges," but still needed to place some limitations on the contours of "liberty" and "property" protected by the Due Process Clause. Liberty entailed "privileges . . . essential to the orderly pursuit of happiness by free men," such as the right to contract, acquire knowledge, rear children, and worship. He went on to claim (wrongly I think) that *Goldberg* was a property-protection case, and that the constitution only protects the security of interests that a person has "a legitimate claim of entitlement to." Welfare recipients, Stewart went on, have a statutory entitlement to benefits, providing the basis for their property claim. "Property interests, of course, are not created by the Constitution. Rather, they are created and their dimensions are defined by existing rules or understandings that stem from an independent source such as state law." Since state law provided no basis for any expectation on Roth's part that he had a right to continue teaching beyond the term of his one-year contract, the Court found he had no Due Process claim.

Perry v. Sindermann,[12] came out the other way, not because of any analytical difference, but because Sindermann claimed he had "de facto" tenure. Though his school had no formal tenure system, the faculty guide provided that it "wishes each faculty member to feel that he has permanent tenure so long as his teaching services are satisfactory and as long as he displays a cooperative attitude." Though the Court did not formally find that Sindermann's firing was unconstitutional, it did remand for further proceedings on whether his expectations of continued employment had a solid basis in state law. These cases set the stage for a further debate among the Justices about the procedural protections to be afforded to those claiming "property" rights in state created entitlements.

---

[11] 408 U.S. 564 (1972).

[12] 408 U.S. 593 (1972).

[2] Opinions of the United States Supreme Court in *Cleveland Board of Education v. Loudermill*

Cleveland Board of Education v. James Loudermill

Supreme Court of the United States
470 U.S. 532, 105 S. Ct. 1487, 84 L. Ed. 2d 494 (1985)

[Note: An amicus curiae brief supporting the Cleveland Board of Education was filed and signed by the Attorneys General from Ohio, Alabama, Arizona, Hawaii, Indiana, Kansas, Michigan, Minnesota, Mississippi, Montana, Nevada, New Hampshire, New Jersey, North Dakota, Oklahoma, Oregon, Pennsylvania, South Dakota, Wisconsin, and Wyoming. Briefs of *amici curiae* supporting Loudermill were filed by the American Civil Liberties Union of Cleveland Foundation, the American Federation of State, County, and Municipal Employees, AFL-CIO, and the National Educational Association.]

Justice WHITE delivered the opinion of the Court.

In these cases we consider what pretermination process must be accorded a public employee who can be discharged only for cause.

I

In 1979 the Cleveland Board of Education . . . hired respondent James Loudermill as a security guard. On his job application, Loudermill stated that he had never been convicted of a felony. Eleven months later, as part of a routine examination of his employment records, the Board discovered that in fact Loudermill had been convicted of grand larceny in 1968. By letter dated November 3, 1980, the Board's Business Manager informed Loudermill that he had been dismissed because of his dishonesty in filling out the employment application. Loudermill was not afforded an opportunity to respond to the charge of dishonesty or to challenge his dismissal. On November 13, the Board adopted a resolution officially approving the discharge.

Under Ohio law, Loudermill was a "classified civil servant." Such employees can be terminated only for cause, and may obtain administrative review if discharged . . . . Loudermill filed an appeal with the Cleveland Civil Service Commission on November 12. The Commission appointed a referee, who held a hearing on January 29, 1981. Loudermill argued that he had thought that his 1968 larceny conviction was for a misdemeanor rather than a felony. The referee recommended reinstatement. On July 20, 1981, the full Commission heard argument and orally announced that it would uphold the dismissal . . . .

. . . Loudermill brought the present suit . . . [claiming that the state regulation] was unconstitutional on its face because it did not provide the employee an opportunity to respond to the charges against him prior to removal. As a result, discharged employees were deprived of liberty and property without due process. The complaint also alleged that the provision was unconstitutional as applied because discharged employees were not given sufficiently prompt postremoval hearings.

Before a responsive pleading was filed, the District Court dismissed for failure to state a claim on which relief could be granted. It held that because the very statute that created the property right in continued employment also specified the procedures for discharge, and because those procedures were followed, Loudermill was, by definition, afforded all the process due.

. . . .

A divided panel of the Court of Appeals for the Sixth Circuit . . . found that . . . [Loudermill] had been deprived of due process. It disagreed with the District Court's original rationale. Instead, it concluded that the compelling private interest in retaining employment, combined with the value of presenting evidence prior to dismissal, outweighed the added administrative burden of a pretermination hearing.

. . . .

II

[Loudermill's] . . . federal constitutional claim depends on [his] . . . having had a property right in continued employment. *Board of Regents v. Roth*, 408 U.S. 564 (1972). If . . . [he] did, the State could not deprive . . . [him] of this property without due process.

Property interests are not created by the Constitution, "they are created and their dimensions are defined by existing rules or understandings that stem from an independent source such as state law . . . ." *Board of Regents v. Roth, supra*, 408 U.S., at 577. The Ohio statute plainly creates such an interest. Respondent . . . [was a] "classified civil service employee," entitled to retain . . . [his] position "during good behavior and efficient service," who could not be dismissed "except . . . for . . . misfeasance, malfeasance, or nonfeasance in office." The statute plainly supports the conclusion, reached by both lower courts, that respondent possessed property rights in continued employment. Indeed, this question does not seem to have been disputed below.[5]

The . . . Board argues, however, that the property right is defined by, and conditioned on, the legislature's choice of procedures for its deprivation. The Board stresses that in addition to specifying the grounds for termination, the statute sets out procedures by which termination may take place. The procedures were adhered to . . . . According to petitioner, "[t]o require additional procedures would in effect expand the scope of the property interest itself."

This argument, which was accepted by the District Court, has its genesis in the plurality opinion in *Arnett v. Kennedy*, 416 U.S. 134 (1974). *Arnett* involved a challenge by a former federal employee to the procedures by which he was dismissed. The plurality reasoned that where the legislation conferring the substantive right also sets out the procedural mechanism for enforcing that right, the two cannot be separated . . . .

. . . .

This view garnered three votes in *Arnett*, but was specifically rejected by the other six Justices. (Opinions of Justices POWELL, BLACKMUN, WHITE, MARSHALL, DOUGLAS and BREN-NAN) Since then, this theory has at times seemed to gather some additional support. More

---

[5] The Cleveland Board of Education now asserts that Loudermill had no property right under state law because he obtained his employment by lying on the application. It argues that had Loudermill answered truthfully he would not have been hired. He therefore lacked a "legitimate claim of entitlement" to the position.

For several reasons, we must reject this submission. First, it was not raised below. Second, it makes factual assumptions—that Loudermill lied, and that he would not have been hired had he not done so—that are inconsistent with the allegations of the complaint and inappropriate at this stage of the litigation, which has not proceeded past the initial pleadings stage. Finally, the argument relies on a retrospective fiction inconsistent with the undisputed fact that Loudermill was hired and did hold the security guard job. The Board cannot escape its constitutional obligations by rephrasing the basis for termination as a reason why Loudermill should not have been hired in the first place.

recently, however, the Court has clearly rejected it. In *Vitek v. Jones*, 445 U.S. 480 (1980), we pointed out that "minimum [procedural] requirements [are] a matter of federal law, they are not diminished by the fact that the State may have specified its own procedures that it may deem adequate for determining the preconditions to adverse official action." This conclusion was reiterated in *Logan v. Zimmerman Brush Co.*, 455 U.S. 422, 432 (1982), where we reversed the lower court's holding that because the entitlement arose from a state statute, the legislature had the prerogative to define the procedures to be followed to protect that entitlement.

In light of these holdings, it is settled that the "bitter with the sweet" approach misconceives the constitutional guarantee. If a clearer holding is needed, we provide it today. The point is straightforward: the Due Process Clause provides that certain substantive rights—life, liberty, and property—cannot be deprived except pursuant to constitutionally adequate procedures. The categories of substance and procedure are distinct. Were the rule otherwise, the Clause would be reduced to a mere tautology. "Property" cannot be defined by the procedures provided for its deprivation any more than can life or liberty. The right to due process is conferred, not by legislative grace, but by constitutional guarantee. While the legislature may elect not to confer a property interest in [public] employment, it may not constitutionally authorize the deprivation of such an interest, once conferred, without appropriate procedural safeguards.

In short, once it is determined that the Due Process Clause applies, "the question remains what process is due." *Morrissey v. Brewer*, 408 U.S. 471 (1972). The answer to that question is not to be found in the Ohio statute.

III

An essential principle of due process is that a deprivation of life, liberty, or property "be preceded by notice and opportunity for hearing appropriate to the nature of the case." *Mullane v. Central Hanover Bank & Trust Co.*, 339 U.S. 306 (1950). We have described "the root requirement" of the Due Process Clause as being "that an individual be given an opportunity for a hearing *before* he is deprived of any significant property interest." *Boddie v. Connecticut*, 401 U.S. 371 (1971) (emphasis in original). This principle requires "some kind of a hearing" prior to the discharge of an employee who has a constitutionally protected property interest in his employment. *Board of Regents v. Roth*, 408 U.S., at 569-570; *Perry v. Sindermann*, 408 U.S. 593, 599 (1972) . . . . Even decisions finding no constitutional violation in termination procedures have relied on the existence of some pretermination opportunity to respond. For example, in Arnett six Justices found constitutional minima satisfied where the employee had access to the material upon which the charge was based and could respond orally and in writing and present rebuttal affidavits . . . .

The need for some form of pretermination hearing, recognized in these cases, is evident from a balancing of the competing interests at stake. These are the private interests in retaining employment, the governmental interest in the expeditious removal of unsatisfactory employees and the avoidance of administrative burdens, and the risk of an erroneous termination. See *Mathews v. Eldridge*, 424 U.S. 319 (1976).

First, the significance of the private interest in retaining employment cannot be gainsaid . . . . While a fired worker may find employment elsewhere, doing so will take some time and is likely to be burdened by the questionable circumstances under which he left his previous job.

Second, some opportunity for the employee to present his side of the case is recurringly of obvious value in reaching an accurate decision. Dismissals for cause will often involve factual disputes. Even where the facts are clear, the appropriateness or necessity of the discharge may not be; in such cases, the only meaningful opportunity to invoke the discretion of the decisionmaker is likely to be before the termination takes effect.

[This case illustrates] . . . these considerations . . . . [G]iven the Commission's ruling we cannot say that [Loudermill's] . . . discharge was mistaken. Nonetheless, in light of the referee's recommendation, neither can we say that a fully informed decisionmaker might not have exercised its discretion and decided not to dismiss him, notwithstanding its authority to do so. In any event, the termination involved arguable issues, and the right to a hearing does not depend on a demonstration of certain success.

The governmental interest in immediate termination does not outweigh these interests . . . . [A]ffording the employee an opportunity to respond prior to termination would impose neither a significant administrative burden nor intolerable delays. Furthermore, the employer shares the employee's interest in avoiding disruption and erroneous decisions; and until the matter is settled, the employer would continue to receive the benefit of the employee's labors. It is preferable to keep a qualified employee on than to train a new one. A governmental employer also has an interest in keeping citizens usefully employed rather than taking the possibly erroneous and counterproductive step of forcing its employees onto the welfare rolls. Finally, in those situations where the employer perceives a significant hazard in keeping the employee on the job, it can avoid the problem by suspending with pay.

IV

The foregoing considerations indicate that the pretermination "hearing," though necessary, need not be elaborate . . . . In general, "something less" than a full evidentiary hearing is sufficient prior to adverse administrative action. Under state law, respondents were later entitled to a full administrative hearing and judicial review. The only question is what steps were required before the termination took effect.

In only one case, *Goldberg v. Kelly*, 397 U.S. 254 (1970), has the Court required a full adversarial evidentiary hearing prior to adverse governmental action. However, as the *Goldberg* Court itself pointed out, that case presented significantly different considerations than are present in the context of public employment. Here, the pretermination hearing need not definitively resolve the propriety of the discharge. It should be an initial check against mistaken decisions— essentially, a determination of whether there are reasonable grounds to believe that the charges against the employee are true and support the proposed action.

The essential requirements of due process, and all that respondents seek or the Court of Appeals required, are notice and an opportunity to respond. The opportunity to present reasons, either in person or in writing, why proposed action should not be taken is a fundamental due process requirement. The tenured public employee is entitled to oral or written notice of the charges against him, an explanation of the employer's evidence, and an opportunity to present his side of the story. To require more than this prior to termination would intrude to an unwarranted extent on the government's interest in quickly removing an unsatisfactory employee.

. . . .

The judgment of the Court of Appeals is affirmed, and the case is remanded for further proceedings consistent with this opinion.

So ordered.

Justice MARSHALL, concurring in part and concurring in the judgment.

I agree wholeheartedly with the Court's express rejection of the theory of due process . . . that a public employee who may be discharged only for cause may be discharged by whatever procedures the legislature chooses. I therefore join Part II of the opinion for the Court. I also agree that, before discharge, the respondent employees were entitled to the opportunity to respond to the charges against them (which is all they requested), and that the failure to accord them that opportunity was a violation of their constitutional rights. Because the Court holds that the respondents were due all the process they requested, I concur in the judgment of the Court.

I write separately, however, to reaffirm my belief that public employees who may be discharged only for cause are entitled, under the Due Process Clause of the Fourteenth Amendment, to more than respondents sought in this case. I continue to believe that before the decision is made to terminate an employee's wages, the employee is entitled to an opportunity to test the strength of the evidence "by confronting and cross-examining adverse witnesses and by presenting witnesses on his own behalf, whenever there are substantial disputes in testimonial evidence," *Arnett v. Kennedy*, (MARSHALL, J., dissenting). Because the Court suggests that even in this situation due process requires no more than notice and an opportunity to be heard before wages are cut off, I am not able to join the Court's opinion in its entirety.

. . . .

Justice BRENNAN, concurring in part and dissenting in part.

Today the Court puts to rest any remaining debate over whether public employers must provide meaningful notice and hearing procedures before discharging an employee for cause. As the Court convincingly demonstrates, the employee's right to fair notice and an opportunity to "present his side of the story" before discharge is not a matter of legislative grace, but of "constitutional guarantee." . . .

Accordingly, I concur in . . . the Court's opinion. I write separately to comment on . . . issues the Court does not resolve today . . . .

. . . [T]he Court today does not prescribe the precise form of required pretermination procedures in cases where an employee disputes the *facts* proffered to support his discharge. The cases at hand involve, as the Court recognizes, employees who did not dispute the facts but had "plausible arguments to make that might have prevented their discharge." In such cases, notice and an "opportunity to present reasons," are sufficient to protect the important interests at stake.

As the Court also correctly notes, other cases "will often involve factual disputes," such as allegedly erroneous records or false accusations. As Justice MARSHALL has previously noted and stresses again today, where there exist not just plausible arguments to be made, but also "substantial disputes in testimonial evidence," due process may well require more than a simple opportunity to argue or deny. The Court acknowledges that what the Constitution requires prior to discharge, in general terms, is pretermination procedures sufficient to provide "an initial check against mistaken decisions—essentially, a determination of whether there are reasonable grounds to believe that the charges against the employee are true and support the proposed action." (emphasis added). When factual disputes are involved, therefore, an employee may deserve a fair opportunity before discharge to produce contrary records or testimony, or even to confront an accuser in front of the decisionmaker. Such an opportunity might not necessitate "elaborate" procedures, but the fact remains that in some cases only such an opportunity to challenge the source or produce contrary evidence will suffice to support a finding that there are "reasonable grounds" to believe accusations are "true."

Factual disputes are not involved in these cases, however . . . . I do not understand Part IV to foreclose the views expressed above or by Justice MARSHALL, with respect to discharges based on disputed evidence or testimony. I therefore join . . . the Court's opinion.

. . . .

Justice REHNQUIST, dissenting.

In *Arnett v. Kennedy* six Members of this Court agreed that a public employee could be dismissed for misconduct without a full hearing prior to termination. A plurality of Justices agreed that the employee was entitled to exactly what Congress gave him, and no more. The Chief Justice, Justice Stewart, and I said:

"Here appellee did have a statutory expectancy that he not be removed other than for 'such cause as will promote the efficiency of [the] service.' But the very section of the statute which granted him that right, a right which had previously existed only by virtue of administrative regulation, expressly provided also for the procedure by which 'cause' was to be determined, and expressly omitted the procedural guarantees which appellee insists are mandated by the Constitution. Only by bifurcating the very sentence of the Act of Congress which conferred upon appellee the right not to be removed save for cause could it be said that he had an expectancy of that substantive right without the procedural limitations which Congress attached to it. In the area of federal regulation of government employees, where in the absence of statutory limitation the governmental employer has had virtually uncontrolled latitude in decisions as to hiring and firing, *Cafeteria Workers v. McElroy*, 367 U.S. 886, 896-897 (1961), we do not believe that a statutory enactment such as the Lloyd-La Follette Act may be parsed as discretely as appellee urges. Congress was obviously intent on according a measure of statutory job security to governmental employees which they had not previously enjoyed, but was likewise intent on excluding more elaborate procedural requirements which it felt would make the operation of the new scheme unnecessarily burdensome in practice. Where the focus of legislation was thus strongly on the procedural mechanism for enforcing the substantive right which was simultaneously conferred, we decline to conclude that the substantive right may be viewed wholly apart from the procedure provided for its enforcement. The employee's statutorily defined right is not a guarantee against removal without cause in the abstract, but such a guarantee as enforced by the procedures which Congress has designated for the determination of cause."

In these cases, the relevant Ohio statute provides in its first paragraph that

"[t]he tenure of every officer or employee in the classified service . . . shall be during good behavior and efficient service and no such officer or employee shall be reduced in pay or position, suspended, or removed, except . . . for incompetency, inefficiency, dishonesty, drunkenness, immoral conduct, insubordination, discourteous treatment of the public, neglect of duty, violation of such sections or the rules of the director of administrative services or the commission, or any other failure of good behavior, or any other acts of misfeasance, malfeasance, or nonfeasance in office."

The very next paragraph of this section of the Ohio Revised Code provides that in the event of suspension of more than three days or removal the appointing authority shall furnish the employee with the stated reasons for his removal. The next paragraph provides that within 10 days following the receipt of such a statement, the employee may appeal in writing to the State Personnel Board of Review or the Commission, such appeal shall be heard within 30 days from the time of its filing, and the Board may affirm, disaffirm, or modify the judgment of the appointing authority.

Thus in one legislative breath Ohio has conferred upon civil service employees such as respondents in these cases a limited form of tenure during good behavior, and prescribed the procedures by which that tenure may be terminated. Here, as in Arnett, "[t]he employee's statutorily defined right is not a guarantee against removal without cause in the abstract, but such a guarantee as enforced by the procedures which [the Ohio Legislature] has designated for the determination of cause." (opinion of REHNQUIST, J.). We stated in Board of Regents v. Roth:

> "Property interests, of course, are not created by the Constitution. Rather, they are created and their dimensions are defined by existing rules or understandings that stem from an independent source such as state law—rules or understandings that secure certain benefits and that support claims of entitlement to those benefits."

We ought to recognize the totality of the State's definition of the property right in question, and not merely seize upon one of several paragraphs in a unitary statute to proclaim that in that paragraph the State has inexorably conferred upon a civil service employee something which it is powerless under the United States Constitution to qualify in the next paragraph of the statute. This practice ignores our duty under Roth to rely on state law as the source of property interests for purposes of applying the Due Process Clause of the Fourteenth Amendment. While it does not impose a federal definition of property, the Court departs from the full breadth of the holding in Roth by its selective choice from among the sentences the Ohio Legislature chooses to use in establishing and qualifying a right.

. . . .

Because I believe that the Fourteenth Amendment of the United States Constitution does not support the conclusion that Ohio's effort to confer a limited form of tenure upon respondents resulted in the creation of a "property right" in their employment, I dissent.

[3] Explanatory Note on Loudermill

Justice Brennan, in his Goldberg v. Kelly opinion, found a basis for deciding in favor of the welfare recipient in the particular situation confronting such a person when payments are terminated, and the process he required grew out of his evaluation of the recipient's circumstances. While the welfare benefits were defined by statute, the rights bestowed by Brennan arose, at least in part, for non-statutory reasons, and the source of legal power came from the Constitution, not state law.

Justice Stewart took a slightly different tack in Roth and Sindermann. He read Goldberg as granting process because of the existence of a statutory entitlement to receive welfare benefits and argued that the Constitution required procedural protection of "property" interests only when entitlements existed as a matter of state law. He used "property" language, concluding that the Constitution required protection only of those assets created by state statutes and instruments. The Constitution did not create property. While the process due was evaluated under Constitutional standards, the property was not. Arguably this was a very Legal Process oriented move. For, a Legal Process advocate might contend, university hiring policies should be legislative in origin, while the resolution of any particular firing decision should be adjudicative.

Justice Rehnquist, dissenting in *Loudermill*, found the Stewart position somewhat strange. He opined that the distinction between substance and procedure inherent in Stewart's analysis made little sense. The protections surrounding any particular asset, he contended, are part of the definition of the asset. To split them was artificial. So, he concluded, we ought to allow the state to define both the asset and the procedural protections, if any, surrounding it.

These three forms of analysis run us around in a circle. If the Realists were correct that substance and procedure are inextricably linked together, that it is not possible to know about an asset unless you understand the legal protections surrounding it, then Rehnquist was correct in arguing that property and process must emanate from the same legal source. But, if Rehnquist was correct that both process and substance emanate from the state, then the Due Process Clause loses meaning, for a state may define an asset in ways that routinely deny process to the owner of an entitlement whenever the state wishes to do something with or to that asset. The only way out of that position is to contend that the Constitution, rather than state law, must be the source of all law defining property situations like *Goldberg, Roth, Sindermann* and *Loudermill.*

But if we do that, as Brennan arguably did, we, in part, return to something like the late nineteenth-century Formalist position claiming judicial supremacy over property definitions, but now without any general understandings about what Constitutional property is. The merry-go-round ride you just took is an allegory for our present intellectual situation in property law.

In an effort to begin your search for new ways of thinking about normative property rules, can you find any assumptions upon which you and your peers are likely to agree? First, will any of you quarrel with the basic idea that property is relational. The debate in these Due Process cases, for example, was about the source for norms, not the fact that human relationships about wealth were at stake. Nor was there much talk about "things" in the opinion. While Rehnquist opined in Loudermill that property was defined by the state, that was hardly the Formalist sort of property the state was designed to protect. Quite the contrary. It was an admission of the role of the state in the formation of valuable assets.

Perhaps you can agree on a few other propositions about property. First, I hope you now see, if you didn't before, that there are relationships between monetary value and process, that imposition of process has costs, and that the decision to deploy a label like "property" carries with it significant legal and political consequences. Reducing process imposes fewer out of pocket costs on the state, but increases the level of insecurity of those claiming they own something called "property." Increasing process imposes more costs on the state or on those dealing with an asset and increases the level of security of those claiming to own something called "property." There are relationships between process and substantive content and meaning.

This continues to be demonstrated by cases before the Supreme Court. In *Gilbert v. Homar,*[13] for example, a public employee was suspended *without* pay after being arrested and charged with a drug offense. The Court unanimously concluded that even though the worker could claim a due process hearing right under *Loudermill*, his suspension without pay before being provided a government hearing was acceptable. The arrest and formal charge filed in a criminal matter, the Court concluded, provided an inherent protection against arbitrary administrative deprivation of Constitutional property interests. No more than a post-suspension review was required.

Second, there are representational issues in property. That is, claims of ownership by individuals, businesses and governments often serve as proxies for the interests of others. Your

---

[13] 520 U.S. 924 (1997).

neighbors have concerns about what you do with your land. Environmental groups are interested in what happens to forest lands owned by paper companies. Voters often wonder about what happens to their tax dollars. Finding an institutional way to listen to the various parties whose interests are at stake in any property dispute is a challenging problem.

Finally, property issues almost always pose inter-generational concerns. What we do today affects those who will inherit this earth. The interests of future generations may be the most important under-represented group in property litigation. And there are economic reasons for that. The value today of the right to receive a dollar in 40 years is quite small. Investors simply have little present economic interest in very long term investment outcomes. There is no money to be made out of concern for the impact seven generations into the future of a decision made today. Those future generations are left out of the picture. Is that a problem? And if so, are there ways to resolve it?

None of these points creates a new set of property norms. But they do give us some parameters within which to work. For example, if property is relational, we can begin to make some sense out of property law by attempting to classify some different sorts of relationships in which assets are thought to be at issue.

I can come up with at least three large categories of property—contract based, market oriented, investment style property, non-commodified property, and the commons. They arise in somewhat different relational settings. Market oriented property, in its purest sense, is the contract-based asset of the Formalist era. It arises as a set of understandings between people. It has value in trade. It is the kind of asset most commonly thought of as "property" by the body politic. Anyone can own it, even the government. It can be a stereo system, land, a job, a baseball card, a copyright, fame, or a million other constructs.

Non-commodifiable property, in its purest guise, is so valuable that it cannot be traded, sold or exchanged. It is often associated with us as people. We will not allow slavery, or sale of organs (at least most of the time) or privacy intrusions of a certain sort. But non-commodifiable assets could also be something more tangible, like the national parks (are they still not for sale?), or a family heirloom.

And then there is the commons, owned by no one in particular and everyone in general. Think of the air, the oceans, culture, or the radio spectrum. A commons is virtually free for the taking and has value when it is possessed or used. And since the commons has value, like the value we place upon air, water, history, or scenery, it is profitable for each of us to use the commons. It is this combination of virtually cost free use and incentives to use that causes people like Christopher Stone[14] to worry about the commons. For if the legal structure does not recognize the commons as a legal entity, it may obtain protection only if the legislature decides to enter the field. And that, the argument goes, is less likely with respect to a commons than it is with other forms of property because the commons is not directly represented in any democratically elected institutions. While people wishing to use the commons will certainly be in legislatures, there may not be anyone arguing on behalf of saving the commons. Furthermore, the commons, absent legislative action, may not partake of any judicial remedies. A commons, perhaps, needs a formally appointed representative in order to increase its ability to obtain redress.

---

[14] In an article that created quite a stir when it was first published, Christopher Stone argued that trees should have standing to sue in the courts. Christopher Stone, *Should Trees Have Standing?—Toward Legal Rights for Natural Objects*, 45 S. CAL. L. REV. 450 (1972). This work is excerpted in RICHARD CHUSED, A PROPERTY ANTHOLOGY 145-154 (2d ed. 1997).

Think about the remainder of this book as an inquiry into these and other basic categories of property.

§ 7.04 Process, Property and Representation Reinforcement

[1] Introduction

In the notes after the *Goldberg v. Kelley* opinions, there is some discussion of the notion that many of the opinions written by Justice Brennan suggest he believed that the courts should reinforce the power and authority of the under-represented in society. Many court decisions of the 1960s and 1970s on race, gender, criminal law and other issues seemed to focus on the difficulties some groups of people had in protecting their interests. The Supreme Court's willingness to structure Equal Protection rules that scrutinized racial and gender classifications more closely than other distinctions give some credence to the contention that the Warren Court Era was heavily influenced by representation reinforcement notions.

The Supreme Court, however, never imbedded the full logic of representation reinforcement in its decisions. When litigants tried to convince the justices that classifications based on poverty, like those on race or gender, should be closely scrutinized, the Court balked. In that realm, at least, reform was going to be left to the legislature. The New Deal era conclusion that the courts should defer to legislative judgment on economic regulatory matters carried the day.

In this final section of the chapter, you will read two cases—one from the state level and another from the Supreme Court. The first, the now famous case of *Shack v. State of New Jersey,* provides a glimpse into the sort anti-poverty programs Congress adopted in the 1960s and 1970s, and displays the ways in which common law property rules were affected by the increased role of government in the lives of workers. The second, *San Antonio v. Rodriguez,* demonstrates the limitations of the representation reinforcement movement in the Supreme Court.

[2] The "Great Society," Trespass Law, and the State

[a] Background to *State of New Jersey v. Shack and Tejeras*

In the spring of 1964, President Lyndon B. Johnson delivered the commencement address at the University of Michigan in Ann Arbor. Reflecting on the enormous post-World War II wealth of the United States and the high expectations that all members of society should be allowed to flourish, he said:

> The challenge of the next half century is whether we have the wisdom to use that wealth to enrich and elevate our national life, and to advance the quality of our American civilization.
>
> Your imagination, your initiative, and your indignation will determine whether we build a society where progress is the servant of our needs, or a society where old values and new visions are buried under unbridled growth. For in your time we have the opportunity to move not only toward the rich society and the powerful society, but upward to the Great Society.
>
> The Great Society rests on abundance and liberty for all.

Johnson's Great Society program led to the enactment of a large number of educational, community action, housing, civil rights and anti-poverty programs. The first nationally funded legal services offices opened as experimental programs funded by the Office of Economic Opportunity. Many of the Great Society reforms were responses to widespread public protests about the conditions of various impoverished groups. Disputes about many major American institutions were rife in the late 1960's. The status of migrant farm workers was no exception. Most of the highly publicized activity occurred in Florida, Texas and California, where Cesar Chavez's efforts to organize workers became a national cause célèbre. But farm worker issues also arose in some smaller growing areas, such as Cumberland County in southern New Jersey. In fact, New Jersey's legislature, partially in response to the national concern over the issue, adopted legislation in the spring of 1967 to strengthen regulation of migrant labor camps in the state.[15] Shortly after this legislation was adopted, the New Jersey Farm Bureau, a private association of growers, sold 4,000 "No Trespassing" signs to its members in an apparent effort to keep antipoverty workers, legal service attorneys, union organizers and newspaper reporters off the farms during the summer.[16] And in December, 1967, Governor Hughes appointed a task force to investigate and report on migrant worker issues.[17]

Ron Sullivan, a reporter for the NEW YORK TIMES and the author of most of the stories on New Jersey migrant workers published in that paper, estimated that in the summer of 1966, about 7,000 black persons migrated from the south to work the New Jersey fields, along with about 5,400 Puerto Ricans. An additional 1,000 persons, mostly from nearby cities like Philadelphia, Camden and Newark, were driven in each day.[18] When the New Jersey Farm Bureau "No Trespassing" signs appeared, the NAACP Legal Defense Fund, deeply interested in the issue because of the large number of black workers, revealed plans to ask federal courts to have the signs removed as a violation of the First Amendment rights of the workers to freely associate with persons of their choice.[19] A short time later the interagency group set up by Governor Hughes to enforce the newly enacted legislation on migrant labor urged that a number of labor camps be closed because of inhumane conditions. Five farmers, including Morris Tedesco who owned the land that was the subject of the *Shack* case, were warned to clean up their camps or face court closure actions. The closure actions were never brought by the state, though migrant workers later confirmed their right to sue the state to demand that migrant camp regulations be enforced.[20]

In 1968, the Governor's task force issued its report on migrant labor, recommending that the state take steps to encourage unionization of the labor force. The notion of constructing state operated housing for migrant laborers was rejected, though such housing had been constructed in the early 1940's by the federal government and seriously considered in New Jersey at about the same time. In any case, the report was never acted upon by the state government. Tensions in the fields grew. By the summer of 1970, guns were being brandished and threats made against

---

[15] *See* 34 N.J. STAT. ANN. § 9A-4.1 *et seq.*

[16] A good portion of the New Jersey migrant worker dispute story was told in the N.Y. TIMES on Sept. 5, 1966, at 11, col. 1; June 11, 1967, at 36, col. 1; June 14, 1967, at 49, col. 8; Aug. 22, 1967, at 1, col. 1; Aug. 23, 1967, at 27, col. 3; Aug. 26, 1967, at 53, col. 1; Aug. 27, 1967, at 53, col. 1; Aug. 29, 1967, at 25, col. 1; Aug. 30, 1967, at 24, col. 4; Aug. 8, 1970, at 19, col. 2; Aug. 17, 1970, at 1, col. 1; and May 12, 1971, at 1, col. 1.

[17] The group eventually produced a report: GOVERNOR'S TASK FORCE ON MIGRANT FARM LABOR, POVERTY IN THE LAND OF PLENTY: THE SEASONAL FARM WORKER IN NEW JERSEY (1968).

[18] N.Y. TIMES, Sept. 5, 1966, at 11, col. 1.

[19] The case was filed, but dismissed on state action grounds. That holding was reversed, but only for a factual hearing on whether state action was present. Peper v. Cedarbrook Farms, Inc., 437 F.2d 1209 (3d Cir. 1971). The case was then dropped. By that time the New Jersey Supreme Court had agreed to review the *Shack* case and the NAACP Legal Defense Fund correctly assumed their interests would prevail in that setting. *See* Casenote, State v. Shack, 46 N.Y.U. L. REV. 834, 840-845 (1971).

[20] Colon v. Tedesco, 125 N.J. Super. 446, 311 A.2d 393 (1973).

antipoverty workers, lawyers and reporters.[21] Frank Tejeras noted, "We got sick and tired of getting pushed out. Often the farmers would come out with guns. I used to kiss my wife and daughter goodbye everyday because I didn't know if I'd be coming home."[22]

On August 6, 1970, Frank Tejeras, a field worker for the Farm Workers Division of the Southern Citizen Organization for Poverty Elimination (SCOPE), went to Tedesco's farm to pick up Tona Rivera, whose face had been slashed some weeks earlier, and take him to the hospital to remove stitches from the wound. The injury was festering because the stitches had been in too long—three weeks. Tejeras passed the "No Trespassing" signs posted along the roadside of the farm and walked up the dirt road toward the migrant camp. Tedesco, rifle in hand, confronted Tejeras and told Tejeras to leave. He left.

Tejeras called Peter Shack, a staff attorney at the Farm Workers Division of Camden Regional Legal Services. The two of them agreed to return to the farm the next day with Ronald Sullivan of the TIMES . At about nine o'clock the next morning Shack, Tejeras and Sullivan (with camera in hand) entered Morris Tedesco's farm. Once again they passed the "No Trespassing" signs posted along the roadside of the farm and walked up the dirt road toward the migrant labor camp.

Tedesco was not pleased. Though without his rifle this time, he was reported to have cursed Shack and Tejeras, said that not "even President Nixon" would be allowed to see the farm, and, when Sullivan tried to take his picture, struck the camera against Sullivan's face and yelled, "I'll smash you for this; I'm going to get you for this. This is my property. You can't come in here looking around!" Shack, Tejeras and Sullivan decided to stay at the farm. State troopers were called and about two hours later all three were arrested and charged with trespass. Later in the day, Tejeras went back to the farm, picked up Rivera and took him to the hospital. Two days later, Tejeras went back to the farm and picked up another worker, Ramon Cruz, whom Shack had wanted to see at the farm. Cruz had suffered a cut on his hand while working in the fields. He was unable to work and had not received wages for a month.

The case against Sullivan was severed from the Shack-Tejeras matter by Judge Steven Kleiner. Kleiner may have been influenced to split the cases by the First Amendment overtones of the Sullivan matter or by the fact that the NEW YORK TIMES had sued Tedesco in tort for damages caused the paper by the battery of its employee, Sullivan. The charges against Sullivan were eventually dropped and the TIMES agreed to dismiss the tort action. The dispute and resultant publicity led to another round of calls for action by state and federal officials against poorly run farms in southern New Jersey and for adoption of legislation guaranteeing government workers and certain other persons access to labor camps. Early the next year, the Justice Department sued for the first time, seeking access to a migrant labor camp to investigate potential violations of civil rights.[23]

---

[21] N.Y. TIMES, Aug. 8, 1970, at 19, col. 2.

[22] Telephone Interview with Frank Tejeras, Aug. 4, 1986.

[23] N.Y. TIMES, Aug. 20, 1970, at 23, col. 1; Aug. 23, 1970, at 39, col. 1; Mar. 14, 1971, at 70, col. 1. *See* Folgueras v. Hassle, 331 F. Supp. 615 (W.D. Mich. 1971).

[b]   Opinion of the New Jersey Supreme Court in *New Jersey v. Shack*

State of New Jersey v. Shack and Tejeras

New Jersey Supreme Court
58 N.J. 297, 277 A.2d 369 (1971)

Max B. Rothman, Camden Regional Services, Inc., for appellants (David H. Dugan, III, Peter K. Shack and Christian B. Peper, Jr. (of the Missouri bar), Camden Regional Legal Services, Inc., attorneys; on the brief).

Samuel J. Serata, Asst. Prosecutor, for respondent (Joseph Tuso, Cumberland County Prosecutor, attorney).

Barry H. Evenchick, Deputy Atty. Gen., for the Atty. Gen. of New Jersey, amicus curiae (George F. Kugler, Jr., Atty. Gen.).

Carl R. Lobel, Trenton, for New Jersey State Office of Legal Services, amicus curiae (Carl F. Bianchi, Trenton, attorney).

Frederick B. Lacey, U.S. Atty., submitted a brief on behalf of the United States, amicus curiae (Jerris Leonard, Asst. Atty. Gen., David L. Norman, Deputy Asst. Atty. Gen., and Joseph B. Scott, attorney, U.S. Dept. of Justice, of the D.C. bar, on the brief).

The opinion of the Court was delivered by

WEINTRAUB, C.J.

Defendants entered upon private property to aid migrant farmworkers employed and housed there. Having refused to depart upon the demand of the owner, defendants were charged with violating N.J.S.A. 2A:170-31 which provides that "[a]ny person who trespasses on any lands . . . after being forbidden so to trespass by the owner . . . is a disorderly person and shall be punished by a fine of not more than $50." Defendants were convicted in the Municipal Court of Deerfield Township and again on appeal in the County Court of Cumberland County on a trial *de novo*. R. 3:23-8(a). We certified their further appeal before argument in the Appellate Division.

Before us, no one seeks to sustain these convictions. The complaints were prosecuted in the Municipal Court and in the County Court by counsel engaged by the complaining landowner, Tedesco. However Tedesco did not respond to this appeal, and the county prosecutor, while defending abstractly the constitutionality of the trespass statute, expressly disclaimed any position as to whether the statute reached the activity of these defendants.

Complainant, Tedesco, a farmer, employs migrant workers for his seasonal needs. As part of their compensation, these workers are housed at a camp on his property.

Defendant Tejeras is a field worker for the Farm Workers Division of the Southwest Citizens Organization for Poverty Elimination, known by the acronym SCOPE, a nonprofit corporation funded by the Office of Economic Opportunity pursuant to an act of Congress, 42 U.S.C.A. §§ 2861-2864. The role of SCOPE includes providing for the "health services of the migrant farm worker."

Defendant Shack is a staff attorney with the Farm Workers Division of Camden Regional Legal Services, Inc., known as "CRLS," also a nonprofit corporation funded by the Office of Economic

Opportunity pursuant to an act of Congress, 42 U.S.C.A. § 2809(a)(3). The mission of CRLS includes legal advice and representation for these workers.

Differences had developed between Tedesco and these defendants prior to the events which led to the trespass charges now before us. Hence when defendant Tejeras wanted to go upon Tedesco's farm to find a migrant worker who needed medical aid for the removal of 28 sutures, he called upon defendant Shack for his help with respect to the legalities involved. Shack, too, had a mission to perform on Tedesco's farm; he wanted to discuss a legal problem with another migrant worker there employed and housed. Defendants arranged to go to the farm together. Shack carried literature to inform the migrant farmworkers of the assistance available to them under federal statutes, but no mention seems to have been made of that literature when Shack was later confronted by Tedesco.

Defendants entered upon Tedesco's property and as they neared the camp site where the farmworkers were housed, they were confronted by Tedesco who inquired of their purpose. Tejeras and Shack stated their missions. In response, Tedesco offered to find the injured worker, and as to the worker who needed legal advice, Tedesco also offered to locate the man but insisted that the consultation would have to take place in Tedesco's office and in his presence. Defendants declined, saying they had the right to see the men in the privacy of their living quarters and without Tedesco's supervision. Tedesco thereupon summoned a State Trooper who, however, refused to remove defendants except upon Tedesco's written complaint. Tedesco then executed the formal complaints charging violations of the trespass statute.

I.

The constitutionality of the trespass statute, as applied here, is challenged on several scores.

It is urged that the First Amendment rights of the defendants and of the migrant farmworkers were thereby offended. Reliance is placed on *Marsh v. Alabama*, 326 U.S. 501 (1946), where it was held that free speech was assured by the First Amendment in a company-owned town which was open to the public generally and was indistinguishable from any other town except for the fact that the title to the property was vested in a private corporation. Hence a Jehovah's Witness who distributed literature on a sidewalk within the town could not be held as a trespasser. . . .

[*Marsh* rests] upon the fact that the property was in fact opened to the general public. There may be some migrant camps with the attributes of the company town in *Marsh* and of course they would come within its holding. But there is nothing of that character in the case before us, and hence there would have to be an extension of *Marsh* to embrace the immediate situation.

Defendants also maintain that the application of the trespass statute to them is barred by the Supremacy Clause of the United States Constitution, Art. VI, cl. 2, and this on the premise that the application of the trespass statute would defeat the purpose of the federal statutes, under which SCOPE and CRLS are funded, to reach and aid the migrant farmworker. The brief of the United States, *amicus curiae*, supports that approach. Here defendants rely upon cases construing the National Labor Relations Act, 29 U.S.C.A. § 151 *et seq.*, and holding that an employer may in some circumstances be guilty of an unfair labor practice in violation of that statute if the employer denies union organizers an opportunity to communicate with his employees at some suitable place upon the employer's premises. *See NLRB v. Babcock and Wilcox Co.*, 351 U.S. 105 (1956). The brief of New Jersey State Office of Legal Services, *amicus curiae*, asserts the workers' Sixth Amendment right to counsel in criminal matters is involved and suggests also that a right to counsel in civil matters is a "penumbra" right emanating from the whole Bill of Rights under the thinking of *Griswold v. Connecticut*, 381 U.S. 479 (1965), or is a privilege of national citizenship protected by the privileges and immunities clause of the Fourteenth Amendment, or is a right "retained by the people" under the Ninth Amendment, citing a dictum in *United Public Workers v. Mitchell*, 330 U.S. 75 (1947).

These constitutional claims are not established by any definitive holding. We think it unnecessary to explore their validity. The reason is that we are satisfied that under our State law the ownership of real property does not include the right to bar access to governmental services available to migrant workers and hence there was no trespass within the meaning of the penal statute. The policy considerations which underlie that conclusion may be much the same as those which would be weighed with respect to one or more of the constitutional challenges, but a decision in nonconstitutional terms is more satisfactory, because the interests of migrant workers are more expansively served in that way than they would be if they had no more freedom than these constitutional concepts could be found to mandate if indeed they apply at all.

II.

Property rights serve human values. They are recognized to that end, and are limited by it. Title to real property cannot include dominion over the destiny of persons the owner permits to come upon the premises. Their well-being must remain the paramount concern of a system of law. Indeed the needs of the occupants may be so imperative and their strength so weak, that the law will deny the occupants the power to contract away what is deemed essential to their health, welfare, or dignity.

Here we are concerned with a highly disadvantaged segment of our society. We are told that every year farmworkers and their families numbering more than one million leave their home areas to fill the seasonal demand for farm labor in the United States. The Migratory Farm Labor Problem in the United States (1969 Report of Subcommittee on Migratory Labor of the United States Senate Committee on Labor and Public Welfare), p. 1. The migrant farmworkers come to New Jersey in substantial numbers. The report just cited places at 55,700 the number of man-months of such employment in our State in 1968. The numbers of workers so employed here in that year are estimated at 1,300 in April; 6,500 in May; 9,800 in June; 10,600 in July; 12,100 in August; 9,600 in September; and 5,500 in October.

The migrant farmworkers are a community within but apart from the local scene. They are rootless and isolated. Although the need for their labors is evident, they are unorganized and without economic or political power. It is their plight alone that summoned government to their aid. In response, Congress provided under Title III-B of the Economic Opportunity Act of 1964 (42 U.S.C.A. § 2701 *et seq.*) for "assistance for migrant and other seasonally employed farmworkers and their families." Section 2861 states "the purpose of this part is to assist migrant and seasonal farmworkers and their families to improve their living conditions and develop skills necessary for a productive and self-sufficient life in an increasingly complex and technological society." Section 2862(b)(1) provides for funding of programs "to meet the immediate needs of migrant and seasonal farmworkers and their families, such as day care for children, education, health services, improved housing and sanitation (including the provision and maintenance of emergency and temporary housing and sanitation facilities), legal advice and representation, and consumer training and counseling." As we have said, SCOPE is engaged in a program funded under this section, and CRLS also pursues the objectives of this section although, we gather, it is funded under § 2809(a)(3), which is not limited in its concern to the migrant and other seasonally employed farmworkers and seeks "to further the cause of justice among persons living in poverty by mobilizing the assistance of lawyers and legal institutions and by providing legal advice, legal representation, counseling, education, and other appropriate services."

These ends would not be gained if the intended beneficiaries could be insulated from efforts to reach them. It is in this framework that we must decide whether the camp operator's rights in his lands may stand between the migrant workers and those who would aid them. The key to that aid is communication. Since the migrant workers are outside the mainstream of the communities in which they are housed and are unaware of their rights and opportunities and of the services available to them, they can be reached only by positive efforts tailored to that end. *The Report of the Governor's Task Force on Migrant Farm Labor* (1968) noted that "One of the major problems related to seasonal farm labor is the lack of adequate direct information with regard to the availability of public services," and that "there is a dire need to provide the workers with basic educational and informational material in a language and style that can be readily understood by the migrant." The report stressed the problem of access and deplored the notion that property rights may stand as a barrier, saying "In our judgment, 'no trespass' signs represent the last dying remnants of paternalistic behavior."

A man's right in his real property of course is not absolute. It was a maxim of the common law that one should so use his property as not to injure the rights of others . . . . Although hardly a precise solvent of actual controversies, the maxim does express the inevitable proposition that rights are relative and there must be an accommodation when they meet. Hence it has long been true that necessity, private or public, may justify entry upon the lands of another.

The subject is not static. As pointed out in 5 Powell, *Real Property* (Rohan 1970) § 745, pp. 493-494, while society will protect the owner in his permissible interests in land, yet

. . . [S]uch an owner must expect to find the absoluteness of his property rights curtailed by the organs of society, for the promotion of the best interests of others for whom these organs also operate as protective agencies. The necessity for such curtailments is greater in a modern industrialized and urbanized society than it was in the relatively simple American society of fifty, 100, or 200 years ago. The current balance between individualism and dominance of the social interest depends not only upon political and social ideologies, but also upon the physical and social facts of the time and place under discussion.

Professor Powell added in § 746, pp. 494-496:

As one looks back along the historic road traversed by the law of land in England and in America, one sees a change from the viewpoint that he who owns may do as he pleases with what he owns, to a position which hesitatingly embodies an ingredient of stewardship; which grudgingly, but steadily, broadens the recognized scope of social interests in the utilization of things . . . .

To one seeing history through the glasses of religion, these changes may seem to evidence increasing embodiments of the golden rule. To one thinking in terms of political and economic ideologies, they are likely to be labeled evidences of "social enlightenment," or of "creeping socialism" or even of "communistic infiltration," according to the individual's assumed definitions and retained or acquired prejudices. With slight attention to words or labels, time marches on toward new adjustments between individualism and the social interests.

This process involves not only the accommodation between the right of the owner and the interests of the general public in his use of his property, but involves also an accommodation between the right of the owner and the right of individuals who are parties with him in consensual transactions relating to the use of the property. Accordingly substantial alterations have been made as between a landlord and his tenant. *See Reste Realty Corp. v. Cooper*, 53 N.J. 444, 251 A.2d 268 (1969); *Marini v. Ireland*, 56 N.J. 130, 265 A.2d 526 (1970).

The argument in this case understandably included the question whether the migrant worker should be deemed to be a tenant and thus entitled to the tenant's right to receive visitors, . . . or whether his residence on the employer's property should be deemed to be merely incidental and in aid of his employment, and hence to involve no possessory interest in the realty . . . .

We see no profit in trying to decide upon a conventional category and then forcing the present subject into it. That approach would be artificial and distorting. The quest is for a fair adjustment of the competing needs of the parties, in the light of the realities of the relationship between the migrant worker and the operator of the housing facility.

Thus approaching the case, we find it unthinkable that the farmer-employer can assert a right to isolate the migrant worker in any respect significant for the worker's well-being. The farmer, of course, is entitled to pursue his farming activities without interference, and this defendants readily concede. But we see no legitimate need for a right in the farmer to deny the worker the opportunity for aid available from federal, State, or local services, or from recognized charitable groups seeking to assist him. Hence representatives of these agencies and organizations may enter upon the premises to seek out the worker at his living quarters. So, too, the migrant worker must be allowed to receive visitors there of his own choice, so long as there is no behavior hurtful to others, and members of the press may not be denied reasonable access to workers who do not object to seeing them.

It is not our purpose to open the employer's premises to the general public if in fact the employer himself has not done so. We do not say, for example, that solicitors or peddlers of all kinds may enter on their own; we may assume for the present that the employer may regulate their entry or bar them, at least if the employer's purpose is not to gain a commercial advantage for himself or if the regulation does not deprive the migrant worker of practical access to things he needs.

And we are mindful of the employer's interest in his own and in his employees' security. Hence he may reasonably require a visitor to identify himself, and also to state his general purpose if the migrant worker has not already informed him that the visitor is expected. But the employer may not deny the worker his privacy or interfere with his opportunity to live with dignity and to enjoy associations customary among our citizens. These rights are too fundamental to be denied on the basis of an interest in real property and too fragile to be left to the unequal bargaining strength of the parties.

It follows that defendants here invaded no possessory right of the farmer-employer. Their conduct was therefore beyond the reach of the trespass statute. The judgments are accordingly reversed and the matters remanded to the County Court with directions to enter judgments of acquittal.

For reversal and remandment: CHIEF JUSTICE WEINTRAUB and JUSTICES JACOBS, FRANCIS, PROCTOR, HALL and SCHETTINO—6.

For affirmance: None.

[c] Explanatory Notes

[*i*] *Events After the Case.* Morris Tedesco reacted strongly to *Shack.* "'We now might as well turn the country over to the Russians,' he said. The decision, he added, will only create more conflict this summer and force the remaining farmers in New Jersey 'to clear out within six months.' "[24] Access problems apparently eased somewhat after the decision. People had more confidence going in, though there was still some resistance.[25] Migrant life itself did not change a whole lot according to Tejeras. But the composition of the work force did. By the mid-1980s the vast majority of the seasonal workers are Puerto Rican. Black migrants from the south were not appearing in large numbers.

[*ii*] *The Role of the State of New Jersey.* The party most obviously interested in whether Shack and Tejeras could enter the farm was the owner, Tedesco, not the State of New Jersey, the named plaintiff in the case. Tedesco could have filed a civil claim against Shack and Tejeras for trespass. But when he called the police to have the visitors removed, the state authorities would not help him without the filing of a criminal complaint. When Tedesco did so, the official power of the state was called upon. At the Municipal Court level, where the first trial was held, state prosecutors generally do not appear in minor criminal cases. The arresting officer or a city attorney usually acts as the prosecutor. In this case, Tedesco actually retained an attorney to present the State's case, a highly unusual step. As the case worked its way up on appeal, Tedesco lost interest in the case, and no one showed up to defend his position. In fact, the named plaintiff, the State of New Jersey, filed an *amicus curiae* brief on the side of Shack and Tejeras! Stranger things have happened, but it is difficult to remember when.

[*iii*] *The Property Contours of the Farm.* Though Tedesco owned a fee simple in the farm, he was said to have limited his own property interest by hiring and housing migrant workers on the property. While the court declined to label the workers "tenants," the analogy was certainly apt in some ways. In both the worker and lease situations, the owner of a fee simple permits others to take possession of certain portions of the fee in return for services or cash. Taking such steps inevitably reduces the fee owner's ability to keep visitors off the farm. At a minimum you would assume that both workers and tenants could invite friends over for a chat.

Three other examples from New Jersey cases illustrate the point. *State of New Jersey v. Kolcz,* 114 N.J. Super. 408, 276 A.2d 595 (1971), involved an attempt by citizens to circulate petitions at the Rossmoor Community, a retirement village, seeking alterations in the form of a municipality's government. The owners of the village caused a trespass action to be brought, but the prosecution was dismissed. Similarly in *Inganamort v. Merker,* 148 N.J. Super. 506, 372 A.2d 1168 (1977), a landlord sought an injunction to halt the distribution of leaflets, prepared by a tenants' association, to the building's residents. The court refused to issue the injunction, holding that such activities were not unreasonable and did not interfere with the operation of the building. In a recent case, the same issue came up in a condominium setting. A private citizens group was allowed to distribute flyers about school board candidates inside three condominium apartment towers containing over a thousand units. *Guttenberg Taxpayers and Rentpayers Association v. Galaxy Towers Condominium Association,* 297 N.J. Super. 404, 688 A.2d 156 (1996).

---

[24] N.Y. TIMES, May 12, 1971, at 1, col. 7.

[25] Telephone Interview with Louis Gutierrez, Field Worker with Camden Regional Legal Services, July 29, 1986.

[*iv*]   *"Public" Private Property.* The ringing statement in the *Shack* opinion that "property rights serve human values," emulates many of the values of both Johnson's Great Society and the Representation Reinforcement notion that courts should protect the interests of the least well represented. It is a far cry from the late nineteenth century Formalist notion that the primary role of government is to protect private contract and property arrangements from outside interference. There are many attributes of the contemporary legal world that take seriously the *Shack* view of property. Some attempts to exclude persons from property, such as those based on racial prejudice, for example, are prohibited by Constitutional or statutory law and apply to virtually all property owners. Even if a person owning property covered by a civil rights statute has the greatest personal dislike for an individual or group, that dislike must be suppressed. But owners of "private" property may also lose their ability to exclude persons from their land for a variety of other reasons. Tedesco, for example, lost his ability to exclude certain persons from his farm because he chose to let other people reside on his property.

Other examples abound. Consider *Streeter v. Brogan*, 113 N.J. Super. 486, 491-493, 274 A.2d 312, 315-316 (1971). Brogan was a disabled Korean War veteran with a stepson serving in the marines. He leased a gas station from Sun Oil Company, where he posted a large sign, saying that the peace symbol, frequently displayed in Vietnam War protests, was a symbol of hate and the Anti-Christ. Streeter and 13 other plaintiffs drove several cars into the station, each emblazoned with the peace symbol, and asked for gas. Brogan refused to serve them. When the plaintiffs refused to leave the station, the police were called. Streeter and the others left under threat of arrest. A short time later they sued Brogan and got their gas. The court wrote, in part:

> Plaintiffs . . . claim the right to service at Brogan's gasoline service station without discrimination, in accordance with the common law rights of the public to accommodations at an inn, including the feeding and stabling of their horses, and to farrier's services in attending to and shoeing horses.
>
> . . . .
>
> Defendant Brogan contends that the extension of the innkeeper's common law duties to the gasoline service station proprietor is not logically warranted. The gasoline service station proprietor does not enjoy the monopoly position which most innkeepers enjoyed at the time their duties were fixed in the middle ages. If the innkeeper cast out a wayfarer, the wayfarer might sleep overnight in a hedgerow. The motor vehicle driver who is refused gasoline at one station may drive nearby to be supplied, to any one of 12 other stations within a half mile radius of Brogan's, for example.
>
> On the other hand, if this court sustains defendant Brogan, the proprietor of each nearby gasoline service station could refuse to supply gasoline to plaintiffs and others displaying the peace symbol on their cars.
>
> Motor vehicles approach being a necessity today. To many people railroad or other public transportation is unavailable. Private motor vehicles provide basic transportation, including transportation to places of employment. As the motor vehicle is a necessity for a large segment of the population, so too is gasoline . . . .
>
> . . . .
>
> The inn survives as the inn or hotel or motel. Its services in feeding and stabling horses, the motor power for transportation before motor vehicles, and the services of the farrier in attending to and shoeing horses, may be viewed as assumed by the gasoline service station

proprietor and garage keeper, who render equivalent fueling and maintenance services for motor vehicles. Transportation would falter and travelers be stranded in a transportation system dominated by the motor vehicle if the gasoline service station proprietor or garage keeper could pick and choose his customers arbitrarily, just as the danger was in a transportation system dependent upon horses whenever there was discrimination by an innkeeper or farrier.

[v] **Caution.** That New Jersey has decided cases in a certain way does not mean that judges in all other states agree. Though there is some federal law governing all states on this subject, the parameters of the right of fee simple owners to exclude are largely left to each state to resolve. Brogan may well have won his case if the station was in another state. It is interesting to note, however, that *Shack* is not totally without company in other jurisdictions. *See State of Washington v. Fox*, 82 Wash. 2d 289, 510 P.2d 230 (1973) (access by attorney and union organizer not trespass).

[d] Problem Notes

[i] **The Right to Exclude.** Setting limitations on the right to exclude is not easy. For each of the following problems, answer two questions. First, how do you think the New Jersey Supreme Court would decide them? Second, how would you decide them? The first question is intended to make you think about the degree to which people with knowledge about legal precedents are able to predict the outcomes of legal disputes. In this setting *Shack* is the precedent. The second question is intended to make you think about how exclusions from property ought to be handled.

(a) Suppose that neither Shack nor Tejeras had any clients among the migrant workers, but wished to enter the farm to distribute leaflets describing the services their organizations offered. Would Tedesco have to admit them? What if Tedesco, rather than owning a farm, owned an apartment building, a shopping center, an office building, or a restaurant?

(b) If newspaper reporters sought to interview and photograph the migrant workers on Tedesco's farm, would they be able to gain entry over Tedesco's objections? A lower New Jersey court deciding a similar case held that the reporters could gain access, but only if such access was reasonably related to legitimate needs of their publication and arranged so as not to interfere with the workers' schedules. *Freedman v. New Jersey State Police*, 135 N.J. Super. 297, 343 A.2d 148 (1975).

Where else may reporters go in New Jersey over the objections of the owner or occupant? How about the rehearsal hall of a symphony orchestra during a practice session? The locker rooms of a professional team after a game? Student lounges at a university dormitory? Faculty lounges in a faculty office building? A classroom? A hospital room? Your apartment or house?

(c) Suppose that the farm workers signed an employment contract with Tedesco stating that the workers agreed to work for Tedesco, to live in certain designated quarters, to receive a certain amount of pay for their labor, and to see visitors only with the express permission of Tedesco and in his presence if he wished. In addition, assume that this contract was read aloud to each worker on the farm before they signed it in whatever language the worker spoke. Would this contract be enforced?

(d) Suppose non-students or staff members wished to enter a private university campus, but not any of its buildings, to distribute political literature. Does the university have to admit them? *See State of New Jersey v. Schmid*, 84 N.J. 535, 423 A.2d 615 (1980), *aff'd sub nom.*

Princeton University v. Schmid, 455 U.S. 100 (1982), in which Princeton's efforts to eject a member of the United States Labor Party failed. Would it make any difference if the literature was racist, anti-semitic, hate mongering garbage? What if a member of the faculty or student body was distributing the literature?

(e) Suppose Shack was a "card counter" in Blackjack, that is, a person who remembers all the cards that have been displayed at a gambling table and makes his bets on the basis of probabilities as altered by the removal of cards played from the deck. Good card counters may, in certain situations, beat gambling houses at their own game. The casinos, of course, make great efforts to detect, and eject, the card counters. May they do so? See *Uston v. Resorts International Hotel, Inc.*, 89 N.J. 163, 445 A.2d 370 (1982), in which the New Jersey Supreme Court refused to permit such ejection. Is there any strong public policy supporting this result?[26]

[*ii*]   *The United States Constitution, Trespass and Institutional Preferences.* In the *Schmid* case mentioned just above, Princeton University claimed, among other things, that its First Amendment rights were violated by persons coming on campus to distribute literature without university permission. Does this make any sense? Who speaks for a university? What if a student, staff member or teacher disagreed with the university President or Board of Governors on some important issue? Could distribution of leaflets describing that difference be controlled by the university? Would it make any difference if the university was affiliated with a particular religious group and the leaflets recommended actions in conflict with that religion's teachings?[27]

[*iii*]   *Natural Law.* Both Johnson's Great Society and the opinion in *Shack* were verbalized in natural laws terms. Johnson often spoke of the value of each human being, the obligation to structure society to allow each person to flourish, and the inherent superiority of human sensibilities over material possessions. Similarly, the ringing statement in the *Shack* opinion—"Property rights serve human values"—affirms that the natural value of each person is more important than the property rights held by Tedesco. While such sentiments may certainly be used to support the Representation Reinforcement Theory's use of courts to protect the least well off, they suggest a far-reaching challenge to the legitimacy of most twentieth century modes of legal thought. For natural law's roots are often in religion, where claims that material wealth takes precedence over claims of human need are received coolly. *Shack* may well mirror such debates, for natural law theory was a backbone of the Civil Rights Movement. Martin Luther King, Jr. was church based and he often claimed that property rights had to give way to the natural law claims for equality and humanity. "One has a moral responsibility to disobey unjust laws," King wrote from the Birmingham jail in 1963. Though the *Shack* court did not speak in religious terms, might it have been making an attempt to use natural law theories of justice to aid its efforts to constrain the impact of the state's trespass statute?

---

[26] The New Jersey State Gambling Commission responded by revising the rules on card shuffling at the Blackjack tables, giving the dealers and casinos authority to use multiple deck card holders and much greater discretion in deciding when to reshuffle decks.

[27] *Cf.* Gay Rights Coalition of Georgetown University v. Georgetown University, 536 A.2d 1 (D.C. 1987), in which the court largely rejected a First Amendment freedom of religion claim by Georgetown University, a Jesuit institution. The court required the university to treat its gay and lesbian student groups like all other student groups, but allowed the school to decline to "recognize" the legitimacy of any group's belief structure and to bar use of the name of the University in the student group's title. The case was brought by the students under a District of Columbia law barring discrimination on the grounds of sexual orientation.

§ 7.05 The Public/Private Distinction and Critical Legal Studies

[1] Notes on the Public/Private Distinction

As you know from prior materials, the distinction between the private and public realms has been terribly important to the development of property law. Early Civic Republicans viewed property as intimately related to the public sphere. Indeed ownership of it was thought essential to the appropriate exercise of public responsibility. By the end of the nineteenth century, the concepts of public and private had largely split apart, with the role of public government being to preserve the operation of a private (largely masculine) economic sphere. That view, in turn, was thoroughly attacked by the Realists who insisted that splitting public and private was part of a larger set of political judgments about how the economy should be run, that the separation was artificial, and that legislative authorities should have the freedom to reconstruct those spheres if they wished.

These shifting attitudes about the importance of public and private economic spheres have been the subject of an enormous amount of academic literature. One of the classic formulations is excerpted below.

Morton J. Horwitz, *The History of the Public/Private Distinction*

130 U. Pa. L. Rev. 1423, 1424-1428 (1982)[28]

Although one can find the origins of the idea of a distinctively private realm in the natural-rights liberalism of Locke and his successors, only in the nineteenth century was the public/private distinction brought to the center of the stage in American legal and political theory. Before this could occur, it was necessary to undermine an earlier tradition of republican thought that had closely identified private virtue and public interest.

The emergence of the market as a central legitimating institution brought the public/private distinction into the core of legal discourse during the nineteenth century. Although, . . . there were earlier anticipations of a distinction between public law and private law, only the nineteenth century produced a fundamental conceptual and architectural division in the way we understand the law. One of the central goals of nineteenth century legal thought was to create a clear separation between constitutional, criminal, and regulatory law—public law—and the law of private transactions—torts, contracts, property, and commercial law.

. . . .

What were the concerns that created a virtual obsession with separating public and private law, both conceptually and practically, during the nineteenth century? Above all was the effort of orthodox judges and jurists to create a legal science that would sharply separate law from politics. By creating a neutral and apolitical system of legal doctrine and legal reasoning free from what was thought to be the dangerous and unstable redistributive tendencies of democratic politics, legal thinkers hoped to temper the problem of "tyranny of the majority." Just as nineteenth-century political economy elevated the market to the status of the paramount institution for distributing rewards on a supposedly neutral and apolitical basis, so too private law came to be understood as a neutral system for facilitating voluntary market transactions

---

[28] Copyright University of Pennsylvania Law Review. Reprinted by permission of the University of Pennsylvania Law Review and Morton J. Horwitz.

and vindicating injuries to private rights. The hostility to statutes expressed by nineteenth-century judges and legal thinkers reflected the view that state regulation of private relations was a dangerous and unnatural public intrusion into a system based on private rights.

The sharp distinction between public and private began to come under attack in reaction to the Supreme Court's 1905 decision in *Lochner v. New York*,[13] constitutionalizing freedom of contract. For the next 30 years, the most brilliant and original legal thinkers America has ever had devoted their energies to exposing the conservative ideological foundations of the public/private distinction. Culminating in the Legal Realist Movement of the 1920's and 1930's, judges such as Holmes, Brandeis, and Cardozo and legal theorists such as Roscoe Pound, Walter Wheeler Cook, Wesley Hohfeld, Robert Lee Hale, Arthur Corbin, Warren Seavey, Morris Cohen, and Karl Llewelyn devoted themselves to attacking the premises behind the public/private distinction.[14] Paralleling arguments then current in political economy, they ridiculed the invisible-hand premise behind any assumption that private law could be neutral and apolitical. All law was coercive and had distributive consequences, they argued. It must therefore be understood as a delegation of coercive public power to individuals, and could only be justified by public policies. Contract, that most "private" of nineteenth-century legal categories, was reconceptualized as simply a delegation of public power that could be justified only by public purposes. Fuller and Perdue's famous 1936 article on contract damages[15] demonstrated that awarding damages for breach of contract could not be deduced from the "logic" of contract or from the will of the parties, but was a state-imposed sanction determined by the choice among policies. *Shelley v. Kraemer*[16] is perhaps the most famous culmination of a generation of successful attacks on the public/private distinction.

By 1940, it was a sign of legal sophistication to understand the arbitrariness of the division of law into public and private realms. No advanced legal thinker of that period, I am certain, would have predicted that forty years later the public/private dichotomy would still be alive and, if anything, growing in influence. What accounts for its surprising vitality?

Until World War II, twentieth-century progressivism emphasized the role of the state in creating institutions that would promote a public interest. In reaction to the spread of totalitarianism, progressivism after World War II capitulated to the argument that any substantive conception of the public interest was simply the first step on the road to totalitarianism. The idea of a public interest thus came to be formulated in the purely proceduralist terms of interest-group pluralism—simply as whatever was the outcome of competition among interest groups. This was, it should be emphasized, a twentieth-century return to a market theory of the public interest—but this time the competitors were groups and the market was the political process.

Earlier, progressivism posited a sharp conflict between a substantive public interest and private self-interest, and regarded a primary function of the state as creating institutions that would transcend private self-interest. Unless the individualism and selfishness that was part of the culture of capitalism could be moderated, they believed, the system could not survive.

---

[13] 198 U.S. 45 (1905).

[14] *See, e.g.*, Cohen, *Property and Sovereignty*, 13 CORNELL L.Q. 8 (1927); Cohen, *The Basis of Contract*, 46 HARV. L. REV. 553 (1933); Hale, *Force and the State: A Comparison of "Political" and "Economic" Compulsion*, 35 COLUM. L. REV. 149 (1935); Pound, *Liberty of Contract*, 18 YALE L.J. 454 (1909).

[15] Fuller & Perdue, *The Reliance Interest in Contract Damages* (pt. 1), 46 YALE L.J. 52 (1936).

[16] 334 U.S. 1 (1948).

Most of the Legal Realists operated out of this political paradigm and understood their task to be the moderation and limitation of private greed and domination.

But once the idea of a substantive public interest began to confront ridicule after World War II, the function of the state came to be redefined as simply a reflection of the sum of the vectors of private conflict. Private self-interest, which under the progressive program was to be kept suspiciously in check, once again became the only legitimate political reality, and the idea of an autonomous public realm began correspondingly to sink into oblivion.

The recent revival of natural-rights individualism in legal and political theory is a symptom of the collapse of a belief in a distinctively public realm standing above private self-interest. It is not only a dangerous symptom of the unraveling of all sense of community, but also a relapse into a predatory and vicious conception of politics.

Yet reality has a funny way of intruding upon theory. The public/private distinction could approximate the actual arrangement of legal and political institutions only in a society and economy of relatively small, decentralized, nongovernmental units. Private power began to become increasingly indistinguishable from public power precisely at the moment, late in the nineteenth century, when large-scale corporate concentration became the norm. The attack on the public/private distinction was the result of a widespread perception that so-called private institutions were acquiring coercive power that had formerly been reserved to governments.

The contemporary erosion of the public/private distinction in many areas of legal doctrine . . . is but another symptom of the passing of that world of nineteenth-century decentralized competitive capitalism that once made that distinction a rough approximation of reality.

The most recent attacks on the public/private distinction have come from the Critical Legal Studies (CLS) Movement. CLS was (and is) an agglomeration of people with quite different perspectives on legal institutions. What initially drew them together was a common belief in indeterminacy. They took seriously the insights of the more radical Realists that rules were subject to dispute, that exceptions to rules often if not always undercut the content of the basic rules, that oral and written language was subject to infinite variation and deconstruction, and that law reflected the allocation of power more than logical, rigorous thought.

While they all believed in some version of the Indeterminacy Principle, they came to that point of view from quite different angles. Some were largely without attachment to any particular, well structured mode of legal thought. Their work was largely "deconstructionist." Their intellectual roots were frequently in existentialism, in which one's belief structure develops out of life's experience. It relishes exercise of freedom as a learning event and denies the utility of pre-existing belief structures. This was not nihilism, but it did make the role of a lawyer quite difficult to grasp. Though much of the CLS writing of this sort was designed to deconstruct doctrine and make clear its indeterminacy, many writing that way actually had a vision of the unempowered driving them. Cutting doctrine down to size was done to expose the nature of power relationships buried beneath the doctrine and open up room for political action.

Many other CLS writers were passionate believers in both indeterminacy and a variety of structured modes of thought. Whether they came out of a Marxist tradition, as many did, a romantic humanist tradition commonly espoused in the sixties, or some other tradition, many brought a highly structured set of beliefs with them. A fundamental problem for them had to be how to make their belief structure co-exist with indeterminacy. At first glance that is an impossible task. What could possibly mediate between belief and deconstruction?

One might take the path that glorifies indeterminacy because it provides lawyers with the ability to act in influential ways. Whatever your foundational belief structure might be, the theory goes, the law is so porous that you are free to move and shake its institutions. There are certainly some historical examples of legal change that lend themselves to that idea. The changes made in landlord-tenant law in cases like *Marini v. Ireland*, which you will read in Chapter 8 (*see* p. 654, below), gutted legal understandings thought impregnable for decades. Words thought to be well defined were given new meanings.

There are other possibilities. Indeterminacy, for example, does not necessarily mean that people never understand anything that other people say. It does not automatically mean that we are incapable of understanding more about each other. Communities with some shared intuitions and meanings might be possible. And those groups might be able to converse at times with other communities. To whatever extent that is so in an indeterminate world, education becomes plausible, political movements become worth the time spent creating them, and the arts become worth reading and listening to. Many offshoots from CLS, especially the various "perspectivist" movements that have arisen among racial, gender, or other groups, make such claims. If one group shares common values and can make others understand something about them, the theory goes, then cultural and legal change becomes manageable.

In sum, many CLS writers were interested in constructing ways of justifying action in the face of linguistic and institutional ambiguity. At a minimum, this was a very hard (perhaps impossible) project. Many found the whole undertaking flawed. The critique that indeterminacy justified anything if enough people believed in doing it and had the power to pull it off was telling to some. If believed, it meant that CLS could not reconstruct a theory that legitimated legal institutions beyond the power they exercised. Indeed, CLS arguably has fallen on hard times in recent years in part because many who sympathize with much of the project are not prepared to deconstruct the meanings of major institutions or of some legal terms, and in part because perspectivists insisting that their cultural situations may be understood undermines indeterminacy. Perspectivist theories are being plumbed, not only because they were a way of creating communities of understanding in a sea of ambiguity, but also because they are thought to be a way of articulating new foundational theories. African Americans, for example, are interested in the way talk about "rights" may provide a protective buffer, even in bad times, against those who are hostile to their cause. And feminists may not be particularly interested in deconstructing either talk about "rights," or the legal meaning of the word "no."

After reading a case like *State of New Jersey v. Shack*, some portions of the Critical Legal Studies critique of the public/private distinction should be visible to you. The use of words like "trespass" or "right to exclude" or "ownership" were not very helpful in telling the court what to do. The legal terms of art at issue in the case were subject to innumerable interpretations. It is, therefore, an appropriate moment to give you a sample of the sort of writing that pushes us to recognize the ambiguity of legal concepts about property. The excerpt that follows is a now classic piece of Critical Legal Studies writing by one of its best known adherents.

Duncan Kennedy, *The Stages of the Decline of the Public/Private Distinction*

130 U. Pa. L. Rev. 1349, 1351-1357 (1982).[29]

An important and exciting moment in the history of a distinction arrives when troublemakers begin to argue that the distinction is incoherent because, no matter how you try to apply it, you end up in a situation of hopeless contradiction. The form of this argument is likely to be as follows: you say that something is X if it has property A, and that it is Y if it has property B. But everything has property A, so everything is X, and the distinction between X and Y has collapsed.

Some fun examples of this involve the public/private distinction. Morris Cohen argued that because both property rights and contract rights were enforced by the state, the so-called rights were really better conceived as delegated public powers, whose exercise should be subject to the rules of public accountability we associate with legislators, rather than with the rules of private accountability we associate with—what else?—property and contract.[9]

. . . .

In *Shelley v. Kraemer* this collapsing tactic succeeded so well that it failed. If state enforcement of the property and contract groundrules of the market was "state action" for fourteenth amendment purposes, then the fourteenth amendment required the states to outlaw any "private" actor who practiced racial discrimination. As seems to happen regularly in the collapsing mode, the extreme consequences that arguably follow from *abolition* of the distinction lead people to pull back and resort to:

Continuumization

Continuumization means that people see most entities (institutions, actors, actions) as "not absolutely one thing or another," rather than reserving this status for a small class of intermediate terms, or collapsing everything into one pole or the other. With the exception of polar situations—passing laws or deciding lawsuits representing the "public" extreme, choosing a toothpaste or making love representing the "private" extreme—everything is "somewhere in the middle." However, it seems intuitively fairly easy to range the things in the middle along a continuum.

Continuumization seems to go along with the disaggregation of the package of legal responses that once seemed to follow "logically" from the choice to categorize an institution one way or another. Institutions in the middle should have rules that are a mixture of public and private modes: for example, sewer districts should have to observe the constitutional prohibition against takings without just compensation but not the constitutional requirement of one-person/one-vote. In continuum consciousness, the ideal is a range of legal responses exactly calibrated to the range of fact situations: an overlay of one continuum on the other.

People who believe in continua tend to explain how they go about deciding what legal response is appropriate for a given institution by listing "factors" that "cut" one way or the other and must be "balanced."

---

[29] Copyright University of Pennsylvania Law Review. Reprinted by permission of the University of Pennsylvania Law Review and Duncan Kennedy.

[9] *See* M. Cohen, *Property and Sovereignty* and *The Basis of Contract*, in Law and the Social Order 41 and 69, 102 (1933); *see also* Brest, *State Action and Liberal Theory: A Casenote on* Flagg Brothers v. Brooks, 130 U. Pa. L. Rev. 1296, 1326-29 (1982).

. . . .

Loopification

Loopification is the most interesting (to me) of all the stages, because it is somewhat hypothetical.

. . . One's consciousness is loopified when the ends of the continuum seem closer to one another, in some moods (for some purposes, in some cases), than either end seems to the middle. Otherwise stated, one's consciousness is loopified when one seems to be able to move by a steady series of steps *around* the whole distinction, ending up where one started without ever reversing direction. Like wow, man.

In the case of the public/private distinction, loopification occurs when one realizes that the private sector includes both the market and the family. We often conceive the family in terms very much like those we apply to the state, and treat the family as a domain "affected with a public interest" to the very extent that it is intensely private. Likewise, we tend to understand the transactions of individual consumers, investors, tenants, and clients as more private than those of large or small businesses, but at the same time conceive of these individual transactions as more, rather than less, amenable to public regulation. All of this produces the following diagram, meant to be representative of the loopification of the public/private distinction.

Loopification of the Public/Private Distinction:

Very large corporations	Small businesses
Lawyers/doctors	Individual workers
Labor unions	Consumers
	Investors
Public utilities	Tenants
	Clients
Port authorities	
School boards	Churches
Local government with home rule	Married persons
Legislators	
Judges	
Executives	Parents

My assertion about this diagram is that you can move around it in a clockwise direction starting at the bottom with the classic state functionaries—legislators, judges, executives—and ending up with parents, feeling as you go that you are always moving in the direction of greater "privateness." Yet at the same time there is a sense in which the sequence eventually brings you back to where you began.

One ends up where one began because of all the ways in which we think of the family and the political community as close together rather than far apart. First, there are many analogies between them. They are both "units of government," rather than markets (though some law and economics types have recently argued for seeing them otherwise). Within them, actors play roles—occupy offices or statuses—which are fiduciary. There are lots of duties and lots of discretion, but neither the duty nor the discretion is like that of market actors. In the family and in the state, we tend to feel that overarching ideals ought to inform every decision, while we conceive the market actor as "free to do whatever she wants so long as she obeys the groundrules."

Second, political philosophy refers constantly to the ideals of the family, and philosophers of the family refer constantly to political ideals. The interpenetration of the two realms of discourse is so thorough that we might better speak of a single political/familial rhetoric. We use the market concept of consent or voluntariness only in a qualified, metaphorical, or "implied" sense in state and family. We temper the notion that you get what you paid for with natural law, natural right, immemorial custom, organic communitarian norms, divine will, and so forth.

Third, the blurring of institutional lines between the state and the family is more obvious than blurring along the market/family or market/state boundaries. It has been common forever to speak of the public functions of the family in producing and socializing "the next generation." Using this and other rationales, the state attempts to determine the content of and then enforce performance of familial roles, both of parents and children. Modern statutory schemes authorize social welfare agencies backed by courts to intervene on no more precise grounds than "the best interests of the child" or the child's "need for supervision." It often seems that the legislator sees parents as a mere adjunct or subagency of the state.

Finally and paradoxically, when people are speaking and thinking of the economy, or "world of work," as the "public sphere," they tend to lump politics, religion and sexuality together as an opposed sphere, into which an employer (for example) has no business intruding. In this perspective, what life in the state has in common with life in the family is that both are quintessentially *private*.

Following out these lines of similarity and difference, one simply loses one's ability to take the public/private distinction seriously as a description, as an explanation, or as a justification of anything.

[2]   A Note on Federal Constitutional Law and State Trespass Cases

Despite the severe critiques of the public/private distinction by Critical Legal Studies writers, it is very much alive in United States Supreme Court cases. A number of cases have arisen about the right of states to prosecute for trespass those who demonstrate inside enclosed shopping malls. The demonstrators, like Shack and Tejeras, claimed that their actions were not covered by state trespass statute or protected by freedom of speech clauses in state constitutions. Such claims have met with mixed success. Some states have provided the demonstrators with protection, provided they do not inconvenience others using the mall facilities. Other states have not. When demonstrators convicted under state law sought federal constitutional protection, however, they were turned aside. In standard First Amendment law, those demonstrating in public forums, such as sidewalks or parks, are constitutionally protected from state prosecution. But when the claim was made that the public forum rules should protect demonstrators inside shopping malls, the Supreme Court held that there was no state action[30] to support a First Amendment claim. *Hudgens v. N.L.R.B.*, 424 U.S. 507 (1976).[31] Since the mall was privately owned, the Court reasoned,

---

[30] Though the First Amendment runs only to actions of Congress, the Supreme Court has applied the same strictures to states by encompassing them within the meaning of the Due Process Clause of the Fourteenth Amendment. State action, therefore, is a prerequisite to claims of First Amendment violations at the state level.

[31] The case involved labor picketers, who also claimed protection under the National Labor Relations Act. The Court agreed that Congress could enact legislation under the Commerce Clause that might allow picketers to march inside of a mall, but refused to find a constitutional basis for compelling that result.

the state trespass laws were only being used to protect private rights. *Marsh v. Alabama*, discussed in the *Shack* opinion, p. 558 above, was distinguished on the grounds that the company town in the case provided all the services of a typical municipality.[32] While a Critical Legal Studies adherent would claim that the distinction between public and private action was completely blurred by the intervention of state policing authority under the trespass statutes, the Court preferred to dwell on the private ownership characteristics of the mall. And claims by someone wishing to reinforce the claims of those seeking recognition of non-majoritarian points of view were told to use public rather than private forums. The utility of the public/private distinction is further called into question as recent court decisions also narrow the scope of permissible activity in places, such as railroad stations and airports, thought until recently to be public forums.[33]

§ 7.06 Poverty, Property Ownership and the Supreme Court

While attempts to convince the Supreme Court to closely scrutinize classifications based on race and gender met with some success in the 1960s and 1970s, the Justices refused to cast a skeptical eye over class distinctions having a serious negative impact on the poor. While Representation Reinforcement theory seemed a descriptively accurate portrayal of the Court's responses to the Civil Rights and Women's Movements, the anti-poverty movement of the Great Society was left to its legislative or state court devices.

As noted earlier in Chapter 6, pp. 523–524 above, a number of state courts have invalidated the property tax systems used to fund public education in most states. Pursuit of state court remedies by school funding reformers was necessitated by the unwillingness of the Supreme Court to treat class distinctions as a basis for searching Equal Protection scrutiny. The 5-4 decision that reached that result, excerpted below, frames both the high water mark for class based Representation Reinforcement theory in the Supreme Court and the transition in modes of thought that occurred in the shift from the Warren to the more conservative Burger Court.[34]

[1]   Opinions of the United States Supreme Court in *San Antonio v. Rodriguez*

[a]   San Antonio Independent School District v. Rodriguez

Supreme Court of the United States
411 U.S. 1, 93 S. Ct. 1278, 36 L. Ed. 2d 16 (1973)

Mr. Justice POWELL delivered the opinion of the Court.

This suit attacking the Texas system of financing public education was initiated by Mexican-American parents whose children attend the elementary and secondary schools in the Edgewood Independent School District, an urban school district in San Antonio, Texas. They brought a class action on behalf of schoolchildren throughout the State who are members of minority groups or who are poor and reside in school districts having a low property tax base. Named as

---

[32] Company provided housing is making something of a comeback. Housing shortages, high housing costs and low unemployment rates are driving the provision of housing. Kirstin Grimsley, *Company Towns Are Back and Booming*, WASHINGTON POST A1, col. 1 (Nov. 27, 1998).

[33] *See, e.g.*, Leron v. National R.R. Passenger Corp., 12 F.3d 388 (2d Cir. 1993), dealing with Penn Station in New York City.

[34] Warren Burger became Chief Justice of the United States Supreme Court in 1969.

defendants[2] were the State Board of Education, the Commissioner of Education, the State Attorney General, and the Bexar County (San Antonio) Board of Trustees . . . . [The District Court] rendered its judgment in a per curiam opinion holding the Texas school finance system unconstitutional under the Equal Protection Clause of the Fourteenth Amendment . . . . For the reasons stated in this opinion, we reverse the decision of the District Court.

I

The first Texas State Constitution, promulgated upon Texas' entry into the Union in 1845, provided for the establishment of a system of free schools. Early in its history, Texas adopted a dual approach to the financing of its schools, relying on mutual participation by the local school districts and the State. As early as 1883, the state constitution was amended to provide for the creation of local school districts empowered to levy ad valorem taxes with the consent of local taxpayers for the "erection . . . of school buildings" and for the "further maintenance of public free schools." Such local funds as were raised were supplemented by funds distributed to each district from the State's Permanent and Available School Funds. The Permanent School Fund, its predecessor established in 1854 with $2,000,000 realized from an annexation settlement, was thereafter endowed with millions of acres of public land set aside to assure a continued source of income for school support. The Available School Fund, which received income from the Permanent School Fund as well as from a state ad valorem property tax and other designated taxes, served as the disbursing arm for most state educational funds throughout the late 1800's and first half of this century. Additionally, in 1918 an increase in state property taxes was used to finance a program providing free textbooks throughout the State.

Until recent times, Texas was a predominantly rural State and its population and property wealth were spread relatively evenly across the State. Sizable differences in the value of assessable property between local school districts became increasingly evident as the State became more industrialized and as rural-to-urban population shifts became more pronounced. The location of commercial and industrial property began to play a significant role in determining the amount of tax resources available to each school district. These growing disparities in population and taxable property between districts were responsible in part for increasingly notable differences in levels of local expenditure for education.

In due time it became apparent to those concerned with financing public education that contributions from the Available School Fund were not sufficient to ameliorate these disparities. Prior to 1939, the Available School Fund contributed money to every school district at a rate of $17.50 per school-age child. Although the amount was increased several times in the early 1940's, the Fund was providing only $46 per student by 1945.

Recognizing the need for increased state funding to help offset disparities in local spending and to meet Texas' changing educational requirements, the state legislature in the late 1940's undertook a thorough evaluation of public education with an eye toward major reform. In 1947, an 18-member committee, composed of educators and legislators, was appointed to explore alternative systems in other States and to propose a funding scheme that would guarantee a

---

[2] The San Antonio Independent School District, whose name this case still bears, was one of seven school districts in the San Antonio metropolitan area that were originally named as defendants. After a pretrial conference, the District Court issued an order dismissing the school districts from the case. Subsequently, the San Antonio Independent School District joined in the plaintiffs' challenge to the State's school finance system and filed an amicus curiae brief in support of that position in this Court.

minimum or basic educational offering to each child and that would help overcome interdistrict disparities in taxable resources. The Committee's efforts led to the passage of the Gilmer-Aikin bills, named for the Committee's co-chairmen, establishing the Texas Minimum Foundation School Program. Today, this Program accounts for approximately half of the total educational expenditures in Texas.

The Program calls for state and local contributions to a fund earmarked specifically for teacher salaries, operating expenses, and transportation costs. The State, supplying funds from its general revenues, finances approximately 80% of the Program, and the school districts are responsible—as a unit—for providing the remaining 20%. The districts' share, known as the Local Fund Assignment, is apportioned among the school districts under a formula designed to reflect each district's relative taxpaying ability. The Assignment is first divided among Texas' 254 counties pursuant to a complicated economic index that takes into account the relative value of each county's contribution to the State's total income from manufacturing, mining, and agricultural activities. It also considers each county's relative share of all payrolls paid within the State and, to a lesser extent, considers each county's share of all property in the State. Each county's assignment is then divided among its school districts on the basis of each district's share of assessable property within the county. The district, in turn, finances its share of the Assignment out of revenues from local property taxation.

The design of this complex system was twofold. First, it was an attempt to assure that the Foundation Program would have an equalizing influence on expenditure levels between school districts by placing the heaviest burden on the school districts most capable of paying. Second, the Program's architects sought to establish a Local Fund Assignment that would force every school district to contribute to the education of its children but that would not by itself exhaust any district's resources. Today every school district does impose a property tax from which it derives locally expendable funds in excess of the amount necessary to satisfy its Local Fund Assignment under the Foundation Program.

In the years since this program went into operation in 1949, expenditures for education—from state as well as local sources—have increased steadily. Between 1949 and 1967, expenditures increased approximately 500%. In the last decade alone the total public school budget rose from $750 million to $2.1 billion and these increases have been reflected in consistently rising per pupil expenditures throughout the State. Teacher salaries, by far the largest item in any school's budget, have increased dramatically—the state-supported minimum salary for teachers possessing college degrees has risen from $2,400 to $6,000 over the last 20 years.

The school district in which appellees reside, the Edgewood Independent School District, has been compared throughout this litigation with the Alamo Heights Independent School District. This comparison between the least and most affluent districts in the San Antonio area serves to illustrate the manner in which the dual system of finance operates and to indicate the extent to which substantial disparities exist despite the State's impressive progress in recent years. Edgewood is one of seven public school districts in the metropolitan area. Approximately 22,000 students are enrolled in its 25 elementary and secondary schools. The district is situated in the core-city sector of San Antonio in a residential neighborhood that has little commercial or industrial property. The residents are predominantly of Mexican-American descent: approximately 90% of the student population is Mexican-American and over 6% is Negro. The average assessed property value per pupil is $5,960—the lowest in the metropolitan area—and the median family income ($4,686) is also the lowest. At an equalized tax rate of $1.05 per $100 of assessed property—the highest in the metropolitan area—the district contributed $26 to the education of each child for the 1967-1968 school year above its Local Fund Assignment for the Minimum Foundation Program. The Foundation Program contributed $222 per pupil for a state-local total of $248. Federal funds added another $108 for a total of $356 per pupil.

Alamo Heights is the most affluent school district in San Antonio. Its six schools, housing approximately 5,000 students, are situated in a residential community quite unlike the Edgewood District. The school population is predominantly "Anglo," having only 18% Mexican-Americans and less than 1% Negroes. The assessed property value per pupil exceeds $49,000, and the median family income is $8,001. In 1967-1968 the local tax rate of $.85 per $100 of valuation yielded $333 per pupil over and above its contribution to the Foundation Program. Coupled with the $225 provided from that Program, the district was able to supply $558 per student. Supplemented by a $36 per-pupil grant from federal sources, Alamo Heights spent $594 per pupil.

Although the 1967-1968 school year figures provide the only complete statistical breakdown for each category of aid, more recent partial statistics indicate that the previously noted trend of increasing state aid has been significant. For the 1970-1971 school year, the Foundation School Program allotment for Edgewood was $356 per pupil, a 62% increase over the 1967-68 school year. Indeed, state aid alone in 1970-1971 equaled Edgewood's entire 1967-1968 school budget from local, state, and federal sources. Alamo Heights enjoyed a similar increase under the Foundation Program, netting $491 per pupil in 1970-1971.[35] These recent figures also reveal the extent to which these two districts' allotments were funded from their own required contributions to the Local Fund Assignment. Alamo Heights, because of its relative wealth, was required to contribute out of its local property tax collections approximately $100 per pupil, or about 20% of its Foundation grant. Edgewood, on the other hand, paid only $8.46 per pupil, which is about 2.4% of its grant. It appears then that, at least as to these two districts, the Local Fund Assignment does reflect a rough approximation of the relative taxpaying potential of each.

Despite these recent increases, substantial interdistrict disparities in school expenditures found by the District Court to prevail in San Antonio and in varying degrees throughout the State[38]

---

[35] Although the Foundation Program has made significantly greater contributions to both school districts over the last several years, it is apparent that Alamo Heights has enjoyed a larger gain. The sizable difference between the Alamo Heights and Edgewood grants is due to the emphasis in the State's allocation formula on the guaranteed minimum salaries for teachers. Higher salaries are guaranteed to teachers having more years of experience and possessing more advanced degrees. Therefore, Alamo Heights, which has a greater percentage of experienced personnel with advanced degrees, receives more state support. In this regard, the Texas Program is not unlike that presently in existence in a number of other States. J. Coones, W. Clune, & S. Sugarman, Private Wealth and Public Education 63-125 (1970). Because more dollars have been given to districts that already spend more per pupil, such Foundation formulas have been described as "anti-equalizing." The formula, however, is anti-equalizing only if viewed in absolute terms. The percentage disparity between the two Texas districts is diminished substantially by state aid. Alamo Heights derived in 1967-1968 almost 13 times as much money from local taxes as Edgewood did. The state aid grants to each district in 1970-1971 lowered the ratio to approximately two to one, i.e., Alamo Heights had a little more than twice as much money to spend per pupil from its combined state and local resources.

[38] The District Court relied on the findings presented in an affidavit submitted by Professor Berke of Syracuse University. His sampling of 110 Texas school districts demonstrated a direct correlation between the amount of a district's taxable property and its level of per-pupil expenditures. But this study found only a partial correlation between a district's median family income and per-pupil expenditures. The study also shows, in the relatively few districts at the extremes, an inverse correlation between percentage of minorities and expenditures.

still exist. And it was these disparities, largely attributable to differences in the amounts of money collected through local property taxation, that led the District Court to conclude that Texas' dual system of public school financing violated the Equal Protection Clause. The District Court held that the Texas system discriminates on the basis of wealth in the manner in which education is provided for its people. Finding that wealth is a "suspect" classification and that education is a "fundamental" interest, the District Court held that the Texas system could be sustained only if the State could show that it was premised upon some compelling state interest. On this issue the court concluded that "[n]ot only are defendants unable to demonstrate compelling state interests . . . they fail even to establish a reasonable basis for these classifications."

Texas virtually concedes that its historically rooted dual system of financing education could not withstand the strict judicial scrutiny that this Court has found appropriate in reviewing legislative judgments that interfere with fundamental constitutional rights or that involve suspect classifications. If, as previous decisions have indicated, strict scrutiny means that the State's system is not entitled to the usual presumption of validity, that the State rather than the complainants must carry a "heavy burden of justification," that the State must demonstrate that its educational system has been structured with "precision," and is "tailored" narrowly to serve legitimate objectives and that it has selected the "less drastic means" for effectuating its objectives, the Texas financing system and its counterpart in virtually every other State will not pass muster. The State candidly admits that "[n]o one familiar with the Texas system would contend that it has yet achieved perfection." Apart from its concession that educational financing in Texas has "defects" and "imperfections," the State defends the system's rationality with vigor and disputes the District Court's finding that it lacks a "reasonable basis."

This, then, establishes the framework for our analysis. We must decide, first, whether the Texas system of financing public education operates to the disadvantage of some suspect class or impinges upon a fundamental right explicitly or implicitly protected by the Constitution, thereby requiring strict judicial scrutiny. If so, the judgment of the District Court should be affirmed. If not, the Texas scheme must still be examined to determine whether it rationally furthers some legitimate, articulated state purpose and therefore does not constitute an invidious discrimination in violation of the Equal Protection Clause of the Fourteenth Amendment.

Categorized by Equalized Property Values, Median Family Income, and State- Local Revenue

Market Value Of Taxable Property Per Pupil	Median Family Income From 1960	Per Cent Minority Pupils	State & Local Revenues Per Pupil
Above $100,000 (10 districts)	$5,900	8%	$815
$100,000-$50,000 (26 districts)	$4,425	32%	$544
$50,000-$30,000 (30 districts)	$4,900	23%	$544
$30,000-$10,000 (40 districts)	$5,050	31%	$462
Below $10,000 (4 districts)	$3,325	79%	$305

Although the correlations with respect to family income and race appear only to exist at the extremes, and although the affiant's methodology has been questioned (see Goldstein, Interdistrict Inequalities in School Financing: A Critical Analysis of Serrano v. Priest and its Progeny, 120 U. Pa. L. Rev. 504, 523-525, nn. 67, 71 (1972)), insofar as any of these correlations is relevant to the constitutional thesis presented in this case we may accept its basic thrust. But see infra, at 1292-1293. For a defense of the reliability of the affidavit, see Berke, Carnevale, Morgan & White, The Texas School Finance Case: A Wrong in Search of a Remedy, 1 J. of L. & Educ. 659 (1972).

II

The District Court's opinion does not reflect the novelty and complexity of the constitutional questions posed by appellees' challenge to Texas' system of school financing. In concluding that strict judicial scrutiny was required, that court relied on decisions dealing with the rights of indigents to equal treatment in the criminal trial and appellate processes, and on cases disapproving wealth restrictions on the right to vote. Those cases, the District Court concluded, established wealth as a suspect classification. Finding that the local property tax system discriminated on the basis of wealth, it regarded those precedents as controlling. It then reasoned, based on decisions of this Court affirming the undeniable importance of education, that there is a fundamental right to education and that, absent some compelling state justification, the Texas system could not stand.

We are unable to agree that this case, which in significant aspects is sui generis, may be so neatly fitted into the conventional mosaic of constitutional analysis under the Equal Protection Clause. Indeed, for the several reasons that follow, we find neither the suspect-classification nor the fundamental-interest analysis persuasive.

A

The wealth discrimination discovered by the District Court in this case, and by several other courts that have recently struck down school-financing laws in other States,[48] is quite unlike any of the forms of wealth discrimination heretofore reviewed by this Court. Rather than focusing on the unique features of the alleged discrimination, the courts in these cases have virtually assumed their findings of a suspect classification through a simplistic process of analysis: since, under the traditional systems of financing public schools, some poorer people receive less expensive educations than other more affluent people, these systems discriminate on the basis of wealth. This approach largely ignores the hard threshold questions, including whether it makes a difference for purposes of consideration under the Constitution that the class of disadvantaged "poor" cannot be identified or defined in customary equal protection terms, and whether the relative—rather than absolute—nature of the asserted deprivation is of significant consequence. Before a State's laws and the justifications for the classifications they create are subjected to strict judicial scrutiny, we think these threshold considerations must be analyzed more closely than they were in the court below.

The case comes to us with no definitive description of the classifying facts or delineation of the disfavored class. Examination of the District Court's opinion and of appellees' complaint, briefs, and contentions at oral argument suggests, however, at least three ways in which the discrimination claimed here might be described. The Texas system of school financing might be regarded as discriminating (1) against "poor" persons whose incomes fall below some identifiable level of poverty or who might be characterized as functionally "indigent," or (2) against those who are relatively poorer than others, or (3) against all those who, irrespective of their personal incomes, happen to reside in relatively poorer school districts.[51] Our task must

---

[48] Serrano v. Priest, 5 Cal. 3d 584, 96 Cal. Rptr. 601, 487 P.2d 1241 (1971); Van Dusartz v. Hatfield, 334 F. Supp. 870 (D.C. Minn. 1971); Robinson v. Cahill, 118 N.J. Super. 223, 287 A.2d 187 (1972); Milliken v. Green, 389 Mich. 1, 203 N.W.2d 457 (1972), rehearing granted, Jan. 1973.

[51] At oral argument and in their brief, appellees suggest that description of the personal status of the residents in districts that spend less on education is not critical to their case. In their view, the Texas system is impermissibly

be to ascertain whether, in fact, the Texas system has been shown to discriminate on any of these possible bases and, if so, whether the resulting classification may be regarded as suspect.

The precedents of this Court provide the proper starting point. The individuals, or groups of individuals, who constituted the class discriminated against in our prior cases shared two distinguishing characteristics: because of their impecunity they were completely unable to pay for some desired benefit, and as a consequence, they sustained an absolute deprivation of a meaningful opportunity to enjoy that benefit. In Griffin v. Illinois, 351 U.S. 12 (1956), and its progeny, the Court invalidated state laws that prevented an indigent criminal defendant from acquiring a transcript, or an adequate substitute for a transcript, for use at several stages of the trial and appeal process. The payment requirements in each case were found to occasion *de facto* discrimination against those who, because of their indigency, were totally unable to pay for transcripts. And the Court in each case emphasized that no constitutional violation would have been shown if the State had provided some "adequate substitute" for a full stenographic transcript.

. . . .

[I]n Bullock v. Carter, 405 U.S. 134 (1972), the Court invalidated the Texas filing-fee requirement for primary elections. Both of the relevant classifying facts found in the previous cases were present there. The size of the fee, often running into the thousands of dollars and, in at least one case, as high as $8,900, effectively barred all potential candidates who were unable to pay the required fee. As the system provided "no reasonable alternative means of access to the ballot," inability to pay occasioned an absolute denial of a position on the primary ballot.

Only appellees' first possible basis for describing the class disadvantaged by the Texas school-financing system—discrimination against a class of definably "poor" persons—might arguably meet the criteria established in these prior cases. Even a cursory examination, however, demonstrates that neither of the two distinguishing characteristics of wealth classifications can be found here. First, in support of their charge that the system discriminates against the "poor," appellees have made no effort to demonstrate that it operates to the peculiar disadvantage of any class fairly definable as indigent, or as composed of persons whose incomes are beneath any designated poverty level. Indeed, there is reason to believe that the poorest families are not necessarily clustered in the poorest property districts. A recent and exhaustive study of school districts in Connecticut concluded that "[i]t is clearly incorrect . . . to contend that the 'poor' live in 'poor' districts . . . . Thus, the major factual assumption of *Serrano*—that the educational financing system discriminates against the 'poor'—is simply false in Connecticut."[53] Defining "poor" families as those below the Bureau of the Census "poverty level," the Connecticut study found, not surprisingly, that the poor were clustered around commercial and industrial areas—those same areas that provide the most attractive sources of property tax income for school districts. Whether a similar pattern would be discovered in Texas is not known, but there is no basis on the record in this case for assuming that the poorest people—defined by reference to any level of absolute impecunity—are concentrated in the poorest districts.

---

discriminatory even if relatively poor districts do not contain poor people. There are indications in the District Court opinion that it adopted this theory of districts discrimination. The opinion repeatedly emphasizes the comparative financial status of districts and early in the opinion it describes appellees' class as being composed of "all . . . children throughout Texas who live in school districts with low property valuations."

[53] Note, A Statistical Analysis of the School Finance Decisions: On Winning Battles and Losing Wars, 81 Yale L.J. 1303, 1328-1329 (1972).

Second, neither appellees nor the District Court addressed the fact that, unlike each of the foregoing cases, lack of personal resources has not occasioned an absolute deprivation of the desired benefit. The argument here is not that the children in districts having relatively low assessable property values are receiving no public education; rather, it is that they are receiving a poorer quality education than that available to children in districts having more assessable wealth. Apart from the unsettled and disputed question whether the quality of education may be determined by the amount of money expended for it,[56] a sufficient answer to appellees' argument is that, at least where wealth is involved, the Equal Protection Clause does not require absolute equality or precisely equal advantages. Nor indeed, in view of the infinite variables affecting the educational process, can any system assure equal quality of education except in the most relative sense. Texas asserts that the Minimum Foundation Program provides an "adequate" education for all children in the State. By providing 12 years of free public-school education, and by assuring teachers, books, transportation, and operating funds, the Texas Legislature has endeavored to "guarantee, for the welfare of the state as a whole, that all people shall have at least an adequate program of education. This is what is meant by 'A Minimum Foundation Program of Education.'" The State repeatedly asserted in its briefs in this Court that it has fulfilled this desire and that it now assures "every child in every school district an adequate education." No proof was offered at trial persuasively discrediting or refuting the State's assertion.

For these two reasons—the absence of any evidence that the financing system discriminates against any definable category of "poor" people or that it results in the absolute deprivation of education—the disadvantaged class is not susceptible of identification in traditional terms.[60]

As suggested above, appellees and the District Court may have embraced a second or third approach, the second of which might be characterized as a theory of relative or comparative discrimination based on family income. Appellees sought to prove that a direct correlation exists between the wealth of families within each district and the expenditures therein for education. That is, along a continuum, the poorer the family the lower the dollar amount of education received by the family's children.

The principal evidence adduced in support of this comparative-discrimination claim is an affidavit submitted by Professor Joele S. Berke of Syracuse University's Educational Finance Policy Institute. The District Court, relying in major part upon this affidavit and apparently accepting the substance of appellees' theory, noted, first, a positive correlation between the wealth of school districts, measured in terms of assessable property per pupil, and their levels of per-pupil expenditures. Second, the court found a similar correlation between district wealth and the personal wealth of its residents, measured in terms of median family income.

---

[56] Each of appellees' possible theories of wealth discrimination is founded on the assumption that the quality of education varies directly with the amount of funds expended on it and that, therefore, the difference in quality between two schools can be determined simplistically by looking at the difference in per-pupil expenditures. This is a matter of considerable dispute among educators and commentators.

[60] An educational financing system might be hypothesized, however, in which the analogy to the wealth discrimination cases would be considerably closer. If elementary and secondary education were made available by the State only to those able to pay a tuition assessed against each pupil, there would be a clearly defined class of "poor" people—definable in terms of their inability to pay the prescribed sum—who would be absolutely precluded from receiving an education. That case would present a far more compelling set of circumstances for judicial assistance than the case before us today. After all, Texas has undertaken to do a good deal more than provide an education to those who can afford it. It has provided what it considers to be an adequate base education for all children and has attempted, though imperfectly, to ameliorate by state funding and by the local assessment program the disparities in local tax resources.

If, in fact, these correlations could be sustained, then it might be argued that expenditures on education—equated by appellees to the quality of education—are dependent on personal wealth. Appellees' comparative-discrimination theory would still face serious unanswered questions, including whether a bare positive correlation or some higher degree of correlation is necessary to provide a basis for concluding that the financing system is designed to operate to the peculiar disadvantage of the comparatively poor, and whether a class of this size and diversity could ever claim the special protection accorded "suspect" classes. These questions need not be addressed in this case, however, since appellees' proof fails to support their allegations or the District Court's conclusions.

Professor Berke's affidavit is based on a survey of approximately 10% of the school districts in Texas. His findings, previously set out in the margin, show only that the wealthiest few districts in the sample have the highest median family incomes and spend the most on education, and that the several poorest districts have the lowest family incomes and devote the least amount of money to education. For the remainder of the districts—96 districts composing almost 90% of the sample—the correlation is inverted, *i.e.*, the districts that spend next to the most money on education are populated by families having next to the lowest median family incomes while the districts spending the least have the highest median family incomes. It is evident that, even if the conceptual questions were answered favorably to appellees, no factual basis exists upon which to found a claim of comparative wealth discrimination.[64]

This brings us, then, to the third way in which the classification scheme might be defined—district wealth discrimination. Since the only correlation indicated by the evidence is between district property wealth and expenditures, it may be argued that discrimination might be found without regard to the individual income characteristics of district residents. Assuming a perfect correlation between district property wealth and expenditures from top to bottom, the disadvantaged class might be viewed as encompassing every child in every district except the district that has the most assessable wealth and spends the most on education. Alternatively, as suggested in Mr. Justice MARSHALL's dissenting opinion, the class might be defined more restrictively to include children in districts with assessable property which falls below the statewide average, or median, or below some other artificially defined level.

However described, it is clear that appellees' suit asks this Court to extend its most exacting scrutiny to review a system that allegedly discriminates against a large, diverse, and amorphous class, unified only by the common factor of residence in districts that happen to have less taxable wealth than other districts. The system of alleged discrimination and the class it defines have none of the traditional indicia of suspectness: the class is not saddled with such disabilities, or subjected to such a history of purposeful unequal treatment, or relegated to such a position of political powerlessness as to command extraordinary protection from the majoritarian political process.

---

[64] Studies in other States have also questioned the existence of any dependable correlation between a district's wealth measured in terms of assessable property and the collective wealth of families residing in the district measured in terms of median family income. Ridenour & Ridenour, Serrano v. Priest: Wealth and Kansas School Finance, 20 Kan. L. Rev. 213, 225 (1972) ("it can be argued that there exists in Kansas almost an inverse correlation: districts with highest income per pupil have low assessed value per pupil, and districts with high assessed value per pupil have low income per pupil"); Davis, Taxpaying Ability: A Study of the Relationship Between Wealth and Income in California Counties, in The Challenge of Change in School Finance, 10th Nat. Educational Assn. Conf. on School Finance 199 (1967) . . ..

We thus conclude that the Texas system does not operate to the peculiar disadvantage of any suspect class.

. . . .

We need not rest our decision, however, solely on the inappropriateness of the strict-scrutiny test. A century of Supreme Court adjudication under the Equal Protection Clause affirmatively supports the application of the traditional standard of review, which requires only that the State's system be shown to bear some rational relationship to legitimate state purposes. This case represents far more than a challenge to the manner in which Texas provides for the education of its children. We have here nothing less than a direct attack on the way in which Texas has chosen to raise and disburse state and local tax revenues. We are asked to condemn the State's judgment in conferring on political subdivisions the power to tax local property to supply revenues for local interests. In so doing, appellees would have the Court intrude in an area in which it has traditionally deferred to state legislatures. This Court has often admonished against such interferences with the State's fiscal policies under the Equal Protection Clause.

. . . .

Questions of federalism are always inherent in the process of determining whether a State's laws are to be accorded the traditional presumption of constitutionality, or are to be subjected instead to rigorous judicial scrutiny. While the maintenance of the principles of federalism is a foremost consideration in interpreting any of the pertinent constitutional provisions under which this Court examines state action, it would be difficult to imagine a case having a greater potential impact on our federal system than the one now before us, in which we are urged to abrogate systems of financing public education presently in existence in virtually every State.

. . . .

[T]o the extent that the Texas system of school financing results in unequal expenditures between children who happen to reside in different districts, we cannot say that such disparities are the product of a system that is so irrational as to be invidiously discriminatory. Texas has acknowledged its shortcomings and has persistently endeavored—not without some success—to ameliorate the differences in levels of expenditures without sacrificing the benefits of local participation. The Texas plan is not the result of hurried, ill-conceived legislation. It certainly is not the product of purposeful discrimination against any group or class. On the contrary, it is rooted in decades of experience in Texas and elsewhere, and in major part is the product of responsible studies by qualified people . . . . In its essential characteristics, the Texas plan for financing public education reflects what many educators for a half century have thought was an enlightened approach to a problem for which there is no perfect solution. We are unwilling to assume for ourselves a level of wisdom superior to that of legislators, scholars, and educational authorities in 50 States, especially where the alternatives proposed are only recently conceived and nowhere yet tested.

. . . .

IV

In light of the considerable attention that has focused on the District Court opinion in this case and on its California predecessor, Serrano v. Priest, 5 Cal. 3d 584, 487 P.2d 1241 (1971), a cautionary postscript seems appropriate. It cannot be questioned that the constitutional judgment reached by the District Court and approved by our dissenting Brothers today would occasion in Texas and elsewhere an unprecedented upheaval in public education. Some commentators have concluded that, whatever the contours of the alternative financing programs that might be devised and approved, the result could not avoid being a beneficial one. But, just as there is nothing simple about the constitutional issues involved in these cases, there is nothing simple or certain about predicting the consequences of massive change in the financing and control of public education. Those who have devoted the most thoughtful attention to the practical ramifications of these cases have found no clear or dependable answers and their scholarship reflects no such unqualified confidence in the desirability of completely uprooting the existing system.

The complexity of these problems is demonstrated by the lack of consensus with respect to whether it may be said with any assurance that the poor, the racial minorities, or the children in over-burdened core-city school districts would be benefited by abrogation of traditional modes of financing education. Unless there is to be a substantial increase in state expenditures on education across the board—an event the likelihood of which is open to considerable question— these groups stand to realize gains in terms of increased per-pupil expenditures only if they reside in districts that presently spend at relatively low levels, i.e., in those districts that would benefit from the redistribution of existing resources. Yet, recent studies have indicated that the poorest families are not invariably clustered in the most impecunious school districts. Nor does it now appear that there is any more than a random chance that racial minorities are concentrated in property-poor districts. Additionally, several research projects have concluded that any financing alternative designed to achieve a greater equality of expenditures is likely to lead to higher taxation and lower educational expenditures in the major urban centers, a result that would exacerbate rather than ameliorate existing conditions in those areas.

These practical considerations, of course, play no role in the adjudication of the constitutional issues presented here. But they serve to highlight the wisdom of the traditional limitations on this Court's function. The consideration and initiation of fundamental reforms with respect to state taxation and education are matters reserved for the legislative processes of the various States, and we do no violence to the values of federalism and separation of powers by staying our hand. We hardly need add that this Court's action today is not to be viewed as placing its judicial imprimatur on the status quo. The need is apparent for reform in tax systems which may well have relied too long and too heavily on the local property tax. And certainly innovative thinking as to public education, its methods, and its funding is necessary to assure both a higher level of quality and greater uniformity of opportunity. These matters merit the continued attention of the scholars who already have contributed much by their challenges. But the ultimate solutions must come from the lawmakers and from the democratic pressures of those who elect them.

Reversed.

[The concurring opinion of Mr. Justice Stewart, the dissenting opinion of Mr. Justice Brennan, and the dissenting opinion of Mr. Justice White with whom Mr. Justice Douglas and Mr. Justice Brennan joined, are all omitted.]

Mr. Justice MARSHALL, with whom Mr. Justice DOUGLAS concurs, dissenting.

The Court today decides, in effect, that a State may constitutionally vary the quality of education which it offers its children in accordance with the amount of taxable wealth located in the school districts within which they reside. The majority's decision represents an abrupt departure from the mainstream of recent state and federal court decisions concerning the unconstitutionality of state educational financing schemes dependent upon taxable local wealth. More unfortunately, though, the majority's holding can only be seen as a retreat from our historic commitment to equality of educational opportunity and as unsupportable acquiescence in a system which deprives children in their earliest years of the chance to reach their full potential as citizens. The Court does this despite the absence of any substantial justification for a scheme which arbitrarily channels educational resources in accordance with the fortuity of the amount of taxable wealth within each district.

In my judgment, the right of every American to an equal start in life, so far as the provision of a state service as important as education is concerned, is far too vital to permit state discrimination on grounds as tenuous as those presented by this record. Nor can I accept the notion that it is sufficient to remit these appellees to the vagaries of the political process which, contrary to the majority's suggestion, has proved singularly unsuited to the task of providing a remedy for this discrimination. I, for one, am unsatisfied with the hope of an ultimate "political" solution sometime in the indefinite future while, in the meantime, countless children unjustifiably receive inferior educations that "may affect their hearts and minds in a way unlikely ever to be undone." Brown v. Board of Education, 347 U.S. 483 (1954). I must therefore respectfully dissent.

. . . .

Authorities concerned with educational quality no doubt disagree as to the significance of variations in per-pupil spending. Indeed, conflicting expert testimony was presented to the District Court in this case concerning the effect of spending variations on educational achievement. We sit, however, not to resolve disputes over educational theory but to enforce our Constitution. It is an inescapable fact that if one district has more funds available per pupil than another district, the former will have greater choice in educational planning than will the latter. In this regard, I believe the question of discrimination in educational quality must be deemed to be an objective one that looks to what the State provides its children, not to what the children are able to do with what they receive. That a child forced to attend an underfunded school with poorer physical facilities, less experienced teachers, larger classes, and a narrower range of courses than a school with substantially more funds—and thus with greater choice in educational planning—may nevertheless excel is to the credit of the child, not the State, cf. Missouri ex rel. Gaines v. Canada, 305 U.S. 337 (1938). Indeed, who can ever measure for such a child the opportunities lost and the talents wasted for want of a broader, more enriched education? Discrimination in the opportunity to learn that is afforded a child must be our standard.

. . . .

The study introduced in the District Court showed a direct inverse relationship between equalized taxable district property wealth and district tax effort with the result that the property-poor districts making the highest tax effort obtained the lowest per-pupil yield.[93] The implications of this situation for local choice are illustrated by . . . comparing the Edgewood and Alamo Heights School Districts. In 1967-1968, Edgewood, after contributing its share to the Local Fund Assignment, raised only $26 per pupil through its local property tax, whereas Alamo Heights was able to raise $333 per pupil. Since the funds received through the Minimum Foundation School Program are to be used only for minimum professional salaries, transportation costs, and operating expenses, it is not hard to see the lack of local choice—with respect to higher teacher salaries to attract more and better teachers, physical facilities, library books, and facilities, special courses, or participation in special state and federal matching funds programs—under which a

_____
[93] See Appendix II.

property-poor district such as Edgewood is forced to labor. In fact, because of the difference in taxable local property wealth, Edgewood would have to tax itself almost nine times as heavily to obtain the same yield as Alamo Heights.[95] At present, then, local control is a myth for many of the local school districts in Texas. As one district court has observed, "rather than reposing in each school district the economic power to fix its own level of per pupil expenditure, the State has so arranged the structure as to guarantee that some districts will spend low (with high taxes) while others will spend high (with low taxes)." Van Dusartz v. Hatfield, 334 F. Supp. 870, 876 (D.C. Minn. 1971).

In my judgment, any substantial degree of scrutiny of the operation of the Texas financing scheme reveals that the State has selected means wholly inappropriate to secure its purported interest in assuring its school districts local fiscal control. At the same time, appellees have pointed out a variety of alternative financing schemes which may serve the State's purported interest in local control as well as, if not better than, the present scheme without the current impairment of the educational opportunity of vast numbers of Texas schoolchildren. I see no need, however, to explore the practical or constitutional merits of those suggested alternatives at this time for, whatever their positive or negative features, experience with the present financing scheme impugns any suggestion that it constitutes a serious effort to provide local fiscal control. If for the sake of local education control, this Court is to sustain interdistrict discrimination in the educational opportunity afforded Texas school children, it should require that the State present something more than the mere sham now before us.

In conclusion, it is essential to recognize that an end to the wide variations in taxable district property wealth inherent in the Texas financing scheme would entail none of the untoward consequences suggested by the Court or by the appellants.

First, affirmance of the District Court's decisions would hardly sound the death knell for local control of education. It would mean neither centralized decisionmaking nor federal court intervention in the operation of public schools. Clearly, this suit has nothing to do with local decisionmaking with respect to educational policy or even educational spending. It involves only a narrow aspect of local control—namely, local control over the raising of educational funds. In fact, in striking down interdistrict disparities in taxable local wealth, the District Court took the course which is most likely to make true local control over educational decision-making a reality for all Texas school districts.

Nor does the District Court's decision even necessarily eliminate local control of educational funding. The District Court struck down nothing more than the continued interdistrict wealth discrimination inherent in the present property tax. Both centralized and decentralized plans for educational funding not involving such interdistrict discrimination have been put forward. The choice among these or other alternatives would remain with the State, not with the federal courts.[98] In this regard, it should be evident that the degree of federal intervention in matters

[95] See Appendix IV.

[98] Centralized educational financing is, to be sure, one alternative. On analysis, though, it is clear that even centralized financing would not deprive local school districts of what has been considered to be the essence of local educational control. Central financing would leave in local hands the entire gamut of local educational policy-making—teachers, curriculum, school sites, the whole process of allocating resources among alternative educational objectives.

A second possibility is the much-discussed theory of district power equalization put forth by Professors Coons, Clune, and Sugarman in their seminal work, Private Wealth and Public Education 201-242 (1970). Such a scheme would truly reflect a dedication to local fiscal control. Under their system, each school district would receive a fixed

of local concern would be substantially less in this context than in previous decisions in which we have been asked effectively to impose a particular scheme upon the States under the guise of the Equal Protection Clause.

Still, we are told that this case requires us "to condemn the State's judgment in conferring on political subdivisions the power to tax local property to supply revenues for local interests." Ante, at 1300. Yet no one in the course of this entire litigation has ever questioned the constitutionality of the local property tax as a device for raising educational funds. The District Court's decision, at most, restricts the power of the State to make educational funding dependent exclusively upon local property taxation so long as there exists interdistrict disparities in taxable property wealth. But it hardly eliminates the local property tax as a source of educational funding or as a means of providing local fiscal control.

The Court seeks solace for its action today in the possibility of legislative reform. The Court's suggestions of legislative redress and experimentation will doubtless be of great comfort to the schoolchildren of Texas' disadvantaged districts, but considering the vested interests of wealthy school districts in the preservation of the status quo, they are worth little more. The possibility of legislative action is, in all events, no answer to this Court's duty under the Constitution to eliminate unjustified state discrimination. In this case we have been presented with an instance of such discrimination, in a particularly invidious form, against an individual interest of large constitutional and practical importance. To support the demonstrated discrimination in the provision of educational opportunity the State has offered a justification which, on analysis, takes on at best an ephemeral character. Thus, I believe that the wide disparities in taxable district property wealth inherent in the local property tax element of the Texas financing scheme render that scheme violative of the Equal Protection Clause.[100]

I would therefore affirm the judgment of the District Court.

---

amount of revenue per pupil for any particular level of tax effort regardless of the level of local property tax base. Appellants criticize this scheme on the rather extraordinary ground that it would encourage poorer districts to overtax themselves in order to obtain substantial revenues for education. But under the present discriminatory scheme, it is the poor districts that are already taxing themselves at the highest rates, yet are receiving the lowest returns.

District wealth reapportionment is yet another alternative which would accomplish directly essentially what district power equalization would seek to do artificially. Appellants claim that the calculations concerning state property required by such a scheme would be impossible as a practical matter. Yet Texas is already making far more complex annual calculations—involving not only local property values but also local income and other economic factors—in conjunction with the Local Fund Assignment portion of the Minimum Foundation School Program. See 5 Governor's Committee Report 43-44.

A fourth possibility would be to remove commercial, industrial, and mineral property from local tax rolls, to tax this property on a statewide basis, and to return the resulting revenues to the local districts in a fashion that would compensate for remaining variations in the local tax bases.

None of these particular alternatives are necessarily constitutionally compelled; rather, they indicate the breadth of choice which would remain to the State if the present interdistrict disparities were eliminated.

[100] Of course, nothing in the Court's decision today should inhibit further review of state educational funding schemes under state constitutional provisions. See Milliken v. Green, 389 Mich. 1, 203 N.W.2d 457 (1972), rehearing granted, Jan. 1973; Robinson v. Cahill, 118 N.J. Super. 223, 287 A.2d 187; 119 N.J. Super. 40, 289 A.2d 569 (1972); cf. Serrano v. Priest, 5 Cal. 3d 584, 487 P.2d 1241 (1971).

[411 US 134]

APPENDIX I TO OPINION OF MARSHALL J., DISSENTING

REVENUES OF TEXAS SCHOOL DISTRICTS CATEGORIZED BY EQUALIZED PROPERTY VALUES AND SOURCE OF FUNDS

CATEGORIES Market Vaule of Taxable Property per Pupil	Local Revenues Per Pupil	State Revenues Per Pupil	State and Local Revenues Per Pupil (Columns 1 and 2)	Federal Revenues Per Pupil	Total Revenues Total Revenues Per Pupil (State-Local-Federal, Columns 1, 2, and 4)
Above $100,00 (10 districts)	$610	$205	$815	$41	$856
$100,00-$50,000 (26 districts)	287	257	544	66	610
$50,00-$30,000 (30 districts)	224	260	484	45	529
$30,00-$10,000 (40 districts)	166	295	461	85	546
Below $10,00 (4 districts)	63	243	306	135	441

Based on Table V to affidavit of Joel S. Berke, App 208, which was prepared on the basis of a sample of 110 selected Texas school districts from data for the 1967-1986 school year.

SAN ANTONIO SCHOOL DISTRICT v RODRIGUEZ
411 US 1, 36 L Ed 2d 16, 93 S Ct 1278

[411 US 135]
APENDIX II TO OPINION OF MARSHALL, J., DISSENTING

TEXAS SCHOOL DISTRICTS CATEGORIZED BY EQUALIZED PROPERTY VALUES,
EQUALIZED TAX RATES, AND YIELD OF RATES

CATEGORIES Market Value of Taxable Property Per Pupil	EQUALIZED TAX RATES ON $100	YIELD PER PUPIL (Equalized Rate Applied to District Market Value)
Above $100,00 (10 districts)	$.31	$585
$100,00-$50,000 (26 districts)	.38	262
$50,00-$30,000 (30 districts)	.55	213
$30,00-$10,000 (40 districts)	.72	162
Below $10,00 (4 districts)	.70	60

Based on Table II to affidavit of Joel S. Berke, App 205, which was prepared on the basis of a sample of 100 selected Texas school districts from data for the 1967-1968 school year.

[411 US 136]

APPENDIX III TO OPINION OF MARSHALL, J., DISSENTING

SELECTED BEXAR COUNTY, TEXAS, SCHOOL DISTRICTS CATEGORIZED BY EQUALIZED PROPERTY VALUATION AND SELECTED INDICATORS OF EDUCATIONAL QUALITY

Selected Districts From High to Low by Market Valuation Per Pupil	Professional Salaries Per Pupil	Per Cent of Teachers With College Degrees	Masters Degrees	Per Cent of Total Staff With Emergency Permits	Student-Counselor Ratios	Professioinal Personnel Per 100 Pupils
ALAMO HEIGHTS	$372	100%	40%	11%	645	4.80
NORTH EAST	288	99	24	7	1,516	4.50
SAN ANTONIO	251	98	29	17	2,320	4.00
NORTH SIDE	258	99	20	17	1,493	4.30
HARLANDALE	243	94	21	22	1,800	4.00
EDGEWOOD	209	96	15	47	3,098	4.06

Based on Table XI to Affidavit of Joel S. Berke, App 220, which was prepared on the basis of a sample of six selected school districts located in Bexar County, Texas, from data for the 1967-1968 school year.

SAN ANTONIO SCHOOL DISTRICT v RODRIGUEZ
36 L Ed 2d 16

[411 US 137]
APPENDIX IV TO OPINION OF MARSHALL, J., DISSENTING

BEXAR COUNTY, TEXAS, SCHOOL DISTRICTS RANKED BY EQUALIZED PROPERTY VALUE AND TAX RATE REQUIRED TO GENERATE HIGHEST YIELD IN ALL DISTRICTS

Districts Ranked from High to Low Market Valuation Per Pupil	Tax Rate Per $100 Needed to Equal Highest Yield
ALAMO HEIGHTS	$0.68
JUDSON	1.04
EAST CENTRAL	1.17
NORTH EAST	1.21
SOMERSET	1.32
SAN ANTONIO	1.56
NORTH SIDE	1.65
SOUTH WEST	2.10
SOUTH SIDE	3.03
HARLANDALE	3.20
SOUTH SAN ANTONIO	5.77
EDGEWOOD	5.76

Based on Table IX to affidavit of Joel S. Berke, App 218, which was prepared on the basis of the 12 school districts located in Bexar County, Texas, from data for the 1967-1968 school year.

[2] Concluding Notes

[a] Judicial Versus Legislative Action

Segregation by economic class and zoning systems are often intermeshed. As noted in the discussion of both *Euclid v. Ambler* (*see* p. 490 above) and the *Mt. Laurel* (*see* p. 516 above) litigation in Chapter 6, many communities may be zoned for uses that are likely to create high property values and low demands for public services. Densely packed urban areas simply could not compete in such an environment. One of the major issues in debates about these problems is whether courts or legislatures should be the final arbiters of such major public policy decisions. A similar debate floats through *Rodriguez*. Should courts closely scrutinize state property taxation systems using either federal or state constitutional standards? If you prefer legislative action because of the broad public policy issues at stake, do you also define yourself as a Legal Process adherent? If, like Justice Marshall, you favor judicial intervention, do you define yourself as a believer in Representation Reinforcement?

[b] Remedy

If you disagree with the result in *Rodriguez*, what remedy would you order? Since any long term solution would have to involve some restructuring of the state's taxation system, would it be appropriate for a court to do more than declare the existing system invalid? Should the court also enjoin collection of taxes under the invalidated plan in order to spur the state legislature to action? If the legislature keeps enacting plans that do not fulfill the requirements of Equal Protection, should the court ever step in and impose a tax plan of its own?

CHAPTER **8**

LANDLORD-TENANT LAW: FROM THE PRIVATE TO THE REGULATED SPHERE

§ 8.01 Introduction

Reading about landlord-tenant law is a useful way of investigating many of the issues taken up in the prior chapter on property law and the post-war administrative state. The central features of nineteenth-century lease law—both procedural and substantive—were in effect in most states when World War II ended. Forty years later, both the procedural and substantive understandings were dramatically different, federal regulatory effects (mostly in civil rights and subsidized housing areas) were quite visible, and state regulation was dramatically greater. Indeed, in one well known article on changes in landlord-tenant law, Mary Ann Glendon concluded that public regulatory law now dominates the area.[1] This chapter tells the story of the transformation of the law of leases from a predominantly private law area to a heavily regulated sphere.

Except for a smattering of items, the contents of this chapter are drawn entirely from New Jersey sources. This selection of materials is designed to provide a clearer understanding of the impact of judicial precedents, the interplay between courts and legislatures, and the development of a body of law over time. The goal is not to learn the law of New Jersey for its own sake, but to use the materials as a vehicle for taking an intense look at how legal institutions operate.

New Jersey is a nice laboratory for several reasons. First, cases and statutes abound; both the courts and the state legislature have been very active in regulating leases. The grist for study is easily available. (To simplify your studies, an appendix of New Jersey landlord–tenant statutes may be found at the end of this text.) Second, the state has been a leader in adopting changes to landlord-tenant law that many other states have emulated. The fact that New Jersey has been a national model makes it a logical jurisdiction for close scrutiny. Third, the procedural system operating in eviction cases in New Jersey is to this day designed, at least in part, to facilitate the speedy resolution of a huge volume of cases. The conflict between demands imposed by enormous caseloads and equitable handling of legal issues appears starkly in the materials. Finally, the state has a long tradition of appointing intelligent, articulate judges to its appellate courts. The opinions available for study are frequently of a higher quality than those from other jurisdictions.[2]

---

[1] Mary Ann Glendon, *The Transformation of American Landlord-Tenant Law*, 23 B.C. L. Rev. 503 (1982).

[2] The tradition goes back to the days of Chief Justice Vanderbilt early in the twentieth century. Governors, regardless of party, have regularly appointed talented people to the bench. In addition, the state Supreme Court frequently uses its authority to temporarily assign judges to various courts to broaden the experience of judges deemed above average. The better trial level judges, for example, are often assigned to sit temporarily on appellate division benches. Promotions up the judicial ladder often follow such temporary assignments.

The chapter examines five major sets of topics. Studying the basic nature of a lease is the first task. The two major cases in the materials discuss the differences between tenants and transient occupants at one end of the spectrum, and lessees and purchasers of cooperative apartments at the other. The next section, on procedural protections in eviction courts, is followed by a detailed look at the relationship between the tenant's obligation to pay rent and the landlord's duty to maintain the rented premises. After a discussion of the limitations on a landlord's ability to terminate a lease, the last portion of the chapter covers a number of potential complexities that may surface when possession of leased property changes hands.

§ 8.02 What is a Lease?: Distinguishing Possessors, Tenants and Owners

[1] Lease Basics: Tenancy Types

A lease entails the transfer of the right to possess and use property for a period of time in return for the payment, usually at regular intervals, of some sort of compensation. Two common forms of leases—term and periodic tenancies—and one unusual form—tenancy at will—are generally recognized in American law. In a *term tenancy*, or *estate for years*, a landlord grants possession of an asset to a tenant for a specific period of time. The period can be of virtually any length, though it is almost always stated as a period of years. No special action needs to be taken to end the lease. At the end of the term the right of the tenant to possess the property automatically terminates, and the reversionary interest of the landlord—the right to regain possession when the lease ends—takes effect. In most states, leases lasting more than one year must be in writing.[3] In some jurisdictions, those for exactly one year must also be written. New Jersey takes the unusual position of requiring leases lasting three or more years to be in writing.[4]

In *periodic tenancies* the parties agree to an arrangement transferring a continuous possessory interest for a recurring term. The length of a periodic arrangement is indefinite. The lease automatically renews itself for another period unless one of the parties takes action—usually a notice ending the arrangement—to terminate the lease.[5] The recurring period can be of any length, but is usually month-to-month or year-to-year. Periodic tenancies frequently arise in settings where there is no written lease.[6] If someone moves into an apartment and pays rent every month, the courts will invariably label the arrangement a month-to-month periodic tenancy. Similarly, if a term tenancy expires, but the tenant continues to pay rent and the landlord continues to accept its payment, most jurisdictions hold that a periodic tenancy arises.[7]

---

[3] In some jurisdictions leases for exactly one year or those for less than a year but ending more than a year from signing must also be written.

[4] N.J. Stat. Ann. § 25:1-12.

[5] In New Jersey, as you will see later in the chapter, the entire common law structure for terminating leases has been replaced by a requirement that landlords show "good cause" for eviction. *See* N.J. Stat. Ann. §§ 2A:18-61.1 to 2A:18:61.3. Assuming there is good cause, a month to month periodic tenancy may be terminated upon one full month's notice. N.J. Stat. Ann. § 2A:18-56.

[6] A writing is usually not required unless the period chosen is long enough to by itself trigger the operation of the statute of frauds.

[7] This result is made explicit by statute in New Jersey. N.J. Stat. Ann. § 46:8-10 provides:

Whenever a tenant whose original term of leasing shall be for a period of one month or longer shall hold over or remain in possession of the demised premises beyond the term of the letting, the tenancy created by or resulting from acceptance of rent by the landlord shall be a tenancy from month to month in the absence of any agreement to the contrary.

Prior to the enactment of this section in 1941, acceptance of rent upon termination of a term tenancy for a year or more resulted in a year-to-year periodic tenancy.

A more unusual lease—the *tenancy at will*—is defined as a possessory interest which is terminable at the will of either the transferor or the transferee and which has no other designated period of duration. Landlords virtually never agree to a tenancy at will. This tenancy usually arises by inference from a situation. For example, a person who moves into a house or apartment for an indefinite period and without an obligation to pay rent on a regular basis is likely to be a tenant at will. At common law a landlord could easily terminate such a lease by self-help eviction, making it more like a hotel guest category than a lease. The most common settings for the tenancy may be roommates or relatives living informally in an apartment or house. In many states, including New Jersey, tenancies at will are now terminable only upon notice.[8]

From time to time, courts also use the misnomer *tenant at sufferance*. Such a "tenant" is one who had a legitimate possessory interest, but wrongfully continued in possession upon termination of the interest. It really isn't a tenancy at all. The only thing that distinguishes a tenant at sufferance from a trespasser is that the coming into possession of a tenant at sufferance is legitimate. Parts of this chapter actually investigate how the status of a tenancy at sufferance arises, for it is only such "tenants" that courts will evict.

The next two cases pose questions about possessory arrangements which don't fit closely with any of the standard tenancies. In both situations, courts are forced to resolve definitional issues in order to decide whether landlord-tenant court has jurisdiction to evict the occupants. To read a bit more about basic tenancy forms, look at ROGER A. CUNNINGHAM, WILLIAM B. STOEBUCK & DALE A. WHITMAN, THE LAW OF PROPERTY 80-83 (2d ed. 1993); JOHN E. CRIBBET & CORWIN W. JOHNSON, PRINCIPLES OF THE LAW OF PROPERTY 54-58 (3d ed. 1989).

[2]   Tenants in Possession Versus Non-Tenants in Possession

[a]   Introduction: Self Help and the Legal Process School

Over the years, New Jersey courts decided a significant number of cases on the status of parties in possession of housing under various circumstances, including some involving employees residing on their employer's property. For example, in *Morris Canal and Banking Company v. Mitchell*,[9] James Mitchell was employed as a lock-tender on a canal. As part of his compensation he was permitted to live in a house "with a garden annexed to it and some vacant land of the company immediately adjoining the lock." A company rule required such persons to leave their houses if they were discharged from employment by the company. Mitchell was discharged in January, 1864, and possession of the house was demanded. When he failed to leave, the canal company sought to dispossess him. The New Jersey Supreme Court, with somewhat cryptic and contradictory reasoning, noted that Mitchell "held under the company and so was their tenant, not at a rent reserved, but as part compensation for his services and only during the time those services were being performed." In such a setting, the court held, Mitchell was *not* entitled to the normal notice and period to vacate granted to most tenants, but the landlord *was* entitled to use the recently enacted summary dispossess proceedings as if Mitchell were a tenant.[10]

---

[8] *See* N.J. STAT. ANN. § 2A:18-56, which requires three months' notice. This notice requirement largely blurs the difference between periodic tenancies and tenancies at will. Indeed, the notice period is shorter for month-to-month tenancies.

[9] 31 N.J.L. 99 (1864).

[10] The summary dispossess statutes provided for a speedy eviction remedy. Thus the employee could be quickly dispossessed without the benefit of the normal notice to quit waiting period granted to typical residential tenants. The decision gave the landlord the best of both worlds.

Mitchell was followed a short time later by another decision which unabashedly held that a household servant living on the employer's grounds was not a tenant for purposes of a summary dispossess proceeding, and that the employee's "removal could be accomplished by the act of the owner, without the aid of any judicial tribunal."[11] This result was apparently followed by the courts well into this century.[12]

The use of self-help to evict employees from their residences was not as socially acceptable after 1960 as it was in the nineteenth century. The very idea of terminating long term property relationships without any judicial or administrative oversight had become very unattractive. One reason for this change in sensibilities was the appearance of the Legal Process School. Pressures such as these eventually led the courts to take another look at the ability to use self-help to remove employees from their living quarters once their jobs ended. The moment for that review arrived in 1980 in *Vasquez v. Glassboro Service Association.*

[b] Opinion of the New Jersey Supreme Court in *Vasquez v. Glassboro Service Association*

Vasquez v. Glassboro Service Association

New Jersey Supreme Court
83 N.J. 86, 415 A.2d 1156 (1980)

Frederick A. Jacob, Millville, for defendants-appellants (Lipman, Antonelli, Batt & Dunlap, Vineland, attorneys).

Michael S. Berger, Haddonfield, Farm Workers Rights Project, Civil Liberties Ed. and Action Fund of American Civil Liberties Union of N.J., for plaintiff-respondent.

The opinion of the court was delivered by

POLLOCK, J.

The primary issue is whether a farm labor service that employs migrant farmworkers from Puerto Rico and provides them with living quarters must dispossess a worker, not by self-help, but in a judicial proceeding after terminating his employment.

Natividad Vasquez, a Puerto Rican farmworker, instituted this action after he was dispossessed without notice following the termination of his employment by Glassboro Service Association, a farm labor service organization. Glassboro had employed Vasquez pursuant to a contract negotiated with the Puerto Rican Department of Labor. The Chancery Division ruled that Glassboro should not have dispossessed Vasquez by self-help, but in a summary dispossess proceeding. The Appellate Division affirmed. We granted certification.

We hold that a farm labor service may not use self-help, but must proceed in a judicial action to dispossess a farmworker who remains in possession of his living quarters after termination of his employment. We reach that conclusion although we hold that a migrant farmworker is

---

[11] McQuade v. Emmons, 38 N.J.L. 397, 400 (1876).

[12] Gray v. Reynolds, 67 N.J.L. 169, 50 A. 670 (1901); Scottish Rite Co. v. Salkowitz, 119 N.J.L. 558, 197 A. 43 (1938); Schuman v. Zurawell, 24 N.J. Misc. 180, 47 A.2d 560 (1946). Other disputes requiring the courts to distinguish tenants from various sorts of possessory interests also arose. Parties fought over the difference between a tenant and a person in possession as a concurrent owner (Corrigan v. Riley, 26 N.J.L. 79 (1856); Sentliffer v. Jacobs, 84 N.J.L. 128, 86 A. 929 (1913)), or as a purchaser of the real estate (Chambers v. Ross, 25 N.J.L. 293 (1855); Nestal v. Schmid, 39 N.J.L. 686 (1877); 405 Monroe Co. v. Asbury Park, 40 N.J. 457, 193 A.2d 115 (1963)).

not a tenant or otherwise included within N.J.S.A. 2A:18-61.1(m) pertaining to the dispossession of certain residential tenants. We hold further that the failure of the Glassboro contract to provide a migrant farmworker with a reasonable opportunity to find shelter before dispossession is against the public policy of the State, and we imply into the contract a provision for a reasonable time to find alternative housing. In resolving a dispute between a farmworker and a labor service, a court may grant time to the worker to find housing, direct the labor service to assist him in obtaining housing or provide him with return passage to Puerto Rico, or order other appropriate relief.

I

Although our analysis is based on facts which occurred in 1976, there is no indication that the essential facts, including the contract, relationships of the parties, or working conditions have changed since that time. Glassboro is a non-profit corporation comprised of farmers who contracted with Glassboro for migrant farm labor. The farmers called Glassboro as they needed workers to pick crops, and Glassboro transported workers from its labor camp to the farms. The length of time that a worker stayed at a farm varied, depending primarily on the time needed to pick a crop. Glassboro paid the worker his wages, and the farmer paid Glassboro for those wages plus a commission for Glassboro's services.

Only men were hired; the workers' families remained in Puerto Rico. Glassboro paid a farmworker $2.40 per hour and charged him $23 per week for meals. The worker agreed to work eight hours a day for six days a week, plus overtime as mutually agreed.

The 1976 contract stated that a worker was to pay for his transportation from Puerto Rico. If he completed his contract, he would be reimbursed for the cost of transportation from and provided return transportation to Puerto Rico. If the worker did not fulfill his contract, Glassboro was not obliged to reimburse him for the cost of transportation. Although the contract provided that Glassboro would furnish a nonnegotiable airplane ticket to Puerto Rico for a worker who became physically unfit, there was no comparable provision for a worker who was fired. The contract period was for 28 weeks, or until December 1, whichever came first.

The contract provided that, if an employee was to be discharged, a hearing was to occur no later than five days after the employee was given notice of termination. The contract did not require a minimum amount of time to elapse between notice and termination of employment.

The contract provided further for administrative review within the Puerto Rican Department of Labor whenever a worker had a complaint "regarding the breach, application, interpretation or compliance" with the contract. If the Secretary of Labor determined that Glassboro had "not adequately remedied the complaint," the Secretary could represent the worker and sue Glassboro.

Pursuant to the contract, Glassboro supplied living quarters for workers at its labor camp in New Jersey. Those quarters consisted of barracks housing up to 30 men. Each worker received a mattress, bedding, and a locker. The barracks were equipped with common toilets, showers, and lavatories. Although some farmers charged the workers for housing while the workers were at the farms, Glassboro did not impose any extra charge for housing at its labor camp. The contract did not require a migrant farmworker to live at Glassboro's labor camp. Nonetheless, the parties contemplated that the farmworker would reside at the labor camp.

In 1976, Vasquez was recruited in Puerto Rico and came to New Jersey to work for Glassboro. According to Glassboro's foreman, Vasquez's work was not satisfactory. On July 19, 1976, the foreman told Vasquez that he was to be discharged. A few hours later Vasquez had his "hearing" with the foreman and a field representative of the Puerto Rican Department of Labor. Thereafter the foreman decided to complete the discharge, a decision Vasquez does not challenge in this action. Although there were vacant spaces at the Glassboro barracks, Vasquez was not permitted to remain overnight. The foreman told him to gather his belongings and leave.

Unable to speak English and without funds to return to Puerto Rico, Vasquez sought the assistance of the Farmworkers Corporation, a federally funded non-profit corporation dedicated to the needs of farmworkers. He also consulted with the Farmworkers Rights Project of the Civil Liberties Education and Action Fund of the American Civil Liberties Union of New Jersey. A Rutgers law student returned with Vasquez to the camp and requested that Vasquez be allowed to remain overnight. The request was refused. Vasquez stayed with a friend who was participating in a job training program conducted by the Farmworkers Corporation.

The Farmworkers Rights Project filed a complaint on July 22, 1976, seeking an order permitting Vasquez to reenter his living quarters and enjoining defendants from depriving him of the use of the quarters except through judicial process. The complaint also sought damages, but Vasquez has abandoned that demand.

The trial court interpreted a provision of *N.J.S.A.* 2A:18-61.1 to apply to Vasquez. *N.J.S.A.* 2A:18-61.1 provides that a landlord may not remove a tenant except by establishing one of enumerated grounds as good cause. *N.J.S.A.* 2A:18-61.1(m) states good cause exists if "[T]he landlord or owner conditioned the tenancy upon and in consideration for the tenant's employment by the landlord or owner as superintendent, janitor or in some other capacity and such employment is being terminated." The court found Vasquez to be included within the phrase "in some other capacity," and ruled that Glassboro reinstate Vasquez to his living quarters.

Although Vasquez has since found housing, other workers have been evicted, one at 3:00 a.m. Shelter for dispossessed migrant farmworkers remains scarce. The Farmworkers Corporation estimates it provides emergency housing for approximately 500 workers each season.

Under the contract, once a worker's employment was ended, he had no right to stay at the camp. Glassboro had no obligation to arrange for alternative shelter. As with Vasquez, within the same day, Glassboro could notify a worker of the termination of his employment, meet with a representative of the Puerto Rican Department of Labor, complete the termination of the employment, and dispossess the employee.

The parties have urged that the dispossession of migrant farmworkers is likely to recur and have requested that we not treat the case as moot. We agree that the public interest requires that we resolve whether a migrant farmworker should be dispossessed from his living quarters through a judicial proceeding.

II

At common law, one who occupied premises as an employee of the owned and received the use of the premises as part compensation for his services or under a contract of employment was not considered a tenant. *See Scottish Rite Co. v. Salkowitz*, 119 *N.J.L.* 558, 197 *A.* 43 (E. & A. 1938) (caretaker who received monthly salary and use of premises was not a tenant but an employee who became a trespasser when his employment ended); *Gray v. Reynolds*, 67 *N.J.L.* 169, 50 *A.* 670 (Sup. Ct. 1901) (agreement for one year between owner and sharecropper does not create landlord-tenant relationship); *McQuade v. Emmons*, 38 *N.J.L.* 397 (Sup. Ct. 1876) (employee who received $25 per month and use of tenant house is a trespasser after end of employment); *Schuman v. Zurawell*, 24 *N.J. Misc.* 180, 47 *A.2d* 560 (Cir. Ct.1946) (apartment superintendent is not a tenant). *But see Morris Canal and Banking Company v. Mitchell*, 31 N.J.L. 99 (Sup. Ct. 1864) (lock tender who used dwelling house as part compensation summarily dispossessed as a tenant).

The statute that the trial court found to be dispositive, *N.J.S.A.* 2A:18-61.1(m), modifies the common law rule by declaring an employee whose housing is conditioned upon employment to be a tenant. Consequently, an employee covered by the statute is entitled to three days' notice prior to institution of an eviction action. *N.J.S.A.* 2A:18-61.2(a). If *N.J.S.A.* 2A:18-61.1(m) applied to Vasquez, he would have been entitled to three days' notice after termination of his employment and before commencement of an eviction action.

The initial question is whether the Legislature intended to include migrant farmworkers in the phrase "in some other capacity" in *N.J.S.A.* 2A:18-61.1(m). Neither the words of the statute nor the legislative history indicates that the Legislature contemplated including farmworkers within that phrase. Consequently, the meaning of the phrase may be gleaned by applying principles of statutory construction. Where general words follow a specific enumeration, the principle of *ejusdem generis* requires that the general words are applicable only to the same class of things already mentioned. In *N.J.S.A.* 2A:18-61.1(m), the general words "in some other capacity" follow the specific enumeration of "superintendent" and "janitor". We determine that, within the meaning of the statute, a farmworker does not belong to the same class of employees as a janitor or superintendent. A farmworker who possesses a mattress and locker in an unpartitioned barracks while waiting to be sent to work on a farm is different from a superintendent or janitor residing with his or her family in an apartment house. The farmworkers are all men who come from Puerto Rico without their families. They live in large barracks with no privacy, sleeping in bunks in an unpartitioned room and sharing toilets and showers. Their occupancy of the barracks is intermittent, since it is a base camp for use while they are awaiting assignment to farms.

Courts in other jurisdictions have considered whether a migrant farmworker is a tenant for the purpose of determining if a right of access should be provided to third parties to visit the migrant farmworker. In *Washington v. Fox*, 82 *Wash.* 2d 289, 510 *P.2d* 230 (Sup. Ct.1973), the court noted that, since the workers paid for the right to live in a labor camp, they were tenants. Accordingly, the court held that an attorney and labor union organizer had the right to visit the farmworker. In *Folgueras v. Hassle*, 331 *F. Supp.* 615 (W.D. Mich. 1971), the court concluded that the farmworkers were tenants even though they did not pay rent. The court noted that the free rent was "one justification for the low wage paid migrant laborers." The workers and their families had exclusive possession of bungalows in the work camp. The court found that the workers had the right to receive visitors such as student coordinators providing social services and doing research.

Migrant farmworkers were described as tenants *sui generis* who had a right of access to information from service organizations and a right to receive visitors in *Franceschina v. Morgan*, 346 *F. Supp.* 833 (S.D. Ind. 1972). In reaching its conclusion, the court stated that it did not matter whether the workers were characterized as tenants or employees. The offer of free rent did not prevent a finding that the workers were entitled to a right of access. The court found that the migrant worker, in effect, paid for the housing because he "swells the pool of agricultural labor in the area, which is to the company's advantage in that it tends to guarantee the flow of crops to its canneries. This is consideration enough, it seems to the Court, to denote the migrant a tenant for the term of the crop season." *Id.* at 838.

These cases from other jurisdictions holding farmworkers to be tenants are distinguishable. They have described farmworkers as tenants in reaching the conclusion that the farmworkers have a right to information and services from third parties. This Court has already ruled, without characterizing migrant farmworkers as tenants, that they are entitled to receive visitors, members of the press, and persons providing charitable and governmental services. *State v. Shack*, 58 *N.J.* 297, 307, 277 *A.2d* 369, 374 (1971). The Court expressly reserved the question before us: "We of course are not concerned here with the right of a migrant [farm]worker to remain on the employer's property after the employment is ended." That issue is before us because Vasquez asserts he is a tenant within *N.J.S.A.* 2A:18-61.1(m). The import of that assertion is that a farm labor service could dispossess a farmworker only after giving notice as required by *N.J.S.A.* 2A:18-61.2 and by recourse to a judicial proceeding in either the superior court or the county district court. *N.J.S.A.* 2A:18-61.1. *See R.* 6:2-1, *R.* 6:3-4, *R.* 6:5-2.

Our analysis of the words of the statute, the absence of any illuminating legislative history, and the application of principles of statutory construction lead to the conclusion that a migrant farmworker is not a tenant within the meaning of *N.J.S.A.* 2A:18-61.1(m). The special characteristics of migrant workers' housing, the absence of a contractual provision for the payment of rent, the lack of privacy, the intermittent occupancy, and the interdependence of employment and housing support this conclusion. Accordingly, we modify the judgment of the Appellate Division insofar as it holds that a migrant farmworker is a tenant within the meaning of the summary dispossess statute. However, our conclusion that Vasquez was not a tenant does not end our inquiry or preclude a finding that a farm labor service may dispossess a migrant farmworker only by judicial process.

III

In ascertaining whether a farmworker is entitled to notice before dispossession, we turn next to the Glassboro contract. As stated above, the contract resulted from negotiations between the Puerto Rican Department of Labor and Glassboro. No migrant farmworker participated directly or through a labor union in the negotiations. The record does not demonstrate whether or not the Puerto Rican Department of Labor has the same interests as the migrant farmworkers. The Puerto Rican Department of Labor may have been concerned also about reducing unemployment in Puerto Rico by finding jobs for its residents on farms in New Jersey. Whatever the interests of the parties to the negotiations, a migrant farmworker was required to accept the contract as presented by Glassboro.

The contract in evidence is written in English. Although Vasquez spoke Spanish only, the record does not show that he received a Spanish translation of the contract. Nonetheless, he signed a copy of the contract.

Once a migrant farmworker came to Glassboro's labor camp in New Jersey, he depended on Glassboro for employment, transportation, food, and housing. He was separated by over 1300 miles from his home and family. Although an American citizen, he was isolated from most citizens in New Jersey by his inability to speak English. An invisible barrier separated a migrant farmworker from the rest of the State as he was shuttled from the labor camp to the farms. The lack of alternative housing emphasized the inequality between Glassboro and the migrant farmworkers. Once his employment ended, a farmworker lost not only his job but his shelter.

The fear of discharge, and with it the loss of income, housing, and return passage to Puerto Rico permeated the contractual relationship. This is the setting in which we measure the contract against the public policy of the State.

. . . .

The courts and Legislature of New Jersey have demonstrated a progressive attitude in providing legal protection for migrant farmworkers. *See, e.g.*, Staff of Senate Subcomm. on Migratory Labor, Comm. on Labor and Public Welfare, 92d Cong., 2d Sess., *Federal and State Statutes Relating to Farmworkers* (Comm. Print 1972). In 1945 the State Legislature passed the Migrant Labor Act which, among other things, regulated housing and imposed sanitation standards for the benefit of migrant workers. *L.* 1945, *c.* 71. That act was amended and the regulation of housing was extended in the Seasonal Farm Labor Act. *L.* 1967, *c.* 91.

In 1971, the Legislature took further action to protect the rights of migrant farmworkers. Growers are required to provide drinking water and toilet facilities. *N.J.S.A.* 34:9A-1 *et seq.*, 37 to 41. The laws require that Spanish interpreters and other personnel be available to assist seasonal workers in matters involving communications with any governmental agency. *N.J.S.A.* 34:9A-7.2. The Legislature also provided for the inspection by state officials of labor camps . . . Enforcement of those statutes "resulted in a marked improvement in living conditions for migrant workers in New Jersey." Office of Agricultural Worker Compliance, New Jersey Department of Labor and Industry, *Status Report* 1 (1978).

In 1979, the federal government . . . assumed responsibility for inspection of many migrant labor camps. However, certain labor camps are still being inspected by New Jersey's Office of Agricultural Worker Compliance for the Federal Employment Service in order to comply with the federal requirement that housing be inspected prior to clearing any orders for interstate recruitment of migrant workers. The constant attention accorded by Congress and the State Legislature demonstrates a legislative concern for the well-being of migrant farmworkers.

In *Shack, supra*, this . . . Court weighed the property rights of the farmer against the rights of the farmworkers to information and services and found that the balance tipped in favor of the farmworker. Underlying that conclusion was recognition of the fundamental right of the farmworker to live with dignity. As in *Shack*, the appropriate result in this case arises from the status and the relationship of the parties.

Later cases have manifested a continuing concern for the plight of the migrant farmworker. In *Freedman v. New Jersey State Police*, 135 *N.J. Super.* 297, 343 *A.* 2d 148 (Law Div. 1975), the right of access of the press to migrant camps was extended to include a college newspaper reporter and photographer.

The enlightened approach of the courts and the Legislature provides the context in which we assess the Glassboro contract and consider how a migrant farmworker should be dispossessed from his living quarters at a labor camp.

A basic tenet of the law of contracts is that courts should enforce contracts as made by the parties. However, application of that principle assumes that the parties are in positions of relative equality and that their consent is freely given. *See Henningsen v. Bloomfield Motors, Inc.*, 32 *N.J.* 358, 386, 161 *A.* 2d 69 (1960). In recent years, courts have become increasingly sensitive to overreaching in contracts where there is an inequality in the status of the parties. In *Shell Oil Co. v. Marinello*, 63 *N.J.* 402, 307 *A.* 2d 598 (1973), this Court found that Shell was the dominant party and could dictate its own terms. Accordingly, the Court "read into" a lease and franchise agreement between a major oil company and one of its dealers a restriction against unilateral termination by the oil company absent good cause. The Court reached that decision from a consideration of the instruments, the relationship between the parties, and the public policy of the State affecting that relationship.

In a variety of other situations, courts have revised contracts where there was an inequality in the bargaining power of the parties . . . . This Court took cognizance of the housing shortage and the inequality in bargaining power of landlords and tenants in *Marini v. Ireland*, 56 *N.J.* 130, 265 *A.2d* 526 (1970). In *Marini*, this Court implied a covenant of habitability into a lease to permit a tenant to deduct the cost of repairing a toilet from rent due a landlord. More recently the inequality in bargaining power between landlord and tenant led this Court to comment that "lease agreements are frequently form contracts of adhesion . . . ." *Trentacost v. Brussel*, 82 *N.J.* 214, 226, 412 *A.2d* 436, 442 (1980). In *Trentacost* the Court concluded that the implied covenant of habitability obliged a landlord to furnish reasonable safeguards, such as a lock on the front door of an apartment building, to protect tenants from foreseeable criminal activity on the premises.

A migrant farmworker has even less bargaining power than a residential tenant. Although the contract did not require a migrant farmworker to live at the labor camp, the realities of his employment forced him to stay at the camp. Residence at the labor camp benefited not only the farmworker, but also Glassboro and its member farmers. It was more convenient for them if the workers resided at the camp: the pool of labor was at hand, and the workers could be transported conveniently to the farms. The contract assured Glassboro that there would be a labor source available on its property.

Under the contract, once a worker's employment was ended, he had no right to stay at the camp. Glassboro's possible need for the bed of a discharged farmworker, particularly during the growing season, is relevant, but not persuasive. In this case, Glassboro had ample space for Vasquez, yet he was turned out of the barracks on the same day he was fired. The interest of neither the migrant farmworker nor the public is served by casting the worker adrift to fend for himself without reasonable time to find shelter.

The status of a worker seeking employment with Glassboro is analogous to that of a consumer who must accept a standardized form contract to purchase needed goods and services. Neither farmworkers nor consumers negotiate the terms of their contracts; both must accept the contracts as presented to them. In both instances, the contracts affect many people as well as the public interest.

. . . .

The absence of a provision in the contract for reasonable time to find housing after termination of his employment bespeaks Glassboro's superior bargaining position. Further, by failing to provide for a reasonable time to find alternative housing, the contract is inconsistent with the enlightened attitude of the Legislature and the courts towards migrant farmworkers.

The crux of this case thus becomes the unconscionability of the contract as it is sought to be enforced against the migrant workers. The unconscionability of the contract inheres not only in its failure to provide a worker with a reasonable opportunity to find alternative housing, but in its disregard for his welfare after termination of his employment. The inherent inequity of the contract arouses a sense of injustice and invokes the equitable powers of the courts. In the absence of any concern demonstrated for the worker in the contract, public policy requires the implication of a provision for a reasonable time to find alternative housing.

IV

At common law, on termination of employment, an employer could dispossess an employee who occupied premises incidental to his employment. *McQuade v. Emmons*, 38 *N.J.L.* 397 (Sup. Ct. 1876). Similarly, a landlord could dispossess peaceably a holdover tenant. *Mershon v. Williams*, 62 *N.J.L.* 779, 42 *A.* 778 (E. & A. 1899); *Todd v. Jackson*, 26 *N.J.L.* 525, (E. & A. 1857). To that extent, both an employer and landlord could use self-help to regain possession peaceably. The advantage to them was that they were assured of prompt restoration of the use of their property. However, an inherent vice in self-help is that it can lead to confrontations and breaches of the peace. *See Thiel v. Bull's Ferry Land Co.*, 58 *N.J.L.* 212, 33 *A.* 281 (Sup. Ct. 1895).

In the absence of self-help, a landlord or employer at common law was remitted to an action in ejectment. The problem with ejectment is that it was slow and expensive. In New Jersey, ejectment has been replaced with a statutory action, *N.J.S.A.* 2A:35-1; however, that action is not a summary proceeding.

With regard to real property occupied solely as a residence, the Legislature has resolved the dilemma by prohibiting entry without consent and by providing a summary dispossess proceeding. *N.J.S.A.* 2A:39-1 and *N.J.S.A.* 2A:18-53 *et seq.* Similarly, the Legislature has provided a summary dispossess proceeding for the removal of residential tenants. *N.J.S.A.* 2A:18-61.2. As explained above, migrant farmworkers are not tenants, and there is no comparable statute providing for their summary dispossession on termination of their employment. In fashioning a suitable remedy, we acknowledge that the realities of the relationship between the migrant worker and a farm labor service are unique and summon a judicial response unrestricted by conventional categories, such as employer-employee and landlord-tenant. *See Shack, supra.* We cannot confine ourselves to traditional actions for possession such as ejectment or summary dispossession.

After oral argument, we requested the parties to submit supplemental briefs analyzing the applicability of the unlawful detainer statute to a farmworker who remains peaceably in possession of his living quarters following termination of his employment. That question had not been presented previously for consideration by the trial court, Appellate Division, or this Court. One type of unlawful detainer statute, *N.J.S.A.*, 2A:39-4, pertains to holdover tenants. Another unlawful detainer statute pertains to persons taking possession "without the consent of the owner or without color of title . . . ." *N.J.S.A.* 2A:39-5. Although a migrant farmworker would qualify under the latter alternative as one who enters without color of title, the question remains whether he has "possession."

At common law, an employee who occupied his employer's premises had no possession of his own, but only the possession of his employer. *McQuade v. Emmons*, 38 *N.J.L.* 397, 399 (Sup. Ct. 1876). Consequently, on termination of his employment, the employee was considered a trespasser.

The meaning of "possession" varies with the context of its use. Comment, *Defects in the Current Forcible Entry and Detainer Laws of the United States and England*, 25 UCLA L. Rev. 1067, 1084 (1978). One writer suggests that "possession can only be usefully defined with reference to the purpose in hand; and that possession may have one meaning in one connection and another meaning in another." Shartel, *Meanings of Possession*, 16 Minn. L. Rev. 611, 612 (1932). Although there are no cases discussing possession under *N.J.S.A.* 2A:39-5, in *Poroznoff v. Alberti*, 161 *N.J. Super.* 414, 391 A.2d 984 (Cty. D. Ct. 1978), aff'd 168 *N.J. Super.* 140,

401 A.2d 1124 (App. Div. 1979), the trial court concluded that a week-to-week resident at a YMCA did not have possession under a related statute pertaining to forcible entry and detainer. Generally, a worker remains at Glassboro's camp only while waiting for assignment to a farm. Together with approximately 30 other men, he shared unpartitioned space in the barracks. We conclude that a migrant farmworker does not have possession of his living quarters within the meaning of N.J.S.A. 2A:39-5 and that the remedy of unlawful detainer is not available.

Even if the unlawful detainer act applied, it provides an imperfect solution to the conflicts between migrant workers and their employers. In an unlawful detainer action, a migrant farmworker could raise equitable defenses relevant to the right of possession, but not to collateral issues.

A migrant worker should be allowed to raise equitable claims or defenses even though they might be considered collateral to the issue of possession. That result is consistent with our conclusion that a tenant may assert equitable as well as legal defenses in a dispossess action. See Marini v. Ireland, 56 N.J. 130, 140, 265 A.2d 526 (1970). It is consistent also with the incorporation by the legislature of equitable considerations into the summary dispossess act by providing in N.J.S.A. 2A:18-55 that proceedings to dispossess a tenant for nonpayment of rent shall stop on payment of the rent. See Vineland Shopping Center, Inc. v. DeMarco, 35 N.J. 459, 469, 173 A.2d 270 (1961). Even after granting a judgment of possession against a tenant, a judge has the statutory authority to stay the issuance of a warrant for removal or a writ of possession. N.J.S.A. 2A:42-106. He may delay eviction for a period no longer than six months "if it shall appear that by the issuance of the warrant or writ the tenant will suffer hardship because of the unavailability of other dwelling accommodations . . . ."

In the absence of a contractual provision or legislation addressing the plight of a migrant farmworker on termination of his employment, the courts, exercising equitable jurisdiction, should devise a remedy to fit the circumstances of each case. Depending on the circumstances, an equitable adjustment of the rights of the parties may vary from one case to another. An appropriate remedy might include time in addition to that implied in the contract, assistance in obtaining alternative housing, return passage to Puerto Rico, or some other form of relief. By abolishing self-help and requiring dispossession through a judicial proceeding, we provide a forum for an equitable resolution of a controversy between a farm labor service and a migrant farmworker on termination of the latter's employment.

We are mindful of the special considerations pertaining to migrant farmworkers and of the need for a prompt resolution of disputes between farmworkers and a farm labour service. In general, a summary action under R. 4:67 should be a more appropriate proceeding than a plenary action. In fact, the present case was instituted on complaint and order to show cause returnable three days later, at which time the court heard testimony, reserved decision, and rendered a written opinion seven days later. We conclude that a dispute concerning the dispossession of a migrant farmworker on termination of his employment, whether instituted by a farm labor service or, as here, by a farmworker, should proceed in a summary manner under R. 4:67.

We affirm the judgment of the Appellate Division as modified and remand the matter to the trial court for the entry of an order consistent with this opinion.

For affirmance: CHIEF JUSTICE WILENTZ and JUSTICES SULLIVAN, PASHMAN, CLIFFORD, SCHREIBER, HANDLER AND POLLOCK—7.

For reversal: None.

[c]   Explanatory Notes: Tenancies and Summary Actions

[*i*]   *Glassboro Service Association.* While the *Vasquez* litigation was pending, Glassboro Service Association was also involved in a lengthy dispute with the United States Labor Department. Unfair labor charges were brought against Glassboro in 1978 for violating a statutory ban on charging workers for transportation when the fees are "for the benefit or convenience of the employer" when payment of such charges has the effect of reducing earnings levels below the minimum wage. Nine years later, Glassboro was found in contempt of court for violating a court order to stop making such charges.[13]

[*ii*]   **State v. Shack** *as Precedent.* The *Vasquez* result was predictable, in part, given the result in *State v. Shack*, p. 557 above. The New Jersey Supreme Court's sympathy with the plight of migrant workers made it likely that Vasquez would obtain some form of protection for his possessory claim to his residence. But the exact nature of the protection afforded Vasquez could not have been anticipated from reading *Shack*. The *Vasquez* dispute could have been characterized in a wide variety of ways and each characterization would have carried a very different set of "legal baggage" along with it. For example, the dispute was arguably a trespass case, like *Shack*. It also could have been characterized as an employment contract dispute, a landlord-tenant dispute, a state constitutional law dispute, a federal constitutional law dispute, a *sui generis* dispute calling for wholly new common law development, or a combination of some of the above.

[*iii*]   *Landlord Remedies.* Before eschewing the landlord-tenant relationship as the model for decision in *Vasquez*, the court discussed the remedies available to a landlord attempting to obtain unpaid rent or to regain possession of property from a tenant. Three varieties of relief were typically available in New Jersey and many other states. First, the landlord could use self-help, either by distraining the goods of a tenant or by peaceably dispossessing a tenant not paying rent. Distraint is the subject of *Callen v. Sherman's, Inc.*, p. 622 below. In *Callen,* decided in 1983, the New Jersey Supreme Court found that the involvement of the sheriff in the operation of the distraint process meant that state action was involved in its use and then went on to hold the remedy unconstitutional. Landlords should have anticipated that result and shied away from using the remedy.

Self-help dispossession, which might escape the state action label, was a risky affair. Failure to follow the statutorily prescribed procedures,[14] or involvement in breaches of the peace, subjected the landlord to suit by the tenant.[15] The riskiness of such activity led many property owners to use the courts to remove tenants and to seek alterations in available proceedings to make them easier and faster to use. During the middle of the nineteenth century, the legislature created a summary dispossess proceeding for landlords as a supplement to the traditional, slow ejectment proceeding.[16] Finally, landlords could sue a non-paying tenant in a typical contract

---

[13] Brock v. Glassboro Service Association, Inc., 107 Lab.Cas. ¶ 34961 (D.N.J. 1987).

[14] New Jersey has long had a forcible entry and detainer statute creating tenant remedies against landlords violating specific self-help guidelines. The legislation is now codified at N.J. STAT. ANN. § 2A:39-1 *et seq.*

[15] For example, in Thiel v. Bull's Ferry Land Co., cited by the court in *Vasquez*, the tenant recovered damages from a landlord who forcibly evicted a tenant who was clearly in breach of the terms of his lease.

[16] That this procedure was made available only to landlords seeking possession of real estate meant that some property owners, such as employers permitting their employees to live on site, were left with a choice between using self-help remedies or seeking a slothful ejectment.

action for damages. This action was useful if the tenant had assets, but in the nineteenth century, as now, most tenants failing to pay rent were not well off. It is therefore understandable that suits for rent have never been the favored remedy for landlords seeking redress from a tenant breaching the terms of a lease.

[*iv*] *A Note on New Jersey Courts.* Summary dispossess actions are brought by landlords in the *Superior Court, Law Division, Special Civil Part.* Before 1991, these actions were brought in the County District Court. Most state court systems usually contain Landlord-Tenant and Small Claims branches. All other actions in New Jersey, such as suits for rent above the small claims court dollar limit, ejectment cases, or summary actions like those mandated by *Vasquez* are brought in the regular *Superior Courts.* These courts, in turn, each have a Law Division and a Chancery Division. Cases seeking primarily legal relief are heard in the Law Division, those seeking equitable relief in Chancery. Appeals go from all these courts to the Superior Court, Appellate Division, and then to the Supreme Court.

[*v*] *The* **Vasquez** *Opinion. Vasquez* presented the New Jersey Supreme Court with some interesting problems. In 1974, the state legislature placed limits on the ability of landlords to use common law rules to evict tenants, including modifications of the rule permitting employers to evict employees from onsite housing. The new language, found in N.J. STAT. ANN. § 2A:18-61.1(m), clearly altered the old employer-employee rule. Nonetheless, the court found that Vasquez was *not* a tenant. Given the court's decision in *Shack,* which demonstrated a strong predilection to provide protections for migrant workers, this result was a bit counter-intuitive. Why did the court reach for a conclusion that migrant workers were not tenants?

The only reason given by the court was a rule of statutory construction. "Where general words follow a specific enumeration," the court noted, "the principle of *ejusdem generis* requires that the general words are applicable only to the same class of things already mentioned." Since the workers were apparently all Spanish speaking and living intermittently in barracks without either private facilities or a contractual obligation to pay rent directly to Glassboro, they were different from superintendents or other employees living in apartments. But there is an equally valid rule of statutory construction cutting in the other direction, for statutes meant to be remedial and beneficial to a class of persons are supposed to be construed liberally so as to provide protection to the protected class. Couldn't the court have used this "rule" to come to the opposite conclusion?

In any case, after finding that there was not a tenancy, the court went on to provide the workers with tenant-like protection anyway! Continuing in the direction *Shack* began and noting the various legislative efforts to provide benefits for migrant workers, the court refused to enforce that part of the employment contract calling for automatic loss of housing rights upon loss of employment, declined to allow self-help eviction, and created a wholly new legal proceeding using Rule 4:67 of the New Jersey Rules of Civil Procedure. This rule provides a procedure applicable to all statutory summary actions for which special rules of court do not exist (special rules exist for landlord-tenant actions) and to other cases, including matters in equity, that need to be resolved speedily. Under Rule 4:67 the plaintiff must file, along with the complaint, a motion to proceed summarily. The motion, served on the defendant along with the complaint, is decided on the return date—the date the defendant is required to answer the complaint. In essence, the New Jersey Supreme Court in *Vasquez* told the lower courts to always grant a motion to proceed summarily in migrant worker dispossess cases.

But that still leaves open the question as to why the court declined to call migrant workers tenants while it provided them with tenant-like protections from use of self-help evictions. Perhaps the court simply believed that the lack of traditional cash rents made it inappropriate to use the lease as the model for handling this transaction. But it is also possible that the court was leery of creating a new form of tenancy in light of the multitude of other rules that result would call into play. In addition to the 1974 statute placing significant limitations upon the ability of landlords to remove tenants, New Jersey also had a myriad of other rules—special notice provisions, security deposit regulations, limitations on assigning and subletting, and special repair obligations, among others. Rather than using a transactional model which would automatically call all of these other rule structures into play, the court may have preferred to retain some flexibility in deciding what sort of a legal structure to create. But while the court may have had good reasons for declining to call the workers tenants, that decision risked forcing landlords to use the slow ejectment process to rid themselves of non-working, non-paying persons. Rather than doing that, the judges crafted a new remedial structure that could operate as fast as a summary dispossess action. Regardless of whether you think the court made the correct policy choices, *Vasquez* surely demonstrates the well-known tendency of the New Jersey Supreme Court to craft creative remedial systems to handle special problems. Selecting the appropriate process was surely the main goal of the court. But would the result be one the Legal Process School would applaud?

[d]   Problem Notes: Other Examples

[*i*]   *Hotel Guests.* After *Vasquez* what right does a hotel have to remove a nonpaying or disruptive guest? In *Poroznoff v. Alberti*, 161 N.J. Super. 414, 391 A.2d 984 (1978), Paul Poroznoff was living on a week-to-week basis in a room at the Young Men's Christian Association in Passaic, New Jersey. In early June, 1978, he was arrested by police for being drunk and disorderly. When he was released and returned to his room, he found it locked. Poroznoff was also told not to return to the building. The court concluded that he was a guest in a hotel and that the Y.M.C.A. was not required to use judicial proceedings to remove him. In deciding this case, the court was confronted with an array of potentially conflicting statutes. One set of statutes governed the eviction and ejectment processes. A second series defined circumstances in which self-help was appropriate. A third group defined hotels and apartments for purposes of various administrative and licensing purposes.

[*A*]   *Summary Dispossession.* The most commonly used eviction statute in New Jersey was (and is) N.J. STAT. ANN. § 2A:18-53, which provided for the summary dispossession of "any lessee or tenant at will or at sufferance, or for a part of a year, or for 1 or more years, of any houses, buildings, lands or tenements" who stays past the end of a lease, fails to pay rent, disturbs the peace and quiet of the premises or violates terms of a lease. This summary dispossess process was limited by N.J. STAT. ANN. § 2A:18-61.1, which required that one of numerous listed grounds be present before a property owner could summarily evict a party. This limiting section, however, did not apply to "owner occupied premises with not more than two rental units or a hotel, motel or other guest house or part thereof rented to a transient guest or seasonal tenant." For purposes of *Poroznoff*, these statutes required resolution of whether the Y.M.C.A., which allowed guests to stay on a week-to-week basis, was an apartment or a hotel.

[*B*]   *Ejectment.* Property owners also could sue in ejectment, a normal civil process lacking the speed of a summary dispossess action. N.J. STAT. ANN. § 2A:35-1 provided that, "Any person claiming the right of possession of real property in the possession of another, or claiming title to such real property," could file an action in a New Jersey trial court. On the face of it, this statute appeared to apply to the *Poroznoff* setting. But an argument could be made that a hotel guest (if that is what Poroznoff was) was not "in possession" of "real property," but only "present" on the land of another as a "guest."

[*C*]   *Forcible Entry and Detainer.* N.J. STAT. ANN. § 2A:39-1 defined those circumstances in which a property owner could use self-help to regain possession from a tenant:

No person shall enter upon or into any real property or estate therein and detain and hold the same, except where entry is given by law, and then only in a peaceable manner. With regard to any real property occupied solely as a residence by the party in possession, such entry shall not be made in any manner without the consent of the party in possession unless the entry and detention is made pursuant to legal process as set out in N.J.S. 2A:18-53 *et seq.* or 2A:35-1 *et seq.*

Poroznoff argued that even if he lacked status as a tenant under N.J. STAT. ANN. §§ 2A:18-53 and 2A:18-61.1, he was a "party in possession" for purposes of N.J. STAT. ANN. § 2A:39-1. If he was correct, then use of self-help was prohibited and the Y.M.C.A. should have used the ejectment process to get him out.

[*D*]   *Administrative Definitions.* Finally, N.J. STAT. ANN. § 55:13A-3(j) defined a hotel as "any building . . . which contains 10 or more units of dwelling space or has sleeping facilities for 25 or more persons and is kept, used, maintained, advertised as, or held out to be, a place where sleeping or dwelling accommodations are available to transient or permanent guests." According to N.J. STAT. ANN. § 55:13A-3(k), a multiple dwelling was "any building . . . in which three or more units of dwelling space are occupied . . . by three or more persons who live independently of each other" provided the building was not registered as a hotel. The purposes for these definitions were different than for the other statutes. Regulating and registering hotels to make sure they are clean, post necessary notices, and meet other code requirements may lead to the creation of a different, perhaps more inclusive, definition of "hotel" than you would expect to find in eviction statutes.

In any case, the court, in a valiant effort to make some sense of this mish-mash of statutes, found that the Y.M.C.A. was a hotel because it held itself out as available for transient guests, that the contractual understanding with Poroznoff was that of an innkeeper and guest, that the building was intended for use as a hotel, and that it was registered with the state as a hotel. Poroznoff was therefore not "in possession" of real estate; the "Y" could toss him out. Did *Vasquez* alter this outcome?

In some more recent cases, persons staying in hotels for a long period of time have been treated as tenants rather than guests. Willa McNeill, for example, was locked out of her hotel room for not paying after staying there for three years. The court distinguished *Poroznoff* as a case dealing with a transient guest and provided McNeill with relief under the Forcible Entry and Detainer Act.[17]

[*ii*]   *Dormitories.* In *Morristown Memorial Hospital v. Wokem Mortgage & Realty Co.*, 192 N.J. Super. 182, 469 A.2d 515 (1983), the hospital leased 26 units in a 140 unit apartment building and then let students and residents involved in the hospital's training programs use them.

---

[17] McNeill v. Estate of Lachman, 285 N.J. Super 212, 666 A.2d 996 (App. Div. 1995). In other cases, a two month resident was treated as a guest in Francis v. Trinidad Motel, 261 N.J. Super. 252, 618 A.2d 873 (App. Div. 1992), while a man living in a hotel for two years with members of his family who attended local schools was treated as a tenant in Williams v. Alexander Hamilton Hotel, 249 N.J. Super. 481, 592 A.2d 644 (App. Div. 1991).

The actual issue in the case was whether a new owner of the building could terminate the arrangement with the hospital, without meeting the limitations of N.J. STAT. ANN. § 2A:18-61.1, the Anti Eviction Act. The court found that the act did not apply on the ground that the agreement between the hospital and the owner was not a residential contract. But what of the residents and students? They worked at the hospital for only one year. May they remain on as tenants and avoid eviction because of the constraints of the Anti Eviction Act? Were they tenants, employees, migrants or guests? Even if the Anti Eviction Act was inapplicable, did *Vasquez* protect them from self-help eviction? Were there any differences between the housing arrangements for medical staff in *Morristown* and a typical dormitory for undergraduate students?

[3]   Tenants in Possession Versus Owners in Possession

[a]   Cooperative Housing and the Proprietary Lease

You may have heard people talk about 99-year leases being the same as full fee simple ownership. While such talk may not reflect reality,[18] there are a number of circumstances in which it is hard to tell the difference between fee and leasehold interests.[19] Cooperative apartment dwellers[20] provide an interesting example. The fee simple absolute in a cooperative is held by a corporation. Fantasize a non-profit cooperative corporation called Get Along Better, Inc. (GAB). When GAB bought or developed the building, they made a down payment for part of the price and financed the rest with a mortgage from Money Bank and Trust Company (Money). When the purchase by GAB was closed, GAB got a deed for the property, paid some money to the prior owner or developer, and conveyed a *mortgage deed* to Money. The mortgage deed provided that if a default in payment on the loan occurred, then Money could foreclose on the building by selling it to raise money to pay off the debt. GAB also signed a *note*. A note is a contract in which a borrower agrees to pay off a loan. A default gives rise, not to a right to foreclose, but to a right to sue for breach of contract on the note. Money, in turn, paid the loan proceeds to the seller. So the transaction, if diagramed, looked something like this:

---

[18] For example, in Hawaii a great deal of very valuable land has been developed under 99-year leases. Many of the leases are now coming up for renewal, causing all sorts of problems for small home owners and large hotel owners. *See* Hawaii Housing Authority v. Midkiff, 467 U.S. 229 (1984), p. 902 below.

[19] Very early in a long term lease, for example, the longevity of the possessory right means the market value of the lease will be almost identical to that of a fee simple.

[20] Don't confuse cooperatives with condominiums. The latter are discussed in some detail along with *Centex v. Boag*, p. 744 below.

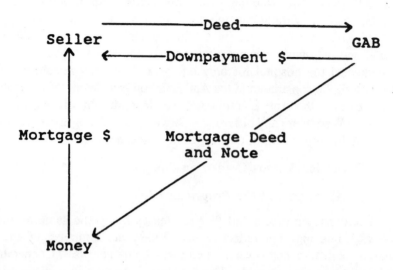

But where did GAB get any money to make its downpayment? And why would a bank rely on its credit and lend it money? The residents of the building helped out on these problems. When Harry and Harriet Homeowner (HHH) decided to buy an apartment in this building, what happened? First, they had to pay a sum of money: to GAB, if HHH were among the original residents of the building, or to the prior residents, if the building had been around for a time. If HHH were among the original residents, this money was used to help GAB make its downpayment to buy the building. Note that the sum paid did not equal the total value of the apartment, but only the "equity" or paid up value of the unit. In addition, HHH signed a lease agreeing to pay GAB "rent" in return for the right to live in the building for indefinitely renewable terms.[21] This "rent" equaled the sum of HHH's proportional share of GAB's monthly mortgage payments to Money, maintenance and upkeep expenses, and other costs involved in running the building. In addition to GAB agreeing to let HHH stay in their apartment indefinitely, HHH also received shares of stock in GAB, Inc. The residents ended up owning GAB and running the building. If we put HHH into the diagram it looks like this:

---

[21] Different building leases carry different terms. Some create long terms, like 99 years, with clauses that permit the Board of Directors of the owning corporation to order payment of different rents if necessary to meet building payments. Others provide for short leases, like one or two years, that are always renewable provided the resident pays the "rent."

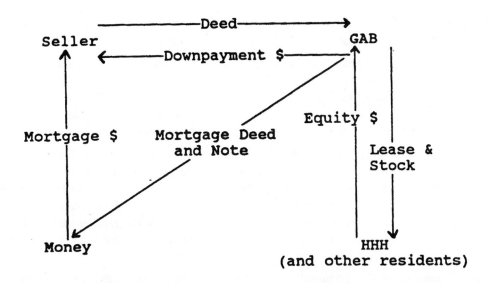

If HHH were not original occupants, they would pay their money to the prior residents, whose lease and shares of stock would be canceled. HHH would then receive a new lease and the stock would be reissued to them.

Under these arrangements, what sort of legal animal is a resident in a cooperative apartment? Perhaps the next case will help you find out.

[b]   Opinion of the New Jersey Superior Court, Appellate Division in *Plaza Road v. Finn*

Plaza Road Cooperative, Inc. v. Finn

New Jersey Superior Court, Appellate Division
201 N.J. Super. 174, 492 A.2d 1072 (1985)

Per Curiam.

We affirm the dismissal of the complaint which sought the summary dispossession of a cooperator-shareholder of a cooperative apartment association under *N.J.S.A.* 2A:18-61.1, substantially for the reasons expressed by Judge B. M. Sween in his written opinion dated November 29, 1983 which we incorporate herein:

This case presents a jurisdictional issue apparently not previously addressed by the courts of this State—is the relationship between a cooperative apartment association and a member-occupant that of a landlord-tenant for purposes of a summary dispossess action in a County District Court?

A cooperative apartment house is a multi-unit dwelling in which each resident has an interest in the entity owning the building and an agreement entitling him to occupy a particular apartment within the building. The interest in the owner-entity is usually that of a stockholder and the occupancy agreement is generally referred to as a "proprietary lease." The difficulty in classifying or defining the owner-occupant status in legal concepts has caused confusion, and a cooperative is frequently described as a building in which each "tenant" "owns" an apartment, an obvious contradiction in terms. The primary issue presented to the court is whether this combination of owner and occupant interests is such that a landlord-tenant relationship no longer exists for the purpose of summary dispossess action jurisdiction in this court.

The conversion of the apartment building and the creation of the legal relationship between the parties in this case is typical of this form of land use. In February 1979, defendant leased an apartment from Plaza Road, Inc., plaintiff's predecessor in title. Thereafter, in late 1981 or early 1982, Plaza Road, Inc. sought to "convert" the apartment building and negotiated a plan of cooperative organization with the tenants and sought the necessary governmental approvals.

Later, defendant entered into an occupancy agreement with her former landlord, which provided for its termination when the plan of cooperative organization was approved, at which time defendant would purchase a membership, purchase one share of stock and enter into a proprietary lease with the cooperative corporation. On or about November 1, 1982, defendant acquired one share of stock in plaintiff cooperative corporation for $41,000 ($6,800 in cash and $34,200 by a mortgage) and entered into an agreement entitled "Owner-Occupant Agreement Proprietary Lease," which gives rise to this litigation.

Plaintiff seeks to invoke the jurisdiction of this court on two grounds: (1) the proprietary lease confers jurisdiction for summary dispossess purposes on the court; and (2) the court has jurisdiction by virtue of the landlord-tenant relationship created by the proprietary lease.

I

Although the proprietary lease provides in paragraph 1(a):

The owner-occupant agrees that any action brought under this agreement for failure to observe any terms or conditions hereunder, including failure to pay rent, shall be brought in the Bergen County District Court as a summary dispossess action under *N.J.S.* 2A:18 and owner-occupant hereby submits to the jurisdiction of this court.

in paragraph 32:

. . . owner-occupant acknowledges that the Essex (sic) County District Court has jurisdiction under this agreement to issue a judgment for possession for the premises which are the subject of this agreement. This shall include, but not be limited to, judgment in a summary dispossess proceeding.

and in paragraph 43:

In addition to submitting to the jurisdiction of the Bergen County District Court, the owner-occupant-lessee agrees to pay L. & F. Co. and/or Plaza Road Cooperative Association, Inc., the following items as part of any judgment, and such amounts are due and includible with any such judgment as if they were due as additional rents, attorney's fee of $75.00, court costs, constable and/or warrant fees, and applicable late charges, as provided for under the terms of all agreements between the parties. it has been long established that no one can confer jurisdiction on a court by private agreement between the parties. The owner-occupant agreement between the parties cannot confer jurisdiction upon the court to hear a summary dispossess action, if a landlord-tenant relationship does not exist between the parties.

II

The provisions of the owner-occupant agreement between the parties may be divided into two categories: (1) those which may be found in any lease agreement setting forth the rights and obligations of the landlord and tenant; and (2) those which become necessary due to the occupants' hybrid position of being both an occupant of a single apartment unit and having an ownership interest in the entire apartment building.

Examples of the former are provisions:

1. Requiring the cooperative association to maintain the exterior and common areas of the building.

2. Defining obligations in case of fire damage to the building.

3. Giving the occupant a right to quiet possession.

4. Establishing rules and regulations concerning conduct on the premises.

5. Limiting who may occupy an apartment.

6. Limiting actions of an occupant which may affect insurance rates.

7. Limiting the occupants' right to make alterations.

8. Defining rights of entry to make repairs.

Examples of the latter are:

1. Defining "rent" as a share of actual carrying charges and maintenance expenses for the building allocated in relation to the total number of shares of the cooperative corporation issued.

2. Limiting the cooperative association's liability for maintaining the public areas and providing insufficient supply of hot and cold water and heat by stating:

The covenants by Co-op herein contained are subject, however, to discretionary power of the Directors to determine from time to time what services and what attendants shall be proper, and the manner of maintaining and operating the building, and also what existing services shall be increased, reduced, changed, modified, or terminated.

3. Giving the "tenant" the right to inspect the "landlord's" books of account by stating:

Co-op shall keep full and correct books of account at its principal office or at such other place as the Directors may from time to time determine, and the same shall be open during all reasonable hours to inspection by the owner-occupant or representative of the owner-occupant. Co-op shall deliver to owner-occupant within a reasonable time after the end of each fiscal year, an annual statement of income and expenses, certified by an independent certified accountant.

4. Promoting a cooperative venture by stating:

Owner-occupant shall always in good faith endeavor to observe and promote the cooperative purposes for the accomplishment of which Co-op is incorporated.

5. Limiting liability of the "landlord" to provide needed services by stating:

Co-op shall not be liable, for any reason, for any failure or insufficiency of heat, or of air conditioning (where air conditioning is supplied or air conditioning equipment maintained by Co-op), water supply, electric current, gas, heat or hot water, or other service to be supplied by Co-op hereunder, or for interference with light, air, view, or other interest of owner-occupant.

6. Granting the "landlord" the unilateral right to terminate the agreement by stating:

If, upon, or at any time after, Co-op shall give to owner-occupant a notice stating that the term hereof will expire on a date at least five days hereafter, the term of this agreement shall expire on the date so fixed in such notice, as fully and completely as if it were the date herein definitely fixed for the expiration of the term. The right, title, and interest of owner-occupant hereunder shall thereupon wholly cease and expire, and owner-occupant hereunder shall thereupon quit and surrender the apartment to the Co-op. It is the intention herein to create a conditional limitation. Co-op shall then have the right to re-enter the apartment and remove all persons and personal property therefrom by any suitable action or proceeding at law or in equity, or by force or otherwise, and to repossess the apartment in its former state, as if this agreement had not been made, and no liability whatsoever shall attach to Co-op by any reason of the exercise of the right of re-entry, repossession, and removal herein granted and reserved.

Among other reasons for giving a notice of termination are:

If owner-occupant shall be in default in the performance of any covenant or provision hereof, including but not limited to the covenant to pay maintenance.

If at any time Co-op shall determine, upon the affirmative vote of two-thirds (2/3) of its then Board of Directors, at a meeting duly called for that purpose, that because of objectionable conduct on the part of owner-occupant or of a person dwelling in or visiting the apartment, repeated after written notice from Co-op, the occupancy of the owner-occupant is undesirable.

However, no notice, in writing or otherwise, need be given owner-occupant prior to any action being taken by Co-op if owner-occupant shall be in default in the payment of any maintenance charge, or additional maintenance charge, or any installment thereof, or of any payment of any moneys due Co-op.

8. Waiving "tenant's" "right of redemption" by stating:

Owner-occupant expressly waives any and all right of redemption in case owner-occupant shall be dispossessed by judgment or warrant of any court or a judge; the words "enter", "re-enter", and "re-entry" as used in this agreement are not restricted to their technical legal meaning, and in the event of a breach or a threatened breach of owner-occupant of any of the covenants or provisions hereof, Co-op shall have the right of injunction and the right to invoke any remedy allowed at law or in equity, as if re-entry, summary proceedings, and other remedies were not herein provided for.

9. Acknowledging that the "tenant" is also a "landlord" and, therefore, waiving certain defenses available to "tenants" in summary dispossess actions, by providing:

Owner-occupant acknowledges the complete control over the premises which are the subject of this agreement, by virtue of the unique position of being a shareholder of the Co-op owner. Therefore, owner-occupant waives any defense available in such proceeding, of "habitability" or otherwise, because of any possible applicable cases, law, rules or regulation of any governmental authority.

Because of the hybrid nature of the interest of an occupant-stockholder-owner in a cooperative apartment building, there have been a great variety of problems concerning cooperative apartments presented to the courts of our land, resulting in varying definitions and solutions. Quotations from cases can be found to support virtually any position. Plaintiff cited and quoted two cases from sister jurisdictions in support of its position. Neither was a summary dispossess action, and in the case of *Hicks v. Bigelow*, 55 A.2d 924 (D.C. Mun. Ct. App. 1947), plaintiff misunderstood (and misquoted) the court saying:

As between the owner of an apartment in a cooperative building and the cooperative corporation, there is a landlord-tenant relationship . . .

but failed to complete the quotation, which reads:

As between plaintiff and the cooperative corporation in form there is a landlord-tenant relationship, but in substance the apartments are owner occupied. The amounts paid by the stockholders as 'rent' really represent the cost of operation, maintenance, etc., of their own property.

and later in the decision, the court said, . . . " . . . the stock was incidental to that purpose and afforded the practical means of combining an ownership interest with a method for sharing proportionately the assessments for maintenance and taxes." The District of Columbia court found the owner-occupant:

. . . has certain proprietary rights which a mere tenant does not have. She has most of the attributes of an owner. She has a voice in management and operation of a building. She has a voice in the selection or approval of other tenant-owners. She has a voice, too, in the important matter of any proposed sale or mortgage of the property. More important, she has the exclusive, personal right to occupy her particular apartment . . .

The issue before the court is not whether a cooperative apartment corporation or one of its owner-occupants can enforce contractual rights in a court of law (obviously they can before a proper forum) but whether it may do so in a summary dispossess action.

Neither plaintiff nor defendant cited any cases from sister jurisdictions on this issue, and the court found the problem discussed only in New York cases. In *Jimerson Housing Co., Inc. v. Butler*, 97 *Misc.* 2d 563, 412 *N.Y.S.* 2d 560 (Civ. Ct. 1978), the court reasoned that:

1. Summary proceedings, as first authorized by statute in New York, were designed as a substitute remedy for the common law action in ejectment, which had become expensive and dilatory, amounting in many cases to a denial of justice.

2. Although the scope of summary proceedings had been enlarged in New York to include parties other than landlords and tenants, it remained an exclusively statutory remedy, in derogation of the common law, and as such had to be strictly construed.

3. The right to maintain summary proceedings must be conferred by statute, and parties to a lease or an occupancy agreement cannot, by agreement, confer such a right nor can it be granted by consent.

4. The relationship of a cooperative corporation and an occupant was not that of a landlord and tenant, regardless of any provision of the occupancy agreement attempting to consensually define it as such.

5. The agreement between a cooperative and an occupant was generally comprised of several components, including a certificate of incorporation, by-laws, shares of stock representing the shareholder-occupant's equity in the corporation, and an occupancy agreement, and the several components must be read together to define the "cooperative interest" or that bundle of rights, privileges, and obligations that determine the relationship between the parties.

6. That since the cooperative corporation's relationship to the occupant was not that of a landlord-tenant, there was no jurisdiction in the Housing Court to entertain a non-payment of

rent petition.[1] However, the New York law is still unsettled as earlier cases came to different conclusions. In *Curtis v. LeMay*, 186 *Misc.* 853, 60 *N.Y.S.*2d 768 (Mun. Ct. 1945), the court permitted a summary dispossess action for an individual who occupied premises as a tenant prior to the creation of the cooperative; and in *930 Fifth Corporation v. King*, 40 *A.D.*2d 140, 338 *N.Y.S.*2d 773 (App. Div. 1972), the court reversed a lower court decision dismissing a dispossess action for breach of a provision in a lease prohibiting pets, although the issue of jurisdiction in a summary dispossess action was apparently not raised; in *Bourgeois v. American Savings Bank*, 63 *Misc.*2d 468, 312 *N.Y.S.*2d 232 (Civ. Ct. 1970), the court found that shareholders in a cooperative corporation were not 'tenants' within the statute authorizing tenants to maintain special proceedings for deposit of rents with third parties for the purpose of making repairs to a building; and in *Adair v. Tookey*, 99 *Misc.*2d 745, 747, 417 *N.Y.S.*2d 185, 187 (Civ. Ct. 1979), the court avoided the issue when deciding the case but noted that New York law was unsettled concerning the right of a cooperative corporation to bring a summary dispossess action against a stockholder-occupant, but cited the *Jimerson* case, noting:

> Cooperative ownership is a rapidly growing housing phenomenon and legislation may be needed to resolve the hybrid quality of the unique nature of property ownership and leasehold.

> The court finds that a cooperative apartment association is a unique form of property ownership which does not fit into common law classifications. It is personalty for purposes of estate distribution; it is real estate for purposes of income tax deductions; and it is governed by corporate law concerning its internal management. It is an entity for the common ownership of property enabling occupant stockholders to own, manage, and operate residential apartments on a nonprofit basis. The rights and obligations of the parties are limited only by their ingenuity in defining their relationship. The relationship is not one of landlord-tenant, and the court has no jurisdiction to hear plaintiff's summary dispossess action.

> The court finds it unnecessary to address issues raised by defendant that the agreement between the parties was "unconscionable" on the grounds that the agreement provided for a waiver of basic rights of a "tenant" to have a "habitable" apartment and the provision cutting off the defendant's "equity of redemption" would result in a forfeiture of defendant's investment in the apartment and its appreciated market value. These issues further illustrate the need for a forum with more comprehensive jurisdiction to deal with the complex relationship between the parties.

> Plaintiff's complaint is dismissed for lack of jurisdiction. We are in accord with Judge Sween's conclusion that a cooperative is a unique form of property ownership and the relationship between the association and a cooperator-shareholder is not that of landlord and tenant for the purpose of a summary dispossess action. Further, as this case involves a jurisdictional issue, our review and affirmance is not precluded by virtue of *N.J.S.A.* 2A:18-59. The dismissal of the complaint is affirmed.

---

[1] Note: This court agrees with the rationale expressed by the Civil Court in *Jimerson Housing Co., Inc. v. Butler*, 97 *Misc.*2d 563, 412 *N.Y.S.*2d 560, as cited in Judge Sween's opinion, although the case was subsequently reversed. 102 *Misc.*2d 423, 425 *N.Y.S.*2d 924 (App. Term 1979). The Appellate Term concluded the relationship between a cooperative and its stockholder is that of landlord and tenant to the extent that the cooperative may maintain a summary proceeding against t he stockholder. *See also Glen Oaks Village Owners, Inc. v. Balwani*, 115 *Misc.*2d 948, 454 *N.Y.S.*2d 802 (Civ. Ct. 1982). However, these decisions are founded on New York case law which in large part did not address the question of jurisdiction in dispossess actions but instead found summary proceedings appropriate for the resolution of other types of cooperative/stockholder disputes. As New Jersey does not have these precedents to guide its characterization of the parties' relationship we decline to follow recent New York case law on this point.

[c] Explanatory Notes

[*i*]   *Financing a Cooperative Purchase.* Mae Finn, the court indicated, purchased her cooperative "for $41,000 ($6,800 in cash and $34,200 by a mortgage)." This statement creates a bit of a puzzle. Recall from the notes before *Finn* describing the nature of a cooperative that the cooperating corporation owns the fee simple in the building and that there is a "blanket" mortgage covering the entire structure. How, then, could Finn obtain a "mortgage" too? She did not have a fee simple in her apartment to use as security, and even if she did, it was already partially encumbered by the blanket mortgage. Finn probably used her proprietary lease and share of stock in the cooperative corporation as security for her loan. If her lender held a mortgage at all,[22] it was a "second" mortgage. That is, if a default in the blanket mortgage occurred causing the building to go into foreclosure, Finn's lender would be second in line, receiving nothing from the proceeds of the foreclosure sale until the main lender was paid off.

[*ii*]   *Finn.* The case itself involved the straightforward issue of whether Finn was a tenant within the meaning of N.J. Stat. Ann. § 2A:18-53. On the surface, she certainly was. There was, after all, a lease. But she was also a part owner of the building, and the lease contained a large array of terms designed to facilitate the organization and operation of the cooperative. These latter characteristics, the court held, meant that the summary dispossess statute did not apply. To the court, Finn was more like an owner than a renter. This was probably consistent with Finn's own perceptions about the nature of the property relationships. Are such perceptions important in working out cases like this? If you thought, before taking this course, that property law was inflexible, rigid and tightly bound by rules, *Finn* should go a long way towards forcing you to rethink your views. The combination of legal concepts involved in this case—lease, fee simple, mortgage, non-profit corporation, servitude and contract—suggests that with a bit of ingenuity, you can create virtually any ownership arrangement you wish.

[*iii*]   *What Happens After Eviction?* If the owner of a cooperative apartment is evicted for failure to pay "rent," what happens to the housing unit left behind? The owner, while no longer in possession, does not automatically lose *all* interest in the residence. Despite the terms of the cooperative documents cutting off a resident's equity of redemption, it is likely that the corporation owning the building may take from the proceeds of such a sale only the amount owed by the evicted resident. Similarly, if the unit was used as collateral for a loan, the sale of the unit to pay off the loan may produce excess funds that will be paid to the defaulting resident. In that sense, eviction of a cooperative owner operates like the foreclosure of a regular mortgage.

[d] Problem Notes

[*i*]   *How Fast is Speedy?* There is no doubt that a nonpaying cooperator may be removed from her apartment. The only issue in *Finn* was whether that removal could occur in the "fast" summary dispossess court, rather than in a regular civil forum by way of ejectment. A summary dispossess case is clearly fast, among the fastest known to the American legal world. But the measuring unit used to evaluate speed in this world should probably be called the "sloth unit" and written as "years per case." The speed of a summary dispossess case is easily expressed

---

[22] Normally a mortgagor (the borrower) uses a fee simple as collateral for the loan. But other real property interests, such as the lease in this case, may also be valuable enough to support a loan. When cooperatives first appeared in the 1920s many banks hesitated to lend on their security. In the northeast, where many of the cooperatives are located, that difficulty has largely been overcome.

in sloth units. The fastest case possible, assuming that the tenant raises no defenses, is about one month, or one-twelfth sloth unit.[23] A judgment for possession, however, does not produce the overdue rent.[24] To get the money, the landlord must bring another civil action or take an offset against a security deposit.

[ii] *Need for Speed.* Given the difficulties of using even a summary action to get possession and the impossibility of using it to get money, isn't the landlord at least entitled to speed? Since ability to continue paying the expenses of running the building depend upon the prompt payment of rent, landlords argue they must be able to quickly rid themselves of unreliable tenants. And if the remedy given landlords in the summary process is not a guarantee of money in the bank, should not cooperatives be able to gain at least the same level of legal protection as traditional landlords? The blanket mortgage covering the whole building can only be paid if all of the residents pay their monthly charges. Their failure to do so creates the risk that the financial structure of the entire cooperative is at risk. So why not permit cooperatives to use a fast remedy to get rid of their non-paying tenants?

[iii] *Need for Sloth.* Most home owners (and condominium owners as well)[25] who default on their mortgages have the benefit of an *equity of redemption* as part of the foreclosure process. Statutes provide that mortgage borrowers have a period of time, say 90 days, to come up with overdue payments or find new financing; only after this redemption period expires may the lender go forward with the foreclosure sale. Even though cooperators do not finance their home purchase the same way, shouldn't there be some hesitancy about kicking anyone out of a home they are buying rather than renting? For most middle class families their home or cooperative is their single most important asset. That fact has driven the development of much of American property and tax law. Indeed federal income tax law generally provides the tax benefits of home ownership to cooperative owners.[26] Why stop providing such protection for cooperators? Is the ability of a tenant to come up with the rent due within three days of the entry of a judgment for possession the equivalent of the "equity of redemption?"

[iv] *Compare Long Term Tenants and Cooperators.* Should tenants be treated differently from cooperators? Should a tenant who has lived in the same place for 12 years have an "equity of redemption?" Even though tenants are not buying their homes, they spend large sums of money on their apartments. Being forced to move is a major disruption. Particularly in areas where good rental housing is both expensive and in short supply, why rush to evict? *Compare* the total unwillingness of the Hawaii Supreme Court, p. 186 above, to provide relief

[23] If the landlord sues fairly quickly, say on the 10th of the month, and the return date (the date when the tenant must appear in court) is 10 days later, New Jersey tenants still have another three days to pay the overdue rent and court costs after a judgment for possession is entered. N.J. STAT. ANN. § 2A:18-57. If payment is not forthcoming, the landlord then has to wait until the sheriff gets around to notifying the tenant of the eviction and actually putting the tenant on the street.

[24] In some states summary actions for possession may be joined with actions for rent. New Jersey does not allow such joinder.

[25] Condominium owners usually purchase their residences with the help of a mortgage loan just like single family home owners. Indeed, one of the major differences between condominium and cooperative owners is that condominium owners each obtain their own loans, while cooperators pay monthly charges large enough to pay their share of the mortgage on the entire building.

[26] Cooperators may deduct from their income their proportionate share of payments made by the cooperative corporation for mortgage interest and local property taxes, just as regular home owners deduct the similar charges they pay directly.

to the Sawadas because the Endos were married *with* the easy route to possession for a landlord dealing with a tenant who has defaulted for only one month on paying rent.

What would you do in *Finn*?

§ 8.03 Procedural Protections in the Eviction Process

[1] History of New Jersey's Dispossess Statutes

New Jersey's original dispossess statutes, enacted in 1795, were modeled almost exactly after English statutes adopted some time before.[27] Section 7 of An Act Concerning Landlords and Tenants[28] provided that where:

> [I]t shall be made to appear to the court where the said suit is depending, by affidavit, or be proved upon the trial, in case the defendant appears, that half a year's rent was due before the declaration was served, and that no sufficient distress was to be found on the demised premises, countervailing the arrears then due, and that the lessor or lessors in ejectment had power to re-enter, then, and in every such case, the lessor or lessors in ejectment shall have judgment and execution, in the same manner, as if the rent in arrears had been legally demanded and re-entry made; and in case the lessee or lessees . . . shall suffer judgment on such ejectment and execution to be executed thereon, without paying the rent and arrears, together with full costs, and without filing any bill or bills for relief in equity, within six calendar months after such execution executed, then, and in such case, the said lessee or lessees . . . shall be barred and foreclosed from all relief or remedy in law or equity . . . and the said landlord or lessor, shall, from thenceforth, hold the same demised premises discharged from such lease.

The statute also contained a provision requiring tenants holding past the end of their term to pay twice the rental value as damages for the period of their unlawful possession.[29] At the same time the legislature passed the Act Concerning Landlords and Tenants, it also adopted legislation on distresses,[30] and waste.[31] No major changes were made for the next half century.[32]

Across the Hudson River in New York, which in 1798 adopted a statute virtually identical to New Jersey's, pressure grew early in the nineteenth century to adopt legislation making it easier to dispossess tenants, particularly those holding over after the end of their leases. The traditional ejectment action was cumbersome and slow. The state Assembly responded in 1820 with a summary dispossess statute. It provided for eviction of holdover tenants and eased the

---

[27] The English antecedent, 4 Geo. II, ch. 28, was adopted in 1731.

[28] Ch. DXXXIV, Acts of the Nineteenth General Assembly of the State of New Jersey 1015, 1017-1018 (Mar. 10, 1795).

[29] Section 5, *Id.* at 1017.

[30] An Act Concerning Distresses, Ch. DXLII, Acts of the Nineteenth General Assembly of the State of New Jersey 1032 (Mar. 16, 1795).

[31] An Act for the Prevention of Waste, Ch. DXLVII, Acts of the Nineteenth General Assembly of the State of New Jersey 1050 (Mar. 17, 1795).

[32] A few minor amendments were adopted. In 1835, the legislature, perhaps under the pressure of bad economic news, passed a provision that goods distressed for rent were not to be sold for 10 days and not to be sold at all if the tenant paid the overdue rent. Two years later this reform was extended to all attachments of tenant's goods, whether by way of distress or other method of execution. The revisions may be found in Elmer, A DIGEST OF THE LAWS OF NEW JERSEY 307 (1838). A further minor change occurred in 1840, when year to year tenancies were deemed terminable on three rather than six months notice to quit. A Further Supplement to the Act Entitled, "An Act Concerning Landlords and Tenants," Acts of the Sixty-Fourth General Assembly of the State of New Jersey 104 (Feb. 28, 1840).

requirements for eviction of non-paying tenants by only requiring proof that the rent was due, a right to re-enter was reserved,[33] and a written demand for the rent was served at least three days before the eviction action was brought.[34] Further amendments were approved in 1840 to prevent landlords from using summary dispossess proceedings to evict tenants with long terms yet to run who had made significant improvements to the property. The ongoing depression of that era convinced the legislature to provide some protections for tenants, especially commercial renters, by forcing landlords to use ejectment whenever a lease for years had more than five years remaining.[35]

Just as New York had used New Jersey as a model for its landlord-tenant legislation in 1798, New Jersey looked to New York for a model when dispossess rules came up for review in Trenton in 1847. In that year, New Jersey adopted a summary dispossess statute almost identical to New York's law.[36] There are no extant legislative journals or reports on New Jersey's legislation. We can only assume that some of the same pressures leading New York to adopt its statute were operating in New Jersey.[37] Since the provision protecting long-term commercial tenants was not included by New Jersey, it is fairly safe to assume that the legislature was more concerned about the difficulty landlords were having in getting rid of non-paying and holdover tenants than with the plight of commercial lessees.

Section 1 of the act provided that any tenant could be removed:

1st. Where such persons shall hold over and continue in possession of the demised premises, or any part thereof, after the expiration of his or her term, and after demand made, and notice in writing given for delivering the possession thereof, by the landlord or his agent, for that purpose.

2d. Where such person shall hold over after any default in the payment of the rent, pursuant to the agreement under which such premises are held, and satisfaction for such rent cannot be obtained by distress of any goods, and a demand of such rent shall have been made, by three days' notice, in writing, requiring the payment of such rent, or the possession of the premises, shall have been served by the person entitled to such rent, upon the person owing the same.

In addition, the legislation forbade all appeals from summary dispossessions. In 1901, this statute was amended to remove the requirement that distress be unavailing.[38] The summary dispossess

---

[33] This requirement means that the lease contained a statement permitting the landlord to re-enter the premises if rent was not paid. Re-entry clauses were a requirement of ejectment actions long before summary dispossess statutes appeared.

[34] An Act to Amend an Act Entitled "An Act Concerning Distresses, Rents, and the Renewal of Leases," Passed Apr. 5, 1813, and for Other Purposes, Ch. 194, Laws of the State of New York 176 (1820). The state courts read back into the statute a requirement that distress be inadequate before summary dispossess procedures could be used. Oakley v. Schoonmaker, 15 N.Y. [Wend.] 226 (1837).

[35] An Act to Amend the Revised Statutes, in Relation to Summary Proceedings to Recover Possession of Demised Premises, Ch. 162, Laws of the State of New York 119 (1840). The reasons for passage of this statute are set forth in Senate Report No. 65, DOCUMENTS OF THE SENATE OF THE STATE OF NEW YORK (1840).

[36] Supplement to an Act Entitled, "An Act Concerning Landlords and Tenants," Acts of the Seventy-First Legislature of the State of New Jersey 142 (Mar. 4, 1847).

[37] There is some support for this in New Jersey court opinions, which validate the use of New York precedents in New Jersey since the statutes of the two states were similar and adopted for like reasons. See, e.g., Smith v. Sinclair, 59 N.J.L. 84 (1896).

[38] In addition, the provisions for serving the demand for possession were altered to read as in the modern codified

process then remained virtually unchanged until 1951 when New Jersey's civil procedure code was entirely re-written. As the summary dispossess process emerged from that process, the appeal provisions were modified to permit appeals on jurisdictional grounds.[39] No major significance was attached to the amendment of the appeal provision when it was adopted. The New Jersey Supreme Court had already held that the legislature was without authority to totally deprive appellate courts of the ability to review jurisdictional issues. Courts have typically claimed that they always have jurisdiction to determine their jurisdiction. In fact, the committee recommending the change in N.J. STAT. ANN. § 2A:18-59 thought it was simply bringing the code into conformity with extant practice.[40] Little did they know what would become of this change when calls for reform of the landlord-tenant court reached their peak in the 1960s and 1970s. *See Marini v. Ireland*, p. 654 below.

[2]   A Note on Federal Constitutional Limitations on the Process of Eviction: The Interplay of Due Process Requirements and the Contours of Common Law Landlord-Tenant Law

After the Supreme Court rendered its decision in *Goldberg v. Kelly*, challenges were made to the contours of summary litigation in various landlord-tenant courts around the country. At first glance, that should seem a bit strange. All *Goldberg* required was a fact-finding hearing prior to termination of welfare benefits. Landlord-tenant court, though fast moving, seemed to provide exactly what *Goldberg* required—a fact-finding hearing prior to eviction. Despite the apparently fair contours of the proceedings, however, landlord-tenant courts were a focus of seething discontent in many urban areas during the 1960s. What was going on?

Personal stories usually don't appear in tomes like this one, but permit me an exception. It may help you understand why urban landlord-tenant courts were such a source of tension during the 1960s. While in law school (I graduated in 1968), I went to visit the landlord-tenant court in Chicago. I watched the long call of cases at the beginning of the court day. Most of the calls went unanswered by tenants, leading to the issuance of default judgments for landlords. When cases finally began to be called where tenants had shown up, they were handled in remarkably rapid fashion. The cases of a single landlord were called *seriatim* so that different landlord lawyers would not have to constantly shuffle back and forth to the dais. Before the landlord lawyers could say anything, the judge usually asked the tenant, "Have you paid the rent?" The answer would generally be, "No." Without waiting for an explanation, the judge would say, "Judgment for [name of plaintiff]. Call the next case." One particularly poignant case has stuck in my mind for these last 30-plus years. The tenant was a very old woman. She was dressed all in white, and wore a hat with a lace veil over her face. When her case was called, she slowly rose from her seat and, cane in hand, began ever so slowly to move her stooped-over self towards the front of the courtroom. When she was about half-way there, the judge asked his question: "Have you paid your rent?" "No, but . . . ." She was interrupted with an award of a judgment by the court before she finished either approaching the bench or her sentence. She continued her slow movement toward the bench and, as the next case was being called, attempted to explain her

---

version of the legislation, N.J. STAT. ANN. § 2A:18-53. An Act to Amend Chapter Sixty-Two of the Laws of One Thousand Eight Hundred and Seventy-Six Entitled "An Act Concerning Landlords and Tenants," Ch. 38, Acts of the One Hundred and Twenty-Fifth Legislature of the State of New Jersey 67 (Mar. 31, 1901).

[39] Title 2A was enacted by this revision and old Title 2 was repealed. Ch. 344, Laws of New Jersey (1951).

[40] *See, e.g.*, Vineland Shopping Center v. DeMarco, 35 N.J. 459, 173 A.2d 270 (1961).

situation to the court. The judge told her to move away because the next case had been called. The bailiff gently led her away. I often wonder what happened to her. [41]

What sort of legal play was I watching? This was more than the operation of a fast, summary proceeding. This was a proceeding in which there seemed to be only one relevant piece of evidence—whether or not rent was paid—and no contest over any other aspects of the landlord-tenant relationship. The summary process was mixing with the substantive content of landlord-tenant law to produce a court that appeared overtly to operate in favor of landlords and without sympathy for the plight of tenants.

The next part of this chapter outlines in some detail the contours of the common law landlord-tenant rules that helped create the landlord-tenant court I visited while in law school. But you should not be surprised that challenges to a system that was not only fast but also unwilling to hear defenses or counterclaims emerged. *Lindsey v. Normet*[42] involved the Oregon summary judicial procedure for evicting tenants under the state's Forcible Entry and Wrongful Detainer statute. Donald and Edna Lindsey withheld payment of rent when their landlord refused to make repairs called for by a public building inspector. Rather than wait to be sued in local landlord-tenant court, they and other tenants filed an action in federal court seeking a declaratory judgment that the state eviction procedure was invalid. Under the state statute, process had to be served not less than two nor more than four days before the trial date, a continuance longer than two days could be granted to a tenant only upon the posting of security for the unpaid rent, the only issue the trial court could hear was whether the allegations in the landlord's complaint were true, [43] and an appeal by a tenant was possible only upon posting of a bond equal to twice the rental value of the property from the time the action was commenced until a final judgment was entered. The Supreme Court concluded that the speedy trial and "no defense" portions of the process were valid. As to the latter, the Court noted:

> The tenant is barred from raising claims in the FED action that the landlord has failed to maintain the premises, but the landlord is also barred from claiming back rent or asserting other claims against the tenant. The tenant is not foreclosed from instituting his own action against the landlord and litigating his right to damages or other relief in that action. [44]

The Court did, however, find the double appeal bond requirement invalid. Though speedy relief to landlords was a valid reason for the state procedure, the penalty imposed on those persons wishing to appeal went beyond what was necessary to provide such relief.

---

[41] You might find it interesting to visit your local landlord-tenant court. They operate somewhat differently now, but it would still be a useful and interesting experience.

[42] 405 U.S. 56 (1972).

[43] A similar limitation existed in New Jersey prior to the decision in Marini v. Ireland, p. 654 below. N.J. STAT. ANN. § 2A:18-53 did not contain the express limitation on issues that could be litigated in the trial that was found in the Oregon statute, but N.J. STAT. ANN. § 2A:18-59 had the same practical effect. That section limited appeals to jurisdiction issues, meaning that until *Marini*, issues other than whether rent had been paid could not be appealed. Trial court Judges got the message and generally did not allow tenants to pursue any housing code or other issues in a summary dispossess case.

[44] A good argument can be made that the Supreme Court decision did not reflect the reality of litigating in a typical urban landlord-tenant court. Though other remedies were theoretically available, the mostly poor tenants appearing in eviction cases virtually never sought such relief. Indeed, even legal services agencies, snowed under with normal eviction cases, rarely brought affirmative contract actions on behalf of tenants. Tenants either raised their defenses in a summary dispossess action or they were evicted.

After the Supreme Court left the central features of summary dispossess statutes intact, tenants' lawyers sought other means of controlling the use of speedy dispossession remedies. Several paths were taken. First, attacks were made, sometimes by relying on state constitutional provisions, on the constitutionality of the procedures used to implement state dispossess remedies, especially service of process practices and self-help remedies. These subjects form the subject matter of the remaining materials in this section. Second, limitations imposed upon the raising of tenant defenses were attacked in state courts and legislatures. The development of tenant defenses to evictions is the subject matter of much of the rest of this chapter. Finally, special attention was paid to government owned or subsidized housing. Since this housing was available only because of actions of state and federal governments, the Fourteenth Amendment imposed limitations upon evictions not applicable to the private sector.

The fairly common practice of posting a summary dispossess complaint and summons on the door of an apartment when no one was home[45] was challenged in *Greene v. Lindsey*.[46] If the papers were removed from the door by someone before the tenants returned home, they would never receive notice of the impending summary dispossess proceedings.[47] Part of the reason for such service of process methods lies in the enormous number of complaints that must be served. For example, in 1984, just over 92,000 cases were filed in the Landlord-Tenant Branch of the District of Columbia Superior Court.[48] With this sort of volume it is difficult to imagine that service of process is routinely done in accordance with the rules. In any case, *Lindsey* involved KY. REV. STAT. § 454.030, which provided:

> If the officer directed to serve notice on the defendant in forcible entry or detainer proceedings cannot find the defendant on the premises mentioned in the writ, he may explain and leave a copy of the notice with any member of the defendant's family thereon over sixteen years of age, and if no such person is found he may serve the notice by posting a copy thereof in a conspicuous place on the premises. The notice shall state the time and place of meeting of the court.

Though posting notice might be satisfactory in many settings, the facts of the *Lindsey* case led the Court to find the statutory procedure invalid. The not infrequent removal of the posted papers by children or other tenants rendered the process an unreasonable method of notification, particularly in light of the availability of the mails as a cheap and readily available alternative. Kentucky, in fact, amended its statute after *Lindsey* to provide for use of the mails.

The United States Supreme Court has not decided a case on the legality of self-help landlord remedies. But the cases it has decided on due process and property rights in consumer remedies[49] formed the backdrop when the New Jersey Supreme Court was confronted with a challenge to the state's self-help distraint statute.

---

[45] It is, of course, possible that such posting also occurred when someone was home. The sheer bulk of complaints that have to be served makes it difficult for process servers to spend much time trying to find the defendants.

[46] 456 U.S. 444 (1982).

[47] When tenants do not show up in landlord-tenant court, the landlord obtains a default judgment. While judgments obtained after faulty service of process theoretically may be re-opened under a local analog to FED. R. CIV. P. 60(b), the first notice some tenants may get of the judgment is a notice that eviction is imminent or the knock of a marshall with the movers.

[48] 1984 ANNUAL REPORT, DISTRICT OF COLUMBIA COURTS 42 (1985).

[49] *See* the discussion in Chapter 7, p. 543 above.

[3]　Opinion of the New Jersey Supreme Court in *Callen v. Sherman's, Inc.*

Callen v. Sherman's, Inc.

New Jersey Supreme Court
92 N.J. 114, 455 A.2d 1102 (1983)

The opinion of the Court was delivered by

POLLOCK, J.

This appeal questions the validity of statutes permitting a landlord to distrain the goods of a commercial tenant for unpaid rent. *N.J.S.A.* 2A:33-1 to -23. Specifically, the appeal presents two issues. The first issue is whether distraint by a municipal constable at the request of a landlord invokes the protection of due process accorded by the fourteenth amendment of the United States Constitution. Implicit in that issue is the further question of whether the acts of the constable are fairly attributable to the state and, therefore, constitute "state action." The second major issue is, if there is state action, whether the statute provides a commercial tenant with sufficient notice and opportunity to be heard to satisfy the constitutional requirement of due process.

The landlord filed a complaint seeking damages for breach of the lease, and the tenant counterclaimed asserting that the distraint was unconstitutional. Before trial, the court found that the tenant had breached the lease and it granted a partial summary judgment on liability for the landlord. At the commencement of the trial, the issues were the damages due the landlord, the liability of the landlord because of the distraint, and damages, if any, due the tenant. The court impaneled a jury and granted the landlord's motion to dismiss the counterclaim as a matter of law. In reaching that conclusion, the trial court reasoned that the actions of the landlord and constable were not state action and, therefore, that the tenant was not entitled to due process under the fourteenth amendment. With the consent of counsel, the court dismissed the jury and proceeded as the trier of fact to determine the damages due the landlord. At the conclusion of the trial, the court entered a judgment against the tenant for unpaid rent in the amount of $7,418.07.

On appeal, the Appellate Division affirmed the damages award for the landlord, but reversed the dismissal of the tenant's counterclaim and remanded the matter for a new trial on the counterclaim. The court found that the distress constituted state action and that the tenants were not afforded due process.

We granted the landlord's petition for certification to review the Appellate Division's determination of the unconstitutionality of the statutes granting a landlord the right to distrain a commercial tenant's goods for unpaid rent. Although we conclude that the statutes are unconstitutional as applied in this case, we find further, in light of all the facts, that the tenant suffered no damages because of the distraint. Consequently, we reverse the judgment of the Appellate Division, thereby reinstating the judgment of the trial court dismissing the counterclaim.

I

Plaintiffs are four individuals trading as Pard Realty, a partnership that owns a commercial building in Little Silver, New Jersey. Pard Realty leased a store in the building to Sherman's, Inc. for an interior decorating retail business. Defendants Florence Karasik and her husband, Jules, principals of Sherman's, guaranteed the lease.

The lease term extended from November 15, 1975 to November 14, 1977, and the total rent was $19,200, payable $800 per month, due in advance on the fifteenth of each month. In the event of a default, the tenant continued to be liable for the monthly rent, but the lease did not provide for the acceleration of the remaining payments. The tenant failed to pay the rent due on October 15, 1976, and in late October or early November advertised with signs at the premises that it was "going out of business." Mr. Callen, on behalf of the landlord, spoke with Mr. Karasik, who said that he could not pay the arrearage and confirmed that he was, in fact, going out of business. On November 12, 1976 the landlord filed its complaint seeking the entire balance due under the lease, $10,400; in fact, however, the actual rent due by November 15 was only $1,600.

After consulting a lawyer, the landlord engaged a municipal constable who distrained the goods in the store by padlocking the premises on December 3, 1976, three weeks after the filing of the complaint. Although the tenant took no action to dissolve the distraint, it notified the United States Small Business Administration (SBA), which held a prior security interest in the personal property and fixtures of the store. The SBA informed the landlord and the constable of its security interest and of the $123,000 balance due on its loan. Pursuant to the SBA's request, the constable turned over the keys to the premises to a representative of a private auctioneer who, on December 13, conducted a public sale of the tenant's property on behalf of the SBA.

On December 15, 1976, the SBA surrendered possession of the premises to the landlord and paid $133 as rent for the period during which it controlled the store. Nothing indicates that the landlord had any knowledge of the SBA's lien on the property at the time of the distraint, and neither the SBA nor the constable is a party to the present action. Shortly after regaining possession of the premises, the landlord advertised for a new tenant, but did not lease the premises until September 30, 1977.

Furthermore, counsel have acknowledged that the certificate of incorporation of Sherman's, Inc. was revoked in 1981 for nonpayment of corporate business taxes. Furthermore, in 1980 Mr. and Mrs. Karasik filed a petition in bankruptcy that included the judgment in favor of the landlord as a liability and the equity, "if any," in the counterclaim as an exempt asset. The trustee in bankruptcy abandoned any interest in that claim, and in 1981 the Karasiks received a discharge in bankruptcy, which declared null and void all judgments.

II

Distraint of a tenant's goods by a landlord may be the sole surviving relic of the early common law's tolerance of self-help. Nonetheless, since at least the thirteenth century, the common law has condoned distraint as an exception to the principle that "self-help is an enemy of the law, a contempt of the king and his court." 2 Pollock & Maitland, *Hist. of Eng. Law* 574 (Cambridge ed. 1968). Other forms of self-help, such as replevin, generally have yielded to the contemporary belief that society is better off if adversaries who cannot otherwise settle their differences proceed before an impartial third-party such as a mediator, arbitrator or judge.

At common law a landlord was allowed only to hold property pending the payment of rents or services. Impounded goods—*e.g.* livestock—were considered to be in the custody of the law. A tenant could not breach the pound and remove the goods, and the landlord could not sell the goods in satisfaction of the debt. Later, statutes permitted the landlord to appraise and sell the goods under official supervision after notice to the tenant. In response to a perceived excess of power in the hands of feudal lords, other statutes were enacted to limit the ability of a lord to distrain. The Statute of Marlebridge, for example, banned unreasonable distraints, gave the tenant the right of replevin and ended distraint for services not due. Bradby, *A Treatise on the Law of Distresses* 8 (1808).

In New Jersey, statutes have provided for distraint since 1795, and the current act, *N.J.S.A.* 2A:33-1 to -23, still exhibits its feudal origins. Although neither the statutes nor the common law has ever specified the form that distraint should take, Bradby, *supra*, at 216-17, padlocking of the tenant's premises has long existed as an accepted method of distraint. *See, Lipinski v. Frank*, 12 *N.J. Misc.* 174, 170 *A.* 608 (1934). No notice or hearing is required before distraint, but a distraining party is liable in damages for an "unreasonable, excessive or wrongful distraint . . . ." *N.J.S.A.* 2A:33-1. Thus, in *Lipinski v. Frank, supra*, a distraint was adjudged to be wrongful when the landlord sold for $50 goods worth $450, although the tenant owed only $45 and offered to pay the amount due.

The New Jersey statute further provides for double damages for goods wrongfully distrained and sold, *N.J.S.A.* 2A:33-17, but awards the landlord double costs if the tenant loses in an action for wrongful distraint. *N.J.S.A.* 2A:33-19. The act exempts from distraint residential premises, *N.J.S.A.* 2A:33-1, and other kinds of property, *N.J.S.A.* 2A:33-6. Unlike the early English common law, the New Jersey statute encourages the participation of a government official from beginning to end: "All sheriffs and constables shall aid in the execution of the provisions of this chapter." *N.J.S.A.* 2A:33-14.

Following the distraint, the goods are impounded and the tenant is liable for treble damages for wrongfully removing them. *N.J.S.A.* 2A:33-16. The statute expressly provides for the assistance to the landlord of a constable or peace officer where the tenant has removed or concealed property subject to distraint. *N.J.S.A.* 2A:33-22.

Once the landlord has effected a distraint on the premises and impounded sufficient goods, the tenant has ten days after receiving notice to commence an action to recover them. Thereafter, on two days' notice, the landlord may have the goods inventoried and appraised by three persons sworn by the county sheriff or local constable. *N.J.S.A.* 2A:33-9. Subsequently, on five days' public notice, the landlord can hold a public sale, *N.J.S.A.* 2A:33-10, the proceeds of which apply toward the satisfaction of rent due and the costs of the distraint and sale. Any surplus money is left with the sheriff or constable for the property owner. The tenant may sue for replevin of distrained goods before sale or later for wrongful distraint and sale. *N.J.S.A.* 2A:33-17. In the absence of such an action, however, the entire procedure may go forward without the involvement of a judge or other impartial third party. The abiding question is whether the statutory distraint procedure comports with fundamental notions of due process under the United States Constitution.

III

To be subject to scrutiny under the due process clause, state action must result in the deprivation of life, liberty or property. Before determining whether the process afforded by the Distress Act meets constitutional standards, the initial question is whether sufficient state action inheres in the distraint by the constable to imperil the constitutional rights of the tenant.

The existence of state action depends "on the relationship between the state and the challenged conduct." *State v. Droutman*, 143 *N.J. Super.* 322, 362 *A.* 2d 1304 (Law Div.1976). An evolving concept, state action is susceptible only to a fluid definition. *See State v. Schmid*, 84 *N.J.* 535, 552, 423 *A.* 2d 615 (discussing state action in the context of first amendment principles as applied to owners of private property). The most recent decision of the United States Supreme Court supports the conclusion that the distraint by the constable resulted in a deprivation by the state. *Lugar v. Edmondson Oil Co.*, 457 *U.S.* 922 (1982).

Lugar involved a Virginia statute allowing creditors to petition the clerk of the court *ex parte* for a writ of attachment against the goods of a debtor. Pursuant to the statutory scheme, the county sheriff executes the writ and a hearing may occur later on the propriety of the attachment. In *Lugar*, after this post-deprivation hearing, the Court dismissed the attachment. The debtor then sued the creditor under 42 *U.S.C.* § 1983 claiming a violation of his constitutional rights. The Court found that the creditor's remedies implicated state action: "Beginning with *Sniadach v. Family Finance Corp.*, 395 *U.S.* 337 (1969), the Court has consistently held that constitutional requirements of due process apply to garnishment and prejudgment attachment procedures whenever officers of the state act jointly with a creditor in securing the property in dispute."

The Court enunciated a two-pronged test for determining whether an action depriving an individual of a constitutional right is "fairly attributable" to the state:

First, the deprivation must be caused by the exercise of some right or privilege created by the state or by a rule of conduct imposed by the state or by a person for whom the state is responsible. In *Sniadach, Fuentes, W. T. Grant* and *North Georgia*, for example, a state statute provided the right to garnish or to obtain prejudgment attachment, as well as the procedure by which the rights could be exercised. Second, the party charged with the deprivation must be a person who may fairly be said to be a state actor. This may be because he is a state official, because he has acted together with or has obtained significant aid from state officials, or because his conduct is otherwise chargeable to the state.[1]

In the distraint in the present case, the landlord and constable acted pursuant to a right created by statute. Although the right to distrain existed at common law, the landlord relied on its rights under the statute in effectuating the distraint. This governmental involvement is mandated by the requirement that sheriffs and constables, if requested, aid in the execution of a distraint. *N.J.S.A.* 2A:33-14. Under the first part of the *Lugar* test, then, the deprivation was caused by a right created or rule imposed by the state.

Next we must determine whether the landlord, in effectuating the distraint, acted in cooperation with a state official. That determination is necessary because the Court has declined to find state action from the mere existence of a body of property law without the involvement of a state official in enforcing that law. *Flagg Bros., Inc. v. Brooks*, 436 *U.S.* 149 (1978). While some scholars believe that regulatory policy can constitute government action, Tribe, *American Constitutional Law*, § 18-7 (1978), *Flagg Bros.* and *Lugar* require the identification of a state actor. In this case, the constable, who padlocked the store and delivered the keys to the SBA, played that part.[2] By carrying out his official duties pursuant to a statutory scheme, the constable was a state actor. We conclude that the conduct of the lessor and constable constitutes state action.

---

[1] The cases cited by the Court, *Sniadach v. Family Fin. Corp.*, 395 *U.S.* 337 (1969); *Fuentes v. Shevin*, 407 *U.S.* 67 (1972); *Mitchell v. W. T. Grant Co.*, 416 *U.S.* 600 (1974), and *North Georgia Finishing, Inc. v. Di-Chem*, 419 *U.S.* 601 (1975), not only illustrate the test for state action, but, as discussed in Part IV, demonstrate that the New Jersey distraint statute fails to satisfy the requirement for due process.

[2] Constables are appointed by the governing body of the municipality for a three-year term. *N.J.S.A.* 40A:9-120. They are required to swear an oath, *N.J.S.A.* 40A:9-124, and post a bond, *N.J.S.A.* 40A:9-125, before taking office. Courts of this State have held constables to be state officers on a number of occasions. Furthermore, as observed by the court in *Van Ness Industries Inc. v. Claremont Painting and Decorating Co.*, 129 *N.J. Super.* 507, 324 *A.* 2d 102 (Ch. Div.1974) sheriffs are constitutional officers under Art. VII, sec. 2, par. 2 of the New Jersey Constitution, further rendering their participation in distraint procedures state action.

That finding, mandated by *Lugar*, is consistent with *King v. South Jersey Nat'l Bank*, 66 *N.J.* 161, 330 *A.*2d 1 (1974). In *King*, we held that no state action was involved in the repossession of an automobile by a creditor without the aid of state officials, pursuant to an agreement between the parties and a provision of the Uniform Commercial Code. *N.J.S.A.* 12A:9-503. As this Court noted in *King*, the Code does not provide expressly for any action by a governmental official in the act of repossession. We found the UCC to be a mere codification of preexisting private rights and "is in effect a passive perpetuation of the common law and as such does not 'significantly' involve the state in the denial of due process rights." Moreover, the statute "permits a creditor to exercise self-help in retaking property in which he possesses a valid security interest. The statute in no way commands the creditor so to do—it simply authorizes. And mere authorization of private conduct does not *ex necessitate* comprise 'state action.' "

The Distress Act does far more than simply permit private action. It authorizes governmental assistance throughout the procedure, *N.J.S.A.* 2A:33-14, and requires governmental assistance in certain circumstances.[3] In the present case, the landlord enlisted the aid of the constable from the inception; it was the constable who effectuated the distraint by padlocking the premises. Those facts and the statutory scheme distinguish the present case from the repossession of an automobile by a private party pursuant to the UCC in *King*.

For similar reasons, *Flagg Bros., Inc.* also is distinguishable. *Flagg Bros.* addressed the constitutionality of the provisions of the UCC pertaining to ware-housemen's liens. The Court rejected the claim that state action was involved, reasoning: "[t]his Court . . . has never held that a State's mere acquiescence in a private action converts that action into that of the State."

Not all state action results in a deprivation of life, liberty or property. At times, it is a difficult and subtle task to determine whether there has been a deprivation sufficient to trigger the procedural protection of the Constitution.

Nonetheless, even a temporary deprivation of property can be a "deprivation" under the Fourteenth Amendment. The padlocking of one's business premises by a municipal constable, although temporary, qualifies as a deprivation of property under this statement. Not only did the distraint preclude the tenant's control of the goods within the store, but it further denied the tenant access to the property in which it held a leasehold estate. We conclude that the tenant was deprived of property within the meaning of the fourteenth amendment.

IV

Having concluded that the distraint by the constable pursuant to the statute invokes the defendant's constitutional rights, we must decide what process is due to the tenant. Both this Court and the Supreme Court of the United States have recognized that due process is a flexible concept, not susceptible to a single definition suitable for all situations. Although that flexibility permits an appropriate accommodation of competing interests, it also injects an element of uncertainty into the determination of whether procedures meet constitutional standards. This uncertainty is reflected in the decisions of the United States Supreme Court over the past thirteen years in considering prejudgment statutory remedies of creditors.

---

[3] A sheriff or constable who effectuates a distraint after request by a landlord is responsible for swearing in the three appraisers. *N.J.S.A.* 2A:33-9. Following the sale of the distrained goods, any proceeds that exceed the debt for rent must be left in the hands of a sheriff or constable for return to the tenant. *N.J.S.A.* 2A:33-10. Furthermore, if a tenant secures property to avoid distraint, the landlord may not distrain without first "calling to his assistance a constable or peace officer, who shall aid and assist therein." *N.J.S.A.* 2A:33-22.

The beginning point for analysis is *Sniadach v. Family Fin. Corp.*, in which the Court struck down a Wisconsin statute allowing creditors to garnish the wages of debtors through a summons issued by the clerk of the court. The statute required the creditor to notify the debtor of the garnishment within ten days and provided the wage earner with the right to a subsequent judicial hearing. The Court acknowledged that those procedures might meet constitutional standards in extraordinary situations, but on considering that wages are "a specialized type of property presenting distinct problems in our economic system," concluded that a predeprivation hearing must be accorded to a wage earner. Obviously impressed by the hardship lost wages can impose on working people, the Court determined that, absent notice and hearing, prejudgment garnishment violates fundamental principles of due process.

Three years later, the Court, in a 4-3 decision, expanded the process that was due debtors in *Fuentes v. Shevin*, striking down Florida and Pennsylvania replevin statutes that allowed for the summary seizure of goods by a state agent upon the *ex parte* application of a creditor and the posting of a security bond in double the value of the property seized. Both statutes allowed the debtor to reclaim possession by posting his own bond within three days of the seizure. Under the Florida statute, the creditor needed to assert only that the debtor was wrongfully detaining the goods and that the creditor was legally entitled to them. The creditor was not required to prove ownership of the goods, but was obliged to prosecute the action against the debtor immediately. Although similar to the Florida scheme, the Pennsylvania statute authorized replevin without requiring the creditor to initiate a prompt court action. Rather, the debtor was permitted to file a demand that the creditor commence an action within twenty days. Thus, under both statutes, debtors were protected in two ways: first, the statute provided some opportunity for a post-deprivation hearing; second, the creditor was required to post a bond in double the value of the property being replevied. However, the Court found these combined protections to be inadequate.

In holding that a predeprivation hearing was required, Justice Stewart, joined by Justices Douglas, Brennan and Marshall, reasoned:

> If the right to notice and a hearing is to serve its full purpose, then, it is clear that it must be granted at a time when the deprivation can still be prevented. At a later hearing, an individual's possessions can be returned to him if they were unfairly or mistakenly taken in the first place. Damages may even be awarded to him for the wrongful deprivation. But no later hearing and no damage award can undo the fact that the arbitrary taking that was subject to the right of procedural due process has already occurred. "This Court has not . . . embraced the general proposition that a wrong may be done if it can be undone."

The Court held further that the posting of a bond was not an adequate substitute for a prior hearing.

Dissenting on behalf of himself, Chief Justice Burger and Justice Blackmun, Justice White concluded that

> much depends on one's perceptions of the practical considerations involved . . . . I cannot say that the likelihood of a mistaken claim of default is sufficiently real or recurring to justify a broad constitutional requirement that a creditor do more than the typical state law requires and permits him to do.

Two years after its decision in *Fuentes*, the Court upheld a Louisiana statute allowing for prejudgment sequestration upon the buyer's default in paying the balance of the purchase price for household goods. *Mitchell v. W. T. Grant Co.*, 416 *U.S.* 600 (1974). As with the Florida statute struck down in *Fuentes*, the creditor was required to post a bond and to pursue the matter in court following the sequestration. The statute did not require the creditor to notify the debtor before seizing the goods, but granted the debtor the right to an immediate post-deprivation hearing seeking dissolution of the writ. Furthermore, the debtor could regain possession of the goods by posting his own bond. Of special importance to the Court was the requirement that, before a writ of sequestration could issue, the creditor file a verified complaint with a judge. The accompanying affidavit must recite specific facts setting forth the nature of the claim, the amount due, and the reason the creditor believed the debtor would dispose of the goods during the pendency of the proceedings.

In the majority opinion, Justice White observed that both the debtor and the creditor had an interest in the goods and that, where only property rights are involved, a post-deprivation hearing can satisfy due process. Justice White undertook to distinguish *Fuentes*, but in a concurring opinion Justice Powell stated that the effect of the majority opinion was to overrule *Fuentes*. Justice Brennan dissented, asserting that the statute was unconstitutional under *Fuentes*. Justice Stewart, joined by Justices Douglas and Marshall, regarded the statute as unconstitutional because it did not provide for notice and hearing. Their dissent stated that the majority had simply rejected the reasoning of the *Fuentes* majority and adopted instead the analysis of the *Fuentes* dissent. Thus, it appeared that, after a life-span of two years, *Fuentes* had expired.

This doubt about the viability of *Fuentes* remained only until the following year, when the Court, again speaking through Justice White, invalidated a Georgia garnishment statute in *North Georgia Finishing, Inc. v. Di-Chem*. In a concurring opinion, Justice Stewart was gratified to note that his report of the demise of *Fuentes* in his concurring opinion in *Mitchell* "seems to have been greatly exaggerated."

Like the Louisiana statute found sufficient in *Mitchell*, the deficient Georgia statute in *North Georgia Finishing* required the creditor to post a bond and file an affidavit to obtain a garnishment. In addition, both statutes permitted the debtor to regain his property by posting his own bond. However, the statutes differed in several respects. First, the Georgia statute did not provide the debtor with the right to an early hearing. Furthermore, the writ could be "issued by a court clerk without notice or opportunity for an early hearing and without participation by a judicial officer." Under the Georgia statute, moreover, the affidavit "need contain only conclusory allegations," and the affiant need not have personal knowledge of the facts. In a concurring opinion, Justice Powell noted with dissatisfaction the resuscitation of *Fuentes* and said that due process would be satisfied if state law required the posting of an adequate bond, establishment before a neutral officer (not necessarily a judge) of the factual basis for the remedy, and a prompt post-garnishment hearing. Justice Blackmun, joined by Chief Justice Burger, in part, and Justice Rehnquist, dissented, arguing in part that the Georgia system afforded commercial entities all the protection required by due process.

The shifting sands of the Supreme Court decisions demonstrate an inconsistency that has been noted by its members and criticized by scholars. Furthermore, each of the majority opinions has inspired a variety of separate opinions, thereby creating an individualized and fragmented body of law. With respect to creditors' preliminary remedies, the Court has been described as being in "serious disarray." Friendly, *Some Kind of Hearing*, 123 *U. Pa. L. Rev.* 1263, 1316 n. 244 (1975). That result is regrettable because it introduces uncertainty in commercial transactions involving not only commercial entities, as in the present case, but also consumers.

Whatever combination of procedures is necessary to meet minimum notice and hearing requirements under the due process clause, the New Jersey statute cannot survive in its present form. No notice and hearing need be given to the lessee before distraint. The tenant is remitted to a subsequent action in replevin for repossession of the goods or for damages suffered because of the excessive distraint. However, the statute contains a built-in disincentive to pursue an action for excessive distraint: the tenant who unsuccessfully pursues such an action is liable to the landlord for double costs. In the meantime, moreover, the tenant will have been deprived of the goods and their value. Before distraint, the lessor need not prove anything to anyone. That is, the lessor is not required to make any showing, either by specific facts or mere conclusions, of his right to distrain. Hence, no judge, court clerk or other impartial officer reviews the lessor's contentions. The landlord is unrestrained in repossessing goods in which he has no ownership interest. No bond or preliminary showing before a third party protects the lessee from an unwarranted taking. In light of the facts of this case, we find the New Jersey statute to be unconstitutional.[6]

Although we limit our holding to a distraint by a constable or sheriff, we note that distraint by a landlord is its functional equivalent. Insofar as the tenant is concerned, he is deprived of possession of his goods no matter who effects the distraint. Landlords would be well advised not to rely on any assumed difference between distraint performed with or without the aid of a constable.

Although we have not previously addressed the constitutionality of *N.J.S.A.* 2A:33-1, the Chancery Division has held that the distraint statute involved state action and failed to meet the requirements of due process. *Van Ness Indus., Inc. v. Claremont Painting and Decorating Co.*, 129 *N.J. Super.* 507, 324 A.2d 102 (Ch. Div.1974); *Porter & Ripa v. 200 Madison Ave. Real Estate*, 159 *N.J. Super.* 317, 387 A. 2d 1248 (Ch. Div.1978), aff'd on other grounds, 167 *N.J. Super.* 48, 400 A. 2d 508 (App. Div.1979). Thus, for over eight years landlords and their attorneys have been on notice that distraint is a doubtful and risky procedure.

V

Notwithstanding our finding that the statute is unconstitutional, we still must determine whether it can be read in a manner consistent with the requirements of due process. As we recently stated, "a court may engage in 'judicial surgery' to excise a constitutional defect or engraft a needed meaning." *Right to Choose v. Byrne*, 91 *N.J.* 287, 311, 450 A. 2d 925 (1982). But whether we should do this "depends on whether the Legislature would have wanted the statute to survive." *United States Chamber of Commerce v. State*, 89 *N.J.* 131, 445 A. 2d 353 (1982).

. . . .

We have no doubt that the Legislature would want this statute to survive. As previously stated, the New Jersey distraint statute has remained virtually unchanged for nearly 200 years. However, its longevity illustrates not only that the statute has stood the test of time, but that it may no longer comport with current concepts of due process. Although self-help was favored long ago

---

[6] Our holding is consistent with out-of-state cases striking down similar statutes that permitted distraint of the property of a residential tenant. *See, e.g., Hall v. Garson*, 468 F.2d 845 (5th Cir. 1972) (invalidating a Texas statute); *Stroemer v. Shevin*, 399 F. Supp. 993 (S.D. Fla. 1973); *Ragin v. Schwartz*, 393 F. Supp. 152 (W.D. Pa. 1975); *Adams v. Joseph F. Sanson Investment Co.*, 376 F. Supp. 61 (D. Nev. 1974); *Shaffer v. Holbrook*, 346 F. Supp. 762 (S.D. W.Va. 1972); *Blocker v. Blackburn*, 228 Ga. 285, 185 S.E.2d 56 (1971). In New Jersey, the relevant statute, *N.J.S.A.* 2A:33-1, was amended in 1971 (*L.* 1971, c. 228, § 1) to eliminate distraint against residential tenants.

as a remedy for landowners, times have changed. Underlying modern procedure is the belief that a society is better off if disputes are resolved in a neutral forum. *See, e.g., N.J.S.A.* 2A:18-53 and -56, which require notice to a residential tenant in a summary dispossess action, and *N.J.S.A.* 2A:18-57, which requires the entry of judgment by the county district court before eviction.

The problem with the challenged statute lies not in the existence of the remedy it accords the landlord, but with the insufficiency of the notice and hearing it affords the tenant. We believe the Legislature would prefer that we preserve the remedy of distraint as long as it is applied fairly. To cure the constitutional deficiencies of the statute, we need only read it in conjunction with the procedural requirements of *R.* 4:52 pertaining to interlocutory relief.[7]

Implicit in *Rule* 4:52 is a dynamic concept of due process, one that requires balancing the interests of the parties in accordance with the circumstances of each case. The rule expressly authorizes an *ex parte* application for a temporary restraining order to prevent immediate and irreparable damage. *R.* 4:52-1(a). Absent those compelling circumstances, notice must be given to a tenant, for example, before issuance of a temporary restraint. Where the court authorizes temporary relief, the tenant has the right to move for dissolution or modification "on 2 days' notice or on such other notice as the court fixes in the order." *Id.* One advantage of a proceeding under *R.* 4:52 is that a neutral third party, a judge, will supervise the distraint, thereby eliminating unwarranted or excessive distraints while adequately protecting the landlord's recourse to the tenant's goods to satisfy a claim for unpaid rent. In most cases, a landlord will have sufficient time to seek judicial approval before distraining a tenant's goods. Therefore, distraint and sale of the goods can proceed as prescribed by the statute, but subject to judicial supervision. Reading the statute in light of *R.* 4:52 does not deprive a lessor of his statutory rights; it merely requires him to proceed with due process. That is, without judicial approval, a lessor simply cannot help himself to a tenant's goods.

In seeking temporary relief, a lessor should proceed under *R.* 4:52 in the Chancery Division by order to show cause, supported by verified complaint or affidavit. Where appropriate, the court may authorize the distraint subject to appropriate terms or grant such other emergent relief as is fair and equitable to the parties. On the return date of the order to show cause, the court should determine the rights of the parties with respect to the possession and sale of the goods pending final hearing. In some instances, the matter may proceed promptly to final hearing.

In the extraordinary case, *e.g.*, where the landlord learns that a tenant is loading his goods onto a truck to avoid a just claim, the landlord still may resort to self-help. The need for relief

---

[7] *R.* 4:52-1(a) provides:

Order to Show Cause with Temporary Restraints. On the filing of a complaint seeking injunctive relief, the plaintiff may apply for an order requiring the defendant to show cause why an interlocutory injunction should not be granted pending the disposition of the action. The order to show cause shall not, however, include any temporary restraints against the defendant unless he has either been given notice of the application or consents thereto or it appears from specific facts shown by affidavit or verified complaint that immediate and irreparable damage will probably result to the plaintiff before notice can be served or informally given and a hearing had thereon. If the order to show cause includes temporary restraints and was issued without notice to the defendant, provision shall be made therein that the defendant shall have leave to move for the dissolution or modification of the restraint on 2 days' notice or on such other notice as the court fixes in the order. The order may further provide for the continuation of the restraint until the further order of the court and shall be returnable within such time after its entry as the court fixes but not exceeding 20 days after the date of its issuance in the case of a resident defendant or 35 days in the case of a non-resident defendant, unless within such time the court on good cause shown extends the time for a like period or unless the defendant consents to an extension for a longer period.

in these circumstances is so compelling that a landlord need not seek judicial approval before availing himself of the statute. A post-deprivation hearing at the request of the tenant under *N.J.S.A.* 2A:33-9 will satisfy the need for due process. By requiring notice and a pre-deprivation hearing in most cases, but permitting self-help and a post-deprivation hearing in extraordinary cases, we remove the constitutional defect and the statute may survive.

VI

Furthermore, we reject the landlord's contention that the tenant waived its constitutional right to due process. Although constitutional rights may be waived in a commercial context, the waiver must be clear. Here, the lease merely provided that the landlord could reenter the premises following default by the tenant and that the landlord could pursue "other remedies . . . as may be permitted by law." That provision can hardly be construed as a waiver of the tenants' constitutional rights. The right of reentry does not authorize a landlord to deprive the tenant of the use of his property until the rent is paid.

VII

We conclude that the distraint by the constable constituted state action entitling the tenant to procedural due process under the United States Constitution. By depriving the tenant of its goods without notice and hearing, the landlord violated the tenant's right to due process. We perceive no useful purpose, however, in remanding the matter for further proceedings. For over a month before the distraint, the tenant had advertised that it was going out of business. At the time of the distraint, the tenant was in default not only under the lease, but also on the loan from the SBA. After the distraint, the tenant took no action to regain possession of the goods or to dissolve the distraint. During the pendency of the proceedings in the courts, the certificate of the corporate tenant has been revoked and the individual guarantors have been discharged in bankruptcy. Under the circumstances, we conclude the appropriate disposition is not to protract the proceedings, but to recognize the reality that the defendants suffered no damage because of the distraint.

That part of the judgment of the Appellate Division that remanded the counterclaim for trial is reversed.

For reversal—Chief Justice Wilentz and Justices Clifford, Schreiber, Handler, Pollock and O'Hern—6.

For affirmance—None.

[4]   Explanatory Notes

[a]   The Judicial Confusion

As the *Callen* court noted, the prior Supreme Court decisions were a mass of confusion. There were two reasons for that. First, the Court had difficulty deciding upon the level of involvement by state officials that was required to fulfill the state action requirement. While you might have expected that the existence of a state statute permitting pre-determination seizures of property would by itself be state action, the Court typically required that some state official participate in the taking of goods. Second, if state action was found, the Court had trouble deciding upon the type of process that was due.

Some of the confusion over the second issue was eliminated after *Callen* was decided in *Connecticut v. Doehr*, 501 U.S. 1 (1991). Connecticut law permitted judges to authorize prejudgment attachment of real property without affording prior notice or the opportunity for a prior hearing to the property owner, and without requiring the party seeking attachment to post a bond to protect the owner's interests. The Court invoked the analysis in *Mathews v. Eldridge*, 424 U.S. 319 (1976), the case forming the analytical backbone of Justice White's opinion in *Cleveland Board of Education v. Loudermill*, excerpted in Chapter 7 above, p. 545. In resolving questions about the sort of process that is due, *Mathews* required the balancing of three factors—the private interest affected by the official action, the risk of an erroneous deprivation of such interest through the procedures used, and the Government's interest, including the function at issue and the fiscal and administrative burdens of any additional procedures. In *Doehr,* noting that the case involved use of state sanctioned procedures by private parties rather than public entities, the Court slightly modified the third *Mathews* factor, analyzing the "interest of the party seeking the prejudgment remedy, with, nonetheless, due regard for any ancillary interest the government may have." Finding no substantial interest in the private party seeking attachment favoring an *ex parte* proceeding, but fearing the risk of error and voicing concern about the importance of the property interest held by the owner, the Court found the Connecticut scheme unconstitutional. The similarities between *Doehr* and *Callen* suggest that the New Jersey Supreme Court probably came to the correct conclusion.

[b] Remedy

As in *Vasquez v. Glassboro Service Association*, p. 594 above, the *Callen* court fashioned relief in a somewhat magical way. After finding the distraint process lacking, the court required landlords to invoke a process much like a motion for a preliminary injunction. But after imposing this obligation on owners, the court declined to require its invocation on the facts before it. The tenants were out of business, the Small Business Administration sold all of the business' assets in an effort to recover the loan it made to the tenant, and the landlord relet the premises without objection from the tenant. It was difficult to find any basis for a monetary remedy. The Karasiks were left only with the "satisfaction" that the distraint statute was limited in its application.

[c] More on Speed

The structure of landlord remedies in existence by the late nineteenth century was based on a need for certainty and speed in results. Imposing more "process" on this structure obviously influences both certainty and speed. In fact, almost all the major developments in landlord-tenant law during the last 20 years involved analysis of the propriety of reform in light of landlords' claims that speed and certainty were required. When you move through the sections of this chapter on various tenant defenses—retaliatory eviction, eviction only for cause, and pleas based on the condition of the premises rented—closely consider the impact of the reforms on the underlying structure of landlord-tenant law. Ultimately you should ponder the wisdom of continued use of a separate judicial forum for landlord-tenant possession disputes.

[5] Problem Notes

[a] State Action

Finding state action was a prerequisite to invalidating the distraint statute under the United States Constitution. There is something a bit peculiar in the court's use of the federal rather than state constitution. Given the confusing status of federal law, one might have expected the court to create a remedy that would have avoided the possibility of reversal by the United States Supreme Court. In any case, the crucial fact in this finding of state action apparently was the use of a constable to accomplish the distraint. You might want to compare this result with *Hudgens v. N.L.R.B.*, pp. 572–573 above. Even though a police officer arrested or threatened to arrest picketers demonstrating inside a shopping mall, the *Hudgens* Court concluded there was no state action. Once again, we are left a bit at sea over the theory of state action justifying these various results. In fact, the *Callen* opinion indicated that the use of a constable may not have been the only basis for finding state action. Near the end of its opinion, the court noted:

> Although we limit our holding to a distraint by a constable or sheriff, we note that distraint by a landlord is its functional equivalent. Insofar as the tenant is concerned, he is deprived of possession of his goods no matter who effects the distraint. Landlords would be well advised not to rely on any assumed difference between distraint performed with or without the aid of a constable.

Does this mean that the existence of the state distraint statutes was the real basis for finding state action? Or was the court simply warning landlords that even though they couldn't completely void the distraint statute under federal law in *Callen*, they would find a way to accomplish the same end under state law if the issue ever arose in another case?

[b]   Other Situations

After *Callen*, may a distraint with or without the assistance of a state official be accomplished without a prior judicial hearing in any of the following circumstances:

[*i*]   *Hotel Guest.* If a hotel guest does not pay his bill, but leaves personal property on the premises, may the owner distrain the guest's goods? Does the threat, presumably extant for any hotel guest, that the room occupant may immediately depart with his property, mean that it is appropriate for a hotelier to use an emergency distraint?

[*ii*]   *Farm Worker.* A farm worker is fired. The farm owner has a rule requiring payment of $50 per week rent once a worker loses his job in order to stay on until new living quarters are found, and that "rent" is not paid.

[*iii*]   *Boarder.* A homeowner rents a room to help pay the mortgage. The boarder doesn't pay.

[c]   Residential versus Commercial Tenants

Callen involved a business. Is there any difference between a distraint in a residential and a commercial setting? Note that the New Jersey legislature amended the distraint statutes in 1971 to prohibit distraints in a residential setting.[50] Was that a wise decision? What is "a residence of the tenant" for purposes of this statute?

[d]   Process Due in Distraints and Summary Evictions

What is the practical difference between distraining goods without a hearing and providing tenants a "hearing" before a court lacking jurisdiction to hear any defenses to an action for

---

[50] The last sentence in N.J. STAT. ANN. § 2A:33-1 now reads:

No distraint shall be permitted for money owed on a lease or other agreement for the occupation of any real property used solely as a residence of the tenant.

possession? If, after *Lindsey v. Normet*, discussed at p. 620 above, the latter process is legitimate, what is wrong with taking goods without a hearing? Is there an argument to be made that no hearing at all is better than a court process holding out a false promise of relief to those unfamiliar with its operation?

[e]   Tenant Defenses to Distraint?

What sort of showing must a landlord make in order to obtain a distraint order from a court? If the owner shows that rent is due, is that enough? What sort of defenses should be available to the distraint petition? Come back to this question after reading more about the availability of tenant defenses generally in the later sections of this chapter.

[f]   Court Setting for Tenants and Non-Tenants

Compare the outcomes of *Vasquez*, p. 594 above, *Finn*, p. 609 above, and it;Callen. When these results are combined, it appears that owners seeking possession from migrant workers and cooperators must go to "fancy" equity courts, while landlords seeking possession from tenants may file in the procedurally restricted landlord-tenant courts. Does this structure make any sense? Why should tenants receive less procedural protection than migrant workers?

§ 8.04   Non-Payment of Rent and the Eviction Process

[1]   Introduction

Most leases terminate either because the tenant fails to pay rent or because the period of occupancy called for in the lease ends. This section investigates the consequences of failing to pay rent. The next section reviews the limitations imposed upon the eviction of tenants who stay in possession after their leases expire.

In the last 20 years, wholesale changes have occurred in the legal rules governing evictions for both non-payment of rent and holding over beyond the end of a lease. While many of the changes were long overdue, the creation of a national legal services program for the poor was a major catalytic event leading to the deluge of landlord-tenant cases that appeared all over the country between 1966 and 1975. In many states, including New Jersey,[51] one of the first areas given concentrated attention by legal service attorneys was reform of eviction law. National conferences on the subject were held in a number of spots between 1965 and 1968,[52] and legal services lawyers were constantly on the lookout for cases that could be used to alter the old rules.

The focus of attention in the non-payment of rent cases was the relationship between the tenant's obligation to pay rent and the landlord's privilege not to repair. The combined operation of common law rules placing the repair obligation on tenants and summary dispossess remedies for non-payment of rent made it virtually impossible for tenants to make demands for repairs. This section of materials first summarizes the pre-1965 structure of rules on payment of rent

---

[51] For a review of the relationship between the creation of the legal services system and the development of New Jersey landlord tenant law, *see* Ventantonio, *"Equal Justice Under Law": The Evolution of a National Commitment to Legal Services for the Poor and a Study of its Impact on New Jersey Landlord-Tenant Law*, 7 SETON HALL L. REV. 233 (1976). For a more general history of legal services, *see* George, *Development of the Legal Services Corporation*, 61 CORNELL L. REV. 681 (1976).

[52] One of the earliest conferences, organized by students at the University of Chicago Law School, was held in 1967 during my second year in law school.

and making of repairs. The last two parts of the section look at the major cases which modified the old rules and the difficulties of maintaining a summary dispossess remedy in the face of demands by tenants for relief from perceived abuses.

For additional readings on the causes for the revolution in landlord-tenant law that occurred in the late 1960s and the early 1970s, read Mary Ann Glendon, *The Transformation of American Landlord-Tenant Law*, 23 B.C. L. REV. 503 (1982); Edward H. Rabin, *The Revolution in Residential Landlord-Tenant Law: Causes and Consequences*, 69 CORNELL L. REV. 517 (1984), both excerpted in RICHARD CHUSED, A PROPERTY ANTHOLOGY 160-180 (2d ed.1997).

[2]   The Traditional Rules: Tenant's Duty to Repair and Landlord's Right to Summarily Dispossess for Non-Payment

Nineteenth-century landlord tenant law was quite strange, given our modern sensibilities. It was strange procedurally (a lot of landlord-tenant law involves procedural issues) and strange substantively. An agricultural, common law English world produced the early law of land leases. In return for virtually unchecked authority to use land, an agricultural tenant agreed to pay rent, to maintain the land, and to return the land in its original condition when the lease expired. Usually the most important asset leased was the land itself. Requiring the tenant to maintain it was probably sensible.

Thus, English law provided for an action in waste—an action by the holder of a reversionary or future interest in fee simple for damage to the value of the reversionary or future interest— against lessees and life tenants,[53] a position absorbed into New Jersey's statutes in 1795.[54] Thus, in *Moore v. Townshend*,[55] the first repair case decided by the New Jersey Supreme Court, the tenant of a glass works was required to pay $550 to the landlord for failing, during the term of the lease, to maintain the glass works and the molds and tools which came with it. Among the few early reported appellate residential lease cases, none involved attempts by landlords to impose an obligation to repair on tenants. But there were a few instances in which tenants attempted to defend suits for rent by arguing that the landlord did not have both the privilege to withhold repairs and the right to claim payment of the rent.

For example, in *Murray v. Albertson*,[56] decided in 1888, the owner of a seaside house rented it for five months beginning on June 1, 1886, for a total rent of $325. After 10 days the tenant abandoned the house, claiming it was unhealthy because the cellar had water in it. There was

---

[53] Originally, only those invested with possession by action of law, such as widows holding dower interests or widowers in possession under curtesy rights, were responsible in waste. Waste actions could not be brought against those holding life estates or leases. The English Parliament responded to perceived abuses of this rule by extending liability to life tenants and lessees. Moore v. Townshend, 33 N.J.L. 284, 300 (1869). There also was a difference between voluntary waste (or in more modern terms, affirmative actions causing harm) and permissive waste (or failure to act or to know of the actions of third parties) for some purposes. Tenants at will, or those in possession for uncertain periods of time and subject to immediate dispossession by the owner, were said not to be liable for permissive waste because of their precarious status.

[54] An Act for the Prevention of Waste, Ch. DXLVII, Acts of the Nineteenth General Assembly of the State of New Jersey, 1050 (Mar. 17, 1795). Section 2 of this act provided:

And be it enacted by the authority aforesaid, That no tenant for life or years, or for any other term, shall, during the term, make or suffer any waste, sale or destruction of houses, gardens, orchards, lands or woods, or any thing belonging to the tenements demised, without special license in writing making mention that he may do it.

[55] 33 N.J.L. 284 (1869).

[56] 50 N.J.L. 167, 13 A. 394 (1888).

no evidence of fraud. Nor was there any evidence that the owner of the house knew of the problem, which was apparently caused by a prior tenant chopping wood in the basement that left a hole in the floor. The tenant did not look in the cellar before taking possession. While there was some authority for the proposition that a party renting a furnished house warranted that the furnishings were reasonably fit for use, the court decided that the landlord was not responsible for making repairs. The tenant, therefore, was obligated to pay the entire rent. [57]

But the outcomes in *Moore* and *Murray* reflected more than the substantive rules about waste and repair obligations. Common law procedural forms also dictated the shape of the litigation. The waste rules operated in a single-issue procedural world. If someone had a legal problem, they filed a writ (today it would be called a complaint) about that problem and litigated the issue. If someone had more than one problem, they filed multiple writs. There were certain defenses to each kind of writ, but counterclaims were unknown. A counterclaim, as we now know it, was only a reason for filing a different writ. At least in a court of law (equity had different and somewhat more flexible pleading rules) the writ system limited your strategic options.

Together the repair rules and the writ system established a legal regime in which suits for unpaid rent were quite separate from suits for breaches of other contracts, including agreements by landlords to keep a premises in good repair. Even if the "contracts" were in the same physical document, they were not thought of as one contract. Indeed, that independence of covenants idea governed not only the law of leases but much of contract law generally. And since different covenants in a lease were said to be independent, breach of one covenant could not be defended by claiming that the other side breached a different covenant. Thus a suit for rent was defendable by a claim of accord and satisfaction (payment), but not by an assertion that the landlord breached any obligation to make repairs. [58] In a simple agricultural world that all made some sense. But in a developing industrial and urban community, it was bound to fall apart. The only question was, when?

"When" turned out to occur in stages. Procedural change began with something called the Field Codes in the 1840s in New York. The Field Codes were the first attempt to remove some of the writ system's baggage, in part by allowing multiple claims and parties. It may not be entirely accidental that summary dispossess remedies began to appear at about the same time as the Field Codes. Procedure does not commonly become a subject of intense scrutiny in state legislatures. Landlords may have struck while the iron was hot. Even though landlords wished to create a narrow procedural remedy much more analogous to the old narrow writ system, they were able to argue that their need for speed justified creating a special remedy even as other civil proceedings were made more all-encompassing and complicated.

In any case, the courts were often resistant to the Field Code reforms, narrowly construing them in many cases to reinstall something like the old writ system. Earth shaking change did

---

[57] As you will see later in this chapter, there is also a problem in the case with the landlord waiting until the lease expired and then suing for all the rent due. Modern cases require not only that landlords keep their residential units in repair, but that they also make reasonable efforts to find a new tenant after an abandonment in order to mitigate damages.

[58] There were rules that allowed tenants to defend actions for rent by claiming that the contractual agreement to pay rent was no longer in effect. If the tenant was *completely* unable to possess the premises, a claim of constructive eviction—in essence a claim that the contract was rescinded—might provide some relief. Discussion on this issue will surface in just a bit. And there is some evidence to support the notion that fraud in the inducement (fraud that induced the tenant to agree to a contract she would otherwise have eschewed) also might release the tenant from the obligation to pay rent.

not occur in many places until the Federal Rules of Civil Procedure were promulgated in 1938 and then copied by many state court systems. Those reforms clearly allowed multiple claims and parties, set up fairly simple rules for the filing of counterclaims, and began the final dissolution of separate courts of law and equity in most states.

The next major set of changes came not in the common law of contracts or leases, but, as described in Chapter 6, p. 475 above, in legislative enactment of housing and building codes, and, starting in 1916 in New York, zoning. The first major tenement house laws were adopted in 1894 and 1901 in New York, and other changes followed, as scandals erupted over lack of maintenance of tenements by famous folks and religious organizations, fires killed people in their apartments and in sweat shops buried in the tenement districts, and rent strikes popped up in the slums. Enforcement of the new standards was accomplished not by enacting changes in the common law, but by setting up bureaucracies and establishing criminal penalties for code violations.[59]

Nonetheless the housing and building codes became the foundation for significant changes in tort law. In *Altz v. Leiberson*,[60] a famous New York case, Judge Benjamin Cardozo authored an opinion significantly altering traditional landlord-tenant liability rules. In conformity with the notion that landlords had no obligation to maintain rented premises, common law cases routinely held that a landlord owed no duty of care to tenants unless the injuries occurred because of defects in common areas, such as hallways and elevators, under the owner's control, of latent defects known to the landlord but not to the tenant, or of defects in premises leased for public purposes. In *Altz*, however, a landlord was held responsible for injuries to a tenant caused by the collapse of a ceiling in a rented apartment.[61] In his opinion, Cardozo used the new housing codes as a basis for redefining the duties owed by landlords to their tenants. The old decisions finding liability when people were injured from falls because the landlord did not light the hallways or repair the steps no longer defined the outer limits of landlord responsibility. When ceilings fell on peoples' heads, payment was forthcoming. When sewer systems were constructed without proper venting so sewer gas seeped into apartments, liability was found.[62]

At about the same time these tort decisions began to appear, contract law was undergoing some massive changes, particularly in commercial transactions. Judge Cardozo was not only a tort reformer; he wrote a famous series of cases affirming the validity of a variety of commercial contracts and treating them as unified deals with dependent covenants. He helped restructure remedy theories to account for the multiplicity of ways in which such unified contracts might

---

[59] For more details of this story, *see* Richard Chused, *Landlord-Tenant Court in New York at the Turn of the Twentieth Century*, in PRIVATE LAW AND SOCIAL INEQUALITY IN THE INDUSTRIAL AGE: COMPARING LEGAL CULTURES IN BRITAIN, FRANCE, GERMANY AND THE UNITED STATES OF AMERICA (Willibald Steinmetz ed., 1999).

[60] 233 N.Y. 16 (1922).

[61] This result reversed the results in earlier cases involving very similar facts. Schwartz v. Apple, 48 N.Y.S. 253 (1897); Kushes v. Ginsburg, 91 N.Y.S. 216 (1904).

[62] There is a remarkable series of cases in New York involving sewer gas seepage. When municipal sewer service was first made available, many buildings were retrofitted with plumbing systems. Installation was often faulty, both because of poor workmanship and because of lack of knowledge about appropriate venting of gases. The early cases provided tenants with no relief. The first breakthrough case provided an early indication of Judge Cardozo's eventual path. In Bradley v. Nestor, 67 How. Prac. 76 (Com. Pleas 1884), a tenant successfully claimed constructive eviction after moving out of a gas filled apartment after a public health administrative order to make repairs was issued. Most of the egregious sewer code violations were repaired by the time Judge Cardozo changed the tort rules.

be breached, and recognized the possibility that one might have the right to breach a part of a contract in response to a prior breach by the other side.[63]

But landlord-tenant law in many jurisdictions did not quickly follow Judge Cardozo's lead. Common law tort rules were still being used in New Jersey until the 1950s, including an opinion written by the late Justice William Brennan when he was an appellate judge in the state.[64] An *Altz*-like result was not rendered by the New Jersey Supreme Court until 1958.[65] Similarly, the idea of independent covenants continued in lease law long after it was dead in contract law.

The result was an anomalous contrast between the contract law of leases and the contract law governing most other transactions, a contrast well demonstrated by *Stewart v. Childs Co.*[66] Childs Co. signed a 20-year lease with Stewart beginning in 1902 for a restaurant and set up "steam apparatus that perfects the coffee" in the basement. The lease contained express covenants that the tenant agreed to pay the $3,000 yearly rent when it fell due and that the landlord guaranteed "that he will at all times during the said lease keep the said cellar waterproof at his own expense." The basement turned out not to be waterproof and the tenant abandoned the premises in 1909. The landlord sued for rent. The court held that the covenant to pay rent and the covenant to keep the basement dry were independent, that the "breach of the covenant to keep the cellar waterproof was not a defense to an action for rent," and that the tenant had to pay the rent when it fell due.

Childs Co. attempted to defend the action, not only by claiming that the dry basement covenant was dependent with the covenant to pay rent, but also that it was *constructively evicted* from the premises. The theory was that the covenant to pay rent, while not dependent with "side" agreements like the dry basement promise, was dependent with the obligation of the landlord to provide the tenant with possession of the property. That minimal level of mutuality was required in order to prevent landlords from renting property, kicking tenants out and suing them for the rent. But even though Childs was not able to operate its coffee equipment or store goods in the basement, the court refused to find constructive eviction. "We are unable to find," the court wrote, "any evidence that shows that the landlord, or by his procurement, did anything with the intention of depriving the tenant of the enjoyment of the premises." The tenant was left to file another case in contract alleging breach of the dry basement covenant, but the rent had to be paid.[67]

While the New Jersey courts held the common law line on constructive eviction, New York gradually liberalized the rule. Rather than looking to the nature of the landlord's intent or actions,

---

[63] Two of the most famous cases are Wood v. Lucy, Lady Duff-Gordon, 222 N.Y. 88, 118 N.E. 214 (1917); Sun Printing and Publishing Ass'n v. Remington Paper and Power Co., Inc., 235 N.Y. 338, 139 N.E. 470 (1923).

[64] Patton v. Texas Co., 13 N.J. Super. 42, 80 A.2d 231 (1951).

[65] In Michaels v. Brookchester, 26 N.J 379, 140 A.2d 199 (1958), the court used building codes as a basis for defining a landlord's duty. Later, the New Jersey Supreme Court took the next logical step in the development of tort rules and imposed a duty on landlords to compensate for injuries caused by their negligence even when state or local statutes did not establish a performance standard as a measuring stick. Braitman v. Overlook Terrace Corp., 68 N.J. 368, 346 A.2d 76 (1975). The court also imposed an implied warranty of fitness on developers of new housing. The most famous of the cases in this line of development was Schipper v. Levitt & Sons, Inc., 44 N.J. 70, 207 A.2d 314 (1965), discussed below at p. 815.

[66] 86 N.J.L. 648, 92 A. 392 (1914).

[67] At common law, this sort of result applied even when the rented premises were destroyed by fire or other calamity. So long as the landlord was blameless the tenant still had to pay rent. Coles v. Celluloid Manufacturing Co., 39 N.J.L. 326 (1877). This particular hardship was remedied in many places by statute in the nineteenth century, including New Jersey. New Jersey's reform was adopted in 1874, and is now codified at N.J. STAT. ANN. §§ 46:8-6 and 46:8-7. This statute effectively requires the landlord, rather than the tenant, to maintain an insurance policy on the premises.

attention was paid to the practical difficulties of using a place for its intended purpose.[68] It is quite possible that the New York courts would have decided *Stewart* differently. Even with the eased rules, however, constructive eviction was still a risky adventure for tenants. If they guessed wrong and moved out, they were stuck with a rent obligation. If they guessed wrong and stayed, they had to use and pay for a lousy place. And even with the eased constructive eviction rules, the action for rent was still a quite limited procedural setting. Because covenants were still independent in such cases, defenses were still limited to accord and satisfaction, constructive eviction and fraud in the inducement.[69]

And that of course is the dilemma. Why did rent law lag so far behind other areas? Why could tenants not claim that landlords had a duty to make repairs defined by building and housing codes and that if they breached that duty, tenants could raise that breach defensively in an action for rent even if they did not leave the premises? In other contract settings, parties could claim that their contract was rescinded after a material breach, or sue for damages in case of a lesser breach. Tenants had the first option in the guise of constructive eviction, but lacked the second. In hindsight, it is not surprising that the common law tort rules changed before the rules about covenants to pay rent. The contingent fee system allowed lawyers to take on cases even when the clients could not normally afford counsel. But lawyers were very unlikely to show up representing tenants in cases involving suits for rent, except in commercial lease cases. The fact that major reforms did begin to occur in the late 1960s just as legal service lawyers showed up in landlord-tenant courts all over the country certainly supports this thesis.

But I suspect something more was involved. Exactly what this more might have been is hard to pinpoint, but let me make some suggestions. First, I think there may be some structural reasons. Commercial tenants probably were represented by counsel not just in rent litigation, but in the drafting of their leases. Some of them probably had safeguard clauses stating that all covenants in the lease should be construed as dependent. Those sorts of agreements were binding and would have eliminated problems like that in *Stewart v. Childs Co.* Perhaps the problems we were talking about did not make much difference in the commercial world.

That leaves the residential setting. We are dealing with an epoch in which debates on Formalism and Realism were in full flower. Was there something about that debate which made it unlikely that lease law reform would be on the table? And second, the Progressives were the likely source of agitation for reform. Were they likely to take on this subject? All of these folks were certainly influenced by the class, race and nativist biases of the time. These biases made them less likely to pay attention to the plight of those not paying rent. But were there other characteristics of Formalism and Realism that might lead their adherents to treat contract and lease law differently?

Formalism in its purist guise would not alter the lease rules we have been looking at. Since all men were juridical equals to the Formalist, they could write in clauses to make various covenants dependent rather than independent. The failure to do so simply meant that the underlying contracts should be enforced. That, after all, was the state's primary job. There was no sympathy here for class distinctions, poverty or language difficulty.

But what about the Realists? Wouldn't they take up this issue? Maybe not. They were highly critical of the Formalist absorption of property into contract law. Remember that it was the

---

[68] Tallman v. Murphy, 120 N.Y. 345, 24 N.E. 716 (1890); Sully v. Schmitt, 147 N.Y. 248 (1895). Lower court opinions then took over, gradually extending constructive eviction rules to include services like heating, sewers and water.

[69] For a fraud in the inducement case, *see* Dennison v. Grove, 52 N.J.L. 144, 19 A.186 (1889).

Constitution's clause about property and due process that was used by the Formalists to resist the encroachment of government regulation of workplace contracts. They diligently worked to undermine the ideas that enforcement of contracts was an apolitical act, that rights in the labor contract were "property," and that workplace risks were mere artifacts of property rights in the wage contract. For their political agenda to work, the Realists had to restructure the legal world so that property, torts, and contracts were potentially different things. These were all different relational arrangements with different purposes and different regulatory needs. The demise of an overarching set of legal rights made it possible to atomize legal concepts and treat different areas as different inquiries. Many Realists actually did that in their professional lives. Indeed, it is remarkable how much time the Realists spent reforming contract law in comparison with other areas. Judge Cardozo and his famous contract and tort cases is the least of it. They spent enormous amounts of time writing model commercial codes. Landlord-tenant law, however, was thought to be about property, not contract, and was never the focus of their attention.

The Realists also had a bias toward legislative activity. Many sympathized with the positive environmentalists urging better tenement house laws, safe water systems, construction of parks and cleaning up of streets. It was possible, they thought, to change people by altering the environment in which they lived. Indeed, it was necessary to change that environment in order to improve the quality of life for most people. It was their hope that widespread legislative action (not piecemeal development of common law rules) was the best hope for mankind. And so the Progressives worked for large scale structural changes like minimum wages laws, uniform acts, tenement house reforms, and zoning laws. They were more interested in making tenement houses livable than they were in changing the rules of lease law. True juridical equals, like Childs Co., could take care of themselves. About that the Formalists and Realists agreed. The less fortunate were best aided by large scale change. The result, perhaps, was a studied lack of attention to rent law.

By the late 1960s, however, rent law was under the microscope. Lack of sympathy for the masses of immigrants and blacks crowding urban areas in the early part of the twentieth century had given way to the Civil Rights Movement and to dramatic expansion of government housing and other programs designed to assist urban areas. When Newark, New Jersey, was torn apart in 1967 by one of the worst urban riots of the decade, the momentum for change was irresistible.[70] The New Jersey Supreme Court went looking for disputes to use as instruments for reform. Although the presence of legal services offices led to a continuous stream of test cases after 1968, the first important step in reform of rent law involved another commercial case with a factual setting remarkably similar to that in *Stewart v. Childs*.

By the 1960s one other major change had altered the litigation scenery of rent litigation. Counterclaims were now routinely available in most civil courts.[71] New Jersey first allowed them in 1912, but the courts so narrowly construed the statute that most counterclaims were still barred.[72] But after the merger of practice in law and equity courts under the New Jersey Constitution of 1947, counterclaim practice approached modern standards. *Stewart v. Childs Co.*

---

[70] After the New Jersey riots of 1967, Governor Richard Hughes appointed a commission to investigate the causes of the disturbances and make recommendations for any actions the state ought to take. The commission's report found that bad housing conditions for the black urban poor was the most frequently mentioned cause of the riots among black citizens. GOVERNOR'S SELECT COMMISSION ON CIVIL DISORDER, REPORT FOR ACTION 55 (1968).

[71] As we will see later, counterclaims are still not available in summary dispossess courts.

[72] *See, e.g.*, Reveruzzi v. Caruso, 86 N.J.L. 556, 91 A. 1022 (1914).

might have been resolved quite differently if counterclaims were available. Even if the covenants to pay rent and keep the basement dry were independent, Childs Co. would have been able to file a counterclaim when it was sued by Stewart.[73] Though that significantly reduced the importance of the independent covenant notion in rent cases, the New Jersey Supreme Court did not hesitate to get rid of independence when it had the chance.

[3]   The Cutting Edge of Reform: Dependent Covenants and Implied Warranties of Habitability

[a]   Opinion of the New Jersey Supreme Court in *Reste v. Cooper*

Reste Realty Corp. v. Cooper

New Jersey Supreme Court
53 N.J. 444, 251 A.2d 268 (1969)

The opinion of the court was delivered by

FRANCIS, J.

Plaintiff-lessor sued defendant-lessee to recover rent allegedly due under a written lease. The suit was based upon a charge that defendant had unlawfully abandoned the premises two and a quarter years before the termination date of the lease. The trial court, sitting without a jury, sustained tenant's defense of constructive eviction and entered judgment for defendant. The Appellate Division reversed, holding (1) the proof did not support a finding of any wrongful act or omission on the part of the lessor sufficient to constitute a constructive eviction, and (2) if such act or omission could be found, defendant waived it by failing to remove from the premises within a reasonable time thereafter. We granted defendant's petition for certification.

On May 13, 1958 defendant Joy M. Cooper, leased from plaintiff's predecessor in title a portion of the ground or basement floor of a commercial (office) building at 207 Union Street, Hackensack, N.J. The term was five years, but after about a year of occupancy the parties made a new five-year lease dated April 1959 covering the entire floor except the furnace room. The leased premises were to be used as "commercial offices" and "not for any other purpose without the prior written consent of the Landlord." More particularly, the lessee utilized the offices for meetings and training of sales personnel in connection with the business of a jewelry firm of which Mrs. Cooper was branch manager at the time. No merchandise was sold there.

A driveway ran along the north side of the building from front to rear. Its inside edge was at the exterior foundation wall of the ground floor. The driveway was not part of Mrs. Cooper's leasehold. Apparently it was provided for use of all tenants. Whenever it rained during the first year of defendant's occupancy, water ran off the driveway and into the offices and meeting rooms either through or under the exterior or foundation wall. At this time Arthur A. Donigian, a member of the bar of this State, had his office in the building. In addition, he was an officer and resident manager of the then corporate-owner. Whenever water came into the leased floor, defendant would notify him and he would take steps immediately to remove it. Obviously Donigian was fully aware of the recurrent flooding. He had some personal files in the furnace room which he undertook to protect by putting them on 2×4's in order to raise them above the floor surface.

---

[73] Indeed, in modern practice, the counterclaim is compulsory under FED. R. CIV. P. 13(a) since it "arises out of the transaction or occurrence that is the subject matter of the opposing party's claim."

When negotiating with defendant for the substitute five-year lease for the larger space, Donigian promised to remedy the water problem by resurfacing the driveway. (It is important to note here that Donigian told Walter T. Wittman, an attorney, who had offices in the building and who later became executor of Donigian's estate, that the driveway needed "regrading and some kind of sealing of the area between the driveway which lay to the north of the premises and the wall." He also told Wittman that the grading was improper and was "letting the water into the basement rather than away from it.") The work was done as promised and although the record is not entirely clear, apparently the seepage was somewhat improved for a time. Subsequently it worsened, but Donigian responded immediately to each complaint and removed the water from the floor.

Donigian died on March 30, 1961, approximately two years after commencement of the second lease. Whenever it rained thereafter and water flooded into the leased floor, no one paid any attention to defendant's complaints, so she and her employees did their best to remove it. During this time sales personnel and trainees came to defendant's premises at frequent intervals for meetings and classes. Sometimes as many as 50 persons were in attendance in the morning and an equal number in the afternoon. The flooding greatly inconvenienced the conduct of these meetings. At times after heavy rainstorms there was as much as two inches of water in various places and "every cabinet, desk and chair had to be raised above the floor." On one occasion jewelry kits that had been sitting on the floor, as well as the contents of file cabinets, became "soaked." Mrs. Cooper testified that once when she was conducting a sales training class and it began to rain, water came into the room making it necessary to move all the chairs and "gear" into another room on the south side of the building. On some occasions the meetings had to be taken to other quarters for which rent had to be paid; on others the meetings were adjourned to a later date. Complaints to the lessor were ignored. What was described as the "crowning blow" occurred on December 20, 1961. A meeting of sales representatives from four states had been arranged. A rainstorm intervened and the resulting flooding placed five inches of water in the rooms. According to Mrs. Cooper it was impossible to hold the meeting in any place on the ground floor; they took it to a nearby inn. That evening she saw an attorney who advised her to send a notice of vacation. On December 21 she asked that the place be cleaned up. This was not done, and after notifying the lessor of her intention she left the premises on December 30, 1961.

Plaintiff acquired the building and an assignment of defendant's lease January 19, 1962. On November 9, 1964 it instituted this action to recover rent for the unexpired term of defendant's lease, *i.e.*, until March 31, 1964.

At trial of the case defendant's proofs showed the facts outlined above. Plaintiff offered very little in the way of contradiction. It seemed to acknowledge that a water problem existed but as defense counsel told the court in his opening statement, he was "prepared to show that the water receded any number of times, and therefore the damage, if it was caused by an act that can be traced to the landlord, [the condition] was not a permanent interference" with the use and enjoyment of the premises. Plaintiff contended further that the water condition would not justify defendant's abandonment of the premises because in the lease she had stipulated that prior to execution thereof she had "examined the demised premises, and accept[ed] them in their [then] condition.., and without any representations on the part of the landlord or its agents as to the present or future condition of the said premises", moreover she had agreed "to keep the demised premises in good condition" and to "redecorate, paint and renovate the said premises as may be necessary to keep them in good repair and good appearance."

The trial judge found that the "testimony is just undisputed and overwhelming that after every rainstorm water flowed into the leased premises of the defendant" and nothing was done to remedy the condition despite repeated complaints to the lessor. He declared also that the condition was intolerable and so substantially deprived the lessee of the use of the premises as to constitute a constructive eviction and therefore legal justification for vacating them.

On this appeal the plaintiff-landlord claims that under the long-settled, law, delivery of the leased premised to defendant-tenant was not accompanied by any implied warranty or covenant of fitness for use for commercial offices or for any other purpose. He asserts also that by express provisions of both the first and second leases (which are identical printed forms, except that the second instrument covers the additional portion of basement floor), the tenant acknowledged having examined the "demised premises," having agreed to accept them in their "present condition," and having agreed to keep them in good repair, which acknowledgment, as a matter of law, has the effect of excluding any such implied warranty or covenant.

It is true that as the law of leasing an estate for years developed historically, no implied warranty or covenant of habitability or fitness for the agreed use was imposed on the landlord. Because the interest of the lessee was considered personal property the doctrine of *caveat emptor* was applied, and in the absence of an express agreement otherwise, or misrepresentation by the lessor, the tenant took the premises "as is." 1 *American Law of Property* (Casner ed. 1952) § 3.45, p. 267; 2 *Powell on Real Property* (1967) ¶ 221[2], p. 185; and see *Faber v. Creswick*, 31 N.J. 234, 238, 156, A.2d 252, 78 A.L.R.2d 1230 (1959); *Michaels v. Brookchester, Inc.*, 26 N.J. 379, 382, 140 A.2d 199 (1958). Modern social and economic conditions have produced many variant uses and types of leases, *e.g.*, sale and leaseback transactions, mortgaging of leasehold interests, shopping center leases, long-term leases. Moreover, an awareness by legislatures of the inequality of bargaining power between landlord and tenant in many cases, and the need for tenant protection, has produced remedial tenement house and multiple dwelling statutes. See *e.g.*, N.J.S.A. 55:13A-1 *et seq.* and the regulations thereunder; see generally Fuerstein and Shustack, *Landlord and Tenant—The Statutory Duty to Repair*, 45 Ill. L. Rev. 205 (1950). It has come to be recognized that ordinarily the lessee does not have as much knowledge of the condition of the premises as the lessor. Building code requirements and violations are known or made known to the lessor, not the lessee. He is in a better position to know of latent defects, structural and otherwise, in a building which might go unnoticed by a lessee who rarely has sufficient knowledge or expertise to see or to discover them. A prospective lessee, such as a small businessman, cannot be expected to know if the plumbing or wiring systems are adequate or conform to local codes. Nor should he be expected to hire experts to advise him. Ordinarily all this information should be considered readily available to the lessor who in turn can inform the prospective lessee. These factors have produced persuasive arguments for reevaluation of the *caveat emptor* doctrine and, for imposition of an implied warranty that the premises are suitable for the leased purposes and conform to local codes and zoning laws. Proponents of more liberal treatment of tenants say, among other things, that if a lease is a demise of land and a sale of an interest in land in the commercial sense, more realistic consideration should be given to the contractual nature of the relationship. See Schoshinski, *Remedies of the Indigent Tenant: Proposal For Change*, 54 Geo. L.J. 519 (1966); Note, 21 Vand. L. Rev. 1117 (1968); and see *Hyland v. Parkside Investment Co., Inc.*, 10 N.J. Misc. 1148, 162 A. 521 (Sup. Ct. 1932); *Pines v. Perssion*, 14 Wis. 2d 590, 111 N.W.2d 409 (1961); and compare, *Schipper v. Levitt & Sons, Inc.*, 44 N.J. 70, 207 A.2d 314 (1965). It will not be necessary to deal at any length with the suggested need for reevaluation and revision of the doctrines of *caveat emptor* and implied warranties in leases beyond consideration of matters projected into the case by the various contentions of the landlord.

Since the language of the two leases is the same, except that the second one describes the larger portion of the basement taken by the tenant, evaluation of the landlord's contentions will be facilitated by first considering the original lease and the factual setting attending its execution. Although the second or substitutionary lease is the controlling instrument, we take this approach in order to focus more clearly upon the effect of the change in the factual setting when the second lease was executed. This course brings us immediately to the landlord's reliance upon the provisions of the first lease (which also appear in the second) that the tenant inspected the "demised premises," accepted them in their "present condition" and agreed to keep them in good condition. The word "premises," construed most favorably to the tenant, means so much of the ground floor as was leased to Mrs. Cooper for commercial offices. The driveway or its surfacing or the exterior wall or foundation under it cannot be considered included as part of the "premises." In any event there is nothing to show that the inspection by Mrs. Cooper of the driveway or the ground floor exterior wall and foundation under it prior to the execution of the first lease would have given or did give her notice that they were so defective as to permit rainwater to flood into the leased portion of the interior. The condition should have been and probably was known to the lessor. If known, there was a duty to disclose it to the prospective tenant. Certainly as to Mrs. Cooper, it was a latent defect, and it would be a wholly inequitable application of *caveat emptor* to charge her with knowledge of it. The attempted reliance upon the agreement of the tenant in both leases to keep the "demised premises" in repair furnishes no support for the landlord's position. The driveway, exterior ground floor wall and foundation are not part of the demised premises. Latent defects in this context, *i.e.*, those the existence and significance of which are not reasonably apparent to the ordinary prospective tenant, certainly were not assumed by Mrs. Cooper. In fact in our judgment present day demands of fair treatment for tenants with respect to latent defects remediable by the landlord, either within the demised premises or outside the demised premises, require imposition on him of an implied warranty against such defects. *See Pines v. Perssion, supra.* Such warranty might be described as a limited warranty of habitability. In any event we need not at this point deal with the scope of the warranty, nor with issues of public policy that might be involved in certain types of cases where express exclusion of such warranty is contained in the lease. *Cf. Henningsen v. Bloomfield Motors, Inc.*, 32 N.J. 358, 396-404, 161 A.2d 69, 75 A.L.R.2d 1 (1960); *Michaels v. Brookchester, Inc., supra*; Uniform Commercial Code, N.J.S. 12A:2-302, N.J.S.A.

In *Pines v. Perssion, supra*, the Supreme Court of Wisconsin after noting that the frame of reference in which the old common law rule operated has undergone a change, declared:

> Legislation and administrative rules, such as the safeplace statute, building codes and health regulations, all impose certain duties on a property owner with respect to the condition of his premises. Thus, the legislature has made a policy judgment—that it is socially (and politically) desirable to impose these duties on a property owner—which has rendered the old common law rule obsolete. To follow the old rule of no implied warranty of habitability of leases would, in our opinion, be inconsistent with the current legislative policy concerning housing standards. The need and social desirability of adequate housing for people in this era of rapid population increases is too important to be rebuffed by that obnoxious legal cliche, *caveat emptor*.

The letting of a one-family home to college students was involved in the case. Although the young men had gone through the house before renting it, the court pointed out they had no way of knowing that the plumbing, heating and wiring systems were defective. Under the circumstances an implied warranty of habitability was said to exist, and its breach by the landlord relieved the tenants of liability for rent, except for such rent as would be reasonable for the one month of their occupancy. Similarly we believe that at the inception of the original lease in the present case, an implied warranty against latent defects existed.

But the landlord says that whatever the factual and legal situation may have been when the original lease was made, the relationship underwent a change to its advantage when the second was executed. This contention is based upon the undisputed fact that in April 1959, after a year of occupancy, defendant, with knowledge that the premises were subject to recurrent flooding, accepted a new lease containing the same provisions as the first one. This acceptance, the argument runs, eliminates any possible reliance upon a covenant or warranty of fitness because the premises were truly taken then "as is." While it is true that a tenant's knowing acceptance of a defective leasehold would normally preclude reliance upon any implied warranties, the landlord's position here is not sustainable because it is asserted in disregard of certain vital facts— the agent's promise to remedy the condition and the existence of an express covenant of quiet enjoyment in the lease.

The evidence is clear that prior to execution of the substitutionary lease, the tenant complained to the owner's agent about the incursion of water whenever it rained. The agent conceded the problem existed and promised to remedy the condition. Relying upon the promise Mrs. Cooper accepted the new lease, and the landlord resurfaced the driveway. Unfortunately, either the work was not sufficiently extensive or it was not done properly because at some unstated time thereafter the water continued to come into the tenant's offices. The complaints about it resumed, and as noted above, until the building manager died he made prompt efforts to remove the water. In our opinion the tenant was entitled to rely upon the promise of its agent to provide a remedy. Thus it cannot be said as a matter of law that by taking the second lease she accepted the premises in their defective condition.

This brings us to the crucial question whether the landlord was guilty of a breach of a covenant which justified the tenant's removal from the premises on December 30, 1961. We are satisfied there was such a breach.

The great weight of authority throughout the country is to the effect that ordinarily a covenant of quiet enjoyment is implied in a lease. 1 *American Law of Property, supra,* § 3.47, pp. 271-272; *Powell on Real Property, supra,* ¶ 225[3], pp. 232-240. The early New Jersey cases laid down the strict rule that such a covenant would not be implied simply from the relationship of landlord and tenant. An express agreement to that effect or the use of words from which it could be implied was required. *May v. Levy,* 88 N.J.L. 351, 353, 95 A. 999 (E. & A. 1915). We need not deal here with problems of current serviceability of that rule because as has been indicated above, the lease in question contains an express covenant of quiet enjoyment for the term fixed. Where there is such a covenant, whether express or implied, and it is breached substantially by the landlord, the courts have applied the doctrine of constructive eviction as a remedy for the tenant. Under this rule any act or omission of the landlord or of anyone who acts under authority or legal right from the landlord, or of someone having superior title to that of the landlord, which renders the premises substantially unsuitable for the purpose for which they are leased, or which seriously interferes with the beneficial enjoyment of the premises, is a breach of the covenant of quiet enjoyment and constitutes a constructive eviction of the tenant.

. . . .

As noted above, the trial court found sufficient interference with the use and enjoyment of the leased premises to justify the tenant's departure and to relieve her from the obligation to pay further rent. In our view the evidence was sufficient to warrant that conclusion, and the Appellate Division erred in reversing it. Plaintiff argued and the Appellate Division agreed that a constructive eviction cannot arise unless the condition interferes with the use in a permanent sense. It is true that the word "permanent" appears in many of the early cases. See *e.g., Stewart v. Childs Co.*, 86 N.J.L. 648, 92 A. 392, L.R.A. 1915C, 649 (E. & A. 1914). But it is equally obvious that permanent does not signify that water in a basement in a case like this one must be an everlasting and unending condition. If its recurrence follows regularly upon rainstorms and is sufficiently serious in extent to amount to a substantial interference with use and enjoyment of the premises for the purpose of the lease, the test for constructive eviction has been met. Additionally in our case, the defective condition of the driveway, exterior and foundation walls which permitted the recurrent flooding was obviously permanent in the sense that it would continue and probably worsen if not remedied. There was no obligation on the tenant to remedy it.

Plaintiff claims further that *Stewart v. Childs Co., supra,* strongly supports its right to recovery. Under the lease in that case the landlord covenanted that at all times he would keep the cellar waterproof. The cellar was known to be necessary to the conduct of the tenant's business. After the business opened, water flooded into the cellar, at times to a depth of two and three feet. There was no doubt the flooding resulted from failure of the landlord to make the place waterproof. But when the tenant moved out, a suit for rent for the unexpired term was instituted and the landlord was allowed to recover. It was held that the agreement to pay rent and the agreement to waterproof the cellar were independent covenants and breach of the covenant to waterproof was not a defense to the action for rent . . . .

We reject the rule of *Stewart v. Childs Co.* and espouse . . . the sensible approach taken in *Pines v. Perssion, supra,* where in addition to the excerpt quoted above, the court said:

> The evidence clearly showed that the implied warranty of habitability was breached. Respondents' covenant to pay rent and appellant's covenant to provide a habitable house were mutually dependent, and thus a breach of the latter by appellant relieved respondents of any liability under the former.

Breach of the implied warranty of habitability was held to constitute failure of consideration on the part of the landlord.

Similarly whether the landlord's default in the present case is treated as a substantial breach of the express covenant of quiet enjoyment resulting in a constructive eviction of the tenant or as a material failure of consideration, (*e.g.,* such failure as amounts to a substantial interference with the beneficial enjoyment of the premises) the tenant's vacation was legal. Thus it is apparent from our discussion that a tenant's right to vacate leased premises is the same from a doctrinal standpoint whether treated as stemming from breach of a covenant of quiet enjoyment or from breach of any other dependent covenant. Both breaches constitute failure of consideration. The inference to be drawn from the cases is that the remedy of constructive eviction probably evolved from a desire by the courts to relieve the tenant from the harsh burden imposed by common law rules which applied principles of *caveat emptor* to the letting, rejected an implied warranty of habitability, and ordinarily treated undertakings of the landlord in a lease as independent covenants. To alleviate the tenant's burden, the courts broadened the scope of the long-recognized implied covenant of quiet enjoyment (apparently designed originally to protect the tenant against ouster by a title superior to that of his lessor) to include the right of the tenant to have the beneficial enjoyment and use of the premises for the agreed term. It was but a short step then to the rule that when the landlord or someone acting for him or by virtue of a right acquired through him causes a substantial interference with that enjoyment and use, the tenant may claim a constructive eviction. In our view, therefore, at the present time whenever a tenant's right to vacate leased premises comes into existence because he is deprived of their beneficial enjoyment and use on account of acts chargeable to the landlord, it is immaterial whether the right is expressed in terms of breach of a covenant of quiet enjoyment, or material failure of consideration, or material breach of an implied warranty against latent defects.

Plaintiff's final claim is that assuming the tenant was exposed to a constructive eviction, she waived it by remaining on the premises for an unreasonable period of time thereafter. The general rule is, of course, that a tenant's right to claim a constructive eviction will be lost if he does not vacate the premises within a reasonable time after the right comes into existence. *Weiss v. I. Zapinsky, Inc.*, 65 N.J. Super. 351, 167 A.2d 802 (App. Div. 1961); *Duncan Development Co. v. Duncan Hardware, Inc.*, 34 N.J. Super. 293, 112 A.2d 274 (App. Div. 1955); 1 *American Law of Property, supra*, § 3.51, p. 282. What constitutes a reasonable time depends upon the circumstances of each case. In considering the problem courts must be sympathetic toward the tenant's plight. Vacation of the premises is a drastic course and must be taken at his peril. If he vacates, and it is held at a later time in a suit for rent for the unexpired term that the landlord's course of action did not reach the dimensions of constructive eviction, a substantial liability may be imposed upon him. That risk and the practical inconvenience and difficulties attendant upon finding and moving to suitable quarters counsel caution.

Here, plaintiff's cooperative building manager died about nine months before the removal. During that period the tenant complained, patiently waited, hoped for relief from the landlord, and tried to take care of the water problem that accompanied the recurring rainstorms. But when relief did not come and the "crowning blow" put five inches of water in the leased offices and meeting rooms on December 20, 1961, the tolerance ended and the vacation came ten days later after notice to the landlord. The trial court found as a fact that under the circumstances such vacation was within a reasonable time, and the delay was not sufficient to establish a waiver of the constructive eviction. We find adequate evidence to support the conclusion and are of the view that the Appellate Division should not have reversed it.[1]

---

[1] Although not necessary to our decision, we note that the New York Supreme Court, Appellate Division, in *E. Esarsee, Inc. v. Holland*, 241 App. Div. 736, 269 N.Y.S. 745 (1934) held that where the condition which caused the constructive eviction, *i.e.*, lack of waterproof exterior walls, was a continuing one, the basis for right to vacate was renewed after each monthly payment of rent.

Also, it is worthy of note that in recent times some courts, recognizing the position of a tenant who claiming constructive eviction moves out before the end of his term, have attempted to neutralize the hazard by authorizing equitable relief. For example in *Charles E. Burt, Inc. v. Seven Grand Corporation*, 340 Mass. 124, 163 N.E.2d 4 (1959), such a tenant was allowed to move in equity to restrain the collection of further rents under the lease, and for rescission of the lease as well as a declaration of nullity. The court indicated further that if the tenant remained in possession until the successful disposition of the action, his liability for intervening rent would be limited to the difference between the lease-fixed rent and the reasonable rental value of the premises in their defective condition. So too in *Pines v. Perssion, supra*, the Wisconsin Supreme Court held that since "there was a [material] failure of consideration, respondents [lessees] are absolved from any liability for rent under the lease and their only liability is for the reasonable rental value of the premises during the time of actual occupancy." In this connection a further application of equitable principles may be worthy of consideration. Where the facts warrant the conclusion that the landlord has breached any dependent covenant of the lease (for example, that of quiet enjoyment) or an implied warranty

For the reasons expressed above, we hold the view that the trial court was correct in deciding that defendant had been constructively evicted from the premises in question, and therefore was not liable for the rent claimed. Accordingly, the judgment of the Appellate Division is reversed and that of the trial court is reinstated.

For reversal: CHIEF JUSTICE WEINTRAUB and JUSTICES JACOBS, FRANCIS, PROCTOR, HALL, SCHETTINO and HANEMAN—7.

For affirmance: None.

[b]   Explanatory Notes: Restructuring Constructive Eviction Theory

[*i*]   **Stewart *Overruled.*** The most obvious outcome of *Reste* was that *Stewart v. Childs Co.* was overruled. But how did the court go about the internment? Surely it is fair to say that the court discussed a number of issues that it did not have to reach in order to decide the case. A warranty that the premises were free of latent defects was implied, the covenant of quiet enjoyment was used as a basis for remaking constructive eviction rules, and an express covenant to repair was said to be dependent with the obligation to pay rent. Any one of these outcomes would have ended the case. Given the breadth of the opinion's language, and the content of footnote 1 at the end of the opinion, tenants' lawyers were optimistic that further reforms were in the offing. That feeling was enhanced by the sources the court relied upon. For those of us working in landlord-tenant related areas at the time, it was obvious that every recent case and article with even a glimmer of reformist prose was referenced. This was one of those unusual opinions that overwhelmed knowledgeable readers with an aura of impending change.

[*ii*]   ***The First Lease.*** The first lease between Reste and Cooper contained a clause requiring the tenant to keep the premises in good condition. But the court found this agreement of no use to the landlord since the location of the defect was "not part of the demised premises." Thus, an implied warranty covering latent defects (note the importation of latency from tort law) applied. In addition, the court strongly suggested that it would impose an implied warranty in all cases, regardless of whether the defect was inside or outside of the leased space and regardless of whether the lease contained a tenant or a landlord repair covenant. But all of this was arguably nothing but important rhetoric. After all, the tenant vacated the place while a different lease was in effect!

[*iii*]   ***The Second Lease.*** When Cooper signed the second lease, she certainly knew about the water problem. But the court used her knowledge, and the oral promise of the owner to correct the problem, to the tenant's advantage. The oral promise to make repairs, even though it was arguably in conflict with clauses in the written lease, became an express part of the entire agreement, the court held, since Cooper relied upon the water proofing covenant in signing the lease. When the "crowning blow" occurred on December 20, 1961, the tenant was entitled to cancel the contract and move out. The court noted that constructive eviction theory operated in implied as well as express warranty situations, that express and implied warranties were "dependent" with the covenant to pay rent, and that the tenant could raise breach of a warranty

---

against latent defects in such manner as to warrant vacation of the premises by the tenant but the tenant is willing to remain in possession and pay a sum representing their reasonable rental value in their defective or reduced-value condition, should he not be entitled to do so for the remainder of the term and to have the court fix the reasonable rental value for that period, or in the alternative have the defective condition repaired or remedied himself and offset the cost against the rent fixed in the lease, provided the expenditure involved would not be unreasonable in light of the value of the leasehold?

as a *defense* to a *claim for rent*.[74] The court did not have to reach all of these issues. They could have simply overruled *Stewart v. Childs Co.* by holding that the tenant's right to possession was so disturbed by the leak that constructive eviction had occurred and cancellation of the contract was appropriate. Implied covenants were not at issue and the covenant of quiet enjoyment of possession, as opposed to an express covenant to repair, was always thought of as dependent with the obligation to pay rent.[75] The court reached out to reform landlord-tenant law. The impact on landlord-tenant law theory was significant. Rent and repair obligations were no longer to be treated as separate contracts, but as parts of a single agreement. Arguments reachable before *Reste* only by way of independent causes of action, or later, counterclaims, became defenses to an action for rent.

[iv]   *Constructive Eviction in the Reformed Context.* Constructive eviction entails risks for tenants. They have to move out to take advantage of the rule. If a court later finds that the decision to vacate was erroneous, rent must be paid. While the post-*Reste* reforms in landlord-tenant law have removed much of this risk by providing defenses to actions for possession for non-payment of rent, some tenants still prefer to move rather than withhold payment of rent and wait for the landlord to sue for possession. At times, tenants may feel they have no choice but to move out. Obstreperous, noisy, or threatening neighbors present particularly difficult problems when landlords refuse to take steps to get rid of such tenants. The courts appear to be protecting tenants who move under such pressure. *See, e.g., Gottdiener v. Hailhot*, 179 N.J. Super. 286, 431 A.2d 851 (1981).

[c]   **Problem Notes: Contract and Property Theory in Leases**

[i]   *The Nature of a Lease.* Is a lease a contract, a conveyance of an interest in land, both a contract and a conveyance, or neither a contract nor a conveyance? Over time, many came to view the traditional common law regime as a "property" system in which the landlord conveys an interest in land largely undisturbed by other arrangements. During the landlord-tenant reform era of the 1970s, many argued that contract law ought to be used as a model for reconstructing the old common law rules. A rarely considered feature of the *Reste* case provides a convenient path into this debate. When Cooper vacated, the landlord did not relet the space to another tenant. The building was sold after Cooper left, and the new owners took an assignment of any extant rights under the Cooper lease. After the lease expired, Cooper was sued for all the unpaid rent. The tenant, as you know, defended the action using a constructive eviction theory; nothing was said about the apparent failure of the landlord to seek another tenant to mitigate his damages after Cooper left.

The remedial path selected by Reste Realty had roots deep in the history of landlord-tenant law. If a tenant abandoned a premises, the landlord had a choice of remedies. He could accept the abandonment, thereby transforming the abandonment into a surrender, and seek a new tenant. He could also refuse to accept the abandonment. The landlord could then sue for the rent as it became due or wait until the end of the term and sue for all the rent at once. In addition, a lessor could rent abandoned space "on the account of the tenant." This remedy permitted the

---

[74] Note well that this case was not an action for possession under the summary dispossess laws. All the court did was undo the restrictive *substantive* contract law of the *Stewart v. Childs* era. It did not alter the *procedural* limitations of the summary eviction proceeding.

[75] By the covenant of quiet enjoyment the landlord agreed to leave the tenant's possession undisturbed. It is breach of this covenant that allows for constructive eviction.

landlord to seek a new occupant and, after notice to the tenant, reduce the tenant's rental obligation by the amount received from the new lessee.

Treating the lease as a conveyance, the notion was that a lease was a unitary conveyance of land in exchange for a price, that the abandonment by the tenant did not act as a reconveyance unless it was accepted by the landlord, and that a landlord was, therefore, free to demand rent as long as the tenant's right to possession was left undisturbed.[76]

But the landlord's right to relet on the tenant's account did not easily mesh with the notion of a lease as a conveyance. The unitary conveyance of land for a price connoted a transfer of a period of possession to the tenant. If the landlord permitted another party to occupy the premises, how could a claim be made that the tenant's right to possession had been left undisturbed? Indeed, the right to relet on the tenant's account was much like the contract notion of mitigating damages. If the lease was a contract and the tenant's failure to pay rent was a breach, then the landlord would only be entitled to receive monetary damages caused by the breach. If a new tenant could be found with reasonable effort, then only the difference between the rent called for in the lease and the amount the landlord could obtain from a new tenant would be attributable to the breach.

After *Reste,* was it appropriate to view the lease as either a conveyance or a contract? Much of the language in the opinion—warranty, dependency, reliance, failure of consideration—was contractual in nature. But the final relief granted was expressed in terms of constructive eviction and other language—latent defects, covenant of quiet enjoyment—reflected tort and property notions. The court declined to select one mode of analysis over another, leaving us with a significant set of theoretical problems to wade through in the rest of this chapter.

[*ii*]   *Historical Bibliography.* This is an appropriate spot to give you an historical bibliography to browse in if you are interested in the reform debates. Some of the more important articles include:

Chase & Taylor, *Landlord and Tenant: A Study in Property and Contract*, 30 Vill. L. Rev. 571 (1985).

Humbach, *The Common-Law Conception of Leasing: Mitigation, Habitability, and Dependence of Covenants*, 60 Wash. U. L.Q. 1213 (1983).

Sarajane Love, *Landlord's Remedies When the Tenant Abandons: Property, Contract, and Leases*, 30 U. Kan. L. Rev. 533 (1982).

Chase, *The Property-Contract Theme in Landlord and Tenant Law: A Critical Commentary on Schoshinski's American Law of Landlord and Tenant*, 13 Rutgers L.J. 189 (1982).

Glendon, *The Transformation of American Landlord-Tenant Law*, 23 B.C. L. Rev. 502 (1982).

Chused, *Contemporary Dilemmas of the* Javins *Defense: A Note on the Need for Procedural Reform in Landlord-Tenant Law*, 67 Geo. L.J. 1385 (1979).

Siegel, *Is the Modern Lease a Contract or a Conveyance?—A Historical Inquiry*, 52 J. Urb. L. 649 (1978).

---

[76] Note that constructive eviction acted as a serious disturbance of the tenant's right to possession and therefore terminated the landlord's right to demand rent. The best review of the consequences of abandonment and the theoretical difficulties presented by the various cases is Jean Love, *Landlord's Remedies When the Tenant Abandons: Property, Contract, and Leases*, 30 U. Kan. L. Rev. 533 (1982).

There are also some earlier pieces that were part of the debate occurring during the era in which landlord-tenant law was being given searching review in the courts. They generally argued that leases were contracts and that the old rules should be accordingly altered. A few of the articles are:

Hicks, *The Contractual Nature of Real Property Leases*, 24 BAYLOR L. REV. 443 (1972).

Note, *Contract Principles and Leases of Realty*, 50 B.U. L. REV. 24 (1970).

Schoshinski, *Remedies of the Indigent Tenant: Proposal for Change*, 54 GEO. L.J. 519 (1966).

Lesar, *The Landlord-Tenant Relation in Perspective: From Status to Contract and Back in 900 Years?*, 9 U. KAN. L. REV. 369 (1961).

Lesar, *Landlord and Tenant Reform*, 35 N.Y.U. L. REV. 1279 (1960).

[4] The Demise of the Old Rules: Merger of Reforms in Substance and Procedure

[a] Introduction: Reform and the Summary Dispossess Process

After *Reste*, several questions were left open. First, the warranty talk in that opinion was mostly about protecting tenants from latent defects. What would have happened if the defect were patent? Second, the defect in that case was not within the premises rented by the tenant. What would have happened if the defect was inside the premises, was patent, and the lease contained a clause requiring the tenant to make repairs? Third, and most importantly, the case did not begin to deal with the structure of litigation in actions for possession filed in landlord-tenant court. *Reste* was an action for rent, not a summary dispossess proceeding brought by the landlord to obtain possession of the premises. Despite the reformist contents of the opinion in *Reste*, there were very few clues about what it meant for the operation of landlord-tenant courts.

The summary dispossess process, in New Jersey and elsewhere, was constructed to minimize defenses, resolve possession questions quickly, and preclude most appeals. Its structure mimicked the common law combination of writs and independent covenants. The primary issue was whether the rent had been paid. Breaches of other covenants could not be used to support defenses. Only issues germane to the payment of rent were relevant to the proceeding. Counterclaims were not available. And, under N.J. STAT. ANN. § 2A:18-59, proceedings were "not appealable except on ground of lack of jurisdiction."

The limitation on appeals created quite a problem for those interested in changing the operation of landlord-tenant court. The standard well-pleaded complaint rule seemed to bar appeals on the warranty issues opened up by *Reste*. Under standard procedural practice, if a complaint contains sufficient allegations to invoke a court's jurisdiction, the case proceeds to trial. If a plaintiff later fails to produce sufficient facts to prove his or her case, the court enters a judgment for the defendant on the merits rather than dismiss for lack of jurisdiction. Look at the language of N.J. STAT. ANN. § 2A:18-53(b) in the Appendix. You should be able to see that in a non-payment of rent case, the landlord has to allege that a landlord-tenant relationship exists between the parties, that the tenant is in possession, and that there is a default in the payment of rent. If those allegations turn out later not to be correct, say because the tenant actually paid the rent and the landlord's agent mistakenly failed to enter the payment in the account books, the court will dismiss the action for possession on the merits. But, under standard practice, that dismissal would not mean the court lacked jurisdiction. So how could a tenant claiming breach of an implied warranty under *Reste* possibly appeal a case after a landlord-tenant court judge concluded that the defense was not available in a summary dispossess proceeding?

There were precious few precedential clues in the New Jersey casebooks. One technique, tried by a few commercial tenants early in the century, was to seek an injunction from an equity court barring a landlord from seeking possession in a summary dispossess action. In *H. Windholz & Son v. Burke*, 131 A. 386 (Ct. Ch. 1925), the tenant obtained an injunction against the landlord's pursuit of a summary dispossess action. The landlord alleged that the tenant breached an agreement not to make alterations without the consent of the landlord and sought possession. The tenant argued that the alterations were made to comply with the health laws and that the landlord had waived all of his objections by accepting rent. The Chancery Court protected the tenant's right to possession, noting among other problems that the district court might lack jurisdiction to entertain a summary dispossess case. That possibility arose because the independent covenant rule underlying *Stewart v. Child Co.* also limited landlords' ability to link the rent covenant with other tenant covenants. In *Smith v. Sinclair*,[77] which was cited by the *Burke* court, the New Jersey Supreme Court held that the landlord-tenant court lacked jurisdiction to entertain an action brought against a tenant for violating covenants against subletting and using the premises only for residential purposes. The *Burke* court then noted that:

> if the district court has jurisdiction, and erroneously should refuse to entertain or uphold the defense of waiver, or any other valid defense, its judgment would be final, the complainant's possession would be lost to it, and its only remedy would be a suit for damages for unlawful ouster. The proceedings are summary. There is no appeal on the merits. The relief the complainant presently stands in need of is the protection of its possession, not damages; and, while the law may grant compensating damages for the injury now threatened, equity prevents the infliction of the injury altogether.

Most tenants did not prevail in their efforts to use chancery to curtail operation of the summary dispossess remedy,[78] but the possibility that a court of equity might intervene led to a fairly continuous string of requests for injunctions. While poor tenants were not going to be able to run to an equity court very often to forestall their evictions, the merger of law and equity proceedings under the 1947 New Jersey Constitution opened the possibility that landlord-tenant courts could hear equitable defenses. That possibility was given a bit of credence by *Vineland Shopping Center, Inc. v. DeMarco*, 35 N.J. 459, 173 A.2d 270 (1961), which summarized the old equity cases in the process of allowing a tenant to delay eviction on equitable grounds.

In *Vineland* a commercial tenant promised to pay sewerage fees, but was sued for possession for failing to do so. In fact the tenant had paid the charges before suit was filed directly to the utility company rather than to the landlord. "The established principle," the New Jersey Supreme Court noted "is that the trial court had jurisdiction if there was evidence from which it could find a statutory basis for removal. If that test is met, the judgment must be affirmed even though it is otherwise infected with error." After summarizing at some length the power of equity courts to bar eviction, noting the efficiency of allowing certain equitable defenses to be raised in order

---

[77] 59 N.J.L. 84, 34 A. 943 (1896).

[78] *See, e.g.*, Galka v. Tide Water Associated Oil Co., 133 N.J. Eq. 137, 30 A.2d 881 (1943); Rankin v. Homestead Golf & Country Club, Inc., 135 N.J. Eq. 160, 37 A. 2d 640 (1944); Westfield Airport, Inc. v. Middlesex-Union Airport Co., Inc., 140 N.J. Eq. 263, 54 A. 2d 204 (1947). For a summary of the use of equity to avoid summary dispossession *see*, Chused, *Contemporary Dilemmas of the Javins Defense: A Note on the Need for Procedural Reform in Landlord-Tenant Law*, 67 GEO. L.J. 1385, 1397-1400 (1979).

to avoid requiring that another action be filed in a different court, and noting that N.J. STAT. ANN. § 2A:18-55 bars eviction after judgment for possession if the tenant pays the rent to the court clerk within three days, the court allowed the appeal and reversed the order for possession obtained by the landlord at the trial level.

There was one interesting, final twist in New Jersey's summary dispossess statue. N.J. STAT. ANN. § 2A:18-60 allowed for summary actions to be removed to a regular civil court if the judge of the regular court "deems [the case] . . . of sufficient importance." Once removed, the limitations on appeal of N.J. STAT. ANN. § 2A:18-59 no longer applied. Before reading the next case, put yourself in the position of a legal services attorney in New Jersey in 1970. A new client, Renatta Osage, has just walked into your office. She gives you a summons and complaint in a summary dispossess action and asks you to help her when her case comes before the local court next week. You take the papers and ask her about her apartment. She says that she has three rooms, one bathroom and a kitchen, that rats and mice can be heard in the walls, that plaster has fallen off of the bathroom and kitchen ceilings because of leaks from upstairs, and that all her requests for repairs have gone unheeded. After she leaves, you re-read *Reste*. You sit at your desk for a time pondering what steps to take in her case. And then you jot down some notes about possible ways to approach her case. Here are your notes:

MEMO TO FILE

Osage Case: Possible Theories for Use in Answer to Summary Dispossess Complaint

a. *Constructive Eviction. Reste* certainly helps, but my client does not want to leave her place. As bad as it is, it is better than the streets. Can I fiddle around with this theory and make it serviceable for someone who wants to stay in her apartment? *See* footnote 1 of the *Reste* opinion.

b. *Implied Warranty.* The *Reste* court talks about implied warranties, but seems to focus on latent defects. My client knew about all the problems before she moved in three years ago. But she didn't have much money and this was the only place she could find.

c. *Illegality.* Though not much talked about, there are some old New Jersey cases which suggest that an illegal lease permits a tenant to abandon possession. Among the most interesting is Stern Holding Co. v. O'Connor, 119 N.J.L. 291, 196 A. 432 (1938). That case involved a lease of land for dumping ashes, street sweepings and other refuse. But a Jersey City ordinance prohibited the dumping of garbage in the city. When the city authorities began enforcing the law, the tenant stopped using the dump and paying rent. He later lost a suit for rent because the court construed the lease to permit the dumping of some items that were not banned by the ordinance. But if I could convince a court that state and local housing codes make it unlawful to lease a premises with violations, would that help me out? Would my client have to move out? Hmmm...

d. *Summary Process Problems. Reste* does not help much on the procedure even if it helps on the substance. There is only one case in New Jersey that permits a tenant to appeal from landlord-tenant court—Vineland Shopping Center v. DeMarco, 35 N.J. 459, 173 A.2d 270 (1961). The decision is fairly recent, but it involved a specific statutory right under N.J. STAT. ANN. § 2A:18-55 to avoid eviction by payment of the overdue money. And that section says that "all proceedings shall be stopped" if payment is made, very strong language to use as a basis for arguing that the landlord-tenant court lacked jurisdiction to evict DeMarco. How can I structure an argument that failure of the landlord-tenant court to consider any of my defenses may be appealed as jurisdictional under N.J. STAT. ANN. § 2A:18-59? After all, I do have to litigate this for appeal.

e. *Long Shot.* Can I remove this thing from landlord-tenant court under N.J. STAT. ANN. § 2A:18-60? So much to ponder in such a short time. Answer due next Monday. Better start by running over in the morning and taking some Polaroids of her place.

f. *Getting in the Answer.* Trials usually occur on the return date. How can I even convince the trial judge to let me file an answer? He is likely to find my request bizarre. Before the return date, I better file a motion to file an answer and brief, an answer, and a brief to make sure the record is in good shape. Guess I should also have emergency appeal papers ready in case the judge orders her ouster without much of a hearing. Late nights coming....

Can you help draft the answer in the Osage matter?

The next case arose in a happenstance manner, very much like the Osage problem. Gordon Lewis, a legal services lawyer was in landlord-tenant court one day with his usual load of cases. A lady was there trying without much success to explain her problems with a toilet. Lewis went up to her and asked if he could help. She said "yes," and the rest, as they say, is history. The brief on appeal was signed by Lewis, but he was too busy to do much of the writing. It was put together by Ken Meiser and Joe Ippolito, then a third year law student at Rutgers University School of Law in Camden, New Jersey.[79] Ippolito was admitted to the bar just before the case was argued before the New Jersey Supreme Court. His name was formally added to the brief when Len Wallach, the attorney arguing the case for Legal Services, moved at the argument to add his name.[80]

[b] Opinion of the New Jersey Supreme Court in *Marini v. Ireland*

Marini v. Ireland

New Jersey Supreme Court
56 N.J. 130, 265 A.2d 526 (1970)

Gordon V. Lewis for appellant (David H. Dugan, III, Newark, Director, Camden Regional Legal Services, Inc., attorney; Joseph V. Ippolito, and Kenneth Meiser, on the brief).

Bartholomew A. Sheehan, Jr., Cherry Hill, for respondent (Hyland, Davis & Reberkenny, Cherry Hill, attorneys).

Richard J. Pilch, Trenton, amicus curiae for the New Jersey State Office of Legal Services (James D. Coffee, Elizabeth, Director).

The opinion of the Court was delivered by

HANEMAN, J.

This matter concerns the appealability of County District Court landlord and tenant dispossess judgments; the scope of a landlord's duty to make repairs; and the right to offset the cost of such repairs against accruing rent on the failure of the landlord to make same, if found to be required.

---

[79] Telephone Interview by Fritz Mulhauser with Ken Meiser, who was a VISTA (Volunteers in Service to America) in the Camden Legal Services Office where the case was handled (Feb. 1998).

[80] Interview by Fritz Mulhauser with Joe Ippolito (Feb. 1998).

On or about April 2, 1969, plaintiff, landlord, and defendant, tenant, entered into a one-year lease for an apartment located in a two-family duplex building at 503-B Rand Street, Camden, New Jersey. The annual rent of $1,140 was agreed to be paid in monthly installments of $95. The lease incorporated a covenant of quiet enjoyment but did not include a specific covenant for repairs.

On or about June 25, 1969, defendant alleges that she discovered that the toilet in the leased apartment was cracked and water was leaking onto the bathroom floor. She further alleges that repeated attempts to inform plaintiff of this condition were unsuccessful. On or about June 27, 1969, defendant hired one Karl T. Bittner, a registered plumber, to repair the toilet. Bittner repaired the toilet at a cost of $85.72, which the tenant paid.

On July 15, 1969, defendant mailed plaintiff a check for $9.28 together with the receipt for $85.72 in payment of the July rent. Plaintiff challenged the offsetting of the cost of the repair and demanded the outstanding $85.72.

When his demands were refused, plaintiff instituted a summary dispossess action for nonpayment of rent in the Camden County District Court pursuant to N.J.S.A. 2A:18-53(b) alleging the nonpayment of the July rent in the amount of $85.72 and August rent of $95. A hearing was had on August 15, 1969. Plaintiff argued that he was entitled to the $85.72 because he had no duty to make repairs and consequently, defendant's payment of the cost of repair could not be offset against rent.

The judge conceived the issue as entirely a legal one and determined that the facts which defendant alleged did not create a duty upon the landlord to make repairs. Thus, without trying out the issues tendered by defendant, he found a default in payment of rent of $85.72 (July) and $95 (August) plus costs and rendered a judgment for possession. Defendant appealed to the Appellate Division.

On August 29, 1969, a judge of the Appellate Division granted a temporary stay of the judgment for possession and the warrant of eviction. The Appellate Division granted a stay pending appeal on September 23, 1969 and ordered defendant to pay all the rents then due except the contested July rent. The Appellate Division also then denied plaintiff's cross-motion to dismiss the appeal. Before the Appellate Division heard argument, this Court certified the case on its own motion. R. 2:12-1.

The issues which evolve on this appeal are: Did defendant's claimed right to offset her cost of repairs against rent raise a "jurisdictional" issue. If the answer to that query is in the affirmative, did the landlord have a duty to repair and may the issue of failure to comply with such duty be raised in a dispossess action. Also involved in the latter question is the right of the tenant to make repairs upon the landlord's failure to so do and the right to offset the cost thereof against rent.

N.J.S.A. 2A:18-53 provides in part:

Any lessee or tenant . . . of any houses, buildings, lands or tenements, . . . may be removed from such premises by the county district court of the county within which such premises are situated, in an action in the following cases:

. . . .

b. Where such person shall hold over after a default in the payment of rent, pursuant to the agreement under which the premises are held.

N.J.S.A. 2A:18-59 reads:

Proceedings had by virtue of this article shall not be appealable except on the ground of lack of jurisdiction. The landlord, however, shall remain liable in a civil action for unlawful proceedings under this article.

As noted, N.J.S.A. 2A:18-59 permits review of the County District Court's judgment only on the question of lack of jurisdiction. Plaintiff rationalizes that as defendant acknowledges that the rent asserted by plaintiff to be due for the month of July was not paid in full as provided in the lease, a defense grounded upon an allegation that the unpaid balance is not owing raises a "meritorious" issue. He states that defendant's contest of the *amount* due directs an attack upon the plaintiff's right to possession rather than an attack upon the jurisdictional basis of his action. Plaintiff argues that the admitted failure to pay *in full* is, in the language of the statute a *"default"* and vests the County District Court with jurisdiction to order a removal of the tenant.

Defendant on the other hand, contends that the County District Court has jurisdiction in dispossess actions only in those factual complexes specified in N.J.S.A. 2A: 18-53—here, for a "default in the payment of rent." The issue of the *amount of rent due*, says defendant, raising as it does the issue of the default alleged by the complaint, is directed at the jurisdiction of the County District Court and a determination rejecting her defense of *non-default*, in whole or part, is therefore appealable under N.J.S.A. 2A:18-59.

The County District Court in the present matter, is vested with jurisdiction as noted, only where there exists a rent default. The complaint must delineate specific allegations of fact giving rise to such a default.

While dealing with the following cases cited in connection with the foregoing, it must be remembered that originally an action for possession was commenced before a justice of the peace by filing an affidavit. Later the jurisdiction was transferred to the District Court, but the action continued to be commenced by the filing of an affidavit. In *Earl v. Krug Baking Co.*, 22 N.J. Misc. 424 (Cir. Ct. 1944), the court said in that connection:

Summary proceedings in the district court for the dispossession of tenants may be described as a statutory substitute for the common law action in ejectment, and although the proceedings are commenced by the filing of the jurisdiction affidavit, that affidavit is nonetheless a complaint in the ordinary acceptation of the term.

Presently the affidavit has been superseded by a complaint. R. 6:3-1. What is said in the following cases concerning affidavits is equally applicable to presently employed complaints. As early as *Fowler v. Roe*, 25 N.J.L. 549 (Sup. Ct. 1856), the court said, at p. 551:

In this summary proceeding before a justice of the peace, to turn one man out of the possession of the premises he occupies, and put another in, the power is delegated by special statutory authority to a court having no jurisdiction to try the title to lands, and can only be exercised where all the prerequisites to its exercise prescribed by the statute appear to exist, and are shown to have been complied with.

Fowler, supra, also held that it must appear from the allegations of the affidavit:

1. That the relation of landlord and tenant exists.

2. That default has been made by the tenant in the payment of rent, according to the terms of the agreement or demise under which he holds.

3. That there are no goods of the tenant on the premises out of which the rent due can be made by distress.

4. That three days' notice in writing has been served by the person entitled to the rent, on the person owing the same, requiring payment or possession.

. . . .

In *Vineland Shopping Center, Inc. v. DeMarco*, 35 N.J. 459 (1961), this Court said in reference to substantiating proof of the pleaded jurisdictional facts:

The established principle is that the trial court had jurisdiction if there was evidence from which it could find a statutory basis for removal. If that test is met, the judgment must be affirmed even though it is otherwise infected with error.

The jurisdictional issue, *i.e.*, the statutory basis for removal, can be twice raised in a dispossess action. First, by motion directed at the complaint for failure to accurately allege the necessary facts with particularity. Second, on trial for failure to adduce adequate proof to corroborate the allegations of the complaint. If the complaint contains adequate factual allegations of default, the issue can be resolved only when proof has been adduced. Failure to furnish either such allegations in the complaint or proof on the trial is sufficient ground to warrant dismissal for lack of jurisdiction.

As noted in *Vineland Shopping Center, Inc. v. DeMarco, supra*, our cases have hewed a line separating the "jurisdictional" issue from the meritorious issue. Confusion arises from this jurisdictional-meritorious dichotomy by reason of the fact that the same proof is required and goes to the same crucial element in each, *i.e.*, proof of the default in rent as alleged in the complaint. Whatever "jurisdiction" means in other settings, here it uniquely connotes the existence of one of the factual situations delineated in N.J.S.A. 2A:18-53. It follows that a finding, by the judge, that there is a default as alleged by the landlord, does not dispose of the meritorious issue alone. It as well disposes of the jurisdictional issue.

The jurisdictional issue of "default" encompasses the question of whether the amount of rent alleged to be in default, is due, unpaid and *owing*, not only whether it is due and unpaid. The mere fact of the tenant's failure to pay rent in full as provided in the lease is not in and of itself a sufficient fact to meet the statutory jurisdictional requisite. Thus a tenant's evidence in substantiation of a defense that there is no default or that the default is not in the amount alleged by the landlord, is admissible on the jurisdictional issue. Consideration must be given not only to a legal defense but as well to an equitable excuse for non-payment, such as confession and avoidance, which would relieve the tenant of the duty of paying and hence make the unpaid rent in whole or part due but not owing and thus not in "default."

That the County District Court "must accept any equitable issue offered to defeat an action within its jurisdiction or to avoid a separate defense to such action" was established by *Vineland Shopping Center, Inc. v. DeMarco, supra*. This duty is imposed on the County District Court not only in connection with proof of cases "within its jurisdiction" but also on the issue of jurisdiction as well. It follows that an equitable defense to the proof of an alleged rent default in a landlord-tenant dispossess proceeding is permissible and facts in support thereof admissible.

There is no logical reason why a tenant who is successful in having a case removed to the Superior Court under N.J.S.A. 2A:18-60 shall have the benefit of equitable defenses to jurisdiction while a tenant who is unsuccessful in seeking to have his case removed from the County District Court to the Superior Court should be limited to legal defenses.[1]

We hold, therefore, that equitable as well as legal defenses asserting payment or absolution from payment in whole or part are available to a tenant in a dispossess action and must be considered by the court. Denial of a motion by defendant directed at the complaint for failure to make adequate factual allegations, or of a motion at the conclusion of the trial for failure to supply proof that the amount of rent alleged in the complaint is in default, both going to the question of jurisdiction, are each appealable.

. . . .

It becomes necessary to consider the merits of defendant's equitable defense that the failure of the landlord to repair the toilet constituted a breach of the covenant of habitability or quiet enjoyment and gave rise to defendant's entitlement to self-help, permitting her to repair the toilet and offset the cost thereof against her rent. We need not concern ourselves with the covenant of quiet enjoyment as will hereafter become apparent.

We are here concerned with the lease of premises for residential purposes. The lease provides:

WITNESSETH, that the said party of the first part hath let, and by these presents doth grant, demise and to farm let unto the said party of the second part, all that contains 4 rooms and bath, apartment situated in the city and county of camden [sic.], state [sic.] of New Jersey, known and designated as 503—B Rand Street.

. . . .

nor use or permit any part thereof to be used for any other purpose than dwelling . . . .

As the lease contains no express covenant to repair, we are obliged to determine whether there arises an implied covenant, however categorized, which would require the landlord to make repairs.

A lease was originally considered a conveyance of an interest in real estate. Thus, the duties and obligations of the parties, implied as well as express, were dealt with according to the law of property and not of the law of contracts. In *Michaels v. Brookchester, Inc.*, 26 N.J. 379 (1958) this Court said:

Historically a lease was viewed as a sale of an interest in land. The concept of *caveat emptor*, applicable to such sales, seemed logically pertinent to leases of land. There was neither an implied covenant of fitness for the intended use nor responsibility in the landlord to maintain

---

[1] N.J.S.A. 2A:18-60 reads:

At any time before an action for the removal of a tenant comes on for trial, either the landlord or person in possession may apply to the superior court, which may, if it deems it of *sufficient importance*, order the cause transferred from the county district court to the superior court. (Emphasis supplied.)

The statute furnishes no guidelines for the solution of the question of what constitutes a case of "sufficient importance." It is self-evident that every tenant removal is of importance to both the landlord and tenant. It could be argued that every such case qualifies for removal to the Superior Court. If a dispossess action is not removed to the Superior Court, appeal by a tenant from an adverse judgment is restricted to the issue of jurisdiction. N.J.S.A. 2A:18-59. If the action is removed to the Superior Court, appeal is not so restricted. Appeal is then available on meritorious grounds as well. *Vineland Shopping Center, Inc. v. DeMarco, supra.* We see no sound reason for any distinction between the right to appeal from a District Court judgment and a Superior Court judgment for possession. It might well be urged that there should be no difference between the scope of review from a District Court judgment and a Superior Court judgment. We are not, however, obliged to pass upon that problem in the matter *sub judice*.

the leased premises. This principle, suitable for the agrarian setting in which it was conceived, lagged behind changes in dwelling habits and economic realities. 1 *American Law of Property* (1952), § 3.78, p. 347. Exceptions to the broad immunity inevitably developed.

The guidelines employed to construe contracts have been modernly applied to the construction of leases.

. . . .

A covenant in a lease can arise only by necessary implication from specific language of the lease or because it is indispensable to carry into effect the purpose of the lease. In determining, under contract law, what covenants are implied, the object which the parties had in view and intended to be accomplished, is of primary importance. The subject matter and circumstances of the letting give at least as clear a clue to the natural intentions of the parties as do the written words. It is of course not the province of the court to make a new contract or to supply any material stipulations or conditions which contravene the agreements of the parties. Terms are to be implied not because

> they are just or reasonable, but rather for the reason that the parties must have intended them and have only failed to express them . . . or because they are necessary to give business efficacy to the contract as written, or to give the contract the effect which the parties, as fair and reasonable men, presumably would have agreed on if, having in mind the possibility of the situation which has arisen, they contracted expressly in reference thereto. See 12 Am. Jur., Contracts, sec. 239; 14 Am. Jur., Covenants, Conditions and Restrictions, sec. 14.

William Berland Realty Co. v. Hahne & Co., 26 N.J. Super. 477, 487, 98 A.2d 124, 129 (Ch. 1953), *modified* 29 N.J. Super. 316, 102 A.2d 686 (App. Div.1954).

So here, the lease expressly described the leased premises as "4 rooms and bath, apartment" and restricted the use thereof for one purpose,—"dwelling." Patently, "the effect which the parties, as fair and reasonable men, presumably would have agreed on," was that the premises were habitable and fit for living. The very object of the letting was to furnish the defendant with quarters suitable for living purposes. This is what the landlord at least impliedly (if not expressly) represented he had available and what the tenant was seeking. In a modern setting, the landlord should, in residential letting, be held to an implied covenant against latent defects, which is another manner of saying, habitability and livability fitness. See *Hyland v. Parkside Investment Co., Inc.*, 10 N.J.Misc. 1148, 162 A. 521 (Sup. Ct.1932). It is a mere matter of semantics whether we designate this covenant one "to repair" or "of habitability and livability fitness." Actually it is a covenant that at the inception of the lease, there are no latent defects in facilities vital to the use of the premises for residential purposes because of faulty original construction or deterioration from age or normal usage. And further it is a covenant that these facilities will remain in usable condition during the entire term of the lease. In performance of this covenant the landlord is required to maintain those facilities in a condition which renders the property livable.

It is eminently fair and just to charge a landlord with the duty of warranting that a building or part thereof rented for residential purposes is fit for that purpose at the inception of the term and will remain so during the entire term. Of course, ancillary to such understanding it must be implied that he has further agreed to repair damage to vital facilities caused by ordinary wear and tear during said term. Where damage has been caused maliciously or by abnormal or unusual use, the tenant is conversely liable for repair. The nature of vital facilities and the extent and type of maintenance and repair required is limited and governed by the type of property rented and the amount of rent reserved. Failure to so maintain the property would constitute a constructive eviction.

It becomes necessary to consider the respective rights and duties which accompany such an implied covenant. We must recognize that historically, the landlord's covenant to alter or repair premises and the tenant's covenant to pay rent were generally regarded as independent covenants. The landlord's failure to perform did not entitle the tenant to make the repair and offset the cost thereof against future rent. It only gave rise to a separate cause of action for breach of covenant. *Duncan Development Co. v. Duncan Hardware, Inc.*, 34 N.J. Super, 293, 112 A.2d 274 (App. Div.1955); *Stewart v. Childs Co.*, 86 N.J.L. 648, 92 A. 392 (E. & A. 1914). This result also eventuated from the application of the law of real estate rather than of contract. The concept of mutually dependent promises was not originally applied to the ascertainment of whether covenants in leases were dependent or independent. However, presently we recognize that covenants are dependent or independent according to the intention of the parties and the good sense of the case.

. . . .

Our courts have on a case by case basis held various lease covenants and covenants to pay rent as dependent and under the guise of a constructive eviction have considered breach of the former as giving the right to the tenant to remove from the premises and terminate his obligation to pay rent.

It is of little comfort to a tenant in these days of housing shortage to accord him the right, upon a constructive eviction, to vacate the premises and end his obligation to pay rent. Rather he should be accorded the alternative remedy of terminating the cause of the constructive eviction where as here the cause is the failure to make reasonable repairs. See *Reste Realty Corporation v. Cooper*, 53 N.J. 444 (1969). This latter course of action is accompanied by the right to offset the cost of such repairs as are reasonable in the light of the value of the leasehold against the rent. His pursuit of the latter form of relief should of course be circumscribed by the aforementioned conditions.

If, therefore, a landlord fails to make repairs and replacements of vital facilities necessary to maintain the premises in a livable condition for a period of time adequate to accomplish such repair and replacements, the tenant may cause the same to be done and deduct the cost thereof from future rents. The tenant's recourse to such self-help must be preceded by timely and adequate notice to the landlord of the faulty condition in order to accord him the opportunity to make the necessary replacement or repair. If the tenant is unable to give such notice after a reasonable attempt, he may nonetheless proceed to repair or replace. This does not mean that the tenant is relieved from the payment of rent so long as the landlord fails to repair. The tenant has only the alternative remedies of making the repairs or removing from the premises upon such a constructive eviction.

We realize that the foregoing may increase the trials and appeals in landlord and tenant dispossess cases and thus increase the burden of the judiciary. By way of warning, however, it should be noted that the foregoing does not constitute an invitation to obstruct the recovery of possession by a landlord legitimately entitled thereto. It is therefore suggested that if the trial of the matter is delayed the defendant may be required to deposit the full amount of unpaid rent in order to protect the landlord if he prevails. Also, an application for a stay of an order of removal on appeal should be critically analyzed and not automatically granted.

In the light of the foregoing we find it unnecessary to pass on defendant's other grounds of appeal.

Reversed and remanded for trial in accordance with the above.

For reversal and remandment: CHIEF JUSTICE WEINTRAUB and JUSTICES JACOBS, FRANCIS, PROCTOR, HALL, SCHETTINO and HANEMAN—7.

For affirmance: None.

[c]   Explanatory Notes

[*i*]   *Procedure.* The court pulled a neat little trick to permit the appeal. Whether rent was in default raised questions about both jurisdiction and the merits. "Whatever," the court wrote, "'jurisdiction' means in other settings, here it uniquely connotes the existence of one of the factual situations delineated in N.J. STAT. ANN. § 2A:18-53. It follows that a finding, by the judge, that there is a default as alleged by the landlord, does not dispose of the meritorious issue alone. It as well disposes of the jurisdictional issue." Since the merits and jurisdiction merged under this logic, the tenant could appeal the merits! Quick and nifty—but surely this was totally out of sync with the original purposes of the summary dispossess proceeding. The old cases worked differently. If the landlord's affidavit contained factual allegations sufficient to fulfill the requirements of N.J. STAT. ANN. § 2A:18-53, then jurisdiction existed and appeals were precluded. It mattered not whether the allegations were true. If the landlord wrongly pursued a summary action, the tenant had a tort action for damages caused by the use of the process under N.J. STAT. ANN. § 2A:18-59. The *Marini* court, by merging jurisdictional *allegations* and *proof* of the merits, ignored the difference between the burden of *pleading* facts sufficient to obtain jurisdiction and the burden of *proving* facts sufficient to win a case.

[*ii*]   *Substance.* Once the court found that it could entertain the appeal, it performed a second major reconstruction of the meaning of N.J. STAT. ANN. § 2A:18-53 by holding that a default in the payment of rent occurred only if the rent was owing. Once the statute was construed this way, the court was free to re-run the reasoning of *Reste*, imply a warranty, and find in favor of the tenant. By doing so, the court not only altered the old nineteenth-century notion that the conveyance of land for a price was a separate contract from the obligation to make repairs, it also moved the merged issues into summary dispossess court where they had never been before.

[*iii*]   *Use of Legislative History.* Use of the old history to criticize the drastic alterations in the original meaning of the summary dispossess statute made in *Marini* is not necessarily a fair way to analyze the opinion. Though the court made mincemeat of the original legislative intent, the continued summary dispossession of tenants without the pretense of a hearing on issues of concern to the defendants had become a major source of urban discontent. The failure of the legislature to respond to that discontent virtually invited a judicial corrective. The interplay between legislative intent (assuming it can be discovered), the passage of time, and the growth of perceptions that the original meaning was no longer appropriate, raised interesting questions about the authority of legislative and judicial bodies. On the one hand, a supporter of legislative authority would argue that the courts are without power to alter original understandings, no matter how outdated. While legislatures are sometimes slow to react, we must accept the negative qualities of legislative governance if democratic procedures are to survive. On the other hand, a supporter of judicial authority would argue that legislative intent is relevant only so long as

the original meaning may rationally be applied to a social setting, that changes in culture may render original legislative meanings irrelevant, and that in such cases the courts must be free to create new meanings. Have you a favorite side? Will you always pick the same side in the debate or will your answer vary depending on the issue?

[*iv*]   *Remedy.* In *Marini,* the court stated that the ability of a tenant to raise defenses in landlord-tenant court "does not mean that the tenant is relieved from the payment of rent so long as the landlord fails to repair. The tenant has only the alternative remedies of making the repairs or removing from the premises upon such a constructive eviction." This narrow statement of remedial alternatives was somewhat surprising in light of the drastic surgery the court performed on the summary dispossess statute and earlier statements in the opinion that all equitable defenses were available in landlord-tenant court. It caused some consternation among the tenants' bar. If removal or repair-and-deduct were the only possible remedies, tenants living in places requiring substantial repairs would be without relief absent their willingness to take enormous monetary risks. The tenants' bar was trying to move the court toward a remedy which would permit tenants to raise defenses in landlord-tenant court without taking any financial risks and without having to move to other living quarters.

[*v*]   *Removal.* As mentioned in the problem notes just before *Marini,* and in the court's opinion, N.J. STAT. ANN. § 2A:18-60 provides for the removal of actions deemed "of sufficient importance" from landlord-tenant court to the Superior Court for trial as a regular civil matter. Before *Marini* was decided, tenant lawyers were unsure what the New Jersey Supreme Court would do with a case challenging the limitations on appeals and tenant defenses in the summary dispossess process. The removal provision provided an alternative method for attempting to obtain appellate review of implied warranty issues. While *Marini* was working its way up the appellate ladder,[81] tenants raising implied warranty defenses in summary dispossess actions were testing the meaning of N.J. STAT. ANN. § 2A:18-60 in *Academy Spires v. Jones,* 108 N.J. Super. 395, 261 A.2d 413 (1970). They requested that their possession actions be removed. The request was denied, *but* the denial came on the ground that landlord-tenant court *did* have jurisdiction to hear habitability defenses related to the rent alleged to be in default! The cases went back to the landlord-tenant court for trial just after *Marini* was decided. The results of that trial are reported in the next opinion in the text.

[d]   Problem Notes

[*i*]   *Rent Deposits.* At the end of the *Marini* opinion, the court noted that if a dispossess trial was likely to be delayed by the use of the new tenant defense they had just created, the tenant could be required to deposit into the court the "full amount of the unpaid rent in order to protect the landlord if he prevails." The court did not discuss this procedure at length in its opinion, but aren't there some serious problems with its use? For example, the summary dispossess action, at least in New Jersey, may be used only to regain possession. Claims for rent may not be joined with the action. If the landlord-tenant court does not have jurisdiction to order the payment of monetary damages, then how can they order the tenant to deposit rent in court to safeguard the landlord's monetary interests? In fact, was not this little "aside" in the

---

[81] Note that the New Jersey Supreme Court certified the case on its own motion while it was pending in the appellate division. This procedure is used only when there is a need for speed and the case is deemed important. It was another sign that the court wished to make some changes in the day-to-day operation of landlord-tenant courts.

opinion an even greater theoretical stretch of the summary dispossess statutes than opening the court to tenant defenses?

Furthermore, even if the court can find a basis for arguing that rent ought to be deposited with the court, why should the full amount of the rent be deposited? If the tenant is likely to prevail on her repair and deduct defense, then requiring her to deposit the full rent makes her pay rent twice, at least for a period of time, once for the repairs and once to the court. Why not make a preliminary inquiry to see if the tenant's defense is a strong one and then reduce the amount of rent deposited to reflect the likelihood that the tenant will ultimately prevail in the case? As a practical matter, should tenants prefer to deposit their rents in court? If they spend the money and lose their case, they will be evicted and open to a fairly large breach of contract action. Do tenant lawyers have an obligation to urge their clients to make rent deposits? Should an attorney urge a deposit even if the client insists that they prefer to move rather than pay? How much of a case's litigation strategy is or should be controlled by the client?

[ii] **Waiver.** At one point the *Marini* court noted that "the lease contains no express covenant to repair, [so] we are obliged to determine whether there arises an implied covenant . . . which would require the landlord to make repairs." Suppose the lease contained express covenants requiring the tenant to make repairs and to return the premises to the landlord in the same condition in which it was leased. Would the *Marini* case have come out any differently? What if the lease contained a clause specifically stating that the tenant waived all rights provided by *Marini v. Ireland*? Would such a clause be enforceable?

[iii] **Waiver and Contract Principles.** It is probably fair to say that the *Marini* implied warranty of habitability may not be waived, at least by a residential tenant. Most other rules found in landlord-tenant law, as well as property law generally, operate only if the parties do nothing to change them. If the warranty may not be waived, then can it really be a contract principle? Since it has the connotation of "right" attached to it as soon as a tenant walks into an apartment, doesn't it take on some of the characteristics of a conveyed property interest? Or is it really a tort concept, one in which landlords owe a certain duty of care to tenants which, if broken, may require payment of damages for diminution in value of property or for personal injury? *Compare Humber v. Morton*, p. 812 below, on new home sale warranties.

[iv] **Commercial Tenants.** Would *Marini* have provided any benefit to the tenant in *Reste Realty v. Cooper*? Suppose that Cooper did not move out of the store, but hired a hydrological engineer to investigate the situation and, in accordance with the recommendations of the engineer, hired a water proofing contractor to make repairs. Assume that the total bill for the engineer and the repairs was $4,000. If Cooper then declined to pay rent until the $4,000 was made up, could a summary dispossess court evict her? Consider the following issues:

(a) Does *Marini* permit the use of repair and deduct for such large repairs?

(b) May Cooper repair areas outside of the area leased in order to obtain a dry interior? Remember that the *Reste* court noted that since the areas where repairs were needed were outside of the leasehold area, Cooper could not be held responsible for maintaining them.

(c) May a commercial tenant like Cooper have access to a *Marini* defense in summary dispossess court? Or is the defense confined to residential tenants?

(d) Would the outcome of the summary dispossess action in this commercial case vary depending upon whether the landlord's promise to repair was express or implied? If you do not think commercial tenants may have access to an implied warranty, then Cooper surely loses. But what about an express covenant? Does a contract theory, rather than a conveyance theory, suggest that all available contractual remedies ought to be raisable in the same forum?

The general issue of application of the implied warranty to commercial tenancies was left open by the New Jersey Supreme Court in 1971. *Kruvant v. Sunrise Market, Inc.,* 58 N.J. 452, 279 A.2d 104 (1971). The issue has not been revisited.

[e] Opinion of the Essex County District Court in *Academy Spires v. Brown*

Academy Spires v. Brown

Essex County, New Jersey County District Court
111 N.J. Super. 477, 268 A.2d 556 (1970)

YANOFF, J.D.C.

This controversy concerns the applicability of *Marini v. Ireland,* 56 N.J. 130, 265 A.2d 526 (1970); *Reste Realty Corp. v. Cooper,* 53 N.J. 444, 251 A.2d 268 (1969), and *Academy Spires v. Jones,* 108 N.J. Super. 395, 261 A.2d 413 (Law Div. 1970), to a multi-family dwelling in which tenant seeks an abatement in rent by reason of landlord's failure to supply services.

Landlord instituted a dispossess proceeding under N.J.S.A. 2A:18-53(b) for nonpayment of rent at the rate of $163.17, of which $156.17 is for the apartment and $7.00 for parking, for the months of December 1969 to March 1970, inclusive, plus a balance of $28.70 for the month of November 1969. Tenant deliberately withheld payment for three months because of alleged failure on the part of landlord to supply services, and denied that any additional rent was unpaid. I find as a fact that the rent for four months has not been paid, and that there is no balance due for November 1969.

Tenant asserts that the rental rate is $135 for the apartment, not $156.17. Landlord's position with relation thereto is that the $156.17 figure is the approved F.H.A. rental for the five-room apartment in question, and I have no reason to question this fact. The evidence shows, however, that the agreement between tenant and landlord's superintendent was that the apartment would rent for $135 per month. The approved F.H.A. amount is merely the maximum permitted rental and the tenant is not bound thereby. 12 U.S.C.A. § 1747c.

Tenant did not move. However, I take judicial notice that there is a great shortage of housing accommodations in Essex County. Evidence Rule 9(1). Therefore, it would be unreasonable to require tenant to move as a prerequisite to abatement of rent. *Marini, supra.*

The apartment in question is on the ninth floor of a complex housing 400 tenants, with a large parking area.

Tenant's defenses fall into two categories: first, that landlord has failed to provide electric illumination in compliance with a Newark ordinance, for the parking lot, by reason of which the agreement for parking lot fee is illegal and unenforceable; and second, invoking *Marini, supra,* that landlord has failed, after notice, to supply essential services, rendering the premises uninhabitable, at least in part, entitling tenant to diminution in rent.

The first problem is determined easily. Factually, there is no evidence that landlord has failed to meet the standards set by section 7:424.6 of the Newark Building Code. Legally, the illegality specified affects only peripheral aspects of landlord's performance in supplying parking space.

This is not a case where the agreement was made for the purpose of violating a statutory prohibition, as in *Brooks v. Cooper*, 50 N.J. Eq. 761, 26 A. 978 (E. & A. 1893). Nor is it a case where a housing code explicitly prohibited rental of premises in violation of the code, as in *Brown v. Southall Realty Co.*, 237 A.2d 834 (D.C. App. 1968), or where a zoning ordinance prohibited the use of the premises for which it was leased . . . . Rather, the facts are that tenant could and did use the parking area, despite the code violation, if any. Indeed, the precise area allotted to tenant was probably well lighted. A more appropriate analogy is *Associated Realities Corp. v. Million Dollar Pier Operating Co.*, 6 N.J. Super. 369, 71 A.2d 545 (App. Div. 1950), in which the lease required tenant to use the premises seven days a week in violation of a "Sunday" law, and it was held that the fact that tenant could operate the premises six days a week overcame the defense of illegality. Accord: *Stern Holding Co. v. O'Connor*, 119 N.J.L. 291, 196 A. 432 (Sup. Ct. 1938). The illegality here was slight; tenant had already gotten the benefit of the parking area, and denial of recovery would amount to forfeiture. In such case landlord should not be denied its price.

Whether *Marini* is authority for tenant's position is more troublesome . . . . The Supreme Court ruled:

1. Tenant could raise the issue of diminution in amount of rent due by reason of landlord's failure to supply services in a dispossess proceeding.

2. A covenant that the premises "were habitable and fit for living" was implied because "indispensable to carry into effect the purpose of the lease". . ..

3. Tenant's covenant to pay rent and landlord's covenant of habitability were not necessarily independent, and could be construed as dependent, "according to the intention of the parties and the good sense of the case" . . . in the context of a dispossess case. It thus followed the logic of *Reste Realty Corp. v. Cooper*, 53 N.J. 444, 251 A.2d 268 (1969), where contract concepts of dependency of obligation and failure of consideration were applied in a case in which tenant had been forced to vacate the premises by landlord's failure to perform an implied covenant of habitability.

In my judgment, these basic principles control this case.

Although there is no written agreement, there was an agreement under which the premises were rented, in which the covenant of habitability was implied.

Tenant asserts this was broken because landlord failed to supply heat and water service to a ninth-story apartment; the incinerator did not function, impairing garbage disposal; the hot water supply failed; water leaked into the bathroom; there were defects in venetian blinds; the plaster in the walls was cracked, and the apartment was unpainted. Some of these clearly go to bare living requirements. In a modern society one cannot be expected to live in a multi-storied apartment building without heat, hot water, garbage disposal or elevator service. Failure to supply such things is a breach of the implied covenant of habitability. Malfunction of venetian blinds, water leaks, wall cracks, lack of painting, at least of the magnitude presented here, go to what may be called "amenities." Living with lack of painting, water leaks and defective venetian blinds may be unpleasant, aesthetically unsatisfying, but does not come within the category of uninhabitability. Such things will not be considered in diminution of the rent.

It is argued that *Marini* is restricted to its facts, and is applicable only when tenant has made the repairs; that tenant's choice is to repair or move out. The court's language in *Marini* . . . , however, must be considered in the light of the facts before the court in *Marini*. On those facts the court granted relief to the tenant. To conclude that on other facts coming within the broad principles enunciated, not only in *Marini* but in *Reste*, the tenant may not have relief, would be to place an emphasis on form, technicality and fiction which has long been foreign to this State.

. . . .

There was conflicting evidence on the question of notice of defect to landlord, but I find this fact in favor of tenant. The superintendent admitted knowledge of nonfunction of heating system, hot water, elevator service and incinerator. The only issue as to these was how long the deficiency existed.

Was the tenant required to make the repairs to this 400-unit complex as a prerequisite to availability of the relief given by *Marini*? If the answer to that question is in the affirmative, *Marini* has no meaning to tenants in multi-family dwellings who need the relief most. Obviously, few such tenants have the means to lay out the capital, and if they do, why should they repair someone else's real estate on the chance of a reduction in rent? It is hard to believe that the Supreme Court intended such a result.

. . . .

The most difficult aspect of this case is determination of the amount of abatement to which tenant is entitled. No expert testimony was produced to show the fair value of the premises without the services which landlord was required to supply. Tenant urges that this be done on a finding of fact that there has been a percentage reduction in use which entitles tenant to a corresponding abatement in rent. There is almost a complete absence of authority on the subject. The Model Residential Landlord-Tenant Code (Tent. Draft 1969), American Bar Foundation, § 2-207(1) (b), would entitle the tenant to withhold one-fourth of the rent accrued during any period when hot water is not supplied. Section 2-207(2) (b) would allow the tenant to procure substitute housing for as long as heat or water is not supplied (between October 1 and May 1), during which time the rent shall abate and the landlord shall be liable for any additional expense incurred by the tenant, up to one-half the amount of the abated rent. In *Charles E. Burt, Inc. v. Seven Grand Corp.*, 340 Mass. 124, 163 N.E.2d 4 (Sup. Jud. Ct. 1959), the court indicated that if the tenant remained in possession until successful disposition of the action, his rent liability would be limited to the difference between the lease-fixed rent and the reasonable rental value of the premises in their defective condition. *Academy Spires v. Jones, supra*, sets forth the same theory.

These approaches are compatible with tenant's position. It is not inconsistent with rules generally applicable in determining damages.

. . . .

Triers of fact daily translate personal injuries into money damages with relatively slight guidelines. Profits lost by reason of breach of contract may be recovered if there are any criteria by which probable profits can be estimated with reasonable certainty.

. . . .

The percentage-diminution approach advocated by tenant seems likely to produce results sufficiently accurate to be compatible with rules as to proof of damages set forth above. I am dubious that use of expert testimony could add to either accuracy or certainty. Certainly, if tenant were required to bear the cost of producing an expert witness, the effectiveness of the relief afforded by *Marini* would be diminished. I therefore accept the percentage abatement theory advocated by tenant.

There is a wide disparity between tenant and landlord's testimony as to the extent of diminution of service, but landlord admits that heat, hot water, elevator service and incinerator use failed at various times during the period December 1969 to March 1970, and that repairs were made from time to time. Had landlord produced records of repair bills, more precise determination of the periods during which service failed might have been possible. Tenant testified that in the child's bedroom there was no heat during the entire period; that complaint was made to the superintendent without avail, and that the child slept in the living room by reason thereof. He testified that there was no hot water for substantial periods in November, December and March, as the result of which water was heated on the stove for bathing; that the living room lacked heat in November and December; that two out of three elevators failed to function in November, December and two weeks in March, and that the incinerator was defective throughout the period.

The superintendent denied that the breakdowns were for such extended periods. He said that the heating system never broke down for more than six-hour periods; that a service repaired the elevators promptly; that the incinerator broke down for a day to a day and one-half in November, and two weeks in December, during which garbage cans were used. He attributed much of the difficulty with the incinerator to vandalism.

I am convinced that tenant exaggerated, and that the superintendent testified from ignorance. I find as a fact that there was a breach of the covenant of habitability, and that the diminution in rent of 25% is a fair amount. There will therefore be a judgment that tenant is indebted to landlord for rent in the amount of $433. If that amount is not paid within three days, a warrant for possession will issue. No costs.

[f] Explanatory Notes

[i] **Marini** *Extended—Withheld Rent as Due, Unpaid and Owing.* In *Marini*, the tenant paid all the rent except the small amount it had taken to make the plumbing repair. But in *Brown*, the tenant withheld *all* rent for four months. Under those circumstances, was there any rational basis for arguing that the tenant had not defaulted on at least *some* of the rent? Picture two situations, one like *Brown* and the other involving a tenant who sent in her rent check less $10 along with a note saying she was angry at the landlord and had therefore kept some of the rent. For purposes of establishing jurisdiction, aren't both cases the same? In both cases, didn't the landlord-tenant court clearly have jurisdiction? And if the court had jurisdiction, would not the tenant be precluded from appealing? Arguably *Marini* takes care of the problem by its holding that rent must be "owing." Figuring out how much is owing may be just as much a "jurisdictional" question as any other rent issue.

[ii] *Illegality as a Way Out of the Jurisdictional Morass.* One way out of the jurisdictional morass was to argue that none of the rent was due. The tenants argued that way, but only as to the parking lot! The court briefly reviewed a series of illegality cases, including a Washington, D.C. case, *Brown v. Southall Realty*, 237 A.2d 834 (D.C. App. 1968), and a New Jersey case, *Stern Holding Co. v. O'Connor*, 119 N.J.L. 291, 196 A. 432 (1938).

Illegality never became a major issue in New Jersey. One of the reasons may have been the experience other jurisdictions had with the defense. For example, in Washington, D.C., a local ordinance made it illegal for a tenant to occupy an apartment that had health and safety code violations. In *Brown v. Southall Realty Co.*, 237 A.2d 834 (D.C. App. 1968), a tenant prevailed on a defense that it was unlawful to collect rent for a violation-riddled housing unit. In addition, the tenant was allowed to retain possession! Did this mean that the landlord was saddled with a non-paying tenant? Tenant lawyers were given some hope that such a dream might actually come true. The year after *Southall* was decided, another illegality case went in favor of the tenant. *Diamond Housing Corp. v. Robinson*, 257 A.2d 492 (D.C. App. 1969). Eighteen months after that action was first brought to landlord-tenant court, but only two months after its resolution on appeal, the landlord served the month-to-month tenant with a notice to quit. The trial court's judgment for Diamond Housing was reversed on appeal on the grounds that the landlord's attempt to terminate the tenancy was an unlawful retaliation against a tenant seeking legal redress.[82] *Robinson v. Diamond Housing Corp.* 150 U.S. App. D.C. 17, 463 F.2d 853 (1972). The court decided that a presumption of retaliation arose where an unexplained attempt to evict followed a successful tenant defense in landlord-tenant court and that a stated desire to take the housing unit off the market did not rebut the presumption.

Was the landlord then stuck with a tenant without any ability to collect rent? Not quite. Other cases indicated that the landlord could recover the equitable value of the tenant's possession. *See, e.g., Davis, Inc. v. Slade*, 271 A.2d 412 (D.C. App. 1970). Thus, a tenant could void a lease for a housing unit with housing code violations and could stay in possession if the value of the premises was paid to the landlord. That is a somewhat uncomfortable theoretical outcome. Why should a tenant be able to remain in a housing unit when it is illegal to rent it? Perhaps the difficulty of justifying these results led New Jersey to select another course. In addition, most jurisdictions in New Jersey did not have ordinances making it illegal to rent housing units with code violations, and landlord-tenant courts lacked jurisdiction to hear a landlord's equitable claim for money.[83]

   [*iii*]   *Rent Diminution.* Even if the tenants had prevailed on their parking lot illegality theory, they still had to deal with their apartment claims. (It is interesting to think about whether the parking and apartment leases were separate contracts with independent covenants; the arguments about them seem to have occurred separately.) The court's judgment was "that tenant is indebted to landlord for rent in the amount of $433. If that amount is not paid within three days, a warrant for possession will issue." But wasn't this clearly phrased erroneously? The judge acted as if he had the authority to issue a judgment for monetary relief. Shouldn't the judge have written something like:

   I find for the tenant on a habitability defense, and find that the actual value of the leased premises for the months in issue equals 75% of the rent called for in the lease. Since none of the rent has been paid for four months, I enter a judgment for the landlord for possession. Should the tenant pay 75% of the rent called for in the lease within the period described by N.J. STAT. ANN. § 2A:18-57, that is, three days, the landlord is enjoined from seeking issuance of the warrant for removal.

Does this rephrasing remove the problem? It does make clear that the court was keeping within its possession-only remedial limits, but doesn't it also make clear that the court had jurisdiction over the case since there was a default in the payment of some rent that was due, unpaid and owing, and that the tenant therefore had no right to appeal in an effort to claim more than a

---

[82] Retaliatory eviction is taken up at p. 692 below.

[83] In Washington, D.C., a landlord may sue for rent if the tenant is personally served with process in the case. Thus, a minor adjustment to permit equitable "rent" claims to be heard let landlords renting illegal apartments pursue rent anyway. The effect was to make the cases into rent abatement cases much like Academy Spires v. Brown.

25% abatement in rent? Or does the claim that even less rent is owing meet the jurisdictional requirement for appeal?

[iv]   **Calculation of Diminished Rent.** The *Brown* court eschewed both exact rent diminution figures like those in the Model Residential Landlord-Tenant Code and expert testimony to determine either the actual market value of the premises or the proportion of the contract rent which was allocated toward the services not provided by the landlord. There is, at least theoretically, a difference between using market value and contract rent as the starting point for analysis. If the rent called for in the lease is very high in relation to the market, then allocating unavailable services on the basis of the lease rent might leave the tenant paying more than the actual value of the premises. If market value is used, then the landlord loses all the benefit of his bargain. If the rent called for is below the market level, then the problems of landlords and tenants are inverted. In practice, the courts rarely take sophisticated testimony and almost always pull a figure somewhat magically out of the air when the time comes to give actual monetary value to the tenant's defenses. *Brown* is a perfect example of this. Despite all the rhetoric, the court simply awarded a 25% diminution without much fanfare. Expert testimony was briefly mentioned and forgotten. The mass production landlord-tenant court was in no position to be drawn into long winded testimonial battles among experts, and the largely poor tenants appearing in that forum could hardly find and pay experts to testify.

[v]   **Implied Warranty Outside of New Jersey.** By the time *Brown* was decided the implied warranty of habitability defense was in existence in a large number of states.[84] At present, virtually every state, either by statute or judicial decision has followed suit. In hindsight, the decision that was the most influential on other courts was *Javins v. First National Realty Corporation*, 138 U.S. App. D.C. 369, 428 F.2d 1071 (1970). The historical sections of that opinion, written by Judge Skelly Wright, led to its ritual citation in virtually every implied warranty case decided since. Excerpts from the opinion follow.

The common law rule absolving the lessor of all obligation to repair originated in the early Middle Ages.[30] Such a rule was perhaps well suited to an agrarian economy; the land was more important[31] than whatever small living structure was included in the leasehold, and the tenant farmer was fully capable of making repairs himself.[32] These historical facts were the

---

[84] For a review of the implied warranty cases of the era, *see* Roger Cunningham, *The New Implied and Statutory Warranties of Habitability in Residential Leases: From Contract to Status*, 16 URB. L. Ann. 3 (1979).

[30] The rule was "settled" by 1485. 3 W. Holdsworth, *A History of English Law* 122-123 (6th ed. 1934). The common law rule discussed in text originated in the even older rule prohibiting the tenant from committing waste. The writ of waste expanded as the tenant's right to possession grew stronger. Eventually, in order to protect the landowner's reversionary interest, the tenant became obligated to make repairs and liable to eviction and damages if he failed to do so.

[31] The land was so central to the original common law conception of a leasehold that rent was viewed as "issuing" from the land: "[T]he governing idea is that the land is bound to pay the rent . . . . We may almost go to the length of saying that the land pays it through [the tenant's] hand." 2 F. Pollock & F. Maitland, *The History of English Law* 131 (2d ed. 1923).

[32] Many later judicial opinions have added another justification of the old common law rule. They have invoked the time-worn cry of *caveat emptor* and argued that a lessee has the opportunity to inspect the premises. On the basis of his inspection, the tenant must then take the premises "as is," according to this reasoning. As an historical matter, the opportunity to inspect was not thought important when the rule was first devised. *See* Note 30 *supra*.

basis on which the common law constructed its rule; they also provided the necessary prerequisites for its application.[33]

Court decisions in the late 1800s began to recognize that the factual assumptions of the common law were no longer accurate in some cases. For example, the common law, since it assumed that the land was the most important part of the leasehold, required a tenant to pay rent even if any building on the land was destroyed.[34] Faced with such a rule and the ludicrous results it produced, in 1863 the New York Court of Appeals declined to hold that an upper story tenant was obliged to continue paying rent after his apartment building burned down.[35] The court simply pointed out that the urban tenant had no interest in the land, only in the attached building.

Another line of cases created an exception to the no-repair rule for short term leases of furnished dwellings. The Massachusetts Supreme Judicial Court, a court not known for its willingness to depart from the common law, supported this exception, pointing out:

> . . . [A] different rule should apply to one who hires a furnished room, or a furnished house, for a few days, or a few weeks or months. Its fitness for immediate use of a particular kind, as indicated by its appointments, is a far more important element entering into the contract than when there is a mere lease of real estate. One who lets for a short term a house provided with all furnishings and appointments for immediate residence may be supposed to contract in reference to a well-understood purpose of the hirer to use it as a habitation . . . . It would be unreasonable to hold, under such circumstances, that the landlord does not impliedly agree that what he is letting is a house suitable for occupation in its condition at the time . . . ."[37]

These as well as other similar cases[38] demonstrate that some courts began some time ago to question the common law's assumptions that the land was the most important feature of a leasehold and that the tenant could feasibly make any necessary repairs himself. Where those assumptions no longer reflect contemporary housing patterns, the courts have created exceptions to the general rule that landlords have no duty to keep their premises in repair.

It is overdue for courts to admit that these assumptions are no longer true with regard to all urban housing. Today's urban[39] tenants, the vast majority of whom live in multiple dwelling

---

[33] Even the old common law courts responded with a different rule for a landlord-tenant relationship which did not conform to the model of the usual agrarian lease. Much more substantial obligations were placed upon the keepers of inns (the only multiple dwelling houses known to the common law). Their guests were interested solely in shelter and could not be expected to make their own repairs. "The modern apartment dweller more closely resembles the guest in an inn than he resembles an agrarian tenant, but the law has not generally recognized the similarity." J. Levi, P. Hablutzel, L. Rosenberg & J. White, *Model Residential Landlord-Tenant Code* 6-7 (Tent. Draft 1969).

[34] *Paradine v. Jane, Aleyn* 26, 82 Eng. Rep. 897 (K.B. 1947); 1 *American Law of Property, supra* Note 11, § 3.103.

[35] *Graves v. Berdan*, 26 N.Y. 498 (1863).

[37] *Ingalls v. Hobbs*, 156 Mass. 348, 31 N.E. 286 (1892).

[38] The cases developing the doctrines of "quiet enjoyment" and "constructive eviction" are the most important. *See* 2 R. Powell, [Real Property], ¶ 225[3]. *See also Gladden v. Walker & Dunlop*, 83 U.S. App. D.C. 224, 168 F.2d 321 (1948) (landlord has duty to maintain portions of apartment "under his control" including plumbing, heating and electrical systems); *J.D. Young Corp. v. McClintic*, Tex. Civ. App., 26 S.W.2d 460 (1930) (implied covenant of fitness in lease of building under construction); *Steefel v. Rothschild*, 179 N.Y. 273, 72 N.E. 112 (1904) (duty to disclose latent defects).

[39] In 1968 more than two thirds of America's people lived in the 228 largest metropolitan areas. Only 5.2% lived on farms. *The World Almanac* 1970 at 251 (L. Long ed.). More than 98% of all housing starts in 1968 were non-farm. *Id.* at 313.

houses, are interested, not in the land, but solely in "a house suitable for occupation." Furthermore, today's city dweller usually has a single, specialized skill unrelated to maintenance work; he is unable to make repairs like the "jack-of-all-trades" farmer who was the common law's model of the lessee. Further, unlike his agrarian predecessor who often remained on one piece of land for his entire life, urban tenants today are more mobile than ever before. A tenant's tenure in a specific apartment will often not be sufficient to justify efforts at repairs. In addition, the increasing complexity of today's dwellings renders them much more difficult to repair than the structures of earlier times. In a multiple dwelling repair may require access to equipment and areas in the control of the landlord. Low and middle income tenants, even if they were interested in making repairs, would be unable to obtain any financing for major repairs since they have no long-term interest in the property.

[g] Problem Notes: What's Impliedly Warranted?

[i] **Javins "Revisionist" History?** Judge Wright took the position in *Javins* that much of the archaic quality of landlord-tenant law arose because leases generally dealt with agricultural land in the last century and law never caught up with the reality of modern urban existence. To some extent, the theory was obviously wrong. Though tenant farming was common in much of the country in the nineteenth century, houses, factories, and other types of property were also frequently leased. The fact that most nineteenth-century New Jersey landlord-tenant cases involved commercial arrangements strongly suggests Wright was in error. The legal roots may have been in rural England, rather than the United States. In addition, one significant land use change, in addition to the dramatic growth of cities, occurred in this century that might have altered attitudes toward the law of leases. Tenement houses and apartment buildings became a staple of American urban existence only in this century. The stacking of people created dangers, particularly from fire, and altered social expectations about the nature of housing as a marketable commodity. Assuming that Wright was wrong in writing that landlord-tenant law was a creation of agricultural commerce in the last century, why did it not become viewed as archaic before the middle of this century? Do any of the following sound reasonable as explanations:

(a) When rich people began to live in apartments in New York and other large cities in the early decades of the century, expectations of other apartment dwellers began slowly to rise. When housing conditions generally rose to a fairly high level in the 1950s, those left behind felt themselves wronged in ways not possible a century before when most people lived in less adequate housing.[85]

(b) General urban reform movements beginning at the turn of the century to improve the quality of the workplace, the cityscape and the home all came to fruition after World War II when the economy had righted itself from the Depression enough to permit the culture to afford rules previously thought luxurious.

(c) It was racial and ethnic. The political process was unable to consider regulations benefiting immigrants and minorities before World War II. It was only with the coming of the civil rights era that reform of housing law could be seriously considered.

(d) The baby boom came, placed enormous strains on the housing market, and made habitation an issue of national concern.

---

[85] Housing quality was generally better during the era in which it became a serious political issue. *See* Edward Rabin, *The Revolution in Residential Landlord-Tenant Law Causes and Consequences*, CORNELL L. REV. 517 (1984), excerpted in RICHARD CHUSED, A PROPERTY ANTHOLOGY 171-180 (2d ed. 1997).

[*ii*] *Defining the Implied Warranty—Uniform Residential Landlord and Tenant Act.*
Defining the implied warranty has not been easy. The National Conference of Commissioners
on Uniform State Laws has taken a stab at it in the following provisions* from the Uniform
Residential Landlord and Tenant Act, adopted in some form in 15 states.

§ 2.104. [Landlord to Maintain Premises]

(a) A landlord shall

(1) comply with the requirements of applicable building and housing codes materially
affecting health and safety;

(2) make all repairs and do whatever is necessary to put and keep the premises in a fit
and habitable condition;

(3) keep all common areas of the premises in a clean and safe condition;

(4) maintain in good and safe working order and condition all electrical, plumbing,
sanitary, heating, ventilating, air-conditioning, and other facilities and appliances, including
elevators, supplied or required to be supplied by him;

(5) provide and maintain appropriate receptacles and conveniences for the removal of
ashes, garbage, rubbish, and other waste incidental to the occupancy of the dwelling unit
and arrange for their removal; and

(6) supply running water and reasonable amounts of hot water at all times and reasonable
heat [between [October 1] and [May 1]] except where the building that includes the dwelling
unit is not required by law to be equipped for that purpose, or the dwelling unit is so
constructed that heat or hot water is generated by an installation within the exclusive control
of the tenant and supplied by a direct public utility connection.

(b) If the duty imposed by paragraph (1) of subsection (a) is greater than any duty imposed
by any other paragraph of that subsection, the landlord's duty shall be determined by reference
to paragraph (1) of subsection (a).

(c) The landlord and tenant of a single family residence may agree in writing that the tenant
perform the landlord's duties specified in paragraphs (5) and (6) of subsection (a) and also
specified repairs, maintenance tasks, alterations, and remodeling, but only if the transaction
is entered into in good faith and not for the purpose of evading the obligations of the landlord.

(d) The landlord and tenant of any dwelling unit other than a single family residence may
agree that the tenant is to perform specified repairs, maintenance tasks, alterations, or
remodeling only if

(1) the agreement of the parties is entered into in good faith and not for the purpose of
evading the obligations of the landlord and is set forth in a separate writing signed by the
parties and supported by adequate consideration;

(2) the work is not necessary to cure noncompliance with subsection (a)(1) of this section;
and

(3) the agreement does not diminish or affect the obligation of the landlord to other tenants
in the premises.

(e) The landlord may not treat performance of the separate agreement described in subsection
(d) as a condition to any obligation or performance of any rental agreement.

---

* Reprinted with the permission of the National Conference of Commissioners on Uniform State Laws.

§ 4.101. [Noncompliance by the Landlord—In General]

(a) Except as provided in this Act, if there is a material noncompliance by the landlord with the rental agreement or a noncompliance with Section 2.104 materially affecting health and safety, the tenant may deliver a written notice to the landlord specifying the acts and omissions constituting the breach and that the rental agreement will terminate upon a date not less than [30] days after receipt of the notice if the breach is not remedied in [14] days, and the rental agreement shall terminate as provided in the notice subject to the following:

(1) If the breach is remedial by repairs, the payment of damages or otherwise and the landlord adequately remedies the breach before the date specified in the notice, the rental agreement shall not terminate by reason of the breach.

(2) If substantially the same act or omission which constituted a prior noncompliance of which notice was given recurs within [6] months, the tenant may terminate the rental agreement upon at least [14 days'] written notice specifying the breach and the date of termination of the rental agreement.

(3) The tenant may not terminate for a condition caused by the deliberate or negligent act or omission of the tenant, a member of his family, or other person on the premises with his consent.

(b) Except as provided in this Act, the tenant may recover actual damages and obtain injunctive relief for any noncompliance by the landlord with the rental agreement or Section 2.104. If the landlord's noncompliance is willful the tenant may recover reasonable attorney's fees.

(c) The remedy provided in subsection (b) is in addition to any right of the tenant arising under Section 4.101(a).

(d) If the rental agreement is terminated, the landlord shall return all security recoverable by the tenant under Section 2.101 and all prepaid rent.

§ 4.105. [Landlord's Noncompliance as Defense to Action for Possession or Rent]

(a) In an action for possession based upon nonpayment of the rent or in an action for rent when the tenant is in possession, the tenant may [counterclaim] for any amount he may recover under the rental agreement or this Act. In that event the court from time to time may order the tenant to pay into court all or part of the rent accrued and thereafter accruing, and shall determine the amount due to each party. The party to whom a net amount is owed shall be paid first from the money paid into court, and the balance by the other party. If no rent remains due after application of this section, judgment shall be entered for the tenant in the action for possession. If the defense or counterclaim by the tenant is without merit and is not raised in good faith, the landlord may recover reasonable attorney's fees.

(b) In an action for rent when the tenant is not in possession, he may [counterclaim] as provided in subsection (a) but is not required to pay any rent into court.

Would *Brown* have been decided the same way if New Jersey had adopted the Uniform Residential Landlord and Tenant Act? How would the parking lot issue have been handled? What about the plaster ceiling cracks and lack of fresh paint?

[*iii*] **Berzito v. Gambino.** The lack of guidance on the scope of the implied warranty eventually became an issue before the New Jersey Supreme Court. In *Berzito v. Gambino*, 63

N.J. 460, 308 A.2d 17 (1973), a tenant sued her landlord for damages arising out of an express contract to make repairs in an apartment. The tenant moved in during September, 1968, under an oral lease calling for a rent of $35 per week. When she moved in, the landlord promised to make the place, which was in deplorable condition, "livable."[86] In June, 1970, the landlord brought a summary dispossess action for non-payment of rent. The tenant's implied warranty defense was successful; the judge abated the rent to $75 per month (about half the contract rent) for the period February 23, 1970, the first week the tenant did not pay rent, through June, 1970. The tenant paid this reduced rent to avoid eviction, but did not pay any more rent from then until November 14, 1970, when she moved out. The tenant then filed a contract action seeking to recover the difference between the contract rent (which she had paid from September, 1968, through February 23, 1970) and $75 for the period of time prior to that covered by the summary dispossess proceeding. The landlord filed a counterclaim for the rent remitted by the summary dispossess court. At trial the tenant obtained a judgment for $973.75 and the counterclaim was dismissed.[87]

When the case came before the New Jersey Supreme Court, three sets of issues were presented. First, the court had to decide whether a tenant who had already paid rent could sue affirmatively in contract for breach of an express promise to repair. Second, if the tenant could sue in contract, the impact of the tenant's successful habitability defense in the summary dispossess case on the contract proceeding had to be resolved. Finally, if the tenant had a cause of action, the court had to decide upon the appropriate theory to use for determining the amount of damages.

Any notion that *Marini* created a basis only for repair-and-deduct relief in summary dispossess proceedings was dissipated. The court held:

[T]he covenant on the part of the tenant to pay rent, and the covenant—whether express or implied—on the part of a landlord to maintain the demised premises in a habitable condition are for all purposes mutually dependent. Accordingly in an action by a landlord for unpaid rent a tenant may plead, by way of defense and set off, a breach by the landlord of his continuing obligation to maintain an adequate standard of habitability . . . .

Furthermore a tenant may initiate an action against his landlord to recover either part or all of a deposit paid upon the execution and delivery of the lease or part or all of the rent thereafter paid during the term, where he alleges that the lessor has broken his covenant to maintain the premises in a habitable condition.

The prior summary dispossess action had a very limited impact on the outcome of the case. As to the months in question in that proceeding, neither party could dispute the outcome. Courts rarely permit parties to reopen judgments once they become final. That meant that the landlord's counterclaim had to be dismissed. But could the tenant use the finding made in the dispossess proceeding that the apartment had housing code violations to her advantage in the contract case? Theoretically the answer was no. Each time period in the lease raised separate issues. Proof that violations existed in one month was not proof that they existed in another month. Thus, the plaintiff was obligated to reprove her case.[88] As a practical matter, however, the proofs were

---

[86] Testimony revealed that windows were boarded up, radiators missing, floors hole ridden, sewers overflowing, rats running, light fixtures missing, and plaster falling.

[87] The tenant paid $2380 before Feb. 23, 1970, when she should have paid only $1200 at the $75 per month rate. The landlord received a credit of $206.25 for the rent that was not paid between June and November, 1970.

[88] This is a basic outcome in all litigation involving the passage of time. Though the evidence submitted in the dispossess case was much like that in the contract case, the only facts found in the dispossess case that were important to its outcome involved the existence of defects during the months in which the tenant had not paid all the rent.

much alike in the two cases. It was not surprising, therefore, that the Supreme Court affirmed the trial court's award of damages on the basis of the same monthly value of $75 that was used in the dispossess case.

Finally, the court tried to adopt some standards for defining the implied warranty:

Not every defect or inconvenience will be deemed to constitute a breach of the covenant of habitability. The condition complained of must be such as truly to render the premises uninhabitable in the eyes of a reasonable person. In *Mease v. Fox*, 200 N.W.2d 791 (1972) the Supreme Court of Iowa considered the same question that is now before us . . . . That opinion set forth the following factors—which we here paraphrase—as meriting consideration in determining whether in fact there has been a breach of the covenant of habitability on the part of the lessor.

1. Has there been a violation of any applicable housing code or building or sanitary regulations?

2. Is the nature of the deficiency or defect such as to affect a vital facility?

3. What is its potential or actual effect upon safety and sanitation?

4. For what length of time has it persisted?

5. What is the age of the structure?

6. What is the amount of rent?

7. Can the tenant be said to have waived the defect or be estopped to complain?

8. Was the tenant in any way responsible for the defective condition?

This list is intended to be suggestive rather than exhaustive. Each case must be governed by its own facts. The result must be just and fair to the landlord as well as the tenant.

Does the *"Mease-Berzito* List" clarify the nature of the implied warranty? Apply it to *Academy Spires v. Brown.*

   [iv]   *Try Out Your Implied Warranty Theory.* Which of the following breach the implied warranty of habitability in New Jersey?

a. A cracked window pane.

b. Three missing tiles from a vinyl tile floor.

c. A sink drain that leaks an average of one pint of fluid daily, an amount easily taken care of by placing a small container under the leaking pipe.

d. Flaking (non-lead) paint and cracked walls.

e. A broken mail box.

f. A broken smoke detector in a rented house in a middle class neighborhood.[89]

g. Defective air conditioning. (Would your answer be different if the building was located in Phoenix?)

h. A broken swimming pool in a rental development charging $1000 per month for a one bedroom apartment.

---

[89] In Dowler v. Boczkowski, 148 N.J. 512, 691 A.2d 314 (1997), the New Jersey Supreme Court found that presence of a non-working smoke detector did not breach the implied warranty because the jurisdiction involved did not require smoke detectors in this sort of building. Do you agree with this result?

[v]   **Self Help and the Constitution.** Compare *Marini* with *Callen v. Sherman's, Inc.*, p. 622 above. If landlords may not use self-help remedies without a judicial hearing prior to the seizure of a tenant's goods, why may tenants use self-help remedies to make repairs before a hearing?

[vi]   **Warranties and Middle Class Housing.** In *Timber Ridge v. Dietz*, 133 N.J. Super. 577, 338 A.2d 21 (1975), Dietz rented a house in a town development. Local authorities ordered the owners to rebuild a retaining wall in the area. During the construction, runoff forced the development's swimming pool to be closed and created a muddy mess around Dietz's house. In order to get into the house, the owners had to set up boards on blocks. When the tenants withheld their rent, a summary dispossess action was filed. The court abated the rent 15% because of the mud problems, but refused to provide any relief for the closed swimming pool.

In the abstract, this result seems plausible as an implied warranty outcome. But the court also found that the tenants had an express contractual right to use of the swimming pool.[90] Given the contractually oriented contours of *Reste Realty v. Cooper*, it seems a bit strange that a court would allow an implied warranty defense to prevail in a summary dispossess action but deny the tenants the right to defend with an *express warranty*. The court concluded that the "tenants' remedy, individually or in combination with other similarly aggrieved tenants, would be best handled in a more conventional legal proceeding . . . . This determination is without prejudice to the tenants' right to seek relief in an action at law for damages, possibly in a class action or in a proceeding in equity, if appropriate." If the case had been an ejectment action, the court would have been forced to deal with the swimming pool issue. Was the actual result an appropriate effort by the judge to maintain the summary nature of landlord-tenant court proceedings? Was the tenant justified in claiming that not all the rent was owing because one of the promised amenities—the swimming pool—was not available? Should the tenant be forced to bring a second action in order to obtain relief for breach of the express promise? Would it have been procedurally better to resolve all of the Dietz's issues in one forum—landlord-tenant court—than to impose the costs of two judicial actions on both the parties and the judicial system?

At a minimum, it is fair to say that the landlord-tenant court is still a court of limited jurisdiction. Counterclaims cannot be brought and, if *Dietz* is correctly decided, there are still some issues that may not be raised in summary dispossess actions. After reading all of these New Jersey cases, do you have any feelings about how the New Jersey Supreme Court would have handled this case if it had been appealed?

[5]   A Conclusory Note on the Warranty of Habitability Cases

The debates that flourished during the era in which the warranty of habitability cases were being rendered displayed arguments from several modes of legal thought. Articles by Mary Ann Glendon and Edward Rabin provide good introduction to the issues.[91] They both argued that some of the major events of that epoch, such as the creation of legal services, the Civil Rights Movement, and a variety of other "rebellions" by people seeing themselves as oppressed in one way or another, created an historic moment in which reform was not only possible, but politically

---

[90] The brochures advertising the development promised a pool as well as other amenities. The court read the contents of the brochure into the contract.

[91] Mary Ann Glendon, *The Transformation of American Landlord Tenant Law*, 23 B.C. L. REV. 503 (1982); Edward Rabin, *The Revolution in Residential Landlord-Tenant Law: Causes and Consequences*, 69 CORNELL L. REV. 517 (1984). Both are excerpted in RICHARD CHUSED, A PROPERTY ANTHOLOGY 160-180 (2d ed. 1997).

necessary. Indeed, Rabin forced us to see how remarkable that moment must have been. For if he was right that the quality of housing occupied by all classes was *better* in 1968 than it ever had been before, the cultural forces at work in the reform movements of the time must have been quite powerful. The reforms were a product of the same forces that motivated Lyndon Johnson's Great Society programs. The heady economy of the post-World War II epoch created very high expectations among all classes that they could attain some version of the American Dream. Though the contrast between rich and poor may have been demographically smaller than in earlier times, that did not stop the plight of the poor from becoming more visible to the body politic. There was a general feeling in that epoch that uplifting the impoverished and downtrodden, both here and around the world, was a positive good.

As we noted when discussing *Goldberg v. Kelly,* p. 530 above, the courts in that historical moment sometimes took on the task of protecting the interests of the under-represented. But note well that to the extent the reforms we have been discussing were part of a Representation Reinforcement movement, there was no theoretical need to provide landlord-tenant court relief for the well-off. Express contract defenses for amenities, which would largely show up in middle and upper class housing did not have to be resolved in landlord-tenant court. Such folks can hire lawyers and use the legal system successfully. It is more difficult for the poor to go on the legal offensive. They wait until they get sued and hope that legal services attorneys can help them. For them, the reforms in landlord tenant court could have significant effect.

There certainly are other ways of characterizing the reforms. Followers of the Legal Process School, for example, might claim the reform mantle. Although they might have preferred that the New Jersey Supreme Court wait for the legislature to redo the eviction process, Glendon argued that the overall picture around the nation, rather than just in New Jersey, involved much more legislative than judicial action. Indeed, we will see in the next section of materials that after *Marini*, most major reform steps in New Jersey were actually adopted by the state legislature rather than the courts.

Some observations about more contemporary modes of legal thought might also be helpful. First, the development of the implied warranty cases provides a nice environment for exploring the determinacy of rules and the problems associated with developing theories to use in contesting strongly entrenched legal norms. The *Marini* case is a perfect example of how seemingly unassailable rules end up being contestable. Viewed this way, the Indeterminacy Principle often espoused by Critical Legal Studies adherents,[92] the idea that rules and meanings are always subject to reconstruction, is not as distressing, or even depressing, as some people make it out to be. Rather than using the idea of indeterminacy to bemoan how ephemeral law is, to castigate Critical Legal thinkers for being nihilists believing in nothing, you might prefer to rejoice in your ability to alter outcomes with intelligent lawyering. Since, for Critical Legal thinkers, an outcome cannot be justified by arguing that the "law" demands it, law is only a manifestation of power relationships in the culture and you are free to use your own aspirations as a baseline for action. In short, Critical Legal Studies can free you, can give you room, to explore and expound upon your own view of the world without fear of being automatically hemmed in by assumptions that certain rules are inalterable.

---

[92] This arm of Critical Legal thinking is much like the Realist's notion that law is a reflection of the exercise of political power. Among other things, Critical Legal thinking adds skepticism about other modes of analysis, such as close textual analysis, science and social science, that Realists often relied upon.

The reforms are also an interesting place to think about the modern Rights Movement, a form of legal discourse you will be exploring in much more detail later in the Takings cases. Landlords might claim that the implied warranty reforms interfered with their property "rights," that their investments in buildings under the pre-*Reste* rules were diminished in value, that the courts and legislatures took "their" money and gave it to tenants by changing the rules, that the whole thing was a "taking" without compensation.

On one level, the point has a certain logic to it. To whatever extent the reforms actually cause a landlord to make repairs that would not otherwise be made, there has been some reallocation of resources. It is not complete, for the value of the repairs partly redounds to the landlord's benefit. It is his building after all. But use of Rights Theory in this context creates a risk that careful thinking about how the landlord-tenant relationship ought to be structured will become more difficult. That happens in two ways. First, deploying the word "rights" to protect landlords rigidifies the property relationship. It makes change difficult if not impossible. And second, talk about landlord's rights omits the claim that tenant's may also claim property "rights." They, after all, have a lease with possessory "rights." To argue that only the landlord has "rights" is to privilege those claims at the expense of the claims of others. To argue that only tenants have rights is to do the opposite. Also note that to claim that both landlords and tenants have rights, rights which are mutually exclusive, is to establish positions with no room for discussion. The political debate freezes. To think of relationships, of the ways in which economic and political power are deployed, makes it easier to get to the important questions than does the use of "rights" vocabulary. "Rights" vocabulary may have other social and cultural benefits, particularly for groups of people who have traditionally been disadvantaged. The point, however, for you to think about is the degree to which the awarding of a "right" serves to freeze debates about reform.

[6] The Impact of Reform on Housing Quality

A great deal of discussion about inequality of bargaining position between landlords and tenants, poor housing quality and low supplies of rental housing appeared in New Jersey's implied warranty opinions. The decisions reflected an undercurrent of hope that modification of Procrustean legal rules would have a beneficial effect on the quantity and quality of rental housing. Several questions are raised by such dreams. First, have the new rules been used often enough to have an impact on the rental housing market? Second, assuming that the new defenses have produced a response in the market, did that response produce better or worse quality housing? Finally, what has happened to housing costs as a result of the reforms?

Several authors studied the usage level and impact of making tenant defenses available in landlord-tenant court. Not surprisingly, the conclusions are mixed. Marilyn Mosier & Richard Soble, in *Modern Legislation, Metropolitan Court, Minuscule Results: A Study of Detroit's Landlord-Tenant Court*, 7 U. MICH. J.L. REFORM 8 (1973), reported on a study begun two years after the Michigan legislature adopted statutes creating implied warranty defenses in actions for rent or possession. They concluded that tenants represented by counsel fared better in court than unrepresented tenants, but that less than 10% of the tenants had attorneys. While some type of court actions may be reasonably easy for *pro se* parties to handle,[93] raising habitability defenses seemed to be too complicated for the tenants routinely appearing in rent and possession actions. The general conclusions of the study were negative. Unrepresented tenants rarely raised defenses.

---

[93] *See* Project, *The Unauthorized Practice of Law and Pro Se Divorce: An Empirical Analysis*, 86 YALE L.J. 104 (1976).

Even if all appearing tenants were provided with counsel, most disputes would not have been influenced. Well over half the cases involved tenants who did not appear at court, thereby defaulting, and almost a quarter of the cases were voluntarily dismissed by landlords, probably because the rent was paid or the tenant had moved. Only about one fifth of the cases were "contested" in the sense that both sides showed up in court, but, as noted, defenses were usually not raised. The authors were skeptical that landlord-tenant court was an appropriate spot to concentrate resources for assaults on poor quality housing.[94]

Two other studies suggested that Mosier & Soble folded their tents too quickly. Allan Heskin, reporting upon his labors in *The Warranty of Habitability Debate: A California Case Study*, 66 CAL. L. REV. 37 (1978), looked not only at court files, but also at legal service office case folders. He found that the implied warranty defense was being used more often than a glance at the court files would indicate. Some cases were settled without the defense being raised in court. Other cases involved use of the defense, even though no formal answer was ever filed by the tenant. Heskin also concluded that the availability of the implied warranty was having some impact on the rate of repair of rental property, but that rents were not significantly altered by use of the defense.

Werner Hirsch, Joel Hirsch & Stephen Margolis, in *Regression Analysis of the Effects of Habitability Laws Upon Rent: An Empirical Observation on the Ackerman-Komesar Debate*, 63 CAL. L. REV. 1098 (1975),[95] like Mosier and Soble, concluded that rent levels did not rise significantly in states with habitability defenses, probably because the defenses were infrequently used. However, states with "receivership statutes" had statistically significant increases in rent levels. Receivership laws provide for judicial appointment of a party to operate a building with significant health and safety problems, and for use of rents to pay for rehabilitation work. New Jersey adopted such a statute in 1971, only one year after *Marini v. Ireland* was decided.[96] A receivership involved an entire building, not just an individual unit, and detailed judicial supervision of a landlord's financial dealings. It may be that fear of the scope and intensity of this form of action generated the rent increases found by Hirsch, Hirsch and Margolis. One might legitimately hypothesize that *widespread and successful* use of tenant defenses would also cause increases in rent.

The studies certainly suggest the difficulty of using predictions of future events as a basis for evaluating the propriety of present day actions. Perhaps it is inappropriate to measure the utility of the widely adopted implied warranty only by reference to its success in improving the quality of housing in the market. There may be other reasons, such as a sense of equity and a notion that all litigants should have a fair opportunity to present important questions to courts in which they routinely appear, which justify the results. In addition, the above discussion of

---

[94] Similar results were reported in another study, Note, *The Great Green Hope: The Implied Warranty of Habitability in Practice*, 28 STAN. L. REV. 729 (1976).

[95] The Ackerman-Komesar Debate involved a long winded discussion on the impact of a variety of land use regulatory models on housing markets. The title of the Werner Hirsch, Joel Hirsch & Stephen Margolis article was referring to the following articles: Bruce Ackerman, *Regulating Slum Housing Markets on Behalf of the Poor: Of Housing Codes, Housing Subsidies and Income Redistribution Policy*, 80 YALE L.J. 1093 (1971); Neil Komesar, *Return to Slumville: A Critique of the Ackerman Analysis of Housing Code Enforcement and the Poor*, 82 YALE L.J. 1175 (1973); Bruce Ackerman, *More on Slum Housing and Redistribution Policy: A Reply to Professor Komesar*, 82 YALE L.J. 1194 (1973). *See also* Richard Markovits, *The Distributive Impact, Allocative Efficiency, and Overall Desirability of Ideal Housing Codes: Some Theoretical Clarifications*, 89 HARV. L. REV. 1815 (1976).

[96] The receivership statute is codified at N.J. STAT. ANN. § 2A:42-85 *et seq.*

implied warranty defenses only scratches the surface of the techniques that could be used to evaluate the relationship between legal rules and market operation.

For example, George Sternlieb, in his classic studies of Newark, New Jersey,[97] argued that the problem of inner-city abandonment was not caused by widespread flight of property owners from the real estate business. Though white owners, perhaps even more of them than usual, left the urban housing market in the 1950s and 1960s, Sternlieb contended, turnover occurs in all businesses. Rather, he contended, the severity of the abandonment problem arose because of the lack of a new generation of buyers among the largely black urban dwellers willing or able to buy even at low prices. Over time, the problem escalated and multiplied. Empty houses, high taxes, high crime rates, and abandonment became a pattern. It was unlikely that habitability defenses would have much of an impact on such a cycle. Sternlieb, of course, argued that strong action was necessary to subsidize the creation of a new generation of inner city property owners. In another approach, Duncan Kennedy argued that there were some circumstances in which it was economically advantageous for landlords to "milk" the housing market before abandoning housing and that consistent enforcement of housing and building codes could reduce the attractiveness of such activity.[98]

A thread runs through virtually all of this literature—the reform of habitability rules will not by itself have much of an impact on housing markets or housing quality. More significant steps—widespread enforcement of public health and safety norms, the infusion of subsidies for below market rate housing, the routine provision of counsel to tenants appearing in landlord-tenant courts or other systematic public intervention—are necessary to improve the quality of housing for those seeking low cost housing.

§ 8.05   Lease Termination: Eviction of a Holdover Tenant and Regulation of a Landlord's Refusal to Renew

[1]   Introduction

From the opening comments in this chapter, you know that different sorts of leases terminate in different ways. Absent changes in common law rules made by statute, a term tenancy ends naturally at the conclusion of the period described in the lease. Many (and in some areas, most) residential leases do not last for a specific term. The parties agree to a periodic tenancy that automatically renews itself for another period unless one of the parties takes action to terminate the lease. Most residential termination cases involve periodic tenancies.

By the second half of the nineteenth century, termination of a periodic tenancy was regulated by quite specific rules about the nature and timing of the notice required to end the arrangement. In *Steffens v. Earl*,[99] for example, the New Jersey Supreme Court confirmed the widely held understandings that notice ending a periodic tenancy could be given for *any* reason by either party, that in cases of tenancies for periods of less than one year the notice had to be given at least one *full* period before the termination date, that for year-to-year tenancies, three months

---

[97] GEORGE STERNLIEB, THE TENEMENT LANDLORD (1969); GEORGE STERNLIEB & ROBERT BURCHELL, RESIDENTIAL ABANDONMENT: THE TENEMENT LANDLORD REVISITED (1973).

[98] Duncan Kennedy, *The Effect of the Warranty of Habitability on Low Income Housing: "Milking" and Class Violence*, 15 FLA. ST. U. L. REV. 485 (1987). This article is excerpted in RICHARD CHUSED, A PROPERTY ANTHOLOGY 180-191 (2d ed. 1997).

[99] 40 N.J.L. 128 (1878).

notice was required,[100] and that periodic tenancies could only terminate at the end of a period. Thus, for the common month-to-month tenancy, a landlord desiring to rent to another party on October 1 had to give notice *before* September 1 that the lease was to end on September 30.[101] As indicated by N.J. STAT. ANN. § 2A:18-56, the requirements as to contents of the notice were very simple. It only had to indicate that the lease was to end on a certain date.[102]

The rules were so simple that very little litigation arose over their application. Disputes over the adequacy of the notice to quit[103] or the timing of its delivery came up from time to time, but most tenants[104] simply moved or paid the new rent when they received a notice to quit. Not even the additional complexities imposed by the details of New Jersey's summary dispossess statute caused much difficulty. N.J. STAT. ANN. § 2A: 18-53(a) provides the landlord-tenant court with jurisdiction to remove a person who "holds over and continues in possession of all or any part of the demised premises after the expiration of his term, and after demand made and written notice given by the landlord or his agent, for delivery of possession thereof." The "demand . . . for delivery of possession" required by this section is different from the notice required to terminate a periodic tenancy, described in N.J. STAT. ANN. § 2A:18-56. Both must be served in order to remove a holdover tenant. In addition, N.J. STAT. ANN. § 2A:18-53(a) requires that the demand for possession be personally served, while a notice to quit may be mailed. As a rule, New Jersey landlords place both the demand for possession and the notice to quit in the same document and try to personally serve it.

The traditional rules also made it fairly easy for a landlord to raise the rent of a periodic tenant. Once the old lease was terminated by the appropriate service of a demand for possession and notice to quit, the landlord simply offered a new tenancy at the higher rent. This offer was usually joined with the demand and notice. The following document, for example, terminated a month-to-month tenancy, issued a demand for possession and offered a new month-to-month tenancy:

---

[100] The requirement for three months notice went into effect in 1840. Prior to then, six months notice was required. These various time limits are now codified in N.J. STAT. ANN. § 2A:18-56.

[101] The requirement that notice be given at least a *full* period prior to the end of the lease means that notice given on Sept. 1 would be one day late.

[102] *See, e.g.,* Bhar Realty Corp. v. Becker, 49 N.J. Super. 585, 140 A.2d 756 (1958).

[103] For example, the courts had to decide whether the notice to quit had to be personally served. In Pennsylvania Railway Co. v. L. Albert & Son, 26 N.J. Super. 508, 98 A.2d 323 (1953), use of the mails was found to be adequate. N.J. STAT. ANN. § 2A:18-56, the modern version of the common law rules on service of the notice to quit, says nothing about the method of service.

[104] Although the rules provided that either side could terminate a periodic tenancy upon giving of proper notice, landlords were more likely to take advantage of the right to terminate.

> Dear Tenant:
>
> This is to notify you that your month-to-month tenancy is terminated as of midnight on September 30, 1896. I demand that you deliver possession of the premises to me on that date.
>
> If you wish to remain in your apartment, I now offer you a new month-to-month periodic tenancy beginning October 1, 1896, at the rent of $32.50 per month. If you would like to accept this offer, you may do so by notifying me directly or by remaining in possession and paying me the new rent on October 1.
>
> > Love,
> > Landlord

The first part of this notice would terminate the old lease and demand possession. If the tenant paid the new rent, that would act as an acceptance of the new arrangements. If the tenant tendered the old rent, she could be evicted.

After World War II, serious disputes arose over the propriety of the common law termination and rent-raising rules. Tenant groups argued that it was unfair to permit a landlord to terminate a tenancy for any reason without any explanation. The first challenges to the rules arose in two somewhat different contexts. First, after World War II the federal government began to construct significant amounts of housing for use by tenants unable to afford market rate apartments. The common law termination rules began to create friction when they were used during the McCarthy Era to evict alleged Communist sympathizers or, somewhat later, to remove tenants protesting housing conditions, rent increases or other management decisions. The Constitutional limitations on state activities reviewed in earlier cases[105] provided a basis for tenants to argue that their due process rights were infringed when public housing authorities, without notification of the reasons, attempted to evict them.

In addition, month-to-month tenants in private housing who sought building inspections or protested in some other way the poor living conditions in their buildings, began to challenge the use of the common law termination rules. When landlords retaliated against such "uppity" tenants by serving them with notices to quit and demands for possession, the courts were confronted with factual settings in which it was very difficult to justify removing the tenants from their housing.

A variety of other social pressures emerged in the 1970s and 1980s that further eroded the common law termination rules. Concern over eviction of the elderly, conversion of rental units to condominiums, high rents and rent controls, and housing shortages, among other matters, have led some states, including New Jersey, to enact statutes that virtually eliminate the right of a landlord to evict a periodic tenant or decline to renew the possessory rights of a term tenant without just cause.

---

[105] Shelley v. Kraemer, p. 445 above; Evans v. Abney, p. 361 above; Kirchberg v. Feenstra, p. 179 above; Goldberg v. Kelley, p. 530 above.

[2]   The Opening Wedge: Public Housing and Political Controversy

[a]   Background to *Kutcher v. Housing Authority*

During the 1950s, the federal government was involved in an extensive effort to control or eliminate the Communist Party of the United States and those allegedly sympathizing with it. Many people believed that the Party had extensive influence in American affairs and that the continued existence of the nation depended on stripping the Party, and those who might sympathize with its aims, of influence. In 1948, the leadership of the Communist Party was indicted for conspiracy to advocate the overthrow of the government of the United States. Their convictions were upheld by the Supreme Court in 1951.[106] Highly publicized Congressional hearings were held by the House Un-American Activities Committee and the Senate Internal Security Committee to investigate the alleged infiltration of Communists into various branches of the executive branch and various public and private organizations.[107] Legislation was adopted requiring the Communist Party and like groups to register and making it a crime to be a member of the Party.[108]

It was in this environment that Representative Ralph W. Gwinn from New York introduced his proposal to prohibit members of subversive groups from living in public housing. In April and May of 1953, Congress was considering the First Independent Offices Appropriation Act for the 1954 fiscal year. The House proposed eliminating all expenditures for public housing, in part because some Representatives thought public housing was Communist and socialist. Gwinn was among this group of House members; he hardly minced his words when he spoke about public housing:

> Mr. Speaker, public housing is, without a doubt, one of the greatest frauds ever put over by Socialist governments.
>
>   . . . .
>
> This political scheme for currying favor and buying votes with taxpayers' savings first appeared in the United States in 1918. That was 2 years after the adoption of the income-tax amendment by which we accepted Karl Marx's program of unlimited Federal taxation; namely, taking from those who save and giving to others according to their needs as vouched for by the politicians.
>
> It was not until the advent of the New Deal, however—specifically, June 27, 1934—that the United States Government elbowed its way into the housing business on a grand scale. From that time down to date thrifty property owners have been forced to assume a mortgage that runs in some cases 60 years and none less than 40 years to pay the bill for this favoritism to the tune of $20 billion. If we would only stop this now, as well as all the other socialistic-communistic programs, we could not only save $10 billion annually but also balance the budget and reduce taxes now.

---

[106] Dennis v. United States, 341 U.S. 494 (1951). The prosecution was under a section of the Smith Act of 1940, presently codified at 18 U.S.C. § 2385 (1970).

[107] Some of the litigation that resulted from these hearings included Quinn v. United States, 349 U.S. 155 (1955); Watkins v. United States, 354 U.S. 178 (1957); Barenblatt v. United States, 360 U.S. 109 (1959).

[108] *See* Subversive Activities Control Act of 1950, 64 Stat. 987; Communist Control Act of 1954, 68 Stat. 907; Communist Party of America v. Subversive Activities Control Board, 367 U.S. 1 (1961); Communist Party v. United States, 331 F.2d 807 (D.C. Cir. 1963); Albertson v. Subversive Activities Control Board, 332 F.2d 317 (D.C. Cir. 1964). The 1954 legislation is still on the books, 50 U.S.C. § 841, *et. seq.* The 1950 legislation was repealed in 1968.

. . . .

The House of Representatives has voted to stop this fraud on the taxpayer, but the Senate hesitates. The time to act is now. For moral, economic and constitutional reasons, the whole gigantic program must be defeated.[109]

Though efforts to eliminate public housing funding failed, Gwinn did manage to insert in the 1952 and 1953 appropriations bills a provision that prohibited members of groups designated as subversive by the Attorney General from living in public housing.[110] That led to the dispute with the Kutcher family's occupancy of a public housing unit in Newark.

In 1952, Hyman Kutcher received a letter from the Newark Housing Authority directing him to sign a "loyalty oath" within three days as a condition for him and his family to continue living in their subsidized apartment. The notice was probably sent because his son, James Kutcher, belonged to the Socialist Workers Party. James, a World War II veteran who lost both his legs in the war, obtained a job at the Veterans Administration upon his release from the hospital in 1945. He was fired four years later because of his Party membership. After seven years of administrative appeals and judicial proceedings, he got his job back; it took two more years to recover back pay. It was in the midst of those proceedings that his father received the "loyalty oath" demand.[111]

[b] Opinion of the New Jersey Supreme Court in *Kutcher v. Housing Authority*

Kutcher v. Housing Authority of the City of Newark

New Jersey Supreme Court
20 N.J. 181, 119 A.2d 1 (1955)

Augustine J. Kelly, Newark, argued the cause for appellant.

Emil Oxfeld, Newark, argued the cause for respondents (Rothbard, Harris & Oxfeld, Newark, attorneys).[112]

The opinion of the court was delivered by

HEHER, JUSTICE.

The plaintiff Hyman Kutcher was a tenant of the Housing Authority of the City of Newark, in Seth Boyden Terrace, a federally-aided low-rent housing project, and the co-plaintiff James Kutcher, Hyman's son, resided there in his father's apartment, when on December 18, 1952 the Authority demanded of the plaintiff Hyman Kutcher, by letter, "a certificate that no member of the family occupying" his apartment "is a member of any organization listed by the Attorney General of the United States as subversive," and set down, it was said, in the form of certificate enclosed. Of this, more hereafter. The addressee was advised that "If you and the members of your family do not belong to any of the organizations listed, have the head of the family sign

---

[109] Cong. Rec., 83rd Cong., 1st Sess., at A2886 (May 25, 1953).

[110] Independent Offices Appropriation Act, 1953, 66 Stat. 393, 403 (July 5, 1952); First Independent Offices Appropriation Act, 1954, 67 Stat. 298, 307 (July 31, 1953).

[111] These and other details of the Kutcher story may be found in BUD SCHULTZ & RUTH SCHULTZ, IT DID HAPPEN HERE: RECOLLECTIONS OF POLITICAL REPRESSION IN AMERICA 175-181 (1989).

[112] Emil Oxfeld, who argued the case for the Kutchers, was a long time member of the New Jersey American Civil Liberties Union and served as its President for a number of years.

the certificate," and the signature witnessed, and return it, dated, within three days, and that the Authority "will be obliged to take action to evict those families who do not file a signed certificate." Reference was made to the proviso of the Independent Offices Appropriation Act of 1953, commonly known as the "Gwinn Amendment," that no housing unit constructed under the United States Housing Act of 1937, as amended, "shall be occupied by a person who is a member of an organization designated as subversive by the Attorney General," and the "foregoing prohibition shall be enforced by the local housing authority."

The plaintiff tenant refused to sign the tendered certificate.

It was stipulated below that the federal and state regulations "require that only those persons or families with income in the lowest income groups be permitted to occupy these dwellings as tenants"; that under the lease the plaintiff tenant "agreed to surrender possession whenever requested to do so by" the Authority, "upon the receipt of thirty days notice in writing," and "Further provision was made . . . for re-entry by the landlord in case of default in any of the provisions of the lease, with or without notice of an intention to do so"; and that the plaintiff Hyman Kutcher "alleges that he is not a member of any organization of (sic) the Attorney General's list and his son" James, who resides in his apartment, "is a member of the Socialist Workers Party, an organization whose name does appear on said list."

Defendant was enjoined from bringing eviction proceedings. The finding was that the proposed certification was not within the requirement of the Gwinn Amendment. Plaintiffs say the Amendment cannot be constitutionally applied to them and, if it be constitutional, the Authority's action was beyond the statute and *ultra vires*. The Authority insists the Amendment is applicable and, moreover, it has "contractual rights" entitled to recognition and protection, "irrespective of [its] motive in asserting those rights," *i.e.*, its contractual right to "terminate the monthly tenancy created by the lease," which it elected to do, "by the giving of the notice as provided in the agreement"; and the tenant having failed to vacate at the time specified in the notice, the court "has no power, under the law of this State, to interfere with the exercise of the rights conferred" upon the Authority "by the contract voluntarily" made by the parties.

The asserted constitutional deficiency, as we understand it, is that the tenant's association with a listed organization does not of itself establish, even *prima facie*, reasonable grounds for belief in the tenant's disloyalty, and a state agency may not "discriminate against members of any such organization solely on the basis of membership therein," nor "arbitrarily prevent any of its citizens from enjoying these statutorily created privileges"; and the "exclusion of otherwise qualified persons solely because of membership in organizations designated as subversive by the Attorney General has no tendency whatever to further" the statutory purpose of eliminating "slums" and providing "housing for persons of low income" and, since association alone, is enough, even though innocent, there is that "indiscriminate classification" which must fall as an exertion of arbitrary power, and the "oath offends due process."

The Supreme Court of Wisconsin lately declared that "there is a complete absence of any congressional finding, of any activity of subversive organizations which threatened the carrying out of federally aided housing projects, to support the enactment of the Gwinn Amendment, or of any evidence produced before congressional committees tending to establish the existence of such evil," and the court "deems the possible harm which might result in suppressing the freedoms of the First Amendment (of the United States Constitution) outweigh any threatened evil posed by the occupation by members of subversive organizations of units in federally aided housing projects," and for that reason the state action taken under the Gwinn Amendment was "unconstitutional and void," and, "as a necessary corollary thereof," it also "violates either sec. 3 or 4, Art. I, of the Wisconsin Constitution or both," which "guarantee the same freedom of speech and right of assembly and petition as do the First and Fourteenth amendments of the United States constitution." *Lawson v. Housing Authority of City of Milwaukee*, 270 Wis. 269, 70 N.W.2d 605 (Sup. Ct. 1955).

. . . .

But there is no occasion to consider the constitutional issue raised; and it is ordinary practice not to undertake the determination of constitutional questions not necessary to the disposition of the cause.

The Gwinn Amendment forbids the occupation of a housing unit of the given class by a person who is a member of an organization designated as "subversive" by the Attorney General. Here, the tenant was required to certify that he was not a member of "any" of the organizations included in the "Consolidated List, Dated November 19, 1952, of Organizations Designated by the Attorney General of the United States as within Executive Order No. 9835," which authorized consideration, "in connection with the determination of disloyalty" of government employees, of various matters including "Membership in, affiliation with or sympathetic association with any foreign or domestic organization, association, movement, group or combination of persons, designated by the Attorney General as (1) totalitarian, (2) fascist, (3) communist, or (4) subversive, or (5) as having adopted a policy of advocating or approving the commission of acts of force or violence to deny other persons their rights under the Constitution of the United States, or (6) as seeking to alter the form of government of the United States by unconstitutional means."

Executive Order 9835 was promulgated by the President on March 21, 1947, as part of the Employees Loyalty Program in the Executive Branch of the Government. The order established a Loyalty Review Board; and it was provided that the Board be "currently furnished" by the Department of Justice with the name of each foreign or domestic organization, association, or combination of persons of the several stated categories, classified by the Attorney General "after appropriate investigation and determination." The Consolidated List thus provided by the Attorney General named 194 organizations. The Consolidated List embodied in the certification demanded here named all these organizations; there were no classes or categories and no indication that the Attorney General had designated any as "subversive." It signified that all had been "designated" by the Attorney General "as within Executive Order No. 9835," nothing more.

For some four years the Attorney General had divided the listed organizations into six categories, only one of which was described as "subversive"; and there were but six so designated in 1948, 12 when the Gwinn Amendment became effective, and 13 when enforcement began. *Rudder v. United States*, 226 F.2d 51 (D.C. Cir. 1955); *Peters v. New York City Housing Authority*, 307 N.Y. 519, 121 N.E.2d 529 (Ct. App. 1954).

Executive Order No. 10450, effective April 27, 1953, revoked Executive Order No. 9835, but the revocatory clause, section 12, requires the Department of Justice to "continue to furnish the information described in paragraph 3 of Part III" of Executive Order No. 9835, classified according to the nature of the organization—"totalitarian, fascist, communist or subversive,"— "but directly to the head of each department and agency."

The refusal of the plaintiff tenant thus to certify non-membership in the organizations named in the Attorney General's Consolidated List, intended for use in screening employees, not tenants, was not a sufficient ground for his eviction from the leased premises. The refusal to deny membership in any organization on the Consolidated List was not proof that the tenant was a member of a subversive organization or one designated as such by the Attorney General. Even proof that the tenant was a member of an organization of the proscribed class, knowing nothing of its character, would not sustain an administrative decision to evict a tenant from public housing. *Rudder v. United States, supra.* As said in *Rudder*, if the Authority had used supposed membership only as "*prima facie* evidence of disqualification," a different question would have been presented . . . . In demanding of the plaintiff tenant a disavowal of membership in organizations named on the Consolidated List other than those "designated as subversive by the Attorney General," the Authority exceeded its powers under the Gwinn Amendment, an enactment that by its very nature is to be strictly construed. As in *Rudder*, this case does not present the question of whether it would be arbitrary to evict the tenant if it were proved that a particular organization was "subversive"; that he was a member of it, and that he was aware of its character.

It is enough to say in conclusion, as in *Rudder*, that "most of the organizations on the Consolidated List were not designated as subversive by the Attorney General," and the plaintiff tenant was not shown to be a member of "any organization."

Insisting upon its contractual right to terminate the tenancy, the Authority invokes the principles that the legal pursuit of one's right, no matter what may be the motive of the promoter of the action, cannot be deemed either illegal or inequitable.

But the Authority cannot act arbitrarily, for, unlike private landlords, it is subject to the requirements of due process. *Rudder v. United States, supra.* Regardless of the existence of an abstract right to public employment, it is "sufficient to say that constitutional protection does extend to the public servant whose exclusion pursuant to a statute is patently arbitrary or discriminatory." *Wieman v. Updegraff*, 344 U.S. 183 (1952). So here, the exclusory action was arbitrary and capricious; and arbitrary exclusion is violative of constitutional precept. The State may not condition a privilege which it may deny altogether on a surrender of constitutional right. Due process and the equal protection of the laws mean equality of treatment under like circumstances and conditions both in the privileges conferred and in the burdens imposed. These constitutional principles secure the individual against an arbitrary exercise of the powers of government.

Affirmed.

WACHENFELD, J., concurring in result.

For affirmance: CHIEF JUSTICE VANDERBILT and JUSTICES HEHER, OLIPHANT, WACHENFELD, BURLING, JACOBS and BRENNAN[113] —7.

For reversal: None.

[c] Explanatory Notes: Due Process and Government Subsidized Housing

[*i*] **Rudder v. United States.** As the *Kutcher* opinion suggested, the Kutcher family was not the only one impacted by the Gwinn Amendment during the 1950s. In *Rudder v. United States*, 226 F.2d 51 (D.C. Cir. 1955), a tenant refused to sign a certificate of non-membership in subversive organizations. Just as in *Kutcher*, the court refused to allow the local public housing authority to use the common law termination rules to arbitrarily evict a tenant, and construed the Gwinn Amendment narrowly to avoid its application to the particular case. The Rudder family

---

[113] Later Justice Brennan of the United States Supreme Court.

was still feeling the impact of the Gwinn Amendment era in the 1980s. In 1977, John Rudder's daughter Miriam was denied a security clearance to work as a research aide with a Congressional committee investigating the assassinations of John and Robert Kennedy and Martin Luther King, Jr. According to newspaper reports and an episode broadcast on "60 Minutes," she was denied clearance because the CIA felt she "was bound to have close bonds of affection" to her parents on whom the FBI had an eight-volume collection of materials. Rudder, who was Black, and his white wife, Doris, were both frequent participants in the Washington, D.C. protest scene of the 1950s and 1960s. As the FBI noted, Rudder was interested in "peace, worldwide disarmament and veterans benefits" and opposed to "the Smith Act, the McCarren Act, General Douglas MacArthur, racial discrimination and the American Legion." He was apparently fired frequently from jobs because the FBI visited his employers shortly after he landed each new job.[114]

[ii] *Due Process and Eviction.* The *Kutcher* case made it clear that government owned housing had to operate within the limitations of the Fourteenth Amendment. The attempt to evict Kutcher failed because the public housing authority, a state agency for Constitutional purposes, acted arbitrarily, and therefore violated the Due Process Clause, when it attempted to extend the Gwinn amendment beyond the meaning intended by Congress. Implicit in this outcome was a requirement that a government landlord must state the reasons for terminating any tenancy. It would be virtually impossible for courts to restrain arbitrary and capricious governmental behavior unless the reasons for evictions were known.

Later cases made this explicit. Indeed, the cases have gone a bit further and required that some form of hearing be held to decide upon contested facts before a public housing authority tenant may be evicted.[115] Prior to the 1970s, protection had been afforded public tenants only for First Amendment-oriented activity. The more expansive reading of the Due Process Clause began with *Goldberg v. Kelly*, discussed at p. 530 above. After public housing tenants began challenging their evictions under the old common law termination rules, the Department of Housing and Urban Development issued regulations imposing eviction procedures on local housing authorities.[116]

The requirement that tenants be notified of the reason for their eviction was later codified.[117] The present version of the statute is the same as that enacted in 1981, except for provisions about speedy eviction for those involved in drug offenses which were added in 1990.[118] 42 U.S.C. §§ 1437(d)(k)-(l) provides as follows:

(k) Administrative grievance procedure regulations: grounds of adverse action, hearing, examination of documents, representation, evidence, decision; judicial hearing; eviction and termination procedures

---

[114] For a summary of the Rudder story, *see Family of "Subversives" Pays a High Price*, WASH. POST, at A1 (Apr. 6, 1981).

[115] *See* Caulder v. Durham Housing Authority, 433 F.2d 998 (4th Cir. 1970); Escalera v. New York City Housing Authority, 425 F.2d 853 (2d Cir. 1970).

[116] The Supreme Court had taken a case to consider the Constitutional limitations on evictions from public housing, but remanded it for further proceedings after HUD issued its first set of regulations. *See* Thorpe v. Housing Authority of the City of Durham, 393 U.S. 268 (1969).

[117] In 1981, when the Department of Housing and Urban Development proposed to significantly reduce the process requirements to terminate tenancies in public housing, Congress responded with a statutory requirement.

[118] For discussion of the due process issues raised by these changes, *see* Robyn Smyers, *High Noon in Public Housing: The Showdown Between Due Process Rights and Good Management Practices in the War on Drugs and Crime*, 30 URB. LAW. 573 (1998).

The Secretary shall by regulation require each public housing agency receiving assistance under this chapter to establish and implement an administrative grievance procedure under which tenants will—

(1) be advised of the specific grounds of any proposed adverse public housing agency action;

(2) have an opportunity for a hearing before an impartial party upon timely request within any period applicable under subsection (*l*) of this section;

(3) have an opportunity to examine any documents or records or regulations related to the proposed action;

(4) be entitled to be represented by another person of their choice at any hearing;

(5) be entitled to ask questions of witnesses and have others make statements on their behalf; and

(6) be entitled to receive a written decision by the public housing agency on the proposed action.

For any grievance concerning an eviction or termination of tenancy that involves any activity that threatens the health, safety, or right to peaceful enjoyment of the premises of other tenants or employees of the public housing agency or any drug-related criminal activity on or off such premises, the agency may (A) establish an expedited grievance procedure as the Secretary shall provide by rule under section 553 of Title 5, or (B) exclude from its grievance procedure any such grievance, in any jurisdiction which requires that prior to eviction, a tenant be given a hearing in court which the Secretary determines provides the basic elements of due process . . . . Such elements of due process shall not include a requirement that the tenant be provided an opportunity to examine relevant documents within the possession of the public housing agency. The agency shall provide to the tenant a reasonable opportunity, prior to hearing or trial, to examine any relevant documents, records, or regulations directly related to the eviction or termination.

(l) Leases; terms and conditions; maintenance; termination

Each public housing agency shall utilize leases which—

(1) do not contain unreasonable terms and conditions;

(2) obligate the public housing agency to maintain the project in a decent, safe, and sanitary condition;

(3) require the public housing agency to give adequate written notice of termination of the lease which shall not be less than—

(A) a reasonable time, but not to exceed 30 days, when the health or safety of other tenants or public housing agency employees is threatened;

(B) 14 days in the case of nonpayment of rent; and

(C) 30 days in any other case;

(4) require that the public housing agency may not terminate the tenancy except for serious or repeated violation of the terms or conditions of the lease or for other good cause;

(5) provide that any criminal activity that threatens the health, safety, or right to peaceful enjoyment of the premises by other tenants or any drug-related criminal activity on or off such premises, engaged in by a public housing tenant, any member of the tenant's household,

or any guest or other person under the tenant's control, shall be cause for termination of tenancy;

(6) specify that with respect to any notice of eviction or termination, notwithstanding any State law, a public housing tenant shall be informed of the opportunity, prior to any hearing or trial, to examine any relevant documents, records, or regulations directly related to the eviction or termination; and

(7) provide that it shall be cause for immediate termination of the tenancy of a public housing tenant if such tenant—

(A) is fleeing to avoid prosecution, or custody or confinement after conviction, under the laws of the place from which the individual flees, for

(1) a crime, or attempt to commit a crime, which is a felony under the laws of the place from which the individual flees, or which, in the case of the State of New Jersey, is a high misdemeanor under the laws of such State; or

(2) is violating a condition of probation or parole imposed under Federal or State law.

For purposes of paragraph (5), the term "drug-related criminal activity" means the illegal manufacture, sale, distribution, use, or possession with intent to manufacture, sell, distribute, or use, of a controlled substance (as defined in section 802 of Title 21).

Do the provisions on removing tenants for drug offenses offend the due process clause?

Note that subsection (*l*)(2) of this statute requires that public housing authorities agree to maintain the premises. Even before such explicit statutory recognition of this obligation, courts in New Jersey had imposed it as a matter of state law. One example is *Housing Authority of City of Newark v. Scott*, 137 N.J. Super. 110, 348 A.2d 195 (1975).

[*iii*]   *Due Process, Rent Increases and Publicly Subsidized Housing.* In addition to eviction cases, courts have also dealt with due process rights in disputes over rent increases and admission to public projects. *See* Note, *Procedural Due Process in Government Subsidized Housing*, 86 HARV. L. REV. 880 (1973). District of Columbia litigation has been particularly interesting. A triumvirate of cases about rent increases was decided in 1973. In *Thompson v. Walter Washington*, 497 F.2d 626 (D.C. Cir. 1973), the court held that tenants must be given notice and an opportunity to participate in the process of official consideration of rent increases by submitting written statements. The case involved traditional public housing like that in *Kutcher*. In a companion case, *Marshall v. Lynn*, 497 F.2d 643 (D.C. Cir. 1973), title to the housing was held by the Linda Pollin Memorial Housing Corporation, and the property was managed by Shannon and Luchs Realty Company. However, the mortgage was insured by the Federal Housing Administration and the interest rate to Pollin was significantly reduced by infusion of government subsidies. In return for the subsidy, Pollin agreed to be regulated by FHA in most matters of operation, including rental charges. The court treated the tenants in *Marshall* like those in *Thompson*.[119] Finally, in *Tenants' Council of Tiber Island-Carrollsburg Square v. Lynn*, 497 F.2d 648 (D.C. Cir. 1973), the court held that tenants had no right to participate in the rent increase process. The tenants, in contrast with those in *Thompson* and *Marshall*, were middle and upper class people. The projects were built on urban renewal land in southwest Washington, D.C. The cost of the urban renewal land was reduced by infusion of federal funds, and the land was sold to private developers. In addition, the projects were financed

---

[119] *Contrast* Burr v. New Rochelle Municipal Housing Authority, 479 F.2d 1165 (2d Cir. 1973).

by an FHA insured, regular market rate mortgage, and were subject to some FHA regulation. The FHA's control, while significantly less complete than in *Marshall*, did include rent level approval. The court found that these controls were initiated primarily to protect the government as insurer of the mortgage, not to provide a legally protected tenant interest in rent levels.

The variety of government subsidy programs displayed in the D.C. cases still exists. While the face of government housing programs has changed from time to time, the basic types of programs outlined above are still operating. The due process and state action problems created by this diversity constantly bedevil the courts. The most recent disputes have involved Section 8 housing, in which subsidies are granted to tenants to live in privately owned buildings. The statutory provisions on termination of Section 8 leases are less comprehensive than those quoted above for publicly owned housing. *See* 42 U.S.C. § 1437(f)(d).[120] The cases seem to require that an administrative hearing be held by the local public housing authority before a person is terminated from the Section 8 program only if judicial eviction proceedings are inadequate.[121]

---

[120] The federal statute reads:

(d) Required provisions and duration of contracts for assistance payments; waiver of limitation

(1) Contracts to make assistance payments entered into by a public housing agency with an owner of existing housing units shall provide (with respect to any unit) that—

(A) the selection of tenants shall be the function of the owner, subject to the provisions of the annual contributions contract between the Secretary and the agency, except that for the certificate and moderate rehabilitation programs only, for the purpose of selecting families to be assisted, the public housing agency may establish, after public notice and an opportunity for public comment, a written system of preferences for selection that is not inconsistent with the comprehensive housing affordability strategy under title I of the Cranston-Gonzalez National Affordable Housing Act [42 U.S.C. § 12701 *et seq.*];

(B)(i) the lease between the tenant and the owner shall be for at least one year or the term of such contract, whichever is shorter, and shall contain other terms and conditions specified by the Secretary;

(ii) during the term of the lease, the owner shall not terminate the tenancy except for serious or repeated violation of the terms a.. conditions of the lease, for violation of applicable Federal, State, or local law, or for other good cause;

(iii) during the term of the lease, any criminal activity that threatens the health, safety, or right to peaceful enjoyment of the premises by other tenant, any criminal activity that threatens the health, safety, or right to peaceful enjoyment of their residences by persons residing in the immediate vicinity of the premises, or any drug-related criminal activity on or near such premises, engaged in by a tenant of any unit, any member of the tenant's household, or any guest or other person under the tenant's control, shall be cause for termination of tenancy;

(iv) any termination of tenancy shall be preceded by the owner's provision of written notice to the tenant specifying the grounds for such action; and

(v) it shall be cause for termination of the tenancy of a tenant if such tenant—

(I) is fleeing to avoid prosecution, or custody or confinement after conviction, under the laws of the place from which the individual flees, for a crime, or attempt to commit a crime, which is a felony under the laws of the place from which the individual flees, or which, in the case of the State of New Jersey, is a high misdemeanor under the laws of such State; or

(II) is violating a condition of probation or parole imposed under Federal or State law;

(C) maintenance and replacement (including redecoration) shall be in accordance with the standard practice for the building concerned as established by the owner and agreed to by the agency; and

(D) the agency and the owner shall carry out such other appropriate terms and conditions as may be mutually agreed to by them.

The regulations enforcing this section make clear that it applies to all lease expiration situations, both term and periodic. *See* 24 C.F.R. § 880.607(b)(1)(iv).

[121] *See* Perry v. Royal Arms Apartments, 729 F.2d 1081 (6th Cir. 1984); Simmons v. Drew, 716 F.2d 1160 (7th Cir. 1983). In *Simmons*, one tenant was evicted for overcrowding after a court hearing and the other was terminated

[*iv*] *Utilities.* Suppose a utility company cuts off service to a tenant without a hearing. Assume further that the tenant claims the utility company has not properly credited payments made, and that all efforts by the tenant to obtain a correction in the bill were unsuccessful. Is the utility company required to provide a hearing before turning off service? The Supreme Court, in *Jackson v. Metropolitan Edison Company*, 419 U.S. 345 (1974), held that state regulation of private utilities did not provide sufficient government involvement to satisfy the state action requirement and trigger the operation of the Due Process Clause.

[*v*] *History of Public Housing.* Public housing has a less than pure image. Pictures of projects being demolished appear much more often on television than stories about well functioning developments. While the scope of procedural protections afforded to the generally poor residents of public projects has increased, so has criticism of government programs. Lawrence Friedman has an interesting explanation for this phenomenon.

Lawrence Friedman, *Public Housing And The Poor: An Overview*

54 CAL. L. REV. 642, 645-647, 649, 651-652 (1966). [122]

It would be a mistake to suppose (if anyone did) that the Wagner-Steagall Act [of 1937] arose solely out of a gradual persuasion of decent-minded people that the slums were odious, crowded, and evil, and that the federal government had a duty to relieve the sufferings of the poor. The social and economic conditions in the slums provided the opportunity, the background, and much of the emotive power of the law. Yet reformers had long dreamed in vain of public housing. And the slums were surely no worse than they had been in the nineteenth century, though possibly they were larger.

In 1937 the country was suffering from a deep and dangerous depression. Fully one-quarter of the work force was unemployed during the worst days of the depression. In the spring of 1933, thirteen to fifteen million were unemployed. Millions of families were barely making a living. The number of "poor people" in the country had been vastly increased; indeed, many of the "poor people" were formerly members of the middle class, who had enjoyed prosperity in the twenties. They retained their middle-class culture and their outlook, their articulateness, their habit of expressing their desires at the polls. There were, therefore, millions of candidates for public housing who did not belong (as later was true) to the class of the "problem poor"; rather they were members of what we might call the submerged middle class. The attractiveness of public housing was enormously enhanced because the potential clientele was itself enormous, composed of millions of relatively articulate citizens, angry and dispirited at their unjust descent into poverty. Public housing was not supported by the dregs of society; a discontented army of men and women of high demands and high expectations stood ready to insist on decent housing from government or at least stood ready to approve and defend it. The political climate was receptive to federal planning and federal housing—not so much as a matter of radical ideology, but out of a demand for positive programs to eliminate the "undeserved" privations of the unaccustomed poor.

Moreover, business was stagnant in the thirties. Programs of social welfare and relief were tested by their ability to create new jobs and prime the business pump as much as by their

---

from the subsidy program after moving out of an apartment. A second administrative hearing was held not to be required for the first tenant, but a first hearing was required for the tenant who vacated.

[122] Reprinted by permission of the California Law Review, Fred B. Rothman & Company, and Lawrence Friedman.

inherent welfare virtues. Public works programs were exceedingly popular for this reason. A vast federal program of house building naturally received the enthusiastic support of manufacturers of building supplies and workers in the building trades. The normal opposition to "socialized" housing made its appearance in debate, but it was weak and somewhat muted. Nonetheless, business support for the act was conditioned upon the act being so structured as to avoid any actual government competition with business. Homes would be built only for those who could not possibly afford to buy them on their own. A clear wall must separate the public and the private sector. This too was only partly ideological. Government, it was felt, should not cut into the markets of private industry; it must stimulate fresh demand and make fresh jobs—otherwise the effect of the program on the economy would be wasted.

During the depression the volume of private housing construction was very low. In 1925, 900,000 housing units were constructed; in 1934, only 60,000. Yet in one sense no housing shortage developed. During much of the depression, plenty of apartments stood vacant. People who were poor doubled up with relatives, lived in "Hoovervilles" and shanties, returned to rural areas, and in general failed to consume the housing supply. Rents were extremely low. The high vacancy rate posed a potential danger for the program. If public construction increased the housing supply during a period in which many dwellings stood vacant, rents would decrease still more and vacancies would increase. In a decade willing to kill baby pigs and impose acreage controls on farmers, one could hardly expect to see government flooding the housing market with new units. And in fact, the Wagner-Steagall Act was careful to avoid the problem of over-supply. No units were to be built without destroying "dwellings . . . substantially equal in number to the number of newly constructed dwellings provided by the project." This provision—the so-called "equivalent elimination" provision—killed two birds with one stone. It neutralized potential opposition from landlords and the housing industry by removing the danger of oversupply; at the same time, by making slum clearance a part of the law, it appealed to those whose desire for public housing stemmed from their loathing of the slums and slum conditions. The Wagner-Steagall Act was thus shaped by the force of concrete social conditions; what emerged was a program geared to the needs of the submerged middle class, tied to slum clearance, and purged of any element of possible competition with business.

. . . .

If this general analysis is correct, what would happen to public housing if a rising standard of living released the submerged middle class from dependence on government shelter? Public housing would be inherited by the permanent poor. The empty rooms would pass to those who had at first been disdained—the unemployed, "problem" families, those from broken homes. The program could adapt only with difficulty to its new conditions, because it had been originally designed for a different clientele. To suit the programs to the needs of the new tenant would require fresh legislation; and yet change would be difficult to enact and to implement precisely because the new clientele would be so poor, so powerless, so inarticulate. The political attractiveness of public housing would diminish. Maladaptations to reality in the program would disenchant housing reformers; they would declare the program a failure and abandon it to search out fresh cures for bad housing and slums.

All this is precisely what has happened . . . . The new tenants were precisely those who had the least power in our society, the least potent voice in the councils of city hall. The middle-class masses, moreover, were spending their sweat and treasure in a wild flight from the slums and their residents. Now that they had attained the status of suburban property owners, they had no intention of giving up their property values and their hard-won status by allowing their former neighbors (and even less desirable people) to move in. The slums were not to follow them into the suburbs. Race and income prejudice was by no means confined to the suburbs. It flourished in the city, too, particularly in the little enclaves of frame houses that formed ethnically homogeneous, proud, and self-contained neighborhoods. These sub-cities would also resist public housing in their midst. Public housing no longer meant homes for less fortunate friends, and neighbors, but rather, intrusions of "foreigners," the problem poor and those least welcome "forbidden neighbors," the lower class Negro. Public housing not only lost its political appeal but what was left of the program was confined to the core of the city. Public housing remained tied to slum clearance and rebuilding out of necessity. The suburbs and the middle-class areas of the city had shut their doors. Vacant land could not be used for sites unless the land happened to lie in skid row or a Negro neighborhood.

[d]   Problem Notes

[*i*]   *Process and Good Cause.* Suppose a local public housing authority followed the federal regulations requiring that tenants be notified of the reasons for their eviction before possession proceedings are initiated, but did not hold any administrative hearings over disputed issues of fact. In addition, assume that the relevant state statutes follow the traditional rules permitting landlords to terminate a lease for any reason, and that the local landlord-tenant court will not hear any evidence on reasons for lease terminations. If requested by a tenant threatened with eviction, should a federal court issue an injunction against further dispossess actions by the public housing authority?

[*ii*]   *Security Deposits.* What due process requirements, if any, govern the taking and repaying of security deposits by a public housing authority?

[*iii*]   *Admission to Subsidized Housing.* Once an application has been filled out and a prospective tenant has met all the statutory and regulatory requirements for entering public housing, does the local public housing authority have any obligations to inform the applicant of the reasons why he or she will not be placed in a subsidized unit? The courts are in conflict over the existence of any property right to which the due process clause may attach procedural protections in this setting.[123]

[3]   Retaliatory Eviction

[a]   Early New Jersey Retaliation Cases

The earliest retaliatory eviction cases involved attempts by landlords to evict tenants who complained to public authorities about the conditions of their apartments. In New Jersey these cases did not find their way to the state Supreme Court. The lower courts were quite receptive to tenants' claims that they should be protected from eviction or huge rent increases[124] if they had sought a housing inspection[125] or had been active in a tenant's association.[126]

---

[123] *Compare* Hill v. Group Three Housing Development Corporation, 799 F.2d 385 (8th Cir. 1985) (no process due) *with* Ressler v. Pierce, 692 F.2d 1212 (9th Cir. 1982); Samuels v. District of Columbia, 770 F.2d 184 (D.C. Cir. 1985) (yes, process due).

[124] E & E Newman, Inc. v. Hallock, 116 N.J. Super 220, 281 A.2d 544 (1971). In this case the landlord attempted to raise the rent from $70 to $200.

[125] PMS Realty Co., Inc. v. Guarino, 126 N.J. Super. 134, 312 A.2d 898 (1973); Alexander Hamilton Savings & Loan Assn. of Paterson v. Whaley, 107 N.J. Super. 89, 257 A.2d 7 (1969).

[126] Engler v. Capital Management Corp., 112 N.J. Super. 445, 271 A.2d 615 (1970).

The strength of the tenant's claims and the unanimity of the courts around the country in protecting lessees from retaliatory activity led the New Jersey legislature to enter the field. They adopted extensive retaliatory eviction legislation in 1971; it is now codified at N.J. STAT. ANN. § 2A:42-10.10 and succeeding sections. One of the first cases to appear after the adoption of this statute was Pohlman v. Metropolitan Trailer Park, Inc. The opinion in that case, reproduced next, provides an interesting context in which to evaluate the circumstances in which retaliation may be said to have occurred and the procedural rules surrounding proof of a landlord's intent to retaliate.

[b]   Opinion of the New Jersey Superior Court in *Pohlman v. Metropolitan Trailer Park*

Pohlman v. Metropolitan Trailer Park, Inc.

New Jersey Superior Court, Chancery Division
126 N.J. Super. 114, 312 A.2d 888 (1973)

KOLE, J.S.C.

Defendant Metropolitan Trailer Park, Inc. is the owner and operator of a trailer park in Moonachie, New Jersey. Defendant June A. Dyer, I, is president of the corporation.

Plaintiffs in this action were mobile home owners who resided in the park until their evictions in late 1970. At issue here is plaintiffs' claim that their evictions were wrongful and warrant the award of compensatory and punitive damages under the Tenant's Reprisal Act, N.J.S.A. 2A:42-10.10 et seq. That Act provides as follows:

No landlord of premises or units to which this act is applicable shall serve a notice to quit upon any tenant or institute any action against a tenant to recover possession of premises, whether by summary dispossess proceedings, civil action for the possession of land, or otherwise:

a. As a reprisal for the tenant's efforts to secure or enforce any rights under the lease or contract, or under the laws of the State of New Jersey or its governmental subdivisions, or of the United States; or

. . . .

c. As a reprisal for the tenant's being an organizer of, a member of, or involved in any activities of, any lawful organization;

. . . .

A landlord shall be subject to a civil action by the tenant for damages and other appropriate relief, including injunctive and other equitable remedies, as may be determined by a court of competent jurisdiction in every case in which the landlord has violated the provisions of this section.

. . . .

Plaintiffs were active, to varying degrees, in the local election campaign in Moonachie in the fall of 1970. During this period the incumbent administration was considering amendment of the municipality's zoning ordinance—in particular, that zoning district in which Metropolitan Trailer Park is located. Without discussing the specific proposals, suffice it to say plaintiffs and defendants had different views as to how the area should be zoned.

This divergence of opinion led plaintiffs to support one mayoral candidate while defendant corporation and its principals supported his opponent. It was clear from the evidence, however, that at least insofar as relevant here, the support of the respective personal candidacies by plaintiffs and defendants was subordinate in importance and incidental to the zoning issue.

I find plaintiffs' evictions were a direct result of their active opposition to defendants on the zoning issue in the fall of 1970. More specifically, I find that the residents evicted were those who, in defendants' view, had clearly aligned themselves against defendants on the zoning issue and that this opposition was the proximate cause of the evictions.

I find, further, that the relationship of each plaintiff to the corporate defendant owner of the trailer park was that of tenant and landlord under the Reprisal Act. Additionally, the exception as to "owner-occupied premises with not more than two rental units" (N.J.S.A. 2A:42-10.13) refers to the entire premises of which a part is rented. It does not refer to a particular rented dwelling unit. Here defendant-landlord, not plaintiffs, is in the position of owner-occupant. The "owner-occupied" premises is the trailer park as a whole. The exception is therefore inapplicable.

The judge who denied the preliminary injunction against the evictions in this case stated that under the Tenant's Reprisal Act the tenants would clearly have a cause of action if they had been evicted for some act that is "germane to the occupancy; and the complaint concerns a violation of some right of occupancy or use acquired by contract, lease or law; or that the organization or activity that involves complaints are actions against the landlord for some unlawful or undesirable act as a landlord."

While such cases are those most clearly within the statute, I find no reported case which limits the statute to matters of dispute between landlord and tenant that are directly involved with the tenant's occupancy. Indeed, there is unqualified language in at least one case which plainly supports the view that a "reprisal" may be found whenever the landlord has retaliated against a tenant for the tenant's exercise of a constitutionally protected right. *See E & E Newman, Inc. v. Hallock*, 116 N.J. Super. 220, 225, 281 A.2d 544 (App. Div.1971).

There is no helpful legislative history on the Tenant's Reprisal Act. Logically, the primary concern of the Legislature was the protection of those tenants who report such matters as housing and health code violations, or band together in tenants' organizations to protest housing-related grievances collectively. See, for example, N.J. Landlord Tenant Relationship Study-Commission, Interim Report, at 19, 20 (1970). Similarly, of course, recent case law involving the rights and obligations of the parties in a landlord-tenant relationship focuses on occupancy-related issues such as inadequate services, unsafe conditions and increased rents. See, for example, *Marini v. Ireland*, 56 N.J. 130, 265 A.2d 526 (1970); *Engler v. Capital Management Corp.*, 112 N.J. Super. 445, 448-449, 271 A.2d 615 (Ch. Div.1970).

It does not necessarily follow, however, that the statute was intended to be limited in application to instances in which a tenant's conduct was directly related to problems of occupancy. To so limit the statute would be contrary to the liberal interpretation given it by the courts, in part resulting from "the beneficial purposes of the legislation in question and the desirable social results intended by the Legislature . . . ." See *Silberg v. Lipscomb*, 117 N.J. Super. 491, 285 A.2d 86 (Cty. Ct. 1971).

Conceding that the primary evil sought to be remedied by the Legislature in enacting N.J.S.A. 2A:42-10.10 was reprisal for the exercise of tenants' "housing" rights, it must still be recognized that the most significant elements in the statute are *rights* and *reprisal*. I find no reason why only certain *rights* should be protected under the statute when the Legislature has failed to clearly express such a limitation. Indeed, the Legislature has chosen to use broad language in several sections of the statute without any indication of an intended limitation thereon. See, for example, N.J.S.A. 2A:42-10.10(a) which prohibits reprisals for a tenant's ". . . efforts to secure or enforce *any rights . . . under the laws of the State of New Jersey or its governmental subdivisions, or of the United States*"; and 2A:42-10.10(c) prohibiting reprisals for ". . . the tenant's being an organizer of, a member of, or involved in any activities of, *any lawful organization.*" (Emphasis added.)

Accordingly, I find the Tenant's Reprisal Act applicable to the case at bar, involving as it does the tenants' exercise of their rights to petition their local government for certain zoning ordinance amendments which they reasonably considered affected their tenancy rights and to communicate their feelings on this matter to their fellow residents similarly situated.

Assuming, *arguendo*, that the Reprisal Act applies only to retaliations for tenants' conduct which is "germane to the occupancy," the result would be the same, for in a very real sense plaintiffs' conduct in this case was germane to their occupancy.

As discussed above, plaintiffs' and defendants' support of the individual candidates for mayor in the fall of 1970 was, on the evidence here, primarily based upon and a function of their respective positions on the zoning issues.

This matter of zoning was not of mere political importance to the parties, nor were they merely interested therein as active citizens. Rather, both plaintiffs and defendants were concerned about the zoning ordinance only insofar as it affected the site of the trailer park. Plaintiffs were apparently seeking zoning protection against a sale of the tract by defendants for an industrial use. Defendants were attempting to block such rezoning to residential uses, in their view in order to prevent the eventual elimination of the trailer park caused by imposition of housing code or other requirements that mobile homes could not possibly meet. In addition, however, defendants had the unexpressed purpose of maintaining the present industrial zoning of the trailer park, thus preserving the site's value.

In essence, then, the controversy was one quite common in a landlord-tenant relationship. To the tenant-mobile home residents the issue was one of security; that is, obtaining such protection as was possible against the threat of defendants' unilateral termination of their occupancy.

The situation was thus not unlike an apartment house tenant's efforts to secure protection against precipitous termination of his tenancy. Indeed, the significance of such protection may be greater to the mobile home owner than to the apartment tenant in view of the former's substantial capital investment in his home, the cost of moving it, and the lack of available sites in the northern New Jersey area for relocation—with respect to which there was ample credible testimony.

Similarly, defendants' position was typical of that frequently experienced by landlords of apartment or other rental premises. In seeking to better their position the residents threatened the economic welfare of the landlord-owner both in terms of current income and, more important, in terms of the value of defendants' capital investment. Defendants' reaction to such threat logically was to seek maintenance of the *status quo.*

Thus, the activities of plaintiffs with respect to the zoning issue had a direct relationship to their occupancy in the park, as they were attempting to secure municipal protection against the unilateral conduct of defendants.

Concededly, a tenant's complaint to the authorities about an existing violation of housing or health laws seems more closely related to the tenants' occupancy than, as here, the tenants' efforts to secure adoption of certain zoning changes. The difference, however, is largely illusory. Had these plaintiffs sought amendment of the housing or health codes then applicable to the park, for example, could it seriously be contended that they would not be entitled to the protection of the Reprisal Act? I think not.

In the present case the absence of zoning protection against a lucrative sale of the tract for industrial use was viewed by plaintiffs as a direct threat to their continued mobile home occupancy. Certainly lawful political activity in response to such a threat—whether real or imagined—is entitled to the same protection as activity designed to secure better housing conditions, rent-leveling protection, or other activities obviously "germane to the occupancy."

The result would be the same even if one assumes the Reprisal Act is inapplicable.

N.J.S.A. 2A:42-10.10 et seq. reveals the Legislature's concern for and intent to protect the rights of residential tenants who, as it has long been recognized, have an unequal bargaining position with the landlord.

There was considerable evidence of the difficulties mobile homeowners encounter in finding a site for their homes. Thus, the fundamental problem of the apartment tenant and mobile homeowner is substantially the same—that is, the housing supply has not kept pace with demand, with the result that the lessor has a markedly superior bargaining position. The lessee's right to move to more suitable premises is simply of little value when such premises are not readily available.

The Legislature has recently recognized the mobile homeowner's position and his need for statutory protection against improper eviction and certain unconscionable conduct by lessors—i. e., by mobile park owners or operators. L.1973, c. 153 (approved May 31, 1973). The Act expressly provides that it is necessary for the welfare of the State and its inhabitants and must be liberally construed to effect its purpose.

Assuming the Tenant's Reprisal Act is inapplicable, the question is whether the retaliatory action of defendants in this case is, nonetheless, wrongful as offensive to the State's public policy.

I conclude that the Mobile Home Owners Rights Act, even though not applicable to the instant case (since it became effective July 1, 1973), and the Tenant's Reprisal Act, N.J.S.A. 2A:42-10.10 et seq., reflect and merely declare the public policy of this State which pre-existed their enactment. *See Engler v. Capital Management Corp., supra; E & E Newman, Inc. v. Hallock, supra. Cf. Shell Oil v. Marinello*, 63 N.J. 402, 307 A.2d 598 (1973); *Berzito v. Gambino*, 63 N.J. 460, 308 A.2d 17 (1973); *Edwards v. Habib*, 397 F.2d 687 (D.C. Cir. 1968).

In view of the foregoing conclusions it is unnecessary to reach the merits of plaintiffs' claims based on the New Jersey Constitution . . . . Similarly, there is no need to rule on plaintiffs' claim that their federal constitutional rights under the 1st, 5th and 14th Amendments have been violated. In any event, it is questionable whether that contention has merit, since there is no showing of governmental involvement in defendants' conduct.

Plaintiffs are entitled to compensatory damages from defendants. No punitive damages are warranted under the facts of this case.

[c] Explanatory Notes

[*i*] *Proof of Retaliation.* As a general proposition, most states now have cases or statutes which protect tenants from evictions sought in retaliation for complaints to local housing code

enforcement officials. Two significant problem areas, however, emerge from the cases. First, what tenant activities may trigger the retaliation rules? And second, what should occur if the landlord has mixed motives—some acceptable and some not—for attempting to remove a tenant?

[A] **Scope of Rule.** *Pohlman* is an example of retaliation for activity not directly related to the tenant's occupancy rights. The court decided that virtually any activity might be treated as a trigger for retaliation provided that the dispute was between the landlord and the tenant. But how far do you think the courts would go? Would the *Pohlman* court protect a tenant in a duplex who was about to marry the landlord's child against his wishes? Suppose that the tenant and the landlord got into an altercation one night when they were both drunk and that the tenant gave the landlord a black eye. Could the landlord terminate the tenancy? Note that the retaliation statute was amended specifically to include mobile home parks after *Pohlman* was decided. *See* N.J. STAT. ANN. § 2A:42-10.13.

[B] **Mixed Motive Cases.** Some of the ambiguity in a mixed motive case may be removed by creating a burden of proof rule. If the landlord must prove that his eviction effort was not retaliatory, presumably the tenant would prevail more often in mixed motive situations. The opposite would be true if the tenant had the burden of proving that the primary intent of the landlord was retaliatory.

An interesting case illustrating the problem arose shortly after New Jersey adopted its retaliatory eviction statute. In *Silberg v. Lipscomb*, 117 N.J. Super. 491, 285 A.2d 86 (1971), the court found that the landlord had valid economic motives and invalid retaliatory motives for evicting some tenants who had filed a receivership action against the landlord. The economic motives related not to loss of money from the tenant action, but to the landlord's desire to remodel the building. Finding that the activation of the remodeling plans had been sped up by the tenant activity, the court held:

> [W]here a landlord, in reaching a decision to evict a tenant, considers as one of the factors favoring that decision the activities of the tenant described in N.J.S.A. 2A:42-10.10, then the notice to quit is a "reprisal" within the meaning of the act, although other factors may also be present or even dominant.

When that ruling was merged with the provisions of N.J. STAT. ANN. § 2A:42-10.12 creating a presumption of retaliation if eviction is sought after the tenant undertakes protected activity, the tenant had to win.

[*ii*] **Term Tenancies and Retaliation.** Retaliation problems also become acute when the landlord refuses to renew a term tenancy and then seeks to evict the tenant at the conclusion of the lease. At common law, landlords are free to refuse to renew a lease for any reason. The tension between this usual rule and the desires of tenants to remain in an apartment after making various complaints about the owner is obvious. The New Jersey statutes resolved this problem by forbidding landlords from substantially altering the terms of a tenancy in retaliation for legitimate tenant protests, and by specifically providing that failure to renew a lease is a substantial alteration of the terms of the tenancy. N.J. STAT. ANN. § 2A:42-10.10(d).

[d] Problem Notes

[*i*] **Retaliation.** How would the New Jersey courts handle the following situations under the retaliatory eviction statute?:

(a) An Orthodox Jewish landlord serves a notice to quit upon a Reform Jewish family living in the upstairs apartment of the landlord's duplex because the tenants refuse to follow Orthodox rules on observance of the Sabbath, such as not using a car, turning electrical switches on or off, or working.

(b) A non-married couple gives birth to a child. The landlord serves them with a notice to quit. The notice states no reasons for its deliverance, but the landlord admits that he does not like unmarried couples living together and has always kept children out of his buildings.

(c) A tenant withholds rent for a swimming pool as in *Timber Ridge v. Dietz*, discussed at p. 676 above. After the landlord sues for possession and wins, the tenant pays the overdue rent within three days to avoid eviction. The following month, however, the tenant withholds rent again for the same reason. The landlord can obviously sue again for possession for non-payment of rent. But if she prefers to rid herself of this "bothersome" tenant, can she serve a notice to quit and remove the tenant for repeated refusals to pay the rent?

(d) A landlord refuses to rent an apartment to a prospective tenant who has been involved in tenant organizing work in other buildings. Does the tenant have a claim arising out of the landlord's refusal to rent?

[*ii*]   *Limitations of Retaliatory Eviction Defense.* If the tenants are likely to lose in any of the examples in the prior note, do you think that is the appropriate result? Should tenants be able to restrict evictions with defenses other than retaliatory eviction? What about "good cause," as in federally subsidized housing settings?

[*iii*]   *Retaliation and Landlord-Tenant Court Jurisdiction.* In New Jersey, prior to the adoption of the retaliatory eviction statute, did the landlord-tenant courts have jurisdiction over claims of retaliation? While the existence of the retaliatory eviction statute mooted the point after 1971, how did the courts get the power to hear such cases before then? Look at N.J. STAT. ANN. § 2A:18-53(a), which allows eviction when a tenant "holds over and continues in possession of all or any part of the demised premises after the expiration of his term." Do you think the New Jersey courts would have construed the word "expiration" to include a lack of retaliation in order to allow for jurisdictional appeals under N.J. STAT. ANN. § 2A:18-59?

[4]   Good Cause For Eviction

[a]   Introduction

As the problem notes just above suggest, there were some situations in which tenancies were terminated for reasons not covered by retaliatory eviction rules. About the same time that retaliatory eviction rules matured, New Jersey and some other states forbade landlords from terminating leases without "good cause."[127] The basic idea of good cause restrictions on evictions

---

[127] Comprehensive good cause restrictions have not been adopted in most states. Though New Jersey does not stand alone in adoption of such legislation, *see, e.g.*, D.C. CODE § 45-2551 (1986), most states have not followed suit. A large number of jurisdictions, however, have adopted restrictions on condominium conversions, permitted localities to adopt rent controls, or protected other classes of citizens (such as the aged) from eviction. In addition, a number of cities have adopted eviction restrictions. No one has done a comprehensive review of such legislation. To date, most of the litigation over good cause eviction provisions has appeared in New Jersey, Washington, D.C., Massachusetts, New York, and California. *See, e.g.*, Administrator of Veterans Affairs v. Valentine, 490 A.2d 1165 (D.C. 1985); E.S. Bills, Inc. v. Tzucanow, 38 Cal. 3d 824, 700 P.2d 1280, 215 Cal. Rptr. 278 (1985); Moulton v. Brookline Rent Control Board, 385 Mass. 228, 431 N.E.2d 225 (1982). The literature in the area is quite sparse, though

has been around since the price and rent control programs implemented during World War II. Every time rent controls have been adopted by one or another governmental unit since the 1940s, eviction restrictions have followed.[128]

Somewhat special pressures arose in New Jersey[129] after World War II to dramatically alter the common law termination rules permitting landlords to evict tenants for any reason. The highly dense population of the state[130] made it difficult to find reasonably priced, good quality rental housing in many areas. After the national rent controls in effect during World War II were lifted, New Jersey, like some other jurisdictions, re-entered the rent and eviction control arena during the Korean War.[131] Repeal of these controls in 1954 left tenancies largely unregulated. But during the late 1960s and early 1970s a powerful statewide organization of tenants developed. The New Jersey Tenant Organization (NJTO)[132] came into being while the nation was faced with double digit inflation rates and soaring housing costs. It lobbied the legislature for a number of tenant

---

a few, not very comprehensive, notes have appeared as the problem has begun to surface. *See* Cornelio, *The Effect of Anti-Eviction Statutes on Foreclosing Mortgages*, 4 ANN. REV. BANKING L. 361 (1985); Salzberg & Zibelman, *Good Cause Eviction*, 21 WILLAMETTE L. REV. 61 (1985); Note, *Just Cause Eviction: Limiting a Landlord's Ability to Evict*, 11 SAN FERN. V. L. Rev. 71 (1983); Case Note, *Osness v. Diamond Estates, Inc.*, 11 UCLA-ALASKA L. REV. 103 (1981).

[128] The reason for this linkage is not difficult to understand. If rent control serves its purpose, tenants pay less than landlords could get in an open market. The regulations therefore create a powerful incentive for landlords to find pliable tenants who will not complain to local authorities. In addition, if a rent control scheme contains a provision that allows a certain rent increase when tenants change (as New York City's did for many years), the incentive to get rid of tenants becomes enormous. If landlords were free to terminate a periodic tenancy or to refuse renewal of a term lease, the rent control scheme could be subverted. Thus, restrictions were adopted to prevent rapid tenant turnover.

[129] Reviewing what has occurred in New Jersey may help you anticipate what other heavily populated states will do in the future. In addition, as the notes after *Kutcher*, p. 683 above, make clear, all government housing is also subject to "good cause" eviction controls. Taking a look at a few of the numerous New Jersey cases may also provide some feel for the settings in which government subsidized landlords may evict tenants.

[130] New Jersey is the most densely populated state in the country. BUREAU OF THE CENSUS, U.S. DEPARTMENT OF COMMERCE, STATISTICAL ABSTRACT OF THE UNITED STATES 1986, at 12 (1985). New Jersey's population density in 1984 was 1,006 persons per square mile. The closest competitors were Rhode Island (912), Massachusetts (741), and Connecticut (647). The District of Columbia, though not a state, is an independent political entity for purposes of landlord tenant law developments. It had a density of 9,886 persons per square mile in 1984.

[131] Ch. 234, N.J. Laws 582 (1950). The statute also contained fairly strict eviction controls. Landlords could obtain a certificate permitting eviction only if the tenant was violating a term of the lease (other than provisions terminating the lease), creating a nuisance, breaking the law, or refusing the landlord access to make repairs, or the landlord needed possession for his own use or to remodel.

[132] The story of the NJTO's successes is laid out in a series of N.Y. TIMES articles: *Jersey Tenants Fight Rent Rises*, at 32, col. 1 (Feb. 15, 1970); *U.S. Rent Freeze Asked by Tenants*, at 34, col. 1 (Oct. 7, 1971); *Fight to Curb Rent Growing Statewide*, at 78, col. 1 (Feb. 6, 1972); *Rent Rises Spur Fight by Tenants*, at 73, col. 1 (Apr. 16, 1972); *Trenton May Face Rent-Curb Debate*, at 49, col. 1 (Sept. 3, 1972); *Rent-Leveling Bill Seems to Be Locked in Committee, Posing Possible '73 Issue*, at 99, col. 1 (Nov. 9, 1972); *Tenant Group Calls '73 Year for a State Rent Bill*, at 98, col. 4 (Dec. 17, 1972); *Cahill Warns Landlords to Adhere to Guidelines*, at 86, col. 1 (Jan. 18, 1973) (Cahill was governor and the guidelines were post price control federal guidelines); *Rent Leveling Measure Sent to Assembly Floor*, at 80, col. 1 (Jan. 30, 1973); *Rent Security Measure Signed*, at 43, col. 7 (July 4, 1973) (reference to security deposit control legislation); *Tenants Enter Political Arena*, at 77, col. 7 (Sept. 23, 1973); *Byrne Endorsed by Tenants' Body*, at 98, col. 3 (Oct. 24, 1973); 4 *Tenant-Rights Bills Win Final Legislative Backing*, at 83, col. 7 (May 17, 1974) (refers to legislation on good cause for eviction, eviction notice, notification by landlord of access to crime insurance, and recordation of identity of building managing agents); *Byrne Signs Tenant Bills, Including Eviction Curbs*, at 90, col. 1 (June 26, 1974).

reforms, including rent controls, restrictions on common law termination rules and condominium conversions, protections for elderly tenants, and a number of other measures.[133] It became such a large group that gubernatorial candidates vigorously sought its endorsement.[134] In 1973, the NJTO endorsed Brendan Byrne, who was elected in part on a platform calling for strong landlord–tenant reforms. In the legislative session following the election four landlord-tenant statutes were adopted with Governor Byrne's support, including an Anti-Eviction Act which required landlords to demonstrate "good cause" before evicting any tenant.[135]

Statewide rent controls were not among the measures adopted in 1974. Pressure to restrain rent increases eased after the federal government adopted rent guidelines in 1970 to deal with the high inflation rates and the state Supreme Court, in 1973, ruled that localities had the authority to adopt their own rent and eviction control ordinances under existing local government statutes.[136] Dozens of rent and eviction control plans were adopted after the decision was announced.[137]

The first major "good cause" eviction case arose while the NJTO was at the peak of its power. It involved a gas station rather than a residential lease. Petroleum product prices were volatile during the 1970s. Prices that had been rising before 1973 rose precipitously after the Arab Oil Boycott of the United States began because of the October, 1973, Israeli-Arab Yom Kippur War. A few of you might recall that people lined up for blocks waiting to put a few gallons of gas in their tanks during the fall of 1973. The U.S. response to the loss of oil imports included enactment of wide-spread controls on the petroleum industry. Price controls, originating in previous economic stabilization measures adopted to stem inflation, were maintained.[138] In addition a program was enacted allocating available supplies of various oil products at levels in proportion with purchases made in 1972.[139] There were also calls for controlling a significant rise in gas station lease terminations as it became more profitable for petroleum distributors to own rather than lease or franchise their outlets. The nation wide price controls expired on April 30, 1974, including those on oil products, but the allocation program was maintained for a bit longer. *Shell Oil Company v. Marinello*, the next case, was decided by the New Jersey Supreme Court just before the oil boycott began, during a period of increasing inflation and substantial realignment of marketing methods by the major oil companies.

---

[133] For a history of the New Jersey Tenant Organization, *see* Baar, *Rent Control in the 1970s: The Case of the New Jersey Tenants' Movement*, 28 HASTINGS L.J. 631 (1977).

[134] NJTO was said to have more than 500,000 members.

[135] N.J. STAT. ANN. § 2A:18-61.1 *et seq.*

[136] Inganamort v. Borough of Fort Lee, 62 N.J. 521, 303 A.2d 298 (1973). Rent control ordinances must provide the landlord with a "just and reasonable return." Helmsley v. Borough of Fort Lee, 78 N.J. 200, 394 A.2d 65 (1978); Mayes v. Jackson Township Rent Leveling Board, 103 N.J. 362, 511 A.2d 589 (1986).

[137] At the time of the decision in *Inganamort*, 18 rent control ordinances were in effect. *Jersey Towns Win on Rent Control*, N.Y. TIMES, at 93, col. 4 (Apr. 5, 1973). Within six months of the decision, that number shot up to about 60. *Tenants Enter Political Arena*, N.Y. TIMES, at 77, col. 7 (Sept. 23, 1973). Today hundreds of cities have rent control in place, including some of the largest municipalities in the country. *See* Edward Rabin, *The Revolution in Residential Landlord Tenant Law: Causes and Consequences*, 69 CORNELL L. REV. 517, 527-529 (1984).

[138] The original controls were adopted under the Economic Stabilization Act, 84 Stat. 799 (1970).

[139] Emergency Petroleum Allocation Act, 87 Stat. 627 (1973).

[b]   Opinion of the New Jersey Supreme Court in *Shell v. Marinello*

Shell Oil Company v. Marinello

New Jersey Supreme Court
63 N.J. 402, 307 A.2d 598 (1973)

The opinion of the Court was delivered by

SULLIVAN, J.

This case involves the interpretation of a lease and a dealer agreement entered into between Shell Oil Company (Shell) and Frank Marinello (Marinello), one of its service station operators, and a determination of the extent of Shell's right to terminate such lease and agreement.

Shell, a major oil company, is a supplier of motor vehicle fuels and automotive lubricants under the trade name "Shell." It also supplies tires, batteries and accessories (TBA) to its dealers for resale. Its products are sold in hundreds of Shell service stations throughout the State. Many of the service station locations are controlled by Shell through long-term leases. In the past, Shell's practice has been not to operate these stations itself, but to lease the station premises to an operator with whom it enters into a dealer or franchise agreement.

This is essentially the relationship before us for consideration. Shell controls a service station located at Route #5 and Anderson Avenue, Fort Lee, Bergen County. In 1959 it leased the station to Marinello, and at the same time entered into a written dealer agreement with the lessee. The original lease was for a one-year term and was regularly renewed in writing for fixed terms. The last lease between Shell and Marinello is dated April 28, 1969 and runs for a three-year term ending May 31, 1972, and from year-to-year thereafter, but is subject to termination by Marinello at any time by giving at least 90 days notice and by Shell at the end of the primary period or of any such subsequent year by giving at least 30 days notice.

The dealer agreement, also originally for a one-year term, was renewed in writing so as to coincide with the existing lease. Each agreement provided that Shell would supply its products to the dealer for resale at the Route #5 service station in question. The last dealer agreement is also dated April 28, 1969, and is for a three-year term ending May 31, 1972 and from year-to-year thereafter, but is subject to termination at any time by giving at least 10 days notice.

By letter dated April 14, 1972, Shell notified Marinello that it was terminating the aforesaid lease and the dealer agreement effective May 31, 1972. Marinello immediately filed suit in the Superior Court, Chancery Division, seeking to have Shell enjoined from taking its proposed action, and asking for reformation of the "agreement" between the parties so as to show a joint venture. Shell on its part, on June 1, 1972, filed a summary dispossess complaint in the District Court for possession of the service station premises alleging that Marinello was holding over and remaining in possession without the consent or permission of Shell.

On motion, the dispossess action was transferred to the Superior Court (N.J.S.A. 2A:18-60) where it was consolidated with and tried with the Chancery suit. After a nine-day trial a decision was rendered in favor of Marinello. The trial court's opinion is reported at 120 N.J. Super. 357, 294 A.2d 253.

In its decision the trial court dealt with three primary issues. It held (1) the newly enacted Franchise Practices Act, N.J.S.A. 56:10-1 et seq., effective December 21, 1971, did not apply to the previously executed renewals of the lease and dealer agreement between Shell and

Marinello; (2) there was an implied covenant in said lease and agreement on the part of Shell not to terminate the relationship without good cause, and these instruments must be reformed to include such covenant; and (3) Marinello had substantially performed his obligations to Shell under these agreements.

Although not necessary to its decision, since it not only granted reformation, but also found that Shell did not have good cause to terminate the lease and dealer agreement, the trial court sustained Marinello's defense of unclean hands in the dispossess action by finding that Shell was guilty of improper and illegal marketing practices (a) by discriminating against Marinello in the tank-wagon prices it charged him, and (b) by tying in increased TBA sales on Marinello's part to a renewal of the lease. These practices were found by the trial court to be violations of the New Jersey Unfair Motor Fuels Act, N.J.S.A. 56:6-19 et seq., and the Robinson-Patman Price Discrimination Act, 15 U.S.C.A. § 13.

Shell appealed from the judgment entered in the consolidated actions. While the appeal was pending unheard in the Appellate Division we ordered direct certification to this Court. R. 2:12-1.

We are in full agreement with the basic determination of the trial court that Shell had no legal right to terminate its relationship with Marinello except for good cause, *i.e.*, the failure of Marinello to substantially comply with his obligations under the lease and dealer agreement. However, we conclude that it was unnecessary to have granted specific reformation of the lease and dealer agreement. The same end result is reached from consideration of the instruments themselves, the relationship between Shell and Marinello created thereby, and the public policy of this State affecting such relationship.

For this reason it is unnecessary for us to deal with the question of reformation, as such, as well as the ancillary issues of parol evidence and the statute of frauds. By the same token, we need not review the trial court's finding that Marinello had established the defense of unclean hands in the dispossess suit filed by Shell. Since our conclusion is that Shell has not shown good cause to terminate its relationship with Marinello, we do not reach the question of equitable defense. *See Vineland Shopping Center, Inc. v. DeMarco*, 35 N.J. 459, 173 A.2d 270 (1961).

Shell argues that its lease of the service station premises to Marinello is independent of its dealer agreement with him, and that its legal rights as a landlord under the lease are absolute and cannot be restricted. This is pure sophistry. The two contractual documents are but part of an integrated business relationship. They were entered into simultaneously, have the same commencement and expiration dates, and expressly refer to the Route #5 service station premises.

These instruments, and the business relationship created thereby, cannot be viewed in the abstract. Shell is a major oil company. It not only controls the supply, but, in this case, the business site. The record shows that while the product itself and the location are prime factors in the profitability of a service station, the personality and efforts of the operator and the good will and clientele generated thereby are of major importance. The amount of fuel, lubricants and TBA a station will sell is directly related to courtesy, service, cleanliness and hours of operation, all dependent on the particular operator.

Marinello testified that when the station was offered to him in 1959 he was told by the Shell representative that the station was run down, but that a good operator could make money and that if he built up the business his future would be in the station. Shell's own witnesses admitted that it was Shell's policy not to terminate its relationship with a lessee-dealer except for good cause, which was described as not running the station in a good and businesslike manner.

Viewing the combined lease and franchise against the foregoing background, it becomes apparent that Shell is the dominant party and that the relationship lacks equality in the respective bargaining positions of the parties. For all practical purposes Shell can dictate its own terms. The dealer, particularly if he has been operating the station for a period of years and built up its business and clientele, when the time for renewal of the lease and dealer agreement comes around, cannot afford to risk confrontation with the oil company. He just signs on the dotted line.

Where there is grossly disproportionate bargaining power, the principle of freedom to contract is non-existent and unilateral terms result. In such a situation courts will not hesitate to declare void as against public policy grossly unfair contractual provisions which clearly tend to the injury of the public in some way *Henningsen v. Bloomfield Motors, Inc.* 32 N.J. 358, 403-404, 161 A.2d 69 (1960).

In *Ellsworth Dobbs, Inc. v. Johnson*, 50 N.J. 528, 553-554, 236 A.2d 843, 856-857 (1967) we said:

> Courts and legislatures have grown increasingly sensitive to imposition, conscious or otherwise, on members of the public by persons with whom they deal, who through experience, specialization, licensure, economic strength or position, or membership in associations created for their mutual benefit and education, have acquired such expertise or monopolistic or practical control in the business transaction involved as to give them an undue advantage. *Henningsen v. Bloomfield Motors, Inc.*, 32 N.J. 358, pp. 388-391, 161 A.2d 69 (1960). Grossly unfair contractual obligations resulting from the use of such expertise or control by the one possessing it, which result in assumption by the other contracting party of a burden which is at odds with the common understanding of the ordinary and untrained member of the public, are considered unconscionable and therefore unenforceable . . . . The perimeter of public policy is an ever increasing one. Although courts continue to recognize that persons should not be unnecessarily restricted in their freedom to contract, there is an increasing willingness to invalidate unconscionable contractual provisions which clearly tend to injure the public in some way.

Applying the foregoing to the case before us, it is clear that the provisions of the lease and dealer agreement giving Shell the right to terminate its business relationship with Marinello, almost at will, are the result of Shell's disproportionate bargaining position and are grossly unfair. That the public is affected in a direct way is beyond question. We live in a motor vehicle age. Supply and distribution of motor vehicle fuels are vital to our economy. In fact the Legislature has specifically concluded that the distribution and sale of motor fuels within this State is affected with a public interest. N.J.S.A. 56:6-19(c).

It is a fallacy to state that the right of termination is bilateral. The oil company can always get another person to operate the station. It is the incumbent dealer who has everything to lose since, even if he had another location to go to, the going business and trade he built up would remain with the old station.

The relationship between Shell and Marinello is basically that of franchise. The lease is an integral part of that same relationship. Our Legislature in enacting the Franchise Practices Act, has declared that distribution and sales through franchise arrangements in New Jersey vitally affect the general economy of the State, the public interest and the public welfare. N.J.S.A. 56:10-2. The Act prohibits a franchisor from terminating, canceling or failing to renew a franchise without good cause which is defined as the failure by the franchisee to substantially comply with the requirements imposed on him by the franchise. N.J.S.A. 56:10-5.

The Act does not directly control the franchise relationship herein since Marinello's last renewal antedates the effective date of the statute. N.J.S.A. 56:10-8. However, the Act reflects the legislative concern over long-standing abuses in the franchise relationship, particularly provisions giving the franchisor the right to terminate, cancel or fail to renew the franchise. To that extent the provisions of the Act merely put into statutory form the extant public policy of this State.

Even on this basis, Shell contends that it had good cause to serve notice of termination on Marinello. Its representatives testified that Marinello did not keep the station in a neat, clean condition, and that frequent complaints to him about station appearance went unheeded. They also said that Marinello did not keep the station open the required period of hours, and that gasoline sales volume for the past three years had become stagnant.

Marinello, on the other hand, produced proof that the appearance of his station was good and the volume of gasoline pumped over the past three years was excellent for a neighborhood station. He said that his hours of operation since 1959 had been 6:30 A.M. to midnight. He asserted that he tried keeping open for 24 hours for a short while, but neighbors complained and Shell told him to stop. He attributed his present difficulties with Shell to his refusal to accede to Shell's request that he lower his price from 3¢ to 5¢ a gallon during an area "gas war" (Marinello said he would have had to absorb a loss from 2¢ to 4¢ a gallon.) He also said that he was told by the assistant district manager for Shell that one of the reasons his lease was not being renewed was he did not buy enough TBA.

The trial court found that Marinello had substantially performed his obligations in a satisfactory manner and had not given Shell any just cause to terminate the lease and franchise. The record amply supports this finding and conclusion. We will not disturb it.

We hold (1) that the lease and dealer agreement herein are integral parts of a single business relationship, basically that of a franchise, (2) that the provision giving Shell the absolute right to terminate on 10 days notice is void as against the public policy of this State, (3) that said public policy requires that there be read into the existing lease and dealer agreement, and all future lease and dealer agreements which may be negotiated in good faith between the parties, the restriction that Shell not have the unilateral right to terminate, cancel or fail to renew the franchise, including the lease, in absence of a showing that Marinello has failed to substantially perform his obligations under the lease and dealer agreement, *i.e.*, for good cause, and (4) that good cause for termination has not been shown in this case.

Based on the foregoing, Marinello's franchise, including his lease, would have legal existence for an indefinite period, subject to his substantially performing his obligations thereunder. We are not called upon to decide whether the relationship is so personal it would not survive Marinello's disability or death. We also reserve the question of the particular remedy to which Marinello would be entitled (injunctive relief or compensatory damages) should Shell in good faith opt to operate the station itself.

The lease and dealer agreement, of course, would be subject to revision to conform with current Shell dealer operational practices for the area. The good faith of the parties and the reasonableness of their respective positions in the negotiations would determine the existence of good cause should the negotiations fail and Shell give notice of termination.

The judgment of the trial court is modified so as to conform with this opinion, and, as modified, is affirmed.

For modification and affirmance: CHIEF JUSTICE WEINTRAUB, JUSTICES JACOBS, PROCTOR, HALL, MOUNTAIN, SULLIVAN and GARVEN—7.

For reversal: None.

[c]   Explanatory Notes: Good Cause for Eviction

[i]   *Commercial Leases and Eviction for Cause.* *Shell* was a somewhat unusual case for two reasons. First, the changing face of the petroleum market during the period in which it was decided created strong pressures not to permit the major oil companies to extract extraordinary profits. Second, the case involved the termination of a franchise within a short period after the state legislature adopted restrictions on franchise terminations. The combination made it somewhat easier for the New Jersey Supreme Court to protect Marinello. But despite the unusual nature of the case, it raised important issues for the future of landlord-tenant law.

Like *Reste Realty v. Cooper,* p. 641 above, *Shell* presented the New Jersey courts with a commercial version of a problem of great concern among residential tenants. And like *Reste,* *Shell* was followed by very significant alterations in residential lease rules. Though the response this time was legislative (*see* N.J. STAT. ANN. § 2A:18-61.1) rather than judicial, the enactments were every bit as important as the *Marini* decision. In addition, just as there are lingering uncertainties about the applicability of the implied warranty rules to commercial tenants, there are still questions about the applicability of "good cause" eviction rules to non-franchise commercial lessees. There is a somewhat entertaining irony about all this. As already noted, most nineteenth-century landlord-tenant litigation involved commercial leases. The old rules did not become unworkable until this century when apartment buildings became common for the first time. Now the dramatic change in residential tenancies has begun to put pressure on the traditional rules still used in commercial leases.[140]

[ii]   *The Anti-Eviction Act.* The Anti-Eviction Act has spawned a deluge of litigation in the New Jersey Courts. Dozens of reported cases exist, with disputes over condominium conversions,[141] pets(!),[142] remodeling,[143] and landlords' desire to use the premises for themselves[144] most frequently surfacing. One other interesting problem has arisen—the ability of a mortgagee to evict tenants in a foreclosure proceeding prior to a judicial sale. In *Guttenberg Savings and Loan Association v. Rivera,* 85 N.J. 617, 428 A.2d 1289 (1981),[145] the Supreme

---

[140] At least one case has declined to apply *Shell* to a non-franchise commercial lease, but the Supreme Court has not yet dealt with the problem. *See* Mintz v. Metropolitan Life Insurance Company, 153 N.J. Super 329, 379 A.2d 526 (1977).

[141] As originally enacted, the Anti-Eviction Act required only six months notice in cases where the owner wished to remove the building from the rental market. In 1975, the act was amended to provide a minimum of three years of protection to pre-conversion tenants in buildings with more than three units and two months of protection to other tenants. *See* Veltri v. Norwood, 195 N.J. Super. 406, 479 A.2d 931 (1984) for a review of the conversion limitations. *See also* Kabakian v. Kobert, 188 N.J. Super. 517, 457 A.2d 1229 (1983).

[142] Young v. Savinon, 201 N.J. Super. 1, 492 A.2d 385 (1985); Royal Associates v. Concannon, 200 N.J. Super. 84, 490 A.2d 357 (1985); Terhune Courts v. Sgambati, 163 N.J. Super. 218, 394 A.2d 416 (1978).

[143] Floral Park Tenants Association v. Project Holding, Inc., 152 N.J. Super 582, 378 A.2d 266 (1977).

[144] Puttrich v. Smith, 170 N.J. Super. 572, 407 A.2d 842 (1979).

[145] *See* Cornelio, *The Effect of Anti-Eviction Statutes on Foreclosing Mortgagees,* 4 ANN. REV. BANKING L. 361 (1985), which discusses the *Guttenberg* case at some length.

Court decided that a foreclosing mortgagee of a residential apartment building may obtain a Superior Court order evicting tenants under leases subordinate to the mortgage without complying with the Anti-Eviction Act. In construing the language in N.J. STAT. ANN. § 2A:18-61.2 prohibiting the entry of a judgment for possession "unless the landlord has made written demand and given written notice" specifying the cause for terminating the tenancy, the court concluded that a mortgagee was not a landlord within the meaning of the statute. The court noted:

> Property law with respect to the rights of a mortgagee vis-a-vis a subordinate tenant strongly supports our analysis of the legislative intent. It is not realistic to believe that the Legislature intended to modify that relationship by the Anti-Eviction Act without some reference to mortgagees. It has long been well settled in this State that upon and after default a mortgagee is entitled to possession of the premises. Until that event the mortgagor is entitled to possession. So long as the mortgage was prior to the tenancy, the mortgagee, upon default, could foreclose on the leasehold and obtain an order for possession against the mortgagor's tenant. When the mortgage precedes the lease, the tenant's rights can rise no higher than those of his landlord, the mortgagor . . . . Since the mortgagee upon default can take possession as against the mortgagor, the same right exists against the mortgagor's tenant. Thus the mortgagee may also repudiate the lease and consider the tenant a trespasser subject to eviction by an action of ejectment. If the Legislature had intended to modify these established fundamental property rights, it would have done so in some straightforward manner.

The result of this case was effectively reversed by N.J. STAT. ANN. § 2A:18-61.3(b)(1) in 1986. Was that a wise legislative judgment?

[iii] *Changing the Terms of a Lease and Raising the Rent Under the Anti-Eviction Act.* From the notes at the beginning of this section of materials, you know that in order to raise the rent of a periodic tenant before the enactment of the Anti-Eviction Act, the landlord had to serve a notice to quit meeting the requirements of N.J. STAT. ANN. § 2A:-56 as well as a demand for possession fulfilling N.J. STAT. ANN. § 2A:18-53(a), and then offer a new tenancy at the higher rent. If, however, the landlord's proffer of a new lease contains changes in the terms of the lease *in addition to* a rent increase, N.J. STAT. ANN. § 2A:18-61.1(i) of the Anti-Eviction Act has been construed to require that the tenant be given one month to accept or reject the changed terms. If acceptance is not forthcoming, then another month's notice must be given under N.J. STAT. ANN. § 2A:61.2(e) before an action for possession may be brought. *Prospect Point Gardens, Inc. v. Timoshenko*, 293 N.J. Super. 459, 681 A.2d 125 (1996). Is there any good policy reason for this procedure?

[iv] *Removal From Landlord-Tenant Court.* As noted in the notes after *Marini v. Ireland*, p. 662 above, it is possible to remove certain actions from landlord-tenant court into the regular civil courts. *See* N.J. STAT. ANN. § 2A:18-60. Indeed, cases involving disputes over title to the property may not be heard in landlord-tenant court. *See* N.J. STAT. ANN. § 2A:18-52. Once a case is removed, all the procedural limitations of landlord-tenant court become irrelevant. Counterclaims may be filed, additional parties added, permanent injunctions requested, and discovery had.

The *Shell* litigation was a particularly interesting setting in which to investigate the impact of the right to remove. If Marinello's motion to remove the possession action was denied, he would have continued to litigate his chancery court action, but without possession. Since the motion was granted, Shell was forced to litigate while Marinello retained possession. By permitting the court to decide the status of the parties pending the outcome of the litigation, the removal motion served the same function as a motion for a preliminary injunction. The availability of removal makes even more intriguing the continued vitality of the limitations on landlord-tenant court practice. Only sophisticated tenants or those with legal assistance will be able to successfully force preliminary decisions on their ability to remain in possession while litigating issues normally not entertained by landlord-tenant courts.

[*v*] ***Caveat—Good Cause Around the Country.*** While most states do provide some sort of protection against retaliatory evictions, most states have *not* adopted good cause for eviction standards. The existence of the good cause limitations on eviction in New Jersey does, however, provide a nice vehicle for inquiring about the wisdom of the regulations. Would you vote for a good cause statute as a legislator?

[*vi*] ***Marinello Denouement.*** My research assistant, Helen Carletta, visited the Shell station in the spring of 1987. Frank Marinello still was running the station, hard by the George Washington Bridge. He received a commendation for good service after the case was decided. As this book goes to press, Frank Marinello is semi-retired, and the station—still selling Shell gasoline—is being run by his son. By the way, the lawyer who handled the case for the Marinellos was a cousin of Frank Marinello.[146]

[d] Problem Notes

[*i*] ***Cooperative Housing.*** Does the Anti-Eviction Act apply to an owner-resident in cooperative housing? Recall[147] that in a cooperative, the building is owned by a corporation and each occupant pays "rent," part of which is used to pay a share of the "blanket" mortgage covering the whole building. What happens if the cooperative defaults on the mortgage?

[*ii*] ***Commercial Leases, Implied Warranties and "Good Cause."*** Should *Marini* and the Anti-Eviction Act be construed or amended to cover all commercial leases? If there are some leases, such as agreements between two sophisticated entities, which should not be covered, are there also some leases that should be covered? Is it possible to draft legislation that adequately describes the difference between covered and non-covered commercial deals?

[*iii*] ***Agricultural Leases.*** Section 2A:18-61.1 of the Anti-Eviction Act has been construed as not applicable to a lease of a farm. *Harden v. Pritzert*, 178 N.J. Super. 237, 428 A.2d 927 (1981). The court found the differences in the description of covered tenancies in N.J. STAT. ANN. §§ 2A:18-53(a) and 2A:18-61.1 telling in holding the former, but not the latter, section applicable to farm leases. As a matter of public policy, should agricultural leases be covered by the Anti-Eviction Act?

[*iv*] ***Economic Effects.*** What might be the economic effects of the Anti-Eviction Act? Suppose, for example, that you owned a 16 unit building that you wished to convert to a condominium? Would you rigidly adhere to the eviction restrictions of the Anti-Eviction Act, or would you take some other steps to speed up the conversion? One alternative is to buy out the tenants. The effect of the Anti-Eviction Act, in such a case, would not necessarily increase the cost of the condominiums when they come onto the market. It might merely transfer to the tenants some of the profit you would otherwise have gained from the conversion. Is it

---

[146] Telephone interview with Mr. Marinello, Dec. 28, 1998.

[147] *See* the prior discussion of cooperatives, p. 607 above.

inappropriate to permit tenants to extract some of a building owner's profits when the building is sold or converted?

[v] **Conversions and the Rental Market.** Many converted condominium units are sold to investors who then rent them. The effect of such a pattern is to restructure the rental market by forcing investors interested in rental properties to own units in scattered locations rather than all in one building and by introducing newly renovated units back into the market at a higher rent. Does this mean that if you want to control rents you also have to control condominium conversions because conversions may be used to evade the rent controls? Similarly, if you want to control conversions but not rent, can that be done without a good cause for eviction statute? If someone wants to convert a building in a state lacking good cause limits on evictions, won't they simply serve notices to quit and empty the place of tenants?

[vi] **Forty-Year Protected Tenancies for the Elderly and Disabled.** In 1981, the Anti-Eviction Act was supplemented by the Senior Citizens and Disabled Protected Tenancy Act.[148] Its major feature provided immunity from eviction for eligible tenants for up to 40 years. A decision affirming the constitutionality of this statute is next in these materials. It involved a building with about 340 units originally purchased for about $6.5 million. By the time of the litigation, about 60 units were still occupied by senior citizens. The others had been sold to new occupants for a total of about $20 million.[149] While reading the opinion, recall the degree of change in property law it represents by comparing it with *Stewart v. Childs Co.*, discussed at p. 638 above.

[e]   Some Thoughts on the Scope of New Jersey Eviction Reforms

New Jersey's reforms in eviction law were quite extensive. They occurred for many of the same reasons that led to the implied warranty of habitability—the arrival of legal services, the emergence of a wide array of demonstrative "rights" movements, including quite extensive efforts to organize poor tenants in both public and private housing, and the felt need to bring landlord-tenant law into line with other areas of the civil law that had undergone significant change in the prior 50 years.

But middle-class pocket book issues played a much large role here than in the implied warranty cases. After World War II, the United States entered into a period of sustained economic growth. We were the only economic game in town for quite some time. Much of Europe, Russia and Asia were devastated by the war. We controlled world markets for most major products. The lack of world-wide competition for our products allowed us to charge high prices and to raise our wages significantly. Real wealth grew at a fast pace across most segments of the culture. By 1960, it was reasonable for young people to assume they could obtain an education and a good job. The expectations of African Americans grew with those of the rest of the population. They expected to be able to improve their lot. Educational doors were beginning to open. Despite all of the continuing racism and segregation, the high flying economy and the successes of the Civil Rights Movement also made it a time of enormous hope for African Americans. Such enhanced expectations made many of us demand the "rights" we were both "entitled to" and "expecting" to receive. I think it is this sort of dynamic that created the phenomenon Edward Rabin described—demands for improved housing conditions at the very time housing conditions

---

[148] Ch. 226, N.J. Laws 862 (1981). It is codified at N.J. STAT. ANN. § 2A:18-61.22 *et seq.*

[149] Attorneys for the building owners provided this cost data.

were probably better than they had ever been. [150] Indeed, almost everyone demanded their "rights" during the 1960s and early 1970s. Expectations were high on all fronts. But, of course, when those high expectations began to be disappointed, anger grew rapidly. The riots in black communities were a not surprising result. It is interesting to note that studies of those arrested during the multitude of urban riots from 1964 through 1973 almost uniformly found that the arrestees were not from the bottom-most rungs of the economic ladder. They were generally job holders who were beginning to work their way up to the middle class. [151] But they were also very angry when their expectations were not fulfilled.

In some places, like New Jersey, reforms moved well beyond the housing quality issues associated with the implied warranty. Rent controls appeared in many places. A few good cause for eviction statutes were adopted. And many places adopted constraints on condominium conversions like those displayed in the next case. I think the roots of these changes were not quite the same as those of implied warranty, or even retaliatory eviction and public housing process reforms. Those pushing for these changes were largely middle class, not lower class. The proponents were moved by their own economic self-interest. Huge inflation rates in the early and mid-1970s scared middle class America. Indeed, there was a national rent control program for a short time during the Nixon years. At the same time, demand for smaller housing units rose as more people delayed marriage, did not marry at all, or split off from pre-existing family units because of divorce. The rise in demand for apartments by people with money fueled an enormous condominium conversion movement. Rental buildings were converted by the hundreds into condominiums. Middle class folks saw their ability to rent good apartments significantly reduced, especially in urban and suburban areas. The overall impact was quite profound as thousands of people with good jobs, but without enough money to make a downpayment on a housing unit or, in places like New York or New Jersey, unable to afford the prices being demanded for condominiums, were threatened with eviction. These folks formed alliances with poor tenants for a time as they came to see their interest in not being evicted as similar to the desires of poor and working class people to be able to stay in a decent place once they found one.

In New Jersey, the middle class tenant's movement was enormous. As the bedroom state for both New York City and Philadelphia and as the most densely populated state in the country, rental living is common among middle as well as working class populations. Tens of thousands of people joined the New Jersey Tenants' Organization. Gubernatorial and legislative candidates came seeking endorsements. Legislative agendas were established and enacted in the early 1980s. The timing also suggests that the historical factors at work were not quite the same as those behind retaliatory eviction and the implied warranty. These reforms in good cause for eviction and condominium conversion rules and other more recent changes were not passed because of some Great Society notion that the impoverished needed support or because of some Legal Process sense that the process of post-*Marini* eviction rules were seriously flawed. These reforms were based on much more standard middle class pocket book issues. Their legitimacy was tested in the next case.

---

[150] Edward Rabin, *The Revolution in Landlord-Tenant Law: Causes and Consequence*, 69 CORNELL L. REV. 517 (1984).

[151] REPORT OF THE NATIONAL ADVISORY COMMISSION ON CIVIL DISORDERS 127-135 (N.Y. TIMES ed. 1968).

[f]　Opinion of the United States Circuit Court in *Troy v. Renna*

Troy Ltd. v. Renna, Commissioner of New Jersey Department of Community Affairs

United States Circuit Court of Appeals, Third Circuit
727 F.2d 287 (1984)

Before GIBBONS and SLOVITER CIRCUIT JUDGES, AND GREEN, DISTRICT JUDGE.*

OPINION OF THE COURT

GIBBONS, CIRCUIT JUDGE:

These are appeals . . . from an order . . . declaring that section 14 of the New Jersey Senior Citizens and Disabled Protected Tenancy Act, N.J.Stat.Ann. § 2A:18-61.11(d) (hereafter the "Tenancy Act"), violates the . . . taking clause of the United States Constitution. The plaintiffs are owners of interests in an apartment complex in Springfield, New Jersey affected by that Act. The defendants are the Commissioner of the New Jersey Department of Community Affairs, the Attorney General of New Jersey, and three tenants in the apartment complex who may be protected by the Tenancy Act.

We hold that the Tenancy Act does not violate the impairment of contracts or taking clause of the United States Constitution. Accordingly, we reverse.

I. Legislative Background

New Jersey regulates its rental housing stock through a comprehensive set of statutes. This discussion begins with an examination of the rental housing legislation in place before 1981 and then moves on to a discussion of the provisions of the Senior Citizens and Disabled Protected Tenancy Act that are in issue here.

A. Prior Legislation

Until 1981, tenants in New Jersey were protected from eviction by provisions of the New Jersey Anti-Eviction Act, N.J.Stat.Ann. §§ 2A:18-61.1 to 61.12. That Act authorized evictions on thirteen prescribed grounds. One of these grounds was a conversion by the owner from rental housing to condominium form of ownership. N.J.Stat.Ann. § 2A:18-61.1(k). Eviction for that purpose, however, required that the owner satisfy several conditions.

An owner converting to condominium ownership must have served a notice of termination three years before the institution of any action for eviction. No action could be instituted until the existing lease expired. N.J.Stat.Ann. § 2A:18-61.2(g). Thus, the Act essentially contained a three-year minimum grace period before eviction. Tenants receiving a three-year notice could, during the eighteen months following its receipt, request that the owner offer to the tenant "the rental of comparable housing . . . ." N.J.Stat.Ann. § 2A:18-61.11(a). Unless the owner located and offered comparable housing, New Jersey courts having jurisdiction over eviction actions were authorized to issue up to five one-year stays of eviction. In practice, therefore, if the owner could not locate comparable housing for the tenant, the grace period before eviction could be extended

---

* Hon. Clifford Scott Green, United States District Judge for the Eastern District of Pennsylvania, sitting by designation.

from three to eight years. After the first stay of eviction, however, the owner could prevent further stays by paying to the tenant a "hardship relocation compensation" equal to five months' rent. N.J.Stat.Ann. § 2A:18-61.11(c). Therefore, after the fourth year following a termination notice—three years plus one stay—owners who could not locate comparable housing were faced with a choice: either they could make a payment to the tenant equal to five months' rent, and thereby prevent additional stays of eviction; or they could make no such payment and continue receiving rent from the tenant for up to four more years.

In addition to the Anti-Eviction Act, several New Jersey statutes governed the conversion of real property to the condominium form of ownership. The New Jersey Condominium Act, N.J.Stat.Ann. §§ 46:8B-1 to 30, provided for conversion of real property to the condominium form by the filing of a master deed meeting certain statutory requirements. N.J.Stat.Ann. § 46:8B-8. When such a master deed is filed, each unit becomes a separate interest in real property. N.J.Stat.Ann. § 46:8B-4. New Jersey also authorized the sale by condominium developers of units created by the filing of a master deed. *See* The Planned Real Estate Development Full Disclosure Act, N.J.Stat.Ann. §§ 45:22A-21 to 42. The Disclosure Act required that a public offering statement be filed with the New Jersey Department of Community Affairs. N.J.Stat.Ann. § 45:22A-28. The Act also authorized the Community Affairs Department to investigate a developer's application, and to register that application upon finding that the developer is likely to comply with the terms of the public offering statement. N.J.Stat.Ann. §§ 45:22A-29-30. The developer's right to offer units for sale to the public was qualified, however, by a provision of the Anti-Eviction Act requiring that tenants must be afforded notice of their option to purchase the units they occupy. N.J.Stat.Ann. § 2A:18-61.8.

B. The Tenancy Act

On July 27, 1981, the New Jersey Legislature enacted the Tenancy Act. The Act's purpose is to enhance the protection of certain senior citizens and disabled persons against evictions resulting from condominium conversions. Legislative findings in the Act recite that the "forced eviction and relocation of elderly persons from their established homes and communities harm the mental and physical health of these senior citizens, . . . affect adversely the social, economic and cultural characteristics of communities of the State, and increase the costs borne by all State citizens . . . ." Although these appeals concern challenges only to Section 14 of the Tenancy Act, various provisions of the Act are interrelated. These provisions fall into three categories: those sections creating a "protected tenancy period"; a section governing rent increases during that period; and a retroactivity section.

1. Protected Tenancy Period

At the heart of the Tenancy Act is a provision is section 4 granting a "protected tenancy status" to "eligible" senior citizens and disabled tenants. Section 3 provides that an eligible "senior citizen tenant" is a tenant in a complex of five or more units who was at least 62 years of age on the date of recordation of the master condominium deed, and who occupied a unit as a principal residence for the prior two years, or who is the surviving spouse of such a tenant. N.J.Stat.Ann. § 2A:18-61.24(a), (f). A recent amendment to this section now provides that an eligible surviving spouse must be at least 50 years of age at the time of the condominium conversion. An eligible "disabled tenant" is a tenant who, on the date of the conversion, was "totally and permanently unable to engage in any substantial gainful activity by reason of any medically determinable physical or mental impairment, including blindness . . . ." N.J.Stat.Ann. § 2A:18-61.24(b).

Eligible tenants may apply under section 7 to an administrative agency for "protected tenancy status" on or before the date of registration of conversion. These tenants qualify for protected tenancy status if their annual household income does not exceed three times the county per capita personal income level. N.J.Stat.Ann. § 2A:18-61.28(c). The "protected tenancy period" conferred by the Act on qualified tenants continues for forty years after the date of conversion. N.J.Stat.Ann. § 2A:18-61.24(h). No action for eviction may be brought against protected tenants during this period. N.J.Stat.Ann. § 2A:18-61.1(k). Thus, the effect of qualifying for a protected tenancy is to obtain the right to remain as a tenant in a converted unit for up to forty years beyond any period already authorized by the Anti-Eviction Act. A protected tenancy status may also be terminated. Section 11 of the Act provides that protected status shall be terminated if the unit is no longer the principal residence of the protected tenant, or if the annual household income of the protected tenant exceeds three times the most recently reported county per capita personal income level. N.J.Stat.Ann. § 2A:18-61.32.

2. Rent Increases During Protected Tenancy

The Tenancy Act also governs the magnitude of rent increases that developers may charge in order to recoup condominium conversion costs. Section 10 of the Act provides that in a municipality without a rent control ordinance in effect, the owner cannot use increased costs due to conversion as a justification for the conscionability of a rent increase in a suit for nonpayment of rent.[4] N.J.Stat.Ann. § 2A:28-61.31. In municipalities with rent control ordinances in effect, the impact of the Tenancy Act is slightly different. In these communities, increased costs due to conversion cannot be used to justify a rent increase in a "fair return or hardship hearing" before a municipal rent board. The Township of Springfield, New Jersey has such a rent control ordinance. That ordinance currently authorizes rent increases of six and one-half percent per year, subject to a number of adjustments. Two such adjustments authorize increases in "Rate of Return" and "hardship" hearings;[5] in these hearings, evidence of increased costs due to conversion would evidently not be permitted. Other adjustments—for example, adjustments reflecting increased property taxes—operate automatically, without hearings; these adjustments would apparently permit the passing on of certain conversion costs.[6]

---

[4] One of the thirteen grounds for eviction under the Anti-Eviction Act is nonpayment of rent after the service of a valid notice of rent increase, "provided the increase in rent is not unconscionable . . . ." N.J.Stat.Ann. § 2A:18-61.1(f). Section 10 of the Tenancy Act prohibits the owner's use of increased costs due to conversion as a justification for the conscionability of a rent increase in such a suit for eviction under section 2(f). Increased conversion costs are those costs that are "solely the result of the conversion," including increased financing or carrying costs, and which "do not add services or amenities not previously provided . . . ." N.J.Stat.Ann. § 2A:18-61.31.

[5] Section 13.6 of the Springfield ordinance authorizes the landlord to apply for a "Rate of Return" increase if the landlord's ratio of operating expenses to gross rents exceeds 60 percent. Section 13.5 authorizes the landlord to apply for a "hardship increase" "[i]n the event that a landlord cannot meet his current expenses for mortgage payments, and-or maintenance or repairs and-or heat-utility expenses . . . ." App. at 56.

[6] Section 13.3.1 authorizes certain capital improvement adjustments. Section 13.4 authorizes the landlord to "seek a tax surcharge from a tenant because of an increase in municipal property taxes." App. at 56. Evidently, neither of these adjustments occurs in a "fair return" or "hardship" hearing. Defendants argue that because section 10 of the Tenancy Act proscribes the passing on of conversion costs in a "fair return or hardship" hearing only, it would have no impact on forms of automatic rent adjustment, including the property-tax pass-through. See App. at 54. Plaintiffs dispute this interpretation of section 10, maintaining that the section forbids any recovery of condominium costs that do not add to the services or amenities of the buildings. Because the issue is not outcome determinative, we have no occasion to pass on this question.

In sum, the applicable rules in Springfield Township permit a condominium owner to receive yearly rent increases of six and one-half percent from each tenant-occupied condominium during the duration of a protected tenancy, and appear to permit the pass-on of certain condominium conversion costs.

3. The Retroactivity Clause

Section 14 of the Tenancy Act permits the retroactive application of the Act in certain circumstances. That section provides that in any action for a stay of eviction, for declaratory judgment, or in any other proceeding under the Anti-Eviction Act:

> the court *may* invoke *some or all* of the provisions of the [Tenancy Act] and grant to a tenant, pursuant to that [Act], a protected tenancy period upon the court's determination that:
>
> (1) The tenant would otherwise qualify as a senior citizen tenant or disabled tenant . . . except that the building or structure in which the dwelling unit is located was converted *prior to the effective date of that* [Act] *and*
>
> (2) The granting of the protected tenancy period as applied to the tenant, giving particular consideration to whether a unit was sold on or before the date that the [Act] takes effect to a bona fide individual purchaser who intended personally to occupy the unit, would not be violative of concepts of fundamental fairness or due process.

N.J.Stat.Ann. § 2A:18-61.11(d). The effect of section 14 is to confer upon the New Jersey courts discretionary authority to recognize a protected tenancy status for certain senior citizens, their spouses, and certain disabled persons who could otherwise have been evicted under the Anti-Eviction Act on three years' notice plus the tender of comparable rental housing or hardship relocation compensation.

If a court declines to grant protected tenancy status, it may nonetheless authorize up to five one-year stays of eviction until comparable rental housing is provided. The owner does not, however, have the option to buy out the interest of the tenant with a "hardship relocation compensation" of five months' rent.

II. Facts and Proceedings in the District Court

Troy Hills of Springfield is a garden apartment complex consisting of 342 residential units. Troy, Ltd. ("Troy") purchased the complex on October 1, 1979. At that time, the complex was occupied by rental tenants. On January 31, 1980, Troy contracted to sell the complex to East Coast Condo Tech, Inc. ("East Coast"), and to take back mortgages on the individual units that would be created by a condominium conversion. On February 28, 1980, Troy filed a master condominium deed, converting its ownership from a single fee to a number of condominium units. East Coast then filed a prospectus with the Department of Community Affairs, which the Department approved, pursuant to the Planned Real Estate Full Disclosure Act, in October of 1980. In January of 1981, East Coast served the three-year notices of eviction required by the Anti-Eviction Act on all tenants in the complex. The Troy-to-East-Coast closing took place on June 28, 1981, one month before the effective date of the Tenancy Act. East Coast became the owner of the separate units; Troy became the mortgagee of those units.

Many units were sold pursuant to the approved prospectus. Among the purchasers of these units are the four individual plaintiffs in this action, John F. King, Jr., Milton Snyder, Morton

Weinberg, and Stephen Forman. Weinberg and Forman executed sales contracts for condominiums before the effective date of the Tenancy Act, but closed these sales after its effective date. King and Snyder both executed sales contracts and closed sales after the Act's effective date.

On November 6, 1981, Troy and East Coast filed this action seeking declaratory and injunctive relief against the enforcement of the Tenancy Act. The complaint named as defendants the New Jersey Community Affairs Commissioner and the Attorney General (the "state defendants") and three tenants who were alleged to claim benefits under the Act as senior citizens (the "tenant defendants"). Counts I and II challenged the rent-control and protected-tenancy provisions of the Act in their prospective application. Count III of the complaint attacked the retroactive operation of section 14. That count averred that section 14 constitutes . . . a taking of property without just compensation, in a variety of respects, principally by aborting the sale of condominium units occupied by tenants who qualify for a protected status, and by denying to the owners of these units "the recovery of the costs of operation and a fair return upon the value of the units." Compl. ¶ 32, App. at 31-32. Count III also alleged a diminution in the value of the complex as security for any mortgage, and an impairment of the ability to obtain further financing on these units.

At the time plaintiffs filed this complaint, the tenant-defendants had not obtained court orders declaring that they qualified for protected tenancy status. Arguing that the district court should not proceed without such a determination, the tenant-defendants filed a motion for abstention on April 10, 1982. The district court denied that motion on April 26. On May 25, Troy and East Coast moved to add the four individual investor-plaintiffs—King, Snyder, Weinberg, and Forman—and moved for partial summary judgment on due process, equal protection, and taking grounds. The state-defendants cross-moved for summary judgment on July 6. The tenant-defendants also filed a cross-motion for summary judgment seeking to dismiss the complaint "insofar as it alleges that [section 14] is unconstitutional."

On December 13, 1982, the district court entered partial summary judgment on that portion of the complaint alleging that the retroactive operation of section 14 violated the taking clauses. Reasoning that the alterations authorized by the Act "amount to a serious disruption of the grantee's expectations," [and that] . . . section 14 applied to premises already converted, [the court held that] it violated the federal constitutional prohibition against uncompensated takings, as interpreted in *Loretto v. Teleprompter Manhattan CATV Corp.*, 458 U.S. 419 (1982).

The district court's order certified that it involves a controlling question of law as to which there is substantial ground for difference of opinion, and that an immediate appeal from it may materially advance the ultimate termination of the litigation. On January 10, 1983, we granted leave to appeal under 28 U.S.C. 1292(b) (1976). We now reverse.

. . . .

IV. The Taking Clause

It has long been settled that since the adoption of the Fourteenth Amendment compensation for private property taken for public uses constitutes an essential element in "due process of law," and that without such compensation the appropriation of private property to public uses, no matter under what form of procedure it is taken, would violate the provisions of the Federal Constitution. It has also been long settled that not every governmental regulation of the uses to which private property may be put is a taking for public use. *See Miller v. Schoene*, 276 U.S.

272 (1928) (statute authorizing destruction of diseased cedar trees); *Village of Euclid v. Ambler Realty Co.*, 272 U.S. 365 (1926) (industrial zoning regulation). The line between permissible police power regulations and impermissible uncompensated takings for public use has not always been easy to discern. In three recent decisions, the Court rejected challenges alleging takings without just compensation. *See Agins v. City of Tiburon*, 447 U.S. 255 (1980); *Penn Central Transp. Co. v. New York City*, 438 U.S. 104 (1978); *Goldblatt v. Town of Hempstead*, 369 U.S. 590 (1962). In *Loretto v. Teleprompter Manhattan C.A.T.V. Corp.*, in contrast, the Court sustained such a challenge. The district court concluded that *Loretto*, rather than *Agins, Penn Central* and *Goldblatt*, controlled. We disagree.

A.

The difficulty which sometimes arises in determining when an uncompensated-taking analysis is appropriate arises out of the failure of courts and litigants to recognize that there is no federal constitutional prohibition against takings, as such. Rather, the Constitution proscribes takings for public use "without just compensation." If adequate compensation is afforded, and if the challenged legislation has a sufficient public purpose to satisfy the demands of equal protection and substantive due process, then it is valid despite the fact that it may change the incidents of ownership in, or even the possession of, private property . . . .

Thus, the fact that the Tenancy Act creates a statutory tenancy for senior citizens and disabled persons that may amount to a "taking" could not, alone, be dispositive of its constitutionality. Both the Anti-Eviction Act and the Tenancy Act provide for compensation to the owner in the form of rent. Until the district court analyzes the compensation features of the statutory scheme to determine whether the level of compensation is adequate, it cannot find an uncompensated taking. No such analysis was made in this case. Indeed, on the summary judgment record on which the court acted, none could be made.

The Supreme Court's recent holding in *Loretto v. Teleprompter Manhattan CATV Corp.* does not compel a different conclusion. *Loretto* addressed the constitutionality of a New York statute requiring owners of rental properties to permit the installation of facilities for cable television transmission owned by cable franchise holders. In that case, the New York Court of Appeals had held that no taking had occurred and had entered judgment for the defendants. The Supreme Court reversed, but remanded for a determination of the question whether the amount of compensation to the owner provided under the New York statutory scheme was adequate. Thus, *Loretto* does not stand for the proposition that an uncompensated-taking challenge to a statute providing for some form of compensation may be decided, in favor of the party challenging the statute, facially without a record. It is clear from the remand in *Loretto* that if the compensation owed by cable franchisees to the owners proved to be adequate, then the New York statute would be constitutional. Plainly, therefore, the summary judgment that section 14 of the Tenancy Act is facially unconstitutional cannot stand.

B.

The appellants also urge that the order appealed from must be reversed because, apart from the absence of findings on "just compensation," the Tenancy Act does not entail a "taking for public use." Instead, they maintain, the Act is a classic economic or social regulation falling outside the ambit of the prohibition against uncompensated takings for public uses . . . .

In *Loretto*, the Supreme Court held that a "permanent physical occupation of property is a taking." The Tenancy Act is clearly not a taking of property under the *Loretto* standard of permanency. Most tenants with a protected status will be 70 years of age (or, if surviving spouses, 58 years of age) before the Tenancy Act comes into play. It is fanciful to imagine that these tenants will occupy their units "permanently." Moreover, the tenancies may terminate by virtue of changing income levels or principal residences, and tenants may be evicted on any of thirteen grounds. *See* N.J.S. 2A:18-61. Finally, the *Loretto* Court itself distinguished state housing legislation authorizing an extension of the tenant's lease. "In none of these cases," the Court held, "did the government authorize the permanent occupation of the landlord's property by a third party." Under these circumstances, the Tenancy Act obviously does not fall within the proscription of *Loretto*.

We also hold that the Tenancy Act is not a taking for a "public use."[12] The installation at issue in *Loretto* is the exemplar of a public use. The challenged New York law authorized an occupation of private property by a common carrier, Teleprompter, engaged in a classic public utility function. The carrier's installation of "crossover" and "noncrossover" cables on the plaintiff's roof, afforded broadcasters a common means of communication with tenants in the plaintiff's building and in the adjacent area. Consequently, *Loretto* cannot reasonably be read without an awareness of the public use involved in the taking. *Loretto* plainly does not hold that a "permanent physical occupation" is a taking without regard for the public use of the property.

Moreover, *Loretto* itself confirmed the age-old distinction between regulation and public use. Writing for the Court, Justice Marshall approved the state government's "broad power to regulate housing conditions in general and the landlord-tenant relationship in particular without paying compensation for all economic injuries that such regulation entails." The Court's citations in support of this longstanding proposition include *Edgar A. Levy Leasing Co. v. Siegel*, 258 U.S. 242 (1922), and *Block v. Hirsh*, 256 U.S. 135 (1921). *Levy* upheld a New York statute similar to the Anti-Eviction Act and the Tenancy Act, placing limits on the landlord's right of action to recover possession from holdover tenants. In *Block*, the Court upheld a District of Columbia ordinance that gave tenants a right of continued occupation following the expiration of their leases. The Court clearly assumed that the creation of the statutory tenancy for private parties was not a taking for public use.[15] Statutory tenancy laws protecting holdover tenants are not takings, but merely regulations of the use to which private property may be put. Such regulations of the use of private property frequently involve costs to the owner. They are nevertheless not deemed

---

[12] "Public use" under the taking clause must be distinguished from "public purpose" as that term is used under the contract clause or in analyzing the scope of the police power. Public uses include, for example, physical occupation by a common carrier engaged in a classic public utility function. *See* note 16 *infra*.

[15] *Loretto* does inform us, however, that even for *public use* a taking within the meaning of the constitution is likely to be found only when the invasion is permanent in character rather than temporary or intermittent. In so holding, the court distinguished cases such as *Transportation Co. v. Chicago*, 99 U.S. 635 (1879) (temporary flooding caused by construction), and cited with approval Professor Michelman's observation that:

> [t]he one incontestable case for compensation (short of formal expropriation) seems to occur when the government deliberately brings it about that its agents, or the public at large, "regularly" use, or "permanently" occupy, space or a thing which theretofore was understood to be under private ownership.

458 U.S. at 427 & n. 5, quoting Michelman, *Property, Utility, and Fairness: Comments on the Ethical Foundations of "Just Compensation" Law*, 80 Harv. L. Rev. 1165, 1184 (1967).

. . . .

to be takings. *E.g., Goldblatt v. Town of Hempstead*, 369 U.S. 590 (1962); *Village of Euclid v. Ambler Realty Co.*, 272 U.S. 365 (1926) (industrial zoning); *see* note 16 *infra. See also* Sax, *Takings and the Police Power*, 74 Yale L.J. 36, 61-76 (1964) (terming the distinction one between government as "enterprise" and government as "mediator").

Where, as here, legislation does not put property to a "public use," it is a constitutional exercise of the state's police power provided, of course, that it satisfies the demands of due process and equal protection. Because the Tenancy Act did not put the plaintiffs' property to public use, but rather regulated its use, the Act is not a taking under the fifth and fourteenth amendments.[16]

The judgment appealed from will be reversed.

[g] Explanatory Notes

[i] *Constitutional Challenges. Renna* is representative of a long string of cases, many cited in the opinion, in which property subject to extensive regulation has not been regarded as "taken" within the meaning of the Fifth Amendment.[152] Some of the more famous taking cases will be read in Chapter 11. While it is not possible to put all of the taking decisions within a consistent theoretical structure, there are three general patterns that the courts seem to have fallen into. First, where there is no physical intrusion by the regulating governmental entity, regulatory activity becomes a taking only when virtually all use of the property has been forbidden. Thus, zoning land solely for park use may be a taking, but limiting the height of buildings to 10 floors is unlikely to constitute a taking. Second, when the state mediates conflicts between owners of property, the form of mediation is unlikely to be a taking even if one owner is severely penalized while another is benefited. Thus, statutes controlling air pollution or requiring subjacent support of neighboring buildings during construction are not takings. Finally, when area wide land use controls are adopted without a procedure for granting hardship variances, the courts are likely to scrutinize the scheme very closely.

From the 1920s until about a decade ago, virtually all major land uses challenged in the Supreme Court survived. *Village of Euclid v. Ambler*, p. 490 above, was the most important case in the 1920s transition from the intense scrutiny of land use controls of the Formalist Era to the judicially restrained review of the New Deal Court. In *Renna*, the continued payment of the

---

[16] It is understandable that the "public use" aspect of the taking clause analysis should become closely identified with the question of the permanent physical nature of the intrusion. Few exercises of the police power require permanent physical intrusion onto private property. In contrast, many public uses—for example, roads, dams, power and communication grids—necessarily involve physical seizure or intrusion. Consequently, most Supreme Court decisions holding governmental action violative of the taking clause have involved both physical intrusion and classic public use. *See, e.g., Portsmouth Harbor Land & Hotel Co. v. United States*, 260 U.S. 327 (1922) (military use); *Western Union Telegraph Co. v. Pennsylvania R.R.*, 195 U.S. 540 (1904) (telegraph lines); *Loretto*, supra. *But see Pennsylvania Coal Co. v. Mahon*, 260 U.S. 393, 414-16 (1922). Most decisions sustaining governmental action, on the other hand, have involved a common exercise of regulatory power. *See Goldblatt v. Town of Hempstead*, 369 U.S. 590 (1962) (safety ordinance banning excavation); *United States v. Central Eureka Mining Co.*, 357 U.S. 155 (1958) (prohibition of mining operations during war emergency regulation not a taking); *Miller v. Schoene*, 276 U.S. 272 (1928) (ordinance requiring destruction of diseased trees); *Village of Euclid v. Ambler Realty Co.*, 272 U.S. 365 (1926) (industrial zoning); *Hadacheck v. Sebastian*, 239 U.S. 394 (1915) (prohibition on operation of brickyard); *Mugler v. Kansas*, 123 U.S. 623 (1887) (prohibition on sale of liquor). *See generally* Note, *Public Use, Private Use, and Judicial Review in Eminent Domain*, 58 N.Y.U. L. Rev. 409 (1983).

[152] There have been other unsuccessful challenges to New Jersey's systematic restrictions on eviction. *See, e.g., Edgewater Investment Associates v. Borough of Edgewater*, 103 N.J. 227, 510 A.2d 1178 (1986); *Puttrich v. Smith*, 170 N.J. Super. 572, 407 A.2d 842 (1979).

landlord by the tenant and the landlord's retention of management control over the property made it very unlikely that a taking would be found.

A useful contrast with *Renna* is provided by the New Jersey rent control cases. While the state Supreme Court has never suggested that rent controls are uniformly invalid, it has voided a system that restricted rent increases to 2.5% and that lacked a workable administrative method for landlords to obtain relief prior to absorbing major losses. In *Helmsley v. Borough of Fort Lee*,[153] the court wrote:

> We share the view of [California and the District of Columbia] that where a rent control scheme will have a foreseeable, widespread confiscatory impact, it is constitutionally necessary to provide a mechanism capable of providing adjustments in maximum rents without a substantially greater incidence and degree of delay than is practically necessary. The landlord of a rent controlled building in Fort Lee must realize inadequate income before it can obtain relief. The confiscation precedes the redress in this case. Some short-term uncompensated confiscation may well be unavoidable under rent control, but it is essential that the severity and duration of such takings be minimized.

Presumably *Renna* would have come out differently if the rent levels of protected elderly tenants were regulated like all units in Fort Lee.

[*ii*]   *Statutory Tenants.* For all practical purposes, protected elderly or disabled tenants in New Jersey have a lifetime guarantee that they may remain in their apartments. Such statutory tenancies turn landlords into virtual public utilities. Just as utility rates are controlled, so are the rent levels of protected tenants. Utilities must provide service to all paying customers, and landlords of protected tenants may not terminate a tenancy without good cause. Utilities must maintain their supply system, while landlords must maintain their apartments. And utilities, like landlords of protected tenants, must obey stringent notice rules in dealing with their customers. For more on this idea, read Mary Ann Glendon, *The Transformation of American Landlord-Tenant Law*, 23 B.C. L. Rev. 503 (1982), excerpted in Richard Chused, A Property Anthology 160-171 (2d ed.1997).

[h]   Problem Notes

[*i*]   *Why Protect the Old to the Exclusion of Others?* Why provide the elderly with greater tenancy protections than other groups? How about single parents with children? Don't they have as much (maybe more) difficulty finding a reasonably priced, high quality place to live? What of the mentally retarded? Should veterans get the same breaks? Does the notion that elderly people have a harder time adjusting to new environments than their younger colleagues justify the protections New Jersey law provides?

[*ii*]   *Taking Problem.* Suppose a state legislature passed a statute permitting a municipality to seize any office building and turn it over to another business entity for their use? Assume that the purpose of the statute was to make it easier for certain towns to attract large new businesses to their areas by avoiding the costly process of assembling large tracts of land or large amounts of unused rental space. Surely there would be constitutional problems with such a statute. First, the lack of compensation would cause the scheme to fail on the altar of the Taking Clause. That problem may be solvable by requiring the new occupant to pay "rent" to the old

---

[153] N.J. 200, 394 A.2d 65 (1978).

owner. Second, some state courts have expressed doubts about the propriety of taking property from one private owner with the sole purpose of giving it to another private owner. The theory is that land may not be taken by the public, even if compensation is paid, unless there is a valid public purpose for the condemnation.[154] Is this office scheme distinguishable from the *Renna* situation?

[*iii*]   ***Switch-a-Tenant.*** If *Renna* was correctly decided, is there anything to prevent a governmental entity from ordering the eviction of an "unprotected" tenant from an apartment and moving a "protected" tenant into the same housing unit? Does the unprotected tenant have any rights protected by the taking clause?

[*iv*]   ***Validity of Selecting Senior Citizens as Protected Class.*** The various provisions of New Jersey law discussed in *Renna* provide detailed protections for senior citizens, including virtual lifetime tenancies, and rent levels determined without regard to property value increases of the building caused by the conversion of other units to condominiums. Although conversion frequently increases property values, rent levels may not be raised to account for increased property tax assessments. In other litigation, the New Jersey Supreme Court has decided that rent control ordinances may not provide "super rent protection" to senior citizens by imposing additional rental obligations on other tenants.[155] Does that mean *Renna* was wrongly decided?

[*v*]   ***A New Protected Class of New Jersey Tenants.*** After Renna was decided, New Jersey adopted legislation protecting a new class of tenants. Under the terms of the Tenant Protection Act of 1992, N.J. Stat. Ann. § 2A:18-61.40 et seq., tenants with incomes below a certain level living in counties losing significant numbers of rental units to condominium or cooperative conversions obtain a protected status, which lasts until the tenant's income rises above the statutory limits or the apartment is vacated. Such tenants may not be evicted and their rents may not be raised an unreasonable amount. Are rationales supporting this form of protected tenancy stronger or weaker than those supporting the system at issue in Renna?

§ 8.06 Tenant Turnover: Departures, Assignments and Subleases

[1] Tenant Departures

The materials in the previous sections of this chapter reviewed some of the problems that arise when a tenant in possession breaches the terms of the lease by not paying rent or by retaining possession beyond the leasehold period. But landlords also have problems with tenants who leave their rented space, either with or without a replacement. This section explores some of these problems. We begin with tenants who leave. To this point, all you know about remedies against departing lessees is that a landlord may seek rent from a tenant who leaves unless there has been a constructive eviction.[156] But the problems of abandonment are much more complex than the constructive eviction rules might lead you to believe. The best summary of the anomalies of the common law legal structure is provided by Professor Sarajane Love in an article excerpted just below.

---

[154] *Compare* Poletown v. Detroit, p. 914 below.

[155] Property Owners Association of North Bergen v. North Bergen Township, 378 A.2d 25, 74 N.J. 327 (1977).

[156] *See Reste Realty v. Cooper*, p. 641 above.

[a]   The Common Law Rules: Abandonment and Surrender

Sarajane Love, *Landlord's Remedies When the Tenant Abandons: Property, Contract, and Leases*

30 U. Kan. L. Rev. 533, 535-540 (1982)[157]

The common law construed the tenant's abandonment as an offer to the landlord to surrender the remainder of the leasehold estate. The landlord's remedies were largely dependent on how he responded to this implied offer of the tenant. He could accept the offer of surrender, but if he did so, it was universally agreed that the tenant's obligation to pay rent for the remainder of the term drowned along with the term itself. On the other hand, the landlord might refuse to accept the offer implied by the abandonment, which in turn opened up two options: he could, consistent with the tenant's interest in the leased premises, stand idly by and sue the tenant for rent as it became due under the terms of the lease; or he could, not so consistent with the tenant's ownership of the leasehold, exercise what is commonly called the tenant's account remedy. Under the tenant's account remedy, the landlord resumed possession of the property for the limited purpose of reletting it to a new tenant. Rent received under the new lease was applied to the defaulting tenant's account. The landlord could then recover from the original tenant any deficiency between the rent promised by him and the rent received by the landlord upon the reletting.

As the above formulation suggests, it was apparently necessary under the common law to determine whether there had been a surrender before addressing the question of whether and how to make the landlord whole for the loss of his rent-paying tenant. Although that may seem to be putting the cart before the horse, it must be remembered that from the earliest times, the common law insisted on a very close association between rent and the tenant's interest in the leased property. It was said that the rent issued from the land, and that the land was bound to pay the rent. Indeed, rent itself was conceived to be very "thinglike," an incorporeal piece of property, so that the landlord's action to recover rent was not an enforcement of an obligation, but the recovery of a thing.[158] Therefore, the medieval landlord had to look to the land for the rent, and if the tenant no longer owned his interest in the land because of a surrender, the tenant had no further obligation to pay rent. So strong was the association between the land and the landlord's right to rent that, even after landlords began routinely to extract from their tenants an express covenant to pay rent to shore up the rental obligation that was inherent in the conveyance of the term, a surrender terminated any liability based on the covenant just as surely as it terminated the liability based on privity of estate between the landlord and tenant . . . .

Against this background, it should not be surprising that it has taxed logic to explain the workings of the tenant's account remedy. How could the tenant still be liable to the landlord when his possession of the leasehold premises was precluded by the presence of a new tenant procured by the landlord?

. . . .

---

[157] Reprinted by permission of Kansas Law Review and Sarajane Love.

[158] [Editor's Note: At some level this made sense because rent was often paid in kind or in services to the landlord during the earliest days of leaseholds.]

An examination of the origins of the tenant's account remedy . . . reveals why the remedy fits so awkwardly into the common law property mold. The tenant's account remedy was not originally a part of the common law. In *Auer v. Penn*,[28] the leading case recognizing the tenant's account remedy, the court's decision was reached through the application of contract rules and was motivated by practical considerations. Property law figures in the opinion only because the court had to refute the tenant's argument that the landlord's reletting had caused a surrender. More convincing to the court than the tenant's surrender argument was the proposition that "one party to a contract cannot rescind it at pleasure." Thus, the tenant could not escape liability by throwing the keys at the landlord's feet and walking away.[30]

Pragmatism, or "good sense," also influenced the court's sanctioning of the remedy. The court emphasized that the landlord's reletting operated to the tenant's benefit, because the landlord could "simply lock the door and lay by and sue the tenant or surety for the whole amount of rent for the whole term for which he has taken it."[32] If the property was relet, however, the tenant's liability was reduced by the amount of rent received under the new lease. The court focused primarily on what was best for the landlord and the tenant, but others have pointed out that the community at large also has a pragmatic stake in promoting the tenant's account remedy. Encouraging the productive use of real property resources benefits the community and has been a constant policy concern in the evolution of property law. Allowing the landlord to relet the abandoned property without being deprived of his remedy against the tenant "renders it more probable that the premises will constantly be in use rather than lie unproductively vacant."

Much of the confusion over the meaning of abandonment, surrender and mitigation described by Professor Love was removed in New Jersey when the Supreme Court applied contractual mitigation rules to cases involved departing tenants. That decision follows.

[b] Opinion of the New Jersey Supreme Court in *Sommer v. Kridel*

Sommer v. Kridel

Supreme Court of New Jersey
74 N.J. 446, 378 A.2d 767 (1977)

The opinion of the court was delivered by

Pashman, J.

We granted certification . . . to consider whether a landlord seeking damages from a defaulting tenant is under a duty to mitigate damages by making reasonable efforts to re-let an apartment wrongfully vacated by the tenant . . . . [T]he Appellate Division held that . . . the landlord

---

[28] 99 Pa. 370 (1882).

[30] Another early tenant's account case, J.C. Meyer & Co. v. Smith, 33 Ark. 627 (1878), like *Auer*, regards the abandoned lease as a breached contract and analogizes to a vendee's breach of a contract for the sale of a chattel. An intriguing light is cast on these courts' unhesitating application of contract rules to the lease by Weinberg, *From Contract to Conveyance: The Law of Landlord and Tenant, 1800-1920* (Part 1), 1980 S. ILL. U. L.J. 29. Professor Weinberg concludes that leases were widely treated as contracts in the eighteenth and nineteenth centuries, and that the systematic analysis of leases as conveyances that appeared in the early twentieth century treatises was in fact a break with the more recent past.

[32] This landlord's option is a standard item in the common law of property, but a departure from the common law of contracts.

. . . could recover rents due under the lease regardless of whether . . . [it] had attempted to re-let the vacated apartments . . . . [The Appellate Division felt bound] by *Joyce v. Bauman*, 113 *N.J.L.* 438, 174 *A.* 693 (E. & A. 1934), a decision by the former Court of Errors and Appeals. We now reverse and hold that a landlord does have an obligation to make a reasonable effort to mitigate damages in such a situation. We therefore overrule Joyce v. Bauman to the extent that it is inconsistent with our decision today.

I

This case was tried on stipulated facts. On March 10, 1972 the defendant, James Kridel, entered into a lease with the plaintiff, Abraham Sommer, owner of the "Pierre Apartments" in Hackensack, to rent apartment 6-L in that building.[1] The term of the lease was from May 1, 1972 until April 30, 1974, with a rent concession for the first six weeks, so that the first month's rent was not due until June 15, 1972.

One week after signing the agreement, Kridel paid Sommer $690. Half of that sum was used to satisfy the first month's rent. The remainder was paid under the lease provision requiring a security deposit of $345. Although defendant had expected to begin occupancy around May 1, his plans were changed. He wrote to Sommer on May 19, 1972, explaining

I was to be married on June 3, 1972. Unhappily the engagement was broken and the wedding plans canceled. Both parents were to assume responsibility for the rent after our marriage. I was discharged from the U.S. Army in October 1971 and am now a student. I have no funds of my own, and am supported by my stepfather.

In view of the above, I cannot take possession of the apartment and am surrendering all rights to it. Never having received a key, I cannot return same to you.

I beg your understanding and compassion in releasing me from the lease, and will of course, in consideration thereof, forfeit the 2 month's rent already paid.

Please notify me at your earliest convenience.

Plaintiff did not answer the letter.

Subsequently, a third party went to the apartment house and inquired about renting apartment 6-L. Although the parties agreed that she was ready, willing and able to rent the apartment, the person in charge told her that the apartment was not being shown since it was already rented to Kridel. In fact, the landlord did not re-enter the apartment or exhibit it to anyone until August 1, 1973. At that time it was rented to a new tenant for a term beginning on September 1, 1973. The new rental was for $345 per month with a six week concession similar to that granted Kridel.

Prior to re-letting the new premises, plaintiff sued Kridel in August 1972, demanding $7,590, the total amount due for the full two-year term of the lease. Following a mistrial, plaintiff filed an amended complaint asking for $5,865, the amount due between May 1, 1972 and September 1, 1973. The amended complaint included no reduction in the claim to reflect the six week concession provided for in the lease or the $690 payment made to plaintiff after signing the agreement. Defendant filed an amended answer to the complaint, alleging that plaintiff breached the contract, failed to mitigate damages and accepted defendant's surrender of the premises. He also counterclaimed to demand repayment of the $345 paid as a security deposit.

---

[1] Among other provisions, the lease prohibited the tenant from assigning or transferring the lease without the consent of the landlord. If the tenant defaulted, the lease gave the landlord the option of re-entering or re-letting, but stipulated that failure to re-let or to recover the full rental would not discharge the tenant's liability for rent.

The trial judge ruled in favor of defendant. Despite his conclusion that the lease had been drawn to reflect "the 'settled law' of this state," he found that "justice and fair dealing" imposed upon the landlord the duty to attempt to re-let the premises and thereby mitigate damages. He also held that plaintiff's failure to make any response to defendant's unequivocal offer of surrender was tantamount to an acceptance, thereby terminating the tenancy and any obligation to pay rent. As a result, he dismissed both the complaint and the counterclaim. The Appellate Division reversed in a per curiam opinion and we granted certification.

. . . .

II

As the lower court . . . found, the weight of authority in this State supports the rule that a landlord is under no duty to mitigate damages caused by a defaulting tenant. See *Joyce v. Bauman, supra; Weiss v. I. Zapinski, Inc.,* 65 *N.J. Super.* 351, 167 *A.*2d 802 (App. Div. 1961); *Heyman v. Linwood Park,* 41 *N.J. Super.* 437, 125 *A.*2d 345 (App. Div. 1956); *Zucker v. Dehm,* 128 *N.J.L.* 435, 26 *A.*2d 564 (Sup. Ct. 1942); *Heckel v. Griese,* 12 *N.J. Misc.* 211, 171 *A.* 148 (Sup. Ct.1934); *Muller v. Beck,* 94 *N.J.L.* 311, 110 *A.* 831 (Sup. Ct.1920); *Tanella v. Rettagliata,* 120 *N.J. Super.* 400, 407, 294 *A.*2d 431 (Cty. Ct. 1972). This rule has been followed in a majority of states, Annot. 21 *A.L.R.*3d 534, § 2[a] at 541 (1968), and has been tentatively adopted in the American Law Institute's Restatement of Property. *Restatement (Second) of Property,* § 11.1(3) (Tent. Draft No. 3, 1975).

Nevertheless, while there is still a split of authority over this question, the trend among recent cases appears to be in favor of a mitigation requirement. *Dushoff v. Phoenix Co.,* 23 *Ariz. App.* 238, 532 *P.*2d 180 (App. 1975); *Hirsch v. Merchants National Bank & Trust Co.,* 336 *N.E.*2d 833 (Ind. App.1975); *Wilson v. Ruhl,* 277 *Md.* 607, 356 *A.*2d 544 (1976) (by statute); *Bernstein v. Seglin,* 184 *Neb.* 673, 171 *N.W.*2d 247 (1969); *Lefrak v. Lambert,* 89 *Misc.*2d 197, 390 *N.Y.S.*2d 959 (N.Y. Cty. Ct.1976); *Howard Stores Corp. v. Rayon Co., Inc.,* 36 *A.D.*2d 911, 320 *N.Y.S.*2d 861 (App. Div.1971); *Ross v. Smigelski,* 42 *Wis.*2d 185, 166 *N.W.*2d 243 (1969).

The majority rule is based on principles of property law which equate a lease with a transfer of a property interest in the owner's estate. Under this rationale the lease conveys to a tenant an interest in the property which forecloses any control by the landlord; thus, it would be anomalous to require the landlord to concern himself with the tenant's abandonment of his own property.

For instance, in *Muller v. Beck, supra,* where essentially the same issue was posed, the court clearly treated the lease as governed by property, as opposed to contract, precepts.[3] The court there observed that the "tenant had an estate for years, but it was an estate qualified by this right of the landlord to prevent its transfer," and that "the tenant has an estate with which the landlord may not interfere." Similarly, in *Heckel v. Griese, supra,* the court noted the absolute nature of the tenant's interest in the property while the lease was in effect, stating that "when the tenant vacated, . . . no one, in the circumstances, had any right to interfere with the

---

[3] It is well settled that a party claiming damages for a breach of contract has a duty to mitigate his loss. *See Frank Stamato & Co. v. Borough of Lodi,* 4 *N.J.* 14, 71 *A.*2d 336 (1950); *Sandler v. Lawn-A-Mat Chem. & Equip. Corp.,* 141 *N.J. Super.* 437, 455, 358 *A.*2d 805 (App. Div.1976); *Wolf v. Marlton Corp.,* 57 *N.J. Super.* 278, 154 *A.*2d 625 (App. Div.1956); 5 *Corbin on Contracts* (1964 ed.), § 1039 at 241 et seq.; *McCormick, Damages,* § 33 at 127 (1935). *See also* N.J. STAT. ANN. 12A:2-708.

defendant's possession of the premises." Other cases simply cite the rule announced in *Muller v. Beck*, supra, without discussing the underlying rationale.

Yet the distinction between a lease for ordinary residential purposes and an ordinary contract can no longer be considered viable. As Professor Powell observed, evolving "social factors have exerted increasing influence on the law of estates for years." 2 *Powell on Real Property* (1977 ed.), § 221[1] at 180-81. The result has been that

> (t)he complexities of city life, and the proliferated problems of modern society in general, have created new problems for lessors and lessees and these have been commonly handled by specific clauses in leases. This growth in the number and detail of specific lease covenants has reintroduced into the law of estates for years a predominantly contractual ingredient.

. . . .

See also Javins v. First National Realty Corp., 138 *U.S.App.D.C.* 369, 373, 428 *F.*2d 1071, 1075 (D.C.Cir.1970); Hicks, "The Contractual Nature of Real Property Leases," 24 *Baylor L.Rev.* 443 (1972); Note, "Right of Lessor to Refuse any Subtenant When Lease Prohibits Transfer Without Consent," 41 *Minn.L.Rev.* 355, 357 (1957).

This Court has taken the lead in requiring that landlords provide housing services to tenants in accordance with implied duties which are hardly consistent with the property notions expressed in *Muller v. Beck, supra,* and *Heckel v. Griese, supra. See Braitman v. Overlook Terrace Corp.,* 68 *N.J.* 368, 346 *A.*2d 76 (1975) (liability for failure to repair defective apartment door lock); *Berzito v. Gambino,* 63 *N.J.* 460, 308 *A.*2d 17 (1973) (construing implied warranty of habitability and covenant to pay rent as mutually dependent); *Marini v. Ireland,* 56 *N.J.* 130, 265 *A.*2d 526 (1970) (implied covenant to repair); *Reste Realty Corp. v. Cooper,* 53 *N.J.* 444, 251 *A.*2d 268 (1969) (implied warranty of fitness of premises for leased purpose). In fact, in *Reste Realty Corp. v. Cooper, supra,* we specifically noted that the rule which we announced there did not comport with the historical notion of a lease as an estate for years. And in *Marini v. Ireland, supra,* we found that the "guidelines employed to construe contracts have been modernly applied to the construction of leases."

Application of the contract rule requiring mitigation of damages to a residential lease may be justified as a matter of basic fairness.[4] Professor McCormick first commented upon the inequity under the majority rule when he predicted in 1925 that eventually

> the logic, inescapable according to the standards of a 'jurisprudence of conceptions' which permits the landlord to stand idly by the vacant, abandoned premises and treat them as the property of the tenant and recover full rent, will yield to the more realistic notions of social advantage which in other fields of the law have forbidden a recovery for damages which the plaintiff by reasonable efforts could have avoided. (McCormick, "The Rights of the Landlord Upon Abandonment of the Premises by the Tenant," 23 *Mich. L. Rev.* 211, 221-22 (1925))

. . . .

The pre-existing rule cannot be predicated upon the possibility that a landlord may lose the opportunity to rent another empty apartment because he must first rent the apartment vacated by the defaulting tenant. Even where the breach occurs in a multi-dwelling building, each

---

[4] We see no distinction between the leases involved in the instant appeals and those which might arise in other types of residential housing. However, we reserve for another day the question of whether a landlord must mitigate damages in a commercial setting.

apartment may have unique qualities which make it attractive to certain individuals. Significantly, in *Sommer v. Kridel,* there was a specific request to rent the apartment vacated by the defendant; there is no reason to believe that absent this vacancy the landlord could have succeeded in renting a different apartment to this individual.

We therefore hold that antiquated real property concepts which served as the basis for the pre-existing rule, shall no longer be controlling where there is a claim for damages under a residential lease. Such claims must be governed by more modern notions of fairness and equity. A landlord has a duty to mitigate damages where he seeks to recover rents due from a defaulting tenant.

If the landlord has other vacant apartments besides the one which the tenant has abandoned, the landlord's duty to mitigate consists of making reasonable efforts to re-let the apartment. In such cases he must treat the apartment in question as if it was one of his vacant stock.

As part of his cause of action, the landlord shall be required to carry the burden of proving that he used reasonable diligence in attempting to re-let the premises. We note that there has been a divergence of opinion concerning the allocation of the burden of proof on this issue. While generally in contract actions the breaching party has the burden of proving that damages are capable of mitigation, here the landlord will be in a better position to demonstrate whether he exercised reasonable diligence in attempting to re-let the premises.

III

The *Sommer v. Kridel* case presents a classic example of the unfairness which occurs when a landlord has no responsibility to minimize damages. Sommer waited 15 months and allowed $4658.50 in damages to accrue before attempting to re-let the apartment. Despite the availability of a tenant who was ready, willing and able to rent the apartment, the landlord needlessly increased the damages by turning her away. While a tenant will not necessarily be excused from his obligations under a lease simply by finding another person who is willing to rent the vacated premises, see, e. g., *Reget v. Dempsey-Tegler & Co.,* 70 *Ill. App.* 2d 32, 216 *N.E.*2d 500 (Ill. App.1966) (new tenant insisted on leasing the premises under different terms); *Edmands v. Rust & Richardson Drug Co.,* 191 *Mass.* 123, 77 *N.E.* 713 (1906) (landlord need not accept insolvent tenant), here there has been no showing that the new tenant would not have been suitable. We therefore find that plaintiff could have avoided the damages which eventually accrued, and that the defendant was relieved of his duty to continue paying rent. Ordinarily we would require the tenant to bear the cost of any reasonable expenses incurred by a landlord in attempting to re-let the premises, but no such expenses were incurred in this case.[5]

. . . .

In assessing whether the landlord has satisfactorily carried his burden, the trial court shall consider, among other factors, whether the landlord, either personally or through an agency, offered or showed the apartment to any prospective tenants, or advertised it in local newspapers. Additionally, the tenant may attempt to rebut such evidence by showing that he proffered suitable tenants who were rejected. However, there is no standard formula for measuring whether the

---

[5] As to defendant's counterclaim for $345, representing the amount deposited with the landlord as a security deposit, we note that this issue has not been briefed or argued before this Court, and apparently has been abandoned. Because we hold that plaintiff breached his duty to attempt to mitigate damages, we do not address defendant's argument that the landlord accepted a surrender of the premises.

landlord has utilized satisfactory efforts in attempting to mitigate damages, and each case must be judged upon its own facts.

IV

The judgment in Sommer v. Kridel is reversed . . . .

For reversal . . . : Chief Justice HUGHES, JUSTICES MOUNTAIN, PASHMAN, CLIFFORD and SCHREIBER and JUDGE CONFORD—6.

For affirmance: None.

[c]   Explanatory Notes

[*i*]   *Abandonment, Surrender and Mitigation.* Ambiguity about the meaning of "surrender" arose in significant part because of the "either-or" quality of common law remedies after abandonment. If a landlord expressly or impliedly accepted an abandonment, thereby creating a surrender, the tenant owed the landlord nothing. Thus, unless the landlord was extremely careful, there was always a risk that taking *any* steps to regain control over possession of the leased premises would be deemed an acceptance of the abandonment. But if the landlord did not accept the abandonment, then the tenant might be responsible for *all* the rent, even though not in possession. In many situations neither solution seemed appropriate. In a number of cases courts not wishing to burden a tenant with all the rent for the remainder of the term struggled to turn abandonments into surrenders. As previously noted by Professor Love, that is why courts were willing to permit landlords to re-let on the tenant's account. The availability of such a remedy created incentives to keep property in productive use, mitigated a tenant's losses, provided landlords with economic redress, and reduced the need for using courts to resolve disputes.

One way out of the abandonment-surrender dilemma, the path apparently selected in *Kridel*, is to simply forget about surrender and "think contract." If a tenant breaches a lease by abandoning, then the landlord has various contract remedies available. If the breach is material (which abandonment surely is), the landlord may cancel the contract. While that ends the contract, it does not necessarily end the landlord's ability to recover losses, at least for the period before cancellation. Quantum meruit forms of equitable relief have long been used to provide landlords with the reasonable value of possession not paid for by the tenant prior to the cancellation.[159] Reasonable value is likely to be the same as rent unless the lease called for an unusual rent or the rental market changed markedly after the lease was signed. In cases where the value of the premises is significantly greater than the lease price, cancellation would be an attractive remedy to a landlord with an abandoned and unpaid for lease.

But given the stability of rent levels during the terms of most leases, the landlord is unlikely to cancel. Some other contract remedy will probably be selected which binds the tenant to the rental obligations for the entire period of the lease. The landlord may choose to sue as each rent installment becomes due, wait until the lease ends and sue for the unpaid rent, or attempt to accelerate the rent for the entire term and sue immediately. In each of these cases, contract

---

[159] There is, of course, the problem of the landlord who waits a long time after the tenant abandons to rescind the lease. In that case, even if the court permits the rescission to go forward, there may not be any obligation on the part of the tenant to pay rent beyond some reasonable period. In any case, this is an extremely unlikely scenario, since the incentive to rescind is greatest when rent levels have risen, a setting not likely to lead the landlord to sit on his hands.

law normally permits the landlord to recover only the difference between the contract (*i.e.* lease) price and the price recoverable in the market, together with any consequential and incidental damages resulting from the breach. Mitigation becomes the (now required) device by which these damages may be measured. If the landlord sues month by month or waits until the end of the lease, he may recover only the difference between the contract rent and the rent obtained from the new tenant. And if the landlord accelerates the total rent anticipating that the tenant has repudiated the entire lease, then the present value of the damages must be discounted by the present value of any rents the landlord is likely to receive through mitigation.[160] In addition, the landlord will be able to recover as consequential or incidental damages the reasonable costs associated with finding a new tenant and making the premises usable.

In all of these contract damage theories, the issue of surrender is unimportant. Absent cancellation, the landlord is always renting on the tenant's account. The need to distinguish between acceptance of abandonment on the one hand, and reletting on either the landlord's or tenant's account on the other, disappears. The court looks only at the difference between an election to cancel and all other remedies.

[*ii*]   *Mitigation in Commercial Cases.* The *Kridel* court left open the issue of whether mitigation will also be required in commercial lease cases, though the overtly contractual nature of the reasoning certainly suggested that mitigation would be obligatory in all cases. So far, the lower courts have been requiring mitigation in commercial cases. *See, e.g., Fanarjian v. Moskowitz,* 237 N.J. Super 395, 568 A.2d 94 (1989).

[*iii*]   *Uniform Residential Landlord-Tenant Act.* The Uniform Residential Landlord-Tenant Act, written in the early 1970s, requires mitigation but places it within the old common law abandonment/surrender structure. The result is quite confusing:

§ 4.203 [Remedies for Absence, Nonuse and Abandonment][*]

. . . .

(c) If the tenant abandons the dwelling unit, the landlord shall make reasonable efforts to rent it at a fair rental. If the landlord rents the dwelling unit for a term beginning before the expiration of the rental agreement, it terminates as of the date of the new tenancy. If the landlord fails to use reasonable efforts to rent the dwelling unit at a fair rental or if the landlord accepts the abandonment as a surrender, the rental agreement is deemed to be terminated by the landlord as of the date the landlord has notice of the abandonment. If the tenancy is from month-to-month or week-to-week, the term of the rental agreement for this purpose is deemed to be a month or a week, as the case may be.

[d]   Problem Notes

[*i*]   *Abandonment and Property Left Behind.* What should be done when a tenant "abandons" a place but leaves property behind? Depending upon how much property is left, the

---

[160] There is some hostility to the notion of permitting the landlord to accelerate all of the rent for an entire term, particularly when the lease has a significant period of time left to run. But this may be the most practical method of handling an abandonment long before a lease expires. It may be more sensible to resolve the entire matter now than to doggedly pursue the dispute for the next 20 (for example) years. My guess is that the hostility to using the doctrine in lease law arises from the notion that the landlord did not have to mitigate and that acceleration therefore meant immediate payment of all rent called for in the contract. Mitigation mitigates that fear.

[*] Reprinted with the permission of the National Conference of Commissioners on Uniform State Laws.

tenant may or may not have breached the terms of the lease. One way to test the tenant's preferences is to file an action for possession. If the tenant does not contest the action, that would give the landlord the right to enter the property and remove any remaining items. In this sort of circumstance, the filing of an action for possession should not be taken as an election by the landlord to rescind the lease. For cases raising this sort of problem, *see Tanella v. Rettagliata,* 120 N.J. Super. 400, 294 A.2d 431 (1972); *56 Glenwood Corp. v. Plotkin,* 248 N.J. Super. 50, 589 A.2d 1380 (1990).

[*ii*]   *Due Process and Mitigation.* In situations like those described in the previous note, the landlord has to deal with a nifty little problem of getting possession of an "abandoned" apartment when the absconding tenant left some property behind. Landlords are no longer free to routinely take a tenant's property away without any judicial process. Although you should wonder about the degree to which this norm is followed in the real world, it sets up an interesting conflict between the moveable "property" owned by the tenant and placed in an apartment and the "contract" agreed to in the form of a lease. Even if the underlying debate over the contract or property status of a lease is resolved in favor of a contract, are there still good reasons why property norms might be applied to some aspects of the landlord-tenant relationship? Should a landlord unsure about whether a tenant has given up possession of an apartment be free to remove personal property from the site without any judicial proceedings?

[*iii*]   *Economic Benefit of Reletting.* Does any of this theorizing about the contractual nature of a lease help decide whether the landlord or the tenant should get the benefit of a reletting after an abandonment when the new tenant pays a *larger* rent than that called for in the original lease? Is this a dispute about different contract theories or about contract as distinguished from property? In *N.J. Industrial Properties, Inc. v. Y.C. & V.L., Inc.,* 100 N.J. 432, 495 A.2d 1320 (1985), the tenant left and failed to pay rent for a time before the landlord found a new tenant at a higher rent. The tenant then claimed that the excess rents paid by the new tenant should be applied to reduce its indebtedness for the period the property was vacant. In a 4-3 vote, the New Jersey Supreme Court held that the benefit of the reletting should accrue only to the landlord and held the tenant responsible for the entire rent left unpaid during the period of vacancy. Both the majority and the dissent claimed to be applying appropriate theories of contract law mitigation.

Traditional contract theory says that the non-breaching party to a contract may recover that amount of damages necessary to return the party to the status it would have occupied had there been no breach. Thus, in a typical case, the difference between the contract price and the amount recovered in a rerenting of the space is an appropriate way of guaranteeing that the landlord gains the same amount of rent it would have received had there not been a breach. But this does not really help very much in a case where the re-renting is for an amount greater than the lease price. The customary market loss damage measure takes care of cases up to the lease price, but says nothing about any excess.

Here are some possible theories—based on both property and contract notions—to apply to the case. Which one would you use?

(a) *Property Version 1.* Since the landlord conveyed an interest in land to the tenant in exchange for rent, the tenant has the use of the premises for the full term. Absent a surrender, the tenant is entitled to the value of the possession for the full term. The landlord has the right to re-let the premises on the tenant's account. But since the landlord's right to gain possession for such purposes arises only because the tenant is not in possession, the landlord rents only for the tenant's benefit. Therefore, the tenant should obtain full credit for all the rent paid during the period, even if that means the landlord owes the tenant money.

(b) *Property Version 2.* Sure, the landlord may re-let on the tenant's account, but that theory arises out of a tenant's abandonment where the landlord has the right to protect his reversion by keeping the property rented and in good condition. Re-letting is therefore partially for the landlord's benefit. While the tenant may claim the amount of rent that is equal to the rent called for by the lease, any amount over the lease rent belongs to the landlord.

(c) *Property Version 3.* The tenant's right to possession is conditioned upon the payment of rent on a monthly basis. While the landlord has conveyed an estate for a term, that term is subject to a condition subsequent that if the rent is not paid for any month, the landlord may attempt to re-let. Until such re-letting occurs, however, possession is available to the tenant and the tenant owes the full rent. Thus the tenant is not entitled to any credit for the four months the property was vacant.

(d) *Contract Version 1.* The landlord has the option of suing for the rent as it becomes due. While he must mitigate damages, no credits will be due the tenant until the landlord's reasonable efforts to mitigate bear fruit. Since the landlord could have sued separately for each month in which the premises were vacant, there is no reason to give the tenant credits for rents received in later months to cover the period when the property was vacant.

(e) *Contract Version 2.* The landlord's duty to mitigate arises out of the basic theory of contract damages that places the non-breaching party in the status he would have occupied had there been no breach. In this case, reasonable efforts to mitigate produced a higher rent for the later portion of the lease term. That higher rent permitted the landlord to recoup for the losses that occurred while the premises were empty. The tenant should therefore obtain the benefit of such rents, at least up to the total he owes the landlord. For if the landlord obtains additional monies from the tenant, he will recover twice because of the breach.

(f) *Contract Version 3.* The landlord's duty to mitigate is designed only to place her in the position she would have occupied absent the breach. Since the landlord agreed in the lease to permit the tenant to assign or sublease for the term of the lease, any benefit obtained from re-letting should go to the tenant. While the landlord could have elected to cancel and thereby to recover the apparent increase in value of the rented premises, she elected not to do so. Therefore, she is entitled only to the benefit of the bargain she has elected to sue upon. The tenant is entitled not only to a credit for the months in which the place was empty, but also to all moneys over and above that owed by the tenant that the landlord has collected from the new tenant during the period of the original tenant's lease.

[2]   Assignments and Subleases

[a]   Introduction

Enforcement of covenants in leases against successors in interest is part of the larger problem of enforcing servitudes covered in Chapter 6. Before going any further, you should read or re-read the introductory materials on enforcement of covenants at law, pp. 409–412 above. From that material, recall that the original rules on servitudes were framed by landlord-tenant law. Leasehold covenants were said to be binding on those in vertical privity—holding the same property interests—as the original landlord or tenant. And assignees, defined as subtenants holding the same interest as the original tenant, were always in vertical privity, while sublessees—those holding less of an interest than the original tenant—were not. This segment of materials explores how these old property rules work in practice and examines the impact of contemporary contractual rules on the liability of both the original and successor parties to a lease. Read the next case carefully. The opinion is short, but quite densely packed. Try to separate the traditional property based privity issues from those in contract.

[b] Opinion of the New Jersey Supreme Court in *Gerber v. Pecht*

Gerber v. Pecht

New Jersey Supreme Court
15 N.J. 29, 104 A.2d 41 (1954)

The opinion of the court was delivered by

JACOBS, J.

The Appellate Division affirmed a judgment for the plaintiff, entered in the Superior Court, Law Division . . . .

The plaintiff's predecessor, as lessor, and the defendant Pecht, as lessee, executed a five-year lease for store premises located in Irvington, New Jersey. The fifth paragraph of the printed terms of the lease prohibited any assignment thereof but a typewritten addition stipulated that "The tenant may assign this lease, provided he gets a written consent from the landlord." On November 9, 1948 the defendant Pecht assigned the lease to Moskowitz; the assignment was made with the plaintiff's written consent and upon condition that the assignor and the assignee were to remain liable on the lease for the balance of its term. On February 14, 1950 Moskowitz assigned the lease to Maria and Wilfred Christensen who agreed to comply with all of its provisions; this assignment was made with the plaintiff's written consent but without the defendant Pecht's consent. After the Christensens had defaulted and had vacated the premises the plaintiff instituted her action against the defendant Pecht and the assignees claiming rent and water charges due under covenants in the lease and damages for breach of a covenant to keep the premises in repair. Summary judgment for rent in the sum of $1,172.50 and water charges in the sum of $45 was entered in the Law Division and the defendant Pecht appealed, contending that upon the first assignment of the lease he became a surety and that upon the second assignment without his consent he was discharged from further liability on the lease.

The assignment of a lease does not relieve the lessee of his contractual undertakings in the lease even though the lessor has consented to the assignment and has accepted rental payments from the assignee. The lessor may, of course, expressly release the lessee from further liability or may engage in conduct which has the same legal effect. Thus the lessor may enter into a direct leasing arrangement with the assignee which effectively establishes a new tenancy relationship while terminating the old. Or the lessor and assignee may, by agreement, materially vary the terms of the original lease with like consequences.

After the defendant Pecht assigned the lease to Moskowitz their relationship *inter se* was comparable to that of principal and surety; they both were liable to the lessor but as between themselves Moskowitz was primarily and Pecht was secondarily liable. Conflicting expressions may be found in the cases as to whether the relationship included the lessor. In *Carrano v. Shoor, supra*, Chief Justice Maltbie adopted the views stated in *Baynton v. Morgan*, 22 Q.B.D. 74 (1888), that the relationship did not include the lessor and that, as regards him, the original lessee "still remained a principal debtor by reason of his covenant to pay rent." [118 Conn. 86, 171 A. 21.] On the other hand, in *Gholson v. Savin*, 137 Ohio St. 551, 31 N.E.2d 858, 862, 139 A.L.R. 75 (Sup. Ct.1941), Judge Hart expressed the rule to be that "when a lease is assigned by the lessee, the assignee becomes the principal obligor for the payment of the rent thereafter accruing and the future performance of the covenants, and the lessee assumes the position of surety toward the lessor." See 1 *American Law of Property*, 311 (1952). While the latter approach has been questioned we need not pursue the matter of labels or nomenclature since we are satisfied that Pecht's claim for discharge of liability must, in any event, rest upon a showing that the second assignment constituted a material and prejudicial variation in the terms of the lease. See *Walker v. Rednalloh Co.*, [299 Mass. 591, 13 N.E.2d 397], where Justice Dolan set forth the principles which we consider to be generally applicable:

> Regardless of the precise analysis of the theories by which the lessee may be relieved of liability by an assignment, the principle is clear that an agreement between the lessor and the assignee materially varying the terms of the original lease will on one theory or another result in the termination of the lessee's covenant to pay rent. The lessee is not discharged, however, by variations which inure to his benefit. Nor is the lessee discharged by agreements between lessor and assignee which may increase the liability of the lessee, but which are permitted by the terms of the original lease, to the benefits of which the assignee is entitled. *Wall v. Hinds*, 4 Gray [Mass.] 256, 266, 267, 64 Am. Dec. 64.

. . . [T]he lease in the instant matter embodied an express provision which authorized the tenant to assign the lease with the landlord's consent. When the defendant Pecht executed his assignment to Moskowitz he did not impose limitations (as he might have) but unconditionally transferred the lease with all of its privileges; included was the provision permitting an assignment. When Moskowitz assigned the lease he complied strictly with its terms; at no time was there any waiver or alteration of its provisions or enlargement of its burdens. Under the circumstances the defendant Pecht may not justly complain about the conduct of the lessor or Moskowitz and is in no position to assert that his consent was a condition precedent to the second assignment . . . .

We find no merit whatever in the appellant's point that the summary judgment should not have included the item for water charges. Under the terms of the lease the defendant Pecht was liable not only for rent but also for water charges and under the pretrial order the plaintiff was entitled, in the event of recovery, to the amounts stipulated on both claims. The judgment entered in the Law Division was entirely proper and is:

Affirmed.

For affirmance: CHIEF JUSTICE VANDERBILT, and JUSTICES HEHER, OLIPHANT, WACHENFELD, BURLING, JACOBS and BRENNAN—7.

For reversal: None.

[c] Explanatory Notes: Payment of Rent by Assignees and Sublessees

[*i*] *Transaction Diagrams.* Here are two diagrams of the transactions in *Gerber*. The first contains only transfers of interests that can be given property labels. The second displays only undertakings that can be given a contractual label.

Diagram Number 1—Property Transactions

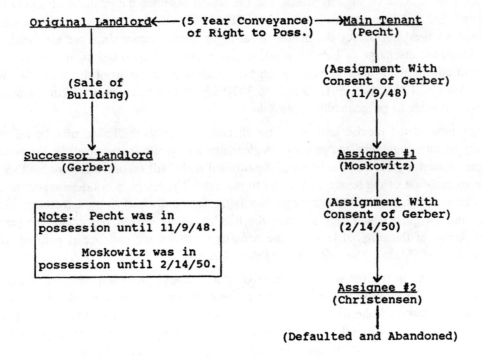

Diagram Number 1--Property Transactions

Original Landlord ←——(5 Year Conveyance)——→ Main Tenant
                     of Right to Poss.)   (Pecht)

(Sale of   (Assignment With
Building)   Consent of Gerber)
                                      (11/9/48)

Successor Landlord   Assignee #1
(Gerber)   (Moskowitz)

Note: Pecht was in   (Assignment With
possession until 11/9/48.   Consent of Gerber)
                                      (2/14/50)
Moskowitz was in
possession until 2/14/50.

                                      Assignee #2
                                      (Christensen)

                                      (Defaulted and Abandoned)

Diagram Number 2—Contract Transactions

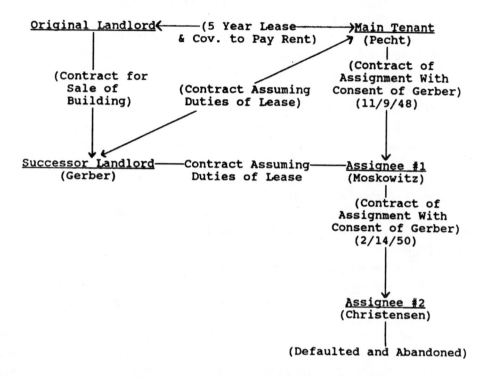

[*ii*] *Property Theories Binding Tenants and Their Assignees to the Obligation to Pay Rent.* At common law it was said that tenants and their assignees[161] were *obligated to pay rent only during the period of their possession.* Thus, independent of any contracts that may have been agreed to, Pecht was responsible for rent until the assignment to Moskowitz on November 9, 1948, Moskowitz was liable for rent for November 9, 1948 to February 14, 1950, and Christensen from February 14, 1950, until the end of possession because of either a surrender or a termination of the lease. This was all described by a set of legal doctrines involving conveyances of property interests and *privity of estate.*

As you know from the material on servitudes in Chapter 6, privity of estate rules governed situations in which there were successor parties to those originally exchanging an interest in land. If there were no successors, disputes were settled by reference to typical property understandings. In *Gerber,* both the Original Landlord and the Main Tenant transferred their interests. If there had not been any contractual understandings other than the lease and assignments, the *Gerber* court would have used privity of estate notions to decide whether a Successor Landlord could collect rent from an Assignee.

To briefly review the common law rules, two sorts of privity of estate were normally discussed—*horizontal privity,* or the relationship between the original parties to the deal, and *vertical privity,* or the relationship between one of the original parties and a successor in interest. *Horizontal privity* was present if the original parties to the conveyance each retained an interest in the land. Thus, in *Gerber,* the Original Landlord and the Main Tenant were in *horizontal privity*

---

[161] An *assignee* is a party who takes the entire remaining interest of the original tenant. If there are any material changes in the agreement from the original lease, the reletting is a sublease rather than an assignment.

with each other because the Original Landlord retained the reversionary interest after the end of the Main Tenant's lease. *Vertical privity* was present if a successor had possession of the same interest in property held by its predecessor. Thus, the Main Tenant, here Pecht, was in *vertical privity* with Assignee #1, here Moskowitz, but only for the period of Moskowitz's possession. And Gerber was also in *vertical privity* with the Original Landlord because Gerber, like Moskowitz, succeeded to all the remaining leasehold interest of the Main Tenant. As long as all three portions of the privity of estate idea (one horizontal and two vertical) were fulfilled, then a Successor Landlord could sue an Assignee in possession for rent.[162]

What was the rationale for this structure of outcomes? If a lease was thought of as a conveyance of an estate in land for a term in exchange for the payment of rent, then it is understandable that rent would be due from someone for the entire term. If a tenant at common law was liable to pay rent for a building heavily damaged by fire because the possessory estate was still thought available, then surely the rent obligation would continue if the occupant of the premises changed. The possessory right belonged to the tenant and that was not alterable without the tenant's permission. The right to receive rent belonged to the landlord and that was not alterable without the landlord's permission.

On this theory, neither the sale of a building by the landlord nor an assignment of all rights and duties under a lease by a tenant disturbed the original understanding between a landlord and a tenant. Rather, such deals merely altered the parties using the original estate conveyed; the estate in land, the lease, remained intact. Since the Original Landlord had no further interest in the building or obligation to the estate, a sale would permit him to exit from the scene. The purchase of the building's fee by the Successor Landlord transferred the full value of the fee to the new owner, including the right to receive rents under any extant leases. Theoretically, the tenant was treated in the same way. When the lease was assigned the Main Tenant was no longer in possession and therefore not the party in privity of estate with the landlord and liable for the rent.

[*iii*]   *Abandonment by Assignees.* The tenant in possession, according to privity of estate theory, was responsible for the rent. Thus, when Christensen abandoned, all the typical landlord remedies came into play. Traditional property theory permitted Gerber to sue for the rent, either month by month or at the end of the term, or relet on the tenant's account. But presumably Christensen was a "deadbeat." Lacking money, he was effectively "judgment proof." So Gerber naturally looked to Pecht and Moskowitz for money. If privity of estate theory didn't help, try contract theory.

[*iv*]   *Contract Theories Binding Main Tenants and Assignees to the Obligation to Pay Rent.* The day-to-day operation of landlord-tenant law operates differently from the privity of estate theory suggested above. It is hard to believe that landlords would routinely permit their Main Tenants to be excused from rent payment obligations simply because of an assignment. Indeed, the Main Tenants of this world are routinely treated as though they had a continuing rent payment obligation that may not be discarded by an assignment. Leases with Main Tenants always contain a *contractual* agreement to pay rent during the *full* term. While the Main Tenant

---

[162] Recall also from Chapter 6 that courts of law also required that two other conditions be fulfilled in order to burden successors to the original parties to a covenant. The covenant had to *touch and concern* the land, that is, relate closely to the interest in land. Private service contracts, for example, might not touch and concern. In addition, the original parties to a covenant had to intend that it bind successors in interest. It should be clear that a promise to pay rent is so central to a lease that there is no difficulty fulfilling the touch and concern or intent requirements.

could let someone else use his property based right of possession if the lease permitted assignments, he was unable to discharge his contractual obligation to pay rent without the permission of the landlord.[163]

Now, what about the contractual obligations of the assignees? For a moment, put aside the assumption contracts between Gerber on the one hand and Pecht and Moskowitz on the other. How might contract law treat the underlying obligations of the parties differently from property theory? Unbound by the notions of an exchange of an estate in land for rent, full assignment of all rights and duties under contract theory established benefits and obligations for the term of the agreement.[164] Thus, an assignee was responsible to her assignor for the life of the assignment. Contract law also provided that the assignment of a duty to pay money to a third party,[165] here the duty assigned to the Assignee to pay rent to Gerber, created a right in the third party to sue the assignee directly. Thus Gerber, as a third party creditor beneficiary of the assignments to Moskowitz and to Christensen, had direct causes of action against each of them for the rent due from the date of their assignments to the *end* of the lease term. Similarly, Pecht would be a third party beneficiary of the assignment from Moskowitz to Christensen. Furthermore, since an assignment of all duties and benefits of a contract did not cancel the original obligation, but only added parties to the arrangement, Gerber could sue Pecht on the original contract, Pecht could sue Moskowitz on their agreement, and Moskowitz could sue Christensen on theirs. In short, all creditors could sue all debtors. While contract law generally placed primary responsibility for rent payment upon the party in possession, inability to collect from that party could lead to suits against the others. The end result was that, since Moskowitz would probably not be able to recover from the "deadbeat" Christensen, Moskowitz would end up holding the bag. That made some sense. The person renting to the defaulting party ought arguably to take the most heat for the difficulties.

Now, return your attention to the assumption contracts in *Gerber*. It is likely that they were sought by Gerber only because of the limitations of privity of estate rules. Those rules limited Gerber to suits against tenants in possession. Though the original lease certainly contained a covenant requiring Pecht to pay rent for the full term, that covenant might not have bound Moskowitz after his possession ended. Thus, the assumption contract between Gerber and Pecht may have been surplusage, but the one with Moskowitz would have meant something. The assumption contract made it clear that the successor tenant took on all the obligations of the lease for its full term. If contract principles governed, however, the general liability rules would probably have made the assumption contracts unnecessary.[166]

[163] As the *Gerber* opinion makes clear, there has been dispute among jurisdictions over who is primarily responsible for rent when an assignee is in possession. Some courts hold that the Main Tenant is primarily liable, while others hold that the assignee is primarily liable.

[164] It is common in contract settings for courts to label as an assignment a transfer of only certain rights or duties under a contract. But what contract law calls an assignment of certain rights or duties under a contract would be a sublease in landlord-tenant law, not an assignment.

[165] Normally an assignee pays rent directly to the landlord, while a sublessee pays to the sublessor. Express statements on the route of payment in a lease may be a factor in whether the arrangement is deemed to be an assignment or a sublease.

[166] There may have been some scenarios in which the assumption contracts were necessary. If, for example, Gerber was not clearly in vertical privity with the Original Landlord, then he might have needed the contracts to reconstruct his ability to claim relief from those in possession.

[v]   *More Pitfalls—Privity of Estate and Subleases.* Additional problems existed under the privity of estate regime if a tenant subleased rather than assigned the possessory rights and rent paying obligations of a lease. Take this set of issues in two bundles. First, there are definitional matters to deal with. What are the differences between assignments and subleases? Second, how does the difference between an assignment and a sublease work out in privity theory?

[A]   *What is a Sublease?* The definitional differences between an assignment and a sublease arise out of the basic notions of privity of estate. A party is in vertical privity with a predecessor in interest only if she takes the same interest held by the predecessor. An assignment, by definition, fulfills this requirement. All other succeeding tenancy interests, that is all *subleases*, do not fulfill this requirement. In most cases, an assignment is a taking of the full term of the lease left to run, while a sublease involves only part of the remaining term. But any substantial variation between the terms of the original lease and the lease taken by the new tenant will cause the new lease to be a sublease rather than an assignment. As in many areas of law, the substance of the arrangement rather than the form will govern the decision. [167]

[B]   *Sublessor's Rental Obligations.* Look again at Diagram Number 1, but replace all the assignments with subleases. Doing that means that no sub-tenant was in vertical privity with Pecht, since none took the same interest held by the Main Tenant. In that case, Gerber could not sue either Moskowitz or Christensen directly for any rent. His remedy was entirely against Pecht. The lack of vertical privity did not relieve Pecht of possession, leaving him as both a tenant of Gerber and a landlord to Moskowitz. Pecht could therefore sue Moskowitz on their sublease arrangement. As between themselves, there is a landlord and tenant relationship. Similarly Moskowitz could sue his sublessee, Christensen, for whatever good it does to sue a "deadbeat." But Pecht has no direct remedy against Christensen, Moskowitz's sublessee, since Christensen is not in vertical privity with Moskowitz.

[vi]   *Statutory Reforms.* The inability of a landlord to sue a sublessee directly for the rent under privity of estate theory and the difficulties of structuring contract theory to accomplish that end, [168] has long been viewed as inequitable. If the Main Tenant was unavailable for some reason, a nineteenth-century landlord was left with the self help remedies of distraint and distress and the possessory remedies of ejectment and summary dispossession. While these remedies gave the landlord access to the premises, they frequently did not provide rent payments. This led to the passage of N.J. STAT. ANN. § 2A:42-4, which permitted a landlord to send a notice to any subtenant, whether assignee or sublessee, demanding payment of rent directly to the landlord. It still is not clear if this statute alters the common law rule that assignees must be in possession in order to be liable directly to the landlord for rent, but it clearly altered the rule that sublessees

---

[167] This notion does cause problems at times. For example, suppose a party leases an entire office building and then breaks it up into smaller areas for re-leasing. If a new tenant pays the same rent as the Main Tenant, but rents less than the whole building for the full term, it is probably still an assignment. But other forms of variation will probably turn the arrangement into a sublease. Typically, for example, the new tenant will pay more rent per square foot than the Main Tenant does to the Original Landlord and, if the building is new, the Main Tenant will agree to pay for some or all of the remodeling necessary to make the rented space usable. For an example of a set of deals that was probably a sublease even though the new tenant rented the premises for the full term left on the lease, *see* 24 Broad Street Corp. v. Quinn, 19 N.J. Super. 21, 87 A.2d 759 (1952). And for a deal the court viewed as an assignment even though the parties called it a sublease, *see* Berkeley Development Co. v. Great Atlantic & Pacific Tea Company, 214 N.J. Super. 227, 518 A.2d 790 (1986).

[168] In contract, third party beneficiary theory probably does not work. The sublessee agrees to pay rent to the sublessor, not the owner of the building.

were never responsible directly to the landlord for rent. For a recent application of this statute, *see Xerox Corporation v. Listmark Computer Systems*, 142 N.J. Super 232, 361 A.2d 81 (1976). The lease in *Xerox* prohibited underletting without the landlord's permission. The clause was violated by the main tenant who subleased a portion of the space and later went bankrupt. Listmark, the sublessee, was held directly responsible to Xerox, the landlord, for the rent due for the share of space it occupied. Xerox thereby avoided the insecurities of the bankruptcy proceeding to recover some of the unpaid rents.

[*vii*] **Subleases and Contract Law.** The property notion of a sublease is a bit anomalous to contract law. Contractual assignments may involve the disposition of less than the entire contract; rights and duties may be separately dealt with. Some deals that might be labeled assignments in contract law may be called subleases in property law. Given the long history in property law where sublessees owe rent to their predecessor tenant, not the building owner, it may be more likely that a sublease contract creates new rent paying obligations rather than assigns the old ones. If we assume that a sublease in property law is like a deal in contract law not involving an assignment, then the rules applied in property and contract turn out to be very much alike. Third party beneficiary theory, which is the basis for suits by landlords against assignees in contract, has no logical application to settings in which the rights and duties of the subtenant are materially different from the original lease. The deals will be treated as two separate contracts. That, in essence, is what property law, prior to the statutory changes mentioned just above, did as well, prohibiting direct suits against sublessees for the rent.

[d] Problem Notes

[*i*] **Abandonment Versus Novation.** There is a notion in contract law that a party may substitute for a prior party. Such contractual *novations* act very much like property assignments. The new tenant, for example, takes the place of the prior tenant, releasing that tenant from all obligations under the contract. When theoreticians look to contract law as a base of ideas useful in reforming landlord-tenant law, why should assignment of lease be treated like contract assignments rather than contract novations? If parties really wanted to avoid a novation, they could simply use contractual language of assignment and assumption to insure the continued liability of the Main Tenant.

[*ii*] **Resolution of the Property Contract Conundrum.** Which body of law—property or contract—should be used to resolve rent disputes between landlords and subtenants? If this problem, like that involving the sorts of defenses that can be raised in summary dispossess actions, is viewed from a procedural perspective, then it is difficult to contend that the property rules make much sense. All they accomplish is the multiplication of lawsuits by prohibiting direct suits against all assignees by landlords.

[*iii*] **More Than a Procedural Issue?** But is procedure the only rational perspective? For example, the New Jersey statute permitting direct landlord suits against sublessees for rent suggests that the possessory rights of a subtenant are so important that payment for them ought not be difficult to obtain. To the extent this is true, a lease becomes something different from other contracts. Contract lovers might respond that the availability of possession to a sublessee might still provide a contract based theory for direct suits for rent by landlords. Would it not be unjust enrichment for a tenant to be able to retain possession without paying for it?

[*iv*] **Assignees, Sublessees and Suits for Possession.** What of suits for possession for non-payment of rent? Remember that regardless of who is in possession under a lease—Main

Tenant, Assignee or Sublessee—a landlord not receiving rent may sue for possession. In "old fashioned" civil procedure parlance, such suits are *in rem*, against the property itself, rather than a party. All the privity of estate theory falls by the wayside in such a case. Thus a landlord may sue for possession when a sublessee is in possession and thereby force the sublessee to pay the rent in order to avoid being thrown out. Does this mean that a lease is a unique entity that neither property nor contract law describes, a unique entity known only to property law, or a contract in which the Seller, in the guise of a Landlord, may seek as a remedy either seizure of "goods" not paid for or the "price?"

[*v*] ***Promises Other than the Obligation to Pay Rent.*** Leases frequently contain many promises other than that to pay rent. There are maintenance obligations, occupancy rules, security deposit deals, restrictions on use, and a host of others. Typically, an assignment involves a transfer of all rights and duties under the lease. But what happens if some rights and duties are passed along to a subtenant, but not others? Consider some of these examples:

(a) The subtenant of a commercial lease agrees to all of the terms of the original lease, including the term, but promises to pay $100 more per month to the Main Tenant. Is the subtenant an assignee or a sublessee? If the lease contains a clause requiring the tenant to maintain the roof of the building, is that clause binding on the subtenant?

(b) Suppose the subtenant agrees to erect a building on empty ground leased for a lengthy term by the Main Tenant under a set of documents in which the subtenant agrees to take an "assignment" of the original lease and to enter into a separate arrangement with the Main Tenant to divide rents that will eventually come in from the new building's tenants after the construction is complete? May the landlord sue the subtenant directly for the original rent?

(c) Suppose a tenant takes a long term lease for a building and then "subleases" to Roxanne. The sublease is exactly the same as the original lease except that it lasts one day less than the original lease. Should that difference operate to make Roxanne a sublessee?

[*vi*] ***Subtenants and the Landlord's Repair Obligations.*** Recall that when a landlord sells a building, the new owner gains the ability to collect rents and the old owner is generally excused from any obligations under the lease. But if a tenant assigns, the original tenant is not excused from the obligation to pay rent. He may be secondarily liable, but he is liable nonetheless. What if a sub-tenant sues under *Berzito v. Gambino*, above at p. 673? Should the sub-tenant be able to collect from all landlords in the chain, provided that Successor Landlords are in vertical privity with their predecessors?

[*vii*] ***Landlord's Refusal to Agree to Assignment or Sublease.*** Courts are reluctant to enforce clauses in leases which totally prohibit assignments or subleases, particularly in long term commercial settings. As a result, most assignment or sublease clauses provide that subletting is permitted with the landlord's consent. If a landlord unreasonably refuses to approve an assignment or a sublease and the main tenant then vacates the premises, the landlord will probably be unable to collect the rent. *See Ringwood Associates, Ltd. v. Jack's of Route 23, Inc.*, 166 N.J. Super. 36, 398 A.2d 1315 (1979). What if an assignee of the main tenant wishes to assign or sublet? How do you decide if the requirement to obtain the landlord's permission is binding on the assignee?

[3] A Note on Security Deposits

A security deposit guarantees the tenant's obligations under the lease, especially the covenant to pay rent. Since a tenant's obligations under a lease are never fully performed until the lease has terminated,[169] the landlord has no obligation to return the deposit until the lease is over. The common phenomenon of tenants using their security deposit to pay the last month's rent occurs for reasons of convenience, not because the landlord is obligated to accept such a process. The "no-duty-to-repay-security-deposit-until-lease-is-over" rule created certain difficulties for common law tenants in recovering their deposits. If a landlord was not forthcoming, the tenant might not know who had the deposit or how to go about collecting it.

At common law, a security deposit arrangement was treated as a set of covenants just like those to pay rent, make repairs or return the premises upon completion of the lease term. And just as a common law landlord could not collect rent directly from a subtenant unless that tenant was in vertical privity with the Main Tenant, a tenant could not recover a security deposit from a landlord who was not in vertical privity with the Original Landlord.[170] If a building was transferred and the security deposits were not turned over to the new owner, the tenants could only recover their money from the original landlord.

The inability of tenants to easily pursue succeeding owners for security deposits unless the new owners took over the deposits and thereby assumed the obligations under the security deposit covenant in the lease, was one of the reasons New Jersey adopted detailed security deposit legislation.[171] The statute requires landlords to hold security deposits in separate interest bearing accounts, notify tenants where the deposits are being held, and transfer the deposit accounts to the new owner if the building is sold. Violations of the security deposit legislation by landlords allow tenants to apply their deposit to rent by withholding rent payments until the deposit is used up.[172] Refusal to refund a deposit after a tenant leaves subjects a landlord to the possibility of double damages, as well as payment of the legal fees expended to recover the deposit.[173] Finally, deposits are limited to a maximum amount of one and one-half times the monthly rent.

The scope of the legislative restrictions imposed on security deposits creates an incentive for landlords to invent new ways of obtaining tenants' money which might not be labeled as security deposits. For example, in *Durante v. Gadino*, 157 N.J. Super. 132, 384 A.2d 575 (1978), the landlord required each tenant to pay a non-refundable fee at the inception of the tenancy for refurbishing, repainting, and repairs due to wear and tear during the tenancy. No typical security deposit was required. The court held that this deposit was not made to secure performance of the lease, but was simply a fee for the specific purpose of refurbishing the apartments.

You should see a series of problems with the *Durante* deposit. First, if the fee was not a security deposit, was it rent? If it was rent, should it be covered by any applicable rent control ordinance. Second, did the *Durante* deposit impose costs on tenants that landlords were obligated to absorb under the implied warranty decisions? Third, did the non-refundable feature of the deposit make

---

[169] Though rent may be fully paid on the first day of the last month of the lease, other obligations, such as the duty to return possession of the premises to the landlord, continue until the term is over.

[170] An example of problems arising because of such a rule was displayed in Kaufman v. Williams, 92 N.J.L. 182, 104 A.2d 202 (E & A 1918).

[171] N.J. Stat. Ann. § 46:8-19 *et seq.*

[172] N.J. Stat. Ann. § 46:8-19.

[173] N.J. Stat. Ann. § 46:8-21.1.

it a liquidated damage clause which imposed costs unrelated to the landlord's actual losses?[174] Higher level New Jersey courts have not dealt with these questions yet.

A Few Final Problems: A landlord comes to you with the following proposals for terms in her standard form lease:

(a) Require a one month security deposit and a $100 per room non-refundable fee for refurbishing, repainting and repair at the end of the tenancy.

(b) Require tenants to pay a $50 fee should they terminate their lease early or fail to accept a proffered renewal lease, such fee to cover advertising and other reletting expenses.

(c) Require tenants to pay a $50 fee whenever they move in or out, such fee to cover the costs of padding the elevator in a highrise building and heating or cooling the lobby area while doors are open.

(d) Require tenants to pay a three month security deposit on garage spaces, which are presently rented for $25 per month.

How would you advise the landlord as to the legality of these various proposals? If any of these clauses, or other ideas you may conjure up, are legal, would you advise amending the Security Deposit Act?

---

[174] In Spialter v. Testa, 162 N.J. Super. 421, 392 A.2d 1265 (1978), the court refused to enforce a clause requiring a tenant to pay 25% of all remaining rent left for the term upon early termination of the lease on the ground that it was an unreasonable liquidated damages provision. This result makes particular sense in light of the obligation of landlords to mitigate damages. The landlord was also hit with double damages and attorney fees for failing to obey the security deposit legislation.

CHAPTER **9**

REAL ESTATE TRANSFERS: THE SUBURBAN EXPLOSION, CONSUMER PROTECTIONS, AND HOME SALES

§ 9.01 Introduction

The Depression had devastating effects on many homeowners. Loss of jobs and deflation made it impossible for many to make loan payments. In addition, home loans often were "balloon" mortgages. Borrowers paid only interest every month for the term of the loan. At the end of the loan term the entire principal fell due.[1] Paying such balloons frequently was impossible. By 1933, over half of all home loans were in default and foreclosures were being filed at a rate of 1,000 per day.[2] Out of such chaos, the modern home sale transaction was born. New Deal Era reorganization of the banking system led to the creation of the Federal Home Loan Bank Board to oversee savings banks. The security of bank deposits was guaranteed by the federal government and savings banks were given the task of making home loans. The use of amortized mortgages requiring constant monthly payments of both principal and interest became standard, removing the financial insecurities of balloon payments. The Federal Housing Administration also began guaranteeing the repayment of approved home loans to banks. After World War II, this program was copied by a guarantee system at the Veterans Administration. By the time of the prolonged economic expansion of the 1950s and 1960s, the construction of the interstate highway system and the stable home mortgage situation allowed for an enormous growth in home ownership rates,[3] booming suburban growth and the proliferation of what has come to be called "urban sprawl."

As the historical materials in Chapter 6 make clear, however, the fast changing housing patterns of the post-war era were highly segregated. Indeed, the major federal agencies involved in regulating the housing industry, as well as major insurance companies, routinely "red-lined" black communities guaranteeing low ratings on loan applications and barring issuance of insurance policies. The contours of both the suburban growth policies and their racial overtones are told in Kenneth T. Jackson's classic 1985 book, THE CRABGRASS FRONTIER: THE SUBURBANIZATION OF THE UNITED STATES. An excerpt from Jackson's work may be found in RICHARD CHUSED, A PROPERTY ANTHOLOGY 407-413 (2d ed. 1997). Another perspective on the story is told in

---

[1] In many situations, the loans were refinanced if the borrower could not pay the entire balloon. During the Depression, of course, new loans were frequently unavailable even for borrowers with jobs and good credit.

[2] KENNETH T. JACKSON, THE CRABGRASS FRONTIER: THE SUBURBANIZATION OF THE UNITED STATES 193 (1985).

[3] The percentage of owner occupied housing units rose from 43.6% in 1940, a rate about 5% lower than the 1890 figures, to 62.9% in 1970. UNITED STATES BUREAU OF THE CENSUS, THE STATISTICAL HISTORY OF THE UNITED STATES FROM COLONIAL TIMES TO THE PRESENT 646 (1976). The rate as of the end of the third quarter of 1998 was 66.8%, confirming that the largest increases in the rate occurred in the post-World War II era. The most recent data may be found at www.census.gov/hhes/www/housing/hvs/historic/histt14.html.

the enormously complex Chicago Buyers League housing discrimination case, which at one point involved allegations of discrimination against all the major home loan regulatory agencies and many real estate developers and sales companies in Chicago.[4]

In more recent times, another series of major changes in the home sale system have appeared. Consumer protection movements of the 1960s and 1970s led to both federal and state controls. Enactment of the Truth in Lending Act[5] in 1968 led to standardization in statements about interest rates and repayment obligations, and passage of the Real Estate Settlement Procedures Act in 1974[6] required the use of a government form for disclosure of all settlement fees, closing charges and other financial aspects of the transaction. At the state level, new home warranties of fitness were imposed on sellers in many jurisdictions, either by the adoption of new statutes or the development of new common law rules.

The final large scale shifts in the contours of the home sale transaction appeared after the banking crises of the 1980s. The largest reorganization of the banking system since the Great Depression led to a merger of the savings and commercial banking systems, the opening of the mortgage lending market to all banks and a host of non-banking financial organizations, and an enormous expansion in the secondary mortgage market. The Federal National Mortgage Association, better known as Fannie Mae, has emerged as a central player in the mortgage market. Volatility in interest rates led to some of the troubles banks faced in the 1980s. Holding mortgages with low interest rates in a time of inflation was not too good for the bottom line. As a result, many banks and other mortgage lenders now prefer to sell their mortgage portfolios to those interested in mortgage backed securities as investments. Fannie Mae performs the role of overseeing these transactions by buying up mortgage portfolios from lenders and selling securities to investors. Lenders are now likely to make their income from the fees they charge to originate loans and to service them by sending out bills and receiving payments. In order to be able to package mortgage backed securities, Fannie Mae will only accept mortgages that are made using forms it finds acceptable. As a result, loans all over the country have become highly standardized.

The goals of this chapter are modest. If you are interested in the details of real estate finance, you should take upper level courses in your last two years of law school. While the cases will display the increasingly regulated nature of the home sale transaction, the focus of the materials is on the basics. We will look at some of the norms surrounding performance of the real estate contract, the nature of a mortgage, the home sale warranty, and the role of the real estate agent.

For additional readings on the basics of real estate transactions, consult ROGER A. CUNNING-HAM, WILLIAM B. STOEBUCK & DALE A. WHITMAN, THE LAW OF PROPERTY 649-758 (2d ed. 1993); JOHN E. CRIBBET & CORWIN W. JOHNSON, PRINCIPLES OF THE LAW OF PROPERTY 159-233 (3d ed. 1989). You might also read Thomas Ulen, *The Efficiency of Specific Performance: Toward a Unified Theory of Contract Remedies,* 83 MICH. L. REV. 341 (1984); Carol M. Rose, *Crystals and Mud in Property Law*, 40 STAN. L. REV. 577 (1988), both excerpted in RICHARD CHUSED, A PROPERTY ANTHOLOGY 303-319 (2d ed. 1997) .

---

[4] See Note, Discriminatory Housing Markets, Racial Unconscionability, and Section 1988: The Contract Buyers League Case, 80 YALE L. J. 516 (1971); Clark v. Universal Builders, 501 F.2d 324 (7th Cir. 1974); Clark v. Universal Builders, 409 F. Supp. 1274 (N.D. Ill. 1976).

[5] 15 U.S.C. § 1601 *et seq.*

[6] 12 U.S.C. § 2601 *et seq.*

§ 9.02 Performance of the Land Sale Contract

[1] Introduction

Concluding a residential lease arrangement is usually a one-document transaction, if indeed any document is used. A standard home sale is a much more complicated transaction. Agreeing on the terms of the sale takes time. Negotiations over price and other parameters of the deal often take many days. After the contract is ratified by both parties, the buyer will pay an earnest money deposit to seal the deal, but final performance of the transaction does not usually occur until two to four months later. During this waiting period, the length of which will be spelled out in the contract,[7] various pre-conditions for final settlement are supposed to be fulfilled. Most buyers, for example, will obtain the right to have the house inspected by an architect or engineer prior to settlement and to void the deal if the inspection reveals significant structural problems. Because of the death-knell quality to many of these clauses, inspections must usually be made very quickly. In areas of the country with termite problems, sellers will be obligated to arrange for a termite inspection and produce a certificate that the structure is free of insects prior to settlement. The buyer will agree to seek financing within a certain period of time. Title searches, usually obtained by the buyer, will have to be performed and title reports submitted to the parties and the lender. Hazard insurance has to be arranged. As each task is performed the contract is often initialed as a sign that the pre-condition has either been fulfilled or waived. In short, the parties will be quite busy between the ratification of the contract and the final settlement of the deal.

With so much to do in a short time, problems can and do occur. People back out of deals, opening up the possibility of breach of contract suits. Deals fall through because of inability to get a loan, discovery of structural flaws or inability of the seller to produce clear title. If the consequences of the deal's failure are not spelled out explicitly in the contract, litigation can result. The standard adage, bandied about in the casebooks and treatises, is that the remedy of specific performance will lie when any party breaches a contract for the sale of real estate. In more contemporary prose, specific performance allows the seller to sue for the price, together with any consequential damages resulting from the breach, and the buyer to obtain an order to transfer title together with any consequential damages.

The standard explanation for the rule is that, even though equitable relief normally is available only when legal relief is inadequate, the unique qualities of each piece of real estate justify recourse to specific performance. The explanation is not very helpful, particularly in a culture full of large apartment buildings with many similar units and mass produced single family housing developments. Providing the seller with specific performance places the burden of reselling a housing unit on the breaching buyer, despite the standard contract rule requiring mitigation of damages. And providing every buyer with specific performance automatically rejects the possibility that some buyers could easily take back their deposit and demand payment of any consequential damages and buy a different dwelling.

The Uniform Land Transactions Act has modified the standard rule a bit, providing that the seller may sue for the price "only if the seller is unable after a reasonable effort to resell it at a reasonable price or the circumstances reasonably indicate the effort will be unavailing."[8] The

---

[7] Unless the terms of the contract provide that time of performance is of the essence of the deal, the time for performance specified in the contract is often extendable for reasonable causes, such as completing paperwork for a loan, making repairs discovered during an engineering inspection, or perfecting title.

[8] UNIF. LAND TRANSACTIONS ACT § 2-506(b), 13 U.L.A. 554 (1977).

Uniform Commissioners recommended that the traditional ability of buyers to obtain specific performance be retained.[9] A few courts have also begun to look more closely at the standard rules. Among the best known of these cases is *Centex v. Boag.*

[2]   Background to *Centex v. Boag*

On Friday, September 13, 1972, Eugene Boag and his wife put down a $525 deposit to buy a new condominium on the 20th floor of a building in Winston Towers, a large development near the Hudson River overlooking Manhattan. A short time after signing the contract, they also delivered a check for $6,870 to cover the rest of the downpayment for the $73,700 unit.

Over the weekend after they signed the contract, the Boags continued to discuss the wisdom of their decision to move to Winston Towers. They were worried about the effect of high rise living on their children. The complex was quite large, containing six buildings with a total of more than 3,600 units. They decided to stop payment on their $6,870 check and not perform the contract. After stopping the check, the Boags contacted an attorney friend, Herbert New, who agreed to help them with their legal problem. According to Eugene Boag, New told them Centex couldn't win a suit attempting to force performance of the contract.[10] The Boags had little to lose. Centex had only $525 of their money. Even if they were forced to buy the unit, Boag was confident it would be easy to resell it. Apartments in the Winston Towers were selling quickly. New forwarded a letter to Centex on September 27, 1972, informing the company that the Boags would not perform their contract.

Because of the fast paced marketing of Winston Towers, Centex could easily have forgotten the whole affair, kept the $525, and sold the apartment to someone else. But Centex, a large conglomerate based in Texas with interests in oil, gas, cement and other businesses in addition to real estate, had a well established company policy of suing on all of their breached real estate contracts. They were used to contracts being scrupulously honored and acted accordingly.[11]

In the opinion you are about to read, the court noted that shortly after signing the condominium contract, Boag was notified by his employer that he was to be transferred to Chicago. If Boag himself is to be believed, this was not quite accurate. He did indeed have a job offer in Chicago, though from a new company. When he told his employer about the offer, he got a raise and decided to stay in the New York area. The Chicago offer was, however, not the decisive factor in the Boags' decision to breach the contract. Concern for their children was central in their thinking. They simply changed their minds after they signed.

[3]   Opinion of the New Jersey Superior Court, Chancery Division in *Centex v. Boag*

Centex Homes Corporation v. Eugene Boag and Virginia D. Boag

New Jersey Superior Court, Chancery Division
128 N.J. Super. 385, 320 A.2d 194 (1974)

GELMAN, J.S.C., Temporarily Assigned.

---

[9] UNIF. LAND TRANSACTIONS ACT § 2-511,13 U.L.A. 559 (1977).

[10] The background information on this case was obtained in a telephone interview with Eugene Boag on Nov. 15, 1986.

[11] This view was expressed both by Boag and by David Carmel, who represented Centex, in an interview on Nov. 9, 1986.

Plaintiff Centex Homes Corporation (Centex) is engaged in the development and construction of a luxury high-rise condominium project in the Boroughs of Cliffside Park and Fort Lee. The project when completed will consist of six 31-story buildings containing in excess of 3600 condominium apartment units, together with recreational buildings and facilities, parking garages and other common elements associated with this form of residential development. As sponsor of the project Centex offers the condominium apartment units for sale to the public and has filed an offering plan covering such sales with the appropriate regulatory agencies of the States of New Jersey and New York.

On September 13, 1972 defendants Mr. & Mrs. Eugene Boag executed a contract for the purchase of apartment unit No. 2019 in the building under construction and known as "Winston Towers 200." The contract purchase price was $73,700, and prior to signing the contract defendants had given Centex a deposit in the amount of $525. At or shortly after signing the contract defendants delivered to Centex a check in the amount of $6,870 which, together with the deposit, represented approximately 10% of the total purchase of the apartment unit. Shortly thereafter Boag was notified by his employer that he was to be transferred to the Chicago, Illinois, area. Under date of September 27, 1972 he advised Centex that he "would be unable to complete the purchase" agreement and stopped payment on the $6,870 check. Centex deposited the check for collection approximately two weeks after receiving notice from defendant, but the check was not honored by defendants' bank. On August 8, 1973 Centex instituted this action in Chancery Division for specific performance of the purchase agreement or, in the alternative, for liquidated damages in the amount of $6,870. The matter is presently before this court on the motion of Centex for summary judgment.

Both parties acknowledge, and our research has confirmed, that no court in this State or in the United States has determined in any reported decision whether the equitable remedy of specific performance will lie for the enforcement of a contract for the sale of a condominium apartment. The closest decision on point is *Silverman v. Alcoa Plaza Associates*, 37 A.D.2d 166, 323 N.Y.S.2d 39 (App. Div. 1971), which involved a default by a contract-purchaser of shares of stock and a proprietary lease in a cooperative apartment building. The seller, who was also the sponsor of the project, retained the deposit and sold the stock and the lease to a third party for the same purchase price. The original purchaser thereafter brought suit to recover his deposit, and on appeal the court held that the sale of shares of stock in a cooperative apartment building, even though associated with a proprietary lease, was a sale of personalty and not of an interest in real estate. Hence, the seller was not entitled to retain the contract deposit as liquidated damages.[1]

As distinguished from a cooperative plan of ownership such as involved in *Silverman*, under a condominium housing scheme each condominium apartment unit constitutes a separate parcel of real property which may be dealt with in the same manner as any real estate. Upon closing of title the apartment unit owner receives a recordable deed which confers upon him the same rights and subjects him to the same obligations as in the case of traditional forms of real estate ownership, the only difference being that the condominium owner receives in addition an undivided interest in the common elements associated with the building and assigned to each unit.

---

[1] Under New York law, if the contract was deemed to be for the sale of realty, the seller could retain the deposit in lieu of damages.

Centex urges that since the subject matter of the contract is the transfer of a fee interest in real estate, the remedy of specific performance is available to enforce the agreement under principles of equity which are well-settled in this state.

The principle underlying the specific performance remedy is equity's jurisdiction to grant relief where the damage remedy at law is inadequate. The text writers generally agree that at the time this branch of equity jurisdiction was evolving in England, the presumed uniqueness of land as well as its importance to the social order of that era led to the conclusion that damages at law could never be adequate to compensate for the breach of a contract to transfer an interest in land. Hence specific performance became a fixed remedy in this class of transactions. *See* 11 *Williston on Contracts* (3d ed. 1968) § 1418A; 5A *Corbin on Contracts* § 1143 (1964). The judicial attitude has remained substantially unchanged and is expressed in *Pomeroy* as follows:

. . . in applying this doctrine the courts of equity have established the further rule that in general the legal remedy of damages is inadequate in all agreements for the sale or letting of land, or of any estate therein; and therefore in such class of contracts the jurisdiction is always exercised, and a specific performance granted, unless prevented by other and independent equitable considerations which directly affect the remedial right of the complaining party. . . [1 Pomeroy, *Equity Jurisprudence* (5th ed. 1941), § 221(b).]

While the inadequacy of the damage remedy suffices to explain the origin of the vendee's right to obtain specific performance in equity, it does not provide a *rationale* for the availability of the remedy at the instance of the vendor of real estate. Except upon a showing of unusual circumstances or a change in the vendor's position, such as where the vendee has entered into possession, the vendor's damages are usually measurable, his remedy at law is adequate and there is no jurisdictional basis for equitable relief. *But see* Restatement, Contracts § 360, comment c.[2] The early English precedents suggest that the availability of the remedy in a suit by a vendor was an outgrowth of the equitable concept of mutuality, *i.e.*, that equity would not specifically enforce an agreement unless the remedy was available to both parties. *See* the discussion in *Stoutenburgh v. Tompkins*, 9 N.J.Eq. 332, 342-346 (Ch.1853); 4 Pomeroy, *Equity Jurisprudence* (5th ed. 1941), § 1405.

So far as can be determined from our decisional law, the mutuality of remedy concept has been the prop which has supported equitable jurisdiction to grant specific performance in actions by vendors of real estate.[3] The earliest reported decision in this State granting specific performance in favor of a vendor is *Rodman v. Zilley*, 1 N.J.Eq. 320 (Ch. 1831), in which the vendee (who was also the judgment creditor) was the highest bidder at an execution sale. In

---

[2] The Restatement's reasoning, as expressed in § 360, comment c amounts to the inconsistent propositions that (1) because the vendor may not have sustained any damage which is actionable at law, specific performance should be granted, and (2) he would otherwise sustain damage equal to the loss of interest on the proceeds of the sale. Yet loss of interest is readily measurable and can be recovered in an action at law, and to the extent that the vendor has sustained no economic injury, there is no compelling reason for equity to grant to him the otherwise extraordinary remedy of specific performance. At the end of the comment, the author suggests that the vendor is entitled to specific performance because that remedy should be mutual, a concept which is substantially rejected as a decisional basis in 372 and 373 of the Restatement.

[3] Another theory has been suggested as a basis for equity's jurisdiction to grant specific performance to a vendor: the vendee's breach constitutes an "equitable conversion" of the purchase price of which the vendee is deemed to be a trustee. See Comment, 10 Villanova L. Rev. 557, 569 (1965); 1 Pomeroy, Equity Jurisprudence, (5th ed. 1941), § 221(b). This view has never been suggested in any reported decision in New Jersey, although it has been alluded to in another context. See Hoagland v. Latourette, 2 N.J.Eq. 254, 256 (Ch. 1839).

his opinion Chancellor Vroom did not address himself to the question whether the vendor had an adequate remedy at law. The first reported discussion of the question occurs in *Hopper v. Hopper*, 16 N.J.Eq. 147 (Ch. 1863), which was an action by a vendor to compel specific performance of a contract for the sale of land. In answer to the contention that equity lacked jurisdiction because the vendor had an adequate legal remedy, Chancellor Green said: ˙

> It constitutes no objection to the relief prayed for, that the application is made by the vendor to enforce the payment of the purchase money, and not by the vendee to compel a delivery of the title. The vendor has not a complete remedy at law. Pecuniary damages for the breach of the contract is not what the complainant asks, or is entitled to receive at the hands of a court of equity. He asks to receive the price stipulated to be paid in lieu of the land. The doctrine is well established that the remedy is mutual, and that the vendor may maintain his bill in all cases where the purchaser could sue for a specific performance of the agreement.

No other *rationale* has been offered by our decisions subsequent to *Hopper*, and specific performance has been routinely granted to vendors without further discussion of the underlying jurisdictional issue. . ..

Our present Supreme Court has squarely held, however, that mutuality of remedy is not an appropriate basis for granting or denying specific performance. *Fleischer v. James Drug Store*, 1 N.J. 138, 62 A.2d 383 (1948); *see also*, Restatement, Contracts § 372; 11 Williston, *Contracts* (3d ed. 1968), § 1433. The test is whether the obligations of the contract are mutual and not whether each is entitled to precisely the same remedy in the event of a breach. In *Fleischer* plaintiff sought specific performance against a cooperative buying and selling association although his membership contract was terminable by him on 60 days' notice. Justice Heher said:

> And the requisite mutuality is not wanting. The contention *contra* rests upon the premise that, although the corporation "can terminate the contract only in certain restricted and unusual circumstances, any 'member' may withdraw at any time by merely giving notice."

> Clearly, there is mutuality of obligation, for until his withdrawal complainant is under a continuing obligation of performance in the event of performance by the corporation. It is not essential that the remedy of specific performance be mutual. . .. The modern view is that the rule of mutuality of remedy is satisfied if the decree of specific performance operates effectively against both parties and gives to each the benefit of a mutual obligation. . ..

> The fact that the remedy of specific enforcement is available to one party to a contract is not in itself a sufficient reason for making the remedy available to the other; but it may be decisive when the adequacy of damages is difficult to determine and there is no other reason for refusing specific enforcement. Restatement, Contracts (1932), sections 372, 373. It is not necessary, to serve the ends of equal justice, that the parties shall have identical remedies in case of breach.

The disappearance of the mutuality of remedy doctrine from our law dictates the conclusion that specific performance relief should no longer be automatically available to a vendor of real estate, but should be confined to those special instances where a vendor will otherwise suffer an economic injury for which his damage remedy at law will not be adequate, or where other equitable considerations require that the relief be granted. As Chancellor Vroom noted in *King v. Morford*, 1 N.J.Eq. 274, 281-282 (Ch. Div. 1831), whether a contract should be specifically enforced is always a matter resting in the sound discretion of the court and

. . . considerable caution should be used in decreeing the specific performance of agreements, and. . . the court is bound to see that it really does the complete justice which it aims at, and which is the ground of its jurisdiction.

Here the subject matter of the real estate transaction—a condominium apartment unit—has no unique quality but is one of hundreds of virtually identical units being offered by a developer for sale to the public. The units are sold by means of sample, in this case model apartments, in much the same manner as items of personal property are sold in the market place. The sales prices for the units are fixed in accordance with schedule filed by Centex as part of its offering plan, and the only variance as between apartments having the same floor plan (of which six plans are available) is the floor level or the building location within the project. In actuality, the condominium apartment units, regardless of their realty label, share the same characteristics as personal property.

From the foregoing one must conclude that the damages sustained by a condominium sponsor resulting from the breach of the sales agreement are readily measurable and the damage remedy at law is wholly adequate. No compelling reasons have been shown by Centex for the granting of specific performance relief and its complaint is therefore dismissed as to the first count.

Centex also seeks money damages pursuant to a liquidated damage clause in its contract with the defendants. It is sufficient to note only that under the language of that clause (which was authored by Centex) liquidated damages are limited to such moneys as were paid by defendant at the time the default occurred. Since the default here consisted of the defendant's stopping payment of his check for the balance of the down-payment, Centex's liquidated damages are limited to the retention of the "moneys paid" prior to that date, or the initial $525 deposit. Accordingly, the second count of the complaint for damage relief will also be dismissed.

[4] Explanatory Notes

[a] Events After the Decision

After Centex lost, it sold Apartment 2015 to someone else. As noted before the opinion, the Boags never moved to Chicago. In fact, the year after they reneged on their decision to buy the apartment in Winston Towers, they bought a resale unit for a higher price in the same complex! Later they bought a townhouse in another Centex development right next door to Winston Towers.

Later decisions in New Jersey continue to follow *Centex's* rejection of the mutuality rule in condominium cases. The seller was denied specific performance in *Mesa Development Corporation v. Meyer*, 260 N.J. Super. 363, 616 A.2d 954 (App. Div. 1992), while the buyer obtained it in *Pruitt v. Graziano*, 215 N.J. Super. 330, 521 A.2d 1313 (App. Div. 1987).

[b] Liquidated Damages

When a contract for the sale of a house is ratified by both parties, the buyer makes an earnest money deposit to bind the deal. In the *Centex* case, the total deposit was $7,395 or about 10% of the price. That amount is not unusual. In some areas that is standard fare. In other places a lesser amount will be paid. In any case, the size of the deposit is fully negotiable between the parties. Five hundred twenty-five dollars of the amount paid by the Boags was apparently given to Centex before the contract was signed to hold the apartment for a short time. The remainder was in the form of a check handed over when the contract was signed. When and if a deal is settled, the earnest money is put toward the downpayment on the house, the amount the buyers will pay in cash rather then through a mortgage. When the Boags reneged, they stopped payment on the check. Since the contract's liquidated damages clause only called for the forfeiture of "moneys paid" to Centex and a check is not deemed paid until the account of the payee is credited with the funds, the Boags lost only $525. If the check had been certified, Centex presumably would have been allowed to keep the funds.

Liquidated damage clauses in real estate contracts are among their most litigated feature. Centex's attorney suggested that the opinion has been read by New Jersey real estate practitioners as a tacit judicial acknowledgment that liquidated damages could legitimately run as high as 10% if the contract was drafted correctly. Centex accordingly altered the terms of its form sales contract to include language liquidating as damages "all money paid or promised to be paid" on the contract.

It is not clear that this change will work as intended. Though some courts routinely allow for liquidated damages on the theory that the money is only part of the amount the seller would normally obtain in a specific performance suit, that reasoning hardly touches the question as to whether the amount forfeited is rationally related to either the nature of the breach or the damages suffered by the seller. Section 339 of the RESTATEMENT (FIRST) of CONTRACTS took the position that liquidated damages clauses operated when the sellers damages were difficult to measure and the liquidated amount was a reasonable estimate of potential damages at the time the contract was signed. That solution is a bit circular. How can a seller's damages be simultaneously difficult to measure and subject to reasonable estimation? Recent cases suggest that courts in many states will independently inquire as to whether, on the particular facts of each case, the amount the seller seeks to liquidate is reasonable. On the *Centex* facts, if the damages suffered by the sellers were well below $7,395, it is unlikely that the New Jersey courts would have required the Boags to forfeit such a large amount.

[c]   Cooling Off Period

In 1977, a few years after *Centex* was decided, New Jersey adopted legislation establishing a seven day "cooling off period" in the sale of real estate developments with more than one hundred units.[12] The enactment provided for large print notices to be given to buyers of their right to cancel the transaction and regain all moneys paid to the seller.

[d]   Specific Performance of Mortgage Commitment Contracts

After a contract for the sale of land is signed, most buyers seek a mortgage loan to finance the bulk of the transaction. Lenders make a "commitment" to issue the loan at closing, and usually ask the borrower to sign the commitment to seal a contractual relationship. Suppose a buyer, after signing a commitment, finds another lender willing to make a commitment at a lower interest rate and refuses to close the deal with the first lender. May the bank obtain specific performance of the loan contract? The traditional answer is "No," on the ground that the damage remedy at law is adequate.[13] That may be true for a typical residential loan. But what of a large deal

---

[12] This bit of regulation was part of The Planned Real Estate Development Full Disclosure Act, N.J. Stat. Ann. § 45:22A-21 *et seq.*, which also required the filing of detailed registration and disclosure statements for large developments offered for sale within the state. Offerings on an interstate basis were previously subjected to similar regulations in the Land Sales Full Disclosure Act, N.J. Stat. Ann. § 45:15-16.2 *et seq.*

[13] Here, as in the land sale contract setting, damages are usually fairly easy to ascertain. The lender may recover any costs expended in preparing to make the loan and the difference, if any, between the value of the loan at the interest rate called for in the commitment and the prevailing interest rate at the time of the breach. In the land sale context, the seller may also obtain any moneys expended preparing for the sale, together with the difference, if any, between the contract sale price and the price eventually obtained for the property from another buyer.

agreed to some time before the breach? Some argue that failure to require performance in this situation creates unnecessary insecurity in the large loan market, particularly where a mortgage broker obtains commitments from a number of lenders to put together a very large loan for a major project. Do you agree? *See* Draper, *The Broken Commitment: A Modern View of the Mortgage Lender's Remedy*, 59 CORNELL L. REV. 418 (1974). While lenders have traditionally been unable to compel performance by borrowers, borrowers have been able to compel lenders to complete their commitments. *See, e.g., Pipkin v. Thomas & Hill, Inc.*, 298 N.C. 278, 258 S.E.2d 778 (1979). This difference in treatment between lenders and borrowers mirrors the no-mutuality result in *Centex*.

[e]   Financing Differences Between Cooperatives and Condominiums

Recall the notes before *Plaza Road Cooperative, Inc. v. Finn*, p. 607 above, which described the property arrangements in a cooperative housing development. While occupants in a cooperative hold proprietary leases and shares of stock in the corporation owning the development, condominium residents hold fee simple interests in their homes. Typically a condominium purchaser buys living space which the building structure surrounds, together with an undivided interest in the common areas, walls, floors and roofs. Condominium owners literally buy a chunk of air. The undivided interest is somewhat different from a common law concurrent estate. Condominium owners could create significant problems if they had the right to partition, sell, or create survivorship interests in their shares of the common areas. States have all adopted statutes requiring that undivided interests in common areas in condominiums be "locked together" with the units in the development. The undivided interests may not be transferred or encumbered unless the housing unit to which the undivided interest is attached is also transferred or encumbered.[14] Condominium buyers usually obtain a mortgage virtually identical to that in a conventional land sale. The condominium is run by an association board whose members are elected (usually by a voting system based on floor space per unit) by the residents who pay monthly fees for maintaining the commonly held parts of the development. The association also usually enforces various parts of the condominium agreements, such as architectural standards, safety rules, and other regulations. In some developments, new owners must also be approved by the board.

[5]   Problem Notes

[a]   Change of Heart

Why should we let the Boags' indecision prevail? Is it difficult to accept the notion that people routinely buy houses impulsively? If such purchases usually are well thought out and undertaken only after a period of introspection, then why not impose the obligation of reselling the housing unit upon the breaching buyer rather than upon the innocent seller? Do any of the following rationales support the result in *Centex*?

---

[14] New Jersey's statute is typical of those in place around the country. N.J. Stat. Ann. § 46:8B-6 provides:

The proportionate undivided interest in the common elements assigned to each unit shall be inseparable from such unit, and any conveyance, lease, devise or other disposition or mortgage or other encumbrance of any unit shall extend to and include such proportionate undivided interest in the common elements, whether or not expressly referred to in the instrument effecting the same. The common elements shall remain undivided and shall not be the object of an action for partition or division. The right of any unit owner to the use of the common elements shall be a right in common with all other unit owners (except to the extent that the master deed provides for limited common elements) to use such common elements in accordance with the reasonable purposes for which they are intended without encroaching upon the lawful rights of the other unit owners.

(1) It is more efficient for a seller to transfer the unit. Placing that obligation on the buyer will result in the need to complete two transactions, with all the attendant settlement costs. Even if the buyers succeed in assigning their contractual rights prior to closing, that is more expensive than simply ignoring the original deal.

(2) The sellers, particularly in large developments, usually have highly routinized settlement procedures. Title has already been searched and financing arrangements have often been made. Since they hold all the information necessary to transfer the housing unit quickly, it is sensible to place the burden upon them to find a new buyer.

(3) The combination of factors described in (a) and (b) above is why sellers of goods normally have an obligation to mitigate damages before seeking the price of the goods from a buyer. Viewed in that light, denying Centex specific performance does nothing more than impose an obligation to mitigate on real estate vendors. *Compare Sommer v. Kridel*, p. 723 above.

[b]   Individuals v. Developers

Assuming you agree with the outcome in *Centex*, should a seller of a single house be treated the same as Centex? While large developers may be able to efficiently and quickly transfer a housing unit, an individual will have to re-advertise the property and absorb (at least in the short run) the costs imposed by a delay in transfer of the house. Rather than routinely deny all sellers specific performance, should the courts investigate the facts of each case to see who is in a better position to absorb the costs associated with delay and resale? Suppose, for example, that you were selling your condominium apartment to Boag, that Boag changed his mind, and that you had already purchased another housing unit in another city. Should Boag be able to avoid performance?

[c]   Efficiency Concerns as Prime Factor in Specific Performance Decisions

Should efficiency concerns be the prime factor in making specific performance decisions? Even though it might be more expensive for reneging buyers to resell a housing unit than a large seller-developer, is there a social cost associated with letting parties escape from "binding" contracts? Do the concepts of "trust" and "commitment" have anything to do with *Centex*? Further, much more detailed, discussion of the role of economics in property law appears in Chapter 10.

[d]   Disputes Over Transfer of Common Areas in Condominiums

There seems to be a never ending stream of cases involving efforts by developers to sell off the risky portions of their projects, while retaining relatively risk free segments of the developments. Management contracts, recreation clubs, and parking lots, for example, provide enticing targets in some settings. Many states have adopted statutes forbidding developers from retaining interests in common areas or in the management of projects after a certain fraction of the units (frequently 75%) have been sold. While separate (but geographically contiguous) organizations, such as country clubs, are still possible, the statutes force organizational independence between the housing projects and other related development.

An interesting twist on this problem arose in *Porter v. Hollander*, 494 F. Supp. 151 (D. Del. 1980). Barbara Porter agreed to sell a condominium unit on the Delaware shore to Morton and Ruth Hollander. The contract simply identified the unit as "Sea Colony #309 Annapolis House, Baltimore Hundred, Sussex County, Delaware" and required that "title conveyed to purchasers shall be good and merchantable, free and clear of all liens and encumbrances, except restrictions of record and existing easements." If title was defective, the deposit was to be returned. The condominium was originally developed under a declaration in which Sea Colony, Inc. *retained* the fee simple interest in the land upon which the project was built, but conveyed to the unit owners a proportionate undivided *leasehold* interest in the land as a common element along with a proportionate fee simple interest in the common elements other than the land. Each owner had the right to purchase a fee simple in their common elements in the land as part of their condominium unit for an extra $5,600. After the Hollanders learned of this situation, they declined to perform the land sale contract, arguing that Delaware condominium law forbade the arrangement and that they were unaware of the leasehold problem when they signed the contract.

The court confronted statutory language almost identical to the New Jersey section quoted above in footnote 14. It first held that the requirement that undivided interests in the "common elements may not be separated from the unit to which such interest pertains" did not prevent developers from creating leasehold interests as common elements to be "locked" together with fee simple interests. The rationale was that the "locking" requirement was designed to benefit unit owners by preventing chaos in land ownership patterns after the condominium was established and that this purpose was not defeated by the leasehold arrangement. Do you agree? As to the second issue—the knowledge of the purchasers and the intention of the parties to the contract—the court remanded the case for a trial on the factual setting in which the contract was signed. Assuming that Delaware follows the traditional rule making specific performance available to sellers as well as buyers in most situations, what facts would you require the Hollanders to demonstrate before releasing them from their contract?

§ 9.03 Risk of Loss Pending Settlement

[1] Introduction: The Traditional Doctrine of Equitable Conversion and the Rise of Contractual Modifications to its Use

The time period between the signing of a real estate contract and its performance usually lasts no more than 90 days. Complex commercial transactions and some residential sales may take longer, but most residential sales move fairly rapidly. Despite the short performance period, a number of problems may arise. One of the parties to the contract may die, the house may be damaged or destroyed, flaws may appear when title is searched, or mortgages may be unattainable on the terms called for by the agreement. Most of these problems are taken care of by specific provisions in real estate contracts. Many contracts provide, for example, that buyers are obligated to make reasonable efforts to obtain financing, but that the contract is voidable if financing cannot be arranged. Standard terms for handling title problems are also in typical land sale contracts. They usually allow the seller a certain amount of time to remedy a flaw, and then release the buyer from all obligations under the contract. Other typical clauses place the risk of loss in case of fire or other calamity on the seller until the deal is completed, and bind successors in interest to the original parties to the terms of the contract.

The insertion of specific contractual provisions in commonly used land sale forms arose not only because various risks needed to be addressed, but also because the typically operative legal concepts did not always meet the parties' needs. As the opinions in the next case illustrate, traditional rules dealing with risk of loss in case of a fire or other catastrophe rested on the equity maxim that the court should treat as done that which ought to be done. Use of the maxim led courts to treat the buyer as the effective owner of the premises during the period between ratification of the contract and full performance of its terms. This rule was dubbed *equitable conversion* since it had the magical effect of converting the real property held by the seller into personal property (the right to receive payment) and the personal property obligation of the buyer to pay money into a right to receive real property.

The doctrine of *equitable conversion* made some sense in the arena in which it was first used—the death of a party to the contract. The old common law rule that a contract terminated upon the death of a party to the agreement was modified at equity where one of the parties to a real estate contract died after the contract was signed but before closing. In such settings, it was frequently in the best interests of both sides to the deal to perform it despite the demise of one party. The courts responded by creating the workable but artificial construct that if a seller died, the estate owned the right to receive cash, and if the buyer died, the estate held real property.

Applying this rubric to a calamity like a fire, however, frequently clashed with normal expectations. If the courts treated as done that which ought to be done, then buyers held real property and bore the risk of its destruction. At least in an urban or commercial setting, most people probably assumed that when they bought a house or other improved property the improvements would be there when they got ready to move in and that the seller should absorb the risk of calamity. If these perceptions are correct, it is not at all surprising that virtually all real estate form contracts contain clauses reversing the traditional rule and placing the risk of loss on the vendor, and that a number of courts have modified the traditional doctrine. The Uniform Land Transaction Act provides that the seller has the risk of loss in most typical settings.[15] As a result, sellers usually maintain insurance coverage on property they sell until settlement has occurred. Buyers arrange for new coverage to begin on the day the deal is closed. The widespread adoption of either contractual modifications or changes in the rules have left courts with fairly narrow classes of cases to resolve—those unusual instances in which the parties to a deal naively say nothing in their contract about allocation of risk of loss and settings in which insurance coverage or payout methods are in doubt. Both contractual omissions and insurance disputes were present in the next case.

[2] Background to *Skelly Oil Company v. Ashmore*

Some of the history of *equitable conversion* is laid out in the opinions in the next case, *Skelly Oil Company v. Ashmore*. But regardless of whether the risk of casualty rules placed the loss on the seller or the buyer, who should get the proceeds of any insurance payout? That was the problem when the grocery store that Tom and Madelyn Ashmore agreed to sell to Skelly Oil Company burned down before their land sale contract was performed.

The Ashmores purchased their one-story concrete block grocery store in Joplin, Missouri, in 1953. It was on the corner of 42nd and Main Streets. A year later, they leased the store to Donald and Mildred Jones for $150 per month and 1% of all gross sales. The Joneses ran the store using the equipment left there by the Ashmores. The lease was to run two years, with an option to renew for another five. It also contained a one-year option to buy for $22,000, but the Joneses let the option expire. They did, however, exercise their right to renew the lease, thereby extending possessory rights through 1961.

When the Ashmores bought the store, Main Street was a typical small town two-lane thoroughfare. During the late 1950s, traffic on Main Street picked up. In 1955, a new road was built connecting Joplin with the new Oklahoma turnpike. Two years later, the state widened Main

---

[15] UNIF. LAND TRANSACTIONS ACT § 2-406, 13 U.L.A. 546 (1977).

Street to a four lane thoroughfare. Demand for gasoline skyrocketed.[16] Within months of Main Street's widening, Skelly's agent, Joe Busby, began negotiations with the Ashmores and a Mr. DeMasters, the owner of a Main Street lot adjacent to Ashmore's store, to buy their land. Contracts for both parcels were eventually signed. The Ashmore parcel ended up in litigation. The DeMasters deal apparently went through easily, for while the appeals in Ashmore's litigation dragged on, Skelly operated a station on DeMasters' lot.

[3] Opinions of the Missouri Supreme Court in *Skelly Oil v. Ashmore*

Skelly Oil Company v. Ashmore

Missouri Supreme Court, En Banc
365 S.W.2d 582 (1963)

HYDE, JUDGE.

This suit for specific performance was transferred by Division Two to the Court en Banc because of the dissent of one of the Judges. . ..

This is a suit by the purchaser, Skelly Oil Company, a corporation, against the vendors, Tom A. Ashmore and Madelyn Ashmore, husband and wife, in two counts. Count One is for the specific performance of a contract to sell the north half of a certain described southwest corner lot (fronting 97 1/2 feet on Main and 195 feet on 42nd Streets) in that part of Joplin lying in Newton County. Count Two seeks an abatement in the purchase price of $10,000, being the proceeds received by the vendors under an insurance policy on a building on the property, which building was destroyed by fire in the interim between the execution of the contract of sale and the time for closing of said sale by the exchange of the $20,000 consideration for the deed to the property. . ... The trial court found the issues in favor of the purchaser, decreed specific performance, and applied the $10,000 insurance proceeds on the $20,000 purchase price. The vendors have appealed.

The vendors acquired this property about 1953, and operated a grocery store in the concrete block building, with fixtures and furniture, and a one story frame "smoke house" thereon. Deeds of trust on the property, securing notes of the vendors to the Bank of Neosho were of record. At all times here material and up to September 30, 1961, the property was leased to Don Jones at a rental of $150 a month. The vendors had a fire insurance policy, with a standard mortgage clause in favor of the Bank of Neosho attached, on the buildings and fixtures, issued February 8, 1958, for a term of one year.

Joe Busby, of the Kansas City office of the Skelly Oil Company real estate department, and Mr. Ashmore conducted the negotiations resulting in the contract of sale. The Ashmores lived in Lawton, Oklahoma. Mr. Ashmore had engaged in the real estate business since 1951. Busby secured the execution of a Skelly printed form of option by the vendors, dated July 31, 1957, for Skelly "to purchase" for the sum of $20,000, "payable in cash upon delivery of deed" said property, "together with the buildings, driveways, and all construction and equipment thereon, at any time before" August 31, 1957. The words "and equipment" were "x-ed" out on said option.

[16] See, GAIL K. RENNER, JOPLIN: FROM MINING TOWN TO URBAN CENTER 77-78 (1985); ROBERTA IRONSIDE, AN ADVENTURE CALLED SKELLY: A HISTORY OF SKELLY OIL COMPANY THROUGH FIFTY YEARS, 1919-1969, at 86 (1970). Information on highway construction was obtained from Gary Ludlam, Chief Designer, District Seven, Missouri Department of Highways and Transportation (Telephone Interview, Feb. 11, 1987).

The option provided in typewriting (referring to the Jones lease): "Purchaser agrees to honor present lease on above property until expiration." The option originally lapsed August 31, 1957. Busby had an agreement for the mutual cancellation of the lease prepared by Skelly's legal department for execution by the Ashmores and Jones, and on August 20 took up securing a cancellation of the lease and possession with Ashmore and his lawyer, Mr. Foulke. Mr. Foulke did not know how long this would take and the option was extended to January 1, 1958. Busby knew Ashmore filed an ejectment suit against Jones, was "patiently waiting" to hear from Mr. Foulke, and on trips to Joplin would inquire if any headway was being made on securing possession. On December 30, the option was extended to March 1, 1958. Skelly's legal department concluded this lease entitled Jones to possession until September 30, 1961. Skelly acquired the property immediately south of the Ashmore property, continued the operation of a service station thereon, and decided to go ahead and exercise the Ashmore option with Jones in possession under his lease and later combine the two properties and erect a service station that required more area than the Ashmore property.

Busby and Ashmore met in Joplin on February 25. Busby informed Ashmore Skelly had decided to purchase under its option with Jones in possession under his lease. The parties orally agreed to certain details, some being mentioned hereinafter in connection with the contract of sale. Busby also informed Ashmore Skelly could not complete the transaction by March 1, and the Ashmores extended the option from March 1 to March 10, 1958. No consideration passed for any extension of the option.

The Bank of Neosho forwarded the abstract of title to Skelly.

The option provided it could be accepted "by giving written notice" to the vendors. By letter to the Ashmores under date of March 4, 1958, Skelly explicitly stated: "This letter is to inform you that Skelly Oil Company does hereby exercise its option to purchase the above described property for the sum of $20,000.00, subject to all the terms and conditions of the above referred to option, and with" further understandings, among others, to the effect: The fixtures and equipment in the store building were to remain the property of the Ashmores; the Ashmores were to assign the Jones lease to Skelly and Skelly was to remit to the Ashmores $5.00 a month for Jones' use of said fixtures and equipment; the Ashmores were to remove said fixtures and equipment within sixty days after the termination of said lease by lapse of time or otherwise, Skelly assuming no responsibility for the repair or physical condition of said fixtures and equipment. The letter also stated that upon approval of the title and the obtaining of necessary permits "we will get in touch with you further toward closing." Immediately following the signature of the purchaser on said letter appears: "ACKNOWLEDGED and AGREED TO This 7th day of March, 1958, Tom A. Ashmore Madelyn Ashmore." The vendors mailed the original thereof to the purchaser.

The latter part of March Busby telephoned to Ashmore in Lawton and they agreed to meet in Joplin on April 16, 1958, to close the transaction.

The concrete block building, furniture and fixtures were destroyed by fire on April 7, 1958, without fault of either party.

Skelly's Kansas City headquarters advised Busby, who was in St. Joseph, on April 7 of the fire. The next day Busby telephoned Ashmore from Kansas City. In this conversation Ashmore said he had insurance on the building and fixtures, naming the company in Kansas City carrying it. Asked on cross-examination whether he told Ashmore the fire would have no effect on the deal, Busby answered: "I told him absolutely not, we would go through with our deal. Q. Just like it was? A. Sure, just like this contract, sir, we're obligated, we can't get out of it." Busby called the insurance company and was informed there was $10,000 insurance on the building and $4,000 on the fixtures. He reported this to the purchaser's legal department. Then, after research, the legal department concluded that Skelly was entitled to have the insurance on the building applied on the purchase price. The closing papers were prepared accordingly.

The closing of the transaction was considered by the parties on April 15, 16 and 17. Busby and Ashmore met on the evening of the 15th. Mr. Winbigler of Skelly's legal department arrived on the 16th. They informed Ashmore they were there to close the purchase of the property; that Skelly thought it was entitled to the insurance proceeds on the building and would like an assignment of the insurance proceeds. When Ashmore disagreed, they informed him Skelly would close the deal and pay him the contract price but would not waive its rights to the insurance proceeds in so doing. Ashmore would not agree to this. They then went to Mr. Foulke's office and informed him of the situation. Mr. Foulke told them he needed time to check into the matter before he could advise his client. Busby and Winbigler returned to Kansas City.

By letter dated April 26, 1958, the Ashmores notified Skelly that the "option agreement" was rescinded "because it was given without consideration and is therefore not binding on us and for the further reason that you have refused to complete the purchase unless we reduce the agreed price, which constitutes a breach of the terms of the agreement."

A month or so later the Phoenix Insurance Company, under the standard mortgage clause, paid the Bank of Neosho the balance due on the vendors' notes, $7,242.46, and $2,757.54, the balance of the $10,000 insurance on the building, to the vendors, and also paid the vendors the $4,000 insurance carried on the furniture and fixtures.

This purchaser's claims are founded on the contract of sale in its letter of March 4, 1958, and the option therein referred to, which letter was "acknowledged and agreed to" by the vendors. Said claims are not based on a mere option to purchase where the improvements on the property were damaged prior to the purchaser's exercise of the option. . ..

The vendors say that the letter and option were prepared by the purchaser and ambiguities and doubts therein are to be resolved in favor of the vendors; that the purchaser paid no consideration for the option or the three extensions; that specific performance will result in inequity, hardship or loss to vendors, and that the trial court's decree of specific performance constitutes an abuse of discretion It is stated that, since there was no binding contract between the parties prior to the letter of March 4, this letter was only an offer to purchase under the terms and conditions in the original option and said letter, which vendors could accept or reject; that the vendors retained possession and the option contained four or more conditions and the letter added others, and because of these "suspensive conditions" the plain intention of the parties was that the purchaser was not to be bound until all these contingencies were met and no specifically enforceable contract existed on April 7, the date of the fire.

We are not impressed with the vendors' broad position that no valid enforceable contract ever existed. The principal suspensive conditions under the option authorized the purchaser to withdraw its acceptance of the option "before the consummation of purchase by payment of the full purchase price" if, sufficiently stated, the purchaser be unable to secure the proper licenses, consents or permits for the erection, maintenance and operation of a service station of a type and according to a ground plan of its choice on the premises, or if any such licenses, consents or permits be revoked, or if the purchaser be enjoined from erecting and operating a service station on said premises. The option called for an abstract showing a merchantable title in the vendors, and the letter of March 4 stated: "Upon approval of title by our Legal Department and our obtaining all necessary permits, we will get in touch with you further toward closing." There was no objection to this condition in the letter and the parties made it definite by orally agreeing the last part of March upon April 16 for the closing date. Under the mentioned suspensive conditions, as well as others of less importance, when the vendors "acknowledged and agreed to" the contract of sale, the purchaser could not act arbitrarily, capriciously or in bad faith in invoking said provisions of the contract; and in consideration of the mutual promises a mutually enforceable contract of sale arose. . .. None of the suspensive conditions entered into the vendors' failure to close the sale on April 16 or their rescission of the contract on April 26. The vendors' only objection to completing the transaction was, as stated in their letter of rescission, "that you have refused to complete the purchase unless we reduce the agreed price," which, of course, refers to the purchaser's claim to the $10,000 insurance proceeds. Mr. Ashmore testified that the only thing that held up the closing of the transaction was Skelly Oil Company's claim to the insurance proceeds.

A further matter concerns the Bank of Neosho, its deeds of trust and the standard mortgage clause of the fire insurance policy under which said mortgagee received $7,242.46 of the insurance proceeds. The standard mortgage clause may be an independent contract between the insurer and the mortgagee, but it was not an entirely disconnected contract in this case as a recovery by the mortgagee paid the debt of the mortgagors secured by this property and inured as much for the mortgagors' benefit as if they had recovered the loss and applied it otherwise. The Bank of Neosho has been paid without objection by either party and has no interest in the subject matter of this litigation. If at one time the mortgagee was a proper party to the suit, there was no objection in the pleadings to its nonjoinder and the fact does not now invalidate any judgment entered or to be entered in this cause.

The contract of sale here involved contained no provision as to who assumed the risk of loss occasioned by a destruction of the building, or for protecting the building by insurance or for allocating any insurance proceeds received therefor. When the parties met to close the sale on April 16, the purchaser's counsel informed vendors and their attorney he was relying on *Standard Oil Co. v. Dye*, 223 Mo. App. 926, 20 S.W.2d 946, for purchaser's claim to the $10,000 insurance proceeds on the building. Purchaser made no claim to the $4,000 paid vendors for the loss of the furniture and fixtures. It is stated in 3 *American Law of Property*, § 11.30, p. 90, that in the circumstances here presented at least five different views have been advanced for allocating the burden of fortuitous loss between vendor and purchaser of real estate. We summarize those mentioned: (1) The view first enunciated in *Paine v. Meller* (Ch. 1801, 6 Ves. Jr. 349, 31 Eng. Reprint 1088) is said to be the most widely accepted; holding that from the time of the contract of sale of real estate the burden of fortuitous loss was on the purchaser even though the vendor retained possession. (2) The loss is on the vendor until legal title is conveyed, although the purchaser is in possession, stated to be a strong minority. (3) The burden of loss should be on the vendor until the time agreed upon for conveying the legal title, and thereafter on the purchaser unless the vendor be in such default as to preclude specific performance, not recognized in the decisions. (4) The burden of the loss should be on the party in possession, whether vendor or purchaser, so considered by some courts. (5) The burden of loss should be on the vendor unless there is something in the contract or in the relation of the parties from which the court can infer a different intention, stating "this rather vague test" has not received any avowed judicial acceptance, although it is not inconsistent with jurisdictions holding the loss is on the vendor until conveyance or jurisdictions adopting the possession test. . ..

We do not agree that we should adopt the arbitrary rule of *Paine v. Meller, supra,* and *Standard Oil Co. v. Dye, supra,* that there is equitable conversion from the time of making a contract for sale and purchase of land and that the risk of loss from destruction of buildings or other substantial part of the property is from that moment on the purchaser. Criticisms of this rule by eminent authorities have been set out in the dissenting opinion of STORCKMAN, J., herein and will not be repeated here.

We take the view stated in an article on *Equitable Conversion by Contract,* 13 Columbia Law Review 369, Dean Harlan F. Stone, later Chief Justice Stone, in which he points out that the only reason why a contract for the sale of land by the owner to another operates to effect conversion is that a court of equity will compel him specifically to perform his contract. He further states:

A preliminary to the determination of the question whether there is equitable ownership of land must therefore necessarily be the determination of the question whether there is a contract which can be and ought to be specifically performed *at the very time when the court is called upon to perform it.* This process of reasoning is, however, reversed in those jurisdictions where the "burden of loss" is cast upon the vendee. The question is whether there shall be a specific performance of the contract, thus casting the burden on the vendee, by compelling him to pay the full purchase price for the subject matter of the contract, a substantial part of which has been destroyed. The question is answered somewhat in this wise: equitable ownership of the vendee in the subject matter of the contract can exist only where the contract is one which equity will specifically perform. The vendee of land is equitably entitled to land; therefore the vendee may be compelled to perform, although the vendor is unable to give in return the performance stipulated for by his contract. The *non sequitur* involved in the proposition that performance may be had because of the equitable ownership of the land by the vendee, which in turn depends upon the right of performance, is evident. The doctrine of equitable conversion, so far as it is exemplified by the authorities hitherto considered, cannot lead to the result of casting the burden of loss on the vendee, since the *conversion depends upon the question whether the contract should in equity be performed.* In all other cases where the vendee is treated as the equitable owner of the land, it is only because the contract is one which equity first determines should be specifically performed.

Whether a plaintiff, in breach of his contract by a default which goes to the essence, as in the case of the destruction of a substantial part of the subject matter of the contract, should be entitled to specific performance, is a question which is answered in the negative in every case except that of destruction of the subject matter of the contract. To give a plaintiff specific performance of the contract when he is unable to perform the contract on his own part, violates the fundamental rule of equity that. . . *equity will not compel a defendant to perform when it is unable to so frame its decree as to compel the plaintiff to give in return substantially what he has undertaken to give* or to do for the defendant.

The rule of casting the "burden of loss" on the vendee by specific performance if justifiable at all can only be explained and justified upon one of two theories: first, that since equity has for most purposes treated the vendee as the equitable owner, it should do so for all purposes, although *this ignores the fact that in all other cases the vendee is so treated only because the contract is either being performed or in equity ought to be performed* or, second, which is substantially the same proposition in a different form, the specific performance which casts the burden on the vendee is an incident to and a consequence of an equitable conversion, whereas in all other equity relations growing out of the contract, the equitable conversion, if it exists, is an incident to and consequence of, a specific performance. Certainly nothing could be more illogical than this process of reasoning. (Emphasis ours.)

For these reasons, we do not agree with the rule that arbitrarily places the risk of loss on the vendee from the time the contract is made. Instead we believe the Massachusetts rule is the proper rule. It is thus stated in *Libman v. Levenson*, 236 Mass. 221, 128 N.E. 13, 22 A.L.R. 560: When "the conveyance is to be made of the whole estate, including both land and buildings, for an entire price, and the value of the buildings constitutes a large part of the total value of the estate, and the terms of the agreement show that they constituted an important part of the subject matter of the contract. . . the contract is to be construed as subject to the implied condition that it no longer shall be binding if, before the time for the conveyance to be made, the buildings are destroyed by fire. The loss by the fire falls upon the vendor, the owner; and if he has not protected himself by insurance, he can have no reimbursement of this loss; but the contract is no longer binding upon either party. If the purchaser has advanced any part of the price, he can recover it back. If the change in the value of the estate is not so great, or if it appears that the buildings did not constitute so material a part of the estate to be conveyed as to result in an annulling of the contract, specific performance may be decreed, *with compensation for any breach of agreement*, or relief may be given in damages." (Emphasis ours.)

An extreme case, showing the unfairness of the arbitrary rule placing all loss on the vendee, is *Amundson v. Severson*, 41 S.D. 377, 170 N.W. 633, where three-fourths of the land sold was washed away by the Missouri River (the part left being of little value) and the vendor brought suit for specific performance. Fortunately for the vendee, he was relieved by the fact that the vendor did not have good title at the time of the loss, although the vendor had procured it as a basis for his suit. However, if the vendor had then held good title even though he did not have the land, the vendee would have been required to pay the full contract price under the loss on the purchaser rule. (Would the vendee have been any better off if the vendor had good title from the start but did not have the land left to convey?) The reason for the Massachusetts rule is that specific performance is based on what is equitable; and it is not equitable to make a vendee pay the vendor for something the vendor cannot give him.

However, the issue in this case is not whether the vendee can be compelled to take the property without the building but whether the vendee is entitled to enforce the contract of sale, with the insurance proceeds substituted for the destroyed building. We see no inequity to defendants in such enforcement since they will receive the full amount ($20,000.00) for which they contracted to sell the property. Their contract not only described the land but also specifically stated they sold it "together with the buildings, driveways and all construction thereon." While the words "Service Station Site" appeared in the caption of the option contract and that no doubt was the ultimate use plaintiff intended to make of the land, the final agreement made by the parties was that plaintiff would take it subject to a lease of the building which would have brought plaintiff about $6,150.00 in rent during the term of the lease. Moreover, defendants' own evidence showed the building was valued in the insurance adjustment at $16,716.00 from which $4,179.00 was deducted for depreciation, making the loss $12,537.00. Therefore, defendants are not in a very good position to say the building was of no value to plaintiff. Furthermore, plaintiff having contracted for the land with the building on it, the decision concerning use or removal of the building, or even for resale of the entire property, was for the plaintiff to make. Statements were in evidence about the use of the building and its value to plaintiff made by its employee who negotiated the purchase but he was not one of plaintiff's chief executive officers nor possessed of authority to bind its board of directors. The short of the matter is that defendants will get all they bargained for; but without the building or its value plaintiff will not.

We therefore affirm the judgment and decree of the trial court.

EAGER, LEEDY and HOLLINGSWORTH, JJ., concur.

WESTHUES, C.J., and DALTON, J., dissent and concur in separate dissenting opinion of STORCKMAN, J.

STORCKMAN, JUDGE (dissenting).

I agree that the parties on March 7, 1958, entered into a valid contract for the transfer of the real estate, but in the circumstances I cannot assent to the holding that the plaintiff is entitled to specific performance on any terms other than those of the purchase contract without reduction in the contract price. . ..

The evidence is convincing that Skelly Oil Company was buying the lot as a site for a service station and that in so using it they not only wanted the Jones's lease terminated but intended to tear down and remove the building in question. The contract documents support this conclusion. Both the option and the letter of acceptance refer to the property as a "service station site" and contain escape clauses permitting Skelly to avoid the purchase agreement if proper permits could not be obtained or if zoning laws prohibited such use. From the time the option was first granted on July 31, 1957, through its various extensions, until the letter of March 4, 1958, Mr. Busby, Skelly's real estate representative, was cooperating with and urging Mr. Ashmore and his attorney to secure a termination of the Jones's lease (which was on the entire property) even to the extent of filing an ejectment suit against the lessee. Then after the fire Skelly's legal department prepared as one of the closing documents an agreement to be executed by the Ashmores and the Jones for mutual cancellation of the lease. The purchase contract calls for an assignment of the Jones's lease by the Ashmores to Skelly and its honoring the lease; but, at the request of Mr. Busby, the Ashmores on April 17, 1958, with the approval of their attorney, executed and delivered to Mr. Busby the mutual cancellation agreement. This conduct is consistent with its prior activities, but is inconsistent with plaintiff's present contention that the building and its rental under the lease represented a substantial part of the consideration for the purchase of the real estate.

Count 1 of the petition is for specific performance in accordance with the terms of the purchase contract; Count 2 seeks a declaration that the defendants hold the $10,000 insurance proceeds in trust for the benefit of the plaintiff and that the defendants be required to pay the proceeds to the plaintiff or that the amount thereof be applied in reduction of the purchase price of the property. Count 2 alleges that the concrete block, single-story building which was used as a grocery store was totally destroyed by fire, that the defendants collected the insurance thereon, and that "said building was a valuable appurtenance on said real estate worth more than $10,000.00 and that its destruction reduced the value of said real estate more than the sum of $10,000.00."

In spite of the issue made by Count 2 as to [the] effect of the destruction of the building upon the value of the real estate, the trial court refused to permit cross-examination of plaintiff's witness to establish that the purpose and intent of Skelly was to remove the building from the premises when the lease was terminated, and the court rejected defendants' offer of proof to the same effect. In this equity action the testimony should have been received. It did not tend to vary or contradict the written contract but dealt with an issue made by plaintiff's petition based on a partial destruction of the subject matter subsequent to the acceptance of the option. Nevertheless, there was other evidence from which it could be reasonably inferred that the use of the real estate as a filling station site necessitated the removal of the building. Mr. Ashmore testified that he originally asked $27,000 for the property but reduced his price on Mr. Busby's representation that the improvements had no value to Skelly and that Skelly would be glad to have Mr. Ashmore remove them.

The plaintiff introduced no evidence of the market value of the property before or after the fire in support of the allegations in Count 2. The amount paid by the insurance company is of little or no benefit as evidence of the actual value of the building because of the valued policy law of Missouri which provides that in case of the total destruction of a building by fire, insurance companies shall not be permitted to deny that the property insured was worth at the time of issuing the policy or policies the full amount for which the property was insured. Sections 379.140 and 379.145, R.S.Mo. 1959, V.A.M.S. Defendants' evidence tended to prove that the real estate was worth more as a site for a service station after the fire than before and that the value of the real estate after the fire was in excess of $20,000.

The claim of neither party is particularly compelling insofar as specific performance in this case is concerned. The destruction of the building by fire, its insurance, and the disposition of the insurance proceeds were matters not contemplated by the parties and not provided for in the purchase contract documents. Skelly's representative did not know that Mr. Ashmore carried insurance on the building until after the fire, and he then told Mr. Ashmore that despite the fire the deal would be closed on the agreed date. Skelly's present claims are an afterthought inconsistent with its conduct throughout the negotiations and prior to the closing date.

In short, as to both Skelly and the Ashmores, the destruction of the insured building was a fortuitous circumstance supplying the opportunity to rid the property of a vexatious lease, to dispose of the building, and at the same time resulting in a windfall of $10,000. And the problem, in fact the only seriously contested issue between the parties, is which of them is to have the advantage of this piece of good fortune. Skelly contracted to pay $20,000 for the property. If it is awarded the $10,000 windfall, it will receive a $20,000 lot for $10,000. If the Ashmores retain the $10,000, they will in fact have realized $30,000 for a piece of property they have agreed to sell for $20,000.

In claiming the proceeds of the Ashmores' fire insurance policy, Skelly did not contend that the value of the real estate as a service station site had decreased. After learning of the fire and the existence of the insurance policy, Skelly's counsel did some research and, as he announced when the parties met in Joplin to close the deal, Skelly was relying on a case he had found, *Standard Oil Company v. Dye*, 223 Mo. App. 926, 20 S.W.2d 946. And in its basic facts the case, admittedly, is quite similar to this one although there were no attendant circumstances such as we have in the present case. As authority for its decision, the court in that case relied almost wholly on *William Skinner & Sons' Shipbuilding & Dry-Dock Co. v. Houghton*, 92 Md. 68, 48 A. 85. The doctrine of these two cases, laboriously evolved from *Paine v. Meller*, (1801) 6 Ves. Jr. 349, 31 Eng.Reprint 1088, is "that a contract to sell real property vests the equitable ownership of the property in the purchaser, with the corollary that any loss by destruction of the property through casualty during the pendency of the contract must be borne by the purchaser." The two-fold rationale of this doctrine is a maxim that "equity regards as done that which should have been done," from which it is said the "vendor becomes a mere trustee, holding the legal title for the benefit of the purchaser or as security for the price." All of the experts and scholars seem to agree that this doctrine and its rationale is misplaced if not unsound. To illustrate *see* only 4 Williston, *Contracts*, §§ 928-943B, pp. 2605-2639. As to the maxim, Williston said, "Only the hoary age and frequent repetition of the maxim prevents a general recognition of its absurdity." As to the corollary, Williston points out that while the purchaser may have an interest in the property, it is equally clear that the vendor likewise has an interest, and as for the vendor's being a trustee for the purchaser observes, "However often the words may be repeated, it cannot be true that the vendor is trustee for the purchaser." *See* also Pound, *The Progress of The Law— Equity*, 33 Harv.L.R. 813, 830.

Nevertheless, adapting this doctrine and following a majority opinion in another English case, *Rayner v. Preston*, (1881) L.R. 18 Ch.Div. 1 (CA), the rule as stated in the *Dye* case has evolved: "Where the purchaser as equitable owner will bear the loss occasioned by a destruction of the property pending completion of the sale, and the contract is silent as to insurance, the rule quite generally followed is that the proceeds of the vendor's insurance policies, even though the purchaser did not contribute to their maintenance, constitute a trust fund for the benefit of the purchaser to be credited on the purchase price of the destroyed property, the theory being that the vendor is a trustee of the property for the purchaser." Many jurisdictions have modified or do not follow this doctrine, some take the view that the vendor's insurance policy is personal to him, and Parliament has enacted a statute which entirely changes the English rule. The rule is not as general as the annotator indicated, and as with the rule upon which it is founded, all the experts agree that it is unsound, their only point of disagreement is as to what the rule should be. *See* 4 Williston, *Contracts*, §§ 928-943; Vance, *Insurance*, § 131, p. 777, and 34 Yale L.J. 87; Vanneman, *Risk of Loss, Between Vendor and Purchaser*, 8 Minn.L.R. 127; Pound, *The Progress of The Law*, 33 Harv.L.R. 813, and the excellent student note to *Standard Oil Co. v. Dye* in 4 Mo.L.R. 290. . ..

Professor Williston was of the view that the risk of loss should follow possession (4 Williston, *Contracts*, §§ 940, 942), and that view has been written into the Uniform Vendor and Purchaser Risk Act, 9C U.L.A., p. 314 and 1960 Supp., p. 82. Eight states have adopted that act and four of those, California, New York, South Dakota, and Oregon, are. . . among the fifteen jurisdictions. . . to follow the *Dye* case. In connection with the factor of possession only, it is an interesting sidelight to note,. . . that this court has held that "Where a vendee thus takes possession of real estate under a title bond from the vendor, and the improvements thereon are destroyed, the loss falls on the vendee." *Walker v. Owen*, 79 Mo.563, 569. If possession is a factor, as that case indicates, the case has not been modified unless what the court said in *Manning v. North British & Merc. Ins. Co.*, 123 Mo. App. 456, 461, 99 S.W. 1095, 1097, is to govern: "Possession is not a necessary requisite to the purchaser enjoying all the profits of his purchase, or standing for its depreciation. A valid contract of sale of real estate puts the equitable title in the vendee, although he may be out of possession."

Vance is of the opinion that a rule of "business usage" should be adopted, but he ruefully adds, "Here we have another instance in which business usage substitutes the insurance money for the insured property, despite the general rule that the two are not legally connected; and, as usual, the courts are sluggishly following business." Vance, *Insurance*, § 131, p. 781. Dean Pound assails Vance's contention that the insurance money is any part of the thing bargained for and he also vigorously attacks the theory that the vendor is a trustee for the vendee. 33 Harv.L.R., 1.c. 829, 830; 4 Mo.L.R., 1.c. 296.

Professor Vanneman has pointed out that the basic problem in all these cases is, "should there be a decree for specific performance at all?" He is of the view that the important and controlling factor should be the intention of the parties. If the building was a material part of the transaction, the vendor intending to sell and the vendee intending to buy "land with a building upon it," the vendee should have the benefit of the insurance. By way of summary, this is his view, "What is the intention of the parties here where incidents of ownership are divided? The court must decide this problem in each case rather than apply a rule of law that possession shows the intent of the parties. Let the matter rest frankly in the court's discretion. This may want in certainty but is not the problem in its nature incapable of settlement by an inflexible rule?. . . Where there is nothing from which a court can infer a different intention let the risk of loss lie with the vendor. Further than this it seems unwise to attempt to formulate a rule. Possession may or may not be a sufficiently controlling element. Since it usually carries other incidents of ownership it would show, in most cases, a reasonably inferable intention to shift the risk of loss, but it may not in a given case as above indicated. It is suggested that in those cases involving additional operative facts each case should be left to the court to decide as its exigencies require, unhampered by rule, thus sacrificing certainty to discretion in order to secure equity and justice in the individual case." 8 Minn.L.R. 141, 143. This view has the merit of avoiding resort to the legal fictions of equitable ownership and trusteeship.

A similar approach to this troublesome question was espoused by Dean Harlan F. Stone in his article entitled, *Equitable Conversion by Contract*, 13 Columbia Law Review 369, 386, wherein he stated: "A preliminary to the determination of the question whether there is equitable ownership of land must therefore necessarily be the determination of the question whether there is a contract which can be and ought to be specifically performed at the very time when the court is called upon to perform it."

Automatic application of the doctrine that "equity regards that as done which ought to be done," in the circumstances of this case, begs the question of *what ought to be done*. Because the insurance proceeds may be a windfall to those legally entitled does not necessarily mean that justice will be accomplished by transferring them elsewhere. The substance of the purchase contract and the use to which the property is to be put must be considered. A resort to equity should involve a consideration of other equitable principles or maxims such as the equally important maxims that "equity follows the law" and "between equal equities the law will prevail."

A valid legal excuse is a sufficient reason for refusal of specific performance. . ... Destruction of a particular thing upon which the contract depends is generally regarded as a legal excuse for nonperformance. . ... In the absence of a contrary provision, if the act to be performed is necessarily dependent on the continued existence of a specific thing, the perishing thereof before the time for performance, without the fault of the promisor, will excuse nonperformance of the contract. This is especially true where, from the nature of the contract, it appears that the parties must, from the beginning, have known that it could not be fulfilled unless when the time for the fulfillment of the contract arrived, some particular specified thing continued to exist. The contract is not, in the absence of any express or implied warranty that the thing shall exist, to be construed as a positive contract, but as subject to an implied condition that the parties shall be excused in case, before breach, performance becomes impossible from the perishing of the thing without default of the contractor.

. . ..

The plaintiff's petition alleges that the building destroyed by fire "was a valuable appurtenance on said real estate worth more than $10,000.00 and that its destruction reduced the value of said real estate more than the sum of $10,000.00." So far as Skelly's use of the property as a service station site is concerned, this allegation cannot be true if Skelly's intent was to tear down and remove the building. On the other hand, if the plaintiff retained the property or sold to an investor who proposed to rent the building for a store or a similar business purpose, then the loss would be substantial and the insurance proceeds would be necessary to restore a suitable building. The petition asserts that "as a matter of law" the defendant held "said $10,000.00 insurance proceeds in trust for the benefit of plaintiff as the vendee of the defendants." I know of no equitable or legal principle that justifies the award of the insurance proceeds automatically to the purchaser in the circumstances of this case.

. . . ..

If plaintiff's contention is that there has been a substantial failure or impairment of the consideration of the contract by reason of the destruction of the building, then I do not think that the Ashmores should be entitled to specific performance, and because of the theory of mutuality it would seem that Skelly would not be entitled to specific performance unless it was willing to perform its legal obligations under the purchase contract as drawn. We would not be justified in making a new contract for the parties to cover the building insurance, and a court of equity will not decree specific performance of a contract that is incomplete, indefinite or uncertain. . . ..

The precise problem presented by this appeal has not heretofore been considered by the supreme court. The facts of this case demonstrate the unsoundness of a rigid and exclusive adherence to the doctrine that equity regards that as done which ought to be done. I would apply general equitable principles and first determine whether Skelly has established by clear, cogent and convincing evidence that it is entitled to have a trust declared in the insurance proceeds in accordance with the allegations of Count 2 of its petition. It is not enough to say that the Ashmores have been unjustly enriched because giving the fund to Skelly would result in its being unjustly enriched. This would result in Skelly acquiring for $10,000 a filling station site for which it solemnly agreed to pay $20,000. Swapping one inequity for another is no justification for disturbing the legal title.

If the subject matter of the purchase contract was not as well or better suited to Skelly's purpose after the fire than it was before, then it appears from the authorities above discussed that Skelly could avoid the contract entirely or that it could clearly establish the amount and manner in which it was damaged. What would the situation be if the building had not been insured or for only a small amount? The fact that the building was insured and the amount thereof are hardly determinative of Skelly's alleged injury.

But Skelly did not after the fire or in this action elect to abandon the contract although the Ashmores gave it the opportunity to do so rather than to sell at the reduced price. It is quite evident that Skelly has received one windfall as the result of the fire in that the lease is terminated and the site can be cleared at less cost. It has not shown itself to be entitled to another, the one now legally vested in the Ashmores. Ideally the purchase contract should be set aside so that the parties could negotiate a new one based on the property in its present condition. But the plaintiff by its election to take title has foreclosed this possibility.

. . . [T]he majority opinion employs conflicting rules or theories. It purports to adopt one but applies another. It professes to repudiate the equitable conversion theory and to adopt unequivocally the Massachusetts rule, stating: "Instead we believe the Massachusetts rule is the proper rule." This rule as shown by the opinion's quotation from *Libman v. Levenson*, 236 Mass.

221, 128 N.E. 13, 22 A.L.R. 560, is that the sales contract will no longer be binding if the buildings are destroyed by fire and "the value of the buildings constitutes a large part of the total value of the estate, and the terms of the agreement show that they constituted an important part of the subject matter of the contract." In the same quotation from the *Libman* case, the circumstances and terms under which specific performance is granted are stated as follows: "If the change in the value of the estate is not so great, or if it appears that the buildings did not constitute so material a part of the estate to be conveyed as to result in an annulling of the contract, specific performance may be decreed, *with compensation for any breach of agreement, or relief may be given in damages.*" Emphasis added.

Obviously the majority opinion did not find that the value of the building constituted "a large part of the total value of the estate" or "an important part of the subject matter of the contract," else it would have declared the sales contract no longer binding under the Massachusetts rule. What it had to find was that the value of the building was not so great or such a material part of the estate to be conveyed as to interfere with the decree of specific performance.

But at this point the majority opinion abandons any pretense of following the Massachusetts rule and switches back to the equitable conversion theory and awards the insurance proceeds as such to the vendee without a determination of compensation for breach or relief to be given in damages. The value of the building for insurance purposes or as a structure to house a retail store is not necessarily the proper measure of the compensation or damages to which the plaintiff is entitled. It might be considerably less than such a figure if Skelly intended to remove the building as soon as it had the legal right to do so. Obviously the Massachusetts rule is not tied in with insurance at all and that is as it should be. Logically the majority opinion should have remanded the case for a determination of the amount of actual damages suffered by Skelly or the compensation to which it is entitled if it still wants specific performance. This is undoubtedly what the Massachusetts rule contemplates. I would find no fault with such a procedure.

Such evidence would also have a bearing on whether specific performance should be decreed at all, which was the first matter to be determined. Actually without such evidence the court does not have any basis for its finding as to the value of the building to the vendee and whether it was "an important part of the subject matter of the contract." Such a determination is a necessary prerequisite to granting or denying specific performance under the Massachusetts rule before the assessment of damages is reached. As the opinion stands, the adoption of the Massachusetts rule is more imaginary than real. The equitable conversion theory is *applied*, not the Massachusetts rule.

The opinion simply awards the *proceeds* of the fire insurance policy. It does not, and could not on the evidence in the present record, ascertain the compensation or damages, if any, to which Skelly is entitled by reason of the destruction of the building. Evidence of this sort was excluded by the trial court. Count 2 of plaintiff's petition claims the insurance proceeds on the theory of a trust fund as a matter of law and that seems to be the basis of the majority opinion's award of the insurance fund to the purchaser. This is the antithesis of the Massachusetts rule which contemplates the ascertainment of the amount of compensation or damages that will assure the vendee receiving the value for which it contracted, and no more.

The statement about Mr. Busby, Skelly's negotiating and contracting agent, in the next to last paragraph of the opinion, overlooks the fact that Mr. Busby, as a witness, could testify as to his authority and the company's intention with respect to the lot. He undoubtedly knew more about this lot than the president of the company or its board of directors. Furthermore, the inference that a company of this size can only be bound by its "chief executive officers" or its board of directors is unsound. The agent has authority to bind the principal within the apparent scope of his authority.

Although the entire court now seems to be in agreement that the theory of equitable conversion should not be adopted and that the equitable rules which should govern are those that require an allowance of compensation or damages to fit the particular case, nevertheless a majority of the court have concurred in an opinion which makes the amount of insurance proceeds the yardstick. This is the rejected doctrine of equitable conversion regardless of the name given to it.

On the present record the plaintiff has failed to show a superior equity in the insurance proceeds under the Massachusetts rule or otherwise, and on well-established equitable principles I would leave the legal title to that fund where it is. I would find against the plaintiff on Count 2 of its petition, but award it specific performance under Count 1 on the condition that it pay to the defendants the agreed purchase price of $20,000 less the amount of compensation or damages, if any, that it could establish against the defendants (not the insurance funds) at a plenary hearing of that issue in the trial court.

[4] Explanatory Notes

[a] Equitable Conversion, Destruction of the Premises, and the Uniform Land Transactions Act

Both the majority and dissenting opinions claimed not to be following the common law (and probably now minority) rule that, absent contrary contractual language, the risk of loss due to fire and casualty was on the buyer. The trend is reflected in the language of the Uniform Land Transactions Act provisions on the question:

Section 2-406. [Risk of Loss, Casualty Loss, Real Estate Other than Leaseholds][17]

(a) This section does not apply to transfers of leaseholds.

(b) Risk of loss or of taking by eminent domain and owner's liabilities remain on the seller until the occurrence of the events specified in subsection (c). In case of a casualty loss or taking by eminent domain while the risk is on the seller:

(1) if the loss or taking results in a substantial failure of the real estate to conform to the contract, the buyer may cancel the contract and recover any portion of the price he has paid, or accept the real estate with his choice of (i) a reduction of the contract price equal to the decrease in fair market value caused by the loss or taking, or (ii) the benefit of the seller's insurance coverage or the eminent domain payment for the loss or taking, but without further right against the seller; or

(2) if the real estate substantially conforms to the contract after the loss or taking, the buyer must accept the real estate, but is entitled to his choice of (i) reduction of the contract price equal to the decrease in fair market value caused by the loss or taking or (ii) the benefit of the seller's insurance coverage or the eminent domain payment with respect to the loss or taking but without further right against the seller.

---

[17] Reprinted by permission of the National Conference of Commissioners on Uniform State Laws.

(c) Risk of loss or taking and owner's liabilities pass to the buyer:

(1) if sale is not to be consummated by means of an escrow, at the earlier of delivery of the instrument of conveyance or transfer of possession of the real estate to him; or

(2) if sale is to be consummated by means of an escrow, at the earlier of transfer of possession or fulfillment of the conditions of the escrow.

(d) Any loss or taking of the real estate after risk of loss or taking has passed to the buyer does not discharge him from his obligations under the contract of purchase.

(e) For the purposes of any provision of law imposing obligations or liabilities upon the holder of legal title, title does not pass to the buyer until he accepts the instrument of conveyance.

[b] Opinion Contracts

The transaction in *Skelly* began with an option contract. Such contracts are often used by parties attempting to assemble areas for development. Rather than create obligations to buy land which may not become part of a larger plot, the assembler pays the owner only to hold the property off the market for a time and give the assembler a right to purchase within that period. While some older cases do hold that option extensions granted without consideration are void, that problem was avoided in *Skelly* by the presence of a signed agreement to conclude the deal. Once the Ashmores signed the letter agreeing to the terms of Skelly's claimed exercise of the option to purchase, a fully enforceable contract existed.

[c] Other Equitable Conversion Examples

In *Zareas v. Smith*, 119 N.H. 534, 404 A.2d 599 (1979), the parties agreed to the sale of a restaurant and two acres of land for $47,000. The contract did not specify a closing date, did not allocate risks in case of casualty, and did not call for apportionment of expenses such as taxes and insurance. As the court said, the contract "can hardly be called a masterpiece of legal writing." Two weeks after the contract was signed, an $8,000 check given the seller by the buyer bounced and the buyer notified the seller that he did not intend to perform the agreement. A month later, the seller, after electing not to sue for specific performance, sued the buyer for damages. Before the case went to trial, but nine months after the contract was signed, the restaurant was completely destroyed by fire. The seller received the proceeds of a $35,000 insurance policy. The main issues for the trial court were to figure out who bore the risk of loss and to decide upon the impact of the insurance policy on the measurement of loss. The court concluded that the seller bore the risk of loss since the contract did not contain a precise closing date and that the proper measure of damages was to be computed using the value of the insurance policy as a reflection of the market price at the time of the buyer's breach. The New Hampshire Supreme Court reversed the insurance holding, noting that the face value of an insurance policy had nothing to do with market value. As indicated above, the contract did not contain a specific time for closing the deal. Suppose the buyer had not breached the contract, that for nine months the parties took no steps to close the deal, that the restaurant burned down, and that the buyer then claimed a credit of $35,000 from the insurance, proffered $12,000 and sought to close the deal. Should specific performance on those terms be available? When contracts do not specify a date for closing, courts will usually allow a "reasonable time" to arrange for performance. If nine months was not reasonable, does that mean that the "do what ought to be done" maxim was inapplicable?

In another New Hampshire case, *In re Estate of Jesseman*, 121 N.H. 313, 429 A.2d 1036 (1981), the vendor under a land sale contract died prior to closing. The will of Norman Jesseman, the vendor, provided first that all of his real property should pass to his wife, and second that the residue of his estate should go in various shares to his wife, daughters, and others. After Jesseman died, the contract of sale was performed by the executrix of his estate, and the proceeds of the sale were paid over entirely to his wife under the first clause. That action was contested by one of the residuary takers. He argued that the property under contract was "equitably converted" to personal property and that it passed under the residuary clause. The court, however, concluded that equitable conversion only operated when a contract was specifically enforceable, that a contingency in this contract requiring the issuance of a building permit for the construction of a two bedroom home was fulfilled *after* Jesseman's death, and that the property was, therefore, still real for purposes of distribution of the estate by the executrix.

[5] Problem Notes

[a] Contract Rights and Insurance Right

Under the Uniform Land Transactions Act provisions excerpted at p. 768 above, the buyer has the option of demanding specific performance despite damage to or destruction of the premises, at its market value or at the contract price less the benefit of the seller's insurance. If the property still substantially conforms to the contract after a casualty, the buyer must perform but at the market price or the contract price less the insurance payout. Apparently the Uniform Land Transactions Act adopts the majority position in *Skelly* that price modification and allocation of insurance are part of the same issue. The *Skelly* minority argued that these issues are not always the same, that there are cases where the value of the premises is not reduced in value to the buyer by destruction or damage to certain facilities, and that allocating insurance proceeds to the buyer when the value of the premises has not been affected by the casualty is inappropriate.

At a minimum, isn't it fair to suggest that the Uniform Land Transactions Act's apparent assumption that valuation and insurance problems are interchangeable may be misplaced in some settings? To the extent that Skelly Oil Company actually wanted to tear down the destroyed building, the value of the property to Skelly may have been unaffected by the fire, even though insurance losses accrued within the terms of the Ashmores' insurance policy. Joe Busby, Skelly's agent seeking to consummate the purchase of the Ashmore property, testified at the trial:

Q. What was the reason for signing. . . [the Jones lease cancellation]?

A. Mr. Ashmore and I discussed it that morning and if we could get an opinion from you we wanted to get this cancellation from Jones and I asked you if you minded if the Ashmores signed this one particular paper and you told him that it was perfectly all right if he signed that one and no more.

Q. You wanted to get that before you went any further with the deal?

A. No, not necessarily. We were ready to close with the previous deal.

Q. Were you ready to close without it?

A. Certainly.

Q. Why did you want it [the cancellation] then?

A. Well,. . . there was no building there and it was just a matter of just getting Jones completely out of the picture. He evidently did not want to pay rent on a vacant property and I did not think Mr. Ashmore or Skelly Oil Company would have rebuilt it.[18]

To work this out a bit more precisely, assume that there was *no* insurance policy in *Skelly* and that the lack of an insurance policy would not have altered Skelly's desire to seek performance from the Ashmores. That performance may have been subject to a right to reduce the price to reflect the reduction, if any, in market value. But a revision in price was highly unlikely to equal the insurance payoff in this case.[19] If that was so, it is somewhat difficult to understand why both the Uniform Land Transactions Act and the *Skelly* majority gave the insurance proceeds to the buyer. The seller obtained the insurance contract, paid the premiums, filed the claims and generally behaved as if its insurable interests were at stake. Did the Ashmores hold the insurance policy in trust for Skelly? Did the court, as the dissent argued, apply the "what-ought-to-be-done-will-be-done" maxim to the insurance policy but not to other aspects of the case? Why should Skelly Oil, which also could have obtained an insurance policy on the buildings after the land sale contract was signed, obtain the benefit of the Ashmore's intelligent decision to maintain an insurance policy? Indeed, think about what the *Skelly* court would have done if the seller and the buyer *both* had insurance coverage on the destroyed building. Would the court have given Skelly the proceeds from both insurance policies? If not, why give Skelly one? In *Skelly* why didn't the court require Skelly to pay Ashmore the premiums it had paid on the insurance policy over the years in return for obtaining the benefit of the policy's payout? If Ashmore paid for the policy, why should Skelly get the proceeds?

[b]   Risk Bearing

Who should bear the risk of loss due to casualty prior to closing? The courts have obviously left the world littered with various approaches to the problem, though the clear contemporary trend is toward placing the risk of loss on the seller, either until the buyer takes possession or the deal is closed. One way of responding to the lack of unanimity is to argue that the various options must not make much difference in most settings. As long as people know what the rule is they will either contract around it or purchase insurance policies to cover whatever risk there is. There certainly is some evidence to suggest that this may be true. Most residential sale contracts do routinely place the risk of loss on sellers and most parties do arrange for the transfer of insurance policies as of the date of closing. If that is so, then isn't the insurance part of the *Skelly* result clearly wrong? If sellers routinely maintain insurance policies up to the date of closing, then shouldn't the world heed that fact and grant them the expected benefit of their insurance contract bargains?

On the other hand, not everyone buys insurance. And in those cases, what should happen? The parties may be naive in not insuring, but that doesn't resolve the legal dispute. Efficiency notions don't really help. The loss has occurred and regardless of who has to bear it, the world at large is unaffected. As between the parties, should it become a simple game of who is better off, with the richer party taking the loss? Should we bow to apparent social norms that the seller "owns" the house until closing? Why not flip a coin in cases where there is no insurance? Or

---

[18] Transcript on Appeal at 92, Skelly Oil Company v. Ashmore, 365 S.W.2d 582 (Mo. 1963) (No. 47911).

[19] There is also an interesting problem in this case about whether the value that should govern is the general market value or the value to the particular party under contract. Those values may have been quite different in the Skelly setting.

even better yet, why not split the difference? Both parties have a stake in the property once a contract has been signed, so let them sink in the same boat. Any suggestions?

§ 9.04 Financing a Real Estate Sale

[1] Introduction

Skelly involved an all cash transaction. Completion of most land sales, however, occurs only after the purchasers obtain a loan from either the seller or a third party. Such loans are typically formalized under one of two legal structures—land sale installment contracts or mortgages. Though mortgage transactions are more common than land sale installment contracts, installment sales are often used in cases where traditional financing is hard to get[20] or in certain communities because of long standing customs. Installment contracts provide that the seller retains title to the property until the buyer completes all payments. If the buyer defaults, sellers usually claim the right *both* to possession of the property and to acceleration of all remaining payments due under the land sale contract. The legality of such contractual terms, which give sellers payment for property they end up not conveying, is the subject of the next case.

There are important differences between deals based on land sale installment contracts and on mortgages. If enforceable, installment contracts give sellers the right to retain any increase in value of the property that accrued between the signing of the contract and any default prior to completion of payments by the buyer.[21] When they recover possession and resell to a new contract buyer, the new price presumably reflects the changed value. Mortgages provide two basic protections to buyers lacking in installment contracts. In case of default, the mortgaged property may be sold, but funds obtained from the sale over and above the amount of the indebtedness and costs of the sale must be paid to the debtor. In addition, the defaulting debtor always has an *equity of redemption*, a period of time in which to seek refinancing and pay off the debt prior to a foreclosure sale. A defaulting mortgagor[22] thus retains the ability to extract any increase in property value that has accrued since the mortgage was obtained.

Given the scope of consumer protections commonly provided mortgage borrowers, it is not surprising that some parties try to invent legal structures which enable "lenders" to charge others for the use of their money, tie up the "borrower's" property, and avoid the debtor protection features of mortgages. Land sale installment contracts may be one such structure, but others also appear from time to time. The second case in this section, *Kawauchi v. Tabata*, investigates the possibility that a lease may also substitute for a mortgage.

Before reading the next two cases, review the following diagram to make sure you understand the nature of a typical mortgage transaction. It will be hard to discern whether installment contracts or leases should sometimes be treated as the equivalent of mortgages without being thoroughly familiar with the standard features of a mortgage. While mortgage credit, like credit under an installment contract, may be extended by a property seller, most mortgages are obtained

[20] In the *Contract Buyers League* litigation discussed at p. 744 above, one of the allegations of the plaintiffs was that defendant housing developers sold on installment contracts with onerous terms to black buyers and on mortgage transactions to white buyers.

[21] They may also saddle sellers with any decrease in value if their defaulting purchasers lack the funds to pay off their contractual obligations. While losses do occasionally accrue, the general trend in real estate values has been upward since the Great Depression.

[22] Remember that a mortgagOR is the borrower and the mortgagEE is the lender. The OR's and EE's follow the path of the mortgage deed, which goes from land purchaser to lender, not the path of the money lent.

from institutional lenders such as insurance companies, banks, or mortgage brokers. When a land sale contract calling for the buyer to obtain mortgage credit from an institutional lender is performed, each party—seller, buyer and lender—has a well defined role. Since the buyer will be using his fee simple interest in the property as security for the mortgage loan, the seller must convey a clear title to the buyer. The price is paid in parts, the downpayment coming from the buyer[23] and the rest of the price from the proceeds of the mortgage. The buyer then conveys an interest in his new fee simple to the lender as security for the extension of mortgage credit. This mortgage deed provides that the lender may sell the property if the loan goes into default. In addition, the buyer signs a note, or contractual obligation, to repay the loan. If a default occurs and the sale of the collateral under the mortgage deed does not produce sufficient funds to pay off the loan, then the lender may sue in contract upon the note for the deficiency.[24] If the mortgage lender is the seller rather than an institutional lender, then the lender and the seller merge in the diagram. In such situations, the seller is said to take a *purchase money mortgage*. In *Skendzel* the question is whether the installment contract between the seller and the buyer should be treated as the equivalent of a purchase money mortgage.

DIAGRAM OF TYPICAL MORTGAGE DEAL

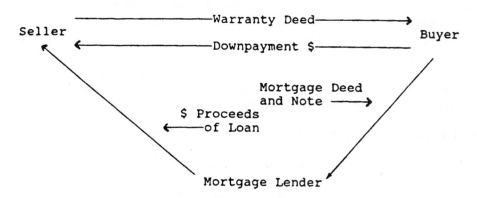

[2]   Installment Sales Contract or Mortgage?

[a]   Background to *Skendzel v. Marshall*

Stanley Burkowski and Mary Skendzel, Polish immigrants to the United States, met and married in Chicago, moved to LaGrange, Indiana, and opened a tavern. They both worked there. Stanley, a "hard, patriarchal man," apparently consumed a good deal of his own spirits.[25] Mary cooked, cleaned and served in the tavern, which gained a reputation for serving good Polish food. Despite being driven hard by her husband, she depended upon him as her connection to the American business and social world. Mary did not read or write English well.

Before Stanley Burkowski died, leaving all of his assets to his wife, Mary Burkowski was befriended by Agnes and Charles Marshall. Agnes Marshall became Mary's confidant and helped

---

[23] The downpayment itself is typically divided in parts, with the earnest money deposit paid upon signing of the original land sale contract being supplemented by additional funds at the closing.

[24] Some jurisdictions prohibit deficiency suits in residential mortgage settings, a position also adopted by the Uniform Land Transactions Act.

[25] The background facts were provided by LeRoy K. Shultess, who represented Mary Skendzel Burkowski during her life and the Marshalls in the litigation you are about to read (Telephone Interview, Nov. 14, 1986).

her bear the burdens of a difficult life. When Stanley died, the Marshalls began to help Mary run the tavern. When Mary later sat down to write her will with attorney LeRoy Shultess, in the Marshall's presence, she announced that she intended to give all of her property to the Marshalls as a sign of her gratitude for their help. Charles and Agnes opposed the idea, insisting that it would not be right for her to disinherit all of her's and Stanley's family. As a result, Josephine Skendzel, Bernice Wysocki, Jean J. Legowski, and Anna J. Blair were named in the will in addition to the Marshalls. Agnes Marshall was the executrix.

In 1958, Mary Burkowski sold the tavern and several other buildings she owned, along with the lake front land on which they stood, to the Marshalls for $36,000 under a land sale installment contract.[26] As the opinion to follow suggests, payments came in somewhat irregularly. Mary paid little attention to that; the Marshalls, after all, were her close friends. After Mary died in 1963, however, the situation changed. The tavern business fell upon hard times, perhaps in part because the cook was gone. In addition, the contract payments no longer went to Mary Burkowski, but to her estate. Though Agnes Marshall, the tavern proprietress, was the executrix of the estate, the takers of the contract payments under the will were the various members of the Skendzel and Burkowski clans included in Mary Burkowski's will.

The will was challenged by these relatives. After a bitter five year legal battle over charges of mental incompetence and undue influence, the will was confirmed. It was at that point, in June, 1968, that Agnes Marshall, in her function as executrix, gave an assignment of Mary Burkowski's rights under the land sale installment contract to the various members of the Skendzel and Burkowski families named in the will. The following year, the various family members filed suit against the Marshalls in their private capacities as the new vendors of the tavern and other property, for defaulting on the land sale installment contract.

[b]   Opinions of the Indiana Supreme Court in *Skendzel v. Marshall*

Skendzel v. Marshall

Indiana Supreme Court
261 Ind. 226, 301 N.E.2d 641 (1973)

HUNTER, JUSTICE.

Petitioners seek transfer to this Court as a result of an adverse ruling by the Court of Appeals. Plaintiff-respondents originally brought suit to obtain possession of certain real estate through the enforcement of a forfeiture clause in a land sale contract. Plaintiff-respondents suffered a negative judgment, from which they appealed. The Court of Appeals reversed, holding that the defendant-petitioners had breached the contract and that the plaintiff-respondents had not waived their right to enforce the forfeiture provisions of the contract.

In December of 1958, Mary Burkowski, as vendor, entered into a land sale contract with Charles P. Marshall and Agnes P. Marshall, as vendees. The contract provided for the sale of certain real estate for the sum of $36,000.00, payable as follows:

$500.00, at the signing, execution and delivery of this contract, the receipt whereof is hereby acknowledged; $500.00 or more on or before the 25th day of December, 1958, and $2500.00 or more on or before the 15th day of January, 1960, and $2500.00 or more on or before the

---

[26] According to Shultess, that was probably a fair price, though he would not have paid that much for the property. The tavern had fallen into some disrepair since Stanley Burkowski died.

15th day of January of each and every year thereafter until the balance of the contract has been fully paid, all without interest and all without relief from valuation and appraisement laws and with attorney fees.

The contract also contained a fairly standard section which provided for the treatment of prepayments—but which the Court of Appeals found to be of particular importance. It provided as follows:

Should Vendees have made prepayments or paid in advance of the payments herein required, said prepayments, if any, shall at any time thereafter be applied in lieu of further principal payments required as herein stated, to the extent of such prepayments only.

The following is the forfeiture/liquidated damages provision of the land sale contract:

It is further agreed that if any default shall be made in the payment of said purchase price or any of the covenants and/or conditions herein provided, and if any such default shall continue for 30 days, then, after the lapse of said 30 days' period, *all moneys and payments previously paid shall, at the option of the Vendor without notice or demand, be and become forfeited and be taken and retained by the Vendor as liquidated damages* and thereupon this contract shall terminate and be of no further force or effect; provided, however, that nothing herein contained shall be deemed or construed to prevent the Vendor from enforcing specific performance of this agreement in the event of any default on the part of the Vendees in complying, observing and performing any of the conditions, covenants and terms herein contained. . .. (Emphasis added.)

The vendor, Mary Burkowski, died in 1963. The plaintiffs in this action are the assignees (under the vendor's will) of the decedent's interests in the contract. They received their assignment from the executrix of the estate of the vendor on June 27, 1968. One year after this assignment, several of the assignees filed their complaint in this action alleging that the defendants had defaulted through non-payment.

The schedule of payments made under this contract was shown by the evidence to be as follows:

Date	Amount Paid	Total of Paid Principal
12/1/1958	$500.00	$500.00
12/25/1958	500.00	1,000.00
3/26/1959	5,000.00	6,000.00
4/5/1960	2,500.00	8,500.00
5/23/1961	2,500.00	11,000.00
4/6/1962	2,500.00	13,500.00
1/15/1963	2,500.00	16,000.00
6/30/1964	2,500.00	18,500.00
2/15/1965	2,500.00	21,000.00

No payments have been made since the last one indicated above—$15,000.00 remains to be paid on the original contract price.

In response to the plaintiff's attempt to enforce the forfeiture provision, the defendants raised the affirmative defense of waiver. The applicable rule is well established and was stated by the Court of Appeals as follows:

Where a contract for the sale and purchase of land contains provisions similar to those in the contract in the case at bar, *the vendor may waive strict compliance with the provisions of the contract by accepting overdue or irregular payments,* and having so done, equity requires the vendor give specific notice of his intent that he will no longer be indulgent and that he will insist on his right of forfeiture unless the default is paid within a reasonable and specified time.

It follows that where the vendor has not waived strict compliance by acceptance of late payments, no notice is required to enforce its provisions.

In essence, the Court of Appeals found that there was no waiver because the vendors were obligated to accept prepayment, and, "the payments made, although irregular in time and amount, were prepayments on the unpaid balance through and including the payment due on January 15, 1965." The Court concluded that up to January 15, 1966, "the vendors waived no rights under the contract, because they were obliged to accept prepayment." and that, "[t]he vendors could not have insisted on forfeiture prior to January 15, 1966, the date of the first missed payment." (We believe the Court of Appeals miscalculated here; the vendors could not have insisted on forfeiture until January 16, 1968.)

If forfeiture is enforced against the defendants, they will forfeit outright the sum of $21,000, or well over one-half the original contract price, as liquidated damages *plus possession.*

Forfeitures are generally disfavored by the law. In fact, ". . . [e]quity abhors forfeitures and beyond any question has jurisdiction, which it will exercise in a proper case to grant relief against their enforcement." 30 C.J.S. *Equity* 56 (1965) and cases cited therein. This jurisdiction of equity to intercede is predicated upon the fact that "the loss or injury occasioned by the default must be susceptible of exact compensation."

Pomeroy defines this doctrine of equitable interference to relieve against penalties and forfeitures as follows:

> Wherever a penalty or a forfeiture *is used merely to secure the payment of a debt*, or the performance of some act, or the enjoyment of some right or benefit, equity, considering the payment, or performance, or enjoyment to be the real thing intended by the agreement, and the penalty or forfeiture to be only an accessory, will relieve against such penalty or forfeiture by awarding compensation instead thereof, proportionate to the damages actually resulting from the non-payment, or non-performance, or non-enjoyment, according to the stipulations of the agreement. The test which determines whether equity will or will not interfere in such cases *is the fact whether compensation can or cannot be adequately made for a breach of the obligation which is thus secured. If the penalty is to secure the mere payment of money, compensation can always be made, and a court of equity will relieve the debtor party upon his paying the principal and interest. . ..*

> The granting of relief in such circumstances is based on the ground that it is wholly against conscience to say that because a man has stipulated for a penalty in case of his omission to do a particular act—*the real object of the parties being the performance of the act*—if he omits to do the act, he shall suffer a loss which is *wholly disproportionate to the injury sustained by the other party.*

Pomeroy, *Equity Jurisprudence*, § 433, 5th Edition (1941). (Emphasis added.)

Paragraph 17 of the contract provides that all prior payments "become forfeited and be taken and retained by the Vendor as liquidated damages." "Reasonable" liquidated damage provisions are permitted by the law. However, the issue before this Court, is whether a $21,000 forfeiture is a "reasonable" measure of damages. If the damages are unreasonable, i.e., if they are disproportionate to the loss actually suffered, they must be characterized as penal rather then compensatory. Under the facts of this case, a $21,000 forfeiture is clearly excessive.

The authors of American Law Reports have provided an excellent analysis of forfeiture provisions in land contracts:

> As is frequently remarked, there is no single rule for the determination of whether a contractual stipulation is one for liquidated damages or a penalty, each case depending largely upon its own facts and equities, and this apothegm is fully applicable to the decisions involving provisions in land contracts for the forfeiture of payments.
>
> There is a plethora of abstract tests and criteria for the determination of the nature of a contractual provision as one for a penalty or liquidated damages, and in most instances the courts struggle valiantly to make the result reached by them accord reasonably well with one or more of the more prominent of these abstract tests. But it must be observed that in the last analysis, these factors and criteria are so vague and indefinite that it is doubtful if they are of much aid in construing a specific contractual provision, even assuming that the court makes a conscious and conscientious effort to apply them. At any rate, a reading of the cases collected herein conveys the impression that the ultimate catalyst is the court's belief as to the equities of the case before it.
>
> Granting this, however, certain tendencies of decision are clearly discernible in the cases. If, for example, the contract involved calls for deferred payments of the purchase price which are relatively small in amount and extend over a number of years, and if it appears that at the time of the purchaser's breach and the consequent invocation of the forfeiture clause by the vendor a comparatively small proportion of the total price remains unpaid, the courts are prone to find that the forfeiture clause was one for a penalty, at least if, as is usually the case, such a holding will tend to give the purchaser another chance to complete the purchase.
>
> On the other hand, if the amount of the payments received by the vendor at the time the purchase was abandoned represents but a small percentage of the total purchase price, and if the purchaser's breach occurred soon after the execution of the agreement (and particularly if the circumstances indicate that the purchase was made for speculative purposes or that the breach represented an effort on the part of the purchaser to escape an unfortunate turn in the market), the courts tend to hold that the forfeiture clause was one for liquidated damages, with the result that the purchaser cannot recover back the payments made. (6 A.L.R.2d 1401 (1949)).

If we apply the specific equitable principle announced above—namely, that the amount paid be considered in relation to the total contract price—we are compelled to conclude that the $21,000 forfeiture as liquidated damages is inconsistent with generally accepted principles of fairness and equity. The vendee has acquired a substantial interest in the property, which, if forfeited, would result in substantial injustice.

Under a typical conditional land contract, the vendor retains legal title until the total contract price is paid by the vendee. Payments are generally made in periodic installments. *Legal* title does not vest in the vendee until the contract terms are satisfied, but equitable title vests in the vendee at the time the contract is consummated. When the parties enter into the contract, all incidents of ownership accrue to the vendee. *Thompson v. Norton* (1860), 14 Ind. 187. The vendee assumes the risk of loss and is the recipient of all appreciation in value. The vendee, as equitable owner, is responsible for taxes. *Stark v. Kreyling* (1934), 207 Ind. 128, 188 N.E. 680. The vendee has a sufficient interest in land so that upon sale of that interest, he holds a vendor's lien. *Baldwin v. Siddons* (1910), 46 Ind. App. 313, 90 N.E. 1055, 92 N.E. 349.

This Court has held, consistent with the above notions of equitable ownership, that a land contract, once consummated constitutes a present sale and purchase. The vendor "has, in effect, exchanged his property for the unconditional obligation of the vendee, the performance of which is secured by the retention of the legal title." *Stark v. Kreyling, supra.* The Court, in effect, views a conditional land contract as a sale with a security interest in the form of legal title reserved by the vendor. Conceptually, therefore, the retention of the title by the vendor is the same as reserving a lien or mortgage. Realistically, vendor-vendee should be viewed as mortgagee-mortgagor. To conceive of the relationship in different terms is to pay homage to form over substance.

The piercing of the transparent distinction between a land contract and a mortgage is not a phenomenon without precedent. In addition to the *Stark* case, there is an abundance of case law from other jurisdictions which lends credence to the position that a land sales contract is in essence a mortgage:

> While the legal title remains in the vendor, the vendee in possession acquires an equitable title and the vendor holds the legal title in trust as it were for the vendee. There is an equitable conversion so that while the heirs of the vendor in case of his death must make conveyance of the legal title, the rights of the vendor under a contract, in case of his death intestate, pass to his representatives rather than to his heirs; the title of the vendee in possession is such that in the event of his death intestate, his interest in the realty descends to his heirs; so that, following the doctrine that equity deems that as done which ought to be done, the vendee in possession for all practical purposes becomes the owner of the property with all the rights of an owner in the operation of it, subject only of course to the terms of the contract; the vendor holds the legal title as security for the performance of the contract, but in effect has a vendor's lien upon the property; the status of the parties is somewhat analogous to that of mortgagor and mortgagee. 3 Pomeroy's *Equity Jurisprudence* (4th Ed.), p. 3042, § 1261.

. . ..

It is also interesting to note that the drafters of the Uniform Commercial Code abandoned the distinction between a conditional sale and a security interest. Section 1-201 of the UCC defines "security interest" as "an interest in personal property or fixtures which secures payment or performance of an obligation. . . retention or reservation of title by a seller of goods notwithstanding shipment or delivery to the buyer is limited in effect to a reservation of 'security interest.' " We can conceive of no rational reason why conditional sales of real estate should be treated any differently.[1]

A conditional land contract in effect creates a vendor's lien in the property to secure the unpaid balance owed under the contract. This lien is closely analogous to a mortgage—in fact, the vendor is commonly referred to as an "equitable mortgagee." In view of this characterization of the vendor as a lienholder, it is only logical that such a lien be enforced through foreclosure

---

[1] In fact, the Commissioners on Uniform State Laws have recognized the transparency of any such distinctions. Section 3-102 of the Uniform Land Transactions Code (working draft of first tentative draft) reads as follows:

> This Article applies to security interests created by contract, including mortgage. . . land sales contract. . . and any other lien or title retention contract intended as security.

We believe this position is entirely consistent with the evolving case law in the area.

proceedings. Such a lien "[has] all the incidents of a mortgage" one of which is the right to foreclose.

There is a multitude of cases upholding the vendor's right to foreclose. The remedy is most often referred to as a foreclosure of an executory contract. (A land contract is "executory" until legal title is actually transferred to the vendee.)

. . ..

The foreclosure of a land sale contract is undeniably comprehended by our Trial Rules. TR. 69(C) IC 1971, 34-5-1-1, deals with the foreclosure of liens upon real estate:

Unless otherwise ordered by the court, *judicial foreclosure of all liens upon real estate shall be conducted under the same rules and the sale procedures applicable to foreclosure of mortgages upon real estate, including without limitation redemption rights, manner and notice of sale, appointment of a receiver, execution of deed to purchaser and without valuation and appraisement.* Judicial lien foreclosures including mortgage foreclosures may be held at any reasonable place stated in the notice of sale. In all cases where a foreclosure or execution sale of realty is not confirmed by the court, the sheriff or other officer conducting the sale shall make a record of his actions therein in his return to be filed promptly with the record of the case and also in the execution docket maintained in the office of the clerk. (Emphasis added.)

The vendor's interest clearly constitutes a "lien upon real estate" and should, therefore, be treated as one. The basic foreclosure statute—that is for mortgages executed after July 1, 1957— provides for a six-month period of redemption, commencing with the filing of the complaint. Additionally, it establishes the procedures attendant to the foreclosure sale. The statute reads as follows:

Mortgages executed after July 1, 1957—Time of issuing execution—Sale—Notices.—In any proceeding for the foreclosure of any mortgage hereafter executed on real estate, no process shall issue for the execution of any such judgment or decree of sale for a period of six [6] months after the filing of a complaint in any such proceeding: Provided, That such period shall be twelve [12] months in any such proceeding for the foreclosure of any mortgage executed prior to July 1, 1957. Thereafter, upon the filing of a praecipe therefor by any judgment creditor in said proceeding a copy of the judgment and decree shall be issued and certified by the clerk under the seal of the court, to the sheriff, who shall thereupon proceed to sell the mortgage premises or so much thereof as may be necessary to satisfy the judgment, interest and costs, at public auction at the door of the courthouse of the county in which said real estate is situated, by advertising the same by publication once each week for three [3] successive weeks in a daily or weekly newspaper of general circulation printed in the English language and published in the county where the real estate is situated, the first of which publications shall be made at least thirty [30] days before the date of sale; and by posting written or printed notices thereof in at least three [3] public places in the township in which the real estate is situated, and at the door of the courthouse of the county: Provided, That if the sheriff be unable to procure the publication of such notice within such county he may dispense with such publication but he shall in his return state his inability to procure such publication and the reason therefor.

TR 69(C) requires that the procedures outlined in the above statute be applied "without limitation" to the "judicial foreclosure of all liens upon real estate." We believe there to be great wisdom in requiring judicial foreclosure of land contracts pursuant to the mortgage statute. Perhaps the most attractive aspect of judicial foreclosure is the period of redemption, during which time the vendee may redeem his interest, possibly through re-financing.

Forfeiture is closely akin to strict foreclosure—a remedy developed by the English courts which did not contemplate the equity of redemption. American jurisdictions, including Indiana, have, for the most part, rejected strict foreclosure in favor of foreclosure by judicial sale:

> The doctrine of strict foreclosure developed in England at a time when real property had, to a great extent, a fixed value; the vastly different conditions in this country, in this respect, led our courts to introduce modifications to the English rules of foreclosure. Generally, in consonance with equity's treatment of a mortgage as essentially a security for the payment of the debt, foreclosure by judicial sale supplanted strict foreclosure as the more equitable mode of effectuating the mutual rights of the mortgagor and mortgagee; and there is at the present time, in the majority of the American states, no strict foreclosure as developed by the English courts—either at law or in equity—by which a mortgagee can be adjudged absolute owner of the mortgaged property. The remedy of the mortgagee is by an action for the sale of the mortgaged premises and an application of the proceeds of such sale to the mortgage debt, and although usually called an action to foreclose, it is totally different in its character and results from a strict foreclosure. The phrase "foreclosure of a mortgage" has acquired, in general, a different meaning from that which it originally bore under the English practice and the common law imported here from England. In this country, the modern meaning of the term "foreclosure" denotes an equitable proceeding for the enforcement of a lien against property in satisfaction of a debt.

55 Am. Jur. 2d, *Mortgages*, 549 (1971).

Guided by the above principles we are compelled to conclude that judicial foreclosure of a land sale contract is in consonance with the notions of equity developed in American jurisprudence. A forfeiture—like a strict foreclosure at common law—is often offensive to our concepts of justice and inimical to the principles of equity. This is not to suggest that a forfeiture is an inappropriate remedy for the breach of all land contracts. In the case of an abandoning, absconding vendee, forfeiture is a logical and equitable remedy. Forfeiture would also be appropriate where the vendee has paid a minimal amount on the contract at the time of default and seeks to retain possession while the vendor is paying taxes, insurance, and other upkeep in order to preserve the premises. Of course, in this latter situation, the vendee will have acquired very little, if any, equity in the property. However, a court of equity must always approach forfeitures with great caution, being forever aware of the possibility of inequitable dispossession of property and exorbitant monetary loss. We are persuaded that forfeiture may only be appropriate under circumstances in which it is found to be consonant with notions of fairness and justice under the law.

In other words, we are holding a conditional land sales contract to be in the nature of a secured transaction, the provisions of which are subject to all proper and just remedies at law and in equity.

Turning our attention to the case at hand, we find that the vendor-assignees were seeking forfeiture, including $21,000 already paid on said contract as liquidated damages and immediate possession. They were, in fact, asking for strict application of the contract terms at law which we believe would have led to unconscionable results requiring the intervention of equity. "Equity delights in justice, but that *not* by halves." (Story, *Eq.Pl.* § 72.) On the facts of this case, we are of the opinion that the trial court correctly refused the remedy sought by the vendor-assignees, but in so refusing it denied all remedial relief to the plaintiffs. Equity will "look upon that as done which ought to have been done." (Story, *Eq.Jur.* § 64(g).) Applying the foregoing maxims to the case at bar, where such parties seek unconscionable results in such an action, equity will treat the subject matter as if the final acts and relief contemplated by the parties were accomplished exactly as they should have been in the first instance. Where discretionary power is not exercised by a trial court, under the mistaken belief that it was without this power, a remand and direction by a court of review is necessary and proper. This is not an unwarranted interference with the trial court's function. Upon appeal to this Court, we have the judicial duty to *sua sponte* direct the trial court to apply appropriate equitable principles in such a case. Consistent with such abovestated rules, this Court has the undeniable authority to remand with guidelines which will give substantial relief to plaintiffs under their secured interests and will prevent the sacrifice of the vendees' equitable lien in the property.

For all of the foregoing reasons, transfer is granted and the cause is reversed and remanded with instructions to enter a judgment of foreclosure on the vendors' lien, pursuant to Trial Rule 69(C) and the mortgage foreclosure statute as modified by Trial Rule 69(C). Said judgment shall include an order for the payment of the unpaid principal balance due on said contract, together with interest at 8% per annum from the date of judgment. The order may also embrace any and all other proper and equitable relief that the court deems to be just, including the discretion to issue a stay of the judicial sale of the property, all pursuant to the provisions of Trial Rule 69(C). Such order shall be consistent with the principles and holdings developed within this opinion.

Reversed and remanded with instructions.

ARTERBURN, C.J., and DEBRULER and PRENTICE, JJ., concur in this opinion on the merits.

GIVAN, J., dissents.

PRENTICE, JUSTICE (concurring).

I have some concern that our opinion herein might be viewed by some as indicating an attitude of indifference towards the rights of contract vendors. Such a view would not be a true reflection.

Because the installment sales contract, with forfeiture provisions, is a widely employed and generally accepted method of commerce in real estate in this state, it is appropriate that a vendee seeking to avoid the forfeiture, to which he agreed, be required to make a clear showing of the inequity of enforcement. In any given transaction anything short of enforcing the forfeiture provision may be a denial of equity to the vendor. It has been set forth in the majority opinion that if the vendee has little or no real equity in the premises, the court should have no hesitancy in declaring a forfeiture. It follows that if the vendee has indicated his willingness to forego his equity, if any, whether by mere abandonment of the premises, by release or deed or by a failure to make a timely assertion of his claim, he should be barred from thereafter claiming an equity.

If the court finds that forfeiture, although provided for by the terms of the contract, would be unjust, it should nevertheless grant the vendor the maximum relief consistent with equity against a defaulting vendee. In so doing, it should consider that, had the parties known that the forfeiture provision would not be enforceable, other provisions for the protection of the vendor doubtlessly would have been incorporated into the agreement. Generally, this would require that the transaction be treated as a note and mortgage with such provisions as are generally included in such documents customarily employed in the community by prudent investors. Terms customarily included in such notes and mortgages but frequently omitted from contracts include provisions for increased interest during periods of default, provision for the acceleration of the due date of the entire unpaid principal and interest upon a default continuing beyond a reasonable grace period, provisions for attorneys' fees and other expenses incidental to foreclosure, for the waiver of relief from valuation and appraisement laws and for receivers.

[c] Explanatory Notes

[*i*] ***Events After Remand.*** After the Indiana Supreme Court rendered the *Skendzel* opinion, the case was remanded back to the trial court. The plaintiffs then contended that the dispute came within the language of the *Skendzel* concurring opinion of Judge Prentice and that foreclosure was inappropriate. The trial court declined to follow that path, instead entering a judgment of foreclosure. That judgment, entered on August 6, 1974, gave the Marshalls 65 days to redeem the property. If redemption did not occur, the property was to be sold. After sale, the plaintiffs were to get the unpaid contract balance of $15,000, delinquent taxes paid by Josephine Skendzel and Bernice Wysocki in the amount of $6,984.97, and attorneys' fees in the amount of $1,000, for a total of $22,984.97 all subject to interest of 8% from the date of the foreclosure judgment. This judgment was appealed, the plaintiffs arguing that the trial court abused its discretion in ordering a foreclosure rather than an ejectment. The appeal failed,[27] as did another effort challenging on due process grounds the failure of the trial judge to take further evidence on the issue of whether foreclosure was appropriate.[28] The continued appeals on already decided issues suggests that the animosity between Agnes Marshall and the relatives of her dead friend was both intense and long lasting. After *Skendzel* was remanded, the Marshalls redeemed the property prior to its being sold at a foreclosure sale.[29]

[*ii*] ***Land Sale Installment Contracts and the Uniform Land Transactions Act.*** The Uniform Land Transactions Act goes a little further than *Skendzel*, requiring the use of foreclosure in all similar situations. The model Act's path to this result rests on its definition of a *security interest*, the all purpose phrase it uses to cover settings in which land is used as collateral for credit:

§ 3-103. [Definitions and Index of Definitions][30]

As used in this Article, unless the context otherwise requires:

. . ..

(7) "Security interest" means an interest in real estate which secures payment or performance of an obligation. If a lease is intended as security to the lessor, the lessor's interest is a security interest. If a seller's retention of legal title to real estate after the buyer enters into possession is intended as security, the seller's interest is a security interest. Whether a transaction is intended as security is to be determined by the facts of each case. However, (i) the inclusion in a lease of an option to purchase at a price not unreasonable in the circumstances at the time of contracting does not of itself indicate the lease is intended for security, and (ii) retention

[27] Skendzel v. Marshall, 263 Ind. 337, 330 N.E.2d 747 (1975).

[28] Skendzel v. Marshall, 264 Ind. 77, 339 N.E.2d 57 (1975).

[29] Telephone Interview with Leroy Shultess (Feb. 18, 1987).

[30] Reprinted by permission of the National Conference of Commissioners on Uniform State Laws.

of the title to real estate by a seller under a contract right to retain title for not more than one year after the buyer enters into possession of the real estate is not a retention for security. [31]

Once a security interest is found, § 3-501 of the Act requires the lender to pursue a foreclosure action. The Act provides one additional protection for debtors in Marshall's position. Section 3-510(b) provides:

> If the debtor is a protected party and the obligation secured is a purchase money security interest, there is no liability for a deficiency, notwithstanding any agreement of the protected party.

A "protected party," defined in § 1-203, includes those who "give a real estate security interest in. . . residential real estate all or a part of which he occupies or intends to occupy as a residence." If operative in *Skendzel*, these provisions would have prevented the plaintiffs from suing for a deficiency, that is, for any portion of the indebtedness not obtained at the foreclosure sale.

   [iii]   **Skendzel *Opinions and the History of Consumer Protection in Mortgage Lending.*** At first blush, it may seem surprising that the Indiana Supreme Court reconfigured the legal structure established by the original land installment sale contract the parties signed. At least in this setting, little sympathy for Formalist "freedom of contract" was displayed. Consumer protection has a long history in mortgage law. And the prevalence of consumer protection enactments during the 1960s and 1970s made it easier for the Indiana Supreme Court to provide Agnes Marshall with some relief.

Early mortgage documents, like the contract terms at stake in *Skendzel*, called for the automatic forfeiture of title by the borrower upon default. Courts of equity first established the notion that borrowers had an equity of redemption to retain their property by full payment of the indebtedness. This equity of redemption provided an important protection against creditors simply seizing possession of property and claiming fee simple ownership. Attempts by creditors to draft waivers of the equity of redemption into their mortgage instruments were resisted by equity courts. As an early American commentator on mortgages wrote:

> No sooner, however, was this equitable principle [of redemption] established than the cupidity of creditors induced them to attempt its invasion, and it was a bold but necessary decision of equity, that the debtor could not, even by the most solemn engagements entered into at the time of the loan, preclude himself from his right to redeem. . . .. In truth it required all the firmness and wisdom of the eminent judges who successively presided in the courts of equity to prevent this equitable jurisdiction being nullified by the artifice of the parties. Accordingly, "Once a mortgage always a mortgage," became one of the most important maxims in this branch of the law; and a strict adherence to it has at all times been enforced. The parties have not been allowed to provide that the deed creating the mortgage shall at any time, or upon the happening of any event, cease to be a mortgage, and become an absolute conveyance. Any agreement or stipulation cutting off the right of redemption has always been held to be utterly void. Even a subsequent release of this right by the mortgagor has always been looked

---

[31] This last clause does not negate the general intention of the section. It is meant to deal with the common situation in which the buyer moves into property prior to closing as a tenant for the convenience of the parties, and then closes the purchase shortly thereafter. That is a routine occurrence when, for one reason or another, the deal cannot be closed before the buyer needs to use the property. Note also the relevance of clause (i) on sale and leaseback to the next case.

upon with suspicion, and sustained only when made for a proper consideration and without oppression on the part of the mortgagee.[32]

This excerpt from Leonard A. Jones' treatise may overstate the level of judicial zealousness in protecting debtors. After equity courts recognized the equity of redemption, creditors succeeded in obtaining the adoption of time limits on the debtor's equity of redemption through the creation of a suit to *foreclose* the equity of redemption. But Jones did touch a central feature of land finance law. Each effort to limit consumer remedies in the mortgage arena has eventually been countered. Thus, the creation of the strict foreclosure remedy, in which the debtor lost all equity in the property once the period of redemption passed, was in turn limited by legislation preventing creditors from retaining foreclosure sale proceeds over and above the amount of the indebtedness.

In any case, one way of looking at *Skendzel* is that it represented the latest debtor response to efforts to use the land sale contract as a device to avoid the borrower's equity of redemption. There is some evidence that the land sale contract became a much more commonly used device in various parts of the country after 1960.[33] Once the perception became widespread that a new device had surfaced to end run the equity of redemption, outcomes like *Skendzel* were predictable.

[iv] *Scope of the* **Skendzel** *Remedy.* Cases raising *Skendzel* issues continue to appear in Indiana.[34] Several involved arguments over whether the debtor had paid enough money on the installment contract to trigger the *Skendzel* foreclosure remedy. Perhaps the most interesting of this series is *Johnson v. Rutoskey*, 472 N.E.2d 620 (Ind. App. 1984). The installment contract in *Johnson* contained a declaration that foreclosure was not required unless the debtor had accrued at least $12,000 in equity on a property purchased for $52,000. At the time of default, just under $12,000 in equity was paid up. Despite the declaration, *Skendzel*'s foreclosure remedy was used.

In a case with a different twist, *Maddox v. Wright*, 489 N.E.2d 133 (Ind. App. 1986), assignment of the purchaser's interest without the consent of Maddox, the seller, was prohibited by the contract. After six years, the buyer, Wright, wished to sell the property. When Wright sought contract payoff information, so that he could arrange a sale of the property, Maddox refused to give the information, saying simply that payments should continue to be paid to his collection agent. Unable to obtain payoff information, Wright assigned his rights under the contract to Fleming, who in turn assigned it to Wesselhoft. Payments were made by the new owner to the collection agent until Maddox told his agent to stop accepting the checks. The new owners then sent their checks directly to Maddox who refused to cash them. Maddox then unsuccessfully sought forfeiture of the property. The court noted that Maddox could not frustrate an effort to prepay the contract by refusing to divulge payoff information and then refuse to accept an assignment when that was the only way the buyer could sell the property to another. To hold otherwise, the court found, would have permitted the seller to impose an unreasonable restraint on alienation.

[v] *Sale of Property Prior to Full Performance of a Land Sale Contract.* The *Maddox* case, described in the prior note, presents an interesting example of a sale of rights under a land

---

[32] L.A. JONES, 1 A TREATISE ON THE LAW OF MORTGAGES OF REAL PROPERTY 7 (1882).

[33] *See* Warren, *California Installment Land Sales Contracts: A Time for Reform*, 9 UCLA L. REV. 608 (1962).

[34] A number of state courts outside of Indiana have also imposed restrictions on the use of land sale installment contracts to avoid the debtor benefits of foreclosure. For a summary of these results, *see* Annotation, *Modern Status of Defaulting Vendee's Right to Recover Contractual Payments Withheld by Vendor as Forfeited*, 4 A.L.R. 4th 993 (1981). For a review of some of the reform efforts, *see Installment Land Contracts: The Illinois Experience and the Difficulties of Incremental Judicial Reform*, 1986 U. ILL. L. REV. 91.

sale installment contract. Contract buyers have two primary ways they may try to sell their asset. First, they can seek a new buyer who is willing to obtain financing from another source, like a bank. In that case, the new buyer (with the help of a loan from a third party) will pay cash at settlement for the property, the old buyer will pay off all remaining indebtedness under the land sale contract, the original seller will then be obligated to transfer title to the old buyer, and the old buyer will then be able to convey good title to the new buyer. Second, the old buyer may seek to assign his rights under the contract to the new buyer. In that case, the transaction operates very much like a lease assignment. The new buyer becomes primarily responsible for payments under the installment contract, but the old buyer is not released from his obligations in case of default. This method may not work well in all cases. If the old buyer has paid a significant portion of the installments due under the contract, then the new buyer will have to have quite a bit of cash if the old buyer is to exit the transaction with fair payment.

[*vi*] *Mortgage Assumptions and Transfers Subject to a Mortgage.* Compare the mortgage setting. When mortgaged property is sold, the old mortgage is usually paid off and a new one obtained by the new buyer. The proceeds from the new loan help pay the purchase price and thereby contribute to paying off the old loan. This is analogous to a payoff of an installment contract and the creation of a new contract between the old and new buyers. But sometimes new institutional loans are hard to get or interest rates are extremely high. Such was the case in the mid-1970s.[35] In such an environment, new buyers are frequently interested in taking over payment of the old mortgage, and, if the outstanding balance due on the old loan is not real high, in getting the old buyer to finance part of the transaction through a purchase money mortgage. In a time of inflation, however, institutional lenders are interested in getting rid of their old loans so they can replace them with mortgages yielding the more recent and higher interest rate. They frequently insert language in their mortgage instruments prohibiting the transfer or encumbering of the property securing the loan without the permission of the lender. In the absence of such language, mortgages may be *assumed* or debtors may sell their property *subject to* a pre-existing mortgage.

[*A*] *Assumptions.* When a new buyer agrees to assume the prior loan and, if required, the lender agrees to the assumption,[36] the new buyer will sign an assumption contract under which the buyer agrees to be bound by the terms of the mortgage deed. The old note is not canceled. Therefore, in case of default, the bank may foreclose and, if there is a deficiency, sue either the old buyer on the old note or the new buyer on the assumption contract. The new buyer is primarily liable.

[*B*] *Purchase Subject to a Mortgage.* When a new buyer purchases property subject to a mortgage, the lender is not involved in the deal. The new buyer simply agrees with the old buyer to buy the land with the mortgage left in force. The lender has no direct recourse against the new buyer, though foreclosure rights under the old mortgage deed are left intact. Lenders don't like *subject to* deals. If the old buyers leave town, the lender is left with no one to sue in case of a deficiency after foreclosure. Frequently mortgage instruments prohibit *subject*

---

[35] The high interest rates also added to the attractiveness of the land sale installment contract. For sellers willing to finance the transaction at an interest rate below the high market level, a land sale contract was seen as an easy way of arranging the deal.

[36] If the mortgage deed is silent on assumption rights or specifically permits assumption, then lender permission is not required. Many mortgage instruments, however, permit assumption only with the permission of the lender.

to transfers and make such transfers without the lender's permission a grounds for immediate foreclosure.

[*vii*]   **Foreclosure Procedures Under the Uniform Land Transactions Act.** Section 3-505 of the Uniform Land Transactions Act outlines the various methods that a lender may use to foreclose. If the security agreement is silent, a judicial sale is required. But if the security agreement permits it, the lender may terminate the debtor's ownership interest in the secured property by exercising a power of sale. Not all states follow the Uniform Land Transactions Act model; judicial sales are required in some places. Where non-judicial sales are permitted, auction sales are generally required to be public and the auction process is heavily regulated.

[*viii*]   **Constitutionality of Non-Judicial Foreclosure.** Given the variety of challenges that have arisen to various self help remedies, including distraint in landlord-tenant law,[37] it should not surprise you that non-judicial foreclosure proceedings have been challenged on due process grounds in a number of places. The challenges have almost uniformly failed on state action grounds. *See, e.g., Charmicor, Inc. v. Deaner,* 572 F.2d 694 (9th Cir. 1979); *Barrera v. Security Building and Investment Corp.,* 519 F.2d 1166 (6th Cir. 1975). Only when a government agency is the lender and foreclosing party has a due process challenge succeeded. *See United States v. Whitney,* 602 F. Supp. 722 (W.D.N.Y. 1985); *Ricker v. United States,* 417 F. Supp. 133 (D. Me. 1976). *But see, Warren v. Government National Mortgage Association,* 611 F.2d 1229 (8th Cir. 1980).

[*ix*]   **Risk of Casualty Loss During the Life of a Land Sale Installment Contract.** Recall that the common law rule placing the risk of casualty loss pending performance of a land sale contract on the buyer has been rejected in many states. Does that also mean that the sellers retain the risk of loss while a land sale *installment* contract is being performed? As a practical matter almost all installment contracts contain language placing the risk of loss on the purchaser, along with other typical home-owner obligations like paying real estate taxes and utility bills. But in that rare case where the contract is silent, wouldn't you expect the risk of loss to be placed on the buyer anyway? If that is so, how should the difference between installment and non-installment land sale contracts be rationalized? Under § 2-406(c) of the Uniform Land Transactions Act, risk of loss passes to the buyer either when the sale is consummated or when the buyer takes possession. State courts that have rejected the common law risk rules seem to follow the Uniform Land Transactions Act's model in installment sales cases.

[d]   Problem Notes

[*i*]   **Forfeiture Shortly After Default by the Buyer.** Even after *Skendzel,* buyers defaulting shortly after performance of a land sale installment contract begins risk forfeiture. Why permit forfeiture in this situation? If the equity of redemption is non-waivable, why permit its waiver when only a small amount has been paid on the contract?

[*ii*]   **Risk Taking and Antipathy to Forfeitures.** Some have argued that the land sale contract, along with its stiff penalties to defaulting buyers, makes it possible for people outside of the conventional housing market to buy housing. The argument goes something like this: Contracts permitting sellers of housing to recover property and resell it upon default are passing along the costs of default only to buyers who actually default, rather than including the cost

---

[37] See Callen v. Sherman's Inc., p. 622 above.

of such risk in the selling price for all purchasers. Only those buyers that actually default lose badly, permitting those who manage to pay regularly to successfully enter the world of home ownership. In addition, selling houses to less well off persons is generally a riskier business than the typical housing market. Sellers in that setting, the argument suggests, ought to be able to assess greater penalties in case of default.

Do you like the argument? Would sellers in the traditional housing market begin to use land sale installment contracts if courts legitimated their forfeiture provisions? If so, does that mean forfeiture provisions should be barred in all situations? Compare the attempt of a cooperative to gain forfeiture rights against a defaulting resident in *Plaza Road Cooperative v. Finn*, p. 609 above.

[*iii*]   *Forfeiture Remedies.* Note that in Indiana, as well as other jurisdictions, defaulting land sale installment contract buyers lose possession of their houses in landlord-tenant court proceedings. New Jersey installment buyers may not be sued in landlord-tenant court. *See* N.J. STAT. ANN. § 2A:18-53, which limits proceedings to those involving a landlord-tenant relationship. Is there any rationality in New Jersey's dispossessing tenants in a "fast" court, while migrant workers, residents of cooperatives and contract buyers must be taken to a "fancy" court?

[*iv*]   *Compare Mitigation.* The forfeiture remedy in land sale installment contracts conflicts with the general notion that parties to breached contracts must mitigate their damages. Mortgages were originally written as fee simples subject to a condition subsequent; that is, the borrower conveyed title to the lender, subject to the conditions that the conveyance would be defeated if the loan was paid off and that it would mature into a fee simple absolute in case of default.[38] Reforms in mortgage law over the last century significantly limited the ability to enforce such conditions. Land sale installment contracts are just modern versions of this old tradition. May installment contract sellers, like common law landlords, escape the general obligation to mitigate damages? Do the same sort of arguments about property and contract that have arisen in academic debates about landlord-tenant law therefore recur in land transfers?

[*v*]   *Mitigation and Retention of Increase in Value.* In a typical sale of goods case, a seller mitigating losses after a purchaser declines to accept delivery of goods gets to keep any surplus money produced by the mitigation or to seek redress from the defaulting purchaser in case there is a deficiency. The same result arose for a landlord mitigating damages after a tenant abandoned. *See N.J. Industrial Properties, Inc. v. Y.C. & V.L. Inc.*, p. 730 above. In those two settings, the transferor of an asset retained the increase in value of the asset, if any, between the date of contracting and the default by the transferee. Thus, mitigation prevents a vendor or landlord from demanding payment before testing the market demand for the relevant product, but it does not automatically give the defaulting party the benefit of a market upswing. Mortgages, however, are structured to both demand mitigation and to provide the borrower with market protection.[39] Sale of goods under a security interest is also treated like a mortgage.[40] Why should parties borrowing under a security interest, whether the collateral is real or personal property, obtain more protection than parties transferring goods without use of a security interest? Is interest

---

[38] Some mortgages are to this day framed in this way.

[39] All is not roses, remember. A declining market leaves a lender with an action against the borrower for a deficiency in many jurisdictions.

[40] *See* U.C.C. § 9-504(2).

received on moneys lent under a security interest a substitute for the market risk-taking normally associated with contract breach cases?

[*vi*] ***"Low Equity" Purchasers and Habitability.*** Many low income "purchasers" of houses under land sale installment contracts are in economic positions quite similar to tenants. They may not stay in their homes for very long or pay off their contracts and obtain a deed. They may be more concerned about the dilapidated state of the house they are "buying" than the possibility of obtaining title many years down the road. Should "purchasers" in such situations be treated as tenants so they can take advantage of the implied warranty of habitability?[41]

[3] Some Thoughts on the Nature of Land Transfer Law

Before investigating another mortgage case, think a bit about the nature of the land transfer law you have read to this point. The rules about specific performance, risk of loss pending settlement and mortgages have all gone through periods in which the law was thought to be well settled and understood. The mutuality rule, allowing both sellers and buyers to seek specific performance, and the doctrine of equitable conversion were followed by decision makers for many years. Only in recent times have some courts begun to rethink the prior understandings. Mortgage rules have gone through a number of transformations. Common law lenders could force forfeitures for a time. Equity courts then intervened, first by allowing borrowers to redeem their equity and later by granting lenders the right to foreclose on the equity of redemption. In the United States, installment sales contracts emerged during the height of the Formalist freedom of contract era in the late nineteenth century, allowing seller-lenders to escape the equity of redemption by inserting forfeiture clauses in their sales documents.[42] This trend has come under criticism in recent decades with many courts treating installment sales contracts as mortgage arrangements and the Restatement (Third) of Mortgages taking the firm position that installment land sale contracts create mortgages.[43] Each period of rule solidity has been followed by an era of flux, only to be followed by another period of solidity. While much of property law has ebbed and flowed in similar patterns, land transfer law has been notorious for such behavior.

Oversimplified a bit, the pattern of change from solidity to flux, or "crystals" to "mud" in the words of a well known article by Carol Rose,[44] reflects constant attempts to Formalize property law. I don't mean Formalism here in the more politicized sense of Freedom of Contract pursued by pre-New Deal Classical Legal Thinkers, but in the methodological sense of seeking a scientific, rationalist legal system. Reducing ambiguity in the operation of legal rules has always been a goal of property law, especially when certainty and transfer of titles is involved. Both owners and buyers of land desire to insure that the assets they buy and sell are marketable. They both think that solid rules make transfers easier and more efficient.

---

[41] One author answered "yes." Eric Freyfogle, *The Installment Land Contract as Lease: Habitability Protections and the Low-Income Purchaser*, 62 N.Y.U. L. REV. 293 (1987).

[42] Much of this history is recounted in a nice article by Grant S. Nelson, *The Contract for Deed as a Mortgage: The Case for the Restatement Approach*, 1998 BYU L. REV. 1111 (1998).

[43] The Restatement provision reads as follows:

§ 3.4 A CONTRACT FOR DEED CREATES A MORTGAGE

(a) A contract for deed is a contract for the purchase and sale of real estate under which the purchaser acquires the immediate right to possession of the real estate and the vendor defers delivery of a deed until a later time to secure all or part of the purchase price.

(b) A contract for deed creates a mortgage.

[44] *Crystals and Mud in Property Law*, 40 STAN. L. REV. 577 (1988).

Carol Rose argues that this theory of efficiency, at least in part, is inaccurate. Solid, or crystalline rules, may ease transfer customs. But the more solid they are, the more likely it is that some people will wish to contract around them. And that immediately introduces the possibility that unsophisticated people will be treated unfairly by rules they fail to take into account. The more often that occurs, the greater the pressure will be to alter the underlying rule. Similarly, if rules are in flux, pressure will grow to solidify understandings to reduce the likelihood of confusion. In addition, Rose argues, both sorts of rules may increase sociability—solid rules by creating better understanding of obligations, particularly among strangers, and rules in flux by allowing for readjustments, especially among those in long term commercial relationships. Rose concludes:

> [I]t is precisely as metaphor or rhetoric that the choice between crystal and mud matters. The lapse of community may occur only infrequently in our everyday lives, but this world of estrangement has had a robust life in our highly individualistic *talk* about politics and economics since the seventeenth century. In the context of that talk of universal individualism, the metaphoric or rhetorical character of crystals and mud has a certain independent significance. However much crystal rules may have a dialogic side like mud, and however much mud rules may lend the certainty of crystal, as *rhetoric*, crystals and mud bear sharply divergent didactic messages. They suggest quite different ways that each self-contained individual should behave and converse with all those other self-contained individuals. Thus, crystal rhetoric suggests that we view friends, family, and fellow citizens from the same cool distance as those we don't know at all, while mud rhetoric suggests that we treat even those to whom we have no real connection with the kind of engagement that we normally reserve for friends and partners. And for this reason—for the sake of the different social didactics, the different modes of conversation and interaction implicit in the two rhetorical styles—we debate endlessly the respective merits of crystals and mud. *

For a more complete exploration of such ideas, read Carol Rose, *Crystals and Mud in Property Law*, 40 STAN. L. REV. 577 (1988), excerpted in RICHARD CHUSED, A PROPERTY ANTHOLOGY 307-319 (2d ed. 1997).

[4] Lease or Mortgage?

[a] Introduction to *Kawauchi v. Tabata*

The opinions of the Hawaii Supreme Court in the next case lay out the facts fairly completely.[45] There is no need to rehearse them here before you read the case. *Kawauchi v. Tabata* involved the most complex factual setting of any case in these materials. It will take some work for you to understand what was going on. The transaction diagrams following the opinions may be helpful. Keep several issues in mind while you study the case. First, recall the definition of "security interest" in Section 3-103(7) of the Uniform Land Transactions Act, p. 782 above. "If a lease is intended as a security to the lessor, the lessor's interest is a security interest," the act provides. But the mere inclusion of an option to purchase in a lease "at a price not unreasonable" is not enough by itself to manifest an intention that the lease is a security interest. The Uniform Land

---

* Republished with the permission of the Standford Law Review, 559 Nathan Abbott Way, Palo Alto, CA 94305. *Crystals and Mud in Property Law,* C. Rose, 1988, Vol. 40. Reproduced by permission of the publisher via Copyright Clearance Center, Inc.

[45] The briefs of the parties filed with the Hawaii Supreme Court contain very similar statements of facts. The court opinions generally mimicked these statements.

Transactions Act clearly recognizes that legal arrangements established under one legal construct, like a lease, may actually serve the purposes of a quite different legal construct, like a mortgage. But it is very indefinite about the circumstances in which the language used in the documents will be "pierced." Think about both the circumstances in which such piercing may occur and the reasons for ignoring the labels attached to a transaction by its participants. Second, compare *Kawauchi v. Tabata* to other cases you have read in which the courts considered, and either accepted or rejected, arguments for protecting parties from the consequences of the deals they made. Recall *Shelley v. Kraemer*, p. 445 above; *Kirchberg v. Feenstra*, p. 179 above; *Nachtrieb v. Harmony Society*, p. 257 above; *Reilly v. Sageser*, p. 123 above; *Vasquez v. Glassboro Service Association*, p. 594 above; *Callen v. Shermans, Inc.*, p. 622 above; and *Skendzel v. Marshall*, p. 774 above. Are there any common threads running through these cases that help you predict when parties may be able to escape from "bad deals." Finally, consider the ethical dilemmas associated with structuring complicated legal transactions involving parties in precarious financial condition. If your client is "taking advantage" of the difficulties of another, are there any ethical obligations to "go easy" on the "other side" to the deal? And if your client is in precarious condition, is there any obligation on your part to structure the deal so there is a chance your client may later be able to escape from it?[46] Or does the obligation run in the other direction, that is to make sure that your client intends to live up to validly executed agreements?

[b] Opinions of the Hawaii Supreme Court in *Kawauchi v. Tabata*

Kawauchi v. Tabata

Hawaii Supreme Court
49 Haw. 160, 413 P.2d 221 (1966)

LEWIS, JUSTICE.

Plaintiffs sued to obtain a declaration that a transaction entered into in 1958 was a mortgage securing a usurious loan, and to establish a right of redemption upon payment of the sum of $90,000 received by them in the transaction, less "all moneys paid on the loan." The court held that the transaction was a sale, coupled with a lease back of the premises and an option to repurchase. Judgment was entered for defendants and plaintiffs appealed.

Plaintiffs are husband and wife. Toichi Kawauchi, the husband, hereinafter will be referred to as "plaintiff." When both plaintiffs are referred to they will be designated as "the Kawauchis." Defendants are a group of ten husbands and wives, hereinafter referred to as the "doctors' group," or "defendants.". . . A bank, hereinafter referred to as "the bank," also was named as a defendant but it is not concerned in the questions at issue.

At the time of the transaction, first and second mortgages on plaintiff's property were about to be foreclosed. Plaintiff had not been able to obtain refinancing. He was, as found by the court, "considered a bad credit risk." The sum of $70,000 was required to save the property from foreclosure. The property was appraised by the court-appointed appraiser at $160,000 and the upset price fixed at $150,000. At the public auction there were no bidders at that price, though

---

[46] In this regard it is interesting to note that Kawauchi began using language like "loan" and "mortgage" when corresponding with various participants to this transaction within a month after the deal was consummated. *See* Opening Brief of Plaintiffs-Appellants at 10, Kawauchi v. Tabata, No. 4399 (Hawaii Supreme Court, 1963). That suggests that he might have been quite aware that his "lease" really was not a lease at all.

previously a written offer of $150,000 had been received by the court. The offer was withdrawn when plaintiff obtained time to pursue the possibility of selling a portion of the property in order to save the balance. This possibility did not materialize.

After the abortive public auction another sale was ordered without an upset price. This order was entered on February 18, 1958, and the sale was advertised for March 26, 1958.

Plaintiff, since the latter part of 1957, had been in touch with Mr. Joseph Ahuna, a stockbroker and real estate broker, whom he had approached to help him get a loan on the property. He was trying to raise $90,000, and was willing to repay $120,000, "something to that effect," as testified by Mr. Ahuna. Plaintiff testified he offered a 30% premium, or $27,000, plus 5 1/2% interest on the $117,000.

On one occasion Mr. Ahuna introduced plaintiff at the bank and unsuccessfully tried to help plaintiff get a bank loan. He also inquired whether, if a lender were found with less than the $90,000 required, such lender could go to the bank and borrow the difference. He ascertained that the bank would not lend money to a mortgagee on the strength of a mortgage held by him.

After plaintiff had visited Mr. Ahuna several times and Mr. Ahuna still did not know of anyone interested in making a loan, plaintiff in February 1958 came in with a proposition the nature of which Mr. Ahuna related as follows:

A. I asked him exactly what he had in mind, and he says, "If you find someone who would like to buy the property, why I would be willing to sell providing the buyer will allow me to lease the property from him on a sort of a sale and lease-back with an option to repurchase the property at the end of three years," and I asked him what he would want for a property that size, and he told me about $90,000, and I remember telling him that $90,000 is pretty cheap in view of the fact that he had previously stated that he thought the property was worth anywhere from $400,000 to $600,000.

Q. When you told him that it was pretty cheap, did he make any reply to that statement?

A. Well, he told me that since the property was due for foreclosure that he was interested in trying to protect his interest and that he would want to sell it with the lease-back and by-back [sic] option, and he agreed that the price of $90,000 was low in relation to his own appraisal of the value of the property, but he stated that because time was short and he needed the money as quickly as possible, he figured that $90,000 would be a very, what you call, an inducing deal for anyone who might be interested in it, and all he wanted was that he be permitted to buy the property back.

I told him that the appraised value was about $160,000 or $175,000. He says he only is interested in enough money to pay off the mortgage and he was confident he would be able to sell the property in view of the development that was upcoming in the Bishop Estate property where the present Star Supermarket is now, and he told me that with the development of that property and surrounding areas that his property value could be enhanced considerably and, if given the chance to buy it back within three years, he could swing it.

And he also stated another reason why he was asking for $90,000 instead of much more was he wanted to be sure that the price is not so high that he could not buy it back later on. In other words, he wanted to sell it and yet make the price to suit him. He stated at that time that he wanted to buy it back for about $117,000, I believe, and with the property value much higher he figured it would be easier for him to arrange financing to buy it back, whereas if he asked for a much higher price it would be difficult to sell and he might not be able to buy it back at a later date.

Sometime after this Dr. Kusunoki called Mr. Ahuna about an investment in stocks, and Mr. Ahuna mentioned plaintiff's proposition as a possible investment. After ascertaining the location of the property, Dr. Kusunoki told Mr. Ahuna "that man must be crazy to want to sell it for $90,000." Mr. Ahuna's testimony continues:

So I told him the reason and he said if the offer was real, and I said yes. He felt that it was a steal. I felt he knew what he was doing and that his actions were based on a calculated risk, and I told Dr. Kusunoki at that time that this fellow feels he can buy it back, and if he couldn't I told him, "You will just fall into a pot of gold."

On the other hand, if he is able to buy it back, I told him, "You will have received a fair lease rental on the property with interest, and no doubt you will be making a profit of somewhere of $25,000 to $30,000.". . ..

The upshot of the matter was that Mr. Ahuna attended a meeting with Dr. Kusunoki and some of his medical associates to explain the proposition. Thereafter, a group of ten was formed, of whom eight put up $5,000, while one put up $4,000 and the tenth $1,000. Mr. Ahuna assisted the group to obtain bank financing for the remaining $45,000. After the bank had tentatively approved the loan to the doctors' group, Mr. Ahuna "having promised Dr. Kusunoki that the deal is as stated" took it upon himself to seek the advice of an attorney he knew[2] as to whether "such a deal was proper." He was advised, as he testified: "'Yes, there have been many deals like that.'"

Mr. Thomas W. Flynn, plaintiff's attorney, drew up the documents to complete the transaction. Mr. Ahuna went with plaintiff to Mr. Flynn's office where, as he testified, they "talked about the deal." Mr. Flynn was the attorney representing plaintiff in the foreclosure proceeding. Mr. Flynn testified that he drew these documents on a request made by "Mr. Ahuna and Mr. Kawauchi both jointly and individually. . .." He further testified: "I had no initiative whatever in this part of the long drawn-out problem of Mr. Kawauchi's mortgage situation, the delinquent mortgage situation."

By the time the transaction had taken shape it was very close to March 26, 1958, the date on which the foreclosure sale was to be held under the supplemental order rescinding the fixing of an upset price. As a temporary measure in order to make funds available to clear the title, the bank made a collateral loan to the doctors' group for two years, secured by the assignment by the doctors' group of a note and mortgage given by the Kawauchis to the doctors' group. This note was in the amount of $117,000, payable over a three-year period in monthly installments of $650, including 5% interest. However, the amount plaintiff was to receive was $90,000, as agreed throughout.

The note and accompanying mortgage were dated March 24, 1958. On the same day the Kawauchis signed a letter addressed to the doctors' group, reading as follows:

Reference is made to the negotiations between us, under which you are willing to enter into an agreement with us so as to prevent the foreclosure sale of our property on North School Street in Honolulu, and which requires you to raise certain funds for the complete transaction. Because of the fact that time is so extremely short, we have had prepared and have delivered

---

[2] This was not plaintiff's attorney, Mr. Flynn, hereinafter mentioned.

to you a mortgage, which mortgage you are assigning to the Bishop National Bank of Hawaii in order to obtain some of the funds required for completion of our transaction. We hereby covenant and agree with you, that this mortgage is a purely temporary arrangement, so that required funds can be raised before the foreclosure deadline, and that the true arrangement or agreement between us will be expressed by the other documents to be prepared hereafter, when time will allow.

Accordingly, we hereby covenant and agree that we will execute and deliver to you a deed of our North School Street property and improvements, it being understood that you will execute back to us a lease of the premises upon the terms and conditions previously agreed to among all of us, which lease will likewise contain a provision allowing us to buy back the property for the sum of $117,000.00 at any time within three years from the date of such deed and lease.

On March 25, 1958, $70,000 was paid into court in the foreclosure proceeding, the sale was canceled, and satisfaction of judgment was entered. In conjunction therewith the court held a hearing the transcript of which shows:

THE COURT: I want the record to show that I received a caller yesterday in regards to this case and he informed me that they were in the process of negotiating with the bank and Mr. Kawauchi. However, they were concerned about the legality of their agreement with Mr. Kawauchi. I informed them that I was not interested in any agreement he might enter, they might enter into with Mr. Kawauchi nor was I interested in any agreement or mortgage they might enter into with the bank.

The only thing I was concerned about was the payment of these judgments and where Mr. Kawauchi got the money from, under what circumstances he got the money, I was not interested in it at all and I advised them if there is any question to contact Mr. Flynn, counsel for Mr. Kawauchi, and he was representing Mr. Kawauchi in this matter and I presume he represents Mr. Kawauchi in any other subsequent or ancillary agreement he might have. Whether they have contacted you, I don't know.

MR. FLYNN: Yes.

On April 1, 1958 the Kawauchis executed a deed of the property, which according to the revenue stamps was for the consideration of $90,000. Thereafter the doctors' group as owners of the property executed a mortgage to the bank for $45,000,[3] the temporary bank loan to the doctors' group was marked "paid," and the March 24, 1958 note and mortgage were returned to plaintiff with the note rubber-stamped "canceled."

After the payment of $70,000 into court, payment of $20,000 was required to complete the promised sum, and this was paid by the doctors' group over a period of time. Of the money thus received, $4,500 or $4,000[4] was paid by plaintiff to Mr. Ahuna as his fee. It further appears that plaintiff made improvements of the property. By the supplemental judgment incorporating the accounting between the parties it was determined that these improvements came to more than $10,000.

A lease for a term of three years from April 1, 1958 was executed by the doctors' group as lessors, and by plaintiff Toichi Kawauchi as lessee, at a monthly rent of $650 payable on the

---

[3] Though the bank was named as a defendant, the validity and priority of its mortgage are not contested.

[4] The fee originally was fixed at $4,500, and plaintiff testified he paid that amount. Mr. Ahuna testified that at plaintiff's request he reduced the fee to $4,000.

21st of each month. It contained an option for the lessee to purchase the property at any time before the termination of the lease for $117,000, less a credit to be computed at the rate of $110 for each month's rent paid under the lease.[5] The $650 monthly payments were made, but at the end of the three-year term plaintiff had not raised the contemplated $117,000 though according to his testimony he had received offers of $350,000 and $400,000 for the property.

Through an attorney, plaintiff in July 1961 sought "an extension of the lease dated April 1, 1958 and the period of the option to re-purchase the property covered thereby, to December 31, 1961." The sum of $12,000 was offered for this extension. This request was denied by a letter of August 28, 1961, and at the same time a notice was given of termination of tenancy as of September 30, 1961. This suit was commenced September 29, 1961.

Plaintiff contends that the court erred in failing to make any finding as to the execution of the note and mortgage of March 24, 1958, and that if the court had taken into account these omitted facts, it would have been forced to view the case as one of subsequent release, without consideration, of an existing equity of redemption. We do not so view the case. The letter of March 24, 1958 constituted a promise by plaintiff to replace the note and mortgage with other instruments. The note, mortgage, deed and lease were parts of a single transaction, and the $90,000 was consideration for the whole. Since the note, mortgage, deed and lease were tied together by the letter there can be no difficulty in connecting them. Therefore the case is one of renunciation of the privilege of redemption at the time of making of the loan (if there was a loan). This brings us to plaintiff's alternative argument, based on the case being one of a deed and defeasance executed at the same time. In this type of case, as stated in Jones, *Mortgages*, § 301 (8th ed.):

When it is once established that the separate instrument is a defeasance, the conveyance assumes the character of a mortgage with the inseparable incident of redemption, which no agreement of the parties, that the estate shall be absolute if the money be not paid at the day fixed, can waive. . ..

The policy back of this rule is explained in section 302 of the same text as follows:

The mortgagor is not allowed to renounce beforehand his privilege of redemption. Generally, every one may renounce any privilege or surrender any right he has; but an exception is made in favor of debtors who have mortgaged their property, for the reason that their necessities often drive them to make ruinous concessions in order to raise money. When one borrows money upon the security of his property, he is not allowed by any form of words to preclude himself for redeeming.

These principles prevail in Hawaii. . ..

Since the right of redemption may not be waived, the form of the instruments cannot control the case if in reality the transaction was a mortgage. As was said in *Hess v. Paulo*, 38 Haw. 279, 286: ". . . [N]either artifice nor form nor superficial declaration of intention will successfully obscure the true nature of the transaction." It is here that the court erred. In finding it to be the intention of all parties[7] that the transaction should constitute a sale subject only to an option

[5] No point is made of the fact that only Toichi Kawauchi, the husband, was a party to this instrument. The letter of March 24, 1958, addressed to the doctors' group and signed by both husband and wife, stated that it was understood the property would be leased back and the lease would contain a provision allowing "us" to buy back the property. Evidently the husband received the option to repurchase in behalf of his wife as well as himself.

[7] The court found not only that all parties intended to enter into a sale transaction, *i.e.*, a conditional sale, but also

to repurchase, the court put undue emphasis on the form of the transaction. We do not doubt that the parties intended the form of words that was used, and intended thereby to cut plaintiff off from all rights unless he exercised his option within the three-year period. But will the court permit this purpose to be accomplished? We must enforce not only the policy against renunciation beforehand of the right of redemption but also the statute against usury.[8] As well explained in *Fiedler v. Darrin*, 50 N.Y. 437, 443:

> . . . [O]ne who deliberately and intentionally secures to himself $1,650 at the end of four months, in return for a present advance of $1,500, cannot avoid the consequences of the act by testifying that he did not intend to take usury; that is, that he intended to give the transaction a different name from that which the law gives it, and call that a purchase and sale which the law calls a loan of money, secured by mortgage. . ..

> . . ..

A separate instrument (here the lease with option to repurchase) is a defeasance if it grants an absolute right to a reconveyance upon payment, is contemporaneous with the deed, and the two together constitute security for a debt. 1 Jones, *Mortgages*, §§ 294-96 (8th ed.). In conformity with the general rule R.L.H.1955, § 196-1, provides:

> *Sec. 196-1. Lien of mortgages; priority*

> Every transfer of an interest in property, real or personal, made as security for the performance of another act or subject to defeasance upon the payment of an obligation. . . is to be deemed a mortgage. . ..

This statute "is comprehensive in scope and should be liberally construed." *Hess v. Paulo, supra.*

Defendants contend that there can be no debt—hence no mortgage—unless the plaintiff was personally liable for repayment of the money. Under this reasoning plaintiff must fail unless defendants could have obtained a personal judgment against him. Some of the writers on the subject afford qualified support for defendants' contention,[9] while others state that the weight of authority is contrary thereto.[10] The court below did not rule that the absence of personal

---

that according to plaintiff's own testimony, he understood on March 24, 1958, that he would have three years within which to buy the property back at $117,000, that if he did not so buy back the property he would lose all rights in the property, and that when he signed the deed he would be passing title to the defendants. We proceed on the premise that plaintiff did so understand.

[8] The usury statute is part of Chapter 191, R.L.H. 1955, 191-3 to 191-6, inclusive. The maximum rate of interest is 1% per month.

In defendants' answer it is averred: "Defendants affirmatively state that Plaintiffs knew that Defendants were unwilling to invest money without a high rate of return, that they were unwilling to enter into a loan transaction because of the law against usury, and that the transaction was intended to be and in fact was a legitimate sale and lease transaction."

[9] 4 Pomeroy, *Equity Jurisprudence*, § 1195 (5th ed.), sets out the view that the existence of a liability on the part of the grantor is a "general criterion,. . . which furnishes a sufficient test in the great majority of cases." 1 Jones, *Mortgages*, § 315 (8th ed.), states that the rights of the parties must be reciprocal, and sec. 316, states that the debt must be one which is enforceable against the person independent of the security. But sec. 90 states that it is not necessary that there be any personal security, and the remedy of the mortgagee may be confined to the land alone.

[10] In 1 Lawrence, *Equity Jurisprudence*, § 170 at 219, it is stated that: "By the weight of authority the existence of an independent in personam remedy against the mortgagor is not essential, a debt chargeable against property only being in effect simply a debt with limited means of satisfaction or enforcement, though some decisions regard such personal liability as essential." Glenn, *Mortgages*, § 5.4, gives it as the rule that "the security nature of a mortgage is in nowise affected by the fact that the mortgagor has refused to bind himself personally for repayment of the debt,"

liability was conclusive, but put considerable stress on the fact that: "There is nothing before this court which indicates any right on the part of the Defendants to compel the payment of any sums of money."

In *Hess v. Paulo, supra*, it is stated. . . that "a test generally accepted as decisive is the mutuality and reciprocity of the remedies of the parties; that is to say, if the grantee enjoys a right, reciprocal to that of the grantor to demand a reconveyance, to compel the latter to pay the consideration named in the stipulation for reconveyance, the transaction is a mortgage, while if he has no such right to compel payment, the transaction is a conditional sale. . .." However, the conclusiveness of this test where personal liability is lacking was not before the court, as there was an outstanding promissory note. The quotation in the opinion continues with recognition of the fact that personal liability is not always regarded as the "*sine qua non*" of a mortgage. It may be regarded simply as "a factor whose existence or nonexistence points strongly to the fact that a conveyance is or is not a mortgage."

. . . ..

. . . [I]n Hess. . . there [was not] any question of usury or of inadequacy of the price figuring in the supposed sale. Where the transaction, if it is a loan, is usurious, the personal liability of the borrower is of no real significance. Under the usury law, R.H.L. 1955, § 191-4, a suit against the borrower personally could produce only the sum advanced, without interest or profit. In this type of case the lender relies on the property for his security, being satisfied that he is protected by its high value in relation to the amount advanced.

. . . ..

Particularly when a question of usury is involved it would be most unrealistic to lay down any absolute requirement that the borrower must be personally liable in order for the transaction to be a mortgage. The result would be to provide a ready avenue of escape from the requirements of the usury law. The absence of personal liability is a factor indicative of a conditional sale but one which nevertheless may be and in this case is outweighed by other circumstances.

. . . ..

Ordinarily we would be guided by the findings of the court below on a matter such as adequacy or inadequacy of the $90,000 advanced in relation to the value of the property. However, the court in its findings ignored the fact that the parties to the transaction dealt on the basis that $90,000 was "a steal." The figure was deliberately set low by the plaintiff in order that he might be able to "buy it back" and defendants knew it. There were no negotiations for a sale at a fair price, and neither side contemplated or intended that plaintiff was to realize the value of the property in this transaction. It is this which unmistakably marks the transaction as a loan.

In the usual case a court is left to infer from the value of the property whether the parties deemed the price to represent the value. Here there is direct evidence that they did not so regard the matter. This overweighs all other circumstances, including absence of personal liability on the part of plaintiff. When the case is judged against the applicable principles of law there is no room for the conclusion that the transaction was a sale.

---

and consistent therewith states in sec. 12 at pp. 60-61 that, though there is a difference of opinion: "The fact that the grantor took back an option merely, which he was not bound to exercise, should not weigh heavily against his contention that a mortgage was really intended, because, as we have seen, a mortgage need not necessarily secure a personal obligation."

The court erred in placing a value of $125,000 on the property on the basis of an appraisal report tucked away in the files of the bank.[12] This appraisal was made for another bank, evidently in connection with efforts of plaintiff to refinance the mortgage under foreclosure. There is no evidence that the parties here involved ever saw it, or if they did that it figured in their negotiations. An employee of the bank, a witness, made "a guess" that it was brought in to the bank by Mr. Ahuna. The bank was taking a mortgage from the doctors' group and it evidently was in that connection that it came into possession of this report. Mr. Ahuna's own opinion was that the property was worth $160,000 to $175,000. This is significant since he was the broker who handled the transaction. He represented to Dr. Kusunoki that he stood to "fall into a pot of gold" if plaintiff couldn't exercise the option. The property also had been appraised by the court-appointed appraiser at $160,000. Though there were no buyers at the auction at the upset price of $150,000, there had been an offer of $150,000 received by the court which fell through only because of plaintiff's unwillingness that the property go at that price. In any event, as we have said, the fact that the parties did not intend the $90,000 to represent the value is established without resort to inferences from the court's own valuation of the property.

It is argued that, in considering the adequacy of the price, plaintiff's option to buy back the property must be taken into consideration. The court below reasoned that "this option and the time that it gave to the Plaintiff had considerable value. . .." Undoubtedly, an option to repurchase would affect the selling price. But it is not possible to approach the matter in that light, because neither the $90,000 nor $117,000 figure was fixed by negotiations seeking to evaluate the property as affected by this provision. The $90,000 represented the amount of money plaintiff required, and the additional $27,000 included in the $117,000 represented the premium he offered to get it.

The court below regarded it as significant that plaintiff received $90,000 when only $70,000 was needed to stop the foreclosure, the court noting that plaintiff received "some money for his own use." Plaintiff, however, was undertaking to make monthly payments of $650 when he had been unable to keep up mortgage payments of $587.50 per month to meet the mortgages under foreclosure. He also had to pay Mr. Ahuna's fee (approximately $4,000). So far as appears, the extra $16,000 was the amount plaintiff deemed that he needed to maintain and improve the property,[13] provide a cushion for monthly payments, and enable plaintiff to carry out his plan, which was to use the three years as a grace period in which to sell the property on the rising market which he expected.

Plaintiff retained possession of the property throughout, at a "rent" which represented 5 1/2% interest on $117,000, or $536.25 per month, plus $110 creditable to the $117,000 sum on "repurchase," or a total of $646.25 rounded out to $650 per month. This is easily seen upon

---

[12] It was stated on the face of this report that the appraisal was "for mortgage loan purposes." The court below reasoned: "That if the figure of $125,000 is taken as a true appraisal of the property and if Plaintiff were able to arrange a loan, the maximum loan based on 60 per cent of the appraised value would have been $75,000. However, even this loan was not available to him because he was a bad credit risk." This was not sound reasoning. Defendants were not figuring on the possibility of a forced sale, as would a bank. Nor were they figuring on receiving only bank interest. Erroneous results were produced by superimposing the conservative approach of a bank on the transaction between plaintiff and the doctors' group, which embraced short cuts and high profits. Even if the property was worth only $125,000, defendants stood to realize from $46,440 to $58,400 at the end of the three-year period, including the monthly payments during the three years, or from 17.2% to 21.6% per annum on the $90,000 advanced.

[13] As seen, plaintiff made improvements of property which came to more than $10,000, according to the supplemental judgment incorporating the accounting between the parties.

comparison of the "lease" with the promissory note of March 24, 1958. On this phase of the argument we agree with plaintiff that the note of March 24, 1958[14] and the accompanying mortgage colored the entire transaction, particularly in view of the letter of March 24, 1958 agreeing that the deed and lease with option to repurchase would be given to take the place of the note and mortgage. The court erred in omitting the documents of March 24, 1958 from consideration, and in failing to consider the agreement as a whole.

Plaintiff not only remained in possession of the property but was active in seeking to have it rezoned. This was in October 1958 and again in 1959. Plaintiff endeavored to have the application for rezoning signed by the doctors' group, as was necessary under the then state of the record. Though plaintiff offered to pay the expenses of this application, there was no reply to his request. Mr. Ahuna acted as agent for collections for the doctors' group, and there is no evidence that they took any interest in the property.

We conclude that the true nature of the transaction was a loan, and that the finding to the contrary was "clearly erroneous" and reversible under H.R.C.P., Rule 52(a), for the reasons we have stated. [*Footnote omitted.*] Were we to hold otherwise our usury statute would be emasculated.

At the same time we agree with certain findings of the court below which are purely factual in nature. These findings show that the entire scheme was instigated by plaintiff, who set up the transaction as a sale, and caused defendants to be approached with that proposition. Defendants were not in the loan business, and would never have considered the transaction except for the manner in which it was presented at plaintiff's instigation. Defendants did not, directly or indirectly, instill the idea that this form of transaction should be used.[16] Mr. Ahuna, as agent

---

[14] It is to be noted that this note was for a three-year loan, the period agreed upon between plaintiff and the doctors' group for winding up the transaction. The bank, however, was making a two-year loan to the doctors' group upon the assignment to the bank of this note and the accompanying mortgage.

[16] We note that plaintiff testified repeatedly that the matter of the deed to the doctors' group entered the transaction only when it appeared that the doctors' group was short of cash, and that the purpose of the deed was to enable the doctors' group to obtain a loan. This must have been, he said, at the time when Mr. Flynn was consulted about preparing the documents. He was contradicted on this point by Mr. Ahuna who, as has been related, testified that plaintiff came to him with the sell and lease-back proposition and thereafter Mr. Ahuna got Dr. Kusunoki interested in the property. Mr. Ahuna was corroborated by the attorney whom he consulted concerning the propriety of such a deal, by defendants themselves who, it was stipulated, if called to testify would testify that they "at no time intended to make a loan. . .," and by Mr. Flynn who testified, as has been noted, that he drew the documents on request and without taking any initiative in the matter. This portion of Mr. Flynn's testimony was given without objection, and we need not get into the disputed portion of Mr. Flynn's testimony which concerns the explanations of the documents made by Mr. Flynn to plaintiff, to which objection was made on the ground of the attorney-client privilege. Accordingly, we have not considered to what extent the court below relied on the disputed testimony, or the admissibility of that testimony.

On the question of when the proposition of a deed and lease back with option to purchase originated the court was amply justified in finding, as it did, that this was before Dr. Kusunoki came into the picture. In addition to the testimony above set out, the circumstances are to be considered. Plaintiff was well aware that he was considered a bad credit risk. He had applied to numerous brokers for help in getting a loan and had learned that investors wanted a big profit; as he testified, "so I figured myself I must make a good offer before I could get a loan, so when I went to see Mr. Ahuna I offered him 30%." Though plaintiff denied knowledge of any question of legality of a 30% premium, and denied having discussed with Mr. Ahuna the proposition of deeding the property and taking a lease back with an option to repurchase, he testified he did discuss such a matter with a Mr. Matsuo; this, according to his testimony, was a matter of helping Mr. Matsuo's hui to borrow money. The probability is that as plaintiff made his rounds he learned that a straight note and mortgage would not be acceptable in the money market he was trying to reach, and so brought in to Mr. Ahuna the proposition to which Mr. Ahuna testified, which Mr. Ahuna in turn relayed to the doctors' group.

of plaintiff in obtaining the money,[17] "promised Dr. Kusunoki that the deal is as stated," that is, a sale, and took steps to check on the matter, consulting an attorney as has been noted. Since the present suit sounds in equity, there is a question whether plaintiff is in an equitable position in seeking to take advantage of his own actions by redeeming the property for only the principal of $90,000 less all payments made, as sought by the prayer for relief contained in his complaint. We proceed to the question of the form of relief to be allowed plaintiff, having disposed of all of the specifications of error which, on our view of the case, are material.

Many authorities hold that one seeking equitable relief from a usurious contract must offer to pay[18] the principal with legal interest. On the other hand. . . there is authority that no interest at all need be paid in case of a usurious contract though the borrower comes into equity seeking relief.

According to some of the courts which require an offer of interest such offer must be, not at the rate prescribed when none is fixed by the contract (here 6% under R.L.H.1955, § 191-1), but instead at the maximum legal rate of interest (here 1% per month under R.L.H.1955, §§ 191-3 and 191-6). However, some require interest at the rate obtaining in the absence of an express contract.

. . ..

In addition to the circumstances heretofore noted there are others to be taken into consideration. Plaintiff had sought an extension of time in which to pay to a date some months after the date on which suit was filed. He filed suit without being ready and able to pay, seeking "an opportunity to raise money" to pay the balance of the loan when determined by the court, "failing which repayment, that the court order a sale of the property upon foreclosure and apportion the proceeds. . .." He had, according to his own testimony, rejected offers which would have enabled him to pay within the agreed time. Plaintiff testified that he refused offers of $350,000 and $400,000 for the property, because "I was asking $475,000 less 5% commission to the broker. . .." Plaintiff was willing to reduce this, but wanted more than the $400,000 offered. He was not ready with the principal, even as computed by him, at the end of the three-year term. He was holding out for his price of over $400,000, intent on making a killing.

We deem it unnecessary to resolve the conflict in the case law of the various states, or to decide what rule is applicable in this jurisdiction in the ordinary case. This is no ordinary case. Proceeding upon the basis that the contract is not void as to all of the interest but is void only as to the interest in excess of 1% per month, and without laying down a rule of general application as to what shall be done in cases not within the terms of section 191-4, we hold that under the circumstances of this case the maxim "he who seeks equity must do equity" requires that the

---

[17] Plaintiff contends Mr. Ahuna was the agent of both parties, but there is no indication that was so during the negotiations for obtaining of the money. *See* 12 C.J.S. *Brokers* § 14; 12 Am. Jur. 2d, *Brokers,* § 67. After the deal was concluded Mr. Ahuna represented the doctors' group in collecting the monthly payments, but that is not material.

[18] While the complaint should set forth an offer to pay in appropriate terms, at this stage of the case we will not hold plaintiff to any exactitude in pleading. The record shows that defendants set forth as their "Third Defense" that "The Complaint fails to state a claim against Defendants upon which relief can be granted," but defendants did not further pursue the contention of insufficiency of plaintiff's pleading. Had they done so, plaintiff might have been granted leave to amend. Under these circumstances we will take a broad view of the averments of the complaint, and will treat the averment that plaintiff seeks the aid of equity to determine the amount remaining due on the loan, as an offer to pay whatever may be required as a condition of equitable relief. While the prayer for relief seeks to redeem the property for only the principal of $90,000 less all payments made, the prayer for relief is not decisive pursuant to H.R.C.P., Rule 54(c).

Kawauchis, in order to redeem the property, pay interest in addition to the principal sum of $90,000 at the maximum rate allowed by law, *i.e.*, 1% per month, to the extent that such rate or a higher rate was contracted for, that is, for the period April 1, 1958 through March 31, 1961.

From and after April 1, 1961, the only provision made was for $650 per month to be paid while plaintiff remained in possession.[25] It was stipulated that of this sum $110 per month was creditable against the $117,000 required for redemption. This credit would apply if the property was redeemed at the $117,000 figure, but our judgment will invalidate more than half of the $27,000 premium included in that figure. The credit provision accordingly is inapplicable. It was not contemplated that such credit would be allowed against the lesser figure. Therefore, $650 per month will be allowed from and after April 1, 1961, for the period plaintiff remained in possession.

We note that there is a dispute as to the period during which plaintiff has remained in possession. This will be for consideration on remand. Plaintiff remained in possession at least until October 8, 1963. For any period during which plaintiff has not been in possession the applicable interest rate will be 6% per annum, pursuant to R.L.H. 1955, § 191-1, there being no contractual rate applicable in such case.

For any period during which defendants have been in possession, they must be deemed mortgagees in possession, and the net rents received by them must be deemed to have been applied on the loan under the principles generally applicable in that situation. *See* 36 Am. Jur., *Mortgages*, § 301 *et seq.* There of course will be a further credit against the amount required to be paid by the Kawauchis, for all payments heretofore made to defendants directly, or in the form of payments on the bank's mortgage. All such credits will be applied first to the interest hereinabove required and then to the $90,000 principal amount, in accordance with the general rule.

The unpaid balance on the bank's mortgage will likewise be a deduction from the amount to be received by defendants. Said mortgage is a valid lien upon the property superior to the rights of either plaintiffs or defendants, as hereinbefore noted. Defendants are entitled to receive from the Kawauchis their promise in writing to assume the bank's mortgage and hold defendants harmless.

We have considered what period of time should be given the Kawauchis in which to redeem and assume the bank's mortgage, also the form of judgment to be entered in the event they do not do so. . . .. Plaintiff is not, any more than the ordinary mortgagor, entitled to the aid of equity

[25] In a supplemental brief filed upon the court ordering argument and putting certain questions "as to the judgment to be entered in the event the transaction is a loan," defendants while not conceding that the transaction was a loan argued upon that assumption in response to the court's questions and contended:

. . . [A]ccording to the intention of the parties, Defendants [upon the non-payment of the $117,000] would have been entitled to the property worth $350,000.00. This value of $350,000.00 is placed as a low value because Plaintiffs were not willing to sell for this price but sought a much higher price for the property.

By contracting to give up all claims to the subject property if not redeemed prior to March 31, 1961, Plaintiffs intended, upon default, to turn over and pay, in property, a sum far in excess of the principal amount plus 1% per month thereon to the present date, for the sum of $90,000.00 plus interest at 1% per month is considerably less than the sum of $350,000.00.

As we have held, a mortgagor cannot renounce beforehand his privilege of redemption. We do not regard the attempt to do so as a contract for interest in the amount agreed to be forfeited in terms of property value, here the difference between $90,000 and $350,000, according to the figures presented.

in obtaining an extension of time in which to pay.[26] The Kawauchis must see to it that defendants are promptly paid the amount secured by the property, which if not paid by them must be paid out of the proceeds of a foreclosure sale to be held without delay.

One more point requires comment, *i.e.*, the matter of attorneys' fees. Whether such fees are allowable pursuant to the bank's mortgage, the lease, or any other contract in writing, and if so whether the same should be allowed and the amount thereof, will be for the court below to determine. Also, in the event of an allowance of such fees to the bank it will be for the court below to determine who shall bear the ultimate burden of the fees. These matters are not determined by this opinion.

Pursuant to the foregoing, the judgment appealed from is reversed and the case remanded for further proceedings consistent with this opinion, including but not limited to (1) determination of the amount to be paid by plaintiff in order to redeem the property, and (2) entry of an order which, in addition to setting forth the amount so determined, shall also provide that, unless such payment be made and a proper instrument assuming the bank's mortgage and holding defendants harmless be furnished within ten days after the entry of such order, an appraisal shall be made and other proceedings taken looking toward and culminating in a foreclosure sale. But if such payment be made and the required instrument furnished within the time prescribed then the Kawauchis shall be adjudged the owners of the property as against the defendants, subject to the rights of the bank.

WIRTZ, JUSTICE, dissenting.

I find myself unable to agree with the conclusion reached by the majority of the court. . ..

By their petition plaintiffs sought to reform the deed and lease with option to repurchase into a mortgage. While such a transaction may be declared to be a security agreement there is a strong presumption that a duly executed, notarized and recorded deed and lease purport to be what they appear to be. Proof negating their obvious nature must be strong, clear and convincing. . ..

There is general agreement that in order to determine whether a deed absolute on its face together with an agreement of reconveyance constitute a mortgage or a conditional sale depends entirely on the intention of the parties at the time of the consummation of the contract.

The concern of the majority about usury which affects the result reached is misplaced in putting the cart before the horse unless the true intent of the parties spells out a security transaction.

. . ..

In considering factors reflecting the intent of the parties the majority recognizes that the absence of personal liability, while not conclusive, is a factor strongly indicative of a conditional sale. However, greater emphasis is placed on the discrepancy between the value of the property and the purported sales price as pointing to a mortgage. While this price, set by plaintiff for his own convenience and regarded by defendants as "a steal,"[2] may appear inadequate as compared with the value of the property, still this inadequacy of the consideration remained only a factor to be considered in determining the intention of the parties. The majority minimizes the conduct

---

[26] As seen, plaintiff has not at any time been ready and able to pay even the principal. According to his own testimony, he rejected offers which would have enabled him to pay within the three-year period. During that period he had a clear right to redeem under the option to repurchase, and was not obstructed by the form of the transaction.

[2] It seems difficult to reconcile the designation of this sales price of $90,000 as "a steal" with the fact that there were no bidders for the property at the public sale originally ordered at the upset price of $150,000. By the same token, the repurchase price of $117,000 was equally "a steal."

and expressions of the parties which are the best indications of intent; the factors considered being merely aids to ascertaining intent where the same is unclear.

The note of March 24, 1958, and accompanying mortgage, as explained by the covering letter of March 24, 1958, which the majority say the trial judge erred in not considering, as they "colored the entire transaction," indicate that the mortgage and note was "a purely temporary arrangement" so that foreclosure could be forestalled and that "the true arrangement or agreement between us" was to be evidenced by a deed and lease with option to repurchase.[3] This points to a conditional sale, which the parties were perfectly free to make, rather than a security transaction.

The majority concedes that the testimony of plaintiff Toichi Kawauchi was hardly worthy of credit when he sought to establish that the transaction was instigated by others than himself. It is no wonder then that the testimony of plaintiffs (who were in straitened circumstances simply through their own greed) was not considered worthy of belief by the chancellor on all material matters concerning the nature of the transaction.

The record shows that plaintiff Toichi Kawauchi, with knowledge that he could not secure a loan in view of his general bad reputation as a debtor, intended a sale from the outset. His agent Ahuna understood that he had been specifically instructed to sell the property with a lease containing an option to repurchase and sought legal assistance to properly carry out the instructions given him by his principal. The letter of March 24, 1958, addressed to the defendants and signed by plaintiffs refers to a deed and lease with option to buy back the property as the "true arrangement or agreement between us." Plaintiffs' then attorney, who drafted the documents involved, fully explained the nature of the transaction to them as one of conditional sale.

Not only did the plaintiffs intend a conditional sales transaction but their actions subsequent to the consummation of the transaction confirm this intent and are inconsistent with the present claim of ownership. Around October of 1958 plaintiff, Mr. Kawauchi, engaged as his attorney a very prominent and reputable attorney who on his behalf addressed a letter of July 7, 1961 to defendants requesting a six months' extension of the option period, offering to pay the sum of $12,000 for such extension, thus placing a value on the option to repurchase, comparably more than the premium originally set for repurchase. The attorney in question, whose repute in legal circles is well known, could hardly have written such a letter on behalf of his client unless, after ascertaining the true nature of the transaction, he considered it a sale subject only to the option to repurchase. Plaintiff, Mr. Kawauchi, in seeking the advice of eminent counsel before making this declaration of his understanding of the transaction cannot now find solace in ignorance of the law.

Plaintiffs' possession of the property was only natural under its lease as tenants and they recognized the ownership of defendants in their request to have the rezoning application signed by them.

It is not disputed that the defendants throughout considered the transaction to be one of a sale with an option to repurchase embodied in the lease back to the plaintiffs. That the defendants never considered that they were making a loan is understandable as they were not in the loan business and there existed no reason, through relationship, friendship or otherwise to make a loan to one whose credit was bad and who could not obtain financing from any regular loan

---

[3] It should be readily apparent that the original mortgage transaction was only an expeditious manner of securing the immediate financing required to avert the foreclosure sale and this "make-shift" transaction was so recognized by all the parties.

institution. It is difficult to imagine that the defendants who are all professional men would want to loan moneys and assume the headache of foreclosure upon default against a person who was even then in default in a foreclosure action.

While the court's allowance of interest on the defendants' investment is a more equitable result than that sought by the plaintiffs, still I do not feel at liberty to use the equitable remedy of reformation to flaunt the clearly expressed intention of the parties to the transaction as one of conditional sale.

Even if the testimony of plaintiffs could be believed that they intended the transaction to be one of security only, it has been held that before a deed absolute on its face can be declared to be a security instrument a court must have found that it was the mutual intent of the parties that the instrument have that effect. The defendants certainly never concurred in any such intent as now conveniently testified to by plaintiffs.

While, had I been the trier of facts, I personally might not have arrived at the conclusion reached by the trial judge in this case, I cannot see my way now to disturb his decision as being "clearly erroneous." Where the evidence can support two diametrically opposed conclusions dependent on credibility, the trial judge's choice between the two permissible views of the weight of the evidence is not "clearly erroneous."

. . ..

On Petition for Rehearing

PER CURIAM

Plaintiffs have petitioned for rehearing contesting the holding that they must pay interest in order to redeem. Main reliance is upon the theory that, by the amendments made by S.L.1931, c. 137, the legislature adopted the usury statute of the State of Washington, with only minor variations, and upon the further proposition that the State also borrowed the construction previously put upon the Washington statute. If so, *Vanasse v. Esterman*, 147 Wash. 300, 265 P. 738, decided in 1928, is clearly in point in support of the conclusion reached in our opinion. . ..

The subject matter of the petition having been fully considered by the court in its opinion, the petition is denied without argument. WIRTZ, J., who dissented from the majority in the original opinion, finds no merit in the petition and joins with the majority in its denial without retreating from the position taken in the dissent.

[c] Explanatory and Problem Notes on *Kawauchi v. Tabata*

[*i*] *Transaction Diagrams*

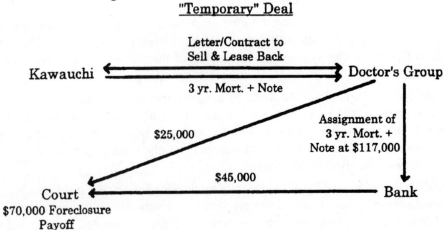

"Temporary" Deal

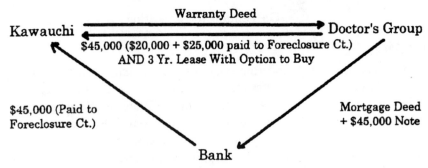

"Permanent" Deal as Characterized by Parties

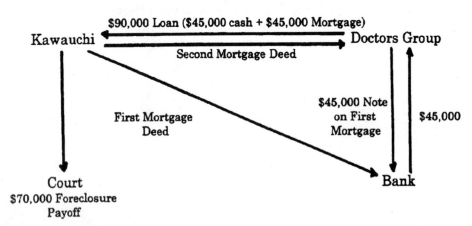

Transaction as Characterized by the Court

[*ii*] *Kawauchi's Initial Financial Position.* Before Ahuna found the group of investing doctors, Kawauchi was in precarious financial position. His credit was not good, all deals to sell the land were either mirages or had fallen through, and a foreclosure action was imminent. Liberty Bank held a first mortgage and Robert M. Tsuchiya held a second mortgage, the total indebtedness amounting to $54,887.26.[47] Liberty and Tsuchiya instituted foreclosure proceedings on July 15, 1957. The property was ordered appraised by the foreclosure court; the value was said to be $160,000. The court therefore set an upset price[48] of $150,000. As noted in the opinions, no bids were made at that level and the sale was rescheduled. Although the actual amount due on the two mortgages was less than $55,000, Kawauchi actually needed about $70,000 to rid himself of the foreclosure threat. Court costs, mortgagee's attorneys fees, additional accrued interest and other costs added significantly to the debt by the time the land was to be foreclosed. The prospect of an auction sale with no upset price was obviously discomfiting. There was a chance that the sale would produce even less than $70,000, leaving Kawauchi with a deficiency to pay off from other assets.

[iii] *The Temporary Deal.* Once the Doctors Group agreed to "rescue" Kawauchi, a fast deal had to be arranged to avoid loss of the land to foreclosure. The temporary deal left fee simple title with Kawauchi, but encumbered by a three year mortgage held by the bank[49] as the assignee of the Doctors Group. Since time was not available to fully perform a land sale by Kawauchi to the Doctors Group, the bank and the Doctors Group had to be satisfied with the temporary expedient of a personal note signed by Kawauchi and payable to the Doctors Group, and an assignment of this note by the Doctors Group to the bank. The assignment at least gave the bank the benefit of the endorsing signatures of the Doctors Group so Kawauchi's tainted credit was not the only prop for the deal.[50] In essence all that happened was that the old mortgage was refinanced, and a contract to enter into a sale and leaseback was agreed to. The mortgage was refinanced by the doctors adding $25,000 to the $45,000 bank loan and paying off the old loan. Kawauchi then signed a three year note for $117,000 at 5 1/2%, payable in monthly installments of $650, along with a contract promising to replace these documents with others later.

Problem: If Kawauchi had backed out of the letter/contract to set up the permanent deal, could the Doctors Group have obtained specific performance relief? Normally the answer would be "Yes," but this case was not typical. The court found the deal to be a mortgage at a usurious interest rate. Put aside for a time the reasons for that result. Did the illegality of the usurious interest called for by the contract make it unenforceable? If the contract itself was unenforceable, how would you have straightened out the chaos such a result would have created? You certainly couldn't leave the parties as they stood, for a *$117,000* note with only *$70,000* of credit actually extended at the time the note was signed was even more usurious than the final deal! Could you put the land back into foreclosure? Not really, since the old lenders were already paid off. Turn the tables. What if the Doctors Group backed out? Could Kawauchi have obtained specific performance at a non-usurious interest rate? Or would the court have concluded that the parties so egregiously misconceived the deals they were making that performance was excused because of mutual mistake?

---

[47] Opening Brief of Plaintiffs-Appellants at 3, Kawauchi v. Tabata, No. 4399 (Hawaii Supreme Court, 1963).

[48] An upset price is an amount below which bids will not be accepted.

[49] According to the court papers the bank was First National Bank of Hawaii.

[50] In negotiable instruments law all endorsers are responsible for the obligation they endorse. If you, for example, endorse a check over to a third party and the check later bounces, you, as well as the party who first wrote the check, are responsible for payment to the third party.

Back to the Case: The temporary deal, of course, was totally unsatisfactory as a permanent arrangement. The bank was unwilling to rely upon a note signed by the Kawauchis and the Doctors Group without any land as security. And the land could not be used as security until title was out of the hands of the Kawauchis. Thus the contract for further action was essential.

[*iv*]   ***The Permanent Deal.*** The contract called for two transactions to occur simultaneously. First, Kawauchi was to sell his land to the Doctors Group for $90,000, with the Doctors Group obtaining financing for 50% of the price from the bank through a conventional first mortgage. Thus, Kawauchi conveyed a warranty deed to the Doctors Group. The Doctors Group paid Kawauchi the $45,000 downpayment ($20,000 in new cash plus the money previously paid to the foreclosure court) and the proceeds of the loan went to Kawauchi (also paid previously to the foreclosure court). That part of the deal was virtually identical to the typical mortgage sale diagramed at the beginning of this section of the text on financing.[51] The only difference between the *Kawauchi* arrangement and typical deals was the lease, the second transaction to be consummated at closing. The three year lease contained the provisions upon which the case turned—a right to repurchase the property for $117,000 within three years. It was the combination of the $27,000 "premium" on the $90,000 purchase price and the 5% interest on $117,000 that ended up being treated as usurious interest.[52] Once these two transactions were completed, all the papers in the temporary deal were canceled.

At least two factual items were crucial to the outcome of the case. First, all sides admitted that the $90,000 price was well below the actual value of the property.[53] Second, Kawauchi had the right to buy back the property at or before the end of the lease term. That right left open the possibility that the Kawauchis' possession would never be terminated. The buy-back right made the sale and leaseback look very much like a *balloon mortgage* in which the mortgagor makes monthly payments lower than required to completely retire the loan during the period of payment, and avoids foreclosure only by tendering a large balloon payment at the end of the loan term. As noted in the introduction to this chapter, such loans were very common before the Great Depression. They are still used where the debtor desires to postpone payment of a large portion of a loan in the hope of obtaining better financing arrangements later.

Problem: Why did the court treat this arrangement as a usurious loan? If the Kawauchis made a bad deal, why not make them stick to it? While the Kawauchis may not have been appealing plaintiffs, it was true that they were in deep financial trouble when the deal was arranged. Usury laws are in part designed to protect people, like the Kawauchis, from digging themselves into deeper holes by agreeing to highly disadvantageous financial deals. If you are uncomfortable with the outcome of the case, is it because you do not like to rescue people as seemingly unattractive as the Kawauchis or because you do not believe that usury laws serve useful social purposes? In any case, once the court concluded that the sale, leaseback and repurchase option

---

[51] Compare the Kawauchi diagram entitled "Permanent Deal as Characterized by Parties" with the diagram at p. 773 above.

[52] *See* footnote 12 in the court's opinion.

[53] Surprisingly, the briefs of the parties were very similar on this factual point. Given the statement in the dissenting opinion criticizing the finding that the $90,000 price was a "steal," I expected the defendants had tried to make something of the "backing and filling" on the actual value of the property by Kawauchi, and the constant inability to actually sell the property. Instead, the defendants claimed that the property was worth about $350,000, and that Kawauchi had lost many opportunities to sell the property because he insisted on a price over $400,000. *See, e.g.,* Supplemental Answering Brief of Defendants-Appellees at 12, Kawauchi v. Tabata, No. 4399 (Hawaii Supreme Court, 1963).

actually were a substitute for a loan transaction, there was little to do but completely restructure the deal and require the Doctors Group to proceed in foreclosure.

[v] *The Deal to the Court.* Reconfiguring the *Kawauchi* transaction was not simple. There were several areas of difficulty. First, the court left title to the land with Kawauchi, while the financial deal was premised on getting title to the Doctors Group. Second, since the bank was unwilling to rely upon Kawauchi's credit in making the deal, Kawauchi never signed a permanent note or mortgage deed for the bank's benefit. Somehow the bank's interest in the deal had to be protected. Third, the $90,000 loan made to Kawauchi came from two sources—half from the bank and half from the Doctors Group. What structure of mortgages could be established to reflect this reality? Finally, the court had to decide what amount of interest, if any, the Doctors Group could charge Kawauchi for their loan.

In working through these problems the sources for the loan funds were crucial. As to the $45,000 actually put up by the bank, Kawauchi would surely be obligated as if he, rather than the Doctors Group, was the first mortgagor. Thus, after recognizing that Kawauchi still held title, it was understandable that the court required Kawauchi formally to *assume* the obligations of the $45,000 bank loan, making him personally liable for the debt. The use of an assumption, rather than wholly reforming the transaction and naming Kawauchi as the only debtor, meant that the bank could sue either the Doctors Group (on the note they signed when the permanent deal was set up) or Kawauchi in case of default.[54] That relieved the bank of some of their concern about relying only upon Kawauchi's credit.

The bank loan of $45,000 was not, of course, interest free. If the court had held that the Doctors Group would not be allowed to charge any interest on their loan to Kawauchi, that would have effectively imposed the interest on the bank's loan upon the Doctors Group. Remember that the Doctors Group used $45,000 of their own money and $45,000 borrowed from the bank to make their $90,000 loan to Kawauchi. In a sense they acted as loan brokers, borrowing money from one source at one interest rate and then relending those funds (along with some of their own money) to Kawauchi at a higher interest rate. On the bank money they relent, they hoped to keep the difference between the bank's rate and their own higher rate as profit. When the court decided that the Doctors Group could charge the maximum legal interest rate of 12%, their brokering function did not entirely fail. They made 12% on the $45,000 of their own money they lent, plus the difference between 12% and the bank's interest rate on the $45,000 from the bank. Perhaps you can view this premium over the bank's rate as the value of the risk they took in dealing with a character like Kawauchi.

All this is made somewhat clearer by the positions on the interest rate question taken by the parties. Kawauchi, arguing that no interest was due on the $90,000 loan, took the position that he could redeem the property in any resulting foreclosure action by paying $90,000, *less* the sum of the amount paid in rent through September, 1961 ($27,300), the amount paid during the pendency of the litigation ($22,061.28 through December, 1965), and other amounts paid while the appeal and remand actions were pending.[55] That position left the interest on the bank loan the total responsibility of the Doctors Group. The Doctors Group took the position that redemption at any subsequent foreclosure required payment of the same amount figured by Kawauchi *plus* 12% interest on $90,000, ($83,700.00 as of December 31, 1965).[56]

---

[54] Compare the discussion of obligations after assumption at p. 785 above.

[55] Supplemental Brief of Plaintiffs-Appellants at 9, Kawauchi v. Tabata, No. 4399 (Hawaii Supreme Court, 1963).

[56] Supplemental Brief of Defendants-Appellees at 7, Kawauchi v. Tabata, No. 4399 (Hawaii Supreme Court, 1963).

In any case, the deal as structured by the court left title with Kawauchi, made the bank a first mortgage lender for $45,000, turned the Doctors Group into a second mortgage lender for $90,000,[57] charged Kawauchi with all legal interest, and forced a remand for an accounting and a new foreclosure action.

[vi] *Cooperative Housing Transaction.* Problem: After reading *Skendzel* and *Kawauchi*, do the labels placed upon a cooperative housing development make sense? Why not treat the purchase of shares of stock and a lease as a purchase money mortgage transaction between the building's corporate owner and the resident buyer? Or, if the resident obtains credit from an outside source to buy the stock and lease, why not call that transaction with an outside lender a second mortgage? Does the cooperative extend "credit" to the resident? Is the rent, at least in part, payment on a debt? Do the leases and shares of stock in the cooperative serve as security for a loan?

[vii] **Kawauchi *on Remand.*** In accordance with the decision of the Hawaii Supreme Court, the *Kawauchi* case was remanded so that the mortgage held by the doctors group could be foreclosed. The trial court found that the debt owed by the Kawauchis amounted to $106,329.13.

This amount was made up of the following items:

Principal on Note:	$ 90,000.00
Interest at 1% per month over that actually paid from 4/1/58 to 3/31/61:	9,000.00
Unpaid rent at $650 per month for 4/1/61 to 9/30/63:	12,129.13
Interest on $90,000 note of .5% per month from 10/1/63 to 5/31/66 (court rate):	14,400.00
Subtotal:	$125,529.13
Less: Credit for rents received by defendant:	(19,200.00)
Total:	$106,329.13

The property was appraised, an upset price of $300,000 was set, and the sale was scheduled for September 14, 1966. No one showed up to make a bid! The sale was reset for October 28, 1966, without an upset price. *Déjà vu.* The sale was held and a "winning" bid of $155,000 was submitted. The motion of the Commissioner holding the sale to confirm it was opposed by Kawauchi on the ground that he had obtained a $150,000 secured loan from the trustees of the Ancient Order of Foresters Friendly Society, a fraternal group! That turned out to be accurate. *Déjà vu.* The court's final judgment, entered on November 15, 1966, ordered payment of the $150,000 loan into court. $106,329.13 was paid as above. In addition, $7,853.48 was paid out in various fees to lawyers and commissioners and $10,574.82 was paid to the First National Bank of Hawaii to repay the remaining principal held by the bank that provided $45,000 to the Doctors Group as part of its "loan" to Kawauchi.[7] That left $25,242.57 from the new $150,000.00 loan

---

[57] Though the total of the two mortgages adds up to $135,000, that is OK. Since the Doctors Group could charge a premium for passing on to Kawauchi the loan they got from the bank, the $135,000 figure actually counts the original $45,000 from the bank twice. Perhaps it would be more correct if the Doctors Group is called a second mortgage lender for $45,000 at 12% plus an amount equal to the difference between 12% and the bank's interest rate on another $45,000.

[7] It strikes me that this outcome may be in error. The payment to the bank was part of the $90,000 paid over to the Doctors Group. Kawauchi should have been given a credit for this amount against the $90,000 principal.

for Kawauchi. Once again Kawauchi managed to snatch victory from the jaws of defeat at the last possible moment. As of a few years ago, the property, in the hills above downtown Honolulu, was developed with a large number of apartments and commercial properties. As far as I know, these structures are not owned by Kawauchi.

[viii] *Other Examples of "Constructed" Mortgages. Kawauchi* certainly does not apply to every sale and lease back transaction involving a debtor in bankruptcy. Where the initial deal is an arm's length transaction at a fair price with reasonable interest rates and no other indication that the arrangement was a loan, it will be enforced as written. That was the result in *Corey v. Loui*, 892 F.2d 829 (1989), a case in which the court found that the original debtor wrongly used the result in *Kawauchi* to try to interfere with a later sale of the property at a favorable price.

But settings in which "investors" risk being called "lenders" because of the way they structure their deals with financially needy property owners do surface from time to time. For example, in *Bermil Corp. v. Sawyer*, 353 So.2d 579 (Fla. App. 1977), a case much like *Kawauchi*, a shopping center owner on the verge of foreclosure conveyed 40% of his $500,000 shopping center in return for a $60,000 foreclosure-avoiding payment and a one-year option to rebuy for $100,000. The deal was treated as if it were a mortgage.

Financial desperation is not the only force causing courts to inquire into the existence of mortgages. Sometimes badly drafted deals raise similar problems. In *Petters Diner, Inc. v. Stellakis*, 202 N.J. Super. 11,493 A.2d 1261 (1985), the owner of a restaurant sold the business for $600,000. The fee simple in the land upon which the restaurant was located was retained by the sellers, but a 25-year lease of the land was included in the deal. The buyers paid $100,000 in cash, and signed a $500,000 note for the rest. The note was secured by the fixtures, equipment and stock in trade of the restaurant. The buyers also assigned the lease back to the sellers to be held in escrow as security for the $500,000 note. Finally, the agreement gave the buyers a five-year option to buy the land upon which the restaurant stood for $350,000. When the buyers notified the sellers of their intention to exercise the option to buy, a major problem suddenly surfaced. The 25-year lease, which had been assigned to the sellers as security for the loan, would no longer be of any consequence since after the exercise of the option the lessee would own the property. That significantly altered the value of the security set aside to cover the $500,000 note. The parties did not anticipate the problem. The court noted that if the assignment of the lease to the seller as security was really a mortgage, then the lease would not disappear after the exercise of the option, but would instead be the equivalent of a mortgage deed. The court remanded for a hearing on what the parties intention was in regard to the assignment of the lease.

[ix] *Federal Income Taxation, Land Transfer and Disguised Mortgages.* Finally, there are several features in the federal tax code that may create incentives to label a transaction a sale and leaseback even when the "true" character of the transaction is a mortgage. Though these incentives have been reduced by tax reforms enacted in the 1980s, they have not been entirely removed. The tax code permits owners of business property to claim as tax deductions expenses associated with renting the assets, such as property taxes, mortgage interest, insurance and utilities. In addition, the tax code permits owners of income producing real estate to claim a depreciation deduction on buildings, structures and equipment placed on the land.[58] This

---

[58] Land itself normally is not depreciable. It is supposed to last forever.

deduction is based on the premise that most structures and equipment deteriorates over time, and that this loss should be reflected in business taxation policy. The deduction, however, almost always permits property owners to claim depreciation at a much faster rate than physical deterioration of the property actually occurs.

Commercial lessees are treated differently. They may not claim depreciation. But they may claim as a deduction from income normal business expenses, such as the rent for their business office. Rent for any particular building may provide larger deductions than expenses and depreciation yield to the owner.[59] For owners of property, that means it may be advantageous to sell their property and lease it back. This becomes most attractive when the property is likely not to be useful or worth very much to the owner in the future, or when the purchaser-lessor is willing to grant the seller-lessee an option to repurchase the building.

The Supreme Court has been confronted with cases of this sort. In *Frank Lyon Co. v. United States*, 435 U.S. 561 (1978), a bank agreed with Lyon to sell and lease back a new bank building being constructed for use by the bank. Due to various state and federal banking regulations, the bank could not construct the bank solely with funds raised on its own credit standing. Worthen (the bank) leased the ground upon which the building was being constructed to Lyon, the rent being nominal for the first 25 years, and in amounts varying from $100,000 to $250,000 a year for the last 50 years of the lease. In addition, Lyon agreed to buy the building as it was constructed by using $500,000 of its own money and the proceeds of a $7,140,000 loan obtained by Lyon from New York Life Insurance Company. Lyon was the only obligor on the mortgage note. Lyon leased the new building back to Worthen. The rents for the first 25 years were exactly equal to the amounts Lyon needed to pay the debt service. Worthen also had an option to buy the building back beginning 11 years after the start of the least at a price which varied year to year, but always equaled the sum of the remaining indebtedness to New York Life, plus $500,000 (Lyon's investment), plus 6% return on the $500,000.

The government contended that Lyon's taking of the interest and depreciation deductions should be disallowed as long as Worthen had an option to repurchase the building. The argument was that Worthen, at least for tax purposes, still owned the building, that Lyon had merely loaned Worthen $500,000, and that Worthen just used Lyon as a conduit for mortgage payments. The Supreme Court disagreed. Justice Blackmun noted for the Court that Lyon undertook a real liability on a large mortgage, invested in a transaction entailing economic risk should Worthen default, and took tax deductions that were going to be available to one party or another regardless of how the transaction was styled.[60] In addition, the parties never treated the $500,000 invested by Lyon as a loan.

The contrast between *Lyon* and *Kawauchi* is interesting. While the reasons for Kawauchi's use of the sale and leaseback form were primarily related to a desperate need for money, that was not so in *Lyon*. While Lyon needed money from a third party to complete its building, the search was not a desperate one. In fact, Lyon had many suitors and took the best offer.

---

[59] This may be especially likely for older buildings which have been largely depreciated for tax purposes. A transfer to a new owner will start depreciation over again for the buyer.

[60] Blackmun may have been wrong on this point. The factual setting probably was one where the United States would have collected more taxes if the deal was viewed as a mortgage. That is, the totality of taxes produced with the depreciation deduction in Lyon's hands and the rent deduction in Worthen's hands may have been smaller than the taxes produced with Lyon a lender and getting *neither* rent *nor* depreciation and Worthen an owner and getting only depreciation.

Furthermore, the policy reasons which led the Hawaii Supreme Court to hold in Kawauchi's favor included a strong desire to enforce the usury statute. In *Lyon*, the government's desire to collect taxes owed it was somewhat tempered by other government requirements that Worthen not construct the building on its own credit standing, and by the lack of any other strong public policy commanding a restructuring of the deal. As Justice Blackmun wrote:

> [W]here, as here, there is a genuine multiple-party transaction with economic substance which is compelled or encouraged by business or regulatory realities, is imbued with tax-independent considerations, and is not shaped solely by tax avoidance features that have meaningless labels attached, the Government should honor the allocation of rights and duties effectuated by the parties. Expressed another way, so long as the lessor retains significant and genuine attributes of the traditional lessor status, the form of the transaction adopted by the parties governs for tax purposes. What those attributes are in any particular case will necessarily depend upon its facts. It suffices to say that, as here, a sale-and-leaseback, in and of itself, does not necessarily operate to deny a taxpayer's claim for deductions.

§ 9.05 Quality of Housing After Sale: Warranties of Fitness, Remedies for Negligent Construction and Installation of Defective Products

[1] Introduction

For most of this century, buyers of residential housing could not obtain relief from sellers if the structures they purchased were of poor quality. They virtually always took their property as they found it. About the same time that courts began to approve tenant defenses in actions for possession for nonpayment of rent, buyers began to succeed in claims against developers of new housing for shoddy construction or installation of defective products. The first case in this section, *Humber v. Morton*, was an important decision in the legal developments that occurred in the late 1960s and early 1970s.[61]

The imposition of implied warranties on developers of new housing, as in *Humber*, left open a large number of other questions. A host of actors in the housing market, such as architects, sellers of used housing, real estate brokers, lenders, and contractors, have also been sued by dissatisfied home buyers. The second case in this section, *Easton v. Strassburger*, involved a dispute with virtually all parties to a land sale.

While reading *Humber* and *Easton*, keep in mind the various liability models that have typically been used in defective product litigation. First, warranties of quality have been imposed in some situations. The consequence of doing so in landlord-tenant law was to provide tenants with the equivalent of a contract damages remedy, either by suing affirmatively or by defending a summary dispossess action. Second, negligence models have been used in some situations where the flaws in the product have caused personal injury or damage to property. The party negligently manufacturing or assembling the product causing the loss is subject to a tort action. Third, various sorts of strict liability remedies have recently become the focus of most defective product tort litigation. The parties in the chain of commerce leading to a defective product's purchase are responsible to the ultimate consumer for any property or personal damage caused by the defect. Under what circumstances should each of these models be used in a real estate sales setting? Or do you think there are other models that should be used?

---

[61] Courts in a substantial majority of states have now imposed some sort of warranty on builder-vendors of new housing. The Florida Supreme Court found 33 such opinions as of 1983. Conklin v. Hurley, 428 So.2d 654 (Fla. 1983).

[2] Opinion of the Texas Supreme Court in *Humber v. Morton*

Humber v. Morton

Texas Supreme Court
426 S.W.2d 554 (1968)

NORVELL, JUSTICE.

The widow Humber brought suit against Claude Morton, alleging that Morton was in the business of building and selling new houses; that she purchased a house from him which was not suitable for human habitation in that the fireplace and chimney were not properly constructed and because of such defect, the house caught fire and partially burned the first time a fire was lighted in the fireplace. Morton defended upon two grounds: that an independent contractor, Johnny F. Mays, had constructed the fireplace and he, Morton, was not liable for the work done by Mays, and that the doctrine of "caveat emptor" applied to all sales of real estate. Upon the first trial of the case (which was to a jury), Mrs. Humber recovered a judgment which was reversed by the Eastland Court of Civil Appeals and the cause remanded for another trial because of an improper submission of the damage issue.

Upon the second trial, defendant Morton filed a motion for summary judgment supported by affidavits, one of which referred to and incorporated therein the statement of the evidence adduced upon the first trial. Plaintiff likewise made a motion for summary judgment. Defendant's motion was granted and that of the plaintiff overruled. Such judgment was affirmed by the Court of Civil Appeals upon the holdings that Mays was an independent contractor and that the doctrine of implied warranty was not applicable to the case. Mrs. Humber, as petitioner, brought the case here, but we shall refer to the parties by their trial court designations.

It conclusively appears that defendant Morton was a "builder-vendor." The summary judgment proofs disclose that he was in the business of building or assembling houses designed for dwelling purposes upon land owned by him. He would then sell the completed houses together with the tracts of land upon which they were situated to members of the house-buying public. There is conflict in the summary judgment proofs as to whether the house sold to Mrs. Humber had been constructed with a dangerously defective fireplace chimney. Construction engineers who testified under oath for Mrs. Humber, as disclosed by the statement of facts upon the first trial which was made a part of the summary judgment record here, stated that the chimney was defective. Mr. Mays, who built the chimney, denied that his work was substandard or deficient in any way.

While there may be other grounds for holding that Mrs. Humber made a case to go to the jury, such as negligence attributable to Morton, failure to inspect and the like, we need not discuss these theories because we are of the opinion that the courts below erred in holding as a matter of law that Morton was not liable to Mrs. Humber because the doctrine of caveat emptor applied to the sale of a new house by a "builder-vendor" and consequently no implied warranty that the house was fit for human habitation arose from the sale. Accordingly, we reverse the judgments of the courts below and remand the cause to the district court for a conventional trial upon the merits.

Mrs. Humber entered into a contract when she bought the house from Morton in May of 1964 and such house, together with the lot upon which it was situated, was conveyed to her. According to Morton, the only warranty contained in the deed was the warranty of title, *i.e.*, "to warrant and forever defend, all and singular, the said premises unto the said Ernestine Humber, her heirs and assigns, . . .," and that he made no other warranty, written or oral, in connection with the sale. While it is unusual for one to sell a house without saying something good about it, and the statement that no warranty was made smacks of a conclusion, we shall assume that such conversation as may have taken place did not involve anything more than mere sales talk or puffing, and that no express warranties, either oral or written, were involved. However, it is undisputed that Morton built the house and then sold it as a new house. Did he thereby impliedly warrant that such house was constructed in a good workmanlike manner and was suitable for human habitation? We hold that he did. Under such circumstances, the law raises an implied warranty.

Preliminary to our discussion of the controlling issue in the case, the applicability of the caveat emptor doctrine, we should notice the reference of the Court of Civil Appeals to Article 1297, Vernon's Ann. Tex. Stats. . .. The statute is not deemed applicable here for a number of reasons. Article 1297 does not say that warranties as to fitness and suitability of structures upon land cannot arise unless expressed in the deed of conveyance. The article relates to covenants which may or may not arise from the use of certain specific words in a conveyance, namely, "grant" or "convey."[2]

This article is part of Title 31, Revised Statutes, relating to conveyances. It relates to covenants of title which arise out of conveyances and not to collateral covenants such as the suitability of a house for human habitation. The presence of a collateral covenant of this type in a deed would be strange indeed. "It is not the office of a deed to express the terms of the contract of sale, but to pass the title pursuant to the contract." 26 C.J.S. *Deeds* § 1, p. 582. The article simply prescribes what covenants may be implied by the use of two designated words, "grant" or "convey." The implied warranty of fitness arises from the sale and does not spring from the conveyance.

It may be that the lower courts were striking at the nonstatutory doctrine of merger under which all prior negotiations with reference to a sale of land are said to be merged in the final transaction between the parties. The doctrine of merger, however, is a matter generally controlled by the intention of the parties. For example: A owns Blackacre and agrees with B to construct a house thereon and then conveys the house and lot to B after the house has been completed. There are numerous cases that an implied covenant or warranty to build in a workmanlike manner is not destroyed by the deed.

If the passage of a deed does not operate to extinguish a warranty, either expressed or implied, in the case of an uncompleted house, it is difficult to understand how the deed could operate to merge and thus destroy an implied warranty raised by law in the case of a sale of a completed new house. It would be a strange doctrine indeed for the law to raise an implied warranty from a sale and then recognize that such warranty could be defeated by the passage of title to the subject matter of the sale. The issue here is not whether the implied warranty was extinguished by a conveyance, but whether such warranty ever came into existence in the first place.

---

[2] Article 1297:

From the use of the word "grant" or "convey," in any conveyance by which an estate of inheritance or fee simple is to be passed, the following covenants, and none other, on the part of the grantor for himself and his heirs to the grantee, his heirs or assigns, are implied, unless restrained by express terms contained in such conveyance:

1. That previous to the time of the execution of such conveyance the grantor has not conveyed the same estate, or any right, title or interest therein, to any person other than the grantee.

2. That such estate is at the time of the execution of such conveyance free from incumbrances.

Such covenants may be sued upon in the same manner as if they had been expressly inserted in the conveyance.

The cases which give some weight to the doctrine of merger in the implied warranty situation hold that the doctrine of caveat emptor applies to sales of real property, thus reducing the "merger" theory to the status of a "unicorn hunting bow." The merger doctrine implies that there is something to merge.

. . ..

We return to the crucial issue in the case—Does the doctrine of caveat emptor apply to the sale of a new house by a builder-vendor?

Originally, the two great systems of jurisprudence applied different doctrines to sales of both real and personal property. The rule of the common law—caveat emptor—was fundamentally based upon the premise that the buyer and seller dealt at arm's length, and that the purchaser had means and opportunity to gain information concerning the subject matter of the sale which were equal to those of the seller. On the other hand, the civil law doctrine—caveat venditor—was based upon the premise that a sound price calls for a sound article; that when one sells an article, he implies that it has value.

Today, the doctrine of caveat emptor as related to sales of personal property has a severely limited application.

In Texas, the doctrine of caveat emptor began its fade-out at an early date. In *Wintz v. Morrison*, 17 Tex. 369 (1856), involving a sale of personal property, the Texas Supreme Court quoted with approval the following from *Story on Sales* as to the trend of 19th century decisions:

> [T]he tendency of all the modern cases of warranty is to enlarge the responsibility of the seller, to construe every affirmation by him to be a warranty, and frequently to imply a warranty on his part, from acts and circumstances, wherever they were relied upon by the buyer. The maxim of *caveat emptor* seems gradually to be restricted in its operation and limited in its dominion, and beset with the circumvallations of the modern doctrine of implied warranty, until it can no longer claim the empire over the law of sales, and is but a shadow of itself. . ..

. . ..

> [I]n numerous common law jurisdictions, the caveat emptor doctrine as applied to the vendor builder new house situation has overstayed its time. . ..

The rapid sickening of the caveat emptor doctrine as applied to sales of new houses was exposed by the *Miller-Perry-Howe-Weck-Jones-Glisan-Carpenter* syndrome.[5] The history of this development is briefly set out in *Carpenter v. Donohoe*, 154 Colo. 78, 388 P.2d 399 (1964), and in more detail by Professor E.F. Roberts in *The Case of the Unwary Home Buyer: The Housing Merchant Did It*, 52 Cornell Law Quarterly 835 (1967). *See also,. . .* Stewart, *Implied Warranties in the Sale of New Houses*, Note, 26 U.Pitt.L.Rev. 862 (1965); Haskell, *The Case for an Implied Warranty of Quality in Sales of Real Property*, 53 Geo.L.J. 633 (1965); Gibson and Lounsberry, *Implied Warranties— Sales of a Completed House*, Comments, 1 Cal. Western L.Rev. 110 (1965); Smith, *Torts, Implied Warranty in Real Estate, Privity Requirement*, Comment, 44 N.Car.L.Rev. 236 (1965); Ramunno, *Implied Warranty of Fitness for Habitation in Sale of Residential Dwellings*, 43 Denver L.Rev. 379 (1966).

---

[5] Miller v. Cannon Hill Estates, Ltd., [1931] 1 All E.R. 93 (K.B.); Perry v. Sharon Dev. Co., [1937] 4 All E.R. 390 (C.A.); Hoye v. Century Builders, Inc., 52 Wash. 2d 830, 329 P.2d 474 (1958); Weck v. A.M. Sunrise Construction Co., 36 Ill. App. 2d 383, 184 N.E.2d 728 (1962); Jones v. Gatewood, 381 P.2d 158 (Okl. 1963); Glisan v. Smolenske, 153 Colo. 274, 387 P.2d 260 (1963); and Carpenter v. Donohoe, 154 Colo. 78, 388 P.2d 399 (1964).

. . ..

While it is not necessary for us to pass upon a situation in which the vendor-purchaser relationship is absent, the case of *Schipper v. Levitt & Sons*, 44 N.J. 70, 207 A.2d 314 (1965), is important as much of the reasoning set forth in the opinion is applicable here. The Supreme Court of New Jersey recognized "the need for imposing on builder-vendors an implied obligation of reasonable workmanship and habitability which survives delivery of the deed." This was a case in which a person other than a purchaser had been injured by a defective water heater which had been installed in a new house by Levitt, the builder-vendor. The opinion. . . proceeded upon the theory of strict liability in tort.[6] The court placed emphasis upon the close analogy between a defect in a new house and a manufactured chattel. The opinion states:

> The law should be based on current concepts of what is right and just and the judiciary should be alert to the never ending need for keeping its common law principles abreast of the times. Ancient distinctions which make no sense in today's society and tend to discredit the law should be readily rejected as they were step by step in *Henningsen* [*Henningsen v. Bloomfield Motors*, 32 N.J. 358, 161 A.2d 69, 75 A.L.R.2d 1 (1960)] and *Santor* [*Santor v. A and M Karagheusian*, 44 N.J. 52, 207 A.2d 305, 16 A.L.R.3d 670 (1965)]. . ..

> When a vendee buys a development house from an advertised model, as in a Levitt or in a comparable project, he clearly relies on the skill of the developer and on its implied representation that the house will be erected in reasonably workmanlike manner and will be reasonably fit for habitation. He has no architect or other professional adviser of his own, he has no real competency to inspect on his own, his actual examination is, in the nature of things, largely superficial, and his opportunity for obtaining meaningful protective changes in the conveyancing documents prepared by the builder vendor is negligible. If there is improper construction such as a defective heating system or a defective ceiling, stairway and the like, the well-being of the vendee and others is seriously endangered and serious injury is foreseeable. The public interest dictates that if such injury does result from the defective construction, its cost should be borne by the responsible developer who created the danger and who is in the better economic position to bear the loss rather than by the injured party who justifiably relied on the developer's skill and implied representation.

If at one time in Texas the rule of caveat emptor had application to the sale of a new house by a vendor-builder, that time is now past. The decisions and legal writings herein referred to afford numerous examples and situations illustrating the harshness and injustice of the rule when applied to the sale of new houses by a builder-vendor,[7] and we need not repeat them here.

---

[6] It is said in the opinion that, "It is true, as Levitt suggests, that cases such as *Carpenter* (388 P.2d 399) involved direct actions by original vendees against their builder vendors and that consequently no questions of privity arose. But it seems hardly conceivable that a court recognizing the modern need for a vendee occupant's right to recover on principles of implied warranty or strict liability would revivify the requirement of privity, which is fast disappearing in the comparable products liability field, to preclude a similar right in other occupants likely to be injured by the builder vendor's default. . .."

[7] In the vendor-builder situation, Professor Roberts seems inclined to agree with Mr. Bumble's estimate of the law and points out that when caveat emptor is retained with regard to the sale of new houses, the law seemingly concerns itself little with a transaction which may and often does involve a purchaser's life savings, yet may afford relief by raising an implied warranty of fitness when one is swindled in the purchase of a two dollar fountain pen. 52 Cornell L.Rev. 835. Similarly, in 111 Solicitors' Journal 22, 1.c.25 (London), it is pointed out that, "the purchaser buying a new house with legal assistance is often less well protected legally than the purchaser buying a chattel without legal assistance." It is further urged that, "The legal profession should have made it their business to insure proper

Obviously, the ordinary purchaser is not in a position to ascertain when there is a defect in a chimney flue, or vent of a heating apparatus, or whether the plumbing work covered by a concrete slab foundation is faulty. It is also highly irrational to make a distinction between the liability of a vendor-builder who employs servants and one who uses independent contractors. The common law is not afflicted with the rigidity of the law of the Medes and the Persians "which altereth not," and as stated in Cardozo in *The Nature of the Judicial Process*, pp. 150-151 (quoted in 415 P.2d 698):

> That court best serves the law which recognizes that the rules of law which grew up in a remote generation may, in the fullness of experience, be found to serve another generation badly, and which discards the old rule when it finds that another rule of law represents what should be according to the established and settled judgment of society, and no considerable property rights have become vested in reliance upon the old rule. . ..[8]

The caveat emptor rule as applied to new houses is an anachronism patently out of harmony with modern home buying practices. It does a disservice not only to the ordinary prudent purchaser but to the industry itself by lending encouragement to the unscrupulous, fly-by-night operator and purveyor of shoddy work.

The judgments of the courts below are reversed and the cause remanded for trial in accordance with this opinion.

GRIFFIN, J., notes his dissent.

[3]   Explanatory Notes

[a]   Uniform Land Transactions Act Provisions on Sale Warranties

The Uniform Land Transactions Act contains the following provisions on implied warranties of quality:

§ 2-309. [Implied Warranty of Quality][62]

(a) Subject to the provisions on risk of loss (§ 2-406), a seller warrants that the real estate will be in at least as good condition at the earlier of the time of the conveyance or delivery of possession as it was on the date the contract was made, reasonable wear and tear excepted.

(b) A seller, other than a lessor, in the business of selling real estate impliedly warrants that the real estate is suitable for the ordinary uses of real estate of its type and that any improvements made or contracted for by him and completed no earlier than 2 years before the date the contract to convey is made will be:

(1) free from defective materials; and

(2) constructed in accordance with applicable law, according to sound engineering and construction standards, and in a workmanlike manner.

---

protection for the purchaser without waiting for building societies to take the initiative" for their own protection since most builders "try to do a good job (but) the reputation of all may be injuriously affected by the low standards of a few."

[8] *See also*, Holmes, Collected Legal Papers, p. 187, quoted in 16 Baylor L.Rev. 263, 277, viz.:

It is revolting to have no better reason for a rule of law than that it was laid down in the time of Henry IV. It is still more revolting if the grounds upon which it was laid down have vanished long since, and the rule persists from blind imitation of the past.

[62] Reprinted by permission of the National Conference of Commissioners on Uniform State Laws.

(c) In addition, a seller in the business of selling real estate warrants to a protected party[63] that an existing use, continuation of which is contemplated by the parties, does not violate applicable law at the earlier of the time of conveyance or delivery of possession.

(d) Warranties imposed by this section may be excluded or modified as specified in the provisions on exclusion or modification of warranties of quality (§ 2-311).

. . ..

§ 2-311. [Exclusion or Modification of Warranties of Quality]

. . ..

(b) Except as limited by subsection (c) with respect to a protected party, implied warranties of quality:

(1) may be excluded or modified by agreement of the parties, and

(2) are excluded by expressions of disclaimer such as "as is," "with all faults," or other language which in common understanding calls the buyer's attention to the exclusion of warranties.

(c) With respect to a protected party, no disclaimer of implied warranties of quality in general language or in the language of the warranty provided in this Act is effective, but a seller may disclaim liability for a specific defect or failure to comply with applicable law if the defect or failure entered into and became part of the basis of the bargain.

(d) Notwithstanding any rule of evidence, written acknowledgment by a protected party that he contracted to buy after the disclosure of a specific defect or failure to comply with applicable law, set forth in the writing and called to his attention before contracting, creates only a presumption that the specific defect or failure was a part of the basis of the bargain and the parties may offer any evidence relevant to that issue.

(e) Any disclaimer of warranties is subject to the provisions on unconscionability (§ 1-311) even though the seller has complied with subsection (b) or (c).

[b]   Scope of Implied Warranty Protection

Schipper v. Levitt & Sons, 44 N.J. 70, 207 A.2d 314 (1965), cited in the *Humber* opinion, was another important early warranty decision. In *Schipper*, the Kreitzer family bought a house in a huge development from Levitt & Sons in 1958. The hot water system was connected directly to the heating system; the hot water came from the furnace boiler without first being mixed with cold water. After the Kreitzers or their guests were burned a couple of times by the water, they put signs up by the bathroom sink warning people to turn on the cold water first. The Schipper family leased the house from the Kreitzers, moving in on August 12, 1960. They called the local utility company on the 15th and were told nothing could be done about the hot water. Their two-year old child was seriously burned the same day. The Schippers sued Levitt, Builders Supply Co. (a Levitt subsidiary that built the house), and York Shipley, Inc. (the manufacturer of the boiler), alleging both negligence and warranty theories. York Shipley was not liable, the court said, because their boiler was in perfect working order and was accompanied with instructions recommending that a mixing valve be installed if domestic hot water was obtained from the boiler. The other defendants were found responsible under an implied warranty theory, despite the fact

---

[63] For the definition of a protected party see p. 783 above.

that negligence was probably provable against the construction company for failing to install a mixing valve.[64]

The Schippers overcame two significant obstacles in winning their case. First, of course, they succeeded in reversing a long series of cases refusing to hold builder-vendors of housing responsible for injuries produced by non-negligently caused flaws in construction. Second, prior plaintiffs had floundered on the shoals of *privity*. Old cases required that parties could collect in negligence only if they were in privity with the defendant. Privity, as in *Gerber v. Pecht*, at p. 732 above, meant that the plaintiff either had to be in a contractual relationship with the defendant or the takers of the same estate in land held by the predecessor in title. The Schippers only had a contractual relationship with the Kreitzers, not Levitt & Sons;[65] they were not in privity of estate with the Levitts since they were only lessees. And the two year old injured child fulfilled none of these requirements. The *Schipper* court ignored the old rules, deciding instead that a duty of care was owed by the builder-vendor to any party logically present in the facility.

[*i*] *Used Housing.* *Humber* and *Schipper* together raise a number of interesting questions about the scope of implied warranty protection. For example, how old does property have to be before the original developer's warranty terminates? The Uniform Land Transactions Act selected a "bright line" test, using a two year time period.[66] But a number of cases have suggested that the longevity of the warranty depends on the facts of each case. Thus, North Carolina courts apply the warranty only to "recently completed" houses, but leave the ultimate finding on recent completion to the trier of fact.[67] This and similar tests used in other jurisdictions leave open the possibility of applying the warranty theory in some used housing situations. Can't a good argument be made that there should be no time limit on the warranty's operation at all? After all, a plaintiff must show that the damages were *caused by* a breach of the warranty. Won't this causation requirement become more and more difficult to fulfill as time passes, placing a "natural" limitation on the scope of the warranty?

[*ii*] *Responsible Parties.* Should anyone other than the builder-vendor be responsible for construction flaws under implied warranty theory? There are cases imposing liability on parties other than builder-vendors. Some of them, however, are really "piercing the corporate veil" situations like *Zaist v. Olson*, p. 326 above. For example, in *Berman v. Watergate West, Inc.*, 391 A.2d 1351 (D.C. App. 1978), the purchaser of a cooperative apartment discovered shortly after moving in that her air conditioning system was not working. It spewed forth such vast amounts of humidity that the bedroom was unusable and various parts of the apartment were damaged by the moisture. Berman, the co-op's buyer, had a large variety of possible defendants. The Watergate Improvements Association (WIA), a partnership, was formed to sponsor the project. A subsidiary of WIA, Watergate Construction Corporation, was formed to construct the building. Another WIA subsidiary, Riverside Realty Corporation, was formed to market the apartments. Watergate West, Inc., the corporate owner of the building itself, was also formed before construction began. WIA controlled Watergate West from its creation until an independent

---

[64] In a negligence action, plaintiffs must normally show that the defendant violated a duty of care owed to the plaintiff by unreasonable behavior. In *Schipper*, the construction company's failure to follow instructions recommending the installation of a mixing valve was strong proof of unreasonable action.

[65] By the way, should the Schippers have been able to collect from their landlords, the Kreitzers?

[66] Note also that § 2-309(b) of the Uniform Land Transactions Act applies to anyone in the business of selling real estate, a provision which would include old housing sold by real estate businesses.

[67] Gaito v. Auman, 313 N.C. 243, 327 S.E.2d 870 (1985).

board of directors was elected by the residents after a large number of the apartments had been sold. Berman selected Riverside Realty Corporation and Watergate West, Inc, as the defendants. The trial court's dismissal was reversed. The District of Columbia Court of Appeals held that warranty theory could be used against any of the developer entities. The cooperative itself, Watergate West, presented a somewhat different problem. It was an empty shell until the units were sold and title to the building was conveyed to it. While admitting that the cooperative might be subject to suit in some cases, the court remanded for trial court consideration of the propriety of joining the cooperative in this case.

Now that it is clear in most jurisdictions that builder vendors impliedly warrant the quality of the housing they construct and sell, plaintiffs will surely seek to apply similar theories to other parties not under the direct control and direction of the primary developer. Architects, lawyers, real estate brokers, contractors, suppliers and lenders will all come under increasing scrutiny. Trying to predict the future is difficult. But it does seem probable that the more closely involved in the planning and development of the project such parties become, the greater will be the risk of liability. *Caveat venditor?*

[c]   Sale of Raw Land

Despite the developments in seller warranty theory, the general rule still is that an implied warranty does not arise when raw land is sold. The courts tend to the view that those buying land for development, whether small or large investors, normally assume greater risks than those buying completed structures. This tendency is obvious in cases where natural forces have led to serious loss or destruction of land. Thus, buyers of seaside property who built houses later damaged by beach erosion have been left without remedies against their vendors.[68] But less obviously risky investments have also trapped unwary buyers. For example, soil conditions which were defective for use of septic systems have usually left land buyers holding the bag.[69]

A couple of interesting cases provide some perspective on the "no-warranty-for-raw-land" idea. In *Stepanov v. Gavrilovich*, 594 P.2d 30 (Alaska 1979), Gavrilovich purchased a tract of land near Anchorage. The land was subdivided into about 150 residential lots. Tests were performed which revealed no permafrost in the area. Builder-vendors then began purchasing lots and constructing houses. The houses later sank due to scattered areas of permafrost not revealed by the prior testing. Heat generated by the houses melted the permafrost and caused the settling. The contractors bought back the damaged units from various buyers and sued Gavrilovich. Testing methods then typically used to detect permafrost were uncertain at best. The court concluded that Gavrilovich had acted reasonably in his search for permafrost, and that the issue was placement of a loss due to unforeseeable flaws in the land. As between the subdivider and the builder-vendors, the court decided the loss should fall on the latter. Compare the status of Gavrilovich with that of Johnny F. Mays, the bricklayer in the *Humber* case. Or compare permafrost to beach erosion.

The other interesting case is *Hinson v. Jefferson*, 287 N.C. 422, 215 S.E.2d 102 (1975). Hinson bought a lot from the Jeffersons subject to a restrictive covenant requiring that the land be used for a single family residence costing not less than $25,000 to construct. The Jeffersons retained ownership of other nearby land. When Hinson was ready to begin construction, the county health

---

[68] *See, e.g.*, Cook v. Salishan Properties, Inc., 279 Or. 333, 569 P.2d 1033 (1977); Conklin v. Hurley, 428 So. 2d 654 (Fla. 1983).

[69] *See, e.g.*, Gamble v. Mai, 300 S.E.2d 110 (W. Va. 1983).

department examined the lot, but refused to issue a permit for a septic system because of drainage and periodic flooding problems. The parties agreed that the drainage and flooding problems were totally unexpected. Installation of a sewer system to solve the problem would have cost several hundred thousand dollars. Hinson then sued the Jeffersons for a return of the $3,500 purchase price of the land. Despite the general rule that sellers of raw land do not impliedly warrant that the land is usable for a certain purpose, the court gave Hinson the relief she sought. The existence of the detailed restrictive covenant requiring that the land be used in a very specific way created an implication that the land could be used for that purpose. Compare swamps with permafrost. Didn't all parties know that the buyers of the land in Alaska intended to use the land for housing construction? Should the covenant really make a difference in *Hinson*?

[d]   Other Quality Assurance Systems

Implied quality warranties are not the only systems that exist to handle the risk of flawed construction. Typical land sale contracts for both new and used housing grant the buyer with a right to have an expert inspect the premises and to cancel the deal if the inspection reveals significant structural flaws. Inspection companies sometimes offer warranties on the main house systems if they find them in good working order. Similarly, some private developers now offer warranties for the main systems in housing units they sell, whether old or new. Inspection systems are also governmentally operated in some places; houses may not be transferred if they fail inspection.

[e]   *Humber* Denouement

The actual plaintiff in *Humber* was the home insurance company of the plaintiff. The insurance company paid Mrs. Humber for the damages to her house caused by the fire and then pursued its remedies against the builder-vendor in the name of Humber.[70] While the appeal on the warranty issue in the case was pending,[71] Mrs. Humber died. At the bench trial after remand, the plaintiff lost. The insurance company lawyer failed to allege or prove that it actually owned the rights to Humber's claim![72] Morton's lawyer, in a later candid chat with the trial judge, was told he would have lost on the merits. The judge believed the plaintiff's claim that the house was constructed with wooden joists running right through the middle of the fireplace chimney.

[4]   Problem Notes

[a]   Liability Theories

Johnny F. Mays, the mason in *Humber* who made the fireplace which caused Ms. Humber's new house to go up in flames, became a bit of a pawn in the litigation. Morton argued that Mays should be solely responsible for the loss. Humber contended that the negligence of a sub-contractor should not excuse the obligation of Morton to provide housing of workmanlike quality. Humber, of course, prevailed. But what about Mays? It is surely true that Morton may try to collect over from Mays. But such an action for payment from Mays will be based on a negligence

---

[70] This information was provided by Jerry R. Hollingsworth, Attorney for Mrs. Humber's insurance company. Telephone Interview (July 2, 1987).

[71] There were actually three appeals in the case. Humber obtained a judgment when the case was first tried, but it was reversed on a jury instruction issue. Morton v. Humber, 399 S.W.2d 831 (Tex. Civ. App. 1966). The results of the second appeal you have read. The third appeal was on the failure of the insurance company to prove it owned the claim.

[72] Telephone Interview with Barry Stone, Attorney for Morton (July 7, 1987).

theory, not warranty theory.[73] That would leave Morton with a more difficult set of litigation obstacles to overcome than a typical warranty plaintiff must hurdle.

Why should there be any difference between the standards used to define liability of a builder-vendor like Morton and a contractor like Mays? Is Morton's deeper pocket (whether full of cash or insurance) more attractive as a source for spreading consumer risks than the presumably shallow pocket of a bricklayer? Is the world better off trying to require builder-vendors to carefully inspect their projects as they are constructed or trying to deter individual workers from operating in an unworkmanlike manner? Does the somewhat limited right of Morton to sue over against contractors mean that we get the best (or worst) of both worlds inspection and individuated deterrence?

[b]   Used Housing

Implied warranties in the sale of new housing touch a fairly small segment of the actual housing stock. Most people who buy houses buy used ones. Should the *Humber* sort of remedy be applied to sellers of used as well as new housing? Doing so would impose liability on a large number of private individuals who sell their houses, either by themselves or with the help of real estate brokers. If such potential liability is unacceptable, then what of real estate brokers and lenders? Should the warranty standards apply to them, with only a negligence standard applied to individuals?

If you think warranties should be imposed for used housing, what sort of warranty would it be? If the furnace is 15 years old when the house is sold, can it be warranted? Should the warranty take the form of a "one-year guarantee" (like you get when you buy a stereo) for all major systems? Is this sort of a warranty one that courts will create? Or will the legislatures have to get involved? If the whole idea of warranties in the sale of used houses strikes you as unworkable, are there any other steps that should be taken to protect home buyers?

[c]   Some Condominium Examples

Conversion of rental apartment buildings to condominiums has been very common in recent decades. Some conversions have gone forward with no renovations at all. The rental units are simply offered for sale. In one such case, *Kelley v. Astor Investors, Inc.*, 106 Ill. 2d 505, 478 N.E.2d 1346 (1985), disgruntled condominium owners sued the developer for damages caused by leaking roofs and other structural defects. The unit owners alleged that promises by the developer to make repairs were not fulfilled, that the developers breached fiduciary obligations while they served as members of the board of the condominium, and that an implied warranty was violated. The case went to the Illinois Supreme Court on the pleadings. The plaintiff's breach of promise theory was left for trial. As to the fiduciary duty count, the plaintiffs were told they had to prove willful misconduct on the part of the developer corporation. Normally such a high level of intention is not required. But the condominium declaration contained an exculpatory clause limiting the liability of board members, whether developers or unit owners, to willful misconduct. Despite language in state statutes imposing fiduciary duties on condominium boards, the court permitted the exculpatory clause to survive. Finally, the implied warranty theory was discarded. No significant refurbishing or renovation was undertaken by the developer. The court

---

[73] Texas law, by the way, treats warranties of quality as tort, not contract, issues. While that seems a bit strange on the face of the language, it is not so strange in the reality. Warranty law in this setting looks very much like product liability rules requiring the seller of a product to pay for any damages caused by a defect in the product.

also noted that the defects were not latent and that some of the unit owners clearly knew about the problems since they were previous renters. In essence the court treated these unit owners like buyers of used single family houses. Is there anything about apartments in a building, as opposed to houses, that makes it more difficult for purchasers to assure themselves of the quality of the units they are buying? Is it logical to ask unit buyers to pay for an inspection of all the main features of an apartment building in addition to the particular unit for sale? Even if you think implied warranties should not be applicable to unrefurbished condominium sales, should disclosure requirements about the building's systems and the financial status of the condominium be imposed?

Compare *Kelley* with *Towers Tenant Association v. Towers Limited Partnership*, 563 F. Supp. 566 (D.D.C. 1983), involving a building that was remodeled. The *Towers* court permitted the plaintiffs to proceed to trial on their theories that the developer breached implied warranties of habitability during the period when some of the plaintiffs were still tenants, and violated implied warranties of quality when the units were sold.[74] Using *Javins v. First National Realty*, discussed at p. 669 above, and *Berman v. Watergate*, discussed at p. 818 above, as starting points, the court held that implied warranties existed during both the pre-and post-conversion periods, and that such warranties could be broken by developers who rehabilitate old as well as build new housing. Does it make sense that an implied warranty of workmanlike quality was imposed in *Towers* when rehabilitation was allegedly defective but not in *Kelley* when allegedly promised repairs were not made at all?

[d]   Warranties in Land Sale Contract or Option to Buy Settings

Suppose Humber was buying her house under an installment land sale contract. Would that change the outcome at all? What if she was occupying the house under a two-year lease with an option to buy at the end of the lease? If the fire occurred during the lease, could the landlord/seller cancel the lease and option under a statute like N.J. STAT. ANN. § 46:8-7 permitting cancellation of leases when buildings are substantially damaged by fire? Or could Humber demand specific performance of the option along with damages under a warranty theory? Is it possible to use warranty theory to alter the traditional equitable conversion rules discussed in *Skelly v. Ashmore*, at p. 756 above?

[5]   Background to *Easton v. Strassburger*

The Strassburgers owned a prime piece of Diablo County, California land backing onto a country club golf course and containing the highest knoll in the area. They, like many before them, wished to build on the top of the knoll. A bulldozer operator was hired to flatten the peak, moving the dirt down the side of the hill. A house was constructed on the top, and on the "bench" created by the bulldozed soil just below the peak, a dressage ring and shed. Later, another substantial house was built in the dressage ring area, along with a swimming pool, and the shed was turned into a guest house. The soil was never compacted or tested for stability.[75]

While the Strassburgers owned the property, two slides occurred. The first was repaired without soil compaction and without notification of local building authorities. The county found out about

---

[74] The plaintiffs were also permitted to pursue a theory based on negligent performance of repairs and renovations. This is based on a traditional tort theory that once a party undertakes an activity, even one not required by law, it must be done in a reasonable manner.

[75] These and many of the following details about the case were obtained from Harry D. Miller, who represented the Eastons on appeal. Telephone Interview (Feb. 25, 1987).

the second slide and gave some advice, which was rejected, about how to repair the damage. When the repairs were finished, the Strassburgers installed a system that watered the soil from underneath, not on the surface, covered the hillside with netting used by nurseries to control surface run off (not netting designed to stabilize filled areas), and replanted the slope with daisies. The landslide that became the catalyst for litigation with the Eastons was made worse by the underground water irrigation system. In the slide occurring six weeks after the Eastons bought the house for $170,000, the slope "fell apart like waterlogged angel food cake."[76]

The Eastons sued virtually everyone associated with the property—the seller's agent, Valley Realty, the Strassburgers, and their various building contractors. The Eastons also had a real estate agent, who was not joined as a defendant, apparently because the plaintiffs thought they would obtain useful testimony for their case. At the trial, it looked doubtful that the plaintiffs would be able to collect from Valley, the Strassburgers' agent. They had sued in fraud. Strassburger apparently made misrepresentations, but there was no proof that Valley's agents made any misstatements about the Strassburgers' property. At the end of the trial, Easton's counsel changed strategy and asked for jury instructions on the negligence theory that eventually won the case for the Eastons. The defense attorneys, in what may have been a serious strategic mistake, made no objection to the jury charge.[77]

[6]   Opinion of the California Court of Appeals in *Easton v. Strassburger*

Easton v. Strassburger

California Court of Appeals, First District, Division 2
152 Cal. App. 3d 90, 199 Cal. Rptr. 383 (1984)

OPINION

KLINE, P.J. —Valley of California, Inc., doing business as Valley Realty (appellant), appeals from a judgment for negligence entered in favor of Leticia M. Easton (respondent). Appellant was one of six defendants in the action, which was brought by respondent for fraud (including negligent misrepresentation) and negligence in the sale of residential property.

FACTS

In the case below, all defendants were found liable to respondent for negligence. However, because Valley Realty alone has appealed, we limit our review of the record only to those facts which affect the liability of that party.

Viewing the evidence in the light most favorable to respondent, as we must, the record discloses the following facts: The property which is the subject of this appeal is a one-acre parcel of land located in the City of Diablo. The property is improved with a 3,000-square-foot home, a swimming pool, and a large guest house. Respondent purchased the property for $170,000 from the Strassburgers in May of 1976 and escrow closed in July of that year. Appellant was the listing broker in the transaction.

---

[76] Telephone Interview with W. Stephen Wilson, Attorney for Valley of California, Inc. (Feb. 20, 1987).

[77] As a general rule, plaintiffs may not change theories in midstream if it would prejudice the ability of the defendants to prepare their case. Since negligence was not an issue until the last minute, it may have been difficult for the Eastons' judgment to sustain appellate review had objection been made to the proposed jury instructions. Without an objection, however, it was virtually impossible to argue that prejudice existed.

Shortly after respondent purchased the property, there was massive earth movement on the parcel. Subsequent slides destroyed a portion of the driveway in 1977 or 1978. Expert testimony indicated that the slides occurred because a portion of the property was fill that had not been properly engineered and compacted. The slides caused the foundation of the house to settle which in turn caused cracks in the walls and warped doorways. After the 1976 slide, damage to the property was so severe that although experts appraised the value of the property at $170,000 in an undamaged condition, the value of the damaged property was estimated to be as low as $20,000. Estimates of the cost to repair the damage caused by the slides and avoid recurrence ranged as high as $213,000.

Appellant was represented in the sale of the property by its agents Simkin and Mourning. It is uncontested that these agents conducted several inspections of the property prior to sale. There is also evidence they were aware of certain "red flags" which should have indicated to them that there were soils problems. Despite this, the agents did not request that the soil stability of the property be tested and did not inform respondent that there were potential soils problems.

During the time that the property was owned by the Strassburgers there was a minor slide in 1973 involving about 10 to 12 feet of the filled slope and a major slide in 1975 in which the fill dropped about 8 to 10 feet in a circular shape 50 to 60 feet across. However, the Strassburgers did not tell Simkin or Mourning anything about the slides or the corrective action they had taken.

Respondent purchased the property without being aware of the soils problems or the past history of slides.

In December of 1976 respondent filed suit against appellant, the Strassburgers, and three other named defendants.[1] As against appellant, respondent alleged causes of action for fraudulent concealment, intentional misrepresentation, and negligent misrepresentation.

Appellant filed a cross-complaint against the Strassburgers seeking full indemnity, or, in the alternative, partial indemnity.

The action was tried before a jury. As to appellant, the judge instructed the jury only as to negligent misrepresentation and simple negligence, since the actions for fraudulent concealment and intentional misrepresentation had been voluntarily dismissed. The jury returned a special verdict finding that all named defendants had been negligent, and assessed damages of $197,000. Negligence was apportioned among the parties under the principles of comparative negligence in the following percentages: Appellant—5 percent; Strassburgers—65 percent; George Sauer and San Ramon Builders—15 percent; H.M. Bull—10 percent. The jury also found a nonparty (a cooperating broker) 5 percent responsible.

Appellant contends that the judgment must be reversed or modified for the following reasons: 1) The trial judge incorrectly instructed the jury on a real estate broker's duty to investigate and disclose defects in property; 2) no expert testimony was produced on two key issues in the case: the standard of care applicable to appellant, and appellant's failure to meet this standard of care; 3) the evidence presented at trial was insufficient to establish that appellant was negligent; 4) the jury based its award on the wrong measure of damages; and 5) appellant was improperly denied indemnity against the Strassburgers.

---

[1] These three defendants San Ramon Builders, George Sauer and H.M. Bull were sued for negligent construction only.

For reasons we shall explain, we find that none of appellant's arguments require reversal of the judgment against it. We agree, however, that appellant was improperly denied indemnification.

DISCUSSION

I.

Appellant's primary contention is that the trial judge committed error by giving the jury an instruction specifying a real estate broker's duty to investigate and disclose defects in property he lists for sale.

In analyzing the validity of this contention, it must be kept in mind that the judgment against appellant was for *simple negligence* only. To establish liability for such negligence, respondent was not required to show that appellant had actual knowledge of the soils problems (as would have been required to prove intentional misrepresentation or fraudulent concealment) or that a misrepresentation had been made as to the soils condition of the property (as is required to establish negligent misrepresentation.) We are concerned here only with the elements of a simple negligence action; that is, whether appellant owed a legal duty to respondent to use due care, whether this legal duty was breached, and finally whether the breach was a proximate cause of appellant's injury.

Whether a defendant owes a duty of due care to a particular plaintiff is a question of law. Appellant does not contend that it was under *no* duty to exercise due care to prevent injury to respondent.[2] Rather, appellant objects to the manner in which this duty was characterized by the trial court. More particularly, appellant challenges the following instruction: "A real estate broker is a licensed person or entity who holds himself out to the public as having particular skills and knowledge in the real estate field. He is under a duty to disclose facts materially affecting the value or desirability of the property that are known to him or which through reasonable diligence should be known to him."

Appellant argues that this instruction elevates a broker's duty beyond the level established by the case law, contending that a broker is only obliged to disclose known facts and has no duty to disclose facts which "should" be known to him "through reasonable diligence." In effect, appellant maintains that a broker has no legal duty to carry out a reasonable investigation of property he undertakes to sell in order to discover defects for the benefit of the buyer. Appellant further argues that since this instruction indicated to the jury that a broker is under such a duty as a matter of law, the giving of the instruction constitutes reversible error.

It is not disputed that current law requires a broker to disclose to a buyer material defects known to the broker but unknown to and unobservable by the buyer. (*Cooper v. Jevne* (1976) 56 Cal. App. 3d 860, 866, 128 Cal. Rptr. 724; *Lingsch v. Savage* (1963) 213 Cal. App. 2d 729, 733; see also regulations of the Department of Real Estate set forth in Cal. Admin. Code, tit. 10, 2785, subd. (a)(3).) The *Cooper* case contains the most complete judicial articulation of the rule: "It is the law of this state that where a real estate broker or agent, representing the seller, knows facts materially affecting the value or the desirability of property offered for sale and these facts are known or accessible only to him and his principal, and the broker or agent also

---

[2] Despite the absence of privity of contract, a real estate agent is clearly under a duty to exercise reasonable care to protect those persons whom the agent is attempting to induce into entering a real estate transaction for the purpose of earning a commission. (Merrill v. Buck (1962) 58 Cal. 2d 552, 561-562, 375 P.2d 304; *see also*, Earp v. Nobmann (1981) 122 Cal. App. 3d 270, 209, 175 Cal. Rptr. 767.)

knows that these facts are not known to or within the reach of the diligent attention and observation of the buyer, the broker or agent is under a duty to disclose these facts to the buyer." If a broker fails to disclose material facts that are known to him he is liable for the intentional tort of "fraudulent concealment" or "negative fraud." As noted, however, appellant's liability was here grounded on negligence rather than fraud. The issue, then, is whether a broker is negligent if he fails to disclose defects which he should have discovered through reasonable diligence. Stated another way, we must determine whether the broker's duty of due care in a residential real estate transaction includes a duty to conduct a reasonably competent and diligent inspection of property he has listed for sale in order to discover defects for the benefit of the buyer.

Admittedly, no appellate decision has explicitly declared that a broker is under a duty to disclose material facts which he should have known. We conclude, however, that such a duty is implicit in the rule articulated in *Cooper* and *Lingsch*, which speaks not only to facts known by the broker, but also and independently to facts that are *accessible* only to him and his principal.[3]

The primary purposes of the *Cooper-Lingsch* rule are to protect the buyer from the unethical broker and seller and to insure that the buyer is provided sufficient accurate information to make an informed decision whether to purchase. These purposes would be seriously undermined if the rule were not seen to include a duty to disclose reasonably discoverable defects. If a broker were required to disclose only known defects, but not also those that are reasonably discoverable, he would be shielded by his ignorance of that which he holds himself out to know. The rule thus narrowly construed would have results inimical to the policy upon which it is based. Such a construction would not only reward the unskilled broker for his own incompetence, but might provide the unscrupulous broker the unilateral ability to protect himself at the expense of the inexperienced and unwary who rely upon him. In any case, if given legal force, the theory that a seller's broker cannot be held accountable for what he does not know but could discover without great difficulty would inevitably produce a disincentive for a seller's broker to make a diligent inspection. Such a disincentive would be most unfortunate, since in residential sales transactions the seller's broker is most frequently the best situated to obtain and provide the most reliable information on the property and is ordinarily counted on to do so.

As one commentator has observed: "Real estate brokers are often in a very commanding position with respect to both sellers and buyers of residential property. The real estate broker's relationship to the buyer is such that the buyer usually expects the broker to protect his interests. This trust and confidence derives from the potential value of the broker's service; houses are infrequently purchased and require a trained eye to determine value and fitness. In addition, financing is often complex. Unlike other commodities, houses are rarely purchased new and there are virtually no remedies for deficiencies in fitness. In some respects the broker-buyer relationship is akin to the attorney-client relationship; the buyer, like the client, relies heavily on another's acquired skill and knowledge, first because of the complexity of the transaction and second because of his own dearth of experience." (Comment, *A Reexamination of the Real Estate Broker-Buyer-Seller Relationship* (1972) 18 Wayne L. Rev. 1343.) Thus, as stated by Judge Cardozo, as he then was, in a different but still relevant context: "The real estate broker is brought by his calling into a relation of trust and confidence. Constant are the opportunities by concealment

---

[3] For reasons we describe presently, where the cause of action is for negligence rather than fraud the undisclosed material facts need not be either actually known by the broker or accessible *only* to him or his principal.

and collusion to extract illicit gains. We know from our judicial records that the opportunities have not been lost. . .. He is accredited by his calling in the minds of the inexperienced or the ignorant with a knowledge greater than their own." (*Roman v. Lobe* (1926) 243 N.Y. 51, 54-55, 152 N.E. 461, 462-463; 50 A.L.R. 1329, 1332 quoted in *Richards Realty Co. v. Real Estate Comr.* (1956) 144 Cal. App. 2d 357, 362, 300 P.2d 893; *see also* Jacobson, *Broker's Liability for Sale of Defective Homes* (1977) 52 L.A. Bar J. 346, 347, 353 and Note, *Real Estate Brokers' Duties to Prospective Purchasers* (1976) B.Y.U. L. Rev. 513, 514-515.)

Definition of the broker's duty to disclose as necessarily including the responsibility to conduct a reasonable investigation thus seems to us warranted by the pertinent realities. Not only do many buyers in fact *justifiably* believe the seller's broker is also protecting their interest in securing and acting upon accurate information[4] and rely upon him, but the injury occasioned by such reliance, if it be misplaced, may well be substantial. However, the broad definition of the duty we adopt is supported not simply by the magnitude of the benefit thus conferred on buyers but also by the relative ease with which the burden can be sustained by brokers. It seems relevant to us, in this regard, that the duty to disclose *that which should be known* is a formally acknowledged professional obligation that it appears many brokers customarily impose upon themselves as an ethical matter.

Thus, the Code of Ethics of the National Association of Realtors includes, *inter alia*, the provision that a broker must not only "avoid. . . concealment of pertinent facts," but "has an affirmative obligation to discover adverse factors that a reasonably competent and diligent investigation would disclose."[6] (National Assn. of Realtors, *Interpretations of the Code of Ethics*

---

[4] *See* Sinclair, *The Duty of the Broker to Purchasers and Prospective Purchasers of Real Property in Illinois* (1981) 69 Ill. Bar J. 260, 263-264, wherein the author states: "In the typical residential real estate transaction, however, the buyer, in particular, may be intentionally or inadvertently led under such circumstances to believe the broker will represent his interest even where he is aware the broker has a listing agreement with the seller. Since the broker's commission is generally paid as a percentage of the sales price, the broker's interest is more closely identified with that of the seller than of the buyer. Where the buyer is unappreciative of the potentially divided loyalty of the broker, he may be lulled into relying on the broker to his significant detriment. Misplaced reliance by the buyer can extend beyond the issue of price to questions regarding quality of title, condition of the premises, and proration of closing costs, property taxes, recording fees, and other expenses."

[6] In fact, one of the examples provided by the association to explain the operation of article 9 is analogous to the facts of this case:

Shortly after REALTOR A negotiated the sale of a home to Buyer B a complaint came to the Board charging REALTOR A with failure to disclose a substantial fact concerning the property. The charge was that the house was not connected to the city sanitary sewage system, but had a septic tank, whereas the buyer claimed he had every reason to believe the house was connected with the sewer line.

In a statement to the Board's Grievance Committee, Buyer B agreed that the subject was not discussed during his various conversations with REALTOR A about the house. However, he pointed out that his own independent inquiries had revealed that the street on which the house was located was "sewered" and he had naturally assumed the house was connected. He had since determined that every other house on the street for several blocks in both directions was connected. He stated that Realtor A, in not having disclosed the exceptional situation, had failed to disclose a pertinent fact.

REALTOR A's defense in a hearing before the Board's Professional Standards Committee was (1) that he did not know that this particular house was not connected with the sewer; (2) that in advertising the house he had not represented it as being connected; (3) that at no time, as Buyer B conceded, had he orally stated that the house was connected; that the fact under discussion was not a "pertinent fact" within the meaning of the Code of Ethics.

The Committee determined that the absence of sewer connection in an area where other houses were connected was a substantial and pertinent fact in the transaction; that the absence of any mention to this fact in advertising or oral representation made it no less pertinent; that ascertaining the failure of previous owners to connect with

(7th ed. 1978) art. 9.) This implicit duty of all real estate agents, regardless whether they are members of the aforementioned association and bound by its Code of Ethics, is reflected in the law. Thus, for example, in *Brady v. Carman* (1960) 179 Cal. App. 2d 63, 3 Cal. Rptr. 612, the court noted that "[t]he defendant. . . is a real estate agent, and as such is supposed to possess ordinary professional knowledge concerning the. . . natural characteristics of the property he is selling. . ., it should have been apparent that the [buyers] were ignorant concerning the nature of an easement and how it could limit their use of the property. . .. [*The broker*] *was obliged as a professional man to obtain information about the easement and make a full disclosure* of the burdens it imposed on the land." It is true that *Brady v. Carman* was an action based on fraud, not, as in the present case, negligence; but we do not conceive that the existence of the professional duty to obtain information described in that case may be allowed to vary with the cause of action.

In sum, we hold that the duty of a real estate broker, representing the seller, to disclose facts, as that fundamental duty is articulated in *Cooper* and *Lingsch*, includes the affirmative duty to conduct a reasonably competent and diligent inspection of the residential[8] property listed for sale and to disclose to prospective purchasers all facts materially affecting the value or desirability of the property that such an investigation would reveal.

With respect to the application of this holding, it is vitally important to keep in mind that in *Cooper* and *Lingsch* the basis of liability was fraud, not negligence. The fundamental duty to disclose set forth in those and other real estate fraud cases has application only where it is alleged that the broker either had actual knowledge of the material facts in issue or that such facts were "accessible *only* to him and his principal," so that the broker may constructively be deemed to have had actual knowledge. The implicit duty to investigate is not considered in those cases simply because it is superfluous to the issue of fraud. However, in cases where, as here, the cause of action is for negligence, not fraud, it need not be alleged or proved that the broker had actual knowledge of the material facts in issue nor that such facts were accessible *only* to him or his principal and that he therefore had constructive knowledge thereof.

The real estate fraud cases also require that the undisclosed material facts be such as "are not known to or within the reach of the diligent attention and observation of the buyer." (*Cooper, supra; Lingsch, supra.*) We decline to place a similar limitation on the duty to investigate here articulated. Such a limitation might, first of all, diminish the broker's incentive to conduct the reasonably competent and diligent inspection which the law seeks to encourage. Furthermore, general principles of comparative negligence provide adequate protection to a broker who neglects to explicitly disclose *manifest* defects. The duty of the seller's broker to diligently investigate

---

the available sewer line was within REALTOR A's obligation under Article 9 of the Code; that he was, therefore, in violation of Article 9.

(National Assn. of Realtors, *supra, Interpretations of the Code of Ethics,* at p. 74.)

It may be observed that the defect in this example—the lack of a conventional sewage connection—would not in the circumstances described likely be as apparent to a broker as the defect at issue in the case at bar.

[8] We express no opinion here whether a broker's obligation to conduct an inspection for defects for the benefit of the buyer applies to the sale of commercial real estate. Unlike the residential home buyer who is often unrepresented by a broker, or is effectively unrepresented because of the problems of dual agency (see; generally, 1 Miller & Starr, *Current Law of Cal. Real Estate* (1983 supp.) § 4.18, pp. 25-29; Comment, *Dual Agency in Residential Real Estate Brokerage: Conflict of Interest and Interests in Conflict* (1982) 12 Golden Gate L. Rev. 379), a purchaser of commercial real estate is likely to be more experienced and sophisticated in his dealings in real estate and is usually represented by an agent who represents only the buyer's interests.

and disclose reasonably discoverable defects to the buyer does not relieve the latter of the duty to exercise reasonable care to protect himself. Cases will undoubtedly arise in which the defect in the property is so clearly apparent that as a matter of law a broker would not be negligent for failure to expressly disclose it, as he could reasonably expect that the buyer's own inspection of the premises would reveal the flaw. In such a case the buyer's negligence *alone* would be the proximate cause of any injury he suffered.

Accordingly, we find that the instruction at issue in this case was legally correct, for, as the trial judge stated to the jury, a seller's broker in a residential real estate transaction *is* "under a duty to disclose facts materially affecting the value or desirability of the property. . . which through reasonable diligence should be known to him."

. . ..

II.

Appellant next contends that the judgment must be reversed because the verdict was not supported by substantial evidence. Again, we cannot agree. The evidence indicates that appellant's agent *had* conducted a limited investigation of the property and that they were aware of "red flags" indicating erosion or settlement problems. There was evidence indicating that one or both of the agents knew that the residence was built on fill and that settlement and erosion problems are commonly associated with such soil. It was additionally established that the agents had seen netting on a slope of the property which had been placed there to repair the slide which occurred most recently prior to the sale. Furthermore, one of the agents testified that he had observed that the floor of a guest house on the property was not level, while the other agent testified that uneven floors were "red flag" indications of soils problems. Although the foregoing does not exhaust the evidence in the record that appellant's agents were on notice of potential soils problems, it is sufficient to establish that there was substantial evidence on the point. Other evidence also established that, despite this notice, the agents did not request that a soils report be prepared, nor take any other significant steps to determine whether there had been slides or other soils problems.

While the evidence did not establish that appellant's agents had actual knowledge of the history of slides and soil problems on the property, such actual knowledge was, as we have said, unnecessary to establish liability for negligence. The jury merely had to conclude—as apparently it did—that a reasonably competent and diligent inspection of the property *would* have uncovered the past history of soils problems. Real estate agents hold themselves out to the public as professionals, and, as such, are required to make reasonable use of their superior knowledge, skills and experience within the area of their expertise. Because such agents are expected to make use of their superior knowledge and skills, which is the reason they are engaged, and because the agents in this case were or should have been alert to the signs of soils problems earlier described, the jury was well within the bounds of reason when it concluded that a reasonably diligent and competent inspection of the property would have included something more than a causal visual inspection and a general inquiry of the owners.

The judgment for negligence against appellant was amply supported by the evidence.

. . ..

VI.

Finally, appellant appeals from the portion of the judgment which denied it a right of indemnity against the sellers of the house, the Strassburgers. Appellant had filed a cross-complaint against the Strassburgers seeking full indemnity, or, in the alternative, partial indemnity based on comparative liability. The issue of indemnity went to the jury. In his instructions to the jury, the trial judge indicated that a person seeking indemnity could not recover if his negligence was "active" as opposed to "passive." The jury explicitly found that appellant's negligence was "active," thus implicitly finding against appellant on the indemnity issue. Appellant argues that as a result of *American Motorcycle Assn. v. Superior Court*, 20 Cal. 3d 578, 578 P.2d 899 (1978), the "active/passive" distinction is no longer tenable, and, in any case, the evidence clearly showed that appellant's negligence was passive.

. . ..

[W]e agree with appellant that the trial judge erred in instructing the jury that a person seeking indemnity cannot recover if his negligence is active as distinguished from passive. . .. In *American Motorcycle* our Supreme Court distinguished between two types of indemnity. The first was the form of equitable indemnity existing before *American Motorcycle*. This form of indemnity provided for *full* indemnification between concurrent tortfeasors where "the relative culpability of the parties [was] sufficiently disparate to warrant placing the entire loss on one party and completely absolving the other." (*American Motorcycle, supra.*) Prior to *American Motorcycle*, the courts struggled to find some linguistic formula that would provide an appropriate test to determine when this form of equitable indemnity was appropriate. Some authorities required that the negligence of the indemnitor be "active," "primary," or "positive," while the negligence of the indemnitee be found "passive," "secondary," or "negative." As the Supreme Court noted, the attempt to create such a precise formula was a futile exercise.

The second type of equitable indemnity was that created by the court in *American Motorcycle*. This form of indemnity "modified" the equitable indemnity doctrine just discussed to permit partial indemnity among concurrent tortfeasors on a comparative fault basis. (*American Motorcycle, supra.*) Although the active-passive distinction may still have some validity where a party is seeking *full* indemnity on the basis of the equitable indemnity doctrine as it existed prior to *American Motorcycle*, this distinction is manifestly inapplicable where a party is seeking partial indemnification on a comparative fault basis. (*See City of Sacramento v. Gemsch Investment Co.* (1981) 115 Cal. App. 3d 869, 875-877, 171 Cal. Rptr. 764.) As the court in *City of Sacramento v. Gemsch* stated with respect to an attempt in that case to draw distinctions between "active" and "passive" negligence: "Substantively, there is no reason to make such distinctions. Whatever the nature of the relative faults, whatever the quantum, it is measurable under *AMA*." We concur. Considering that appellant's cross-complaint against the Strassburgers sought partial indemnity based on comparative liability (as well as full indemnity), it was error for the judge to instruct without qualification that a party seeking indemnity cannot recover if his negligence is deemed to be "active."

. . ..

The portion of the judgment denying appellant a right to partial indemnity as against the Strassburger cross-defendants is reversed, and the cause remanded to the trial court with instructions to enter judgment in favor of appellant on this issue consistent with the views expressed in this opinion and the law of partial indemnity as developed in *American Motorcycle* and its progeny. In all other respects the judgment is affirmed.

MILLER, J., and SMITH, J., concurred.

Appellant's petition for a hearing by the Supreme Court was denied May 31, 1984. MOSK, J., and LUCAS, J., were of the opinion that the petition should be granted.

[7]   Explanatory Notes

[a]   California Legislative Response to *Easton*

The *Easton* decision caused great concern among California real estate agents. The year after *Easton* was decided, the California legislature adopted a bill, drafted by the California Association of Realtors,[78] requiring all sellers of real property, and their agents, to deliver written disclosure statements to prospective buyers prior to signing a real estate sales contract. A form for use by sellers and agents is contained in the statute. It requires a detailed listing of all facilities on the property and disclosure of any known defects or malfunctions. Sellers must declare (through the use of questions which may be answered only Yes or No) whether they are aware if any of a long list of defects is present on the property they desire to transfer, including "Any settling from any cause, or slippage, sliding or other soil problems." Agents must only declare they have made a "reasonably competent and diligent visual inspection of the accessible areas of the property" and state any problems that inspection reveals. It is clear from the face of the legislation that most of the disclosure burden is placed upon the property owner rather than the agent. Failure to abide by the disclosure statute does not void a real estate sale. The only penalty is liability for any "actual damages suffered by a transferee."[79] The statute appears to have had its intended effect of releasing real estate brokers from a duty to independently investigate the statements made by sellers on the quality disclosure forms. *See,* for example, *Robinson v. Grossman,* 67 Cal. App. 4th 634, 67 Cal. Rptr. 380 (1997).

[b]   Interplay of Real Estate Agent's Duty and Comparative Negligence Rules

Valley of California, Inc. was found liable, jointly and severally, on a negligence theory. They either were aware or, given their general expertise in real estate matters, should have been aware of the soil problems, and unreasonably failed to disclose them to the Eastons. The "red flags" were, according to the court, too numerous for Valley to escape responsibility. There were cracks, uneven floors and indications of repairs. In addition, the house was located on a ledge that was obviously man made. Under those circumstances, a duty to investigate problems and to reveal any defects to the buyers arose.

The comparative negligence judgment obtained by the Eastons placed 65% of the responsibility for the damages upon the Strassburgers, 25% on the Strassburger's various building contractors, 5% on the Strassburger's real estate broker (Valley), and 5% on the buyer's broker.[80] Since this was joint and several liability, the plaintiffs could execute the *entire* judgment against any party found responsible. If such execution required a party to pay more than their share of the damages they were relegated to an action for contribution from one of the other defendants. This system gives plaintiffs the right to seek the deepest pocket and let the defendants fight over allocation of the loss. Thus, if the Strassburgers had money, other parties (like Valley of California) paying the judgment could recover from them. The Strassburgers, after all, were found

---

[78] Telephone Interview with Harry D. Miller, Attorney for the Eastons (Feb. 25, 1987).

[79] CAL. CIV. CODE §§ 1102.6, 1102.13.

[80] The Eastons did not sue their broker but the jury found against them anyway! This part of the judgment was simply ignored by the trial and appellate courts.

to have fraudulently misled the Eastons. But the Strassburgers declared bankruptcy after the case was decided, and have never paid any of the judgment. As it worked out, Valley of California paid the Eastons all of the judgment.[81] Valley, now Coldwell Banker, managed to collect a small portion of the damages from one of the Strassburgers' building contractors. They also sued the Easton's real estate agent, alleging the same theory Easton prevailed on against Valley, and collected half the remaining obligation.[82]

[c]   Liability Theories

The negligence theory used against Valley was different from the warranty rule used in *Humber v. Morton*. Valley of California was not responsible for all defects on an implied warranty theory, but only for those they should have known about but failed to disclose to the buyers. Indeed, on the face of the typical implied warranty case, the Eastons would have lost against both Valley and Strassburger. The house was not new, leaving Easton to take the house "as is."

[d]   Some Other Cases

The Longs bought a house. The basement was completely flooded (up to the rafters!) 8 days after closing. In *Long v. Brownstone Real Estate Co.*, 484 A.2d 126 (Pa. Super. 1984), the court held that the sellers and their agent had a duty to disclose prior floodings and that the presence of a water line in the basement six inches above the floor did not relieve the defendants of liability for flooding of the magnitude alleged by the plaintiffs.

Even investors have succeeded in some cases. The Amatos relied upon representations made by *their* broker that property they were about to buy was producing profits. In reality it was a bust. The property was condemned shortly after the Amato's bought it. They sought relief on the theories that the broker breached his fiduciary duty to the buyers and misrepresented the condition of the property. Despite the facts that the broker only passed along to the Amatos statements made by the seller's broker and that the Amatos never went to look at the property before buying it, the attempts of the broker to have the case dismissed on summary judgment failed. *Amato v. Rathbun Realty, Inc.*, 98 N.M. 231, 647 P.2d 433 (1982).

[8]   Problem Notes

[a]   The Broker's Fiduciary Role in a Real Estate Transaction

Real estate sellers generally hire the real estate brokers and pay their commissions. Home buyers usually do not hire their own brokers. As a day-to-day matter, therefore, real estate agents usually have fiduciary obligations only to their client-sellers. The buyer is "befriended" by the agent but not "defended." The Code of Ethics and Standards of Practice of the National Association of Realtors states the basic obligation of a realtor this way:

ARTICLE 7

In accepting employment as an agent, the realtor pledges himself to protect and promote the interests of the client. This obligation of absolute fidelity to the client's interests is primary, but it does not relieve the realtor of the obligation to treat fairly all parties to the transaction.

Fulfilling the obligation of "absolute fidelity" to a client while treating all other parties "fairly" creates a difficult, if not impossible, ethical task for a real estate agent. Buyers often assume

---

[81] Telephone Interview with W. Stephen Wilson, Attorney for Valley of California, Inc. (Feb. 20, 1987).

[82] Telephone Interview with Harry D. Miller, Attorney for Easton (Feb. 25, 1987).

that the broker is helping them. In theory, at least, brokers representing sellers but helping buyers may breach their fiduciary obligations.[83] For example, if the Strassburgers' agent revealed concerns over soil conditions to the Eastons, would that have breached the fiduciary duty owed to the client? Must a seller's real estate agent notify (preferably in writing?) any potential buyer that the agency relationship requires the realtor to act in the best interest of the seller and that buyers should contact other agents or lawyers for advice on the wisdom of their actions? Would such notice avoid the potential conflicts of interest inherent in a typical deal orchestrated by an agent?

[b]   The Facilitator, Rather than Fiduciary, Model

After *Easton* should we abandon all pretense that a real estate broker is a fiduciary of the seller in favor of a model of the broker as "facilitator" of a deal in which the primary focus is the broker's interest in obtaining a sale's commission? Does the "facilitator" model reflect what actually happens now in many real estate transactions? In such a world what steps would you take to protect sellers and buyers? Would notice of defects to sellers and buyers, like that now required in California, be enough? How about notice from agents to sellers and buyers that the agent's primary interest is in facilitating a deal so a commission may be obtained?

[c]   Transactions in Which Both Sides Have Brokers

Note that the Eastons, contrary to the typical pattern, *did* have their own broker! While still not typical, buyers are obtaining their own agents more frequently now than in prior years.[84] Does *Easton* suggest that the buyer's, as well as the seller's, broker is liable in negligence for failing to detect flaws they should have known about on a reasonable inspection? In fact, since the buyers had their own broker, why did Valley of California have any duty at all to inspect the house on behalf of the buyers? Did the court have its fiduciary obligations backwards? How would the case have come out if both brokers had been parties? Can a "facilitator" model work when both sides have agents? Are multiple models necessary depending on the number of agents involved? Is it possible to develop a workable set of ethical rules to meet the varying settings in which agents may work?

[d]   Scope of Liability

Is *Easton* just a way of evading the inability to hold sellers of used houses to the strictures of implied warranty theory? There is no proof that the real estate agent actually knew of the soil problems in *Easton*. But the court imposed a duty to inquire when "red flags" suggested there were problems. If negligence existed on these facts, then doesn't negligence exist any time a defect should have been noticed but wasn't? And if the real estate agents are liable in these cases, then aren't sellers clearly responsible? After all, Valley of California was given a right of contribution against Strassburger. If all this is true, then the only task left is for courts to define the nature of the defects sellers and their agents should normally be aware of. That leaves room for taking the age and condition of used housing into account, right? Or, is *Easton* just

---

[83] For general reading on the role of real estate agents, *see* Currier, *Finding the Broker's Place in the Typical Residential Real Estate Transaction*, 33 FLA. L. REV. 655 (1981); Comment, *Protecting the Real Estate Consumer: Traditional Theories of Liability Revisited, and a Look at Nebraska's Proposed Real Estate Consumers Protection Act*, 65 NEB. L. REV. 188 (1986).

[84] DeMuth, *Buyers Hiring Real Estate Brokers to Represent Their Own Interests*, WASH. POST, at G1, col. 4 (Sept. 20, 1986).

an example of egregious, fraudulent behavior by sellers that led to enormous losses and a sharp judicial response? Would you have voted for the post *Easton* legislation lowering the level of care of real estate brokers in return for seller disclosures? Is this result more or less likely to provide relief to buyers who deal with unscrupulous private sellers?

[e] Obtaining Leases Through Agents

Is there any theory under which a lessor's real estate agent is liable to a tenant for breach of the landlord's implied warranty of habitability? Must an agent reveal defects in an apartment to prospective tenants? Should a tenant add her landlord's agent to any suit brought under *Berzito v. Gambino,* p. 673 above.

[f] Standard of Care

Should real estate brokers be held only to a negligence level of care in dealing with buyers? Compare the status of sellers, masons, architects and real estate agents.

[g] Other Actors

Compare the underground irrigation system installed by the Strassburgers with the hot water system in *Schipper*, discussed at p. 817 above. If the maker of the irrigation system did not include warnings about steep slope installations in its packaging, would it be partially responsible for the Eastons' losses? Or should the real estate brokers have realized upon inspection that the irrigation system should never have been installed?

In *Ferentchak v. Village of Frankfort*, 105 Ill. 2d 474, 475 N.E.2d 822 (1985), the buyers of a home with a consistently flooded basement sued the civil engineer who designed the surface water drainage system in the development. The court refused to find the engineer responsible, holding that the engineer's contract with the developer only required the setting of minimum foundation grade levels and that they had no duty to inquire beyond the terms of their contractual understandings. Would *Easton* require a different outcome in California, at least in those cases where the engineer discovered that a certain minimum foundation grade level was highly desirable to protect future home owners?

§ 9.06 Note on Transaction Costs: Closing Charges, Broker's Commissions, Attorney's Fees and Title Assurance

Many of the institutional complexities involved in completing even the most standard of real estate transactions involve systems for discovering and using information—about the state of the title, the quality of any structures, the financial status of the buyer, and the availability of financing. Idealized markets are said by economists to be most efficient in settings where all parties involved in transactions have perfect knowledge of the circumstances surrounding their deals. Lack of information imposes costs on the parties, reduces the likelihood of rational decision making, increases the costs of policing for misbehavior and, at times, produces a call for government regulation. The information-based impediments to the completion of a real estate transaction have led to all of these sorts of costs, as well as government regulation. The brief summary of some of these issues that follows is intended to be both informational and an introduction to some of the issues taken up in the next chapter on the relationships between law and economics.

Closing a residential real estate transaction is very expensive. During the early 1970s, a widespread perception arose that the high costs were due, at least in part, to lack of an informed consuming public and inadequate price competition in the various industries servicing residential sales. A study by the Department of Housing and Urban Development and the Veterans Administration of the closing costs involved in a sample of federally insured or supported loan transactions revealed that sales of houses in 1971 with an average price of $19,397 led to closing costs averaging $1,937, or about 10% of the price.[85] This figure included all closing related charges, including real estate commissions, title insurance, points on loans, and apportionment of prepaid items like real estate taxes and insurance. In addition, the study revealed very substantial differences in the closing costs in various parts of the country.[86]

The perceived scope of the problem led to the adoption of the Real Estate Settlement Procedures Act (RESPA) of 1974,[87] which requires the transmittal of a statement of charges to the buyer and seller at closing. The Act was supposed to provide information in an understandable way to consumers of real estate services, leading to more informed actions by consumers and to greater price competition. As a practical matter, the Act probably has had only a small impact. The statement of charges is not given to the buyer until just before or at closing, though estimates must be given much earlier. Unless buyers shop around and request detailed price listings from those servicing their transactions, they will be unable to intelligently use the information provided under RESPA to reduce the cost of their real estate purchases. In addition, there is a general understanding that price competition does not determine the level of charges imposed for some important settlement items. The title insurance industry, like insurance generally, is exempt from operation of federal antitrust laws. Real estate brokerage commissions rarely fall below 6% of the price of the house; in some areas they are now 7%. Many think the indications of price fixing in the real estate brokerage industry are high.[88] As the prices of housing have risen in recent decades, the use of a percent-of-price method to determine some settlement fees and virtually all brokerage commissions has caused costs to rise quite rapidly. Since the real estate commission

---

[85] This figure was a bit inflated since it included prorated charges such as property taxes and transfer taxes imposed by governments that were not directly attributable to the costs of closing the real estate transaction. But it did include a real estate brokerage commission, then usually about 6% and now 7% in some cases. The commission, obviously the most important single cost, is also the one arguably most susceptible to price fixing. There have been a number of cases brought against real estate brokers charging that they fixed prices.

[86] A summary of the study may be found in Additional Views of Senator Proxmire, Senate Report No. 866, Committee on Banking, Housing and Urban Affairs, 93rd Cong., 2nd Sess., at 13-18 (1974).

[87] 12 U.S.C. § 2601 et seq.

[88] See, e.g., Erxleben, In Search of Price and Service Competition in Residential Real Estate Brokerage: Breaking the Cartel, 56 WASH. L. REV. 179 (1981); Owen, Kickbacks, Specialization, Price Fixing, and Efficiency in Residential Real Estate Markets, 29 STAN. L. REV. 931 (1977); LOS ANGELES REGIONAL OFFICE, FEDERAL TRADE COMMISSION, 1 THE RESIDENTIAL REAL ESTATE BROKERAGE INDUSTRY 12-19 (1983). Owen, after studying the California real estate market, argued that the greatest impediment to cost reduction was price fixing among real estate agents. He also suggested that competition could be induced in the title insurance industry by permitting and encouraging title insurance companies to pay agents rebates for referring customers. Owen theorized that competition among agents would force this rebate savings to be passed along to customers. If commissions are price fixed, would it be likely that agents would lower their rates in return for relatively small kickbacks? Erxleben attributed the high brokerage rates to a combination of factors, including the use of multiple listing services (data bases with houses of member brokers listed) with fixed commission splitting if the listing leads to a sale and with membership restricted to non-discount brokers, inability of local officials to police the large number of brokers, the difficulty of proving intentional conspiratorial action to fix prices, and lack of customer sophistication. The entry of national brokerage houses, such as Merrill Lynch, Century 21 and others, in recent years may create a different market structure. Save for Remax, it has not led to much price cutting, either to drive the local brokers out of the market or to increase the national brokers' share of the business pie.

is the single largest charge in most transactions, controlling it is central to the control of residential settlement costs. But for the most part, brokerage fees are unregulated.

Once in a while, attempts surface to control closing costs, usually through the use of state antitrust statutes. Some of these disputes involved the "packaging" of virtually all parts of a closing—real estate agent, title search, escrow agent, lender and even decorator.[89] Rather than reducing transactions costs by taking advantage of the efficiencies of scale, especially in title searching, plaintiffs have charged that developers increase fees and take advantage of their "captive" audience of buyers. Packaged deals are not the only "traditions" in the real estate industry that have been subjected to judicial scrutiny. Attorneys and mortgage lenders, as well as real estate brokers and escrow companies, have surfaced in the disputes.

In *Goldfarb v. Virginia State Bar*, 421 U.S. 773 (1975), the Supreme Court held that Virginia Bar Association minimum fee schedules operated to fix prices in violation of the antitrust laws. The Goldfarbs inquired of numerous lawyers about their charges for acting as counsel in a home purchase. All of them felt bound by the minimum fee schedules. In addition, Virginia banks routinely required a lawyer to certify title thereby making it impossible for the Goldfarbs to close their deal without the services of an attorney.

A related problem formed the setting for *Forrest v. Capital Building and Loan Association*, 385 F. Supp. 831 (M.D. La. 1973).[90] Forrest, an attorney, alleged that local banks unlawfully tied legal and notarial services to the tying product—mortgage money. That is, he charged that local banks unlawfully merged products by requiring borrowers to sign documents prepared by attorneys selected annually by the banks' boards of directors. In contrast to *Goldfarb*, the borrower's attorney could not serve that function, though such counsel could provide other services not required by the bank. The plaintiff, who was not selected as a bank counsel, sued. The court found that there was no tying arrangement. The banks were simply hiring their own counsel, and passing the costs along to their customers. The lawyers' clients were the banks, not the borrowers. The use of bank counsel was part of the mortgage package; counsel was required to insure that the bank (not the borrowers) got good security for its loan.

Packaging loan and real estate brokerage services has become more and more popular, particularly as national brokerage companies have become commonplace. In New Jersey, the linkage of real estate sales and lending services spawned a major bureaucratic battle among banks, real estate brokers, mortgage brokers, and state regulatory agencies. When banks offered to either pay commissions to real estate brokers placing loans with them or to purchase loans issued by real estate brokers, the Mortgage Bankers Association (MBA) sued, seeking the issuance of regulations prohibiting such practices. MBA argued that state law barred real estate agents from accepting commissions from more than one side to a transaction and that state regulatory bodies were obligated to regulate any activity that permitted agents to accept a commission from a seller and a lender in the same transaction. The dispute boiled its way up to the state Supreme Court, which concluded that the administrative proceedings undertaken to consider various regulations violated the state's administrative procedure act. The issues were sent back to both the banking and real estate regulatory agencies for further proceedings. *Mortgage Bankers Association of New Jersey v. New Jersey Real Estate Commission*, 102 N.J. 176, 506 A.2d 733 (1986). Related issues

---

[89] *See, e.g.*, MacManus v. A.E. Realty Partners, 146 Cal. App. 3d 275, 194 Cal. Rptr. 567 (1983); Saxer v. Phillip Morris, Inc., 54 Cal. App. 3d 7, 126 Cal. Rptr. 327 (1975).

[90] *Forrest* was affirmed *per curiam*, 504 F.2d 891 (5th Cir. 1974). A case much like *Forrest*, with the same result, is Foster v. Maryland State Savings and Loan Association, 590 F.2d 928 (D.C. Cir. 1978).

were still being litigated a decade later. *Mortgage Bankers Association of New Jersey v. New Jersey Real Estate Commission*, 283 N.J. Super. 233, 661 A.2d 832 (App. Div. 1995).

One of the reasons why costs are difficult to control is that there are so many actors working in a typical residential real estate sale. Each of them has very distinct interests and needs. Sellers like to make a profit, lenders watch out for their security interest, real estate brokers want to insure payment of their commissions, attorneys want their fees paid, and those searching and insuring titles want payment for their services. There is a great deal of variation in local community customs about how the closing drama plays out and which party pays for which services. But in all locations, the complexity of the transaction has led to the creation of two industries other than real estate mortgage lending—escrow agents who theoretically manage the drama, hold and disburse funds, and, of course, take their cut of the pie, and title searchers who research title documents, report to all the parties in the deal, and issue some form of insurance policy about the quality of the title conveyed.[91]

In most real estate transactions, a party is hired by the participants[92] to hold money and documents while the deal is being completed. Buyers, for example, generally do not want sellers to hold their earnest money deposits pending closing; a neutral third party is better. When the deed has been prepared, someone must hold it until the sale price has been paid. When the price has been paid and the deed delivered, the mortgage deed must be conveyed. While most of these things happen at about the same time, someone must have the responsibility for organizing the sale, distributing the funds and recording the various documents. The escrow function is performed by a variety of people in different places. In some areas, lawyers take on that role. In others, escrow companies, title insurance companies, banks, or real estate agents take on the task.

The primary reason for the proliferation of institutions surrounding real property transfers is the need to insure either that good title is exchanged, or that losses are covered should title be flawed. Both the lender and the buyer have obvious concern about the strength of the seller's claims of ownership. Although most sales are by warranty deed, banks and buyers are generally unwilling to rely upon the contractual promises contained in such a deed as the only basis for obtaining solid security for their loans.[93] Thus, a series of systems have arisen to gather information about land titles and to insure for the small risk of a title flaw.

The basic data systems are publicly subsidized and operated. Deeds and other title documents are filed, and kept open for public inspection, at local Recorder of Deeds offices. The deeds are usually indexed in Grantor and Grantee lists. To search title, the seller in the deal under review is searched for in the Grantee index. His or her Grantor is then searched for in the Grantee index, and so on as far back as state statutes require.[94] Then the searcher goes back the other way using the Grantor index. Other relevant records are kept at probate courts (trusts and wills),

---

[91] In some places these functions have merged. In Washington, D.C., title insurance companies frequently act as escrow agents as well as title searchers and title insurers.

[92] In most places the custom has the buyer selecting the agent since most funds held in escrow come from the buyer.

[93] The mere fact that the seller may leave the area after the settlement is enough to make any contract action arising from breach of a promise to convey good title of dubious value.

[94] Marketable title acts have reduced the period to be searched down to 40 years or less. Older title flaws are deemed waived. Periods in the west tend to be shorter, probably because of the desire to quickly resolve the numerous title disputes that arose during the opening of the western territories to settlement by non-Indians.

real estate tax offices, and civil courts (liens, judgments, eminent domain proceedings and land ownership disputes). If the instruments are all found, and when read, all sound, title is deemed clear. If a hole is found, title will be deemed unmarketable, triggering remedies described in the real estate contract. Title reports also list any encumbrances, such as covenants or easements. If unexpected encumbrances surface, title may also be unmarketable. Someone has to search for all the records and aggregate the data whenever a title is transferred.

Great variety exists in the ways this raw data is gathered and analyzed. In some places, particularly rural locations, attorneys (or their employees) do everything. They search the records, evaluate the title and "certify" the marketability of the title. In case of error, buyers sue the lawyers in negligence or the seller on the title warranties in the deed. Lawyers rely on malpractice insurance to cover them in case they make mistakes. In other places, commercial operations aggregate the records and prepare an abstract of title. Private attorneys then evaluate the abstract and certify the title. Still other locales use either of the above methods, but replace the certification process with title insurance. Title insurance companies have taken over the entire process in some places. Many maintain title "factories" with up to date aggregations of local records, usually in better condition and more highly automated than public record depositories. But regardless of the system used, fees must be paid for the title search and guarantee.[95]

Finally, a few places use the Torrens system, which operates much like a typical automobile title system. When a car is sold, the old title is taken into the local department of motor vehicles office, canceled, and a new title is issued to the new owner. Title is controlled not by recording a series of documents and searching these documents each time the car is transferred, but by recycling registration at each transfer. Land titles could be organized in a similar fashion by giving each parcel a registration number and controlling title with a public bureaucracy. Title insurance companies and attorneys have very little relevance to this system. Though it sounds like Nirvana, there are problems here too. Such a system is very expensive to start up. Before the public bureaucracy could gain control of any particular title, that title would have to be searched and all potential defects eliminated. Only clean titles may be put into the system at start up if it is to work correctly. You can imagine what it would be like to search every title in a large city prior to switching over to Torrens. In addition, this system is publicly operated and supported. The non-public title assurance systems are "free" to taxpayers, at least until they buy a house. Most local governments have been unwilling to pay for the start up costs and the ongoing operational costs of a Torrens system. In addition, efforts to establish Torrens registration systems run into strong opposition from the existing title assurance industry. The possibility of computerized title records has also dampened enthusiasm for the Torrens system. If all the records for any particular parcel can be retrieved quickly from a data base, perhaps a more efficient title assurance system will develop.

Title recording and research systems are not the only title safeguards commonly used. Warranty deeds commonly used in real estate transactions contain five covenants. Three are violated, if

---

[95] Some proposals have been made to reduce these costs. Dale Whitman, in *Optimizing Land Title Assurance Systems*, 42 GEO. WASH. L. REV. 40 (1973), suggested reducing search duplication by making public all prior title searches; requiring that all title insurance policies be assignable to succeeding purchasers, requiring that all land surveys be recorded to avoid repetitious surveys, computerizing all land records, reducing marketable title act time periods down to 20 or 30 years, standardizing land documents, recording data by tract in addition to the names of the grantors and grantees, consolidating title "factories" already in existence, and changing to the Torrens system (discussed in the text just after this note) with an initial infusion of federal funds. These recommendations are still relevant. *See also* John L. McCormack, *Torrens and Recording: Land Title Assurance in the Computer Age*, 18 WM. MITCHELL L. REV. 61 (1982); Gresham, *The Residential Real Estate Transfer Process: A Functional Critique*, 23 EMORY L.J. 421 (1973).

at all, at the time of conveyance. These warrant that the seller is in possession of a fee simple absolute (covenant of seisin), has the present ability to convey, and is conveying a fee free of encumbrances not of record, such as liens, easements and covenants. In addition, sellers usually warrant that the buyer will be able to quietly enjoy possession of the property and that a paramount title holder will not disturb the buyer's possession. These two covenants provide a future remedy in damages should a violation of one of the first three covenants lead to eviction from some or all of the land.

Many jurisdictions have adopted statutory forms for warranty deeds. The District of Columbia Code, for example, provides that the language "do hereby grant" is sufficient to pass a fee simple absolute. The traditional "and his heirs" language is not necessary.[96] In addition, the phrase "warrant specially" has the same effect in the District of Columbia "as if the grantor had covenanted that he, his heirs, devisees and personal representatives will forever warrant and defend the said property unto the grantee, his heirs, devisees, personal representatives, and assigns against the claims and demands of the grantor and all persons claiming or to claim by, through, or under him."[97] Such statutory forms have largely substituted for the common law warranties.

---

[96] D.C. CODE ANN. 45-301.

[97] D.C. CODE ANN. 45-305.

CHAPTER 10

WASTE AND NUISANCE LAW: ECONOMICS AND THE LAW OF
PROPERTY

§ 10.01 Introduction

In Chapter 7, it was mentioned that members of the Legal Process School were descendants of, or at least reacted to, the Realists. They agreed with the Realists that it was impossible to find a body of substantive principles of justice all could accept. So they looked for a system of institutional legitimacy, hoping to use generally accepted principles about the appropriate ways to solve problems as a neutral basis for justifying the exercise of power by various parts of the legal system. The same dearth of theoretical justifications for the exercise of legal power leading to the rise of the Legal Process School led others to seek non-legal analytical systems that might provide guidance to courts, legislatures and executives. The most prominent of the new modes of thought emerged from Law and Economics scholars. Many claimed a mantle similar to that of the Legal Process School, contending that economic theories, rather than institutional competence, were the appropriate, non-normative, source of principles that could justify legal decisions. They noted, and correctly so, that Realists were enamored of the social sciences. Refusing to view law itself as a science, they sought a basis for rule making in the needs of people and searched for those needs using emerging social sciences. Contemporary use of economics in law is a descendant of these Realist traditions.

The claims of the Law and Economics School, like the claims made by other modes of thought studied here, are subject to some serious limitations. First, the claim that economics is non-normative is troublesome. The utilitarian claim fundamental to some economic literature—that the world is better off making choices that maximize wealth—is itself a normative claim.[1] Indeed, many of those criticizing use of economics as a tool for resolving legal disputes call upon some of the same arguments the Realists used in their debates with late nineteenth-and early twentieth-century Formalists. In response, much recent law and economics literature relies less on pure *laissez faire* theories, focuses more on the extent to which assumptions of rational decision making actually govern people's economic choices, or states that its goal is minimalist—to provide a realistic structure within which political choices may be made.

This chapter is structured to provide an introduction to some of the basic economic analysis that is now being used in various legal fields. The goal is to allow you to test the notion that

---

[1] As used by many of its adherents, economics creates a bias towards free markets. The bias often takes on the tone that making use of markets is the "correct" solution to a variety of problems. That claim inevitably becomes normative. The debate about economics and normative discourse is the subject of a famous article by Arthur Leff, *Economic Analysis of Law: Some Realism About Nominalism,* 60 VA. L. REV. 451 (1974). You will find a short excerpt from the article a bit later in the chapter.

economic inquiries may sometimes help structure decision making. We begin with a well known case about access to sunlight along the beach in Miami, Florida.

§ 10.02 Additional Readings

For basic materials on the law of waste and nuisance, read ROGER A. CUNNINGHAM, WILLIAM B. STOEBUCK & DALE A. WHITMAN, THE LAW OF PROPERTY 157-186, 417-435 (2d ed. 1993).

The law and economics literature is vast. Those interested in perusing some of the most widely read work on nuisance and related questions can look at Ronald Coase, *The Problem of Social Cost,* 3 J.L. & ECON. 1 (1960); Garrett Hardin, *The Tragedy of the Commons,* 162 SCIENCE 1243 (1968); RICHARD POSNER, ECONOMIC ANALYSIS OF LAW 10-40 (1972); Guido Calabresi & Douglas Melamed, *Property Rules, Liability Rules, and Inalienability: One View of the Cathedral,* 85 HARV. L. REV. 1089 (1972); Robert Ellickson, *Alternatives to Zoning: Covenants, Nuisance Rules, and Fines as Land Use Controls,* 40 U. CHI. L. REV. 681 (1973); Edward Rabin, *Rethinking Basic Assumptions,* 63 VA. L. REV. 1299 (1977); A. Mitchell Polinksy, *Resolving Nuisance Disputes: The Simple Economics of Injunctive and Damage Remedies,* 32 STAN. L. REV. 1075 (1980); Jeff Lewin, *Compensated Injunctions and the Evolution of Nuisance Law,* 71 IOWA L. REV. 775 (1986); James Krier & Stewart Schwab, *Property Rules and Liability Rules: The Cathedral in a New Light,* 70 N.Y.U. L. REV. 440 (1995); Louis Kaplow & Steven Shavell, *Property Rules Versus Liability Rules: An Economic Analysis,* 109 HARV. L. REV. 713 (1996). Jeff Lewin's article contains a very helpful summary of all the major writings written before 1986.

The articles by Hardin, and Calabresi & Melamed are excerpted in RICHARD CHUSED, A PROPERTY ANTHOLOGY 387-394 (2d ed. 1997).

§ 10.03 The First Problem: Access to Sunlight

[1] Background to *Fontainebleau Hotel Corp. v. Forty-Five Twenty-Five, Inc.*

The Sans Souci Hotel was owned by Harry Mufson and Ben Novack during its heyday after World War II. Novack handled the "back of the house."[2] He was a bit hard of hearing, so it made some sense for him to run the day-to-day behind-the-scenes part of the operation. Mufson was the "front man." He fraternized with the guests, ran the public portions of the business, and not surprisingly, got all the glory. Despite their different roles, Mufson and Novack worked together tolerably well. Their relationship soured, however, after Novack got married. Running the back of the house became less and less acceptable. In 1950, Mufson and Novack decided to sell the hotel and split up.

After the sale of the Sans Souci, Mufson returned to his family's business, the Jefferson Stores. They were a "high class K-Mart" sort of operation in Dade County. Novack wanted to stay in the hotel business. He "took a liking" to the Firestone Estate at Collins Avenue and 44th Street in Miami Beach. Though the Firestone family was quite attached to the spot, Novack "charmed" them into selling so he could build a first class hotel. Ground was broken for the Fontainebleau on January 5, 1954; a gala opening was held on December 18 of the same year. The 600-plus

---

[2] This is the language of Harold Gardner, who served as Public Relations Director of the Fontainebleau Hotel between 1954 and 1959, and after a year's stint working in a Hollywood hotel, returned to Miami Beach to work at the Eden Roc. He was gracious enough to spin out the story of the litigation in delightfully colorful terms. My rendering of his tale in the text hardly does it justice. At the time of my interview with him, he worked for the Deauville Hotel in Miami Beach. Telephone Interview (Aug. 6, 1987).

room hotel was an immediate hit. It was continually full during its first year. Fontainebleau became a household word along the east coast.

Novack's newfound fame as a first class hotelier grated on Harry Mufson. Though a number of potential hotel sites existed at that point in Miami Beach's history, Mufson selected a plot right next door to the Fontainebleau for his re-entry into the hotel business. The 375 room Eden Roc was constructed during 1955 and 1956. Though it was a smaller operation than the Fontainebleau, it had a classier style. Mufson used his old "front man" experience to the fullest to insure that his guests got personalized, high quality service. The Fontainebleau had glitz and throngs of people; the Eden Roc had class. Both did well.

But the old feud would not die. Looking for more controversy as well as business, Novack decided to construct a large ballroom and a huge addition in order to attract convention bookings. Though he had a number of possible locations on his land for the addition, he decided to build a 14 story tower just to the south of Eden Roc's swimming pool. In addition, the north wall of the tower facing the Eden Roc was a windowless mass of solid cement painted gray. The next case resulted.

View of the North Wall of the Fontainebleau from
the Eden Rock Swimming Pool

[2] Opinion of the Florida Court of Appeal in *Fontainebleau Hotel v. Forty-Five Twenty-Five*

Fontainebleau Hotel Corp. v. Forty-Five Twenty-Five, Inc.

Florida District Court of Appeal, Third District
114 So.2d 357 (1959)

PER CURIAM.

This is an interlocutory appeal from an order temporarily enjoining the appellants from continuing with the construction of a fourteen-story addition to the Fontainebleau Hotel, owned and operated by the appellants. Appellee, plaintiff below, owns the Eden Roc Hotel, which was constructed in 1955, about a year after the Fontainebleau, and adjoins the Fontainebleau on the north. Both are luxury hotels, facing the Atlantic Ocean. The proposed addition to the Fontainebleau is being constructed twenty feet from its north property line, 130 feet from the mean high water mark of the Atlantic Ocean, and 76 feet 8 inches from the ocean bulkhead line. The 14-story tower will extend 160 feet above grade in height and is 416 feet long from east to west. During the winter months, from around two o'clock in the afternoon for the remainder of the day, the shadow of the addition will extend over the cabana, swimming pool, and sunbathing areas of the Eden Roc, which are located in the southern portion of its property.

In this action, plaintiff-appellee sought to enjoin the defendants-appellants from proceeding with the construction of the addition to the Fontainebleau (it appears to have been roughly eight stories high at the time suit was filed), alleging that the construction would interfere with the light and air on the beach in front of the Eden Roc and cast a shadow of such size as to render the beach wholly unfitted for the use and enjoyment of its guests, to the irreparable injury of the plaintiff; further, that the construction of such addition on the north side of defendants' property, rather than the south side, was actuated by malice and ill will on the part of the defendants' president toward the plaintiff's president; and that the construction was in violation of a building ordinance requiring a 100-foot setback from the ocean. It was also alleged that the construction would interfere with the easements of light and air enjoyed by plaintiff and its predecessors in title for more than twenty years and "impliedly granted by virtue of the acts of the plaintiff's predecessors in title, as well as under the common law and the express recognition of such rights by virtue of Chapter 9837, Laws of Florida 1923 . . . ." Some attempt was also made to allege an easement by implication in favor of the plaintiff's property, as the dominant, and against the defendants' property, as the servient, tenement.

The defendants' answer denied the material allegations of the complaint, pleaded laches and estoppel by judgment.

The chancellor heard considerable testimony on the issues made by the complaint and the answer and, as noted, entered a temporary injunction restraining the defendants from continuing with the construction of the addition. His reason for so doing was stated by him, in a memorandum opinion, as follows:

> In granting the temporary injunction in this case the Court wishes to make several things very clear. The ruling is not based on any alleged presumptive title nor prescriptive right of the plaintiff to light and air nor is it based on any deed restrictions nor recorded plats in the title of the plaintiff nor of the defendant nor of any plat of record. It is not based on any zoning ordinance nor on any provision of the building code of the City of Miami Beach nor

on the decision of any court, *nisi prius* or appellate. It is based solely on the proposition that no one has a right to use his property to the injury of another. In this case it is clear from the evidence that the proposed use by the Fontainebleau will materially damage the Eden Roc. There is evidence indicating that the construction of the proposed annex by the Fontainebleau is malicious or deliberate for the purpose of injuring the Eden Roc, but it is scarcely sufficient, standing alone, to afford a basis for equitable relief.

This is indeed a novel application of the maxim *sic utere tuo ut alienum non laedas*. This maxim does not mean that one must never use his own property in such a way as to do any injury to his neighbor. It means only that one must use his property so as not to injure the lawful *rights* of another . . . .

No American decision has been cited, and independent research has revealed none, in which it has been held that—in the absence of some contractual or statutory obligation—a landowner has a legal right to the free flow of light and air across the adjoining land of his neighbor. Even at common law, the landowner had no legal right, in the absence of an easement or uninterrupted use and enjoyment for a period of 20 years, to unobstructed light and air from the adjoining land. And the English doctrine of "ancient lights" has been unanimously repudiated in this country.

There being, then, no legal right to the free flow of light and air from the adjoining land, it is universally held that where a structure serves a useful and beneficial purpose, it does not give rise to a cause of action, either for damages or for an injunction under the maxim *sic utere tuo ut alienum non laedas,* even though it causes injury to another by cutting off the light and air and interfering with the view that would otherwise be available over adjoining land in its natural state, regardless of the fact that the structure may have been erected partly for spite.

We see no reason for departing from this universal rule. If, as contended on behalf of plaintiff, public policy demands that a landowner in the Miami Beach area refrain from constructing buildings on his premises that will cast a shadow on the adjoining premises, an amendment of its comprehensive planning and zoning ordinance, applicable to the public as a whole, is the means by which such purpose should be achieved. (No opinion is expressed here as to the validity of such an ordinance, if one should be enacted pursuant to the requirements of law. *Cf. City of Miami Beach v. State ex rel. Fontainebleau Hotel Corp.,* Fla. App. 1959, 108 So.2d 614, 619.) But to change the universal rule—and the custom followed in this state since its inception—that adjoining landowners have an equal right under the law to build to the line of their respective tracts and to such a height as is desired by them (in the absence, of course, of building restrictions or regulations) amounts, in our opinion, to judicial legislation. As stated in *Musumeci v. Leonardo,* [77 R.I. 255, 75 A.2d 177], "So use your own as not to injure another's property is, indeed, a sound and salutary principle for the promotion of justice, but it may not and should not be applied so as gratuitously to confer upon an adjacent property owner incorporeal rights incidental to his ownership of land which the law does not sanction."

We have also considered whether the order here reviewed may be sustained upon any other reasoning, conformable to and consistent with the pleadings, regardless of the erroneous reasoning upon which the order was actually based. We have concluded that it cannot.

The record affirmatively shows that no statutory basis for the right sought to be enforced by plaintiff exists. The so-called Shadow Ordinance enacted by the City of Miami Beach at plaintiff's behest was held invalid in *City of Miami Beach v. State ex rel. Fontainebleau Hotel Corp., supra.* It also affirmatively appears that there is no possible basis for holding that plaintiff has an easement for light and air, either express or implied, across defendants' property, nor any prescriptive right thereto—even if it be assumed, arguendo, that the common-law right of prescription as to "ancient lights" is in effect in this state. And from what we have said heretofore in this opinion, it is perhaps superfluous to add that we have no desire to dissent from the unanimous holding in this country repudiating the English doctrine of ancient lights.

The only other possible basis—and, in fact, the only one insisted upon by plaintiff in its brief filed here, other than its reliance upon the law of private nuisance as expressed in the maxim *sic utere tuo ut alienum non laedas* —for the order here reviewed is the alleged violation by defendants of the setback line prescribed by ordinance. The plaintiff argues that the ordinance applicable to the Use District in which plaintiff's and defendants' properties are located, prescribing "a front yard having a depth of not less than one hundred (100) feet, measured from the ocean, . . . ," should be and has been interpreted by the City's zoning inspector as requiring a setback of 100 feet from an established ocean bulkhead line. As noted above, the addition to the Fontainebleau is set back only 76 feet 8 inches from the ocean bulkhead line, although it is 130 feet from the ocean measured from the mean high water mark.

While the chancellor did not decide the question of whether the setback ordinance had been violated, it is our view that, even if there was such a violation, the plaintiff would have no cause of action against the defendants based on such violation. The application of simple mathematics to the sun studies filed in evidence by plaintiff in support of its claim demonstrates conclusively that to move the existing structure back some 23 feet from the ocean would make no appreciable difference in the problem which is the subject of this controversy. The construction of the 14-story addition is proceeding under a permit issued by the city pursuant to the mandate of this court in *City of Miami Beach v. State ex rel. Fontainebleau Hotel Corp., supra,* which permit authorizes completion of the 14-story addition according to a plan showing a 76-foot setback from the ocean bulkhead line. Moreover, the plaintiff's objection to the distance of the structure from the ocean appears to have been made for the first time in the instant suit, which was filed almost a year after the beginning of the construction of the addition, at a time when it was roughly eight stories in height, representing the expenditure by defendants of several million dollars. In these circumstances, it is our view that the plaintiff has stated no cause of action for equitable relief based on the violation of the ordinance—assuming, arguendo, that there has been a violation.

Since it affirmatively appears that the plaintiff has not established a cause of action against the defendants by reason of the structure here in question, the order granting a temporary injunction should be and it is hereby reversed with directions to dismiss the complaint.

Reversed with directions.

HORTON, C.J., and CARROLL, CHAS, J., and CABOT, TED, Associate Judge concur.

[3] Explanatory Notes on the Law and Facts

[a] *Fontainebleau I* and *II*

The opinion in *Fontainebleau Hotel v. Forty-Five Twenty-Five* [*Fontainebleau II*] mentioned *City of Miami Beach v. State of Florida ex rel. Fontainebleau Hotel Corp.* [*Fontainebleau I*], 108 So.2d 614 (Fla. App. 1959). *Fontainebleau I* was brought by the Fontainebleau hotel as a mandamus action to compel the issuance of a building permit for its planned hotel expansion.

Miami Beach had refused to issue a permit[3] because the plans violated a recently enacted ordinance that required a building fronting on the ocean to be no higher than 30 feet or one-half the distance from the property line to the beach front side of the building, whichever was greater. As the *Fontainebleau II* court noted, the addition to the Fontainebleau Hotel was 160 feet tall, but only 76 feet, 8 inches from the property line. The *Fontainebleau I* court, affirming the decision of the trial judge, held that Miami Beach lacked authority to adopt the ordinance.[4] The *Fontainebleau II* case was filed after the trial judge issued the writ of mandamus directing that the building permit issue. It was arguably unfair, therefore, for the *Fontainebleau II* court to criticize the Eden Roc for waiting until after construction began to bring its lawsuit. It may have made strategic sense to await the outcome of the building permit litigation before starting a new lawsuit. Why pay for such litigation if it might be unnecessary? On the other hand, once the writ of mandamus issued and the trial and appellate courts declined to stay the issuance of the writ, the owners of the Eden Roc had virtually no chance of halting construction while they contested the actions of the Fontainebleau.

[b]   Events After the Decision

After the Eden Roc lost its legal efforts to stop the Fontainebleau addition, it built a new swimming pool east of the old one and closer to the ocean. It was far enough east to be in the sunlight for a good part of those winter days when the sun was low in the southerly sky. In addition the hotel "dressed up" its roof area so that parties, cocktails and the like could be had overlooking the beach. Indeed, when news of the dispute hit the media, the Eden Roc was more than willing to let news photographers go up to the roof to snap shots of the "wall" behind happily drinking patrons of the Eden Roc.[5]

[c]   Prescriptive Rights to Air and Light

Fontainebleau II is the best known of a number of cases which have rejected attempts to create prescriptive rights of access to air and light. Though concerns over renewable energy resources has led to a lot of recent thought about solar access rights,[6] the case law displays little change.[7]

---

[3] A permit was issued for the first three floors of the building, about which there was no dispute. The first three floors did not exceed the 30 foot height limit of the ordinance.

[4] The grounds for the decision were narrow, based on a prior state Supreme Court holding that cities lacked authority to adopt ordinances requiring that buildings be set back a certain distance from lot lines.

[5] Telephone Interview with Harold Gardner (Aug. 6, 1987).

[6] By and large, American courts have long rejected the English notion of Ancient Lights, which provided prescriptive access to air and light. For more information on English and American rules on access to light and air, *see* Adrian Bradbrook, *Future Directions in Solar Access Protection,* 19 ENVTL. L. 167 (1988); Williams, *Solar Access and Property Rights: A Maverick Analysis,* 11 CONN. L. REV. 430 (1979); Comment, *Solar Energy and Restrictive Covenants: The Conflict Between Public Policy and Private Zoning,* 67 CAL. L. REV. 350 (1979); Dean & Miller, *Utilities at the Dawn of a Solar Age,* 53 N.D. L. REV. 329 (1977); Moskowitz, *Legal Access to Light: The Solar Energy Imperative,* 9 NAT. RESOURCES LAW. 177 (1976); Zillman & Deeny, *Legal Aspects of Solar Energy Development,* 1976 ARIZ. ST. L.J. 25; Eisenstadt & Utton, *Solar Rights and Their Effect on Solar Heating and Cooling,* 16 NAT. RESOURCES J. 363 (1976).

[7] No American court has decided that prescriptive rights to air or light exist. For some recent decisions, *see* Hill v. Beach Co., 279 S.C. 313, 306 S.E.2d 604 (1983); Wolford v. Thomas, 190 Cal. App. 3d 347, 235 Cal. Rptr. 422 (1987). The first case involved obstruction of beach views, the second urban view changes caused by building additions. There has been some movement to permit nuisance actions for interference with solar energy facilities. *See* Tenn v. 889 Associates, Ltd, 127 N.H. 321, 500 A.2d 366 (1985); Prah v. Maretti, 108 Wis.2d 223, 321 N.W.2d 182 (1982). *But see* Sher v. Leiderman, 181 Cal. App. 3d 867, 226 Cal. Rptr. 698 (1986). There also has been some legislative development. The California Solar Shade Control Act was the subject of discussion in Sher v. Leiderman, 181 Cal. App. 3d 867, 226 Cal. Rptr. 698 (1986).

Concern that those building first in American cities could block neighboring land owners from using their land by installing side windows appeared to motivate much of the nineteenth-century opposition to creating air and light access rights.

[d] Nuisance

The court rejected nuisance as well as prescriptive easement theory as a basis for relief in *Fontainebleau II,* noting that nuisance law has nothing to say so long as a property owner acts "so as not to injure the lawful *rights* of another." The court's reasoning was a bit circular. The right to expand the Fontainebleau Hotel was lawful only because the court refused to question prior decisions on ancient lights and nuisance. Furthermore, reliance on the uniform rejection by American courts of the English prescription doctrine of ancient lights as a basis for calling the Fontainebleau expansion lawful was misplaced; it is difficult to understand how prescription rules have anything to do with the meaning of lawfulness for purposes of nuisance law.

The most prominent decision on solar energy facilities and nuisance law has come from the Wisconsin Supreme Court—*Prah v. Maretti,* 108 Wis. 2d 223, 321 N.W.2d 182 (1982). Prah built a solar house. The owner of land next door planned to construct a house which would have cast shadows on some of Prah's facilities. The trial court's dismissal of the nuisance complaint was reversed and the case remanded for trial. The court noted that earlier desires to permit urban development without impediments from air and light access rights had been replaced by concerns over rapid land development and alternative energy sources.

[4] Problem Notes on Law and Facts

[a] Prescription

Even if you think that some protection should be provided to those investing in solar energy devices, is prescription the best way to go about it? Does it seem strange to argue that use of a solar energy device on your own land is adverse to the interests of a neighbor? And what about the length of time needed to perfect a prescriptive right? Isn't that a risky basis on which to develop alternative energy sources? Compare *Confederated Salish and Kootenai Tribes v. Vulles,* p. 84 above.

[b] Legislative Protections for Solar Energy Devices

Is legislative action needed to provide some predictable basis for knowing whether investment in solar energy facilities is worthwhile? While *Prah v. Maretti* was pending, the Wisconsin legislature adopted an act permitting local communities to create a land use permit system for those installing solar energy systems. Those with permits would then be protected from other conflicting land uses.[8] California has also adopted legislation protecting solar devices from growth of trees or shrubs.[9]

[c] Nuisance

What of nuisance law? Does the broadly stated nuisance rule—one must not use property to injure the property of another—provide a secure and predictable footing for resolving any dispute,

---

[8] WIS. STAT. ANN. § 66.032. Further information about the legislation may be found in Comment, *Wisconsin Recognizes the Power of the Sun:* Prah v. Maretti *and the Solar Access Act,* 1983 WIS. L. REV. 1263.

[9] CAL. PUB. RES. CODE § 25980 *et seq.* One court has held that passive solar devices, such as windows facing south with masonry in the background to absorb and hold solar energy, are not covered by the California legislation. *Sher v. Leiderman,* 181 Cal. App. 3d 867, 226 Cal. Rptr.698 (1986).

let alone one on alternative energy investments? Might economics provide some footholds in this sea of ambiguity? That is the subject of the next set of notes.

[5] *Fontainebleau* as an Economic Problem

The classic article on economics and nuisance disputes, *Property Rules, Liability Rules, and Inalienability,* was published by Guido Calabresi and Douglas Melamed in 1972.[10] They broke down nuisance problems into two areas of inquiry—assignment of the entitlement, or legal right to behave in a certain way, and protection of the entitlement by use of a "liability rule" or a "property rule." Liability rules award damages; property rules rely on injunctions. In this structure, four classes of outcomes may be reached. In the *Fontainebleau* case, for example, the Fontainebleau could be given the entitlement to build its addition protected by either a liability rule or a property rule, or the Eden Roc could be given the entitlement protected by either a liability rule or a property rule. The process of awarding the entitlement and deciding upon the remedy, Calabresi and Melamed argued, may involve a number of inquiries, including economic efficiency, distributional goals, and other considerations of justice and morality. Their primary aim, however, was to test the idea that once various costs are taken into account, economic efficiency may lead us to prefer one outcome rather than another.

Let's give the *Fontainebleau* setting some hypothetical numbers to play with in order to work through the use of entitlement theory in a fairly simple situation. First, assume that at the time the decision was made to enlarge the Fontainebleau Hotel, that the addition had a value of $20 million. This value would not be the cost of construction, but the present value of the income stream the addition would generate for the hotel.[11] Second, assume that the Fontainebleau had adequate space to construct a similarly sized addition in an attractive way without shading the Eden Roc pool, but that this plan would have cost more to build and reduced the present value of the addition from $20 million to $19 million. Third, assume that the impact on the Eden Roc of the ugly appearance of the hotel addition and its shading of the Eden Roc swimming pool reduced the present value of the Eden Roc Hotel by $2 million. Fourth, assume that the negative impact on the Eden Roc of the unattractive, sun shading addition could be reduced to $1.5 million by constructing a second swimming pool to the east of the old one.[12] Under these assumptions, what should a court do?

To begin, think about the case as it stood before construction started on the addition. After construction began, the monetary assumptions made above would surely change. Asking the Fontainebleau to tear down a partially completed building, for example, would impose significant costs. So if the Eden Roc seeks to bar construction of the addition, what should a court do? One way to think about it is to ask which outcome would lead to the greatest community wealth— the addition as planned without a new Eden Roc pool, the addition as planned with a new Eden

---

[10] 85 HARV. L. REV. 1089 (1972).

[11] *Present value* is a simple concept. If you put a dollar in the bank today and let it sit for, say 30 years, it will grow in value to say $10. The rate of growth will depend on prevailing interest rates. In this little example, the present value of the right to receive $10 in 30 years under prevailing interest rates is one dollar. As interest rates rise, the present value of the right to receive money in the future goes *down*. That is one of the impacts of high inflation. In addition, the use of present values absorbs the costs of construction into calculation by amortizing them over the life of the improvement. Present value calculates not the value of the gross income produced by the addition, but the net income.

[12] Like the value of the addition to the Fontainebleau, this number is in terms of present values. It, therefore, automatically takes the costs of construction into account by amortizing them over the life of the improvement.

Roc pool, or the more attractive addition on a different site without a new Eden Rock pool. Given the assumptions, we can figure this out.

Addition without new Eden Roc pool:

Increase in value of Fontainebleau	$20,000,000
Decrease in value of Eden Roc	-2,000,000
Result	$18,000,000

Addition with new Eden Roc pool:

Increase in value of Fontainebleau	$20,000,000
Decrease in value of Eden Roc	-1,500,000
Result	$18,500,000

Attractive addition in different location:

Increase in value of Fontainebleau	$19,000,000
Decrease in value of Eden Roc	0
Result	$19,000,000

If community wealth is the ultimate goal and no other costs existed, the last of the three outcomes would be preferred. Can that result be reached? For starters, assume there are no transactions costs of any sort involved in making trades between the parties or in constructing facilities. We will come back to the impact of this crucial assumption later.

First note, that if the Fontainebleau builds its unattractive, sun shading addition, the Eden Roc will always build a new swimming pool. The Eden Roc is $500,000 to the good by going ahead with a second pool. So the problem boils down to whether we can reach the result that the Fontainebleau builds an attractive addition elsewhere on its land. Under the entitlement system, we can award the right to stop the addition to the Eden Roc protected by either a property or liability rule or the right to build the addition to the Fontainebleau protected by either a property or liability rule. What happens under each option?

Eden Roc Entitlement with a Liability Rule: This outcome would allow the Eden Roc to recover damages if the Fontainebleau builds the unattractive addition. The damages would be $1.5 million. Rather than pay that amount the Fontainebleau would build its addition more attractively in another spot and reduce the value of its addition by only $1 million.

Eden Roc Entitlement with a Property Rule: This outcome would allow the Eden Roc to enjoin construction of the unattractive addition. Though the Fontainebleau would have the right to buy its way out of the injunction in a trade, it would have to pay at least $1.5 million to do so. Rather than pay, they would build the attractive addition in a different spot.

Fontainebleau Entitlement with a Liability Rule: This outcome would allow the Fontainebleau to build its addition and protect that decision by the right to receive damages. The damages for halting construction would be $1 million, the reduction in value occasioned by a location shift of the project. Since the Eden Roc would be better off by $1.5 million if the shift occurred, it would be willing to pay the Fontainebleau $1 million to move the project. The result after trade would be that the hotel would be moved, but the Eden Roc would pay the Fontainebleau $1 million to reach that result.

Fontainebleau Entitlement with a Property Rule: This outcome would allow the Fontainebleau to enjoin any interference with its project. The Eden Roc would be able to purchase the injunction.

It would have to pay at least $1 million to do so. In contrast to the outcome just above, however, the cost of the trade is not limited by the amount of liability to $1 million. The Eden Roc would be willing to pay up to just less than $1.5 million to move the project. A deal presumably would be reached at somewhere between $1 and $1.5 million, and the hotel would be built in a different spot.

The various outcomes can be summarized in an "entitlements table":

Fontainebleau Entitlements Table

Entitlement Goes To:	Remedy	Result After Trade
Eden Roc	Liability Rule (Damages)	Hotel Moves to New Spot. Eden Roc Pays Nothing.
Eden Roc	Property Rule (Injunction)	Hotel Moves to New Spot. Eden Roc Pays Nothing.
Fontainebleau	Liability Rule (Damages)	Hotel Moves to New Spot. Eden Roc pays Font. $1 million.
Fontainebleau	Property Rule (Injunction)	Hotel Moves to New Spot. Eden Roc pays Font. up to $1.5 million.

There are two characteristics of this table which are worth special note. First, the final result is the same in all outcomes—the addition gets moved to a new spot. This occurs because of two factors—the values built into the problem making the loss to Eden Rock larger than the cost of moving the Fontainebleau addition to a different spot, and the assumption that trade is cost free and frictionless. Second, the distributional outcomes are *not* the same. Depending upon which outcome you select, the total amount of increase in value held by both parties ($19 million) stays the same, but the amounts each entity holds varies. If the Eden Roc holds the entitlement, the value of its hotel stays the same and the value of the Fontainebleau rises by $19 million. If the Fontainebleau has the entitlement, the present value of the Eden Roc falls by either $1 million or somewhere between $1 and $1.5 million, and that of the Fontainebleau rises by an identical amount.

These outcomes reflect the results of the Coase Theorem[13] —the assignment of legal rights will not affect the ultimate outcome of a legal dispute if the transaction costs of trade between the parties is zero. The more conservative law and economics advocates have taken this result and argued that in order to avoid transaction costs inherent in trade, while retaining the maximum possible social wealth between the parties to a nuisance dispute, the entitlement should usually be awarded to the party who would purchase it, and this award should be protected by a liability rule. The idea is that even if transactions costs are non-zero, community wealth will be maximized by structuring the outcome to avoid the need for a transaction. The best known advocate for this position is Richard Posner. It is explained more fully in RICHARD POSNER, ECONOMIC ANALYSIS OF LAW 10-40 (1972). Thus, in the *Fontainebleau* example we have been playing with,

---

[13] The theorem was first described in Ronald Coase, *The Problem of Social Cost,* 3 J. L. & ECON. 1 (1960).

Posner would award the entitlement to the Eden Roc to avoid what would be, given the animosity between the parties, considerable transaction costs associated with a trade.

Many have critiqued the Posner position, arguing that its utility is reduced by our inability to precisely value preferences, the existence of transaction costs imposed by outsiders to the litigation, the existence of uncounted costs or benefits of the litigants' behavior on those not before the court, and the importance of justice considerations not taken into account by entitlements theory. Indeed, a recent study of twenty nuisance cases has found that no post-judgment bargaining of entitlements or remedies occured in any of them. Animosity betweeen the parties, together with unwillingness to deal in rights associated with nuisances precluded the making of any deals. Ward Farnsworth, *Do Parties to Nuisance Cases Bargain After Judgment? A Glimpse Inside the Cathedral,* 66 U. CHI. L. REV. 373 (1999). The antipathy present in the *Fontainbleau* case, it turns out, may be typical. At this point, an excerpt from a broad brush critique is printed below. More specific issues will be taken up in the discussion surrounding the problems taken up in the remaining pages of this chapter—the law of waste and pollution nuisances.

[6]   A Broad Brushed Critique of Law and Economics

When Richard Posner's book, ECONOMIC ANALYSIS OF LAW came out in 1972, it generated a large number of reviews. One of the most trenchant was written by Arthur Leff, now viewed as an early standard bearer for the Critical Legal Studies movement. Leff himself did not live long enough to see the influence his views would have. He died of cancer at a young age in 1981.

Arthur Leff, *Economic Analysis of Law: Some Realism About Nominalism*

60 VA. L. REV. 451, 453-458, 477-482 (1974)[14]

The Way We Live Today

Let us start with a couple of vicious intellectual parodies. Once upon a time there was Formalism. The law itself was a deductive system, with unquestionable premises leading to ineluctable conclusions. It was, potentially at least, all consistent and pervasive. Oh, individual judges messed up, and even individual professors, and their misperceptions and mispronouncements needed rationalization, connection, and correction. But that was the proper job of one of the giants we had in the earth in those days. The job of legal commentators, and *a fortiori* of treatise writers, was to find the consistent thread in the inconsistent statements of others and pull it all together along the seam of what was implicit in "the logic of the system." When you found enough threads and pulled them just hard enough, you made a very neat bag . . . .

Then, out of the hills, came the Realists. What their messianic message was has never been totally clear. But it is generally accepted that, at least in comparison to the picture of their predecessors which they drew for themselves, they were much more interested in the way law actually functioned in society. There were *men* in law, and the law created by men had an effect on other men in society. The critical questions were hence forward no longer to be those of systematic consistency, but of existential reality. You could no longer criticize law in terms of logical operations, but only in terms of operational logic.

---

[14] Reprinted by permission of the Virginia Law Review Association and Fred B. Rothman & Co.

Now such a move, while liberating, was also ultimately terrifying. For if you were interested in a society, and with law as an operative variable within that society, you would have to find out something about that subject matter and those operations. You would, it seems, have to become an empiricist. That, as we shall see, is no picnic when the facts you are searching out are social facts. But there is a worse worry yet. If you no longer are allowed to believe in a deductive system, if criticism is no longer solely logical, you no longer can avoid the question of *premises*. Premises, in terms of logic, are just that: those things you don't talk about. But if you are under an obligation to talk about non-foreordained conclusions, you must start to talk about non-given starting points. Any (mostly implicit) assumptions that one's premises in some mysterious manner are at least congruent with the commands of the universe would (and did) come under increasing pressure. If "good" were seen solely in terms of effects, the only good premises were those that came up with good effects. Thus, by dropping formalism we (quite rightly) fell into the responsibility of good and evil.

But not, alas, the knowledge thereof. While all this was going on, most likely conditioning it in fact, the knowledge of good and evil, as an intellectual subject, was being systematically and effectively destroyed. The historical fen through which ethical wanderings led was abolished in the early years of this century (not for the first time, but very clearly this time); normative thought crawled out of the swamp and died in the desert. There arose a great number of schools of ethics—axiological, materialistic, evolutionary, intuitionist, situational, existentialist, and so on—but they all suffered the same fate: either they were seen to be ultimately premised on some intuition (buttressed or not by nosecounts of those seemingly having the same intuitions), or they were even more arbitrary than that, based solely on some "for the sake of argument" premises. I will put the current situation as sharply and nastily as possible: there is today no way of "proving" that napalming babies is bad except by asserting it (in a louder and louder voice), or by defining it as so, early in one's game, and then later slipping it through, in a whisper, as a conclusion.

Now this is a fact of modern intellectual life so well and painfully known as to be one of the few which is simultaneously horrifying and banal. As I said, I raise it here only because it seems so very important both in explaining and understanding Posner's book, and the impulse in current legal scholarship it exemplifies.

Let us say you found yourself facing a universe normatively empty and empirically overflowing. What I suppose you would want most to do, if you wanted to talk at all, would be to find some grid you could place over this buzzing data to generate a language which would at the same time provide a critical terminology ("X is bad because . . .") and something in terms of which the criticism could be made (that is, something to follow the "because . . ."). Now "because it is" is a bit naked as a satisfactory explanation. "Because you won't get to Y that way" is better, but when you make "good" teleological, you rather promptly run into "what's so great about Y?" It is hardly convincing if you explain the goodness of X in terms of the desirability of Y if you can't say anything more about Y than that it is desirable. You might just as well skip the intervening step and stick with X, saying all the pretty things about it itself, rather than about its product.

But what if you said X wasn't "good" or anything like that, that is, wasn't normative at all? What if you described X solely in empirical terms, for instance, X is what people, as a matter of fact, want. That way you can get to the well-known neo-Panglossian position of classic utilitarianism: while all is not for the best (because the best is what people want and they don't have it yet), the best is still nothing more than what they do want. Admittedly, this is just an example of one of the now-classic normative copouts—essentially, "good" becomes just a function of nosecounting—but it does have the advantage of providing a ready-made critical vocabulary: because there is now a clear area between what people want and what they have, while you can no longer say that doing anything is bad, you *can* say of some things that they are being done badly.

Of course, you still haven't solved all your intellectual (or practical) problems. The world may no longer be normatively empty (you've filled it by definitional fiat), but it is still full of all sorts of puzzling things. You have, that is, solved only one difficult problem. True, you need no longer ask if people *ought* to desire other things than they do desire, for those desires are the measure of all things. But what do people (some or all and is that relevant?) desire? If you don't know that, then you can't criticize what they presently have, or what they are right now doing, with reference to their failure to reach that desire. That is, while you are now working with *is* -terms only (you have escaped the dreaded *ought*), they are, as a matter of fact, very difficult matters of fact: what indeed *is* of "value" must be known before one rates the "efficiency" in getting there. Thus it is possible that all you have ended up doing is substituting for the arbitrariness of ethics the impossibilities of epistemology.[9]

Now all of the above is but by way of introduction to Posner's solution to these scarifying problems.[10] He does indeed solve the normative "oughtness" problems by the neo-Panglossian move: good is defined as that which is in fact desired. But then he makes a very pretty move, one that renders his work, and work like it, so initially attractive to the dwellers of the box: in place of what one might have expected (and feared)—a complex regimen for an empirical investigation of human wants and values—he puts a single-element touchstone, so narrow a view of the critical empirical question as to be, essentially, a definition. "What people want" is presented in such a way that while it is in form empirical, it is almost wholly non-falsifiable by anything so crude as fact.

To follow this initially attractive development in legal criticism (for purposes both of admiration and scorn), one will have to master the critical early moves. The first and most basic is "the assumption that man is a rational maximizer of his ends in life . . . ." As Posner points out, this assumption "is no stronger than that most people in most affairs of life are guided by what they conceive to be their self-interest and that they choose means reasonably (not perfectly) designed to promote it."

. . . . In other words, since people are rationally self-interested, what they *do* shows what they value, and their willingness to pay for what they value is proof of their rational self-interest. Nothing merely empirical could get in the way of such a structure because it is definitional. That is why the assumptions can predict how people behave: in *these* terms there

---

[9] This may be a not quite fair, but close enough, description of utilitarian ethics in general.

[10] A note on the relationship between this book and economic analysis in general is necessary at this point. Am I talking about Posner's particular brand of economics, or something wider? More precisely, am I commenting upon and sometimes criticizing a "school" of economic analysis, or the thing in itself? My uncertain answer is that I really don't know, for I am not really widely enough acquainted with enough of the literature to be able to make any independent contribution to any "schools" controversy. I certainly do not think that the downward sloping demand curve is some kind of "political" tenet of the "Chicago School." But good economists disagree about many things, many of which are relevant to what I say here. Thus, whenever I refer herein to "economic analysis," even in lower case, let it be taken as having no necessarily wider application than to its particular context, that is, the book under review.

is no other way they can behave.[19] If, for instance, a society dentist raises his prices and thereby increases his gross volume of business, it is no violation of the principle of inverse relation between price and quantity. It only proves that the buyers now perceive that they are buying something else which they now value more highly, "society dentistry," say, rather than "mere" dentistry. And if circularity isn't sufficient, the weak version of the rational maximization formula ("most people in most affairs of life . . . choose means reasonably (not perfectly) designed . . . .") has the effect of chewing up and spitting out any discordant empirical data anyway. Any puzzling observation fed into that kind of definition will always be able to find a "most," or a "reasonably," way out.[20]

Thus what people do is good, and its goodness can be determined by looking at what it is they do. In place of the more arbitrary normative "goods" of Formalism, *and* in place of the more complicated empirical "goods" of Realism, stands the simple definitionally circular "value" of Posner's book. If human desire itself becomes normative (in the sense that it cannot be criticized), and if human desire is made definitionally identical with certain human acts, then those human acts are also beyond criticism in normative or efficiency terms; everyone is doing as best he can exactly what he set out to do which, by definition, is "good" for him. In those terms, it is not at all surprising that economic analyses have "considerable power in predicting how people in fact behave."[21]

. . . .

Smuggling Normatives: How To Win for Friends and Influential People

. . . For all of his claims to non-normativity, it is obvious that there is at least one value *qua* value that directs and informs Posner's whole analysis. God (and history) knows it's one that does him credit: individual human freedom. One could, I suppose, treat Posner's making his whole structure balance on a definition of value in terms of individual human desire as hypothetical or accidental, but that would be silly. As normatives go, freedom is a good good, and there's no reason for anyone to be embarrassed by its espousal. For Posner, freedom— individual freedom—is a merit good, and why not; it's certainly no worse than, say, equality.

But having said that human freedom is the subterranean value upon which *Economic Analysis of Law* stands, and having praised that foundation, I cannot bring myself to stop. I know I

---

[19] This may also help to answer George Stigler's question why, though professional bliss awaits anyone who proves false the "law of demand," no one has yet done so. Academic knighthood does *not* await anyone who merely violates someone else's system of definitions. *See* G. STIGLER, THE THEORY OF PRICE 24 (3d ed. 1966). For a short but elegant discussion of the empirical status of certain basic economic hypotheses, *see* P. SAMUELSON, FOUNDATIONS OF ECONOMIC ANALYSIS 90-92 (1947).

[20] It is painful to point this out to an economist-lawyer, but most reasonably adequate sociologists would blush to present any such standard as part of a research matrix for an empirical study. Compare P. Samuelson, *supra* note 19, at 92:

Nevertheless . . . the modern utility theory with all its qualifications is not in a technical sense *meaningless*. It *is* a hypothesis which places definite restrictions upon demand functions and price-quantity data; these could be refuted or verified under ideal observational conditions. One should have thought that these empirical implications would have been the sole end of the theorists who have concerned themselves with these matters. Strangely enough, means and ends have been so confused that only a small fraction of the literature has been concerned with this problem even indirectly; moreover, in this there are scarcely half a dozen papers in which valid demand restrictions have been developed. (Emphasis in original.)

[21] . . . That is often the problem with heuristically simplified models; when you think you are describing a curve, you are really describing the graph paper.

should. Normative premises are just that; they don't get any more proved by being talked about. But I am just not up to resisting the modern moralist's temptation: even if I cannot say anything sensible about the choice of an intuitionist good, I shall nonetheless run on a while about the logical consistency and intellectual elegance of its deployment.[70]

All right, let us consider, one last time, Posner's key definitional paragraph:

> Despite the use of terms like "value" and "efficiency," economics cannot tell us how society should be managed. Efficiency is a technical term: it means exploiting economic resources in such a way that human satisfaction as measured by aggregate consumer willingness to pay for goods and services is maximized. Value too is defined by willingness to pay. Willingness to pay is in turn a function of the existing distribution of income and wealth in the society. Were income and wealth distributed in a different pattern, the pattern of demands might also be different and efficiency would require a different deployment of our economic resources. The economist cannot tell us whether the existing distribution of income and wealth is just, although he may be able to tell us something about the costs of altering it as well as about the distributive consequences of various policies. Nor can he tell us whether, assuming the existing distribution is just, consumer satisfaction should be the dominant value of society. The economist's competence in a discussion of the legal system is limited to predicting the effect of legal rules and arrangements on value and efficiency, in their strict technical senses, and on the existing distribution of income and wealth.[71]

In such a system whatever is, is. If you do not "buy" something, you are *unwilling* to do so. There is no place for the word or concept "unable." Thus, in this system, there is nothing which is coerced. For instance, let us say that a starving man approaches a loaf of bread held by an armed baker. Another potential buyer is there. The baker institutes an auction; he wants cash only (having too great doubts about the starveling's health to be interested in granting credit). The poor man gropes in his pockets and comes up with a dollar. The other bidder immediately takes out $1.01 and makes off with the bread. Now under Posner's definitional system we must say that the "value" of the bread was no more than a dollar to the poor man because he was "unwilling" to pay more than that. An observer not bound within that particular definitional structure might find it somehow more illuminating to characterize the poor man's failure as being the result of being unable to pay more than a dollar. But one cannot, consistent with Posner's system, say any such thing. One's actual power is irrelevant.

Now, if one were to suggest that one's basic definitional structure ought to be altered to take account of a possible critical distinction between two empirically discernible kinds of "unwillingness"—to confront the possible effect of various kinds and levels of brute necessity upon will—one would not be changing the *realm* of definition. That is, no attempt would thereby be made to generate some normative definition of value. If one defines value in terms of objective willingness to pay (*i.e.*, actually paying), to see those acts as ambiguous across certain ranges of actualization is not to call them better or worse, but only more complex.

---

[70] Let me nonetheless make clear that proving logical inconsistency within an ethical system has no effect at all on its "validity." The propositions (1) $A > B$; (2) $B > C$; (3) $C > A$ are logically incoherent; they are not evil. And for any closet Kantians among you, it should be pointed out that the proposition, "Act always as if under a general law applicable to all mankind except Morris Schwelb" is pretty silly, but hardly immoral. That is, there is no meta-ethical rule that morality be logically elegant, or even comprehensible.

[71] Posner 4-5.

But let us pass all that. A man is entitled to his own definitional structures for his own "non-normative" deductions. It is, after all, not very useful to tell Richard that unarmed Morris' fleeing a battlefield in the face of an armored division coming his way is not "cowardice" when Richard has just written "'Cowardice' is defined as fleeing a battlefield in the face of an armored division coming one's way." All you can say is that if you had the defining to do, you might have defined cowardice somewhat differently. And that is not really to the point.

If, however, one thinks intellectual consistency is worth talking about, it is worth pointing out that a similar argument can, perhaps must, be made if one applies Posner's definitional structure to political decisions. There are two ways to put the case. One is that if the poor man is forever to be deemed "unwilling" to buy, then the individual (rich or not) must be deemed "unwilling" to change or leave the political system, and so we will not hear his complaints about being coerced. That is tempting, but maybe it would be more instructive to say no more than that in both cases, he is "unwilling" to pay the price charged. The poor man could grab the bread (and risk being shot); the political man, unsatisfied with his lot, could revolt and seek to form his own polity (and risk getting squashed). In each case, all that stands in his way is a serious worry about his likelihood of success, given the inequality of power between him and the others.

What this all means is that Posner has not played fair with the question of power, or inequalities thereof. He has made a very common move: *after* something of value has been distributed he has defined *taking* as illicit and *keeping* (except when paid) as in tune with the expressed wishes of the universe. It is not as if force is never to be used; Posner assumes, indeed commands, its use against theft. One of the purposes of the state is to detect the terrible inefficiencies of non-consensual transfers by having the government really smash those who persist in such behavior. But by and large the government is to have no role in even annoying those who choose to exclude others from what they already have. Keepers keepers, so to speak.

But why is that? Let us say I am naturally superior to a rich man in taking things, either by my own strength or by organizing aggregations of others (call them governments) to do my will. I am not much of a trader, but I'm one hell of a grabber. That's just the way things are. Is there any way to criticize my activities except from the standpoint of taste (or some other normative proposition)? It would be inefficient to allow violent acquisitions? How can one know that? All of Posner's arguments about the efficiency-inducing effects of private property assume only that someone has the right to use and exclude, not that it be any particular person. If force, organized or not, were admissible as a method of acquisition there is no reason to assume that eventual equilibrium would not be reached, albeit in different hands than it presently rests. After all, as Posner would be the first to tell you, "force" is just an expenditure. If a man is "willing" to pay that price, and the other party is "unwilling" to pay the price of successful counterforce, we have an "efficient" solution. That is, we are "exploiting economic resources in such a way that human satisfaction as measured by aggregate consumer willingness to pay for goods and services is maximized."

In brief, there seems to be some normative content in Posner's neo-Panglossianism after all. Only some kinds of inequality are to be accepted as an unquestionable *grundnorm* upon which to base efficiency analyses.[75] The transfers that come about against a background of

---

[75] Posner is ostentatiously close-mouthed about how wealth inequalities may originally have occurred and been perpetuated. *See Posner* 10-15 for the relevant void. It is certainly possible that some of this ground-state material inequality is directly or indirectly the result of prior force, applied individually or politically. For an illuminating and sophisticated discussion of "entitlements," initial and other, *see* Calabresi & Melamed, *Property Rules, Liability Rules, and Inalienability: One View of the Cathedral,* 85 HARV. L. REV. 1089, 1090-93 (1972).

wealth inequality are fine; any that come about against a background of inequality in strength, or the power to organize and apply strength, are unjustifiable. Some inequalities are apparently more equal than others—and all without reference to any apparent normative criterion at all.

Conclusion

There is none, and that's the point. We all know that all value is not a sole function of willingness to pay, and that it's a grievous mistake to use a tone which implies (while the words deny) that it is. Man may be the measure of all things, but he is not beyond measurement himself.[76] I don't know how one talks about it, but napalming babies *is* bad, and so is letting them or even their culpable parents starve, freeze, or merely suffer plain miserable discomfort while other people, more "valuable" than they are or not, freely choose snowmobiles and whipped cream. Whatever is wrong with all that, it is only partly statistical. People are neither above reproach, nor are they ever just "sunk costs." *And "the law" has always known it; that is the source of its tension and complexity.* If economic efficiency is part of the common law (and it is), so is *fiat justitia, ruat coelum.*[77]

Thus, though one *can* graph (non-interpersonally comparable) marginal utilities for money which are the very picture of geometric nymphomania,[78] we still preserve our right to say to those whose personalities generate such curves, "You swine," or "When did you first notice this anal compulsion overwhelming you?" or even "Beware the masses." And indeed "the law," even "the common law," has on impulses like those often said, even against efficiency—"Sorry buddy, you lose."

I admit that it is not easy these days to be a moralist *manqué,* when what it is that one lacks is any rational and coherent way to express one's intuitions. That's why it is, today, so very hard to be a thinking lawyer. But I will tell you this: substituting definitions for both facts and values is not notably likely to fill the echoing void. Much as I admire the many genuine insights of American Legal Nominalism, I think we shall have to continue wrestling with a universe filled with too many things about which we understand too little and then evaluate them against standards we don't even have. That doesn't mean that any of us— especially bright, talented and sensitive people like Richard Posner—should stop what they are doing and gaze silently into the buzz. What he is doing and has done (including this book) enriches us all. But (to get back to where we started) he (and all of us) should keep in mind what I think is the most lovely moment in *Don Quixote.* When asked by a mocking Duke if he actually believes in the real existence of his lady Dulcinea, the Don replies:

> This is not one of those cases where you can prove a thing conclusively. I have not begotten or given birth to my lady, although I contemplate her as she needs must be . . . .[79]

One can understand the impulse, and be touched by the attempt, but the world is never as it needs must be. If it ever so seems, it is not the thing illuminated one is seeing, but the light.

---

[76] Man may even be changeable. God forbid that human nature should be inalterable—and there is even some theological warrant for the suggestion that He did.

[77] There is also the cognate aesthetic position, which may also be a delusion, that the "value" of art is not solely a function of price, even if price is taken to be a function of human evaluation.

[78] *See Posner* 216-17. The graph actually drawn at page 217 shows only mild greed. Posner's text promised a graph which compared the marginal utilities of a millionaire and a pauper. Had that actually been drawn, the nastiness of the situation would have been much more apparent.

[79] M. CERVANTES, DON QUIXOTE, Part II, ch. XXXII (S. Putnam transl. 1949).

§ 10.04 Waste: Property Use Conflicts Over Time

[1] Background to *Baker v. Weedon*

Nuisance-like land use conflicts arise in a variety of settings. There is potential for litigation any time uses of two different property interests come into conflict. While the label "nuisance" is usually applied only to disputes between neighboring land owners, analytically similar issues arise when servient tenements complain about the activities of the owner of servitudes or when owners of remainder interests disagree with the actions of the life tenant. This section deals with discord in this last situation—property divided over time between the holder of a life estate and the owners of a remainder.

The fact statement in the *Baker v. Weedon* opinion gives a reasonably full explanation of the story, but there are a few additional items that might interest you. As you will read, this is a tale about land left to a robust young wife for life and distant relatives in remainder. The land is located near Corinth, Mississippi, a town which had just under 12,000 people in 1990. While not a very large place, its growth made the land Anna Plaxico Weedon was entitled to use for her life fairly valuable. After 1964, when a highway bypass around town was run through the Weedon farm, land investors got very interested in buying the place. Anna Weedon was by then an impoverished woman living in the same farmhouse (without electricity or running water) that had been on the land for a century.

One day Anna Weedon showed up at the offices of William L. Sharp, a local attorney.[15] Sharp had heard various rumors that people were interested in buying the old Weedon place, but had never met Weedon. She asked him to try to sell the farm for her. Sharp then filed a lawsuit, seeking to force a judicial sale of the land. His request for a sale was granted by the Alcorn County Chancery Division in an unreported opinion, and the holders of the remainder took an appeal.

Anna Weedon's first husband had two prior wives and four children. His marriage tree, depicted in the following chart, may help you decipher the appellate opinion.

---

[15] My thanks of Mr. Sharp, of Sharp & Fisher in Corinth, Mississippi, for describing some of the details of the case. Telephone Interviews (July 11 and Aug. 14, 1986).

WEEDON MARRIAGE TREE

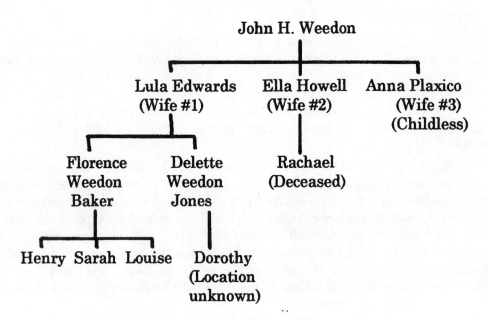

John H. Weedon

Lula Edwards
(Wife #1)

Ella Howell
(Wife #2)

Anna Plaxico
(Wife #3)
(Childless)

Florence
Weedon
Baker

Delette
Weedon
Jones

Rachael
(Deceased)

Henry Sarah Louise

Dorothy
(Location
unknown)

[2] Opinion of the Mississippi Supreme Court in *Baker v. Weedon*

Baker v. Weedon

Mississippi Supreme Court
262 So.2d 641 (1972)

PATTERSON, JUSTICE:

This is an appeal from a decree of the Chancery Court of Alcorn County. It directs a sale of land affected by a life estate and future interests with provision for the investment of the proceeds. The interest therefrom is to be paid to the life tenant for her maintenance. We reverse and remand.

John Harrison Weedon was born in High Point, North Carolina. He lived throughout the South and was married twice prior to establishing his final residence in Alcorn County. His first marriage to Lula Edwards resulted in two siblings, Mrs. Florence Weedon Baker and Mrs. Delette Weedon Jones. Mrs. Baker was the mother of three children, Henry Baker, Sarah Baker Lyman and Louise Virginia Baker Heck, the appellants herein. Mrs. Delette Weedon Jones adopted a daughter, Dorothy Jean Jones, who has not been heard from for a number of years and whose whereabouts are presently unknown.

John Weedon was next married to Ella Howell and to this union there was born one child, Rachel. Both Ella and Rachel are now deceased.

Subsequent to these marriages John Weedon bought Oakland Farm in 1905 and engaged himself in its operation. In 1915 John, who was then 55 years of age, married Anna Plaxico, 17 years of age. This marriage, though resulting in no children, was a compatible relationship. John and Anna worked side by side in farming this 152.95-acre tract of land in Alcorn County. There can be no doubt that Anna's contribution to the development and existence of Oakland

Farm was significant. The record discloses that during the monetarily difficult years following World War I she hoed, picked cotton and milked an average of fifteen cows per day to protect the farm from financial ruin.

While the relationship of John and Anna was close and amiable, that between John and his daughters of his first marriage was distant and strained. He had no contact with Florence, who was reared by Mr. Weedon's sister in North Carolina, during the seventeen years preceding his death. An even more unfortunate relationship existed between John and his second daughter, Delette Weedon Jones. She is portrayed by the record as being a nomadic person who only contacted her father for money, threatening on several occasions to bring suit against him.

With an obvious intent to exclude his daughters and provide for his wife Anna, John executed his last will and testament in 1925. It provided in part:

Second; I give and bequeath to my beloved wife, Anna Plaxico Weedon all of my property both real, personal and mixed during her natural life and upon her death to her children, if she has any, and in the event she dies without issue then at the death of my wife Anna Plaxico Weedon I give, bequeath and devise all of my property to my grandchildren, each grandchild sharing equally with the other.

Third; In this will I have not provided for my daughters, Mrs. Florence Baker and Mrs. Delette Weedon Jones, the reason is, I have given them their share of my property and they have not looked after and cared for me in the latter part of my life.

Subsequent to John Weedon's death in 1932 and the probate of his will, Anna continued to live on Oakland Farm. In 1933 Anna, who had been urged by John to remarry in the event of his death, wed J. E. Myers. This union lasted some twenty years and produced no offspring which might terminate the contingent remainder vested in Weedon's grandchildren by the will.

There was no contact between Anna and John Weedon's children or grandchildren from 1932 until 1964. Anna ceased to operate the farm in 1955 due to her age and it has been rented since that time. Anna's only income is $1000 annually from the farm rental, $300 per year from sign rental and $50 per month by way of social security payments. Without contradiction Anna's income is presently insufficient and places a severe burden upon her ability to live comfortably in view of her age and the infirmities therefrom.

In 1964 the growth of the city of Corinth was approaching Oakland Farm. A right-of-way through the property was sought by the Mississippi State Highway Department for the construction of U.S. Highway 45 bypass. The highway department located Florence Baker's three children, the contingent remaindermen by the will of John Weedon, to negotiate with them for the purchase of the right-of-way. Dorothy Jean Jones, the adopted daughter of Delette Weedon Jones, was not located and due to the long passage of years, is presumably dead. A decree proconfesso was entered against her.

Until the notice afforded by the highway department the grandchildren were unaware of their possible inheritance. Henry Baker, a native of New Jersey, journeyed to Mississippi to supervise their interests. He appears, as was true of the other grandchildren, to have been totally sympathetic to the conditions surrounding Anna's existence as a life tenant. A settlement of $20,000 was completed for the right-of-way bypass of which Anna received $7500 with which to construct a new home. It is significant that all legal and administrative fees were deducted from the shares of the three grandchildren and not taxed to the life tenant. A contract was executed in 1970 for the sale of soil from the property for $2500. Anna received $1000 of this sum which went toward completion of payments for the home.

There was substantial evidence introduced to indicate the value of the property is appreciating significantly with the nearing completion of U.S. Highway 45 bypass plus the growth of the city of Corinth. While the commercial value of the property is appreciating, it is notable that the rental value for agricultural purposes is not. It is apparent that the land can bring no more for agricultural rental purposes than the $1000 per year now received.

The value of the property for commercial purposes at the time of trial was $168,500. Its estimated value within the ensuing four years is placed at $336,000, reflecting the great influence of the interstate construction upon the land. Mr. Baker, for himself and other remaindermen, appears to have made numerous honest and sincere efforts to sell the property at a favorable price. However, his endeavors have been hindered by the slowness of the construction of the bypass.

Anna, the life tenant and appellee here, is 73 years of age and although now living in a new home, has brought this suit due to her economic distress. She prays that the property, less the house site, be sold by a commissioner and that the proceeds be invested to provide her with an adequate income resulting from interest on the trust investment. She prays also that the sale and investment management be under the direction of the chancery court.

The chancellor granted the relief prayed by Anna under the theory of economic waste. His opinion reflects:

> . . . [T]he change of the economy in this area, the change in farming conditions, the equipment required for farming, and the age of this complainant leaves the real estate where it is to all intents and purposes unproductive when viewed in light of its capacity and that a continuing use under the present conditions would result in economic waste.

The contingent remaindermen by the will, appellants here, were granted an interlocutory appeal to settle the issue of the propriety of the chancellor's decree in divesting the contingency title of the remaindermen by ordering a sale of the property.

The weight of authority reflects a tendency to afford a court of equity the power to order the sale of land in which there are future interests. Simes, *Law of Future Interest,* section 53 (2d ed. 1966), states:

> By the weight of authority, it is held that a court of equity has the power to order a judicial sale of land affected with a future interest and an investment of the proceeds, where this is necessary for the preservation of all interests in the land. When the power is exercised, the proceeds of the sale are held in a judicially created trust. The beneficiaries of the trust are the persons who held interests in the land, and the beneficial interests are of the same character as the legal interests which they formally held in the land.

This Court has long recognized that chancery courts do have jurisdiction to order the sale of land for the prevention of waste . . . .

While Mississippi and most jurisdictions recognize the inherent power of a court of equity to direct a judicial sale of land which is subject to a future interest, nevertheless the scope of this power has not been clearly defined. It is difficult to determine the facts and circumstances which will merit such a sale.

It is apparent that there must be "necessity" before the chancery court can order a judicial sale. It is also beyond cavil that the power should be exercised with caution and only when the need is evident . . . [such as] where the freehold estate [is] deteriorating and the income therefrom [is] insufficient to pay taxes and maintain the property. In [such cases] . . . this court [has] approved a judicial sale to preserve and maintain the estate. The appellants argue, therefore, that since Oakland Farm is not deteriorating and since there is sufficient income from rental to pay taxes, a judicial sale by direction of the court was not proper.

The unusual circumstances of this case persuade us to the contrary. We are of the opinion that deterioration and waste of the property is not the exclusive and ultimate test to be used in determining whether a sale of land affected by future interest is proper, but also that consideration should be given to the question of whether a sale is necessary for the best interest of all the parties, that is, the life tenant and the contingent remaindermen. This "necessary for the best interest of all parties" rule is gleaned from Rogers, *Removal of Future Interest Encumbrances— Sale of the Fee Simple Estate,* 17 Vanderbilt L. Rev. 1437 (1964); Simes, *Law of Future Interest, supra*; Simes and Smith, *The Law of Future Interests,* § 1941 (1956); and appears to have the necessary flexibility to meet the requirements of unusual and unique situations which demand in justice an equitable solution.

Our decision to reverse the chancellor and remand the case for his further consideration is couched in our belief that the best interest of all the parties would not be served by a judicial sale of the entirety of the property at this time. While true that such a sale would provide immediate relief to the life tenant who is worthy of this aid in equity, admitted by the remaindermen, it would nevertheless under the circumstances before us cause great financial loss to the remaindermen.

We therefore reverse and remand this cause to the chancery court, which shall have continuing jurisdiction thereof, for determination upon motion of the life tenant, if she so desires, for relief by way of sale of a part of the burdened land sufficient to provide for her reasonable needs from interest derived from the investment of the proceeds. The sale, however, is to be made only in the event the parties cannot unite to hypothecate the land for sufficient funds for the life tenant's reasonable needs. By affording the options above we do not mean to suggest that other remedies suitable to the parties which will provide economic relief to the aging life tenant are not open to them if approved by the chancellor. It is our opinion, shared by the chancellor and acknowledged by the appellants, that the facts suggest an equitable remedy. However, it is our further opinion that this equity does not warrant the remedy of sale of all of the property since this would unjustly impinge upon the vested rights of the remaindermen.

[3]   Explanatory Notes

[a]   Later Events

After the Mississippi Supreme Court remanded the matter, the Chancery Division ordered that the bulk of the land be sold, and instructed that the proceeds of the sale be held in trust for Anna Plaxico Weedon for her life. About 110 acres were sold. Several tracts were sold in small parcels, but the bulk of the acreage went to Hall Printing Company, which then printed (among other things) The National Geographic and Playboy. The rest of the land was retained, including five acres surrounding her new home. As of 1988, she still lived there. According to Anna Weedon's attorney, the trust income provided her a "comfortable living." Upon her death, the trust will be distributed in accordance with the terms of John Weedon's will.

[b]   Use *Baker v. Weedon* to Review Some Future Interest Terminology

Label the various interests created by the Weedon will in Anna Plaxico, her children, and John Weedon's grandchildren. Be careful to take into account the fact that the will provided that after the death of Anna, the land should first go to the children of Anna, not the children of Weedon's marriage with Anna, and only later to the grandchildren of Weedon. What would the interests be if Anna Plaxico Weedon had a child? The answer to this question might not be clear. For example, would her children have to survive her? If so, their interest would be contingent upon survival. If not, their interest would be vested subject to open upon the birth of additional children. At the time the case was decided, what interest was held by the grandchildren of John Weedon?

[c]   Decree Proconfesso Against Delette Weedon Jones

The court noted that a decree proconfesso was entered against Delette Weedon Jones. This is a device for handling cases when the whereabouts of an interested party is not known. Attempts will be made to find the party and notice will be placed in newspapers published in the last known location of the missing person. If no response is made, the court will proceed with the case without the participation of the missing person.

[d]   Sale of Unproductive Land

The Uniform Principal and Income Act, which has been adopted by Mississippi, contains a section on the disposition of unproductive land. Section 12 of the Uniform Act, as codified in Mississippi, provides:

§ 91-17-25. Underproductive property.

(1) Except as otherwise provided in this section, a portion of the net proceeds of sale of any part of principal which has not produced an average net income of at least one per cent (1%) per year of its inventory value for more than a year (including as income the value of any beneficial use of the property by the income beneficiary) shall be treated as delayed income to which the income beneficiary is entitled as provided in this section. The net proceeds of sale are the gross proceeds received, including the value of any property received in substitution for the property disposed of, less the expenses, including capital gains tax, if any, incurred in disposition and less any carrying charge paid while the property was underproductive.

(2) The sum allocated as delayed income is the difference between the net proceeds and the amount which, had it been invested at simple interest at four per cent (4%) per year while the property was underproductive, would have produced the net proceeds. This sum, plus any carrying charges and expenses previously charged against income while the property was underproductive, less any income received by the income beneficiary from the property and less the value of any beneficial use of the property by the income beneficiary, is income, and the balance is principal.

(3) An income beneficiary or his estate is entitled to delayed income under this section as if it accrued from day to day during the time he was a beneficiary.

(4) If principal subject to this section is disposed of by conversion into property which cannot be apportioned easily, including land or mortgages (for example, realty acquired by or in lieu of foreclosure), the income beneficiary is entitled to the net income from any property or

obligation into which the original principal is converted while the substituted property or obligation is held. If within five (5) years after the conversion the substituted property has not been further converted into easily apportionable property, no allocation as provided in this section shall be made.

This statute certainly suggests that the Mississippi state legislature anticipated that settings like *Baker* might necessitate some unusual rules about allocation between principal and income. But does it help resolve the actual case?

[e] Present and Future Values

The land held for life by Anna Plaxico Weedon was said to be worth $168,500 at the time of the trial. The court found that its value four years later probably was going to be about $336,000. That sounds like a huge difference. In most cases, doubling the sale price in four years would be a very significant rate of return. But if inflation was quite high, say just under 20% annually, then receipt of $336,000 in four years would be worth about the same as getting $168,500 today. The present value of the right to receive money in the future must, therefore, be discounted by some assumed inflation rate in order to get a true picture of the value of the right. This sort of problem is basic to a full understanding of the impact of a result like *Baker v. Weedon.*

From the table just below you can see the effect inflation assumptions have on valuations of the present worth of the right to receive $336,000 in four years:

Present Value of Future Right to Money	Inflation Rate Assumed	Value in Four Years
$247,000	8%	$336,000
$256,000	7%	$336,000
$266,000	6%	$336,000
$276,000	5%	$336,000

Thus, if the land had been sold for $168,500 in the year of the trial and inflation was 8% during the following four years, the actual loss to the capital held in trust would have been the difference between the sale price and the present value of the right to receive $336,000 in four years, or $247,000. The loss would therefore be just under $90,000. In the actual case, the loss did not really occur since the land was not sold until after the litigation was completed. The delay caused by the litigation served the owners of the remainder well. It eventually also served Anna Plaxico Weedon well, though she had to put up with years of privation before she finally was able to obtain a better income stream from her property. Given her age, that was not clearly a good bargain.

[4] Notes on *Baker v. Weedon* as a Nuisance Problem

Was the decision to sell most of the land the appropriate one? If the land's value was rising (as Weedon's attorney indicates it was) at the time of the sale, was it not in the best interests of the owners of the remainder to delay selling the property? Are they entitled to the most money they can make or the most money consistent with the ability of the owner of the life estate to obtain income from the asset? If the latter, how do you mediate the differing economic interests of the two sets of owners?[16] Is it a "reasonable" substitute for the owners of the remainder that the amount of money received for the land will increase in size over time if investments prove to be wisely made? These sorts of problems are endemic whenever land is split between a present possessory interest and a future interest.

To focus your analysis a bit, consider three slightly different situations. In each case assume that the land as it is being used by the holder of the life estate is not producing income at a typical rate. Then assume in one setting (the actual case) that the market value of the fee simple in the land was rising significantly faster than the general rate of return on most other investments. Suppose in a second setting that the value of the land was rising at about the same rate as most other common investments. And finally, suppose that the value of the land was rising more slowly than the general rate of return on typical investments. How would you decide the case in each of these situations?

The issues are complicated by some of the standard rules mediating the rights of those owning present possessory and future interests. In theory, the owner of the life estate has the right to receive income from the property, while leaving the value of the asset itself intact for the owner of the remainder. In common law days, some fairly detailed rules emerged on some questions. Life tenants of wood lots, for example, could take out wood from the ground or perhaps a tree every now and then in order to obtain fuel for daily needs, but general timbering was barred. Present possessors could take exposed coal for daily use, but could not open up a new mine. In the contemporary financial world with its array of alternative investments, the issues have become much more complex.

For example, suppose Terry Testator wills a $1,000 bond producing 6% in interest per year (that is, $60) to Lillian Life for life, and then to Reginald Remainder. Who gets what? The easy answer is to say that Lillian gets $60 per year and when she dies, Reginald gets the bond. But what if average interest rates at the time Terry Testator dies are 10%? Should some adjustment be made to reflect the wide variation between the interest rate on the bond and the prevailing market rate? For example, could Lillian demand that a portion of the $1000 principal be paid to her as interest?[17] Or what if interest rates are only 4% when Terry Testator dies? Should Reginald be able to force the sale of the bond to insure a higher capital balance when Lillian Life dies? The list of problems is endless. Stock splits, tax benefits from certain forms of investment, sale of securities and transfer of real property each cause difficulties for determination of the difference between income and capital. Potential conflicts in the interests of life estate and future interest owners exist in virtually every case.

---

[16] There also is potential for non-economic conflicts in cases like this. The trustee for the money generated by the land sales appointed by the court was the attorney for Anna Plaxico Weedon. Was that the proper appointment? Is he not trustee for both Anna and the later takers? If so, are his interests neutral enough to justify the appointment? The creation of bright line rules for allocating receipts to income or capital do not resolve the potential conflict of interest. If the trustee invests in income producing investments, capital gains may be low. On the other hand, investments producing good capital increases may yield low income streams. Does it make a difference that, as the case actually worked its way towards a conclusion, the designation of Weedon's attorney as trustee was approved by all the parties involved in the case?

[17] Note that sale of the bond does not solve the problem. If it were sold, the bond would not fetch a price of $1,000. Since interest rates are higher than when the bond was first purchased, the value of the bond on the securities market is probably *down* to about $600. (10% of $600 is about $60.) The price would not fall so far if the bond is due to mature shortly and produce its full paper value of $1,000 to the owner. In any case, selling the bond might not be in the best interest of Reginald, particularly if lots of people are predicting that interest rates will fall shortly, driving the price of the bond up. (Yes, there is an inverse relationship between interest rates and bond prices.)

Many states have adopted statutory provisions in an effort to mediate some of these disputes. Rather than attempting to attribute some of the "income" to "principal" or "principal" to "income" when the rate of return or increase in value of an asset are significantly different than usual, the statutes try to establish formal rules to classify various sorts of payments. For example, the Uniform Principal and Income Act, adopted in some version by most jurisdictions, simply provides that rent and interest payments are almost always income.[18] Since most decisions allocating money between income and principal are made by trustees, the Act also gives trust settlors the right to grant their designated trustees discretion to allocate credits or debits to income or capital and to administer the trust assets. The provision on trusts reads as follows:

Section 2: Duty of Trustee as to Receipts and Expenditures

(a) A trust shall be administered with due regard to the respective interests of income beneficiaries and remaindermen. A trust is so administered with respect to the allocation of receipts and expenditures if a receipt is credited or an expenditure is charged to income or principal or partly to each—

(1) in accordance with the terms of the trust instrument, notwithstanding contrary provisions of this Act;

(2) in the absence of any contrary terms of the trust instrument, in accordance with the provisions of this Act; or

(3) if neither of the preceding rules of administration is applicable, in accordance with what is reasonable and equitable in view of the interests of those entitled to income as well as of those entitled to principal, and in view of the manner in which men of ordinary prudence, discretion and judgment would act in the management of their own affairs.

(b) If the trust instrument gives the trustee discretion in crediting a receipt or charging an expenditure to income or principal or partly to each, no inference of imprudence or partiality arises from the fact that the trustee has made an allocation contrary to a provision of this Act.[19]

But such statutes can't answer all the questions. The guidelines for trustees are very broad. In addition, not all land splits between a life tenant and remainder interests are held in trust. These, of course, were the problems in *Baker*. Return to the three fact settings this note began with—low income for the life tenant with high, typical and low market values for the fee simple in the land. In order to convey the full fee simple, the interests of both Anna Plaxico Weedon and John Weedon's grandchildren must be hypothecated (merged) and sold together. In contrast to concurrent owners, neither the life tenant nor the owners of the remainder may force a sale of the fee.[20] In entitlement terms, there usually is no right to force a sale! The first of three problem settings is a case like *Baker*, where there apparently was no room for the parties to reach agreement on a hypothecated sale. The owners of the remainder were interested in waiting

---

[18] UNIF. PRINCIPAL AND INCOME ACT § 3, 7B U.L.A. 154 (1962 Act).

[19] UNIF. PRINCIPAL AND INCOME ACT § 2, 7B U.L.A. 151 (1962 Act). Reprinted with permission of the National Conference of Commissioners on Uniform State Laws.

[20] The wisdom of that rule is open to debate. At least for land, there has been some historical reluctance to force a life tenant out of possession, though during the first few decades of the nineteenth century, some states began to force women to take their dower interest in cash. Even though they can't force a sale, the life tenant and remainder person may each sell their own interest—life estate or remainder. But in *Baker* that was not likely to produce a good price. No one knew exactly when Anna would die. The prediction problem, together with the broken up quality of the interests, probably lowered the price for each part.

while the value of the land rose. The life tenant wanted the money now. In the other two settings, the likelihood of a deal rises. If the land value is not rising faster than the market for other sorts of investments and the income being produced is low, the life tenant might be able to convince the owners of the future interest to sell, especially if a little bonus payment is added. And in the third setting, where the price is falling and the income is low, both sides should be interested in selling.

So the most interesting setting is that of the *Baker* case. In economic terms, if the goal was to maximize the value of the litigant community and minimize transaction costs, the court would have ordered a sale of the land, but delayed it for four years. If the goal was to provide immediate relief to the life tenant, then immediate sale was in order. Put another way, there was a trade off between delay and the size of the income stream to the life tenant. Since the owners of the remainder make the most money by waiting, they have no monetary incentive to make a deal with the life tenant.[21] And so it is not surprising that the life-tenant sued to force a sale, in essence alleging that the unwillingness of the grandchildren to approve a sale was causing her economic harm. The factual setting is therefore similar to that in *Fontainebleau.*

You can work out a possible solution using the same sort of entitlement structure we used in *Fontainebleau.* Think of the entitlement in issue as the right to have or block an adequate income stream to the life tenant, and again assume that the parties will be able to make a deal after the court issues its decree. The most wealth for the litigant community is created by delaying the sale for four years. But different remedies would have produced quite different distributional outcomes. As the following table suggests, awarding Anna Plaxico the entitlement would have led the remainder persons to buy the right to delay sale of the land by making payments to the life tenant. Awarding an injunction to Anna—in essence the right to force immediate sale—would give Anna greater bargaining power and the potential for larger payments.

Baker Entitlements Table

Entitlement Goes To:	Remedy	Result After Trade
Life Tenant	Liability Rule (Damages)	Sale Delayed. Damages to life tenant.
Life Tenant	Property Rule (Injunction)	Sale Delayed. Damages plus Bonus paid.
Remainder People	Liability Rule (Damages)	Sale Delayed.
Remainder People	Property Rule (Injunction)	Sale Delayed.

As the *Baker* case finally worked out, the grandchildren really "won," even though the courts eventually ordered sale of most of the land. The time delay allowed the land value to rise. Anna was denied access to a higher income stream while the case was being heard and appealed. Simply

---

[21] The deals they did make don't change this conclusion. The highway condemnation award fell into their laps and had to be divided. Sale of the gravel did not alter the overall value of the site at all. Both Anna and her deceased husband's grandchildren had an incentive to sell the gravel and split the proceeds. The grandchildren may have been perfectly nice to Anna Plaxico, but they apparently were not willing to forego the ultimate benefit of a delayed sale.

put, the transaction costs to Anna were very high. The inability to force a sale deprived her of bargaining power and cost her dearly. She won the battle but lost the war.

In an ideal world, perhaps, this sort of outcome would get us to think of a new rule that would prevent the Annas of this world from losing in the future due to delay. Is it possible to draft a legal principle that describes her situation so well that she would be able to recover damages if the remainder people did not pay her off? Does the outcome of the actual case do that? Will the next Anna be able to get damages if her remainder people refuse to agree to either sale of the fee simple or payment to her of a larger income stream?

§ 10.05 Nuisance

[1]   The *Boomer* Litigation

[a]   Transaction Costs

In this section of the chapter, we will investigate two important issues in the resolution of nuisance disputes—the impact of transaction costs and the propriety of awarding injunctive or damages relief. We will use two cases—*Boomer v. Atlantic Cement Company* and *Spur v. Del Webb*—to focus on these issues.

Begin with the following problem on transaction costs. The facts are taken from A. Mitchell Polinsky's quite useful introductory book on law and economics, AN INTRODUCTION TO LAW AND ECONOMICS (1983).[22] He posits a problem in which there are five residents near a polluting factory. The pollution causes each resident $75 in damages. The pollution can be eliminated either by installation of some equipment by the factory at a cost of $150 or by the installation of equipment in each home at a cost of $50. In a transaction cost free world, the best result is for the factory to install equipment at a cost of $150. That step is cheaper than the total $250 cost for the residents to equip their homes and prevents a total of $375 ($75 for each resident) in damages to the residents. If you create an entitlement table for this example, you will see that regardless of who gets the entitlement, the pollution control equipment will be installed at the factory. The distributional results will vary, but the curative step taken will be the same.

Now, Polinsky suggests, add one additional fact. Suppose that it costs each resident—in financial, social and psychological terms—$60 to try to work with the other four neighbors to solve the pollution problem. Then what will happen? You can make another entitlement table and see what happens. You will discover that if you award the entitlement to the factory, then each resident will spend $50 to install equipment at home because it costs more to work with the neighbors. If you award the entitlement to the residents . . . . Well, actually you can't reach that result because it costs each resident $60 to pursue legal relief. Suit will never be filed. The residents will each install equipment in their houses even though they have the legal claim to an entitlement to be free of pollution. In this example, transaction costs get in the way of an "efficient" solution.[23] If, therefore, you alter the assumption in the Coase Theorem that transaction costs are zero, efficient results will not always prevail. By the way, you might want to play around with this same problem and assume that the cost of seeking a solution with neighbors is only $40.

---

[22] *See* pp. 11-14.

[23] If the residents knew ahead of time that they were *sure* to win their litigation and therefore be able to force the installation of equipment at the factory that removed the $75 cost imposed by the pollution, they would go ahead. But such certainty of results rarely if ever exits in the legal system. In addition, costs of suit are not usually known prior to the institution of litigation.

Keep the transaction cost problem in mind while you read the next case.

[b] Background of *Boomer v. Atlantic Cement Company*

The most complete story behind *Boomer v. Atlantic Cement Company* has been told by Daniel Farber. An excerpt from his work follows.

Daniel A. Farber, *Reassessing* Boomer: *Justice, Efficiency and Nuisance Law*

in PROPERTY LAW AND LEGAL EDUCATION:
ESSAYS IN HONOR OF JOHN E. CRIBBET 8-11
(Peter Hay & Michael H. Hoeflich eds., 1988).[24]

Atlantic Cement began construction of its plant in May of 1961. The area was unzoned at the time. Operations began in September of 1961, after Atlantic had invested more than $40 million in this plant, including the most effective available pollution control. The area was described as follows by a real estate expert:

> Prior to the purchase by the Atlantic Cement Company, this property in the area is about a mile and a half or two miles north of the Village of Ravena, which was in a state of transition from rural to suburban living, with individual houses built presently along Route 9W with a smattering of commercial enterprises dotted here and there. When I say commercial, I'm referring principally to gasoline service stations or a motel or a drive-in theatre.

All the plaintiffs had owned and occupied their properties prior to the ground-breaking for the plant.

Atlantic's impact on its neighbors was drastic. For example, Floyd and Barbara Millious lived in an eight-room ranch-style house 900 feet from the cement plant, and even closer to an overhead conveyer used to move rocks from the quarry to the plant. Atlantic's quarry was a half mile to the west. According to the Milliouses, the blasting had caused large cracks in the walls, ceiling, and exterior of their home. Moreover, the fine dust blowing onto their property covered everything with what they described as a "plastic-like" coating, which they found impossible to remove. Similar property damage was reported by Joseph and Carrie Ventura, who owned a Cape Cod house about the same distance from the plant and conveyer.

Kenneth and Delores Livengood lived farther from the cement plant but closer to the quarry. Delores Livengood's testimony vividly describes the effects of the blasting on their daily lives, as in this episode in March of 1967:

> Well, we were sitting on the floor in the living room, playing a game when they had this awful tremble, and to me the house seemed like the whole house was rocking, and I would see the lamp shades vibrating and it just scared the children. That was one of the times that they just got up and started to run for the basement. And I didn't go out the door because I knew what it was. I heard the big blast, but the whole house just rocked and I just wondered if it was going to stop. It was terrible.

---

[24] Copyright 1988 by the Board of Trustees of the University of Illinois. Reprinted with the permission of the University of Illinois Press and the author.

At least one dairy farm, owned by Avie Kinley, was near the plant. The 283 acre farm consisted of a house, barns, two silos and three tenant houses.

The area was also used by small businesses such as Oscar and June Boomer's automobile junk yard, which was just north of the main plant. They owned about eight acres, on which the Boomers sold used car parts and did auto body and fender work. Mr. Boomer had apparently hoped that his two sons would carry on the family business, but the viability of the business was threatened by the vibration and heavy dust.

The Coach House Restaurant, owned and operated by Theodore and Miriam Richard, was within seven hundred feet of the cement company's stock pile. Before 1961, the restaurant was surrounded by evergreens, and the Coach House served cocktails and sandwiches to its customers outside on the lawn. According to one expert witness, the Coach House had just completed a lengthy start-up period. With the mortgage paid off, it was just about to become profitable when the cement plant opened.

The record also contains considerable information about the cement company and its operations. The company was formed as the Burwill Realty Company in 1959, presumably to facilitate the acquisition of property by concealing the purchaser's plans. Just before construction of the plant began, the name was changed to the Atlantic Cement Company. Although this was the company's only plant, it had distribution centers from Boston to Florida, served either by rail or barge. The quarry included some 1544 acres. The plant normally employed about four hundred people (though there was a strike at the time of the trial), with annual wages of about $3 million. The assessed value of the plant was about half of the assessed value of the township.

The blasting involved something called the "millisecond delay" procedure. Rather than setting off one large blast, a series of blasts would be used to remove one layer after another, so that one layer of rock would be falling away just as the next blast went off. The dust collection equipment, which had cost over $2 million, was said to be the best in the country.

[c] Opinions of the New York Court of Appeals in _Boomer v. Atlantic Cement Company_

Boomer v. Atlantic Cement Company, Inc.

New York Court of Appeals
26 N.Y.2d 219, 257 N.E.2d 870, 309 N.Y.S.2d 312 (1970)

BERGAN, JUDGE.

Defendant operates a large cement plant near Albany. These are actions for injunction and damages by neighboring land owners alleging injury to property from dirt, smoke and vibration emanating from the plant. A nuisance has been found after trial, temporary damages have been allowed; but an injunction has been denied.

The public concern with air pollution arising from many sources in industry and in transportation is currently accorded ever wider recognition accompanied by a growing sense of responsibility in State and Federal Governments to control it. Cement plants are obvious sources of air pollution in the neighborhoods where they operate.

But there is now before the court private litigation in which individual property owners have sought specific relief from a single plant operation. The threshold question raised by the division of view on this appeal is whether the court should resolve the litigation between the parties now before it as equitably as seems possible; or whether, seeking promotion of the general public welfare, it should channel private litigation into broad public objectives.

A court performs its essential function when it decides the rights of parties before it. Its decision of private controversies may sometimes greatly affect public issues. Large questions of law are often resolved by the manner in which private litigation is decided. But this is normally an incident to the court's main function to settle controversy. It is a rare exercise of judicial power to use a decision in private litigation as a purposeful mechanism to achieve direct public objectives greatly beyond the rights and interests before the court.

Effective control of air pollution is a problem presently far from solution even with the full public and financial powers of government. In large measure adequate technical procedures are yet to be developed and some that appear possible may be economically impracticable.

It seems apparent that the amelioration of air pollution will depend on technical research in great depth; on a carefully balanced consideration of the economic impact of close regulation; and of the actual effect on public health. It is likely to require massive public expenditure and to demand more than any local community can accomplish and to depend on regional and interstate controls.

A court should not try to do this on its own as a by-product of private litigation and it seems manifest that the judicial establishment is neither equipped in the limited nature of any judgment it can pronounce nor prepared to lay down and implement an effective policy for the elimination of air pollution. This is an area beyond the circumference of one private lawsuit. It is a direct responsibility for government and should not thus be undertaken as an incident to solving a dispute between property owners and a single cement plant—one of many—in the Hudson River valley.

The cement making operations of defendant have been found by the court at Special Term to have damaged the nearby properties of plaintiffs in these two actions. That court, as it has been noted, accordingly found defendant maintained a nuisance and this has been affirmed at the Appellate Division. The total damage to plaintiffs' properties is, however, relatively small in comparison with the value of defendant's operation and with the consequences of the injunction which plaintiffs seek.

The ground for the denial of injunction, notwithstanding the finding both that there is a nuisance and that plaintiffs have been damaged substantially, is the large disparity in economic consequences of the nuisance and of the injunction. This theory cannot, however, be sustained without overruling a doctrine which has been consistently reaffirmed in several leading cases in this court and which has never been disavowed here, namely that where a nuisance has been found and where there has been any substantial damage shown by the party complaining an injunction will be granted.

The rule in New York has been that such a nuisance will be enjoined although marked disparity be shown in economic consequence between the effect of the injunction and the effect of the nuisance.

The problem of disparity in economic consequence was sharply in focus in *Whalen v. Union Bag & Paper Co.*, 208 N.Y. 1, 101 N.E. 805. A pulp mill entailing an investment of more than a million dollars polluted a stream in which plaintiff, who owned a farm, was "a lower riparian owner." The economic loss to plaintiff from this pollution was small. This court, reversing the Appellate Division, reinstated the injunction granted by the Special Term against the argument of the mill owner that in view of "the slight advantage to plaintiff and the great loss that will be inflicted on defendant" an injunction should not be granted. "Such a balancing of injuries cannot be justified by the circumstances of this case," Judge Werner noted. He continued: "Although the damage to the plaintiff may be slight as compared with the defendant's expense of abating the condition, that is not a good reason for refusing an injunction."

Thus the unconditional injunction granted at Special Term was reinstated. The rule laid down in that case, then, is that whenever the damage resulting from a nuisance is found not "unsubstantial," *viz.*, $100 a year, injunction would follow. This states a rule that had been followed in this court with marked consistency (*McCarty v. Natural Carbonic Gas Co.*, 189 N.Y. 40, 81 N.E. 549; *Strobel v. Kerr Salt Co.*, 164 N.Y. 303, 58 N.E. 142; *Campbell v. Seaman*, 63 N.Y. 568).

. . . .

Although the court at Special Term and the Appellate Division held that injunction should be denied, it was found that plaintiffs had been damaged in various specific amounts up to the time of the trial and damages to the respective plaintiffs were awarded for those amounts. The effect of this was, injunction having been denied, plaintiffs could maintain successive actions at law for damages thereafter as further damage was incurred.

The court at Special Term also found the amount of permanent damage attributable to each plaintiff, for the guidance of the parties in the event both sides stipulated to the payment and acceptance of such permanent damage as a settlement of all the controversies among the parties. The total of permanent damages to all plaintiffs thus found was $185,000. This basis of adjustment has not resulted in any stipulation by the parties.

This result at Special Term and at the Appellate Division is a departure from a rule that has become settled; but to follow the rule literally in these cases would be to close down the plant at once. This court is fully agreed to avoid that immediately drastic remedy; the difference in view is how best to avoid it.

One alternative is to grant the injunction but postpone its effect to a specified future date to give opportunity for technical advances to permit defendant to eliminate the nuisance; another is to grant the injunction conditioned on the payment of permanent damages to plaintiff which would compensate them for the total economic loss to their property present and future caused by defendant's operations. For reasons which will be developed the court chooses the latter alternative.

If the injunction were to be granted unless within a short period—*e.g.*, 18 months—the nuisance be abated by improved methods, there would be no assurance that any significant technical improvement would occur.

The parties could settle this private litigation at any time if defendant paid enough money and the imminent threat of closing the plant would build up the pressure on defendant. If there were no improved techniques found, there would inevitably be applications to the court at Special Term for extensions of time to perform on showing of good faith efforts to find such techniques.

Moreover, techniques to eliminate dust and other annoying by-products of cement making are unlikely to be developed by any research the defendant can undertake within any short period, but will depend on the total resources of the cement industry nationwide and throughout the world. The problem is universal wherever cement is made.

For obvious reasons the rate of the research is beyond control of defendant. If at the end of 18 months the whole industry has not found a technical solution a court would be hard put to close down this one cement plant if due regard be given to equitable principles.

On the other hand, to grant the injunction unless defendant pays plaintiffs such permanent damages as may be fixed by the court seems to do justice between the contending parties. All of the attributions of economic loss to the properties on which plaintiff's complaints are based will have been redressed.

The nuisance complained of by these plaintiffs may have other public or private consequences, but these particular parties are the only ones who have sought remedies and the judgment proposed will fully redress them. The limitation of relief granted is a limitation only within the four corners of these actions and does not foreclose public health or other public agencies from seeking proper relief in a proper court.

It seems reasonable to think that the risk of being required to pay permanent damages to injured property owners by cement plant owners would itself be a reasonable effective spur to research for improved techniques to minimize nuisance.

The power of the court to condition on equitable grounds the continuance of an injunction on the payment of permanent damages seems undoubted.

. . . .

There is some parallel to the conditioning of an injunction on the payment of permanent damages in the noted "elevated railway cases" (*Pappenheim v. Metropolitan El. Ry. Co.,* 128 N.Y. 436, 28 N.E. 518 and others which followed). Decisions in these cases were based on the finding that the railways created a nuisance as to adjacent property owners, but in lieu of enjoining their operation, the court allowed permanent damages.

Judge Finch, reviewing these cases in *Ferguson v. Village of Hamburg,* 272 N.Y. 234, 5 N.E.2d 801, said: "The courts decided that the plaintiffs had a valuable right which was being impaired, but did not grant an absolute injunction or require the railway companies to resort to separate condemnation proceedings. Instead they held that a court of equity could ascertain the damages and grant an injunction which was not to be effective unless the defendant failed to pay the amount fixed as damages for the past and permanent injury inflicted."

Thus it seems fair to both sides to grant permanent damages to plaintiffs which will terminate this private litigation. The theory of damage is the "servitude on land" of plaintiffs imposed by defendant's nuisance. (*See United States v. Causby,* 328 U.S. 256, 261, 262, 267, 66 S. Ct. 1062, 90 L. Ed. 1206, where the term "servitude" addressed to the land was used by Justice Douglas relating to the effect of airplane noise on property near an airport.)

The judgment, by allowance of permanent damages imposing a servitude on land, which is the basis of the actions, would preclude future recovery by plaintiffs or their grantees.

This should be placed beyond debate by a provision of the judgment that the payment by defendant and the acceptance by plaintiffs of permanent damages found by the court shall be in compensation for a servitude on the land.

Although the Trial Term has found permanent damages as a possible basis of settlement of the litigation, on remission the court should be entirely free to re-examine this subject. It may again find the permanent damage already found; or make new findings.

The orders should be reversed, without costs, and the cases remitted to Supreme Court, Albany County to grant an injunction which shall be vacated upon payment by defendant of such amounts of permanent damage to the respective plaintiffs as shall for this purpose be determined by the court.

JASEN, JUDGE (dissenting).

I agree with the majority that a reversal is required here, but I do not subscribe to the newly enunciated doctrine of assessment of permanent damages, in lieu of an injunction, where substantial property rights have been impaired by the creation of a nuisance.

. . . .

The harmful nature and widespread occurrence of air pollution have been extensively documented. Congressional hearings have revealed that air pollution causes substantial property damage, as well as being a contributing factor to a rising incidence of lung cancer, emphysema, bronchitis and asthma.[2]

The specific problem faced here is known as particulate contamination because of the fine dust particles emanating from defendant's cement plant. The particular type of nuisance is not new, having appeared in many cases for at least the past 60 years.

It is interesting to note that cement production has recently been identified as a significant source of particulate contamination in the Hudson Valley.[3] This type of pollution, wherein very small particles escape and stay in the atmosphere, has been denominated as the type of air pollution which produces the greatest hazard to human health.[4] We have thus a nuisance which not only is damaging to the plaintiffs,[5] but also is decidedly harmful to the general public.

I see grave dangers in overruling our long-established rule of granting an injunction where a nuisance results in substantial continuing damage. In permitting the injunction to become inoperative upon the payment of permanent damages, the majority is, in effect, licensing a continuing wrong. It is the same as saying to the cement company, you may continue to do harm to your neighbors so long as you pay a fee for it. Furthermore, once such permanent damages are assessed and paid, the incentive to alleviate the wrong would be eliminated, thereby continuing air pollution of an area without abatement.

It is true that some courts have sanctioned the remedy here proposed by the majority in a number of cases,[6] but none of the authorities relied upon by the majority are analogous to the situation before us. In those cases, the courts, in denying an injunction and awarding money damages, grounded their decision on a showing that the use to which the property was intended

---

[2] See U.S. Cong., Senate Comm. on Public Works, Special Subcomm. on Air and Water Pollution, Air Pollution 1966, 89th Cong., 2d Sess., 1966, at pp. 22-24; U.S. Cong., Senate Comm. on Public Works, Special Subcomm. on Air and Water Pollution, Air Pollution 1968, 90th Cong., 2d Sess., 1968, at pp. 850, 1084.

[3] New York State Bureau of Air Pollution Control Services, Air Pollution Capital District, 1968, at p. 8.

[4] J. Ludwig, *Air Pollution Control Technology: Research and Development on New and Improved Systems,* 33 Law & Contemp. Prob., 217, 219 (1968).

[5] There are seven plaintiffs here who have been substantially damaged by the maintenance of this nuisance. The trial court found their total permanent damages to equal $185,000.

[6] See *United States v. Causby,* 328 U.S. 256; *Kentucky-Ohio Gas Co. v. Bowling.* 264 Ky. 470, 477, 95 S.W.2d 1; *Northern Indiana Public Service Co. v. W. J. & M.S. Vesey,* 210 Ind. 338, 200 N.E. 620; *City of Amarillo v. Ware,* 120 Tex. 456, 40 S.W.2d 57; *Pappenheim v. Metropolitan El. Ry. Co.,* 128 N.Y. 436, 28 N.E. 518; *Ferguson v. Village of Hamburg,* 272 N.Y. 234, 5 N.E.2d 801.

to be put was primarily for the public benefit. Here, on the other hand, it is clearly established that the cement company is creating a continuing air pollution nuisance primarily for its own private interest with no public benefit.

This kind of inverse condemnation may not be invoked by a private person or corporation for private gain or advantage. Inverse condemnation should only be permitted when the public is primarily served in the taking or impairment of property. The promotion of the interest of the polluting cement company has, in my opinion, no public use or benefit.

Nor is it constitutionally permissible to impose [a] servitude on land, without consent of the owner, by payment of permanent damages where the continuing impairment of the land is for a private use. This is made clear by the State Constitution (art. I, § 7, subd. [a]) which provides that "[p]rivate property shall not be taken for *public use* without just compensation" (emphasis added). It is, of course, significant that the section makes no mention of taking for a *private* use.

In sum, then, by constitutional mandate as well as by judicial pronouncement, the permanent impairment of private property for private purposes is not authorized in the absence of clearly demonstrated public benefit and use.

I would enjoin the defendant cement company from continuing the discharge of dust particles upon its neighbors' properties unless, within 18 months, the cement company abated this nuisance.[7]

It is not my intention to cause the removal of the cement plant from the Albany area, but to recognize the urgency of the problem stemming from this stationary source of air pollution, and to allow the company a specified period of time to develop a means to alleviate this nuisance.

I am aware that the trial court found that the most modern dust control devices available have been installed in defendant's plant, but, I submit, this does not mean that *better* and more effective dust control devices could not be developed within the time allowed to abate the pollution.

Moreover, I believe it is incumbent upon the defendant to develop such devices, since the cement company, at the time the plant commenced production (1962), was well aware of the plaintiffs' presence in the area, as well as the probable consequences of its contemplated operation. Yet, it still chose to build and operate the plant at this site.

In a day when there is a growing concern for clean air, highly developed industry should not expect acquiescence by the courts, but should, instead, plan its operations to eliminate contamination of our air and damage to its neighbors.

Accordingly, the orders of the Appellate Division, insofar as they denied the injunction, should be reversed, and the actions remitted to Supreme Court, Albany County to grant an injunction to take effect 18 months hence, unless the nuisance is abated by improved techniques prior to said date.

FULD, C.J., and BURKE and SCILEPPI, JJ., concur with BERGAN, J.

JASEN, J., dissents in part and votes to reverse in a separate opinion.

BREITEL and GIBSON, JJ., taking no part.

---

[7] The issuance of an injunction to become effective in the future is not an entirely new concept. For instance, in *Schwarzenbach v. Oneonta Light & Power Co.*, 207 N.Y.671, 100 N.E. 1134, an injunction against the maintenance of a dam spilling water on plaintiff's property was issued to become effective one year hence.

[d]   Explanatory Notes on Law and Facts

    [*i*]   *Events After Remand.* The *Boomer* appeal was actually a consolidation of several cases pending against Atlantic Cement Company. All of the litigants except one settled their differences after the Court of Appeals opinion was rendered, with Atlantic Cement agreeing to pay a total of $466,250.00 in permanent damages.[25] Avie Kinley, owner of a 283-acre dairy farm, was the only party to go to trial; he obtained an award of $175,000.[26] The actual judgment entered in the case was $244,487.56, once interest and costs were included. At the Kinley trial, Atlantic Cement claimed that it had installed additional water spraying devices in the conveyor system between the quarry and the factory and spent $1.6 million on additional pollution control equipment. Once all the litigation was over, Atlantic Cement sought reimbursement for the settlement costs and Kinley judgment—a total of $710,737.56—from its insurance carriers, Fidelity & Casualty Company of New York and Travelers Indemnity Company. The insurance companies resisted payment on the ground that the judgment and settlements resulted from intentional injuries caused by Atlantic; the insurance policies excluded coverage for intentional torts. The New York courts eventually held that the insurance policy covered the *Boomer* losses, but remanded for a trial on the reasonableness of the settlements agreed to by Atlantic Cement.[27]

    [*ii*]   The Boomer *Case as a Private Nuisance Action.* The New York Court of Appeals treated *Boomer* as a private nuisance action. While admitting that the consequences of cement factory pollution were widely felt, the court refused to look beyond the needs of the litigants before it unless public officials took steps to join as parties to the action. Several reasons can be offered for this outcome. First, the plaintiffs did not pursue the case as a class action.[28] There were a number of property owners who had causes of action against Atlantic Cement who were not before the court. Pursuing the case as a public nuisance without their presence might have raised some nice procedural questions.[29] Second, the pollution had an impact on many persons who were not property owners. Employees were certainly interested in the outcome of the case. And the pollution probably had diverse impacts on many people living and working outside the immediate vicinity of the factory. Finally, the court was reluctant to take upon itself the decision to treat the case as a public nuisance action. The importance of the cement industry to the Hudson Valley area meant the case was a political hot potato. If cement pollution was to be the object of public censure, the court wanted state authorities to join them in the limelight.

    [*iii*]   The Boomer *Outcome.* Once the court decided to treat the *Boomer* case as a private nuisance action, the factual view became quite narrowly focused on the interests of the parties

---

  [25] Atlantic Cement Company, Inc. v. Fidelity & Casualty Company of New York, 91 A.D.2d 412, 459 N.Y.S.2d 425 (1983).

  [26] Boomer v. Atlantic Cement Co., Inc. 72 Misc.2d 834, 340 N.Y.S.2d 97 (1972), *affirmed sub nom.* Kinley v. Atlantic Cement Co., 42 A.D.2d 496, 349 N.Y.S.2d 199 (1973).

  [27] Atlantic Cement Company, Inc. v. Fidelity & Casualty Company of New York, 91 A.D.2d 412, 459 N.Y.S.2d 425 (1983), *affirmed,* 63 N.Y.2d 798, 471 N.E.2d 142, 481 N.Y.S.2d 329 (1984).

  [28] It is not clear that typical rules of civil procedure would have permitted this case to be handled as a class action. While the liability issues were similar for all members of a property owning class, damage issues were quite different case to case. In addition, if some property owners came to the area after the cement factory opened, the defenses to the nuisance claims might be different for various members of the class. *See* FED. R. CIV. P. 23.

  [29] For example, should a court dealing with a public nuisance case be obligated to notify all landowners in the area of the litigation? Would the result of a public nuisance action bind those parties severely effected by the pollution who were not parties to the case?

involved in the litigation. Two facts may have been crucial to the outcome in that setting—the cement factory was the second to the area and, in addition, was worth much more than the assets held by the plaintiffs.

        [A]   *Order of Arrival.* Why should the order of arrival to the scene of the nuisance make any difference? The factory's presence reduced the value of neighboring property below what they paid for it. Those owners who arrived after the cement factory began operating paid a price for their land that was discounted by the impact of the defendant's polluting activity. An argument can be made, therefore, that if any of the plaintiffs came to the area knowing of the existence of the cement factory, they should not be entitled to any economic relief for the pollution of their land. Their predecessors in title, who received a reduced price for their land, were the real damaged parties. While the court clearly could have reached the conclusion that the cement factory was a nuisance regardless of the order in which the parties arrived on the scene, the actual facts made it fairly easy for the judges to agree that the plaintiffs had an *entitlement* to clean air.

        [B]   *Relative Worth of the Parties.* Despite concluding that the plaintiffs were entitled to relief, the *Boomer* court refused to grant them an injunction against the operation of the cement factory. This portion of the decision was clearly influenced by the enormous investment made by Atlantic Cement in its facility and the importance of the factory jobs to the surrounding community. The apparent lack of technology to clean up the pollution[30] meant, at least to the court, that an injunction threatened the factory's existence. Damages were one thing, but a shut down was quite another. Whether the court's judgment was correct is one of the subjects taken up in the next set of notes.

        [iv]   *The* **Boomer** *Dissent.* Judge Jasen, much like Judge Benjamin in dissent in *Ginsberg v. Yeshiva of Far Rockaway,* p. 465 above, argued that the decision to award damages was state action and served as a taking in violation of the Constitution because the award of property interests to Atlantic Cement did not serve a valid *public* purpose. "[T]he permanent impairment of private property for private purposes is not authorized in the absence of clearly demonstrated public benefit and use." While Judge Jasen's position did not prevail, you might want to consider whether his theory would apply to other well known legal doctrines:

    (a) Adverse possession or prescription, in which title to property interests goes to trespassers because of the intervention of state legislatures adopting statutes of limitations and courts deciding cases.

    (b) Specific performance of contracts for the sale of land in which buyers gain full title to land despite claims by sellers that specific performance is unwarranted.

    (c) State constitutions, statutes or court decisions which provide demonstrators with a right to go upon land of another with picket signs.

    (d) The Rule Against Perpetuities which voids an interest in land despite a clear intention on the part of the grantor to create it.

Is private property being taken for private purposes in any of these cases?

---

[30] Though note well the company's expenditure of $1.6 million on additional pollution control equipment after *Boomer* was rendered.

[e] Notes on Transactions Costs and Remedies

[*i*] *Transaction Costs.* In the notes before *Boomer,* a problem invented by A. Mitchell Polinsky was used to suggest some of the impacts that transactions costs might have on the willingness of parties to seek solutions to their problems or to pursue litigation. It is easy to see how far reaching such an effect may be. In many air pollution settings, individuals are unable to pursue any standard forms of legal redress. Sources for automobile pollution, for example, are widely scattered and beyond the ability of any one of us to control. Many large, single source polluters have effects far beyond the area where their businesses are located. Developing a legal strategy to pursue them is quite a daunting task. In short, the simple Polinsky example is a metaphor for a quite standard set of problems.

In the *Boomer* setting, however, the psychological, social and economic barriers to seeking redress from Atlantic Cement Company were overcome. The reasons for that are evident in the factual background described in the Daniel Farber excerpt reprinted just before the opinion. While the court left the impression that the major problem involved dust pollution, the litigants told stories about quite serious impacts from dynamiting in the quarry supplying the factory with raw material. The plaintiffs were quite literally shaken into action. While the result suggests that the preclusive effect of transaction costs sometimes may be overcome, they still left their mark on the litigants. If the legal fees paid in *Boomer* followed typical practice, the attorney collected at least one-third of the amounts paid by Atlantic Cement.[31] It, therefore, is not clear whether the plaintiffs actually received full compensation for their losses.

When all of the transaction costs are taken into account, an intriguing remedy problem results. If there are certain sorts of groups, such as pollution victims, that you wish to encourage to file lawsuits, increasing the amounts of money litigation might produce is one way to do that. A variety of systems are actually in use in various settings that serve this sort of purpose. They include statutes awarding attorneys fees to prevailing parties, allowing for bonus awards in certain sorts of high risk litigation, or providing citizens with a share of any moneys recovered if they produce information leading to successful government actions against wrongdoers. Should any of these sorts of techniques be used in cases like *Boomer*?

[*ii*] *Relief.* As noted in the opening segment of this chapter, some of the early law and economics literature opined that remedies were in some sense superfluous. The nineteenth-century noxious use nuisance test, for example, was not necessarily helpful, for even in cases where activity was enjoined, the Coase theorem suggested, a bargain would be struck between the litigants which would eliminate the injunction *if* the enjoined use was worth more than the entitlement held by the owners of the injunction. Thus, in a case like *Boomer,* the issuance of an injunction against the cement factory would lead, not to the end of dust pollution, but to the transfer of a sum of money to the pollutees. Some, such as Posner, then argued that we might as well award the property entitlement represented by an injunction to the more valuable use in order to avoid the costs of determining damages or organizing a sale of an injunction at a later time. And if the pollutee must be rewarded, Posner argued, a damage award rather than an injunction should be used to avoid later transaction costs associated with a sale of an entitlement awarded to the damaged party.

---

[31] A standard contingent fee paid after a trial is one-third. Many retainer agreements will increase that amount to 40% or 50% if an appeal is required.

Since this initial run of articles, mountains of materials have been written about nuisance. Many authors have argued that the economic outcomes are not as clear as Posner's work suggested. They have noted that transaction costs will sometimes produce inefficient results or prevent the pursuit and resolution of disputes, that psychological, political or other usually non-monetized obstacles to the making of deals exist, that some costs associated with a nuisance are not represented by the litigants before the courts, that even if deals are made we may be more interested in the income redistribution accomplished by that deal than in the costs of making a transaction, that some things or aspects of our personal selves should not be for sale, or that discussion of the economic content of nuisance law leads us to ignore moral or ethical considerations. But regardless of the views taken by this array of writers, they all paid homage in some way to the central point made by the early authors—that the issuance of an injunction does not *automatically* lead to a halt in the enjoined activity, because injunctions, like other forms of property, may sometimes be sold. In light of this conclusion, the *Boomer* court's conclusion that issuing an injunction threatened shutdown of the cement factory probably was significantly overstated.

Though injunctions may be sold, their issuance may still have quite different consequences from a damage award. The propriety of using one or the other form of relief has been a major topic of debate in the literature. Here is an excerpt from one effort to describe the differences between damages and injunctions and to suggest settings in which one or another might be used.

A. Mitchell Polinsky, *Resolving Nuisance Disputes: The Simple Economics of Injunctive and Damage Remedies*[32]

32 STAN. L. REV. 1075, 1076-1080, 1110-1112 (1980)

The resolution of nuisance disputes may, following Calabresi and Melamed,[5] be viewed as involving two steps. First, a determination must be made as to who is entitled to prevail. The polluter can be granted the right to pollute, or the pollutee can be granted the right to be free from pollution. Then, in the language of Calabresi and Melamed, a decision must be made whether to protect the entitlement by a "property rule" or a "liability rule." The former grants the holder of the entitlement an injunction, while the latter awards him damages determined by some collective authority such as a court. Thus, in their framework, there are four possible types of solutions, depending on who is given the entitlement and how it is protected.[6]

Most recent legal commentaries on nuisance law have strongly recommended the use of damages rather than injunctions. Whether court decisions also favor the damage remedy is unclear, although many commentators perceive a trend in this direction.[8]

---

[32] Copyright 1980 by the Board of Trustees of the Leland Stanford Junior University. Reprinted by permission of Stanford Law Review and A. Mitchell Polinsky.

[5] Calabresi & Melamed, *Property Rules, Liability Rules, and Inalienability: One View of the Cathedral*, 85 HARV. L. REV. 1089 (1972).

[6] These solutions are a property rule with the entitlement held by the polluter; a property rule with the entitlement held by the pollutee; a liability rule with the entitlement held by the polluter; and a liability rule with the entitlement held by the pollutee.

[8] The leading modern American cases illustrating the use of damage remedies are *Boomer v. Atlantic Cement Co.*, 26 N.Y.2d 219, 257 N.E.2d 870, 309 N.Y.S.2d 312 (1970), and *Spur Indus., Inc. v. Del E. Webb Dev. Co.*, 108 Ariz. 178, 494 P.2d 700 (1972) . . . .

. . . .

Three arguments have been suggested for this preference; I will refer to these as the extortion, strategic behavior, and "bonus payment" arguments.

The first argument against injunctive remedies is that they allow the plaintiff to "extort" the defendant. This possibility arises whenever the potential cost that enforcement of the injunction would impose on the defendant exceeds the loss borne by the plaintiff if the activity in question occurs. Suppose, for example, that operation of a plant injures a pollutee by $1,000 while the polluter would lose $10,000 in profits if the plant were shut down by an injunction. Because the defendant may be willing to pay up to his entire potential profit to prevent the shutdown, the plaintiff might be able to exact compensation well in excess of his actual damages. Under a damage remedy, however, the court dictates the plaintiff's compensation—presumably $1,000 in this example—leaving no scope for extortion.

Note that the extortion argument relates to the goal of distributional equity, not economic efficiency. In the previous example, it is efficient for the plant to continue to operate since the gains are $10,000 while the costs are only $1,000. If, because of the threat of an injunction, the polluter pays the pollutee $9,000 in order to continue operating, this may be inequitable, but it is not inefficient.

The second argument against injunctive remedies—the strategic behavior argument—concerns the consequences for economic efficiency of *unsuccessful* extortion. Strategic behavior consists of bargaining conduct in which a party, perhaps misperceiving his opponent's bargaining position, holds out for a settlement that is never reached (or that is reached after undue delay or negotiation cost). Under an injunctive remedy, strategic behavior may prevent the parties from reaching an efficient resolution of the dispute. In the previous example, the plaintiff might hold out for $8,000 while the defendant, also behaving strategically, might refuse to pay anything over $5,000. As a result, the plaintiff might enforce the injunction and shut down the defendant's plant (at least for some period). In contrast, a damage award seems to overcome strategic behavior problems because the defendant does not have to obtain the consent of the plaintiff. In the example, the defendant presumably would choose to pay any court-determined damage award under $10,000 and keep his plant in operation.

The third argument for damage remedies—the "bonus payment" argument—is offered less frequently than the other two arguments. Once it has been decided to use a damage remedy for either of the other reasons, it is possible to pursue additional distributional goals by making the defendant's liability more or less than the plaintiff's actual damages. In the example, suppose the plaintiff is poorer than the defendant and a more equal distribution of income is desired. The damage award could be augmented by a "bonus payment" to achieve the precise amount of redistribution preferred. If redistribution by other means—such as the income tax system—is costlier (in an efficiency sense), then using a damage remedy to achieve this end may be appropriate. Under the injunctive remedy, on the other hand, distributional outcomes are uncertain. For example, extortion may lead the defendant to pay the plaintiff any amount between $1,000 and $10,000. The actual sum will depend on the parties' relative bargaining strengths. Alternatively, strategic behavior may lead to enforcement of the injunction, forcing the defendant to shut down, with a loss of $10,000 to him and a gain of $1,000 in pollution damage avoided to the plaintiff.

These three arguments amount to the proposition that damage remedies are better able to achieve the efficient outcome (by avoiding strategic behavior) and to promote the desired distributional outcome (by avoiding extortion and allowing bonus payments).

. . . [H]owever, . . . in realistic circumstances the preference for damage remedies is not always justified. In terms of achieving efficiency, . . . damage remedies are just as susceptible to strategic behavior problems as injunctive remedies when, realistically, courts cannot correctly determine actual damages. And in terms of achieving distributional equity, . . . damage remedies are not nearly as flexible distributionally as is usually presumed. Damage remedies are still preferable in some circumstances, but injunctive remedies are superior in other circumstances.

. . . .

The first argument against injunctive remedies was that they allowed the plaintiff to "extort" the defendant, that is, to obtain compensation possibly far in excess of the plaintiff's actual damages. But in the framework of this article, "excess" compensation simply means that the plaintiff is sharing the gains from trade with the defendant. Neither party is "entitled" to these gains in the first place; rather, the desirability of those transfers depends on the distributional goal society wishes to promote. If the distributional goal strongly favors the plaintiff and if redistribution by other means is costly, then excess compensation may be desirable.

Even if the distributional effects of extortion are undesirable, turning from injunctive remedies to damages does not necessarily avoid them. If the court has imperfect information and is likely to understate the plaintiff's damages, then the defendant can "extort" the plaintiff in two ways. First, since the defendant's output will initially exceed the efficient output when damages are understated, the plaintiff will have an incentive to bribe the defendant to reduce output. But the defendant can hold out for more than his lost profits, thereby extorting the plaintiff. Moreover, the defendant can threaten to increase output beyond his profit maximizing output, thereby extorting the plaintiff in a different way. Thus, the extortion argument against the injunctive remedy may be misguided even on its own terms if one accepts the realistic assumption that the court underestimates the plaintiff's damages.

The second argument for damage remedies concerned the efficiency consequences of unsuccessful extortion. According to this argument, strategic behavior under the injunctive remedy might lead to the enforcement of the injunction when enforcement was inefficient. Given strategic behavior, this criticism is valid whenever the entitlement point does not coincide with the efficient outcome. However, the same type of criticism applies at least as forcefully to the damage remedy when, as frequently happens, courts underestimate the plaintiff's damages. As noted in the previous paragraph, when damages are understated, the defendant can employ strategic behavior to extort the plaintiff in two ways: He can reject the plaintiff's "bribe" to reduce output, or he can carry out threats to increase output. Either way, the efficiency loss from strategic behavior under the damage remedy could be larger than the efficiency loss under the injunctive remedy.

The third argument favoring damage remedies was that they are distributionally more flexible—the liability schedule apparently can be precisely adjusted to allow overcompensation ("bonus payments") or undercompensation to achieve desired distributional results. In contrast, it was noted, the distributional outcome under the injunctive remedy is uncertain because of strategic behavior. However, damage remedies are potentially superior in pursuing distributional goals only when the courts have perfect information about the plaintiff's actual damages. Even then, the distributional flexibility of damage remedies is quite limited. It was shown that liability schedules that overcompensate the plaintiff are subject to the same kinds of strategic behavior problems that arise under the injunctive remedy. Moreover, no advantage accrues to using a liability schedule that undercompensates the plaintiff. And when, as can realistically be assumed, courts understate damages, the distributional advantages of the damage remedy may disappear altogether.

. . . Under none of the assumptions examined are damage remedies unambiguously favored, except, possibly, when there are many victims. And under the most realistic set of assumptions—strategic behavior, costly redistribution, and understated damages—the argument could easily go either way.

Though neither remedy can be established conclusively as superior in the abstract, the better remedy in practice may be clear depending on the circumstances. Suppose, for example, that efficiency is of paramount concern. If it seems that the parties would act strategically, and the court knows the victim's damages but not the injurer's benefits, the damage remedy is clearly superior. Inadequate information about the injurer's benefits would prevent the court from accurately setting the entitlement at the efficient point, so that the injunctive remedy will fail because of strategic behavior. However, by assigning an absolute entitlement to the victim and using a damage remedy with liability equal to actual damages, the efficient outcome can be guaranteed.

On the other hand, if the court lacks information about both damages and benefits, then an argument can be made for the injunctive remedy. The argument is especially strong if the efficiency loss from too little activity by the injurer is small relative to the loss from excessive activity. Under the injunctive remedy, the court could give an absolute entitlement to the victim and know that, at worst, the parties will remain at the entitlement point because of bargaining failure. Under the damage remedy, however, the court's lack of information may well result in a liability schedule which leads the injurer to engage in too much activity, especially if the injurer carries out extortion threats. This could easily result in a much larger efficiency loss.

Bringing distributional issues back into consideration may simplify the choice of remedy. For example, if the distributional goal does not strongly favor one party and the court knows the victim's damages and the injurer's benefits, then the damage remedy with liability equal to actual damages is preferable. It can reach the efficient outcome and simultaneously redistribute income to the desired extent. However, if the distributional goal strongly favors one party and efficiency is less important, an injunctive remedy may be better.

While the arguments developed in this article cannot provide a unique answer— indeed, that is the point of the article—they may help clarify the goals in resolving nuisance disputes and, given the goals, the principles relevant to choosing the better remedy.

————————

Apply some of Polinsky's thoughts to the *Boomer* case. Are there reasons to award an injunction rather than damages? Daniel Farber, in the same article that is excerpted before the *Boomer* opinion, argued that the behavior of Atlantic Cement was so egregious that some form of serious financial or punitive sanction should have been imposed on the company. One goal of imposing such relief would be to create incentives to entice the Atlantic Cement Companies of this world to purchase properties likely to pose land use conflicts with their planned use before they undertake their projects, or locate elsewhere if the purchases can't be made. If Atlantic Cement had acquired a buffer zone of land around their planned factory, much like those planning Dulles International Airport outside of Washington, D.C. did many years ago, problems could have been avoided.

What sort of remedy might serve this goal? To start your thinking, assume that the present value of the Atlantic Cement Company quarry and factory was $30 million, that the total amount of actual damage to each of the five[33] nearby neighbors was $150,000, for a total of $750,000, that transaction costs for each of the neighbors were $50,000, for a total of $250,000, and that whatever impediments existed to joint action among the neighbors had been overcome by the chance to recover significant damage awards. Look over the resulting entitlement table:

Boomer Entitlement Table

Entitlement to:	Remedy	Result
Atlantic Cement	Liability Rule (Damages)	Dust Pollution and Shakes. No Payment to Neighbors.
Atlantic Cement	Property Rule (Injunction)	Dust Pollution and Shakes. No Payment to Neighbors.
Neighbors	Liability Rule (Damages)	Dust Pollution and Shakes. Atlantic Pays $750,000
Neighbors	Property Rule (Injunction)	Dust Pollution and Shakes. Atlantic Pays Between $1 million and $30 million[34]

If you think the plaintiffs should receive more than their actual losses, then granting them an injunction is certainly one way to do it. The injunction would allow the neighbors to seek some of the value of the factory in addition to their losses and costs as part of any settlement. Would you allow that result?

If you think the potential premium an injunction would provide is too large, but an award of standard damages is too small, what remedy would you impose? Should nuisance courts make "bonus" awards, even when punitive damages can't be awarded because the defendant's actions were not taken with malice? In the actual case, the final amount paid out by Atlantic Cement was probably higher than the actual losses to the plaintiffs. In the cryptic ending of the *Boomer* opinion, the court vacated the $185,000 damage award entered by the court below and said simply that the trial court could "make new findings." That opening apparently led Atlantic Cement to increase its settlement offers and allowed Kinley to win a significant award on retrial. The rationales for the final amounts are not known.

To help you pull various threads of thought together, do you think courts should award damages in amounts greater than actual losses for any of the following reasons:

[33] I have changed the facts just a bit to ease review.

[34] Presumably the neighbors would not settle for less than their actual losses plus their transaction costs. That is why the minimum settlement price is set at $1 million rather than $750,000.

(a) It is appropriate to create fiscal deterrents to the location of polluting industries in populated areas.

(b) The pollution in *Boomer* had an impact on many persons other than plaintiffs or other nearby landowners. But many of these other persons could not bring a nuisance action. Employees, even if their health was affected, probably hesitated to sue their boss. Those outside the range of heavy pollution effects probably lacked standing to sue at all. A larger award was therefore necessary in order to pass along the *true* costs of the pollution to Atlantic. An award of such a premium creates the appropriate incentive for an efficient judgment about the value of entering the cement business and should be awarded even though the amounts paid to the actual plaintiffs are well above their actual losses and transaction costs.

(c) Even if present pollution technology could not halt the dust from spreading outside the factory, the award of actual damages does not create a large enough incentive for the development of pollution controls by Atlantic and other cement manufacturers. Given the harm caused by the industry, low levels of expenditures on pollution research cannot be justified.

(d) Grappling with pollution is expensive for potential plaintiffs. Additional damages are needed to assist with attorney's fees, court costs, expert witness fees and other typical costs associated with bringing a lawsuit. In addition, people are difficult to organize. Since cases like *Boomer* are best brought by groups, additional incentives are necessary to overcome the normal human impediments to community organization.

[*iii*]   *Distributional Issues.* If you want to award more than actual damages, do you want the "right" people to collect the money? If harm to future generations or to parties other than the polluted landowners is used as the basis for increasing the award, why give the premium to the landowners? If a desire for more pollution research drives the award, why not accomplish that purpose by forcing the companies to pay outsiders for research or imposing penalties upon pollution causing industries spending less than a certain amount on research? Could a court award a damage premium and establish a trust fund for pollution research or seek out those persons who might actually be entitled to monetary awards?

[*iv*]   *Free Riders.* A *free rider* takes advantage of the gains resulting from expenditures by another party. After the *Boomer* litigation is completed, suppose another neighbor makes a demand upon Atlantic Cement Company that they stop dust pollution and dynamite damage. Would the remedy originally granted to the plaintiffs in the lawsuit have an impact on the response of Atlantic Cement? If the original parties were awarded a specific sum of money, whether actual losses or actual losses with some sort of bonus, the new case presumably would move right along to its own independent conclusion.[35] If the first trial resulted in an injunction against Atlantic Cement which the company then purchased at a premium price, the second case might result in a similar result with the need to make another premium payment. If there were enough potential plaintiffs around lying in wait, the company could end up paying quite a lot. One way to avoid this sort of effect is to use the class action device to preclude action by later plaintiffs. But many class actions don't allow all parties to be precluded from participation in another case and *Boomer*-like settings may not be eligible for class action treatment. In other cases would the possibility of a free rider lead you to forgo use of the injunctive remedy?

---

[35] The late filer might gain some benefits from the results of the first case. For example, there might be some collateral estoppel impact resulting from the facts found in the first trial that could be used again without much factual digging. There might also be some negative effects. There would, for example, be precedential impact from the initial decision about the appropriate form of relief. But the cases probably would be largely independent of one another.

[**v**] *Injunctive Relief, Site Assemblage Problems, and the Impact of Condemnation.*
A party holding an injunction against the operation of a valuable enterprise functions economically very much like an entity holding a crucial parcel in an area being bought up for development.
Suppose, for example, that Site Assembly Inc. (SAI), a real estate company, is attempting to
assemble a site for a new office building in the middle of a large city. SAI has managed to
purchase all but one parcel out of the dozen or so that were under separate ownership when
the assemblage process began. Unfortunately, the single holdout parcel is crucial to future
development, since it is in the middle of the block and reaches back to an alley which can be
closed only if all land on both sides of it is owned by the same party. There are no typical rules
permitting SAI or any other developer to compel the holdout owner either to sell or to agree
to a certain price. Just as a holdout plaintiff holding an entitlement under an injunction in a setting
like *Boomer* may ask for a premium before selling, the holdout parcel owner may demand a
share of the value of the development project over and above the value of the land if left
undeveloped. If you think a holdout parcel owner should not be able to extract a significant part
of the development value from the developer, then you should favor some compulsory sale
process. If you think that the holdout owner ought to be able to get as much as possible from
the developer, then you would leave things as they are. In either case, compare your views on
the holdout situation with your views in the nuisance-injunction setting. If you would permit
a holdout owner to extract more than actual loss or value in one case but not the other, explain
why.

One way to avoid a holdout problem is to make condemnation available to the party wishing
to assemble land (or end an injunction for that matter). Governments assembling large sites for
public use condemn all the needed parcels at once, paying standard, non-holdout prices, for each
one. Urban renewal projects, highway and school construction, park development and many other
public endeavors proceed this way. In general, private parties are not given access to the
condemnation power, though utility companies often may use it to assemble rights of way.[36]
Should the condemnation power ever be used to circumvent the issuance of injunctions or the
impact of holdouts on private development? Was there any real functional difference between
the damage award in *Boomer* and a condemnation? Didn't both end the ability of the plaintiffs
to seek a holdout level price for selling their rights? Was the dissenter in *Boomer* therefore
correct?

[**vi**] *Public Regulation.* Putting all of the problems from these notes together provides
some sense about the sorts of situations in which public regulation is likely to arise. When it
is hard for individual citizens to control actions of large enterprises or large numbers of nuisance
makers, transaction costs are high, incentives for "proper" development of land are hard to create,
free rider problems exist, and damages provide too little relief and injunctions grant too much,
political pressure for government intervention is likely to be high.

[2] The *Spur* Litigation

[a] The Commons

In a brief but famous essay, Garrett Hardin's *The Tragedy of the Commons,* 162 SCIENCE 1243
(1968), Hardin described an economic dilemma about herdsmen using a common field. Each

---

[36] Those purchasing land cleared in urban renewal projects also get the advantage of a price lowered by use of
the condemnation power. *See Berman v. Parker,* at p. 900 below.

herdsman gains positive economic benefit from adding one more animal to his flock. The result is that the field is over grazed. Hardin noted that the same phenomenon drives those in advanced societies to overuse supplies of commonly available resources, including air and water.[37] Caring for such *public goods* requires either a common understanding about the appropriate levels of use,[38] or some form of public regulation. The next case is a particularly good example of problems in the commons. It arose because of urban sprawl reaching into areas long used in agricultural ways that made life uncomfortable for suburban home owners. For a lengthy history of development of Sun City, Arizona, as a retirement and resort community, *see* JOHN M. FINDLAY, MAGIC LANDS: WESTERN CITYSCAPES AND AMERICAN CULTURE AFTER 1940, at 160-213 (1992). Conflicts over Sun City developments continue to appear. The most recent controversies have arisen as Del Webb builds on other large sites near Luke Air Force Base, one of the largest air force training bases in the country. About three-quarters of the noise complaints come from Sun City residents.[39]

[b] Opinion of the Arizona Supreme Court in *Spur v. Del Webb*

Spur Industries, Inc. v. Del E. Webb Development Co.

Arizona Supreme Court
108 Ariz. 178, 494 P.2d 700 (1972)

CAMERON, VICE CHIEF JUSTICE.

From a judgment permanently enjoining the defendant, Spur Industries, Inc., from operating a cattle feedlot near the plaintiff Del E. Webb Development Company's Sun City, Spur appeals. Webb cross-appeals. Although numerous issues are raised, we feel that it is necessary to answer only two questions. They are:

1. Where the operation of a business, such as a cattle feedlot is lawful in the first instance, but becomes a nuisance by reason of a nearby residential area, may the feedlot operation be enjoined in an action brought by the developer of the residential area?

2. Assuming that the nuisance may be enjoined, may the developer of a completely new town or urban area in a previously agricultural area be required to indemnify the operator of the feedlot who must move or cease operation because of the presence of the residential area created by the developer?

The facts necessary for a determination of this matter on appeal are as follows. The area in question is located in Maricopa County, Arizona, some 14 to 15 miles west of the urban area of Phoenix, on the Phoenix-Wickenburg Highway, also known as Grand Avenue. About two miles south of Grand Avenue is Olive Avenue which runs east and west. 111th Avenue runs

---

[37] A similar problem arises in intellectual property. If a book is free for everyone to copy, then sales of the "official" version will decline. Copyright, in part, is designed to structure markets to provide a market for material that would otherwise be public goods—free for use at little or no cost.

[38] In a recent essay commenting on Hardin's, George Monbiot noted that many cultures were able to manage their grazing commons by maintaining nomadic life styles or obeying norms of behavior about temperate use of resources. When common lands are enclosed, Monbiot suggested, controlling use levels gets more difficult. *The Tragedy of Enclosure,* 273 SCIENTIFIC AMERICAN 159 (1994).

[39] Jennifer Barrett, *Luke's Losing Ground: Development Clouds Future of Fighter Base,* THE ARIZONA REPUBLIC (Nov. 6, 1997).

north and south as does the Agua Fria River immediately to the west. See Exhibits A and B below.

Farming started in this area about 1911. In 1929, with the completion of the Carl Pleasant Dam, gravity flow water became available to the property located to the west of the Agua Fria River, though land to the east remained dependent upon well water for irrigation. By 1950, the only urban areas in the vicinity were the agriculturally related communities of Peoria, El Mirage, and Surprise located along Grand Avenue. Along 111th Avenue, approximately one mile south of Grand Avenue and 1½ miles north of Olive Avenue, the community of Youngtown was commenced in 1954. Youngtown is a retirement community appealing primarily to senior citizens.

In 1956, Spur's predecessors in interest, H. Marion Welborn and the Northside Hay Mill and Trading Company, developed feedlots, about ½ mile south of Olive Avenue, in an area between the confluence of the usually dry Agua Fria and New Rivers. The area is well suited for cattle feeding and in 1959, there were 25 cattle feeding pens or dairy operations within a 7 mile radius of the location developed by Spur's predecessors. In April and May of 1959, the Northside Hay Mill was feeding between 6,000 and 7,000 head of cattle and Welborn approximately 1,500 head on a combined area of 35 acres.

In May of 1959, Del Webb began to plan the development of an urban area to be known as Sun City. For this purpose, the Marinette and the Santa Fe Ranches, some 20,000 acres of farmland, were purchased for $15,000,000 or $750.00 per acre. This price was considerably less than the price of land located near the urban area of Phoenix, and along with the success of Youngtown was a factor influencing the decision to purchase the property in question.

By September 1959, Del Webb had started construction of a golf course south of Grand Avenue and Spur's predecessors had started to level ground for more feedlot area. In 1960, Spur purchased the property in question and began a rebuilding and expansion program extending both to the north and south of the original facilities. By 1962, Spur's expansion program was completed and had expanded from approximately 35 acres to 114 acres. See Exhibit A . . . .

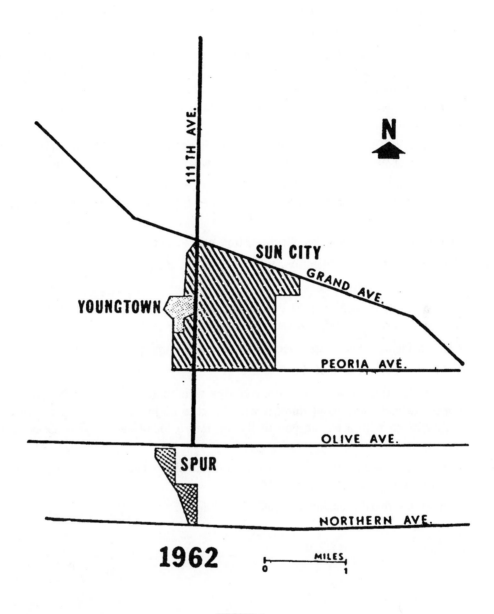

EXHIBIT A

Accompanied by an extensive advertising campaign, homes were first offered by Del Webb in January 1960 and the first unit to be completed was south of Grand Avenue and approximately 2½ miles north of Spur. By 2 May 1960, there were 450 to 500 houses completed or under construction. At this time, Del Webb did not consider odors from the Spur feed pens a problem and Del Webb continued to develop in a southerly direction, until sales resistance became so great that the parcels were difficult if not impossible to sell. Thomas E. Breen, Vice President and General Manager of the housing division of Del Webb, testified at deposition as follows:

Q: Did you ever have any discussions with Tony Cole at or about the time the sales office was opened south of Peoria concerning the problem in sales as the development came closer towards the feed lots?

A: Not at the time that that facility was opened. That was subsequent to that.

Q: All right, what is it that you recall about conversations with Cole on that subject?

A: Well, when the feed lot problem became a bigger problem, which, really, to the best of my recollection, commenced to become a serious problem in 1963, and there was some talk about not developing that area because of sales resistance, and to my recollection we shifted—we had planned at that time to the eastern portion of the property, and it was a consideration.

Q: Was any specific suggestion made by Mr. Cole as to the line of demarcation that should be drawn or anything of that type exactly where the development should cease?

A: I don't recall anything specific as far as the definite line would be, other than, you know, that it would be advisable to stay out of the southwestern portion there because of sales resistance.

Q: And to the best of your recollection, this was in about 1963?

A: That would be my recollection, yes.

. . . .

Q: As you recall it, what was the reason that the suggestion was not adopted to stop developing towards the southwest of the development?

A: Well, as far as I know, that decision was made subsequent to that time.

Q: Right. But I mean at that time?

A: Well, at that time what I am really referring to is more of a long-range planning than immediate planning, and I think it was the case of just trying to figure out how far you could go with it before you really ran into a lot of sales resistance and found a necessity to shift the direction.

Q: So the plan was to go as far as you could until the resistance got to the point where you couldn't go any further?

A: I would say that is reasonable, yes.

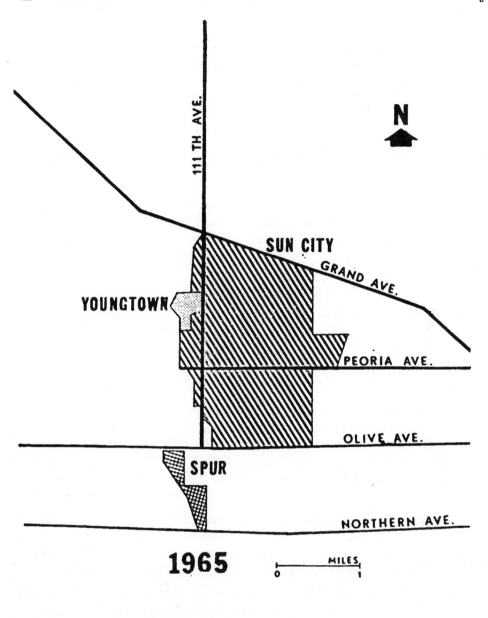

EXHIBIT B

By December 1967, Del Webb's property had extended south to Olive Avenue and Spur was within 500 feet of Olive Avenue to the north. See Exhibit B above. Del Webb filed its original complaint alleging that in excess of 1,300 lots in the southwest portion were unfit for development for sale as residential lots because of the operation of the Spur feedlot.

Del Webb's suit complained that the Spur feeding operation was a public nuisance because of the flies and the odor which were drifting or being blown by the prevailing south to north wind over the southern portion of Sun City. At the time of the suit, Spur was feeding between 20,000 and 30,000 head of cattle, and the facts amply support the finding of the trial court that the feed pens had become a nuisance to the people who resided in the southern part of Del Webb's development. The testimony indicated that cattle in a commercial feedlot will produce 35 to 40 pounds of wet manure per day, per head, or over a million pounds of wet manure per day for 30,000 head of cattle, and that despite the admittedly good feedlot management and good housekeeping practices by Spur, the resulting odor and flies produced an annoying if not unhealthy situation as far as the senior citizens of southern Sun City were concerned. There is no doubt that some of the citizens of Sun City were unable to enjoy the outdoor living which Del Webb had advertised and that Del Webb was faced with sales resistance from prospective purchasers as well as strong and persistent complaints from the people who had purchased homes in that area.

Trial was commenced before the court with an advisory jury. The advisory jury was later discharged and the trial was continued before the court alone. Findings of fact and conclusions of law were requested and given. The case was vigorously contested, including special actions in this court on some of the matters. In one of the special actions before this court, Spur agreed to, and did, shut down its operation without prejudice to a determination of the matter on appeal. On appeal the many questions raised were extensively briefed.

It is noted, however, that neither the citizens of Sun City nor Youngtown are represented in this lawsuit and the suit is solely between Del E. Webb Development Company and Spur Industries, Inc.

MAY SPUR BE ENJOINED?

The difference between a private nuisance and a public nuisance is generally one of degree. A private nuisance is one affecting a single individual or a definite small number of persons in the enjoyment of private rights not common to the public, while a public nuisance is one affecting the rights enjoyed by citizens as a part of the public. To constitute a public nuisance, the nuisance must affect a considerable number of people or an entire community or neighborhood.

Where the injury is slight, the remedy for minor inconveniences lies in an action for damages rather than in one for an injunction. Moreover, some courts have held, in the "balancing of conveniences" cases, that damages may be the sole remedy. *See Boomer v. Atlantic Cement Co.,* 26 N.Y.2d 219, 309 N.Y.S.2d 312, 257 N.E.2d 870, 40 A.L.R.3d 590 (1970).

Thus, it would appear from the admittedly incomplete record as developed in the trial court, that, at most, residents of Youngtown would be entitled to damages rather than injunctive relief.

We have no difficulty, however, in agreeing with the conclusion of the trial court that Spur's operation was an enjoinable public nuisance as far as the people in the southern portion of Del Webb's Sun City were concerned.

§ 36-601, subsec. A reads as follows:

§ 36-601. Public nuisances dangerous to public health

A. The following conditions are specifically declared public nuisances dangerous to the public health:

1. Any condition or place in populous areas which constitutes a breeding place for flies, rodents, mosquitoes and other insects which are capable of carrying and transmitting disease-causing organisms to any person or persons.

By this statute, before an otherwise lawful (and necessary) business may be declared a public nuisance, there must be a "populous" area in which people are injured:

. . . [I]t hardly admits a doubt that, in determining the question as to whether a lawful occupation is so conducted as to constitute a nuisance as a matter of fact, the locality and surroundings are of the first importance. (Citations omitted.) A business which is not per se a public nuisance may become such by being carried on at a place where the health, comfort, or convenience of a populous neighborhood is affected . . . . What might amount to a serious nuisance in one locality by reason of the density of the population, or character of the neighborhood affected, may in another place and under different surroundings be deemed proper and unobjectionable . . . .

MacDonald v. Perry, 32 Ariz. 39, 255 P. 494 (1927).

It is clear that as to the citizens of Sun City, the operation of Spur's feedlot was both a public and a private nuisance. They could have successfully maintained an action to abate the nuisance. Del Webb, having shown a special injury in the loss of sales, had a standing to bring suit to enjoin the nuisance. The judgment of the trial court permanently enjoining the operation of the feedlot is affirmed.

MUST DEL WEBB INDEMNIFY SPUR?

A suit to enjoin a nuisance sounds in equity and the courts have long recognized a special responsibility to the public when acting as a court of equity:

§ 104. Where public interest is involved.

Courts of equity may, and frequently do, go much further both to give and withhold relief in furtherance of the public interest than they are accustomed to go when only private interests are involved. Accordingly, the granting or withholding of relief may properly be dependent upon considerations of public interest . . . .

27 Am. Jur.2d, *Equity,* page 626.

In addition to protecting the public interest, however, courts of equity are concerned with protecting the operator of a lawfully, albeit noxious, business from the result of a knowing and willful encroachment by others near his business.

In the so-called "coming to the nuisance" cases, the courts have held that the residential landowner may not have relief if he knowingly came into a neighborhood reserved for industrial or agricultural endeavors and has been damaged thereby:

Plaintiffs chose to live in an area uncontrolled by zoning laws or restrictive covenants and remote from urban development. In such an area plaintiffs cannot complain that legitimate agricultural pursuits are being carried on in the vicinity, nor can plaintiffs, having chosen to build in an agricultural area, complain that the agricultural pursuits carried on in the area depreciate the value of their homes. The area being *primarily agricultural,* any opinion reflecting the value of such property must take this factor into account. The standards affecting the value of residence property in an urban setting, subject to zoning controls and controlled planning techniques, cannot be the standards by which agricultural properties are judged.

People employed in a city who build their homes in suburban areas of the county beyond the limits of a city and zoning regulations do so for a reason. Some do so to avoid the high taxation rate imposed by cities, or to avoid special assessments for street, sewer and water projects. They usually build on improved or hard surface highways, which have been built either at state or county expense and thereby avoid special assessments for these improvements. It may be that they desire to get away from the congestion of traffic, smoke, noise, foul air and the many other annoyances of city life. But with all these advantages in going beyond the area which is zoned and restricted to protect them in their homes, they must be prepared to take the disadvantages.

Dill v. Excel Packing Company, 183 Kan. 513, 331 P.2d 539 (1958).

. . . .

Were Webb the only party injured, we would feel justified in holding that the doctrine of "coming to the nuisance" would have been a bar to the relief asked by Webb, and, on the other hand, had Spur located the feedlot near the outskirts of a city and had the city grown toward the feedlot, Spur would have to suffer the cost of abating the nuisance as to those people locating within the growth pattern of the expanding city.

. . . .

There was no indication in the instant case at the time Spur and its predecessors located in western Maricopa County that a new city would spring up, full-blown, alongside the feeding operation and that the developer of that city would ask the court to order Spur to move because of the new city. Spur is required to move not because of any wrongdoing on the part of Spur, but because of a proper and legitimate regard of the courts for the rights and interests of the public.

Del Webb, on the other hand, is entitled to the relief prayed for (a permanent injunction), not because Webb is blameless, but because of the damage to the people who have been encouraged to purchase homes in Sun City. It does not equitably or legally follow, however, that Webb, being entitled to the injunction, is then free of any liability to Spur if Webb has in fact been the cause of the damage Spur has sustained. It does not seem harsh to require a developer, who has taken advantage of the lesser land values in a rural area as well as the availability of large tracts of land on which to build and develop a new town or city in the area, to indemnify those who are forced to leave as a result.

Having brought people to the nuisance to the foreseeable detriment of Spur, Webb must indemnify Spur for a reasonable amount of the cost of moving or shutting down. It should be noted that this relief to Spur is limited to a case wherein a developer has, with foreseeability, brought into a previously agricultural or industrial area the population which makes necessary the granting of an injunction against a lawful business and for which the business has no adequate relief.

It is therefore the decision of this court that the matter be remanded to the trial court for a hearing upon the damages sustained by the defendant Spur as a reasonable and direct result of the granting of the permanent injunction. Since the result of the appeal may appear novel and both sides have obtained a measure of relief, it is ordered that each side will bear its own costs.

Affirmed in part, reversed in part, and remanded for further proceedings consistent with this opinion.

HAYS, C.J., STRUCKMEYER and LOCKWOOD, JJ., and UDALL, Retired Justice.

[c] Explanatory Notes

[*i*] **Spur.** *Spur* is the only case of note to award a *compensated injunction* to a "successful" nuisance plaintiff. That is, Del Webb was granted an injunction against further operation of the feedlot, but at the cost of paying the cost of moving the feedlot. Some have suggested that there is something quite special about this result.[40] But in many ways the case was like *Boomer.* Think of Atlantic Cement and Del Webb as similar parties on one side, and Boomer and Spur as similar parties on the other side. Both Atlantic Cement and Del Webb came to areas with established land use patterns and introduced a new, "disruptive" activity. Boomer and Spur represent the "traditional" use patterns. In each case, the new, larger, more costly undertaking was permitted to continue its activities as long as it paid damages to the "traditional" users. The procedural setting of the cases certainly differed. The "traditional" use was represented by the plaintiff in *Boomer,* but by the defendant in *Spur.* The new user was labeled a nuisance in *Boomer,* while the old user was called a nuisance in *Spur.* But the end result of each case was quite similar—the entitlement was awarded to the "traditional" user and the new user was required to pay damages.

[*ii*] **Measure of Damages.** The *Spur* court held that Del Webb had to indemnify Spur "for a reasonable amount of the cost of moving or shutting down." How should this damage measure be determined? If Spur wished to move its operation to another location, Del Webb presumably had to pay for the purchase of the new land, the installation of new fixtures and buildings, and lost profits during the transition period. A good argument may also be made that Webb should pay more than compensatory damages in this case. Given the costs of litigation, including the suits described in the next note brought by residents against Spur, compensatory damages would hardly repay Spur. In addition, Webb elected to develop land that was unsuitable for residential use. Perhaps others should be deterred from undertaking similar developments in the future by requiring Del Webb to pay a large amount in damages. In any case, after the remand in *Spur* the case was settled for an amount "in the millions."[41] Spur did relocate and operated a new feedlot until about 10 years ago.

[*iii*] **The Residents of Sun City.** The *Spur* court indicated that Del Webb had to pay damages because it enticed such a large number of residents to the area even though difficulty with odors and flies from the feed lots was foreseeable. Indeed, while *Spur* was being decided by the Arizona Supreme Court, over 400 property owners in Sun City were seeking damages from Spur in other lawsuits because of Spur's cattle feeding operation.[42] After *Spur* was decided, Spur, as defendant in the actions brought by Sun City residents, filed a third party complaint against Del E. Webb Development Company claiming indemnity from Webb for any damages Spur might have to pay to Sun City residents.[43] The Arizona Supreme Court later confirmed that Spur had the right to file the third party complaint.[44]

---

[40] Jeff Lewin spends quite a bit of time on this question in his article, *Compensated Injunctions and the Evolution of Nuisance Law,* 71 IOWA L. REV. 775 (1986).

[41] Fritz Mulhauser, Georgetown University Law Center Class of 2002, one of my property students, got interested in the case and called John Lundin, one of the attorneys for Spur. He did not recall the exact amount of the settlement. Telephone Interview (Apr. 8, 1998).

[42] For a different view of the residents, there is a long article on the "culture" of Sun Cities that have been constructed around the country by Del Webb. *See* the piece by Frances Fitzgerald, in THE NEW YORKER 54 (Apr. 25, 1983).

[43] This was the Arizona equivalent of an impleader filed under FED. R. CIV. P. 14.

[44] Spur Feeding Co. v. Superior Court of Maricopa County, 109 Ariz. 105, 505 P.2d 1377 (1973).

Did the residents have a claim against either Spur or Webb? The outcome of *Spur* probably gave those Sun City residents living in the area *before* the decision was rendered two economic benefits. First, the cost of their housing units probably did not include any anticipated costs associated with the *Spur* litigation. Second, to the extent that the feedlots depressed housing prices in the area, the termination of the feed lots instantly made their housing units more valuable. Those arriving *after* the litigation was over gained neither of these advantages. Should a portion of the costs associated with the *Spur* litigation have been "taxed" against the older residents so that the new residents effectively paid the same amounts for their housing units? As with some of the possible damage systems discussed after *Boomer,* the benefits of the *Spur* outcome may not necessarily be distributed to the economically most deserving parties. Though the *Spur* court's preservation of the more valuable of the two enterprises may have been economically efficient, it paid little attention to the distributional impact of its decision. In any case, after *Spur* was decided, were there any damages left to give to the residents? Perhaps they are entitled to damages for the unpleasant living experience they endured while the feedlot existed, but surely they are not entitled to any money for lowering of property values once the feedlot was gone unless they sold out when prices were down. Given the *Spur* court's reasoning, any damages should probably come from Webb's pockets. Compare the implied warranty of fitness decisions like *Humber v. Morton,* p. 812 above.

[*iv*] ***Preservation of Agricultural Land.*** The continued encroachment of urban and suburban development into agricultural areas has led a number of states to adopt legislation designed to save agricultural land uses.[45] Typical legislation has reduced property tax rates for agricultural land[46] or zoned land for agricultural uses only. Some jurisdictions have also purchased or condemned the value of non-agricultural use of farm property or permitted the owner of agricultural land to sell the development potential to others for use on non-agricultural land. In either case, the farm owner is left with land that is usable only for agricultural purposes; the development potential is owned either by the public or private developers. In those schemes involving transfer of the farm's development rights to others, the purchasers of the development rights are allowed to build on non-agricultural land at more intense levels than is otherwise permitted by typical zoning regulations.[47]

In 1981 Arizona enacted legislation which probably reversed that part of *Spur* holding the feed lot to be a nuisance. The preamble to the enactment reads:

> The legislature declares that agricultural operations conducted on farmland in urbanizing areas are often subject to nuisance lawsuits and that the litigation encourages and even forces the premature removal of the land from agricultural uses. In this act, it is the intent of the legislature to ensure that agricultural operations conducted on farmland be adequately protected from nuisance litigation.

---

[45] *See* Alexander A. Reinert, *The Right to Farm: Hog-Tied and Nuisance-Bound,* 73 N.Y.U. L. Rev. 1694 (1998); Margaret Rosso Grossman & Thomas G. Fischer, *Protecting the Right to Farm: Statutory Limits on Nuisance Actions Against the Farmer,* 1983 Wis. L. Rev. 95; Jacqueline P. Hand, *Right-to-Farm Laws: Breaking New Ground in the Preservation of Farmland,* 45 U. Pitt. L. Rev. 289 (1984); Note, *The Arizona Agricultural Nuisance Protection Act,* 1982 Ariz. St. L.J. 689.

[46] The vast majority of states have such legislation. *See* Hand, note 45 above, at 293. Hand noted that 48 states had property tax relief acts.

[47] *Compare Penn Central v. City of New York,* p. 948 below, a transferred development rights case where severance of development rights from the rest of the real estate was used to preserve historical building rather than a farm.

The relevant sections of the Arizona Revised Statutes read as follows:

Section 3-311. Definitions

In this chapter, unless the context otherwise requires:

1. "Agricultural operations" means all activities by the owner, lessee, agent, independent contractor and supplier conducted on any facility for the production of crops, livestock, poultry, livestock products or poultry products.

2. "Farmland" means land devoted primarily to the production for commercial purposes of livestock or agricultural commodities.

Section 3-312. Agricultural operations; nuisance liability

A. Agricultural operations conducted on farmland that are consistent with good agricultural practice and established prior to surrounding non-agricultural uses are presumed to be reasonable and do not constitute a nuisance unless the agricultural operation has a substantial adverse effect on the public health and safety.

B. Agricultural operations undertaken in conformity with federal, state and local laws and regulations are presumed to be good agricultural practice and not adversely affecting the public health and safety.

Decide *Spur* under this statute. If the feedlot prevails, then it gains an entitlement to remain despite the encroachment of developments like Del Webb's and the concomitant ability to demand some of Del Webb's potential profit before selling out. If the feedlot elects to stay and not sell, may the residents of Sun City sue in nuisance even though Del Webb may not?

[d]   Problem Notes

[*i*]   *Measure of Damages for Spur.* As noted above, the *Spur* court gave fairly vague guidelines on how to measure the damages Webb had to pay to Spur for its injunction. "Webb," the court said, "must indemnify Spur for a reasonable amount of the cost of moving or shutting down." Which of the following items are included in this damage theory?

(a) Attorney's fees and court costs to defray the costs of the nuisance litigation.

(b) Assuming Spur moved farther out of town, the greater costs to transport cattle to and from the feedlot resulting from the less convenient location.

(c) Punitive damages because of the intentional actions of Webb.

(d) The mortgage payments and other carrying charges on the old farm during the period of transition from old to new location.

(e) Lost profits resulting from the business disruption associated with the move.

Can you think of other problem areas?

[*ii*]   *Webb Coming to the Nuisance.* The *Spur* court forced Del Webb to buy its injunction because it developed property in an area beset with difficulties. Implicit in this conclusion is the idea that Webb should have purchased Spur's land before beginning its mammoth project. Having failed to buy out Spur, Webb was then caught in a vice. It couldn't sell any more houses and Spur, seeing the control it had over future development, had the economic power to demand a greater price for its land than Webb would have had to pay before development began. Under these circumstances, isn't it appropriate to let Spur obtain more than

just moving costs from Webb as a warning to others that they had better buy out inconsistent land uses before beginning their own projects? Recall the notes after *Boomer* on premiums and holdouts. If Spur could have demanded a premium as a holdout seller, then why not give it a premium in the nuisance litigation?

[*iii*]   *What to Do With the Old Land?* If Spur decides to move, but wishes to keep its old site, how should that be handled? Should Webb be given a credit for the cost to Spur of the old land or the present value of the old land? If Spur decides to sell the old feedlot site and makes a large profit on the sale, should Spur retain the entire profit or should Webb gain a credit for the profit Spur makes on the sale?

[*iv*]   *Agricultural Land.* If you wanted to minimize the loss of agricultural land to urban and suburban development, what sorts of land use controls would you adopt?

[*v*]   *Ground Water.* If industrial use of ground water supplies causes either loss of water in other wells or subsidence of land, who, if anyone, should be able to sue in nuisance? For a fairly recent case confirming the existence of a nuisance cause of action in such a situation, *see Friendswood Development Co. v. Smith-Southwest Industries,* 576 S.W.2d 21 (Tex. 1978).

[*vi*]   *The Commons Revisited.* Can a market be used to control use of a commons? Some recent pollution control regimes establish the maximum amounts of certain materials that may be released into the air in an area, award certificates to those companies that reduce their polluting levels below certain levels, and allow those certificates to be sold to other companies needing the right to add to their polluting levels. So a company that installs efficient pollution control equipment would be able to sell to another company that wishes to expand its operations. What do you think of such systems?

CHAPTER **11**

PROPERTY THEORY AND THE SUPREME COURT SINCE THE NEW DEAL

§ 11.01 Introduction

The scope of land use regulation by federal, state and local governments is enormous. The federal government actually owns one-third of the land in the mainland United States, mostly in the western half of the country. In addition, Congress has adopted legislation on water pollution, flood controls, interstate land sales, real estate settlements, race and gender discrimination, mining, grazing and timbering on federal lands, national parks, wildlife zones, Native American lands and a host of other problems. State and local governments have passed an even longer list of land use measures, including zoning statutes, building codes, environmental regulations, consumer protection statutes, anti-discrimination laws, and historic preservation programs. Prior sections of the text have discussed many such regulatory schemes.

The breadth of topics covered by land use controls is much too large to cover comprehensively in a first year survey course. The purpose of this chapter, therefore, is to pull together some of the basic themes that emerge in legal discourse when public land use controls are at issue. The courts have focused on two large questions when dealing with the constitutionality of land use controls—the validity of the public purposes served by the regulation and the extent to which property may be regulated without offending the Takings Clause. [1] The vast sweep of the questions suggests that great difficulty awaits anyone attempting to create easily stated rules or bright signposts for use in deciding land use disputes. Indeed, the Supreme Court lamented in *Penn Central Transportation Company v. City of New York*, p. 955 below, that it, "quite simply, has been unable to develop any set formula for determining when justice and fairness require that economic injuries caused by public action be compensated by the government, rather than remain disproportionately concentrated on a few persons." The themes discussed here, therefore, must be viewed, not as definitive answers to long simmering disputes over the appropriate limits to place upon government control of property, but as suggestions for creating analytical models for your own use.

§ 11.02 Public Purpose and the Eminent Domain Power

[1] Introduction

It is hornbook law that land use regulations or decisions to use the eminent domain power must be supported by a valid public purpose. Between the time *Euclid v. Ambler* was decided

---

[1] Though some states have construed their constitutions to place greater limits on their government's regulation of land than those limits which the United States Supreme Court has read into the federal Constitution, the basic questions posed are the same.

and the 1980s, the Supreme Court typically refrained from closely scrutinizing the rationales used by localities to support their land use or condemnation actions. For example, in *Berman v. Parker*,[2] the owner of a parcel of land at 712 4th Street, S.W., in Washington, D.C., challenged the D.C. Redevelopment Land Agency's condemnation of the land for an urban renewal project. The urban renewal program called for the condemnation of "blighted" areas, the demolition of most existing structures, and the resale of the land to private parties for redevelopment. The federal government subsidized the condemnation and destruction of existing structures to help reduce the land's resale price and thereby entice new developers to the area. The landowner in *Berman* argued that the Constitution forbade the taking of private property for resale to private parties. The Supreme Court disagreed:

> The first project undertaken under the [Urban Renewal] Act relates to Project Area B in Southwest Washington, D.C. In 1950 the Planning Commission prepared and published a comprehensive plan for the District. Surveys revealed that in Area B, 64.3% of the dwellings were beyond repair, 18.4% needed major repairs, only 17.3% were satisfactory; 57.8% of the dwellings had outside toilets, 60.3% had no baths, 29.3% lacked electricity, 82.2% had no wash basins or laundry tubs, 83.8% lacked central heating. In the judgment of the District's Director of Health it was necessary to redevelop Area B in the interests of public health. The population of Area B amounted to 5,012 persons, of whom 97.5% were Negroes.

> . . . .

> In the present case, Congress and its authorized agencies attack the problem of the blighted parts of the community on an area rather than on a structure-by-structure basis. That . . . is opposed by appellants. They maintain that since their building does not imperil health or safety nor contribute to the making of a slum or a blighted area, it cannot be swept into a redevelopment plan by the mere dictum of the Planning Commission or the Commissioners.[3] The particular uses to be made of the land in the project were determined with regard to the needs of the particular community. The experts concluded that if the community were to be healthy, if it were not to revert again to a blighted or slum area, as though possessed of a congenital disease, the area must be planned as a whole. It was not enough, they believed, to remove existing buildings that were unsanitary or unsightly. It was important to redesign the whole area so as to eliminate the conditions that cause slums—the over crowding of dwellings, the lack of parks, the lack of adequate streets and alleys, the absence of recreational areas, the lack of light and air, the presence of outmoded street patterns. . . . The entire area needed redesigning so that a balanced, integrated plan could be developed for the region, including not only new homes but also schools, churches, parks, streets, and shopping centers. In this way it was hoped that the cycle of decay of the area could be controlled and the birth of future slums prevented. Such diversification in future use is plainly relevant to the maintenance of the desired housing standards and therefore within congressional power.[4]

Though *Berman* and other cases suggest a great reluctance on the part of the Supreme Court to inquire deeply into the rationality of purposes claimed by state and local governments to support

---

[2] 348 U.S. 26 (1954).

[3] [Editor's Note: At the time of *Berman*, the District of Columbia had no City Council or other elected legislative body. Rather a body of Commissioners were appointed by various federal officials to serve as the city's legislature. The city presently has an elected Mayor and City Council, though their Acts are subject to Congressional review. The District also has no voting members in either house of Congress.]

[4] 348 U.S. at 30, 34-35.

their regulatory actions, some state courts have been more willing to intervene under their own constitutions. This section opens with a recent case on the federal public purpose requirement that revisits some of the issues raised in *Berman v. Parker*. That is followed by a prominent state court dispute on the appropriate scope of community regulatory authority.

For additional reading on the public purpose requirement, look at Thomas W. Merrill, *The Economics of Public Use*, 72 CORNELL L. REV. 61 (1986). Merrill applies economic analysis to the public purpose requirement and spends quite a bit of time discussing all the cases in this section of the text. An excerpted version of the work may be found in RICHARD CHUSED, A PROPERTY ANTHOLOGY 483-499 (2d ed. 1997).

[2] Public Purpose and The Federal Constitution

[a] Background to *Hawaii Housing Authority v. Midkiff*

Ground leases are a common feature of the Hawaiian real estate scene. During the nineteenth century, when outsiders gradually took over most of the state's land from the Native Hawaiians,[5] real estate became heavily concentrated among a very small group of mostly non-Native owners. At the time *Hawaiian Housing Authority v. Midkiff* was litigated, the state government controlled about 39% of Hawaii's land area, the federal government a bit under 10%, and only 72 private owners held 47%. That left less than 5% of the land for others to own in a state with a population of about one million.[6]

The large landowners, including the State of Hawaii, found it much more profitable to ground lease rather than sell fee interests in usable property. The severity of the land ownership concentration eventually led the Hawaii legislature to adopt a statute permitting the state to condemn fee simple interests in ground leased residential developments and resell them to the residents.[7] The Constitutionality of that enactment was the subject of the next case, *Hawaii Housing Authority v. Midkiff*. The legislature found that the shortage of fee simple lands available on the market caused prices for such land to rise. And the monopoly-like controls exercised by the large landowners enabled them to exact high prices or stringent terms for leasehold property as well. As the Hawaii Legislature noted in the Preamble to the legislation challenged in *Midkiff*:

> The shortage of single-family, residential, fee simple property, and the restriction on the people of a real choice between fee simple and leasehold residential property have in turn caused land prices for both fee simple and leasehold residential lots to become artificially inflated and have enabled lessors to include in residential leases terms and conditions that are financially disadvantageous to the lessees, restrict unduly their freedom to enjoy their leasehold estates and are weighted heavily in favor of the landlord as against the lessees.

The Bishop Estate is the largest of Hawaii's landed charitable estates and one of the largest land holders in Hawaii, owning about 9% of the state's land area. Midkiff, the respondent before the Supreme Court, was one of the estate's trustees. The Estate was established in 1874 under the will of Princess Bernice Pauahi Bishop, which named five westerners as trustees to manage or sell the vast lands for the support of two schools giving admissions preference to Native Hawaiians, and for "the support and education of orphans, and others in indigent circumstances,

---

[5] For a history of that period, *see* Neil M. Levy, *Native Hawaiian Land Rights*, 63 CAL. L. REV. 848 (1975).

[6] Brief for the Hou Hawaiians as *Amici Curiae* at 32 in Midkiff v. Hawaiian Housing Authority (1987).

[7] HAW. REV. STAT. § 516-1 *et seq.*

giving the preference to Hawaiians."[8] About 90% of the Estate's lands are leased for long terms for residential, agricultural, commercial and industrial purposes.[9] And the Estate generally declined to use its authority to "support . . . others in indigent circumstances, giving the preference to Hawaiians" to provide land at low prices to Natives of the islands. The failure of the Bishop Estate, or other large landed charitable estates in Hawaii, to modify its ground lease policies was one of the reasons why the legislation permitting condemnation of fee simple interests in ground leased residential lands was made expressly applicable to lands held in trust, terms of the trust to the contrary notwithstanding.[10] The stage was thus set for the Bishop Estate to challenge the validity of the condemnation scheme.

[b]   Opinions of the United States Supreme Court in *Hawaii Housing Authority v. Midkiff*

Hawaii Housing Authority v. Midkiff

United States Supreme Court
467 U.S. 229, 104 S.Ct. 2321, 81 L. Ed. 2d 186 (1984)

JUSTICE O'CONNOR delivered the opinion of the Court.

The Fifth Amendment of the United States Constitution provides, in pertinent part, that "private property [shall not] be taken for public use, without just compensation." These cases present the question whether the Public Use Clause of that Amendment, made applicable to the States through the Fourteenth Amendment, prohibits the State of Hawaii from taking, with just compensation, title in real property from lessors and transferring it to lessees in order to reduce the concentration of ownership of fees simple in the State. We conclude that it does not.

I

A

The Hawaiian Islands were originally settled by Polynesian immigrants from the western Pacific. These settlers developed an economy around a feudal land tenure system in which one island high chief, the ali'I nui, controlled the land and assigned it for development to certain subchiefs. The subchiefs would then reassign the land to other lower ranking chiefs, who would administer the land and govern the farmers and other tenants working it. All land was held at the will of the ali'I nui and eventually had to be returned to his trust. There was no private ownership of land. See generally Brief for Office of Hawaiian Affairs as *Amicus Curiae* 3-5.

Beginning in the early 1800's, Hawaiian leaders and American settlers repeatedly attempted to divide the lands of the kingdom among the crown, the chiefs, and the common people. These efforts proved largely unsuccessful, however, and the land remained in the hands of a few. In the mid-1960's, after extensive hearings, the Hawaii Legislature discovered that, while the State and Federal Governments owned almost 49% of the State's land, another 47% was in the hands of only 72 private landowners. See Brief for the Hou Hawaiians and Maui Loa, Chief of the Hou Hawaiians, as *Amici Curiae* 32. The legislature further found that 18 landholders, with tracts

---

[8] Levy, note 5 above at 870-873.

[9] *Id.* at 871.

[10] HAW. REV. STAT. § 516-4.

of 21,000 acres or more, owned more than 40% of this land and that on Oahu, the most urbanized of the islands, 22 landowners owned 72.5% of the fee simple titles. The legislature concluded that concentrated land ownership was responsible for skewing the State's residential fee simple market, inflating land prices, and injuring the public tranquility and welfare.

To redress these problems, the legislature decided to compel the large landowners to break up their estates. The legislature considered requiring large landowners to sell lands which they were leasing to homeowners. However, the landowners strongly resisted this scheme, pointing out the significant federal tax liabilities they would incur. Indeed, the landowners claimed that the federal tax laws were the primary reason they previously had chosen to lease, and not sell, their lands. Therefore, to accommodate the needs of both lessors and lessees, the Hawaii Legislature enacted the Land Reform Act of 1967 (Act), Haw. Rev. Stat., ch. 516, which created a mechanism for condemning residential tracts and for transferring ownership of the condemned fees simple to existing lessees. By condemning the land in question, the Hawaii Legislature intended to make the land sales involuntary, thereby making the federal tax consequences less severe while still facilitating the redistribution of fees simple.

Under the Act's condemnation scheme, tenants living on single-family residential lots within developmental tracts at least five acres in size are entitled to ask the Hawaii Housing Authority (HHA) to condemn the property on which they live. Haw. Rev. Stat. §§ 516-1(2), (11), 516-22 (1977). When 25 eligible tenants,[1] or tenants on half the lots in the tract, whichever is less, file appropriate applications, the Act authorizes HHA to hold a public hearing to determine whether acquisition by the State of all or part of the tract will "effectuate the public purposes" of the Act. § 516-22. If HHA finds that these public purposes will be served, it is authorized to designate some or all of the lots in the tract for acquisition. It then acquires, at prices set either by condemnation trial or by negotiation between lessors and lessees,[2] the former fee owners' full "right, title, and interest" in the land. § 516-25.

After compensation has been set, HHA may sell the land titles to tenants who have applied for fee simple ownership. HHA is authorized to lend these tenants up to 90% of the purchase price, and it may condition final transfer on a right of first refusal for the first 10 years following sale. §§ 516-30, 516-34, 516-35. If HHA does not sell the lot to the tenant residing there, it may lease the lot or sell it to someone else, provided that public notice has been given. § 516-28. However, HHA may not sell to any one purchaser, or lease to any one tenant, more than one lot, and it may not operate for profit. §§ 516-28, 516-32. In practice, funds to satisfy the condemnation awards have been supplied entirely by lessees. See App. 164. While the Act authorizes HHA to issue bonds and appropriate funds for acquisition, no bonds have issued and HHA has not supplied any funds for condemned lots.

B

In April 1977, HHA held a public hearing concerning the proposed acquisition of some of appellees' lands. HHA made the statutorily required finding that acquisition of appellees' lands would effectuate the public purposes of the Act. Then, in October 1978, it directed appellees

---

[1] An eligible tenant is one who, among other things, owns a house on the lot, has a bona fide intent to live on the lot or be a resident of the State, shows proof of ability to pay for a fee interest in it, and does not own residential land elsewhere nearby. Haw. Rev. Stat. §§ 516-33(3), (4), (7) (1977).

[2] See § 516-56 (Supp. 1983). In either case, compensation must equal the fair market value of the owner's leased fee interest § 516-1(14). The adequacy of compensation is not before us.

to negotiate with certain lessees concerning the sale of the designated properties. Those negotiations failed, and HHA subsequently ordered appellees to submit to compulsory arbitration.

Rather than comply with the compulsory arbitration order, appellees filed suit, in February 1979, in United States District Court, asking that the Act be declared unconstitutional and that its enforcement be enjoined. The District Court temporarily restrained the State from proceeding against appellees' estates. Three months later, while declaring the compulsory arbitration and compensation formulae provisions of the Act unconstitutional,[3] the District Court refused preliminarily to enjoin appellants from conducting the statutory designation and condemnation proceedings. Finally, in December 1979, it granted partial summary judgment to appellants, holding the remaining portion of the Act constitutional under the Public Use Clause. See 483 F. Supp. 62 (Haw. 1979). The District Court found that the Act's goals were within the bounds of the State's police powers and that the means the legislature had chosen to serve those goals were not arbitrary, capricious, or selected in bad faith.

The Court of Appeals for the Ninth Circuit reversed. 702 F.2d 788 (CA9 1983). . . . [T]he Court of Appeals determined that the Act could not pass the requisite judicial scrutiny of the Public Use Clause. It found that the transfers contemplated by the Act were unlike those of takings previously held to constitute "public uses" by this Court. The court further determined that the public purposes offered by the Hawaii Legislature were not deserving of judicial deference. The court concluded that the Act was simply "a naked attempt on the part of the state of Hawaii to take the private property of A and transfer it to B solely for B's private use and benefit." One judge dissented.

On applications of HHA and certain private appellants who had intervened below, this Court noted probable jurisdiction. We now reverse.

. . . .

II

A

The starting point for our analysis of the Act's constitutionality is the Court's decision in *Berman v. Parker*, 348 U.S. 26 (1954). In *Berman*, the Court held constitutional the District of Columbia Redevelopment Act of 1945. That Act provided both for the comprehensive use of the eminent domain power to redevelop slum areas and for the possible sale or lease of the condemned lands to private interests. In discussing whether the takings authorized by that Act were for a "public use," the Court stated:

>We deal, in other words, with what traditionally has been known as the police power. An attempt to define its reach or trace its outer limits is fruitless, for each case must turn on its own facts. The definition is essentially the product of legislative determinations addressed to the purposes of government, purposes neither abstractly nor historically capable of complete definition. Subject to specific constitutional limitations, when the legislature has spoken, the public interest has been declared in terms well-nigh conclusive. In such cases the legislature,

---

[3] As originally enacted, lessor and lessee had to commence compulsory arbitration if they could not agree on a price for the fee simple title. Statutory formulae were provided for the determination of compensation. The District Court declared both the compulsory arbitration provision and the compensation formulae unconstitutional. No appeal was taken from these rulings, and the Hawaii Legislature subsequently amended the statute to provide only for mandatory negotiation and for advisory compensation formulae. These issues are not before us.

not the judiciary, is the main guardian of the public needs to be served by social legislation, whether it be Congress legislating concerning the District of Columbia . . . or the States legislating concerning local affairs . . . . This principle admits of no exception merely because the power of eminent domain is involved . . . .

The Court explicitly recognized the breadth of the principle it was announcing, noting:

> Once the object is within the authority of Congress, the right to realize it through the exercise of eminent domain is clear. For the power of eminent domain is merely the means to the end. . . . . Once the object is within the authority of Congress, the means by which it will be attained is also for Congress to determine. Here one of the means chosen is the use of private enterprise for redevelopment of the area. Appellants argue that this makes the project a taking from one businessman for the benefit of another businessman. But the means of executing the project are for Congress and Congress alone to determine, once the public purpose has been established.

The "public use" requirement is thus coterminous with the scope of a sovereign's police powers.

. . . .

To be sure, the Court's cases have repeatedly stated that one person's property may not be taken for the benefit of another private person without a justifying public purpose, even though compensation be paid. . . . But where the exercise of the eminent domain power is rationally related to a conceivable public purpose, the Court has never held a compensated taking to be proscribed by the Public Use Clause.

On this basis, we have no trouble concluding that the Hawaii Act is constitutional. The people of Hawaii have attempted, much as the settlers of the original 13 Colonies did,[5] to reduce the perceived social and economic evils of a land oligopoly traceable to their monarchs. The land oligopoly has, according to the Hawaii Legislature, created artificial deterrents to the normal functioning of the State's residential land market and forced thousands of individual homeowners to lease, rather than buy, the land underneath their homes. Regulating oligopoly and the evils associated with it is a classic exercise of a State's police powers. We cannot disapprove of Hawaii's exercise of this power.

Nor can we condemn as irrational the Act's approach to correcting the land oligopoly problem. The Act presumes that when a sufficiently large number of persons declare that they are willing but unable to buy lots at fair prices the land market is malfunctioning. When such a malfunction is signaled, the Act authorizes HHA to condemn lots in the relevant tract. The Act limits the number of lots any one tenant can purchase and authorizes HHA to use public funds to ensure that the market dilution goals will be achieved. This is a comprehensive and rational approach to identifying and correcting market failure.

Of course, this Act, like any other, may not be successful in achieving its intended goals. But "whether *in fact* the provision will accomplish its objectives is not the question: the [constitutional requirement] is satisfied if . . . the . . . [state] Legislature *rationally could have believed* that the [Act] would promote its objective." *Western & Southern Life Ins. Co. v. State Bd. Of*

---

[5] After the American Revolution, the colonists in several States took steps to eradicate the feudal incidents with which large proprietors had encumbered land in the Colonies. *See, e.g.*, Act of May 1779, 10 Henning's Statutes At Large 64, ch. 13 § 6 (1822) (Virginia statute); Divesting Act of 1779, 1775-1781 Pa. Acts 258, ch. 139 (1782) (Pennsylvania statute). Courts have never doubted that such statutes served a public purpose. *See, e.g., Wilson v. Iseminger*, 185 U.S. 55, 60-61 (1902); *Stewart v. Gorter*, 70 Md. 242, 244-245, 16 A. 644, 645 (1889).

Equalization, 451 U.S. 648, 671-672 (1981). When the legislature's purpose is legitimate and its means are not irrational, our cases make clear that empirical debates over the wisdom of takings—no less than debates over the wisdom of other kinds of socioeconomic legislation—are not to be carried out in the federal courts. Redistribution of fees simple to correct deficiencies in the market determined by the state legislature to be attributable to land oligopoly is a rational exercise of the eminent domain power. Therefore, the Hawaii statute must pass the scrutiny of the Public Use Clause.

B

The Court of Appeals read our cases to stand for a much narrower proposition. First, it read our "public use" cases, especially *Berman*, as requiring that government possess and use property at some point during a taking. Since Hawaiian lessees retain possession of the property for private use throughout the condemnation process, the court found that the Act exacted takings for private use. Second, it determined that these cases involved only "the review of . . . *congressional* determination[s] that there was a public use, *not* the review of . . . state legislative determination[s]." Because state legislative determinations are involved in the instant cases, the Court of Appeals decided that more rigorous judicial scrutiny of the public use determinations was appropriate. The court concluded that the Hawaii Legislature's professed purposes were mere "statutory rationalizations." We disagree with the Court of Appeals' analysis.

The mere fact that property taken outright by eminent domain is transferred in the first instance to private beneficiaries does not condemn that taking as having only a private purpose. The Court long ago rejected any literal requirement that condemned property be put into use for the general public. "It is not essential that the entire community, nor even any considerable portion, . . . directly enjoy or participate in any improvement in order [for it] to constitute a public use." *Rindge Co. v. Los Angeles*, 262 U.S., at 707. "[W]hat in its immediate aspect [is] only a private transaction may . . . be raised by its class or character to a public affair." *Block v. Hirsh*, 256 U.S., at 155. As the unique way titles were held in Hawaii skewed the land market, exercise of the power of eminent domain was justified. The Act advances its purposes without the State's taking actual possession of the land. In such cases, government does not itself have to use property to legitimate the taking; it is only the taking's purpose, and not its mechanics, that must pass scrutiny under the Public Use Clause.

Similarly, the fact that a state legislature, and not the Congress, made the public use determination does not mean that judicial deference is less appropriate.[7] Judicial deference is required because, in our system of government, legislatures are better able to assess what public purposes should be advanced by an exercise of the taking power. State legislatures are as capable as Congress of making such determinations within their respective spheres of authority. *See Berman v. Parker*, 348 U.S., at 32. Thus, if a legislature, state or federal, determines there are substantial reasons for an exercise of the taking power, courts must defer to its determination that the taking will serve a public use. . . .

The State of Hawaii has never denied that the Constitution forbids even a compensated taking of property when executed for no reason other than to confer a private benefit on a particular

---

[7] It is worth noting that the Fourteenth Amendment does not itself contain an independent "public use" requirement. Rather, that requirement is made binding on the States only by incorporation of the Fifth Amendment's Eminent Domain Clause through the Fourteenth Amendment's Due Process Clause. *See Chicago, B. & Q. R. Co. v. Chicago*, 166 U.S. 226 (1897). It would be ironic to find that state legislation is subject to greater scrutiny under the incorporated "public use" requirement than is congressional legislation under the express mandate of the Fifth Amendment.

private party. A purely private taking could not withstand the scrutiny of the public use requirement; it would serve no legitimate purpose of government and would thus be void. But no purely private taking is involved in these cases. The Hawaii Legislature enacted its Land Reform Act not to benefit a particular class of identifiable individuals but to attack certain perceived evils of concentrated property ownership in Hawaii—a legitimate public purpose. Use of the condemnation power to achieve this purpose is not irrational. Since we assume for purposes of these appeals that the weighty demand of just compensation has been met, the requirements of the Fifth and Fourteenth Amendments have been satisfied. Accordingly, we reverse the judgment of the Court of Appeals, and remand these cases for further proceedings in conformity with this opinion.

It is so ordered.

JUSTICE MARSHALL took no part in the consideration or decision of these cases.

[c]   Explanatory Notes

[*i*]   *The Land Structure at Stake in* **Midkiff.** A significant portion of Hawaii's land was encumbered by ground leases. The owners of the structures on the land had to pay ground rents to the lessors. When the leases terminated, the building owners lost their investments if lease renewals were not agreed to. The concentration of ownership of the ground leases among a very small class of people permitted virtual monopoly pricing policies to occur. In addition, the widespread existence of leases made it very difficult for people to elect to purchase houses unencumbered by leases. At renewal time, the lessors had a degree of economic power very much like the holdout seller in the land assembly problem discussed above at p. 885.

[*ii*]   *Standards for Judicial Review of Economic Regulation Since the New Deal.* The Fifth Amendment to the Constitution provides that a person's private property may not be "taken for public use, without just compensation." In her opinion for the Court, Justice O'Connor granted Congress and state legislative bodies broad authority to define the meaning of "public use." She noted that the "public use" requirement is "coterminous with the scope of a sovereign's police power" to legislate for the public welfare and that "where the exercise of the eminent domain power is rationally related to a conceivable public purpose, the Court has never held a compensated taking to be proscribed by the Public Use Clause." This sweeping language reads very much like the Court's New Deal Era holdings reversing use of Substantive Due Process to embed Formalist visions of freedom of contract into the Constitution and bestowing broad authority on Congress to regulate the economy. In *N.L.R.B v. Jones & Laughlin Steel Corp.*, 301 U.S. 1 (1937), for example, the Court opined that Congress had the power to adopt all appropriate legislation to regulate interstate commerce and that such power was "plenary." Justice Sutherland's opinion in *Euclid v. Ambler*, p. 490 above, permitting local communities to adopt zoning statutes was a bit more grudging. "If the validity of the legislative classification for zoning purposes be fairly debatable," he wrote, "the legislative judgment must be allowed to control." In sum, from the New Deal Era through the decision in *Midkiff*, the Supreme Court rarely scrutinized with great care the public purpose for any land use regulatory scheme.

[*iii*]   *Family and Land Use Regulations.* The opinions in *Berman v. Parker* and *Midkiff* were not the only ones countenancing broad land use regulatory authority at the state and federal levels. Perhaps the broadest statements on the public purpose requirement ever to come from

the Supreme Court appeared in a case involving regulation of quite personal life style choices. *Belle Terre v. Boraas*, 416 U.S. 1 (1974) involved a challenge to local regulations restricting all land in a small community to single family residential use and defining "family" to include only "one or more persons related by blood, adoption or marriage, living and cooking together as a single housekeeping unit, exclusive of household servants. A number of persons but not exceeding two (2) living and cooking together as a single housekeeping unit though not related by blood, adoption, or marriage shall be deemed to constitute a family." Six university students argued that the regulation violated rights of free association, privacy and equal protection. Their challenge failed, the Court writing:

> A quiet place where yards are wide, people few, and motor vehicles restricted are legitimate guidelines in a land use project addressed to family needs. This goal is a permissible one within *Berman v. Parker*. The police power is not confined to elimination of filth, stench, and unhealthy places. It is ample to lay out zones where family values, youth values, and the blessing of quiet seclusion and clean air make the area a sanctuary for people.

Despite such broad language, a particularly sympathetic family forced the Court to take a closer look at the intersection of family policy and land use controls. An East Cleveland ordinance limited occupancy of a dwelling unit to members of a family and defined family to include a single person living alone, a head of household and spouse, unmarried children (provided they did not have children), parents of the head of the household or the spouse of the head of the household, and no more than one married child or child with children. Inez Moore lived with her son and her two grandsons. One of the grandsons was the child of the son living with her, the other was a cousin of her son who came to live with the Moores after his mother died. Inez Moore's conviction and $25 fine for violating the East Cleveland ordinance was reversed. *Moore v. City of East Cleveland*, 431 U.S. 494 (1977). Justice Powell writing for himself and three other members of the Court, distinguished *Boraas* because it involved unrelated individuals. While hesitant to second-guess the desire of East Cleveland to minimize overcrowding and traffic congestion from multiple member households, Powell noted:

> Appropriate limits on substantive due process come not from drawing arbitrary lines but rather from careful respect for the teachings of history and solid recognition of the basic values that underlie our society. Our decisions establish that the Constitution protects the sanctity of the family precisely because the institution of the family is deeply rooted in the Nation's history and tradition. It is through the family that we inculcate and pass down many of our most cherished values, moral and cultural.

Powell went on to include the extended family in his tradition based reasoning process, presumably excluding from Constitutional protection unmarried and unrelated cohabitants of any sexual persuasion. Justice Stevens concurred in the result, but on the ground that *Euclid v. Ambler*, p. 490 above, still left room for voiding enactments which were not police power regulations on behalf of public health, safety, morals or general welfare. Four Justices dissented.[11]

---

[11] For commentary on the Constitution, land use and family privacy, *see* Bruce C. Hafen, *The Constitutional Status of Marriage, Kinship and Sexual Privacy—Balancing Individual and Social Interests*, 81 MICH. L. REV. 463 (1983); J. Gregory Richards, *Zoning for Direct Social Control*, 1982 DUKE L.J. 761; Kenneth Karst, *The Freedom of Intimate Association*, 89 YALE L.J. 624 (1980).

[d]   Problem Notes

[*i*]   ***Public-Private Distinction Revisited*** Is it possible to analyze cases like *Midkiff* by trying to distinguish between condemnations pursued for the benefit of private parties and those undertaken for public benefit? That is, can you rationally distinguish a regulatory scheme designed to benefit the public from one calculated to help private parties? There were certainly elements of both private gain and public benefit in *Midkiff*. Can this layering of purposes be handled by a "relative" rule, one that inquires into the degree to which private or public needs are served by a condemnation? Or is there a better way of thinking about the sorts of government actions that should not be sanctioned? This issue resurfaces in dramatic fashion in the next case involving the condemnation of Poletown for the construction of a General Motors assembly factory.

[*ii*]   ***Condemnation and Notions of Equality.*** Is condemnation inherently fatal to any concept of economic equality? Even though condemnees receive payment for the property interests they lose to government action, the compensation required by the Constitution is the value of the asset in the market, not including money for relocation costs, business losses or psychological disruption.[12] Can it ever be "equal" to lose your house or business in this way?

[*iii*]   ***Condemnation and Distributional Fairness.*** The eminent domain power is used to obtain land for construction of many public facilities—parks, roads, schools, and monuments, among others. Is it possible to justify these actions on the theory that they help large numbers of people, but do not make anyone else worse off in the process? Is that argument plausible without payment for relocation, business or psychological losses?

[*iv*]   ***Concepts of Ownership and Intrusion.*** Should any of the following public actions offend the Constitution?

(a) Adoption of a regulation banning from a particular zone in a community all persons under the age of 18? How about under the age of 52, the typical cut off point for developments for senior citizens?

(b) Adoption of a regulation requiring all sexually oriented businesses to stay within a small zone in the downtown area of a large city.[13]

(c) Adoption of a regulation prohibiting citizens from operating businesses in their homes which require no employees.

(d) Condemnation of a private house for use by the president of the largest business in town as part of a much larger package of actions designed to keep the business from relocating.

---

[12] In response to the some of the unfairness caused by a market value based payment system, Congress adopted the Relocation Assistance Act of 1971, now codified at 42 U.S.C. § 4601 *et seq.*, granting additional payments to persons and businesses forced to move because of eminent domain proceedings brought by federal agencies or state agencies with federal funds. Section 4622 grants payments for moving expenses, losses from destruction of tangible personal property, search costs for new business locations and up to $10,000 in lost business profits. Section 4623 provides for up to $22,500 in payments to persons who lose homes purchased not less than 180 days prior to the condemnation for such expenses as closing costs, purchase of a comparable dwelling and additional mortgage loan interest. Section 4624 deals with tenants and persons not covered by § 4623 and grants of up to $5,250 to pay rent in a new dwelling or to make a downpayment on a home.

[13] *Compare* Young v. American Mini Theatres, Inc., 427 U.S. 50 (1976), which by a 5-4 vote approved a Detroit ordinance dispersing such businesses by requiring them to keep certain distances from each other and from schools, churches, and residential areas despite allegations that the requirements essentially banned sexually oriented businesses from most of the city.

(e) Adoption of a state statute granting condemnation authority to privately owned utility companies, cable television operators and universities.

[*v*]   ***"Religious" Families and Zoning.*** Suppose a religion required its members to live together in groups of at least 10 people. After *Belle Terre* and *Moore*, could a town ban such communes from single family residential zones? In *City of Chula Vista v. Pagard*, 97 Cal. App. 3d 627, 159 Cal. Rptr. 29 (1979), an ordinance very much like the one in *Belle Terre* was enforced against such a group, despite arguments that it infringed on the fundamental right to freely exercise religious beliefs. The court noted that towns were free to ban all temples and churches from residential zones and that if the ordinance interfered with religious worship, it did so only incidentally through an otherwise valid regulation. Was the court correct? *Compare Serbian Eastern Orthodox Diocese v. Milivojevich*, discussed at p. 267 above; *Ginsberg v. Yeshiva of Far Rockaway*, p. 465.

[*vi*]   ***Public Purpose, State Action, and Racial Preferences.*** The Bishop Estate lands at issue in *Midkiff* were held under a trust instrument requiring that benefits be distributed with preferences for Native Hawaiians. *Compare* this trust with the covenants in *Shelley v. Kraemer*, p. 445 above. Is there anything Constitutionally infirm about judicial enforcement of the trust's preferences? And what of state action? The land is privately held, but the dead or departed trustees are replaced by vote of the members of the Hawaii Supreme Court supposedly acting in their individual, not official, capacity, and the trust owns a vast portion of the state. Do these facts mean that federal Constitutional limitations control the estate's operation?

[e]   Some Jurisprudential Commentary Supporting New Deal Regulatory Authority

The following excerpt is taken from a very prominent jurisprudential work by John Rawls. Use it to stimulate your own thoughts about the appropriate scope of public authority to regulate land. Rawls begins from an ahistorical original position, in which citizens are thoughtful but totally without social place, historical moment or political view. His work then unfolds a theory of justice that persons in that stance would reach. The central conclusion he reaches is that persons in the original position would conclude that "social and economic inequalities, for example inequalities of wealth and authority, are just only if they result in compensating benefits for everyone, and in particular for the least advantaged members of society." Use of such jurisprudence in contemporary society requires that sensitive attention be paid not only to the distribution of wealth among those now living, but also to the availability of resources to those that will follow. After reading this selection, consider what Rawls' reaction would have been to the *Midkiff* regulatory scheme.

JOHN RAWLS, A THEORY OF JUSTICE 11-15, 284-287, 293 (1971)[14]

THE MAIN IDEA OF THE THEORY OF JUSTICE

My aim is to present a conception of justice which generalizes and carries to a higher level of abstraction the familiar theory of the social contract as found, say, in Locke, Rousseau, and Kant. In order to do this we are not to think of the original contract as one to enter a particular society or to set up a particular form of government. Rather, the guiding idea is

---

[14] Reprinted by permission of the publisher from *A Theory of Justice* by John Rawls, Cambridge, Mass.: Harvard University Press, Copyright @1971 by the President and Fellows of Harvard College.

that the principles of justice for the basic structure of society are the object of the original agreement. They are the principles that free and rational persons concerned to further their own interests would accept in an initial position of equality as defining the fundamental terms of their association. These principles are to regulate all further agreements; they specify the kinds of social cooperation that can be entered into and the forms of government that can be established. This way of regarding the principles of justice I shall call justice as fairness.

Thus we are to imagine that those who engage in social cooperation choose together, in one joint act, the principles which are to assign basic rights and duties and to determine the division of social benefits. Men are to decide in advance how they are to regulate their claims against one another and what is to be the foundation charter of their society. Just as each person must decide by rational reflection what constitutes his good, that is, the system of ends which it is rational for him to pursue, so a group of persons must decide once and for all what is to count among them as just and unjust. The choice which rational men would make in this hypothetical situation of equal liberty, assuming for the present that this choice problem has a solution, determines the principles of justice.

In justice as fairness the original position of equality corresponds to the state of nature in the traditional theory of the social contract. This original position is not, of course, thought of as an actual historical state of affairs, much less as a primitive condition of culture. It is understood as a purely hypothetical situation characterized so as to lead to a certain conception of justice. Among the essential features of this situation is that no one knows his place in society, his class position or social status, nor does any one know his fortune in the distribution of natural assets and abilities, his intelligence, strength, and the like. I shall even assume that the parties do not know their conceptions of the good or their special psychological propensities. The principles of justice are chosen behind a veil of ignorance. This ensures that no one is advantaged or disadvantaged in the choice of principles by the outcome of natural chance or the contingency of social circumstances. Since all are similarly situated and no one is able to design principles to favor his particular condition, the principles of justice are the result of a fair agreement or bargain. For given the circumstances of the original position, the symmetry of everyone's relations to each other, this initial situation is fair between individuals as moral persons, that is, as rational beings with their own ends and capable, I shall assume, of a sense of justice. The original position is, one might say, the appropriate initial status quo, and thus the fundamental agreements reached in it are fair. This explains the propriety of the name "justice as fairness": it conveys the idea that the principles of justice are agreed to in an initial situation that is fair. The name does not mean that the concepts of justice and fairness are the same, any more than the phrase "poetry as metaphor" means that the concepts of poetry and metaphor are the same.

. . . .

In working out the conception of justice as fairness one main task clearly is to determine which principles of justice would be chosen in the original position. To do this we must describe this situation in some detail and formulate with care the problem of choice which it presents. . . . . It may be observed, however, that once the principles of justice are thought of as arising from an original agreement in a situation of equality, it is an open question whether the principle of utility would be acknowledged. Offhand it hardly seems likely that persons who view themselves as equals, entitled to press their claims upon one another, would agree to a principle which may require lesser life prospects for some simply for the sake of a greater sum of advantages enjoyed by others. Since each desires to protect his interests, his capacity to advance his conception of the good, no one has a reason to acquiesce in an enduring loss for himself in order to bring about a greater net balance of satisfaction. In the absence of strong and lasting benevolent impulses, a rational man would not accept a basic structure merely because it maximized the algebraic sum of advantages irrespective of its permanent effects on his own basic rights and interests. Thus it seems that the principle of utility is incompatible with the conception of social cooperation among equals for mutual advantage. It appears to be inconsistent with the idea of reciprocity implicit in the notion of a well-ordered society. Or, at any rate, so I shall argue.

I shall maintain instead that the persons in the initial situation would choose two rather different principles: the first requires equality in the assignment of basic rights and duties, while the second holds that social and economic inequalities, for example inequalities of wealth and authority, are just only if they result in compensating benefits for everyone, and in particular for the least advantaged members of society. These principles rule out justifying institutions on the grounds that the hardships of some are offset by a greater good in the aggregate. It may be expedient but it is not just that some should have less in order that others may prosper. But there is no injustice in the greater benefits earned by a few provided that the situation of persons not so fortunate is thereby improved. The intuitive idea is that since everyone's well-being depends upon a scheme of cooperation without which no one could have a satisfactory life, the division of advantages should be such as to draw forth the willing cooperation of everyone taking part in it, including those less well situated. Yet this can be expected only if reasonable terms are proposed. The two principles mentioned seem to be a fair agreement on the basis of which those better endowed, or more fortunate in their social position, neither of which we can be said to deserve, could expect the willing cooperation of others when some workable scheme is a necessary condition of the welfare of all. Once we decide to look for a conception of justice that nullifies the accidents of natural endowment and the contingencies of social circumstance as counters in quest for political and economic advantage, we are led to these principles. They express the result of leaving aside those aspects of the social world that seem arbitrary from a moral point of view.

. . . .

THE PROBLEM OF JUSTICE BETWEEN GENERATIONS

We must now consider the question of justice between generations. There is no need to stress the difficulties that this problem raises. It subjects any ethical theory to severe if not impossible tests. Nevertheless, the account of justice as fairness would be incomplete without some discussion of this important matter. The problem arises in the present context because the question is still open whether the social system as a whole, the competitive economy surrounded by the appropriate family of background institutions, can be made to satisfy the two principles of justice. The answer is bound to depend, to some degree anyway, on the level at which the social minimum is to be set. But this in turn connects up with how far the present generation is bound to respect the claims of its successors.

. . . .

Finding a just savings principle is one aspect of this question. Now I believe that it is not possible, at present anyway, to define precise limits on what the rate of savings should be. How the burden of capital accumulation and of raising the standard of civilization and culture is to be shared between generations seems to admit of no definite answer. It does not follow, however, that certain bounds which impose significant ethical constraints cannot be formulated. As I have said, a moral theory characterizes a point of view from which policies are to be assessed; and it may often be clear that a suggested answer is mistaken even if an alternative doctrine is not ready to hand.

. . . .

Now the contract doctrine looks at the problem from the standpoint of the original position. The parties do not know to which generation they belong or, what comes to the same thing, the stage of civilization of their society. They have no way of telling whether it is poor or relatively wealthy, largely agricultural or already industrialized, and so on. The veil of ignorance is complete in these respects. Thus the persons in the original position are to ask themselves how much they would be willing to save at each stage of advance on the assumption that all other generations are to save at the same rates. That is, they are to consider their willingness to save at any given phase of civilization with the understanding that the rates they propose are to regulate the whole span of accumulation. In effect, then, they must choose a just savings principle that assigns an appropriate rate of accumulation to each level of advance. Presumably this rate changes depending upon the state of society. When people are poor and saving is difficult, a lower rate of saving should be required; whereas in a wealthier society greater savings may reasonably be expected since the real burden is less. Eventually once just institutions are firmly established, the net accumulation required falls to zero. At this point a society meets its duty of justice by maintaining just institutions and preserving their material base.

. . . .

We can now see that persons in different generations have duties and obligations to one another just as contemporaries do. The present generation cannot do as it pleases but is bound by the principles that would be chosen in the original position to define justice between persons at different moments of time. In addition, men have a natural duty to uphold and to further just institutions and for this the improvement of civilization up to a certain level is required. The derivation of these duties and obligations may seem at first a somewhat farfetched application of the contract doctrine. Nevertheless these requirements would be acknowledged in the original position, and so the conception of justice as fairness covers these matters without any change in its basic idea.

[3] The Public Purpose Requirement at the State Level

[a] Introduction to the *Poletown* Condemnation Case

The condemnation power of the cities of Detroit and Hamtramck was used to clear 465 acres for the construction of a new General Motors assembly plant. The area condemned was a lower middle class area in fairly good condition occupied by a large ethnic population. Many small businesses in the community were hard hit. While residents were generally able to find suitable new housing, about three quarters of the small businesses in the area did not ever reopen.[15] Opposition to the condemnation in *Poletown* led to nationwide publicity about the uprooting of an area the size of a small city.[16] Even if General Motors needed somewhere to locate a new

[15] Blonston, *Poletown, The Profits, The Loss,* in *Detroit Magazine: A Special Issue,* DETROIT FREE PRESS (Nov. 22, 1981).

[16] Three of the many stories that appeared in papers across the country may be found in the NEW YORK TIMES

facility, there was widespread wonderment that our culture would permit such a remarkable intrusion into the lives of a townsworth of people to proceed virtually unchecked. Many condemnations now proceed under "quick take" statutes in which the fee is transferred to the condemning public entity almost immediately upon certification by a court that there is a valid basis for the taking to proceed. The government does not have to wait until a final determination is made on the amount of the compensation that must be paid before it takes possession. If there is disagreement over the amount of compensation, that issue, and that issue alone, goes to trial. By the time *Poletown* was decided, most of the area was vacant. As people agreed to accept compensation awards, they moved out and their houses or businesses were torn down. Even if the case had been decided the other way, a virtually empty area would have been left behind.

[b]   Opinions of the Michigan Supreme Court in *Poletown v. Detroit*

Poletown Neighborhood Council v. The City of Detroit and the Detroit Economic Development Corporation

Supreme Court of Michigan
410 Mich. 894, 304 N.W.2d 455 (1981)

PER CURIAM.

This case arises out of a plan by the Detroit Economic Development Corporation to acquire, by condemnation if necessary, a large tract of land to be conveyed to General Motors Corporation as a site for construction of an assembly plant. The plaintiffs, a neighborhood association and several individual residents of the affected area, brought suit in Wayne Circuit Court to challenge the project on a number of grounds, not all of which have been argued to this Court. Defendants' motions for summary judgment were denied pending trial on a single question of fact: whether the city abused its discretion in determining that condemnation of plaintiffs' property was necessary to complete the project.

The trial lasted 10 days and resulted in a judgment for defendants and an order on December 9, 1980, dismissing plaintiffs' complaint. The plaintiffs filed a claim of appeal with the Court of Appeals on December 12, 1980, and an application for bypass with this Court on December 15, 1980.

We granted a motion for immediate consideration and an application for leave to appeal prior to decision by the Court of Appeals to consider the following questions:

Does the use of eminent domain in this case constitute a taking of private property for private use and, therefore, contravene Const. 1963, Art. 10, § 2?

Did the court below err in ruling that cultural, social and historical institutions were not protected by the Michigan Environmental Protection Act?

We conclude that these questions must be answered in the negative and affirm the trial court's decision.

---

at A1, col. 1 (Sept. 15, 1980); A14, col. 1 (Dec. 10, 1980); A14, col. 5 (Apr. 4, 1981). The story is told at length in JEANIE WYLIE, POLETOWN: A COMMUNITY BETRAYED (1989). A documentary available on video has also been made about Poletown. INFORMATION FACTORY, INC., POLETOWN LIVES! (1983).

I

This case raises a question of paramount importance to the future welfare of this state and its residents: Can a municipality use the power of eminent domain granted to it by the Economic Development Corporations Act, M.C.L. § 125.1601 *et seq.* M.S.A. § 5.3520(1) *et. seq.*, to condemn property for transfer to a private corporation to build a plant to promote industry and commerce, thereby adding jobs and taxes to the economic base of the municipality and state?

Const. 1963, Art. 10, § 2, states in pertinent part that "[p]rivate property shall not be taken for public use without just compensation therefor being first made or secured in a manner prescribed by law." Art. 10, § 2 has been interpreted as requiring that the power of eminent domain not be invoked except to further a public use or purpose.[1] . . . The term "public use" has not received a narrow or inelastic definition by this Court in prior cases.[2] Indeed, this Court has stated that "[a] public use changes with changing conditions of society" and that "[t]he right of the public to receive and enjoy the benefit of the use determines whether the use is public or private."[3]

The Economic Development Corporations Act is a part of the comprehensive legislation dealing with planning, housing and zoning whereby the State of Michigan is attempting to provide for the general health, safety, and welfare through alleviating unemployment, providing economic assistance to industry, assisting the rehabilitation of blighted areas, and fostering urban redevelopment.

Section 2 of the act provides:

There exists in this state the continuing need for programs to alleviate and prevent conditions of unemployment, and that it is accordingly necessary to assist and retain local industries and commercial enterprises to strengthen and revitalize the economy of this state and its municipalities; that accordingly it is necessary to provide means and methods for the encouragement and assistance of industrial and commercial enterprises in locating, purchasing, constructing, reconstructing, modernizing, improving, maintaining, repairing, furnishing, equipping, and expanding in this state and in its municipalities; and that it is also necessary to encourage the location and expansion of commercial enterprises to more conveniently provide needed services and facilities of the commercial enterprises to municipalities and the residents thereof. *Therefore, the powers granted in this act constitute the performance of essential public purposes and functions for this state and its municipalities.* M.C.L. § 125.1602; M.S.A. § 5.3520(2). (Emphasis added.)

To further the objectives of this act, the legislature has authorized municipalities to acquire property by condemnation in order to provide industrial and commercial sites and the means of transfer from the municipality to private users. M.C.L. § 125.1622; M.S.A. § 5.3520(22).

Plaintiffs-appellants do not challenge the declaration of the legislature that programs to alleviate and prevent conditions of unemployment and to preserve and develop industry and commerce are essential public purposes. Nor do they challenge the proposition that legislation to accomplish

---

[1] *Shizas v. Detroit*, 333 Mich. 44, 50, 52 N.W.2d 589 (1952).

[2] *City of Center Line v. Michigan Bell Telephone Co.*, 387 Mich. 260, 196 N.W.2d 144 (1972); *Gregory Marina, Inc. v. Detroit*, 378 Mich. 364, 144 N.W.2d 503 (1966); and *In re Slum Clearance*, 331 Mich. 714, 50 N.W.2d 340 (1951).

[3] *Hays v. Kalamazoo*, 316 Mich. 443, 453-454, 25 N.W.2d 787, 169 A.L.R. 1218 (1947), quoting from 37 Am. Jur., Municipal Corporations, § 120, pp. 734-735.

this purpose falls within the Constitutional grant of general legislative power to the legislature in Const. 1963, Art. 4, § 51, which reads as follows:

> The public health and general welfare of the people of the state are hereby declared to be matters of primary public concern. The legislature shall pass suitable laws for the protection and promotion of the public health.

What plaintiffs-appellants do challenge is the constitutionality of using the power of eminent domain to condemn one person's property to convey it to another private person in order to bolster the economy. They argue that whatever incidental benefit may accrue to the public, assembling land to General Motors' specifications for conveyance to General Motors for its uncontrolled use in profit making is really a taking for private use and not a public use because General Motors is the primary beneficiary of the condemnation.

The defendants-appellees contend, on the other hand, that the controlling public purpose in taking this land is to create an industrial site which will be used to alleviate and prevent conditions of unemployment and fiscal distress. The fact that it will be conveyed to and ultimately used by a private manufacturer does not defeat this predominant public purpose.

. . . .

The Legislature has determined that governmental action of the type contemplated here meets a public need and serves an essential public purpose. The Court's role after such a determination is made is limited.

The determination of what constitutes a public purpose is primarily a legislative function, subject to review by the courts when abused, and the determination of the legislative body of that matter should not be reversed except in instances where such determination is palpable and manifestly arbitrary and incorrect. *Gregory Marina, Inc. v. Detroit*, 378 Mich. 364, 396, 144 N.W.2d 503 (1966). The United States Supreme Court has held that when a legislature speaks, the public interest has been declared in terms "well-nigh conclusive." *Berman v. Parker*, 348 U.S. 26, 32, 75 S. Ct. 98, 102, 99 L. Ed. 27 (1954).

The Legislature has delegated the authority to determine whether a particular project constitutes a public purpose to the governing body of the municipality involved. The plaintiffs concede that this project is the type contemplated by the Legislature and that the procedures set forth in the Economic Development Corporations Act have been followed. This further limits our review.

In the court below, the plaintiffs-appellants challenged the necessity for the taking of the land for the proposed project. In this regard the city presented substantial evidence of the severe economic conditions facing the residents of the city and state, the need for new industrial development to revitalize local industries, the economic boost the proposed project would provide, and the lack of other adequate available sites to implement the project.

. . . .

When there is such public need, the abstract right (of an individual) to make use of his own property in his own way is compelled to yield to the general comfort and protection of community, and to a proper regard to relative rights in others. Eminent domain is an inherent power of the sovereign of the same nature as, albeit more severe than, the power to regulate the use of land through zoning or the prohibition of public nuisances.

In the instant case the benefit to be received by the municipality invoking the power of eminent domain is a clear and significant one and is sufficient to satisfy this Court that such a project was an intended and a legitimate object of the Legislature when it allowed municipalities to exercise condemnation powers even though a private party will also, ultimately, receive a benefit as an incident thereto.

The power of eminent domain is to be used in this instance primarily to accomplish the essential public purposes of alleviating unemployment and revitalizing the economic base of the community. The benefit to a private interest is merely incidental.

Our determination that this project falls within the public purpose, as stated by the Legislature, does not mean that every condemnation proposed by an economic development corporation will meet with similar acceptance simply because it may provide some jobs or add to the industrial or commercial base. If the public benefit was not so clear and significant, we would hesitate to sanction approval of such a project. The power of eminent domain is restricted to furthering public uses and purposes and is not to be exercised without substantial proof that the public is primarily to be benefited. Where, as here, the condemnation power is exercised in a way that benefits specific and identifiable private interests, a court inspects with heightened scrutiny the claim that the public interest is the predominant interest being advanced. Such public benefit cannot be speculative or marginal but must be clear and significant if it is to be within the legitimate purpose as stated by the Legislature. We hold this project is warranted on the basis that its significance for the people of Detroit and the state has been demonstrated.

II

Plaintiffs' complaint also alleged that the proposed project violates the Michigan Environmental Protection Act (MEPA), M.C.L. § 691.1201 *et seq.*; M.S.A. § 14.528(201) *et seq.*, because it "will have a major adverse impact on the adjoining social and cultural environment which is referred to as Poletown." The trial court dismissed this claim, stating that "'social and cultural environments' are matters not within the purview of the MEPA and outside its legislative intent." We agree.

. . . .

The decision of the trial court is affirmed.

. . . .

No costs, a public question being involved.

COLEMAN, C.J., and MOODY, LEVIN, KAVANAGH and WILLIAMS, JJ., concur. FITZGERALD, J. (dissenting).

This Court today decides that the power of eminent domain permits the taking of private property with the object of transferring it to another private party for the purpose of constructing and operating a factory, on the ground that the employment and other economic benefits of this privately operated industrial facility are such as to satisfy the "public use" requirement for the exercise of eminent domain power. Because I believe the proposed condemnation clearly exceeds the government's authority to take private property through the power of eminent domain, I dissent.

I

In the spring of 1980, General Motors Corporation informed the City of Detroit that it would close its Cadillac and Fisher Body plants located within the city in 1983. General Motors offered to build an assembly complex in the city, if a suitable site could be found. General Motors set four criteria for the approval of a site: an area of between 450 and 500 acres; a rectangular shape (3/4 mile by 1 mile); access to a long-haul railroad line; and access to the freeway system. The city evaluated a number of potential sites and eventually made an in-depth study of nine sites. Eight of the sites were found not to be feasible,[1] and the ninth, with which we are concerned, was recommended. It occupies approximately 465 acres in the cities of Detroit and Hamtramck.[2] A plan was developed to acquire the site, labeled the Central Industrial Park, under the Economic Development Corporations Act. As authorized by the statute, the project plan contemplated the use of condemnation to acquire at least some of the property within the site.

This action was brought by several residents faced with the loss of their property to condemnation as part of the project. After an expedited trial on the merits, the circuit court entered judgment for the defendants,[4] the effect of which is to allow the pending condemnation actions under the Michigan "quick take" statute to proceed.

We granted the plaintiffs' application for leave to appeal prior to decision by the Court of Appeals and on January 29, 1981, issued an injunction prohibiting the city from proceeding with certain aspects of the condemnations pending decision in this case.

On this appeal, the plaintiffs do not challenge the city's compliance with the applicable statutes. Nor do they seek review of the circuit court's finding that the city did not abuse its discretion in the selection of the Central Industrial Park site over the possible alternative sites that it had studied. Rather, the appeal is limited to the plaintiffs' claims that acquisition of the site through condemnation is illegal as the taking of private property for private use, and that the circuit court erred in ruling that cultural, social, and historical institutions are not protected by the Michigan Environmental Protection Act.

The majority rejects both claims. I concur with the discussion of the environmental protection act issue, but disagree with the analysis of the eminent domain question.

II

The city attaches great importance to the explicit legislative findings in the Economic Development Corporations Act that unemployment is a serious problem and that it is necessary to encourage industry in order to revitalize the economy of this state, and to the legislative declaration that the use of eminent domain power pursuant to a project under the act, "shall be considered necessary for public purposes and for the benefit of the public." It is undeniable that such legislative pronouncements are entitled to great deference. However, determination whether a taking is for a public or a private use is ultimately a judicial question. Through the years, this Court has not hesitated to declare takings authorized by statute not to be for public use in appropriate cases. This is as it must be, since if a legislative declaration on the question of public use were conclusive, citizens could be subjected to the most outrageous confiscation of property for the benefit of other private interests without redress. Thus, while mindful of the expression of the legislative view of the appropriateness of using the eminent domain power in the

---

[1] Indeed, according to the Draft Environmental Impact Statement prepared by the city, none of the other eight sites studied met even the four basic criteria specified by General Motors.

[2] Although approximately 145 of the 465 acres of the project lie within the City of Hamtramck, this case involves only the portion of the project located in Detroit.

[4] Actually there are two defendants, the city and its economic development corporation . . . . However, under . . . [the] statute it is the municipality that exercises the eminent domain power within the project.

circumstances of this case, this Court has the responsibility to determine whether the authorization is lawful.

. . . .

III

Our approval of the use of eminent domain power in this case takes this state into a new realm of takings of private property; there is simply no precedent for this decision in previous Michigan cases. There were several early cases in which there was an attempt to transfer property from one private owner to another through the condemnation power pursuant to express statutory authority. *Board of Health v. Van Hoesen*, 87 Mich. 533, 49 N.W. 894 (1891); *Ryerson v. Brown*, 35 Mich. 333 (1877). In each case, the proposed taking was held impermissible.

The city places great reliance on a number of slum clearance cases here and elsewhere in which it has been held that the fact that the property taken is eventually transferred to private parties does not defeat a claim that the taking is for a public use. *E.g., In re Slum Clearance*, 331 Mich. 714, 50 N.W.2d 340 (1951); *Ellis v. City of Grand Rapids*, 257 F. Supp. 564 (W.D. Mich., 1966). Despite the superficial similarity of these cases to the instant one based on the ultimate disposition of the property, these decisions do not justify the condemnation proposed by the city.[9] The public purpose that has been found to support the slum clearance cases is the benefit to the public health and welfare that arises from the elimination of existing blight, even though the ultimate disposition of the property will benefit private interests. As we said in *In re Slum Clearance, supra*:

> It seems to us that the public purpose of slum clearance is in any event the one *controlling* purpose of the condemnation. The jury were not asked to decide any necessity to condemn the parcels involved for any purpose of resale, but only for slum clearance . . . .
>
> . . . (T)he resale (abating part of the cost of clearance) is not a primary purpose and is incidental and ancillary to the primary and real purpose of clearance. 331 Mich. 720. (Emphasis in original.)

However, in the present case the transfer of the property to General Motors after the condemnation cannot be considered incidental to the taking. It is only through the acquisition and use of the property by General Motors that the "public purpose" of promoting employment can be achieved. Thus, it is the economic benefits of the project that are incidental to the private use of the property.

The city also points to decisions that have found the objective of economic development to be a sufficient "public purpose" to support the expenditure of public funds in aid of industry. *Advisory Opinion on Constitutionality of 1975 PA 301*, 400 Mich. 270, 254 N.W.2d 528 (1977); *City of Gaylord v. Gaylord City Clerk*, 378 Mich. 273, 144 N.W.2d 460 (1966). What constitutes a public purpose in a context of governmental taxing and spending power cannot be equated with the use of that term in connection with eminent domain powers. The potential risk of abuse in the use of eminent domain power is clear. Condemnation places the burden of aiding industry on the few, who are likely to have limited power to protect themselves from the excesses of legislative enthusiasm for the promotion of industry. The burden of taxation is distributed on

---

[9] The city did not proceed under the urban renewal statutes that were the basis for the earlier decisions, and it has never sought to justify the taking of the land for this project on the ground that the area is a "slum" or "blighted" area.

the great majority of the population, leading to a more effective check on improvident use of public funds.

IV

The courts of other states have occasionally dealt with proposals to use condemnation to transfer property from one set of private owners to others, justified on the ground that the resulting economic benefits provide the requisite public use of public purpose. Some decisions have upheld the use of eminent domain powers on that basis;[11] others have found the proposed taking to exceed the power of the government to take private property.[12] While these cases are instructive, they are not controlling of the disposition of this case. Each is presented against the background of a particular state's constitutional and statutory framework. The peculiar facts of the development projects involved also make it difficult to compare them with the present case. In addition, each is decided in the context of that state's body of case law which may have given either a broad or a narrow interpretation to the term "public use."

Despite the limited value of decisions in other states, several points can be made. First, while it is difficult and perhaps futile to categorize individual states as utilizing a "broad" or "narrow" interpretation of "public use" for condemnation purposes, Michigan law seems most consistent with that of states that give a more limited construction to the term. While our decisions have sometimes used the phrase "public purpose" (a phrase often associated with a broad interpretation), the result of our decisions has been to limit the eminent domain power to situations in which direct governmental use is to be made of the land or in which the private recipient will use it to serve the public. The slum clearance cases are really the only significant departure from these principles, and, as noted above, those decisions have been sustained only because of the conclusion that the clearing of a blighted area is a public use. In this respect, the scope of "public use" in Michigan is quite similar to that in states that have rejected development projects on the theory that they would improve general economic conditions. . . .

Second, it is worth noting that [other] . . . cases . . . are distinguishable in that in each it was the governmental unit that selected the site in question for commercial or industrial development. By contrast, the project before us was initiated by General Motors Corporation's solicitation of the city for its aid in locating a factory site.

---

[11] *Prince George's County v. Collington Crossroads, Inc.*, 275 Md. 171, 339 A.2d 278 (1975), involved an attempt by a county to condemn land for an industrial park along major highways. In *City of Minneapolis v. Wurtele*, 291 N.W.2d 386 (Minn., 1980), the city council designated a portion of the downtown area as a "development district" pursuant to statutory authority. The city chose a developer for the project and sought to use condemnation to acquire the land.

[12] In *City of Owensboro v. McCormick*, 581 S.W.2d 3 (Ky., 1979), the Supreme Court of Kentucky held unconstitutional an act authorizing a governmental unit to condemn private property in order to convey it through a local industrial development authority for private development for industrial and commercial purposes. The Supreme Judicial Court of Maine rendered an advisory opinion in *Opinion of the Justices*, 152 Me. 440, 131 A.2d 904 (1957), that the Legislature could not authorize a municipality to use the power of eminent domain to acquire private property for industrial development through transfer to other private enterprises. The use of eminent domain power to acquire land for a privately developed convention center was found impressible in *Karesh v. City Council of the City of Charleston*, 271 S.C. 339, 247 S.E.2d 342 (1978), and a plan for the use of condemnation to acquire land for an industrial development district was struck down in *Hogue v. Port of Seattle*, 54 Wash. 2d 799, 341 P.2d 171 (1959).

V

The majority relies on the principle that the concept of public use is an evolving one; however, I cannot believe that this evolution has eroded our historic protection against the taking of private property for private use to the degree sanctioned by this Court's decision today. The decision that the prospect of increased employment, tax revenue, and general economic stimulation makes a taking of private property for transfer to another private party sufficiently "public" to authorize the use of the power of eminent domain means that there is virtually no limit to the use of condemnation to aid private businesses. Any business enterprise produces benefits to society at large. Now that we have authorized local legislative bodies to decide that a different commercial or industrial use of property will produce greater public benefits than its present use, no homeowner's, merchant's or manufacturer's property, however productive or valuable to its owner, is immune from condemnation for the benefit of other private interests that will put it to a "higher" use.[15] As one prominent commentator has written:

> It often happens that the erection of a large factory will be of more benefit to the whole community in which it is planned to build it than any strictly public improvement which the inhabitants of the place could possibly undertake; but even if the plan was blocked by the refusal of the selfish owner of a small but necessary parcel of land to part with it at any price, the public mind would instinctively revolt at any attempt to take such land by eminent domain. 2A Nichols, *Eminent Domain* § 7.61(1) (rev. 3d ed.).

The condemnation contemplated in the present action goes beyond the scope of the power of eminent domain in that it takes private property for private use. I would reverse the judgment of the circuit court.

RYAN, J., concurs.

RYAN, JUSTICE (dissenting).

This is an extraordinary case.

The reverberating clang of its economic, sociological, political, and jurisprudential impact is likely to be heard and felt for generations. By its decision, the Court has altered the law of eminent domain in this state in a most significant way and, in my view, seriously jeopardized the security of all private property ownership.

This case will stand, . . . despite the sound intentions of the majority, for judicial approval of municipal condemnation of private property for private use. This is more than an example of a hard case making bad law—it is, in the last analysis, good faith but unwarranted judicial imprimatur upon government action taken under the policy of the end justifying the means.

My separate views are set down some days after the Court's 5-to-2 decision has been made and announced and the controlling and dissenting opinions of my colleagues released. I take this unusual step for a number of reasons:

---

[15] It would be easy to sustain the proposed project because of its large size and the extent of the claimed benefits to flow from it. The estimate is that approximately 6150 persons would be employed in the factory itself, with the generation of substantial other employment, business activity, and tax revenue as a result. However, it must be remembered that the dislocations and other costs of the project are also massive. The project plan indicates that a total of 3438 persons will be displaced by the project, that it will require the destruction of 1176 structures, and that the cost of the project to the public sector will be nearly $200,000,000.

The speed with which this case was submitted, argued, considered and decided has meant preparation of opinions which, in my view, do not adequately address the constitutional issues involved.

The ever-broadening audience for which we write may profit from a longer and more detailed analysis of the unique facts which generated this litigation in order to appreciate the economic, social, and political context in which, in my view, our constitutional precedents have been disregarded.

Because this case so remarkably alters our jurisprudence, it is worthwhile to trace our precedent from the beginning and to note with care where and how, from this dissenting perspective, the Court departed from it.

Finally, it seems important to describe in detail for the bench and bar who may address a comparable issue on a similarly stormy day, how easily government, in all of its branches, caught up in the frenzy of perceived economic crisis, can disregard the rights of the few in allegiance to the always disastrous philosophy that the end justifies the means.

I

The real controversy which underlies this litigation concerns the propriety of condemning private property for conveyance to another private party because the use of it by the new owner promises greater public "benefit" than the old use. The controversy arises in the context of economic crisis. While unemployment is high throughout the nation, it is of calamitous proportions throughout the state of Michigan, and particularly in the City of Detroit, whose economic lifeblood is the now foundering automobile industry. It is difficult to overstate the magnitude of the crisis. Unemployment in the state of Michigan is at 14.2%. In the City of Detroit it is at 18%, and among black citizens it is almost 30%. The high cost of doing business in Michigan generally has driven many manufacturers out of this state and to the so-called sunbelt states on a continuing basis during the past several years. Nowhere is the exodus more steady or more damaging than from the Metropolitan Detroit area. It is appropriate to take judicial notice of the fact that the view is widely held that the Chrysler Corporation, headquartered in Detroit, is "on the ropes," surviving only because of hundreds of millions of dollars of federally insured loans. It is likewise appropriate to note judicially the commonly known and readily verifiable fact that the Ford Motor Company, the American Motors Corporation and the General Motors Corporation have all, within days, reported for the previous year the largest financial losses in their histories.

A new national administration and a reconstituted Congress are struggling to find acceptable means to assist the American automotive industry to compete with the overseas automobile manufacturing competition which is largely accountable for domestic automobile industry losses. To meet that competition, domestic manufacturers are finding it necessary to construct new manufacturing facilities in order to build redesigned, lighter and more economical cars. That means new factories and new factory locations.

. . . .

The desirability of a "new generation facility" to enable General Motors Corporation in particular to recoup its losses and recapture its competitive edge is clear in view of the fact that for decades General Motors has been operating two manufacturing facilities in the City of Detroit of the "old generation" vintage.

. . . .

For those reasons and others, General Motors concluded that it would terminate its Cadillac and Fisher Body manufacturing operations at the old facilities in Detroit by 1983 and build a new plant. Needless to say, the fundamental consideration governing the location of the new facility was the corporation's enlightened self-interest as a private, profit-making enterprise.

It was in this economic context, fueled with talk of removal of its long-established Cadillac and Fisher Body manufacturing operations from the Detroit area and the construction of a new 3-million-square-foot plant in a sunbelt state, that in 1980 General Motors made its first overture to the City of Detroit about finding a suitable plant site in the city.[2]

. . . .

It was, of course, evident to all interested observers that the removal by General Motors of its Cadillac manufacturing operations to a more favorable economic climate would mean the loss to Detroit of at least 6,000 jobs as well as the concomitant loss of literally thousands of allied and supporting automotive design, manufacture and sales functions. There would necessarily follow, as a result, the loss of millions of dollars in real estate and income tax revenues. The darkening picture was made even bleaker by the operation of other forces best explained by the social sciences, including the city's continuing loss of its industrial base and the decline of its population.[4]

Thus it was to a city with its economic back to the wall that General Motors presented its highly detailed "proposal" for construction of a new plant in a "green field" location in the City of Detroit. In addition to the fact that Detroit had virtually no "green fields," the requirements of the "proposal" were such that it was clear that no existing location would be suitable unless the city acquired the requisite land one way or another and did so within the General Motors declared time schedule. The corporation told the city that it must find or assemble a parcel 450 to 500 acres in size with access to long-haul railroad lines and a freeway system with railroad marshaling yards within the plant site. As both General Motors and the city knew at the outset,

---

[2] Testifying before the circuit court in this matter, Coleman A. Young, Mayor of the City of Detroit, stated:

Q (By Mr. Honigman): When did you first undertake to study this situation?

A: It was after a visit to my office by the chairman of the board of General Motors, Tom Murphy, several months ago, in which he indicated that General Motors was interested in building a plant within the city limits, if we could provide the cleared land. I had previously requested from both Ford and General Motors, as well as Chrysler, that if in the future they had any plans to expand or build new plants, that the City of Detroit be given the first opportunity. Mr. Murphy's visit was in reaction to that previous request.

[4] Moreover, the problem is not indigenous to Detroit, but part of the broader migration of business and people from the older, industrial cities of the Northeast and Midwest to the so-called sunbelt; to Detroit's Mayor Young those factors impressed the project with symbolic value of national dimension:

I think it transcends in its economic and social potential for this community the Renaissance or any other development that has taken place. What we have here is a development that is being watched by older industrial cities in the midwest and northeast across the Nation. . . . If we can assemble this land, doing justice to those who live there, both the merchants and the residents, and provide a strengthening industrial base for our state, I think we can open up an approach for other northern industrial cities who are landlocked as we are, who have lost population, to relocate and to reassemble and to attract industry . . . . I consider it of great importance, the ability of this city to survive, and to the ability of other cities in the industrial belt, that is the midwest, and the northeast, all these cities face exactly the same problem as Detroit does, escalating unemployment and decreasing population, the exodus of industry. Trial Testimony of Mayor Coleman A. Young.

As compelling as these concerns are, they hardly support the constitutionality of the governmental action at issue here.

no such "green field" existed. Unquestionably cognizant of its immense political and economic power, General Motors also insisted that it must receive title to the assembled parcel by May 1, 1981.

In a most impressive demonstration of governmental efficiency, the City of Detroit set about its task of meeting General Motors' specifications. Nine possible sites were identified and suggested to General Motors. Only one was found adequate—a parcel consisting of 465 acres straddling the Detroit-Hamtramck border that has come to be known as Central Industrial Park (CIP).

In July, 1980, the general outlines of the proposal to condemn property to meet General Motors' demands were submitted to the Detroit Common Council, which promptly approved the boundaries of CIP. The city had already begun to purchase property in contemplation of CIP's establishment. Approval of the CIP boundaries by the Common Council set in motion other activities: surveying in the area was begun, appraisals of the affected properties were made, and two major documents were prepared: "Project Plan: Central Industrial Park" and "Draft Environmental Impact Statement: Central Industrial Park, The Cities of Detroit and Hamtramck, Michigan" (EIS). On September 30, 1980, the completed project plan was approved by the Detroit Economic Development Corporation. Two weeks later a public hearing was held on the then proposed CIP and the next day, October 15, 1980, the Environmental Impact Statement was issued. On October 29, 1980 the Detroit Community and Economic Development Department, . . . sent a letter to the Detroit Common Council recommending that the council approve the project plan with suggested amendments for the CIP. Two days later, the council followed the recommendation, passed a resolution approving the project plan with minor modifications, and declared in the resolution "that said project constitutes a public purpose" and "is hereby determined to be for the use and benefit of the public." On November 3, 1980 the mayor of the City of Detroit signed the resolution.

Behind the frenzy of official activity was the unmistakable guiding and sustaining, indeed controlling, hand of the General Motors Corporation. The city administration and General Motors worked in close contact during the summer and autumn of 1980 negotiating the specifics for the new plant site. The negotiations culminated in a letter dated October 8, 1980 from Thomas A. Murphy, Chairman of the Board of Directors of General Motors, to Mayor Coleman A. Young and Mr. Howard Woods, Chairmen of the Economic Development Corporations of the cities of Detroit and Hamtramck, respectively.[6]

---

[6] So clearly does the letter demonstrate the control being exercised over the condemnation project by General Motors, that it is reproduced here in its entirety.

GENERAL MOTORS CORPORATION
October 8, 1980

The Honorable Coleman A. Young,   Mr. Howard Woods,
Chairman   Chairman
Economic Development Corp   Economic Development Corp.
of the City of Detroit   of the City of Hamtramck
Detroit, Michigan 48226   Hamtramck, Michigan 48212

Gentlemen:

This letter will confirm General Motors' public statements and our many discussions held during the last several months, and will serve to express the commitment of General Motors Corporation to the cities of Detroit and Hamtramck to cause an automotive assembly plant to be built on the Detroit/Hamtramck site if the site criteria requirements detailed on the attachment to this letter are accomplished.

These site criteria have been prepared by General Motors' Site Selection Committee, and are the requirements necessary for General Motors to construct and complete an assembly plant by May 1, 1983.

Attached to the letter from Mr. Murphy were eight pages of "site criteria requirements," all established by General Motors, to which the cities of Detroit and Hamtramck were required to agree, as a condition precedent to General Motors' "enter[ing] into a *mutually* satisfactory development agreement with the Economic Development Corporations." (Emphasis added.) The cities agreed.

Among the more publicized of the criteria imposed by General Motors was the requirement that "[t]itle to the entire site and the rail marshaling yard must be vested in the City of Detroit by May 1, 1981." In light of that demand, the uncommon speed and efficiency with which the city moved to establish CIP and initiate proceedings to condemn the affected property is more understandable.

It is the less publicized site criteria prescribed by General Motors, however, and incorporated in the approved project plan by the City of Detroit, which suggest the withering economic clout of the country's largest auto firm. An example is the requirement that the economic development corporations, which are nothing more than the alter egos of the municipalities involved, must "provide for the construction and upgrading of site perimeter roads." This entails relocation and extension of East Grand Boulevard, which now runs through CIP; the widening of existing roads and construction of new roads to form a ring road around CIP; "[a]ppropriate modification of I-94 access ramps and service roads;" and erection of an "[a]ppropriate street lighting system around the perimeter road." The projected cost of these improvements is $23.5 million. In addition, it was decreed that "General Motors will not be responsible for absorbing the penalty of approximately $3.5 million for underground (utility) service versus overhead service, as required by the Public Lighting Department of the City of Detroit." Furthermore, the economic development corporations agreed "[t]o dispose of, at their expense, hazardous and toxic waste materials which are found on the site." Of course, the cities are also required by law to pay

---

If the site criteria are acceptable to the Economic Development Corporations, please indicate your acknowledgment to that effect by executing and returning the attached copy of this letter to us by October 31, 1980.

General Motors Corporation will then enter into a mutually satisfactory development agreement with the Economic Development Corporations. A draft of this development agreement should be delivered to General Motors Corporation by November 30, 1980 and shall set forth the conditions for satisfaction of the site criteria and specify, among other matters, the financing methods, procedures and timing required to complete the development of the site. When the conditions of the site criteria are satisfied as provided for in the development agreement, General Motors Corporation will purchase the site and cause an automotive assembly plant of approximately 3,000,000 square feet, and employing approximately 6,000 people, to be built upon this site.

We know how difficult it is to accomplish a project of this magnitude without inconveniencing some individuals. However, we know that this site presents the fewest such problems of any location in the city. I also know you will address the concerns of the individuals in the area with great care and concern. I firmly believe the prospect of retaining some 6,000 jobs, and the attendant revitalization of these communities, is a tremendous challenge. But it also is an opportunity and a responsibility which none of us can ignore. Working together, in a spirit of cooperation, I feel confident we can accomplish it.

Very truly yours,

(s) T.A. Murphy

Thomas A. Murphy Chairman
Attachments

The undersigned have examined the site criteria as specified and hereby accept the terms and conditions thereof:

Economic Development Corp. of City of Detroit	Economic Development Corporation of City of Hamtramck
Coleman A. Young, Chairman	Howard Woods, Chairman

just compensation to those dislocated by CIP. In all, the projected public cost of preparing a site agreeable to the board of directors of General Motors is over $200 million.[7] Remarkably, the site will be sold to General Motors for little more than $8 million.[8]

The long shadow of this public accommodation of a private manufacturing development was adumbrated by a provision in the site criteria document, attached to GM Chairman Murphy's letter, which states:

Taxes

The Cities of Detroit and Hamtramck shall establish a Plant Rehabilitation District pursuant to the terms of Public Act 198 Michigan Acts of 1974, as amended, being M.C.L. § 207.551 *et seq.*; M.S.A. § 7.800(1) *et seq.*, which shall include maximum allowable tax abatement under said law for a period of 12 years.

The evidence then is that what General Motors wanted, General Motors got. The corporation conceived the project, determined the cost, allocated the financial burdens, selected the site, established the mode of financing, imposed specific deadlines for clearance of the property and taking title, and even demanded 12 years of tax concessions.[9]

From the beginning, construction of the new assembly plant in Detroit was characterized by the city administration as a do or die proposition. Accordingly, the city, aided by the Michigan "quick-take" statute, marshaled and applied its resources and power to insure that CIP was a

---

[7] A "Statement of Project Cost" is found in the Project Plan:

Statement of Project Cost

A. The following are the projected public sector costs associated with the project:

Acquisition	$62,000,000
Relocation	25,000,000
Demolition	35,000,000
Roads	23,500,000
Rail	12,000,000
Other Site Preparation	38,700,000
Professional Services	3,500,000
Total	$199,700,000

Project Plan, p. 11.

When the Detroit Common Council approved the Project Plan, the cost of relocation was increased to $25,750,000, bringing the total public sector cost to over $200 million.

[8] The attachment to the letter discussed in the text . . . contains the following provision:

Marketable title shall be conveyed to General Motors Corporation by Warranty Deeds, on a phased basis . . . for a total consideration equal to $18,000 multiplied by the number of acres of the plant site . . . .

[9] What is reported here is not meant to denigrate either the role or the good faith of General Motors Corporation. It is a private, profit-making enterprise. Its managers are answerable to a demanding board of directors who, in turn, have a fiduciary obligation to the corporation's shareholders. It is struggling to compete worldwide in a depressed economy. It is a corporation having a history, especially in recent years, of a responsible, even admirable, "social conscience." In fact, this project may well entail compromises of sound business dictates and concomitant financial sacrifices to avoid the worsening unemployment and economic depression which would result if General Motors were to move from the state of Michigan as other major employers have. The point here is not to criticize General Motors, but to relate accurately the facts which attended the city's decision to condemn private property to enable General Motors to build a new plant in Detroit and to "set the scene" in which, as will be seen hereafter, broad-based support for the project was orchestrated in the state, fostering a sense of inevitability and dire consequence if the plan was not approved by all concerned. General Motors is not the villain of the piece.

fait accompli before meaningful objection could be registered [11] or informed opposition organized. Faced with the unacceptable prospect of losing two automotive plants and the jobs that go with them, the city chose to march in fast lock-step with General Motors to carve a "green field" out of an urban setting which ultimately required sweeping away a tightly-knit residential enclave of first-and second-generation Americans, for many of whom their home was their single most valuable and cherished asset and their stable ethnic neighborhood the unchanging symbol of the security and quality of their lives.

It is easy to underestimate the overwhelming psychological pressure which was brought to bear upon property owners in the affected area, especially the generally elderly, mostly retired and largely Polish-American residents of the neighborhood which has come to be called Poletown. As the new plant site plans were developed and announced, the property condemnation proceedings under the "quick-take" statute begun and the demolitionist's iron ball razed neighboring commercial properties such as the already abandoned Chrysler Dodge Main plant, a crescendo of supportive applause sustained the city and General Motors and their purpose. Labor leaders, bankers, and businessmen, including those for whom a new GM plant would mean new economic life, were joined by radio, television, newspaper and political opinion-makers in extolling the virtues of the bold and innovative fashion in which, almost overnight, a new and modern plant would rise from a little known inner-city neighborhood of minimal tax base significance. The promise of new tax revenues, retention of a mighty GM manufacturing facility in the heart of Detroit, new opportunities for satellite businesses, retention of 6,000 or more jobs, and concomitant reduction of unemployment, all fostered a community-wide chorus of support for the project. It was in such an atmosphere that the plaintiffs sued to enjoin the condemnation of their homes.

The judiciary, cognizant of General Motors' May 1 deadline for the city's taking title to all of the property, moved at flank speed. The circuit court conducted a trial on defendants' motion to dismiss plaintiffs' complaint from November 17 to December 2, 1980, and the decision to dismiss the complaint was made on December 9, 1980. Application for leave to appeal prior to decision by the Court of Appeals was received in this Court on December 15, 1980. However, the trial transcript was not received by us until January 5, 1981. We promptly convened, conferred, and granted leave to appeal on January 29, 1981. The case was argued on March 3, 1981.

In less than two weeks, the lead opinions were filed by this Court and released. It is in such circumstances that we were asked to decide, and did decide, an important constitutional issue having towering implications both for the individual plaintiff property owners and for the City of Detroit and the state alike, to say nothing of the impact upon our jurisprudence.

I now turn to set down separately my understanding of the law which governs this case and the outcome it ought to have dictated. My disagreement with my colleagues in the majority, while vigorous, is nonetheless respectful. Vigorous, because I think the unintended jurisprudential mischief which has been done, if not soon rectified, will have echoing effects far beyond this case, and respectful because the crushing burden of litigation which this Court must address daily

---

[11] This approach was reflected in and abetted by an amendment to the Project Plan approved by the Detroit Common Council on October 31, 1980. The amendment reads as follows: "The intent of the development plan is to encourage relocation from the project area within 90 days of notification by the City to vacate. In order for property owners and tenants, however, to be informed of the latest date allowed for vacating the premises within a particular area of the project, dates shall be posted monthly by the City at the District Council office and shall be included in the District Council newsletters."

did not afford adequate time for sufficient consideration of the complex constitutional issues involved within the two-week deadline the Court set for itself for submission, consideration, and decision of the case.

II

The Issue

Stripped of the justifying adornments which have universally attended public description of this controversy, the central jurisprudential issue is the right of government to expropriate property from those who do not wish to sell for the use and benefit of a strictly private corporation. It is not disputed that this action was authorized by statute. The question is whether such authorization is constitutional.

. . . .

III

Public Use and Public Purpose Distinguished

Section 2 of Art. 10 of the state constitution, the taking clause, provides in pertinent part, "[p]rivate property shall not be taken for public *use* without just compensation." (Emphasis added.) Although not stated affirmatively, it is axiomatic that the provision proscribes the taking of private property for private use. . . .

Not to be confused is a separate provision of our constitution respecting an altogether different governmental power, one not in question in this case—the power of taxation. That provision limits the use of the power, including the expenditure of tax revenues, to "public purposes." . . . Const. 1963, Art. 7, § 21.

Well over a century ago, a clear line of demarcation was drawn between the powers of eminent domain and taxation, setting the jurisprudence of the taking clause and, if you will, the "taxing clause" on separate, independent courses. What is "public" for one is not necessarily "public" for the other . . . . *People ex rel. Detroit & Howell R. Co. v. Salem Twp. Board*, 20 Mich. 452, 477-478 (1870) (Cooley, J.).

The distinction established by Justice Cooley in *Salem* has been consistently maintained by this Court . . . until now. It is in failing to make this distinction that, in my view, the Court loses its way.

The issue before the *Salem* court was whether townships could use tax revenues to lend credit to a private railroad company for the purpose of building a railway line; that is, is railroad construction a public purpose? The Court answered no. . . . Concededly, much has changed since . . . 1870. For example, the concept of public purpose as it relates to government's taxing power has been greatly enlarged. In fact, in *Salem*, Justice Cooley construed the concept of public purpose (taxation) more narrowly than the concept of public use (eminent domain).[16]

This right (of eminent domain), it has been held, may be exercised on behalf of railways in the hands of private parties. But there can be no doubt, I think, that this holding was a considerable modification of common law principles.

---

[16] This can be explained by the fact that the comparison was done in the context of railroad building for which exception to general eminent domain principles was made in the common law.

The railroad exception, like those pertaining to other instrumentalities of public transport and commerce such as canals, highways, and bridges, which may in effect permit private companies to exercise the power of eminent domain, are historical aberrations justified by "overriding public necessity." *See generally* Part IV, *infra.*

. . . .

As a general proposition . . . "public purpose" (taxation) has been construed less restrictively than "public use" (eminent domain). The distinction is fully justified. The character of governmental interference with the individual in the case of taxation is wholly different from the case of eminent domain. The degree of compelled deprivation of property is manifestly less intrusive in the former case: it is one thing to disagree with the purposes for which one's tax money is spent; it is quite another to be compelled to give up one's land and be required, as in this case, to leave what may well be a lifelong home and community.

The distinction is further reflected in the Legislature's proper role, as we have defined it, in describing the ambits of the terms. . . . [D]ecisions of this Court abound with . . . statements of deference to legislative determinations respecting the boundaries of "public purpose" . . . . The eminent domain cases, on the other hand, evince no like commitment to minimal judicial review. Instead, it has always been the case that this Court has accorded little or no weight to legislative determinations of "public use."

. . . .

The majority also relies on *Berman v. Parker*, 348 U.S. 26, 32, 75 S. Ct. 98, 99 L. Ed. 27 (1954), . . . where the United States Supreme Court said, "The role of the judiciary in determining whether (the) power (of eminent domain) is being exercised for a public purpose is an extremely narrow one."

The Court's reliance on *Berman* is particularly disingenuous. The case stands for minimal judicial review of acts of Congress by federal courts with respect to application of the Fifth Amendment taking clause, which per se applies only to the federal government.

It is certainly true that the Fifth Amendment taking clause is incorporated in the Fourteenth Amendment due process clause and applies to the states. *E.g., Penn Central Transportation Co. v. New York City*, 438 U.S. 104, 122 (1978). It is also true that in construing the Fourteenth Amendment the United States Supreme Court has adopted a deferential standard of review. But deference is paid not to the decisions of state legislatures but to the judgments of state courts pertaining to the public use question in the context of state law. The distinction is critical and, in this case, makes the whole difference.

. . . .

That the United States Supreme Court would defer to the decisions of Congress while interpreting the Fifth Amendment or to this Court while interpreting the Fourteenth Amendment on the issue of public use, is no logical support for the proposition that this Court, in construing the Michigan constitution, should defer to the judgment of the Michigan Legislature.

In point of fact, this Court has never employed the minimal standard of review in an eminent domain case which is adopted by the majority in this case. Notwithstanding explicit legislative findings, this Court has always made an independent determination of what constitutes a public use for which the power of eminent domain may be utilized.

. . . .

IV

Eminent Domain and Private Corporations

As a general rule, when the object of eminent domain is to take land for ultimate conveyance to a private corporation to use as it sees fit, the state constitution will forbid it as a taking for private use. . . . Accordingly, land may not be condemned for private corporations engaged in the business of water-power mills, *Ryerson v. Brown*, 35 Mich. 333 (1877); cemeteries, *Board of Health v. Van Hoesen*, 87 Mich. 533, 49 N.W. 894 (1891); or general retail, *Shizas v. Detroit*, 333 Mich. 44, 52 N.W.2d 589 (1952). In this case, land has been condemned solely for a private corporation engaged in the business of manufacturing automobiles.

A

It is plain, of course, that condemnation of property for transfer to private corporations is not wholly proscribed. For many years, and probably since the date of Michigan's statehood, an exception to the general rule has been recognized. The exception, which for ease of reference might be denominated the instrumentality of commerce exception, has permitted condemnation for the establishment or improvement of the avenues of commerce—highways, railroads, and canals, for example—and can be traced to the common law where it was considered an exception to a general rule.

. . . .

It cannot for an instant be maintained, however, nor has anyone suggested, that the case before us falls within the instrumentality of commerce exception.

In fact, the only authorities that even arguably support or justify the use of eminent domain in this case are the "slum clearance" cases. *In re Slum Clearance*, 331 Mich. 714, 50 N.W.2d 340 (1951); *General Development Corp. v. City of Detroit*, 322 Mich. 495, 33 N.W.2d 919 (1948); *In re Jeffries Homes Housing Project*, 306 Mich. 638, 11 N.W.2d 272 (1943); *In re Brewster Street Housing Site*, 291 Mich. 313, 289 N.W. 493 (1939). These cases hold that slum clearance is a public use for which eminent domain may be employed. The distinction, however, between those cases and the one at hand is evident. The fact that the private developers in the cited cases, to whom the city sold the cleared land, eventually benefited from the projects does not lend validity to the condemnation under consideration here. Justice Fitzgerald, in his dissenting opinion, correctly stresses the observation of the *In re Slum Clearance* Court that in those cases the object of eminent domain was found, and the decision to exercise the power was made, entirely apart from considerations relating to private corporations.

. . . .

The inapplicability of the slum clearance cases is evident. In the case before us the reputed public "benefit" to be gained is inextricably bound to ownership, development and use of the property in question by one, and only one, private corporation, General Motors, and then only in the manner prescribed by the corporation. The public "benefit" claimed by defendant to result can be achieved only if condemnation is executed upon an area, within a timetable, essentially for a price, and entirely for a purpose determined not by any public entity, but by the board of directors of General Motors. There may never be a clearer case than this of condemning land for a private corporation.

B

As discussed above, land may not be condemned for a private corporation save for those cases falling within what I have called the instrumentality of commerce exception. This has been the unwavering rule in this state for well over a century. It may be argued, however, that the fact that the case before us lies outside the exception does not end the inquiry if the reasons justifying the existing exception are present here. I turn now to determine whether such reasons exist.

Examination of the cases involving the instrumentality of commerce exception reveal that three common elements appear in those decisions that go far toward explicating and justifying the use of eminent domain for private corporations: 1) public necessity of the extreme sort, 2) continuing accountability to the public, and 3) selection of land according to facts of independent public significance.

1.

Public Necessity of the Extreme Sort Otherwise Impracticable: The Indispensability of Collective Action

To justify the exception, this Court has relied on a principle expressed in varying phraseology such as "overriding public necessity,"[19] "necessity . . . otherwise impracticable,"[20] and "necessity of the extreme sort."[21] The principle has to do not so much with public benefit, which is to a greater or lesser extent invariably present, as with the indispensability of compelled expropriation of property to the very existence of the enterprise pursued by the private corporation. The principle, as valid today as when stated years ago, is that "[e]very branch of needful industry has a right to exist," *People ex rel. Detroit & Howell R. Co., supra*, 482. With regard to highways, railroads, canals, and other instrumentalities of commerce, it takes little imagination to recognize that without eminent domain these essential improvements, all of which require particular configurations of property narrow and generally straight ribbons of land would be "otherwise impracticable;" they would not exist at all.

. . . .

The production of automobiles certainly entails public benefits. Nevertheless, it could hardly be contended that the existence of the automotive industry or the construction of a new General Motors assembly plant requires the use of eminent domain.

---

[19] *People ex rel. Detroit & Howell R. Co. v. Salem Township Board*, 20 Mich. 452, 480 (1870).

[20] *Id.* 481.

[21] *Ryerson v. Brown*, 35 Mich. 333, 339 (1877).

This type of necessity, which goes to the legal question of public use, should not be confused with "public necessity" as that term is used in § 6 of the Michigan "quick-take" statute, which pertains to a question of fact and provides, in pertinent part:

[T]he determination of public necessity by (a public) agency shall be binding on the court in the absence of a showing of fraud, error of law, or abuse of discretion. M.C.L. § 213.56(2); M.S.A. § 8.265(6)(2).

This question of fact is concerned with the need to condemn particular land to achieve a given object. The minimal standard of judicial review set out in the statute above is the usual one for questions of fact.

But whether eminent domain may be employed at all to bring about that object is an entirely distinct inquiry, a question of law for the courts respecting the ambit of the constitutional term of art "public use."

Hence, if an object is ruled not to be a public use, the factual question of public necessity is obviated.

Instead, what defendants are really claiming is that eminent domain is required for the existence of a new General Motors assembly plant within the city limits of Detroit in order to comply with the specifications of General Motors. This is an altogether different argument, acceptance of which would vitiate the requirement of "necessity of the extreme sort" and significantly alter the balance between governmental power and private property rights struck by the people and embodied in the taking clause. Just as ominously, it would work a fundamental shift in the relative force between private corporate power and individual property rights having the sanction of the state.

2.

Continuing Accountability to the Public:
A Condition for the Use of Public Power

Another circumstance common to the instrumentality of commerce cases justifying condemnation for private corporations is the retention of some measure of government control over the operation of the enterprise after it has passed into private hands. For example, railroad companies entitled to invoke eminent domain are subject to a panoply of regulations, such as seeing to it that the public has equal and fair access to use of the railroad.

. . . .

A fuller explication of the principle of public accountability was made in *Board of Health of Portage Twp. v. Van Hoesen*, 87 Mich. 533, 539, 49 N.W. 894 (1891) (establishment of cemeteries by private corporation is not a public use):

> To justify the condemnation of lands for a private corporation, not only must the purpose be one in which the public has an interest, but *the state must have a voice in the manner in which the public may avail itself of that use*. . . . The use which the public is to have of such property must be fixed and definite. The general public must have a right to a certain definite use of the private property, on terms and for charges fixed by law, and the owner of the property must be compelled by law to permit the general public to enjoy it. It will not suffice that the general prosperity of the community is promoted by the taking of private property from the owner, and transferring its title and control to a corporation, to be used by such corporation as its private property, uncontrolled by law as to its use. (Emphasis added.)

. . . .

Whether or not one subscribes to the fiction that, in the instrumentality of commerce cases, the private corporation is merely a public agent, it is clear that public control of the use of land after transfer to the private entity invests the taking with far greater public attributes than would exist without the control and fortifies the justification for the abridgment of individual property rights in those cases.

One of the reasons advanced by the defendants as justification of the taking in this case, and adopted by the majority, is the claim of alleviation of unemployment. Even assuming, arguendo, that employment per se is a "necessity of the extreme sort," there are no guarantees from General Motors about employment levels at the new assembly plant. General Motors has made representations about the number of employees who will work at the new plant, and I certainly do not doubt the good faith of those representations. But the fact of the matter is that once CIP is sold to General Motors, there will be no public control whatsoever over the management, or operation, or conduct of the plant to be built there. General Motors will be accountable not to the public, but to its stockholders. Who knows what the automotive industry will look like in 20 years, or even 10? For that matter, who knows what cars will look like then? For all that can be known now, in light of present trends, the plant could be fully automated in 10 years. Amid these uncertainties, however, one thing is certain. The level of employment at the new GM plant will be determined by private corporate managers primarily with reference, not to the rate of regional unemployment, but to profit.

By permitting the condemnation in this case, this Court has allowed the use of the public power of eminent domain without concomitant public accountability.

3.

Choosing the Land: Facts of Independent Public Significance

The third element common to our cases has to do with the recognition that when property is condemned for a private corporation, determination of the specific land to be condemned is made without reference to the private interests of the corporation. The determination is based instead upon criteria related to the public interest.

. . . .

Without belaboring the obvious, the location of CIP is, to say the least, solely a result of conditions laid down by General Motors, which were designed to further its private, pecuniary interest. These are facts of private significance.

The three elements discussed above are not recognized by the majority, which instead has tied the concept of public use to the existence of a public benefit. Yet, the principles inhering in the precedent demonstrate that, although public benefit is a necessary condition, it is itself an insufficient condition for the existence of a public use.

From now on "the protean concept of public benefit" will be the sole criterion by which we are to adjudge the constitutionality of employing eminent domain for private corporations. The concept of public benefit is indeed protean. It is also nebulous. The state taking clause has now been placed on a spectrum that admits of no principles and therefore no limits.

V

Conclusion

. . . .

[A] more general principle, consonant with prior decisions of this Court and entirely contrary to the holding of the majority here, is contained in the state taking clause: the right to own and occupy land will not be subordinated to private corporate interests unless the use of the land condemned by or for the corporation is invested with public attributes sufficient to fairly deem the corporate activity governmental. . . .

The majority opinion stands in contravention of the well established and constant jurisprudence of the taking clause of the Michigan constitution. Present economic conditions notwithstanding, I can discern no principled ground on which their decision can be reconciled with the body of law interpreting the state taking clause. Their decision would be less dangerous were there a sound basis for the change in the law, or even claim of one. However, since the arguments were directed toward justifying the condemnation in question on the basis of present law, understandably no reasons for a change in the law were offered.

I noted earlier that the concept of public purpose, which describes the bounds of the state's taxing power, has undergone significant expansion over the course of the last century. Now it is common for the state to aid private corporations, directly or indirectly, through the use of public revenues. The most conspicuous recent example is the $150 million loan to the Chrysler Corporation. Chrysler, of course, also received federally guaranteed loans.

There are at least two compelling considerations that weigh decisively against the similar expansion of "public use" accomplished so precipitously by the majority.

First, as discussed earlier, the deprivations of property that result from the exercise of the powers of taxation and eminent domain are different in kind. Eminent domain is a far more intrusive power. Like taxation, it can entail financial loss, although "just compensation" is required. But more important, it can entail, as it did in this case, intangible losses, such as severance or personal attachments to one's domicile and neighborhood and the destruction of an organic community of a most unique and irreplaceable character.

Second, when the private corporation to be aided by eminent domain is as large and influential as General Motors, the power of eminent domain, for all practical purposes, is in the hands of the private corporation. The municipality is merely the conduit. In contrast, the broader view of the notion of "public purpose" has not effected a comparable transfer of the power of taxation to the private sector. Government still determines how tax liability is computed and how and under what conditions tax revenues are spent.

Eminent domain is an attribute of sovereignty. When individual citizens are forced to suffer great social dislocation to permit private corporations to construct plants where they deem it most profitable, one is left to wonder who the sovereign is.

The sudden and fundamental change in established law effected by the Court in this case, entailing such a significant diminution of constitutional rights, cannot be justified as a function of judicial construction; the only proper vehicle for change of this dimension is a constitutional amendment. What has been done in this case can be explained by the overwhelming sense of inevitability that has attended this litigation from the beginning; a sense attributable to the combination and coincidence of the interests of a desperate city administration and a giant corporation willing and able to take advantage of the opportunity that presented itself. The justification for it, like the inevitability of it, has been made to seem more acceptable by the "team spirit" chorus of approval of the project which has been supplied by the voices of labor, business, industry, government, finance, and even the news media. Virtually the only discordant sounds of dissent have come from the minuscule minority of citizens most profoundly affected by this case, the Poletown residents whose neighborhood has been destroyed.

With this case the Court has subordinated a constitutional right to private corporate interests. As demolition of existing structures on the future plant site goes forward, the best that can be hoped for, jurisprudentially, is that the precedential value of this case will be lost in the accumulating rubble.

. . . .

[c] Notes on *Poletown*

[*i*] *Costs and Benefits of Condemnation.* The most obvious benefit of condemnation in a case like *Poletown* is the ability to assemble large amounts of land without having to pay

holdout prices to land owners aware of the project and willing to play hardball with the developer. Indeed, if a public entity can purchase land on the open market there is little need to pay the additional costs of starting a condemnation proceeding to obtain land. In an interesting article, Thomas Merrill found that most condemnations occur only when governments are confronted with the prospects of a holdout or some other (to use Merrill's terminology) "thin market" that raises the costs of buying land on the open market. Thomas W. Merrill, *The Economics of Public Use*, 72 CORNELL L. REV. 61 (1986). But he then goes on to wonder whether condemnations like those in *Poletown* are justified. While they occur in thin markets, the parties most directly benefiting from the condemnations may be private institutions in a position to extract significant amounts of money from the state in exchange for the condemned land. When the state ends up paying more out to the beneficiary of the condemnation action than it saves by avoiding the ability of owners to holdout for higher prices for their land in a thin market, Merrill argues that the condemnation does not serve a valid public purpose. How would this sort of analysis work out in cases like *Berman v. Parker*, discussed at p. 900 above, or *Hawaii Housing Authority v. Midkiff*, p. 902 above?

[*ii*] **Denouement.** As of a decade ago, the General Motors factory was operating, employment in the plant was at about 3,000 workers, property taxes were said to be coming in at a better than planned rate because of the installation of a great deal of robotic equipment, and federal economic development loans used to support the project were being paid off. The City of Detroit viewed the project as a great success and was involved in a similar plan to provide expansion room for a Chrysler Corporation engine factory. This project drew virtually no national attention. The Poletown plan involved the demolition of over 1700 structures, the Chrysler plan about 800.[17] The engine factory is scheduled for completion soon. A $250 million expansion of the Poletown General Motors plant was completed in 1996.

§ 11.03 Contemporary Land Use Controls and The Takings Problem

[1] Introduction

Since the decisions in *Euclid v. Ambler*, p. 490 above, and *Berman v. Parker*, p. 900 above, confirmed the breadth of police power authority to zone and redevelop property, an extensive array of zoning and land use controls have been adopted. Sewer and water crises have led to moratoria on construction in some areas,[18] historic preservation has come of age, major decreases in permitted densities have been adopted along with contests among developers interested in using the development rights that remain,[19] bonus programs have permitted increased densities in return

---

[17] Telephone Interview with Ronald Flies, Department of Community and Economic Development, City of Detroit (July 31, 1987).

[18] *See, e.g.* Charles v. Diamond, 41 N.Y.2d 318, 392 N.Y.S.2d 594, 360 N.E.2d 1295 (1977).

[19] Montgomery County in Maryland ran one of the best known such programs in the Bethesda business district just northwest of Washington, D.C. When the metropolitan area's subway system was under construction in the 1970s, the central business district in Bethesda, a planned stop on the subway, was rezoned. The ordinance did not locate development rights on each lot but created a ceiling for the total amount of development that could occur on a list of available sites, required a mix of commercial and residential uses and asked developers to submit proposals to local authorities for review. A set of projects was then selected. They are now all under construction or built and the subway is running. The remaining parcels available for development were then effectively downzoned to low density commercial use. The results, to this author's eyes, are mixed, but much better than most downtown areas. The quality of architecture is, on the whole, better than average and some of it is outstanding. There are a number of well designed public spaces and amenities and the overall density level of residents and businesses is high enough to create excitement and low enough to prevent total paralysis in public services and traffic.

for the construction of public amenities,[20] property tax abatement programs have been adopted in order to preserve agricultural land uses, environmental controls have become commonplace, and on and on. Since it is impossible in an introductory text such as this to cover them all, I have selected a few of the more intriguing Supreme Court cases for study. In the last several decades, some of the recently invented land use control techniques came before the Court, including historic preservation, environmental controls, and bonus programs. These and other programs all raise potential Takings Clause problems, the subject of this section of the chapter.

A number of land use cases in addition to *Euclid* were decided before the post-World War II boom began, but two—*Pennsylvania Coal Company v. Mahon*, 260 U.S. 393 (1922), and *Causby v. United States*, 328 U.S. 256 (1946)—were particularly important in establishing the vocabulary of disputes under the Takings Clause of the Fifth Amendment. In *Mahon* the Court invalidated Pennsylvania regulations prohibiting the removal of pillars from an underground mine. Justice Holmes, writing for the Court in *Mahon*, crafted the following oft quoted passage to justify the outcome:

> Government hardly could go on if to some extent values incident to property could not be diminished without paying for every such change in the general law. As long recognized some values are enjoyed under an implied limitation and must yield to the police power. But obviously the implied limitation must have its limits or the contract and due process clauses are gone. One fact for consideration in determining such limits is the extent of the diminution. When it reaches a certain magnitude, in most if not in all cases there must be an exercise of eminent domain and condemnation to sustain the act. So the question depends upon the particular facts. The greatest weight is given to the judgment of the legislature but it always is open to interested parties to contend that the legislature has gone beyond its constitutional power.

> This is the case of a single private house. No doubt there is a public interest even in this, as there is in every purchase and sale and in all that happens within the commonwealth. Some existing rights may be modified even in such a case. But usually in ordinary private affairs the public interest does not warrant much of this kind of interference. A source of damage to such a house is not a public nuisance even if similar damage is inflicted on others in different places. The damage is not common or public. The extent of the public interest is shown by the statute to be limited, since the statute ordinarily does not apply to land when the surface is owned by the owner of the coal. Furthermore, it is not justified as a protection of personal safety. That could be provided for by notice. Indeed the very foundation of this bill is that the defendant gave timely notice of its intent to mine under the house. On the other hand the extent of the taking is great. It purports to abolish what is recognized in Pennsylvania as an estate in land—a very valuable estate—and what is declared by the Court below to be a contract hitherto binding the plaintiffs. If we were called upon to deal with the plaintiff's position alone we should think it clear that the statute does not disclose a public interest sufficient to warrant so extensive a destruction of the defendant's constitutionally protected rights.

> . . . .

> The rights of the public in a street purchased or laid out by eminent domain are those that it has paid for. If in any case its representatives have been so short sighted as to acquire only

---

[20] This method has been used to entice the construction of theaters in the Times Square area in New York City and hotels near the convention center in Washington, D.C., to name just two. Many major cities have such programs.

surface rights without the right of support we see no more authority for supplying the latter without compensation than there was for taking the right of way in the first place and refusing to pay for it because the public wanted it very much. The protection of private property in the Fifth Amendment presupposes that it is wanting for public use, but provides that it shall not be taken for such use without compensation. . . .

The general rule at least is that while property may be regulated to a certain extent, if regulation goes too far it will be recognized as a taking. It may be doubted how far exceptional cases, like the blowing up of a house to stop a conflagration, go—and if they go beyond the general rule, whether they do not stand as much upon tradition as upon principle. In general it is not plain that a man's misfortunes or necessities will justify his shifting the damages to his neighbor's shoulders. We are in danger of forgetting that a strong public desire to improve the public condition is not enough to warrant achieving the desire by a shorter cut than the constitutional way of paying for the change. . . .

We assume, of course, that the statute was passed upon the conviction that an exigency existed that would warrant it, and we assume that an exigency exists that would warrant the exercise of eminent domain. But the question at bottom is upon whom the loss of the changes desired should fall. So far as private persons or communities have seen fit to take the risk of acquiring only surface rights, we cannot see that the fact that their risk has become a danger warrants the giving to them greater rights than they bought.

Courts have had difficulty dealing with *Mahon* ever since it was decided. It established a substantive due process balancing test between "regulation" under the "police power" and control that goes "too far."[21] The open ended qualities of the test make it easy to describe *Euclid*'s approval of zoning as a classic example of the notion that "mere regulation" under the "police power" is constitutionally permissible despite the limitations of the Takings Clause. But this rhetorical formulation creates a number of problems.

For example, work backwards from the notion that governments have the power to condemn land for a public purpose. The Fifth Amendment, which provides "nor shall private property be taken for public purpose, without just compensation," was originally drafted, not to control land use regulation, but to prevent land seizures like those made during both the colonial era and the early years of the United States.[22] Property confiscations did occur in our early history and the clause was intended to stop the practice. Regulatory actions, like controlling the sale of land in the western territories, requiring the establishment of land title systems, modifying dower or creating new forms of ownership like married women's estates effected land. Such legal structures were not originally seen as potential Takings problems. Their adoption raised issues about the authority of Congress under the Contracts Clause[23] and the Due Process Clause,

---

[21] For more details on the history of the *Mahon* case, read Joseph F. DeMento, *Mining the Archives of* Pennsylvania Coal: *Heaps of Constitutional Mischief*, 11 J. LEGAL HIST. 396 (1990). An excerpt from this work may be found in RICHARD CHUSED, A PROPERTY ANTHOLOGY 461-468 (2d ed. 1997).

[22] A large literature on the history of the Takings Clause now exists. Among the more interesting articles are John F. Hart, *Colonial Land Use Law and Its Significance for Modern Takings Doctrine*, 109 HARV. L. REV. 1252 (1996); William Michael Treanor, *The Original Understanding of the Takings Clause and the Political Process*, 95 COLUM. L. REV. 782 (1995).

[23] Art. I, § 10, cl. 1, prohibits adoption of laws "impairing the Obligation of Contracts."

but not the Takings Clause. The major issue was often stated in terms of the reasonableness of retroactive legislation, not the need for compensation.[24]

In this century, however, the reasonableness and compensation problems have merged. As urban land use controls grew in intensity before the Great Depression,[25] retroactivity became only one of many concerns. The rhetoric used by the Supreme Court in both *Mahon* and *Euclid* continued to distinguish between reasonable and unreasonable regulation under the police power, but the arguments raised by land owners began to sound more and more like contentions that their land had been seized for public use without the payment of compensation. The difficulty was implicit in *Mahon* itself. Note well that the remedy obtained by the Pennsylvania Coal Company was not compensation, as if their mineral interest had been taken, but an injunction against enforcement of the regulation, as if their Due Process rights had been violated. *Euclid* reflected the same dilemma. The remedy sought was an injunction, even though the allegations in the complaint read as if Ambler Realty had been deprived of rights to exploit its land. Even the reasoning of the opinion—the nuisance analogy—relies on reasonableness as an inextricable part of the standard used to decide whether losses caused by regulation were Constitutional.

But one day, a problem had to arise in which injunctive relief was inappropriate. The most prominent of such disputes were the so-called airport cases—claims by landowners living under approaches to airport runways that jet aircraft noise effectively took their property in violation of the Constitution.[26] The most famous of these cases was *Causby v. United States*. Those courts agreeing with the plaintiffs' contentions knew that they could not enjoin operation of a major government airbase or publicly operated commercial airport. These facilities, like the factory in *Boomer v. Atlantic Cement Company*, p. 871 above, were just too important to shut down. Nor were the courts willing to issue injunctions allowing private owners living under runway approaches to extract bonus payments from airport authorities before agreeing to sell their entitlements. Awarding compensation for a taking was the only alternative.[27] The same balancing-of-factors approach that so typically governed decision making in Substantive Due Process cases and early land use cases like *Mahon* and *Euclid* was used in the airport cases even though the remedy was labeled as compensation for an unconstitutional taking.

We are still attempting to discover the difference between mere regulation and unreasonable government actions or takings. One of the first comprehensive post-World War II academic attempts to make some sense out of the problem was written by Frank Michelman in 1967. It quickly became a classic that wielded significant influence over the Warren Court's thinking about takings law. Calling upon a long tradition of utilitarian jurisprudence and well understood

---

[24] For an exhaustive survey of early Contract Clause and Taking Clause cases, *see* Steven A. Siegel, *Understanding the Nineteenth Century Contract Clause: The Role of the Property-Privilege Distinction and "Takings" Clause Jurisprudence,* 60 S. Cal. L. Rev. 1 (1986).

[25] John Hart, in his work cited above at note 22, argues that, contrary to the general impression of many lawyers and judges, quite intrusive land use regulation existed from the very early days of our history. But the scope of regulation clearly grew in the first decades of the twentieth century and drew quite a bit of attention from Formalists and Freedom of Contract adherents.

[26] Even though a number of old urban airports, such as Washington, D.C.'s National Airport, Boston's Logan Airport, Chicago's Midway Airport and New York's LaGuardia Airport, were located near densely populated areas, widespread complaints about noise did not arise until after World War II. Civilian jet airplanes proliferated after the war, noise complaints grew in intensity, and new airports were located outside of densely populated areas.

[27] Use of nuisance law by the private litigants against the government entities operating the airports was often barred by sovereign immunity doctrines.

conceptions of fairness, Michelman concluded that the Takings Clause was intended to remedy disadvantageous or painful treatment caused by collective decision making. His work discussed many of the streams of legal thought previously discussed in this text—the Formalist call for bright line rules, the Realist desire to enhance legislative power, the Legal Process adherent's concerns about institutional legitimacy, and the Representation Reinforcer's desire to protect the under represented and perhaps unfairly treated land owner. An excerpt from the work follows.

Frank I. Michelman, *Property, Utility and Fairness: Comments on the Ethical Foundations of "Just Compensation" Law*

80 HARV. L. REV. 1165, 1224-1239 (1967).[28]

We have, in effect, been searching for a useful and satisfying way to identify the "evil" supposedly combated by the constitutional just compensation provisions, and have now suggested equating it with a capacity of some collective actions to imply that someone may be subjected to immediately disadvantageous or painful treatment for no other apparent reason, and in accordance with no other apparent principle, than that someone else's claim to satisfaction has been ranked as intrinsically superior to his own.

The discussion has also shown why avoidance of this evil is not the same thing as avoidance of all social action having capricious redistributive effects. The reasons begin with the universal acknowledgment that some collective constraint on individual free choice is necessary in order to minimize the frustrations produced by people's concurrent quests for fulfillment, and to exploit fully the potential benefits from human interaction; and that social control, therefore, can ultimately lead to fuller achievement by each of his own ends. It is true that collective action which depends for its legitimacy on such understandings must look ultimately to the furtherance of *everyone's* attainment of his own ends, without "discrimination," and that this latter requirement would most obviously be met if a way were found to distribute the benefits and costs associated with each collective measure so that each person would share equally in the net benefit. But such perfection is plainly unattainable. Efficiency-motivated collective measures will regularly inflict on countless people disproportionate burdens which cannot practically be erased by compensation settlements. In the face of this difficulty, it seems we are pleased to believe that we can arrive at an acceptable level of assurance that *over time* the burdens associated with collectively determined improvements will have been distributed "evenly" enough so that everyone will be a net gainer. The function of a compensation practice, as here viewed, is to fulfill a strongly felt need to maintain that assurance at an "acceptable" level—to justify the general expectations of long-run "evenness." If one feels impelled to refer this need back to a social interest in maximizing production, what we have called a utilitarian approach to compensation will be the result. If, however, the need is accepted on its own terms and for its own sake, as simply rooted in the condition of being a human person, then justice or fairness, rather than utility, will seem to be the key to compensation. The two approaches may lead to different results in some situations, but in general decisions made under their guidance turn on much the same factors—the disproportionateness of the harm a measure inflicts on individuals, the likelihood that those harmed were in a position to extract balancing concessions, the clarity with which efficiency demands the measure, and so forth. In what follows, I shall often treat the two approaches as parallel, and use the word "fairness" to signify also that apparent evenhandedness which a utilitarian approach may be understood as requiring.

---

[28] Reprinted by permission of the Harvard Law Review Association and Frank I. Michelman.

If it truly is important for society to subordinate its pursuit of efficiency to a discipline aimed at preventing outrages to fairness, then it may be worth asking whether the constitutional just compensation provisions present any hazard to sound social functioning. These provisions attract attention as the visible, formal expressions of society's commitment to fairness as a constraint on its pursuit of efficiency. The question is whether their magnetism is an energizing force, or a mesmerizing one. If it induces the habit of waiting upon the courts to administer a fairness discipline, and if courts are less than fully equal to the task or cannot perform it without serious damage to their effectiveness in other spheres, then there is cause for concern.

To argue at length for the unamazing proposition that the true purpose of the just compensation rule is to forestall evils associated with unfair treatment, is to imply that the proposition, for all its obviousness, is insufficiently understood or recognized in practice. We should, then, consider carefully the extent to which the "fairness" or utility rationale is already reflected, even if inexplicitly, in the judicial doctrines which presently compose the main corpus of our just compensation lore. My conclusion is that these doctrines do significantly reflect the line of thought which has been elaborated in these pages, and that this approach, indeed, derives some indirect support from its power to explain much that is otherwise mysterious about the doctrines. Nevertheless, the courts fall too far short of adequate performance to be left without major assistance from other quarters.

A. Physical Invasion

It will be recalled that the factor of physical invasion has a doctrinal potency often troublesome on two counts. First, private losses otherwise indistinguishable from one another may, as in the flight nuisance cases, be classified for compensability purposes according to whether they are accompanied by a physical invasion, even though that seems a purely fortuitous circumstance. Second, purely nominal harms—such as many which accompany street-widenings or subterranean utility installations—are automatically deemed compensable if accompanied by governmental occupation of private property, in apparent contradiction of the principle that the size of the private loss is a critically important variable. Both these seeming oddities may now seem easier to understand.

Actual, physical use or occupation by the public of private property may make it seem rather specially likely that the owner is sustaining a distinctly disproportionate share of the cost of some social undertaking. Moreover, there probably will be no need, in such a case, to trace remote consequences in order to arrive at a reasonable appraisal of the gravity of the owner's loss—a loss which is relatively likely to be practically determinable and expressible as a dollar amount. Furthermore, to limit compensation to those whose possessions have been physically violated, while in a sense arbitrary, may at least furnish a practical, defensible, impersonal line between compensable and non compensable impositions—one which makes it possible to compensate on some occasions without becoming mired in the impossible task of compensating all disproportionately burdened interests.

. . . .

But this justification for a physical invasion criterion is really rather weak. The capacity for such a criterion to minimize settlement costs is beyond question, but its capacity to distinguish, even crudely, between significant and insignificant losses is too puny to be taken seriously. A rule that no loss is compensable unless accompanied by physical invasion would be patently unacceptable. A physical invasion test, then, can never be more than a convenience for identifying *clearly compensable* occasions. It cannot justify dismissal of any occasion as *clearly non compensable*. But in that case, the significance of the settlement-cost-saving feature is sharply diminished. We find ourselves accepting the disadvantage of a test requiring compensation on many occasions where losses in truth seem relatively insignificant and bearable, in return for the convenience of having a simple way to identify some—but by no means all—compensable occasions. This seems a questionable bargain.

There may be a way of shoring up the physical invasion test—viewing it as a way of identifying some but not all compensable occasions—if we are inclined to take a utilitarian rather than an "absolute" view of fairness. This requires some reflection on psychic phenomena. Physical possession doubtless is the most cherished prerogative, and the most dramatic index, of ownership of tangible things. Sophisticated rationalizations and assurances of overall evenness which may stand up as long as one's possessions are unmolested may wilt before the stark spectacle of an alien, uninvited presence in one's territory. The psychological shock, the emotional protest, the symbolic threat to all property and security, may be expected to reach their highest pitch when government is an unabashed invader. Perhaps, then, the utilitarian might say that as long as courts must fend with compensability issues, to lay great stress on the polar circumstance of a permanent or regular physical use or occupation by the public is sound judicial practice—even though, at the same time and in a broader view, to discriminate on such a basis seems unacceptably arbitrary.

It is this evident arbitrariness which seems to require outright disapproval of the physical invasion criterion if we judge it by the standards of "absolute" fairness. For, true as may be the utilitarian controller's judgment that physical invasion raises special risks to the sense of security he wishes to inculcate, the rational actors of the fairness model must be expected to see that the relevant comparison is between large losses and small losses—not between those which are and are not accompanied by partial evictions.

B. Diminution of Value

Earlier we found it hard to understand why compensability should be thought to turn on a comparison of the size of the claimant's loss with the preexisting value of that spatially defined piece of property to which the loss in value seems to be specifically attached. It can now be suggested that judicial reliance on such comparisons reflects a utilitarian approach to compensability, as qualified by some special behavioral assumptions.

The method of identifying compensable harms on the basis of the degree to which "the affected piece" of property is devalued offers several parallels to that of discriminating on the basis of physical invasion. Both methods, though they seem obtuse and illogical so long as the purpose of compensation is broadly stated to be that of preventing capricious redistributions, gain in plausibility given the more refined statement that the purpose of compensation is to prevent a special kind of suffering on the part of people who have grounds for feeling themselves the victims of unprincipled exploitation. Moreover, the appeal of both methods rests ultimately in administrative expediency, in their defining classes of cases whose members will (a) usually be easy to identify and (b) usually, under certain behavioral suppositions, present a particularly strong subjective need for compensation.

As applied to the diminution of value test, these statements require explanation. We may begin by noticing a refinement, not mentioned earlier, which might initially seem only to deepen the mystery. It will be recalled that Justice Holmes, writing for the Court in the famous

Pennsylvania Coal case, held that a restriction on the extraction of coal, which effectively prevented the petitioner from exercising certain mining rights which it owned, was a taking of property and so could be enforced only upon payment of compensation. Holmes intimated strongly that the separation in ownership of the mining rights from the balance of the fee, prior to enactment of the restriction, was critically important to the petitioner's victory. But why should this be so? We can see that if one owns mining rights only, but not the residue of the fee, then a regulation forbidding mining totally devalues the owner's stake in "that" land. But is there any reason why it should matter whether one owns, in addition to mining rights, residually rights in the same parcel (which may be added to the denominator so as probably to reduce the fraction of value destroyed below what is necessary for compensability) or residuary rights in some other parcel (which will not be added to the denominator)?

The significance of this question is confirmed by its pertinency to many comparable judicial performances. There is, for example, the widespread rule requiring compensation to the owner of an equitable servitude (such as a residential building restriction) when the government destroys the servitude's value by acquiring the burdened land and then using that land in violation of the private restriction embodied in the servitude. Vis-à-vis the servitude owner, the government cannot be said in the narrow sense to have "taken" any property. It has not, as in the air easement cases, engaged in an activity which would be an actionable eviction if privately instigated. It is not affirmatively exploiting any prerogative formerly held by the owner of the servitude. It is simply engaging in activity which, absent the servitude, might have been a nuisance; but government does not usually come under an automatic obligation to compensate whenever it maintains a nuisance. Yet many courts award compensation to persons deprived by government action of the benefits of private building restrictions, without asking any questions about how much value, or what fraction of some value, has been destroyed. Thus, government activity, on land adjacent to the complainant's, which would otherwise give rise to no claim to compensation, may support such a claim if it violates a building restriction of which the complainant is a beneficiary. If a justification exists for such a difference in treatment, it would seem to be that one's psychological commitment to his explicit, formally carved out, appurtenant rights in another's land is much more sharply focused and intense, and much nearer the surface of his consciousness, than any reliance he places on his general claim to be safeguarded against nuisances. This proposition, if valid, would not affect the "fairness" of non compensation, but it means that a utilitarian, with his eye on the actual long term psychological effects of his decisions, will be wary of denying compensation to the affronted servitude owner.

. . . .

The "fraction of value destroyed" test, to recapitulate, appears to proceed by first trying to isolate some "thing" owned by the person complaining which is affected by the imposition. Ideally, it seems, one traces the incidence of the imposition and then asks what "thing" is likely to be identified by the owner as "the thing" affected by this measure? Once having thus found the denominator of the fraction, the test proceeds to ask what proportion of the value or prerogatives formerly attributed by the claimant to that thing has been destroyed by the measure. If practically all, compensation is to be paid.

All this suggests that the common way of stating the test under discussion—in terms of a vaguely located critical point on a sliding scale—is misleading (though certainly a true representation of the language repeatedly used by Holmes). The customary labels—magnitude of the harm test, or diminution of value test—obscure the test's foundations by conveying the idea that it calls for an arbitrary pinpointing of a critical proportion (probably lying somewhere between fifty and one hundred percent). More sympathetically perceived, however, the test poses not nearly so loose a question of degree; it does not ask "how much," but rather (like the physical-occupation test) it asks "whether or not"; whether or not the measure in question can easily be seen to have practically deprived the claimant of some distinctly perceived, sharply crystallized, investment-backed expectation.

. . . .

C. Balancing

Earlier it was argued that while the process of striking a balance between a compensation claimant's losses and "society's" net gains would reveal the *efficiency* of the measure responsible for those losses and gains, it would be inconclusive as to compensability. By viewing compensation as a response to the demands of fairness we can now see that the "balancing" approach, while certainly inconclusive, is not entirely irrelevant to the compensability issue.

What fairness (or the utilitarian test) demands is assurance that society will not act deliberately so as to inflict painful burdens on some of its members unless such action is "unavoidable" in the interest of long-run, general well-being. Society violates that assurance if it pursues a doubtfully efficient course and, at the same time, refuses compensation for resulting painful losses. In this situation, even a practical impossibility of compensating will leave the sense of fairness unappeased, since it is unfair, and harmful to those expectations of the property owner that society wishes to protect, to proceed with measures which seem certain to cause painful individual losses while not clearly promising any net social improvement. In short, where compensability is the issue the "balancing" test is relevantly aimed at discovering not whether a measure is or is not efficient, but whether it is *so obviously* efficient as to quiet the potential outrage of persons "unavoidably" sacrificed in its interest. This conclusion does not, of course, detract from our earlier conclusion that even the clear and undisputed efficiency of a measure does not sufficiently establish its fairness in the absence of compensation.

D. Harm and Benefit

For clarity of analysis the most important point to be made about asking whether a restrictive measure requires a man to "benefit" his neighbors or only stops him from "harming" them is that this distinction (insofar as it is relevant and valid at all) is properly addressed to an issue different from, and antecedent to the issue of "compensation" as we have now come to view it. We concluded earlier that the harm-benefit distinction was illusory as long as efficiency was to be taken as the justifying purpose of a collective measure. But we have for many pages past been treating the compensation problem as one growing out of a need to reconcile efficiency with the protection of fair, or socially useful, expectations. The issue we have been trying to clarify does not exist apart from the collective pursuit of efficiency. In this scheme of things, the office of the harm-benefit distinction cannot be to help resolve that issue. But the distinction, properly understood, does have a related use. It helps us to identify certain situations which, although in most obvious respects they resemble paradigm compensability problems, can be treated as raising no compensation issues *because the collective measures involved are not grounded solely in considerations of efficiency.*

The core of truth in the harm-prevention/benefit-extraction test—and the reason for its strong intuitive appeal—emerges when we recognize that some use restrictions can claim a justification having nothing to do with the question of what use of the available resources is the most efficient. If someone, without my consent, takes away a valuable possession of mine, he is said to have stolen and is called a thief. When theft occurs, society usually will do what it can to make the thief restore to the owner the thing stolen or its equivalent, either because "commutative justice" so requires or because it is felt that there will be an intolerable threat to stable, productive social existence unless society sets its face against the unilateral decisions of thieves that they should have what is in the possession of others. The case is not essentially different if I own a residence in a pleasant neighborhood and you open a brickworks nearby. In pursuit of your own welfare you have by your own fiat deprived me of some of mine. Society, by closing the brickworks, simply makes you give back the welfare you grabbed; and, since you were not authorized in the first place to make distributional judgments as between you and me, you have no claim to compensation. The whole point of society's intervention negates any claim to compensation.

The point, then, is that the appeal of the tendered distinction between antinuisance measures and public benefit measures lies in the fact that the activities curbed by the first sort of measure are much more likely to have been "theft-like" in their origin than are activities restricted by the second sort. Measures of the "public benefit" type can usually be justified *only* in terms of efficiency, a justification which leaves the compensation issue unresolved, while "antinuisance" measures may be justified by considerations of commutative justice, or of the protection of orderly decision making, which negate any possible claim to compensation.

It should be clear, however, that no sharp distinction is thus established between the two types of measures. Activity which is obviously detrimental to others at the time regulations are adopted may have been truly innocent when first instigated. Failure to act upon this plain truth is responsible for some of the most violently offensive decisions not to compensate. The brickyard case is the undying classic. The yard is established out of sight, hearing, and influence of any other activity whatsoever. The city expands, and eventually engulfs the brickyard. The brickmaker is then ordered to desist. That order reduces the market value of his land from 800,000 dollars to 60,000 dollars. There is no question here of disgorging ill-gotten gains; brickmaking is a worthy occupation, and at the time of its establishment the yard generated no nuisance. No incompatibility with any use of other land was apparent. To say that the brickmaker should have foreseen the emergence of the incompatibility is fantastic when the conclusion depending from that premise is that we may now destroy his investment without compensating him. It would be no less erratic for society to explain to a homeowner, as it bulldozed his house out of the way of a new public school or pumping station, that he should have realized from the beginning that congestion would necessitate these facilities and that topographical factors have all along pointed unerringly in the direction of his lot.

Just as the compensation issue raised by an ostensibly nuisance-curbing regulation cannot always be dismissed by assuming that the owner's claim is no stronger than a thief's or a gambler's, so conversely it will often be wholly appropriate to deny compensation because that assumption does hold, even though the measure occasioning the private loss seems to fall within the class of restrictions on "innocent" activity for the enrichment of the public.

Suppose I buy scenic land along the highway during the height of public discussion about the possibility of forbidding all development of such land, and the market clearly reflects awareness that future restrictions are a significant possibility. If restrictions are ultimately adopted, have I a claim to be compensated in the amount of the difference between the land's value with restrictions and its value without them? Surely this would be a weak claim. I bought land which I knew might be subjected to restrictions; and the price I paid should have been discounted by the possibility that restrictions would be imposed. Since I got exactly what I meant to buy, it perhaps can be said that society has affected no redistribution so far as I am concerned, any more than it does when it refuses to refund the price of my losing sweepstakes ticket.

In sum, then, it would appear that losses inflicted by "nuisance prevention" may raise serious questions of compensation, while losses fixed by "public benefit" measures may not even involve any redistribution. If that is so, then surely we ought to be wary of any compensation rule which treats as determinative the distinction between the two types of measures. Such a rule has over generalized from relevant considerations which are somewhat characteristic of, but not logically or practically inseparable from, measures in one or the other class. If the relevant considerations can be kept in view without the oversimplified rule, then the oversimplified rule is merely a menace to just decision and should be dismissed.

Clarity of analysis is, at any rate, greatly improved by treating these considerations as logically antecedent to compensability issues. If efficiency-motivated social action has a painfully uneven distributional side-effect, the issue of compensability must be faced and resolved. But social action which merely corrects prior, unilaterally determined redistributions, or brings a deliberate gamble to its denouement, raises no question of compensability. The true office of the harm-prevention/benefit-extraction dichotomy is, then, to help us decide whether a potential occasion of compensation exists at all. If one does, the compensability discussion must proceed from that point.

Michelman's use of the phrase "distinctly perceived, sharply crystallized, investment-backed expectations" to describe the situations in which compensation should be paid became a central organizing feature of Justice Brennan's opinion in the Grand Central Terminal litigation, the most widely known Takings opinion of the Warren Court era.

[2] The Grand Central Terminal Litigation

[a] Introduction

Penn Central Transportation Company v. City of New York, was widely viewed as a crucial Constitutional test for the historic preservation movement. The Warren Court had begun to disappear, with Justices Burger, Rehnquist and Stevens replacing more liberal jurists. Preservationists were worried. Creation of historic districts had been subjected to judicial scrutiny prior to *Penn Central*.[29] But designation of individual buildings, rather than districts, as historic had never been thoroughly tested. Preserving single buildings did not create the same "chic" ambience, and resulting economic returns, so prevalent in neighborhoods like New Orleans' French Quarter, San Francisco's Russian Hill, Washington, D.C.'s Georgetown, or New York City's Greenwich Village. The building involved in the dispute—Grand Central Terminal—was extremely well known and the amounts of development money at stake were enormous.

---

[29] The best known case was probably Maher v. City of New Orleans, 516 F.2d 1051 (5th Cir. 1975), which involved the Vieux Carre Historic District, more commonly known as the French Quarter.

The Supreme Court's opinion contains a reasonably complete history of the case. What it does not portray is the nature of the aesthetic and planning choices Penn Central's building proposals presented to New York City. In order to fill that gap, here are a few pictures of Grand Central in various settings. First, as noted in the *Penn Central* opinion, Grand Central Terminal was built with support columns for an office building over the terminal's main concourse. Here is an architect's rendering of how that building was to look:

THE ORIGINAL ARCHITECTS PLAN [30]

The building Penn Central proposed to build over the terminal was much larger than that planned by the original architects. The 2.4 million square foot Pan Am Building (now the Met Life Building), constructed just north of the terminal's main concourse and completed in 1963, was then the largest commercial building in the world. [31] Penn Central's plan dwarfed even the Pan Am structure in size. Some sense of the proposed building's scale is evident in the renderings of the Breuer I and Breuer II plans mentioned in the Court's opinion. [32]

---

[30] W.D. Middleton, *Grand Central: The World's Greatest Railway Terminal* 136 (1977). Photographs obtained from The Architectural Forum, Marcel Breuer & Associates and the Library of Congress reprinted by permission of William D. Middleton.

[31] *Id.* at 105.

[32] *Id.* at 134-135.

Breuer I   Breuer II

Grand Central Terminal is a vast structure. It encompasses not only the above grade building that was the subject of *Penn Central*, but also an enormous maze of underground facilities and tracks. The station has two levels of tracks and track platforms, stretching from Lexington Avenue, on the east, almost to Madison Avenue, two city blocks to the west, and from 43rd Street, on the south, to 50th Street on the north. In addition, subway platforms run under the southern end of the terminal building at 42nd Street. To the north of Grand Central Terminal is the Pan Am Building which has direct connections to the terminal circulation system, as well as about 15 square blocks of office buildings along Madison Avenue constructed on air rights over the double level of tracks and track platforms. Some of the air rights buildings located near the terminal are still owned by Penn Central or its subsidiaries, but most of the structures to the north of the terminal are now owned by other companies.

[b]   Opinions of the United States Supreme Court in *Penn Central Transportation Company v. City of New York*

Penn Central Transportation Company v. City of New York

United States Supreme Court
438 U.S. 104, 98 S. Ct. 2646, 57 L. Ed. 2d 631 (1978)

Mr. Justice Brennan delivered the opinion of the Court.

The question presented is whether a city may, as part of a comprehensive program to preserve historic landmarks and historic districts, place restrictions on the development of individual historic landmarks—in addition to those imposed by applicable zoning ordinances—without effecting a "taking" requiring the payment of "just compensation." Specifically, we must decide whether the application of New York City's Landmarks Preservation Law to the parcel of land occupied by Grand Central Terminal has "taken" its owners' property in violation of the Fifth and Fourteenth Amendments.

I

A

Over the past 50 years, all 50 States and over 500 municipalities have enacted laws to encourage or require the preservation of buildings and areas with historic or aesthetic importance.[1] These nationwide legislative efforts have been precipitated by two concerns. The first is recognition that, in recent years, large numbers of historic structures, landmarks, and areas have been destroyed[2] without adequate consideration of either the values represented therein or the possibility of preserving the destroyed properties for use in economically productive ways. The second is a widely shared belief that structures with special historic, cultural, or architectural significance enhance the quality of life for all. Not only do these buildings and their workmanship represent the lessons of the past and embody precious features of our heritage, they serve as examples of quality for today. "[H]istoric conservation is but one aspect of the much larger problem, basically an environmental one, of enhancing—or perhaps developing for the first time—the quality of life for people."[4]

---

[1] *See* National Trust for Historic Preservation, *A Guide to State Historic Preservation Programs* (1976); National Trust for Historic Preservation, *Directory of Landmark and Historic District Commissions* (1976). In addition to these state and municipal legislative efforts, Congress has determined that "the historical and cultural foundations of the Nation should be preserved as a living part of our community life and development in order to give a sense of orientation to the American people," National Historic Preservation Act of 1966, 80 Stat. 915, 16 U.S.C. § 470(b) (1976 ed.), and has enacted a series of measures designed to encourage preservation of sites and structures of historic, architectural, or cultural significance. *See* generally Gray, *The Response of Federal Legislation to Historic Preservation*, 36 Law & Contemp. Prob. 314 (1971).

[2] Over one-half of the buildings listed in the Historic American Buildings Survey, begun by the Federal Government in 1933, have been destroyed. *See* Costonis, *The Chicago Plan: Incentive Zoning and the Preservation of Urban Landmarks*, 85 Harv. L. Rev. 574, 574 n. 1 (1972), citing Huxtable, "Bank's Building Plan Sets Off Debate on 'Progress,' " *N.Y. Times*, Jan. 17, 1971, section 8, p. 1, col. 2.

[4] Gilbert, *Introduction, Precedents for the Future*, 36 Law & Contemp. Prob. 311, 312 (1971), quoting address by Robert Stipe, 1971 Conference on Preservation Law, Washington, D.C., May 1, 1971 (unpublished text, pp. 6-7).

New York City, responding to similar concerns and acting pursuant to a New York State enabling Act,[5] adopted its Landmarks Preservation Law in 1965. *See* N.Y.C. Admin. Code, ch. 8-A, § 205-1.0 *et seq.* (1976). The City acted from the conviction that "the standing of [New York City] as a world-wide tourist center and world capital of business, culture and government" would be threatened if legislation were not enacted to protect historic landmarks and neighborhoods from precipitate decisions to destroy or fundamentally alter their character. § 205-1.0(a). The city believed that comprehensive measures to safeguard desirable features of the existing urban fabric would benefit its citizens in a variety of ways: *e.g.*, fostering "civic pride in the beauty and noble accomplishments of the past"; protecting and enhancing "the city's attractions to tourists and visitors"; "support[ing] and stimul[ating] business and industry"; "strengthen[ing] the economy of the city"; and promoting "the use of historic districts, landmarks, interior landmarks and scenic landmarks for the education, pleasure and welfare of the people of the city." § 205-1.0(b).

The New York City law is typical of many urban landmark laws in that its primary method of achieving its goals is not by acquisitions of historic properties,[6] but rather by involving public entities in land-use decisions affecting these properties and providing services, standards, controls, and incentives that will encourage preservation by private owners and users. While the law does place special restrictions on landmark properties as a necessary feature to the attainment of its larger objectives, the major theme of the law is to ensure the owners of any such properties both a "reasonable return" on their investments and maximum latitude to use their parcels for purposes not inconsistent with the preservation goals.

The operation of the law can be briefly summarized. The primary responsibility for administering the law is vested in the Landmarks Preservation Commission (Commission), a broad based, 11-member agency[8] assisted by a technical staff. The Commission first performs the function, critical to any landmark preservation effort, of identifying properties and areas that have "a special character or special historical or aesthetic interest or value as part of the development, heritage or cultural characteristics of the city, state or nation." § 207-1.0(n); *see* § 207-1.0(h). If the Commission determines, after giving all interested parties an opportunity to be heard, that a building or area satisfies the ordinance's criteria, it will designate a building to be a "landmark," § 207-1.0(n),[9] situated on a particular "landmark site," § 207-1.0(o),[10] or will designate an area

---

[5] *See* N.Y.Gen.Mun.Law § 96-a (McKinney 1977). It declares that it is the public policy of the State of New York to preserve structures and areas with special historical or aesthetic interest or value and authorizes local governments to impose reasonable restrictions to perpetuate such structures and areas.

[6] The consensus is that widespread public ownership of historic properties in urban settings is neither feasible nor wise. Public ownership reduces the tax base, burdens the public budget with costs of acquisitions and maintenance, and results in the preservation of public buildings as museums and similar facilities, rather than as economically productive features of the urban scene. *See* Wilson & Winkler, *The Response of State Legislation to Historic Preservation*, 36 Law & Contemp. Prob. 329, 330-331, 339-340 (1971).

[8] The ordinance creating the Commission requires that it include at least three architects, one historian qualified in the field, one city planner or landscape architect, one realtor, and at least one resident of each of the city's five boroughs. N.Y.C. Charter § 534 (1976). In addition to the ordinance's requirements concerning the composition of the Commission, there is, according to a former chairman, a "prudent tradition" that the Commission include one or two lawyers, preferably with experience in municipal government, and several laymen with no specialized qualifications other than concern for the good of the city. Goldstone, *Aesthetics in Historic Districts*, 36 Law & Contemp. Prob. 379, 384-385 (1971).

[9] "'Landmark.' Any improvement, any part of which is thirty years old or older, which has a special character or special historical or aesthetic interest or value as part of the development, heritage or cultural characteristics of

to be a "historic district," § 207-1.0(h).[11] After the Commission makes a designation, New York City's Board of Estimate, after considering the relationship of the designated property "to the master plan, the zoning resolution, projected public improvements and any plans for the renewal of the area involved," § 207-2.0(g)(1), may modify or disapprove the designation, and the owner may seek judicial review of the final designation decision. Thus far, 31 historic districts and over 400 individual landmarks have been finally designated,[12] and the process is a continuing one.

Final designation as a landmark results in restrictions upon the property owner's options concerning use of the landmark site. First, the law imposes a duty upon the owner to keep the exterior features of the building "in good repair" to assure that the law's objectives not be defeated by the landmark's falling into a state of irremediable disrepair. *See* § 207-10.0(a). Second, the Commission must approve in advance any proposal to alter the exterior architectural features of the landmark or to construct any exterior improvement on the landmark site, thus ensuring that decisions concerning construction on the landmark site are made with due consideration of both the public interest in the maintenance of the structure and the landowner's interest in use of the property. *See* §§ 207-4.0 to 207-9.0.

In the event an owner wishes to alter a landmark site, three separate procedures are available through which administrative approval may be obtained. First, the owner may apply to the Commission for a "certificate of no effect on protected architectural features": that is, for an order approving the improvement or alteration on the ground that it will not change or affect any architectural feature of the landmark and will be in harmony therewith. *See* § 207-5.0. Denial of the certificate is subject to judicial review.

Second, the owner may apply to the Commission for a certificate of "appropriateness." *See* § 207-6.0. Such certificates will be granted if the Commission concludes—focusing upon aesthetic, historical, and architectural values—that the proposed construction on the landmark site would not unduly hinder the protection, enhancement, perpetuation, and use of the landmark. Again, denial of the certificate is subject to judicial review. Moreover, the owner who is denied either a certificate of no exterior effect or a certificate of appropriateness may submit an alternative or modified plan for approval. The final procedure—seeking a certificate of appropriateness on the ground of "insufficient return," see § 207-8.0—provides special

---

the city, state or nation and which has been designated as a landmark pursuant to the provisions of this chapter." § 207-1.0(n).

[10] "'Landmark site.' An improvement parcel or part thereof on which is situated a landmark and any abutting improvement parcel or part thereof used as and constituting part of the premises on which the landmark is situated, and which has been designated as a landmark site pursuant to the provisions of this chapter." § 207-1.0(o).

[11] "'Historic district.' Any area which: (1) contains improvements which: (a) have a special character or special historical or aesthetic interest or value; and (b) represent one or more periods or styles of architecture typical of one or more eras in the history of the city; and (c) cause such area, by reason of such factors, to constitute a distinct section of the city; and (2) has been designated as a historic district pursuant to the provisions of this chapter." § 207-1.0(h). The Act also provides for the designation of a "scenic landmark," *see* § 207-1.0(w), and an "interior landmark." *See* § 207-1.0(m).

[12] *See* Landmarks Preservation Commission of the City of New York, *Landmarks and Historic Districts* (1977). Although appellants are correct in noting that some of the designated landmarks are publicly owned, the vast majority are, like Grand Central Terminal, privately owned structures.

mechanisms, which vary depending on whether or not the landmark enjoys a tax exemption,[13] to ensure that designation does not cause economic hardship.

Although the designation of a landmark and landmark site restricts the owner's control over the parcel, designation also enhances the economic position of the landmark owner in one significant respect. Under New York City's zoning laws, owners of real property who have not developed their property to the full extent permitted by the applicable zoning laws are allowed to transfer development rights to contiguous parcels on the same city block. *See* New York City, Zoning Resolution Art. I, ch. 2, § 12-10 (1978) (definition of "zoning lot"). A 1968 ordinance gave the owners of landmark sites additional opportunities to transfer development rights to other parcels. Subject to a restriction that the floor area of the transferee lot may not be increased by more than 20% above its authorized level, the ordinance permitted transfers from a landmark parcel to property across the street or across a street intersection. In 1969, the law governing the conditions under which transfers from landmark parcels could occur was liberalized, see New York City Zoning Resolutions 74-79 to 74-793, apparently to ensure that the Landmarks Law would not unduly restrict the development options of the owners of Grand Central Terminal. *See* Marcus, *Air Rights Transfers in New York City*, 36 Law & Contemp. Prob. 372, 375 (1971). The class of recipient lots was expanded to include lots "across a street and opposite to another lot or lots which except for the intervention of streets or street intersections f[or]m a series extending to the lot occupied by the landmark building[, provided that] all lots [are] in the same ownership." New York City Zoning Resolution 74-79 (emphasis deleted).[14] In addition, the 1969

---

[13] If the owner of a non-tax-exempt parcel has been denied certificates of appropriateness for a proposed alteration and shows that he is not earning a reasonable return on the property in its present state, the Commission and other city agencies must assume the burden of developing a plan that will enable the landmark owner to earn a reasonable return on the landmark site. The plan may include, but need not be limited to, partial or complete tax exemption, remission of taxes, and authorizations for alterations, construction, or reconstruction appropriate for and not inconsistent with the purposes of the law. § 207 8.0(c). The owner is free to accept or reject a plan devised by the Commission and approved by the other city agencies. If he accepts the plan, he proceeds to operate the property pursuant to the plan. If he rejects the plan, the Commission may recommend that the city proceed by eminent domain to acquire a protective interest in the landmark, but if the city does not do so within a specified time period, the Commission must issue a notice allowing the property owner to proceed with the alteration or improvement as originally proposed in his application for a certificate of appropriateness.

Tax-exempt structures are treated somewhat differently. They become eligible for special treatment only if four preconditions are satisfied: (1) the owner previously entered into an agreement to sell the parcel that was contingent upon the issuance of a certificate of approval; (2) the property, as it exists at the time of the request, is not capable of earning a reasonable return; (3) the structure is no longer suitable to its past or present purposes; and (4) the prospective buyer intends to alter the landmark structure. In the event the owner demonstrates that the property in its present state is not earning a reasonable return, the Commission must either find another buyer for it or allow the sale and construction to proceed.

But this is not the only remedy available for owners of tax-exempt landmarks. As the case at bar illustrates, see *infra*, . . . , if an owner files suit and establishes that he is incapable of earning a "reasonable return" on the site in its present state, he can be afforded judicial relief. Similarly, where a landmark owner who enjoys a tax exemption has demonstrated that the landmark structure, as restricted, is totally inadequate for the owner's "legitimate needs," the law has been held invalid as applied to that parcel. *See Lutheran Church v. City of New York*, 35 N.Y.2d 121, 359 N.Y.S.2d 7, 316 N.E.2d 305 (1974).

[14] To obtain approval for a proposed transfer, the landmark owner must follow the following procedure. First, he must obtain the permission of the Commission which will examine the plans for the development of the transferee lot to determine whether the planned construction would be compatible with the landmark. Second, he must obtain the approbation of New York City's Planning Commission which will focus on the effects of the transfer on occupants of the buildings in the vicinity of the transferee lot and whether the landmark owner will preserve the landmark. Finally, the matter goes to the Board of Estimate, which has final authority to grant or deny the application. *See also* Costonis, *supra* n.2, at 585-586 (1972).

amendment permits, in highly commercialized areas like midtown Manhattan, the transfer of all unused development rights to a single parcel. *Ibid.*

B

This case involves the application of New York City's Landmarks Preservation Law to Grand Central Terminal (Terminal). The Terminal, which is owned by the Penn Central Transportation Co. and its affiliates (Penn Central), is one of New York City's most famous buildings. Opened in 1913, it is regarded not only as providing an ingenious engineering solution to the problems presented by urban railroad stations, but also as a magnificent example of the French beaux-arts style.

The Terminal is located in midtown Manhattan. Its south façade faces 42d Street and that street's intersection with Park Avenue. At street level, the Terminal is bounded on the west by Vanderbilt Avenue, on the east by the Commodore Hotel, and on the north by the Pan-American Building. Although a 20-story office tower, to have been located above the Terminal, was part of the original design, the planned tower was never constructed.[15] The Terminal itself is an eight-story structure which Penn Central uses as a railroad station and in which it rents space not needed for railroad purposes to a variety of commercial interests. The Terminal is one of a number of properties owned by appellant Penn Central in this area of midtown Manhattan. The others include the Barclay, Biltmore, Commodore, Roosevelt, and Waldorf-Astoria Hotels, the Pan-American Building and other office buildings along Park Avenue, and the Yale Club. At least eight of these are eligible to be recipients of development rights afforded the Terminal by virtue of landmark designation.

On August 2, 1967, following a public hearing, the Commission designated the Terminal a "landmark" and designated the "city tax block" it occupies a "landmark site."[16] The Board of Estimate confirmed this action on September 21, 1967. Although appellant Penn Central had opposed the designation before the Commission, it did not seek judicial review of the final designation decision.

On January 22, 1968, appellant Penn Central, to increase its income, entered into a renewable 50-year lease and sublease agreement with appellant UGP Properties, Inc. (UGP), a wholly owned subsidiary of Union General Properties, Ltd., a United Kingdom corporation. Under the terms of the agreement, UGP was to construct a multistory office building above the Terminal. UGP promised to pay Penn Central $1 million annually during construction and at least $3 million annually thereafter. The rentals would be offset in part by a loss of some $700,000 to $1 million in net rentals presently received from concessionaires displaced by the new building.

Appellants UGP and Penn Central then applied to the Commission for permission to construct an office building atop the Terminal. Two separate plans, both designed by architect Marcel Breuer and both apparently satisfying the terms of the applicable zoning ordinance, were submitted to the Commission for approval. The first, Breuer I, provided for the construction of

---

[15] The Terminal's present foundation includes columns, which were built into it for the express purpose of supporting the proposed 20-story tower.

[16] The Commission's report stated:

Grand Central Station, one of the great buildings of America, evokes a spirit that is unique in this City. It combines distinguished architecture with a brilliant engineering solution, wedded to one of the most fabulous railroad terminals of our time. Monumental in scale, this great building functions as well today as it did when built. In style, it represents the best of the French Beaux Arts. Record 2240.

a 55-story office building, to be cantilevered above the existing façade and to rest on the roof of the Terminal. The second, Breuer II Revised,[17] called for tearing down a portion of the Terminal that included the 42d Street façade, stripping off some of the remaining features of the Terminal's façade, and constructing a 53-story office building. The Commission denied a certificate of no exterior effect on September 20, 1968. Appellants then applied for a certificate of "appropriateness" as to both proposals. After four days of hearings at which over 80 witnesses testified, the Commission denied this application as to both proposals.

The Commission's reasons for rejecting certificates respecting Breuer II Revised are summarized in the following statement: "To protect a Landmark, one does not tear it down. To perpetuate its architectural features, one does not strip them off." Record 2255. Breuer I, which would have preserved the existing vertical facades of the present structure, received more sympathetic consideration. The Commission first focused on the effect that the proposed tower would have on one desirable feature created by the present structure and its surroundings: the dramatic view of the Terminal from Park Avenue South. Although appellants had contended that the Pan-American Building had already destroyed the silhouette of the south façade and that one additional tower could do no further damage and might even provide a better background for the façade, the Commission disagreed, stating that it found the majestic approach from the south to be still unique in the city and that a 55-story tower atop the Terminal would be far more detrimental to its south façade than the Pan-American Building 375 feet away. Moreover, the Commission found that from closer vantage points the Pan Am Building and the other towers were largely cut off from view, which would not be the case of the mass on top of the Terminal planned under Breuer I. In conclusion, the Commission stated:

> [We have] no fixed rule against making additions to designated buildings—it all depends on how they are done. . . . But to balance a 55-story office tower above a flamboyant Beaux-Arts façade seems nothing more than an aesthetic joke. Quite simply, the tower would overwhelm the Terminal by its sheer mass. The "addition" would be four times as high as the existing structure and would reduce the Landmark itself to the status of a curiosity.

> Landmarks cannot be divorced from their settings—particularly when the setting is a dramatic and integral part of the original concept. The Terminal, in its setting, is a great example of urban design. Such examples are not so plentiful in New York City that we can afford to lose any of the few we have. And we must preserve them in a meaningful way—with alterations and additions of such character, scale, materials and mass as will protect, enhance and perpetuate the original design rather than overwhelm it.

Id., at 2251.[18]

Appellants did not seek judicial review of the denial of either certificate. Because the Terminal site enjoyed a tax exemption, remained suitable for its present and future uses, and was not the

---

[17] Appellants also submitted a plan, denominated Breuer II, to the Commission. However, because appellants learned that Breuer II would have violated existing easements, they substituted Breuer II Revised for Breuer II, and the Commission evaluated the appropriateness only of Breuer II Revised.

[18] In discussing Breuer I, the Commission also referred to a number of instances in which it had approved additions to landmarks: "The office and reception wing added to Gracie Mansion and the school and church house added to the 12th Street side of the First Presbyterian Church are examples that harmonize in scale, material and character with the structures they adjoin. The new Watch Tower Bible and Tract Society building on Brooklyn Heights, though completely modern in idiom, respects the qualities of its surroundings and will enhance the Brooklyn Heights Historic District, as Butterfield House enhances West 12th Street, and Breuer's own Whitney Museum its Madison Avenue locale." Record 2251.

subject of a contract of sale, there were no further administrative remedies available to appellants as to the Breuer I and Breuer II Revised plans. *See* n. 13, *supra*. Further, appellants did not avail themselves of the opportunity to develop and submit other plans for the Commission's consideration and approval. Instead, appellants filed suit in New York Supreme Court, Trial Term, claiming, *inter alia*, that the application of the Landmarks Preservation Law had "taken" their property without just compensation in violation of the Fifth and Fourteenth Amendments and arbitrarily deprived them of their property without due process of law in violation of the Fourteenth Amendment. Appellants sought a declaratory judgment, injunctive relief barring the city from using the Landmarks Law to impede the construction of any structure that might otherwise lawfully be constructed on the Terminal site, and damages for the "temporary taking" that occurred between August 2, 1967, the designation date, and the date when the restrictions arising from the Landmarks Law would be lifted. The trial court granted the injunctive and declaratory relief, but severed the question of damages for a "temporary taking."[20]

Appellees appealed, and the New York Supreme Court, Appellate Division, reversed. 50 A.D.2d 265, 377 N.Y.S.2d 20 (1975). . . . The New York Court of Appeals affirmed. 42 N.Y.2d 324, 366 N.E.2d 1271 (1977). That court summarily rejected any claim that the Landmarks Law had "taken" property without "just compensation," indicating that there could be no "taking" since the law had not transferred control of the property to the city, but only restricted appellants' exploitation of it. In that circumstance, the Court of Appeals held that appellants' attack on the law could prevail only if the law deprived appellants of their property in violation of the Due Process Clause of the Fourteenth Amendment. Whether or not there was a denial of substantive due process turned on whether the restrictions deprived Penn Central of a "reasonable return" on the "privately created and privately managed ingredient" of the Terminal.[23] The Court of Appeals concluded that the Landmarks Law had not effected a denial of due process because: (1) the landmark regulation permitted the same use as had been made of the Terminal for more than half a century; (2) the appellants had failed to show that they could not earn a reasonable return on their investment in the Terminal itself; (3) even if the Terminal proper could never operate at a reasonable profit some of the income from Penn Central's extensive real estate holdings in the area, which include hotels and office buildings, must realistically be imputed to the Terminal; and (4) the development rights above the Terminal, which had been made transferable to numerous sites in the vicinity of the Terminal, one or two of which were suitable for the construction of office buildings, were valuable to appellants and provided "significant, perhaps 'fair,' compensation for the loss of rights above the terminal itself."

---

[20] Although that court suggested that any regulation of private property to protect landmark values was unconstitutional if "just compensation" were not afforded, it also appeared to rely upon its findings: first, that the cost to Penn Central of operating the Terminal building itself, exclusive of purely railroad operations, exceeded the revenues received from concessionaires and tenants in the Terminal; and second, that the special transferable development rights afforded Penn Central as an owner of a landmark site did not "provide compensation to plaintiffs or minimize the harm suffered by plaintiffs due to the designation of the Terminal as a landmark."

[23] The Court of Appeals suggested that in calculating the value of the property upon which appellants were entitled to earn a reasonable return, the "publicly created" components of the value of the property—*i.e.*, those elements of its value attributable to the "efforts of organized society" or to the "social complex" in which the Terminal is located—had to be excluded. However, since the record upon which the Court of Appeals decided the case did not, as that court recognized, contain a basis for segregating the privately created from the publicly created elements of the value of the Terminal site and since the judgment of the Court of Appeals in any event rests upon bases that support our affirmance *see infra*, we have no occasion to address the question whether it is permissible or feasible to separate out the "social increments" of the value of property. *See* Costonis, *The Disparity Issue: A Context for the Grand Central Terminal Decision*, 91 Harv. L. Rev. 402, 416-417 (1977).

. . . .

We noted probable jurisdiction. We affirm.

II

The issues presented by appellants are (1) whether the restrictions imposed by New York City's law upon appellants' exploitation of the Terminal site effect a "taking" of appellants' property for a public use within the meaning of the Fifth Amendment, which of course is made applicable to the States through the Fourteenth Amendment, and, (2), if so, whether the transferable development rights afforded appellants constitute "just compensation" within the meaning of the Fifth Amendment. We need only address the question whether a "taking" has occurred.[25]

A

Before considering appellants' specific contentions, it will be useful to review the factors that have shaped the jurisprudence of the Fifth Amendment injunction "nor shall private property be taken for public use, without just compensation." The question of what constitutes a "taking" for purposes of the Fifth Amendment has proved to be a problem of considerable difficulty. While this Court has recognized that the Fifth Amendment's guarantee . . . [is] designed to bar Government from forcing some people alone to bear public burdens which, in all fairness and justice, should be borne by the public as a whole, this Court, quite simply, has been unable to develop any "set formula" for determining when "justice and fairness" require that economic injuries caused by public action be compensated by the government, rather than remain disproportionately concentrated on a few persons. *See Goldblatt v. Hempstead*, 369 U.S. 590, 594 (1962). Indeed, we have frequently observed that whether a particular restriction will be rendered invalid by the government's failure to pay for any losses proximately caused by it depends largely "upon the particular circumstances [in that] case." *United States v. Central Eureka Mining Co.*, 357 U.S. 155, 168 (1958); *see United States v. Caltex, Inc.*, 344 U.S. 149 (1952).

In engaging in these essentially ad hoc, factual inquiries, the Court's decisions have identified several factors that have particular significance. The economic impact of the regulation on the claimant and, particularly, the extent to which the regulation has interfered with distinct investment-backed expectations are, of course, relevant considerations. *See Goldblatt v. Hempstead, supra*, 369 U.S., at 594. So, too, is the character of the governmental action. A "taking" may more readily be found when the interference with property can be characterized as a physical invasion by government, *see, e.g., United States v. Causby*, 328 U.S. 256 (1946), than when interference arises from some public program adjusting the benefits and burdens of economic life to promote the common good.

"Government hardly could go on if to some extent values incident to property could not be diminished without paying for every such change in the general law," *Pennsylvania Coal Co. v. Mahon*, 260 U.S. 393 (1922), and this Court has accordingly recognized, in a wide variety of contexts, that government may execute laws or programs that adversely affect recognized economic values. Exercises of the taxing power are one obvious example. A second are the decisions in which this Court has dismissed "taking" challenges on the ground that, while the challenged government action caused economic harm, it did not interfere with interests that were

---

[25] As is implicit in our opinion, we do not embrace the proposition that a "taking" can never occur unless government has transferred physical control over a portion of a parcel.

sufficiently bound up with the reasonable expectations of the claimant to constitute "property" for Fifth Amendment purposes. *See, e.g., United States v. Willow River Power Co.*, 324 U.S. 499 (1945) (interest in high-water level of river for runoff for tailwaters to maintain power head is not property); *United States v. Chandler-Dunbar Water Power Co.*, 229 U.S. 53 (1913) (no property interest can exist in navigable waters); Sax, *Takings and the Police Power*, 74 Yale L.J. 36, 61-62 (1964).

More importantly for the present case, in instances in which a state tribunal reasonably concluded that "the health, safety, morals, or general welfare" would be promoted by prohibiting particular contemplated uses of land, this Court has upheld land-use regulations that destroyed or adversely affected recognized real property interests. *See Nectow v. Cambridge*, 277 U.S. 183, 188 (1928). Zoning laws are, of course, the classic example, *see Euclid v. Ambler Realty Co.*, 272 U.S. 365 (1926) (prohibition of industrial use); *Gorieb v. Fox*, 274 U.S. 603 (1927) (requirement that portions of parcels be left unbuilt); *Welch v. Swasey*, 214 U.S. 91 (1909) (height restriction), which have been viewed as permissible governmental action even when prohibiting the most beneficial use of the property.

Zoning laws generally do not affect existing uses of real property, but "taking" challenges have also been held to be without merit in a wide variety of situations when the challenged governmental actions prohibited a beneficial use to which individual parcels had previously been devoted and thus caused substantial individualized harm. *Miller v. Schoene*, 276 U.S. 272 (1928), is illustrative. In that case, a state entomologist, acting pursuant to a state statute, ordered the claimants to cut down a large number of ornamental red cedar trees because they produced cedar rust fatal to apple trees cultivated nearby. Although the statute provided for recovery of any expense incurred in removing the cedars, and permitted claimants to use the felled trees, it did not provide compensation for the value of the standing trees or for the resulting decrease in market value of the properties as a whole. A unanimous Court held that this latter omission did not render the statute invalid. The Court held that the State might properly make "a choice between the preservation of one class of property and that of the other" and since the apple industry was important in the State involved, concluded that the State had not exceeded "its constitutional powers by deciding upon the destruction of one class of property [without compensation] in order to save another which, in the judgment of the legislature, is of greater value to the public."

Again, *Hadacheck v. Sebastian*, 239 U.S. 394 (1915), upheld a law prohibiting the claimant from continuing his otherwise lawful business of operating a brickyard in a particular physical community on the ground that the legislature had reasonably concluded that the presence of the brickyard was inconsistent with neighboring uses. . . .

Goldblatt v. Hempstead, supra, is a recent example. There, a 1958 city safety ordinance banned any excavations below the water table and effectively prohibited the claimant from continuing a sand and gravel mining business that had been operated on the particular parcel since 1927. The Court upheld the ordinance against a "taking" challenge, although the ordinance prohibited the present and presumably most beneficial use of the property and had, like the regulations in *Miller* and *Hadacheck*, severely affected a particular owner. The Court assumed that the ordinance did not prevent the owner's reasonable use of the property since the owner made no showing of an adverse effect on the value of the land. Because the restriction served a substantial public purpose, the Court thus held no taking had occurred. It is, of course, implicit in *Goldblatt* that a use restriction on real property may constitute a "taking" if not reasonably necessary to the effectuation of a substantial public purpose, *see Nectow v. Cambridge, supra;* or perhaps if it has an unduly harsh impact upon the owner's use of the property.

Pennsylvania Coal Co. v. Mahon, 260 U.S. 393 (1922), is the leading case for the proposition that a state statute that substantially furthers important public policies may so frustrate distinct investment-backed expectations as to amount to a "taking." There the claimant had sold the surface rights to particular parcels of property, but expressly reserved the right to remove the coal thereunder. A Pennsylvania statute, enacted after the transactions, forbade any mining of coal that caused the subsidence of any house, unless the house was the property of the owner of the underlying coal and was more than 150 feet from the improved property of another. Because the statute made it commercially impracticable to mine the coal, and thus had nearly the same effect as the complete destruction of rights claimant had reserved from the owners of the surface land, the Court held that the statute was invalid as effecting a "taking" without just compensation. *See* generally Michelman, *Property, Utility, and Fairness: Comments on the Ethical Foundations of "Just Compensation" Law*, 80 Harv. L. Rev. 1165, 1229-1234 (1967).

Finally, government actions that may be characterized as acquisitions of resources to permit or facilitate uniquely public functions have often been held to constitute "takings." *United States v. Causby*, 328 U.S. 256 (1946), is illustrative. In holding that direct overflights above the claimant's land, that destroyed the present use of the land as a chicken farm, constituted a "taking," *Causby* emphasized that Government had not "merely destroyed property [but was] using a part of it for the flight of its planes." *See also Griggs v. Allegheny County*, 369 U.S. 84 (1962) (overflights held a taking); *Portsmouth Co. v. United States*, 260 U.S. 327 (1922) (United States military installations' repeated firing of guns over claimant's land is a taking); *United States v. Cress*, 243 U.S. 316 (1917) (repeated floodings of land caused by water project is taking); but *see YMCA v. United States*, 395 U.S. 85 (1969) (damage caused to building when federal officers who were seeking to protect building were attacked by rioters held not a taking). *See* generally Michelman, *supra*, at 1226-1229; Sax, *Takings and the Police Power*, 74 Yale L.J. 36 (1964).

B

In contending that the New York City law has "taken" their property in violation of the Fifth and Fourteenth Amendments, appellants make a series of arguments, which, while tailored to the facts of this case, essentially urge that any substantial restriction imposed pursuant to a landmark law must be accompanied by just compensation if it is to be constitutional. Before considering these, we emphasize what is not in dispute. Because this Court has recognized, in a number of settings, that States and cities may enact land-use restrictions or controls to enhance the quality of life by preserving the character and desirable aesthetic features of a city, *see New Orleans v. Dukes*, 427 U.S. 297 (1976); *Young v. American Mini Theatres, Inc.*, 427 U.S. 50 (1976); *Village of Belle Terre v. Boraas*, 416 U.S. 1 (1974); *Berman v. Parker*, 348 U.S. 26 (1954); *Welch v. Swasey*, 214 U.S., at 108, appellants do not contest that New York City's objective of preserving structures and areas with special historic, architectural, or cultural significance is an entirely permissible governmental goal. They also do not dispute that the restrictions imposed on its parcel are appropriate means of securing the purposes of the New York City law. Finally, appellants do not challenge any of the specific factual premises of the decision below. They accept for present purposes both that the parcel of land occupied by Grand Central Terminal must, in its present state, be regarded as capable of earning a reasonable return,[26]

---

[26] Both the Jurisdictional Statement 7-8, n. 7, and Brief for Appellants 8 n. 7 state that appellants are not seeking review of the New York courts' determination that Penn Central could earn a "reasonable return" on its investment

and that the transferable development rights afforded appellants by virtue of the Terminal's designation as a landmark are valuable, even if not as valuable as the rights to construct above the Terminal. In appellants' view none of these factors derogate from their claim that New York City's law has effected a "taking."

They first observe that the airspace above the Terminal is a valuable property interest, citing *United States v. Causby, supra.* They urge that the Landmarks Law has deprived them of any gainful use of their "air rights" above the Terminal and that, irrespective of the value of the remainder of their parcel, the city has "taken" their right to this superadjacent airspace, thus entitling them to "just compensation" measured by the fair market value of these air rights.

Apart from our own disagreement with appellants' characterization of the effect of the New York City law, the submission that appellants may establish a "taking" simply by showing that they have been denied the ability to exploit a property interest that they heretofore had believed was available for development is quite simply untenable. Were this the rule, this Court would have erred not only in upholding laws restricting the development of air rights, *see Welch v. Swasey, supra,* but also in approving those prohibiting both the subjacent, *see Goldblatt v. Hempstead,* 369 U.S. 590 (1962), and the lateral, *see Gorieb v. Fox,* 274 U.S. 603 (1927), development of particular parcels.[27] "Taking" jurisprudence does not divide a single parcel into discrete segments and attempt to determine whether rights in a particular segment have been entirely abrogated. In deciding whether a particular governmental action has effected a taking, this Court focuses rather both on the character of the action and on the nature and extent of the interference with rights in the parcel as a whole—here, the city tax block designated as the "landmark site."

Secondly, appellants, focusing on the character and impact of the New York City law, argue that it effects a "taking" because its operation has significantly diminished the value of the Terminal site. Appellants concede that the decisions sustaining other land-use regulations, which, like the New York City law, are reasonably related to the promotion of the general welfare, uniformly reject the proposition that diminution in property value, standing alone, can establish a "taking," *see Euclid v. Ambler Realty Co.,* 272 U.S. 365 (1926) (75% diminution in value caused by zoning law); *Hadacheck v. Sebastian,* 239 U.S. 394 (1915) (87 1/2% diminution in value), and that the "taking" issue in these contexts is resolved by focusing on the uses the regulations permit. *See also Goldblatt v. Hempstead, supra.* Appellants, moreover, also do not dispute that a showing of diminution in property value would not establish a taking if the restriction had been imposed as a result of historic-district legislation, *see* generally *Maher v. New Orleans,* 516 F.2d 1051 (CA5 1975), but appellants argue that New York City's regulation of individual landmarks is fundamentally different from zoning or from historic-district legislation because the controls imposed by New York City's law apply only to individuals who own selected properties.

---

in the Terminal. Although appellants suggest in their reply brief that the factual conclusions of the New York courts cannot be sustained unless we accept the rationale of the New York Court of Appeals, *see* Reply Brief for Appellants 12 n. 15, it is apparent that the findings concerning Penn Central's ability to profit from the Terminal depend in no way on the Court of Appeals' rationale.

[27] These cases dispose of any contention that might be based on *Pennsylvania Coal Co. v. Mahon,* 260 U.S. 393, 43 S.Ct. 158, 67 L.Ed. 322 (1922), that full use of air rights is so bound up with the investment-backed expectations of appellants that governmental deprivation of these rights invariably—*i.e.,* irrespective of the impact of the restriction on the value of the parcel as a whole—constitutes a "taking." Similarly, *Welch, Goldblatt,* and *Gorieb* illustrate the fallacy of appellants' related contention that a "taking" must be found to have occurred whenever the land-use restriction may be characterized as imposing a "servitude" on the claimant's parcel.

Stated baldly, appellants' position appears to be that the only means of ensuring that selected owners are not singled out to endure financial hardship for no reason is to hold that any restriction imposed on individual landmarks pursuant to the New York City scheme is a "taking" requiring the payment of "just compensation." Agreement with this argument would, of course, invalidate not just New York City's law, but all comparable landmark legislation in the Nation. We find no merit in it.

It is true, as appellants emphasize, that both historic-district legislation and zoning laws regulate all properties within given physical communities whereas landmark laws apply only to selected parcels. But, contrary to appellants' suggestions, landmark laws are not like discriminatory, or "reverse spot," zoning: that is, a land-use decision which arbitrarily singles out a particular parcel for different, less favorable treatment than the neighboring ones. In contrast to discriminatory zoning, which is the antithesis of land-use control as part of some comprehensive plan, the New York City law embodies a comprehensive plan to preserve structures of historic or aesthetic interest wherever they might be found in the city, and as noted, over 400 landmarks and 31 historic districts have been designated pursuant to this plan.

Equally without merit is the related argument that the decision to designate a structure as a landmark "is inevitably arbitrary or at least subjective, because it is basically a matter of taste," Reply Brief for Appellants 22, thus unavoidably singling out individual landowners for disparate and unfair treatment. The argument has a particularly hollow ring in this case. For appellants not only did not seek judicial review of either the designation or of the denials of the certificates of appropriateness and of no exterior effect, but do not even now suggest that the Commission's decisions concerning the Terminal were in any sense arbitrary or unprincipled. But, in any event, a landmark owner has a right to judicial review of any Commission decision, and, quite simply, there is no basis whatsoever for a conclusion that courts will have any greater difficulty identifying arbitrary or discriminatory action in the context of landmark regulation than in the context of classic zoning or indeed in any other context.[29]

Next, appellants observe that New York City's law differs from zoning laws and historic-district ordinances in that the Landmarks Law does not impose identical or similar restrictions on all structures located in particular physical communities. It follows, they argue, that New York City's law is inherently incapable of producing the fair and equitable distribution of benefits and burdens of governmental action which is characteristic of zoning laws and historic-district legislation and which they maintain is a constitutional requirement if "just compensation" is not to be afforded. It is, of course, true that the Landmarks Law has a more severe impact on some landowners than on others, but that in itself does not mean that the law effects a "taking." Legislation designed to promote the general welfare commonly burdens some more than others. The owners of the brickyard in *Hadacheck*, of the cedar trees in *Miller v. Schoene*, and of the gravel and sand mine in *Goldblatt v. Hempstead*, were uniquely burdened by the legislation sustained in those cases.[30]

---

[29] When a property owner challenges the application of a zoning ordinance to his property, the judicial inquiry focuses upon whether the challenged restriction can reasonably be deemed to promote the objectives of the community land-use plan, and will include consideration of the treatment of similar parcels. See generally *Nectow v. Cambridge*, 277 U.S. 183 (1928). When a property owner challenges a landmark designation or restriction as arbitrary or discriminatory, a similar inquiry presumably will occur.

[30] Appellants attempt to distinguish these cases on the ground that, in each, government was prohibiting a "noxious" use of land and that in the present case, in contrast, appellants' proposed construction above the Terminal would be beneficial. We observe that the uses in issue in *Hadacheck, Miller,* and *Goldblatt* were perfectly lawful in themselves. They involved no "blameworthiness, . . . moral wrongdoing or conscious act of dangerous risktaking which induce[d

Similarly, zoning laws often affect some property owners more severely than others but have not been held to be invalid on that account. For example, the property owner in *Euclid* who wished to use its property for industrial purposes was affected far more severely by the ordinance than its neighbors who wished to use their land for residences.

In any event, appellants' repeated suggestions that they are solely burdened and unbenefited is factually inaccurate. This contention overlooks the fact that the New York City law applies to vast numbers of structures in the city in addition to the Terminal—all the structures contained in the 31 historic districts and over 400 individual landmarks, many of which are close to the Terminal.[31] Unless we are to reject the judgment of the New York City Council that the preservation of landmarks benefits all New York citizens and all structures, both economically and by improving the quality of life in the city as a whole—which we are unwilling to do—we cannot conclude that the owners of the Terminal have in no sense been benefited by the Landmarks Law. Doubtless appellants believe they are more burdened than benefited by the law, but that must have been true, too, of the property owners in *Miller, Hadacheck, Euclid,* and *Goldblatt.*

Appellants' final broad-based attack would have us treat the law as an instance, like that in *United States v. Causby,* in which government, acting in an enterprise capacity, has appropriated part of their property for some strictly governmental purpose. Apart from the fact that *Causby* was a case of invasion of airspace that destroyed the use of the farm beneath and this New York City law has in nowise impaired the present use of the Terminal, the Landmarks Law neither exploits appellants' parcel for city purposes nor facilitates nor arises from any entrepreneurial operations of the city. The situation is not remotely like that in *Causby* where the airspace above the property was in the flight pattern for military aircraft. The Landmarks Law's effect is simply to prohibit appellants or anyone else from occupying portions of the airspace above the Terminal, while permitting appellants to use the remainder of the parcel in a gainful fashion. This is no more an appropriation of property by government for its own uses than is a zoning law prohibiting, for "aesthetic" reasons, two or more adult theaters within a specified area, *see Young v. American Mini Theatres, Inc.,* 427 U.S. 50 (1976), or a safety regulation prohibiting excavations below a certain level. *See Goldblatt v. Hempstead.*

C

Rejection of appellants' broad arguments is not, however, the end of our inquiry, for all we thus far have established is that the New York City law is not rendered invalid by its failure to provide "just compensation" whenever a landmark owner is restricted in the exploitation of property interests, such as air rights, to a greater extent than provided for under applicable zoning laws. We now must consider whether the interference with appellants' property is of such a

---

society] to shift the cost to a pa[rt]icular individual." Sax, *Takings and the Police Power,* 74 Yale L.J. 36, 50 (1964). These cases are better understood as resting not on any supposed "noxious" quality of the prohibited uses but rather on the ground that the restrictions were reasonably related to the implementation of a policy—not unlike historic preservation—expected to produce a widespread public benefit and applicable to all similarly situated property.

Nor, correlatively, can it be asserted that the destruction or fundamental alteration of a historic landmark is not harmful. The suggestion that the beneficial quality of appellants' proposed construction is established by the fact that the construction would have been consistent with applicable zoning laws ignores the development in sensibilities and ideals reflected in landmark legislation like New York City's.

[31] There are some 53 designated landmarks and 5 historic districts or scenic landmarks in Manhattan between 14th and 59th Streets. *See* Landmarks Preservation Commission, *Landmarks and Historic Districts* (1977).

magnitude that "there must be an exercise of eminent domain and compensation to sustain [it]." *Pennsylvania Coal Co. v. Mahon, supra.* That inquiry may be narrowed to the question of the severity of the impact of the law on appellants' parcel, and its resolution in turn requires a careful assessment of the impact of the regulation on the Terminal site.

Unlike the governmental acts in *Goldblatt, Miller, Causby, Griggs,* and *Hadacheck,* the New York City law does not interfere in any way with the present uses of the Terminal. Its designation as a landmark not only permits but contemplates that appellants may continue to use the property precisely as it has been used for the past 65 years: as a railroad terminal containing office space and concessions. So the law does not interfere with what must be regarded as Penn Central's primary expectation concerning the use of the parcel. More importantly, on this record, we must regard the New York City law as permitting Penn Central not only to profit from the Terminal but also to obtain a "reasonable return" on its investment.

Appellants, moreover, exaggerate the effect of the law on their ability to make use of the air rights above the Terminal in two respects.[33] First, it simply cannot be maintained, on this record, that appellants have been prohibited from occupying *any* portion of the airspace above the Terminal. While the Commission's actions in denying applications to construct an office building in excess of 50 stories above the Terminal may indicate that it will refuse to issue a certificate of appropriateness for any comparably sized structure, nothing the Commission has said or done suggests an intention to prohibit *any* construction above the Terminal. The Commission's report emphasized that whether any construction would be allowed depended upon whether the proposed addition "would harmonize in scale, material and character with [the Terminal]." Record 2251. Since appellants have not sought approval for the construction of a smaller structure, we do not know that appellants will be denied any use of any portion of the airspace above the Terminal.[34]

Second, to the extent appellants have been denied the right to build above the Terminal, it is not literally accurate to say that they have been denied *all* use of even those pre-existing air rights. Their ability to use these rights has not been abrogated; they are made transferable to at least eight parcels in the vicinity of the Terminal, one or two of which have been found suitable for the construction of new office buildings. Although appellants and others have argued that New York City's transferable development-rights program is far from ideal,[35] the New York courts here supportably found that, at least in the case of the Terminal, the rights afforded are valuable. While these rights may well not have constituted "just compensation" if a "taking" had occurred, the rights nevertheless undoubtedly mitigate whatever financial burdens the law has imposed on appellants and, for that reason, are to be taken into account in considering the impact of regulation.

On this record, we conclude that the application of New York City's Landmarks Law has not effected a "taking" of appellants' property. The restrictions imposed are substantially related to the promotion of the general welfare and not only permit reasonable beneficial use of the landmark site but also afford appellants opportunities further to enhance not only the Terminal site proper but also other properties.

---

[33] Appellants, of course, argue at length that the transferable development rights, while valuable, do not constitute "just compensation." Brief for Appellants 36-43.

[34] Counsel for appellants admitted at oral argument that the Commission has not suggested that it would not, for example, approve a 20-story office tower along the lines of that which was part of the original plan for the Terminal. *See* Tr. of Oral Arg. 19.

[35] *See* Costonis, *supra* n. 2, at 585-589.

Affirmed.

MR. JUSTICE REHNQUIST, with whom THE CHIEF JUSTICE and MR. JUSTICE STEVENS join, dissenting.

Of the over one million buildings and structures in the city of New York, appellees have singled out 400 for designation as official landmarks.[1] The owner of a building might initially be pleased that his property has been chosen by a distinguished committee of architects, historians, and city planners for such a singular distinction. But he may well discover, as appellant Penn Central Transportation Co. did here, that the landmark designation imposes upon him a substantial cost, with little or no offsetting benefit except for the honor of the designation. The question in this case is whether the cost associated with the city of New York's desire to preserve a limited number of "landmarks" within its borders must be borne by all of its taxpayers or whether it can instead be imposed entirely on the owners of the individual properties.

Only in the most superficial sense of the word can this case be said to involve "zoning." Typical zoning restrictions may, it is true, so limit the prospective uses of a piece of property as to diminish the value of that property in the abstract because it may not be used for the forbidden purposes. But any such abstract decrease in value will more than likely be at least partially offset by an increase in value which flows from similar restrictions as to use on neighboring properties. All property owners in a designated area are placed under the same restrictions, not only for the benefit of the municipality as a whole but also for the common benefit of one another. In the words of Mr. Justice Holmes, speaking for the Court in *Pennsylvania Coal Co. v. Mahon*, 260 U.S. 393 (1922), there is "an average reciprocity of advantage."

Where a relatively few individual buildings, all separated from one another, are singled out and treated differently from surrounding buildings, no such reciprocity exists. The cost to the property owner which results from the imposition of restrictions applicable only to his property and not that of his neighbors may be substantial—in this case, several million dollars—with no comparable reciprocal benefits. And the cost associated with landmark legislation is likely to be of a completely different order of magnitude than that which results from the imposition of normal zoning restrictions. Unlike the regime affected by the latter, the landowner is not simply prohibited from using his property for certain purposes, while allowed to use it for all other purposes. Under the historic-landmark preservation scheme adopted by New York, the property owner is under an affirmative duty to *preserve* his property *as a landmark* at his own expense. To suggest that because traditional zoning results in some limitation of use of the property zoned, the New York City landmark preservation scheme should likewise be upheld, represents the ultimate in treating as alike things which are different. The rubric of "zoning" has not yet sufficed to avoid the well-established proposition that the Fifth Amendment bars the Government from forcing some people alone to bear public burdens which, in all fairness and justice, should be borne by the public as a whole.

---

[1] A large percentage of the designated landmarks are public structures (such as the Brooklyn Bridge, City Hall, the Statute of Liberty and the Municipal Asphalt Plant) and thus do not raise Fifth Amendment taking questions. See Landmarks Preservation Commission of the City of New York, *Landmarks and Historic Districts* (1977 and Jan. 10, 1978, Supplement). Although the Court refers to the New York ordinance as a *comprehensive* program to preserve *historic* landmarks, the ordinance is not limited to historic buildings and gives little guidance to the Landmarks Preservation Commission in its selection of landmark sites. Section 207-1.0(n) of the Landmarks Preservation Law, as set forth in N.Y.C. Admin. Code, ch. 8-A (1976), requires only that the selected landmark be at least 30 years old and possess "a special character or special historical or aesthetic interest or value as part of the development, heritage or cultural characteristics of the city, state or nation."

. . . .

I

The Fifth Amendment provides in part: "nor shall private property be taken for public use, without just compensation." In a very literal sense, the actions of appellees violated this constitutional prohibition. Before the city of New York declared Grand Central Terminal to be a landmark, Penn Central could have used its "air rights" over the Terminal to build a multistory office building, at an apparent value of several million dollars per year. Today, the Terminal cannot be modified in *any* form, including the erection of additional stories, without the permission of the Landmark Preservation Commission, a permission which appellants, despite good-faith attempts, have so far been unable to obtain. Because the Taking Clause of the Fifth Amendment has not always been read literally, however, the constitutionality of appellees' actions requires a closer scrutiny of this Court's interpretation of the three key words in the Taking Clause—"property," "taken," and "just compensation."

A

Appellees do not dispute that valuable property rights have been destroyed. . . . While neighboring landowners are free to use their land and "air rights" in any way consistent with the broad boundaries of New York zoning, Penn Central, absent the permission of appellees, must forever maintain its property in its present state.[5] The property has been thus subjected to a nonconsensual servitude not borne by any neighboring or similar properties.

B

Appellees have thus destroyed—in a literal sense, "taken"—substantial property rights of Penn Central. . . . But an examination of the two exceptions where the destruction of property does *not* constitute a taking demonstrates that a compensable taking has occurred here.

1

As early as 1887, the Court recognized that the government can prevent a property owner from using his property to injure others without having to compensate the owner for the value of the forbidden use. . . . Thus, there is no "taking" where a city prohibits the operation of a brickyard within a residential area, *see Hadacheck v. Sebastian*, 239 U.S. 394 (1915), or forbids excavation for sand and gravel below the water line, *see Goldblatt v. Hempstead*, 369 U.S. 590 (1962). Nor is it relevant, where the government is merely prohibiting a noxious use of property, that the government would seem to be singling out a particular property owner. *Hadacheck, supra*, at 413, 36 S.Ct., at 146.[8]

---

[5] In particular, Penn Central cannot increase the height of the Terminal. This Court has previously held that the "air rights" over an area of land are "property" for purposes of the Fifth Amendment. *See United States v. Causby*, 328 U.S. 256 (1946) ("air rights" taken by low-flying airplanes); *Griggs v. Allegheny County*, 369 U.S. 84 (1962) (same); *Portsmouth Harbor Land & Hotel Co. v. United States*, 260 U.S. 327 (1922) (firing of projectiles over summer resort can constitute taking). *See also Butler v. Frontier Telephone Co.*, 186 N.Y. 486, 79 N.E. 716 (1906) (stringing of telephone wire across property constitutes a taking).

[8] Each of the cases cited by the Court for the proposition that legislation which severely affects some landowners but not others does not effect a "taking" involved noxious uses of property. *See Hadacheck; Miller v. Schoene*, 276 U.S. 272 (1928); *Goldblatt*.

The nuisance exception to the taking guarantee is not coterminous with the police power itself. The question is whether the forbidden use is dangerous to the safety, health, or welfare of others . . . .

Appellees are not prohibiting a nuisance. The record is clear that the proposed addition to the Grand Central Terminal would be in full compliance with zoning, height limitations, and other health and safety requirements. Instead, appellees are seeking to preserve what they believe to be an outstanding example of beaux-arts architecture. Penn Central is prevented from further developing its property basically because *too good* a job was done in designing and building it. The city of New York, because of its unadorned admiration for the design, has decided that the owners of the building must preserve it unchanged for the benefit of sightseeing New Yorkers and tourists.

Unlike land-use regulations, appellees' actions do not merely *prohibit* Penn Central from using its property in a narrow set of noxious ways. Instead, appellees have placed an *affirmative* duty on Penn Central to maintain the Terminal in its present state and in "good repair." Appellants are not free to use their property as they see fit within broad outer boundaries but must strictly adhere to their past use except where appellees conclude that alternative uses would not detract from the landmark. While Penn Central may continue to use the Terminal as it is presently designed, appellees otherwise "exercise complete dominion and control over the surface of the land," *United States v. Causby*, 328 U.S. 256 (1946), and must compensate the owner for his loss. Property is taken in the constitutional sense when inroads are made upon an owner's use of it to an extent that, as between private parties, a servitude has been acquired. . . .

2

Even where the government prohibits a noninjurious use, the Court has ruled that a taking does not take place if the prohibition applies over a broad cross section of land and thereby "secure[s] an average reciprocity of advantage." *Pennsylvania Coal Co. v. Mahon, supra.* [10] It is for this reason that zoning does not constitute a "taking." While zoning at times reduces *individual* property values, the burden is shared relatively evenly and it is reasonable to conclude that on the whole an individual who is harmed by one aspect of the zoning will be benefited by another.

Here, however, a multimillion dollar loss has been imposed on appellants; it is uniquely felt and is not offset by any benefits flowing from the preservation of some 400 other "landmarks" in New York City. Appellees have imposed a substantial cost on less than one one-tenth of one percent of the buildings in New York City for the general benefit of all its people. It is exactly this imposition of general costs on a few individuals at which the "taking" protection is directed. The Fifth Amendment

prevents the public from loading upon one individual more than his just share of the burdens of government, and says that when he surrenders to the public something more and different from that which is exacted from other members of the public, a full and just equivalent shall be returned to him.

---

[10] Appellants concede that the preservation of buildings of historical or aesthetic importance is a permissible objective of state action. Brief for Appellants 12. *Cf. Berman v. Parker*, 348 U.S. 26 (1954); *United States v. Gettysburg Electric R. Co.*, 160 U.S. 668 (1896).

For the reasons noted in the text, historic *zoning*, as has been undertaken by cities, such as New Orleans, may well not require compensation under the Fifth Amendment.

Monongahela Navigation Co. v. United States, 148 U.S. 312, 325 (1893).

. . . .

As Mr. Justice Holmes pointed out in *Pennsylvania Coal Co. v. Mahon*, "the question at bottom" in an eminent domain case "is upon whom the loss of the changes desired should fall." The benefits that appellees believe will flow from preservation of the Grand Central Terminal will accrue to all the citizens of New York City. There is no reason to believe that appellants will enjoy a substantially greater share of these benefits. If the cost of preserving Grand Central Terminal were spread evenly across the entire population of the city of New York, the burden per person would be in cents per year—a minor cost appellees would surely concede for the benefit accrued. Instead, however, appellees would impose the entire cost of several million dollars per year on Penn Central. But it is precisely this sort of discrimination that the Fifth Amendment prohibits.[12]

Appellees in response would argue that a taking only occurs where a property owner is denied *all* reasonable value of his property.[13] The Court has frequently held that, even where a destruction of property rights would not *otherwise* constitute a taking, the inability of the owner to make a reasonable return on his property requires compensation under the Fifth Amendment. But the converse is not true. A taking does not become a noncompensable exercise of police power simply because the government in its grace allows the owner to make some "reasonable" use of his property. It is the character of the invasion, not the amount of damage resulting from it, so long as the damage is substantial, that determines the question whether it is a taking. . . .

C

Appellees, apparently recognizing that the constraints imposed on a landmark site constitute a taking for Fifth Amendment purposes, do not leave the property owner empty-handed. As the Court notes, the property owner may theoretically "transfer" his previous right to develop the landmark property to adjacent properties if they are under his control. Appellees have coined this system "Transfer Development Rights," or TDR's.

Of all the terms used in the Taking Clause, "just compensation" has the strictest meaning. The Fifth Amendment does not allow simply an approximate compensation but requires a full and perfect equivalent for the property taken. . . .

Appellees contend that, even if they have "taken" appellants' property, TDR's constitute "just compensation." Appellants, of course, argue that TDR's are highly imperfect compensation. Because the lower courts held that there was no "taking," they did not have to reach the question

---

[12] The fact that the Landmarks Preservation Commission may have allowed additions to a relatively few landmarks is of no comfort to appellants. Nor is it of any comfort that the Commission refuses to allow appellants to construct any additional stories because of their belief that such construction would not be aesthetic.

[13] Difficult conceptual and legal problems are posed by a rule that a taking only occurs where the property owner is denied all reasonable return on his property. Not only must the Court define "reasonable return" for a variety of types of property (farmlands, residential properties, commercial and industrial areas), but the Court must define the particular property unit that should be examined. For example, in this case, if appellees are viewed as having restricted Penn Central's use of its "air rights," *all* return has been denied. *See Pennsylvania Coal Co. v. Mahon*, 260 U.S. 393 (1922). The Court does little to resolve these questions in its opinion. Thus, at one point, the Court implies that the question is whether the restrictions have "an unduly harsh impact upon the owner's use of the property," at another point, the question is phrased as whether Penn Central can obtain "a 'reasonable return' on its investment," and, at yet another point, the question becomes whether the landmark is "economically viable."

of whether or not just compensation has already been awarded. The New York Court of Appeals' discussion of TDR's gives some support to appellants:

> The many defects in New York City's program for development rights transfers have been detailed elsewhere. . . . The area to which transfer is permitted is severely limited [and] complex procedures are required to obtain a transfer permit.

And in other cases the Court of Appeals has noted that TDR's have an "uncertain and contingent market value" and do "not adequately preserve" the value lost when a building is declared to be a landmark. *French Investing Co. v. City of New York*, 39 N.Y.2d 587, 350 N.E.2d 381 (1976). On the other hand, there is evidence in the record that Penn Central has been offered substantial amounts for its TDR's. Because the record on appeal is relatively slim, I would remand to the Court of Appeals for a determination of whether TDR's constitute a "full and perfect equivalent for the property taken."[14]

II

Over 50 years ago, Mr. Justice Holmes, speaking for the Court, warned that the courts were "in danger of forgetting that a strong public desire to improve the public condition is not enough to warrant achieving the desire by a shorter cut than the constitutional way of paying for the change." *Pennsylvania Coal Co. v. Mahon, supra.* The Court's opinion in this case demonstrates that the danger thus foreseen has not abated. The city of New York is in a precarious financial state, and some may believe that the costs of landmark preservation will be more easily borne by corporations such as Penn Central than the overburdened individual taxpayers of New York. But these concerns do not allow us to ignore past precedents construing the Eminent Domain Clause to the end that the desire to improve the public condition is, indeed, achieved by a shorter cut than the constitutional way of paying for the change.

[c] Events After the Supreme Court Decision

Disputes swirled for decades after the Supreme Court rendered its opinion over use of the Grand Central Terminal air rights. While the litigation was pending, the scope of development rights bandied about as transferable from the terminal to other sites was 2.3 million square feet. As it turns out, this number may have been about twice as large as is really available. One sale of 74,665 square feet was completed for use in an office building on Park Avenue across the street from the terminal. A zoning change further reduced the available amount to just under 2 million square feet,[33] or enough space to build a 35-40 story office building covering an entire

---

[14] The Court suggests that if appellees are held to have "taken" property rights of landmark owners, not only the New York City Landmarks Preservation Law, but "all comparable landmark legislation in the Nation" must fall. This assumes, of course, that TDR's are not "just compensation" for the property rights destroyed. It also ignores the fact that many States and cities in the Nation have chosen to preserve landmarks by purchasing or condemning restrictive easements over the facades of the landmarks and are apparently quite satisfied with the results. See, e.g., Ore. Rev. Stat. §§ 271.710, 271.720 (1977); Md. Ann. Code, Art. 41, § 181A (1978); Va. Code §§ 10-145.1 and 10-138(e) (1978); Richmond, Va., City Code §§ 21-23 et seq. (1975). The British National Trust has effectively used restrictive easements to preserve landmarks since 1937. See National Trust Act, 1937, 1 Edw. 8 and 1 Geo. 6 ch. lvii, §§ 4 and 8. Other States and cities have found that tax incentives are also an effective means of encouraging the private preservation of landmark sites. See, e.g. Conn. Gen. Stat. § 12-127a (1977); Ill. Rev. Stat., ch.24, § 11-48.2-6 (1976); Va. Code § 10-139 (1978). The New York City Landmarks Preservation Law departs drastically from these traditional, and constitutional, means of preserving landmarks.

[33] Gottlieb, *Zoning Fight Again Imperils Grand Central*, N.Y. TIMES, Oct. 14, 1986, at B 11, col. 5; Horsley, *In the Air Over Midtown: Builders New Arena*, N.Y. TIMES, Feb. 11, 1979, § 8, at p. 1, col. 4.

football field, including the end zones. Two other disputes before the New York City Planning Commission had the potential to reduce the total available space by another 1.1 million square feet. The Pan Am Building, which is over 500,000 square feet above present zoning limits, may be treated as part of the Grand Central Terminal site, thereby reducing the total development potential transferable to other locations. In addition, the original square footage figures were calculated on the assumption that the Park Avenue overpass above 42nd Street and the roadway around the terminal were also part of the terminal site. If the road is separated from the site, the development potential for the site would take another significant dip.

In November, 1983, Penn Central Corporation announced plans to sell 1.5 million square feet of the air rights to First Boston Real Estate Company for an office tower at 383 Madison Avenue, the location of a 14 story building about four blocks north of the terminal.[34] The original proposal called for the construction of a 140 story tower, the maximum allowed using transferred rights. The project was scaled down to 74 floors, about twice the size allowed under present zoning,[35] a building which would still require the use of about 800,000 square feet of the rights transferred from Penn Central. One major roadblock stood in the way of the project's construction. The landmark preservation rules allowed transfer of rights only to sites adjacent to, directly across the street from or cat-e-corner to either the landmark or any contiguous sites owned by the same party. Though the site is an air rights block over the terminal's double decked tracks north of the terminal building, it and several other intervening parcels were sold when Penn Central went through bankruptcy proceedings in the 1970s. The bankruptcy sales did not, however, include subsurface rights to the tracks, which were retained by the railroad. Penn Central and First Boston argued that these sub surface rights should be included in defining the site and parcels contiguous to the terminal for landmark purposes. Penn Central threatened to return to court if it was denied permission to sell air rights to First Boston for use at 383 Madison Avenue, arguing that it was not being permitted an adequate return on the terminal and its airspace and seeking once again to construct a large building atop the terminal itself. Since the price to be paid by First Boston for the air rights was well over $80 million, you can understand why Penn Central would be willing to litigate some more.

Though the design for the proposed First Boston building was praised by some, there was widespread concern about the wisdom of building yet another huge building in midtown Manhattan. Paul Goldberger, architecture critic for the *New York Times*, noted, "[T]here is a peculiar irony to this—for when more air rights are sold, . . . we get larger and larger buildings that create a physical climate of gigantism, antithetical and even hostile to the purpose of landmarks preservation in the first place."[36] Extending air rights north by using the underground tracks was not approved. The entire terminal just underwent an extensive restoration and renovation. The Main Concourse and Oyster Bar have been returned to their previous grandeur.[37]

---

[34] Horsley, *Air Rights Bought at Grand Central,* N.Y. TIMES, Nov. 26, 1983, at p. 1, col.1.

[35] At that point, New York City zoning rules permitted large buildings in the Madison Avenue area. The construction of a large number of towers led to significant changes in zoning rules in an effort to shift development pressures to the West side of Manhattan.

[36] Goldberger, *When Air Rights Go Underground,* N.Y. TIMES, Dec. 21, 1986, § II, at p. 1, col. 1. For an earlier and longer statement about over building in Manhattan, *see* Goldberger, *The Limits of Urban Growth,* N.Y. TIMES, Nov. 14, 1982 (Magazine), at 46.

[37] For a summary of the restoration, look at Shawn Kennedy, *Bringing Symmetry and Logic Back to 'New York's Living Room,'* N.Y. TIMES, Nov. 26, 1995, (Metro Sunday) at 41.

[d]   Some Thoughts on the Grand Central Terminal Litigation

Here are some thoughts on the New York Court of Appeals decision, Justice Brennan's majority opinion and Justice Rehnquist's dissenting opinion in the Grand Central Terminal litigation. The New York Court of Appeals did two things of note.[38] First, drawing on some of the history of Takings jurisprudence discussed in the notes before the *Penn Central* opinion, it insisted that most land use litigation is simply substantive due process litigation. In essence, the court treated land the same as any other economic asset for constitutional purposes. If stocks and bonds may be regulated, then why not land? Second, the New York Court of Appeals argued that part of the value of the Grand Central Terminal was attributable to government investment. As to that share of the terminal's value, the court opined, Penn Central was not entitled to a reasonable rate of return.

It is interesting that, at least on the surface of his opinion, Justice Brennan rejected the first conclusion of the New York Court of Appeals and evaded the second. But on a closer look, he may actually agree with the substance of both. Perhaps he had to reject the central features of the lower court opinion in order to craft a majority in the Supreme Court.

In any case, Justice Brennan organized his opinion around several basic assumptions. First, he argued, the parcel at stake in the litigation was the entire Grand Central Terminal site. Indeed, the content of his argument probably reflected a feeling that the parcel was the terminal site together with the areas to which development rights could be transferred. Second, he posited that the regulations at issue were "general" rather than "individualized." Finally, his analytical structure accepted the New Dealish point of view that legislatures may take reasonable steps to protect the general welfare, even when negative results accrue to individual land owners. Only when Michelman's distinct, investment backed expectations were significantly diminished was Justice Brennan prepared to find a taking.

This overall view actually mirrors the general structure of much post-New Deal analysis of Commerce Clause legislation. That is, Congress, the Supreme Court has held, has significant latitude to both define the nature of perceived social ills and select the best solutions to cure them. Brennan basically said the same thing in *Penn Central*. Even though he refused to abide the notion that the case was a Substantive Due Process case, he construed the Takings Clause as containing the same basic allocations of power between executive and legislative branches as those buried in Substantive Due Process.

In hindsight his willingness to think about the case as a Takings Clause dispute rather than a Substantive Due Process case has come back to haunt the Court's liberals. The conservatives now on the Court have been free to work on more recent takings cases without fear that their invalidation of regulations would undo the central holdings of the New Deal Court. The present Court has not had to worry about the repercussions that might flow from a return to much more Formalist notions about regulating the entire economy.

Justice Brennan's opinion took a slightly different tack in its discussion of public values, though it reached a result quite similar to that of the New York Court's public investment idea. Brennan, despite all of the ad hoc factor analysis in his opinion, paid a lot of attention to the notion of distinct investment backed expectations of land owners. Michelman developed that idea as a way of thinking about takings from either a Utilitarian or a Kantian point of view, that is from either a distributional or an individual fairness perspective. Distributionally, Michelman wrote in Pareto

---

[38] Some hints about the contours of the decision may be found in footnotes 20 and 23 in Justice Brennan's opinion.

Optimality terms, hoping to find ways of insuring fairness by reducing negative impacts on individual owners. Thoughts about fairness led him in the same direction—concern about the impact of singling out individuals and forcing them to bear losses for the benefit of the larger community. In both models, the notion of disaffection costs—the economic and political costs of making individuals feel they have been unfairly treated—was central. It is easy to see when someone's pocket book has been hurt. But Michelman was also concerned with the political disaffection associated with unfair regulation. It is possible, for example, to see how economically similar regulatory schemes might have different disaffection costs. A zoning regulation that downzones a parcel by 25% might be perceived as quite different from a zoning regulation that zones 25% of a parcel for park land use only. While both rules have the same economic impact, the park rule's exclusion of the owner from control over possession might cause higher disaffection costs. Preventing someone from using land at all is likely to be seen as more arbitrary than distributing use rights more evenly.

It was considerations like these, I think, that led Justices Brennan and Rehnquist to battle so furiously in their opinions over whether the historic preservation regulations were general or specific. For if regulation is general rather than specific, the expectations and therefore the disaffection costs of a single land owner are less likely to be at issue. If policy preferences are strongly held by the general public, then expectations about land development might logically be tempered by such generally prevailing notions of propriety. The idea of distinct investment backed expectations, which Justice Brennan took from Michelman, was constructed as a kind of rule device for implementing notions of fairness and disaffection.

One way of reading this device is to suggest that part of the risk calculation made by investors involves the likelihood of regulation. To the extent that regulation affects the prices of things people invest in, the impact of regulation gets buried in the prices for assets and can have no deleterious economic or taking impacts in most cases. But that approach can also be a bootstrapping proposition, for integrating the likelihood of regulation into the risk calculus is to assume the answer to the question posed; it automatically means that regulation is usually not a taking.[39]

But maybe there is another approach. Justice Brennan, in contrast to the New York Court of Appeals, did not make use of the "socialist," publicly developed parts of the terminal complex. In fact he seemed to reject that aspect of the New York Court of Appeals' decision. But the expectations construct arguably served the same purpose. Think about the way Justice Brennan referred to the writings of Joseph Sax.[40] Sax argued that any action by a property owner causing a negative effect on another land owner or on the public can be regulated free of inhibition under the Taking Clause. While it may be that Sax carried his argument too far,[41] the point he made is one Justice Brennan empathized with, at least in part.

Brennan, who surely knew that the incentive to redevelop historic sites in places like Manhattan would lead to loss of old architecture absent public intervention, cited Sax to support the proposition that some court decisions dismissed takings challenges in disputes involving water

---

[39] Such bootstrapping was overtly deemed acceptable to Justice Kennedy in Lucas v. South Carolina Coastal Council, 505 U.S. 1003 (1992), a later takings case reproduced at p. 1043 below.

[40] Joseph Sax, *Takings and the Police Power*, 74 YALE L.J. 36 (1964); Joseph Sax, *Takings, Private Property and Public Rights*, 81 YALE L.J. 149 (1971).

[41] There are, for example, any number of settings where land uses cause conflicts when "late comers" arrive, as in *Boomer* or *Spur*. For constitutional purposes, it shouldn't make a difference how the land use conflict occurred?

access because the regulation "did not interfere with interests that were sufficiently bound up with the reasonable expectations of the claimant to constitute 'property' for Fifth Amendment purposes." That is, there are some things people may wish to do with land that are not "property" because one cannot have a distinct, investment backed expectation to do them.

For Sax, and for Justice Brennan, one type of thing that may not be property is a "commons," an asset, as noted earlier, that is available to many at no or low cost and is valuable to all who have access to it. History in general and specific historic sites, like the air and the oceans, may be a "commons," a "public good," something of value potentially available to each of us for free or at very low cost and subject to destruction if left unregulated. That is a situation which creates concerns about protection of history. For the low price charged for use of history and viewing of an extant architectural masterpiece means that incentives for its destruction might be much higher than those for its protection. For Sax, that meant that legislative decisions allocating or prohibiting use of a commons had to be free from the threat of a takings finding. That is, the common asset—air, water or history—may not be thought of as property for takings purposes; at least for purposes of takings jurisprudence, it is a non-commodity.

Justice Brennan's vision of a social construct surrounding investment backed expectations, therefore, may not have been just a sense of mutual need or common feeling. He may have sensed that some things are so important that they are subject neither to destruction nor to individualized market choices. He was not writing about things like knowledge that should be in the public domain for all of us to use. Rather, he was looking to protect some publicly available aspects of our world by permitting the state to remove them from traditional property rubrics, to place them in a "savings account" to be carefully spent, or spent, if at all, only by the state, to put them outside the arena of economic risk taking by creating expectations that they may not become objects of investment. Important manifestations of cultural history should not be for sale, Justice Brennan might have been arguing; its preservation is an issue of importance to multiple generations; its present market value is an inadequate measure of the generational issues at stake.

This, of course, is the sort of rubric John Rawls wrote about in the THEORY OF JUSTICE excerpt reprinted above. Rawls, a jurisprude writing what was in essence a justification for the New Deal and The Great Society, started his thinking by putting all people behind the veil of ignorance and reached a conclusion much like Michelman and Justice Brennan. Since none of us behind the veil would know about our economic status, we would, Rawls argued, set a minimum floor for all of us in order to protect ourselves. And, he went on, our ignorance about our generational place would also lead us to establish a savings principle to insure that one generation would not use so many assets that later generations are left economically stranded. Perhaps historic preservation rules are one form of savings principle.

In sum, Justice Brennan may have been trying to do more than simply deciding the appropriate point of balance between general welfare and individual needs. He may also have been trying to resolve another set of difficult problems about the sorts of assets which are appropriate parts of any market based system under the Constitution, about the necessity for non-commodification—state control of assets that should not be part of any market system and that should not be the subject of private risk calculations. In short, what he did ended up having very much the same impact as the New York Court of Appeals decision.

Justice Rehnquist's opinion began with quite different assumptions. First, he assumed that the parcel at stake was limited to the air rights above Grand Central Terminal. The transferable development rights associated with the designation of the terminal as historic were only relevant to the justness of the compensation for the air rights, not to the size of the parcel. Second, he opined that the regulations were not general, but singled out the owners of the terminal for distinctly different treatment. Finally, he assumed that significant negative effects on a single land owner arising from non-comprehensive regulations will be a taking unless one of two exceptions is present. To avoid a taking, the owner's use must be noxious, or the regulation must create a mutual reciprocity of advantage, a kind of constitutional neighborhood scheme in which benefits and burdens are generally distributed among the owners in a significant area. And so, a Rehnquist-like vision of the case may be stated something like this:

> Landowners negatively effected by land use regulations which single them out for special treatment may claim a taking unless they use their land for a noxious purpose, or as members of a neighborhood obtain area wide benefits from the regulatory activities.

When his opinion is summarized this way, it is clear that the opinions of Justices Brennan and Rehnquist are vastly different. Indeed, you might ask how two people sitting on the same court hearing the same arguments could factually characterize the same case in such different ways. It is clear that these judges brought different world views to their work. Are there ways of describing what was going on?

First, although Justices Brennan and Rehnquist brought many different perspectives to bear on their work, there are some aspects of these two opinions that are alike. For both of them, the thoughts of ordinary lay observers of the legal scene are quite important. Each took quite seriously the notion that Michelman's disaffection costs were useful in defining the areas of regulatory activity forbidden to the state. Or, thinking about the cases in equality terms, both Justices took the view that one land owner may not be singled out in a way significantly different from others. Though their starting assumptions differed in many ways, both justices were writing about disaffection costs.

Justice Rehnquist started his analysis of disaffection costs with the assumption that most people will define their own economic interests to benefit themselves (thereby rejecting Rawls out of hand) and that commonplace property labels will be used to describe any harms they perceive. While this may be an overly simplistic view of the attitudes of sophisticated Manhattan real estate developers, this method of reification does filter through his opinion. Thus, Rehnquist concluded, the owners of the Grand Central Terminal felt aggrieved by the historic site designation and the "thing" harmed was "their air rights." Indeed, this view was central to his opinion, for it was only when perceptions of individualized economic harm were at issue, that his theory operated.

While Justice Rehnquist began his analysis of disaffection by inquiring into the nature of the "thing" affected by the regulation, Justice Brennan began with an analysis of the benefits bestowed upon the public by the regulation. Disaffection was a possible consequence of regulation, not an inherent limitation upon it. Brennan assumed people perceive value not just in their own self interest, but also in the well being of others. This perspective, like that of Justice Rehnquist, also required that the views of ordinary observers be taken seriously, for the general public benefit may be unconstitutional in its reach if individual expectations were too harshly treated.

The points of view of Justices Brennan and Rehnquist also were different. Their "ordinary languages" of disaffection were not the same. They looked to different segments of the population to define ordinary lay observers and the nature of self-interest. Justice Rehnquist's ordinary observer was quite Formalist—closely linked to his property, affronted by reduced abilities to profit and cognizant of the legally defined labels and distinct characteristics of each of the sticks in his property bundle. Justice Brennan's ordinary observer was much more Realist—less wedded to particularized images of property, more willing to permit use of property for public purposes and less attuned to sophisticated legal terminology. Nonetheless, both inevitably relied upon some view of the perceptions of the body politic in reaching their conclusions about the takings problem.

[e] Problem Notes

[i] *Transferred Development Rights.* Transferred development rights (TDRs) take full advantage of the power of local governments to zone. After *Euclid*, zoning was routinely used to place upper limits on land development. Absent a later rezoning, land owners in some areas lost their ability to develop projects to the maximum level the market would have permitted in the absence of regulation. In recent decades, it began to dawn on large numbers of local government officials that the economic value extracted from the market by zoning could be used for other policy objectives. Some of the extracted value could be offered back as incentives for the creation of desired land use patterns. Thus, New York City permitted larger buildings in Times Square if they contained theaters and some states permitted farmers near suburban development to sell their development rights in return for promises to maintain land in its agricultural use.[42] Transferring development rights brought *Euclid* full circle. The value extracted by zoning but, according to the *Euclid* Court, not unconstitutionally taken, became the vehicle by which public authorities could "purchase" desired land uses without any direct payments from their operating budgets. Some early scholarship in this area, particularly two articles by John Costonis, recommended use of TDRs in historic preservation.[43] The recommendation was not without its opponents. One particularly trenchant critique, found in Note, *Development Rights Transfer in New York City*, 82 YALE L.J. 338, 370-372 (1972), contained these thoughts:[44]

[C]ertain conclusions from New York's experience with the technique are already clear. and these are worth pondering by any city contemplating its adoption. First, development rights transfer is not a *necessary* device for saving landmarks, where the municipal landmarks commission has other preservation powers and is willing to employ them. Second, it is not a *reliable* device for landmark preservation, because it depends on the local market for new office space. This market may well be glutted through over building or, ironically, through the extensive utilization of other . . . bonus provisions in the municipal zoning ordinance. Third, it is not even a *serviceable* device over the long run, unless the city intends to abandon effective limits on the intensity of development. Only new and bigger office towers and apartments can absorb the transferred rights, and this necessarily means increased residential and employee densities.

Finally, development rights transfer is a *pernicious* device in today's congested cities. Whether from landmarks, mid block brownstones, or municipal buildings, unused rights will always flow to those areas where the commercial advantages of concentration make transfer economically attractive. If this existing concentration is attended by its usual effects—if the

---

[42] Montgomery County, in Maryland just north of Washington, D.C., adopted a comprehensive plan that downzoned substantial areas used for agriculture and permitted owners to sell their remaining development rights for use in designated areas of the county. The plan has caused some controversy, particularly in the areas targeted for use of the transferred development rights. *See* Armao, *Montgomery Sees a Building Battle, Issue: Land Rights Transfer,* WASHINGTON POST, May 18, 1987, at A1, col. 5.

[43] John Costonis, *The Chicago Plan: Incentive Zoning and the Preservation of Urban Landmarks*, 85 HARV. L. REV. 574 (1972); John Costonis, *Development Rights Transfer: An Exploratory Essay*, 83 YALE L.J. 75 (1973).

[44] Reprinted by permission of the Yale Law Journal Company.

subways and buses are overloaded; the streets, clogged; the air, polluted; and the few remaining open spaces, in the perpetual shadow of surrounding office or apartment towers—then development rights transfer can only make life more miserable.

In the final analysis, debate on the merits of development rights transfer is really an argument about the optimal size of buildings in the central city.

. . . .

[P]roponents of transfer schemes can argue with some conviction that this new zoning practice "is defensible in planning terms." But whatever the planning terms, the results of urban concentration are increasingly intolerable in human terms, and a zoning device aimed at increasing that concentration deserves censure rather than praise.

What do you think of transferred development rights?

[*ii*] *Transferred Development Rights and* **Euclid.** One of the criticisms levied against some TDR schemes is the lack of marketability of the rights. In the *Penn Central* setting, for example, the TDRs were usable only on adjacent parcels owned by the owner of the site designated historic. If the owner of the historic site could not arrange to purchase an adjacent site, the rights would be virtually useless. Suppose that New York City adopted a scheme which made it possible for the owner of any individually designated historic site (not in any historic district) to sell their development rights, measured by the difference between the level of use permitted by the zoning rules and the level of use permitted as an historic site, to any party for use on any property located in a large area of midtown Manhattan. Suppose further that after about 15 years of operation, opposition began to surface to the continued construction of development rights buildings larger than normal zoning rules permitted. In response to the opposition, imagine that New York City took two steps. First it rezoned midtown Manhattan, reducing the permitted density level of non-development rights buildings in the zone by 20%. Second, it reduced by 20% the amount of bonus space that ownership of each development right produced when attached to a site. Would either or both of these new regulations be unconstitutional? Think about the reactions of Justice Brennan, Justice Rehnquist, and Frank Michelman.

[*iii*] *A Problem—Interstate Highway Cloverleafs.* Picture two property owners— Wanda Wealthy and Max Middling. All the relevant planners decide to build a new interstate highway in the community where Wealthy and Middling own property. A major dispute arises over where to locate the community's cloverleaf. After much discussion, the powers that be decide to locate the interchange right on top of Middling's land. Wealthy's parcel is located just to one side of the proposed cloverleaf. As soon as the plan is finalized, Wealthy is inundated with offers to buy her land. She holds out for a year and then sells to a shopping center developer for approximately five times what she would have obtained had her land been condemned for the cloverleaf. Middling's land is condemned. He is paid a value for typical agricultural land in the area. Is it appropriate for Wealthy to end up with five times as much money per acre as Middling? Is there an eminent domain theory that takes the potentially large shifts resulting from land use decisions into account? Note well that zoning decisions sometimes have effects very much like this clover-leaf problem. May a local government require land owners whose property is made more valuable by land use decisions to pay those whose land is devalued by land use decisions?[45]

---

[45] For commentary on the large scale exchanges in value resulting from public regulation of land, *see* Donald Hagman, *Compensable Regulation: A Way of Dealing With Wipeouts From Land Use Controls?* 54 U. Det. J. Urb. L. 45 (1976).

[*iv*]   ***Problem—Bonus Plans.*** Part of the historic preservation scheme at issue in *Penn Central* involved the transfer of Grand Central Terminal's unusable air rights to other sites owned by Penn Central. Could a major urban area use the bonus plan method to downzone all downtown land to one story commercial use, with additional density of up to 50 floors permitted if certain amenities were included in the building or "donated" to the city? Here are some possible amenities and "donations":

(a) Public plazas at ground level.

(b) Free office space for non-profit and public interest groups.

(c) Public meeting rooms.

(d) Donation of space on the first two floors for a public school.

(e) Construction of subsidized housing or contribution of funds for such housing on other sites.

(f) Installation of artworks in public spaces.

(g) Submission of designs to public authorities for reviews of architectural and aesthetic quality.

(h) Installation of a sewer system or other "infrastructure."

Could any of these items be required without the granting of bonus density rights?

[*v*]   ***Problem—Required Maintenance.*** May an ordinance require an owner of a designated historic structure to restore and maintain it, even if that means that substantial sums of money must be spent? An attempt to require restoration of an historic building in Rye, New York, was frustrated by a decision holding that the city lacked authority to adopt such an ordinance. *FGL & L Property Corp. v. City of Rye*, 66 N.Y.2d 111, 485 N.E.2d 986, 495 N.Y.S.2d 321 (1985). The court avoided the constitutional question. How would you decide it? Is there a difference between forcing a property owner to spend money to fix a building code violation and requiring an owner to restore a rundown historic structure? What expectations have "crystallized" about maintenance and repair obligations?

[*vi*]   ***Sewer Assessment Districts.*** In some areas without sewer and water service, the only way to obtain the installation of such facilities is to "voluntarily" form a sewer district and agree to be assessed for the installation of pipelines to hook into the local sewage treatment facility. Suppose that a bunch of landowners in an area zoned for residential and commercial use, but presently used only for farming, petitioned for the installation of sewer lines in anticipation of future development, that assessments were levied and the sewer pipes installed, and that the area was then downzoned to agricultural uses. Assuming that the agricultural use zoning was lawful, could the owners recover their sewer assessments? The answer was "No" in *Furey v. City of Sacramento*, 780 F.2d 1448 (9th Cir. 1986). The court argued that the assessment was not really a public action, but a private investment by the landowners. Since there was no public compulsion involved in the expenditures, there was no possibility of a taking. Is this public-private distinction an acceptable way of resolving the dispute? Expenditures on a building are "private," but if the building is condemned the "public" must pay for it. Why isn't the downzoning in *Furey* the equivalent of an eminent domain action? Does Michelman's crystallized investment backed expectation theory help with this sort of a dispute?

[*vii*]   ***Investment Backed Expectations and Urban Growth.*** Two of the cases referred to by Justice Brennan in his *Penn Central* opinion involved situations much like *Spur v. Del Webb*, p. 887 above. *Hadacheck v. Sebastian*, 239 U.S. 394 (1915) involved a law which barred brick yards from residential zones. The brick yard in the litigation had been in the area for many years and found itself in difficulty after the previously rural area became residential. Similarly, a long standing open pit sand and gravel mining business was closed in *Goldblatt v. Hempstead*, 369 U.S. 590 (1962) after the area lost its rural character. In both cases, long standing business investments were lost. Should the courts have required compensation in these cases for the same reasons that Del Webb had to pay Spur? Are these the sort of cases in which economic expectations have crystallized and disaffection costs for the property owners are quite high?

§ 11.04 Physical Invasion and Takings Law: The *Loretto* Litigation

[1] Introduction

The contours of takings law have changed quite dramatically since the Grand Central Terminal litigation was resolved. In one sense, this was perfectly predictable. As discussed earlier, at p. 788 much of property law has gone through periods of rigidity and flexibility—from crystals to mud and back again in the language of Carol Rose.[46] After Justice Brennan's musings about the *ad hoc* quality of takings law in *Penn Central*, we might have expected the Court to seek out some bright line rules about Constitutional property law. The three dissenters in *Penn Central*—Justices Burger, Stevens and Rehnquist—were joined by another conservative jurist—Sandra Day O'Connor—in 1980. The shifts in Court personnel had their first noticeable impact on takings jurisprudence in 1982 in *Loretto v. Teleprompter Manhattan CATV Corp.* Ironically the opinion in the case was written by Justice Marshall, an occurrence arguably as remarkable as Justice Sutherland's authorship of *Euclid v. Ambler Realty* 56 years before. He was joined by the three dissenters in *Penn Central*, Justice O'Connor and Justice Powell, who had voted with the majority in the prior case.

[2] Opinions of the United States Supreme Court in *Loretto v. Teleprompter Manhattan CATV Corp.*

Loretto v. Teleprompter Manhattan CATV Corp.

United States Supreme Court
458 U.S. 419, 102 S. Ct. 3164, 73 L. Ed. 2d 868 (1982)

JUSTICE MARSHALL delivered the opinion of the Court.

This case presents the question whether a minor but permanent physical occupation of an owner's property authorized by government constitutes a "taking" of property for which just compensation is due under the Fifth and Fourteenth Amendments of the Constitution. New York law provides that a landlord must permit a cable television company to install its cable facilities upon his property. N.Y. Exec. Law § 828(1) (McKinney Supp. 1981-1982). In this case, the cable installation occupied portions of appellant's roof and the side of her building. The New York Court of Appeals ruled that this appropriation does not amount to a taking. Because we conclude that such a physical occupation of property is a taking, we reverse.

---

[46] *Crystals and Mud in Property Law*, 40 STAN. L. REV. 577 (1988).

I

Appellant Jean Loretto purchased a five-story apartment building located at 303 West 105th Street, New York City, in 1971. The previous owner had granted appellees Teleprompter Corp. and Teleprompter Manhattan CATV (collectively Teleprompter) permission to install a cable on the building and the exclusive privilege of furnishing cable television (CATV) services to the tenants. The New York Court of Appeals described the installation as follows:

> On June 1, 1970 Teleprompter installed a cable slightly less than one-half inch in diameter and of approximately 30 feet in length along the length of the building about 18 inches above the roof top, and directional taps, approximately 4 inches by 4 inches, on the front and rear of the roof. By June 8, 1970 the cable had been extended another 4 to 6 feet and cable had been run from the directional taps to the adjoining building at 305 West 105th Street.

Teleprompter also installed two large silver boxes along the roof cables. The cables are attached by screws or nails penetrating the masonry at approximately two-foot intervals, and other equipment is installed by bolts.

Initially, Teleprompter's roof cables did not service appellant's building. They were part of what could be described as a cable "highway" circumnavigating the city block, with service cables periodically dropped over the front or back of a building in which a tenant desired service. Crucial to such a network is the use of so-called "crossovers"—cable lines extending from one building to another in order to reach a new group of tenants.[2] Two years after appellant purchased the building, Teleprompter connected a "noncrossover" line—*i.e.*, one that provided CATV service to appellant's own tenants—by dropping a line to the first floor down the front of appellant's building.

Prior to 1973, Teleprompter routinely obtained authorization for its installations from property owners along the cable's route, compensating the owners at the standard rate of 5% of the gross revenues that Teleprompter realized from the particular property. To facilitate tenant access to CATV, the State of New York enacted § 828 of the Executive Law, effective January 1, 1973. Section 828 provides that a landlord may not "interfere with the installation of cable television facilities upon his property or premises," and may not demand payment from any tenant for permitting CATV, or demand payment from any CATV company "in excess of any amount which the [State Commission on Cable Television] shall, by regulation, determine to be reasonable."[3]

---

[2] The Court of Appeals defined a "crossover" more comprehensively as occurring:

[W]hen (1) the line servicing the tenants in a particular building is extended to adjacent or adjoining buildings, (2) an amplifier which is placed on a building is used to amplify signals to tenants in that building and in a neighboring building or buildings, and (3) a line is placed on a building, none of the tenants of which are provided CATV service, for the purpose of providing service to an adjoining or adjacent building.

[3] New York Exec. Law § 828 (McKinney Supp. 1981-1982) provides in part:

1. No landlord shall

a. interfere with the installation of cable television facilities upon his property or premises, except that a landlord may require:

i. that the installation of cable television facilities conform to such reasonable conditions as are necessary to protect the safety, functioning and appearance of the premises, and the convenience and well-being of other tenants;

ii. that the cable television company or the tenant or a combination thereof bear the entire cost of the installation, operation or removal of such facilities; and

iii. that the cable television company agree to indemnify the landlord for any damage caused by the installation, operation or removal of such facilities.

The landlord may, however, require the CATV company or the tenant to bear the cost of installation and to indemnify for any damage caused by the installation. Pursuant to § 828(1)(b), the State Commission has ruled that a one-time $1 payment is the normal fee to which a landlord is entitled. *In the Matter of Implementation of Section 828 of the Executive Law*, No. 90004, Statement of General Policy (New York State Commission on Cable Television, Jan. 15, 1976) (Statement of General Policy), App. 51-52; Clarification of General Policy (Aug. 27, 1976), App. 68-69. The Commission ruled that this nominal fee, which the Commission concluded was equivalent to what the landlord would receive if the property were condemned pursuant to New York's Transportation Corporations Law, satisfied constitutional requirements "in the absence of a special showing of greater damages attributable to the taking." Statement of General Policy, App. 52.

Appellant did not discover the existence of the cable until after she had purchased the building. She brought a class action against Teleprompter in 1976 on behalf of all owners of real property in the State on which Teleprompter has placed CATV components, alleging that Teleprompter's installation was a trespass and, insofar as it relied on § 828, a taking without just compensation. She requested damages and injunctive relief.[4] Appellee City of New York, which has granted Teleprompter an exclusive franchise to provide CATV within certain areas of Manhattan, intervened. The Supreme Court, Special Term, granted summary judgment to Teleprompter and the city, upholding the constitutionality of § 828 in both crossover and noncrossover situations. The Appellate Division affirmed without opinion.

On appeal, the Court of Appeals, over dissent, upheld the statute. The court concluded that the law requires the landlord to allow both crossover and noncrossover installations but permits him to request payment from the CATV company under § 828(1)(b), at a level determined by the State Cable Commission, only for noncrossovers. The court then ruled that the law serves a legitimate police power purpose—eliminating landlord fees and conditions that inhibit the development of CATV, which has important educational and community benefits. Rejecting the argument that a physical occupation authorized by government is necessarily a taking, the court stated that the regulation does not have an excessive economic impact upon appellant when measured against her aggregate property rights, and that it does not interfere with any reasonable investment-backed expectations. Accordingly, the court held that § 828 does not work a taking of appellant's property. Chief Judge Cooke dissented, reasoning that the physical appropriation of a portion of appellant's property is a taking without regard to the balancing analysis courts ordinarily employ in evaluating whether a regulation is a taking.

In light of its holding, the Court of Appeals had no occasion to determine whether the $1 fee ordinarily awarded for a noncrossover installation was adequate compensation for the taking. Judge Gabrielli, concurring, agreed with the dissent that the law works a taking but concluded that the $1 presumptive award, together with the procedures permitting a landlord to demonstrate a greater entitlement, affords just compensation. We noted probable jurisdiction.

---

b. demand or accept payment from any tenant, in any form, in exchange for permitting cable television service on or within his property or premises, or from any cable television company in exchange therefor in excess of any amount which the commission shall, by regulation, determine to be reasonable; or

c. discriminate in rental charges, or otherwise, between tenants who receive cable television service and those who do not.

[4] Class-action status was granted in accordance with appellant's request, except that owners of single-family dwellings on which a CATV component had been placed were excluded. Notice to the class has been postponed, however, by stipulation.

II

The Court of Appeals determined that § 828 serves the legitimate public purpose of "rapid development of and maximum penetration by a means of communication which has important educational and community aspects," and thus is within the State's police power. We have no reason to question that determination. It is a separate question, however, whether an otherwise valid regulation so frustrates property rights that compensation must be paid. *See Penn Central Transportation Co. v. New York City*, 438 U.S. 104, 98 S. Ct. 2646, 57 L. Ed. 2d 631 (1978). We conclude that a permanent physical occupation authorized by government is a taking without regard to the public interests that it may serve. Our constitutional history confirms the rule, recent cases do not question it, and the purposes of the Takings Clause compel its retention.

A

In *Penn Central Transportation Co. v. New York City, supra*, the Court surveyed some of the general principles governing the Takings Clause. The Court noted that no "set formula" existed to determine, in all cases, whether compensation is constitutionally due for a government restriction of property. Ordinarily, the Court must engage in "essentially ad hoc, factual inquiries." But the inquiry is not standardless. The economic impact of the regulation, especially the degree of interference with investment-backed expectations, is of particular significance. "So, too, is the character of the governmental action. A 'taking' may more readily be found when the interference with property can be characterized as a physical invasion by government, than when interference arises from some public program adjusting the benefits and burdens of economic life to promote the common good."

As *Penn Central* affirms, the Court has often upheld substantial regulation of an owner's use of his own property where deemed necessary to promote the public interest. At the same time, we have long considered a physical intrusion by government to be a property restriction of an unusually serious character for purposes of the Takings Clause. Our cases further establish that when the physical intrusion reaches the extreme form of a permanent physical occupation, a taking has occurred. In such a case, "the character of the government action" not only is an important factor in resolving whether the action works a taking but also is determinative.

When faced with a constitutional challenge to a permanent physical occupation of real property, this Court has invariably found a taking.[5] As early as 1872, in *Pumpelly v. Green Bay Co.*, 13 Wall. (80 U.S.) 166, this Court held that the defendant's construction, pursuant to state authority, of a dam which permanently flooded plaintiff's property constituted a taking. A unanimous Court stated, without qualification, that "where real estate is actually invaded by superinduced additions of water, earth, sand, or other material, or by having any artificial structure placed on it, so as

---

[5] Professor Michelman has accurately summarized the case law concerning the role of the concept of physical invasions in the development of takings jurisprudence:

At one time it was commonly held that, in the absence of explicit expropriation, a compensable "taking" could occur *only* through physical encroachment and occupation. The modern significance of physical occupation is that courts, while they sometimes do hold nontrespassory injuries compensable, *never* deny compensation for a physical takeover. The one incontestable case for compensation (short of formal expropriation) seems to occur when the government deliberately brings it about that its agents, or the public at large, "regularly" use, or "permanently" occupy, space or a thing which theretofore was understood to be under private ownership.

Michelman, *Property, Utility, and Fairness: Comments on the Ethical Foundations of "Just Compensation" Law*, 80 Harv. L. Rev. 1165, 1184 (1967). . . .

to effectually destroy or impair its usefulness, it is a taking, within the meaning of the Constitution." . . .

Since these early cases, this Court has consistently distinguished between flooding cases involving a permanent physical occupation, on the one hand, and cases involving a more temporary invasion, or government action outside the owner's property that causes consequential damages within, on the other. A taking has always been found only in the former situation.[7] . . .

More recent cases confirm the distinction between a permanent physical occupation, a physical invasion short of an occupation, and a regulation that merely restricts the use of property. In *United States v. Causby*, 328 U.S. 256 (1946), the Court ruled that frequent flights immediately above a landowner's property constituted a taking, comparing such over flights to the quintessential form of a taking:

> If, by reason of the frequency and altitude of the flights, respondents could not use this land for any purpose, their loss would be complete. It would be as complete as if the United States had entered upon the surface of the land and taken exclusive possession of it.

As the Court further explained,

> We would not doubt that, if the United States erected an elevated railway over respondents' land at the precise altitude where its planes now fly, there would be a partial taking, even though none of the supports of the structure rested on the land. The reason is that there would be an intrusion so immediate and direct as to subtract from the owner's full enjoyment of the property and to limit his exploitation of it.

The Court concluded that the damages to the respondents "were not merely consequential. They were the product of a direct invasion of respondents' domain."

. . . .

Although this Court's most recent cases have not addressed the precise issue before us, they have emphasized that physical *invasion* cases are special and have not repudiated the rule that any permanent physical *occupation* is a taking. The cases state or imply that a physical invasion is subject to a balancing process, but they do not suggest that a permanent physical occupation would ever be exempt from the Takings Clause.

Penn Central Transportation Co. v. New York City, as noted above, contains one of the most complete discussions of the Takings Clause. The Court explained that resolving whether public action works a taking is ordinarily an ad hoc inquiry in which several factors are particularly significant—the economic impact of the regulation, the extent to which it interferes with investment-backed expectations, and the character of the governmental action. The opinion does not repudiate the rule that a permanent physical occupation is a government action of such a

---

[7] Early commentators viewed a physical occupation of real property as the quintessential deprivation of property. *See, e.g.,* 1 W. Blackstone, *Commentaries* 139; J. Lewis, *Law of Eminent Domain in the United States* 197 (1888) ("Any invasion of property, except in case of necessity . . ., either upon, above or below the surface, and whether temporary or permanent, is a *taking:* as by constructing a ditch through it, passing under it by a tunnel, laying gas, water or sewer pipes in the soil, or extending structures over it, as a bridge or telephone wire" (footnote omitted; emphasis in original)); 1 P. Nichols, *Law of Eminent Domain* 282 (2d ed. 1917).

unique character that it is a taking without regard to other factors that a court might ordinarily examine.[9]

. . . .

Another recent case underscores the constitutional distinction between a permanent occupation and a temporary physical invasion. In *PruneYard Shopping Center v. Robins*, 447 U.S. 74 (1980), the Court upheld a state constitutional requirement that shopping center owners permit individuals to exercise free speech and petition rights on their property, to which they had already invited the general public. The Court emphasized that the State Constitution does not prevent the owner from restricting expressive activities by imposing reasonable time, place, and manner restrictions to minimize interference with the owner's commercial functions. Since the invasion was temporary and limited in nature, and since the owner had not exhibited an interest in excluding all persons from his property, "the fact that [the solicitors] may have 'physically invaded' [the owners'] property cannot be viewed as determinative."[11]

. . . .

B

The historical rule that a permanent physical occupation of another's property is a taking has more than tradition to commend it. Such an appropriation is perhaps the most serious form of invasion of an owner's property interests. To borrow a metaphor, the government does not simply take a single "strand" from the "bundle" of property rights: it chops through the bundle, taking a slice of every strand.

Property rights in a physical thing have been described as the rights "to possess, use and dispose of it." *United States v. General Motors Corp.*, 323 U.S. 373, 378 (1945). To the extent that the government permanently occupies physical property, it effectively destroys *each* of these rights. First, the owner has no right to possess the occupied space himself, and also has no power to exclude the occupier from possession and use of the space. The power to exclude has traditionally been considered one of the most treasured strands in an owner's bundle of property rights.[12]

---

[9] The City of New York and the opinion of the Court of Appeals place great emphasis on *Penn Central's* reference to a physical invasion "by government," and argue that a similar invasion by a private party should be treated differently. We disagree. A permanent physical occupation authorized by state law is a taking without regard to whether the State, or instead a party authorized by the State, is the occupant. *See, e.g., Pumpelly v. Green Bay Co.*, 13 Wall. (80 U.S.) 166, 20 L. Ed. 557 (1872). Penn Central *simply holds that in cases of physical invasion short of permanent appropriation, the fact that the government itself commits an invasion from which it directly benefits is one relevant factor in determining whether a taking has occurred.*

[11] Teleprompter's reliance on labor cases requiring companies to permit access to union organizers, *see, e.g., Hudgens v. NLRB*, 424 U.S. 507 (1976); *Central Hardware Co. v. NLRB*, 407 U.S. 539 (1972); *NLRB v. Babcock & Wilcox Co.*, 351 U.S. 105 (1956), is similarly misplaced. As we recently explained:

[T]he allowed intrusion on property rights is limited to that necessary to facilitate the exercise of employees' § 7 rights [to organize under the National Labor Relations Act]. After the requisite need for access to the employer's property has been shown, the access is limited to (i) union organizers; (ii) prescribed nonworking areas of the employer's premises; and (iii) the duration of the organization activity. In short, the principle of accommodation announced in *Babcock* is limited to labor organization campaigns, and the "yielding" of property rights it may require is both temporary and limited.

Central Hardware Co., supra, at 545, 92 S.Ct., at 2242.

[12] The permanence and absolute exclusivity of a physical occupation distinguish it from temporary limitations on the right to exclude. Not every physical *invasion* is a taking. As *PruneYard Shopping Center v. Robins*, 447 U.S.

Second, the permanent physical occupation of property forever denies the owner any power to control the use of the property; he not only cannot exclude others, but can make no nonpossessory use of the property. Although deprivation of the right to use and obtain a profit from property is not, in every case, independently sufficient to establish a taking, it is clearly relevant. Finally, even though the owner may retain the bare legal right to dispose of the occupied space by transfer or sale, the permanent occupation of that space by a stranger will ordinarily empty the right of any value, since the purchaser will also be unable to make any use of the property.

Moreover, an owner suffers a special kind of injury when a *stranger* directly invades and occupies the owner's property. As Part II-A, *supra*, indicates, property law has long protected an owner's expectation that he will be relatively undisturbed at least in the possession of his property. To require, as well, that the owner permit another to exercise complete dominion literally adds insult to injury. *See* Michelman, *Property, Utility, and Fairness: Comments on the Ethical Foundations of "Just Compensation" Law*, 80 Harv. L. Rev. 1165, 1228, and n. 110 (1967). Furthermore, such an occupation is qualitatively more severe than a regulation of the *use* of property, even a regulation that imposes affirmative duties on the owner, since the owner may have no control over the timing, extent, or nature of the invasion.

The traditional rule also avoids otherwise difficult line-drawing problems. Few would disagree that if the State required landlords to permit third parties to install swimming pools on the landlords' rooftops for the convenience of the tenants, the requirement would be a taking. If the cable installation here occupied as much space, again, few would disagree that the occupation would be a taking. But constitutional protection for the rights of private property cannot be made to depend on the size of the area permanently occupied. Indeed, it is possible that in the future, additional cable installations that more significantly restrict a landlord's use of the roof of his building will be made. Section 828 requires a landlord to permit such multiple installations.[14]

Finally, whether a permanent physical occupation has occurred present relatively few problems of proof. The placement of a fixed structure on land or real property is an obvious fact that will rarely be subject to dispute. Once the fact of occupation is shown, of course, a court should consider the *extent* of the occupation as one relevant factor in determining the compensation due.[15] For that reason, moreover, there is less need to consider the extent of the occupation in determining whether there is a taking in the first instance.

---

74 (1980); *Kaiser Aetna v. United States*, 444 U.S. 164 (1979), and the intermittent flooding cases reveal, such temporary limitations are subject to a more complex balancing process to determine whether they are a taking. The rationale is evident: they do not absolutely dispossess the owner of his rights to use, and exclude others from, his property.

The dissent objects that the distinction between a permanent physical occupation and a temporary invasion will not always be clear. This objection is overstated, and in any event is irrelevant to the critical point that a permanent physical occupation *is* unquestionably a taking. In the antitrust area, similarly, this Court has not declined to apply a *per se* rule simply because a court must, at the boundary of the rule, apply the rule of reason and engage in a more complex balancing analysis.

[14] Although the City of New York has granted an exclusive franchise to Teleprompter, it is not required to do so under state law, *see* N.Y. Exec. Law § 811 *et seq.* (McKinney Supp. 1981-1982), and future changes in technology may cause the city to reconsider its decision. Indeed, at present some communities apparently grant nonexclusive franchises. Brief for National Satellite Cable Association *et al.* as *Amici Curiae* 21.

[15] In this case, the Court of Appeals noted testimony preceding the enactment of § 828 that the landlord's interest in excluding cable installation "consists entirely of insisting that some negligible unoccupied space remain unoccupied." The State Cable Commission referred to the same testimony in establishing a $1 presumptive award. Statement of General Policy, App. 48.

C

Teleprompter's cable installation on appellant's building constitutes a taking under the traditional test. The installation involved a direct physical attachment of plates, boxes, wires, bolts, and screws to the building, completely occupying space immediately above and upon the roof and along the building's exterior wall.[16]

In light of our analysis, we find no constitutional difference between a crossover and a noncrossover installation. The portions of the installation necessary for both crossovers and noncrossovers permanently appropriate appellant's property. Accordingly, each type of installation is a taking.

Appellees raise a series of objections to application of the traditional rule here. Teleprompter notes that the law applies only to buildings used as rental property, and draws the conclusion that the law is simply a permissible regulation of the use of real property. We fail to see, however, why a physical occupation of one type of property but not another type is any less a physical occupation. Insofar as Teleprompter means to suggest that this is not a permanent physical invasion, we must differ. So long as the property remains residential and a CATV company wishes to retain the installation, the landlord must permit it.[17]

Teleprompter also asserts the related argument that the State has effectively granted a tenant the property right to have a CATV installation placed on the roof of his building, as an appurtenance to the tenant's leasehold. The short answer is that § 828(1)(a) does not purport to give the *tenant* any enforceable property rights with respect to CATV installation, and the lower courts did not rest their decisions on this ground.[18] Of course, Teleprompter, not appellant's

---

A number of the dissent's arguments—that § 828 "likely increases both the building's resale value and its attractiveness on the rental market," and that appellant might have no alternative use for the cable-occupied space—may also be relevant to the amount of compensation due. It should be noted, however, that the first argument is speculative and is contradicted by appellant's testimony that she and "the whole block" would be able to sell their buildings for a higher price absent the installation. App. 100.

[16] It is constitutionally irrelevant whether appellant (or her predecessor in title) had previously occupied this space, since a "landowner owns at least as much of the space above the ground as he can occupy or use in connection with the land." *United States v. Causby, supra,* at 264.

The dissent asserts that a taking of about one-eighth of a cubic foot of space is not of constitutional significance. The assertion appears to be factually incorrect, since it ignores the two large silver boxes that appellant identified as part of the installation. App. 90; Loretto Affidavit in Support of Motion for Summary Judgment (Apr. 21, 1978), Appellants' Appendix in No. 8300/76 (N.Y. App.), p. 77. Although the record does not reveal their size, appellant states that they are approximately 18" x 2" x 6", Brief for Appellant 6 n.*, and appellees do not dispute this statement. The displaced volume, then, is in excess of 1 1\2 cubic feet. In any event, these facts are not critical: whether the installation is a taking does not depend on whether the volume of space it occupies is bigger than a bread box.

[17] It is true that the landlord could avoid the requirements of § 828 by ceasing to rent the building to tenants. But a landlord's ability to rent his property may not be conditioned on his forfeiting the right to compensation for a physical occupation. Teleprompter's broad "use-dependency" argument proves too much. For example, it would allow the government to require a landlord to devote a substantial portion of his building to vending and washing machines, with all profits to be retained by the owners of these services and with no compensation for the deprivation of space. It would even allow the government to requisition a certain number of apartments as permanent government offices. The right of a property owner to exclude a stranger's physical occupation of his land cannot be so easily manipulated.

[18] We also decline to hazard an opinion as to the respective rights of the landlord and tenant under state law *prior* to enactment of § 828 to use the space occupied by the cable installation, an issue over which the parties sharply disagree.

tenants, actually owns the installation. Moreover, the government does not have unlimited power to redefine property rights. . . .

Finally, we do not agree with appellees that application of the physical occupation rule will have dire consequences for the government's power to adjust landlord-tenant relationships. This Court has consistently affirmed that States have broad power to regulate housing conditions in general and the landlord-tenant relationship in particular without paying compensation for all economic injuries that such regulation entails. . . . Consequently, our holding today in no way alters the analysis governing the State's power to require landlords to comply with building codes and provide utility connections, mailboxes, smoke detectors, fire extinguishers, and the like in the common area of a building. So long as these regulations do not require the landlord to suffer the physical occupation of a portion of his building by a third party, they will be analyzed under the multifactor inquiry generally applicable to nonpossessory governmental activity. *See Penn Central Transportation Co. v. New York City*, 438 U.S. 104, 98 S. Ct. 2646, 57 L. Ed. 2d 631 (1978).

III

Our holding today is very narrow. We affirm the traditional rule that a permanent physical occupation of property is a taking. In such a case, the property owner entertains a historically rooted expectation of compensation, and the character of the invasion is qualitatively more intrusive than perhaps any other category of property regulation. We do not, however, question the equally substantial authority upholding a State's broad power to impose appropriate restrictions upon an owner's *use* of his property.

Furthermore, our conclusion that § 828 works a taking of a portion of appellant's property does not presuppose that the fee which many landlords had obtained from Teleprompter prior to the law's enactment is a proper measure of the value of the property taken. The issue of the amount of compensation that is due, on which we express no opinion, is a matter for the state courts to consider on remand.

The judgment of the New York Court of Appeals is reversed, and the case is remanded for further proceedings not inconsistent with this opinion.

It is so ordered.

JUSTICE; BLACKMUN with whom JUSTICE BRENNAN and JUSTICE WHITE join, dissenting. . . .

In a curiously anachronistic decision, the Court today acknowledges its historical disavowal of set formulae in almost the same breath as it constructs a rigid *per se* takings rule: "a permanent physical occupation authorized by government is a taking without regard to the public interest that it may serve." To sustain its rule against our recent precedents, the Court erects a strained and untenable distinction between "temporary physical invasions," whose constitutionality concededly "is subject to a balancing process," and "permanent physical occupations," which are "taking[s] without regard to other factors that a court might ordinarily examine."

In my view, the Court's approach "reduces the constitutional issue to a formalistic quibble" over whether property has been "permanently occupied" or "temporarily invaded." Sax, *Takings and the Police Power*, 74 Yale L.J. 36, 37 (1964). The Court's application of its formula to the facts of this case vividly illustrates that its approach is potentially dangerous as well as misguided. Despite its concession that "States have broad power to regulate . . . the landlord-tenant relationship . . . without paying compensation for all economic injuries that such regulation entails," the Court uses its rule to undercut a carefully considered legislative judgment concerning landlord-tenant relationships. I therefore respectfully dissent.

I

Before examining the Court's new takings rule, it is worth reviewing what was "taken" in this case. At issue are about 36 feet of cable one-half inch in diameter and two 4" x 4" x 4" metal boxes. Jointly, the cable and boxes occupy only about one-eighth of a cubic foot of space on the roof of appellant's Manhattan apartment building. When appellant purchased that building in 1971, the "physical invasion" she now challenges had already occurred.[2] Appellant did not bring this action until about five years later, demanding 5% of appellee Teleprompter's gross revenues from her building, and claiming that the operation of N.Y. Exec. Law § 828 (McKinney Supp. 1981-1982) "took" her property. The New York Supreme Court, the Appellate Division, and the New York Court of Appeals all rejected that claim, upholding § 828 as a valid exercise of the State's police power.

The Court of Appeals held that

the State may proscribe a trespass action by landlords generally against a cable TV company which places a cable and other fixtures on the roof of any landlord's building, in order to protect the right of the tenants of rental property, who will ultimately have to pay any charge a landlord is permitted to collect from the cable TV company, to obtain TV service in their respective apartments.

In so ruling, the court applied the multi-factor balancing test prescribed by this Court's recent Takings Clause decisions.

. . . .

II

Given that the New York Court of Appeals' straightforward application of this Court's balancing test yielded a finding of no taking, it becomes clear why the Court now constructs a *per se* rule to reverse. The Court can escape the result dictated by our recent takings cases only by resorting to bygone precedents and arguing that "permanent physical occupations" somehow differ qualitatively from all other forms of government regulation.

. . . .

---

[2] In January 1968, appellee Teleprompter signed a 5-year installation agreement with the building's previous owner in exchange for a flat fee of $50. Appellee installed both the 30-foot main cable and its 4-to 6-foot "crossover" extension in June 1970. For two years after taking possession of the building and the appurtenant equipment, appellant did not object to the cable's presence. Indeed, despite numerous inspections, appellant had never even noticed the equipment until Teleprompter first began to provide cable television service to one of her tenants. Nor did appellant thereafter ever specifically ask Teleprompter to remove the components from her building. App. 107, 108, 110.

Although the Court alludes to the presence of "two large silver boxes" on appellant's roof, the New York Court of Appeals' opinion nowhere mentions them, nor are their dimensions stated anywhere in the record.

A

The Court's recent Takings Clause decisions teach that *nonphysical* government intrusions on private property, such as zoning ordinances and other land-use restrictions, have become the rule rather than the exception. Modern government regulation exudes intangible "externalities" that may diminish the value of private property far more than minor physical touchings. Nevertheless, as the Court recognizes, it has often upheld substantial regulation of an owner's use of his own property where deemed necessary to promote the public interest.

Precisely because the extent to which the government may injure private interests now depends so little on whether or not it has authorized a "physical contact," the Court has avoided *per se* takings rules resting on outmoded distinctions between physical and nonphysical intrusions. As one commentator has observed, a takings rule based on such a distinction is inherently suspect because "its capacity to distinguish, even crudely, between significant and insignificant losses is too puny to be taken seriously." Michelman, *Property, Utility, and Fairness: Comments on the Ethical Foundations of "Just Compensation" Law*, 80 Harv. L. Rev. 1165, 1227 (1967).

Surprisingly, the Court draws an even finer distinction today—between "temporary physical invasions" and "permanent physical occupations." When the government authorizes the latter type of intrusion, the Court would find "a taking without regard to the public interests" the regulation may serve. Yet an examination of each of the three words in the Court's "permanent physical occupation" formula illustrates that the newly-created distinction is even less substantial than the distinction between physical and nonphysical intrusions that the Court already has rejected.

First, what does the Court mean by "permanent"? Since all "temporary limitations on the right to exclude" remain "subject to a more complex balancing process to determine whether they are a taking," the Court presumably describes a government intrusion that lasts forever. But as the Court itself concedes, § 828 does not require appellant to permit the cable installation forever, but only "[s]o long as the property remains residential and a CATV company wishes to retain the installation." This is far from "permanent."

The Court reaffirms that "States have broad power to regulate housing conditions in general and the landlord-tenant relationship in particular without paying compensation for all economic injuries that such regulation entails." Thus, § 828 merely defines one of the many statutory responsibilities that a New Yorker accepts when she enters the rental business. If appellant occupies her own building, or converts it into a commercial property, she becomes perfectly free to exclude Teleprompter from her one-eighth cubic foot of roof space. But once appellant chooses to use her property for rental purposes, she must comply with all reasonable government statutes regulating the landlord-tenant relationship. If § 828 authorizes a "permanent" occupation, and thus works a taking "without regard to the public interests that it may serve," then all other New York statutes that require a landlord to make physical attachments to his rental property also must constitute takings, even if they serve indisputably valid public interests in tenant protection and safety.[7]

---

[7] *See e.g.*, N.Y. Mult. Dwell. Law § 35 (McKinney 1974) (requiring entrance doors and lights); § 36 (windows and skylights for public halls and stairs); § 50-a (Supp. 1982) (locks and intercommunication systems); § 50-c (lobby attendants); § 51-a (peepholes); § 51-b (elevator mirrors); § 53 (fire escapes); § 57 (bells and mail receptacles); § 67(3) (fire sprinklers). *See also Queenside Hills Realty Co. v. Saxl*, 328 U.S. 80, 66 S. Ct. 850, 90 L. Ed. 1096 (1946) (upholding constitutionality of New York fire sprinkler provision).

The Court denies that its theory invalidates these statutes, because they "do not require the landlord to suffer the physical occupation of a portion of his building by a third party." But surely this factor cannot be determinative, since the Court simultaneously recognizes that temporary invasions by third parties are not subject to a *per se* rule. Nor can the qualitative difference arise from the incidental fact that, under § 828, Teleprompter, rather than appellant or her tenants, owns the cable installation. If anything, § 828 leaves appellant better off than do other housing statutes, since it ensures that her property will not be damaged esthetically or physically without burdening her with the cost of buying or maintaining the cable.

In any event, under the Court's test, the "third party" problem would remain even if appellant herself owned the cable. So long as Teleprompter continuously passed its electronic signal through the cable, a litigant could argue that the second element of the Court's formula—a "physical touching" by a stranger—was satisfied and that § 828 therefore worked a taking.[8] Literally read, the Court's test opens the door to endless metaphysical struggles over whether or not an individual's property has been "physically" touched. It was precisely to avoid permitting technicalities of form to dictate consequences of substance, that the Court abandoned a "physical contacts" test in the first place.

Third, the Court's talismanic distinction between a continuous "occupation" and a transient "invasion" finds no basis in either economic logic or Takings Clause precedent. In the landlord-tenant context, the Court has upheld against takings challenges rent control statutes permitting "temporary" physical invasions of considerable economic magnitude. . . . Moreover, precedents record numerous other "temporary" officially authorized invasions by third parties that have intruded into an owner's enjoyment of property far more deeply than did Teleprompter's long-unnoticed cable. *See, e.g., PruneYard Shopping Center v. Robins*, 447 U.S. 74, 100 S. Ct. 2035, 64 L. Ed. 2d 741 (1980) (leafletting and demonstrating in busy shopping center). . . .

In sum, history teaches that takings claims are properly evaluated under a multifactor balancing test. By directing that all "permanent physical occupations" automatically are compensable, "without regard to whether the action achieves an important public benefit or has only minimal economic impact on the owner," the Court does not further equity so much as it encourages litigants to manipulate their factual allegations to gain the benefit of its *per se* rule. I do not relish the prospect of distinguishing the inevitable flow of certiorari petitions attempting to shoehorn insubstantial takings claims into today's "set formula."

These statutes specify in far greater detail than § 828 what types of physical facilities a New York landlord must provide his tenants and where he must provide them. *See, e.g.* N.Y. Mult. Dwell. Law § 75 (McKinney 1974) (owners of multiple dwellings must provide "proper appliances to receive and distribute an adequate supply of water," including "a proper sink with running water and with a two-inch waste and trap"); § 35 (owners of multiple dwellings with frontage exceeding 22 feet must provide "at least two lights, one at each side of the entrance way, with an aggregate illumination of one hundred fifty watts or equivalent illumination"); § 50-a(2) (Supp. 1981-1982) (owners of Class A multiple dwellings must provide intercommunication system "located at an automatic self-locking door giving public access to the main entrance hall or lobby").

Apartment building rooftops are not exempted. *See* § 62 (landlords must place parapet walls and guardrails on their roofs "three feet six inches or more in height above the level of such area").

[8] Indeed, appellant's counsel made precisely this claim at oral argument. Urging the rule which the Court now adopts, appellant's counsel suggested that a taking would result even if appellant owned the cable. "[T]he precise location of the easement [taken by Teleprompter changes] from the surface of the roof to inside the wire. . . . [T]he wire itself is owned by the landlord, but the cable company has the right to pass its signal through the wire without compensation to the landlord, for its commercial benefit." Tr. of Oral Arg. 15.

B

Setting aside history, the Court also states that the permanent physical occupation authorized by § 828 is a *per se* taking because it uniquely impairs appellant's powers to dispose of, use, and exclude others from, her property. In fact, the Court's discussion nowhere demonstrates how § 828 impairs these private rights in a manner *qualitatively* different from other garden-variety landlord-tenant legislation.

The Court first contends that the statute impairs appellant's legal right to dispose of cable-occupied space by transfer and sale. But that claim dissolves after a moment's reflection. If someone buys appellant's apartment building, but does not use it for rental purposes, that person can have the cable removed, and use the space as he wishes. In such a case, appellant's right to dispose of the space is worth just as much as if § 828 did not exist.

Even if another landlord buys appellant's building for rental purposes, § 828 does not render the cable-occupied space valueless. As a practical matter, the regulation ensures that tenants living in the building will have access to cable television for as long as that building is used for rental purposes, and thereby likely increases both the building's resale value and its attractiveness on the rental market.[9]

In any event, § 828 differs little from the numerous other New York statutory provisions that require landlords to install physical facilities "permanently occupying" common spaces in or on their buildings. As the Court acknowledges, the States traditionally—and constitutionally—have exercised their police power "to require landlords to . . . provide utility connections, mailboxes, smoke detectors, fire extinguishers, and the like in the common area of a building." Like § 828, these provisions merely ensure tenants access to services the legislature deems important, such as water, electricity, natural light, telephones, intercommunication systems, and mail service. A landlord's dispositional rights are affected no more adversely when he sells a building to another landlord subject to § 828, than when he sells that building subject only to these other New York statutory provisions.

The Court also suggests that § 828 unconstitutionally alters appellant's right to control the *use* of her one-eighth cubic foot of roof space. But other New York multiple dwelling statutes not only oblige landlords to surrender significantly larger portions of common space for their tenants' use, but also compel the *landlord*—rather than the tenants or the private installers—to pay for and to maintain the equipment. For example, New York landlords are required by law to provide and pay for mailboxes that occupy more than five times the volume that Teleprompter's cable occupies on appellant's building. If the State constitutionally can insist that appellant make this sacrifice so that her tenants may receive mail, it is hard to understand why the State may not require her to surrender less space, *filled at another's expense*, so that those same tenants can receive television signals.

For constitutional purposes, the relevant question cannot be solely *whether* the State has interfered in some minimal way with an owner's use of space on her building. Any intelligible takings inquiry must also ask whether the *extent* of the State's interference is so severe as to constitute a compensable taking in light of the owner's alternative uses for the property.[10]

---

[9] In her pretrial deposition, appellant conceded not only that owners of other apartment buildings thought that the cable's presence had enhanced the market value of their buildings, App. 102-103, but also that her own tenants would have been upset if the cable connection had been removed. *Id.*, at 107, 108, 110.

[10] For this reason, the Court provides no support for its *per se* rule by asserting that the State could not require

Appellant freely admitted that she would have had no other use for the cable-occupied space, were Teleprompter's equipment not on her building.

The Court's third and final argument is that § 828 has deprived appellant of her "power to exclude the occupier from possession and use of the space" occupied by the cable. This argument has two flaws. First, it unjustifiably assumes that appellant's tenants have no countervailing property interest in permitting Teleprompter to use that space.[11] Second, it suggests that the New York Legislature may not exercise its police power to affect appellant's common-law right to exclude Teleprompter even from one-eighth cubic foot of roof space. But this Court long ago recognized that new social circumstances can justify legislative modification of a property owner's common-law rights, without compensation, if the legislative action serves sufficiently important public interests.

. . . .

III

In the end, what troubles me most about today's decision is that it represents an archaic judicial response to a modern social problem. Cable television is a new and growing, but somewhat controversial, communications medium. . . . The New York Legislature not only recognized, but also responded to, this technological advance by enacting a statute that sought carefully to balance the interests of all private parties. New York's courts in this litigation, with only one jurist in dissent, unanimously upheld the constitutionality of that considered legislative judgment.

This Court now reaches back in time for a *per se* rule that disrupts that legislative determination.[12] Like Justice Black, I believe that "the solution of the problems precipitated by . . . technological advances and new ways of living cannot come about through the application of rigid constitutional restraints formulated and enforced by the courts." *United States v. Causby*, 328 U.S., at 274, 66 S.Ct., at 1072 (dissenting opinion). I would affirm the judgment and uphold the reasoning of the New York Court of Appeals.

---

landlords, without compensation, "to permit third parties to install swimming pools," or vending and washing machines, for the convenience of tenants. Presumably, these more intrusive government regulations would create difficult takings problems even under our traditional balancing approach. Depending on the character of the governmental action, its economic impact, and the degree to which it interfered with an owner's reasonable investment-backed expectations, among other things, the Court's hypothetical examples might or might not constitute takings. These examples hardly prove, however, that a permanent physical occupation that works a *de minimis* interference with a private property interest is a taking *per se.*

[11] It is far from clear that, under New York law, appellant's tenants would lack all property interests in the few square inches on the exterior of the building to which Teleprompter's cable and hardware attach. Under modern landlord-tenant law, a residential tenancy is not merely a possessory interest in specified space, but also a contract for the provision of a package of services and facilities necessary and appurtenant to that space. *See* R. Schoshinski, *American Law of Landlord and Tenant* § 3:14 (1980). A modern urban tenant's leasehold often includes not only contractual, but also statutory rights, including the rights to an implied warranty of habitability, rent control, and such services as the landlord is obliged by statute to provide.

[12] Happily, the Court leaves open the question whether § 828 provides landlords like appellant sufficient compensation for their actual losses. Since the State Cable Television Commission's regulations permit higher than nominal awards if a landlord makes "a special showing of greater damages," App. 52, the concurring opinion in the New York Court of Appeals found that the statute awards just compensation. ("[I]t is obvious that a landlord who actually incurs damage to his property or is restricted in the use to which he might put that property will receive compensation commensurate with the greater injury.") If, after the remand following today's decision, this minor physical invasion is declared to be a taking deserving little or no compensation, the net result will have been a large expenditure of judicial resources on a constitutional claim of little moment.

[3] Explanatory Notes

[a] Events After Remand

After the Supreme Court decision in *Loretto*, the case was remanded to the New York Court of Appeals. They, in turn, sent the dispute back to the New York State Cable Television Commission with instructions to hold fact finding hearings on the amount of compensation that property owners with cable wiring equipment on their buildings should receive.[47] The right to seek compensation has not been frequently invoked. The Cable Television Commission has continued to operate on the presumption that $1.00 is an appropriate award to a landlord for a cable television hookup.[48] That presumption was followed when the *Loretto* dispute was reviewed by the Commission. The award of $1.00 was appealed to the New York State courts, which affirmed the small payment in unpublished opinions.[49]

Despite the theoretical importance of the Supreme Court's *Loretto* opinion, it has had virtually no impact on cable regulation in New York. The prospect of individual compensation proceedings for each property owner has made it extremely unlikely that property owners will routinely seek compensation. Not only must they prove that a *valuable* asset has been taken, but they must also pay the legal and other fees to obtain a hearing. The property owners originally hoped that the entire matter could be taken care of in one case. *Loretto* was filed as a class action. The property owners attempted to convince the courts that the liability issue was the same for all property owners, and that the level of required compensation could be determined on a basis immediately applicable to all. The Supreme Court noted that prior to the adoption of § 828, many property owners received payments of 5% of the cable TV revenues generated by tenant hookups on their property as payment for permission to install the cable equipment.[50] That was the measure of relief sought by the plaintiffs as a class in *Loretto*. Once the case was sent back for individual hearings on the value of the property "taken" by § 828, it became unprofitable for most owners to undertake a multitude of administrative and judicial proceedings. The costs of such hearings far outweighed any benefits the owners might ultimately receive. Loretto won the battle and lost the war. The careful statements at the end of Justice Marshall's majority opinion emphasizing that damages were yet to be determined suggests that the Justices knew they were deciding a case where the amounts in issue were small. Given the variety of important cases the Court must decide each year, one wonders why they decided to review *Loretto* at all.

[b] Academic Reaction to *Loretto*

Despite the apparent insignificance of *Loretto* to the residents of New York, the case caused a major stir in the legal academy. Most of the commentary was critical. The Court's reasoning

---

[47] Loretto v. Teleprompter Manhattan CATV Corp., 58 N.Y.2d 143, 446 N.E.2d 428 (1983).

[48] Telephone Interview with Anne Dalton, Cable Television Municipal Consultant, Commission on Cable Television of the City of New York (July 2, 1987). For the first 10 years of cable regulation in the state, no one applied for compensation. In the last few years, a handful of applications have been filed. Only one landlord is known to have received an award larger than $1.00, but that award involved payment for damages done to the building when the equipment was installed.

[49] Telephone Interview with Michael Gruen, Counsel to Jean Loretto (June 11, 1987). Loretto herself no longer owns the building, but she does retain an interest in the litigation. As an aside, Michael Gruen is the same Michael Gruen involved in *Gruen v. Gruen*, p. 243 above.

[50] Prior to the *Loretto* litigation, Teleprompter tried to get owners to sign a standard form five year contract which bound the owners to the 5% fee along with a $5.00 one-time hookup fee each time a tenant subscribed to the service. Joint Appendix Filed in the United States Supreme Court in *Loretto v. Teleprompter*, at 32 (1981).

was deemed to be out of character with Supreme Court precedent. The century had never witnessed a *per se* rule requiring compensation in any land use regulatory setting. Justice Marshall's authorship of the opinion surprised many. The labeling of Michelman's summary of the physical invasion cases as an accurate summary (see footnote 5) without any further comments about his unwillingness to use them as a basis for establishing a bright line test was seen as disingenuous. And, finally, the failure of the Court to speak to the interests of tenants in the outcome of the case was said to be strange at best and wrong-headed at worst. Here is a brief sample of the last form of critique, taken from an article by John Costonis, *Presumptive and Per Se Takings: A Decisional Model for the Taking Issue*, 58 N.Y.U. L. REV. 465 516-518 (1983).*

In the Court's view, *Loretto* was a simple two-class affair which pitted the right of landlords to exclude (conceived of largely in terms of the dominion interest) against the right of "strangers," the cable companies, to enter and place their "property" for profit upon landlords' "property." The . . . inquiry would suggest instead that section 828 benefited two other classes—tenants and cable service subscribers generally—and that the New York legislature intentionally subordinated the interests of cable companies to those of tenants and cable subscribers. The statute regulates landlord-tenant relations by preventing landlords from obstructing tenants' receipt of cable television and thereby facilitates the development of a medium which promises important communications and education benefits to tenants and to other cable subscribers statewide. While obviously essential to this scheme, the access rights that section 828 grants to cable companies are but a means to these ends, not ends in themselves.

Moreover, contrary to the Court's portrayal, the class of "property" burdened is apartment buildings, not cable-occupied space. This class of property is unique in two ways: the manner in which rights, including the right to exclude outsiders, are held in it, and the legal relationship between the owners and occupants of the building. At to the first, rights of exclusion are *already* divided between landlords and tenants. Tenants hold both exclusive possessory rights to their apartments (which generally make up most of the building's interior) and nonexclusive easements to many of the building's interior and exterior common spaces. Section 828 simply enlarged the nonexclusive easements of tenants to include cable-occupied space as an additional appurtenance to the leaseholds of the tenants. To characterize the cable companies as "strangers" to the landlords' "property," therefore, is to misunderstand the three-cornered relationship among landlords, tenants, and cable companies envisaged by the legislature. Under the legislative scheme, cable companies were acting as tenants' business invitees; their access rights to the cable-occupied space were derivative of and subordinate to the tenants' access to this same space.

[c]   Permanent Occupation Versus Temporary Physical Invasion

In his majority opinion in *Loretto*, Justice Marshall drew a line between permanent occupations and temporary physical invasions, claiming that takings arise after the former but not the latter. He distinguished a number of cases from the situation in *Loretto*, including *Hudgens v. N.L.R.B.*, 424 U.S. 507 (1976) and *PruneYard Shopping Center v. Robins*, 447 U.S. 74 (1980). *Hudgens* is discussed at p. 572 above in the notes after *Shack v. State of New Jersey*. Both *Hudgens* and *PruneYard* involved claims by shopping center owners that they had the right to eject picketers from their establishments. While the Supreme Court held in *Hudgens* that the state action

---

* Reprinted with permission of the New York University Law Review and the author.

requirement barred use of the First Amendment to protect labor picketers on private property, later proceedings under federal labor laws provided similar safeguards for the demonstrators. The owners of the PruneYard Shopping Center brought an action claiming that holdings of the California courts invoking state constitutional provisions to bar eviction of picketers from areas normally open to the public constituted a Taking of property in violation of the Fifth Amendment to the United States Constitution.

Justice Rehnquist, writing for the majority in *PruneYard*, admitted that "one of the essential sticks in the bundle of property rights is the right to exclude others," but concluded that state protection of free expression in shopping centers "clearly does not amount to an unconstitutional infringement of appellants' property rights under the Taking Clause. There is nothing to suggest that preventing appellants from prohibiting this sort of activity will unreasonably impair the value or use of their property as a shopping center." Justice Marshall joined in Justice Rehnquist's opinion and added a separate concurrence of his own. Marshall noted his continued disagreement with the holding of *Hudgens* that trespass convictions of those picketing on private land open to the public did not involve state action. He went on to note that PruneYard's argument amounted:

> to no less than a suggestion that the common law of trespass is not subject to revision by the State, notwithstanding the California Supreme Court's finding that state-created rights of expressive activity would be severely hindered if shopping centers were closed to expressive activities by members of the public. If accepted, that claim would represent a return to the era of *Lochner v. New York*, 198 U.S. 45 (1905), when common law rights were also found immune from revision by State or Federal Government. Such an approach would freeze the common law as it has been constructed by the courts, perhaps at its 19th century state of development. It would allow no room for change in response to changes in circumstance. The Due Process Clause does not require such a result.

In *Loretto*, Justice Marshall distinguished *PruneYard*, claiming that the intrusion into the shopping center was "temporary and limited in nature," that "the owner had not exhibited an interest in excluding all persons from the property," and that the physical invasion by the picketers was therefore not determinative.

Justice Marshall was certainly correct that the picketers in *PruneYard* were not always present, while the cable television boxes were continually attached to the roof of Loretto's apartment building. But can that be the determining factor in the outcome of the case? After all, property typically is not defined by the presence or absence of people or objects in particular places, but by the existence of rights to do things on or use property in certain ways. An easement, or servitude as we are beginning to say, creating a right of way over the land of another exists regardless of whether a person happens to be in the right of way at any particular moment. So one way of thinking about *PruneYard* is that the state of California requires the owners of shopping centers to permanently dedicate to the public an easement in their passage ways for use by those carrying picket signs in ways that do not disrupt the normal commercial operation of the establishment. If viewed that way, *PruneYard* arguably involved a much more significant permanent physical invasion than *Loretto*. In short, the only way to make any sense of the *Loretto* outcome is to focus on the physical presence of objects, not the standard ways in which people think about the meaning of interests in property.

[d]   Another Example of *Loretto*-Style Takings Analysis

Hodel v. Irving, 481 U.S. 704 (1987), involved § 207 of the Indian Land Consolidation Act of 1983 which provided that an undivided fractional interest in any tract of land within a reservation escheated to the tribe "if such interest represents 2 per centum or less of the total acreage in such tract and has earned to its owner less than $100 in the preceding year before it is due to escheat." The statute was adopted to ameliorate the impact of widespread fragmented ownership of lands distributed in the end of the nineteenth century under the Allotment Acts.[51] By the 1960s, 12 million acres were held in fractionated ownership with over a quarter of this land held by more than six heirs. One example cited by the court involved a tract of 40 acres worth $8,000 producing $1,080 of annual income with 439 owners, two thirds of whom received less than $1.00 per year. The largest owner received $82.85 annually, the smallest received one cent every 177 years. The Court recognized that Congress had a strong and valid interest in merging such fractionated land holdings. But it found that the total abolition of both testate and intestate succession rights constituted a taking, regardless of the value of the share to be escheated.[52] Too many sticks were taken from the property bundle, the Court opined. The Justices did suggest, however, that Congress could limit intestate succession rights to certain fractional interests, or establish procedures for the escheat of unclaimed interests.

[4]   Problem Note: Permanent Physical Occupation

Are any of the following situations covered by the "permanent physical occupation" test of *Loretto*:

(a) A building code requirement that every housing unit contain at least 150 square feet for each occupant.

(b) A building code requirement that every housing unit contain a bathroom.

(c) A building code requirement that at least one operating smoke detector be installed by property owners on each floor of every house, in each unit in an apartment building, and in public areas on each floor of every apartment building.

(d) A zoning regulation forbidding all construction more than 20 feet above grade in an area extending one-half mile from the end of an airport runway.

(e) A zoning regulation covering a steep hillside residential area imposing strict height limitations so that every house has a majestic view down to the valley floor.

(f) A regulation adopted for aesthetic reasons covering only historic districts forbidding the installation of any television dish antennae.

(g) A housing code section prohibiting any house in a two acre single family residential zone from occupying more than 25% of the square footage of any lot.

(h) A statute covering coastal zones requiring that anyone owning a parcel within 100 yards of the ocean must set aside a 3 foot wide walking area running from the sand beach to the nearest access road for use by members of the public wishing to gain access to the beach. This setting is similar to that in *Nollan v. Coastal Commission*, p. 1004 below.

---

[51] These acts are discussed at p. 49 above.

[52] Justices Stevens and White concurred, but only on the theory that the statute provided inadequate notice and hearing rights prior to the escheat of potentially abandoned property.

(i) A state court decision, like that in *New Jersey v. Shack*, p. 557 above, requiring a farm owner, or any other property owner, to let reporters, lawyers, doctors, priests and teachers visit resident employees during non-working hours.

(j) A requirement that electric utilities must allow cable TV operators to hang cables on their utility poles. *See FCC v. Florida Power Corp.*, noted just below.

[5]   Some Additional Thoughts on *Loretto*

It is quite difficult to explain Justice Marshall's position in *Loretto*. It was out of kilter with economic need and didn't conform with his acceptance of Justice Brennan's opinion in *Penn Central*. We have already noted, p. 938 above, that Takings Law has some of the characteristics of nuisance law. It allows private litigants to seek damages when public actions have negative effects on privately owned land. It requires governments to internalize some of the costs of regulation, much like private businesses must sometimes internalize the costs of creating land use conflicts with their neighbors. We have also noted that there are some important differences between Takings and nuisance law, especially when an entitlement protected by an injunction is awarded to a private citizen against a government. For in that setting, the state may simply elect to condemn the property of the person awarded the entitlement, cutting off the ability of the entitlement holder to demand a premium price to waive rights under an injunction.

The economic impact of the New York cable regulation can be conceptualized in the same sorts of terms. Its intended purpose was to cut off the ability of landlords to extract part of the value of deals made between tenants and cable companies when cable service was installed. It did that in two ways—by awarding cable companies an entitlement to install service equipment for tenants similar to entitlements held by telephone and other utility companies, and by cutting off the ability of landlords owning properties needed by cable companies to complete their wiring scheme on a block to demand hold out prices for installation of crossover lines. This combination of regulatory effects is quite similar to the impact of federal rules requiring telephone utilities to allow cable television companies to hang wires on telephone poles for a fee established by the Federal Communications Commission, a statute which was unanimously approved by the Supreme Court in 1987 in an opinion written by Justice Marshall.[53]

Placing *Loretto* in a consistent structure with Justice Brennan's opinion in *Penn Central* is extremely difficult, if not impossible. The structure of Brennan's argument in *Penn Central*—that regulation of the totality of economic interests held by a landowner is valid unless it disturbs distinct investment based expectations—did not fit the *Loretto* outcome. The effect on the entire parcel owned by Loretto was quite minimal. Indeed a good argument may be made that the regulation actually increased the value of the building by guaranteeing to all prospective tenants that cable television, like telephone and electrical services, would always be obtainable. Even if Loretto had strong investment based expectations about productive economic use of her property, the small volumes of space occupied by the cable equipment hardly altered them. Furthermore, the boxes could be moved to accommodate her future needs.

The only way Loretto could have made an argument that Justice Brennan might have listened to would have been to claim that she bought the building at a price that included the right to take 5% of the gross cable receipts paid by the tenants to Teleprompter. Barring her ability to collect those funds every year therefore destroyed a distinct investment based expectation. But I suspect that Justice Brennan would have answered by saying that no one can have a legitimate

---

[53] Federal Communications Commission v. Florida Power Commission, 480 U.S. 245 (1987).

expectation to seek part of the value of a transaction between others—tenants and utility providers. Furthermore, Brennan might have claimed, loss of that income was offset by increases in the value of the property.

Frank Michelman might have put the case in a slightly different way, but his structure also suggests the case was wrongly decided. For example, as he noted in his article, the use of a bright line rule preventing physical intrusion by the state might avoid serious disaffection costs—those costs associated with citizen antagonism to or cynicism about the political process. While that argument has some superficial appeal as a way of resolving the *Loretto* dilemma, it ignores the disaffection costs imposed upon the tenants by precluding control over the ways landlords deal with cable television companies. Indeed, the most surprising part of Marshall's opinion was his apparent lack of concern about the tenants. I presume he would have sided with all of the tenant reforms you read about earlier. Yet his opinion is curiously lacking in recognition of all those changes.

Perhaps Justice Marshall was concerned about privacy intrusions. While the ringing rhetoric in his opinion about precluding permanent government intrusions into privately owned spaces may have its roots in privacy talk, the factual setting suggests that only the tenant's privacy was really at stake, and that the New York statute was in part designed to preserve tenants' ability to gain access to cable TV. The landlord's intrusion generated complaint of "That's my roof!" rings a bit hollow. Tenants also have a claim to possessory property rights in the common areas of the buildings they rent space in. If Justice Marshall's views were generated by privacy concerns, they were quite Formalist in tone. The building "belongs" to the landlord, he would have had to think, and the state has no right to "occupy" the landlord's property.

Justice Rehnquist's *Penn Central* dissent is much easier to merge with *Loretto*. Rehnquist, you'll recall, structured his *Penn Central* argument by presuming that the narrowest relevant definition of an asset, once encumbered by significant regulation not affecting all nearby parcels, was constitutionally taken unless the use regulated was noxious or the regulation provided a mutual reciprocity of advantage.[54] He began his analysis by defining the object of regulation as "air rights" and asking whether the regulations took that property interest. Justice Brennan, by contrast, began his analysis by assuming that the totality of interests held by Penn Central in the area was the subject of regulation, thereby expanding the value of the assets subjected to state control and reducing the likelihood of a significant diminution in value. This little "trick"—defining the nature of the property interest at issue narrowly or broadly depending on your underlying views on the Takings Clause—has been a fairly constant characteristic of Takings litigation since the decision in *Penn Central.*

In any case, Justice Rehnquist might have characterized Justice Marshall's views as saying that the air space occupied by the little boxes—the narrowest description of the regulated property regulated by the state—was "taken," that the regulation was not designed to prevent a noxious use, and that taking *all* of a parcel—here the space occupied by the boxes—does not create a mutual reciprocity of advantage. The counter of course, is that this regulation actually created a substantial reciprocity of advantage since it burdened all owners in the area, maintained or increased property values and made apartments more attractive for rental.

---

[54] Note well that the latter exception will virtually never apply under this test, because Rehnquist stated its predicate on the assumption that the regulation does not affect all neighboring land. Under those circumstances it is difficult to see how there could ever be a mutual reciprocity of advantage in single site regulations.

After all this, I hope you can see why the *Loretto* opinion was a bit of a shocker when it was rendered. It was a significant change of pace from *Penn Central* and written by an unlikely author. Perhaps it is not surprising that Justice Rehnquist's eulogy for Justice Marshall referred to only two cases, one of which was *Loretto*. [55]

§ 11.05 Environmental Controls, Land Use "Trades," Changing Cultural Norms and the Conservative Court

[1] Introduction

Three major Takings cases were decided in 1987. In combination, they initiated a significant shift in the contours of Supreme Court jurisprudence. The first in the triad of decisions—*Keystone Bituminous Coal Association v. DeBenedictis*, 480 U.S. 470 (1987)—forced the Court to revisit its famous decision in *Pennsylvania Coal v. Mahon*, p. 936 above, while the second—*First English Evangelical Lutheran Church of Glendale v. County of Los Angeles*—sought guidance on the circumstances in which compensatory rather than injunctive relief should be awarded in Takings cases. The opinion in *Nollan v. California Coastal Commission*—the last of the three cases—may auger the most dramatic change in Takings law since Justice Sutherland's decision in *Euclid v. Ambler Realty*. This introductory section presents some information about *Keystone* and *First English* in order to provide a complete picture of the legal and jurisprudential context in which the *Nollan* case was litigated.

[a] *Keystone Bituminous Coal Association v. DeBenedictis*

In 1966, the Pennsylvania legislature concluded that its mine subsidence regulations were inadequate and adopted a new set of standards. [56] One of the new rules required that underground miners leave 50% of the coal in place in areas under public buildings, noncommercial buildings generally used by the public, dwellings and cemeteries. When the statute was challenged, the plaintiffs claimed that Pennsylvania law on estates in land recognized a specific, transferable "support estate." This interest in land could be sold by a surface owner to the owner of mineral rights, thereby waiving any right to sue if a mine collapse caused damage to buildings or other features on the surface of the land. Many deeds transferring mineral interests between 1890 and 1920 contained explicit transfers of the support estate from the owner of the surface to the mineral rights owner. The subsidence controls enacted by Pennsylvania's legislature, the plaintiffs argued, took the rights they had purchased in the support estate.

In the notes after *Loretto*, p. 994 above, there was discussion of the predisposition of those finding land use controls to be Takings to narrowly define the property interests subject to regulation. Those validating land use controls usually define the property interests at stake quite broadly. This sort of manipulation of the constitutional meaning of "property" occurred in both The Grand Central Terminal litigation and in *Loretto*. The *Keystone* plaintiffs attempted to use this tendency by claiming that the support estate was the subject of Pennsylvania's subsidence regulatory scheme and that the scheme effectively barred miners from removing any of the coal

---

[55] Chief Justice William Rehnquist, *Remarks at the Funeral of Justice Thurgood Marshall*, reprinted in FED. NEWS SERV., Jan. 28, 1993.

[56] Pennsylvania was not the only jurisdiction to adopt mining controls in this era. Strip mining legislation was adopted by Congress and some states. Coal operators also challenged the validity of these controls on the ground that their mineral rights were taken without the payment of just compensation. The Supreme Court denied those claims. Hodel v. Virginia Surface Mining and Reclamation Association, 452 U.S. 264 (1981); Hodel v. Indiana, 452 U.S. 314 (1981).

within the boundaries of the support estate. The existence of this support estate, an interest in land unique to Pennsylvania law, may have been a central factor in the reasoning of Justice Holmes' *Mahon* opinion. If he thought that disaffection costs were influenced by common perceptions about the meaning of property interests, and that *all* of an interest in land was subject to regulation, then a Taking outcome was not a surprise. This sort of logic required that each interest in property be "conceptually severed"[57] from other related interests and analyzed for Takings purposes independently of any other economic interests the parties may hold. If this is what Justice Holmes did in *Mahon*, the plaintiffs contended, the Court should do it again in *Keystone*.

Although Justice Rehnquist and three of his colleagues[58] agreed with that argument and opined that the Pennsylvania regulations were a Taking, Justice Stevens, writing for a slim, one-vote majority, rejected the claim. He posited that *Mahon* was distinguishable in two ways and, therefore, not a controlling precedent. First, he pointed to the purposes written into the Subsidence Statute by the Pennsylvania legislature. "None of the indicia," Stevens wrote, "of a statute enacted solely for the benefit of private parties identified in Justice Holmes' opinion [in *Mahon*] are present here." The Subsidence Act, by requiring that subsidence damage be repaired, was designed to protect the surface for everyone, not merely to reimburse surface owners for their private losses. Thus, Stevens argued, Pennsylvania's efforts to prevent subsidence fit neatly into the most traditional of reasons for upholding land use controls—the prevention of nuisances.

The second distinguishing factor, Justice Stevens claimed, rested on the finding in *Mahon* that the regulations "made mining of certain coal commercially impracticable. In this case, by contrast, petitioners have not shown any deprivation significant enough to satisfy the heavy burden placed upon one alleging a regulatory taking." He pointed out that "petitioners have not even pointed to a single mine that can no longer be mined for profit." The attempt by Keystone to narrowly define their property interest was rejected. The coal that had to be left in place was not "a separate segment of property for takings law purposes."

If the distinctions drawn between *Mahon* and *Keystone* seem weak, your skepticism is probably well placed. The dissenters, in a strongly worded opinion, countered that the Kohler Act at stake in *Mahon* was clearly adopted with public as well as private purposes within the legislature's purview. Justice Rehnquist's protestation that "We should hesitate to allow a regulation based on essentially economic concerns to be insulated from the dictates of the Fifth Amendment by labeling it nuisance regulation," rang a bit hollow in light of the actual impact of surface subsidence. But he returned to stronger ground when he reminded the majority that *Mahon* was clearly based on the assumption that Pennsylvania treated the support estate as a separate property interest and that Stevens' refusal to abide by that prior holding rendered his second distinction meaningless.

The bickering among the Justices over the significance of *Mahon* left little room for discussion of other issues. The venerable quality of Justice Holmes' opinion led the Justices to argue about precedent and largely ignore other larger Takings issues. *Keystone* was actually a nice setting in which to think carefully about the meaning of the Michelman-*Penn Central* notion of crystallized investment backed expectations. For Michelman the language invoked an effort to avoid capricious redistributions of wealth, capricious in the sense of preventing "a special kind

---

[57] This phrase was coined by Margaret Jane Radin in an important article, *The Liberal Conception of Property: Cross Currents in the Jurisprudence of Takings*, 88 COLUM. L. REV. 1667 (1988).

[58] Justices Powell, O'Connor and Scalia.

of suffering on the part of people who have grounds for feeling themselves the victims of unprincipled exploitation." Michelman argued that Holmes, the author of the *Mahon* opinion, felt that Pennsylvania's separate treatment of the support estate was crucial to the outcome of the case. To the extent that Stevens ignored that factor, Michelman would presumably argue that he misread *Mahon*.[59]

Despite the fact that Justice Stevens was not very artistic in his handling of *Mahon*, Keystone's crystallized expectations were difficult to fathom. On the one hand, Keystone argued that they fully expected their rights in underground coal to be defined by the outcome of *Mahon*, a sturdy precedent of long standing. On the other hand, Stevens could have pointed to the vast change in cultural understandings about the environment, land use controls, and public regulation that has occurred since the beginning of this century. Such wholesale changes make it difficult to believe that Keystone could reasonably have anticipated being bound by the same expectations as their brethren six decades earlier. The notion of expectations as used in taking litigation must encompass the prospects for alterations in community norms. For only those, in Michelman's terms, who have grounds for feeling exploited may justifiably claim a breach of the Constitution.

The gradual alteration of expectations about appropriate uses of land, both in the community and among individual property owners, is, therefore, something of a bootstrapping affair. When *Euclid* was decided, a certain level of public concern had arisen over planning policies in urban America. Those concerns presumably altered expectations of investors enough to Constitutionally legitimate the enactment of public controls. Both prior legislative enactments dealing with subdivisions, plats, housing standards and the like, and widespread consideration of the Standard Zoning Enabling Act were then deemed sufficient to make any reasonable real estate investor take the possibility of regulation into account when making investment decisions. Once the public regulatory path was entered, investment expectations continued to be changed both by public perceptions about social ills and by the actions of governments in enforcing and tinkering with previously enacted land use controls. With careful planning, government itself may lay the groundwork for further statutory limitations on land use. While this sort of bootstrapping may be an inevitable part of any system of Takings law that tries to accommodate changing social preferences, *Keystone* suggested that at least four Justices were unwilling to allow changing expectations to alter the economic fate of land owners at least in cases where the regulation sharply narrowed the use of a well defined estate in land.

[b]   *First English Evangelical Lutheran Church of Glendale v. County of Los Angeles*

Changing expectations about the permissible scope of land use regulations also may lead some jurisdictions to overreach. Problems may arise when corrective action by the courts is slow to arrive and the only relief afforded to the aggrieved owner is an injunction against continued use of the unfair regulation. Why, land owners asked, should they not receive some compensation for the period of time they were unable to use their land while their legal challenges were being heard? That problem was presented in a quite abstract way in *First English*. First English owned some land along the canyon banks of Middle Fork of Mill Creek in a national forest. They ran a campground there for retreats and other events. After a major forest fire denuded many of the slopes in the upper reaches of the canyon, the ground's water absorption capacity plummeted and flood danger increased. A major rainstorm in 1978 flooded the canyon and destroyed the

---

[59] This is not to say that Michelman would have sided with Justice Rehnquist in *Keystone*. He might well have wanted to overrule *Mahon*.

campground. The following year the County of Los Angeles adopted legislation barring construction of any facilities in the area until the forest regrew. First English sued. They did not seek to enjoin operation of the statute, but rather sought just compensation for a temporary taking beginning when the legislation was adopted and ending when it was repealed or no longer needed. The California courts refused to entertain the compensation claim, dismissing the claim on the pleadings. Interim, emergency regulations like this flood damage prevention measure presented no Takings problem they said. The Supreme Court reversed. Justice Rehnquist, writing for a six-Justice majority, concluded that there was no reason to preclude compensatory relief just because the regulation was temporary. Leases may be condemned, he argued, suggesting that substantial, short term regulatory impacts might also produce compensatory relief in an appropriate case. Justice Stevens dissented, complaining that the temporary taking issue should not be resolved by the court without first deciding whether the underlying regulatory scheme was a Taking.

Both of the land use regulations at issue in *Keystone* and *First English* relied upon changes in land use practices—growth in environment expectations in *Keystone* and the impact of a forest fire and flood in *First English*. While the investment backed expectations theory of Michelman and Brennan was constructed in part to simplify approvals of land use controls despite vast changes in environmental, cultural and legal practice, more Formalist visions of property ownership would bar use of changing social norms as a basis for approving intense government regulation. The value of an investment at the time of purchase, rather than any later arising public policy, would drive Takings jurisprudence. Robert Nozick, one of the best known conservative critics of Michelman, Brennan, and John Rawls, articulated a detailed theory designed to solidify property claims and reduce the importance of shifts in cultural norms. Here is an excerpt.

ROBERT NOZICK, ANARCHY, STATE AND UTOPIA 149-155 (1974)[60]

The minimal state is the most extensive state that can be justified. Any state more extensive violates people's rights. Yet many persons have put forth reasons purporting to justify a more extensive state. . . . I shall focus upon those generally acknowledged to be most weighty and influential, to see precisely wherein they fail. In this chapter we consider the claim that a more extensive state is justified, because necessary (or the best instrument) to achieve distributive justice. . . .

The term "distributive justice" is not a neutral one. Hearing the term "distribution," most people presume that some thing or mechanism uses some principle or criterion to give out a supply of things. Into this process of distributing shares some error may have crept. So it is an open question, at least, whether *re*distribution should take place; whether we should do again what has already been done once, though poorly. However, we are not in the position of children who have been given portions of pie by someone who now makes last minute adjustments to rectify careless cutting. There is no *central* distribution, no person or group entitled to control all the resources, jointly deciding how they are to be doled out. What each person gets, he gets from others who give to him in exchange for something, or as a gift. In a free society, diverse persons control different resources, and new holdings arise out of the voluntary exchanges and actions of persons. There is no more a distributing or distribution of shares than there is a distributing of mates in a society in which persons choose whom

---

they shall marry. The total result is the product of many individual decisions which the different individuals involved are entitled to make. Some uses of the term "distribution," it is true, do not imply a previous distributing appropriately judged by some criterion (for example, "probability distribution"); nevertheless, despite the title of this chapter, it would be best to use a terminology that clearly is neutral. We shall speak of people's holdings; a principle of justice in holdings describes (part of) what justice tells us (requires) about holdings. . . .

THE ENTITLEMENT THEORY

The subject of justice in holdings consists of three major topics. The first is the *original acquisition of holdings*, the appropriation of unheld things. This includes the issues of how unheld things may come to be held, the process, or processes, by which unheld things may come to be held, the things that may come to be held by these processes, the extent of what come to be held by a particular process, and so on. We shall refer to the complicated truth about this topic, which we shall not formulate here, as the principle of justice in acquisition. The second topic concerns the *transfer of holdings* from one person to another. By what processes may a person transfer holdings to another? How may a person acquire a holding from another who holds it? Under this topic come general descriptions of voluntary exchange, and gift and (on the other hand) fraud, as well as reference to particular conventional details fixed upon in a given society. The complicated truth about this subject (with placeholders for conventional details) we shall call the principle of justice in transfer. (And we shall suppose it also includes principles governing how a person may divest himself of a holding, passing it into an unheld state.)

If the world were wholly just, the following inductive definition would exhaustively cover the subject of justice in holdings.

1. A person who acquires a holding in accordance with the principle of justice in acquisition is entitled to that holding.

2   A person who acquires a holding in accordance with the principle of justice in transfer, from someone else entitled to the holding, is entitled to the holding.

3. No one is entitled to a holding except by (repeated) applications of 1 and 2.

The complete principle of distributive justice would say simply that a distribution is just if everyone is entitled to the holdings they possess under the distribution.

A distribution is just if it arises from another just distribution by legitimate means. The legitimate means of moving from one distribution to another are specified by the principle of justice in transfer. The legitimate first "moves" are specified by the principle of justice in acquisition. Whatever arises from a just situation by just steps is itself just. The means of change specified by the principle of justice in transfer preserve justice. As correct rules of inference are truth-preserving, and any conclusion deduced via repeated application of such rules from only true premises is itself true, so the means of transition from one situation to another specified by the principle of justice in transfer are justice-preserving, and any situation actually arising from repeated transitions in accordance with the principle from a just situation is itself just. The parallel between justice-preserving transformations and truth-preserving transformations illuminates where it fails as well as where it holds. That a conclusion could have been deduced by truth-preserving means from premises that are true suffices to show its truth. That from a just situation a situation *could* have arisen via justice-preserving means does *not* suffice to show its justice. The fact that a thief's victims voluntarily *could* have presented him with gifts does not entitle the thief to his ill-gotten gains. Justice in holdings is historical; it depends upon what actually has happened. We shall return to this point later.

Not all actual situations are generated in accordance with the two principles of justice in holdings: the principle of justice in acquisition and the principle of justice in transfer. Some people steal from others, or defraud them, or enslave them, seizing their product and preventing them from living as they choose, or forcibly exclude others from competing in exchanges. None of these are permissible modes of transition from one situation to another. And some persons acquire holdings by means not sanctioned by the principle of justice in acquisition. The existence of past injustice (previous violations of the first two principles of justice in holdings) raises the third major topic under justice in holdings; the rectification of injustice in holdings. If past injustice has shaped present holdings in various ways, some identifiable and some not, what now, if anything, ought to be done to rectify these injustices? What obligations do the performers of injustice have toward those whose position is worse than it would have been had the injustice not been done? Or, than it would have been had compensation been paid promptly? How, if at all, do things change if the beneficiaries and those made worse off are not the direct parties in the act of injustice, but, for example, their descendants? Is an injustice done to someone whose holding was itself based upon an unrectified injustice? How far back must one go in wiping clean the historical slate of injustices? What may victims of injustice permissibly do in order to rectify the injustices being done to them, including the many injustices done by persons acting through their government? I do not know of a thorough or theoretically sophisticated treatment of such issues. Idealizing greatly, let us suppose theoretical investigation will produce a principle of rectification. This principle uses historical information about previous situations and injustices done in them (as defined by the first two principles of justice and rights against interference), and information about the actual course of events that flowed from these injustices, until the present, and it yields a description (or descriptions) of holdings in the society. The principle of rectification presumably will make use of its best estimate of subjunctive information about what would have occurred (or a probability distribution over what might have occurred, using the expected value) if the injustice had not taken place. If the actual description of holdings turns out not to be one of the descriptions yielded by the principle, then one of the descriptions yielded must be realized.

The general outlines of the theory of justice in holdings are that the holdings of a person are just if he is entitled to them by the principles of justice in acquisition and transfer, or by the principle of rectification of injustice (as specified by the first two principles). If each person's holdings are just, then the total set (distribution) of holdings is just. . . .

HISTORICAL PRINCIPLES AND END-RESULT PRINCIPLES

The general outlines of the entitlement theory illuminate the nature and defects of other conceptions of distributive justice. The entitlement theory of justice in distribution is *historical*; whether a distribution is just depends upon how it came about. In contrast, *current time-slice principles* of justice hold that the justice of a distribution is determined by how things are distributed (who has what) as judged by some *structural* principle(s) of just distribution. A utilitarian who judges between any two distributions by seeing which has the greater sum of utility and, if the sums tie, applies some fixed equality criterion to choose the more equal distribution, would hold a current time-slice principle of justice. As would someone who had a fixed schedule of trade-offs between the sum of happiness and equality. According to a current time-slice principle, all that needs to be looked at, in judging the justice of a distribution, is who ends up with what; in comparing any two distributions one need look only at the matrix presenting the distributions. No further information need be fed into a principle of justice. It is a consequence of such principles of justice that any two structurally identical distributions are equally just. (Two distributions are structurally identical if they present the same profile, but perhaps have different persons occupying the particular slots. My having ten and your having five, and my having five and your having ten are structurally identical distributions.) Welfare economics is the theory of current time-slice principles of justice. The subject is conceived as operating on matrices representing only current information about distribution. This, as well as some of the usual conditions (for example, the choice of distribution is invariant under relabeling of columns), guarantees that welfare economics will be a current time-slice theory, with all of its inadequacies.

Most persons do not accept current time-slice principles as constituting the whole story about distributive shares. They think it relevant in assessing the justice of a situation to consider not only the distribution it embodies, but also how that distribution came about. If some persons are in prison for murder or war crimes, we do not say that to assess the justice of the distribution in the society we must look only at what this person has, and that person has, and that person has, . . . at the current time. We think it relevant to ask whether someone did something so that he *deserved* to be punished, deserved to have a lower share. Most will agree to the relevance of further information with regard to punishments and penalties. Consider also desired things. One traditional socialist view is that workers are entitled to the product and full fruits of their labor; they have earned it; a distribution is unjust if it does not give the workers what they are entitled to. Such entitlements are based upon some past history. No socialist holding this view would find it comforting to be told that because the actual distribution *A* happens to coincide structurally with the one he desires *D, A* therefore is no less just than *D*; it differs only in that the "parasitic" owners of capital receive under *A* what the workers are entitled to under *D*, and the workers receive under *A* what the owners are entitled to under *D*, namely very little. This socialist rightly, in my view, holds onto the notions of earning, producing, entitlement, desert, and so forth, and he rejects current time-slice principles that look only to the structure of the resulting set of holdings. (The set of holdings resulting from what? Isn't it implausible that how holdings are produced and come to exist has no effect at all on who should hold what?) His mistake lies in his view of what entitlements arise out of what sorts of productive processes.

We construe the position we discuss too narrowly by speaking of *current* time-slice principles. Nothing is changed if structural principles operate upon a time sequence of current time-slice profiles and, for example, give someone more now to counterbalance the less he has had earlier. A utilitarian or an egalitarian or any mixture of the two over time will inherit the difficulties of his more myopic comrades. He is not helped by the fact that *some* of the information others consider relevant in assessing a distribution is reflected, unrecoverable, in past matrices. Henceforth, we shall refer to such unhistorical principles of distributive justice, including the current time-slice principles, as *end-result principles* or *end-state principles*.

In contrast to end-result principles of justice, *historical principles* of justice hold that past circumstances or actions of people can create differential entitlements or differential deserts to things. An injustice can be worked by moving from one distribution to another structurally identical one, for the second, in profile the same, may violate people's entitlements or deserts; it may not fit the actual history.

[2] Background to *Nollan v. California Coastal Commission*

An old beach front cottage on Faria Beach in Ventura County a bit over 50 miles northwest of Los Angeles had been in Marilyn Nollan's family for over 40 years. For many years the family used the cottage as a summer residence. In more recent times it was rented to summer vacationers. But by 1981, the small single story cottage was so unsafe and dilapidated it could not be used. It was also out of character with the Faria Beach area which was changing from a cabin vacation spot to a family residential area.[61]

Marilyn Nollan and her husband, James, hired an architect and made plans to tear down the old cottage and replace it with a modern two story home for themselves and their two children. They hoped to move from their home in Los Angeles where James worked as an assistant city attorney.[62] The planned new home contained about three times the floor area of the old cabin and, together with paved areas and other improvements, covered just under 90% of the 2800 square foot lot as opposed to about two-thirds for the old cottage.[63] The plans left only about three feet of the lot on each side of the house unbuilt upon. The house to the west went right up to the property line and that to the east went to within two feet of the line. The hurdle the Nollans faced before they could build their new house was gaining the approval of the California Coastal Commission, which was charged with regulating new development to protect public access to Pacific Ocean beaches. The Coastal Commission was established as part of a legislative effort to comply with Article X, Section 4 of the California Constitution:

> No individual, partnership, or corporation claiming or possessing the frontage or tidal lands of a harbor, bay inlet, estuary, or other navigable water in this State shall be permitted to exclude the right of way to such water whenever it is required for any public purpose . . . and the Legislature shall enact such laws as will give the most liberal construction to the provision, so that access to the navigable waters of this State shall always be attainable for the people thereof.

Section 30212 of the California Public Resources Code, part of the legislation implementing the constitutional provision, required those undertaking new development projects to provide for public access to the beach. It provided:

> (a) Public access from the nearest public roadway to the shoreline and along the coast shall be provided in new development projects except where (1) it is inconsistent with public safety, military security needs, or the protection of fragile coastal resources, (2) adequate access exists nearby, or (3) agriculture would be adversely affected. Dedicated accessways shall not be required to be opened to public use until a public agency or private association agrees to accept responsibility for maintenance and liability of the accessway.

---

[61] Joint Appendix in the United States Supreme Court at 43, 278, 302, 310-311, Nollan v. California Coastal Commission, 483 U.S. 825 (1987).

[62] Savage, *Court Rejects State Rule on Beach Access,* LOS ANGELES TIMES, June 27, 1987, at pt. 1, p. 1, col.4; Joint Appendix, note 61 above, at 310.

[63] Joint Appendix, note 61 above, at 43, 57. The buildable lot area did not include a 10-foot frontage between the front house line and the Pacific Coast Highway, and a 17-foot span to the seawall. The latter area in essence became the back yard.

(b) For purposes of this section, "new development" does not include:

(1) Replacement of any structure . . . .

(2) The demolition and reconstruction of a single-family residence; provided, that the reconstructed residence shall not exceed either the floor area, height or bulk of the former structure by more than 10 percent, and that the reconstructed residence shall be sited in the same location on the affected property as the former structure.

(3) Improvements to any structure which do not change the intensity of its use, which do not increase either the floor area, height, or bulk of the structure by more than 10 percent, which do not block or impede public access, and which do not result in a seaward encroachment by the structure.

. . . .

The Nollans applied for a building permit from the Commission on February 25, 1982, and the initial hearing was held about two months later. The permit request was approved, provided that:

Prior to the issuance of the Coastal Development Permit, the applicants shall record, in a form and manner approved by the Executive Director, a deed restriction acknowledging the right of the public to pass and repass across the subject properties in an area bounded by the mean high tide line at one end, to the toe of the revetment at the other end.[64]

This requirement was consistent with those imposed on other owners in the area. Of the 43 building permits issued for new developments on shoreline lots in the Faria Beach Tract after 1979 when administrative regulations allowing such a requirement were adopted, none were issued without the beach easement condition. The Faria family, former owners of the tract and former lessors to the Nollans, also felt the beach easement policy was appropriate. The Nollans were the first land owners in the area to object to it.

The Nollans' decision to protest the condition imposed on the grant of their permit led to five years of litigation in the California courts, the Coastal Commission and, eventually, the United States Supreme Court. By the time the dispute got to the high Court, § 30212 had been construed by the state courts to cover the Nollans' project. Their argument that adequate access to the beach for purposes of § 30212 was provided by Faria County Park, about one-half mile to the west and an area called the "Cove" about one-third mile to the east[65] was rejected. Both the Commission and the courts countered that the Faria Beach area was becoming a virtual wall of substantial houses on relatively small lots between the Pacific Coast Highway and the beach, that guarantees of lateral beach access were basic to continued public perception that the Pacific Ocean beaches were available for general use, and that access between the seawall and the mean high tide line was necessary to maintain public use of the beach because of wide variations in daily tidal levels.[66]

---

[64] Jurisdictional Statement at 7, Nollan v. California Coastal Commission, 483 U.S. 825 (1987). The "revetment" noted in the text is a seawall located about eight feet inland from the high tide line.

[65] Joint Appendix, note 61 above, at 49.

[66] Nollan v. California Coastal Commission, 177 Cal. App. 3d 719, 223 Cal. Rptr. 28 (1986). *See also* Grupe v. California Coastal Commission, 166 Cal. App. 3d 148, 212 Cal. Rptr. 578 (1985), a case relied on in *Nollan* with very similar facts.

[3]   Opinions of the United States Supreme Court in *Nollan v. California Coastal Commission*

Nollan v. California Coastal Commission

United States Supreme Court
483 U.S. 825, 107 S. Ct. 3141, 97 L. Ed. 2d 677 (1987)

SCALIA, J., delivered the opinion of the Court, in which REHNQUIST, C.J., and WHITE, POWELL, and O'CONNOR, JJ., joined.

James and Marilyn Nollan appeal from a decision of the California Court of Appeal ruling that the California Coastal Commission could condition its grant of permission to rebuild their house on their transfer to the public of an easement across their beachfront property. The California Court rejected their claim that imposition of that condition violates the Takings Clause of the Fifth Amendment, as incorporated against the States by the Fourteenth Amendment. We noted probable jurisdiction.

I

The Nollans own a beachfront lot in Ventura County, California. A quarter-mile north of their property is Faria County Park, an oceanside public park with a public beach and recreation area. Another public beach area, known locally as "the Cove," lies 1,800 feet south of their lot. A concrete seawall approximately eight feet high separates the beach portion of the Nollans' property from the rest of the lot. The historic mean high tide line determines the lot's oceanside boundary.

The Nollans originally leased their property with an option to buy. The building on the lot was a small bungalow, totaling 504 square feet, which for a time they rented to summer vacationers. After years of rental use, however, the building had fallen into disrepair, and could no longer be rented out.

The Nollans' option to purchase was conditioned on their promise to demolish the bungalow and replace it. In order to do so, under California Public Resources Code §§ 30106, 30212, and 30600 (West 1986), they were required to obtain a coastal development permit from the California Coastal Commission. On February 25, 1982, they submitted a permit application to the Commission in which they proposed to demolish the existing structure and replace it with a three-bedroom house in keeping with the rest of the neighborhood.

The Nollans were informed that their application had been placed on the administrative calendar, and that the Commission staff had recommended that the permit be granted subject to the condition that they allow the public an easement to pass across a portion of their property bounded by the mean high tide line on one side, and their seawall on the other side. This would make it easier for the public to get to Faria County Park and the Cove. The Nollans protested imposition of the condition, but the Commission overruled their objections and granted the permit subject to their recordation of a deed restriction granting the easement.

On June 3, 1982, the Nollans filed a petition for writ of administrative mandamus asking the Ventura County Superior Court to invalidate the access condition. They argued that the condition could not be imposed absent evidence that their proposed development would have a direct adverse impact on public access to the beach. The court agreed, and remanded the case to the Commission for a full evidentiary hearing on that issue.

On remand, the Commission held a public hearing, after which it made further factual findings and reaffirmed its imposition of the condition. It found that the new house would increase blockage of the view of the ocean, thus contributing to the development of "a 'wall' of residential structures" that would prevent the public "psychologically . . . from realizing a stretch of coastline exists nearby that they have every right to visit." The new house would also increase private use of the shorefront. These effects of construction of the house, along with other area development, would cumulatively "burden the public's ability to traverse to and along the shorefront." Therefore the Commission could properly require the Nollans to offset that burden by providing additional lateral access to the public beaches in the form of an easement across their property. The Commission also noted that it had similarly conditioned 43 out of 60 coastal development permits along the same tract of land, and that of the 17 not so conditioned, 14 had been approved when the Commission did not have administrative regulations in place allowing imposition of the condition, and the remaining 3 had not involved shorefront property.

The Nollans filed a supplemental petition for a writ of administrative mandamus with the Superior Court, in which they argued that imposition of the access condition violated the Takings Clause of the Fifth Amendment, as incorporated against the States by the Fourteenth Amendment. The Superior Court ruled in their favor on statutory grounds, finding, in part to avoid "issues of constitutionality," that the California Coastal Act of 1976, Cal. Pub. Res. Code Ann. § 30000 *et seq.*, authorized the Commission to impose public access conditions on coastal development permits for the replacement of an existing single-family home with a new one only where the proposed development would have an adverse impact on public access to the sea. App. 419. In the Court's view, the administrative record did not provide an adequate factual basis for concluding that replacement of the bungalow with the house would create a direct or cumulative burden on public access to the sea. Accordingly, the Superior Court granted the writ of mandamus and directed that the permit condition be struck.

The Commission appealed to the California Court of Appeal. While that appeal was pending, the Nollans satisfied the condition on their option to purchase by tearing down the bungalow and building the new house, and bought the property. They did not notify the Commission that they were taking that action.

The Court of Appeal reversed the Superior Court. It disagreed with the Superior Court's interpretation of the Coastal Act, finding that it required that a coastal permit for the construction of a new house whose floor area, height or bulk was more than 10% larger than that of the house it was replacing be conditioned on a grant of access. It also ruled that the requirement did not violate the Constitution under the reasoning of an earlier case of the Court of Appeal, *Grupe v. California Coastal Comm'n*, 166 Cal. App. 3d 148, 212 Cal. Rptr. 578 (1985). In that case, the court had found that so long as a project contributed to the need for public access, even if the project standing alone had not created the need for access, and even if there was only an indirect relationship between the access exacted and the need to which the project contributed, imposition of an access condition on a development permit was sufficiently related to burdens created by the project to be constitutional. The Court of Appeal ruled that the record established that that was the situation with respect to the Nollans' house. It ruled that the Nollans' taking claim also failed because, although the condition diminished the value of the Nollans' lot, it did not deprive them of all reasonable use of their property. Since, in the Court of Appeal's view, there was no statutory or constitutional obstacle to imposition of the access condition, the Superior Court erred in granting the writ of mandamus. The Nollans appealed to this Court, raising only the constitutional question.

II

Had California simply required the Nollans to make an easement across their beachfront available to the public on a permanent basis in order to increase public access to the beach, rather than conditioning their permit to rebuild their house on their agreeing to do so, we have no doubt there would have been a taking. To say that the appropriation of a public easement across a landowner's premises does not constitute the taking of a property interest but rather, (as JUSTICE BRENNAN contends) "a mere restriction on its use," is to use words in a manner that deprives them of all their ordinary meaning. Indeed, one of the principal uses of the eminent domain power is to assure that the government be able to require conveyance of just such interests, so long as it pays for them.

Perhaps because the point is so obvious, we have never been confronted with a controversy that required us to rule upon it, but our cases' analysis of the effect of other governmental action leads to the same conclusion. We have repeatedly held that, as to property reserved by its owner for private use, "the right to exclude [others is] 'one of the most essential sticks in the bundle of rights that are commonly characterized as property.' " *Loretto v. Teleprompter Manhattan CATV Corp.*, 458 U.S. 419 (1982), quoting *Kaiser Aetna v. United States*, 444 U.S. 164, 176 (1979). In *Loretto* we observed that where governmental action results in "[a] permanent physical occupation" of the property, by the government itself or by others, "our cases uniformly have found a taking to the extent of the occupation, without regard to whether the action achieves an important public benefit or has only minimal economic impact on the owner." We think a "permanent physical occupation" has occurred, for purposes of that rule, where individuals are given a permanent and continuous right to pass to and fro, so that the real property may continuously be traversed, even though no particular individual is permitted to station himself permanently upon the premises.[1]

. . . .

Given, then, that requiring uncompensated conveyance of the easement outright would violate the Fourteenth Amendment, the question becomes whether requiring it to be conveyed as a condition for issuing a land use permit alters the outcome. We have long recognized that land use regulation does not effect a taking if it "substantially advance[s] legitimate state interests" and does not "den[y] an owner economically viable use of his land," *Agins v. Tiburon*, 447 U.S. 255, 260, 100 S. Ct. 2138, 2141, 65 L. Ed. 2d 106 (1980). . . . Our cases have not elaborated on the standards for determining what constitutes a "legitimate state interest" or what type of connection between the regulation and the state interest satisfies the requirement that the former "substantially advance" the latter.[3] They have made clear, however, that a broad range of

---

[1] The holding of *PruneYard Shopping Center v. Robins*, 447 U.S. 74 (1980), is not inconsistent with this analysis, since there the owner had already opened his property to the general public, and in addition permanent access was not required. The analysis of *Kaiser Aetna v. United States*, 444 U.S. 164 (1979), is not inconsistent because it was affected by traditional doctrines regarding navigational servitudes. Of course neither of those cases involved, as this one does, a classic right-of-way easement.

[3] Contrary to Justice Brennan's claim, our opinions do not establish that these standards are the same as those applied to due process or equal-protection claims. To the contrary, our verbal formulations in the takings field have generally been quite different. We have required that the regulation "substantially advance" the "legitimate state interest" sought to be achieved, *Agins v. Tiburon*, 447 U.S. 255 (1980), not that "the State *'could rationally have decided'* the measure adopted might achieve the State's objective." . . . [T]here is no reason to believe (and the language of our cases gives some reason to disbelieve) that so long as the regulation of property is at issue the standards for takings challenges, due process challenges, and equal protection challenges are identical; any more than there is any reason to believe

governmental purposes and regulations satisfies these requirements. *See Agins v. Tiburon, supra,* (scenic zoning); *Penn Central Transportation Co. v. New York City, supra* (landmark preservation); *Euclid v. Ambler Realty Co.,* 272 U.S. 365 (1926) (residential zoning); Laitos and Westfall, *Government Interference with Private Interests in Public Resources,* 11 Harv. Envtl. L. Rev. 1, 66 (1987). The Commission argues that among these permissible purposes are protecting the public's ability to see the beach, assisting the public in overcoming the "psychological barrier" to using the beach created by a developed shorefront, and preventing congestion on the public beaches. We assume, without deciding, that this is so—in which case the Commission unquestionably would be able to deny the Nollans their permit outright if their new house (alone, or by reason of the cumulative impact produced in conjunction with other construction)[4] would substantially impede these purposes, unless the denial would interfere so drastically with the Nollans' use of their property as to constitute a taking. *See Penn Central Transportation Co. v. New York City, supra.*

The Commission argues that a permit condition that serves the same legitimate police-power purpose as a refusal to issue the permit should not be found to be a taking if the refusal to issue the permit would not constitute a taking. We agree. Thus, if the Commission attached to the permit some condition that would have protected the public's ability to see the beach notwithstanding construction of the new house—for example, a height limitation, a width restriction, or a ban on fences—so long as the Commission could have exercised its police power (as we have assumed it could) to forbid construction of the house altogether, imposition of the condition would also be constitutional. Moreover (and here we come closer to the facts of the present case), the condition would be constitutional even if it consisted of the requirement that the Nollans provide a viewing spot on their property for passersby with whose sighting of the ocean their new house would interfere. Although such a requirement, constituting a permanent grant of continuous access to the property, would have to be considered a taking if it were not attached to a development permit, the Commission's assumed power to forbid construction of the house in order to protect the public's view of the beach must surely include the power to condition construction upon some concession by the owner, even a concession of property rights, that serves the same end. If a prohibition designed to accomplish that purpose would be a legitimate exercise of the police power rather than a taking, it would be strange to conclude that providing the owner an alternative to that prohibition which accomplishes the same purpose is not.

The evident constitutional propriety disappears, however, if the condition substituted for the prohibition utterly fails to further the end advanced as the justification for the prohibition. When that essential nexus is eliminated, the situation becomes the same as if California law forbade shouting fire in a crowded theater, but granted dispensations to those willing to contribute $100 to the state treasury. While a ban on shouting fire can be a core exercise of the State's police power to protect the public safety, and can thus meet even our stringent standards for regulation

---

that so long as the regulation of speech is at issue the standards for due process challenges, equal protection challenges, and First Amendment challenges are identical. *Goldblatt v. Hempstead,* 369 U.S. 590 (1962), does appear to assume that the inquiries are the same, but that assumption is inconsistent with the formulations of our later cases.

[4] If the Nollans were being singled out to bear the burden of California's attempt to remedy these problems, although they had not contributed to it more than other coastal landowners, the State's action, even if otherwise valid, might violate either the incorporated Takings Clause or the Equal Protection Clause. One of the principal purposes of the Takings Clause is "to bar Government from forcing some people alone to bear public burdens which, in all fairness and justice, should be borne by the public as a whole." *Armstrong v. United States,* 364 U.S. 40, 49, 80 S. Ct. 1563, 1569, 4 L. Ed. 2d 1554 (1960). But that is not the basis of the Nollans' challenge here.

of speech, adding the unrelated condition alters the purpose to one which, while it may be legitimate, is inadequate to sustain the ban. Therefore, even though, in a sense, requiring a $100 tax contribution in order to shout fire is a lesser restriction on speech than an outright ban, it would not pass constitutional muster. Similarly here, the lack of nexus between the condition and the original purpose of the building restriction converts that purpose to something other than what it was. The purpose then becomes, quite simply, the obtaining of an easement to serve some valid governmental purpose, but without payment of compensation. Whatever may be the outer limits of "legitimate state interests" in the takings and land use context, this is not one of them. In short, unless the permit condition serves the same governmental purpose as the development ban, the building restriction is not a valid regulation of land use but an out-and-out plan of extortion.[5]

III

The Commission claims that it concedes as much, and that we may sustain the condition at issue here by finding that it is reasonably related to the public need or burden that the Nollans' new house creates or to which it contributes. We can accept, for purposes of discussion, the Commission's proposed test as to how close a "fit" between the condition and the burden is required, because we find that this case does not meet even the most untailored standards. The Commission's principal contention to the contrary essentially turns on a play on the word "access." The Nollans' new house, the Commission found, will interfere with "visual access" to the beach. That in turn (along with other shorefront development) will interfere with the desire of people who drive past the Nollans' house to use the beach, thus creating a "psychological barrier" to "access." The Nollans' new house will also, by a process not altogether clear from the Commission's opinion but presumably potent enough to more than offset the effects of the psychological barrier, increase the use of the public beaches, thus creating the need for more "access." These burdens on "access" would be alleviated by a requirement that the Nollans provide "lateral access" to the beach.

Rewriting the argument to eliminate the play on words makes clear that there is nothing to it. It is quite impossible to understand how a requirement that people already on the public beaches be able to walk across the Nollans' property reduces any obstacles to viewing the beach created by the new house. It is also impossible to understand how it lowers any "psychological barrier" to using the public beaches, or how it helps to remedy any additional congestion on them caused by construction of the Nollans' new house. We therefore find that the Commission's imposition of the permit condition cannot be treated as an exercise of its land use power for any of these purposes. Our conclusion on this point is consistent with the approach taken by every other court that has considered the question, with the exception of the California state courts.

. . . .

We are left, then, with the Commission's justification for the access requirement unrelated to land use regulation:

---

[5] One would expect that a regime in which this kind of leveraging of the police power is allowed would produce stringent land-use regulation which the State then waives to accomplish other purposes, leading to lesser realization of the land-use goals purportedly sought to be served than would result from more lenient (but nontradeable) development restrictions. Thus, the importance of the purpose underlying the prohibition not only does not *justify* the imposition of unrelated conditions for eliminating the prohibition, but positively militates against the practice.

Finally, the Commission notes that there are several existing provisions of pass and repass lateral access benefits already given by past Faria Beach Tract applicants as a result of prior coastal permit decisions. The access required as a condition of this permit is part of a comprehensive program to provide continuous public access along Faria Beach as the lots undergo development or redevelopment.

App. 68. That is simply an expression of the Commission's belief that the public interest will be served by a continuous strip of publicly accessible beach along the coast. The Commission may well be right that it is a good idea, but that does not establish that the Nollans (and other coastal residents) alone can be compelled to contribute to its realization. Rather, California is free to advance its "comprehensive program," if it wishes, by using its power of eminent domain for this "public purpose," *see* U.S. Const., Amdt. V; but if it wants an easement across the Nollans' property, it must pay for it.

Reversed.

JUSTICE BRENNAN with whom JUSTICE MARSHALL joins, dissenting.

Appellants in this case sought to construct a new dwelling on their beach lot that would both diminish visual access to the beach and move private development closer to the public tidelands. The Commission reasonably concluded that such "buildout," both individually and cumulatively, threatens public access to the shore. It sought to offset this encroachment by obtaining assurance that the public may walk along the shoreline in order to gain access to the ocean. The Court finds this an illegitimate exercise of the police power, because it maintains that there is no reasonable relationship between the effect of the development and the condition imposed.

The first problem with this conclusion is that the Court imposes a standard of precision for the exercise of a State's police power that has been discredited for the better part of this century. Furthermore, even under the Court's cramped standard, the permit condition imposed in this case directly responds to the specific type of burden on access created by appellants' development. Finally, a review of those factors deemed most significant in takings analysis makes clear that the Commission's action implicates none of the concerns underlying the Takings Clause. The Court has thus struck down the Commission's reasonable effort to respond to intensified development along the California coast, on behalf of landowners who can make no claim that their reasonable expectations have been disrupted. The Court has, in short, given appellants a windfall at the expense of the public.

I

The Court's conclusion that the permit condition imposed on appellants is unreasonable cannot withstand analysis. First, the Court demands a degree of exactitude that is inconsistent with our standard for reviewing the rationality of a state's exercise of its police power for the welfare of its citizens. Second, even if the nature of the public access condition imposed must be identical to the precise burden on access created by appellants, this requirement is plainly satisfied.

A

There can be no dispute that the police power of the States encompasses the authority to impose conditions on private development. *See, e.g., Agins v. Tiburon,* 447 U.S. 255 (1980); *Penn Central Transportation Co. v. New York City,* 438 U.S. 104 (1978); *Gorieb v. Fox,* 274 U.S. 603 (1927).

It is also by now commonplace that this Court's review of the rationality of a State's exercise of its police power demands only that the State *"could rationally have decided"* that the measure adopted might achieve the State's objective. *Minnesota v. Clover Leaf Creamery Co.*, 449 U.S. 456, 466 (1981) (emphasis in original).[1] In this case, California has employed its police power in order to condition development upon preservation of public access to the ocean and tidelands. The Coastal Commission, if it had so chosen, could have denied the Nollans' request for a development permit, since the property would have remained economically viable without the requested new development. Instead, the State sought to accommodate the Nollans' desire for new development, on the condition that the development not diminish the overall amount of public access to the coastline. Appellants' proposed development would reduce public access by restricting visual access to the beach, by contributing to an increased need for community facilities, and by moving private development closer to public beach property. The Commission sought to offset this diminution in access, and thereby preserve the overall balance of access, by requesting a deed restriction that would ensure "lateral" access: the right of the public to pass and repass along the dry sand parallel to the shoreline in order to reach the tidelands and the ocean. In the expert opinion of the Coastal Commission, development conditioned on such a restriction would fairly attend to both public and private interests.

The Court finds fault with this measure because it regards the condition as insufficiently tailored to address the precise type of reduction in access produced by the new development. The Nollans' development blocks visual access, the Court tells us, while the Commission seeks to preserve lateral access along the coastline. Thus, it concludes, the State acted irrationally. Such a narrow conception of rationality, however, has long since been discredited as a judicial arrogation of legislative authority.

. . . .

---

1 . . . .

Notwithstanding the suggestion otherwise, *ante*, at n. 3, our standard for reviewing the threshold question whether an exercise of the police power is legitimate is a uniform one. As we stated over 25 years ago in addressing a takings challenge to government regulation:

The term "police power" connotes the time-tested conceptional limit of public encroachment upon private interests. Except for the substitution of the familiar standard of "reasonableness," this Court has generally refrained from announcing any specific criteria. The classic statement of the rule in *Lawton v. Steele*, 152 U.S. 133, 137 (1894), is still valid today: " . . . [I]t must appear, first, that the interests of the public . . . require [government] interference; and, second, that the means are reasonably necessary for the accomplishment of the purpose, and not unduly oppressive upon individuals." Even this rule is not applied with strict precision, for this Court has often said that "debatable questions as to reasonableness are not for the courts but for the legislature . . ." *E.g., Sproles v. Binford*, 286 U.S. 374, 388 (1932). *Goldblatt v. Hempstead*, 369 U.S. 590, 594-595 (1962).

. . . .

Our phraseology may differ slightly from case to case—*e.g.*, regulation must "substantially advance," *Agins v. Tiburon*, 447 U.S. 255, 260 (1980), or be "reasonably necessary to," *Penn Central Transportation Co. v. New York City*, 438 U.S. 104, 127 (1978), the government's end. These minor differences cannot, however, obscure the fact that the inquiry in each case is the same.

Of course, government action may be a valid exercise of the police power and still violate specific provisions of the Constitution. Justice Scalia is certainly correct in observing that challenges founded upon these provisions are reviewed under different standards. Our consideration of factors such as those identified in *Penn Central, supra*, for instance, provides an analytical framework for protecting the values underlying the Takings Clause, and other distinctive approaches are utilized to give effect to other constitutional provisions. This is far different, however, from the use of different standards of review to address the threshold issue of the rationality of government action.

The Court's demand for this precise fit is based on the assumption that private landowners in this case possess a reasonable expectation regarding the use of their land that the public has attempted to disrupt. In fact, the situation is precisely the reverse: it is private landowners who are the interlopers. The public's expectation of access considerably antedates any private development on the coast. Article X, Section 4 of the California Constitution, adopted in 1879, declares:

No individual, partnership, or corporation, claiming or possessing the frontage or tidal lands of a harbor, bay, inlet, estuary, or other navigable water in this State, shall be permitted to exclude the right of way to any such water whenever it is required for any public purpose, nor to destroy or obstruct the free navigation of such water; and the Legislature shall enact such laws as will give the most liberal construction to this provision, so that access to the navigable waters of this State shall always be attainable for the people thereof.

It is therefore private landowners who threaten the disruption of settled public expectations. Where a private landowner has had a reasonable expectation that his or her property will be used for exclusively private purposes, the disruption of this expectation dictates that the government pay if it wishes the property to be used for a public purpose. In this case, however, the State has sought to protect *public* expectations of access from disruption by private land use. The State's exercise of its police power for this purpose deserves no less deference than any other measure designed to further the welfare of state citizens.

Congress expressly stated in passing the CZMA that "[i]n light of competing demands and the urgent need to protect and to give high priority to natural systems in the coastal zone, present state and local institutional arrangements for planning and regulating land and water uses in such areas are inadequate." 16 U.S.C. § 1451(h). It is thus puzzling that the Court characterizes as a "non-land-use justification," the exercise of the police power to "'provide continuous public access along Faria Beach as the lots undergo development or redevelopment.'" The Commission's determination that certain types of development jeopardize public access to the ocean, and that such development should be conditioned on preservation of access, is the essence of responsible land use planning. The Court's use of an unreasonably demanding standard for determining the rationality of state regulation in this area thus could hamper innovative efforts to preserve an increasingly fragile national resource.

B

Even if we accept the Court's unusual demand for a precise match between the condition imposed and the specific type of burden on access created by the appellants, the State's action easily satisfies this requirement. First, the lateral access condition serves to dissipate the impression that the beach that lies behind the wall of homes along the shore is for private use only. It requires no exceptional imaginative powers to find plausible the Commission's point that the average person passing along the road in front of a phalanx of imposing permanent residences, including the appellants' new home, is likely to conclude that this particular portion of the shore is not open to the public. If, however, that person can see that numerous people are passing and repassing along the dry sand, this conveys the message that the beach is in fact open for use by the public. Furthermore, those persons who go down to the public beach a quarter-mile away will be able to look down the coastline and see that persons have continuous access to the tidelands, and will observe signs that proclaim the public's right of access over the dry sand. The burden produced by the diminution in visual access—the impression that the beach is not open to the public—is thus directly alleviated by the provision for public access over the dry sand. The Court therefore has an unrealistically limited conception of what measures could reasonably be chosen to mitigate the burden produced by a diminution of visual access.

The second flaw in the Court's analysis of the fit between burden and exaction is more fundamental. The Court assumes that the only burden with which the Coastal Commission was concerned was blockage of visual access to the beach. This is incorrect.[4] The Commission specifically stated in its report in support of the permit condition that "[t]he Commission finds that the applicants' proposed development would present an increase in view blockage, *an increase in private use of the shorefront*, and that this impact would burden the public's ability to traverse to and along the shorefront." It declared that the possibility that "the public may get the impression that the beachfront is no longer available for public use" would be "due to *the encroaching nature of private use immediately adjacent to the public use, as well as* the visual 'block' of increased residential build-out impacting the visual quality of the beach-front."

The record prepared by the Commission is replete with references to the threat to public access along the coastline resulting from the seaward encroachment of private development along a beach whose mean high tide line is constantly shifting. As the Commission observed in its report, "The Faria Beach shoreline fluctuates during the year depending on the seasons and accompanying storms, and the public is not always able to traverse the shoreline below the mean high tide line." As a result, the boundary between publicly owned tidelands and privately owned beach is not a stable one, and "[t]he existing seawall is located very near to the mean high water line." When the beach is at its largest, the seawall is about 10 feet from the mean high tide mark; "[d]uring the period of the year when the beach suffers erosion, the mean high water line appears to be located either on or beyond the existing seawall." Expansion of private development on appellants' lot toward the seawall would thus "increase private use immediately adjacent to public tidelands, which has the potential of causing adverse impacts on the public's ability to traverse the shoreline." As the Commission explained:

> The placement of more private use adjacent to public tidelands has the potential of creating conflicts between the applicants and the public. The results of new private use encroachment into boundary/buffer areas between private and public property can create situations in which landowners intimidate the public and seek to prevent them from using public tidelands because of disputes between the two parties over where the exact boundary between private and public ownership is located. If the applicants' project would result in further seaward encroachment of private use into an area of clouded title, new private use in the subject encroachment area could result in use conflict between private and public entities on the subject shorefront.

The deed restriction on which permit approval was conditioned would directly address this threat to the public's access to the tidelands. It would provide a formal declaration of the public's right of access, thereby ensuring that the shifting character of the tidelands, and the presence of private development immediately adjacent to it, would not jeopardize enjoyment of that right.[5]

---

[4] This may be because the State in its briefs and at argument contended merely that the permit condition would serve to preserve overall public access, by offsetting the diminution in access resulting from the project, such as, *inter alia*, blocking the public's view of the beach. The State's position no doubt reflected the reasonable assumption that the Court would evaluate the rationality of its exercise of the police power in accordance with the traditional standard of review, and that the Court would not attempt to substitute its judgment about the best way to preserve overall public access to the ocean at the Faria Family Beach Tract.

[5] As the Commission's *Public Access (Shoreline) Interpretative Guidelines* state:

The imposition of the permit condition was therefore directly related to the fact that appellant's development would be "located along a unique stretch of coast where lateral access is inadequate due to the construction of private residential structures and shoreline protective devices along a fluctuating shoreline." The deed restriction was crafted to deal with the particular character of the beach along which appellants sought to build, and with the specific problems created by expansion of development toward the public tidelands. In imposing the restriction, the State sought to ensure that such development would not disrupt the historical expectation of the public regarding access to the sea.[6]

The Court is therefore simply wrong that there is no reasonable relationship between the permit condition and the specific type of burden on public access created by the appellants' proposed development. Even were the Court desirous of assuming the added responsibility of closely monitoring the regulation of development along the California coast, this record reveals rational public action by any conceivable standard.

II

The fact that the Commission's action is a legitimate exercise of the police power does not, of course, insulate it from a takings challenge, for when "regulation goes too far it will be recognized as a taking." *Pennsylvania Coal Co. v. Mahon*, 260 U.S. 393, 43 S. Ct. 158, 67 L. Ed. 322 (1922). Conventional takings analysis underscores the implausibility of the Court's holding, for it demonstrates that this exercise of California's police power implicates none of the concerns that underlie our takings jurisprudence.

In reviewing a Takings Clause claim, we have regarded as particularly significant the nature of the governmental action and the economic impact of regulation, especially the extent to which regulation interferes with investment-backed expectations. *Penn Central, supra.* The character of the government action in this case is the imposition of a condition on permit approval, which allows the public to continue to have access to the coast. The physical intrusion permitted by the deed restriction is minimal. The public is permitted the right to pass and re-pass along the coast in an area from the seawall to the mean high tide mark. This area is at its *widest* 10 feet, which means that *even without the permit condition*, the public's right of access permits it to pass on average within a few feet of the seawall. Passage closer to the 8-foot high rocky seawall

---

[T]he provision of lateral access recognizes the potential for conflicts between public and private use and creates a type of access that allows the public to move freely along all the tidelands in an area that can be clearly delineated and distinguished from private use areas. . . . Thus the "need" determination set forth in P[ublic] R[esources] C[ode] 30212(a)(2) should be measured in terms of providing access that buffers public access to the tidelands from the burdens generated on access by private development.

[6] The Court suggests that the risk of boundary disputes "is inherent in the right to exclude others from one's property," and thus cannot serve as a purpose to support the permit condition. The Commission sought the deed restriction, however, not to address a generalized problem inherent in any system of property, but to address the *particular* problem created by the shifting high-tide line along Faria Beach. Unlike the typical area in which a boundary is delineated reasonably clearly, the very problem on Faria Beach is that the boundary is *not* constant. The area open to public use therefore is frequently in question, and, as the discussion, *supra*, demonstrates, the Commission clearly tailored its permit condition precisely to address this specific problem.

The Court acknowledges that the Nollans' seawall could provide "a clear demarcation of the public easement," and thus avoid merely shifting "the location of the boundary dispute further on to the private owner's land." It nonetheless faults the Commission because every property subject to regulation may not have this feature. This case, however, is a challenge to the permit condition *as applied to the Nollans' property*, so the presence or absence of seawalls on other property is irrelevant.

will make the appellants even less visible to the public than passage along the high tide area farther out on the beach. The intrusiveness of such passage is even less than the intrusion resulting from the required dedication of a sidewalk in front of private residences, exactions which are commonplace conditions on approval of development. Furthermore, the high tide line shifts throughout the year, moving up to and beyond the seawall, so that public passage for a portion of the year would either be impossible or would not occur on appellant's property. Finally, although the Commission had the authority to provide for either passive or active recreational use of the property, it chose the least intrusive alternative: a mere right to pass and repass.[8] As this Court made clear in *PruneYard Shopping Center v. Robins*, 447 U.S. 74, 100 S. Ct. 2035, 64 L. Ed. 2d 741 (1980), physical access to private property in itself creates no takings problem if it does not "unreasonably impair the value or use of [the] property." Appellants can make no tenable claim that either their enjoyment of their property or its value is diminished by the public's ability merely to pass and re-pass a few feet closer to the seawall beyond which appellants' house is located.

PruneYard is also relevant in that we acknowledged in that case that public access rested upon a "state constitutional . . . provision that had been construed to create rights to the use of private property by strangers." In this case, of course, the State is also acting to protect a state constitutional right. The constitutional provision guaranteeing public access to the ocean states that "the Legislature shall enact such laws as will give *the most liberal construction to this provision* so that access to the navigable waters of this State shall be always attainable for the people thereof." Cal. Const., Art. X, § 4. This provision is the explicit basis for the statutory directive to provide for public access along the coast in new development projects, Cal. Pub. Res. Code Ann. § 30212 (1986), and has been construed by the state judiciary to permit passage over private land where necessary to gain access to the tidelands. *Grupe v. California Coastal Comm'n*, 166 Cal. App. 3d 148, 212 Cal. Rptr. 578 (1985). The physical access to the perimeter of appellants' property at issue in this case thus results directly from the State's enforcement of the state constitution.

Finally, the character of the regulation in this case is not unilateral government action, but a condition on approval of a development request submitted by appellants. The State has not sought to interfere with any pre-existing property interest, but has responded to appellants' proposal to intensify development on the coast. Appellants themselves chose to submit a new development application, and could claim no property interest in its approval. They were aware that approval of such development would be conditioned on preservation of adequate public

---

[8] The Commission acted in accordance with its *Guidelines* both in determining the width of the area of passage, and in prohibiting any recreational use of the property. The *Guidelines* state that it may be necessary on occasion to provide for less than the normal 25-foot wide access way along the dry sand when this may be necessary to "protect the privacy rights of adjacent property owners." They also provide this advice in selecting the type of public use that may be permitted:

Pass and Repass. Where topographic constraints of the site make use of the beach dangerous, where habitat values of the shoreline would be adversely impacted by public use of the shoreline or where the accessway may encroach closer than 20 feet to a residential structure, the accessway may be limited to the right of the public to pass and repass along the access area. For the purposes of these guidelines, pass and repass is defined as the right to walk and run along the shoreline. This would provide for public access along the shoreline but would not allow for any additional use of the accessway. Because this severely limits the public's ability to enjoy the adjacent state owned tidelands by restricting the potential use of the access areas, this form of access dedication should be used only where necessary to protect the habitat values of the site, where topographic constraints warrant the restriction, or where it is necessary to protect the privacy of the landowner.

access to the ocean. The State has initiated no action against appellants' property; had the Nollans' not proposed more intensive development in the coastal zone, they would never have been subject to the provision that they challenge.

Examination of the economic impact of the Commission's action reinforces the conclusion that no taking has occurred. Allowing appellants to intensify development along the coast in exchange for ensuring public access to the ocean is a classic instance of government action that produces a "reciprocity of advantage." *Pennsylvania Coal, supra.* Appellants have been allowed to replace a one-story 521-square-foot beach home with a two-story 1,674-square-foot residence and an attached two-car garage, resulting in development covering 2,464 square feet of the lot. Such development obviously significantly increases the value of appellants' property; appellants make no contention that this increase is offset by any diminution in value resulting from the deed restriction, much less that the restriction made the property less valuable than it would have been without the new construction. Furthermore, appellants gain an additional benefit from the Commission's permit condition program. They are able to walk along the beach beyond the confines of their own property only because the Commission has required deed restrictions as a condition of approving other new beach developments. Thus, appellants benefit both as private landowners and as members of the public from the fact that new development permit requests are conditioned on preservation of public access.

Ultimately, appellants' claim of economic injury is flawed because it rests on the assumption of entitlement to the full value of their new development. Appellants submitted a proposal for more intensive development of the coast, which the Commission was under no obligation to approve, and now argue that a regulation designed to ameliorate the impact of that development deprives them of the full value of their improvements. Even if this novel claim were somehow cognizable, it is not significant. "[T]he interest in anticipated gains has traditionally been viewed as less compelling than other property-related interests." *Andrus v. Allard*, 444 U.S. 51, 100 S. Ct. 318, 62 L. Ed. 2d 210 (1979).

With respect to appellants' investment-backed expectations, appellants can make no reasonable claim to any expectation of being able to exclude members of the public from crossing the edge of their property to gain access to the ocean. . . . In this case, the state constitution explicitly states that no one possessing the "front-age" of any "navigable water in this State, shall be permitted to exclude the right of way to such water whenever it is required for any public purpose." Cal. Const., Art. X, § 4. The state Code expressly provides that, save for exceptions not relevant here, "[p]ublic access from the nearest public roadway to the shoreline and along the coast shall be provided in new development projects." Cal. Pub. Res. Code Ann. § 30212 (1986). The Coastal Commission *Interpretative Guidelines* make clear that fulfillment of the Commission's constitutional and statutory duty require that approval of new coastline development be conditioned upon provisions ensuring lateral public access to the ocean. At the time of appellants' permit request, the Commission had conditioned all 43 of the proposals for coastal new development in the Faria Family Beach Tract on the provision of deed restrictions ensuring lateral access along the shore. Finally, the Faria family had leased the beach property since the early part of this century, and "the Faria family and their lessees [including the Nollans] had not interfered with public use of the beachfront within the Tract, so long as public use was limited to pass and re-pass lateral access along the shore." California therefore has clearly established that the power of exclusion for which appellants seek compensation simply is not a strand in the bundle of appellants' property rights, and appellants have never acted as if it were. Given this state of affairs, appellants cannot claim that the deed restriction has deprived them of a reasonable expectation to exclude from their property persons desiring to gain access to the sea.

Even were we somehow to concede a pre-existing expectation of a right to exclude, appellants were clearly on notice when requesting a new development permit that a condition of approval would be a provision ensuring public lateral access to the shore. Thus, they surely could have had no expectation that they could obtain approval of their new development and exercise any right of exclusion afterward.

. . . .

Standard Takings Clause analysis thus indicates that the Court employs its unduly restrictive standard of police power rationality to find a taking where neither the character of governmental action nor the nature of the private interest affected raise any takings concern. The result is that the Court invalidates regulation that represents a reasonable adjustment of the burdens and benefits of development along the California coast.

III

The foregoing analysis makes clear that the State has taken no property from appellants. Imposition of the permit condition in this case represents the State's reasonable exercise of its police power. The Coastal Commission has drawn on its expertise to preserve the balance between private development and public access, by requiring that any project that intensifies development on the increasingly crowded California coast must be offset by gains in public access. Under the normal standard for review of the police power, this provision is eminently reasonable. Even accepting the Court's novel insistence on a precise *quid pro quo* of burdens and benefits, there is a reasonable relationship between the public benefit and the burden created by appellants' development. The movement of development closer to the ocean creates the prospect of encroachment on public tidelands, because of fluctuation in the mean high tide line. The deed restriction ensures that disputes about the boundary between private and public property will not deter the public from exercising its right to have access to the sea.

Furthermore, consideration of the Commission's action under traditional takings analysis underscores the absence of any viable takings claim. The deed restriction permits the public only to pass and repass along a narrow strip of beach, a few feet closer to a seawall at the periphery of appellants' property. Appellants almost surely have enjoyed an increase in the value of their property even with the restriction, because they have been allowed to build a significantly larger new home with garage on their lot. Finally, appellants can claim the disruption of no expectation interest, both because they have no right to exclude the public under state law, and because, even if they did, they had full advance notice that new development along the coast is conditioned on provisions for continued public access to the ocean.

Fortunately, the Court's decision regarding this application of the Commission's permit program will probably have little ultimate impact either on this parcel in particular or the Commission program in general. A preliminary study by a Senior Lands Agent in the State Attorney General's Office indicates that the portion of the beach at issue in this case likely belongs to the public. Since a full study had not been completed at the time of appellants' permit application, the deed restriction was requested "without regard to the possibility that the applicant is proposing development on public land." Furthermore, analysis by the same Land Agent also indicated that the public had obtained a prescriptive right to the use of Faria Beach from the seawall to the ocean.[12] The Superior Court explicitly stated in its ruling against the Commission on the permit condition issue that "no part of this opinion is intended to foreclose the public's opportunity to adjudicate the possibility that public rights in [appellants'] beach have been acquired through prescriptive use."

With respect to the permit condition program in general, the Commission should have little difficulty in the future in utilizing its expertise to demonstrate a specific connection between provisions for access and burdens on access produced by new development. Neither the Commission in its report nor the State in its briefs and at argument highlighted the particular threat to lateral access created by appellants' development project. In defending its action, the State emphasized the general point that *overall* access to the beach had been preserved, since the diminution of access created by the project had been offset by the gain in lateral access. This approach is understandable, given that the State relied on the reasonable assumption that its action was justified under the normal standard of review for determining legitimate exercises of a State's police power. In the future, alerted to the Court's apparently more demanding requirement, it need only make clear that a provision for public access directly responds to a particular type of burden on access created by a new development. Even if I did not believe that the record in this case satisfies this requirement, I would have to acknowledge that the record's documentation of the impact of coastal development indicates that the Commission should have little problem presenting its findings in a way that avoids a takings problem.

Nonetheless it is important to point out that the Court's insistence on a precise accounting system in this case is insensitive to the fact that increasing intensity of development in many areas calls for farsighted, comprehensive planning that takes into account both the interdependence of land uses and the cumulative impact of development. As one scholar has noted:

> Property does not exist in isolation. Particular parcels are tied to one another in complex ways, and property is more accurately described as being inextricably part of a network of relationships that is neither limited to, nor usefully defined by, the property boundaries with which the legal system is accustomed to dealing. Frequently, use of any given parcel of property is at the same time effectively a use of, or a demand upon, property beyond the border of the user.

Sax, *Takings, Private Property, and Public Rights*, 81 Yale L.J. 149, 152 (1971). As Congress has declared, "The key to more effective protection and use of the land and water resources of the coastal zone [is for the states to] develo[p] land and water use programs for the coastal zone, including unified policies, criteria, standards, methods, and processes for dealing with land and water use decisions of more than local significance." 16 U.S.C. § 1451(i). This is clearly a call for a focus on the overall impact of development on coastal areas. State agencies therefore require considerable flexibility in responding to private desires for development in a way that guarantees the preservation of public access to the coast. They should be encouraged to regulate development in the context of the overall balance of competing uses of the shoreline. The Court today does precisely the opposite, overruling an eminently reasonable exercise of an expert state agency's judgment, substituting its own narrow view of how this balance should be struck. Its reasoning is hardly suited to the complex reality of natural resource protection in the twentieth century.

---

[12] The report of the Senior Land Agent stated: Based on my past experience and my investigation to date of this property it is my opinion that the area seaward of the revetment at 3822 Pacific Coast Highway, Faria Beach, as well as all the area seaward of the revetments built to protect the Faria Beach community, if not publicly owned, has been impliedly dedicated to the public for passive recreational use.

I can only hope that today's decision is an aberration, and that a broader vision ultimately prevails.[14]

I dissent.

JUSTICE BLACKMUN, dissenting.

[Opinion omitted.]

JUSTICE STEVENS, with whom JUSTICE BLACKMUN joins, dissenting.

The debate between the Court and Justice Brennan illustrates an extremely important point concerning government regulation of the use of privately owned real estate. Intelligent, well-informed public officials may in good faith disagree about the validity of specific types of land use regulation. Even the wisest lawyers would have to acknowledge great uncertainty about the scope of this Court's takings jurisprudence. Yet, because of the Court's remarkable ruling in *First English Evangelical Lutheran Church v. Los Angeles County*, 482 U.S. 304 (1987), local governments and officials must pay the price for the necessarily vague standards in this area of the law.

In his dissent in *San Diego Gas & Electric Co. v. San Diego*, 450 U.S. 621 (1981), Justice Brennan proposed a brand new constitutional rule. He argued that a mistake such as the one that a majority of the Court believes that the California Coastal Commission made in this case should automatically give rise to pecuniary liability for a "temporary taking." Notwithstanding the unprecedented chilling effect that such a rule will obviously have on public officials charged with the responsibility for drafting and implementing regulations designed to protect the environment and the public welfare, six Members of the Court recently endorsed Justice Brennan's novel proposal. *See First English Evangelical Lutheran Church, supra.*

I write today to identify the severe tension between that dramatic development in the law and the view expressed by Justice Brennan's dissent in this case that the public interest is served by encouraging state agencies to exercise considerable flexibility in responding to private desires for development in a way that threatens the preservation of public resources. I like the hat that Justice Brennan has donned today better than the one he wore in *San Diego*, and I am persuaded that he has the better of the legal arguments here. Even if his position prevailed in this case, however, it would be of little solace to land-use planners who would still be left guessing about how the Court will react to the next case, and the one after that. As this case demonstrates, the rule of liability created by the Court in *First English* is a short-sighted one. Like Justice Brennan, I hope "that a broader vision ultimately prevails."

I respectfully dissent.

[4] Some Thoughts About *Nollan*

Much of property law is about time—lifetimes, time divisions, the time value of money, and history. The longevity of the economic and cultural interests studied in a property course is the main thing that distinguishes it from all of the others you take as a first year student. In various

---

[14] I believe that States should be afforded considerable latitude in regulating private development, without fear that their regulatory efforts will often be found to constitute a taking. "*If* . . . regulation denies the property owner the use and enjoyment of his land and is found to effect a 'taking'," however, I believe that compensation is the appropriate remedy for this constitutional violation. *San Diego Gas & Electric Co. v. San Diego*, 450 U.S. 621, 656 (1981) (BRENNAN, J., dissenting) (emphasis added). I therefore see my dissent here as completely consistent with my position in *First English Evangelical Church v. Los Angeles County*, 482 U.S. 304 (1987).

spots in this text, you have studied agreements—not the legality of their formation so much as their impact upon later generations. You have studied process—not only for the way it organizes a legal system but also for its utility in protecting values accumulated over time. You have studied torts—not just as a way of redressing wrongs, but as a device for structuring investment incentives over long periods of time. And you have studied constitutional law—partly as an inquiry into the structure of government, but mostly as a way of investigating the place of property concepts in our political history.

Time and history are clearly relevant to the ways the Supreme Court has talked about the Takings Clause. Justice Rehnquist's views, for example, seem to encode prior experience into the Takings Clause, creating significant obstacles to the redefinition of economic obligations in later generations. Investments made some time ago are given a major role even if cultural expectations about them have changed dramatically in the intervening years. Put in another, and perhaps more provocative way, Rehnquistian Takings analysis does not view cultural change as one of the major types of risk that investors must take into account when they make property decisions.

Justice Brennan, on the other hand, suggested in *Penn Central* that he was willing to set aside some areas as regulated "commons," as areas unavailable to individuals for use in markets, as areas to be saved for future generations. And he was willing to warn people that changing cultural values may have a significant impact on the value of their property holdings. As attitudes about the environment change, so may an owner's ability to exploit an asset. For Justice Brennan, the risks of government regulation were part of the risk calculus every investor had to make before electing to purchase and deciding to continue holding an asset. Indeed the existence of regulation created expectations of still more regulation to come.

The opinions in *Nollan v. California Coastal Commission*, like those in *Penn Central*, embody different conceptions of time. Much in *Nollan* mirrored the prior opinions of Justices Brennan and Rehnquist in *Penn Central*. Think, for example, of the ways the Justices described the nature of the property interests at stake in the cases. In *Penn Central* Rehnquist said the case was about air rights, while Brennan wrote about the entire terminal site. Rehnquist conceptually severed the air rights from the rest of the parcel, just as Holmes conceptually severed the support estate from the rest of the mineral interests held by Pennsylvania Coal. Once conceptually severed from the rest of the assets owned by the party being subjected to regulation by the state, Rehnquist treated the case as one that affected only the conceptually severed interest. Doing that made it much easier to argue that the entire property interest of the regulated party was "taken." Brennan declined to do that. Rehnquist enshrined the historical, legal descriptions of traditional estates and interests in property—air rights—and surrounded such legal terms of art with enormous symbolic importance. They became the vehicles by which Rehnquist determined whether disaffection costs existed. Brennan looked beyond the legal vocabulary to investigate the nature of the investment portfolio at issue in the case. He was less concerned with the history of estates in land or the way people reacted to particularized bits of legal vocabulary than he was with the history of an investor's investment expectations in a portfolio of interests.

Justice Scalia pushed the conceptual analysis of Justice Rehnquist's *Penn Central* opinion one step further in *Nollan*. He presumed that if the state wished only to control lateral access along the beach, an easement was taken. Not only did he conceptually sever the access rights from the rest of Nollan's parcel, but he also *assumed* the takings answer that Rehnquist agonized over at some length in his *Penn Central* dissent. He made an assumption out of what even Rehnquist thought was contestable in the Grand Central Terminal litigation.

After Justice Scalia eliminated lateral access as an issue from the case without discussing the merits of the assumption that requiring conveyance of lateral access rights was a Taking, he left himself what was arguably an easier task—getting rid of the idea that lateral access contributes to better ocean views and reduces psychological barriers to recognition of the beach as a public gathering place. Stating the issue in the case that way made California's regulation seem silly. How, Scalia claimed, could California argue with a straight face that requiring the Nollans to sign over an easement contributed to the ability of citizens to view the ocean from the road? Posing the issue that way made it easy for him to find that there was no substantial link between the purposes for the state regulation and the solution adopted by the California Coastal Commission. As a useful adjunct, it also allowed him to enunciate a test requiring a substantial link between regulation and its goals, a test that buried any hope that land use controls would be treated in the future like other legislation controlling the economy. The broad vision of public purpose and low level of judicial scrutiny seen in cases like *Euclid v. Ambler*, p. 490 above; *Belle Terre v. Boraas*, discussed p. 908 above; or *Hawaii Housing Authority v. Midkiff*, p. 902 above, was not called upon to rescue the *Nollan* accessway dedication program.

At the end of his opinion, Justice Scalia concluded that the lack of a substantial link between the contents of the access regulation and its goals meant that the dedication requirement imposed on the Nollans was simply a disguised grab of lateral access, a result that he assumed at the outset violated the Takings Clause under *Loretto*. In short, once Scalia stated what for him was obvious—lateral access is a clear taking—then Nollan had to win. When all was said and done, Justice Scalia left himself two ways to attack regulation of land in the future—a substantive due process theory attacking the nexus between a regulation and its purpose, and a Takings theory using conceptual severance and a broad vision of *Loretto*.

Justice Scalia, like Justice Rehnquist, looked mostly to the justness of prior transfers of title in his analysis. He gave the formal, historical status of ownership extant prior to the enforcement of the land use controls on the Nollans enormous influence in his jurisprudence. No credence was given to the notion that cultural expectations or shifts in ideologies supported changes in Constitutional analysis. The idea that the state may bargain with a landowner over the use of property was not acceptable to Scalia. All the recent publicity about the risks of construction on fragile shore lines, and the need for public regulation to reduce public expenditures after hurricanes and other natural disasters was unimportant in defining investment expectations. Present time analysis was wholly dependent on the validity of prior historical understandings about ownership of specific interests in land, here easements.

Justice Brennan, dissenting in *Nollan*, assumed that certain elements of our surroundings, such as views of or access along beaches and oceans, may be excluded from market control and saved for future generations, that each generation may initiate steps inhibiting the actions of later owners. His view of history was less formal than Justice Scalia's. Shifts in cultural judgments created a much more substantial foundation for enacting limitations on use of property than they did for Scalia.

This debate between Justice Brennan on one side and Justices Rehnquist and Scalia on the other is like (though not completely like) the jurisprudential debate between Rawls and Nozick. Rawls theory began on a largely ahistorical note. When behind the veil, people did not even know which generation they were from. They only knew they had been born. His search was for a justification for redistribution, for an ahistorical basis for allowing each generation to alter the expectations of the generation that preceded it. He used the veil to construct a rule that we would all vote, as it were, for legal norms precluding us from making the least well off worse off. Not knowing our own economic or generational situation, we would structure a world that created a minimum floor for everyone. In some ways Rawls tried to find a jurisprudential outlet for many of the political conclusions reached by the moderate Realists, New Dealers, and Great Society advocates. Justice Brennan may have been reaching for something like that idea, while still paying attention to the negative consequences of redistribution—to disaffection costs—at least when the worst off are effected, and perhaps in other circumstances as well.

Nozick argued that Rawls created an unacceptable end-result theory devoid of concepts of current justice. He argued that the creation of distributional rules behind the veil was in fact quite different from the notion of redistribution of assets already in circulation in an extant culture. Nozick used this notion as a starting point for structuring a different theory of justice, one based on the idea that a claim of ownership is just if the transfers leading to that ownership were themselves just. While bowing to history as a basis for determining present day justice, this theory actually enshrined extant distributions as presumptively just and made it difficult to undertake any redistribution unless it was done to rectify past unjust transfers. That surely is similar to what Justice Scalia did in *Nollan*. In many ways both Scalia and Nozick represent the conservative wing of a new form of "rights"-based advocacy now used by conservative thinkers.[67]

The jurisprudential debate, therefore, like the debate among the Justices, is about the power of history to bind our present-day legal structure. Are we willing to qualify the power of history by allowing redistributions to improve the status of the least well off?[68] Or will such efforts be trumped by claims that distributions justly arising in the past are unalterable?

[5]   Problem Notes

[a]   What's New in Scalia's Opinion?

There are two characteristics of Justice Scalia's opinion that may portend some change in takings jurisprudence. First, Brennan correctly pointed out at the beginning of his dissent that the Supreme Court routinely required state or local governments to fulfill a very minimal public purpose test—whether the government "could rationally have decided that the measure adopted might achieve" a valid objective. Scalia's test inquired whether the land use regulation "substantially advances legitimate state interests and does not deny an owner economically viable use of his land," a verbal construct that appears less sympathetic to government controls. Second, Scalia followed through on his apparent threat to scrutinize more closely the purposes underlying local controls by examining in detail the interests the California Coastal Commission claimed supported its conditional grant of a building permit to the Nollans. While Brennan was willing

---

[67] It may be worth a brief pause to think about Rawls and Nozick as commentators on gender, race and ethnicity. For example, what would Nozick have to say about modern claims by Native Americans that their property was unjustly taken by European settlers in the seventeenth and following centuries? Is a rectification principle in order? Or what about the continuing cultural consequences of slavery or the refusal of the culture to recognize property rights of married women? Do prior unjust distributions justify redistribution? Do changing conceptions of what "unjust" means have any influence on the content of the rectification principle? Does history turn out to be relevant anyway?

[68] Or think about Rawls' savings principle and Native American culture. Many traditional Native American cultures have strong affinities to nature. Can we learn a savings principle from that? Many traditional Native American cultures also attempt to resolve problems by thinking about the consequences of their actions for many generations into the future. It is impossible to know exactly what the "correct" answers are when acting under such constraints. All you can do is the best you can do. But the idea does suggest a quite different cultural mind set from that of the majority American culture.

to give credence to the most tenuous of connections between the lateral beach easement and the public's need to view the beach, Scalia eliminated one purpose—actual access—as patently frivolous and dismissed the others as obviously unrelated to the building permit condition. If the *Penn Central* case, or one like it, came before the Supreme Court, today, would Justice Scalia invalidate the single site historic designation system?

[b]   Takings and the Due Process Clause

Earlier materials, p. 935 above, noted the difficulties in distinguishing between the Supreme Court's reasoning in Takings Clause and Due Process Clause cases. This debate surfaced in *Nollan.* Justice Scalia, in footnote 3, argued that the Takings and Due Process Clauses do not operate under the same general standard. Justice Brennan responded in footnote 1 in his dissent that he never contended that Takings and Due Process cases were the same, but only that judicial scrutiny of the public purposes claimed to support regulation of either land or other aspects of the economy should be quite restrained.[69] Though both Justices Scalia and Brennan say that Taking and Due Process cases are different, are they correct?

[c]   Revisit *Oregon ex rel. Thornton v. Hay*

Take another look at *Oregon ex. Rel. Thornton v. Hay,* p. 105 above in Chapter 1. Suppose that the result in the case was wholly novel to the law of Oregon, an unexpected delight to beach lovers everywhere. After *Nollan,* would that result constitute a Taking? Was Justice Brennan accurate when he noted that prescription by the public will probably lead to Nollan's loss of the beach between the high tide line and the seawall?

[d]   Revisit *New Jersey v. Shack*

Revisit the New Jersey Supreme Court's opinion in *New Jersey v. Shack,* p. 557 above. After *Nollan,* may the New Jersey Supreme Court still require owners of migrant farms to grant access to various private persons claiming a need to visit with employees? The United States Supreme Court has held that California may require shopping center owners to permit demonstrations on the portions of their property open to the public. *PruneYard Shopping Center v. Robins,* discussed p. 990 above. Justice Scalia, in footnote 1 of his opinion in *Nollan,* contended that *PruneYard* was not inconsistent with *Nollan* because the shopping center was already open to the public and the access granted was not permanent. Justice Brennan, of course, argued that *PruneYard* supported California's beach access permit condition in *Nollan.* In neither case, he argued, did the access unreasonably impair the value of the property. Is there a difference between an "easement" to demonstrate at a shopping center during business hours and an "easement" to walk along a beach above the high tide line and below the seawall?

[e]   Revisit Justice Scalia's Opinion

In his *Nollan* opinion, Justice Scalia noted:

[I]f the [California Coastal] Commission attached to the permit some condition that would have protected the public's ability to see the beach notwithstanding construction of the new

---

[69] Public purposes are relevant to exercise of the eminent domain power because every condemnation must be supported by a valid public purpose. In other economic regulation cases, the Court has also insisted that the Due Process clause requires that legislatures, whether state or federal, enact statutes that are *reasonably* related to some valid public purpose. Justice Scalia expressed a more stringent relationship test in *Nollan.* Obviously the more closely the Court scrutinizes public purposes, the more likely it is that either the Takings Clause or the Due Process Clause will be invoked to invalidate legislation.

house—for example, a height limitation, a width restriction, or a ban on fences—so long as the Commission could have exercised its police power (as we have assumed it could) to forbid construction of the house altogether, imposition of the condition would also be constitutional. Moreover (and here we come closer to the facts of the present case), the condition would be constitutional even if it consisted of the requirement that the Nollans provide a viewing spot on their property for passersby with whose sighting of the ocean their new house would interfere.

How can these sentiments be squared with Scalia's opening remarks that labeling as mere regulation a requirement that all waterfront owners grant a lateral beach easement to the public deprives words "of all their ordinary meaning?" Isn't a scenic view easement like a beach access easement? Is the public's interest in a scenic view stronger than its concern over beach access? Was *Nollan* a case about public intrusions into possessory interests, a case about the public interest requirement of taking law discussed in the prior section of materials, a case about both issues, or a case about neither set of concerns?

[f]   Some Landlord–Tenant Examples of Government "Taking" "Possession"

As you discovered in the landlord-tenant materials, a number of states have adopted restrictions on property owners' ability to evict tenants or convert buildings to condominiums. Why isn't a statute that prohibits conversion, or forbids an owner from occupying the unit herself, invalid? One constitutional challenge to a statute that effectively barred a condominium unit owner from removing a tenant failed in *Flynn v. City of Cambridge*, 383 Mass. 152, 418 N.E.2d 335 (1981). What would the Supreme Court do? Isn't occupancy as important a stick in the bundle as inheritance? Do *Nollan* and *Loretto* suggest that *Flynn* was wrongly decided?

Another interesting case involved claims by tenants for compensation when they were removed from their apartments by public authorities after the discovery of very serious housing code violations. In *Devines v. Maier*, 665 F.2d 138 (7th Cir. 1981), the Circuit Court found that the leasehold interests of the tenants were taken and remanded the case for determination of what compensation was just. Arguments by the City of Milwaukee that occupancy of unsafe apartments was illegal were unavailing since, the court decided, public authorities were actively involved in the decision to label a building uninhabitable and to remove its occupants. The court also noted that the tenants lost their entire bundle of rights in the building, while the owner lost only the right to receive rents, not the fee simple. Thus, what was a taking for the tenants might not be a taking for the landlord. What would the Supreme Court do with this sort of dispute?

[g]   Rent Control

In *Pennell v. City of San Jose*, 485 U.S. 1 (1988), a rent control ordinance contained features typical of many similar statutes around the country, including a provision entitling landlords to seek rent increases in order to maintain acceptable rates of return. But it had one novel feature which became the focus of the litigation. Tenants could challenge rent increases of more than 8% on financial hardship grounds and obtain rollbacks, even if that reduced the overall rate of return to the landlord from the building. Justice Rehnquist, writing for a 6-2 majority, rebuffed the facial challenge to the tenant hardship provision. Justice Scalia wrote the dissent. Are there any differences between a tenant hardship provision, a beach access condition, or a mandatory cable attachment standard?

[6]   Background to *Dolan v. City of Tigard*

The Dolan family lived in Portland, Oregon, and owned 11 hardware and lighting stores in the city and its surrounding area. John Dolan first came to public attention in the late 1980s when he was instrumental in blocking a plan to spruce up the downtown area of Tigard. The plan would have forced the Dolans to close their Tigard store. The town wanted to purchase the land and use it for other purposes. After voters rejected the urban renewal plans, the town proceeded with another project to create a park in the Fanno Creek flood plain. When the Dolans sought permission to enlarge their A-Boy store in Tigard, they were asked to dedicate land to the public for the park in return for the right to enlarge their business. John Dolan decided to resist the dedication request. He died before the Supreme Court decided the case, but his son Daniel continued the dispute.[70]

A-Boy West Store Viewed From the North Side of Main Street

---

[70] The story may be found in Paul Barrett, *A Store Owner's Squabble With a City Tests Government's Right to Private Land*, WALL ST. J. Mar. 23, 1994.

A-Boy West Store Viewed from the Main Street Bridge Over Fanno Creek

[7]   Opinions of the United States Supreme Court in *Dolan v. Tigard*

Florence Dolan v. City of Tigard

Supreme Court of the United States
512 U.S. 374, 114 S. Ct. 2309, 129 L. Ed. 2d 304 (1994)

REHNQUIST, C.J., delivered the opinion of the Court, in which O'CONNOR, SCALIA, KENNEDY, and THOMAS, JJ., joined.

Petitioner challenges the decision of the Oregon Supreme Court which held that the city of Tigard could condition the approval of her building permit on the dedication of a portion of her property for flood control and traffic improvements. We granted certiorari to resolve a question left open by our decision in *Nollan v. California Coastal Comm'n*, 483 U.S. 825 (1987), of what is the required degree of connection between the exactions imposed by the city and the projected impacts of the proposed development.

I

The State of Oregon enacted a comprehensive land use management program in 1973. The program required all Oregon cities and counties to adopt new comprehensive land use plans that were consistent with the statewide planning goals. The plans are implemented by land use regulations which are part of an integrated hierarchy of legally binding goals, plans, and regulations. Pursuant to the State's requirements, the city of Tigard, a community of some 30,000 residents on the southwest edge of Portland, developed a comprehensive plan and codified it in its Community Development Code (CDC). The CDC requires property owners in the area zoned Central Business District to comply with a 15% open space and landscaping requirement, which limits total site coverage, including all structures and paved parking, to 85% of the parcel. After the completion of a transportation study that identified congestion in the Central Business District as a particular problem, the city adopted a plan for a pedestrian/bicycle pathway intended to encourage alternatives to automobile transportation for short trips. The CDC requires that new development facilitate this plan by dedicating land for pedestrian pathways where provided for in the pedestrian/bicycle pathway plan.[1]

The city also adopted a Master Drainage Plan (Drainage Plan). The Drainage Plan noted that flooding occurred in several areas along Fanno Creek, including areas near petitioner's property. The Drainage Plan also established that the increase in impervious surfaces associated with continued urbanization would exacerbate these flooding problems. To combat these risks, the Drainage Plan suggested a series of improvements to the Fanno Creek Basin, including channel excavation in the area next to petitioner's property. Other recommendations included ensuring that the floodplain remains free of structures and that it be preserved as greenways to minimize flood damage to structures. The Drainage Plan concluded that the cost of these improvements should be shared based on both direct and indirect benefits, with property owners along the waterways paying more due to the direct benefit that they would receive. . . .

Petitioner Florence Dolan owns a plumbing and electric supply store located on Main Street in the Central Business District of the city. The store covers approximately 9,700 square feet on the eastern side of a 1.67-acre parcel, which includes a gravel parking lot. Fanno Creek flows through the southwestern corner of the lot and along its western boundary. The year-round flow of the creek renders the area within the creek's 100-year floodplain virtually unusable for commercial development. The city's comprehensive plan includes the Fanno Creek floodplain as part of the city's greenway system.

Petitioner applied to the city for a permit to redevelop the site. Her proposed plans called for nearly doubling the size of the store to 17,600 square feet, and paving a 39-space parking lot. The existing store, located on the opposite side of the parcel, would be razed in sections as construction progressed on the new building. In the second phase of the project, petitioner proposed to build an additional structure on the northeast side of the site for complementary businesses, and to provide more parking. The proposed expansion and intensified use are consistent with the city's zoning scheme in the Central Business District.

The City Planning Commission granted petitioner's permit application subject to conditions imposed by the city's CDC. The CDC establishes the following standard for site development review approval: "Where landfill and/or development is allowed within and adjacent to the 100-year floodplain, the city shall require the dedication of sufficient open land area for greenway adjoining and within the floodplain. This area shall include portions at a suitable elevation for

---

[1] The CDC . . . provides: "The development shall facilitate pedestrian/bicycle circulation if the site is located on a street with designated bikepaths or adjacent to a designated greenway/open space/park. Specific items to be addressed [include]: (i) Provision of efficient, convenient and continuous pedestrian and bicycle transit circulation systems, linking developments by requiring dedication and construction of pedestrian and bikepaths identified in the comprehensive plan. If direct connections cannot be made, require that funds in the amount of the construction cost be deposited into an account for the purpose of constructing paths."

the construction of a pedestrian/bicycle pathway within the floodplain in accordance with the adopted pedestrian/bicycle plan." Thus, the Commission required that petitioner dedicate the portion of her property lying within the 100-year floodplain for improvement of a storm drainage system along Fanno Creek and that she dedicate an additional 15-foot strip of land adjacent to the floodplain as a pedestrian/bicycle pathway. The dedication required by that condition encompasses approximately 7,000 square feet, or roughly 10% of the property. In accordance with city practice, petitioner could rely on the dedicated property to meet the 15% open space and landscaping requirement mandated by the city's zoning scheme. The city would bear the cost of maintaining a landscaped buffer between the dedicated area and the new store.

Petitioner requested variances from the CDC standards. Variances are granted only where it can be shown that, owing to special circumstances related to a specific piece of the land, the literal interpretation of the applicable zoning provisions would cause "an undue or unnecessary hardship" unless the variance is granted. Rather than posing alternative mitigating measures to offset the expected impacts of her proposed development, as allowed under the CDC, petitioner simply argued that her proposed development would not conflict with the policies of the comprehensive plan. The Commission denied the request.

The Commission made a series of findings concerning the relationship between the dedicated conditions and the projected impacts of petitioner's project. First, the Commission noted that "[i]t is reasonable to assume that customers and employees of the future uses of this site could utilize a pedestrian/bicycle pathway adjacent to this development for their transportation and recreational needs." The Commission noted that the site plan has provided for bicycle parking in a rack in front of the proposed building and "[i]t is reasonable to expect that some of the users of the bicycle parking provided for by the site plan will use the pathway adjacent to Fanno Creek if it is constructed." In addition, the Commission found that creation of a convenient, safe pedestrian/bicycle pathway system as an alternative means of transportation "could offset some of the traffic demand on [nearby] streets and lessen the increase in traffic congestion."

The Commission went on to note that the required floodplain dedication would be reasonably related to petitioner's request to intensify the use of the site given the increase in the impervious surface. The Commission stated that the "anticipated increased storm water flow from the subject property to an already strained creek and drainage basin can only add to the public need to manage the stream channel and floodplain for drainage purpose." Based on this anticipated increased storm water flow, the Commission concluded that "the requirement of dedication of the floodplain area on the site is related to the applicant's plan to intensify development on the site." The Tigard City Council approved the Commission's final order, subject to one minor modification; the City Council reassigned the responsibility for surveying and marking the floodplain area from petitioner to the city's engineering department.

Petitioner appealed to the Land Use Board of Appeals (LUBA) on the ground that the city's dedication requirements were not related to the proposed development, and, therefore, those requirements constituted an uncompensated taking of their property under the Fifth Amendment. In evaluating the federal taking claim, LUBA assumed that the city's findings about the impacts of the proposed development were supported by substantial evidence. Given the undisputed fact that the proposed larger building and paved parking area would increase the amount of impervious surfaces and the runoff into Fanno Creek, LUBA concluded that "there is a 'reasonable relationship' between the proposed development and the requirement to dedicate land along Fanno Creek for a greenway." With respect to the pedestrian/bicycle pathway, LUBA noted the

Commission's finding that a significantly larger retail sales building and parking lot would attract larger numbers of customers and employees and their vehicles. It again found a "reasonable relationship" between alleviating the impacts of increased traffic from the development and facilitating the provision of a pedestrian/bicycle pathway as an alternative means of transportation.

The Oregon Court of Appeals affirmed, rejecting petitioner's contention that in *Nollan v. California Coastal Comm'n*, 483 U.S. 825 (1987), we had abandoned the "reasonable relationship" test in favor of a stricter "essential nexus" test. The Oregon Supreme Court affirmed. The court also disagreed with petitioner's contention that the *Nollan* Court abandoned the "reasonably related" test. Instead, the court read *Nollan* to mean that an "exaction is reasonably related to an impact if the exaction serves the same purpose that a denial of the permit would serve." The court decided that both the pedestrian/bicycle pathway condition and the storm drainage dedication had an essential nexus to the development of the proposed site. Therefore, the court found the conditions to be reasonably related to the impact of the expansion of petitioner's business. We granted certiorari because of an alleged conflict between the Oregon Supreme Court's decision and our decision in *Nollan*.

II

. . . One of the principal purposes of the Takings Clause is "to bar Government from forcing some people alone to bear public burdens which, in all fairness and justice, should be borne by the public as a whole." *Armstrong v. United States*, 364 U.S. 40, 49 (1960). Without question, had the city simply required petitioner to dedicate a strip of land along Fanno Creek for public use, rather than conditioning the grant of her permit to redevelop her property on such a dedication, a taking would have occurred. *Nollan*. Such public access would deprive petitioner of the right to exclude others, "one of the most essential sticks in the bundle of rights that are commonly characterized as property." *Kaiser Aetna v. United States*, 444 U.S. 164, 176 (1979).

On the other side of the ledger, the authority of state and local governments to engage in land use planning has been sustained against constitutional challenge as long ago as our decision in *Euclid v. Ambler Realty Co.*, 272 U.S. 365 (1926). "Government hardly could go on if to some extent values incident to property could not be diminished without paying for every such change in the general law." *Pennsylvania Coal Co. v. Mahon*, 260 U.S. 393, 413 (1922). A land use regulation does not effect a taking if it "substantially advance[s] legitimate state interests" and does not "den[y] an owner economically viable use of his land." *Agins v. Tiburon*, 447 U.S. 255, 260 (1980).[6]

The sort of land use regulations discussed in the cases just cited, however, differ in two relevant particulars from the present case. First, they involved essentially legislative determinations classifying entire areas of the city, whereas here the city made an adjudicative decision to condition petitioner's application for a building permit on an individual parcel. Second, the conditions imposed were not simply a limitation on the use petitioner might make of her own parcel, but a requirement that she deed portions of the property to the city. In *Nollan* we held that governmental authority to exact such a condition was circumscribed by the Fifth and Fourteenth Amendments. . . . . [T]he government may not require a person to give up a constitutional right, here the right to receive just compensation when property is taken for a public

---

[6] There can be no argument that the permit conditions would deprive petitioner "economically beneficial us[e]" of her property as she currently operates a retail store on the lot. Petitioner assuredly is able to derive some economic use from her property.

use in exchange for a discretionary benefit conferred by the government where the property sought has little or no relationship to the benefit.

Petitioner contends that the city has forced her to choose between the building permit and her right under the Fifth Amendment to just compensation for the public easements. Petitioner does not quarrel with the city's authority to exact some forms of dedication as a condition for the grant of a building permit, but challenges the showing made by the city to justify these exactions. She argues that the city has identified "no special benefits" conferred on her, and has not identified any "special quantifiable burdens" created by her new store that would justify the particular dedications required from her which are not required from the public at large.

III

In evaluating petitioner's claim, we must first determine whether the "essential nexus" exists between the "legitimate state interest" and the permit condition exacted by the city. If we find that a nexus exists, we must then decide the required degree of connection between the exactions and the projected impact of the proposed development. We were not required to reach this question in *Nollan*, because we concluded that the connection did not meet even the loosest standard. Here, however, we must decide this question.

A

We addressed the essential nexus question in *Nollan.* . . . We resolved . . . that the Coastal Commission's regulatory authority was set completely adrift from its constitutional moorings when it claimed that a nexus existed between visual access to the ocean and a permit condition requiring lateral public access along the Nollan's beachfront lot. How enhancing the public's ability to "traverse to and along the shorefront" served the same governmental purpose of "visual access to the ocean" from the roadway was beyond our ability to countenance. The absence of a nexus left the Coastal Commission in the position of simply trying to obtain an easement through gimmickry, which converted a valid regulation of land use into "an out-and-out plan of extortion."

No such gimmicks are associated with the permit conditions imposed by the city in this case. Undoubtedly, the prevention of flooding along Fanno Creek and the reduction of traffic congestion in the Central Business District qualify as the type of legitimate public purposes we have upheld. It seems equally obvious that a nexus exists between preventing flooding along Fanno Creek and limiting development within the creek's 100-year floodplain. Petitioner proposes to double the size of her retail store and to pave her now-gravel parking lot, thereby expanding the impervious surface on the property and increasing the amount of stormwater run-off into Fanno Creek.

The same may be said for the city's attempt to reduce traffic congestion by providing for alternative means of transportation. In theory, a pedestrian/bicycle pathway provides a useful alternative means of transportation for workers and shoppers: "Pedestrians and bicyclists occupying dedicated spaces for walking and/or bicycling . . . remove potential vehicles from streets, resulting in an overall improvement in total transportation system flow." A. Nelson, *Public Provision of Pedestrian and Bicycle Access Ways: Public Policy Rationale and the Nature of Private Benefits* 11, Center for Planning Development, Georgia Institute of Technology, Working Paper Series (Jan. 1994). *See also*, Intermodal Surface Transportation Efficiency Act of 1991, Pub. L. 102-240, 105 Stat. 1914; (recognizing pedestrian and bicycle facilities as necessary components of any strategy to reduce traffic congestion).

B

The second part of our analysis requires us to determine whether the degree of the exactions demanded by the city's permit conditions bear the required relationship to the projected impact of petitioner's proposed development. . . . Here the Oregon Supreme Court deferred to what it termed the "city's unchallenged factual findings" supporting the dedication conditions and found them to be reasonably related to the impact of the expansion of petitioner's business.

The city required that petitioner dedicate "to the city as Greenway all portions of the site that fall within the existing 100-year floodplain [of Fanno Creek] . . . and all property 15 feet above [the floodplain] boundary." In addition, the city demanded that the retail store be designed so as not to intrude into the greenway area. The city relies on the Commission's rather tentative findings that increased stormwater flow from petitioner's property "can only add to the public need to manage the [floodplain] for drainage purposes" to support its conclusion that the "requirement of dedication of the floodplain area on the site is related to the applicant's plan to intensify development on the site."

The city made the following specific findings relevant to the pedestrian/bicycle pathway: "In addition, the proposed expanded use of this site is anticipated to generate additional vehicular traffic thereby increasing congestion on nearby collector and arterial streets. Creation of a convenient, safe pedestrian/bicycle pathway system as an alternative means of transportation could offset some of the traffic demand on these nearby streets and lessen the increase in traffic congestion."

The question for us is whether these findings are constitutionally sufficient to justify the conditions imposed by the city on petitioner's building permit. Since state courts have been dealing with this question a good deal longer than we have, we turn to representative decisions made by them.

In some States, very generalized statements as to the necessary connection between the required dedication and the proposed development seem to suffice. *See, e.g., Billings Properties, Inc. v. Yellowstone County*, 144 Mont. 25, 394 P.2d 182 (1964); *Jenad, Inc. v. Scarsdale*, 18 N.Y.2d 78, 218 N.E.2d 673 (1966). We think this standard is too lax to adequately protect petitioner's right to just compensation if her property is taken for a public purpose.

Other state courts require a very exacting correspondence, described as the "specifi[c] and uniquely attributable" test. The Supreme Court of Illinois first developed this test in *Pioneer Trust & Savings Bank v. Mount Prospect*, 22 Ill. 2d 375, 380, 176 N.E.2d 799, 802 (1961). Under this standard, if the local government cannot demonstrate that its exaction is directly proportional to the specifically created need, the exaction becomes "a veiled exercise of the power of eminent domain and a confiscation of private property behind the defense of police regulations." We do not think the Federal Constitution requires such exacting scrutiny, given the nature of the interests involved.

A number of state courts have taken an intermediate position, requiring the municipality to show a "reasonable relationship" between the required dedication and the impact of the proposed development. Typical is the Supreme Court of Nebraska's opinion in *Simpson v. North Platte*, 206 Neb. 240, 245, 292 N.W.2d 297, 301 (1980), where that court stated: "The distinction, therefore, which must be made between an appropriate exercise of the police power and an improper exercise of eminent domain is whether the requirement has some reasonable relationship or nexus to the use to which the property is being made or is merely being used as an excuse for taking property simply because at that particular moment the landowner is asking the city for some license or permit." Thus, the court held that a city may not require a property owner to dedicate private property for some future public use as a condition of obtaining a building permit when such future use is not "occasioned by the construction sought to be permitted."

. . . .

We think the "reasonable relationship" test adopted by a majority of the state courts is closer to the federal constitutional norm than either of those previously discussed. But we do not adopt it as such, partly because the term "reasonable relationship" seems confusingly similar to the term "rational basis" which describes the minimal level of scrutiny under the Equal Protection Clause of the Fourteenth Amendment. We think a term such as "rough proportionality" best encapsulates what we hold to be the requirement of the Fifth Amendment. No precise mathematical calculation is required, but the city must make some sort of individualized determination that the required dedication is related both in nature and extent to the impact of the proposed development.[8]

. . . We turn now to analysis of whether the findings relied upon by the city here, first with respect to the floodplain easement, and second with respect to the pedestrian/bicycle path, satisfied these requirements.

It is axiomatic that increasing the amount of impervious surface will increase the quantity and rate of storm-water flow from petitioner's property. Therefore, keeping the floodplain open and free from development would likely confine the pressures on Fanno Creek created by petitioner's development. In fact, because petitioner's property lies within the Central Business District, the Community Development Code already required that petitioner leave 15% of it as open space and the undeveloped floodplain would have nearly satisfied that requirement. But the city demanded more. It not only wanted petitioner not to build in the floodplain, but it also wanted petitioner's property along Fanno Creek for its Greenway system. The city has never said why a public greenway, as opposed to a private one, was required in the interest of flood control.

The difference to petitioner, of course, is the loss of her ability to exclude others. As we have noted, this right to exclude others is "one of the most essential sticks in the bundle of rights that are commonly characterized as property." *Kaiser Aetna*, 444 U.S., at 176. It is difficult to see why recreational visitors trampling along petitioner's floodplain easement are sufficiently related to the city's legitimate interest in reducing flooding problems along Fanno Creek, and the city has not attempted to make any individualized determination to support this part of its request.

The city contends that [the] recreational easement along the Greenway is only ancillary to the city's chief purpose in controlling flood hazards. It further asserts that unlike the residential

---

[8] Justice Stevens' dissent takes us to task for placing the burden on the city to justify the required dedication. He is correct in arguing that in evaluating most generally applicable zoning regulations, the burden properly rests on the party challenging the regulation to prove that it constitutes an arbitrary regulation of property rights. *See, e.g., Euclid v. Ambler Realty Co.*, 272 U.S. 365 (1926). Here, by contrast, the city made an adjudicative decision to condition petitioner's application for a building permit on an individual parcel. In this situation, the burden properly rests on the city. *See Nollan*, 483 U.S., at 836. This conclusion is not, as he suggests, undermined by our decision in *Moore v. East Cleveland*, 431 U.S. 494 (1977), in which we struck down a housing ordinance that limited occupancy of a dwelling unit to members of a single family as violating the Due Process Clause of the Fourteenth Amendment. The ordinance at issue in *Moore* intruded on choices concerning family living arrangements, an area in which the usual deference to the legislature was found to be inappropriate.

property at issue in *Nollan*, petitioner's property is commercial in character and therefore, her right to exclude others is compromised. . . . The city maintains that "[t]here is nothing to suggest that preventing [petitioner] from prohibiting [the easements] will unreasonably impair the value of [her] property as a [retail store]." *PruneYard Shopping Center v. Robins*, 447 U.S. 74, 83 (1980).

Admittedly, petitioner wants to build a bigger store to attract members of the public to her property. She also wants, however, to be able to control the time and manner in which they enter. The recreational easement on the Greenway is different in character from the exercise of state-protected rights of free expression and petition that we permitted in *PruneYard*. In *PruneYard*, we held that a major private shopping center that attracted more than 25,000 daily patrons had to provide access to persons exercising their state constitutional rights to distribute pamphlets and ask passersby to sign their petitions. We based our decision, in part, on the fact that the shopping center "may restrict expressive activity by adopting time, place, and manner regulations that will minimize any interference with its commercial functions." By contrast, the city wants to impose a permanent recreational easement upon petitioner's property that borders Fanno Creek. Petitioner would lose all rights to regulate the time in which the public entered onto the Greenway, regardless of any interference it might pose with her retail store. Her right to exclude would not be regulated, it would be eviscerated.

If petitioner's proposed development had somehow encroached on existing greenway space in the city, it would have been reasonable to require petitioner to provide some alternative greenway space for the public either on her property or elsewhere. . . . But that is not the case here. We conclude that the findings upon which the city relies do not show the required reasonable relationship between the floodplain easement and the petitioner's proposed new building.

With respect to the pedestrian/bicycle pathway, we have no doubt that the city was correct in finding that the larger retail sales facility proposed by petitioner will increase traffic on the streets of the Central Business District. The city estimates that the proposed development would generate roughly 435 additional trips per day. Dedications for streets, sidewalks, and other public ways are generally reasonable exactions to avoid excessive congestion from a proposed property use. But on the record before us, the city has not met its burden of demonstrating that the additional number of vehicle and bicycle trips generated by the petitioner's development reasonably relate to the city's requirement for a dedication of the pedestrian/bicycle pathway easement. The city simply found that the creation of the pathway "could offset some of the traffic demand . . . and lessen the increase in traffic congestion."

As Justice Peterson of the Supreme Court of Oregon explained in his dissenting opinion, however, "[t]he findings of fact that the bicycle pathway system 'could offset some of the traffic demand' is a far cry from a finding that the bicycle pathway system will, or is likely to, offset some of the traffic demand." No precise mathematical calculation is required, but the city must make some effort to quantify its findings in support of the dedication for the pedestrian/bicycle pathway beyond the conclusory statement that it could offset some of the traffic demand generated.

IV

Cities have long engaged in the commendable task of land use planning, made necessary by increasing urbanization particularly in metropolitan areas such as Portland. The city's goals of reducing flooding hazards and traffic congestion, and providing for public greenways, are laudable, but there are outer limits to how this may be done. "A strong public desire to improve the public condition [will not] warrant achieving the desire by a shorter cut than the constitutional way of paying for the change." *Pennsylvania Coal*, 260 U.S., at 416.

The judgment of the Supreme Court of Oregon is reversed, and the case is remanded for further proceedings consistent with this opinion.

It is so ordered.

JUSTICE STEVENS, with whom JUSTICE BLACKMUN and JUSTICE GINSBURG join, dissenting.

The record does not tell us the dollar value of petitioner Florence Dolan's interest in excluding the public from the greenway adjacent to her hardware business. The mountain of briefs that the case has generated nevertheless makes it obvious that the pecuniary value of her victory is far less important than the rule of law that this case has been used to establish. It is unquestionably an important case.

Certain propositions are not in dispute. The enlargement of the Tigard unit in Dolan's chain of hardware stores will have an adverse impact on the city's legitimate and substantial interests in controlling drainage in Fanno Creek and minimizing traffic congestion in Tigard's business district. That impact is sufficient to justify an outright denial of her application for approval of the expansion. The city has nevertheless agreed to grant Dolan's application if she will comply with two conditions, each of which admittedly will mitigate the adverse effects of her proposed development. The disputed question is whether the city has violated the Fourteenth Amendment to the Federal Constitution by refusing to allow Dolan's planned construction to proceed unless those conditions are met. The Court is correct in concluding that the city may not attach arbitrary conditions to a building permit or to a variance even when it can rightfully deny the application outright. I also agree that state court decisions dealing with ordinances that govern municipal development plans provide useful guidance in a case of this kind. Yet the Court's description of the doctrinal underpinnings of its decision, the phrasing of its fledgling test of "rough proportionality," and the application of that test to this case run contrary to the traditional treatment of these cases and break considerable and unpropitious new ground.

I

Candidly acknowledging the lack of federal precedent for its exercise in rulemaking, the Court purports to find guidance in . . . "representative" state court decisions. To do so is certainly appropriate. The state cases the Court consults, however, either fail to support or decidedly undermine the Court's conclusions in key respects.

First, although discussion of the state cases permeates the Court's analysis of the appropriate test to apply in this case, the test on which the Court settles is not naturally derived from those courts' decisions. The Court recognizes as an initial matter that the city's conditions satisfy the "essential nexus" requirement announced in *Nollan v. California Coastal Comm'n*, because they serve the legitimate interests in minimizing floods and traffic congestions. The Court goes on, however, to erect a new constitutional hurdle in the path of these conditions. In addition to showing a rational nexus to a public purpose that would justify an outright denial of the permit, the city must also demonstrate "rough proportionality" between the harm caused by the new land use and the benefit obtained by the condition. The Court also decides for the first time that the city has the burden of establishing the constitutionality of its conditions by making an "individualized determination" that the condition in question satisfies the proportionality requirement.

Not one of the state cases cited by the Court announces anything akin to a "rough proportionality" requirement. For the most part, moreover, those cases that invalidated municipal ordinances did so on state law or unspecified grounds roughly equivalent to *Nollan*'s "essential nexus" requirement. . . . One case purporting to apply the strict "specifically and uniquely attributable" test established by *Pioneer Trust & Savings Bank v. Mount Prospect*, 22 Ill. 2d 375, 176 N.E.2d 799 (1961), nevertheless found that test was satisfied because the legislature had decided that the subdivision at issue created the need for a park or parks. *Billings Properties, Inc. v. Yellowstone County*, 144 Mont. 25, 33-36, 394 P.2d 182, 187-188 (1964). . . . Although 4 of the 12 opinions mention the Federal Constitution, two of those only in passing, it is quite obvious that neither the courts nor the litigants imagined they might be participating in the development of a new rule of federal law. Thus, although these state cases do lend support to the Court's reaffirmance of *Nollan*'s reasonable nexus requirement, the role the Court accords them in the announcement of its newly minted second phase of the constitutional inquiry is remarkably inventive.

In addition, the Court ignores the state courts' willingness to consider what the property owner gains from the exchange in question. The Supreme Court of Wisconsin, for example, found it significant that the village's approval of a proposed subdivision plat "enables the subdivider to profit financially by selling the subdivision lots as home-building sites and thus realizing a greater price than could have been obtained if he had sold his property as unplatted lands." *Jordan v. Village of Menomonee Falls*, 28 Wis. 2d 608, 619-620; 137 N.W.2d 442, 448 (1965). The required dedication as a condition of that approval was permissible "[i]n return for this benefit." . . . In this case, moreover, Dolan's acceptance of the permit, with its attached conditions, would provide her with benefits that may well go beyond any advantage she gets from expanding her business. As the United States pointed out at oral argument, the improvement that the city's drainage plan contemplates would widen the channel and reinforce the slopes to increase the carrying capacity during serious floods, "confer[ring] considerable benefits on the property owners immediately adjacent to the creek."

The state court decisions also are enlightening in the extent to which they required that the entire parcel be given controlling importance. All but one of the cases involve challenges to provisions in municipal ordinances requiring developers to dedicate either a percentage of the entire parcel (usually 7 or 10 percent of the platted subdivision) or an equivalent value in cash (usually a certain dollar amount per lot) to help finance the construction of roads, utilities, schools, parks and playgrounds. In assessing the legality of the conditions, the courts gave no indication that the transfer of an interest in realty was any more objectionable than a cash paymen . . . . Instead, the courts uniformly examined the character of the entire economic transaction.

II

It is not merely state cases, but our own cases as well, that require the analysis to focus on the impact of the city's action on the entire parcel of private property. In *Penn Central Transportation Co. v. New York City*, 438 U.S. 104 (1978), we stated that takings jurisprudence "does not divide a single parcel into discrete segments and attempt to determine whether rights in a particular segment have been entirely abrogated." Instead, this Court focuses "both on the character of the action and on the nature and extent of the interference with rights in the parcel as a whole." *Andrus v. Allard*, 444 U.S. 51 (1979), reaffirmed the nondivisibility principle outlined in *Penn Central*, stating that "[a]t least where an owner possesses a full 'bundle' of property rights, the destruction of one 'strand' of the bundle is not a taking, because the aggregate must be viewed in its entirety."[3] . . . Although limitation of the right to exclude others undoubtedly constitutes a significant infringement upon property ownership, restrictions on that right do not alone constitute a taking, and do not do so in any event unless they "unreasonably impair the value or use" of the property. *PruneYard Shopping Center v. Robins*, 447 U.S. 74, 82-84 (1980).

The Court's narrow focus on one strand in the property owner's bundle of rights is particularly misguided in a case involving the development of commercial property. As Professor Johnston has noted: "The subdivider is a manufacturer, processor, and marketer of a product; land is but one of his raw materials. In subdivision control disputes, the developer is not defending hearth and home against the king's intrusion, but simply attempting to maximize his profits from the sale of a finished product. As applied to him, subdivision control exactions are actually business regulations." Johnston, *Constitutionality of Subdivision Control Exactions: The Quest for A Rationale*, 52 Cornell L. Q. 871, 923 (1967). The exactions associated with the development of a retail business are likewise a species of business regulation that heretofore warranted a strong presumption of constitutional validity.

In Johnston's view, "if the municipality can demonstrate that its assessment of financial burdens against subdividers is rational, impartial, and conducive to fulfillment of authorized planning objectives, its action need be invalidated only in those extreme and presumably rare cases where the burden of compliance is sufficiently great to deter the owner from proceeding with his planned development." The city of Tigard has demonstrated that its plan is rational and impartial and that the conditions at issue are "conducive to fulfillment of authorized planning objectives." Dolan, on the other hand, has offered no evidence that her burden of compliance has any impact at all on the value or profitability of her planned development. Following the teaching of the cases on which it purports to rely, the Court should not isolate the burden associated with the loss of the power to exclude from an evaluation of the benefit to be derived from the permit to enlarge the store and the parking lot.

The Court's assurances that its "rough proportionality" test leaves ample room for cities to pursue the "commendable task of land use planning," even twice avowing that "[n]o precise mathematical calculation is required," are wanting, given the result that test compels here. Under the Court's approach, a city must not only "quantify its findings," and make "individualized determination[s]" with respect to the nature and the extent of the relationship between the conditions and the impact, but also demonstrate "proportionality." The correct inquiry should instead concentrate on whether the required nexus is present and venture beyond considerations of a condition's nature or germaneness only if the developer establishes that a concededly germane condition is so grossly disproportionate to the proposed development's adverse effects that it manifests motives other than land use regulation on the part of the city. The heightened requirement the Court imposes on cities is even more unjustified when all the tools needed to resolve the questions presented by this case can be garnered from our existing case law.

III

Applying its new standard, the Court finds two defects in the city's case. First, while the record would adequately support a requirement that Dolan maintain the portion of the floodplain on

---

[3] Similarly, in *Keystone Bituminous Coal Assn. v. DeBenedictis*, 480 U.S. 470, 498-499 (1987), we concluded that "[t]he 27 million tons of coal do not constitute a separate segment of property for takings law purposes" and that "[t]here is no basis for treating the less than 2% of petitioners' coal as a separate parcel of property."

her property as undeveloped open space, it does not support the additional requirement that the floodplain be dedicated to the city. Second, while the city adequately established the traffic increase that the proposed development would generate, it failed to quantify the offsetting decrease in automobile traffic that the bike path will produce. Even under the Court's new rule, both defects are, at most, nothing more than harmless error.

In her objections to the floodplain condition, Dolan made no effort to demonstrate that the dedication of that portion of her property would be any more onerous than a simple prohibition against any development on that portion of her property. Given the commercial character of both the existing and the proposed use of the property as a retail store, it seems likely that potential customers "trampling along petitioner's floodplain," are more valuable than a useless parcel of vacant land. Moreover, the duty to pay taxes and the responsibility for potential tort liability may well make ownership of the fee interest in useless land a liability rather than an asset. That may explain why Dolan never conceded that she could be prevented from building on the floodplain. The City Attorney also pointed out that absent a dedication, property owners would be required to "build on their own land" and "with their own money" a storage facility for the water runoff. Dolan apparently "did have that option," but chose not to seek it. If Dolan might have been entitled to a variance confining the city's condition in a manner this Court would accept, her failure to seek that narrower form of relief at any stage of the state administrative and judicial proceedings clearly should preclude that relief in this Court now.

The Court's rejection of the bike path condition amounts to nothing more than a play on words. Everyone agrees that the bike path "could" offset some of the increased traffic flow that the larger store will generate, but the findings do not unequivocally state that it will do so, or tell us just how many cyclists will replace motorists. Predictions on such matters are inherently nothing more than estimates. Certainly the assumption that there will be an offsetting benefit here is entirely reasonable and should suffice whether it amounts to 100 percent, 35 percent, or only 5 percent of the increase in automobile traffic that would otherwise occur. If the Court proposes to have the federal judiciary micromanage state decisions of this kind, it is indeed extending its welcome mat to a significant new class of litigants. Although there is no reason to believe that state courts have failed to rise to the task, property owners have surely found a new friend today.

IV

The Court has made a serious error by abandoning the traditional presumption of constitutionality and imposing a novel burden of proof on a city implementing an admittedly valid comprehensive land use plan. Even more consequential than its incorrect disposition of this case, however, is the Court's resurrection of a species of substantive due process analysis that it firmly rejected decades ago.

The Court . . . [applies] the same kind of substantive due process analysis . . . frequently identified with a better known case that accorded similar substantive protection to a baker's liberty interest in working 60 hours a week and 10 hours a day. *See Lochner v. New York*, 198 U.S. 45 (1905).[9] Later cases have interpreted the Fourteenth Amendment's substantive protection

---

[9] The *Lochner* Court refused to presume that there was a reasonable connection between the regulation and the state interest in protecting the public health. A similar refusal to identify a sufficient nexus between an enlarged building with a newly paved parking lot and the state interests in minimizing the risks of flooding and traffic congestion proves fatal to the city's permit conditions in this case under the Court's novel approach.

against uncompensated deprivations of private property by the States as though it incorporated the text of the Fifth Amendment's Takings Clause. *See, e.g., Keystone Bituminous Coal Assn. v. DeBenedictis*, 480 U.S. 470 (1987). There was nothing problematic about that interpretation in cases enforcing the Fourteenth Amendment against state action that involved the actual physical invasion of private property. *See Loretto v. Teleprompter Manhattan CATV Corp.*, 458 U.S. 419 (1982). Justice Holmes charted a significant new course, however, when he opined that a state law making it "commercially impracticable to mine certain coal" had "very nearly the same effect for constitutional purposes as appropriating or destroying it." *Pennsylvania Coal Co. v. Mahon*, 260 U.S. 393 (1922). The so-called "regulatory takings" doctrine that the Holmes dictum kindled has an obvious kinship with the line of substantive due process cases that *Lochner* exemplified. Besides having similar ancestry, both doctrines are potentially open-ended sources of judicial power to invalidate state economic regulations that Members of this court view as unwise or unfair.

. . . .

The Court has decided to apply its heightened scrutiny to a single strand—the power to exclude—in the bundle of rights that enables a commercial enterprise to flourish in an urban environment. That intangible interest is undoubtedly worthy of constitutional protection much like the grandmother's interest in deciding which of her relatives may share her home in *Moore v. East Cleveland*, 431 U.S. 494 (1977). Both interests are protected from arbitrary state action by the Due Process Clause of the Fourteenth Amendment. It is, however, a curious irony that Members of the majority in this case would impose an almost insurmountable burden of proof on the property owner in the *Moore* case while saddling the city with a heightened burden in this case. In its application of what is essentially the doctrine of substantive due process, the Court confuses the past with the present. On November 13, 1922, the village of Euclid, Ohio, adopted a zoning ordinance that effectively confiscated 75 percent of the value of property owned by the Ambler Realty Company. Despite its recognition that such an ordinance "would have been rejected as arbitrary and oppressive" at an earlier date, the Court (over the dissent of Justices Van Devanter, McReynolds and Butler) upheld the ordinance. Today's majority should heed the words of Justice Sutherland: "Such regulations are sustained, under the complex conditions of our day, for reasons analogous to those which justify traffic regulations, which, before the advent of automobiles and rapid transit street railways, would have been condemned as fatally arbitrary and unreasonable. And in this there is no inconsistency, for while the meaning of constitutional guaranties never varies, the scope of their application must expand or contract to meet the new and different conditions which are constantly coming within the field of their operation. In a changing world, it is impossible that it should be otherwise."

In our changing world one thing is certain: uncertainty will characterize predictions about the impact of new urban developments on the risks of floods, earthquakes, traffic congestion, or environmental harms. When there is doubt concerning the magnitude of those impacts, the public interest in averting them must outweigh the private interest of the commercial entrepreneur. If the government can demonstrate that the conditions it has imposed in a land-use permit are rational, impartial and conducive to fulfilling the aims of a valid land-use plan, a strong presumption of validity should attach to those conditions. The burden of demonstrating that those conditions have unreasonably impaired the economic value of the proposed improvement belongs squarely on the shoulders of the party challenging the state action's constitutionality. That allocation of burdens has served us well in the past. The Court has stumbled badly today by reversing it.

I respectfully dissent.

JUSTICE SOUTER, dissenting.

This case, like *Nollan v. California Coastal Comm'n*, 483 U.S. 825 (1987), invites the Court to examine the relationship between conditions imposed by development permits, requiring landowners to dedicate portions of their land for use by the public, and governmental interests in mitigating the adverse effects of such development. *Nollan* declared the need for a nexus between the nature of an exaction of an interest in land (a beach easement) and the nature of governmental interests. The Court treats this case as raising a further question, not about the nature, but about the degree, of connection required between such an exaction and the adverse effects of development. The Court's opinion announces a test to address this question, but as I read the opinion, the Court does not apply that test to these facts, which do not raise the question the Court addresses.

First, as to the floodplain and Greenway, the Court acknowledges that an easement of this land for open space (and presumably including the five feet required for needed creek channel improvements) is reasonably related to flood control, but argues that the "permanent recreational easement" for the public on the Greenway is not so related. If that is so, it is not because of any lack of proportionality between permit condition and adverse effect, but because of a lack of any rational connection at all between exaction of a public recreational area and the governmental interest in providing for the effect of increased water runoff. That is merely an application of *Nollan*'s nexus analysis. As the Court notes, "[i]f petitioner's proposed development had somehow encroached on existing greenway space in the city, it would have been reasonable to require petitioner to provide some alternative greenway space for the public." But that, of course, was not the fact, and the city of Tigard never sought to justify the public access portion of the dedication as related to flood control. It merely argued that whatever recreational uses were made of the bicycle path and the one foot edge on either side, were incidental to the permit condition requiring dedication of the 15-foot easement for an 8-foot-wide bicycle path and for flood control, including open space requirements and relocation of the bank of the river by some five feet. It seems to me such incidental recreational use can stand or fall with the bicycle path, which the city justified by reference to traffic congestion. As to the relationship the Court examines, between the recreational easement and a purpose never put forth as a justification by the city, the Court unsurprisingly finds a recreation area to be unrelated to flood control.

Second, as to the bicycle path, the Court again acknowledges the "theor[etically]" reasonable relationship between "the city's attempt to reduce traffic congestion by providing [a bicycle path] for alternative means of transportation," and the "correct" finding of the city that "the larger retail sales facility proposed by petitioner will increase traffic on the streets of the Central Business District." The Court only faults the city for saying that the bicycle path "could" rather than "would" offset the increased traffic from the store. That again, as far as I can tell, is an application of *Nollan*, for the Court holds that the stated connection ("could" offset) between traffic congestion and bicycle paths is too tenuous; only if the bicycle path "would" offset the increased traffic by some amount, could the bicycle path be said to be related to the city's legitimate interest in reducing traffic congestion.

I cannot agree that the application of *Nollan* is a sound one here, since it appears that the Court has placed the burden of producing evidence of relationship on the city, despite the usual rule in cases involving the police power that the government is presumed to have acted constitutionally.* Having thus assigned the burden, the Court concludes that the City loses based on one word ("could" instead of "would"), and despite the fact that this record shows the connection the Court looks for. Dolan has put forward no evidence that the burden of granting a dedication for the bicycle path is unrelated in kind to the anticipated increase in traffic congestion, nor, if there exists a requirement that the relationship be related in degree, has Dolan shown that the exaction fails any such test. The city, by contrast, calculated the increased traffic flow that would result from Dolan's proposed development to be 435 trips per day, and its Comprehensive Plan, applied here, relied on studies showing the link between alternative modes of transportation, including bicycle paths, and reduced street traffic congestion . . . . *Nollan*, therefore, is satisfied, and on that assumption the city's conditions should not be held to fail a further rough proportionality test or any other that might be devised to give meaning to the constitutional limits. As Members of this Court have said before, "the common zoning regulations requiring subdividers to . . . dedicate certain areas to public streets, are in accord with our constitutional traditions because the proposed property use would otherwise be the cause of excessive congestion." *Pennell v. San Jose*, 485 U.S. 1, 20 (1988) (Scalia, J., concurring in part and dissenting in part). The bicycle path permit condition is fundamentally no different from these.

In any event, on my reading, the Court's conclusions about the city's vulnerability carry the Court no further than *Nollan* has gone already, and I do not view this case as a suitable vehicle for taking the law beyond that point. The right case for the enunciation of takings doctrine seems hard to spot.

[8]   Events on Remand in *Tigard*

In December, 1997, the City of Tigard and the Dolan family agreed to a $1.5 million settlement.[71] The amount settled all economic matters between the parties, including payment by the City of Tigard for the bike path they wished to construct along Fanno Creek and resolution of a claim by the Dolan family that the long delay in settling their claim amounted to a temporary taking under *First English Evangelical Lutheran Church of Glendale v. County of Los Angeles*.[72] In February of the following year, Dan Dolan submitted permit applications with the City of Tigard to demolish the old store and construct two new buildings—a new store and an office building available for renting to local businesses.[73] The article announcing the event also contained some local commentary from some Tigard citizens welcoming the opportunity to get rid of the ugly old sign and store. Four months later, a ground breaking ceremony was held, with Dan Dolan decked out in a tuxedo and exulting in the long sought victory over the town.[74] His attorney, Dorothy Cofield, called the dispute "one of the most important cases in property rights in 50 years." And Bill Sizemore, then a Republican candidate for governor, contended

---

* *See, e.g., Goldblatt v. Hempstead*, 369 U.S. 590, 594-596 (1962). The majority characterizes this case as involving an "adjudicative decision" to impose permit conditions, *ante*, at 16, n. 8, but the permit conditions were imposed pursuant to Tigard's Community Development Code. The adjudication here was of Dolan's requested variance from the permit conditions otherwise required to be imposed by the Code. This case raises no question about discriminatory, or "reverse spot" zoning, which "singles out a particular parcel for different, less favorable treatment than the neighboring ones." *Penn Central Transp. Co. v. New York City*, 438 U.S. 104, 132 (1978).

[71] *Dolan Family's Lawsuit Against Tigard Ends with $1.5 Million Payment*, PORTLAND OREGONIAN, Dec. 11, 1997.

[72] This case is discussed at p. 997 above.

[73] Emily Tsao, *A Boy Sign and Store in Tigard Bound for Extinction*, PORTLAND OREGONIAN, Feb. 12, 1998.

[74] Emily Tsao, *Turn of Spade Caps Property Rights Case*, PORTLAND OREGONIAN, June 9, 1998.

that "Property rights are the cornerstone of a free society. We Americans are not free if the government can take someone's property without just compensation." Dolan's celebration was a bit premature. A few weeks later the parties were back in court.[75] The city held up the building permit, claiming that two small parts of the planned building overlapped the bike easement called for in the earlier settlement. In fairly short order, the local court ordered the city to issue the building permit, holding that they had been on notice of the building location for a long time and should have caught the problem earlier.[76] As this volume goes to press, the new buildings are under construction.

[9] Some Thoughts on *Dolan*

Rehnquist used the distinction between Takings and exercise of the police power in Holmes' famous opinion in *Mahon* as a starting point for his work in *Dolan*. In the process he seemed to affirm the continuing vitality of *Euclid* and used the difference between area wide regulation and specific site regulation as the central core of his analytical structure. Perhaps he used the distinction between area wide land use controls and specific site regulation as a mirror for the *Mahon* distinction between exercise of the police power and Takings. In any case, his conclusion that the dispute involved a single site led him to frame the issue in the case as one requiring an investigation of the nexus required between regulatory means and ends. Though he found the public purposes expressed by the Oregon authorities in the case perfectly valid, he could not justify all of the means used to put those purposes into effect. Tigard was allowed to ban building (at least on part of the Dolan's land) within a certain distance of the creek, but Justice Rehnquist could not find a rough proportionality between a valid public purpose and the dedications Tigard wished to exact. The proportionality inquiry focussed particularly on the harms imposed upon and benefits extended to Dolan. Once past the no build in the flood plain rule, Rehnquist found the level of harm to Dolan (loss of the right to exclude) far greater than any related benefit the public in general or Dolan in particular might gain from the dedications.

The *Dolan* outcome, together with that in *Nollan*, leaves open to question the continuing ability of land use authorities to use the value of restrictions imposed on land as bargaining chips for further concessions from developers, or to use the building permit process to obtain concessions that would otherwise be unattainable. This sort of bargaining process between government and owner goes on constantly in the land use world. In many ways it is central to modern regulatory systems. Any time a builder wants to do things in a way somewhat different from what is allowed "as of right" under the zoning statutes, a bargaining process opens up between planners and owners. Indeed, some modern zoning schemes don't really zone. They establish the parameters of a bargaining process between public regulators and private developers over the shape of the uses to be built. Can this still be done?

For example, before the Washington, D.C. area's subway system was built through Bethesda, a suburban community just to the northwest of the city, the county government adopted a scheme allowing a certain amount of new square footage to be constructed in the town's commercial corridor. But the amount they allowed was less than the amount that could have been built if every available parcel was developed to the previously allowed zoning maximum. Those who wished to construct new projects in anticipation of the subway were asked to submit proposals to the land use authorities. The authorities then selected what they thought were the best plans

---

[75] Emily Tsao, *Tigard, A-Boy Owners Head Back to Court*, PORTLAND OREGONIAN, June 25, 1998.

[76] Emily Tsao, *Judge Orders Tigard to Cooperate with A-Boy*, PORTLAND OREGONIAN, July 2, 1998.

and turned the others down. The zoning in those parts of the area not covered by approved projects was then effectively lowered to a low density that was likely to guarantee the continued existence of the buildings then in existence. As you might expect, the accepted plans contained plazas and open spaces, restaurant courtyards, enhanced subway entrances, higher quality architecture and lower densities than the ones not accepted. While some of the remaining sites have since been rebuilt with two and three story shops, many still have the old, pre-subway buildings in use.

What would the court do with this plan today? Is this area wide zoning or specific site planning? Is the use of public authority to "extract" or "extort" public amenities legitimate? Would Rehnquist or Scalia find it lawful for a town like Bethesda to use the value of its power to regulate in ways that create incentives to "donate" things to the public? Is the requisite means and ends linkage present in light of the fact that owners who lost the planning contest saw their lands effectively downzoned? Is this redistribution of wealth and the resulting imposition of losses on only some of the parcels scattered throughout the Bethesda business district an area wide regulation or a process imposing single site controls?

At the other end of Rehnquist's opinion in *Dolan*, that part in which he opined that flood control was a valid public purpose, how far will he be willing to go? What of a desire to control density in order to maximize the efficiency of transportation? Is Portland, Oregon's attempt to create a green belt around the city to avoid sprawl valid? Or put another way, may valid public purposes put into effect with substantially related means still produce a takings problem if the value of land is reduced almost to zero?

For more information on land use "trades" and public policy, read Carol Rose, *Planning and Dealing: Piecemeal Land Controls as a Problem of Local Legitimacy*, 71 CAL. L. REV. 837 (1983).

[10]   Problem Notes

[a]   The *Dolan* Core

Shortly after finishing its recitation of the factual and procedural history of the case, the *Dolan* Court wrote:

> The sort of land use regulations discussed in . . . [*Euclid v. Ambler*], however, differ in two relevant particulars from the present case. First, they involved essentially legislative determinations classifying entire areas of the city, whereas here the city made an adjudicative decision to condition petitioner's application for a building permit on an individual parcel. Second, the conditions imposed were not simply a limitation on the use petitioner might make of her own parcel, but a requirement that she deed portions of the property to the city.

This statement echoes almost exactly the sentiment expressed by Justice Rehnquist at the beginning of his opinion in the Grand Central Terminal litigation.[77] Selecting a particular property owner for regulatory attention, he contended in both *Penn Central* and *Dolan*, significantly increased the likelihood for arbitrary behavior by imposing the costs of regulation on one owner and focussing the impact of disaffection costs. Imposition of a more stringent standard of judicial review, therefore, was designed to protect individuals from the power of the state. Is *Penn Central* still a viable precedent?

---

[77] You might want to return to his statement at p. 962 above.

[b] *Nollan* Revisited

The *Dolan* majority claimed that it was answering a question left unresolved by *Nollan*—the nature of the nexus required between regulatory purpose and the regulated property. The majority opined: "In evaluating petitioner's claim, we must first determine whether the 'essential nexus' exists between the 'legitimate state interest' and the permit condition enacted by the city. If we find that a nexus exists, we must then decide the required degree of connection between the exactions and the projected impact of the proposed development. We were not required to reach this question in *Nollan*, because we concluded that the connection did not meet even the loosest standard." Is there a difference between these two issues—nexus and degree of connection? Or did the Court simply take *Dolan* as an opportunity to refine or toughen the rational basis test it enunciated in *Nollan*?

[c] Facial and As–Applied Review

One theme coursing through the Taking cases involves the character of the attack made by a property owner on the regulation. *Euclid, Penn Central* and *Keystone*, among others, were all treated as facial attacks. The Court used that status as a way of granting legislatures some degree of discretion to structure their regulatory activities and justifying a reluctance to interfere with legislative judgments. Justice Rehnquist, in his *Penn Central* dissent, complained that the designation of Grand Central Terminal as an historic structure was really not general legislation—that deference to legislative decisions was not appropriate when a single site is uniquely burdened by regulatory action. In *Dolan*, Justice Rehnquist returned to that theme, using the notion that the dispute involved an adjudicative action as a basis for refusing to defer to legislative judgment. Is there really a difference between legislative and adjudicative action in a case like this? Was Justice Stevens correct in noting that Dolan was being subjected to a general regulatory scheme, indeed a scheme that was more general than the one in *Penn Central*? If so, why should the fact that Dolan's request for a variance (the adjudicative process I presume) was denied alter the standard used to judicially review a land use regulatory action? Or was Justice Rehnquist just preparing the way for a more general alteration of Taking jurisprudence when the next facial attack comes before the court?

[d] Rent Control

Suppose a municipality adopts a rent control law and that its public purpose is claimed to be a desire to provide housing for low and moderate income residents. After the rent control plan has been in effect for a time, a study reveals that 30% of the residents of rent controlled housing have low or moderate incomes. Can the rent control scheme survive the analytical demands of *Nollan* and *Dolan*? In a 4-3 decision the California Supreme Court said "yes." *Santa Monica Beach Ltd. v. Superior Court of Los Angeles County*, 19 Cal. 4th 952, 968 P.2d 993 (1999). Was that the correct result?

[e] Remand

The Supreme Court did not command the Oregon courts to enter a finding that a taking had occurred. It remanded the dispute for further proceedings consistent with the *Dolan* opinion. If the Oregon Supreme Court remanded the case to the trial court for further proceedings in order to give Tigard a chance to meet the burden of proof newly imposed upon it by the *Tigard* opinion, what would happen? Could the new proportionality standard be met? Is this latest Supreme court result as serious an obstacle to the adoption of land use controls as Justice Stevens fears?

§ 11.06 Regulatory Preclusion of Future Wipeouts

[1] Introduction to *Lucas v. South Carolina Coastal Council*

Public concern about the use, preservation and longevity of ocean front property has increased dramatically in recent decades. Large numbers of people have moved to coastal regions and development of lowland areas has increased significantly. Storms that used to roll in across largely empty beaches "reconstruct" the topography much as they always have, but now at the cost of billions of dollars in damages to buildings, utility infrastructure and public facilities. Erosion has reduced the size of many Atlantic coast beaches. The public is now spending many millions of dollars annually to reconstruct beaches in important urban and vacation areas.

Beginning in the 1970s, Congress and coastal state legislatures began adopting laws designed to control new construction, create large buffer zones between the ocean waters and sites open for construction, and require local communities to refuse permission to rebuild structures destroyed by natural forces. It was this sort of legislation that gave rise to the next case.

[2] Opinions of the United States Supreme Court in *Lucas v. South Carolina Coastal Council*

David H. Lucas v. South Carolina Coastal Council

United States Supreme Court
505 U.S. 1003, 112 S. Ct. 2886, 120 L. Ed. 2d 798 (1992)

SCALIA, J., delivered the opinion of the Court, in which REHNQUIST, C.J., and WHITE, O'CONNOR, and THOMAS, JJ., joined.

In 1986, petitioner David H. Lucas paid $975,000 for two residential lots on the Isle of Palms in Charleston County, South Carolina, on which he intended to build single-family homes. In 1988, however, the South Carolina Legislature enacted the Beachfront Management Act, S.C. Code s 48-39-250 et seq. (Supp. 1990) (Act), which had the direct effect of barring petitioner from erecting any permanent habitable structures on his two parcels. See s 48-39-290(A). A state trial court found that this prohibition rendered Lucas's parcels "valueless." App. to Pet. for Cert. 37. This case requires us to decide whether the Act's dramatic effect on the economic value of Lucas's lots accomplished a taking of private property under the Fifth and Fourteenth Amendments requiring the payment of "just compensation." U.S. Const., Amdt. 5.

I

A

South Carolina's expressed interest in intensively managing development activities in the so-called "coastal zone" dates from 1977 when, in the aftermath of Congress's passage of the federal Coastal Zone Management Act of 1972, 86 Stat. 1280, as amended, 16 U.S.C. § 1451 et seq., the legislature enacted a Coastal Zone Management Act of its own. See S.C. Code § 48-39-10 et seq. (1987). In its original form, the South Carolina Act required owners of coastal zone land that qualified as a "critical area" (defined in the legislation to include beaches and immediately adjacent sand dunes, § 48-39-10(J)) to obtain a permit from the newly created South Carolina Coastal Council (respondent here) prior to committing the land to a "use other than the use the critical area was devoted to on [September 28, 1977]." § 48-39-130(A).

In the late 1970's, Lucas and others began extensive residential development of the Isle of Palms, a barrier island situated eastward of the City of Charleston. Toward the close of the development cycle for one residential subdivision known as "Beachwood East," Lucas in 1986 purchased the two lots at issue in this litigation for his own account. No portion of the lots, which were located approximately 300 feet from the beach, qualified as a "critical area" under the 1977 Act; accordingly, at the time Lucas acquired these parcels, he was not legally obliged to obtain a permit from the Council in advance of any development activity. His intention with respect to the lots was to do what the owners of the immediately adjacent parcels had already done: erect single-family residences. He commissioned architectural drawings for this purpose.

The Beachfront Management Act brought Lucas's plans to an abrupt end. Under that 1988 legislation, the Council was directed to establish a "baseline" connecting the landward-most "point[s] of erosion . . . during the past forty years" in the region of the Isle of Palms that includes Lucas's lots. § 48-39-280(A)(2) (Supp. 1988).[1] In action not challenged here, the Council fixed this baseline landward of Lucas's parcels. That was significant, for under the Act construction of occupiable improvements[2] was flatly prohibited seaward of a line drawn 20 feet landward of, and parallel to, the baseline, § 48-39-290(A) (Supp. 1988). The Act provided no exceptions.

B

Lucas promptly filed suit in the South Carolina Court of Common Pleas, contending that the Beachfront Management Act's construction bar effected a taking of his property without just compensation. Lucas did not take issue with the validity of the Act as a lawful exercise of South Carolina's police power, but contended that the Act's complete extinguishment of his property's value entitled him to compensation regardless of whether the legislature had acted in furtherance of legitimate police power objectives. Following a bench trial, the court agreed. Among its factual determinations was the finding that "at the time Lucas purchased the two lots, both were zoned for single-family residential construction and . . . there were no restrictions imposed upon such use of the property by either the State of South Carolina, the County of Charleston, or the Town of the Isle of Palms." The trial court further found that the Beachfront Management Act decreed a permanent ban on construction insofar as Lucas's lots were concerned, and that this prohibition "deprive[d] Lucas of any reasonable economic use of the lots, . . . eliminated the unrestricted right of use, and render[ed] them valueless." The court thus concluded that Lucas's properties had been "taken" by operation of the Act, and it ordered respondent to pay "just compensation" in the amount of $1,232,387.50.

The Supreme Court of South Carolina reversed. It found dispositive what it described as Lucas's concession "that the Beachfront Management Act [was] properly and validly designed to preserve . . . South Carolina's beaches." Failing an attack on the validity of the statute as such, the court believed itself bound to accept the "uncontested . . . findings" of the South

---

[1] This specialized historical method of determining the baseline applied because the Beachwood East subdivision is located adjacent to a so called "inlet erosion zone" (defined in the Act to mean "a segment of shoreline along or adjacent to tidal inlets which is influenced directly by the inlet and its associated shoals," S.C. Code § 48-39-270(7) (Supp. 1988)) that is "not stabilized by jetties, terminal groins, or other structures," § 48-39-280(A)(2). For areas other than these unstabilized inlet erosion zones, the statute directs that the baseline be established "along the crest of the primary oceanfront sand dune." § 48-39-280(A)(1).

[2] The Act did allow the construction of certain nonhabitable improvements, e.g., "wooden walkways no larger in width than six feet," and "small wooden decks no larger than one hundred forty-four square feet." §§ 48-39-290(A)(1) and (2) (Supp. 1988).

Carolina legislature that new construction in the coastal zone—such as petitioner intended—threatened this public resource. The Court ruled that when a regulation respecting the use of property is designed "to prevent serious public harm," (*citing, inter alia, Mugler v. Kansas*, 123 U.S. 623 (1887)), no compensation is owing under the Takings Clause regardless of the regulation's effect on the property's value.

Two justices dissented. They acknowledged that our *Mugler* line of cases recognizes governmental power to prohibit "noxious" uses of property—i.e., uses of property akin to "public nuisances"—without having to pay compensation. But they would not have characterized the Beachfront Management Act's "primary purpose [as] the prevention of a nuisance." To the dissenters, the chief purposes of the legislation, among them the promotion of tourism and the creation of a "habitat for indigenous flora and fauna," could not fairly be compared to nuisance abatement. As a consequence, they would have affirmed the trial court's conclusion that the Act's obliteration of the value of petitioner's lots accomplished a taking.

We granted certiorari.

II

As a threshold matter, we must briefly address the Council's suggestion that this case is inappropriate for plenary review. After briefing and argument before the South Carolina Supreme Court, but prior to issuance of that court's opinion, the Beachfront Management Act was amended to authorize the Council, in certain circumstances, to issue "special permits" for the construction or reconstruction of habitable structures seaward of the baseline. According to the Council, this amendment renders Lucas's claim of a permanent deprivation unripe, as Lucas may yet be able to secure permission to build on his property. "[The Court's] cases," we are reminded, "uniformly reflect an insistence on knowing the nature and extent of permitted development before adjudicating the constitutionality of the regulations that purport to limit it." Because petitioner "has not yet obtained a final decision regarding how [he] will be allowed to develop [his] property," *Williamson County Regional Planning Comm'n of Johnson City v. Hamilton Bank*, 473 U.S. 172, 190 (1985), the Council argues that he is not yet entitled to definitive adjudication of his takings claim in this Court.

We think these considerations would preclude review had the South Carolina Supreme Court rested its judgment on ripeness grounds, as it was (essentially) invited to do by the Council. The South Carolina Supreme Court shrugged off the possibility of further administrative and trial proceedings, however, preferring to dispose of Lucas's takings claim on the merits. This unusual disposition does not preclude Lucas from applying for a permit under the 1990 amendment for future construction, and challenging, on takings grounds, any denial. But it does preclude, both practically and legally, any takings claim with respect to Lucas's past deprivation, *i.e.*, for his having been denied construction rights during the period before the 1990 amendment. See generally *First English Evangelical Lutheran Church of Glendale v. County of Los Angeles*, 482 U.S. 304 (1987). Without even so much as commenting upon the consequences of the South Carolina Supreme Court's judgment in this respect, the Council insists that permitting Lucas to press his claim of a past deprivation on this appeal would be improper, since "the issues of whether and to what extent [Lucas] has incurred a temporary taking . . . have simply never been addressed." Yet Lucas had no reason to proceed on a "temporary taking" theory at trial, or even to seek remand for that purpose prior to submission of the case to the South Carolina Supreme Court, since as the Act then read, the taking was unconditional and permanent. Moreover, given the breadth of the South Carolina Supreme Court's holding and judgment, Lucas would plainly be unable (absent our intervention now) to obtain further state-court adjudication with respect to the 1988-1990 period.

In these circumstances, we think it would not accord with sound process to insist that Lucas pursue the late-created "special permit" procedure before his takings claim can be considered ripe. Lucas has properly alleged Article III injury-in-fact in this case, with respect to both the pre-1990 and post-1990 constraints placed on the use of his parcels by the Beachfront Management Act.[3] . . . We leave for decision on remand, of course, the questions left unaddressed by the South Carolina Supreme Court as a consequence of its categorical disposition.

III

A

Prior to Justice Holmes' exposition in *Pennsylvania Coal Co. v. Mahon*, 260 U.S. 393 (1922), it was generally thought that the Takings Clause reached only a "direct appropriation" of property, *Legal Tender Cases*, 12 Wall. 457, 551 (1871), or the functional equivalent of a "practical ouster of [the owner's] possession." *Transportation Co. v. Chicago*, 99 U.S. 635 (1879). Justice Holmes recognized in *Mahon*, however, that if the protection against physical appropriations of private property was to be meaningfully enforced, the government's power to redefine the range of interests included in the ownership of property was necessarily constrained by constitutional limits. If, instead, the uses of private property were subject to unbridled, uncompensated qualification under the police power, "the natural tendency of human nature [would be] to extend the qualification more and more until at last private property disappear[ed]." These considerations gave birth in that case to the oft-cited maxim that, "while property may be regulated to a certain extent, if regulation goes too far it will be recognized as a taking."

Nevertheless, our decision in *Mahon* offered little insight into when, and under what circumstances, a given regulation would be seen as going "too far" for purposes of the Fifth Amendment. In 70-odd years of succeeding "regulatory takings" jurisprudence, we have generally eschewed any "'set formula'" for determining how far is too far, preferring to "engag[e] in . . . essentially ad hoc, factual inquiries," *Penn Central Transportation Co. v. New York City*, 438 U.S. 104, 124 (1978). We have, however, described at least two discrete categories of regulatory action as compensable without case-specific inquiry into the public interest advanced in support of the restraint. The first encompasses regulations that compel the property owner to suffer a physical "invasion" of his property. In general (at least with regard to permanent invasions), no matter how minute the intrusion, and no matter how weighty the public purpose behind it, we have required compensation. For example, in *Loretto v. Teleprompter Manhattan CATV Corp.*, 458 U.S. 419 (1982), we determined that New York's law requiring landlords to allow television cable companies to place cable facilities in their apartment buildings constituted a taking, id., at 435-440, 102 S. Ct., at 3175-3178, even though the facilities occupied at most only 1 1\2 cubic feet of the landlords' property. *See also United States v. Causby*, 328 U.S. 256 (1946).

---

[3] Justice BLACKMUN insists that this aspect of Lucas's claim is "not justiciable," because Lucas never fulfilled his obligation under *Williamson County Regional Planning Comm'n v. Hamilton Bank of Johnson City*, 473 U.S. 172 (1985), to "submi[t] a plan for development of [his] property" to the proper state authorities. But such a submission would have been pointless, as the Council stipulated below that no building permit would have been issued under the 1988 Act, application or no application. . . .

The second situation in which we have found categorical treatment appropriate is where regulation denies all economically beneficial or productive use of land. *See Nollan v. California Coastal Comm'n*, 483 U.S. 825, 834 (1987); *Keystone Bituminous Coal Assn. v. DeBenedictis*, 480 U.S. 470, 495 (1987); *Hodel v. Virginia Surface Mining & Reclamation Assn., Inc.*, 452 U.S. 264 (1981).[4] As we have said on numerous occasions, the Fifth Amendment is violated when land-use regulation does not substantially advance legitimate state interests or denies an owner economically viable use of his land.[7]

We have never set forth the justification for this rule. Perhaps it is simply, as Justice Brennan suggested, that total deprivation of beneficial use is, from the landowner's point of view, the equivalent of a physical appropriation. *See San Diego Gas & Electric Co. v. San Diego*, 450 U.S., at 652 (Brennan, J., dissenting). . . . Surely, at least, in the extraordinary circumstance when no productive or economically beneficial use of land is permitted, it is less realistic to indulge our usual assumption that the legislature is simply "adjusting the benefits and burdens of economic life," *Penn Central Transportation Co.*, 438 U.S., at 124, in a manner that secures an "average reciprocity of advantage" to everyone concerned. *Pennsylvania Coal Co. v. Mahon*, 260 U.S., at 415. And the functional basis for permitting the government, by regulation, to affect property values without compensation—that "Government hardly could go on if to some extent

---

[4] We will not attempt to respond to all of Justice BLACKMUN'S mistaken citation of case precedent. Characteristic of its nature is his assertion that the cases we discuss here stand merely for the proposition "that proof that a regulation does not deny an owner economic use of his property is sufficient to defeat a facial taking challenge" and not for the point that "denial of such use is sufficient to establish a taking claim regardless of any other consideration." The cases say, repeatedly and unmistakably, that "[t]he test to be applied in considering [a] facial [takings] challenge is fairly straightforward. A statute regulating the uses that can be made of property effects a taking if it denies an owner economically viable use of his land." *Keystone*, 480 U.S., at 495. Justice BLACKMUN describes that rule (which we do not invent but merely apply today) as "alter[ing] the long-settled rules of review" by foisting on the State "the burden of showing [its] regulation is not a taking." This is of course wrong. Lucas had to do more than simply file a lawsuit to establish his constitutional entitlement; he had to show that the Beachfront Management Act denied him economically beneficial use of his land. Our analysis presumes the unconstitutionality of state land-use regulation only in the sense that any rule with exceptions presumes the invalidity of a law that violates it . . . . Justice BLACKMUN'S real quarrel is with the substantive standard of liability we apply in this case, a long-established standard we see no need to repudiate.

[7] Regrettably, the rhetorical force of our "deprivation of all economically feasible use" rule is greater than its precision, since the rule does not make clear the "property interest" against which the loss of value is to be measured. When, for example, a regulation requires a developer to leave 90% of a rural tract in its natural state, it is unclear whether we would analyze the situation as one in which the owner has been deprived of all economically beneficial use of the burdened portion of the tract, or as one in which the owner has suffered a mere diminution in value of the tract as a whole. (For an extreme—and, we think, unsupportable—view of the relevant calculus, *see Penn Central Transportation Co. v. New York City*, 42 N.Y.2d 324, 333-334, 366 N.E.2d 1271, 1276-1277 (1977), *aff'd*, 438 U.S. 104 (1978), where the state court examined the diminution in a particular parcel's value produced by a municipal ordinance in light of total value of the taking claimant's other holdings in the vicinity.) Unsurprisingly, this uncertainty regarding the composition of the denominator in our "deprivation" fraction has produced inconsistent pronouncements by the Court. *Compare Pennsylvania Coal Co. v. Mahon*, 260 U.S. 393, 414 (1922), *with Keystone Bituminous Coal Assn. v. DeBenedictis*, 480 U.S. 470, 497-502 (1987) (nearly identical law held not to effect a taking). The answer to this difficult question may lie in how the owner's reasonable expectations have been shaped by the State's law of property—*i.e.*, whether and to what degree the State's law has accorded legal recognition and protection to the particular interest in land with respect to which the takings claimant alleges a diminution in (or elimination of) value. In any event, we avoid this difficulty in the present case, since the "interest in land" that Lucas has pleaded (a fee simple interest) is an estate with a rich tradition of protection at common law, and since the South Carolina Court of Common Pleas found that the Beachfront Management Act left each of Lucas's beachfront lots without economic value.

values incident to property could not be diminished without paying for every such change in the general law,"—does not apply to the relatively rare situations where the government has deprived a landowner of all economically beneficial uses.

On the other side of the balance, affirmatively supporting a compensation requirement, is the fact that regulations that leave the owner of land without economically beneficial or productive options for its use—typically, as here, by requiring land to be left substantially in its natural state—carry with them a heightened risk that private property is being pressed into some form of public service under the guise of mitigating serious public harm. *See, e.g., Annicelli v. South Kingstown*, 463 A.2d 133, 140-141 (R.I. 1983) (prohibition on construction adjacent to beach justified on twin grounds of safety and "conservation of open space"); *Morris County Land Improvement Co. v. Parsippany-Troy Hills Township*, 40 N.J. 539, 552-553, 193 A.2d 232, 240 (1963) (prohibition on filling marshlands imposed in order to preserve region as water detention basin and create wildlife refuge). As Justice Brennan explained: "From the government's point of view, the benefits flowing to the public from preservation of open space through regulation may be equally great as from creating a wildlife refuge through formal condemnation or increasing electricity production through a dam project that floods private property." *San Diego Gas & Elec. Co., supra*, 450 U.S., at 652 (Brennan, J., dissenting). The many statutes on the books, both state and federal, that provide for the use of eminent domain to impose servitudes on private scenic lands preventing developmental uses, or to acquire such lands altogether, suggest the practical equivalence in this setting of negative regulation and appropriation.

We think, in short, that there are good reasons for our frequently expressed belief that when the owner of real property has been called upon to sacrifice all economically beneficial uses in the name of the common good, that is, to leave his property economically idle, he has suffered a taking.[8]

B

The trial court found Lucas's two beachfront lots to have been rendered valueless by respondent's enforcement of the coastal-zone construction ban.[9] Under Lucas's theory of the

[8] Justice STEVENS criticizes the "deprivation of all economically beneficial use" rule as "wholly arbitrary", in that "[the] landowner whose property is diminished in value 95% recovers nothing," while the landowner who suffers a complete elimination of value "recovers the land's full value." This analysis errs in its assumption that the landowner whose deprivation is one step short of complete is not entitled to compensation. Such an owner might not be able to claim the benefit of our categorical formulation, but, as we have acknowledged time and again, "[t]he economic impact of the regulation on the claimant and . . . the extent to which the regulation has interfered with distinct investment-backed expectations" are keenly relevant to takings analysis generally. *Penn Central Transportation Co. v. New York City*, 438 U.S. 104, 124 (1978). It is true that in at least some cases the landowner with 95% loss will get nothing, while the landowner with total loss will recover in full. But that occasional result is no more strange than the gross disparity between the landowner whose premises are taken for a highway (who recovers in full) and the landowner whose property is reduced to 5% of its former value by the highway (who recovers nothing). Takings law is full of these "all-or-nothing" situations. Justice STEVENS similarly misinterprets our focus on "developmental" uses of property (the uses proscribed by the Beachfront Management Act) as betraying an "assumption that the only uses of property cognizable under the Constitution are developmental uses." We make no such assumption. Though our prior takings cases evince an abiding concern for the productive use of, and economic investment in, land, there are plainly a number of noneconomic interests in land whose impairment will invite exceedingly close scrutiny under the Takings Clause. *See, e.g., Loretto v. Teleprompter Manhattan CATV Corp.*, 458 U.S. 419, 436 (1982) (interest in excluding strangers from one's land).

[9] This finding was the premise of the Petition for Certiorari, and since it was not challenged in the Brief in Opposition we decline to entertain the argument in respondent's brief on the merits that the finding was erroneous. Instead, we decide the question presented under the same factual assumptions as did the Supreme Court of South Carolina.

case, which rested upon our "no economically viable use" statements, that finding entitled him to compensation. Lucas believed it unnecessary to take issue with either the purposes behind the Beachfront Management Act, or the means chosen by the South Carolina Legislature to effectuate those purposes. The South Carolina Supreme Court, however, thought otherwise. In its view, the Beachfront Management Act was no ordinary enactment, but involved an exercise of South Carolina's "police powers" to mitigate the harm to the public interest that petitioner's use of his land might occasion. By neglecting to dispute the findings enumerated in the Act[10] or otherwise to challenge the legislature's purposes, petitioner "concede[d] that the beach/dune area of South Carolina's shores is an extremely valuable public resource; that the erection of new construction, inter alia, contributes to the erosion and destruction of this public resource; and that discouraging new construction in close proximity to the beach/dune area is necessary to prevent a great public harm." In the court's view, these concessions brought petitioner's challenge within a long line of this Court's cases sustaining against Due Process and Takings Clause challenges the State's use of its "police powers" to enjoin a property owner from activities akin to public nuisances. *See Mugler v. Kansas*, 123 U.S. 623 (1887) (law prohibiting manufacture of alcoholic beverages); *Hadacheck v. Sebastian*, 239 U.S. 394 (1915) (law barring operation

---

[10] The legislature's express findings include the following:

The General Assembly finds that:

(1) The beach/dune system along the coast of South Carolina is extremely important to the people of this State and serves the following functions:

(a) protects life and property by serving as a storm barrier which dissipates wave energy and contributes to shoreline stability in an economical and effective manner;

(b) provides the basis for a tourism industry that generates approximately two-thirds of South Carolina's annual tourism industry revenue which constitutes a significant portion of the state's economy. The tourists who come to the South Carolina coast to enjoy the ocean and dry sand beach contribute significantly to state and local tax revenues;

(c) provides habitat for numerous species of plants and animals, several of which are threatened or endangered. Waters adjacent to the beach/dune system also provide habitat for many other marine species;

(d) provides a natural health environment for the citizens of South Carolina to spend leisure time which serves their physical and mental well-being.

(2) Beach/dune system vegetation is unique and extremely important to the vitality and preservation of the system.

(3) Many miles of South Carolina's beaches have been identified as critically eroding.

(4)... [D]evelopment unwisely has been sited too close to the [beach/dune] system. This type of development has jeopardized the stability of the beach/dune system, accelerated erosion, and endangered adjacent property. It is in both the public and private interests to protect the system from this unwise development.

(5) The use of armoring in the form of hard erosion control devices such as seawalls, bulkheads, and rip-rap to protect erosion-threatened structures adjacent to the beach has not proven effective. These armoring devices have given a false sense of security to beachfront property owners. In reality, these hard structures, in many instances, have increased the vulnerability of beachfront property to damage from wind and waves while contributing to the deterioration and loss of the dry sand beach which is so important to the tourism industry.

(6) Erosion is a natural process which becomes a significant problem for man only when structures are erected in close proximity to the beach/dune system. It is in both the public and private interests to afford the beach/dune system space to accrete and erode in its natural cycle. This space can be provided only by discouraging new construction in close proximity to the beach/dune system and encouraging those who have erected structures too close to the system to retreat from it.

. . .

(8) It is in the state's best interest to protect and to promote increased public access to South Carolina's beaches for out-of-state tourists and South Carolina residents alike.

S.C. Code § 48-39-250 (Supp. 1991).

of brick mill in residential area); *Miller v. Schoene*, 276 U.S. 272 (1928) (order to destroy diseased cedar trees to prevent infection of nearby orchards); *Goldblatt v. Hempstead*, 369 U.S. 590 (1962) (law effectively preventing continued operation of quarry in residential area).

It is correct that many of our prior opinions have suggested that "harmful or noxious uses" of property may be proscribed by government regulation without the requirement of compensation. For a number of reasons, however, we think the South Carolina Supreme Court was too quick to conclude that that principle decides the present case. The "harmful or noxious uses" principle was the Court's early attempt to describe in theoretical terms why government may, consistent with the Takings Clause, affect property values by regulation without incurring an obligation to compensate—a reality we nowadays acknowledge explicitly with respect to the full scope of the State's police power. We made this very point in *Penn Central Transportation Co.*, where, in the course of sustaining New York City's landmarks preservation program against a takings challenge, we rejected the petitioner's suggestion that *Mugler* and the cases following it were premised on, and thus limited by, some objective conception of "noxiousness": "[T]he uses in issue in *Hadacheck*, *Miller*, and *Goldblatt* were perfectly lawful in themselves. They involved no 'blameworthiness, . . . moral wrongdoing or conscious act of dangerous risk-taking which induce[d society] to shift the cost to a pa[rt]icular individual.' Sax, *Takings and the Police Power*, 74 Yale L.J. 36, 50 (1964). These cases are better understood as resting not on any supposed 'noxious' quality of the prohibited uses but rather on the ground that the restrictions were reasonably related to the implementation of a policy—not unlike historic preservation—expected to produce a widespread public benefit and applicable to all similarly situated property." 438 U.S., at 133-134, n. 30. "Harmful or noxious use" analysis was, in other words, simply the progenitor of our more contemporary statements that "land-use regulation does not effect a taking if it substantially advance[s] legitimate state interests . . . ." *Nollan, supra*, 483 U.S., at 834; *see also Penn Central Transportation Co., supra*, 438 U.S., at 127; *Euclid v. Ambler Realty Co.*, 272 U.S. 365, 387-388 (1926).

The transition from our early focus on control of "noxious" uses to our contemporary understanding of the broad realm within which government may regulate without compensation was an easy one, since the distinction between "harm-preventing" and "benefit-conferring" regulation is often in the eye of the beholder. It is quite possible, for example, to describe in either fashion the ecological, economic, and aesthetic concerns that inspired the South Carolina legislature in the present case. One could say that imposing a servitude on Lucas's land is necessary in order to prevent his use of it from "harming" South Carolina's ecological resources; or, instead, in order to achieve the "benefits" of an ecological preserve.[11] . . . Whether one or

---

[11] In the present case, in fact, some of the "[South Carolina] legislature's 'findings' " to which the South Carolina Supreme Court purported to defer in characterizing the purpose of the Act as "harm-preventing," seem to us phrased in "benefit-conferring" language instead. For example, they describe the importance of a construction ban in enhancing "South Carolina's annual tourism industry revenue," in "provid[ing] habitat for numerous species of plants and animals, several of which are threatened or endangered," and in "provid[ing] a natural healthy environment for the citizens of South Carolina to spend leisure time which serves their physical and mental well-being." It would be pointless to make the outcome of this case hang upon this terminology, since the same interests could readily be described in "harm-preventing" fashion. Justice BLACKMUN, however, apparently insists that we must make the outcome hinge (exclusively) upon the South Carolina Legislature's other, "harm-preventing" characterizations, focusing on the declaration that "prohibitions on building in front of the setback line are necessary to protect people and property from storms, high tides, and beach erosion." He says "[n]othing in the record undermines [this] assessment," apparently seeing no significance in the fact that the statute permits owners of existing structures to remain (and even to rebuild if their structures are not "destroyed beyond repair," S.C. Code Ann. § 48-39-290(B)), and in the fact that the 1990 amendment authorizes the Council to issue permits for new construction in violation of the uniform prohibition, *see* S.C. Code § 48-39-290(D)(1) (Supp.1991).

the other of the competing characterizations will come to one's lips in a particular case depends primarily upon one's evaluation of the worth of competing uses of real estate . . . . A given restraint will be seen as mitigating "harm" to the adjacent parcels or securing a "benefit" for them, depending upon the observer's evaluation of the relative importance of the use that the restraint favors. . . . Whether Lucas's construction of single-family residences on his parcels should be described as bringing "harm" to South Carolina's adjacent ecological resources thus depends principally upon whether the describer believes that the State's use interest in nurturing those resources is so important that any competing adjacent use must yield.

When it is understood that "prevention of harmful use" was merely our early formulation of the police power justification necessary to sustain (without compensation) any regulatory diminution in value; and that the distinction between regulation that "prevents harmful use" and that which "confers benefits" is difficult, if not impossible, to discern on an objective, value-free basis; it becomes self-evident that noxious-use logic cannot serve as a touchstone to distinguish regulatory "takings"—which require compensation—from regulatory deprivations that do not require compensation. *A fortiori* the legislature's recitation of a noxious-use justification cannot be the basis for departing from our categorical rule that total regulatory takings must be compensated. If it were, departure would virtually always be allowed. The South Carolina Supreme Court's approach would essentially nullify *Mahon*'s affirmation of limits to the noncompensable exercise of the police power.

Where the State seeks to sustain regulation that deprives land of all economically beneficial use, we think it may resist compensation only if the logically antecedent inquiry into the nature of the owner's estate shows that the proscribed use interests were not part of his title to begin with.[14] This accords, we think, with our "takings" jurisprudence, which has traditionally been guided by the understandings of our citizens regarding the content of, and the State's power over, the "bundle of rights" that they acquire when they obtain title to property. It seems to us that the property owner necessarily expects the uses of his property to be restricted, from time to time, by various measures newly enacted by the State in legitimate exercise of its police powers; "[a]s long recognized, some values are enjoyed under an implied limitation and must yield to the police power." *Pennsylvania Coal Co. v. Mahon*, 260 U.S., at 413. And in the case of personal property, by reason of the State's traditionally high degree of control over commercial dealings, he ought to be aware of the possibility that new regulation might even render his property economically worthless (at least if the property's only economically productive use is sale or manufacture for sale). In the case of land, however, we think the notion pressed by the Council that title is somehow held subject to the "implied limitation" that the State may subsequently eliminate all economically valuable use is inconsistent with the historical compact recorded in the Takings Clause that has become part of our constitutional culture.[15]

---

[14] . . . Justice STEVENS would "loo[k] to the generality of a regulation of property" to determine whether compensation is owing. The Beachfront Management Act is general, in his view, because it "regulates the use of the coastline of the entire state." There may be some validity to the principle Justice STEVENS proposes, but it does not properly apply to the present case . . . . Perhaps such a law—the generally applicable criminal prohibition on the manufacturing of alcoholic beverages challenged in *Mugler* comes to mind—cannot constitute a compensable taking. But a regulation specifically directed to land use . . . [does not acquire] immunity by plundering landowners generally . . . . Justice STEVENS' approach renders the Takings Clause little more than a particularized restatement of the Equal Protection Clause.

[15] After accusing us of "launch[ing] a missile to kill a mouse," Justice BLACKMUN expends a good deal of throw-weight of his own upon a noncombatant, arguing that our description of the "understanding" of land ownership that informs the Takings Clause is not supported by early American experience. That is largely true, but entirely irrelevant.

Where "permanent physical occupation" of land is concerned, we have refused to allow the government to decree it anew (without compensation), no matter how weighty the asserted "public interests" involved, *Loretto v. Teleprompter Manhattan CATV Corp.*, 458 U.S., at 426—though we assuredly would permit the government to assert a permanent easement that was a pre-existing limitation upon the landowner's title. . . . We believe similar treatment must be accorded confiscatory regulations, i.e., regulations that prohibit all economically beneficial use of land: Any limitation so severe cannot be newly legislated or decreed (without compensation), but must inhere in the title itself, in the restrictions that background principles of the State's law of property and nuisance already place upon land ownership. A law or decree with such an effect must, in other words, do no more than duplicate the result that could have been achieved in the courts—by adjacent landowners (or other uniquely affected persons) under the State's law of private nuisance, or by the State under its complementary power to abate nuisances that affect the public generally, or otherwise.[16]

On this analysis, the owner of a lake bed, for example, would not be entitled to compensation when he is denied the requisite permit to engage in a landfilling operation that would have the effect of flooding others' land. Nor the corporate owner of a nuclear generating plant, when it is directed to remove all improvements from its land upon discovery that the plant sits astride an earthquake fault. Such regulatory action may well have the effect of eliminating the land's only economically productive use, but it does not proscribe a productive use that was previously permissible under relevant property and nuisance principles. The use of these properties for what are now expressly prohibited purposes was always unlawful, and (subject to other constitutional limitations) it was open to the State at any point to make the implication of those background principles of nuisance and property law explicit. *See* Michelman, *Property, Utility, and Fairness, Comments on the Ethical Foundations of "Just Compensation" Law*, 80 Harv. L. Rev. 1165, 1239-1241 (1967). In light of our traditional resort to "existing rules or understandings that stem from an independent source such as state law" to define the range of interests that qualify for protection as "property" under the Fifth (and Fourteenth) amendments, *Board of Regents of State Colleges v. Roth*, 408 U.S. 564, 577 (1972), this recognition that the Takings Clause does not require compensation when an owner is barred from putting land to a use that is proscribed by those "existing rules or understandings" is surely unexceptional. When, however, a regulation that declares "off-limits" all economically productive or beneficial uses of land goes beyond what the relevant background principles would dictate, compensation must be paid to sustain it.

The "total taking" inquiry we require today will ordinarily entail (as the application of state nuisance law ordinarily entails) analysis of, among other things, the degree of harm to public lands and resources, or adjacent private property, posed by the claimant's proposed activities,

---

The practices of the States prior to incorporation of the Takings and Just Compensation Clauses—which, as Justice BLACKMUN acknowledges, occasionally included outright physical appropriation of land without compensation—were out of accord with any plausible interpretation of those provisions. Justice BLACKMUN is correct that early constitutional theorists did not believe the Takings Clause embraced regulations of property at all, but even he does not suggest (explicitly, at least) that we renounce the Court's contrary conclusion in *Mahon*. Since the text of the Clause can be read to encompass regulatory as well as physical deprivations (in contrast to the text originally proposed by Madison, see Speech Proposing Bill of Rights (June 8, 1789), in 12 J. Madison, *The Papers of James Madison* 201 (C. Hobson, R. Rutland, W. Rachal, & J. Sisson ed. 1979) ("No person shall be . . . obliged to relinquish his property, where it may be necessary for public use, without a just compensation"), we decline to do so as well.

[16] The principal "otherwise" that we have in mind is litigation absolving the State (or private parties) of liability for the destruction of "real and personal property, in cases of actual necessity, to prevent the spreading of a fire" or to forestall other grave threats to the lives and property of others.

the social value of the claimant's activities and their suitability to the locality in question, and the relative ease with which the alleged harm can be avoided through measures taken by the claimant and the government (or adjacent private landowners) alike. The fact that a particular use has long been engaged in by similarly situated owners ordinarily imports a lack of any common-law prohibition (though changed circumstances or new knowledge may make what was previously permissible no longer so). So also does the fact that other landowners, similarly situated, are permitted to continue the use denied to the claimant.

It seems unlikely that common-law principles would have prevented the erection of any habitable or productive improvements on petitioner's land; they rarely support prohibition of the "essential use" of land. The question, however, is one of state law to be dealt with on remand. We emphasize that to win its case South Carolina must do more than proffer the legislature's declaration that the uses Lucas desires are inconsistent with the public interest, or the conclusory assertion that they violate a common-law maxim such as *sic utere tuo ut alienum non laedas*. As we have said, a "State, by *ipse dixit*, may not transform private property into public property without compensation . . . ." *Webb's Fabulous Pharmacies, Inc. v. Beckwith*, 449 U.S. 155, 164 (1980). Instead, as it would be required to do if it sought to restrain Lucas in a common-law action for public nuisance, South Carolina must identify background principles of nuisance and property law that prohibit the uses he now intends in the circumstances in which the property is presently found. Only on this showing can the State fairly claim that, in proscribing all such beneficial uses, the Beachfront Management Act is taking nothing.[18]

. . . .

The judgment is reversed and the cause remanded for proceedings not inconsistent with this opinion.

So ordered.

JUSTICE KENNEDY, concurring in the judgment.

The case comes to the Court in an unusual posture, as all my colleagues observe. After the suit was initiated but before it reached us, South Carolina amended its Beachfront Management Act to authorize the issuance of special permits at variance with the Act's general limitations. Petitioner has not applied for a special permit but may still do so. The availability of this alternative, if it can be invoked, may dispose of petitioner's claim of a permanent taking. As I read the Court's opinion, it does not decide the permanent taking claim, but neither does it foreclose the Supreme Court of South Carolina from considering the claim or requiring petitioner to pursue an administrative alternative not previously available.

The potential for future relief does not control our disposition, because whatever may occur in the future cannot undo what has occurred in the past. The Beachfront Management Act was enacted in 1988. It may have deprived petitioner of the use of his land in an interim period. If this deprivation amounts to a taking, its limited duration will not bar constitutional relief. It is well established that temporary takings are as protected by the Constitution as are permanent

---

[18] Justice BLACKMUN decries our reliance on background nuisance principles at least in part because he believes those principles to be as manipulable as we find the "harm prevention"/"benefit conferral" dichotomy. There is no doubt some leeway in a court's interpretation of what existing state law permits—but not remotely as much, we think, as in a legislative crafting of the reasons for its confiscatory regulation. We stress that an affirmative decree eliminating all economically beneficial uses may be defended only if an objectively reasonable application of relevant precedents would exclude those beneficial uses in the circumstances in which the land is presently found.

ones. *First English Evangelical Lutheran Church of Glendale v. County of Los Angeles*, 482 U.S. 304 (1987).

. . . .

The South Carolina Court of Common Pleas found that petitioner's real property has been rendered valueless by the State's regulation. The finding appears to presume that the property has no significant market value or resale potential. This is a curious finding, and I share the reservations of some of my colleagues about a finding that a beach front lot loses all value because of a development restriction. While the Supreme Court of South Carolina on remand need not consider the case subject to this constraint, we must accept the finding as entered below. Accepting the finding as entered, it follows that petitioner is entitled to invoke the line of cases discussing regulations that deprive real property of all economic value.

The finding of no value must be considered under the Takings Clause by reference to the owner's reasonable, investment-backed expectations. *Penn Central Transportation Co. v. New York City*, 438 U.S. 104 (1978). The Takings Clause, while conferring substantial protection on property owners, does not eliminate the police power of the State to enact limitations on the use of their property. *Mugler v. Kansas*, 123 U.S. 623 (1887). The rights conferred by the Takings Clause and the police power of the State may coexist without conflict. Property is bought and sold, investments are made, subject to the State's power to regulate. Where a taking is alleged from regulations which deprive the property of all value, the test must be whether the deprivation is contrary to reasonable, investment-backed expectations.

There is an inherent tendency towards circularity in this synthesis, of course; for if the owner's reasonable expectations are shaped by what courts allow as a proper exercise of governmental authority, property tends to become what courts say it is. Some circularity must be tolerated in these matters, however, as it is in other spheres. The definition, moreover, is not circular in its entirety. The expectations protected by the Constitution are based on objective rules and customs that can be understood as reasonable by all parties involved.

In my view, reasonable expectations must be understood in light of the whole of our legal tradition. The common law of nuisance is too narrow a confine for the exercise of regulatory power in a complex and interdependent society. *Goldblatt v. Hempstead*, 369 U.S. 590 (1962). The State should not be prevented from enacting new regulatory initiatives in response to changing conditions, and courts must consider all reasonable expectations whatever their source. The Takings Clause does not require a static body of state property law; it protects private expectations to ensure private investment. I agree with the Court that nuisance prevention accords with the most common expectations of property owners who face regulation, but I do not believe this can be the sole source of state authority to impose severe restrictions. Coastal property may present such unique concerns for a fragile land system that the State can go further in regulating its development and use than the common law of nuisance might otherwise permit.

The Supreme Court of South Carolina erred, in my view, by reciting the general purposes for which the state regulations were enacted without a determination that they were in accord with the owner's reasonable expectations and therefore sufficient to support a severe restriction on specific parcels of property. The promotion of tourism, for instance, ought not to suffice to deprive specific property of all value without a corresponding duty to compensate. Furthermore, the means as well as the ends of regulation must accord with the owner's reasonable expectations. Here, the State did not act until after the property had been zoned for individual lot development and most other parcels had been improved, throwing the whole burden of the regulation on the remaining lots. This too must be measured in the balance. *See Pennsylvania Coal Co. v. Mahon*, 260 U.S. 393 (1922).

With these observations, I concur in the judgment of the Court.

JUSTICE BLACKMUN, dissenting.

Today the Court launches a missile to kill a mouse.

The State of South Carolina prohibited petitioner Lucas from building a permanent structure on his property from 1988 to 1990. Relying on an unreviewed (and implausible) state trial court finding that this restriction left Lucas' property valueless, this Court granted review to determine whether compensation must be paid in cases where the State prohibits all economic use of real estate. According to the Court, such an occasion never has arisen in any of our prior cases, and the Court imagines that it will arise "relatively rarely" or only in "extraordinary circumstances." Almost certainly it did not happen in this case.

Nonetheless, the Court presses on to decide the issue, and as it does, it ignores its jurisdictional limits, remakes its traditional rules of review, and creates simultaneously a new categorical rule and an exception (neither of which is rooted in our prior case law, common law, or common sense). I protest not only the Court's decision, but each step taken to reach it. More fundamentally, I question the Court's wisdom in issuing sweeping new rules to decide such a narrow case. Surely, as Justice KENNEDY demonstrates, the Court could have reached the result it wanted without inflicting this damage upon our Taking Clause jurisprudence.

My fear is that the Court's new policies will spread beyond the narrow confines of the present case. For that reason, I, like the Court, will give far greater attention to this case than its narrow scope suggests—not because I can intercept the Court's missile, or save the targeted mouse, but because I hope perhaps to limit the collateral damage.

I

A

In 1972 Congress passed the Coastal Zone Management Act. 16 U.S.C. § 1451 *et seq.* The Act was designed to provide States with money and incentives to carry out Congress' goal of protecting the public from shoreline erosion and coastal hazards. In the 1980 Amendments to the Act, Congress directed States to enhance their coastal programs by "[p]reventing or significantly reducing threats to life and the destruction of property by eliminating development and redevelopment in high-hazard areas."[1]

South Carolina began implementing the congressional directive by enacting the South Carolina Coastal Zone Management Act of 1977. Under the 1977 Act, any construction activity in what was designated the "critical area" required a permit from the Council, and the construction of any habitable structure was prohibited. The 1977 critical area was relatively narrow.

---

[1] The country has come to recognize that uncontrolled beachfront development can cause serious damage to life and property. Hurricane Hugo's September 1989 attack upon South Carolina's coastline, for example, caused 29 deaths and approximately $6 billion in property damage, much of it the result of uncontrolled beachfront development. *See* Zalkin, *Shifting Sands and Shifting Doctrines: The Supreme Court's Changing Takings Doctrine and South Carolina's Coastal Zone Statute*, 79 Cal. L. Rev. 205, 212-213 (1991). The beachfront buildings are not only themselves destroyed in such a storm, "but they are often driven, like battering rams, into adjacent inland homes." Moreover, the development often destroys the natural sand dune barriers that provide storm breaks.

This effort did not stop the loss of shoreline. In October 1986, the Council appointed a "Blue Ribbon Committee on Beachfront Management" to investigate beach erosion and propose possible solutions. In March 1987, the Committee found that South Carolina's beaches were "critically eroding," and proposed land-use restrictions. In response, South Carolina enacted the Beachfront Management Act on July 1, 1988. S.C. Code § 48-39-250 *et seq.* (Supp. 1990). The 1988 Act did not change the uses permitted within the designated critical areas. Rather, it enlarged those areas to encompass the distance from the mean high watermark to a setback line established on the basis of "the best scientific and historical data" available.[2]

B

Petitioner Lucas is a contractor, manager, and part owner of the Wild Dune development on the Isle of Palms. He has lived there since 1978. In December 1986, he purchased two of the last four pieces of vacant property in the development.[3] The area is notoriously unstable. In roughly half of the last 40 years, all or part of petitioner's property was part of the beach or flooded twice daily by the ebb and flow of the tide. Between 1957 and 1963, petitioner's property was under water. Between 1963 and 1973 the shoreline was 100 to 150 feet onto petitioner's property. In 1973 the first line of stable vegetation was about halfway through the property. Between 1981 and 1983, the Isle of Palms issued 12 emergency orders for sandbagging to protect property in the Wild Dune development. Determining that local habitable structures were in imminent danger of collapse, the Council issued permits for two rock revetments to protect condominium developments near petitioner's property from erosion; one of the revetments extends more than halfway onto one of his lots.

C

The South Carolina Supreme Court found that the Beach Management Act did not take petitioner's property without compensation. The decision rested on two premises that until today were unassailable—that the State has the power to prevent any use of property it finds to be harmful to its citizens, and that a state statute is entitled to a presumption of constitutionality.

The Beachfront Management Act includes a finding by the South Carolina General Assembly that the beach/dune system serves the purpose of "protect[ing] life and property by serving as a storm barrier which dissipates wave energy and contributes to shoreline stability in an economical and effective manner." The General Assembly also found that "development unwisely has been sited too close to the [beach/dune] system. This type of development has jeopardized the stability of the beach/dune system, accelerated erosion, and endangered adjacent property."

If the state legislature is correct that the prohibition on building in front of the setback line prevents serious harm, then, under this Court's prior cases, the Act is constitutional. "Long ago it was recognized that all property in this country is held under the implied obligation that the owner's use of it shall not be injurious to the community, and the Takings Clause did not transform that principle to one that requires compensation whenever the State asserts its power to enforce

---

[2] The setback line was determined by calculating the distance landward from the crest of an ideal oceanfront sand dune which is forty times the annual erosion rate.

[3] The properties were sold frequently at rapidly escalating prices before Lucas purchased them. Lot 22 was first sold in 1979 for $96,660, sold in 1984 for $187,500, then in 1985 for $260,000, and, finally, to Lucas in 1986 for $475,000. He estimated its worth in 1991 at $650,000. Lot 24 had a similar past. The record does not indicate who purchased the properties prior to Lucas, or why none of the purchasers held on to the lots and built on them.

it." *Keystone Bituminous Coal Assn. v. DeBenedictis*, 480 U.S. 470, 491-492 (1987). The Court consistently has upheld regulations imposed to arrest a significant threat to the common welfare, whatever their economic effect on the owner. *See e.g., Goldblatt v. Hempstead*, 369 U.S. 590, 592-593 (1962); *Euclid v. Ambler Realty Co.*, 272 U.S. 365 (1926); *Mugler v. Kansas*, 123 U.S. 623 (1887).

Petitioner never challenged the legislature's findings that a building ban was necessary to protect property and life. Nor did he contend that the threatened harm was not sufficiently serious to make building a house in a particular location a "harmful" use, that the legislature had not made sufficient findings, or that the legislature was motivated by anything other than a desire to minimize damage to coastal areas. Indeed, petitioner objected at trial that evidence as to the purposes of the setback requirement was irrelevant. The South Carolina Supreme Court accordingly understood petitioner not to contest the State's position that "discouraging new construction in close proximity to the beach/dune area is necessary to prevent a great public harm," and "to prevent serious injury to the community." The court considered itself "bound by these uncontested legislative findings . . . [in the absence of] any attack whatsoever on the statutory scheme."

Nothing in the record undermines the General Assembly's assessment that prohibitions on building in front of the setback line are necessary to protect people and property from storms, high tides, and beach erosion. Because that legislative determination cannot be disregarded in the absence of such evidence, *see, e.g., Euclid*, 272 U.S., at 388 and because its determination of harm to life and property from building is sufficient to prohibit that use under this Court's cases, the South Carolina Supreme Court correctly found no taking.

II

My disagreement with the Court begins with its decision to review this case. This Court has held consistently that a land-use challenge is not ripe for review until there is a final decision about what uses of the property will be permitted. The ripeness requirement is not simply a gesture of good-will to land-use planners. In the absence of a final and authoritative determination of the type and intensity of development legally permitted on the subject property, and the utilization of state procedures for just compensation, there is no final judgment, and in the absence of a final judgment there is no jurisdiction.

. . . .

The Court admits that the 1990 amendments to the Beachfront Management Act allowing special permits preclude Lucas from asserting that his property has been permanently taken. The Court agrees that such a claim would not be ripe because there has been no final decision by respondent on what uses will be permitted. The Court, however, will not be denied: it determines that petitioner's "temporary takings" claim for the period from July 1, 1988, to June 25, 1990, is ripe. But this claim also is not justiciable.

From the very beginning of this litigation, respondent has argued that the courts: "lac[k] jurisdiction in this matter because the Plaintiff has sought no authorization from Council for use of his property, has not challenged the location of the baseline or setback line as alleged in the Complaint and because no final agency decision has been rendered concerning use of his property or location of said baseline or setback line." Although the Council's plea has been ignored by every court, it is undoubtedly correct.

Under the Beachfront Management Act, petitioner was entitled to challenge the setback line or the baseline or erosion rate applied to his property in formal administrative, followed by judicial, proceedings. Because Lucas failed to pursue this administrative remedy, the Council never finally decided whether Lucas' particular piece of property was correctly categorized as a critical area in which building would not be permitted. This is all the more crucial because Lucas argued strenuously in the trial court that his land was perfectly safe to build on, and that his company had studies to prove it. If he was correct, the Council's final decision would have been to alter the setback line, eliminating the construction ban on Lucas' property.

That petitioner's property fell within the critical area as initially interpreted by the Council does not excuse petitioner's failure to challenge the Act's application to his property in the administrative process. The claim is not ripe until petitioner seeks a variance from that status.

Even if I agreed with the Court that there were no jurisdictional barriers to deciding this case, I still would not try to decide it. The Court creates its new taking jurisprudence based on the trial court's finding that the property had lost all economic value.[6] This finding is almost certainly erroneous. Petitioner still can enjoy other attributes of ownership, such as the right to exclude others, "one of the most essential sticks in the bundle of rights that are commonly characterized as property." *Kaiser Aetna v. United States*, 444 U.S. 164, 176 (1979). Petitioner can picnic, swim, camp in a tent, or live on the property in a movable trailer . . . . Petitioner also retains the right to alienate the land, which would have value for neighbors and for those prepared to enjoy proximity to the ocean without a house.

Yet the trial court, apparently believing that "less value" and "valueless" could be used interchangeably, found the property "valueless." The court accepted no evidence from the State on the property's value without a home, and petitioner's appraiser testified that he never had considered what the value would be absent a residence. The appraiser's value was based on the fact that the "highest and best use of these lots . . . [is] luxury single family detached dwellings." The trial court appeared to believe that the property could be considered "valueless" if it was not available for its most profitable use. Absent that erroneous assumption, I find no evidence in the record supporting the trial court's conclusion that the damage to the lots by virtue of the restrictions was "total." I agree with the Court that it has the power to decide a case that turns on an erroneous finding, but I question the wisdom of deciding an issue based on a factual premise that does not exist in this case, and in the judgment of the Court will exist in the future only in "extraordinary circumstance[s]."

Clearly, the Court was eager to decide this case.[7] But eagerness, in the absence of proper jurisdiction, must—and in this case should have been—met with restraint.

---

[6] Respondent contested the findings of fact of the trial court in the South Carolina Supreme Court, but that court did not resolve the issue. This Court's decision to assume for its purposes that petitioner had been denied all economic use of his land does not, of course, dispose of the issue on remand.

[7] The Court overlooks the lack of a ripe and justiciable claim apparently out of concern that in the absence of its intervention Lucas will be unable to obtain further adjudication of his temporary-taking claim. The Court chastises respondent for arguing that Lucas's temporary-taking claim is premature because it failed "so much as [to] commen[t]" upon the effect of the South Carolina Supreme Court's decision on petitioner's ability to obtain relief for the 2-year period, and it frets that Lucas would "be unable (absent our intervention now) to obtain further state-court adjudication with respect to the 1988-1990 period." Whatever the explanation for the Court's intense interest in Lucas' plight when ordinarily we are more cautious in granting discretionary review, the concern would have been more prudently expressed by vacating the judgment below and remanding for further consideration in light of the 1990 amendments. At that point, petitioner could have brought a temporary-taking claim in the state courts.

III

The Court's willingness to dispense with precedent in its haste to reach a result is not limited to its initial jurisdictional decision. The Court also alters the long-settled rules of review.

The South Carolina Supreme Court's decision to defer to legislative judgments in the absence of a challenge from petitioner comports with one of this Court's oldest maxims: "the existence of facts supporting the legislative judgment is to be presumed." *United States v. Carolene Products Co.,* 304 U.S. 144 (1938). Indeed, we have said the legislature's judgment is "well-nigh conclusive." *Berman v. Parker,* 348 U.S. 26 (1954). *See also Euclid,* 272 U.S., at 388 ("If the validity of the legislative classification for zoning purposes be fairly debatable, the legislative judgment must be allowed to control").

Accordingly, this Court always has required plaintiffs challenging the constitutionality of an ordinance to provide some factual foundation of record that contravenes the legislative findings. In the absence of such proof, the presumption of constitutionality must prevail. We only recently have reaffirmed that claimants have the burden of showing a state law constitutes a taking. *See Keystone Bituminous Coal,* 480 U.S., at 485.

Rather than invoking these traditional rules, the Court decides the State has the burden to convince the courts that its legislative judgments are correct. Despite Lucas' complete failure to contest the legislature's findings of serious harm to life and property if a permanent structure is built, the Court decides that the legislative findings are not sufficient to justify the use prohibition. Instead, the Court "emphasize[s]" the State must do more than merely proffer its legislative judgments to avoid invalidating its law. In this case, apparently, the State now has the burden of showing the regulation is not a taking. The Court offers no justification for its sudden hostility toward state legislators, and I doubt that it could.

IV

The Court does not reject the South Carolina Supreme Court's decision simply on the basis of its disbelief and distrust of the legislature's findings. It also takes the opportunity to create a new scheme for regulations that eliminate all economic value. From now on, there is a categorical rule finding these regulations to be a taking unless the use they prohibit is a background common-law nuisance or property principle.

A

I first question the Court's rationale in creating a category that obviates a "case-specific inquiry into the public interest advanced," if all economic value has been lost. If one fact about the Court's taking jurisprudence can be stated without contradiction, it is that "the particular circumstances of each case" determine whether a specific restriction will be rendered invalid by the government's failure to pay compensation. This is so because although we have articulated certain factors to be considered, including the economic impact on the property owner, the ultimate conclusion necessarily requires a weighing of private and public interests. When the government regulation prevents the owner from any economically valuable use of his property, the private interest is unquestionably substantial, but we have never before held that no public interest can outweigh it. Instead the Court's prior decisions uniformly reject the proposition that diminution in property value, standing alone, can establish a taking. *Penn Central Transp. Co. v. New York City,* 438 U.S. 104, 131 (1978).

This Court repeatedly has recognized the ability of government, in certain circumstances, to regulate property without compensation no matter how adverse the financial effect on the owner may be. More than a century ago, the Court explicitly upheld the right of States to prohibit uses of property injurious to public health, safety, or welfare without paying compensation: "A prohibition simply upon the use of property for purposes that are declared, by valid legislation, to be injurious to the health, morals, or safety of the community, cannot, in any just sense, be deemed a taking or an appropriation of property." *Mugler v. Kansas*, 123 U.S. 623 (1887). On this basis, the Court upheld an ordinance effectively prohibiting operation of a previously lawful brewery, although the "establishments will become of no value as property."

Mugler was only the beginning in a long line of cases. . . . In *Hadacheck v. Sebastian*, 239 U.S. 394 (1915), the Court upheld an ordinance prohibiting a brickyard, although the owner had made excavations on the land that prevented it from being utilized for any purpose but a brickyard. In *Miller v. Schoene*, 276 U.S. 272 (1928), the Court held that the Fifth Amendment did not require Virginia to pay compensation to the owner of cedar trees ordered destroyed to prevent a disease from spreading to nearby apple orchards. The "preferment of [the public interest] over the property interest of the individual, to the extent even of its destruction, is one of the distinguishing characteristics of every exercise of the police power which affects property." . . . More recently, in *Goldblatt,* the Court upheld a town regulation that barred continued operation of an existing sand and gravel operation in order to protect public safety. 369 U.S., at 596. "Although a comparison of values before and after is relevant," the Court stated, "it is by no means conclusive." . . .

The Court recognizes that "our prior opinions have suggested that 'harmful or noxious uses' of property may be proscribed by government regulation without the requirement of compensation," but seeks to reconcile them with its categorical rule by claiming that the Court never has upheld a regulation when the owner alleged the loss of all economic value. Even if the Court's factual premise were correct, its understanding of the Court's cases is distorted. In none of the cases did the Court suggest that the right of a State to prohibit certain activities without paying compensation turned on the availability of some residual valuable use.[12] Instead, the cases depended on whether the government interest was sufficient to prohibit the activity, given the significant private cost.[13]

. . . .

---

[12] *Miller v. Schoene*, 276 U.S. 272 (1928), is an example. In the course of demonstrating that apple trees are more valuable than red cedar trees, the Court noted that red cedar has "occasional use and value as lumber." But the Court did not discuss whether the timber owned by the petitioner in that case was commercially saleable, and nothing in the opinion suggests that the State's right to require uncompensated felling of the trees depended on any such salvage value. To the contrary, it is clear from its unanimous opinion that the *Schoene* Court would have sustained a law requiring the burning of cedar trees if that had been necessary to protect apple trees in which there was a public interest: the Court spoke of preferment of the public interest over the property interest of the individual, "to the extent even of its destruction."

[13] The Court seeks to disavow the holdings and reasoning of *Mugler* and subsequent cases by explaining that they were the Court's early efforts to define the scope of the police power. There is language in the earliest taking cases suggesting that the police power was considered to be the power simply to prevent harms. Subsequently, the Court expanded its understanding of what were government's legitimate interests. But it does not follow that the holding of those early cases—that harmful and noxious uses of property can be forbidden whatever the harm to the property owner and without the payment of compensation—was repudiated. To the contrary, as the Court consciously expanded the scope of the police power beyond preventing harm, it clarified that there was a core of public interests that overrode any private interest. *See Keystone Bituminous Coal*, 480 U.S., at 491, n. 20.

B

Ultimately even the Court cannot embrace the full implications of its per se rule: it eventually agrees that there cannot be a categorical rule for a taking based on economic value that wholly disregards the public need asserted. Instead, the Court decides that it will permit a State to regulate all economic value only if the State prohibits uses that would not be permitted under "background principles of nuisance and property law."[15]

Until today, the Court explicitly had rejected the contention that the government's power to act without paying compensation turns on whether the prohibited activity is a common-law nuisance.[16] The brewery closed in *Mugler* itself was not a common-law nuisance, and the Court specifically stated that it was the role of the legislature to determine what measures would be appropriate for the protection of public health and safety. In upholding the state action in *Miller*, the Court found it unnecessary to "weigh with nicety the question whether the infected cedars constitute a nuisance according to common law; or whether they may be so declared by statute." . . . Instead the Court has relied in the past, as the South Carolina Court has done here, on legislative judgments of what constitutes a harm.[17]

The Court rejects the notion that the State always can prohibit uses it deems a harm to the public without granting compensation because "the distinction between 'harm-preventing' and 'benefit-conferring' regulation is often in the eye of the beholder." Since the characterization will depend "primarily upon one's evaluation of the worth of competing uses of real estate," the Court decides a legislative judgment of this kind no longer can provide the desired "objective, value-free basis" for upholding a regulation. The Court, however, fails to explain how its proposed common law alternative escapes the same trap.

The threshold inquiry for imposition of the Court's new rule, "deprivation of all economically valuable use," itself cannot be determined objectively. As the Court admits, whether the owner has been deprived of all economic value of his property will depend on how "property" is defined. The "composition of the denominator in our 'deprivation' fraction," is the dispositive inquiry. Yet there is no "objective" way to define what that denominator should be. "We have long

---

[15] Although it refers to state nuisance and property law, the Court apparently does not mean just any state nuisance and property law. Public nuisance was first a common-law creation, . . . but by the 1800s in both the United States and England, legislatures had the power to define what is a public nuisance, and particular uses often have been selectively targeted . . . . The Court's references to "common-law" background principles, however, indicate that legislative determinations do not constitute "state nuisance and property law" for the Court.

[16] Also, until today the fact that the regulation prohibited uses that were lawful at the time the owner purchased did not determine the constitutional question. The brewery, the brickyard, the cedar trees, and the gravel pit were all perfectly legitimate uses prior to the passage of the regulation. *See Mugler, Hadacheck, Miller,* and *Goldblatt.* This Court explicitly acknowledged in *Hadacheck* that "[a] vested interest cannot be asserted against [the police power] because of conditions once obtaining. To so hold would preclude development and fix a city forever in its primitive conditions."

[17] The Court argues that finding no taking when the legislature prohibits a harmful use, such as the Court did in *Mugler* and the South Carolina Supreme Court did in the instant case, would nullify *Pennsylvania Coal.* Justice Holmes, the author of *Pennsylvania Coal,* joined *Miller v. Schoene* six years later. In *Miller,* the Court adopted the exact approach of the South Carolina Court: It found the cedar trees harmful, and their destruction not a taking, whether or not they were a nuisance. Justice Holmes apparently believed that such an approach did not repudiate his earlier opinion. Moreover, this Court already has been over this ground five years ago, and at that point rejected the assertion that *Pennsylvania Coal* was inconsistent with *Mugler, Hadacheck, Miller,* or the others in the string of "noxious use" cases, recognizing instead that the nature of the State's action is critical in takings analysis. *Keystone Bituminous Coal,* 480 U.S., at 490.

understood that any land-use regulation can be characterized as the'total' deprivation of an aptly defined entitlement . . . . Alternatively, the same regulation can always be characterized as a mere'partial' withdrawal from full, unencumbered ownership of the landholding affected by the regulation . . . ." Michelman, *Takings*, 1987, 88 Colum. L. Rev. 1600, 1614 (1988).

. . . .

Even more perplexing, however, is the Court's reliance on common-law principles of nuisance in its quest for a value-free taking jurisprudence. In determining what is a nuisance at common law, state courts make exactly the decision that the Court finds so troubling when made by the South Carolina General Assembly today: they determine whether the use is harmful. Common-law public and private nuisance law is simply a determination whether a particular use causes harm . . . . There is nothing magical in the reasoning of judges long dead. They determined a harm in the same way as state judges and legislatures do today. If judges in the 18th and 19th centuries can distinguish a harm from a benefit, why not judges in the 20th century, and if judges can, why not legislators? There simply is no reason to believe that new interpretations of the hoary common law nuisance doctrine will be particularly "objective" or "value-free." Once one abandons the level of generality of *sic utere tuo ut alienum non laedas*, one searches in vain, I think, for anything resembling a principle in the common law of nuisance.

C

Finally, the Court justifies its new rule that the legislature may not deprive a property owner of the only economically valuable use of his land, even if the legislature finds it to be a harmful use, because such action is not part of the "long recognized" "understandings of our citizens." These "understandings" permit such regulation only if the use is a nuisance under the common law. Any other course is "inconsistent with the historical compact recorded in the Takings Clause." It is not clear from the Court's opinion where our "historical compact" or "citizens' understanding" comes from, but it does not appear to be history.

The principle that the State should compensate individuals for property taken for public use was not widely established in America at the time of the Revolution. "The colonists . . . inherited . . . a concept of property which permitted extensive regulation of the use of that property for the public benefit—regulation that could even go so far as to deny all productive use of the property to the owner if, as Coke himself stated, the regulation 'extends to the public benefit . . . for this is for the public, and every one hath benefit by it.' " F. Bosselman, D. Callies & J. Banta, *The Taking Issue* 80-81 (1973) (hereinafter Bosselman). *See also* Treanor, *The Origins and Original Significance of the Just Compensation Clause of the Fifth Amendment*, 94 Yale L.J. 694, 697, n. 9 (1985).

Even into the 19th century, state governments often felt free to take property for roads and other public projects without paying compensation to the owners. *See* M. Horwitz, *The Transformation of American Law*, 1780-1860, pp. 63-64 (1977) (hereinafter Horwitz); Treanor, 94 Yale L.J., at 695. As one court declared in 1802, citizens "were bound to contribute as much of [land], as by the laws of the country, were deemed necessary for the public convenience." *M'Clenachan v. Curwin*, 3 Yeates 362, 373 (Pa. 1802). There was an obvious movement toward establishing the just compensation principle during the 19th century, but "there continued to be a strong current in American legal thought that regarded compensation simply as a 'bounty given . . . by the State' out of 'kindness' and not out of justice." Horwitz 65.

Although, prior to the adoption of the Bill of Rights, America was replete with land use regulations describing which activities were considered noxious and forbidden, *see* Bender, T*he Takings Clause: Principles or Politics?*, 34 Buffalo L. Rev. 735, 751 (1985); L. Friedman, *A History of American Law* 66-68 (1973), the Fifth Amendment's Taking Clause originally did not extend to regulations of property, whatever the effect.[23] Most state courts agreed with this narrow interpretation of a taking. "Until the end of the nineteenth century . . . jurists held that the constitution protected possession only, and not value." Siegel, *Understanding the Nineteenth Century Contract Clause: The Role of the Property-Privilege Distinction and "Takings" Clause Jurisprudence*, 60 S. Cal. L. Rev. 1, 76 (1986); Bosselman 106. Even indirect and consequential injuries to property resulting from regulations were excluded from the definition of a taking.

Even when courts began to consider that regulation in some situations could constitute a taking, they continued to uphold bans on particular uses without paying compensation, notwithstanding the economic impact, under the rationale that no one can obtain a vested right to injure or endanger the public.[24] In the *Coates* cases, for example, the Supreme Court of New York found no taking in New York's ban on the interment of the dead within the city, although "no other use can be made of these lands." *Coates v. City of New York*, 7 Cow. 585, 592 (N.Y. 1827). . . .

. . . .

In short, I find no clear and accepted "historical compact" or "understanding of our citizens" justifying the Court's new taking doctrine. Instead, the Court seems to treat history as a grab-bag of principles, to be adopted where they support the Court's theory, and ignored where they do not. If the Court decided that the early common law provides the background principles for interpreting the Taking Clause, then regulation, as opposed to physical confiscation, would not be compensable. If the Court decided that the law of a later period provides the background principles, then regulation might be compensable, but the Court would have to confront the fact that legislatures regularly determined which uses were prohibited, independent of the common law, and independent of whether the uses were lawful when the owner purchased. What makes the Court's analysis unworkable is its attempt to package the law of two incompatible eras and peddle it as historical fact.[26]

V

The Court makes sweeping and, in my view, misguided and unsupported changes in our taking doctrine. While it limits these changes to the most narrow subset of government regulation—those

---

[23] James Madison, author of the Taking Clause, apparently intended it to apply only to direct, physical takings of property by the Federal Government. *See* Treanor, *The Origins and Original Significance of the Just Compensation Clause of the Fifth Amendment*, 94 Yale L.J. 694, 711 (1985) . . . .

[24] For this reason, the retroactive application of the regulation to formerly lawful uses was not a controlling distinction in the past. "Nor can it make any difference that the right is purchased previous to the passage of the by-law," for "[e]very right, from an absolute ownership in property, down to a mere easement, is purchased and holden subject to the restriction, that it shall be so exercised as not to injure others. Though, at the time, it be remote and inoffensive, the purchaser is bound to know, at his peril, that it may become otherwise." Coates v. City of New York, 7 Cow. 585, 605 (N.Y. 1827).

[26] The Court asserts that all early American experience, prior to and after passage of the Bill of Rights, and any case law prior to 1897 are "entirely irrelevant" in determining what is "the historical compact recorded in the Takings Clause." Nor apparently are we to find this compact in the early federal taking cases, which clearly permitted prohibition of harmful uses despite the alleged loss of all value, whether or not the prohibition was a common-law nuisance, and whether or not the prohibition occurred subsequent to the purchase. I cannot imagine where the Court finds its "historical compact," if not in history.

that eliminate all economic value from land—these changes go far beyond what is necessary to secure petitioner Lucas' private benefit. One hopes they do not go beyond the narrow confines the Court assigns them to today.

I dissent.

JUSTICE STEVENS, dissenting.

Today the Court restricts one judge-made rule and expands another. In my opinion it errs on both counts. Proper application of the doctrine of judicial restraint would avoid the premature adjudication of an important constitutional question. Proper respect for our precedents would avoid an illogical expansion of the concept of "regulatory takings."

I

As the Court notes, South Carolina's Beachfront Management Act has been amended to permit some construction of residences seaward of the line that frustrated petitioner's proposed use of his property. Until he exhausts his right to apply for a special permit under that amendment, petitioner is not entitled to an adjudication by this Court of the merits of his permanent takings claim.

It is also not clear that he has a viable "temporary takings" claim. If we assume that petitioner is now able to build on the lot, the only injury that he may have suffered is the delay caused by the temporary existence of the absolute statutory ban on construction. We cannot be sure, however, that that delay caused petitioner any harm because the record does not tell us whether his building plans were even temporarily frustrated by the enactment of the statute. Thus, on the present record it is entirely possible that petitioner has suffered no injury-in-fact even if the state statute was unconstitutional when he filed this lawsuit.

It is true, as the Court notes, that the argument against deciding the constitutional issue in this case rests on prudential considerations rather than a want of jurisdiction. I think it equally clear, however, that a Court less eager to decide the merits would [not c]avalierly dismiss . . . the doctrine of judicial restraint . . . [. T]he Court today tersely announces that "we do not think it prudent to apply that prudential requirement here." I respectfully disagree and would save consideration of the merits for another day. Since, however, the Court has reached the merits, I shall do so as well.

II

In its analysis of the merits, the Court starts from the premise that this Court has adopted a "categorical rule that total regulatory takings must be compensated," and then sets itself the task of identifying the exceptional cases in which a State may be relieved of this categorical obligation. The test the Court announces is that the regulation must do no more than duplicate the result that could have been achieved under a State's nuisance law. Under this test the categorical rule will apply unless the regulation merely makes explicit what was otherwise an implicit limitation on the owner's property rights.

In my opinion, the Court is doubly in error. The categorical rule the Court establishes is an unsound and unwise addition to the law and the Court's formulation of the exception to that rule is too rigid and too narrow.

The Categorical Rule

As the Court recognizes, *Pennsylvania Coal Co. v. Mahon*, 260 U.S. 393 (1922), provides no support for its—or, indeed, any—categorical rule. To the contrary, Justice Holmes recognized that such absolute rules ill fit the inquiry into "regulatory takings." Thus, in the paragraph that contains his famous observation that a regulation may go "too far" and thereby constitute a taking, the Justice wrote: "As we already have said, this is a question of degree—and therefore cannot be disposed of by general propositions." What he had "already . . . said" made perfectly clear that Justice Holmes regarded economic injury to be merely one factor to be weighed: "One fact for consideration in determining such limits is the extent of the diminution [of value.] So the question depends upon the particular facts."

Nor does the Court's new categorical rule find support in decisions following *Mahon*. Although in *dicta* we have sometimes recited that a law "effects a taking if [it] . . . denies an owner economically viable use of his land," Agins v. Tiburon, 447 U.S. 255, 260 (1980), our rulings have rejected such an absolute position. We have frequently—and recently—held that, in some circumstances, a law that renders property valueless may nonetheless not constitute a taking. *See, e.g., Goldblatt v. Hempstead*, 369 U.S. 590 (1962); *Miller v. Schoene*, 276 U.S. 272 (1928); *Hadacheck v. Sebastian*, 239 U.S. 394 (1915); *Mugler v. Kansas*, 123 U.S. 623 (1887). . . .

In addition to lacking support in past decisions, the Court's new rule is wholly arbitrary. A landowner whose property is diminished in value 95% recovers nothing, while an owner whose property is diminished 100% recovers the land's full value. The case at hand illustrates this arbitrariness well. The Beachfront Management Act not only prohibited the building of new dwellings in certain areas, it also prohibited the rebuilding of houses that were "destroyed beyond repair by natural causes or by fire." Thus, if the homes adjacent to Lucas' lot were destroyed by a hurricane one day after the Act took effect, the owners would not be able to rebuild, nor would they be assured recovery. Under the Court's categorical approach, Lucas (who has lost the opportunity to build) recovers, while his neighbors (who have lost both the opportunity to build and their homes) do not recover. The arbitrariness of such a rule is palpable.

Moreover, because of the elastic nature of property rights, the Court's new rule will also prove unsound in practice. In response to the rule, courts may define "property" broadly and only rarely find regulations to effect total takings. This is the approach the Court itself adopts in its revisionist reading of venerable precedents. We are told that—notwithstanding the Court's findings to the contrary in each case—the brewery in *Mugler*, the brickyard in *Hadacheck*, and the gravel pit in *Goldblatt* all could be put to "other uses" and that, therefore, those cases did not involve total regulatory takings.[3]

On the other hand, developers and investors may market specialized estates to take advantage of the Court's new rule. The smaller the estate, the more likely that a regulatory change will effect a total taking. Thus, an investor may, for example, purchase the right to build a multi-family home on a specific lot, with the result that a zoning regulation that allows only single-family

---

[3] Of course, the same could easily be said in this case: Lucas may put his land to "other uses"—fishing or camping, for example—or may sell his land to his neighbors as a buffer. In either event, his land is far from "valueless." This highlights a fundamental weakness in the Court's analysis: its failure to explain why only the impairment of "economically beneficial or productive use," of property is relevant in takings analysis. I should think that a regulation arbitrarily prohibiting an owner from continuing to use her property for bird-watching or sunbathing might constitute a taking under some circumstances; and, conversely, that such uses are of value to the owner. Yet the Court offers no basis for its assumption that the only uses of property cognizable under the Constitution are developmental uses.

homes would render the investor's property interest "valueless."[4] In short, the categorical rule will likely have one of two effects: Either courts will alter the definition of the "denominator" in the takings "fraction," rendering the Court's categorical rule meaningless, or investors will manipulate the relevant property interests, giving the Court's rule sweeping effect. To my mind, neither of these results is desirable or appropriate, and both are distortions of our takings jurisprudence.

Finally, the Court's justification for its new categorical rule is remarkably thin. The Court mentions in passing three arguments in support of its rule; none is convincing. First, the Court suggests that "total deprivation of feasible use is, from the landowner's point of view, the equivalent of a physical appropriation." This argument proves too much. From the "landowner's point of view," a regulation that diminishes a lot's value by 50% is as well "the equivalent" of the condemnation of half of the lot. Yet, it is well established that a 50% diminution in value does not by itself constitute a taking. *See Euclid v. Ambler Realty Co.*, 272 U.S. 365 (1926). Thus, the landowner's perception of the regulation cannot justify the Court's new rule.

Second, the Court emphasizes that because total takings are "relatively rare" its new rule will not adversely affect the government's ability to "go on." This argument proves too little. Certainly it is true that defining a small class of regulations that are per se takings will not greatly hinder important governmental functions—but this is true of any small class of regulations. The Court's suggestion only begs the question of why regulations of this particular class should always be found to effect takings.

Finally, the Court suggests that "regulations that leave the owner . . . without economically beneficial . . . use . . . carry with them a heightened risk that private property is being pressed into some form of public service." As discussed more fully below, I agree that the risks of such singling out are of central concern in takings law. However, such risks do not justify a per se rule for total regulatory takings. There is no necessary correlation between "singling out" and total takings: a regulation may single out a property owner without depriving him of all of his property, *see e.g., Nollan v. California Coastal Comm'n*, 483 U.S. 825 (1987); and it may deprive him of all of his property without singling him out, *see e.g., Mugler v. Kansas*, 123 U.S. 623 (1887); *Hadacheck v. Sebastian*, 239 U.S. 394 (1915). What matters in such cases is not the degree of diminution of value, but rather the specificity of the expropriating act. For this reason, the Court's third justification for its new rule also fails.

In short, the Court's new rule is unsupported by prior decisions, arbitrary and unsound in practice, and theoretically unjustified. In my opinion, a categorical rule as important as the one established by the Court today should be supported by more history or more reason than has yet been provided.

The Nuisance Exception

Like many bright-line rules, the categorical rule established in this case is only "categorical" for a page or two in the U.S. Reports. No sooner does the Court state that "total regulatory takings must be compensated," than it quickly establishes an exception to that rule.

---

[4] This unfortunate possibility is created by the Court's subtle revision of the "total regulatory takings" dicta. In past decisions, we have stated that a regulation effects a taking if it "denies an owner economically viable use of his land," indicating that this "total takings" test did not apply to other estates. Today, however, the Court suggests that a regulation may effect a total taking of any real property interest.

The exception provides that a regulation that renders property valueless is not a taking if it prohibits uses of property that were not "previously permissible under relevant property and nuisance principles." The Court thus rejects the basic holding in *Mugler v. Kansas*, 123 U.S. 623 (1887). There we held that a state-wide statute that prohibited the owner of a brewery from making alcoholic beverages did not effect a taking, even though the use of the property had been perfectly lawful and caused no public harm before the statute was enacted. We squarely rejected the rule the Court adopts today: "It is true, that, when the defendants . . . erected their breweries, the laws of the State did not forbid the manufacture of intoxicating liquors. But the State did not thereby give any assurance, or come under an obligation, that its legislation upon that subject would remain unchanged. [T]he supervision of the public health and the public morals is a governmental power, 'continuing in its nature,' and 'to be dealt with as the special exigencies of the moment may require;' . . . 'for this purpose, the largest legislative discretion is allowed, and the discretion cannot be parted with any more than the power itself.' "

Under our reasoning in *Mugler*, a state's decision to prohibit or to regulate certain uses of property is not a compensable taking just because the particular uses were previously lawful. Under the Court's opinion today, however, if a state should decide to prohibit the manufacture of asbestos, cigarettes, or concealable firearms, for example, it must be prepared to pay for the adverse economic consequences of its decision. One must wonder if Government will be able to "go on" effectively if it must risk compensation "for every such change in the general law." *Mahon.*

The Court's holding today effectively freezes the State's common law, denying the legislature much of its traditional power to revise the law governing the rights and uses of property. Until today, I had thought that we had long abandoned this approach to constitutional law. More than a century ago we recognized that "the great office of statutes is to remedy defects in the common law as they are developed, and to adapt it to the changes of time and circumstances." *Munn v. Illinois*, 94 U.S. 113 (1877). As Justice Marshall observed about a position similar to that adopted by the Court today: "If accepted, that claim would represent a return to the era of *Lochner v. New York*, 198 U.S. 45 (1905), when common-law rights were also found immune from revision by State or Federal Government. Such an approach would freeze the common law as it has been constructed by the courts, perhaps at its 19th-century state of development. It would allow no room for change in response to changes in circumstance. The Due Process Clause does not require such a result." *PruneYard Shopping Center v. Robins*, 447 U.S. 74 (1980) (concurring opinion).

Arresting the development of the common law is not only a departure from our prior decisions; it is also profoundly unwise. The human condition is one of constant learning and evolution—both moral and practical. Legislatures implement that new learning; in doing so they must often revise the definition of property and the rights of property owners. Thus, when the Nation came to understand that slavery was morally wrong and mandated the emancipation of all slaves, it, in effect, redefined "property." On a lesser scale, our ongoing self-education produces similar changes in the rights of property owners: New appreciation of the significance of endangered species, the importance of wetlands, and the vulnerability of coastal lands, shapes our evolving understandings of property rights.

Of course, some legislative redefinitions of property will effect a taking and must be compensated—but it certainly cannot be the case that every movement away from common law does so. There is no reason, and less sense, in such an absolute rule. We live in a world in which changes in the economy and the environment occur with increasing frequency and importance.

If it was wise a century ago to allow Government " 'the largest legislative discretion' " to deal with " 'the special exigencies of the moment,' " *Mugler*, it is imperative to do so today. The rule that should govern a decision in a case of this kind should focus on the future, not the past.[5]

. . . .

The Court's categorical approach rule will, I fear, greatly hamper the efforts of local officials and planners who must deal with increasingly complex problems in land-use and environmental regulation. As this case—in which the claims of an individual property owner exceed $1 million— well demonstrates, these officials face both substantial uncertainty because of the ad hoc nature of takings law and unacceptable penalties if they guess incorrectly about that law.

Viewed more broadly, the Court's new rule and exception conflict with the very character of our takings jurisprudence. We have frequently and consistently recognized that the definition of a taking cannot be reduced to a "set formula" and that determining whether a regulation is a taking is "essentially [an] ad hoc, factual inquir[y]." *Penn Central Transportation Co. v. New York City*, 438 U.S. 104 (1978). This is unavoidable, for the determination whether a law effects a taking is ultimately a matter of fairness and justice, and necessarily requires a weighing of private and public interests. The rigid rules fixed by the Court today clash with this enterprise: "fairness and justice" are often disserved by categorical rules.

III

It is well established that a takings case "entails inquiry into [several factors:] the character of the governmental action, its economic impact, and its interference with reasonable investment-backed expectations." *PruneYard*, 447 U.S., at 83. The Court's analysis today focuses on the last two of these three factors: the categorical rule addresses a regulation's "economic impact," while the nuisance exception recognizes that ownership brings with it only certain "expectations." Neglected by the Court today is the first, and in some ways, the most important factor in takings analysis: the character of the regulatory action.

The Just Compensation Clause was designed to bar Government from forcing some people alone to bear public burdens which, in all fairness and justice, should be borne by the public as a whole. Accordingly, one of the central concerns of our takings jurisprudence is preventing the public from loading upon one individual more than his just share of the burdens of government. We have, therefore, in our takings law frequently looked to the generality of a regulation of property.

For example, in the case of so-called "developmental exactions," we have paid special attention to the risk that particular landowners might "b[e] singled out to bear the burden" of a broader problem not of his own making. *Nollan*. Similarly, in distinguishing between the Kohler Act (at issue in *Mahon*) and the Subsidence Act (at issue in *Keystone*), we found it significant that the regulatory function of the latter was substantially broader. Unlike the Kohler Act, which simply transferred back to the surface owners certain rights that they had earlier sold to the coal companies, the Subsidence Act affected all surface owners—including the coal companies— equally. Perhaps the most familiar application of this principle of generality arises in zoning cases.

---

[5] Even measured in terms of efficiency, the Court's rule is unsound. The Court today effectively establishes a form of insurance against certain changes in land-use regulations. Like other forms of insurance, the Court's rule creates a "moral hazard" and inefficiencies: In the face of uncertainty about changes in the law, developers will overinvest, safe in the knowledge that if the law changes adversely, they will be entitled to compensation. *See* generally Farber, *Economic Analysis and Just Compensation*, 12 Int'l Rev. of Law & Econ. 125 (1992).

A diminution in value caused by a zoning regulation is far less likely to constitute a taking if it is part of a general and comprehensive land-use plan, *see Euclid v. Ambler Realty Co.*, 272 U.S. 365 (1926); conversely, "spot zoning" is far more likely to constitute a taking, *see Penn Central*, 438 U.S., at 132.

The presumption that a permanent physical occupation, no matter how slight, effects a taking is wholly consistent with this principle. A physical taking entails a certain amount of "singling out." Consistent with this principle, physical occupations by third parties are more likely to effect takings than other physical occupations. Thus, a regulation requiring the installation of a junction box owned by a third party, *Loretto v. Teleprompter Manhattan CATV Corp.*, 458 U.S. 419 (1982), is more troubling than a regulation requiring the installation of sprinklers or smoke detectors; just as an order granting third parties access to a marina, *Kaiser Aetna v. United States*, 444 U.S. 164 (1979), is more troubling than an order requiring the placement of safety buoys in the marina.

. . . .

In considering Lucas' claim, the generality of the Beachfront Management Act is significant. The Act does not target particular landowners, but rather regulates the use of the coastline of the entire State. Indeed, South Carolina's Act is best understood as part of a national effort to protect the coastline, one initiated by the Federal Coastal Zone Management Act of 1972. Pursuant to the Federal Act, every coastal State has implemented coastline regulations. Moreover, the Act did not single out owners of undeveloped land. The Act also prohibited owners of developed land from rebuilding if their structures were destroyed, and what is equally significant, from repairing erosion control devices, such as seawalls. In addition, in some situations, owners of developed land were required to "renouris[h] the beach . . . on a yearly basis with an amount . . . of sand . . . not . . . less than one and one-half times the yearly volume of sand lost due to erosion." In short, the South Carolina Act imposed substantial burdens on owners of developed and undeveloped land alike. This generality indicates that the Act is not an effort to expropriate owners of undeveloped land.

Admittedly, the economic impact of this regulation is dramatic and petitioner's investment-backed expectations are substantial. Yet, if anything, the costs to and expectations of the owners of developed land are even greater: I doubt, however, that the cost to owners of developed land of renourishing the beach and allowing their seawalls to deteriorate effects a taking. The costs imposed on the owners of undeveloped land, such as petitioner, differ from these costs only in degree, not in kind.

The impact of the ban on developmental uses must also be viewed in light of the purposes of the Act. The legislature stated the purposes of the Act as "protect[ing], preserv[ing], restor[ing] and enhanc[ing] the beach/dune system" of the State not only for recreational and ecological purposes, but also to "protec[t] life and property." The State, with much science on its side, believes that the "beach/dune system [acts] as a buffer from high tides, storm surge, [and] hurricanes." This is a traditional and important exercise of the State's police power, as demonstrated by Hurricane Hugo, which in 1989, caused 29 deaths and more than $6 billion in property damage in South Carolina alone.

In view of all of these factors, even assuming that petitioner's property was rendered valueless, the risk inherent in investments of the sort made by petitioner, the generality of the Act, and the compelling purpose motivating the South Carolina Legislature persuade me that the Act did not effect a taking of petitioner's property.

Accordingly, I respectfully dissent.

Statement of Justice SOUTER.

I would dismiss the writ of certiorari in this case as having been granted improvidently. After briefing and argument it is abundantly clear that an unreviewable assumption on which this case comes to us is both questionable as a conclusion of Fifth Amendment law and sufficient to frustrate the Court's ability to render certain the legal premises on which its holding rests.

The petition for review was granted on the assumption that the state by regulation had deprived the owner of his entire economic interest in the subject property. Such was the state trial court's conclusion, which the state supreme court did not review. It is apparent now that in light of our prior cases, the trial court's conclusion is highly questionable. While the respondent now wishes to contest the point, the Court is certainly right to refuse to take up the issue, which is not fairly included within the question presented, and has received only the most superficial and one-sided treatment before us.

Because the questionable conclusion of total deprivation cannot be reviewed, the Court is precluded from attempting to clarify the concept of total (and, in the Court's view, categorically compensable) taking on which it rests, a concept which the Court describes, as so uncertain under existing law as to have fostered inconsistent pronouncements by the Court itself. Because that concept is left uncertain, so is the significance of the exceptions to the compensation requirement that the Court proceeds to recognize. This alone is enough to show that there is little utility in attempting to deal with this case on the merits.

The imprudence of proceeding to the merits in spite of these unpromising circumstances is underscored by the fact that, in doing so, the Court cannot help but assume something about the scope of the uncertain concept of total deprivation, even when it is barred from explicating total deprivation directly. Thus, when the Court concludes that the application of nuisance law provides an exception to the general rule that complete denial of economically beneficial use of property amounts to a compensable taking, the Court will be understood to suggest (if it does not assume) that there are in fact circumstances in which state-law nuisance abatement may amount to a denial of all beneficial land use as that concept is to be employed in our takings jurisprudence under the Fifth and Fourteenth Amendments. The nature of nuisance law, however, indicates that application of a regulation defensible on grounds of nuisance prevention or abatement will quite probably not amount to a complete deprivation in fact. The nuisance inquiry focuses on conduct, not on the character of the property on which that conduct is performed, and the remedies for such conduct usually leave the property owner with other reasonable uses of his property . . . . Indeed, it is difficult to imagine property that can be used only to create a nuisance, such that its sole economic value must presuppose the right to occupy it for such seriously noxious activity.

The upshot is that the issue of what constitutes a total deprivation is being addressed by indirection, and with uncertain results, in the Court's treatment of defenses to compensation claims. While the issue of what constitutes total deprivation deserves the Court's attention, as does the relationship between nuisance abatement and such total deprivation, the Court should confront these matters directly. Because it can neither do so in this case, nor skip over those preliminary issues and deal independently with defenses to the Court's categorical compensation rule, the Court should dismiss the instant writ and await an opportunity to face the total deprivation question squarely. Under these circumstances, I believe it proper for me to vote to dismiss the writ, despite the Court's contrary preference.

[3] Events After Remand

On remand, the South Carolina Supreme Court found there was a temporary taking between 1988 and 1992. The case was sent back to the trial court for further proceedings to determine the amount of damages Lucas was to receive. Further proceedings over the grant or denial of a special permit were not precluded. *Lucas v. South Carolina Coastal Council*, 424 S.E.2d 484 (1992). In the summer of 1993, a settlement was reached. South Carolina paid Lucas $425,000 for each lot, along with legal fees, interest on the investment from 1988 and other miscellaneous costs, for a total of 1.5 million dollars. In order to recoup some of the funds, the state planned to sell the lots for development! The state, accused by some of hypocrisy for selling the land, noted that if the lots ever flooded again, it could force the owners to tear down any buildings. The two lots sit among a row of million dollar houses in the nearly finished Wild Dune community. For more of the story, *see Accord Ends Fight Over Use of Land*, WASHINGTON POST, July 17, 1993, at E1, col. 4.

[4] Analytical Thoughts on *Lucas*

In *Lucas,* Scalia created a second presumptive takings rule to add to the permanent physical invasion test of *Loretto*—a presumption of a taking when all the value of land is removed by state regulation. He took a quite remarkable journey in getting to this result. First, he sniped at *Mahon*, Holmes' venerable conservative precedent you might have assumed he would leave alone. He condemned *Mahon* to the purgatory of ambiguity, a step Justice Rehnquist refused to take in *Dolan*. Second, he established a new path out of the difficult *Mahon* problem of distinguishing between valid regulation and invalid diminution in value. And finally, he used that new path out of the *Mahon* world to describe a quite striking rule defining confiscatory takings.

As you must know by now, it is difficult, maybe impossible, to distinguish between a valid regulation and an invalid taking. The lines drawn by the Court between these categories have been wavy at best and full of gaping holes at worst. Sensing that problem, felt by people of all political stripes, Justice Scalia critiqued *Mahon* and argued that it was time for the Court to settle in with some more usable rules. Discarding the old noxious use test, which Scalia argued led both to approval of too many regulations by balancing the harms and benefits of various land uses and to an impractical legal test, he began a search for new bright line rules.

The search for more easily applied rules led him to create a presumption of a taking when the value of land is reduced to nothing. After stating that rule he dropped an intriguing, and I think important, footnote—number 7. In that note he first confessed that there was some ambiguity in even his bright line test because there were usually a number of ways to construct the contours of the property that was being subjected to regulation. As an example of an "extreme" solution to the problem Justice Scalia cited the state court opinion in *Penn Central*, which, he said, "examined the diminution in a particular parcel's value produced by a municipal ordinance in light of the total value of the taking claimant's other holdings in the vicinity." Note well that Justice Brennan may have done the same thing in his Supreme Court opinion. It is hard not to believe that Scalia dislikes the *Penn Central* outcome.

In an effort to avoid such "extremes," Scalia went on in the footnote to say that "the answer to this difficult question may lie in how the owner's reasonable expectations have been shaped by the state's law of property—*i.e.*, whether and to what degree the state's law has accorded legal recognition and protection to the particular interest in land with respect to which the takings claimant alleges a diminution in (or elimination of) value."

Note well how this is likely to work. Taking the *claimant's* allegations about the nature of the *particular* property interests being regulated seriously means that there is a high likelihood that many (perhaps all?) of the complaints filed in takings cases will claim that all of a particular interest in property has been taken. The only limitation on a plaintiff's ability to make such an allegation is the availability of an appropriate, Formalist, property label in the body of a state's law. Thus in *Mahon*, the coal company alleged that the "support estate" was taken. And in *Penn Central* the allegation was that "air rights" were taken. In *Nollan* it was an "easement," and in *Lucas* it was a "fee simple absolute."

In each of these cases, there were other ways of describing the situation, ways that paid attention to the economic content of the investments under review rather than the nature of a particularized interest labeled by state law as property. *Mahon* involved a large mine, *Penn Central* a huge complex of buildings, *Nollan* a house on a beach, and *Lucas* a major housing development with a number of large homes. The Realist approach of Justices Brennan and Blackmun, who paid attention to the economic content of the entire portfolio of investments at issue in the litigation, was rejected by Justice Scalia. His approach allows most takings plaintiffs to construct a complaint with supportable allegations that their cases involve a taking of all of the value of an interest in land. The general trend of the reviews in the academic literature of this case has been to minimize its importance, to call it a case of narrow application dealing only with total wipeouts. But Justice Blackmun may have been justified in voicing concern early in his dissent that the missile launched by Justice Scalia was powerful enough to kill more than a mouse.

Once Scalia established that he was going to work with the contours of particularized property interests defined by state law, the rest of the opinion was an attempt to tell us how to discover what the contents of those particularized property interests were. The dissenters, of course, accused Scalia of establishing a bright line rule and then writing a big exception to it. That is certainly a plausible critique, but maybe he simply was defining his vision of property for us. That seems to be the tenor of his statement that "where the state seeks to sustain regulation that deprives land of all economically beneficial use, we think it may resist compensation only if the logically antecedent inquiry into the nature of the owner's estate shows that the proscribed use interests were not part of his title to begin with." Put another way, if the property owner owns the property right being regulated, the state must pay to obtain it.

This is an extraordinarily narrow view of the Takings Clause.[78] When all was said and done, there was a significant difference between Justice Scalia's approach and the old noxious use test, which allowed the state to prohibit certain uses of land, even if that prohibition destroyed the value of a site. The noxious use test contemplated that changes in cultural values might justify alteration of land use policies. Uses not noxious yesterday could become noxious tomorrow. Temperance could be declared a public value and bars could be closed, quarries could be banned, and brickyards could be wiped out. Justice Scalia refused to make that accommodation to

---

[78] It is one that arguably mimics the views of Richard Epstein, in his 1995 book TAKINGS: PRIVATE PROPERTY AND THE POWER OF EMINENT DOMAIN. The Takings Clause, Epstein argued, means exactly what it says. If someone has a particularized interest in land the state may not take some or all of it for free. Indeed, Epstein argued, the only power a state needs other than the right to keep order is the "right to force exchanges of property rights that leave individuals with rights more valuable than those they have been deprived of." In essence that means that compensation is always required. Indeed, to Epstein, the primary reason for public land use regulation is to get rid of free riding and holdouts by use of the condemnation power.

historical change. If a stick was in the property bundle when title passed to the owner before the court, then the state was not free to regulate that stick later, even if attitudes about land use changed in the interim. If taken to its logical conclusion, *Euclid* and *Penn Central* would both fall by the wayside. Robert Nozick would be proud.

Justice Kennedy rejected that approach. While concurring in the result because the state failed to properly consider the economic expectations of the property owner, Kennedy was careful to reject a rigid, Formalist definition of expectations. Indeed, he made the interesting observation that investment based expectations of regulation may bootstrap us into acceptance of more regulation and that a certain amount of such bootstrapping was acceptable. The dissents of Justices Blackmun and Stevens attacked Justice Scalia more directly, noting the illogic involved in rejecting the noxious use exception only to replace it with one equally vague.

Pulling back a bit from this case, Justices Scalia and Rehnquist have now covered a wide range of takings settings. Little room may be left to maneuver for those interested in affirming widespread land use regulation. Public purpose is subject to close scrutiny after *Nollan*. The state must demonstrate a substantial nexus between the purpose for its regulation and the content of its actions. On the takings side, two presumptive taking rules now govern—permanent physical invasion and loss of virtually all value. There are apparently no exceptions to the first and a narrow historically driven outer limit to the second. And another area of widespread discussion— zoning by trade, exchange and bargaining—is constrained by *Nollan*'s strict scrutiny of purpose, *Dolan*'s placement of a burden on the public to demonstrate a tight link between purpose and action, *Loretto*'s permanent physical invasion test, and, I suspect, by a *Lucas* test that only rights not owned at the outset are subject to regulation.

This structure has the potential to limit the operation of an enormous array of land use controls and many environmental regulations. Whether the Court will go that far is certainly subject to doubt. Whether Justices Scalia and Rehnquist can hold a majority together in future cases is unclear. The views of Justice Breyer are largely unknown and the opinions of Justices Kennedy and Souter in *Lucas* leave some doubts about where they are headed. But it is clear that takings law has changed dramatically in the last 20 years. As Justice Stevens noted in his dissent, the development of the line of recent cases you have been reading is similar to the rise of the Freedom of Contract cases at the end of the nineteenth and the beginning of the twentieth centuries. A particular vision of history and *laissez faire* economics is once again being enshrined in constitutional language. It is being done in such a way that many attempts to regulate land are of tenuous validity. And since much of present day environmental law involves issues about land—beach controls, pollution controls, attempts to preserve agricultural land, limitations on urban sprawl—these decisions have the potential to create significant conflicts between the Court and Congress. That is not occurring now because Congress is conservative. But that will not be true forever, at least on environmental questions. And when Congress shifts, it will be interesting to see what the Court lets it do.

You might also begin to speculate what the reaction will eventually be to the rise of Takings law as a Formalist barrier to environmental controls. In mode of legal thought terms, what will be the analog to the Realist movement in the coming decades? How will people go about attacking the present conservative agenda of the Court? Many Realists relied on the social sciences to prescribe solutions to the problems posed by the Great Depression. Will the next generation rely upon "real" scientists to convince the political world that the court is endangering the planet? Will this be part of a larger search for basic moral and ethical principles to govern the use and allocation of resources?

The *Lucas* opinion pays a great deal of attention to the history of Takings law. For some analysis of this area, read William Treanor, *The Original Understanding of the Takings Clause and the Political Process*, 95 COLUM. L. REV. 782 (1995), excerpted in RICHARD CHUSED, A PROPERTY ANTHOLOGY 468-482 (2d ed. 1997).

[5] Problem Notes

[a] Takings and Politics

The opinions of conservatives like Justices Rehnquist and Scalia suggest they are quite concerned about the likelihood that governments will abuse the rights of property owners. Since the New Deal, the courts have left the vast bulk of responsibility for setting public policy in other areas of the economy to federal, state and local legislative bodies. Is there any justification for the courts to scrutinize property regulatory schemes more closely than other economic controls? Why shouldn't we just rely on the electoral process to remove from office those who tread too harshly on various ownership interests

[b] Takings, Original Understanding and Conservative Judging

If those drafting the Takings Clause intended it to bar only complete confiscations of property, should conservative jurists follow that historical understanding?

[c] Takings and Risk

Those investing in property take risks, such as the possibility that a natural disaster will destroy their assets. Should the Takings Clause be used to provide risk takers with government "insurance" in cases where regulations do not allow reconstruction of buildings on fragile lands? What is the relationship between the Takings Clause and investment risk for Justice Scalia?

§ 11.07 Summary of Suggested Readings on Takings

A number of articles have been excerpted or referred to in this chapter. Here is a summary of those articles, as well as a few others that might be of interest. Excerpts of all of them may be found in RICHARD CHUSED, A PROPERTY ANTHOLOGY 428-583 (2d ed. 1997).

Robert C. Ellickson, *Controlling Chronic Misconduct in City Spaces: Of Panhandlers, Skid Rows, and Public-Space Zoning*, 105 YALE L. J. 1165 (1996).

Jerold Kayden, *Zoning for Dollars: New Rules for an Old Game? Comments on the* Municipal Art Society *and* Nollan *Cases*, 39 WASH. U. J. URB. & CONTEMP. L.3 (1991).

Thomas Merrill, *The Economics of Public Use*, 72 CORNELL L. Rev. 61 (1986).

Frank Michelman, *Property, Utility, and Fairness: Comments on the Ethical Foundations of "Just Compensation" Law*, 80 HARV. L. REV. 1165 (1967).

Jeremy Paul, *The Hidden Structure of Takings Law*, 64 S. CAL. L. REV. 1393 (1991).

Carol M. Rose, *Planning and Dealing: Piecemeal Land Controls as a Problem of Local Legitimacy*, 71 CAL. L. REV. 837 (1983).

William Simon, *Social Republic Property*, 38 UCLA L. REV. 1335 (1991).

Joseph Singer, *The Reliance Interest in Property Law*, 40 STAN. L. REV. 614 (1988).

William Treanor, *The Original Understanding of the Takings Clause and the Political Process*, 95 COLUM. L. REV. 782 (1995).

CHAPTER 12

AUTONOMY AND COMMUNITY: PROPERTY IN HUMAN BEINGS

§ 12.01 Introduction

This concluding chapter investigates the relationships between our human selves, our realms of autonomy, our need for community, and concepts of property. Three sets of legal problems taken from different historical moments are used to frame the discussion. In an effort to ensure that you as a reader must take the humanity of the characters in each drama into account, the cases are surrounded with detailed information about the people involved in each legal dispute. The chapter begins with slavery. Justice Taney's opinion in the *Dred Scott Case* was not only an important part of the build-up to the Civil War, but a far reaching statement about the impact of slavery on our political, legal and cultural life. The second segment of the chapter explores the burgeoning right of publicity, beginning with the ancestral case supporting the right— *Associated Press v. International News Service*—and ending with *Martin Luther King, Jr., Center for Social Change v. American Heritage Products*, a classic judicial exploration of the parameters of our power to control use of our personalities for commercial purposes. The chapter ends with two cases that explore the extent of our right to make property claims for parts of our bodies. In all three settings—slavery, publicity rights and bodily tissues—difficult questions constantly surface about the relationships between law and justice, the interplay of autonomy and community, and the role markets play in the development of property theory.

§ 12.02 Persons as Property: Slavery and the *Dred Scott* Decision

[1] History of the Case

The *Dred Scott* case did not, of course, appear magically. Though there are many inexplicable or puzzling events in the background of the case, slavery was a potent political issue. If this case had not appeared, some other similar dispute may have reached the Supreme Court. After 1830, compromise on slavery became increasingly difficult. From 1831, when the first issue of William Lloyd Garrison's abolitionist newspaper *The Liberator* appeared and the Nat Turner rebellion occurred, southerners reacted with increasing stridency to attempts to control slavery and northerners replied with mounting opposition. Federal policy established by the Jacksonian Democrat coalition during the 1830s clearly opposed granting full citizenship to freed blacks, let alone slaves.

Almost total polarization between north and south arose over the Wilmot Proviso, first offered in 1846 by Representative David Wilmot of Pennsylvania. The Proviso would have barred slavery in all territories acquired in the Mexican-American War then in progress. Many southerners were horrified at the prospect of establishing vast areas of free territory. The states that would be carved out of such areas were highly likely to become free states, creating the possibility of a Congress with a strong anti-slavery majority. Versions of the Wilmot Proviso were offered in a number of circumstances for the rest of the decade, tying up organization of the far western territories until 1850, when California was admitted as a free state. That admission effectively nullified the Missouri Compromise, which was designed to insure that a fairly equal number of slave and free states would enter the Union over time, and convinced many Southern politicians that their only hope was to preserve state sovereignty to decide upon slavery issues. From the time Dred Scott first sued for his freedom in the state courts of Missouri in 1846, until the Supreme Court agreed to review the dispute in 1854, it became clear to partisans on both sides of the slavery question that the Supreme Court might be the institution which would resolve the state sovereignty issue.[1]

Dred Scott was born in Virginia around the turn of the nineteenth century, entering life as the property of Peter Blow. The Blow family moved to St. Louis, Missouri, around 1831. Shortly after his arrival in Missouri and not too long before Peter Blow died, Scott was sold to Dr. John Emerson. Emerson joined the Army in 1833 and was ordered to service at Fort Armstrong in Rock Island, Illinois.[2] The move to Illinois was a crucial fact in the later litigation. Illinois was a free state, located at the western end of what was the Northwest Territory. The Northwest Ordinance of 1787, adopted under the Articles of Confederation, prohibited slavery in the Territory.[3] All of the states eventually carved out of the area became free states, in part because of the heritage established by the Ordinance. At the time Scott went to Illinois as Emerson's slave, a line of Missouri Supreme Court decisions had held that taking up residence with a slave in a free state freed the slave, even if the master eventually returned, slave in tow, to Missouri. Once free, always free—that was the rule.[4] And only one year before Scott sued, the Missouri state legislature passed a statute recodifying a long extant judicial procedure for handling claims by slaves for their freedom.[5]

Emerson served in Illinois for several years before moving on to the Wisconsin Territory, where Scott met and married Harriet Robinson, the slave of an army major. The Wisconsin Territory was also a free area, being part of what was originally the Louisiana Territory north of the Missouri Compromise demarcation line.[6] Emerson was later transferred south to Louisiana, but

---

[1] For a thorough study of the place of the *Dred Scott* case in the lengthy slavery dispute, *see* DON E. FEHRENBACHER, THE DRED SCOTT CASE: ITS SIGNIFICANCE IN AMERICAN LAW AND POLITICS (1978) [hereinafter Fehrenbacher] or the shorter abridged version of the book entitled SLAVERY, LAW, AND POLITICS: THE DRED SCOTT CASE IN HISTORICAL PERSPECTIVE (1981).

[2] WALTER EHRLICH, THEY HAVE NO RIGHTS: DRED SCOTT'S STRUGGLE FOR FREEDOM 9-17 (1979) [hereinafter cited as Ehrlich].

[3] An Ordinance for the Government of the Territory of the United States North West of the River Ohio, 32 JOURNALS OF THE CONTINENTAL CONGRESS 334 (July 13, 1787).

[4] Rachael, a woman of color, v. Walker, 4 Mo. 350 (1836); Vincent (a man of color) v. Duncan, 2 Mo. 214 (1830); La Grange, alias Isidore, v. Chouteau, 2 Mo. 20 (1828); Winny v. Whitesides alias Prewitt, 1 Mo. 472 (1824). The most frequently contested issue in these cases was whether master and slave had been gone from a slave state long enough to support the slave's claim for freedom. The *Walker* case, decided in 1836, was very close on its facts to the *Dred Scott* situation.

[5] Chapter 69, REVISED STATUTES OF THE STATE OF MISSOURI 531-534 (1845). Virtually the same statute appears in all prior Missouri codes. A DIGEST OF THE LAWS OF MISSOURI TERRITORY 210-211 (1818); 1 LAWS OF THE STATE OF MISSOURI, REVISED & DIGESTED 404-406 (1825); REVISED STATUTES OF MISSOURI 284-286 (1835).

[6] Nonetheless, Harriet Scott (nee Robinson) became the property of Emerson by agreement of the masters. Ehrlich, note 2 above, at 20-21. The spot where Emerson was located in the Wisconsin Territory is presently in the state of Minnesota.

he left the Scotts behind in the Wisconsin Territory hired out to others. While in Louisiana, Emerson married Elizabeth Irene Sanford, the sister of John Sanford, the eventual named defendant in the Supreme Court case. The Scotts then joined the Emersons in Louisiana. After further army assignments in the Wisconsin Territory and Florida, the Emersons and Scotts returned to St. Louis.[7]

Emerson died in 1843, leaving all his property to his wife *for her life*, with the *remainder* to his daughter, Henrietta Sanford Emerson.[8] The will also gave Mrs. Emerson the *power to encroach* upon the interest of the remainder to provide for her own maintenance or for the education of Henrietta.[9] George Davenport and John Sanford were named as *executors* of Emerson's estate.[10] A few years after Emerson's death, Dred and Harriet Scott instituted actions for their freedom in accordance with the procedure re-codified by the Missouri legislature in 1845.

The long line of Missouri cases supporting the "once free, always free" rule seemed to assure that the Scotts would win their cases. At the trial, however, an evidentiary problem arose. A Mr. Samuel Russell was put on the stand by the Scott's counsel to establish that John Emerson's wife, Irene Emerson, still held them as slaves at the time they brought their cases. He testified that he had hired out the Scotts from Mrs. Emerson. When cross examined, Russell revealed that his wife actually did the hiring, and that he merely paid money to Mr. Alexander Sanford, Irene Emerson's father, presuming it was for the Scotts' labor. The trial judge then ruled that Russell's testimony was hearsay[11] and instructed the jury that if the Scotts had not proven their case from other evidence, a verdict should be entered for the defendant. The jury so found. A motion for a new trial was made on the Scotts' behalf and the motion was granted.[12] An attempt by Mrs. Emerson to appeal the grant of a new trial was rebuffed by the Missouri Supreme Court on the grounds that the case had not been completed at the trial level and an appeal was premature.[13]

The second trial did not take place until 1850. The plaintiffs' main case was the same as at the first trial, except that Mrs. Russell testified instead of Mr. Russell in order to avoid the hearsay

---

[7] Ehrlich, note 2 above, at 22–28.

[8] Ehrlich, note 2 above, at 28. These basic notions in property law were reviewed in Chapter 5. In the case of slaves, the owner of the life estate generally received the income and service produced by the slave and (if the slave was female) the slave's offspring. If the slave was sold, the life estate owner got only the income produced by the proceeds of the sale. *Compare Baker v. Weedon*, p. 860 above.

[9] Ehrlich, note 2 above, at 28. *Powers* were discussed above in Chapter 2. Review the case of *Givens v. Givens*, p. 135 above. In the Emerson situation, Mr. Emerson wished to give his wife some flexibility to grapple with unexpected circumstances. If she needed money for her own use, he trusted her enough to give her the authority to sell some of his assets rather than save them for their daughter.

[10] An *executor* is a person named in a will to manage the affairs of the deceased person's estate. This task usually does not last too long. The executor must gather all the assets of the dead person, pay any bills unpaid at the person's death, and with court permission distribute the remaining assets in accordance with the wishes expressed in the will. If a person dies intestate, a person (usually called an *administrator or administratrix*) is appointed by the court to undertake the same sort of tasks, except that the assets are distributed under state intestate succession laws rather than the will.

[11] Hearsay evidence, or statements uttered by a non-witness and submitted to the court for the truth of the matters asserted in the statement, is not always inadmissible. Many exceptions exist in the modern evidence rules in every jurisdiction.

[12] Ehrlich, note 2 above, at 42-49.

[13] Emerson v. Harriet (of color), 11 Mo. 413 (1848); Emerson v. Dred Scott (of color), 11 Mo. 413 (1848).

problem. The defendant, however, raised the point that Emerson was under military law while in Illinois, not civil law, and that the former did not act to free the Scotts even if the latter did. This exact point had been rejected in prior Missouri cases,[14] and the verdict went to the plaintiffs.[15]

A second appeal was taken, with the military versus civil law question the primary focus of the briefs. By this time, Mrs. Emerson had moved to Massachusetts, married an abolitionist and left the Scott matter in the hands of her brother John Sanford. The Scotts were left in the court's charge to be hired out as the judge approved. Funds raised by such hirings were held by the court, to be awarded to the eventual winner of the case. Changes in both the makeup of the Missouri Supreme Court due to election turnover and the influence of an increasingly aggressive proslavery Southern ideology emphasizing state sovereignty eventually led to the reversal of the trial court's decision and a rejection of the "once free always free" rule. The case was rebriefed after the 1851 election, and for the first time, counsel for Mrs. Emerson challenged the correctness of the old case law and raised the possibility that Missouri need not pay attention to federal regulations on slavery contained in the Northwest Ordinance or the Missouri Compromise.[16]

This time the Missouri Supreme Court reversed, denying the Scotts their freedom. The "once free, always free" rule was discarded. Each state, the court opined, had the authority to decide the law on removed slaves returned to its territory, without regard to the content of federal territorial regulations.

> An attempt has been made to show, that the comity shown to the laws of other States, is a matter of discretion, to be determined by the courts of that State in which the laws are proposed to be enforced. If it is a matter of discretion, that discretion must be controlled by circumstances. Times are not now as they were when the former decisions on this subject were made. Since then not only individuals but States have been possessed with a dark and fell spirit in relation to slavery, whose gratification is sought in the pursuit of measures, whose inevitable consequences must be the overthrow and destruction of our government. Under such circumstances it does not behoove the State of Missouri to show the least countenance to any measure which might gratify this spirit. She is willing to assume her full responsibility for the existence of slavery within her limits, nor does she seek to share or divide it with others. Although we may, for our own sakes, regret that the avarice and hard-heartedness of the progenitors of those who are now so sensitive on the subject, ever introduced the institution among us, yet we will not go to them to learn law, morality or religion on the subject.[17]

While the Missouri Supreme Court was deciding the case, a new case was filed on behalf of the Scotts in federal court under the diversity jurisdiction, with John Sanford as the defendant, rather than Mrs. Irene (Sanford Emerson) Chafee. The state court case was remanded to the trial court after the state Supreme Court issued its opinion, and held in abeyance pending the outcome of the new federal litigation. It is not totally clear why the new federal action was filed, but suspicions abound. Dred Scott was by then working in the law offices of his attorneys, Charles E. LaBeaume and Roswell M. Field, two abolitionists, hired out to them by the trial court in St. Louis that had originally decided Scott should be freed.[18] Both sides in the *Scott* case may

---

[14] Rachael, a woman of color, v. Walker, 4 Mo. 350, 354 (1836).

[15] Ehrlich, note 2 above, at 52.

[16] Ehrlich, note 2 above, at 61-65.

[17] Scott, a man of color, v. Emerson, 15 Mo. 576, 586-587 (1852).

[18] Ehrlich, note 2 above, at 75.

have seen it as a perfect vehicle for a Supreme Court test of an issue that could be framed as one of state sovereignty over slavery—whether Missouri had to abide by the "once free, always free" rule in effect in Missouri prior to the *Scott* case. There are several indications that the federal case was collusive "test" litigation, but no one has ever found conclusive evidence that it was. First, the case went forward on a *stipulated* statement of facts.[19] That sort of procedure is sometimes indicative of a setting in which both sides to a case desire to avoid long fact finding hearings and quickly get to the issues at hand. But it can also be used as a way of reducing costs. Second, it is not at all clear that the defendant, John Sanford, actually owned the Scotts.[20] No evidence of transfer from Irene Chafee to Sanford has come to light and the Scotts did not appear in the probate inventory filed when he died shortly after the Supreme Court rendered its decision.[21] So it is possible that if the Scotts' attorneys, LaBeaume and Field, really wanted to free them, they could simply have bought them from the Chafees. Remember that Mrs. Chafee had the power to encroach upon the corpus of her first husband's estate. And even if there were doubts about the legality of using the power to free the Scotts, Mrs. Emerson and her daughter could each have sold their individual interests in the Scotts to the attorneys.[22] Finally, the shift of the case to the federal courts was the only way to ensure a definitive test of the impact of federal territorial statutes on the status of freed Blacks returned to slave states.[23] The state Scott litigation did not definitively raise the federal statutory or Constitutional aspects of the "once free, always free" rule, though the Missouri Supreme Court's opinion certainly exhibited hostility to the use of either the Northwest Ordinance or the Missouri Compromise to support the Scotts' claims for freedom. In addition, state law provided a recognized procedure for establishing jurisdiction over suits brought by slaves seeking their freedom. But in the federal courts, the diversity statute, not the Missouri procedure, would govern the power of the court to hear the

---

[19] A *stipulation* is an agreement about some aspect of a case by both sides to the litigation. It is often a fact or facts that form the basis for a stipulation, though other portions of a case are also the subject of such documents. The stipulation included a statement that John Sanford, not Irene Sanford Chafee, the remarried wife of John Emerson, owned Dred Scott. There is some evidence that both sides knew that to be false, since Scott was under the control of the Missouri state court system. Perhaps Sanford was named in order not to embarrass Irene Chafee's husband, Calvin Chafee, an important Massachusetts Republican. *Id.* at 181.

[20] It is also possible that Sanford was serving as next friend for Irene Chafee in order to get around her inability to sue or be sued as a married woman. But there is no indication in the court record that this occurred. Indeed, it is unclear how much the Chafees knew about the case when it was originally filed.

[21] Fehrenbacher, note 1 above, at 273.

[22] The Emerson will did state that Mrs. Emerson had the power to encroach for her own needs or for the education of their daughter. But freeing Scott as a political statement might arguably be outside the scope of such a power. However, a sale of the separate interests of mother and daughter would not have called upon the power. Even though Henrietta Emerson held only a remainder, that was a transferable interest. In this case, the interest was held by a minor, since Henrietta was born in 1843 and was therefore only 10 years old when the federal *Scott* case was filed. But Henrietta's interests were in the control of her parents, and even if her mother did not use her power to encroach on the corpus, the remainder interest of Henrietta could have been sold and the proceeds held for Henrietta's later use.

[23] Additional evidence that this was thought to be the important issue when the case was first filed in federal court is that the "once free, always free" problem had just arisen in a somewhat different setting before the Supreme Court. In Strader v. Graham, 51 U.S. (10 How.) 82 (1852), the Supreme Court held that the Northwest Ordinance ban on slavery lasted only so long as the area was a territory. Once some or all of the area became a state, the state's constitution governed. Thus the issue of "once free, always free" was not decided because there was no federal law relevant to the status of the slave in that case. Scott, however, had traveled to both Illinois, which was governed by the outcome of *Strader* and Wisconsin, which was governed by the Missouri Compromise, making him a viable vehicle to test either configuration of the "once free, always free" rule.

case. The defendants were therefore in a position to assert that Scott lacked the ability to sue in the federal courts because he was not a citizen of Missouri for diversity purposes. That is exactly what the defendants did, filing a *plea in abatement*, or motion to dismiss, challenging the subject matter jurisdiction of the federal court.[24] Regardless of whether the two sides colluded to produce the law suit, its rise through the federal system turned out to be a major turning point in the history of American slavery.

The federal trial judge held that Scott was a citizen of the state of Missouri for diversity purposes. The court did not decide whether the Scotts could claim the protection of any Constitutional rights bestowed on citizens. It only concluded that they were, at a minimum, citizens for purposes of the diversity jurisdiction. Moving beyond this limited outcome would have resulted in challenges to a number of extant legal practices. At the time of this decision, the property rights of a master in slaves was much clearer than the citizenship of a freed slave. Only five states, all in New England, allowed black men to vote. Others excluded them from public schools, restricted employment opportunities, and treated them as non-citizens.[25]

On the merits, however, the district court decided that a slave's status as a slave was not changed upon entry into a free state, but only suspended, and that each state retained discretion, or sovereignty, to decide whether to apply the laws of sister states or territories altering the status of slaves residing within their boundaries. If the federal government could not abolish slavery within a state, he reasoned, it could not deprive owners of their property because they entered a federal territory. With this much decided, the case was appealed to the United States Supreme Court, where arguments were first heard in February, 1856.

The contention that the Missouri Compromise was unconstitutional was apparently introduced into the case for the first time when it reached the Supreme Court. The defendants contended not merely that Missouri was not bound to recognize Scott's status as a freed man upon his return to Missouri with Emerson from either Illinois or Wisconsin, but that Scott was never freed at all because Congress lacked the authority to regulate slavery in the territories. The Court, apparently dead-locked on an underlying jurisdictional point, asked that the case be reargued, limited to two questions—whether the trial court's decision on the plea in abatement could properly be reviewed, given that the defendants had litigated the merits after the trial judge ruled he had jurisdiction,[26] and whether black persons were state citizens and therefore able to sue in federal courts. By the time the case was argued a second time in 1856, it had begun to receive widespread notoriety. When the Supreme Court sat to hear the second set of arguments, the first standing room only crowd in the history of the litigation was present.[27]

---

[24] Ehrlich argued that the citizenship defense was not a calculated part of any "test" case, that there is no evidence for any deal on that issue prior to the case being filed, that the use of citizenship as a defense was an honest effort by the defendant to rid himself of unwanted litigation. Ehrlich, note 2 above, at 85. If Sanford did not own the Scotts, Ehrlich's theory is difficult to accept since Sanford could have gotten rid of the case by simply noting he did not own Scott.

[25] Mark Graber, *Desperately Ducking Slavery: Dred Scott and Contemporary Constitutional Theory*, 14 CONST. COMMENT 271, 284 (1997). Recent scholarship has also contended that the circumstances of Harriet Scott might have made for a better claim for freedom than that of her husband. Issues specifically related to her status became invisible as the case wore on. Lea Vandervelde and Sandhya Subramanian, *Mrs. Dred Scott*, 106 YALE L. J. 1033 (1997).

[26] Recall that the defendants filed a plea in abatement on the ground that Scott was not a citizen of Missouri for diversity purposes and therefore without ability to sue in federal court. It was common practice in the nineteenth century that if you lost such a plea and litigated the merits of your claim, you waived the issue raised in the plea in abatement. Thus, the Supreme Court's instructions for reargument asked the litigants to discuss the applicability of this procedural waiver rule to the *Scott* case as well as the claim that Scott lacked state citizenship and therefore could not sue.

[27] Ehrlich, note 2 above, at 117.

[2]   Opinions of The United States Supreme Court in *Dred Scott v. Sanford*

Dred Scott v. John F. A. Sanford

United States Supreme Court
60 U.S. (19 How.) 393, 15 L. Ed. 691 (1857)

Mr. CHIEF JUSTICE TANEY delivered the opinion of the court.

This case has been twice argued. After the argument at the last term, differences of opinion were found to exist among the members of the court; and as the questions in controversy are of the highest importance, and the court was at that time much pressed by the ordinary business of the term, it was deemed advisable to continue the case, and direct a re-argument on some of the points, in order that we might have an opportunity of giving to the whole subject a more deliberate consideration. It has accordingly been again argued by counsel, and considered by the court; and I now proceed to deliver its opinion.

There are two leading questions presented by the record:

1. Had the Circuit Court of the United States jurisdiction to hear and determine the case between these parties? And

2. If it had jurisdiction, is the judgment it has given erroneous or not?

The plaintiff in error, who was also the plaintiff in the court below, was, with his wife and children, held as slaves by the defendant, in the State of Missouri; and he brought this action in the Circuit Court of the United States for that district, to assert the title of himself and his family to freedom.

The declaration is in the form usually adopted in that State to try questions of this description, and contains the averment necessary to give the court jurisdiction; that he and the defendant are citizens of different States; that is, that he is a citizen of Missouri, and the defendant a citizen of New York.

The defendant pleaded in abatement to the jurisdiction of the court, that the plaintiff was not a citizen of the State of Missouri, as alleged in his declaration, being a negro of African descent, whose ancestors were of pure African blood, and who were brought into this country and sold as slaves.

To this plea the plaintiff demurred, and the defendant joined in demurrer. The court overruled the plea, and gave judgment that the defendant should answer over. And he thereupon put in sundry pleas in bar, upon which issues were joined; and at the trial the verdict and judgment were in his favor. Whereupon the plaintiff brought this writ of error.

Before we speak of the pleas in bar, it will be proper to dispose of the questions which have arisen on the plea in abatement.

That plea denies the right of the plaintiff to sue in a court of the United States, for the reasons therein stated.

If the question raised by it is legally before us, and the court should be of opinion that the facts stated in it disqualify the plaintiff from becoming a citizen, in the sense in which that word is used in the Constitution of the United States, then the judgment of the Circuit Court is erroneous, and must be reversed.

It is suggested, however, that this plea is not before us; and that as the judgment in the court below on this plea was in favor of the plaintiff, he does not seek to reverse it, or bring it before the court for revision by his writ of error; and also that the defendant waived this defense by pleading over, and thereby admitted the jurisdiction of the court.

But, in making this objection, we think the peculiar and limited jurisdiction of courts of the United States has not been adverted to. This peculiar and limited jurisdiction has made it necessary, in these courts, to adopt different rules and principles of pleading, so far as jurisdiction is concerned, from those which regulate courts of common law in England, and in the different States of the Union which have adopted the common-law rules. . . . Hence, when a plaintiff sues in a court of the United States, it is necessary that he should show, in his pleading, that the suit he brings is within the jurisdiction of the court, and that he is entitled to sue there.

. . . .

In this case, the citizenship is averred, but it is denied by the defendant in the manner required by the rules of pleading, and the fact upon which the denial is based is admitted by the demurrer. And, if the plea and demurrer, and judgment of the court below upon it, are before us upon this record, the question to be decided is, whether the facts stated in the plea are sufficient to show that the plaintiff is not entitled to sue as a citizen in a court of the United States.

We think they are before us. The plea in abatement and the judgment of the court upon it, are a part of the judicial proceedings in the Circuit Court, and are there recorded as such; and a writ of error always brings up to the superior court the whole record of the proceedings in the court below. . . . And this being the case. . .it becomes, therefore, our duty to decide whether the facts stated in the plea are or are not sufficient to show that the plaintiff is not entitled to sue as a citizen in a court of the United States.

This is certainly a very serious question, and one that now for the first time has been brought for decision before this court. But it is brought here by those who have a right to bring it, and it is our duty to meet it and decide it.

The question is simply this: Can a negro, whose ancestors were imported into this country, and sold as slaves, become a member of the political community formed and brought into existence by the Constitution of the United States, and as such become entitled to all the rights, and privileges, and immunities, guaranteed by that instrument to the citizen? One of which rights is the privilege of suing in a court of the United States in the cases specified in the Constitution.

It will be observed, that the plea applies to that class of persons only whose ancestors were negroes of the African race, and imported into this country, and sold and held as slaves. The only matter in issue before the court, therefore, is, whether the descendants of such slaves, when they shall be emancipated, or who are born or parents who had become free before their birth, are citizens of a State, in the sense in which the word citizen is used in the Constitution of the United States. And this being the only matter in dispute on the pleadings, the court must be understood as speaking in this opinion of that class only, that is, of those persons who are the descendants of Africans who were imported into this country, and sold as slaves.

The situation of this population was altogether unlike that of the Indian race. The latter, it is true, formed no part of the colonial communities, and never amalgamated with them in social connections or in government. But although they were uncivilized, they were yet a free and independent people, associated together in nations or tribes, and governed by their own laws. Many of these political communities were situated in territories to which the white race claimed the ultimate right of dominion. But that claim was acknowledged to be subject to the right of the Indians to occupy it as long as they thought proper, and neither the English nor colonial Governments claimed or exercised any dominion over the tribe or nation by whom it was occupied, nor claimed the right to the possession of the territory, until the tribe or nation consented to cede it. These Indian Governments were regarded and treated as foreign Governments, as much so as if an ocean had separated the red man from the white; and their freedom has constantly been acknowledged, from the time of the first emigration to the English colonies to the present day, by the different Governments which succeeded each other. Treaties have been negotiated with them, and their alliance sought for in war; and the people who compose these Indian political communities have always been treated as foreigners not living under our Government. It is true that the course of events has brought the Indian tribes within the limits of the United States under subjection to the white race; and it has been found necessary, for their sake as well as our own, to regard them as in a state of pupilage, and to legislate to a certain extent over them and the territory they occupy. But they may, without doubt, like the subjects of any become citizens of a State, and of the United States; and if an individual should leave his nation or tribe, and take up his abode among the white population, he would be entitled to all the rights and privileges which would belong to an emigrant from any other foreign people.

We proceed to examine the case as presented by the pleadings.

The words "people of the United States" and "citizens" are synonymous terms, and mean the same thing. They both describe the political body who, according to our republican institutions, form the sovereignty, and who hold the power and conduct the Government through their representatives. They are what we familiarly call the "sovereign people," and every citizen is one of this people, and a constituent member of this sovereignty. The question before us is, whether the class of persons described in the plea in abatement compose a portion of this people, and are constituent members of this sovereignty? We think they are not, and that they are not included, and were not intended to be included, under the word "citizens" in the Constitution, and can therefore claim none of the rights and privileges which that instrument provides for and secures to citizens of the United States. On the contrary, they were at that time considered as a subordinate and inferior class of beings, who had been subjugated by the dominant race, and, whether emancipated or not, yet remained subject to their authority, and had no rights or privileges but such as those who held the power and the Government might choose to grant them.

It is not the province of the court to decide upon the justice or injustice, the policy or impolicy, of these laws. The decision of that question belonged to the political or law-making power; to those who formed the sovereignty and framed the Constitution. The duty of the court is, to interpret the instrument they have framed, with the best lights we can obtain on the subject, and to administer it as we find it, according to its true intent and meaning when it was adopted.

In discussing this question, we must not confound the rights of citizenship which a State may confer within its own limits, and the rights of citizenship as a member of the Union. It does not by any means follow, because he has all the rights and privileges of a citizen of a State, that he must be a citizen of the United States. He may have all of the rights and privileges of the citizen of a State, and yet not be entitled to the rights and privileges of a citizen in any other State. For, previous to the adoption of the Constitution of the United States, every State had the undoubted right to confer on whomsoever it pleased the character of citizen, and to endow him with all its rights. But this character of course was confined to the boundaries of the State, and gave him no rights or privileges in other States beyond those secured to him by the laws of nations and the comity of States. Nor have the several States surrendered the power of conferring these rights and privileges by adopting the Constitution of the United States. Each State may still confer them upon an alien, or any one it thinks proper, or upon any class or description of persons; yet he would not be a citizen in the sense in which that word is used in the Constitution of the United States, nor entitled to sue as such in one of its courts, nor to the privileges and immunities of a citizen in the other States. The rights which he would acquire would be restricted to the State which gave them. The Constitution has conferred on Congress the right to establish an uniform rule of naturalization, and this right is evidently exclusive, and has always been held by this court to be so. Consequently, no State, since the adoption of the Constitution, can by naturalizing an alien invest him with the rights and privileges secured to a citizen of a State under the Federal Government, although, so far as the State alone was concerned, he would undoubtedly be entitled to the rights of a citizen, and clothed with all the rights and immunities which the Constitution and laws of the State attached to that character.

It is very clear, therefore, that no State can, by any act or law of its own, passed since the adoption of the Constitution, introduce a new member into the political community created by the Constitution of the United States. It cannot make him a member of this community by making him a member of its own. And for the same reason it cannot introduce any person, or description of persons, who were not intended to be embraced in this new political family, which the Constitution brought into existence, but were intended to be excluded from it.

The question then arises, whether the provisions of the Constitution, in relation to the personal rights and privileges to which the citizen of a State should be entitled, embraced the negro African race, at that time in this country, or who might afterwards be imported, who had then or should afterwards be made free in any State; and to put it in the power of a single State to make him a citizen of the United States, and endue him with the full rights of citizenship in every other State without their consent? Does the Constitution of the United States act upon him whenever he shall be made free under the laws of a State, and raised there to the rank of a citizen, and immediately clothe him with all the privileges of a citizen in every other State, and in its own courts?

The court think the affirmative of these propositions cannot be maintained. And if it cannot, the plaintiff in error could not be a citizen of the State of Missouri, within the meaning of the Constitution of the United States, and, consequently, was not entitled to sue in its courts.

. . . .

In the opinion of the court, the legislation and histories of the times, and the language used in the Declaration of Independence, show, that neither the class of persons who had been imported as slaves, nor their descendants, whether they had become free or not, were then acknowledged as a part of the people, nor intended to be included in the general words used in that memorable instrument.

It is difficult at this day to realize the state of public opinion in relation to that unfortunate race, which prevailed in the civilized and enlightened portions of the world at the time of the Declaration of Independence, and when the Constitution of the United States was framed and adopted. But the public history of every European nation displays it in a manner too plain to be mistaken.

They had for more than a century before been regarded as beings of an inferior order, and altogether unfit to associate with the white race, either in social or political relations; and so far inferior, that they had no rights which the white man was bound to respect; and that the negro might justly and lawfully be reduced to slavery for his benefit. He was bought and sold, and treated as an ordinary article of merchandise and traffic, whenever a profit could be made by it. This opinion was at that time fixed and universal in the civilized portion of the white race. It was regarded as an axiom in morals as well as in politics, which no one thought of disputing, or supposed to be open to dispute; and men in every grade and position in society daily and habitually acted upon it in their private pursuits, as well as in matters of public concern, without doubting for a moment the correctness of this opinion.

. . . .

The language of the Declaration of Independence . . . would seem to embrace the whole human family, and if they were used in a similar instrument at this day would be so understood. But it is too clear for dispute, that the enslaved African race were not intended to be included, and formed no part of the people who framed and adopted this declaration; for if the language, as understood in that day, would embrace them, the conduct of the distinguished men who framed the Declaration of Independence would have been utterly and flagrantly inconsistent with the principles they asserted; and instead of the sympathy of mankind, to which they so confidently appealed, they would have deserved and received universal rebuke and reprobation.

Yet the men who framed this declaration were great men—high in literary acquirements—high in their sense of honor, and incapable of asserting principles inconsistent with those on which they were acting. They perfectly understood the meaning of the language they used, and how it would be understood by others; and they knew that it would not in any part of the civilized world be supposed to embrace the negro race, which, by common consent, had been excluded from civilized Governments and the family of nations, and doomed to slavery. They spoke and acted according to the then established doctrines and principles, and in the ordinary language of the day, and no one misunderstood them. The unhappy black race were separated from the white by indelible marks, and laws long before established, and were never thought of or spoken of except as property, and when the claims of the owner or the profit of the trader were supposed to need protection.

This state of public opinion had undergone no change when the Constitution was adopted. . . .

. . . .

[T]here are two clauses in the Constitution which point directly and specifically to the negro race as a separate class of persons, and show clearly that they were not regarded as a portion of the people or citizens of the Government then formed.

One of these clauses reserves to each of the thirteen States the right to import slaves until the year 1808, if it thinks proper. And the importation which it thus sanctions was unquestionably of persons of the race of which we are speaking, as the traffic in slaves in the United States had always been confined to them. And by the other provision the States pledge themselves to each other to maintain the right of property of the master, by delivering up to him any slave who may have escaped from his service, and be found within their respective territories. By the first above-mentioned clause, therefore, the right to purchase and hold this property is directly sanctioned and authorized for twenty years by the people who framed the Constitution. And by the second, they pledge themselves to maintain and uphold the right of the master in the manner specified, as long as the Government they then formed should endure. And these two provisions show, conclusively, that neither the description of persons therein referred to, nor their descendants, were embraced in any of the other provisions of the Constitution; for certainly these two clauses were not intended to confer on them or their posterity the blessings of liberty, or any of the personal rights so carefully provided for the citizen.

. . . .

And if we turn to the legislation of the States where slavery had worn out, or measures taken for its speedy abolition, we shall find the same opinions and principles equally fixed and equally acted upon.

Thus, Massachusetts, in 1786, passed a law . . . [forbidding] the marriage of any white person with any negro, Indian, or mulatto, and inflicts a penalty of fifty pounds upon any one who shall join them in marriage; and declares all such marriages absolutely null and void, and degrades thus the unhappy issue of the marriage by fixing upon it the stain of bastardy. . . .

So, too, in Connecticut. We refer . . . to the legislation of this State, because it was not only among the first to put an end to slavery within its own territory, but was the first to fix a mark of reprobation upon the African slave trade.

. . . .

The legislation of the States therefore shows, in a manner not to be mistaken, the inferior and subject condition of that race at the time the Constitution was adopted, and long afterwards, throughout the thirteen States by which that instrument was framed; and it is hardly consistent with the respect due to these States, to suppose that they regarded at that time, as fellow-citizens and members of the sovereignty, a class of beings whom they had thus stigmatized; whom, as we are bound, out of respect to the State sovereignties, to assume they had deemed it just and necessary thus to stigmatize, and upon whom they had impressed such deep and enduring marks of inferiority and degradation; or, that when they met in convention to form the Constitution, they looked upon them as a portion of their constituents, or designed to include them in the provisions so carefully inserted for the security and protection of the liberties and rights of their citizens. It cannot be supposed that they intended to secure to them rights, and privileges, and rank, in the new political body throughout the Union, which every one of them denied within the limits of its own dominion. More especially, it cannot be believed that the large slaveholding States regarded them as included in the word citizens, or would have consented to a Constitution which might compel them to receive them in that character from another State. For if they were so received, and entitled to the privileges and immunities of citizens, it would exempt them from the operation of the special laws and from the police regulations which they considered to be necessary for their own safety. It would give to persons of the negro race, who were recognised as citizens in any one State of the Union, the right to enter every other State whenever they pleased, singly or in companies, without pass or passport, and without obstruction, to sojourn there as long as they pleased, to go where they pleased at every hour of the day or night without molestation, unless they committed some violation of law for which a white man would be punished; and it would give them the full liberty of speech in public and in private upon all subjects upon which its own citizens might speak; to hold public meetings upon political affairs, and to keep and carry arms wherever they went. And all of this would be done in the face of the subject race of the same color, both free and slaves, and inevitably producing discontent and insubordination among them, and endangering the peace and safety of the State.

. . . .

Besides, this want of foresight and care would have been utterly inconsistent with the caution displayed in providing for the admission of new members into this political family. For, when they gave to the citizens of each State the privileges and immunities of citizens in the several States, they at the same time took from the several States the power of naturalization, and confined that power exclusively to the Federal Government. No State was willing to permit another State to determine who should or should not be admitted as one of its citizens, and entitled to demand equal rights and privileges with their own people, within their own territories. The right of naturalization was therefore, with one accord, surrendered by the States, and confided to the Federal Government. And this power granted to Congress to establish an uniform rule of *naturalization* is, by the well-understood meaning of the word, confined to persons born in a foreign country, under a foreign Government. It is not a power to raise to the rank of a citizen any one born in the United States, who, from birth or parentage, by the laws of the country, belongs to an inferior and subordinate class. And when we find the States guarding themselves from the indiscreet or improper admission by other States of emigrants from other countries, by giving the power exclusively to Congress, we cannot fail to see that they could never have left with the States a much more important power—that is, the power, of transforming into citizens a numerous class of persons, who in that character would be much more dangerous to the peace and safety of a large portion of the Union, than the few foreigners one of the States might improperly naturalize.

. . . .

But it is said that a person may be a citizen, and entitled to that character, although he does not possess all the rights which may belong to other citizens; as, for example, the right to vote, or to hold particular offices; and that yet, when he goes into another State, he is entitled to be recognised there as a citizen, although the State may measure his rights by the rights which it allows to persons of a like character or class resident in the State, and refuse to him the full rights of citizenship.

This argument overlooks the language of the provision in the Constitution of which we are speaking.

Undoubtedly, a person may be a citizen, that is, a member of the community who form the sovereignty, although he exercises no share of the political power, and is incapacitated from holding particular offices. Women and minors, who form a part of the political family, cannot vote; and when a property qualification is required to vote or hold a particular office, those who have not the necessary qualification cannot vote or hold the office, yet they are citizens.

. . . .

But so far as mere rights of person are concerned, the provision in question is confined to citizens of a State who are temporarily in another State without taking up their residence there. It gives them no political rights in the State, as to voting or holding office, or in any other respect. For a citizen of one State has no right to participate in the government of another. But if he ranks as a citizen in the State to which he belongs, within the meaning of the Constitution of the United States, then, whenever he goes into another State, the Constitution clothes him, as to the rights of person, with all the privileges and immunities which belong to citizens of the State. And if persons of the African race are citizens of a State, and of the United States, they would be entitled to all of these privileges and immunities in every State, and the State could not restrict them; for they would hold these privileges and immunities under the paramount authority of the Federal Government, and its courts would be bound to maintain and enforce them, the Constitution and laws of the State to the contrary notwithstanding. And if the States could limit or restrict them, or place the party in an inferior grade, this clause of the Constitution would be unmeaning, and could have no operation; and would give no rights to the citizen when in another State. He would have none but what the State itself chose to allow him. This is evidently not the construction or meaning of the clause in question. It guaranties rights to the citizen, and the State cannot withhold them. And these rights are of a character and would lead to consequences which make it absolutely certain that the African race were not included under the name of citizens of a State, and were not in the contemplation of the framers of the Constitution when these privileges and immunities were provided for the protection of the citizen in other States.

. . . .

And upon a full and careful consideration of the subject, the court is of opinion, that, upon the facts stated in the plea in abatement, Dred Scott was not a citizen of Missouri within the meaning of the Constitution of the United States, and not entitled as such to sue in its courts; and, consequently, that the Circuit Court had no jurisdiction of the case, and that the judgment on the plea in abatement is erroneous.

We are aware that doubts are entertained by some of the members of the court, whether the plea in abatement is legally before the court upon this writ of error; but if that plea is regarded as waived, or out of the case upon any other ground, yet the question as to the jurisdiction of the Circuit Court is presented on the face of the bill of exception itself, taken by the plaintiff at the trial; for he admits that he and his wife were born slaves, but endeavors to make out his title to freedom and citizenship by showing that they were taken by their owner to certain places, hereinafter mentioned, where slavery could not by law exist, and that they thereby became free, and upon their return to Missouri became citizens of that State.

. . . .

But, before we proceed to examine this part of the case, it may be proper to notice an objection taken to the judicial authority of this court to decide it; and it has been said, that as this court has decided against the jurisdiction of the Circuit Court on the plea in abatement, it has no right to examine any question presented by the exception; and that anything it may say upon that part of the case will be extra-judicial, and mere obiter dicta.

This is a manifest mistake; there can be no doubt as to the jurisdiction of this court to revise the judgment of a Circuit Court, and to reverse it for any error apparent on the record, whether it be the error of giving judgment in a case over which it had no jurisdiction, or any other material error; and this, too, whether there is a plea in abatement or not.

. . . .

It is true that the result either way, by dismissal or by a judgment for the defendant, makes very little, if any, difference in a pecuniary or personal point of view to either party. But the fact that the result would be very nearly the same to the parties in either form of judgment, would not justify this court in sanctioning an error in the judgment which is patent on the record, and which, if sanctioned, might be drawn into precedent, and lead to serious mischief and injustice in some future suit.

We proceed, therefore, to inquire whether the facts relied on by the plaintiff entitled him to his freedom.

. . . .

In considering this part of the controversy, two questions arise: 1. Was he, together with his family, free in Missouri by reason of the stay in the territory of the United States hereinbefore mentioned? And 2. If they were not, is Scott himself free by reason of his removal to Rock Island, in the State of Illinois, as stated in the above admissions?

We proceed to examine the first question.

The act of Congress, upon which the plaintiff relies, declares that slavery and involuntary servitude, except as a punishment for crime, shall be forever prohibited in all that part of the territory ceded by France, under the name of Louisiana, which lies north of thirty-six degrees thirty minutes north latitude, and not included within the limits of Missouri. And the difficulty which meets us at the threshold of this part of the inquiry is, whether Congress was authorized to pass this law under any of the powers granted to it by the Constitution; for if the authority is not given by that instrument, it is the duty of this court to declare it void and inoperative, and incapable of conferring freedom upon any one who is held as a slave under the laws of any one of the States.

The counsel for the plaintiff has laid much stress upon that article in the Constitution which confers on Congress the power "to dispose of and make all needful rules and regulations respecting the territory or other property belonging to the United States;" but, in the judgment of the court, that provision has no bearing on the present controversy, and the power there given, whatever it may be, is confined, and was intended to be confined, to the territory which at that time belonged to, or was claimed by, the United States, and was within their boundaries as settled by the treaty with Great Britain, and can have no influence upon a territory afterwards acquired from a foreign Government. It was a special provision for a known and particular territory, and to meet a present emergency, and nothing more.

. . . .

This view of the subject is confirmed by the manner in which the present Government of the United States dealt with the subject as soon as it came into existence. . . .

[A]mong the earliest laws passed under the new Government, is one reviving the ordinance of 1787, which had become inoperative and a nullity upon the adoption of the Constitution. This law introduces no new form or principles for its government, but recites, in the preamble, that it is passed in order that this ordinance may continue to have full effect, and proceeds to make only those rules and regulations which were needful to adapt it to the new Government, into whose hands the power had fallen. It appears, therefore, that this Congress regarded the purposes to which the land in this Territory was to be applied, and the form of government and principles of jurisprudence which were to prevail there, while it remained in the Territorial state, as already determined on by the States when they had full power and right to make the decision; and that the new Government, having received it in this condition, ought to carry substantially into effect the plans and principles which had been previously adopted by the States, and which no doubt the States anticipated when they surrendered their power to the new Government. And if we regard this clause of the Constitution as pointing to this Territory, with a Territorial Government already established in it, which had been ceded to the States for the purposes hereinbefore mentioned—every word in it is perfectly appropriate and easily understood, and the provisions it contains are in perfect harmony with the objects for which it was ceded, and with the condition of its government as a Territory at the time. We can, then, easily account for the manner in which the first Congress legislated on the subject—and can also understand why this power over the territory was associated in the same clause with the other property of the United States, and subjected to the like power of making needful rules and regulations. But if the clause is construed in the expanded sense contended for, so as to embrace any territory acquired from a foreign nation by the present Government, and to give it in such territory a despotic and unlimited power over persons and property, such as the confederated States might exercise in their common property, it would be difficult to account for the phraseology used, when compared with other grants of power—and also for its association with the other provisions in the same clause.

. . . .

This brings us to examine by what provision of the Constitution the present Federal Government, under its delegated and restricted powers, is authorized to acquire territory outside of the original limits of the United States, and what powers it may exercise therein over the person or property of a citizen of the United States, while it remains a Territory, and until it shall be admitted as one of the States of the Union.

. . . .

The power to expand the territory of the United States by the admission of new States is plainly given; and in the construction of this power by all the departments of the Government, it has been held to authorize the acquisition of territory, not fit for admission at the time, but to be admitted as soon as its population and situation would entitle it to admission. It is acquired to become a State, and not to be held as a colony and governed by Congress with absolute authority; and as the propriety of admitting a new State is committed to the sound discretion of Congress, the power to acquire territory for that purpose, to be held by the United States until it is in a suitable condition to become a State upon an equal footing with the other States, must rest upon the same discretion.

. . . .

But until that time arrives, it is undoubtedly necessary that some Government should be established, in order to organize society, and to protect the inhabitants in their persons and property; and as the people of the United States could act in this matter only through the Government which represented them, and through which they spoke and acted when the Territory was obtained, it was not only within the scope of its powers, but it was its duty to pass such laws and establish such a Government as would enable those by whose authority they acted to reap the advantages anticipated from its acquisition, and to gather there a population which would enable it to assume the position to which it was destined among the States of the Union. The power to acquire necessarily carries with it the power to preserve and apply to the purposes for which it was acquired. The form of government to be established necessarily rested in the discretion of Congress. It was their duty to establish the one that would be best suited for the protection and security of the citizens of the United States, and other inhabitants who might be authorized to take up their abode there, and that must always depend upon the existing condition of the Territory, as to the number and character of its inhabitants, and their situation in the Territory. . . .

But the power of Congress over the person or property of a citizen can never be a mere discretionary power under our Constitution and form of Government. The powers of the Government and the rights and privileges of the citizen are regulated and plainly defined by the Constitution itself. And when the Territory becomes a part of the United States, the Federal Government enters into possession in the character impressed upon it by those who created it. It enters upon it with its powers over the citizen strictly defined, and limited by the Constitution, from which it derives its own existence, and by virtue of which alone it continues to exist and act as a Government and sovereignty. It has no power of any kind beyond it; and it cannot, when it enters a Territory of the United States, put off its character, and assume discretionary or despotic powers which the Constitution has denied to it. It cannot create for itself a new character separated from the citizens of the United States, and the duties it owes them under the provisions of the Constitution. The Territory being a part of the United States, the Government and the citizen both enter it under the authority of the Constitution, with their respective rights defined and marked out; and the Federal Government can exercise no power over his person or property, beyond what that instrument confers, nor lawfully deny any right which it has reserved.

. . . .

For example, no one, we presume, will contend that Congress can make any law in a Territory respecting the establishment of religion, or the free exercise thereof, or abridging the freedom of speech or of the press, or the right of the people of the Territory peaceably to assemble, and to petition the Government for the redress of grievances.

. . . .

The powers over person and property of which we speak are not only not granted to Congress, but are in express terms denied, and they are forbidden to exercise them. And this prohibition is not confined to the States, but the words are general, and extend to the whole territory over which the Constitution gives it power to legislate, including those portions of it remaining under Territorial Government, as well as that covered by States. It is a total absence of power everywhere within the dominion of the United States, and places the citizens of a Territory, so far as these rights are concerned, on the same footing with citizens of the States, and guards them as firmly and plainly against any inroads which the General Government might attempt, under the plea of implied or incidental powers. And if Congress itself cannot do this—if it is beyond the powers conferred on the Federal Government—it will be admitted, we presume, that it could not authorize a Territorial Government to exercise them. It could confer no power on any local Government, established by its authority, to violate the provisions of the Constitution.

It seems, however, to be supposed, that there is a difference between property in a slave and other property, and that different rules may be applied to it in expounding the Constitution of the United States. And the laws and usages of nations, and the writings of eminent jurists upon the relation of master and slave and their mutual rights and duties, and the powers which Governments may exercise over it, have been dwelt upon in the argument.

. . . .

Now, as we have already said in an earlier part of this opinion, upon a different point, the right of property in a slave is distinctly and expressly affirmed in the Constitution. The right to traffic in it, like an ordinary article of merchandise and property, was guarantied to the citizens of the United States, in every State that might desire it, for twenty years. And the Government in express terms is pledged to protect it in all future time, if the slave escapes from his owner. This is done in plain words—too plain to be misunderstood. And no word can be found in the Constitution which gives Congress a greater power over slave property, or which entitles property of that kind to less protection than property of any other description. The only power conferred is the power coupled with the duty of guarding and protecting the owner in his rights.

Upon these considerations, it is the opinion of the court that the act of Congress which prohibited a citizen from holding and owning property of this kind in the territory of the United States north of the line therein mentioned, is not warranted by the Constitution, and is therefore void; and that neither Dred Scott himself, nor any of his family, were made free by being carried into this territory; even if they had been carried there by the owner, with the intention of becoming a permanent resident.

We have so far examined the case, as it stands under the Constitution of the United States, and the powers thereby delegated to the Federal Government.

But there is another point in the case which depends on State power and State law. And it is contended, on the part of the plaintiff, that he is made free by being taken to Rock Island, in the State of Illinois, independently of his residence in the territory of the United States; and being so made free, he was not again reduced to a state of slavery by being brought back to Missouri.

Our notice of this part of the case will be very brief; for the principle on which it depends was decided in this court, upon much consideration, in the case of *Strader et al. v. Graham*, reported in 10th Howard, 82. In that case, the slaves had been taken from Kentucky to Ohio, with the consent of the owner, and afterwards brought back to Kentucky. And this court held that their *status* or condition, as free or slave, depended upon the laws of Kentucky, when they were brought back into that State, and not of Ohio; and that this court had no jurisdiction to revise the judgment of a State court upon its own laws. This was the point directly before the court, and the decision that this court had not jurisdiction turned upon it, as will be seen by the report of the case.

So in this case. As Scott was a slave when taken into the State of Illinois by his owner, and was there held as such, and brought back in that character, his *status*, as free or slave, depended on the laws of Missouri, and not of Illinois.

It has, however, been urged in the argument, that by the laws of Missouri he was free on his return, and that this case, therefore, cannot be governed by the case of *Strader et al. v. Graham*, where it appeared, by the laws of Kentucky, that the plaintiffs continued to be slaves on their return from Ohio. But whatever doubts or opinions may, at one time, have been entertained upon this subject, we are satisfied, upon a careful examination of all the cases decided in the State courts of Missouri referred to, that it is now firmly settled by the decisions of the highest court in the State, that Scott and his family upon their return were not free, but were, by the laws of Missouri, the property of the defendant; and that the Circuit Court of the United States had no jurisdiction, when, by the laws of the State, the plaintiff was a slave, and not a citizen.

Moreover, the plaintiff, it appears, brought a similar action against the defendant in the State court of Missouri, claiming the freedom of himself and his family upon the same grounds and the same evidence upon which he relies in the case before the court. The case was carried before the Supreme Court of the State; was fully argued there; and that court decided that neither the plaintiff nor his family were entitled to freedom, and were still the slaves of the defendant; and reversed the judgment of the inferior State court, which had given a different decision. If the plaintiff supposed that this judgment of the Supreme Court of the State was erroneous, and that this court had jurisdiction to revise and reverse it, the only mode by which he could legally bring it before this court was by writ of error directed to the Supreme Court of the State, requiring it to transmit the record to this court. If this had been done, it is too plain for argument that the writ must have been dismissed for want of jurisdiction in this court. The case of *Strader and others v. Graham* is directly in point; and, indeed, independent of any decision, the language of the 25th section of the act of 1789 is too clear and precise to admit of controversy.

But the plaintiff did not pursue the mode prescribed by law for bringing the judgment of a State court before this court for revision, but suffered the case to be remanded to the inferior State court, where it is still continued, and is, by agreement of parties, to await the judgment of this court on the point. All of this appears on the record before us, and by the printed report of the case.

And while the case is yet open and pending in the inferior State court, the plaintiff goes into the Circuit Court of the United States, upon the same case and the same evidence, and against the same party, and proceeds to judgment, and then brings here the same case from the Circuit Court, which the law would not have permitted him to bring directly from the State court. And if this court takes jurisdiction in this form, the result, so far as the rights of the respective parties are concerned, is in every respect substantially the same as if it had in open violation of law entertained jurisdiction over the judgment of the State court upon a writ of error, and revised and reversed its judgment upon the ground that its opinion upon the question of law was erroneous. It would ill become this court to sanction such an attempt to evade the law, or to exercise an appellate power in this circuitous way, which it is forbidden to exercise in the direct and regular and invariable forms of judicial proceedings.

Upon the whole, therefore, it is the judgment of this court, that it appears by the record before us that the plaintiff in error is not a citizen of Missouri, in the sense in which that word is used in the Constitution; and that the Circuit Court of the United States, for that reason, had no jurisdiction in the case, and could give no judgment in it. Its judgment for the defendant must, consequently, be reversed, and a mandate issued, directing the suit to be dismissed for want of jurisdiction.

[3] Explanatory Notes

[a] Events After the Case

Within a week of the Supreme Court's decision, the Springfield, Massachusetts *Argus*, a paper with Democratic Party politics, revealed that Dr. Calvin Chafee, the Republican Congressman from the area, the wife of Irene Sanford Chafee, and a supposed abolitionist, was a slaveholder. Chafee wrote a letter published in the *Springfield Daily Republican* that, when he met and married Irene Emerson he did not know that she owned slaves. He also claimed to have learned of his relationship to the *Dred Scott* case only a short time before the Supreme Court handed down its opinions. Chafee and his wife signed quit claim deeds turning over all their rights in the Scotts to Taylor Blow in St. Louis. Their formal transfer of property rights in the Scotts adds further credence to the claim some historians have made that Sanford, the defendant in the *Dred Scott* litigation, was not a proper party. Blow formally emancipated them on May 26, 1857.[28] Scott died the following year. A headstone was not erected on his grave until the centennial of the *Dred Scott* decision.[29]

[b] The Various Dred Scott Opinions

Every judge on the Supreme Court wrote an opinion in the *Dred Scott* case, the first instance since *Marbury v. Madison*, 5 U.S. (1 Cranch) 137 (1803), in which an act of Congress was found unconstitutional. The various opinions make fascinating reading, but they are simply too long

---

[28] Under Missouri law manumission had to be accomplished by a citizen of the state. The conveyance of the Scotts to Blow was done to meet this requirement.

[29] Ehrlich, note 2 above, at 183.

to include here. Chief Justice Taney's opinion contained three main segments. In the first, he argued that the defendant's plea in abatement was properly before the court. Then he concluded that Dred Scott was not a citizen of the United States and therefore could not file a diversity action in federal court. Finally, he contended that Scott was not freed by the terms of the Missouri Compromise, because that act was unconstitutional, or by the old "once free, always free" rule Missouri followed until it decided the *Dred Scott* case.

When all the other opinions are carefully read, it turns out that a majority of the court did *not* agree with Taney that the defendant's plea in abatement was properly before the Justices! Despite the fact that Taney's opinion is labeled as the Opinion of the Court, it wasn't quite so. Justices Wayne and Daniel basically agreed with Taney on all major issues. Justices McLean and Curtis filed dissents in which they disagreed with Taney on most major issues, including the plea in abatement. The other four judges took a variety of stances. Justice Nelson evaded decision on the plea in abatement issue. He opined that the case was easily resolved by reference to the Missouri decision declining to enforce the "once free, always free" rule, making it unnecessary to resolve the other issues. Nelson agreed with Taney that the result below should be affirmed, but he declined to concur in Taney's opinion. Justice Grier concurred with Nelson and with that part of Taney's opinion finding the Missouri Compromise invalid. But he too evaded the plea in abatement question. Justice Catron wrote that the plea in abatement issue was not before the Court, that, as a result, the prima facie case of jurisdiction pleaded in the complaint permitted the Supreme Court to entertain the case, that Congress *did* have authority to regulate slavery in territories generally, but that the terms of the Louisiana Purchase Treaty with France made it unlawful to disturb rights in property, including slaves, in the Louisiana Territory. Lastly, Justice Campbell, who concurred only in the court's judgment, not the Taney opinion, also evaded the plea in abatement issue. He wrote that the case should be decided in accordance with Missouri law and that Congress lacked authority to alter that law.

Thus, Taney only had two other judges—Wayne and Daniel—who explicitly agreed with him that the issue of citizenship raised by the plea in abatement was properly before the Court. One other judge—Catron—argued that since the plea was *not* before the court the jurisdiction as alleged in the complaint provided a basis for proceeding. That made at most four judges who agreed that the Court could proceed on that issue, for two others dissented and three others evaded the question.

This nose counting is not unimportant. Ever since *Dred Scott* was decided, Taney has been subjected to withering criticism on the ground that the portions of his opinion on the Missouri Compromise were *obiter dicta*, or opinions unnecessary to the result. That criticism may be partially unfair. The defendant's plea in abatement argued that from the face of the complaint, the court lacked diversity jurisdiction because Scott was black and therefore not a citizen of Missouri. The trial court held that Scott was a citizen of Missouri for diversity purposes. If, despite Taney's opinion, the Supreme Court's view was that the plea in abatement was waived by the defendant's pursuit of a full trial in the case, then there could be no dispute about the legitimacy of the trial court hearing evidence as to whether Scott was free.

In thinking about this problem, recognize that there is a difference between a ruling made on the jurisdiction of a court based only on the allegations in a complaint and one made after a full fact finding hearing. The defendants first contended, in their plea in abatement, that Scott's race meant that there was no state citizenship for diversity purposes. The trial court declined to accept that proposition, reasoning instead that Scott's status for diversity purposes was not the same as a general inquiry into the rights of citizens. Having lost the contention that the court lacked jurisdiction, the defendant then defended the case on the merits. It was that step that got him into trouble. For the old procedural rules forced the defendant to either appeal the plea in abatement or waive that issue and go to trial. Taney declined to follow that practice, noting instead that the jurisdiction of the federal courts was limited and that subject matter jurisdiction was therefore always open to challenge. If there was not a Supreme Court majority for reversing the first part of the trial court's rulings on the plea of abatement, then the Court *had* to discuss Scott's status as a slave in order to decide the jurisdictional claims. While that portion of Taney's opinion saying that the court is always free to review the entire record below was, therefore, very misleading, it was probably not inappropriate for him to get to the question of Scott's status as a slave.

That, however, does not mean that Taney's opinion on the jurisdictional issue is not subject to criticism. The lower federal court had framed the issue about diversity as one of state citizenship. Taney turned the issue into one of federal citizenship, declaring first that a party had to be a federal citizen before gaining the right to sue or be sued in a federal court, and then declaring that Scott, even if a free man, could not be a federal citizen. It is clear, therefore, that Taney could have decided this case without reaching out to find the Missouri Compromise invalid. By concluding that not only slaves but all black persons lacked citizenship for diversity purposes, and that any attempt in the Missouri Compromise to bar that result was unconstitutional, he ranged far and wide through federal slavery law. It is the breadth of this result that has led to the scathing criticism of the Court. Their attempt to definitively deal with the slavery question caused them to invalidate a Compromise which Congress had already decided to ignore,[30] decide upon the status of all blacks, even those in northern states, and ignore a resolution of the case which would have been much more moderate in its impact.

[c] Scope of the Case

The *Dred Scott* case could be the subject of discussion in a number of other courses. Constitutional Law obviously plays a large role in the case. The appellate litigation is almost entirely about diversity jurisdiction, a matter routinely discussed in Civil Procedure. And the notion that the Supreme Court could have simply applied Missouri law to the citizenship question and left well enough alone, raises problems commonplace to both Civil Procedure and Choice of Law courses. If no other lesson emerges from a reading of the case, it should be clear that the demarcation lines between your first year courses are somewhat artificial. Interesting litigation rarely pigeon-holes itself into the same boxes you study in law school. Though that creates some confusion at this point in your careers, it also creates a challenge as you try to integrate your first year work into some sort of a coherent pattern.

One example of the interplay may help you out a bit. As already noted, the Court could have decided *Dred Scott* by applying Missouri law to the citizenship question. This would, of course, have resulted in potentially different citizenship rules from state to state. At one level, that seems unwise. Perhaps citizenship is the sort of thing that should be uniform across the country. But an incredible array of areas are left to the varying impulses of the states for resolution, including most basic property rules. While it seems immoral today to view the *Scott* case as a property

---

[30] Recall that the admission of California in 1850 had for all practical purposes repealed the Missouri Compromise demarcation line. The line, though tattered from years of rivalry over slavery, had been reaffirmed before the California question in an 1844 Congressional resolution annexing the territories claimed by Texas.

dispute, that is what it was. Somehow we manage to survive in a world in which property rules differ in significant ways from jurisdiction to jurisdiction, as well as from epoch to epoch. While that may create some anxiety in law students, it is also a feature of the legal system that provides very interesting textures for study. At a minimum, we are given enough alternative methods for solving various problems that we can argue about which way is best to use over the long run.

[4]   The Nature of Citizenship and Personhood After the *Dred Scott* Era

The consequences of owning people were vast. Since people can act on thoughtful impulses, a complex system of control had to be erected in the slave states to avoid disintegration of the slave system. One example may provide some insight into the ways such control systems operated. In Taney's *Dred Scott* opinion, he wrote with incredulity of the possibility that black persons might actually have the freedom to move about the country. "It cannot be believed," he wrote, that the slaveholding states would have consented to a Constitution entitling black persons to citizenship. "For if they were so received, and entitled to the privileges and immunities of citizens, it would exempt them from the operation of the special laws and from the police regulations which they considered to be necessary for their own safety. It would give persons of the negro race, who were recognized as citizens in any one State of the Union, the right to enter every other State whenever they pleased, singly or in companies, without pass or passport, and without obstruction, to sojourn there as long as they pleased, to go where they pleased at every hour of the day or night without molestation, unless they committed some violation of law."

This passage suggests only the barest outlines of the pervasive systems used to control the movement of all black persons in the south prior to the Civil War, including organized posse systems for returning persons to their masters or homes and disciplining those who were insolent to whites or moved about without passes. At times, the operation of such "patroller" systems led to litigation. For if a slave was harmed unlawfully by patrollers, the master might sue for his losses. *See, e.g., Tate v. O'Neal*, 3 N.C. 220 (1821).

At different points in his opinion, Taney compared the status of black persons with Native Americans and with women and children. In brief, Taney contended that tribes were treated as "foreign nations" and that the members of these nations could be naturalized like citizens immigrating here from any other civilized nation. You might want to compare these sentiments with those of Chief Justice Marshall in *Johnson v. McIntosh*, p. 8 above, and *Worcester v. Georgia*, p. 36 above. Women, Taney noted, despite their inability to vote, were still members of the political community, while freed black persons were not. This suggests he would have been quite comfortable with the result in *Bradwell v. State of Illinois*, p. 163 above. The ways in which Taney carefully parsed the Constitutional status of various groups provides only a bare bones suggestion of the ways racial, ethnic, gender and class differences were pervasively used to justify various methods of social control.

As slavery and coverture waned after the Civil War, the search for new conceptions of citizenship and personhood became enormously complex. Development of constituent aspects of liberty, such as the right to contract for one's labor and to own property, were the first steps in removing from our jurisprudence the notion that persons of any sort may be owned lock, stock and barrel by any other person. In short, it was not obvious from our early culture that ownership of persons was unjust. In more recent times, that central idea—the inalienability of persons—has become the cornerstone of a new set of jurisprudential theories. Margaret Jane Radin is one of the most important creative spirits of personhood theory. An excerpt from one of her articles follows. Those interested in a more complete exposition of Radin's ideas should read her recently published book, CONTESTED COMMODITIES (1996).

Margaret Jane Radin, *Market Inalienability*
100 HARV. L. REV. 1849, 1903-1908 (1987)[31]

Noncommodification and an Ideal of Human Flourishing

1. Rethinking Personhood: Freedom, Identity, Contextuality.—Because of the ideological heritage of the subject/object dichotomy, we tend to view things internal to the person as inalienable and things external as freely alienable. Because of the ideological heritage of negative liberty, we also tend to think of inalienabilities as paternalistic. A better view of personhood, one that does not conceive of the self as pure subjectivity standing wholly separate from an environment of pure objectivity, should enable us to discard both the notion that inalienabilities relate only to things wholly subjective or internal and the notion that inalienabilities are paternalistic.

In searching for such a better view, it is useful to single out three main, overlapping aspects of personhood: freedom, identity, and contextuality. The freedom aspect of personhood focuses on will, or the power to choose for oneself. In order to be autonomous individuals, we must at least be able to act for ourselves through free will in relation to the environment of things and other people. The identity aspect of personhood focuses on the integrity and continuity of the self required for individuation. In order to have a unique individual identity, we must have selves that are integrated and continuous over time. The contextuality aspect of personhood focuses on the necessity of self-constitution in relation to the environment of things and other people. In order to be differentiated human persons, unique individuals, we must have relationship with the social and natural world.

A better view of personhood—a conception of human flourishing that is superior to the one implied by universal commodification—should present more satisfactory views of personhood in each of these three aspects. I am not seeking here to elaborate a complete view of personhood. Rather, I focus primarily on a certain view of contextuality and its consequences: the view that connections between the person and her environment are integral to personhood. I also suggest that to the extent we have already accepted certain views of freedom, identity, and contextuality, we are committed to a view of personhood that rejects universal commodification.

Universal commodification conceives of freedom as negative liberty, indeed as negative liberty in a narrow sense, construing freedom as the ability to trade everything in free markets. In this view, freedom is the ability to use the will to manipulate objects in order to yield the greatest monetizable value. Although negative liberty has had difficulty with the hypothetical problem of free choice to enslave oneself, even negative liberty can reject the general notion of commodification of persons: the person cannot be an entity exercising free will if it is a manipulable object of monetizable value.

A more positive meaning of freedom starts to emerge if one accepts the contextuality aspect of personhood. Contextuality means that physical and social contexts are integral to personal

---

[31] Copyright 1987 by the Harvard Law Review Association. Reprinted by permission of the Harvard Law Review Association and Margaret Jane Radin.

individuation, to self-development. Even under the narrowest conception of negative liberty, we would have to bring about the social environment that makes trade possible in order to become the persons whose freedom consists in unfettered trades of commodified objects. Under a broader negative view that conceives of freedom as the ability to make oneself what one will, contextuality implies that self-development in accordance with one's own will requires one to will certain interactions with the physical and social context because context can be integral to self-development. The relationship between personhood and context requires a positive commitment to act so as to create and maintain particular contexts of environment and community. Recognition of the need for such a commitment turns toward a positive view of freedom, in which the self-development of the individual is linked to pursuit of proper social development, and in which proper self-development, as a requirement of personhood, could in principle sometimes take precedence over one's momentary desires or preferences.

Universal commodification undermines personal identity by conceiving of personal attributes, relationships, and philosophical and moral commitments as monetizable and alienable from the self. A better view of personhood should understand many kinds of particulars—one's politics, work, religion, family, love, sexuality, friendships, altruism, experiences, wisdom, moral commitments, character, and personal attributes—as integral to the self. To understand any of these as monetizable or completely detachable from the person—to think, for example, that the value of one person's moral commitments is commensurate or fungible with those of another, or that the "same" person remains when her moral commitments are subtracted—is to do violence to our deepest understanding of what it is to be human.

To affirm that work, politics, or character is integral to the person is not to say that persons cease to be persons when they dissociate themselves from their jobs, political engagements, or personal attributes. Indeed, the ability to dissociate oneself from one's particular context seems integral to personhood. But if we must recognize the importance of the ability to detach oneself, we must recognize as well that interaction with physical and social contexts is also integral to personhood. One's surroundings—both people and things—can become part of who one is, of the self. From our understanding that attributes and things can be integral to personhood, which stems mainly from our understanding of identity and contextuality, and from our rejection of the idea of commodification of the person, which stems mainly from our understanding of freedom, it follows that those attributes and things identified with the person cannot be treated as completely commodified. Hence, market-inalienability may attach to things that are personal.

2. Protecting Personhood: Noncommodification of Personal Rights, Attributes, and Things.—. . .We are now in a better position to understand how conceiving of personal things as commodities does violence to personhood, and to explore the problem of knowing what things are personal.

. . . .

To conceive of something personal as fungible . . . assumes that persons cannot freely give of themselves to others. At best they can bestow commodities. At worst—in universal commodification—the gift is conceived of as a bargain. Conceiving of gifts as bargains not only conceives of what is personal as fungible, it also endorses the picture of persons as profit-maximizers. A better view of personhood should conceive of gifts not as disguised sales, but rather as expressions of the interrelationships between the self and others. To relinquish something to someone else by gift is to give of yourself. Such a gift takes place within a personal relationship with the recipient, or else it creates one. Commodification stresses separateness both between ourselves and our things and between ourselves and other people. To postulate personal interrelationship and communion requires us to postulate people who can yield personal things to other people and not have them instantly become fungible. Seen this way, gifts diminish separateness. This is why (to take an obvious example) people say that sex bought and paid for is not the same "thing" as sex freely shared. Commodified sex leaves the parties as separate individuals and perhaps reinforces their separateness; they only engage in it if each individual considers it worthwhile. Noncommodified sex ideally diminishes separateness; it is conceived of as a union because it is ideally a sharing of selves.

Not everything with which someone may subjectively identify herself should be treated legally or morally as personal. Otherwise the category of personal things might collapse into "consumer surplus": anything to which someone attached high subjective value would be personal. The question whether something is personal has a normative aspect: whether identifying oneself with something—constituting oneself in connection with that thing—is justifiable. What makes identifying oneself with something justifiable, in turn, is an appropriate connection to our conception of human flourishing. More specifically, such relationships are justified if they can form part of an appropriate understanding of freedom, identity, and contextuality. A proper understanding of contextuality, for example, must recognize that, although personhood is fostered by relations with people and things, it is possible to be involved too much, or in the wrong way, or with the wrong things.

To identify something as personal, it is not enough to observe that many people seem to identify with some particular kind of things, because we may judge such identification to be bad for people. An example of a justifiable kind of relationship is people's involvement with their homes. This relationship permits self-constitution within a stable environment. An example of an unjustifiable kind of relationship is the involvement of the robber baron with an empire of "property for power." The latter is unjustified because it ties into a conception of the person we can recognize as inferior: the person as self-interested maximizer of manipulative power.

There is no algorithm or abstract formula to tell us which items are (justifiably) personal. A moral judgment is required in each case.

[5]   The Post Civil War Era: The Transition to Freedom

In the years immediately after the Civil War, important alterations in the Constitutional and statutory status of black persons were adopted. The Thirteenth Amendment abolishing slavery was ratified in 1865. Shortly thereafter, the Civil Rights Act of 1866[32] passed Congress. This act declared that all persons born in the United States were citizens of the United States and that all citizens "of every race and color, without regard to any previous condition of slavery" had the "same right . . . to make and enforce contracts, to sue, be parties, and give evidence, to inherit, purchase, lease, sell, hold, and convey real and personal property . . . as is enjoyed by white citizens . . . ." During the Congressional debates on this act, doubts were expressed that the second section of the Thirteenth Amendment provided Congress with authority to pass the bill. President Andrew Johnson, whose veto of the bill was overridden by Congress, expressed the same point of view.

---

[32] An Act to Protect All Persons in the United States in Their Civil Rights, and Furnish the Means of Their Vindication, 14 Stat. 27 (1866). This act is currently codified at 42 U.S.C. §§ 1981, 1982 and 18 U.S.C. § 242. Section 1981 became the subject of *Jones v. Mayer*, discussed at p. 502 above.

Such expressions of doubt led Congress to draw up another amendment designed in part to validate the Civil Rights Act of 1866. The Fourteenth Amendment was passed by Congress and ratified by sufficient states by 1868. In 1870, the Fifteenth Amendment, or suffrage amendment, was ratified and Congress passed another civil rights act, mostly containing provisions enforcing the Fifteenth Amendment.[33] Further Civil Rights legislation was adopted in 1871 and 1875,[34] before the election of Hayes in the close election of 1876, and the withdrawal of Northern troops from the South shortly thereafter, ended the Reconstruction Era. Not until 1957 was another major piece of Civil Rights legislation adopted by Congress.

While the major civil rights debates were raging in Congress and state legislative halls after the Civil War, a number of lesser noted legal difficulties were appearing for black persons in their transition from slave to freed status. Since much of the normal legal structure was inapplicable to slaves, it was inevitable that the post-war era would create disputes over the status of slave marriages, the legitimacy of slave children, inheritance of property by slaves from blacks freed before the war was over, and countless other issues. The next case provides a brief glimpse at these sorts of problems.

[6] A Transition Case

Bristow Bugg v. Walter Towner

Georgia Supreme Court
41 Ga. 315 (1870)

Towner brought ejectment against Bugg. He showed by his deed and by his oath, that in 1855 he bought the lot, had been in possession from that date up to 1863, when he left the country, leaving Bugg, as his slave, in possession, with a promise to Bugg that no wages would be required from him if he would keep intruders off the place, keep it in good order and pay Towner's taxes till his return; that Bugg did not pay the taxes, nor keep said place in good order, and when he returned, after emancipation, refused to give him possession. It came out in evidence that Bugg furnished part of the money which paid his price when Towner bought him. The defense offered to show by Bugg and by admissions of Towner, that Bugg's former master was dead and Bugg was about to be sold and begged Towner to buy him, let him repay the price and then be actually free, though nominally Towner's slave; that Towner agreed to this, bought him and Bugg repaid the price, and that Towner agreed to buy this place for Bugg, let Bugg pay for it, and to hold the title for Bugg's benefit, and that Bugg did so pay for it and had occupied it as his own. All this testimony was ruled out, upon the ground that while Bugg was a slave he could not make a contract. The plaintiff had a verdict for the premises in dispute. Bugg moved for a new trial, because of the rejection of said evidence. The case hung fire, but finally a new trial was refused, and that is assigned as error.

The only description of Towner's deed in the bill of exceptions, was this: "Plaintiff then offered deed from Zemula Walker, dated December, 1855, to Walker Towner, made by attorney-in-fact,

---

[33] An Act to Enforce the Rights of Citizens of the United States to Vote in the Several States of this Union, and for Other Purposes, 16 Stat. 140 (1870).

[34] An Act to Enforce the Provisions of the Fourteenth Amendment to the Constitution of the United States, and for Other Purposes, 17 Stat. 13 (1871); An Act to Protect All Citizens in Their Civil and Legal Rights, 18 Stat. 335 (1875). Part of the 1871 legislation is now codified at 42 U.S.C. § 1983 and provides the statutory basis for a substantial number of cases now filed each year in the federal courts.

Joseph Burch. The power and the deed both offered and admitted by the Court in evidence, the deed being to the land in dispute." The certificate to the bill of exceptions was in the usual form. But the brief of evidence had never been agreed to by counsel, and the Judge had approved it in these words only: "I cannot be supposed to recollect the testimony (after a year's time) given in before me on the trial, yet I believe this brief is correct in substance. I know that all testimony going to prove a contract with a slave, as to freedom and purchasing land with proceeds of his labor, was ruled out by me on the trial." Defendant's counsel moved to dismiss the writ of error, because said deed was not copied in the bill of exceptions, and because the Judge had not certified that the evidence was correctly set forth. The motion was overruled.

By the Court—BROWN, C.J., delivering the opinion.

By the Act of 1818, Cobb's New Digest, page 991, every will, *deed*, contract, agreement or stipulation, or other instrument in writing, or by way of parol, whether by way of trust or otherwise, made for the purpose of effecting or endeavoring to effect the manumission of any slave or slaves, either directly, by conferring or attempting to confer freedom on such slave or slaves, or *indirectly*, or *virtually*, by allowing and securing, or attempting to allow or secure to such slave or slaves, the privilege of working for himself, free from the control of the owner, or enjoying the profits of his labor, are declared to be utterly *null* and *void.*

In this case, the defendant sought to attack the deed which was the foundation of plaintiff's title, by showing that it was made in aid of a contract between plaintiff and defendant, by which plaintiff, for a consideration, undertook to emancipate the defendant, who was then his slave, *in* this State, and to locate him upon the tract of land in dispute, which defendant alleges was paid for with his money, and the deed taken in the name of the plaintiff for his use and benefit, in furtherance of this illegal design. If such was the fact, and the defendant was placed in possession of the land by the plaintiff, with intent to evade the law and carry out the illegal purpose, we hold that the Courts of this State, under the rule repeatedly announced by this Court, will not aid plaintiff to recover the possession of the land from the defendant. If the defendant's version of the case is correct, the parties were engaged in an illegal transaction, in violation of the laws and public policy of this State, in existence at that time. And it makes no difference whether the illegal transaction is *malum prohibitum* or *malum in se.* In neither case will the Courts of this State interfere to grant relief to either party. But they will leave the parties where they find them, no matter whether the illegality of the contract appears from the plaintiff's case, or is set up by way of defense.

It is objected that the defendant should not be heard, to set up the illegality of the transaction for his own benefit. The reply is, that Courts sustain such a defense, not for the sake of the defendant, but upon general principles of public policy. In *Holman vs. Johnson*, Cowper 343, Lord Mansfield uses the following language, which has heretofore been approved and adopted by this court, as a correct statement of the rule on this subject:

"The objection that a contract is immoral or illegal, as between plaintiff and defendant, sounds at all times very ill in the mouth of the defendant. It is not for his sake, however, that the objection is ever allowed, but it is founded on general principles of policy, which the defendant has the advantage of, contrary to real justice, as between him and the plaintiff, by accident, if I may so say. The principle of public policy is this, *ex dolo malo non oritur actio.* No Court will lend its aid to a man upon an illegal or an immoral act. If from the plaintiff's own statement, or otherwise, the cause of action appears to arise *ex turpi causa*, or the transgression of a positive law of this country, then the Courts say he has no right to be assisted. It is upon that ground the Court goes, not for the sake of the defendant, but because it will not lend its aid to such a plaintiff. So if the plaintiff and defendant should change sides and the defendant were to bring his action against the plaintiff, the latter would then have the advantage of it, for where both are equally at fault, *potior est conditio defendentis*."

The object of the rule is to discourage and discountenance all illegal and immoral transactions, which violate sound public policy, and not to aid or favor *either party*. And we see no good reason why the defendant should not be heard to set up this defense to defeat the plaintiff's action. It matters not how the fact is brought to the attention of the Court; whenever it is ascertained, the law denies its aid to either party, it leaves them where it finds them, it closes its temples against them, and says, your "polluted hands shall not touch the pure fountains of justice."

We hold that the Court erred in this case, in ruling out the evidence, offered by the defendant, to show that this purchase was in fact made for his benefit, while he was a slave, and that the land was paid for in whole, or in part, by his money, and that he was placed in possession by the plaintiff in furtherance of such illegal transaction. We do not know how far the evidence, if admitted, would have gone to establish these facts; but, if it had been sufficient, we hold that plaintiff had no right to the assistance of the Court to recover the possession of the premises from the defendant.

Judgment reversed.

[7]   Explanatory Notes

[a]   *Bristow Bugg v. Walter Towner*

This case may also be viewed as a "pox on both your houses" dispute, save for the fact that the status quo left Bugg with possession of the land. The Court used a traditional equity rule by declining to enforce an *illegal* contract for the benefit of either party, thereby washing its hands of the whole affair. This *clean hands* approach may have a certain appeal in some settings, but it may also cause courts to ignore policy considerations that favor one party or another. For example, suppose in this case that Towner was in possession of the property and Bugg was the plaintiff. Should the emancipation of Bugg by the Thirteenth Amendment make it possible for him to enforce a previously illegal contract? Or should Bugg be able to use for his benefit another traditional rule of equity granting title to land to the person providing the funds for its purchase? Or perhaps another common property rule might be applicable; if you agree to sell something that you do not presently own, but come into ownership of it later, you will be obligated to transfer the asset to the party you previously agreed to sell it to. Rather than viewing the case as one involving an illegal contract, why not conceive of it as the disposition of an *after acquired* asset?

[b]   Other Examples of Transition Problems

Attempts of freed slaves to claim property of relatives freed before the general emancipation ran into the problem that slaves could not inherit any property. Even frauds committed by guardians of freed slaves did not always lead to successful claims by freed slaves. *Compare Munroe v. Phillips* 64 Ga. 32 (1879), *with Woods v. Pearce*, 68 Ga. 160 (1881). The interplay between intestate succession and legitimacy of children of slave marriages arose in *Gilbert v. Edwards*, 74 S.W. 959 (Civ. App. Tex. 1903); *Tobin v. Gentry*, 208 S.W. 325 (Ct. App. Ky. 1919); *Rankin v. Dunn*, 49 S.W.2d 1018 (Ct. App. Ky. 1932). Some states adopted statutes after the Civil War declaring certain slave marriages lawful and their offspring legitimate in an effort to cope with these problems. Related problems arose when relatives of deceased persons stayed on "family" land without any clear right to do so. Adverse possession problems arose in such cases. *See, e.g., Dingle v. Mitchell*, 20 S.C. 202 (1883).

The *Bugg* opinion, together with the other examples of transition problems explored in these notes, is indicative of both the harsh realities associated with denying persons the right to own property and the difficulties associated with providing new members of the political community with a basic set of legal tools. Agreements with slaves could be ignored without peril prior to emancipation and, as it turned out, agreements made with ex-slaves while they were in bondage could also be ignored without peril after emancipation. The impacts of slavery lasted far beyond the time period in which it was lawful.

§ 12.03 Rights in Personalities

[1] The Foundation of the Right to Publicity: *International News Service v. Associated Press*

[a] History of the Case

The Associated Press was founded in 1845 as a cooperative association of newspapers to gather and distribute descriptions of events to media in the United States. The recent invention of the telegraph had dramatically sped up distribution of news around the country. Newspaper publishers, unable individually to pay for the installation and management of widespread electronic networks, pooled their resources and formed Associated Press. Three sister news services were based in Europe—Wolff in Berlin, Reuters in London, and Havas in Paris.[35] These three had carved up much of the world into territories in which each had monopoly authority over news distribution. In fact, in 1893 Associated Press purchased from Reuters exclusive rights to cover news in the United States and its possessions. Associated Press was given the reciprocal right to use news releases wired to it by the three European organizations from their respective territories.[36]

On September 8, 1914, Melville Stone, the general manager of Associated Press, received a cable from *La Nación*, a major newspaper in Buenos Aires, asking for the text of German communiques and official news of World War I. Associated Press, restricted by its 1893 agreements with the European news services to gathering news in the United States, did not respond to the cable. *La Nación* then sought help from smaller American news agencies, including United Press Associations which, unrestrained by any agreements with the European news cartel, agreed to take on the South American paper as its client. Other breaches in the cartel followed. Shortly thereafter it collapsed and a number of American news services, including both the Associated Press and the International News Service, began to send news cables to the United States from the war theater.

The opening of the war theater to the news services was not complete. Wartime government censors still demanded control over the content of dispatches sent to the United States from the various countries at war in Europe. Indeed, American war authorities also exercised such control once our own troops became involved in the hostilities. Because of what the British government

---

[35] Kent Cooper, Barriers Down: The Story of the News Agency Epoch 6-7 (1942).
[36] *Id.* at 16-19.

termed "continued garbling of messages and breach of faith,"[37] International News Service was barred from obtaining any news or using cables running from England after November 17, 1916. The British censors accused International News Service of distributing unapproved stories. A number of other countries in Europe followed Britain's lead.

Despite the ban, International News Service continued sending dispatches on the war to its American newspapers as if nothing unusual had occurred. Shortly thereafter, Kent Cooper, Associated Press Traffic Chief, received a tip from a discharged employee of International News in Cleveland that one B.E. Cushing, a member of the staff of the *Cleveland News* (an Associated Press paper), was selling Associated Press war news to the International News Service. Cooper traveled to Cleveland, obtained affidavits confirming the story, and gave them to Melville Stone in the New York office of Associated Press. On January 4, 1917, Associated Press sued International News Service in the United States District Court for the Southern District of New York seeking to enjoin International News Service from appropriating the news from Associated Press.

The International News Service never denied the Cushing story. Indeed, it admitted it before the trial court.[38] Their strategy was to try to convince the trial court judge, Augustus N. Hand, that Associated Press was also less than an angelic enterprise.[39] International News Service took the position that their papers were free to take any fact published by an Associated Press paper as a "tip," confirm its veracity and send that fact out as a "new" story over its own wires, and that Associated Press, like International News Service, routinely operated in this fashion.

Prior to the invention of the telegraph and the investment of large sums of money on world wide news communication systems, newspapers routinely took news articles from other newspapers and republished them. It was the primary way that news spread across the country. Indeed, it was viewed by some as a compliment when their stories were picked up by other papers.[40] In hindsight it should not be surprising that the "tip" practice continued after the telegraph was invented and that, given the scope of investment in telegraph systems, disputes would eventually arise over the legitimacy of using "tips." Remember that newspapers were easily the primary medium of mass communication during World War I. Television was the subject matter of science fiction, radio was just emerging from the labs,[41] commercial airline flights became a reality only in the 1920s, and telephones and automobiles were luxury items. Cities each had many newspapers with bevies of hawkers in downtown streets. Competition for advertisers and buyers was fierce. Blaring headlines on front pages were frequently changed to reflect the latest "hot" stories. Shouts of "EXTRA! EXTRA! READ ALL ABOUT IT!" were part of the normal blare of urban life. The concept of "hot" news might seem strange to you, but it had its reality on the streets. Associated Press, which admitted that it followed the "tip"

---

[37] OLIVER GRAMLING, AP: THE STORY OF NEWS 285 (1940).

[38] Associated Press v. International News Service, 240 F. 983, 986 (S.D.N.Y. 1917). The Associated Press also had fairly convincing proof that at least two employees of the International News Service offices in New York regularly went to the offices of the New York American, an Associated Press paper, to read and copy war stories. *Id.* at 988.

[39] International News Service did argue that the news dispatches turned over to it by Cushing were rephrased before publication. That argument carried little weight with Hand, both because Cushing violated his obligations to his employer by cooperating with International News Service and because there was precious little evidence that the dispatches were in fact rewritten before they were reused.

[40] Gramling, note 37 above, at 285.

[41] The first commercial stations appeared in the early 1920s.

practice, apparently decided that creation of property rights in the volatile news business was important enough to risk the continued vitality of the nineteenth-century "tip" system.

There is evidence that Associated Press knew when it filed the case that it would be placed in the position of arguing against one of its own business practices. First, the "tip" system was widespread. Melville Stone, who caused the case to be filed, certainly knew that if he attempted to stop International News Service from using Associated Press news as "tips," the worm would turn.[42] Second, it was probably impossible for any single news service to stop the practice. If, for example, Associated Press stopped using other news service stories, they might lose customers to other services willing to continue the practice. Finally, Stone stated publicly that he wanted to establish a "property right" in news. He felt it was the only way to protect the news service industry. Earlier attempts to use the copyright statutes to grant protection to news had failed.[43] Stone's focus on the need for "property right" protection led him to ignore the potential benefits of the revisions made to the United States Copyright Law in 1909.[44] While the factual content of news stories was still not protected by copyright, the expressive content could not be copied. Thus, the Copyright Act of 1909 let the "tip" practice continue while providing a basis for controlling the plagiarism of previously published stories.

Judge Hand, perhaps like any sensible judge, found the case difficult. He posed the issues like this:

> It is evident. . .that both sides think news, *when published* by any subscribers to a competing news agency, may properly be investigated, and, if verified, the result of the verification may be sold. . . . [T]he real matter for consideration is whether news gathered and sold to a newspaper, which publishes it, can be used after publication by a competing news agency, either as a tip for further investigation or as authentic news for immediate distribution before sufficient time has elapsed for the news to be published within the territory in which the gatherer is engaged in the general dissemination of news.[45]

Hand agreed with Associated Press that news was the product of the labor and capital of the gatherer, and that its use by others for any purpose, whether as a "tip" or as a story, deprived the gatherer "of the very thing which is of value to him, namely the power to control the sale of the news he has gathered until sufficient time has elapsed to enable it to be published by

[42] In fact, Associated Press had previously been involved in litigation of this sort. At the turn of the century, it was sued by the Tribune Company of Chicago. The Tribune failed in this case to stop Associated Press from cabling Tribune stories to its member papers. Tribune Company of Chicago v. Associated Press, 116 F. 126 (C.C.N.D. Ill. 1900). The case, however, was brought on a copyright theory, an issue not raised by Associated Press in its case against International News Service.

[43] A very old case had held that newspapers could not be copyrighted. Clayton v. Stone, 5 F. Cas. 999 (C.C.S.D.N.Y. 1829) (No. 2,872). Efforts to reverse that result in Congress were made in the 1890s, but legislation was never adopted. Clayton v. Stone was reaffirmed in the courts at the turn of the twentieth century, both in a newspaper context (Tribune Company of Chicago v. Associated Press, 116 F. 126 (C.C.N.D. Ill. 1900)), and in a wire service context (National Telegraph News Company v. Western Union Telegraph Company, 119 F. 294 (7th Cir. 1902)). Only after International News Service v. Associated Press was decided by the United States Supreme Court (the opinion following this historical segment), did opinions begin to appear affirming the copyrightability of the expressive, but not factual, content of articles appearing in newspapers. An example was Chicago Record-Herald Company v. Tribune Association, 275 F. 797 (7th Cir. 1921). Such results permitted the facts of a story to be reprinted elsewhere, but not the way in which the facts were expressed in the article. Protection of expressive content of newspapers was also given support by the adoption of a complete revision of the federal copyright statute in 1909.

[44] Section 5(b) of that Act made specific reference to newspapers as copyrightable.

[45] Associated Press v. International News Service, 240 F. 983, 991-992 (S.D.N.Y. 1917).

all the newspapers he supplies."[46] But Hand only enjoined International News Service from abstracting Associated Press News *before* its publication by an Associated Press paper. The "tip"—or reuse of published news—issue,[47] he felt, was one of first impression, and not so clear cut that he was free to grant an injunction against its continued use.[48]

Note well how the original dispute had become transformed by the time Hand issued his opinion on March 29, 1917. What was filed as a test case over the use of "tips" had become buried in a procedural dispute about the propriety of issuing a preliminary injunction. There will be more on injunctions in the notes following the *Associated Press* opinion. For now, simply note that a court may justifiably hesitate to stop a litigant from behaving in a certain way while a case is pending if there is doubt about who will eventually win the case. The procedural debate also served to hide a tense relationship between the major players. There is significant evidence that Melville Stone, the head of Associated press, and William Randolph Hearst, the head of International News Service, did not get along. It is hard to believe that Stone was upset when his employee, Kent Cooper, brought him affidavits confirming that International News Service was using Associated Press stories.

Hearst was actually in a very strange position. While he had helped create the International News Service, he was also the largest subscriber to the Associated Press. Over the years many of his newspapers paid millions for its services. Nonetheless some of his papers could not gain membership in the Associated Press because of organizational rules requiring 80% yes votes for the admission of any paper in competition with an existing member. Partially in response to this system, Hearst set up his own news service for his papers. In any case, Hearst thought Stone had an "obsession" with the notion of creating a "property right" in news, and insisted that the whole matter could have been resolved short of litigation if Stone had only talked to Hearst about the matter. Hearst even argued that the final result of the case in the United States Supreme Court was favorable to his position against a "property right" in news. Stone, of course, disagreed.[49] Perhaps the final decision on who "won" the case should be left up to you.[50]

---

[46] *Id.* at 991.

[47] Hand actually saw no difference between using news as a "tip" or as a story. Since stories could be rapidly confirmed with electronic technology, the economic effects of the two uses of news were no different. But the newness of the issue led him to be cautious about issuing an injunction.

[48] *Id.* at 996.

[49] There is a certain irony in this whole situation, since Hearst himself used the Associated Press rules when it was to his advantage against papers competing in areas where he owned Associated Press publication. KENT COOPER, KENT COOPER AND THE ASSOCIATED PRESS: AN AUTOBIOGRAPHY 195-199 (1959).

[50] Before getting to the United States Supreme Court, the dispute traveled through the United States Circuit Court of Appeals for the Second Circuit, sitting in New York. Both sides appealed, International News Service from the order barring it from abstracting news stories prior to their publication and Associated Press from Judge Hand's refusal to enjoin the use of stories after publication. No particularly interesting new facts emerged from the opinion of that court, Associated Press v. International News Service, 245 F. 244 (2d Cir. 1917), although some of its reasoning will be referred to in the notes at the end of the Supreme Court opinion. The Second Circuit opinion was rendered on June 21. The case, as you can see, moved fairly rapidly through the courts. It was viewed as an important matter.

[b] United States Supreme Court Opinions in *International News Service v. Associated Press*

International News Service v. Associated Press

United States Supreme Court
248 U.S. 215, 39 S. Ct. 68, 63 L. Ed. 211 (1918)

Mr. Justice Pitney delivered the opinion of the court.

The parties are competitors in the gathering and distribution of news and its publication for profit in newspapers throughout the United States. The Associated Press, which was complainant in the District Court, is a cooperative organization, incorporated under the Membership Corporations Law of the State of New York, its members being individuals who are either proprietors or representatives of about 950 daily newspapers published in all parts of the United States.

. . . Complainant gathers in all parts of the world, by means of various instrumentalities of its own, by exchange with its members, and by other appropriate means, news and intelligence of current and recent events of interest to newspaper readers and distributes it daily to its members for publication in their newspapers. The cost of the service, amounting approximately to $3,500,000 per annum, is assessed upon the members and becomes a part of their costs of operation, to be recouped, presumably with profit, through the publication of their several newspapers. Under complainant's by-laws each member agrees upon assuming membership that news received through complainant's service is received exclusively for publication in a particular newspaper, language, and place specified in the certificate of membership, that no other use of it shall be permitted, and that no member shall furnish or permit anyone in his employ or connected with his newspaper to furnish any of complainant's news in advance of publication to any person not a member. And each member is required to gather the local news of his district and supply it to the Associated Press and to no one else.

Defendant is a corporation organized under the laws of the State of New Jersey, whose business is the gathering and selling of news to its customers and clients, consisting of newspapers published throughout the United States, under contracts by which they pay certain amounts at stated times for defendant's service. It has wide-spread news-gathering agencies; the cost of its operations amounts, it is said, to more than $2,000,000 per annum; and it serves about 400 newspapers located in the various cities of the United States and abroad, a few of which are represented, also, in the membership of the Associated Press.

The parties are in the keenest competition between themselves in the distribution of news throughout the United States; and so, as a rule, are the newspapers that they serve, in their several districts.

. . . .

The bill was filed to restrain the pirating of complainant's news by defendant in three ways: First, by bribing employees of newspapers published by complainant's members to furnish Associated Press news to defendant before publication, for transmission by telegraph and telephone to defendant's clients for publication by them; Second, by inducing Associated Press members to violate its by-laws and permit defendant to obtain news before publication; and Third, by copying news from bulletin boards and from early editions of complainant's newspapers and selling this, either bodily or after rewriting it, to defendant's customers.

The District Court, upon consideration of the bill and answer, with voluminous affidavits on both sides, granted a preliminary injunction under the first and second heads; but refused at that stage to restrain the systematic practice admittedly pursued by defendant, of taking news bodily from the bulletin boards and early editions of complainant's newspapers and selling it as its own. The court expressed itself as satisfied that this practice amounted to unfair trade, but as the legal question was one of first impression it considered that the allowance of an injunction should await the outcome of an appeal. Both parties having appealed, the Circuit Court of Appeals sustained the injunction order so far as it went, and upon complainant's appeal modified it and remanded the cause with directions to issue an injunction also against any bodily taking of the words or substance of complainant's news until its commercial value as news had passed away. The present writ of certiorari was then allowed.

The only matter that has been argued before us is whether defendant may lawfully be restrained from appropriating news taken from bulletins issued by complainant or any of its members, or from newspapers published by them, for the purpose of selling it to defendant's clients. Complainant asserts that defendant's admitted course of conduct in this regard both violates complainant's property right in the news and constitutes unfair competition in business. And notwithstanding the case has proceeded only to the stage of a preliminary injunction, we have deemed it proper to consider the underlying questions, since they go to the very merits of the action and are presented upon facts that are not in dispute. As presented in argument, these questions are: 1. Whether there is any property in news; 2. Whether, if there be property in news collected for the purpose of being published, it survives the instant of its publication in the first newspaper to which it is communicated by the news-gatherer; and 3. Whether defendant's admitted course of conduct in appropriating for commercial use matter taken from bulletins or early editions of Associated Press publications constitutes unfair competition in trade.

The federal jurisdiction was invoked because of diversity of citizenship, not upon the ground that the suit arose under the copyright or other laws of the United States. Complainant's news matter is not copyrighted. It is said that it could not, in practice, be copyrighted, because of the large number of dispatches that are sent daily; and, according to complainant's contention, news is not within the operation of the copyright act. Defendant, while apparently conceding this, nevertheless invokes the analogies of the law of literary property and copyright, insisting as its principal contention that, assuming complainant has a right of property in its news, it can be maintained (unless the copyright act be complied with) only by being kept secret and confidential, and that upon the publication with complainant's consent of uncopyrighted news by any of complainant's members in a newspaper or upon a bulletin board, the right of property is lost, and the subsequent use of the news by the public or by defendant for any purpose whatever becomes lawful.

. . . .

In considering the general question of property in news matter, it is necessary to recognize its dual character, distinguishing between the substance of the information and the particular form or collocation of words in which the writer has communicated it.

No doubt news articles often possess a literary quality, and are the subject of literary property at the common law; nor do we question that such an article, as a literary production, is the subject of copyright by the terms of the act as it now stands. In an early case at the circuit Mr. Justice Thompson held in effect that a newspaper was not within the protection of the copyright acts of 1790 and 1802 (*Clayton v. Stone*, 2 Paine, 382; 5 Fed. Cas. No. 2872). But the present act is broader; it provides that the works for which copyright may be secured shall include "all the writings of an author," and specifically mentions "periodicals, including newspapers." Act of March 4, 1909, c. 320, §§ 4 and 5. Evidently this admits to copyright a contribution to a newspaper, notwithstanding it also may convey news; and such is the practice of the copyright office, as the newspapers of the day bear witness.

But the news element—the information respecting current events contained in the literary production—is not the creation of the writer, but is a report of matters that ordinarily are *publici juris*; it is the history of the day. It is not to be supposed that the framers of the Constitution, when they empowered Congress "to promote the progress of science and useful arts, by securing for limited times to authors and inventors the exclusive right to their respective writings and discoveries" (Const., Art I, § 8, par. 8), intended to confer upon one who might happen to be the first to report a historic event the exclusive right for any period to spread the knowledge of it.

We need spend no time, however, upon the general question of property in news matter at common law, or the application of the copyright act, since it seems to us the case must turn upon the question of unfair competition in business. And, in our opinion, this does not depend upon any general right of property analogous to the common-law right of the proprietor of an unpublished work to prevent its publication without his consent; nor is it foreclosed by showing that the benefits of the copyright act have been waived. We are dealing here not with restrictions upon publication but with the very facilities and processes of publication. The peculiar value of news is in the spreading of it while it is fresh; and it is evident that a valuable property interest in the news, as news, cannot be maintained by keeping it secret. Besides, except for matters improperly disclosed, or published in breach of trust or confidence, or in violation of law, none of which is involved in this branch of the case, the news of current events may be regarded as common property. What we are concerned with is the business of making it known to the world, in which both parties to the present suit are engaged. That business consists in maintaining a prompt, sure, steady, and reliable service designed to place the daily events of the world at the breakfast table of the millions at a price that, while of trifling moment to each reader, is sufficient in the aggregate to afford compensation for the cost of gathering and distributing it, with the added profit so necessary as an incentive to effective action in the commercial world. The service thus performed for newspaper readers is not only innocent but extremely useful in itself, and indubitably constitutes a legitimate business. The parties are competitors in this field; and, on fundamental principles, applicable here as elsewhere, when the rights or privileges of the one are liable to conflict with those of the other, each party is under a duty so to conduct its own business as not unnecessarily or unfairly to injure that of the other.

Obviously, the question of what is unfair competition in business must be determined with particular reference to the character and circumstances of the business. The question here is not so much the rights of either party as against the public but their rights as between themselves. And although we may and do assume that neither party has any remaining property interest as against the public in uncopyrighted news matter after the moment of its first publication, it by no means follows that there is no remaining property interest in it as between themselves. For, to both of them alike, news matter, however little susceptible of ownership or dominion in the absolute sense, is stock in trade, to be gathered at the cost of enterprise, organization, skill, labor, and money, and to be distributed and sold to those who will pay money for it, as for any other merchandise. Regarding the news, therefore, as but the material out of which both parties are seeking to make profits at the same time and in the same field, we hardly can fail to recognize that for this purpose, and as between them, it must be regarded as *quasi* property, irrespective of the rights of either as against the public.

In order to sustain the jurisdiction of equity over the controversy, we need not affirm any general and absolute property in the news as such. The rule that a court of equity concerns itself only in the protection of property rights treats any civil right of a pecuniary nature as a property right; and the right to acquire property by honest labor or the conduct of a lawful business is as much entitled to protection as the right to guard property already acquired. It is this right that furnishes the basis of the jurisdiction in the ordinary case of unfair competition.

The question, whether one who has gathered general information or news at pains and expense for the purpose of subsequent publication through the press has such an interest in its publication as may be protected from interference, has been raised many times, although never, perhaps, in the precise form in which it is now presented.

Board of Trade v. Christie Grain & Stock Co., 198 U.S. 236, 250, related to the distribution of quotations of prices on dealings upon a board of trade, which were collected by plaintiff and communicated on confidential terms to numerous persons under a contract not to make them public. This court held that, apart from certain special objections that were overruled, plaintiff's collection of quotations was entitled to the protection of the law; that, like a trade secret, plaintiff might keep to itself the work done at its expense, and did not lose its right by communicating the result to persons, even if many, in confidential relations to itself, under a contract not to make it public; and that strangers should be restrained from getting at the knowledge by inducing a breach of trust.

In *National Tel. News Co. v. Western Union Tel. Co.*, 119 Fed. Rep. 294, the Circuit Court of Appeals for the Seventh Circuit dealt with news matter gathered and transmitted by a telegraph company, and consisting merely of a notation of current events having but a transient value due to quick transmission and distribution; and, while declaring that this was not copyrightable although printed on a tape by tickers in the offices of the recipients, and that it was a commercial not a literary product, nevertheless held that the business of gathering and communicating the news—the service of purveying it—was a legitimate business, meeting a distinctive commercial want and adding to the facilities of the business world, and partaking of the nature of property in a sense that entitled it to the protection of a court of equity against piracy.

Other cases are cited, but none that we deem it necessary to mention.

Not only do the acquisition and transmission of news require elaborate organization and a large expenditure of money, skill, and effort; not only has it an exchange value to the gatherer, dependent chiefly upon its novelty and freshness, the regularity of the service, its reputed reliability and thoroughness, and its adaptability to the public needs; but also, as is evident, the news has an exchange value to one who can misappropriate it.

The peculiar features of the case arise from the fact that, while novelty and freshness form so important an element in the success of the business, the very processes of distribution and publication necessarily occupy a good deal of time. Complainant's service, as well as defendant's, is a daily service to daily newspapers; most of the foreign news reaches this country at the Atlantic seaboard, principally at the City of New York, and because of this, and of time differentials due to the earth's rotation, the distribution of news matter throughout the country is principally from east to west; and, since in speed the telegraph and telephone easily outstrip the rotation of the earth, it is a simple matter for defendant to take complainant's news from bulletins or early editions of complainant's members in the eastern cities and at the mere cost of telegraphic transmission cause it to be published in western papers issued at least as early as those served by complainant. Besides this, and irrespective of time differential, irregularities in telegraphic transmission on different lines, and the normal consumption of time in printing and distributing the newspaper, result in permitting pirated news to be placed in the hands of defendant's readers sometimes simultaneously with the service of competing Associated Press papers, occasionally even earlier.

Defendant insists that when, with the sanction and approval of complainant, and as the result of the use of its news for the very purpose for which it is distributed, a portion of complainant's members communicate it to the general public by posting it upon bulletin boards so that all may read, or by issuing it to newspapers and distributing it indiscriminately, complainant no longer has the right to control the use to be made of it; that when it thus reaches the light of day it becomes the common possession of all to whom it is accessible; and that any purchaser of a newspaper has the right to communicate the intelligence which it contains to anybody and for any purpose, even for the purpose of selling it for profit to newspapers published for profit in competition with complainant's members.

The fault in the reasoning lies in applying as a test the right of the complainant as against the public, instead of considering the rights of complainant and defendant, competitors in business, as between themselves. The right of the purchaser of a single newspaper to spread knowledge of its contents gratuitously, for any legitimate purpose not unreasonably interfering with complainant's right to make merchandise of it, may be admitted; but to transmit that news for commercial use, in competition with complainant—which is what defendant has done and seeks to justify—is a very different matter. In doing this defendant, by its very act, admits that it is taking material that has been acquired by complainant as the result of organization and the expenditure of labor, skill, and money, and which is salable by complainant for money, and that defendant in appropriating it and selling it as its own is endeavoring to reap where it has not sown, and by disposing of it to newspapers that are competitors of complainant's members is appropriating to itself the harvest of those who have sown. Stripped of all disguises, the process amounts to an unauthorized interference with the normal operation of complainant's legitimate business precisely at the point where the profit is to be reaped, in order to divert a material portion of the profit from those who have earned it to those who have not; with special advantage to defendant in the competition because of the fact that it is not burdened with any part of the expense of gathering the news. The transaction speaks for itself, and a court of equity ought not to hesitate long in characterizing it as unfair competition in business.

The underlying principle is much the same as that which lies at the base of the equitable theory of consideration in the law of trusts—that he who has fairly paid the price should have the beneficial use of the property. It is no answer to say that complainant spends its money for that which is too fugitive or evanescent to be the subject of property. That might, and for the purposes of the discussion we are assuming that it would, furnish an answer in a common-law controversy. But in a court of equity, where the question is one of unfair competition, if that which complainant has acquired fairly at substantial cost may be sold fairly at substantial profit, a competitor who is misappropriating it for the purpose of disposing of it to his own profit and to the disadvantage of complainant cannot be heard to say that it is too fugitive or evanescent to be regarded as property. It has all the attributes of property necessary for determining that a misappropriation of it by a competitor is unfair competition because contrary to good conscience.

The contention that the news is abandoned to the public for all purposes when published in the first newspaper is untenable. Abandonment is a question of intent, and the entire organization of the Associated Press negatives such a purpose. The cost of the service would be prohibitive if the reward were to be so limited. No single newspaper, no small group of newspapers, could sustain the expenditure. Indeed, it is one of the most obvious results of defendant's theory that, by permitting indiscriminate publication by anybody and everybody for purposes of profit in competition with the news-gatherer, it would render publication profitless, or so little profitable as in effect to cut off the service by rendering the cost prohibitive in comparison with the return. The practical needs and requirements of the business are reflected in complainant's by-laws which have been referred to. Their effect is that publication by each member must be deemed not by any means an abandonment of the news to the world for any and all purposes, but a publication for limited purposes; for the benefit of the readers of the bulletin or the newspaper as such; not for the purpose of making merchandise of it as news, with the result of depriving complainant's other members of their reasonable opportunity to obtain just returns for their expenditures.

It is to be observed that the view we adopt does not result in giving to complainant the right to monopolize either the gathering or the distribution of the news, or, without complying with the copyright act, to prevent the reproduction of its news articles; but only postpones participation by complainant's competitor in the processes of distribution and reproduction of news that it has not gathered, and only to the extent necessary to prevent that competitor from reaping the fruits of complainant's efforts and expenditure, to the partial exclusion of complainant, and in violation of the principle that underlies the maxim *sic utere tuo*, etc.

It is said that the elements of unfair competition are lacking because there is no attempt by defendant to palm off its goods as those of the complainant, characteristic of the most familiar, if not the most typical, cases of unfair competition. But we cannot concede that the right to equitable relief is confined to that class of cases. In the present case the fraud upon complainant's rights is more direct and obvious. Regarding news matter as the mere material from which these two competing parties are endeavoring to make money, and treating it, therefore, as *quasi* property for the purposes of their business because they are both selling it as such, defendant's conduct differs from the ordinary case of unfair competition in trade principally in this that, instead of selling its own goods as those of complainant, it substitutes misappropriation in the place of misrepresentation, and sells complainant's goods as its own.

Besides the misappropriation, there are elements of imitation, of false pretense, in defendant's practices. The device of rewriting complainant's news articles, frequently resorted to, carries its own comment. The habitual failure to give credit to complainant for that which is taken is significant. Indeed, the entire system of appropriating complainant's news and transmitting it as a commercial product to defendant's clients and patrons amounts to a false representation to them and to their newspaper readers that the news transmitted is the result of defendant's own investigation in the field. But these elements, although accentuating the wrong, are not the essence of it. It is something more than the advantage of celebrity of which complainant is being deprived.

The doctrine of unclean hands is invoked as a bar to relief; it being insisted that defendant's practices against which complainant seeks an injunction are not different from the practice attributed to complainant, of utilizing defendant's news published by its subscribers. At this point it becomes necessary to consider a distinction that is drawn by complainant, and, as we understand it, was recognized by defendant also in the submission of proofs in the District Court, between two kinds of use that may be made by one news agency of news taken from the bulletins and newspapers of the other. The first is the bodily appropriation of a statement of fact or a news article, with or without rewriting, but without independent investigation or other expense. This form of pirating was found by both courts to have been pursued by defendant systematically with respect to complainant's news, and against it the Circuit Court of Appeals granted an injunction. This practice complainant denies having pursued, and the denial was sustained by the finding of the District Court. It is not contended by defendant that the finding can be set aside, upon the proofs as they now stand. The other use is to take the news of a rival agency as a "tip" to be investigated, and if verified by independent investigation the news thus gathered is sold. This practice complainant admits that it has pursued and still is willing that defendant shall employ.

. . . .

As to securing "tips" from a competing news agency, the District Court, while not sanctioning the practice, found that both parties had adopted it in accordance with common business usage, in the belief that their conduct was technically lawful, and hence did not find in it any sufficient ground for attributing unclean hands to complainant. The Circuit Court of Appeals found that the tip habit, though discouraged by complainant, was "incurably journalistic," and that there was "no difficulty in discriminating between the utilization of 'tips' and the bodily appropriation of another's labor in accumulating and stating information."

We are inclined to think a distinction may be drawn between the utilization of tips and the bodily appropriation of news matter, either in its original form or after rewriting and without independent investigation and verification; whatever may appear at the final hearing, the proofs as they now stand recognize such a distinction; both parties avowedly recognize the practice of taking tips, and neither party alleges it to be unlawful or to amount to unfair competition in business.

. . . .

In the case before us, in the present state of the pleadings and proofs, we need go no further than to hold, as we do, that the admitted pursuit by complainant of the practice of taking news items published by defendant's subscribers as tips to be investigated, and, if verified, the result of the investigation to be sold—the practice having been followed by defendant also, and by news agencies generally—is not shown to be such as to constitute an unconscientious or inequitable attitude towards its adversary so as to fix upon complainant the taint of unclean hands, and debar it on this ground from the relief to which it is otherwise entitled.

There is some criticism of the injunction that was directed by the District Court upon the going down of the mandate from the Circuit Court of Appeals. In brief, it restrains any taking or gainfully using of the complainant's news, either bodily or in substance, from bulletins issued by the complainant or any of its members, or from editions of their newspapers, *"until its commercial value as news to the complainant and all of its members has passed away."* The part complained of is the clause we have italicized; but if this be indefinite, it is no more so than the criticism. Perhaps it would be better that the terms of the injunction be made specific, and so framed as to confine the restraint to an extent consistent with the reasonable protection of complainant's newspapers, each in its own area and for a specified time after its publication, against the competitive use of pirated news by defendant's customers. But the case presents practical difficulties; and we have not the materials, either in the way of a definite suggestion of amendment, or in the way of proofs, upon which to frame a specific injunction; hence, while not expressing approval of the form adopted by the District Court, we decline to modify it at this preliminary stage of the case, and will leave that court to deal with the matter upon appropriate application made to it for the purpose.

The decree of the Circuit Court of Appeals will be

Affirmed.

MR. JUSTICE HOLMES, concurring:

When an uncopyrighted combination of words is published there is no general right to forbid other people repeating them—in other words there is no property in the combination or in the thoughts or facts that the words express. Property, a creation of law, does not arise from value, although exchangeable—a matter of fact. Many exchangeable values may be destroyed intentionally without compensation. Property depends upon exclusion by law from interference, and a person is not excluded from using any combination of words merely because someone has used it before, even if it took labor and genius to make it. If a given person is to be prohibited from making the use of words that his neighbors are free to make some other ground must be found. One such ground is vaguely expressed in the phrase unfair trade. This means that the words are repeated by a competitor in business in such a way as to convey a misrepresentation that materially injures the person who first used them, by appropriating credit of some kind which the first user has earned. The ordinary case is a representation by device, appearance, or other indirection that the defendant's goods come from the plaintiff. But the only reason why it is actionable to make such a representation is that it tends to give the defendant an advantage in his competition with the plaintiff and that it is thought undesirable that an advantage should be gained in that way. Apart from that the defendant may use such unpatented devices and uncopyrighted combinations of words as he likes. The ordinary case, I say, is palming off the defendant's product as the plaintiff's but the same evil may follow from the opposite falsehood— from saying, whether in words or by implication, that the plaintiff's product is the defendant's, and that, it seems to me, is what has happened here.

Fresh news is got only by enterprise and expense. To produce such news as it is produced by the defendant represents by implication that it has been acquired by the defendant's enterprise and at its expense. When it comes from one of the great news-collecting agencies like the Associated Press, the source generally is indicated, plainly importing that credit; and that such a representation is implied may be inferred with some confidence from the unwillingness of the defendant to give the credit and tell the truth. If the plaintiff produces the news at the same time that the defendant does, the defendant's presentation impliedly denies to the plaintiff the credit of collecting the facts and assumes that credit to the defendant. If the plaintiff is later in western cities it naturally will be supposed to have obtained its information from the defendant. The falsehood is a little more subtle, the injury a little more indirect, than in ordinary cases of unfair trade, but I think that the principle that condemns the one condemns the other. It is a question of how strong an infusion of fraud is necessary to turn a flavor into a poison. The dose seems to me strong enough here to need a remedy from the law. But as, in my view, the only ground of complaint that can be recognized without legislation is the implied misstatement, it can be corrected by stating the truth; and a suitable acknowledgment of the source is all that the plaintiff can require. I think that within the limits recognized by the decision of the Court the defendant should be enjoined from publishing news obtained from the Associated Press for hours after publication by the plaintiff unless it gives express credit to the Associated Press; the number of hours and the form of acknowledgment to be settled by the District Court.

MR. JUSTICE MCKENNA concurs in this opinion.

MR. JUSTICE BRANDEIS dissenting.

There are published in the United States about 2,500 daily papers. More than 800 of them are supplied with domestic and foreign news of general interest by the Associated Press—a corporation without capital stock which does not sell news or earn or seek to earn profits, but serves merely as an instrumentality by means of which these papers supply themselves at joint expense with such news. Papers not members of the Associated Press depend for their news of general interest largely upon agencies organized for profit.[2] Among these agencies is the International News Service which supplies news to about 400 subscribing papers. It has, like the Associated Press, bureaus and correspondents in this and foreign countries; and its annual expenditure in gathering and distributing news is about $2,000,000. Ever since its organization in 1909, it has included among the sources from which it gathers news, copies (purchased in the open market) of early editions of some papers published by members of the Associated Press and the bulletins publicly posted by them. These items, which constitute but a small part of the news transmitted to its subscribers, are generally verified by the International News Service before transmission; but frequently items are transmitted without verification; and occasionally even without being re-written. In no case is the fact disclosed that such item was suggested by or taken from a paper or bulletin published by an Associated Press Member.

No question of statutory copyright is involved. The sole question for our consideration is this: Was the International News Service properly enjoined from using, or causing to be used gainfully, news of which it acquired knowledge by lawful means (namely, by reading publicly posted bulletins or papers purchased by it in the open market) merely because the news had been originally gathered by the Associated Press and continued to be of value to some of its members, or because it did not reveal the source from which it was acquired?

The "ticker" cases, the cases concerning literary and artistic compositions, and cases of unfair competition were relied upon in support of the injunction. But it is admitted that none of those cases affords a complete analogy with that before us. The question presented for decision is new; and it is important.

News is a report of recent occurrences. The business of the news agency is to gather systematically knowledge of such occurrences of interest and to distribute reports thereof. The Associated Press contended that knowledge so acquired is property, because it costs money and labor to produce and because it has value for which those who have it not are ready to pay; that it remains property and is entitled to protection as long as it has commercial value as news; and that to protect it effectively the defendant must be enjoined from making, or causing to be made, any gainful use of it while it retains such value. An essential element of individual property is the legal right to exclude others from enjoying it. If the property is private, the right of exclusion may be absolute; if the property is affected with a public interest, the right of exclusion is

---

[2] *The Associated Press*, by Frank B. Noyes, Sen. Doc. No. 27, 63d Cong., 1st sess. In a brief filed in this court by counsel for the Associated Press the number of its members is stated to be 1030. Some members of the Associated Press are also subscribers to the International News Service.

Strictly the member is not the publishing concern, but an individual who is the sole or part owner of a newspaper, or an executive officer of a company which owns one. By-laws, Article II, § 1.

qualified. But the fact that a product of the mind has cost its producer money and labor, and has a value for which others are willing to pay, is not sufficient to ensure to it this legal attribute of property. The general rule of law is, that the noblest of human productions—knowledge, truths ascertained, conceptions, and ideas—become, after voluntary communication to others, free as the air to common use. Upon these incorporeal productions the attribute of property is continued after such communication only in certain classes of cases where public policy has seemed to demand it. These exceptions are confined to productions which, in some degree, involve creation, invention, or discovery. But by no means all such are endowed with this attribute of property. The creations which are recognized as property by the common law are literary, dramatic, musical, and other artistic creations; and these have also protection under the copyright statutes. The inventions and discoveries upon which this attribute of property is conferred only by statute, are the few comprised within the patent law. There are also many other cases in which courts interfere to prevent curtailment of plaintiff's enjoyment of incorporeal productions; and in which the right to relief is often called a property right, but is such only in a special sense. In those cases, the plaintiff has no absolute right to the protection of his production; he has merely the qualified right to be protected as against the defendant's acts, because of the special relation in which the latter stands or the wrongful method or means employed in acquiring the knowledge or the manner in which it is used. Protection of this character is afforded where the suit is based upon breach of contract or of trust or upon unfair competition.

The knowledge for which protection is sought in the case at bar is not of a kind upon which the law has heretofore conferred the attributes of property; nor is the manner of its acquisition or use nor the purpose to which it is applied, such as has heretofore been recognized as entitling a plaintiff to relief.

First: Plaintiff's principal reliance was upon the "ticker" cases; but they do not support its contention. The leading cases on this subject rest the grant of relief, not upon the existence of a general property right in news, but upon the breach of a contract or trust concerning the use of news communicated; and that element is lacking here. In *Board of Trade v. Christie Grain & Stock Co.*, 198 U.S. 236, 250, the court said the Board "does not lose its rights by communicating the result [the quotations] to persons, even if many, in confidential relations to itself, under a contract not to make it public, and strangers to the trust will be restrained from getting at the knowledge by inducing a breach of trust and using knowledge obtained by such a breach."

. . . .

If the news involved in the case at bar had been posted in violation of any agreement between the Associated Press and its members, questions similar to those in the "ticker" cases might have arisen. But the plaintiff does not contend that the posting was wrongful or that any papers were wrongfully issued by its subscribers. On the contrary it is conceded that both the bulletins and the papers were issued in accordance with the regulations of the plaintiff. Under such circumstances, for a reader of the papers purchased in the open market, or a reader of the bulletins publicly posted, to procure and use gainfully, information therein contained, does not involve inducing anyone to commit a breach either of contract or of trust, or committing or in any way abetting a breach of confidence.

Second: Plaintiff also relied upon the cases which hold that the common-law right of the producer to prohibit copying is not lost by the private circulation of a literary composition, the delivery of a lecture, the exhibition of a painting, or the performance of a dramatic or musical composition. These cases rest upon the ground that the common law recognizes such productions as property which, despite restricted communication, continues until there is a dedication to the public under the copyright statutes or otherwise. But they are inapplicable for two reasons. (1) At common law, as under the copyright acts, intellectual productions are entitled to such protection only if there is underneath something evincing the mind of a creator or originator, however modest the requirement. The mere record of isolated happenings, whether in words or by photographs not involving artistic skill, are denied such protection. (2) At common law, as under the copyright acts, the element in intellectual productions which secures such protection is not the knowledge, truths, ideas, or emotions which the composition expresses, but the form or sequence in which they are expressed; that is, some new collocation of visible or audible points,—of lines, colors, sounds, or words. An author's theories, suggestions, and speculations, or the systems, plans, methods, and arrangements of an originator, derive no such protection from the statutory copyright of the book in which they are set forth; and they are likewise denied such protection at common law.

That news is not property in the strict sense is illustrated by the case of *Sports and General Press Agency, Ltd., v. "Our Dogs" Publishing Co., Ltd.*, [1916] 2 K.B. 880, where the plaintiff, the assignee of the right to photograph the exhibits at a dog show, was refused an injunction against defendant who had also taken pictures of the show and was publishing them. The court said that, except in so far as the possession of the land occupied by the show enabled the proprietors to exclude people or permit them on condition that they agree not to take photographs (which condition was not imposed in that case), the proprietors had no exclusive right to photograph the show and could therefore grant no such right. And, it was further stated that, at any rate, no matter what conditions might be imposed upon those entering the grounds, if the defendant had been on top of a house or in some position where he could photograph the show without interfering with the physical property of the plaintiff, the plaintiff would have no right to stop him. If, when the plaintiff creates the event recorded, he is not entitled to the exclusive first publication of the news (in that case a photograph) of the event, no reason can be shown why he should be accorded such protection as to events which he simply records and transmits to other parts of the world, though with great expenditure of time and money.

Third: If news be treated as possessing the characteristics not of a trade secret, but of literary property, then the earliest issue of a paper of general circulation or the earliest public posting of a bulletin which embodies such news would, under the established rules governing literary property, operate as a publication, and all property in the news would then cease. Resisting this conclusion, plaintiff relied upon the cases which hold that uncopyrighted intellectual and artistic property survives private circulation or a restricted publication; and it contended that in each issue of each paper, a restriction is to be implied that the news shall not be used gainfully in competition with the Associated Press or any of its members. There is no basis for such an implication. But it is also well settled that where the publication is in fact a general one, even express words of restriction upon use are inoperative. In other words, a general publication is effective to dedicate literary property to the public, regardless of the actual intent of its owner. In the cases dealing with lectures, dramatic and musical performances, and art exhibitions, upon which plaintiff relied, there was no general publication in print comparable to the issue of daily newspapers or the unrestricted public posting of bulletins. The principles governing those cases differ more or less in application, if not in theory, from the principles governing the issue of printed copies; and in so far as they do differ, they have no application to the case at bar.

Fourth: Plaintiff further contended that defendant's practice constitutes unfair competition, because there is "appropriation without cost to itself of values created by" the plaintiff; and it is upon this ground that the decision of this court appears to be based. To appropriate and use for profit, knowledge and ideas produced by other men, without making compensation or even acknowledgment, may be inconsistent with a finer sense of propriety; but, with the exceptions indicated above, the law has heretofore sanctioned the practice. Thus it was held that one may ordinarily make and sell anything in any form, may copy with exactness that which another has produced, or may otherwise use his ideas without his consent and without the payment of compensation, and yet not inflict a legal injury; and that ordinarily one is at perfect liberty to find out, if he can by lawful means, trade secrets of another, however valuable, and then use the knowledge so acquired gainfully, although it cost the original owner much in effort and in money to collect or produce.

Such taking and gainful use of a product of another which, for reasons of public policy, the law has refused to endow with the attributes of property, does not become unlawful because the product happens to have been taken from a rival and is used in competition with him. The unfairness in competition which hitherto has been recognized by the law as a basis for relief, lay in the manner or means of conducting the business; and the manner or means held legally unfair, involves either fraud or force or the doing of acts otherwise prohibited by law. In the "passing off" cases (the typical and most common case of unfair competition), the wrong consists in fraudulently representing by word or act that defendant's goods are those of plaintiff. In the other cases, the diversion of trade was effected through physical or moral coercion, or by inducing breaches of contract or of trust or by enticing away employees. In some others, called cases of simulated competition, relief was granted because defendant's purpose was unlawful; namely, not competition but deliberate and wanton destruction of plaintiff's business.

That competition is not unfair in a legal sense, merely because the profits gained are unearned, even if made at the expense of a rival, is shown by many cases besides those referred to above. He who follows the pioneer into a new market, or who engages in the manufacture of an article newly introduced by another, seeks profits due largely to the labor and expense of the first adventurer; but the law sanctions, indeed encourages, the pursuit. He who makes a city known through his product, must submit to sharing the resultant trade with others who, perhaps for that reason, locate there later. . . . One bearing a name made famous by another is permitted to enjoy the unearned benefit which necessarily flows from such use, even though the use proves harmful to him who gave the name value.

The means by which the International News Service obtains news gathered by the Associated Press is also clearly unobjectionable. It is taken from papers bought in the open market or from bulletins publicly posted. No breach of contract. . .or of trust. . .and neither fraud nor force, is involved. The manner of use is likewise unobjectionable. No reference is made by word or by act to the Associated Press, either in transmitting the news to subscribers or by them in publishing it in their papers. Neither the International News Service nor its subscribers is gaining or seeking to gain in its business a benefit from the reputation of the Associated Press. They are merely using its product without making compensation.

That, they have a legal right to do; because the product is not property, and they do not stand in any relation to the Associated Press, either of contract or of trust, which otherwise precludes such use. The argument is not advanced by characterizing such taking and use a misappropriation.

It is also suggested, that the fact that defendant does not refer to the Associated Press as the source of the news may furnish a basis for the relief. But the defendant and its subscribers, unlike members of the Associated Press, were under no contractual obligation to disclose the source of the news; and there is no rule of law requiring acknowledgment to be made where uncopyrighted matter is reproduced. The International News Service is said to mislead its subscribers into believing that the news transmitted was originally gathered by it and that they in turn mislead their readers. There is, in fact, no representation by either of any kind. Sources of information are sometimes given because required by contract; sometimes because naming the source gives authority to an otherwise incredible statement; and sometimes the source is named because the agency does not wish to take the responsibility itself of giving currency to the news. But no representation can properly be implied from omission to mention the source of information except that the International News Service is transmitting news which it believes to be credible.

. . . .

Fifth: The great development of agencies now furnishing country-wide distribution of news, the vastness of our territory, and improvements in the means of transmitting intelligence, have made it possible for a news agency or newspapers to obtain, without paying compensation, the fruit of another's efforts and to use news so obtained gainfully in competition with the original collector. The injustice of such action is obvious. But to give relief against it would involve more than the application of existing rules of law to new facts. It would require the making of a new rule in analogy to existing ones. The unwritten law possesses capacity for growth; and has often satisfied new demands for justice by invoking analogies or by expanding a rule or principle. This process has been in the main wisely applied and should not be discontinued. Where the problem is relatively simple, as it is apt to be when private interests only are involved, it generally proves adequate. But with the increasing complexity of society, the public interest tends to become omnipresent; and the problems presented by new demands for justice cease to be simple. Then the creation or recognition by courts of a new private right may work serious injury to the general public, unless the boundaries of the right are definitely established and wisely guarded. In order to reconcile the new private right with the public interest, it may be necessary to prescribe limitations and rules for its enjoyment; and also to provide administrative machinery for enforcing the rules. It is largely for this reason that, in the effort to meet the many new demands for justice incident to a rapidly changing civilization, resort to legislation has latterly been had with increasing frequency.

The rule for which the plaintiff contends would effect an important extension of property rights and a corresponding curtailment of the free use of knowledge and of ideas; and the facts of this case admonish us of the danger involved in recognizing such a property right in news, without imposing upon news-gatherers corresponding obligations. A large majority of the newspapers and perhaps half the newspaper readers of the United States are dependent for their news of general interest upon agencies other than the Associated Press. The channel through which about 400 of these papers received, as the plaintiff alleges, "a large amount of news relating to the European war of the greatest importance and of intense interest to the newspaper reading public" was suddenly closed. The closing to the International News Service of these channels for foreign news (if they were closed) was due not to unwillingness on its part to pay the cost of collecting the news, but to the prohibitions imposed by foreign governments upon its securing news from their respective countries and from using cable or telegraph lines running therefrom. For aught that appears, this prohibition may have been wholly undeserved; and at all events the 400 papers and their readers may be assumed to have been innocent. For aught that appears, the International

News Service may have sought then to secure temporarily by arrangement with the Associated Press the latter's foreign news service. For aught that appears, all of the 400 subscribers of the International News Service would gladly have then become members of the Associated Press, if they could have secured election thereto.[15] It is possible, also, that a large part of the readers of these papers were so situated that they could not secure prompt access to papers served by the Associated Press. The prohibition of the foreign governments might as well have been extended to the channels through which news was supplied to the more than a thousand other daily papers in the United States not served by the Associated Press; and a large part of their readers may also be so located that they can not procure prompt access to papers served by the Associated Press.

A legislature, urged to enact a law by which one news agency or newspaper may prevent appropriation of the fruits of its labors by another, would consider such facts and possibilities and others which appropriate enquiry might disclose. Legislators might conclude that it was impossible to put an end to the obvious injustice involved in such appropriation of news, without opening the door to other evils, greater than that sought to be remedied. Such appears to have been the opinion of our Senate which reported unfavorably a bill to give news a few hours' protection;[16] and which ratified, on February 15, 1911, the convention adopted at the Fourth International American Conference;[17] and such was evidently the view also of the signatories to the International Copyright Union of November 13, 1908;[18] as both these conventions expressly exclude news from copyright protection.

---

[15] According to the by-laws of the Associated Press no one can be elected a member without the affirmative vote of at least four-fifths of all the members of the corporation or the vote of the directors. Furthermore, the power of the directors to admit anyone to membership may be limited by a right of protest to be conferred upon individual members. *See* By-laws, Article III, § 6.

The members of this Corporation may, by an affirmative vote of seven-eights of all the members, confer upon a member (with such limitations as may be at the time prescribed) a right of protest against the admission of new members by the Board of Directors. The right of protest, within the limits specified at the time it is conferred, shall empower the members holding it to demand a vote of the members of the Corporation on all applications for the admission of new members within the district for which it is conferred except as provided in Section 2 of this Article.

[16] Senate Bill No. 1728, 48th Cong., 1st sess. The bill provides:

That any daily or weekly newspaper, or any association of daily or weekly newspapers, published in the United States or any of the Territories thereof, shall have the sole right to print, issue, and sell, for the term of eight hours, dating from the hour of going to press, the contents of said daily or weekly newspaper, or the collected news of said newspaper association, exceeding one hundred words.

Sec. 2. That for any infringement of the copyright granted by the first section of this act the party injured may sue in any court of competent jurisdiction and recover in any proper action the damages sustained by him from the person making such infringement, together with the costs of suit.

It was reported on April 18, 1884, by the Committee on the Library, without amendment, and that it ought not to pass. Journal of the Senate, 48th Cong., 1st sess., p. 548. No further action was apparently taken on the bill.

When the copyright legislation of 1909, finally enacted as Act of March 4, 1909, c. 320, 35 Stat. 1075, was under consideration, there was apparently no attempt to include news among the subjects of copyright. Arguments before the Committees on Patents of the Senate and House of Representatives on Senate Bill No. 6330 and H.R. Bill No. 19853, 59th Cong., 1st sess., June 6, 7, 8, and 9, and December 7, 8, 10, and 11, 1906; Hearings on Pending Bills to Amend and Consolidate Acts Respecting Copyright, March 26, 27 and 28, 1908.

[17] 38 Stat. 1785, 1789, Article 2.

[18] Bowker, *Copyright: Its History and its Law*, pp. 330, 612, 613. See the similar provisions in the Berne Convention (1886) and the Paris Convention (1896). *Id.*, pp. 612, 613.

In 1898 Lord Herschell introduced in Parliament a bill, § 11 of which provides: "Copyright in respect of a newspaper

Or legislators dealing with the subject might conclude, that the right to news values should be protected to the extent of permitting recovery of damages for any unauthorized use, but that protection by injunction should be denied, just as courts of equity ordinarily refuse (perhaps in the interest of free speech) to restrain actionable libels, and for other reasons decline to protect by injunction mere political rights; and as Congress has prohibited courts from enjoining the illegal assessment or collection of federal taxes. If a legislature concluded to recognize property in published news to the extent of permitting recovery at law, it might, with a view to making the remedy more certain and adequate, provide a fixed measure of damages, as in the case of copyright infringement.[22]

Or again, a legislature might conclude that it was unwise to recognize even so limited a property right in published news as that above indicated; but that a news agency should, on some conditions, be given full protection of its business; and to that end a remedy by injunction as well as one for damages should be granted, where news collected by it is gainfully used without permission. If a legislature concluded, (as at least one court has held, *New York & Chicago Grain & Stock Exchange v. Board of Trade*, 127 Illinois, 153) that under certain circumstances news-gathering is a business affected with a public interest, it might declare that, in such cases, news should be protected against appropriation, only if the gatherer assumed the obligation of supplying it, at reasonable rates and without discrimination, to all papers which applied therefor. If legislators reached that conclusion, they would probably go further, and prescribe the conditions under which and the extent to which the protection should be afforded; and they might also provide the administrative machinery necessary for ensuring to the public, the press, and the news agencies, full enjoyment of the rights so conferred.

Courts are ill-equipped to make the investigations which should precede a determination of the limitations which should be set upon any property right in news or of the circumstances under which news gathered by a private agency should be deemed affected with a public interest. Courts would be powerless to prescribe the detailed regulations essential to full enjoyment of the rights conferred or to introduce the machinery required for enforcement of such regulations. Considerations such as these should lead us to decline to establish a new rule of law in the effort to redress a newly-disclosed wrong, although the propriety of some remedy appears to be clear.

[c] Explanatory Notes

[*i*] *Preliminary Injunction Questions.* In *Associated Press*, the plaintiff asked the court to order International News Service to stop using Associated Press news releases throughout the pendency of the litigation. While courts rarely stop anybody from doing anything immediately upon the filing of a complaint,[51] they do issue *preliminary injunctions* from time to time. Such

---

shall apply only to such parts of the newspaper as are compositions of an original literary character, to original illustrations therein, *and to such news and information as have been specially and independently obtained.*" (Italics ours.) House of Lords, Sessional Papers, 1898, vol. 3, Bill No. 21. Birrell, *Copyright in Books*, p. 210. But the bill was not enacted, and in the English law as it now stands there is no provision giving even a limited copyright in news as such. Act of December 16, 1911, 1 and 2 Geo. V, c. 46.

[22] Act of March 4, 1909, § 25, c. 320, 35 Stat. 1075, 1081, provides as to the liability for the infringement of a copyright, that, "in the case of a newspaper reproduction of a copyrighted photograph such damages shall not exceed the sum of two hundred dollars nor be less than the sum of fifty dollars"; and that in the case of infringement of a copyrighted newspaper the damages recoverable shall be one dollar for every infringing copy, but shall not be less than $250 nor more than $5,000.

[51] A *temporary restraining order* (TRO) is available, although it is not used much. Courts are extremely reluctant

orders are issued only after an opportunity has been given to both sides to present their versions of the circumstances to the court, by the use of either witnesses or affidavits. The issuance of a preliminary injunction governs the behavior of the parties only until the case is finally decided or settled. Courts are sometimes hesitant to issue such an injunction. For if the final result of the case turns out to be different from the impulses which led to the issuance of the preliminary injunction, unnecessary harm will be caused the enjoined party. Although similar injuries might result to a party who fails to obtain the issuance of a preliminary injunction but eventually wins a case, the perhaps natural human instinct not to alter the status quo unless it seems necessary tends to obscure that reality for many judges.[52]

In *Associated Press*, the importance of the procedural issues surrounding preliminary injunctions was much diminished. Most of the facts were not in dispute between the parties. International News Service admitted taking Associated Press stories and Associated Press admitted using other services' stories as "tips." The only factual dispute involved International News Service's allegation that Associated Press copied other services' stories verbatim and used them. The trial court found little support for that and, in addition, wrote an opinion which argued that there was no real difference in the effect of verbatim copying of published stories and use of published stories as "tips." Under these circumstances, the appellate courts saw little need to worry about the preliminary injunction problem. Since all, or virtually all, the facts had come out in the voluminous affidavits the parties submitted at the time the preliminary injunction was argued in the trial court, there was virtually no likelihood that the ultimate outcome of the case would differ from the first round. The Supreme Court, in essence, merged the hearing on the final merits of the case with the hearing on the preliminary injunction, an option now specifically made available to the federal courts by Federal Rule of Civil Procedure 65.

[ii]   *Choice of Law Questions.* In his majority opinion, Justice Pitney wrote that "federal jurisdiction was invoked because of diversity of citizenship, not upon the ground that the suit arose under the copyright or other laws of the United States." Since the Supreme Court decision in *Erie v. Tompkins*, 304 U.S. 64 (1938), federal district courts have used the choice of law rules of the forum state to resolve issues about what law to apply in the case. *International News Service* was decided prior to *Erie* in the days when district courts hearing diversity cases were free to apply "general federal common law." The change in approach to choice of law issues mirrored a number of changes in modes of legal thought between the end of the nineteenth century and the New Deal Era. The Formalist notion that law was scientific, rational, knowable and predictable had given way in the face of Realist insistence that law was subject to cultural forces, part of the political milieu of its time, widely variant, and riddled with policy variations. The Formalist sense that law could be unified had given way to a more realistic feeling that variations among the states were endemic. Recognition of the importance of those variations and acceptance of the power of the states to impose them on litigants was part of the underlying mind set leading to choice of law reforms. To the degree that *International News Service* was itself a Realist

---

to issue orders when only one side has been given an opportunity to marshal its forces before the time for the court hearing arrives. Most TROs are issued in emergency situations with very little time for presentation of proofs and are effective for a very short time. Continued effect of the order beyond an initial period of time (such as 10 days) almost always requires a court hearing in which it is possible for factual information to be presented to the court by both sides.

[52] For one of a number of articles criticizing the hesitancy of courts to see the similarities between the issuance and non-issuance of preliminary injunctions, *see* Leubsdorf, *The Standard for Preliminary Injunctions*, 91 HARV. L. REV. 525 (1978).

opinion in its reliance upon the parameters of specific relationships to define economic relationships, it was a precursor to the demise of the general federal common law. A case like *International News Service* would simply not be accepted for review by the Supreme Court today. It would be viewed as completely a matter of local law.

[*iii*]   *The Case on Appeal.* By the time the case wound its way to the United States Supreme Court, some of the issues had fallen away. Recall that the plaintiffs made three series of allegations against the defendants—bribery, inducement to breach a contract, and sale of copied news releases. International News Service petitioned the Supreme Court to review only the copying issue. That decision is understandable; most litigants would prefer not to defend allegations of bribery and contract breach inducement (especially when they were true!) before that Court. While the decision is understandable, it further illustrates the way in which strategic decisions made by attorneys and litigants filter the nature of the materials judges actually see when deciding disputes.

In any case, while Judge Augustus Hand was reluctant to enjoin the copying of news releases because he felt it was too difficult to distinguish between the copying and "tipster" issues, the United States Court of Appeals for the Second Circuit, which heard the case on appeal from Hand before it reached the Supreme Court, had no such hesitancy. Judge Hough, writing for a 2-1 majority, found "no difficulty in discriminating between the utilization of 'tips' and the bodily appropriation of another's labor in accumulating and stating information."[53] Having made such a distinction, and having removed the "hard" issue of "tips," it was perhaps easy for the court to write that "any bodily taking for sale of plaintiff's news, without other labor than the perception thereof, before the reasonable reward of industry is secured . . ., is an unlawful invasion of property rights, and any sale thereof in competition with plaintiff under pretense of individual gathering thereof is a tort of the nature of unfair competition. . . ."

[*iv*]   *Justice Pitney's Opinion.* Thus, the case found its way to the United States Supreme Court. Mr. Justice Pitney, the author of the Court's majority opinion, wrote that the words "property" and "copyright" were not at issue in the case, even though the litigants framed the issues in these terms, as did Judge Hough for the United States Court of Appeals for the Second Circuit. He preferred to use the words "unfair competition" and "quasi property" to label the dispute. The labels themselves provide little guidance as to what the Court had in mind, though each of you surely has some notions about the meanings of all this vocabulary. Pitney provided one important clue as to what he meant, when he wrote that the fault in the defendant's reasoning "lies in applying as a test the right of the complainant as against the public, instead of considering the rights of complainant and defendant, competitors in business, as between themselves." Pitney's notion was that property was not an object or specific right, but a combination of interests with a composition heavily dependent on the facts and the nature of the involved parties. Property was a way of defining relationships among individuals, groups, organizations, business and the government. Pitney's use of the word "quasi" property was not so much an effort to define a new kind of property as it was an attempt to underscore the possibility that one party, *A*, may have rights against another party, *B*, which a third party, *C*, may not have against *B*.

At one level, this is all patently obvious. If *B* runs into *A*'s house and throws *A*'s television set through the window, *A* may certainly recover the amount of the damages from *B*. But just because *C* happened to be walking by at the time of *B*'s rampage does not provide *C* with any

---

[53] Associated Press v. International News Service, 245 F. 244, 247 (2d Cir. 1917).

right to sue *B* for the same damages. At another level, it is not obvious at all. Many of you probably entered law school thinking that property was easy to define—something visible, something tangible—and that ownership of property provided one with certain clear cut rights against everyone in the world. This view, however, could not be further from reality. "Ownership" of "property" does not mean the same thing all the time, even with the same asset. You may be able to keep a stranger out of your house, but not a policewoman. You may be able to copy news service releases for your personal use, but you may not be able to sell them to another newspaper. You may be able to video tape a movie off the television, but you may not be able to sell that tape to me. The variations on these themes are endless, and thus capable of generating considerable contention about what "property" may really be.

[d] Property Concepts in the Realist Era

Chapter 6 opened with some discussion of the transition in property concepts that occurred between the end of the nineteenth and the beginning of the twentieth centuries. A number of Realists wrote what are now classic articles on the relational, political and economic underpinnings of property. In many ways, the *International News Service* case was a model of Realist analysis. That became clear in the decade after the case was decided when Morris Cohen, one of a coterie of Realists who wrote about property, penned the classic article *Property and Sovereignty*. [54]

Cohen argued that claims of property ownership staked out realms of power and sovereignty, and that a variety of theories had been used to justify such claims. They included ancient theories arising out of use and occupation of land, Lockean notions about expenditure of labor and investment justifying the assertion of dominion and control over any resulting products, ideas of privacy and personality supporting claims of autonomous rights over oneself and objects of a personal nature, and economic theories calling for ownership rights as part of a set of incentives designed to encourage the efficient use of resources. While Hale argued that all property, regardless of the theory used to justify its existence, was subject to the needs of the public for regulation and control of abuses, the outline of theories he constructed was one that encapsulated many of the issues discussed in this text.

The *Associated Press* opinion arguably relies upon three of the four analytical props discussed by Cohen—occupancy, labor and economics. Associated Press claimed a possessory like interest in its hot news and invested a great deal of money, time and resources in creating its news distribution network. Justice Pitney argued that the law should provide support for the level of incentives required to motivate entrepreneurs to create efficient news gathering systems. Indeed, Justice Brandeis also claimed that maintenance of monetary incentives for the production of news was crucial to the free flow of information. The two Justices differed only in the appropriate way in which to guarantee the widespread dissemination of news.

The validity of their assumption that use of private economic incentives was the only, or at least the best, way to encourage distribution of information is subject to nettlesome questions. If ability to produce income is the basic measure of the worthiness of news, are there forms of news that will rarely if ever be printed? Should the gathering of news be regulated so that all papers or other media wishing to use a news service may gain access to its stories upon the payment of a fee? Such a system would make wire services something like a public utility, an

---

[54] Morris R. Cohen, *Property and Sovereignty*, 13 CORNELL L. Q. 8 (1927). The article is excerpted in RICHARD CHUSED, A PROPERTY ANTHOLOGY 89-97 (2d ed. 1997).

outcome which has in fact occurred since the 1944 antitrust verdict against Associated Press. Should wire services be deemed so important that public subsidies ought to be used for their support in order to reduce the cost to the media of developing and disseminating information? This option, too, has come to pass in the form of federal funding support for public radio and television news and information features. The Supreme Court's decision to invest news gathering with some attributes of private property was therefore imbued with a series of assumptions about both the importance of news and the most appropriate mechanisms for insuring its dissemination as a marketable product.

An enormous number of cases have been decided since *Associated Press* involving allegations that one or another product was copied and sold without permission. Most of the opinions reported between 1918 and 1950 involved consumer goods or attempts by one or another media to piggy-back on someone else's product.[55] In an early case, for example, Associated Press found itself back in court seeking to enjoin KVOS, a station in Bellingham, Washington, from broadcasting news releases. The Ninth Circuit Court of Appeals ordered an injunction to issue.[56] The Ninth Circuit noted that radio news did compete with papers for advertisers, that use of the Associated Press stories gave to the public "free" news which might cause them not to purchase papers, that the news was still "hot" in the Bellingham area when the radio broadcasts occurred, and that no efforts to independently confirm the stories were made.

Another famous early case, *Cheney Bros. v. Doris Silk Corp.* 35 F.2d 279 (2d Cir. 1929), involved allegations that silk designs were being copied in cloth manufactured and sold by the defendant. The designs were seasonal and quite ephemeral in the market—here today, gone tomorrow. The court declined to issue an injunction, in part because it was unsympathetic to *International News Service*, citing Justice Brandeis' dissenting opinion in the case as that with the greater wisdom. But the court was also reluctant to intervene in long standing practices in the fashion industry of "knocking off" new products shortly after the big name designers hit the streets with their most recent wares. Interestingly enough, the copyright law now clearly covers fabric designs. However, general "styles" in fashion, such as shape, length, tightness of fit, and the like, are not covered by copyright. You all are aware of how quickly new fads lead to a rash of new products in the same genre. Would the rationale of *International News Service* reach any of this activity? Isn't a "tip" much like a style? You take the "tip," "research" its authenticity, and "publish" a "new" story, much like you take the "style," "rework" its lines slightly, and "produce" a "new" product.

None of the cases like *KVOS* or *Cheney Bros.* involved the fourth sort of property in Morris Cohen's typology—that based on personality or personhood. Not until the advent of baseball cards did the fame of a person become the object of judicial attention. Suppose a baseball player

---

[55] For more information, you might want to sample among these articles. Terrell & Smith, *Publicity, Liberty, and Intellectual Property: A Conceptual and Economic Analysis of the Inheritability Issue*, 34 EMORY L.J. 1 (1985); Hoffman, *The Right of Publicity—Heirs' Right, Advertisers' Windfall, or Courts' Nightmare?*, 31 DEPAUL L. REV. 1 (1981); Felcher & Rubin, *The Descendability of the Right of Publicity: Is There Commercial Life After Death*, 89 YALE L.J. 1125 (1980); Comment, *The Right of Publicity vs. The First Amendment: Reconciling the Conflict Between a Proprietary Interest of the Plaintiff and the Constitutional Guarantee of Free Speech*, 27 VILL. L. REV. 1205 (1982); Note, *The Right of Publicity Revisited: Reconciling Fame, Fortune, and Constitutional Rights*, 62 B.U. L. REV. 965 (1982); Note, *An Assessment of the Copyright Model in Right of Publicity Cases*, 70 CAL. L. REV. 786 (1982).

[56] Associated Press v. KVOS, Inc., 80 F.2d 575 (9th Cir. 1935). The result was later reversed by the Supreme Court, but on the ground that the federal courts lacked jurisdiction to hear the case in the first place, not on the merits of the unfair competition claim. KVOS, Inc. v. Associated Press, 299 U.S. 269 (1936).

signed a contract granting a bubble gum manufacturer the *exclusive* right to use his photograph in connection with sale of the gum. What would happen if a rival bubble gum manufacturer induced the same player to sign a second contract authorizing the use of the player's photograph in the sale of the rival's bubble gum? Does *Associated Press* cover this situation? Remember that the allegations that International News Service induced and bribed Associated Press employees to provide news "under the counter" never came up for review by the Supreme Court. Is it proper to assume that the Supreme Court would have decided the bribery and inducement issues in favor of Associated Press and applied similar logic to the bubble gum case?

Make the bubble gum case a little more difficult. Assume that the rival gum manufacturer did not induce a player to sign a second contract, but that the rival purchased rights under a second contract from another party, and that the rival did not participate in any way in obtaining the ball player's signature on the second contract. In legal terminology, the rival was an *assignee* of rights under a contract originally obtained by someone else. May the rival use the ball player's photographs? In one of the most famous misappropriation cases ever decided, *Haelan Laboratories, Inc. v. Topps Chewing Gum, Inc.*, 202 F.2d 866 (2d Cir. 1953), the rival company holding rights under a contract assignment was enjoined from using the photograph of a ball player who had previously signed an exclusive rights contract with the rival's competitor. Did *Associated Press* compel this result? The *Haelan* case was the first step in a gradual transformation of unfair competition theory into a right of publicity. That is the next topic for discussion.

[2]   Development of the Right to Publicity: *Martin Luther King, Jr., Center for Social Change v. American Heritage Products*

[a]   The Nascent Right of Publicity

The two litigants in *Haelan Laboratories v. Topps Chewing Gum* were in the business of selling bubble gum with baseball cards inserted in each package. Haelan signed contracts with ball players and agreed to pay them for the exclusive right to use their pictures in bubble gum inserts. The dispute arose when Topps later obtained contracts with some of the same players. Haelan sued. Topps took the position that the ball players' contracts with Haelan only released Haelan from liability for invasions of privacy resulting from publication of the pictures, that the right of privacy was not assignable, and that therefore no exclusive "property" rights were established by the contracts. The United States Court of Appeals for the Second Circuit disagreed:

> We think that, in addition to and independent of that right of privacy. . ., a man has a right in the publicity value of his photograph, *i.e.*, the right to grant the exclusive privilege of publishing his picture, and that such a grant may validly be made "in gross," *i.e.*, without an accompanying transfer of a business or of anything else. Whether it be labeled a "property" right is immaterial; for here, as often elsewhere, the tag "property" simply symbolizes the fact that courts enforce a claim which has pecuniary worth.

> This right might be called a "right of publicity." For it is common knowledge that many prominent persons (especially actors and ball-players), far from having their feelings bruised through public exposure of their likenesses, would feel sorely deprived if they no longer received money for authorizing advertisements, popularizing their countenances, displayed in newspapers, magazines, busses, trains and subways. This right of publicity would usually yield them no money unless it could be made the subject of an exclusive grant which barred any other advertiser from using their pictures.

Although the case was not explicitly decided on an *International News Service* based "unfair competition" or "misappropriation" theory, it is quite difficult to separate such an idea from publicity rights.[57] In both *International News Service* and *Haelan*, allegations were made that the defendants induced persons to breach contracts, in the first case by paying off employees of Associated Press and in the second by signing ball players already under contract with Haelan. Both cases involved product mimicry, competitive enterprises, and the use of intangible "assets" developed through the expenditure of money, time and effort.

But there were also some important differences between the two cases. Most notably, the photographs used by Topps were not the same as those used by Haelan. Nor can the use of photographs be easily analogized to the "tip" problem in *International News Service*. The case moved the protection of intangible "assets" to a somewhat different plane. Even if you can imagine a way of describing the outer limits of the "rule" established by *International News Service*, what can be done to describe this "right of publicity"? Indeed, the cases decided after *Haelan* expanded the right into a number of areas other than the use of pictures associated with the sale of products. Courts have approved the use of the right in protecting stage names,[58] characterizations created by performers,[59] and theatrical performances.[60] And the right of publicity has spawned disputes over the propriety of activity normally protected by the First Amendment, including movies, stage plays,[61] political campaigns,[62] and television news programs.[63] Some famous characters, including Howard Hughes, Elizabeth Taylor, Jane Fonda, and J.D. Salinger have even tried to stop the publication of biographies written without their permission on the ground that such books violated both their rights to privacy and publicity.[64]

In addition to the significant expansion of the right of publicity that has occurred in the last 40 years, courts have also been forced to grapple with the inheritability of the right. A number of cases have arisen in which the heirs of deceased persons claimed the right to control the use of their ancestors' personality or likeness. Most of you naturally assume that you may do pretty much what you want with your "property." Buying, selling, altering, destroying, or disposing of it at death, are actions you take for granted. But most common forms of property, such as clothes, stereo equipment, cars, and houses, are quite different from intangible "property" like that at stake in a right of publicity case. In the cases involving intangibles, such as *International*

[57] The trial judge in *Haelan* dismissed all the claims, including one framed on unfair competition. The plaintiffs, however, did not appeal the unfair competition aspect of the case. If the plaintiffs had appealed on that issue, it would have been interesting to see how the court would have handled the problem.

[58] Estate of Presley v. Russen, 513 F. Supp. 1339 (D.N.J. 1981).

[59] Price v. Worldvision Enterprises, Inc. 455 F. Supp. 252 (S.D.N.Y. 1978).

[60] Zacchini v. Scripps-Howard Broadcasting Co., 433 U.S. 562 (1977).

[61] Joplin Enterprises v. Allen, 795 F. Supp. 349 (W.D. Wash. 1992); Groucho Marx Productions, Inc. v. Day and Night Company, Inc., 689 F.2d 317 (2d Cir. 1981).

[62] Paulsen v. Personality Posters, Inc., 59 Misc. 2d 444, 299 N.Y.S.2d 501 (Sup. Ct. 1968); Keep Thomson for Governor Committee v. Citizens for Gallen Committee, 457 F. Supp. 957 (D.N.H. 1978).

[63] Zacchini v. Scripps-Howard Broadcasting Co., 433 U.S. 562 (1977).

[64] Rosemont Enterprises, Inc. v. Random House, Inc., 58 Misc. 2d 1, 294 N.Y.S.2d 122 (Sup. Ct. 1968) (Hughes). Reports on Taylor and Fonda may be found at sec. 2, p. 1, col. 6 in the Nov. 21, 1982, issue of the NEW YORK TIMES and sec. C, p. 1, col. 1 of the Apr. 25, 1982, issue of the WASHINGTON POST, respectively. Salinger v. Random House, 811 F.2d 90 (2d Cir. 1987). Salinger eschewed use of a publicity rights claim, perhaps because of the failure of Hughes, Taylor and Fonda in stopping "unauthorized" stories about themselves. Salinger did, however, use an "unfair competition" theory based on the author's use of phrases, such as "he says," attributing direct statements to Salinger. Salinger also claimed copyright infringement, a theory upon which he prevailed.

News Service v. Associated Press, the courts are forced into asking very basic questions about the nature of property itself. Should a claim of right be given the status of "property"? If this claim raises "property" issues, what sort of "property" "rights" should attach? Can the claim be bought and sold, destroyed, waived, disposed of at death? Will the claim, like land, be presumed to last forever? Such issues are the grist of the next case.

[b]   History of *Martin Luther King v. American Heritage Products*

Martin Luther King, Jr. was assassinated on April 4, 1968; he died *intestate*, that is, without a will. Georgia, like all other states, had statutes describing in some detail who got the property of a person dying intestate. According to the law in effect at the time of King's death, his property passed to his wife, Coretta Scott King, and his children, with each person taking an equal share.[65] In addition, the statutes provided for the designation of a person (usually called an *Administrator* or, in the case of a woman, an *Administratrix*) to manage the affairs of the dead person's estate until the property is all distributed. If there is a surviving spouse, he or she is almost always chosen to manage an estate's affairs. It was therefore not surprising that Coretta Scott King ended up managing her deceased husband's estate. In most cases, the job ends fairly quickly. The property is distributed and the estate is closed. King died with very little property. If he had not been so well known, his estate also would have been quickly closed. But in King's case, there was a strong desire among surviving relatives and close associates to control the use of his fame for the benefit of his family and the civil rights movement. The estate therefore set up a formal procedure for the licensing of those wishing to use Dr. King's likeness[66] and began to write letters demanding royalties when parties used his likeness without the estate's permission. Proceeds from the licensing process help support the family and the Martin Luther King, Jr. Center for Social Change. The Center does not have an automatic right to share in the proceeds of Dr. King's estate. Rather, King's heirs have agreed to the disbursement of funds from the estate to the Center.

Applications for use of King's image arrive in a steady stream at the Atlanta offices of the Center for Social Change. Among the 1980 applications was one from James F. Bolen and his son James E. Bolen, filed on behalf of B & S Sales, Inc., seeking permission to market a plastic figure with a bust of Dr. King sitting on top of a casket. The license request was denied. Those controlling the permission process all thought the item lacked the requisite good taste to justify granting a license. The Bolens went ahead and marketed the item anyway. Ads for the product appeared in the November and December, 1980, issues of Ebony Magazine. A reprint of one such ad may be found below. When the product's existence came to the attention of King's associates in Atlanta, a lawsuit was brought.

---

[65] At King's death the Georgia Code of 1933 was in effect. Since then, the state's statutes have been recodified, but the intestate succession laws were left unchanged. The present provisions of the intestate succession law may be found at GA. CODE ANN. § 53-4-1 to -8.

[66] A similar process was set up to license the copyrighted works of Dr. King. A number of his speeches had been published before his death. The validity of the copyrights in some of the most important works, including the I Have a Dream Speech, was confirmed in a celebrated copyright case, King v. Mister Maestro, Inc., 224 F. Supp. 101 (S.D.N.Y. 1963). That result, in turn, recently was rejected in Estate of Martin Luther King, Jr., Inc. v. CBS, Inc., 13 F. Supp. 2d 1347 (N.D. Ga. 1998).

The case presented counsel for Dr. King's estate, Mr. Archer D. Smith III,[67] with certain problems. Many of the prior cases dealing with the inheritability of the right of publicity required that the *heirs* or *legatees*[68] could control the personage of their deceased compatriot only if the right had been exercised during the life of the famous person. While King was certainly a very famous individual, he had not exploited his renown by selling posters, advertising products, producing plays or movies, or demanding money for television appearances. Any attempt to base the case against the Bolens only on the right of publicity was therefore very risky.

As a result the complaint in the case pursued a number of different angles, including allegations that the name of the Center for Social Change was used without authorization, that the advertisements for the product contained false and misleading statements,[69] that the excerpts from King speeches in some advertisements for the product infringed copyrights, and last (but as it turned out, not least), that the distribution of the product violated "common law property rights to the exclusive use of the image and likeness of Dr. King" held by his estate. When the King estate sought a preliminary injunction, the trial court agreed that the defendants had violated

---

[67] Much of the information in these notes was graciously provided by Mr. Smith, as well as his colleague Mr. Ty Bridges, and Mr. Isaac Farris, Dr. King's brother-in-law. I appreciate their help in providing some of the background of the case.

[68] The technical legal uses of the words "heir" and "legatee" are slightly different. Heirs are those who take property in accordance with a state's intestate succession laws. Legatees are those designated in a will to take the personal property (generally movable and intangible assets, not land) of a deceased person. A *devisee* takes land under a will.

[69] For example, the ad says that a portion of the price of the item was to be given to the Center, but it does not say that the amount contemplated was only $.90 per sale. A formal mechanism for turning over that money was never established.

valid copyrights, pursued deceptive trade practices and appropriated the likeness of Dr. King. An injunction was issued barring the use of the name of the Center for Social Change in ads promoting the sale of the bust and any further printing or distribution of the copyright infringing pamphlets and ads. The court refused, however, to bar the sale of the plastic bust, noting that King had not commercially exploited his right of publicity while alive.[70]

The plaintiffs appealed the refusal of the trial court to bar the sale of the plastic bust. In a somewhat unusual procedure, the Eleventh Circuit Court of Appeals certified a series of questions to the Georgia Supreme Court for resolution. The federal courts routinely take diversity jurisdiction over cases involving state law issues. Normally in such cases, the federal courts must do the best they can to figure out what state law is. A few states, however, have created procedures permitting the federal courts to certify perplexing issues to the state courts for resolution. Once that has been done, the federal court receives an opinion answering the certified questions and proceeds to decide the case. That is what happened here. The opinion reproduced next is the opinion of the Georgia Supreme Court answering questions certified to it by the Eleventh Circuit.

[c]   The Georgia Supreme Court Opinion in *Martin Luther King Jr., Center for Social Change v. American Heritage Products*

Martin Luther King, Jr., Center for Social Change v. American Heritage Products

Georgia Supreme Court
250 Ga. 135, 296 S.E.2d 697 (1982)

HILL, PRESIDING JUSTICE.

These are certified questions regarding the "right of publicity". The certification comes from the United States Court of Appeals for the Eleventh Circuit. The facts upon which the questions arise are as follows:

The plaintiffs are the Martin Luther King, Jr., Center for Social Change (the Center),[2] Coretta Scott King, as administratrix of Dr. King's estate, and Motown Record Corporation, the assignee of the rights to several of Dr. King's copyrighted speeches. Defendant James F. Bolen is the sole proprietor of a business known as B & S Sales, which manufactures and sells various plastic products as funeral accessories. Defendant James E. Bolen, the son of James F. Bolen, developed the concept of marketing a plastic bust of Dr. Martin Luther King, Jr., and formed a company, B & S Enterprises, to sell the busts, which would be manufactured by B & S Sales. B & S Enterprises was later incorporated under the name of American Heritage Products, Inc.

Although Bolen sought the endorsement and participation of the Martin Luther King, Jr. Center for Social Change, Inc., in the marketing of the bust, the Center refused Bolen's offer. Bolen pursued the idea, nevertheless, hiring an artist to prepare a mold and an agent to handle the promotion of the product. Defendant took out two half-page advertisements in the November and December 1980 issues of Ebony magazine, which purported to offer the bust as "an exclusive memorial" and "an opportunity to support the Martin Luther King, Jr., Center for Social change." The advertisement stated that "a contribution from your order goes to the King Center for Social

---

[70] Martin Luther King, Jr. Center for Social Change, Inc. v. American Heritage Products, Inc., 508 F. Supp. 854, 864 (N.D. Ga. 1981). The court did not find that honorariums received by King for some speaking engagements amounted to exploitation of his fame.

[2] The Center is a non-profit corporation which seeks to promote the ideals of Dr. King.

Change." Out of the $29.95 purchase price, defendant Bolen testified he set aside 3% or $.90, as a contribution to the Center. The advertisement also offered "free" with the purchase of the bust a booklet about the life of Dr. King entitled "A Tribute to Dr. Martin Luther King, Jr."

In addition to the two advertisements in Ebony, defendant published a brochure or pamphlet which was inserted in 80,000 copies of newspapers across the country. The brochure reiterated what was stated in the magazine advertisements, and also contained photographs of Dr. King and excerpts from his copyrighted speeches. The brochure promised that each "memorial" (bust) is accompanied by a Certificate of Appreciation "testifying that a contribution has been made to the Martin Luther King, Jr., Center for Social Change."

Defendant James E. Bolen testified that he created a trust fund for that portion of the earnings which was to be contributed to the Center. The trust fund agreement, however, was never executed, and James E. Bolen testified that this was due to the plaintiffs' attorneys' request to cease and desist from all activities in issue. Testimony in the district court disclosed that money had been tendered to the Center, but was not accepted by its governing board. Also, the district court found that, as of the date of the preliminary injunction, the defendants had sold approximately 200 busts and had outstanding orders for 23 more.

On November 21, 1980, and December 19, 1980, the plaintiffs demanded that the Bolens cease and desist from further advertisements and sales of the bust, and on December 31, 1980, the plaintiffs filed a complaint in the United States District Court for the Northern District of Georgia. The district court held a hearing on the plaintiffs' motion for a preliminary injunction and the defendants' motion to dismiss the complaint. The motion to dismiss was denied and the motion for a preliminary injunction was granted in part and denied in part. The motion for an injunction sought (1) an end to the use of the Center's name in advertising and marketing the busts, (2) restraint of any further copyright infringement and (3) an end to the manufacture and sale of the plastic busts. The defendants agreed to discontinue the use of the Center's name in further promotion. Therefore, the court granted this part of the injunction. The district court found that the defendants had infringed the King copyrights and enjoined all further use of the copyrighted material.

In ruling on the third request for injunction, the court confronted the plaintiffs' claim that the manufacture and sale of the busts violated Dr. King's right of publicity which had passed to his heirs upon Dr. King's death. The defendants contended that no such right existed, and hence, an injunction should not issue. The district court concluded that it was not necessary to determine whether the "right of publicity" was devisable in Georgia because Dr. King did not commercially exploit this right during his lifetime. As found by the district court, the evidence of exploitation by Dr. King came from his sister's affidavit which stated that he had received "thousands of dollars in the form of honorariums from the use of his name, likeness, literary compositions, and speeches." The district court further found that "Dr. King apparently sold his copyrights in several speeches to Motown Records Corporation."

On plaintiffs' appeal of the partial denial of the preliminary injunction, the Eleventh Circuit Court of Appeals has certified the following questions:

(1) Is the "right of publicity" recognized in Georgia as a right distinct from the right of privacy?

(2) If the answer to question (1) is affirmative, does the "right to publicity" survive the death of its owner? Specifically, is the right inheritable and devisable?

(3) If the answer to question (2) is also affirmative, must the owner have commercially exploited the right before it can survive his death?

(4) Assuming the affirmative answers to questions (1), (2) and (3), what is the guideline to be followed in defining commercial exploitation and what are the evidentiary prerequisites to a showing of commercial exploitation?

As noted by the Eleventh Circuit, this case raises questions concerning the laws of Georgia as to which there are no controlling precedents directly on point. In addition to being novel in this jurisdiction, the questions are legally alluring. Under these twin circumstances, it is necessary in the first instance to consider how the answers to the questions apply to other fact situations, and tempting in the second instance to include those considerations in writing. Hopefully having considered the various ramifications, we will resist to the extent possible the temptation to answer more than has been asked.

The right of publicity may be defined as a celebrity's right to the exclusive use of his or her name and likeness. *Price v. Hal Roach Studios, Inc.*, 400 F. Supp. 836, 843 (S.D.N.Y. 1975); *Estate of Presley v. Russen*, 513 F. Supp. 1339, 1353 (D.N.J. 1981), and cases cited. The right is most often asserted by or on behalf of professional athletes, comedians, actors and actresses, and other entertainers. This case involves none of those occupations. As is known to all, from 1955 until he was assassinated on April 4, 1968, Dr. King, a Baptist minister by profession, was the foremost leader of the civil rights movement in the United States. He was awarded the Nobel Prize for Peace in 1964. Although not a public official, Dr. King was a public figure, and we deal in this opinion with public figures who are neither public officials nor entertainers. Within this framework, we turn to the questions posed.

1. Is the "right of publicity" recognized in Georgia as a right distinct from the right of privacy?

Georgia has long recognized the right of privacy. Following denial of the existence of the right of privacy in a controversial decision by the New York Court of Appeals in *Roberson v. Rochester Folding-Box Co.*, 171 N.Y. 538, 64 N.E. 442 (1902), the Georgia Supreme Court became the first such court to recognize the right of privacy in *Pavesich v. New England Life Ins. Co.*, 122 Ga. 190, 50 S.E. 68 (1905). *See* Prosser, Law of Torts, pp. 802-804 (1971).

In *Pavesich v. New England Life Ins. Co., supra*, the picture of an artist was used without his consent in a newspaper advertisement of the insurance company. Analyzing the right of privacy, this court held: "The publication of a picture of a person, without his consent, as a part of an advertisement, for the purpose of exploiting the publisher's business, is a violation of the right of privacy of the person whose picture is reproduced, and entitles him to recover without proof of special damage." If the right to privacy had not been recognized, advertisers could use photographs of private citizens to promote sales and the professional modeling business would not be what it is today.

In the course of its opinion the *Pavesich* court said several things pertinent here. It noted that the commentators on ancient law recognized the right of personal liberty, including the right to exhibit oneself before the public at proper times and places and in a proper manner. As a corollary, the court recognized that the right of personal liberty included the right of a person not to be exhibited before the public, saying: "The right to withdraw from the public gaze at such times as a person may see fit, when his presence in public is not demanded by any rule of law is also embraced within the right of personal liberty. Publicity in one instance and privacy in the other is each guaranteed. If personal liberty embraces the *right of publicity*, it no less embraces the correlative right of privacy; and this is no new idea in Georgia law."

Recognizing the possibility of a conflict between the right of privacy and the freedoms of speech and press, this court said: "There is in the publication of one's picture for advertising purposes not the slightest semblance of an expression of an idea, a thought, or an opinion, within the meaning of the constitutional provision which guarantees to a person the right to publish his sentiments on any subject." The defendants in the case now before us make no claim under these freedoms and we find no violation thereof.

Observing in dicta that the right of privacy in general does not survive the death of the person whose privacy is invaded, the *Pavesich* court said: "While the right of privacy is personal, and may die with the person, we do not desire to be understood as assenting to the proposition that the relatives of the deceased can not, in a proper case, protect the memory of their kinsman, not only from defamation, but also from an invasion into the affairs of his private life after his death. This question is not now involved, but we do not wish anything said to be understood as committing us in any way to the doctrine that against the consent of relatives the private affairs of a deceased person may be published and his picture or statue exhibited."

Finding that Pavesich, although an artist, was not recognized as a public figure, the court said: "It is not necessary in this case to hold, nor are we prepared to do so, that the mere fact that a man has become what is called a public character, either by aspiring to public office, or by holding public office, or by exercising a profession which places him before the public, or by engaging in a business which has necessarily a public nature, gives to every one the right to print and circulate his picture." Thus, although recognizing the right of privacy, the *Pavesich* court left open the question facing us involving the likeness of a public figure.[3]

. . . .

The right of publicity is not absolute. In *Hicks v. Casablanca Records*, 464 F. Supp. 426 (S.D.N.Y. 1978), the court held that a fictional novel and movie concerning an unexplained eleven-day disappearance by Agatha Christie, author of numerous mystery novels, were permissible under the first amendment. On the other hand, in *Zacchini v. Scripps-Howard Broadcasting Co.*, 433 U.S. 562, 97 S.Ct. 2849, 53 L. Ed.2d 965 (1977), a television station broadcast on its news program plaintiff's 15-second "human cannonball" flight filmed at a local fair. The Supreme Court held that freedom of the press does not authorize the media to broadcast a performer's entire act without his consent, just as the media could not televise a stage play, prize fight or baseball game without consent. Quoting from Kalven, *Privacy in Tort Law—Were Warren and Brandeis Wrong?*, 31 Law & Contemp. Prob. 326, 332 (1966), the Court said: "The rationale for [protecting the right of publicity] is the straight-forward one of preventing unjust enrichment by the theft of good will. No social purpose is served by having the defendant get free some aspect of the plaintiff that would have market value and for which he would normally pay."

The right of publicity was first recognized in Georgia by the Court of Appeals in *Cabaniss v. Hipsley*, 114 Ga. App. 367, 151 S.E.2d 496 (1966). There the court held that the plaintiff,

---

[3] Following *Pavesich, supra*, this court has continued to recognize the right of privacy. In *Bazemore v. Savannah Hospital*, 171 Ga. 257, 155 S.E. 194 (1930), the court held that the parents of a child born with his heart outside his body, who died following surgery, could maintain a suit for invasion of their privacy against the hospital, a photographer and a newspaper which respectively allowed, photographed and published a nude post mortem picture of the child.

On the other hand, in *Waters v. Fleetwood*, 212 Ga. 161, 91 S.E.2d 344 (1956), it was held that the mother of a 14-year-old murder victim could not recover for invasion of the mother's privacy from a newspaper which published and sold separately photographs of her daughter's body taken after it was removed from a river. There the court found that publication and reproduction for sale of a photograph incident to a matter of public interest or to a public investigation could not be a violation of anyone's right of privacy.

an exotic dancer, could recover from the owner of the Atlanta Playboy Club for the unauthorized use of the dancer's misnamed photograph in an entertainment magazine advertising the Playboy Club. Although plaintiff had had her picture taken to promote her performances, she was not performing at the Playboy Club. The court used Dean William L. Prosser's four-pronged analysis of the right of privacy, saying:

> . . . Dean Prosser has analyzed the many privacy cases in an article entitled *Privacy*, published in 48 Calif. L. Rev. 383 (1960), and in reviewing the cases he suggests that the invasion of privacy is in reality a complex of four loosely related torts; that there are four distinct kinds of invasion of four different interests of plaintiff; that there are four disparate torts under a common name. These four torts may be described briefly as: (1) intrusion upon the plaintiff's seclusion or solitude, or into his private affairs; (2) public disclosure of embarrassing private facts about the plaintiff; (3) publicity which places the plaintiff in a false light in the public eye; (4) appropriation, for the defendant's advantage, of the plaintiff's name or likeness.

Finding no violation of the first three rights of privacy, the court found a violation of the fourth, saying:

> Unlike intrusion, disclosure, or false light, appropriation does not require the invasion of something secret, secluded or private pertaining to plaintiff, nor does it involve falsity. It consists of the appropriation, for the defendant's benefit, use or advantage, of the plaintiff's name or likeness. . . . "The interest protected [in the 'appropriation' cases] is not so much a mental as a proprietary one, in the exclusive use of the plaintiff's name and likeness as an aspect of his identity."

Although Ms. Hipsley was an entertainer (*i.e.*, a public figure), the court found she was entitled to recover from the Playboy Club (but not from the magazine which published the Club's ad) for the unauthorized use of her photograph. However the court noted a difference in the damages recoverable in traditional right of privacy cases as opposed to right of publicity cases saying:

> Recognizing, as we do, the fundamental distinction between causes of action involving injury to feelings, sensibilities or reputation and those involving an appropriation of rights in the nature of property rights for commercial exploitation, it must necessarily follow that there is a fundamental distinction between the two classes of cases in the measure of damages to be applied. In the former class (which we take to include the intrusion, disclosure, and false light aspects of the privacy tort), general damages are recoverable without proof of special damages. In the latter class, the measure of damages is the value of the use of the appropriated publicity.

In *McQueen v. Wilson*, 117 Ga. App. 488, 161 S.E.2d 63, *reversed on other grounds*, 224 Ga. 420, 162 S.E.2d 313 (1968), the Court of Appeals upheld the right of an actress, Butterfly McQueen, who appeared as "Prissie" in the movie *Gone With the Wind*, to recover for the unauthorized use of her photograph, saying: "Both before and since *Pavesich* it has been recognized that the appropriation of another's identity, picture, papers, name or signature without consent and for financial gain might be a tort for which an action would lie. . . ."

Thus, the courts in Georgia have recognized the rights of private citizens, *Pavesich, supra*, as well as entertainers, *Cabaniss* and *McQueen, supra*, not to have their names and photographs used for the financial gain of the user without their consent, where such use is not authorized as an exercise of freedom of the press. We know of no reason why a public figure prominent in religion and civil rights should be entitled to less protection than an exotic dancer or a movie actress. Therefore, we hold that the appropriation of another's name and likeness, whether such likeness be a photograph or sculpture, without consent and for the financial gain of the appropriator is a tort in Georgia, whether the person whose name and likeness is used is a private citizen, entertainer, or as here a public figure who is not a public official.

In *Pavesich, supra*, this right not to have another appropriate one's photograph was denominated the right of privacy; in *Cabaniss v. Hipsley, supra*, it was the right of publicity. Mr. Pavesich was not a public figure; Ms. Hipsley was. We conclude that while private citizens have the right of privacy, public figures have a similar right of publicity, and that the measure of damages to a public figure for violation of his or her right of publicity is the value of the appropriation to the user. As thus understood the first certified question is answered in the affirmative.

2. Does the "right of publicity" survive the death of its owner (*i.e.*, is the right inheritable and devisable)?

Although the *Pavesich* court expressly did not decide this question, the tenor of that opinion is that the right to privacy at least should be protectable after death.

The right of publicity is assignable during the life of the celebrity, for without this characteristic, full commercial exploitation of one's name and likeness is practically impossible. That is, without assignability the right of publicity could hardly be called a "right." Recognizing its assignability, most commentators have urged that the right of publicity must also be inheritable. . . .

The courts that have considered the problem are not as unanimous. In *Price v. Hal Roach Studios, Inc., supra*, the court reasoned that since the right of publicity was assignable, it survived the deaths of Stanley Laurel and Oliver Hardy. Other decisions from the Southern District of New York recognize the descendibility of the right of publicity, which has also been recognized by the Second Circuit Court of Appeals.

In *Factors Etc., Inc. v. Pro Arts, Inc.*, 579 F.2d 215 (2d Cir.1978), Elvis Presley had assigned his right of publicity to Boxcar Enterprises, which assigned that right to Factors after Presley's death. Defendant Pro Arts published a poster of Presley entitled "In Memory." In affirming the grant of injunction against Pro Arts, the Second Circuit Court of Appeals said: "The identification of this exclusive right belonging to Boxcar as a transferable property right compels the conclusion that the right survives Presley's death. The death of Presley, who was merely the beneficiary of an income interest in Boxcar's exclusive right, should not in itself extinguish Boxcar's property right. Instead, the income interest, continually produced from Boxcar's exclusive right of commercial exploitation, should inure to Presley's estate at death like any other intangible property right. To hold that the right did not survive Presley's death, would be to grant competitors of Factors, such as Pro Arts, a windfall in the form of profits from the use of Presley's name and likeness. At the same time, the exclusive right purchased by Factors and the financial benefits accruing to the celebrity's heirs would be rendered virtually worthless."

In *Lugosi v. Universal Pictures*, 25 Cal. 3d 813, 160 Cal. Rptr. 323, 603 P.2d 425 (1979), the Supreme Court of California, in a 4 to 3 decision, declared that the right of publicity expires upon the death of the celebrity and is not descendible. Bela Lugosi appeared as Dracula in Universal Picture's movie by that name. Universal had acquired the movie rights to the novel by Bram Stoker. Lugosi's contract with Universal gave it the right to exploit Lugosi's name and likeness in connection with the movie. The majority of the court held that Lugosi's heirs could not prevent Universal's continued exploitation of Lugosi's portrayal of Count Dracula after his death. The court did not decide whether Universal could prevent unauthorized third parties from exploitation of Lugosi's appearance as Dracula after Lugosi's death.

In *Memphis Development Foundation v. Factors Etc., Inc.*, 616 F.2d 956 (6th Cir. 1980), Factors, which had won its case against Pro Arts in New York (*see* above), lost against the Memphis Development Foundation under the Court of Appeals for the Sixth Circuit's interpretation of Tennessee law. There, the Foundation, a nonprofit corporation, planned to erect a statute of Elvis Presley in Memphis and solicited contributions to do so. Donors of $25 or more received a small replica of the proposed statue. The Sixth Circuit reversed the grant of an injunction favoring Factors, holding that a celebrity's right of publicity was not inheritable even where that right had been exploited during the celebrity's life.[4] The court reasoned that although recognition of the right of publicity during life serves to encourage effort and inspire creative endeavors, making the right inheritable would not. The court also was concerned with unanswered legal questions which recognizing inheritability would create. We note, however, that the court was dealing with a non-profit foundation attempting to promote Presley's adopted home place, the City of Memphis. The court was not dealing, as we do here, with a profit making endeavor.

In *Estate of Presley v. Russen, supra*, the court found in favor of descendibility,. . .saying: "If the right is descendible, the individual is able to transfer the benefits of his labor to his immediate successors and is assured that control over the exercise of the right can be vested in a suitable beneficiary. 'There is no reason why, upon a celebrity's death, advertisers should receive a windfall in the form of freedom to use with impunity the name or likeness of the deceased celebrity who may have worked his or her entire life to attain celebrity status. The financial benefits of that labor should go to the celebrity's heirs. . . .' "

For the reasons which follow we hold that the right of publicity survives the death of its owner and is inheritable and devisable. Recognition of the right of publicity rewards and thereby encourages effort and creativity. If the right of publicity dies with the celebrity, the economic value of the right of publicity during life would be diminished because the celebrity's untimely death would seriously impair, if not destroy, the value of the right of continued commercial use. Conversely, those who would profit from the fame of a celebrity after his or her death for their own benefit and without authorization have failed to establish their claim that they should be the beneficiaries of the celebrity's death. Finally, the trend since the early common law has been to recognize survivability, notwithstanding the legal problems which may thereby arise. We therefore answer question 2 in the affirmative.

3. Must the owner of the right of publicity have commercially exploited that right before it can survive?

Exploitation is understood to mean commercial use by the celebrity other than the activity which made him or her famous, *e.g.*, an inter vivos transfer of the right to the use of one's name and likeness.

The requirement that the right of publicity be exploited by the celebrity during his or her lifetime in order to render the right inheritable arises from the case involving Agatha Christie, *Hicks v. Casablanca Records, supra*. . . .

However,. . .the finding that exploitation during life was necessary to inheritability was actually unnecessary to that decision.

---

[4] The Second Circuit has now accepted the Sixth Circuit's interpretation of Tennessee law. *Factors Etc., Inc. v. Pro Arts, Inc.*, 652 F.2d 278 (2d Cir. 1981).

Nevertheless, the *Hicks* dicta has been relied upon. See *Groucho Marx Productions, Inc. v. Day & Night Co.*, 523 F. Supp. 485, 490 (S.D.N.Y. 1981).[5] However, in this case, involving the Marx brothers, it was found that, although Leo and Adolpho Marx ("Chico" and "Harpo") had not made inter vivos or specific testamentary dispositions of their rights, they had earned their livelihoods by exploiting the unique characters they created and thus had exploited their rights to publicity so as to make such rights descendible. Thus, even in the Southern District of New York where the requirement arose, exploitation beyond the "activity which made him or her famous" is not now required.

The cases which have considered this issue involved entertainers. The net result of following them would be to say that celebrities and public figures have the right of publicity during their lifetimes (as others have the right of privacy), but only those who contract for bubble gum cards, posters and tee shirts have a descendible right of publicity upon their deaths. That we should single out for protection after death those entertainers and athletes who exploit their personae during life, and deny protection after death to those who enjoy public acclamation but did not exploit themselves during life, puts a premium on exploitation. Having found that there are valid reasons for recognizing the right of publicity during life, we find no reason to protect after death only those who took commercial advantage of their fame.

Perhaps this case more than others brings the point into focus. A well known minister may avoid exploiting his prominence during life because to do otherwise would impair his ministry. Should his election not to take commercial advantage of his position during life ipso facto result in permitting others to exploit his name and likeness after his death? In our view, a person who avoids exploitation during life is entitled to have his image protected against exploitation after death just as much if not more than a person who exploited his image during life.[6]

Without doubt, Dr. King could have exploited his name and likeness during his lifetime. That this opportunity was not appealing to him does not mean that others have the right to use his name and likeness in ways he himself chose not to do. Nor does it strip his family and estate of the right to control, preserve and extend his status and memory and to prevent unauthorized exploitation thereof by others. Here, they seek to prevent the exploitation of his likeness in a manner they consider unflattering and unfitting. We cannot deny them this right merely because Dr. King chose not to exploit or commercialize himself during his lifetime.

Question 3 is answered in the negative, and therefore we need not answer question 4.

Certified questions 1 and 2 answered in the affirmative, question 3 answered in the negative, and question 4 not answered.

All the Justices concur, except WELTNER, J., who concurs specially.

WELTNER, JUSTICE, concurring specially.

I concur specially because, although this matter is one of certified questions, I believe that the complaint states a claim upon which relief can be granted. I disagree most decidedly with

---

[5] On appeal of this case, the Second Circuit reversed, finding the law of California applicable, where, as noted above, the right of publicity is not inheritable. *Groucho Marx Productions, Inc. v. Day & Night Co.*, 689 F.2d 317 (2d Cir. 1982).

[6] Although the conclusion reached in answer to question 2 was based in part upon commercial considerations, and our answer to question 3 is based upon the absence of exploitation, the reasoning supporting the answer to question 3 also supports the answer to question 2.

the substantive portion of the majority opinion, for reason that it generates more unsettling questions than it resolves.

In this opinion, we have taken the "right of privacy" as enumerated in *Pavesich, supra*, and added thereto a new thing, now called a "right of publicity." That seems to me to be more an exercise in verbal juxtaposition than a careful examination of legal issues and practical results.

At heart, the whole body of tort law is but an expression of what the community perceives to be the civil, as opposed to moral or ethical, responsibility of its members to each other. That concept changes with the cumulative experiences and assessments of succeeding generations, through constitutional, legislative, and judicial pronouncement. And well it should, for, in Thomas Jefferson's words, "Laws and institutions must go hand in hand with the progress of the human mind."

Pavesich, as example, found that it was contrary to good conscience (the conscience, that is, of the community as delineated and declared by this Court) that New England Life Insurance Company, for financial gain, might expropriate an aspect of the personality of Paolo Pavesich by the unauthorized publication of his photograph. That conduct did not meet community standards, as assayed by our Court in the year 1905. Because a remedy must need be provided, we became the first high court in the Republic to "discover" a new right—the right to privacy.

. . . .

There can be little difficulty in approaching this case in precisely the same manner. I believe we would correctly assess community concepts of responsibility in declaring that the complaint alleges conduct on the part of the defendants which, if true, would be, simply put, unconscionable. Conduct which is unconscionable under all the facts and circumstances of a given case is conduct which demands remedy. Thus we are saved the rigors and toils and perils of creating some new "right" and then declaring that it, like some Cardiff Giant, has been there all the while, waiting to be unearthed.

I would, therefore, answer the questions of the United States Court of Appeals in this manner: "The complaint in this case states a claim upon which relief can be granted." The authority for this response is no new "right," but this ancient remedy: "An action for money had and received lies in all cases where another has received money which the plaintiff, ex aequo et bono, is entitled to recover and which the defendant is not entitled in good conscience to retain." *Fain v. Neal*, 97 Ga. App. 497, 498, 103 S.E.2d 437 (1958).

Why, then, this exercise?

Because in proclaiming this new "right of publicity," we have created an open-ended and ill-defined force which jeopardizes a right of unquestioned authenticity—free speech. It should be noted that our own constitutional provision, Art. I, Sec. I, Par. IV, Constitution of Georgia (Code Ann. § 2-104), traces its lineage to the first Constitution of our State, in 1777, antedating the First Amendment by fourteen years. Its language is plain and all-encompassing: "No law shall ever be passed to curtail, or restrain the liberty of speech, or of the press; any person may speak, write and publish his sentiments, on all subjects, being responsible for the abuse of that liberty." Its authority is firmly established.

But the majority says that the fabrication and commercial distribution of a likeness of Dr. King is not "speech," thereby removing the inquiry from the ambit of First Amendment or Free Speech inquiries.

To this conclusion I most vigorously dissent. When our Constitution declares that anyone may "speak, write and publish his sentiments, on all subjects" it does not confine that freedom exclusively to verbal expression. Human intercourse is such that ofttimes the most powerful of expressions involve no words at all, *e.g.*, Jesus before Pilate; Thoreau in the Concord jail; King on the bridge at Selma.

Do not the statutes of the Confederate soldiers which inhabit so many of our courthouse squares express the sentiments of those who raised them?

Are not the busts of former chief justices, stationed within the rotunda of this very courthouse, expressions of sentiments of gratitude and approval?

Is not the portrait of Dr. King which hangs in our Capitol an expression of sentiment?

Manifestly so.

If, then, a two-dimensional likeness in oil and canvas is an expression of sentiment, how can it be said that a three-dimensional likeness in plastic is *not?*

But, says the majority, our new right to publicity is violated only in cases involving financial gain.

Did the sculptors of our Confederate soldiers, and of our chief justices, labor without gain? Was Dr. King's portraitist unpaid for his work?

If "financial gain" is to be the watershed of violation *vel non* of this new-found right, it cannot withstand scrutiny. It is rare, indeed, that any expression of sentiment beyond casual conversation is not somehow connected, directly or indirectly, to "financial gain." For example, a school child wins a $25 prize for the best essay on Dr. King's life. Is this "financial gain?" Must the child then account for the winnings?

The essay, because of its worth, is reprinted in a commercial publication. Must the publisher account?

The publication is sold on the newsstand. Must the vendor account?

The majority will say "free speech." Very well. The same child wins a $25 prize in the school art fair. His creation—a bust of Dr. King.

Must he account?

The local newspaper prints a photograph of the child and of his creation. Must it account?

The school commissions replicas of the bust to raise money for its library. Must it account?

UNICEF reproduces the bust on its Christmas cards. Must it account?

Finally, a purely commercial venture undertakes to market replicas of the bust under circumstances similar to those of this case. Must it account?

Obviously, the answers to the above questions will vary, and properly so, because the circumstances posited are vastly different. The dividing line, however, cannot be fixed upon the presence or absence of "financial gain." Rather, it must be grounded in the community's judgment of what, *ex aequo et bono*, is unconscionable.

Were it otherwise, this "right of publicity," fully extended, would eliminate scholarly research, historical analysis, and public comment, because food and shelter, and the financial gain it takes to provide them, are still essentials of human existence.

Were it otherwise, no newspaper might identify any person or any incident of his life without accounting to him for violation of his "right to publicity."

Were it otherwise, no author might refer to any event in history wherein his reference is identifiable to any individual (or his heirs!) without accounting for his royalties.

. . . .

A careful analysis of the right of free speech yields conclusions not inconsistent with the above. *All* speech is not "free," in the sense of being immune from all consequence.

Over the years our law has imposed and sustained restraints—criminal, equitable, and remedial—upon forms of speech which *inter alia* include: treason, pornography, inciting to riot, fighting words, defamation, criminal conspiracy and criminal solicitation, false official statements, and perjury.

It is undeniable that the acts controlled by these sanctions can be that of "speaking, writing, or publishing of sentiments." Yet, we have little difficulty in excluding proper cases from the privileged realm of "free speech" because *in each such instance* the calculable evil of its license plainly outweighs the potential evil of its prohibition.

As example, the community deems it "better" (and the courts so declare it) that treason be controlled than that an untrammeled free speech should give license to treasonable conduct.

Each lawful restraint finds its legitimacy, then, *not* because it is laid against some immutable rule (like the weights and measures of the Bureau of Standards) but because it is perceived that it would be irresponsible to the interest of the community—to the extent of being *unconscionable*—that such conduct go unrestrained.

The doctrine of unjust enrichment finds its genesis in such a reckoning. It can be applied to just such a matter as that before us. Were we to do so, we could avoid entering the quagmire of combining considerations of "right of privacy," "right of publicity," and considerations of *inter vivos* exploitation. We would also retain our constitutional right of free speech uncluttered and uncompromised by these new impediments of indeterminate application.

And we could sanction relief *in this case*—where relief is plainly appropriate.

[d]   Explanatory Notes

Before posing some interesting problems to wrestle with, three sets of notes may help you put the *King* case in some perspective. First, the courts in some publicity cases have attempted to articulate reasons for legitimating both the underlying right of publicity and its inheritability. Working through some of these rationales may aid evaluation of the cases. Second, the dilemmas posed by some of the right to publicity cases have led to the adoption of statutes in several states. Their provisions may also provide some structure for organizing your thoughts. Third, as previously mentioned, publicity rights have surfaced in an enormous variety of settings. A description of some of the more interesting (or humorous) cases might provide some sense of the difficulty of the issues facing the courts.

[i]   *Judicial Rationales for Publicity Rights*

[A]   *The Right of Publicity.* The *King* court, quoting Kalven, argued that the right of publicity prevents unjust enrichment by the theft of good will, and that no social purpose is served by permitting a party to "get free some aspect of the plaintiff that would have market value and for which he would normally pay." This was said to be different from the interests protected by the right to privacy, where the courts evaluate injuries to feelings, sensibilities and reputation. Does the theft of good will argument really work? "Normalcy" in receiving payments may depend upon a court's willingness to affirm the existence of protected rights in the good will. The mere incantation of the notion that you should not be able to get something of value for free assumes the result you want to reach.

There are at least two other explanations for the result, one based on commonly held notions of work and value, and the other on theoretical notions about the economic incentives necessary to foster creativity. There is a thread of feeling common to both *Associated Press* and *King* that an asset of value was created through hard work and dedication and that outsiders ought not be permitted to make money off such labor. This reasoning operates on the unmentioned assumption that hard work pays off, and the commonly held view that, when the payoff arrives, sharing the wealth is not required. Neither the assumption that hard work pays off, nor the view that payoffs should be owned exclusively by the recipient is clearly and demonstrably true. But much American cultural mythology is built upon the continued vitality of such "truths." Given Martin Luther King's lifetime devotion to the needs of others, reliance on such ideas is peculiarly ironic in the *King* case. Nonetheless, the *King* opinion may simply reflect the crass cultural understanding that the Kings have no obligation to share anything with the Bolens.

At a more dispassionate, theoretical level, it is possible that the "real" issue involves analysis of the circumstances in which our culture wishes to establish incentives for the creation and maintenance of intellectual property. Much of copyright law, for example, is based less on an aspiration to provide money to artists and authors, than it is on a desire to use the availability of money as an incentive for the creation of works beneficial to the culture at large. A system which focuses on remuneration of creative people for its own sake would *always* require payment whenever an artistic work was used by someone other than the author or artist. A system based on a desire to make intellectual property as useful as possible to as many people as possible will at times focus on ways to distribute freely a product in spite of the author's wish to restrain its use. What sort of mold does the right of publicity fit into? Is this a right which arises simply because we wish to compensate people for the use of a product created after much work and time? Or is it a right which arises because as a culture we wish to have it both ways—create an incentive to be famous, but not so big an incentive that we can never make use of a famous person's image?

[*B*]   *Inheritability.* Once a person has died, the reasons for protecting publicity rights become seriously attenuated. If courts protect publicity rights because of some proprietary notion about work and payoffs, the death of the laborer makes it more difficult to allocate payoffs arriving in the future. If a desire to structure incentives for the creation of works beneficial to society underlays the judicial protection of publicity rights, the death of the creator terminates the utility of the incentive. In fact, if incentive for creativity is the goal, publicity rights should arguably not be inheritable since the continued vitality of the deceased person's personality makes it *more expensive* for other creative talents to craft new works.

Then why protect rights in the likenesses of dead people? What of reputational and privacy concerns? If our desire is simply to pay a person for the worth of their reputation, then little is to be gained by permitting the right of publicity to be inherited. Much like the right to privacy, when the person dies, the claim on society for protection disappears. What of concern for family, a grouping of abiding importance in the rhetoric of American culture? If inheritability of the publicity rights increases the incentives for the production of beneficial intellectual properties, then a rationale may exist for permitting the successors of famous persons to control the future disposition of fame. How large an incentive need this be? Will famous people be more creative if they know their heirs will be able to control their fame? And does this rationale even fit a case like *King* where relatives were not the primary beneficiaries of King's publicity rights? Even if creativity is increased by inheritability, some outer time limit on publicity rights would still be required. At some point, adding on more years to the length of a right's existence provides no real incentive to the creativity of living persons. Rather it creates a legal structure with no present incentive effects but with unknown, and perhaps negative, impacts on the ability of future generations to create intellectual works.

The copyright law has responded to this inter-generational dilemma by setting a maximum length of time for the existence of a copyright—the life of the author or artist plus 70 years. But courts grappling with the right of publicity have generally not engrafted such a precise time limit on the right. Indeed, many would say that courts do not have the "right" to establish such precise limits. That, so the argument goes, may only be done by a legislative body. Regardless of whether this supposed difference between judicial and legislative rule making power has any real substance to it, there can be little doubt that courts have hesitated to decide cases that precisely. That hesitancy creates a real problem. How can a right be judicially created in circumstances in which an end to the right is probably called for, but the courts have repeatedly refused to describe the end point?

Note well that if you think the right of publicity ought to end at some point in the future (think of restrictions on the making of King busts a century from now, long after the Martin Luther King, Jr. monument has been constructed in monument-filled Washington, D.C.), a species of "property" would be created that is quite different from land. We normally assume that land will be here forever, even if the present owners will not. But such an assumption need not be made about all forms of property. Indeed, one of the major purposes of this course is to get you to understand the degree to which different sorts of property exist and different sorts of legal structures arise to govern their use.

[ii] *Examples of State Statutes*

[A] *Tennessee.* One of the most interesting series of publicity rights cases involved Elvis Presley. Shortly after Presley died in 1977, Pro Arts, Inc. purchased the copyright in a photograph of Presley. They enlarged the photo, placed the words "IN MEMORY . . ." in the upper left corner, the words "1935-1977" at the bottom, and had it on the market only three days after Presley died. Factors Etc., Inc., which held contractual rights to Presley's likeness,[71] sued Pro Arts, seeking to preliminarily enjoin the sale and distribution of the poster. The requested injunction was granted by the trial court, and the result was affirmed on appeal. The case later went back before the trial court for a decision on the issuance of a permanent injunction. As you might expect, the permanent injunction was issued, and the case went back up on appeal a second time. By that time the waters had been muddied by another Presley case decided by the Sixth Circuit Court of Appeals in which it was decided that the right of publicity was not inheritable.[72] When the *Pro Arts* case came back before the Second Circuit, the court decided

---

[71] Presley entered into a contract with Colonel Tom Parker granting Parker rights to his likeness. Parker in turn had contracted with Boxcar Enterprises to exploit Presley's likeness. Two days after Presley died, the rights held by Boxcar were transferred to Factors Etc., Inc. *See* Factors Etc., Inc. v. Pro Arts, Inc., 579 F.2d 215 (2d Cir. 1978).

[72] Memphis Development Foundation v. Factors Etc., Inc. 616 F.2d 956 (6th Cir. 1980).

that it had correctly used state rather than federal law to decide the case, but that it had erred in applying New York rather than Tennessee law in the original appeal. After all, almost all the basic facts in the case arose in Tennessee. The Second Circuit then deferred to the Sixth Circuit's analysis as to the content of Tennessee law and reversed the issuance of the injunction against Pro Arts![73]

All the confusion over the legitimacy of the various claims to a piece of the Presley action apparently caught the eye of the Tennessee legislature. It adopted the publicity rights statute reproduced below. Pay particular attention to §§ 47-25-1103 and 47-25-1104(b)(2). The first provides that all persons have a right of publicity. The second provision guarantees that the right will last at least 10 years after death, and terminates the right only when it has gone unused for at least two years after this minimum period has expired. Would you vote for this statute?[74]

The Tennessee Personal Rights Protection Act
TENN. CODE ANN. §§ 47-25-1101, et. seq.

§ 47-25-1102. Definitions.—As used in this part, unless the context otherwise requires:

(1) "Definable group" means an assemblage of individuals existing or brought together with or without interrelation, orderly form or arrangement, including but not limited to, a crowd at any sporting event, a crowd in any street or public building, the audience at any theatrical or stage production, a glee club, or a baseball team;

(2) "Individual" means human being, living or dead;

(3) "Likeness" means the use of an image of an individual for commercial purposes;

(4) "Person" means any firm, association, partnership, corporation, joint stock company, syndicate, receiver, common law trust, conservator, statutory trust or any other concern by whatever name known or however organized, formed or created, and includes not-for-profit corporations, associations, educational and religious institutions, political parties, community, civic or other organizations; and

(5) "Photograph" means any photograph or photographic reproduction, still or moving, or any videotape or live television transmission, of any individual, so that the individual is readily identifiable.

§ 47-25-1103. Property right in use of name, photograph, likeness.—(a) Every individual has a property right in the use of his name, photograph or likeness in any medium in any manner.

(b) The individual rights provided for in subsection (a) shall constitute property rights and shall be freely assignable and licensable, and shall not expire upon the death of the individual so protected, whether or not such rights were commercially exploited by the individual during the individual's lifetime, but shall be descendible to the executors, assigns, heirs, or devisees of the individual so protected by this part.

---

[73] Factors Etc., Inc. v. Pro Arts, Inc., 652 F.2d 278 (2d Cir. 1981).

[74] After this statute was adopted the Tennessee courts were given another opportunity to decide upon the inheritability questions in a case involving events occurring prior to the adoption of the statute. The Tennessee Court of Appeals decided that publicity rights were descendible in another Presley dispute. State of Tennessee ex rel. The Elvis Presley International Memorial Foundation v. Crowell, 733 S.W.2d 89 (Tenn. App. 1987).

§ 47-25-1104. Exclusivity and duration of right.—(a) The rights provided for in this part shall be deemed exclusive to the individual, subject to the assignment or licensing of such rights as provided in § 47-25-1103, during such individual's lifetime and to the executors, heirs, assigns or devisees for a period of ten (10) years after the death of the individual.

(b) (1) Commercial exploitation of the property right by any executor, assignee, heir, or devisee if the individual is deceased shall maintain the right as his exclusive property until such right is terminated as provided in this subsection (b).

(2) The exclusive right to commercial exploitation of the property rights is terminated by proof of the non-use of the name, likeness, or image of any individual for commercial purposes by an executor, assignee, heir or devisee to such use for a period of two (2) years subsequent to the initial ten (10) year period following the individual's death.

§ 47-25-1105. Unauthorized use prohibited.—(a) Any person who knowingly uses or infringes upon the use of another individual's name, photograph, or likeness in any medium, in any manner directed to any person other than such individual, as an item of commerce for purposes of advertising products, merchandise, goods, or services, or for purposes of fund raising, solicitation of donations, purchases of products, merchandise, goods, or services, without such individual's prior consent, or, in the case of a minor, the prior consent of such minor's parent or legal guardian, or in the case of a deceased individual, the consent of the executor or administrator, heirs, or devisees of such deceased individual, shall be liable to a civil action.

(b) In addition to the civil action authorized by this section and the remedies set out in § 47-25-1106, any person who commits unauthorized use as defined in subsection (a) commits a Class C misdemeanor.

(c) It is no defense to the unauthorized use defined in subsection (a) that the photograph includes more than one (1) individual so identifiable; provided, that the individual or individuals complaining of the use shall be represented as individuals per se rather than solely as members of a definable group represented in the photograph.

(d) If an unauthorized use as defined in subsection (a) is by means of products, merchandise, goods or other tangible personal property, all such property is declared contraband and subject to seizure by, and forfeiture to, the state in the same manner as is provided by law for the seizure and forfeiture of other contraband items.

§ 47-25-1106. Remedies.—(a) The chancery and circuit court having jurisdiction for any action arising pursuant to this part may grant injunctions on such terms as it may deem reasonable to prevent or restrain the unauthorized use of an individual's name, photograph or likeness.

(b) At any time while an action under this part is pending, the court may order the impounding, on such terms as it may deem reasonable, of all materials or any part thereof claimed to have been made or used in violation of the individual's rights, and such court may enjoin the use of all plates, molds, matrices, masters, tapes, film negatives, or other articles by means of which such materials may be reproduced.

(c) As part of a final judgment or decree, the court may order the destruction or other reasonable disposition of all materials found to have been made or used in violation of the individual's rights, and of all plates, molds, matrices, masters, tapes, film negatives, or other articles by means of which such materials may be reproduced.

(d) An individual is entitled to recover the actual damages suffered as a result of the knowing use or infringement of such individual's rights and any profits that are attributable to such use or infringement which are not taken into account in computing the actual damages. Profit or lack thereof by the unauthorized use or infringement of an individual's rights shall not be a criteria of determining liability.

(e) The remedies provided for in this section are cumulative and shall be in addition to any others provided for by law.

§ **47-25-1107. Exemptions.**—(a) It shall be deemed a fair use and no violation of an individual's rights shall be found, for purposes of this part, if the use of a name, photograph or likeness is in connection with any news, public affairs, or sports broadcast or account.

(b) The use of a name, photograph or likeness in a commercial medium shall not constitute a use for purpose of advertising or solicitation solely because the material containing such use is commercially sponsored or contains paid advertising. Rather it shall be a question of fact whether or not the use of the complainant individual's name, photograph or likeness was so directly connected with the commercial sponsorship or with the paid advertising as to constitute a use for purposes of advertising or solicitation.

(c) Nothing in this section shall apply to the owners or employees of any medium used for advertising, including, but not limited to, newspapers, magazines, radio and television stations, billboards, and transit ads, who have published or disseminated any advertisement or solicitation in violation of this part unless it is established that such owners or employees had knowledge of the unauthorized use of the individual's name, photograph, or likeness as prohibited by this section.

[*B*]   *California.* Compare the Tennessee statute with that of California, which limits the right of publicity to 50 years after death and provides for the precise family members who have the right to control the disposition of a dead person's likeness in the absence of an agreement made by the personality before death. CAL. CIV. CODE § 990. The statute, adopted in 1984, has the effect of overruling those California court decisions which had declined to make the right of publicity inheritable. California thereby followed the general trend then emerging throughout the county to create inheritance rights in fame.

California Civil Code § 990

§ **990. Deceased personality's name, voice, signature, photograph or likeness; unauthorized use; damages and profits from use; persons entitled to exercise rights; successors in interest or licensees; registration of claim; uses not requiring consent**

(a) Any person who uses a deceased personality's name, voice, signature, photograph, or likeness, in any manner, on or in products, merchandise, or goods, or for purposes of advertising or selling, or soliciting purchases of, products, merchandise, goods, or services, without prior consent from the person or persons specified in subdivision (c), shall be liable for any damages sustained by the person or persons injured as a result thereof. In addition, in any action brought under this section, the person who violated the section shall be liable to the injured party or parties in an amount equal to the greater of seven hundred fifty dollars ($750) or the actual damages suffered by the injured party or parties, as a result of the unauthorized use, and any profits from the unauthorized use that are attributable to the use and are not taken into account in computing the actual damages. In establishing these profits, the injured party or parties shall be required to present proof only of the gross revenue attributable to the use and the person who violated the section is required to prove his or her deductible expenses. Punitive damages may also be awarded to the injured party or parties. The prevailing party or parties in any action under this section shall also be entitled to attorneys' fees and costs.

(b) The rights recognized under this section are property rights, freely transferable, in whole or in part, by contract or by means of trust or testamentary documents, whether the transfer occurs before the death of the deceased personality, by the deceased personality or his or her transferees, or, after the death of the deceased personality, by the person or persons in whom the rights vest under this section or the transferees of that person or persons.

(c) The consent required by this section shall be exercisable by the person or persons to whom the right of consent (or portion thereof) has been transferred in accordance with subdivision (b), or if no such transfer has occurred, then by the person or persons to whom the right of consent (or portion thereof) has passed in accordance with subdivision (d).

(d) Subject to subdivisions (b) and (c), after the death of any person, the rights under this section shall belong to the following person or persons and may be exercised, on behalf of and for the benefit of all of those persons, by those persons who, in the aggregate, are entitled to more than a one-half interest in the rights:

(1) The entire interest in those rights belong to the surviving spouse of the deceased personality unless there are any surviving children or grandchildren of the deceased personality, in which case one-half of the entire interest in those rights belong to the surviving spouse.

(2) The entire interest in those rights belong to the surviving children of the deceased personality and to the surviving children of any dead child of the deceased personality unless the deceased personality has a surviving spouse, in which case the ownership of a one-half interest in rights is divided among the surviving children and grandchildren.

(3) If there is no surviving spouse, and no surviving children or grandchildren, then the entire interest in those rights belong to the surviving parent or parents of the deceased personality.

(4) The rights of the deceased personality's children and grandchildren are in all cases divided among them and exercisable in the manner provided in Section 240 of the Probate Code according to the number of the deceased personality's children represented; the share of the children of a dead child of a deceased personality can be exercised only by the action of a majority of them.

(e) If any deceased personality does not transfer his or her rights under this section by contract, or by means of a trust or testamentary document, and there are no surviving persons as described in subdivision (d), then the rights set forth in subdivision (a) shall terminate.

(f) (1) A successor-in-interest to the rights of a deceased personality under this section or a licensee thereof may not recover damages for a use prohibited by this section that occurs before the successor-in-interest or licensee registers a claim of the rights under paragraph (2).

(2) Any person claiming to be a successor-in-interest to the rights of a deceased personality under this section or a licensee thereof may register that claim with the Secretary of State on a form prescribed by the Secretary of State and upon payment of a fee of ten dollars ($10). The form shall be verified and shall include the name and date of death of the deceased

personality, the name and address of the claimant, the basis of the claim, and the rights claimed.

(3) Upon receipt and after filing of any document under this section, the Secretary of State may microfilm or reproduce by other techniques any of the filings or documents and destroy the original filing or document. The microfilm or other reproduction of any document under the provision of this section shall be admissible in any court of law. The microfilm or other reproduction of any document may be destroyed by the Secretary of State 50 years after the death of the personality named therein.

(4) Claims registered under this subdivision shall be public records.

(g) No action shall be brought under this section by reason of any use of a deceased personality's name, voice, signature, photograph, or likeness occurring after the expiration of 50 years from the death of the deceased personality.

(h) As used in this section, "deceased personality" means any natural person whose name, voice, signature, photograph, or likeness has commercial value at the time of his or her death, whether or not during the lifetime of that natural person the person used his or her name, voice, signature, photograph, or likeness on or in products, merchandise or goods, or for purposes of advertising or selling, or solicitation of purchase of, products, merchandise, goods or service. A "deceased personality" shall include, without limitation, any such natural person who has died within 50 years prior to January 1, 1985.

(i) As used in this section, "photograph" means any photograph or photographic reproduction, still or moving, or any video tape or live television transmission, of any person, such that the deceased personality is readily identifiable. A deceased personality shall be deemed to be readily identifiable from a photograph when one who views the photograph with the naked eye can reasonably determine who the person depicted in the photograph is.

(j) For purposes of this section, a use of a name, voice, signature, photograph, or likeness in connection with any news, public affairs, or sports broadcast or account, or any political campaign, shall not constitute a use for which consent is required under subdivision (a).

(k) The use of a name, voice, signature, photograph, or likeness in a commercial medium shall not constitute a use for which consent is required under subdivision (a) solely because the material containing the use is commercially sponsored or contains paid advertising. Rather it shall be a question of fact whether or not the use of the deceased personality's name, voice, signature, photograph, or likeness was so directly connected with the commercial sponsorship or with the paid advertising as to constitute a use for which consent is required under subdivision (a).

(l) Nothing in this section shall apply to the owners or employees of any medium used for advertising, including, but not limited to, newspapers, magazines, radio and television networks and stations, cable television systems, billboards, and transit ads, by whom any advertisement or solicitation in violation of this section is published or disseminated, unless it is established that the owners or employees had knowledge of the unauthorized use of the deceased personality's name, voice, signature, photograph, or likeness as prohibited by this section.

(m) The remedies provided for in this section are cumulative and shall be in addition to any others provided for by law.

(n) This section shall not apply to the use of a deceased personality's name, voice, signature, photograph, or likeness, in any of the following instances:

(1) A play, book, magazine, newspaper, musical composition, film, radio or television program, other than an advertisement or commercial announcement not exempt under paragraph (4).

(2) Material that is of political or newsworthy value.

(3) Single and original works of fine art.

(4) An advertisement or commercial announcement for a use permitted by paragraph (1), (2), or (3).

[iii]   *Some Other Examples of Publicity Rights Cases*

[A]   *Groucho Marx Productions, Inc. v. Day and Night Company, Inc.,* 689 F.2d 317 (2d Cir. 1982). Persons claiming to be the owners of the right of publicity held during life by Groucho, Chico, and Harpo Marx sought damages for the performance of a play on Broadway which closely mimicked the styles of the dead comics. The play itself was new material, but the characters were dressed and made up like the Marx Brothers, and they took on the mannerisms and comic styles of the famous trio. The parties argued about the applicability of the First Amendment to the protection of creative dramatic works, but the court avoided that issue. It held that California law governed the decision of the case and that California law did not provide for the survival of publicity rights. The case was decided before California's publicity rights legislation was adopted.

[B]   *John W. Carson v. Here's Johnny Portable Toilets, Inc.,* 698 F.2d 831 (6th Cir. 1983). As you may know, the late evening Johnny Carson show opened with an introduction by Ed McMahon. He named the evening's guests and finished his introduction with a fairly grotesque, prolonged, loud, "Heeeeeeeeeeeeeeeeeeeeeeere's Johnny!" Carson then strolled onto the stage to the boisterous applause of a well prompted audience. The defendants, who were in the portable toilet business, argued that they had not used the actual name or likeness of Johnny Carson on their product. But the court held that the bond of recognition between McMahon's introduction and Johnny Carson was so strong that the right of publicity was violated by the use of the label "Here's Johnny" for the portable toilets. Did Johnny Carson, therefore, have a monopoly on jokes about himself?

[C]   *The Flying Cannonball.* In *Hugo Zacchini v. Scripps-Howard Broadcasting Co.,* 433 U.S. 562 (1977), Hugo Zacchini, the Human Cannonball,[75] sued the owners of WEWS-TV in Cleveland for broadcasting a video tape of his act on the local Eyewitness News, despite being warned not to shoot the 200-foot shot. The Ohio Supreme Court held that the Human Cannonball failed to allege a cause of action because the TV station had a First Amendment right to report matters of public interest. 47 Ohio St. 2d 224, 351 N.E.2d 454 (1976). The United States Supreme Court reversed, stating that the display of the complete cannon shot on the tube posed "a substantial threat to the economic value of that performance." The station either had to pay

---

[75] Hugo was not the only flying cannon ball. Five of the seven sons of Ildebrando Zacchini, an Italian gymnast of the early twentieth century, ended up being shot out of a cannon at 90 miles per hour. The family came up with the act in 1922. John Ringling saw them in Copenhagen at Tivoli Gardens and brought them to the United States in 1929 to perform with the Ringling Brothers, Barnum & Bailey Circus. The five brothers, and later some of their children, continued the act with various circuses. Hugo Zacchini was the son of Edmondo Zacchini, the last of the family to perform. That curtain call came on Aug. 29, 1991. The last living flying cannonball, Mario Zacchini, one of the original five brothers, died on Jan. 28, 1999 in Tampa, Florida, at the age of 87. Glenn Collins, *Mario Zacchini, Sensational Human Cannonball, Dies at 87*, N.Y. TIMES, Feb. 3, 1999, at A21, col. 3.

Zacchini to broadcast the entire shot, or report the event without using a tape of the complete act. Three of the dissenters in the case, which was decided on a vote of 5-4, argued that the First Amendment protected the station unless there was clear commercial exploitation of the act.

[e]   Problem Notes

[*i*]   *Political Humor and the Right of Publicity.* During the presidential election campaign of 1980, Thomas Shadyac, the owner of an outfit called Punch Posters, printed a poster with a hand-waving figure looking much like Ronald Reagan dressed in a Ronald McDonald outfit, standing in front of a restaurant looking much like a McDonald's Restaurant under a double arch looking much like those at McDonald's Restaurants. Under the hand-waving figure was the name "Ronald McReagan," instead of Ronald McDonald. On the double arch was a phrase, much like those that used to appear on McDonald's arches indicating how many hamburgers had been sold to date by the chain. On the poster the sign on the arches said "Ronald's: Over 69 Years Old," instead of "McDonald's: Over 16 Billion Sold." Finally, at the top of the poster was the phrase, "Give Ronald a Job He Can Handle." Punch Posters was sued by McDonald's, which (according to the newspaper accounts) alleged that the poster abused both Reagan and the company trademarks. An injunction was issued against the further sale of the poster. WASHINGTON POST, Oct. 3, 1980, at Section B, p. 1, col. 5. Is the law humorless? Can McDonald's sue on behalf of Reagan? If not, could Reagan have obtained an injunction on his own behalf?

[*ii*]   *Humorless Politics and Publicity.* In *Nixon v. Warner Communications*, 435 U.S. 589 (1978), Warner Communications sued to obtain copies of the tapes admitted into evidence during the Watergate trial of Nixon's advisors. Warner wanted to use the copies for broadcast and sale to the public. The Supreme Court described one of the arguments made by Nixon to prevent release of the tapes as follows:

> [Nixon] argues that he has a property interest in the sound of his own voice, an interest that respondents intend to appropriate unfairly. In respondents' view, our decision in *Nixon v. Administrator of General Services*, 433 U.S. 425 (1977), upholding the constitutionality of the Presidential Recordings Act, divested petitioner of any property rights in the tapes that could be asserted against the general public. Petitioner insists however, that respondents' point is not fully responsive to his argument. Petitioner is not asserting a proprietary right in the tapes themselves. He likens his interest to that of a third party whose voice is recorded in the course of a lawful wiretap by police officers and introduced into evidence on tape. In petitioner's view, use of one's voice as evidence in a criminal trial does not give rise to a license for commercial exploitation.

The Supreme Court did not answer the question of Nixon's rights in the commercial use of his voice; the case was decided on other grounds. After reading *International News Service* and *King*, how would you decide the unanswered issue? Nixon is now dead. Should that make a difference? Now re-answer the same questions, but assume that you are a history professor at a university. Compare this dispute with ones in which famous singers have successfully objected to the use of voice mimes in product commercials. *Waits v. Frito-Lay, Inc.,* 978 F.2d 1093 (9th Cir. 1992); *Midler v. Ford Motor Co.,* 849 F.2d 460 (9th Cir. 1988).

[*iii*]   *Imitation is the Sincerest Form of Flattery—Or Is It?* Onassis v. Christian Dior-New York, Inc., 122 Misc. 2d 603, 472 N.Y.S.2d 254 (Sup. Ct. 1984), involved an advertisement

promoting Dior products with a picture of a group of famous people. Most of the people in the picture were real. But a "look alike," Barbara Reynolds, stood in for Jacqueline Kennedy Onassis. I have seen the advertisement. Take my word for it that Reynolds' picture was a spitting image of Onassis. Onassis sued and won. Does that mean that all imitators must change their acts to other forms of comedy?

[*iv*]   ***Commercial Exploitation and Publicity Rights.*** Here are the facts of a wonderful case, *Columbia Broadcasting System v. DeCosta*, 377 F.2d 315 (1st Cir. 1977), in which DeCosta "donated" his personality to his community. Given the right of publicity cases that have been decided since 1977, would you, like the First Circuit Court of Appeals, still deny him relief?[76]

The story of this case—more bizarre than most television serial installments—is one of "coincidence" run riot. The plaintiff, of Portuguese parents, is a Rhode Island mechanic whose formal education ceased after the fourth grade. During the Depression, having tired of factory work, he hopped a freight for the West, lived in hobo jungles, and eventually became a range hand on a Texas ranch. After two years of riding and roping he returned to Rhode Island to work as a mechanic and later received training as a motor machinist in the Coast Guard. But he retained his passion for all things western. In 1947 he began to participate in rodeos, horse shows, horse auctions, and parades.

From the beginning plaintiff indulged a penchant for costume. He was already equipped with a moustache. He soon settled on a black shirt, black pants, and a flat-crowned black hat. He had acquired a St. Mary's medal at a parade and affixed this to his hat. He adopted the name Paladin after an onlooker of Italian descent had hurled an epithet at him containing the word "Paladino." On looking up the word Paladin in a dictionary he found it meant "champion of Knights" and was content that people began so to call him. One day when he had donned his costume in preparation for a horse show, and was about to mount his horse, one of a group waiting for him shouted "Have Gun Will Travel," a cry immediately picked up by the children present.

The finishing touches were a chess knight, bought for fifteen cents at an auction, which plaintiff thought was a good symbol, and which he used on a business card along with the words "Have," "Gun," "Will," "Travel," and "Wire Paladin, N. Court St., Cranston, R. I.", hand-printed with separate rubber stamps; a silver copy of the chess piece on his holster; and an antique derringer strapped under his arm. So accoutered, he would appear in parades, the openings and finales of rodeos, auctions, horse shows, and a pony ring he once operated. From time to time at rodeos he would stage a western gunfight, featuring his quick draw and the timely use of his hidden derringer. He would pass out photographs of himself and cards— printed versions soon replacing the rubber-stamped ones. Hospitals, drug stores, barber shops, sports shops, diners—all were the repositories of his cards, some 250,000 of them. Children clamored for the cards, and clustered about him to the extent that he was likened to the Pied Piper and Gene Autry. This was perhaps one of the purest promotions ever staged, for plaintiff did not seek anything but the entertainment of others. He sold no product, services, or institution, charged no fees, and exploited only himself.

Ten years after he had begun to live his avocational role of Paladin, he and his friends saw the first CBS television production of "Have Gun Will Travel," starring mustachioed Richard

---

[76] Mr. DeCosta eventually recovered $3.5 million, but relief came in a trademark infringement case. *'Night Knight*, N.Y. Times, Sept. 29, 1991, at E8, col. 1.

Boone, who played the part of an elegant knight errant of the Old West, always on the side of Good—for a fee. The television Paladin also wore a black costume, a flat-crowned black hat bearing an oval silver decoration, and a silver chess knight on his holster, and announced himself with a card featuring a chess piece virtually—if not absolutely—identical with the plaintiff's and the words "HAVE GUN WILL TRAVEL, WIRE PALADIN, SAN FRANCISCO." The series was notably successful; it appeared in 225 first-run episodes in the United States, was licensed in foreign countries, and by the time of trial had grossed in excess of fourteen million dollars.

[v] **World Famous Persons and Their Fame.** A bitter family feud has recently erupted over the use of Pablo Picasso's name. Claude Picasso, his surviving son and administrator of his estate, has sold the right to use of the artist's name to PSA Peugot–Citroën. The French automaker plans to use the name on a new car. Marina Picasso, granddaughter of the artist, has sued to bar such use of her ancestor's name. "I cannot tolerate that the name of my grandfather and of my father be used to sell something as banal as a car," she is reported to have said. "He was a genius who is now being exploited outrageously. His name, his very soul, should not be used for any ends other than art." The estate has also licensed use of the Picasso name for a new restaurant in Bellagio Hotel in Las Vegas. For more details on the Picasso dispute *see* Alan Riding, *A family Feud Over a Picasso (On Wheels),* NEW YORKTIMES, B1, col. 3 (April 19, 1999). Can people ever become so well important and well known that their names become public "property?" Was Martin Luther King such a person?

[f]   Some Closing Thoughts on the *King* Case and the Right of Publicity

Victor DeCosta's search for relief from CBS and that of Martin Luther King's successors for some remedy against American Heritage Products are closely related disputes. In both cases, the central characters literally gave themselves away to their constituents and supporters.[77] They behaved far differently from the contemporary sports figures who sell themselves for all sorts of advertising purposes.[78] Neither had a desire to exploit a market. And yet in each case, part of the relief sought was a declaration that the owners of rights in their publicity had control over the economic exploitation of their fame. Applying the logic of *International News Service* to these claims may well stretch to the breaking point. Why should a theory based on control over the marketing of products have any application to the status of people who refused to market themselves?

The *King* opinion was written on the assumption that those running King's estate had to choose between attempting to protect his fame as best they could and abandoning control over his fame to the public domain. That is a very Formalist assumption. If you assume that private ordering should be protected from interference by the government, you might conclude that King's failure to privately order anything means that no product needing protection from interference by others exists. Anyone should be free to make contracts about himself free from legal constraint.

---

[77] King apparently made some small amounts from speeches and copyrights in his works, but the Georgia Supreme Court treated those as unimportant.

[78] Cases involving famous sports figures, entertainers and performers are commonplace. Some of the most recent involved Joe Montana (Montana v. San Jose Mercury News, Inc. 40 Cal. Rptr. 639 (1995)), the 1969 World Champion New York Mets (Shamsky v. Garan, Inc., 632 N.Y.S.2d 930 (1995)), Elvis Presley (Elvis Presley Enterprises v. Capece, 141 F.3d 188 (5th Cir. 1998)), Fred Astaire's wife Robyn Astaire (Astaire v. Best Film Video Corp., 116 F.3d 1297 (9th Cir. 1997)), and Woody Allen (Allen v. Men's World Outlet, 679 F. Supp. 360 (S.D.N.Y. 1988)).

But what if you take a different view and think about personhood and products? Shouldn't King have had the ability to stop someone from commercially using his name because it demeaned the meaning of his life? And in searching for a rule to protect King's privacy or personhood, aren't you really seeking to prevent the creation of a market rather than to allow one to operate. A personhood rule, after all, is about precluding the use of one's fame, not obtaining payment for it. So if the motivation for King having a publicity right arises primarily out of personhood concerns, then the Center for Social Change should be able to obtain relief against American Heritage, but it should also have been unable to commercially exploit King in any other, less junky way! I suspect, however, that the Center wants to have it both ways—stop the junk and make money in good taste. Is it clear they should be allowed to do that?

Clearly we have made a paradigm shift from *International News Service* to the *King* case. We have reached a confusing point where market based theories are used to handle disputes over rights which arguably should be structured as non-marketable commodities.[79] In the final segment of this chapter, the materials quite explicitly explore the idea that some forms of property should be intentionally left outside of a market sphere. And that exploration is done by thinking about the human body, not as the object of slave ownership, but as the repository of assets so valuable that they should not be for sale.

§ 12.04 Personhood, Property and Markets

[1] Introduction

Can it, or should it, be said that we own ourselves? That is the central question posed by the materials in this section. Ownership of one person by another has been illegal since the Civil War. In a theoretical sense, that came to mean that we could make property like claims for the value of our labor. But in this century, the linkages between property, personhood and value have moved far beyond our work.

The law obviously provides each of us with significant "rights" to exclude others from interfering with our physical and mental integrity. Criminal and civil penalties for assault and battery or Constitutional protections from unreasonable searches and seizures immediately come to mind. Similarly, we each retain the ability to "use" our bodies in quite far ranging ways, just as owners of tangible assets may use their property for a profusion of purposes. Our personalities are now protected by publicity rights. The scope of our "right" to control private intimate behavior has grown substantially. But as with most typical forms of property, the right to "exclude" others from our physical selves or to use our bodies in certain ways is not absolute. Compulsory vaccination and inoculation laws, marriage license blood tests and, now, AIDS testing are a few examples. There also are significant limitations on our ability to use our own tissues as we please. Consider prostitution controls, drug laws, and, more recently, bans on the sale of transplantable tissues. And, of course, recent developments in medical technology have made our bodies into containers of valuable tissues, transplantable organs and genetic information. What are these developments going to do to the core meanings of "property?"

---

[79] The notion that the right of publicity has moved far beyond its originally intended purposes has been the subject of quite a bit of commentary. For a recent version, *see* Arlen Langvardt, *The Troubling Implications of a Right of Publicity "Wheel" Spun out of Control*, 45 U. KAN. L. REV. 329 (1997). The wheel reference in the title is to the well known case involving Vanna White of Wheel of Fortune fame, White v. Samsung Electronics Am., Inc., 971 F.2d 1395 (9th Cir. 1992), which involved a claim against an advertisement using an evening gown clad, blonde wigged robot turning letters on a mock game show.

The "property-ness" of our physical, rather than reputational, selves is the subject of the next case, *Florida v. Powell.*[80] It was a dispute between relatives of two deceased young persons and a coroner who removed corneas from the two bodies without the permission of any next of kin. While reading this case, think about four quite different models for approaching the problems it presents. The first model would treat the corneas of dead people as in the public domain. Once people die, they have no need for their corneas. The compelling needs of blind people, the argument would go, suggest that coroners should be able to remove corneas without hindrance to help living people. A second approach would treat corneas as transferable, but only by way of gift. They would be treated as aspects of generosity and kept out of a market environment. Third, you could treat corneas as marketable commodities, available for sale to the highest bidder. And finally, why not think of corneas as so valuable that they are not available for transfer under any circumstances? Like the heart of a living person, they would be permanently linked to the body of their "owner."

For some readings on these problems, consult MARGARET JANE RADIN, CONTESTED COMMODI-TIES (1998); Stephen Schnably, *Property and Pragmatism: A Critique of Radin's Theory of Property and Personhood*, 45 STAN. L. REV. 347 (1993); Susan Rose-Ackerman, *Inalienability and the Theory of Property Rights*, 85 COLUM. L. REV. 931 (1985); Margaret Jane Radin, *Personhood and Property*, 34 STAN. L. REV. 957 (1982).

[2] Opinions of the Florida Supreme Court in *State of Florida v. Powell*

State of Florida v. Powell

Florida Supreme Court
497 So.2d 1188 (1986)

Jim Smith, Atty. Gen. and Kenneth McLaughlin, Asst. Atty. Gen., Tallahassee, for State of Florida.

Alan C. Sundberg, George N. Meros, Jr. and F. Townsend Hawkes of Carlton, Fields, Ward, Emmanuel, Smith and Cutler, Tallahassee, for Medical Eye Bank, Inc., North Florida Lions Eye Bank, Inc., and Florida Lions Eye Bank, Inc.

Andrew G. Pattillo, Jr. and Russell W. LaPeer of Patillo and McKeever, Ocala, for William H. Shutze, M.D., Thomas M. Techman, M.D., and Keith Gauger.

Craig A. Dennis of Perkins & Collins, Tallahassee, for Florida Society of Ophthalmology, Inc.

Donald W. Weidner, Associate Gen. Counsel, Jacksonville, for Florida Medical Association, Inc.

Robert A. Ginsburg, Dade Co. Atty. and Robert L. Blake, Asst. Co. Atty., Public Health Division, Jackson Memorial Hospital, Miami, for Dade County, intervenor.

Jerome J. Bornstein and Mark P. Lang, Staff Counsel, American Civil Liberties, Orlando, and Stephen T. Maher, American Civil Liberties Union Foundation of Florida, Inc., University of Miami School of Law, Coral Gables, for Wade Powell and Freda Powell.

James T. Reich, and Jack Singbush of Jack Singbush, P.A., Ocala, for Erwin White and Susan White.

---

[80] The story of the case is well described in the opinion. A background history is not really necessary.

Frederick H. von Unwerth of Kilpatrick & Cody, Washington, D.C., for the Eye Bank Association of America, Inc., amicus curiae.

Melinda L. McNichols of Arky, Freed, Stearns, Watson, Greer and Weaver, P.A., Miami, for Reverend Thomas J. Price, amicus curiae.

Benedict P. Kuehne of Bierman, Sonnett, Shohat and Sale, P.A., Miami, for the Rabbinical Association of Greater Miami, Temple Beth Or, and Rabbi Rami Shapiro, Ph.D., amicus curiae.

OVERTON, JUSTICE.

This is a petition to review a circuit court order finding unconstitutional section 732.9185, Florida Statutes (1983), which authorizes medical examiners to remove corneal tissue from decedents during statutorily required autopsies when such tissue is needed for transplantation. The statute prohibits the removal of the corneal tissue if the next of kin objects, but does not require that the decedent's next of kin be notified of the procedure. The Fifth District Court of Appeal certified that this case presents a question of great public importance requiring immediate resolution by this Court. We accept jurisdiction pursuant to article V, section 3(b)(5), Florida Constitution, and, for the reasons expressed below, find that the statute is constitutional.

The challenged statute provides:

Corneal removal by medical examiners.—

(1) In any case in which a patient is in need of corneal tissue for a transplant, a district medical examiner or an appropriately qualified designee with training in ophthalmologic techniques may, upon request of any eye bank authorized under s. 732.918, provide the cornea of a decedent whenever all of the following conditions are met:

(a) A decedent who may provide a suitable cornea for the transplant is under the jurisdiction of the medical examiner and an autopsy is required in accordance with s. 406.11.

(b) No objection by the next of kin of the decedent is known by the medical examiner.

(c) The removal of the cornea will not interfere with the subsequent course of an investigation or autopsy.

(2) Neither the district medical examiner nor his appropriately qualified designee nor any eye bank authorized under s. 732.918 may be held liable in any civil or criminal action for failure to obtain consent of the next of kin.

The trial court decided this case by summary judgment. The facts are not in dispute. On June 15, 1983, James White drowned while swimming at the city beach in Dunellon, Florida. Associate Medical Examiner Dr. Thomas Techman, who is an appellant in this cause, performed an autopsy on James' body at Leesburg Community Hospital. On July 11, 1983, Anthony Powell died in a motor vehicle accident in Marion County. Medical Examiner Dr. William H. Shutze, who is also an appellant in this cause, performed an autopsy on Anthony's body. In each instance, under the authority of section 732.9185, the medical examiner removed corneal tissue from the decedent without giving notice to or obtaining consent from the parents of the decedent.

James' and Anthony's parents, who are the appellees in this case, each brought an action claiming damages for the alleged wrongful removal of their son's corneas and seeking a judgment declaring section 732.9185 unconstitutional.[1] The actions were subsequently consolidated.

---

[1] The Whites named as defendants Shutze, Techman, Keith Gauger, who is an investigator for the medical examiner's office in that district, and the State of Florida. The Powells named as defendants Shutze and the Monroe Regional

In its judgment, the trial court noted that section 732.9185 "has as its purpose the commendable and laudable objective of providing high quality cornea tissue to those in need of same," but declared the statute unconstitutional on the grounds that it (1) deprives survivors of their fundamental personal and property right to dispose of their deceased next of kin in the same condition as lawful autopsies left them, without procedural or Substantive Due Process of law; (2) creates an invidious classification which deprives survivors of their right to equal protection; and (3) permits a taking of private property by state action for a non-public purpose, in violation of article X, section 6(a), of the Florida Constitution. The court concluded that the state has no compelling interest in non-consensual removal of appellees' decedents' corneal tissue that outweighs the survivors' right to dispose of their sons' bodies in the condition death left them. For the reasons expressed below, we reject these findings.

In addressing the issue of the statute's constitutionality, we begin with the premise that a person's constitutional rights terminate at death. *See Roe v. Wade*, 410 U.S. 113 (1973); *Silkwood v. Kerr-McGee Corp.*, 637 F.2d 743 (10th Cir. 1980), *cert. denied*, 454 U.S. 833 (1981). If any rights exist, they belong to the decedent's next of kin.

Next, we recognize that a legislative act carries with it the presumption of validity and the party challenging a statute's constitutionality must carry the burden of establishing that the statute bears no reasonable relation to a permissible legislative objective.

In determining whether a permissible legislative objective exists, we must review the evidence arising from the record in this case.

The unrebutted evidence in this record establishes that the State of Florida spends approximately $138 million each year to provide its blind with the basic necessities of life. At present, approximately ten percent of Florida's blind citizens are candidates for cornea transplantation, which has become a highly effective procedure for restoring sight to the functionally blind. As advances are made in the field, the number of surgical candidates will increase, thereby raising the demand for suitable corneal tissue. The increasing number of elderly persons in our population has also created a great demand for corneas because corneal blindness often is age-related. Further, an affidavit in the record states:

> Corneal transplants are particularly important in newborns. The brain does not learn to see if the cornea is not clear. There is a critical period in the first few months of life when the brain "learns to see." If the cornea is not clear, the brain not only does not "learn to see," but the brain loses its ability to "learn to see." Hence, corneal transplant in children must be made as soon as practicable after the problem is discovered. Without the medical examiner legislation, there would be virtually no corneal tissue available for infants and these children would remain forever blind.

The record reflects that the key to successful corneal transplantation is the availability of high-quality corneal tissue and that corneal tissue removed more than ten hours after death is generally unsuitable for transplantation. The implementation of section 732.9185 in 1977 has, indisputably, increased both the supply and quality of tissue available for transplantation. Statistics show that,

Medical Center. Dade County, The Medical Eye Bank, Inc., North Florida Lions Eye Bank, Inc., Florida Lions Eye Bank, Inc., Florida Medical Association, Inc., Florida Society of Ophthalmology, Inc., and Eye Bank Association of America, Inc., were each permitted to intervene as parties in support of the constitutionality of section 732.9185. The Reverend Thomas J. Price of the Florida Conference of United Methodist Churches and the Rabbinical Association of Greater Miami filed amicus briefs in support of the appellees' position.

in 1976, only 500 corneas were obtained in Florida for transplantation while, in 1985, more than 3,000 persons in Florida had their sight restored through corneal transplantation surgery.

The record also demonstrates that a qualitative difference exists between corneal tissue obtained through outright donation and tissue obtained pursuant to section 732.9185. In contrast to the tissue donated by individuals, which is largely unusable because of the advanced age of the donor at death, approximately eighty to eighty-five percent of tissue obtained through medical examiners is suitable for transplantation. The evidence establishes that this increase in the quantity and quality of available corneal tissue was brought about by passage of the statute and is, in large part, attributable to the fact that section 732.9185 does not place a duty upon medical examiners to seek out the next of kin to obtain consent for cornea removal. An affidavit in the record reveals that, before legislation authorized medical examiners in California to remove corneas without the consent of the next of kin, the majority of the families asked by the Los Angeles medical examiner's office responded positively; however, approximately eighty percent of the families could not be located in sufficient time for medical examiners to remove usable corneal tissue from the decedents.

An autopsy is a surgical dissection of the body; it necessarily results in a massive intrusion into the decedent. This record reflects that cornea removal, by comparison, requires an infinitesimally small intrusion which does not affect the decedent's appearance. With or without cornea removal, the decedent's eyes must be capped to maintain a normal appearance.

Our review of section 732.9185 reveals certain safeguards which are apparently designed to limit cornea removal to instances in which the public's interest is greatest and the impact on the next of kin the least: corneas may be removed only if the decedent is under the jurisdiction of the medical examiner; an autopsy is mandated by Florida law; and the removal will not interfere with the autopsy or an investigation of the death. Further, medical examiners may not automatically remove tissue from all decedents subject to autopsy; rather, a request must be made by an eye bank based on a present need for the tissue.

We conclude that this record clearly establishes that this statute reasonably achieves the permissible legislative objective of providing sight to many of Florida's blind citizens.

We next address the trial court's finding that section 732.9185 deprives appellees of a fundamental property right. All authorities generally agree that the next of kin have no property right in the remains of a decedent. Although, in *Dunahoo v. Bess*, 146 Fla. 182, 200 So. 541 (1941), this Court held that a surviving husband had a "property right" in his wife's body which would sustain a claim for negligent embalming, we subsequently clarified our position to be consistent with the majority view that the right is limited to "possession of the body. . .for the purpose of burial, sepulture or other lawful disposition," and that interference with this right gives rise to a tort action.[3] *Kirksey v. Jernigan*, 45 So.2d 188, 189 (Fla. 1950). More recently, we affirmed the district court's determination that the next of kin's right in a decedent's remains is based upon "the personal right of the decedent's next of kin to bury the body rather than any property right in the body itself." *Jackson v. Rupp*, 228 So.2d 916, 918 (Fla. 4th DCA 1969), *affirmed*, 238 So.2d 86 (Fla.1970). The view that the next of kin has no property right but merely

[3] The American Law Institute sets forth the tort of interfering with the "right of burial" as follows: "One who intentionally, recklessly or negligently removes, withholds, mutilates or operates upon the body of a dead person or prevents its proper interment or cremation is subject to liability to a member of the family of the deceased who is entitled to the disposition of the body." Restatement (Second) of Torts § 868 (1979).

a limited right to possess the body for burial purposes is universally accepted by courts and commentators.

. . . .

The Maryland Court of Appeals has summarized the law as follows:

It is universally recognized that there is no property in a dead body in a commercial or material sense.

[I]t is not part of the assets of the estate (though its disposition may be affected by the provision of the will); it is not subject to replevin; it is not property in a sense that will support discovery proceedings; it may not be held as security for funeral costs; it cannot be withheld by an express company, or returned to the sender, where shipped under a contract calling for cash on delivery; it may not be the subject of a gift *causa mortis*; it is not common law larceny to steal a corpse. Rights in a dead body exist ordinarily only for purposes of burial and, except with statutory authorization, for no other purpose.

Snyder v. Holy Cross Hosp., 30 Md. App. 317 at 328 n. 12, 352 A.2d 334 at 340, quoting P.E. Jackson, *The Law of Cadavers and of Burial and Burial Places* (2d ed. 1950).

Under the facts and circumstances of these cases, we find no taking of private property by state action for a non-public purpose in violation of article X, section 6, of the Florida Constitution. We note that the right to bring an action in tort does not necessarily invoke constitutional protections. Decisions of the United States Supreme Court have clearly established that the loss of a common law right by legislative act does not automatically operate as a deprivation of substantive due process. Tort actions may be restricted when necessary to obtain a permissible legislative objective.

Appellees also assert that their right to control the disposition of their decedents' remains is a fundamental right of personal liberty protected against unreasonable governmental intrusion by the due process clause. Appellees argue that, because the statute permits the removal of a decedent's corneas without reference to his family's preferences, it infringes upon a right, characterized as one of religion, family, or privacy, which is fundamental and must be subjected to strict scrutiny. Appellees rely upon a line of decisions from the United States Supreme Court which recognize the freedom of personal choice in matters of family life as one of the liberties protected by the due process clause.

Appellees also point out that the United States Supreme Court has found rights to personal privacy in connection with activities relating to marriage, *Boddie v. Connecticut*, 401 U.S. 371 (1971); procreation, *Skinner v. Oklahoma*, 316 U.S. 535 (1942); contraception, *Griswold v. Connecticut*, 381 U.S. 479 (1965); abortion, *Roe v. Wade*; and child-rearing and education, *Pierce v. Society of Sisters*, 268 U.S. 510 (1925). According to appellees, the theme which runs through these cases, and which compels the invalidation of section 732.9185, is the protection from governmental interference of the right of free choice in decisions of fundamental importance to the family.

We reject appellees' argument. The cases cited recognize only freedom of choice concerning personal matters involved in existing, ongoing relationships among living persons as fundamental or essential to the pursuit of happiness by free persons. We find that the right of the next of kin to a tort claim for interference with burial, established by this Court in *Dunahoo*, does not rise to the constitutional dimension of a fundamental right traditionally protected under either the United States or Florida Constitution. Neither federal nor state privacy provisions protect an individual from every governmental intrusion into one's private life, especially when a statute addresses public health interests. . . .

The record contains no evidence that the appellees' objections to the removal of corneal tissues for human transplants are based on any fundamental tenets of their religious beliefs. The very concept of ordered liberty precludes allowing every person to make his own standards on matters of conduct in which society as a whole has important interests.

. . . .

In conclusion, we hold that section 732.9185 is constitutional because it rationally promotes the permissible state objective of restoring sight to the blind.[4] In so holding, we note that laws regarding the removal of human tissues for transplantation implicate moral, ethical, theological, philosophical, and economic concerns which do not readily lend themselves to analysis within a traditional legal frame-work. Applying constitutional standards of review to section 732.9185 obscures the fact that at the heart of the issue lies a policy question which calls for a delicate balancing of societal needs and individual concerns more appropriately accomplished by the legislature.

For the reasons expressed, we reverse the trial court's order and remand this cause to the trial court with directions to enter judgment consistent with this opinion.

McDONALD, C.J., AND ADKINS, BOYD, EHRLICH AND BARKETT, JJ., concur.

SHAW, JUSTICE, dissenting.

Before setting out my disagreements with the substance of the majority opinion, it is necessary to first clarify the procedural posture of these cases.

The Whites brought a complaint in four counts against appellants Gauger, Techman and Shutze concerning the circumstances surrounding an autopsy and cornea removal performed on their teenage son following his accidental drowning on 15 June 1983. Techman and Shutze are medical doctors and, respectively, an assistant medical examiner and the medical examiner in the Fifth Judicial Circuit. Gauger is a non-medical investigator in Marion County. As amended in four counts, the complaint alleges, inter alia, as follows. Count I alleges that the Whites had objected to the autopsy and any alteration of their son's body; that no cause of death other than accidental drowning was reasonable in that five persons, including an off-duty highway patrolman, had witnessed the drowning; that appellant Shutze had established a policy and mechanism for performing autopsies on all drowning victims contrary to section 406.11, Florida Statutes (1981); that decisions on autopsies in Marion County are made by Gauger, a private employee of Shutze & Techman P.A., who obtains and transports bodies to Lake County where autopsies are performed; that appellant Shutze permitted Gauger to falsely represent himself as a member of the medical examiner's staff; that Shutze & Techman P.A. performed formed autopsies on a piecework basis and directly benefited from the number of autopsies performed; that the autopsy was performed contrary to section 872.04, Florida Statutes (1981); that appellant Gauger was untrained in ophthalmology and unqualified to be designated under section 732.9185, Florida Statutes (1981), as a person to provide corneas; that conditions precedent to removal of corneas under section 732.9185 were not met; and that the Whites have suffered damages by reason of

---

[4] Courts in Georgia and Michigan have upheld the constitutionality of cornea removal statutes similar to Florida's. *See Georgia Lions Eye Bank, Inc. v. Lavant*, 255 Ga. 60, 335 S.E.2d 127 (1985), *cert. denied*, 475 U.S. 1084, 106 S. Ct. 1464, 89 L. Ed. 2d 721 (1986); *Tillman v. Detroit Receiving Hospital*, 138 Mich. App. 683, 360 N.W.2d 275 (1984).

extreme mental pain and anguish for which compensatory and punitive damages should be paid. Counts II and III are actions pursuant to chapter 86, Florida Statutes (1981), seeking declaratory judgments as to the Whites' rights, duties, and privileges under sections 732.9185 and 406.11 which allege that both sections are unconstitutional both facially and as applied. Count IV is an action alleging violation of civil rights under Title 42, U.S.C. § 1983 and the United States Constitution.

The Powells also brought a complaint in four counts against appellants Shutze and Monroe Regional Medical Center (MRMC) concerning the autopsy and cornea removal performed on their twenty-year-old son following his death in a single vehicle accident on 11 July 1983. Count I alleges that appellants performed an arbitrary, capricious and unlawful autopsy and removed corneas without meeting the conditions precedent of section 732.9185. Count II alleges that section 732.9185 is facially unconstitutional and directly contrary to section 732.910, *et seq.*, Florida Statutes (1981). Counts III and IV allege mental anguish and financial loss caused by, respectively, appellants Shutze and MRMC.

The two cases were consolidated and came before the trial judge on motions for summary judgment. In the order under appeal, the trial judge found that section 406.11 was constitutional on its face and as applied, but that section 732.9185 was facially unconstitutional. The trial judge did not rule on a motion that section 732.9185 was unconstitutional as applied. The order comes directly to us on the certification of the Fifth District Court of Appeal that it contains a question of great public importance which requires immediate resolution.

The only question legitimately before us is whether the trial court erred in granting a summary judgment that section 732.9185 is facially unconstitutional. In the present posture of the case, we are not presented with the issues of whether sections 406.11 and 732.9185 were complied with in performing these autopsies and cornea removals, of whether the two sections have been constitutionally applied, of whether section 406.11 is facially constitutional, of whether any or all of the appellants are liable, and of the Whites' rights, duties and privileges under sections 406.11 and 732.9185. Without specifying that it is addressing the narrow issue of the *facial* constitutionality of section 732.9185, the majority opinion addresses a wide range of issues which are only tenuously related to the narrow issue before us. The majority then reverses and remands with directions that a judgment for appellants (defendants) be entered. In my view this disposition is completely premature. My review of the record indicates there are substantial questions of material fact which preclude entry of summary judgments for the defendants.

The thrust of the majority opinion appears to be that the state and its agents have an unqualified right to the body of a decedent provided at some point the remains of the remains are turned over to the next of kin. I do not believe this is the law. I am persuaded, as was the trial judge below, that since time immemorial it has been the duty and the right of the next of kin to take control, possession, and custody of the body and remains of a deceased family member. These duties and rights, predicated on religious, moral, and philosophical grounds, were recognized at common law and were not totally surrendered to the state when our constitutions were adopted. These rights are not only reserved to the people under article I, section 1 of the Florida Constitution, but are affirmatively protected as religious, liberty, and privacy rights under article I, sections 3, 9, and 23 and by various statutes of the state.

. . . .

These personal rights of the next of kin are qualified only by the overriding police power of the state to regulate the care and disposition of dead bodies for the protection of public health and welfare. I have no doubt that the state may require an autopsy when there is a founded suspicion that death was by criminal action, when there is a likelihood that the death was caused by a communicable disease, or, even, when the death is simply inexplicable and the cause needs to be determined. I do not agree that the agents of the state may be constitutionally granted carte blanche to conduct autopsies based on whim, bureaucratic convenience, curiosity, pecuniary gain, or "policy." A significant question of material fact is whether the agents exceeded their statutory authority and we should have this issue resolved before we address the constitutionality of the statutes. The record consists largely of a series of depositions and affidavits taken or given in connection with the Whites' complaint and with the motions for summary judgments. The Powells' complaint was filed well after the Whites' complaint and contains little of record.

. . . .

Attempting to recount all of the significant questions of material fact which appear on the face of this record would be excessively burdensome and would be of little benefit at this stage of the proceedings. Moreover, any list would likely be incomplete. It is appropriate, however, to refer to several as illustrative of the issues not yet addressed. The two overarching issues are, first, whether the policies and practices of the medical examiner's office followed in these two cases are consistent with the provisions of sections 406.11 and 732.9185. Second, assuming the statutes were complied with, were they constitutionally applied. Section 925.09, Florida Statutes (1981), authorizes the state attorney to have an autopsy performed when "it is necessary in determining whether or not death was the result of a crime." Two significant questions of material fact engendered by this section are whether these two autopsies, and accompanying cornea removals, were performed under the authority of the state attorney, and, if so, was that authority legally exercised. Section 406.11(1) authorizes the medical examiner to perform such autopsies as he deems necessary to determine the cause of death. An additional question of material fact is whether the medical examiner's office has a policy or practice of performing autopsies on all accident victims, specifically drowning and vehicle accident victims. . . . Significant questions of material fact also arise in connection with section 732.9185. Two general questions, with numerous subsidiary questions, are whether the conditions precedent to cornea removal were present and whether the provisions of section 732.9185 were followed. The issue of the constitutionality of sections 406.11 and 732.9185, as applied, is inchoate at this stage of the proceeding.

The legislature is apparently of the view, contrary to the majority, that a decedent's next of kin have the right to possess and control the decedent's body and that both the decedent and next of kin may control the removal and donation of human organs. The various provisions of chapter 245, Florida Statutes (1981), titled *Disposition of Dead Bodies*, are grounded on the right of the next of kin to claim control and possession of dead bodies. Section 245.07 appears to rule out the state's use of dead bodies for the advancement of medical science unless the bodies are unclaimed or donated under section 245.11.[1] On the question of the donation and removal of organs, chapter 732, part X, Florida Statutes (1985), authorizes and establishes programs whereby both the decedent and survivors may donate organs of a decedent. Section 732.912 is particularly pertinent. Subsection (1) authorizes the donation of organs by will; subsection (2) authorizes the donation of a decedent's organs by next of kin in a priority order and also

---

[1] This does not mean that medical science may not be advanced as a *by-product* of autopsies which are legally conducted for other reasons under § 406.11. It does suggest, however, that advancement of medical science, without more, is not legal justification for conducting an autopsy on bodies which come into the hands of the medical examiner.

recognizes the right of next of kin to veto the removal or donation of organs. Moreover, section 732.9185(1)(b) itself recognizes the right of the next of kin to veto the donation of the cornea.[2] The crucial point is that part X of chapter 732 is grounded on the right of the decedent and next of kin to control the removal and disposition of organs taken from the body of the decedent. If this is not so, part X is grounded on air. It is a conundrum in that it is simply not legally possible nor permissible to donate or control the donation of an article which does not belong to the donor.

I agree that these cases present issues of great public importance which may, at some point, require this Court's attention. At this point, however, there is substantial doubt that sections 406.11 and 732.9185 have been correctly interpreted and applied by the cognizant authorities in Marion County. The issues presented by these suits, particularly the counts requesting a declaratory judgment of the rights, duties, and privileges of the next of kin, are likely to be with us a long time and to become even more intense as medical science advances and organ transplants increase in number. I am simply not prepared to rush to judgment on issues as important as these based on a summary judgment. These issues are important, but we are not a legislative body rushing to enact emergency legislation to meet an urgent state need before the end of a legislative session. These cases should be remanded with instructions that the trial go forward and a record be developed.

[3] Explanatory Notes

[a] The Plaintiffs' Theories

The plaintiffs in *Powell* used three different theories to argue that Florida's corneal removal statute violated the United States Constitution. First, they contended that the right of next of kin to dispose of the remains of their relatives was a "fundamental personal and property right" protected by the Due Process Clause of the Constitution. Second, they asserted that the statute classified next of kin "invidiously" in violation of the Equal Protection Clause. Finally, they claimed that the taking of corneal tissue for public use without payment of compensation violated the Takings Clause.

[i] *Fundamental Rights and Privacy.* From prior materials in this text, you know that the Due Process Clause has taken on at least two roles. On its face, the clause would seem to require that judicial and administrative procedures operate fairly. This process-oriented version of the clause has been supplemented by "Substantive Due Process" litigation involving challenges to the rationality of government actions. The courts have opined on many occasions that government programs must be rationally operated in light of the purposes they are meant to serve. And the rationality of government actions will be given particularly close scrutiny when a fundamental right is threatened. The *Powell* court noted that the United States Supreme Court has decided a series of cases protecting from state interference choices made by family members about their intimate lives. Even though these cases only dealt with living persons, the plaintiffs hoped that the courts would see them as persuasive analogies for use in constraining the right of Florida to control the disposition of corneal tissue. To the extent that the Constitutional law

---

[2] Section 732.9185(1)(b) states: "[n]o objection by the next of kin of the decedent is known by the medical examiner." Subsection (2) provides that the medical examiner will not be held liable for "failure to obtain consent of the next of kin." The words "failure to obtain" suggest an unsuccessful effort. These provisions are apparently being interpreted as authority not to seek consent from next of kin who are physically present and readily available to grant or deny consent. Is that the legislative intent? The trial court should hear arguments and address this point.

of privacy protects intimate sensibilities, they argued, relatives' rights in the remains of their kin should be protected from serious intrusions by the state.

[ii] **Invidious Classifications.** Governments routinely classify people in a variety of ways. Most such classifications are thought innocuous, and many others usually pass muster with only limited scrutiny. In cases involving racial or gender classifications, courts use the Equal Protection Clause as a basis for close scrutiny of the regulatory regimes. Thus, racial classifications must generally be supported by a compelling public interest, and gender distinctions must have a fair and substantial relation to an important state interest. Furthermore, the burden of demonstrating the validity of such suspect or near-suspect classifications is generally placed on the government, not the party claiming a Constitutional violation. But for most distinctions, the courts require only that the government have some rational basis for making the classification. Once the *Powell* court found that fundamental rights were not at issue and that the public benefits of the corneal removal statute were substantial, it became virtually impossible for the plaintiffs to prevail in their Equal Protection challenge.

[iii] **Taking Law.** In *Powell*, corneal tissue was "taken" from bodies of the plaintiffs' relatives in order to further an important public purpose—reducing the prevalence of blindness. The tissue was obviously valuable in more than a medical sense. Absent the ability to routinely remove corneas during autopsies, a thriving market for the usable tissue of deceased persons might have cropped up. If such potential economic value exists, why could corneal tissue simply be taken without payment of any compensation to those affronted by the practice? The *Powell* court's response simply was to deny that next of kin retained any property right in the bodies of their deceased relatives. Next of kin retained only the rights to gain possession of the body for purposes of burial and the right to recover damages for mental distress if the body was handled in an undignified or disrespectful manner. The basis for these rights lay in personal and religious sensibilities about dead bodies and public health requirements about speedy burial, rather than a desire to commercialize cadavers. Furthermore, states routinely override or limit the right of kin to gain possession of a body if an important public need will be served. Thus, autopsies may be performed in certain circumstances, such as homicide investigations, even over strong religious objections from next of kin.[81] In *Powell*, the plaintiffs' inability to argue that the removal of corneas caused them economic harm made it quite difficult to raise a taking claim. While their sensibilities were offended, their purses were not. In addition, compare the difficulties of making a traditional taking argument with the contention of Margaret Radin, in the excerpt at p. 1097 above, that property *not* for sale may have characteristics making its worth incalculable.

For commentary on *Powell,* see Comment, *Toward the Right of Commerciality: Recognizing Property Rights in the Commercial Value of Human Tissue,* 34 UCLA L. Rev. 207 (1986).

[b] Another Approach to Corneal Seizures

In *Brotherton v. Cleveland,* 923 F.2d 477 (6th Cir. 1991), a spouse claimed there were Constitutional infirmities in the taking of corneas from the body of her husband without her permission. Rather than claiming that she was protected by the Takings Clause or that the corneal rules were arbitrary, she argued that she had an entitlement to the body entitling her to procedural protections prior to the removal of the corneas. The court concluded that she had an entitlement under Ohio law to the body of her husband for purposes of burial and for purposes of dignitary

---

[81] *See* Snyder v. Holy Cross Hospital, 30 Md. App. 317, 352 A.2d 334 (1976).

protection from mutilation, that this entitlement was "property" for purposes of the Due Process Clause, and that she was entitled to procedural protections prior to removal of the corneas.[82]

[c]   Analogous Sets of Legal Precedents

As Justice Overton noted in his majority opinion in *Powell*, no extant set of legislative or judicial materials dealt precisely with the legitimacy of removing corneal tissue during autopsies. (The *Associated Press* and *Martin Luther King* courts, of course, also lacked much authoritative precedent.) But there were a number of bundles of legal materials dealing with areas analogous to those in *Powell* that might have proved helpful in resolving the case. Some, such as the right of next of kin to gain possession of a body for disposal, have already been mentioned. There were others.

[*i*]   *Will Writing Authority.* Most states recognize the right of every person to give directions for disposing of their body in a will. Even here, burial instructions which are deemed highly inappropriate by relatives and courts may be overridden. Once again, public sensibilities seem to both guarantee acceptance of most personal decisions on how to handle our bodies at death and to limit our ability to make bizarre or outlandish requests. In *Powell*, there were no wills. The monetary assets of the deceased persons passed to various relatives in accordance with state intestate succession statutes. One also could look to the intestate succession statutes for some guidance as to who should have authority to resolve questions about tissue donation.

[*ii*]   *Theft and Conversion.* The stealing or retention of assets owned by others provides a basis for both criminal and civil actions. But the use of these rules virtually requires that the asset stolen or converted be a transferable commodity, a "property" asset. The traditional unwillingness to impart "property"-ness to dead human tissue made efforts to analogize to theft or conversion statutes difficult. If you feel that the removal of corneal tissue was like a theft of a tangible asset, then you must seriously consider the relevance of property concepts to the *Powell* dispute.

[d]   The Uniform Anatomical Gift Act

The Uniform Anatomical Gift Act, adopted in a large number of states, allows any person 18 years of age or older to make an anatomical gift, limit a gift to specific purposes, or refuse to make a gift. Anatomical gifts must be in writing and signed by the donor. Unless a person has left behind a signed refusal to make a gift, a relative may authorize a gift. The relative authorized to make that decision is the first available person on a list that begins with a surviving spouse, and continues with child, parent, sibling, grandparent and guardian.[83] The Act then provides:

§ 4. Authorization by Medical Examiner[84]

(a) The medical examiner may release and permit the removal of a part from a body within that official's custody, for transplantation or therapy, if:

---

[82] Whaley v. County of Tuscola, 58 F.3d 1111 (6th Cir. 1995) follows *Brotherton.*

[83] If a spouse is available and refuses to make a gift, medical authorities may not pursue others lower on the list.

[84] ANATOMICAL GIFT ACT (1987) § 4, 8A U.L.A. 43. The proposal allows for the words coroner or public health official to be substituted for medical examiner if appropriate to the legal structure in a particular jurisdiction. Reprinted with the permission of the National Conference of Commissioners on Uniform State Laws.

(1) the official has received a request for the part from a hospital, physician, surgeon, or procurement organization;

(2) the official has made a reasonable effort, taking into account the useful life of the part, to locate and examine the decedent's medical records and inform persons listed in Section 3(a)[85] of their option to make, or object to making, an anatomical gift;

(3) the official does not know of a refusal or contrary indication by the decedent or objection by a person having priority to act as listed in Section 3(a);

(4) the removal will be by a physician, surgeon, or technician; but in the case of eyes, by one of them or by an enucleator;

(5) the removal will not interfere with any autopsy or investigation;

(6) the removal will be in accordance with accepted medical standards; and

(7) cosmetic restoration will be done, if appropriate.

. . . .

The provisions set out above are worth comparing with other areas of the law. Gift law, for example, normally requires that the donor intend to make a gift and actually transfer the asset during life in order for the gift to be complete and enforceable. *See Gruen v. Gruen*, p. 243 above. It makes obvious sense to waive the actual delivery requirement and substitute a document. But gifts may not normally be made on our behalf by those surviving us. As an interesting aside, most hospitals and physicians will ask permission of next of kin before removing organs from a decedent even if an organ donor card has been signed.

[e] National Organ Transplant Act of 1984

In the fall of 1983, H. Barry Jacobs established a company in Virginia to buy and sell kidneys. The reaction was swift. Within six months, Virginia banned the practice.[86] Shortly thereafter, Congress adopted the National Organ Transplant Act of 1984.[87] The act, an effort to encourage, organize and financially support organ donation for transplantation, also contained provisions prohibiting the for-profit sale of most human tissue for transplantation. The prohibitory part of the scheme presently provides:

42 U.S.C. § 274e. Prohibition of organ purchases

(a) Prohibition

It shall be unlawful for any person to knowingly acquire, receive, or otherwise transfer any human organ for valuable consideration for use in human transplantation if the transfer affects interstate commerce.

(b) Penalties

Any person who violates subsection (a) of this section shall be fined not more than $50,000 or imprisoned not more than five years, or both.

(c) Definitions

---

[85] This section contains the list of prioritized relatives who may make a donation in the absence of a prior gift by the deceased.

[86] Note, *Regulating the Sale of Human Organs*, 71 VA. L. REV. 1015 (1985).

[87] Pub. L. No. 98-507, 98 Stat. 2339 (1984).

For purposes of subsection (a) of this section:

(1) The term "human organ" means the human (including fetal) kidney, liver, heart, lung, pancreas, bone marrow, cornea, eye, bone, and skin or any subpart thereof and any other human organ (or any subpart thereof, including that derived from a fetus) specified by the Secretary of Health and Human Services by regulation.

(2) The term "valuable consideration" does not include the reasonable payments associated with the removal, transportation, implantation, processing, preservation, quality control, and storage of a human organ or the expenses of travel, housing, and lost wages incurred by the donor of a human organ in connection with the donation of the organ.

The Senate Labor and Human Resources Committee gave the following reasons for recommending adoption of the above section:

It is the sense of the Committee that individuals or organizations should not profit by the sale of human organs for transplantation. This is not meant to include blood and blood derivatives, which can be replenished and whose donation does not compromise the health of the donor. The current state of the law is uncertain with regard to the sale of organs, and the Committee believes that legislation is necessary to clarify this issue. The Committee believes that human body parts should not be viewed as commodities; however, recognizing that laws governing medical treatment, consent, definition of death, autopsy, burial, and the disposition of dead bodies is exclusively state law, the proscription in this legislation relates only to interstate commerce.[88]

[4]   Problem Notes

[a]   Other Related Problems

A variety of circumstances have forced us to decide whether to attribute property-like characteristics to our physical selves, whether living or dead. Here are a few examples:

[i]   *Slavery.* Though slavery has departed from these shores, it is not an institution that has disappeared from the globe. In our own culture, vast dislocations and conflicts occurred over the decision to end the practice.

[ii]   *"Amateur" Athletics.* Athletics has become much more than just fun. The best among us make a good living playing games with their bodies. But the notion of "sport" rather than profession still pulls and tugs some portions of the athletic world. Big time college sports and the Olympic Games are constantly wrestling with the conflict between the need to entice good athletes to compete and the desires to create high quality educational environments or foster international good will.

[iii]   *Sale of Cemetery Plots and Protection of Cemeteries.* General revulsion greets news of cemetery desecrations. Will legal institutions respond to the strength of our reactions with property-like rules, such as those surrounding trespass? Or do tort principles better redress the wrongs to our sensibilities occasioned by such action?

[iv]   *Medical Study and Research.* Both living and dead human tissue is required for medical study and research. Should medical schools be permitted to accept only gifts or unclaimed

---

[88] S. Rep. No. 98-382, at 16-17 (Apr. 6, 1984), *reprinted in* 1984 U.S.C.C.A.N. 3982-3983.

cadavers for use in anatomy? Or should we permit them to purchase ourselves while living for later use? What of tissues taken from the living for research? Should such tissues be marketable? Does it make a difference if the tissues are naturally replenishable, like blood or bone marrow? What of organ pairs, such as kidneys, when a healthy person needs only one?

[*v*] ***Physical Injuries Caused by Others.*** Does our willingness to evaluate injuries for purposes of tort litigation mean that we should be willing to consider marketing our physical selves? Such evaluation in tort cases is usually accomplished by totaling up medical bills and permitting juries or judges to place a value on the pain and suffering of the injured party.

[*vi*] ***Genetic Counseling and Reproduction.*** Sperm has been sold for many years, frequently by medical students, to sperm banks for artificially inseminating women married to infertile men. The practice of inserting genetic material in wombs has now expanded to a variety of other settings, using both male and female genetic material. But sale of genetic material by women has not been as prominent. Is there a gender bias at work here? Are the physical risks of ova removal so much greater than sperm donation that market formation should be discouraged?

[*vii*] ***Surrogate Parenting.*** Women have sold the right to use their wombs for carrying a fetus to term, usually for around $10,000, to married couples. Sometimes the surrogate mother also sells her genetic material. At other times genetic material from each of the married partners is fertilized and inserted in the surrogate. Is this a market that should be encouraged?

[b] Harvesting Organs from the Dead

42 U.S.C. § 274e, quoted at p.1164 above, does not distinguish between organs taken from the living and organs taken from the dead. Why should relatives, charged with the authority of taking possession of and burying their dead, not be able to sell transplantable organs? Why should a person writing his or her will not be able to direct that organs be harvested from their bodies at death and sold in order to increase the size of the estate available for distribution to relatives, friends or charities? If famous people may control the monetary disposition of their renown in a will, why not their kidneys? Suppose, for example, that Martin Luther King, Jr. or Elvis Presley had died with a will asking that their organs be sold and the proceeds donated to a specific charity.

[c] Concepts of Property: Commodification

The notion that corneal or other human tissues could be property was unthinkable a short time ago. The technology of transplantation has created economic value where none previously existed. Put yourself to the test on the meaning of "property" by asking whether a person may be guilty of theft for "stealing" corneas from a tissue storage facility?[89] If so, is there a difference between "property" as a commodity for criminal law purposes and "property" as a commodity for civil law purposes?

---

[89] Steve Maher, Counsel for the Powells, reported that such a criminal case was brought in Florida. Telephone Interview with Steve Maher, Counsel for the Powells (Aug. 5, 1987). Prosecutors charged five defendants with intercepting corneas intended for a Tampa tissue bank and selling them in Saudi Arabia, Argentina and other countries. Each defendant was charged with second degree grand theft, of which an essential element is the taking of property worth more than $100 and less than $20,000. Petitioners' Reply Brief in Support of Grant of Writ of Certiorari in the United States Supreme Court at 5, Powell v. State of Florida, *cert. denied*, 481 U.S. 1059 (1987).

[d]   Concepts of Property: Personhood and Quasi Property

Justice Pitney's opinion in *International News Service* used the language "quasi-property" to help define the economic relationship between the competing news agencies and to differentiate the dealings between the news services from their relationships with the rest of the world. What are the differences, if any, between Pitney's concept of quasi-property and Radin's use of personhood to define certain forms of property? Should corneas be viewed as essential parts of personhood and protected from transfer? Should corneas be treated as completely non-transferable, or transferable only with the permission of the "owner."

[e]   Termination of Constitutional Rights at Death

The *Powell* court insisted that Constitutional rights terminate at death. Was the court correct? The courts have said that citizens whose Constitutional rights have been violated may sue the responsible government officials for damages. If you were unlawfully fired from a government job because of your race and died the day after the discharge, would your cause of action against the government die with you? The cause of action would probably be taken over by your estate and any money collected would be distributed in accordance with the terms of your will or under intestate succession laws. Though the violation occurred when you were alive, the right to sue does not end with your life. If you carry a statement around with you clearly stating that you are *not* an organ donor, but corneal tissue is taken from you anyway after you die, would such a violation of an instrument written during your life end simply because you died? If control of human remains is thought of as a right retained not only by next of kin but also by each of us prior to our deaths, was it appropriate for the *Powell* court to assume that Constitutional rights die when we do?

[f]   Weighing Human Needs

In *State of New Jersey v. Shack*, p. 557 above, the New Jersey Supreme Court issued the now famous statement, "Property rights serve human values." Would the *Shack* court use this ringing declaration as a basis for concluding that all transplantable tissue in the body of a dead person should be freely available for use in surgery to treat still living persons? Should the needs of the living uniformly take precedence over the "rights" of the dead? Wouldn't a rule presuming that transplantable organs may be harvested from the dead solve the present shortages of transplant tissues?

[5]   Introduction to the *Moore* Litigation

On October 20, 1976, John Moore's spleen was removed by doctors at the U.C.L.A. School of Medicine as part of a treatment regime for leukemia. Prior to the operation, he signed a consent form allowing the medical staff to perform the splenectomy and related procedures. Subsequently he had regular treatment sessions and checkups, at which blood and other substances were removed from his body. The particular structure of his blood made it a potentially valuable resource for the development of therapies for leukemia and other diseases. After the operation, in fact, a patent was issued to the Regents of the University of California for a cell line derived from Mr. Moore's blood. The cell line produced interferon and other useful products. Moore then sued, alleging, among other things, that he was never informed that his tissue would be used for the production of marketable products, and that the university and its staff had converted his property for their own use and violated obligations of trust and honesty due to patients. Moore asked for ownership rights in the patent, damages for the value of the assets taken from him, and punitive damages for the allegedly willful and deceitful behavior of the defendants.

[6] Opinions of the California Supreme Court in *Moore v. Regents of the University of California*

John Moore v. The Regents of the University Of California

Supreme Court of California
51 Cal.3d 120, 793 P.2d 479, 271 Cal. Rptr. 146 (1990)

PANELLI, J.

I. INTRODUCTION

We granted review in this case to determine whether plaintiff has stated a cause of action against his physician and other defendants for using his cells in potentially lucrative medical research without his permission. Plaintiff alleges that his physician failed to disclose preexisting research and economic interests in the cells before obtaining consent to the medical procedures by which they were extracted. The superior court sustained all defendants' demurrers to the third amended complaint, and the Court of Appeal reversed. We hold that the complaint states a cause of action for breach of the physician's disclosure obligations, but not for conversion.

II. FACTS

Our only task in reviewing a ruling on a demurrer is to determine whether the complaint states a cause of action. Accordingly, we assume that the complaint's properly pleaded material allegations are true and give the complaint a reasonable interpretation by reading it as a whole and all its parts in their context. . . .

The plaintiff is John Moore (Moore), who underwent treatment for hairy-cell leukemia at the Medical Center of the University of California at Los Angeles (UCLA Medical Center). The five defendants are: (1) Dr. David W. Golde (Golde), a physician who attended Moore at UCLA Medical Center; (2) the Regents of the University of California (Regents), who own and operate the university; (3) Shirley G. Quan, a researcher employed by the Regents; (4) Genetics Institute, Inc. (Genetics Institute); and (5) Sandoz Pharmaceuticals Corporation and related entities (collectively Sandoz).

Moore first visited UCLA Medical Center on October 5, 1976, shortly after he learned that he had hairy-cell leukemia. After hospitalizing Moore and "withdr[awing] extensive amounts of blood, bone marrow aspirate, and other bodily substances," Golde confirmed that diagnosis. At this time all defendants, including Golde, were aware that "certain blood products and blood components were of great value in a number of commercial and scientific efforts" and that access to a patient whose blood contained these substances would provide "competitive, commercial, and scientific advantages."

On October 8, 1976, Golde recommended that Moore's spleen be removed. Golde informed Moore "that he had reason to fear for his life, and that the proposed splenectomy operation. . .was necessary to slow down the progress of his disease." Based upon Golde's representations, Moore signed a written consent form authorizing the splenectomy.

Before the operation, Golde and Quan "formed the intent and made arrangements to obtain portions of [Moore's] spleen following its removal" and to take them to a separate research unit. Golde gave written instructions to this effect on October 18 and 19, 1976. These research activities "were not intended to have. . .any relation to [Moore's] medical. . .care." However, neither Golde nor Quan informed Moore of their plans to conduct this research or requested his permission. Surgeons at UCLA Medical Center, whom the complaint does not name as defendants, removed Moore's spleen on October 20, 1976.

Moore returned to the UCLA Medical Center several times between November 1976 and September 1983. He did so at Golde's direction and based upon representations "that such visits were necessary and required for his health and well-being, and based upon the trust inherent in and by virtue of the physician-patient relationship . . . ." On each of these visits Golde withdrew additional samples of "blood, blood serum, skin, bone marrow aspirate, and sperm." On each occasion Moore traveled to the UCLA Medical Center from his home in Seattle because he had been told that the procedures were to be performed only there and only under Golde's direction.

"In fact, [however,] throughout the period of time that [Moore] was under [Golde's] care and treatment,. . .the defendants were actively involved in a number of activities which they concealed from [Moore] . . . ." Specifically, defendants were conducting research on Moore's cells and planned to "benefit financially and competitively. . .[by exploiting the cells] and [their] exclusive access to [the cells] by virtue of [Golde's] ongoing physician-patient relationship . . . ."

Sometime before August 1979, Golde established a cell line from Moore's T-lymphocytes.[2] On January 30, 1981, the Regents applied for a patent on the cell line, listing Golde and Quan as inventors. "[B]y virtue of an established policy. . ., [the] Regents, Golde, and Quan would share in any royalties or profits. . .arising out of [the] patent." The patent issued on March 20, 1984, naming Golde and Quan as the inventors of the cell line and the Regents as the assignee of the patent. (U.S. Patent No. 4,438,032 (Mar. 20, 1984).)

The Regent's patent also covers various methods for using the cell line to produce lymphokines. Moore admits in his complaint that "the true clinical potential of each of the lymphokines. . .[is]

---

[2] A T-lymphocyte is a type of white blood cell. T-lymphocytes produce lymphokines, or proteins that regulate the immune system. Some lymphokines have potential therapeutic value. If the genetic material responsible for producing a particular lymphokine can be identified, it can sometimes be used to manufacture large quantities of the lymphokine through the techniques of recombinant DNA. (See generally U.S. Congress, Office of Technology Assessment, New Developments in Biotechnology: Ownership of Human Tissues and Cells (1987) at pp. 31-46 (hereafter OTA Report); see also fn. 29, post.)

While the genetic code for lymphokines does not vary from individual to individual, it can nevertheless be quite difficult to locate the gene responsible for a particular lymphokine. Because T-lymphocytes produce many different lymphokines, the relevant gene is often like a needle in a haystack. (OTA Rep., supra, at p. 42.) Moore's T-lymphocytes were interesting to the defendants because they overproduced certain lymphokines, thus making the corresponding genetic material easier to identify. (In published research papers, defendants and other researchers have shown that the overproduction was caused by a virus, and that normal T-lymphocytes infected by the virus will also overproduce. See fn. 30, post.)

Cells taken directly from the body (primary cells) are not very useful for these purposes. Primary cells typically reproduce a few times and then die. One can, however, sometimes continue to use cells for an extended period of time by developing them into a "cell line," a culture capable of reproducing indefinitely. This is not, however, always an easy task. "Longterm growth of human cells and tissues is difficult, often an art," and the probability of succeeding with any given cell sample is low, except for a few types of cells not involved in this case. (OTA Rep., supra, at p. 5.)

difficult to predict, [but]. . .competing commercial firms in these relevant fields have published reports in biotechnology industry periodicals predicting a potential market of approximately $3.01 Billion Dollars by the year 1990 for a whole range of [such lymphokines] . . . ."

With the Regents' assistance, Golde negotiated agreements for commercial development of the cell line and products to be derived from it. Under an agreement with Genetics Institute, Golde "became a paid consultant" and "acquired the rights to 75,000 shares of common stock." Genetics Institute also agreed to pay Golde and the Regents "at least $330,000 over three years, including a pro-rata share of [Golde's] salary and fringe benefits, in exchange for. . .exclusive access to the materials and research performed" on the cell line and products derived from it. On June 4, 1982, Sandoz "was added to the agreement," and compensation payable to Golde and the Regents was increased by $110,000. "[T]hroughout this period,. . .Quan spent as much as 70 [percent] of her time working for [the] Regents on research" related to the cell line.

Based upon these allegations, Moore attempted to state 13 causes of action.[4] . . .[T]he superior court sustained a general demurrer to the entire complaint. . .

With one justice dissenting, the Court of Appeal reversed . . . ..

III. DISCUSSION

A. Breach of Fiduciary Duty and Lack of Informed Consent

Moore repeatedly alleges that Golde failed to disclose the extent of his research and economic interests in Moore's cells before obtaining consent to the medical procedures by which the cells were extracted. These allegations, in our view, state a cause of action against Golde for invading a legally protected interest of his patient. This cause of action can properly be characterized either as the breach of a fiduciary duty to disclose facts material to the patient's consent or, alternatively, as the performance of medical procedures without first having obtained the patient's informed consent.

Our analysis begins with three well-established principles. First, a person of adult years and in sound mind has the right, in the exercise of control over his own body, to determine whether or not to submit to lawful medical treatment. Second, the patient's consent to treatment, to be effective, must be an informed consent. Third, in soliciting the patient's consent, a physician has a fiduciary duty to disclose all information material to the patient's decision.

These principles lead to the following conclusions: (1) a physician must disclose personal interests unrelated to the patient's health, whether research or economic, that may affect the physician's professional judgment; and (2) a physician's failure to disclose such interests may give rise to a cause of action for performing medical procedures without informed consent or breach of fiduciary duty.

. . . .

It is important to note that no law prohibits a physician from conducting research in the same area in which he practices. Progress in medicine often depends upon physicians, such as those

---

[4] (1) "Conversion"; (2) "lack of informed consent"; (3) "breach of fiduciary duty"; (4) "fraud and deceit"; (5) "unjust enrichment"; (6) "quasi-contract"; (7) "bad faith breach of the implied covenant of good faith and fair dealing"; (8) "intentional infliction of emotional distress"; (9) "negligent misrepresentation"; (10) "intentional interference with prospective advantageous economic relationships"; (11) "slander of title"; (12) "accounting"; and (13) "declaratory relief."

practicing at the university hospital where Moore received treatment, who conduct research while caring for their patients.

Yet a physician who treats a patient in whom he also has a research interest has potentially conflicting loyalties. This is because medical treatment decisions are made on the basis of proportionality—weighing the benefits *to the patient* against the risks *to the patient.* . . . A physician who adds his own research interests to this balance may be tempted to order a scientifically useful procedure or test that offers marginal, or no, benefits to the patient. The possibility that an interest extraneous to the patient's health has affected the physician's judgment is something that a reasonable patient would want to know in deciding whether to consent to a proposed course of treatment. It is material to the patient's decision and, thus, a prerequisite to informed consent.

. . . .

Accordingly, we hold that a physician who is seeking a patient's consent for a medical procedure must, in order to satisfy his fiduciary duty and to obtain the patient's informed consent, disclose personal interests unrelated to the patient's health, whether research or economic, that may affect his medical judgment.

. . . .

Moore admits in his complaint that defendants disclosed they "were engaged in strictly academic and purely scientific medical research . . . ." However, Golde's representation that he had no financial interest in this research became false, based upon the allegations, at least by May 1979, when he "began to investigate and initiate the procedures. . .for [obtaining] a patent" on the cell line developed from Moore's cells.

In these allegations, Moore plainly asserts that Golde concealed an economic interest in the postoperative procedures. Therefore, applying the principles already discussed, the allegations state a cause of action for breach of fiduciary duty or lack of informed consent.

. . . .

B. Conversion

Moore also attempts to characterize the invasion of his rights as a conversion—a tort that protects against interference with possessory and ownership interests in personal property. He theorizes that he continued to own his cells following their removal from his body, at least for the purpose of directing their use, and that he never consented to their use in potentially lucrative medical research. Thus, to complete Moore's argument, defendants' unauthorized use of his cells constitutes a conversion. As a result of the alleged conversion, Moore claims a proprietary interest in each of the products that any of the defendants might ever create from his cells or the patented cell line.

No court, however, has ever in a reported decision imposed conversion liability for the use of human cells in medical research.[15] While that fact does not end our inquiry, it raises a flag of caution. In effect, what Moore is asking us to do is to impose a tort duty on scientists to investigate the consensual pedigree of each human cell sample used in research. To impose such a duty, which would affect medical research of importance to all of society, implicates policy

---

[15] The absence of such authority cannot simply be attributed to recent developments in technology. The first human tumor cell line, which still is widely used in research, was isolated in 1951. (OTA Rep., supra, at p. 34.)

concerns far removed from the traditional, two-party ownership disputes in which the law of conversion arose.[17] Invoking a tort theory originally used to determine whether the loser or the finder of a horse had the better title, Moore claims ownership of the results of socially important medical research, including the genetic code for chemicals that regulate the functions of every human being's immune system.

. . . .

[W]e first consider whether the tort of conversion clearly gives Moore a cause of action under existing law. We do not believe it does. Because of the novelty of Moore's claim to own the biological materials at issue, to apply the theory of conversion in this context would frankly have to be recognized as an extension of the theory. Therefore, we consider next whether it is advisable to extend the tort to this context.

1. Moore's Claim Under Existing Law

"To establish a conversion, plaintiff must establish an actual interference with his *ownership* or *right of possession*. . . . Where plaintiff neither has title to the property alleged to have been converted, nor possession thereof, he cannot maintain an action for conversion." (*Del E. Webb Corp. v. Structural Materials Co.* (1981) 123 Cal. App. 3d 593, 610-611, italics added.)

Since Moore clearly did not expect to retain possession of his cells following their removal,[20] to sue for their conversion he must have retained an ownership interest in them. But there are several reasons to doubt that he did retain any such interest. First, no reported judicial decision supports Moore's claim, either directly or by close analogy. Second, California statutory law drastically limits any continuing interest of a patient in excised cells. Third, the subject matters of the Regents' patent—the patented cell line and the products derived from it—cannot be Moore's property.

Neither the Court of Appeal's opinion, the parties' briefs, nor our research discloses a case holding that a person retains a sufficient interest in excised cells to support a cause of action for conversion. We do not find this surprising, since the laws governing such things as human tissues,[21] transplantable organs,[22] blood,[23] fetuses,[24] pituitary glands,[25] corneal tissue,[26] and

---

[17] Conversion arose out of the common law action of trover. "We probably do not have the earliest examples of its use, but they were almost certainly cases in which the finder of lost goods did not return them, but used them himself, or disposed of them to someone else. . . . By 1554 the allegations of the complaint had become more or less standardized: that the plaintiff was possessed of certain goods, that he casually lost them, that the defendant found them, and that the defendant did not return them, but instead 'converted them to his own use.' From that phrase in the pleading came the name of the tort." (Prosser & Keeton, Torts (5th ed. 1984) § 15, p. 89.)

[20] In his complaint, Moore does not seek possession of his cells or claim the right to possess them. This is consistent with Health and Safety Code section 7054.4, which provides that "human tissues. . .following conclusion of scientific use shall be disposed of by interment, incineration, or any other method determined by the state department [of health services] to protect the public health and safety."

[21] See Health and Safety Code section 7054.4 (fn. 20, ante).

[22] See the Uniform Anatomical Gift Act, Health and Safety Code section 7150 et seq. The act permits a competent adult to "give all or part of [his] body" for certain designated purposes, including "transplantation, therapy, medical or dental education, research, or advancement of medical or dental science." (Health & Saf. Code, §§ 7151, 7153.) The act does not, however, permit the donor to receive "valuable consideration" for the transfer. (Health & Saf. Code, § 7155.)

[23] See Health and Safety Code section 1601 et seq., which regulates the procurement, processing, and distribution of human blood. Health and Safety Code section 1606 declares that "[t]he procurement, processing, distribution, or

dead bodies[27] deal with human biological materials as objects sui generis, regulating their disposition to achieve policy goals rather than abandoning them to the general law of personal property. It is these specialized statutes, not the law of conversion, to which courts ordinarily should and do look for guidance on the disposition of human biological materials.

Lacking direct authority for importing the law of conversion into this context, Moore relies, as did the Court of Appeal, primarily on decisions addressing privacy rights. One line of cases involves unwanted publicity. (*Lugosi v. Universal Pictures* (1979) 25 Cal. 3d 813; *Motschenbacher v. R. J. Reynolds Tobacco Company* (9th Cir. 1974) 498 F.2d 821 [interpreting Cal. law].) These opinions hold that every person has a proprietary interest in his own likeness and that unauthorized, business use of a likeness is redressible as a tort. But in neither opinion did the authoring court expressly base its holding on property law. Each court stated, following Prosser, that it was "pointless" to debate the proper characterization of the proprietary interest in a likeness. For purposes of determining whether the tort of conversion lies, however, the characterization of the right in question is far from pointless. Only property can be converted.

Not only are the wrongful-publicity cases irrelevant to the issue of conversion, but the analogy to them seriously misconceives the nature of the genetic materials and research involved in this case. Moore, adopting the analogy originally advanced by the Court of Appeal, argues that "[i]f the courts have found a sufficient proprietary interest in one's persona, how could one not have a right in one's own genetic material, something far more profoundly the essence of one's human uniqueness than a name or a face?" However, as the defendants' patent makes clear—and the complaint, too, if read with an understanding of the scientific terms which it has borrowed from the patent—the goal and result of defendants' efforts has been to manufacture lymphokines.[29]

---

use of whole blood, plasma, blood products, and blood derivatives for the purpose of injecting or transfusing the same. . .is declared to be, for all purposes whatsoever, the rendition of a service. . .and shall not be construed to be, and is declared not to be, a sale. . .for any purpose or purposes whatsoever."

[24] See Health and Safety Code section 7054.3: "Notwithstanding any other provision of law, a recognizable dead human fetus of less than 20 weeks uterogestation not disposed of by interment shall be disposed of by incineration."

[25] See Government Code section 27491.46: "The coroner [following an autopsy] shall have the right to retain pituitary glands solely for transmission to a university, for use in research or the advancement of medical science" (id., subd. (a)) or "for use in manufacturing a hormone necessary for the physical growth of persons who are, or may become, hypopituitary dwarfs . . ."(id., subd. (b)).

[26] See Government Code section 27491.47: "The coroner may, in the course of an autopsy [and subject to specified conditions], remove. . .corneal eye tissue from a body . . ."(id., subd. (a)) for "transplant, therapeutic, or scientific purposes" (id., subd. (a)(5)).

[27] See Health and Safety Code section 7000 et seq. While the code does not purport to grant property rights in dead bodies, it does give the surviving spouse, or other relatives, "[t]he right to control the disposition of the remains of a deceased person, unless other directions have been given by the decedent . . . ." (Health & Saf. Code, § 7100.)

[29] Inside the cell, a gene produces a lymphokine (see fn. 2, ante) by attracting protein molecules, which bond to form a strand of "messenger RNA" (mRNA) in the mirror image of the gene. The mRNA strand then detaches from the gene and attracts other protein molecules, which bond to form the lymphokine that the original gene encoded. (OTA Rep., supra, at pp. 38-44.)

In the laboratory, scientists sometimes use genes to manufacture lymphokines by cutting a gene from the chromosome and grafting it onto the chromosome of a bacterium. The resulting chromosome is an example of "recombinant DNA," or DNA composed of genetic material from more than one individual or species. As the bacterium lives and reproduces, the engrafted gene continues to produce the lymphokine that the gene encodes. (OTA Rep., supra, at pp. 41-44, 158.)

It can be extremely difficult to identify the gene that carries the code for a particular lymphokine. "Since the amount of DNA in a human cell is enormous compared to the amount present in an individual gene, the search for any single gene within a cell is like searching for a needle in a haystack." (OTA Rep., supra, at p. 42.) As the Regents' patent

Lymphokines, unlike a name or a face, have the same molecular structure in every human being and the same, important functions in every human being's immune system. Moreover, the particular genetic material which is responsible for the natural production of lymphokines, and which defendants use to manufacture lymphokines in the laboratory, is also the same in every person; it is no more unique to Moore than the number of vertebrae in the spine or the chemical formula of hemoglobin.[30]

. . . [O]ne may earnestly wish to protect privacy and dignity without accepting the extremely problematic conclusion that interference with those interests amounts to a conversion of personal property. Nor is it necessary to force the round pegs of "privacy" and "dignity" into the square hole of "property" in order to protect the patient, since the fiduciary-duty and informed-consent theories protect these interests directly by requiring full disclosure.

The next consideration that makes Moore's claim of ownership problematic is California statutory law, which drastically limits a patient's control over excised cells. Pursuant to Health and Safety Code section 7054.4, "[n]otwithstanding any other provision of law, recognizable anatomical parts, human tissues, anatomical human remains, or infectious waste following conclusion of scientific use shall be disposed of by interment, incineration, or any other method determined by the state department [of health services] to protect the public health and safety." Clearly the Legislature did not specifically intend this statute to resolve the question of whether a patient is entitled to compensation for the nonconsensual use of excised cells. A primary object of the statute is to ensure the safe handling of potentially hazardous biological waste materials.[33] Yet one cannot escape the conclusion that the statute's practical effect is to limit, drastically, a patient's control over excised cells. By restricting how excised cells may be used and requiring their eventual destruction, the statute eliminates so many of the rights ordinarily attached to property that one cannot simply assume that what is left amounts to "property" or "ownership" for purposes of conversion law.

---

application explains, the significance of a cell that overproduces mRNA is to make the difficult search for a particular gene unnecessary. (U.S. Patent No. 4,438,032 (Mar. 20, 1984) at col. 2.) If one has an adequate source of mRNA—the gene's mirror image—it can be used to make a copy, or clone, of the original gene. The cloned gene can then be used in recombinant DNA, as already described, for large-scale production of lymphokines. (Id., at col. 3.)

[30] By definition, a gene responsible for producing a protein found in more than one individual will be the same in each. It is precisely because everyone needs the same basic proteins that proteins produced by one person's cells may have therapeutic value for another person. (See generally OTA Rep., supra, at pp. 38-40.) Thus, the proteins that defendants hope to manufacture—lymphokines such as interferon—are in no way a "likeness" of Moore.

Because all normal persons possess the genes responsible for production of lymphokines, it is sometimes possible to make normal cells into overproducers. (See OTA Rep., supra, at p. 55.) According to a research paper to which defendants contributed, Moore's cells overproduced lymphokines because they were infected by a virus, HTLV-II (human T-cell leukemia virus type II). (Chen, Quan & Golde, Human T-cell Leukemia Virus Type II Transforms Normal Human Lymphocytes (Nov. 1983) 80 Proceedings Nat. Acad. Sci. USA 7006.) The same virus has been shown to transform normal T-lymphocytes into overproducers like Moore's. (Ibid.)

[33] The policy of keeping biological materials in safe hands has substantial relevance to this case. The catalog of the American Type Culture Collection, an organization that distributes cell lines to researchers, gives this warning about the cell line derived from Moore's T-lymphocytes: Because "[t]he cells. . .contain a replication competent genome of Human T Cell Leukemia Virus II (HTLV-II) [i.e., genetic material capable of reproducing the virus]. . ., they must be handled as potentially biohazardous material under P-II [level II] containment." (American Type Culture Collection, Catalogue of Cell Lines and Hybridomas (6th ed. 1988) p. 176.) Level II containment is a standard established by the National Institutes of Health and the Center for Disease Control for handling hazardous biological materials. The level II standard requires, among other things, the use of a biological safety cabinet when the cell line is manipulated, and the autoclaving (sterilization by heat) and disposal of contaminated materials. (Id., at p. xi.)

It may be that some limited right to control the use of excised cells does survive the operation of this statute. There is, for example, no need to read the statute to permit "scientific use" contrary to the patient's expressed wish.[34] A fully informed patient may always withhold consent to treatment by a physician whose research plans the patient does not approve. That right, however, as already discussed, is protected by the fiduciary-duty and informed-consent theories.

Finally, the subject matter of the Regents' patent—the patented cell line and the products derived from it—cannot be Moore's property. This is because the patented cell line is both factually and legally distinct from the cells taken from Moore's body. Federal law permits the patenting of organisms that represent the product of "human ingenuity," but not naturally occurring organisms. (*Diamond v. Chakrabarty* (1980) 447 U.S. 303, 309-310.) Human cell lines are patentable because "[l]ong-term adaptation and growth of human tissues and cells in culture is difficult—often considered an art. . .," and the probability of success is low. (OTA Rep., supra, at p. 33; see fn. 2, ante.) It is this inventive effort that patent law rewards, not the discovery of naturally occurring raw materials. Thus, Moore's allegations that he owns the cell line and the products derived from it are inconsistent with the patent, which constitutes an authoritative determination that the cell line is the product of invention. Since such allegations are nothing more than arguments or conclusions of law, they of course do not bind us.

2. Should Conversion Liability Be Extended?

As we have discussed, Moore's novel claim to own the biological materials at issue in this case is problematic, at best. Accordingly, his attempt to apply the theory of conversion within this context must frankly be recognized as a request to extend that theory. While we do not purport to hold that excised cells can never be property for any purpose whatsoever, the novelty of Moore's claim demands express consideration of the policies to be served by extending liability rather than blind deference to a complaint alleging as a legal conclusion the existence of a cause of action.

There are three reasons why it is inappropriate to impose liability for conversion based upon the allegations of Moore's complaint. First, a fair balancing of the relevant policy considerations counsels against extending the tort. Second, problems in this area are better suited to legislative resolution. Third, the tort of conversion is not necessary to protect patients' rights. For these reasons, we conclude that the use of excised human cells in medical research does not amount to a conversion.

Of the relevant policy considerations, two are of overriding importance. The first is protection of a competent patient's right to make autonomous medical decisions. That right, as already discussed, is grounded in well-recognized and long-standing principles of fiduciary duty and informed consent. This policy weighs in favor of providing a remedy to patients when physicians act with undisclosed motives that may affect their professional judgment. The second important

---

[34] The dissent argues that the term "scientific use" in Health and Safety Code section 7054.4 excludes "commercial exploitation"; in effect, according to the dissent, the statute says "scientific use" but means "not-for-profit scientific use." There is, however, no reason to believe that the Legislature intended to make such a distinction. Nor is the distinction likely to be meaningful or practical in this context—"a relationship of unparalled intimacy between universities and biotechnology companies . . . ." Unless research necessarily ceases to be "scientific" when directed to the development of marketable products, a proposition we cannot accept, the distinction between academic and commercial "use" of human tissues has no logical bearing on the statute, which permits all "scientific use." Shedding no light on the Legislature's intent, philosophical issues about "scientists bec[oming] entrepreneurs" are best debated in another forum.

policy consideration is that we not threaten with disabling civil liability innocent parties who are engaged in socially useful activities, such as researchers who have no reason to believe that their use of a particular cell sample is, or may be, against a donor's wishes.

To reach an appropriate balance of these policy considerations is extremely important. . . .. We need not, however, make an arbitrary choice between liability and nonliability. Instead, an examination of the relevant policy considerations suggests an appropriate balance: Liability based upon existing disclosure obligations, rather than an unprecedented extension of the conversion theory, protects patients' rights of privacy and autonomy without unnecessarily hindering research.

To be sure, the threat of liability for conversion might help to enforce patients' rights indirectly. This is because physicians might be able to avoid liability by obtaining patients' consent, in the broadest possible terms, to any conceivable subsequent research use of excised cells. Unfortunately, to extend the conversion theory would utterly sacrifice the other goal of protecting innocent parties. Since conversion is a strict liability tort, it would impose liability on all those into whose hands the cells come, whether or not the particular defendant participated in, or knew of, the inadequate disclosures that violated the patient's right to make an informed decision. In contrast to the conversion theory, the fiduciary-duty and informed-consent theories protect the patient directly, without punishing innocent parties or creating disincentives to the conduct of socially beneficial research.

Research on human cells plays a critical role in medical research. This is so because researchers are increasingly able to isolate naturally occurring, medically useful biological substances and to produce useful quantities of such substances through genetic engineering. These efforts are beginning to bear fruit. Products developed through biotechnology that have already been approved for marketing in this country include treatments and tests for leukemia, cancer, diabetes, dwarfism, hepatitis-B, kidney transplant rejection, emphysema, osteoporosis, ulcers, anemia, infertility, and gynecological tumors, to name but a few. (Note, *Source Compensation for Tissues and Cells Used in Biotechnical Research: Why a Source Shouldn't Share in the Profits* (1989) 64 Notre Dame L. Rev. 628 & fn. 1 (hereafter Note, Source Compensation); see also OTA Rep., supra, at pp. 58-59.)

The extension of conversion law into this area will hinder research by restricting access to the necessary raw materials. Thousands of human cell lines already exist in tissue repositories, such as the American Type Culture Collection and those operated by the National Institutes of Health and the American Cancer Society. These repositories respond to tens of thousands of requests for samples annually. Since the patent office requires the holders of patents on cell lines to make samples available to anyone, many patent holders place their cell lines in repositories to avoid the administrative burden of responding to requests. (OTA Rep., supra, at p. 53.) At present, human cell lines are routinely copied and distributed to other researchers for experimental purposes, usually free of charge. This exchange of scientific materials, which still is relatively free and efficient, will surely be compromised if each cell sample becomes the potential subject matter of a lawsuit. (OTA Rep., supra, at p. 52.)

. . . .

In deciding whether to create new tort duties we have in the past considered the impact that expanded liability would have on activities that are important to society, such as research. For example, in *Brown v. Superior Court*, supra, 44 Cal. 3d 1049, the fear that strict product liability would frustrate pharmaceutical research led us to hold that a drug manufacturer's liability should not be measured by those standards. We wrote that, "[i]f drug manufacturers were subject to strict liability, they might be reluctant to undertake research programs to develop some pharmaceuticals that would prove beneficial or to distribute others that are available to be marketed, because of the fear of large adverse monetary judgments."

As in *Brown*, the theory of liability that Moore urges us to endorse threatens to destroy the economic incentive to conduct important medical research. If the use of cells in research is a conversion, then with every cell sample a researcher purchases a ticket in a litigation lottery. Because liability for conversion is predicated on a continuing ownership interest, "companies are unlikely to invest heavily in developing, manufacturing, or marketing a product when uncertainty about clear title exists." (OTA Rep., supra, at p. 27.) In our view, borrowing again from *Brown*, "[i]t is not unreasonable to conclude in these circumstances that the imposition of a harsher test for liability would not further the public interest in the development and availability of these important products."

Indeed, this is a far more compelling case for limiting the expansion of tort liability than *Brown*. In *Brown*, eliminating strict liability made it more difficult for plaintiffs to recover actual damages for serious physical injuries resulting from their mothers' prenatal use of the drug diethylstilbestrol (DES). In this case, by comparison, limiting the expansion of liability under a conversion theory will only make it more difficult for Moore to recover a highly theoretical windfall. Any injury to his right to make an informed decision remains actionable through the fiduciary-duty and informed-consent theories.

If the scientific users of human cells are to be held liable for failing to investigate the consensual pedigree of their raw materials, we believe the Legislature should make that decision. Complex policy choices affecting all society are involved, and legislatures, in making such policy decisions, have the ability to gather empirical evidence, solicit the advice of experts, and hold hearings at which all interested parties present evidence and express their views. Legislative competence to act in this area is demonstrated by the existing statutes governing the use and disposition of human biological materials. Legislative interest is demonstrated by the extensive study recently commissioned by the United States Congress. (OTA Rep., supra.) Commentators are also recommending legislative solutions. (See Danforth, *Cells, Sales, and Royalties: The Patient's Right to a Portion of the Profits* (1988) 6 Yale L. & Pol'y Rev. 179, 198-201; Note, *Source Compensation*, supra, 64 Notre Dame L. Rev. at pp. 643-645.)

Finally, there is no pressing need to impose a judicially created rule of strict liability, since enforcement of physicians' disclosure obligations will protect patients against the very type of harm with which Moore was threatened. So long as a physician discloses research and economic interests that may affect his judgment, the patient is protected from conflicts of interest. Aware of any conflicts, the patient can make an informed decision to consent to treatment, or to withhold consent and look elsewhere for medical assistance. As already discussed, enforcement of physicians' disclosure obligations protects patients directly, without hindering the socially useful activities of innocent researchers.

For these reasons, we hold that the allegations of Moore's third amended complaint state a cause of action for breach of fiduciary duty or lack of informed consent, but not conversion.

. . . .

LUCAS, C. J., and EAGLESON and KENNARD, JJ., concur.

ARABIAN, Justice, concurring.

I join in the views cogently expounded by the majority. I write separately to give voice to a concern that I believe informs much of that opinion but finds little or no expression therein. I speak of the moral issue.

Plaintiff has asked us to recognize and enforce a right to sell one's own body tissue for profit. He entreats us to regard the human vessel—the single most venerated and protected subject in any civilized society—as equal with the basest commercial commodity. He urges us to commingle the sacred with the profane. He asks much.

My learned colleague, Justice Mosk, in an impressive if ultimately unpersuasive dissent, recognizes the moral dimension of the matter. "[O]ur society," he writes, "acknowledges a profound ethical imperative to respect the human body as the physical and temporal expression of the unique human persona." He concludes, however, that morality militates in favor of recognizing plaintiff's claim for conversion of his body tissue. Why? Essentially, he answers, because of these defendants' moral shortcomings, duplicity and greed. Let them be compelled, he argues, to disgorge a portion of their ill-gotten gains to the uninformed individual whose body was invaded and exploited and without whom such profits would not have been possible.

I share Justice Mosk's sense of outrage, but I cannot follow its path. His eloquent paean to the human spirit illuminates the problem, but not the solution. Does it uplift or degrade the "unique human persona" to treat human tissue as a fungible article of commerce? Would it advance or impede the human condition, spiritually or scientifically, by delivering the majestic force of the law behind plaintiff's claim? I do not know the answers to these troubling questions, nor am I willing—like Justice Mosk—to treat them simply as issues of "tort" law, susceptible of judicial resolution.

. . . .

Whether, as plaintiff urges, his cells should be treated as property susceptible to conversion is not, in my view, ours to decide. The question implicates choices which not only reflect, but which ultimately define our essence. A mark of wisdom for us as expositors of the law is the recognition that we cannot cure every ill, mediate every dispute, resolve every conundrum. Sometimes, as Justice Brandeis said, "the most important thing we do, is not doing."[1]

Where then shall a complete resolution be found? Clearly the Legislature, as the majority opinion suggests, is the proper deliberative forum. Indeed, a legislative response creating a licensing scheme, which establishes a fixed rate of profit sharing between researcher and subject, has already been suggested. (*Danforth*, supra, 6 Yale L. & Pol'y Rev. at pp. 198-201.) Such an arrangement would not only avoid the moral and philosophical objections to a free market operation in body tissue, but would also address stated concerns by eliminating the inherently coercive effect of a waiver system and by compensating donors regardless of temporal circumstances.

The majority view is not unmindful of the seeming injustice in a result that denies plaintiff a claim for conversion of his body tissue, yet permits defendants to retain the fruits thereof. As we have explained, the reason for our holding is essentially twofold: First, plaintiff in this matter is not without a remedy; he remains free to pursue defendants on a breach-of-fiduciary-duty theory, as well as, perhaps, other tort claims not before us. Second, a judicial pronouncement, while supple, is not without its limitations. Courts cannot and should not seek to fashion a remedy

---

[1] Bickel, The Least Dangerous Branch (1962) page 71.

for every "heartache and the thousand natural shocks that flesh is heir to."[2] Sometimes, the discretion of forbearance is the better part of responsive valor. This is such an occasion.

BROUSSARD, Justice, concurring and dissenting.

Given the novel scientific setting in which this case arises and the considerable interest this litigation has engendered within the medical research community and the public generally, it is easy to lose sight of the fact that the specific allegations on which the complaint in this case rests are quite unusual, setting this matter apart from the great majority of instances in which donated organs or cells provide the raw materials for the advancement of medical science and the development of new and beneficial medical products. Ordinarily, when a patient consents to the use of a body part for scientific purposes, the potential value of the excised organ or cell is discovered only through subsequent experimentation or research, often months or years after the removal of the organ. In this case, however, the complaint alleges that plaintiff's doctor recognized the peculiar research and commercial value of plaintiff's cells before their removal from plaintiff's body. Despite this knowledge, the doctor allegedly failed to disclose these facts or his interest in the cells to plaintiff, either before plaintiff's initial surgery or throughout the ensuing seven-year period during which the doctor continued to obtain additional cells from plaintiff's body in the course of periodic medical examinations.

The majority opinion, of course, is not oblivious to the significance of these unusual allegations. It relies on those allegations in concluding that the complaint states a cause of action for breach of fiduciary duty. I concur fully in that holding.

When it turns to the conversion cause of action, however, the majority opinion fails to maintain its focus on the specific allegations before us. Concerned that the imposition of liability for conversion will impede medical research by innocent scientists who use the resources of existing cell repositories—a factual setting not presented here—the majority opinion rests its holding, that a conversion action cannot be maintained, largely on the proposition that a patient generally possesses no right in a body part that has already been removed from his body. Here, however, plaintiff has alleged that defendants interfered with his legal rights before his body part was removed. Although a patient may not retain any legal interest in a body part after its removal when he has properly consented to its removal and use for scientific purposes, it is clear under California law that before a body part is removed it is the patient, rather than his doctor or hospital, who possesses the right to determine the use to which the body part will be put after removal. If, as alleged in this case, plaintiff's doctor improperly interfered with plaintiff's right to control the use of a body part by wrongfully withholding material information from him before its removal, under traditional common law principles plaintiff may maintain a conversion action to recover the economic value of the right to control the use of his body part. Accordingly, I dissent from the majority opinion insofar as it rejects plaintiff's conversion cause of action.

. . . .

If this were a typical case in which a patient consented to the use of his removed organ for general research purposes and the patient's doctor had no prior knowledge of the scientific or commercial value of the patient's organ or cells, I would agree that the patient could not maintain a conversion action. In that common scenario, the patient has abandoned any interest in the removed organ and is not entitled to demand compensation if it should later be discovered that the organ or cells have some unanticipated value. I cannot agree, however, with the majority

[2] Shakespeare, Hamlet, act III, scene 1.

that a patient may never maintain a conversion action for the unauthorized use of his excised organ or cells, even against a party who knew of the value of the organ or cells before they were removed and breached a duty to disclose that value to the patient. Because plaintiff alleges that defendants wrongfully interfered with his right to determine, prior to the removal of his body parts, how those parts would be used after removal, I conclude that the complaint states a cause of action under traditional, common law conversion principles.

In analyzing the conversion issue, the majority properly begins with the established requirements of a common law conversion action, explaining that a plaintiff is required to demonstrate an actual interference with his "ownership or right of possession" in the property in question. Although the majority opinion, at several points, appears to suggest that a removed body part, by its nature, may never constitute "property" for purposes of a conversion action, there is no reason to think that the majority opinion actually intends to embrace such a broad or dubious proposition. If, for example, another medical center or drug company had stolen all of the cells in question from the UCLA Medical Center laboratory and had used them for its own benefit, there would be no question but that a cause of action for conversion would properly lie against the thief, and the majority opinion does not suggest otherwise. Thus, the majority's analysis cannot rest on the broad proposition that a removed body part is not property, but rather rests on the proposition that a patient retains no ownership interest in a body part once the body part has been removed from his or her body.

The majority opinion fails to recognize, however, that, in light of the allegations of the present complaint, the pertinent inquiry is not whether a patient generally retains an ownership interest in a body part after its removal from his body, but rather whether a patient has a right to determine, before a body part is removed, the use to which the part will be put after removal. Although the majority opinion suggests that there are "reasons to doubt" that a patient retains "any" ownership interest in his organs or cells after removal, the opinion fails to identify any statutory provision or common law authority that indicates that a patient does not generally have the right, before a body part is removed, to choose among the permissible uses to which the part may be put after removal. On the contrary, the most closely related statutory scheme—the Uniform Anatomical Gift Act (Health & Saf. Code, § 7150 et seq.)—makes it quite clear that a patient does have this right.

. . . .

Thus, unlike the majority, I conclude that under established common law principles the facts alleged in the complaint state a cause of action for conversion.

. . . .

Finally, the majority's analysis of the relevant policy considerations tellingly omits a most pertinent consideration. In identifying the interests of the patient that are implicated by the decision whether to recognize a conversion cause of action, the opinion speaks only of the "patient's right to make autonomous medical decisions" and fails even to mention the patient's interest in obtaining the economic value, if any, that may adhere in the subsequent use of his own body parts. Although such economic value may constitute a fortuitous "windfall" to the patient, the fortuitous nature of the economic value does not justify the creation of a novel exception from conversion liability which sanctions the intentional misappropriation of that value from the patient.

This last point reveals perhaps the most serious flaw in the majority's public policy analysis in this case. It is certainly arguable that, as a matter of policy or morality, it would be wiser to prohibit any private individual or entity from profiting from the fortuitous value that adheres in a part of a human body, and instead to require all valuable excised body parts to be deposited in a public repository which would make such materials freely available to all scientists for the betterment of society as a whole. The Legislature, if it wished, could create such a system, as it has done with respect to organs that are donated for transplantation. To date, however, the Legislature has not adopted such a system for organs that are to be used for research or commercial purposes, and the majority opinion, despite some oblique suggestions to the contrary, emphatically does not do so by its holding in this case. Justice Arabian's concurring opinion suggests that the majority's conclusion is informed by the precept that it is immoral to sell human body parts for profit. But the majority's rejection of plaintiff's conversion cause of action does not mean that body parts may not be bought or sold for research or commercial purposes or that no private individual or entity may benefit economically from the fortuitous value of plaintiff's diseased cells. Far from elevating these biological materials above the marketplace, the majority's holding simply bars *plaintiff*, the source of the cells, from obtaining the benefit of the cells' value, but permits *defendants*, who allegedly obtained the cells from plaintiff by improper means, to retain and exploit the full economic value of their ill-gotten gains free of their ordinary common law liability for conversion.

Because I conclude that plaintiff's complaint states a cause of action for conversion under traditional common law principles, I dissent from the majority opinion insofar as it rejects such a claim.

MOSK, Justice, dissenting.

I dissent.

Contrary to the principal holding of the Court of Appeal, the majority conclude that the complaint does not—in fact cannot—state a cause of action for conversion. I disagree with this conclusion . . . . For convenience I shall discuss the six premises of the majority's conclusion in the order in which they appear.

1.

The majority first take the position that Moore has no cause of action for conversion under existing law because he retained no "ownership interest" in his cells after they were removed from his body.

. . . .

The majority cite several statutes regulating aspects of the commerce in or disposition of certain parts of the human body, and conclude in effect that in the present case we should also "look for guidance" to the Legislature rather than to the law of conversion. Surely this argument is out of place in an opinion of the highest court of this state. As the majority acknowledge, the law of conversion is a creature of the common law. The inherent capacity of the common law for growth and change is its most significant feature. . . .

Especially is this true in the field of torts. I need not review the many instances in which this court has broken fresh ground by announcing new rules of tort law: time and again when a new rule was needed we did not stay our hand merely because the matter was one of first impression.

. . . .

2.

The majority's second reason for doubting that Moore retained an ownership interest in his cells after their excision is that "California statutory law . . . drastically limits a patient's control over excised cells." For this proposition the majority rely on Health and Safety Code section 7054.4 . . . . The majority concede that the statute was not meant to directly resolve the question whether a person in Moore's position has a cause of action for conversion, but reason that it indirectly resolves the question by limiting the patient's control over the fate of his excised cells . . . .

First, in my view the statute does not authorize the principal use that defendants claim the right to make of Moore's tissue, i.e., its commercial exploitation. . . .

By its terms, section 7054.4 permits only "scientific use" of excised body parts and tissue before they must be destroyed. . . . I would agree that "scientific use" at least includes routine postoperative examination of excised tissue conducted by a pathologist for diagnostic or prognostic reasons (e.g., to verify preoperative diagnosis or to assist in determining postoperative treatment). I might further agree that "scientific use" could be extended to include purely scientific study of the tissue by a disinterested researcher for the purpose of advancing medical knowledge—provided of course that the patient gave timely and informed consent to that use. It would stretch the English language beyond recognition, however, to say that commercial exploitation of the kind and degree alleged here is also a usual and ordinary meaning of the phrase "scientific use."

. . . .

Secondly, even if section 7054.4 does permit defendants' commercial exploitation of Moore's tissue under the guise of "scientific use," it does not follow that—as the majority conclude—the statute "eliminates so many of the rights ordinarily attached to property" that what remains does not amount to "property" or "ownership" for purposes of the law of conversion.

The concepts of property and ownership in our law are extremely broad . . . [and] abstract: rather than referring directly to a material object such as a parcel of land or the tractor that cultivates it, the concept of property is often said to refer to a "bundle of rights" that may be exercised with respect to that object—principally the rights to possess the property, to use the property, to exclude others from the property, and to dispose of the property by sale or by gift . . . . But the same bundle of rights does not attach to all forms of property. For a variety of policy reasons, the law limits or even forbids the exercise of certain rights over certain forms of property. For example, both law and contract may limit the right of an owner of real property to use his parcel as he sees fit. Owners of various forms of personal property may likewise be subject to restrictions on the time, place, and manner of their use. Limitations on the disposition of real property, while less common, may also be imposed. Finally, some types of personal property may be sold but not given away,[9] while others may be given away but not sold,[10] and still others may neither be given away nor sold.[11]

---

[9] A person contemplating bankruptcy may sell his property at its "reasonably equivalent value," but he may not make a gift of the same property. (See 11 U.S.C. § 548(a).)

[10] A sportsman may give away wild fish or game that he has caught or killed pursuant to his license, but he may not sell it. (Fish & G. Code, §§ 3039, 7121.). . .

[11] E.g., a license to practice a profession, or a prescription drug in the hands of the person for whom it is prescribed.

In each of the foregoing instances, the limitation or prohibition diminishes the bundle of rights that would otherwise attach to the property, yet what remains is still deemed in law to be a protectible property interest. . . . The same rule applies to Moore's interest in his own body tissue: even if we assume that section 7054.4 limited the use and disposition of his excised tissue in the manner claimed by the majority, Moore nevertheless retained valuable rights in that tissue. Above all, at the time of its excision he at least had the right to do with his own tissue whatever the defendants did with it: i.e., he could have contracted with researchers and pharmaceutical companies to develop and exploit the vast commercial potential of his tissue and its products. Defendants certainly believe that their right to do the foregoing is not barred by section 7054.4 and is a significant property right, as they have demonstrated by their deliberate concealment from Moore of the true value of his tissue, their efforts to obtain a patent on the Mo cell line, their contractual agreements to exploit this material, their exclusion of Moore from any participation in the profits, and their vigorous defense of this lawsuit. The Court of Appeal summed up the point by observing that "Defendants' position that plaintiff cannot own his tissue, but that they can, is fraught with irony." It is also legally untenable. As noted above, the majority cite no case holding that an individual's right to develop and exploit the commercial potential of his own tissue is not a right of sufficient worth or dignity to be deemed a protectible property interest. In the absence of such authority—or of legislation to the same effect—the right falls within the traditionally broad concept of property in our law.

3.

The majority's third and last reason for their conclusion that Moore has no cause of action for conversion under existing law is that "the subject matter of the Regents' patent—the patented cell line and the products derived from it—cannot be Moore's property." The majority then offer a dual explanation: "This is because the patented cell line is both *factually* and *legally* distinct from the cells taken from Moore's body." Neither branch of the explanation withstands analysis.

First, in support of their statement that the Mo cell line is "factually distinct" from Moore's cells, the majority assert that "Cells change while being developed into a cell line and continue to change over time," and in particular may acquire an abnormal number of chromosomes. No one disputes these assertions, but they are nonetheless irrelevant. . . . Even if the cells of the Mo cell line in fact have an abnormal number of chromosomes, at the present stage of this case we do not know if that fact has any bearing whatever on their capacity to produce proteins; yet it is in the commercial exploitation of that capacity—not simply in their number of chromosomes—that Moore seeks to assert an interest. For all that appears, therefore, the emphasized fact is a distinction without a difference.

Second, the majority assert in effect that Moore cannot have an ownership interest in the Mo cell line because defendants patented it. The majority's point wholly fails to meet Moore's claim that he is entitled to compensation for defendants' unauthorized use of his bodily tissues *before* defendants patented the Mo cell line: defendants undertook such use immediately after the splenectomy on October 20, 1976, and continued to extract and use Moore's cells and tissue at least until September 20, 1983; the patent, however, did not issue until March 20, 1984, more than seven years after the unauthorized use began. Whatever the legal consequences of that event, it did not operate retroactively to immunize defendants from accountability for conduct occurring long before the patent was granted.

. . . .

4.

Having concluded—mistakenly, in my view—that Moore has no cause of action for conversion under existing law, the majority next consider whether to "extend" the conversion cause of action to this context. . . .

. . . .

In . . . my view whatever merit the majority's . . . policy consideration may have is outweighed by two contrary considerations, i.e., policies that are promoted by recognizing that every individual has a legally protectible property interest in his own body and its products. First, our society acknowledges a profound ethical imperative to respect the human body as the physical and temporal expression of the unique human persona. One manifestation of that respect is our prohibition against direct abuse of the body by torture or other forms of cruel or unusual punishment. Another is our prohibition against indirect abuse of the body by its economic exploitation for the sole benefit of another person. The most abhorrent form of such exploitation, of course, was the institution of slavery. Lesser forms, such as indentured servitude or even debtor's prison, have also disappeared. Yet their specter haunts the laboratories and boardrooms of today's biotechnological research-industrial complex. It arises wherever scientists or industrialists claim, as defendants claim here, the right to appropriate and exploit a patient's tissue for their sole economic benefit—the right, in other words, to freely mine or harvest valuable physical properties of the patient's body: "Research with human cells that results in significant economic gain for the researcher and no gain for the patient offends the traditional mores of our society in a manner impossible to quantify. Such research tends to treat the human body as a commodity—a means to a profitable end. The dignity and sanctity with which we regard the human whole, body as well as mind and soul, are absent when we allow researchers to further their own interests without the patient's participation by using a patient's cells as the basis for a marketable product." (Danforth, supra, 6 Yale L. & Pol'y Rev. at p. 190, fn. omitted.)

A second policy consideration adds notions of equity to those of ethics. Our society values fundamental fairness in dealings between its members, and condemns the unjust enrichment of any member at the expense of another. This is particularly true when, as here, the parties are not in equal bargaining positions. We are repeatedly told that the commercial products of the biotechnological revolution hold the promise of tremendous profit. In the case at bar, for example, the complaint alleges that the market for the kinds of proteins produced by the Mo cell line was predicted to exceed $3 billion by 1990. These profits are currently shared exclusively between the biotechnology industry and the universities that support that industry. . . . Thus the complaint alleges that because of his development of the Mo cell line defendant Golde became a paid consultant of defendant Genetics Institute and acquired the rights to 75,000 shares of that firm's stock at a cost of 1 cent each; that Genetics Institute further contracted to pay Golde and the Regents at least $330,000 over 3 years, including a pro rata share of Golde's salary and fringe benefits; and that defendant Sandoz Pharmaceuticals Corporation subsequently contracted to increase that compensation by a further $110,000.

There is, however, a third party to the biotechnology enterprise—the patient who is the source of the blood or tissue from which all these profits are derived. While he may be a silent partner, his contribution to the venture is absolutely crucial: as pointed out above, but for the cells of Moore's body taken by defendants there would have been no Mo cell line at all. Yet defendants deny that Moore is entitled to any share whatever in the proceeds of this cell line. This is both inequitable and immoral. As Dr. Thomas H. Murray, a respected professor of ethics and public policy, testified before Congress, "the person [who furnishes the tissue] should be justly compensated. . . . If biotechnologists fail to make provision for a just sharing of profits with the person whose gift made it possible, the public's sense of justice will be offended and no one will be the winner." (Murray, *Who Owns the Body? On the Ethics of Using Human Tissue for Commercial Purposes* (Jan.-Feb. 1986) IRB: A Review of Human Subjects Research, at p. 5.)[21]

. . . In short, as the Court of Appeal succinctly put it, "If this science has become science for profit, then we fail to see any justification for excluding the patient from participation in those profits."

5.

The majority's second reason for declining to extend the conversion cause of action to the present context is that "the Legislature should make that decision." I do not doubt that the Legislature is competent to act on this topic. The fact that the Legislature may intervene if and when it chooses, however, does not in the meanwhile relieve the courts of their duty of enforcing—or if need be, fashioning—an effective judicial remedy for the wrong here alleged. . . . To do so would be to abdicate pro tanto our responsibility over a body of law—torts— that is particularly a creature of the common law. And such reluctance to act would be especially unfortunate at the present time, when the rapid expansion of biotechnological science and industry makes resolution of these issues an increasingly pressing need.

The inference I draw from the current statutory regulation of human biological materials, moreover, is the opposite of that drawn by the majority. By selective quotation of the statutes the majority seem to suggest that human organs and blood cannot legally be sold on the open market—thereby implying that if the Legislature were to act here it would impose a similar ban on monetary compensation for the use of human tissue in biotechnological research and development. But if that is the argument, the premise is unsound: contrary to popular misconception, it is not true that human organs and blood cannot legally be sold.

As to organs, the majority rely on the Uniform Anatomical Gift Act for the proposition that a competent adult may make a post mortem gift of any part of his body but may not receive "valuable consideration" for the transfer. But the prohibition of the UAGA against the sale of a body part is much more limited than the majority recognize: by its terms the prohibition applies only to sales for "transplantation" or "therapy." Yet a different section of the UAGA authorizes the transfer and receipt of body parts for such additional purposes as "medical or dental education, research, or advancement of medical or dental science." No section of the UAGA prohibits anyone from selling body parts for any of those additional purposes; by clear implication, therefore, such sales are legal. Indeed, the fact that the UAGA prohibits no sales of organs other than sales for "transplantation" or "therapy" raises a further implication that it is also legal for anyone to sell human tissue to a biotechnology company for research and development purposes.

With respect to the sale of human blood the matter is much simpler: there is in fact no prohibition against such sales. The majority rely on Health and Safety Code section 1606, which provides in relevant part that the procurement and use of blood for transfusion "shall be construed

---

[21] The quoted view of Dr. Murray stands in stark contrast to the majority's disparaging remark that describes Moore's right to share in these profits as "a highly theoretical windfall."

to be, and is declared to be . . . the rendition of a service . . . and shall not be construed to be, and is declared not to be, a sale . . . ." There is less here, however, than meets the eye: the statute does not mean that a person cannot sell his blood or, by implication, that his blood is not his property . . . . The reason is plain: "No State or Federal statute prohibits the sale of blood, plasma, semen, or other replenishing tissues if taken in nonvital amounts. Nevertheless, State laws usually characterize these paid transfers as the provision of services rather than the sale of a commodity . . . . [¶] The primary legal reason for characterizing these transactions as involving services rather than goods is to avoid liability for contaminated blood products under either general product liability principles or the [Uniform Commercial Code's] implied warranty provisions." (OTA Rep., supra, at p. 76, fn. omitted.). . .Thus despite the statute relied on by the majority, it is perfectly legal in this state for a person to sell his blood for transfusion or for any other purpose—indeed, such sales are commonplace, particularly in the market for plasma. (See OTA Rep., supra, at p. 121.)

It follows that the statutes regulating the transfers of human organs and blood do not support the majority's refusal to recognize a conversion cause of action for commercial exploitation of human blood cells without consent. On the contrary, because such statutes treat both organs and blood as property that can legally be sold in a variety of circumstances, they impliedly support Moore's contention that his blood cells are likewise property for which he can and should receive compensation, and hence are protected by the law of conversion.

6.

The majority's final reason for refusing to recognize a conversion cause of action on these facts is that "there is no pressing need" to do so because the complaint also states another cause of action that is assertedly adequate to the task; that cause of action is "the breach of a fiduciary duty to disclose facts material to the patient's consent or, alternatively,. . .the performance of medical procedures without first having obtained the patient's informed consent." Although last, this reason is not the majority's least; in fact, it underlies much of the opinion's discussion of the conversion cause of action, recurring like a leitmotiv throughout that discussion.

. . . .

The remedy [for nondisclosure] is largely illusory. "[A]n action based on the physician's failure to disclose material information sounds in negligence. As a practical matter, however, it may be difficult to recover on this kind of negligence theory because the patient must prove a *causal connection* between his or her injury and the physician's failure to inform." (Martin & Lagod, *Biotechnology and the Commercial Use of Human Cells: Toward an Organic View of Life and Technology* (1989) 5 Santa Clara Computer & High Tech L.J. 211, 222, fn. omitted, italics added.) There are two barriers to recovery. First, "the patient must show that if he or she had been informed of all pertinent information, he or she would have declined to consent to the procedure in question." (Ibid.) As we explained in the seminal case of *Cobbs v. Grant* (1972) 8 Cal. 3d 229, 245, "There must be a causal relationship between the physician's failure to inform and the injury to the plaintiff. Such a causal connection arises only if it is established that had revelation been made consent to treatment would not have been given."

The second barrier to recovery is still higher, and is erected on the first: it is not even enough for the plaintiff to prove that he personally would have refused consent to the proposed treatment if he had been fully informed; he must also prove that in the same circumstances *no reasonably prudent person* would have given such consent. The purpose of this "objective" standard is evident: "Since at the time of trial the uncommunicated hazard has materialized, it would be surprising if the patient-plaintiff did not claim that had he been informed of the dangers he would have declined treatment. Subjectively he may believe so, with the 20/20 vision of hindsight, but we doubt that justice will be served by placing the physician in jeopardy of the patient's bitterness and disillusionment. Thus an objective test is preferable: i.e., what would a prudent person in the patient's position have decided if adequately informed of all significant perils." (*Cobbs v. Grant*, supra, 8 Cal. 3d 229, 245.)

. . . .

[Furthermore,] the nondisclosure cause of action is inadequate for the task that the majority assign to it [in] that it fails to solve half the problem before us: it gives the patient only the right to *refuse* consent, i.e., the right to prohibit the commercialization of his tissue; it does not give him the right to *grant* consent to that commercialization on the condition that he share in its proceeds. . . .

Reversing the words of the old song, the nondisclosure cause of action thus accentuates the negative and eliminates the positive: the patient can say no, but he cannot say yes and expect to share in the proceeds of his contribution. Yet as explained above, there are sound reasons of ethics and equity to recognize the patient's right to participate in such benefits. The nondisclosure cause of action does not protect that right; to that extent, it is therefore not an adequate substitute for the conversion remedy, which does protect the right.

. . . .

[7] Notes

[a] Events After the Moore Decision

The results in *Moore* left John Moore with the equivalent of a medical malpractice claim. Under California law, damages in such claims were limited to actual losses plus $250,000 for pain and suffering. Since Moore had no physical injury or lost earnings as a result of the actions of his doctors, Moore exited the appellate review with "significantly diminished economic expectations." The case was eventually settled, but for much less money than would have been produced by a successful conversion claim. JUDITH C. AREEN, PATRICIA A. KING, STEVEN GOLDBERG, LARRY O. GOSTIN & ALEXANDER CAPRON, LAW SCIENCE & MEDICINE 911 (2d ED.1996).

[b] Preembryos

Perhaps the most famous dispute over human tissue arose in *Davis v. Davis*, 842 S.W.2d 588 (Tenn. 1992). *Davis* was a case in which a divorcing couple—Junior and Mary Davis—quarreled over custody of "preembryos"—cryogenically protected fertilized eggs waiting to be implanted in Mary Sue Davis' womb. Mary wished to take possession of the preembryos and implant them. Junior Davis had no interest in being the father of new children born to his ex-spouse. After years of litigation, Junior Davis was finally awarded possession of the preembryos and they were destroyed. Can preembryos be thought of as "property?" A number of other related disputes have arisen about control and possession of human genetic material. For one summary read Cynthia Gorney, *The Real-Life Dilemmas of Frozen Embryos,* WASH. POST, July 26, 1989, at B1, col. 1.

[c] Genetic Codes

As the composition of the human genome is gradually unraveled, the day is approaching when the genetic blueprint for each of us will be discoverable. Should these blueprints be deemed to be the "property" of their "owners?" Should we have the right to transfer our genetic codes to others, either as a gift or by way of sale?

[d] Commodities and Non-Commodities

How should we think of John Moore's cancerous cells? Were they a commodity available for sale to the first person who took possession of them? Should the labor and efforts of the researchers who turned Moore's cells into therapeutic tools be rewarded by giving them an interest in the cell line? Should therapeutic items like Moore's cells be deemed non-marketable commodities? Or should we simply create a market in cells that anyone may use to purchase a therapy?

APPENDIX I

THE CONSTITUTION OF THE UNITED STATES OF AMERICA

We the People of the United States, in Order to form a more perfect Union, establish Justice, insure domestic Tranquility, provide for the common defence, promote the general Welfare, and secure the Blessings of Liberty to ourselves and our Posterity, do ordain and establish this Constitution for the United States of America.

ARTICLE I

Section 1. All legislative Powers herein granted shall be vested in a Congress of the United States, which shall consist of a Senate and House of Representatives.

Section 2. [1] The House of Representatives shall be composed of Members chosen every second Year by the People of the several States, and the Electors in each State shall have the Qualifications requisite for Electors of the most numerous Branch of the State Legislature.

[2] No Person shall be a Representative who shall not have attained to the Age of twenty five Years, and been seven Years a Citizen of the United States, and who shall not, when elected, be an Inhabitant of that State in which he shall be chosen.

[3] Representatives and direct Taxes shall be apportioned among the several States which may be included within this Union, according to their respective Numbers, which shall be determined by adding to the whole Number of free Persons, including those bound to Service for a Term of Years, and excluding Indians not taxed, three fifths of all other Persons. The actual Enumeration shall be made within three Years after the first Meeting of the Congress of the United States, and within every subsequent Term of ten Years, in such Manner as they shall by Law direct. The Number of Representatives shall not exceed one for every thirty Thousand, but each State shall have at Least one Representative; and until such enumeration shall be made, the State of New Hampshire shall be entitled to chuse three, Massachusetts eight, Rhode Island and Providence Plantations one, Connecticut five, New York six, New Jersey four, Pennsylvania eight, Delaware one, Maryland six, Virginia ten, North Carolina five, South Carolina five, and Georgia three.

[4] When vacancies happen in the Representation from any State, the Executive Authority thereof shall issue Writs of Election to fill such Vacancies.

[5] The House of Representatives shall chuse their Speaker and other Officers; and shall have the sole Power of Impeachment.

Section 3. [1] The Senate of the United States shall be composed of two Senators from each State, chosen by the Legislature thereof, for six Years; and each Senator shall have one Vote.

[2] Immediately after they shall be assembled in Consequence of the first Election, they shall be divided as equally as may be into three Classes. The Seats of the Senators of the first Class shall be vacated at the Expiration of the Second Year, of the second Class at the Expiration of the fourth Year, and of the third Class at the Expiration of the sixth Year, so that one third may be chosen every second Year; and if Vacancies happen by Resignation, or otherwise, during

the Recess of the Legislature of any State, the Executive thereof may make temporary Appointments until the next Meeting of the Legislature, which shall then fill such Vacancies.

[3] No Person shall be a Senator who shall not have attained to the Age of thirty Years, and been nine Years a Citizen of the United States, and who shall not, when elected, be an Inhabitant of that State for which he shall be chosen.

[4] The Vice President of the United States shall be President of the Senate, but shall have no Vote, unless they be equally divided.

[5] The Senate shall chuse their other Officers, and also a President pro tempore, in the Absence of the Vice President, or when he shall exercise the Office of President of the United States.

[6] The Senate shall have the sole Power to try all Impeachments. When sitting for that Purpose, they shall be on Oath or Affirmation. When the President of the United States is tried, the Chief Justice shall preside: And no Person shall be convicted without the Concurrence of two thirds of the Members present.

[7] Judgment in Cases of Impeachment shall not extend further than to removal from Office, and disqualification to hold and enjoy any Office of honor, Trust, or profit under the United States: but the Party convicted shall nevertheless be liable and subject to Indictment, Trial, Judgment, and Punishment, according to Law.

Section 4. [1] The Times, Places and Manner of holding Elections for Senators and Representatives, shall be prescribed in each State by the Legislature thereof; but the Congress may at any time by Law make or alter such Regulations, except as to the Places of chusing Senators.

[2] The Congress shall assemble at least once in every Year, and such Meeting shall be on the first Monday in December, unless they shall by Law appoint a different Day.

Section 5. [1] Each House shall be the Judge of the Elections, Returns, and Qualifications of its own Members, and a Majority of each shall constitute a Quorum to do Business; but a smaller Number may adjourn from day to day, and may be authorized to compel the Attendance of absent Members, in such Manner, and under such Penalties as each House may provide.

[2] Each House may determine the Rules of its Proceedings, punish its Members for disorderly Behavior, and, with the Concurrence of two thirds expel a Member.

[3] Each House shall keep a Journal of its Proceedings, and from time to time publish the same, excepting such Parts as may in their Judgment require Secrecy; and the Yeas and Nays of the Members of either House on any question shall, at the Desire of one fifth of those Present, be entered on the Journal.

[4] Neither House, during the Session of Congress, shall, without the Consent of the other, adjourn for more than three days, nor to any other Place than that in which the two Houses shall be sitting.

Section 6. [1] The Senators and Representatives shall receive a Compensation for their Services, to be ascertained by Law, and paid out of the Treasury of the United States. They shall in all Cases, except Treason, Felony and Breach of the Peace, be privileged from Arrest during their Attendance at the Session of their respective Houses, and in going to and returning from the same; and for any Speech or Debate in either House, they shall not be questioned in any other Place.

[2] No Senator or Representative shall, during the Time for which he was elected, be appointed to any civil Office under the Authority of the United States, which shall have been created, or the Emoluments whereof shall have been increased during such time; and no Person holding any Office under the United States, shall be a Member of either House during his Continuance in Office.

Section 7. [1] All Bills for raising Revenue shall originate in the House of Representatives; but the Senate may propose or concur with Amendments as on other Bills.

[2] Every Bill which shall have passed the House of Representatives and the Senate, shall, before it become a Law, be presented to the President of the United States; If he approve he shall sign it, but if not he shall return it, with his Objections to the House in which it shall have originated, who shall enter the Objections at large on their Journal, and proceed to reconsider it. If after such Reconsideration two thirds of that House shall agree to pass the Bill, it shall be sent together with the Objections, to the other House, by which it shall likewise be reconsidered, and if approved by two thirds of that House, it shall become a Law. But in all such Cases the Votes of both Houses shall be determined by yeas and Nays, and the Names of the Persons voting for and against the Bill shall be entered on the Journal of each House respectively. If any Bill shall not be returned by the President within ten Days (Sundays excepted) after it shall have been presented to him, the Same shall be a Law, in like Manner as if he had signed it, unless the Congress by their Adjournment prevent its return in which Case it shall not be a Law.

[3] Every Order, Resolution, or Vote, to which the Concurrence of the Senate and House of Representatives may be necessary (except on a question of Adjournment) shall be presented to the President of the United States; and before the Same shall take Effect, shall be approved by him, or being disapproved by him, shall be repassed by two thirds of the Senate and House of Representatives, according to the rules and Limitations prescribed in the Case of a Bill.

Section 8. [1] The Congress shall have Power To lay and collect Taxes, Duties, Imposts and Excises, to pay the Debts and provide for the common Defence and general Welfare of the United States; but all Duties, Imposts and Excises shall be uniform throughout the United States;

[2] To borrow money on the credit of the United States;

[3] To regulate Commerce with foreign Nations, and among the several States, and with the Indian Tribes;

[4] To establish an uniform Rule of Naturalization, and uniform Laws on the subject of Bankruptcies throughout the United States;

[5] to coin Money, regulate the Value thereof, and of foreign Coin, and fix the Standard of Weights and Measures;

[6] To provide for the Punishment of counterfeiting the Securities and current Coin of the United States;

[7] To Establish Post Offices and Post Roads;

[8] To promote the Progress of Science and useful Arts, by securing for limited Times to Authors and Inventors the exclusive Right to their respective Writings and Discoveries;

[9] To constitute Tribunal inferior to the supreme Court;

[10] To define and punish Piracies and Felonies committed on the high Seas, and Offenses against the Law of Nations;

[11] To declare War, grant Letters of Marque and Reprisal, and make Rules concerning Captures on Land and Water;

[12] To raise and support Armies, but no Appropriation of Money to that Use shall be for a longer Term than two Years;

[13] To provide and maintain a Navy;

[14] To make Rules for the Government and Regulation of the land and naval Forces;

[15] To provide for calling forth the Militia to execute the Laws of the Union, suppress Insurrections and repel Invasions;

[16] To provide for organizing, arming, and disciplining, the Militia, and for governing such Part of them as may be employed in the Service of the United States, reserving to the States respectively, the Appointment of the Officers, and the Authority of training the Militia according to the discipline prescribed by Congress;

[17] To exercise exclusive Legislation in all Cases whatsoever, over such District (not exceeding ten Miles square) as may, by Cession of particular States, and the Acceptance of Congress, become the Seat of the Government of the United States, and to exercise like Authority over all Places purchased by the Consent of the Legislature of the State in which the Same shall be, for the Erection of Forts, Magazines, Arsenals, dock-Yards, and other needful Buildings;—And

[18] To make all Laws which shall be necessary and proper for carrying into Execution the foregoing Powers, and all other Powers vested by this Constitution in the Government of the United States, or in any Department or Officer thereof.

Section 9. [1] The Migration or Importation of Such Persons as any of the States now existing shall think proper to admit, shall not be prohibited by the Congress prior to the Year one thousand eight hundred and eight, but a Tax or duty may be imposed on such Importation, not exceeding ten dollars for each Person.

[2] The privilege of the Writ of Habeas Corpus shall not be suspended, unless when in Cases of Rebellion or Invasion the public Safety may require it.

[3] No Bill of Attainder or ex post facto Law shall be passed.

[4] No Capitation, or other direct, Tax shall be laid, unless in Proportion to the Census or Enumeration herein before directed to be taken.

[5] No Tax or Duty shall be laid on Articles exported from any State.

[6] No Preference shall be given by any Regulation of Commerce or Revenue to the Ports of one State over those of another: nor shall Vessels bound to, or from, one State be obliged to enter, clear, or pay Duties in another.

[7] No money shall be drawn from the Treasury, but in Consequence of Appropriations made by Law; and a regular Statement and Account of the Receipts and Expenditures of all public Money shall be published from time to time.

[8] No Title of Nobility shall be granted by the United States: And no Person holding any Office of Profit or Trust under them, shall, without the Consent of the Congress, accept of any present, Emolument, Office, or Title, of any kind whatever, from any King, Prince, or foreign State.

Section 10. [1] No State shall enter into any Treaty, Alliance, or Confederation; grant Letters of Marque and Reprisal; coin Money; emit Bills of Credit; make any Thing but gold and silver Coin a Tender in Payment of Debts; pass any Bill of Attainder, ex post facto Law, or Law impairing the Obligation of Contracts, or grant any Title of Nobility.

[2] No State shall, without the Consent of the Congress, lay any Imposts or Duties on Imports or Exports, except what may be absolutely necessary for executing it's inspection Laws: and the net Produce of all Duties and Imposts, laid by any State on Imports or Exports, shall be for the Use of the Treasury of the United States; and all such Laws shall be subject to the Revision and Controul of the Congress.

[3] No State shall, without the Consent of Congress, lay any Duty of Tonnage, keep Troops, or Ships of War in time of Peace, enter into any Agreement or Compact with another State, or with a foreign Power, or engage in War, unless actually invaded, or in such imminent Danger as will not admit of delay.

ARTICLE II

Section 1. [1] The executive Power shall be vested in a President of the United States of America. He shall hold his Office during the Term of four Years, and, together with the Vice President, chosen for the same Term, be elected, as follows:

[2] Each State shall appoint, in such Manner as the Legislature thereof may direct, a Number of Electors, equal to the whole Number of Senators and Representatives to which the State may be entitled in the Congress; but no Senator or Representative, or Person holding an Office of Trust or Profit under the United States, shall be appointed an Elector.

[3] The Electors shall meet in their respective States, and vote by Ballot for two Persons, of whom one at least shall not be an Inhabitant of the same State with themselves. And they shall make a List of all the Persons voted for, and of the Number of Votes for each; which List they shall sign and certify, and transmit sealed to the Seat of the Government of the United States, directed to the President of the Senate. The President of the Senate shall, in the Presence of the Senate and House of Representatives, open all the Certificates, and the Votes shall then be counted. The Person having the greatest Number of Votes shall be the President, if such Number be a Majority of the whole Number of Electors appointed; and if there be more than one who have such Majority, and have an equal Number of Votes, then the House of Representatives shall immediately chuse by Ballot one of them for President; and if no Person have a Majority, then from the five highest on the List the said House shall in like Manner chuse the President. But in chusing the President, the Votes shall be taken by States the Representation from each State having one Vote; A quorum for this Purpose shall consist of a Member or Members from two thirds of the States, and a Majority of all the States shall be necessary to a Choice. In every Case, after the Choice of the President, the Person having the greater Number of Votes of the Electors shall be the Vice President. But if there should remain two or more who have equal Votes, the Senate shall chuse from them by Ballot the Vice President.

[4] The Congress may determine the Time of chusing the Electors, and the Day on which they shall give their Votes; which Day shall be the same throughout the United States.

[5] No person except a natural born Citizen, or a Citizen of the United States, at the time of the Adoption of this Constitution, shall be eligible to the Office of President; neither shall any Person be eligible to that Office who shall not have attained to the Age of thirty five Years, and been fourteen Years a Resident within the United States.

[6] In case of the removal of the President from Office, or of his Death, Resignation or Inability to discharge the Powers and Duties of the said Office, the Same shall devolve on the Vice President, and the Congress may by Law provide for the Case of Removal, Death, Resignation or Inability, both of the President and Vice President, declaring what Officer shall then act as President, and such Officer shall act accordingly, until the Disability be removed, or a President shall be elected.

[7] The President shall, at stated Times, receive for his Services, a Compensation, which shall neither be increased nor diminished during the Period for which he shall have been elected, and he shall not receive within that Period any other Emolument from the United States, or any of them.

[8] Before he enter on the Execution of his Office, he shall take the following Oath or Affirmation: "I do solemnly swear (or affirm) that I will faithfully execute the Office of President of the United States, and will to the best of my Ability, preserve, protect and defend the Constitution of the United States."

Section 2. [1] The President shall be Commander in Chief of the Army and Navy of the United States, and of the militia of the several States, when called into the actual Service of the United States; he may require the Opinion, in writing, of the principal Officer in each of the Executive Departments, upon any Subject relating to the Duties of their respective Offices, and he shall have Power to grant Reprieves and Pardons for Offenses against the United States, except in Cases of Impeachment.

[2] He shall have Power, by and with the Advice and Consent of the Senate to make Treaties, provided two thirds of the Senators present concur; and he shall nominate, and by and with the Advice and Consent of the Senate, shall appoint Ambassadors, other public Ministers and Consuls, Judges of the supreme Court, and all other Officers of the United States, whose Appointments are not herein otherwise provided for, and which shall be established by Law; but the Congress may be Law vest the Appointment of such inferior Officers, as they think proper, in the President alone, in the Courts of Law, or in the Heads of Departments.

[3] The President shall have Power to fill up all Vacancies that may happen during the Recess of the Senate, by granting Commissions which shall expire at the End of their next Session.

Section 3. He shall from time to time give to the Congress Information of the State of the Union, and recommend to their Consideration such Measures as he shall judge necessary and expedient; he may, on extraordinary Occasions, convene both Houses, or either of them, and in Case of Disagreement between them, with Respect to the Time of Adjournment, he may adjourn them to such Time as he shall think proper; he shall receive Ambassadors and other public Ministers; he shall take Care that the Laws be faithfully executed, and shall Commission all the Officers of the United States.

Section 4. The President, Vice President and all civil Officers of the United States, shall be removed from Office on Impeachment for, and Conviction of, Treason, Bribery, or other high Crimes and Misdemeanors.

ARTICLE III

Section 1. The judicial Power of the United States, shall be vested in one supreme Court, and in such inferior Courts as the Congress may from time to time ordain and establish. The Judges, both of the supreme and inferior Courts, shall hold their Offices during good Behaviour, and shall, at stated Times, receive for their Services a Compensation, which shall not be diminished during their Continuance in Office.

Section 2. [1] The judicial Power shall extend to all Cases, in Law and Equity, arising under this Constitution, the Laws of the United States, and Treaties made, or which shall be made, under their Authority;—to all Cases affecting Ambassadors, other public Ministers and Consuls;—to all Cases of admiralty and maritime Jurisdiction;—to Controversies to which the United States shall be a Party;—to Controversies between two or more States;—between a State and Citizens of another State;—between Citizens of different States;—between Citizens of the same State claiming Lands under the Grants of different States, and between a State, or the Citizens thereof, and foreign States, Citizens or Subjects.

[2] In all Cases affecting Ambassadors, other public Ministers and Consuls, and those in which a State shall be a Party, the supreme Court shall have original Jurisdiction. In all the other Cases before mentioned, the supreme Court shall have appellate Jurisdiction, both as to Law and Fact, with such Exceptions, and under such Regulations as the Congress shall make.

[3] The trial of all Crimes, except in Cases of Impeachment, shall be by Jury; and such Trial shall be held in the State where the said Crimes shall have been committed; but when not committed within any State, the Trial shall be at such Place or Places as the Congress may by Law have directed.

Section 3. [1] Treason against the United States, shall consist only in levying War against them, or, in adhering to their Enemies, giving them Aid and Comfort. No Person shall be convicted of Treason unless on the Testimony of two Witnesses to the same overt Act, or on Confession in open Court.

[2] The Congress shall have Power to declare the Punishment of Treason, but no Attainder of Treason shall work Corruption of Blood, or Forfeiture except during the Life of the Person attainted.

ARTICLE IV

Section 1. Full Faith and Credit shall be given in each State to the public Acts, Records, and judicial Proceedings of every other State. And the Congress may by general Laws prescribe the Manner in which such Acts, Records and Proceedings shall be proved, and the Effect thereof.

Section 2. [1] The Citizens of each State shall be entitled to all Privileges and Immunities of Citizens in the several States.

[2] A Person charged in any State with Treason, Felony, or other Crime, who shall flee from Justice, and be found in another State, shall on demand of the executive Authority of the State from which he fled, be delivered up, to be removed to the State having Jurisdiction of the Crime.

[3] No Person held to Service or Labour in one State, under the Laws thereof, escaping into another, shall, in Consequence of any Law or Regulation therein, be discharged from such Service or Labour, but shall be delivered up on Claim of the Party to whom such Service or Labour may be due.

Section 3. [1] New States may be admitted by the Congress into this Union; but no new State shall be formed or erected within the Jurisdiction of any other State; nor any State be formed by the Junction of two or more States, or Parts of States, without the Consent of the Legislatures of the States concerned as well as of the Congress.

[2] The Congress shall have Power to dispose of and make all needful Rules and Regulations respecting the Territory or other Property belonging to the United States; and nothing in this Constitution shall be so construed as to Prejudice any Claims of the United States, or of any particular State.

Section 4. The United States shall guarantee to every State in this Union a Republican Form of Government, and shall protect each of them against Invasion; and on Application of the Legislature, or of the Executive (when the Legislature cannot be convened) against domestic Violence.

ARTICLE V

The Congress, whenever two thirds of both Houses shall deem it necessary, shall propose Amendments to this Constitution, or, on the Application of the Legislatures of two thirds of the several States, shall call a Convention for proposing Amendments, which, in either Case, shall be valid to all Intents and Purposes, as part of this Constitution, when ratified by the Legislatures of three fourths of the several States, or by Conventions in three fourths thereof, as the one or the other Mode of Ratification may be proposed by the Congress; Provided that no Amendment which may be made prior to the Year One thousand eight hundred and eight shall in any Manner affect the first and fourth Clauses in the Ninth Section of the first Article; and that no State, without its Consent, shall be deprived of its equal Suffrage in the Senate.

ARTICLE VI

[1] All Debts contracted and Engagements entered into, before the Adoption of this Constitution shall be as valid against the United States under this Constitution, as under the Confederation.

[2] This Constitution, and the Laws of the United States which shall be made in Pursuance thereof; and all Treaties made, or which shall be made, under the Authority of the United States, shall be the supreme Law of the Land; and the Judges in every State shall be bound thereby, any Thing in the Constitution or Laws of any State to the Contrary notwithstanding.

[3] The Senators and Representatives before mentioned, and the Members of the several State Legislatures, and all executive and judicial Officers, both of the United States and of the several States, shall be bound by Oath or Affirmation, to support this Constitution; but no religious Test shall ever be required as a Qualification to any Office or public Trust under the United States.

ARTICLE VII

The Ratification of the Conventions of nine States shall be sufficient for the Establishment of this Constitution between the States so ratifying the Same.

ARTICLES IN ADDITION TO, AND AMENDMENT OF, THE CONSTITUTION OF THE UNITED STATES OF AMERICA, PROPOSED BY CONGRESS, AND RATIFIED BY THE LEGISLATURES OF THE SEVERAL STATES PURSUANT TO THE FIFTH ARTICLE OF THE ORIGINAL CONSTITUTION.

AMENDMENT I [1791]

Congress shall make no law respecting an establishment of religion, or prohibiting the free exercise thereof; or abridging the freedom of speech, or of the press; or the right of the people peaceably to assemble, and to petition the Government for a redress of grievances.

Amendment II [1791]

A well regulated Militia, being necessary to the security of a free State, the right of the people to keep and bear Arms, shall not be infringed.

Amendment III [1791]

No Soldier shall, in time of peace be quartered in any house, without the consent of the Owner, nor in time of war, but in a manner to be prescribed by law.

Amendment IV [1791]

The right of the people to be secure in their persons, houses, papers, and effects, against unreasonable searches and seizures, shall not be violated, and no Warrants shall issue, but upon probable cause, supported by Oath or affirmation, and particularly describing the place to be searched, and the persons or things to be seized.

Amendment V [1791]

No person shall be held to answer for a capital, or otherwise infamous crime, unless on a presentment or indictment of a Grand Jury, except in cases arising in the land or naval forces, or in the Militia, when in actual service in time of War or public danger; nor shall any person be subject for the same offence to be twice put in jeopardy of life or limb; nor shall be compelled in any criminal case to be a witness against himself, nor be deprived of life, liberty, or property, without due process of law; nor shall private property be taken for public use, without just compensation.

Amendment VI [1791]

In all criminal prosecutions, the accused shall enjoy the right to a speedy and public trial, by an impartial jury of the State and district wherein the crime shall have been committed, which district shall have been previously ascertained by law, and to be informed of the nature and cause of the accusation; to be confronted with the witnesses against him; to have compulsory process for obtaining witnesses in his favor, and to have the Assistance of Counsel for his defence.

Amendment VII [1791]

In Suits at common law, where the value in controversy shall exceed twenty dollars, the right of trial by jury shall be preserved, and no fact tried by jury, shall be otherwise re-examined in any Court of the United States, than according to the rules of the common law.

Amendment VIII [1791]

Excessive bail shall not be required, nor excessive fines imposed, nor cruel and unusual punishments inflicted.

Amendment IX [1791]

The enumeration in the Constitution, of certain rights, shall not be construed to deny or disparage others retained by the people.

AMENDMENT X [1791]

The powers not delegated to the United States by the Constitution, nor prohibited by it to the States, are reserved to the States respectively, or to the people.

AMENDMENT XI [1798]

The Judicial power of the United States shall not be construed to extend to any suit in law or equity, commenced or prosecuted against one of the United States by Citizens of another State, or by Citizens or Subjects of any Foreign State.

AMENDMENT XII [1804]

The Electors shall meet in their respective states and vote by ballot for President and Vice-President, one of whom, at least, shall not be an inhabitant of the same state with themselves; they shall name in their ballots the person voted for as President, and in distinct ballots the person voted for as Vice-President, and they shall make distinct lists of all persons voted for as President, and of all persons voted for as Vice-President, and of the number of votes for each, which lists they shall sign and certify, and transmit sealed to the seat of the government of the United States, directed to the President of the Senate;—The President of the Senate shall, in the presence of the Senate and House of Representatives, open all the certificates and the votes shall then be counted;—The person having the greatest number of votes for President, shall be the President, if such number be a majority of the whole number of Electors appointed; and if no person have such majority, then from the persons having the highest numbers not exceeding three on the list of those voted for as President, the House of Representatives shall choose immediately, by ballot, the President. But in choosing the President, the votes shall be taken by states, the representation from each state having one vote; a quorum for this purpose shall consist of a member or members from two-thirds of the states, and a majority of all the states shall be necessary to a choice. And if the House of Representatives shall not choose a President whenever the right of choice shall devolve upon them before the fourth day of March next following, then the Vice-President shall act as President, as in the case of the death or other constitutional disability of the President.—The person having the greatest number of votes as Vice-President, shall be the Vice-President, if such number be a majority of the whole number of Electors appointed, and if no person have a majority, then from the two highest numbers on the list, the Senate shall choose the Vice-President; a quorum for the purpose shall consist of two-thirds of the whole number of Senators, and a majority of the whole number shall be necessary to a choice. But no person constitutionally ineligible to the office of President shall be eligible to that of Vice-President of the United States.

AMENDMENT XIII [1865]

Section 1. Neither slavery nor involuntary servitude, except as a punishment for crime whereof the party shall have been duly convicted, shall exist within the United States, or any place subject to their jurisdiction.

Section 2. Congress shall have power to enforce this article by appropriate legislation.

AMENDMENT XIV [1868]

Section 1. All persons born or naturalized in the United States, and subject to the jurisdiction thereof, are citizens of the United States and of the State wherein they reside. No State shall make or enforce any law which shall abridge the privileges or immunities of citizens of the United States; nor shall any State deprive any person of life, liberty, or property, without due process of law; nor deny to any person within its jurisdiction the equal protection of the laws.

Section 2. Representatives shall be apportioned among the several States according to their respective numbers, counting the whole number of persons in each State, excluding Indians not taxed. But when the right to vote at any election for the choice of electors for President and Vice President of the United States, Representatives in Congress, the Executive and Judicial officers of a State, or the members of the Legislature thereof, is denied to any of the male inhabitants of such State, being twenty-one years of age, and citizens of the United States, or in any way abridged, except for participation in rebellion, or other crime, the basis of representation therein shall be reduced in the proportion which the number of such male citizens shall bear to the whole number of male citizens twenty-one years of age in such State.

Section 3. No person shall be a Senator or Representative in Congress, or elector of President and Vice President, or hold any office, civil or military, under the United States, or under any State, who having previously taken an oath, as a member of Congress, or as an officer of the United States, or as a member of any State legislature, or as an executive or judicial officer of any State, to support the Constitution of the United States, shall have engaged in insurrection or rebellion against the same, or given aid or comfort to the enemies thereof. But Congress may by a vote of two-thirds of each House, remove such disability.

Section 4. The validity of the public debt of the United States, authorized by law, including debts incurred for payment of pensions and bounties for services in suppressing insurrection or rebellion, shall not be questioned. But neither the United States nor any State shall assume or pay any debt or obligation incurred in aid of insurrection or rebellion against the United States, or any claim for the loss or emancipation of any slave; but all such debts, obligations and claims shall be held illegal and void.

Section 5. The Congress shall have power to enforce, by appropriate legislation, the provisions of this article.

Amendment XV [1870]

Section 1. The right of citizens of the United States to vote shall not be denied or abridged by the United States or by any State on account of race, color, or previous condition of servitude.

Section 2. The Congress shall have power to enforce this article by appropriate legislation.

Amendment XVI [1913]

The Congress shall have power to lay and collect taxes on incomes, from whatever source derived, without apportionment among the several States, and without regard to any census or enumeration.

Amendment XVII [1913]

[1] The Senate of the United States shall be composed of two Senators from each State, elected by the people thereof, for six years; and each Senator shall have one vote. The electors in each State shall have the qualifications requisite for electors of the most numerous branch of the State legislatures.

[2] When vacancies happen in the representation of any State in the Senate, the executive authority of such State shall issue writs of election to fill such vacancies: *Provided*, That the legislature of any State may empower the executive thereof to make temporary appointments until the people fill the vacancies by election as the legislature may direct.

[3] This amendment shall not be so construed as to affect the election or term of any Senator chosen before it becomes valid as part of the Constitution.

AMENDMENT XVIII [1919]

Section 1. After one year from the ratification of this article the manufacture, sale, or transportation of intoxicating liquors within, the importation thereof into, or the exportation thereof from the United States and all territory subject to the jurisdiction thereof for beverage purposes is hereby prohibited.

Section 2. The Congress and the several States shall have concurrent power to enforce this article by appropriate legislation.

Section 3. This article shall be inoperative unless it shall have been ratified as an amendment to the Constitution by the legislatures of the several States, as provided in the Constitution, within seven years from the date of the submission hereof to the States by the Congress.

AMENDMENT XIX [1920]

[1] The right of citizens of the United States to vote shall not be denied or abridged by the United States or by any State on account of sex.

[2] Congress shall have power to enforce this article by appropriate legislation.

AMENDMENT XX [1933]

Section 1. The terms of the President and Vice President shall end at noon on the 20th day of January, and the terms of Senators and Representatives at noon on the 3d day of January, of the years in which such terms would have ended if this article had not been ratified; and the terms of their successors shall then begin.

Section 2. The Congress shall assemble at least once in every year, and such meeting shall begin at noon on the 3d day of January, unless they shall by law appoint a different day.

Section 3. If, at the time fixed for the beginning of the term of the President, the President elect shall have died, the Vice President elect shall become President. If the President shall not have been chosen before the time fixed for the beginning of his term, or if the President elect shall have failed to qualify, then the Vice President elect shall act as President until a President shall have qualified; and the Congress may by law provide for the case wherein neither a President elect nor a Vice President elect shall have qualified, declaring who shall then act as President, or the manner in which one who is to act shall be selected, and such person shall act accordingly until a President or Vice President shall have qualified.

Section 4. The Congress may by law provide for the case of the death of any of the persons from whom the House of Representatives may choose a President whenever the right of choice shall have devolved upon them, and for the case of the death of any of the persons from whom the Senate may choose a Vice President whenever the right of choice shall have devolved upon them.

Section 5. Sections 1 and 2 shall take effect on the 15th day of October following the ratification of this article.

Section 6. This article shall be inoperative unless it shall have been ratified as an amendment to the Constitution by the legislatures of three-fourths of the several States within seven years from the date of its submission.

AMENDMENT XXI [1933]

Section 1. The eighteenth article of amendment to the Constitution of the United States is hereby repealed.

Section 2. The transportation or importation into any State, Territory, or possession of the United States for delivery or use therein of intoxicating liquors, in violation of the laws thereof, is hereby prohibited.

Section 3. This article shall be inoperative unless it shall have been ratified as an amendment to the Constitution by conventions in the several States, as provided in the Constitution, within seven years from the date of the submission hereof to the States by the Congress.

AMENDMENT XXII [1951]

Section 1. No person shall be elected to the office of the President more than twice, and no person who has held the office of President, or acted as President, for more than two years of a term to which some other person was elected President shall be elected to the office of President more than once. But this Article shall not apply to any person holding the office of President when this Article was proposed by the Congress, and shall not prevent any person who may be holding the office of President, or acting as President, during the term within which this Article becomes operative from holding the office of President or acting as President during the remainder of such term.

Section 2. This article shall be inoperative unless it shall have been ratified as an amendment to the Constitution by the legislatures of three-fourths of the several States within seven years from the date of its submission to the States by the Congress.

AMENDMENT XXIII [1961]

Section 1. The District constituting the seat of Government of the United States shall appoint in such manner as the Congress may direct:

A number of electors of President and Vice President equal to the whole number of Senators and Representatives in Congress to which the District would be entitled if it were a State, but in no event more than the least populous state; they shall be in addition to those appointed by the states, but they shall be considered, for the purposes of the election of President and Vice President, to be electors appointed by a state; and they shall meet in the District and perform such duties as provided by the twelfth article of amendment.

Section 2. The Congress shall have power to enforce this article by appropriate legislation.

AMENDMENT XXIV [1964]

Section 1. The right of citizens of the United States to vote in any primary or other election for President or Vice President, for electors for President or Vice President, or for Senator or

Representative in Congress, shall not be denied or abridged by the United States or any State by reason of failure to pay any poll tax or other tax.

Section 2. The Congress shall have power to enforce this article by appropriate legislation.

AMENDMENT XXV [1967]

Section 1. In case of the removal of the President from office or of his death or resignation, the Vice President shall become President.

Section 2. Whenever there is a vacancy in the office of the Vice President, the President shall nominate a Vice President who shall take office upon confirmation by a majority vote of both Houses of Congress.

Section 3. Whenever the President transmits to the President pro tempore of the Senate and the Speaker of the House of Representatives his written declaration that he is unable to discharge the powers and duties of his office, and until he transmits to them a written declaration to the contrary, such powers and duties shall be discharged by the Vice President as Acting President.

Section 4. Whenever the Vice President and a majority of either the principal officers of the executive departments or of such other body as Congress may by law provide, transmit to the President pro tempore of the Senate and the Speaker of the House of Representatives their written declaration that the President is unable to discharge the powers and duties of his office, the Vice President shall immediately assume the powers and duties of the office as Acting President.

Thereafter, when the President transmits to the President pro tempore of the Senate and the Speaker of the House of Representatives his written declaration that no inability exists, he shall resume the powers and duties of his office unless the Vice President and a majority of either the principal officers of the executive department or of such other body as Congress may by law provide, transmit within four days to the President pro tempore of the Senate and the Speaker of the House of Representatives their written declaration and the President is unable to discharge the powers and duties of his office. Thereupon Congress shall decide the issue, assembling within forty-eight hours for that purpose if not in session. If the Congress, within twenty-one days after receipt of the latter written declaration, or, if Congress is not in session, within twenty-one days after Congress is required to assemble, determines by two-thirds vote of both Houses that the President is unable to discharge the powers and duties of his office, the Vice President shall continue to discharge the same as Acting President; otherwise, the President shall resume the powers and duties of his office.

AMENDMENT XXVI [1971]

Section 1. The right of citizens of the United States, who are eighteen years of age or older, to vote shall not be denied or abridged by the United States or by any State on account of age.

Section 2. The Congress shall have power to enforce this article by appropriate legislation.

APPENDIX II

NEW JERSEY LANDLORD-TENANT MATERIALS

NEW JERSEY LANDLORD TENANT COURT RULES

RULES OF COURT
PART VI
RULES GOVERNING PRACTICE IN THE
LAW DIVISION, SPECIAL CIVIL PART

RULE 6:2. PROCESS

6:2-1. Form of Summons

. . . [I]n landlord tenant actions for the recovery of premises, [and] forcible entry and detainer actions . . ., in lieu of directing the defendant to file his answer, it shall require him to appear and state his defense at a certain time and place, to be therein specified, which time shall be not less than 10 days in summary dispossess actions, and 5 days in other actions, nor more than 30 days from the date of service of the summons, and shall notify the defendant that upon failure to do so, judgment by default may be rendered for the relief demanded in the complaint.

. . . .

6:2-3. Service of Process

. . . .

(b) Manner of Service. Service of process within this State shall be made in accordance with R. 4:4-4,[1] . . . except that, in landlord and tenant actions, service of process shall be by ordinary mail and by either delivery personally pursuant to R. 4:4-4 or by affixing a copy of the summons and complaint on the door of the subject premises.

. . . .

RULE 6:3. PLEADINGS, MOTIONS AND PARTIES

6:3-1. Applicability of Superior Court Rules

. . . [N]o answer shall be permitted in summary actions between landlord and tenant. . . .

. . . .

6:3-4. Summary Actions Between Landlord and Tenant

Summary actions between landlord and tenant for the recovery of premises and forcible entry and detainer actions shall not be joined with any other cause of action, nor shall a defendant in such proceedings file a counterclaim or a third-party complaint.

---

[1] Rule 4:4-4(a), (b), and (c) contain provisions for service of process upon individuals, minors, incompetents, corporations, partnerships, and associations.

. . . .

RULE 6:4. PROCEEDINGS BEFORE TRIAL

6:4-1. Transfer of Actions

. . . .

(g) Transfer of Landlord/Tenant Action. A motion to transfer a summary action for the recovery of premises to the Law Division pursuant to N.J.S. 2A:18-60, shall be made by serving and filing the original of said motion with the Clerk of the Special Part no later than the last court day prior to the date set for trial. The motion shall be returnable in the Special Civil Part on the trial date, or such date thereafter as the court may determine in its discretion or upon application by the respondent for more time to prepare a response to the motion. Upon the filing of the motion, the Special Civil Part shall take no further action pending disposition of the motion. If the motion is granted the Clerk shall transmit the record . . . [to the Law Division]. If the motion is denied, the court shall set the action expeditiously for summary hearing.

. . . .

RULE 6:5. TRIALS

6:5-2. Notice of Trial; Assignment for Trial

. . . .

(b) Landlord and Tenant Actions. Summary actions between landlord and tenant shall be placed on a separate list on the calendar and shall be heard on the return day unless adjourned by the court, or by consent with the approval of the court.

. . . .

RULE 6:6. JUDGMENT

6:6-3. Judgment by Default

. . . .

(b) Entry by Clerk; Judgment for Possession. In summary actions between landlord and tenant for the recovery of premises, judgment for possession may be entered by the clerk on affidavit if the defendant fails to appear, plead or otherwise defend, and is not a minor or incompetent person.

NEW JERSEY STATUTES

TITLE 2A: ADMINISTRATION OF CIVIL AND CRIMINAL JUSTICE

SUBTITLE 4. CIVIL ACTIONS

CHAPTER 18: CIVIL ACTIONS IN SPECIAL CIVIL PART

ARTICLE 9: PROCEEDINGS BETWEEN LANDLORD AND TENANT

A. GENERAL PROVISIONS

2A:18-51. Tenancy created by agent; termination by owner; recovery of possession or rentals

If real estate is leased by an agent of the owner thereof, in his own name or as agent, the owner, his assignee or grantee may terminate the tenancy as the agent might do. The owner or his duly authorized agent, assignee or grantee may institute and maintain proceedings to recover the possession or the rentals thereof in their own names or in the name of the former agent, in the same manner and with the same effect as though the real estate had been leased in their own names.

2A:18-52. Dismissal of action involving title of land

If upon trial of a landlord and tenancy proceeding the plaintiff shall not be able to prove, by lease or other evidence, his right to the possession of the premises claimed by him without proving title to lands, tenements and hereditaments, the cause shall be dismissed, provided however that an assignee or grantee of a landlord may, at the trial or hearing, offer in evidence a deed or other writing for the purpose of showing the assignment or grant by the landlord. Furthermore a deed or other writing may be received for the purpose of showing the right to possession of the premises for the recovery of which the proceedings are brought.

B. SUMMARY ACTIONS FOR RECOVERY OF PREMISES

2A:18-53. Removal of tenant in certain cases; jurisdiction

Except for residential lessees and tenants included in [section 2A:18-61.1] . . . of this act,[2] any lessee or tenant at will or at sufferance, or for a part of a year, or for 1 or more years, of any houses, buildings, lands or tenements, and the assigns, undertenants or legal representatives of such tenant or lessee, may be removed from such premises by the Superior Court, Law Division, Special Civil Part[3] in an action in the following cases:

a. Where such person holds over and continues in possession of all or any part of the demised premises after the expiration of his term, and after demand made and written notice given by the landlord or his agent, for delivery of possession thereof. The notice shall be served either personally upon the tenant or such person in possession by giving him a copy thereof or by leaving a copy of the same at his usual place of abode with a member of his family above the age of 14 years.

---

[2] The reference to 2A:18-61.1 was added in 1974 when the Anti-Eviction Act was adopted.

[3] Prior to 1991, these actions were brought in the County District Court.

b. Where such person shall hold over after a default in the payment of rent, pursuant to the agreement under which the premises are held.

c. Where such person (1) shall be so disorderly as to destroy the peace and quiet of the landlord or the other tenants or occupants living in said house or the neighborhood, or (2) shall willfully destroy, damage or injure the premises, or (3) shall constantly violate the landlord's rules and regulations governing said premises, provided, such rules have been accepted in writing by the tenant or are made a part of the lease; or (4) shall commit any breach or violation of any of the covenants or agreements in the nature thereof contained in the lease for the premises where a right of re-entry is reserved in the lease for a violation of such covenants or agreements, and shall hold over and continue in possession of the demised premises or any part thereof, after the landlord or his agent for that purposes has caused a written notice of the termination of said tenancy to be served upon said tenant, and a demand that said tenant remove from said premises within 3 days from the service of such notice. The notice shall specify the cause of the termination of the tenancy, and shall be served either personally upon the tenant or such person in possession by giving him a copy thereof, or by leaving a copy thereof at his usual place of abode with some member of his family above the age of 14 years.

2A:18-54. Notices and summons; substituted service; service by posting

Where for any reason, any of the notices required by section 2A:18-53 of this title, cannot be served as provided in said section or a summons and complaint cannot be served as in other actions, such notices or summons and complaint may be served upon any person actually occupying the premises, either personally or by leaving same with a member of his family above the age of 14 years, or when admission to the premises is denied or the tenant or occupant and all members of his family above the age of 14 years are absent from the premises, or there is no person actually occupying them, the officer or other person may post or affix a copy of the same upon the door or other conspicuous part of such premises. Such posting shall be deemed to be lawful service.

2A:18-55. Discontinuance upon payment into court of rent in arrears; receipt

If, in actions instituted under paragraph "b" of section 2A:18-53 of this title, the tenant or person in possession of the demised premises shall at any time on or before entry of final judgment, pay to the clerk of the court the rent claimed to be in default, together with the accrued costs of the proceedings, all proceedings shall be stopped. The receipt of the clerk shall be evidence of such payment.

The clerk shall forthwith pay all moneys so received to the landlord, his agent or assigns.

2A:18-56. Proof of notice to quit prerequisite to judgment

No judgment for possession in cases specified in paragraph "a" of section 2A:18-53 of this Title shall be ordered unless:

a. The tenancy, if a tenancy at will or from year to year, has been terminated by the giving of 3 months' notice to quit, which notice shall be deemed to be sufficient; or

b. The tenancy, if a tenancy from month to month, has been terminated by the giving of 1 months' notice to quit, which notice shall be deemed to be sufficient; or

c. The tenancy, if for a term other than at will, from year to year, or from month to month, has been terminated by the giving of one term's notice to quit, which notice shall be deemed to be sufficient; and

d. It shall be shown to the satisfaction of the court by due proof that the notice herein required has been given.

2A:18-57. Judgment for possession; warrant for removal; issuance

If no sufficient cause is shown to the contrary when the action comes on for trial, the court shall issue its warrant to any officer of the court, commanding him to remove all persons from the premises, and to put the claimant into full possession thereof, and to levy and make the costs out of the goods and chattels of the person in possession.

No warrant of removal shall issue until the expiration of 3 days after entry of judgment for possession, except as provided in [N.J.S. 2A:42-10.16 and 10.17] . . . of this Title.

2A:18-58. Execution of warrant; use of force

An officer, to whom a warrant is issued by virtue of this article, shall obey the command of and faithfully execute the same, and may, if necessary to the execution thereof, use such force as may be necessary.

2A:18-59. Review; landlord liable for unlawful proceedings

Proceedings had by virtue of this article shall not be appealable except on ground of lack of jurisdiction. The landlord, however, shall remain liable in a civil action for unlawful proceedings under this article.

2A:18-59.1. Terminally ill tenant; stay of eviction

Notwithstanding the provisions of any other law to the contrary, the county district court or the Superior Court may authorize and review one year stays of eviction during which the tenant shall be entitled to renew the lease at its term of expiration, subject to reasonable changes proposed to the tenant by the landlord in written notice, whenever:

a. The tenant fulfills all the terms of the lease and removal is sought under subsection a. of N.J.S. 2A:18-53 where a residential tenant holds over after written notice for delivery of possession; and

b. The tenant has a terminal illness which illness has been certified by a licensed physician; and

c. There is substantial likelihood that the tenant would be unable to search for, rent and move to a comparable alternative rental dwelling unit without serious medical harm; and

d. The tenant has been a tenant of the landlord for at least two years prior to the issuance of the stay.

In reviewing a petition for a stay of eviction, the court shall specifically consider whether the granting of the stay of eviction would cause an undue hardship to the landlord because of the landlord's financial condition or any other factor relating to the landlord's ownership of the premises.[4]

2A:18-59.2. Inapplicability of act to hotel, motel or guest house rented to transient guest or seasonal tenant or to residential health care facility

[Section 2A:18-59.1] . . . shall not apply to a hotel, motel or other guest house, or part thereof, rented to a transient guest or seasonal tenant, or a residential health care facility. . ..

---

[4] This section took effect in 1984.

2A:18-60. *Removal of proceedings into superior court*

At any time before an action for the removal of a tenant comes on for trial, either the landlord or person in possession may apply to the superior court, which may, if it deems it of sufficient importance, order the cause transferred from the Special Civil Part to the Law Division.

2A:18-61. *Trial by Jury*

A summary action for the removal of a tenant, commenced in the Special Civil Part but transferred to the Law Division shall be tried before a jury, unless a jury is waived.

2A:18-61.1. *Removal of residential tenants; grounds*[5]

No lessee or tenant or the assigns, under-tenants or legal representatives of such lessee or tenant may be removed by the Superior Court from any house, building, mobile home or land in a mobile home park or tenement leased for residential purposes, other than (1) owner-occupied premises with not more than two rental units or a hotel, motel or other guest house or part thereof rented to a transient guest or seasonal tenant; (2) a dwelling unit which is held in trust on behalf of a member of the immediate family of the person or persons establishing the trust, provided that the member of the immediate family on whose behalf the trust is established permanently occupies the unit; and (3) a dwelling unit which is permanently occupied by a member of the immediate family of the owner of that unit, provided, however, that exception (2) and (3) shall apply only in cases in which the member of the immediate family has a developmental disability, except upon establishment of one of the following grounds as good cause:

a. The person fails to pay rent due and owing under the lease whether the same be oral or written;

b. The person has continued to be, after written notice to cease, so disorderly as to destroy the peace and quiet of the occupants or other tenants living in said house or neighborhood;

c. The person has willfully or by reason of gross negligence caused or allowed destruction, damage or injury to the premises;

d. The person has continued, after written notice to cease, to substantially violate or breach any of the landlord's rules and regulations governing said premises, provided such rules and regulations are reasonable and have been accepted in writing by the tenant or made a part of the lease at the beginning of the lease term;

e. (1) The person has continued, after written notice to cease, to substantially violate or breach any of the covenants or agreements contained in the lease for the premises where a right of reentry is reserved to the landlord in the lease for a violation of such covenant or agreement, provided that such covenant or agreement is reasonable and was contained in the lease at the beginning of the lease term;

(2) In public housing under the control of a public housing authority or redevelopment agency, the person has substantially violated or breached any of the covenants or agreements contained in the lease for the premises pertaining to illegal uses of controlled dangerous substances, or other illegal activities, whether or not a right of reentry is reserved to the landlord in the lease for violation of such covenant or agreement, provided that such covenant or agreement conforms

---

[5] This section, together with 2A:18-61.2, 61.3, 61.4 and 61.5, made up the Anti-Eviction Act adopted in 1974. As the other sections now attached to it attest, substantial additions have been made to the act since its adoption. The original act has also been amended to account for other changes in condominium conversion rules and for special protections for elderly and disabled persons.

to federal guidelines regarding such lease provisions and was contained in the lease at the beginning of the lease term.

f. The person has failed to pay rent after a valid notice to quit and notice of increase in said rent, provided the increase in rent is not unconscionable and complies with any and all other laws or municipal ordinances governing rent increases;

g. The landlord or owner (1) seeks to permanently board up or demolish the premises because he has been cited by local or State housing inspectors for substantial violations affecting the health and safety of tenants and it is economically unfeasible for the owner to eliminate the violations; (2) seeks to comply with local or State housing inspectors who have cited him for substantial violations affecting the health and safety of tenants and it is unfeasible to so comply without removing the tenant; simultaneously with service of notice of eviction pursuant to this clause, the landlord shall notify the Department of Community Affairs of the intention to institute proceedings and shall provide the department with such other information as it may require pursuant to rules and regulations. The department shall inform all parties and the court of its view with respect to the feasibility of compliance without removal of the tenant and may in its discretion appear and present evidence; (3) seeks to correct an illegal occupancy because he has been cited by local or State housing inspectors and it is unfeasible to correct such illegal occupancy without removing the tenant; or (4) is a governmental agency which seeks to permanently retire the premises from the rental market pursuant to a redevelopment or land clearance plan in a blighted area. . ..

h. The owner seeks to retire permanently the residential building or the mobile home park from residential use or use as a mobile home park, provided this paragraph shall not apply to circumstances covered under paragraph g. of this section;

i. The landlord or owner proposes, at the termination of a lease, reasonable changes of substance in the terms and conditions of the lease, including specifically any change in the term thereof, which the tenant, after written notice, refuses to accept; provided that in cases where a tenant has received a notice of termination pursuant to section [2A:18-61.2(g)] . . ., or has a protected tenancy status pursuant to section [2A:18-61.30] of the "Senior Citizens and Disabled Protected Tenancy Act," . . . or pursuant to [2A:18-61.40] of the "Tenant Protection Act of 1992," . . . the landlord or owner shall have the burden of proving that any change in the terms and conditions of the lease, rental or regulations both is reasonable and does not substantially reduce the rights and privileges to which the tenant was entitled prior to the conversion;

j. The person, after written notice to cease, has habitually and without legal justification failed to pay rent which is due and owing;

k. The landlord or owner of the building or mobile home park is converting from the rental market to a condominium, cooperative or fee simple ownership of two or more dwelling units or park sites, except as hereinafter provided in subsection l. Where the tenant is being removed pursuant to this subsection, no warrant for possession shall be issued until this act has been complied with. No action for possession shall be brought pursuant to this subsection against a senior citizen tenant or disabled tenant with protected tenancy status pursuant to the "Senior Citizen and Disabled Protected Tenancy Act," . . . [2A:18-61.22 et seq.], or against a qualified tenant under the "Tenant Protection Act of 1992" . . . [2A:18-61.40 et seq.] as long as the agency has not terminated the protected tenancy status or the protected tenancy period has not expired;

l. (1) The owner of a building or mobile home park, which is constructed as or being converted to a condominium, cooperative or fee simple ownership, seeks to evict a tenant or sublessee whose initial tenancy began after the master deed, agreement establishing the cooperative or subdivision plat was recorded, because the owner has contracted to sell the unit to a buyer who seeks to personally occupy it and the contract for sale calls for the unit to be vacant at the time of closing. However, no action shall be brought against a tenant under paragraph (1) of this subsection unless the tenant was given a statement in accordance with section [2A:18-61.9] . . . of this . . . act;

(2) The owner of three or less condominium or cooperative units seeks to evict a tenant whose initial tenancy began by rental from an owner of three or less units after the master deed or agreement establishing the cooperative was recorded, because the owner seeks to personally occupy the unit, or has contracted to sell the unit to a buyer who seeks to personally occupy it and the contract for sale calls for the unit to be vacant at the time of closing;

(3) The owner of a building of three residential units or less seeks to personally occupy a unit, or has contracted to sell the residential unit to a buyer who wishes to personally occupy it and the contract for sale calls for the unit to be vacant at the time of closing;

m. The landlord or owner conditioned the tenancy upon and in consideration for the tenant's employment by the landlord or owner as superintendent, janitor or in some other capacity and such employment is being terminated.

n. The person has been convicted of or pleaded guilty to, or if a juvenile, has been adjudicated delinquent on the basis of an act which if committed by an adult would constitute an offense . . . involving the use, possession, manufacture, dispensing or distribution of a controlled dangerous substance, controlled dangerous substance analog or drug paraphernalia within the meaning of that act within or upon the leased premises or the building or complex of buildings and land appurtenant thereto, or the mobile home park, in which those premises are located, and has not in connection with his sentence for that offense either (1) successfully completed or (2) been admitted to and continued upon probation while completing, a drug rehabilitation program . . .; or, being the tenant or lessee of such leased premises, knowingly harbors or harbored therein a person who has been so convicted or has so pleaded, or otherwise permits or permitted such a person to occupy those premises for residential purposes, whether continuously or intermittently, except that this subsection shall not apply to a person harboring or permitting a juvenile to occupy the premises if the juvenile has been adjudicated delinquent upon the basis of an act which if committed by an adult would constitute the offense of use or possession under the said act. No action for removal may be brought pursuant to this subsection more than two years after the date of the adjudication or conviction or more than two years after the person's release from incarceration whichever is the later.

o. The person has been convicted of or pleaded guilty to, or if a juvenile, has been adjudicated delinquent on the basis of an act which if committed by an adult would constitute an offense . . . involving assault, or terroristic threats against the landlord, a member of the landlord's family or an employee of the landlord; or, being the tenant or lessee of such leased premises, knowingly harbors or harbored therein a person who has been so convicted or has so pleaded, or otherwise permits or permitted such a person to occupy those premises for residential purposes, whether continuously or intermittently. No action for removal may be brought pursuant to this subsection more than two years after the adjudication or conviction or more than two years after the person's release from incarceration whichever is the later.

p. The person has been found, by a preponderance of the evidence, liable in a civil action for removal commenced under this act for an offense . . . involving theft of property located on the leased premises from the landlord, the leased premises or other tenants residing in the leased premises, or . . . involving assault or terroristic threats against the landlord, a member of the landlord's family or an employee of the landlord, or . . . involving the use, possession, manufacture, dispensing or distribution of a controlled dangerous substance, controlled dangerous substance analog or drug paraphernalia within the meaning of that act within or upon the leased premises or the building or complex of buildings and land appurtenant thereto, or the mobile home park, in which those premises are located, and has not in connection with his sentence for that offense either (1) successfully completed or (2) been admitted to and continued upon probation while completing a drug rehabilitation program . . .; or, being the tenant or lessee of such leased premises, knowingly harbors or harbored therein a person who committed such an offense, or otherwise permits or permitted such a person to occupy those premises for residential purposes, whether continuously or intermittently, except that this subsection shall not apply to a person who harbors or permits a juvenile to occupy the premises if the juvenile has been adjudicated delinquent upon the basis of an act which if committed by an adult would constitute the offense of use or possession . . ..

q. The person has been convicted of or pleaded guilty to, or if a juvenile, has been adjudicated delinquent on the basis of an act which if committed by an adult would constitute an offense . . . involving theft of property from the landlord, the leased premises or other tenants residing in the same building of complex; or being the tenant or lessee of such leased premises, knowingly harbors therein a person who has been so convicted or has so pleaded, or otherwise permits such a person to occupy those premises for residential purposes, whether continuously or intermittently.

For purposes of this section, (1) "developmental disability" means any disability which is defined as . . . by the "Developmentally Disabled Rights Act of 1977"; (2) "member of the immediate family" means a person's spouse, parent, child or sibling, or a spouse, parent, child or sibling of any of them; and (3) "permanently" occupies or occupied means that the occupant maintains no other domicile at which the occupant votes, pays rent or property taxes or at which rent or property taxes are paid on the occupant's behalf.

2A:18-61.1a. Legislative findings and intent[6]

The Legislature finds that:

a. Acute State and local shortages of supply and high levels of demand for residential dwellings have motivated removal of blameless tenants in order to directly or indirectly profit from conversion to higher income rental or ownership interest residential use.

b. This has resulted in unfortunate attempts to displace tenants employing pretexts, stratagems or means other than those provided pursuant to the intent of State eviction laws designated to fairly balance and protect rights of tenants and landlords.

c. These devices have circumvented the intent of current State eviction laws by failing to utilize available means to avoid displacement such as: protected tenancies; rights to purchase; rent affordability protection; full disclosures relevant to eviction challenges; and, stays of eviction where relocation is lacking.

d. It is in the public interest of the State to maintain for citizens the broadest protections available under State eviction laws to avoid such displacement and resultant loss of affordable housing which, due to housing's uniqueness as the most costly and difficult to change necessity

---

[6] Sections 2A:18-61.1a-f, An Act to Prevent the Use of Certain Pretexts that Cause Tenants to Vacate Premises, took effect in 1986.

of life, causes overcrowding, unsafe and unsanitary conditions, blight, burdens on community services, wasted resources, homelessness, emigration from the State and personal hardship which is particularly severe for vulnerable seniors, the disabled, the frail, minorities, large families and single parents.

e. Such personal hardship includes, but is not limited to: economic loss, time loss, physical and emotional stress and in some cases severe emotional trauma, illness, homelessness or other irreparable harm resulting from strain of eviction controversy; relocation search and moving difficulty; employment, education, family and social disruption; relocation and empty unit security hazards, relocation to premises of less affordability, capacity, accessibility and physical or environmental quality; and relocation adjustment problems particularly of the blind or other disabled citizens.

. . . .

2A:18-61.1b. Eviction alleging permanent retirement of premises from residential use; presumptions and conditions; contents of notice

If an owner seeks an eviction alleging permanent retirement of the premises from residential use pursuant to . . . [N.J.S. 2A:18-61.1] and if, pursuant to land use law, nonresidential use of the premises is not permitted as a principal permitted use or is limited to accessory, conditional or public use, a rebuttable presumption is created that the premises are not and will not be permanently retired from residential use. Residential premises that are unoccupied, boarded up or otherwise out of service shall not be deemed retired from residential use unless they are converted to a principal permitted nonresidential use. No tenant shall be evicted pursuant to . . . [N.J.S. 2A:18-61.1] if any State or local permit or approval required by law for the nonresidential use is not obtained. Nothing contained in this section shall be deemed to require obtaining a certificate of occupancy for the proposed use prior to an eviction. The detail specified in notice given pursuant to . . . [N.J.S. 2A:18-61.2] shall disclose the proposed nonresidential use to which the premises are to be permanently retired.

2A:18-61.1c. Application for registration of conversion pursuant to "Planned Real Estate Development Full Disclosure Act"; time of approval; provision of copy of notice of termination to tenant to department of community affairs

The Department of Community Affairs shall not approve an application for registration of conversion pursuant to "The Planned Real Estate Development Full Disclosure Act," . . . [N.J.S. 45:22A-21 et seq.] for any premises for a period of five years following the date on which any dwelling unit in the premises becomes vacant after notice has been given that the owner seeks to permanently board up or demolish the premises or seeks to retire permanently the premises from residential use pursuant to . . . [N.J.S. 2A:18-61.1(g)(1) or (h)]. Within five days of the date on which any owner provides notice of termination to a tenant pursuant to . . . [N.J.S. 2A:18-61.1(g)(1) or (h)], the owner shall provide a copy of the notice to the Department of Community Affairs.

2A:18-61.1d. Municipality with rent control; personal occupancy after vacation after notice to board up or demolish or to retire permanently from residential use; maximum rent; increases; providing copy of notice of termination to municipality

In a municipality which has an ordinance regulating rents in effect, if a dwelling unit in the premises becomes vacated after notice has been given that the owner seeks to permanently board up or demolish the premises or seeks to retire permanently the premises from residential use pursuant to . . . [N.J.S. 2A:18-61.1 (g)(1) or (h)] and if any time thereafter an owner permits the personal occupancy of the premises, the maximum rent authorized for a unit in the premises shall not exceed the rent that would have been authorized for that unit if there had been no vacancy or change of tenancy for the unit. Increased costs which occur during the period of vacancy, which are solely the result of the premises being vacated, closed and reoccupied and which do not add services or amenities not previously provided, or which add new services or amenities whose costs significantly reduce the affordability of the premises, shall not be used as a basis for any rent increase pursuant to any municipal rent regulation provision, fair return or hardship hearing before a municipal rent board or any appeal from such determination. Increased costs of new services and amenities create a rebuttable presumption that they significantly reduce the affordability of the premises, if they result in a doubling of the rent increases otherwise permitted by law during the period of vacancy. Within five days of the date on which any owner provides notice of termination to a tenant pursuant to . . . [N.J.S. 2A:18-61.1(g)(1) or (h)], the owner shall provide a copy of the notice to the municipal agency responsible for administering the regulation of rents in the municipality. The owner's notice to the municipal agency shall also include a listing of the current tenants and rents for each dwelling unit in the premises, unless the owner has previously submitted to the municipal agency a listing which is still current.

2A:18-61.1e. Intention to return premises to residential use after vacation by tenant after notice; notice to and rights of former tenant; transmittal of notice to municipality; failure to give notice; liability for civil penalty, damages, attorney fees and costs; enforcement; jurisdiction

If a dwelling unit becomes vacated after notice has been given that the owner seeks to permanently board up or demolish the premises or seeks to retire permanently the premises from residential use pursuant to . . . [N.J.S. 2A:18-61.1(g)(1) or (h)] and if at any time thereafter an owner instead seeks to return the premises to residential use, the owner shall provide the former tenant:

a. Written notice 90 days in advance of any return to residential use or any agreement for possession of the unit by any other party, which notice discloses the owner's intention to return the unit to residential use and all appropriate specifics;

b. The right to return to possession of the vacated unit or, if return is not available, the right to possession of affordable housing relocation in accord with the standards and criteria set forth for comparable housing as defined by . . . [N.J.S. 2A:18-61.7]; and

c. In the case of a conversion, the right to a protected tenancy pursuant to the "Senior Citizens and Disabled Protected Tenancy Act" . . . [N.J.S. 2A:18-61.22 et seq.], or pursuant to the "Tenant Protection Act of 1992" . . . [N.J.S. 2A:18-61.40 et seq.] if the former tenant would have at the time of the conversion been eligible for a protected tenancy under either of those acts, had the former tenant not vacated the premises.

The 90-day notice shall disclose the tenant's rights pursuant to this section and the method for the tenant's response to exercise these rights. A duplicate of the notice shall be transmitted within the first five days of the 90-day period to the rent board in the municipality or the municipal clerk, if there is no rent board. Notwithstanding the provisions of . . . [N.J.S. 2A:18-61.6(c)], damages awarded shall not be trebled where possession has been returned in accord with this section; nor shall any damages be awarded as provided for in . . . [N.J.S. 2A:18-61.6(e)]. An owner who fails to provide a former tenant a notice of intention to return to residential use pursuant to this section is liable to a civil penalty of not less than $2,500.00 or more than $10,000.00 for each offense, and shall also be liable in treble damages, plus attorney fees and costs of suit, for any loss or expenses incurred by a former tenant as a result of that failure. . .. No owner shall be liable for a penalty pursuant to this section if the unit is returned to residential use more than five years after the date the premises are vacated or if the owner made every reasonable effort to locate the former tenant and provide the notice, including, but not limited to, the employment of a qualified professional locator service, where no return receipt is obtained from the former tenant.

In any action under this section, the court shall, in addition to damages, award any other appropriate legal or equitable relief.

. . . .

2A:18-61.2. *Removal of residential tenants; required notice; contents; service*

No judgment of possession shall be entered for any premises covered by section [2A:18-61.1] . . . except in the nonpayment of rent under paragraph a. or f. of [N.J.S. 2A:18-61.1] . . ., unless the landlord has made written demand and given written notice for delivery of possession of the premises. The following notice shall be required:

a. For an action alleging disorderly conduct under paragraph b. of section [2A:18-61.1] . . ., or injury to the premises under paragraph c. of section [2A:18-61.1] . . . or any grounds under paragraph m., n., o. or p. of section [2A:18-61.1] . . ., three days' notice prior to the institution of the action for possession;

b. For an action alleging continued violation of rules and regulations under paragraph d. of section [2A:18-61.1] . . ., or substantial breach of covenant under paragraph e. of section [2A:18-61.1] . . ., or habitual failure to pay rent, one month's notice prior to the institution of the action for possession;

c. For an action alleging any grounds under paragraph g. of section [2A:18-61.1] . . ., three months' notice prior to the institution of the action;

d. For an action alleging permanent retirement under paragraph h. of section [2A:18-61.1] . . ., 18 months' notice[7] prior to the institution of the action, and provided that, where there is a lease in effect, no action may be instituted until the lease expires;

e. For an action alleging refusal of acceptance of reasonable lease changes under paragraph i. of section [2A:18-61.1] . . ., one month's notice prior to institution of the action;

f. For an action alleging any grounds under paragraph l. of section [2A:18-61.1] . . ., two months' notice prior to the institution of the action, and provided that, where there is a written lease in effect, no action shall be instituted until the lease expires;

g. For an action alleging any grounds under paragraph k. of section [2A:18-61.1] . . ., three years' notice prior to the institution of action, and provided that where there is a written lease in effect, no action shall be instituted until the lease expires.

h. In public housing under the control of a public housing authority or redevelopment agency, for an action alleging substantial breach of contract under paragraph (2) of subsection e. of [N.J.S. 2A:18-61.1] . . ., the period of notice required prior to the institution of an action for possession shall be in accordance with federal regulations pertaining to public housing leases.

The notice in each of the foregoing instances shall specify in detail the cause of the termination of the tenancy and shall be served either personally upon the tenant or lessee or such person

---

[7] The period was extended from 6 to 18 months in 1986.

in possession by giving him a copy thereof, or by leaving a copy thereof at his usual place of abode with some member of his family above the age of 14 years, or by certified mail; if the certified letter is not claimed, notice shall be sent by regular mail.

2A:18-61.3. Residential lease; eviction or failure to renew by landlord or by owner's or landlord's successor in ownership or possession; necessity for good cause or other grounds

a. No landlord may evict or fail to renew any lease of any premises covered by section [2A:18-61.1] . . . except for good cause as defined in section [2A:18-61.1]. . ..

b. A person who was a tenant of a landlord in premises covered by section . . . [N.J.S. 2A:18-61.1] may not be removed by any order or judgment for possession from the premises by the owner's or landlord's successor in ownership or possession except:

(1) For good cause in accordance with the requirements . . . [of 2A:18-61.1 et seq.]; or

(2) For proceedings in premises where federal law supersedes applicable State law governing removal of occupants; or

(3) For proceedings where removal of occupants is sought by an authorized State or local agency pursuant to eminent domain or code or zoning enforcement laws and which comply with applicable relocation laws. . ..

Where the owner's or landlord's successor in ownership or possession is not bound by the lease entered into with the former tenant and may offer a different lease to the former tenant, nothing in this . . . act shall limit that right.[8]

2A:18-61.3a. Mobile home parks; restrictions on "for sale" signs; prohibition

No mobile home park owner or operator may evict a mobile home resident for posting in or on his mobile home a "for sale" sign or similar notice of the private sale of the mobile home. Nor may a mobile home park owner or operator prohibit or unreasonably restrict such posting by any means, including but not limited to, rules and regulations of the mobile home park of written leases or rental agreements between the park owner or operator and mobile home residents.[9]

2A:18-61.4. Waiver of rights by provision in lease; unenforceability

Any provision in a lease whereby any tenant covered by section [2A:18-61.1] . . . agrees that his tenancy may be terminated or not renewed for other than good cause as defined in section [2A:18-61.1] . . ., or whereby the tenant waives any other rights under this act shall be deemed against public policy and unenforceable.

2A:18-61.5. Severability

If any section, subsection, paragraph, sentence or other part of this act is adjudged unconstitutional or invalid, such judgment shall not affect, impair or invalidate the remainder of this act, but shall be confined in its effect to the section, subsection, paragraph, sentence or other part of this act directly involved in the controversy in which said judgment shall have been rendered.

---

[8] Subsection (b) of this section was adopted in 1986.

[9] This section went into effect in 1984. The Commerce and Industry Committee of the New Jersey Assembly recommended passage of this section in order to prevent park owners "from subverting the freedom of sale provisions of N.J.S.A. 46:8C-3" by refusing permission to home owners to place for sale signs on the property where the home is located. The referenced section of the statutes eliminates the right of a park owner to act as agent in all sales of mobile homes within his park.

2A:18-61.6. Vacation of premises by tenant after notice; failure of owner to meet conditions of grounds stated or to advise prospective owner by sale, lease or conveyance in writing notice was given or to obtain eviction by use of unauthorized or illegal cause; liability for civil damages, attorney fees and costs; exemptions

a. Where a tenant vacates the premises after being given a notice alleging the owner seeks to personally occupy the premises under section [2A:18-61.1(1)] . . . and the owner thereafter arbitrarily fails to personally occupy the premises for a total of at least six months, or arbitrarily fails to execute the contract for sale, but instead permits personal occupancy of the premises by another tenant or instead permits registration of conversion of the premises by the Department of Community Affairs pursuant to "The Planned Real Estate Development Full Disclosure Act," . . . [N.J.S. 45:22A-21 et seq.], such owner shall be liable to the former tenant in a civil action for three times the damages plus the tenant's attorney fees and costs.

b. If an owner purchases the premises pursuant to a contract requiring the tenant to vacate in accordance with section [2A:18-61.1(1)] . . . and thereafter arbitrarily fails to personally occupy the premises for a total of at least six months, but instead permits personal occupancy of the premises by another tenant or instead permits registration of conversion of the premises by the Department of Community Affairs pursuant to . . . [N.J.S. 45:22A-21 et seq.], such owner-purchaser shall be liable to the former tenant in a civil action for three times the damages plus the tenant's attorney fees and costs.

c. If a tenant vacates a dwelling unit after notice has been given alleging that the owner seeks to permanently board up or demolish the premises or to retire permanently the premises from residential use pursuant to . . . [N.J.S. 2A:18-61.1 (g)(1) or (h)] and instead, within five five years following the date on which the dwelling unit or the premises becomes vacant, an owner permits residential use of the vacated premises, the owner shall be liable to the former tenant in a civil action for three times the damages plus the tenant's attorney fees and costs of suit.

An owner of any premises where notice has been given pursuant to . . . [N.J.S. 2A:18-61.1(g)(1) or (h)] who subsequently seeks to sell, lease or convey the property to another shall, before executing any lease, deed or contract for such conveyance, advise in writing the prospective owner that such notice was given and that the owners of the property are subject to the liabilities provided in this subsection and . . . [N.J.S. 2A:18-61.1c and d]. Whoever fails to so advise a prospective owner prior to the execution of the contract of sale, lease or conveyance is liable to a civil penalty of not less than $2,500.00 or more than $10,000.00 for each offense, and shall also be liable in treble damages, plus attorney fees and costs of suit, for any loss or expenses incurred by a new owner of the property as a result of that failure. . ..

d. If a tenant vacates a dwelling unit after receiving from an owner an eviction notice (1) purporting to compel by law the tenant to vacate the premises for cause or purporting that if the tenant does not vacate the premises, the tenant shall be compelled by law to vacate the premises for cause; and (2) using a cause that is clearly not provided by law or using a cause that is based upon a lease clause which is contrary to law pursuant to . . . [N.J.S. 46:8-48]; and (3) misrepresenting that, under the facts alleged, the tenant would be subject to eviction, the owner shall be liable to the former tenant in a civil action for three times the damages plus the tenant's attorney fees and costs. An owner shall not be liable under this subsection for alleging any cause for eviction which, if proven, would subject the tenant to eviction pursuant to . . . [N.J.S. 2A:18-53 or 2A:18-61.1].

In any action under this section the court shall, in addition to damages, award any other appropriate legal or equitable relief. For purposes of . . . [N.J.S. 2A:18-61.1] the term "owner" includes, but is not limited to, lessee, successor owner and lessee and other successors in interest.

. . . .

2A:18-61.7. Definitions

As used in this act:[10]

a. "Comparable housing or park site" means housing that is (1) decent, safe, sanitary, and in compliance with all local and State housing codes; (2) open to all persons regardless of race, creed, national origin, ancestry, marital status or sex; and (3) provided with facilities equivalent to that provided by the landlord in the dwelling unit or park site in which the tenant then resides in regard to each of the following: (a) apartment size including number of rooms or park site size, (b) rent range, (c) apartment's major kitchen and bathroom facilities, and (d) special facilities necessary for the handicapped or infirmed; (4) located in an area not less desirable than the area in which the tenant then resides in regard to each of the following: (a) accessibility to the tenant's place of employment, (b) accessibility of community and commercial facilities, and (c) environmental quality and conditions; and (5) in accordance with additional reasonable criteria which the tenant has requested in writing at the time of making any request under this act.

b. "Condominium" means a condominium as defined in the "Condominium Act," [N.J.S. 46:8B-1 et seq.]. . ..

c. "Cooperative" means a housing corporation or association which entitles the holder of a share or membership interest thereof to possess and occupy for dwelling purposes a house, apartment or other structure owned or leased by said corporation or association, or to lease or purchase a dwelling constructed or to be constructed by said corporation or association.

d. "Mobile home park" means any park, including a trailer park or camp, equipped to handle mobile homes sited on a year-round basis.

2A:18-61.8 Conversion of multiple dwelling into condominium, cooperative or fee simple ownership; notice to and rights of tenants

Any owner who intends to convert a multiple dwelling . . . other than a hotel or motel, or a mobile home park into a condominium or cooperative, or to fee simple ownership of the several dwelling units or park sites shall give the tenants 60 days' notice of his intention to convert and the full plan of the conversion prior to serving notice, provided for in section . . . [N.J.S. 2A:18-61.2]. A duplicate of the first such 60-day notice and full plan shall be transmitted to the clerk of the municipality at the same time. In the notice of intention to convert tenants shall be notified of their right to purchase ownership in the premises at a specified price in accordance with this section, and their other rights as tenants under this act in relation to the conversion of a building or park to a condominium, cooperative or fee simple ownership. A tenant in occupancy at the time of the notice of intention to convert shall have the exclusive right to purchase his unit, the shares of stock allocated thereto or the park site, as the case may be, for the first 90 days after such notice that such purchase could be made during which time the unit or site shall not be shown to a third party unless the tenant has in writing waived the right to purchase.

---

[10] This section, along with succeeding sections up to and including 2A:18-61.12 were part of an act adopted in 1975 to regulate rights of tenants in conversion projects.

2A:18-61.9. Notice to tenant after master deed or agreement to establish cooperative

Any owner who establishes with a person an initial tenancy after the master deed or agreement establishing the cooperative was recorded shall provide to such person at the time of applying for tenancy and at the time of establishing any rental agreement a separate written statement as follows:

STATEMENT

THIS BUILDING (PARK) IS BEING CONVERTED TO OR IS A CONDOMINIUM OR COOPERATIVE (OR FEE SIMPLE OWNERSHIP OF THE SEVERAL DWELLING UNITS OR PARK SITES). YOUR TENANCY CAN BE TERMINATED UPON 60 DAYS' NOTICE IF YOUR APARTMENT (PARK SITE) IS SOLD TO A BUYER WHO SEEKS TO PERSONALLY OCCUPY IT. IF YOU MOVE OUT AS A RESULT OF RECEIVING SUCH A NOTICE, AND THE LANDLORD ARBITRARILY FAILS TO COMPLETE THE SALE, THE LANDLORD SHALL BE LIABLE FOR TREBLE DAMAGES AND COURT COSTS.

The parenthesized words shall be omitted or substituted for preceding words where appropriate. Such statement shall also be reproduced as the the first clause in any written lease provided to such person.

2A:18-61.10. Removal of tenant to allow conversion to cooperative or condominium; moving expense compensation

Any tenant receiving notice under section [2A:18-61.2(g)] . . . who is not evicted for any cause under this act other than under section [2A:18-61.2(g)] . . . shall receive from the owner moving expense compensation or waiver of payment of 1 month's rent.

2A:18-61.11. Comparable housing; offer of rental; stay of eviction; alternative compensation; senior citizen and disabled protected tenancy period

a. Tenants receiving notice under section [2A:18-61.2(g)] . . . may request of the landlord within 18 full months after receipt of such notice, and the landlord shall offer to the tenant, personally or through an agent, the rental of comparable housing or park site and a reasonable opportunity to examine and rent such comparable housing or park site. In any proceeding under subsection k. of section [2A:18-61.1] . . . instituted following the expiration of notice required under section [2A:18-61.2(g)] . . ., the owner shall prove that a tenant was offered such comparable housing or park site and provided such reasonable opportunity to examine and rent such housing or park site as requested pursuant to this section. The court shall authorize 1 year stays of eviction with reasonable rent increases until such time as the court is satisfied that the tenant has been offered comparable housing or park site and provided a reasonable opportunity to examine and rent such housing or park site as requested pursuant to this section. However, in no case shall more than five such stays be granted.

b. The court shall automatically renew any 1 year stay of eviction in any case where the landlord failed to allege to the court within 1 year of a prior stay that the tenant was offered a reasonable opportunity to examine and rent comparable housing or park site within such prior year.

c. However the court shall not authorize any further stays at any time after one such stay has been authorized when the owner has also provided a tenant with hardship relocation compensation or waiver of payment of 5 months' rent.

d. On or after the effective date of the "Senior Citizens and Disabled Protected Tenancy Act," . . . [N.J.S. 2A:18-61.22 et seq.], notwithstanding the provisions of subsection a. of this section, where the court has jurisdiction pursuant to that subsection, whether by virtue of the authorization by the court of a stay of eviction or by virtue of any other proceedings required or instituted pursuant to [this act or the "Senior Citizens and Disabled Protected Tenancy Act,"] . . . or in any action for declaratory judgment, the court may invoke some or all of the provisions of the "Senior Citizens and Disabled Protected Tenancy Act" and grant to a tenant, pursuant to that amendatory and supplementary act, a protected tenancy period upon the court's determination that:

(1) The tenant would otherwise qualify as a senior citizen tenant or disabled tenant pursuant to that amendatory and supplementary act, except that the building or structure in which the dwelling unit is located was converted prior to the effective date of that amendatory and supplementary act; and

(2) The granting of the protected tenancy period as applied to the tenant, giving particular consideration to whether a unit was sold on or before the date that the amendatory and supplementary act takes effect to a bona fide individual purchaser who intended personally to occupy the unit, would not be violative of concepts of fundamental fairness or due process. Where a court declines to grant a protected tenancy status, it shall nevertheless order such hardships stays as authorized by subsections a. and b. of this section until comparable relocation housing is provided. The hardship relocation compensation alternative of subsection c. of this section shall not be applicable in this situation.

2A:18-61.12. Rules and regulations

In accordance with the "Administrative Procedure Act" (. . . 52:14B-1 et seq.), the Department of Community Affairs shall adopt rules and regulations setting forth procedures required to be followed by landlords in providing tenants a reasonable opportunity to examine and rent comparable housing and setting forth procedures and content for information required to be disclosed to tenants regarding such procedures, the rights and responsibilities of tenants under this act, and the plans and proposals of landlords which may affect any tenant in order to maximize tenants' ability to exercise rights provided under this act. Any rules and regulations adopted under this section shall only be applicable to tenants and owners of a building or mobile home park which is being, or is about to be converted from the rental market to a condominium, cooperative or to fee simple ownership of the several dwelling units or park sites, or to any mobile home park being permanently retired from the rental market.

2A:18-61.22. Short Title

This amendatory and supplementary act shall be known and may be cited as the "Senior Citizens and Disabled Protected Tenancy Act."[11]

2A:18-61.23. Legislative findings and declarations

The Legislature finds that research studies have demonstrated that the forced eviction and relocation of elderly persons from their established homes and communities harm the mental and physical health of these senior citizens, and that these disruptions in the lives of older persons affect adversely the social, economic and cultural characteristics of communities of the State, and increase the costs borne by all State citizens in providing for their public health, safety and welfare. These conditions are particularly serious in light of the rising costs of home ownership, and are of increasing concern where rental housing is converted into condominiums or

---

[11] The act, sections 2A:18-61.22 to 61.39, was adopted in 1981.

cooperatives which senior citizens on fixed limited incomes cannot afford, an occurrence which is becoming more and more frequent in this State under prevailing economic circumstances. The Legislature, therefore, declares that it is in the public interest of the State to avoid the forced eviction and relocation of senior citizen tenants wherever possible, specifically in those instances where rental housing market conditions and particular financial circumstances combine to diminish the ability of senior citizens to obtain satisfactory comparable housing within their established communities, and where the eviction action is the result not of any failure of the senior citizen tenant to abide by the terms of a lease or rental agreement, but of the owner's decision advantageously to dispose of residential property through the device of conversion to a condominium or cooperative.

The Legislature further finds that it is in the public interest of the State to avoid the forced eviction and the displacement of the handicapped wherever possible because of their limited mobility and the limited number of housing units which are suitable for their needs.

The Legislature further declares that in the service of this public interest it is appropriate that qualified senior citizen tenants and disabled tenants be accorded a period of protected tenancy, during which they shall be entitled to the fair enjoyment of the dwelling unit within the converted residential structure, to continue for such time, up to 40 years, as the conditions and circumstances which make necessary such protected tenancy shall continue.

The Legislature further finds that the promotion of this public interest is possible only if senior citizen tenants and disabled tenants are protected during this period from alterations in the terms of the tenancy or rent increases which are the result solely of an owner's decision to convert.

2A:18-61.24. Definitions

As used in this amendatory and supplementary act:

a. "Senior citizen tenant" means a person who is at least 62 years of age on the date of the conversion recording for the building or structure in which is located the dwelling unit of which he is a tenant, or the surviving spouse of such a person if the person should die after the owner files the conversion recording and the surviving spouse is at least 50 years of age at the time of the filing; provided that the building or structure has been the principal residence of the senior citizen tenant or the spouse for at least one year immediately preceding the conversion recording or the death or that the building or structure is the principal residence of the senior citizen tenant or the spouse under the terms of a lease for a period of more than one year, as the case may be;

b. "Disabled tenant" means a person who is, on the date of the conversion recording for the building or structure in which is located the dwelling unit of which he is a tenant, totally and permanently unable to engage in any substantial gainful activity by reason of any medically determinable physical or mental impairment, including blindness, or a person who has been honorably discharged or released under honorable circumstances from active service in any branch of the United States Armed Forces and who is rated as having a 60% disability or higher as a result of that service pursuant to any federal law administered by the United States Veterans' Act; provided that the building or structure has been the principal residence of the disabled tenant for at least one year immediately preceding the conversion recording or that the building or structure is the principal residence of the disabled tenant under the terms of a lease for a period of more than one year. For the purposes of this subsection, "blindness" means central visual acuity of $20/200$ or less in the better eye with the use of correcting lens. An eye which is accompanied by a limitation in the fields of vision such that the widest diameter of the visual field subtends an angle no greater than 20 degrees shall be considered as having a central visual acuity of $^{20}/_{200}$ or less;

c. "Tenant's annual household income" means the total income from all sources during the last full calendar year for all members of the household who reside in the dwelling unit at the time the tenant applies for protected tenant status, whether or not such income is subject to taxation by any taxing authority;

d. "Application for registration of conversion" means an application for registration filed with the Department of Community Affairs in accordance with "The Planned Real Estate Development Full Disclosure Act," . . . [N.J.S. 45:22A-21 et seq.];

e. "Registration of conversion" means an approval of an application for registration by the Department of Community Affairs in accordance with "The Planned Real Estate Development Full Disclosure Act" . . .;

f. "Convert" means to convert one or more buildings or structures or a mobile home park containing in the aggregate not less than 5 dwelling units or mobile home sites or pads from residential rental use to condominium, cooperative, planned residential development or separable fee simple ownership of the dwelling units or of the mobile home sites or pads;

g. "Conversion recording" means the recording with the appropriate county officer of a master deed for condominium or a deed to a cooperative corporation for a cooperative or the first deed of sale to a purchaser of an individual unit for a planned residential development or separate fee simple ownership of the dwelling units;

h. "Protected tenancy period" means, except as otherwise provided in section [2A:18-61.32] . . ., the 40 years following the conversion recording for the building or structure in which is located the dwelling unit of the senior citizen tenant or disabled tenant.

2A:18-61.25. Protected tenancy status; conversion of dwelling unit of eligible senior citizen or disabled tenant

Each eligible senior citizen tenant or disabled tenant shall be granted a protected tenancy status with respect to his dwelling unit whenever the building or structure in which that unit is located shall be converted. The protected tenancy status shall be granted upon proper application and qualification pursuant to the provisions of this amendatory and supplementary act.

2A:18-61.26. Administrative agency

The governing body of the municipality may authorize a municipal board, agency or officer to act as its administrative agency for the purposes of this amendatory and supplementary act or may enter into a contractual agreement with a county office on aging or a similar agency to act as its administrative agency for purposes of this amendatory and supplementary act. In the absence of such authorization or contractual agreement, this amendatory and supplementary act shall be administered by a municipal board whose principal responsibility concerns the regulation of residential rents or, if no such board exists, by the municipal clerk.

2A:18-61.27. Notice of intention to register for conversion to administrative agency or officer and to tenants; contents; affidavit of proof of notice to tenants

The owner of any building or structure who, after the effective date of this amendatory and supplementary act, seeks to convert any premises, shall, prior to his filing of the application for registration of conversion with the Department of Community Affairs, notify the administrative agency or officer responsible for administering this amendatory and supplementary act of his intention to so file. The owner shall supply the agency or officer with a list of every tenant residing in the premises, with stamped envelopes addressed to each tenant and with sufficient copies of the notice to tenants and application form for protected tenancy status. Within 10 days thereafter, the administrative agency or officer shall notify each residential tenant in writing of the owner's intention and of the applicability of the provisions of this amendatory and supplementary act and shall provide him with a written application form. The agency's or officer's notice shall be substantially in the following form:

NOTICE

THE OWNER OF YOUR APARTMENT HAS NOTIFIED (insert name of municipality) OF HIS INTENTION TO CONVERT TO A CONDOMINIUM OR COOPERATIVE. THE LEGISLATURE HAS PROVIDED THAT, IF YOU ARE A SENIOR CITIZEN, 62 YEARS OF AGE OR OLDER, OR DISABLED, YOU MAY BE ENTITLED TO A PROTECTED TENANCY PERIOD. PROTECTED TENANCY MEANS THAT YOU CANNOT BE EVICTED BECAUSE OF THE CONVERSION. YOU MAY BE ELIGIBLE:

(1) IF YOU ARE 62, OR WILL SOON BE 62, OR IF YOU ARE DISABLED; AND

(2) IF YOU HAVE LIVED IN YOUR APARTMENT FOR AT LEAST ONE YEAR OR IF THE LEASE ON YOUR APARTMENT IS FOR A PERIOD OF MORE THAN ONE YEAR; AND

(3) IF YOUR HOUSEHOLD INCOME IS LESS THAN (insert current income figure for county as established by section [2A:18-61.28(c)] . . . of this amendatory and supplementary act). IF YOU WISH THIS PROTECTION, SEND IN THE APPLICATION FORM BY (insert date 60 days after municipality's mailing) TO THE (insert name and address of administrative agency). FOR FURTHER INFORMATION CALL (insert phone number of administrative agency) OR (insert phone number of Department of Community Affairs)

IF YOU DO NOT APPLY YOU CAN BE EVICTED BY YOUR LANDLORD UPON PROPER NOTICE.

The Department of Community Affairs shall not accept any application for registration of conversion for any building or structure unless included in the application is proof that the agency or officer notified the tenants prior to the application for registration. The proof shall be by affidavit or in such other form as the department shall require.

2A:18-61.28. Application for eligibility; determination; grounds; written notice of eligibility to tenant and to owner

Within 30 days after receipt of an application for protected tenancy status by a tenant, the administrative agency or officer shall make a determination of eligibility. It shall send written notice of eligibility to each senior citizen tenant or disabled tenant who:

a. Applied therefor on or before the date of registration of conversion by the Department of Community Affairs; and,

b. Qualifies as an eligible senior citizen tenant or disabled tenant pursuant to this amendatory and supplementary act; and,

c. Has an annual household income that does not exceed an amount equal to three times the County per capita personal income, as last reported by the Department of Labor and Industry on the basis of the U.S. Department of Commerce's Bureau of Economic Analysis data, or $50,000, whichever is greater; and,

d. Has occupied the premises as his principal residence for at least one year or has a lease on the premises for a period longer than one year.

The department shall adjust the county per capita personal income to be used in subsection c. of this section if there is a difference of one or more years between (1) the year in which the last reported county per capita personal income was based and (2) the last year in which the tenant's annual household income is based. The county per capita personal income shall be adjusted by the department by an amount equal to the number of years of the difference above times the average increase or decrease in the county per capita personal income for three years, including in the calculation the current year reported and the three immediately preceding years.

The administrative agency or officer shall likewise send a notice of denial with reasons to any tenant whom it determines to be ineligible. The owner shall be notified of those tenants who are determined to be eligible and ineligible.

The administrative agency or officer may require that the application include such documents and information as may be necessary to establish that the tenant is eligible for a protected tenancy status under the provisions of this amendatory and supplementary act and shall require such application to be submitted under oath. The Department of Community Affairs may be regulation adopt forms for application for protected tenancy status and notification of eligibility or ineligibility or adopt such other regulations for the procedure of determining eligibility as it determines are necessary.

2A:18-61.29. Registration of conversion; approval after proof of notice of eligibility to tenants

No registration of conversion shall be approved until the Department of Community Affairs receives proof that the administrative agency or officer has made determinations and notified all tenants who applied for protected tenancy status within the initial 60-day period of their eligibility or lack of eligibility. The proof shall be by affidavit or in such other form as the department may require.

The department may grant registrations of conversion for applications pending on the effective date of this amendatory and supplementary act upon the implementation of a procedure whereby any eligible tenant may make application for protected tenancy status in a manner comparable to that specified in sections [2A:18-61.27 and 2A:18-61.28] . . . of this amendatory and supplementary act.

2A:18-61.30. Protected tenancy status; applicability after notice of eligibility and filing of conversion recording

Protected tenancy status shall not be applicable to any eligible tenant until such time as the owner has filed his conversion recording. The protected tenancy status shall automatically apply as soon as a tenant receives notice of eligibility and the landlord files his conversion recording. The conversion recording shall not be filed until after the registration of conversion.

2A:18-61.31. Rent increases; limitations

In a municipality which does not have a rent control ordinance in effect, no evidence of increased costs which are solely the result of the conversion, including but not limited to any increase in financing or carrying costs, and which do not add services or amenities not previously provided shall be used as a basis to establish the reasonableness of a rent increase under section [2A:18-61.1(f)]. . ..

In a municipality which has a rent control ordinance in effect, a rent increase for a tenant with a protected tenancy status, or for any tenant to whom notice of termination pursuant to section [2A:18-61.2(g)] . . . has been given, shall not exceed the increase authorized by the ordinance for rent controlled units. Increased costs which are solely the result of a conversion, including but not limited to any increase in financing or carrying costs, and which do not add services or amenities not previously provided shall not be passed directly through to these tenants as surcharges or pass-throughs on the rent, shall not be used as the basis for a rent increase, and shall not be used as a basis for an increase in a fair return or hardship hearing before a municipal rent board or on any appeal from such determination.

2A:18-61.32. *Termination of protected tenancy status; grounds; removal; procedures*

The administrative agency or officer shall terminate the protected tenancy status immediately upon finding that:

a. The dwelling unit is no longer the principal residence of the senior citizen tenant or disabled tenant; or

b. The tenant's annual household income, or the average of the tenant's annual household income for the current year, computed on an annual basis, and the tenant's annual household income for the 2 preceding years, whichever is less, exceeds an amount equal to three times the county per capital personal income as last reported by the Department of Labor and Industry on the basis of the U.S. Department of Commerce's Bureau of Economic Analysis data, or $50,000, whichever is greater.

The department shall adjust the county per capita personal income to be used in subsection b. of this section if there is a difference of one or more years between (1) the year in which the last reported county per capita personal income was based and (2) the last year in which the tenant's annual household income is based. The county per capita personal income shall be adjusted by the department by an amount equal to the number of years of the difference above times the average increase or decrease in the county per capita personal income for three years, including in the calculation the current year reported and the three immediately preceding years.

Upon the termination of the protected tenancy status by the administrative agency or officer, the senior citizen tenant or disabled tenant may be removed from the dwelling unit pursuant to [section 2A:18-61.1 et seq.] . . ., except that all notice and other times set forth therein shall be calculated and extend from the date of the expiration or termination of the protected tenancy period, or the date of the expiration of the last lease entered into with the senior citizen tenant or disabled tenant during the protected tenancy period, whichever shall be later.

If the administrative agency determines pursuant to this section that a tenant is no longer qualified for protected tenancy under this act, the administrative agency shall proceed to determine the eligibility of that tenant under the "Tenant Protection Act of 1992," . . . or, in any case in which the administrative agency is not the same as the agency administering that other act in the municipality, refer the case to the appropriate administrative agency for such determination. If the tenant is found to be eligible under the "Tenant Protection Act of 1992," . . . his protected tenancy status shall be continued. The protected tenancy status of the tenant shall remain in full force pending such determination.

2A:18-61.33. *Termination upon purchase of unit by senior citizen or disabled tenant*

In the event that a senior citizen tenant or disabled tenant purchases the dwelling unit he occupies, the protected tenancy status shall terminate immediately upon purchase.

2A:18-61.34. Informing prospective purchaser of act; contract or agreement for sale; clause informing of application of act and acknowledgment by purchaser

Any public offering statement for a conversion as required by "The Planned Real Estate Development Full Disclosure Act," . . . [45:22A-21 et seq.], shall clearly inform the prospective purchaser of the provisions of this amendatory and supplementary act, including, but not limited to, the provisions concerning eviction, rent increases and leases. Any contract or agreement for sale of a converted unit shall contain a clause in 10-point bold type or larger that the contract is subject to the terms of this amendatory and supplementary act concerning eviction and rent increases and an acknowledgment that the purchaser has been informed of these terms.

2A:18-61.35. Fee

A municipality is authorized to charge an owner a fee which may vary according to the size of the building to cover the cost of providing the services required by this amendatory and supplementary act.

2A:18-61.36. Agreement by tenant to waive rights; deemed against public policy and unenforceable

Any agreement whereby the tenant waives any rights under [this act] . . . shall be deemed to be against public policy and unenforceable.

2A:18-61.37. Severability

If any section, subsection, paragraph, sentence or other part of this amendatory and supplementary act is adjudged unconstitutional or invalid, such judgment shall not affect, impair or invalidate the remainder of this act, but shall be confined in its effect to the section, subsection, paragraph, sentence or other part of this act directly involved in the controversy in which said judgment shall have been rendered.

2A:18-61.38. Rules and regulations

The Department of Community Affairs is authorized to adopt such rules and regulations as may be necessary to implement the provisions of this amendatory and supplementary act.

2A:18-61.39. Liberal construction of act

This amendatory and supplementary act shall be liberally construed to effectuate the purposes thereof.

Editorial Note on N.J.S. 2A:18-61.40 *et seq.*: In 1992, New Jersey adopted the Tenant Protection Act, N.J.S. 2A:18-61.40 et seq. This act contains provisions much like those excerpted just above protecting the tenancies of disabled and elderly tenants. To save space the statute is not reproduced here. The General Assembly described its provisions as follows:

The protected tenancy authorized under this bill is available to tenants who reside in qualified counties and who meet certain other eligibility requirements.

Under the bill a qualified county is either a county which (1) has a high population and population density, (therefore has limited land available for the development of new low and moderate income rental units) or (2) has experience significant reductions in the availability of rental dwellings due to the conversions of those units into condominium and cooperative properties.

To meet the population/population density qualification, a county must have a population in excess of 500,000 and a population density in excess of 8,500 per square mile. To qualify under the reduction in available rental unit criterion, the Commissioner of Community Affairs must certify that during the preceding 10 years the county has lost: (1) an aggregate of at least 10,000 rental units due to conversions in any three consecutive years and (2) at least 5,000 rental units due to conversions in at least one of those three years.

. . . .

Tenants who reside in qualified counties would be eligible for the protected tenancy authorized under this bill if: (1) they have lived in their unit for at least one year before the conversion and (2) either are 75 years of age or older; disabled; or have an income below a certain level. (The income standards set forth in the bill range from $31,400 for a single individual to $64,300 for a household of 8 or more, but are subject to adjustment annually based upon the Consumer Price Index.)

The protected tenancy provided by this legislation lasts until the tenant dies the tenant's income rises above the protected levels, or the tenant buys the housing unit he or she is living in.

SUBTITLE 6. SPECIFIC CIVIL ACTIONS

CHAPTER 33. DISTRESS

2A:33-1. Authorized distraints; liability for wrongful distraint; prohibition on money owed on lease of residence

Distraints may be taken when authorized by law; but no unreasonable, excessive or wrongful distraint shall be taken, and for any such taking, the distraining party shall be liable in damages to the party aggrieved.

No distraint shall be permitted for money owed on a lease or other agreement for the occupation of any real property used solely as a residence of the tenant.[12]

2A:33-2. Place of impounding chattels

Chattels distrained or taken by distress, at one time, for any cause whatsoever, shall be impounded together or the distraining party be liable in treble damages to the party aggrieved.

2A:33-3. Exemptions

Property to the value of $500, to be selected by the person distrained against or as provided in section 2A:33-12 of this title, and all wearing apparel shall be exempt from distraint. This section shall be inapplicable in the case of the impounding and distraint of straying domestic animals.

2A:33-4. Impounding of strays

Cattel or other domestic animals found straying on the property of any person other than their owner, causing damage to such property, may be distrained and impounded to secure reimbursement for such damage.

2A:33-5. Distraint for levying of penalty inflicted or money directed to be paid by law; warrant and sale by judge or magistrate

Where any judge or magistrate is required or authorized to issue a warrant of distress for the levying of a penalty inflicted, or sum of money directed to be paid by any law, and no mode is provided for the disposal of the distress, the judge or magistrate may order the chattels, to

---

[12] This sentence was added to 2A:33-1 in 1971.

be so distrained, sold and disposed of within the time to be limited in the warrant, which time shall not be less than 4 nor more than 10 days, unless the penalty or sum of money, together with reasonable charges, to be taxed by the judge or magistrate, of taking and keeping the distress, be sooner paid.

Reasonable charges of taking, keeping and selling the distress, to be taxed as aforesaid, shall be deducted by the officer making the distress out of moneys arising from the sale, and the overplus, if any, after such charges, and also said penalty or sum of money shall be satisfied and paid, shall be returned on demand to the owner of the chattels so distrained. The officer executing the warrant shall show the same to the person whose chattels are distrained, and give him a copy thereof.

2A:33-6. Property subject to distraint for rent

A landlord or his duly authorized agent may, for arrears of rent, distrain:

a. The goods and chattels of his tenant, found upon the demised premises, except such as are by law exempt from distraint and except the goods and chattels of another in possession of the tenant;

b. The live stock of his tenant, found upon the demised premises or upon premises appurtenant thereto, except the property of another in the tenant's possession; and

c. All products of the soil severed from the soil and remaining upon any part of the land charged with such rent; and

d. All fruits or products of the soil, growing or being upon the demised premises, which the landlord or his agent may sever and remove from such premises to a safe and proper place on the premises or, if there be no such place thereon, to some other place to be procured by the landlord, due notice of which place shall be given to the tenant or left at his place of abode.

The property so subject to distraint shall be appraised, sold and disposed of at the time and in the manner provided in this chapter.

2A:33-7. Limitation of right to distrain for rent

No landlord shall at one time distrain for more than 1 year's arrears of rent, and such distraint shall be made within 6 months after the rent becomes due, or, if the rent is payable in installments, within 6 months after the entire year's rent has become due.

2A:33-8. Distraint after term or estate ended

A person having rent in arrear and due upon a lease for term of life, years, or at will ended or determined, may distrain for the same after determination of the respective leases, in the same manner as he might have done if the lease had not been ended or determined.

The distress shall be made within 6 calendar months after the determination of the lease, and during the continuance of the landlord's title or interest, and during the possession of the tenant from whom the arrears became due, or if the landlord's title and interest shall have ceased, or the tenant has removed from the leasehold premises, then within 30 days after the end and determination of the term of tenancy, but not thereafter.

2A:33-9. Time for owner of distrained property to take action; inventory and appraisal; aid of officers

If the tenant or owner of property distrained for rent shall not, within 10 days next after the distress taken and after notice thereof, and of the cause of the taking, has been left at the main dwelling house or other most conspicuous place on the premises charged with the rent distrained for, commence an action or otherwise lawfully proceed to recover possession of said property or set aside or end the distraint, the person distraining may, after the distress, notice and expiration of 10 days, on 2 days' notice to the tenant, cause the goods and chattels to be inventoried and appraised by 3 sworn appraisers.

The sheriff of the county, or a constable of the place wherein the distress shall be taken, shall aid and assist therein and shall summon 3 appraisers for such service and shall swear them well and truly to appraise the same, at the true and intrinsic value thereof, according to their best understanding.

2A:33-10. Sale of distrained property; notice

After the inventory and appraisement, the person distrained for rent shall sell at public vendue the property so distrained. He shall give 5 days' public notice by advertising the articles to be sold and the time and place of sale, in at least 3 of the most public places in the municipality where the distress shall be made, and sell the same for the best price that can be secured towards satisfaction of the rent and charges of the distress, appraisement and sale, leaving the overplus, if any, with the sheriff or constable for the owner's use.

2A:33-11. Impounding and sale on premises

A person lawfully distraining for rent may impound or otherwise secure the articles distrained so made, on the part of the premises most convenient for the purpose, and may appraise, sell and dispose of the same thereon in like manner as a distress taken for rent off the premises. A person may go upon the place where the articles are impounded or secured, in order to view, appraise, buy or remove the same on account of the purchaser thereof.

2A:33-12. Selection of articles to be exempted; when by appraisers

From the inventory of the property appraised, the tenant, or in his absence, his agent, attorney, or member of his family, may select articles, the value of which, according to the appraisement, shall not exceed $500. If the tenant, or member of his family, his agent or attorney, cannot readily be found, the selection may be made by the appraisers to be reserved for the family's use.

2A:33-13. Procedure if landlord fails to proceed with appraisement; selection

If the landlord, his attorney or agent shall not, within 2 days after being served with a written request from his tenant so to do, proceed and have the distrained property appraised, the tenant may, after 5 days' notice thereof to this landlord, his attorney or agent, apply to the sheriff or a constable of the county and have the property inventoried and appraised. The property reserved for the use of the family of the tenant may thereupon be selected as provided by section 2A:33-12 of this title.

2A:33-15. Distress for residue

When the value of the property distrained shall not amount to the full value of the arrears further distraints may be made from time to time, for the residue of the arrears. Any such further distress shall be made within the time limited by this chapter.

2A:33-16. Pound breach or rescue; remedy; damages

A person aggrieved by any pound breach or rescue of any property distrained for rent and impounded or otherwise secured by virtue of this chapter, shall in an action at law recover treble damages and costs of any action against the offender or the owner of the property distrained, if it be afterwards found to have come into his use or possession.

2A:33-17. Wrongful distress and sale for rent; remedy

If a distress and sale shall be made for rent not in fact due the person distraining or for whom the distress is taken, the owner of the property distrained, shall be entitled to recover double the value of the property so distrained and sold, together with full costs of any action.

2A:33-18. Wrongful acts after distraint for rent; remedy; damages

When a distress is made for rent justly due and an irregularity or unlawful act shall afterwards be done by the party distraining, or his agent, the distress shall not therefore be deemed unlawful nor the party making it deemed a trespasser ab initio. The party aggrieved thereby shall be entitled to recover full satisfaction for the special damage sustained thereby, and no more. When the plaintiff shall recover such damages, he shall be entitled to his full costs, the same as in other cases of costs.

2A:33-19. Actions against distrainor; double costs in certain cases

In any action brought to recover damages for an alleged wrongful distress or wrongful act after distraint, a defendant, in whose favor judgment is rendered, shall be entitled to recover double costs.

2A:33-20. Distraint of property removed; bona fide purchasers

Where property of a tenant, subject to be distrained for accrued and unpaid rent, payable or to become payable, is removed from the demised premises, the landlord may, within thirty days next after such removal, distrain such property notwith standing its removal, unless it shall have been sold to a purchaser for a valuable consideration without knowledge of the landlord's right to distrain.

2A:33-21. Liability of tenant for removing or concealing property subject to distraint

Any tenant who removes or conceals any of his personal property subject to distraint by his landlord, with intent to delay, hinder, or defraud said landlord, shall be liable for the damages resulting therefrom, to his landlord; and in any action to recover such damages if it shall appear that the action of the tenant was willful, the landlord shall be entitled to recover double damages.

2A:33-22. Seizure of property locked up; breaking and entering

When property is removed by a tenant and put in any place locked up, fastened or otherwise secured, to prevent the said property from being distrained for arrears of rent, the landlord, first calling to his assistance a constable or peace officer, who shall aid and assist therein, may, in the daytime, break open and enter the place, and distrain the said property for the arrears of rent as he might have done if the said property had been put in an open place.

If the place where the said property is secured is a dwelling house, oath shall first be made before some judge or magistrate, of a reasonable ground to suspect that the said property is therein.

2A:33-23. Remedy where rent apportionable

Wherever rent is legally or equitably apportionable between successive owners or landlords or their representatives, any person entitled to a proportion of such rent shall be entitled to distrain therefor in the same manner as though such person was entitled to receive the full rent.

CHAPTER 35
POSSESSION OF AND TITLE TO REAL PROPERTY

2A:35-1. Jurisdiction in real property possessory actions

Any person claiming the right of possession of real property in the possession of another, or claiming title to such real property, shall be entitled to have his rights determined in an action in the superior court.

2A:35-2. Damages; limitations

In any such action, the plaintiff shall be entitled to recover from the defendant any and all incidental damages, including mesne profits, and the full value of the use and occupation of the premises for the time, not exceeding 6 years, before the commencement of the action, during which the defendant was in possession thereof.

2A:35-3. Allowances for improvements; limitations

Where permanent improvements have been made on the premises in good faith, under circumstances entitling the defendant to have the value thereof allowed to him, the court may allow the same to be set off against the damages of the plaintiff, but only to the extent of such damages.

CHAPTER 39
FORCIBLE ENTRY AND DETAINER

2A:39-1. Unlawful entry prohibited

No person shall enter upon or into any real property or estate therein and detain and hold the same, except where entry is given by law, and then only in a peaceable manner. With regard to any real property occupied solely as a residence by the party in possession, such entry shall not be made in any manner without the consent of the party in possession unless the entry and detention is made pursuant to legal process as set out in N.J.S. 2A:18-53 et seq. or 2A:35-1 et seq.[13]

2A:39-2. Forcible or unlawful entry and detainer defined

If any person shall enter upon or into real property and detain or hold the same with force, whether or not any person be in it, by any kind of violence whatsoever, or by threatening to kill, maim or beat the party in possession, or by such words, circumstances or action as have a natural tendency to excite fear or apprehension of danger, or by putting out of doors, or carrying away the goods of the party in possession, or by entering peaceably and then, by force or frightening by threats, or by other circumstances of terror, turning the party out of possession, such person shall be guilty of a forcible entry and detainer within the meaning of this chapter. With regard to any real property occupied solely as a residence by the party in possession, if any person shall enter upon or into said property and detain or hold same in any manner without the consent of the party in possession unless the entry is made pursuant to legal process as set out in N.J.S. 2A:18-53 et seq. or 2A:35-1 et seq., such person shall be guilty of an unlawful entry and detainer within the meaning of this chapter.[14]

---

[13] The last sentence in this section was added in 1971.

[14] The last sentence in this section was added in 1971.

2A:39-3. Forcible detainer defined

No person lawfully or peaceably entering upon or into any real property shall hold or keep the same with force; and whatever words or circumstances, conduct or actions, as will make an entry forcible under this chapter shall also make a detainer forcible.

2A:39-4. Unlawful detainer defined

If any tenant or other person in possession of any real property under a tenant, shall willfully and without force, hold over any such real property after demand and notice in writing given for the delivery of the possession thereof by a lessor or the person to whom the remainder or reversion of such real estate shall belong, such tenant or other person, so holding over, shall be guilty of an unlawful detainer.

2A:39-5. Unlawful detainer; notice

A person taking possession of real property, without the consent of the owner or without color of title, and willfully and without force holding or detaining the same after demand and written notice given for the delivery of the possession thereof, by the owner or person entitled to possession or right to possession shall be guilty of an unlawful detainer.

2A:39-6. Jurisdiction

Any forcible unlawful entry and detainer, forcible detainer and unlawful detainer as defined in this chapter shall be cognizable before the district court or the Superior Court, and the court may hear and determine an action therefor in a summary manner.

2A:39-7. Title not inquired into; defense of 3 years possession

Title shall not be an issue in any action commenced under this chapter. 3 years peaceable possession by the defendant shall be a defense to the action.

2A:39-8. Recovery of damages and possession of property; treble damages in lieu of possession

In any action under this chapter, a plaintiff recovering judgment shall be entitled to possession of the real property and shall recover all damages proximately caused by the unlawful entry and detainer including court costs and reasonable attorney's fees. When a return to possession would be an inappropriate remedy, treble damages shall be awarded in lieu thereof. The judgment may be enforced against either party in a summary manner by any process necessary to secure complete compliance therewith, including the payment of the costs.

CHAPTER 42
LANDLORD AND TENANT; RIGHTS AND REMEDIES

ARTICLE 1: LIEN OF LANDLORD

2A:42-1. Landlord's lien for rent; amount; taking goods or chattels to satisfy

No goods or chattels whatsoever, in or upon any real property leased for any term of life or lives, years or years, at will or otherwise, shall be liable to be taken, by virtue of any execution, attachment or other process, unless the party suing out the same shall, before the removal of such goods or chattels from the premises by virtue of such process, pay to the landlord of such premises all rent, not exceeding 1 year's rent, due for such premises at the time of the taking of such goods or chattels by virtue of such process, or which shall have accrued up to the day of the removal of the goods and chattels from the premises. If by the terms of the tenancy, the day of payment of the rent shall not have arrived, a rebate of interest shall be made on the sum not payable.

If the arrears of rent shall exceed 1 year's rent, the party at whose action such process is sued out may, upon paying the landlord 1 year's rent, proceed to execute his process.

The sheriff or other officer shall levy and pay to the plaintiff, as well the money so paid for rent as the money to be made by virtue of such process.

2A:42-2. Levy subject to landlord's lien; time of sale; notice

If any goods or chattels, in or upon any real property as provided by section 2A:42-1 of this title, shall be taken by virtue of any execution, attachment or other process and removed from the premises, the same shall not be sold by the sheriff or other officer so taking and removing them until 10 days after such removal, and not then unless the party at whose action such goods or chattels are so taken shall, before the sale thereof, pay to the landlord of such premises, such sum as he may be entitled to receive for rent under the provisions of said section 2A:42-1, provided the landlord shall, before the expiration of the 10 days above-mentioned, give notice to the sheriff or other officer holding such process of the amount of rent in arrear, and claim the same. Such notice may be served by delivering the same to the sheriff or other officer, or by leaving a copy thereof at his usual place of abode.

2A:42-3. Goods and chattels removed openly and in daytime; notice to defendant

No such goods and chattels shall be removed from the leased premises by the sheriff or other officer, except openly and in the daytime, and not then unless such officer shall, at the time of such removal, give notice thereof to the defendant, or, in his absence, to some person of his family residing on such premises, of such removal.

ARTICLE 2: LIABILITY FOR RENT AND PENALTIES FOR HOLDING OVER

2A:42-4. Undertenant's liability for rent

When premises shall be underlet by any tenant, the undertenant shall be liable to the lessor or landlord for the rent which shall accrue from and after notice in writing served for that purpose upon the undertenant, or which shall be unpaid by the undertenant at the time of such notice, and the lessor or landlord shall have all the remedy for the recovery of the same by distress; but the rent to be paid by such undertenant shall in no case exceed the amount agreed to be paid by the first tenant. If only a part of the premises shall be underlet, payment shall be required only for the part underlet, at a rate proportioned to the rent agreed to be paid by the first tenant or lessee.

2A:42-5. Holding over by tenant after giving notice of quitting; double rent recoverable

If a tenant of real estate shall give notice of his intention to quit the premises by him held at a time specified in such notice, and shall not deliver up the possession of such real estate at the time specified in the notice, such tenant, his executors or administrators, shall, from such time, pay to his landlord or lessor, his heirs or assigns, double the rent which he should otherwise have paid, to be levied, sued for and recovered at the same time and in the same manner as the single rent before the giving of such notice could be levied, sued for and recovered. Such double rent shall continue to be paid during all the time such tenant shall continue in possession after the giving of such notice.

2A:42-6. Willful holding over by tenant after the expiration of term; notice to deliver possession; penalty

When a tenant for any term or any other person coming into possession of any real estate by, from or under, or by collusion with such tenant, willfully holds over any such real estate after the determination of such term and after demand made and notice in writing for delivering the possession thereof, given by his landlord or lessor, or by the person to whom the remainder or reversion of such real estate shall belong, the person so holding over shall, for and during the time he so holds over or keeps the person entitled out of possession of such real estate pay to the person so kept out of possession, his executors, administrators or assigns, at the rate of double the yearly value of the real estate so detained, for so long a time as the same is detained. Such amount shall be recoverable by an action in any court of competent jurisdiction.

2A:42-6.1. Five day grace period for payment of rent

A person to whom rent is due and payable on the first of the month upon a lease or other agreement shall allow a period of 5 days grace in which the rent due shall be paid. No delinquency or other late charge shall be made which includes the 5-day grace period.

2A:42-6.2. Violations; disorderly persons

Any person violating the provisions of this act[15] shall be a disorderly person.

2A:42-6.3. Application of act only to senior citizens

The provisions of this act[16] shall only be applicable to premises rented or leased by senior citizens receiving Social Security Old Age Pensions, Railroad Retirement Pensions or other governmental pensions in lieu of Social Security Old Age Pensions.

ARTICLE 3: CIVIL ACTION FOR RE-ENTRY

2A:42-7. Action for possession for nonpayment of rent; service of summons

A landlord or lessor to whom 1 year's rent in arrear is due, and who shall have the right to re-enter the demised premises for non-payment thereof, may without a formal demand or re-entry, institute an action for the possession of such premises. If the summons in the action cannot be served in the usual manner, the landlord or lessor may affix the same upon the demised premises in a conspicuous place thereon, which affixing shall be deemed legal service thereof. The service or affixing shall take the place of a demand and re-entry.

2A:42-8. Judgment and execution bar to relief; except appeal

A lessee or other person claiming or deriving title under a lease who suffers judgment in said action for possession and execution to be executed thereon, without paying the rent and arrears, together with costs and without filing any complaint for equitable relief within 6 months after the execution is executed, shall be barred and foreclosed from all relief or remedy other than by appeal from the judgment, and the landlord or lessor shall, from thenceforth hold the demised premises discharged from the lease.

2A:42-9. Dismissal on payment of rent and costs; resumption of lease

If the tenant or his assignee shall at any time before the trial in the action for possession of the demised premises, pay or tender to the lessor or landlord, his executor, administrator or

---

[15] This act includes only sections 2A:42-6.1 to 6.3.

[16] This act includes only sections 2A:42-6.1 to 6.3.

attorney, or pay into the court where the action for possession of the demised premises shall be pending, all the rents and arrears, together with the costs, all further proceedings in the action shall be dismissed. If the lessee, his executors, administrators or assigns, shall be granted equitable relief, he shall have, hold and enjoy the demised lands, according to the lease thereof made, without a new lease being made to him, provided the court shall so adjudge.

2A:42-10. Rights of mortgagee; payment of rent and costs

Nothing contained in sections 2A:42-7 and 2A:42-8 of this title shall extend to bar the right of a mortgagee of such lease, or any party thereof, who shall not be in possession, if he shall, within 6 months after judgment is obtained and execution executed, pay all rent in arrear, costs and damages sustained by the lessor, or person entitled to the remainder or reversion and perform the covenants and agreements which on the part and behalf of the first lessee should be performed.

. . . .

2A:42-10.6. Warrant or writ for recovery of premises not under rent control; issuance; stay

Notwithstanding any other provisions of law, in any action brought by a landlord against a tenant to recover possession of premises or unit used for dwelling purposes, to which this act[17] is applicable, whether by summary dispossess proceedings, civil action for the possession of land, or otherwise, the judge of the court having jurisdiction shall use sound discretion in the issuance of a warrant or writ for removal or writ of possession, and if it shall appear that by the issuance of the warrant or writ the tenant will suffer hardship because of the unavailability of other dwelling accommodations the judge may stay the issuance of the warrant or writ and cause the same to issue at such time as he shall deem proper under the circumstances, but in no case shall such judge stay the issuance of any such warrant or writ for possession for a longer period than 6 months after the date of entry of the judgment of possession; provided, however, that in no case shall the issuance of the warrant or writ be stayed or the stay thereof be longer continued, as the case may be, if the tenant should (a) fail to pay to the landlord all arrears in rent and the amount that would have been payable as rent if the tenancy had continued, together with the accrued costs of the action; or (b) during the stay, fail to continue to pay to the landlord the amount of rent that would be due if the tenancy had continued; or (c) during the stay, become so disorderly as to destroy the peace and quiet of the other tenants living in the same building or in the neighborhood; or (d) during the stay, willfully destroy, damage or injure the premises.

2A:42-10.7. Rent payments not to create new tenancy

In no event shall any payment made by the tenant to the landlord for continued occupancy of any premises or unit, as provided in section [2A:42-10.6] . . ., be deemed to create a new tenancy.

2A:42-10.8. Applicability

This act shall apply to all actions and proceedings by a landlord against a tenant to recover possession of premises used for dwelling purposes for which warrants or writs of removal shall not have been satisfied, but this act shall not be operative as to any premises under rent control.

. . . .

2A:42-10.10. Reprisal as unlawful grounds for civil action for re-entry; action for damages or other appropriate relief by tenant

---

[17] This act includes sections 2A:42-10.6 to 10.8.

No landlord of premises or units to which this act[18] is applicable shall serve a notice to quit upon any tenant or institute any action against a tenant to recover possession of premises, whether by summary dispossess proceedings, civil action for possession of land, or otherwise:

a. As a reprisal for the tenant's efforts to secure or enforce any rights under the lease or contract, or under the laws of the State of New Jersey or its governmental subdivisions, or of the United States; or

b. As a reprisal for the tenant's good faith complaint to a governmental authority of the landlord's alleged violation of any health or safety law, regulation, code or ordinance, or State law or regulation which has as its objective the regulation of premises used for dwelling purposes; or

c. As a reprisal for the tenant's being an organizer of, a member of, or involved in any activities of, any lawful organization; or

d. On account of the tenant's failure or refusal to comply with the terms of the tenancy as altered by the landlord, if the landlord shall have altered substantially the terms of the tenancy as a reprisal for any actions of the tenant set forth in subsection a, b, and c of [this section]. . .. Substantial alteration shall include the refusal to renew a lease or to continue a tenancy of the tenant without cause.

Under subsection b of this section the tenant shall originally bring his good faith complaint to the attention of the landlord or his agent and give the landlord a reasonable time to correct the violation before complaining to a governmental authority.

A landlord shall be subject to a civil action by the tenant for damages and other appropriate relief, including injunctive and other equitable remedies, as may be determined by a court of competent jurisdiction in every case in which the landlord has violated the provisions of this section.

2A:42-10.11. Grounds for judgment for tenant in unlawful action for possession by landlord

In any action brought by a landlord against a tenant to recover possession of premises or units to which this act is applicable, whether by summary dispossess proceedings, civil action for the possession of land, or otherwise, judgment shall be entered for the tenant if the tenant shall establish that the notice to quit, if any, or the action to recover possession was intended for any of the reasons set forth in subsections a, b, c, or d of section [2A:42-10.10] . . . of this act.

2A:42-10.12. Rebuttable presumption; notice to quit or alteration of tenancy as reprisal

In any action or proceeding instituted by or against a tenant, the receipt by the tenant of a notice to quit or any substantial alteration of the terms of the tenancy without cause after:

a. The tenant attempts to secure or enforce any rights under the lease or contract, or under the laws of the State of New Jersey, or its governmental subdivisions, or of the United States; or

b. The tenant, having brought a good faith complaint to the attention of the landlord and having given him a reasonable time to correct the alleged violation, complains to a governmental authority with a report of the landlord's alleged violation of any health or safety law, regulation, code or ordinance; or

---

[18] This act, adopted in 1970, includes sections 2A:42-10.10 to 10.15.

c. The tenant organizes, becomes a member of, or becomes involved in any activities of, any lawful organization; or

d. Judgment under section [2A:42-10.11] . . . of this act is entered for the tenant in a previous action for recovery of premises between the parties; shall create a rebuttable presumption that such notice or alteration is a reprisal against the tenant for making such attempt, report, complaint, or for being an organizer of, a member of, or involved in any activities of, any lawful organization. No reprisal shall be presumed under this section based upon the failure of a landlord to renew a lease or tenancy when so requested by a tenant if such request is made sooner than 90 days before the expiration date of the lease or tenancy, or the renewal date set forth in the lease agreement, whichever later occurs.

2A:42-10.13. Application of act to rental premises for dwelling purposes

This act shall apply to all rental premises or units used for dwelling purposes except owner-occupied premises with not more than two rental units. Mobile home spaces and mobile homes shall constitute rental premises under this act.

2A:42-10.14. Severability

If any provision of this act or the application thereof to any person or circumstances or the exercise of any power or authority thereunder is held invalid or contrary to law, such holding shall not affect other provisions or applications of the act which can be given effect without the invalid provisions or applications or affect other exercises of power or authority under said provisions not contrary to law, and to this end the provisions of this act are declared to be severable.

2A:42-10.15. Short Title

This act shall be known and may be cited as "The Fair Eviction Notice Act."

2A:42-10.16. Summary dispossess proceedings; warrant for possession; requirements[19]

In any proceeding for the summary dispossession of a tenant, warrant for possession issued by a court of appropriate jurisdiction:

a. Shall include a notice to the tenant of any right to apply to the court for a stay of execution of the warrant, together with a notice advising that the tenant may be eligible for temporary housing assistance or other social services and that the tenant should contact the appropriate county welfare agency, at the address and telephone number given in the notice, to determine eligibility; and

b. Shall be executed not earlier than the third day following the day of personal service upon the tenant by the appropriate court officer. In calculating the number of days hereby required, Saturday, Sunday and court holidays shall be excluded; and

c. Shall be executed during the hours of 8 a.m. to 6 p.m., unless the court, for good cause shown, otherwise provides in its judgment for possession.

Whenever a written notice, in accordance with the provisions of subsection a., is given to the tenant by the court, this shall constitute personal service in accordance with the provisions of subsection b.

The Superior Court, Law Division, Special Civil Part shall retain jurisdiction for a period of 10 days subsequent to the actual execution of the warrant for possession for the purpose of hearing applications by the tenant for lawful relief.

---

[19] This section was originally enacted in 1974.

2A:42-10.17. Warrant for removal; disorderly or destructive residential seasonal tenant[20]

The provisions of any other law to the contrary notwithstanding, in any action alleging habitual violation of section . . . [2A;18-61.1(b)], or violation of section . . . [2A:18-61.1(c)], brought by a landlord against a tenant to recover possession of any furnished unit leased or rented for seasonal use in any premises of five or fewer units, the court having jurisdiction shall issue a warrant for removal within 2 days from judgment for possession. Such a warrant for removal may be stayed only upon consent by the landlord. For the purposes of this act "seasonal use" means use for a term of not more than 125 consecutive days for residential purposes by a person having a permanent place of residence elsewhere. "Seasonal use" does not mean use as living quarters for seasonal, temporary or migrant farm workers in connection with any work or place where work is being performed. The landlord shall have the burden of proving that the use of the unit is seasonal.

ARTICLE 4: ACTIONS FOR RENT

2A:42-11. Action for rent

A person to whom rent is due upon a lease or other agreement may bring an action for such rent whether the term of the letting be for a definite term or for life or otherwise.

. . . .

2A:42-13. Action for use and occupation; parol agreement for rent

The landlord, his heirs or assigns, may, where the agreement is not in writing, recover a reasonable satisfaction for the real estate, held or occupied by the defendant, in an action for the use and occupation of what was so held or enjoyed.

No such action shall be defeated by a parol lease or agreement whereon a certain rent was reserved, but no damages may be recovered in excess of the amount of the rent so reserved.

ARTICLE 5: RENT CONTROL

2A:42-14 to 2A:42-73

[1949 Rent Control Act expired.]

2A:42-74. Legislative findings[21]

The Legislature finds:

(a) Many citizens of the State of New Jersey are required to reside in multiple dwelling units which fail to meet minimum standards of safety and sanitation and are compelled to pay rents disproportionate to the value of the facilities and services received;

(b) It is essential to the health, safety and general welfare of the people of the State that owners of substandard multiple dwelling units be encouraged to provide safe and sanitary housing accommodations for the public to whom such accommodations are offered;

(c) It is necessary, in order to insure the improvement of substandard multiple dwelling units, to authorize the governing bodies of municipalities to enact and impose rent controls on

---

[20] This section was adopted in 1979.

[21] 2A:42-74 to 2A:42-84, providing among other things for placing certain apartments into receivership, were adopted in 1966.

substandard multiple dwelling units until such dwelling units satisfy minimum standards of safety and sanitation.

2A:42-75. Definitions

The following terms whenever used or referred to in this act shall have the following respective meanings for the purposes of this act, unless a different meaning clearly appears from the context.

(a) "Public officer" shall mean the officer, officers, board or body who is or are authorized by ordinances adopted hereunder to exercise the powers prescribed by such ordinances and by this act.

(b) "Owner" shall mean the holder or holders of the title in fee simple.

(c) "Parties in interest" shall mean all individuals, associations and corporations who have interests of record in a multiple dwelling, and who are in actual possession thereof and any person authorized to receive rents payable for housing space in a multiple dwelling.

(d) "Multiple dwelling" means and includes any building or structure and land appurtenant thereto containing 3 or more apartments or rented or offered for rent to 3 or more tenants or family units.

(e) "Housing space" means that portion of a multiple dwelling rented or offered for rent for living or dwelling purposes in which cooking equipment is supplied, and includes all privileges, services, furnishings, furniture, equipment, facilities, and improvements connected with the use or occupancy of such portion of the property. The term shall not mean or include public housing or dwelling space in any hotel, motel or established guest house, commonly regarded as a hotel, motel or established guest house, as the case may be, in the community in which it is located.

(f) "Bureau of Housing" means the Bureau of Housing in the State Department of Conservation and Economic Development.

(g) "Substandard multiple dwelling" means any multiple dwelling determined to be substandard by the public officer.

2A:42-76. Promulgation of state housing code; scope of standards

Within 60 days following the effective date of this act the Bureau of Housing shall promulgate a State Housing Code which shall be effective in any municipality adopting an ordinance under this act. Said code shall set standards consistent with minimum health and safety requirements and covering, but not limited to, matters such as water supply, plumbing, garbage storage, lighting, ventilation, heating, egress, maintenance and use and occupancy.

2A:42-77. Authority to adopt ordinance regulating rents and possession of space in substandard multiple dwellings; provisions

Whenever the governing body of a municipality finds that the health and safety of residents of that municipality are impaired or threatened by the existence of substandard multiple dwellings, it may adopt an ordinance setting forth such a finding and providing for the regulation of rents and the possession of rental space in substandard multiple dwellings. Such ordinance shall include in its provisions that:

(a) A public officer be designated or appointed to exercise the powers prescribed by the ordinance.

(b) Whenever it appears by preliminary investigation that a multiple dwelling is substandard the public officer shall cause a complaint to be served upon the owner of and parties in interest in such multiple dwelling, stating the reasons why said multiple dwelling is deemed to be substandard and setting a time and place for hearing before the public officer. The owners and parties in interest shall be given the right to file an answer and to appear and give testimony. The rules of evidence shall not be controlling in hearings before the public officer.

(c) If, after notice and hearing, the public officer determines the multiple dwelling under consideration is substandard he shall state his findings in writing and shall issue and cause to be served upon the owner or other person entitled to receive said rents an order requiring that such repairs, alterations or improvements necessary to bring such property up to minimum standards be made within a reasonable time.

(d) Failure to complete such repairs, alterations or improvements within a reasonable time as fixed by the public officer shall be cause to impose rent control on the substandard multiple dwelling.

(e) In establishing maximum rents which may be charged for housing space in a multiple dwelling subject to rent control, the permissible rents shall be sufficient to provide the owner or other person entitled to receive said rents with a fair net operating income from the multiple dwelling. The net operating income shall not be considered less than fair if it is 20% or more of the annual income in the case of a multiple dwelling containing less than 5 dwelling units or is 15% or more in the case of a multiple dwelling containing 5 or more dwelling units. In determining the fair net operating income, the public officer shall consider the following items of expense: heating fuel, utilities, payroll, janitorial materials, real estate taxes, insurance, interior painting and decorating, depreciation, and repairs and replacements and additions to furniture and furnishings which expenses shall be deducted from the annual income derived from the multiple dwelling. All items of expense and the amount of annual income shall be certified by the owner or other person entitled to receive said rents on forms provided by the public officer.

(f) The imposition of rent control on any substandard multiple dwelling shall not operate to impair leases existing at the time of the adoption of an ordinance under this act, but shall take effect at the expiration of the term of any such lease and shall remain in effect thereafter so long as the multiple dwelling is subject to rent control.

(g) It shall be unlawful for any person to demand or receive any rent in excess of the maximum rent established for housing space in multiple dwelling subject to rent control or to demand possession of the space or evict a tenant for refusal to pay rent in excess of the established maximum rent. The owner or other person entitled to receive said rents shall not be prevented, however, from exercising his rights to obtain possession of housing space from a tenant as a result of the tenant's violation of law or contract and the owner or other person entitled to receive said rents shall be provided reasonable grounds to obtain possession of premises for his own personal use and occupancy and for purposes of substantially altering, remodeling or demolishing the multiple dwelling.

(h) Whenever the public officer finds that a multiple dwelling subject to rent control is no longer substandard he shall so inform the governing body and rent control on said multiple dwelling shall be removed.

2A:42-78. Registration of owners and management of multiple dwellings

Any ordinance adopted under this act may provide for the registration of the owners and management of every multiple dwelling in the municipality. Such registration shall be with the clerk of the municipality upon forms prescribed by and furnished by the municipality. Every such registration form shall include the name and address of the owner and the name and address of an agent in charge of the premises residing in the municipality.

2A:42-79. Failure to comply with order for repair, alteration or improvement; appointment of receiver

Any ordinance adopted under this act may provide that in the event the owner of a substandard multiple dwelling fails to comply with an order for repair, alteration or improvement after notice and reasonable opportunity to do so and where such failure to comply results in the continuation of a condition or conditions harmful to the health and safety of the occupants of the multiple dwelling or to the general public, the public officer may, by and with the approval of the governing body of the municipality, bring an action in the Superior Court, or, in cases involving property located in municipalities in counties of the first class that have established full-time municipal housing courts, in the municipal housing court of the municipality in which that property is located, to be appointed receive ex officio of the rents and income from such property and expend the same for the purpose of making such repairs, alterations or improvements as are necessary to correct said harmful condition or conditions. The said rents and income so collected by the said receiver shall also be available for the payment of such costs of receivership, as may be adjudged by the court, and for the payment to the municipality of any fines or penalties which may have been imposed on the owner for violations of the ordinance and which have not been paid by the person liable therefor. The court may proceed in the action in a summary manner or otherwise. Such receiver shall not be required to give bond and shall be appointed only for the said purposes.

2A:42-80. Appointment of agent to collect rents and income

Upon his appointment, the receiver, by and with the approval of the governing body of such municipality, in all cases where the real property in question is encumbered by a first mortgage shall appoint such first mortgagee, if such mortgagee is a proper person and is willing to accept such appointment, as the receiver's agent to collect the rents and income from such real property and manage the same and in all other cases the receiver, by and with the approval of the governing body of such municipality may designate the person in charge or management of such real property or some other competent person as the receiver's agent to collect the rents and income from such real property and manage the same, which mortgagee or other person shall account promptly to the receiver for the rents and income so collected; provided, however, that if the mortgagee or other persons so designated is derelict in collecting or accounting for such rents and income or in the management of such real property, the receiver shall apply to the court for the removal of such designated mortgagee or other person, upon notice in writing to him, and the court upon removing such designated mortgagee or other person, in its discretion, may designate another person to collect the rents and income from such real property and manage the same and account to the receiver for the rents and income of such real property as aforesaid.

2A:42-81. Allowance of fees for receiver or counsel

In any such receivership no fees shall be allowed the receiver or his counsel for action as such receiver or counsel.

2A:42-82. Receivership procedure

Except as other provided herein, the procedure in respect to any such receivership shall be as in the case of receiverships to secure the payment of delinquent taxes, penalties, interest, costs and expenses wherein a collector of taxes of a municipality or other officer of the municipality is such receiver. In any receivership proceeding under this act, the court shall have jurisdiction to make such orders and directions to the receiver as may be necessary to effectuate the purposes of this act and to conserve the real property during the pendency of the receivership.

2A:42-83. Injunctive relief for persons aggrieved

Any person aggrieved by an order issued by a public officer under this act may, within 60 days after the posting and service of such order, bring an action for injunctive relief to restrain the public officer from carrying out the provisions of the order and for any other appropriate relief. The court may proceed in the action in a summary manner or otherwise. The remedy herein provided shall be exclusive, and no person affected by an order of the public officer shall be entitled to recover any damages for action taken pursuant thereto, or because of noncompliance by any person with any order of the public officer.

2A:42-84. Construction of act; powers as additional and supplemental

Nothing in this act shall be construed to abrogate or impair the powers of the courts or of any department of any municipality to enforce any provisions of its charter or its ordinances or regulations, nor to prevent or punish violations thereof; and the powers conferred by this act shall be in addition and supplemental to the powers conferred by any other law.

Editorial Note on N.J.S. 2A:42-84.1 *et seq.*: In 1987, New Jersey exempted some newly constructed apartment units from rent controls. See N.J.S. 2A:42-84.1 et seq.

ARTICLE 6: ACTIONS, ETC., FOR MAINTENANCE OF SAFE AND SANITARY HOUSING

2A:42-85. Legislative Findings[22]

The Legislature finds:

a. Many citizens of the State of New Jersey are required to reside in dwelling units which fail to meet minimum standards of safety and sanitation;

b. It is essential to the health, safety and general welfare of the people of the State that owners of substandard dwelling units be encouraged to provide safe and sanitary housing accommodations for the public to whom such accommodations are offered;

c. It is necessary, in order to insure the improvement of substandard dwelling units, to authorize the tenants dwelling therein to deposit their rents with a court appointed administrator until such dwelling units satisfy minimum standards of safety and sanitation. . ..

2A:42-86. Definitions

The following terms whenever used or referred to in this act shall have the following respective meanings, unless a different meaning clearly appears from the context.

(a) "Public officer" shall mean the officer, officers, board or body who is or are authorized by the governing body of a municipality to supervise the physical condition of dwellings within such municipality pursuant to this act.

(b) "Owner" shall mean the holder or holders of the title in fee simple.

(c) "Parties in interest" shall mean all individuals, associations and corporations who have interests of record in a dwelling, and who are in actual possession thereof and any person authorized to receive rents payable for housing space in a dwelling.

---

[22] This receivership act was adopted in 1971.

(d) "Dwelling" means and includes all rental premises or units used for dwelling purposes except owner-occupied premises with not more than two rental units.

(e) "Housing space" means that portion of a dwelling rented or offered for rent for living or dwelling purposes in which cooking equipment is supplied, and includes all privileges, services, furnishings, furniture, equipment, facilities, and improvements connected with the use or occupancy of such portion of the property. The term shall not mean or include public housing or dwelling space in any hotel, motel or established quest house, commonly regarded as a hotel, motel or established quest house, as the case may be, in the community in which it is located.

(f) [Deleted]

(g) [Deleted]

(h) "Substandard dwelling" means any dwelling determined to be substandard by the public officer.

(i) "State Housing Code" means the code adopted by the Department of Community Affairs pursuant to . . . 2A:42-74 et seq.

2A:42-87. Jurisdiction; venue

A proceeding by a public officer, tenant, or tenants of a dwelling for a judgment directing the deposit of rents into court and their use for the purpose of remedying conditions in substantial violation of the standards of fitness for human habitation established under the State or local housing codes or regulations . . . may be maintained in a court of competent jurisdiction. The place of trial of the proceeding shall be within the county in which the real property or a portion thereof from which the rents issue is situated. In cases involving real property located in municipalities in counties of the first class that have established full-time municipal housing courts, the proceedings may be brought in the municipal housing court of the municipality in which the property is located.

2A:42-88. Grounds for actions

. . . The public officer or any tenant occupying a dwelling may maintain a proceeding as provided in this act, upon the grounds that there exists in such dwellings or in housing space thereof a lack of heat or of running water or of light or of electricity or of adequate sewage disposal facilities, or any other condition or conditions in substantial violation of the standards of fitness for human habitation established under the State or local housing or health codes or regulations or any other condition dangerous to life, health or safety.

. . . .

2A:42-89. Institution of action; service and notice of petition

a. A proceeding prescribed by this act shall be commenced by the service of a petition and notice of a petition. A notice of petition may be issued only by a judge or a clerk of the court.

b. Notice of the proceeding shall be given to the nonpetitioning tenant occupying the dwelling by affixing a copy of the petition upon a conspicuous part of the subject dwelling.

2A:42-90. Contents of petition

The petition shall:

a. Set forth material facts showing that there exists in such dwelling or any housing space thereof one or more of the following: (1) a lack of heat or of running water or of light or electricity or of adequate sewage disposal facilities; . . . any other condition or conditions in substantial violation of the standards of fitness for human habitation established under the State or local housing or health codes or regulations; or (5) any other condition dangerous to life, health or safety.

b. Set forth that the facts shown in subsection a. of this section have been brought to the attention of the owner or any individual designated by him as the manager of said dwelling and that he has failed to take any action thereon within a reasonable period.

c. Set forth that the petitioner is a tenant of the subject dwelling or is the public officer of the municipality in which the subject dwelling is located. . ..

d. Set forth a brief description of the nature of the work required to remove or remedy the condition and an estimate as to the cost thereof.

e. Set forth the amount of rent due from each petitioning tenant, if any, monthly.

f. State the relief sought.

2A:42-91. Defenses to action

It shall be a sufficient defense to the proceeding, if the owner or any mortgagee or lienor of record establishes that:

a. The condition or conditions alleged in the petition did not in fact exist or that such condition or conditions have been removed or remedied; or

b. Such condition or conditions have been caused maliciously or by abnormal or unusual use by a petitioning tenant or tenants or members of the family or families of such petitioner or petitioners.

c. Any tenant or resident of the dwelling has refused entry to the owner or his agent to a portion of the premises for the purpose of correcting such condition or conditions.

2A:42-92. Judgment; service upon nonpetitioning tenants; deposit of rents with clerk of court

The court shall proceed in a summary manner and shall render a judgment either:

a. Dismissing the petition for failure to affirmatively establish the allegations thereof or because of the affirmative establishment by the owner or a mortgagee or lienor of record of a defense or defenses specified in this act; or

b. Directing that (1) the rents due on the date of the entry of such judgment from the petitioning tenant, if any, and the rents due on the dates of service of the judgment on all other tenants occupying such dwelling, from such other tenants, shall be deposited with the clerk of the court; (2) any rents to become due in the future from such petitioner and from all other tenants occupying such dwelling shall be deposited with such clerk as they fall due; (3) such deposited rents shall be used, subject to the court's direction, to the extent necessary to remedy the condition or conditions alleged in the petition and (4) upon the completion of such work in accordance with such judgment, any remaining surplus shall be turned over to the owner, together with a complete accounting of the rents deposited and the costs incurred; and granting such other and further relief as to the court may seem just and proper. A certified copy of such judgment shall be served personally upon each nonpetitioning tenant occupying such dwelling. If personal service on any such nonpetitioning tenant cannot be made with due diligence, service on such tenant shall be made by affixing a certified copy of such judgment on the entrance door of such tenant's apartment and, in addition, within 1 day after such affixing, by sending a certified copy thereof by registered mail, return receipt requested, to such tenant. Any right of the owner or parties in interest of such dwelling to collect such rent moneys from any petitioning tenant of such dwelling on or after the date of entry of such judgment, and from any nonpetitioning tenant of such dwelling on or after the date of service of such judgment on such nonpetitioning tenant as herein provided, shall be void and unenforceable to the extent that such petitioning or nonpetitioning tenant, as the case may be, has deposited such moneys with the clerk of the court in accordance with the terms of such judgment, regardless of whether such right of the owner arises from a lease, contract, agrement or understanding heretofore or hereafter made or entered into or arises as a matter of law from the relationship of the parties or otherwise. Any such rent moneys received by the owner or parties in interest shall be deposited immediately with the clerk of the court by such owner or parties in interest. It shall be a valid defense in any action or proceeding against any such tenant to recover possession of real property for the nonpayment of rent or for use or occupation to prove that the rent alleged to be unpaid was deposited with the clerk of the court in accordance with the terms of a judgment entered under this section.

2A:42-93. Order permitting performance of work in lieu of judgment; security; failure to exercise due diligence; hearing; judgment; appointment of administrator; powers

a. If, after a trial, the court shall determine that the facts alleged in the petition have been affirmatively established by the petitioner, that no defense thereto specified in this act has been affirmatively established by the owner or a mortgagee or lienor of record, and that the facts alleged in the petition warrant the granting of the relief sought, and if the owner or any mortgagee or lienor of record or parties in interest in the property, shall apply to the court to be permitted to remove or remedy the conditions specified in such petition and shall (1) demonstrate the ability promptly to undertake the work required; and (2) post security for the performance thereof within the time, and in the amount and manner deemed necessary by the court, then the court, in lieu of rendering judgment as provided in this act, may issue an order permitting such person to perform the work within a time fixed by the court.

b. If, after the issuance of an order pursuant to subdivision a. of this section, but before the time fixed in such order for the completion of the work prescribed therein, it shall appear to the petitioner that the person permitted to do the same is not proceeding with due diligence, the petitioners may apply to the court on notice to those persons who have appeared in the proceeding for a hearing to determine whether judgment should be rendered immediately as provided in subdivision c. of this section.

c. If, upon a hearing authorized in subdivision b. hereof, the court shall determine that such owner, mortgagee, lienor or parties in interest is not proceeding with due diligence, or upon the failure of such owner, mortgagee, lienor or parties in interest to complete the work in accordance with the provisions of said order, the court shall render a final judgment appointing an administrator as authorized in this act. Such judgment shall direct the administrator to apply the security posted by such person to the removing or remedying of the condition or conditions specified in the petition. In the event that the amount of such security should be insufficient for such purpose, such judgment shall direct the deposit of rents with the clerk, as authorized by this act, to the extent of such deficiency. In the event that such security should exceed the amount required to remove or remedy such condition or conditions, such judgment shall direct the administrator to file with the court, upon completion of the work prescribed therein, a full accounting of the amount of such security and the expenditures made pursuant to such judgment, and to turn over such surplus to the person who posted such security, together with a copy of such accounting.

d. The court is authorized and empowered, in implementing a judgment rendered pursuant to this act, to appoint an administrator who may be a public officer of the municipality wherein the subject dwelling is situated, an incorporated or unincorporated association, or other responsible person or persons, except that no owner, mortgagee or lienor of the subject dwelling shall be appointed an administrator of said dwelling.

The administrator is authorized and empowered, subject to the court's direction, to receive from the clerk such amounts of rent moneys or security deposited with said clerk as may be necessary to remove or remedy the condition or conditions specified in the judgment.

2A:42-94. Accounts of receipts and expenditures; presentation or settlement; notice

The court shall require the keeping of written accounts itemizing the receipts and expenditures under an order issued pursuant to this act, which shall be open to inspection by the owner, any mortgagee or lienor or parties in interest in such receipts or expenditures. Upon motion of the court or the administrator or of the owner, any mortgagee or lienor of record or of parties in interest, the court may require a presentation or settlement of the accounts with respect thereto. Notice of a motion for presentation or settlement of such accounts shall be served on the owner, any mortgagee or other lienor of record who appeared in the proceeding and any parties in interest in such receipts or expenditures.

2A:42-95. Compensation of administrator; bond

The court may allow from the rent moneys or security on deposit a reasonable amount for the services of an administrator appointed under the provisions of this act. The administrator so appointed shall furnish a bond, the amount and form of which shall be approved by the court. The cost of such bond shall be paid from the moneys so deposited.

2A:42-96. Waiver of provisions of act

Any provision of a lease or other agreement whereby an provision of this act for the benefit of a tenant, resident or occupant of a dwelling is waived, shall be deemed against public policy and shall be void.

ARTICLE 7. DISCRIMINATION IN RENTING

2A:42-100. Source of lawful income or rent payment as grounds for refusal to rent or lease

No person, firm or corporation or any agent, officer or employee thereof shall refuse to rent or lease any house or apartment to another person because of the source of any lawful income received by the person or the source of any lawful rent payment to be paid for the house or apartment. This section shall not apply to any owner-occupied house containing not more than two dwelling units. Nothing contained in this section shall limit the ability of a person, firm or corporation or any agent, officer or employee thereof to refuse to rent or lease any house or apartment because of the credit worthiness of the person or persons seeking to rent a house or apartment.

2A:42-101. Family with children under 14 as grounds for refusal to rent or lease; birth of child as grounds for cancellation of rent; exemption

No person, firm or corporation or any agent, officer or employee thereof shall refuse to rent or lease any house or apartment to another person because his family includes children under 14 years of age or shall make an agreement, rental or lease of any house or apartment which provides that the agreement, rental or lease shall be rendered null and void upon the birth of a child. This section shall not apply to any State or Federally financed or assisted housing project constructed for occupancy by senior citizens or to any property located in a retirement subdivision as defined in the "Retirement Community Full Disclosure Act" [45:22A-1 et seq.] . . . or to any owner-occupied house containing not more than two dwelling units.

TITLE 46: PROPERTY

SUBTITLE 2. REAL PROPERTY ONLY

CHAPTER 8. LEASEHOLD ESTATES; LANDLORD AND TENANT

46:8-2. Grantees or assignees of leased real estate or reversions thereof; rights same as those of original lessors

From and after November tenth, one thousand seven hundred and ninety-seven, all persons and bodies politic and corporate, being grantees or assignees of any real estate, let to lease, or of the reversions thereof from any person, and the heirs, executors, administrators, successors and assigns of such grantees or assignees, shall have and enjoy the like advantages against the lessees, their executors, administrators and assigns, by entry for non-payment of rent, or for waste, or other forfeitures; and also shall have and enjoy all the covenants, conditions and agreements contained in their leases, demises or grants, against the lessees, their executors, administrators and assigns, as the lessors themselves, or their heirs, ought or might have had or enjoyed at any time.

46:8-3. Lessees of real estate; rights against grantees of reversion

From and after November tenth, one thousand seven hundred and ninety-seven, all lessees of real estate for a term of years, life or lives, their executors, administrators or assigns, shall have the like action and advantage against all persons and bodies politic and corporate, their heirs, successors and assigns, who have or shall have any gift or grant of the reversions of such real estate so let, or any part thereof, for any condition, covenant or agreement contained in their leases, as the same lessees, or any of them, ought or might have had against such lessors, and their heirs, excepting the right to recover upon any warranty of title by deed or implied by law.

. . . .

46:8-6. Injuries by fire to buildings on leased premises; repair by landlord

Whenever any building or buildings erected on leased premises shall be injured by fire, without the fault of the lessee, the landlord shall repair the same as speedily as possible. In default of such repair the rent shall cease until such time as the building or buildings shall be put in complete repair. This section shall not extend or apply to cases wherein the parties have otherwise stipulated in their agreement of lease.

46:8-7. Buildings on leased premises totally destroyed by fire or otherwise; lease terminated

Whenever any building or buildings erected on leased premises shall be totally destroyed by fire or otherwise, without the fault of the lessee, the rent shall be paid up to the time of such destruction, and then, and from thenceforth, the lease shall cease and come to an end. This section shall not extend or apply to cases wherein the parties have otherwise stipulated in their agreement of lease.

. . . .

46:8-9. Three months' notice to tenant to quit sufficient

In all cases where a tenant is or may be entitled by law to notice to quit the leased premises, or order to determine his tenancy, three months' notice in writing to quit shall be deemed and taken to be sufficient.

46:8-9.1. Death of lessee of dwelling place or spouse; termination of lease; notice to lessor; time for vacation of property[23]

Any lease for a term of one or more years of a property that has been leased and used by the lessee solely for the purpose of providing a dwelling place for himself, or for himself and his family, may be terminated prior to the expiration date thereof, in the event of the death of such lessee or in the event of the death of such lessee or his spouse, as the case may be, upon notice duly given by such lessee or by the executor or administrator of his estate or by the surviving spouse in the event that such lease was executed jointly by husband and wife. Such termination shall take effect on the fortieth day following the receipt by the lessor of written notice thereof, and the rent shall be paid up to the time of such termination, whereupon the lease shall cease and come to and end. The property shall be vacated and possession shall be turned over the lessor at least five working days prior to the fortieth day following receipt by the lessor of written notice. The provisions of this act shall not apply to any lease the terms whereof shall explicitly provide otherwise.

46:8-9.2. Disabling illness or accident of lessee or spouse; termination of lease

A lease for a term of one or more years of a property that has been leased and used by the lessee solely for the purpose of providing a dwelling place for himself, or himself and his family, may be terminated prior to the expiration date thereof if the lessee or his spouse, or both, suffer a disabling illness or accident, upon notice duly given by the lessee or his spouse, on a form to be provided by the Director of the Division of Housing in the Department of Community Affairs, which form shall include: a. certification of a treating physician that the lessee or spouse is unable to continue to engage in gainful employment; b. proof of loss of income; and c. proof that any pension, insurance or other subsidy to which the lessee or his spouse is entitled is insufficient to supplement the income of the lessee or his spouse so that the rent on the property in question can be paid and that the income is necessary for payment of the rent. The termination shall take effect on the fortieth day following the receipt by the lessor of written notice thereof, and the rent shall be paid up to the time of termination, whereupon the lease shall cease and come to an end. The property shall be vacated and possession shall be turned over to the lessor at least five working days prior to the fortieth day following receipt by the lessor of written notice. The provisions of this section shall not apply to any lease the terms whereof shall explicitly provide otherwise.

. . . .

46:8-10. Tenant holding over; tenancy from month to month

Whenever a tenant whose original term of leasing shall be for a period of one month or longer shall hold over or remain in possession of the demised premises beyond the term of the letting, the tenancy created by or resulting from acceptance of rent by the landlord shall be a tenancy from month to month in the absence of any agreement to the contrary.

. . . .

---

[23] This and the following section were adopted in 1971.

46:8-19. Deposit to secure performance of lease; investment of deposit; interest rights; notice requirements; failure to provide notice[24]

Whenever money or other form of security shall be deposited or advanced on a contract, lease or license agreement for the use or rental of real property as security for performance of the contract, lease or agreement or to be applied to payments upon such contract, lease or agreement when due, such money or other form of security, until repaid or so applied including the tenant's portion of the interest or earnings accumulated thereon as hereinafter provided, shall continue to be the property of the person making such deposit or advance and shall be held in trust by the person with whom such deposit or advance shall be made for the use in accordance with the terms of the contract, lease or agreement and shall not be mingled with the personal property or become an asset of the person receiving the same. The person receiving money so deposited or advanced shall:

a. (1) Invest that money in shares of an insured money market fund established by an investment company based in this State and registered under the "Investment Company Act of 1940," . . . 15 U.S.C. Section 80a-1 et seq., whose shares are registered under the "Securities Act of 1933," . . . 15 U.S.C. Section 77a et seq., and the only investments of which fund are instruments maturing in one year or less, or (2) deposit that money in a State or federally chartered bank, savings bank or savings and loan association in this State insured by an agency of the federal government in an account bearing a variable rate of interest, which shall be established at least quarterly, which is similar to the average rate of interest on active interest bearing money market transaction accounts paid by the bank or association . . . or equal to similar accounts of an investment company described in paragraph (1) of this subsection, less an amount not to exceed 1% per annum of the amount so invested or deposited for the costs of servicing and processing the account.

This subsection shall not apply to persons receiving money for less than 10 rental units except where required by the Commissioner of Banking by rule or regulation. The commissioner shall apply the provisions of this subsection to some or all persons receiving money for less than 10 rental units where the commissioner finds that it is practicable to deposit or invest the money received with an investment company or State or federally chartered bank, savings bank or savings and loan association in accordance with this subsection. Except as expressly provided herein, nothing in this subsection shall affect or modify the rights or obligations of persons receiving money for rental premises or units, tenants, licensees or contractees under any other law.

b. Persons not required to invest or deposit money in accordance with subsection a. of this section shall deposit such money in a State or federally chartered bank, savings bank or savings and loan association in this State insured by an agency of the federal government in an account bearing interest at the rate currently paid by such institutions and associations on time or savings deposits.

The person investing the security deposit pursuant to subsection a. or b. of this section shall thereupon notify in writing each of the persons making such security deposit or advance, giving the name and address of the investment company, State or federally chartered bank, savings bank or savings and loan association in which the deposit or investment of security money is made, and the amount of such deposit.

---

[24] Sections 46:8-19 to 46:8-26, dealing with security deposits, were originally enacted in 1967.

All of the money so deposited or advanced may be deposited or invested by the person receiving the same in one interest-bearing or dividend yielding account as long as he complies with all the other requirements of this act.

The person receiving money so deposited or so advanced shall be entitled to receive as administrative expenses a sum equivalent to 1% per annum thereon or 12.5% of the aggregate interest yield on the security deposit, whichever is greater, less the amount of any service fee charged by an investment company, a State or federally chartered bank, savings bank or savings and loan association for money deposited pursuant to this section, which shall be in lieu of all other administrative and custodial expenses. The balance of the interest or earnings paid thereon by the investment company, State or federally chartered bank, savings bank or savings and loan association, hereinafter referred to as tenant's portion, shall belong to the person making the deposit or advance and shall be permitted to compound to the benefit of the tenant, or be paid to the tenant in cash, or be credited toward the payment of rent due on the renewal or anniversary of said tenant's lease.

In the event the person receiving a security deposit fails to invest or deposit the security money in the manner required under this section or notify the tenant of the name and address of the investment company, State or federally chartered bank, savings bank or savings and loan association in which the deposit or investment of such security is made, and the amount thereof, within 30 days after receipt of same from the tenant, . . . the tenant may give written notice to the person receiving the same that such security money be applied on account of rent payment or payments due or to become due from the tenant, and thereafter the tenant shall be without obligation to make any further security deposit and the person receiving the money so deposited shall not be entitled to make further demand for a security deposit.

. . . .

46:8-20. Conveyance, assignment, foreclosure or bankruptcy; disposition of security deposit plus interest or earnings

Any person, whether the owner or lessee of the property leased, who or which has or hereafter shall have received from a tenant or licensee a sum of money as a deposit or advance of rental as security for the full performance by such tenant or licensee of the terms of his contract, lease or license agreement, or who or which has or shall have received the same from a former owner or lessee, shall, upon conveying such property or assigning his or its lease to another, or upon the conveyance of such property to another person by a court in action to foreclose a mortgage thereon, at the time of the delivery of the deed or instrument or assignment, or within five days thereafter, or in the event of the insolvency or bankruptcy of the person receiving said deposit, within five days after the making and entry of an order of the court discharging the receiver or trustee, deal with the security deposit by turning over to his or its grantee or assignee, or to the purchaser at the foreclosure sale the sum so deposited, plus the tenant's portion of the interest or earnings accumulated thereon, and notify the tenant or licensee by registered or certified mail of such turning over and the name and address of such grantee, assignee, or purchaser.

46:8-21. Release of former owner or lessee from liability; liability of transferee

Any owner or lessee turning over to his or its grantee, assignee, or to a purchaser of the leased premises at a foreclosure sale the amount of such security deposit, plus the tenant's portion of the interest or earnings accumulated thereon, is hereby relieved of and from liability to the tenant or licensee for the repayment thereof; and the transferee of such security deposit, plus the tenant's portion of the interest or earnings accumulated thereon, is hereby made responsible for the return thereof to the tenant or licensee, in accordance with the terms of the contract, lease, or agreement unless he or it shall thereafter and before the expiration of the term of the tenant's lease or licensee's agreement, transfer such security deposit to another, pursuant to section [46:8-20] . . . and give the requisite notice in connection therewith as provided thereby.

46:8-21.1. Return of deposit; expiration of lease or displacement; resumption of occupancy; repayment of deposit; penalty for failure to return

Within 30 days after the termination of the tenant's lease or licensee's agreement, the owner or lessee shall return by personal delivery, registered or certified mail the sum so deposited plus the tenant's portion of the interest or earnings accumulated thereon, less any charges expended in accordance with the terms of a contract, lease, or, agreement to the tenant or licensee, or, in the case of a lease terminated pursuant to . . . 46:8-9.1, the executor or administrator of the estate of the tenant or licensee or the surviving spouse of the tenant or licensee so terminating the lease. The interest or earnings and any such deductions shall be itemized and the tenant, licensee, executor, administrator or surviving spouse notified thereof by personal delivery, registered or certified mail.

Within five business days after a. the tenant is caused to be displaced by fire, flood, condemnation, or evacuation, and b. an authorized public official posts the premises with a notice prohibiting occupancy, or c. any building inspector, in consultation with a relocation officer, where applicable, has certified within 48 hours that displacement is expected to continue longer than seven days and has so notified the owner or lessee in writing, the owner or lessee shall have available and return to the tenant or the tenant's designated agent upon his demand the sum so deposited plus the tenant's portion of the interest or earnings accumulated thereon, less any charges expended in accordance with the terms of the contract, lease or agreement and less any rent due and owing at the time of displacement.

Such net sum shall continue to be available to be returned upon demand during normal business hours for a period of 30 days at a location in the same municipality in which the subject leased property is located and shall be accompanied by an itemized statement of interest or earnings and any deductions. The owner of lessee may, by mutual agreement with the municipal clerk, have the municipal clerk of the municipality in which the subject leased property is located return said net sum in the same manner. Within three business days after receiving notification of the displacement, the owner or lessee shall provide written notice to a displaced tenant by personal delivery or mail to the tenant's last known address. Such notice shall include, but not be limited to, the location at which and the hours and days during which said net sum shall be available to him. The owner or lessee shall provide a duplicate notice in the same manner to the relocation officer. Where a relocation officer has not been designated, the duplicate notice shall be provided to the municipal clerk. When the last known address of the tenant is that from which he was displaced and the mailbox of that address is not accessible during normal business hours, the owner or lessee shall also post such notice at each exterior public entrance of the property from which the tenant was displaced. Any such net sum not demanded by and returned to the tenant or the tenant's designated agent within the period of 30 days shall be redeposited or reinvested by the owner of lessee in any appropriate interest bearing or divided yielding account in the same investment company, State or federally chartered bank, savings bank or savings and loan association from which it was withdrawn.

In the event that said displaced tenant resumes occupancy of the premises, said tenant shall redeliver to the owner or lessee one-third of the security deposit immediately, one-third in 30 days and one-third in 60 days from the date of reoccupancy. Upon the failure of said tenant to make such payments of the security deposit, the owner or lessee may institute legal action for possession of the premises in the same manner that authorized for nonpayment of rent.

In any action by a tenant, licensee, executor, administrator or surviving spouse for the return of moneys due under this section, the court upon finding for the tenant, licensee, executor, administrator or surviving spouse shall award recovery of double the amount of said moneys, together with full costs of any action and, in the court's discretion, reasonable attorney's fees.

46:8-21.2. Limitation an amount of deposit

An owner or lessee may not require more than a sum equal to 1 1/2 times 1 month's rental according to the terms of contract, lease, or agreement as a security for the use or rental of real property used for dwelling purposes.

. . . .

46:8-22. Enforcement of trust by civil action

Any trust arising under the provisions of this act shall be enforceable by a civil action in a court of competent jurisdiction and that court shall have jurisdiction to make any appropriate order or judgment both pendente lite and final to fully effectuate the purposes of this act.

46:8-23. Statutory trust upon insolvency or bankruptcy of person receiving security deposit

In the event of the insolvency or bankruptcy of the person receiving the said moneys, the claim of the person who paid the said moneys shall constitute a statutory trust with respect to any moneys so received and not previously expended in accordance with the terms of the contract, lease or agreement.

46:8-24. Waiver by depositor prohibited

Any provision of such a contract, lease or agreement whereby a person who so deposits or advances money waives any provision of this act is absolutely void.

46:8-25. Unlawful diversion of trust funds; penalty

Any person party to said contract, lease or agreement, or any agent of said persons, or any officer of a corporation receiving said moneys, who, with knowledge that such moneys constitute trust funds, unlawfully diverts or consents to an unlawful diversion of such moneys shall be a disorderly person and subject to a fine of not less than $200.00 or by imprisonment for not more than 30 days, or both.

46:8-26. Application of act

The provisions of this act shall apply to all rental premises or units used for dwelling purposes except owner-occupied premises with not more than two rental units where the tenant has failed to provide 30 days written notice to the landlord invoking the provisions of this act.

46:8-27. Landlord and project defined

The term "landlord", as used in this act,[25] shall mean the person or persons who own or purport to own, or exercise control of any building or project in which there is rented or offered for rent housing space for living or dwelling purposes under either a written or oral lease, provided that this definition shall not include owner-occupied two unit premises. This definition shall

_____

[25] This act, adopted in 1974, includes sections 46:8-27 to 46:8-37.

include but not be limited to any multiple dwelling subject to the "Hotel and Multiple Dwelling Law" . . . [55:13A-1 et seq.].

The term "project" as used in this act shall mean a group of buildings which are or are represented to be under common or substantially common ownership and which stand on a single parcel of land or parcels of land which are contiguous and which group of buildings is named, designated or advertised as a common entity.

The contiguity of such parcels shall not be adversely affected by public rights-of-way incidental to such buildings.

46:8-28. Certificate of registration; filing; contents

Every landlord shall, within 30 days following the effective date of this act, or at the time of the creation of the first tenancy in any newly constructed or reconstructed building, file with the clerk of the municipality in which the residential property is situated in the case of a one-dwelling unit rental or a two-dwelling unit non-owner occupied premises, or with the Bureau of Housing Inspection in the Department of Community Affairs in the case of a multiple dwelling . . ., a certificate of registration on forms prescribed by the Commissioner of Community Affairs, which shall contain the following information:

a. The name and address of the record owner or owners of the premises and the record owner or owners of the rental business if not the same persons. In the case of a partnership the names of general partners shall be provided;

b. If the record owner is a corporation, the name and address of the registered agent and corporate officers of said corporation;

c. If the address of any record owner is not located in the county in which the premises are located, the name and address of a person who resides in the county in which the premises are located and is authorized to accept notices from a tenant and to issue receipts therefor and to accept service of process on behalf of the record owner;

d. The name and address of the managing agent of the premises, if any;

e. The name and address, including the dwelling unit, apartment or room number of the superintendent, janitor, custodian or other individual employed by the record owner or managing agent to provide regular maintenance service, if any;

f. The name, address and telephone number of an individual representative of the record owner or managing agent who may be reached or contacted at any time in the event of an emergency affecting the premises or any unit of dwelling space therein, including such emergencies as the failure of any essential service or system, and who has the authority to make emergency decisions concerning the building and any repair thereto or expenditure in connection therewith;

g. The name and address of every holder of a recorded mortgage on the premises;

h. If fuel oil is used to heat the building and the landlord furnishes the heat in the building, the name and address of the fuel oil dealer servicing the building and the grade of fuel oil used.

. . . .

46:8-28.2. Certificate of registration; amendment; filing

Every landlord required to file a certificate of registration as described in section . . . [46:8-28] shall file an amended certificate of registration within 20 days after any change in the information required to be included thereon. No fee shall be required for the filing of an amendment except where the ownership of the premises is changed.

. . . .

46:8-29. Certificate of registration and amendments; providing to occupants and tenants

Within 30 days following the effective date hereof, and at the time of the creation of a new tenancy, every landlord shall provide each occupant or tenant in his building or project a copy of the certificate of registration required by section . . . [46:8-28]. If an amended certificate is filed the landlord shall furnish each occupant or tenant with a copy of the amended certificate within 7 days after the amended certificate is filed. . ..

. . . .

46:8-31. Action by tenant; jurisdiction of landlord not in compliance with act

In any action in the Superior Court, Law Division, Special Civil Part or municipal court by an occupant or tenant or to recover penalties against a landlord who has not complied with this act and who cannot be served within the county or municipality, the summons and complaint may be served by certified and regular mail upon the record owner at the last address listed in the tax records of either the municipality or county. Service of such summons and complaint by certified and regular mail shall be effective to bring the landlord before the Superior Court, Law Division, Special Civil Part or municipal court even if it were not served within the county or municipality in which the court issuing the summons is located.

. . . .

46:8-33. Action for possession by landlord; compliance with act

In any action for possession instituted by a landlord who has failed to comply with the provisions of this act, no judgment for possession shall be entered until there has been compliance. The court shall continue such case for up to 90 days and if there has not been compliance within such period, the action shall be dismissed.

46:8-34. Jurisdiction of county district court; amounts under $3,000.00

The Superior Court, Law Division, Special Civil Part shall have jurisdiction over any action between a landlord and tenant where the amount in controversy is $3,000.00 or less.

46:8-35. Violations; penalty; enforcement; disposition

Any landlord who shall violate any provision of this act shall be liable to a penalty of not more than $500.00 for each offense, recoverable by a summary proceeding under the "Penalty Enforcement Law" . . . [2A:58-1 et seq.]. . ..

46:8-36. Waiver of rights by agreement; unenforceability

Any written or oral provision in any agreement whereby any tenant waives any rights under this act shall be deemed against public policy and unenforceable.

. . . .

46:8-43. Short title

This act[26] shall be known and may be cited as "The Truth-in-Renting Act."

46:8-44. Definitions

---

[26] This act includes sections 46:8-43 to 46:8-49.

As used in this act:

a. "Landlord" means any person who rents or leases or offers to rent or lease, for a term of at least 1 month, dwelling units, except dwelling units in rental premises containing not more than two such units, or in owner-occupied premises of not more than three dwelling units, or in hotels, motels or other guest houses serving transient or seasonal guests.

b. "Department" means the Department of Community Affairs.

c. "Commissioner" means the Commissioner of the Department of Community Affairs.

46:8-45. Statement of legal rights and responsibilities of tenants and landlords of rental dwelling units; promulgation; distribution; effect

a. The department shall, as soon as practicable and annually thereafter, after public hearing, prepare and make available at cost to the public a statement, in a form and size suitable for posting and distributing pursuant to the provisions of this act, of the primary, clearly established legal rights and responsibilities of tenants and landlords of rental dwelling units. This statement shall be printed in both the English and Spanish languages. The statement shall serve as an informational document, and nothing therein shall be construed as binding on or affecting a judicial determination under section [46:8-48] . . . of this act of what constitutes a lease provision which violates clearly established legal rights of tenants or responsibilities of landlords.

b. Where practical considerations make it necessary for the department to limit the extent of the statement items to be included shall be selected on the basis of the importance of their inclusion in protecting the rights of the public.

46:8-46. Statement; distribution and posting by landlords

Every landlord shall distribute one copy of the statement prepared and made available pursuant to the provisions of this act to each of their tenants within 30 days after it has been made available by the department and shall thereafter provide a copy of the current statement to each new tenant at or prior to the time he assumes occupancy of the dwelling. In addition, every landlord shall keep a copy of the current statement posted in one or more locations so that the statement is prominent and accessible to all his tenants.

46:8-47. Violations; penalty; collection and enforcement

Any landlord who violates any provisions of this act, contrary to the legal rights of tenants, shall be liable to a penalty of not more $100.00 for each offense. Such penalty shall be collected and enforced by summary proceedings pursuant to the Penalty Enforcement Law (N.J.S. 2A:58-1 et seq.). . ..

46:8-48. Offer of or entry into lease in violation of rights of tenants; termination of lease; exception

No landlord shall offer to any tenant or prospective tenant or enter into any written lease after the effective date of this act which includes a lease provision which violates clearly established legal rights of tenants or responsibilities of landlords as established by the law of this State at the time the lease is signed. A tenant shall have the right to petition a court of competent jurisdiction to terminate a lease containing any such provision. Nothing contained herein shall limit any rights of remedies a tenant may have under a lease.

No landlord shall be liable to any penalty under section [46:8-47] . . . nor any lease termination by a tenant under [this section] . . ., for any lease provision in violation of [this section] . . .

where the proposal to include such lease provision originated from the tenant and not such landlord.

46:8-49. Waiver of right to receive or refusal to accept statement; effect

No waiver or refusal by a tenant of his right to receive a copy of the statement as provided herein shall alter the responsibilities of the landlord under any provision of this act.

TABLE OF CASES

[Principal Cases appear in *italics;* Cases cited or discussed by the author appear in Roman type. References are to pages.]

[Principal Cases appear in *italics;* Cases cited or discussed by the author appear in Roman type. References are to pages.]

[Principal Cases appear in *italics;* Cases cited or discussed by the author appear in Roman type. References are to pages.]

C

[Principal Cases appear in *italics;* Cases cited or discussed by the author appear in Roman type. References are to pages.]

[Principal Cases appear in *italics;* Cases cited or discussed by the author appear in Roman type. References are to pages.]

[Principal Cases appear in *italics;* Cases cited or discussed by the author appear in Roman type. References are to pages.]

[Principal Cases appear in *italics;* Cases cited or discussed by the author appear in Roman type. References are to pages.]

[Principal Cases appear in *italics;* Cases cited or discussed by the author appear in Roman type. References are to pages.]

[Principal Cases appear in *italics;* Cases cited or discussed by the author appear in Roman type. References are to pages.]

[Principal Cases appear in *italics;* Cases cited or discussed by the author appear in Roman type. References are to pages.]

L

[Principal Cases appear in *italics;* Cases cited or discussed by the author appear in Roman type. References are to pages.]

[Principal Cases appear in *italics;* Cases cited or discussed by the author appear in Roman type. References are to pages.]

[Principal Cases appear in *italics;* Cases cited or discussed by the author appear in Roman type. References are to pages.]

[Principal Cases appear in *italics;* Cases cited or discussed by the author appear in Roman type. References are to pages.]

[Principal Cases appear in *italics;* Cases cited or discussed by the author appear in Roman type. References are to pages.]

[Principal Cases appear in *italics;* Cases cited or discussed by the author appear in Roman type. References are to pages.]

[Principal Cases appear in *italics;* Cases cited or discussed by the author appear in Roman type. References are to pages.]

[Principal Cases appear in *italics;* Cases cited or discussed by the author appear in Roman type. References are to pages.]

X

Y

Z

INDEX

[References are to pages.]

A

[References are to pages.]

[References are to pages.]

[References are to pages.]

COOPERATIVE/CONDOMINIUM HOUSING—Cont.
Financing
 Generally . . . 615
 Differences between cooperatives and condominiums . . 752
Long term tenants compared . . . 616–617
Performance of sales contract . . . 746–754
Proprietary leases . . . 607–615
Sales contract, performance of . . . 746–754
Warranties of habitability, applicability to conversions of . . . 821–822

COPYRIGHTS
Newsmatter . . . 1105–1124

CORPORATIONS
Generally . . . 311–313; 315–316
Establishing, requirements for . . . 315
General incorporation statutes . . . 312–313
Historical development . . . 311–313
Liability insulation feature of . . . 315–316
Piercing the corporate veil
 Generally . . . 316; 333; 337–338
 Bartle v. Home Owners Co-operative Inc., . . . 335–336
 Capitalization of corporation as factor in . . . 334
 Commonality as factor in . . . 333–334
 Deception as factor in . . . 334–335
 Operation as separate legal entities as factor in . . . 334
 Torts and . . . 336
 Zaist v. Olson, court opinion in . . . 326–333
State corporate charters . . . 311–312

COVENANTS
Generally . . . 356; 409–412
Dependent covenants . . . 641–649
Enforcement . . . 412; 422
Independence of covenants, traditional rule on . . . 636–638
Notice requirements
 Background of case . . . 414–418
 Gaskin v. Harris, court opinion in . . . 419–421
Privity of estate . . . 410–411
Property restrictions
 Corrigan v. Buckley, court opinion in . . . 439–442
 Explanatory notes . . . 442–443
Property restrictions based on race (See RACIAL DISCRIMINATION)
Racial restrictions (See RACIAL DISCRIMINATION)
Restatement Third of Property . . . 412–413
Run with the land
 Generally . . . 412
 Notice requirements and . . . 414–421
Touch and concern the land . . . 412; 421–422

CREDITORS
Married women's property, creditor protection for . . . 175
Partnership property, rights to . . . 324
Tenancy by the entirety and (See TENANCY BY THE ENTIRETY)

CRITICAL LEGAL STUDIES MOVEMENT (CLS)
Generally . . . 568–572; 677

CURTESY
Generally . . . 145

CUSTOM DOCTRINE
Generally . . . 103
Coastal areas, applicability to . . . 103; 104–113

CY PRES RULES
Generally . . . 368–369

D

DAMAGES
Abandonment cases, landlord's responsibility for mitigation of damages in (See ABANDONMENT, subhead: Mitigation of damages, landlord's responsibility for)
Nuisance actions (See NUISANCE)

DAWES ACT
Generally . . . 5; 49–50
Contemporary consequences of . . . 49–51
Court opinion; U.S. Supreme Court
 Recent cases . . . 76–78
 Yakima Indian Nation cases . . . 51–73
Takings clause, applicability of . . . 78
Yakima Indian Nation cases . . . 51–76
Zoning rights . . . 51–78

DEEDS
Generally . . . 16
Quit claim deed . . . 119–127; 128–129
Warranty deeds . . . 838–839

DEVISEE
Defined . . . 342

DEVISES
Equitable distribution principle, applicability of . . . 198–203

DISABLED PERSONS
Protected tenancy status of . . . 710; 712–721

DISCRIMINATION
Definitions of . . . 371
Gender bias (See GENDER BIAS)
Racial discrimination (See RACIAL DISCRIMINATION)
Religious discrimination . . . 475

DIVORCE
Community property states . . . 142; 195–198; 203–204
Equitable distribution (See EQUITABLE DISTRIBUTION)
Family partnership, dissolution of . . . 316–325
Marital property states (See MARITAL PROPERTY)
Testamentary dispositions, effect on . . . 250

DOWER
Generally . . . 145–146

DUE PROCESS CONSIDERATIONS
Generally . . . 528
Abandonment, mitigation of . . . 730
Consumer protection . . . 543–544
Contemporary views on property and . . . 544–554

[References are to pages.]

ESCHEAT
Harmony Society case, applicability to . . . 280; 282

ESTATES IN LAND
Generally . . . 339–340
Fee simple estates (See FEE SIMPLE ESTATES)
Future interests (See FUTURE INTERESTS)

ESTOPPEL
Adverse possession cases, applicability to . . . 91

EVICTION
Anti-Eviction Act . . . 707–709
Appealability of dispossess judgments
    Generally . . . 651–653
    Explanatory notes . . . 661–662
    Marini v. Ireland, court opinion in . . . 654–661
Commercial leases
    Constructive eviction . . . 641–649
    Distraint of goods for unpaid rent of commercial tenant
    . . . 622–632
    Good cause . . . 703–707; 709
Constructive eviction
    Defense to nonpayment of rent . . . 641–649
    Explanatory notes . . . 648–649
    Modern context, in . . . 649
    Reste v. Cooper, court opinion in . . . 641–648
    Traditional rules . . . 638–639
Cooperatives . . . 607–615
Distraint . . . 622–634
Dormitory residents . . . 606–607
Due process considerations (See DUE PROCESS CONSIDER-
ATIONS)
Ejectment . . . 605–606
Forcible entry and detainer . . . 606
Good cause
    Generally . . . 700–702
    Explanatory notes . . . 707–709
    Shell Oil Company v. Marinello, court opinion in . . . .
    703–707
Historical background . . . 617–619
Hotel guests, of . . . 605
Migrant farm worker, of . . . 594–605
Notice requirements for dispossession of migrant farm worker
. . . 594–605
Procedural protections
    Callen v. Sherman's, Inc., court opinion in . . . 622–631
    Due process considerations . . . 619–621
    Explanatory notes . . . 631–632
    Historical background . . . 617–619
Public housing, evictions from . . . 543
Reforms, impact of . . . 710–711
Remedial alternatives available to tenants . . . 662
Removal of action from landlord-tenant court . . 662; 708–709
Rent, nonpayment of (See RENT)
Retaliatory eviction
    Early cases . . . 694–695
    Explanatory notes . . . 698–699
    Jurisdiction . . . 700
    Limitations of defense . . . 700

EVICTION—Cont.
Retaliatory eviction—Cont.
    Pohlman v. Metropolitan Trailer Park, court opinion in
    . . . 695–698
    Proof of retaliation . . . 698–699
    Term tenancies and . . . 699
Self-help eviction
    Generally . . . 593–594; 603–604
    Migrant farm worker, availability for dispossession of
    . . . 594–605
Summary dispossession
    Generally . . . 605
    Appealability (See subhead: Appealability of dispossess
    judgments)
    Cooperative-shareholder, of . . . 609–615
    Historical background . . . 617–619
    Reform of . . . 651–654
    Rent deposits . . . 662–663
    Speed of . . . 615–616
    Tenant remedies . . . 662

EXCLUSIONARY ZONING
Federal race discrimination law, challenges based on
    Generally . . . 501–504
    Huntington NAACP v. Town of Huntington, court opinion
    in . . . 504–515
State constitutional provisions, challenges based on
    Generally . . . 516–517
    Britton v. Town of Chester . . . 517–523
    Explanatory notes . . . 523–524
Zoning incentives and . . . 523–524

EXECUTORY INTERESTS
Generally . . . 342–343; 345

EXPENSES, RECOVERABILITY OF
Generally . . . 130–131

F

FAMILIAL STATUS
Discrimination based on . . . 185

FEE SIMPLE ESTATES
Absolute
    Generally . . . 340–341; 356–357
    "Heirs", use of word . . . 341–342
Chart of . . . 344
Condition subsequent, subject to
    Generally . . . 343; 356–357
    State action and . . . 358
Defeasible fee simple . . . 396–407
Executory limitation, subject to . . . 343–344
Fee simple determinable
    Generally . . . 342–343
    Park land deeded with reversion conditioned on racial
    restrictions . . . 350–358
Leases (See LEASES)
Life estates (See LIFE ESTATES)
Racial restrictions, park land deeded with reversion conditioned
on . . . 350–358

[References are to pages.]

[References are to pages.]

[References are to pages.]

[References are to pages.]

[References are to pages.]

PUBLICITY RIGHTS
Generally . . . 1126–1128; 1151–1152
California statute . . . 1145–1148
Carson decision . . . 1148
Commercial exploitation and . . . 1150–1151
Development of publicity rights . . . 1126–1152
Flying Cannonball decision . . . 1148–1149
Foundation of publicity rights . . . 1103–1126
Imitators, treatment of . . . 1149–1150
Inheritability of
　Generally . . . 1127–1128; 1141–1142; 1151–1152
　Background of case . . . 1128–1130
　Explanatory notes . . . 1140–1149
　Martin Luther King, Jr., Center for Social Change v. American Heritage Products, court opinion in 1130–1140
Judicial rationales for . . . 1140–1141
Marx Brothers decision . . . 1148
Newsmatter, property rights in
　Generally . . . 1124–1126
　Background of case . . . 1103–1106
　Explanatory notes . . . 1121–1124
　International News Service v. Associated Press, court opinion in . . . 1107–1121
Nixon tapes, rights in . . . 1149
Political humor and . . . 1149
State statutes
　California . . . 1145–1148
　Tennessee . . . 1142–1145
Tennessee statute . . . 1142–1145

PUBLIC/PRIVATE DISTINCTION
Generally . . . 566
Decline of, stages of . . . 570–572
Historical background . . . 566–569
Takings context, in . . . 909

PUBLIC TRUST DOCTRINE
Generally . . . 103
Coastal areas, applicability to . . . 103; 104–113
Oregon ex rel. Thornton v. Hay, court opinion in . . 104–112
Tidelands, applicability to . . . 103

PURCHASE MONEY MORTGAGE
Generally . . . 773

PURCHASE MONEY RESULTING TRUST
Generally . . . 452–453

Q

QUIT CLAIM DEEDS
Generally . . . 119–127; 128–129

R

RACIAL DISCRIMINATION
Class-based zoning (See EXCLUSIONARY ZONING)
Covenants, property restrictions in
　Generally . . . 436–438

RACIAL DISCRIMINATION—Cont.
Covenants, property restrictions in—Cont.
　Corrigan v. Buckley, court opinion in . . . 439–442
　Explanatory notes . . . 442–443
Definitions of . . . 371
Equitable servitudes, property restrictions in
　Background of case . . . 443–445
　Explanatory notes . . . 451–454
　Shelley v. Kraemer . . . 445–451
Exclusionary zoning (See EXCLUSIONARY ZONING)
Fee simple determinable deed of park conditioned on racial restrictions
　Analysis of case . . . 355–358
　Background of case . . . 350–352
　Charlotte Park and Recreation Commission v. Barringer, court opinion in . . . 352–355
Future interest in park with reversion based on racial restrictions
　Background of case . . . 358–360
　Evans v. Abney, court opinion in . . . 361–368
　Subsequent events . . . 370
Housing; class-based zoning (See EXCLUSIONARY ZONING)
Parks, use of
　Fee simple determinable with reversion based on racial restriction (See subhead: Fee simple determinable deed of park conditioned on racial restrictions)
　Future interest with reversion based on racial restriction (See subhead: Future interest in park with reversion based on racial restrictions)
Property restrictions
　Covenants, in (See subhead: Covenants, property restrictions in)
　Equitable servitudes, in (See subhead: Equitable servitudes, property restrictions in)
　Zoning schemes (See subhead: Zoning schemes)
Zoning schemes
　Generally . . . 483–485
　Buchanan v. Warley, court opinion in . . . 478–483
　Class-based zoning (See EXCLUSIONARY ZONING)
　Exclusionary zoning (See EXCLUSIONARY ZONING)
　Historical background . . . 476–477

REALISM
Generally . . . 393–395
Due process and property . . . 539–543
Lease law reforms and . . . 639–640
Post-World War II era . . . 527–530
Property concepts in Realist era . . . 1124–1126
Racial covenants and . . . 442–443
Servitudes Restatement, formalism-realism debate in drafting of . . . 432–436
Zoning and land use controls . . . 500–501

REAL PROPERTY
Brokers (See BROKERS)
Ownership (See OWNERSHIP OF PROPERTY)
Sales (See SALES OF REAL PROPERTY)
Transfers (See TRANSFERS OF LAND INTERESTS)

RELIGION
Generally . . . 475

[References are to pages.]

[References are to pages.]

[References are to pages.]